GENERAL MOTORS FULL-SI... 1988-96 REPAIR MANUAL

President Dean F. Morgantini, S.A.E.
Vice President–Finance Barry L. Beck
Vice President–Sales Glenn D. Potere

Executive Editor Kevin M. G. Maher
Production Manager Ben Greisler, S.A.E.
Project Managers Michael Abraham, George B. Heinrich III, Will Kessler, A.S.E., Richard Schwartz

Editor Thomas A. Mellon

CHILTON™ Automotive Books
PUBLISHED BY **W. G. NICHOLS, INC.**

Manufactured in USA

1020 Andrew Drive
West Chester, PA 19380
ISBN 0-8019-8798-9
Library of Congress Catalog Card No. 96-84179
4567890123 7654321098

Contents

Contents

SAFETY NOTICE

Proper service and repair procedures are vital to the safe, reliable operation of all motor vehicles, as well as the personal safety of those performing repairs. This manual outlines procedures for servicing and repairing vehicles using safe, effective methods. The procedures contain many NOTES, CAUTIONS and WARNINGS which should be followed along with standard procedures to eliminate the possibility of personal injury or improper service which could damage the vehicle or compromise its safety.

It is important to note that the repair procedures and techniques, tools and parts for servicing motor vehicles, as well as the skill and experience of the individual performing the work vary widely. It is not possible to anticipate all of the conceivable ways or conditions under which vehicles may be serviced, or to provide cautions as to all of the possible hazards that may result. Standard and accepted safety precautions and equipment should be used when handling toxic or flammable fluids, and safety goggles or other protection should be used during cutting, grinding, chiseling, prying, or any other process that can cause material removal or projectiles.

Some procedures require the use of tools specially designed for a specific purpose. Before substituting another tool or procedure, you must be completely satisfied that neither your personal safety, nor the performance of the vehicle will be endangered.

Although information in this manual is based on industry sources and is complete as possible at the time of publication, the possibility exists that some vehicle manufacturers made later changes which could not be included here. While striving for total accuracy, W. G. Nichols, Inc. cannot assume responsibility for any errors, changes or omissions that may occur in the compilation of this data.

PART NUMBERS

Part numbers listed in this reference are not recommendations by Chilton for any product by brand name. They are references that can be used with interchange manuals and aftermarket supplier catalogs to locate each brand supplier's discrete part number.

SPECIAL TOOLS

Special tools are recommended by the vehicle manufacturer to perform their specific job. Use has been kept to a minimum, but where absolutely necessary, they are referred to in the text by the part number of the tool manufacturer. These tools can be purchased, under the appropriate part number, from your local dealer or regional distributor, or an equivalent tool can be purchased locally from a tool supplier or parts outlet. Before substituting any tool for the one recommended, read the SAFETY NOTICE at the top of this page.

ACKNOWLEDGMENTS

Portions of the materials contained herein have been reprinted with the permission of General Motors Corporation, Service Technology Group.

1

ROUTINE MAINTENANCE

HOW TO USE THIS BOOK

Chilton's Repair Manual for the 1/2, 3/4 and 1 ton Chevrolet and GMC Pick-ups, Blazers, Jimmys, Tahoe, Yukons and Suburbans from 1988 to 1996, is intended to help you learn more about the inner workings of your vehicle while saving you money on its upkeep and operation.

The beginning of the book will likely be referred to the most, since that is where you will find information for maintenance and tune-up. The other sections deal with the more complex systems of your vehicle. Operating systems from engine through brakes are covered to the extent that the average do-it-yourselfer becomes mechanically involved. This book will not explain such things as rebuilding a differential for the simple reason that the expertise required and the investment in special tools make this task uneconomical. It will, however, give you detailed instructions to help you change your own brake pads and shoes, replace spark plugs, and perform many more jobs that can save you money, give you personal satisfaction and help you avoid expensive problems.

A secondary purpose of this book is a reference for owners who want to understand their vehicle and/or their mechanics better. In this case, no tools at all are required.

Where to Begin

Before removing any bolts, read through the entire procedure. This will give you the overall view of what tools and supplies will be required. There is nothing more frustrating than having to walk to the bus stop on Monday morning because you were short one bolt on Sunday afternoon. So read ahead and plan ahead. Each operation should be approached logically and all procedures thoroughly understood before attempting any work.

All sections contain adjustments, maintenance, removal and installation procedures, and in some cases, repair or overhaul procedures. When repair is not considered practical, we tell you how to remove the part and then how to install the new or rebuilt replacement. In this way, you at least save the labor costs. Backyard repair of some components is just not practical.

Avoiding Trouble

Many procedures in this book require you to "label and disconnect . . . " a group of lines, hoses or wires. Don't be lulled into thinking you can remember where everything goes — you won't. If you hook up vacuum or fuel lines incorrectly, the vehicle will run poorly, if at all. If you hook up electrical wiring incorrectly, you may instantly learn a very expensive lesson.

You don't need to know the official or engineering name for each hose or line. A piece of masking tape on the hose and a piece on its fitting will allow you to assign your own label such as the letter A or a short name. As long as you remember your own code, the lines can be reconnected by matching similar letters or names. Do remember that tape will dissolve in gasoline or other fluids; if a component is to be washed or cleaned, use another method of identification. A permanent felt-tipped marker can be very handy for marking metal parts. Remove any tape or paper labels after assembly.

Maintenance or Repair?

It's necessary to mention the difference between maintenance and repair. Maintenance includes routine inspections, adjustments, and replacement of parts which show signs of normal wear. Maintenance compensates for wear or deterioration. Repair implies that something has broken or is not working. A need for repair is often caused by lack of maintenance. Example: draining and refilling the automatic transmission fluid is maintenance recommended by the manufacturer at specific mileage intervals. Failure to do this can ruin the transmission/transaxle, requiring very expensive repairs. While no maintenance program can prevent items from breaking or wearing out, a general rule can be stated: MAINTENANCE IS CHEAPER THAN REPAIR.

Two basic mechanic's rules should be mentioned here. First, whenever the left side of the vehicle or engine is referred to, it is meant to specify the driver's side. Conversely, the right side of the vehicle means the passenger's side. Second, most screws and bolts are removed by turning counterclockwise, and tightened by turning clockwise.

Safety is always the most important rule. Constantly be aware of the dangers involved in working on an automobile and take the proper precautions. See the information in this section regarding SERVICING YOUR VEHICLE SAFELY and the SAFETY NOTICE on the acknowledgment page.

Avoiding the Most Common Mistakes

Pay attention to the instructions provided. There are 3 common mistakes in mechanical work:

1. Incorrect order of assembly, disassembly or adjustment. When taking something apart or putting it together, performing steps in the wrong order usually just costs you extra time; however, it CAN break something. Read the entire procedure before beginning disassembly. Perform everything in the order in which the instructions say you should, even if you can't immediately see a reason for it. When you're taking apart something that is very intricate, you might want to draw a picture of how it looks when assembled at one point in order to make sure you get everything back in its proper position. We will supply exploded views whenever possible. When making adjustments, perform them in the proper order; often, one adjustment affects another, and you cannot expect even satisfactory results unless each adjustment is made only when it cannot be changed by any other.

2. Overtorquing (or undertorquing). While it is more common for overtorquing to cause damage, undertorquing may allow a fastener to vibrate loose causing serious damage. Especially when dealing with aluminum parts, pay attention to torque specifications and utilize a torque wrench in assembly. If a torque figure is not available, remember that if you are using the right tool to perform the job, you will probably not have to strain yourself to get a fastener tight enough. The pitch of most threads is so slight that the tension you put on

the wrench will be multiplied many times in actual force on what you are tightening. A good example of how critical torque is can be seen in the case of spark plug installation, especially where you are putting the plug into an aluminum cylinder head. Too little torque can fail to crush the gasket, causing leakage of combustion gases and consequent overheating of the plug and engine parts. Too much torque can damage the threads or distort the plug, changing the spark gap.

There are many commercial products available for ensuring that fasteners won't come loose, even if they are not torqued just right (a very common brand is Loctite®). If you're worried about getting something together tight enough to hold, but loose enough to avoid mechanical damage during assembly, one of these products might offer substantial insurance. Before choosing a threadlocking compound, read the label on the package and make sure the product is compatible with the materials, fluids, etc. involved.

3. Crossthreading. This occurs when a part such as a bolt is screwed into a nut or casting at the wrong angle and forced. Crossthreading is more likely to occur if access is difficult. It helps to clean and lubricate fasteners, then to start threading with the part to be installed positioned straight in. Then, start the bolt, spark plug, etc. with your fingers. If you encounter resistance, unscrew the part and start over again at a different angle until it can be inserted and turned several times without much effort. Keep in mind that many parts, especially spark plugs, have tapered threads, so that gentle turning will automatically bring the part you're threading to the proper angle, but only if you don't force it or resist a change in angle. Don't put a wrench on the part until it's been tightened a couple of turns by hand. If you suddenly encounter resistance, and the part has not seated fully, don't force it. Pull it back out to make sure it's clean and threading properly.

Always take your time and be patient; once you have some experience, working on your vehicle may well become an enjoyable hobby.

TOOLS AND EQUIPMENT

See Figures 1, 2, 3, 4, 5, 6, 7, 8, 9, 10, 11, 12, 13 and 14

Naturally, without the proper tools and equipment it is impossible to properly service your vehicle. It would also be virtually impossible to catalog every tool that you would need to perform all of the operations in this book. Of course, It would be unwise for the amateur to rush out and buy an expensive set of tools on the theory that he/she may need one or more of them at some time.

The best approach is to proceed slowly, gathering a good quality set of those tools that are used most frequently. Don't be misled by the low cost of bargain tools. It is far better to spend a little more for better quality. Forged wrenches, 6 or 12-point sockets and fine tooth ratchets are by far preferable to their less expensive counterparts. As any good mechanic can tell you, there are few worse experiences than trying to work on a vehicle with bad tools. Your monetary savings will be far outweighed by frustration and mangled knuckles.

Begin accumulating those tools that are used most frequently: those associated with routine maintenance and tune-up. In addition to the normal assortment of screwdrivers and pliers, you should have the following tools:

- Wrenches/sockets and combination open end/box end wrenches in sizes from $1/8$-$3/4$ in. or 3mm-19mm (depending on whether your vehicle uses standard or metric fasteners) and a $13/16$ in. or $5/8$ in. spark plug socket (depending on plug type).

➡If possible, buy various length socket drive extensions. Universal-joint and wobble extensions can be extremely useful, but be careful when using them, as they can change the amount of torque applied to the socket.

- Jackstands for support.
- Oil filter wrench.
- Spout or funnel for pouring fluids.
- Grease gun for chassis lubrication (unless your vehicle is not equipped with any grease fittings — for details, please refer to information on Fluids and Lubricants found later in this section).
- Hydrometer for checking the battery (unless equipped with a sealed, maintenance-free battery).
- A container for draining oil and other fluids.
- Rags for wiping up the inevitable mess.

In addition to the above items there are several others that are not absolutely necessary, but handy to have around. These include Oil Dry® (or an equivalent oil absorbent gravel — such as cat litter) and the usual supply of lubricants, antifreeze and fluids, although these can be purchased as needed. This is a basic list for routine maintenance, but only your personal needs and desire can accurately determine your list of tools.

After performing a few projects on the vehicle, you'll be amazed at the other tools and non-tools on your workbench. Some useful household items are: a large turkey baster or siphon, empty coffee cans and ice trays (to store parts), ball of twine, electrical tape for wiring, small rolls of colored tape for tagging lines or hoses, markers and pens, a note pad, golf tees (for plugging vacuum lines), metal coat hangers or a roll

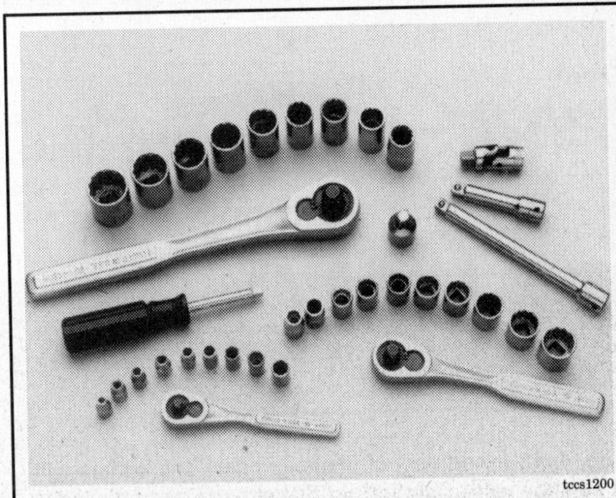

Fig. 1 All but the most basic procedures will require an assortment of ratchets and sockets

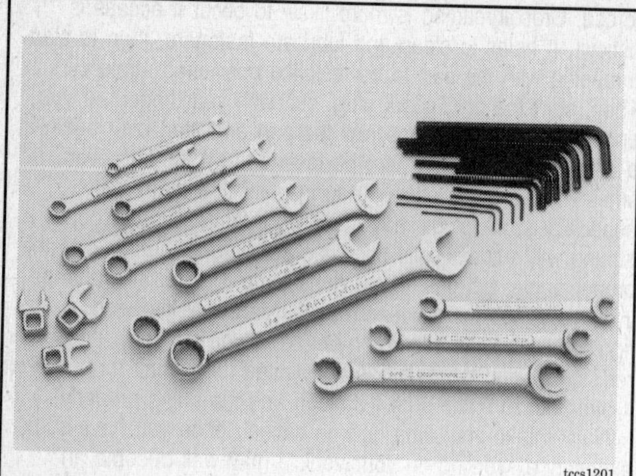

Fig. 2 In addition to ratchets, a good set of wrenches and hex keys will be necessary

Fig. 3 A hydraulic floor jack and a set of jackstands are essential for lifting and supporting the vehicle

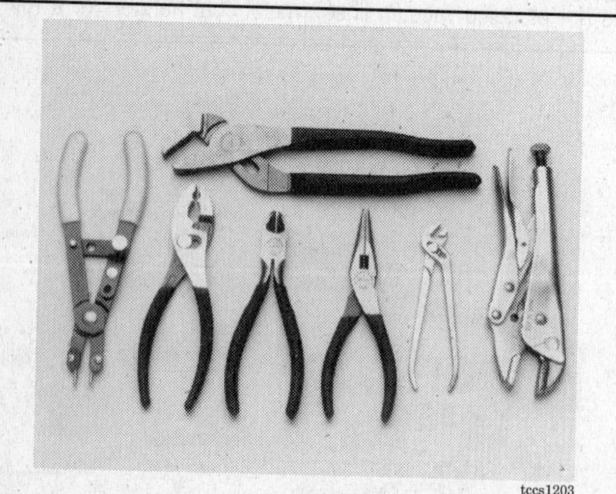

Fig. 4 An assortment of pliers, grippers and cutters will be handy, especially for old rusted parts and stripped bolt heads

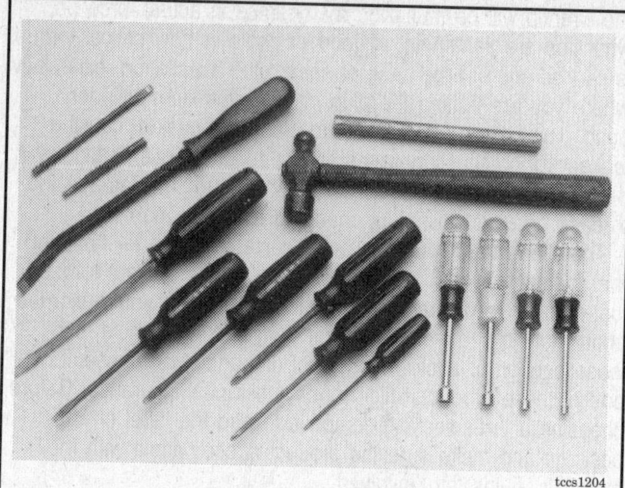

Fig. 5 Various drivers, chisels and prybars are great tools to have in your toolbox

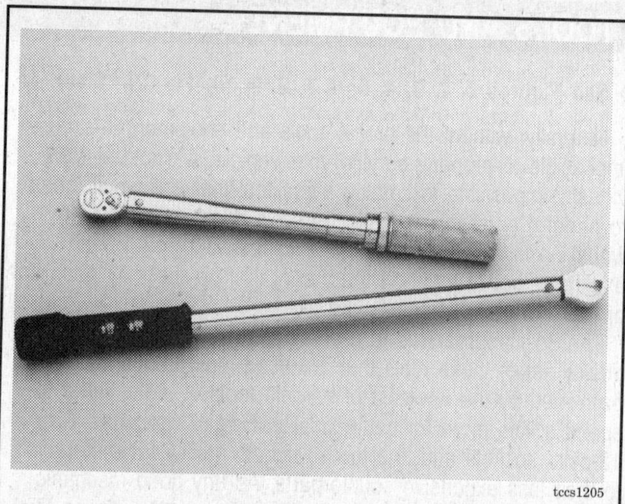

Fig. 6 Many repairs will require the use of a torque wrench to assure the components are properly fastened

of mechanics's wire (to hold things out of the way), dental pick or similar long, pointed probe, a strong magnet, and a small mirror (to see into recesses and under manifolds).

A more advanced set of tools, suitable for tune-up work, can be drawn up easily. While the tools are slightly more sophisticated, they need not be outrageously expensive. There are several inexpensive tach/dwell meters on the market that are every bit as good for the average mechanic as a professional model. Just be sure that it goes to a least 1200-1500 rpm on the tach scale and that it works on 4, 6 and 8-cylinder engines. (If you have one or more vehicles with a diesel engine, a special tachometer is required since diesels don't use spark plug ignition systems). The key to these purchases is to make them with an eye towards adaptability and wide range. A basic list of tune-up tools could include:

- Tach/dwell meter.
- Spark plug wrench and gapping tool.
- Feeler gauges for valve or point adjustment. (Even if your vehicle does not use points or require valve adjustments, a feeler gauge is helpful for many repair/overhaul procedures).

tccs1209

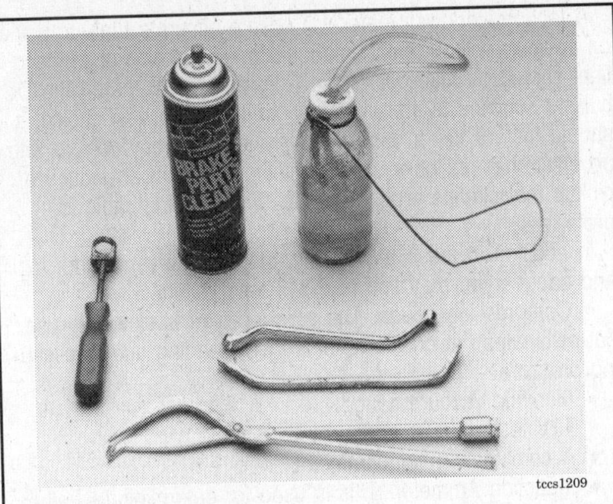

Fig. 7 Although not always necessary, using specialized brake tools will save time

tccs1210

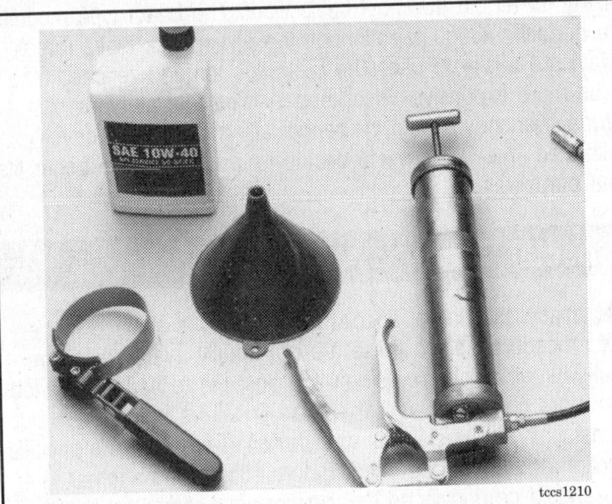

Fig. 8 A few inexpensive lubrication tools will make maintenance easier

tccs1211

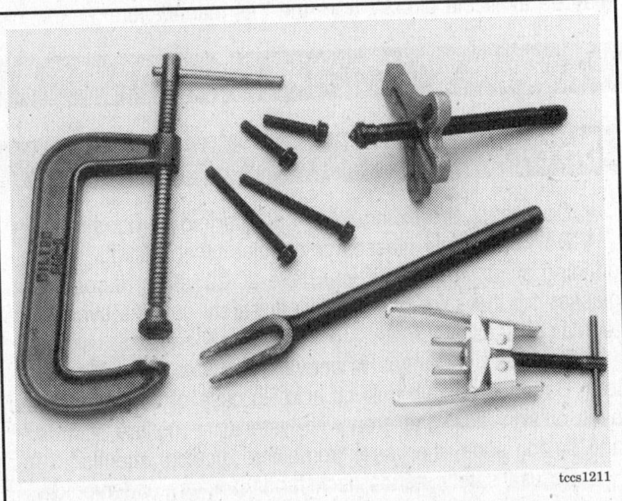

Fig. 9 Various pullers, clamps and separator tools are needed for many larger, more complicated repairs

tccs1212

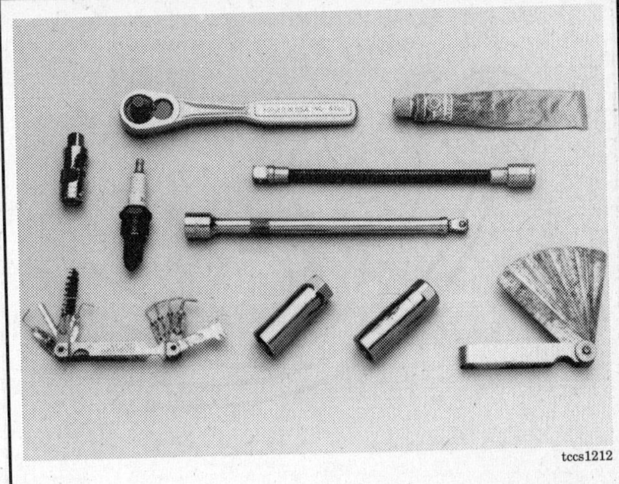

Fig. 10 A variety of tools and gauges should be used for spark plug gapping and installation

tccs1001

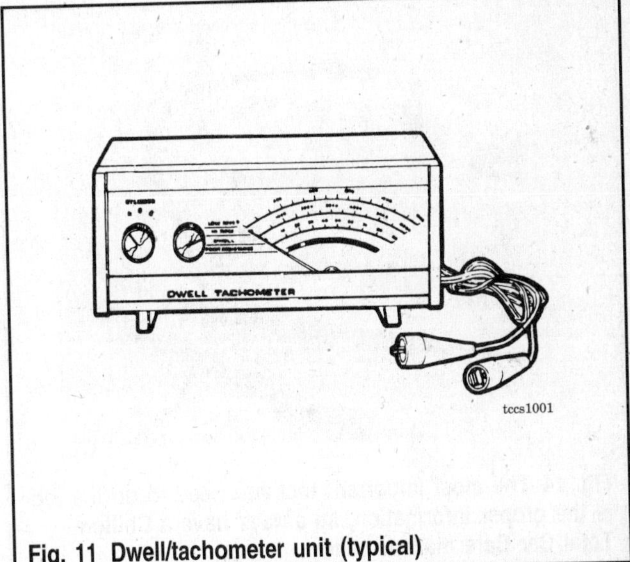

Fig. 11 Dwell/tachometer unit (typical)

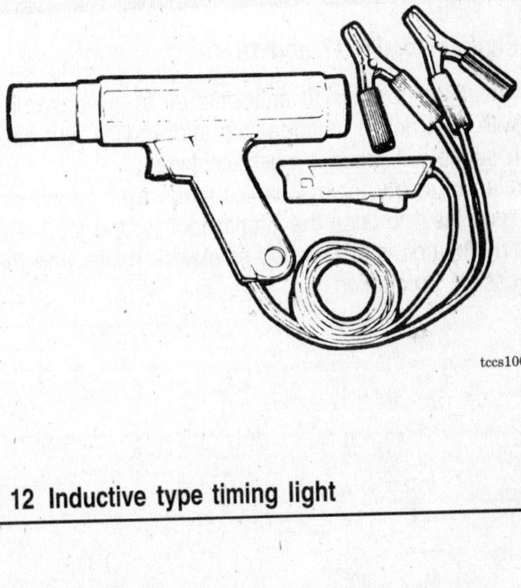

tccs1002

Fig. 12 Inductive type timing light

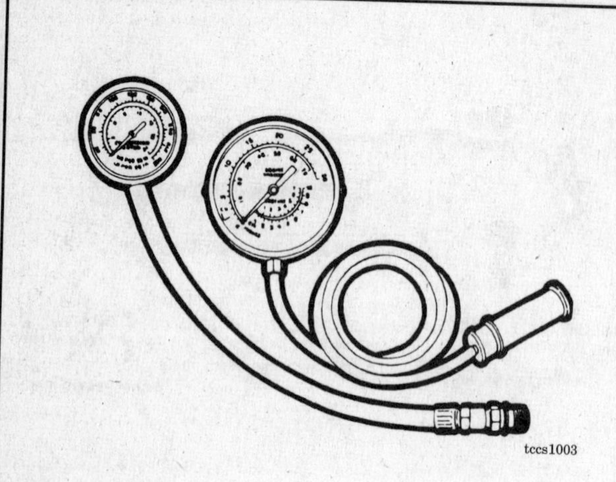

Fig. 13 Compression gauge and a combination vacuum/fuel pressure test gauge

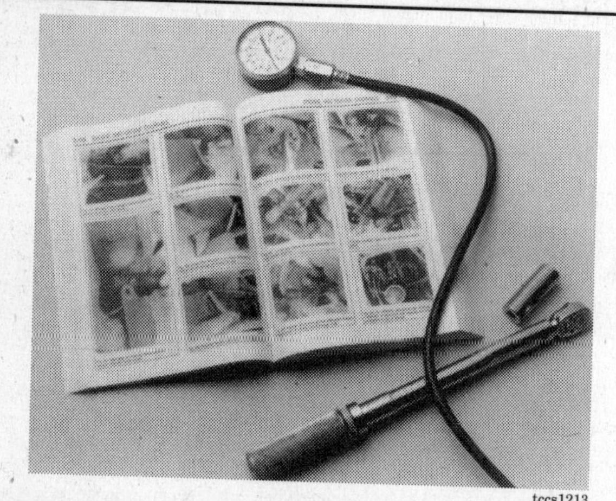

Fig. 14 The most important tool you need to do the job is the proper information, so always have a Chilton Total Car Care manual handy

A tachometer/dwell meter will ensure accurate tune-up work on vehicles without electronic ignition. The choice of a timing light should be made carefully. A light which works on the DC current supplied by the vehicle's battery is the best choice; it should have a xenon tube for brightness. On any vehicle with an electronic ignition system, a timing light with an inductive pickup that clamps around the No. 1 spark plug cable is preferred.

In addition to these basic tools, there are several other tools and gauges you may find useful. These include:

- Compression gauge. The screw-in type is slower to use, but eliminates the possibility of a faulty reading due to escaping pressure.
- Manifold vacuum gauge.
- 12V test light.
- A combination volt/ohmmeter
- Induction Ammeter. This is used for determining whether or not there is current in a wire. These are handy for use if a wire is broken somewhere in a wiring harness.

As a final note, you will probably find a torque wrench necessary for all but the most basic work. The beam type models are perfectly adequate, although the newer click types (breakaway) are easier to use. The click type torque wrenches tend to be more expensive. Also keep in mind that all types of torque wrenches should be periodically checked and/or recalibrated. You will have to decide for yourself which better fits your purpose.

Special Tools

Normally, the use of special factory tools is avoided for repair procedures, since these are not readily available for the do-it-yourself mechanic. When it is possible to perform the job with more commonly available tools, it will be pointed out, but occasionally, a special tool was designed to perform a specific function and should be used. Before substituting another tool, you should be convinced that neither your safety nor the performance of the vehicle will be compromised.

Special tools can usually be purchased from an automotive parts store or from your dealer. In some cases special tools may be available directly from the tool manufacturer.

SERVICING YOUR VEHICLE SAFELY

➧ **See Figures 15, 16, 17 and 18**

It is virtually impossible to anticipate all of the hazards involved with automotive maintenance and service, but care and common sense will prevent most accidents.

The rules of safety for mechanics range from "don't smoke around gasoline," to "use the proper tool for the job." The trick to avoiding injuries is to develop safe work habits and to take every possible precaution.

Do's

- Do keep a fire extinguisher and first aid kit handy.
- Do wear safety glasses or goggles when cutting, drilling, grinding or prying, even if you have 20-20 vision. If you wear glasses for the sake of vision, wear safety goggles over your regular glasses.
- Do shield your eyes whenever you work around the battery. Batteries contain sulfuric acid. In case of contact with the eyes or skin, flush the area with water or a mixture of water and baking soda, then seek immediate medical attention.
- Do use safety stands (jackstands) for any undervehicle service. Jacks are for raising vehicles; jackstands are for making sure the vehicle stays raised until you want it to come down. Whenever the vehicle is raised, block the wheels remaining on the ground and set the parking brake.

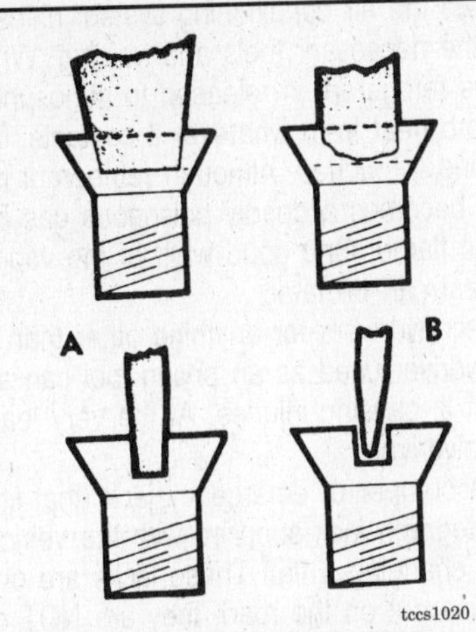

Fig. 15 Screwdrivers should be kept in good condition to prevent injury or damage which could result if the blade slips from the screw

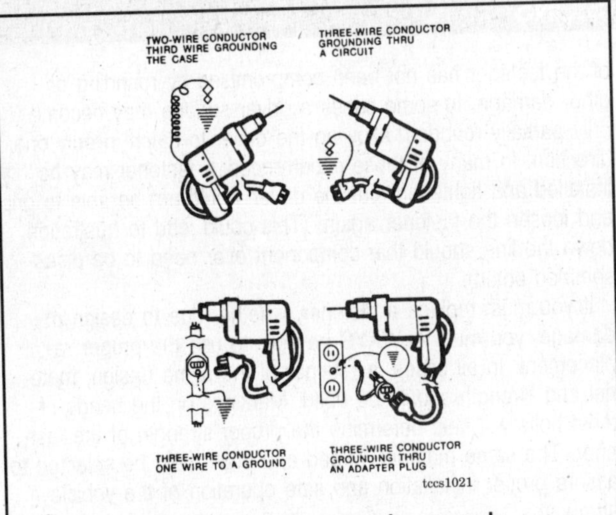

Fig. 16 Power tools should always be properly grounded

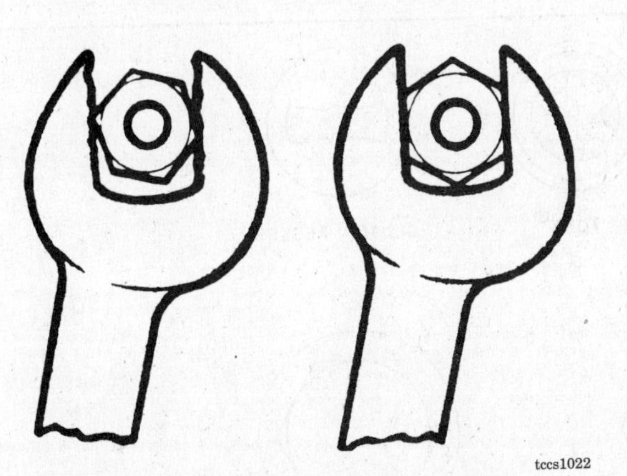

Fig. 17 Using the correct size wrench will help prevent the possibility of rounding-off a nut

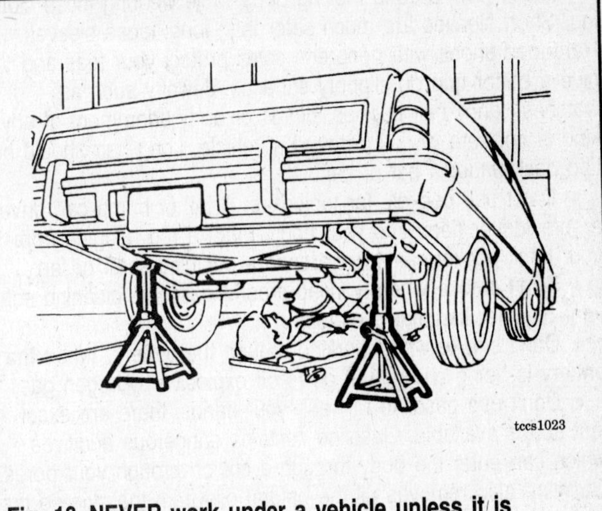

Fig. 18 NEVER work under a vehicle unless it is supported using safety stands (jackstands)

• Do use adequate ventilation when working with any chemicals or hazardous materials. Like carbon monoxide, the asbestos dust resulting from some brake lining wear can be hazardous in sufficient quantities.

• Do disconnect the negative battery cable when working on the electrical system. The secondary ignition system contains EXTREMELY HIGH VOLTAGE. In some cases it can even exceed 50,000 volts.

• Do follow manufacturer's directions whenever working with potentially hazardous materials. Most chemicals and fluids are poisonous if taken internally.

• Do properly maintain your tools. Loose hammerheads, mushroomed punches and chisels, frayed or poorly grounded electrical cords, excessively worn screwdrivers, spread wrenches (open end), cracked sockets, slipping ratchets, or faulty droplight sockets can cause accidents.

• Likewise, keep your tools clean; a greasy wrench can slip off a bolt head, ruining the bolt and often harming your knuckles in the process.

• Do use the proper size and type of tool for the job at hand. Do select a wrench or socket that fits the nut or bolt. The wrench or socket should sit straight, not cocked.

• Do, when possible, pull on a wrench handle rather than push on it, and adjust your stance to prevent a fall.

• Do be sure that adjustable wrenches are tightly closed on the nut or bolt and pulled so that the force is on the side of the fixed jaw.

• Do strike squarely with a hammer; avoid glancing blows.

• Do set the parking brake and block the drive wheels if the work requires a running engine.

Don'ts

• Don't run the engine in a garage or anywhere else without proper ventilation — EVER! Carbon monoxide is poisonous; it takes a long time to leave the human body and you can build up a deadly supply of it in your system by simply breathing in a little every day. You may not realize you are slowly poisoning yourself. Always use power vents, windows, fans and/or open the garage door.

• Don't work around moving parts while wearing loose clothing. Short sleeves are much safer than long, loose sleeves. Hard-toed shoes with neoprene soles protect your toes and give a better grip on slippery surfaces. Jewelry such as watches, fancy belt buckles, beads or body adornment of any kind is not safe working around a vehicle. Long hair should be tied back under a hat or cap.

• Don't use pockets for toolboxes. A fall or bump can drive a screwdriver deep into your body. Even a rag hanging from your back pocket can wrap around a spinning shaft or fan.

• Don't smoke when working around gasoline, cleaning solvent or other flammable material.

• Don't smoke when working around the battery. When the battery is being charged, it gives off explosive hydrogen gas.

• Don't use gasoline to wash your hands; there are excellent soaps available. Gasoline contains dangerous additives which can enter the body through a cut or through your pores. Gasoline also removes all the natural oils from the skin so that bone dry hands will suck up oil and grease.

• Don't service the air conditioning system unless you are equipped with the necessary tools and training. When liquid or compressed gas refrigerant is released to atmospheric pressure it will absorb heat from whatever it contacts. This will chill or freeze anything it touches. Although refrigerant is normally non-toxic, R-12 becomes a deadly poisonous gas in the presence of an open flame. One good whiff of the vapors from burning refrigerant can be fatal.

• Don't use screwdrivers for anything other than driving screws! A screwdriver used as an prying tool can snap when you least expect it, causing injuries. At the very least, you'll ruin a good screwdriver.

• Don't use a bumper or emergency jack (that little ratchet, scissors, or pantograph jack supplied with the vehicle) for anything other than changing a flat! These jacks are only intended for emergency use out on the road; they are NOT designed as a maintenance tool. If you are serious about maintaining your vehicle yourself, invest in a hydraulic floor jack of at least a 1½ ton capacity, and at least two sturdy jackstands.

FASTENERS, MEASUREMENTS AND CONVERSIONS

Bolts, Nuts and Other Threaded Retainers

➧ See Figures 19, 20, 21 and 22

Although there are a great variety of fasteners found in the modern car or truck, the most commonly used retainer is the threaded fastener (nuts, bolts, screws, studs, etc). Most threaded retainers may be reused, provided that they are not damaged in use or during the repair. Some retainers (such as stretch bolts or torque prevailing nuts) are designed to deform when tightened or in use and should not be reinstalled.

Whenever possible, we will note any special retainers which should be replaced during a procedure. But you should always inspect the condition of a retainer when it is removed and replace any that show signs of damage. Check all threads for rust or corrosion which can increase the torque necessary to achieve the desired clamp load for which that fastener was originally selected. Additionally, be sure that the driver surface of the fastener has not been compromised by rounding or other damage. In some cases a driver surface may become only partially rounded, allowing the driver to catch in only one direction. In many of these occurrences, a fastener may be installed and tightened, but the driver would not be able to grip and loosen the fastener again. (This could lead to frustration down the line should that component ever need to be disassembled again).

If you must replace a fastener, whether due to design or damage, you must ALWAYS be sure to use the proper replacement. In all cases, a retainer of the same design, material and strength should be used. Markings on the heads of most bolts will help determine the proper strength of the fastener. The same material, thread and pitch must be selected to assure proper installation and safe operation of the vehicle afterwards.

Thread gauges are available to help measure a bolt or stud's thread. Most automotive and hardware stores keep gauges available to help you select the proper size. In a pinch,

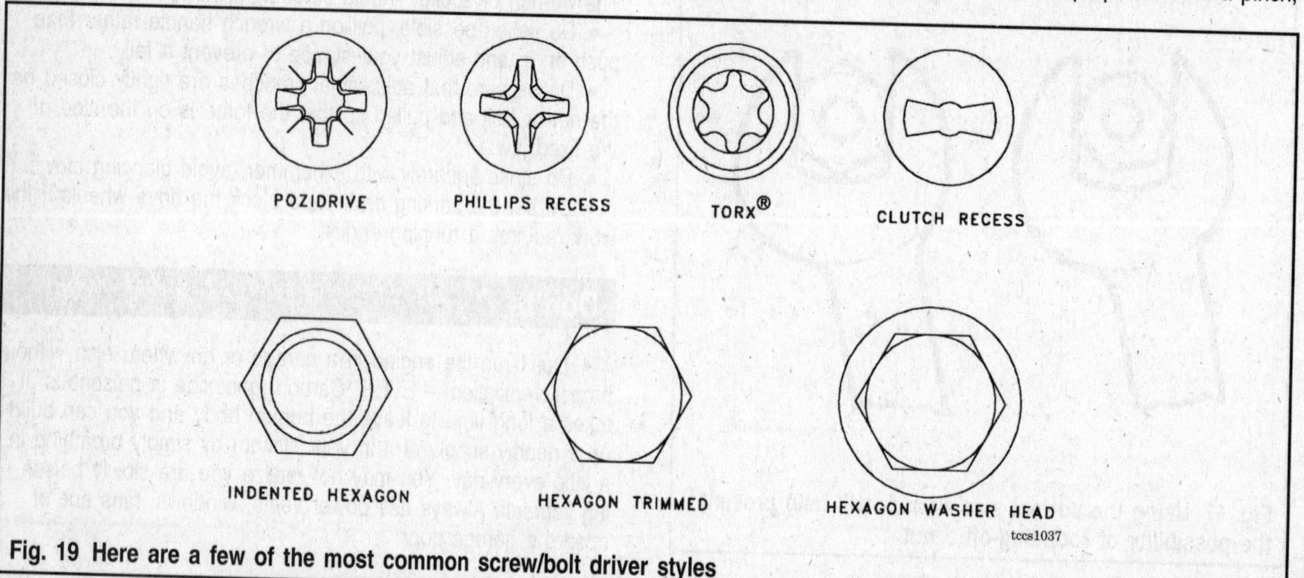

Fig. 19 Here are a few of the most common screw/bolt driver styles

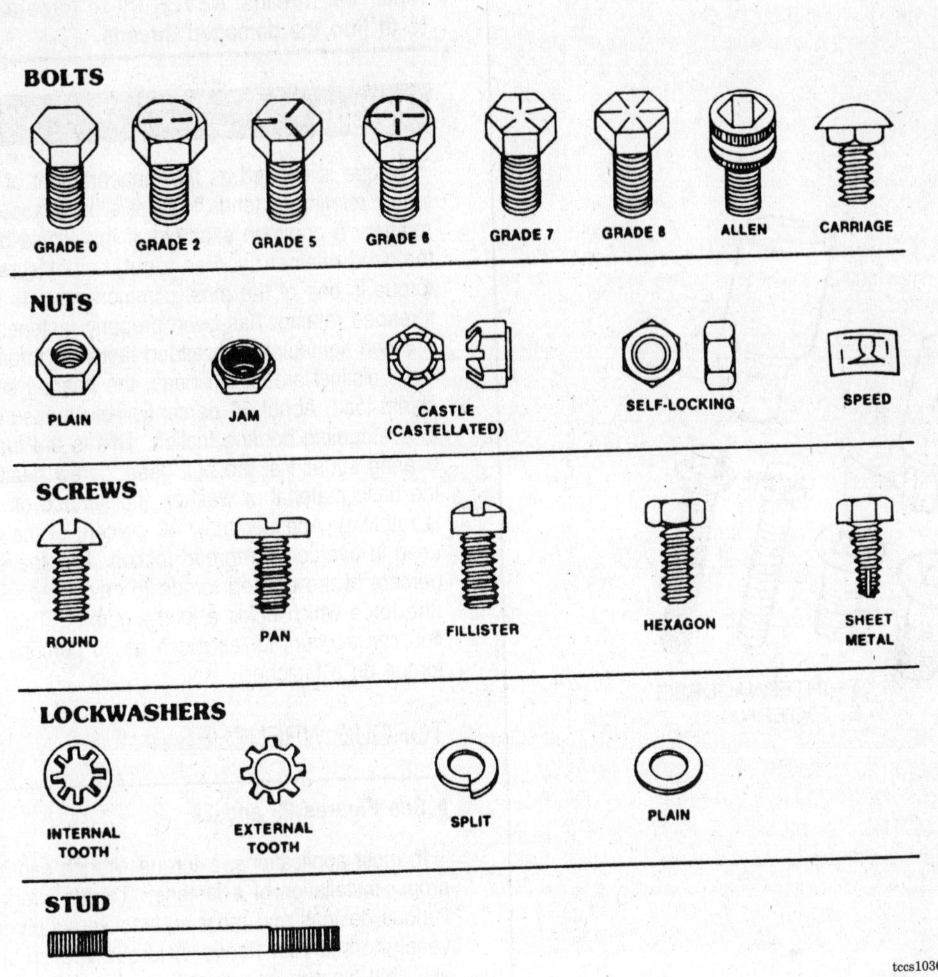

Fig. 20 There are many different types of threaded retainers found on vehicles

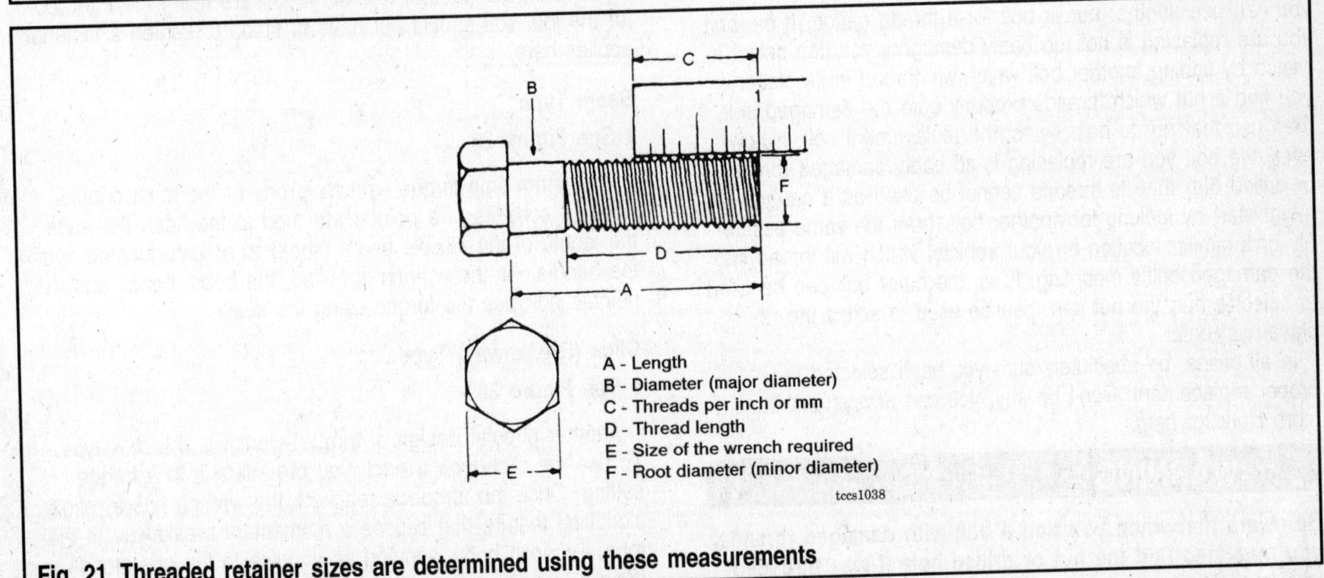

Fig. 21 Threaded retainer sizes are determined using these measurements

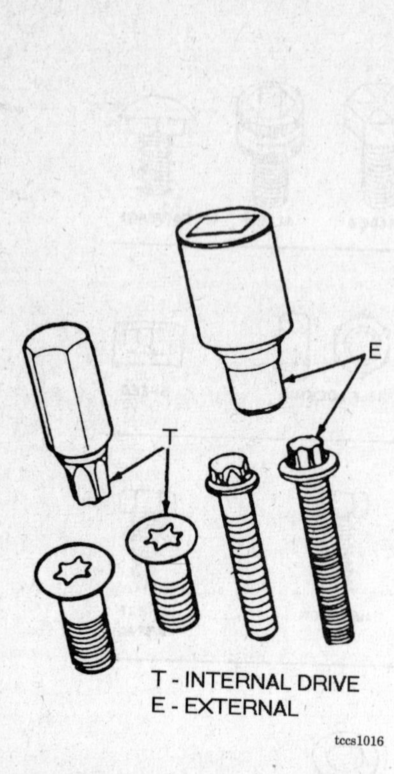

Fig. 22 Special fasteners such as these Torx® head bolts are used by manufacturers to discourage people from working on vehicles without the proper tools

you can use another nut or bolt for a thread gauge. If the bolt you are replacing is not too badly damaged, you can select a match by finding another bolt which will thread in its place. If you find a nut which threads properly onto the damaged bolt, then use that nut to help select the replacement bolt. If however, the bolt you are replacing is so badly damaged (broken or drilled out) that its threads cannot be used as a gauge, you might start by looking for another bolt (from the same assembly or a similar location on your vehicle) which will thread into the damaged bolt's mounting. If so, the other bolt can be used to select a nut; the nut can then be used to select the replacement bolt.

In all cases, be absolutely sure you have selected the proper replacement. Don't be shy, you can always ask the store clerk for help.

WARNING

Be aware that when you find a bolt with damaged threads, you may also find the nut or drilled hole it was threaded into has also been damaged. If this is the case, you may have to drill and tap the hole, replace the nut or otherwise repair the threads. NEVER try to force a replacement bolt to fit into the damaged threads.

Torque

Torque is defined as the measurement of resistance to turning or rotating. It tends to twist a body about an axis of rotation. A common example of this would be tightening a threaded retainer such as a nut, bolt or screw. Measuring torque is one of the most common ways to help assure that a threaded retainer has been properly fastened.

When tightening a threaded fastener, torque is applied in three distinct areas, the head, the bearing surface and the clamp load. About 50 percent of the measured torque is used in overcoming bearing friction. This is the friction between the bearing surface of the bolt head, screw head or nut face and the base material or washer (the surface on which the fastener is rotating). Approximately 40 percent of the applied torque is used in overcoming thread friction. This leaves only about 10 percent of the applied torque to develop a useful clamp load (the force which holds a joint together). This means that friction can account for as much as 90 percent of the applied torque on a fastener.

TORQUE WRENCHES

See Figures 23 and 24

In most applications, a torque wrench can be used to assure proper installation of a fastener. Torque wrenches come in various designs and most automotive supply stores will carry a variety to suit your needs. A torque wrench should be used any time we supply a specific torque value for a fastener. A torque wrench can also be used if you are following the general guidelines in the accompanying charts. Keep in mind that because there is no worldwide standardization of fasteners, the charts are a general guideline and should be used with caution. Again, the general rule of "if you are using the right tool for the job, you should not have to strain to tighten a fastener" applies here.

Beam Type

See Figure 25

The beam type torque wrench is one of the most popular types. It consists of a pointer attached to the head that runs the length of the flexible beam (shaft) to a scale located near the handle. As the wrench is pulled, the beam bends and the pointer indicates the torque using the scale.

Click (Breakaway) Type

See Figure 26

Another popular design of torque wrench is the click type. To use the click type wrench you pre-adjust it to a torque setting. Once the torque is reached, the wrench has a reflex signalling feature that causes a momentary breakaway of the torque wrench body, sending an impulse to the operator's hand.

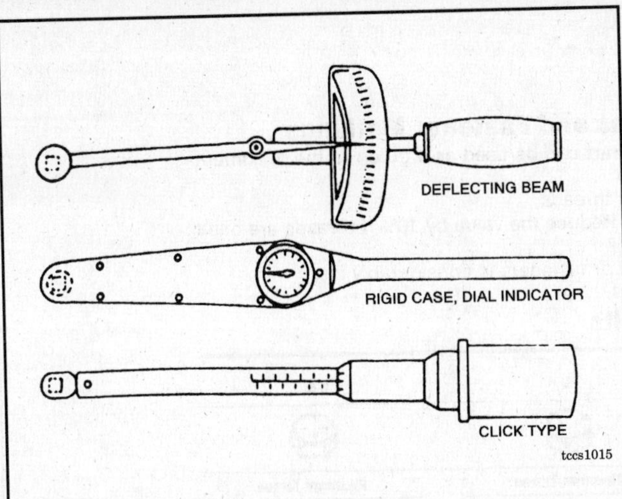

Fig. 23 Various styles of torque wrenches are usually available at your local automotive supply store

Pivot Head Type

➧ See Figures 26 and 27

Some torque wrenches (usually of the click type) may be equipped with a pivot head which can allow it to be used in areas of limited access. BUT, it must be used properly. To hold a pivot head wrench, grasp the handle lightly, and as you pull on the handle, it should be floated on the pivot point. If the handle comes in contact with the yoke extension during the process of pulling, there is a very good chance the torque readings will be inaccurate because this could alter the wrench loading point. The design of the handle is usually such as to make it inconvenient to deliberately misuse the wrench.

➡It should be mentioned that the use of any U-joint, wobble or extension will have an effect on the torque readings, no matter what type of wrench you are using. For the most accurate readings, install the socket directly on the wrench driver. If necessary, straight extensions (which hold a socket directly under the wrench driver) will have the least effect on the torque reading. Avoid any extension that alters the length of the wrench from the handle to the head/driving point (such as a crow's foot). U-joint or Wobble extensions can greatly affect the readings; avoid their use at all times.

Rigid Case (Direct Reading)

➧ See Figure 28

A rigid case or direct reading torque wrench is equipped with a dial indicator to show torque values. One advantage of these wrenches is that they can be held at any position on the wrench without affecting accuracy. These wrenches are often preferred because they tend to be compact, easy to read and have a great degree of accuracy.

TORQUE ANGLE METERS

➧ See Figure 29

Because the frictional characteristics of each fastener or threaded hole will vary, clamp loads which are based strictly on torque will vary as well. In most applications, this variance is not significant enough to cause worry. But, in certain applications, a manufacturer's engineers may determine that more precise clamp loads are necessary (such is the case with many aluminum cylinder heads). In these cases, a torque angle method of installation would be specified. When installing fasteners which are torque angle tightened, a predetermined seating torque and standard torque wrench are usually used first to remove any compliance from the joint. The fastener is then tightened the specified additional portion of a turn measured in degrees. A torque angle gauge (mechanical protractor) is used for these applications.

Standard and Metric Measurements

Throughout this manual, specifications are given to help you determine the condition of various components on your vehicle, or to assist you in their installation. Some of the most common measurements include length (in. or cm/mm), torque (ft. lbs., inch lbs. or Nm) and pressure (psi, in. Hg, kPa or mm Hg). In most cases, we strive to provide the proper measurement as determined by the manufacturer's engineers.

Though, in some cases, that value may not be conveniently measured with what is available in your toolbox. Luckily, many of the measuring devices which are available today will have two scales so the Standard or Metric measurements may easily be taken. If any of the various measuring tools which are available to you do not contain the same scale as listed in the specifications, use the accompanying conversion factors to determine the proper value.

The conversion factor chart is used by taking the given specification and multiplying it by the necessary conversion factor. For instance, looking at the first line, if you have a measurement in inches such as "free-play should be 2 in." but your ruler reads only in millimeters, multiply 2 in. by the conversion factor of 25.4 to get the metric equivalent of 50.8mm. Likewise, if the specification was given only in a Metric measurement, for example in Newton Meters (Nm), then look at the center column first. If the measurement is 100 Nm, multiply it by the conversion factor of 0.738 to get 73.8 ft. lbs.

Standard Torque Specifications and Fastener Markings

In the absence of specific torques, the following chart can be used as a guide to the maximum safe torque of a particular size/grade of fastener.

- There is no torque difference for fine or coarse threads.
- Torque values are based on clean, dry threads. Reduce the value by 10% if threads are oiled prior to assembly.
- The torque required for aluminum components or fasteners is considerably less.

U.S. Bolts

SAE Grade Number / Number of lines always 2 less than the grade number.	1 or 2			5			6 or 7		
	Maximum Torque			Maximum Torque			Maximum Torque		
Bolt Size (Inches)—(Thread)	**Ft./Lbs.**	**Kgm**	**Nm**	**Ft./Lbs.**	**Kgm**	**Nm**	**Ft./Lbs.**	**Kgm**	**Nm**
¼—20	5	0.7	6.8	8	1.1	10.8	10	1.4	13.5
—28	6	0.8	8.1	10	1.4	13.6			
5/16—18	11	1.5	14.9	17	2.3	23.0	19	2.6	25.8
—24	13	1.8	17.6	19	2.6	25.7			
⅜—16	18	2.5	24.4	31	4.3	42.0	34	4.7	46.0
—24	20	2.75	27.1	35	4.8	47.5			
7/16—14	28	3.8	37.0	49	6.8	66.4	55	7.6	74.5
—20	30	4.2	40.7	55	7.6	74.5			
½—13	39	5.4	52.8	75	10.4	101.7	85	11.75	115.2
—20	41	5.7	55.6	85	11.7	115.2			
9/16—12	51	7.0	69.2	110	15.2	149.1	120	16.6	162.7
—18	55	7.6	74.5	120	16.6	162.7			
⅝—11	83	11.5	112.5	150	20.7	203.3	167	23.0	226.5
—18	95	13.1	128.8	170	23.5	230.5			
¾—10	105	14.5	142.3	270	37.3	366.0	280	38.7	379.6
—16	115	15.9	155.9	295	40.8	400.0			
⅞— 9	160	22.1	216.9	395	54.6	535.5	440	60.9	596.5
—14	175	24.2	237.2	435	60.1	589.7			
1— 8	236	32.5	318.6	590	81.6	799.9	660	91.3	894.8
—14	250	34.6	338.9	660	91.3	849.8			

Metric Bolts

Relative Strength Marking / Bolt Markings	4.6, 4.8			8.8		
	Maximum Torque			Maximum Torque		
Bolt Size Thread Size x Pitch (mm)	**Ft./Lbs.**	**Kgm**	**Nm**	**Ft./Lbs.**	**Kgm**	**Nm**
6 x 1.0	2–3	.2–.4	3–4	3–6	4–.8	5–8
8 x 1.25	6–8	.8–1	8–12	9–14	1.2–1.9	13–19
10 x 1.25	12–17	1.5–2.3	16–23	20–29	2.7–4.0	27–39
12 x 1.25	21–32	2.9–4.4	29–43	35–53	4.8–7.3	47–72
14 x 1.5	35–52	4.8–7.1	48–70	57–85	7.8–11.7	77–110
16 x 1.5	51–77	7.0–10.6	67–100	90–120	12.4–16.5	130–160
18 x 1.5	74–110	10.2–15.1	100–150	130–170	17.9–23.4	180–230
20 x 1.5	110–140	15.1–19.3	150–190	190–240	26.2–46.9	160–320
22 x 1.5	150–190	22.0–26.2	200–260	250–320	34.5–44.1	340–430
24 x 1.5	190–240	26.2–46.9	260–320	310–410	42.7–56.5	420–550

tccs1098

Fig. 24 Standard and metric bolt torque specifications based on bolt strengths — WARNING: use only as a guide

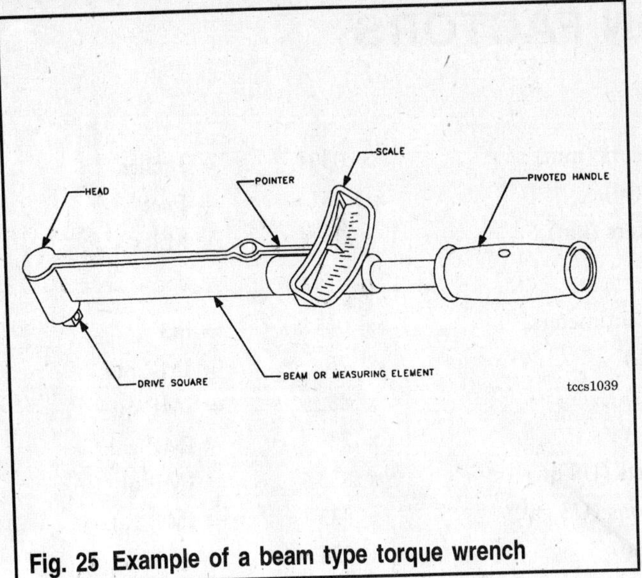

Fig. 25 Example of a beam type torque wrench

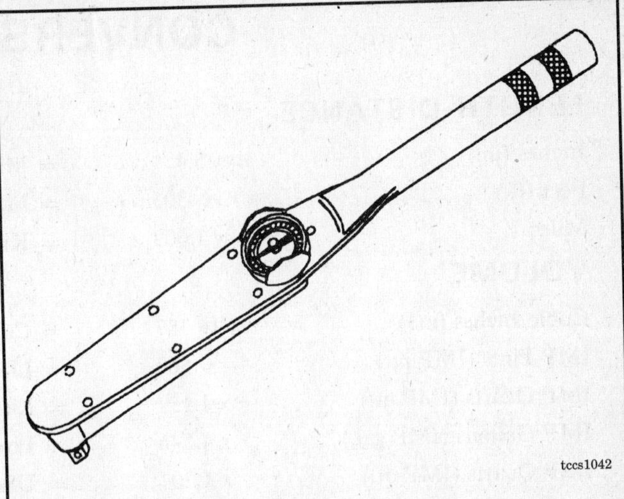

Fig. 28 The rigid case (direct reading) torque wrench uses a dial indicator to show torque

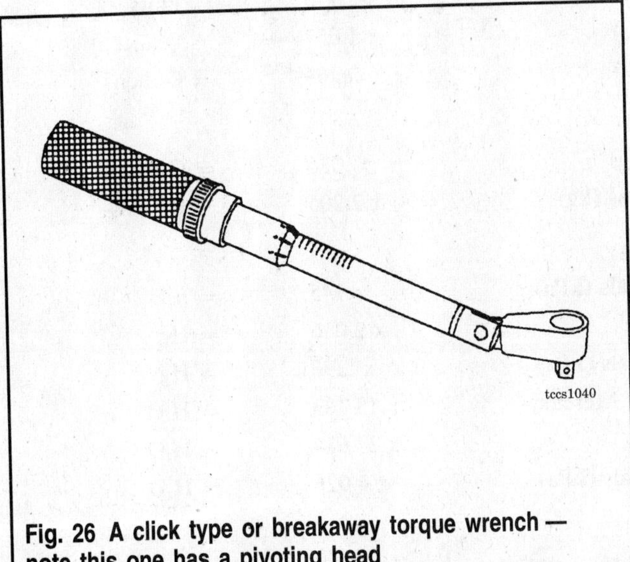

Fig. 26 A click type or breakaway torque wrench — note this one has a pivoting head

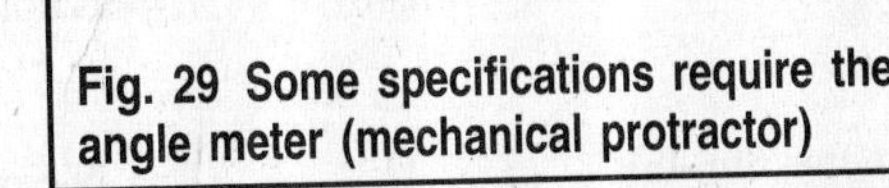

Fig. 29 Some specifications require the use of a torque angle meter (mechanical protractor)

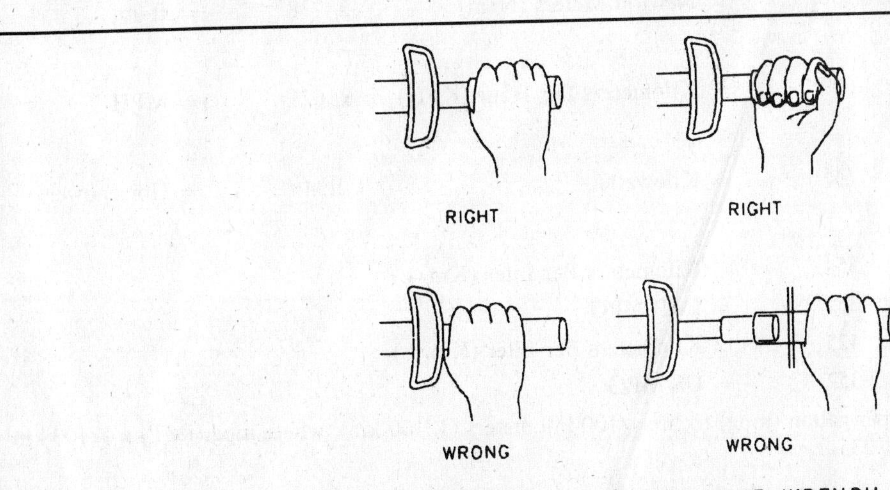

Fig. 27 Torque wrenches with pivoting heads must be grasped and used properly to prevent an incorrect reading

CONVERSION FACTORS

LENGTH–DISTANCE

Inches (in.)	x 25.4	= Millimeters (mm)	x .0394	= Inches
Feet (ft.)	x .305	= Meters (m)	x 3.281	= Feet
Miles	x 1.609	= Kilometers (km)	x .0621	= Miles

VOLUME

Cubic Inches (in3)	x 16.387	= Cubic Centimeters	x .061	= in3
IMP Pints (IMP pt.)	x .568	= Liters (L)	x 1.76	= IMP pt.
IMP Quarts (IMP qt.)	x 1.137	= Liters (L)	x .88	= IMP qt.
IMP Gallons (IMP gal.)	x 4.546	= Liters (L)	x .22	= IMP gal.
IMP Quarts (IMP qt.)	x 1.201	= US Quarts (US qt.)	x .833	= IMP qt.
IMP Gallons (IMP gal.)	x 1.201	= US Gallons (US gal.)	x .833	= IMP gal.
Fl. Ounces	x 29.573	= Milliliters	x .034	= Ounces
US Pints (US pt.)	x .473	= Liters (L)	x 2.113	= Pints
US Quarts (US qt.)	x .946	= Liters (L)	x 1.057	= Quarts
US Gallons (US gal.)	x 3.785	= Liters (L)	x .264	= Gallons

MASS–WEIGHT

Ounces (oz.)	x 28.35	= Grams (g)	x .035	= Ounces
Pounds (lb.)	x .454	= Kilograms (kg)	x 2.205	= Pounds

PRESSURE

Pounds Per Sq. In. (psi)	x 6.895	= Kilopascals (kPa)	x .145	= psi
Inches of Mercury (Hg)	x .4912	= psi	x 2.036	= Hg
Inches of Mercury (Hg)	x 3.377	= Kilopascals (kPa)	x .2961	= Hg
Inches of Water (H_2O)	x .07355	= Inches of Mercury	x 13.783	= H_2O
Inches of Water (H_2O)	x .03613	= psi	x 27.684	= H_2O
Inches of Water (H_2O)	x .248	= Kilopascals (kPa)	x 4.026	= H_2O

TORQUE

Pounds–Force Inches (in–lb)	x .113	= Newton Meters (N·m)	x 8.85	= in–lb
Pounds–Force Feet (ft–lb)	x 1.356	= Newton Meters (N·m)	x .738	= ft–lb

VELOCITY

Miles Per Hour (MPH)	x 1.609	= Kilometers Per Hour (KPH)	x .621	= MPH

POWER

Horsepower (Hp)	x .745	= Kilowatts	x 1.34	= Horsepower

FUEL CONSUMPTION*

Miles Per Gallon IMP (MPG)	x .354	= Kilometers Per Liter (Km/L)
Kilometers Per Liter (Km/L)	x 2.352	= IMP MPG
Miles Per Gallon US (MPG)	x .425	= Kilometers Per Liter (Km/L)
Kilometers Per Liter (Km/L)	x 2.352	= US MPG

*It is common to covert from miles per gallon (mpg) to liters/100 kilometers (1/100 km), where mpg (IMP) x 1/100 km = 282 and mpg (US) x 1/100 km = 235.

TEMPERATURE

Degree Fahrenheit (°F)	= (°C x 1.8) + 32
Degree Celsius (°C)	= (°F − 32) x .56

tccs1044

SERIAL NUMBER IDENTIFICATION

Vehicle

➧ See Figures 30 and 31

The Vehicle Identification Number (VIN) plate is mounted on the driver's side of the instrument panel, and is visible through the windshield.

The models covered in this book are full size C/K trucks including the Tahoe, Blazer, Jimmy, Yukon and Suburban. Starting in 1992 the Blazer was renamed the Blazer/Tahoe and Jimmy the Jimmy/Yukon.

The 5th digit on the vehicle identification number is the vehicle line and chassis type:

- C and R are 2-wheel drive conventional cabs
- V and K are 4-wheel drive conventional cabs

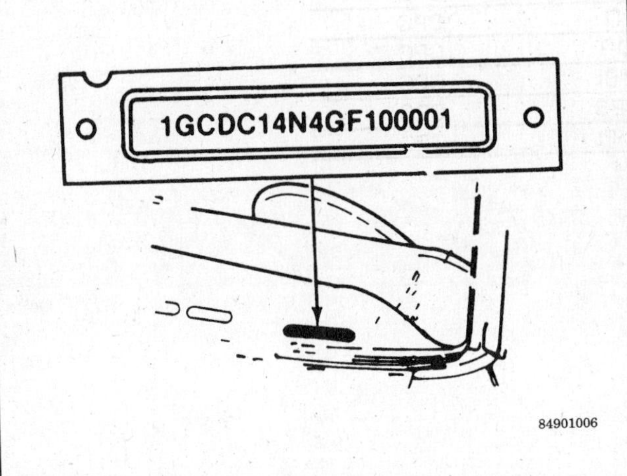

Fig. 30 The Vehicle Identification Number (VIN) is visible through the windshield

Engine

➧ See Figures 32, 33, 34, 35 and 36

On the 4.8L, inline 6-cylinder engine, the engine identification number is found on a machined pad on the left side of the block, just rear of center, below the engine side cover.

On the 1988-92 4.3L V6 engine, the engine identification number is found on a machined pad on the block, at the front just below the right side cylinder head.

On the 1993-96 4.3L V6 engine, the engine identification number is found on a machined pad on the rear of the cylinder block, below and behind the left cylinder head where the engine mates with the bellhousing.

On V8 gasoline engines, the engine identification number is usually found on a machined pad on the block, at the front just below the right side cylinder head. The engine identification number is sometimes also found on a machined pad on the left, rear upper side of the block, where the engine mates with the bellhousing.

On V8 diesel engines, the engine identification number is found on a machined pad on the front of the block, between the left cylinder head and the thermostat housing, and/or on a machined pad on the left rear of the block, just behind the left cylinder head. The engine number is broken down as follows: Example — F1210TFA

- F — Manufacturing Plant. F-Flint and T-Tonawanda
- 12 — Month of Manufacture (December)
- 10 — Day of Manufacturer (Tenth)
- T — Truck engine
- FA — Transmission and Engine Combination

Transmission

➧ See Figures 37, 38, 39 and 40

The Muncie 117mm 4-speed transmission is numbered on the rear of the case, above the output shaft.

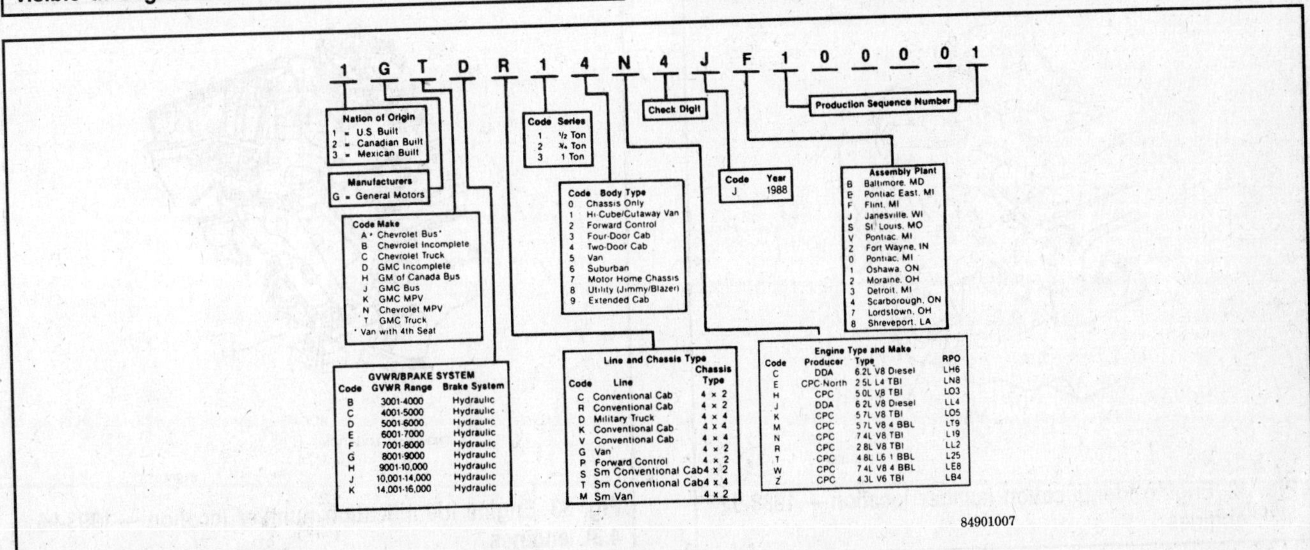

Fig. 31 Vehicle Identification number decoding

VEHICLE IDENTIFICATION CHART

8th digit	Liters	Cu. in. (cc)	Cyl.	Fuel Sys.	Eng. Mfg.
		Engine Code			
Z	4.3	263 (4293)	6	TBI	CPC
W	4.3	263 (4293)	6	MFI	CPC
T	4.8	292 (4785)	6	1BC	CPC
H	5.0	305 (4999)	8	4BC	CPC
H	5.0	305 (4999)	8	TBI	CPC
M	5.0	305 (4999)	8	MFI	CPC
K	5.7	350 (5735)	8	TBI	CPC
R	5.7	350 (5735)	8	MFI	CPC
C	6.2	379 (6210)	8	D	DDA
J	6.2	379 (6210)	8	D	DDA
F	6.5	395 (6473)	8	D	CPC
F	6.5	395 (6473)	8	D-T/HO	CPC
P	6.5	395 (6473)	8	D	CPC
S	6.5	395 (6473)	8	D-T	CPC
N	7.4	454 (7440)	8	TBI	CPC
W	7.4	454 (7440)	8	4BC	CPC
J	7.4	454 (7440)	8	MFI	CPC

Model Year	
10th digit	Year
J	1988
K	1989
L	1990
M	1991
N	1992
P	1993
R	1994
S	1995
T	1996

TBI-Throttle body injection
BC-Barrel carburetor
D-Diesel
10th digit corresponds with the year code
8th digit corresponds with the engine code

D-T/HO-Diesel Turbo/High output
CPC-Chevrolet/Pontiac/Canada
DDA-Detroit Diesel Allison
MFI-Multiport fuel injection

87981c01

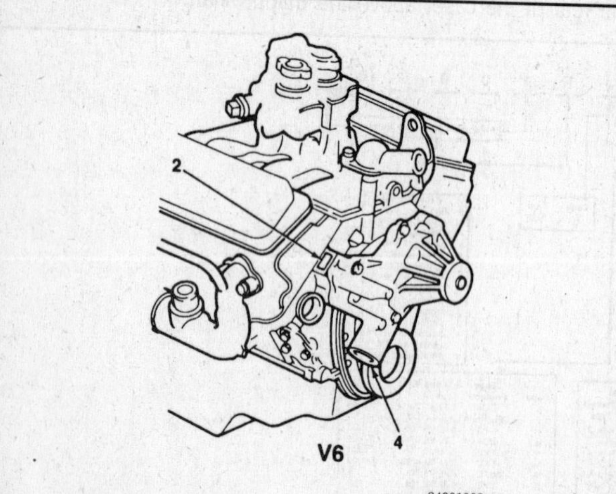

Fig. 32 Engine identification number location — 1988-92 4.3L engines

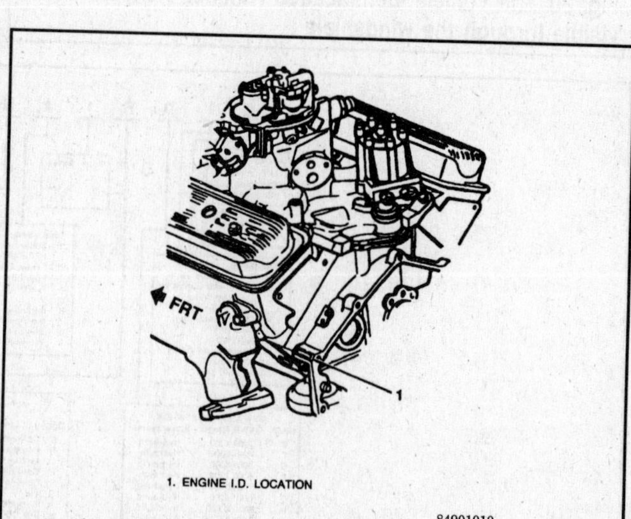

Fig. 33 Engine identification number location — 1993-96 4.3L engines

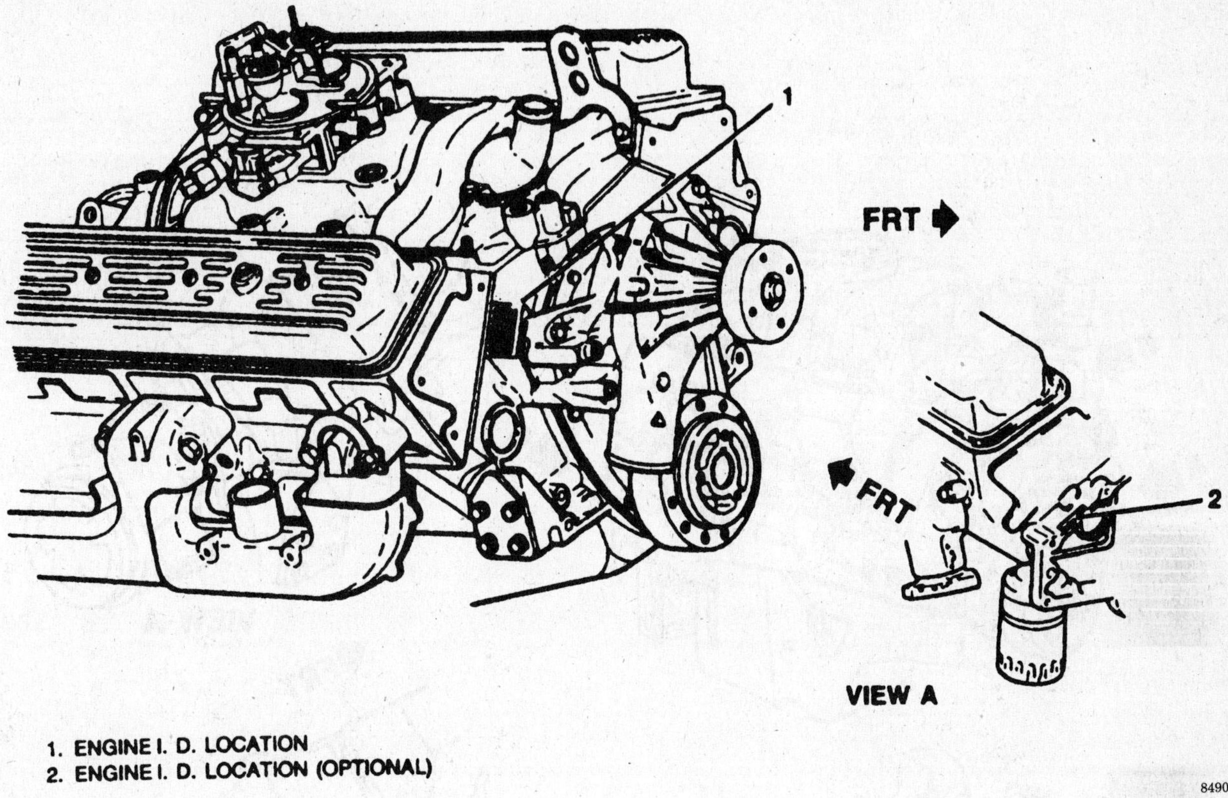

FRT

VIEW A

1. ENGINE I. D. LOCATION
2. ENGINE I. D. LOCATION (OPTIONAL)

84901011

Fig. 34 Engine identification number location — 5.0L, 5.7L engines

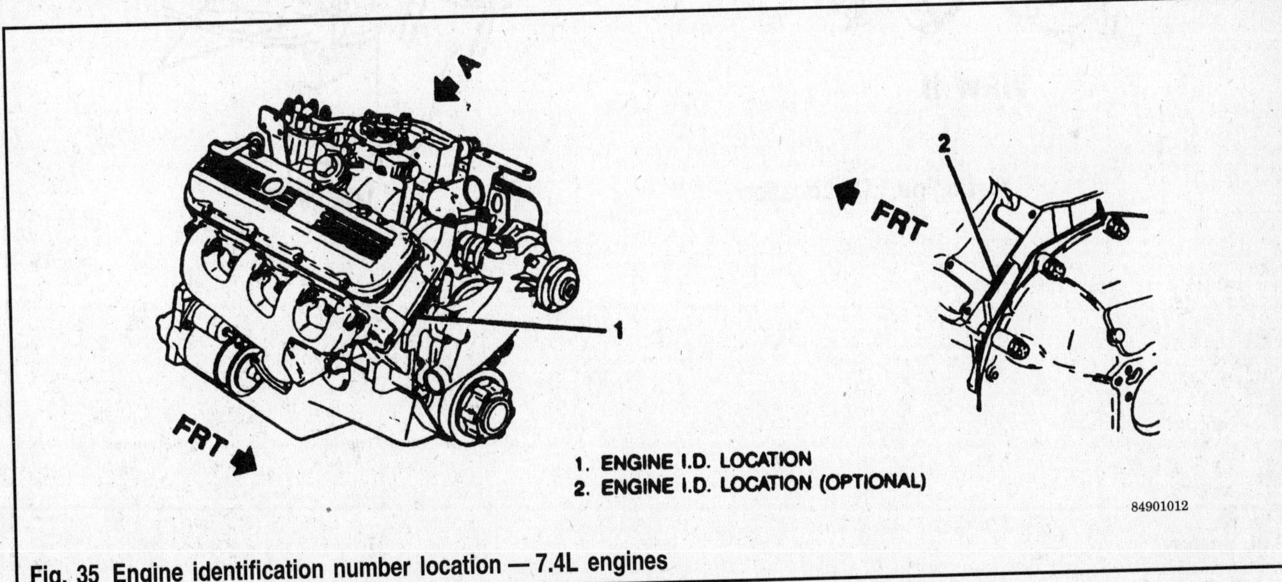

Fig. 35 Engine identification number location — 7.4L engines

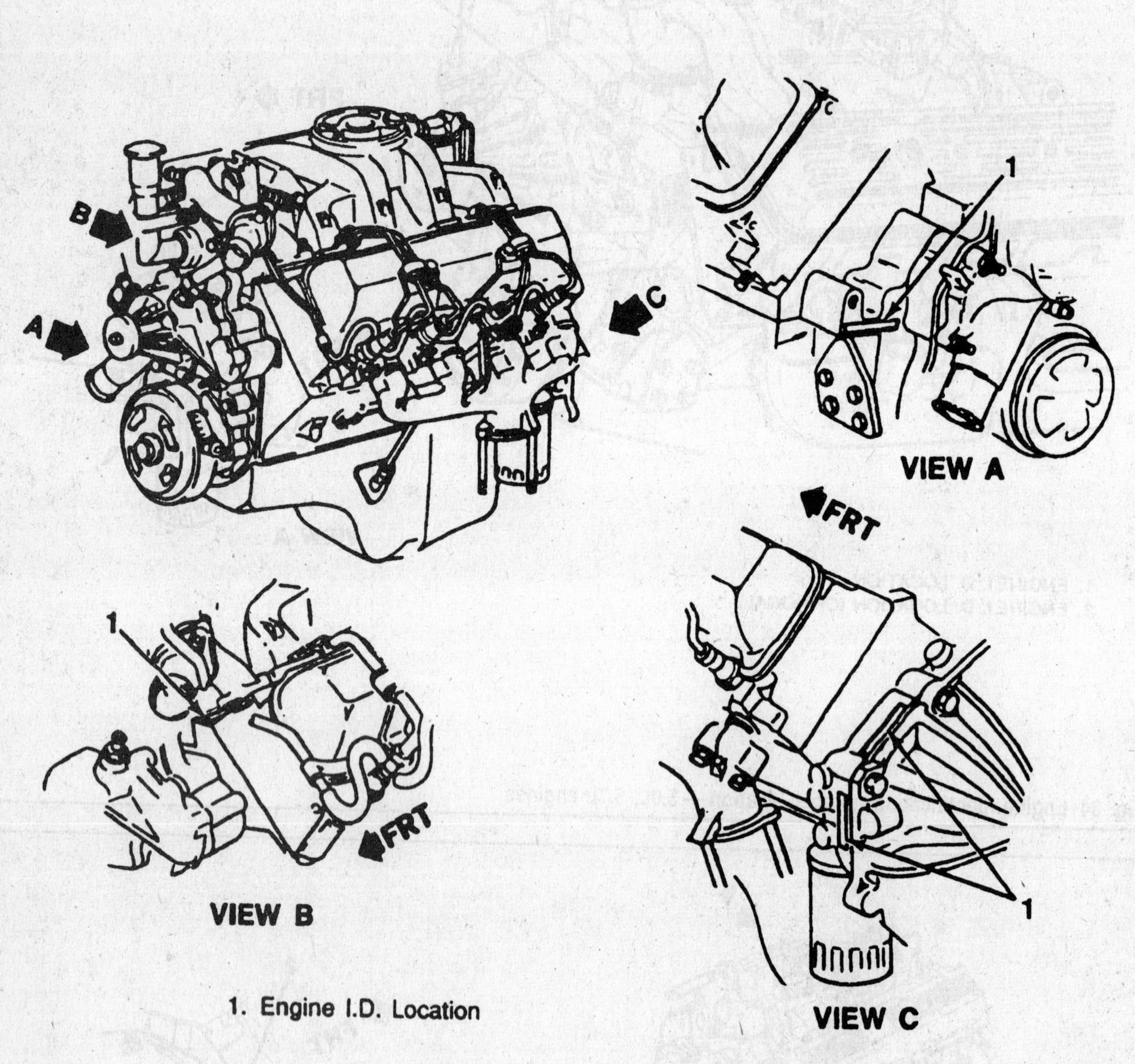

Fig. 36 Engine identification number location — 6.2L, 6.5L engines

ENGINE IDENTIFICATION

Year	Model	Engine Displacement Liters (cc)	Engine Series (ID/VIN)	Fuel System	No. of Cylinders	Engine Type
1988	All	4.3 (4293)	Z	TBI	V6	OHV
	All	4.8 (4785)	T	1BC	L6	OHV
	All	5.0 (4998)	H	4BC	V8	OHV
	All	5.7 (5735)	K	4BC	V8	OHV
	All	6.2 (6243)	C/J	D	V8	OHV
	All	7.4 (7439)	N	TBI	V8	OHV
	All	7.4 (7439)	W	4BC	V8	OHV
1989	All	4.3 (4293)	Z	TBI	V6	OHV
	All	4.8 (4785)	T	1BC	L6	OHV
	All	5.0 (4998)	H	TBI	V8	OHV
	All	5.7 (5735)	K	TBI	V8	OHV
	All	6.2 (6243)	C/J	D	V8	OHV
	All	7.4 (7439)	N	TBI	V8	OHV
	All	7.4 (7439)	W	4BC	V8	OHV
1990	All	4.3 (4293)	Z	TBI	V6	OHV
	All	5.0 (4998)	H	TBI	V8	OHV
	All	5.7 (5735)	K	TBI	V8	OHV
	All	6.2 (6243)	C/J	D	V8	OHV
	All	7.4 (7439)	N	TBI	V8	OHV
1991	All	4.3 (4293)	Z	TBI	V6	OHV
	All	5.0 (4998)	H	TBI	V8	OHV
	All	5.7 (5735)	K	TBI	V8	OHV
	All	6.2 (6243)	C/J	D	V8	OHV
	All	7.4 (7439)	N	TBI	V8	OHV
1992	All	4.3 (4293)	Z	TBI	V6	OHV
	All	5.0 (4998)	H	TBI	V8	OHV
	All	5.7 (5735)	K	TBI	V8	OHV
	All	6.2 (6243)	C/J	D	V8	OHV
	All	6.5 (6489)	F	D	V8	OHV
	All	7.4 (7439)	N	TBI	V8	OHV
1993	All	4.3 (4293)	Z	TBI	V6	OHV
	All	5.0 (4998)	H	TBI	V8	OHV
	All	5.7 (5735)	K	TBI	V8	OHV
	All	6.2 (6243)	C/J	D	V8	OHV
	All	6.5 (6489)	F	D	V8	OHV
	All	7.4 (7439)	N	TBI	V8	OHV

87981C03

ENGINE IDENTIFICATION

Year	Model	Engine Displacement Liters (cc)	Engine Series (ID/VIN)	Fuel System	No. of Cylinders	Engine Type
1994	All	4.3 (4293)	Z	TBI	V6	OHV
	All	5.0 (4998)	H	TBI	V8	OHV
	All	5.7 (5735)	K	TBI	V8	OHV
	All	6.5 (6489)	F	D-T/HO	V8	OHV
	All	6.5 (6489)	P	D	V8	OHV
	All	6.5 (6489)	S	D-T	V8	OHV
	All	7.4 (7439)	N	TBI	V8	OHV
1995	All	4.3 (4293)	Z	TBI	V6	OHV
	All	5.0 (4998)	H	TBI	V8	OHV
	All	5.7 (5735)	K	TBI	V8	OHV
	All	6.5 (6489)	F	D-T	V8	OHV
	All	6.5 (6489)	P	D	V8	OHV
	All	6.5 (6489)	S	D-T	V8	OHV
	All	7.4 (7439)	N	TBI	V8	OHV
1996	All	4.3 (4293)	W	CSFI	V6	OHV
	All	5.0 (4998)	M	CSFI	V8	OHV
	All	5.7 (5735)	R	CSFI	V8	OHV
	All	6.5 (6489)	F	D-T	V8	OHV
	All	6.5 (6489)	S	D-T	V8	OHV
	All	7.4 (7439)	J	MFI	V8	OHV

TBI-Throttle Body Injection
1BC-1 Barrel Carburetor
4BC-4 Barrel Carburetor
D-Diesel

D-T-Diesel Turbo
D-T/HO-Diesel Turbo/High Output
MFI-Multi-Port Fuel Injection
CSFI-Central Sequential Fuel Injection

87981ca3

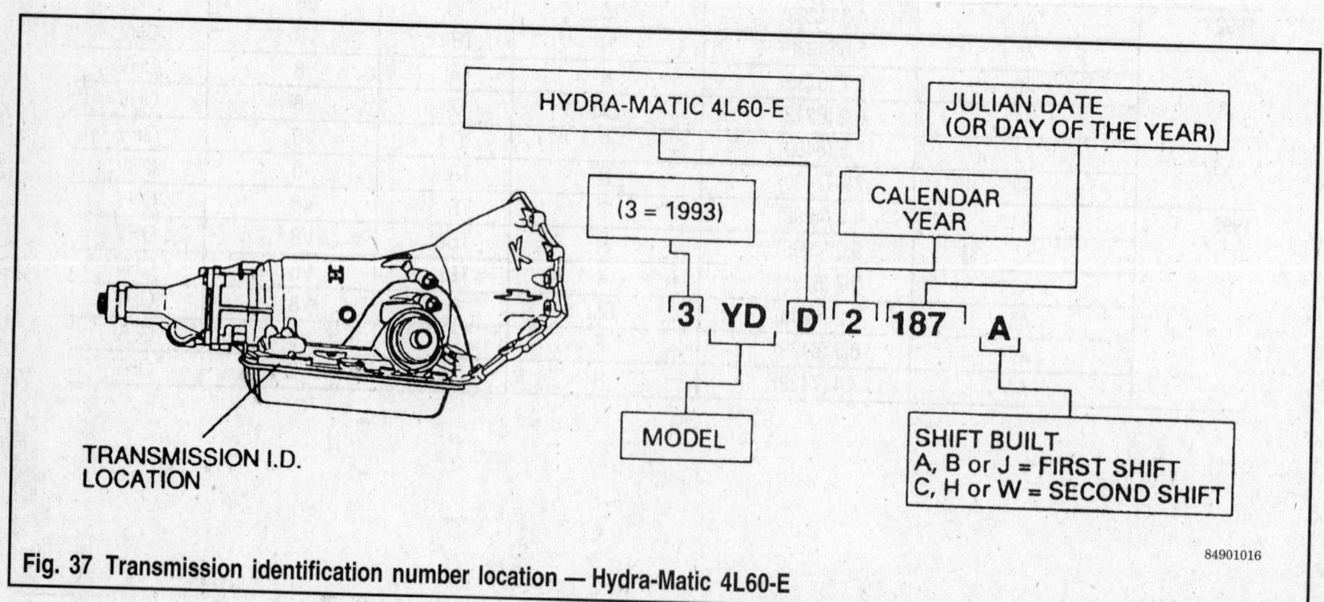

Fig. 37 Transmission identification number location — Hydra-Matic 4L60-E

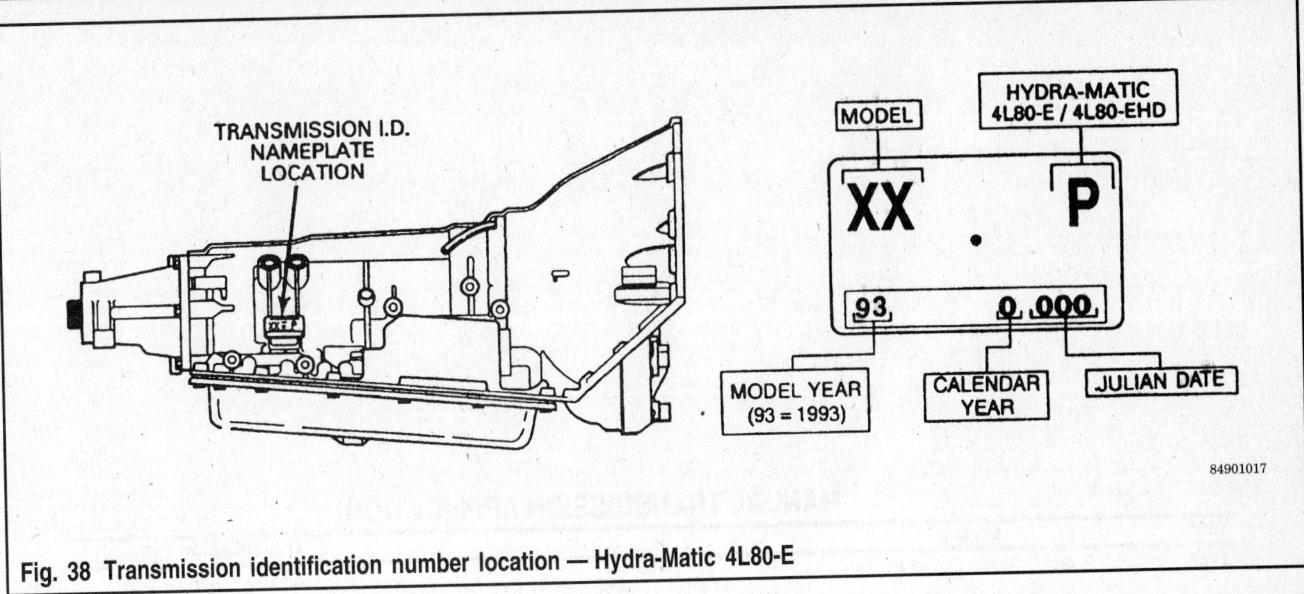

Fig. 38 Transmission identification number location — Hydra-Matic 4L80-E

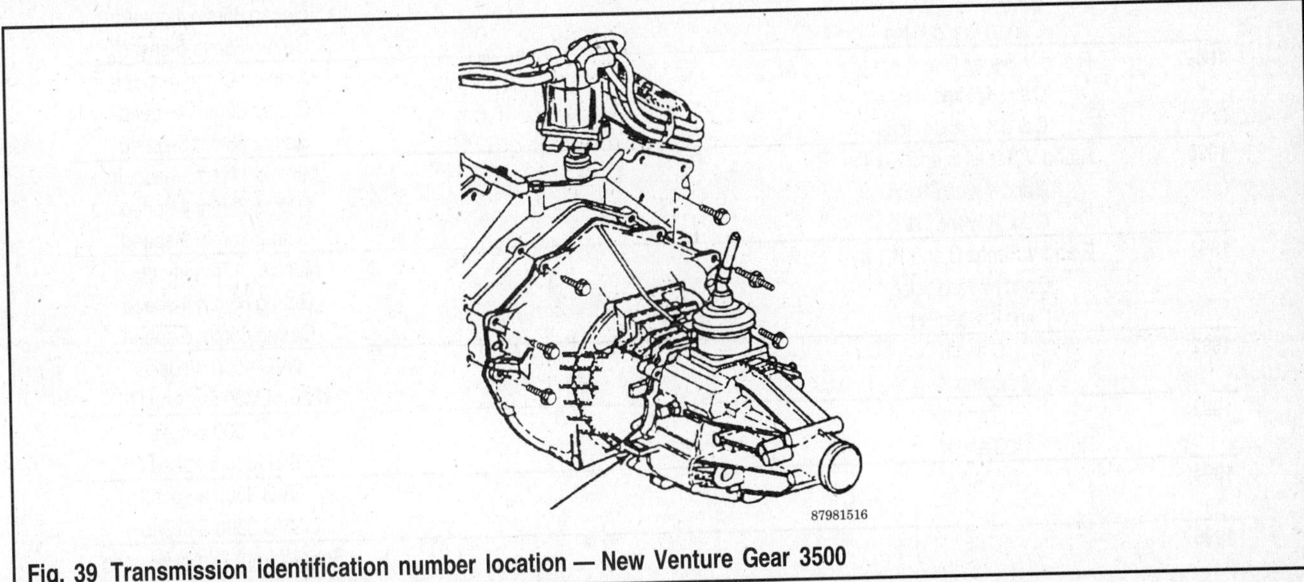

Fig. 39 Transmission identification number location — New Venture Gear 3500

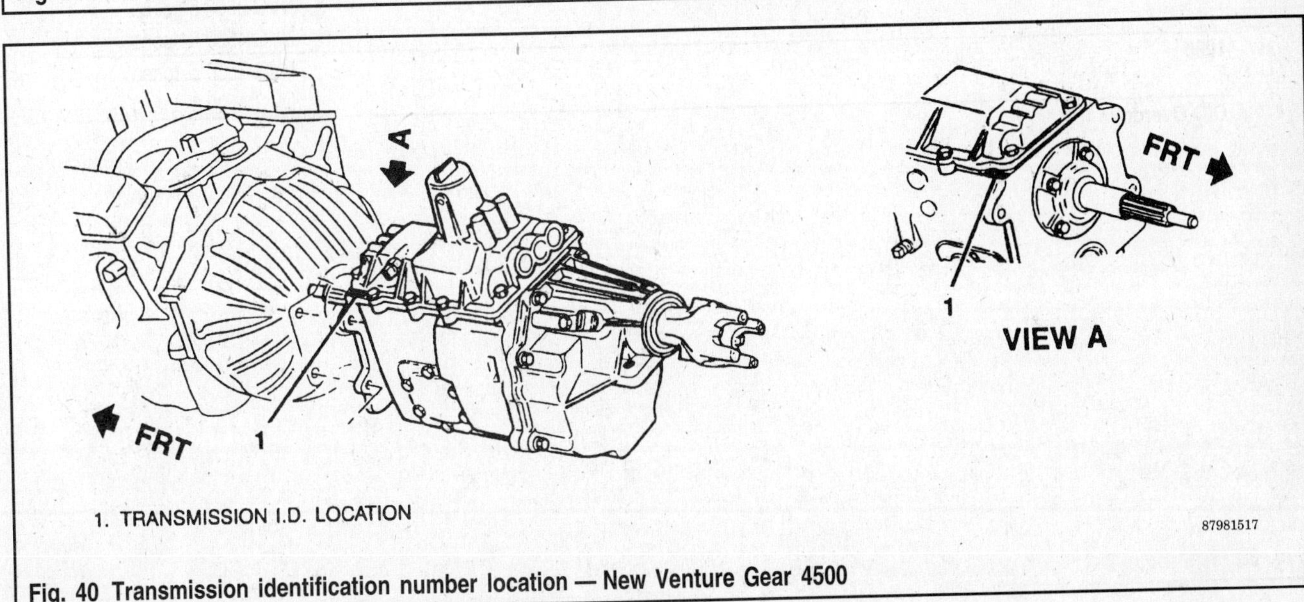

Fig. 40 Transmission identification number location — New Venture Gear 4500

MANUAL TRANSMISSION APPLICATION

Year	Models	Transmission Type
1988	R and V Series C and K 1 ton	Muncie 117mm 4-speed
	C and K ½ and ¾ ton	Getrag 85mm 4-speed
	C and K ½ and ¾ ton	Getrag 85mm 5-speed
1989	R and V Series C and K 1 ton	Muncie 117mm 4-speed
	C and K ½ and ¾ ton	Getrag 85mm 4-speed
	C and K ½ and ¾ ton	Getrag 85mm 5-speed
1990	R and V Series C and K 1 ton	Muncie 117mm 4-speed
	C and K ½ and ¾ ton	Getrag 85mm 4-speed
	C and K ½ and ¾ ton	Getrag 85mm 5-speed
1991	R and V Series C and K 1 ton	Muncie 117mm 4-speed
	C and K ½ and ¾ ton	Getrag 85mm 4-speed
	C and K ½ and ¾ ton	Getrag 85mm 5-speed
1992	C and K	NVG 4500 5-speed
	C and K	NVG 5LM60 5-speed O/D
1993	C and K	NVG 4500 5-speed
	C and K	NVG 5LM60 5-speed O/D
1994	All	NVG 4500 5-speed
		NVG 3500 5-speed
1995	All	Borg-Warner 77mm 5-speed
		NVG 3500 5-speed
		NVG 4500 5-speed
1996	All	NVG 3500 5-speed
		NVG 4500 5-speed

O/D-Overdrive

87981C05

AUTOMATIC TRANSMISSION APPLICATION

Year	Models	Transmission Type
1988	All	Turbo Hydra-Matic 400 3-speed Turbo Hydra-Matic 700-R4 4-speed
1989	All	Turbo Hydra-Matic 400 3-speed Turbo Hydra-Matic 700-R4 4-speed
1990	All	Turbo Hydra-Matic 400 3-speed Turbo Hydra-Matic 700-R4 4-speed
1991	All	Hydra-matic 4L60E Hydra-matic 4L80E
1992	All	Hydra-matic 4L60E Hydra-matic 4L80E
1993	All	Hydra-matic 4L60E Hydra-matic 4L80E
1994	All	Hydra-matic 4L60E Hydra-matic 4L80E
1996	All	Hydra-matic 4L60E Hydra-matic 4L80E

87981C04

The 4-Speed 85mm and 5-Speed 85mm transmissions are numbered on the right rear of the case.

The NVG 3500 5-speed transmissions are numbered on the top, left side of the case, near the bellhousing.

The NVG 4500 5-speed transmissions are numbered on the top, left side of the case, near the bellhousing.

The NVG 5LM60 5-speed transmissions are numbered on the lower left side, about halfway back on the case.

The Hydra-Matic automatic transmissions are identified by a plate attached to the right side, which is stamped with the serial number.

Drive Axle

The drive axle serial number is stamped on the axle shaft housing, where it connects to the differential housing.

Front axles on four wheel drive models are marked on the front of the left axle tube.

Transfer Case

➧ **See Figures 41 and 42**

All transfer cases have a build tag attached to the case.

On the NP205, it is attached to the bolt retaining the Power Take Off (PTO) cover.

On the NP231, NP233 and NP241, it is attached to the rear case half.

On the NV241 and NV243, it is attached to the rear case half.

On the Borg Warner 4401/4470, it is attached to an extension housing bolt.

Service Parts Identification Label

➧ **See Figure 43**

The service parts identification label, commonly known as the option list, is usually located on the inside of the glove compartment door. On some trucks, you may have to look for it on an inner fender panel. The label lists the vehicle serial number, wheelbase, all Regular Production Options (RPOs) and all special equipment. Probably, the most valuable piece of information on this label is the paint code, a useful item when you have occasion to need paint.

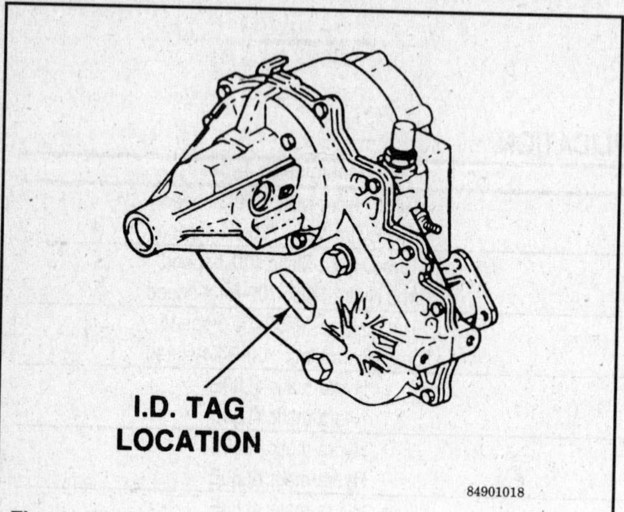

Fig. 41 Transfer case identification number location — NP241

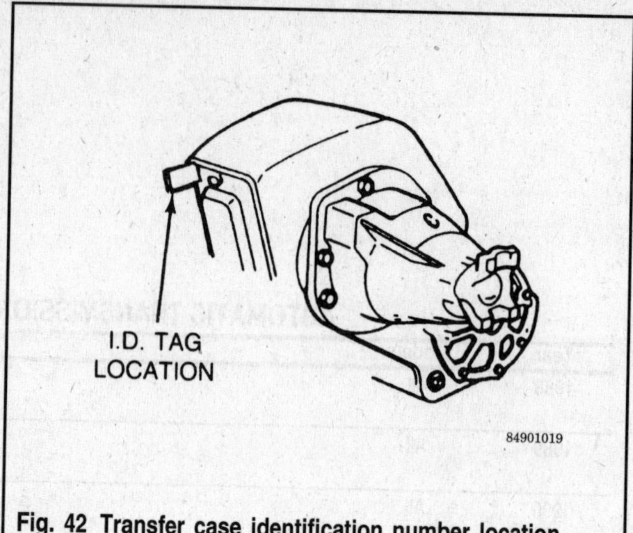

Fig. 42 Transfer case identification number location — NP205

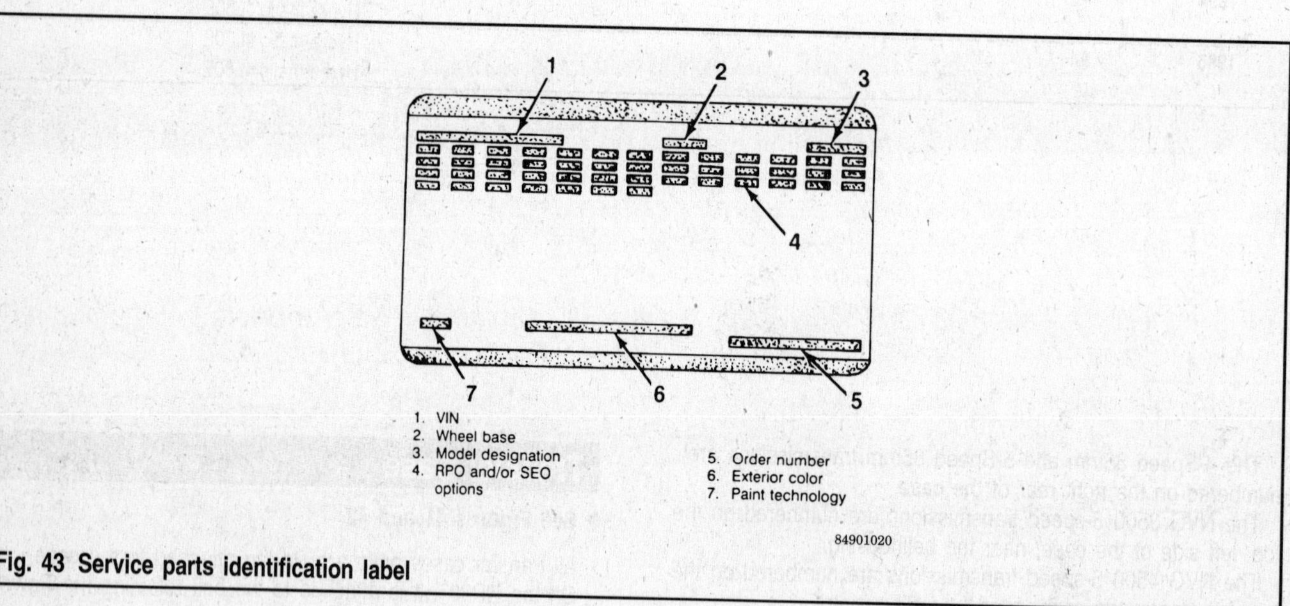

Fig. 43 Service parts identification label

FRONT DRIVE AXLE APPLICATION

Year	Models	Axle Type
1988	K 15/25 Series	GMC 8¼ in. Ring Gear Independant Front Axle
	V 10/15 and 20/25 Series	GMC 8½ in. Ring Gear
	K 35 Series	GMC 9¼ in. Ring Gear Independant Front Axle
	V 30/35 Series	Dana 60 Series 9¾ in. Ring Gear
1989	K 15/25 Series	GMC 8¼ in. Ring Gear Independant Front Axle
	V 10/15 and 20/25 Series	GMC 8½ in. Ring Gear
	K 35 Series	GMC 9¼ in. Ring Gear Independant Front Axle
	V 30/35 Series	Dana 60 Series 9¾ in. Ring Gear
1990	K 15/25 Series	GMC 8¼ in. Ring Gear Independant Front Axle
	V 10/15 and 20/25 Series	GMC 8½ in. Ring Gear
	K 35 Series	GMC 9¼ in. Ring Gear Independant Front Axle
	V 30/35 Series	Dana 60 Series 9¾ in. Ring Gear
1991	K 15/25 Series	GMC 8¼ in. Ring Gear Independant Front Axle
	V 10/15 and 20/25 Series	GMC 8½ in. Ring Gear
	K 35 Series	GMC 9¼ in. Ring Gear Independant Front Axle
	V 30/35 Series	Dana 60 Series 9¾ in. Ring Gear
1992	K 15/25 Series	GMC 8¼ in. Ring Gear Independant Front Axle
	K 35 Series	GMC 9¼ in. Ring Gear Independant Front Axle
1992	K 15/25 Series	GMC 8¼ in. Ring Gear Independant Front Axle
	K 35 Series	GMC 9¼ in. Ring Gear Independant Front Axle
1993	K 15/25 Series	GMC 8¼ in. Ring Gear Independant Front Axle
	K 35 Series	GMC 9¼ in. Ring Gear Independant Front Axle
1994	K Series	GMC 8¼ in. Ring Gear Independant Front Axle
	K Series	GMC 9¼ in. Ring Gear Independant Front Axle

87981C06

FRONT DRIVE AXLE APPLICATION

Year	Models	Axle Type
1995	K Series	GMC 8¼ in. Ring Gear Independant Front Axle
	K Series	GMC 9¼ in. Ring Gear Independant Front Axle
1996	K Series	GMC 8¼ in. Ring Gear Independant Front Axle
	K Series	GMC 9¼ in. Ring Gear Independant Front Axle

87981ca6

REAR AXLE APPLICATION

Year	Models	Axle Type
1988	R, C Series ½ ton	GM 8½ Ring Gear Semi-Floating
	R, V, C, K Series ½ ton	GM 9½ in. Ring Gear Semi-Floating
	R, V, C, K Series ¾ and 1 ton	GM 10½ in. Ring Gear Full-Floating
	R, V, C, K Series ¾ ton	Dana 9¾ in. Ring Gear Full-Floating
	R, V, C, K Series ¾ and 1 ton	Dana 10½ in. Ring Gear Full-Floating
1989	R, C Series ½ ton	GM 8½ Ring Gear Semi-Floating
	R, V, C, K Series ½ ton	GM 9½ in. Ring Gear Semi-Floating
	R, V, C, K Series ¾ and 1 ton	GM 10½ in. Ring Gear Full-Floating
	R, V, C, K Series ¾ ton	Dana 9¾ in. Ring Gear Full-Floating
	R, V, C, K Series ¾ and 1 ton	Dana 10½ in. Ring Gear Full-Floating
1990	R, C Series ½ ton	GM 8½ Ring Gear Semi-Floating
	R, V, C, K Series ½ ton	GM 9½ in. Ring Gear Semi-Floating
	R, V, C, K Series ¾ and 1 ton	GM 10½ in. Ring Gear Full-Floating
	R, V, C, K Series ¾ ton	Dana 9¾ in. Ring Gear Full-Floating
	R, V, C, K Series ¾ and 1 ton	Dana 10½ in. Ring Gear Full-Floating
1991	R, C Series ½ ton	GM 8½ Ring Gear Semi-Floating
	R, V, C, K Series ½ ton	GM 9½ in. Ring Gear Semi-Floating
	R, V, C, K Series ¾ and 1 ton	GM 10½ in. Ring Gear Full-Floating
	R, V, C, K Series ¾ ton	Dana 9¾ in. Ring Gear Full-Floating
	R, V, C, K Series ¾ and 1 ton	Dana 10½ in. Ring Gear Full-Floating
	C, K Series	Rockwell 12 in. Ring Gear Full-Floating

87981C07

REAR AXLE APPLICATION

Year	Models	Axle Type
1992	C Series ½ ton	GM 8½ Ring Gear Semi-Floating
	C, K Series ½ ton	GM 9½ in. Ring Gear Semi-Floating
	C, K Series ¾ and 1 ton	GM 10½ in. Ring Gear Full-Floating
	C, K Series ¾ ton	Dana 9¾ in. Ring Gear Full-Floating
	C, K Series ¾ and 1 ton	Dana 10½ in. Ring Gear Full-Floating
	C, K Series	Rockwell 12 in. Ring Gear Full-Floating
1993	C Series ½ ton	GM 8½ Ring Gear Semi-Floating
	C, K Series ½ ton	GM 9½ in. Ring Gear Semi-Floating
	C, K Series ¾ and 1 ton	GM 10½ in. Ring Gear Full-Floating
	C, K Series ¾ ton	Dana 9¾ in. Ring Gear Full-Floating
	C, K Series ¾ and 1 ton	Dana 10½ in. Ring Gear Full-Floating
	C, K Series	Rockwell 12 in. Ring Gear Full-Floating
1994	C, K Series	GM 8½ Ring Gear Semi-Floating
	C, K Series	GM 9½ in. Ring Gear Semi-Floating
	C, K Series	Dana 9¾ in. Ring Gear Full-Floating
	C, K Series	Dana 10½ in. Ring Gear Full-Floating
	C, K Series	Dana 11 in. Ring Gear Full-Floating
1995	C, K Series	GM 8½ Ring Gear Semi-Floating
	C, K Series	GM 9½ in. Ring Gear Semi-Floating
	C, K Series	GM 10½ in. Ring Gear Full-Floating
	C, K Series	Dana 11 in. Ring Gear Full-Floating
1996	C, K Series	GM 8½ in. Ring Gear Semi-Floating
	C, K Series	GM 9½ in. Ring Gear Semi-Floating
	C, K Series	Dana 11 in. Ring Gear Full-Floating

87981C08

TRANSFER CASE APPLICATION

Year	Models	Transfer Case Type
1988	V 30/3500	New Process 205
	V 10/15, 20/25	New Process 208
	All K Series	New Process 241
1989	V 30/3500	New Process 205
	V 10/15, 20/25	New Process 241
	K Series, exc. K 30 with DRW	New Process 241
	K Series DRW	Borg-warner 1370
1990	V 30/3500	New Process 205
	V 10/15, 20/25	New Process 241
	K Series DRW	Borg-warner 1370
1991	V 30/3500	New Process 205
	K Series, exc. K 30 with DRW	New Process 241
	K Series DRW	Borg-warner 1370
	K30	Borg-warner 4470
1992	K Series, exc. K 30 with DRW	New Process 241
	K30	Borg-warner 4470
	K30	Borg-warner 4401
1993	K Series, exc. K 30 with DRW	New Process 241
	K30	Borg-warner 4470
	K30	Borg-warner 4401
1994	All	New Process 241
	All	Borg-warner 4470
	All	Borg-warner 4401
1995	All	New Process 241
	All	New Process 233
	All	New Process 231
	All	Borg-warner 4470
	All	Borg-warner 4401
	All	Borg-warner 4472
1996	All	New Process 241
	All	New Process 243
	All	Borg-warner 4470
	All	Borg-warner 4401

DRW-Dual Rear Wheels

87981C09

ROUTINE MAINTENANCE AND TUNE-UP

Proper maintenance is the key to long and trouble-free vehicle life. As a conscientious owner and driver, set aside a Saturday morning, say once a month, to check or replace items which could cause major problems later. Keep your own personal log to jot down which services you performed, how much the parts cost you, the date, and the exact odometer reading at the time. Keep all receipts for such items as engine oil and filters, so that they may be referred to in case of related problems or to determine operating expenses. As a do-it-yourselfer, these receipts are the only proof you have that the required maintenance was performed. In the event of a warranty problem, these receipts will be invaluable.

The literature provided with your vehicle when it was originally delivered includes the factory recommended maintenance schedule. If you no longer have this literature, replacement copies are usually available from the dealer. A maintenance schedule is provided later in this section, in case you do not have the factory literature.

Air Cleaner

➧ See Figures 44, 45, 46 and 47

The element should be replaced at the recommended intervals shown in the Maintenance Intervals chart later in this section. If your truck is operated under severely dusty conditions or severe operating conditions, more frequent changes will certainly be necessary. Inspect the element at least twice a year. Early spring and early fall are always good times for inspection. Remove the element and check for any perforations or tears in the filter. Check the cleaner housing for signs of dirt or dust that may have leaked through the filter element or in through the snorkel tube. Position a droplight on one side of the element and look through the filter at the light. If no glow of light can be seen through the element material, replace the filter. If holes in the filter element are apparent or signs of dirt seepage through the filter are evident, replace the filter.

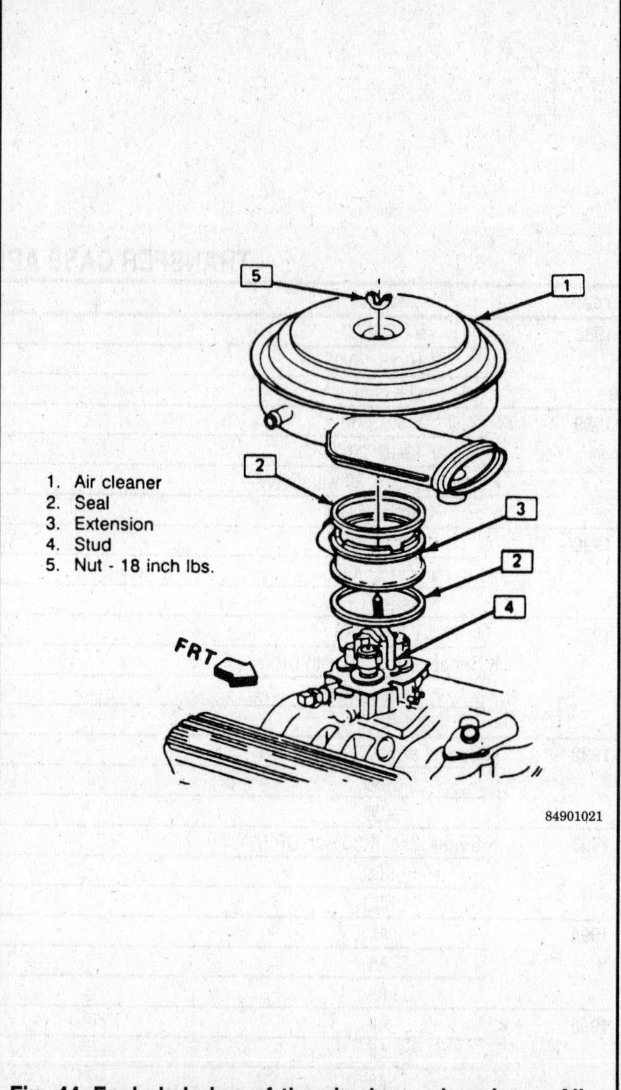

Fig. 44 Exploded view of the air cleaner housing — All 1988-92 gasoline engines exc. 7.4L

REMOVAL & INSTALLATION

➧ See Figures 48, 49, 50, 51 and 52

1. Loosen the wingnut(s) and lift off the housing cover. On the 6.5L diesel, lift the wire tabs to release the retaining clips and separate the two case halves.
2. On the 6.5L diesel, position the cover with the air cleaner flexible hose off to the side.
3. Withdraw the element from the housing and discard it.
4. With a clean rag, remove any dirt or dust from the front cover and also from the element seating surface.

To install:

5. Position and install the new filter element so that it seats properly in the housing.
6. On the 6.5L diesel, position the cover with the attached hose over the element and snap the retaining clips into place. On all other engines, install the housing lid and tighten the wingnut(s) to about 18 inch lbs. (2 Nm).

WARNING

Do not drive the vehicle with air cleaner removed. Doing so will allow dirt and a variety of other foreign particles to enter the engine and cause damage and wear. Also, backfiring could cause a fire in the engine compartment.

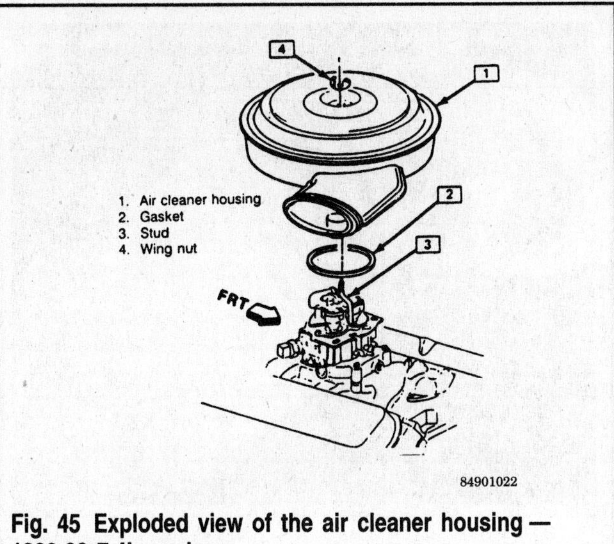

Fig. 45 Exploded view of the air cleaner housing — 1988-92 7.4L engines

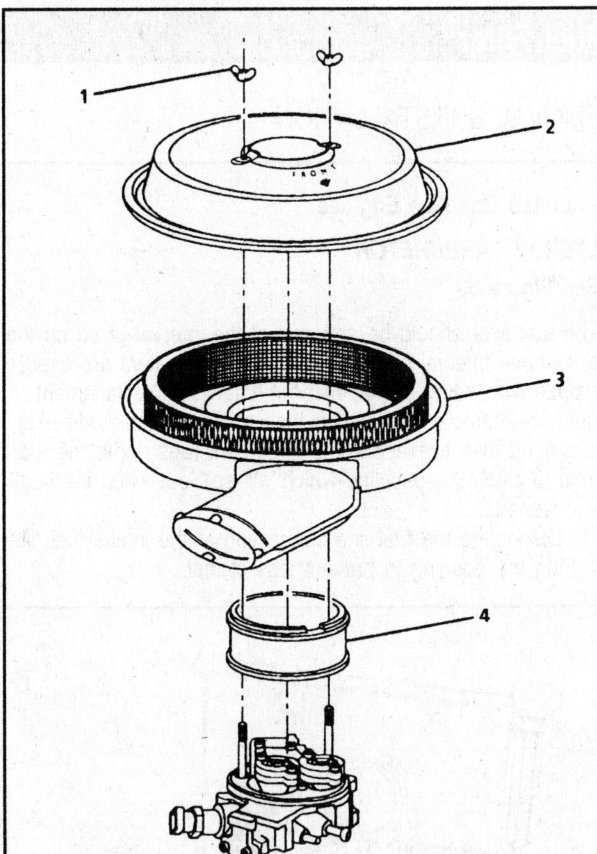

Fig. 46 Exploded view of the air cleaner housing — 1993 gasoline engines

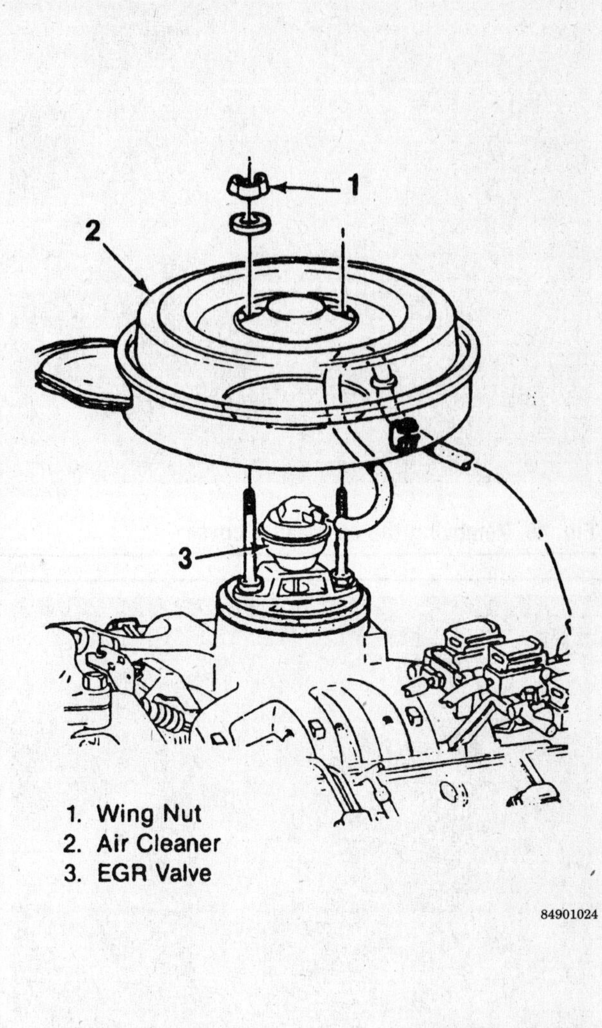

Fig. 47 Exploded view of the air cleaner housing — 6.2L diesel engines

Fig. 48 Loosen the wingnut and remove it from the air cleaner cover

Fig. 49 Removing the air cleaner cover

Fig. 50 Remove the old air cleaner element

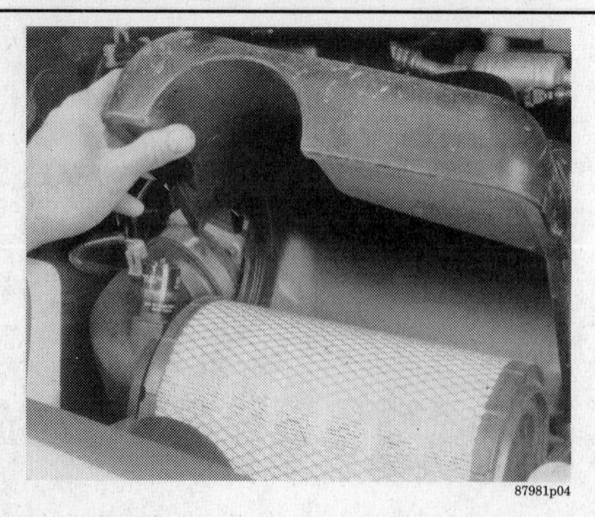

Fig. 51 On newer vehicles lift up the air cleaner cover — 1996 truck shown

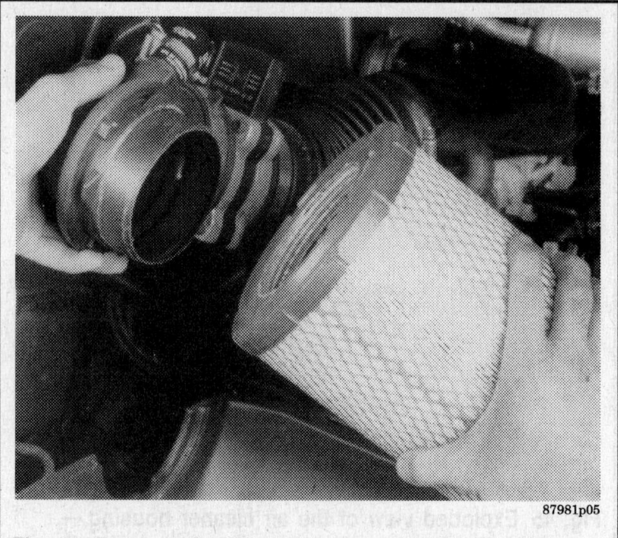

Fig. 52 Remove the filter element — 1996 truck shown

Fuel Filter

REMOVAL & INSTALLATION

Carbureted Gasoline Engines

FILTER IN CARBURETOR

See Figure 53

The fuel filter should be serviced at the interval given on the Maintenance Interval chart. Two types of fuel filters are used, a bronze type and a paper element type. Filter replacement should be attempted only when the engine is cold. Additionally, it is a good idea to place some absorbent rags under the fuel fittings to catch the gasoline which will spill out when the lines are loosened.

1. Disengage the fuel line connection at the intake fuel filter nut. Plug the opening to prevent loss of fuel.

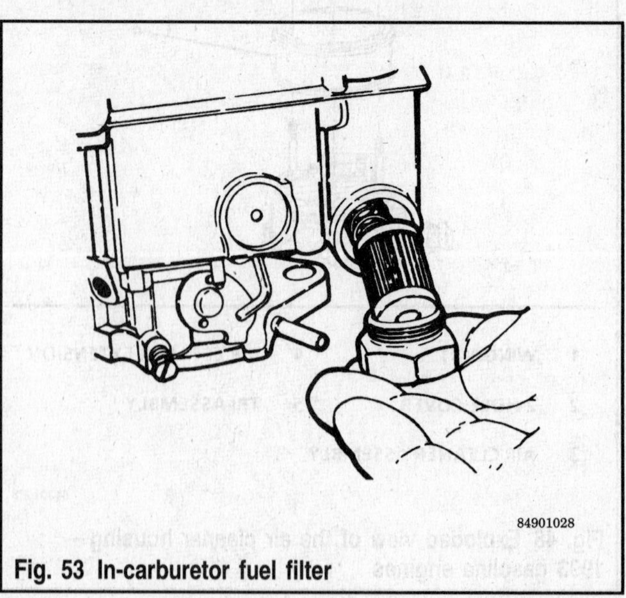

Fig. 53 In-carburetor fuel filter

2. Remove the intake fuel filter nut from the carburetor with a 1 in. open end wrench (or adjustable wrench).
3. Remove the filter element and spring.
4. Check the element for restrictions by blowing on the cone end. Air should pass freely.
5. Clean or replace the element, as necessary.

To install:

6. Install the element spring, then the filter element in the carburetor. Bronze filters should have the small section of the cone facing out.
7. Install a new gasket on the intake fuel nut. Install the nut in the carburetor body and tighten securely.
8. Install the fuel line and tighten the connector.

INLINE FILTER

Some trucks may have an inline filter. This is a can-shaped device located in the fuel line between the pump and the carburetor. It may be made of either plastic or metal. To replace the filter:

1. Place some absorbent rags under the filter. Remember, it will be full of gasoline when removed.
2. Use a pair of pliers to expand the clamp on one end of the filter, then slide the clamp down past the point to which the filter pipe extends in the rubber hose. Do the same with the other clamp.
3. Gently twist and pull the hoses free of the filter pipes. Remove and discard the old filter.

➡Most replacement filters come with new hoses that should be installed with a new filter.

4. Install the new filter into the hoses, slide the clamps back into place, and check for leaks with the engine idling.

Fuel Injected Gasoline Engines

➧ See Figures 54, 55 and 56

The inline filter on the fuel injected models is found along the frame rail.

1. You must first relieve the fuel system pressure as follows:
   a. Disconnect the negative battery cable.
   b. Loosen the filler cap.
   c. Connect a fuel pressure gauge to the fuel pressure tap. Wrap a shop towel around the fitting while connecting the gauge to avoid spilling fuel.
   d. Connect a bleed hose to the gauge and insert the other end into a suitable container for storing fuel.
   e. Open the valve and bleed the system pressure.

✲✲CAUTION

The 220 TBI unit used on the V6 and V8 engines contains a constant bleed feature in the pressure regulator that relieves pressure any time the engine is turned off. Therefore, no special relief procedure is required, however, a small amount of fuel may be released when the fuel line is disconnected. To reduce the chance of personal injury, cover the fuel line with cloth to collect the fuel and then place the cloth in an approved container.

2. Disconnect the fuel lines.
3. Remove the fuel filter from the retainer or mounting bolt.

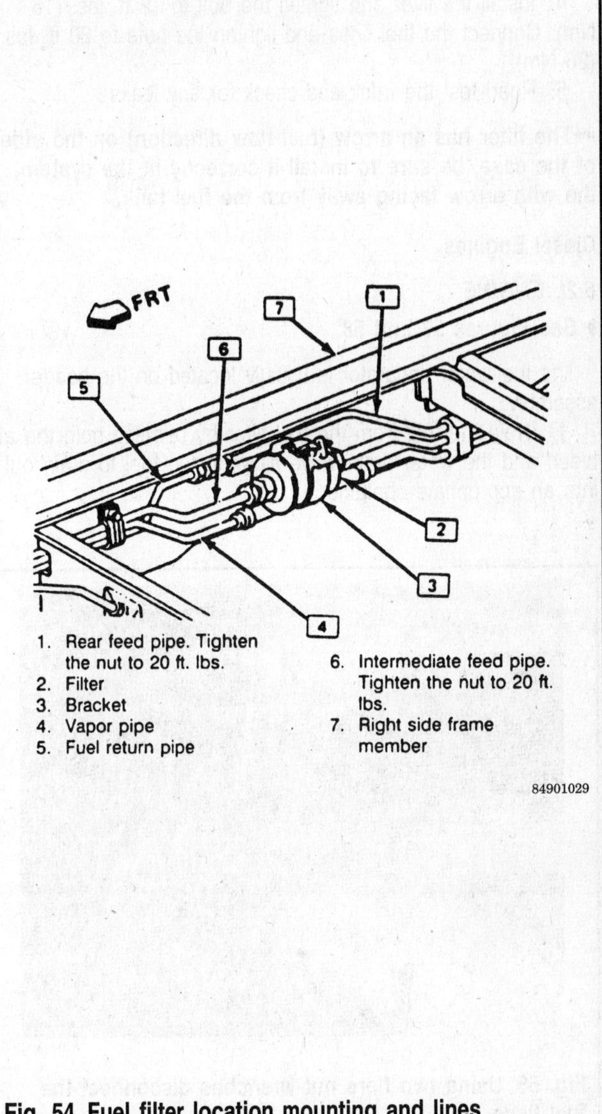

Fig. 54 Fuel filter location mounting and lines

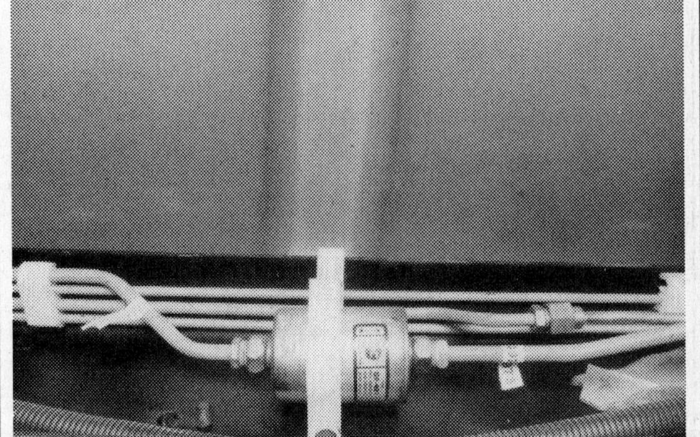

Fig. 55 The fuel filter is found along the frame rail

To install:

4. Install the filter and tighten the bolt to 12 ft. lbs. (16 Nm). Connect the fuel lines and tighten the nuts to 20 ft. lbs. (26 Nm).
5. Road test the truck and check for any leaks.

➡**The filter has an arrow (fuel flow direction) on the side of the case, be sure to install it correctly in the system, the with arrow facing away from the fuel tank.**

Diesel Engines

6.2L ENGINE

See Figures 57 and 58

The fuel/water separator is usually located on the header assembly.

1. Drain the fuel from the fuel filter by opening both the air bleed and the water drain valve allowing the fuel to drain out into an appropriate container.

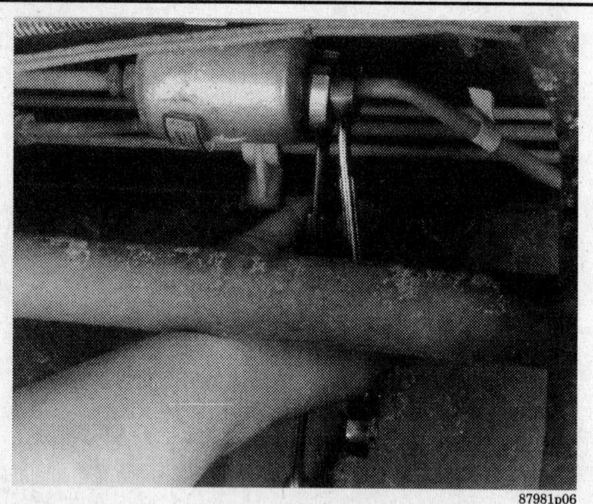

87981p06

Fig. 56 Using two flare nut wrenches disconnect the fuel lines

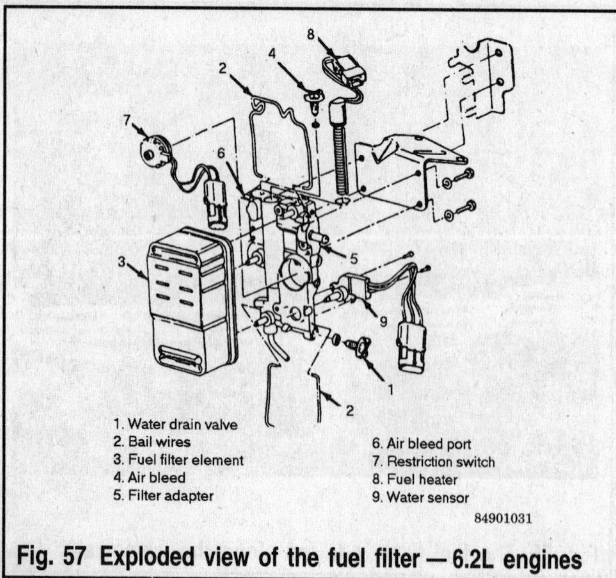

Fig. 57 Exploded view of the fuel filter — 6.2L engines

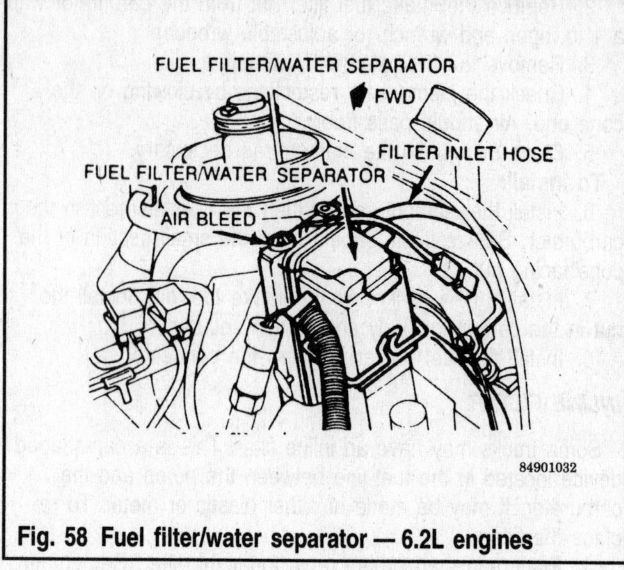

Fig. 58 Fuel filter/water separator — 6.2L engines

2. Remove the fuel tank cap to release any pressure or vacuum in the tank.
3. Unstrap both bail wires with a screwdriver and remove the filter.

To install:

4. Before installing the new filter, insure that both filter mounting plate fittings are clear of dirt.
5. Install the new filter, snap into place with the bail wires.
6. Close the water drain valve and open the air bleed valve. Connect a 1/8 in. (3mm) I.D. hose to the air bleed port and place the other end into a suitable container.
7. Disconnect the fuel injection pump shut off solenoid wire.
8. Crank the engine for 10-15 seconds, then wait one minute for the starter motor to cool. Repeat until clear fuel is observed coming from the air bleed.

➡**If the engine is to be cranked, or starting attempted with the air cleaner removed, care must be taken to prevent dirt from being pulled into the air inlet manifold which could result in engine damage.**

9. Close the air bleed valve, reconnect the injection pump solenoid wire and replace the fuel tank cap.
10. Start the engine, allow it to idle for 5 minutes and check the fuel filter for leaks.

6.5L ENGINE

See Figure 59

1. Remove the fuel tank cap to release any pressure or vacuum in the tank.
2. Spin off the element nut at the top of the filter — it looks like a large knurled knob.
3. Lift the filter element out of the header assembly.

To install:

4. Clean the mating surfaces on the header assembly and the filter. Align the widest key slot in the element cap with that in the header assembly, push the element down until the two surfaces make contact, then tighten the nut by hand.
5. Open the air bleed valve on top of the filter assembly. Connect a hose to the bleeder valve and insert the other end into a suitable glass container.

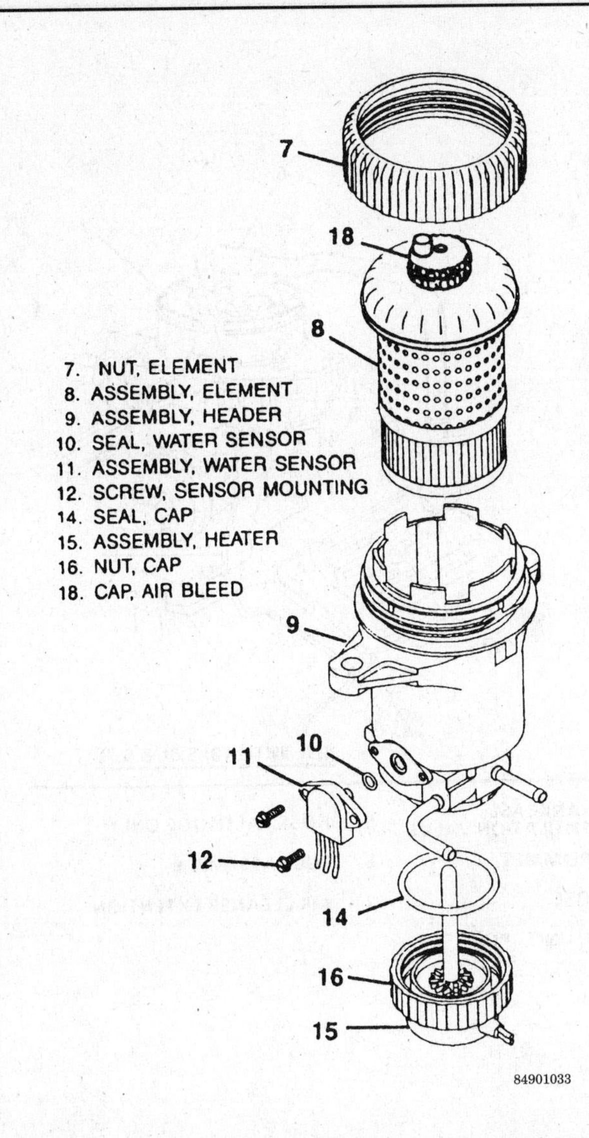

Fig. 59 Exploded view of the fuel filter — 6.5L engines

6. Disconnect the fuel injection pump shut-down solenoid wire, then crank the engine in 10-15 second intervals until clear, clean fuel is coming out of the hose.

➡**Wait about one minute between cranking intervals!**

7. Remove the hose and close the bleeder valve.
8. Connect the shut-down solenoid wire and install the fuel cap. Start the engine and allow it to idle for a few minutes. Check for leaks.

PCV Valve

➧ See Figures 60 and 61

➡**Diesel engines do not utilize a PCV system.**

The PCV valve, which is the heart of the positive crankcase ventilation system, should be changed as noted in the Maintenance Intervals chart at the end of this section. The main thing to keep in mind is that the valve should be free of dirt and residue and should be in working order. As long as the valve is not showing signs of becoming damaged or gummed up, it should perform its function properly. When the valve becomes sticky and will not operate freely, it should be replaced.

The PCV valve is used to control the rate at which crankcase vapors are returned to the intake manifold. The action of the valve plunger is controlled by intake manifold vacuum and the spring. During deceleration and idle, when manifold vacuum is high, it overcomes the tension of the valve spring and the plunger bottoms in the manifold end of the valve housing. Because of the valve construction, it reduces, but does not stop, the passage of vapors to the intake manifold. When the engine is lightly accelerated or operated at constant speed, spring tension matches intake manifold vacuum pull and the plunger takes a mid-position in the valve body, allowing more vapors to flow into the manifold.

The valve is either mounted on the valve cover or in the line which runs from the intake manifold to the crankcase. Do not attempt to adjust or repair the valve. If the valve is faulty, replace it.

TESTING

➧ See Figure 62

An inoperative PCV system will cause rough idling, sludge and oil dilution. In the event erratic idle, never attempt to compensate by disconnecting the PCV system. Disconnecting the PCV system will adversely affect engine ventilation. It could also shorten engine life through the buildup of sludge.

1. With the engine idling, remove the PCV valve from the rocker cover or line. If the valve is not plugged, a hissing sound will be heard. A strong vacuum should be felt when you place your finger over the valve.
2. Reinstall the PCV valve and allow about a minute for pressure to drop.
3. Remove the crankcase intake air cleaner. Cover the opening in the rocker cover with a piece of stiff paper. The paper should be sucked against the opening with noticeable force.
4. With the engine stopped, remove the PCV valve and shake it. A rattle or clicking should be heard to indicate that the valve is free.
5. If the system meets the tests in Steps 1, 2, 3, and 4 (above), no further service is required, unless replacement is specified in the Maintenance Intervals Chart. If the system does not meet the tests, the valve should be replaced with a new one.

➡**Do not attempt to clean a PCV valve.**

6. After checking and/or servicing the Crankcase Ventilation System, any components that do not allow passage or air to the intake manifold should be replaced.

REMOVAL & INSTALLATION

➧ See Figures 63 and 64

1. Remove the PCV valve from the cylinder head cover or from the manifold-to-crankcase hose.
2. Visually inspect all hose connections and hoses for cracks, clogs or deterioration and replace as necessary.

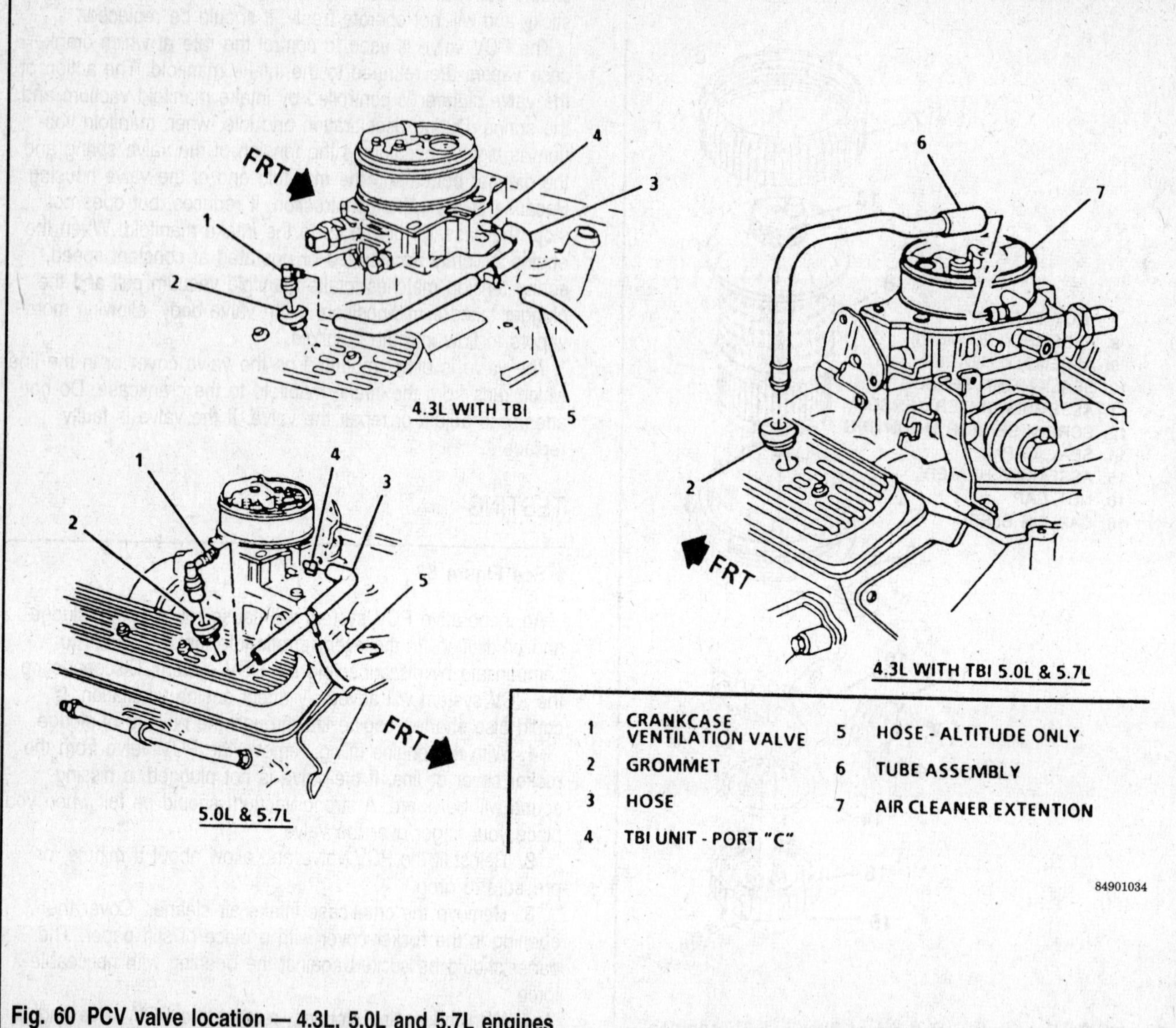

Fig. 60 PCV valve location — 4.3L, 5.0L and 5.7L engines

Crankcase Depression Regulator and Flow Control Valve

SERVICING

➡This system is found only on diesel engines

▸ See Figures 65 and 66

The Crankcase Depression Regulator (CDR) is designed to scavenge crankcase vapors in basically the same manner as the PCV valve on gasoline engines. The valve is located by the right cylinder head cover. On this system, the valve and filter are replaced as an assembly.

The ventilation pipes and tubes should also be cleaned and replaced as wear and tear dictates.

➡Do not attempt to test the crankcase controls on these diesels. Instead, clean the valve cover filter assembly and vent pipes and check the vent pipes. Replace the breather cap assembly every 30,000 miles (48,000 km). Replace all rubber fittings as required every 15,000 miles (24,000 km).

Evaporative Canister

SERVICING

The only regular maintenance that need be performed on the evaporative emission canister is to regularly change the filter (on those 1988-90 models which utilize one; 1991-96 trucks do not have a canister filter) and check the condition of the hoses. If any hoses need replacement, use only hoses which are marked EVAP. No other type should be used.

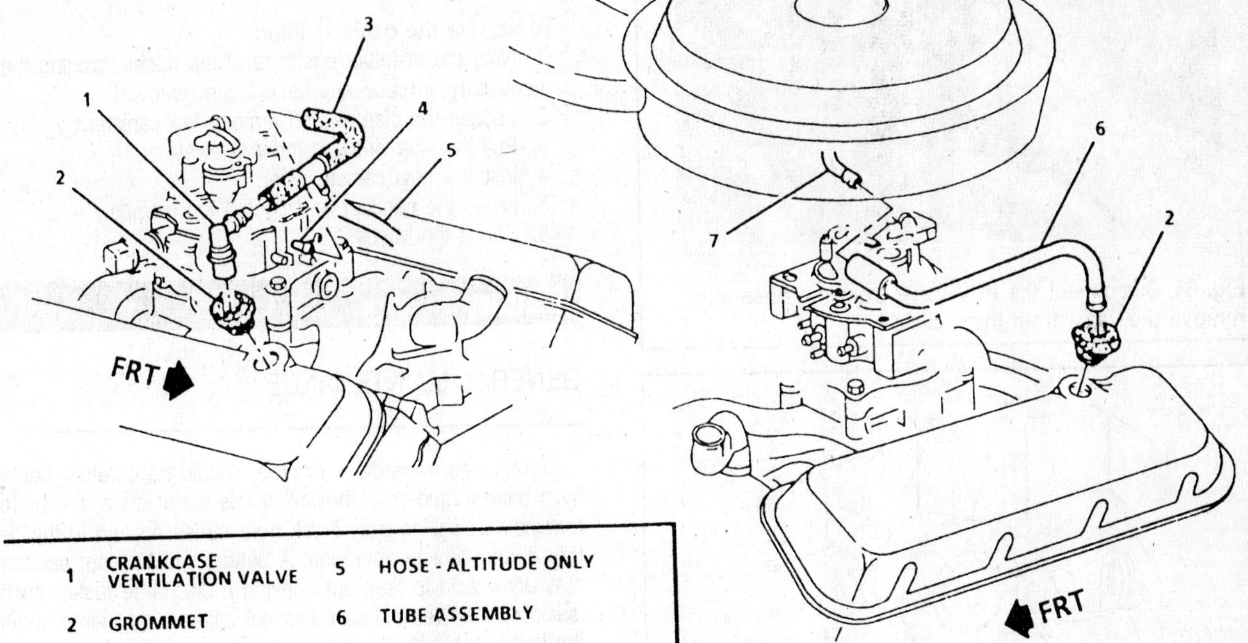

1 CRANKCASE VENTILATION VALVE
2 GROMMET
3 HOSE
4 TBI UNIT - PORT "C"
5 HOSE - ALTITUDE ONLY
6 TUBE ASSEMBLY
7 AIR CLEANER FITTING

FRT

84901035

Fig. 61 PCV valve locations — 7.4L engines

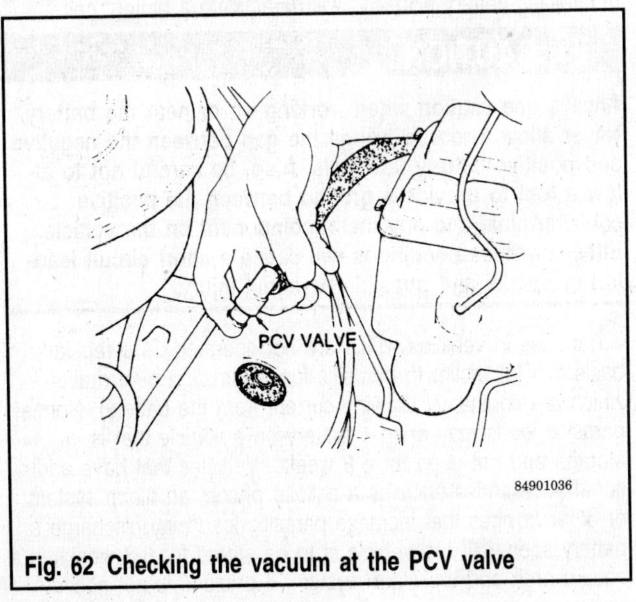

Fig. 62 Checking the vacuum at the PCV valve

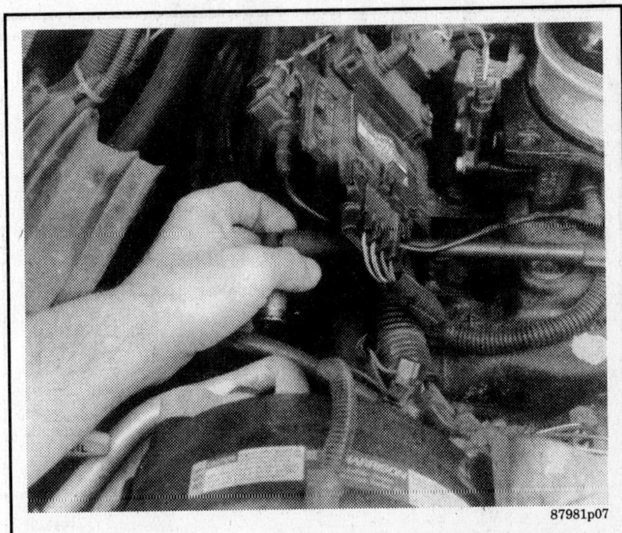

Fig. 63 Pull the PCV valve out of the cylinder head

Fig. 64 Disconnect the PCV valve from the hose and remove the valve from the vehicle

1 CDR VALVE
2 INTAKE MANIFOLD
3 HOSE
4 RIGHT VALVE COVER

84901038

Fig. 65 CDR valve — 6.2L engine

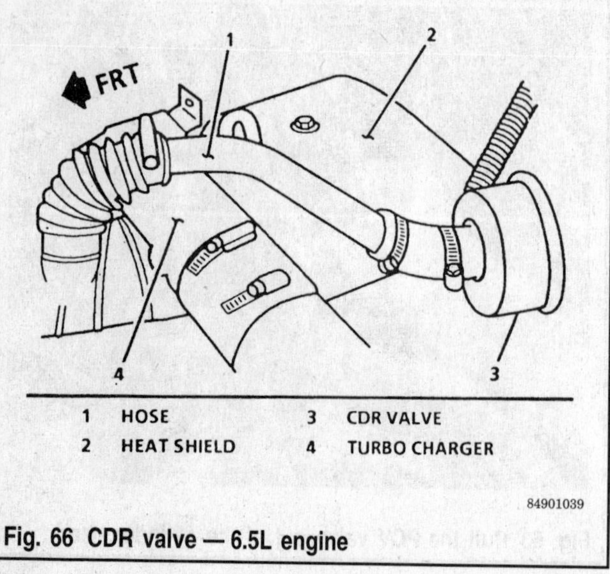

Fig. 66 CDR valve — 6.5L engine

Whenever the vapor vent hose is replaced, the restrictor adjacent to the canister should also be replaced.

The evaporative emission canister is located on the left side of the engine compartment, with a filter located in its bottom (if applicable).

➡**For further information on the evaporative emission system, please refer to Section 4.**

To service the canister filter:

1. Note the installed positions of the hoses, tagging them as necessary, in case any have to be removed.
2. Loosen the clamps and remove the canister.
3. Pull the filter out and throw it away.
4. Install a new canister filter.
5. Install the canister and tighten the clamps.
6. Check the hoses.

Battery

GENERAL MAINTENANCE

All batteries, regardless of type, should be carefully secured by a battery hold-down device. If this is not done, the battery terminals or casing may crack from stress applied to the battery during vehicle operation. A battery which is not secured may allow acid to leak out, making it discharge faster; such leaking corrosive acid can also eat away components under the hood. A battery that is not sealed must be checked periodically for electrolyte level. You cannot add water to a sealed maintenance-free battery (though not all maintenance-free batteries are sealed), but a sealed battery must also be checked for proper electrolyte level as indicated by the color of the built-in hydrometer "eye."

Keep the top of the battery clean, as a film of dirt can completely discharge a battery that is not used for long periods. A solution of baking soda and water may be used for cleaning, but be careful to flush this off with clear water. DO NOT let any of the solution into the filler holes. Baking soda neutralizes battery acid and will de-activate a battery cell.

****CAUTION**

Always use caution when working on or near the battery. Never allow a tool to bridge the gap between the negative and positive battery terminals. Also, be careful not to allow a tool to provide a ground between the positive cable/terminal and any metal component on the vehicle. Either of these conditions will cause a short circuit leading to sparks and possible personal injury.

Batteries in vehicles which are not operated on a regular basis can fall victim to parasitic loads (small current drains which are constantly drawing current from the battery). Normal parasitic loads may drain a battery on a vehicle that is in storage and not used for 6-8 weeks. Vehicles that have additional accessories such as a cellular phone, an alarm system or other devices that increase parasitic load may discharge a battery sooner. If the vehicle is to be stored for 6-8 weeks in a secure area and the alarm system, if present, is not necessary, the negative battery cable should be disconnected at the onset of storage to protect the battery charge.

Remember that constantly discharging and recharging will shorten battery life. Take care not to allow a battery to be needlessly discharged.

BATTERY FLUID

See Figures 67, 68 and 69

CAUTION

Battery electrolyte contains sulfuric acid. If you should splash any on your skin or in your eyes, flush the affected area with plenty of clear water. If it lands in your eyes, get medical help immediately.

The fluid (sulfuric acid solution) contained in the battery cells will tell you many things about the condition of the battery. Because the cell plates must be kept submerged below the fluid level in order to operate, maintaining the fluid level is extremely important. And, because the specific gravity of the acid is an indication of electrical charge, testing the fluid can be an aid in determining if the battery must be replaced. A battery in a vehicle with a properly operating charging system should require little maintenance, but careful, periodic inspection should reveal problems before they leave you stranded.

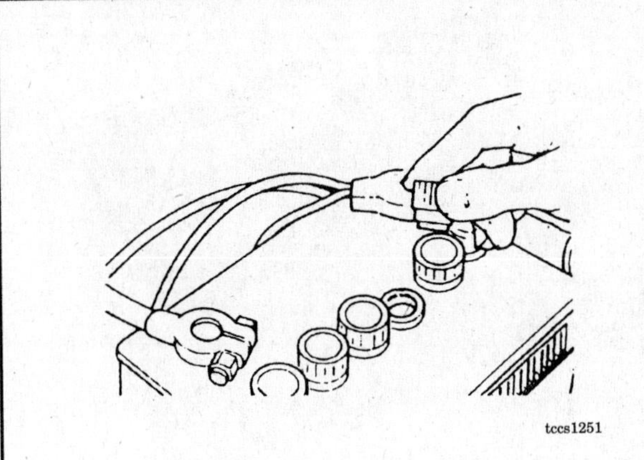

Fig. 67 On non-maintenance free batteries, the level can be checked through the case on translucent batteries; the cell caps must be removed on other models

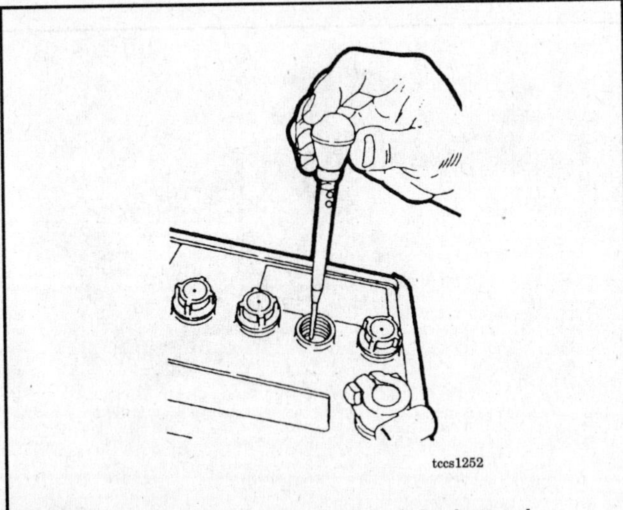

Fig. 68 Check the specific gravity of the battery's electrolyte with a hydrometer

Fluid Level

Check the battery electrolyte level at least once a month, or more often in hot weather or during periods of extended vehicle operation. On non-sealed batteries, the level can be checked either through the case on translucent batteries or by removing the cell caps on opaque-cased types. The electrolyte level in each cell should be kept filled to the split ring inside each cell, or the line marked on the outside of the case.

If the level is low, add only distilled water through the opening until the level is correct. Each cell is separate from the others, so each must be checked and filled individually. Distilled water should be used, because the chemicals and minerals found in most drinking water are harmful to the battery and could significantly shorten its life.

If water is added in freezing weather, the vehicle should be driven several miles to allow the water to mix with the electrolyte. Otherwise, the battery could freeze.

Although some maintenance-free batteries have removable cell caps for access to the electrolyte, the electrolyte condition and level on all sealed maintenance-free batteries must be checked using the built-in hydrometer "eye." The exact type of eye varies between battery manufacturers, but most apply a sticker to the battery itself explaining the possible readings. When in doubt, refer to the battery manufacturer's instructions to interpret battery condition using the built-in hydrometer.

Although the readings from built-in hydrometers found in sealed batteries may vary, a green eye usually indicates a properly charged battery with sufficient fluid level. A dark eye is normally an indicator of a battery with sufficient fluid, but one which may be low in charge. And a light or yellow eye is usually an indication that electrolyte supply has dropped below the necessary level for battery (and hydrometer) operation. In this last case, sealed batteries with an insufficient electrolyte level must usually be discarded.

Specific Gravity

As stated earlier, the specific gravity of a battery's electrolyte level can be used as an indication of battery charge. At least once a year, check the specific gravity of the battery. It should be between 1.20 and 1.26 on the gravity scale. Most auto supply stores carry a variety of inexpensive battery testing hydrometers. These can be used on any non-sealed battery to test the specific gravity in each cell.

The battery testing hydrometer has a squeeze bulb at one end and a nozzle at the other. Battery electrolyte is sucked into the hydrometer until the float is lifted from its seat. The specific gravity is then read by noting the position of the float. If gravity is low in one or more cells, the battery should be slowly charged and checked again to see if the gravity has come up. Generally, if after charging, the specific gravity between any two cells varies more than 50 points (0.50), the

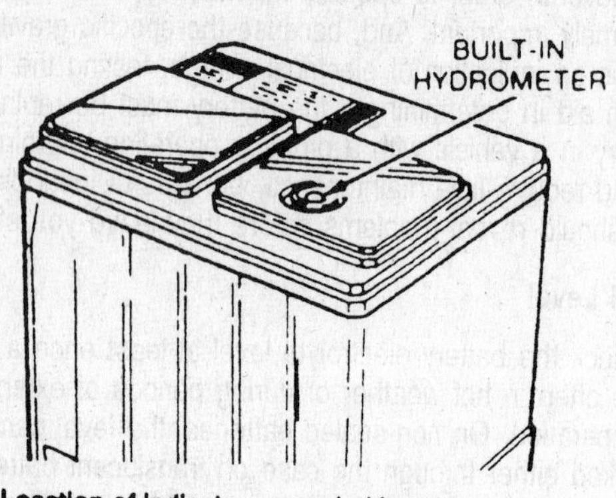

Location of indicator on sealed battery

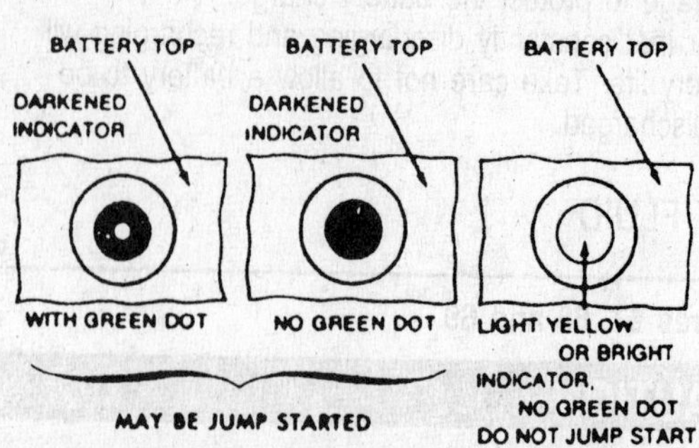

Check the appearance of the charge indicator on top of the battery before attempting a jump start; if it's not green or dark, do not jump start the car

tccs1253

Fig. 69 A typical sealed (maintenance-free) battery with a built-in hydrometer — NOTE that the hydrometer eye may vary between battery manufacturers; always refer to the battery's label

battery should be replaced as it can no longer produce sufficient voltage to guarantee proper operation.

On sealed batteries, the built-in hydrometer is the only way of checking specific gravity. Again, check with your battery's manufacturer for proper interpretation of its built-in hydrometer readings.

CABLES

➧ See Figures 70, 71, 72, 73, 74 and 75

Once a year (or as necessary), the battery terminals and the cable clamps should be cleaned. Loosen the clamps and remove the cables, negative cable first. On batteries with posts on top, the use of a puller specially made for this purpose is recommended. These are inexpensive and available in most auto parts stores. Side terminal battery cables are secured with a small bolt.

Clean the cable clamps and the battery terminal with a wire brush, until all corrosion, grease, etc., is removed and the metal is shiny. It is especially important to clean the inside of

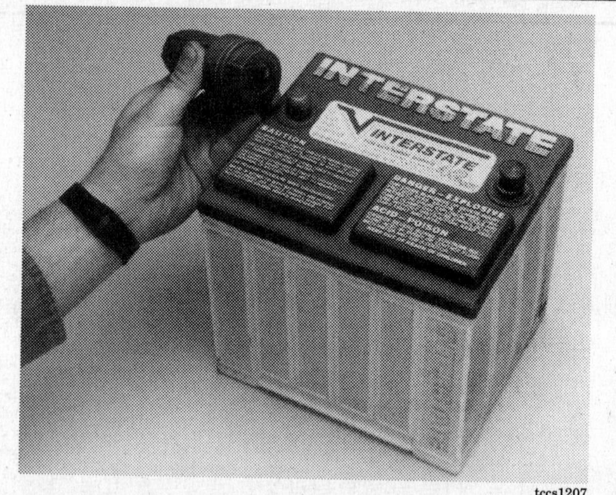

tccs1207

Fig. 71 The underside of this special battery tool has a wire brush to clean post terminals

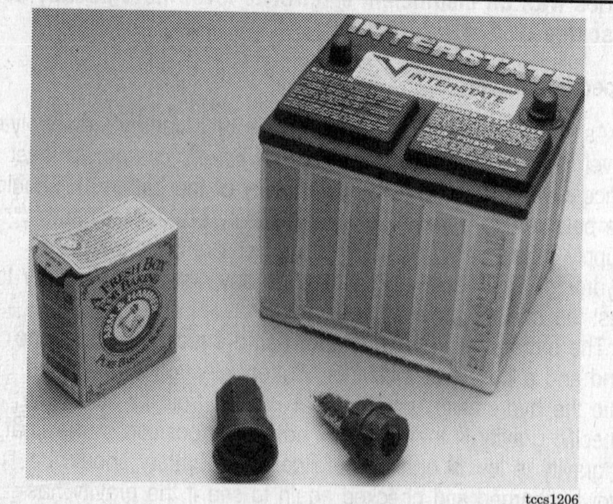

tccs1206

Fig. 70 Maintenance is performed with household items and with special tools like this post cleaner

tccs1208

Fig. 72 Place the tool over the terminals and twist to clean the post

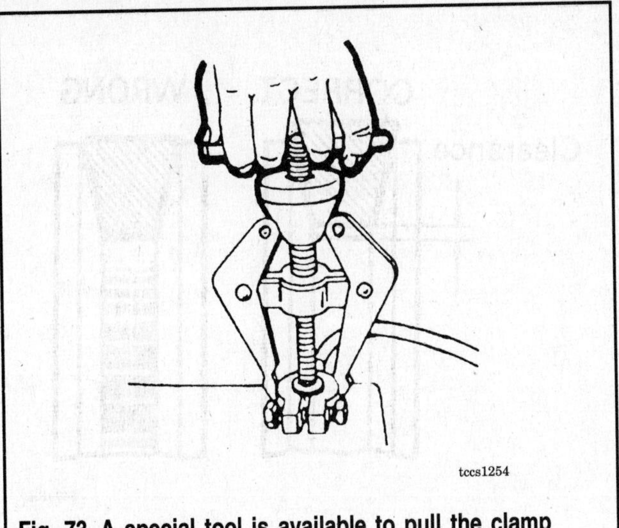

Fig. 73 A special tool is available to pull the clamp from the post

the clamp (an old knife is useful here) thoroughly, since a small deposit of foreign material or oxidation there will prevent a sound electrical connection and inhibit either starting or charging. Special tools are available for cleaning these parts, one type for conventional top post batteries and another type for side terminal batteries.

Before installing the cables, loosen the battery hold-down clamp or strap, remove the battery and check the battery tray. Clear it of any debris, and check it for soundness (the battery tray can be cleaned with a baking soda and water solution). Rust should be wire brushed away, and the metal given a couple coats of anti-rust paint. Install the battery and tighten the hold-down clamp or strap securely. Do not overtighten, as this can crack the battery case.

After the clamps and terminals are clean, reinstall the cables, negative cable last; DO NOT hammer the clamps onto post batteries. Tighten the clamps securely, but do not distort

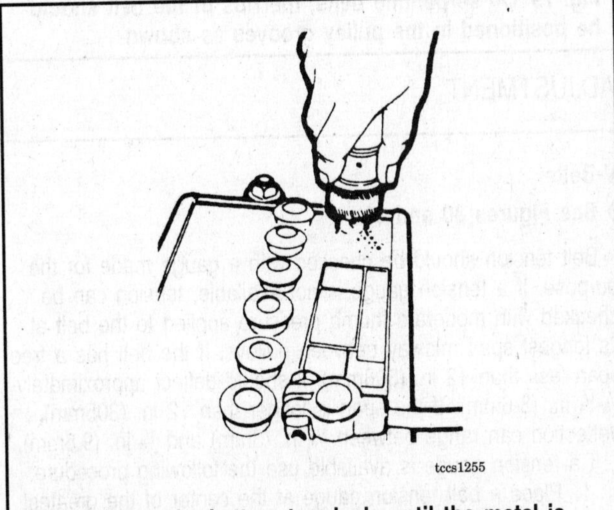

Fig. 74 Clean the battery terminals until the metal is shiny

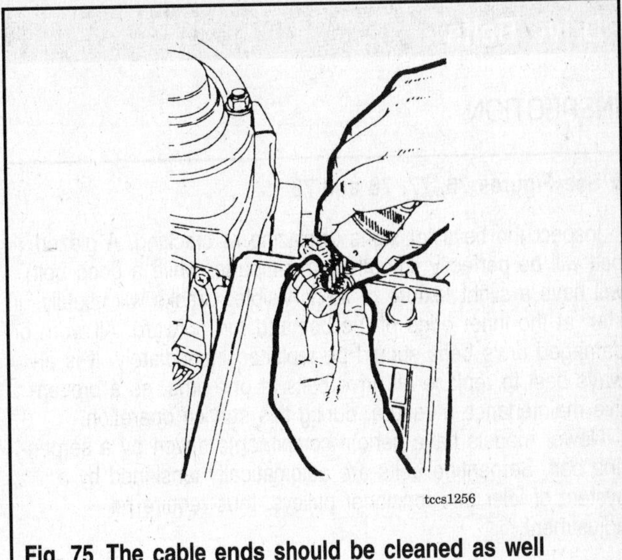

Fig. 75 The cable ends should be cleaned as well

them. Give the clamps and terminals a thin external coating of grease after installation, to retard corrosion.

Check the cables at the same time that the terminals are cleaned. If the cable insulation is cracked or broken, or if the ends are frayed, the cable should be replaced with a new cable of the same length and gauge.

CHARGING

****CAUTION**

The chemical reaction which takes place in all batteries generates explosive hydrogen gas. A spark can cause the battery to explode and splash acid. To avoid serious personal injury, be sure there is proper ventilation and take appropriate fire safety precautions when connecting, disconnecting, or charging a battery and when using jumper cables.

A battery should be charged at a slow rate to keep the plates inside from getting too hot. However, if some maintenance-free batteries are allowed to discharge until they are almost "dead," they may have to be charged at a high rate to bring them back to "life." Always follow the charger manufacturer's instructions on charging the battery.

REPLACEMENT

When it becomes necessary to replace the battery, select one with a rating equal to or greater than the battery originally installed. Deterioration and just plain aging of the battery cables, starter motor, and associated wires makes the battery's job harder in successive years. The slow increase in electrical resistance over time makes it prudent to install a new battery with a greater capacity than the old.

Drive Belts

INSPECTION

➧ **See Figures 76, 77, 78 and 79**

Inspect the belts for signs of glazing or cracking. A glazed belt will be perfectly smooth from slippage, while a good belt will have a slight texture of fabric visible. Cracks will usually start at the inner edge of the belt and run outward. All worn or damaged drive belts should be replaced immediately. It is always best to replace all drive belts at one time, as a preventive maintenance measure, during this service operation.

Newer models have certain components driven by a serpentine belt. Serpentine belts are automatically tensioned by a system of idler and tensioner pulleys, thus require no adjustment.

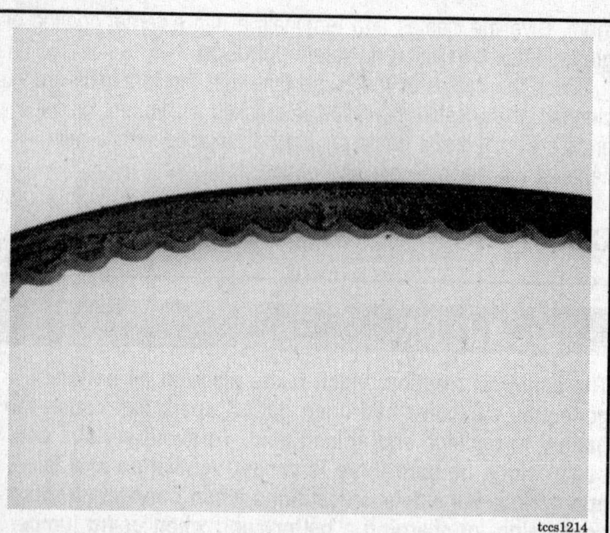

Fig. 76 An example of a healthy drive belt

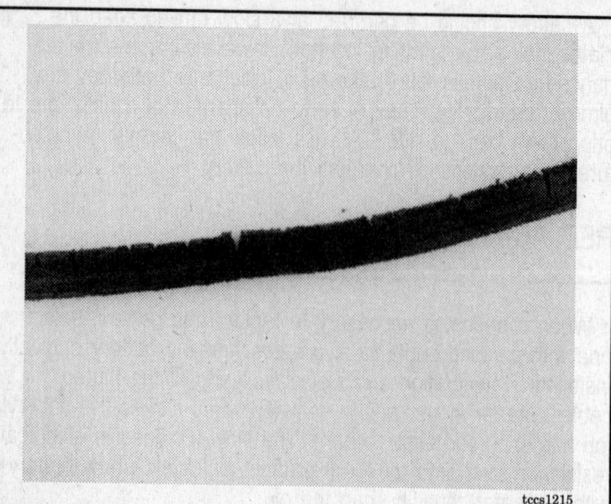

Fig. 77 The deep cracks in this belt will cause it to flex, building up heat that will eventually lead to failure

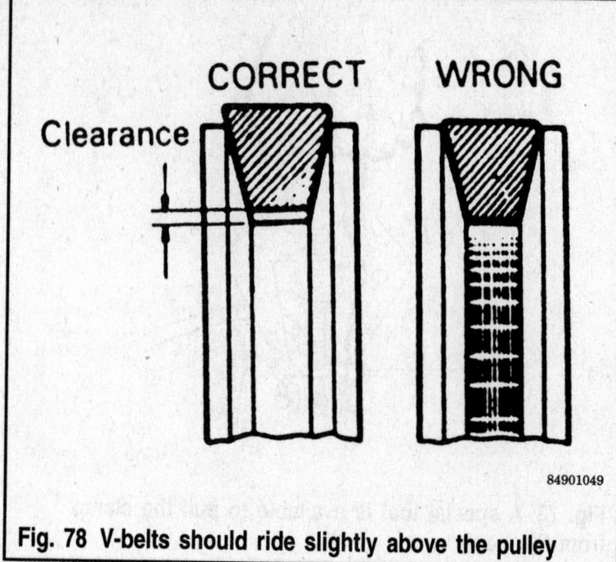

Fig. 78 V-belts should ride slightly above the pulley

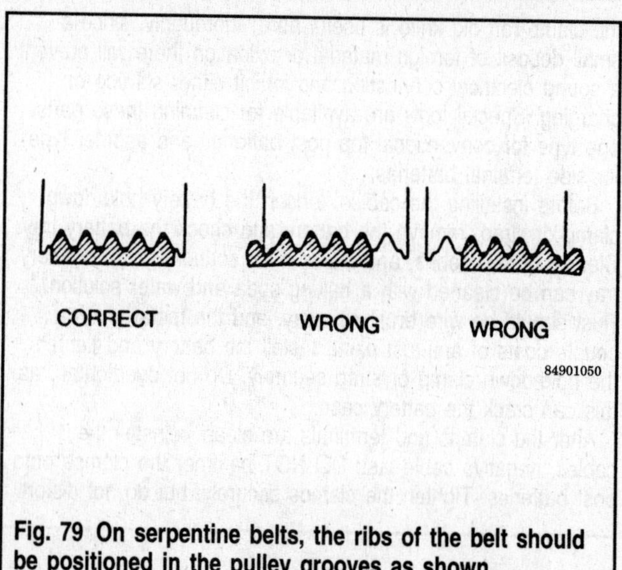

Fig. 79 On serpentine belts, the ribs of the belt should be positioned in the pulley grooves as shown

ADJUSTMENT

V-Belts

➧ **See Figures 80 and 81**

Belt tension should be checked with a gauge made for the purpose. If a tension gauge is not available, tension can be checked with moderate thumb pressure applied to the belt at its longest span midway between pulleys. If the belt has a free span less than 12 in. (305mm), it should deflect approximately $\frac{1}{8}$-$\frac{1}{4}$ in. (3-6mm). If the span is longer than 12 in. (305mm), deflection can range between $\frac{1}{8}$ in. (3mm) and $\frac{3}{8}$ in. (9.5mm).

If a tension gauge is available use the following procedure:

1. Place a belt tension gauge at the center of the greatest span of a warm, not hot, drive belt and measure the tension.
2. If the belt is not within the specification, loosen the component mounting bracket and adjust to specification.
3. Run the engine at idle for 15 minutes to allow the belt to reseat itself in the pulleys.

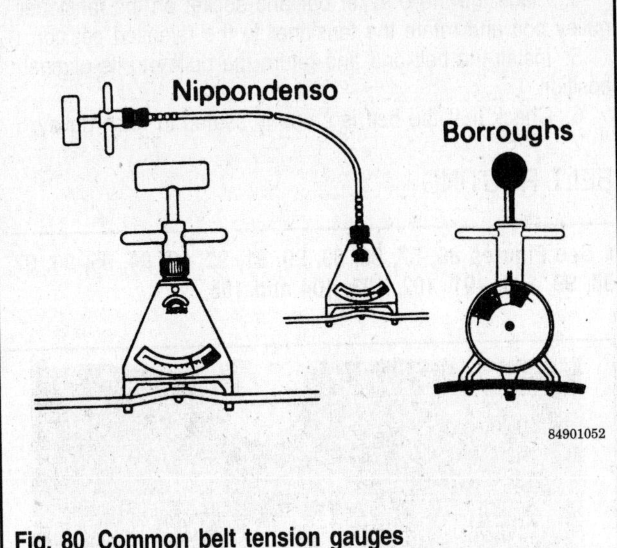

Fig. 80 Common belt tension gauges

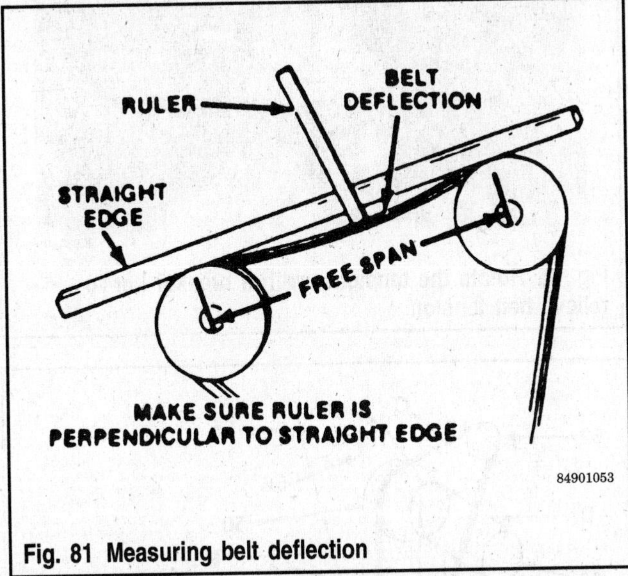

Fig. 81 Measuring belt deflection

4. Allow the drive belt to cool and re-measure the tension. Adjust as necessary to meet the following specifications:

- V6, V8 gasoline engines: used — 90 ft. lbs. (122Nm); new — 135 ft. lbs. (183 Nm).
- 6 — 4.8L: used — 90 ft. lbs. (122 Nm); new — 169 ft. lbs. (229 Nm).
- V8 — 6.2L/6.5L diesel: used — 67 ft. lbs. (90 Nm); new — 146 ft. lbs. (197 Nm).

➡A belt is considered "used' after 15 minutes of operation.

Serpentine Drive Belts

The serpentine belt tension can be checked by simply observing the belt acceptable belt wear range indicator located on the tensioner spindle. If the belt does not meet the specified range, it must be replaced.

REMOVAL & INSTALLATION

V-Belts

➧ See Figures 82, 83 and 84

1. Loosen the driven accessory's pivot and mounting bolts. Remove the belt.
2. Install the belt. Move the accessory toward or away from the engine until the tension is correct. You can use a wooden hammer handle, or broomstick, as a lever, but do not use anything metallic, such as a prybar. Certain models may utilize an adjusting bolt to do this work for you. Simply loosen the mounting bolt and turn the adjuster!
3. Tighten the bolts and recheck the tension. If new belts have been installed, run the engine for a few minutes, then recheck and readjust as necessary.

It is better to have belts too loose than too tight, because overtight belts will lead to bearing failure, particularly in the water pump and alternator. However, loose belts place an ex-

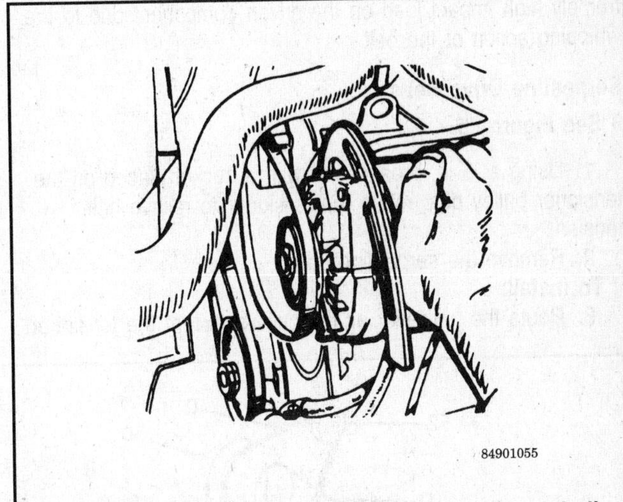

Fig. 82 Push the component toward the engine and slip off the belt

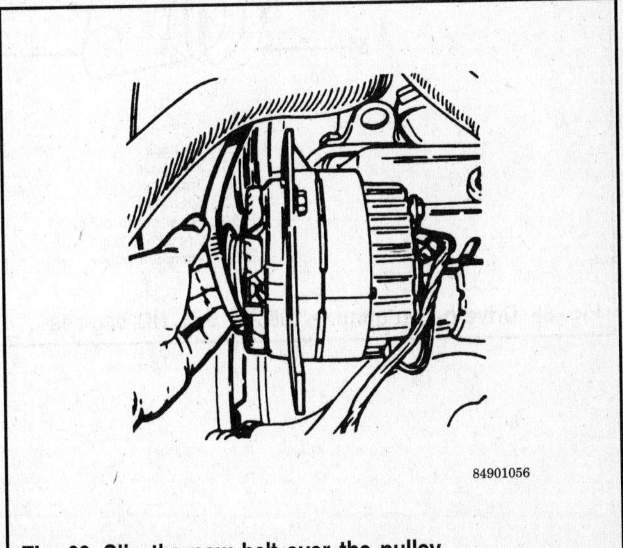

Fig. 83 Slip the new belt over the pulley

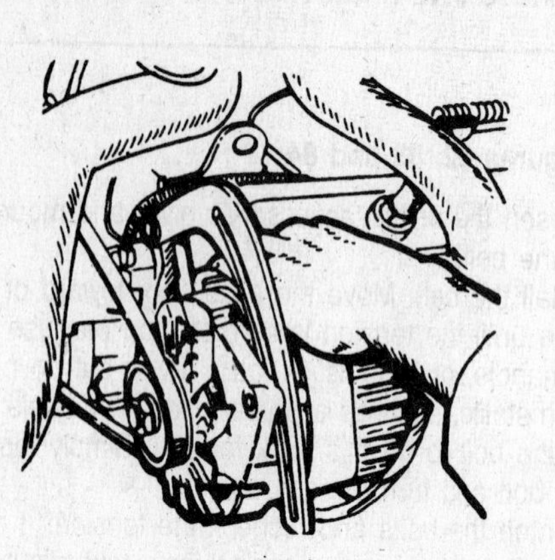

Fig. 84 Pull outward on the component and tighten the adjusting and mounting bolts

tremely high impact load on the driven component due to the whipping action of the belt.

Serpentine Drive Belts

➧ See Figure 85

1. Using a ½ in. breaker bar with a socket placed on the tensioner pulley bolt, rotate the tensioner to relieve belt tension.
2. Remove the serpentine belt.

To install:

3. Route the belt over all the pulleys except the tensioner.
4. Place the the breaker bar and socket on the tensioner pulley bolt and rotate the tensioner to the released position.
5. Install the belt and and return the pulley to its original position.
6. Check that the belt is properly seated in each pulley.

BELT ROUTING

➧ See Figures 86, 87, 88, 89, 90, 91, 92, 93, 94, 95, 96, 97, 98, 99, 100, 101, 102, 103, 104 and 105

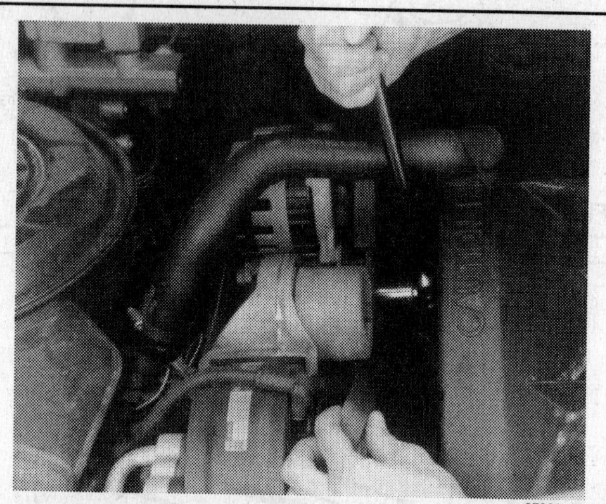

87981p09

Fig. 85 Rotate the tensioner with a breaker bar to relieve belt tension

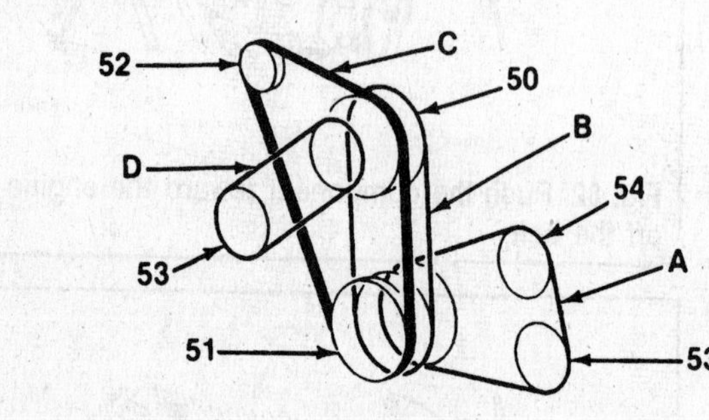

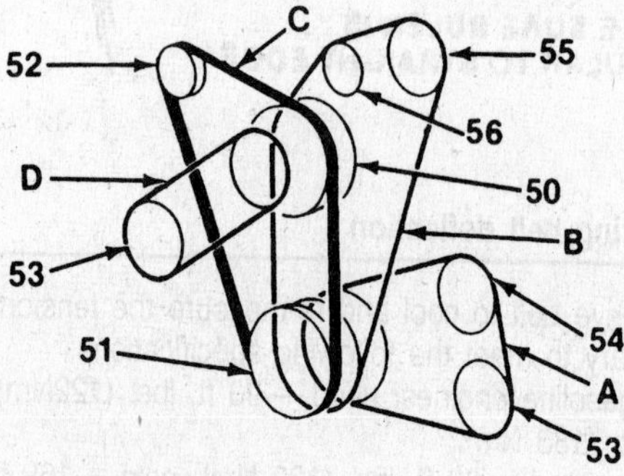

A. 1st track
B. 2nd track
C. 3rd track
D. 4th track
50. Water pump pulley
51. Crankshaft pulley
52. Alternator pulley
53. AIR pump pulley
54. Power steering pump pulley
55. Air conditioning compressor pulley
56. Idler pulley

84901058

Fig. 86 Drive belt routing — 1988-90 5.7L HD engines

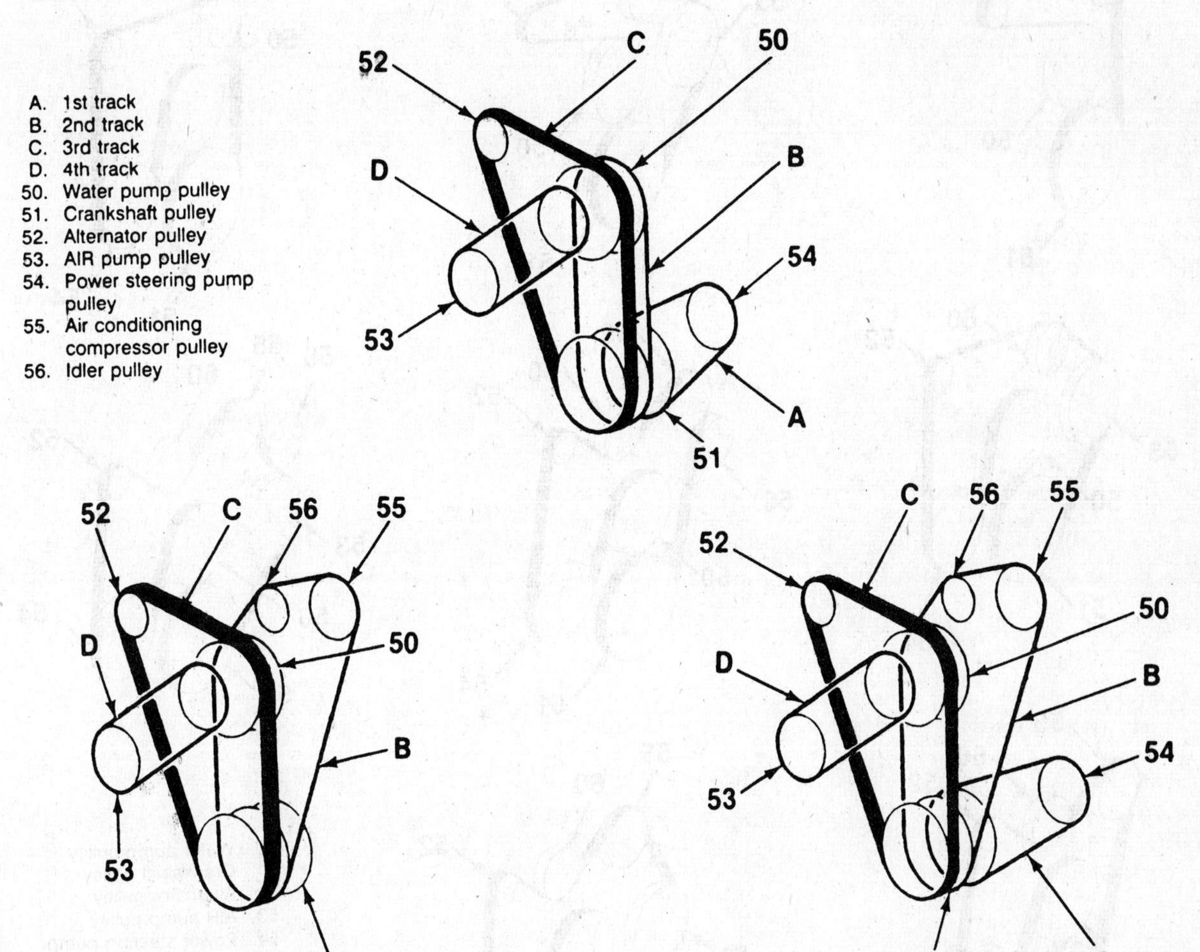

Fig. 87 Drive belt routing — 1988-90 5.7L, 6.2L engines

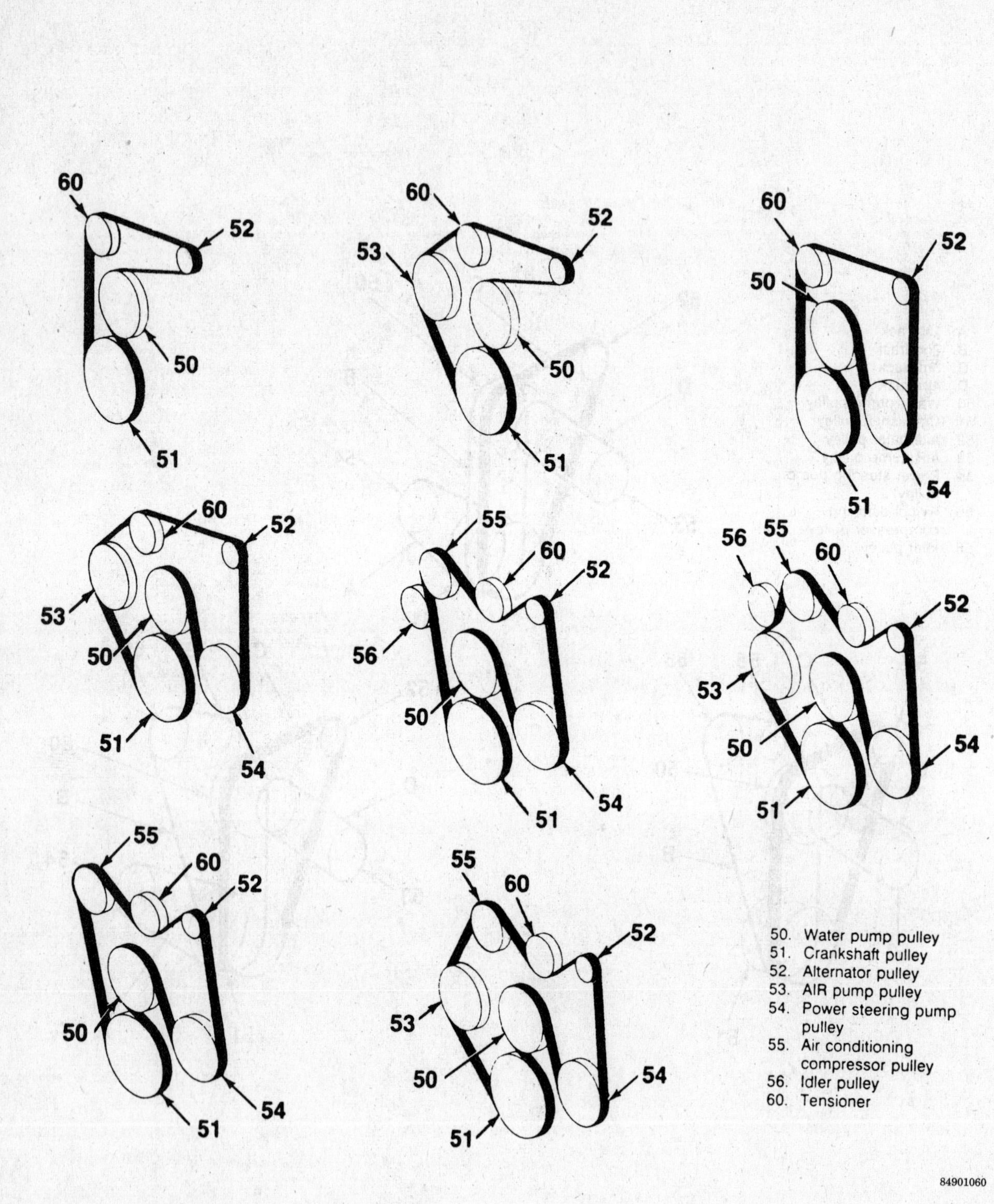

Fig. 88 Drive belt routing — 1988-90 4.3L, 5.0L and 7.4L engines

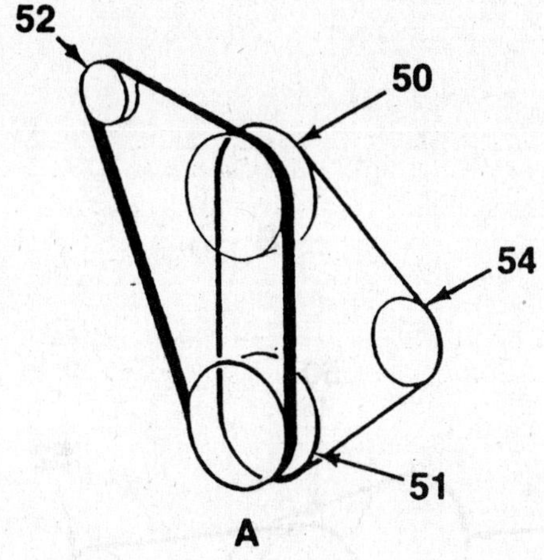

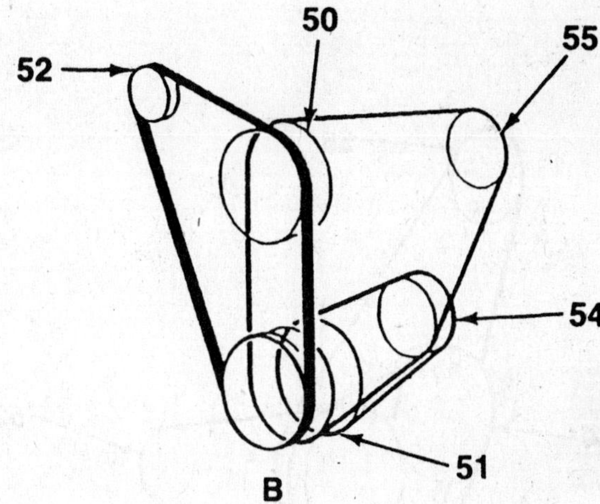

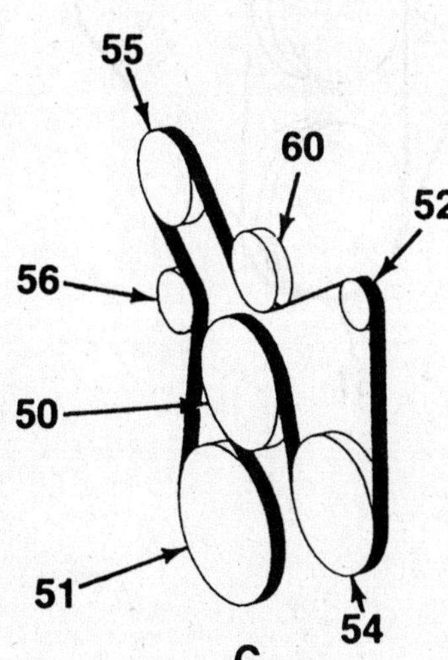

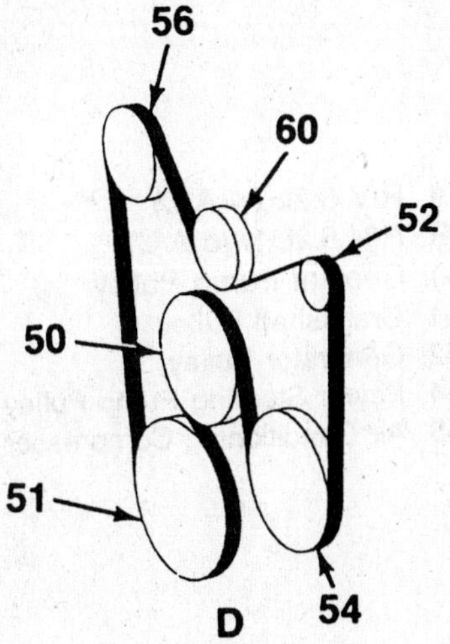

A. R/V3 5.7L (W/O A/C)
B. R/V35.7L (W A/C)
C. R/V1,2 5.7L (W A/C)
D. R/V1,2 5.7L (W/O A/C)
50. Coolant Pump Pulley
51. Crankshaft Pulley
52. Generator Pulley
54. Power Steering Pump Pulley
55. Air Conditioning Compressor Pulley
56. Idler Pulley
60. Tensioner

84901061

Fig. 89 Drive belt routing — 1991 5.7L engines, R/V series

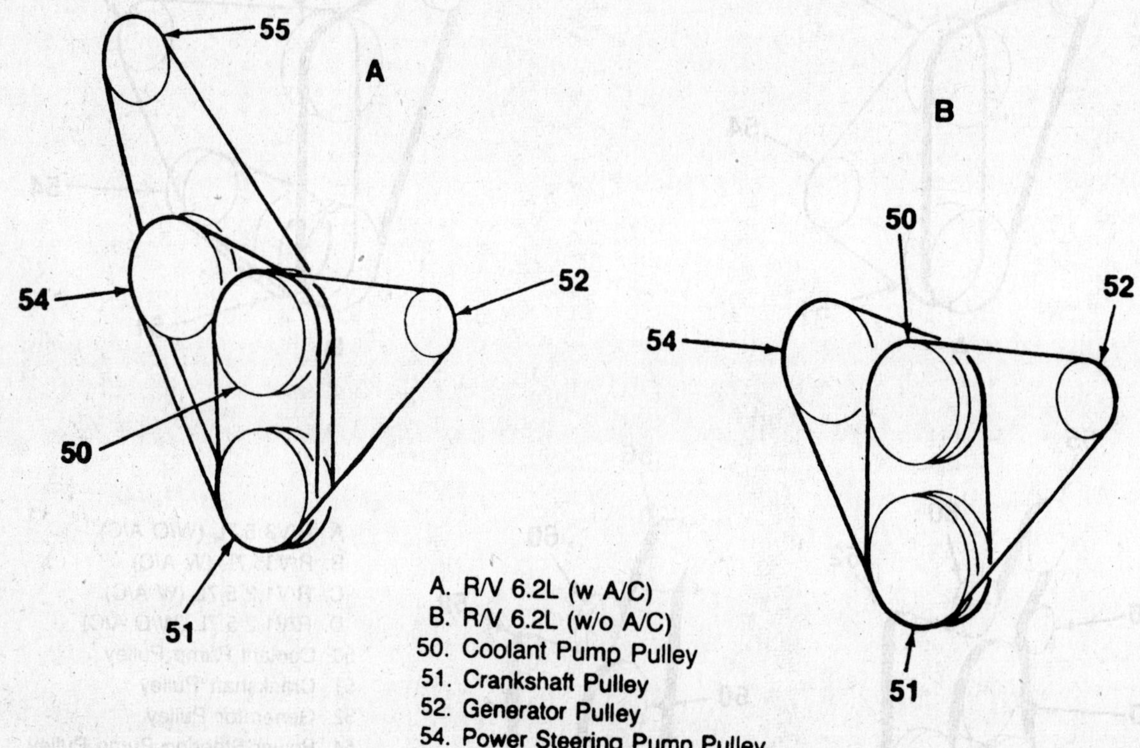

Fig. 90 Drive belt routing — 1991 6.2L engines, R/V series

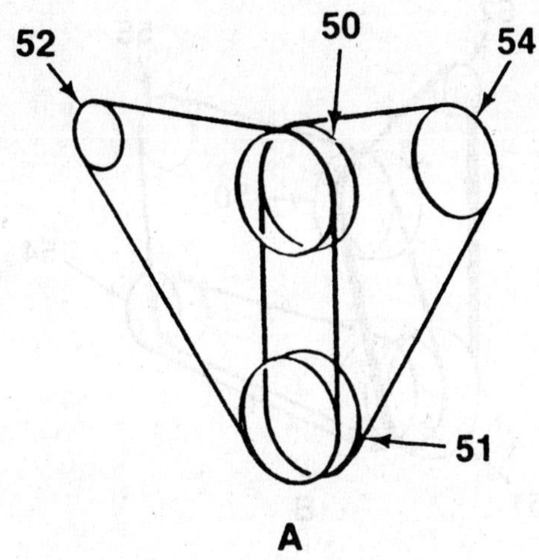

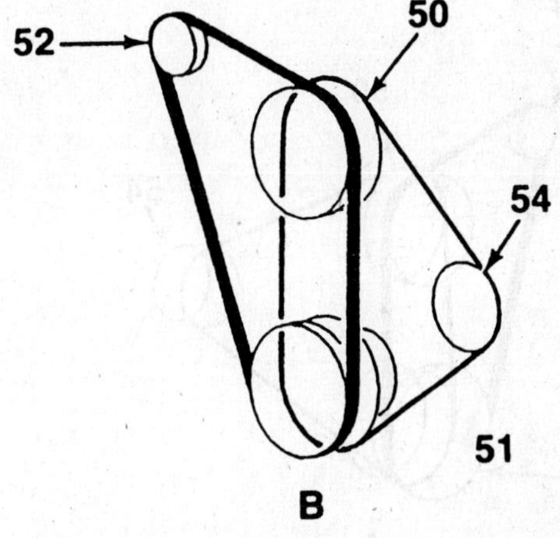

A. P3 6.26 HD (W P/S, P/B Pump)
B. P3 4.3L, 5.7L (W P/S)
C. P3 5.7L (W P/S and A/C)
50. Coolant Pump Pulley
51. Crankshaft Pulley
52. Generator Pulley
54. Power Steering Pump Pulley
55. Air Conditioning Compressor Pulley
56. Idler Pulley

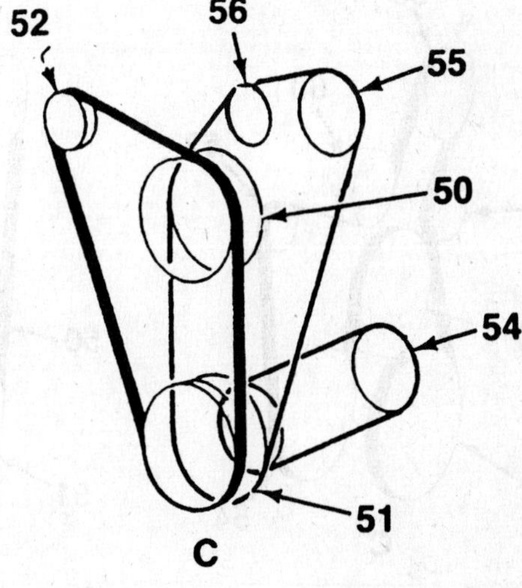

84901063

Fig. 91 Drive belt routing — 1991 6.2L HD, 4.3L engines

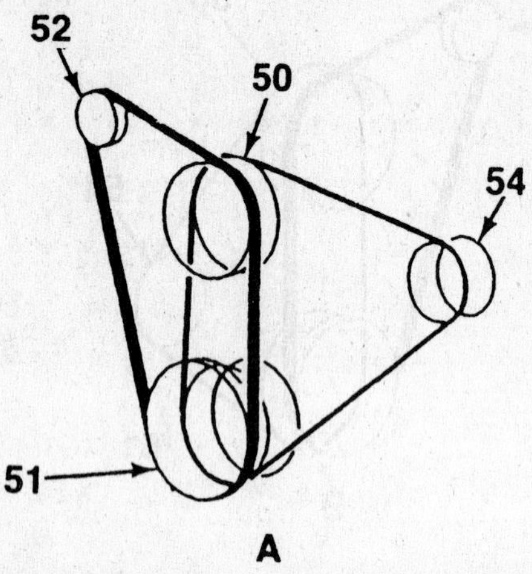

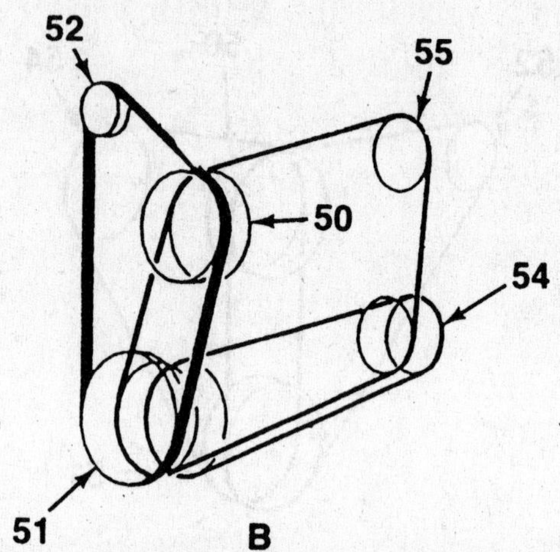

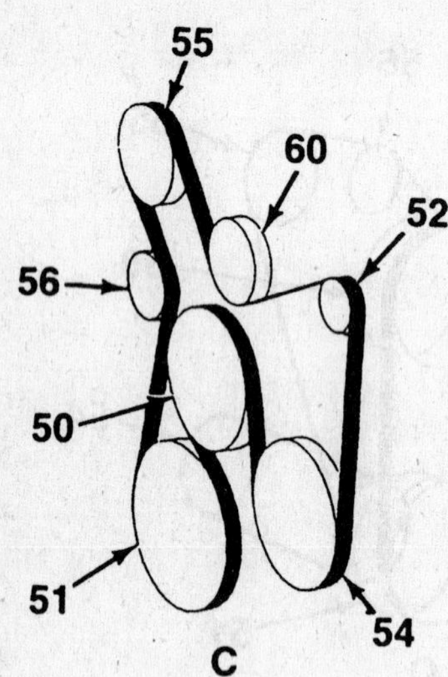

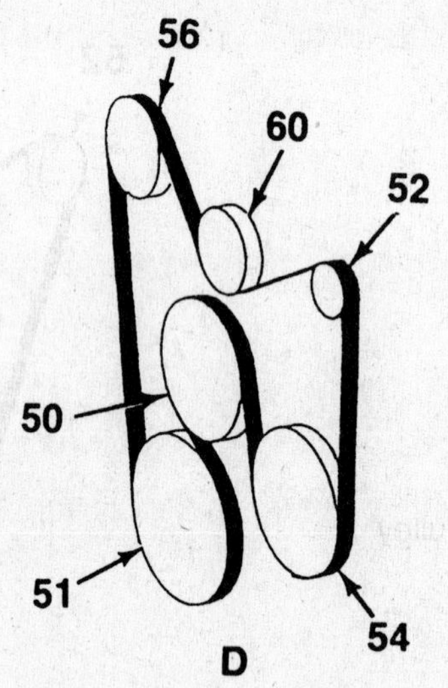

A. R/V3 7.4L (W/O A/C)
B. R/V3 7.4L (W A/C)
C. R2 7.4L (W A/C)
D. R2 7.4L (W/O A/C)
50. Coolant Pump Pulley
51. Crankshaft Pulley
52. Generator Pulley
54. Power Steering Pump Pulley
55. Air Conditioning Compressor Pulley
56. Idler Pulley
60. Tensioner

84901064

Fig. 92 Drive belt routing — 1991 7.4L engines, R/V series

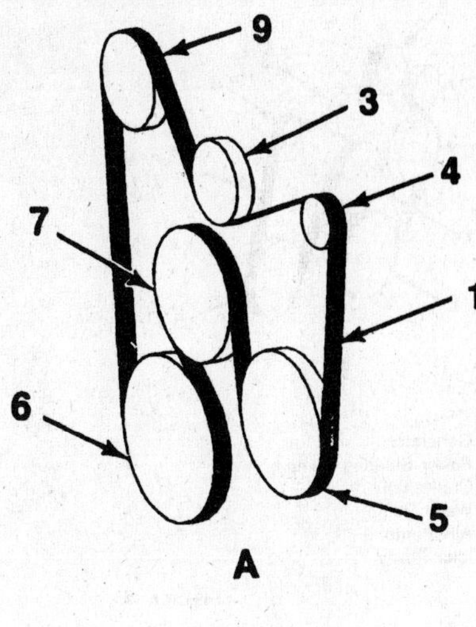

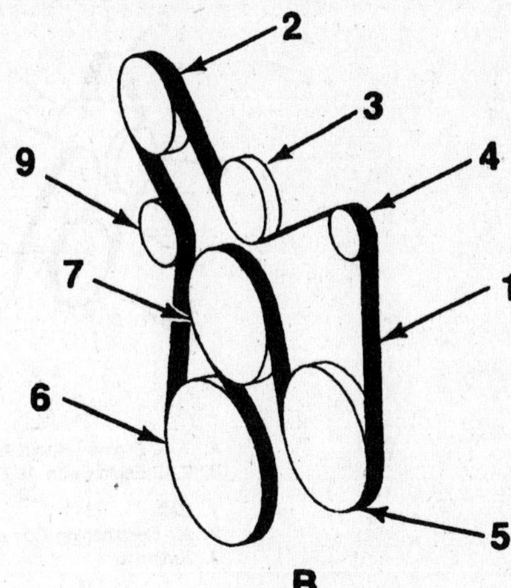

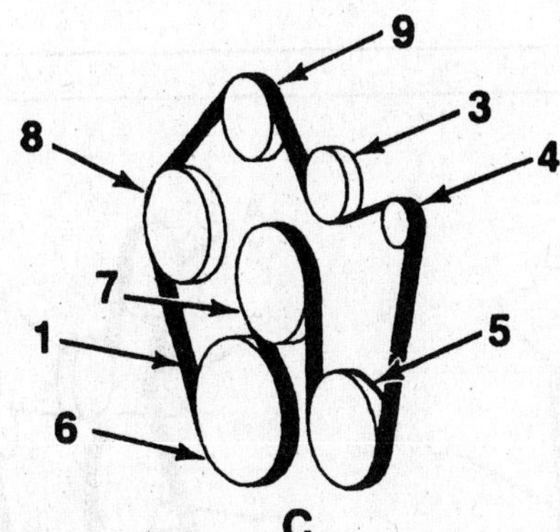

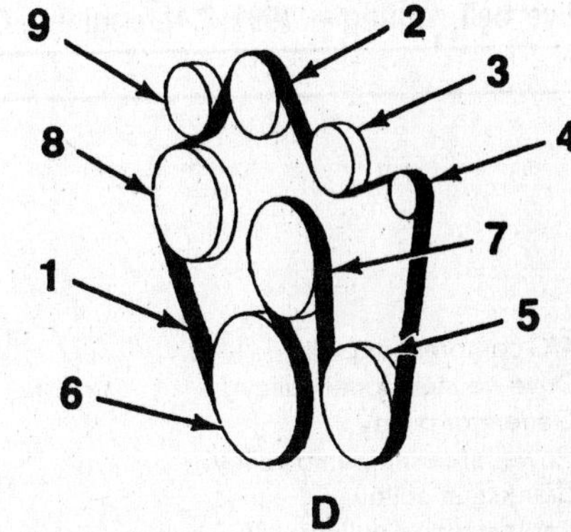

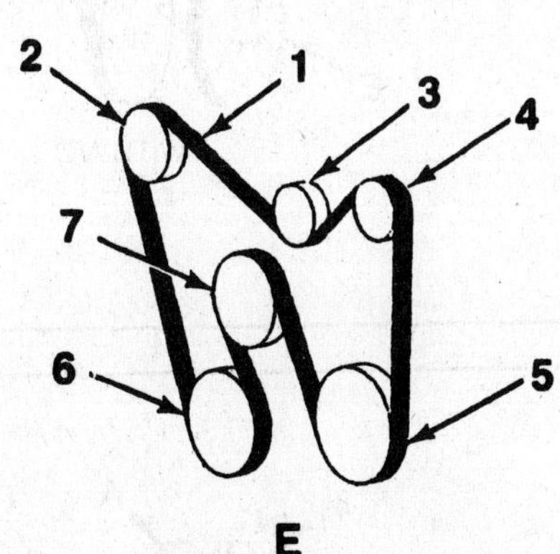

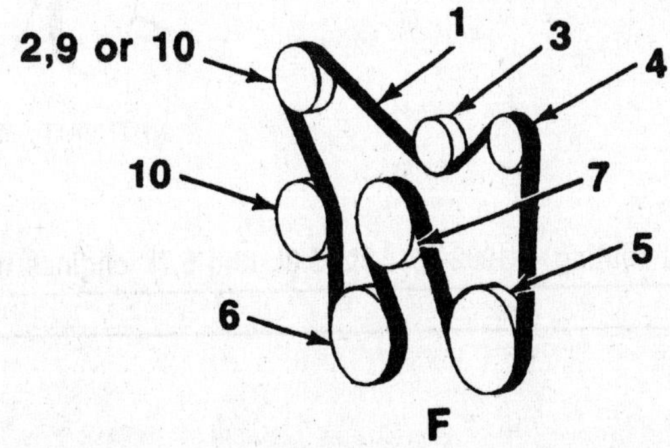

1. Belt
2. Air Conditioning Compressor
3. Tensioner
4. Generator
5. Power Steering Pump
6. Crankshaft
7. Coolant Pump
8. AIR Pump
9. Idler Pulley

* 4.3L, 5.0L, 5.7L Engines
A. With Power Steering Pump
B. With Power Steering Pump and A/C Compressor
C. With Power Steering Pump and AIR Pump
D. With Power Steering Pump and AIR Pump and A/C Compressor

* 6.2L Diesel Engines
E. With Air Conditioning
F. With Air Conditioning or Vacuum Pump or Idler Pulley

84901069

Fig. 93 Drive belt routing — 1991 4.3L, 5,0L, 5.7L and 6.2L engines, C/K series

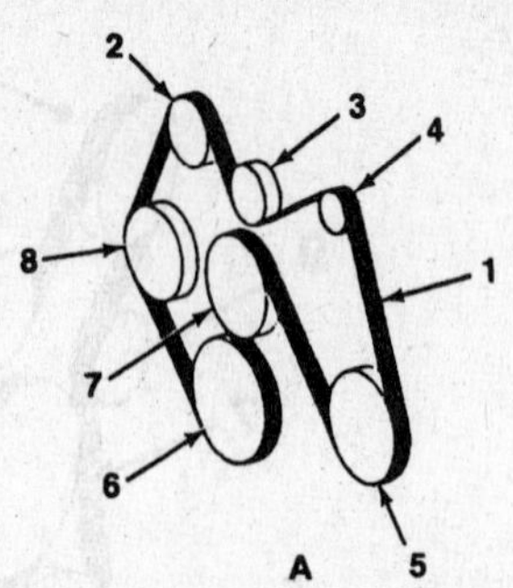

A. 7.4L Engine without Air Conditioning
B. 7.4L Engine with Air Conditioning

1. Belt
2. Air Conditioning Compressor
3. Tensioner
4. Generator
5. Power Steering Pump
6. Crankshaft
7. Water Pump
8. AIR Pump
9. Idler Pulley

84901070

Fig. 94 Drive belt routing — 1991 7.4L engines, C/K series

A. A/C compressor pulley
B. Drive belt tensioner pulley
C. Generator pulley
D. Power steering pump pulley
E. Crankshaft pulley
F. Coolant pump pulley
H. Idler pulley

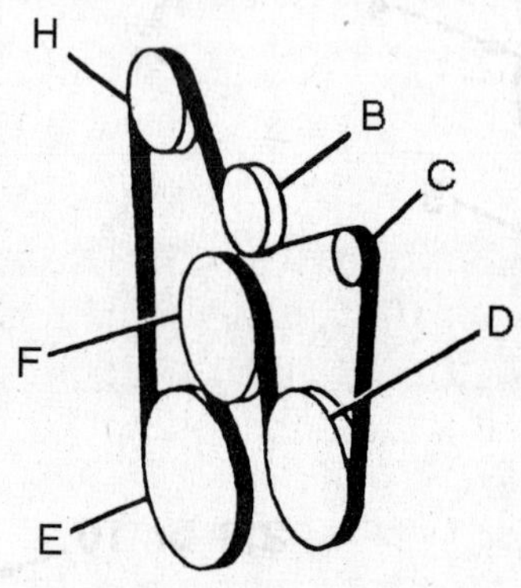

WITHOUT A/C

WITH A/C

84901065

Fig. 95 Drive belt routing — 1992-93 4.3L, 5.0L and 5.7L engines w/o AC

A. A/C compressor pulley
B. Drive belt tensioner pulley
C. Generator pulley
D. Power steering pump pulley
E. Crankshaft pulley
F. Coolant pump pulley
H. Idler pulley
I. A.I.R. pump pulley

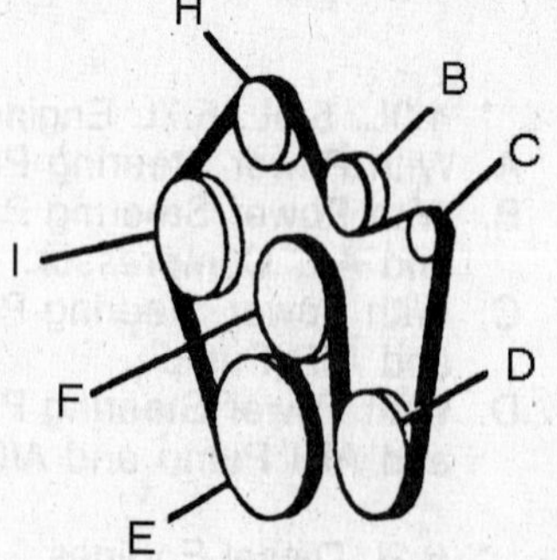

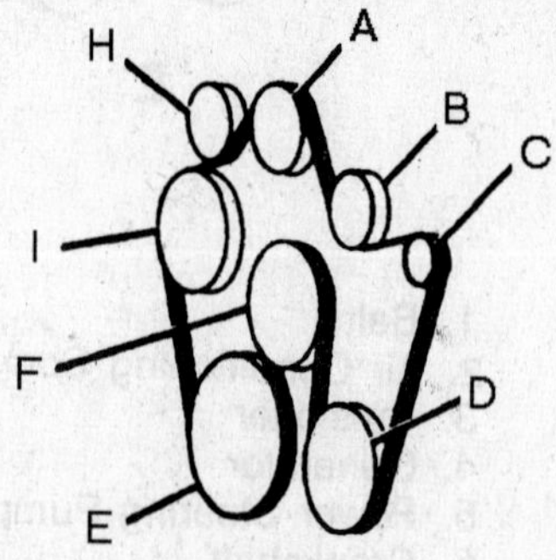

84901066

Fig. 96 Drive belt routing — 1992-93 4.3L and 5.7L engines w/AC

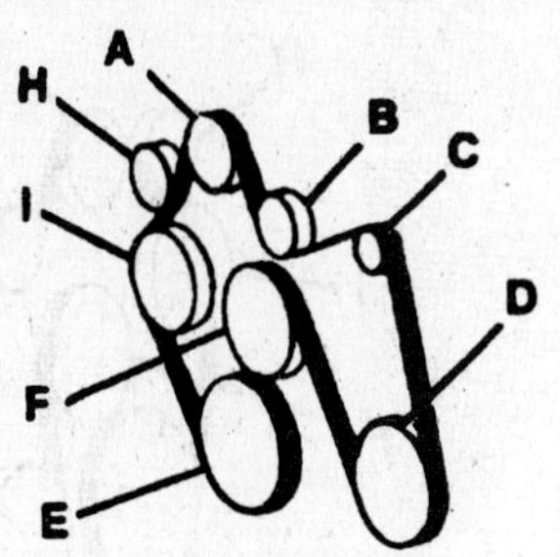

C1 WITH A/C

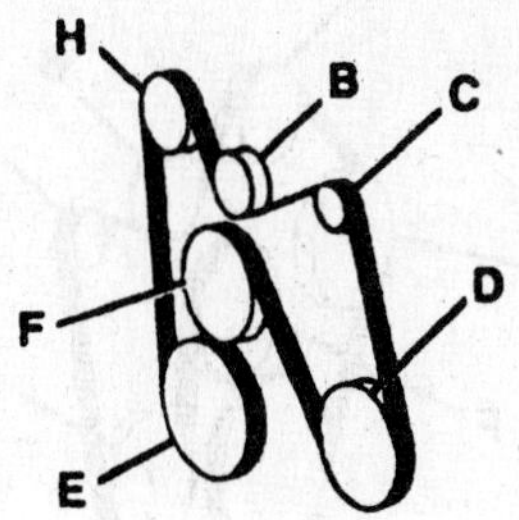

CK 2,3 WITHOUT A/C

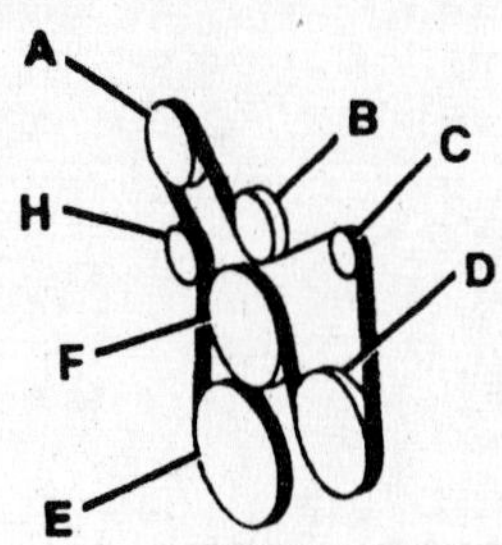

CK 2,3 WITH A/C

A. PULLEY, A/C COMPRESSOR
B. PULLEY, DRIVE BELT TENSIONER
C. PULLEY, GENERATOR
D. PULLEY, POWER STEERING PUMP
E. PULLEY, CRANKSHAFT
F. PULLEY, COOLANT PUMP
H. PULLEY, IDLER
I. PULLEY, A.I.R. PUMP

84901067

Fig. 97 Drive belt routing — 1992-93 7.4L engines

A. PULLEY, A/C COMPRESSOR
B. PULLEY, DRIVE BELT TENSIONER
C. PULLEY, GENERATOR
D. PULLEY, POWER STEERING PUMP
E. PULLEY, CRANKSHAFT
F. PULLEY, COOLANT PUMP
G. PULLEY, VACUUM PUMP
H. PULLEY, IDLER

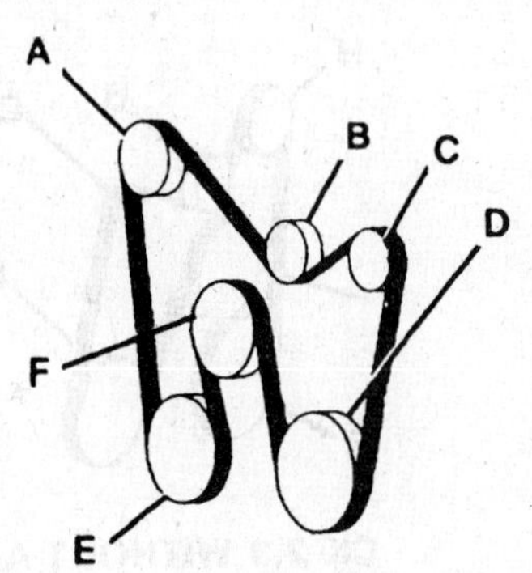

WITH A/C

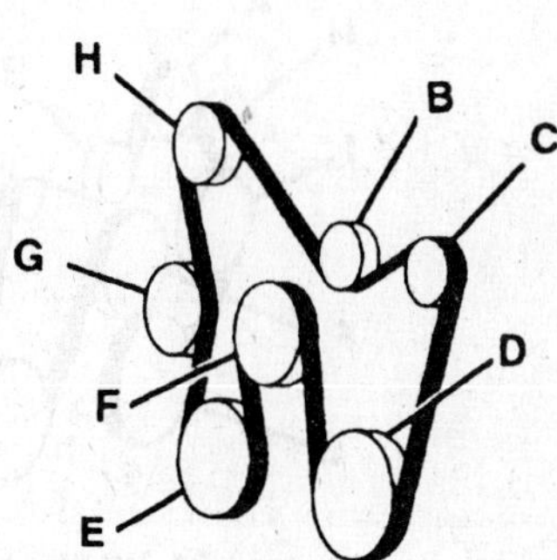

WITHOUT A/C

84901068

Fig. 98 Drive belt routing — 1992-93 6.2L and 6.5L engines

A. PULLEY, A/C COMPRESSOR
B. PULLEY, DRIVE BELT TENSIONER
C. PULLEY, GENERATOR
D. PULLEY, POWER STEERING PUMP
E. PULLEY, CRANKSHAFT
F. PULLEY, COOLANT PUMP
H. PULLEY, IDLER

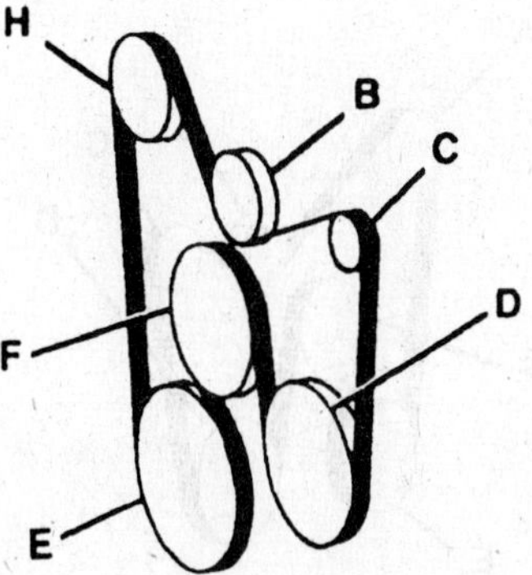

WITHOUT A/C

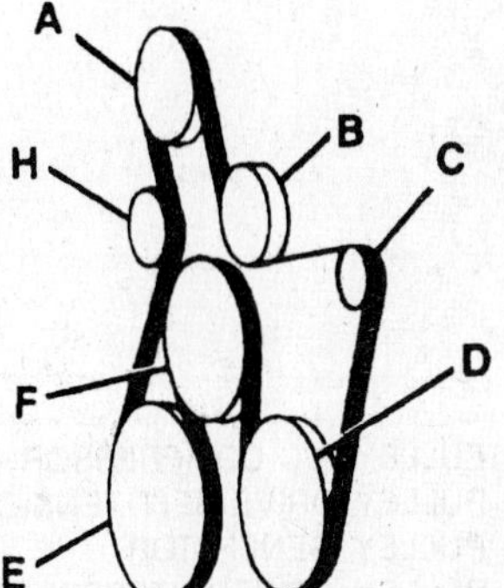

WITH A/C

87981533

Fig. 99 Drive belt routing — 1994-95 4.3L, 5.0L and 5.7L engines, C/K series (without A.I.R.)

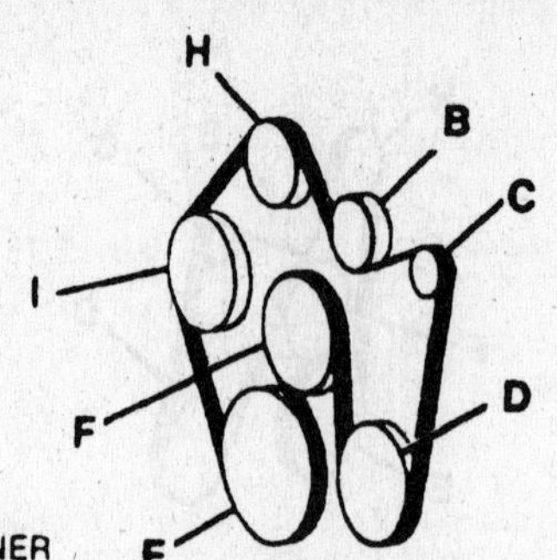

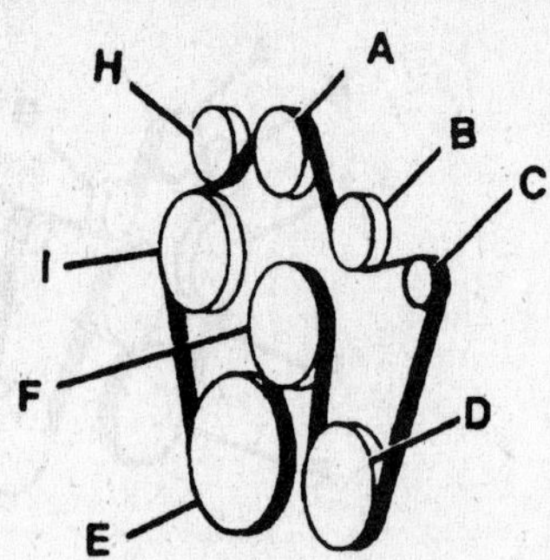

A. PULLEY, A/C COMPRESSOR
B. PULLEY, DRIVE BELT TENSIONER
C. PULLEY, GENERATOR
D. PULLEY, POWER STEERING
E. PULLEY, CRANKSHAFT
F. PULLEY, COOLANT PUMP
H. PULLEY, IDLER
I. PULLEY, A.I.R. PUMP

87981534

Fig. 100 Drive belt routing — 1994-95 4.3L, 5.0L and 5.7L engines, C/K series (with A.I.R.)

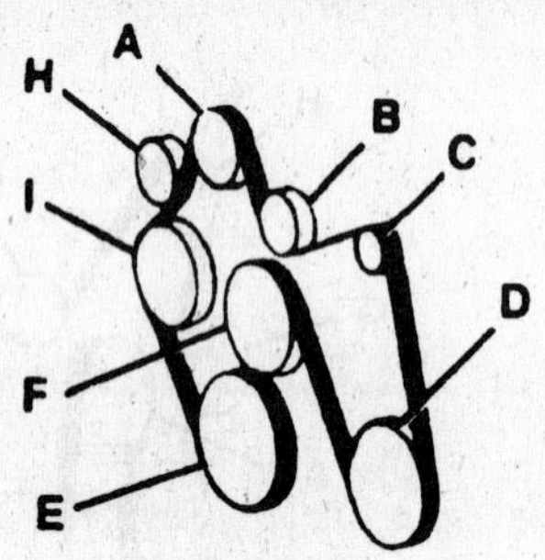

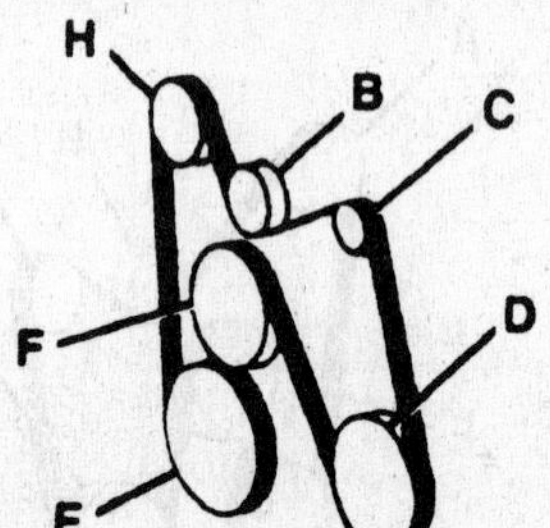

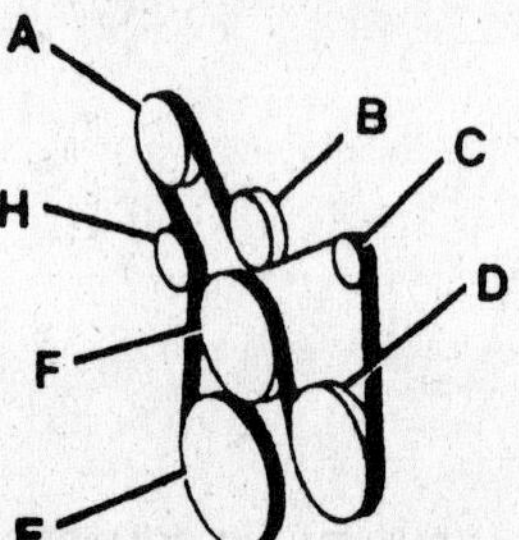

A. PULLEY, A/C COMPRESSOR
B. PULLEY, DRIVE BELT TENSIONER
C. PULLEY, GENERATOR
D. PULLEY, POWER STEERING PUMP
E. PULLEY, CRANKSHAFT
F PULLEY, COOLANT PUMP
H. PULLEY, IDLER
I. PULLEY, A.I.R. PUMP

87981535

Fig. 101 Drive belt routing — 1994-95 7.4L engines, C1, C/K 2,3 series

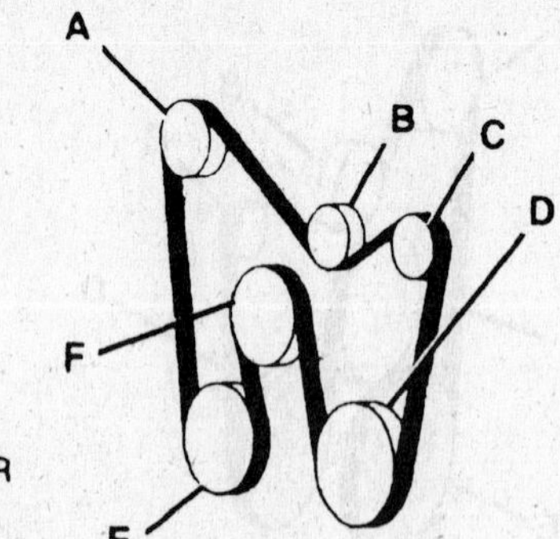

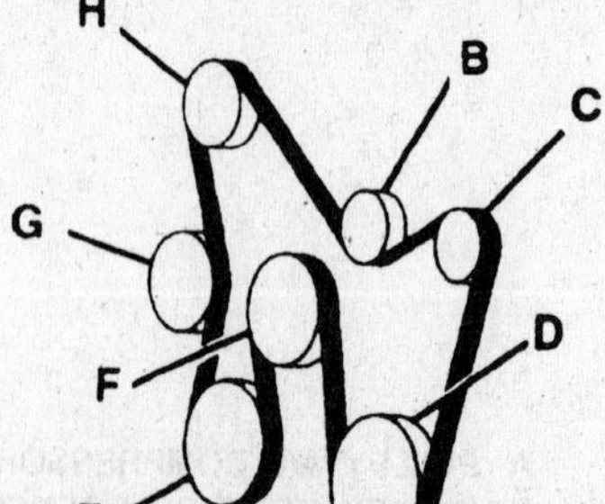

A. PULLEY, A/C COMPRESSOR
B. PULLEY, DRIVE BELT TENSIONER
C. PULLEY, GENERATOR
D. PULLEY, POWER STEERING PUMP
E. PULLEY, CRANKSHAFT
F. PULLEY, COOLANT PUMP
G. PULLEY, VACUUM PUMP
H. PULLEY, IDLER

87981536

Fig. 102 Drive belt routing — 1994-95 Diesel engines

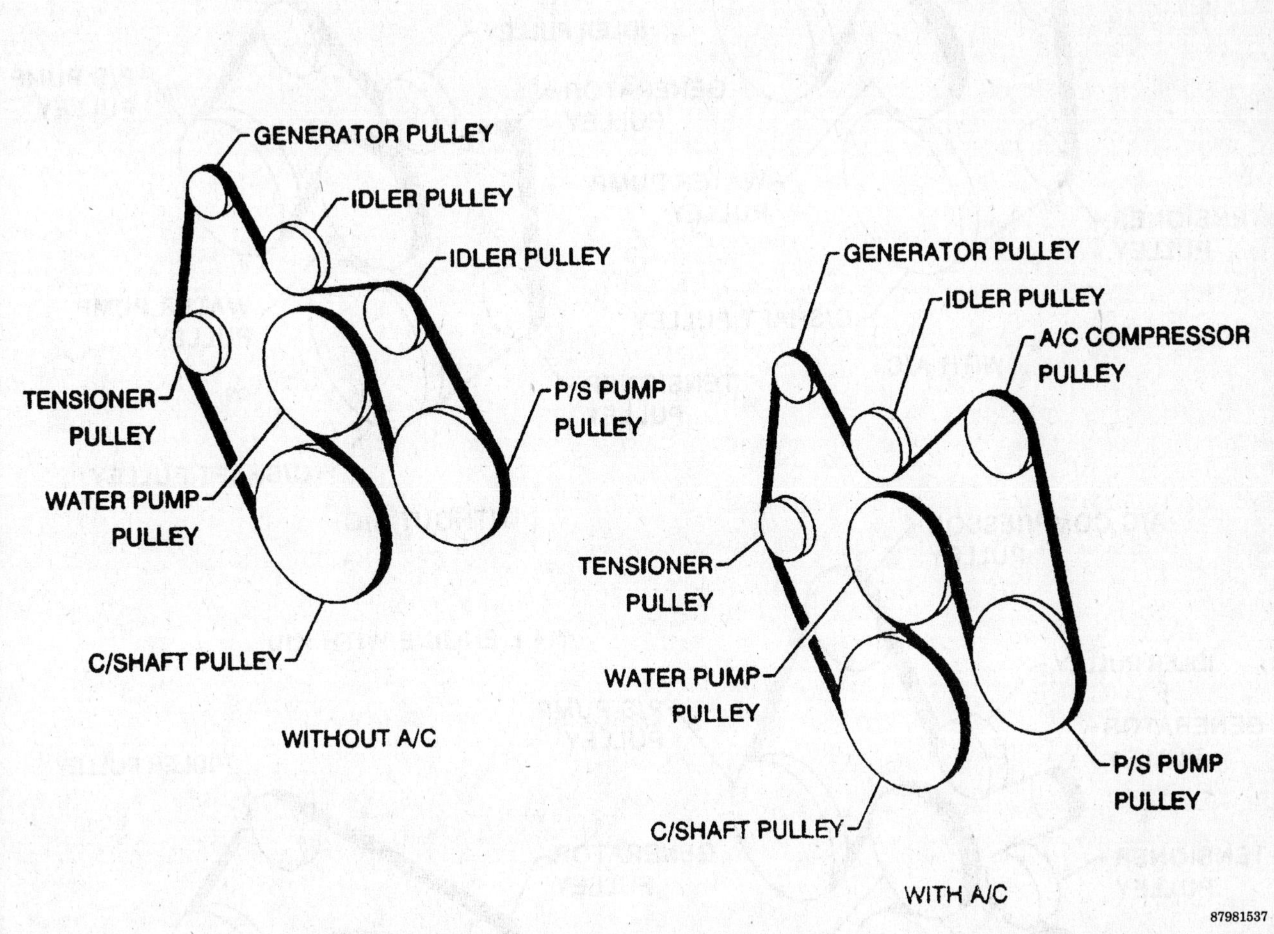

Fig. 103 Drive belt routing — 1996 4.3L, 5.0L and 5.7L engines

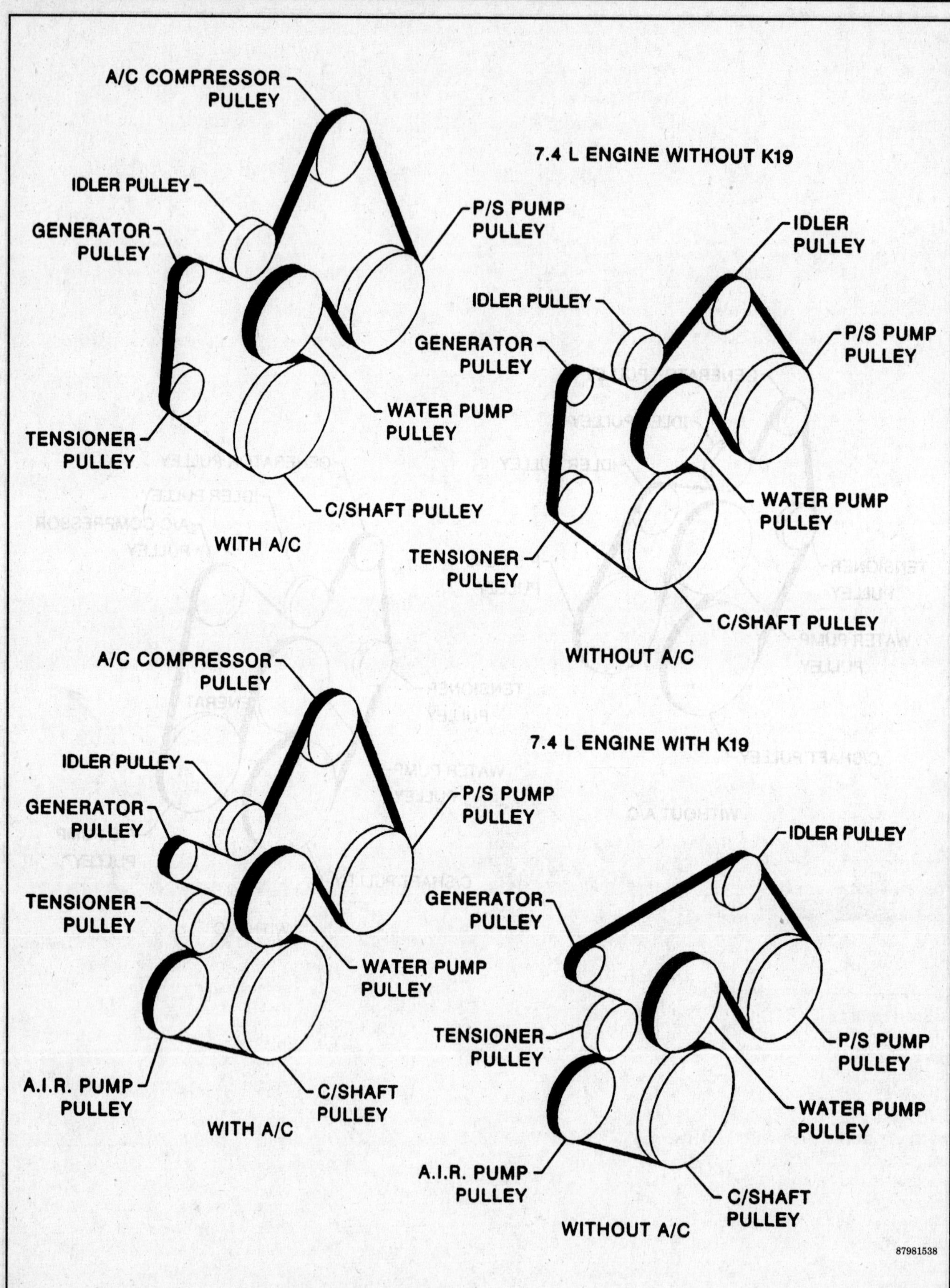

Fig. 104 Drive belt routing — 1996 7.4L engines C/K series

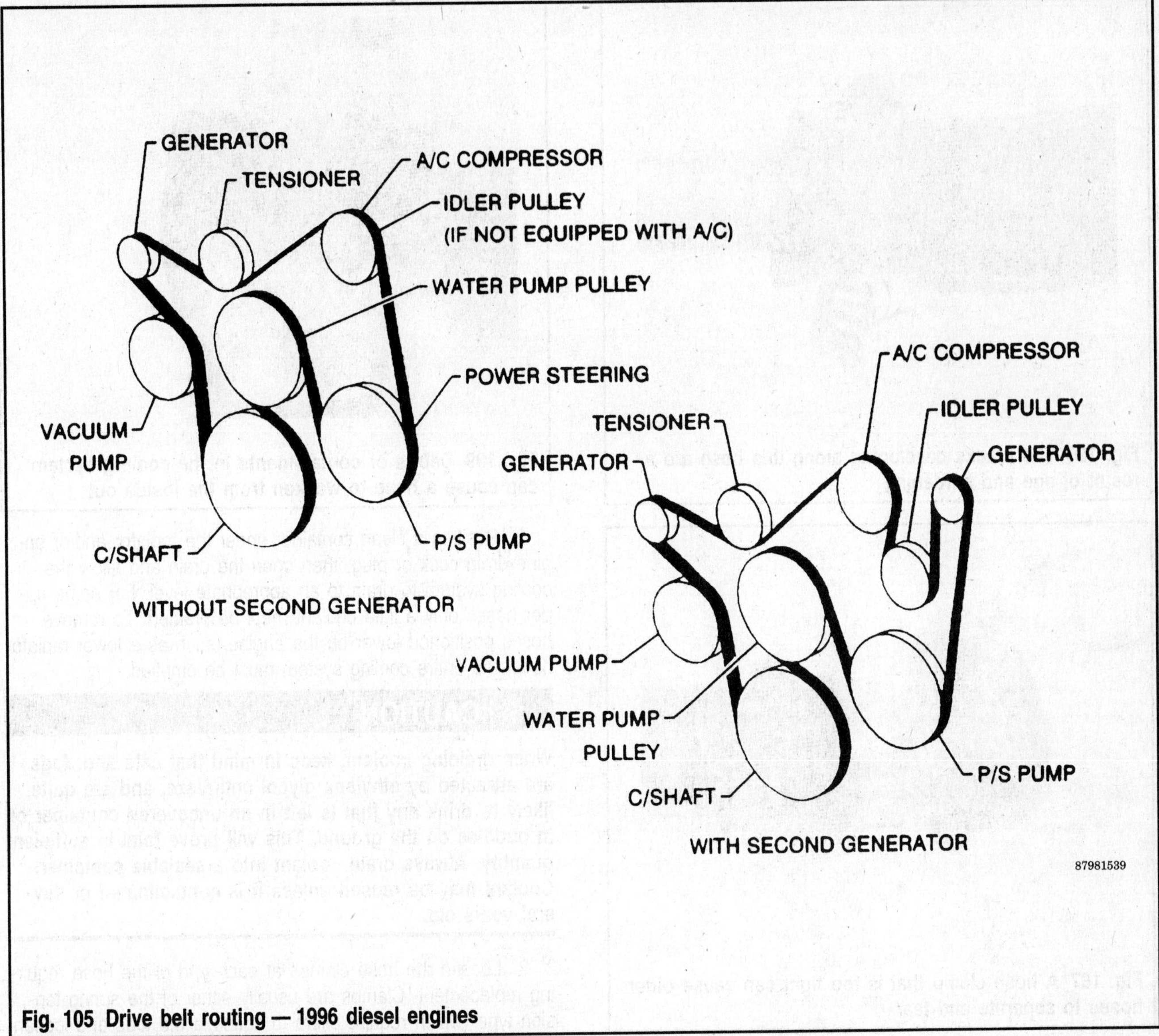

Fig. 105 Drive belt routing — 1996 diesel engines

Hoses

INSPECTION

➧ See Figures 106, 107, 108 and 109

Upper and lower radiator hoses along with the heater hoses should be checked for deterioration, leaks and loose hose clamps at least every 15,000 miles (24,000 km). It is also wise to check the hoses periodically in early spring and at the beginning of the fall or winter when you are performing other maintenance. A quick visual inspection could discover a weakened hose which might have left you stranded if it had remained unrepaired.

Whenever you are checking the hoses, make sure the engine and cooling system is cold. Visually inspect for cracking, rotting or collapsed hoses, replace as necessary. Run your hand along the length of the hose. If a weak or swollen spot is noted when squeezing the hose wall, the hose should be replaced.

REMOVAL & INSTALLATION

➧ See Figures 110, 111, 112 and 113

1. Remove the radiator pressure cap.

⁂CAUTION

Never remove the pressure cap while the engine is running or personal injury from scalding hot coolant or steam may result. If possible, wait until the engine has cooled to remove the pressure cap. If this is not possible, wrap a thick cloth around the pressure cap and turn it slowly to the stop. Step back while the pressure is released from the cooling system. When you are sure all the pressure has been released, still using the cloth, turn and remove the cap.

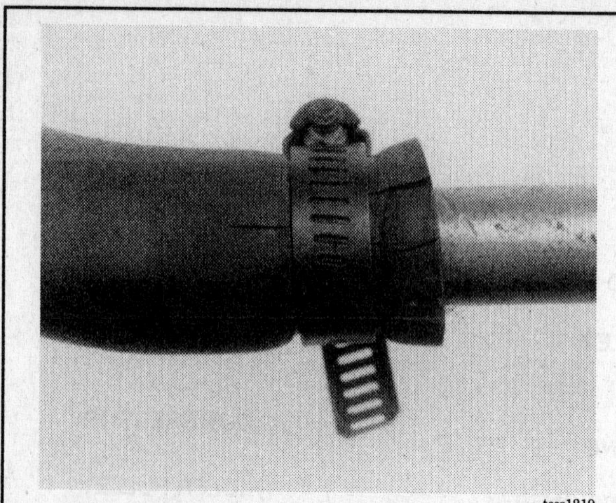

tccs1219

Fig. 106 The cracks developing along this hose are a result of age and hardening

tccs1220

Fig. 107 A hose clamp that is too tight can cause older hoses to separate and tear

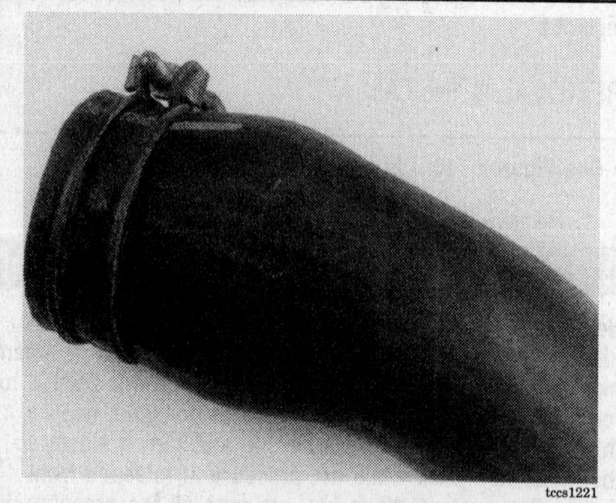

tccs1221

Fig. 108 A soft, spongy hose like this is identifiable by the swollen section at the clamp

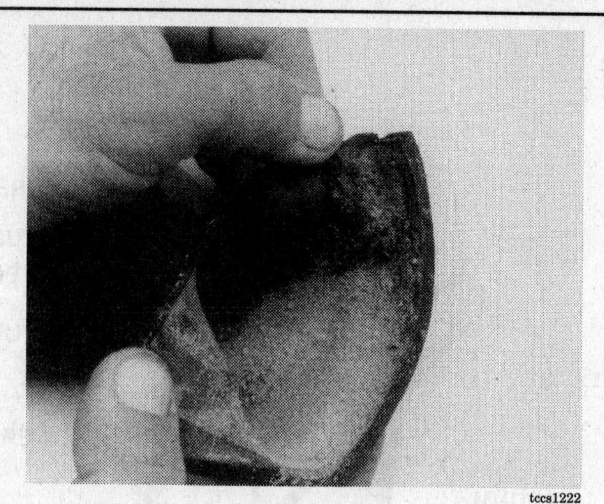

tccs1222

Fig. 109 Debris or contaminants in the cooling system can cause a hose to weaken from the inside out

2. Position a clean container under the radiator and/or engine drain cock or plug, then open the drain and allow the cooling system to drain to an appropriate level. For some upper hoses only a little coolant must be drained. To remove hoses positioned lower on the engine, such as a lower radiator hose, the entire cooling system must be emptied.

****CAUTION**

When draining coolant, keep in mind that cats and dogs are attracted by ethylene glycol antifreeze, and are quite likely to drink any that is left in an uncovered container or in puddles on the ground. This will prove fatal in sufficient quantity. Always drain coolant into a sealable container. Coolant may be reused unless it is contaminated or several years old.

3. Loosen the hose clamps at each end of the hose requiring replacement. Clamps are usually either of the spring tension type (which require pliers to squeeze the tabs and loosen) or of the screw tension type (which require screw or hex driv-

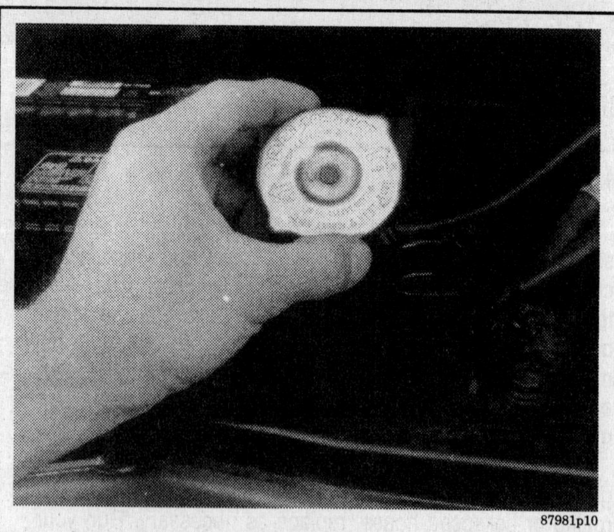

87981p10

Fig. 110 Remove the radiator cap

87981p11

Fig. 111 Loosen the hose clamps at each end of the hose requiring replacement and remove the hose

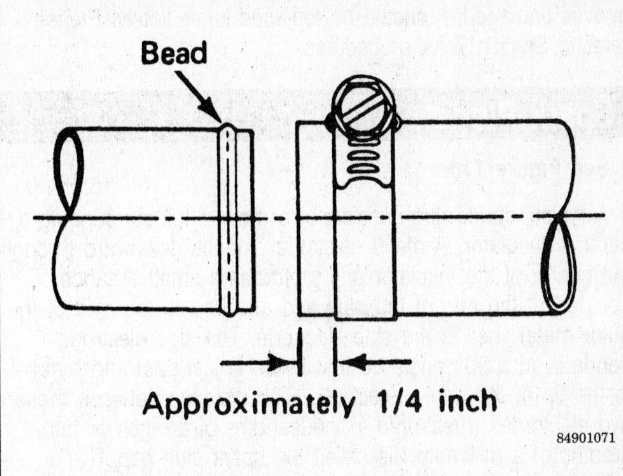

Fig. 112 Position the hose clamp so that it is about 1/4 in. from the end of the hose

ers to loosen). Pull the clamps back on the hose away from the connection.

4. Twist, pull and slide the hose off the fitting taking care not to damage the neck of the component from which the hose is being removed.

➡If the hose is stuck at the connection, do not try to insert a screwdriver or other sharp tool under the hose end in an effort to free it, as the connection and/or hose may become damaged. Heater connections especially may be easily damaged by such a procedure. If the hose is to be replaced, use a single-edged razor blade to make a slice along the portion of the hose which is stuck on the connection, perpendicular to the end of the hose. Do not cut deep so as to prevent damaging the connection. The hose can then be peeled from the connection and discarded.

5. Clean both hose mounting connections. Inspect the condition of the hose clamps and replace them, if necessary.

To install:

6. Dip the ends of the new hose into clean engine coolant to ease installation.

7. Slide the clamps over the replacement hose, then slide the hose ends over the connections into position.

8. Position and secure the clamps at least 1/4 in. (6.35mm) from the ends of the hose. Make sure they are located inside the raised bead of the connector.

9. Close the radiator or engine drains and properly refill the cooling system with the clean drained engine coolant or a suitable mixture of ethylene glycol coolant and water.

10. If available, install a pressure tester and check for leaks. If a pressure tester is not available, run the engine until normal operating temperature is reached (allowing the system to naturally pressurize), then check for leaks.

CAUTION

If you are checking for leaks with the system at normal operating temperature, BE EXTREMELY CAREFUL not to touch any moving or hot engine parts. Once temperature has been reached, shut the engine OFF, and check for leaks around the hose fittings and connections which were removed earlier.

87981p12

Fig. 113 Properly refill the cooling system with a suitable mixture of ethylene glycol coolant and water

CV-Boots

INSPECTION

See Figures 114 and 115

The CV (Constant Velocity) boots on four wheel drive models should be checked for damage each time the oil is changed and any other time the vehicle is raised for service. These boots keep water, grime, dirt and other damaging matter from entering the CV-joints. Any of these could cause early CV-joint failure which can be expensive to repair. Heavy grease thrown around the inside of the front wheel(s) and on the brake caliper can be an indication of a torn boot. Thoroughly check the boots for missing clamps and tears. If the boot is damaged, it should be replaced immediately. Please refer to Section 7 for procedures.

Spark Plugs

➧ **See Figure 116**

A typical spark plug consists of a metal shell surrounding a ceramic insulator. A metal electrode extends downward through the center of the insulator and protrudes a small distance. Located at the end of the plug and attached to the side of the outer metal shell is the side electrode. The side electrode bends in at a 90° angle so that its tip is just past and parallel to the tip of the center electrode. The distance between these two electrodes (measured in thousandths of an inch or hundredths of a millimeter) is called the spark plug gap.

The spark plug does not produce a spark but instead provides a gap across which the current can arc. The coil produces anywhere from 20,000 to 50,000 volts (depending on the type and application) which travels through the wires to the spark plugs. The current passes along the center electrode and jumps the gap to the side electrode, and in doing so, ignites the air/fuel mixture in the combustion chamber.

TCCS1011

Fig. 114 CV-Boots must be inspected periodically for damage

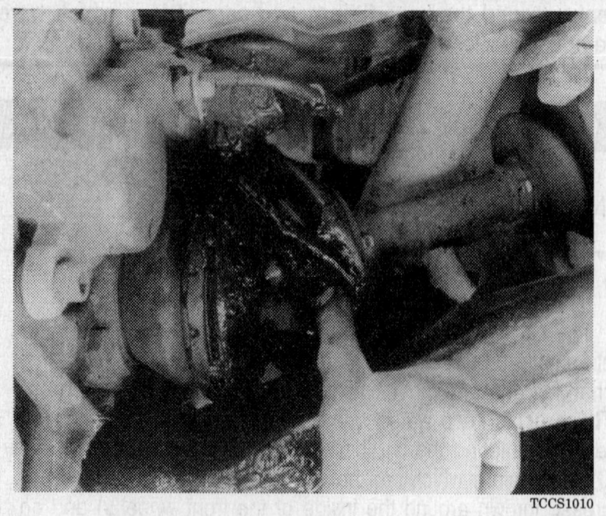

TCCS1010

Fig. 115 A torn boot should be replaced immediately

SPARK PLUG HEAT RANGE

➧ **See Figure 117**

Spark plug heat range is the ability of the plug to dissipate heat. The longer the insulator (or the farther it extends into the engine), the hotter the plug will operate; the shorter the insulator (the closer the electrode is to the block's cooling passages) the cooler it will operate. A plug that absorbs little heat and remains too cool will quickly accumulate deposits of oil and carbon since it is not hot enough to burn them off. This leads to plug fouling and consequently to misfiring. A plug that absorbs too much heat will have no deposits but, due to the excessive heat, the electrodes will burn away quickly and might possibly lead to preignition or other ignition problems. Preignition takes place when plug tips get so hot that they glow sufficiently to ignite the air/fuel mixture before the actual spark occurs. This early ignition will usually cause a pinging during low speeds and heavy loads.

The general rule of thumb for choosing the correct heat range when picking a spark plug is: if most of your driving is long distance, high speed travel, use a colder plug; if most of your driving is stop and go, use a hotter plug. Original equipment plugs are generally a good compromise between the 2 styles and most people never have the need to change their plugs from the factory-recommended heat range.

REMOVAL & INSTALLATION

➡**Remove the spark plugs and wires one at a time to avoid confusion and miswiring during installation.**

1. Disconnect the negative battery cable, and if the vehicle has been run recently, allow the engine to thoroughly cool.
2. Carefully twist the spark plug wire boot to loosen it, then pull upward and remove the boot from the plug. Be sure to

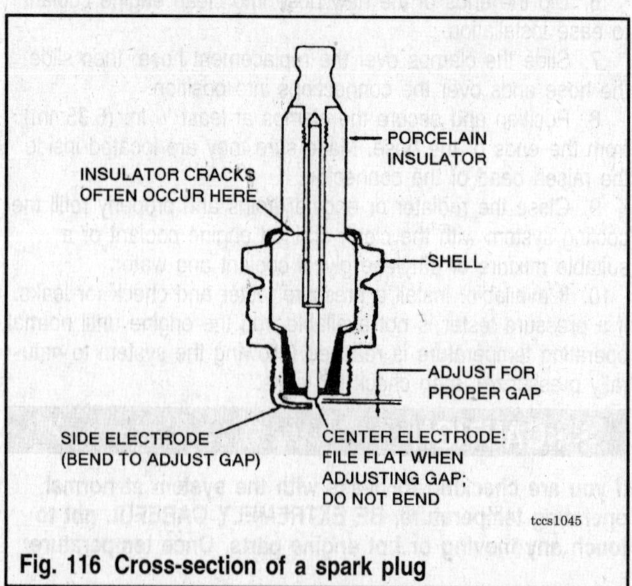

Fig. 116 Cross-section of a spark plug

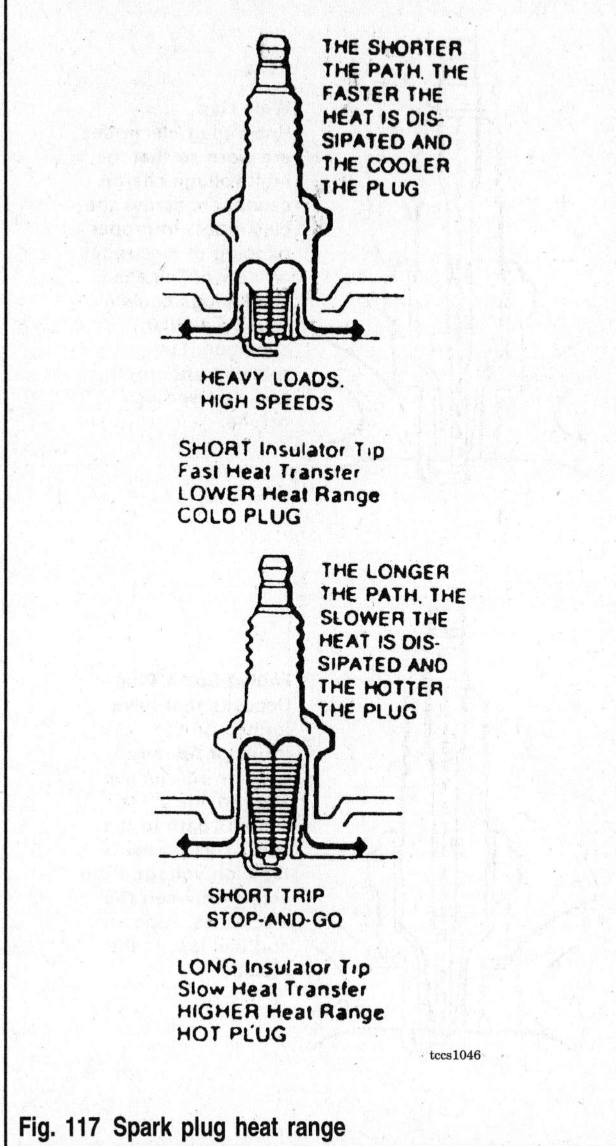

Fig. 117 Spark plug heat range

pull on the boot and not on the wire, otherwise the connector located inside the boot may become separated.

3. Using compressed air, blow any water or debris from the spark plug well to assure that no harmful contaminants are allowed to enter the combustion chamber when the spark plug is removed. If compressed air is not available, use a rag or a brush to clean the area.

➡Remove the spark plugs when the engine is cold, if possible, to prevent damage to the threads. If removal of the plugs is difficult, apply a few drops of penetrating oil or silicone spray to the area around the base of the plug, and allow it a few minutes to work.

4. Using a spark plug socket that is equipped with a rubber insert to properly hold the plug, turn the spark plug counterclockwise to loosen and remove the spark plug from the bore.

✲✲WARNING

Be sure not to use a flexible extension on the socket. Use of a flexible extension may allow a shear force to be applied to the plug. A shear force could break the plug off in the cylinder head, leading to costly and frustrating repairs.

To install:

5. Inspect the spark plug boot for tears or damage. If a damaged boot is found, the spark plug wire must be replaced.

6. Using a wire feeler gauge, check and adjust the spark plug gap. When using a gauge, the proper size should pass between the electrodes with a slight drag. The next larger size should not be able to pass while the next smaller size should pass freely.

7. Carefully thread the plug into the bore by hand. If resistance is felt before the plug is almost completely threaded, back the plug out and begin threading again. In small to reach areas, an old spark plug wire and boot could be used as a threading tool. The boot will hold the plug while you twist the end of the wire and the wire is supple enough to twist before it would allow the plug to crossthread.

✲✲WARNING

Do not use the spark plug socket to thread the plugs. Always carefully thread the plug by hand or using an old plug wire to prevent the possibility of cross-threading and damaging the cylinder head bore.

8. Carefully tighten the spark plug. If the plug you are installing is equipped with a crush washer, seat the plug, then tighten about 1/4 turn to crush the washer. If you are installing a tapered seat plug, tighten the plug to specifications provided by the vehicle or plug manufacturer.

9. Apply a small amount of silicone dielectric compound to the end of the spark plug lead or inside the spark plug boot to prevent sticking, then install the boot to the spark plug and push until it clicks into place. The click may be felt or heard, then gently pull back on the boot to assure proper contact.

INSPECTION & GAPPING

➧ See Figures 118, 119, 120, 121, 122, 123, 124, 125, 126 and 127

Check the plugs for deposits and wear. If they are not going to be replaced, clean the plugs thoroughly. Remember that any kind of deposit will decrease the efficiency of the plug. Plugs can be cleaned on a spark plug cleaning machine, which can sometimes be found in service stations, or you can do an acceptable job of cleaning with a stiff brush. If the plugs are cleaned, the electrodes must be filed flat. Use an ignition points file, not an emery board or the like, which will leave deposits. The electrodes must be filed perfectly flat with sharp edges; rounded edges reduce the spark plug voltage by as much as 50%.

Tracking Arc
High voltage arcs between a fouling deposit on the insulator tip and spark plug shell. This ignites the fuel/air mixture at some point along the insulator tip, retarding the ignition timing which causes a power and fuel loss.

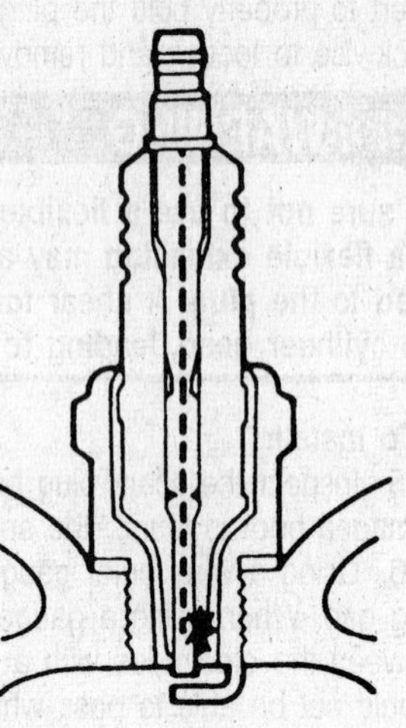

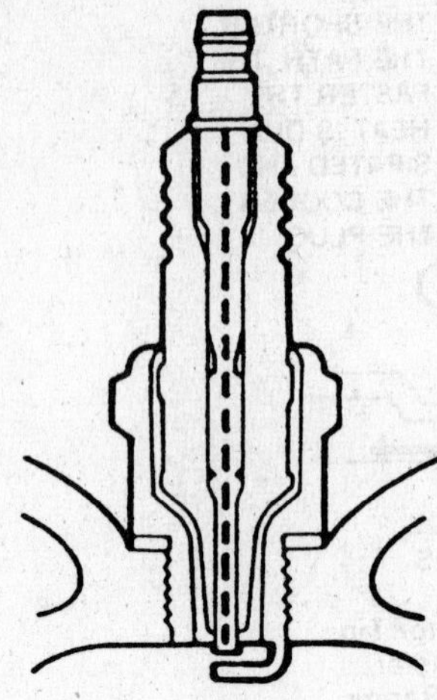

Wide Gap
Spark plug electrodes are worn so that the high voltage charge cannot arc across the electrodes. Improper gapping of electrodes on new or "cleaned" spark plugs could cause a similar condition. Fuel remains unburned and a power loss results.

Flashover
A damaged spark plug boot, along with dirt and moisture, could permit the high voltage charge to short over the insulator to the spark plug shell or the engine. AC's buttress insulator design helps prevent high voltage flashover.

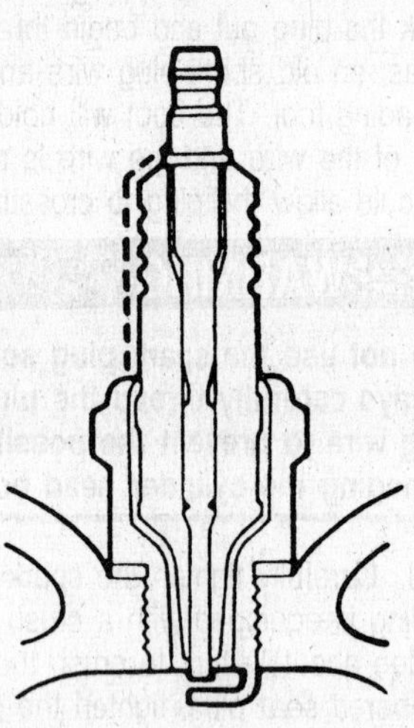

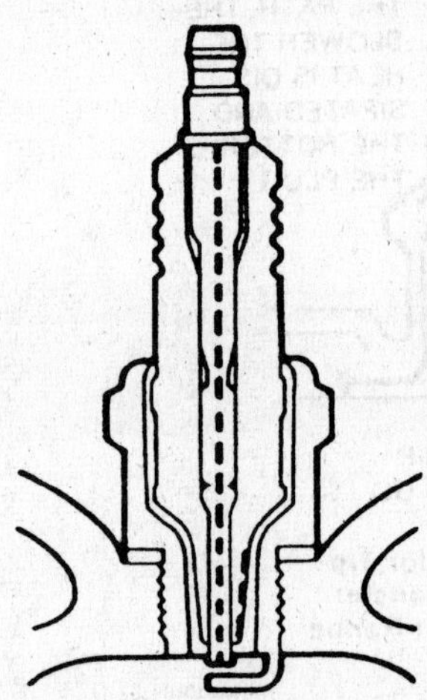

Fouled Spark Plug
Deposits that have formed on the insulator tip may become conductive and provide a "shunt" path to the shell. This prevents the high voltage from arcing between the electrodes. A power and fuel loss is the result.

Bridged Electrodes
Fouling deposits between the electrodes "ground out" the high voltage needed to fire the spark plug. The arc between the electrodes does not occur and the fuel air mixture is not ignited. This causes a power loss and exhausting of raw fuel.

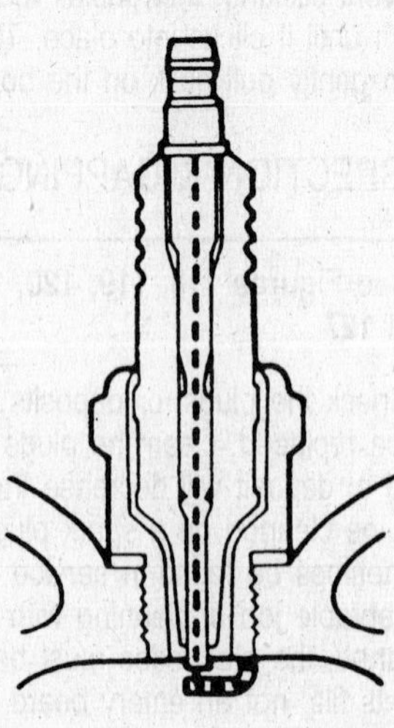

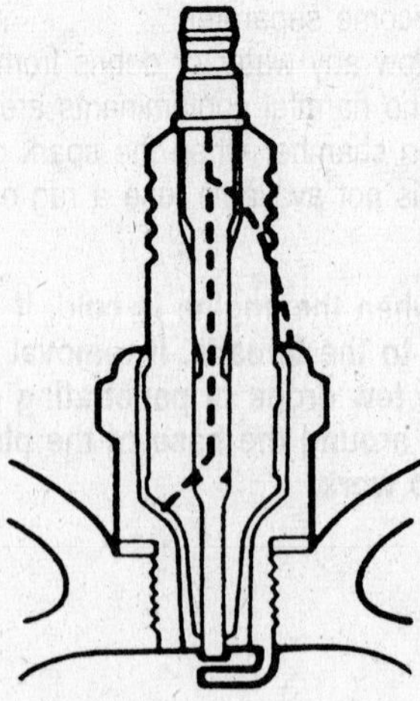

Cracked Insulator
A crack in the spark plug insulator could cause the high voltage charge to "ground out." Here, the spark does not jump the electrode gap and the fuel air mixture is not ignited. This causes a power loss and raw fuel is exhausted.

tccs2001

Fig. 118 Used spark plugs which show damage may indicate engine problems

tccs2135

Fig. 119 A normally worn spark plug should have light tan or gray deposits on the firing tip

tccs2136

Fig. 120 A carbon fouled plug, identified by soft, sooty, black deposits

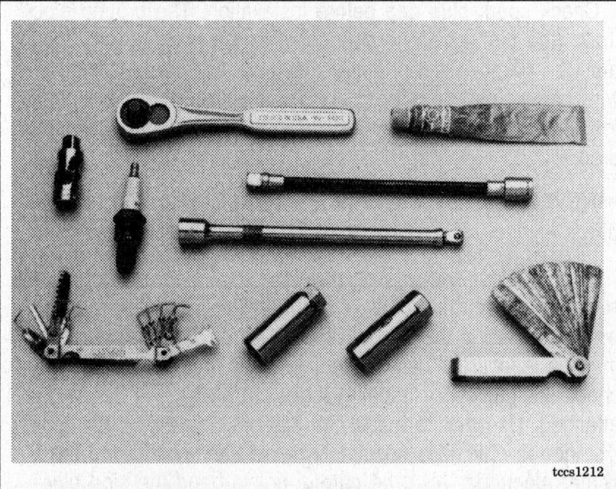

tccs1212

Fig. 121 A variety of tools and gauges are needed for spark plug service

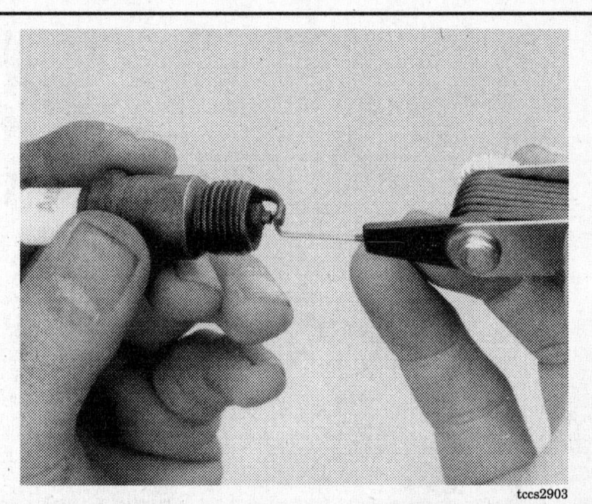

tccs2903

Fig. 122 Checking the spark plug gap with a feeler gauge

tccs2137

Fig. 123 A physically damaged spark plug may be evidence of severe detonation in that cylinder

tccs2138

Fig. 124 An oil fouled spark plug indicates an engine allowing excessive oil to enter the chamber

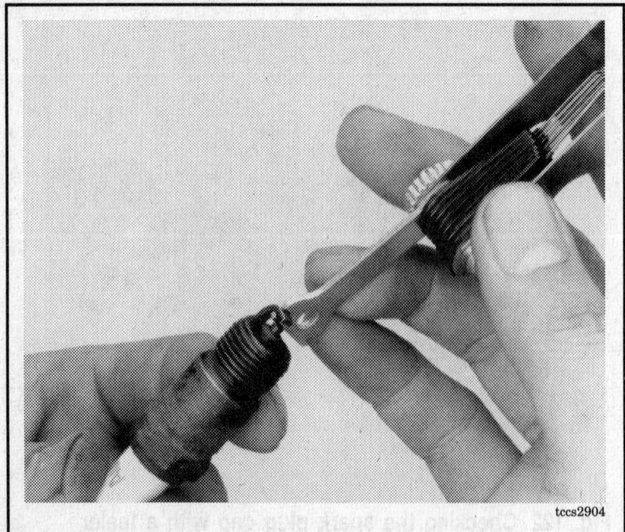

tccs2904

Fig. 125 Adjusting the spark plug gap

Check spark plug gap before installation. The ground electrode (the L-shaped one connected to the body of the plug) must be parallel to the center electrode and the specified size wire gauge (please refer to the Tune-Up Specifications chart for details) must pass between the electrodes with a slight drag.

➡NEVER adjust the gap on a used platinum type spark plug.

Always check the gap on new plugs as they are not always set correctly at the factory. Do not use a flat feeler gauge when measuring the gap on a used plug, because the reading may be inaccurate. A wire type gapping tool is the best way to check the gap. Wire gapping tools usually have a bending tool attached. Use that to adjust the side electrode until the proper distance is obtained. Absolutely never attempt to bend the center electrode. Also, be careful not to bend the side electrode too far or too often as it may weaken and break off within the engine, requiring removal of the cylinder head to retrieve it.

Fig. 126 This spark plug has been left in the engine too long, as evidenced by the extreme gap

Fig. 127 A bridged plug caused by excessive carbon or oil build-up on the plug

Spark Plug Wires

TESTING

➧ **See Figures 128 and 129**

At every tune-up/inspection, visually check the spark plug cables for burns cuts, or breaks in the insulation. Check the boots and the nipples on the distributor cap and coil. Replace any damaged wiring.

Every 50,000 miles (80,000 km) or 60 months, the resistance of the wires should be checked with an ohmmeter. Wires with excessive resistance will cause misfiring, and may make the engine difficult to start in damp weather.

To check resistance:

1. Remove the distributor cap, leaving the wires in place.
2. Connect one lead of an ohmmeter to an electrode within the cap.
3. Connect the other lead to the corresponding spark plug terminal (remove it from the spark plug for this test).

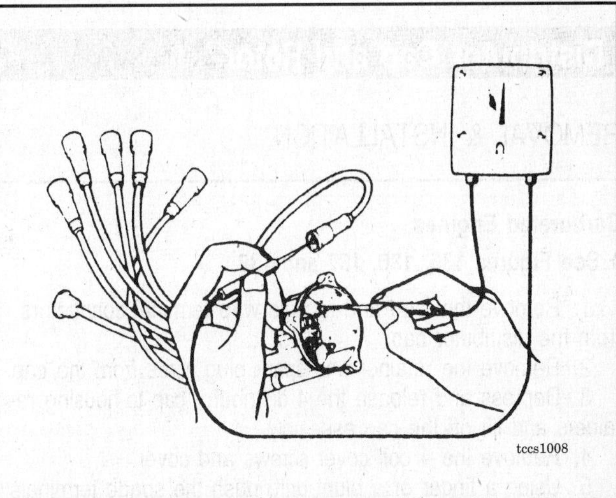

Fig. 128 Checking plug wire resistance through the distributor cap with an ohmmeter

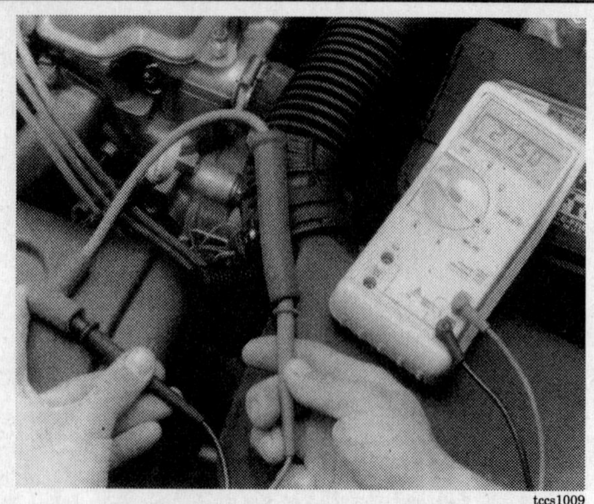

tccs1009

Fig. 129 Checking individual plug wire resistance with an digital ohmmeter

4. Replace any wire which shows a resistance over 30,000 ohms. Generally speaking, however, resistance should not be over 25,000 ohms, and 30,000 ohms must be considered the outer limit of acceptability.

It should be remembered that resistance is also a function of length. The longer the wire, the greater the resistance. Thus, if the wires on your truck are longer than the factory originals, the resistance will be higher, possibly outside these limits.

REMOVAL & INSTALLATION

➧ See Figures 130, 131, 132, 133 and 134

When installing new wires, replace them one at a time to avoid mixups. Start by replacing the longest one first.

1. Remove the spark plug wire by gripping the boot firmly and disengaging the wire from the spark plug and the distributor.
2. Install the boot of the new wire firmly over the spark plug. Route the wire over the same path as the original.

Distributor Cap and Rotor

REMOVAL & INSTALLATION

Carbureted Engines

➧ See Figures 135, 136, 137 and 138

1. Remove the feed and module wire terminal connectors from the distributor cap.
2. Remove the retainer and spark plug wires from the cap.
3. Depress and release the 4 distributor cap-to-housing retainers and lift off the cap assembly.
4. Remove the 4 coil cover screws and cover.
5. Using a finger or a blunt drift, push the spade terminals up out of the distributor cap.
6. Remove all 4 coil screws and lift the coil, coil spring and rubber seal washer out of the cap coil cavity.
7. Remove the two rotor attaching screws (if equipped) and rotor.
8. Using a new distributor cap and rotor, reverse the above procedures to assemble, being sure to clean and lubricate the rubber seal washer with dielectric lubricant.

Fuel Injected Engines

1. Tag and remove the spark plug wires.
2. Loosen the cap retaining fasteners and remove the cap.
3. Remove the rotor from the distributor shaft.
4. Installation is the reverse of removal.

INSPECTION

1. Remove the distributor cap and rotor as described in this section.
2. Check the cap for wear, electrode cracks or damage. Replace if defective.
3. Check the rotor for cracks and wear. Replace if defective.

Ignition Timing

GENERAL INFORMATION

➡This procedure does not apply to diesel engines

Ignition timing is the measurement, in degrees of crankshaft rotation, of the point at which the spark plugs fire in each of the cylinders. It is measured in degrees before or after Top Dead Center (TDC) of the compression stroke. Ignition timing is controlled by turning the distributor in the engine.

Ideally, the air/fuel mixture in the cylinder will be ignited by the spark plug just as the piston passes TDC of the compression stroke. If this happens, this piston will be beginning the power stroke just as the compressed and ignited air/fuel mixture starts to expand. The expansion of the air/fuel mixture then forces the piston down on the power stroke and turns the crankshaft.

Because it takes a fraction of a second for the spark plug to ignite the gases in the cylinder, the spark plug must fire a little before the piston reaches TDC. Otherwise, the mixture will not be completely ignited as the piston passes TDC and the full benefit of the explosion will not be used by the engine. The timing measurement is given in degrees of crankshaft rotation before the piston reaches TDC (BTDC). If the setting for the ignition timing is 5 degrees BTDC, the spark plug must fire 5 degrees before that piston reaches TDC. This only holds true, however, when the engine is at idle speed.

As the engine speed increases, the pistons go faster. The spark plugs have to ignite the fuel even sooner if it is to be completely ignited when the piston reaches TDC. To do this, the distributor has a means to advance the timing of the spark as the engine speed increases.

If the ignition is set too far advanced (BTDC), the ignition and expansion of the fuel in the cylinder will occur too soon and tend to force the piston down while it is still traveling up. This causes engine ping. If the engine is too far retarded after TDC (ATDC), the piston will have already passed TDC and

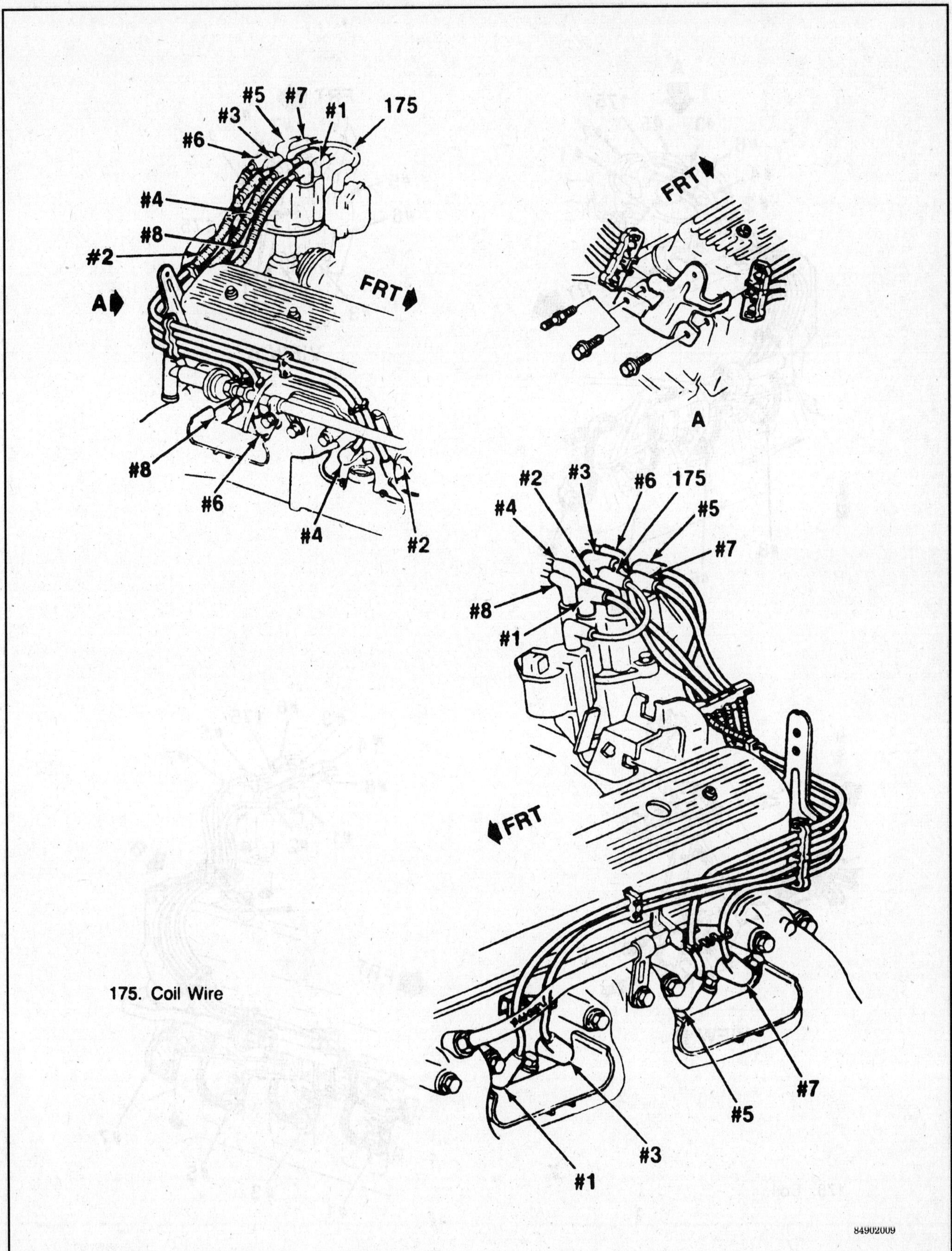

Fig. 130 Spark plug wire routing — 5.7L R/V Series

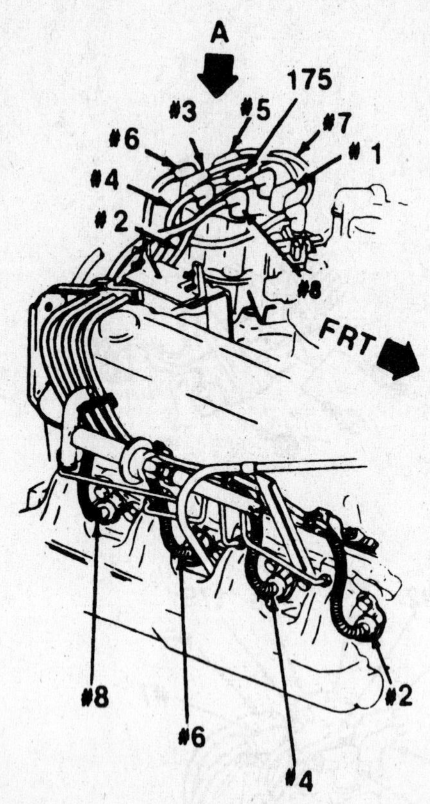

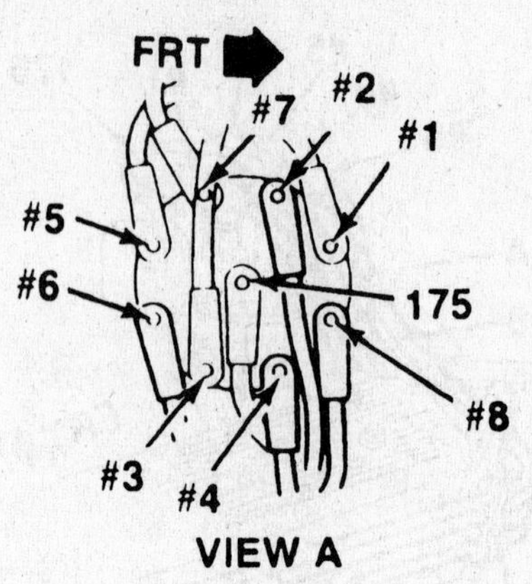

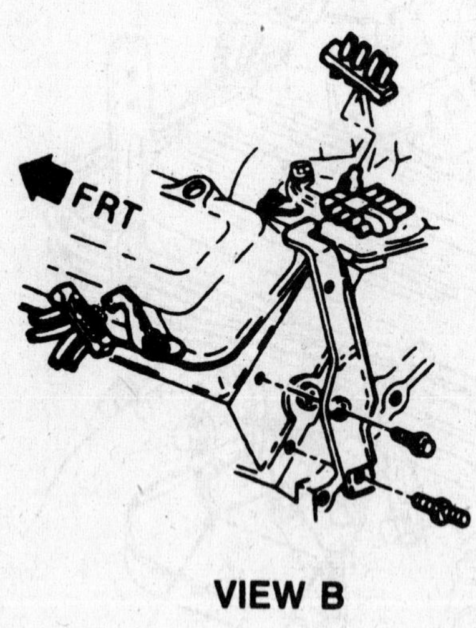

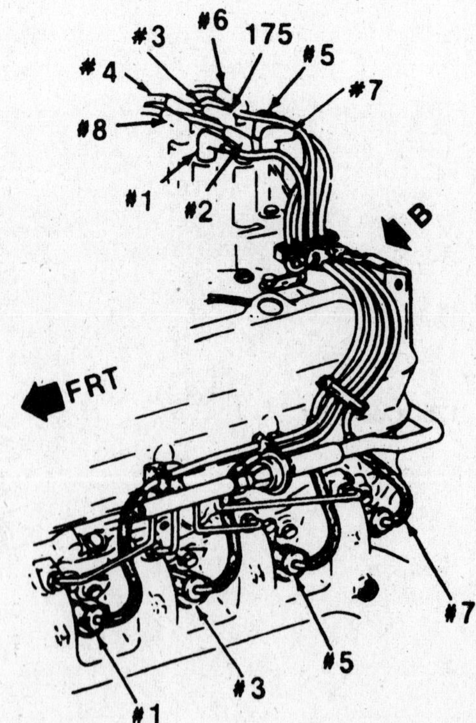

175. Coil

84902010

Fig. 131 Spark plug wire routing — 7.4L R/V Series

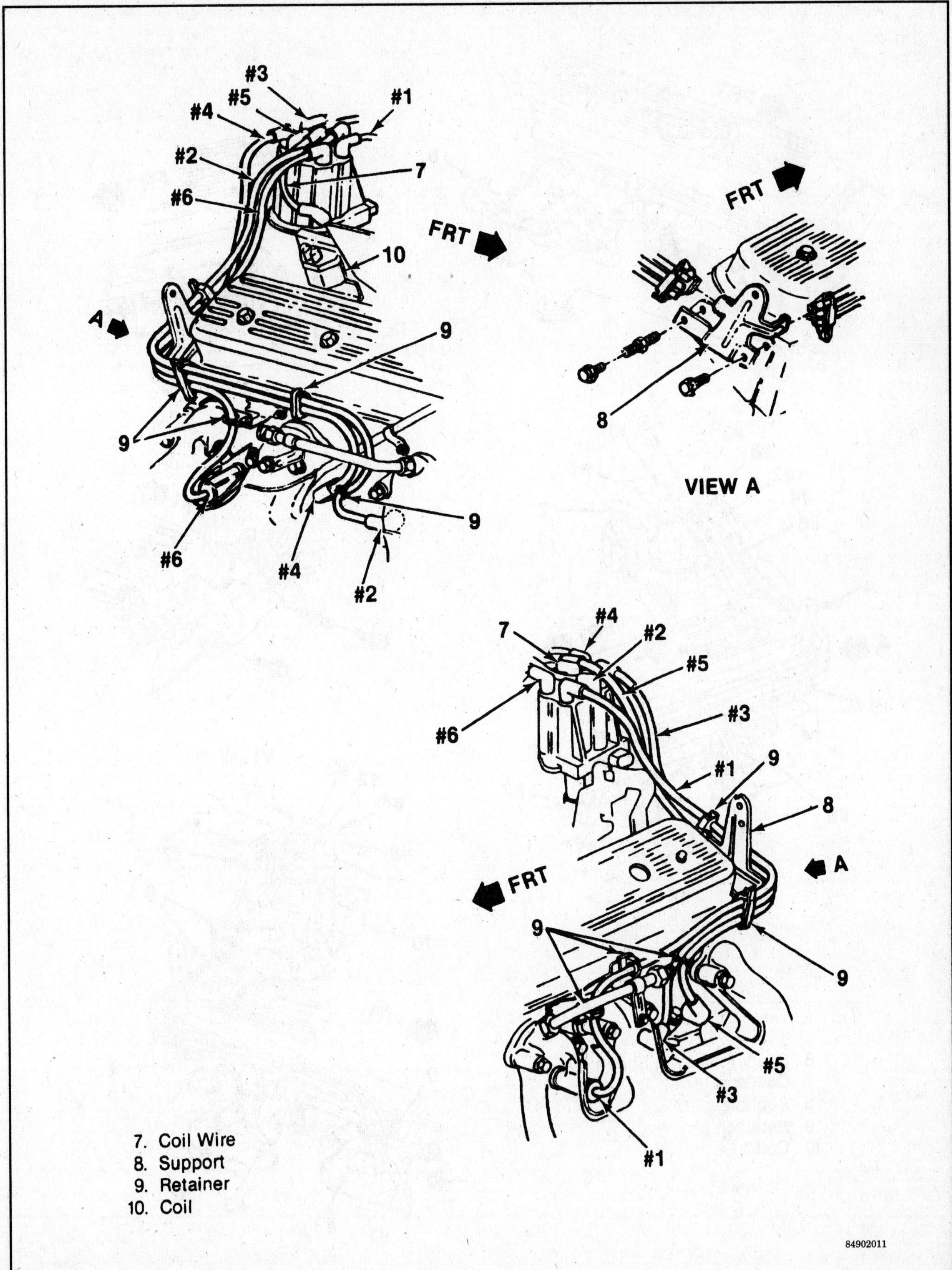

Fig. 132 Spark plug wire routing — 4.3L C/K Series

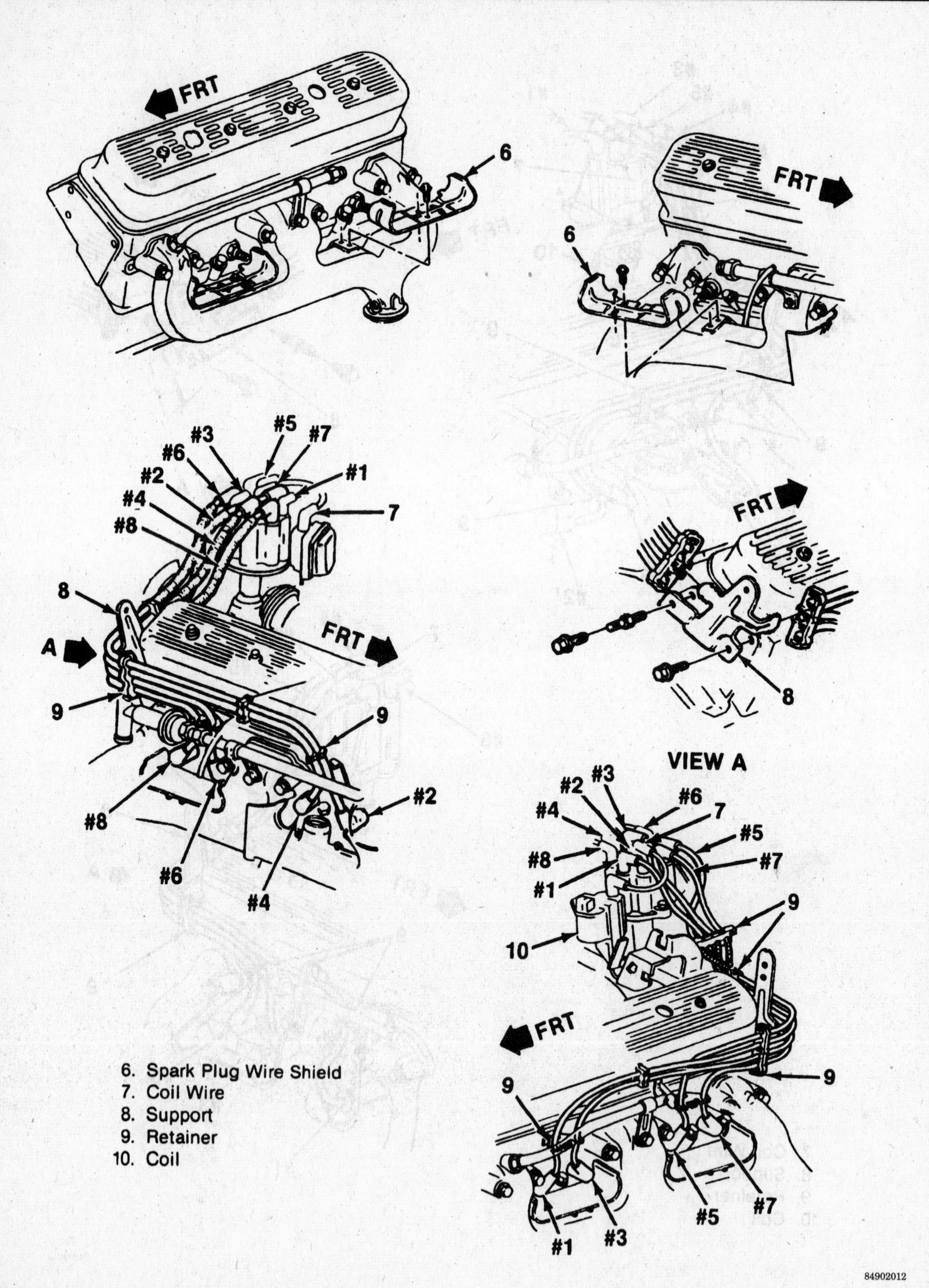

Fig. 133 Spark plug wire routing — 5.0, 5.7L C/K Series

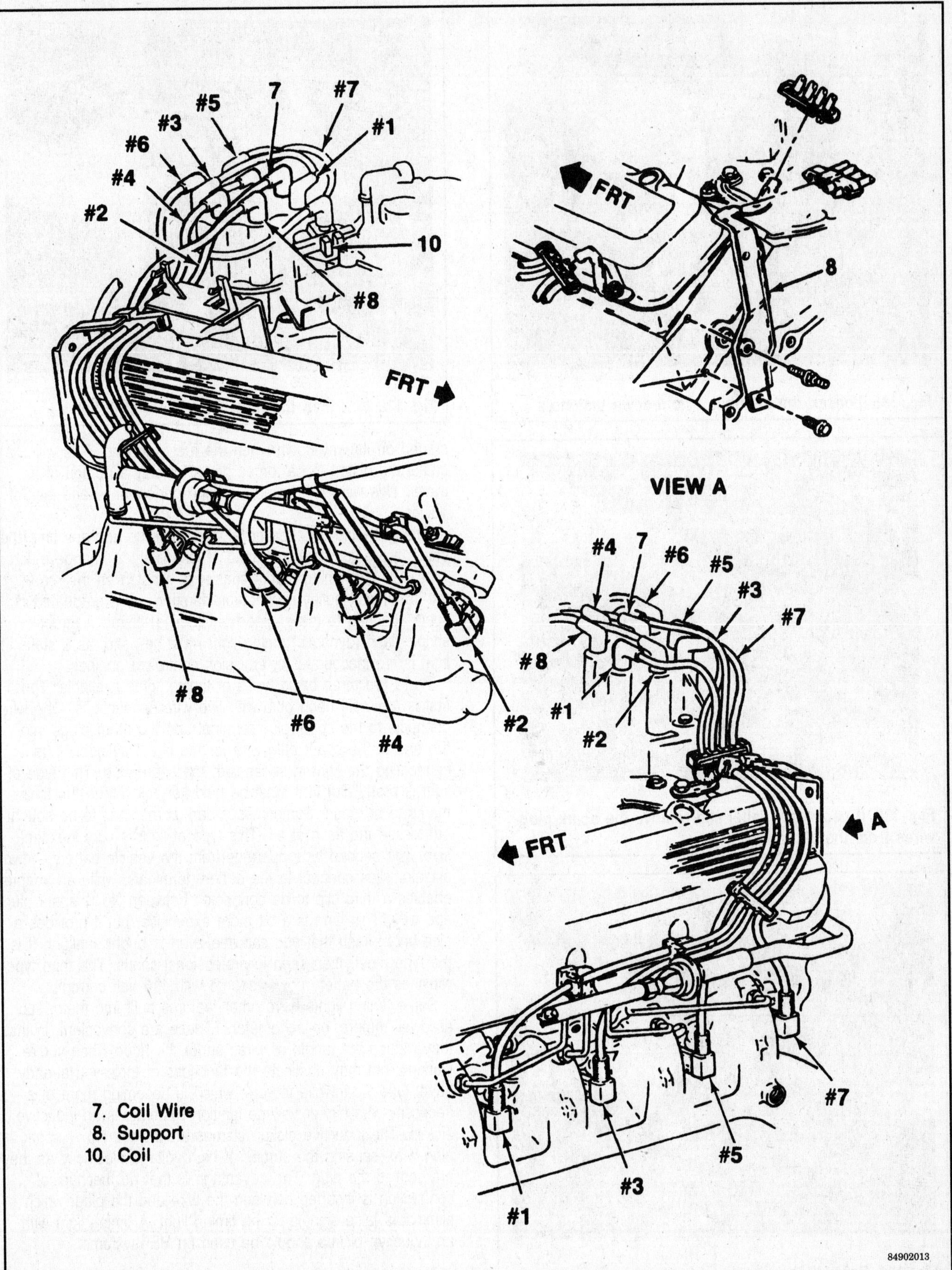

Fig. 134 Spark plug wire routing — 7.4L C/K Series

Fig. 135 Loosen the distributor hold-down fasteners

Fig. 136 If necessary, label and remove the spark plug wires from the distributor cap

Fig. 137 Remove the distributor cap . . .

Fig. 138 . . . then the rotor from the distributor

started on its way down when the fuel is ignited. This will cause the piston to be forced down for only a portion of its travel. This will result in poor engine performance and lack of power.

Timing should be checked at each tune-up and any time the points are adjusted or replaced. It isn't likely to change much with HEI. The timing marks consist of a notch on the rim of the crankshaft pulley or vibration damper and a graduated scale attached to the engine front (timing) cover. A stroboscopic flash (dynamic) timing light must be used, as a static light is too inaccurate for emission controlled engines.

There are three basic types of timing lights available. The first is a simple neon bulb with two wire connections. One wire connects to the spark plug terminal and the other plugs into the end of the spark plug wire for the No. 1 cylinder, thus connecting the light in series with the spark plug. This type of light is pretty dim and must be held very closely to the timing marks to be seen. Sometimes a dark corner has to be sought out to see the flash at all. This type of light is very inexpensive. The second type operates from the vehicle battery — two alligator clips connect to the battery terminals, while an adapter enables a third clip to be connected between No. 1 spark plug and wire. This type is a bit more expensive, but it provides a nice bright flash that you can see even in bright sunlight. It is the type most often seen in professional shops. The third type replaces the battery power source with 115 volt current.

Some timing lights have other features built into them, such as dwell meters, or tachometers. These are convenient, in that they reduce the tangle of wires under the hood when you're working, but may duplicate the functions of tools you already have. One worthwhile feature, which is becoming more of a necessity with higher voltage ignition systems, is an inductive pickup. The inductive pickup clamps around the No. 1 spark plug wire, sensing the surges of high voltage electricity as they are sent to the plug. The advantage is that no mechanical connection is inserted between the wire and the plug, which eliminates false signals to the timing light. A timing light with an inductive pickup should be used on HEI systems.

CHECKING AND ADJUSTMENT

HEI Systems

1. Start the engine and allow it to reach operating temperature. Stop the engine and connect the timing light to the No. 1 (left front) spark plug wire, at the plug or at the distributor cap. You can also use the No. 6 wire, if it is more convenient. Numbering is illustrated in this section.

➡Do not pierce the plug wire insulation with HEI; it will cause a miss. The best method is an inductive pickup timing light.

2. Clean off the timing marks and mark the pulley or damper notch and timing scale with white chalk.
3. Disconnect and plug the vacuum line at the distributor on models with a carburetor. This is done to prevent any distributor vacuum advance. On fuel injected models, disengage the timing connector which comes out of the harness conduit next to the distributor, this will put the system in the bypass mode. Check the underhood emission sticker for any other hoses or wires which may need to be disconnected.
4. Start the engine and adjust the idle speed to that specified on the Underhood Emissions label. With automatic transmission, set the specified idle speed in Park. It will be too high, since it is normally (in most cases) adjusted in Drive. You can disconnect the idle solenoid, if any, to get the speed down. Otherwise, adjust the idle speed screw.

The tachometer connects to the **TACH** terminal on the distributor and to a ground on models with a carburetor. On models with fuel injection, the tachometer connects to the **TACH** terminal on the ignition coil. Some tachometers must connect to the **TACH** terminal and to the positive battery terminal. Some tachometers won't work with HEI.

✲✲WARNING

Never ground the HEI TACH terminal; serious system damage will result.

5. Aim the timing light at the pointer marks. Be careful not to touch the fan, because it may appear to be standing still. If the pulley or damper notch isn't aligned with the proper timing mark (see the Underhood Emissions label), the timing will have to be adjusted.

➡TDC or Top Dead Center corresponds to 0°B, or BTDC, or Before Top Dead Center may be shown as BEFORE. A, or ATDC, or After Top Dead Center may be shown as AFTER.

6. Loosen the distributor base clamp locknut. You can buy trick wrenches which make this task a lot easier.
7. Turn the distributor slowly to adjust the timing, holding it by the body and not the cap. Turn the distributor in the direction of rotor rotation to retard, and against the direction of rotation to advance.
8. Tighten the locknut. Check the timing again, in case the distributor moved slightly as you tightened it.
9. Reinstall the distributor vacuum line or the timing connector. Correct the idle speed.
10. Stop the engine and disconnect the timing light.

Distributor Ignition (DI) Systems

1995 MODELS

➡Refer to the underhood label for the proper timing setting.

1. Engage the parking brake, block the wheels and set the transmission in P.
2. Disconnect the Ignition Control (IC) system by disengaging the "set timing connector". This is a single wire sealed connector that has a tan with black stripe lead. This wire comes out of the wiring harness below the heater case.
3. With the ignition switch **OFF**, connect the timing light pickup lead to the No. 1 spark plug wire.
4. Start the engine and point the timing light at the timing mark on the balancer or pulley and check the timing.
5. If the timing is not within specifications refer to the underhood emission sticker, loosen the distributor hold-down bolt. Slowly rotate the distributor until the proper timing setting is achieved.
6. Tighten the hold-down bolt and recheck the timing.
7. Turn the ignition **OFF**, remove the timing light and engage the "set timing" connector.

1996 MODELS

The ignition timing is preset and cannot be adjusted. If the distributor position is moved crossfiring may be induced. To check distributor position the following:

➡An OBD II compliant scan tool is required for this procedure

1. With the ignition **OFF** install scan tool to the Data Link Connector (DLC).
2. Start the engine and bring the vehicle to operating temperature.
3. Monitor cam retard on the scan tool.
4. If cam retard is between -2° and +2° the distributor is properly adjusted.
5. If cam retard is not between -2° and +2° the distributor must adjusted.

GASOLINE ENGINE TUNE-UP SPECIFICATIONS

Year	Engine ID/VIN	Engine Displacement Liters (cc)	Spark Plugs Gap (in.)	Ignition Timing (deg.) MT	Ignition Timing (deg.) AT	Fuel Pump (psi)	Idle Speed (rpm) MT	Idle Speed (rpm) AT	Valve Clearance In.	Valve Clearance Ex.
1988	Z	4.3 (4293)	0.040	①	①	9-13	700	700	HYD	HYD
	T	4.8 (4785)	0.035	8B	8B	5.0	700	700	HYD	HYD
	H	5.0 (4999)	0.045	4B	4B	4.0-6.5	700	700	HYD	HYD
	K	5.7 (5735)	0.045	4B	4B	4.0-6.5	700	700	HYD	HYD
	N	7.4 (7440)	0.045	4B	4B	9-13	700	700	HYD	HYD
	W	7.4 (7440)	0.045	4B	4B	4.0-6.5	700	700	HYD	HYD
1989	Z	4.3 (4293)	0.040	①	①	9-13	700	700	HYD	HYD
	T	4.8 (4785)	0.035	8B	8B	5.0	700	700	HYD	HYD
	H	5.0 (4999)	0.045	4B	4B	4.0-6.5	700	700	HYD	HYD
	K	5.7 (5735)	0.045	4B	4B	4.0-6.5	700	700	HYD	HYD
	N	7.4 (7440)	0.045	4B	4B	9-13	700	700	HYD	HYD
	W	7.4 (7440)	0.045	4B	4B	4.0-6.5	700	700	HYD	HYD
1990	Z	4.3 (4293)	0.040	①	①	9-13	①	①	HYD	HYD
	T	4.8 (4785)	0.035	①	①	9-13	①	①	HYD	HYD
	H	5.0 (4999)	0.045	①	①	9-13	①	①	HYD	HYD
	K	5.7 (5735)	0.045	①	①	9-13	①	①	HYD	HYD
	N	7.4 (7440)	0.045	①	①	9-13	①	①	HYD	HYD
	W	7.4 (7440)	0.045	①	①	5.0	①	①	HYD	HYD
1991	Z	4.3 (4293)	0.040	①	①	9-13	①	①	HYD	HYD
	H	5.0 (4999)	0.045	①	①	9-13	①	①	HYD	HYD
	K	5.7 (5735)	0.045	①	①	9-13	①	①	HYD	HYD
	N	7.4 (7440)	0.045	①	①	9-13	①	①	HYD	HYD
1992	Z	4.3 (4293)	0.035	①	①	9-13	①	①	HYD	HYD
	H	5.0 (4999)	0.045	①	①	9-13	①	①	HYD	HYD
	K	5.7 (5735)	0.045	①	①	9-13	①	①	HYD	HYD
	N	7.4 (7440)	0.045	①	①	9-13	①	①	HYD	HYD
1993	Z	4.3 (4293)	0.035	①	①	9-13	①	①	HYD	HYD
	H	5.0 (4999)	0.045	①	①	9-13	①	①	HYD	HYD
	K	5.7 (5735)	0.045	①	①	9-13	①	①	HYD	HYD
	N	7.4 (7440)	0.045	①	①	9-13	①	①	HYD	HYD
1994	Z	4.3 (4293)	0.035	①	①	9-13	①	①	HYD	HYD
	H	5.0 (4999)	0.045	①	①	9-13	①	①	HYD	HYD
	K	5.7 (5735)	0.045	①	①	9-13	①	①	HYD	HYD
	N	7.4 (7440)	0.045	①	①	9-13	①	①	HYD	HYD
1995	Z	4.3 (4293)	0.035	①	①	9-13	①	①	HYD	HYD
	H	5.0 (4999)	0.045	①	①	9-13	①	①	HYD	HYD
	K	5.7 (5735)	0.045	①	①	9-13	①	①	HYD	HYD
	N	7.4 (7440)	0.045	①	①	9-13	①	①	HYD	HYD
1996	W	4.3 (4293)	0.035	①	①	60-66	①	①	HYD	HYD
	M	5.0 (4999)	0.045	①	①	60-66	①	①	HYD	HYD
	R	5.7 (5735)	0.045	①	①	60-66	①	①	HYD	HYD
	J	7.4 (7440)	0.045	①	①	60-66	①	①	HYD	HYD

NOTE: The Vehicle Emission Control Information label often reflects specification changes made during production. The label figures must be used if they differ from those in this chart.

B - Before top dead center

HYD - Hydraulic

① Refer to underhood label for exact setting

87981C10

DIESEL ENGINE TUNE-UP SPECIFICATIONS

Year	Engine ID/VIN	Engine Displacement cu. in. (cc)	Valve Clearance Intake (in.)	Valve Clearance Exhaust (in.)	Intake Valve Opens (deg.)	Injection Pump Setting (deg.)	Injection Nozzle Pressure (psi) New	Injection Nozzle Pressure (psi) Used	Idle Speed (rpm)	Cranking Compression Pressure (psi)
1988	C	6.2 (6210)	HYD	HYD	②	①	1600	1500	②	NA
	J	6.2 (6210)	HYD	HYD	②	①	1600	1500	②	NA
1989	C	6.2 (6210)	HYD	HYD	②	①	1600	1500	②	NA
	J	6.2 (6210)	HYD	HYD	②	①	1600	1500	②	NA
1990	C	6.2 (6210)	HYD	HYD	②	①	1600	1500	②	NA
	J	6.2 (6210)	HYD	HYD	②	①	1600	1500	②	NA
1991	C	6.2 (6210)	HYD	HYD	②	①	1600	1500	②	NA
	J	6.2 (6210)	HYD	HYD	②	①	1600	1500	②	NA
1992	C	6.2 (6210)	HYD	HYD	②	①	1600	1500	②	NA
	F	6.5 (6473)	HYD	HYD	②	②	1600	1500	②	NA
	J	6.2 (6210)	HYD	HYD	②	①	1600	1500	②	NA
1993	C	6.2 (6210)	HYD	HYD	②	①	1600	1500	②	NA
	F	6.5 (6473)	HYD	HYD	①	①	1600	1500	①	NA
	J	6.2 (6210)	HYD	HYD	②	①	1600	1500	②	NA
1994	F	6.5 (6473)	HYD	HYD	①	①	1600	1500	①	NA
	P	6.5 (6473)	HYD	HYD	①	①	1800	1700	①	NA
	S	6.5 (6473)	HYD	HYD	①	①	1800	1700	①	NA
1995	F	6.5 (6473)	HYD	HYD	①	①	1600	1500	①	NA
	P	6.5 (6473)	HYD	HYD	①	①	1800	1700	①	NA
	S	6.5 (6473)	HYD	HYD	①	①	1800	1700	①	NA
1996	F	6.5 (6473)	HYD	HYD	①	①	1600	1500	①	NA
	P	6.5 (6473)	HYD	HYD	①	①	1800	1700	①	NA

NOTE: The Vehicle Emission Control Information label often reflects specification changes made during production. The label figures must be used if they differ from those in this chart

HYD - Hydraulic

NA - Not Available

① Set by aligning marks on top of engine front cover and injection pump flange

② Refer to underhood label

87981C11

6. With the engine **OFF** loosen the distributor hold-down bolt.

7. Start the engine and check the cam retard reading. Rotate the distributor counterclockwise to compensate for a negative reading and clockwise to compensate for a positive reading.

8. Momentarily raise the engine speed to over 1000 RPM and check the cam retard reading.

9. If the proper reading is not achieved repeat Steps 7 and 8.

10. When the proper reading has been achieved tighten the distributor hold-down bolt and disconnect the scan tool.

Valve Lash

All engines covered in this guide are equipped with hydraulic valve lifters. Engines so equipped operate with zero clearance in the valve train. Because of this the rocker arms are non-adjustable. The hydraulic lifters themselves do not require any adjustment as part of the normal tune-up, although they occasionally become noisy (especially on high mileage engines) and need to be replaced. In the event of cylinder head removal or any operation that requires disturbing or removing the rocker arms, the rocker arms have to be adjusted. Please refer to Section 3.

Idle Speed and Mixture Adjustments

CARBURETED ENGINES

Mixture screws are concealed under staked-in plugs. Idle mixture is adjustable only during carburetor overhaul, and requires the addition of propane as an artificial mixture enricher. For these reasons, mixture adjustments are not considered part of routine maintenance. Refer to Section 5 for these procedures.

4.8L Engines

➧ See Figure 139

CURB IDLE SPEED

With the idle speed solenoid energized, turn the solenoid body to establish the curb idle speed shown on your underhood sticker.

BASE IDLE SPEED

With the solenoid wire disconnected, turn the 1/8 in. hex head solenoid plunger adjusting screw to establish the base idle speed shown on your underhood sticker.

5.7L Engines

➧ See Figures 140 and 141

1. All adjustments should be made with the engine at normal operating temperature, air cleaner on, choke open, and air conditioning off, unless otherwise noted. Set the parking brake and block the rear wheels. Automatic transmissions should be set in Drive, manuals in Neutral, unless otherwise noted in the procedures or on the emission control label.
2. Refer to the underhood emission sticker and prepare the vehicle for adjustment as specified on the sticker. On models without a solenoid, turn the idle speed screw to obtain the idle speed listed in the underhood emission control label. On models with a solenoid, turn the solenoid screw to obtain the idle speed listed in the underhood emission control label. Disconnect the wire at the air conditioning compressor and turn the air conditioning on. Rev the engine momentarily to fully extend the solenoid plunger. Turn the solenoid screw to obtain the solenoid idle speed listed on the underhood emission sticker. Reconnect the air conditioning wire at the compressor.

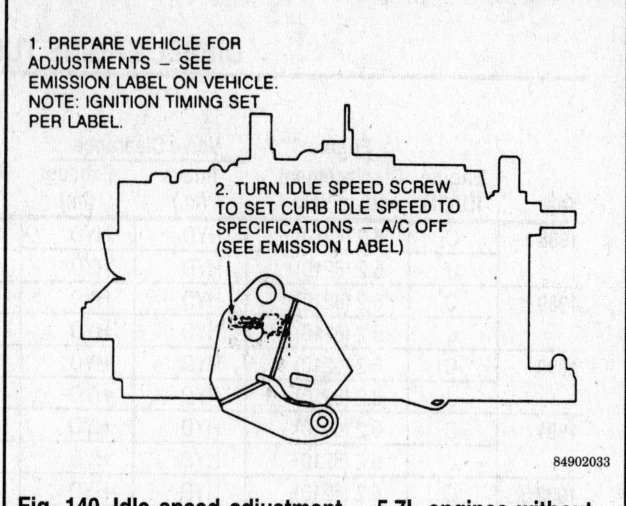

Fig. 140 Idle speed adjustment — 5.7L engines without solenoid

GASOLINE FUEL INJECTED ENGINES

The fuel injected vehicles are controlled by a computer which supplies the correct amount of fuel during all engine operating conditions and controls idle speed; no adjustment is necessary or possible.

DIESEL FUEL INJECTION

Idle Speed Adjustment

➧ See Figure 142

➡A special tachometer suitable for diesel engines must be used. A gasoline engine type tach will not work with the diesel engine.

1. Set the parking brake and block the drive wheels.
2. Run the engine up to normal operating temperature. The air cleaner must be mounted and all accessories turned off.
3. Install the diesel tachometer as per the manufacturer's instructions.
4. Adjust the low idle speed screw on the fuel injection pump to the specification listed on the underhood label in Neutral or P for both manual and automatic transmissions.

➡All idle speeds are to be set within 25 rpm of the specified values.

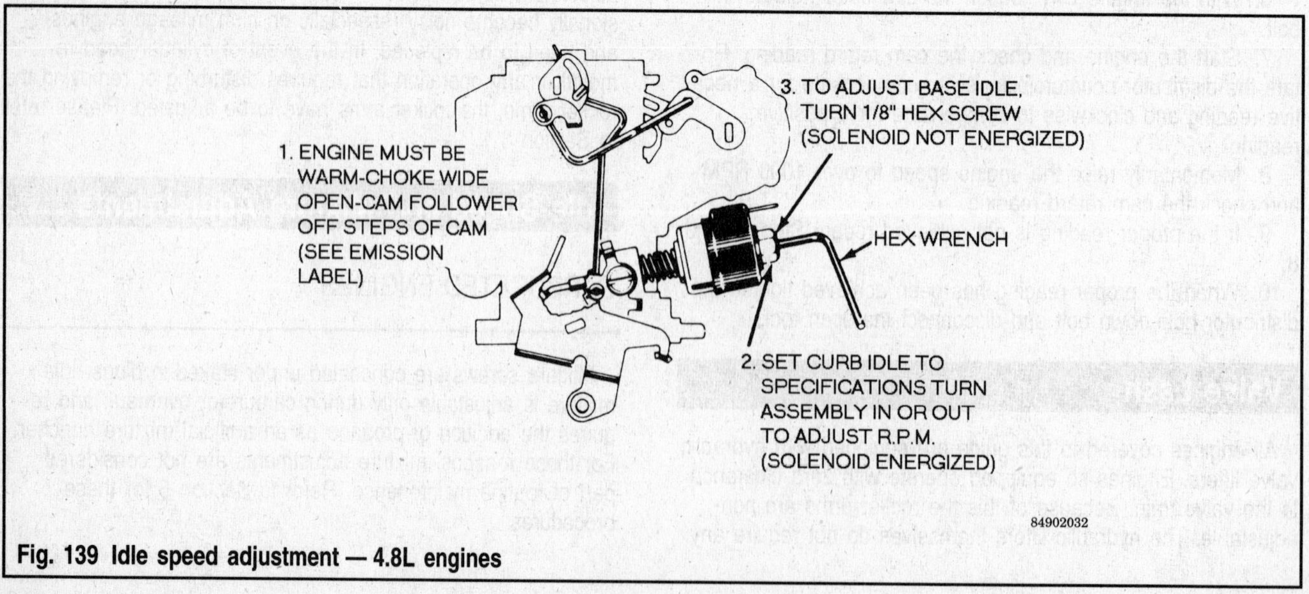

Fig. 139 Idle speed adjustment — 4.8L engines

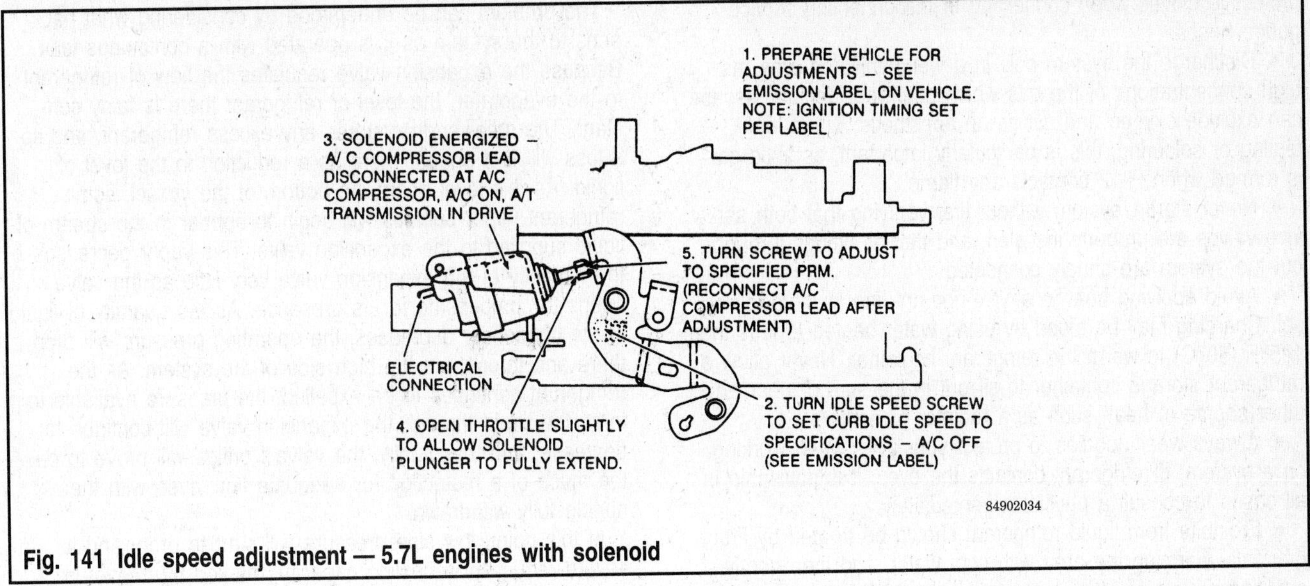

Fig. 141 Idle speed adjustment — 5.7L engines with solenoid

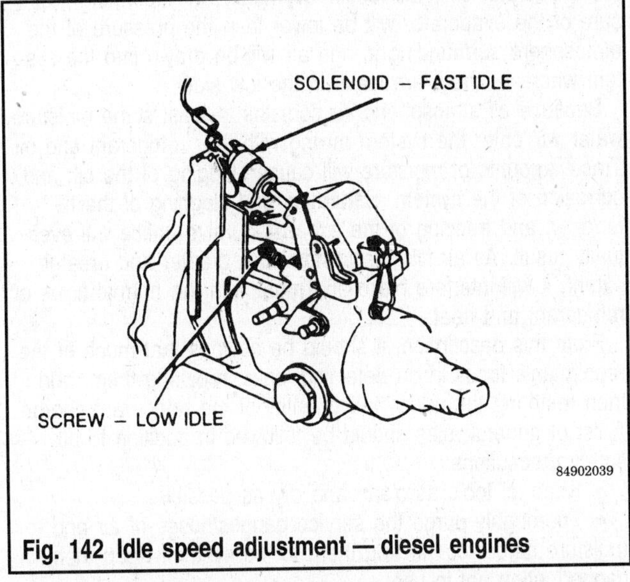

Fig. 142 Idle speed adjustment — diesel engines

5. Adjust the fast idle speed as follows:
   a. Remove the connector from the fast idle solenoid. Use an insulated jumper wire from the battery positive terminal to the solenoid terminal to energize the solenoid.
   b. Open the throttle momentarily to ensure that the fast idle solenoid plunger is energized and fully extended.
   c. Adjust the extended plunger by turning the hex-head screw to an engine speed of 800 rpm (check the underhood label) in Neutral.
   d. Remove the jumper wire and reinstall the connector to the fast idle solenoid.
6. Disconnect and remove the tachometer.

Air Conditioning

➡Be sure to consult the laws in your area before servicing the air conditioning system. In most areas, it is illegal to perform repairs involving refrigerant unless the work is done by a certified technician. Also, it is quite likely that you will not be able to purchase refrigerant without proof of certification.

SAFETY PRECAUTIONS

There are two major hazards associated with air conditioning systems and they both relate to the refrigerant gas. First, the refrigerant gas (R-12 or R-134a) is an extremely cold substance. When exposed to air, it will instantly freeze any surface it comes in contact with, including your eyes. The other hazard relates to fire (if your vehicle is equipped with R-12. Although normally non-toxic, the R-12 gas becomes highly poisonous in the presence of an open flame. One good whiff of the vapor formed by burning R-12 can be fatal. Keep all forms of fire (including cigarettes) well clear of the air conditioning system.

Because of the inherent dangers involved with working on air conditioning systems, these safety precautions must be strictly followed.

- Avoid contact with a charged refrigeration system, even when working on another part of the air conditioning system or vehicle. If a heavy tool comes into contact with a section of tubing or a heat exchanger, it can easily cause the relatively soft material to rupture.
- When it is necessary to apply force to a fitting which contains refrigerant, as when checking that all system couplings are securely tightened, use a wrench on both parts of the fitting involved, if possible. This will avoid putting torque on refrigerant tubing. (It is also advisable to use tube or line wrenches when tightening these flare nut fittings.)

➡R-12 refrigerant is a chlorofluorocarbon which, when released into the atmosphere, can contribute to the depletion of the ozone layer in the upper atmosphere. Ozone filters out harmful radiation from the sun.

- Do not attempt to discharge the system without the proper tools. Precise control is possible only when using the service gauges and a proper A/C refrigerant recovery station. Wear protective gloves when connecting or disconnecting service gauge hoses.

- Discharge the system only in a well ventilated area, as high concentrations of the gas which might accidentally escape can exclude oxygen and act as an anesthetic. When leak testing or soldering, this is particularly important, as toxic gas is formed when R-12 contacts any flame.
- Never start a system without first verifying that both service valves are properly installed, and that all fittings throughout the system are snugly connected.
- Avoid applying heat to any refrigerant line or storage vessel. Charging may be aided by using water heated to less than 125°F (50°C) to warm the refrigerant container. Never allow a refrigerant storage container to sit out in the sun, or near any other source of heat, such as a radiator or heater.
- Always wear goggles to protect your eyes when working on a system. If refrigerant contacts the eyes, it is advisable in all cases to consult a physician immediately.
- Frostbite from liquid refrigerant should be treated by first gradually warming the area with cool water, and then gently applying petroleum jelly. A physician should be consulted.
- Always keep refrigerant drum fittings capped when not in use. If the container is equipped with a safety cap to protect the valve, make sure the cap is in place when the can is not being used. Avoid sudden shock to the drum, which might occur from dropping it, or from banging a heavy tool against it. Never carry a drum in the passenger compartment of a vehicle.
- Always completely discharge the system into a suitable recovery unit before painting the vehicle (if the paint is to be baked on), or before welding anywhere near refrigerant lines.
- When servicing the system, minimize the time that any refrigerant line or fitting is open to the air in order to prevent moisture or dirt from entering the system. Contaminants such as moisture or dirt can damage internal system components. Always replace O-rings on lines or fittings which are disconnected. Prior to installation coat, but do not soak, replacement O-rings with suitable compressor oil.

GENERAL SERVICING PROCEDURES

➡It is recommended, and possibly required by law, that a qualified technician perform the following services.

⁂WARNING

Some of the vehicles covered by this manual may be equipped with R-134a refrigerant systems, rather than R-12. Be ABSOLUTELY SURE what type of system you are working on before attempting to add refrigerant. Use of the wrong refrigerant or oil will cause damage to the system.

The most important aspect of air conditioning service is the maintenance of a pure and adequate charge of refrigerant in the system. A refrigeration system cannot function properly if a significant percentage of the charge is lost. Leaks are common because the severe vibration encountered underhood in an automobile can easily cause a sufficient cracking or loosening of the air conditioning fittings; allowing, the extreme operating pressures of the system to force refrigerant out.

The problem can be understood by considering what happens to the system as it is operated with a continuous leak. Because the expansion valve regulates the flow of refrigerant to the evaporator, the level of refrigerant there is fairly constant. The receiver/drier stores any excess refrigerant, and so a loss will first appear there as a reduction in the level of liquid. As this level nears the bottom of the vessel, some refrigerant vapor bubbles will begin to appear in the stream of liquid supplied to the expansion valve. This vapor decreases the capacity of the expansion valve very little as the valve opens to compensate for its presence. As the quantity of liquid in the condenser decreases, the operating pressure will drop there and throughout the high side of the system. As the refrigerant continues to be expelled, the pressure available to force the liquid through the expansion valve will continue to decrease, and, eventually, the valve's orifice will prove to be too much of a restriction for adequate flow even with the needle fully withdrawn.

At this point, low side pressure will start to drop, and a severe reduction in cooling capacity, marked by freeze-up of the evaporator coil, will result. Eventually, the operating pressure of the evaporator will be lower than the pressure of the atmosphere surrounding it, and air will be drawn into the system wherever there are leaks in the low side.

Because all atmospheric air contains at least some moisture, water will enter the system mixing with the refrigerant and oil. Trace amounts of moisture will cause sludging of the oil, and corrosion of the system. Saturation and clogging of the filter/drier, and freezing of the expansion valve orifice will eventually result. As air fills the system to a greater and greater extent, it will interfere more and more with the normal flows of refrigerant and heat.

From this description, it should be obvious that much of the repairman's focus in on detecting leaks, repairing them, and then restoring the purity and quantity of the refrigerant charge. A list of general rules should be followed in addition to all safety precautions:

- Keep all tools as clean and dry as possible.
- Thoroughly purge the service gauges/hoses of air and moisture before connecting them to the system. Keep them capped when not in use.
- Thoroughly clean any refrigerant fitting before disconnecting it, in order to minimize the entrance of dirt into the system.
- Plan any operation that requires opening the system beforehand, in order to minimize the length of time it will be exposed to open air. Cap or seal the open ends to minimize the entrance of foreign material.
- When adding oil, pour it through an extremely clean and dry tube or funnel. Keep the oil capped whenever possible. Do not use oil that has not been kept tightly sealed.
- Purchase refrigerant intended for use only in automatic air conditioning systems.
- Completely evacuate any system that has been opened for service, or that has leaked sufficiently to draw in moisture and air. This requires evacuating air and moisture with a good vacuum pump for at least one hour. If a system has been open for a considerable length of time it may be advisable to evacuate the system for up to 12 hours (overnight).
- Use a wrench on both halves of a fitting that is to be disconnected, so as to avoid placing torque on any of the refrigerant lines.

• When overhauling a compressor, pour some of the oil into a clean glass and inspect it. If there is evidence of dirt, metal particles, or both, flush all refrigerant components with clean refrigerant before evacuating and recharging the system. In addition, if metal particles are present, the compressor should be replaced.
• Schrader valves may leak only when under full operating pressure. Therefore, if leakage is suspected but cannot be located, operate the system with a full charge of refrigerant and look for leaks from all Schrader valves. Replace any faulty valves.

Additional Preventive Maintenance

USING THE SYSTEM

The easiest and most important preventive maintenance for your A/C system is to be sure that it is used on a regular basis. Running the system for five minutes each month (no matter what the season) will help assure that the seals and all internal components remain lubricated.

ANTIFREEZE

See Figure 143

In order to prevent heater core freeze-up during A/C operation, it is necessary to maintain a proper antifreeze protection. Use a hand-held antifreeze tester (hydrometer) to periodically check the condition of the antifreeze in your engine's cooling system.

➡Antifreeze should not be used longer than the manufacturer specifies.

RADIATOR CAP

For efficient operation of an air conditioned vehicle's cooling system, the radiator cap should have a holding pressure which meets manufacturer's specifications. A cap which fails to hold these pressures should be replaced.

CONDENSER

Any obstruction of or damage to the condenser configuration will restrict the air flow which is essential to its efficient operation. It is therefore a good rule to keep this unit clean and in proper physical shape.

tccs1233

Fig. 143 An antifreeze tester can be use to determine the freezing and boiling level of the coolant

➡Bug screens which are mounted in front of the condenser (unless they are original equipment) are regarded as obstructions.

CONDENSATION DRAIN TUBE

This single molded drain tube expels the condensation, which accumulates on the bottom of the evaporator housing, into the engine compartment. If this tube is obstructed, the air conditioning performance can be restricted and condensation buildup can spill over onto the vehicle's floor.

SYSTEM INSPECTION

➡R-12 refrigerant is a chlorofluorocarbon which, when released into the atmosphere, can contribute to the depletion of the ozone layer in the upper atmosphere. Ozone filters out harmful radiation from the sun.

The easiest and often most important check for the air conditioning system consists of a visual inspection of the system components. Visually inspect the air conditioning system for refrigerant leaks, damaged compressor clutch, compressor drive belt tension and condition, plugged evaporator drain tube, blocked condenser fins, disconnected or broken wires, blown fuses, corroded connections and poor insulation.

A refrigerant leak will usually appear as an oily residue at the leakage point in the system. The oily residue soon picks up dust or dirt particles from the surrounding air and appears greasy. Through time, this will build up and appear to be a heavy dirt impregnated grease. Most leaks are caused by damaged or missing O-ring seals at the component connections, damaged charging valve cores or missing service gauge port caps.

For a thorough visual and operational inspection, check the following:

1. Check the surface of the radiator and condenser for dirt, leaves or other material which might block air flow.
2. Check for kinks in hoses and lines. Check the system for leaks.
3. Make sure the drive belt is under the proper tension. When the air conditioning is operating, make sure the drive belt is free of noise or slippage.
4. Make sure the blower motor operates at all appropriate positions, then check for distribution of the air from all outlets with the blower on **HIGH**.

➡Keep in mind that under conditions of high humidity, air discharged from the A/C vents may not feel as cold as expected, even if the system is working properly. This is because the vaporized moisture in humid air retains heat more effectively than does dry air, making the humid air more difficult to cool.

5. Make sure the air passage selection lever is operating correctly. Start the engine and warm it to normal operating temperature, then make sure the hot/cold selection lever is operating correctly.

DISCHARGING, EVACUATING AND CHARGING

Discharging, evacuating and charging the air conditioning system must be performed by a properly trained and certified mechanic in a facility equipped with refrigerant recovery/recycling equipment that meets SAE standards for the type of system to be serviced.

If you don't have access to the necessary equipment, we recommend that you take your vehicle to a reputable service station to have the work done. If you still wish to perform repairs on the vehicle, have them discharge the system, then take your vehicle home and perform the necessary work. When you are finished, return the vehicle to the station for evacuation and charging. Just be sure to cap ALL A/C system fittings immediately after opening them and keep them protected until the system is recharged.

Windshield Wipers

➧ See Figures 144, 145, 146, 147, 148, 149, 150, 151, 152 and 153

ELEMENT CARE AND REPLACEMENT

For maximum effectiveness and longest element life, the windshield and wiper blades should be kept clean. Dirt, tree sap, road tar and so on will cause streaking, smearing and blade deterioration if left on the glass. It is advisable to wash the windshield carefully with a commercial glass cleaner at least once a month. Wipe off the rubber blades with the wet rag afterwards. Do not attempt to move wipers across the windshield by hand; damage to the motor and drive mechanism will result.

To inspect and/or replace the wiper blades, place the wiper switch in the **LOW** speed position and the ignition switch in the **ACC** position. When the wiper blades are approximately vertical on the windshield, turn the ignition switch to **OFF**.

Examine the wiper blades. If they are found to be cracked, broken or torn, they should be replaced immediately. Replacement intervals will vary with usage, although ozone deterioration usually limits blade life to about one year. If the wiper pattern is smeared or streaked, or if the blade chatters across the glass, the elements should be replaced. It is easiest and most sensible to replace the elements in pairs.

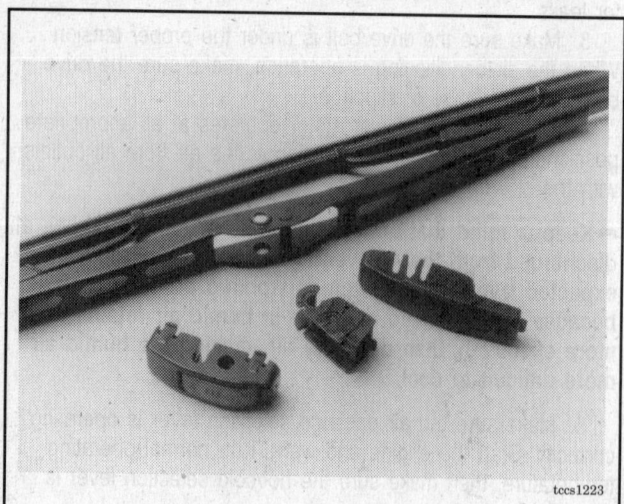
tccs1223

Fig. 144 Bosch® wiper blade and fit kit

tccs1224

Fig. 145 Lexor® wiper blade and fit kit

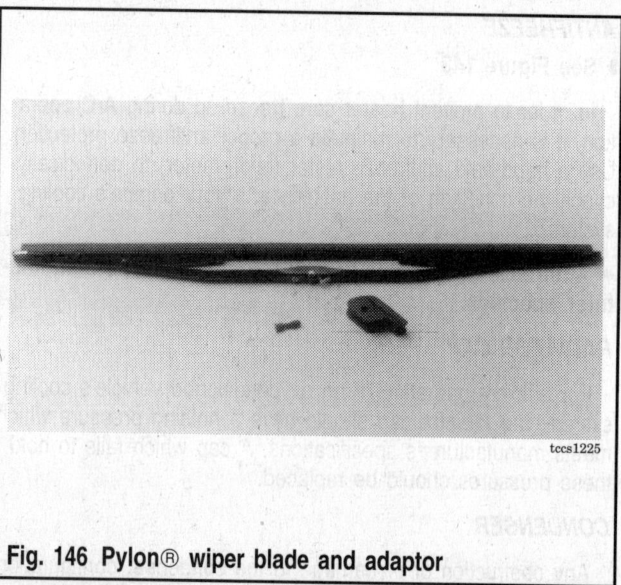
tccs1225

Fig. 146 Pylon® wiper blade and adaptor

If your vehicle is equipped with aftermarket blades, there are several different types of refills and your vehicle might have any kind. Aftermarket blades and arms rarely use the exact same type blade or refill as the original equipment. Here are some typical aftermarket blades, not all may be available for your vehicle:

The Anco® type uses a release button that is pushed down to allow the refill to slide out of the yoke jaws. The new refill slides back into the frame and locks in place.

Some Trico® refills are removed by locating where the metal backing strip or the refill is wider. Insert a small screwdriver blade between the frame and metal backing strip. Press down to release the refill from the retaining tab.

Other types of Trico® refills have two metal tabs which are unlocked by squeezing them together. The rubber filler can

tccs1226

Fig. 147 Trico® wiper blade and fit kit

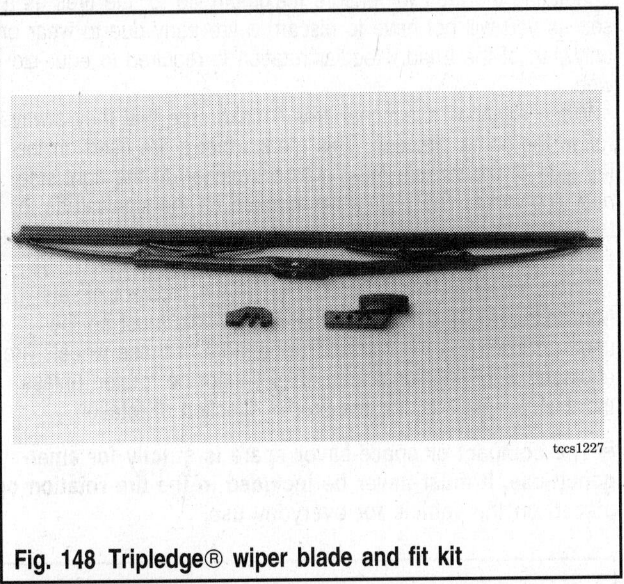

tccs1227

Fig. 148 Tripledge® wiper blade and fit kit

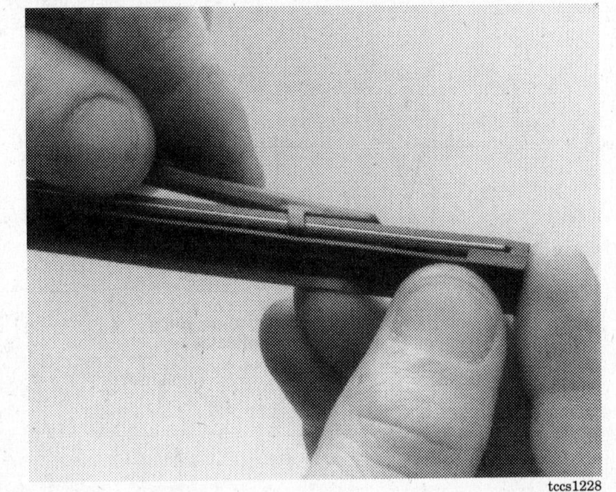

tccs1228

Fig. 149 To remove and install a Lexor® wiper blade, slip the old insert off and slide the new one on

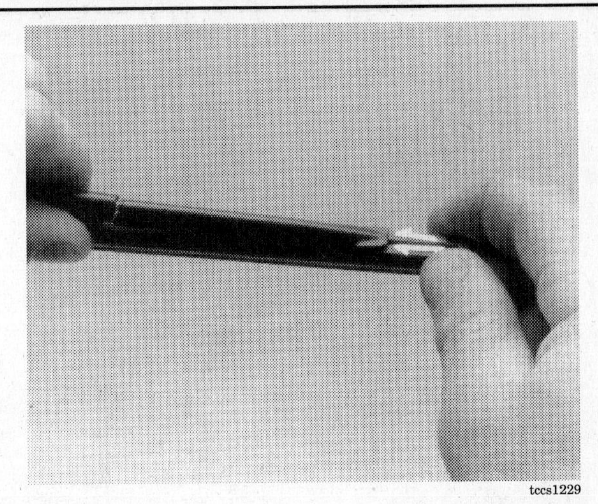

tccs1229

Fig. 150 On Pylon® wiper blade inserts, the clip at the end has to be removed prior to sliding the insert off

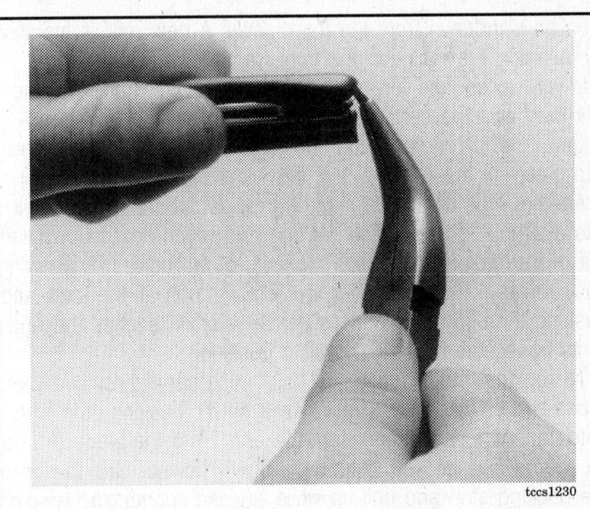

tccs1230

Fig. 151 On Trico® wiper blades, the tab at the end of the blade must be turned up . . .

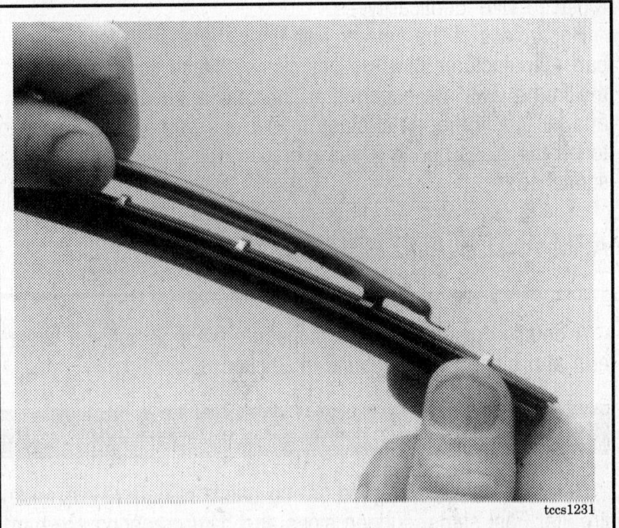

tccs1231

Fig. 152 . . . then the insert can be removed

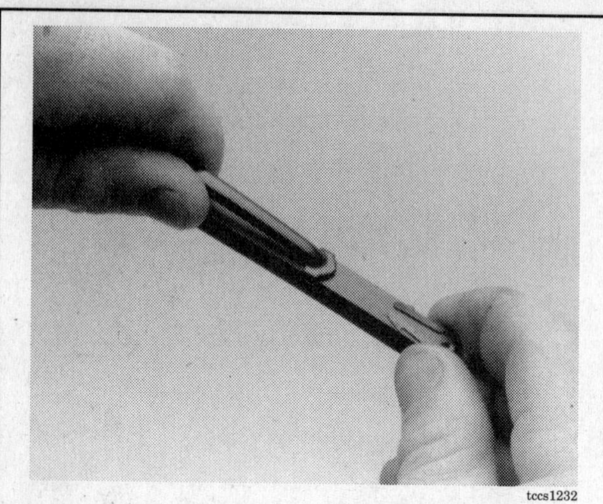

Fig. 153 The Tripledge® wiper blade insert is removed and installed using a securing clip

then be withdrawn from the frame jaws. A new refill is installed by inserting the refill into the front frame jaws and sliding it rearward to engage the remaining frame jaws. There are usually four jaws; be certain when installing, that the refill is engaged in all of them. At the end of its travel, the tabs will lock into place on the front jaws of the wiper blade frame.

Another type of refill is made from polycarbonate. The refill has a simple locking device at one end which flexes downward out of the groove into which the jaws of the holder fit, allowing easy release. By sliding the new refill through all the jaws and pushing through the slight resistance when it reaches the end of its travel, the refill will lock into position.

To replace the Tridon® refill, it is necessary to remove the wiper arm or blade. This refill has a plastic backing strip with a notch about 1 in. (25mm) from the end. Hold the blade (frame) on a hard surface so the frame is tightly bowed. Grip the tip of the backing strip and pull up while twisting counterclockwise. The backing strip will snap out of the retaining tab. Do this for the remaining tabs until the refill is free of the arm. The length of these refills is molded into the end and they should be replaced with identical types.

Regardless of the type of refill used, be sure to follow the part manufacturer's instructions closely. Make sure that all of the frame jaws are engaged as the refill is pushed into place and locked. If the metal blade holder and frame are allowed to touch the glass during wiper operation, the glass will be scratched.

ARM AND BLADE REPLACEMENT

A detailed description and procedure for replacing the wiper arm and blade may be found in Section 6.

Tires and Wheels

Common sense and good driving habits will afford maximum tire life. Fast starts, sudden stops and hard cornering are hard on tires and will shorten their useful life span. Make sure that you don't overload the vehicle or run with incorrect pressure in the tires. Both of these practices will increase tread wear.

Inspect your tires frequently. Be especially careful to watch for bubbles in the tread or sidewall, deep cuts or under-inflation. Replace any tires with bubbles in the sidewall. If cuts are so deep that they penetrate to the cords, discard the tire. Any cut in the sidewall of a radial tire renders it unsafe. Also look for uneven tread wear patterns that may indicate the front end is out of alignment or that the tires are out of balance.

TIRE ROTATION

See Figures 154 and 155

Tires must be rotated periodically to equalize wear patterns that vary with a tire's position on the vehicle. Tires will also wear in an uneven way as the front steering/suspension system wears to the point where the alignment should be reset.

Rotating the tires will ensure maximum life for the tires as a set, as you will not have to discard a tire early due to wear on only part of the tread. Regular rotation is required to equalize wear.

When rotating "directional tires," make sure that they always roll in the same direction. This means that a tire used on the left side of the vehicle must not be switched to the right side and vice-versa. These tires are marked on the sidewall as to the direction of rotation; observe the mark when reinstalling the tire(s).

Some styled or "mag" wheels may have different offsets front to rear. In these cases, the rear wheels must not be used up front and vice-versa. Furthermore, if these wheels are equipped with directional tires, they cannot be rotated unless the tire is remounted for the proper direction of rotation.

➡The compact or space-saver spare is strictly for emergency use. It must never be included in the tire rotation or placed on the vehicle for everyday use.

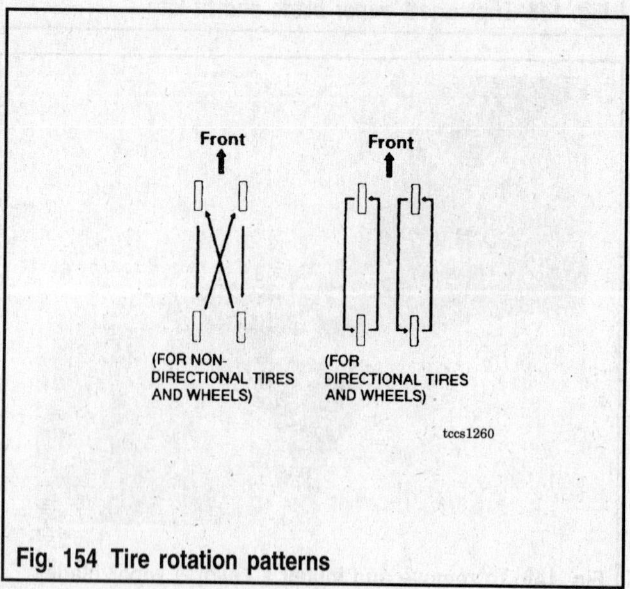

Fig. 154 Tire rotation patterns

Fig. 155 Some tires are directional and can only be rotated to the front or rear of the vehicle

TIRE DESIGN

See Figure 156

For maximum satisfaction, tires should be used in sets of four. Mixing of different types (radial, bias-belted, fiberglass belted) must be avoided. In most cases, the vehicle manufacturer has designated a type of tire with which the vehicle was designed for best performance. Your first choice when replacing tires should be to use the same type of tire as the manufacturer recommends.

When radial tires are used, tire sizes and wheel diameters should be selected to maintain ground clearance and tire load capacity equivalent to the original specified tire. Radial tires should always be used in sets of four.

CAUTION

Radial tires should never be used on only the front axle.

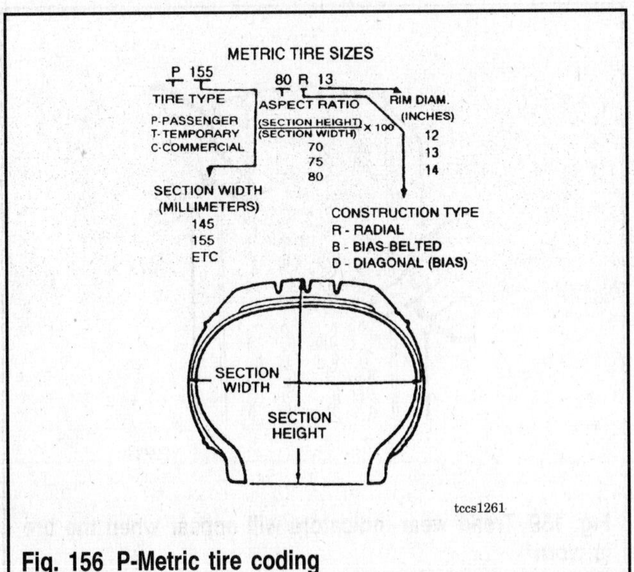

Fig. 156 P-Metric tire coding

When selecting tires, pay attention to the original size as marked on the tire. Most tires are described using an industry size code sometimes referred to as P-Metric. This allows the exact identification of the tire specifications, regardless of the manufacturer. If selecting a different tire size or brand, remember to check the installed tire for any sign of interference with the body or suspension while the vehicle is stopping, turning sharply or heavily loaded.

Snow Tires

Good radial tires can produce a big advantage in slippery weather, but in snow, a street radial tire does not have sufficient tread to provide traction and control. The small grooves of a street tire quickly pack with snow and the tire behaves like a billiard ball on marble floor. The more open, chunky tread of a snow tire will self-clean as the tire turns, providing much better grip on snowy surfaces.

To satisfy municipalities requiring snow tires during weather emergencies, most snow tires carry either an M + S designation after the tire size stamped on the sidewall or the designation "all-season." In general, no change in tire size is necessary when buying snow tires.

Most manufacturers strongly recommend the use of 4 snow tires on their vehicles for reasons of stability. If snow tires are fitted only to the drive wheels, the opposite end of the vehicle may become very unstable under braking or turning on slippery surfaces. This instability can lead to unpleasant endings if the driver can't counteract the slide in time.

Note that snow tires, whether 2 or 4, will affect vehicle handling in all non-snow situations. The stiffer, heavier snow tires will noticeably change the turning and braking characteristics of the vehicle. Once the snow tires are installed, you must re-learn the behavior of the vehicle and drive accordingly.

Consider buying extra wheels on which to mount the snow tires. Once done, the "snow wheels" can be installed and removed as needed. This eliminates the potential damage to tires or wheels from seasonal removal and installation. Even if your vehicle has styled wheels, see if inexpensive steel wheels are available. Although the look of the vehicle will change, the expensive wheels will be protected from salt, curb hits and pothole damage.

TIRE STORAGE

If they are mounted on wheels, store the tires at proper inflation pressure. All tires should be kept in a cool, dry place. If they are stored in the garage or basement, do not let them stand on a concrete floor; set them on strips of wood, a mat or a large stack of newspaper. Keeping them away from direct moisture is of paramount importance. Tires should not be stored upright, but in a flat position.

INSPECTION

See Figures 157, 158, 159, 160 and 161

The importance of proper tire inflation cannot be overemphasized. A tire employs air as part of its structure. It is designed around the supporting strength of the air at a specified pressure. For this reason, improper inflation drastically reduces the tires's ability to perform as intended. A tire will lose some air in day-to-day use; having to add a few pounds of air periodically is not necessarily a sign of a leaking tire.

Two items should be a permanent fixture in every glove compartment: an accurate tire pressure gauge and a tread depth gauge. Check the tire pressure (including the spare) regularly with a pocket type gauge. Too often, the gauge on the end of the air hose at your corner garage is not accurate because it suffers too much abuse. Always check tire pressure when the tires are cold, as pressure increases with temperature. If you must move the vehicle to check the tire inflation, do not drive more than a mile before checking. A cold tire is generally one that has not been driven for more than three hours.

A plate or sticker is normally provided somewhere in the vehicle (door post, hood, tailgate or trunk lid) which shows the proper pressure for the tires. Never counteract excessive pressure build-up by bleeding off air pressure (letting some air out). This will cause the tire to run hotter and wear quicker.

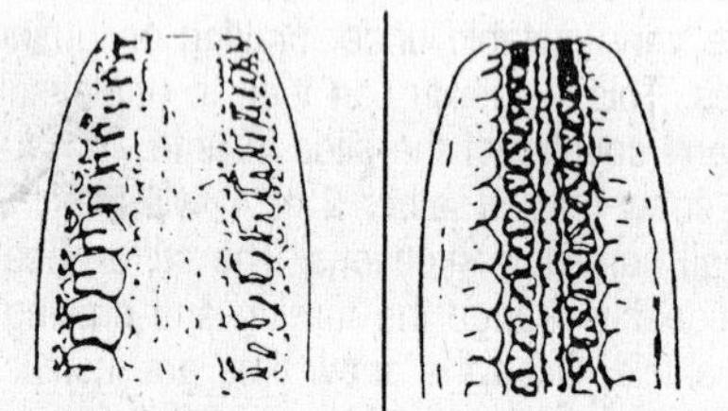

Fig. 157 Examples of inflation-related tire wear patterns

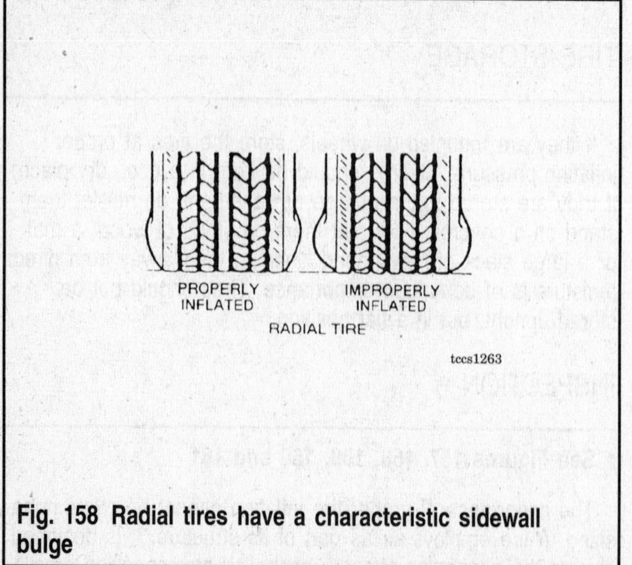

Fig. 158 Radial tires have a characteristic sidewall bulge

****CAUTION**

Never exceed the maximum tire pressure embossed on the tire! This is the pressure to be used when the tire is at maximum loading, but it is rarely the correct pressure for everyday driving. Consult the owner's manual or the tire pressure sticker for the correct tire pressure.

Once you've maintained the correct tire pressures for several weeks, you'll be familiar with the vehicle's braking and handling personality. Slight adjustments in tire pressures can fine-tune these characteristics, but never change the cold pressure specification by more than 2 psi. A slightly softer tire pressure will give a softer ride but also yield lower fuel mileage. A slightly harder tire will give crisper dry road handling but can cause skidding on wet surfaces. Unless you're fully attuned to the vehicle, stick to the recommended inflation pressures.

All tires made since 1968 have built-in tread wear indicator bars that show up as 1/2 in. (13mm) wide smooth bands across the tire when 1/16 in. (1.5mm) of tread remains. The appearance of tread wear indicators means that the tires should be replaced. In fact, many states have laws prohibiting the use of tires with less than this amount of tread.

You can check your own tread depth with an inexpensive gauge or by using a Lincoln head penny. Slip the Lincoln penny (with Lincoln's head upside-down) into several tread grooves. If you can see the top of Lincoln's head in 2 adjacent grooves, the tires have less than 1/16 in. (1.5mm) tread left and should be replaced. You can measure snow tires in the same manner by using the "tails" side of the Lincoln penny. If you can see the top of the Lincoln memorial, it's time to replace the snow tires.

CARE OF SPECIAL WHEELS

If you have invested money in magnesium, aluminum alloy or sport wheels, special precautions should be taken to make

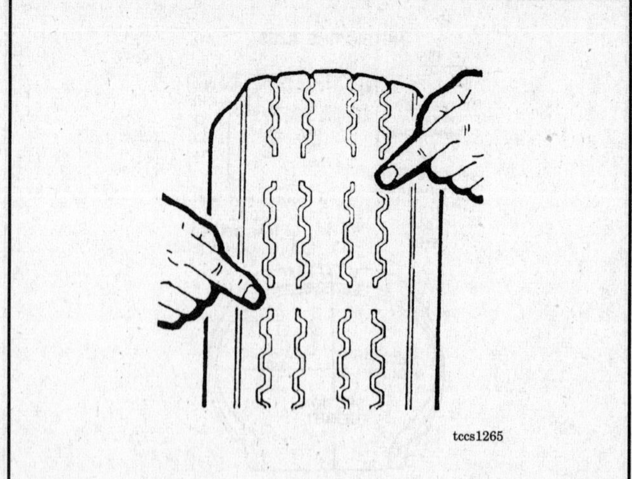

Fig. 159 Tread wear indicators will appear when the tire is worn

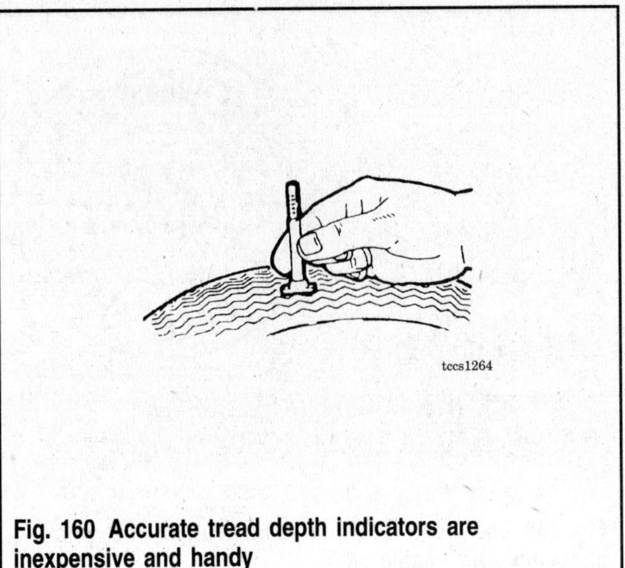

Fig. 160 Accurate tread depth indicators are inexpensive and handy

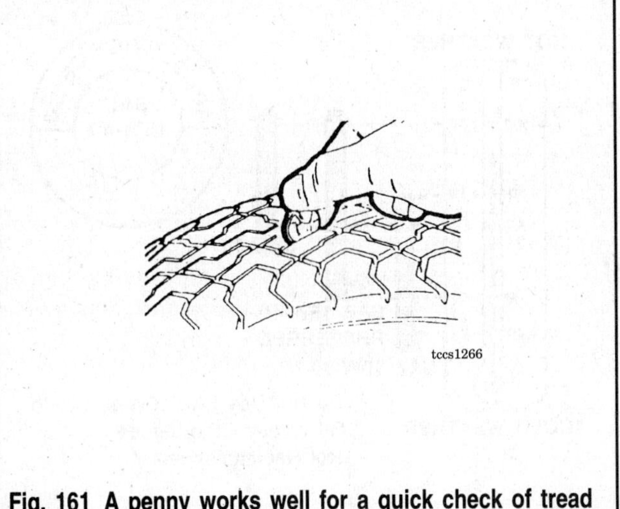

Fig. 161 A penny works well for a quick check of tread depth

sure your investment is not wasted and that your special wheels look good for the life of the vehicle.

Special wheels are easily damaged and/or scratched. Occasionally check the rims for cracking, impact damage or air leaks. If any of these are found, replace the wheel. But in order to prevent this type of damage and the costly replacement of a special wheel, observe the following precautions:

- Use extra care not to damage the wheels during removal, installation, balancing, etc. After removal of the wheels from the vehicle, place them on a mat or other protective surface. If they are to be stored for any length of time, support them on strips of wood. Never store tires and wheels upright; the tread may develop flat spots.
- When driving, watch for hazards; it doesn't take much to crack a wheel.
- When washing, use a mild soap or nonabrasive dish detergent (keeping in mind the detergent tends to remove wax). Avoid cleansers with abrasives or the use of hard brushes. There are many cleaners and polishes for special wheels.
- If possible, remove the wheels during the winter. Salt and sand used for snow removal can severely damage the finish of a wheel.
- Make certain the recommended lug nut torque is never exceeded or the wheel may crack. Never use snow chains on special wheels; severe scratching will occur.

FLUIDS AND LUBRICANTS

Fluid Disposal

Used fluids such as engine oil, transmission fluid, anti-freeze and brake fluid are hazardous wastes and must be disposed of properly. Before draining any fluids, consult with the local authorities; in many areas, waste oil, etc. is being accepted as part of recycling programs. A number of service stations and auto parts stores are also accepting waste fluids for recycling.

Be sure of the recycling center's policies before draining any fluids, as many will not accept different fluids that have been mixed together, such as oil and anti-freeze.

Fuel and Oil Recommendations

OIL

See Figures 162, 163 and 164

The Society of Automotive Engineers (SAE) grade number indicates the viscosity of the engine oil; its resistance to flow at a given temperature. The lower the SAE grade number, the lighter the oil. For example, the mono-grade oils begin with SAE 5 weight, which is a thin light oil, and continue in viscosity up to SAE 80 or 90 weight, which are heavy gear lubricants. These oils are also known as 'straight weight', meaning they are of a single viscosity, and do not vary with engine temperature.

Multi-viscosity oils offer the important advantage of being adaptable to temperature extremes. These oils have designations such as 10W-40, 20W-50, etc. The 10W-40 means that in winter (the "W" in the designation) the oil acts like a thin 10 weight oil, allowing the engine to spin easily when cold and offering rapid lubrication. Once the engine has warmed up, however, the oil acts like a straight 40 weight, maintaining good lubrication and protection for the engine's internal components. A 20W-50 oil would therefore be slightly heavier than and not as ideal in cold weather as the 10W-40, but would offer better protection at higher rpm and temperatures because when warm it acts like a 50 weight oil. Whichever oil viscosity you choose when changing the oil, make sure you are anticipating the temperatures your engine will be operating in until the oil is changed again. Refer to the oil viscosity chart for oil recommendations according to temperature.

The American Petroleum Institute (API) designation indicates the classification of engine oil used under certain given operating conditions. Only oils designated for use "Service SG" or greater should be used. Oils of the SG type perform a variety of functions inside the engine in addition to the basic function as a lubricant. Through a balanced system of metallic detergents and polymeric dispersants, the oil prevents the formation of high and low temperature deposits and also keeps sludge and particles of dirt in suspension. Acids, particularly sulfuric acid, as well as other by-products of combustion, are neutralized. Both the SAE grade number and the APE designation can be found on top of the oil can.

Diesel engines also require SG or greater engine oil. In addition, the oil must qualify for a CC or greater rating. The API has a number of different diesel engine ratings, including CB, CC, and CD. Any of these other oils are fine as long as the designation CC appears on the can along with them. Do not use oil labeled only SG or only CC. Both designations must always appear together.

For recommended oil viscosities, refer to the chart. Note that 10W-30 and 10W-40 grade oils are not recommended for sustained high speed driving when the temperature rises above the indicated limit.

Fig. 163 Look for the API oil identification label when choosing your engine oil

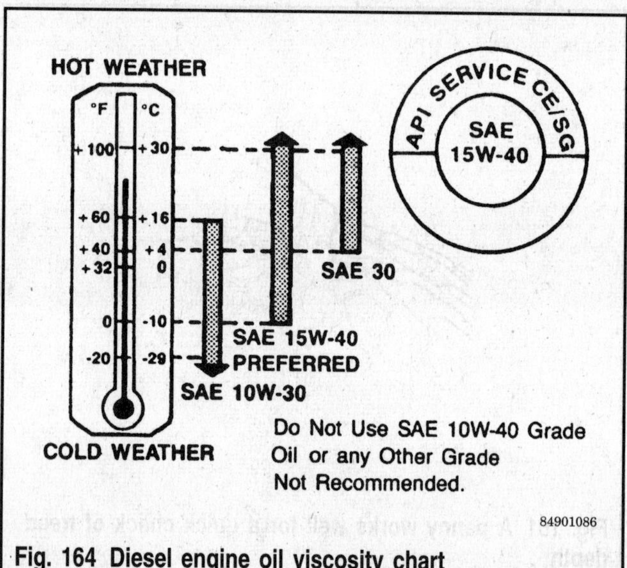

Fig. 164 Diesel engine oil viscosity chart

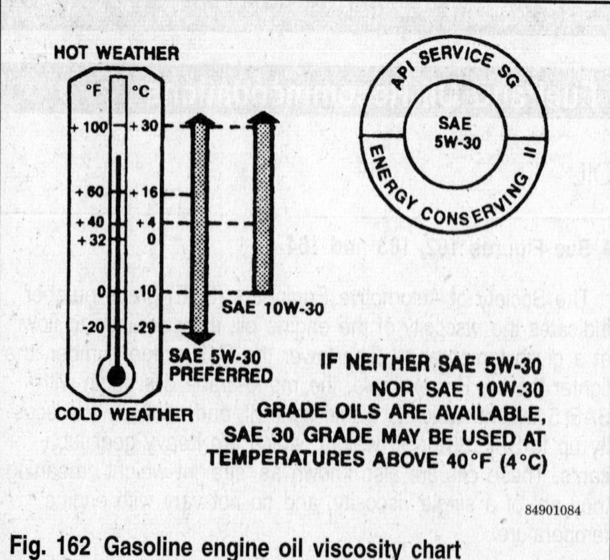

Fig. 162 Gasoline engine oil viscosity chart

Synthetic Oil

There are many excellent synthetic and fuel-efficient oils currently available that can provide better gas mileage, longer service life, and in some cases better engine protection. These benefits do not come without a few hitches, however; the main one being the price of synthetic oils, which is three or four times the price per quart of conventional oil.

Synthetic oil is not for every truck and every type of driving, so you should consider your engine's condition and your type of driving. Also, check your truck's warranty conditions regarding the use of synthetic oils.

Brand new engines are a wrong candidate for synthetic oil. The synthetic oils are so slippery that they can prevent the proper break-in of new engines; most manufacturers recommend that you wait until the engine is properly broken in; 3000 miles (4800 km), before using synthetic oil. Also, if your truck is leaking oil past old seals you'll have a much greater leak problem with synthetics.

Consider your type of driving. If most of your accumulated mileage is high speed, highway type driving, the more expen-

RECOMMENDED LUBRICANTS

Component	Lubricant
Engine Oil	API SG/CE ①
Coolant	Ethylene Glycol Anti-Freeze
Manual Transmission Muncie 117mm Getrag 85mm NVG 4500 NVG 5LM60	 API GL5, SAE 80W-90 Synchromesh Transmission Fluid Castrol Syntorq GL-4 Synchromesh Transmission Fluid
Automatic Transmission	AFT Dexron® II ①
Transfer Case	
Differential	API GL-5, SAE 80W-90
Master Cylinder	DOT 3 Brake Fluid
Power Steering	GM Power Steering Fluid
Manual Steering Gear	GM Lubricant
Multi-Purpose Grease	NLGI #2

① Or its superceding fluid type.

84901151

sive synthetic oils may be a benefit. Extended highway driving gives the engine a chance to warm up, accumulating less acids in the oil and putting less stress on the engine over the long run. Under these conditions, the oil change interval can be extended (as long as your oil filter can last the extended life of the oil) up to the advertised mileage claims of the synthetics. Trucks with synthetic oils may show increased fuel economy in highway driving, due to less internal friction. However, many automotive experts agree that 50,000 miles (80,000 km) is too long to keep any oil in your engine.

FUEL

Gasoline Engines

It is important to use fuel of the proper octane rating in your truck. Octane rating is based on the quantity of anti-knock compounds added to the fuel and it determines the speed at which the gas will burn. The lower the octane rating, the faster it burns. The higher the octane, the slower the fuel will burn and a greater percentage of compounds in the fuel prevent spark ping (knock), detonation and preignition (dieseling).

As the temperature of the engine increases, the air/fuel mixture exhibits a tendency to ignite before the spark plug is fired. If fuel of an octane rating too low for the engine is used, this will allow combustion to occur before the piston has completed its compression stroke, thereby creating a very high pressure very rapidly.

Fuel of the proper octane rating, for the compression ratio and ignition timing of your truck, will slow the combustion process sufficiently to allow the spark plug enough time to ignite the mixture completely and smoothly. Many non-catalyst models are designed to run on regular fuel. The use of some super-premium fuel is no substitution for a properly tuned and maintained engine. Chances are that if your engine exhibits any signs of spark ping, detonation or pre-ignition when using regular fuel, the ignition timing should be checked against specifications or the cylinder head should be removed for decarbonizing.

Vehicles equipped with catalytic converters must use UNLEADED GASOLINE ONLY. Use of unleaded fuel shortened the life of spark plugs, exhaust systems and EGR valves and can damage the catalytic converter. Most converter equipped models are designed to operate using unleaded gasoline with a minimum rating of 87 octane. Use of unleaded gas with octane ratings lower than 87 can cause persistent spark knock which could lead to engine damage.

Light spark knock may be noticed when accelerating or driving up hills. The slight knocking may be considered normal (with 87 octane) because the maximum fuel economy is obtained under condition of occasional light spark knock. Gasoline with an octane rating higher than 87 may be used, but it is not necessary (in most cases) for proper operation.

If spark knock is constant, when using 87 octane, at cruising speeds on level ground, ignition timing adjustment may be required.

➡Your engine's fuel requirement can change with time, mainly due to carbon buildup, which changes the compression ratio. If your engine pings, knocks or runs on, switch to a higher grade of fuel. Sometimes just changing brands will cure the problem. If it becomes necessary to retard the timing from specifications, don't change it more than a few degrees. Retarded timing will reduce power output and fuel mileage and will increase the engine temperature.

Diesel Engines

Diesel engines require the use of diesel fuel. At no time should gasoline be substituted. Two grades of diesel fuel are manufactured, #1 and #2, although #2 grade is generally more available. Better fuel economy results from the use of #2 grade fuel. In some northern parts of the U.S. and in most parts of Canada, #1 grade fuel is available in the winter or a winterized blend of #2 grade is supplied in winter months. When the temperature falls below 20°F (-7°C), #1 grade or winterized #2 grade fuel are the only fuels that can be used. Cold temperatures cause unwinterized #2 to thicken (it actually gels), blocking the fuel lines and preventing the engine from running.

- Do not use home heating oil in your truck.
- Do not use ether or starting assist fluids in your truck.
- Do not use any fuel additives recommended for use in gasoline engines.

It is normal that the engine noise level is louder during the warm-up period in winter. It is also normal that whitish/blue smoke may be emitted from the exhaust after starting and during warm-up. The amount of smoke depends upon the outside temperature.

OPERATION IN FOREIGN COUNTRIES

If you plan to drive your truck outside the United States or Canada, there is a possibility that fuels will be too low in antiknock quality and could produce engine damage. It is wise to consult with local authorities upon arrival in a foreign country to determine the best fuels available.

Engine

**CAUTION

Prolonged and repeated skin contact with used engine oil, with no effort to remove the oil, may be harmful. Always follow these simple precautions when handling used motor oil:

- Avoid prolonged skin contact with used motor oil.
- Remove oil from skin by washing thoroughly with soap and water or waterless hand cleaner. Do not use gasoline, thinners or other solvents.
- Avoid prolonged skin contact with oil-soaked clothing.

OIL LEVEL CHECK

➧ See Figures 165, 166 and 167

Every time you stop for fuel, check the engine oil as follows:

1. Park the truck on level ground.
2. When checking the oil level it is best for the engine to be at operating temperature, although checking the oil immediately after a stopping will lead to a false reading. Wait a few minutes after turning off the engine to allow the oil to drain back into the crankcase.
3. Open the hood and locate the dipstick which is on the left side of the engine. Pull the dipstick from its tube, wipe it clean and reinsert it.
4. Pull the dipstick out again and, holding it horizontally, read the oil level. The oil should be between the **FULL** or **OPERATING RANGE** and **ADD** or **ADD OIL** marks on the dipstick.
5. If the oil is below the **ADD** mark, add oil of the proper viscosity through the capped opening on the top of the cylinder head cover. See the "Oil and Fuel Recommendations"chart in this section for the proper viscosity and rating of oil to use.
6. Reinsert the dipstick and check the oil level again after adding any oil. Be careful not to overfill the crankcase. Approximately one quart of oil will raise the level from the **ADD** to the **FULL**. Excess oil will generally be consumed at an accelerated rate.

OIL AND FILTER CHANGE

➧ See Figures 168, 169, 170 and 171

The oil should be changed every 7500 miles (12,000 km). General Motors recommends changing the oil filter with every other oil change; we suggest that the filter be changed with every oil change. There is approximately 1 quart of dirty oil left remaining in the old oil filter if it is not changed! A few dollars more every year seems a small price to pay for extended engine life — so change the filter every time you change the oil!

The oil drain plug is located on the bottom, rear of the oil pan (bottom of the engine, underneath the truck).

The mileage figures given are the recommended intervals assuming normal driving and conditions. If your truck is being used under dusty, polluted or off-road conditions, change the

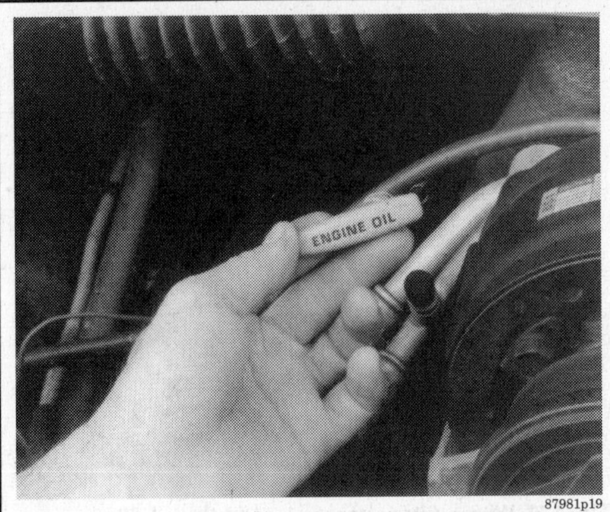

87981p19

Fig. 165 Remove the oil dipstick and check the oil level

87981p20

Fig. 166 Remove the oil filler cap

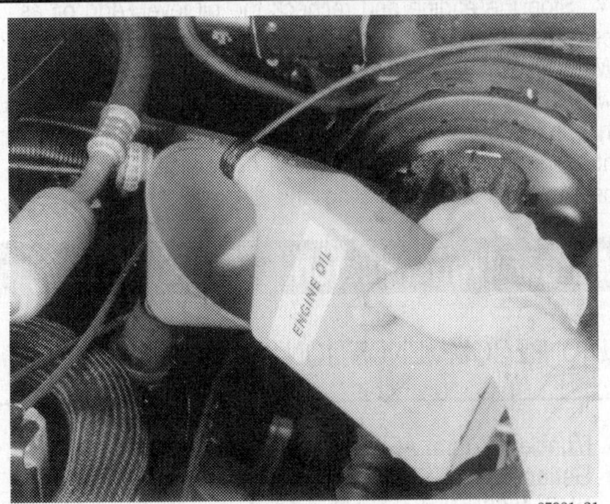

87981p21

Fig. 167 Using a funnel add the proper grade and viscosity of oil

oil and filter more frequently than specified. The same goes for trucks driven in stop-and-go traffic or only for short distances. Always drain the oil after the engine has been running long enough to bring it to normal operating temperature. Hot oil will flow easier and more contaminants will be removed along with the oil than if it were drained cold. To change the oil and filter:

➡If the engine is equipped with an oil cooler, this will also have to be drained, using the drain plug. Be sure to add enough oil to fill the cooler in addition to the engine.

1. Warm the oil by running the engine for a short period of time or at least until the needle on the temperature gauge rises above the **C** mark. This will make the oil flow more freely from the oil pan.
2. Park on a level surface, apply the parking brake and block the wheels.
3. Stop the engine. Raise the hood and remove the oil filler cap from the top of the valve cover. This allows the air to enter the engine as the oil drains. Remove the dipstick, wipe it off and set it aside.
4. Position a suitable oil drain pan under the drain plug.

➡All diesel and gasoline engines hold approximately 5-8 quarts of oil (give or take), so choose a drain pan that exceeds this amount to allow for movement of the oil when the pan is pulled from under the vehicle. This will prevent time lost to the cleaning up of messy oil spills.

5. With the proper size socket or wrench (DO NOT use pliers or vise grips), loosen the drain plug. Back out the drain plug while maintaining a slight upward force on it to keep the oil from running out around it (and your hand). Allow the oil to drain into the drain pan.

✲✲CAUTION

The engine oil will be hot. Keep your arms, face and hands away from the oil as it is draining.

6. Remove the drain pan and wipe any excess oil from the area around the hole using a clean rag.

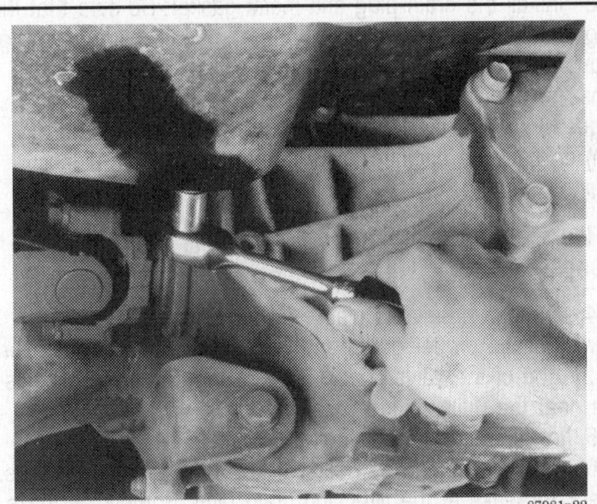
87981p22

Fig. 168 With the proper size socket loosen the drain plug

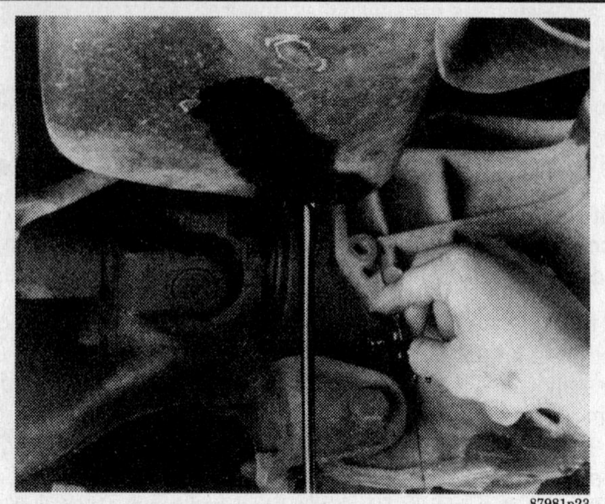

87981p23

Fig. 169 Remove the drain plug while maintaining a slight upward force to keep the oil from running out

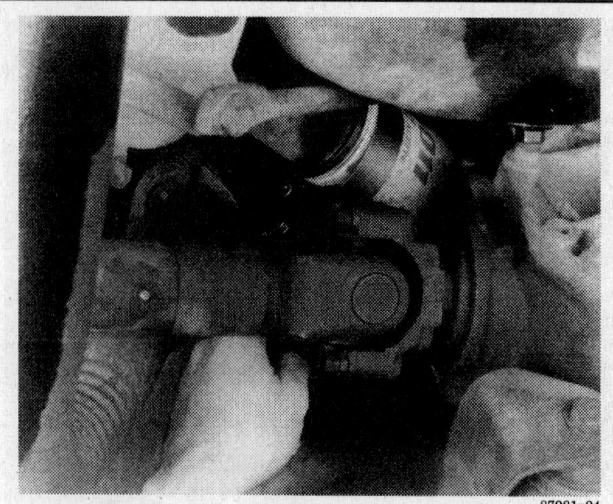

87981p24

Fig. 170 With a filter wrench, loosen the oil filter counterclockwise

7. Clean the threads of the drain plug and the drain plug gasket to remove any sludge deposits that may have accumulated.
8. Place the drain pan under the oil filter location to prevent spilling any oil from the filter on to the ground.
9. With a filter wrench, loosen the oil filter counterclockwise and back the filter off the filter post the rest of the way by hand. Keep the filter end up so that the oil does not spill out. Tilt the filter into the drain pan to drain the oil.
10. Remove the drain pan from under the vehicle and position it off to the side.
11. With a clean rag, wipe off the filter seating surface to ensure a proper seal. Make sure that the old gasket is not stuck to the seating surface. If it is, remove it and thoroughly clean the seating surface of the old gasket material.
12. Open a container of new oil and smear some of this oil onto the rubber gasket of the new oil filter. Get a feel for where the filter post is and start the filter by hand until the gasket contacts the seat. Turn the filter an additional 3/4 turn with your hand.
13. Install the drain plug and metal gasket. Be sure that the plug is tight enough that the oil does not leak out, but not tight enough to strip the threads. Over time you will develop a sense of what the proper tightness of the drain plug is. If a torque wrench is available, tighten the plug to 20 ft. lbs. (27 Nm) on gasoline engines or 30 ft. lbs. (40 Nm) on diesel engines.

➡Replace the drain plug gasket at every third or fourth oil change.

14. Through a suitable plastic or metal funnel, add clean new oil of the proper grade and viscosity through the oil filler on the top of the valve cover. Be sure that the oil level registers near the (full) mark on the dipstick.
15. Install and tighten the oil filler cap.
16. Start the engine and allow it to run for several minutes. Check for leaks at the filter and drain plug. Sometimes leaks will not be revealed until the engine reaches normal operating temperature.

TCCS1901

Fig. 171 Before installing a new oil filter, coat the rubber gasket with clean oil

17. Stop the engine and recheck the oil level. Add oil as necessary.

When you have finished this job, you will notice that you now possess several quarts of dirty oil. The best thing to do with it is to pour it into plastic jugs, such as milk or anti-freeze containers. Then, find a gas station or service garage which accepts waste oil for recycling and dispose of it there.

Manual Transmission

FLUID RECOMMENDATION

- Muncie 117mm: API GL-5, SAE 80W-90
- Getrag 85mm: Syncromesh Transmission Fluid
- NVG 4500: Castrol Syntorq GL-4
- NVG 5LM60: Syncromesh Transmission Fluid
- NVG 3500: Syncromesh Transmission Fluid

FLUID LEVEL CHECK

➧ See Figure 172

Check the lubricant level at least twice a year, even more frequently if driven in deep water.

1. With the truck parked on a level surface, remove the filler plug from the side of the transmission case. Be careful not to take out the drain plug at the bottom.
2. If lubricant begins to trickle out of the hole, there is enough. If not, carefully insert a finger (watch out for sharp threads) and check that the level is up to the edge of the hole.
3. If not, add sufficient lubricant with a funnel and tube, or a squeeze bulb to bring it to the proper level. You can also use a common kitchen baster.
4. Install the plug and tighten to 17 ft. lbs. (23 Nm) on the Muncie and Getrag; 30 ft. lbs. (40 Nm) on NVG 4500; and 46 ft. lbs. (60 Nm) on the NVG 5LM60. Road test the truck and check for any leaks.

DRAIN AND REFILL

No intervals are specified for changing the transmission lubricant, but it is a good idea on a used vehicle, one that has been worked hard, or one driven in deep water. The vehicle should be on a level surface and the lubricant should be at operating temperature.

1. Position the truck on a level surface.
2. Place a pan of sufficient capacity under the transmission drain plug.
3. Remove the upper (fill) plug to provide a vent opening.
4. Remove the lower (drain) plug and let the lubricant drain out.

✲✲CAUTION

The oil will be hot! Be careful when you remove the plug or you'll be taking a bath in hot gear oil.

5. Install the drain plug and tighten to 17 ft. lbs. (23 Nm) on the Muncie and Getrag; 30 ft. lbs. (40 Nm) on NVG 4500; and 46 ft. lbs. (60 Nm) on the NVG 5LM60.
6. Add lubricant with a suction gun or squeeze bulb.
7. Reinstall the filler plug. Run the engine and check for leaks.

Automatic Transmission

FLUID RECOMMENDATIONS

Use Dexron II® or its superceding fluid type.

FLUID LEVEL CHECK

➧ See Figures 173, 174 and 175

Check the level of the fluid at least once a month. The fluid level should be checked with the engine at normal operating temperature and running. If the truck has been running at high speed for a long period, in city traffic on a hot day, or pulling a trailer, let it cool down for about thirty minutes before checking the level.

1. Park the truck on a level surface with the engine idling. Shift the transmission into **P** and set the parking brake.
2. Remove the dipstick (on newer models, you may have to flip up the handle first), wipe it clean and reinsert if firmly. Be sure that it has been pushed all the way in.
3. Remove the dipstick and check the fluid level while holding it horizontally. All models have a HOT and a COLD side to the dipstick.
   - **COLD**: the fluid level should fall in this range when the engine has been running for only a short time.
   - **HOT**: the fluid level should fall in this range when the engine has reached normal running temperatures.
4. Early models have two dimples below the ADD mark, the level should be between these when the engine is cold.
5. If the fluid level is not within the proper area on either side of the dipstick, pour ATF into the dipstick tube. This is

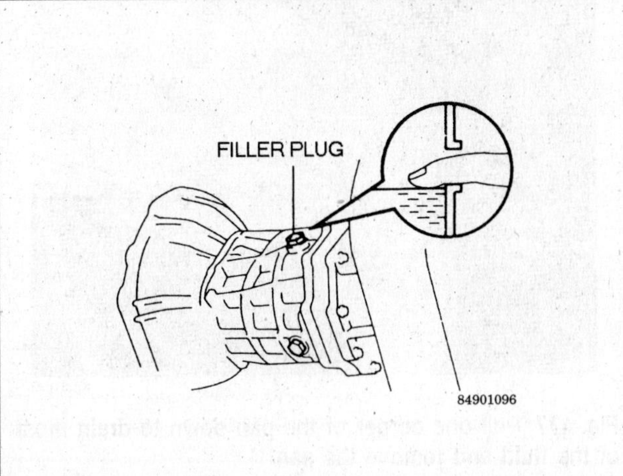

Fig. 172 Use your finger to check the oil level in the manual transmission

Fig. 173 Remove the dipstick to check the transmission fluid level

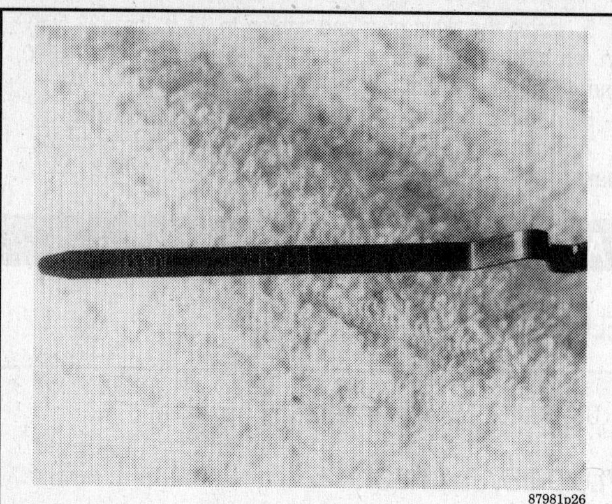

87981p26

Fig. 174 Hold the dipstick horizontally and check the fluid level

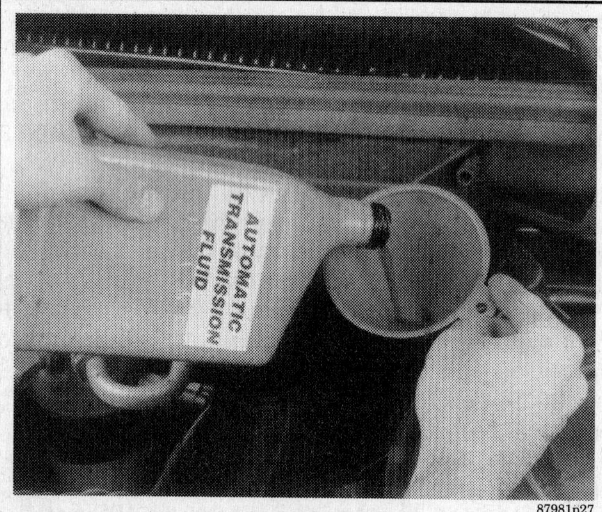

87981p27

Fig. 175 Use a funnel to add transmission fluid

easily done with the aid of a funnel. Check the level often as you are filling the transmission. Be extremely careful not to overfill it. Overfilling will cause slippage, seal damage and overheating. Approximately one pint of ATF will raise the level from one notch to the other.

CAUTION

The fluid on the dipstick should always be a bright red color. It if is discolored (brown or black), or smells burnt, serious transmission troubles, probably due to overheating, should be suspected. The transmission should be inspected by a qualified service technician to locate the cause of the burnt fluid.

DRAIN AND REFILL

See Figures 176, 177, 178, 179 and 180

1. The fluid should be drained with the transmission warm. It is easier to change the fluid if the truck is raised somewhat from the ground, but this is not always easy without a lift. The transmission must be level for it to drain properly.
2. Place a shallow pan underneath to catch the transmission fluid (about 5 pints). Loosen all the pan bolts, then pull one corner down to drain most of the fluid. If it sticks, VERY CAREFULLY pry the pan loose. You can buy aftermarket drain plug kits that makes this operation a bit less messy, once installed.

If the fluid removed smells burnt, serious transmission troubles, probably due to overheating, should be suspected.

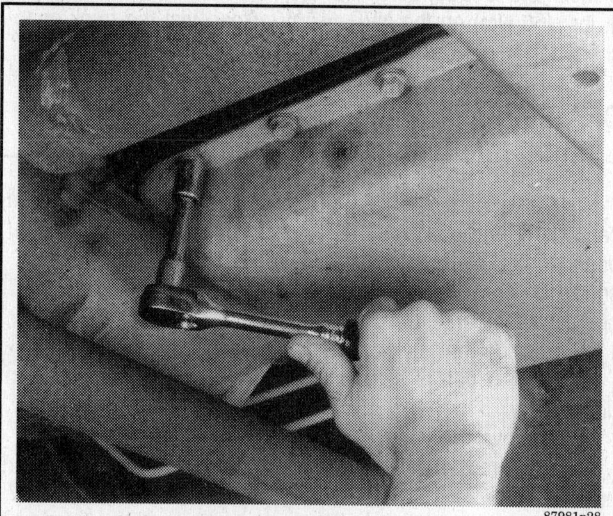

87981p28

Fig. 176 Loosen all the pan bolts

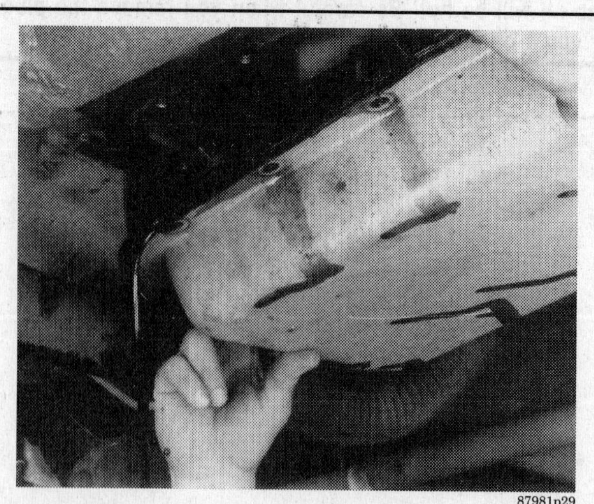

87981p29

Fig. 177 Pull one corner of the pan down to drain most of the fluid and remove the pan

87981p30

Fig. 178 Remove the old pan gasket and clean both gasket mating surfaces

3. Remove the pan bolts and empty out the pan. On some models, there may not be much room to get at the screws at the front of the pan.
4. Clean the pan with solvent and allow it to air dry. If you use a rag to wipe it out, you risk leaving bits of lint and threads in the transmission.
5. Remove the filter or strainer retaining bolts. On the Turbo Hydra-Matic 400, there are two screws securing the filter or screen to the valve body. A reusable strainer may be found on some models. The strainer may be cleaned in solvent and air dried thoroughly. The filter and gasket must be replaced.

To install:

6. Install a new gasket and filter.
7. Install a new gasket on the pan, and tighten the bolts evenly to 12 ft. lbs. (16 Nm) in a crisscross pattern.
8. Add DEXRON®II or its superceding type of transmission fluid through the dipstick tube. The correct amount is in the Capacities Chart. Do not overfill.

87981p31

Fig. 179 Remove the filter from the transmission

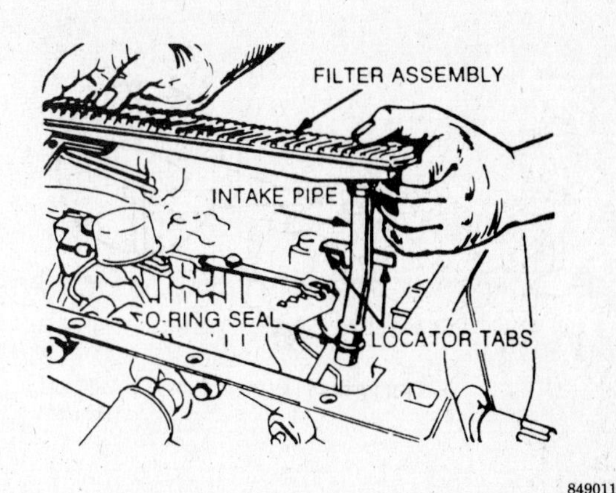

Fig. 180 Check the condition of the O-ring and replace it as necessary

9. With the gearshift lever in **Park**, start the engine and let it idle. Do not race the engine.
10. Move the gearshift lever through each position, holding the brakes. Return the lever to **Park**, and check the fluid level with the engine idling. The level should be between the two dimples on the dipstick, about 1/4 in. (6mm) below the ADD mark. Add fluid, if necessary.
11. Check the fluid level after the truck has been driven enough to thoroughly warm up the transmission. If the transmission is overfilled, the excess must be drained off. Overfilling causes aerated fluid, resulting in transmission slippage and probable damage.

Transfer Case

FLUID RECOMMENDATIONS

Use Dexron II® or its superceding fluid type on models through 1994. On 1995-96 models, use Dexron III®.

FLUID LEVEL CHECK

➧ See Figure 181

Check the four wheel drive transfer case lubricant at least twice a year.

1. With the truck parked on a level surface, remove the filler plug from the rear of the transfer case (behind the transmission). Be careful not to take out the drain plug at the bottom.
2. If lubricant trickles out, there is enough. If not, carefully insert a finger and check that the level is up to the edge of the hole, EXCEPT in full time four wheel drive cases which should be 1/2 in. (13mm) below the hole.
3. Lubricant may be added, if necessary, with a funnel and tube, or a squeeze bulb.
4. Tighten the plug to 18 ft. lbs. (25 Nm).

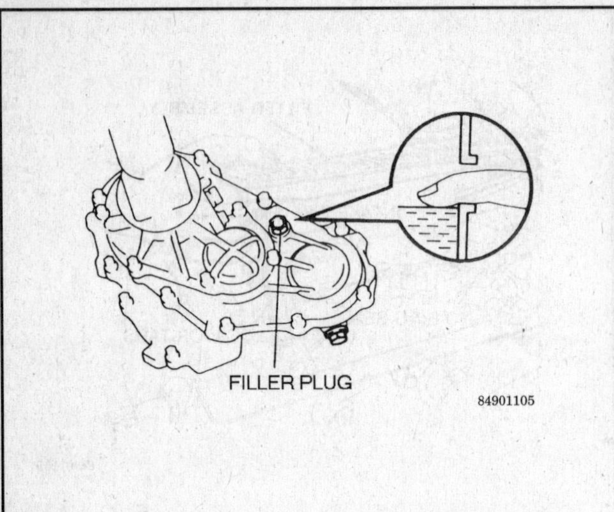

Fig. 181 Check the transfer case fluid level with your finger

DRAIN AND REFILL

1. With the transfer case warmed up, park on a level surface.
2. Slide a pan of a least 6 pts. capacity under the case drain plug.
3. Remove the filler plug from the rear of the transfer case (behind the transmission). Remove the drain plug from the bottom.
4. Wipe the area clean and install the drain plug.
5. Add lubricant with a suction gun or squeeze bulb.
6. When the lubricant level is up to the bottom of the filler hole, install the plug and tighten it to specifications.
   - 4401 and 4470 models: 18 ft. lbs. (25 Nm).
   - NV241 and NV243 models: 35 ft. lbs. (47 Nm).

Front and Rear Drive Axles

FLUID RECOMMENDATIONS

Front axles use SAE 80W-90, GL-5 Gear Lubricant. Rear axles use SAE 80W-90 gear oil. Posi-traction axles must use special lubricant available from dealers and most auto parts stores. If the special fluid is not used, noise, uneven operation, and damage will result. There is also a Posi-traction additive used to cure noise and slippage. Posi-traction axles have an identifying tag, as well as a warning sticker near the jack or on the rear wheel well.

FLUID LEVEL CHECK

See Figures 182 and 183

The oil level in the front and/or rear differentials should be checked at least twice a year. If driven in deep water it should be checked immediately afterward. The fluid level in the front axle should be ½ in. (13mm) below the filler plug opening. The fluid level in the rear axle should be up to the bottom of the filler plug opening. Lubricant may be added with a suction gun or squeeze bulb.

1. Park on level ground.
2. Remove the filler plug from the differential housing cover.
3. If lubricant trickles out there is enough. If not, carefully insert a finger and check that the level is up to the bottom of the hole. Locking front hubs should be run in the LOCK position for at least 10 miles (10 km) each month to assure proper lubrication to the front axle.
4. Fill with the proper fluid, install the plug and tighten to:

REAR:
- 8½ in. — 25 ft. lbs. (34 Nm)
- 9½ and 10½ in. — 19 ft. lbs. (24 Nm)
- 9¾-10½ in. — 10 ft. lbs. (14 Nm)
- 12 in. — 35 ft. lbs. (47 Nm)

FRONT:
- All — 80 ft. lbs. (110 Nm)

DRAIN AND REFILL

See Figures 184, 185 and 186

No intervals are specified for changing axle lubricant, but it is a good idea every year or so. If you have driven in water over the axle vents, change the fluid immediately.

1. Park the vehicle on the level with the axles at normal operating temperature.
2. Place a pan of at least 6 pints capacity under the differential housing.
3. Remove the filler plug.
4. If you have a drain plug, remove it. If not, unbolt and remove the differential cover.
5. Install the drain plug, or differential cover. Use a new gasket if the differential cover has been removed.
6. Install the drain plug and tighten it so it will not leak. Do not overtighten.

➡It is usually a good idea to replace the gasket at this time.

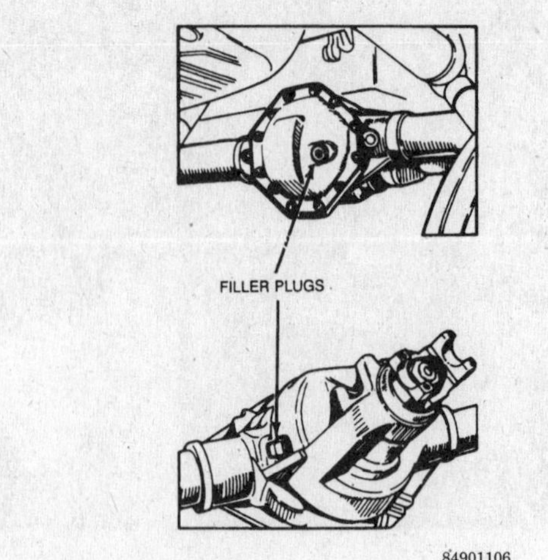

Fig. 182 The rear differential filler plug may be in either of these locations

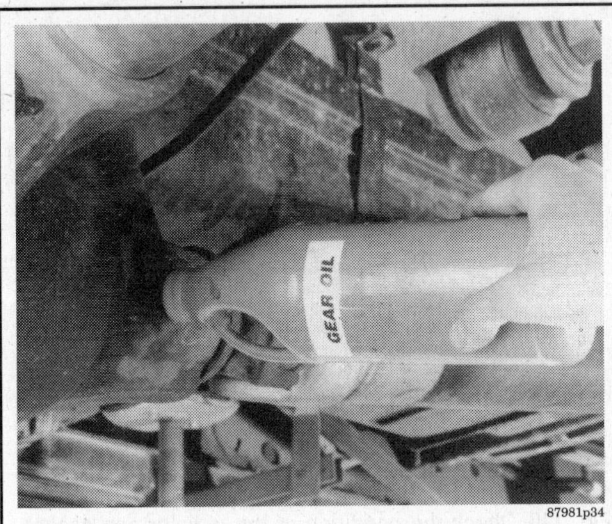

87981p34

Fig. 183 If necessary, fill with the proper fluid

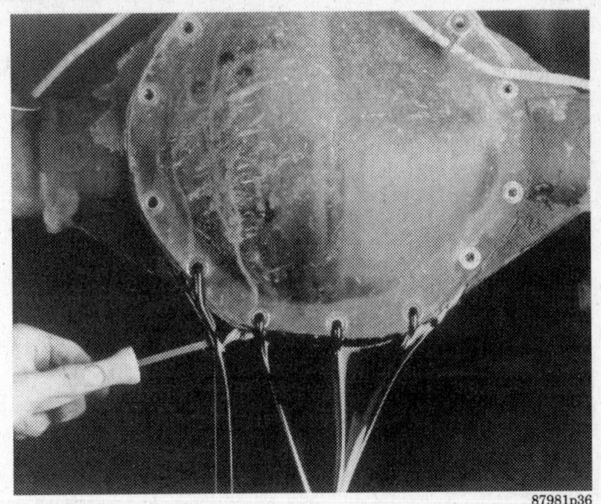

87981p36

Fig. 185 After removing the bolts carefully pry the bottom of the cover off and drain the fluid

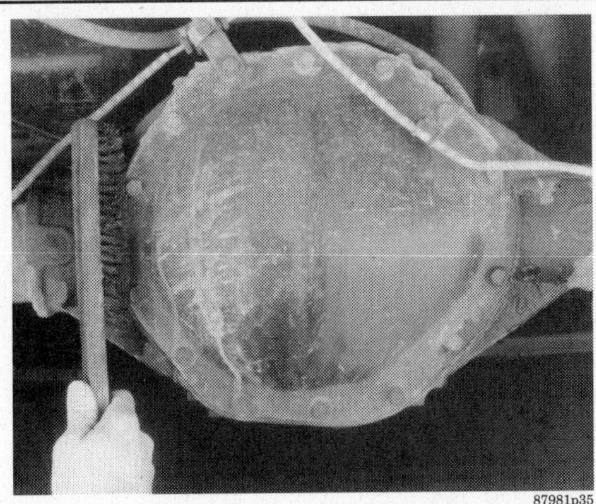

87981p35

Fig. 184 Using a wire brush clean the bolts and edges of the differential cover

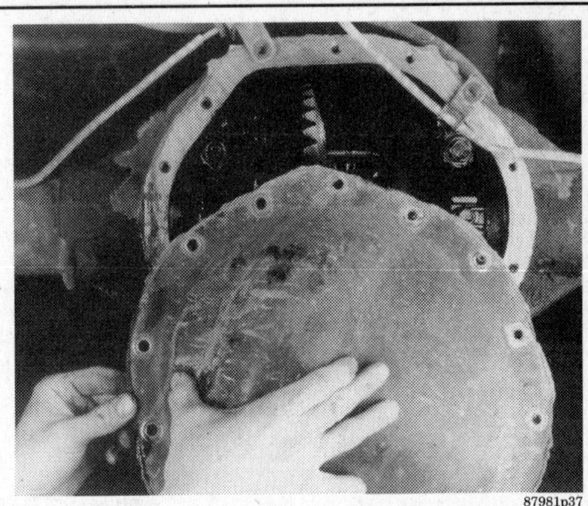

87981p37

Fig. 186 After the oil has drained remove the differential cover

7. Refill the differential with the proper lubricant — do not overfill!
8. Install the filler plug and tighten both plugs to:

REAR:

- 8½ in. — 25 ft. lbs. (34 Nm)
- 9½ and 10½ in. — 19 ft. lbs. (24 Nm)
- 9¾-10½ in. — 10 ft. lbs. (14 Nm)
- 12 in. — 35 ft. lbs. (47 Nm)

FRONT:

- All: 80 ft. lbs. (110 Nm)

9. Road test the truck and check for any leaks.

Cooling System

See Figures 187, 188, 189, 190 and 191

The cooling system was filled at the factory with a high quality coolant solution that is good for year around operation and protects the system from freezing down to -20°F (-29°C) (-32°F/36°C in Canada). It is good for two full calendar years or 24,000 miles (38,500 km), whichever occurs first, provided that the proper concentration of coolant is maintained.

The hot coolant level should be at the FULL HOT mark on the expansion tank and the cold coolant level should be at the FULL COLD mark on the tank. Do not remove the radiator cap to check the coolant level.

FLUID RECOMMENDATIONS

Coolant mixture in Chevy/GMC trucks is 50/50 ethylene glycol and water for year round use. Use a good quality antifreeze with water pump lubricants, rust inhibitors and other corrosion inhibitors along with acid neutralizers.

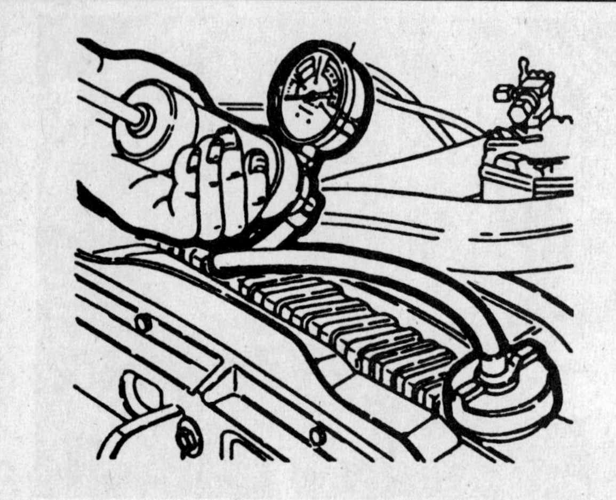

Fig. 187 The system should be pressure-tested once a year

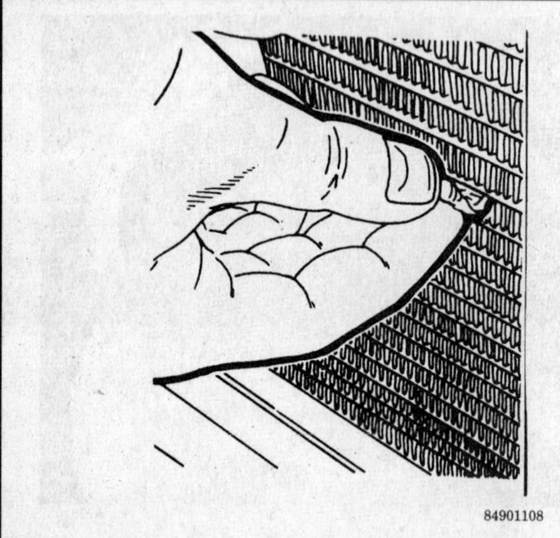

Fig. 188 Remove any debris from the radiator's cooling fins

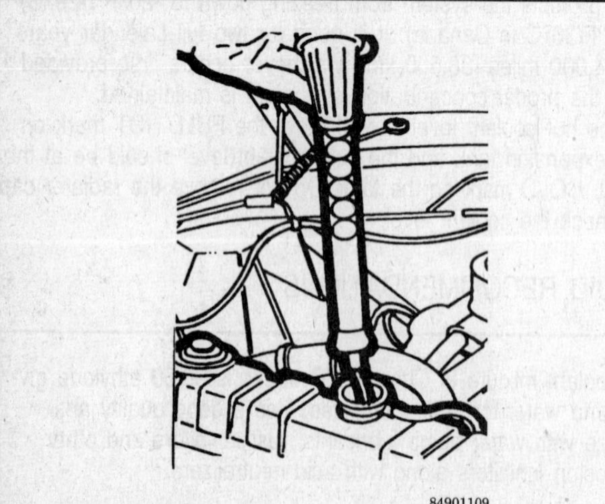

Fig. 189 Coolant condition can be checked with an inexpensive tester

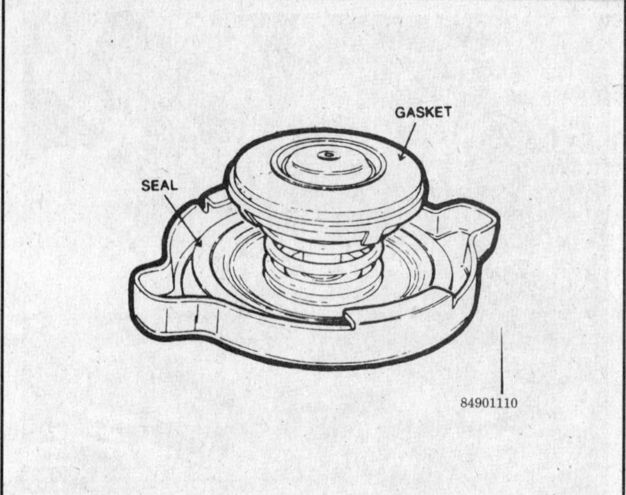

Fig. 190 Check the condition of the radiator cap gasket and seal

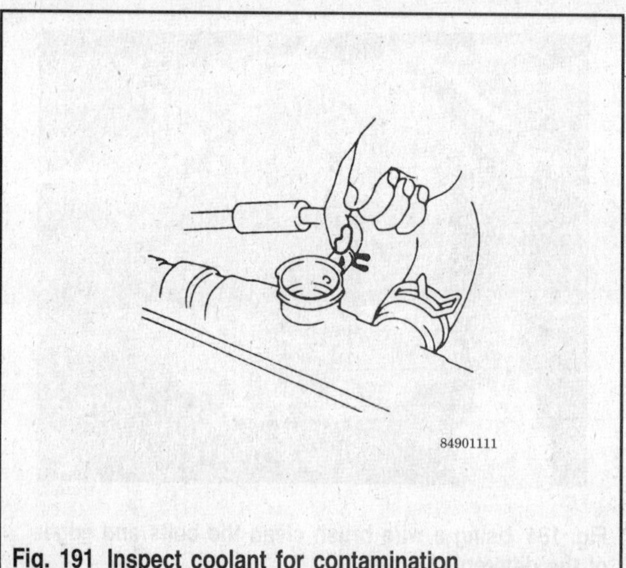

Fig. 191 Inspect coolant for contamination

FLUID LEVEL CHECK

1. Check the level on the see-through expansion tank.

✱✱CAUTION

The radiator coolant is under pressure when hot. To avoid the danger of physical harm, coolant level should be checked or replenished only when the engine is cold. To remove the radiator cap when the engine is hot, first cover the cap with a thick rag, or wear a heavy glove for protection. Press down on the cap slightly and slowly turn it counterclockwise until it reaches the first stop. Allow all the pressure to vent (indicated when the hissing sound stops). When the pressure is released, press down on the cap and continue to rotate it counterclockwise. Some radiator caps have a lever for venting the pressure, but you should still exercise extreme caution when removing the cap.

2. Check the level and, if necessary, add coolant through the expansion tank to the proper level. Use a 50/50 mix of ethylene glycol anti-freeze and water. Alcohol or methanol base coolants are not recommended. Anti-freeze solutions should be used, even in summer, to prevent rust and to take advantage of the solution's higher boiling point compared to plain water. This is imperative on air conditioned trucks; the heater core can freeze if it isn't protected. Coolant should be added through the coolant recovery tank, not the radiator filler neck.

WARNING

Never add large quantities of cold coolant to a hot engine! A cracked engine block may result!

Each year the cooling system should be serviced as follows:

- Wash the radiator cap and filler neck with clean water.
- Check the coolant for proper level and freeze protection.
- Have the system pressure tested 15 psi. (103 kPa), If a replacement cap is installed, be sure that it conforms to the original specifications.
- Tighten the hose clamps and inspect all hoses. Replace hoses that are swollen, cracked or otherwise deteriorated.
- Clean the frontal area of the radiator core and the air conditioning condenser, if so equipped.

DRAINING AND FLUSHING

The cooling system in you truck accumulates some internal rust and corrosion in its normal operation. A simple method of keeping the system clean is known as flushing the system. It is performed by circulating a can of radiator flush through the system, and then draining and refilling the system with the normal coolant. Radiator flush is marketed by several different manufacturers, and is available in cans at auto departments, parts stores, and many hardware stores. This operation should be performed every 30,000 miles (48,000 km)or once a year.

CAUTION

When draining the coolant, keep in mind that cats and dogs are attracted by ethylene glycol anti-freeze, and are quite likely to drink any that is left in an uncovered container or in puddles on the ground. This will prove fatal in sufficient quantity. Always drain the coolant into a sealable container. Coolant should be reused unless it is contaminated or several years old.

1. Drain the existing anti-freeze and coolant. Open the radiator and engine drain petcocks (located near the bottom of the radiator and engine block, respectively), or disconnect the bottom radiator hose at the radiator outlet.
2. Close the petcock or reconnect the lower hose and fill the system with water — hot water if the system has just been run.
3. Add a can of quality radiator flush to the radiator or recovery tank, following any special instructions on the can.
4. Idle the engine as long as specified on the can of flush, or until the upper radiator hose gets hot.
5. Drain the system again. There should be quite a bit of scale and rust in the drained water.
6. Repeat this process until the drained water is mostly clear.
7. Close all petcocks and connect all hoses.
8. Flush the coolant recovery reservoir with water and leave empty.
9. Determine the capacity of your truck's cooling system (see Capacities specifications in this guide). Add a 50/50 mix of ethylene glycol anti-freeze and water to provide the desired protection.
10. Run the engine to operating temperature, then stop the engine and check for leaks. Check the coolant level and top up if necessary.
11. Check the protection level of your anti-freeze mix with an anti-freeze tester (a small, inexpensive syringe type device available at any auto parts store). The tester has five or six small colored balls inside, each of which signify a certain temperature rating. Insert the tester in the recovery tank and suck just enough coolant into the syringe to float as many individual balls as you can (without sucking in too much coolant and floating all the balls at once). A table supplied with the tester will explain how many floating balls equal protection down to a certain temperature (three floating balls might mean the coolant will protect your engine down to +5°F (-15°C), for example.

Brake Master Cylinder

FLUID RECOMMENDATIONS

See Figure 192

Use only Heavy Duty Brake fluid meeting or exceeding DOT 3 standards.

FLUID LEVEL CHECK

See Figures 193 and 194

Chevrolet and GMC trucks are equipped with a dual braking system, allowing a vehicle to be brought to a safe stop in the event of failure in either front or rear brakes. The dual master cylinder has 2 entirely separate reservoirs, one connected to the front brakes and the other connected to the rear brakes. In the event of failure in either portion, the remaining part is not affected. Fluid level in the master cylinder should be checked on a regular basis.

The master cylinder is mounted to the left side of the firewall.

1. Clean all of the dirt from around the cover of the master cylinder.
2. Be sure that the vehicle is resting on a level surface.
3. Carefully pry the clip from the top of the master cylinder to release the cover. On some later models, just pull up on the tabs.
4. The fluid level should be approximately 1/4 in. (6mm) from the top of the master cylinder or at least above the **MIN** mark. If not, add fluid until the level is correct. Replacement fluid should be Delco Supreme No. 11, DOT 3, or its

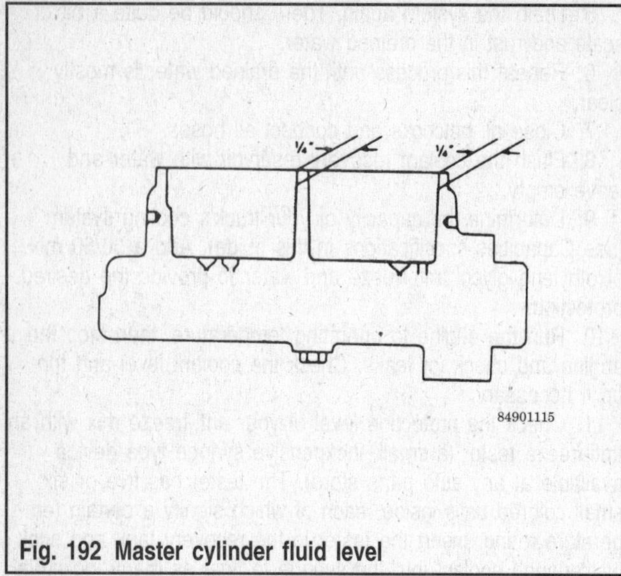

Fig. 192 Master cylinder fluid level

equivalent. It is normal for the fluid level to fall as the disc brake pads wear.

WARNING

Brake fluid dissolves paint! It also absorbs moisture from the air. Never leave a container or the master cylinder uncovered any longer than necessary!

5. Install the cover of the master cylinder. On most models there is a rubber gasket under the cover, which fits into 2 slots on the cover. Be sure that this is seated properly.
6. Push the clip back into place and be sure that it seats in the groove on the top of the cover.

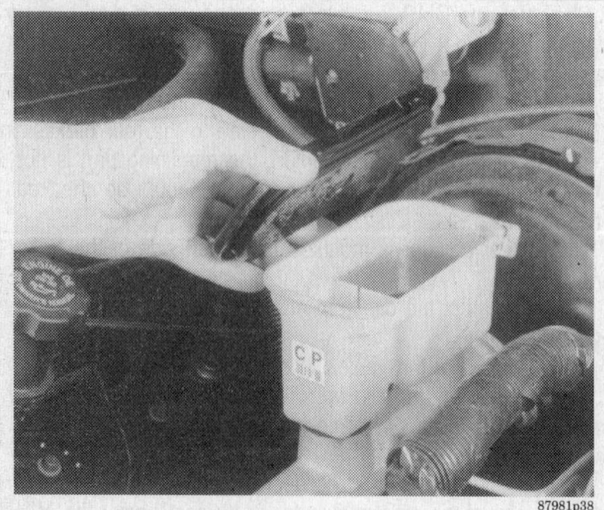

Fig. 193 Remove the master cylinder cover

Fig. 194 Add brake fluid until the level is correct

Clutch Master Cylinder

FLUID RECOMMENDATIONS

Use only Heavy Duty Brake fluid meeting DOT 3 standards.

FLUID LEVEL CHECK

The clutch master cylinder is located on the firewall in the engine compartment.

1. Clean all of the dirt from around the cover of the master cylinder.
2. Be sure that the vehicle is resting on a level surface.
3. Carefully remove the cover from the master cylinder.
4. The fluid level should be approximately 1/4 in. (6mm) from the top of the master cylinder or at least above the **MIN** mark. If not, add fluid until the level is correct. Replacement fluid should be Delco Supreme No. 11, DOT 3, or its equivalent.
5. Install the cover of the master cylinder.

Power Steering Pump

FLUID RECOMMENDATION

Use GM Power Steering fluid, or its equivalent.

FLUID LEVEL CHECK

See Figures 195, 196 and 197

Check the dipstick in the pump reservoir when the fluid is at operating temperature. The fluid should be between the **HOT** and **COLD** marks. If the fluid is at room temperature, the fluid should be between the **ADD** and **COLD** marks. The fluid does not require periodic changing.

On systems with a remote reservoir, the level should be maintained approximately 1/2-1 in. (13-25mm) from the top with the wheels in the full left turn position.

Steering Gear

FLUID RECOMMENDATIONS

Use GM Lubricant (part No. 1051052).

FLUID LEVEL CHECK

No lubrication is needed for the life of the gear, except in the event of seal replacement or overhaul, when the gear should be refilled with a 13 oz. container of Steering Gear

87981p40

Fig. 195 Remove the power steering pump dipstick

87981p41

Fig. 196 Hold the dipstick horizontally and check the power steering fluid level

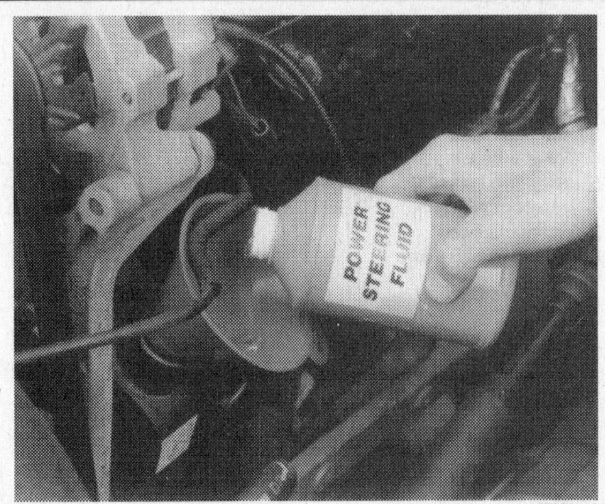

87981p42

Fig. 197 Add power steering fluid to the pump and fill it to the proper level

Lubricant (Part No. 1051052) which meets GM Specification GM 4673M, or its equivalent.

Chassis Greasing

See Figures 198, 199, 200, 201 and 202

Refer to the diagrams for chassis points to be lubricated. Not all vehicles have all the fittings illustrated. Water resistant EP chassis lubricant (grease) conforming to GM specification 6031-M should be used for all chassis grease points.

Every year or 7500 miles (12,067 km) the front suspension ball joints, both upper and lower on each side of the truck, must be greased. Most trucks covered in this guide should be equipped with grease nipples on the ball joints, although some may have plugs which must be removed and nipples fitted.

WARNING

Do not pump so much grease into the ball joint that excess grease squeezes out of the rubber boot. This destroys the watertight seal.

1. Raise up the front end of the truck and safely support it with jackstands. Block the rear wheels and firmly apply the parking brake.
2. If the truck has been parked in temperatures below 20°F (-7°C) for any length of time, park it in a heated garage for an hour or so until the ball joints loosen up enough to accept the grease.
3. Depending on which front wheel you work on first, turn the wheel and tire outward, either full-lock right or full-lock left. You now have the ends of the upper and lower suspension control arms in front of you; the grease nipples are visible pointing up (top ball joint) and down (lower ball joint) through the end of each control arm.
4. If the nipples are not accessible enough, remove the wheel and tire.
5. Wipe all dirt and crud from the nipples or from around the plugs (if installed). If plugs are on the truck, remove them and install grease nipples in the holes (nipples are available in various thread sizes at most auto parts stores).

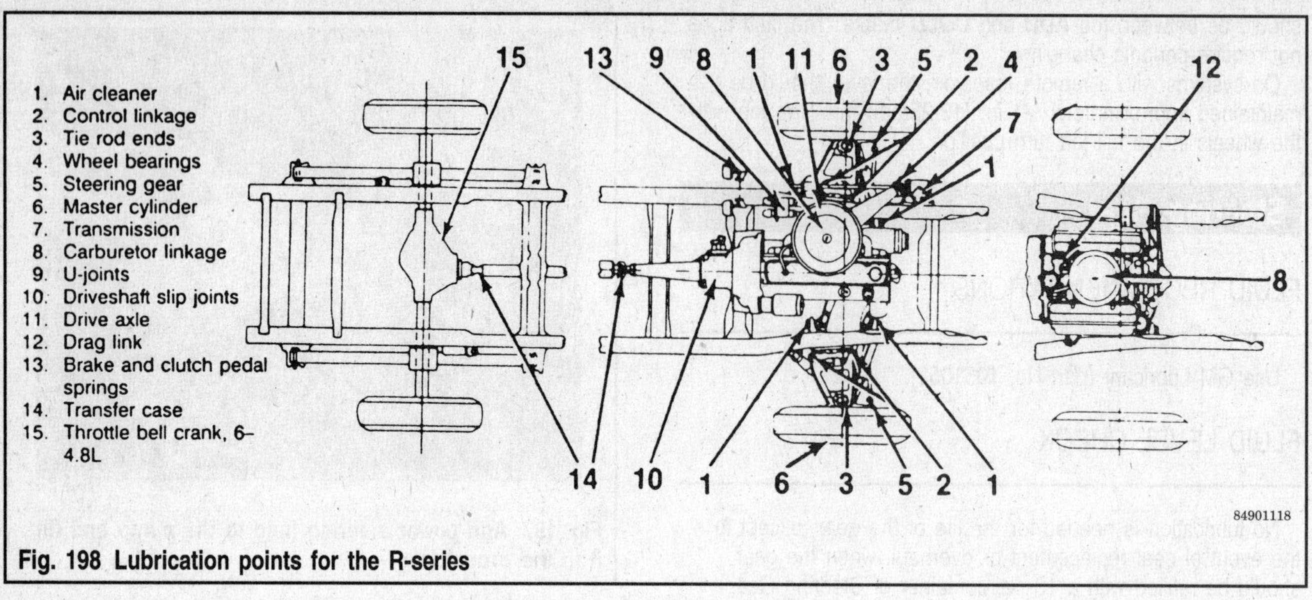

Fig. 198 Lubrication points for the R-series

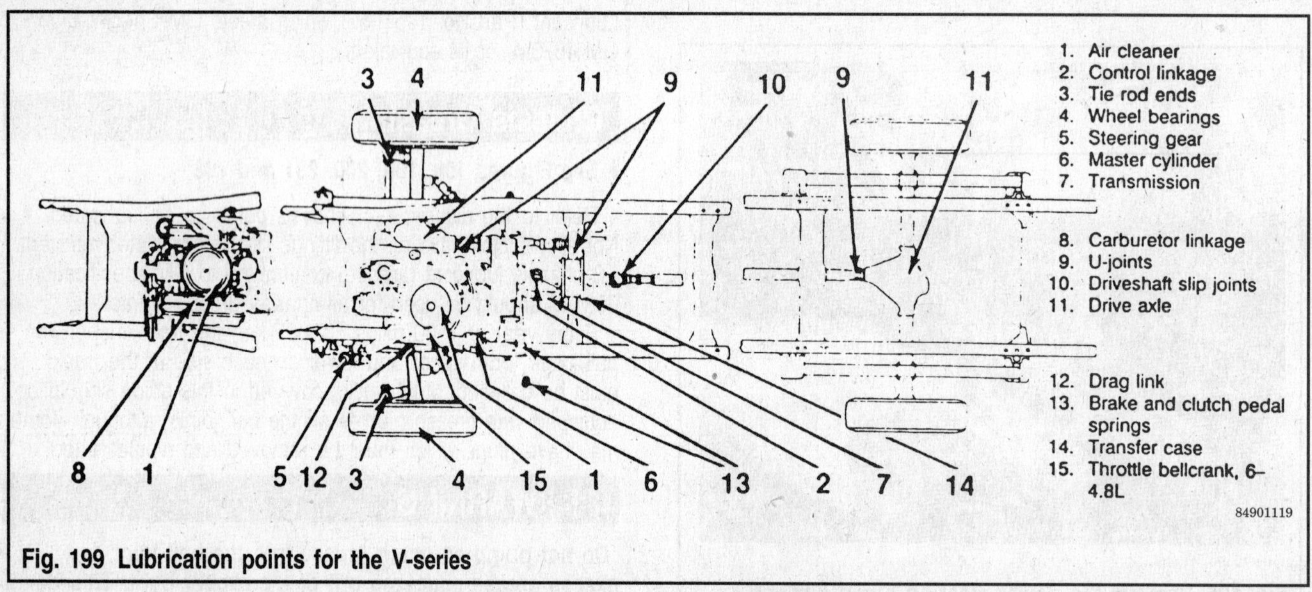

Fig. 199 Lubrication points for the V-series

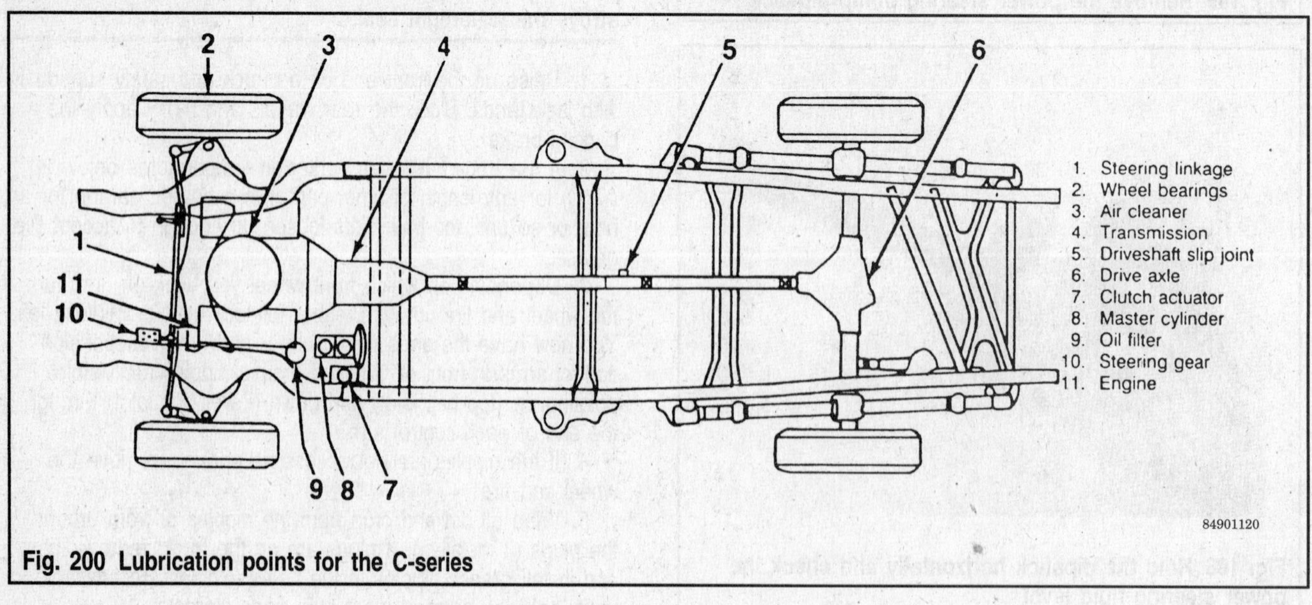

Fig. 200 Lubrication points for the C-series

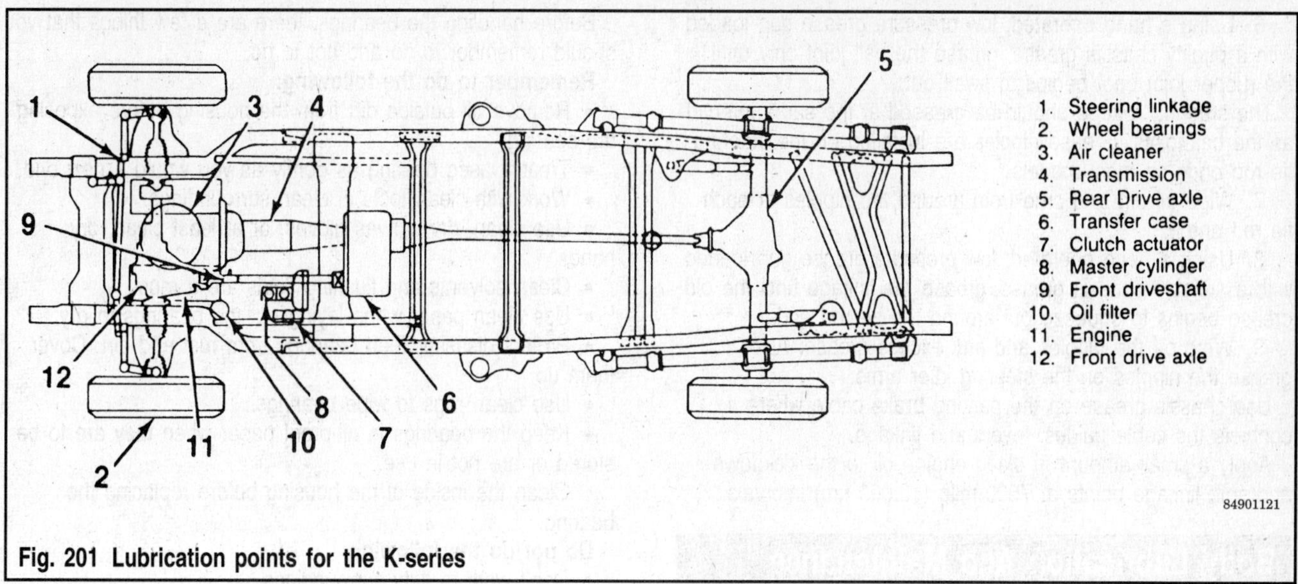

Fig. 201 Lubrication points for the K-series

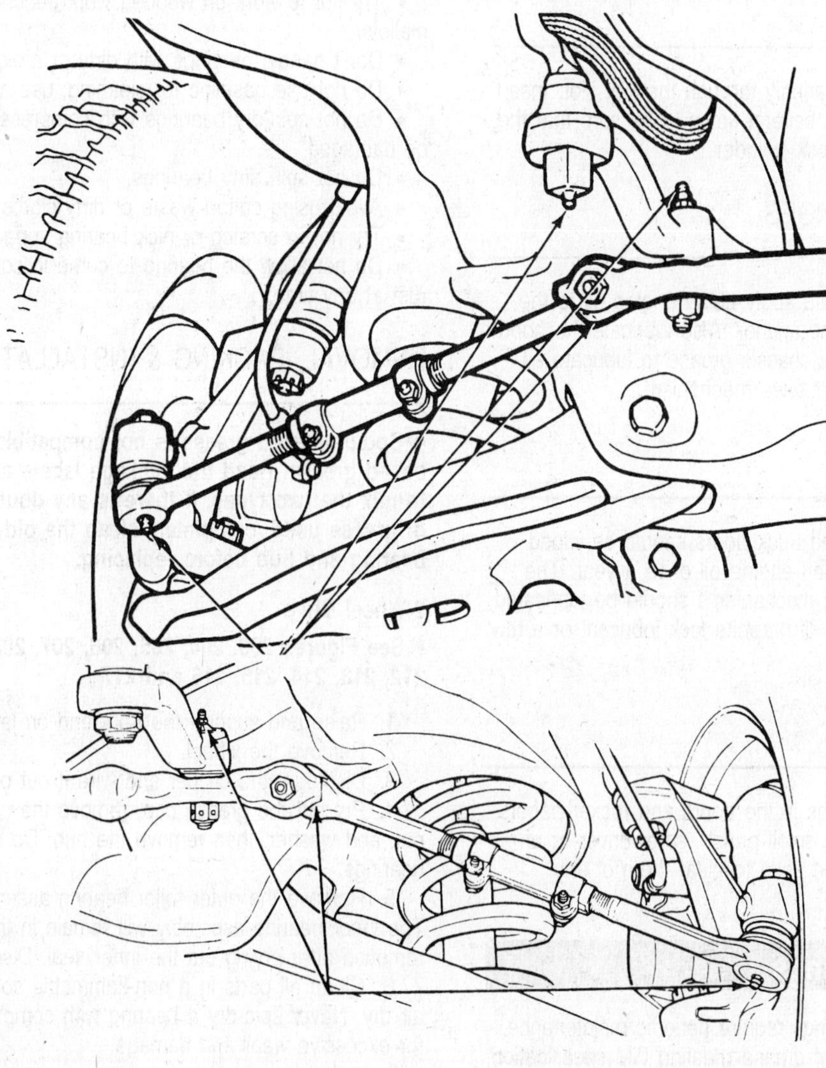

84901122

Fig. 202 Front lubrication fittings — C/K series

6. Using a hand operated, low pressure grease gun loaded with a quality chassis grease, grease the ball joint only until the rubber joint boot begins to swell out.

The steering linkage should be greased at the same interval as the ball joints. Grease nipples are installed on the steering tie rod ends on most models.

7. Wipe all dirt and crud from around the nipples at each tie rod end.
8. Using a hand operated, low pressure grease gun loaded with a suitable chassis grease, grease the linkage until the old grease begins to squeeze out around the tie rod ends.
9. Wipe off the nipples and any excess grease. Also grease the nipples on the steering idler arms.

Use chassis grease on the parking brake cable where it contacts the cable guides, levers and linkage.

Apply a small amount of clean engine oil to the kickdown and shift linkage points at 7500 mile (12,000 km) intervals.

Body Lubrication And Maintenance

LOCK CYLINDERS

Apply graphite lubricant sparingly through the key slot. Insert the key and operate the lock several times to be sure that the lubricant is worked into the lock cylinder.

HOOD LATCH AND HINGES

Clean the latch surfaces and apply clean engine oil to the latch pilot bolts and the spring anchor. Also lubricate the hood hinges with engine oil. Use a chassis grease to lubricate all the pivot points in the latch release mechanism.

DOOR HINGES

The gas tank filler door and truck doors should be wiped clean and lubricated with clean engine oil once a year. The door lock cylinders and latch mechanisms should be lubricated periodically with a few drops of graphite lock lubricant or a few shots of silicone spray.

BODY DRAIN HOLES

Be sure that the drain holes in the doors and rocker panels are cleared of obstruction. A small punch, screwdriver or unbent wire coat hanger can be used to clear them of any debris.

Front Wheel Bearings

Only the front wheel bearings require periodic maintenance. A premium high melting point grease meeting GM specification 6031-M must be used. Long fiber type greases must not be used. This service is recommended at the intervals in the Maintenance Intervals Chart or whenever the truck has been driven in water up to the hubs.

Before handling the bearings, there are a few things that you should remember to do and not to do.

Remember to do the following:

- Remove all outside dirt from the housing before exposing the bearing.
- Treat a used bearing as gently as you would a new one.
- Work with clean tools in clean surroundings.
- Use clean, dry canvas gloves, or at least clean, dry hands.
- Clean solvents and flushing fluids are a must.
- Use clean paper when laying out the bearings to dry.
- Protect disassembled bearings from rust and dirt. Cover them up.
- Use clean rags to wipe bearings.
- Keep the bearings in oil-proof paper when they are to be stored or are not in use.
- Clean the inside of the housing before replacing the bearing.

Do not do the following:

- Don't work in dirty surroundings.
- Don't use dirty, chipped or damaged tools.
- Try not to work on wooden work benches or use wooden mallets.
- Don't handle bearings with dirty or moist hands.
- Do not use gasoline for cleaning; use a safe solvent.
- Do not spin-dry bearings with compressed air. They will be damaged.
- Do not spin dirty bearings.
- Avoid using cotton waste or dirty cloths to wipe bearings.
- Try not to scratch or nick bearing surfaces.
- Do not allow the bearing to come in contact with dirt or rust at any time.

REMOVAL, PACKING & INSTALLATION

➡Sodium-based grease is not compatible with lithium-based grease. Read the package labels and be careful not to mix the two types. If there is any doubt as to the type of grease used, completely clean the old grease from the bearing and hub before replacing.

2-Wheel Drive

▶ See Figures 203, 204, 205, 206, 207, 208, 209, 210, 211, 212, 213, 214, 215, 216 and 217

1. Raise and support the front end on jackstands.
2. Remove the wheel.
3. Dismount the caliper and wire it out of the way.
4. Pry out the grease cap, remove the cotter pin, spindle nut, and washer, then remove the hub. Do not drop the wheel bearings.
5. Remove the outer roller bearing assembly from the hub. The inner bearing assembly will remain in the hub and may be removed after prying out the inner seal. Discard the seal.
6. Clean all parts in a non-flammable solvent and let them air dry. Never spin-dry a bearing with compressed air! Check for excessive wear and damage.

To install:

7. Using a hammer and drift, remove the bearing races from the hub. They are driven out from the inside out. When

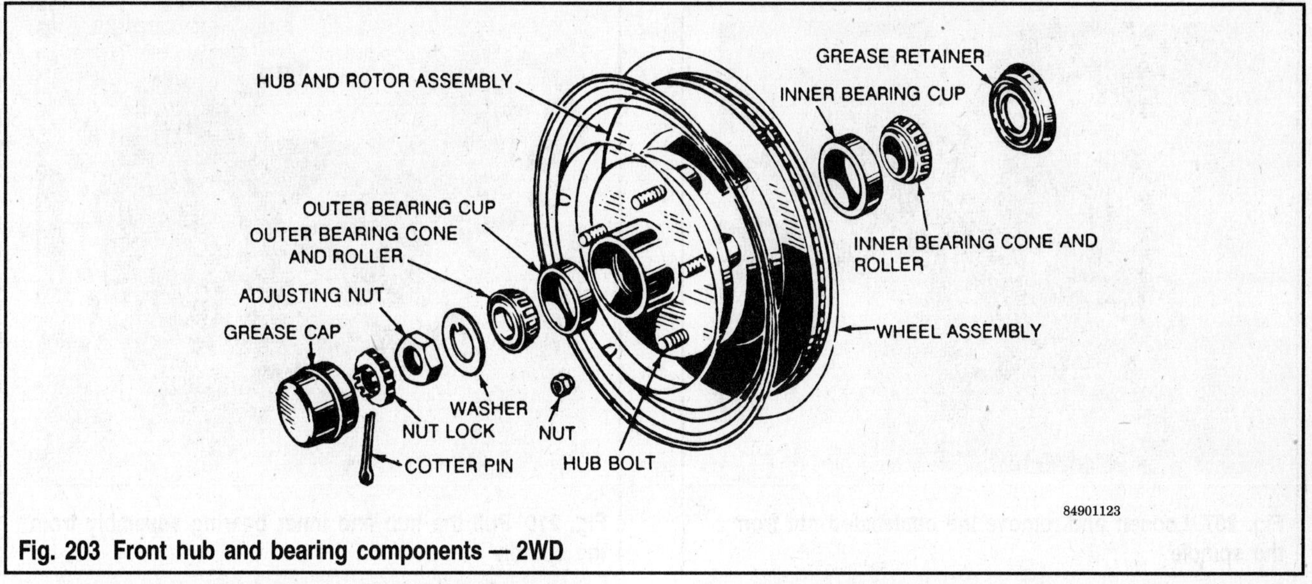

Fig. 203 Front hub and bearing components — 2WD

Fig. 204 Pry the dust cap from the hub taking care not to distort or damage its flange

Fig. 206 If difficulty is encountered, gently tap on the pliers with a hammer to help free the cotter pin

Fig. 205 Once the bent ends are cut, grasp the cotter pin and pull or pry it free of the spindle

installing new races, make sure that they are not cocked and that they are fully seated against the hub shoulder.

8. Pack both wheel bearings using high melting point wheel bearing grease for disc brakes. Ordinary grease will melt and ooze out ruining the pads. Bearings should be packed using a cone-type wheel bearing greaser tool. If one is not available they may be packed by hand.

9. Place a healthy glob of grease in the palm of one hand and force the edge of the bearing into it so that the grease fills the bearing. Do this until the whole bearing is packed.

10. Place the inner bearing in the hub and install a new inner seal, making sure that the seal flange faces the bearing race.

11. Carefully install the wheel hub over the spindle.

12. Using your hands, firmly press the outer bearing into the hub. Install the spindle washer and nut.

13. Spin the wheel hub by hand and tighten the nut until it is just snug; 12 ft. lbs. (16 Nm).

Fig. 207 Loosen and remove the castellated nut from the spindle

Fig. 208 Remove the washer from the spindle

Fig. 209 With the nut and washer out of the way, the outer bearing may be removed from the hub

Fig. 210 Pull the hub and inner bearing assembly from the spindle

Fig. 211 Use a small prytool to remove the old inner bearing seal

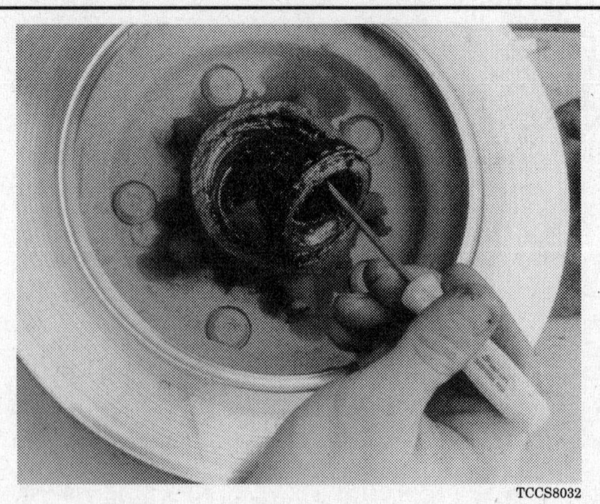

Fig. 212 With the seal removed, the inner bearing may be withdrawn from the hub

Fig. 213 Thoroughly pack the bearing with fresh, high temperature wheel-bearing grease before installation

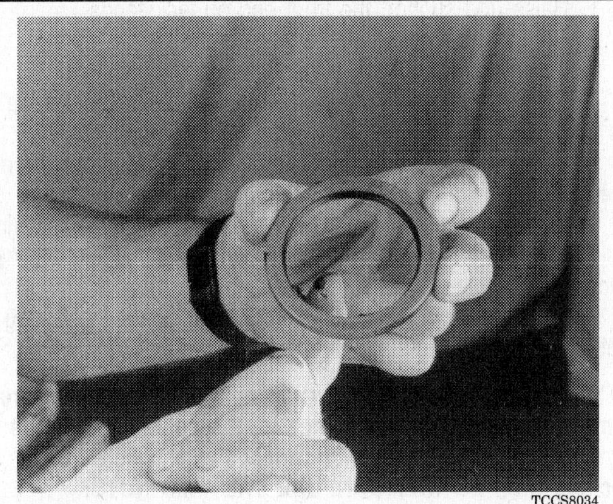

Fig. 214 Apply a thin coat of fresh grease to the new inner bearing seal lip

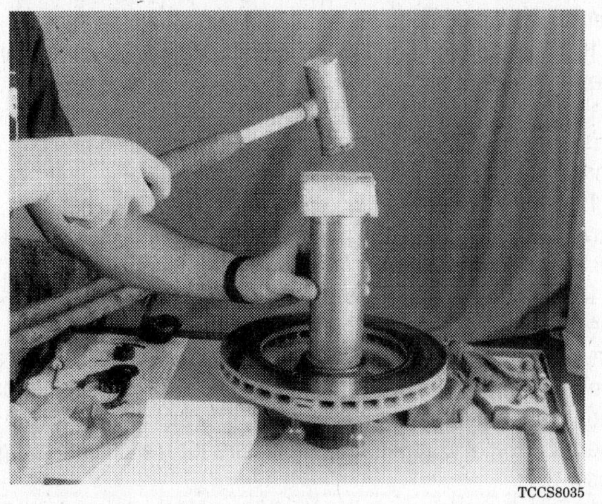

Fig. 215 Use a suitably sized driver to install the inner bearing seal to the hub

Fig. 216 Tighten the nut to specifications while gently spinning the wheel, then adjust the bearing

Fig. 217 After the bearings are adjusted, install the dust cap by gently tapping on the flange

14. Back off the nut until it is loose, then tighten it finger tight. Loosen the nut until either hole in the spindle lines up with a slot in the nut and insert a new cotter pin.
15. There should be 0.001-0.005 in. (0.025-0.127mm) end-play on 1988-90 models. On 1991-96 models, end-play should be 0.005-0.008 in. (0.013-0.20mm) on HD models. This can be measured with a dial indicator, if you wish.
16. Replace the dust cap, wheel and tire.

4-Wheel Drive

V-SERIES

See Figures 218, 219 and 220

➡Before starting you'll need a special wheel bearing nut socket for your 1/2 inch drive ratchet. These sockets are available through auto parts stores and catalogs. You can't do this job properly without it! You'll also need a 1/2 inch drive torque wrench, a clean container, like a shoe box, for the parts as you remove them and PLENTY of paper towels handy.

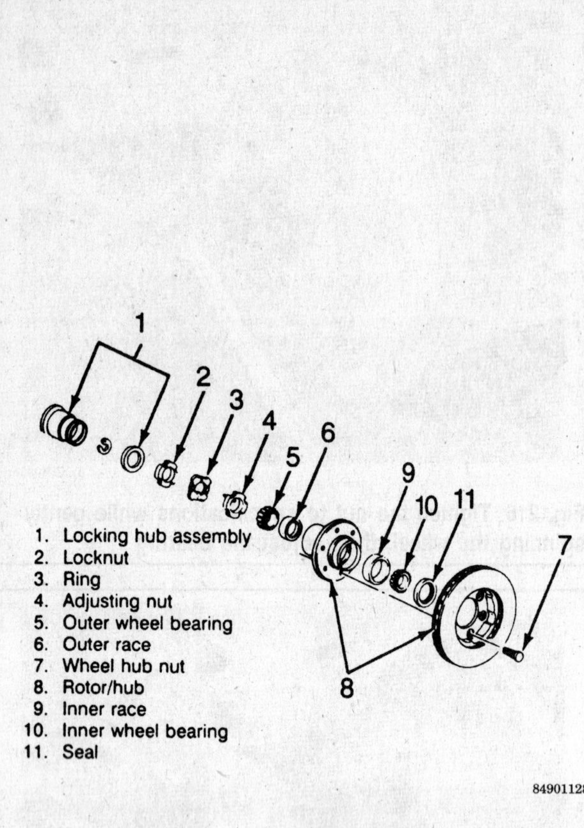

Fig. 218 Exploded view of the V10/1500 and V20/2500 series front hub and bearing assembly

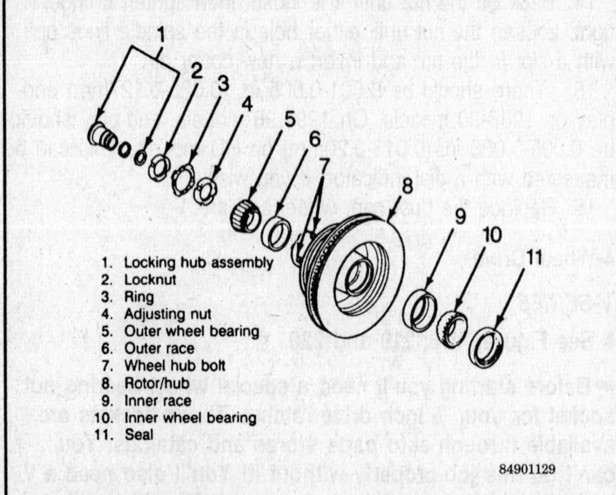

Fig. 219 Exploded view of the V30/3500 series front hub and bearing assembly

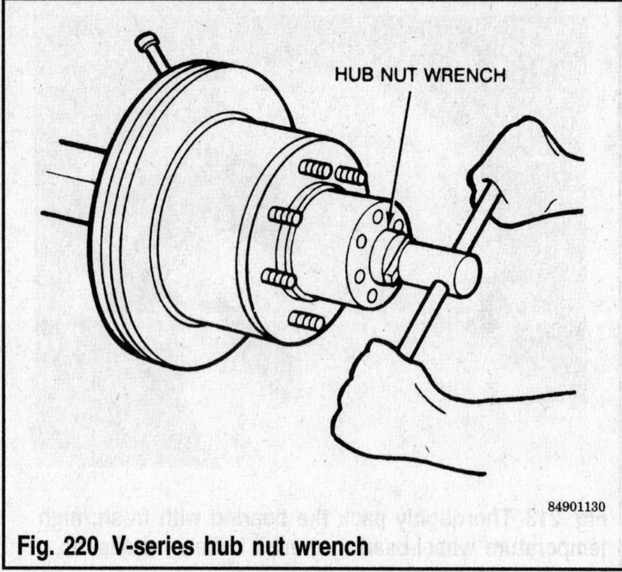

Fig. 220 V-series hub nut wrench

1. Raise and support the front end on jackstands.
2. Remove the wheels.
3. Remove the hubs. See the Section 7.
4. Wipe the inside of the hub to remove as much grease as possible.
5. Using your bearing nut socket, remove the locknut from the spindle.
6. With the locknut off you'll be able to see the locking ring on the adjusting nut. Remove the locking ring. A tool such as a dental pick will make this easier.
7. Using the special socket, remove the bearing adjusting nut.

➡You'll notice that the adjusting nut and the locknut are almost identical. The difference is, the adjusting nut has a small pin on one side which indexes with a hole in the locking ring. DO NOT CONFUSE THE TWO NUTS!

8. Dismount the brake caliper and suspend it out of the way, without disconnecting the brake line. See Section 9.
9. Pull the hub off of the spindle. The outer bearing will tend to fall out as soon as it clears the spindle, so have a hand ready to catch it.
10. If you are going to reuse the outer bearing, place it on a clean surface.
11. Position the hub, face up, on 2 wood blocks placed under opposite sides of the rotor. Have a paper towel positioned under the hub.
12. Using a hardened wood dowel or a hammer handle, drive out the inner bearing and seal. If your are going to reuse the inner bearing, move it to a clean area. Discard the seal.
13. If the bearings are being replaced, you'll have to replace the races. The races are pressed into the hub, but you can drive them out. With the hub in position on the blocks, use a long drift and hammer evenly around the outside diameter of the inner bearing race until it is free. Discard the race. Turn the hub over and repeat this procedure for the outer bearing race.
14. wash the bearings in a non-flammable solvent and let them air-dry. Never use compressed air to spin-dry the bearings!

15. If either bearing shows any sign of damage, rust, heat blueing or excessive looseness, both bearings in that hub must be replaced as a set. If bearings are replaced, the races MUST be replaced also!

➡If the bearings show signs of heat blueing, wipe the spindle clean and check for heat blueing on the spindle surface. If the spindle shows large areas of heat blueing, it should be replaced.

16. Wash out the hub with solvent and wipe it clean. Check the races. If they show signs of wear, pitting, cracking, rusting or heat blueing, they, along with the bearings, must be replaced.
17. Coat the race and its bore in the hub with high temperature wheel bearing grease.
18. Position the race in the bore and start gently tapping it into place. There are drivers made for this purpose, but you can do it with a blunt drift and hammer. Just tap evenly around the race as you drive it into place so that it doesn't cock in the bore.
19. Drive the race in until it is fully seated against the shoulder in the bore. You can tell that it's fully seated in 2 ways:
   a. Your hammer blows will sound differently when the race seats against the shoulder.
   b. The grease you applied to the bore will be squeezed out below the race as the race seats against the shoulder.

➡Either race can be installed first.

20. Pack the bearings thoroughly with high temperature wheel bearing grease. An inexpensive wheel bearing packing tool is available at most auto parts stores. The tool has a grease fitting which utilizes a grease gun and completely packs the bearing. You can, however, pack a bearing reasonably well without the tool:
   a. Open the container of grease.
   b. Force the bearing down into the container, first on one side, then the other, until grease squeezes out among the rollers.
   c. Place a large blob of grease in the palm of one hand and force the bearing into the grease to squeeze out any air cavities among the rollers. When you're satisfied that each bearing is completely packed, place them on a clean paper towel, in a clean area, and cover them with another clean paper towel.
21. Pack the area of the hub, between the races, with wheel bearing grease.
22. Place the inner bearing in its race and position a new seal in the hub bore. Gently tap around the outer diameter of the seal with a plastic mallet until the seal is flush with the end of the bore.
23. Carefully place the hub assembly on the spindle. Take care to avoid damaging the seal on the spindle threads. Make sure the hub is all the way on the spindle.
24. Place the outer bearing on the spindle and slide it into place in its race.
25. Thread the adjusting nut on the spindle until it contacts the outer bearing.

✲✲WARNING

Make sure you are using the adjusting nut. Remember, it has a small pin on one side. That pin must face outwards, towards you!

26. Using the special socket and the torque wrench:
   a. Tighten the adjusting nut to 50 ft. lbs. (67 Nm) while rotating the hub.
   b. Back off the adjusting nut until it is loose.
   c. While rotating the hub, tighten the adjusting nut to 35 ft. lbs. (48 Nm) for automatic locking hubs or 50 ft. lbs. (67 Nm) for manual locking hubs.
   d. Back off the adjusting nut $\frac{1}{4}$-$\frac{3}{8}$ of a turn for automatic hubs or $\frac{1}{6}$-$\frac{1}{4}$ of a turn for manual hubs.
27. Coat the locking ring with wheel bearing grease. Place the locking ring on the spindle. There is a tab on the inner diameter of the ring which must fit in the slot on the top of the spindle. Slide the locking ring in until it contacts the adjusting nut. The pin on the adjusting nut must enter one of the holes in the locking ring. You can tell that the locking ring is seated properly when you see the grease on the ring get pushed out of one of the holes by the pin, and the ring does not rock from side-to-side when you press on either side with your finger. If the locking ring and pin don't index, take note of how far off they are, pull the ring off the spindle and turn the nut, either by hand or with the socket, just enough for a good fit. Try the locking ring again.
28. When the locking ring engages the adjusting nut pin properly, your bearing adjustment is set. Thread the locknut onto the spindle until it contacts the locking ring.
29. Tighten the locknut to at least 160 ft. lbs. (216 Nm). This locknut ensures that the locking ring and adjusting nut don't move. Over-tightening the locknut has no effect on the bearing adjustment.
30. Install the locking hub.
31. Install the caliper.
32. Install the wheel.

K-SERIES

These axles have integral hub/bearing assemblies. No periodic service is required. See Section 7 for disassembly details.

TRAILER TOWING

➧ **See Figures 221 and 222**

General Recommendations

Your vehicle was primarily designed to carry passengers and cargo. It is important to remember that towing a trailer will place additional loads on your vehicle's engine, drive train, steering, braking and other systems. However, if you find decide to tow a trailer, using the proper equipment is a must.

Local laws may require specific equipment such as trailer brakes or fender mounted mirrors. Check your local laws.

Recommended Equipment Checklist

Equipment	Class I Trailers Under 2,000 pounds	Class II Trailers 2,000-3,500 pounds	Class III Trailers 3,500-6,000 pounds	Class IV Trailers 6,000 pounds and up
Hitch	Frame or Equalizing	Equalizing	Equalizing	Fifth wheel Pick-up truck only
Tongue Load Limit**	Up to 200 pounds	200-350 pounds	350-600 pounds	600 pounds and up
Trailer Brakes	Not Required	Required	Required	Required
Safety Chain	3/16" diameter links	1/4" diameter links	5/16" diameter links	—
Fender Mounted Mirrors	Useful, but not necessary	Recommended	Recommended	Recommended
Turn Signal Flasher	Standard	Constant Rate or heavy duty	Constant Rate or heavy duty	Constant Rate or heavy duty
Coolant Recovery System	Recommended	Required	Required	Required
Transmission Oil Cooler	Recommended	Recommended	Recommended	Recommended
Engine Oil Cooler	Recommended	Recommended	Recommended	Recommended
Air Adjustable Shock Absorbers	Recommended	Recommended	Recommended	Recommended
Flex or Clutch Fan	Recommended	Recommended	Recommended	Recommended
Tires	***	***	***	***

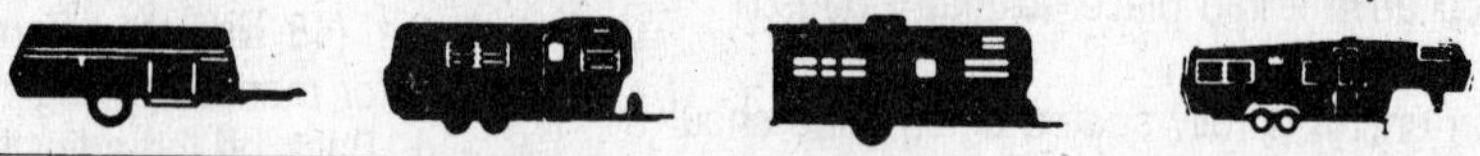

NOTE The information in this chart is a guide Check the manufacturer's recommendations for your car if in doubt

*Local laws may require specific equipment such as trailer brakes or fender mounted mirrors .Check your local laws Hitch weight is usually 10-15% of trailer gross weight and should be measured with trailer loaded

**Most manufacturer's do not recommend towing trailers of over 1,000 pounds with compacts Some intermediates cannot tow Class III trailers

***Check manufacturer's recommendations for your specific car trailer combination

—Does not apply

84901131

Fig. 221 Recommended trailer towing equipment

Trailer Weight

The weight of the trailer is the most important factor. A good weight-to-horsepower ratio is about 35:1, 35 lbs. of Gross Combined Weight (GCW) for every horsepower your engine develops. Multiply the engine's rated horsepower by 35 and subtract the weight of the vehicle passengers and luggage. The result is the approximate ideal maximum weight you should tow, although a a numerically higher axle ratio can help compensate for heavier weight.

Hitch (Tongue) Weight

Figure the hitch weight to select a proper hitch. Hitch weight is usually 9-11% of the trailer gross weight and should be measured with the trailer loaded. Hitches fall into various categories: those that mount on the frame and rear bumper, the bolt-on or weld-on distribution type used for larger trailers. Axle mounted or clamp-on bumper hitches should never be used.

Check the gross weight rating of your trailer. Tongue weight is usually figured as 10% of gross trailer weight. Therefore, a trailer with a maximum gross weight of 2000 lbs. will have a maximum tongue weight of 200 lbs. Class I trailers fall into this category. Class II trailers are those with a gross weight rating of 2000-3000 lbs., while Class III trailers fall into the 3500-6000 lbs. category. Class IV trailers are those over 6000 lbs. and are for use with fifth wheel trucks, only.

When you've determined the hitch that you'll need, follow the manufacturer's installation instructions, exactly, especially when it comes to fastener torques. The hitch will subjected to a lot of stress and good hitches come with hardened bolts. Never substitute an inferior bolt for a hardened bolt.

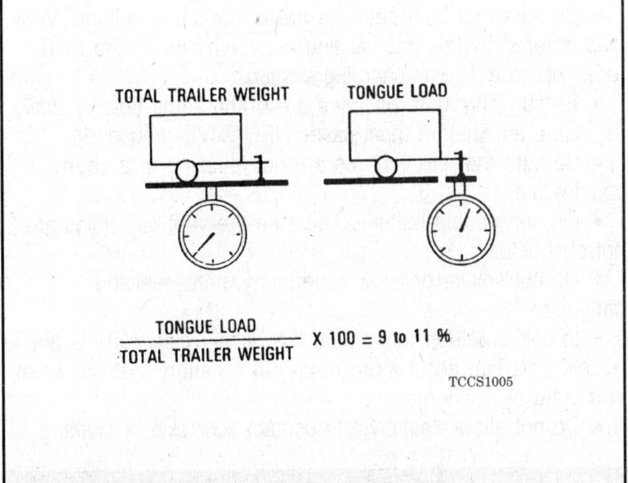

Fig. 222 Calculating proper tongue weight for you trailer

Cooling

ENGINE

One of the most common, if not THE most common, problems associated with trailer towing is engine overheating. If you have a standard cooling system, without an expansion tank, you'll definitely need to get an aftermarket expansion tank kit, preferably one with at least a 2 quart capacity. These kits are easily installed on the radiator's overflow hose, and come with a pressure cap designed for expansion tanks.

Another helpful accessory for vehicles using a belt-driven radiator fan is a flex fan. These fans are large diameter units are designed to provide more airflow at low speeds, with blades that have deeply cupped surfaces. The blades then flex, or flatten out, at high speed, when less cooling air is needed. These fans are far lighter in weight than stock fans, requiring less horsepower to drive them. Also, they are far quieter than stock fans. If you do decide to replace your stock fan with a flex fan, note that if your vehicle has a fan clutch, a spacer will be needed between the flex fan and water pump hub.

Aftermarket engine oil coolers are helpful for prolonging engine oil life and reducing overall engine temperatures. Both of these factors increase engine life. While not absolutely necessary in towing Class I and some Class II trailers, they are recommended for heavier Class II and all Class III towing. Engine oil cooler systems consists of an adapter, screwed on in place of the oil filter, a remote filter mounting and a multi-tube, finned heat exchanger, which is mounted in front of the radiator or air conditioning condenser.

TRANSMISSION

An automatic transmission is usually recommended for trailer towing. Modern automatics have proven reliable and, of course, easy to operate, in trailer towing. The increased load of a trailer, however, causes an increase in the temperature of the automatic transmission fluid. Heat is the worst enemy of an automatic transmission. As the temperature of the fluid increases, the life of the fluid decreases.

It is essential, therefore, that you install an automatic transmission cooler. The cooler, which consists of a multi-tube, finned heat exchanger, is usually installed in front of the radiator or air conditioning compressor, and hooked in-line with the transmission cooler tank inlet line. Follow the cooler manufacturer's installation instructions.

Select a cooler of at least adequate capacity, based upon the combined gross weights of the vehicle and trailer.

Cooler manufacturers recommend that you use an aftermarket cooler in addition to, and not instead of, the present cooling tank in your radiator. If you do want to use it in place of the radiator cooling tank, get a cooler at least two sizes larger than normally necessary.

➡A transmission cooler can, sometimes, cause slow or harsh shifting in the transmission during cold weather, until the fluid has a chance to come up to normal operating temperature. Some coolers can be purchased with or retrofitted with a temperature bypass valve which will allow fluid flow through the cooler only when the fluid has reached above a certain operating temperature.

Handling A Trailer

Towing a trailer with ease and safety requires a certain amount of experience. It's a good idea to learn the feel of a trailer by practicing turning, stopping and backing in an open area such as an empty parking lot.

TOWING THE VEHICLE

General Information

2-WHEEL DRIVE

Chevrolet and GMC trucks can be towed on all four wheels (flat towed) at speeds of less than 35 mph (56 km), for distances less than 50 miles (80 km), providing that the axle, driveline and engine/transmission are normally operable. The transmission should be in Neutral, the engine off, the steering unlocked, and the parking brake released.

The rear wheels must be raised off the ground or the driveshaft disconnected when the transmission if not operating properly, or when speeds of over 35 mph (56 km) will be used or when towing more than 50 miles. (80 km).

Do not attach chains to the bumpers or bracketing. All attachments must be made to the structural members. Safety chains should be used. It should also be remembered that power steering and brake assists will not be working with the engine off.

4-WHEEL DRIVE

➧ See Figure 223

Refer to the illustration for details in towing your vehicle.

Remember that the power steering and power brakes will not have their power assist with the engine off. The only safe way to tow is with a tow bar. The steering column must be unlocked and the parking brake released. Attachments should be made to the frame and to the bumper or its brackets. Safety chains are also required.

JUMP STARTING A DEAD BATTERY

Whenever a vehicle is jump started, precautions must be followed in order to prevent the possibility of personal injury. Remember that batteries contain a small amount of explosive hydrogen gas which is a by-product of battery charging. Sparks should always be avoided when working around batteries, especially when attaching jumper cables. To minimize the possibility of accidental sparks, follow the procedure carefully.

⁂CAUTION

NEVER hook the batteries up in a series circuit or the entire electrical system will go up in smoke, especially the starter!

Cars equipped with a diesel engine may utilize two 12 volt batteries. If so, the batteries are connected in a parallel circuit (positive terminal to positive terminal, negative terminal to negative terminal). Hooking the batteries up in parallel circuit increases battery cranking power without increasing total battery voltage output. Output remains at 12 volts. On the other hand, hooking two 12 volt batteries up in a series circuit (positive terminal to negative terminal, positive terminal to negative terminal) increases total battery output to 24 volts (12 volts plus 12 volts).

Jump Starting Precautions

- Be sure that both batteries are of the same voltage. Vehicles covered by this manual and most vehicles on the road today utilize a 12 volt charging system.
- Be sure that both batteries are of the same polarity (have the same terminal, in most cases NEGATIVE grounded).
- Be sure that the vehicles are not touching or a short could occur.
- On serviceable batteries, be sure the vent cap holes are not obstructed.
- Do not smoke or allow sparks anywhere near the batteries.
- In cold weather, make sure the battery electrolyte is not frozen. This can occur more readily in a battery that has been in a state of discharge.
- Do not allow electrolyte to contact your skin or clothing.

Gasoline Engines

➧ See Figure 224

1. Make sure that the voltages of the 2 batteries are the same. Most batteries and charging systems are of the 12 volt variety.
2. Pull the jumping vehicle (with the good battery) into a position so the jumper cables can reach the dead battery and

FRONT WHEELS OFF THE GROUND	
FULL TIME (4 X 4) AUTOMATIC TRANSMISSION	PART TIME (4 X 4) MANUAL TRANSMISSION
1. TRANSFER CASE IN NEUTRAL 2. TRANSMISSION IN PARK 3. MAXIMUM SPEED 35 MPH 4. MAXIMUM DISTANCE 50 MILES NOTE: For distances over 50 miles, disconnect rear propshaft at rear axle carrier and secure in safe position.	1. TRANSFER CASE IN 2 H 2. TRANSMISSION IN NEUTRAL 3. MAXIMUM SPEED 35 MPH 4. MAXIMUM DISTANCE 50 MILES NOTE: For distances over 50 miles, disconnect the rear propshaft at rear axle carrier and secure in safe position.
REAR WHEELS OFF THE GROUND	
CAUTION: When towing a vehicle in this position, the steering wheel should be secured to keep the front wheels in a straight ahead position.	
FULL TIME (4 X 4)	PART TIME (4 X 4)
1. TRANSFER CASE IN NEUTRAL 2. TRANSMISSION IN PARK 3. MAXIMUM SPEED 35 MPH 4. MAXIMUM DISTANCE 50 MILES NOTE: For distances over 50 miles, disconnect front propshaft at front axle carrier and secure in safe position.	1. TRANSFER CASE IN 2 H 2. TRANSMISSION IN NEUTRAL 3. MAXIMUM SPEED 35 MPH 4. MAXIMUM DISTANCE 50 MILES NOTE: For distances over 50 miles, disconnect the front propshaft at front axle carrier and secure in safe position.
ALL FOUR WHEELS ON GROUND	
FULL TIME (4 X 4)	PART TIME (4 X 4)
1. TRANSFER CASE IN NEUTRAL 2. TRANSMISSION IN PARK NOTE: Do not exceed speed as per State laws for towing vehicles.	1. TRANSFER CASE IN 2 H 2. TRANSMISSION IN NEUTRAL 3. MAXIMUM SPEED 35 MPH 4. MAXIMUM DISTANCE 50 MILES NOTE: For speeds or distances greater than above, both propshafts must be disconnected at the axle carrier end and secured in a safe position. It is recommended that both propshafts be removed and stored in the vehicle. NOTE: Do not exceed speeds as per State laws for towing vehicles.

84901132

Fig. 223 Four wheel drive towing procedures

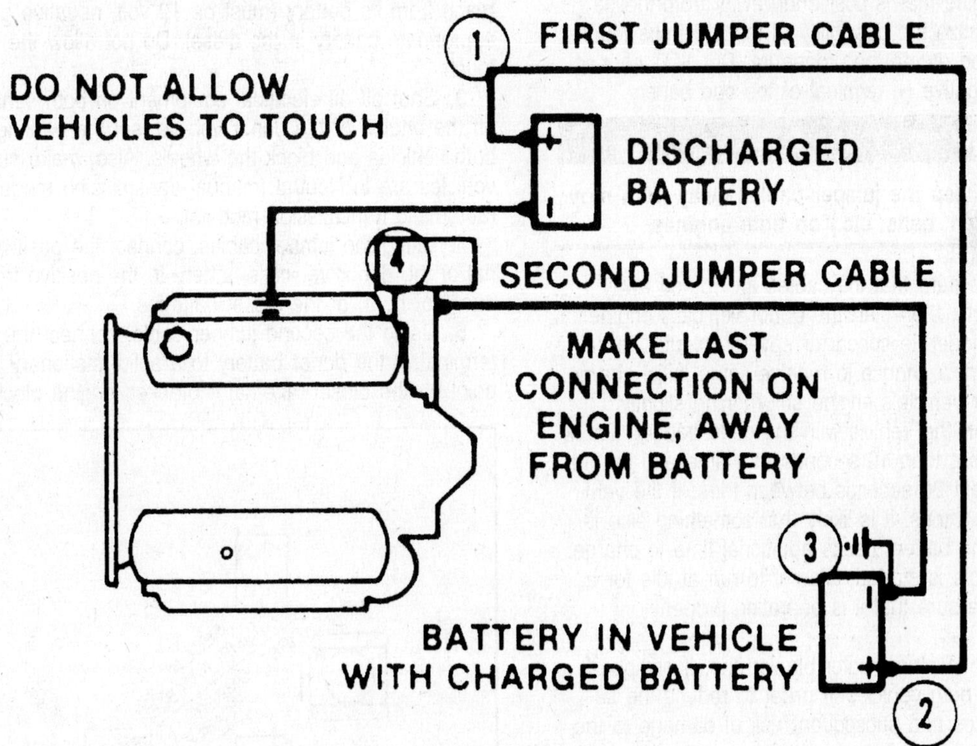

Fig. 224 Connect the jumper cables to the batteries and engine in the order shown

that vehicle's engine. Make sure that the vehicles do NOT touch.

3. Place the transmissions of both vehicles in Neutral or Park, as applicable, then firmly set their parking brakes.

➡If necessary for safety reasons, the hazard lights on both vehicles may be operated throughout the entire procedure without significantly increasing the difficulty of jumping the dead battery.

4. Turn all lights and accessories off on both vehicles. Make sure the ignition switches on both vehicles are turned to the **OFF** position.

5. Cover the battery cell caps with a rag, but do not cover the terminals.

6. Make sure the terminals on both batteries are clean and free of corrosion or proper electrical connection will be impeded. If necessary, clean the battery terminals before proceeding.

7. Identify the positive (+) and negative (-) terminals on both battery posts.

8. Connect the first jumper cable to the positive (+) terminal of the dead battery, then connect the other end of that cable to the positive (+) terminal of the booster (good) battery.

9. Connect one end of the other jumper cable to the negative (-) terminal on the booster battery and the other cable clamp to an engine bolt head, alternator bracket or other solid, metallic point on the engine with the dead battery. Try to pick a ground on the engine that is positioned away from the battery in order to minimize the possibility of the 2 clamps touching should one loosen during the procedure. DO NOT connect this clamp to the negative (-) terminal of the bad battery.

✱✱CAUTION

Be very careful to keep the jumper cables away from moving parts (cooling fan, belts, etc.) on both engines.

10. Check to make sure that the cables are routed away from any moving parts, then start the donor vehicle's engine. Run the engine at moderate speed for several minutes to allow the dead battery a chance to receive some initial charge.

11. With the donor vehicle's engine still running slightly above idle, try to start the vehicle with the dead battery. Crank the engine for no more than 10 seconds at a time and let the starter cool for at least 20 seconds between tries. If the vehicle does not start in 3 tries, it is likely that something else is also wrong or that the battery needs additional time to charge.

12. Once the vehicle is started, allow it to run at idle for a few seconds to make sure that it is operating properly operating.

13. Turn on the headlights, heater blower and, if equipped, the rear defroster of both vehicles in order to reduce the severity of voltage spikes and subsequent risk of damage to the vehicles' electrical systems when the cables are disconnected. This step is especially important to late model vehicles equipped with computer control modules.

14. Carefully disconnect the cables in the reverse order of connection. Start with the negative cable that is attached to the engine ground, then the negative cable on the donor battery. Disconnect the positive cable from the donor battery and finally, disconnect the positive cable from the formerly dead battery. Be careful when disconnecting the cables from the positive terminals not to allow the alligator clips to touch any metal on either vehicle or a short and sparks will occur.

Diesel Engines

➧ **See Figure 225**

All GM V8 diesels are equipped with two 12 volt batteries. The batteries are connected in parallel circuit (positive terminal to positive terminal, negative terminal to negative terminal). Hooking the batteries up in parallel circuit increases battery cranking power without increasing total battery voltage output (12 volts). On the other hand, hooking two 12 volt batteries up in a series circuit (positive terminal to negative terminal, positive terminal to negative terminal) increases total battery output to 24 volts (12 volts + 12 volts).

✱✱CAUTION

NEVER hook the batteries up in a series circuit or the entire electrical system will go up in smoke.

In the event that a dual battery diesel must be jump started, use the following procedure.

1. Open the hood and locate the batteries. On GM diesels, the manufacturer usually suggests using the battery on the driver's side of the truck to make the connection.

2. Position the donor vehicle so that the jumper cables will reach from its battery (must be 12 volt, negative ground) to the appropriate battery in the diesel. Do not allow the vehicles to touch.

3. Shut off all electrical equipment on both vehicles. Turn off the engine of the donor vehicle, set the parking brakes on both vehicles and block the wheels. Also, make sure both vehicles are in Neutral (manual transmission models) or Park (automatic transmission models).

4. Using the jumper cables, connect the positive (+) terminal of the donor vehicle's battery to the positive terminal of one (not both) of the diesel batteries.

5. Using the second jumper cable, connect the negative (-) terminal of the donor battery to a solid, stationary, metallic point on the diesel (alternator bracket, engine block, etc.). Be

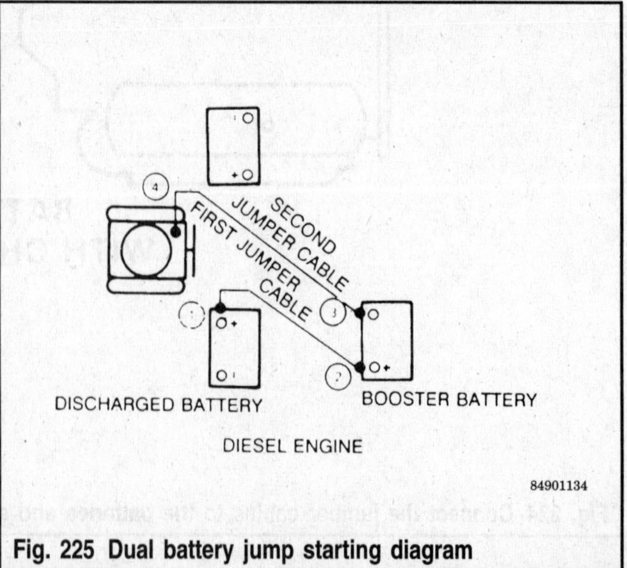

Fig. 225 Dual battery jump starting diagram

very careful to keep the jumper cables away from moving parts (cooling fan, alternator belt, etc.) on both vehicles.

6. Start the engine of the donor can and run it at moderate speed.

7. Start the engine of the diesel.

8. When the diesel starts, disconnect the battery cables in the reverse order of attachment.

JACKING

➧ **See Figures 226, 227, 228, 229, 230 and 231**

Your vehicle was supplied with a jack for emergency road repairs. This jack is fine for changing a flat tire or other operations not requiring you to go beneath the vehicle. If it is used in an emergency situation, carefully follow the instructions provided either with the jack or in your owner's manual. Do not attempt to use the jack in any places other than specified by the vehicle manufacturer. Always block the diagonally opposite wheel when using a jack.

A more convenient way of jacking is the use of a garage or floor jack. You may use the floor jack to raise your GM full size truck.

Never place the jack under the radiator, engine or transmission components. Severe and expensive damage will result when the jack is raised. Additionally, never jack under the floorpan or bodywork; the metal will deform.

Whenever you plan to work under the vehicle, you must support it on jackstands or ramps. Never use cinder blocks or stacks of wood to support the vehicle, even if you're only going to be under it for a few minutes. Never crawl under the vehicle when it is supported only by the tire-changing jack or other floor jack.

➡**Always position a block of wood on top of the jack or stand to protect the finish when lifting or supporting the vehicle.**

Small hydraulic, screw, or scissors jacks are satisfactory for raising the vehicle. Drive-on trestles or ramps are also a handy and safe way to both raise and support the vehicle. Be careful though, some ramps may be too steep to drive your vehicle onto without scraping the front bottom panels. Never support the vehicle on any suspension member (unless specifically instructed to do so by a repair manual) or underbody panel.

The following safety points cannot be overemphasized:

- Always block the opposite wheel or wheels to keep the vehicle from rolling off the jack.
- When raising the front of the vehicle, firmly apply the parking brake.
- Always use jackstands to support the vehicle when you are working underneath. Place the stands beneath the scissors jacking brackets. Before climbing underneath, rock the vehicle a bit to make sure it is firmly supported.

87981p43

Fig. 226 Raising the front of the vehicle using a hydraulic jack

87981p44

Fig. 227 Raising the rear of the vehicle using a hydraulic jack

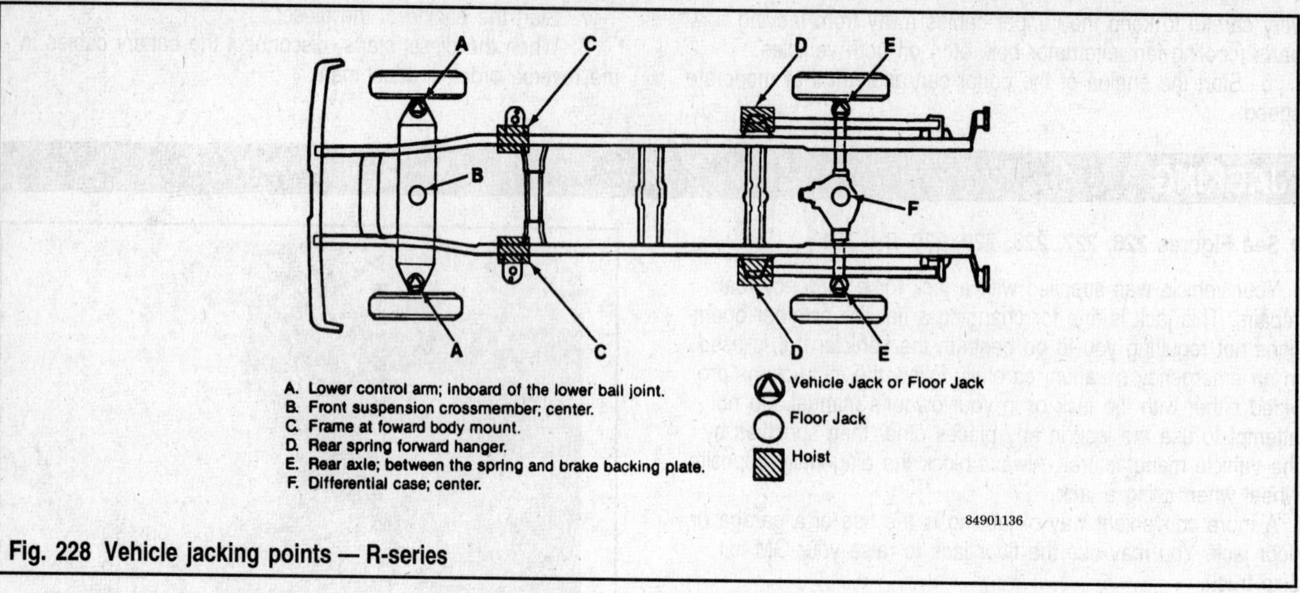

Fig. 228 Vehicle jacking points — R-series

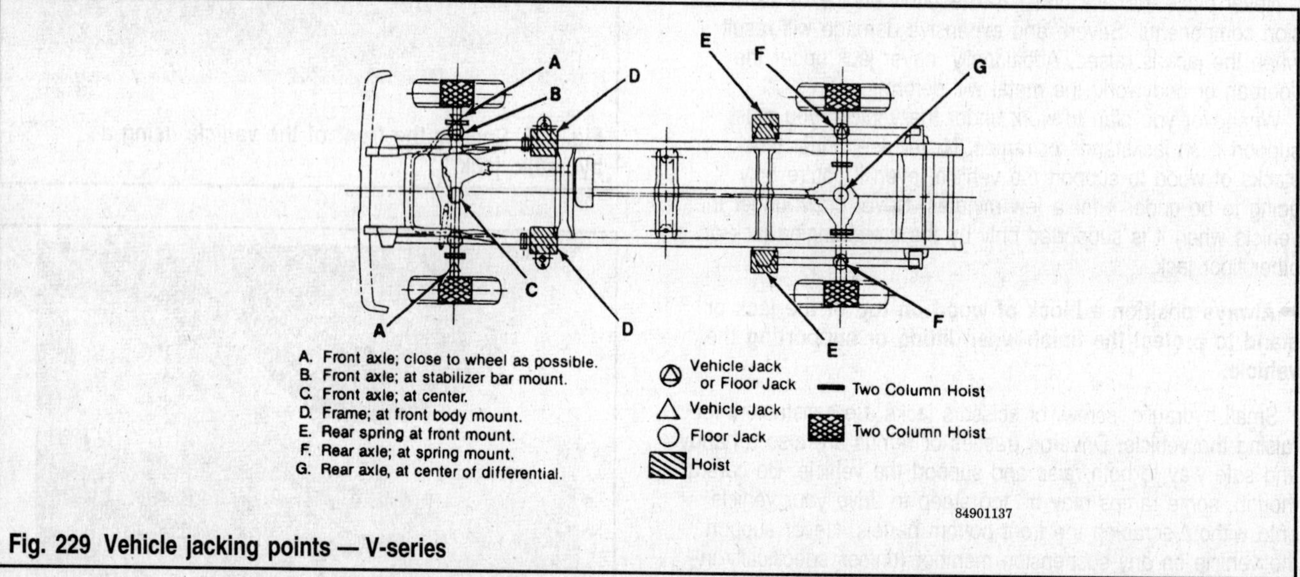

Fig. 229 Vehicle jacking points — V-series

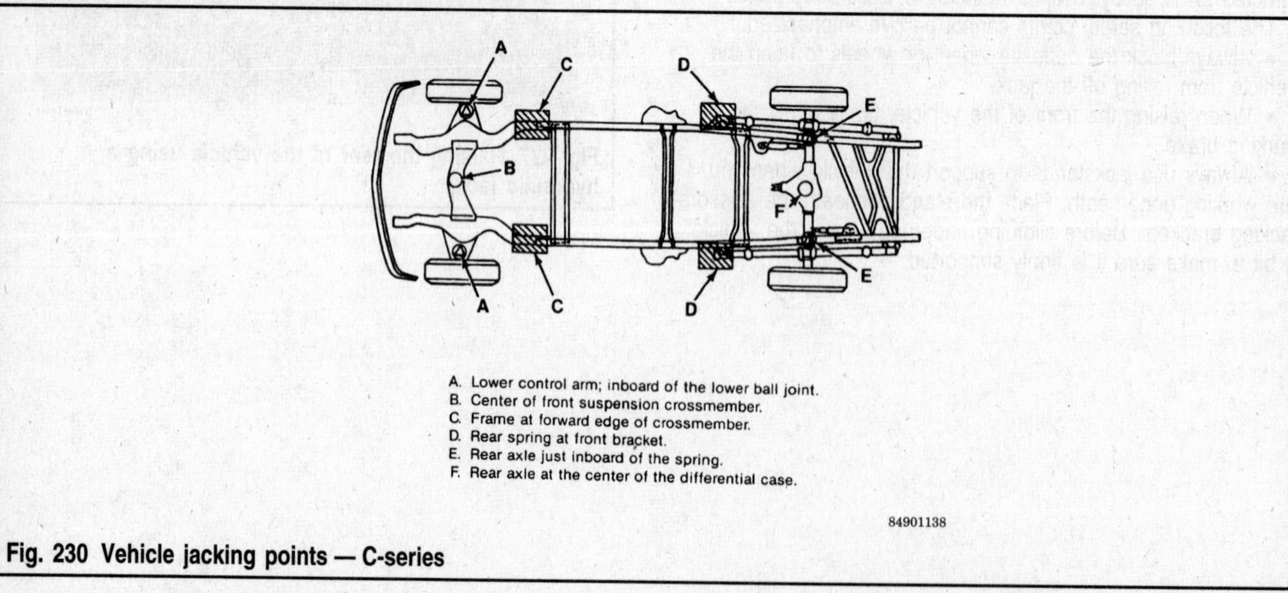

Fig. 230 Vehicle jacking points — C-series

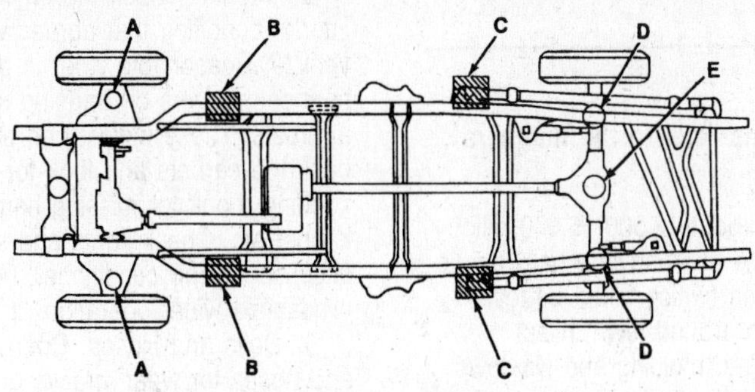

Fig. 231 Vehicle jacking points — K-series

HOW TO BUY A USED VEHICLE

Many people believe that a two or three year old used car or truck is a better buy than a new vehicle. This may be true as most new vehicles suffer the heaviest depreciation in the first two years and, at three years old, a vehicle is usually not old enough to present a lot of costly repair problems. But keep in mind, when buying a non-warranted automobile, there are no guarantees. Whatever the age of the used vehicle you might want to purchase, this section and a little patience should increase your chances of selecting one that is safe and dependable.

Tips

1. First decide what model you want, and how much you want to spend.
2. Check the used car lots and your local newspaper ads. Privately owned vehicles are usually less expensive, however, you may not get a warranty that, in many cases, comes with a used vehicle purchased from a lot. Of course, some aftermarket warranties may not be worth the extra money, so this is a point you will have to debate and consider based on your priorities.
3. Never shop at night. The glare of the lights make it easy to miss faults on the body caused by accident or rust repair.
4. Try to get the name and phone number of the previous owner. Contact him/her and ask about the vehicle. If the owner of a lot refuses this information, look for a vehicle somewhere else.

A private seller can tell you about the vehicle and maintenance. But remember, there's no law requiring honesty from private citizens selling used vehicles. There is a law that forbids tampering with or turning back the odometer mileage. This includes both the private citizen and the lot owner. The law also requires that the seller or anyone transferring ownership of the vehicle must provide the buyer with a signed statement indicating the mileage on the odometer at the time of transfer.

5. You may wish to contact the National Highway Traffic Safety Administration (NHTSA) to find out if the vehicle has ever been included in a manufacturer's recall. Write down the year, model and serial number before you buy the vehicle, then contact NHTSA (there should be a 1-800 number that your phone company's information line can supply). If the vehicle was listed for a recall, make sure the needed repairs were made.
6. Refer to the Used Vehicle Checklist in this section and check all the items on the vehicle you are considering. Some items are more important than others. Only you know how much money you can afford for repairs, and depending on the price of the vehicle, may consider performing any needed work yourself. Beware, however, of trouble in areas that will affect operation, safety or emission. Problems in the Used Vehicle Checklist break down as follows:
   - Numbers 1-8: Two or more problems in these areas indicate a lack of maintenance. You should beware.
   - Numbers 9-13: Problems here tend to indicate a lack of proper care, however, these can usually be corrected with a tune-up or relatively simple parts replacement.
   - Numbers 14-17: Problems in the engine or transmission can be very expensive. Unless you are looking for a project, walk away from any vehicle with problems in 2 or more of these areas.
7. If you are satisfied with the apparent condition of the vehicle, take it to an independent diagnostic center or mechanic for a complete check. If you have a state inspection program, have it inspected immediately before purchase, or specify on the bill of sale that the sale is conditional on passing state inspection.
8. Road test the vehicle — refer to the Road Test Checklist in this section. If your original evaluation and the road test agree — the rest is up to you.

USED VEHICLE CHECKLIST

See Figure 232

The numbers on the illustrations refer to the numbers on this checklist.

1. Mileage: Average mileage is about 12,000-15,000 miles per year. More than average mileage may indicate hard usage or could indicate many highway miles (which could be less detrimental than half as many tough around town miles).
2. Paint: Check around the tailpipe, molding and windows for overspray indicating that the vehicle has been repainted.
3. Rust: Check fenders, doors, rocker panels, window moldings, wheelwells, floorboards, under floormats, and in the trunk for signs of rust. Any rust at all will be a problem. There is no way to permanently stop the spread of rust, except to replace the part or panel.

If rust repair is suspected, try using a magnet to check for body filler. A magnet should stick to the sheet metal parts of the body, but will not adhere to areas with large amounts of filler.

4. Body appearance: Check the moldings, bumpers, grille, vinyl roof, glass, doors, trunk lid and body panels for general overall condition. Check for misalignment, loose hold-down clips, ripples, scratches in glass, welding in the trunk, severe misalignment of body panels or ripples, any of which may indicate crash work.
5. Leaks: Get down and look under the vehicle. There are no normal leaks, other than water from the air conditioner condenser.
6. Tires: Check the tire air pressure. One old trick is to pump the tire pressure up to make the vehicle roll easier. Check the tread wear, open the trunk and check the spare too. Uneven wear is a clue that the front end may need an alignment.
7. Shock absorbers: Check the shock absorbers by forcing downward sharply on each corner of the vehicle. Good shocks will not allow the vehicle to bounce more than once after you let go.
8. Interior: Check the entire interior. You're looking for an interior condition that agrees with the overall condition of the vehicle. Reasonable wear is expected, but be suspicious of new seat covers on sagging seats, new pedal pads, and worn armrests. These indicate an attempt to cover up hard use. Pull back the carpets and look for evidence of water leaks or flooding. Look for missing hardware, door handles, control knobs, etc. Check lights and signal operations. Make sure all accessories (air conditioner, heater, radio, etc.) work. Check windshield wiper operation.
9. Belts and Hoses: Open the hood, then check all belts and hoses for wear, cracks or weak spots.
10. Battery: Low electrolyte level, corroded terminals and/or cracked case indicate a lack of maintenance.
11. Radiator: Look for corrosion or rust in the coolant indicating a lack of maintenance.
12. Air filter: A severely dirty air filter would indicate a lack of maintenance.
13. Ignition wires: Check the ignition wires for cracks, burned spots, or wear. Worn wires will have to be replaced.
14. Oil level: If the oil level is low, chances are the engine uses oil or leaks. Beware of water in the oil (there is probably a cracked block or bad head gasket), excessively thick oil (which is often used to quiet a noisy engine), or thin, dirty oil with a distinct gasoline smell (this may indicate internal engine problems).
15. Automatic Transmission: Pull the transmission dipstick out when the engine is running. The level should read FULL, and the fluid should be clear or bright red. Dark brown or black fluid that has distinct burnt odor, indicates a transmission in need of repair or overhaul.
16. Exhaust: Check the color of the exhaust smoke. Blue smoke indicates, among other problems, worn rings. Black smoke can indicate burnt valves or carburetor problems. Check the exhaust system for leaks; it can be expensive to replace.
17. Spark Plugs: Remove one or all of the spark plugs (the most accessible will do, though all are preferable). An engine in good condition will show plugs with a light tan or gray deposit on the firing tip.

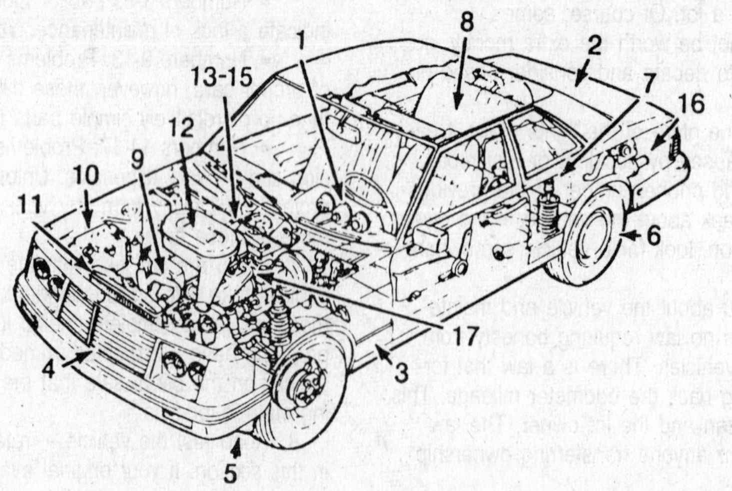

Fig. 232 Each of the numbered items should be checked when purchasing a used vehicle

ROAD TEST CHECKLIST

1. Engine Performance: The vehicle should be peppy whether cold or warm, with adequate power and good pickup. It should respond smoothly through the gears.

2. Brakes: They should provide quick, firm stops with no noise, pulling or brake fade.

3. Steering: Sure control with no binding harshness, or looseness and no shimmy in the wheel should be expected. Noise or vibration from the steering wheel when turning the vehicle means trouble.

4. Clutch (Manual Transmission/Transaxle): Clutch action should give quick, smooth response with easy shifting. The clutch pedal should have free-play before it disengages the clutch. Start the engine, set the parking brake, put the transmission in first gear and slowly release the clutch pedal. The engine should begin to stall when the pedal is $\frac{1}{2}$-$\frac{3}{4}$ of the way up.

5. Automatic Transmission/Transaxle: The transmission should shift rapidly and smoothly, with no noise, hesitation, or slipping.

6. Differential: No noise or thumps should be present. Differentials have no normal leaks.

7. Driveshaft/Universal Joints: Vibration and noise could mean driveshaft problems. Clicking at low speed or coast conditions means worn U-joints.

8. Suspension: Try hitting bumps at different speeds. A vehicle that bounces excessively has weak shock absorbers or struts. Clunks mean worn bushings or ball joints.

9. Frame/Body: Wet the tires and drive in a straight line. Tracks should show two straight lines, not four. Four tire tracks indicate a frame/body bent by collision damage. If the tires can't be wet for this purpose, have a friend drive along behind you and see if the vehicle appears to be traveling in a straight line.

GASOLINE ENGINES WITH LIGHT DUTY EMISSIONS— MAINTENANCE SCHEDULE I

Item No.	Service	3	6	7.5	9	12	15	18	21	22.5	24	27	30	33	36	37.5	39	42	45	48	51	52.5	54	57	60
	Kilometers (000)	5	10	12.5	15	20	25	30	35	37.5	40	45	50	55	60	62.5	65	70	75	80	85	87.5	90	95	100
1	Engine Oil Change*—Every 3 Months, or	+	+		+	+	+	+	+		+	+	+	+	+		+	+	+	+	+		+	+	+
	Oil Filter Change*—Every 3 Months, or	+	+		+	+	+	+	+		+	+	+	+	+		+	+	+	+	+		+	+	+
2	Chassis Lubrication—Every 12 Months, or	+	+		+	+	+	+	+		+	+	+	+	+		+	+	+	+	+		+	+	+
3	Clutch Fork Ball Stud Lubrication												+												+
5	Cooling System Service*—Every 24 Months or												+												+
6	Air Cleaner Filter Replacement*												+												+
7	Front Wheel Bearing Repack						+						+						+						+
8	Transmission Service																								
10	Fuel Filter Replacement*												+												+
11	Spark Plugs Replacement*												+												+
12	Spark Plug Wire Inspection*																								+
14	Electronic Vacuum Regulator Valve (EVRV) Inspection*																								+
15	Engine Timing Check*																								+
16	Fuel Tank, Cap and Lines Inspection*																								+
18	Engine Accessory Drive Belt(s) Inspection*																								+
24	Tire and Wheel Rotation																								
25	Drive Axle Service																								
26	Brake Systems Inspection																								

(Column headings 3 … 60 are Miles (000).)

FOOTNOTES:
*An Emission Control Service

THE SERVICES SHOWN ON THIS CHART UP TO 60,000 MILES (100 000 km) ARE TO BE DONE AFTER 60,000 MILES AT THE SAME INTERVALS.

87981cx1

GASOLINE ENGINES WITH LIGHT DUTY EMISSIONS— MAINTENANCE SCHEDULE II

Item No.	Service / Miles (000)	3	6	7.5	9	12	15	18	21	22.5	24	27	30	33	36	37.5	39	42	45	48	51	52.5	54	57	60
	Kilometers (000)	5	10	12.5	15	20	25	30	35	37.5	40	45	50	55	60	62.5	65	70	75	80	85	87.5	90	95	100
1	Engine Oil Change*—Every 12 Months, or			•			•			•			•			•			•			•			•
	Oil Filter Change*—Every 12 Months, or			•						•						•						•			
2	Chassis Lubrication—Every 12 Months, or			•			•			•			•			•			•			•			•
3	Clutch Fork Ball Stud Lubrication												•												•
5	Cooling System Service*—Every 24 Months or												•												•
6	Air Cleaner Filter Replacement*												•												•
7	Front Wheel Bearing Repack												•												•
8	Transmission Service																								
10	Fuel Filter Replacement*																								•
11	Spark Plugs Replacement*												•												•
12	Spark Plug Wire Inspection*																								•
14	Electronic Vacuum Regulator Valve (EVRV) Inspection*																								•
15	Engine Timing Check*																								•
16	Fuel Tank, Cap and Lines Inspection*																								•
18	Engine Accessory Drive Belt(s) Inspection*																								•
24	Tire and Wheel Rotation																								
25	Drive Axle Service																								
26	Brake Systems Inspection																								

FOOTNOTES:
*An Emission Control Service

THE SERVICES SHOWN ON THIS CHART UP TO 60,000 MILES (100 000 km) ARE TO BE DONE AFTER 60,000 MILES AT THE SAME INTERVALS.

87981x1a

GASOLINE ENGINES WITH HEAVY DUTY EMISSIONS— MAINTENANCE SCHEDULE I

Item No.	Service	Miles (000)	3	6	9	12	15	18	21	24	27	30	33	36	39	42	45	48	51	54	57	60
		Kilometers (000)	5	10	15	20	25	30	35	40	45	50	55	60	65	70	75	80	85	90	95	100
1	Engine Oil Change*—Every 3 Months, or		+	+	+	+	+	+	+	+	+	+	+	+	+	+	+	+	+	+	+	+
	Oil Filter Change*—Every 3 Months, or		+	+	+	+	+	+	+	+	+	+	+	+	+	+	+	+	+	+	+	+
2	Chassis Lubrication—Every 12 Months, or		+	+	+	+	+	+	+	+	+	+	+	+	+	+	+	+	+	+	+	+
3	Clutch Fork Ball Stud Lubrication											+										+
5	Cooling System Service*—Every 24 Months or									+								+				
6	Air Cleaner Filter Replacement▲*									+								+				
7	Front Wheel Bearing Repack					+				+				+				+				
8	Transmission Service																					
10	Fuel Filter Replacement*					+				+				+				+				+
11	Spark Plugs Replacement*										+									+		
12	Spark Plug Wire Inspection*																					+
13	EGR System Inspection*																					+
14	Electronic Vacuum Regulator Valve (EVRV) Inspection*													+								
15	Engine Timing Check▲*									+								+				
16	Fuel Tank, Cap and Lines Inspection*																					+
17	Thermostatically Controlled Air Cleaner Inspection▲*									+								+				
18	Engine Accessory Drive Belt(s) Inspection*					+				+				+				+				+
19	Evaporative Control System Inspection*																					+
20	Shields and Underhood Insulation Inspection▲■					+				+				+				+				+
21	Air Intake System Inspection▲■									+								+				
22	Thermostatically Controlled Engine Cooling Fan Check ▲■— Every 12 Months or					+				+				+				+				+
24	Tire and Wheel Rotation																					
25	Drive Axle Service																					
26	Brake Systems Inspection																					

FOOTNOTES:
* An Emission Control Service
▲ Also a Noise Emission Control Service
■ Applicable only to vehicles sold in the United States

THE SERVICES SHOWN ON THIS CHART UP TO 60,000 MILES (100 000 km) ARE TO BE DONE AFTER 60,000 MILES AT THE SAME INTERVALS.

87981cx2

GASOLINE ENGINES WITH HEAVY DUTY EMISSIONS— MAINTENANCE SCHEDULE II

Item No.	Service	3	6	9	12	15	18	21	24	27	30	33	36	39	42	45	48	51	54	57	60
	Miles (000)	3	6	9	12	15	18	21	24	27	30	33	36	39	42	45	48	51	54	57	60
	Kilometers (000)	5	10	15	20	25	30	35	40	45	50	55	60	65	70	75	80	85	90	95	100
1	Engine Oil Change*—Every 12 Months, or		•		•		•		•		•		•		•		•		•		•
	Oil Filter Change*—Every 12 Months, or		•				•				•				•				•		
2	Chassis Lubrication—Every 12 Months, or		•		•		•		•		•		•		•		•		•		•
3	Clutch Fork Ball Stud Lubrication										•										•
5	Cooling System Service*—Every 24 Months or								•								•				
6	Air Cleaner Filter Replacement▲*								•								•				
7	Front Wheel Bearing Repack								•								•				
8	Transmission Service																				
10	Fuel Filter Replacement*								•								•				
11	Spark Plugs Replacement*									•									•		
12	Spark Plug Wire Inspection*																				•
13	EGR System Inspection*																				•
14	Electronic Vacuum Regulator Valve (EVRV) Inspection*																				•
15	Engine Timing Check▲*								•								•				
16	Fuel Tank, Cap and Lines Inspection*																				•
17	Thermostatically Controlled Air Cleaner Inspection▲*								•								•				
18	Engine Accessory Drive Belt(s) Inspection*				•				•				•				•				•
19	Evaporative Control System Inspection*																				•
20	Shields and Underhood Insulation Inspection▲■				•				•				•				•				•
21	Air Intake System Inspection▲■								•								•				
22	Thermostatically Controlled Engine Cooling Fan Check ▲■— Every 12 Months or				•				•				•				•				•
24	Tire and Wheel Rotation																				
25	Drive Axle Service																				
26	Brake Systems Inspection																				

FOOTNOTES:
* An Emission Control Service
▲ Also a Noise Emission Control Service
■ Applicable only to vehicles sold in the United States

THE SERVICES SHOWN ON THIS CHART UP TO 60,000 MILES (100 000 km) ARE TO BE DONE AFTER 60,000 MILES AT THE SAME INTERVALS.

87981cx3

6.2L AND 6.5L DIESEL ENGINES—MAINTENANCE SCHEDULE I†

Item No.	Service	2.5	5	7.5	10	12.5	15	17.5	20	22.5	25	27.5	30	32.5	35	37.5	40	42.5	45	47.5	50	52.5	55	57.5	60
	Kilometers (000)	4	8	12	16	20	24	28	32	36	40	44	48	52	56	60	64	68	72	76	80	84	88	92	96
1	Engine Oil Change*—Every 3 Months, or	+	+	+	+	+	+	+	+	+	+	+	+	+	+	+	+	+	+	+	+	+	+	+	+
	Oil Filter Change*—Every 3 Months, or	+	+	+	+	+	+	+	+	+	+	+	+	+	+	+	+	+	+	+	+	+	+	+	+
2	Chassis Lubrication—Every 12 Months, or	+	+	+	+	+	+	+	+	+	+	+	+	+	+	+	+	+	+	+	+	+	+	+	+
3	Clutch Fork Ball Stud Lubrication												+												+
4	Engine Idle Speed Adjustment*		+										+												+
5	Cooling System Service*—Every 24 Months or												+												+
6	Air Cleaner Filter Replacement*★																								
7	Front Wheel Bearing Repack						+						+						+						+
8	Transmission Service																								
9	CDRV System Inspection*																								+
10	Fuel Filter Replacement*												+												+
13	EGR System Inspection*																								+
18	Drive Belt(s) Inspection																								+
20	Shields and Underhood Insulation Inspection■▲				+				+				+				+				+				+
21	Air Intake System Inspection■▲				+				+				+				+				+				+
22	Thermostatically Controlled Engine Cooling Fan Check■▲—Every 12 Months or				+				+				+				+				+				+
23	Exhaust Pressure Regulator Valve Inspection*																								+
24	Tire and Wheel Rotation																								
25	Drive Axle Service																								
26	Brake Systems Inspection																								

(Column headings 2.5–60 are Miles (000).)

FOOTNOTES:

★ Change filter every 15,000 miles (24 000 km), except when operating in dusty conditions. Dusty conditions may require more frequent filter replacement. Extreme dust and dirt operating conditions (off-road), may require the air filter to be checked as often as every 300 miles (483 km) and replaced as necessary.

* An Emission Control Service

■ Applicable only to trucks sold in the United States.

▲ Also, a Noise Control Service (applicable to vehicles with engine VIN Code J).

† This maintenance schedule applies to all diesel engines available.

THE SERVICES SHOWN ON THIS CHART UP TO 60,000 MILES (100 000 km) ARE TO BE DONE AFTER 60,000 MILES AT THE SAME INTERVALS.

87981cx4

6.2L AND 6.5L DIESEL ENGINES— **MAINTENANCE SCHEDULE II†**

Item No.	Service	Miles (000)	2.5	5	7.5	10	12.5	15	17.5	20	22.5	25	27.5	30	32.5	35	37.5	40	42.5	45	47.5	50	52.5	55	57.5	60
		Kilometers (000)	4	8	12	16	20	24	28	32	36	40	44	48	52	56	60	64	68	72	76	80	84	88	92	96
1	Engine Oil Change*—Every 12 Months, or			•		•		•		•		•		•		•		•		•		•		•		•
	Oil Filter Change*—Every 12 Months, or			•		•		•		•		•		•		•		•		•		•		•		•
2	Chassis Lubrication—Every 12 Months, or			•		•		•		•		•		•		•		•		•		•		•		•
3	Clutch Fork Ball Stud Lubrication													•												•
4	Engine Idle Speed Adjustment*			•										•												•
5	Cooling System Service*—Every 24 Months or													•												•
6	Air Cleaner Filter Replacement*													•												•
7	Front Wheel Bearing Repack													•												•
8	Transmission Service																									
9	CDRV System Inspection*																									•
10	Fuel Filter Replacement*													•												•
13	EGR System Inspection*																									•
18	Drive Belt(s) Inspection																									•
20	Shields and Underhood Insulation Inspection■▲					•				•				•				•				•				•
21	Air Intake System Inspection■▲					•				•				•				•				•				•
22	Thermostatically Controlled Engine Cooling Fan Check■▲—Every 12 Months or					•				•				•				•				•				•
23	Exhaust Pressure Regulator Valve Inspection*																									•
24	Tire and Wheel Rotation																									
25	Drive Axle Service																									
26	Brake Systems Inspection																									

FOOTNOTES:
* An Emission Control Service
■ Applicable only to trucks sold in the United States.
▲ Also, a Noise Control Service (applicable to vehicles with engine VIN Code J).
† This maintenance schedule applies to all diesel engines available.

THE SERVICES SHOWN ON THIS CHART UP TO 60,000 MILES (100 000 km) ARE TO BE DONE AFTER 60,000 MILES AT THE SAME INTERVALS.

87981x4a

CAPACITIES

Year	Engine ID/VIN	Engine Displacement Liters (cc)	Engine Oil with Filter (qts.)	Transmission (pts.) 4-Spd	5-Spd	Auto.	Transfer Case (pts.)	Drive Axle Front (pts.)	Rear (pts.)	Fuel Tank (gal.)	Cooling System (qts.) w/AC	wo/AC
1988	Z	4.3 (4293)	5.0	①	3.6	②	-	-	③	⑤	10.9	10.9
	T	4.8 (4785)	5.0	①	-	②	⑥	④	③	⑤	13.8	13.8
	H	5.0 (4998)	5.0	①	3.6	②	1.4	1.75	③	⑤	18.0	17.5
	K	5.7 (5735)	5.0	①	3.6	②	⑥	④	③	⑤	25.0	25.0
	C/J	6.2 (6243)	7.0	-	3.6	②	⑥	④	③	⑤	25.0	25.0
	N/W	7.4 (7439)	6.0	-	-	②	⑥	④	③	⑤	25.0	25.0
1989	Z	4.3 (4293)	5.0	①	3.6	②	-	-	③	⑤	10.9	10.9
	T	4.8 (4785)	5.0	①	-	②	⑥	④	③	⑤	13.8	13.8
	H	5.0 (4998)	5.0	①	3.6	②	1.4	1.75	③	⑤	18.0	17.5
	K	5.7 (5735)	5.0	①	3.6	②	⑥	④	③	⑤	18.0	17.5
	C/J	6.2 (6243)	7.0	-	3.6	②	⑥	④	③	⑤	25.0	25.0
	N/W	7.4 (7439)	6.0	-	-	②	⑥	④	③	⑤	25.0	25.0
1990	Z	4.3 (4293)	5.0	①	3.6	②	-	-	③	⑧	10.9	10.9
	H	5.0 (4998)	5.0	①	3.6	②	1.4	1.75	③	⑧	18.0	17.5
	K	5.7 (5735)	5.0	①	3.6	②	⑦	④	③	⑧	18.0	18.0
	C/J	6.2 (6243)	7.0	-	3.6	②	⑦	④	③	⑧	25.0	25.0
	N	7.4 (7439)	6.0	-	-	②	⑦	④	③	⑧	25.0	25.0
1991	Z	4.3 (4293)	5.0	①	⑩	②	-	-	③	⑧	10.9	10.9
	H	5.0 (4998)	5.0	①	⑩	②	⑪	④	③	⑧	18.0	17.5
	K	5.7 (5735)	5.0	①	⑩	②	⑪	④	③	⑧	18.0	17.5
	C/J	6.2 (6243)	7.0	-	⑩	②	⑪	④	③	⑧	25.0	25.0
	N	7.4 (7439)	7.0	-	-	②	⑪	④	③	⑧	25.0	25.0
1992	Z	4.3 (4293)	4.5	-	-	10.0	-	-	③	⑧	11.0	11.0
	H	5.0 (4998)	5.0	-	⑫	10.0	⑪	④	③	⑧	18.0	17.5
	K	5.7 (5735)	5.0 ⑨	-	⑫	10.0	⑪	④	③	⑧	18.0 ⑬	17.5 ⑬
	C/J	6.2 (6243)	7.0	-	⑫	10.0	⑪	④	③	⑧	25.0	25.0
	F	6.5 (6489)	7.0	-	⑫	10.0	⑪	④	③	⑧	26.5	26.5
	N	7.4 (7439)	7.0	-	⑫	10.0	⑪	④	③	⑧	25.0 ⑭	23.0 ⑭
1993	Z	4.3 (4293)	4.5	-	⑫	10.0	-	-	③	⑧	11.0	11.0
	H	5.0 (4998)	5.0	-	⑫	10.0	⑲	④	③	⑧	18.0	17.5
	K	5.7 (5735)	5.0 ⑨	-	⑫	10.0	⑲	④	③	⑧	18.0 ⑬	17.5 ⑬
	C/J	6.2 (6243)	7.0	-	⑫	10.0	⑲	④	③	⑧	25.0	25.0
	F	6.5 (6489)	7.0	-	⑫	10.0	⑲	④	③	⑧	26.5	26.5
	N	7.4 (7439)	7.0 ⑨	-	⑫	10.0	⑲	④	③	⑧	25.0 ⑭	23.0 ⑭
1994	Z	4.3 (4293)	5.0	-	⑩	10.0	-	④	③	⑧	11.0	11.0
	H	5.0 (4998)	5.0	-	⑩	10.0	⑲	④	③	⑧	11.0	11
	K	5.7 (5735)	5.7 ⑨	-	⑩	10.0	⑲	④	③	⑧	18.0 ⑬	17.5 ⑬
	F/P/S	6.5 (6489)	7.0	-	⑩	10.0	⑲	④	③	⑧	18.0	17.5
	N	7.4 (7439)	7.0 ⑨	-	⑩	10.0	⑲	④	③	⑧	25.0 ⑬	23.0 ⑭

87981C12

CAPACITIES

Year	Engine ID/VIN	Engine Displacement Liters (cc)	Engine Oil with Filter (qts.)	Transmission (pts.)			Transfer Case (pts.)	Drive Axle		Fuel Tank (gal.)	Cooling System (qts.)	
				4-Spd	5-Spd	Auto.		Front (pts.)	Rear (pts.)		w/AC	wo/AC
1995	Z	4.3 (4293)	5.0	-	(18)	(2)	-	-	(3)	(8)	11.0	11.0
	H	5.0 (4998)	5.0	-	(18)	(2)	(19)	(4)	(3)	(8)	18.0	17.5
	K	5.7 (5735)	5.0 (9)	-	(18)	(2)	(19)	(4)	(3)	(8)	18.0	17.5
	F/P/S	6.5 (6489)	7.0	-	(18)	(2)	(19)	(4)	(3)	(8)	26.5	26.5
	N	7.4 (7439)	5.0 (9)	-	(18)	(2)	(19)	(4)	(3)	(8)	25.0	25.0
1996	W	4.3 (4293)	4.5	-	(18)	(17)	-	-	(3)	(8)	13.0	13.0
	M	5.0 (4998)	5.0	-	(18)	(17)	(19)	(4)	(3)	(8)	18.0	17.5
	R	5.7 (5735)	5.0 (9)	-	(18)	(17)	(19)	(4)	(3)	(8)	20.0 (16)	17.5 (16)
	F/P/S	6.5 (6489)	7.0	-	(18)	(17)	(19)	(4)	(3)	(8)	27.5	27.5
	J	7.4 (7439)	7.0 (#)	-	(18)	(17)	(19)	(4)	(3)	(8)	27.5 (14)	27.5 (14)

*Drain and refill

(1) 117mm: 8.4 pts.
85mm: 3.6 pts.

(2) THM400/480LE: 8.4 pts.
THM700-R4/4L60: 10.00 pts.

(3) 8¼ in. : 4.2 pts.
9½ in. 5.5 : pts.
10½ in. : 5.5 pts.
Dana.
11 in. : 8.2 pts.

(4) 15/25 Series: 3.5 pts.
35 Series : 4.4 pts

(5) Standard : 26 gal.
Optional : 34 gal.

(6) 15/25 Series : 1.4 pts.
35 Series : 2.75 pts.

(7) 15/25 Series :2.3 pts.
35 Series: 2.75 pts.

(8) Pick-up : Short-26: Long-34.
Chassis cab : Side-22; Rear-32.
1992-96 C3500 HD: Side-23 ; Rear-31.

(9) C3500 HD : 6.0 qts.

(10) 85mm : 3.6 pts.
NVG 4500 : 9.5 pts.

(11) K1/K2 : 2.8 pts.
K3 : 5.5 pts.

(12) NVG 4500 : 8.0 pts.
NVG 3500 : 4.4 pts.

(13) C3500 HD : w/AC-27; w/o AC-26.5

(14) C3500 HD : w/AC-28.5 ; w/o AC-26.5

(15) C3500 HD: 8 qts.

(16) C3500 HD : w/AC-27 ; w/AC-26.5

(17) 4L60 : 10.00 pts.
4L80E :15.4 pts.

(18) T-5 : 5.92 pts.
3500 : 4.4 pts.
4500 : 8.00 pts.

(19) 241 /243 : 4.5 pts.
233/231 : 2.5 pts.
4401/4470 : 6.6 pts.
4472 : 2.6 pts.

87981C13

ENGLISH TO METRIC CONVERSION: LENGTH

To convert inches (ins.) to millimeters (mm): multiply number of inches by 25.4

To convert millimeters (mm) to inches (ins.): multiply number of millimeters by .04

Inches	Decimals	Milli-meters	Inches to millimeters inches	mm	Inches	Decimals	Milli-meters	Inches to millimeters inches	mm
1/64	0.051625	0.3969	0.0001	0.00254	33/64	0.515625	13.0969	0.6	15.24
1/32	0.03125	0.7937	0.0002	0.00508	17/32	0.53125	13.4937	0.7	17.78
3/64	0.046875	1.1906	0.0003	0.00762	35/64	0.546875	13.8906	0.8	20.32
1/16	0.0625	1.5875	0.0004	0.01016	9/16	0.5625	14.2875	0.9	22.86
5/64	0.078125	1.9844	0.0005	0.01270	37/64	0.578125	14.6844	1	25.4
3/32	0.09375	2.3812	0.0006	0.01524	19/32	0.59375	15.0812	2	50.8
7/64	0.109375	2.7781	0.0007	0.01778	39/64	0.609375	15.4781	3	76.2
1/8	0.125	3.1750	0.0008	0.02032	5/8	0.625	15.8750	4	101.6
9/64	0.140625	3.5719	0.0009	0.02286	41/64	0.640625	16.2719	5	127.0
5/32	0.15625	3.9687	0.001	0.0254	21/32	0.65625	16.6687	6	152.4
11/64	0.171875	4.3656	0.002	0.0508	43/64	0.671875	17.0656	7	177.8
3/16	0.1875	4.7625	0.003	0.0762	11/16	0.6875	17.4625	8	203.2
13/64	0.203125	5.1594	0.004	0.1016	45/64	0.703125	17.8594	9	228.6
7/32	0.21875	5.5562	0.005	0.1270	23/32	0.71875	18.2562	10	254.0
15/64	0.234375	5.9531	0.006	0.1524	47/64	0.734375	18.6531	11	279.4
1/4	0.25	6.3500	0.007	0.1778	3/4	0.75	19.0500	12	304.8
17/64	0.265625	6.7469	0.008	0.2032	49/64	0.765625	19.4469	13	330.2
9/32	0.28125	7.1437	0.009	0.2286	25/32	0.78125	19.8437	14	355.6
19/64	0.296875	7.5406	0.01	0.254	51/64	0.796875	20.2406	15	381.0
5/16	0.3125	7.9375	0.02	0.508	13/16	0.8125	20.6375	16	406.4
21/64	0.328125	8.3344	0.03	0.762	53/64	0.828125	21.0344	17	431.8
11/32	0.34375	8.7312	0.04	1.016	27/32	0.84375	21.4312	18	457.2
23/64	0.359375	9.1281	0.05	1.270	55/64	0.859375	21.8281	19	482.6
3/8	0.375	9.5250	0.06	1.524	7/8	0.875	22.2250	20	508.0
25/64	0.390625	9.9219	0.07	1.778	57/64	0.890625	22.6219	21	533.4
13/32	0.40625	10.3187	0.08	2.032	29/32	0.90625	23.0187	22	558.8
27/64	0.421875	10.7156	0.09	2.286	59/64	0.921875	23.4156	23	584.2
7/16	0.4375	11.1125	0.1	2.54	15/16	0.9375	23.8125	24	609.6
29/64	0.453125	11.5094	0.2	5.08	61/64	0.953125	24.2094	25	635.0
15/32	0.46875	11.9062	0.3	7.62	31/32	0.96875	24.6062	26	660.4
31/64	0.484375	12.3031	0.4	10.16	63/64	0.984375	25.0031	27	690.6
1/2	0.5	12.7000	0.5	12.70					

ENGLISH TO METRIC CONVERSION: TORQUE

To convert foot-pounds (ft. lbs.) to Newton-meters: multiply the number of ft. lbs. by 1.3

To convert inch-pounds (in. lbs.) to Newton-meters: multiply the number of in. lbs. by .11

in lbs	N-m	in lbs	N-m	in lbs	N-m	in lbs	N-m	in lbs	N-m
0.1	0.01	1	0.11	10	1.13	19	2.15	28	3.16
0.2	0.02	2	0.23	11	1.24	20	2.26	29	3.28
0.3	0.03	3	0.34	12	1.36	21	2.37	30	3.39
0.4	0.04	4	0.45	13	1.47	22	2.49	31	3.50
0.5	0.06	5	0.56	14	1.58	23	2.60	32	3.62
0.6	0.07	6	0.68	15	1.70	24	2.71	33	3.73
0.7	0.08	7	0.78	16	1.81	25	2.82	34	3.84
0.8	0.09	8	0.90	17	1.92	26	2.94	35	3.95
0.9	0.10	9	1.02	18	2.03	27	3.05	36	4.07

tccs1c02

ENGLISH TO METRIC CONVERSION: TORQUE

Torque is now expressed as either foot-pounds (ft./lbs.) or inch-pounds (in./lbs.). The metric measurement unit for torque is the Newton-meter (Nm). This unit—the Nm—will be used for all SI metric torque references, both the present ft./lbs. and in./lbs.

ft lbs	N-m	ft lbs	N-m	ft lbs	N-m	ft lbs	N-m
0.1	0.1	33	44.7	74	100.3	115	155.9
0.2	0.3	34	46.1	75	101.7	116	157.3
0.3	0.4	35	47.4	76	103.0	117	158.6
0.4	0.5	36	48.8	77	104.4	118	160.0
0.5	0.7	37	50.7	78	105.8	119	161.3
0.6	0.8	38	51.5	79	107.1	120	162.7
0.7	1.0	39	52.9	80	108.5	121	164.0
0.8	1.1	40	54.2	81	109.8	122	165.4
0.9	1.2	41	55.6	82	111.2	123	166.8
1	1.3	42	56.9	83	112.5	124	168.1
2	2.7	43	58.3	84	113.9	125	169.5
3	4.1	44	59.7	85	115.2	126	170.8
4	5.4	45	61.0	86	116.6	127	172.2
5	6.8	46	62.4	87	118.0	128	173.5
6	8.1	47	63.7	88	119.3	129	174.9
7	9.5	48	65.1	89	120.7	130	176.2
8	10.8	49	66.4	90	122.0	131	177.6
9	12.2	50	67.8	91	123.4	132	179.0
10	13.6	51	69.2	92	124.7	133	180.3
11	14.9	52	70.5	93	126.1	134	181.7
12	16.3	53	71.9	94	127.4	135	183.0
13	17.6	54	73.2	95	128.8	136	184.4
14	18.9	55	74.6	96	130.2	137	185.7
15	20.3	56	75.9	97	131.5	138	187.1
16	21.7	57	77.3	98	132.9	139	188.5
17	23.0	58	78.6	99	134.2	140	189.8
18	24.4	59	80.0	100	135.6	141	191.2
19	25.8	60	81.4	101	136.9	142	192.5
20	27.1	61	82.7	102	138.3	143	193.9
21	28.5	62	84.1	103	139.6	144	195.2
22	29.8	63	85.4	104	141.0	145	196.6
23	31.2	64	86.8	105	142.4	146	198.0
24	32.5	65	88.1	106	143.7	147	199.3
25	33.9	66	89.5	107	145.1	148	200.7
26	35.2	67	90.8	108	146.4	149	202.0
27	36.6	68	92.2	109	147.8	150	203.4
28	38.0	69	93.6	110	149.1	151	204.7
29	39.3	70	94.9	111	150.5	152	206.1
30	40.7	71	96.3	112	151.8	153	207.4
31	42.0	72	97.6	113	153.2	154	208.8
32	43.4	73	99.0	114	154.6	155	210.2

tccs1c03

ENGLISH TO METRIC CONVERSION: FORCE

Force is presently measured in pounds (lbs.). This type of measurement is used to measure spring pressure, specifically how many pounds it takes to compress a spring. Our present force unit (the pound) will be replaced in SI metric measurements by the Newton (N). This term will eventually see use in specifications for electric motor brush spring pressures, valve spring pressures, etc.

To convert pounds (lbs.) to Newton (N): multiply the number of lbs. by 4.45

lbs	N	lbs	N	lbs	N	oz	N
0.01	0.04	21	93.4	59	262.4	1	0.3
0.02	0.09	22	97.9	60	266.9	2	0.6
0.03	0.13	23	102.3	61	271.3	3	0.8
0.04	0.18	24	106.8	62	275.8	4	1.1
0.05	0.22	25	111.2	63	280.2	5	1.4
0.06	0.27	26	115.6	64	284.6	6	1.7
0.07	0.31	27	120.1	65	289.1	7	2.0
0.08	0.36	28	124.6	66	293.6	8	2.2
0.09	0.40	29	129.0	67	298.0	9	2.5
0.1	0.4	30	133.4	68	302.5	10	2.8
0.2	0.9	31	137.9	69	306.9	11	3.1
0.3	1.3	32	142.3	70	311.4	12	3.3
0.4	1.8	33	146.8	71	315.8	13	3.6
0.5	2.2	34	151.2	72	320.3	14	3.9
0.6	2.7	35	155.7	73	324.7	15	4.2
0.7	3.1	36	160.1	74	329.2	16	4.4
0.8	3.6	37	164.6	75	333.6	17	4.7
0.9	4.0	38	169.0	76	338.1	18	5.0
1	4.4	39	173.5	77	342.5	19	5.3
2	8.9	40	177.9	78	347.0	20	5.6
3	13.4	41	182.4	79	351.4	21	5.8
4	17.8	42	186.8	80	355.9	22	6.1
5	22.2	43	191.3	81	360.3	23	6.4
6	26.7	44	195.7	82	364.8	24	6.7
7	31.1	45	200.2	83	369.2	25	7.0
8	35.6	46	204.6	84	373.6	26	7.2
9	40.0	47	209.1	85	378.1	27	7.5
10	44.5	48	213.5	86	382.6	28	7.8
11	48.9	49	218.0	87	387.0	29	8.1
12	53.4	50	224.4	88	391.4	30	8.3
13	57.8	51	226.9	89	395.9	31	8.6
14	62.3	52	231.3	90	400.3	32	8.9
15	66.7	53	235.8	91	404.8	33	9.2
16	71.2	54	240.2	92	409.2	34	9.4
17	75.6	55	244.6	93	413.7	35	9.7
18	80.1	56	249.1	94	418.1	36	10.0
19	84.5	57	253.6	95	422.6	37	10.3
20	89.0	58	258.0	96	427.0	38	10.6

tccs1c04

ENGLISH TO METRIC CONVERSION: LIQUID CAPACITY

Liquid or fluid capacity is presently expressed as pints, quarts or gallons, or a combination of all of these. In the metric system the liter (l) will become the basic unit. Fractions of a liter would be expressed as deciliters, centiliters, or most frequently (and commonly) as milliliters.

To convert pints (pts.) to liters (l): multiply the number of pints by .47
To convert liters (l) to pints (pts.): multiply the number of liters by 2.1
To convert quarts (qts.) to liters (l): multiply the number of quarts by .95

To convert liters (l) to quarts (qts.): multiply the number of liters by 1.06
To convert gallons (gals.) to liters (l): multiply the number of gallons by 3.8
To convert liters (l) to gallons (gals.): multiply the number of liters by .26

gals	liters	qts	liters	pts	liters
0.1	0.38	0.1	0.10	0.1	0.05
0.2	0.76	0.2	0.19	0.2	0.10
0.3	1.1	0.3	0.28	0.3	0.14
0.4	1.5	0.4	0.38	0.4	0.19
0.5	1.9	0.5	0.47	0.5	0.24
0.6	2.3	0.6	0.57	0.6	0.28
0.7	2.6	0.7	0.66	0.7	0.33
0.8	3.0	0.8	0.76	0.8	0.38
0.9	3.4	0.9	0.85	0.9	0.43
1	3.8	1	1.0	1	0.5
2	7.6	2	1.9	2	1.0
3	11.4	3	2.8	3	1.4
4	15.1	4	3.8	4	1.9
5	18.9	5	4.7	5	2.4
6	22.7	6	5.7	6	2.8
7	26.5	7	6.6	7	3.3
8	30.3	8	7.6	8	3.8
9	34.1	9	8.5	9	4.3
10	37.8	10	9.5	10	4.7
11	41.6	11	10.4	11	5.2
12	45.4	12	11.4	12	5.7
13	49.2	13	12.3	13	6.2
14	53.0	14	13.2	14	6.6
15	56.8	15	14.2	15	7.1
16	60.6	16	15.1	16	7.6
17	64.3	17	16.1	17	8.0
18	68.1	18	17.0	18	8.5
19	71.9	19	18.0	19	9.0
20	75.7	20	18.9	20	9.5
21	79.5	21	19.9	21	9.9
22	83.2	22	20.8	22	10.4
23	87.0	23	21.8	23	10.9
24	90.8	24	22.7	24	11.4
25	94.6	25	23.6	25	11.8
26	98.4	26	24.6	26	12.3
27	102.2	27	25.5	27	12.8
28	106.0	28	26.5	28	13.2
29	110.0	29	27.4	29	13.7
30	113.5	30	28.4	30	14.2

tccs1c05

ENGLISH TO METRIC CONVERSION: PRESSURE

The basic unit of pressure measurement used today is expressed as pounds per square inch (psi). The metric unit for psi will be the kilopascal (kPa). This will apply to either fluid pressure or air pressure, and will be frequently seen in tire pressure readings, oil pressure specifications, fuel pump pressure, etc.

To convert pounds per square inch (psi) to kilopascals (kPa): multiply the number of psi by 6.89

Psi	kPa	Psi	kPa	Psi	kPa	Psi	kPa
0.1	0.7	37	255.1	82	565.4	127	875.6
0.2	1.4	38	262.0	83	572.3	128	882.5
0.3	2.1	39	268.9	84	579.2	129	889.4
0.4	2.8	40	275.8	85	586.0	130	896.3
0.5	3.4	41	282.7	86	592.9	131	903.2
0.6	4.1	42	289.6	87	599.8	132	910.1
0.7	4.8	43	296.5	88	606.7	133	917.0
0.8	5.5	44	303.4	89	613.6	134	923.9
0.9	6.2	45	310.3	90	620.5	135	930.8
1	6.9	46	317.2	91	627.4	136	937.7
2	13.8	47	324.0	92	634.3	137	944.6
3	20.7	48	331.0	93	641.2	138	951.5
4	27.6	49	337.8	94	648.1	139	958.4
5	34.5	50	344.7	95	655.0	140	965.2
6	41.4	51	351.6	96	661.9	141	972.2
7	48.3	52	358.5	97	668.8	142	979.0
8	55.2	53	365.4	98	675.7	143	985.9
9	62.1	54	372.3	99	682.6	144	992.8
10	69.0	55	379.2	100	689.5	145	999.7
11	75.8	56	386.1	101	696.4	146	1006.6
12	82.7	57	393.0	102	703.3	147	1013.5
13	89.6	58	399.9	103	710.2	148	1020.4
14	96.5	59	406.8	104	717.0	149	1027.3
15	103.4	60	413.7	105	723.9	150	1034.2
16	110.3	61	420.6	106	730.8	151	1041.1
17	117.2	62	427.5	107	737.7	152	1048.0
18	124.1	63	434.4	108	744.6	153	1054.9
19	131.0	64	441.3	109	751.5	154	1061.8
20	137.9	65	448.2	110	758.4	155	1068.7
21	144.8	66	455.0	111	765.3	156	1075.6
22	151.7	67	461.9	112	772.2	157	1082.5
23	158.6	68	468.8	113	779.1	158	1089.4
24	165.5	69	475.7	114	786.0	159	1096.3
25	172.4	70	482.6	115	792.9	160	1103.2
26	179.3	71	489.5	116	799.8	161	1110.0
27	186.2	72	496.4	117	806.7	162	1116.9
28	193.0	73	503.3	118	813.6	163	1123.8
29	200.0	74	510.2	119	820.5	164	1130.7
30	206.8	75	517.1	120	827.4	165	1137.6
31	213.7	76	524.0	121	834.3	166	1144.5
32	220.6	77	530.9	122	841.2	167	1151.4
33	227.5	78	537.8	123	848.0	168	1158.3
34	234.4	79	544.7	124	854.9	169	1165.2
35	241.3	80	551.6	125	861.8	170	1172.1
36	248.2	81	558.5	126	868.7	171	1179.0

tccs1c06

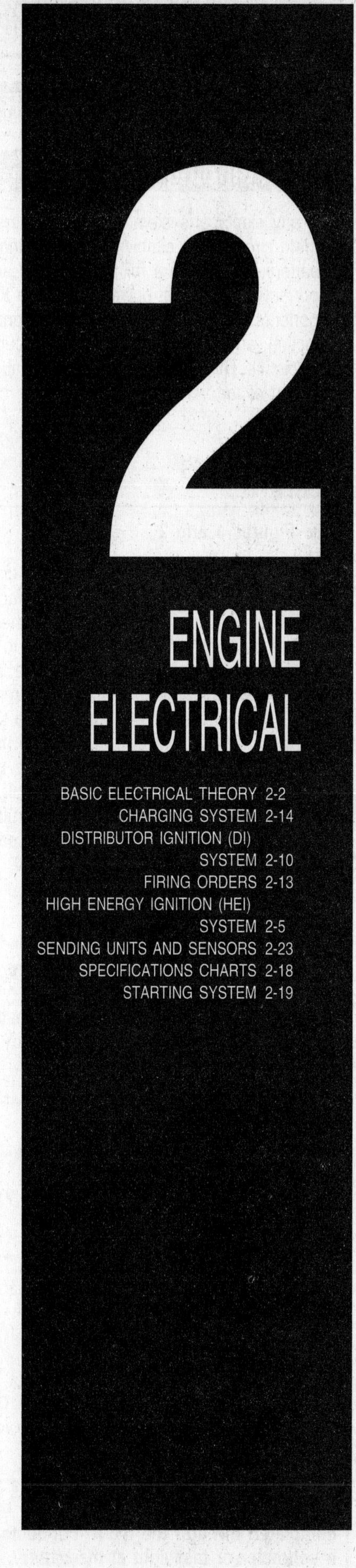

2 ENGINE ELECTRICAL

BASIC ELECTRICAL THEORY

Understanding Electricity

For any electrical system to operate, there must be a complete circuit. This simply means that the power flow from the battery must make a full circle. When an electrical component is operating, power flows from the battery to the components, passes through the component (load) causing it to function, and returns to the battery through the ground path of the circuit. This ground may be either another wire or a metal part of the vehicle (depending upon how the component is designed).

BASIC CIRCUITS

See Figures 1 and 2

Perhaps the easiest way to visualize a circuit is to think of connecting a light bulb (with two wires attached to it) to the battery. If one of the two wires was attached to the negative post (-) of the battery and the other wire to the positive post (+), the circuit would be complete and the light bulb would illuminate. Electricity could follow a path from the battery to the bulb and back to the battery. It's not hard to see that with longer wires on our light bulb, it could be mounted anywhere on the vehicle. Further, one wire could be fitted with a switch so that the light could be turned on and off. Various other items could be added to our primitive circuit to make the light flash, become brighter or dimmer under certain conditions, or advise the user that it's burned out.

Ground

Some automotive components are grounded through their mounting points. The electrical current runs through the chassis of the vehicle and returns to the battery through the ground (-) cable; if you look, you'll see that the battery ground cable connects between the battery and the body of the vehicle.

Load

Every complete circuit must include a "load" (something to use the electricity coming from the source). If you were to connect a wire between the two terminals of the battery (DON'T do this, but take out word for it) without the light bulb, the battery would attempt to deliver its entire power supply from one pole to another almost instantly. This is a short circuit. The electricity is taking a short cut to get to ground and is not being used by any load in the circuit. This sudden and uncontrolled electrical flow can cause great damage to other components in the circuit and can develop a tremendous amount of heat. A short in an automotive wiring harness can develop sufficient heat to melt the insulation on all the surrounding wires and reduce a multiple wire cable to one sad lump of plastic and copper. Two common causes of shorts are broken insulation (thereby exposing the wire to contact with surrounding metal surfaces or other wires) or a failed switch (the pins inside the switch come out of place and touch each other).

Switches and Relays

Some electrical components which require a large amount of current to operate also have a relay in their circuit. Since these circuits carry a large amount of current (amperage or amps), the thickness of the wire in the circuit (wire gauge) is also greater. If this large wire were connected from the load to the control switch on the dash, the switch would have to carry the high amperage load and the dash would be twice as large to accommodate wiring harnesses as thick as your wrist. To prevent these problems, a relay is used. The large wires in the circuit are connected from the battery to one side of the relay and from the opposite side of the relay to the load. The relay is normally open, preventing current from passing through the circuit. An additional, smaller wire is connected from the relay to the control switch for the circuit. When the control switch is turned on, it grounds the smaller wire to the relay and completes its circuit. The main switch inside the relay closes, sending power to the component without routing the main

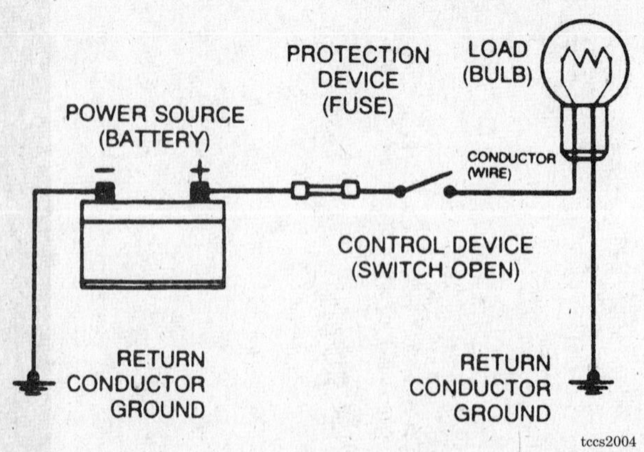

Fig. 1 Here is an example of a simple automotive circuit. When the switch is closed, power from the positive battery terminal flows through the fuse, then the switch and to the load (light bulb), the light illuminates and then, the circuit is completed through the return conductor and the vehicle ground. If the light did not work, the tests could be made with a voltmeter or test light at the battery, fuse, switch or bulb socket

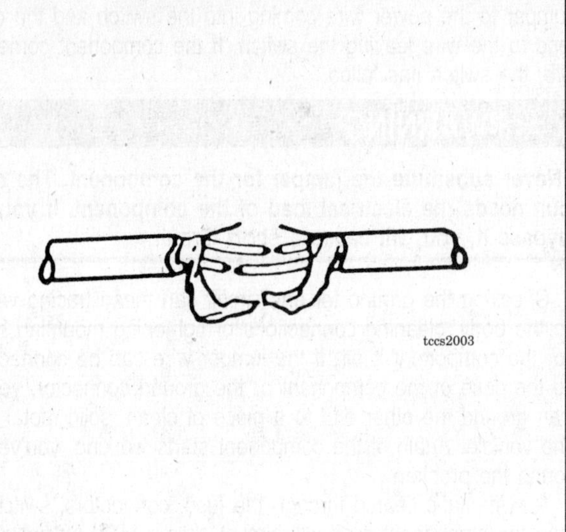

Fig. 2 Damaged insulation can allow wires to break (causing an open circuit) or touch (causing a short)

power through the inside of the vehicle. Some common circuits which may use relays are the horn, headlights, starter and rear window defogger systems.

Protective Devices

It is possible for larger surges of current to pass through the electrical system of your vehicle. If this surge of current were to reach the load in the circuit, it could burn it out or severely damage it. To prevent this, fuses, circuit breakers and/or fusible links are connected into the supply wires of the electrical system. These items are nothing more than a built-in weak spot in the system. It's much easier to go to a known location (the fusebox) to see why a circuit is inoperative than to dissect 15 feet of wiring under the dashboard, looking for what happened.

When an electrical current of excessive power passes through the fuse, the fuse blows (the conductor melts) and breaks the circuit, preventing the passage of current and protecting the components.

A circuit breaker is basically a self repairing fuse. It will open the circuit in the same fashion as a fuse, but when either the short is removed or the surge subsides, the circuit breaker resets itself and does not need replacement.

A fuse link (fusible link or main link) is a wire that acts as a fuse. One of these is normally connected between the starter relay and the main wiring harness under the hood. Since the starter is usually the highest electrical draw on the vehicle, an internal short during starting could direct about 130 amps into the wrong places. Consider the damage potential of introducing this current into a system whose wiring is rated at 15 amps and you'll understand the need for protection. Since this link is very early in the electrical path, it's the first place to look if nothing on the vehicle works, but the battery seems to be charged and is properly connected.

TROUBLESHOOTING

➧ See Figures 3, 4 and 5

Electrical problems generally fall into one of three areas:

- The component that is not functioning is not receiving current.
- The component is receiving power but is not using it or is using it incorrectly (component failure).
- The component is improperly grounded.

The circuit can be can be checked with a test light and a jumper wire. The test light is a device that looks like a pointed screwdriver with a wire on one end and a bulb in its handle. A jumper wire is simply a piece of wire with alligator clips or special terminals on each end. If a component is not working,

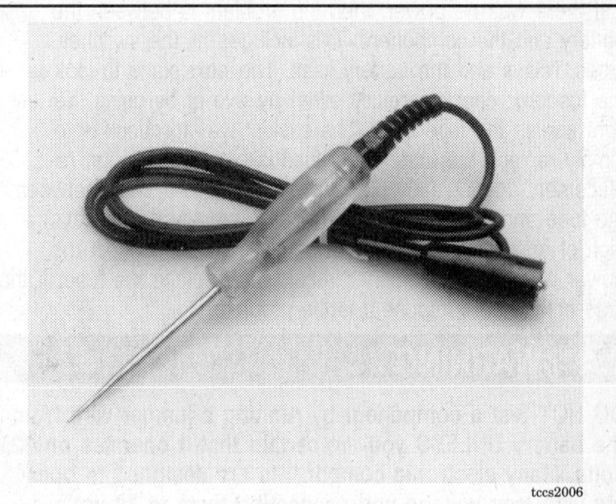

Fig. 3 A 12 volt test light is useful when checking parts of a circuit for power

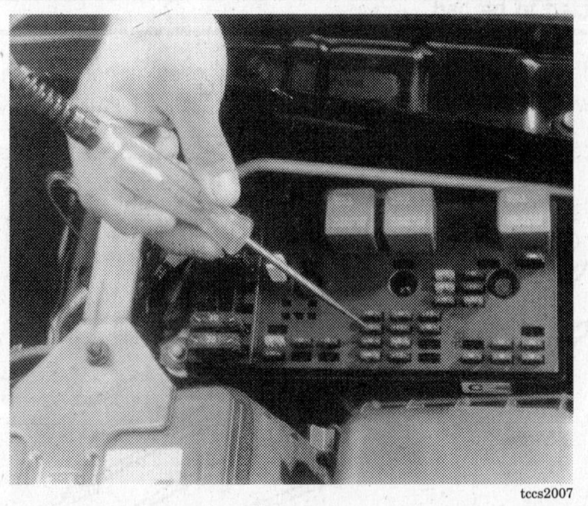

Fig. 4 Here, someone is checking a circuit by making sure there is power to the component's fuse

you must follow a systematic plan to determine which of the three causes is the villain.

1. Turn ON the switch that controls the item not working.

➡**Some items only work when the ignition switch is turned ON.**

2. Disconnect the power supply wire from the component.
3. Attach the ground wire of a test light or a voltmeter to a good metal ground.
4. Touch the end probe of the test light (or the positive lead of the voltmeter) to the power wire; if there is current in the wire, the light in the test light will come on (or the voltmeter will indicate the amount of voltage). You have now established that current is getting to the component.
5. Turn the ignition or dash switch **OFF** and reconnect the wire to the component.

If there was no power, then the problem is between the battery and the component. This includes all the switches, fuses, relays and the battery itself. The next place to look is the fusebox; check carefully either by eye or by using the test light across the fuse clips. The easiest way to check is to simply replace the fuse. If the fuse is blown, and upon replacement, immediately blows again, there is a short between the fuse and the component. This is generally (not always) a sign of an internal short in the component. Disconnect the power wire at the component again and replace the fuse; if the fuse holds, the component is the problem.

****WARNING**

DO NOT test a component by running a jumper wire from the battery UNLESS you are certain that it operates on 12 volts. Many electronic components are designed to operate with less voltage and connecting them to 12 volts could destroy them. Jumper wires are best used to bypass a portion of the circuit (such as a stretch of wire or a switch) that DOES NOT contain a resistor and is suspected to be bad.

If all the fuses are good and the component is not receiving power, find the switch for the circuit. Bypass the switch with the jumper wire. This is done by connecting one end of the jumper to the power wire coming into the switch and the other end to the wire leaving the switch. If the component comes to life, the switch has failed.

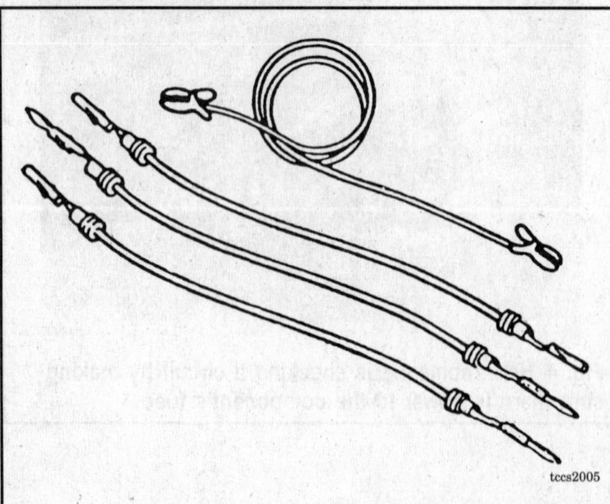

Fig. 5 Jumper wires with various connectors are handy for quick electrical testing

****WARNING**

Never substitute the jumper for the component. The circuit needs the electrical load of the component. If you bypass it, you will cause a short circuit.

Checking the ground for any circuit can mean tracing wires to the body, cleaning connections or tightening mounting bolts for the component itself. If the jumper wire can be connected to the case of the component or the ground connector, you can ground the other end to a piece of clean, solid metal on the vehicle. Again, if the component starts working, you've found the problem.

A systematic search through the fuse, connectors, switches and the component itself will almost always yield an answer. Loose and/or corroded connectors, particularly in ground circuits, are becoming a larger problem in modern vehicles. The computers and on-board electronic (solid state) systems are highly sensitive to improper grounds and will change their function drastically if one occurs.

Remember that for any electrical circuit to work, ALL the connections must be clean and tight.

➡**For more information on Understanding and Troubleshooting Electrical Systems, please refer to Section 6 of this manual.**

Battery, Starting and Charging Systems

BASIC OPERATING PRINCIPLES

Battery

The battery is the first link in the chain of mechanisms which work together to provide cranking of the automobile engine. In most modern vehicles, the battery is a lead/acid electrochemical device consisting of six 2v subsections (cells) connected in series so the unit is capable of producing approximately 12v of electrical pressure. Each subsection consists of a series of positive and negative plates held a short distance apart in a solution of sulfuric acid and water.

The two types of plates are of dissimilar metals. This sets-up a chemical reaction, and it is this reaction which produces current flow from the battery when its positive and negative terminals are connected to an electrical accessory such as a lamp or motor. The continued transfer of electrons would eventually convert the sulfuric acid to water, and make the two plates identical in chemical composition. As electrical energy is removed from the battery, its voltage output tends to drop. Thus, measuring battery voltage and battery electrolyte composition are two ways of checking the ability of the unit to supply power. During engine cranking, electrical energy is removed from the battery. However, if the charging circuit is in good condition and the operating conditions are normal, the power removed from the battery will be replaced by the alternator which will force electrons back through the battery, reversing the normal flow, and restoring the battery to its original chemical state.

Starting System

The battery and starting motor are linked by very heavy electrical cables designed to minimize resistance to the flow of current. Generally, the major power supply cable that leaves the battery goes directly to the starter, while other electrical system needs are supplied by a smaller cable. During starter operation, power flows from the battery to the starter and is grounded through the vehicle's frame/body or engine and the battery's negative ground strap.

The starter is a specially designed, direct current electric motor capable of producing a great amount of power for its size. One thing that allows the motor to produce a great deal of power is its tremendous rotating speed. It drives the engine through a tiny pinion gear (attached to the starter's armature), which drives the very large flywheel ring gear at a greatly reduced speed. Another factor allowing it to produce so much power is that only intermittent operation is required of it. Thus, little allowance for air circulation is necessary, and the windings can be built into a very small space.

The starter solenoid is a magnetic device which employs the small current supplied by the start circuit of the ignition switch. This magnetic action moves a plunger which mechanically engages the starter and closes the heavy switch connecting it to the battery. The starting switch circuit usually consists of the starting switch contained within the ignition switch, a neutral safety switch or clutch pedal switch, and the wiring necessary to connect these in series with the starter solenoid or relay.

The pinion, a small gear, is mounted to a one way drive clutch. This clutch is splined to the starter armature shaft. When the ignition switch is moved to the **START** position, the solenoid plunger slides the pinion toward the flywheel ring gear via a collar and spring. If the teeth on the pinion and flywheel match properly, the pinion will engage the flywheel immediately. If the gear teeth butt one another, the spring will be compressed and will force the gears to mesh as soon as the starter turns far enough to allow them to do so. As the solenoid plunger reaches the end of its travel, it closes the contacts that connect the battery and starter, then the engine is cranked.

As soon as the engine starts, the flywheel ring gear begins turning fast enough to drive the pinion at an extremely high rate of speed. At this point, the one-way clutch begins allowing the pinion to spin faster than the starter shaft so that the starter will not operate at excessive speed. When the ignition switch is released from the starter position, the solenoid is de-energized, and a spring pulls the gear out of mesh interrupting the current flow to the starter.

Some starters employ a separate relay, mounted away from the starter, to switch the motor and solenoid current on and off. The relay replaces the solenoid electrical switch, but does not eliminate the need for a solenoid mounted on the starter used to mechanically engage the starter drive gears. The relay is used to reduce the amount of current the starting switch must carry.

Charging System

The automobile charging system provides electrical power for operation of the vehicle's ignition system, starting system and all electrical accessories. The battery serves as an electrical surge or storage tank, storing (in chemical form) the energy originally produced by the engine driven generator. The system also provides a means of regulating output to protect the battery from being overcharged and to avoid excessive voltage to the accessories.

The storage battery is a chemical device incorporating parallel lead plates in a tank containing a sulfuric acid/water solution. Adjacent plates are slightly dissimilar, and the chemical reaction of the two dissimilar plates produces electrical energy when the battery is connected to a load such as the starter motor. The chemical reaction is reversible, so that when the generator is producing a voltage (electrical pressure) greater than that produced by the battery, electricity is forced into the battery, and the battery is returned to its fully charged state.

Newer automobiles use alternating current generators or alternators, because they are more efficient, can be rotated at higher speeds, and have fewer brush problems. In an alternator, the field usually rotates while all the current produced passes only through the stator winding. The brushes bear against continuous slip rings. This causes the current produced to periodically reverse the direction of its flow. Diodes (electrical one way valves) block the flow of current from traveling in the wrong direction. A series of diodes is wired together to permit the alternating flow of the stator to be rectified back to 12 volts DC for use by the vehicle's electrical system.

The voltage regulating function is performed by a regulator. The regulator is often built in to the alternator; this system is termed an integrated or internal regulator.

HIGH ENERGY IGNITION (HEI) SYSTEM

Description And Operation

▸ **See Figures 6 and 7**

The General Motors HEI system is a pulse-triggered, transistorized controlled, inductive discharge ignition system. The entire HEI system (except for the ignition coil) is contained within the distributor cap.

The distributor, in addition to housing the mechanical and vacuum advance mechanisms, contains the electronic control module, and the magnetic triggering device. The magnetic pick-up assembly contains a permanent magnet, a pole piece with internal teeth, and a pick-up coil (not to be confused with the ignition coil).

In the HEI system, as in other electronic ignition systems, the breaker points have been replaced with an electronic switch — a transistor — which is located within the control module. This switching transistor performs the same function the points did in an conventional ignition system. It simply turns coil primary current on and off at the correct time. Essentially then, electronic and conventional ignition systems operate on the same principle.

The module which houses the switching transistor is controlled (turned on and off) by a magnetically generated impulse induced in the pick-up coil. When the teeth of the rotating

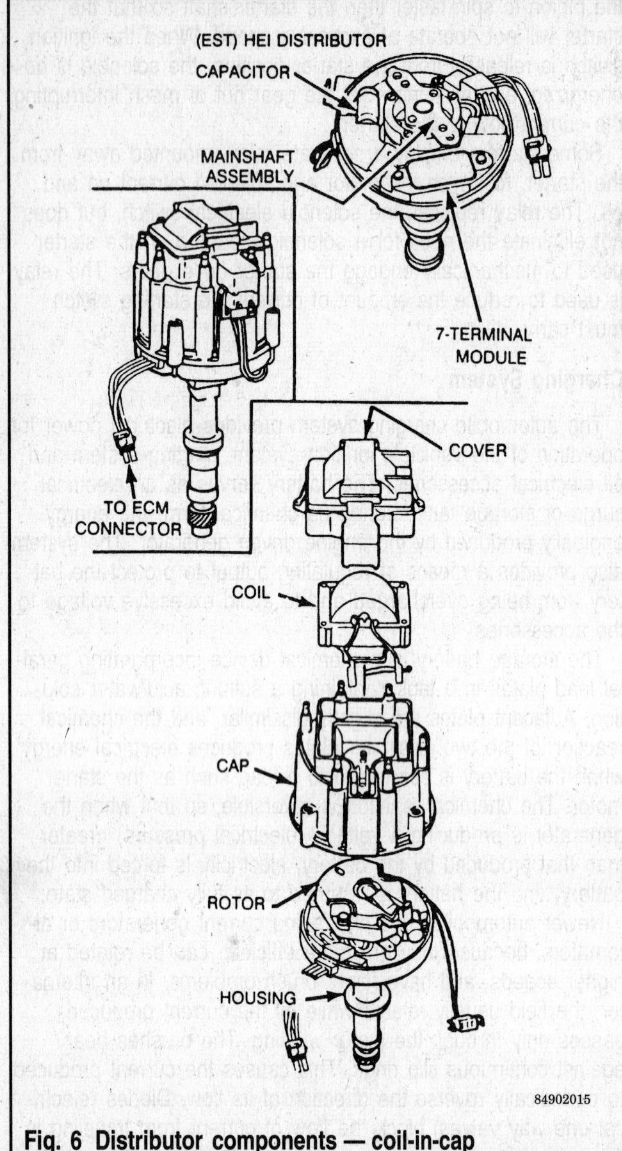

Fig. 6 Distributor components — coil-in-cap

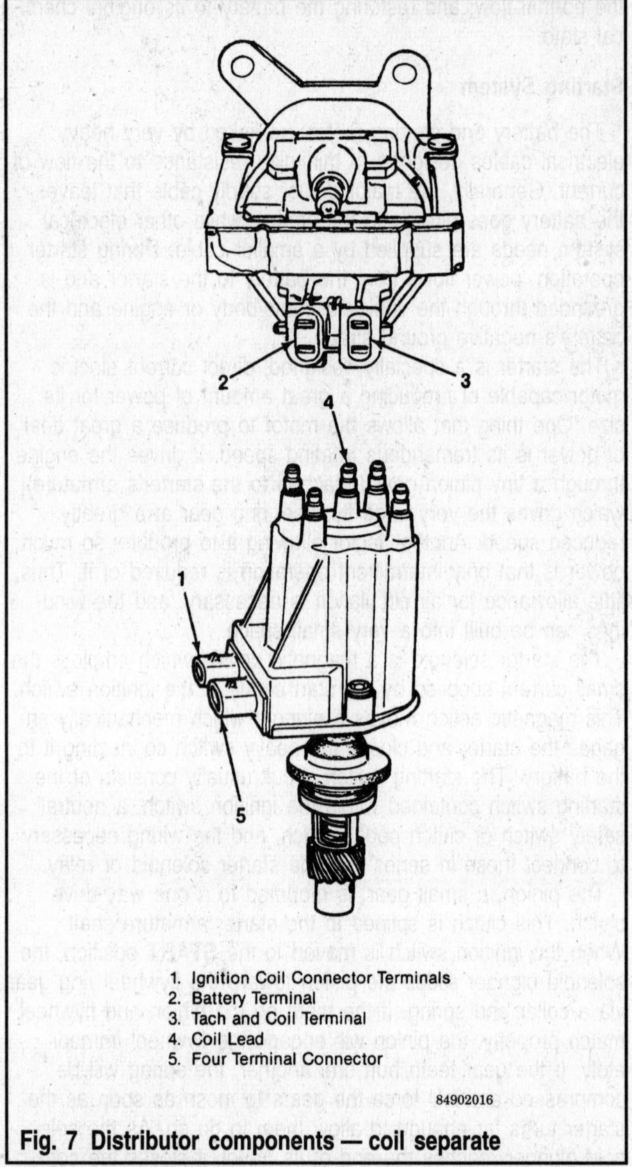

Fig. 7 Distributor components — coil separate

timer align with the teeth of the pole piece, the induced voltage in the pick-up coil signals the electronic module to open the coil primary circuit. The primary current then decreases, and a high voltage is induced in the ignition coil secondary windings which is then directed through the rotor and high voltage leads (spark plug wires) to fire the spark plugs.

In essence then, the pick-up coil module system simply replaces the conventional breaker points and condenser. The condenser found within the distributor is for radio suppression purposes only and has nothing to do with the ignition process. The module automatically controls the dwell period, increasing it with increasing engine speed. Since dwell is automatically controlled, it cannot be adjusted. The module itself is non-adjustable and non-repairable and must be replaced if found defective.

HEI SYSTEM PRECAUTIONS

Before going on to troubleshooting, it might be a good idea to take note of the following precautions:

Timing Light Use

Inductive pick-up timing lights are the best kind to use if your truck is equipped with HEI. Timing lights which connect between the spark plug and the spark plug wire occasionally (not always) give false readings.

Spark Plug Wires

The plug wires used with HEI systems are of a different construction than conventional wires. When replacing them, make sure you get the correct wires, since conventional wires won't carry the voltage. Also, handle them carefully to avoid cracking or splitting them and never pierce them.

Tachometer Use

Not all tachometers will operate or indicate correctly when used on a HEI system. While some tachometers may give a reading, this does not necessarily mean the reading is correct. In addition, some tachometers hook up differently from others. If you can't figure out whether or not your tachometer will work on your truck, check with the tachometer manufacturer.

HEI Systems Testers

Instruments designed specifically for testing HEI systems are available from several tool manufacturers. Some of these will even test the module itself. However, the tests given in the following section will require only an ohmmeter and a voltmeter.

Diagnosis and Testing

The symptoms of a defective component within the HEI system are exactly the same as those you would encounter in a conventional system. Some of these symptoms are:

- Hard or no Starting
- Rough Idle
- Fuel Poor Economy
- Engine misses under load or while accelerating

If you suspect a problem in the ignition system, there are certain preliminary checks which you should carry out before you begin to check the electronic portions of the system. First, it is extremely important to make sure the vehicle battery is in a good state of charge. A defective or poorly charged battery will cause the various components of the ignition system to read incorrectly when they are being tested. Second, make sure all wiring connections are clean and tight, not only at the battery, but also at the distributor cap, ignition coil, and at the electronic control module.

SECONDARY SPARK TEST

Since the only change between electronic and conventional ignition systems is in the distributor component area, it is imperative to check the secondary ignition circuit first. If the secondary circuit checks out properly, then the engine condition is probably not the fault of the ignition system. To check the secondary ignition system, perform a simple spark test.

1. Remove one of the plug wires and insert some sort of extension in the plug socket. An old spark plug with the ground electrode removed makes a good extension.
2. Hold the wire and extension about 1/4 in. (.009mm) away from the block and crank the engine. If a normal spark occurs, then the problem is most likely not in the ignition system.
3. Check for fuel system problems, or fouled spark plugs.
4. If, however, there is no spark or a weak spark, then further ignition system testing will have to be done. Troubleshooting techniques fall into two categories, depending on the nature of the problem. The categories are (1) Engine cranks, but won't start or (2) Engine runs, but runs rough or cuts out.

Engine Fails to Start

1. If the engine won't start, perform a spark test as described earlier. If no spark occurs, check for the presence of normal battery voltage at the battery (**BAT**) terminal in the distributor cap. The ignition switch must be in the **ON** position for this test.
2. If battery voltage is not present, this indicates an open circuit in the ignition primary wiring leading to the distributor. In this case, you will have to check wiring continuity back to the ignition switch using a test light.
3. If there is battery voltage at the **BAT** terminal, but no spark at the plugs, then the problem lies within the distributor assembly. Go on to test the ignition coil.

Engine Runs, but Runs Roughly or Cuts Out

1. Make sure the plug wires are in good shape first. There should be no obvious cracks or breaks. You can check the plug wires with an ohmmeter, but do not pierce the wires with a probe.
2. If the plug wires are OK, remove the cap assembly, and check for moisture, cracks, chips, or carbon tracks, or any other high voltage leaks or failures.
3. Replace the cap if you find any defects. Make sure the timer wheel rotates when the engine is cranked. If everything is all right so far, go on to test the ignition coil.

IGNITION COIL

Carbureted Engines

1. Connect an ohmmeter between the **TACH** and **BAT** terminals in the distributor cap. The primary coil resistance should be less than one ohm (zero or nearly zero).
2. To check the coil secondary resistance, connect an ohmmeter between the rotor button and the **BAT** terminal. Then connect the ohmmeter between the ground terminal and the rotor button. The resistance in both cases should be between 6000 and 30,000 ohms.
3. Replace the coil only if the readings in Step 1 and 2 are infinite.

➡These resistance checks will not disclose shorted coil windings. This condition can be detected only with scope analysis or a suitably designed coil tester. If these instruments are unavailable, replace the coil with a known good coil as a final coil test.

Fuel Injected Engines

See Figure 8

1. Tag and disconnect the distributor lead and wiring from the coil.
2. Connect an ohmmeter as shown in Step 1 of the accompanying illustration. Place the ohmmeter on the high scale. The reading should be infinite.
3. Connect an ohmmeter as shown in Step 2 of the same illustration. Place the ohmmeter on the low scale. The reading should be very low or zero. If not replace the coil.
4. Connect an ohmmeter as shown in Step 3 of the same illustration. Place the ohmmeter on the high scale. The meter should not read infinite. If it does replace the coil.
5. Connect the distributor lead and wiring.

PICK-UP COIL

See Figures 9, 10 and 11

1. To test the pick-up coil, first disconnect the white and green module leads. Set the ohmmeter on the high scale and connect it between a ground and either the white or green

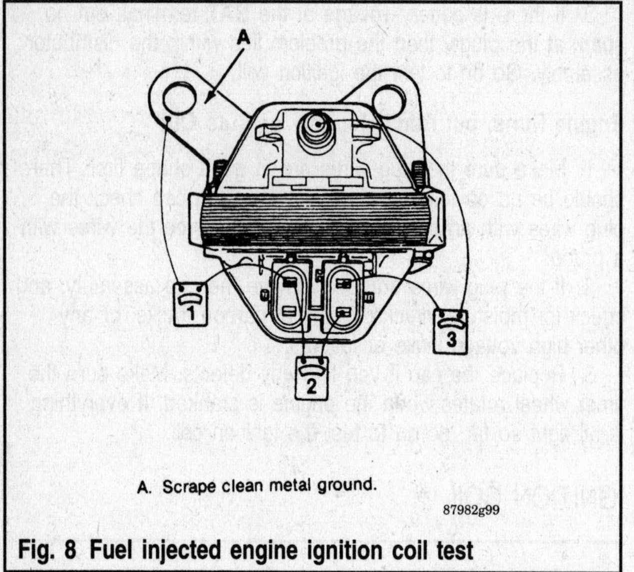

Fig. 8 Fuel injected engine ignition coil test

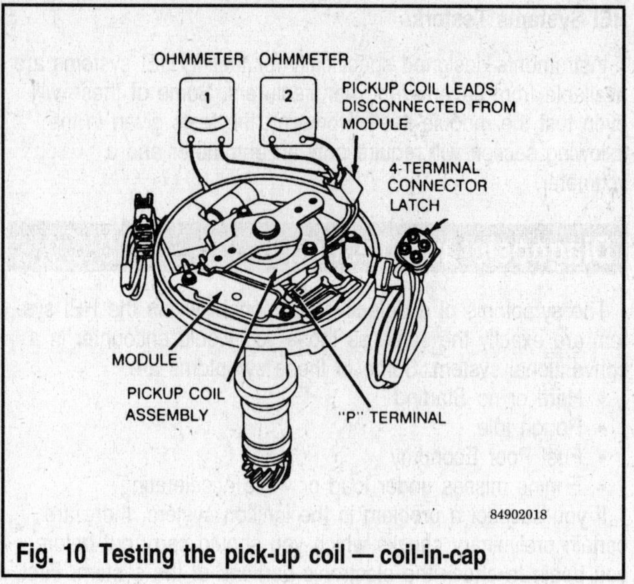

Fig. 10 Testing the pick-up coil — coil-in-cap

lead. Any resistance measurement less than infinity requires replacement of the pick-up coil.

2. Pick-up coil continuity is tested by connecting the ohmmeter (on low range) between the white and green leads. Normal resistance is between 500 and 1500 ohms. Move the vacuum advance arm while performing this test. This will detect any break in coil continuity. Such a condition can cause intermittent misfiring. Replace the pick-up coil if the reading is outside the specified limits.

3. If no defects have been found at this time, and you still have a problem, then the module will have to be checked. If you do not have access to a module tester, the only possible alternative is a substitution test. If the module fails the substitution test, replace it.

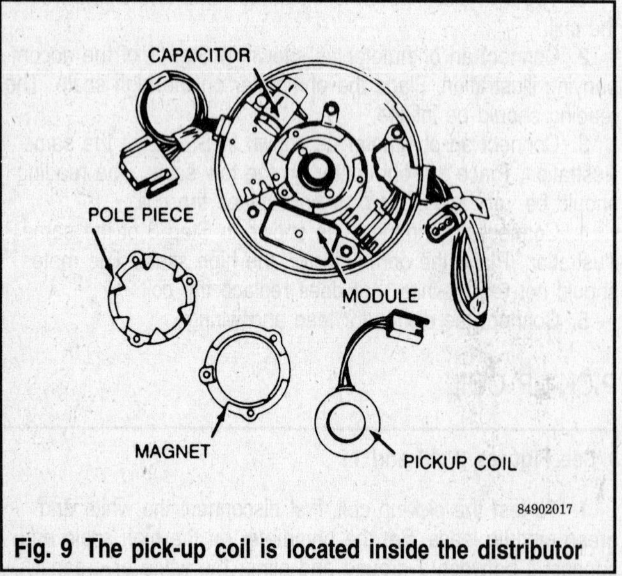

Fig. 9 The pick-up coil is located inside the distributor

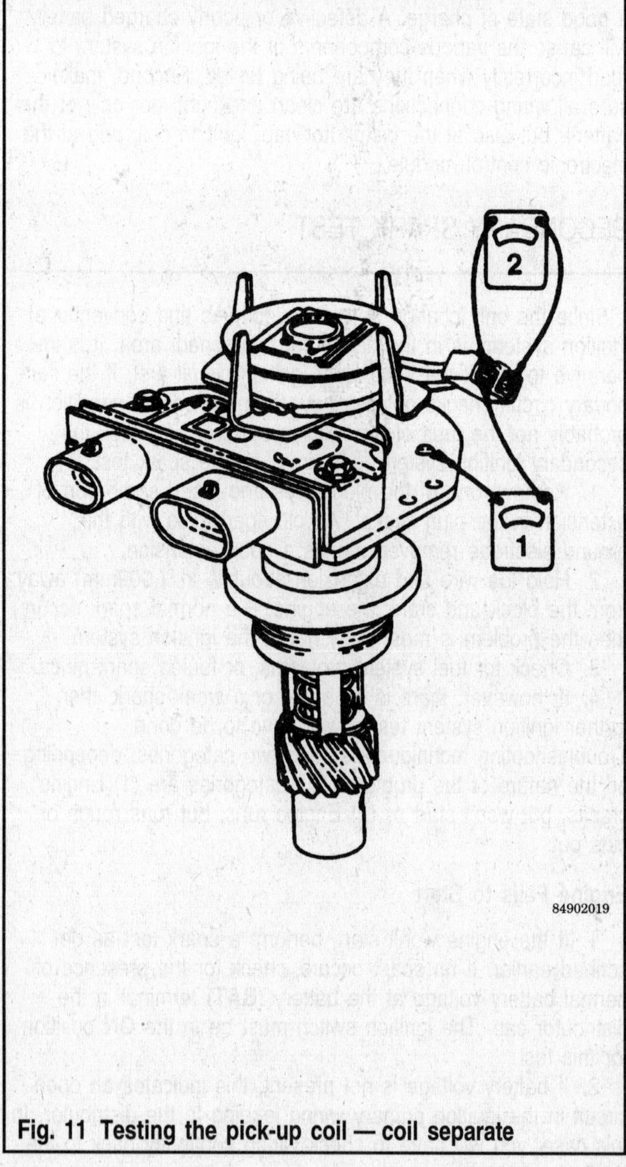

Fig. 11 Testing the pick-up coil — coil separate

Ignition Coil

REMOVAL & INSTALLATION

Carbureted Engines

➧ See Figure 12

1. Disconnect the feed and module wire terminal connectors from the distributor cap.
2. Remove the ignition set retainer.
3. Remove the 4 coil cover-to-distributor cap screws and coil cover.
4. Remove the 4 coil-to-distributor cap screws.
5. Using a blunt drift, press the coil wire spade terminals up out of distributor cap.
6. Lift the coil up out of the distributor cap.
7. Remove and clean the coil spring, rubber seal washer and coil cavity of the distributor cap.

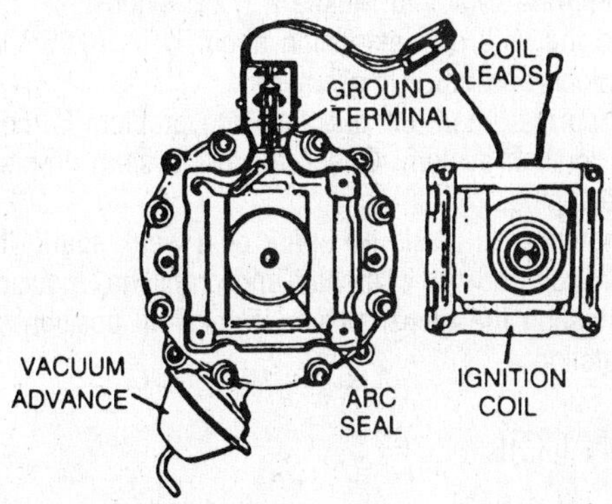

Fig. 12 Check the condition of the arc seal under the coil

8. Coat the rubber seal with a dielectric lubricant furnished in the replacement ignition coil package.
9. Reverse the above procedures to install.

Fuel Injected Engines

➧ See Figure 13

1. Make sure that the ignition switch is in the **OFF** position.
2. Tag and disconnect the coil wire and the connector on the side of the coil.
3. Remove the nuts holding the coil and bracket assembly to the engine and lift out the coil. The coil is riveted to the bracket, to remove it will require drilling the rivets and punching them out.
4. Position the coil on the engine and tighten the nuts.
5. Connect the coil wire and electrical connectors.

Vacuum Advance Unit

REMOVAL & INSTALLATION

1. Remove the distributor cap and rotor as previously described.
2. Disconnect the vacuum hose from the vacuum advance unit.
3. Remove the two vacuum advance retaining screws, pull the advance unit outward, rotate and disengage the operating rod from its tang.
4. Reverse the above procedure to install.

Module

REMOVAL & INSTALLATION

➧ See Figure 14

1. Remove the distributor cap and rotor as previously described.

Fig. 13 Be careful not to break the locktabs when unplugging the connectors

2. Disconnect the harness connector and pickup coil spade connectors from the module. Be careful not to damage the wires when removing the connector.

3. Remove the two screws and module from the distributor housing.

4. Coat the bottom of the new module with dielectric silicone lubricant. This is usually supplied with the new module. Reverse the above procedure to install.

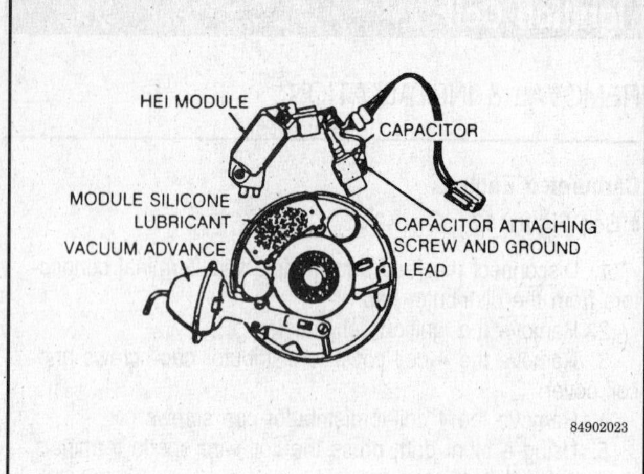

Fig. 14 Be sure to coat the mating surfaces with silicone lubricant

DISTRIBUTOR IGNITION (DI) SYSTEM

General Information

The distributor Ignition system (DI) consists of the distributor, hall effect switch (camshaft position sensor), ignition coil, secondary wires, spark plugs, knock sensor and the crankshaft position sensor. The system is controlled by the Vehicle Control Module (VCM). The VCM using information from various engine sensors, controls the spark timing, dwell, and the firing of the ignition coil. It is used on the 1993-96 models.

Diagnosis and Testing

The symptoms of a defective component within the DI system are exactly the same as those you would encounter in a conventional or HEI system. Some of these symptoms are:

- Hard or no Starting
- Rough Idle
- Fuel Poor Economy
- Engine misses under load or while accelerating

If you suspect a problem in the ignition system, there are certain preliminary checks which you should carry out before you begin to check the electronic portions of the system. First, it is extremely important to make sure the vehicle battery is in a good state of charge. A defective or poorly charged battery will cause the various components of the ignition system to read incorrectly when they are being tested. Second, make sure all wiring connections are clean and tight, not only at the battery, but also at the distributor cap, ignition coil, and at the electronic control module.

1. Check the cap for tiny holes and carbon tracks as follows.
   a. Remove the cap and place an ohmmeter lead on the cap terminal.
   b. Use the other lead to probe all the other terminals and the center carbon ball.
2. If the readings are not infinite, the cap must be replaced.

SECONDARY SPARK TEST

It is imperative to check the secondary ignition circuit first. If the secondary circuit checks out properly, then the engine condition is probably not the fault of the ignition system. To check the secondary ignition system, perform a simple spark test.

1. Remove one of the plug wires and insert some sort of extension in the plug socket. An old spark plug with the ground electrode removed makes a good extension.
2. Hold the wire and extension about ¼ in. (0.25mm) away from the block and crank the engine.
3. If a normal spark occurs, then the problem is most likely not in the ignition system. Check for fuel system problems, or fouled spark plugs.
4. If, however, there is no spark or a weak spark, then test the ignition coil and the camshaft and crankshaft position sensors. For testing the camshaft and crankshaft position sensors, refer to Section 4.

IGNITION COIL

➧ See Figure 15

➡Make sure the ignition switch is OFF

1. Tag and disconnect the wires from the ignition coil.
2. Using a digital ohmmeter set on the high scale, probe the the ignition coil as shown in Step 1 of the accompanying illustration.
3. The reading should be infinite. If not replace the coil.
4. Using the low scale of the ohmmeter, probe the the ignition coil as shown in Step 2 of the accompanying illustration. The reading should be 0.1 ohms, if not replace the coil.
5. Using the high scale of the ohmmeter, probe the ignition coil as shown in Step 3 of the accompanying illustration. The reading should be 5k-25k ohms, if not replace the coil.
6. Reconnect the wires to the ignition coil.

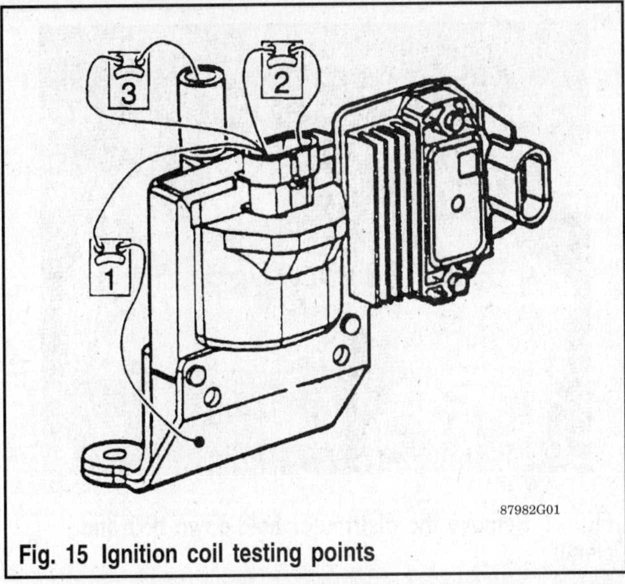

Fig. 15 Ignition coil testing points

Ignition Coil

REMOVAL & INSTALLATION

See Figures 16, 17 and 18

1. Tag and disengage the wiring connectors from the coil and the the coil wire.
2. Unfasten the retainers securing the coil bracket and coil to the manifold.
3. Remove the coil and bracket and drill out the two rivets securing the coil to the bracket.
4. Remove the coil from the bracket.

To install:

➡The replacement coil kit may come with the two screws to attach the coil to the bracket. If not, you must supply your own screws.

5. Fasten the coil to the bracket using two screws.

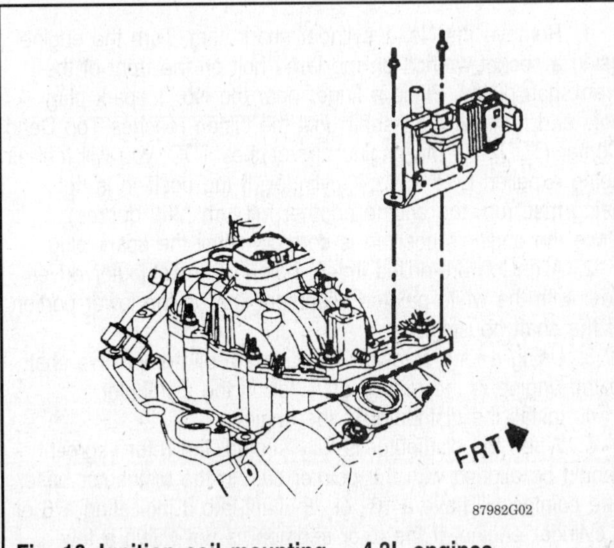

Fig. 16 Ignition coil mounting — 4.3L engines

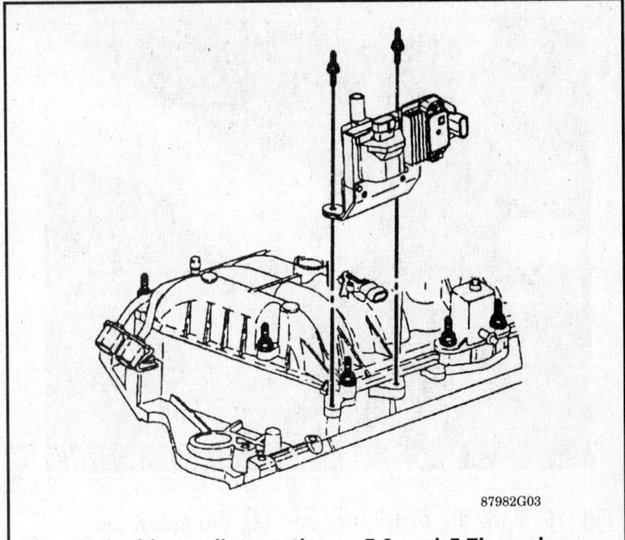

Fig. 17 Ignition coil mounting — 5.0 and 5.7L engines

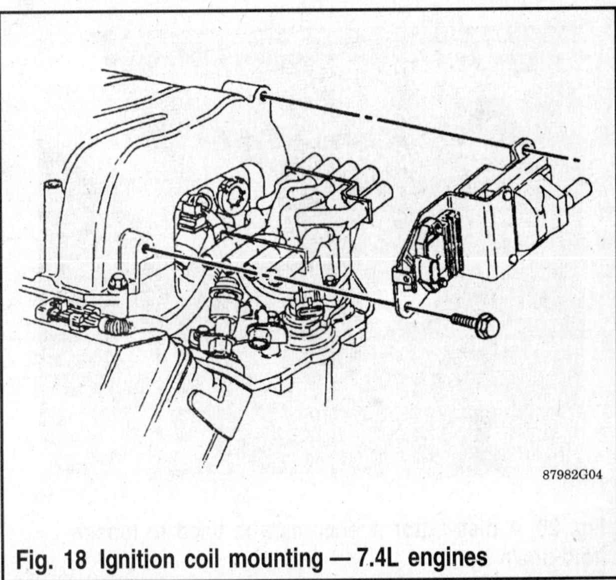

Fig. 18 Ignition coil mounting — 7.4L engines

6. Fasten the coil and bracket to the manifold. Tighten the retainers to 20 ft. lbs. (27 Nm).
7. Engage the coil wire and the wiring connectors to the coil.

Distributor

REMOVAL

See Figures 19, 20, 21 and 22

1. Disconnect the negative battery cable.
2. Tag and remove the spark plug wires and the coil leads from the distributor.
3. Disengage the electrical connector at the base of the distributor.
4. Loosen the distributor cap fasteners and remove the cap.

87982p21

Fig. 19 Mark the distributor and tag the spark plug wires

87982p23

Fig. 21 Remove the distributor hold-down bolt and clamp

87982p22

Fig. 20 A distributor wrench can be used to loosen hold-down bolt

87982p24

Fig. 22 Be sure to mark the distributor position before removing it

5. Using a marker, matchmark the rotor-to-housing and housing-to-engine block positions so that they can be matched during installation.
6. Loosen and remove the distributor hold-down bolt.
7. Remove the distributor from the engine.

INSTALLATION

Engine Not Disturbed

1. Install the distributor in the engine making sure that the matchmarks are properly aligned.
2. Install the hold-down bolt and tighten the bolt to 20 ft. lbs. (27 Nm).
3. Install the distributor cap and engage the electrical connector at the base of the distributor.
4. Install the spark plug wires and coil leads.
5. Connect the negative battery cable.

Engine Disturbed.

1. Remove the No. 1 cylinder spark plug. Turn the engine using a socket wrench on the large bolt on the front of the crankshaft pulley. Place a finger near the No. 1 spark plug hole and turn the crankshaft until the piston reaches Top Dead Center (TDC). As the engine approaches TDC, you will feel air being expelled by the No. 1 cylinder. If the position is not being met, turn the engine another full turn (360 degree). Once the engine's position is correct, install the spark plug.
2. Align the pre-drilled indent hole in the distributor driven gear with the white painted alignment line on the lower portion of the shaft housing.
3. Using a long screwdriver, align the oil pump drive shaft in the engine in the mating drive tab in the distributor.
4. Install the distributor in the engine.
5. When the distributor is fully seated, the rotor segment should be aligned with the pointer cast in the distributor base. The pointer will have a "6" or "8" cast into it indicating a 6 or 8 cylinder engine. If the rotor segment is not within a few degrees of the pointer, the distributor gear may be off a tooth

or more. If this is the case repeat the process until the rotor aligns with the pointer.

6. Install the cap and fasten the mounting screws.

7. Tighten the distributor mounting bolt to 20 ft. lbs. (27 Nm).

8. Engage the electrical connections and the spark plug wires.

Crankshaft Position Sensor

For information on the crankshaft position sensor, please refer to Section 4.

Camshaft Position Sensor

For information on the camshaft position sensor, please refer to Section 4.

FIRING ORDERS

➧ See Figure 23

➡To avoid confusion, always remove and tag the spark plug wires one at a time.

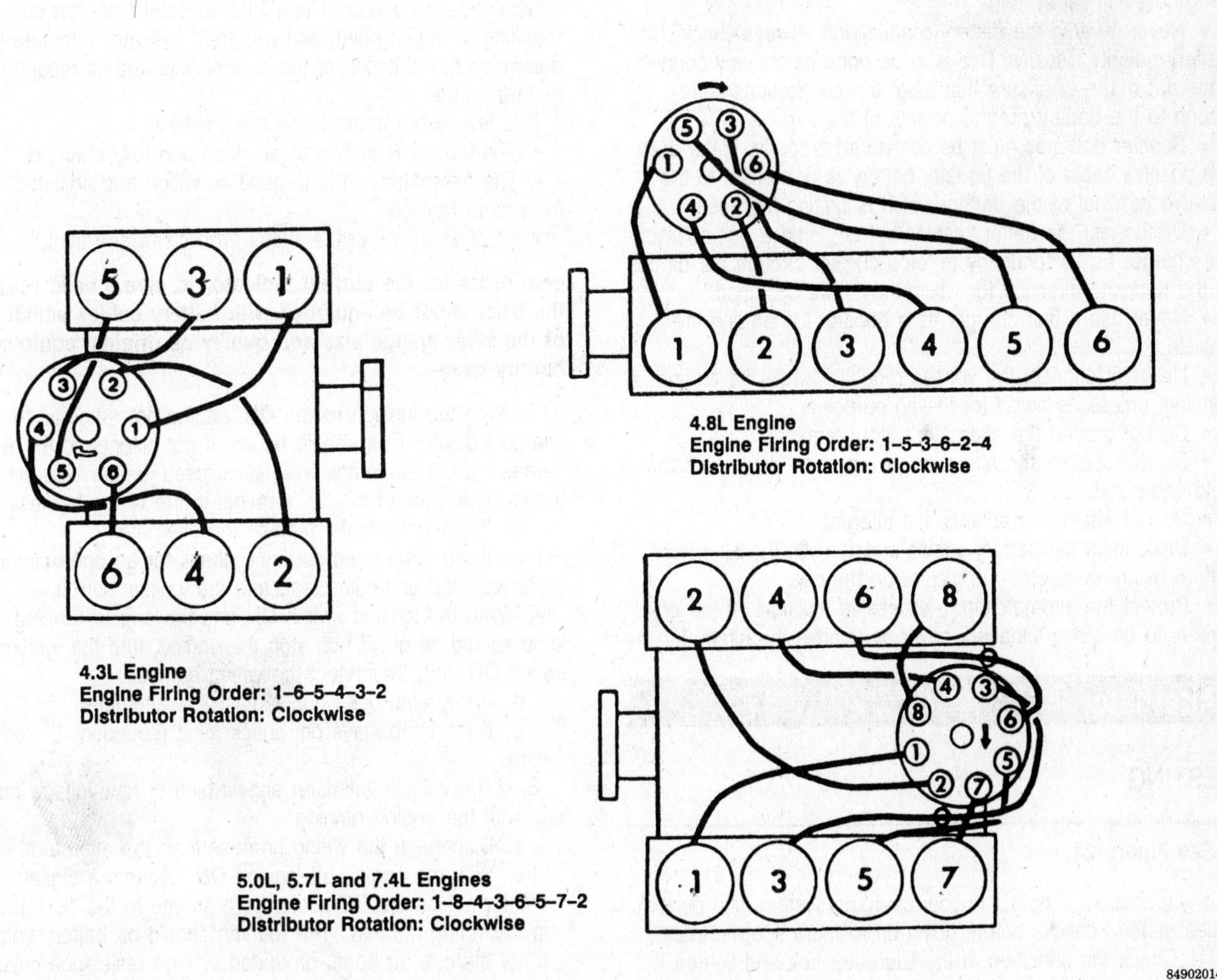

Fig. 23 Firing orders

CHARGING SYSTEM

General Information

The automobile charging system provides electrical power for operation of the vehicle's ignition and starting systems and all the electrical accessories. The battery serves as an electrical surge or storage tank, storing (in chemical form) the energy originally produced by the engine driven generator. The system also provides a means of regulating generator output to protect the battery from being overcharged and to avoid excessive voltage to the accessories.

Alternator Precautions

To prevent damage to the alternator and regulator, the following precautionary measures must be taken when working with the electrical system.

- Never reverse the battery connections. Always check the battery polarity visually. This is to be done before any connections are made to ensure that all of the connections correspond to the battery ground polarity of the car
- Booster batteries must be connected properly. Make sure the positive cable of the booster battery is connected to the positive terminal of the battery which is getting the boost
- Disconnect the battery cables before using a fast charger; the charger has a tendency to force current through the diodes in the opposite direction for which they were designed.
- Never use a fast charger as a booster for starting the vehicle
- Never disconnect the voltage regulator while the engine is running, unless as noted for testing purposes.
- Do not ground the alternator output terminal
- Do not operate the alternator on an open circuit with the field energized
- Do not attempt to polarize the alternator
- Disconnect the battery cables and remove the alternator before using an electric arc welder on the car
- Protect the alternator from excessive moisture. If the engine is to be steam cleaned, cover or remove the alternator

Alternator

TESTING

➧ **See Figure 24**

If you suspect a defect in your charging system, first perform these general checks before going on to more specific tests.

1. Check the condition of the alternator belt and tighten it if necessary.
2. Clean the battery cable connections at the battery. Make sure the connections between the battery wires and the battery clamps are good. Reconnect the negative terminal only and proceed to the next step.
3. With the key **OFF**, insert a test light between the positive terminal on the battery and the disconnected positive battery terminal clamp. If the test light comes on, there is a short in the electrical system of the truck. The short must be repaired before proceeding. If the light does not come on, proceed to the next step.

➡If the truck is equipped with an electric clock, the clock must be disconnected.

4. Check the charging system wiring for any obvious breaks or shorts.
5. Check the battery to make sure it is fully charged and in good condition.

There are many possible ways in which the charging system can malfunction. Often the source of a problem is difficult to diagnose, requiring special equipment and a good deal of experience. This is usually not the case, however, where the charging system fails completely and causes the dash board warning light to come on or the battery to become dead. To troubleshoot a complete system failure only two pieces of equipment are needed: a test light, to determine that current is reaching a certain point; and a current indicator (ammeter), to determine the direction of the current flow and its measurement in amps.

This test works under three assumptions:

- The battery is known to be good and fully charged
- The alternator belt is in good condition and adjusted to the proper tension
- All connections in the system are clean and tight.

➡In order for the current indicator to give a valid reading, the truck must be equipped with battery cables which are of the same gauge size and quality as original equipment battery cables.

6. With the ignition switch **ON**, engine not running, the charge indicator light should be on. If not disengage the wiring harness at the alternator and use a fused jumper wire with a 5-amp fuse, ground the "L" terminal in the wiring harness.
   a. If the lamp lights, replace the alternator.
   b. If the lamp does not light, check for an open circuit between the grounding lead and the ignition switch.
7. With the ignition switch **ON** and the engine running, the lamp should be off. If not, stop the engine, turn the ignition switch **ON**, and disconnect the wiring harness.
   a. If the lamp goes out, replace the alternator.
   b. If the lamp stays on, check for a grounded "L" terminal wire.
8. If the vehicle voltmeter shows high or low voltage readings with the engine running:
   a. Disengage the wiring harness from the alternator.
   b. With the engine off ignition **ON**, connect a digital multimeter set on the DC scale, from ground to the "L' terminal in the wiring harness. The reading should be battery voltage, if not there is an open, grounded or high resistance circuit between the terminal and the battery. Repair this circuit before performing any more tests.
9. Engage the harness connect to the alternator and run the engine at 2500 RPM with the accessories off.
10. Measure the voltage at the battery. If it is above 16 volts, replace the alternator.
11. With the engine off, connect an ammeter at the alternator output terminal. The ammeter must have the capability to measure 115 amps of current.

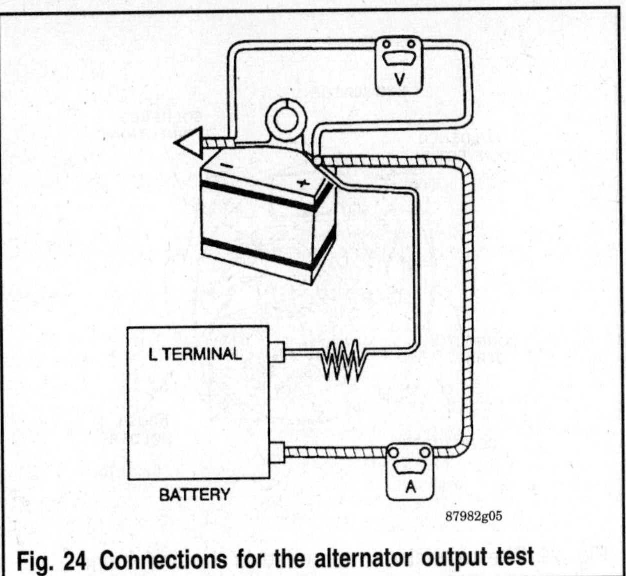

Fig. 24 Connections for the alternator output test

12. Connect a digital multimeter set on the DC scale across the alternator and a carbon pile across the battery.
  a. Run the engine at 2500 RPM, turn on all the accessories and load the battery with a carbon pile to obtain maximum amperage. Maintain voltage at 13 volts or more.
  b. If the output is within 15 amps of the rated output, the alternator is OK. Refer to the alternator specifications in this section.
  c. If the output is not within 15 amps, the alternator must be replaced.

REMOVAL & INSTALLATION

See Figures 25, 26, 27 and 28

1. Disconnect the negative battery cable.
2. Disconnect and tag all wiring to the alternator.
3. Remove the alternator brace bolt.
4. Remove the drive belt.
5. Support the alternator and remove the mounting bolts. Remove the alternator.

Fig. 25 Loosen and remove the nut securing the wire

Fig. 26 Don't break the locktab securing the harness connector in the alternator

Fig. 27 Loosen and remove the alternator retaining bolts . . .

Fig. 28 . . .then remove the alternator from the vehicle

To install:

6. Install the unit and tighten the bolts to the following torques:

On 4.3L, 4.8L, 5.0L and 5.7L engines:

- Top (right) mount bolt: 18 ft. lbs (25 Nm)
- Lower (left) mount bolt: 37 ft. lbs (50 Nm)
- Bracket bolt: 18 ft. lbs (25 Nm)

On 7.4L engines:

- Lower mount bolt: 18 ft. lbs (25 Nm)
- Upper mount bolt: 37 ft. lbs (50 Nm)
- Upper bracket bolt: 18 ft. lbs (25 Nm)
- Lower bracket bolt: 24 ft. lbs (33 Nm)

On 6.2L and 6.5L diesel engines:

- Top mount bolt: 18 ft. lbs (25 Nm)
- Lower mount nut: 17 ft. lbs (23 Nm)
- Bracket bolt: 18 ft. lbs (25 Nm)

7. Reconnect the wire at the alternator.
8. Reconnect the negative battery cable.
9. Adjust the belt to have ½ in. (13mm) depression under thumb pressure on its longest run.

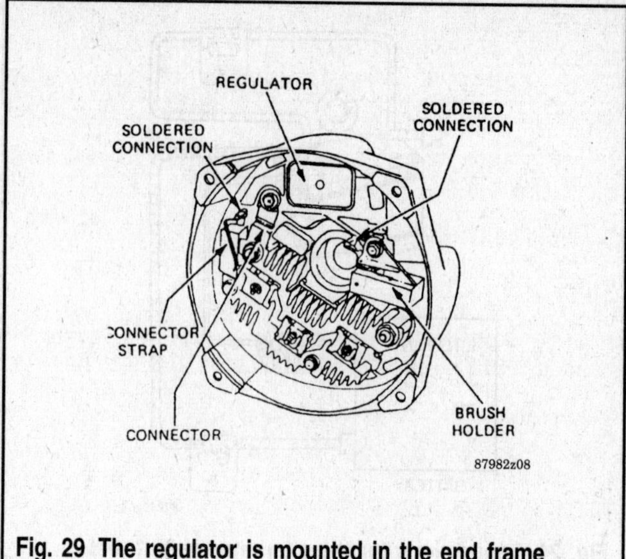

Fig. 29 The regulator is mounted in the end frame

Regulator

The voltage regulator works with the battery and alternator to comprise the charging system. As the voltage regulator's name implies, it regulates the voltage output of the alternator to a safe level (so the alternator does not overcharge the battery). A properly working regulator also prevents excessive voltage from burning out wiring, bulbs and other electrical components. All models covered in this manual are equipped with integral regulators, which are built into the alternator case. The regulators are solid state and require no maintenance or adjustment.

REMOVAL & INSTALLATION

See Figures 29 and 30

1. Remove the alternator from the vehicle. Scribe marks on the end frames to facilitate assembly. Remove the through bolts and separate the end frames.
2. Remove the cover rivets or pins and remove the cover.
3. Unsolder the stator leads at the three terminals on the rectifier bridge. Avoid excessive heat, as damage to the assembly will occur. Remove the stator.
4. Remove the brush holder screw. Disconnect the terminal and remove the brush holder assembly.
5. Unsolder and pry open the terminal between the regulator and the rectifier bridge. Remove the terminal and the retaining screws. Remove the regulator and the rectifier bridge from the end frame.

To install:

6. Position the brushes in the brush holder and retain them in place using a brush retainer wire or equivalent.
7. Assembly is the reverse of disassembly. Be sure to remove the brush retainer wire when the alternator has been reassembled.

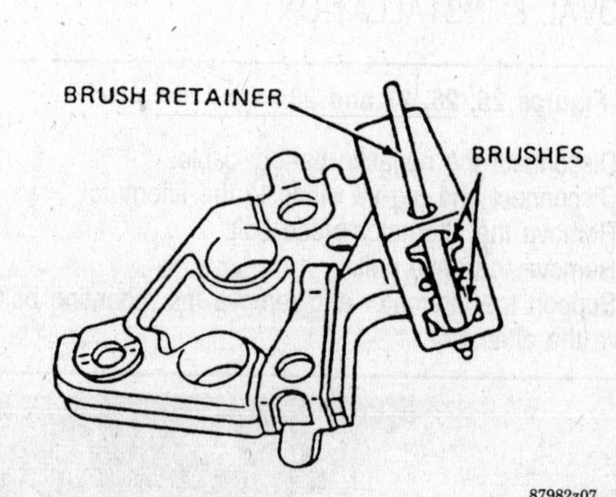

Fig. 30 The brushes can be retained with a wire in the holder

Battery

REMOVAL & INSTALLATION

➧ See Figure 31

1. Disconnect the negative battery cable terminal and then the positive cable terminal. Special pullers are available to remove clamp type battery terminals.

➡To avoid sparks, always disconnect the negative battery cable first, and reconnect it last.

2. Remove the hold-down clamp.
3. Remove the battery, being careful not to spill the acid.

CAUTION

Spilled acid can be neutralized with a baking soda/water solution. If you somehow get acid in your eyes, flush with lots of water and immediately consult a physician.

To install:

4. Clean the cable terminals of any corrosion, using a wire brush tool or an old jackknife inside and out.
5. Install the battery. Position the hold-down clamp and tighten it to 13 ft. lbs. (17 Nm) on 1988-90 models and 18 ft. lbs. (25 Nm) in 1991-96 models.
6. Connect the positive and then the negative cable terminal. Do not hammer them in place. The terminals should be coated lightly (externally) with grease or petroleum jelly to prevent corrosion. Tighten them to 11 ft. lbs. (15 Nm) on side terminal batteries or 13 ft. lbs. (17 Nm) on top terminal batteries.

WARNING

Make absolutely sure that the battery is connected properly before you start the engine! Reversed polarity can destroy your alternator and regulator in a matter of seconds!

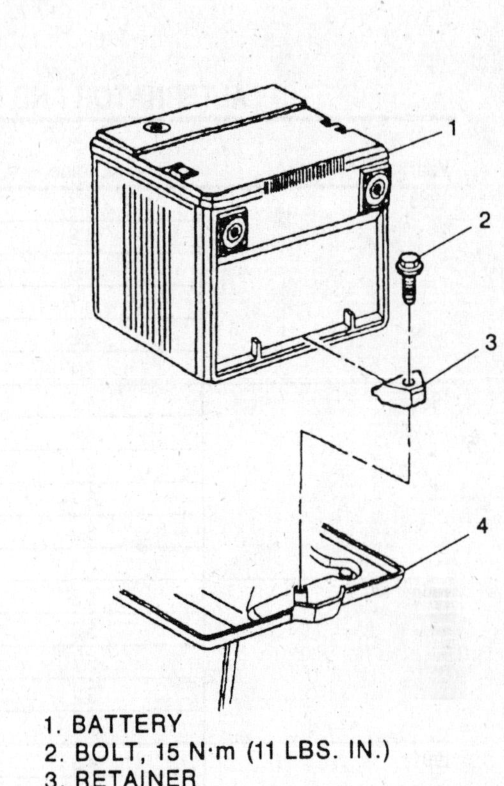

Fig. 31 Exploded view of the battery retaining system

ALTERNATOR AND REGULATOR SPECIFICATIONS

Year	Engine	Alternator Amps	Regulated Volts @ 77 F
1988	4.3	85	13.5-16.0
	4.8	85	13.5-16.0
	5.0	85	13.5-16.0
	5.7	105	13.5-16.0
	6.2	85	13.5-16.0
	7.4	100	13.5-16.0
1989	4.3	85	13.5-16.0
	4.8	85	13.5-16.0
	5.0	85	13.5-16.0
	5.7	105	13.5-16.0
	6.2	85	13.5-16.0
	7.4	100	13.5-16.0
1990	4.3	100	13.5-16.0
	5.0	100	13.5-16.0
	5.7	105	13.5-16.0
	6.2	100	13.5-16.0
	7.4	100	13.5-16.0
1991	4.3	100	13.5-16.0
	5.0	100	13.5-16.0
	5.7	105	13.5-16.0
	6.2	100	13.5-16.0
	7.4	100	13.5-16.0
1992	4.3	100	13.5-16.0
	5.0	100	13.5-16.0
	5.7	100	13.5-16.0
	6.2	100	13.5-16.0
	6.5	100	13.5-16.0
	7.4	105	13.5-16.0
1993	4.3	100	13.5-16.0
	5.0	100	13.5-16.0
	5.7	100	13.5-16.0
	6.2	105	13.5-16.0
	6.5	100	13.5-16.0
	7.4	105	13.5-16.0
1994	4.3	100	13.5-16.0
	5.0	100	13.5-16.0
	5.7	100	13.5-16.0
	6.2	100	13.5-16.0
	6.5	100	13.5-16.0
	7.4	105	13.5-16.0

87982c01

ALTERNATOR AND REGULATOR SPECIFICATIONS

Year	Engine	Alternator Amps	Regulated Volts @ 77 F
1995	4.3	100	13.5-16.0
	5.0	100	13.5-16.0
	5.7	100	13.5-16.0
	6.5	100	13.5-16.0
	7.4	100	13.5-16.0
1996	4.3	105	13.5-16.0
	5.0	105	13.5-16.0
	5.7	105	13.5-16.0
	6.5	105	13.5-16.0
	7.4	105	13.5-16.0

87982c02

STARTING SYSTEM

Starter

The starting motor is a specially designed, direct current electric motor capable of producing a great amount of power for its size. One thing that allows the motor to produce a great deal of power is its tremendous rotating speed. It drives the engine through a tiny pinion gear (attached to the starter's armature), which drives the very large flywheel ring gear at a greatly reduced speed. Another factor allowing it to produce so much power is that only intermittent operation is required of it. Thus, little allowance for air circulation is required, and the windings can be built into a very small space.

REMOVAL & INSTALLATION

See Figures 32, 33, 34, 35, 36 and 37

The following is a general procedure for all trucks covered in this manual, and may vary slightly depending on model and series.

1. Disconnect the negative battery cable at the battery.
2. Raise and support the vehicle.
3. Disconnect and tag all wires at the solenoid terminal.

Reinstall all nuts as soon as they are removed, since the thread sizes are different.

4. Remove the front bracket from the starter and the mounting bolts. On engines with a solenoid heat shield, remove the front bracket upper bolt and detach the bracket from the starter.
5. Remove the front bracket bolt or nut. Lower the starter, front end first, then remove the unit from the truck.

To install:

6. Position the starter and tighten all bolts as follows:

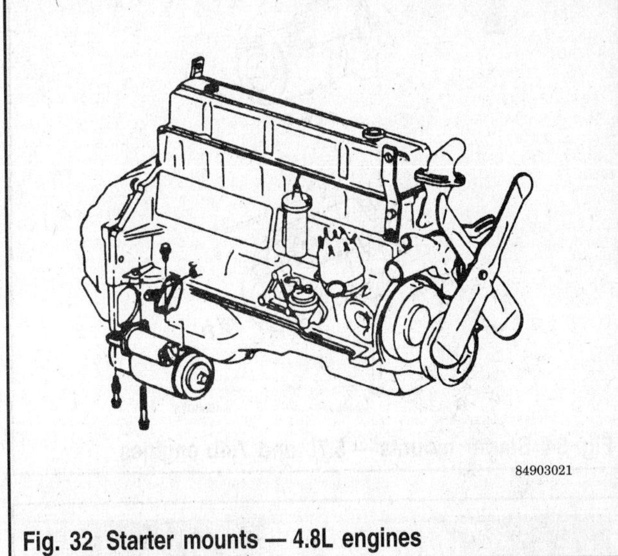
84903021

Fig. 32 Starter mounts — 4.8L engines

R/V Series:
- Thru-bolts: 40 ft. lbs. (54 Nm)
- Bracket bolt: 30 ft. lbs. (41 Nm)
- Nut (gas): 11 ft. lbs. (15 Nm)
- Nut (diesel): 90 inch lbs. (10 Nm)

C/K Series:
- Thru-bolts: 35 ft. lbs. (45 Nm)
- Bracket bolt (diesel): 24 ft. lbs. (33 Nm)
- Nut (diesel): 75 inch lbs. (8.5 Nm)

7. Reconnect all wires.

SHIMMING THE STARTER

See Figures 38, 39 and 40

Starter noise during cranking and after the engine fires is often a result of too much or too little distance between the starter pinion gear and the flywheel. A high pitched whine

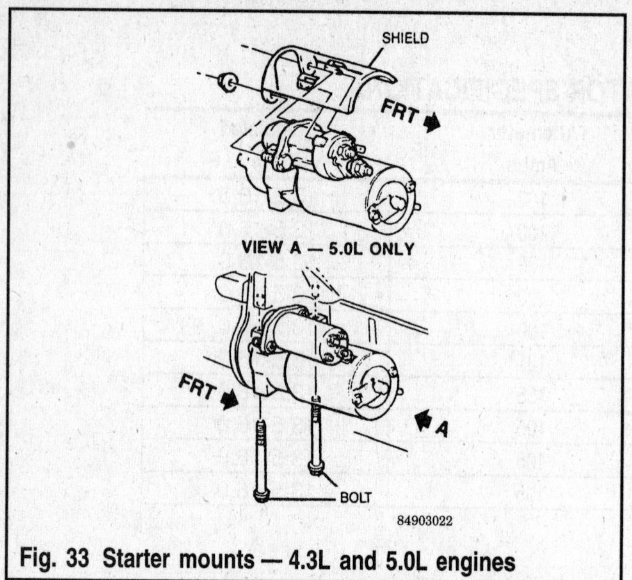

Fig. 33 Starter mounts — 4.3L and 5.0L engines

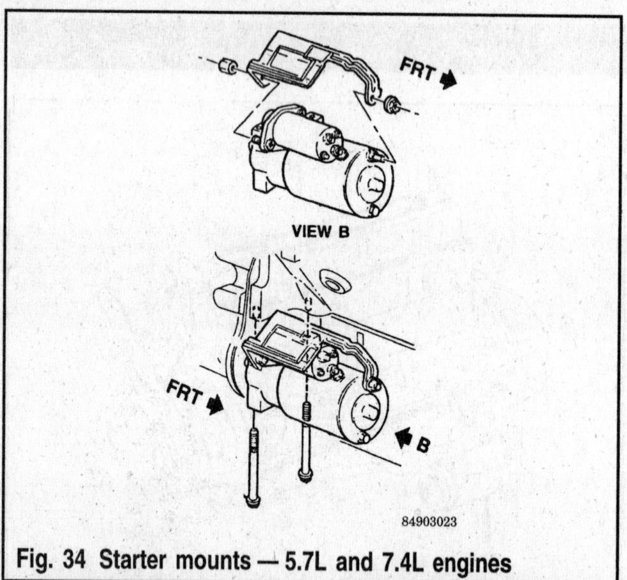

Fig. 34 Starter mounts — 5.7L and 7.4L engines

Fig. 35 Disconnect the negative battery cable

Fig. 36 Remove the starter retaining bolts

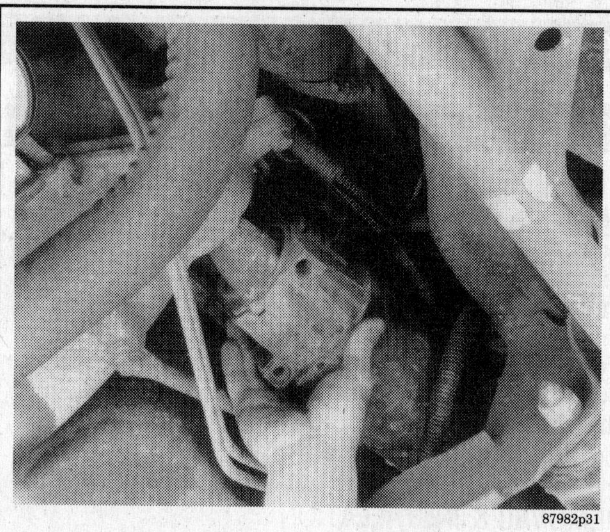

Fig. 37 Remove the starter from the vehicle

during cranking (before the engine fires) can be caused by the pinion and flywheel being too far apart. Likewise, a whine after the engine starts (as the key is released) is often a result of the pinion-flywheel relationship being too close. In both cases flywheel damage can occur. Shims are available in 0.015 in. (0.3mm) sizes to properly adjust the starter on its mount. You will also need a flywheel turning tool, available at most auto parts stores or from most auto tool store or salesperson.

If your truck's starter emits the above noises, follow the shimming procedure:

1. Disconnect the negative battery cable.
2. Remove the flywheel inspection cover on the bottom of the bellhousing.
3. Using the flywheel turning tool, turn the flywheel and examine the flywheel teeth. If damage is evident, the flywheel should be replaced.
4. Insert a screwdriver into the small hole in the bottom of the starter and move the starter pinion and clutch assembly so the pinion and flywheel teeth mesh. If necessary, rotate the flywheel so that a pinion tooth is directly in the center of the

two flywheel teeth and on the centerline of the two gears, as shown in the accompanying illustration.

5. Check the pinion-to-flywheel clearance by using a 0.020 in. (0.5mm) wire gauge (a spark plug wire gauge may work here, or you can make your own). Make sure you center the pinion tooth between the flywheel teeth and the gauge — NOT in the corners, as you may get a false reading. If the clearance is under this minimum, shim the starter away from the flywheel by adding shim(s) one at a time to the starter mount. Check clearance after adding each shim.

6. If the clearance is a good deal over 0.020 in. (0.5mm) — in the vicinity of 0.050 in. (1.3mm) plus, shim the starter towards the flywheel. Broken or severely mangled flywheel teeth are also a good indicator that the clearance here is too great. Shimming the starter towards the flywheel is done by adding shims to the outboard starter mounting pad only. Check the clearance after each shim is added. A shim of 0.015 in. (0.3mm) at this location will decrease the clearance about 0.010 in. (0.2mm).

SOLENOID REPLACEMENT

1. Disconnect the negative battery cable.
2. Remove the screw and washer from the field strap terminal.
3. Remove the two solenoid-to-housing retaining screws and the motor terminal bolt.
4. Remove the solenoid by twisting the unit 90 degrees.
5. To replace the solenoid, reverse the above procedure. Make sure the return spring is on the plunger, and rotate the solenoid unit into place on the starter.

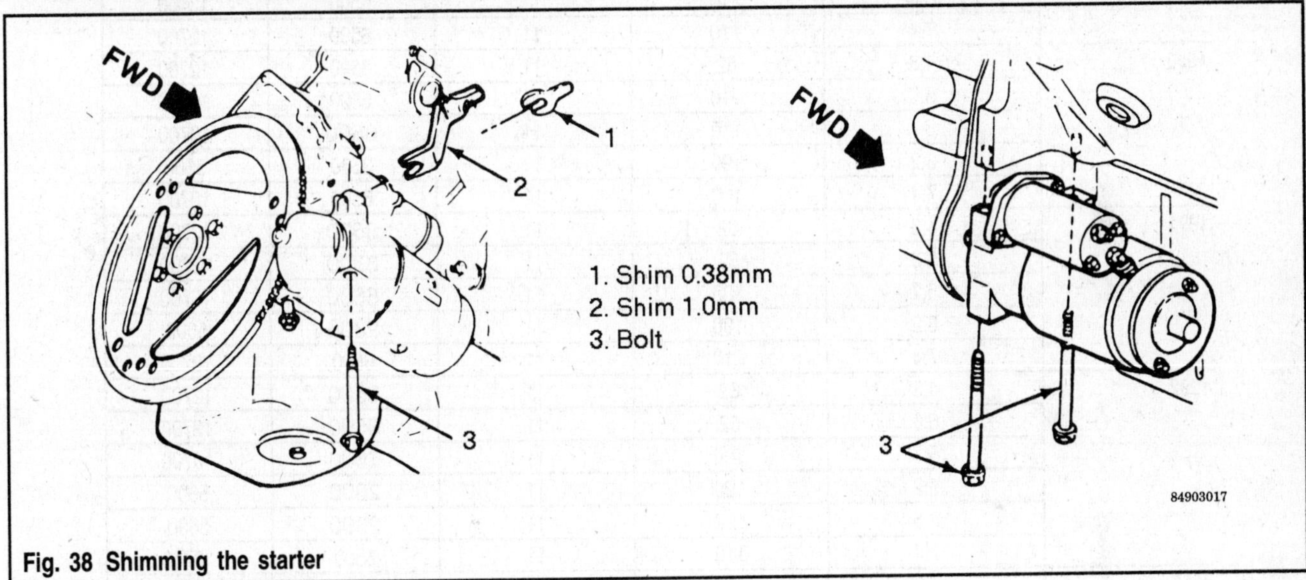

Fig. 38 Shimming the starter

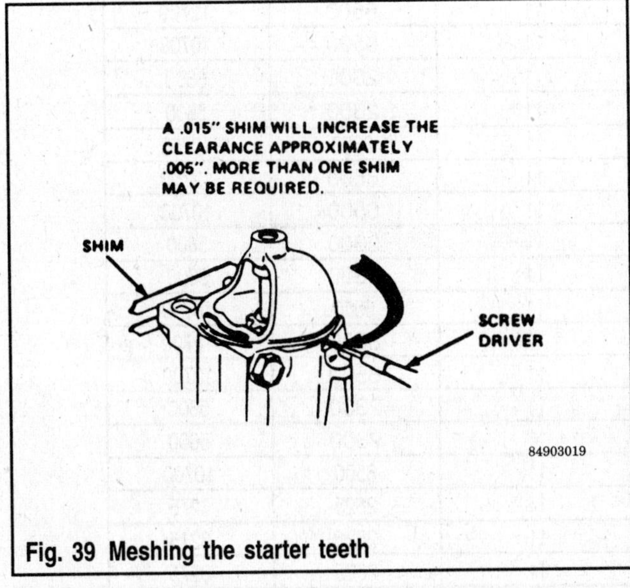

Fig. 39 Meshing the starter teeth

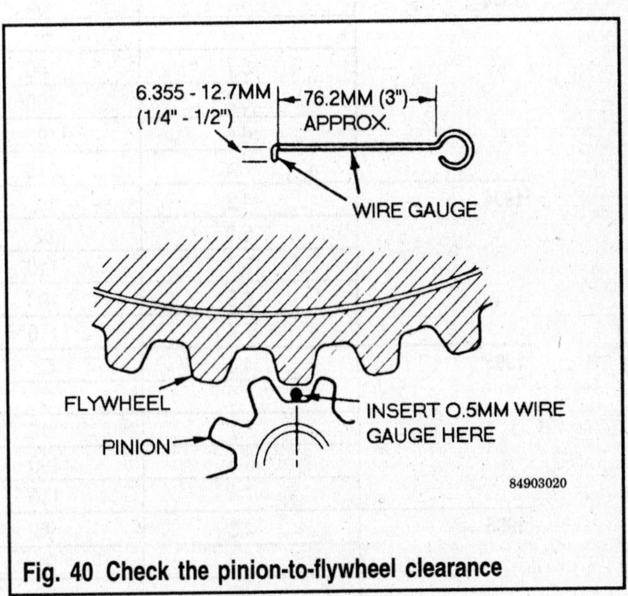

Fig. 40 Check the pinion-to-flywheel clearance

STARTER SPECIFICATIONS

Year	Engine	Max. Amps	No-Load Test @ 10 Volts		
			Max. Volts	Min. RPM	Max. RPM
1988	4.3	110	11	6500	10700
	4.8	90	11	6500	10700
	5.0	110	11	6500	10700
	5.7	110	11	6500	10700
	6.2	210	11	6500	13400
	7.4	110	11	6500	10700
1989	4.3	110	11	6500	10700
	4.8	90	11	6500	10700
	5.0	110	11	6500	10700
	5.7	110	11	6500	10700
	6.2	210	11	6500	13400
	7.4	110	11	6500	10700
1990	4.3	62	11	8500	12700
	5.0	110	11	6500	10700
	5.7	110	11	6500	10700
	6.2	190	11	3500	5600
	7.4	110	11	6500	10700
1991	4.3	62	11	8500	12700
	5.0	62	11	8500	12700
	5.7	100	11	6500	10700
	6.2	190	11	2300	5600
	7.4	110	11	6500	10700
1992	4.3	62	11	8500	12700
	5.0	62	11	8500	12700
	5.7	100	11	6500	10700
	6.2	190	11	2300	5600
	6.5	190	11	2300	5600
	7.4	110	11	6500	10700
1993	4.3	62	11	8500	12700
	5.0	62	11	8500	12700
	5.7	100	11	6500	10700
	6.2	190	11	2300	5600
	6.5	190	11	2300	5600
	7.4	110	11	6500	10700
1994	4.3	62	11	8500	12700
	5.0	62	11	6500	10700
	5.7	110	11	2300	5600
	6.5	190	11	2300	5600
	7.4	110	11	6500	10700
1995	4.3	62	11	8500	12700
	5.0	62	11	8500	12700
	5.7	110	11	2300	5600
	6.5	190	11	2300	5600
	7.4	110	11	6500	10700
1996	4.3	95	11	2825	3275
	5.0	95	11	2825	3275
	5.7	95	11	2825	3275
	6.5	190	11	2300	5600
	7.4	95	11	2825	3275

87982c03

SENDING UNITS AND SENSORS

The sensors covered in this section are not related to engine control. They are for gauges and warning lights only. For sensors related to engine control refer to Electronic Engine Controls in Section 4.

Coolant Temperature Sensor

OPERATION

The coolant temperature sensor changes resistance as the coolant temperature increases and decreases.

REMOVAL & INSTALLATION

➧ **See Figures 41, 42, 43 and 44**

1. Disconnect the negative battery cable and drain the engine coolant.
2. Disconnect the sensor electrical lead and unscrew the sensor. The coolant sensor can be found on the front, left side of the engine block, visible through, or below, the manifold.

To install:

3. Install the sensor and tighten it to 17 ft. lbs. (23 Nm). Connect the electrical lead.
4. Connect the battery cable and fill the engine with coolant.

Oil Pressure Sender

OPERATION

The oil pressure sender relays to the dash gauge the oil pressure in the engine.

REMOVAL & INSTALLATION

1. Disconnect the negative battery cable and drain the engine oil.
2. Disconnect the sensor electrical lead and unscrew the sensor. The sensor can be found on the top side of the engine, near the distributor.

To install:

3. Coat the first two or three threads with sealer. Install the sensor and tighten until snug. Engage the electrical lead.
4. Connect the battery cable and fill the engine with oil.

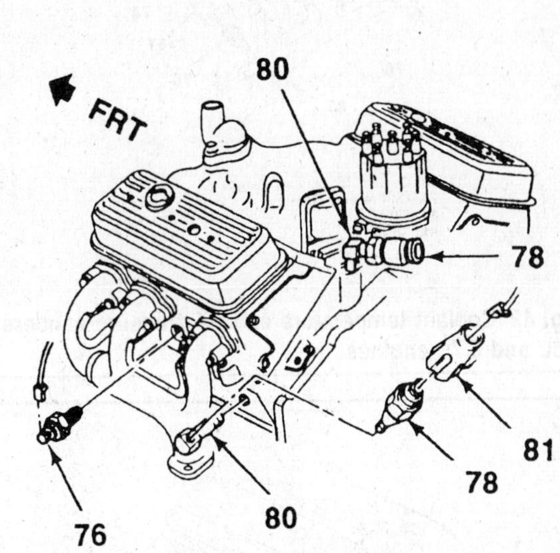

76. Coolant Temperature Sensor
78. Oil Pressure Sensor
80. Fitting
81. Shield

84903027

Fig. 41 Coolant temperature and oil pressure senders — 4.3L engines

Auxiliary Fan Switch

OPERATION

The auxiliary fan circuit contains the auxiliary fan, coolant temperature sensor and a relay. When the sensor reaches a predetermined temperature, it closes the circuit to the relay. This energizes the relay sending 12 volts to the auxiliary fan. When the temperature decreases below the setpoint of the sensor, the circuit opens and the voltage is no longer applied to the auxiliary fan.

REMOVAL & INSTALLATION

1. Disconnect the negative battery cable.

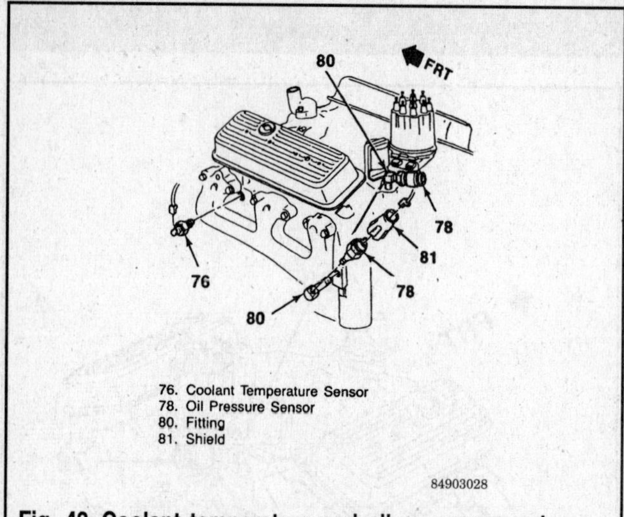

Fig. 42 Coolant temperature and oil pressure senders — 5.0L and 5.7L engines

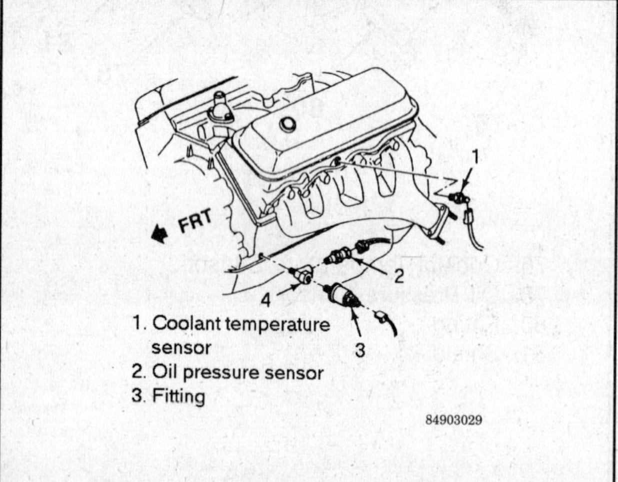

Fig. 43 Coolant temperature and oil pressure senders — 7.4L engines

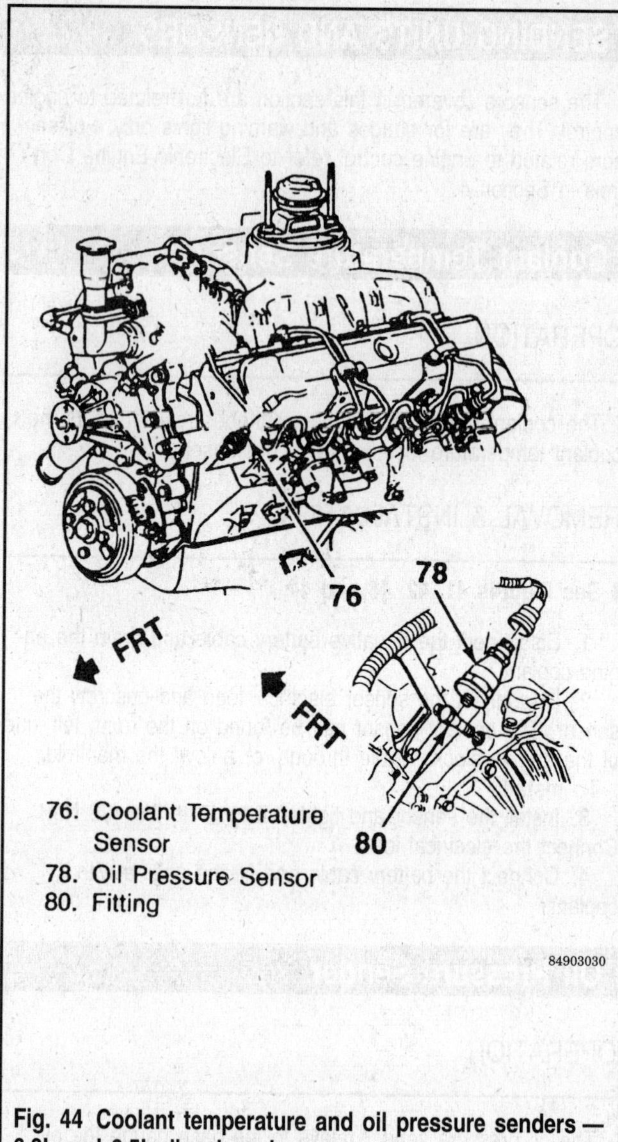

Fig. 44 Coolant temperature and oil pressure senders — 6.2L and 6.5L diesel engines

2. Disconnect the sensor electrical lead and unscrew the sensor. The sensor can be found on the right side of the engine.

To install:

3. Install the sensor or relay and connect the electrical lead.
4. Connect the battery cable.

Low Coolant Monitoring System

OPERATION

A sensor located in the overflow tank signals the module when a low coolant condition exists. The module relays this to the dash.

REMOVAL & INSTALLATION

Module

1. Disconnect the negative battery cable.
2. Remove the glove box and disengage the electrical connector.
3. Remove the module from the instrument panel by pulling it straight out.
4. Installation is the reverse of removal.

Sensor

1. Remove the overflow tank.
2. Remove the sensor and the grommet.
3. Installation is the reverse of removal.

3
ENGINE AND ENGINE OVERHAUL
ENGINE MECHANICAL 3-2
EXHAUST SYSTEM 3-109
SPECIFICATIONS CHARTS 3-6

ENGINE MECHANICAL

Description

4.8L ENGINES

The 4.8L, inline 6-cylinder engine, is an overhead valve design with cast iron head and block. The crankshaft is supported by 7 main bearings with the thrust taken on No. 7. The camshaft is driven directly by the crankshaft and rides in 4 bearings. Hydraulic lifters are used with pushrods and ball-type rocker arms. The valve guides are integral. The pistons are cast aluminum and the pins are press-fit floating type. The connecting rods are forged steel.

4.3L ENGINES

The 4.3L engines are 90° V6 type, overhead valve, water cooled, with cast iron block and heads. The crankshaft is supported by four precision insert main bearings, with crankshaft thrust taken at the No. 4 (rear) bearing. The camshaft is supported by four plain bearings and is chain driven. Motion from the camshaft is transmitted to the valves by hydraulic lifters, pushrods, and ball type rocker arms. The valve guides are integral in the cylinder head. The connecting rods are forged steel, with precision insert type crankpin bearings. The piston pins are a press fit in the connecting rods. The pistons are cast aluminum alloy and the piston pins are a floating fit in the piston.

5.0L AND 5.7L ENGINES

The small block family of V8 engines, 5.0L and 5.7L, are derived from the innovative design of the original 1955 265 cu in. Chevrolet V8. This engine introduced the ball mounted rocker arm design, replacing the once standard shaft mounted rocker arms. There is extensive interchangeability of components among these engines, extending to the several other small block displacement sizes available.

7.4L ENGINES

The 7.4L engine is known as the Mark IV engine or big block. This engine features unusual cylinder heads, in that the intake and exhaust valves are canted at the angle at which their respective port enters the cylinder. The big block cylinder heads use ball joint rockers similar to those on the small block engines.

6.2L AND 6.5L ENGINES

The 6.2L diesel was introduced for the trucks in 1983. This engine is built by GM's Detroit Diesel Division. Designed from the start as a diesel, it utilizes robust features such as four-bolt main bearing caps. The new-generation 6.5L engine is also available.

Engine Overhaul Tips

Most engine overhaul procedures are fairly standard. In addition to specific parts replacement procedures and specifications for your individual engine, this section is also a guide to acceptable rebuilding procedures. Examples of standard rebuilding practice are given and should be used along with specific details concerning your particular engine.

Competent and accurate machine shop services will ensure maximum performance, reliability and engine life. In most instances it is more profitable for the do-it-yourself mechanic to remove, clean and inspect the component, buy the necessary parts and deliver these to a shop for actual machine work.

On the other hand, much of the rebuilding work (crankshaft, block, bearings, piston rods, and other components) is well within the scope of the do-it-yourself mechanic's tools and abilities. You will have to decide for yourself the depth of involvement you desire in an engine repair or rebuild.

TOOLS

The tools required for an engine overhaul or parts replacement will depend on the depth of your involvement. With a few exceptions, they will be the tools found in a mechanic's tool kit (see Section 1 of this manual). More in-depth work will require some or all of the following:

- A dial indicator (reading in thousandths) mounted on a universal base
- Micrometers and telescope gauges
- Jaw and screw-type pullers
- Scraper
- Valve spring compressor
- Ring groove cleaner
- Piston ring expander and compressor
- Ridge reamer
- Cylinder hone or glaze breaker
- Plastigage®
- Engine stand

The use of most of these tools is illustrated in this chapter. Many can be rented for a one-time use from a local parts jobber or tool supply house specializing in automotive work.

Occasionally, the use of special tools is called for. See the information on Special Tools and the Safety Notice in the front of this book before substituting another tool.

INSPECTION TECHNIQUES

Procedures and specifications are given in this chapter for inspecting, cleaning and assessing the wear limits of most major components. Other procedures such as Magnaflux® and Zyglo® can be used to locate material flaws and stress cracks. Magnaflux® is a magnetic process applicable only to ferrous materials. The Zyglo® process coats the material with a fluorescent dye penetrant and can be used on any material.

Checking for suspected surface cracks can be more readily made using spot check dye. The dye is sprayed onto the suspected area, wiped off and the area sprayed with a developer. Cracks will show up brightly.

OVERHAUL TIPS

Aluminum has become extremely popular for use in engines, due to its low weight. Observe the following precautions when handling aluminum parts:

- Never hot tank aluminum parts (the caustic hot tank solution will eat the aluminum.
- Remove all aluminum parts (identification tag, etc.) from engine parts prior to the tanking.
- Always coat threads lightly with engine oil or anti-seize compounds before installation, to prevent seizure.
- Never overtorque bolts or spark plugs especially in aluminum threads.

Stripped threads in any component can be repaired using any of several commercial repair kits (Heli-Coil®, Microdot®, Keenserts®, etc.).

When assembling the engine, any parts that will be exposed to frictional contact must be prelubed to provide lubrication at initial start-up. Any product specifically formulated for this purpose can be used, but engine oil is not recommended as a prelube in most cases.

When semi-permanent (locked, but removable) installation of bolts or nuts is desired, threads should be cleaned and coated with Loctite® or another similar, commercial non-hardening sealant.

REPAIRING DAMAGED THREADS

See Figures 1, 2, 3, 4 and 5

Several methods of repairing damaged threads are available. Heli-Coil® (shown here), Keenserts® and Microdot® are among the most widely used. All involve basically the same principle — drilling out stripped threads, tapping the hole and installing a prewound insert — making welding, plugging and oversize fasteners unnecessary.

Two types of thread repair inserts are usually supplied: a standard type for most inch coarse, inch fine, metric course and metric fine thread sizes and a spark lug type to fit most spark plug port sizes. Consult the individual tool manufacturer's catalog to determine exact applications. Typical thread repair kits will contain a selection of prewound threaded inserts, a tap (corresponding to the outside diameter threads of the insert) and an installation tool. Spark plug inserts usually differ because they require a tap equipped with pilot threads and a combined reamer/tap section. Most manufacturers also supply blister-packed thread repair inserts separately in addition to a master kit containing a variety of taps and inserts plus installation tools.

Before attempting to repair a threaded hole, remove any snapped, broken or damaged bolts or studs. Penetrating oil can be used to free frozen threads. The offending item can usually be removed with locking pliers or using a screw/stud

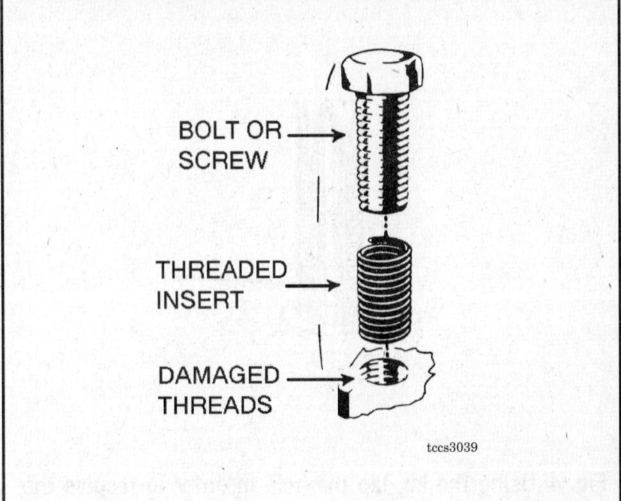

Fig. 1 Damaged bolt hole threads can be replaced with thread repair inserts

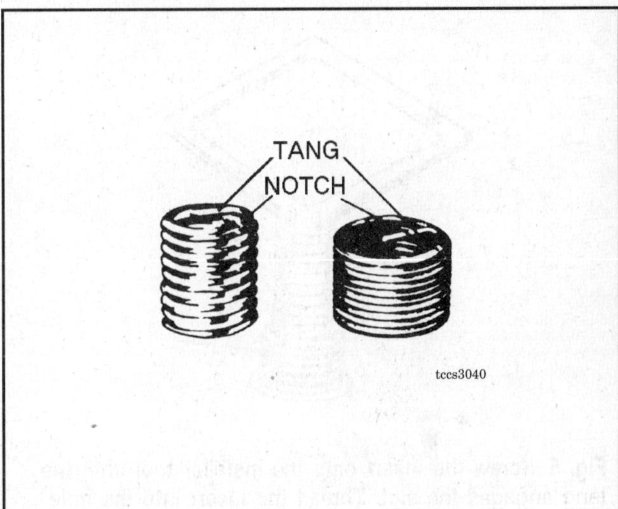

Fig. 2 Standard thread repair insert (left), and spark plug thread insert

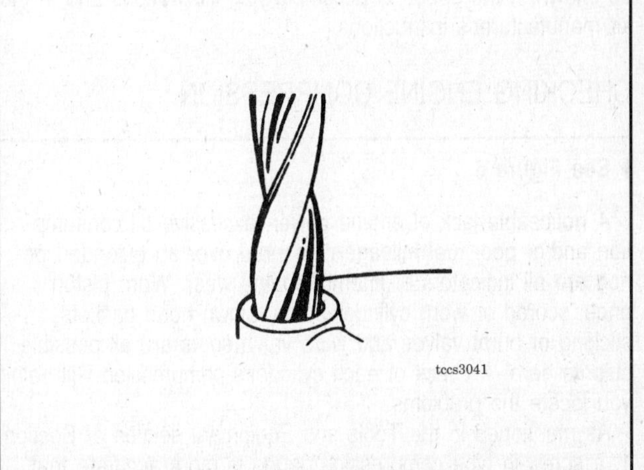

Fig. 3 Drill out the damaged threads with the specified size bit. Be sure to drill completely through the hole or to the bottom of a blind hole

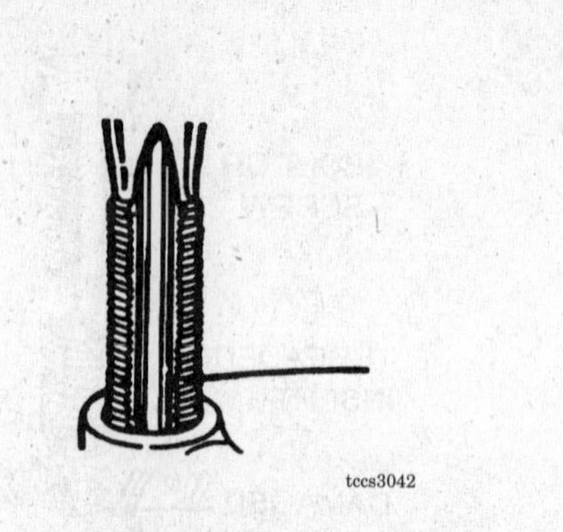

Fig. 4 Using the kit, tap the hole in order to receive the thread insert. Keep the tap well oiled and back it out frequently to avoid clogging the threads.

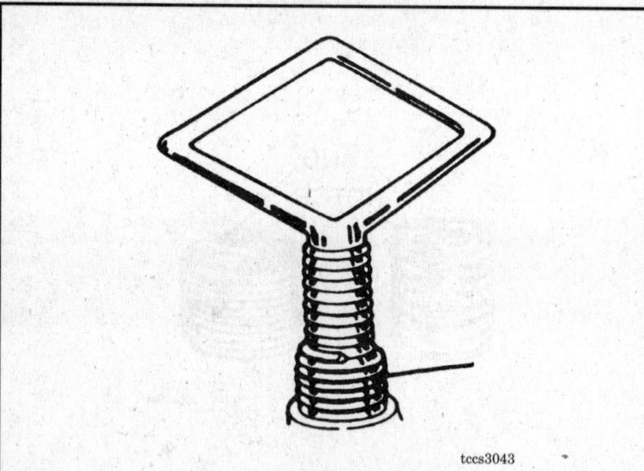

Fig. 5 Screw the insert onto the installer tool until the tang engages the slot. Thread the insert into the hole until it is ¼-½ turn below the top surface, then remove the tool and break off the tang using a punch.

extractor. After the hole is clear, the thread can be repaired, as shown in the series of accompanying illustrations and in the kit manufacturer's instructions.

CHECKING ENGINE COMPRESSION

See Figure 6

A noticeable lack of engine power, excessive oil consumption and/or poor fuel mileage measured over an extended period are all indicators of internal engine wear. Worn piston rings, scored or worn cylinder bores, blown head gaskets, sticking or burnt valves and worn valve seats are all possible culprits here. A check of each cylinder's compression will help you locate the problems.

As mentioned in the Tools and Equipment section of Section 1, a screw-in type compression gauge is more accurate that the type you simply hold against the spark plug hole, although it takes slightly longer to use. It's worth it to obtain a more accurate reading. Follow the procedures below for gasoline and diesel engine trucks.

Gasoline Engines

1. Warm up the engine to normal operating temperature.
2. Remove all spark plugs.
3. Disconnect the high tension lead from the ignition coil.
4. Fully open the throttle either by operating the throttle linkage by hand or by having an assistant floor the accelerator pedal.
5. Screw the compression gauge into the No. 1 spark plug hole until the fitting is snug.

Be careful not to crossthread the plug hole.

6. Ask an assistant to depress the accelerator pedal fully on both carbureted and fuel injected trucks. Then, while you read the compression gauge, ask the assistant to crank the engine two or three times in short bursts using the ignition switch.
7. Read the compression gauge at the end of each series of cranks, and record the highest of these readings. Repeat this procedure for each of the engine's cylinders. Compare the highest reading of each cylinder to the compression pressure specification in the Tune-Up Specifications chart in Section 1. The specs in this chart are maximum values.

A cylinder's compression pressure is usually acceptable if it is not less than 80% of maximum. The difference between each cylinder should be no more than 12-14 psi (82-96 kPa).

8. If a cylinder is unusually low, pour a tablespoon of clean engine oil into the cylinder through the spark plug hole and repeat the compression test. If the compression comes up after adding the oil, it appears that the cylinder's piston rings or bore are damaged or worn. If the pressure remains low, the valves may not be seating properly (a valve job is needed), or the head gasket may be blown near that cylinder. If compression in any two adjacent cylinders is low, and if the addition of oil doesn't help the compression, there is leakage past the head gasket. Oil and coolant water in the combustion chamber can result from this problem. There may be evidence of water droplets on the engine dipstick when a head gasket has blown.

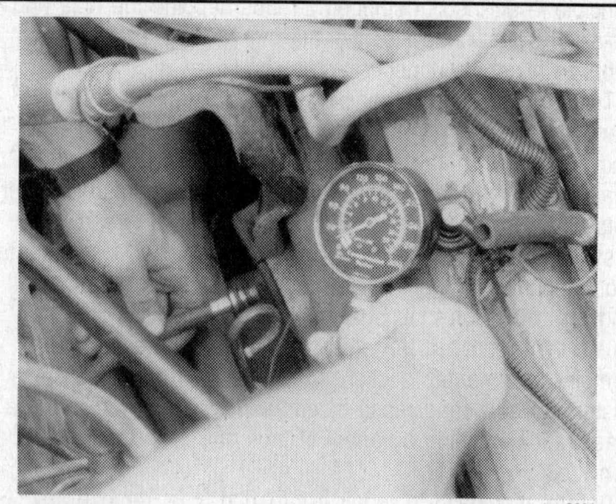

Fig. 6 A screw-in type compression gauge is more accurate and easier to use without an assistant

Diesel Engines

➧ See Figures 7 and 8

1. Warm up and stop the engine. Remove the air cleaner and cover the opening.
2. Disconnect the wire (usually pink) fuel solenoid terminal of the injection pump.
3. Disconnect the electrical leads from the glow plugs and then remove the glow plugs.

✲✲WARNING

Make sure the load wire is not grounded.

➡A special compression gauge and adaptor suitable for diesel engines (because these engines have much greater compression pressures) must be used. Use SST J 26999 (gauge) and J 26999-10 (adapter) or their equivalents to measure the compression pressure.

4. Install and tighten the adapter into glow plug opening and connect a compression gauge to the adapter.
5. While you read the compression gauge, have an assistant crank the engine in short bursts using the ignition switch (allow about six puffs).

➡The battery must be fully charged to produce a revolution of at least 250 rpm.

6. Read the compression gauge at the end of each series of cranks, and record the highest of these readings. Repeat this procedure for each of the engine's cylinders. Compare the highest reading of each cylinder to the compression pressure specification in the Tune-Up Specifications chart in Section 1. The specifications given in this chart are maximum values.

A cylinder's compression pressure is usually acceptable if it is not less than 80% of maximum. The difference between any two cylinders should be no more than 12-14 psi. (82-96 kPa).

✲✲WARNING

DO NOT add oil to the cylinders while performing a compression test!

7. Remove the compression gauge and adapter.
8. Reinstall the glow plugs and reconnect the fuel solenoid wire connector.

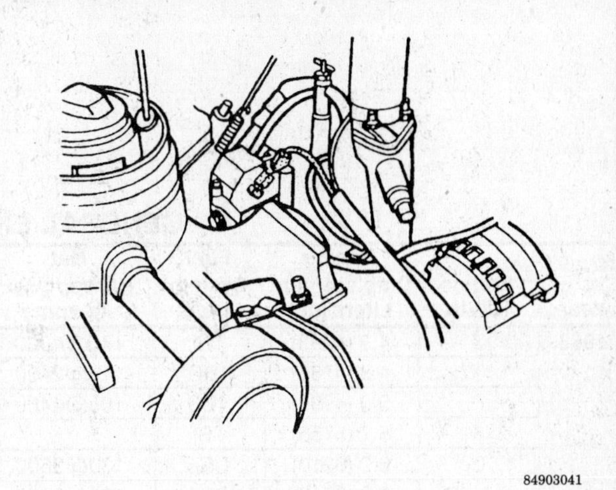

Fig. 7 Disconnect the fuel solenoid terminal wire at the injection pump — diesel engines

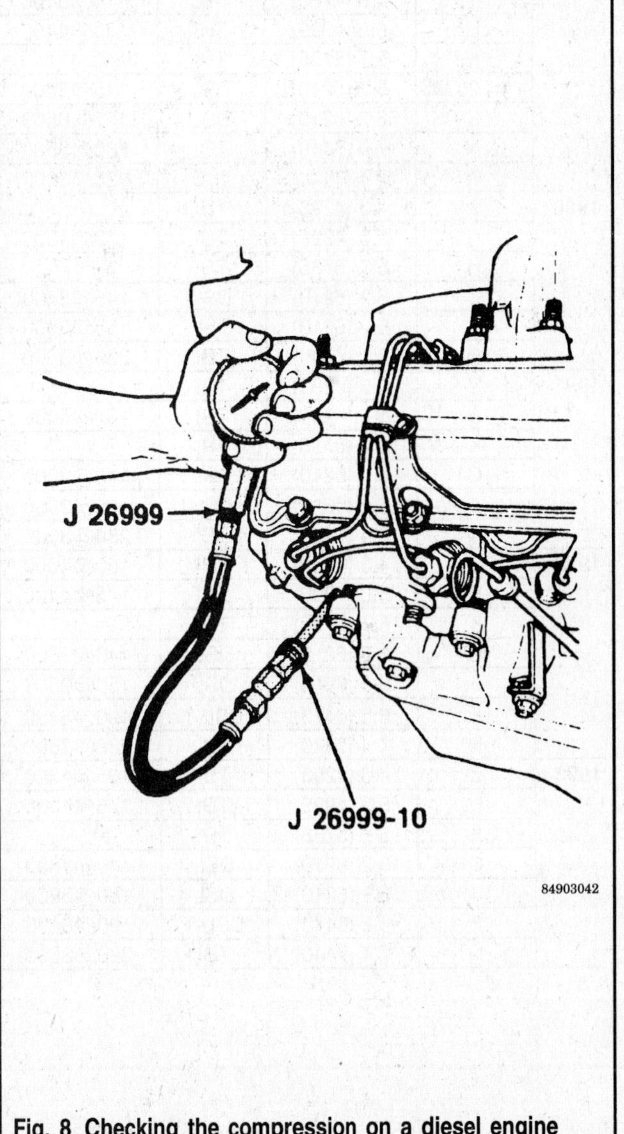

Fig. 8 Checking the compression on a diesel engine

GENERAL ENGINE SPECIFICATIONS

Year	Engine ID/VIN	Engine Displacement Liters (cc)	Fuel System Type	Net Horsepower @ rpm	Net Torque @ rpm (ft. lbs.)	Bore x Stroke (in.)	Com-pression Ratio	Oil Pressure @ rpm
1988	Z	4.3 (4293)	TBI	145@4000	230@2400	4.00x3.48	9.3:1	30@2000
	T	4.8 (4785)	1BC	115@3400	215@1600	3.88x4.12	8.0:1	50@2000
	H	5.0 (4999)	4BC	165@4400	240@2000	3.74x3.48	9.0:1	18@2000
	K	5.7 (5735)	TBI	(1)	(2)	4.00x3.48	8.5:1	18@2000
	C	6.2 (6210)	DSL	130@3600	240@2000	3.98x3.80	21.0:1	35@2000
	J	6.2 (6210)	DSL	135@3600	240@2000	3.98x3.80	21.0:1	35@2000
	N	7.4 (7440)	TBI	230@3600	385@1600	4.25x4.00	8.0:1	40@2000
	W	7.4 (7440)	4BC	240@3800	375@3200	4.25x4.00	8.0:1	40@2000
1989	Z	4.3 (4293)	TBI	145@4000	230@2400	4.00x3.48	9.3:1	30@2000
	T	4.8 (4785)	1BC	115@3400	215@1600	3.88x4.12	8.0:1	50@2000
	H	5.0 (4999)	TBI	170@4400	270@2400	3.74x3.48	9.0:1	18@2000
	K	5.7 (5735)	TBI	(3)	(4)	4.00x3.48	8.5:1	18@2000
	C	6.2 (6210)	DSL	145@3600	255@1900	3.98x3.80	21.0:1	35@2000
	J	6.2 (6210)	DSL	155@3500	257@2000	3.98x3.80	21.0:1	35@2000
	N	7.4 (7440)	TBI	230@3600	385@1600	4.25x4.00	8.0:1	40@2000
	W	7.4 (7440)	4BC	230@3600	370@2800	4.25x4.00	8.0:1	40@2000
1990	Z	4.3 (4293)	TBI	(1)	(2)	4.00x3.48	9.3:1 (7)	18@2000
	H	5.0 (4999)	TBI	170@4000	270@2400	3.74x3.48	9.0:1 (7)	18@2000
	K	5.7 (5735)	TBI	(3)	(4)	4.00x3.48	8.5:1 (7)	18@2000
	C	6.2 (6210)	DSL	145@3600	255@1900	3.98x3.80	21.0:1	35@2000
	J	6.2 (6210)	DSL	155@3500	257@2000	3.98x3.80	21.0:1	35@2000
	N	7.4 (7440)	TBI	230@3600	385@1600	4.25x4.00	8.0:1	40@2000
1991	Z	4.3 (4293)	TBI	(1)	(2)	4.00x3.48	9.3:1 (7)	18@2000 (9)
	H	5.0 (4999)	TBI	170@4400	270@2400	3.74x3.48	9.0:1	18@2000 (9)
	K	5.7 (5735)	TBI	(3)	(4)	4.00x3.48	8.5:1 (8)	18@2000 (9)
	C	6.2 (6210)	DSL	145@3600	255@1900	3.98x3.80	21.0:1	35@2000
	J	6.2 (6210)	DSL	155@3600	257@2000	3.98x3.80	21.0:1	35@2000
	N	7.4 (7440)	TBI	230@3600	385@1600	4.25x4.00	8.0:1	40@2000
1992	Z	4.3 (4293)	TBI	160@4000	235@2400	4.00x3.48	9.3:1	18@2000 (9)
	H	5.0 (4999)	TBI	175@4400	270@2400	3.74x3.48	9.0:1	18@2000 (9)
	K	5.7 (5735)	TBI	(3)	(4)	4.00x3.48	8.5:1 (8)	18@2000 (9)
	C	6.2 (6210)	DSL	140@3600	255@1900	3.98x3.80	21.3:1	35@2000
	J	6.2 (6210)	DSL	150@3500	280@2000	3.98x3.80	21.3:1	350@2000
	F	6.5 (6473)	DSL-T	190@3400	380@1700	4.05x3.80	21.0:1	40-45@2000
	N	7.4 (7440)	TBI	230@3600 (5)	385@1600 (6)	4.25x4.00	8.0:1	40@2000
1993	Z	4.3 (4293)	TBI	165@4000	235@2000	4.00x3.48	9.3:1	18@2000 (9)
	H	5.0 (4999)	TBI	175@4000	270@2400	3.74x3.48	9.0:1	18@2000 (9)
	K	5.7 (5735)	TBI	(3)	(4)	4.00x3.48	8.5:1 (8)	18@2000 (9)
	C	6.2 (6210)	DSL	140@3600	255@1900	3.98x3.80	21.3:1	35@2000
	J	6.2 (6210)	DSL	150@3600	280@2000	3.98x3.80	21.3:1	35@2000
	F	6.5 (6473)	DSL-T	190@3400	380@1700	4.05x3.80	21.0:1	40-45@2000
	N	7.4 (7440)	TBI	230@3600 (5)	385@1600 (6)	4.25x4.00	8.0:1	40@2000

87983c01

GENERAL ENGINE SPECIFICATIONS

Year	Engine ID/VIN	Engine Displacement Liters (cc)	Fuel System Type	Net Horsepower @ rpm	Net Torque @ rpm (ft. lbs.)	Bore x Stroke (in.)	Com-pression Ratio	Oil Pressure @ rpm
1994	Z	4.3 (4293)	TBI	160@4000	235@2400	4.00x3.48	9.1:1	18@2000 (9)
	H	5.0 (4999)	TBI	175@4200	265@2800	3.74x3.48	9.0:1	18@2000 (9)
	K	5.7 (5735)	TBI	200@4000	310@2400	4.00x3.48	9.1:1 (8)	18@2000 (9)
	F	6.5 (6473)	DSL	140@3600	255@1900	4.05x3.80	21.5:1	40-45@2000
	P	6.5 (6473)	DSL	150@3600	280@2000	4.06x3.82	21.5:1	40-45@2000
	S	6.5 (6473)	DSL	190@3400	380@1700	4.06x3.82	21.5:1	40-45@2000
	N	7.4 (7440)	TBI	230@3600 (5)	385@1600 (6)	4.25x4.00	8.0:1	40@2000
1995	Z	4.3 (4293)	TBI	160@4000	235@2400	4.00x3.48	9.1:1	18@2000 (9)
	H	5.0 (4999)	TBI	175@4200	265@2800	3.74x3.48	9.0:1	18@2000 (9)
	K	5.7 (5735)	TFI	200@4000	310@2400	4.00x3.48	9.1:1	18@2000 (9)
	F	6.5 (6473)	DSL	140@3600	255@1900	4.05x3.80	21.5:1	40-45@2000
	P	6.5 (6473)	DSL	150@3600	280@2000	4.06x3.82	21.5:1	40-45@2000
	S	6.5 (6473)	DSL	190@3400	380@1700	4.06x3.82	21.5:1	40-45@2000
	N	7.4 (7440)	TBI	230@3600 (5)	385@1600 (6)	4.25x4.00	8.0:1	40@2000
1996	W	4.3 (4293)	MFI	200@4400	255@2800	4.00x3.48	9.2:1	18@2000 (9)
	M	5.0 (4999)	MFI	230@4600	285@2800	3.74x3.48	9.4:1	18@2000 (9)
	R	5.7 (5735)	MFI	255@4600	330@2800	4.00x3.48	9.4:1	18@2000 (9)
	F	6.5 (6473)	DSL	180@3400 (10)	360@1800 (11)	4.06x3.82	21.5:1	40-45@2000
	P	6.5 (6473)	DSL	180@3400 (10)	360@1800 (11)	4.06x3.82	21.5:1	40-45@2000
	S	6.5 (6473)	DSL	180@3400 (10)	360@1800 (11)	4.06x3.82	21.5:1	40-45@2000
	J	7.4 (7440)	MFI	290@4000 (10)	410@3200 (11)	4.25x4.00	9.0:1	25@2000

TBI - Throttle body fuel injection
BC - Barrel carburetor
DSL - Diesel
1- C/K pick-up-160@4000
C/K pick-up-155@4000
2- C/K pick-up-235@2400
C/K H.D. pick-up-230@2400
3- Below 8500 GVWR: 210@4000
C/K pick-up-155@4000
4- Below 8500 GVWR: 300@2800
Above 8500 GVWR: 300@2400
5- 454SS-255@4000
6- 454SS-405@2400
7- H.D.-8.6:1
8- H.D.-8.3:1
9- Minimum psi
10- H.D.-190@3400
11- H.D.-385@1800

87983c02

VALVE SPECIFICATIONS

Year	Engine ID/VIN	Engine Displacement Liters (cc)	Seat Angle (deg.)	Face Angle (deg.)	Spring Test Pressure (lbs. @ in.)	Spring Installed Height (in.)	Stem-to-Guide Clearance (in.)		Stem Diameter (in.)	
							Intake	Exhaust	Intake	Exhaust
1988	Z	4.3 (4293)	46	45	194-206@ 1.25	1.72	0.0010-0.0027	0.0010-0.0027	0.3410-0.3417	0.3410-0.3417
	T	4.8 (4785)	46	45	175@1.26	1.66	0.0010-0.0027	0.0015-0.0032	0.3410-0.3417	0.3410-0.3417
	H	5.0 (4999)	46	45	76-84@1.70	1.72	0.0010-0.0027	0.0010-0.0027	0.3410-0.3417	0.3410-0.3417
	K	5.7 (5735)	46	45	76-84@1.70	1.72	0.0010-0.0027	0.0010-0.0027	0.3410-0.3417	0.3410-0.3417
	M	5.7 (5735)	46	45	76-84@1.70	1.72	0.0010-0.0027	0.0010-0.0027	0.3410-0.3417	0.3410-0.3417
	C/J	6.2 (6210)	46	45	80@1.81	1.81	0.0010-0.0027	0.0010-0.0027	0.3414	0.3414
	N	7.4 (7440)	46	45	74-86@1.80	1.80	0.0010-0.0027	0.0012-0.0029	0.3410-0.3417	0.3410-0.3417
	W	7.4 (7440)	46	45	74-86@1.80	1.80	0.0010-0.0027	0.0012-0.0029	0.3410-0.3417	0.3410-0.3417
1989	Z	4.3 (4293)	46	45	194-206@ 1.25	1.72	0.0010-0.0027	0.0010-0.0027	0.3410-0.3417	0.3410-0.3417
	T	4.8 (4785)	46	45	175@1.26	1.66	0.0010-0.0027	0.0015-0.0032	0.3410-0.3417	0.3410-0.3417
	H	5.0 (4999)	46	45	76-84@1.70	1.72	0.0010-0.0027	0.0010-0.0027	0.3410-0.3417	0.3410-0.3417
	K	5.7 (5735)	46	45	76-84@1.70	1.72	0.0010-0.0027	0.0010-0.0027	0.3410-0.3417	0.3410-0.3417
	C/J	6.2 (6210)	46	45	80@1.81	1.81	0.0010-0.0027	0.0010-0.0027	0.3414	0.3414
	N	7.4 (7440)	46	45	76-84@1.70	1.80	0.0010-0.0027	0.0012-0.0029	0.3410-0.3417	0.3410-0.3417
	W	7.4 (7440)	46	45	76-84@1.70	1.80	0.0010-0.0027	0.0012-0.0029	0.3410-0.3417	0.3410-0.3417
1990	Z	4.3 (4293)	46	45	194-206@ 1.25	1.72	0.0010-0.0027	0.0010-0.0027	0.3410-0.3417	0.3410-0.3417
	T	4.8 (4785)	46	45	175@1.26	1.66	0.0010-0.0027	0.0015-0.0032	0.3410-0.3417	0.3410-0.3417
	H	5.0 (4999)	46	45	76-84@1.70	1.72	0.0010-0.0027	0.0010-0.0027	0.3410-0.3417	0.3410-0.3417
	K	5.7 (5735)	46	45	70-84@1.70	1.72	0.0010-0.0027	0.0010-0.0027	0.3410-0.3417	0.3410-0.3417
	C/J	6.2 (6210)	46	45	80@1.81	1.81	0.0010-0.0027	0.0010-0.0027	0.3414	0.3414
	N	7.4 (7440)	46	45	74-86@1.80	1.80	0.0010-0.0027	0.0012-0.0029	0.3410-0.3417	0.3410-0.3417
	W	7.4 (7440)	46	45	74-86@1.80	1.80	0.0010-0.0027	0.0012-0.0029	0.3410-0.3417	0.3410-0.3417

87983c03

VALVE SPECIFICATIONS

Year	Engine ID/VIN	Engine Displacement Liters (cc)	Seat Angle (deg.)	Face Angle (deg.)	Spring Test Pressure (lbs. @ in.)	Spring Installed Height (in.)	Stem-to-Guide Clearance (in.)		Stem Diameter (in.)	
							Intake	Exhaust	Intake	Exhaust
1991	Z	4.3 (4293)	46	45	194-206@ 1.25	1.72	0.0010-0.0027	0.0010-0.0027	0.3410-0.3417	0.3410-0.3417
	H	5.0 (4999)	46	45	76-84@1.70	1.72	0.0010-0.0027	0.0010-0.0027	0.3410-0.3417	0.3410-0.3417
	K	5.7 (5735)	46	45	76-84@1.70	1.72	0.0010-0.0027	0.0010-0.0027	0.3410-0.3417	0.3410-0.3417
	C/J	6.2 (6210)	46	45	80@1.81	1.81	0.0010-0.0027	0.0010-0.0027	0.3414	0.3414
	N	7.4 (7440)	46	45	74-86@1.80	1.80	0.0010-0.0027	0.0012-0.0029	0.3410-0.3417	0.3410-0.3417
1992	Z	4.3 (4293)	46	45	194-206@ 1.25	1.72	0.0010-0.0027	0.0010-0.0027	NA	NA
	H	5.0 (4999)	46	45	76-84@1.70	1.72	0.0010-0.0027	0.0010-0.0027	NA	NA
	K	5.7 (5735)	46	45	76-84@1.70	1.72	0.0010-0.0027	0.0010-0.0027	NA	NA
	C/J	6.2 (6210)	46	45	230@1.39	1.81	0.0010-0.0027	0.0010-0.0027	NA	NA
	F	6.5 (6473)	46	45	230@1.39	1.81	0.0010-0.0027	0.0010-0.0027	NA	NA
	N	7.4 (7440)	46	45	74-86@1.80	1.80	0.0010-0.0027	0.0012-0.0029	NA	NA
1993	Z	4.3 (4293)	46	45	194-206@ 1.25	1.72	0.0010-0.0027	0.0010-0.0027	NA	NA
	H	5.0 (4999)	46	45	76-84@1.70	1.72	0.0010-0.0027	0.0010-0.0027	NA	NA
	K	5.7 (5735)	46	45	76-84@1.70	1.72	0.0010-0.0027	0.0010-0.0027	NA	NA
	C/J	6.2 (6210)	46	45	230@1.39	1.81	0.0010-0.0027	0.0010-0.0027	NA	NA
	F	6.5 (6473)	46	45	230@1.39	1.81	0.0010-0.0027	0.0010-0.0027	NA	NA
	N	7.4 (7440)	46	45	74-86@1.80	1.80	0.0010-0.0027	0.0012-0.0029	NA	NA
1994	Z	4.3 (4293)	46	45	194-206@ 1.25	1.72	0.0010-0.0027	0.0010-0.0027	NA	NA
	H	5.0 (4999)	46	45	76-84@1.70	1.72	0.0010-0.0027	0.0010-0.0027	NA	NA
	K	5.7 (5735)	46	45	76-84@1.70	1.72	0.0010-0.0027	0.0010-0.0027	NA	NA
	F	6.5 (6473)	46	45	230@1.39	1.81	0.0010-0.0027	0.0010-0.0027	NA	NA
	P	6.5 (6473)	46	45	230@1.39	1.81	0.0010-0.0027	0.0010-0.0027	NA	NA
	S	6.5 (6473)	46	45	230@1.39	1.81	0.0010-0.0027	0.0010-0.0027	NA	NA
	N	7.4 (7440)	46	45	74-86@1.80	1.80	0.0010-0.0027	0.0012-0.0029	NA	NA

87983c04

VALVE SPECIFICATIONS

Year	Engine ID/VIN	Engine Displacement Liters (cc)	Seat Angle (deg.)	Face Angle (deg.)	Spring Test Pressure (lbs. @ in.)	Spring Installed Height (in.)	Stem-to-Guide Clearance (in.) Intake	Stem-to-Guide Clearance (in.) Exhaust	Stem Diameter (in.) Intake	Stem Diameter (in.) Exhaust
1995	Z	4.3 (4293)	46	45	194-206@ 1.25	1.72	0.0010-0.0027	0.0010-0.0027	NA	NA
	H	5.0 (4999)	46	45	76-84@1.70	1.72	0.0010-0.0027	0.0010-0.0027	NA	NA
	K	5.7 (5735)	46	45	76-84@1.70	1.72	0.0010-0.0027	0.0010-0.0027	NA	NA
	F	6.5 (6473)	46	45	230@1.39	1.81	0.0010-0.0027	0.0010-0.0027	NA	NA
	P	6.5 (6473)	46	45	230@1.39	1.81	0.0010-0.0027	0.0010-0.0027	NA	NA
	S	6.5 (6473)	46	45	230@1.39	1.81	0.0010-0.0027	0.0010-0.0027	NA	NA
	N	7.4 (7440)	46	45	74-86@ 1.80	1.80	0.0010-0.0027	0.0010-0.0027	NA	NA
1996	W	4.3 (4293)	46	45	194-206@ 1.25	1.72	0.0010-0.0027	0.0010-0.0027	NA	NA
	M	5.0 (4999)	46	45	76-84@ 1.70	1.72	0.0010-0.0027	0.0010-0.0027	NA	NA
	R	5.7 (5735)	46	45	76-84@ 1.70	1.72	0.0010-0.0027	0.0010-0.0027	NA	NA
	F	6.5 (6473)	46	45	230@1.39	1.81	0.0010-0.0027	0.0010-0.0027	NA	NA
	P	6.5 (6473)	46	45	230@1.39	1.81	0.0010-0.0027	0.0010-0.0027	NA	NA
	S	6.5 (6473)	46	45	230@1.39	1.81	0.0010-0.0027	0.0010-0.0027	NA	NA
	J	7.4 (7440)	46	45	74-86@ 1.8	1.80	0.0010-0.0027	0.0010-0.0027	NA	NA

NA - Not Available

87983c05

CAMSHAFT SPECIFICATIONS

All measurements given in inches.

Year	Engine ID/VIN	Engine Displacement Liters (cc)	Journal Diameter 1	2	3	4	5	Elevation In.	Ex.	Bearing Clearance	Camshaft End Play
1988	Z	4.3 (4293)	1.8682-1.8692	1.8682-1.8692	1.8682-1.8692	1.8682-1.8692	NA	0.3570	0.3900	0.0010-0.0030	0.0040-0.0120
	T	4.8 (4785)	1.8677-1.8697	1.8677-1.8697	1.8677-1.8697	1.8677-1.8697	NA	0.2313-0.2317	0.2313-0.2317	NA	0.0030-0.0080
	H	5.0 (4999)	1.8682-1.8692	1.8682-1.8692	1.8682-1.8692	1.8682-1.8692	1.8682-1.8692	0.2484	0.2667	NA	0.0040-0.0120
	K	5.7 (5735)	1.8682-1.8692	1.8682-1.8692	1.8682-1.8692	1.8682-1.8692	1.8682-1.8692	0.2600	0.2733	NA	0.0040-0.0120
	C	6.2 (6210)	2.1633-2.1642	2.1633-2.1642	2.1633-2.1642	2.1633-2.1642	2.0067-2.0089	0.2808	0.2808		NA
	J	6.2 (6210)	2.1633-2.1642	2.1633-2.1642	2.1633-2.1642	2.1633-2.1642	2.0067-2.0089	0.2808	0.2808		NA
	N	7.4 (7440)	1.9482-1.9492	1.9482-1.9492	1.9482-1.9492	1.9482-1.9492	1.9482-1.9492	0.2341-0.2345	0.2529-0.2531	NA	NA
	W	7.4 (7440)	1.9482-1.9492	1.9482-1.9492	1.9482-1.9492	1.9482-1.9492	1.9482-1.9492	0.2341-0.2345	0.2529-0.2531	NA	NA
1989	Z	4.3 (4293)	1.8682-1.8692	1.8682-1.8692	1.8682-1.8692	1.8682-1.8692	NA	0.3570	0.3900	0.0010-0.0030	0.0040-0.0120
	T	4.8 (4785)	1.8677-1.8697	1.8677-1.8697	1.8677-1.8697	1.8677-1.8697	NA	0.2313-0.2317	0.2313-0.2317	NA	0.0030-0.008
	H	5.0 (4999)	1.8682-1.8692	1.8682-1.8692	1.8682-1.8692	1.8682-1.8692	1.8682-1.8692	0.2484	0.2667	NA	0.0040-0.0120
	K	5.7 (5735)	1.8682-1.8692	1.8682-1.8692	1.8682-1.8692	1.8682-1.8692	1.8682-1.8692	0.2600	0.2733	NA	0.0040-0.0120
	C	6.2 (6210)	2.1633-2.1642	2.1633-2.1642	2.1633-2.1642	2.1633-2.1642	2.0067-2.0089	0.2808	0.2808		NA
	J	6.2 (6210)	2.1633-2.1642	2.1633-2.1642	2.1633-2.1642	2.1633-2.1642	2.0067-2.0089	0.2808	0.2808		NA
	N	7.4 (7440)	1.9482-1.9492	1.9482-1.9492	1.9482-1.9492	1.9482-1.9492	1.9482-1.9492	0.2341-0.2345	0.2529-0..2531	NA	NA
	W	7.4 (7440)	1.9482-1.9492	1.9482-1.9492	1.9482-1.9492	1.9482-1.9492	1.9482-1.9492	0.2341-0.2345	0.2529-0..2531	NA	NA
1990	Z	4.3 (4293)	1.8682-1.8692	1.8682-1.8692	1.8682-1.8692	1.8682-1.8692	NA	0.3570	0.3900	0.0010-0.0030	0.004-0.012
	H	5.0 (4999)	1.8682-1.8692	1.8682-1.8692	1.8682-1.8692	1.8682-1.8692	1.8682-1.8692	0.2484	0.2667	NA	0.0040-0.0120
	K	5.7 (5735)	1.8682-1.8692	1.8682-1.8692	1.8682-1.8692	1.8682-1.8692	1.8682-1.8692	0.2600	0.2733	NA	0.0040-0.0120
	C	6.2 (6210)	2.1633-2.1642	2.1633-2.1642	2.1633-2.1642	2.1633-2.1642	2.0067-2.0089	0.2808	0.2808		NA
	J	6.2 (6210)	2.1633-2.1642	2.1633-2.1642	2.1633-2.1642	2.1633-2.1642	2.0067-2.0089	0.2808	0.2808		NA
	N	7.4 (7440)	1.9482-1.9492	1.9482-1.9492	1.9482-1.9492	1.9482-1.9492	1.9482-1.9492	0.2341-0.2345	0.2529-0.2531	NA	NA
	W	7.4 (7440)	1.9482-1.9492	1.9482-1.9492	1.9482-1.9492	1.9482-1.9492	1.9482-1.9492	0.2341-0.2345	0.2529-0.2531	NA	NA

87983c06

CAMSHAFT SPECIFICATIONS

All measurements given in inches.

Year	Engine ID/VIN	Engine Displacement Liters (cc)	Journal Diameter 1	2	3	4	5	Elevation In.	Ex.	Bearing Clearance	Camshaft End Play
1991	Z	4.3 (4293)	1.8682-1.8692	1.8682-1.8692	1.8682-1.8692	1.8682-1.8692	NA	0.3570	0.3900	0.0010-0.0030	0.0040-0.0120
	H	5.0 (4999)	1.8682-1.8692	1.8682-1.8692	1.8682-1.8692	1.8682-1.8692	NA	0.2484	0.2667	NA	0.0040-0.0120
	K	5.7 (5735)	1.8682-1.8692	1.8682-1.8692	1.8682-1.8692	1.8682-1.8692	NA	0.2600	0.2733	NA	0.0040-0.0120
	C	6.2 (6210)	2.1633-2.1642	2.1633-2.1642	2.1633-2.1642	2.1633-2.1642	2.0067-2.0089	0.2808	0.2808		NA
	J	6.2 (6210)	2.1633-2.1642	2.1633-2.1642	2.1633-2.1642	2.1633-2.1642	2.0067-2.0089	0.2808	0.2808		NA
	N	7.4 (7440)	1.9482-1.9492	1.9482-1.9492	1.9482-1.9492	1.9482-1.9492	1.9482-1.9492	0.2341-0.2345	0.2529-0.2531	NA	NA
1992	Z	4.3 (4293)	1.8682-1.8692	1.8682-1.8692	1.8682-1.8692	1.8682-1.8692	NA	0.2340	0.2570	0.0010-0.0030	0.0040-0.0120
	H	5.0 (4999)	1.8682-1.8692	1.8682-1.8692	1.8682-1.8692	1.8682-1.8692	1.8682-1.8692	0.2336	0.2565	NA	0.0040-0.0120
	K	5.7 (5735)	1.8682-1.8692	1.8682-1.8692	1.8682-1.8692	1.8682-1.8692	1.8682-1.8692	0.2565	0.2690	NA	0.0040-0.0120
	C	6.2 (6210)	2.1633-2.1642	2.1633-2.1642	2.1633-2.1642	2.1633-2.1642	2.0067-2.0089	0.2808	0.2808	0.0010-0.0040	0.0020-0.0120
	J	6.2 (6210)	2.1633-2.1642	2.1633-2.1642	2.1633-2.1642	2.1633-2.1642	2.0067-2.0089	0.2808	0.2808	0.0010-0.0040	0.0020-0.0120
	F	6.5 (6473)	2.1642-2.1663	2.1642-2.1663	2.1642-2.1663	2.1642-2.1663	2.0067-2.0089	0.2808	0.2808	NA	0.0020-0.0120
	N	7.4 (7440)	1.9482-1.9492	1.9482-1.9492	1.9482-1.9492	1.9482-1.9492	1.9482-1.9492	0.2341-0.2345	0.2529-0.2531	NA	NA
1993	Z	4.3 (4293)	1.8682-1.8692	1.8682-1.8692	1.8682-1.8692	1.8682-1.8692	NA	0.2340	0.2570	0.0010-0.0030	0.0040-0.0120
	H	5.0 (4999)	1.8682-1.8692	1.8682-1.8692	1.8682-1.8692	1.8682-1.8692	1.8682-1.8692	0.2336	0.2565	NA	0.0040-0.0120
	K	5.7 (5735)	1.8682-1.8692	1.8682-1.8692	1.8682-1.8692	1.8682-1.8692	1.8682-1.8692	0.2565	0.2690	NA	0.0040-0.0120
	C	6.2 (6210)	2.1633-2.1642	2.1633-2.1642	2.1633-2.1642	2.1633-2.1642	2.0067-2.0089	0.2808	0.2808	0.0010-0.0040	0.0020-0.0120
	J	6.2 (6210)	2.1633-2.1642	2.1633-2.1642	2.1633-2.1642	2.1633-2.1642	2.0067-2.0089	0.2808	0.2808	0.0010-0.0040	0.0020-0.0120
	F	6.5 (6473)	2.1642-2.1663	2.1642-2.1663	2.1642-2.1663	2.1642-2.1663	2.0067-2.0089	0.2808	0.2808	NA	0.0020-0.0120
	N	7.4 (7440)	1.9482-1.9492	1.9482-1.9492	1.9482-1.9492	1.9482-1.9492	1.9482-1.9492	0.2341-0.2345	0.2529-0.2531	NA	NA

87983c07

CAMSHAFT SPECIFICATIONS

All measurements given in inches.

Year	Engine ID/VIN	Engine Displacement Liters (cc)	Journal Diameter 1	2	3	4	5	Elevation In.	Ex.	Bearing Clearance	Camshaft End Play
1994	Z	4.3 (4293)	1.8682-1.8692	1.8682-1.8692	1.8682-1.8692	1.8682-1.8692	NA	0.234	0.257	0.0010-0.0030	0.0040-0.0120
	H	5.0 (4999)	1.8682-1.8692	1.8682-1.8692	1.8682-1.8692	1.8682-1.8692	1.8682-1.8692	0.2336	0.2565	NA	0.0040-0.0120
	K	5.7 (5735)	1.8682-1.8692	1.8682-1.8692	1.8682-1.8692	1.8682-1.8692	1.8682-1.8692	0.2565	0.2690	NA	0.0040-0.0120
	F	6.5 (6473)	2.1642-2.1663	2.1642-2.1663	2.1642-2.1663	2.1642-2.1663	2.0067-2.0089	0.2808	0.2808	NA	0.0020-0.0120
	P	6.5 (6473)	2.1642-2.1663	2.1642-2.1663	2.1642-2.1663	2.1642-2.1663	2.0067-2.0089	0.2808	0.2808	NA	0.0020-0.0120
	S	6.5 (6473)	2.1642-2.1663	2.1642-2.1663	2.1642-2.1663	2.1642-2.1663	2.0067-2.0089	0.2808	0.2808	NA	0.0020-0.0120
	N	7.4 (7440)	1.9482-1.9492	1.9482-1.9492	1.9482-1.9492	1.9482-1.9492	1.9482-1.9492	0.2341-0.2345	0.2529-0.2531	NA	NA
1995	Z	4.3 (4293)	1.8682-1.8692	1.8682-1.8692	1.8682-1.8692	1.8682-1.8692	NA	0.2340	0.2570	0.0010-0.0030	0.0040-0.0120
	H	5.0 (4999)	1.8682-1.8692	1.8682-1.8692	1.8682-1.8692	1.8682-1.8692	1.8682-1.8692	0.2336	0.2565	NA	0.0040-0.0120
	K	5.7 (5735)	1.8682-1.8692	1.8682-1.8692	1.8682-1.8692	1.8682-1.8692	1.8682-1.8692	0.2565	0.2690	NA	0.0040-0.0120
	F	6.5 (6473)	2.1642-2.1663	2.1642-2.1663	2.1642-2.1663	2.1642-2.1663	2.0067-2.0089	0.2808	0.2808	NA	0.0020-0.0120
	P	6.5 (6473)	2.1642-2.1663	2.1642-2.1663	2.1642-2.1663	2.1642-2.1663	2.0067-2.0089	0.2808	0.2808	NA	0.0020-0.0120
	S	6.5 (6473)	2.1642-2.1663	2.1642-2.1663	2.1642-2.1663	2.1642-2.1663	2.0067-2.0089	0.2808	0.2808	NA	0.0020-0.0120
	N	7.4 (7440)	1.9482-1.9492	1.9482-1.9492	1.9482-1.9492	1.9482-1.9492	1.9482-1.9492	0.2341-0.2345	0.2529-0.2531	NA	NA
1996	W	4.3 (4293)	1.8677-1.8697	1.8677-1.8697	1.8677-1.8697	1.8677-1.8697	NA	0.2340	0.2570	NA	0.001-0.009
	M	5.0 (4999)	1.9477-1.9497	1.9477-1.9497	1.9477-1.9497	1.9477-1.9497	1.9477-1.9497	0.2821	0.2843	NA	NA
	R	5.7 (5735)	1.9477-1.9497	1.9477-1.9497	1.9477-1.9497	1.9477-1.9497	1.9477-1.9497	0.2821	0.2843	NA	NA
	F	6.5 (6473)	2.1658-2.1680	2.1658-2.1680	2.1658-2.1680	2.1658-2.1680	2.0082-2.0104	0.2810	0.2810	NA	0.0020-0.012
	S	6.5 (6473)	2.1658-2.1680	2.1658-2.1680	2.1658-2.1680	2.1658-2.1680	2.0082-2.0104	0.2810	0.2810	NA	0.0020-0.012
	J	7.4 (7440)	1.9477-1.9497	1.9477-1.9497	1.9477-1.9497	1.9477-1.9497	1.9477-1.9497	0.2821	0.2843	NA	NA

NA - Not Available

87983c08

CRANKSHAFT AND CONNECTING ROD SPECIFICATIONS

All measurements are given in inches.

Year	Engine ID/VIN	Engine Displacement Liters (cc)	Crankshaft Main Brg. Journal Dia.	Crankshaft Main Brg. Oil Clearance	Crankshaft Shaft End-play	Crankshaft Thrust on No.	Connecting Rod Journal Diameter	Connecting Rod Oil Clearance	Connecting Rod Side Clearance
1988	Z	4.3 (4293)	②	③	0.0020-0.0060	3	2.2487-2.2497	0.0013-0.0035	0.0060-0.0140
	T	4.8 (4785)	2.2979-2.2994	④	0.0020-0.0060	7	2.0990-2.1000	0.0010-0.0026	0.0060-0.0170
	H	5.0 (4999)	②	③	0.0020-0.0060	5	2.0988-2.0998	0.0013-0.0035	0.0060-0.0140
	K	5.7 (5735)	②	③	0.0020-0.0060	5	2.0988-2.0998	0.0013-0.0035	0.0060-0.0140
	C	6.2 (6210)	⑤	⑥	0.0020-0.0070	3	2.3980-2.3990	0.0017-0.0039	0.0070-0.0240
	J	6.2 (6210)	⑤	⑥	0.0020-0.0070	3	2.3980-2.3990	0.0017-0.0039	0.0070-0.0240
	N	7.4 (7440)	⑦	⑧	0.0060-0.0100	5	2.1990-2.2000	0.0009-0.0025	0.0130-0.0230
	W	7.4 (7440)	⑦	⑧	0.0060-0.0100	5	2.1990-2.2000	0.0009-0.0025	0.0130-0.0230
1989	Z	4.3 (4293)	②	③	0.0020-0.0060	3	2.2487-2.2497	0.0013-0.0035	0.0060-0.0140
	T	4.8 (4785)	2.2979-2.2994	④	0.0020-0.0060	7	2.0990-2.1000	0.0010-0.0026	0.0060-0.0170
	H	5.0 (4999)	②	③	0.0020-0.0060	5	2.0988-2.0998	0.0013-0.0035	0.0060-0.0140
	K	5.7 (5735)	②	③	0.0020-0.0060	5	2.0988-2.0998	0.0013-0.0035	0.0060-0.0140
	C	6.2 (6210)	⑤	⑥	0.0020-0.0070	3	2.3980-2.3990	0.0017-0.0039	0.0070-0.0240
	J	6.2 (6210)	⑤	⑥	0.0020-0.0070	3	2.3980-2.3990	0.0017-0.0039	0.0070-0.0240
	N	7.4 (7440)	⑦	⑧	0.0060-0.0100	5	2.1990-2.2000	0.0009-0.0025	0.0130-0.0230
	W	7.4 (7440)	⑦	⑧	0.0060-0.0100	5	2.1990-2.2000	0.0009-0.0025	0.0130-0.0230
1990	Z	4.3 (4293)	②	③	0.0020-0.0060	3	2.2487-2.2497	0.0013-0.0035	0.0060-0.0140
	H	5.0 (4999)	②	③	0.0020-0.0060	5	2.0988-2.0998	0.0013-0.0035	0.0060-0.0140
	K	5.7 (5735)	②	③	0.0020-0.0060	5	2.0988-2.0998	0.0013-0.0035	0.0060-0.0140
	C	6.2 (6210)	⑤	⑥	0.0020-0.0070	3	2.3980-2.3990	0.0017-0.0039	0.0070-0.0240
	J	6.2 (6210)	⑤	⑥	0.0020-0.0070	3	2.3980-2.3990	0.0017-0.0039	0.0070-0.0240
	N	7.4 (7440)	⑦	⑧	0.0060-0.0100	5	2.1990-2.2000	0.0009-0.0025	0.0130-0.0230
	W	7.4 (7440)	⑦	⑧	0.0060-0.0100	5	2.1990-2.2000	0.0009-0.0025	0.0130-0.0230

87983c09

CRANKSHAFT AND CONNECTING ROD SPECIFICATIONS

All measurements are given in inches.

		Engine	Crankshaft				Connecting Rod		
Year	Engine ID/VIN	Displacement Liters (cc)	Main Brg. Journal Dia.	Main Brg. Oil Clearance	Shaft End-play	Thrust on No.	Journal Diameter	Oil Clearance	Side Clearance
1991	Z	4.3 (4293)	②	③	0.0020-0.0060	3	2.2487-2.2497	0.0013-0.0035	0.0060-0.0140
	H	5.0 (4999)	②	③	0.0020-0.0060	5	2.0988-2.0998	0.0013-0.0035	0.0060-0.0140
	K	5.7 (5735)	②	③	0.0020-0.0060	5	2.0988-2.0998	0.0013-0.0035	0.0060-0.0140
	C	6.2 (6210)	④	⑤	0.0020-0.0070	3	2.3980-2.3990	0.0017-0.0039	0.0070-0.0240
	J	6.2 (6210)	④	⑤	0.0020-0.0070	3	2.3980-2.3990	0.0017-0.0039	0.0070-0.0240
	N	7.4 (7440)	⑥	⑦	0.004-0.011	5	2.1990-2.2000	0.0009-0.0025	0.0130-0.0230
1992	Z	4.3 (4293)	②	③	0.0020-0.0060	3	2.2487-2.2497	0.0013-0.0035	0.0060-0.0140
	H	5.0 (4999)	②	③	0.0020-0.0060	5	2.0988-2.0998	0.0013-0.0035	0.0060-0.0140
	K	5.7 (5735)	②	③	0.0020-0.0060	5	2.0988-2.0998	0.0013-0.0035	0.0060-0.0140
	C	6.2 (6210)	④	⑤	0.0020-0.0070	3	2.3980-2.3990	0.0017-0.0039	0.0070-0.0240
	J	6.2 (6210)	④	⑤	0.0020-0.0070	3	2.3980-2.3990	0.0017-0.0039	0.0070-0.0240
	F	6.5 (6473)	④	⑤	0.0020-0.0070	3	2.3980-2.3990	0.0017-0.0039	0.0070-0.0240
	N	7.4 (7440)	⑥	⑦	0.004-0.011	5	2.1990-2.2000	0.0009-0.0025	0.0130-0.0230
1993	Z	4.3 (4293)	②	③	0.0020-0.0060	3	2.2487-2.2497	0.0013-0.0035	0.0060-0.0140
	H	5.0 (4999)	②	③	0.0020-0.0060	3	2.2487-2.2497	0.0013-0.0035	0.0060-0.0140
	K	5.7 (5735)	②	③	0.0020-0.0060	3	2.2487-2.2497	0.0013-0.0035	0.0060-0.0140
	C	6.2 (6210)	④	⑤	0.0020-0.0070	3	2.3980-2.3990	0.0017-0.0039	0.0070-0.0240
	J	6.2 (6210)	④	⑤	0.0020-0.0070	3	2.3980-2.3990	0.0017-0.0039	0.0070-0.0240
	F	6.5 (6473)	④	⑤	0.0020-0.0070	3	2.3980-2.3990	0.0017-0.0039	0.0070-0.0240
	N	7.4 (7440)	⑥	⑦	0.004-0.011	5	2.1990-2.2000	0.0009-0.0025	0.0130-0.0230

87983c10

CRANKSHAFT AND CONNECTING ROD SPECIFICATIONS

All measurements are given in inches.

		Engine	Crankshaft				Connecting Rod		
Year	Engine ID/VIN	Displacement Liters (cc)	Main Brg. Journal Dia.	Main Brg. Oil Clearance	Shaft End-play	Thrust on No.	Journal Diameter	Oil Clearance	Side Clearance
1994	Z	4.3 (4293)	②	③	0.0020-0.0060	3	2.2487-2.2497	0.0013-0.0035	0.0060-0.0140
	H	5.0 (4999)	②	③	0.0020-0.0080	5	2.0988-2.0998	0.0013-0.0035	0.0060-0.0140
	K	5.7 (5735)	②	③	0.0020-0.0080	5	2.0988-2.0998	0.0013-0.0035	0.0060-0.0140
	F	6.5 (6473)	⑤	④	0.0040-0.0100	3	2.3980-2.3990	0.0018-0.0035	0.0070-0.0250
	P	6.5 (6473)	⑤	④	0.0040-0.0100	3	2.3980-2.3990	0.0018-0.0035	0.0070-0.0250
	S	6.5 (6473)	⑤	④	0.0040-0.0100	3	2.3980-2.3990	0.0018-0.0035	0.0070-0.0250
	N	7.4 (7440)	⑥	⑦	0.004-0.011	5	2.1990-2.2000	0.0009-0.0025	0.0130-0.0230
1995	Z	4.3 (4293)	②	③	0.0020-0.0060	3	2.2487-2.2497	0.0013-0.0035	0.0060-0.0140
	H	5.0 (4999)	②	③	0.0020-0.0080	5	2.0988-2.0998	0.0013-0.0035	0.0060-0.0140
	K	5.7 (5735)	②	③	0.0020-0.0080	5	2.0988-2.0998	0.0013-0.0035	0.0060-0.0140
	F	6.5 (6473)	④	⑤	0.0040-0.0100	3	2.3980-2.3990	0.0018-0.0035	0.0070-0.0250
	P	6.5 (6473)	④	⑤	0.0040-0.0100	3	2.3980-2.3990	0.0018-0.0035	0.0070-0.0250
	S	6.5 (6473)	④	⑤	0.0040-0.0100	3	2.3980-2.3990	0.0018-0.0035	0.0070-0.0250
	N	7.4 (7440)	⑥	⑦	0.004-0.011	5	2.1990-2.2000	0.0009-0.0025	0.0130-0.0230
1996	W	4.3 (4293)	⑪	⑧	0.0020-0.0060	4	2.2487-2.2497	0.0013-0.0035	0.0060-0.0140
	M	5.0 (4999)	①	⑩	0.0020-0.0080	5	2.0988-2.0998	0.0013-0.0035	0.0060-0.0140
	R	5.7 (5735)	①	⑩	0.0020-0.0080	5	2.0988-2.0998	0.0013-0.0035	0.0060-0.0140
	F	6.5 (6473)	⑫	⑦	0.0040-0.0100	3	2.3980-2.3990	0.0018-0.0035	0.0070-0.0250
	S	6.5 (6473)	⑫	⑦	0.0040-0.0100	3	2.3980-2.3990	0.0018-0.0035	0.0070-0.0250
	J	7.4 (7440)	①	⑩	0.004-0.011	5	2.1990-2.2000	0.0009-0.0025	0.0130-0.0230

1 Three dots: 2.64728-2.64
  Two dots: 2.64759-2.64790
  One dot: 2.64790-2.6482:

2 No. 1: 2.4484-2.4493
  Nos. 2-3: 2.4481-2.4490
  No. 4: 2.4479-2.4488

3 No. 1: 0.0008-0.0020
  Nos. 2-3: 0.0011-0.0023
  No. 4: 0.0017-0.0032

4 Nos. 1-6: 0.0010-0.0024
  No. 7: 0.0016-0.0035

5 Nos. 1-4:: 2.9495-2.9504
  No. 5: 2.9493-2.9502

6 Nos. 1-4: 0.0083
  No. 5: 0.0055-0.0093

7 Nos. 1-4: 2.7481-2.7490
  No. 5: 2.7476-2.7486

8 Nos. 1-4: 0.0013-0.0025
  No. 5: 0.0024-0.0040

9 Two dots: 1.9983-1.9989
  One dot: 1.9989-1.9994

10 No. 1: 0.0007-0.0021
  Nos. 2-4: 0.0009-0.0024
  No. 5: 0.0010-0.0027

11 No. 1: 2.4488-2.4495
  Nos. 2-3: 2.4485-2.4494
  No. 5: 0.0010-0.0027

12 Blue-
  Nos. 1-4: 2.9517-2.9520
  No. 5: 2.9515-2.9518
  Orange or Red
  Nos. 1-4: 2.9520-2.9524
  No. 5: 2.9518-2.9522
  White-
  Nos. 1-4: 2.9524-2.9527
  No. 5: 2.9522-2.9525

87983c11

PISTON AND RING SPECIFICATIONS

All measurements are given in inches.

Year	Engine ID/VIN	Engine Displacement Liters (cc)	Piston Clearance	Ring Gap: Top Compression	Ring Gap: Bottom Compression	Ring Gap: Oil Control	Ring Side Clearance: Top Compression	Ring Side Clearance: Bottom Compression	Ring Side Clearance: Oil Control
1988	Z	4.3 (4293)	0.0007-0.0017	0.010-0.020	0.010-0.025	0.015-0.055	0.0012-0.0032	0.0012-0.0032	0.0020-0.0070
	T	4.8 (4785)	0.0026-0.0036	0.010-0.020	0.010-0.020	0.015-0.055	0.0020-0.0040	0.0020-0.0040	0.0050-0.0055
	H	5.0 (4999)	0.0007-0.0017	0.010-0.020	0.010-0.025	0.015-0.055	0.0012-0.0032	0.0012-0.0032	0.0020-0.0070
	K	5.7 (5735)	0.0007-0.0017	0.010-0.020	0.010-0.025	0.015-0.055	0.0012-0.0032	0.0012-0.0032	0.0020-0.0070
	C	6.2 (6210)	①	0.012-0.022	0.030-0.039	0.010-0.020	0.0030-0.0070	0.0300-0.0390	0.0020-0.0040
	J	6.2 (6210)	①	0.012-0.022	0.030-0.039	0.010-0.020	0.0030-0.0070	0.0300-0.0390	0.0020-0.0040
	N	7.4 (7440)	0.0030-0.0040	0.010-0.020	0.010-0.020	0.015-0.055	0.0017-0.0032	0.0017-0.0032	0.0050-0.0065
	W	7.4 (7440)	0.0030-0.0040	0.010-0.020	0.010-0.020	0.015-0.055	0.0017-0.0032	0.0017-0.0032	0.0050-0.0065
1989	Z	4.3 (4293)	0.0007-0.0017	0.010-0.020	0.010-0.025	0.015-0.055	0.0012-0.0032	0.0012-0.0032	0.0020-0.0070
	T	4.8 (4785)	0.0026-0.0036	0.010-0.020	0.010-0.020	0.015-0.055	0.0020-0.0040	0.0020-0.0040	0.0050-0.0055
	H	5.0 (4999)	0.0007-0.0017	0.010-0.020	0.010-0.025	0.015-0.055	0.0012-0.0032	0.0012-0.0032	0.0020-0.0070
	K	5.7 (5735)	0.0007-0.0017	0.010-0.020	0.010-0.025	0.015-0.055	0.0012-0.0032	0.0012-0.0032	0.0020-0.0070
	C	6.2 (6210)	①	0.012-0.022	0.030-0.039	0.010-0.020	0.0030-0.0070	0.0300-0.0390	0.0020-0.0040
	J	6.2 (6210)	①	0.012-0.022	0.030-0.039	0.010-0.020	0.0030-0.0070	0.0300-0.0390	0.0020-0.0040
	N	7.4 (7440)	0.0030-0.0040	0.010-0.018	0.016-0.024	0.015-0.055	0.0017-0.0032	0.0017-0.0032	0.0050-0.0065
	W	7.4 (7440)	0.0030-0.0040	0.010-0.018	0.016-0.024	0.015-0.055	0.0017-0.0032	0.0017-0.0032	0.0050-0.0065
1990	Z	4.3 (4293)	0.0007-0.0017	0.010-0.020	0.010-0.025	0.015-0.055	0.0012-0.0032	0.0012-0.0032	0.0020-0.0070
	T	4.8 (4785)	0.0026-0.0036	0.010-0.020	0.010-0.020	0.015-0.055	0.0020-0.0040	0.0020-0.0040	0.0050-0.0055
	H	5.0 (4999)	0.0007-0.0017	0.010-0.020	0.010-0.025	0.015-0.055	0.0012-0.0032	0.0012-0.0032	0.0020-0.0070
	K	5.7 (5735)	0.0007-0.0017	0.010-0.020	0.010-0.025	0.015-0.055	0.0012-0.0032	0.0012-0.0032	0.0020-0.0070
	C	6.2 (6210)	①	0.012-0.022	0.030-0.039	0.010-0.020	0.0030-0.0070	0.0020-0.0030	0.0020-0.0040
	J	6.2 (6210)	①	0.012-0.022	0.030-0.039	0.010-0.020	0.0030-0.0070	0.0020-0.0030	0.0020-0.0040
	N	7.4 (7440)	0.0030-0.0040	0.010-0.018	0.016-0.024	0.015-0.055	0.0017-0.0032	0.0017-0.0032	0.0050-0.0065

87983c12

PISTON AND RING SPECIFICATIONS

All measurements are given in inches.

Year	Engine ID/VIN	Engine Displacement Liters (cc)	Piston Clearance	Ring Gap			Ring Side Clearance		
				Top Compression	Bottom Compression	Oil Control	Top Compression	Bottom Compression	Oil Control
1991	Z	4.3 (4293)	0.0007-0.0017	0.010-0.020	0.010-0.025	0.015-0.055	0.0012-0.0032	0.0012-0.0032	0.0020-0.0070
	H	5.0 (4999)	0.0007-0.0017	0.010-0.020	0.010-0.025	0.015-0.055	0.0012-0.0032	0.0012-0.0032	0.0020-0.0070
	K	5.7 (5735)	0.0007-0.0017	0.010-0.020	0.010-0.025	0.015-0.055	0.0012-0.0032	0.0012-0.0032	0.0020-0.0070
	C	6.2 (6210)	①	0.012-0.022	0.030-0.039	0.010-0.020	0.0030-0.0070	0.0300-0.0400	0.0020-0.0040
	J	6.2 (6210)	①	0.012-0.022	0.030-0.039	0.010-0.020	0.0030-0.0070	0.0300-0.0400	0.0020-0.0040
	N	7.4 (7440)	0.0030-0.0040	0.010-0.018	0.016-0.024	0.010-0.030	0.0012-0.0029	0.0012-0.0029	0.0050-0.0065
1992	Z	4.3 (4293)	0.0007-0.0017	0.010-0.020	0.010-0.025	0.015-0.055	0.0012-0.0032	0.0012-0.0032	0.0020-0.0070
	H	5.0 (4999)	0.0007-0.0017	0.010-0.020	0.018-0.026	0.010-0.030	0.0012-0.0032	0.0012-0.0032	0.0020-0.0070
	K	5.7 (5735)	0.0007-0.0017	0.010-0.020	0.018-0.026	0.010-0.030	0.0012-0.0032	0.0012-0.0032	0.0020-0.0070
	C	6.2 (6210)	②	0.012-0.022	0.030-0.039	0.010-0.020	0.0030-0.0070	0.0300-0.0400	0.0020-0.0040
	J	6.2 (6210)	②	0.012-0.022	0.030-0.039	0.010-0.020	0.0030-0.0070	0.0300-0.0400	0.0020-0.0040
	F	6.5 (6473)	②	0.010-0.020	0.030-0.039	0.010-0.023	0.0030-0.0070	0.0300-0.0400	0.0020-0.0040
	N	7.4 (7440)	0.0030-0.0042	0.010-0.018	0.016-0.024	0.010-0.030	0.0012-0.0029	0.0012-0.0029	0.0050-0.0065
1993	Z	4.3 (4293)	0.0007-0.0017	0.010-0.020	0.010-0.025	0.015-0.055	0.0012-0.0032	0.0012-0.0032	0.0020-0.0070
	H	5.0 (4999)	0.0007-0.0021	0.010-0.020	0.018-0.026	0.010-0.030	0.0012-0.0032	0.0012-0.0032	0.0020-0.0070
	K	5.7 (5735)	0.0007-0.0021	0.010-0.020	0.018-0.026	0.010-0.030	0.0012-0.0032	0.0012-0.0032	0.0020-0.0070
	C	6.2 (6210)	②	0.010-0.020	0.030-0.039	0.010-0.020	④	0.0015-0.0030	0.0015-0.0035
	J	6.2 (6210)	②	0.010-0.020	0.030-0.039	0.010-0.020	④	0.0015-0.0030	0.0015-0.0035
	F	6.5 (6473)	③	0.010-0.020	0.030-0.039	0.010-0.020	④	0.0015-0.0030	0.0015-0.0035
	N	7.4 (7440)	0.0003-0.0042	0.010-0.018	0.016-0.024	0.010-0.030	0.0012-0.0029	0.0012-0.0029	0.0050-0.0065

87983c13

PISTON AND RING SPECIFICATIONS

All measurements are given in inches.

				Ring Gap			Ring Side Clearance		
Year	Engine ID/VIN	Engine Displacement Liters (cc)	Piston Clearance	Top Compression	Bottom Compression	Oil Control	Top Compression	Bottom Compression	Oil Control
1994	Z	4.3 (4293)	0.0007-0.0017	0.010-0.020	0.010-0.025	0.015-0.055	0.0012-0.0032	0.0012-0.0032	0.0020-0.0070
	H	5.0 (4999)	0.0007-0.0021	0.010-0.020	0.018-0.026	0.010-0.030	0.0012-0.0032	0.0012-0.0032	0.0020-0.0070
	K	5.7 (5735)	0.0007-0.0021	0.010-0.020	0.018-0.026	0.010-0.030	0.0012-0.0032	0.0012-0.0032	0.0020-0.0070
	F	6.5 (6473)	②	0.010-0.020	0.030-0.039	0.010-0.020	③	0.0015-0.0030	0.0015-0.0035
	P	6.5 (6473)	②	0.010-0.020	0.030-0.039	0.010-0.020	③	0.0015-0.0030	0.0015-0.0035
	S	6.5 (6473)	②	0.010-0.020	0.030-0.039	0.010-0.020	③	0.0015-0.0030	0.0015-0.0035
	N	7.4 (7440)	0.0018-0.0030	0.010-0.018	0.016-0.024	0.010-0.030	0.0012-0.0029	0.0012-0.0029	0.0050-0.0065
1995	Z	4.3 (4293)	0.0007-0.0017	0.010-0.020	0.010-0.025	0.015-0.055	0.0012-0.0032	0.0012-0.0032	0.0020-0.0070
	H	5.0 (4999)	0.0007-0.0021	0.010-0.020	0.018-0.026	0.010-0.030	0.0012-0.0032	0.0012-0.0032	0.0020-0.0070
	K	5.7 (5735)	0.0007-0.0021	0.010-0.020	0.018-0.026	0.010-0.030	0.0012-0.0032	0.0012-0.0032	0.0020-0.0070
	F	6.5 (6473)	①	0.010-0.020	0.030-0.039	0.010-0.020	③	0.0015-0.0030	0.0015-0.0035
	P	6.5 (6473)	①	0.010-0.020	0.030-0.039	0.010-0.020	③	0.0015-0.0030	0.0015-0.0035
	S	6.5 (6473)	①	0.010-0.020	0.030-0.039	0.010-0.020	③	0.0015-0.0030	0.0015-0.0035
	N	7.4 (7440)	0.0018-0.0030	0.010-0.018	0.016-0.024	0.010-0.030	0.0012-0.0029	0.0012-0.0029	0.0050-0.0065
1996	W	4.3 (4293)	0.0007-0.0017	0.010-0.020	0.010-0.025	0.015-0.055	0.0012-0.0032	0.0012-0.0032	0.0020-0.0070
	M	5.0 (4999)	0.0007-0.0021	0.010-0.020	0.018-0.026	0.010-0.030	0.0012-0.0032	0.0012-0.0032	0.0020-0.0070
	R	5.7 (5735)	0.0007-0.0021	0.010-0.020	0.018-0.026	0.010-0.030	0.0012-0.0032	0.0012-0.0032	0.0020-0.0070
	F	6.5 (6473)	②	0.010-0.020	0.030-0.039	0.010-0.020	0.0015-0.0031	0.0015-0.0031	0.0016-0.0035
	S	6.5 (6473)	②	0.010-0.020	0.030-0.039	0.010-0.020	0.0015-0.0031	0.0015-0.0031	0.0016-0.0035
	J	7.4 (7440)	0.0018-0.0030	0.010-0.018	0.016-0.024	0.010-0.030	0.0012-0.0029	0.0012-0.0029	0.0050-0.0065

① Bohn piston Nos. 1-6: 0.0035-0.0045
Bohn piston Nos. 7-8: 0.0040-0.0050
Zollner piston Nos. 1-6: 0.0044-0.0054
Zollner piston Nos. 7-8: 0.0049-0.0059

② 1-6-0.0037-0.0047
7-8-0.0042-. 0.0052

③ Bore Nos. 1-6: 0.0037-0.0047
Nos. 7-8: 0.0042-0.0052
Keystone type ring

87983c14

TORQUE SPECIFICATIONS

All readings in ft. lbs.

Year	Engine ID/VIN	Engine Displacement Liters (cc)	Cylinder Head Bolts	Main Bearing Bolts	Rod Bearing Bolts	Crankshaft Damper Bolts	Flywheel Bolts	Manifold		Spark Plugs	Lug Nut
								Intake	Exhaust		
1988	Z	4.3 (4293)	65	80	45	70	75	36	⑦	22	90
	T	4.8 (4785)	95 ①	65	44	50	110	⑤	⑤	17-27	90
	H	5.0 (4999)	65	④	45	70	60	35	⑦	17-27	90
	K	5.7 (5735)	65	④	45	70	60	35	⑦	17-27	90
	C	6.2 (6210)	②	③	48	200	60	31	25	-	90
	J	6.2 (6210)	②	③	48	200	65	31	26	-	90
	N	7.4 (7440)	80	110	48	85	65	30	25	17-27	90
	W	7.4 (7440)	80	110	50	85	65	30	25	22	90
1989	Z	4.3 (4293)	65	80	45	70	75	36	⑦	22	90
	T	4.8 (4785)	95 ①	65	44	50	110	⑤	⑤	17-27	90
	H	5.0 (4999)	65	④	45	70	60	35	⑦	17-27	90
	K	5.7 (5735)	65	④	45	70	60	35	⑦	17-27	90
	C	6.2 (6210)	②	③	48	200	60	31	25	-	90
	J	6.2 (6210)	②	③	48	200	65	31	26	-	90
	N	7.4 (7440)	80	110	48	85	65	30	25	17-27	90
	W	7.4 (7440)	80	110	50	85	65	30	25	22	90
1990	Z	4.3 (4293)	65	80	45	70	75	36	⑦	22	90
	H	5.0 (4999)	65	④	45	70	60	35	⑦	17-27	120
	K	5.7 (5735)	65	④	45	70	60	35	⑦	17-27	120
	C	6.2 (6210)	②	③	48	200	60	31	26	-	120
	J	6.2 (6210)	②	③	48	200	60	31	26	-	120
	N	7.4 (7440)	80	110	50	85	65	30	20	17-27	120
1991	Z	4.3 (4293)	65	75	20 ⑥	75	75	36	⑦	22	120
	H	5.0 (4999)	65	④	45	70	75	35	⑦	15	120
	K	5.7 (5735)	65	④	45	70	60	35	⑦	15	120
	C	6.2 (6210)	②	③	48	200	66	31	-	-	120
	J	6.2 (6210)	②	③	48	200	66	31	-	-	120
	N	7.4 (7440)	80	100	48	85	65	40	40	22	120
1992	Z	4.3 (4293)	65	75	20 ⑥	70	75	36	⑦	22	120
	H	5.0 (4999)	65	④	45	70	75	35	⑦	15	120
	K	5.7 (5735)	65	④	45	70	75	35	⑦	15	120
	C	6.2 (6210)	②	③	48	200	66	31	26	-	120
	J	6.2 (6210)	②	③	48	200	66	31	26	-	120
	F	6.5 (6473)	②	③	48	200	66	31	26	-	120
	N	7.4 (7440)	80	100	48	85	65	40	40	22	120
1993	Z	4.3 (4293)	65	75	20 ⑥	70	75	36	⑦	22	120
	H	5.0 (4999)	65	④	45	70	75	35	⑦	15	120
	K	5.7 (5735)	65	④	45	70	75	35	⑦	15	120
	C	6.2 (6210)	②	③	48	200	66	31	26	-	120
	J	6.2 (6210)	②	③	48	200	66	31	26	-	120
	F	6.5 (6473)	②	③	48	200	66	31	26	-	120
	N	7.4 (7440)	80	100	48	85	65	40	40	22	120
1994	Z	4.3 (4293)	65	75	20 ⑥	70	75	36	⑦	22	120
	H	5.0 (4999)	65	④	45	70	75	35	⑦	15	120
	K	5.7 (5735)	65	④	45	70	75	35	⑦	15	120
	F	6.5 (6473)	②	③	48	200	66	31	26	-	120
	P	6.5 (6473)	②	③	48	200	66	31	26	-	120
	S	6.5 (6473)	②	③	48	200	66	31	26	-	120
	N	7.4 (7440)	80	100	48	85	65	40	40	22	120
1995	Z	4.3 (4293)	65	75	20 ⑥	70	75	36	⑦	22	120
	H	5.0 (4999)	65	④	45	70	75	35	⑦	15	120
	K	5.7 (5735)	65	④	45	70	75	35	⑦	15	120
	F	6.5 (6473)	②	③	48	200	66	31	26	-	120
	P	6.5 (6473)	②	③	48	200	66	31	26	-	120
	S	6.5 (6473)	②	③	48	200	66	31	26	-	120
	N	7.4 (7440)	80	100	48	85	65	40	40	22	120

87983c15

TORQUE SPECIFICATIONS

All readings in ft. lbs.

Year	Engine ID/VIN	Engine Displacement Liters (cc)	Cylinder Head Bolts	Main Bearing Bolts	Rod Bearing Bolts	Crankshaft Damper Bolts	Flywheel Bolts	Manifold Intake	Manifold Exhaust	Spark Plugs	Lug Nut
1996	W	4.3 (4293)	(8)	77	20 (6)	74	74	(10)	(12)	15	140
	M	5.0 (4999)	(8)	(9)	20 (6)	74	74	(10)	(12)	15	140
	R	5.7 (5735)	(8)	(9)	20 (6)	74	74	(10)	(12)	15	140
	F	6.5 (6473)	(2)	(3)	48	200	66	31	26	-	140
	S	6.5 (6473)	(2)	(3)	48	200	66	31	26	-	140
	J	7.4 (7440)	85	100	45	110	67	40	30	22	140

(1) Left front bolt: 85 ft. lbs.
(2) 1st: 20 ft. lbs.
2nd: 50 ft. lbs.
3rd: 1/4 turn
(3) Inner bolts: 110 ft. lbs.
Outer bolts: 100 ft. lbs.
(4) Outer bolts on #2, 3, 4: 70 ft. lbs.
All other bolts: 80 ft. lbs.
(5) Intake-to-exhaust: 44 ft. lbs.
Manifold-to-cylinder head: 38 ft. lbs
(6) Plus an additional 60° turn
Tubular stainless steel: 26 ft. lbs
(7) Center bolts: 26 ft. lbs.
All others: 20 ft. lbs.
(8) 1st: 22 ft. lbs
Final pass:
Short bolt: plus an additional 55° turn
Medium bolt: plus an additional 65° turn
Long bolt: plus an additional 75° turn
(9) Outer bolts: 67 ft. lbs.
Inner bolts: 74 ft. lbs.
(10) 1st: 27 inch. lbs.
2nd: 106 inch. lbs
3rd: 11 ft. lbs.
(11) 1st: 11 ft. lbs
2nd: 22 ft. lbs.

87983C16

Engine

REMOVAL & INSTALLATION

⁂CAUTION

When draining the coolant, keep in mind that cats and dogs are attracted by ethylene glycol antifreeze, and are quite likely to drink any that is left in an uncovered container or in puddles on the ground. This will prove fatal in sufficient quantity. Always drain the coolant into a sealable container. Coolant should be reused unless it is contaminated or several years old.

4.8L Engines

See Figures 9, 10 and 11

1. Matchmark and remove the hood.
2. Disconnect the negative battery cable.
3. Remove the battery.
4. Drain the cooling system.
5. Drain the engine oil.
6. Disconnect the accelerator cable from the carburetor throttle lever.
7. On trucks with automatic transmission, remove the detent cable from the throttle lever.
8. Remove the air cleaner assembly.
9. Mark and disconnect all necessary electrical wiring from the engine.
10. Mark and disconnect all necessary vacuum hoses from the engine.
11. Disconnect the radiator hoses at the radiator.
12. Disconnect the heater hoses at the engine.
13. Remove the radiator.

⁂CAUTION

Please refer to Section 1 before discharging the compressor or disconnecting air conditioning lines. Damage to the air conditioning system or personal injury could result. Consult your local laws concerning refrigerant discharge and recycling. In many areas it may be illegal for anyone but a certified technician to service the A/C system. Always use an approved recovery station when discharging the air conditioning.

14. On trucks with air conditioning, discharge the system using an approved recovery/recycling machine.
15. Remove the air conditioning condenser.
16. Remove the fan assembly and water pump pulley.
17. Disconnect and plug the fuel line at the fuel pump.
18. Raise and support the truck on jackstands.
19. Remove the starter.
20. Remove the flywheel cover.
21. Disconnect the exhaust pipe from the exhaust manifold.
22. Support the weight of the engine with a shop crane and remove the engine mount through-bolts.
23. If equipped with an automatic transmission, remove the torque converter-to-flexplate bolts.
24. If equipped with 4WD, unbolt the strut rods at the engine mounts.
25. Remove the bellhousing-to-engine retaining bolts.
26. Support the transmission with a floor jack.
27. Using the shop crane, carefully remove the engine from the vehicle.

To install:

28. Using the shop crane, carefully lower the engine into the truck.
29. Install the bellhousing-to-engine retaining bolts. Tighten the bolts to 30 ft. lbs. (40 Nm).
30. Remove the floor jack.
31. If equipped with 4WD, bolt the strut rods to the engine mounts. Tighten the bolts to 45 ft. lbs. (61 Nm).

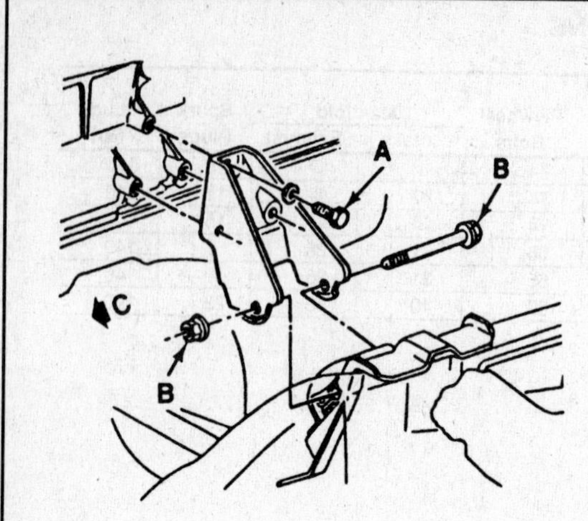

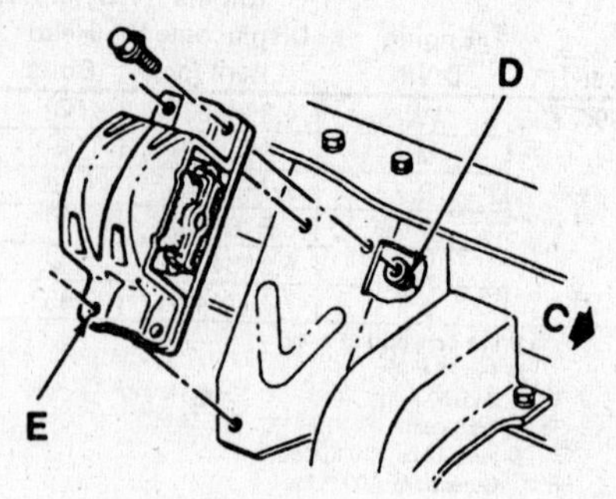

Fig. 9 Front engine mounts — 4.8L engines, 10/1500 series

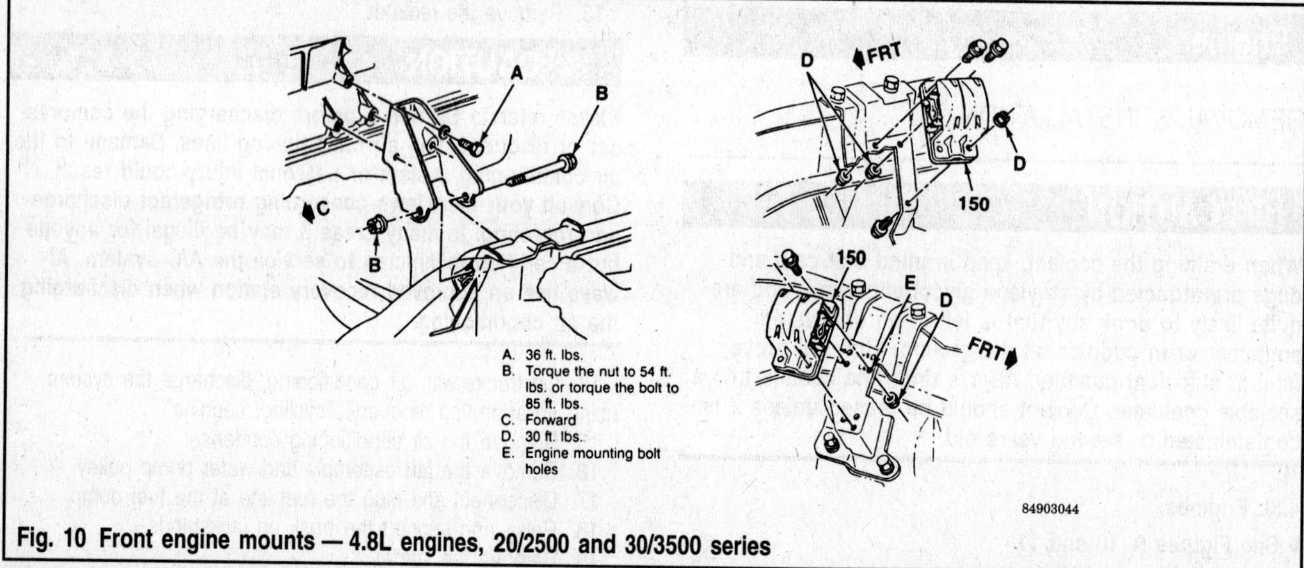

Fig. 10 Front engine mounts — 4.8L engines, 20/2500 and 30/3500 series

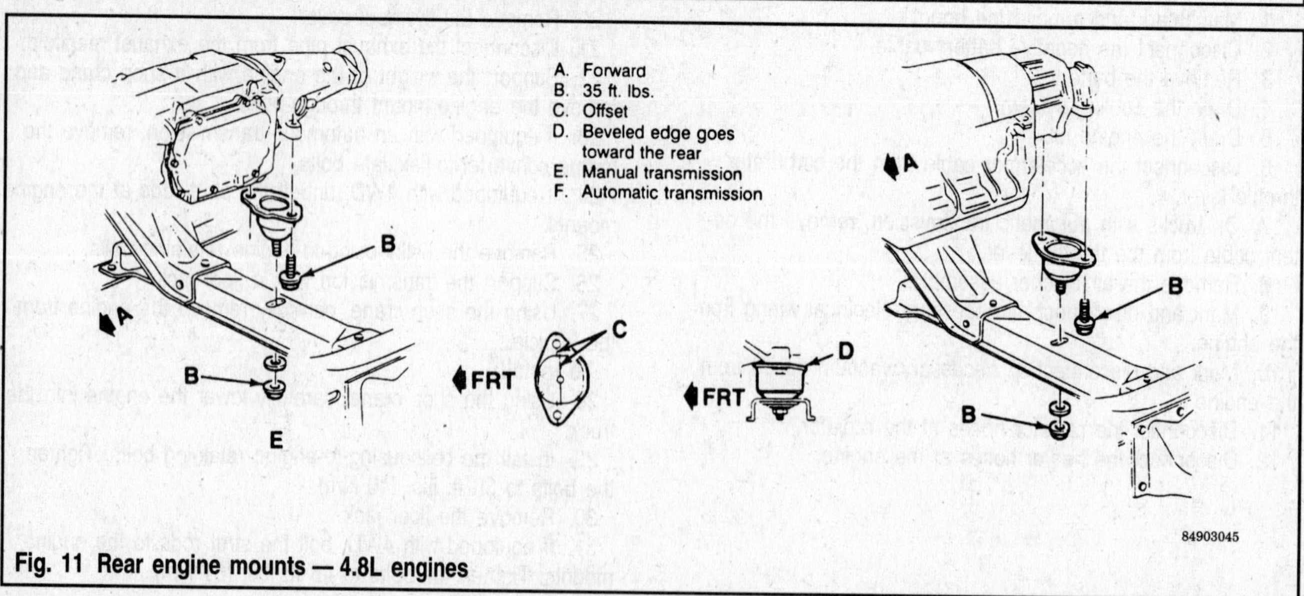

Fig. 11 Rear engine mounts — 4.8L engines

32. If equipped with an automatic transmission, install the torque converter-to-flexplate bolts. Tighten the bolts to 40 ft. lbs. (54 Nm).
33. Install the engine mount through-bolts. Tighten them to 60 ft. lbs. (81 Nm). Remove the shop crane.
34. Connect the exhaust pipe at the exhaust manifold. Tighten the nuts to 20 ft. lbs. (27 Nm).
35. Install the flywheel cover.
36. Install the starter.
37. Lower the truck.
38. Connect the fuel line at the fuel pump.
39. Install the fan assembly and water pump pulley.
40. Install the air conditioning condenser.
41. Install the radiator.
42. Connect the heater hoses at the engine.
43. Connect the radiator hoses at the radiator.
44. Connect all vacuum hoses.
45. Connect all electrical wiring.
46. On trucks with automatic transmission, connect the detent cable at the throttle lever.
47. Connect the accelerator cable at the carburetor throttle lever.
48. Fill the cooling system.
49. Fill the engine crankcase with oil.

CAUTION

The EPA warns that prolonged contact with used engine oil may cause a number of skin disorders, including cancer! You should make every effort to minimize you exposure to used engine oil. Protective gloves should be worn when changing the oil. Wash your hands and any other exposed skin areas as soon as possible after exposure to used engine oil. Soap and water, or waterless hand cleaner should be used.

50. Install the battery.
51. Connect the negative battery cable.
52. Evacuate and charge the air conditioning system.
53. Install air cleaner assembly.
54. Install the hood.

4.3L, 5.0L and 5.7L Engines

See Figures 12 and 13

1. Disconnect the negative battery cable.
2. Remove the hood.
3. Drain the cooling system.
4. Remove the air cleaner assembly.
5. Remove the accessory drive belt, fan and water pump pulley.
6. Remove the radiator and shroud.

CAUTION

Please refer to Section 1 before discharging the compressor or disconnecting air conditioning lines. Damage to the air conditioning system or personal injury could result. Consult your local laws concerning refrigerant discharge and recycling. In many areas it may be illegal for anyone but a certified technician to service the A/C system. Always use an approved recovery station when discharging the air conditioning.

7. On vehicles with air conditioning, discharge the system using an approved recovery/recycling machine.
8. Remove the air conditioning condenser.
9. Disconnect the heater hoses at the engine.
10. Disconnect the accelerator, cruise control and detent linkage (if equipped).
11. Disconnect the air conditioning compressor, (if equipped), and lay aside.
12. Remove the power steering pump and lay aside.
13. Disconnect the engine wiring harness from the engine.
14. Disconnect and tag the fuel line(s) from the intake manifold to the rear of the block.
15. Disconnect and tag the vacuum lines from the intake manifold.
16. Remove the distributor.
17. Raise the vehicle and support it safely.
18. Drain the engine oil.
19. Disconnect the exhaust pipes from the manifold.
20. Disconnect the strut rods at the engine mountings, (if equipped).
21. Remove the flywheel or torque converter cover.
22. Disconnect the wiring along the oil pan rail.
23. Remove the starter.
24. Disconnect the wire for the fuel gauge.
25. On vehicles equipped with automatic transmission, remove the converter-to-flexplate bolts.
26. Lower the vehicle and suitably support the transmission. Attach a suitable lifting fixture to the engine.
27. Remove the bell housing-to-engine bolts.
28. Remove the rear engine mounting-to-frame bolts and the front through-bolts and remove the engine.

CAUTION

The EPA warns that prolonged contact with used engine oil may cause a number of skin disorders, including cancer! You should make every effort to minimize you exposure to used engine oil. Protective gloves should be worn when changing the oil. Wash your hands and any other exposed skin areas as soon as possible after exposure to used engine oil. Soap and water, or waterless hand cleaner should be used.

To install:

29. Raise the vehicle and support it safely.
30. Lower the engine and install the engine mounting bolts. Tighten the mounting bolts as follows:

1988-96 4.3L C/K Series
- Front mount bolts: 44 ft. lbs. (59 Nm)
- Front through-bolt: 70 ft. lbs. (95 Nm)
- Front mount nut: 50 ft. lbs. (68 Nm)
- Rear mount bolts: 35 ft. lbs. (47 Nm)

1988-91 4.3L R/V Series
- Front mount bolts: 36 ft. lbs. (48 Nm)
- Front mount nut: 33 ft. lbs. (45 Nm)
- Front through-bolt: 70 ft. lbs. (95 Nm)
- Front through-bolt nut: 50 ft. lbs. (68 Nm)
- Rear mount bolts: 35 ft. lbs. (47 Nm)

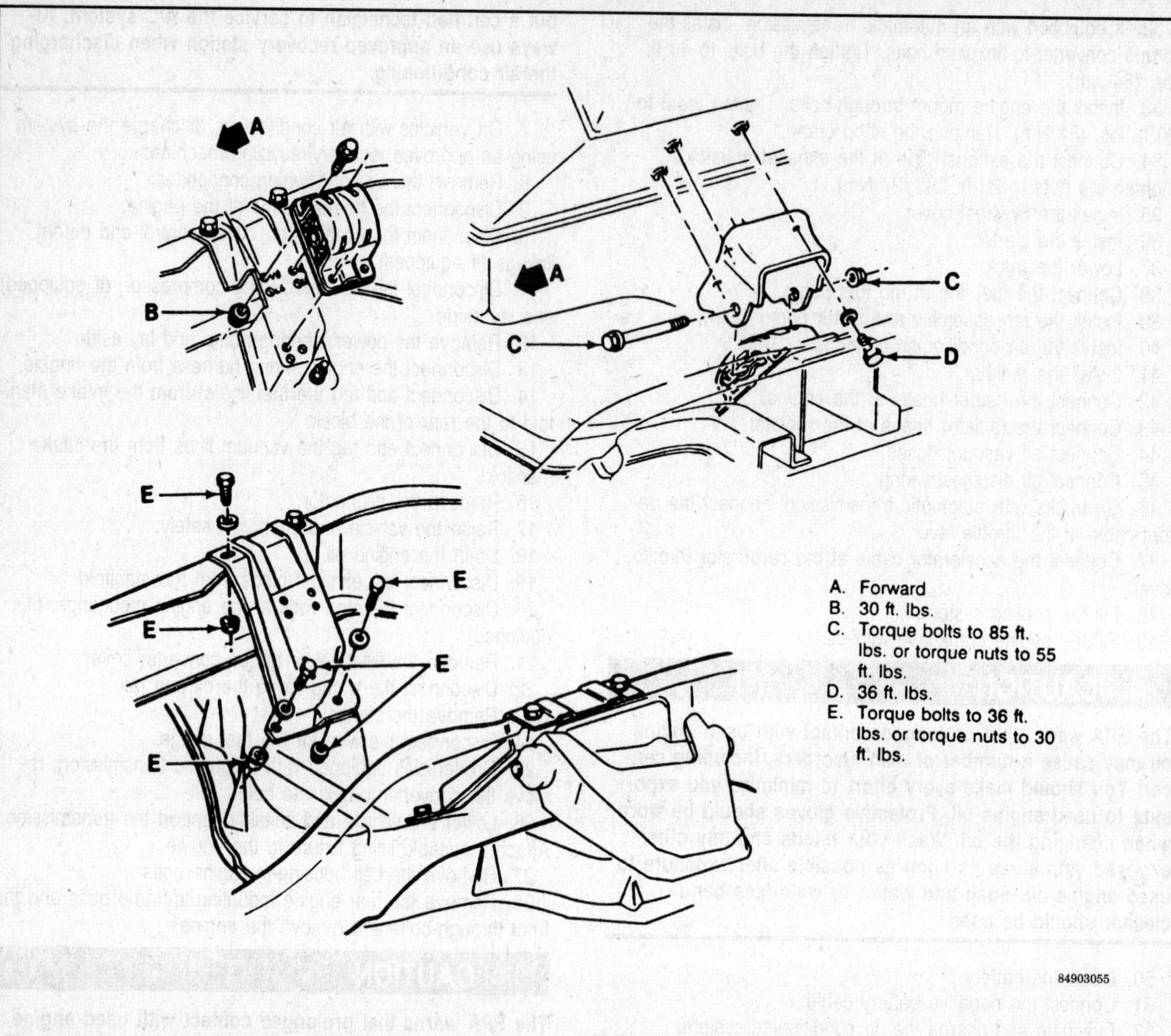

A
B
C
D
E
A. Forward
B. 30 ft. lbs.
C. Torque bolts to 85 ft. lbs. or torque nuts to 55 ft. lbs.
D. 36 ft. lbs.
E. Torque bolts to 36 ft. lbs. or torque nuts to 30 ft. lbs.
84903055

Fig. 12 Front engine mounts — 5.0 and 5.7L shown, others similar

A. Forward
B. 36 ft. lbs.
C
D
ALL MODELS EXCEPT WITH THM 400
VIEW C
ALL MODELS WITH THM 400
VIEW D
84903057

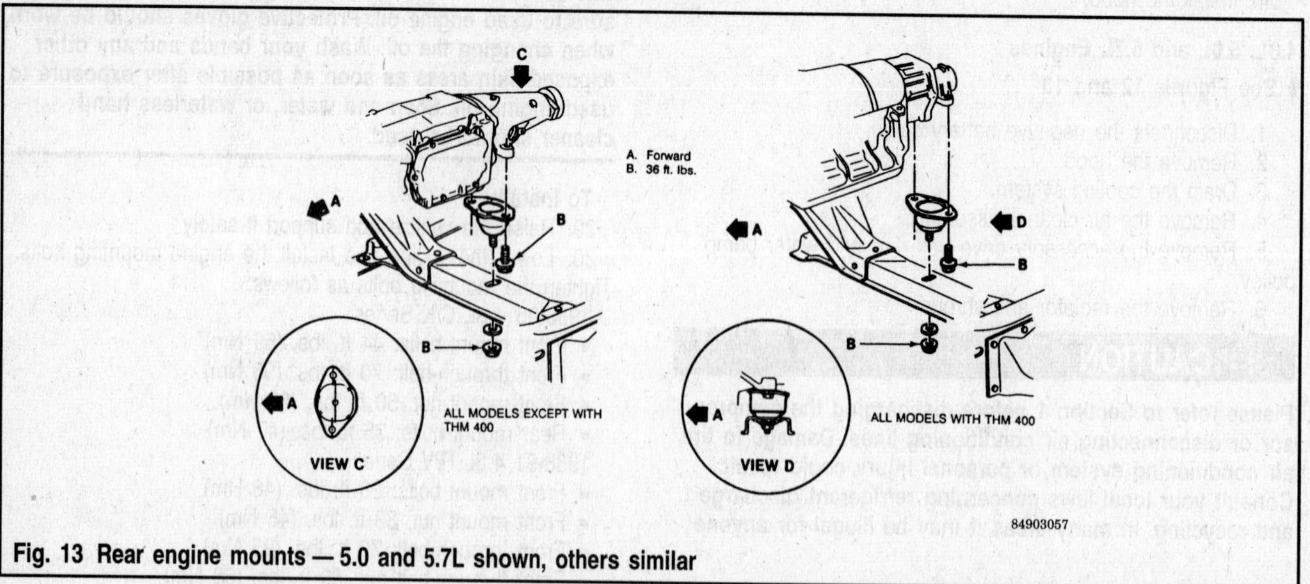

Fig. 13 Rear engine mounts — 5.0 and 5.7L shown, others similar

1988-91 5.0L and 5.7L engines

- Front mount bolts: 36 ft. lbs. (48 Nm)
- Front mount nut: 30 ft. lbs. (40 Nm)
- Front through-bolt: 85 ft. lbs. (115 Nm)
- Front through-bolt nut: 55 ft. lbs. (75 Nm)
- Rear mount bolt/nut (R Series): 35 ft. lbs. (47 Nm)
- Rear mount bolt (V Series): 40 ft. lbs. (54 Nm)
- Rear mount nut (V Series): 36 ft. lbs. (48 Nm)

1992-96 5.0L and 5.7L C/K Series

- Front mount frame bolt: 44 ft. lbs. (59 Nm)
- Front mount frame nut: 33 ft. lbs. (45 Nm)
- Front through-bolt: 70 ft. lbs. (95 Nm)
- Front through-bolt nut: 50 ft. lbs. (68 Nm)
- Front mount engine bolt: 38 ft. lbs. (51 Nm)
- Rear mount bolts: 35 ft. lbs. (47 Nm)

31. Install the bell housing-to-engine bolts and tighten to 35 ft. lbs. (47 Nm).
32. Remove the transmission support.
33. Install the converter-to-flex bolts and torque to 35 ft. lbs. (47 Nm).
34. Install the fuel gauge wiring and starter.
35. Install the flywheel or torque converter cover.
36. Connect the strut rods at the engine mountings, (if equipped).
37. Install the exhaust pipes at the manifold.
38. Lower the vehicle.
39. Install the distributor.
40. Connect the vacuum lines to the intake manifold.
41. Install the fuel line.
42. Connect the engine wiring harness.
43. Install the power steering pump.
44. Connect the air conditioning compressor.
45. Connect the accelerator, cruise control and detent linkage.
46. Connect the heater hoses.
47. Install the radiator and shroud.
48. Install the accessory drive belts.
49. Install the hood.
50. Install the proper quantity and grade of coolant and engine oil.
51. Connect the negative battery cable.

7.4L Engines

➧ See Figures 14 and 15

1. Remove the hood.
2. Disconnect the negative battery cable.
3. Drain the cooling system.
4. Remove the air cleaner assembly.
5. Remove the radiator and fan shroud.
6. Disconnect and tag all necessary engine wiring.
7. Disconnect the accelerator, cruise control and TVS linkage.
8. Disconnect the fuel supply lines.
9. Disconnect all necessary vacuum wires.
10. Disconnect the air conditioning compressor and lay aside. Do not disconnect the lines.
11. Dismount the power steering pump and position it out of the way. It's not necessary to disconnect the fluid lines.
12. Raise the vehicle and support it on jackstands.
13. Disconnect the exhaust pipes from the manifold.
14. Remove the starter.
15. Remove the torque converter cover.
16. Remove the converter-to-flexplate bolts.
17. Lower the vehicle and suitably support the transmission. Attach a suitable lifting fixture to the engine.
18. Remove the bellhousing-to-engine bolts.
19. Remove the rear engine mounting-to-frame bolts and the front through-bolts and remove the engine.

To install:

20. Lower the engine and install the engine mounting bolts. Tighten the mounting bolts as follows:

1988-91 C/K Series

- Front mount frame bolt: 36 ft. lbs. (48 Nm)
- Front mount engine bolt: 45 ft. lbs. (60 Nm)
- Front through-bolt: 70 ft. lbs. (95 Nm)
- Front through-bolt nut: 50 ft. lbs. (68 Nm)
- Rear mount bolts: 36 ft. lbs. (48 Nm)

1988-91 R/V Series

- Front mount bolts: 36 ft. lbs. (48 Nm)
- Front mount nut: 30 ft. lbs. (40 Nm)
- Front through-bolt: 85 ft. lbs. (115 Nm)
- Front through-bolt nut: 55 ft. lbs. (75 Nm)
- Rear mount bolt/nut (R Series): 35 ft. lbs. (47 Nm)
- Rear mount bolt (V Series): 40 ft. lbs. (54 Nm)
- Rear mount nut (V Series): 36 ft. lbs. (48 Nm)

1992-96 C/K Series

- Front mount frame bolt: 44 ft. lbs. (59 Nm)
- Front mount frame nut: 33 ft. lbs. (45 Nm)
- Front through-bolt: 70 ft. lbs. (95 Nm)
- Front through-bolt nut: 50 ft. lbs. (68 Nm)
- Front mount engine bolt: 38 ft. lbs. (51 Nm)
- Rear mount bolts: 35 ft. lbs. (47 Nm)

21. Install the bellhousing-to-engine bolts and tighten to 35 ft. lbs. (47 Nm).
22. Remove the engine lifting fixture and transmission jack.
23. Raise the vehicle and support it on jackstands.
24. Install the converter-to-flexplate bolts and tighten them to 35 ft. lbs. (47 Nm).
25. Install the fuel gauge wiring and starter.
26. Install the torque converter cover.
27. Install the starter.

✲✲CAUTION

The EPA warns that prolonged contact with used engine oil may cause a number of skin disorders, including cancer! You should make every effort to minimize you exposure to used engine oil. Protective gloves should be worn when changing the oil. Wash your hands and any other exposed skin areas as soon as possible after exposure to used engine oil. Soap and water, or waterless hand cleaner should be used.

28. Install the exhaust pipes at the manifold.
29. Lower the vehicle.
30. Install the power steering pump.
31. Install the air conditioning compressor.
32. Install all vacuum hoses.
33. Install the fuel supply line.
34. Connect the accelerator, cruise control and TVS linkage.
35. Connect the engine wiring.
36. Install the radiator and fan shroud.
37. Install the air cleaner.

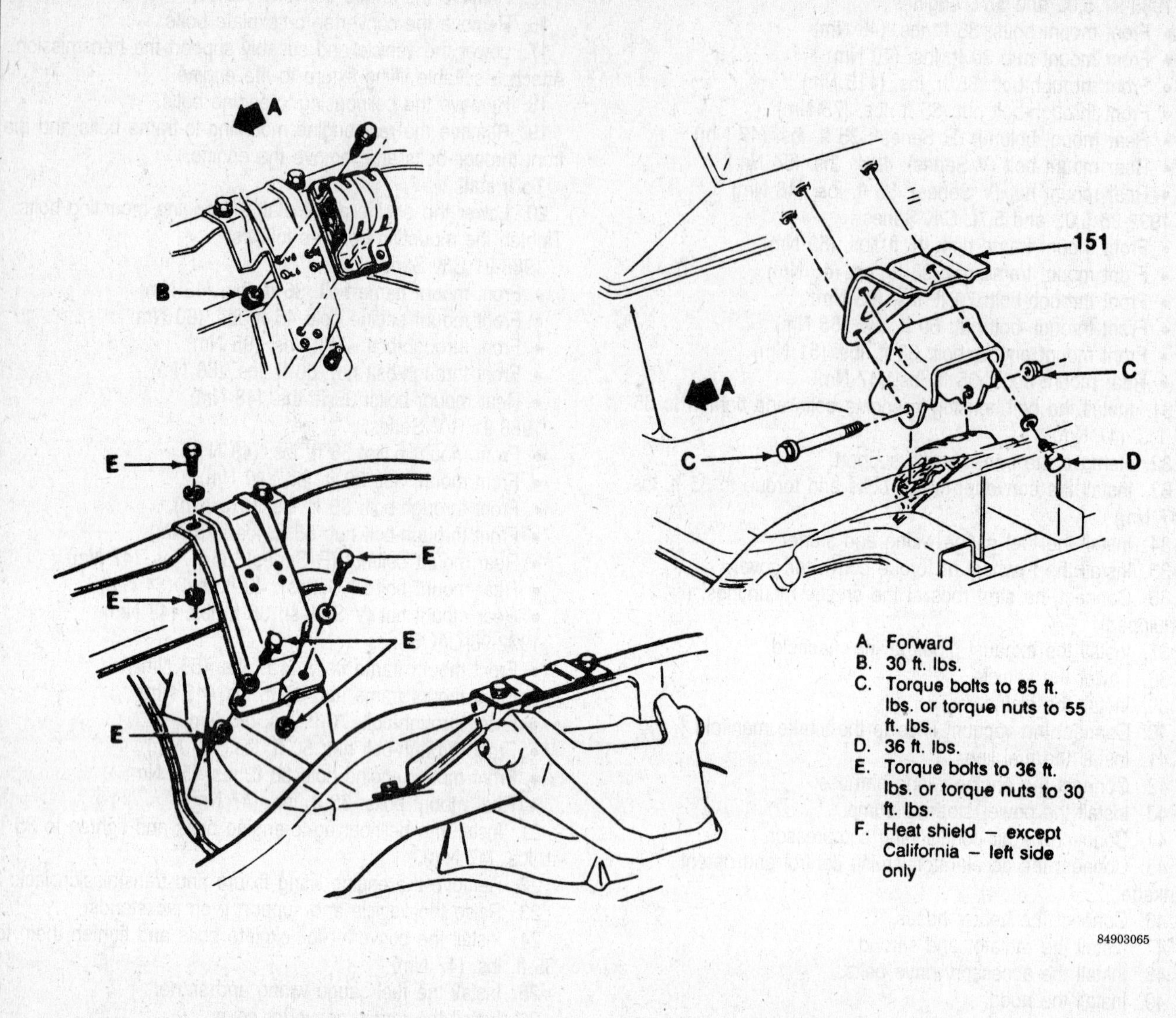

A
B
E
E
E
E
E
A
151
C
C
D
A. Forward
B. 30 ft. lbs.
C. Torque bolts to 85 ft. lbs. or torque nuts to 55 ft. lbs.
D. 36 ft. lbs.
E. Torque bolts to 36 ft. lbs. or torque nuts to 30 ft. lbs.
F. Heat shield – except California – left side only
84903065

Fig. 14 Front engine mounts — 7.4L engines

C
A
B
A. 40 ft. lbs.
B. 36 ft. lbs.
C. Forward
84903069

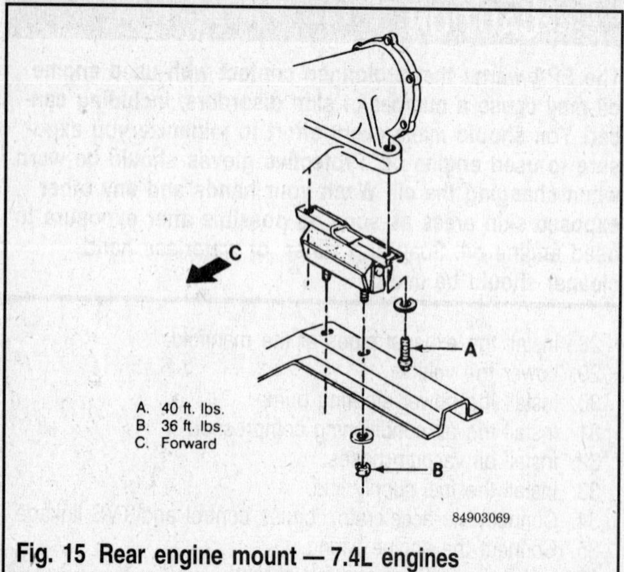

Fig. 15 Rear engine mount — 7.4L engines

38. Install the hood.
39. Connect the negative battery cable.
40. Install the proper quantity and grade of coolant.

6.2L and 6.5L Diesel Engines

See Figures 16 and 17

CAUTION

When draining the coolant, keep in mind that cats and dogs are attracted by ethylene glycol antifreeze, and are quite likely to drink any that is left in an uncovered container or in puddles on the ground. This will prove fatal in sufficient quantity. Always drain the coolant into a sealable container. Coolant should be reused unless it is contaminated or several years old.

1. Disconnect the negative battery cable.
2. Raise the vehicle and support it safely.
3. Remove the flywheel or torque converter cover.

4. On vehicles equipped with automatic transmission, remove the converter-to-flexplate bolts.
5. Disconnect the exhaust pipes from the manifold.
6. Remove the starter.
7. Remove the bellhousing bolts.
8. Remove the engine mounting through-bolts.
9. Disconnect the block heater wiring.
10. Disconnect the wiring harness, transmission cooler lines, and a battery cable clamp at the oil pan.
11. Disconnect the fuel return lines at the engine.
12. Disconnect the oil cooler lines at the engine.
13. Lower the vehicle.
14. Remove the hood.
15. Drain the cooling system.
16. Remove the air cleaner and cover the mouth of the intake manifold.
17. Remove the alternator wires and clips.
18. Disconnect the wiring at the injector pump.
19. Disconnect the wiring from the rocker cover including the glow plug wires.
20. Disconnect the EGR/EPR solenoids, glow plug controller and temperature solenoid and move the harness aside.
21. Disconnect the left or right ground strap.
22. Remove the upper fan shroud and fan.
23. Disconnect the power steering pump and reservoir and lay to one side.
24. Disconnect the accelerator, cruise control and detent cables at the injection pump.
25. Disconnect the heater hose at the engine.
26. Remove the radiator.
27. Support the transmission with a suitable jack.
28. Remove the engine.

To install:

29. Lower the engine and install the engine mounting bolts. Tighten as follows:
- Front mount bolt: 44 ft. lbs. (59 Nm)
- Front mount nut: 33 ft. lbs. (45 Nm)
- Bracket-to-block bolt: 38 ft. lbs. (51 Nm)
- Through-bolt: 70 ft. lbs. (95 Nm)
- Through-bolt nut: 50 ft. lbs. (68 Nm)

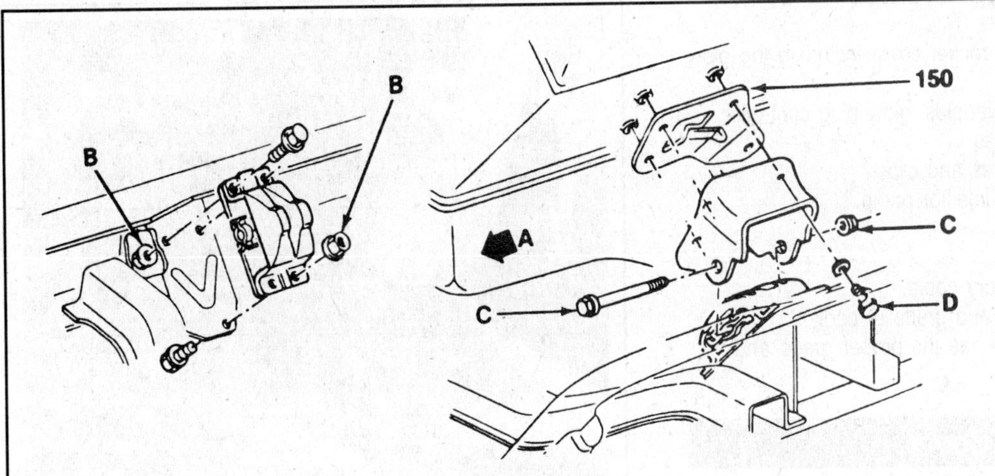

Fig. 16 Front engine mounts — 6.2L/6.5L engines

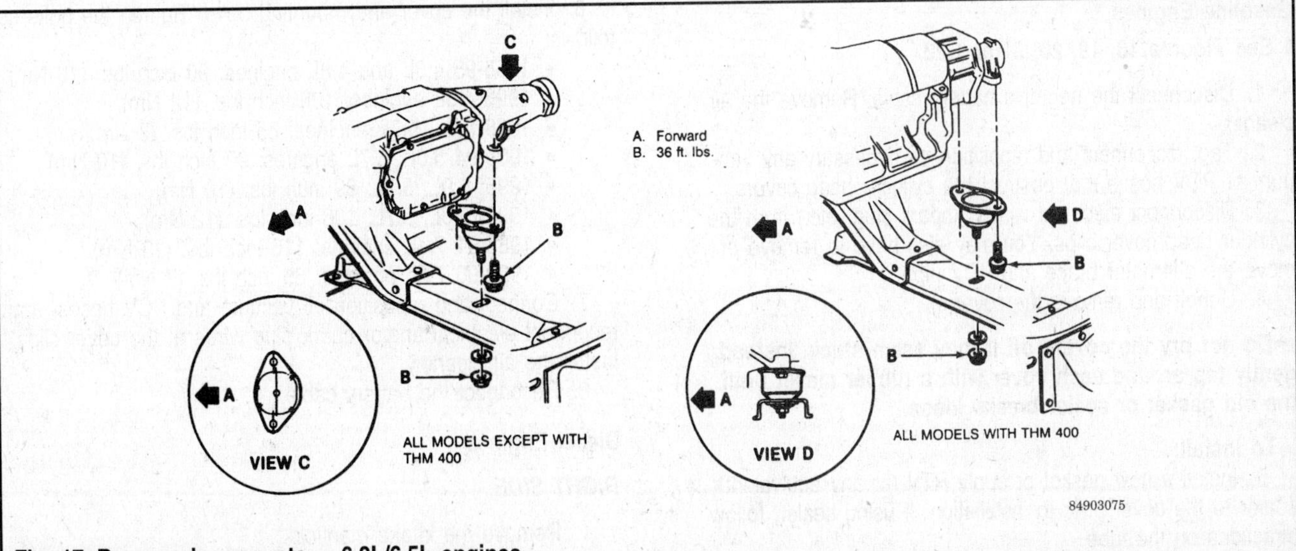

Fig. 17 Rear engine mounts — 6.2L/6.5L engines

30. Install the bellhousing-to-engine bolts and tighten to 30 ft. lbs. (40 Nm).
31. Remove the engine lifting fixture and transmission jack.
32. Raise the vehicle and support it on jackstands.
33. Install the converter-to-flexplate bolts and tighten to 35 ft. lbs. (47 Nm).
34. Install the fuel gauge wiring and starter.
35. Install the flywheel or torque converter cover.
36. Install the starter.
37. Install the exhaust pipes at the manifold.
38. Connect the wiring harness, transmission cooler lines, and a battery cable clamp at the oil pan.
39. Connect the fuel return lines at the engine.
40. Connect the oil cooler lines at the engine.
41. Lower the vehicle.
42. Install the radiator.
43. Install the heater hose to the engine.
44. Connect the accelerator, cruise control and detent cables at the injection pump.
45. Connect the power steering pump and reservoir.
46. Install the fan and the upper fan shroud.
47. Install the ground strap.
48. Connect the wiring to the rocker cover including the glow plug wires.
49. Connect the EGR/EPR solenoids, glow plug controller and temperature solenoid harness.
50. Connect the alternator wires and clips.
51. Connect the wiring at the injector pump.
52. Install the air cleaner.
53. Install the hood.
54. Connect the negative battery cable.
55. Install the proper quantity and grade of coolant.
56. Ensure that the crankcase has the proper grade and quantity of oil.

Valve/Cylinder Head Cover

REMOVAL & INSTALLATION

Gasoline Engines

➧ See Figures 18, 19, 20, 21 and 22

1. Disconnect the negative battery cable. Remove the air cleaner.
2. Tag, disconnect and reposition as necessary any vacuum or PCV hoses that obstruct the cylinder head covers.
3. Disconnect electrical wire(s) (spark plug, etc.) from the cylinder head cover clips. You may also have to remove or move the alternator brace and PCV pipe.
4. Unbolt and remove the cover(s).

➡Do not pry the covers off if they seem stuck. Instead, gently tap around each cover with a rubber mallet until the old gasket or sealer breaks loose.

To install:

5. Install a new gasket or apply RTV (or any equivalent) sealer to the cover prior to installation. If using sealer, follow directions on the tube.

87983p28

Fig. 18 Unfasten and remove the cover bolts

87983p30

Fig. 19 Remove the old gasket material

6. Install the cover and mounting bolts. Tighten the bolts as follows:
   - 1988-95 4.3L and 4.8L engines: 90 inch lbs. (10 Nm)
   - 1996 4.3L engines: 106 inch lbs. (12 Nm)
   - 1988 5.0L, 5.7L engines: 65 inch lbs. (7 Nm)
   - 1989-94 5.0L, 5.7L engines: 90 inch lbs. (10 Nm)
   - 1995: 5.0L, 5.7L: 89 inch lbs. (10 Nm)
   - 1996: 5.0L, 5.7L: 106 inch lbs. (12 Nm)
   - 1988-91 7.4L engines: 115 inch lbs. (13 Nm)
   - 1992-96 7.4L engines: 65 inch lbs. (7 Nm)
7. Connect and reposition all vacuum and PCV hoses, and reconnect electrical and/or spark plug wires at the cover clips. Install the air cleaner.
8. Reconnect the battery cable.

Diesel Engines

RIGHT SIDE

1. Remove the intake manifold.

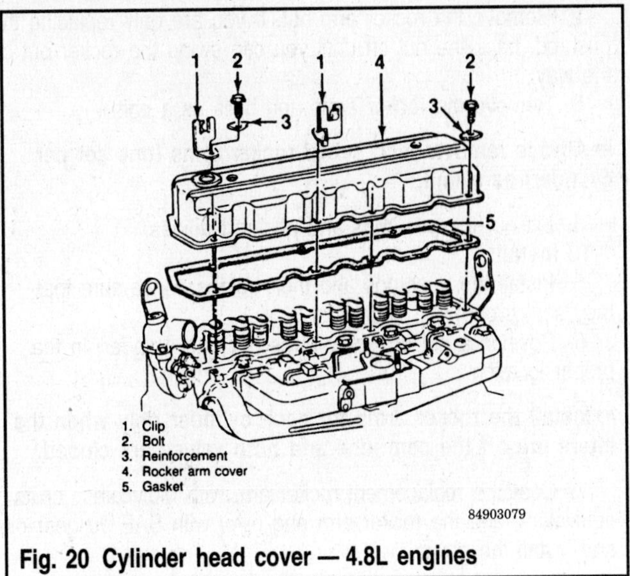

Fig. 20 Cylinder head cover — 4.8L engines

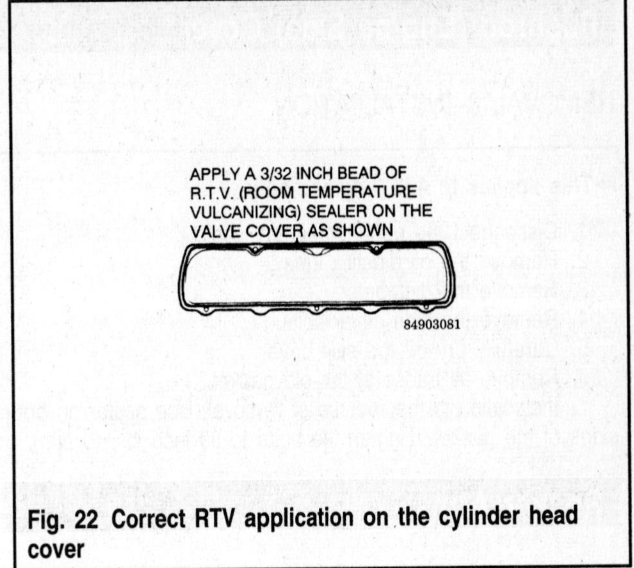

Fig. 22 Correct RTV application on the cylinder head cover

2. Remove the fuel injection lines for all except the No. 5 and No. 7 injectors.
3. Disconnect the glow plug wires.
4. Remove the wiring harness from the clip.
5. Remove the CDR valve.
6. Remove the cover bolts.
7. Remove the cover. If the cover sticks, jar it loose with a plastic or rubber mallet. NEVER pry it loose!
8. Installation is the reverse of removal. Clean all old RTV gasket material from the mating surfaces. Apply a 5/16 in. (8mm) bead of sealer to the head mating surfaces. Tighten the cover bolts to 16 ft. lbs. (22 Nm).

LEFT SIDE

1. Remove the intake manifold.
2. Remove the fuel injection lines.
3. On trucks with air conditioning, remove the upper fan shroud.
4. On trucks with air conditioning, remove the compressor drive belt.
5. On trucks with air conditioning, remove the left exhaust manifold.
6. Remove the dipstick tube
7. On trucks with air conditioning, dismount the compressor and move it out of the way. It may be possible to avoid disconnecting the refrigerant lines. If not, Discharge the system and disconnect the lines. Cap all openings at once. See Section 1 for discharging procedures.
8. Remove the dipstick tube front bracket from the stud.
9. Remove the wiring harness brackets.
10. Remove the rocker arm cover bolts and fuel return bracket.
11. Remove the cover. If the cover sticks, jar it loose with a plastic or rubber mallet. NEVER pry it loose!
12. Installation is the reverse of removal. Clean all old RTV gasket material from the mating surfaces. Apply a 5/16 in. (8 mm) bead of sealer to the head mating surfaces. Tighten the cover bolts to 16 ft. lbs. (22 Nm).

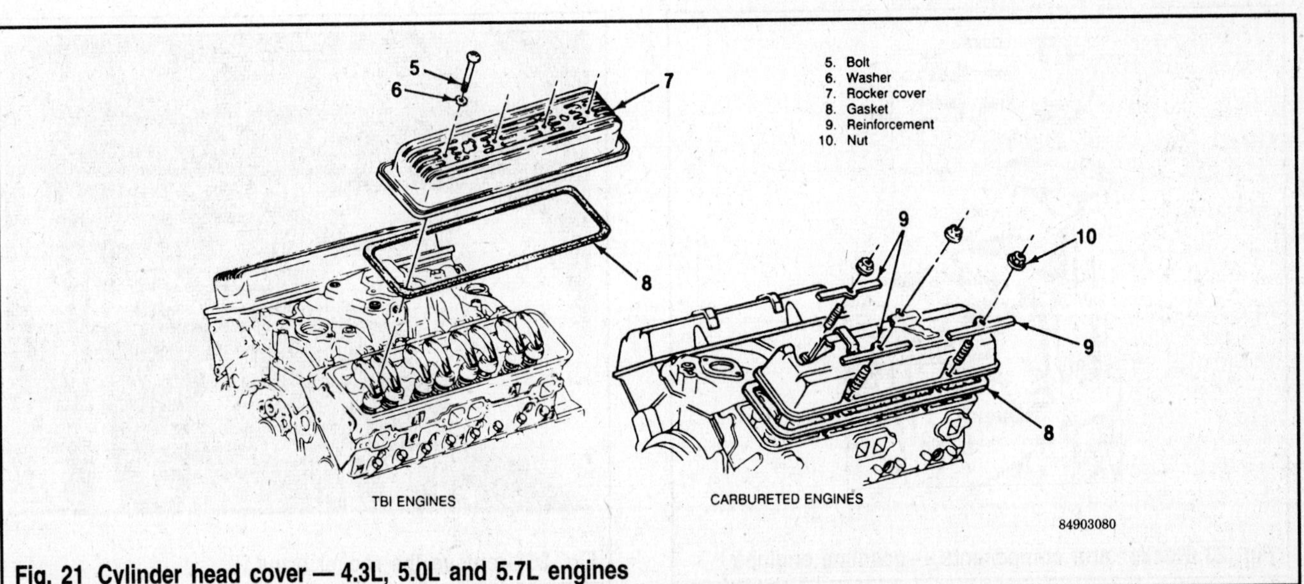

Fig. 21 Cylinder head cover — 4.3L, 5.0L and 5.7L engines

Pushrod (Engine Side) Cover

REMOVAL & INSTALLATION

➡This applies to 4.8L engines only

1. Disconnect the negative battery cable.
2. Remove the oil dipstick tube.
3. Remove the distributor.
4. Remove the side cover bolts.
5. Carefully pry off the side cover.
6. Remove all traces of the old gasket.
7. Installation is the reverse of removal. Use sealer on both sides of the gasket. Tighten the bolts to 80 inch lbs. (9 Nm).

Rocker Arms

REMOVAL & INSTALLATION

4.8L Engines

➧ See Figure 23

1. Remove the rocker arm cover.
2. Remove the rocker arm nut.
3. Remove the rocker arm and ball.

To install:

4. Coat the replacement rocker arm with Molykote® or its equivalent, and the rocker arm and pivot with SAE 90 gear oil, and install the pivots.
5. Install the nut. See the valve lash adjustment procedure later in this section.
6. Install the cover.

4.3L, 5.0L, 5.7L and 7.4L Engines

➧ See Figures 24, 25, 26 and 27

1. Remove the cylinder head cover.
2. Remove the rocker arm nut. If you are only replacing the pushrod, back the nut off until you can swing the rocker out of the way.
3. Remove the rocker arms and balls as a unit.

➡Always remove each set of rocker arms (one set per cylinder) as a unit.

4. Lift out the pushrods and pushrod guides.

To install:

5. Install the pushrods and their guides. Make sure that they seat properly in each lifter.
6. Position a set of rocker arms (for one cylinder) in the proper location.

➡Install the rocker arms for each cylinder only when the lifters are off the cam lobe and both valves are closed.

7. Coat the replacement rocker arm with Molykote® or its equivalent, and the rocker arm and pivot with SAE 90 gear oil, and install the pivots.

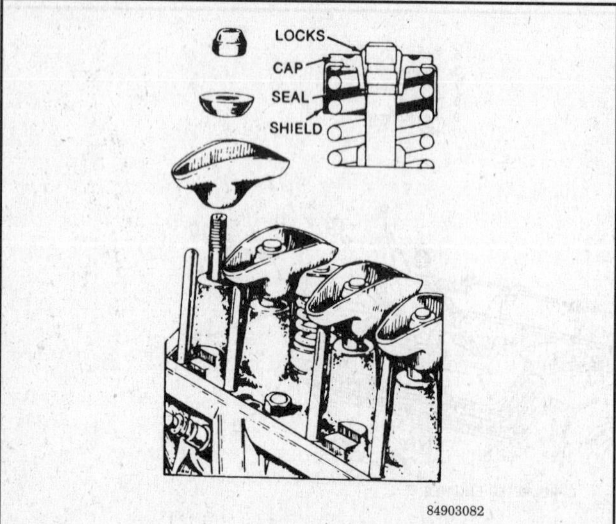

Fig. 23 Rocker arm components — gasoline engines

Fig. 24 Remove the rocker arm nut

Fig. 25 Remove the rocker arms

8. Install the nuts and tighten alternately as detailed in the valve lash adjustment procedure later in this section.

6.2L and 6.5L Diesel Engines

See Figures 28 and 29

Rotate the engine until the mark on the crankshaft balancer is at 2 o'clock. Rotate the crankshaft counterclockwise 3 ½ in. (88mm) aligning the crankshaft balancer mark with the first lower water pump bolt, about 12:30. This will ensure that no valves are close to a piston crown

1. Remove the cylinder head cover.
2. The rocker assemblies are mounted on two short rocker shafts per cylinder head, with each shaft operating four rockers. Remove the two bolts which secure each rocker shaft assembly, and remove the shaft. Mark the shafts so they can be installed in their original locations.
3. Remove the pushrods. The pushrods MUST be installed in the original direction! A paint stripe usually identifies the upper end of each rod, but if you can't see it, make sure to mark each rod yourself.
4. Insert a small prybar into the end of the rocker shaft bore and break off the end of the nylon retainers. Pull off the retainers with pliers and then slide off the rockers.

To install:

5. Make sure first that the rocker arms and springs go back on the shafts in the exact order in which they were removed. Its a good idea to coat them with engine oil.
6. Center the rockers on the corresponding holes in the shaft and install new plastic retainers using a ½ in. (13mm) drift.
7. Install the pushrods with their marked ends up.
8. Install the rocker shaft assemblies and make sure that the ball ends of the pushrods seat themselves in the rockers.
9. Rotate the engine clockwise until the mark on the torsional damper aligns with the **0** on the timing tab. Rotate the engine counterclockwise 3½ in. (88mm) measured at the damper. You can estimate this by checking that the mark on the damper is now aligned with the FIRST lower water pump

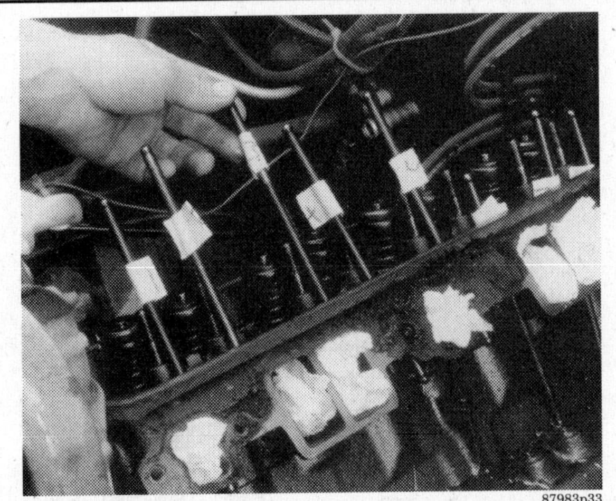

Fig. 26 Tag the pushrods before removal as they must be installed in the same order

Fig. 27 A piece of cardboard may be used to hold the pushrods in order

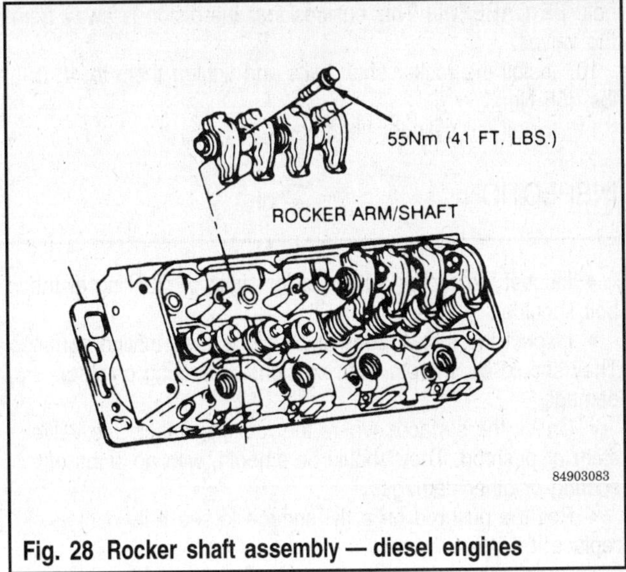

Fig. 28 Rocker shaft assembly — diesel engines

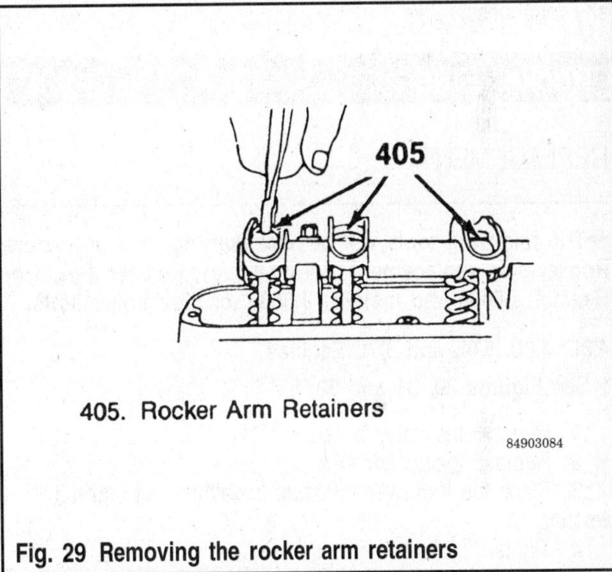

Fig. 29 Removing the rocker arm retainers

bolt. BE CAREFUL! This ensures that the piston is away from the valves.

10. Install the rocker shaft bolts and tighten them to 40 ft. lbs. (55 Nm).

11. Install the cylinder head cover.

INSPECTION

- Inspect the rocker arm bolts for signs of cracking at the bolt shoulder.
- Inspect the rocker arms and balls at their mating surfaces. They should be smooth, with no signs of scoring or other damage.
- Check the surfaces where the rocker contacts the valve stem or pushrod. They should be smooth, with no signs of scoring or other damage.
- Roll the pushrod on a flat surface to see if its bent—replace it if it is.
- Check the ends of the pushrods for signs of scoring or any roughness.

Rocker Stud

REPLACEMENT

➡The following tools will be necessary for this procedure: Rocker stud replacement tool J-5802-01, Reamer J-5715 or Reamer J-6036 and Installer J-6880, or their equivalents.

4.3L, 4.8L, 5.0L and 5.7L Engines

See Figures 30, 31 and 32

1. Remove the valve cover.
2. Remove the rocker arm.
3. Place the tool over the stud. Install the nut and flat washer.
4. Tighten the nut to remove the stud.

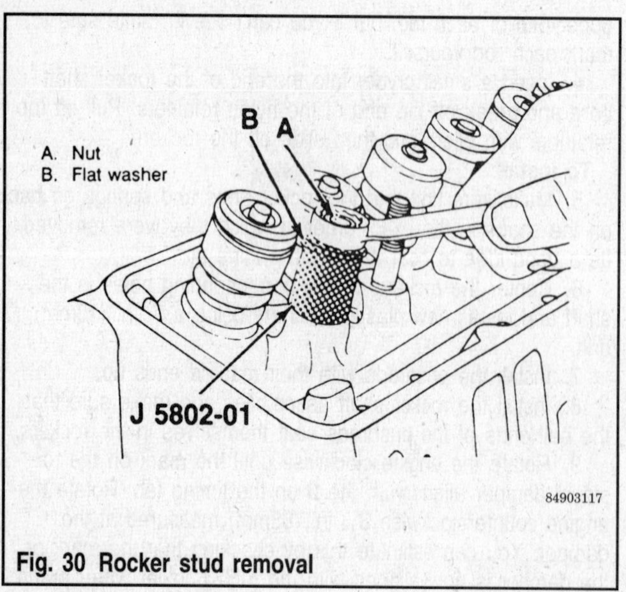

Fig. 30 Rocker stud removal

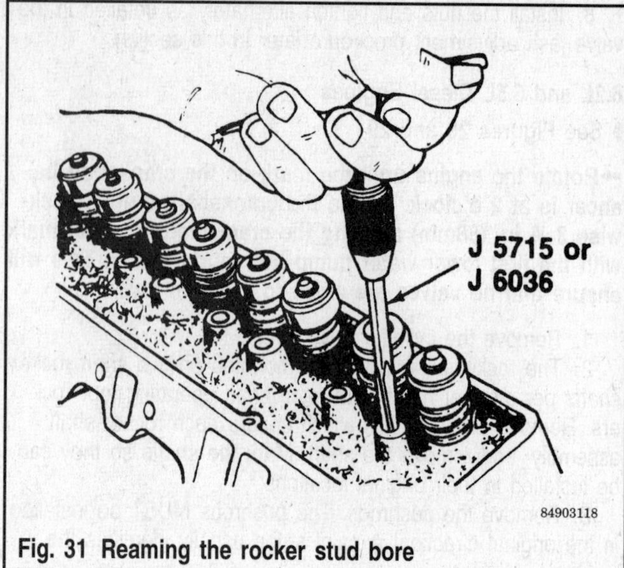

Fig. 31 Reaming the rocker stud bore

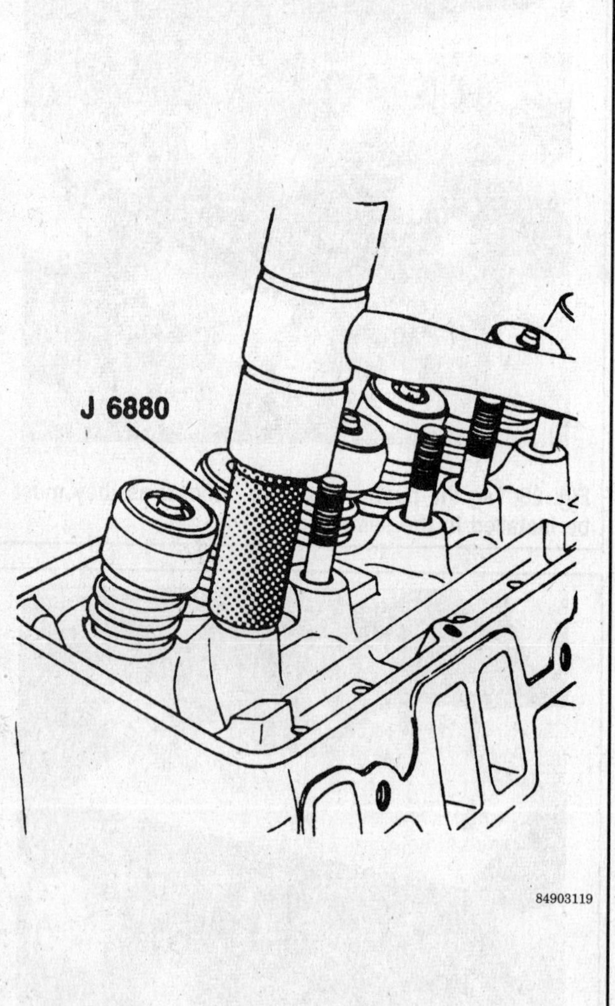

Fig. 32 Rocker stud installation

To install:

5. Using one of the reamers, ream the stud hole as necessary.
6. Coat the lower end of the new stud with SAE 80W-90 gear oil.
7. Using the installing tool, install the new stud. The stud is properly installed when the tool bottoms on the cylinder head.
8. Install the rocker arm(s) and adjust the valves.
9. Install the cover.

7.4L Engines

1. Remove the valve cover.
2. Remove the rocker arm.
3. Using a deep socket, unscrew the stud.
4. To install, simply reverse the removal procedures. Tighten the stud to 50 ft. lbs. (68 Nm). Adjust the valves.

Thermostat

****CAUTION**

When draining the coolant, keep in mind that cats and dogs are attracted by ethylene glycol antifreeze, and are quite likely to drink any that is left in an uncovered container or in puddles on the ground. This will prove fatal in sufficient quantity. Always drain the coolant into a sealable container. Coolant should be reused unless it is contaminated or several years old.

REMOVAL & INSTALLATION

Gasoline Engines

See Figures 33, 34, 35, 36, 37, 38, 39 and 40

1. Drain the radiator until the coolant is below the thermostat level (below the level of the intake manifold).
2. Remove the water outlet elbow assembly from the engine. Remove the thermostat from the engine, or, on the 4.8L, from inside the adapter elbow.

To install:

3. Clean the gasket surfaces on the water outlet elbow and the intake manifold. Use a new gasket when installing the elbow to the manifold.
4. Install the new thermostat making sure the spring side is inserted into the engine, or, on the 4.8L, downward into the thermostat housing. Tighten the thermostat housing bolts to 20 ft. lbs. (28 Nm). On the 4.3L, 5.0L, 5.7L tighten the studs to 21 ft. lbs. (28 Nm). On the 7.4L tighten the bolts to 27 ft. lbs. (37 Nm).
5. Refill the cooling system. Start the engine and check for leaks.

6.2L and 6.5L Diesel Engines

See Figures 41 and 42

1. Remove the upper fan shroud.
2. Drain the cooling system to a point below the thermostat.
3. Remove the engine oil dipstick tube brace and the oil fill brace.

87983p35

Fig. 33 Remove the thermostat housing bolts

87983p36

Fig. 34 Remove the thermostat housing from the engine

87983p37

Fig. 35 Remove the thermostat from the housing

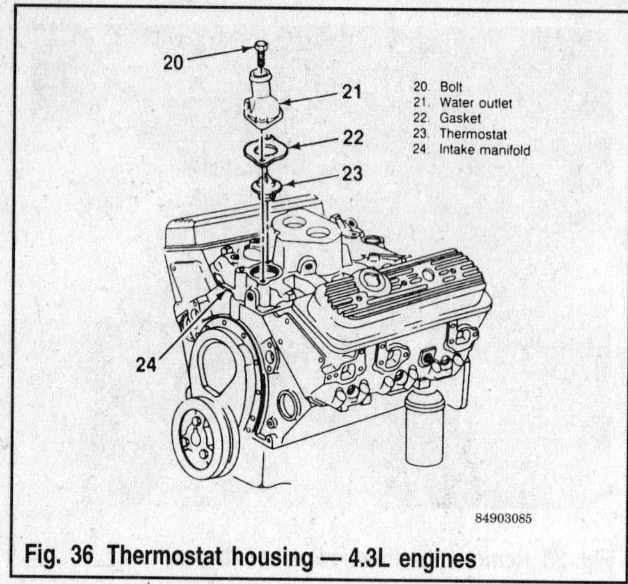

Fig. 36 Thermostat housing — 4.3L engines

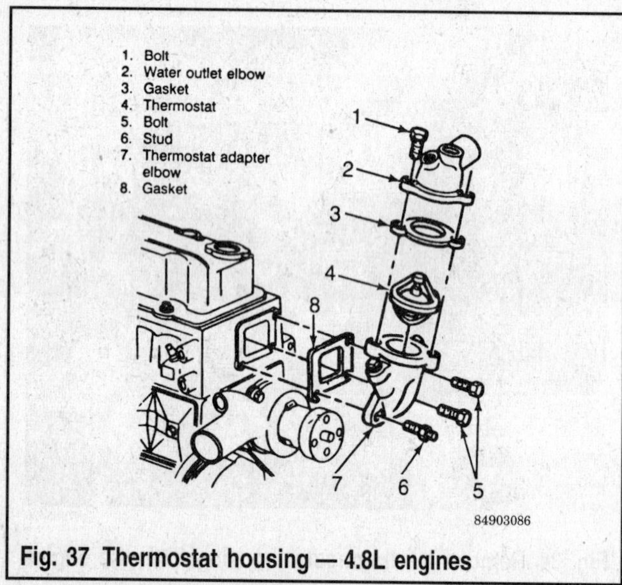

Fig. 37 Thermostat housing — 4.8L engines

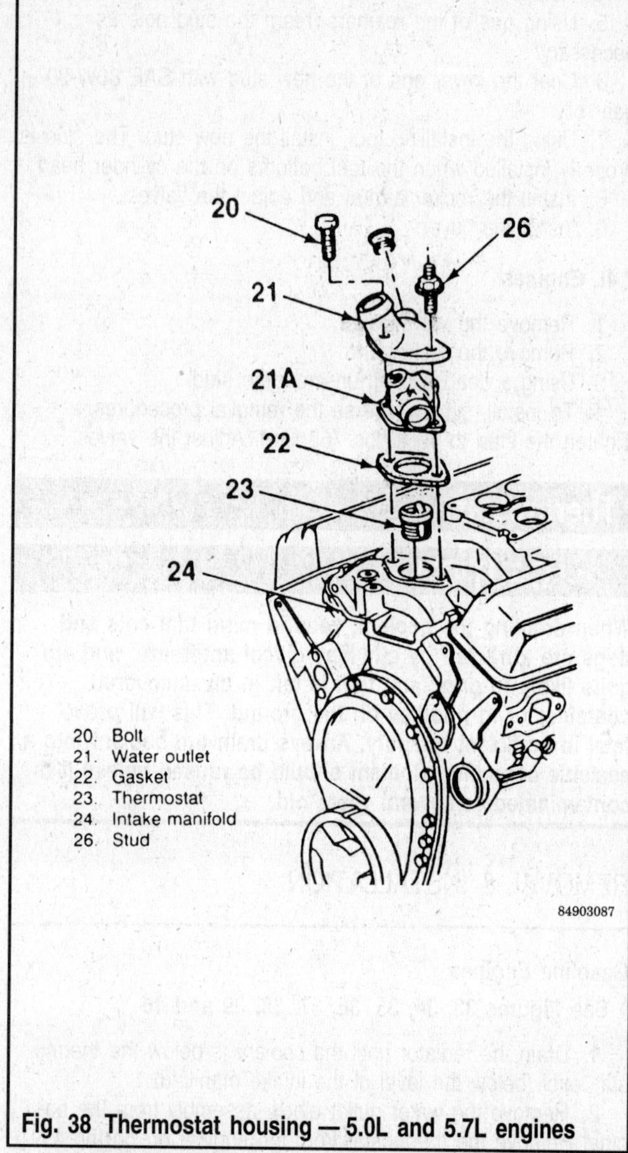

Fig. 38 Thermostat housing — 5.0L and 5.7L engines

4. Remove the upper radiator hose.
5. Remove the water outlet.
6. Remove the thermostat and gasket.
7. Installation is the reverse of removal.
8. Use a new gasket coated with sealer, Make sure that the spring end of the thermostat is in the engine. Tighten the bolts to 35 ft. lbs. (47 Nm) on 1988-91 models and 31 ft. lbs. (42 Nm) on 1992-96 models.

Overflow Tank

REMOVAL & INSTALLATION

➧ See Figure 43

1. Drain the cooling system to a point below the level of the tank.
2. Disconnect the overflow hose from the radiator.
3. Disconnect the return hose from the tank.
4. Remove the tank's mounting screw and bolt and lift the tank from the truck.

To install:

5. Install the tank and tighten the bolt.
6. Connect the return and overflow hoses.
7. Fill the cooling system.

Thermostat Housing Crossover

REMOVAL & INSTALLATION

➧ See Figures 44 and 45

➡This is found on the 6.2 and 6.5L diesel engines only.

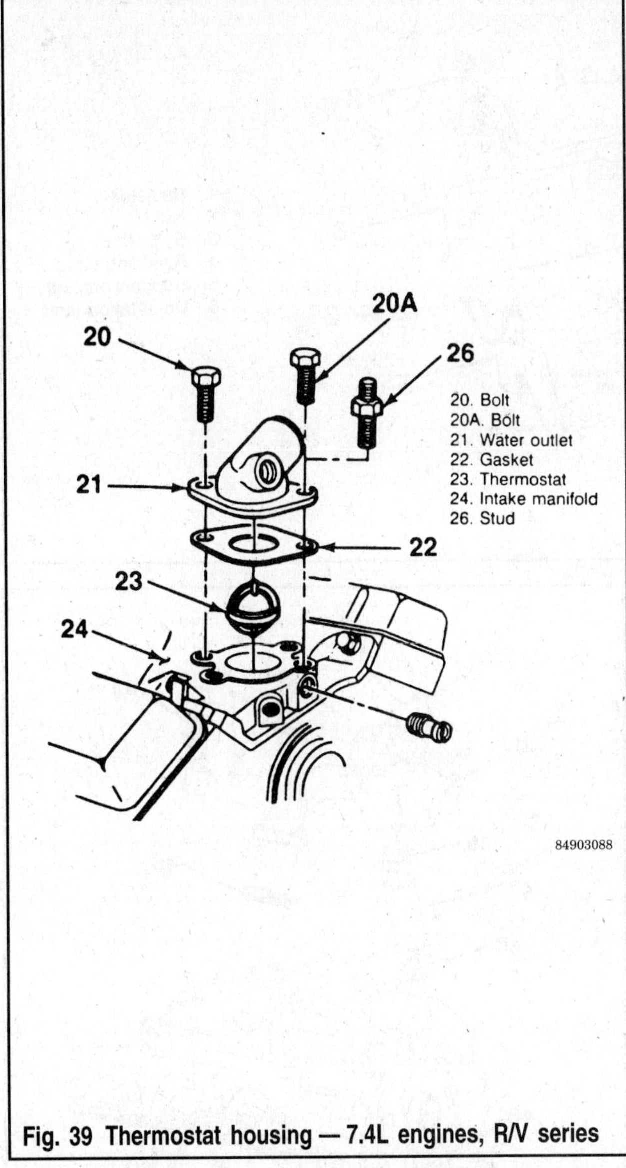

Fig. 39 Thermostat housing — 7.4L engines, R/V series

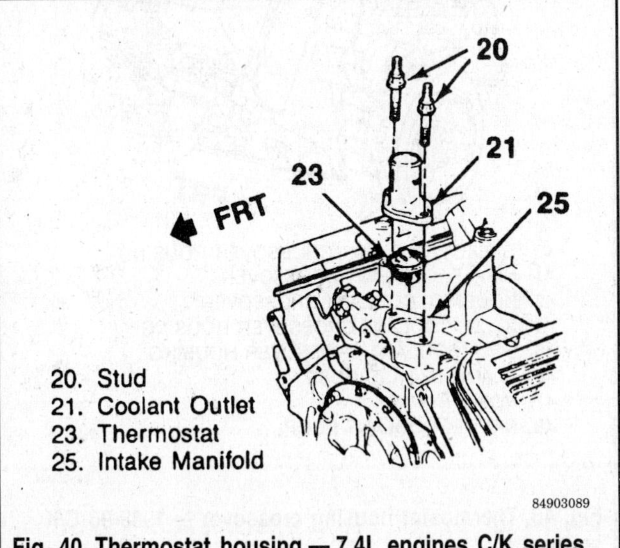

Fig. 40 Thermostat housing — 7.4L engines C/K series

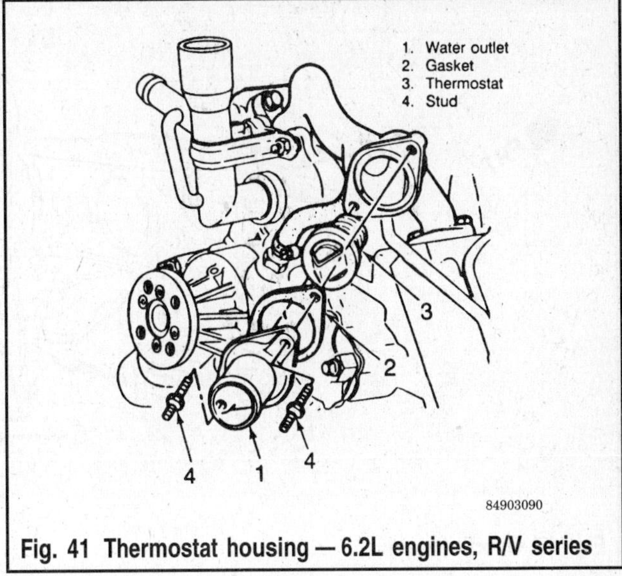

Fig. 41 Thermostat housing — 6.2L engines, R/V series

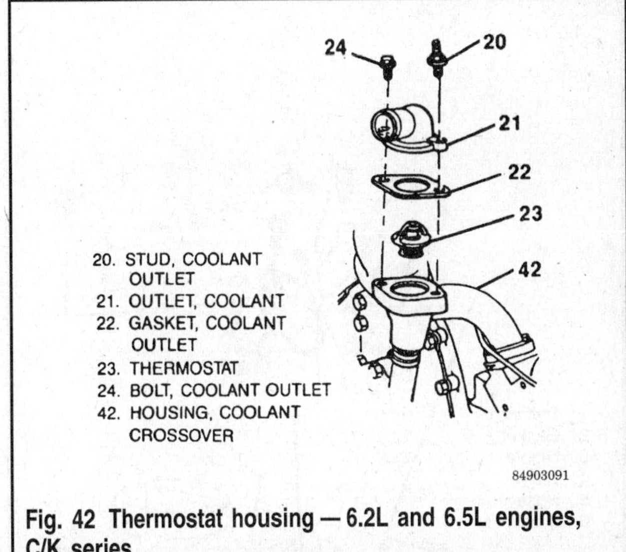

Fig. 42 Thermostat housing — 6.2L and 6.5L engines, C/K series

1. Drain the cooling system.

CAUTION

When draining the coolant, keep in mind that cats and dogs are attracted by ethylene glycol antifreeze, and are quite likely to drink any that is left in an uncovered container or in puddles on the ground. This will prove fatal in sufficient quantity. Always drain the coolant into a sealable container. Coolant should be reused unless it is contaminated or several years old.

2. Remove the engine cover.
3. Remove the air cleaner and CDR valve.
4. Remove the air cleaner resonator and bracket.
5. Remove the upper fan shroud.
6. Remove the upper alternator bracket.
7. Remove the bypass hose.
8. Remove the upper radiator hose.
9. Disconnect the heater hose.
10. Remove the attaching bolts and lift out the crossover.

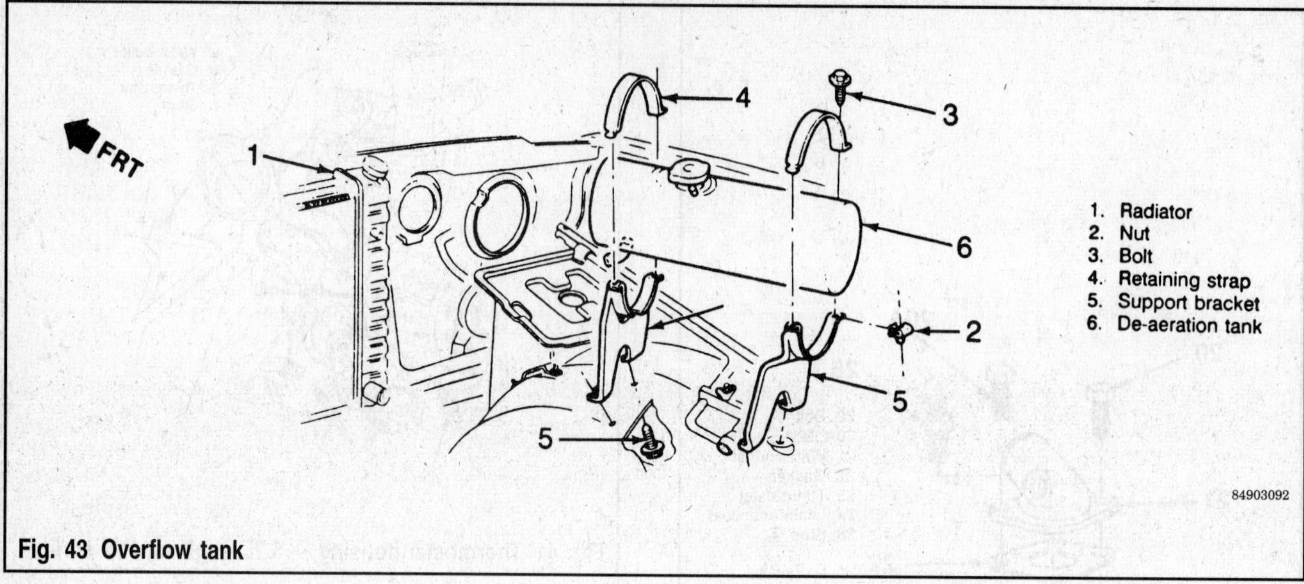

Fig. 43 Overflow tank

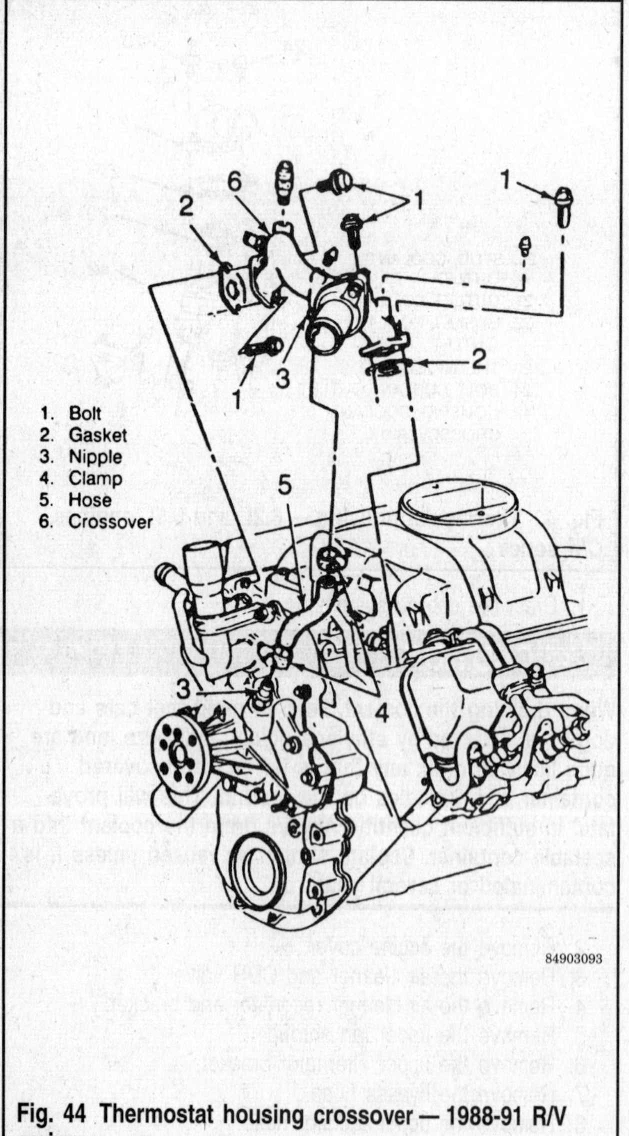

Fig. 44 Thermostat housing crossover — 1988-91 R/V series

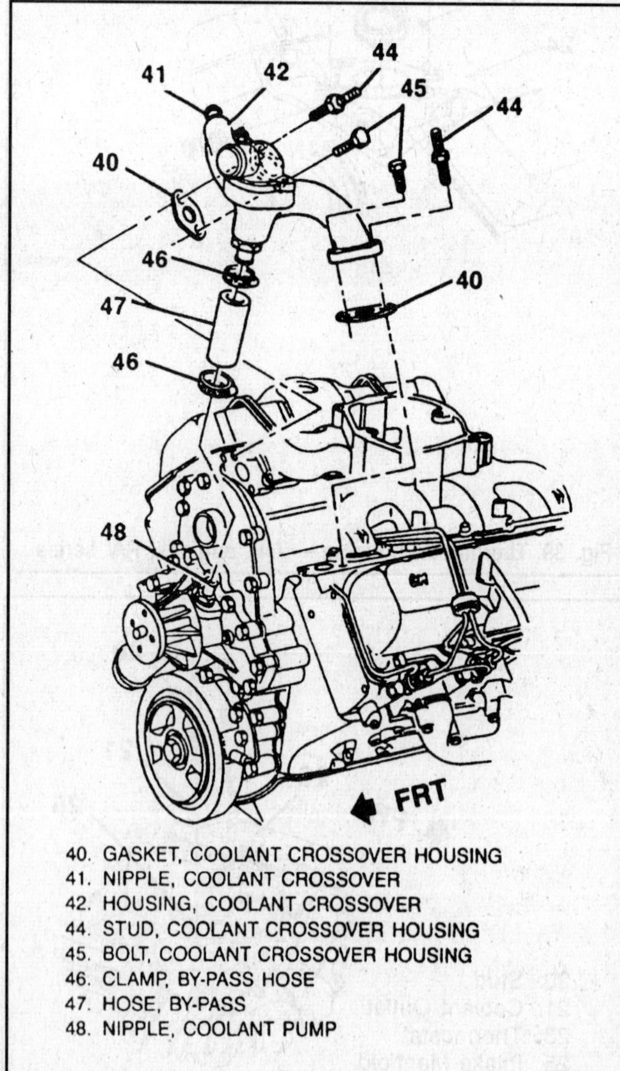

Fig. 45 Thermostat housing crossover — 1988-96 C/K series

To install:

11. Thoroughly clean the mating surfaces.
12. Position the crossover, using new gaskets coated with sealer.
13. Install the attaching bolts and tighten them to 35 ft. lbs. (47 Nm) on 1988-91 engines, or 31 ft. lbs. (42 Nm) on 1992-96 engines.
14. Connect the heater hose.
15. Install the upper radiator hose.
16. Install the bypass hose.
17. Install the upper alternator bracket.
18. Install the upper fan shroud.
19. Install the air cleaner resonator and bracket.
20. Install the air cleaner and the CDR valve.
21. Install the engine cover.
22. Fill the cooling system.

Upper Intake Manifold

REMOVAL & INSTALLATION

4.3L Engines

1996 MODELS

The intake manifold assembly is a two-piece design. The upper portion is made from a composite material and the lower portion is cast-aluminum. The throttle body attaches to the upper manifold. The lower manifold has an Exhaust Gas Recirculation (EGR) port cast into the manifold for mixture of exhaust gases with the fuel and air mixture. The EGR valve bolts into the lower intake manifold.

The Central Sequential Multiport Fuel Injection (CSFI) system uses multiple injectors to meter and distribute fuel to each engine cylinder. The CSFI unit is retained by a bracket bolted to the lower intake manifold. The fuel meter body also houses the pressure regulator. Metal inlet and outlet fuel lines and nylon delivery tubes connect to the CSFI unit. The delivery tubes independently distribute fuel to each cylinder through nozzles located at the port entrance of each manifold runner where the fuel is atomized.

****CAUTION**

Fuel injection systems remain under pressure, even after the engine has been turned OFF. The fuel system pressure must be relieved before disconnecting any fuel lines. Failure to do so may result in fire and/or personal injury.

1. Disconnect the negative battery cable.
2. Drain the cooling system.
3. Remove the air cleaner intake duct.
4. Remove the wiring harness connectors and brackets and move them aside.
5. Disconnect the throttle linkage and bracket from the upper intake manifold.
6. Remove the cruise control cable (if equipped).
7. Remove the brake booster vacuum hose at the upper intake manifold.
8. Remove the ignition coil and bracket.
9. Remove the purge solenoid and bracket.

➡Note the location of the manifold bolts and studs before removal for reassembly in their original positions.

10. Remove the intake manifold bolts and studs.

➡Do not disassemble the CSFI unit.

11. Remove the upper intake manifold.

To install:

12. Install the upper intake manifold gasket.
13. Install the upper intake manifold.

➡When installing the upper intake manifold be careful not to pinch the injector wires between the upper and lower intake manifolds.

14. Install the upper intake manifold mounting bolts and studs in the same locations as prior to removal.
15. Tighten the bolts and studs in a crisscross pattern to 88 inch lbs. (10 Nm).
16. Install the purge solenoid and bracket.
17. Install the ignition coil and bracket.
18. Install the throttle linkage and bracket to the upper intake manifold.
19. Install the throttle linkage cable.
20. Install the cruise control cable (if equipped).
21. Install the wiring harness connectors and brackets.
22. Install the air cleaner intake duct.
23. Connect the negative battery cable.
24. Start the vehicle and verify no leaks.

5.0 and 5.7L Engines

The 5.0L and 5.7L engines use a two-piece intake manifold design. The upper portion is made from a composite material and lower portion is cast-aluminum. The throttle body attaches to the upper manifold. The lower manifold has an Exhaust Gas Recirculation (EGR) port cast into the manifold for mixture of exhaust gases with the fuel and air mixture. The EGR valve bolts to the lower intake manifold.

The Central Sequential Multiport Fuel Injection (CSFI) system uses multiple injectors to meter and distribute fuel to each engine cylinder. The CSFI unit is retained by a bracket bolted to the lower intake manifold. The fuel meter body also houses the pressure regulator. Metal inlet and outlet fuel lines and nylon delivery tubes connect to the CSFI unit. The delivery tubes independently distribute fuel to each cylinder through nozzles located at the port entrance of each manifold runner where the fuel is atomized.

Note that the lower intake manifold gaskets are NOT reusable on the 5.0L and 5.7L engines.

****CAUTION**

Fuel injection systems remain under pressure, even after the engine has been turned OFF. The fuel system pressure must be relieved before disconnecting any fuel lines. Failure to do so may result in fire and/or personal injury.

1. Disconnect the negative battery cable.
2. Remove the air cleaner intake duct.
3. Remove the wiring harness connectors and brackets and move them aside.

4. Disconnect the throttle linkage and bracket from the upper intake manifold.
5. Remove the cruise control cable (if equipped).
6. Remove the PCV valve and hose.
7. Remove the ignition coil and bracket.
8. Remove the purge solenoid and bracket.

➡Note the location of the manifold bolts and studs before removal for reassembly in their original positions.

9. Remove the intake manifold bolts and studs.

➡Do not disassemble the CSFI unit.

10. Remove the upper intake manifold.

To install:

11. Install the upper intake manifold gasket.
12. Install the upper intake manifold.

➡When installing the upper intake manifold be careful not to pinch the injector wires between the upper and lower intake manifolds.

13. Install the upper intake manifold mounting bolts and studs in the same locations as prior to removal.
14. Tighten the bolts and studs in a crisscross patern in 2 steps first to 45 inch lbs. (5 Nm) then to 83 inch lbs. (10 Nm).
15. Install the purge solenoid and bracket.
16. Install the ignition coil and bracket.
17. Install the throttle linkage and bracket to the upper intake manifold.
18. Install the throttle linkage cable.
19. Install the cruise control cable (if equipped).
20. Install the wiring harness connectors and brackets.
21. Install the air cleaner intake duct.
22. Connect the negative battery cable.
23. Start the vehicle and verify no leaks.

7.4L Engines

1996 MODELS

▸ See Figure 46

In 1996, the 7.4L engine was changed from Throttle Body Fuel Injection (TBI) to Sequential Fuel Injection (SFI). The intake manifold was changed to a two-piece unit. The upper half, often called a "plenum" mounts the throttle body assembly. The lower half of the intake manifold, which bolts to the cylinder heads, contains the fuel rail and injectors. Use care when working with light alloy parts. Work as clean as possible to prevent dirt and foreign material from entering the engine.

1. Disconnect the negative battery cable.
2. Remove the air cleaner intake duct.
3. Remove the wiring harness connectors and brackets and move them aside.
4. Remove the throttle and cruise control linkage (if equipped).
5. Remove the throttle body electrical connectors.
6. Remove the PCV valve and hose.
7. Remove the EGR inlet tube.
8. Remove the purge solenoid and connectors.
9. Remove the ignition coil and bracket.
10. Remove the #8 spark plug wire from the distributor.

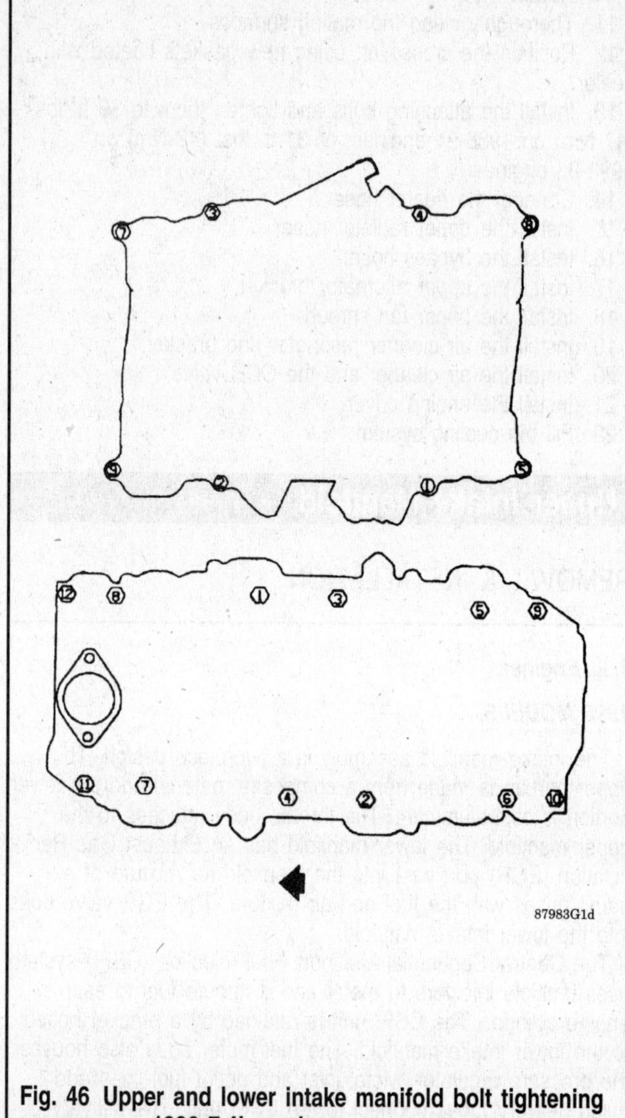

Fig. 46 Upper and lower intake manifold bolt tightening sequence — 1996 7.4L engines

11. Remove the upper intake manifold bolts and remove the upper intake manifold.

To install:

12. Clean all parts well. Clean all traces of gasket from the sealing surfaces.
13. Install a new upper intake manifold gasket.
14. Carefully place the upper intake manifold into position.
15. Install the upper intake manifold bolts and tighten them in sequence to 17 ft. lbs. (22 Nm). Install the two corner bolts first to help align the two halves.
16. Connect the #8 spark plug wire.
17. Install the ignition coil and bracket.
18. Install the purge canister and connectors.
19. Install the EGR inlet tube.
20. Install the PCV valve and hose.
21. Install the throttle body electrical connectors.
22. Install the throttle and cruise control linkage and bracket.
23. Install the wiring harness connectors and brackets.
24. Install the air cleaner intake duct.

Lower Intake Manifold

➡For the 4.8L engine, please refer to the Combination Manifold procedure.

REMOVAL & INSTALLATION

4.3L Engines

1988-95 MODELS

➧ See Figures 47, 48 and 49

1. Disconnect the negative battery cable. Drain the cooling system.
2. Remove the air cleaner assembly.

➡Mark the relationship of the distributor and rotor for proper reassembly

3. Remove the distributor.
4. Disconnect the accelerator and cruise control cables with their brackets.
5. Remove the rear air conditioner compressor bracket, the alternator bracket and the idler pulley bracket at the manifold.
6. Disconnect all electrical connections and vacuum lines from the manifold. Remove the EGR valve if necessary.
7. Disconnect the fuel line at the intake manifold.
8. Remove the heater pipe.
9. Disconnect the upper radiator hose and pull it off.
10. Tag and disconnect the power brake vacuum pipe and the EGR vacuum line.
11. Tag and disconnect the coil wires and if necessary remove the coil.
12. Remove the sensors and bracket on the right side. Disconnect the wiring harness on the right side and position it out of the way.

➡Mark the location of the intake manifold studs for proper reassembly

13. Remove the intake manifold bolts. Remove the manifold and the gaskets. Remember to reinstall the O-ring between the

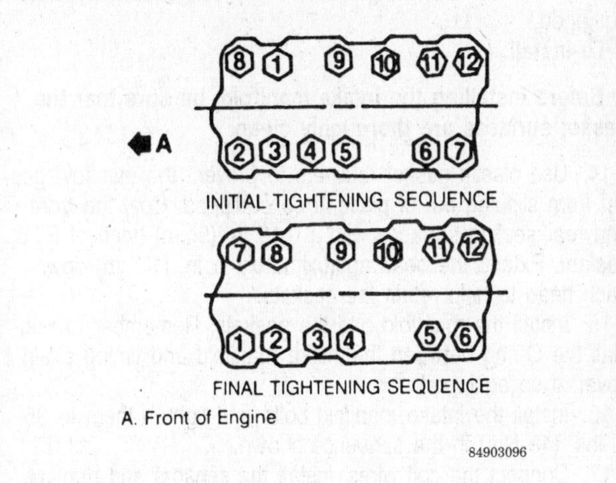

Fig. 48 Intake manifold bolt tightening sequence — 1988-91 4.3L engines

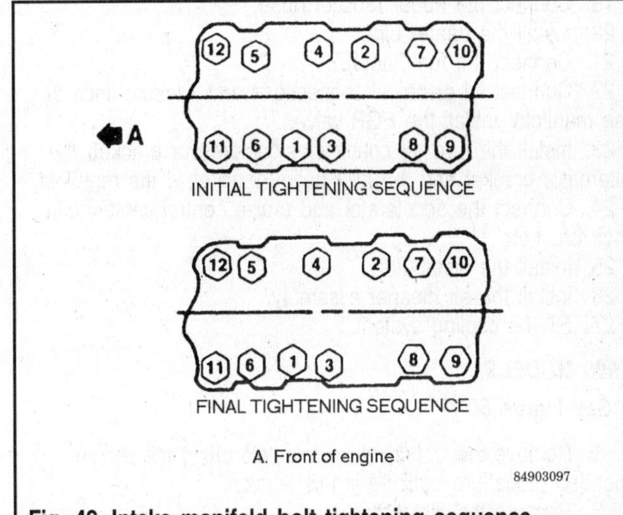

Fig. 49 Intake manifold bolt tightening sequence — 1992-95 4.3L engines

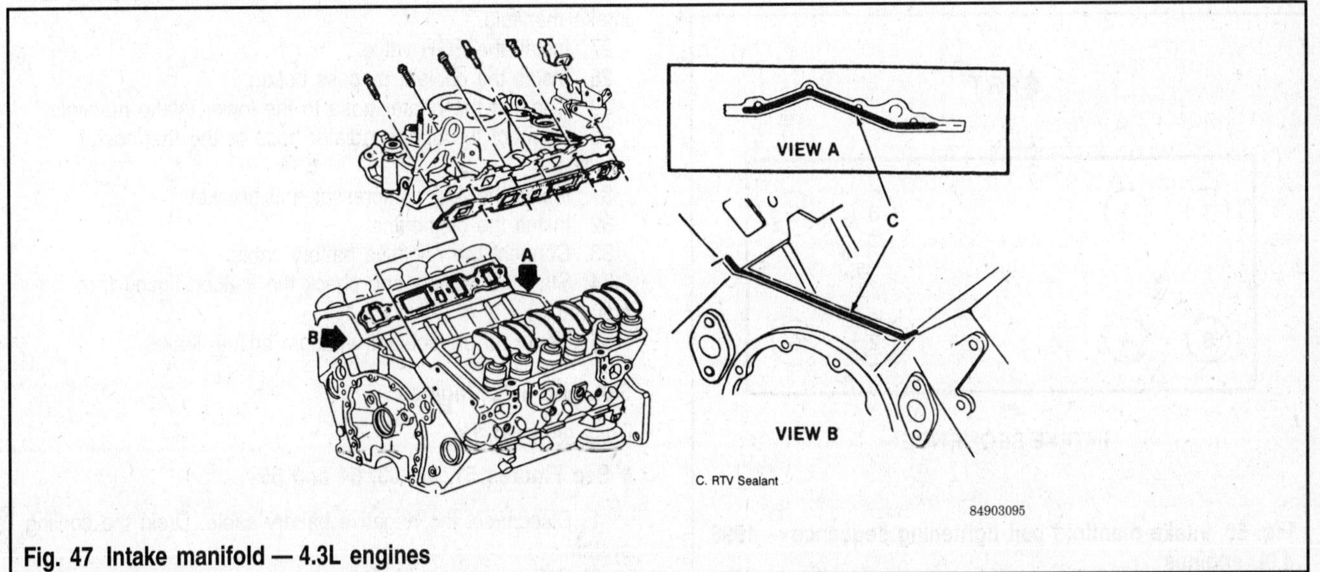

Fig. 47 Intake manifold — 4.3L engines

intake manifold and timing chain cover during assembly, if so equipped.

To install:

➡Before installing the intake manifold, be sure that the gasket surfaces are thoroughly clean.

14. Use plastic gasket retainers to prevent the manifold gasket from slipping out of place, if so equipped. Coat the front and rear sealing surfaces with a 0.19 in. (5mm) bead of RTV sealant. Extend the bead approximately ½ in. (13mm) down each head to help retain the gaskets.
15. Install the manifold and the gaskets. Remember to reinstall the O-ring between the intake manifold and timing chain cover, if so equipped.
16. Install the intake manifold bolts and tighten them to 35 ft. lbs. (48 Nm) in the sequence shown.
17. Connect the coil wires. Install the sensors and bracket on the right side. Connect the wiring harness.
18. Connect the power brake vacuum pipe and the EGR vacuum line.
19. Connect the upper radiator hose.
20. Install the heater pipe.
21. Connect the fuel line(s).
22. Connect all electrical connections and vacuum lines at the manifold. Install the EGR valve.
23. Install the rear air conditioner compressor bracket, the alternator bracket and the idler pulley bracket at the manifold.
24. Connect the accelerator and cruise control cables with their brackets.
25. Install the distributor.
26. Install the air cleaner assembly.
27. Fill the cooling system.

1996 MODELS

➧ See Figure 50

1. Remove the upper intake manifold using the recommended procedure outlined in this section.
2. Remove the distributor.
3. Disconnect the upper radiator hose from the thermostat housing.

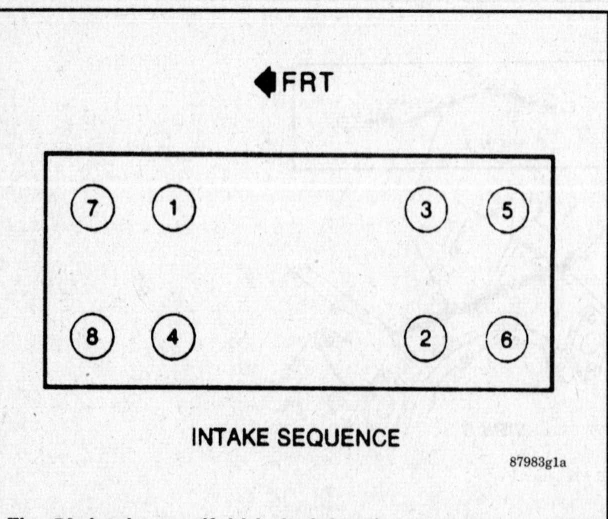

Fig. 50 Intake manifold bolt tightening sequence — 1996 4.3L engines

4. Disconnect the heater hose from the lower intake manifold.
5. Remove the coolant by-pass hose.
6. Remove the EGR valve.
7. Disconnect the fuel pressure and return lines from the lower intake manifold.
8. Disconnect the wiring harnesses and brackets from the lower manifold.
9. Remove the transmission oil level indicator and tube, if equipped.
10. Remove the EGR tube, clamp and bolt.
11. Remove the PCV valve and hose.
12. Remove the A/C compressor and bracket, but do NOT disconnect the lines. Move the compressor out of the way. Take care not to kink the A/C lines.
13. Loosen the compressor mounting bracket and slide it forward, but do NOT remove it.
14. Remove the lower intake manifold bolts.
15. Remove the lower intake manifold.

To install:

16. Clean all gasket surfaces completely.
17. Install the intake manifold gaskets with the port blocking plates facing the rear. Factory gaskets should have the words "This Side Up" visable.
18. Apply gasket sealer to the front and rear sealing surfaces of the engine block. Extend the sealer approximately ½-inch (13mm) onto the heads.
19. Install the lower intake manifold.
20. Apply sealer to the lower intake manifold bolts prior to installation.
21. Install the bolts and tighten in sequence and in 3 steps as follows:
    a. First step to 26 inch lbs. (3 Nm).
    b. Second step to 106 inch lbs. (12 Nm).
    c. Final step to 11 ft. lbs. (15 Nm).
22. Install the PCV valve and hose.
23. Install the EGR tube, clamp and bolt.
24. Install the transmission oil level indicator and tube, if equipped.
25. Connect the wiring harnesses and brackets to the lower manifold.
26. Connect the fuel pressure and return lines to the lower intake manifold.
27. Install the EGR valve.
28. Install the coolant by-pass hose.
29. Connect the heater hose to the lower intake manifold.
30. Connect the upper radiator hose to the thermostat housing.
31. Install the A/C compressor and bracket.
32. Install the distributor.
33. Connect the negative battery cable.
34. Start the vehicle and check the ignition timing (not adjustable).
35. Verify no oil, coolant, vacuum or fuel leaks.

5.0L and 5.7L Engines

1988-95 MODELS

➧ See Figures 51, 52, 53, 54 and 55

1. Disconnect the negative battery cable. Drain the cooling system.
2. Remove the air cleaner assembly.

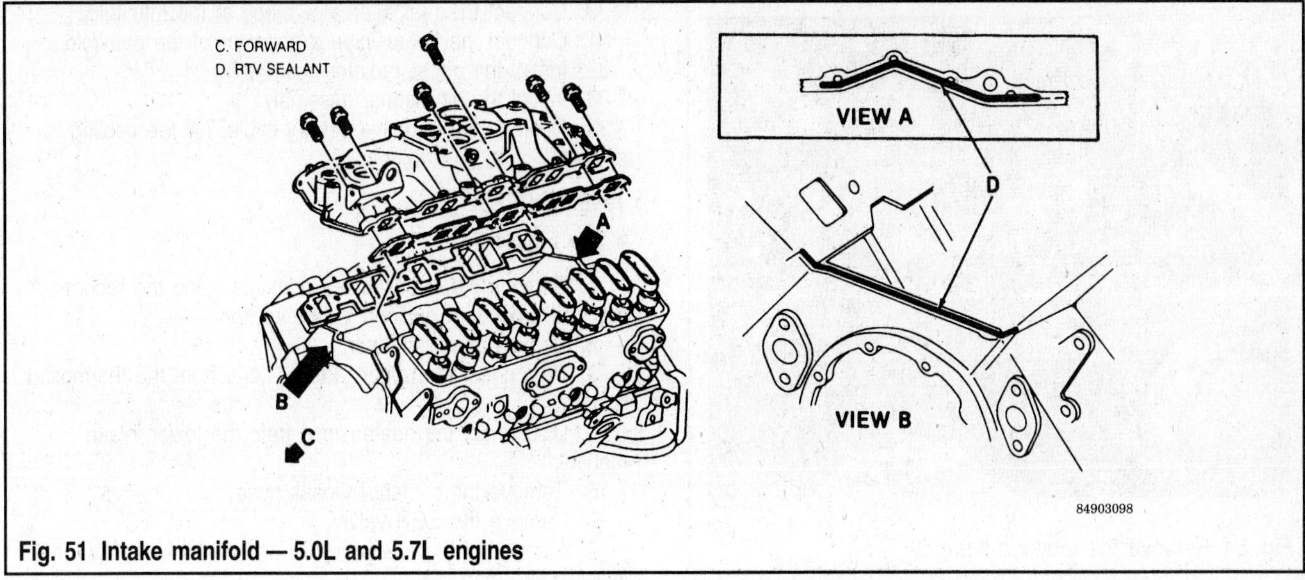

Fig. 51 Intake manifold — 5.0L and 5.7L engines

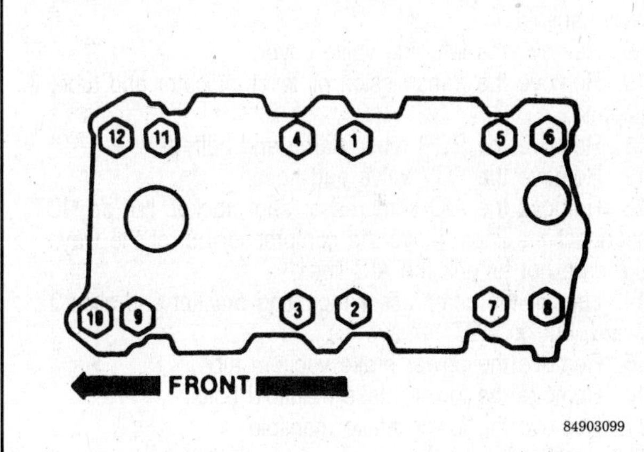

Fig. 52 Intake manifold bolt tightening sequence — 1988-95 5.0L and 5.7L engines

3. Remove the upper radiator hose from the thermostat housing.
4. Disconnect the heater pipe at the rear of the manifold.
5. Disconnect the rear alternator brace at the manifold.
6. Disengage all electrical connections and vacuum lines from the manifold. Remove the EGR valve if necessary.

➡Mark the relationship of the distributor and rotor for proper reassembly

7. Remove the distributor.
8. Disconnect the fuel line at the intake manifold.
9. Remove the accelerator and cruise control linkage.
10. Remove the air conditioner compressor rear bracket.
11. Remove the brake booster vacuum pipe and then disconnect the coil wires.
12. Remove the emission control sensors and their bracket from the right side.
13. Remove the fuel line bracket at the rear of the manifold and position the fuel lines out of the way.
14. Remove the bracket behind the idler pulley.
15. Remove the carburetor or TBI unit if necessary. Refer to Section 5 for this procedure.

➡Mark the location of the intake manifold studs for proper reassembly

16. Remove the intake manifold bolts. Remove the manifold and the gaskets. Remember to reinstall the O-ring between the intake manifold and timing chain cover during assembly, if so equipped.

To install:

➡Before installing the intake manifold, be sure that the gasket surfaces are thoroughly clean.

17. Use plastic gasket retainers to prevent the manifold gasket from slipping out of place, if so equipped. Place a $^3/_{16}$ in. (5mm) bead of RTV type silicone sealer on the front and rear ridges of the cylinder block-to-manifold mating surfaces. Extend the bead $^1/_2$ in. (13mm) up each cylinder head to seal and retain the manifold side gaskets.

Fig. 53 Remove the intake manifold retaining bolts

87983p39

Fig. 54 Remove the intake manifold

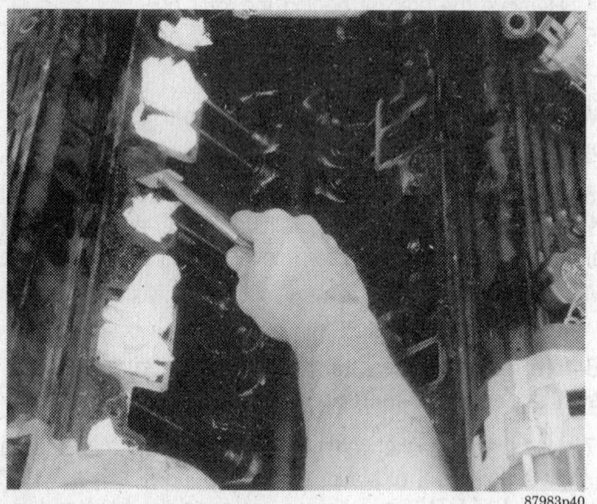

87983p40

Fig. 55 Using a scraper clean the intake manifold gasket mating surfaces

18. Install the manifold and the gaskets. Remember to reinstall the O-ring between the intake manifold and timing chain cover, if so equipped.
19. Install the intake manifold bolts and tighten in the proper sequence. Tighten to 35 ft. lbs. (48Nm).
20. Install the carburetor or TBI unit if removed. Refer to Section 5 for this procedure.
21. Install the bracket behind the idler pulley.
22. Install the fuel line bracket at the rear of the manifold.
23. Install the emission control sensors and their bracket on the right side.
24. Install the brake booster vacuum pipe and then connect the coil wires.
25. Install the air conditioner compressor rear bracket.
26. Install the accelerator and cruise control linkage.
27. Install the fuel line and bracket.
28. Install the distributor.
29. Engage all electrical connections and vacuum lines at the manifold. Install the EGR valve.
30. Connect the rear alternator brace at the manifold.
31. Connect the heater pipe to the rear of the manifold.
32. Install the upper radiator hose.
33. Install the air cleaner assembly.
34. Connect the negative battery cable. Fill the cooling system.

1996 MODELS

➧ See Figure 56

1. Remove the upper intake manifold using the recommended procedure outlined in this section.
2. Remove the distributor.
3. Disconnect the upper radiator hose from the thermostat housing.
4. Disconnect the heater hose from the lower intake manifold.
5. Remove the coolant by-pass hose.
6. Remove the EGR valve.
7. Disconnect the fuel pressure and return lines from the lower intake manifold.
8. Disconnect the wiring harnesses and brackets from the lower manifold.
9. Remove the left side valve cover.
10. Remove the transmission oil level indicator and tube, if equipped.
11. Remove the EGR tube, clamp and bolt.
12. Remove the PCV valve and hose.
13. Remove the A/C compressor and bracket, but do NOT disconnect the lines. Move the compressor out of the way. Take care not to kink the A/C lines.
14. Loosen the compressor mounting bracket and slide it forward, but do NOT remove it.
15. Remove the power brake vacuum tube.
16. Remove the lower intake manifold bolts.
17. Remove the lower intake manifold.

To install:

18. Clean all gasket surfaces completely.
19. Install the intake manifold gaskets with the port blocking plates facing the rear. Factory gaskets should have the words "This Side Up" visible.

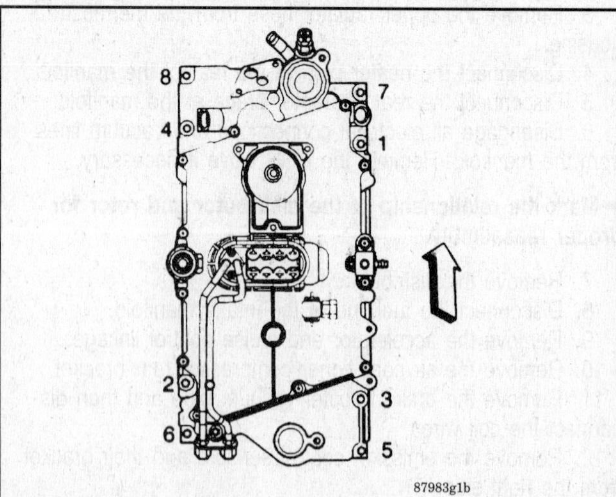

87983g1b

Fig. 56 Intake manifold bolt tightening sequence — 1996 5.0L and 5.7L engines

20. Apply gasket sealer to the front and rear sealing surfaces of the engine block. Extend the sealer approximately ½-inch (13mm) onto the heads.
21. Install the lower intake manifold.
22. Apply sealer to the lower intake manifold bolts prior to installation.
23. Install the bolts and tighten in sequence and in 3 steps as follows:
  a. First step to 71 inch lbs. (8 Nm).
  b. Second step to 106 inch lbs. (12 Nm).
  c. Final step to 11 ft. lbs. (15 Nm).
24. Install the power brake vacuum tube.
25. Install the PCV valve and hose.
26. Install the EGR tube, clamp and bolt.
27. Install the transmission oil level indicator and tube, if equipped.
28. Install the left side valve cover.
29. Connect the wiring harnesses and brackets to the lower manifold.
30. Connect the fuel pressure and return lines to the lower intake manifold.
31. Install the EGR valve.
32. Install the coolant by-pass hose.
33. Connect the heater hose to the lower intake manifold.
34. Connect the upper radiator hose to the thermostat housing.
35. Install the A/C compressor and bracket.
36. Install the distributor.
37. Connect the negative battery cable.
38. Start the vehicle and check the ignition timing (not adjustable).
39. Verify no oil, coolant, vacuum or fuel leaks.

6.2L and 6.5L Diesel Engines

See Figure 57

1. Disconnect both batteries.
2. Remove the air cleaner assembly.
3. Remove the crankcase ventilator tubes, and disconnect the secondary fuel filter lines. Remove the secondary filter and adaptor.
4. Remove the thermostat bolts and the upper radiator hose.
5. Loosen the vacuum pump hold-down clamp and rotate the pump to gain access to the nearest manifold bolt.
6. Remove the EPR/EGR boost solenoids and bracket, if equipped. Tag and disconnect the EGR and crankcase vent hoses.
7. Remove the heater hose bracket, tag and disconnect any vacuum lines and electrical connections as necessary.
8. If equipped with a turbocharger remove the long pencil brace.
9. Remove the fuel line brackets and ground straps.
10. Remove the rear air conditioning bracket, if equipped.
11. Remove the intake manifold bolts. The injection line clips are retained by these bolts.
12. Remove the intake manifold.

➡If the engine is to be further serviced with the manifold removed, install protective covers over the intake ports.

To install:

13. Clean the manifold gasket surfaces on the cylinder heads and install new gaskets before installing the manifold.

➡The gaskets have an opening for the EGR valve on light duty installations. An insert covers this opening on heavy duty installations.

14. Install the manifold. Tighten the bolts in the sequence illustrated to 32 ft. lbs. (42 Nm).
15. The secondary filter must be filled with clean diesel fuel before it is reinstalled.
16. Install the rear air conditioning bracket, if equipped.
17. Install the ground straps and fuel line brackets.
18. Install the turbocharger pencil brace, if equipped.
19. Engage any electrical connections and vacuum hoses that were removed.
20. Install the EPR/EGR valve bracket. Reconnect the hoses.
21. Tighten the vacuum pump hold-down clamp.
22. Install the upper radiator hose and the thermostat bolts.
23. Install the secondary filter and adaptor.
24. Connect the secondary fuel filter lines.

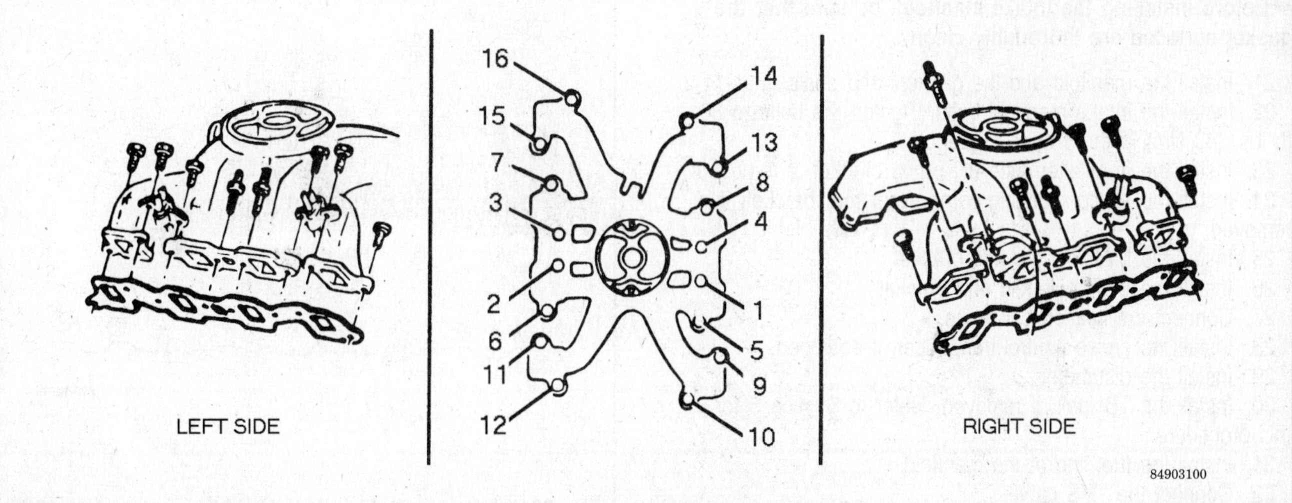

Fig. 57 Intake manifold bolt tightening sequence — diesel engines (6.2L shown)

25. Install the crankcase ventilator tubes.
26. Install the air cleaner assembly.
27. Connect both batteries.

7.4L Engines

1988-95 MODELS

See Figures 58, 59 and 60

1. Disconnect the battery.
2. Drain the cooling system.
3. Remove the air cleaner assembly.
4. Remove the upper radiator hose, thermostat housing and the bypass hose, if necessary.
5. Disconnect the heater hose and pipe.
6. Tag and disconnect all electrical connections and vacuum lines from the manifold and move them to the side.
7. Disconnect the accelerator linkage.
8. Disconnect the cruise control cable, if equipped.
9. Disconnect the TVS cable.
10. Remove the fuel line at the manifold.
11. Remove the TBI unit, if necessary. Refer to Section 5 for this procedure.

Mark the relationship of the distributor and rotor for proper reassembly

12. Remove the distributor, if necessary.
13. Remove the cruise control transducer, if equipped.
14. Disconnect the ignition coil wires and remove the coil if necessary.
15. Remove the EGR solenoid and bracket.
16. Remove the MAP sensor and bracket.
17. Remove the air conditioning compressor rear bracket.
18. Remove the front alternator/AIR pump bracket, if necessary.
19. Remove the intake manifold bolts.
20. Remove the manifold and the gaskets and seals.

Remember to reinstall the O-ring between the intake manifold and timing chain cover during assembly, if so equipped.

To install:

Before installing the intake manifold, be sure that the gasket surfaces are thoroughly clean.

21. Install the manifold and the gaskets and seals.
22. Install the intake manifold bolts. Tighten the bolts to 30 ft. lbs. (40 Nm) in the proper sequence.
23. Install the front alternator/AIR pump bracket, if removed.
24. Install the air conditioning compressor rear bracket, if removed.
25. Install the MAP sensor and bracket.
26. Install the EGR solenoid and bracket.
27. Connect the ignition coil wires.
28. Install the cruise control transducer, if equipped.
29. Install the distributor.
30. Install the TBI unit, if removed. Refer to Section 5 for this procedure.
31. Install the fuel line at the manifold.
32. Connect the TVS cable.
33. Connect the cruise control cable, if equipped.
34. Connect the accelerator linkage.

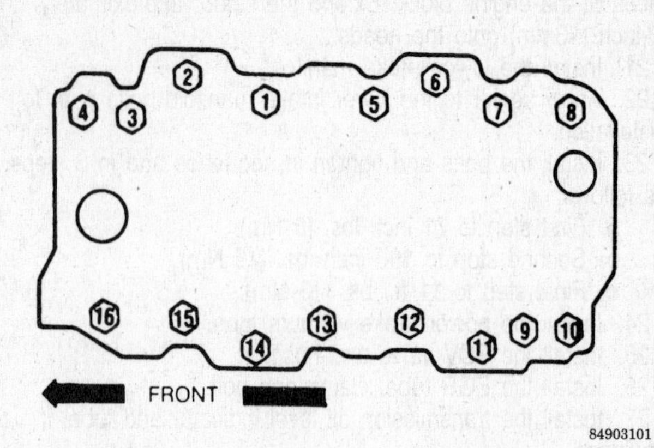

Fig. 58 Intake manifold bolt tightening sequence — 1988-90 7.4L engines

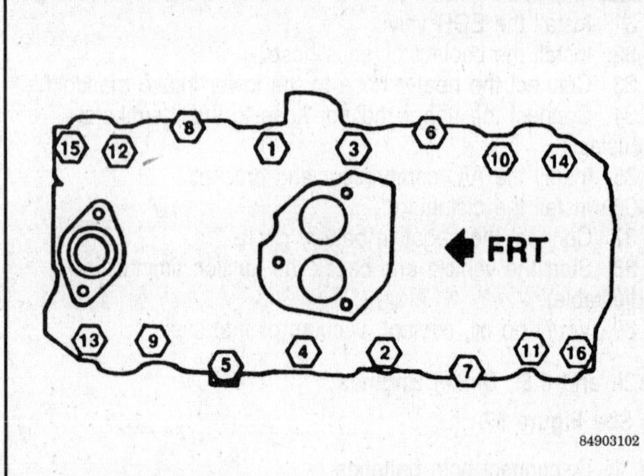

Fig. 59 Intake manifold bolt tightening sequence — 1991-94 7.4L engines

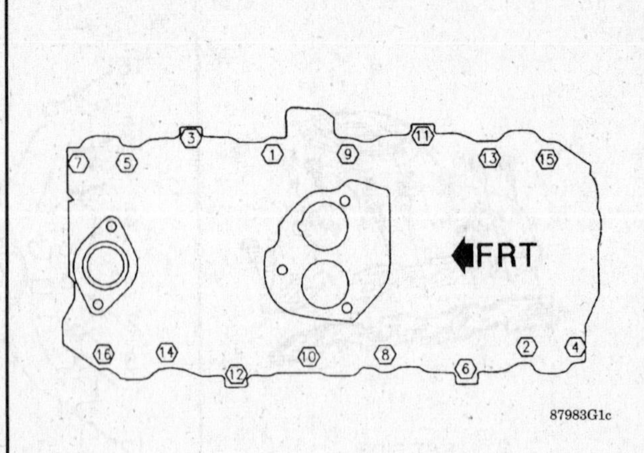

Fig. 60 Intake manifold bolt tightening sequence — 1995 7.4L engines

35. Connect all electrical connections and vacuum lines at the manifold.
36. Connect the heater hose and pipe.
37. Install the upper radiator hose, thermostat housing and the bypass hose.
38. Install the air cleaner assembly.
39. Fill the cooling system.
40. Connect the battery.

1996 MODELS

See Figure 46

1. Have the A/C system discharged. Recover the refrigerant using the appropriate recycling equipment.
2. Remove the upper intake manifold using the recommended procedure outlined in this section.
3. Remove the A/C lines at the compressor.
4. Remove the distributor using the recommended procedure. Mark the relationship of the distributor housing and rotor for proper reassembly.
5. Drain the engine coolant. Remove the upper radiator hose at the thermostat housing.
6. Disconnect the heater hose from the manifold.
7. Disconnect the fuel line brackets and rail.
8. Disconnect the water pump by-pass hose.
9. Remove the lower intake manifold bolts and remove the lower intake manifold and gaskets.

To install:

10. Clean all parts well:
    a. Clean all traces of gasket from the sealing surfaces.
    b. Inspect for cracks, broken flanges and gasket surface damage.
    c. Clean excessive carbon buildup in the exhaust passages.
    d. Clean scale and deposits from the coolant passages.
    e. Clean the EGR passage of carbon deposits.
11. Install the gaskets to the cylinder head in their proper position. Factory-type gaskets should be stamped "This Side Up".
12. Install the front and rear intake manifold seals to the block.
13. Apply a $^{3}/_{16}$-inch (5mm) bead of RTV GM #1052289, or equivalent, to the four seal corners of the block. Extend the bead approximately $^{1}/_{2}$-inch (13mm) up the cylinder head to seal and retain the gaskets.
14. Carefully place the lower intake manifold into position on the engine.
15. Apply sealer, GM #1052080, or equivalent, to the lower intake manifold bolts. Install the lower manifold bolts and tighten them in sequence to 30 ft. lbs. (40 Nm).
16. Install the water pump by-pass hose.
17. Install the wiring harness connectors and brackets.
18. Install the fuel line brackets and fuel rail.
19. Install the heater hose.
20. Install the upper radiator hose.
21. Install the A/C lines to the compressor.
22. Install the distributor. Note the relationship of the distributor housing and rotor made at disassembly.
23. Install the upper intake manifold using the procedure in this section.
24. Fill the cooling system.

➡The 1996 models should have come with DEX-COOL™. This orange-color coolant is low in silicates and is designed to protect the aluminum components in the cooling system.

25. Connect the negative battery cable.
26. Start the engine. Check for coolant, oil and vacuum leaks and for proper engine operation.
27. Have the A/C system recharged.

Exhaust Manifold

➡For the 4.8L engine, please refer to the Combination Manifold procedure.

REMOVAL & INSTALLATION

4.3L Engines

See Figure 61

On some engines, tab locks are used on the front and rear pairs of bolts on each exhaust manifold. When removing the bolts, straighten the tabs from beneath the truck using a suitable tool. When installing the tab locks, bend the tabs against the sides of the bolt, not over the top of the bolt.

1988-94 MODELS

1. Disconnect the negative battery cable. Remove the air cleaner assembly.
2. Raise the vehicle and support it with jackstands.
3. Remove the hot air shroud, (if so equipped). Disconnect the exhaust pipe at the manifold.
4. Lower the truck.
5. Disconnect the O_2 sensor wire on the left side manifold. Do not remove the sensor unless you intend to replace it.
6. Disconnect the rear power steering pump bracket at the left manifold.
7. Remove the heat stove pipe on the right side manifold.
8. Remove the AIR hose at the check valve.
9. Remove the manifold bolts and remove the manifold(s). Some models have lock tabs on the front and rear manifold bolts which must be removed before removing the bolts. These tabs can be bent with a drift pin.

To install:

10. Clean both the manifold and cylinder block mating surfaces and install the manifold. Install the flat washers and then the tab washers and insert the bolts. Tighten the two center bolts to 26 ft. lbs. (36 Nm); the outside bolts to 20 ft. lbs. (28 Nm) and then bend the tab washers against the bolt heads.
11. Install the AIR hose at the check valve.
12. Install the heat stove pipe on the right side manifold.
13. Connect the rear power steering pump bracket at the left manifold.
14. Connect the O_2 sensor wire on the left side manifold.
15. Raise the truck and support it with jackstands.
16. Connect the exhaust pipe at the manifold. Install the hot air shroud.
17. Lower the truck.

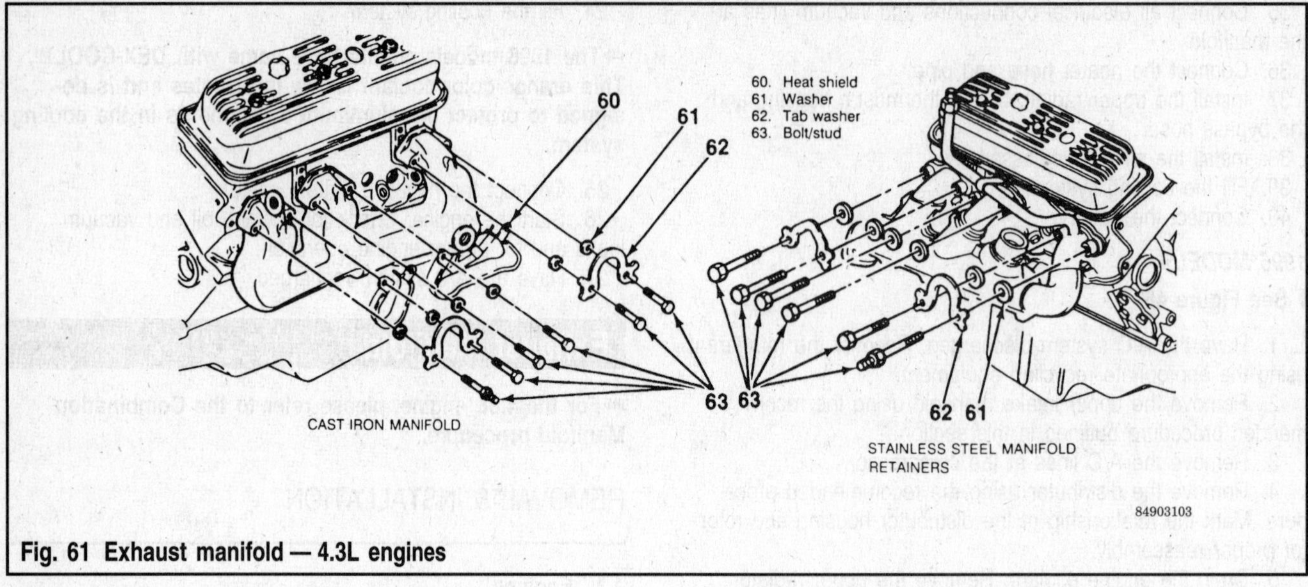

Fig. 61 Exhaust manifold — 4.3L engines

18. Install the air cleaner. Connect the negative battery cable.

1995-96 MODELS

1. Disconnect the negative battery cable. Remove the air cleaner assembly.
2. Raise the vehicle and support it with jackstands.
3. Remove the hot air shroud, (if so equipped). Disconnect the exhaust pipe at the manifold.
4. Lower the truck.
5. Unfasten the manifold retainers and remove the manifold.

To install:

6. Install the manifold and tighten the retainers in the following sequence:
   - Bolts on the center exhaust tube: 26 ft. lbs. (36 Nm)
   - Bolts on the front and rear exhaust tubes: 20 ft. lbs. (28 Nm)
7. Bend the tab washers over the bolts.
8. Raise the vehicle and support it with jackstands.
9. Install the exhaust pipe at the manifold.
10. Install the hot air shroud, If equipped.
11. Lower the vehicle.

5.0L and 5.7L Engines

➧ See Figures 62, 63, 64, 65 and 66

On some engines, tab locks are used on the front and rear pairs of bolts on each exhaust manifold. When removing the bolts, straighten the tabs from beneath the truck using a suitable tool. When installing the tab locks, bend the tabs against the sides of the bolt, not over the top of the bolt.

1. Disconnect the negative battery cable. Remove the air cleaner.
2. Raise the truck and support it with jackstands.
3. Remove the hot air shroud, (if so equipped). Disconnect the exhaust pipe at the manifold.
4. Lower the truck.
5. Disconnect the O_2 sensor wire on the left side manifold. Do not remove the sensor unless you intend to replace it.
6. Remove the AIR hose at the check valve.
7. Remove the heat stove pipe on the right side manifold.

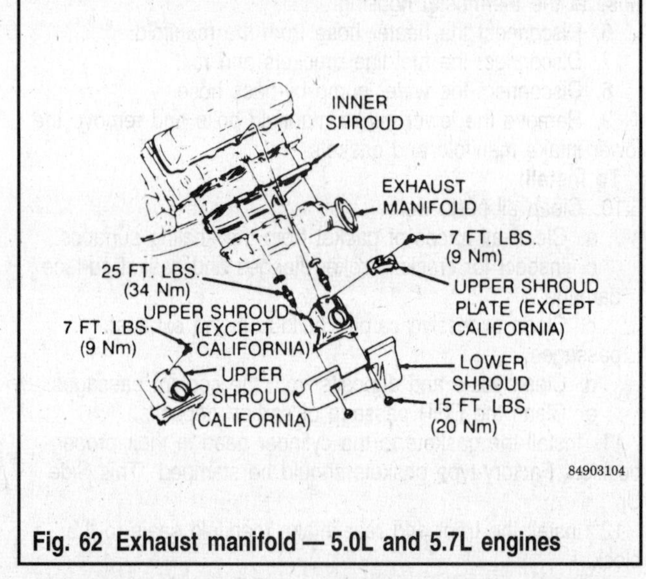

Fig. 62 Exhaust manifold — 5.0L and 5.7L engines

8. Disconnect the rear power steering pump bracket at the left manifold.
9. Remove the dipstick tube bracket on the right manifold.
10. Remove the manifold bolts and remove the manifold(s). Some models have locktabs on the front and rear manifold bolts which must be removed before removing the bolts. These tabs can be bent with a drift pin or needlenose pliers.

To install:

11. Clean both the manifold and cylinder block mating surfaces and install the manifold. Install the flat washers and then the tab washers and insert the bolts. Tighten the two center bolts to 26 ft. lbs. (36 Nm); the outside bolts to 20 ft. lbs. (28 Nm) and then bend the tab washers against the bolt heads.
12. Install the dipstick tube bracket on the right manifold.
13. Connect the rear power steering pump bracket at the left manifold.
14. Install the heat stove pipe on the right side manifold.
15. Install the AIR hose at the check valve.
16. Connect the O2 sensor wire on the left side manifold.
17. Raise the truck and support it with jackstands.

18. Connect the exhaust pipe at the manifold. Install the hot air shroud.
19. Lower the truck.
20. Install the air cleaner. Connect the negative battery cable.

7.4L Engines

RIGHT SIDE

1. Disconnect the negative battery cable.
2. Remove the heat stove pipe.
3. Remove the dipstick tube.
4. Disconnect the AIR hose at the check valve.
5. Remove the spark plugs.
6. Disconnect the exhaust pipe at the manifold.
7. Remove the manifold bolts and spark plug heat shields.
8. Remove the manifold.

To install:

9. Clean the mating surfaces.
10. Clean the stud threads.

87983p27

Fig. 63 Remove the exhaust pipe from the manifold

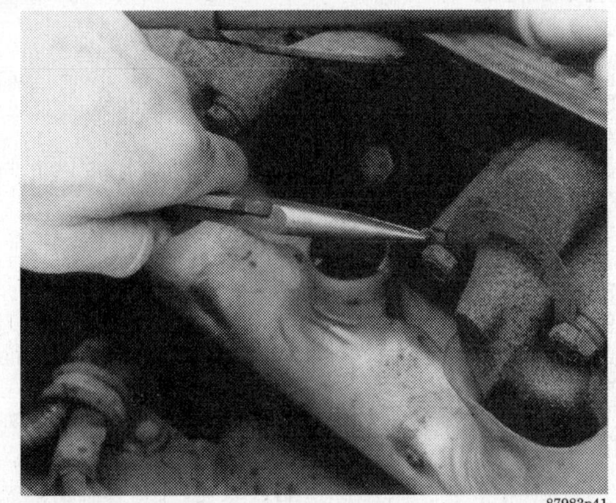

87983p41

Fig. 64 Use a pair of needlenose pliers to bend back the locktabs on the exhaust manifold

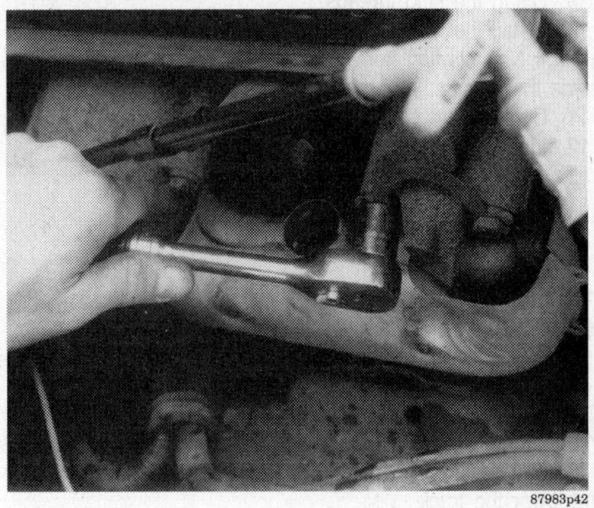

87983p42

Fig. 65 Loosen and remove the exhaust manifold bolts

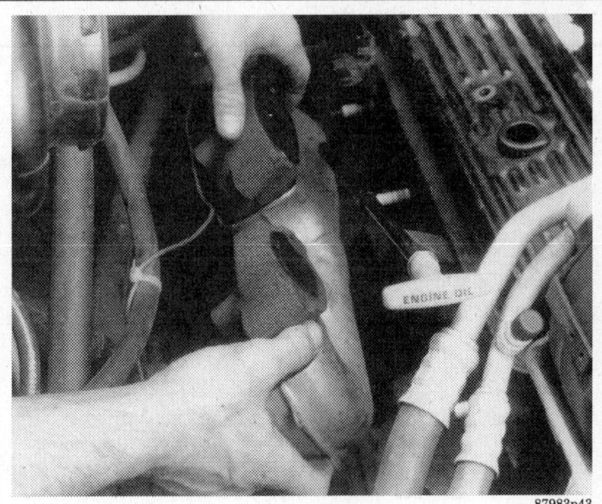

87983p43

Fig. 66 Remove the exhaust manifold

11. Install the manifold and bolts. Tighten the bolts to 40 ft. lbs. (54 Nm) starting from the center bolts and working towards the outside.
12. Connect the exhaust pipe at the manifold.
13. Install the spark plugs.
14. Connect the AIR hose at the check valve.
15. Install the dipstick tube.
16. Install the heat stove pipe.
17. Connect the battery.

LEFT SIDE

1. Disconnect the negative battery cable.
2. Disconnect the oxygen sensor wire.
3. Disconnect the AIR hose at the check valve.
4. Remove the spark plugs.
5. Disconnect the exhaust pipe at the manifold.
6. Remove the manifold bolts and spark plug heat shields.
7. Remove the manifold.

To install:

8. Clean the mating surfaces.

9. Clean the stud threads.
10. Install the manifold and bolts. Tighten the bolts to 40 ft. lbs. (54 Nm) starting from the center bolts and working towards the outside.
11. Connect the exhaust pipe at the manifold.
12. Install the spark plugs.
13. Connect the AIR hose at the check valve.
14. Connect the oxygen sensor wire.
15. Connect the battery.

6.2L and 6.5L Diesel Engines

RIGHT SIDE

See Figures 67 and 68

1. Disconnect the batteries.
2. Jack up the vehicle and safely support it with jackstands.
3. Disconnect the exhaust pipe from the manifold flange and lower the truck.
4. Disconnect the glow plug wires.
5. Remove the air cleaner duct bracket.

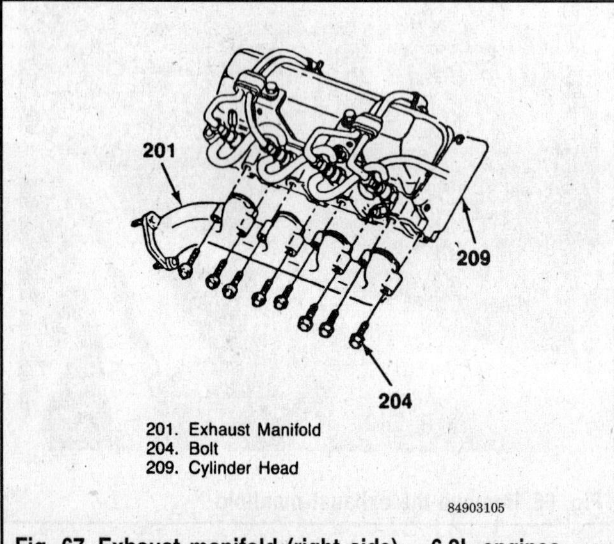

Fig. 67 Exhaust manifold (right side) — 6.2L engines

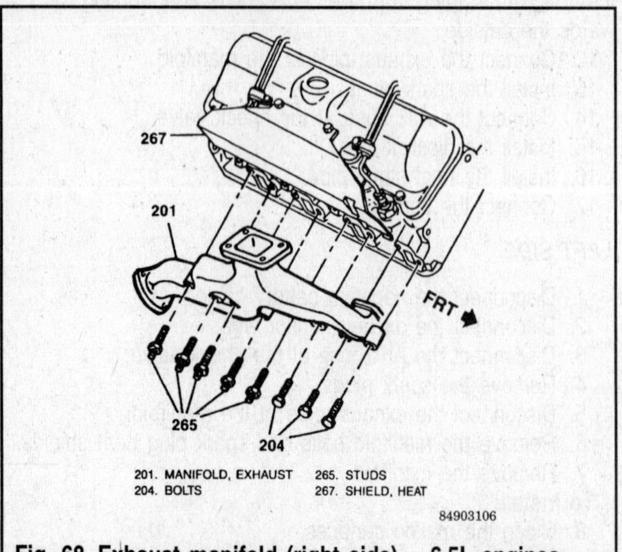

Fig. 68 Exhaust manifold (right side) — 6.5L engines

6. Remove the glow plug wires.
7. Remove the turbocharger on the 6.5L, if equipped.
8. Remove the manifold bolts and remove the manifold.

To install:

9. Clean all mating surfaces and install the manifold. Tighten the bolts to 26 ft. lbs. (35 Nm).
10. Install the turbocharger on the 6.5L, if equipped.
11. Install the glow plugs.
12. Install the air cleaner duct bracket.
13. Connect the glow plug wires.
14. Raise the vehicle and support it with jackstands.
15. Connect the exhaust pipe to the manifold flange and lower the truck.
16. Connect the batteries.

LEFT SIDE

See Figure 69

1. Disconnect the batteries, negative cable first.
2. Remove the dipstick tube nut, and remove the dipstick tube.
3. Disconnect the glow plug wires.
4. Raise the vehicle and safely support it with jackstands.
5. Disconnect the exhaust pipe at the manifold flange.
6. Remove the manifold bolts. Remove the manifold from underneath the truck.

To install:

7. Install the manifold and tighten the bolts to 25 ft. lbs. (35 Nm).
8. Connect the exhaust pipe to the manifold flange.
9. Lower the vehicle and connect the glow plug wires.
10. Install the dipstick tube and tighten the nut.
11. Connect the batteries, positive cable first.

Combination Manifold

REMOVAL & INSTALLATION

4.8L Engines

See Figure 70

1. Disconnect the negative battery cable.
2. Remove the air cleaner.
3. Disconnect the throttle controls at the bellcrank.
4. Remove the carburetor.
5. Disconnect and label the fuel and vacuum lines from the manifold.
6. Remove the AIR pump and bracket.
7. Disconnect the PCV hose.
8. Disconnect the exhaust pipe.
9. Remove the manifold heat stove.
10. Remove the clamps, bolts and washers and remove the combination manifold.
11. Separate the manifolds by removing the bolts and nuts.

To install:

12. Clean the mating surfaces.
13. Clean the stud threads.
14. Assemble the manifolds with a new gasket and leave the nuts finger-tight.
15. Install a new gasket over the manifold studs on the cylinder head and install the manifold assembly.

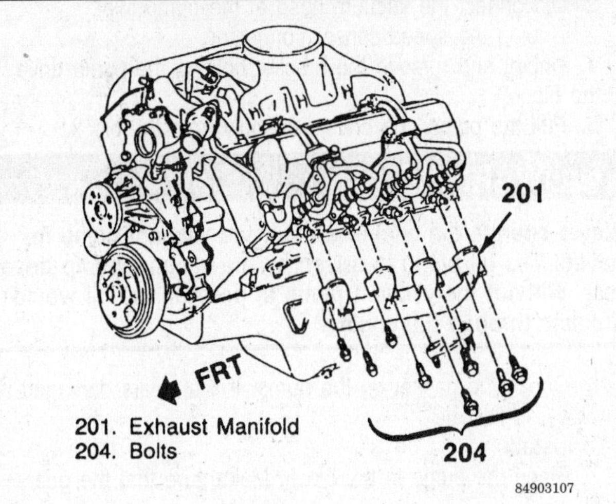

Fig. 69 Exhaust manifold (left side) — 6.2L and 6.5L engines

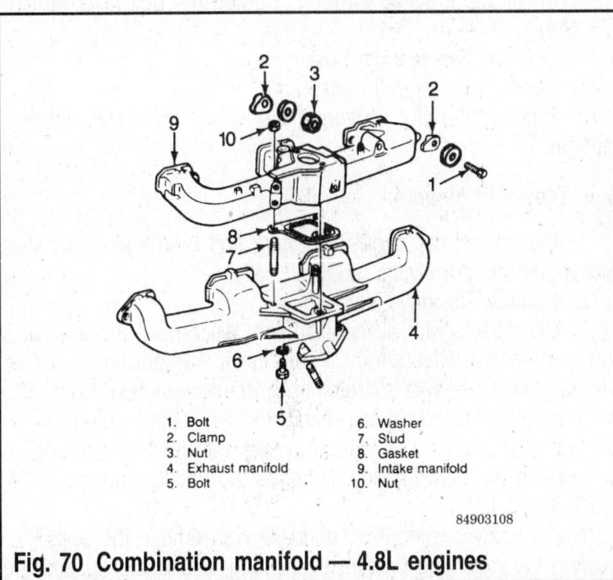

Fig. 70 Combination manifold — 4.8L engines

16. Install the bolts, clamps and nuts.

➡**Always tighten the manifold-to-cylinder head bolts and nuts to 38 ft. lbs. (52 Nm) before tightening the manifold center bolts and nuts to 44 ft. lbs. (60 Nm).**

17. Install the manifold heat stove.
18. Connect the exhaust pipe.
19. Connect the PCV hose.
20. Install the AIR pump and bracket.
21. Connect the fuel and vacuum lines from the manifold.
22. Install the carburetor.
23. Connect the throttle controls at the bellcrank.
24. Install the air cleaner.
25. Connect the negative battery cable.

Turbocharger

REMOVAL & INSTALLATION

➡**This applies to 6.5L diesel engines only.**

See Figure 71

1. Disconnect the negative battery cables.
2. Remove the upper intake manifold cover.
3. Loosen the two clamps and then remove the air intake duct from between the air cleaner and the turbocharger.
4. Disconnect the oil feed line at the top of the turbocharger.
5. Remove the self-tapping screw that holds the CDR valve vent tube bracket to the top of the turbocharger and then remove the valve and tube.
6. Remove the three bolts and then lift off the heat shield.
7. Tag and remove the vacuum hose to the waste gate actuator.
8. Remove the turbocharger braces.
9. Remove the hose clamps at the intake extension/turbocharger compressor connected hose.
10. Remove the fasteners securing the air cleaner housing where it attaches to the wheel arch and slide it off the duct.
11. Remove the right front tire.
12. Pry out the five plastic retainers and pull out the wheelwell splash shield.
13. Loosen the clamp that holds the exhaust pipe to the turbocharger.
14. Disconnect the oil drain tube at the turbocharger, loosen the four mounting bolts and lift the turbocharger out through the wheel opening.

To install:

15. Clean all mating surfaces and coat any turbocharger fasteners with anti-sieze compound.
16. Position the unit on the exhaust manifold and tighten the bolts to 37 ft. lbs. (50 Nm), on 1988-95 models. On 1996 models tighten the bolts to 43 ft. lbs. (58 Nm).
17. Connect the oil drain tube to the bottom of the turbocharger with a new flange gasket and tighten the bolts to 19 ft. lbs. (26 Nm).
18. Install the hose clamps at the intake extension/turbocharger compressor connected hose.
19. Install the turbocharger braces. Tighten the long brace nut to 26 ft. lbs. (34 Nm) and the long brace bolt to 37 ft. lbs. (50 Nm). Tighten the short brace bolts to 19 ft. lbs. (25 Nm).
20. Install the vacuum hose to the waste gate actuator.
21. Drip 1-2cc of engine oil into the oil feed hole on top of the unit and then rotate the compressor wheel by hand. This will pre-lube the bearings. Connect the oil feed line and tighten the bolts to 13 ft. lbs. (17 Nm).
22. Tighten the exhaust elbow clamp to 71 inch lbs. (8 Nm).
23. Unplug the injection pump fuel shut-down solenoid connector at the pump or at the harness and then crank the engine for about 15 seconds. This will prime the oil system. DO NOT START THE ENGINE!
24. Install the wheel splash shield and the tire.
25. Install the heat shield and tighten the bolts to 56 inch lbs. (6 Nm). Be sure to use Loctite® or its equivalent.

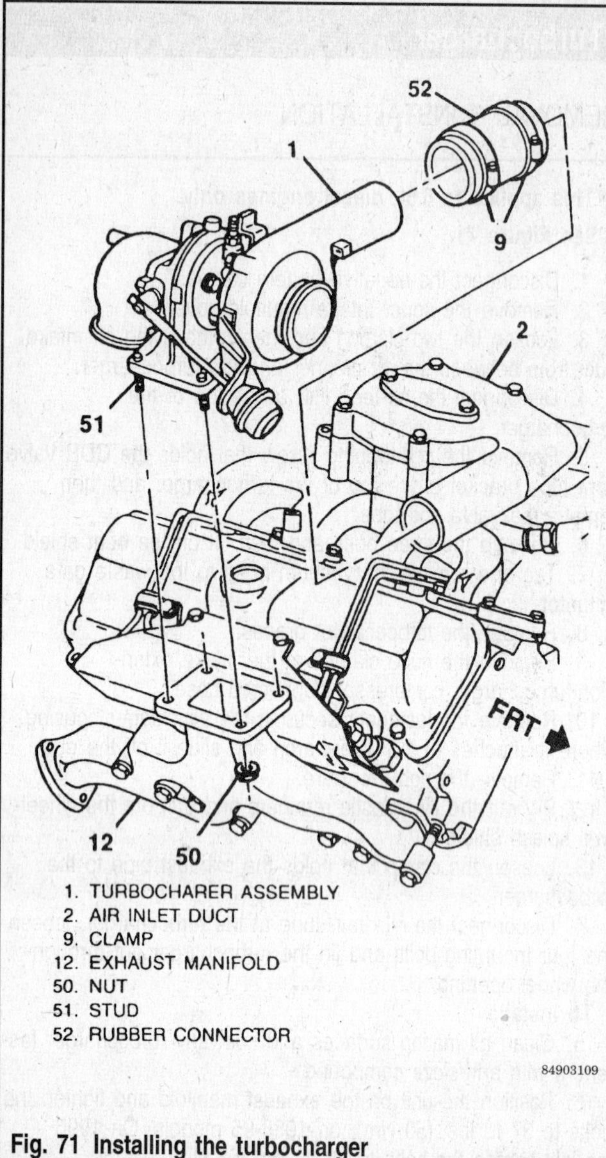

Fig. 71 Installing the turbocharger

26. Install the air cleaner and intake ducts. Tighten the clamps to 15 inch lbs. (2 Nm).
27. Install the intake manifold cover bolts and tighten to 90 inch lbs. (11Nm).
28. Install the CDR valve and tube, making sure to tighten the self-tapping screw securely.
29. Connect the negative battery cables.

Vacuum Pump

REMOVAL & INSTALLATION

6.2L Diesel Engines

1. Remove the air cleaner. Cover the intake with a cloth.
2. Disconnect the vacuum hose at the pump inlet.
3. Unplug the speed sensor connector.
4. Unbolt and remove the bracket holding the pump drive to the block.
5. Pull the pump and drive assembly from the block.

WARNING

Never operate the engine without the vacuum pump installed! The oil pump is driven by the vacuum pump drive gear. Without the vacuum pump in position, no oil would circulate through the engine.

6. Check the gasket on the pump. If it appears damaged in any way, replace it.

To install:

7. Place the pump in the block. Make sure that the gears mesh.
8. Rotate the pump so that the inlet tube faces front. The pump should be on a 20° angle.
9. Install the bracket and bolt. Tighten the bolt to 20 ft. lbs. (27 Nm).
10. Connect the vacuum hose.
11. Connect the speed sensor.
12. Remove the cloth covering the intake and install the air cleaner.

6.5L Diesel Engines

1. Disconnect the negative battery and then make sure that the engine control switch is OFF.
2. Remove the drive belt.
3. On models with air conditioning, disconnect the lead at the compressor. Remove the compressor and position it out of the way with the lines still attached. Pull the vacuum hose off the pipe. Remove the through-bolt and two nuts holding the bracket to the engine — you can reach the lower nut through the hole in the pump pulley. Remove the vacuum pump, bracket and belt
4. On models without air conditioning, remove the bolts holding the mounting bracket to the engine and the nut holding it to the stud, then remove the pump.

To install:

5. On models without air conditioning, tighten the pump-to-bracket bolts to 20 ft. lbs. (27 Nm) and the bracket-to-engine bolts/nuts to 30 ft. lbs. (40 Nm).
6. On models with air conditioning, tighten the bolts to 30 ft. lbs. (40 Nm) and the nuts to 22 ft. lbs. (30 Nm).
7. Tighten the air conditioner compressor bolt to 30 ft. lbs. (40 Nm).
8. Install the drive belt.
9. Connect the negative battery cable.

Radiator

REMOVAL & INSTALLATION

CAUTION

When draining the coolant, keep in mind that cats and dogs are attracted by ethylene glycol antifreeze, and are quite likely to drink any that is left in an uncovered container or in puddles on the ground. This will prove fatal in sufficient quantity. Always drain the coolant into a sealable container. Coolant should be reused unless it is contaminated or several years old.

Gasoline Engines

See Figures 72, 73, 74 and 75

1. Drain the cooling system.
2. Disconnect the radiator upper and lower hoses and, if applicable, the transmission coolant lines. Remove the coolant recovery system line, if so equipped.
3. Remove the oil coolant lines, if equipped.
4. Remove the radiator upper panel if so equipped.
5. If there is a radiator shroud in front of the radiator, the radiator and shroud are removed as an assembly.
6. If there is a fan shroud, remove the shroud attaching screws and let the shroud hang on the fan.
7. Remove the radiator attaching bolts and remove the radiator.

To install:

8. Install the radiator. Install the upper panel, if removed.
9. Install and tighten the shroud bolts to 71 inch lbs. (9 Nm).
10. Tighten the engine oil cooler pipe bolts to 18 ft. lbs. (24 Nm) and the transmission oil cooler bolts to 19 ft. lbs. (26 Nm).

Diesel Engines

1. Drain the cooling system.

87983p45

Fig. 73 Remove the radiator upper panel

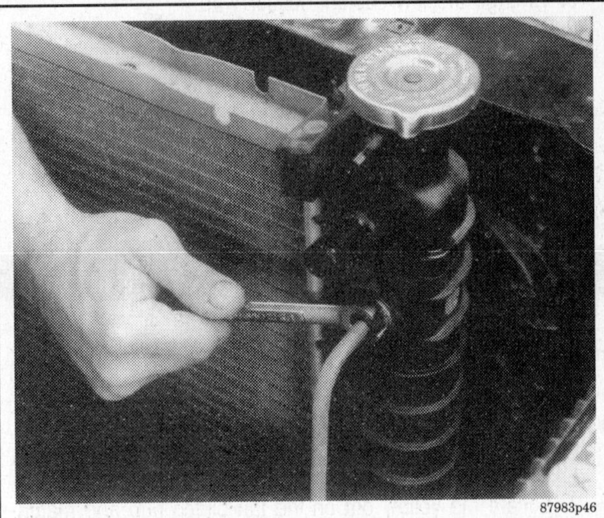

87983p46

Fig. 74 Disconnect the transmission cooler lines

87983p44

Fig. 72 Remove the radiator upper panel fasteners

87983p23

Fig. 75 After the fasteners are removed, lift the radiator from the vehicle

2. Remove the air intake snorkel.
3. Remove the windshield washer bottle.
4. Remove the hood release cable.
5. Remove the upper fan shroud.
6. Disconnect the upper radiator hose.
7. Disconnect the transmission cooler lines.
8. Unplug the low coolant sensor wire.
9. Disconnect the overflow hose.
10. Disconnect the engine oil cooler lines.
11. Disconnect the lower radiator hose.
12. Remove the brake master cylinder. See Section 9.
13. Remove the fasteners securing the radiator, then remove the radiator from the vehicle.

To install:

14. Position the radiator at its mounting points and install its retainers. Tighten to 71 inch. lbs. (9 Nm).
15. Install the brake master cylinder.
16. Connect the lower radiator hose.
17. Connect the engine oil cooler lines.
18. Connect the overflow hose.
19. Engage the low coolant sensor wire.
20. Connect the transmission cooler lines.
21. Connect the upper radiator hose.
22. Install the upper fan shroud.
23. Install the hood release cable.
24. Install the windshield washer bottle.
25. Install the air intake snorkel.
26. Fill the cooling system.

Engine Fan

REMOVAL & INSTALLATION

➧ See Figures 76, 77 and 78

1. Disconnect the negative battery cable.
2. Locate the yellow dot on the fan clutch hub and matchmark the water pump pulley.
3. Remove the radiator shroud.
4. Remove the drive belt, if necessary.
5. Remove the four fan clutch-to-water pump pulley nuts and lift out the fan/clutch assembly.
6. Remove the fan clutch bolts and separate the fan from the clutch.

To install:

7. Install the the fan on the fan clutch and tighten the bolts to 17 ft. lbs. (23 Nm).
8. Position the fan/clutch assembly on the water pump pulley so that the reference marks on each hub align. Tighten the nuts to 18 ft. lbs. (24 Nm).
9. Install the fan shroud.
10. Connect the battery cable.

Auxiliary Cooling Fan

REMOVAL & INSTALLATION

1. Remove the grille.
2. Unplug the fan harness connector.
3. Remove the fan-to-brace bolts and lift out the fan.
4. Installation is the reverse of removal. Tighten the bolts to 53 ft. lbs. (72 Nm).

TESTING

➧ See Figures 79 and 80

For testing the auxiliary cooling fan, refer to the cooling fan circuit illustration and the diagnosis chart.

Water Pump

REMOVAL & INSTALLATION

✳✳CAUTION

When draining the coolant, keep in mind that cats and dogs are attracted by ethylene glycol antifreeze, and are quite likely to drink any that is left in an uncovered container or in puddles on the ground. This will prove fatal in sufficient quantity. Always drain the coolant into a sealable container. Coolant should be reused unless it is contaminated or several years old.

4.8L Engines

➧ See Figure 81

1. Disconnect the negative battery cable.
2. Drain the radiator.
3. Loosen the alternator and other accessories at their adjusting points, and remove the fan belts from the fan pulley.
4. Remove the fan, fan clutch and pulley.
5. Remove any accessory brackets that might interfere with water pump removal.
6. Disconnect the hose from the water pump inlet and the heater hose from the nipple on the pump. Remove the bolts, pump assembly and old gasket from the timing chain cover.

To install:

7. Make sure the gasket surfaces on the pump and engine block are clean.
8. Install the pump assembly with a new gasket. Tighten the bolts to 15 ft. lbs. (20 Nm).
9. Connect the hose between the water pump inlet and the nipple on the pump.
10. Install any accessory brackets.
11. Install the fan and pulley.
12. Install and adjust the alternator and other accessories.
13. Install the fan belts from the fan pulley.
14. Fill the cooling system.
15. Connect the battery.

4.3L, 5.0L, 5.7L and 7.4L Engines

➧ See Figures 82, 83, 84, 85, 86, 87 and 88

1. Disconnect the negative battery cable.
2. Drain the radiator. Remove the upper fan shroud.
3. Remove the drive belt(s).

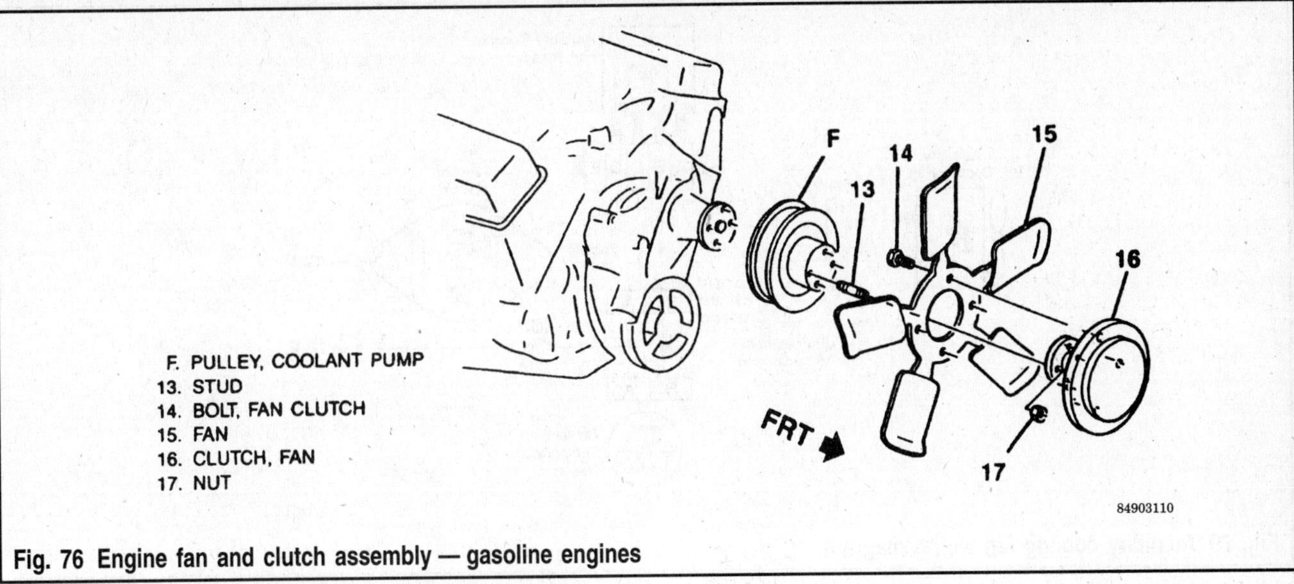

Fig. 76 Engine fan and clutch assembly — gasoline engines

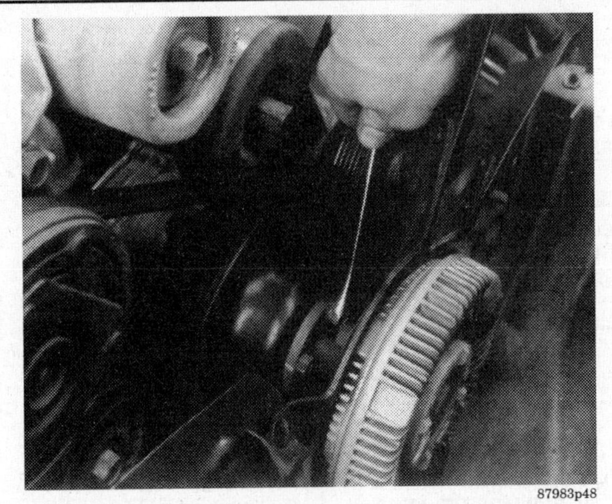

Fig. 77 Remove the four fan clutch-to-water pump pulley nuts and lift out the fan/clutch assembly

4. Remove the alternator and other accessories, if necessary.
5. Remove the fan, fan clutch and pulley.
6. Remove any accessory brackets that might interfere with water pump removal.
7. Disconnect the lower radiator hose from the water pump inlet and the heater hose from the nipple on the pump. On the 7.4L engine, remove the bypass hose.
8. Remove the bolts, then pull the water pump assembly away from the timing cover.

To install:

9. Clean all old gasket material from the timing chain cover.
10. Install the pump assembly with a new gasket. Tighten the bolts to 30 ft. lbs. (41 Nm).
11. Connect the hose between the water pump inlet and the nipple on the pump. Connect the heater hose and the bypass hose (7.4L only).
12. Install the fan, fan clutch and pulley.
13. Install and adjust the alternator and other accessories, if necessary.
14. Install the drive belt (s). Install the upper radiator shroud

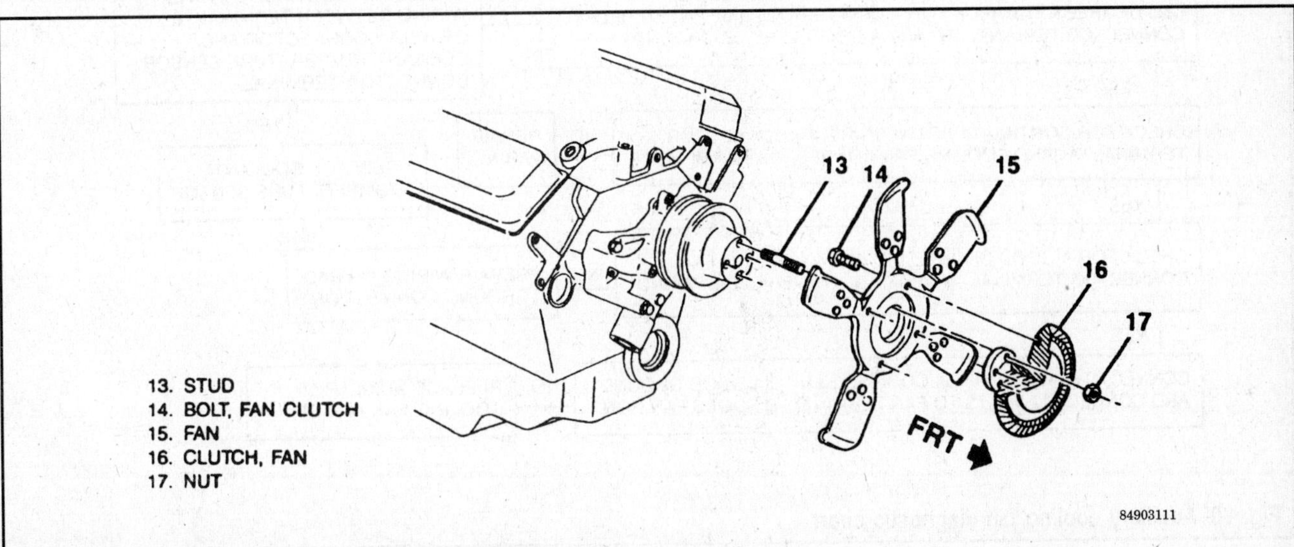

Fig. 78 Engine fan and clutch assembly — diesel engines

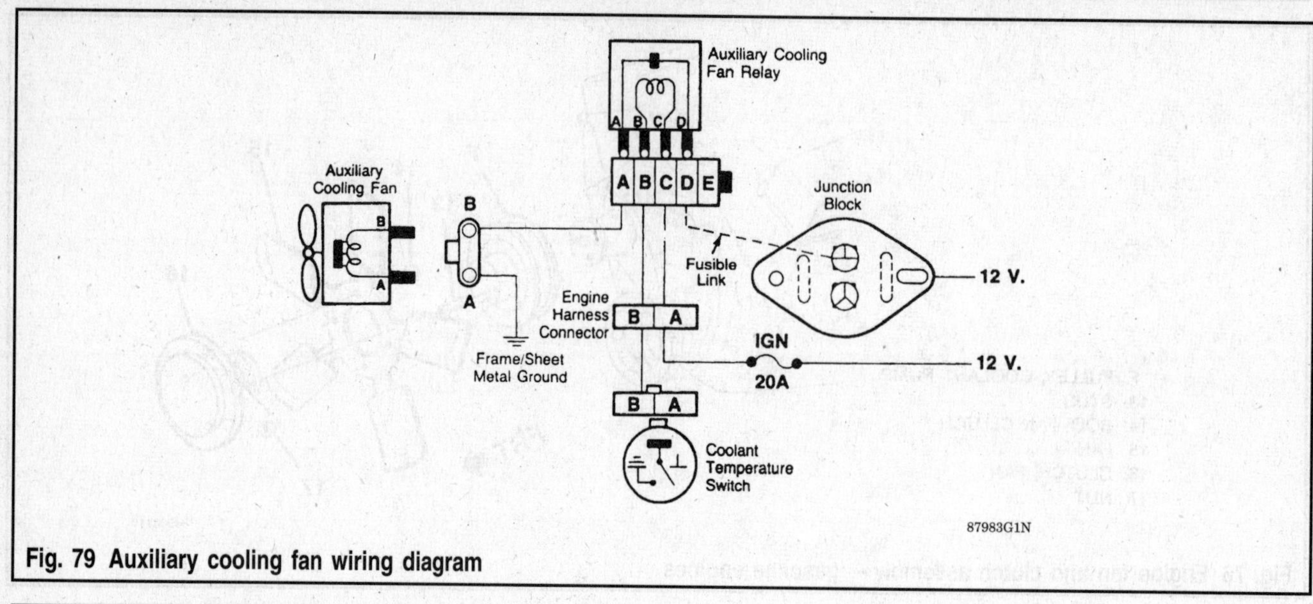

Fig. 79 Auxiliary cooling fan wiring diagram

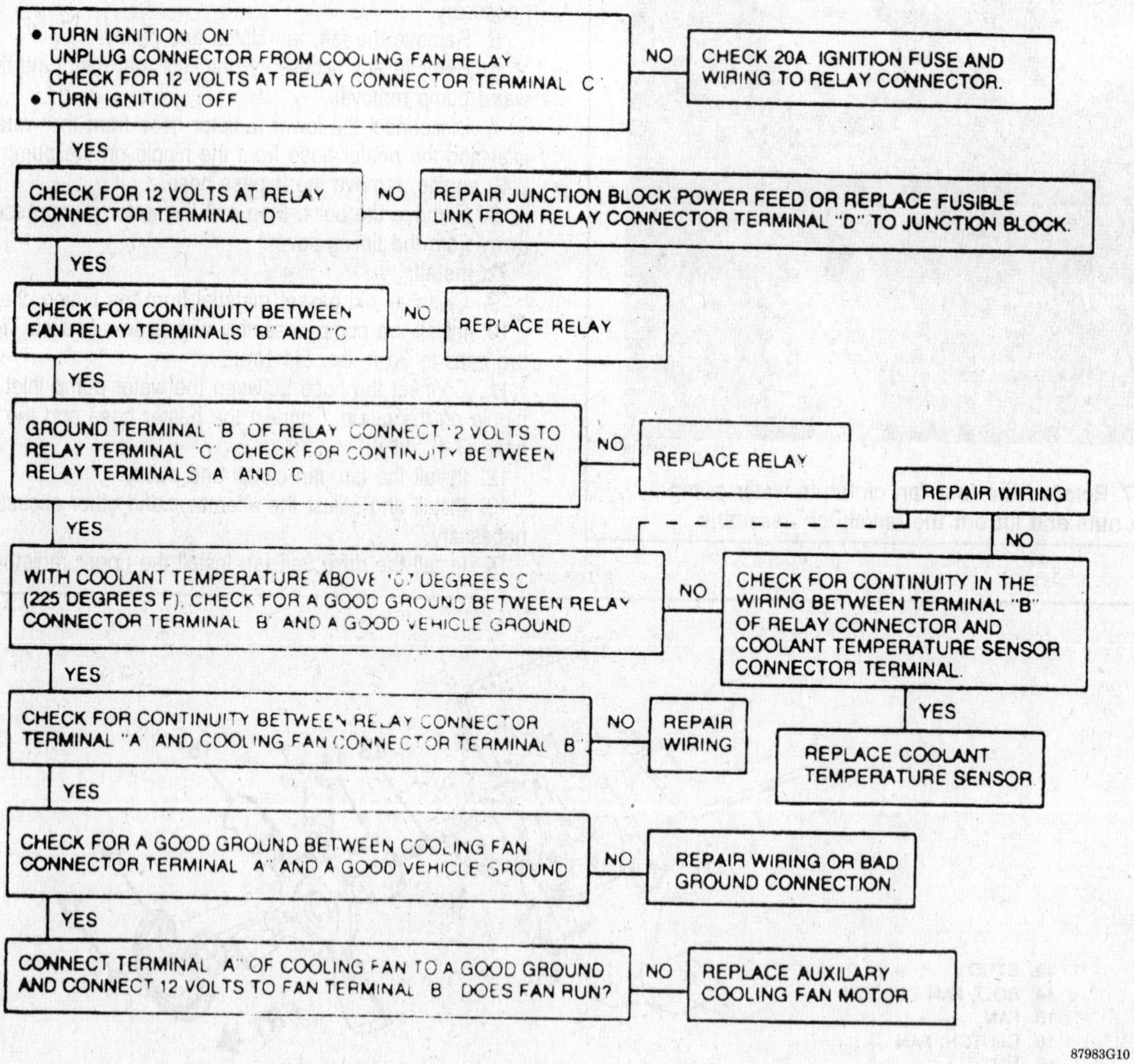

- • TURN IGNITION "ON"
  UNPLUG CONNECTOR FROM COOLING FAN RELAY
  CHECK FOR 12 VOLTS AT RELAY CONNECTOR TERMINAL "C"
  • TURN IGNITION "OFF"
  - NO → CHECK 20A IGNITION FUSE AND WIRING TO RELAY CONNECTOR.
  - YES ↓
- CHECK FOR 12 VOLTS AT RELAY CONNECTOR TERMINAL "D"
  - NO → REPAIR JUNCTION BLOCK POWER FEED OR REPLACE FUSIBLE LINK FROM RELAY CONNECTOR TERMINAL "D" TO JUNCTION BLOCK.
  - YES ↓
- CHECK FOR CONTINUITY BETWEEN FAN RELAY TERMINALS "B" AND "C"
  - NO → REPLACE RELAY
  - YES ↓
- GROUND TERMINAL "B" OF RELAY. CONNECT 12 VOLTS TO RELAY TERMINAL "C". CHECK FOR CONTINUITY BETWEEN RELAY TERMINALS "A" AND "D"
  - NO → REPLACE RELAY
  - YES ↓
- WITH COOLANT TEMPERATURE ABOVE 107 DEGREES C (225 DEGREES F). CHECK FOR A GOOD GROUND BETWEEN RELAY CONNECTOR TERMINAL "B" AND A GOOD VEHICLE GROUND
  - NO → CHECK FOR CONTINUITY IN THE WIRING BETWEEN TERMINAL "B" OF RELAY CONNECTOR AND COOLANT TEMPERATURE SENSOR CONNECTOR TERMINAL.
    - NO → REPAIR WIRING
    - YES → REPLACE COOLANT TEMPERATURE SENSOR
  - YES ↓
- CHECK FOR CONTINUITY BETWEEN RELAY CONNECTOR TERMINAL "A" AND COOLING FAN CONNECTOR TERMINAL "B"
  - NO → REPAIR WIRING
  - YES ↓
- CHECK FOR A GOOD GROUND BETWEEN COOLING FAN CONNECTOR TERMINAL "A" AND A GOOD VEHICLE GROUND
  - NO → REPAIR WIRING OR BAD GROUND CONNECTION.
  - YES ↓
- CONNECT TERMINAL "A" OF COOLING FAN TO A GOOD GROUND AND CONNECT 12 VOLTS TO FAN TERMINAL "B". DOES FAN RUN?
  - NO → REPLACE AUXILARY COOLING FAN MOTOR

87983G10

Fig. 80 Auxiliary cooling fan diagnostic chart

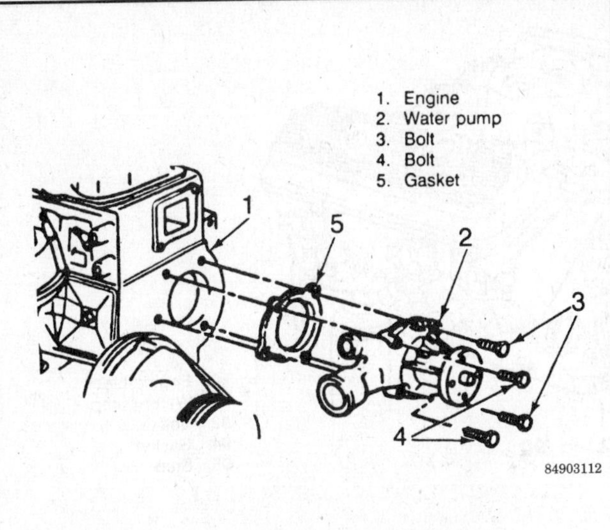

Fig. 81 Water pump installation — 4.8L engines

15. Fill the cooling system. Connect the battery.

6.2L and 6.5L Diesel Engines

➧ See Figure 89

1. Disconnect the batteries, negative cable first.
2. Remove the fan and fan shroud.
3. Drain the radiator.
4. If the vehicle is equipped with air conditioning, remove the air conditioning hose bracket nuts.
5. Remove the oil filler tube.
6. Remove the drive belt(s).
7. Remove the generator pivot bolt and remove the generator lower bracket.
8. Remove the vacuum pump and bracket.
9. Remove the power steering pump bracket.
10. Disconnect the bypass hose and the lower radiator hose.
11. Remove the water pump bolts.
12. Remove the water pump plate and gasket and water pump.

Fig. 82 Disconnect the lower radiator hose from the water pump inlet

Fig. 84 Remove the water pump from the vehicle

Fig. 83 Remove the water pump attaching bolts

Fig. 85 Using a scraper, clean the old gasket from both mating surfaces of the water pump

90. Engine block
91. Water pump
92. Bolt
94. Gasket
95. Stud

84903113

Fig. 86 Water pump installation — 4.3L engines

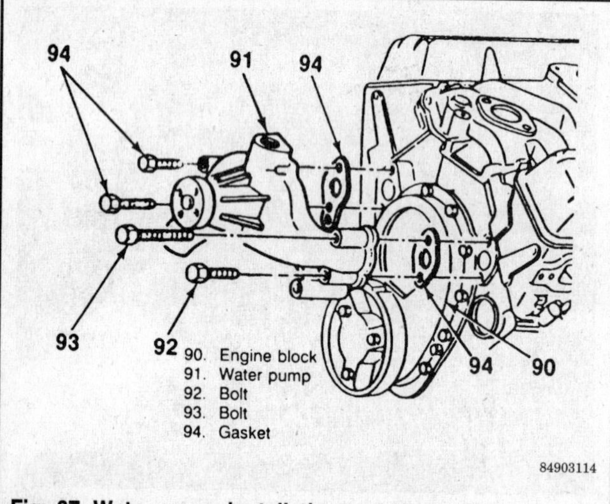

Fig. 87 Water pump installation — 5.0L and 5.7L engines

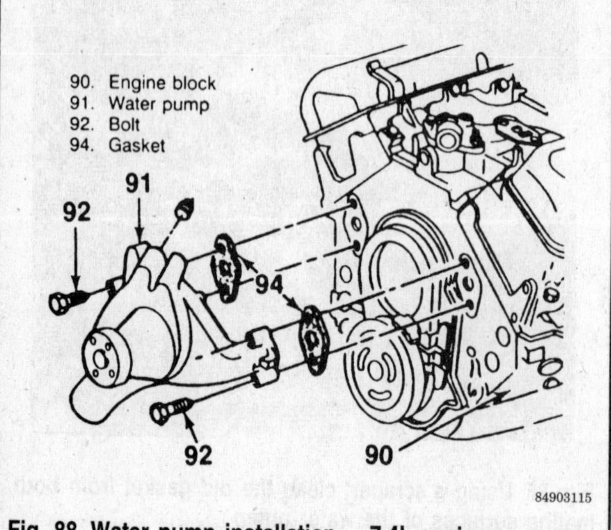

Fig. 88 Water pump installation — 7.4L engines

13. If the pump gasket is to be replaced, remove the plate attaching bolts to the water pump and remove (and replace) the gasket.

To install:

14. When installing the pump, the flanges must be free of oil. Apply an anaerobic sealer (GM part #1052357 or equivalent) as shown in the accompanying illustration.

➡**The sealer must be wet to the touch when the bolts are tightened.**

15. Attach the water pump and plate assembly. Tighten the bolts to 17 ft. lbs. (23 Nm), except the three lower right side bolts. Tighten these three to 31 ft. lbs. (42 Nm).
16. Connect the bypass hose and the lower radiator hose.
17. Install the power steering pump mounting bracket.
18. Install the generator lower bracket.
19. Install the generator pivot bolt.
20. Install the drive belt (s).
21. Install the oil filler tube.
22. If the vehicle is equipped with air conditioning, install the air conditioning hose bracket nuts.
23. Fill the radiator.
24. Install the fan and fan shroud.
25. Connect the batteries.

Cylinder Head

REMOVAL & INSTALLATION

✲✲CAUTION

When draining the coolant, keep in mind that cats and dogs are attracted by ethylene glycol antifreeze, and are quite likely to drink any that is left in an uncovered container or in puddles on the ground. This will prove fatal in sufficient quantity. Always drain the coolant into a sealable container. Coolant should be reused unless it is contaminated or several years old.

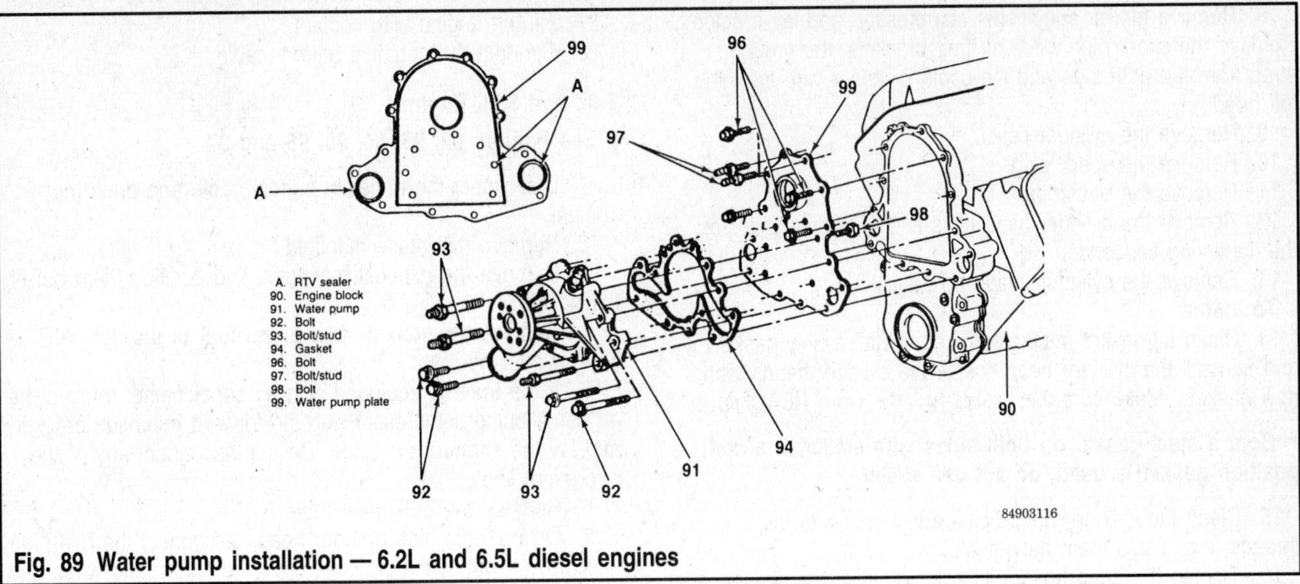

Fig. 89 Water pump installation — 6.2L and 6.5L diesel engines

4.8L Engines

➧ See Figure 90

1. Disconnect the negative battery cable and unbolt it at the engine.
2. Drain the cooling system.
3. Remove the air cleaner assembly.
4. Disconnect the fuel line at the carburetor.
5. Disconnect the accelerator and transmission linkages.
6. Mark and disconnect all required electrical and vacuum lines.
7. Remove the combination manifold assembly retaining bolts.
8. Remove the combination manifold from the engine.
9. Remove the cylinder head cover.
10. Remove the rocker arms and pushrods. Keep them in order for re-installation.
11. If equipped, disconnect the AIR injection hose at the check valve.
12. Disconnect the upper radiator hose at the thermostat housing.
13. Remove the cylinder head retaining bolts.
14. With the aid of an assistant, lift the cylinder head from the engine.

To install:

15. Thoroughly clean both the head and block surfaces.
16. Install a new head gasket on the block. If an all steel gasket is used, coat both sides with sealer. If a composition gasket is used, do not use sealer. Position the gasket on the block with the bead up.
17. With the aid of an assistant, lower the cylinder head onto the engine.
18. Coat the threads of the head bolts with sealer and install them. Tighten the bolts, in 3 equal steps, in the sequence shown, to 95 ft. lbs. (129 Nm) for all but the left front (No. 12) bolt. Tighten that one to 85 ft. lbs. (115 Nm).
19. Connect the upper radiator hose at the thermostat housing.
20. Connect the AIR injection hose at the check valve.
21. Install the rocker arms and pushrods. Adjust the valves.
22. Install the cylinder head cover.

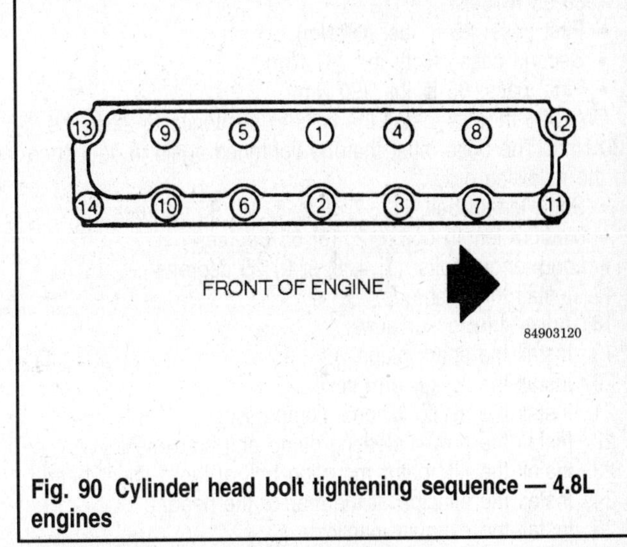

Fig. 90 Cylinder head bolt tightening sequence — 4.8L engines

23. Install the combination manifold.
24. Connect all electrical and vacuum lines.
25. Connect the accelerator and transmission linkages.
26. Connect the fuel line at the carburetor.
27. Install air cleaner assembly.
28. Fill the cooling system.
29. Install the negative battery cable.

4.3L Engines

➧ See Figure 91

1. Disconnect the negative battery cable.
2. Drain the coolant.
3. Remove the intake manifold.
4. Remove the exhaust manifold.
5. Remove the air pipe at the rear of the right cylinder head.
6. Remove the alternator mounting bolt at the right cylinder head.
7. Remove the power steering pump and brackets from the left cylinder head, and lay them aside.

8. Remove the air conditioner compressor, and lay it aside. Remove the spark plug wires at their brackets, the ground strap from the right side and the coolant sensor wire from the left head.
9. Remove the cylinder cover.
10. Remove the spark plugs.
11. Remove the pushrods.
12. Remove the cylinder head bolts in the reverse order of the tightening sequence.
13. Remove the cylinder head and gasket.

To install:

14. Clean all gasket mating surfaces, install a new gasket and reinstall the cylinder head. Install the cylinder heads using new gaskets. Make sure the gasket has the word **HEAD** up.

➡Coat a steel gasket on both sides with sealer. If a composition gasket is used, do not use sealer.

15. Clean the cylinder head bolts, apply sealer to the threads, and install them hand-tight.
16. Tighten the head bolts a little at a time in the sequence shown. Tighten the bolts in three stages:

1988-95 models:

- First pass: 25 ft. lbs. (34 Nm)
- Second pass: 45 ft. lbs. (61 Nm)
- Final pass: 65 ft. lbs. (90 Nm)

On 1996 models install the bolts in sequence to 22 ft. lbs. (30 Nm). The bolts must then be tightened again in sequence in the following order:

- Short length bolt: (11, 7, 3, 2, 6, 10) 55 degrees
- Medium length bolt: (12, 13) 65 degrees
- Long length bolts: (1, 4, 8, 5, 9) 75 degrees

17. Install the pushrods.
18. Adjust the rocker arms.
19. Install the spark plugs.
20. Install the rocker arm cover.
21. Install the air conditioner compressor.
22. Install the power steering pump and brackets.
23. Install the alternator mounting bolt at the cylinder head.
24. Install the air pipe at the rear of the head.
25. Install the exhaust manifold.
26. Install the intake manifold.
27. Fill the engine with coolant.
28. Connect the negative battery cable.

5.0L and 5.7L Engines

➧ See Figures 92, 93, 94, 95, 96 and 97

1. Disconnect the negative battery cable and drain the coolant.
2. Remove the intake manifold.
3. Remove the exhaust manifolds and position them out of the way.
4. Remove the ground strap at the rear of the right AIR pipe, If equipped.
5. If the truck is equipped with air conditioning, remove the air conditioning compressor and the forward mounting bracket and lay the compressor aside. Do not disconnect any of the refrigerant lines.
6. Remove the EGR inlet tube.
7. On the right side cylinder head, disconnect the fuel pipe and move it out of the way. Remove the spark plug wires and disconnect the wiring harness bracket.
8. Remove the nut and stud attaching the main accessory bracket to the cylinder head. You may have to loosen the remaining bolts and studs in order to remove the head.
9. Tag and disconnect the coolant sensor wire. Remove the spark plug wire bracket.
10. Remove the cylinder head covers. Remove the spark plugs.
11. Back off the rocker arm nuts and pivot the rocker arms out of the way so that the pushrods can be removed. Identify the pushrods so that they can be installed in their original positions.
12. Remove the cylinder head bolts in the reverse order of the tightening sequence and then remove the heads.

To install:

13. Inspect the cylinder head and block mating surfaces. Clean all old gasket material.
14. Install the cylinder heads using new gaskets. Install the gaskets with the word **HEAD** up.

➡Coat a steel gasket on both sides with sealer. If a composition gasket is used, do not use sealer.

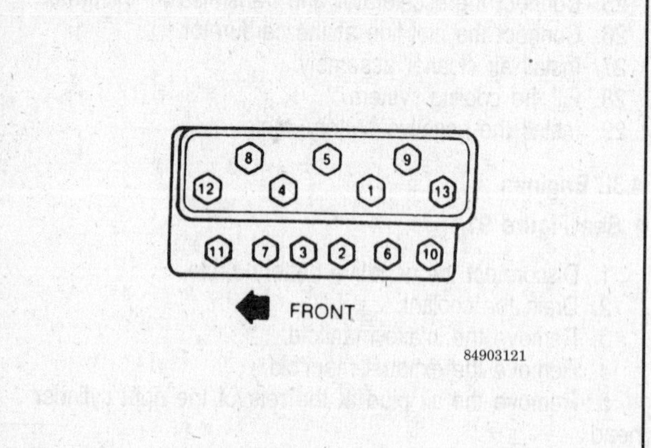

Fig. 91 Cylinder head bolt tightening sequence — 1988-96 4.3L engines

Fig. 92 Using a breaker bar remove the cylinder head bolts in the reverse order of the tightening sequence

Fig. 93 After removing all the cylinder head bolts remove the cylinder head

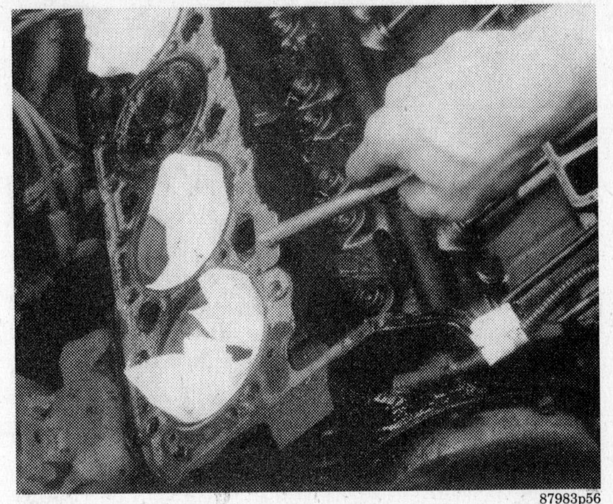

Fig. 95 Using a scraper remove the old gasket residue from both mating surfaces

15. Clean the bolts, apply sealer to the threads, and install them hand-tight.

16. Tighten the cylinder head bolts a little at a time, in the sequence shown. Tighten the bolts in three stages:

1988-95 models.

- First pass: 25 ft. lbs. (34 Nm)
- Second pass: 45 ft. lbs. (61 Nm)
- Final pass: 65 ft. lbs. (90 Nm)

On 1996 models install the bolts in sequence to 22 ft. lbs. (30 Nm). The bolts must then be tightened again in sequence in the following order:

- Short length bolt: (3, 4, 7, 8, 11, 12, 15, 16) 55 degrees
- Medium length bolt: (14, 17) 65 degrees
- Long length bolts: (1, 2, 5, 6, 9, 10, 13) 75 degrees

17. Install the pushrods so that they are in their original positions. Swing the rocker arms into position and tighten the bolts.

18. Install the cylinder head covers. Install the spark plugs.

19. Connect the coolant sensor wire. Install the spark plug wire bracket.

20. Install main accessory bracket to the cylinder head.

21. Install the EGR vent tube.

22. Connect the fuel pipe. Install the spark plug wires and Connect the wiring harness bracket.

23. Install the air conditioning compressor and the forward mounting bracket.

24. Connect the ground strap to the rear of the right AIR pipe.

25. Install the exhaust manifolds.

26. Install the intake manifold.

27. Connect the negative battery cable and fill the engine with coolant.

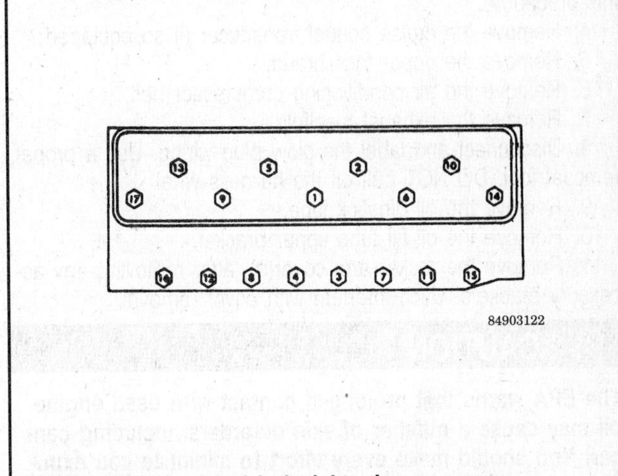

Fig. 96 Cylinder head bolt tightening sequence — 1988-96 5.0L and 5.7L engines

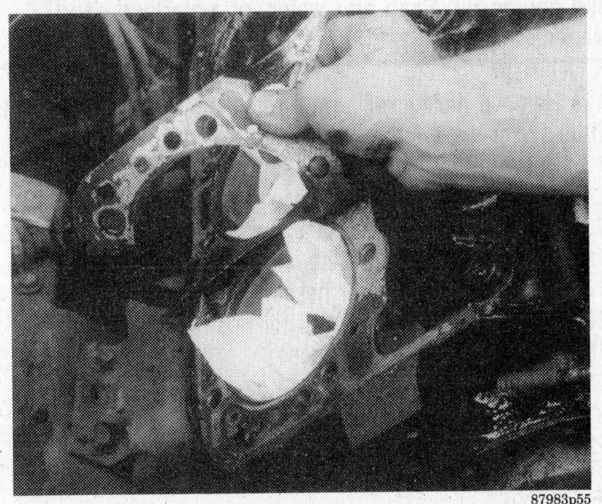

Fig. 94 Remove and discard the old cylinder head gasket

6.2L and 6.5L Diesel Engines

➧ See Figure 98

RIGHT SIDE

1. Disconnect the negative battery cable. Drain the cooling system.

2. Remove the intake manifold.

Fig. 97 Using a torque wrench, tighten the cylinder head bolts in sequence

3. Remove the fuel injection lines. Refer to Section 5 for this procedure.
4. Remove the cruise control transducer (if so equipped).
5. Remove the upper fan shroud.
6. Remove the air conditioning compressor belt.
7. Remove the exhaust manifold.
8. Disconnect and label the glow plug wiring. Use a proper removal tool. DO NOT pull on the harness wire!
9. Remove the oil dipstick tube.
10. Remove the oil fill tube upper bracket.
11. Remove the rocker arm cover(s), after removing any accessory brackets which interfere with cover removal.

CAUTION

The EPA warns that prolonged contact with used engine oil may cause a number of skin disorders, including cancer! You should make every effort to minimize you exposure to used engine oil. Protective gloves should be worn when changing the oil. Wash your hands and any other exposed skin areas as soon as possible after exposure to used engine oil. Soap and water, or waterless hand cleaner should be used.

12. Remove the rocker arm assemblies. It is a good practice to number or mark the parts to avoid interchanging them.
13. Remove the pushrods. Keep them in order.
14. Remove the air cleaner resonator and bracket.
15. Remove the automatic transmission dipstick and tube.
16. Drain the cooling system.
17. Disconnect the heater hoses at the head.
18. Disconnect the upper radiator hose.
19. Disconnect the bypass hose.
20. Remove the alternator upper bracket.
21. Remove the coolant crossover pipe and thermostat.
22. Remove the head bolts.
23. Remove the cylinder head.

To install:

24. Clean the mating surfaces of the head and block thoroughly.
25. Install a new head gasket on the engine block. Do NOT coat the gaskets with any sealer on either engine. The gaskets have a special coating that eliminates the need for sealer. The use of sealer will interfere with this coating and cause leaks. Install the cylinder head onto the block.
26. Clean the head bolts thoroughly. The left rear head bolt must be installed into the head prior to head installation. Coat the threads and heads of the head bolts with sealing compound (GM part #1052080 or equivalent) before installation. Tighten the head bolts in three stages: 20 ft. lbs. (25 Nm); 50 ft. lbs. (68 Nm) and finally, 1/4 turn more.
27. Install the coolant crossover pipe and thermostat.
28. Install the alternator upper bracket.
29. Connect the bypass hose.
30. Connect the upper radiator hose.
31. Connect the heater hoses at the head.
32. Install the automatic transmission dipstick and tube.
33. Install the air cleaner resonator and bracket.
34. Install the pushrods.
35. Install the rocker arm assemblies.
36. Adjust the valves.
37. Install the rocker arm cover(s).
38. Install the oil fill tube upper bracket.
39. Install the oil dipstick tube.
40. Connect the glow plug wiring.
41. Install the exhaust manifold.
42. Install the air conditioning compressor belt.
43. Install the upper fan shroud.
44. Install the cruise control transducer.
45. Install the fuel injection lines. See Section 5.
46. Install the intake manifold.
47. Fill the cooling system and connect the battery cable.

LEFT SIDE

1. Disconnect the negative battery cable and drain the cooling system.
2. Remove the intake manifold.
3. Remove the fuel injection lines. See Section 5.
4. Remove the cruise control transducer.
5. Remove the upper fan shroud.
6. Remove the air conditioning compressor belt.
7. Remove the exhaust manifold.
8. Remove the power steering pump lower adjusting bolts.

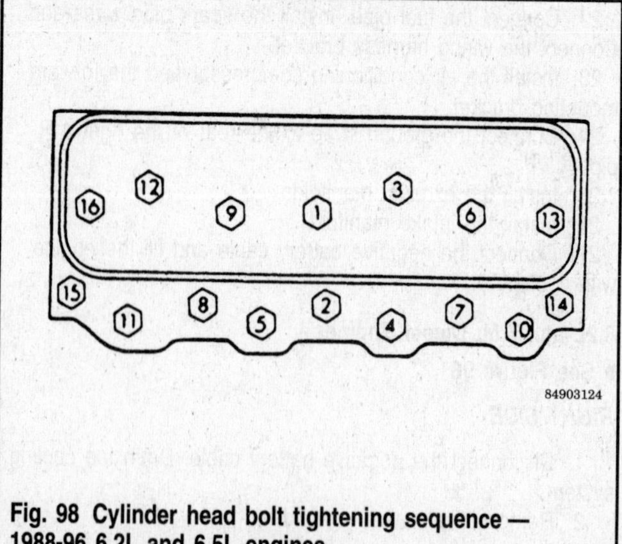

Fig. 98 Cylinder head bolt tightening sequence — 1988-96 6.2L and 6.5L engines

9. Disconnect and label the glow plug wiring.
10. Remove the air conditioning compressor and position it out of the way. DO NOT DISCONNECT ANY REFRIGERANT LINES!
11. Remove the power steering pump and position it out of the way. DO NOT DISCONNECT THE FLUID LINES!
12. Remove the oil dipstick tube.
13. Disconnect the transmission detent cable.
14. Remove the glow plug controller and bracket.
15. Remove the rocker arm cover(s), after removing any accessory brackets which interfere with cover removal.
16. Remove the rocker arm assemblies. It is a good practice to number or mark the parts to avoid interchanging them.
17. Remove the pushrods. Keep them in order.
18. Remove the air cleaner resonator and bracket.
19. Remove the automatic transmission dipstick and tube.
20. Remove the alternator upper bracket.
21. Remove the coolant crossover pipe and thermostat.
22. Remove the head bolts.
23. Remove the cylinder head.

To install:

24. Clean the mating surfaces of the head and block thoroughly.
25. Install a new head gasket on the engine block. Do NOT coat the gaskets with any sealer on either engine. The gaskets have a special coating that eliminates the need for sealer. The use of sealer will interfere with this coating and cause leaks. Install the cylinder head onto the block.
26. Clean the head bolts thoroughly. The left rear head bolt must be installed into the head prior to head installation. Coat the threads and heads of the head bolts with sealing compound (GM part #1052080 or equivalent) before installation. Tighten the head bolts in three stages: 20 ft. lbs. (25 Nm); 50 ft. lbs. (68 Nm) and finally, 1/4 turn more.
27. Install the coolant crossover pipe and thermostat.
28. Install the alternator upper bracket.
29. Install the automatic transmission dipstick and tube.
30. Install the air cleaner resonator and bracket.
31. Install the pushrods.
32. Install the rocker arm assemblies.
33. Adjust the valves.
34. Install the rocker arm cover(s).
35. Install the oil fill tube upper bracket.
36. Install the oil dipstick tube.
37. Connect the glow plug wiring.
38. Install the compressor.
39. Install the power steering pump.
40. Install the glow plug controller.
41. Install the exhaust manifold.
42. Connect the detent cable.
43. Install the air conditioning compressor belt.
44. Install the upper fan shroud.
45. Install the cruise control transducer.
46. Install the fuel injection lines. See Section 5.
47. Install the intake manifold.
48. Connect the battery cable and fill the cooling system.

7.4L Engines

➧ See Figure 99

1. Disconnect the negative battery cable and drain the cooling system.
2. Remove the intake manifold.
3. Remove the exhaust manifolds.
4. Remove the alternator and bracket.
5. Remove the AIR pump, if equipped.
6. If the vehicle is equipped with air conditioning, remove the air conditioning compressor and the forward mounting bracket and lay the compressor aside. Do not disconnect any of the refrigerant lines.
7. Remove the rocker arm cover.
8. Remove the spark plugs.
9. Remove the AIR pipes at the rear of the head, if equipped.
10. Disconnect the ground strap at the rear of the head.
11. Disconnect the temperature sensor wire.
12. Back off the rocker arm nuts and pivot the rocker arms out of the way so that the pushrods can be removed. Identify the pushrods so that they can be installed in their original positions.
13. Remove the cylinder head bolts and remove the heads.

To install:

14. Thoroughly clean the mating surfaces of the head and block. Clean the bolt holes thoroughly.
15. Install the cylinder heads using new gaskets. Install the gaskets with the word **HEAD** up.

➡Coat a steel gasket on both sides with sealer. If a composition gasket is used, do not use sealer.

16. Clean the bolts, apply sealer to the threads, and install them hand-tight.
17. Tighten the head bolts a little at a time in the sequence shown. Tighten the bolts in three stages: 30 ft. lbs. (40 Nm), 60 ft. lbs. (80 Nm) and finally to 80 ft. lbs. (110 Nm).
18. Install the intake and exhaust manifolds.
19. Install the pushrods.
20. Install the rocker arms and adjust them as described in this section.
21. Connect the temperature sensor wire.
22. Connect the ground strap at the rear of the head.
23. Install the AIR pipes at the rear of the head.
24. Install the spark plugs.
25. Install the rocker arm cover.

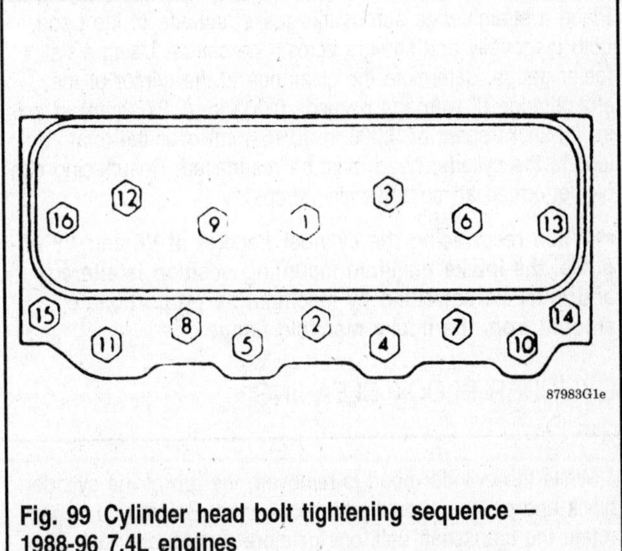

Fig. 99 Cylinder head bolt tightening sequence — 1988-96 7.4L engines

26. Install the air conditioning compressor and the forward mounting bracket.
27. Install the AIR pump.
28. Install the alternator.
29. Connect the battery cable and refill the cooling system.

CLEANING AND INSPECTION

➧ See Figures 100 and 101

➡Any diesel cylinder head work should be handled by a reputable machine shop familiar with diesel engines. Disassembly, valve lapping, and assembly can be completed by the following engine procedures.

One the complete valve train has been removed from the cylinder head(s), the head itself can be inspected, cleaned and machined (if necessary). Set the head(s) on a clean work space, so the combustion chambers are facing up. Begin cleaning the chambers and ports with a hardwood chisel or other non-metallic tool (to avoid nicking or gouging the chamber, ports, and especially the valve seats). Chip away the major carbon deposits, then remove the remainder of carbon with a wire brush fitted to an electric drill. A fine-bristled rifle bore cleaning brush will also work well.

➡Be sure that the carbon is actually removed, rather than just burnished.

After decarbonizing is completed, take the head(s) to a machine shop and have the head hot tanked. In this process, the head is lowered into a hot chemical bath that very effectively cleans all grease, corrosion, and scale from all internal and external head surfaces. Also have the machinist check the valve seats and recut them if necessary. When you bring the clean head(s) home, place them on a clean surface. Completely clean the entire valve train with solvent.

RESURFACING

➧ See Figures 102 and 103

Lay the head down with the combustion chambers facing up. Place a straightedge across the gasket surface of the head, both diagonally and straight across the center. Using a flat feeler gauge, determine the clearance at the center of the straightedge. If warpage exceeds 0.003 in. (0.0762mm) in a 6 in. (152mm) span, or 0.006 in. (0.152mm) over the total length, the cylinder head must be resurfaced. Resurfacing can be performed at most machine shops.

➡When resurfacing the cylinder head(s) of V6 and V8 engines, the intake manifold mounting position is altered, and must be corrected by machining a proportionate amount from the intake manifold flange.

CYLINDER BLOCK CLEANING

While the cylinder head is removed, the top of the cylinder block and pistons should also be cleaned. Before you begin, rotate the crankshaft until one or more pistons are flush with the top of the block. Carefully stuff clean rags into the cylin-

tccs3133

Fig. 101 An electric drill equipped with a wire wheel will expedite complete gasket removal

tccs3134

Fig. 102 Check the cylinder head for warpage along the center using a straightedge and a feeler gauge

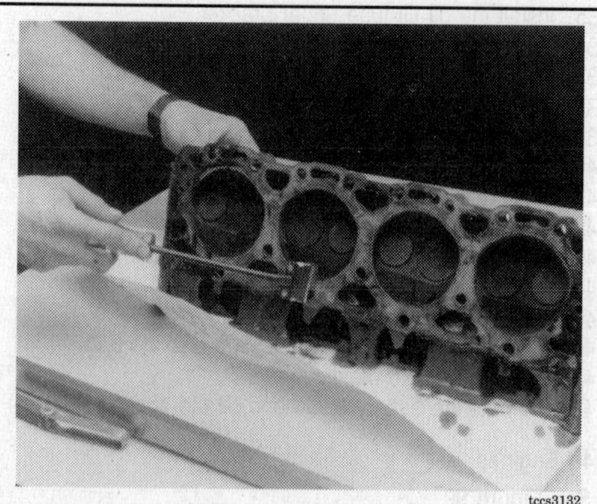
tccs3132

Fig. 100 Use a gasket scraper to remove the bulk of the old head gasket from the mating surface

Fig. 103 Be sure to check for warpage across the cylinder head at both diagonals

Fig. 104 Use a valve spring compressor tool to relieve spring tension from the valve caps

ders in which the pistons are down. This will help keep grit and carbon chips out during cleaning. Using care not to gouge or scratch the block-to-head mating surface and the piston top(s), clean away any old gasket material with a wire brush and/or scraper. On the piston tops, make sure you are actually removing the carbon and not merely burnishing it.

Remove the rags from the down cylinders after you have wiped the top of the block with a solvent soaked rag. Rotate the crankshaft until the other pistons come up flush with the top of the block, and clean those pistons.

➡Because you have rotated the crankshaft, you will have to re-time the engine following the procedure listed later in this section. Make sure you wipe out each cylinder thoroughly with a solvent-soaked rag, to remove all traces of grit, before the head is reassembled to the block.

Valves

REMOVAL & INSTALLATION

See Figures 104, 105, 106, 107, 108, 109, 110 and 111

1. Remove the head(s), and place on a clean surface.
2. Using a suitable spring compressor (for pushrod type overhead valve engines), compress the valve spring and remove the valve spring cap key. Release the spring compressor and remove the valve spring and cap (and valve rotator on some engines).

➡Use care in removing the keys. They are easily lost.

3. Remove the valve seals from the intake valve guides. Throw these old seals away, as you'll be installing new seals during reassembly.
4. Slide the valves out of the head from the combustion chamber side.
5. Make a holder for the valves out of a piece of wood or cardboard. Make sure you number each hole in the cardboard to keep the valves in proper order. Slide the valves out of the

Fig. 105 A magnet may be helpful in removing the valve keepers

head from the combustion chamber side. They MUST be installed as they were removed.

New valve seals must be installed when the valve train is put back together. Certain seals slip over the valve stem and guide boss, while others require that the boss be machined. Teflon® guide seals are available. Check with a machinist and/or automotive parts store for a suggestion on the proper seals to use.

➡Remember that when installing valve seals, a small amount of oil must be able to pass the seal to lubricate the valve guides; otherwise, excessive wear will result.

To install:

6. Lubricate the valve stems with clean engine oil.
7. Install the valves in the cylinder head, one at a time, as numbered.
8. Lubricate and position the seals and valve springs, again a valve at a time.
9. Install the spring retainers, and compress the springs.
10. With the valve key groove exposed above the compressed valve spring, wipe some wheel bearing grease around the groove. This will retain the keys as you release the spring compressor.
11. Using needlenose pliers (or your fingers), place the keys in the key grooves. The grease should hold the keys in place. Slowly release the spring compressor. The valve cap or rotator will raise up as the compressor is released, retaining the keys.
12. Install the rocker assembly, and install the cylinder head(s).

INSPECTION

➧ See Figures 112, 113, 114, 115, 116, 117 and 118

Inspect the valve faces and seats (in the head) for pits, burned spots and other evidence of poor seating. If a valve face is in such bad shape that the head of the valve must be ground in order to true up the face, discard the valve because the sharp edge will run too hot. The correct angle for valve faces is 45°. We recommend the refacing be done at a reputable machine shop.

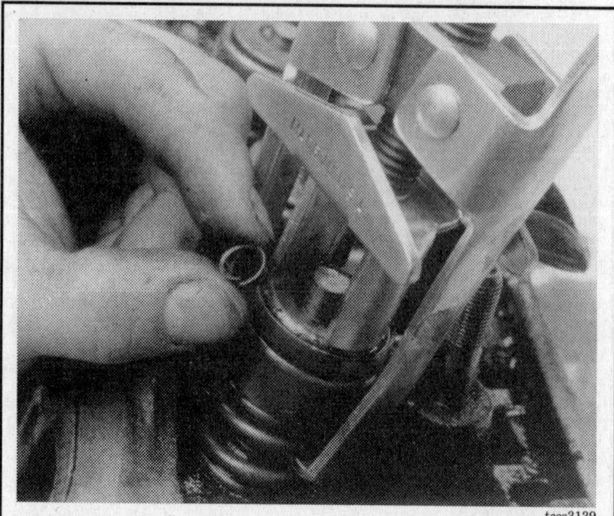

tccs3139

Fig. 106 Be careful not to lose the valve keepers

tccs3810

Fig. 107 Remove the spring from the valve stem in order to access the seal

tccs3140

Fig. 108 Once the spring has been removed, the O-ring may be removed from the valve stem

Fig. 109 Remove the valve stem seal from the cylinder head

Fig. 110 Invert the cylinder head and withdraw the valve from the cylinder head bore

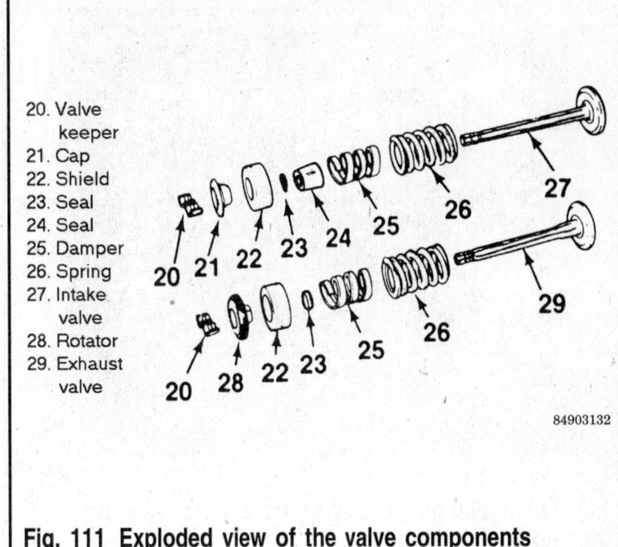

Fig. 111 Exploded view of the valve components

Check the valve stem for scoring and burned spots. If not noticeably scored or damaged, clean the valve stem with solvent to remove all gum and varnish. Clean the valve guides using solvent an an expanding wire type valve guide cleaner. If you have access to a dial indicator for measuring valve stem-to-guide clearance, mount it so that the stem of the indicator is at 90° to the valve stem, and as close to the valve guide as possible. Move the valve off its seat, and measure the valve guide-to-stem clearance by rocking the stem back and forth to actuate the dial indicator. Measure the valve stems using a micrometer, and compare to specifications to determine whether stem or guide wear is responsible for the excess clearance. If a dial indicator and micrometer are not available to you, take your cylinder head and valves to a reputable machine shop for inspection.

Some of the engines covered in this guide are equipped with valve rotators, which double as valve spring caps. In normal operation the rotators put a certain degree of wear on the tip of the valve stem. This wear appears as concentric rings on the stem tip. However, if the rotator is not working properly, the wear may appear as straight notches or **X** patterns across

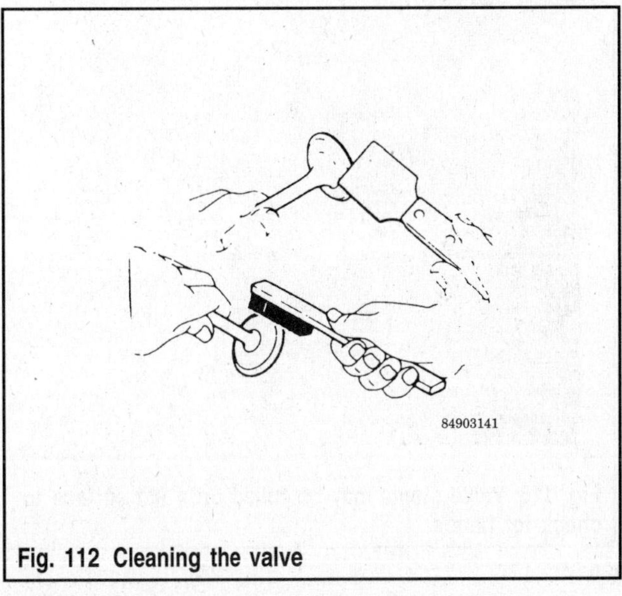

Fig. 112 Cleaning the valve

tccs3142

Fig. 113 A dial gauge may be used to check valve stem-to-guide clearance

the valve stem tip. Whenever the valves are removed from the cylinder head, the tips should be inspected for improper pattern, which could indicate valve rotator problems. Valve stem tips will have to be ground flat if rotator patterns are severe.

REFACING

Valve refacing should only be handled by a reputable machine shop, as the experience and equipment needed to do the job are beyond that of the average owner/mechanic. During the course of a normal valve job, refacing is necessary when simply lapping the valves into their seats will not correct the seat and face wear. When the valves are reground (resurfaced), the valve seats must also be recut, again requiring special equipment and experience.

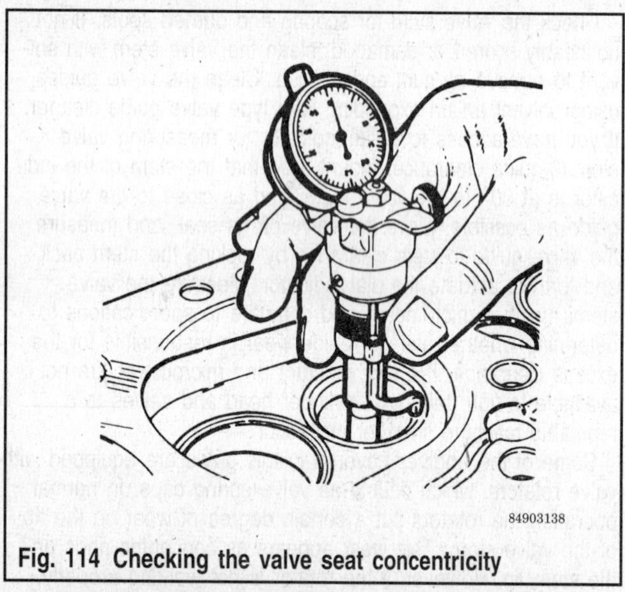
84903138

Fig. 114 Checking the valve seat concentricity

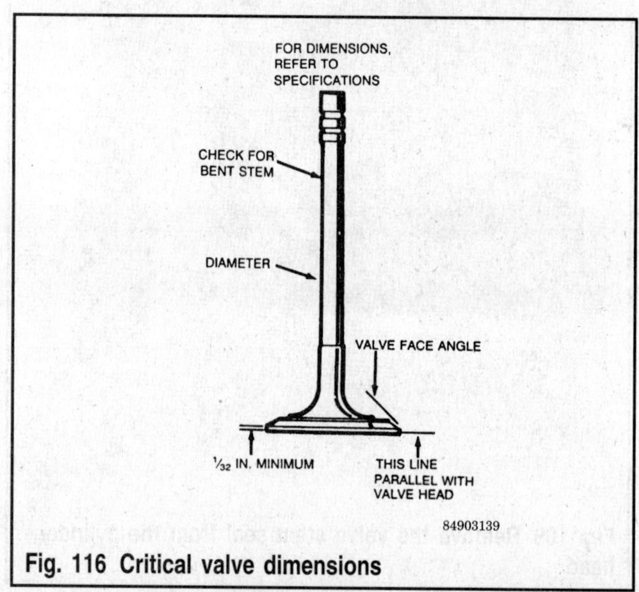

84903139

Fig. 116 Critical valve dimensions

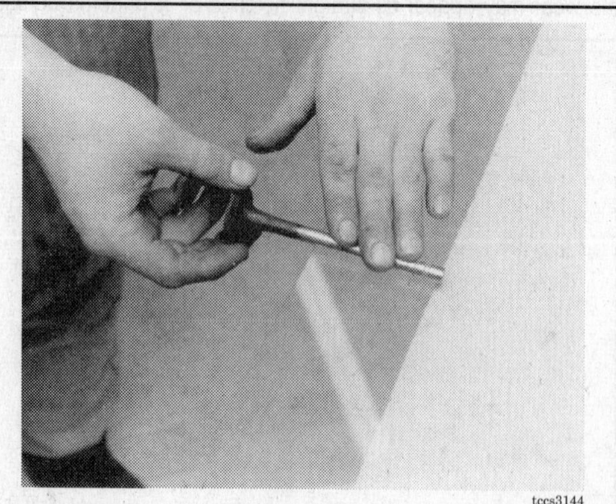
tccs3144

Fig. 115 Valve stems may be rolled on a flat surface to check for bends

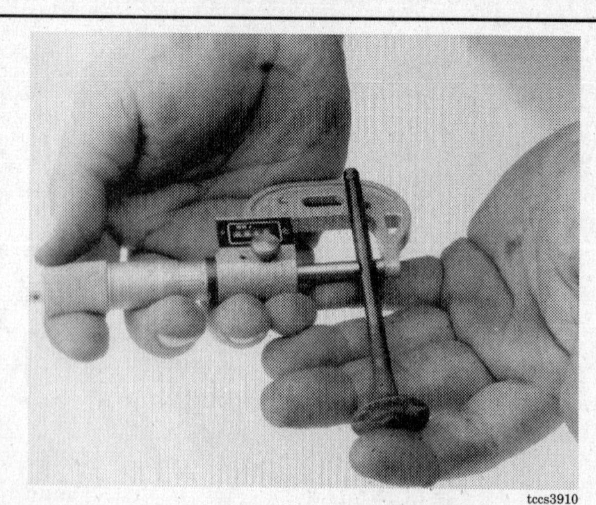
tccs3910

Fig. 117 Use a micrometer to check the valve stem diameter

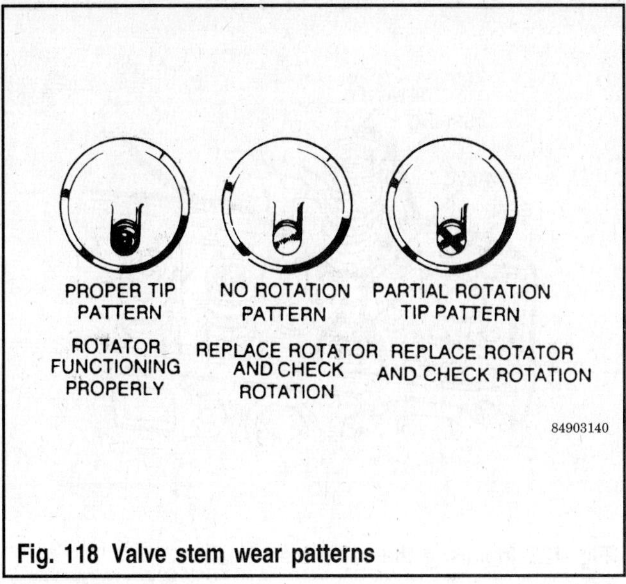

Fig. 118 Valve stem wear patterns

VALVE LAPPING

See Figures 119 and 120

After machine work has been performed on the valves, it may be necessary to lap the valve to assure proper contact. For this, you should first contact your machine shop to determine if lapping is necessary. Some machine shops will perform this for you as part of the service, but the precision machining which is available today often makes lapping unnecessary. Additionally, the hardened valves/seats used in modern automobiles may make lapping difficult or impossible. If your machine shop recommends that you lap the valves, proceed as follows:

1. Set the cylinder head on the workbench, combustion chamber side up. Rest the head on wooden blocks on either end, so there are two or three inches between the tops of the valve guides and the bench.
2. Lightly lube the valve stem with clean engine oil. Coat the valve seat completely with valve grinding compound. Use just enough compound that the full width and circumference of the seat are covered.
3. Install the valve in its proper location in the head. Attach the suction cup end of the valve lapping tool to the valve head. It usually helps to put a small amount of saliva into the suction cup to aid it sticking to the valve.
4. Rotate the tool between the palms, changing position and lifting the tool often to prevent grooving. Lap the valve in until a smooth, evenly polished seat and valve face are evident.
5. Remove the valve from the head. Wipe away all traces of grinding compound from the valve face and seat. Wipe out the port with a solvent soaked rag, and swab out the valve guide with a piece of solvent soaked rag to make sure there are no traces of compound grit inside the guide. This cleaning is important.
6. Proceed through the remaining valves, one at a time. Make sure the valve faces, seats, cylinder ports and valve guides are clean before reassembling the valve train.

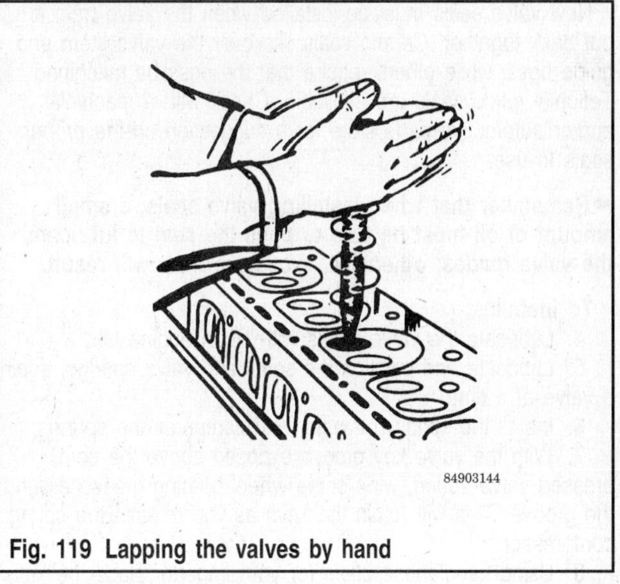

Fig. 119 Lapping the valves by hand

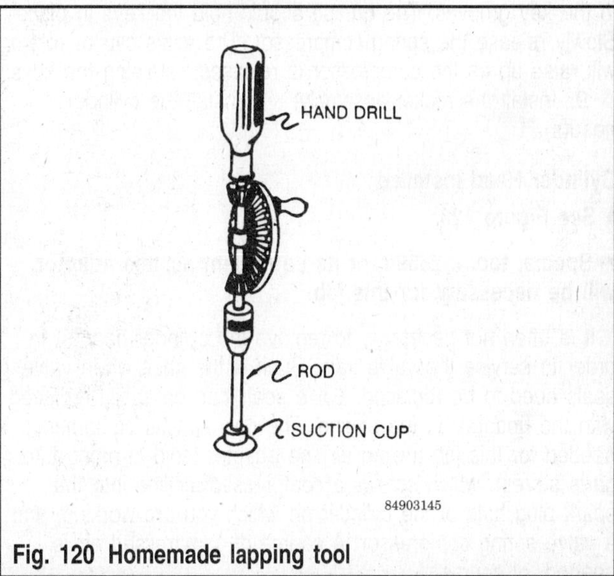

Fig. 120 Homemade lapping tool

Valve Stem Seals

REMOVAL & INSTALLATION

Cylinder Head Removed

See Figures 121 and 122

1. Remove the head(s), and place on a clean surface.
2. Using a suitable spring compressor (for pushrod type overhead valve engines), compress the valve spring and remove the valve spring cap key. Release the spring compressor and remove the valve spring and cap (and valve rotator on some engines).

➡Use care in removing the keys. They are easily lost.

3. Remove the valve seals from the intake valve guides. Throw these old seals away, as you'll be installing new seals during reassembly.

New valve seals must be installed when the valve train is put back together. Certain seals slip over the valve stem and guide boss, while others require that the boss be machined. Teflon® guide seals are available. Check with a machinist and/or automotive parts store for a suggestion on the proper seals to use.

➡Remember that when installing valve seals, a small amount of oil must be able to pass the seal to lubricate the valve guides; otherwise, excessive wear will result.

To install:

4. Lubricate the valve stems with clean engine oil.
5. Lubricate and position the seals and valve springs, again a valve at a time.
6. Install the spring retainers, and compress the springs.
7. With the valve key groove exposed above the compressed valve spring, wipe some wheel bearing grease around the groove. This will retain the keys as you release the spring compressor.
8. Using needlenose pliers (or your fingers), place the keys in the key grooves. The grease should hold the keys in place. Slowly release the spring compressor. The valve cap or rotator will raise up as the compressor is released, retaining the keys.
9. Install the rocker assembly, and install the cylinder head(s).

Cylinder Head Installed

▶ See Figure 123

➡Special tool J-23590, or its equivalent air line adaptor, will be necessary for this job.

It is often not necessary to remove the cylinder head(s) in order to service the valve train. Such is the case when valve seals need to be replaced. Valve seals can be easily replaced with the head(s) on the engine. The only special equipment needed for this job are an air line adapter (sold in most auto parts stores), which screws a compressed air line into the spark plug hole of the cylinder on which you are working, and a valve spring compressor. A source of compressed air is needed, of course.

1. Remove the cylinder head cover.

Fig. 121 With the valve spring out of the way, the valve stem seals may now be replaced

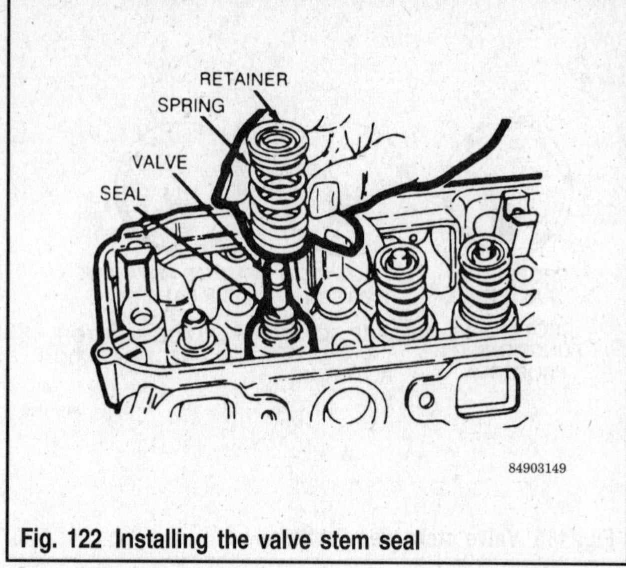

Fig. 122 Installing the valve stem seal

2. Remove the spark plug, rocker arm and pushrod on the cylinder(s) to be serviced.
3. Position the engine so that both valves are closed.
4. Install air line adapter (GM tool No. J-23590 or equivalent) into the spark plug hole. Turn on the air compressor to apply compressed air into the cylinder. This keeps the valves up in place.

➡Set the regulator of the air compressor at least 50 psi (344 kPa) to ensure adequate pressure.

5. Using the valve spring compressor, compress the valve spring and remove the valve keys and keepers, the valve spring and damper.
6. Remove the valve stem seal.
7. To reassemble, oil the valve stem and new seal. Install a new seal over the valve stem. Set the spring, damper and keeper in place. Compress the spring. Coat the keys with grease to hold them onto the valve stem and install the keys, making sure they are seated fully in the keeper. Reinstall the cylinder head cover after adjusting the valves, as outlined in this section.

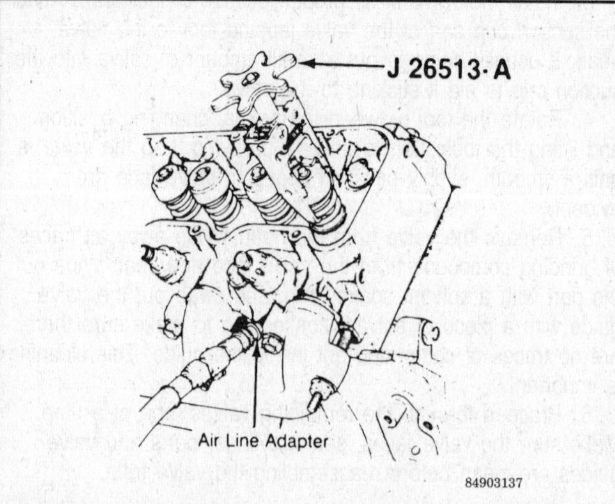

Fig. 123 Compressing the valve springs with the head installed

Valve Springs

REMOVAL & INSTALLATION

Please refer to the procedure for valve removal and installation.

INSPECTION

▶ **See Figures 124, 125, 126 and 127**

Valve spring squareness, length and tension should be checked while the valve train is disassembled. Place each valve spring on a flat surface next to a steel square. Measure the length of the spring, and rotate it against the edge of the square to measure distortion. If spring length varies (by comparison) by more than 0.06 in. (1.6mm) or if distortion exceeds 0.06 in. (1.6mm), replace the spring.

Spring tension must be checked on a spring tester. Springs used on most engines should be within one pound of each other when tested at their specified installed heights.

Valve Seats

REMOVAL & INSTALLATION

The valve seats in these engines are not removable. Refer all servicing of the valve seats to a qualified machine shop.

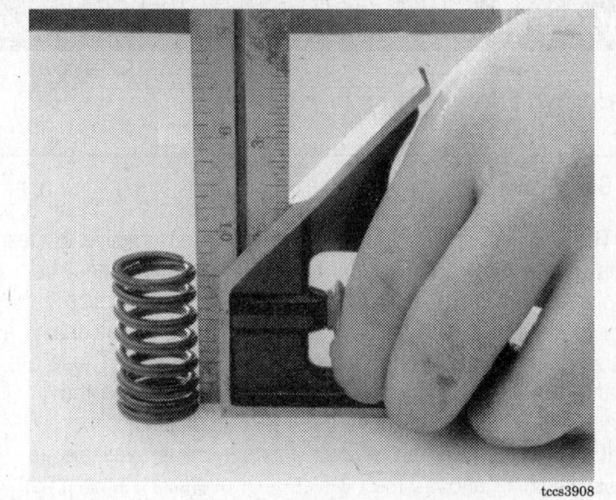

tccs3908

Fig. 125 Check the valve spring for squareness on a flat service; a carpenter's square can be used

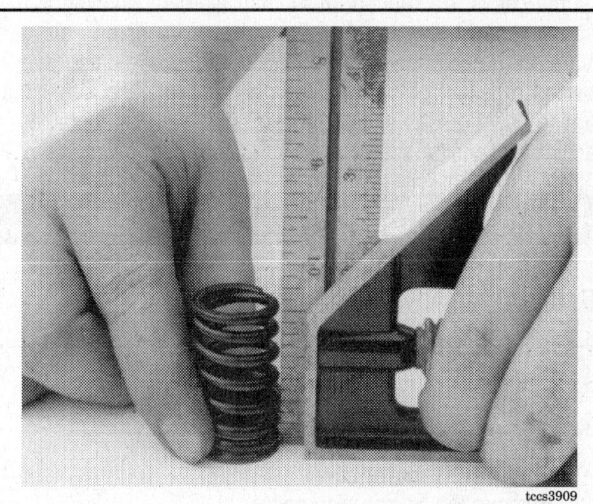

tccs3909

Fig. 126 The valve spring should be straight up and down when placed like this

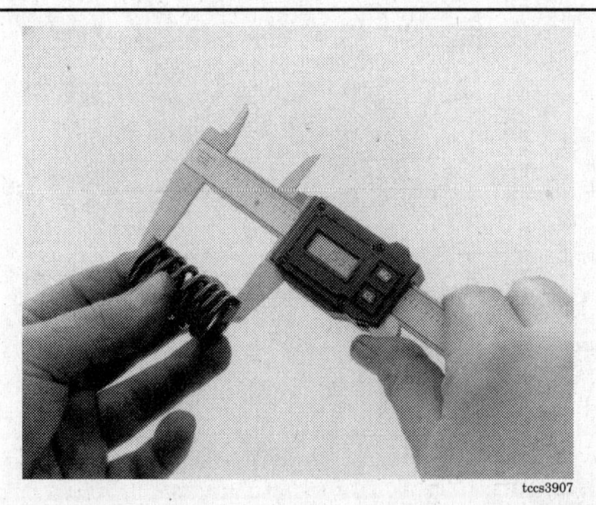

tccs3907

Fig. 124 Use a caliper gauge to check the valve spring free-length

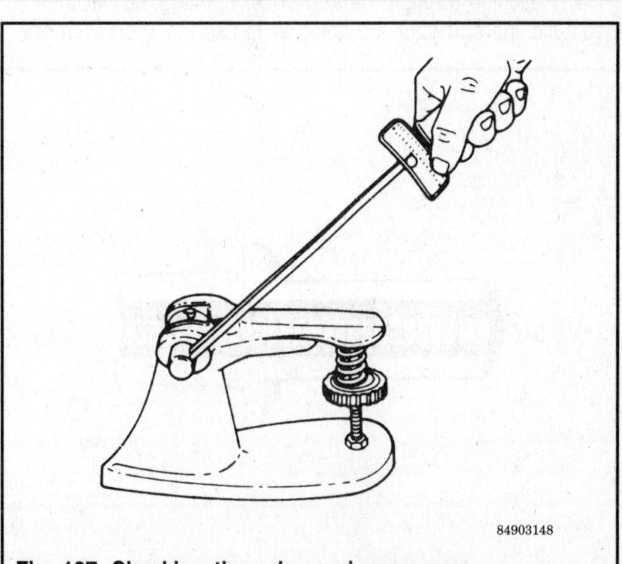

84903148

Fig. 127 Checking the valve spring pressure

Valve Guides

REMOVAL & INSTALLATION

➧ See Figure 128

The engines covered in this guide use integral valve guides. That is, they are a part of the cylinder head and cannot be replaced. The guides can, however, be reamed oversize if they are found to be worn past an acceptable limit. Occasionally, a valve guide bore will be oversize as manufactured. These are marked on the inboard side of the cylinder heads on the machined surface just above the intake manifold.

If the guides must be reamed (this service is available at most machine shops), then valves with oversize stems must be fitted. Valves are usually available in 0.001 in. (0.025mm), 0.003 in. (0.076mm), and 0.005 in. (0.12mm) stem oversizes. Valve guides which are not excessively worn or distorted may, in some cases, be knurled rather than reamed. Knurling is a process in which the metal on the valve guide bore is displaced and raised, thereby reducing clearance. Knurling also provides excellent oil control. The option of knurling rather than reaming valve guides should be discussed with a reputable machinist or engine specialist.

Hydraulic Lifters

REMOVAL & INSTALLATION

➧ See Figure 129

4.8L Engines

1. Remove the rocker cover.
2. Remove the engine side cover.
3. Back off the rocker arm adjusting nuts and remove the pushrods. Keep them in order for installation.
4. Reaching through the side cover opening, lift out the hydraulic lifters. If your are going to re-use the lifters, remove them one at a time and mark each one for installation. They **must** be re-installed in the same locations.

If a lifter is stuck, it can be removed with a grasping-type lifter tool, available form most auto parts stores.

5. Inspect each lifter thoroughly. If any of them shows any signs of wear, heat bluing or damage, replace the whole set.

To install:

6. Install and coat each lifter with engine oil supplement.
7. Install the remaining components by reversing the removal procedure.
8. Once installation is complete, adjust the valves as described in the valve lash procedure.

4.3L, 5.0L, 5.7L and 7.4L Engines

1. Remove the cylinder head cover.
2. Remove the intake manifold.
3. Back off the rocker arm adjusting nuts and remove the pushrods. Keep them in order for installation.
4. Remove the lifter retainer bolts, retainer and restrictor.
5. Remove the lifters. If your are going to re-use the lifters, remove them one at a time and mark each one for installation.

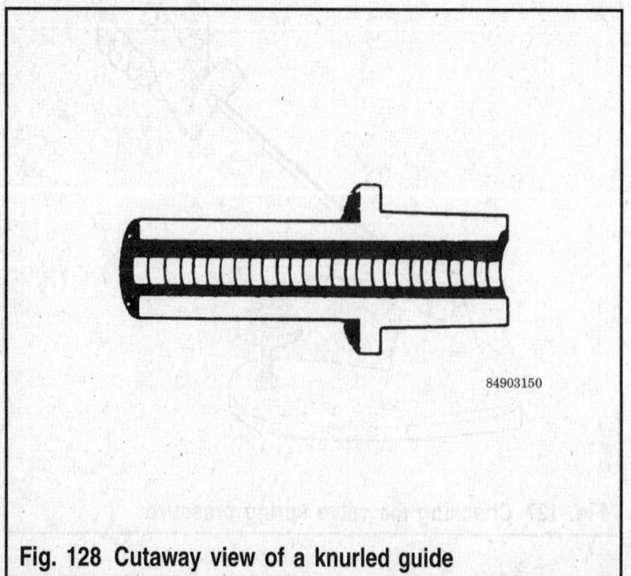

Fig. 128 Cutaway view of a knurled guide

Fig. 129 Stuck lifters must be freed using a slide hammer type lifter removal tool

They **must** be re-installed in the same locations. If a lifter is stuck, it can be removed with a grasping-type lifter tool, available from most auto parts stores.

6. Inspect each lifter thoroughly. If any of them shows any signs of wear, heat bluing or damage, replace the whole set.

7. Coat each lifter with engine oil supplement prior to installation. Tighten the retainer bolts to 12 ft. lbs. (16 Nm). Adjust the valves as described in the valve lash procedure.

6.2L and 6.5L Diesel Engines

➧ See Figure 130

1. Remove the cylinder head cover.
2. Remove the rocker arm shaft, rocker arms and pushrods. Keep all parts in order and properly identified for installation.
3. Remove the clamps and lifter guide plates.
4. Remove the lifters by reaching through the access holes in the cylinder head with a magnetic lifter tool. If you are are going to re-use the lifters, remove them one at a time and mark each one for installation. They **must** be re-installed in the same locations. If a lifter is stuck, it can be removed with a grasping-type lifter tool, available form most auto parts stores.

To install:

5. Inspect each lifter thoroughly. If any of them shows any signs of wear, heat bluing or damage, replace the whole set.

➡Some engines will have both standard and 0.010 in. (.0039mm) oversize lifters. The oversized lifters will have "10" etched into the side. The block will be stamped "OS" on the cast pad next to the lifter bore. and on the top rail of the crankcase above the lifter bore.

⁎⁎WARNING

New lifters must be primed before installation. Damage to the lifters and engine will result if new lifters are installed dry!

6. Prime new lifters by immersing them in clean kerosene or diesel fuel and working the lifter plunger while the unit is submerged.

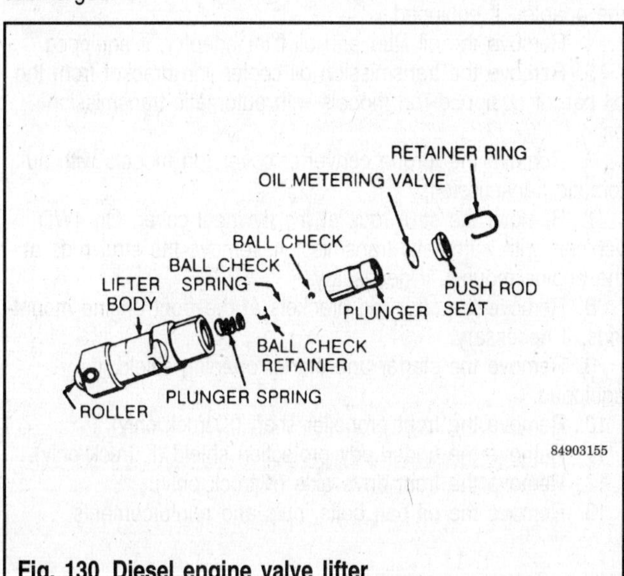

Fig. 130 Diesel engine valve lifter

7. Prior to installation, coat the lifter roller with engine oil supplement. Re-used lifters must be installed in their original positions!
8. Install the lifters.
9. Install the guide plates and clamps. Tighten the clamp bolts to 18 ft. lbs. (26 Nm).
10. After all the clamps are installed, turn the crankshaft by hand, 2 full turns (720°) to ensure free movement of the lifters in the guide plates. If the crankshaft won't turn, one or more lifters may be jamming in the guide plates.
11. The remainder of assembly the the reverse of disassembly.

Valve Lash

All engines described in this book use hydraulic lifters, which require no periodic adjustment. In the event of cylinder head removal or any operation that requires disturbing the rocker arms, the rocker arms will have to be adjusted.

ADJUSTMENT

4.8L Engines

1. Remove the rocker arm cover.
2. Mark the distributor housing at the No. 1 and No. 6 wire positions and remove the cap.
3. Turn the crankshaft until the rotor points to the No. 1 position. The following valves can be adjusted:
   - No. 1 exhaust and intake
   - No. 2 intake
   - No. 3 exhaust
   - No. 4 intake
   - No. 5 exhaust

To adjust a valve, back off the adjusting nut until lash (play) is felt at the pushrod. Tighten the nut just until all lash is removed. This can be determined by rotating the pushrod with your fingers. When all lash is removed, the pushrod will stop rotating. When all play is removed, tighten the nut 1 full turn (360°).

4. Rotate the crankshaft until the rotor points to the No. 6 position. The following valves can be adjusted:
   - No. 2 exhaust
   - No. 3 intake
   - No. 4 exhaust
   - No. 5 intake
   - No. 6 intake and exhaust
5. Install the distributor cap.
6. Install the rocker cover.

V6 and V8 Engines

➧ See Figure 131

1. Remove the rocker covers and gaskets.
2. Crank the engine until the mark on the damper aligns with the **TDC** or **0** mark on the timing tab and the engine is in No. 1 firing position. This can be determined by placing your finger on the No. 1 cylinder valves as the marks align. If the valves do not move, it is in No. 1 firing position. If the valves move, it is in No. 6 firing position (No. 4 on the V6) and the crankshaft should be rotated 1 more revolution to the No. 1

firing position. To adjust a valve, back off the adjusting nut until lash (play) is felt at the pushrod. Tighten the nut just until all lash is removed. This can be determined by rotating the pushrod with your fingers. When all lash is removed, the pushrod will stop rotating. When all play is removed, tighten the nut 1 full turn (360°).

3. With the engine in No. 1 firing position, the following valves can be adjusted:

V6 Engines

- Exhaust — 1, 5, 6,
- Intake — 1, 2, 3,

V8 Engines

- Exhaust — 1,3,4,8
- Intake — 1,2,5,7

4. Crank the engine 1 full revolution until the marks are again in alignment. This is No. 6 firing position (No. 4 on the V6). The following valves can now be adjusted:

V6 Engines

- Exhaust — 2, 3, 4
- Intake — 4, 5, 6

V8 Engines

- Exhaust — 2,5,6,7
- Intake — 3,4,6,8

5. Reinstall the rocker arm covers using new gaskets.
6. Install the distributor cap and wire assembly.

Oil Pan

REMOVAL & INSTALLATION

4.3L Engines

See Figure 132

A one-piece oil pan gasket is used.

1. Disconnect the negative battery cable. Raise the vehicle, support it safely, and drain the engine oil.
2. Remove the exhaust crossover pipe, if necessary.

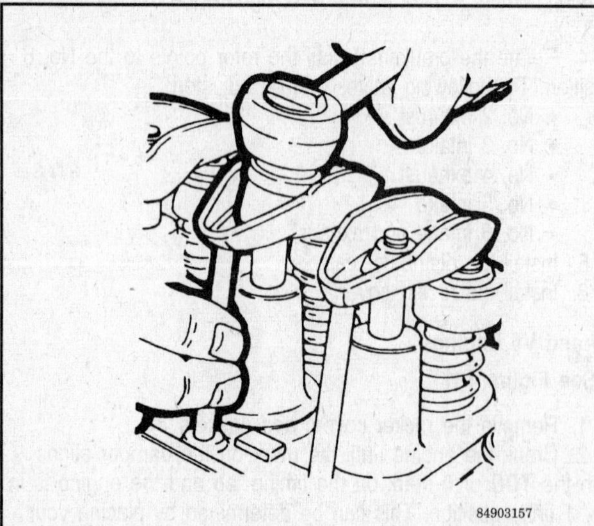

84903157

Fig. 131 Adjusting the valve — gasoline engines

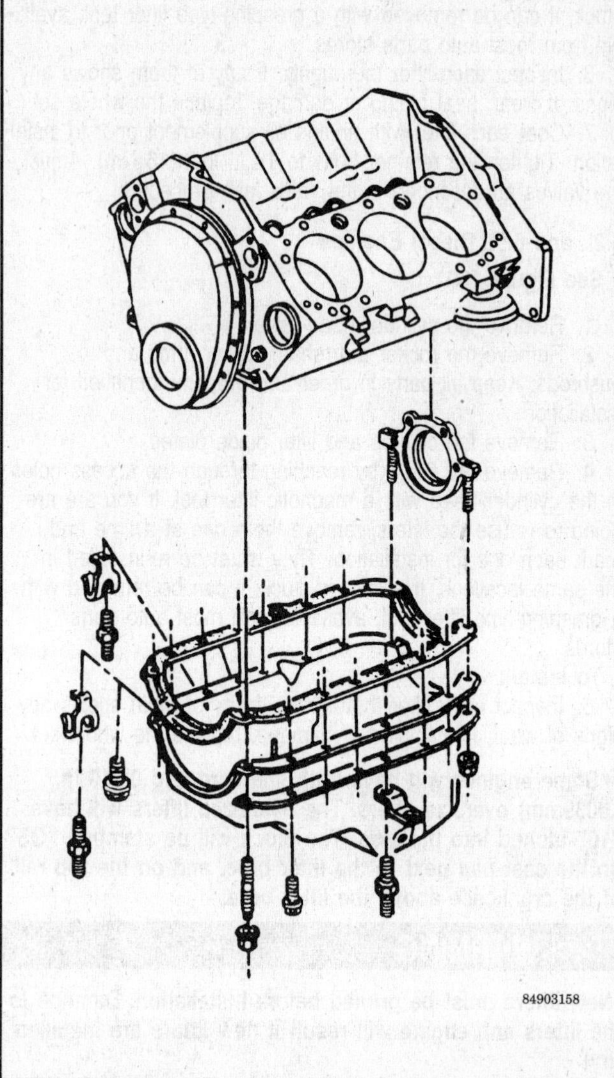

84903158

Fig. 132 Exploded view of the oil pan — 4.3L engines

3. Remove the oil cooler lines from the oil pan and from the adaptor, if equipped.
4. Remove the oil filter and oil filter adaptor, if equipped.
5. Remove the transmission oil cooler line bracket from the oil pan, if equipped (on models with automatic transmission only).
6. Remove the torque converter cover (on models with automatic transmission).
7. Remove the strut rods at the flywheel cover. On 4WD vehicles with automatic transmission, remove the strut rods at the engine mounts, if necessary.
8. Remove the strut rod brackets at the front engine mountings, if necessary.
9. Remove the starter and starter opening shield, If equipped.
10. Remove the front propeller shaft (K truck only).
11. Remove the underbody protection shield (K truck only).
12. Remove the front drive axle (K truck only).
13. Remove the oil pan bolts, nuts and reinforcements.

14. Remove the oil pan and gaskets.

:*:*CAUTION

The EPA warns that prolonged contact with used engine oil may cause a number of skin disorders, including cancer! You should make every effort to minimize you exposure to used engine oil. Protective gloves should be worn when changing the oil. Wash your hands and any other exposed skin areas as soon as possible after exposure to used engine oil. Soap and water, or waterless hand cleaner should be used.

To install:

15. Thoroughly clean all gasket surfaces and install a new gasket, using only a small amount of sealer at the front and rear corners of the oil pan.
16. Install the oil pan and new gaskets.
17. Install the oil pan bolts, nuts and reinforcements. Tighten the pan bolts to 100 inch lbs. (11 Nm). Tighten the nuts at the corners to 17 ft. lbs. (23 Nm).
18. Install the transmission oil cooler line bracket (on models with automatic transmission).
19. Install oil filter adaptor, oil cooler and the oil filter.
20. Install the front drive axle (K trucks only).
21. Install the front propeller shaft (K trucks only).
22. Install the underbody protection shields (K trucks only).
23. Install the starter and opening shield.
24. Install the strut rod brackets at the front engine mountings, if removed.
25. Install the strut rods at the flywheel cover, if removed.
26. Install the torque converter cover (on models with automatic transmission), if removed.
27. Install the exhaust crossover pipe, if removed.
28. Connect the negative battery cable.
29. Fill the crankcase.

4.8L Engines

1. Disconnect the negative battery cable.
2. Raise and support the truck on jackstands.
3. Drain the engine oil.
4. Remove the flywheel cover.
5. Remove the starter assembly.
6. Remove the engine mount through-bolts from the engine front mounts.
7. Using a floor jack under the damper, raise the engine enough to remove the oil pan.
8. Remove the oil pan retaining bolts. Remove the oil pan from the engine. You may have to break loose the pan with a soft mallet.
9. Thoroughly clean the mating surfaces of the pan and block. If the lips of the pan are bent, straighten them.
10. Installation is the reverse of the removal procedure. Use new gaskets and seals. Tighten the pan-to-front cover bolts to 45 inch lbs. (5 Nm). Tighten the $\frac{1}{4}$ in. pan-to-block bolts to 80 inch lbs. (9 Nm) and the $\frac{5}{16}$ in. bolts to 14 ft. lbs. (19 Nm).
11. Fill the engine with the proper grade and viscosity of engine oil and check for leaks.

5.0L and 5.7L Engines

2WD MODELS

1. Disconnect the negative battery cable. Drain the cooling system. Drain the engine oil.
2. Remove the oil dipstick and tube.
3. If necessary remove the exhaust pipe crossover.
4. If equipped with automatic transmission, remove the converter housing pan and the transmission oil cooler line retainer from the bracket.
5. Remove the oil filter and the oil filter adaptor.
6. Remove the starter brace and bolt and swing the starter aside. On 4WD vehicles with automatic transmission, remove the strut rods at the engine mounts, if necessary.
7. Remove the oil pan and discard the gaskets.
8. Installation is the reverse of removal. Clean all gasket surfaces and use new gaskets to assemble. Use gasket sealer to retain side gaskets to the cylinder block. Install a new oil pan rear seal in the rear main bearing cap slot with the ends butting the side gaskets. Install a new front seal in the crankcase front cover with the ends butting the side gaskets. Tighten the pan bolts to 100 inch lbs. (11 Nm). Tighten the nuts at the corners to 17 ft. lbs. (23 Nm). Fill the engine with oil and check for leaks.

4WD MODELS

See Figures 133, 134, 135, 136, 137, 138, 139, 140 and 141

1. Disconnect the negative battery cable. Raise the vehicle, support it safely, and drain the engine oil.
2. Remove the exhaust crossover pipe, if necessary.
3. Oil cooler lines from the oil pan and from the adaptor, if equipped.
4. Oil filter and oil filter adaptor, if equipped.
5. Remove the transmission oil cooler line bracket from the oil pan, if equipped (on models with automatic transmission only).
6. Remove the strut rods at the flywheel cover. On 4WD vehicles with automatic transmission, remove the strut rods at the engine mounts, if necessary.

87983p58

Fig. 133 Remove the bolts from the oil filter adaptor

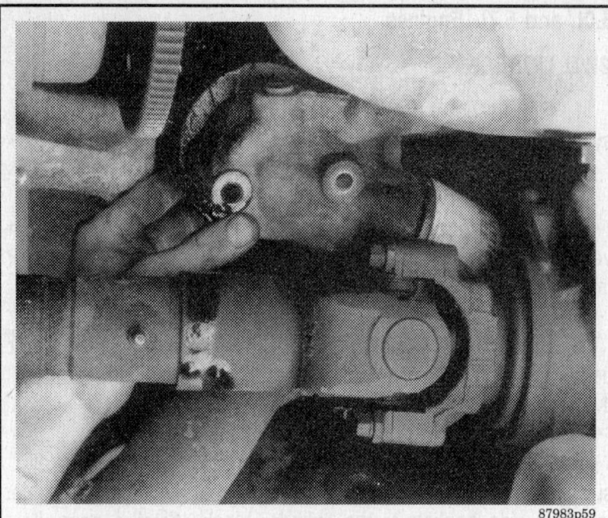
87983p59

Fig. 134 Remove the oil filter and adaptor

7. Remove the torque converter cover (on models with automatic transmission).

8. Remove the strut rod brackets at the front engine mountings, if necessary.

9. Remove the starter and starter opening shield, If equipped.

10. Remove the front propeller shaft (K truck only).

11. Remove the underbody protection shield (K truck only).

12. Remove the front drive axle (K truck only);

  a. Two right side bolts and nuts.
  b. One left side upper bolt and nut.
  c. Rotate the front drive axle forward.
  d. Turn the front wheels to the left.
  e. Allow the front axle to drop, this will allow for extra clearance (if needed).

13. Remove the oil pan bolts, nuts and reinforcements.

87983p61

Fig. 136 Remove the strut rods

14. Remove the oil pan and gaskets.

CAUTION

The EPA warns that prolonged contact with used engine oil may cause a number of skin disorders, including cancer! You should make every effort to minimize you exposure to used engine oil. Protective gloves should be worn when changing the oil. Wash your hands and any other exposed skin areas as soon as possible after exposure to used engine oil. Soap and water, or waterless hand cleaner should be used.

To install:

15. Thoroughly clean all gasket surfaces and install a new gasket, using only a small amount of sealer at the front and rear corners of the oil pan.

16. Install the oil pan and new gaskets.

17. Install the oil pan bolts, nuts and reinforcements. Tighten the pan bolts to 100 inch lbs. (11 Nm). Tighten the nuts at the corners to 17 ft. lbs. (23 Nm).

87983p60

Fig. 135 Remove the strut rod fasteners

87983p62

Fig. 137 Remove the torque convertor cover

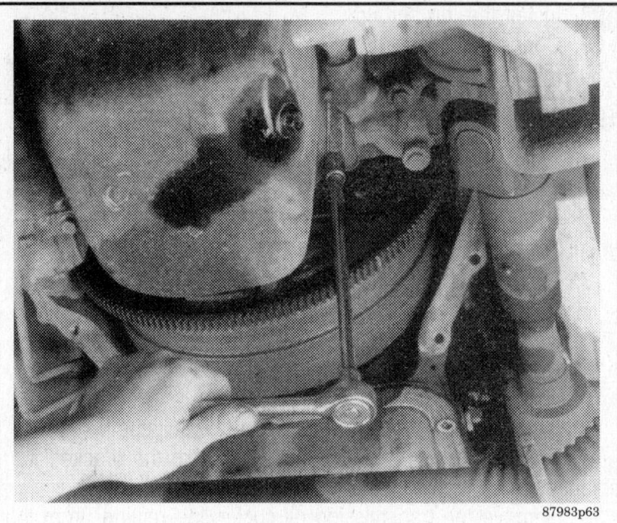

Fig. 138 Remove the oil pan bolts and nuts

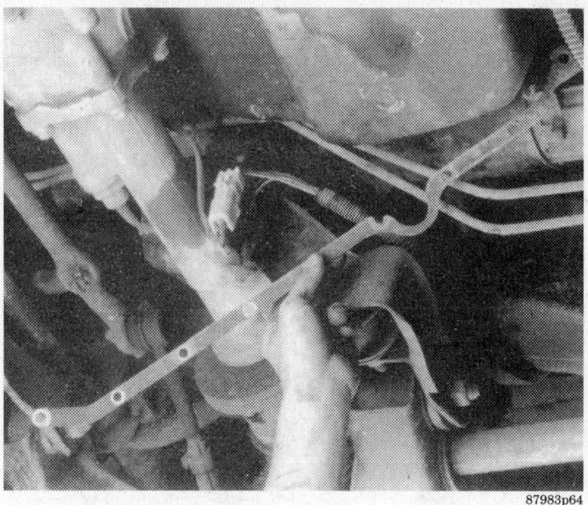

Fig. 139 Remove the oil pan reinforcements

18. Install the transmission oil cooler line bracket (on models with automatic transmission).
19. Install oil filter adaptor, oil cooler and the oil filter.
20. Install the front drive axle (K trucks only).
21. Install the front propeller shaft (K trucks only).
22. Install the underbody protection shields (K trucks only).
23. Install the starter and opening shield.
24. Install the strut rod brackets at the front engine mountings, if removed.
25. Install the strut rods at the flywheel cover, if removed.
26. Install the torque converter cover (on models with automatic transmission), if removed.
27. Install the exhaust crossover pipe, if removed.
28. Connect the negative battery cable.
29. Fill the crankcase.

7.4L Engines

1988-94 MODELS

See Figure 142

1. Disconnect the battery.
2. Remove the fan shroud.
3. Remove the air cleaner.
4. Remove the distributor cap.
5. Raise and support the front end on jackstands.
6. Drain the engine oil.
7. Remove the converter housing pan. On 4WD vehicles with automatic transmission, remove the strut rods at the engine mounts.
8. Remove the oil filter.
9. Remove the oil pressure line.
10. Support the engine with a floor jack.

WARNING

Do not place the jack under the pan, sheet metal or pulley!

11. Remove the engine mount through-bolts.
12. Raise the engine just enough to remove the pan.
13. Remove the oil pan and discard the gaskets.

Fig. 140 Remove the oil pan from the vehicle

Fig. 141 Remove the old gasket from both mating surfaces

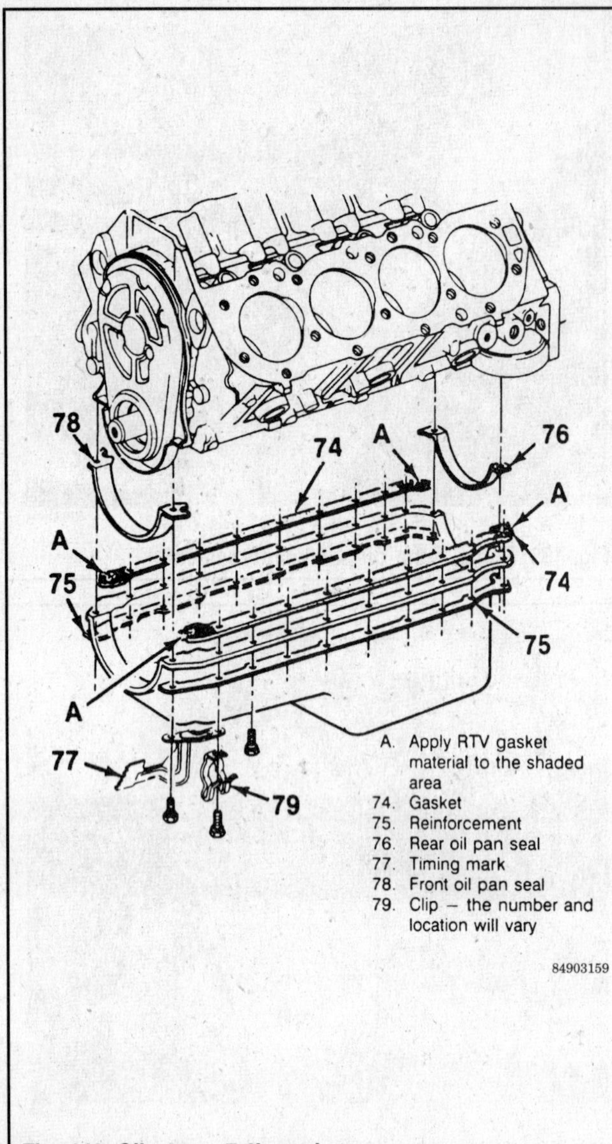

Fig. 142 Oil pan — 7.4L engines

To install:

14. Clean all mating surfaces thoroughly.
15. Apply RTV gasket material to the front and rear corners of the gaskets.
16. Coat the gaskets with adhesive sealer and position them on the block.
17. Install the rear pan seal in the pan with the seal ends mating with the gaskets.
18. Install the front seal on the bottom of the front cover, pressing the locating tabs into the holes in the cover.
19. Install the oil pan.
20. Install the pan bolts, clips and reinforcements. Tighten the pan-to-cover bolts to 70 inch lbs. (8 Nm); the pan-to-block bolts to 13 ft. lbs. (18 Nm).
21. Lower the engine onto the mounts.
22. Install the engine mount through-bolts.
23. Install the oil pressure line.
24. Install the oil filter.
25. Install the converter housing pan.
26. Install the distributor cap.
27. Install the air cleaner.
28. Install the fan shroud.
29. Connect the battery.
30. Fill the crankcase.

1995-96 MODELS

1. Disconnect the negative battery cable and remove the oil level indicator and tube.
2. Raise the vehicle, support it safely with jackstands and drain the oil.
3. Remove the front propeller shaft (K truck only).
4. Remove the underbody protection shield (K truck only).
5. Remove the front drive axle (K truck only).
6. Remove the flywheel/torque convertor cover.
7. Remove the exhaust crossover pipe.
8. Remove the oil filter and adaptor, if equipped.
9. Remove the oil cooler line retainer from the bracket, if equipped.
10. Remove the transmission oil cooler line retainer from the bracket, if equipped.
11. Remove the oil pan bolts, nuts and strut rods, if equipped.
12. Remove the oil pan and gasket.

To install:

13. Thoroughly clean all gasket surfaces and install a new gasket, using only a small amount of sealer at the front and rear corners of the oil pan.
14. Install the oil pan and new gaskets.
15. Install the oil pan bolts, nuts and strut rods. Tighten the pan bolts and nuts to 18 ft. lbs. (25 Nm).
16. Install the transmission oil cooler line bracket (on models with automatic transmission).
17. Install oil filter adaptor, oil cooler and the oil filter.
18. Install the front drive axle (K trucks only).
19. Install the front propeller shaft (K trucks only).
20. Install the underbody protection shields (K trucks only).
21. Install the starter and opening shield.
22. Install the strut rod brackets at the front engine mountings, if removed.
23. Install the strut rods at the flywheel cover, if removed.
24. Install the torque converter cover (on models with automatic transmission), if removed.
25. Install the exhaust crossover pipe, if removed.
26. Connect the negative battery cable.
27. Fill the crankcase.

6.2L and 6.5L Diesel Engines

➧ **See Figure 143**

1988-94 MODELS

1. Remove the vacuum pump and drive (with air conditioning or the oil pump drive (without air conditioning).
2. Disconnect the batteries and remove the engine oil dipstick.
3. Remove the upper radiator support and fan shroud.
4. Raise and support the truck. Drain the oil.
5. Remove the flywheel cover. On 4WD vehicles with automatic transmission, remove the strut rods at the engine mounts.
6. Disconnect the exhaust and crossover pipes, if necessary.
7. Remove the oil cooler lines at the filter base.

8. Remove the starter assembly. Support the engine with a jack.
9. Remove the engine mounts from the block.
10. Raise the front of the engine and remove the oil pan.

To install:

11. Using new gaskets coated with sealer, position the oil pan on the block and install the bolts. Tighten the bolts to 89 inch lbs. (10 Nm), except for the two rear bolts. Tighten them to 17 ft. lbs. (23 Nm).
12. Install the engine mounts.
13. Remove the jack.
14. Install the starter assembly.
15. Install the oil cooler lines at the filter base.
16. Connect the exhaust and crossover pipes.
17. Install the flywheel cover.
18. Install the upper radiator support and fan shroud.
19. Connect the batteries.
20. Install the engine oil dipstick.
21. Install the vacuum pump and drive (with air conditioning or the oil pump drive (without air conditioning).
22. Fill the crankcase.

1995-96 MODELS

1. Disconnect the batteries and remove the engine oil dipstick.
2. Raise the vehicle, support it with jackstands and drain the engine oil.
3. Remove the flywheel cover. On 4WD vehicles with automatic transmission, remove the strut rods at the engine mounts.
4. Remove the oil level tube.
5. Remove the oil cooler line clip.
6. Remove the oil pan bolts, pan and gasket.

To install:

7. Using new gaskets coated with sealer, position the oil pan on the block and install the bolts. Tighten the bolts to 89 inch lbs. (10 Nm), except for the two rear bolts. Tighten them to 17 ft. lbs. (23 Nm).
8. Install the oil cooler line clip.
9. Install the oil level tube.
10. Install the flywheel cover.

A. RTV sealant
110. Oil pump
111. Bolt
112. Oil pan rear seal

84903160

Fig. 143 Oil pan — 6.2L engines

11. Connect the batteries.
12. Install the dipstick.
13. Fill the crankcase.

Oil Pump

REMOVAL & INSTALLATION

4.3L, 5.0L, 5.7L and 7.4L Engines

See Figures 144, 145 and 146

1. Remove the oil pan.
2. Remove the bolt attaching the pump to the rear main bearing cap. Remove the pump and the extension shaft, which will come out behind it.

To install:

3. If the pump has been disassembled, is being replaced, or for any reason oil has been removed from it, it must be

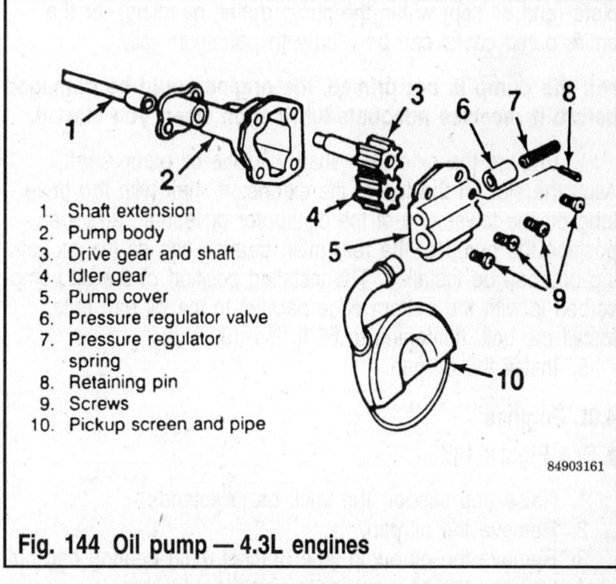

Fig. 144 Oil pump — 4.3L engines

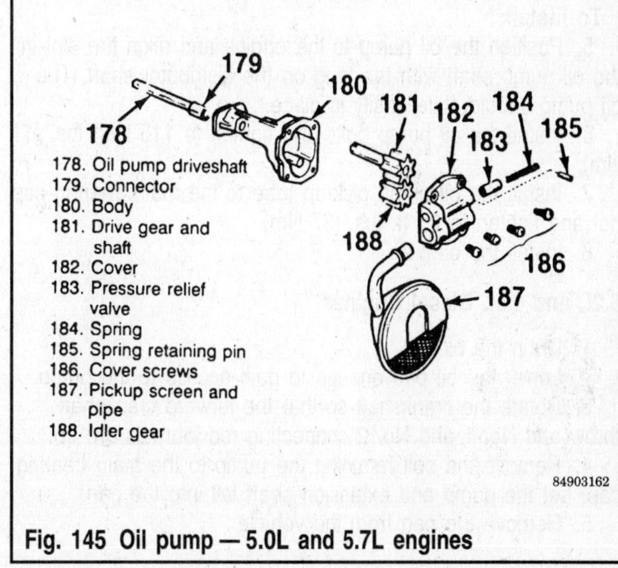

Fig. 145 Oil pump — 5.0L and 5.7L engines

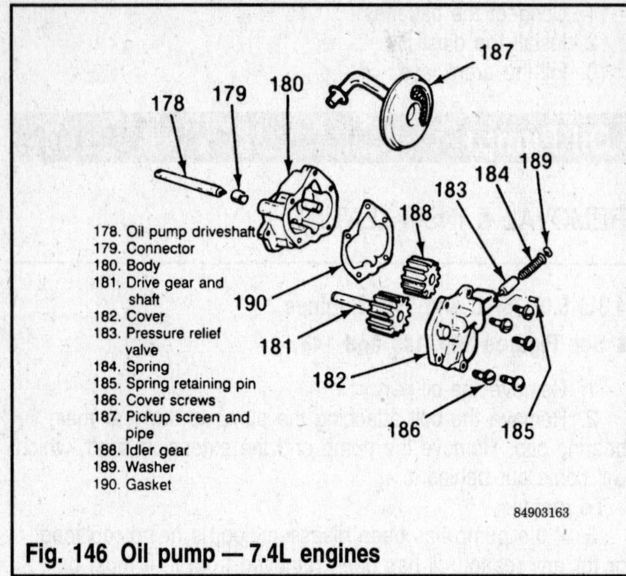

Fig. 146 Oil pump — 7.4L engines

primed. It can either be filled with oil before installing the cover plate (and oil kept within the pump during handling), or the entire pump cavity can be filled with petroleum jelly.

➡If the pump is not primed, the engine could be damaged before it receives adequate lubrication when you start it.

4. Engage the extension shaft with the oil pump shaft. Align the slot on the top of the extension shaft with the drive tang on the lower end of the distributor driveshaft, and then position the pump at the rear main bearing cap so the mounting bolt can be installed. The installed position of the oil pump screen is with the bottom edge parallel to the oil pan rails. Install the bolt, tightening to 65 ft. lbs. (90 Nm).
5. Install the oil pan.

4.8L Engines

➧ See Figure 147

1. Raise and support the truck on jackstands.
2. Remove the oil pan.
3. Remove the oil pump tube bracket main bearing cap nut.
4. Remove the oil pump bolts and the oil pump.

To install:

5. Position the oil pump to the engine and align the slot in the oil pump shaft with the tang on the distributor shaft. The oil pump should slide easily in place.
6. Install the oil pump bolts and tighten to 115 inch lbs. (11 Nm).
7. Install the oil pump pick-up tube to the main bearing cap nut and tighten to 25 ft. lbs. (37 Nm).
8. Install the oil pan.

6.2L and 6.5L Diesel Engines

1. Drain the oil.
2. Lower the oil pan enough to gain access to the pump.
3. Rotate the crankshaft so that the forward crankshaft throw and No. 1 and No. 2 connecting rod journals are up.
4. Remove the bolt retaining the pump to the main bearing cap. Let the pump and extension shaft fall into the pan.
5. Remove the pan from the vehicle.

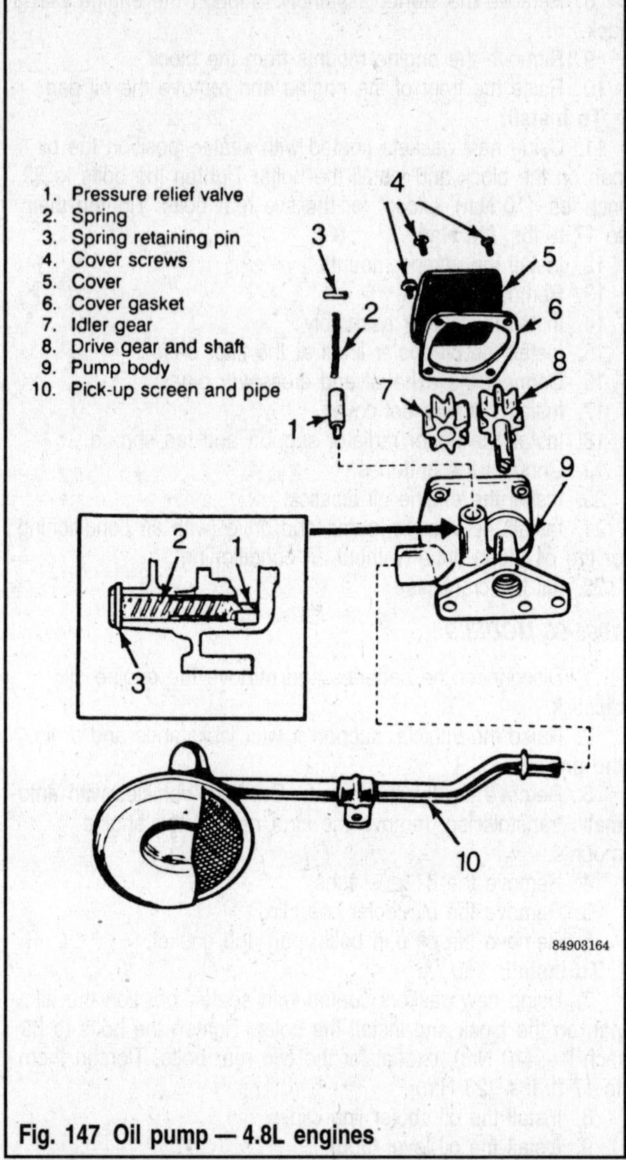

Fig. 147 Oil pump — 4.8L engines

To install:

6. Maneuver the pan, pump and extension shaft into position.
7. Position the pump on the bearing cap.
8. Align the extension shaft hex with the drive hex on the oil pump drive or vacuum pump. The pump should push easily into place. Install the pump and tighten the bolt to 65 ft. lbs. (90 Nm).
9. Install the pan and fill the engine with oil.

INSPECTION

1. Inspect the pump body for wear, cracks or other damage.
2. Inspect the inside of the pump cover for cracks or wear that might allow oil to leak past the gear ends.
3. Inspect the gears for wear.
4. Inspect the drive gear and shaft for improper fit in the pump body.

5. Inspect the pick-up screen and pipe for damage and/or loose fit.
6. Check that the pressure regulator valve slides freely in its bore without sticking or binding.
7. Oil pump gears, cover and body are serviced as a unit. If any single part is damaged, replace the entire assembly.

OVERHAUL

4.8L Engines

1. Remove the cover screws and lift off the cover. Discard the gasket.
2. Matchmark the gear teeth for installation purposes.
3. Remove the drive gear and shaft.
4. Remove the idler gear.
5. Remove the spring retaining pin.
6. Remove the spring.
7. Remove the pressure relief valve.
8. If replacement is necessary, remove the pickup screen and pipe. The pipe is a press-fit.
9. Check all parts for wear and/or damage. Check the gears for looseness and wear. Check the drive gear and shaft for looseness and wear. If any parts are suspect, replace them. The gears, cover and body are not serviced separately. The regulator valve should slide freely in its bore without sticking or binding.

To assemble:

10. Install the pressure relief valve.
11. Install the spring.
12. Install the spring retaining pin.
13. Install the drive gear and shaft.
14. Install the idler gear with the smooth side of the gear towards the cover opening. Align the matchmarks.
15. Install a new gasket with the cover. Tighten the cover screws to 70 inch lbs. (8 Nm).

Except 4.8L Engines

1. Remove the oil pump driveshaft extension.
2. Remove the cotter pin, spring and the pressure regulator valve.

➡Place your thumb over the pressure regulator bore before removing the cotter pin, as the spring is under pressure.

3. Remove the oil pump cover attaching screws and remove the oil pump cover and gasket. Clean the pump in solvent or kerosene, and wash out the pickup screen.
4. Remove the drive gear and the idler gear from the pump body.
5. Check the gears for scoring and other damage. Install the gears if in good condition or replace them if damaged. Check gear end clearance by placing a straightedge over the gears and measuring the clearance between the straightedge and the gasket surface with a feeler gauge. End clearance is 0.002 in. (0.051mm) to 0.0065 in. (0.165mm). If end clearance is excessive, check for scores in the cover that would bring the total clearance over the specs.
6. Check the gear side clearance by inserting the feeler gauge between the gear teeth and the side of the pump body. Clearance should be between 0.002 in. (0.051mm) and 0.005 in. (0.127mm).

To assemble:

7. Pack the inside of the pump completely with petroleum jelly. DO NOT USE ENGINE OIL. The pump MUST be primed this way or it will not produce any oil pressure when the engine is started.
8. Install the cover screws and tighten alternately and evenly to 8 ft. lbs. (11 Nm).
9. Position the pressure valve into the pump cover, closed end first, then install the spring and retaining pin.

➡When assembling the driveshaft extension into the driveshaft, the end of the extension nearest the washers must be inserted into the driveshaft.

10. Insert the driveshaft extension through the opening in the main bearing cap and block until the shaft mates into the distributor drive gear.
11. Install the pump onto the rear main bearing cap and install the attaching bolts. Tighten the bolts to 35 ft. lbs. (47 Nm).
12. Install the pan and fill the engine with oil.

Crankshaft Damper

REMOVAL & INSTALLATION

See Figures 148, 149 and 150

➡A torsional damper puller tool is required to perform this procedure.

1. Disconnect the negative battery cable.
2. Remove the fan shroud assembly.
3. Remove the fan belts, fan and pulley.
4. If necessary, remove the radiator.
5. Remove the accessory drive pulley (crankshaft pulley on diesel engines).
6. Remove the torsional damper bolt.

87983p67

Fig. 148 Remove the accessory drive pulley bolts

87983p68

Fig. 149 Remove the accessory drive pulley and the damper bolt from the vehicle

87983p69

Fig. 150 Remove the crankshaft damper using the puller tool

7. Remove the torsional damper using tool # J-39046 or its equivalent puller.

➡Make sure you do not lose the crankshaft key, if it has been removed.

To install:

8. Coat the crankshaft stub with engine oil.
9. Position the crankshaft key if one was used. If you pulled the crank seal, replace it with the open end facing in.

➡The inertial weight section of the damper is attached to the hub with a rubber-like material. The correct installation procedures, with the proper tools, MUST be followed or the resultant movement of the inertial weight will destroy the tuning of the damper!

10. Thread the stud on the tool into the end of the crankshaft.
11. Position the damper on the shaft and tap it into place with a plastic mallet (lightly!). Make sure the key is in place by securing it with a little RTV sealant.
12. Install the bearing, washer and nut and then turn the nut until the damper is pulled into position. Remove the tool.
13. Make sure the damper is all the way on, then install the bolt. Tighten the bolt as follows:
    - 4.3L, 5.0L & 5.7L engines: 70 ft. lbs. (95 Nm)
    - 4.8L engine: 50 ft. lbs. (70 Nm)
    - 6.2L & 6.5L engine: 200 ft. lbs. (270 Nm)
    - 7.4L engine: 85 ft. lbs. (115 Nm)
14. Install the remaining components and road test the truck.

Timing Chain Cover

REMOVAL & INSTALLATION

4.3L, 5.0L and 5.7L Engines

➧ See Figures 151, 152, 153, 154, 155, 156, 157, 158 and 159

1. Drain the cooling system. On V8 engines, drain the oil and remove the oil pan.
2. Remove the crankshaft pulley and damper. Remove the water pump. Remove the screws holding the timing case cover to the block and remove the cover and gaskets.
3. Use a suitable tool to pry the old seal out of the front face of the cover.

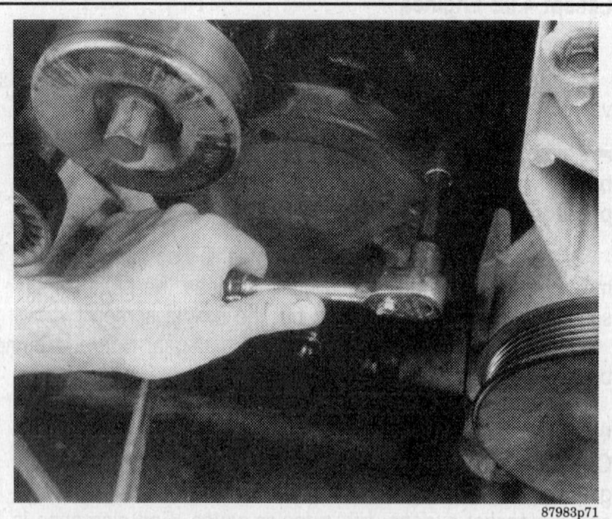
87983p71

Fig. 151 Remove the timing cover bolts

87983p72

Fig. 152 Remove the timing cover from the engine

87983p74

Fig. 154 Installing the new seal in the front cover

To install:

4. Install the new seal so that the open end is toward the inside of the cover.

➡**Coat the lip of the new seal with oil prior to installation.**

5. Check that the timing chain oil slinger is in place against the crankshaft sprocket.
6. Apply sealer to the front cover as shown in the accompanying illustration. Install the cover carefully onto the locating dowels.
7. Tighten the attaching screws to 124 inch lbs. (14 Nm) on the 4.3L and 100 inch lbs. (11 Nm) on the 5.0L and 5.7L.
8. Install the remaining components and fill the engine with oil and coolant. Road test the truck.

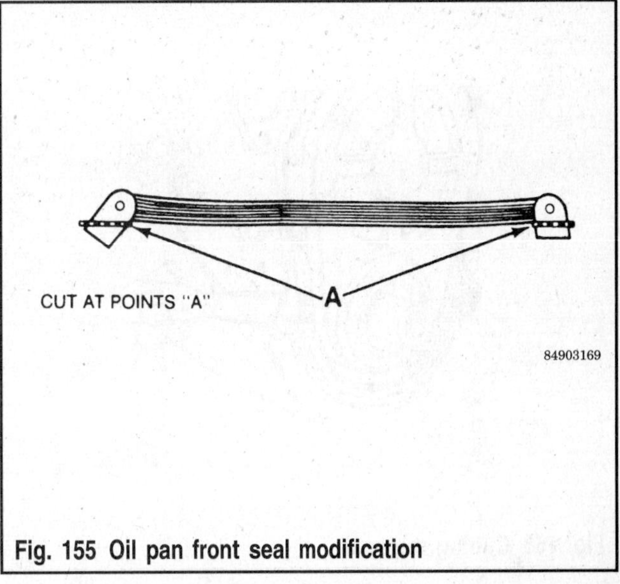

84903169

Fig. 155 Oil pan front seal modification

7.4L Engines

➡**Special tool J-22102, or its equivalent seal driver, will be necessary for this job.**

1. Disconnect the negative battery cable.
2. Drain the cooling system.

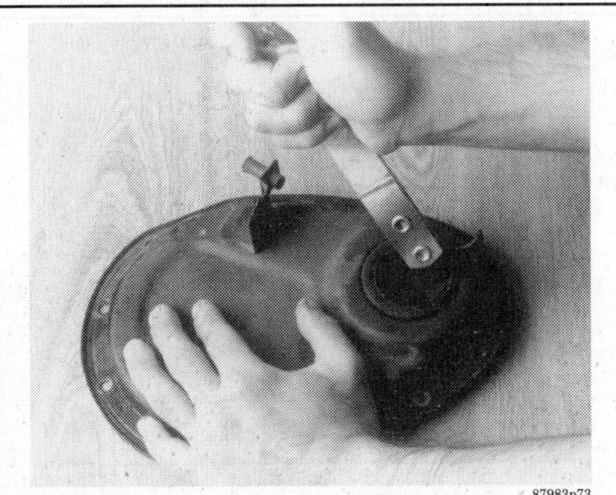
87983p73

Fig. 153 Using a seal puller remove the old seal from the front cover

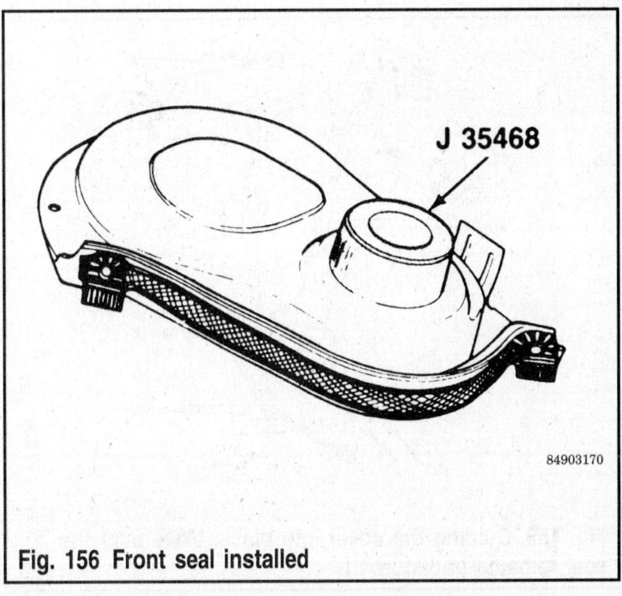

84903170

Fig. 156 Front seal installed

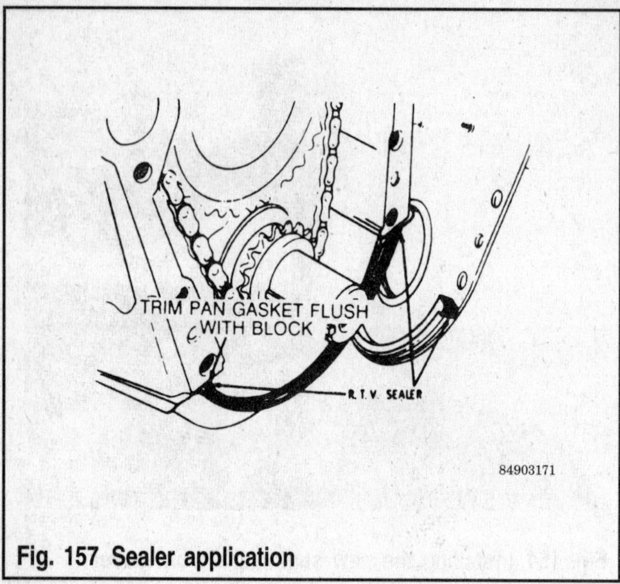

Fig. 157 Sealer application

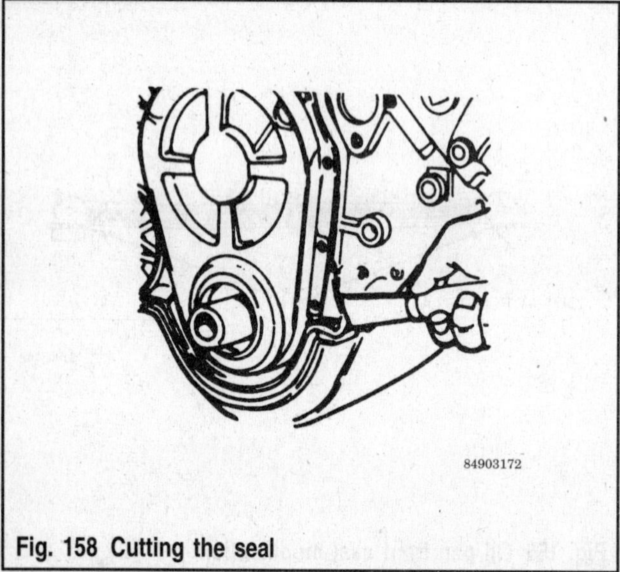

Fig. 158 Cutting the seal

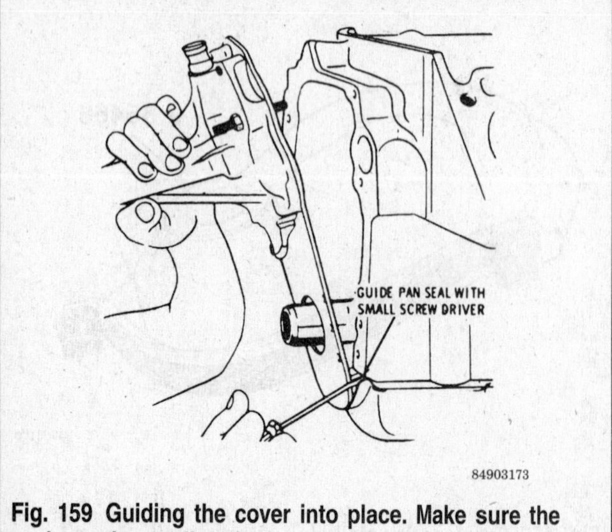

Fig. 159 Guiding the cover into place. Make sure the seal remains undisturbed

3. Remove the water pump.
4. Remove the crankshaft pulley and damper.
5. Remove the oil pan-to-front cover bolts.
6. Remove the screws holding the timing case cover to the block, pull the cover forward enough to cut the front oil pan seal. Cut the seal flush with the block on both sides.
7. Pull off the cover and gaskets.
8. Use a suitable tool to pry the old seal out of the front face of the cover.

To install:

9. Using seal driver J-22102, or equivalent, install the new seal so that the open end is toward the inside of the cover.

➡Coat the lip of the new seal with oil prior to installation.

10. Install a new front pan seal, cutting the tabs off.
11. Coat a new cover gasket with adhesive sealer and position it on the block.
12. Apply a 1/8 in. (bead of RTV gasket material to the front cover. Install the cover carefully onto the locating dowel.
13. Tighten the attaching screws to 96 inch lbs. (11 Nm).
14. Tighten the cover-to-pan bolts to 70 inch lbs. (8 Nm).
15. Install the damper.
16. Install the water pump.
17. Connect the battery cables and fill the cooling system.

6.2L and 6.5L Diesel Engines

➧ See Figure 160

1. Drain the cooling system.
2. Remove the water pump.
3. Rotate the crankshaft to align the marks on the injection pump driven gear and the camshaft gear as shown in the illustration.
4. Scribe a mark aligning the injection pump flange and the front cover.
5. Remove the crankshaft pulley and torsional damper.
6. Remove the front cover-to-oil pan bolts (4).
7. Remove the two fuel return line clips.
8. Remove the injection pump retaining nuts from the front cover.
9. Remove the baffle. Remove the remaining cover bolts, and remove the front cover.

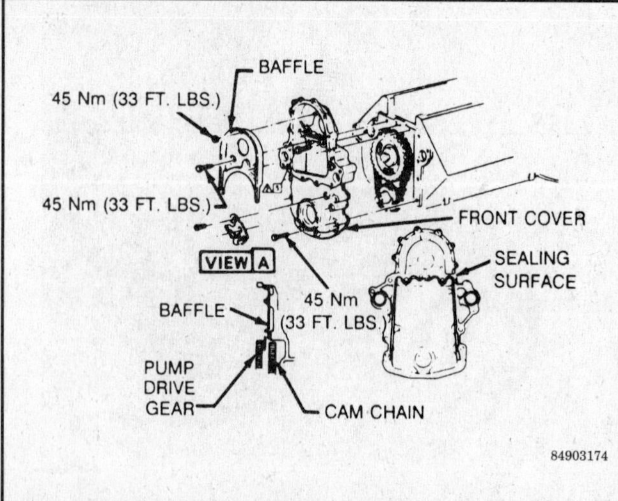

Fig. 160 Front cover installation showing sealer application — diesel engines

10. If the front cover oil seal is to be replaced, it can now be pried out of the cover with a suitable prying tool. Press the new seal into the cover evenly.

➡The oil seal can also be replaced with the front cover installed. Remove the torsional damper first, then pry the old seal out of the cover using a suitable prying tool. Use care not to damage the surface of the crankshaft. Install the new seal evenly into the cover and install the damper.

To install:

11. To install the front cover, first clean both sealing surfaces until all traces of old sealer are gone. Apply a 3/32 in. (2mm) bead of sealant (GM sealant #1052357 or equivalent) to the sealing surface as shown in the illustration. Apply a bead of RTV type sealer to the bottom portion of the front cover which attached to the oil pan. Install the front cover.
12. Install the baffle.
13. Install the injection pump, making sure the scribe marks on the pump and front cover are aligned.
14. Install the injection pump driven gear, making sure the marks on the cam gear and pump are aligned. Be sure the dowel pin and the three holes on the pump flange are also aligned.
15. Install the fuel line clips, the front cover-to-oil bolts, and the torsional damper and crankshaft pulley. Tighten the pan bolts to 89 inch lbs. (10 Nm), the cover-to-block bolts to 33 ft. lbs. (45 Nm), the baffle bolts and nut to 33 ft. lbs. (45 Nm), the injection pump nuts to 31 ft. lbs. (42 Nm) and the injection pump bolts to 17 ft. lbs. (23 Nm).

Timing Gear Cover and Seal

REMOVAL & INSTALLATION

4.8L Engines

1. Disconnect the negative battery cable.
2. Drain the cooling system.
3. Remove the water pump.
4. Remove the crankshaft pulley and damper.
5. Remove the oil pan-to-front cover bolts.
6. Remove the screws holding the timing case cover to the block, pull the cover forward enough to cut the front oil pan seal. Cut the seal flush with the block on both sides.
7. Pull off the cover and gaskets.
8. Use a suitable tool to pry the old seal out of the front face of the cover.

To install:

9. Lubricate the new seal lip with engine oil and using a seal centering tool and installer J-23042, or equivalent, press the new seal into place. Leave the tool in position on the seal.
10. Install a new front pan seal, cutting the tabs off.
11. Coat a new cover gasket with adhesive sealer and position it on the block.
12. Apply a 1/8in. (3.17mm) bead of RTV gasket material to the front cover. Install the cover carefully in place with the centering tool still attached.
13. Tighten the timing gear cover to block bolts to 80 inch lbs. (9 Nm).
14. Tighten the cover-to-pan bolts to 45 inch lbs. (6 Nm).
15. Install the damper.
16. Install the water pump.
17. Connect the battery cables and fill the cooling system.

Timing Chain

REMOVAL & INSTALLATION

4.3L, 5.0L, 5.7L and 7.4L Engines

See Figures 161, 162, 163, 164 and 165

1. Remove the radiator, water pump, the torsional damper and the crankcase front cover. This will allow access to the timing chain.
2. Crank the engine until the timing marks on both sprockets are nearest each other and in line between the shaft centers.
3. On 1996 vehicles remove the crankshaft position sensor reluctor ring. On 7.4L engines tool J-41371 or its equivalent puller must be used to remove the reluctor ring.
4. Take out the bolts that hold the camshaft gear to the camshaft. This gear is a light press fit on the camshaft and will come off easily. It is located by a dowel. The chain comes off with the camshaft gear.

➡A gear puller will be required to remove the crankshaft gear.

To install:

5. Without disturbing the position of the engine, mount the new crankshaft gear on the shaft, and mount the chain over the camshaft gear. Arrange the camshaft gear in such a way that the timing marks will line up between the shaft centers and the camshaft locating dowel will enter the dowel hole in the cam sprocket.
6. Place the cam sprocket, with its chain mounted over it, in position on the front of the truck and pull up with the three bolts that hold it to the camshaft.
7. After the gears are in place, turn the engine two full revolutions to make certain that the timing marks are in correct

87983p75

Fig. 161 Crank the engine until the timing marks on both sprockets are in line

87983p76

Fig. 162 Remove the camshaft gear retaining bolts

87983p78

Fig. 164 A gear puller will be required to remove the crankshaft gear

87983p77

Fig. 163 Remove the camshaft gear and timing chain

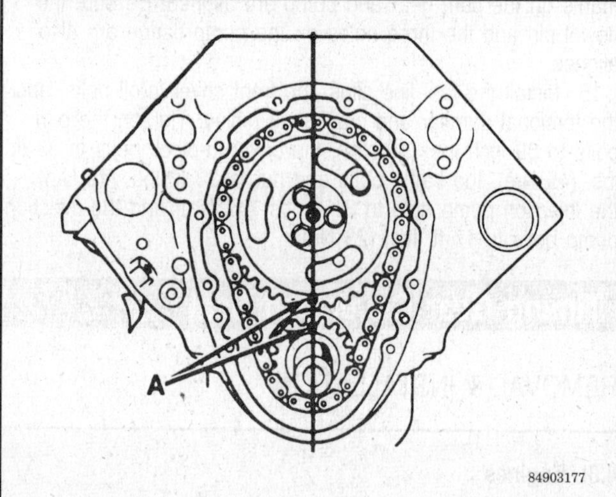

84903177

Fig. 165 Timing mark alignment — 4.3L, 5.0L, 5.7L and 7.4L engines

alignment between the shaft centers. Tighten the camshaft sprocket bolts (and nut on the 4.3L) to 21 ft. lbs. (28 Nm). On the 7.4L, tighten them to 20 ft. lbs. (26 Nm).

➡When installing the crankshaft position sensor you must use install a new oil ring seal onto the sensor.

8. Install the crankshaft position sensor reluctor ring onto the crankshaft until it is firmly seated against the crankshaft sprocket. On 1996 7.4L vehicles replace the reluctor ring with a new component.

9. Install the front cover, torsional damper, water pump and the radiator.

End-play of the camshaft is zero.

6.2L and 6.5L Diesel Engines

➧ See Figures 166 and 167

1. Remove the front cover.

2. Remove the bolt and washer attaching the camshaft gear and the injection pump gear. Crank the engine until the timing marks on both sprockets are nearest each other and inline between the shaft centers.

3. Remove the camshaft sprocket, timing chain and crankshaft sprocket as a unit.

To install:

4. Install the camshaft sprocket, timing chain and crankshaft sprocket as a unit, aligning the timing marks on the sprockets as shown in the illustration. Tighten the camshaft gear bolt to 75 ft. lbs. (100 Nm).

5. Rotate the crankshaft 360° so that the camshaft gear and the injection pump gear are aligned as shown in the illustration (accompanying the diesel Front Cover Removal Procedure). Tighten the bolt to 17 ft. lbs. (23 Nm).

6. Install the front cover as previously detailed. The injection pump must be re-timed since the timing chain assembly was removed. See Section 5 for this procedure.

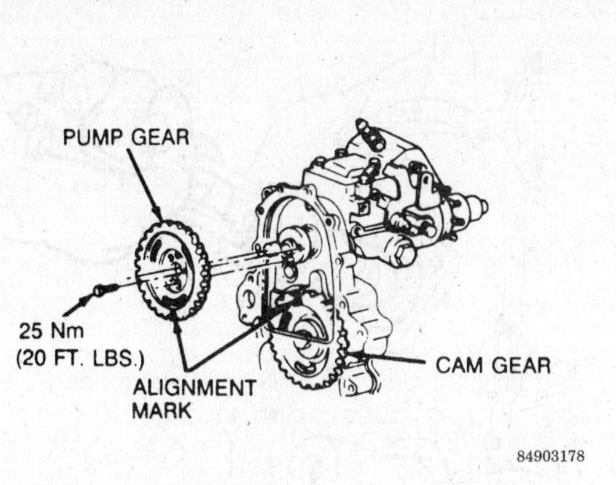

Fig. 166 Timing mark alignment — 6.2L and 6.5L engines

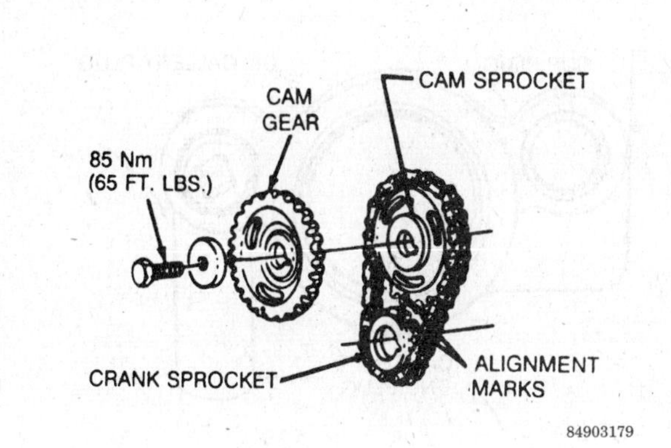

Fig. 167 Timing chain installation — 6.2L and 6.5L engines

Timing Gears

REMOVAL & INSTALLATION

4.8L Engines

➧ **See Figure 168**

The camshaft on these engines is gear driven, unlike the chain driven V6 and V8 engines. The camshaft must be removed to replace the gear.

1. Disconnect the negative battery cable. Remove the camshaft and place in an arbor press.

➡**Support the camshaft gear not the thrust plate.**

2. Press the gear off of the camshaft and remove the thrust plate and the spacer.

To install:

3. Support the camshaft at the front journal with tool J-22912-01 or equivalent, and mount the camshaft in a press.
4. Lubricate the thrust plate with engine oil.
5. Install the key if removed.
6. Install the spacer making sure the chamfer in the spacer faces toward the journal radius.
7. Install the thrust plate.
8. Install the camshaft gear on with the timing mark to the outside and press the gear on until it bottoms on the spacer.
9. Remove the camshaft from the press.

➡**The clearance between the camshaft and thrust plate should be 0.003-0.008 in.**

Camshaft

REMOVAL & INSTALLATION

4.3L, 5.0L and 5.7L Engines

➧ **See Figures 169, 170, 171, 172 and 173**

1. Disconnect the negative battery cable.

⁂CAUTION

When draining engine coolant, keep in mind that cats and dogs are attracted to ethylene glycol antifreeze and could drink any that is left in an uncovered container or in puddles on the ground. This will prove fatal in sufficient quantity. Always drain coolant into a sealable container. Coolant should be reused unless it is contaminated or is several years old.

2. Drain the coolant and remove the radiator.
3. If the vehicle is equipped with a mechanical fuel pump remove it.
4. Disconnect the throttle cable and the air cleaner.
5. Remove the drive belt(s), loosen the alternator bolts and move the alternator to one side.

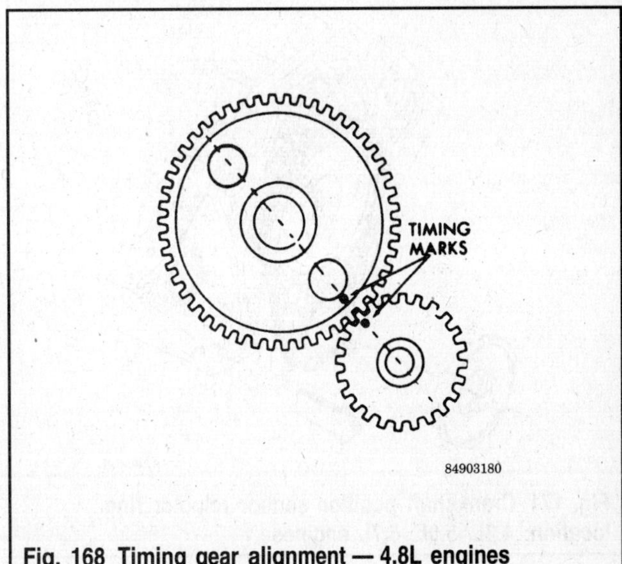

Fig. 168 Timing gear alignment — 4.8L engines

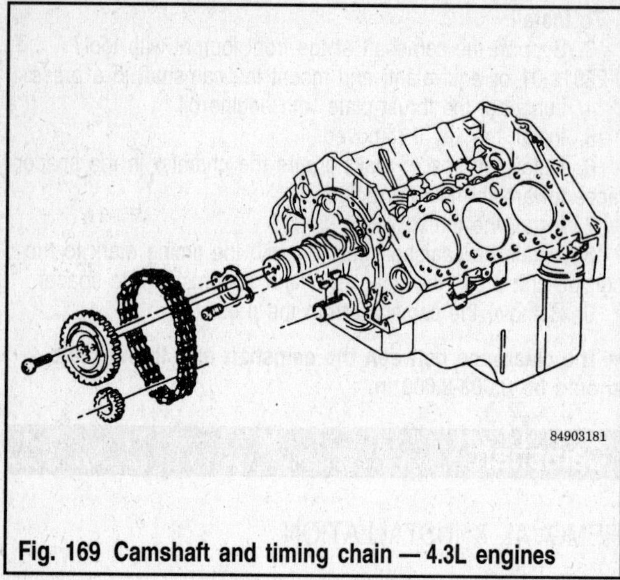

Fig. 169 Camshaft and timing chain — 4.3L engines

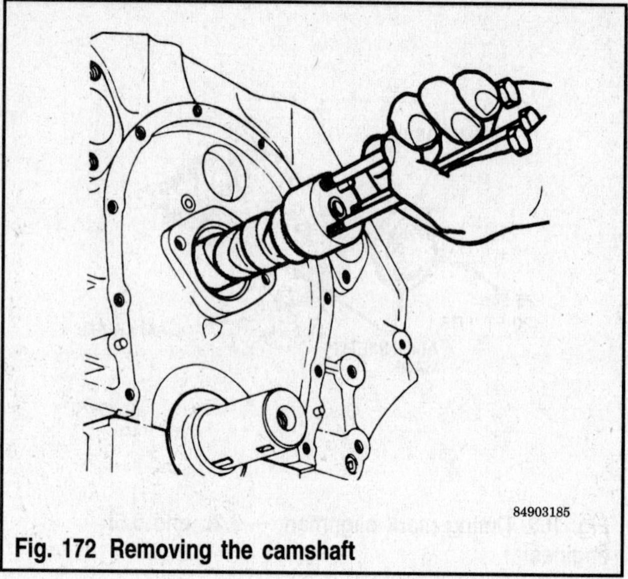

Fig. 172 Removing the camshaft

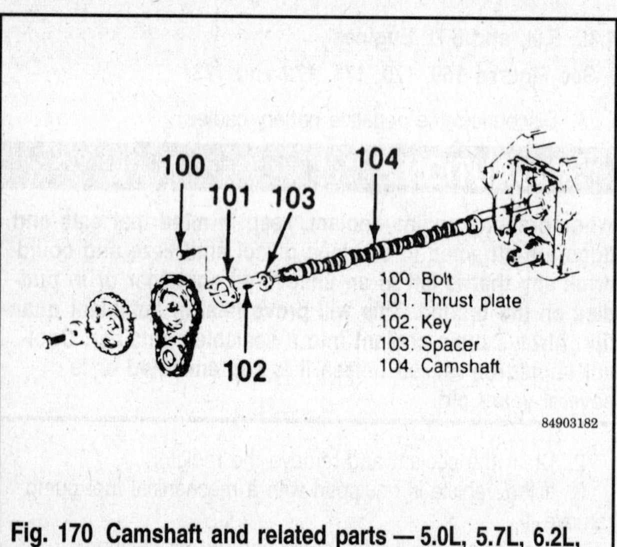

Fig. 170 Camshaft and related parts — 5.0L, 5.7L, 6.2L, 6.5L and 7.4L engines

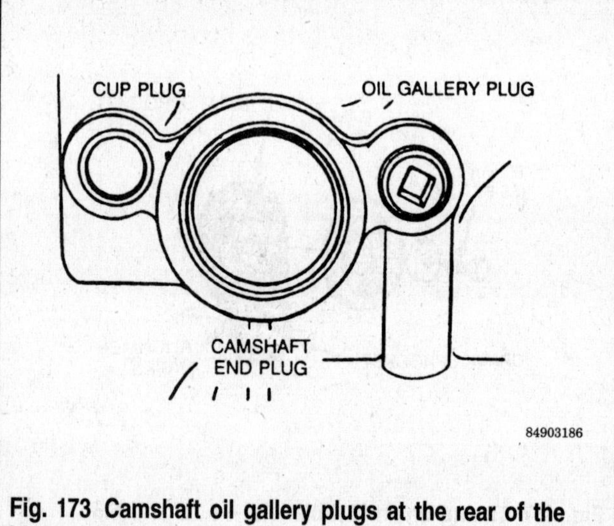

Fig. 173 Camshaft oil gallery plugs at the rear of the block

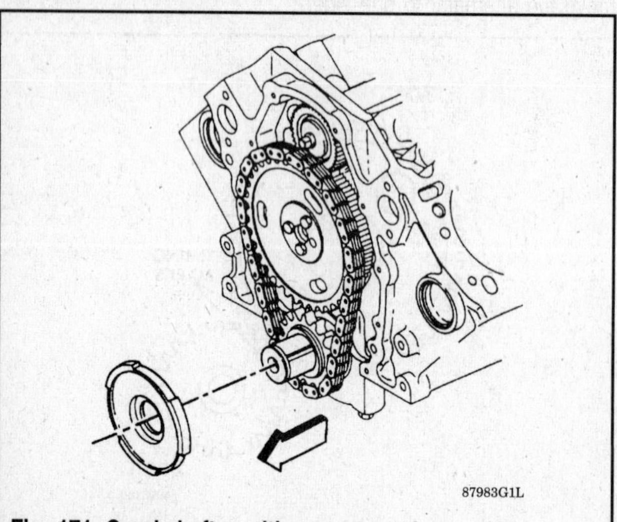

Fig. 171 Crankshaft position sensor reluctor ring location: 4.3L, 5.0L, 5.7L engines

6. Remove the power steering pump from its brackets and move it out of the way.
7. Remove the air conditioning compressor from its brackets and move the compressor out of the way without disconnecting the lines.
8. Disconnect the hoses from the water pump.
9. Disengage and tag the electrical and vacuum connections.
10. Mark the distributor as to location in the block. Remove the distributor.
11. Raise the truck and drain the oil.
12. Remove the exhaust crossover pipe and starter motor.
13. Disconnect the exhaust pipe at the manifold.
14. Remove the torsional damper and pulley.
15. Support the engine and remove the front motor mounts.
16. Remove the flywheel inspection cover.
17. Remove the oil pan.
18. Support the engine by placing wooden blocks between the exhaust manifolds and the front crossmember.
19. Remove the front cover.

20. Remove the cylinder head covers.
21. Remove the intake manifold, oil filler pipe, and temperature sending switch.
22. Mark the lifters, pushrods, and rocker arms as to location so that they may be installed in the same position. Remove these parts.

****CAUTION**

Please refer to Section 1 before discharging the compressor or disconnecting air conditioning lines. Damage to the air conditioning system or personal injury could result. Consult your local laws concerning refrigerant discharge and recycling. In many areas it may be illegal for anyone but a certified technician to service the A/C system. Always use an approved recovery station when discharging the air conditioning.

23. If the truck is equipped with air conditioning, discharge the air conditioning system and remove the condenser.
24. On carbureted engines remove the fuel pump eccentric, camshaft gear, oil slinger, and timing chain.
25. Remove the camshaft thrust plate (on front of camshaft) on the 4.3L.
26. Install 2 or 3 $^5/_{16}$-18 bolts, 4-5 in. (101-127mm) long, into the threaded holes in the end of the shaft. Carefully remove the camshaft from the engine.
27. Inspect the camshaft for signs of excessive wear or damage.

To install:

28. Liberally coat camshaft and bearing with heavy engine oil, engine assembly lubricant or engine oil supplement, and carefully insert the cam into the engine.
29. Align the timing marks on the camshaft and crankshaft gears. (refer to timing chain removal and installation).
30. Install the distributor using the locating marks made during removal. If any problems are encountered, refer to distributor removal and installation.
31. Install the camshaft thrust plate (on front of camshaft) on the 4.3L. Tighten the bolts to 105 inch lbs. (12 Nm).
32. Install the timing chain, oil slinger, camshaft gear, and fuel pump eccentric.
33. Install the condenser. If the truck is equipped with air conditioning, charge the air conditioning system.
34. Install the lifters, pushrods, and rocker arms.
35. Install the temperature sending switch.
36. Install the oil filler pipe.
37. Install the intake manifold.
38. Install the cylinder head covers.
39. Install the front cover.
40. Install the oil pan.
41. Install the front motor mounts.
42. Remove the wood blocks.
43. Install the flywheel inspection cover.
44. Install the torsional damper and pulley.
45. Connect the exhaust pipe at the manifold.
46. Install the exhaust crossover pipe.
47. Install the starter motor.
48. Install the flywheel inspection cover.
49. Connect the electrical wiring.
50. Connect all vacuum connections.
51. Connect the hoses at the water pump.
52. Install the air conditioning compressor.
53. Install the timing indicator.
54. Install the power steering pump.
55. Install the alternator and drive belt (s).
56. Connect the throttle cable.
57. Install the air cleaner.
58. Install the fuel pump, if removed.
59. Install the radiator.
60. Connect the battery.
61. Fill the crankcase.
62. Fill the cooling system.

4.8L Engines

See Figures 173, 174 and 175

1. Remove the grille. Remove the radiator hoses and remove the radiator.
2. Remove the hydraulic lifters.
3. Remove the timing gear cover.
4. Remove the fuel pump.
5. Remove the distributor.
6. Align the timing marks on the camshaft and crankshaft gears.
7. Remove the camshaft thrust plate bolts.
8. Support and carefully remove the camshaft.
9. If either the camshaft or the camshaft gear is being renewed, the gear must be pressed off the camshaft. The replacement parts must be assembled in the same way. When placing the gear on the camshaft, press the gear onto the shaft until it bottoms against the gear spacer ring. The end clearance of the thrust plate should be 0.003-0.008 in. -0.031mm)

To install:

10. Pre-lube the camshaft lobes with clean engine oil or engine oil supplement, and then install the camshaft assembly in the engine. Be careful not to damage the bearings.
11. Turn the crankshaft and the camshaft gears so that the timing marks align. Push the camshaft into position and install and tighten the thrust plate bolts to 80 inch lbs. (9 Nm).
12. Check camshaft and crankshaft gear runout with a dial indicator. Camshaft gear runout should not exceed 0.004 in. (0.012mm) and crankshaft gear run-out should not be above 0.003 in. (0.011mm).
13. Using a dial indicator, check the backlash at several points between the camshaft and crankshaft gear teeth. Backlash should be 0.004-0.006 inches. (0.015-0.023mm).
14. Install the timing gear cover.
15. Install the distributor.
16. Install the fuel pump.
17. Install the valve lifters and the pushrods.
18. Install the radiator and fill with coolant.

7.4L Engines

See Figures 170, 172, 173 and 176

1. Disconnect the negative battery cable.
2. Remove the air cleaner.
3. Remove the grille.
4. Remove the air conditioning compressor from its brackets and move the compressor out of the way without disconnecting the lines.
5. Drain the cooling system.
6. Remove the fan shroud and radiator.

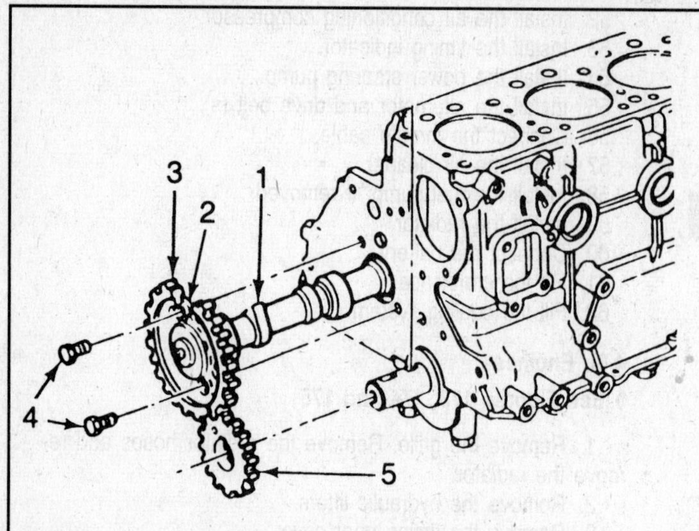

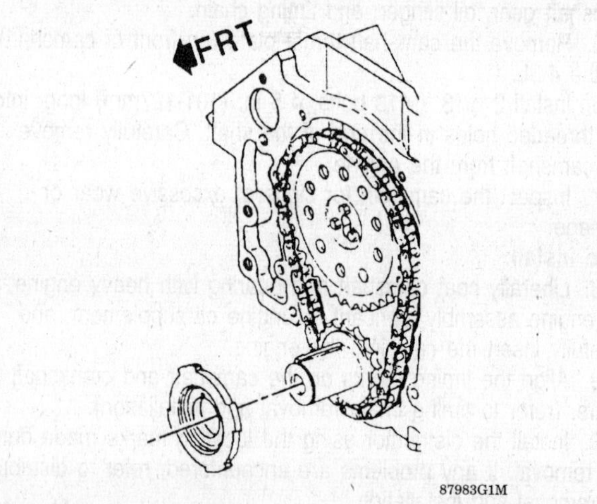

Fig. 174 Camshaft and related parts — 4.8L engines

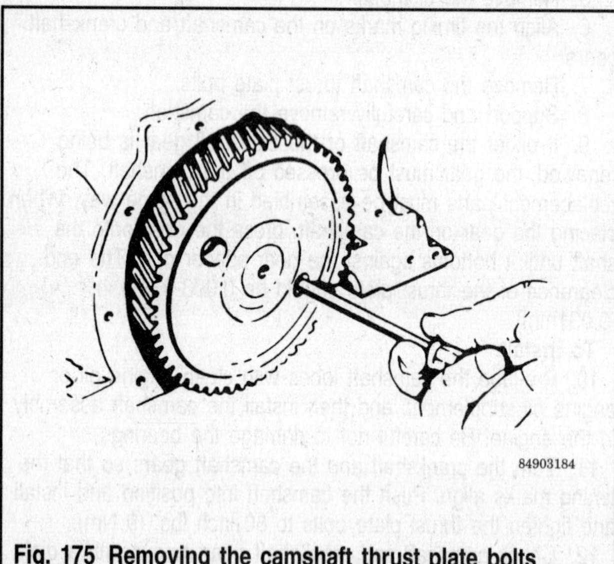

Fig. 175 Removing the camshaft thrust plate bolts

Fig. 176 Crankshaft position sensor reluctor ring location — 7.4L engines

7. Remove the drive belt(s), loosen the alternator bolts and move the alternator to one side.
8. Remove the cylinder head covers.
9. Disconnect the hoses from the water pump.
10. Remove the water pump.
11. Remove the torsional damper and pulley.
12. Remove the front cover.
13. Mark the distributor as to location in the block. Remove the distributor.
14. Remove the intake manifold.
15. Mark the lifters, pushrods, and rocker arms as to location so that they may be installed in the same position. Remove these parts.
16. Rotate the camshaft so that the timing marks align.
17. Remove the camshaft sprocket bolts.
18. Pull the camshaft sprocket and timing chain off. The sprocket is a tight fit, so you'll have to tap it loose with a plastic mallet.
19. Install two 5/16 in.-18 bolts in the holes in the front of the camshaft and carefully pull the camshaft from the block.

To install:

20. Liberally coat camshaft and bearing with heavy engine oil or engine assembly lubricant and insert the cam into the engine.
21. Install the distributor using the locating marks made during removal. (If any problems are encountered, refer to distributor removal and installation)
22. Install the camshaft sprocket bolts and tighten them to 20 ft. lbs. (27 Nm).
23. Install the lifters, pushrods, and rocker.
24. Install the intake manifold.
25. Install the front cover.
26. Install the torsional damper and pulley.
27. Install the water pump.
28. Connect the hoses at the water pump.
29. Install the cylinder head covers.
30. Install the alternator and drive belt(s).
31. Install the fan shroud and radiator.
32. Fill the cooling system.
33. Install the air conditioning compressor.

34. Install the grille.
35. Install the air cleaner.
36. Connect the battery.

6.2L and 6.5L Diesel Engines

See Figures 170, 172 and 173

1. Disconnect the negative battery cable.
2. Raise the truck and safely support it with jackstands.
3. Drain the cooling system, including the block.
4. Disconnect the exhaust pipes at the manifolds. Remove the fan shroud.
5. Lower the truck.
6. Remove the radiator and fan.
7. Remove the vacuum pump and the intake manifolds as previously detailed.
8. Remove the injection pump and fuel lines. Make sure you cap all injection lines to prevent dirt from entering the system, and tag the lines for later installation.
9. Remove the water pump.
10. Remove the injection pump drive gear.
11. Scribe a mark aligning the line on the injection pump flange to the front cover.
12. Remove the injection pump from the cover.
13. Remove the power steering pump and the generator and lay them aside.
14. If the truck is equipped with air conditioning, remove the compressor (with the lines attached) and position it out of the way.
15. Remove the cylinder head covers.
16. Remove the rocker shaft assemblies and pushrods. Place the pushrods in order in a rack (easily by punching holes in a piece of heavy cardboard and numbering the holes) so that they can be installed in correct order.
17. Remove the thermostat housing and the crossover from the cylinder heads.
18. Remove the cylinder heads as previously detailed, with the exhaust manifolds attached.
19. Remove the valve lifter clamps, guide plates and valve lifters. Place these parts in a rack so they can be installed in the correct order.
20. Remove the front cover.
21. Remove the timing chain assembly.
22. Remove the fuel pump. Remove the front engine mount through-bolts.
23. Remove the camshaft retainer plate.

CAUTION

Please refer to Section 1 before discharging the compressor or disconnecting air conditioning lines. Damage to the air conditioning system or personal injury could result. Consult your local laws concerning refrigerant discharge and recycling. In many areas it may be illegal for anyone but a certified technician to service the A/C system. Always use an approved recovery station when discharging the air conditioning.

24. If the truck is equipped with air conditioning, discharge the air conditioning system and remove the condenser. Have an assistant help in lifting the condenser out of the way.
25. Remove the camshaft by carefully sliding it out of the block.

Whenever a new camshaft installed, GM recommends replacing all the valve lifters, as well as the oil filter. The engine oil must be changed. These measures will help ensure proper wear characteristics of the new camshaft.

To install:

26. Coat the camshaft lobes with Molykote® or an equivalent lube. Liberally tube the camshaft journals with clean engine oil and install the camshaft carefully.
27. Install the camshaft retainer plate and tighten the bolts to 17 ft. lbs. (23 Nm).
28. Install the front engine mount bolts and tighten them to 70 ft. lbs. (95 Nm). Tighten the nut to 50 ft. lbs. (70 Nm).
29. Install the fuel pump.
30. Install the timing chain assembly.
31. Install the front cover.
32. Install the valve lifters, guide plates and clamps, and rotate the crankshaft so that the lifters are free to travel.
33. Install the cylinder heads.
34. Install the pushrods in their original order. Install the rocker shaft assemblies, then install the cylinder head covers.
35. Install the injection pump to the front cover, making sure the lines on the pump and the scribe line on the front cover are aligned.
36. Install the injection pump driven gear, making sure the gears are aligned. Re-time the injection pump.
37. Install the air conditioning condenser. Charge the system. See Section 1.
38. Install the thermostat housing and the crossover.
39. Install the compressor.
40. Install the power steering pump.
41. Install the alternator.
42. Install the water pump.
43. Install the vacuum pump.
44. Install the intake manifolds.
45. Install the radiator and fan.
46. Install the fan shroud.
47. Connect the exhaust pipes at the manifolds.
48. Fill the cooling system and connect the battery.

INSPECTION

Run-Out

See Figure 177

Camshaft runout should be checked when the camshaft has been removed from the engine. An accurate dial indicator is needed for this procedure; engine specialists and most machine shops have this equipment. If you have access to a dial indicator, or can take your camshaft to someone who does, measure the camshaft bearing journal runout. If the runout exceeds the limit replace the camshaft.

Lobe Height

See Figures 178 and 179

Use a micrometer to check camshaft (lobe) height, making sure the anvil and the spindle of the micrometer are positioned

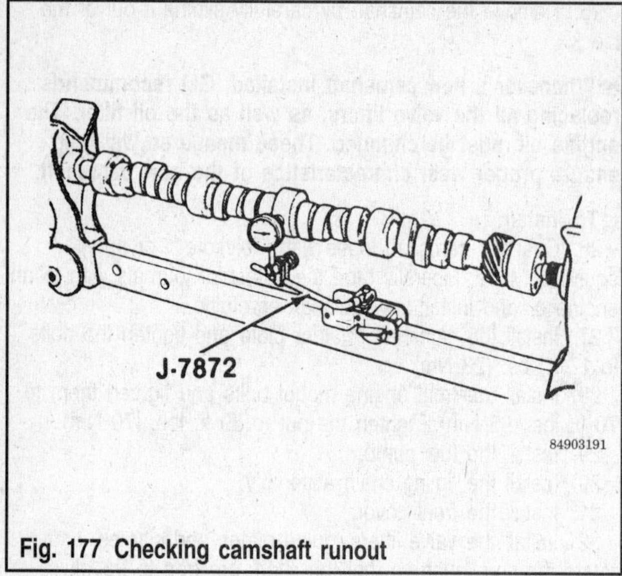

Fig. 177 Checking camshaft runout

directly on the heel and tip of the camshaft lobe as shown in the accompanying illustration.

End-Play

➧ See Figure 180

After the camshaft has been installed, end-play should be checked. The camshaft sprocket should be installed on the cam. Use a dial gauge to check the end-play, by moving the camshaft forward and backward. End-play specifications should be as noted in the Camshaft Specifications chart.

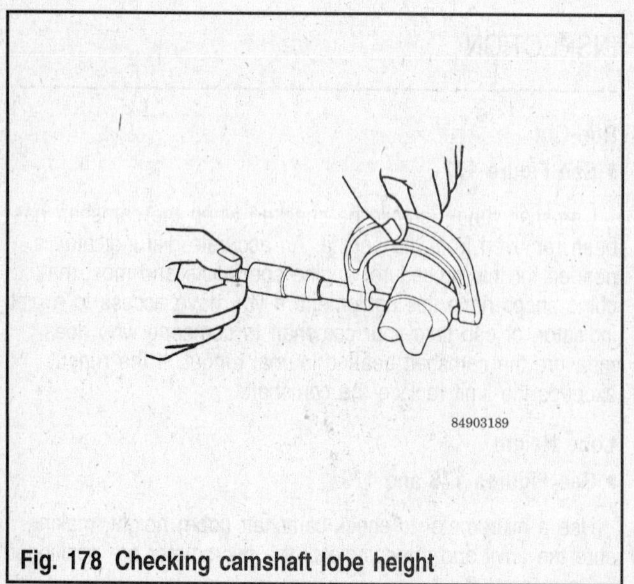

Fig. 178 Checking camshaft lobe height

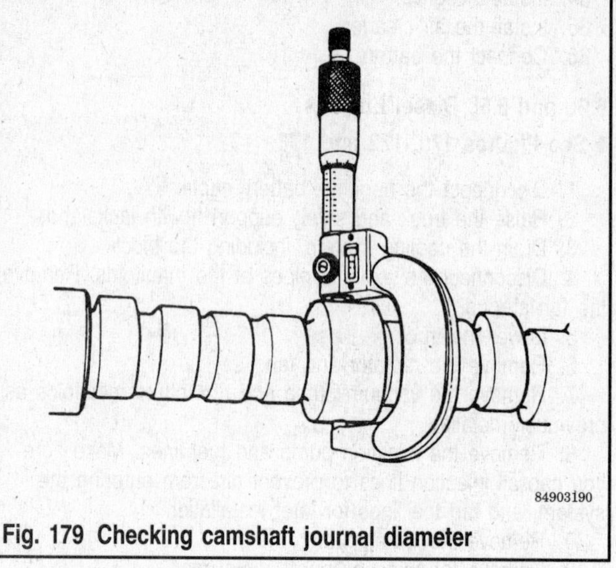

Fig. 179 Checking camshaft journal diameter

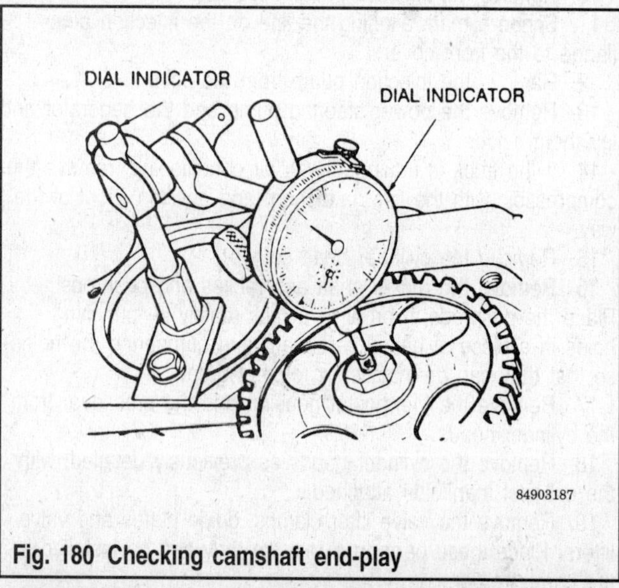

Fig. 180 Checking camshaft end-play

Camshaft Bearings

REMOVAL & INSTALLATION

➧ See Figures 181, 182, 183, 184 and 185

If excessive camshaft wear is found, or if the engine is completely rebuilt, the camshaft bearings should be replaced.

➡**The front and rear bearings should be removed last, and installed first. Those bearings act as guides for the other bearings and pilot.**

1. Drive the camshaft rear plug from the block.
2. Assemble the removal puller with its shoulder on the bearing to be removed. Gradually tighten the puller nut until the bearing is removed.
3. Remove the remaining bearings, leaving the front and rear for last. To remove these, reverse the position of the puller, so as to pull the bearings towards the center of the

block. Leave the tool in this position, pilot the new front and rear bearings on the installer, and pull them into position.

4. Return the puller to its original position and pull the remaining bearings into position.

➡You must make sure that the oil holes of the bearings and block align when installing the bearings. If they don't align, the camshaft will not get proper lubrication and may seize or at least be seriously damaged. To check for correct oil hole alignment, use a piece of brass rod with a 90° bend in the end as shown in the illustration. Check all oil hole openings. The wire must enter each hole, or the hole is not properly aligned.

5. Replace the camshaft rear plug, and stake it into position. On the diesel, coat the outer diameter of the new plug with GM sealant #1052080 or equivalent, and install it flush to $\frac{1}{32}$ in. (0.794mm) deep.

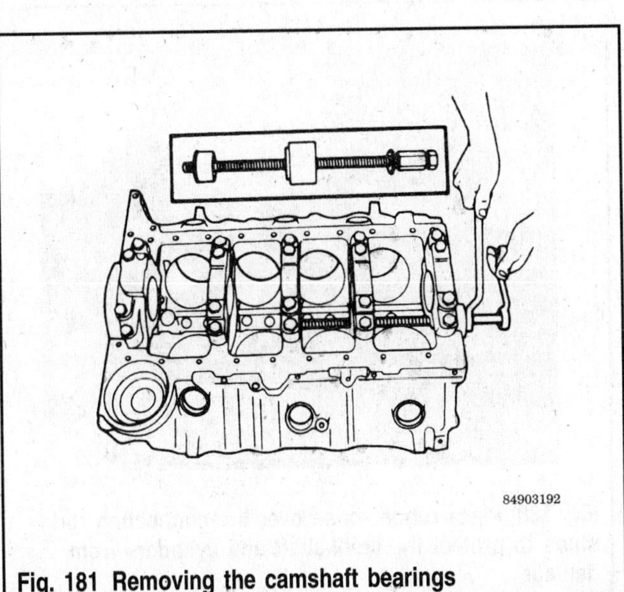

Fig. 181 Removing the camshaft bearings

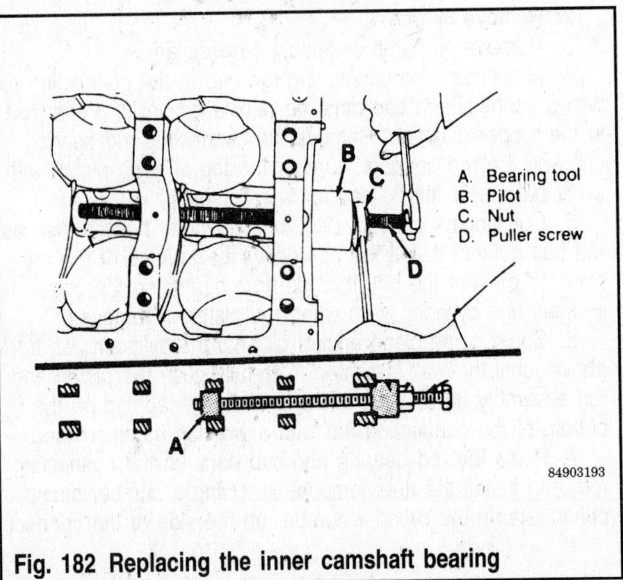

Fig. 182 Replacing the inner camshaft bearing

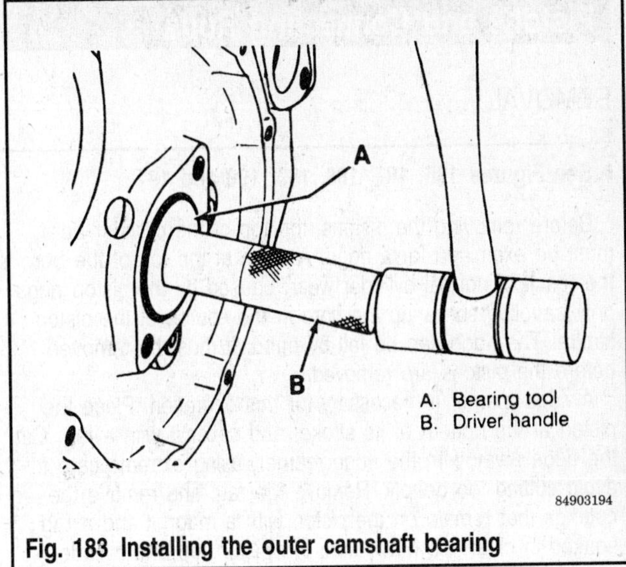

Fig. 183 Installing the outer camshaft bearing

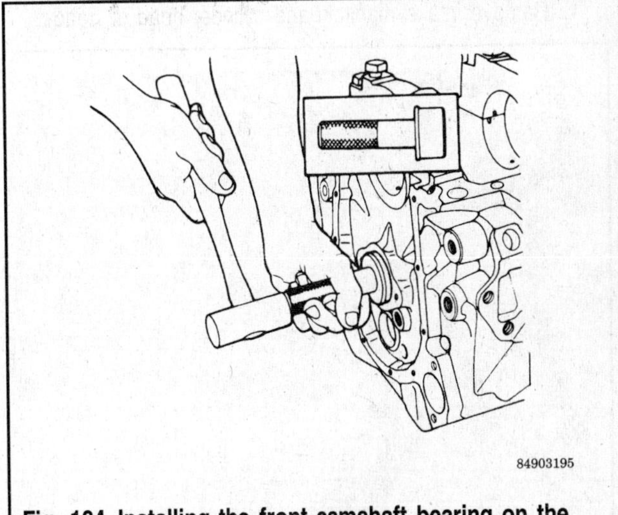

Fig. 184 Installing the front camshaft bearing on the diesel. The bearing tool is shown in the inset

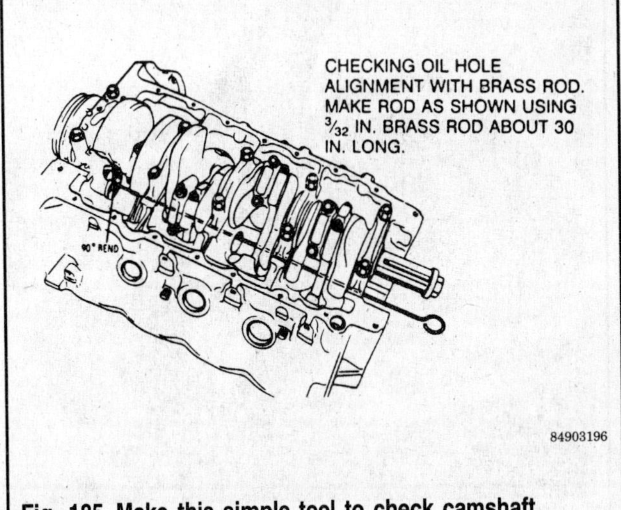

Fig. 185 Make this simple tool to check camshaft bearing oil hole alignment

Pistons and Connecting Rods

REMOVAL

➧ See Figures 186, 187, 188, 189, 190 and 191

Before removing the pistons, the top of the cylinder bore must be examined for a ridge. A ridge at the top of the bore is the result of normal cylinder wear, caused by the piston rings only traveling so far up the bore in the course of the piston stroke. The ridge can be felt by hand. It must be removed before the pistons are removed.

A ridge reamer is necessary for this operation. Place the piston at the bottom of its stroke, and cover it with a rag. Cut the ridge away with the ridge reamer, using extreme care to avoid cutting too deeply. Remove the rag, and remove the cuttings that remain on the piston with a magnet and a rag soaked in clean oil. Make sure the piston top and cylinder bore are absolutely clean before moving the piston.

1. Remove intake manifold and cylinder head or heads.

Fig. 186 Remove the ridge from the cylinder bore using a ridge cutter

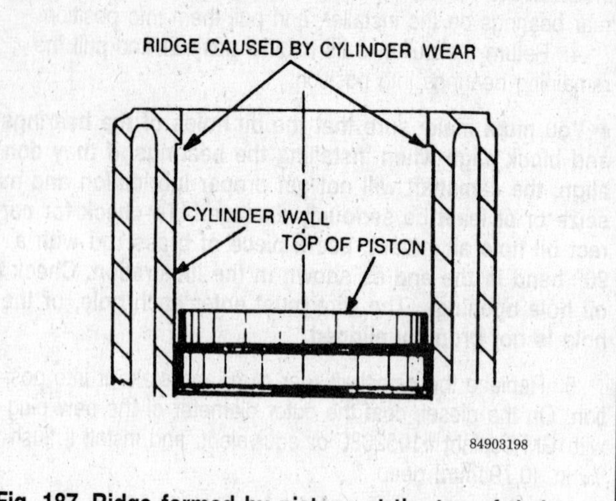

Fig. 187 Ridge formed by pistons at the top of their travel

Fig. 188 Place rubber hose over the connecting rod studs to protect the crankshaft and cylinders from damage

2. Remove oil pan.
3. Remove oil pump assembly if necessary.
4. Matchmark the connecting rod cap to the connecting rod with a scribe. Each cap must be reinstalled on its proper rod in the proper direction. Remove the connecting rod bearing cap and the rod bearing. Number the top of each piston with silver paint or a felt tip pen for later assembly.
5. Cut lengths of $^3/_8$ in. (9.53mm) diameter hose to use as rod bolt guides. Install the hose over the threads of the rod bolts, to prevent the bolt threads from damaging the crankshaft journals and cylinder walls when the piston is removed.
6. Squirt some clean engine oil onto the cylinder wall from above, until the wall is coated. Carefully push the piston and rod assembly up and out of the cylinder by tapping on the bottom of the connecting rod with a wooden hammer hand
7. Place the rod bearing and cap back on the connecting rod, and install the nuts temporarily. Using a number stamp or punch, stamp the cylinder number on the side of the connect-

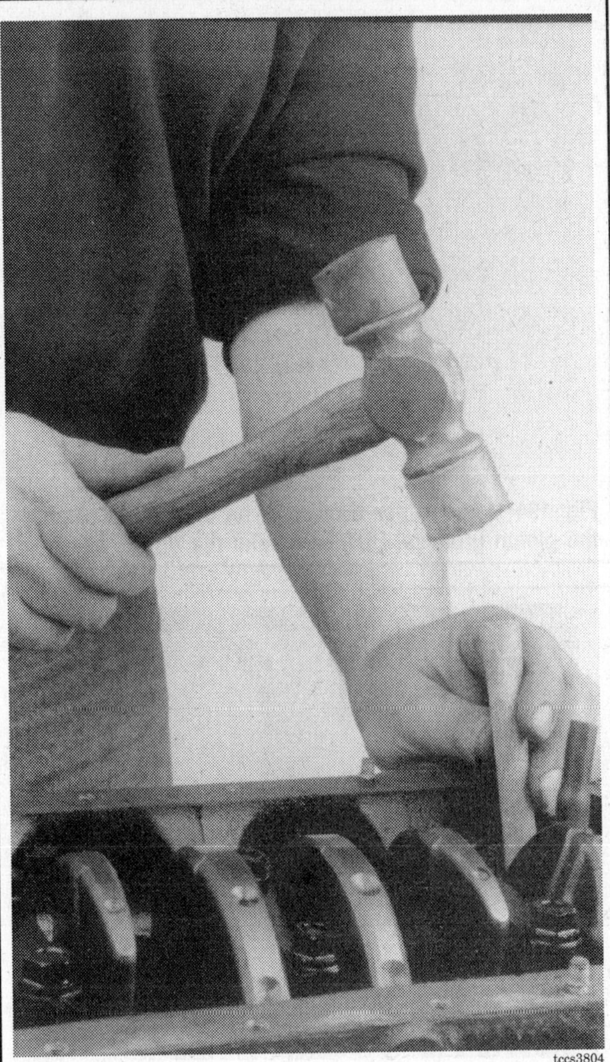
tccs3804

Fig. 189 Carefully tap the piston out of the bore using a wooden dowel

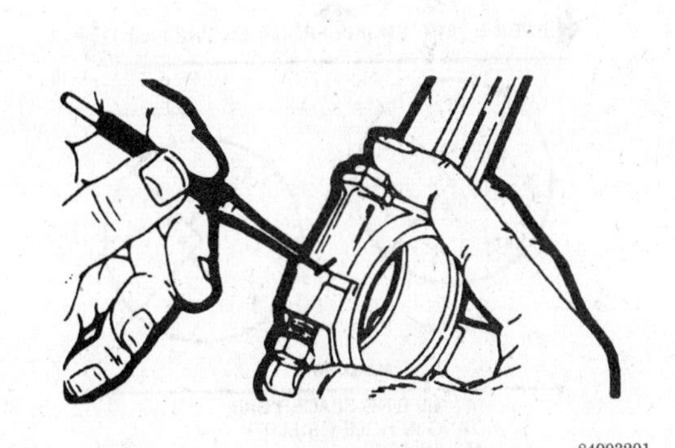
84903201

Fig. 190 Match the connecting rods to their cap with a scribe mark

tccs3914

Fig. 191 Installing the piston into the block using a ring compressor and the handle of a hammer

ing rod and cap. This will help keep the proper piston and rod assembly on the proper cylinder.

➡On all V8 engines, starting at the front, the right bank cylinders are numbered 2-4-6-8 and the left bank 1-3-5-7. On the 4.3L V6 engine even number cylinders 2-4-6 are in the right bank, odd number cylinders 1-3-5 are in the left bank, when viewed from the rear of the engine. The 4.8L is numbered from front to back.

8. Remove remaining pistons in similar manner.

CLEANING & INSPECTION

Piston Ring

▶ See Figures 192, 193, 194, 195, 196, 197 and 198

A piston ring expander is necessary for removing piston rings without damaging them; any other method (screwdriver blades, pliers, etc.) usually results in the rings being bent, scratched or distorted, or the piston itself being damaged. When the rings are removed, clean the ring grooves using an appropriate ring groove cleaning tool, using care not to cut too deeply. Thoroughly clean all carbon and varnish from the piston with a non-caustic solvent.

✲✲CAUTION

Do not use a wire brush or caustic solvent (acids, etc.) on pistons.

Inspect the pistons for scuffing, scoring, cracks, pitting, or excessive ring groove wear. If these are evident, the piston must be replaced.

The piston should also be checked in relation to the cylinder diameter. Using a telescoping gauge and micrometer, or a dial gauge, measure the cylinder bore diameter perpendicular to the piston pin, 2½ in. (63.5mm) below the cylinder block deck (surface where the block mates with the heads). Then, with the micrometer, measure the piston perpendicular to its wrist pin on the skirt. The difference between the two measurements is the piston clearance. If the clearance is within specifications

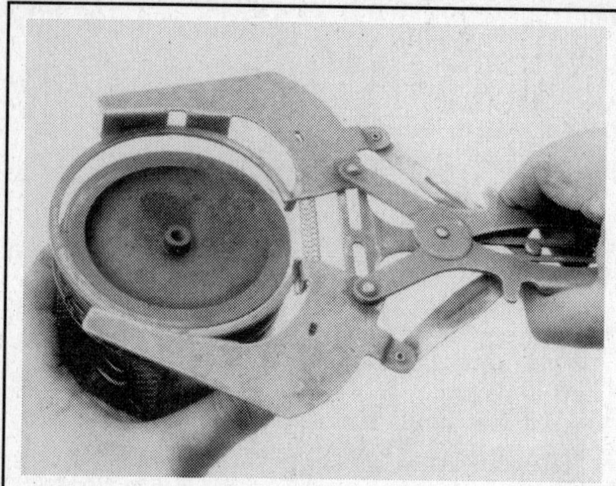

Fig. 192 Use a ring expander tool to remove the piston rings

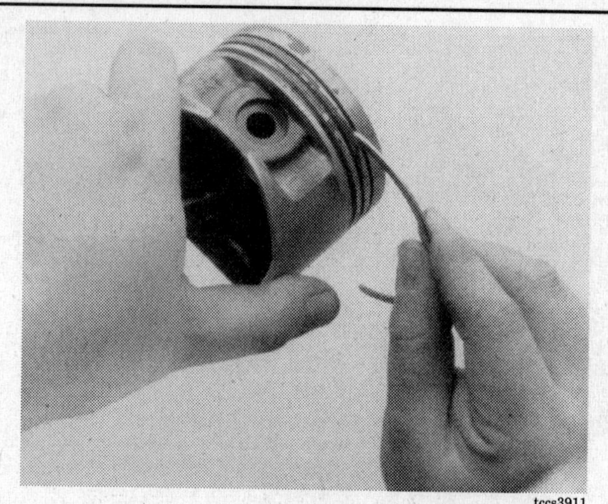

Fig. 194 You can use a piece of an old ring to clean the piston grooves, BUT be careful the ring is sharp

Fig. 193 Clean the piston grooves using a ring groove cleaner

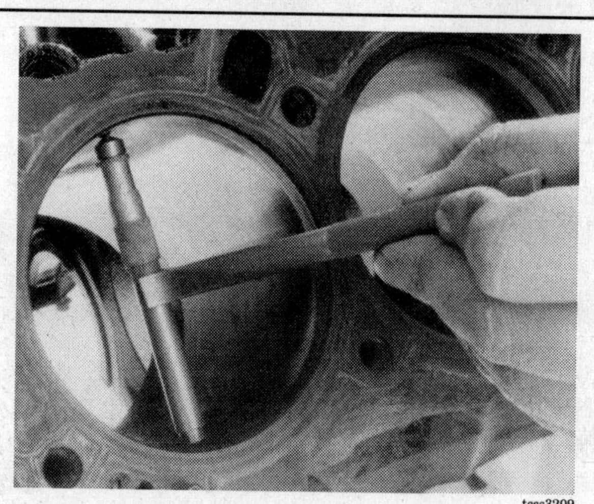

Fig. 195 A telescoping gauge may be used to measure the cylinder bore diameter

or slightly below (after the cylinders have been bored or honed), finish honing is all that is necessary. If the clearance is excessive, try to obtain a slightly larger piston to bring clearance to within specifications. If this is not possible, obtain the first oversize piston and bore the cylinder to size. Generally, if the cylinder bore is tapered 0.005 in. (0.127mm) or more or is out-of-round 0.003 in. (0.0762mm) or more, it is advisable to rebore for the smallest possible oversize piston and rings.

After measuring, mark pistons with a felt-tip for reference and for assembly.

Piston Ring End Gap

➧ See Figure 199

Piston ring end gap should be checked while the rings are removed from the pistons. Incorrect end gap indicates that the wrong size rings are being used; ring breakage could occur.

Compress the piston rings to be used in a cylinder, one at a time, into that cylinder. Squirt clean oil into the cylinder, so that the rings and the top 2 in. (51mm) of cylinder wall are

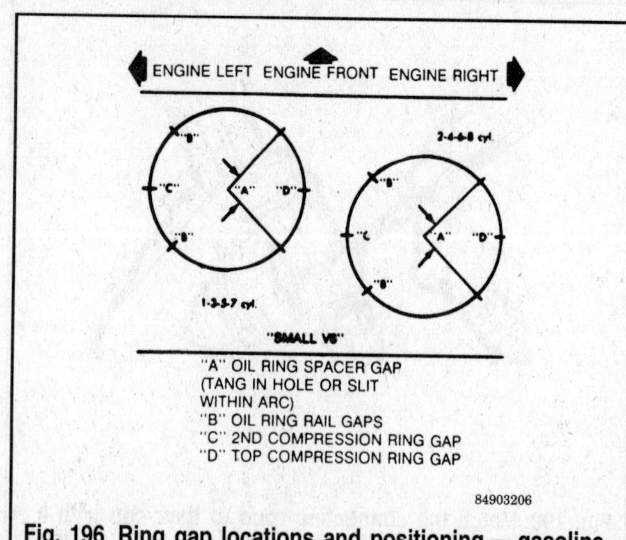

Fig. 196 Ring gap locations and positioning — gasoline engines. Some have a notch at the 12 o'clock position

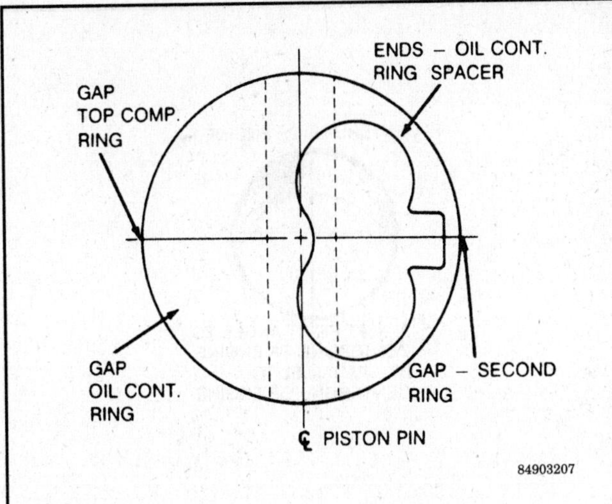

Fig. 197 Ring gap locations and positioning — diesel engines

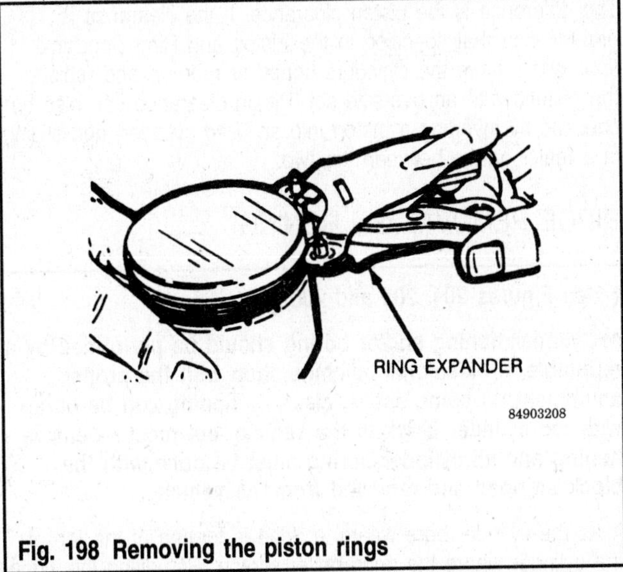

Fig. 198 Removing the piston rings

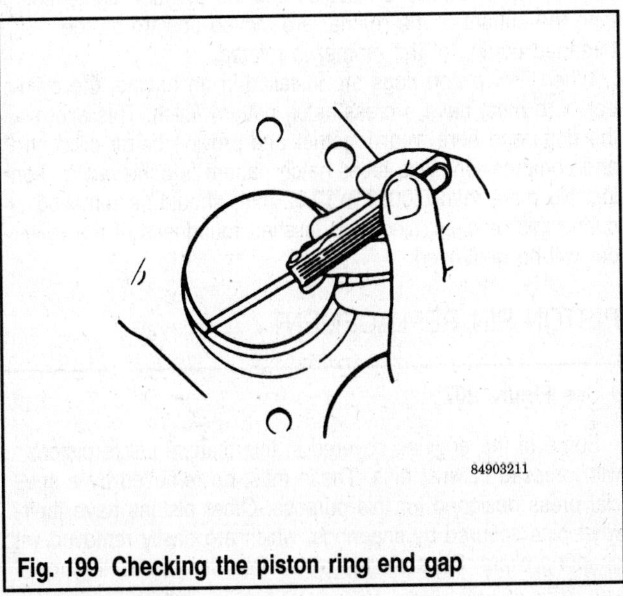

Fig. 199 Checking the piston ring end gap

coated. Using an inverted piston, press the rings approximately 1 in. (25.4mm) below the deck of the block (on diesels, measure ring gap clearance with the ring positioned at the bottom of ring travel in the bore). Measure the ring end gap with a feeler gauge, and compare to the Ring Gap chart in this section. Carefully pull the ring out of the cylinder and file the ends squarely with a fine file to obtain the proper clearance.

Piston Ring Side Clearance

See Figure 200

Check the piston to see that the ring grooves and oil return holes have been properly cleaned. Slide a piston ring into its groove, and check the side clearance with a feeler gauge. On gasoline engines, make sure you insert the gauge between the ring and its lower land (lower edge of the groove), because any wear that occurs forms a step at the inner portion of the lower land. On diesels, insert the gauge between the ring and the upper land. If the piston grooves have worn to the extent that relatively high steps exist on the lower land, the piston should be replaced, because these will interfere with the operation of the new rings and ring clearances will be excessive.

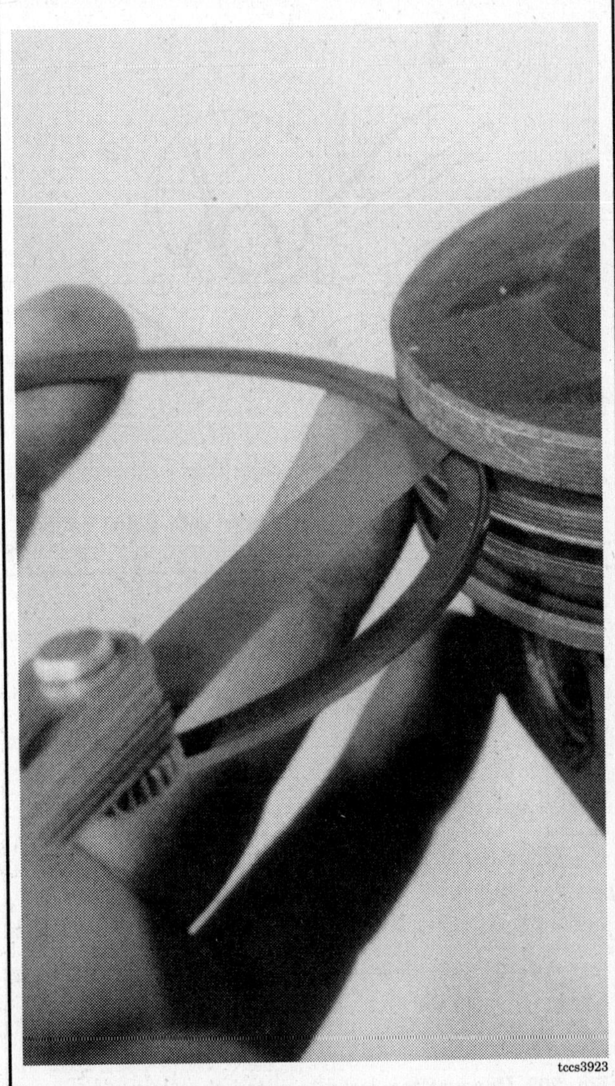

Fig. 200 Checking the ring-to-ring groove clearance

Pistons rings are not furnished in oversize widths to compensate for ring groove wear.

Cylinder Bore

➧ See Figures 201, 202 and 203

Place a rag over the crankshaft journals. Wipe out each cylinder with a clean, solvent-soaked rag. Visually inspect the cylinder bores for roughness, scoring or scuffing; also check the bores by feel. Measure the cylinder bore diameter with an inside micrometer, or a telescope gauge and micrometer. Measure the bore at points parallel and perpendicular to the engine centerline at the top (below the ridge) and bottom of the bore. Subtract the bottom measurements from the top to determine cylinder taper.

Measure the piston diameter with a micrometer; since this micrometer may not be part of your tool kit as it is necessarily large, you have to have the pistons miked at a machine shop. Take the measurements at right angles to the wrist pin center line, about an inch down the piston skirt from the top. Compare this measurement to the bore diameter of each cylinder.

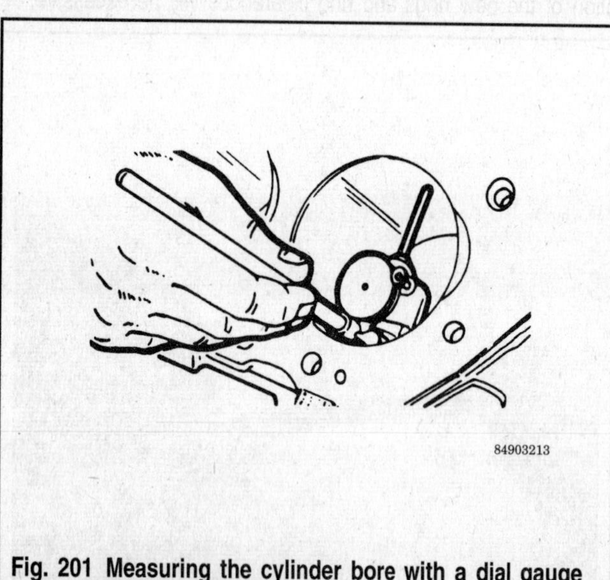

Fig. 201 Measuring the cylinder bore with a dial gauge

Fig. 202 Measure the piston's outer diameter using a micrometer

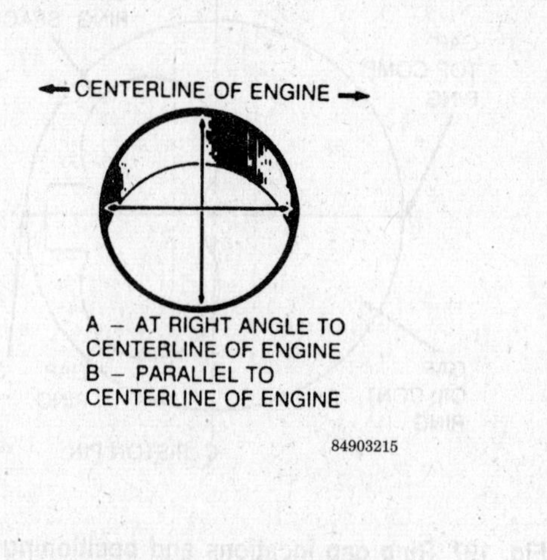

Fig. 203 Cylinder bore measuring points

The difference is the piston clearance. If the clearance is greater than that specified in the Piston and Ring Specifications chart, have the cylinders honed or rebored and replace the pistons with an oversize set. Piston clearance can also be checked by inverting a piston into an oiled cylinder, and sliding in a feeler gauge between the two.

RIDGE REMOVAL and HONING

➧ See Figures 204, 205 and 206

➡Cylinder honing and/or boring should be performed by a reputable, professional machine shop with the proper equipment. In some cases, clean-up honing can be done with the cylinder block in the vehicle, but most extensive honing and all cylinder boring must be done with the block stripped and removed from the vehicle.

As the cylinder bore wears, a ridge is formed at the top of the cylinder where the rings never scrape. Removing this ridge makes piston removal easier and prevents damage to the rings. A ridge reamer is installed into the cylinder, tightened, then the cutters of the reamer are moved upward as the threaded portion of the reamer is rotated.

When new piston rings are installed in an engine, the cylinder bore must have a cross-hatch pattern finish. This allows the rings and bore wear together and provide better oil control and compression. This cross-hatch pattern is achieved by honing. No more than 0.0008 in (0.02 mm) should be removed during this process, since the finished roundness of the cylinder will be destroyed.

PISTON PIN REPLACEMENT

➧ See Figure 207

Some of the engines covered in this manual utilize pistons with pressed in wrist pins. These must be removed by a special press designed for this purpose. Other pistons have their wrist pins secured by snaprings, which are easily removed with snapring pliers. Separate the piston from the connecting rod.

tccs3915

Fig. 204 Remove the ridge from the cylinder bore using a ridge cutter

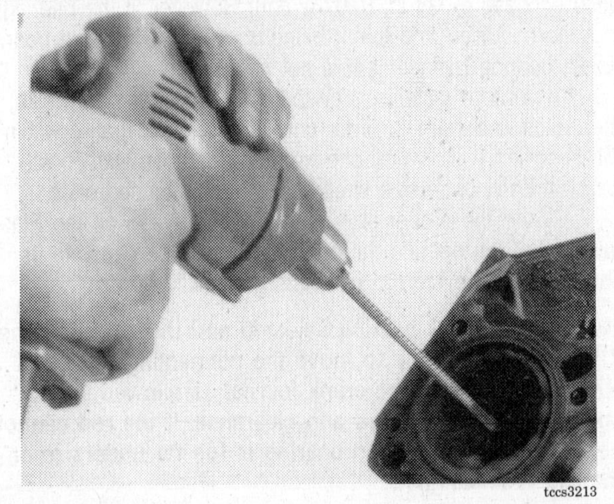
tccs3213

Fig. 205 Removing cylinder glazing using a flexible hone

tccs3216

Fig. 206 A properly cross-hatched cylinder bore

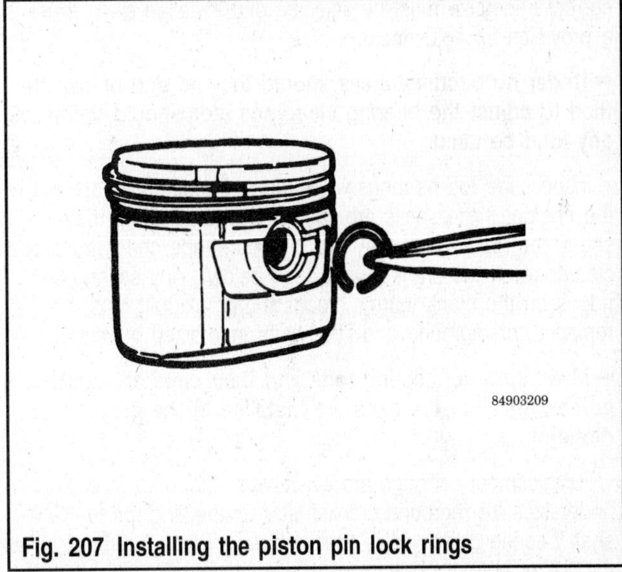
84903209

Fig. 207 Installing the piston pin lock rings

To install:

On engines that utilize pistons with pressed in wrist pins a special press must be used to install the pins. On the pistons that have their wrist pins secured by snaprings, engage the piston and connecting rod. Install the piston pin and snapring.

ROD BEARING REPLACEMENT

➧ **See Figures 208, 209, 210, 211 and 212**

Connecting rod bearings for the engine covered in this manual consist of two halves or shells which are interchangable in the rod and cap. When the shells are placed in position, the ends extend slightly beyond the rod and cap surfaces. As the rod bolts are tightened, the shells will be capped tightly in place to insure positive seating and to prevent turning. A tang holds the shells in place.

If a rod bearing becomes noisy or is worn so that its clearance on the crank journal is sloppy, a new bearing of the

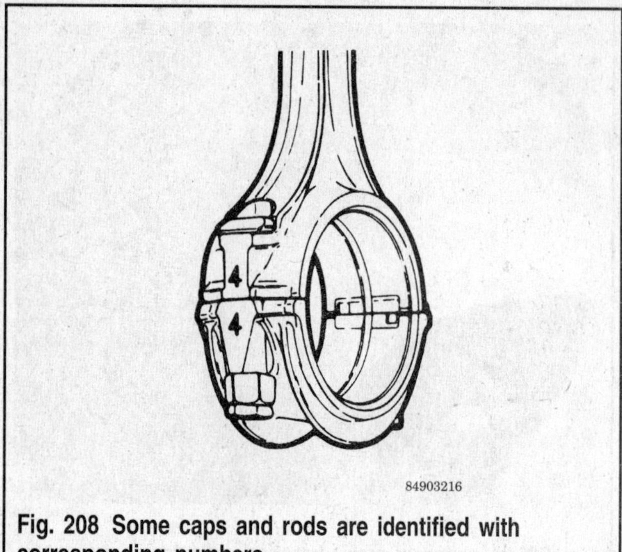

Fig. 208 Some caps and rods are identified with corresponding numbers

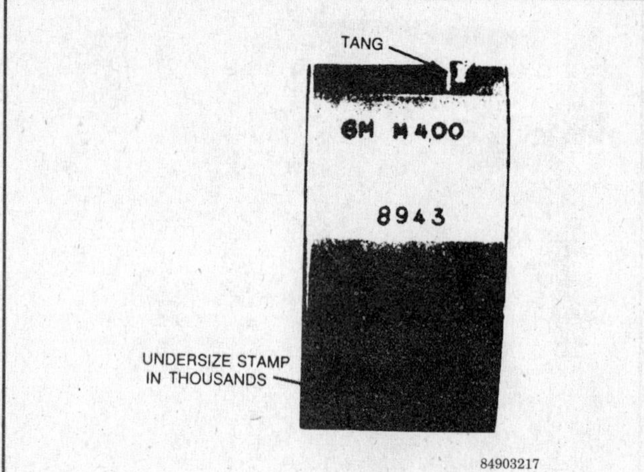

Fig. 209 Undersize marks are stamped on the bearing shells. The tang fits into the notches on the rod and cap

correct undersize must be selected and installed since there is a provision for adjustment.

➡Under no circumstances should the rod end or cap be filed to adjust the bearing clearance, nor should shims of any kind be used.

Inspect the rod bearings while the rod assemblies are out of the engine. If the shells are scored or show flaking, they should be replaced. If they are in good shape check for proper clearance on the crank journal (see below). Any scoring or ridges on the crank journal means the crankshaft must be replaced, or reground and fitted with undersized bearings.

➡Make sure connecting rods and their caps are kept together, and that the caps are installed in the proper direction.

Replacement bearings are available in standard size, and in undersizes for reground crankshafts. Connecting rod-to-crankshaft bearing clearance is checked using Plastigage® at either the top or bottom of each crank journal. The Plastigage® has a range of 0.001-0.003 in. (0.0254-0.0762mm).

1. Remove the rod cap with the bearing shell. Completely clean the bearing shell and the crank journal, and blow any oil from the oil hole in the crankshaft; Plastigage® is soluble in oil.
2. Place a piece of Plastigage® lengthwise along the bottom center of the lower bearing shell, then install the cap with shell. Tighten the bolt or nuts to specification. DO NOT turn the crankshaft with Plastigage® in the bearing.
3. Remove the bearing cap with the shell. The flattened Plastigage® will be found sticking to either the bearing shell or crank journal. Do not remove it yet.
4. Use the scale printed on the Plastigage® envelope to measure the flattened material at its widest point. The number within the scale which most closely corresponds to the width of the Plastigage® indicates bearing clearance in thousandths of an inch.
5. Check the specifications chart in this section for the desired clearance. It is advisable to install a new bearing if clearance exceeds 0.003 in. (0.0762mm). However, if the bearing is in good condition and is not being checked because of bearing noise, bearing replacement is not necessary.

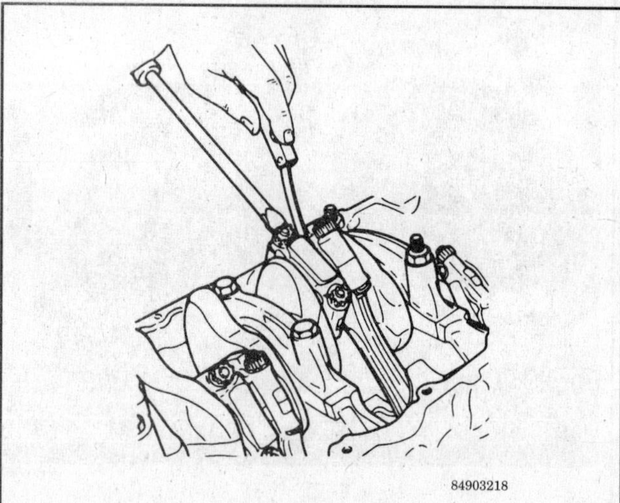

Fig. 210 Checking the connecting rod side clearance. Use a small prybar to carefully spread the rods

6. If you are installing new bearings, try a standard size, then each undersize in order until one is found that is within the specified limits when checked for clearance with Plastigage®. Each undersize shell has its size stamped on it.
7. When the proper size shell is found, clean off the Plastigage®, oil the bearing thoroughly, reinstall the cap with its shell and tighten the rod bolt nuts to specification.

➡With the proper bearing selected and the nuts tightened, it should be possible to move the connecting rod back and forth freely on the crank journal as allowed by the specified connecting rod and clearance. If the rod cannot be moved, either the rod bearing is too far undersize or the rod is misaligned.

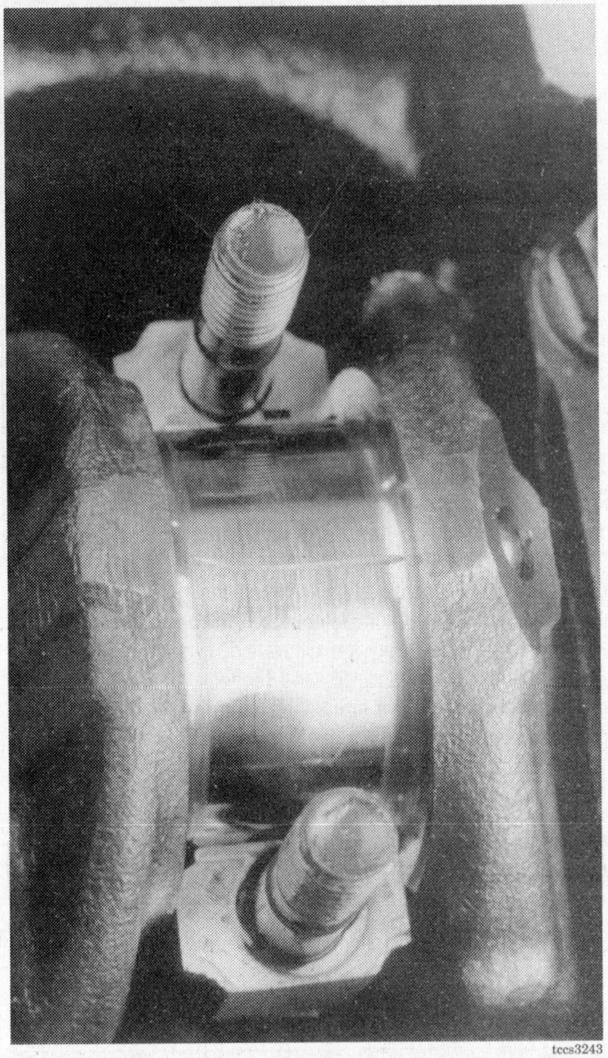

Fig. 211 Apply a strip of gauging material to the bearing journal, then install and torque the cap

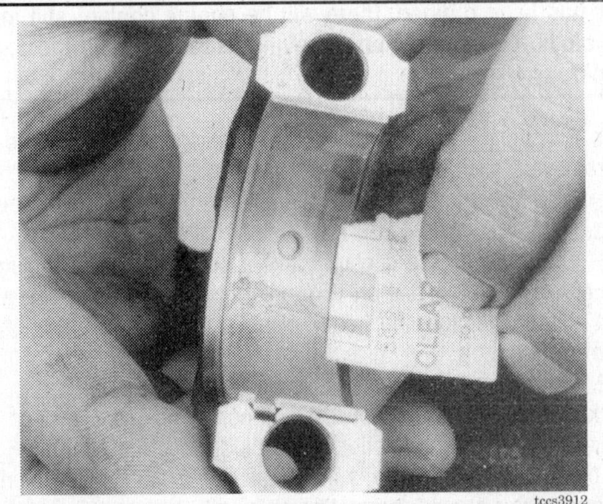

Fig. 212 After the cap is removed again, use the scale supplied with the gauge material to check clearances

IDENTIFICATION AND POSITIONING

See Figures 213, 214 and 215

On all gasoline engines, the notch on the piston will face the front of the engine for assembly. The chamfered corners of the bearing caps should face toward the front of the left bank and toward the rear of the right bank, and the boss on the connecting rod should face toward the front of the engine for the right bank and to the rear of the engine on the left bank.

On the diesel, install the piston and rod assemblies with the rod bearing tang slots on the side opposite the camshaft.

On various engines, the piston compression rings are marked with a dimple, a letter **T**, a letter **O**, **GM** or the word **TOP** to identify the side of the ring which must face toward the top of the piston.

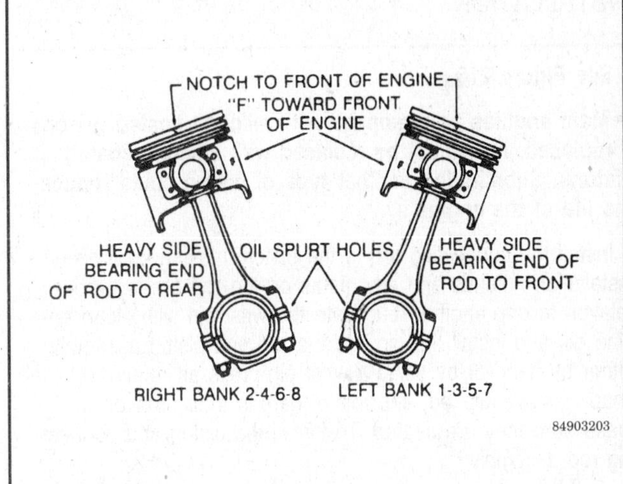

Fig. 213 Piston and connecting rod positioning — 4.3L, 5.0L and 5.7L engines

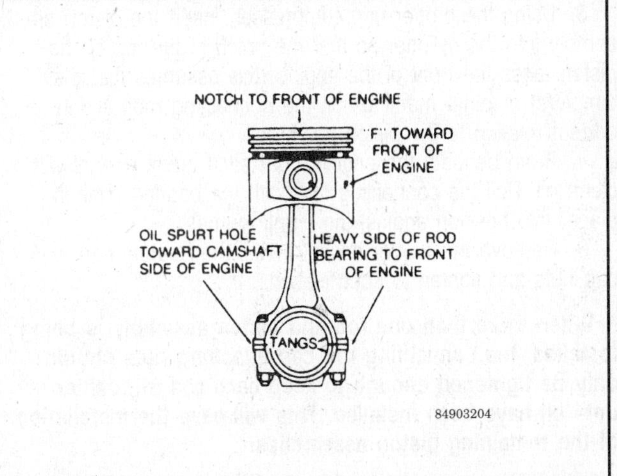

Fig. 214 Piston and connecting rod positioning — 4.8L engines

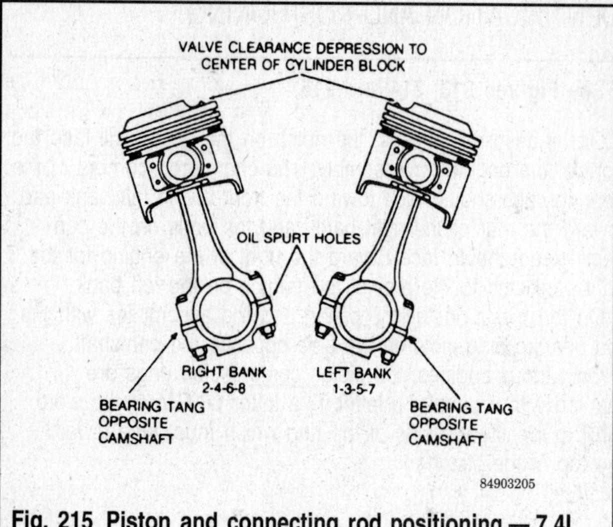

Fig. 215 Piston and connecting rod positioning — 7.4L engines

Fig. 216 Installing the piston into the block using a ring compressor and the handle of a hammer

INSTALLATION

See Figure 216

➡Most engines are equipped with silicone coated pistons. If replaced, they must be replaced with silicone coated pistons. Substituting another type of piston could reduce the life of the engine.

Install the connecting rod to the piston, making sure piston installation notches and any marks on the rod are in proper relation to one another. Lubricate the wrist pin with clean engine oil, and install the pin into the rod and piston assembly, either by hand or by using a wrist pin press as required. Install snaprings if equipped, and rotate them in their grooves to make sure they are seated. To install the piston and connecting rod assembly:

1. Make sure connecting rod big end bearings (including end cap) are of the correct size and properly installed.
2. Fit rubber hoses over the connecting rod bolts to protect the crankshaft journals. Coat the rod bearings with clean oil.
3. Using the proper ring compressor, insert the piston assembly into the cylinder so that the notch in the top of the piston faces the front of the engine (this assumes that the dimple(s) or other markings on the connecting rods are in correct relation to the piston notch(es).
4. From beneath the engine, coat each crank journal with clean oil. Pull the connecting rod, with the bearing shell in place, into position against the crank journal.
5. Remove the rubber hoses. Install the bearing cap and cap nuts and tighten to specification.

➡When more than one rod and piston assembly is being installed, the connecting rod cap attaching nuts should only be tightened enough to keep each rod in position until all have been installed. This will ease the installation of the remaining piston assemblies.

6. Check the clearance between the sides of the connecting rods and the crankshaft using a feeler gauge. Spread the rods slightly with a screwdriver to insert the gauge. If clearance is below the minimum tolerance, the rod may be machined to provide adequate clearance. If clearance is excessive, substitute an unworn rod, and recheck. If clearance is still outside specifications, the crankshaft must be welded and reground or replaced.
7. Replace the oil pump if removed and the oil pan.
8. Install the cylinder head(s) and intake manifold.

Freeze Plugs

REMOVAL & INSTALLATION

See Figures 217 and 218

CAUTION

Removing the freeze plug may cause personal injury if the engine is not completely cooled down. Even after the radiator has been drained, there will be engine coolant still in the block. Use care when removing assembly from the block.

To remove an engine freeze plug, accessories may have to be removed, such as the starter motor, motor mount, etc. Remove an obstruction before attempting to remove the freeze plug.

1. Drain the engine coolant, drive a chisel through the plug and pry outward. Or drill an 1/8in. hole into the plug and use a dent puller to remove the freeze plug.

To install:

2. Coat the new plug with silicone sealer and clean the block mating surface free of rust and corrosion. Using a deep socket the size of the interior of the plug, drive the plug into the block until the plug lip is flush with the cylinder block. Run silicone sealer around the mating area.
3. Fill the engine with coolant and check for leaks.

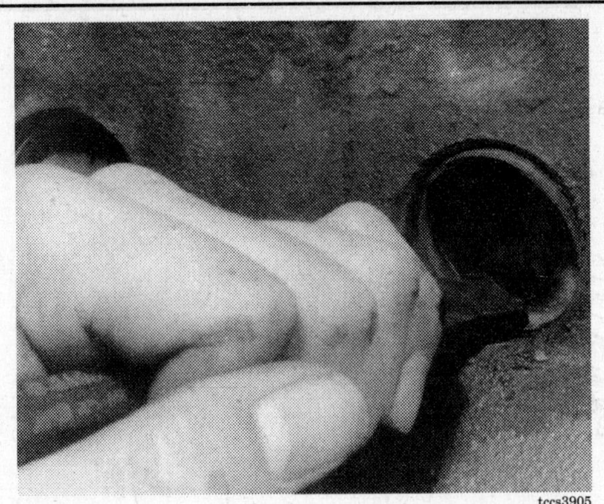

Fig. 217 Using a punch and hammer, the freeze plug can be loosened in the block

Fig. 218 Once the freeze plug has been loosened, it can be removed from the block

Engine Block Heater

REMOVAL & INSTALLATION

See Figure 219

CAUTION

Removing the block heater may cause personal injury if the engine is not completely cooled down. Even after the radiator has been drained, there will be engine coolant still in the block. Use care when removing assembly from the block.

To remove an engine block heater, accessories may have to be removed, such as the starter motor, motor mount, etc. Remove an obstruction before attempting to remove the freeze plug.

1. Disconnect the negative battery cable.
2. Drain the engine coolant, disconnect the electrical connector, loosen the retaining screw and remove the heater from the block.
3. Coat the O-ring with engine oil and clean the block mating surface free of rust and corrosion. Install the heater and tighten the retaining screw. Connect the electrical and negative battery cable.

Rear Main Oil Seal

REMOVAL & INSTALLATION

4.8L Engines

See Figures 220, 221, 222, 223 and 224

The rear main bearing oil seal, both halves, can be removed without removal of the crankshaft. Always replace the upper and lower halves together.

1. Raise and support the truck on jackstands.
2. Drain the oil.
3. Remove the oil pan.
4. Remove the rear main bearing cap.
5. Remove the old oil seal from its groove in the cap, prying from the bottom using a suitable tool.
6. Coat a new seal half completely with clean engine oil, and insert it into the bearing cap groove. Keep the oil off of the parting line surface, as this surface is treated with glue. Gradually push the seal with a hammer handle until the seal is rolled into place.
7. To remove the upper half of the old seal, use a small hammer and a soft, blunt punch to tap one end of the oil seal out until it protrudes far enough to be removed with needle-nosed pliers.
8. Push the new seal into place with the lip toward the front of the engine.
9. Install the bearing cap and tighten the bolts to a loose fit; do not final-torque.
10. With the cap fitted loosely, move the crankshaft first to the rear and then to the front with a rubber mallet. This will properly position the thrust bearing.
11. Tighten the bearing cap to a final torque of 65 ft. lbs. (90 Nm).
12. Install the oil pan.

1988-90 7.4L Engines

See Figures 220, 221, 222, 223 and 224

1. Remove the oil pan, oil pump and rear main bearing cap.
2. Remove the oil seal from the bearing cap by prying it out with a suitable tool.
3. Remove the upper half of the seal with a small punch. Drive it around far enough to be gripped with pliers.

To install:

4. Clean the crankshaft and bearing cap.
5. Coat the lips and bead of the seal with light engine oil, keeping oil from the ends of the seal.
6. Position the fabricated tool between the crankshaft and seal seat.

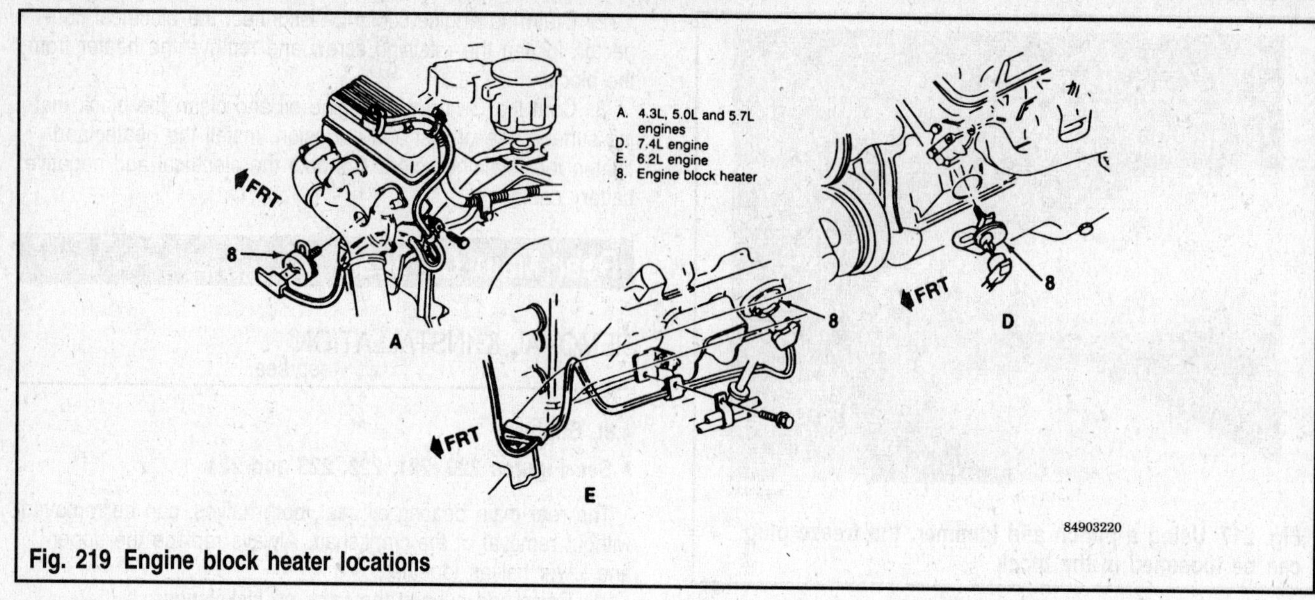

Fig. 219 Engine block heater locations

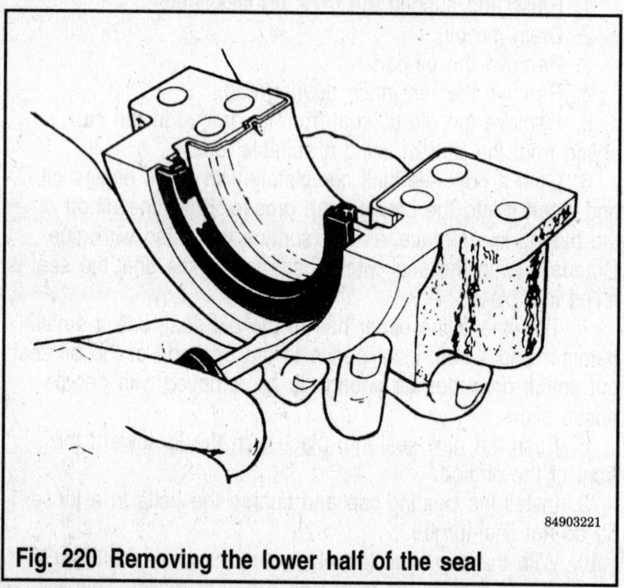

Fig. 220 Removing the lower half of the seal

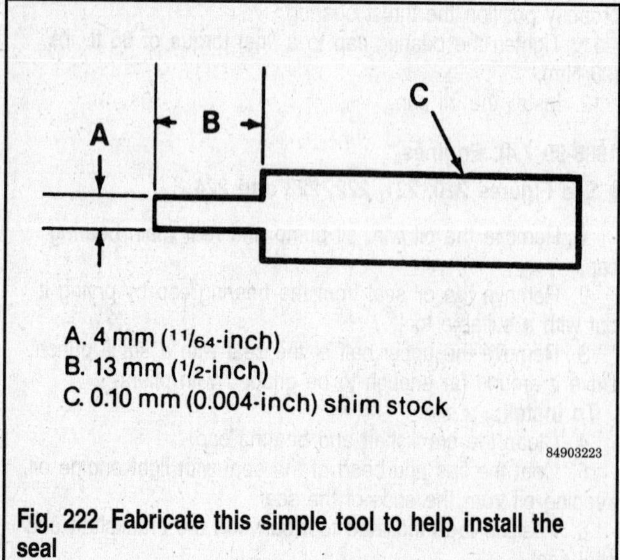

Fig. 222 Fabricate this simple tool to help install the seal

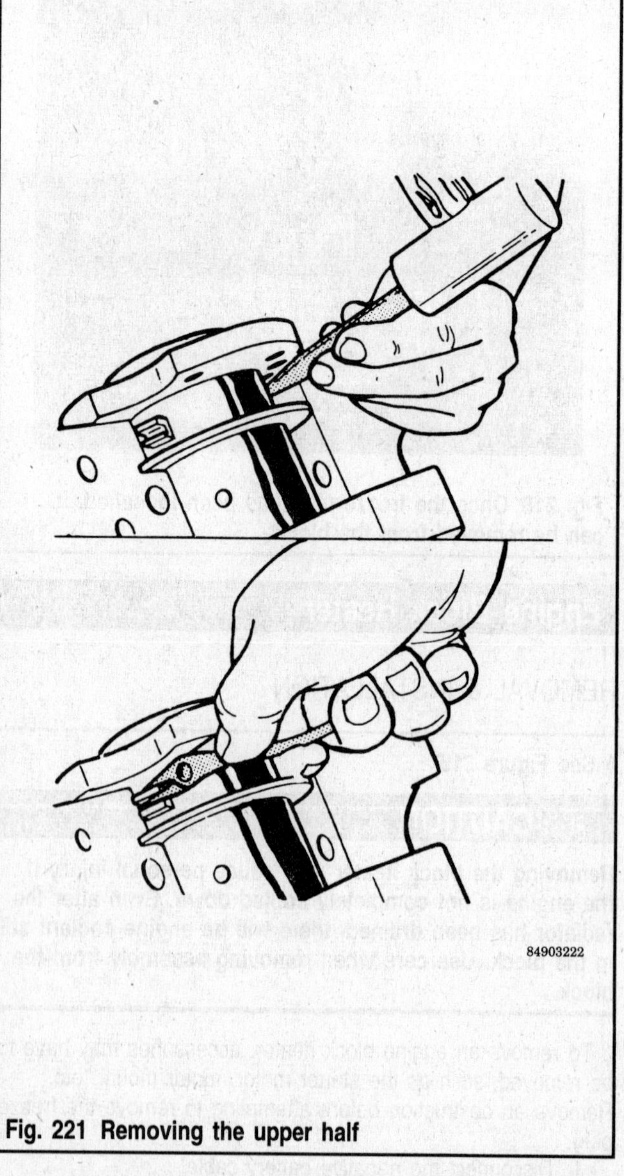

Fig. 221 Removing the upper half

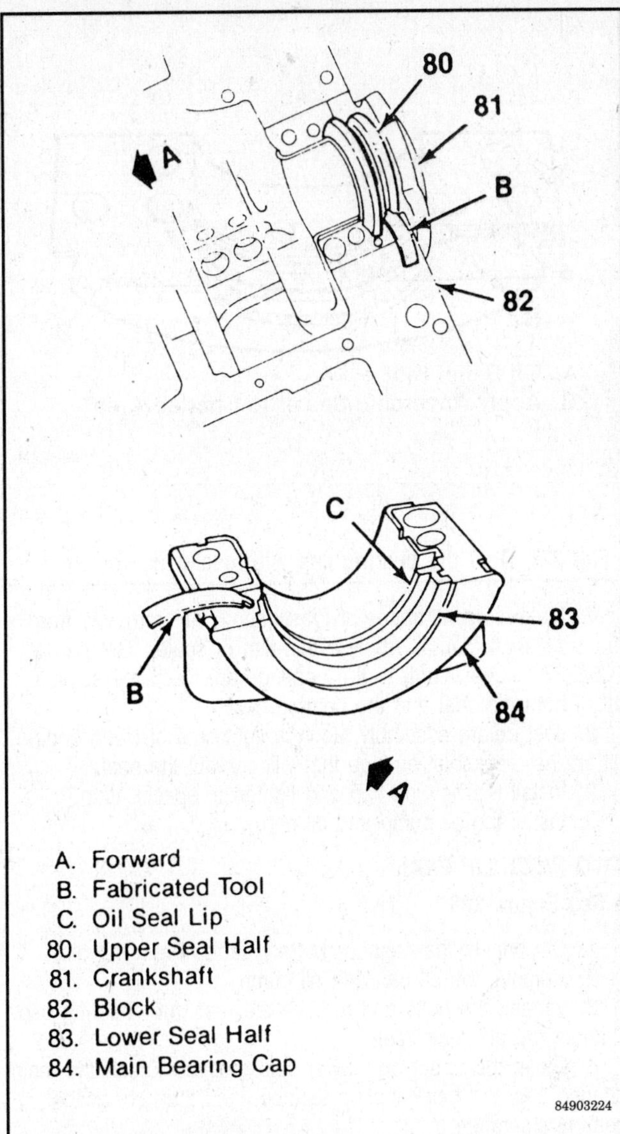

Fig. 223 Installing the new seal

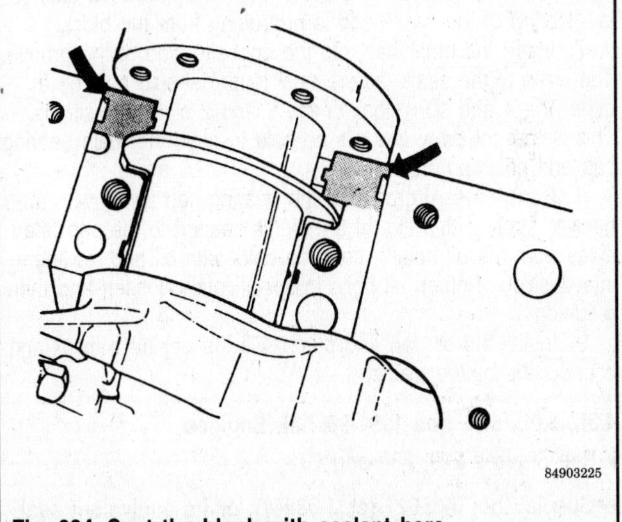

Fig. 224 Coat the block with sealant here

7. Position the seal between the crankshaft and tip of the tool so that the seal bead contacts the tip of the tool. The oil seal lip should face forward.
8. Roll the seal around the crankshaft using the tool to protect the seal bead from the sharp corners of the crankcase.
9. The installation tool should be left installed until the seal is properly positioned with both ends flush with the block.
10. Remove the tool.
11. Install the other half of the seal in the bearing cap using the tool in the same manner as before. Light thumb pressure should install the seal.
12. Install the bearing cap with sealant applied to the mating areas of the cap and block. Keep sealant from the ends of the seal.
13. Tighten the main bearing cap retaining bolts to 10 ft. lbs. (14 Nm). Tap the end of the crankshaft first rearward, then forward with a lead hammer. This will line up the rear main bearing and the crankshaft thrust surfaces. Tighten the main bearing cap 110 ft. lbs. (150 Nm).
14. Install the oil pump.
15. Install the oil pan.

6.2L Diesel Engines

ROPE SEAL

See Figures 225, 226 and 227

The crankshaft need not be removed to replace the rear main bearing upper oil seal. The lower seal is installed in the bearing cap.

Engines are originally equipped with a rope-type seal. This should be replaced with the lip-type seal available as a service replacement.

1. Drain the crankcase oil and remove the oil pan and rear main bearing cap.
2. Using a special main seal tool or a tool that can be made from a dowel (see illustration), drive the upper seal into its groove on each side until it is tightly packed. This is usually $^{1}/_{4}$-$^{3}/_{4}$ in. (6-19mm).
3. Measure the amount the seal was driven up on one side. Add $^{1}/_{16}$ in. (2mm) and cut another length from the old seal. Use the main bearing cap as a holding fixture when cutting the seal as illustrated. Carefully trim protruding seal.
4. Work these two pieces of seal up into the cylinder block on each side with two nailsets or small screwdrivers. Using the packing tool again, pack these pieces into the block, then trim the flush with a razor blade or hobby knife as shown. Do not scratch the bearing surface with the razor.

It may help to use a bit of oil on the short pieces of the rope seal when packing it into the block.

5. Apply Loctite® # 496 sealer or equivalent to the rear main bearing cap and install the rope seal. Cut the ends of the seal flush with the cap.
6. Check to see if the rear main cap with the new seal will seat properly on the block. Place a piece of Plastigage® on the rear main journal, install the cap and tighten to 70 ft. lbs. (94 Nm). Remove the cap and check the Plastigage® against specifications. If out of specs, recheck the end of the seal for fraying that may be preventing the cap from seating properly.

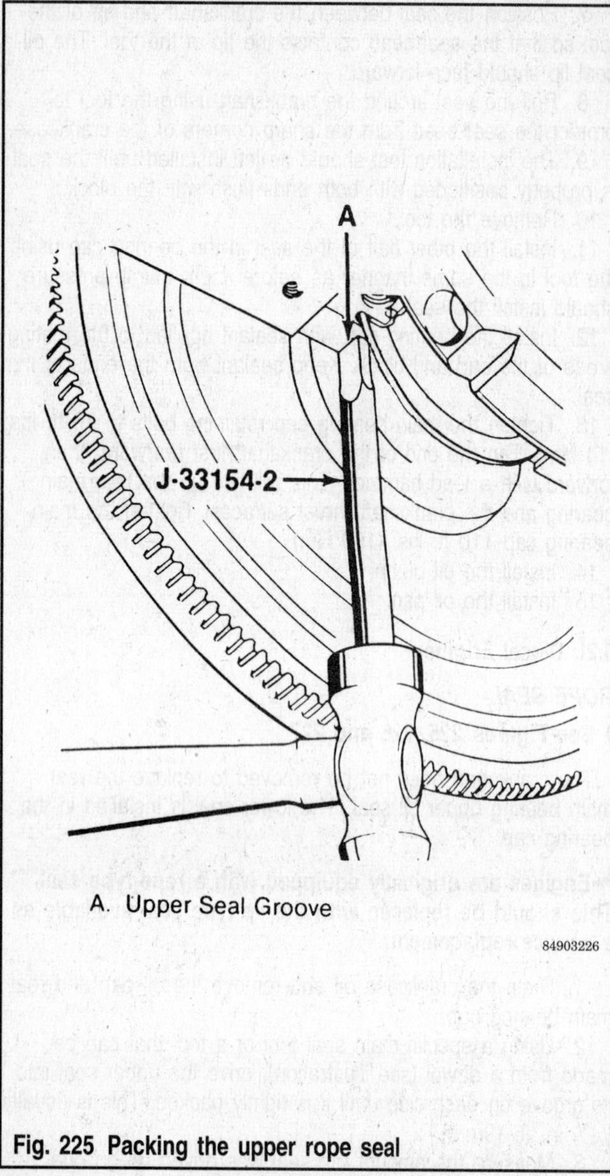

Fig. 225 Packing the upper rope seal

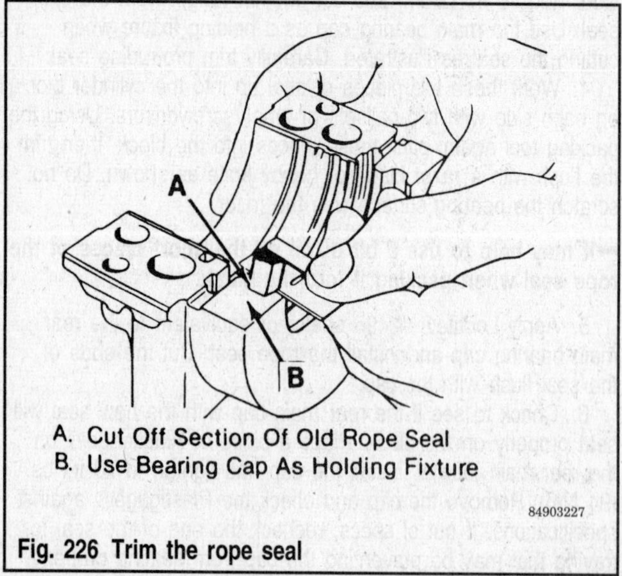

Fig. 226 Trim the rope seal

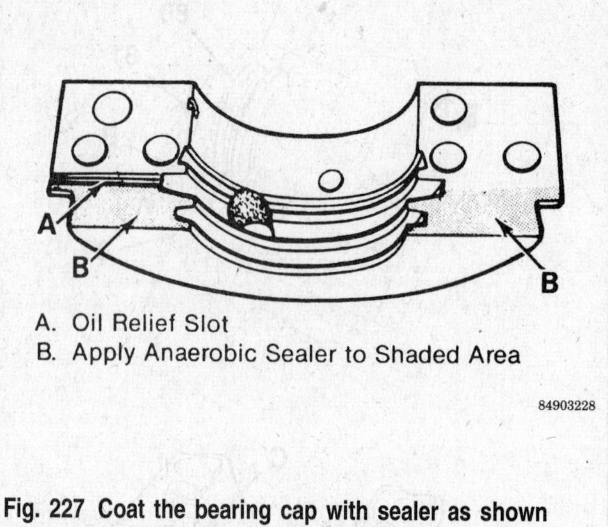

Fig. 227 Coat the bearing cap with sealer as shown

7. Make sure all traces of Plastigage® are removed from the crankshaft journal. Apply a thin film of sealer (GM part # 1052357 or equivalent) to the bearing cap. Keep the sealant off of both the seal and the bearing.
8. Just before assembly, apply a light coat of clean engine oil on the crankshaft surface that will contact the seal.
9. Install the bearing cap and tighten to specification.
10. Install the oil pump and oil pan.

TWO PIECE LIP SEAL

➧ See Figure 228

1. Disconnect the negative battery cable. Drain the oil.
2. Remove the oil pan and oil pump.
3. Loosen the bolts and remove the rear main bearing cap. Pull out the old rope seal.
4. Clean the upper and lower seal grooves. Clean the main bearing cap and block mating surfaces and then check the bearing clearance.
5. Coat the inner side of the seal halves where they contact the crankshaft and slide them into position.
6. Roll one seal half into the cylinder block groove until ½ in. (13mm) of the seal's end is protruding from the block.
7. Insert the other half into the opposite side of the groove. The ends of the seals (where they touch) should now be at either the 4 and 10 o'clock or the 8 and 2 o'clock positions. This is the only way you will be able to align the main bearing cap and seal lips properly!
8. Coat the seal groove in the bearing cap lightly with adhesive. Apply a thin film of anaerobic sealant to the cap (stay away from the oil hole!!), coat the bolts with oil and tap them into position. Tighten all bolts to specification, loosen and then retighten.
9. Install the oil pan and pump. Fill the engine with oil and connect the battery cable.

4.3L, 5.0L, 5.7L and 1991-96 7.4L Engines

➧ See Figures 229, 230 and 231

➡Special tool J-35621 (or J-38841), or its equivalent seal installer, will be necessary for this job.

1. Remove the transmission.

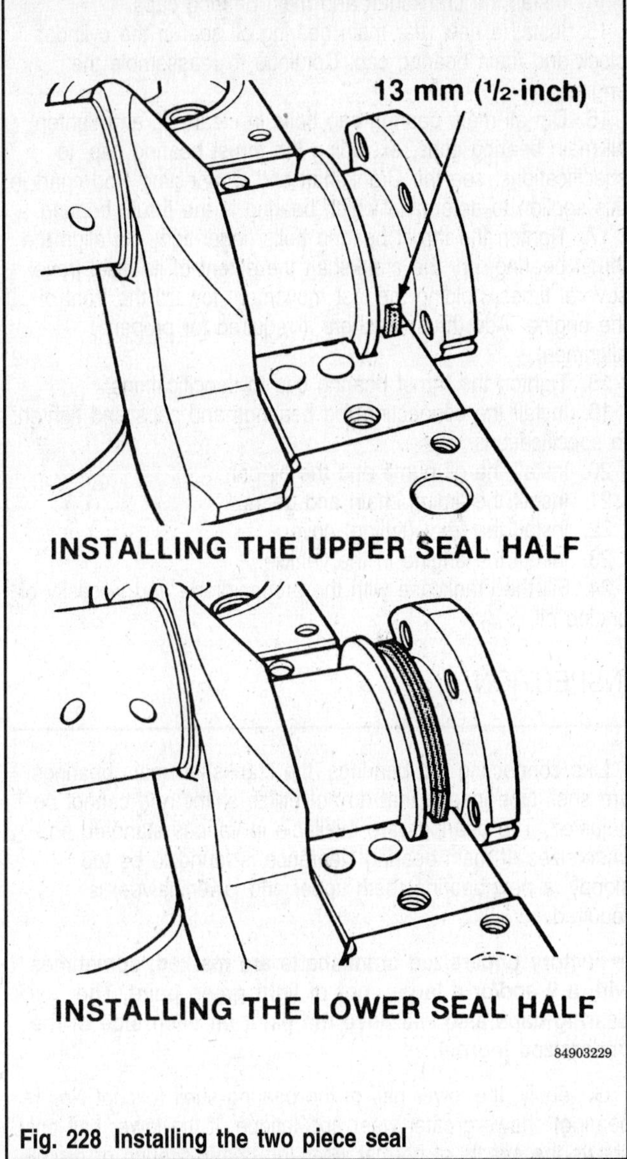

Fig. 228 Installing the two piece seal

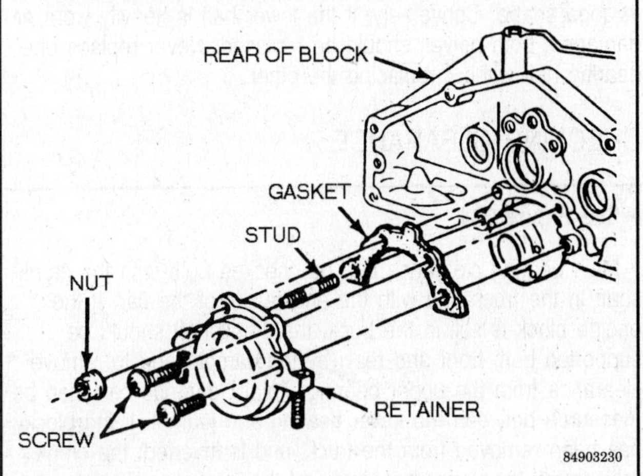

Fig. 229 Rear main seal and retainer — 4.3L, 5.0L and 5.7L engines

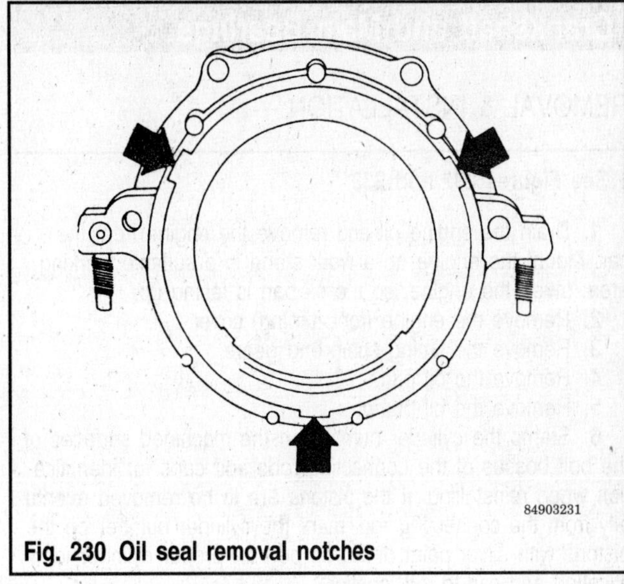

Fig. 230 Oil seal removal notches

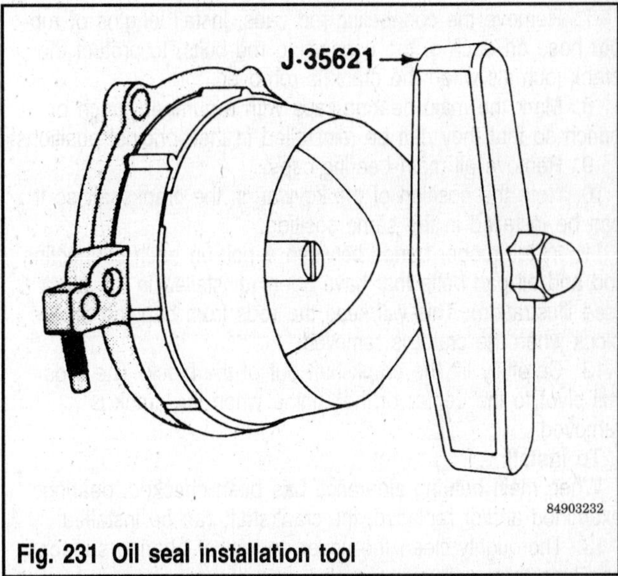

Fig. 231 Oil seal installation tool

2. With manual transmission, remove the clutch.
3. Remove the flywheel or flexplate.
4. Insert a small prying tool in the notches provided in the seal retainer and pry out the old seal. Be VERY CAREFUL to avoid nicking or scratching the sealing surfaces of the crankshaft.

To install:

5. Coat the inner and outer diameters of the new seal with clean engine oil.
6. Using seal tool J-35621, or equivalent, position the seal on the tool.
7. Thread the attaching screws into the holes in the crankshaft end and tighten them securely with a screwdriver.
8. Turn the installer handle until it bottoms.
9. Remove the tool.
10. Install the flywheel/flexplate, clutch and transmission.

Crankshaft and Main Bearings

REMOVAL & INSTALLATION

▶ See Figures 232 and 233

1. Drain the engine oil and remove the engine from the car. Mount the engine on a work stand in a suitable working area. Invert the engine, so the oil pan is facing up.
2. Remove the engine front (timing) cover.
3. Remove the timing chain and gears.
4. Remove the oil pan.
5. Remove the oil pump.
6. Stamp the cylinder number on the machined surfaces of the bolt bosses of the connecting rods and caps for identification when reinstalling. If the pistons are to be removed eventually from the connecting rod, mark the cylinder number on the pistons with silver paint or felt tip pen for proper cylinder identification and cap-to-rod location.
7. Remove the connecting rod caps. Install lengths of rubber hose on each of the connecting rod bolts, to protect the crank journals when the crank is removed.
8. Mark the main bearing caps with a number punch or punch so that they can be reinstalled in their original positions.
9. Remove all main bearing caps.
10. Note the position of the keyway in the crankshaft so it can be installed in the same position.
11. Install rubber bands between a bolt on each connecting rod and oil pan bolts that have been reinstalled in the block (see illustration). This will keep the rods from banging on the block when the crank is removed.
12. Carefully lift the crankshaft out of the block. The rods will pivot to the center of the engine when the crank is removed.

To install:

When main bearing clearance has been checked, bearings examined and/or replaced, the crankshaft can be installed.

13. Thoroughly clean the upper and lower bearing surfaces, and lube them with clean engine oil.

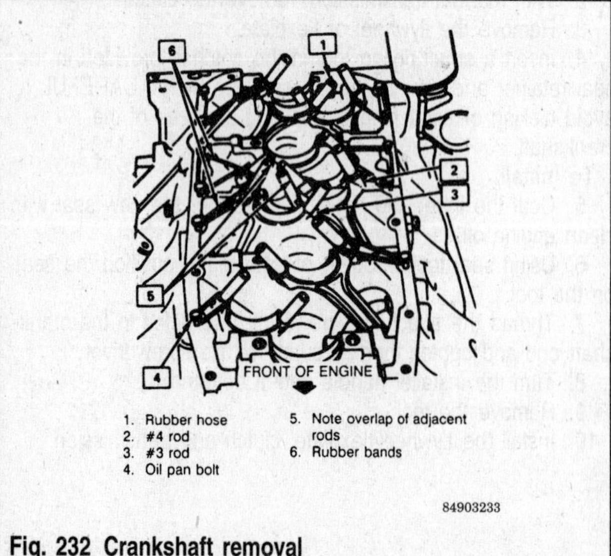

Fig. 232 Crankshaft removal

14. Install the crankshaft and main bearing caps.
15. Install a new rear main bearing oil seal in the cylinder block and main bearing cap. Continue to reassemble the engine.
16. Dip all main bearing cap bolts in clean oil, and tighten all main bearing caps, excluding the thrust bearing cap, to specifications. see the Crankshaft and Connecting Rod chart in this section to determine which bearing is the thrust bearing.
17. Tighten the thrust bearing bolts finger-tight. To align the thrust bearing, pry the crankshaft the extent of its axial travel several times, holding the last movement toward the front of the engine. Add thrust washers if required for proper alignment.
18. Tighten the thrust bearing cap to specifications.
19. Install the connecting rod bearings and caps and tighten to specifications.
20. Install the oil pump and the oil pan.
21. Install the timing chain and gears.
22. Install the front (timing) cover.
23. Install the engine in the vehicle.
24. Fill the crankcase with the proper grade and viscosity of engine oil.

INSPECTION

Like connecting rod bearings, the crankshaft main bearings are shell type inserts that do not utilize shims and cannot be adjusted. The bearings are available in various standard and undersizes. If main bearing clearance is found to be too sloppy, a new bearing (both upper and lower halves) is required.

➡Factory undersized crankshafts are marked, sometimes with a 9 and/or a large spot of light green paint. The bearing caps also will have the paint on each side of the undersized journal.

Generally, the lower half of the bearing shell (except No. 1 bearing) shows greater wear and fatigue. If the lower half only shows the effects of normal wear (no heavy scoring or discoloration), it can usually be assumed that the upper half is also in good shape. Conversely, if the lower half is heavily worn or damaged, both halves should be replaced. Never replace one bearing half without replacing the other.

CHECKING CLEARANCE

▶ See Figure 234

Main bearing clearance can be checked both with the crankshaft in the truck and with the engine out of the car. If the engine block is still in the truck, the crankshaft should be supported both front and rear (by the damper and to remove clearance from the upper bearing. Total clearance can then be measured between the lower bearing and journal. If the block has been removed from the truck, and is inverted, the crank will rest on the upper bearings and the total clearance can be measured between the lower bearing and journal. Clearance is

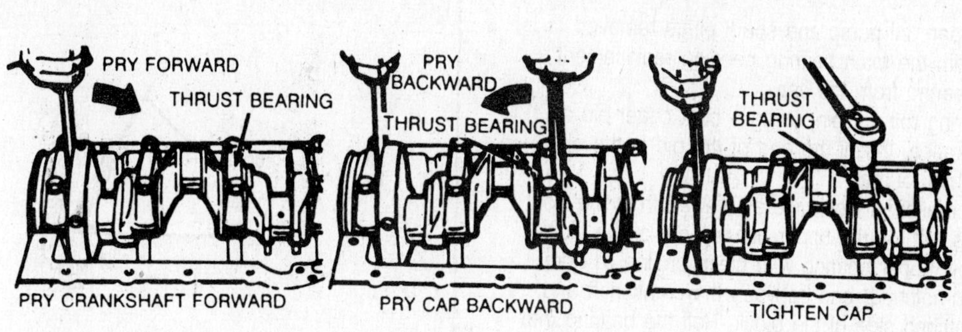

Fig. 233 Aligning the crankshaft thrust bearing

checked in the same manner as the connecting rod bearings, with Plastigage®.

➡Crankshaft bearing caps and bearing shells should NEVER be filed flush with the cap-to-block mating surface to adjust for wear in the old bearings. Always install new bearings.

1. If the crankshaft has been removed, install it (block removed from truck). If the block is still in the truck, remove the oil pan and oil pump. Starting with the rear bearing cap, remove the cap and wipe all oil from the crank journal and bearing cap.
2. Place a strip of Plastigage® the full width of the bearing, (parallel to the crankshaft), on the journal.

⁂WARNING

Do not rotate the crankshaft while the gaging material is between the bearing and the journal!

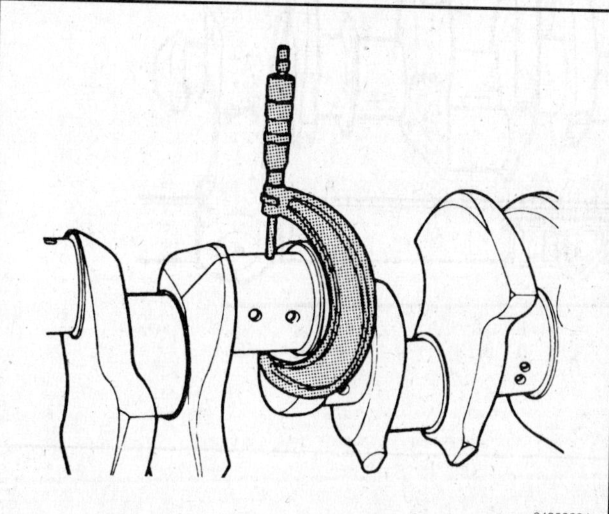

Fig. 234 Measuring the crankshaft bearing journals

3. Install the bearing cap and evenly tighten the cap bolts to specification.
4. Remove the bearing cap. The flattened Plastigage® will be sticking to either the bearing shell or the crank journal.
5. Use the graduated scale on the Plastigage® envelope to measure the material at its widest point.

➡If the flattened Plastigage® tapers toward the middle or ends, there is a difference in clearance indicating the bearing or journal has a taper, low spot or other irregularity. If this is indicated, measure the crank journal with a micrometer.

6. If bearing clearance is within specifications, the bearing insert is in good shape. Replace the insert if the clearance is not within specifications. Always replace both upper and lower inserts as a unit.
7. Standard, 0.001 in. (0.0254mm) or 0.002 in. (0.051mm) undersize bearings should produce the proper clearance. If these sizes still produce too sloppy a fit, the crankshaft must be reground for use with the next undersize bearing. Recheck all clearances after installing new bearings.
8. Replace the rest of the bearings in the same manner. After all bearings have been checked, rotate the crankshaft to make sure there is no excessive drag. When checking the No. 1 main bearing, loosen the accessory drive belts (engine in truck) to prevent a tapered reading with the Plastigage®.

MAIN BEARING REPLACEMENT

Engine Out of Truck

1. Remove and inspect the crankshaft.
2. Remove the main bearings from the bearing saddles in the cylinder block and main bearing caps.

To install:

3. Coat the bearing surfaces of the new, correct size main bearings with clean engine oil and install them in the bearing saddles in the block and in the main bearing caps.
4. Install the crankshaft. See Crankshaft removal and installation.

Engine in Truck

➧ See Figure 235

1. With the oil pan, oil pump and spark plugs removed, remove the cap from the main bearing needing replacement and remove the bearing from the cap.
2. Make a bearing roll out pin, using a bent cotter pin as shown in the illustration. Install the end of the pin in the oil hole in the crankshaft journal.
3. Rotate the crankshaft clockwise as viewed from the front of the engine. This will roll the upper bearing out of the block.
4. Lube the new upper bearing with clean engine oil and insert the plain (un-notched) end between the crankshaft and the indented or notched side of the block. Roll the bearing into place, making sure that the oil holes are aligned. Remove the roll pin from the oil hole.
5. Lube the new lower bearing and install the main bearing cap. Install the main bearing cap, making sure it is positioned in proper direction with the matchmarks in alignment.
6. Tighten the main bearing cap bolts to specification. Refer to the crankshaft removal and installation.

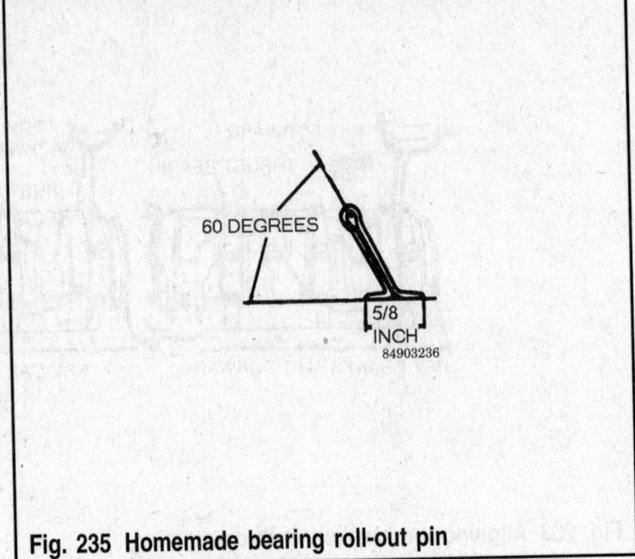

Fig. 235 Homemade bearing roll-out pin

CRANKSHAFT END-PLAY

➧ See Figures 236 and 237

When main bearing clearance has been checked, bearings examined and/or replaced, the crankshaft can be installed. Thoroughly clean the upper and lower bearing surfaces, and lube them with clean engine oil. Install the crankshaft and main bearing caps.

1. To check crankshaft end-play, pry the crankshaft to the extreme rear of its axial travel, then to the extreme front of its travel.
2. Using a feeler gauge, measure the end-play at the front of the rear main bearing.
3. End-play may also be measured at the thrust bearing.

Fig. 236 Measuring the crankshaft runout

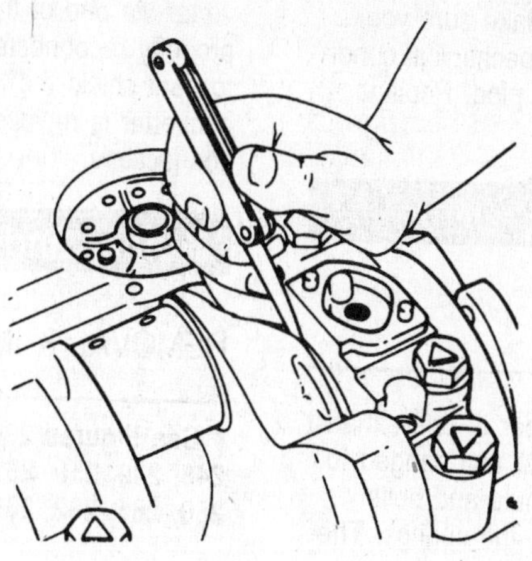

Fig. 237 Measuring the crankshaft end-play

Flywheel and Ring Gear

REMOVAL & INSTALLATION

The ring gear is an integral part of the flywheel and is not replaceable. To remove the flywheel:

1. Remove the transmission.
2. Remove the six bolts attaching the flywheel to the crankshaft flange. Remove the flywheel.
3. Inspect the flywheel for cracks, and inspect the ring gear for burrs or worn teeth. Replace the flywheel if any damage is apparent. Remove burrs with a mill file.
4. Install the flywheel. The flywheel will only attach to the crankshaft in one position, as the bolt holes are unevenly spaced. Install the bolts and tighten to specification. Refer to the torque specification chart.

EXHAUST SYSTEM

General Information

➡Safety glasses should be worn at all times when working on or near the exhaust system. Older exhaust systems will almost always be covered with loose rust particles which will shower you when disturbed. These particles are more than a nuisance and could injure your eye.

Whenever working on the exhaust system always keep the following in mind:

- Check the complete exhaust system for open seams, holes loose connections, or other deterioration which could permit exhaust fumes to seep into the passenger compartment.
- The exhaust system is usually supported by free-hanging rubber mountings which permit some movement of the exhaust system, but does not permit transfer of noise and vibration into the passenger compartment. Do not replace the rubber mounts with solid ones.
- Before removing any component of the exhaust system, ALWAYS squirt a liquid rust dissolving agent onto the fasteners for ease of removal. A lot of knuckle skin will be saved by following this rule. It may even be wise to spray the fasteners and allow them to sit overnight.

✲✲CAUTION

Allow the exhaust system to cool sufficiently before spraying a solvent exhaust fasteners. Some solvents are highly flammable and could ignite when sprayed on hot exhaust components.

- Annoying rattles and noise vibrations in the exhaust system are usually caused by misalignment of the parts. When aligning the system, leave all bolts and nuts loose until all parts are properly aligned, then tighten, working from front to rear.
- When installing exhaust system parts, make sure there is enough clearance between the hot exhaust parts and pipes and hoses that would be adversely affected by excessive heat. Also make sure there is adequate clearance from the floor pan to avoid possible overheating of the floor.

Crossover Pipe

REMOVAL & INSTALLATION

The crossover pipe (used on V-type engines only) is typically connected to the manifolds by flanged connections or collars.

In some cases, bolts that are unthreaded for part of their length are used in conjunction with springs. Make sure you install the springs and that they are in good mechanical condition (no broken coils) when installing the new pipe. Replace ring type seals, also.

Headpipe

REMOVAL & INSTALLATION

The headpipe is typically attached to the rear of one exhaust manifold with a flange or collar type connector and flanged to the front of the catalytic converter. Remove nuts and bolts and, if springs are used to maintain the seal, the springs. The pipe may then be separated from the rest of the system at both flanges.

Replace ring seals; inspect springs and replace them if any coils are broken.

Catalytic Converter

REMOVAL & INSTALLATION

➧ See Figure 238

CAUTION

Be very careful when working on or near the converter! External temperatures can reach 1,500°F (816°C) and more, causing severe burns! Removal or installation should only be performed on a cold exhaust system.

1. Remove bolts at the flange at the rear end, then loosen nuts and remove U-clamp
2. Slide the catalytic convertor out of the outlet pipe.
3. Installation is the reverse of removal.

Replace all ring seals. In some cases, you'll have to disconnect an air line coming from the engine compartment before catalyst removal. In some cases, a hanger supports the converter via one of the flange bolts. Make sure the hanger gets properly reconnected. Also, be careful to retain all parts used to heat shield the converter and reinstall them. Make sure the converter is replaced for proper direction of flow and air supply connections.

Muffler and Tailpipes

REMOVAL & INSTALLATION

➧ See Figures 239, 240, 241, 242, 243, 244, 245, 246, 247, 248, 249, 250, 251, 252, 253, 254, 255, 256, 257, 258, 259, 260, 261, 262, 263, 264, 265, 266 and 267

These units are typically connected by flanges at the rear of the converter and at either end of mufflers either by an original weld or by U-clamps working over a pipe connection in which one side of the connection is slightly larger than the other. You may have to cut the original connection and use the pipe expander to allow the original equipment exhaust pipe to be fitted over the new muffler. In this case, you'll have to purchase new U-clamps to fasten the joints. GM recommends that whenever you replace a muffler, all parts to the rear of the muffler in the exhaust system must be replaced. Also, all slip joints rearward of the converter should be coated with sealer before they are assembled.

Be careful to connect all U-clamps or other hanger arrangements so the exhaust system will not flex. Assemble all parts loosely and rotate parts inside one another or clamps on the pipes to ensure proper routing of all exhaust system parts to avoid excessive heating of the floorpan, fuel lines and tank, etc. Also, make sure there is clearance to prevent the system from rattling against spring shackles, the differential, etc. You may be able to bend long pipes slightly by hand to help get enough clearance, if necessary.

While disassembling the system, keep your eye open for any leaks or for excessively close clearance to any brake system parts. Inspect the brake system for any sort of heat damage and repair as necessary.

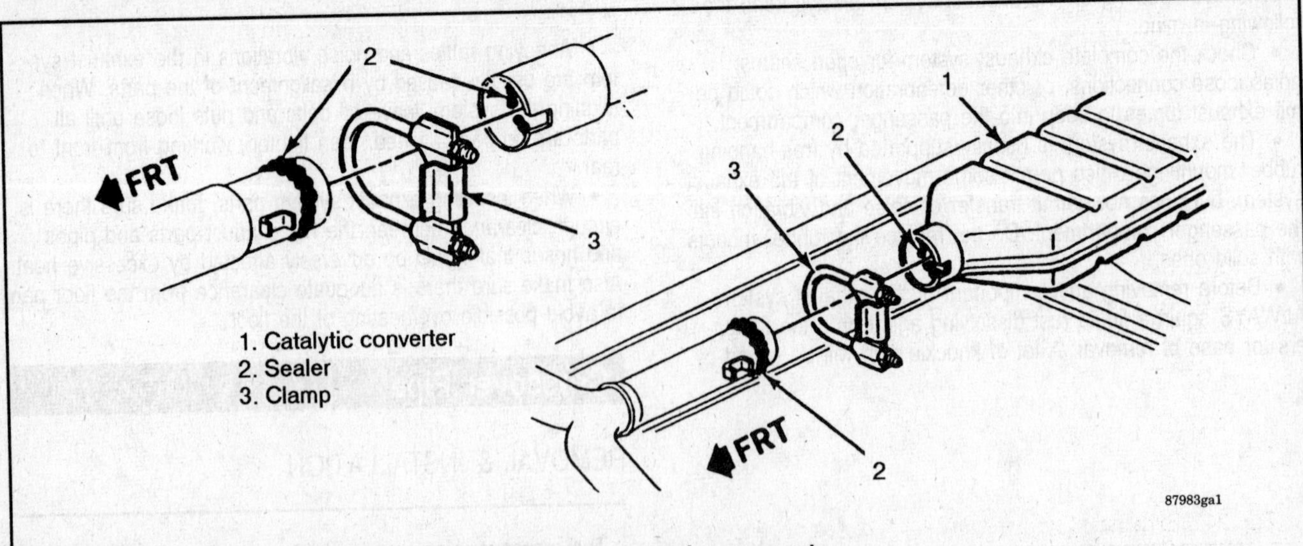

Fig. 238 Exploded view of the three way catalytic convertor and components

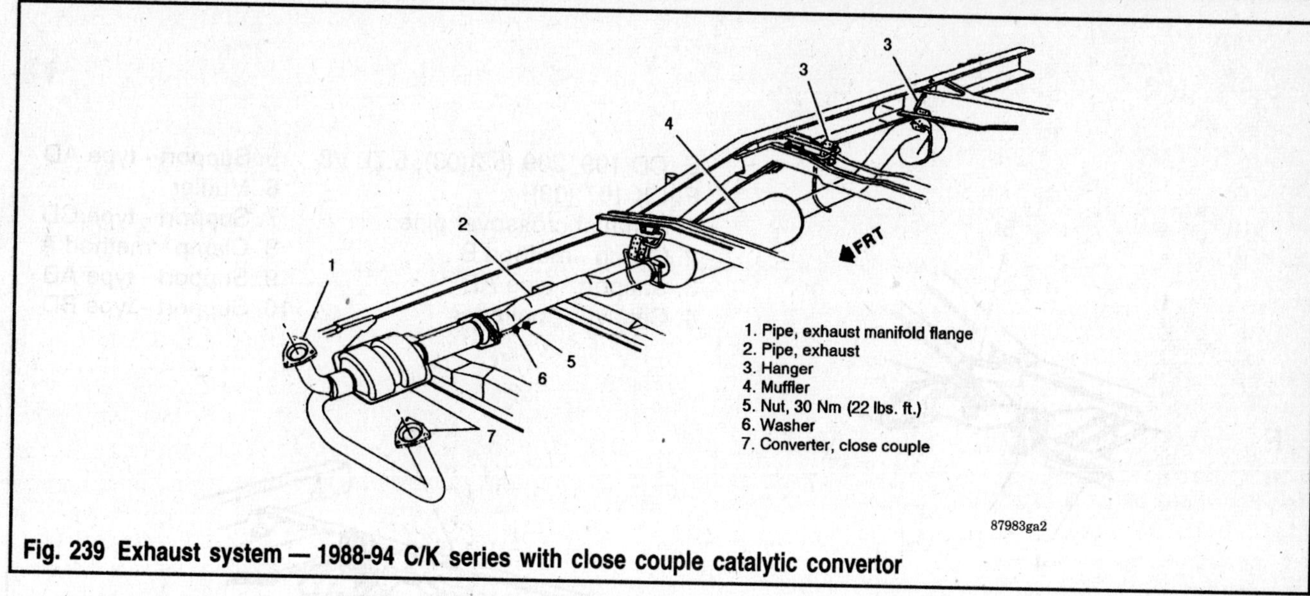

Fig. 239 Exhaust system — 1988-94 C/K series with close couple catalytic convertor

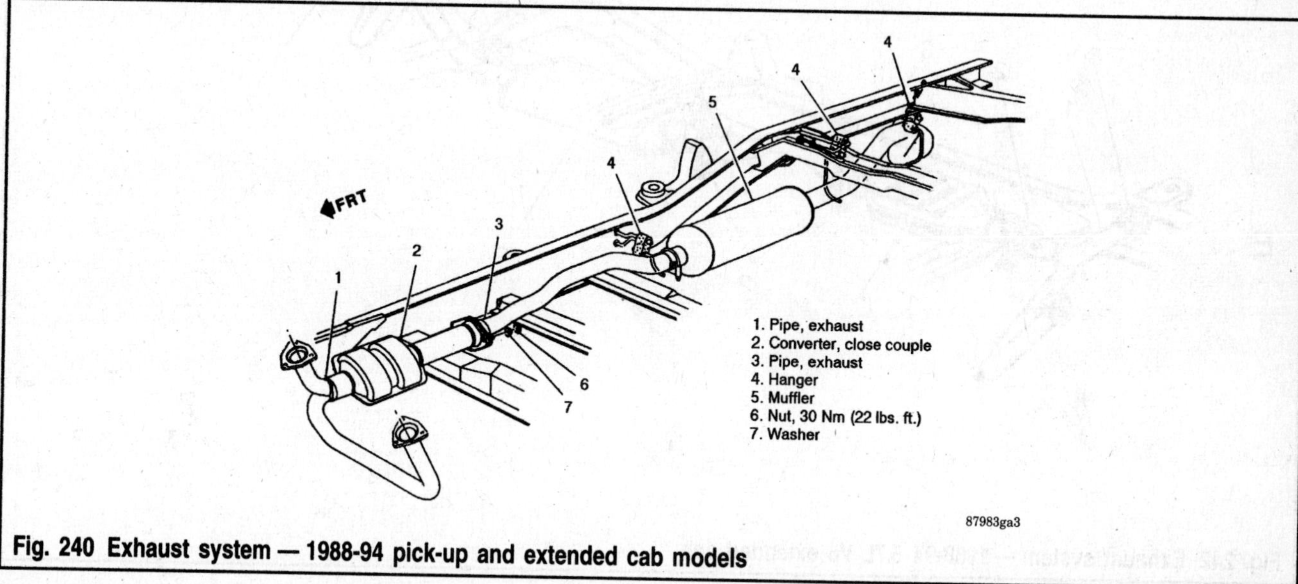

Fig. 240 Exhaust system — 1988-94 pick-up and extended cab models

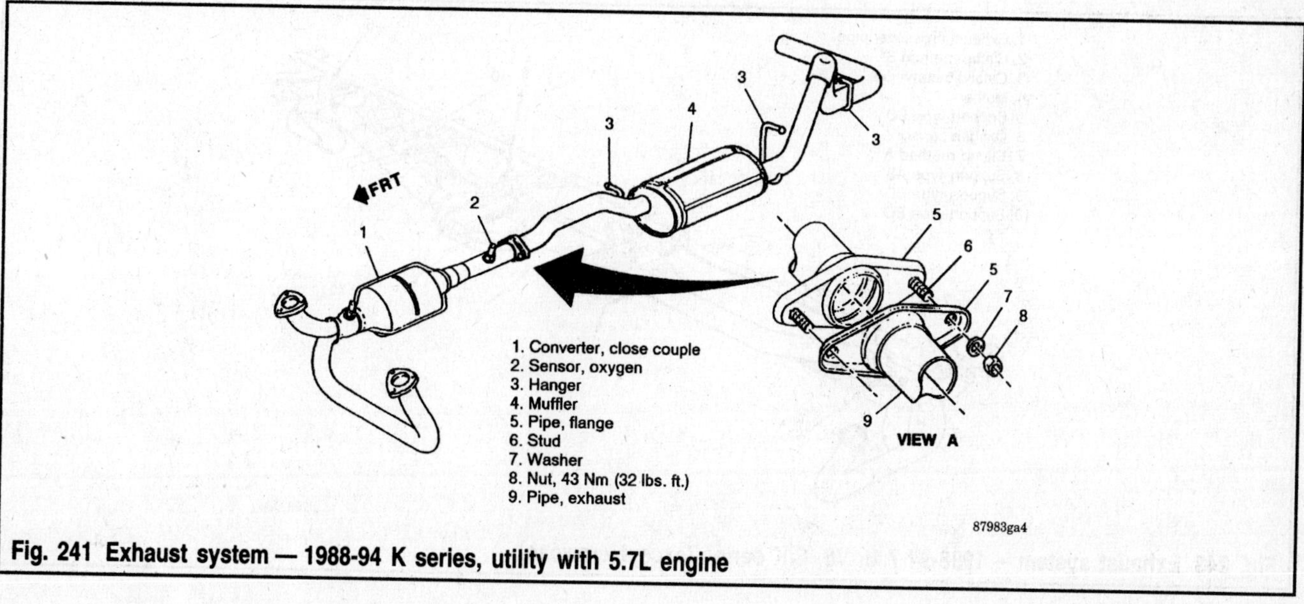

Fig. 241 Exhaust system — 1988-94 K series, utility with 5.7L engine

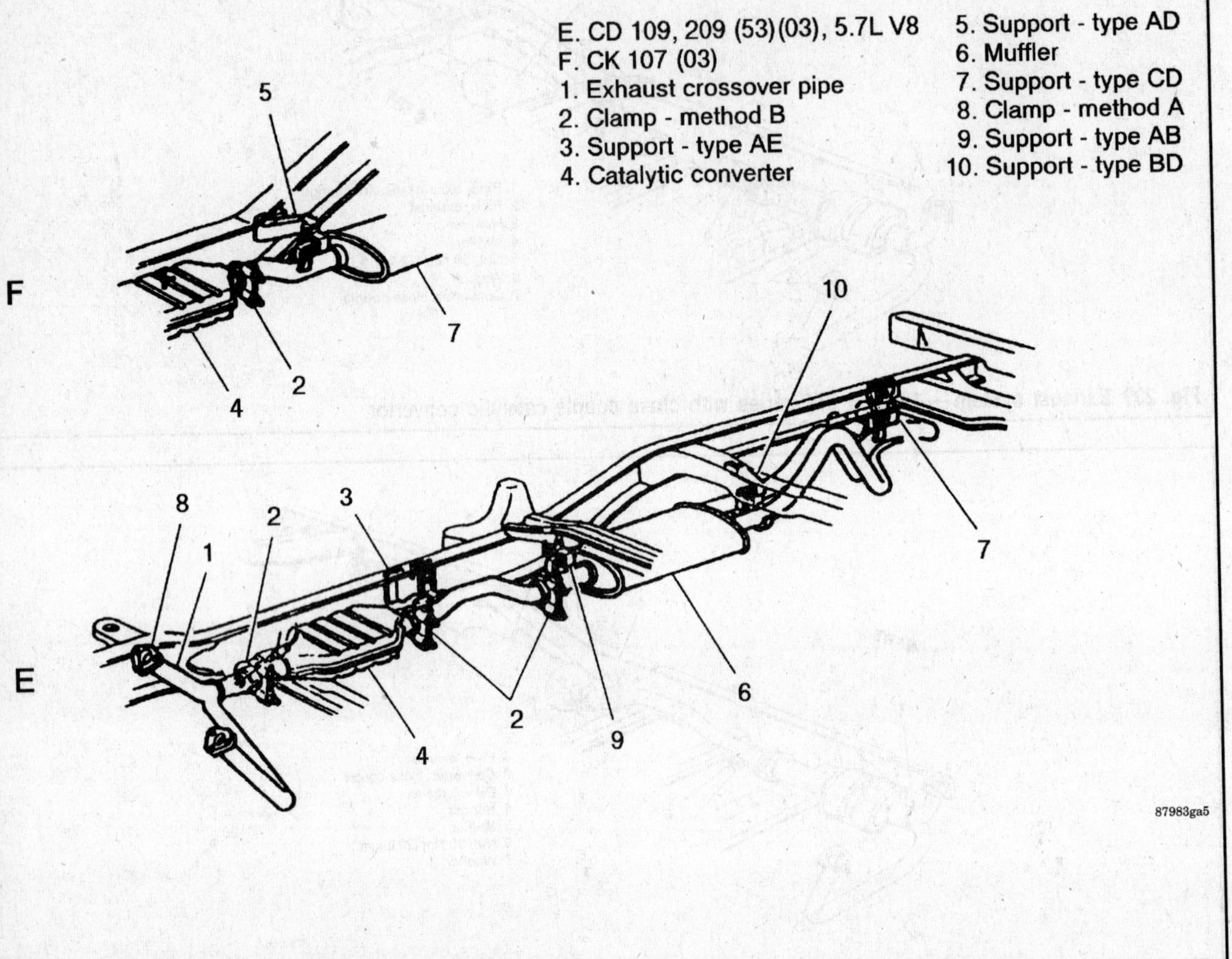

E. CD 109, 209 (53)(03), 5.7L V8
F. CK 107 (03)
1. Exhaust crossover pipe
2. Clamp - method B
3. Support - type AE
4. Catalytic converter
5. Support - type AD
6. Muffler
7. Support - type CD
8. Clamp - method A
9. Support - type AB
10. Support - type BD
F
E
87983ga5

Fig. 242 Exhaust system — 1988-94 5.7L V8 extended cab

1. Exhaust crossover pipe
2. Clamp-method B
3. Catalytic converter
4. Muffler
5. Support-type CD
6. Oxygen sensor
7. Clamp-method A
8. Support-type AB
9. Support-type BD
10. Support-type BC
87983ga6

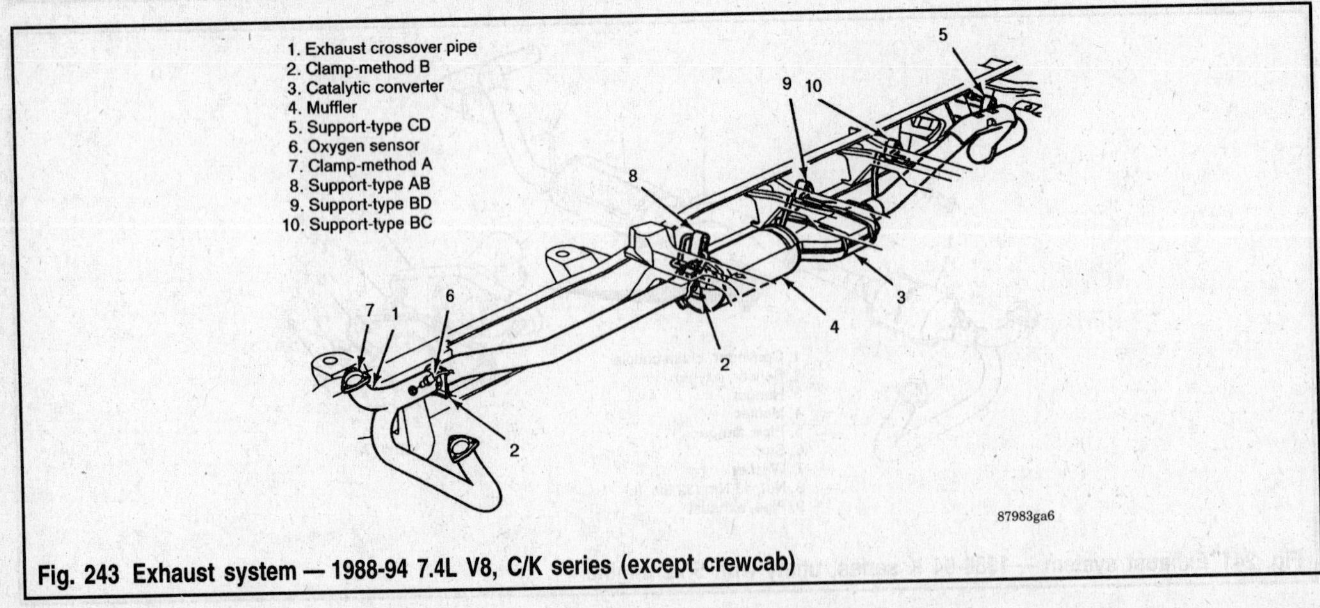

Fig. 243 Exhaust system — 1988-94 7.4L V8, C/K series (except crewcab)

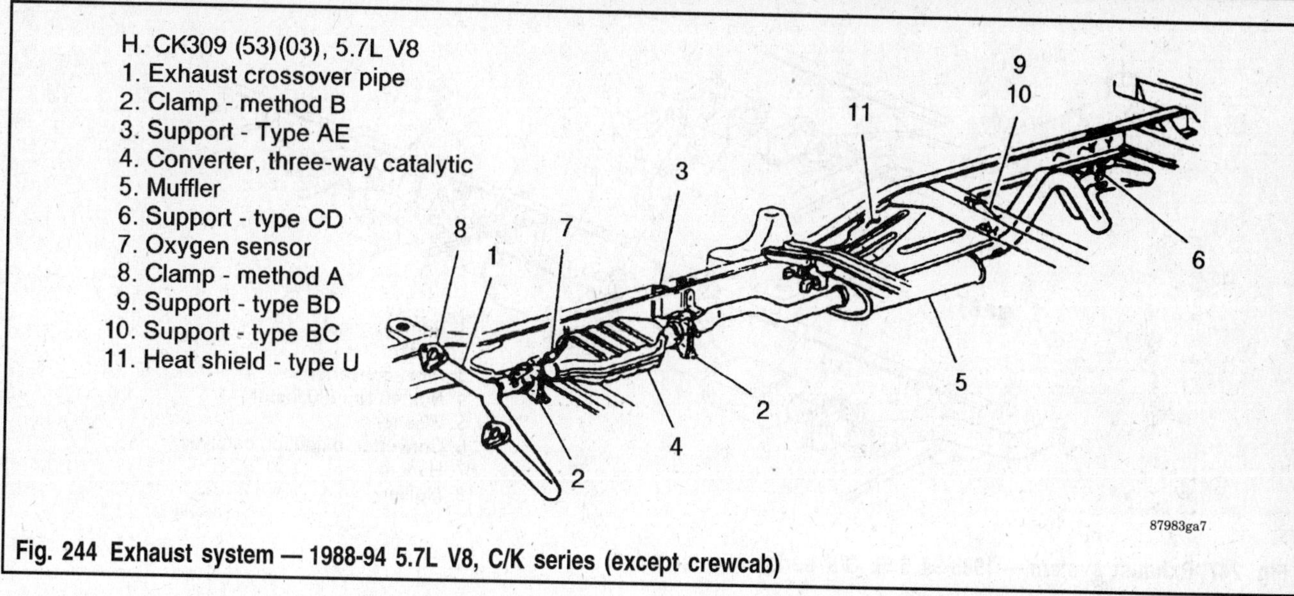

Fig. 244 Exhaust system — 1988-94 5.7L V8, C/K series (except crewcab)

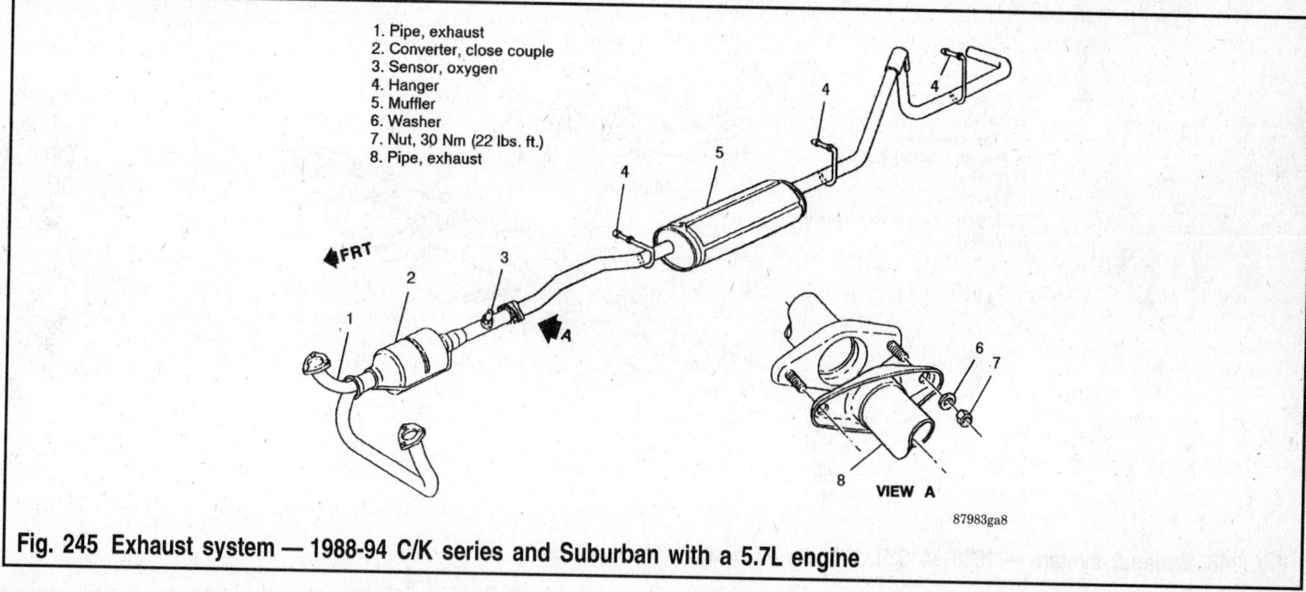

Fig. 245 Exhaust system — 1988-94 C/K series and Suburban with a 5.7L engine

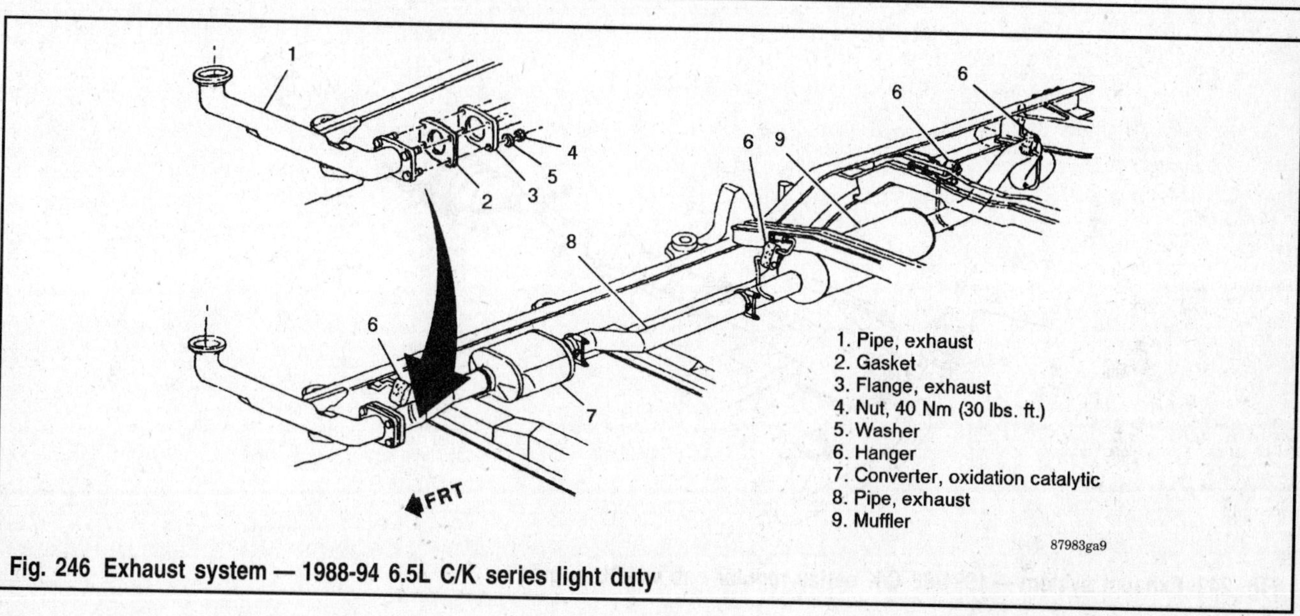

Fig. 246 Exhaust system — 1988-94 6.5L C/K series light duty

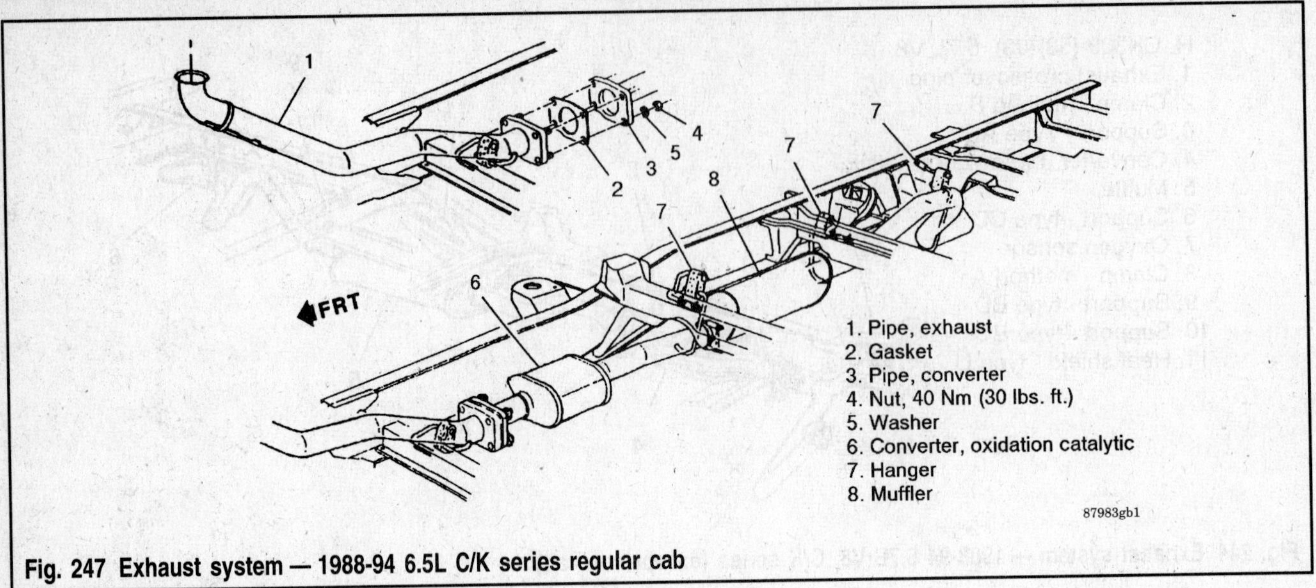

Fig. 247 Exhaust system — 1988-94 6.5L C/K series regular cab

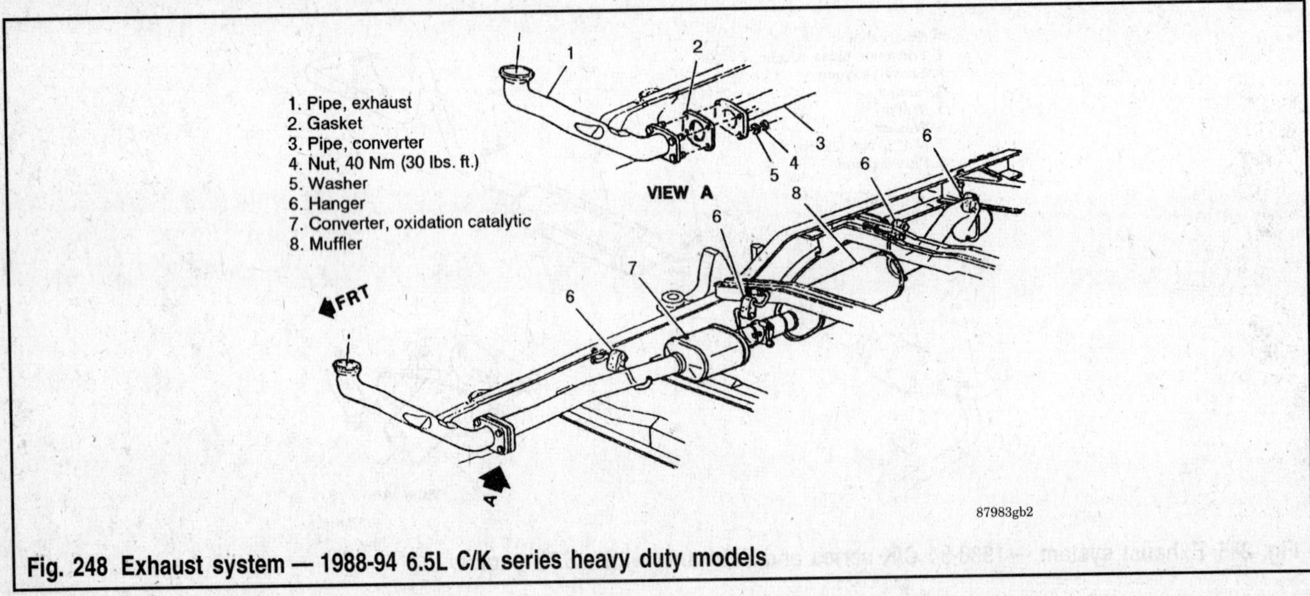

Fig. 248 Exhaust system — 1988-94 6.5L C/K series heavy duty models

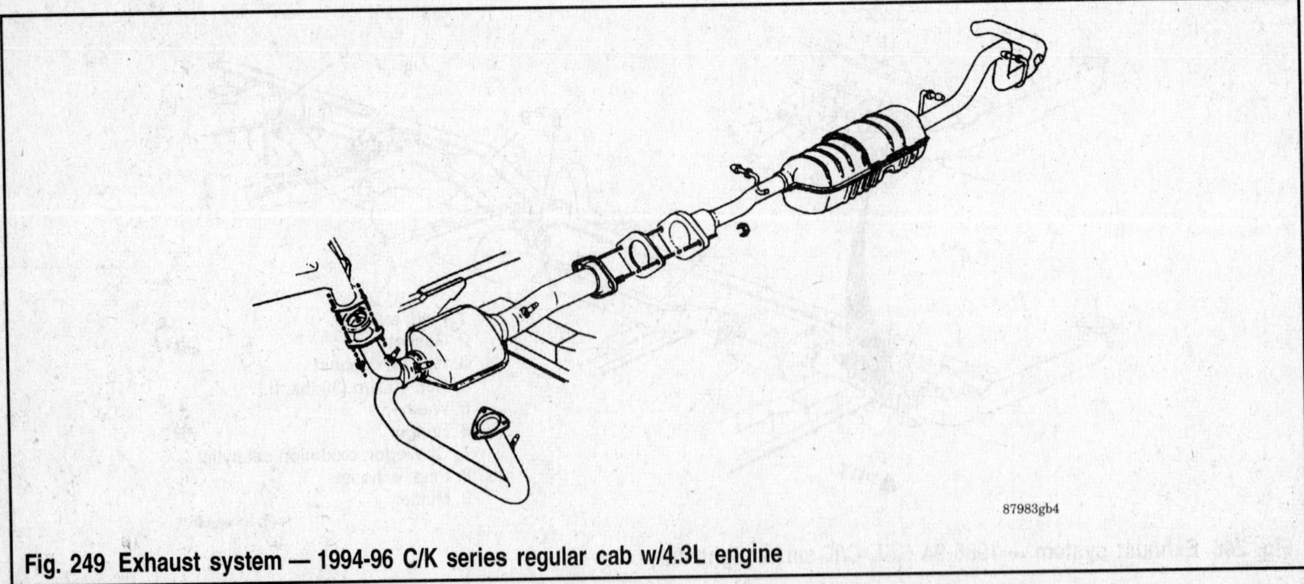

Fig. 249 Exhaust system — 1994-96 C/K series regular cab w/4.3L engine

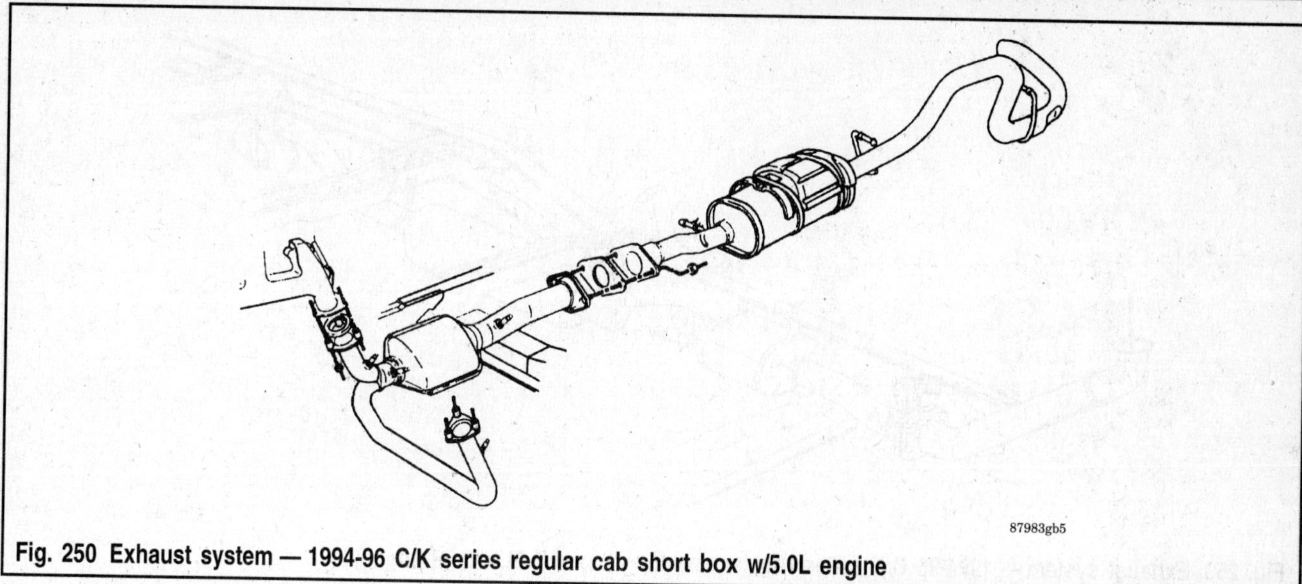

Fig. 250 Exhaust system — 1994-96 C/K series regular cab short box w/5.0L engine

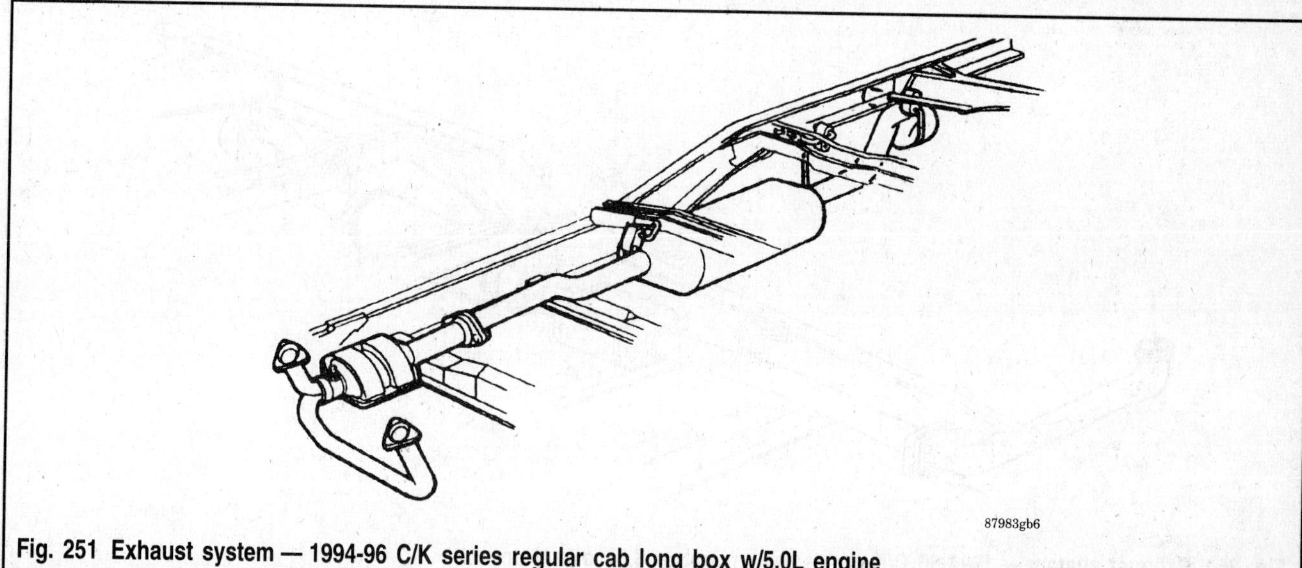

Fig. 251 Exhaust system — 1994-96 C/K series regular cab long box w/5.0L engine

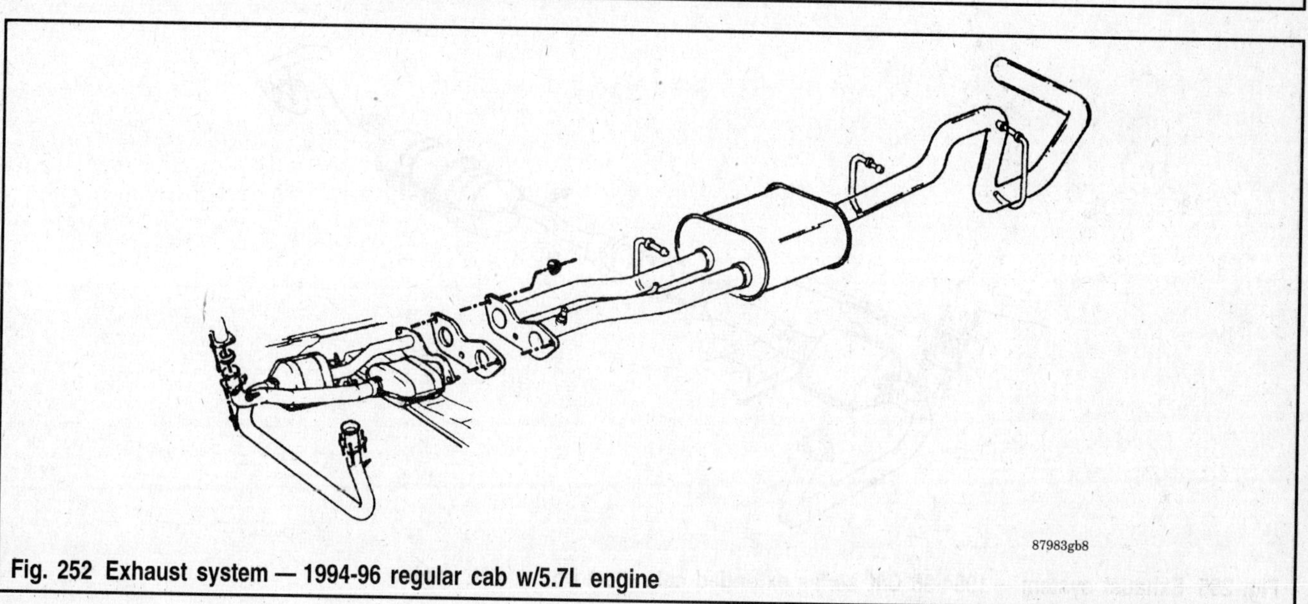

Fig. 252 Exhaust system — 1994-96 regular cab w/5.7L engine

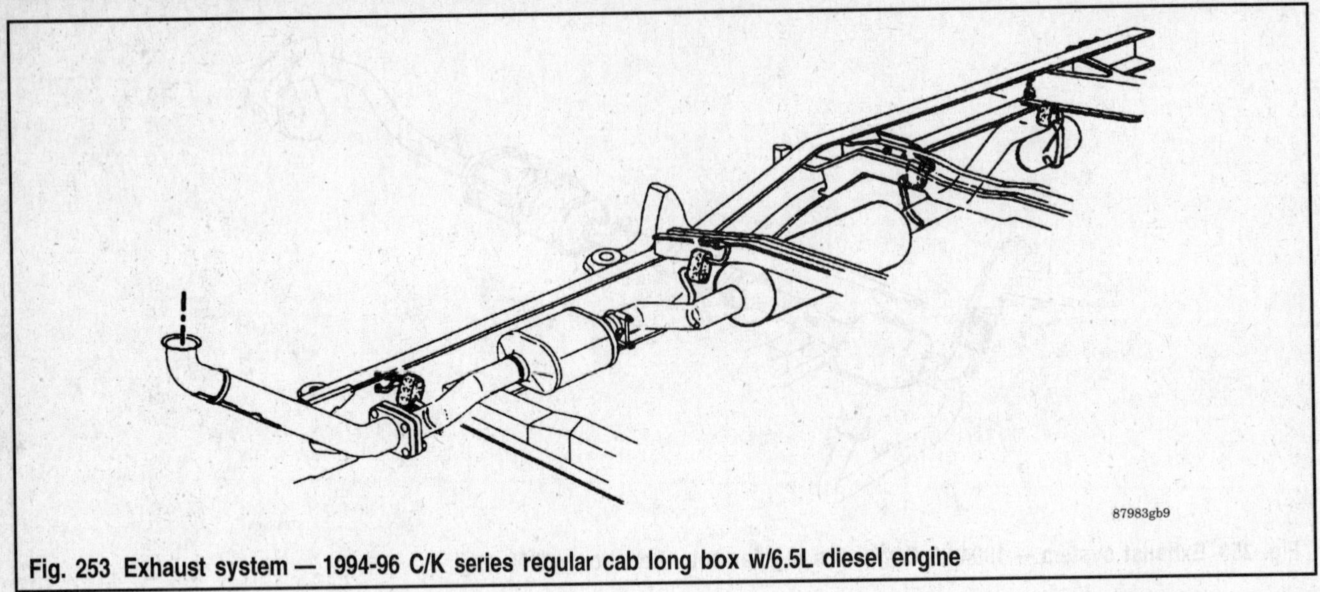

Fig. 253 Exhaust system — 1994-96 C/K series regular cab long box w/6.5L diesel engine

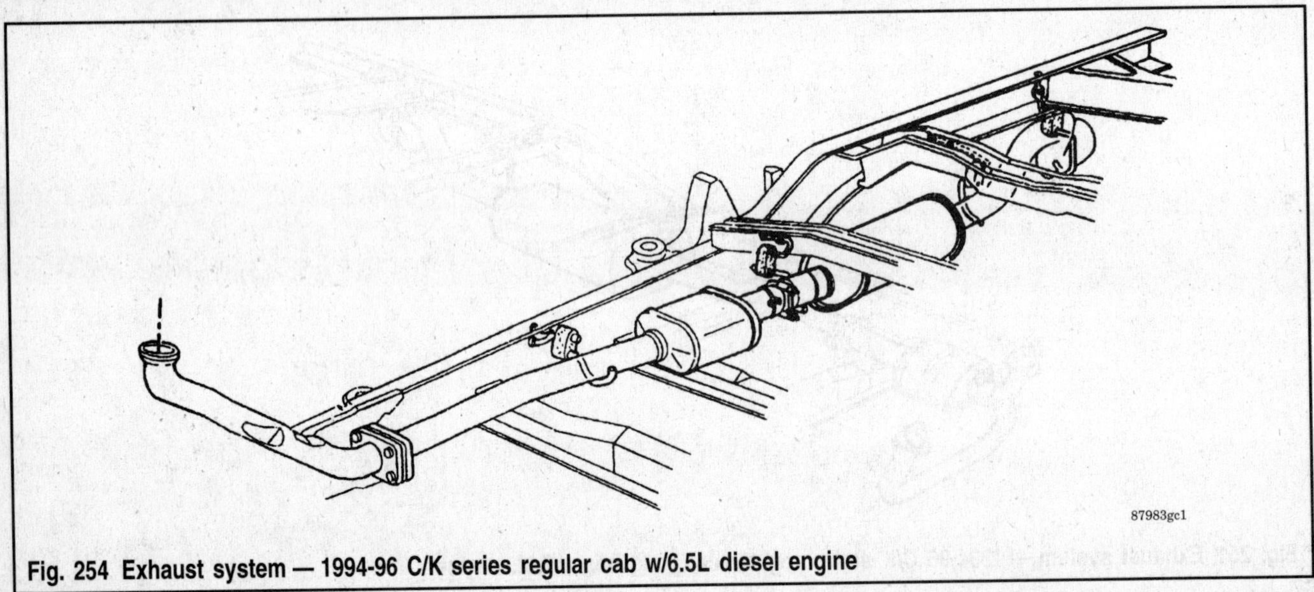

Fig. 254 Exhaust system — 1994-96 C/K series regular cab w/6.5L diesel engine

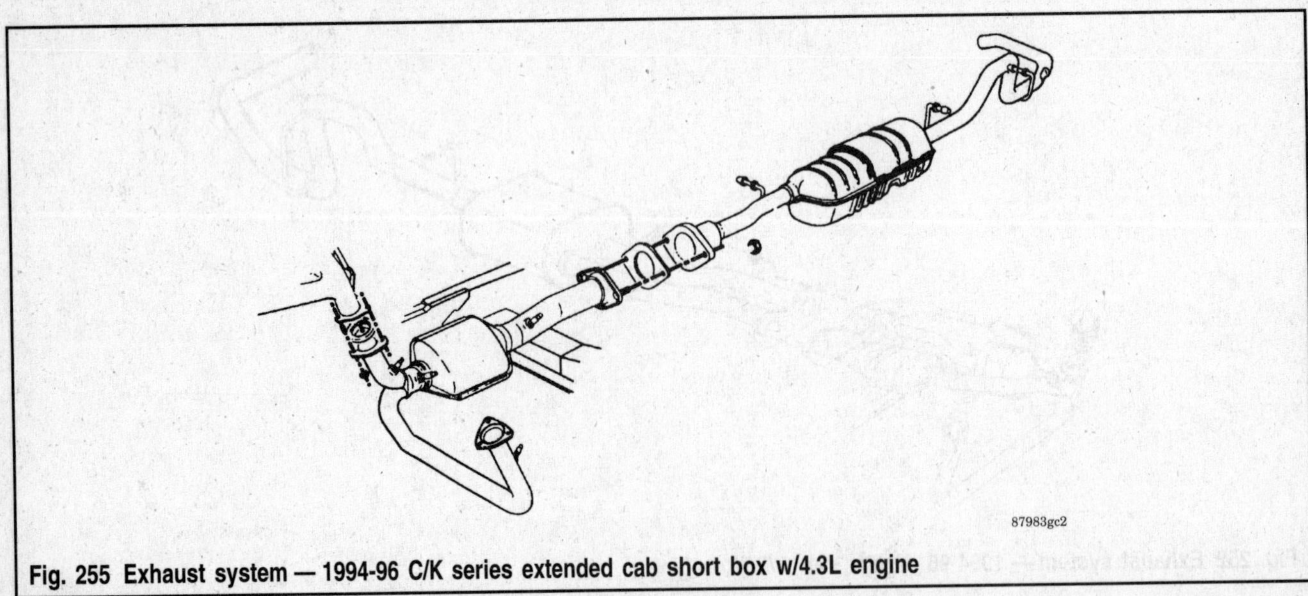

Fig. 255 Exhaust system — 1994-96 C/K series extended cab short box w/4.3L engine

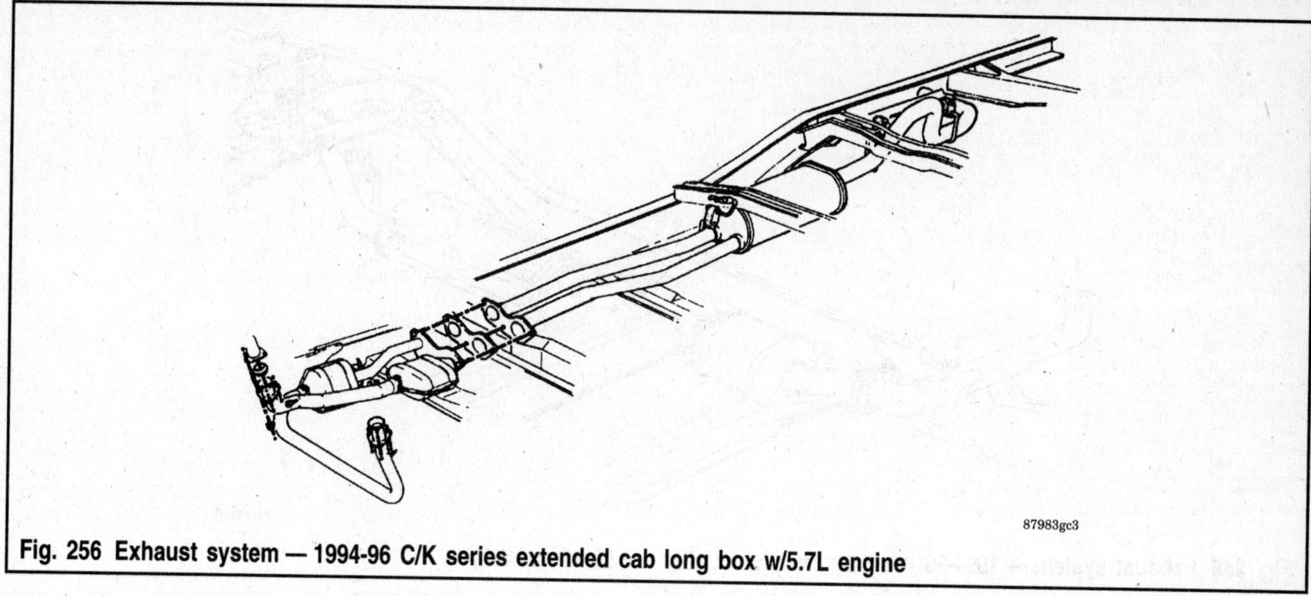

Fig. 256 Exhaust system — 1994-96 C/K series extended cab long box w/5.7L engine

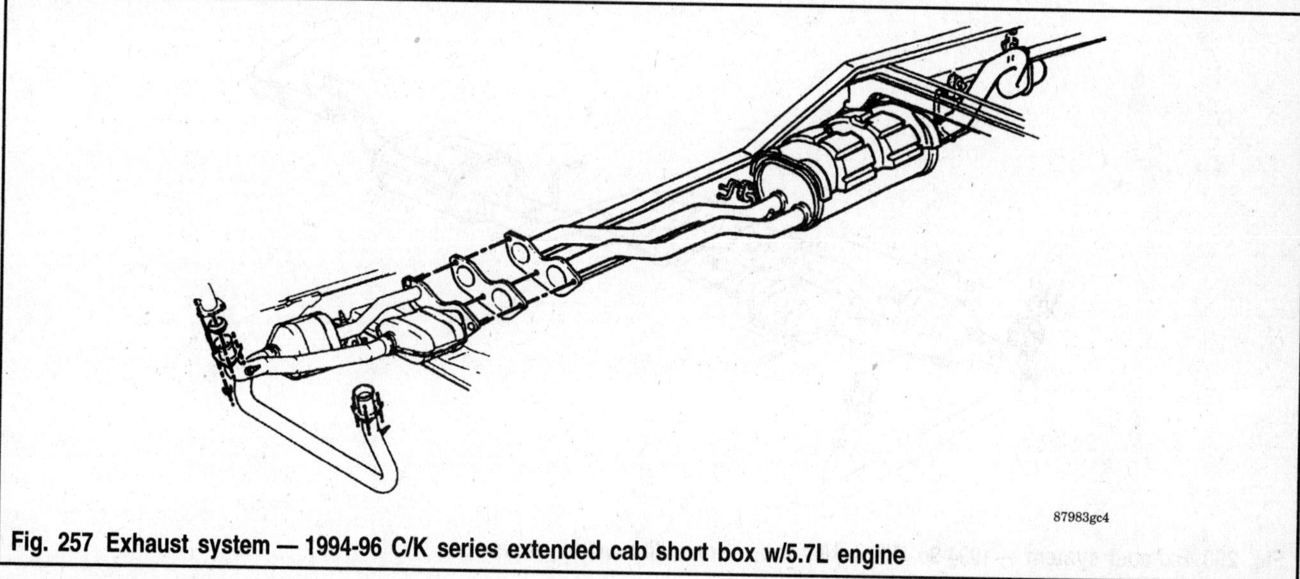

Fig. 257 Exhaust system — 1994-96 C/K series extended cab short box w/5.7L engine

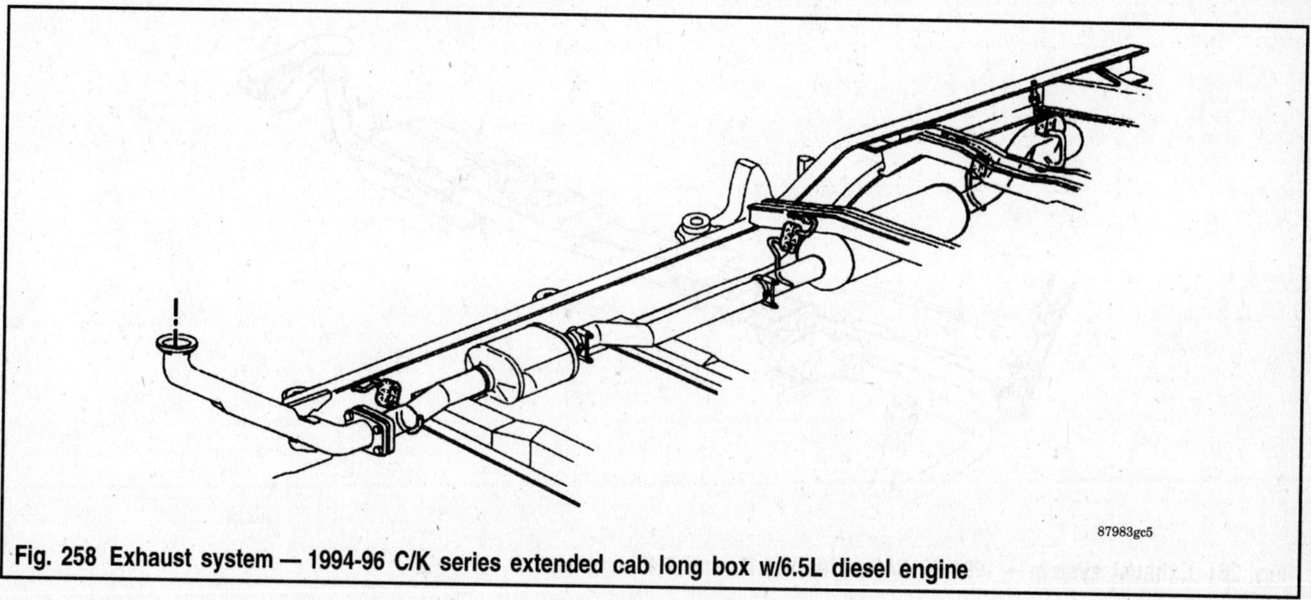

Fig. 258 Exhaust system — 1994-96 C/K series extended cab long box w/6.5L diesel engine

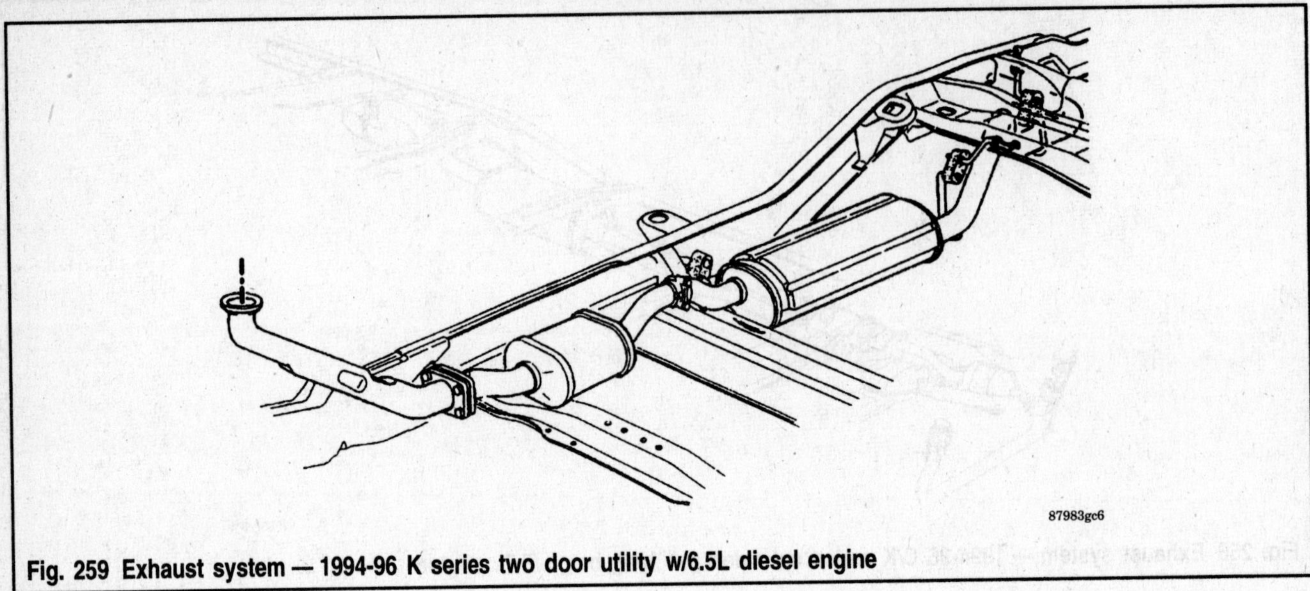

Fig. 259 Exhaust system — 1994-96 K series two door utility w/6.5L diesel engine

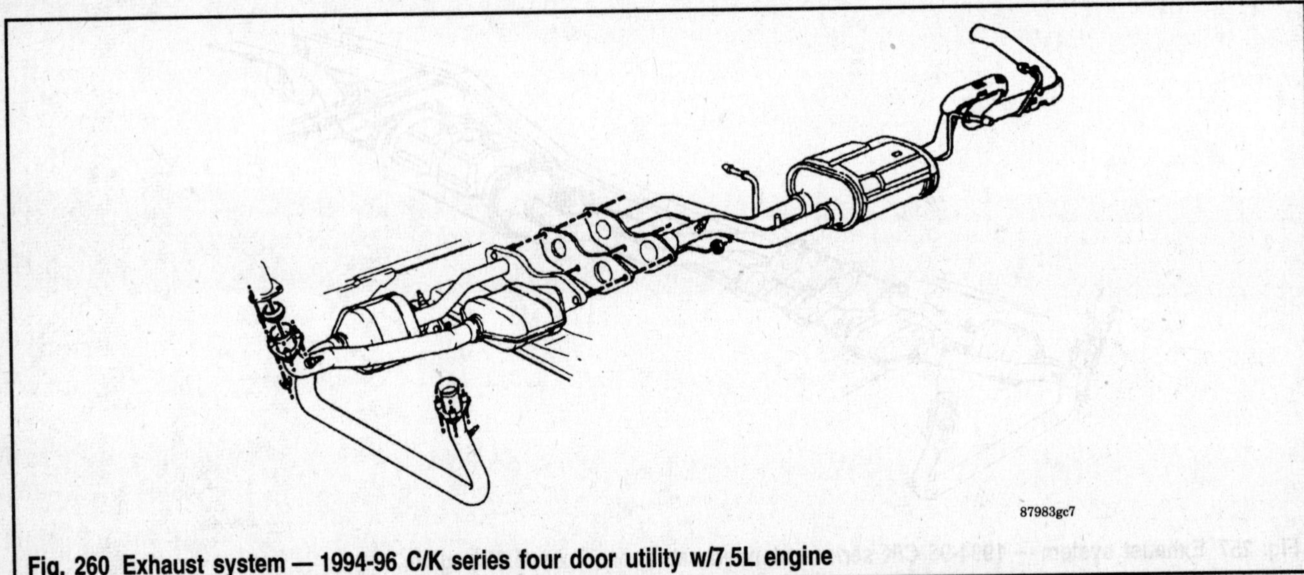

Fig. 260 Exhaust system — 1994-96 C/K series four door utility w/7.5L engine

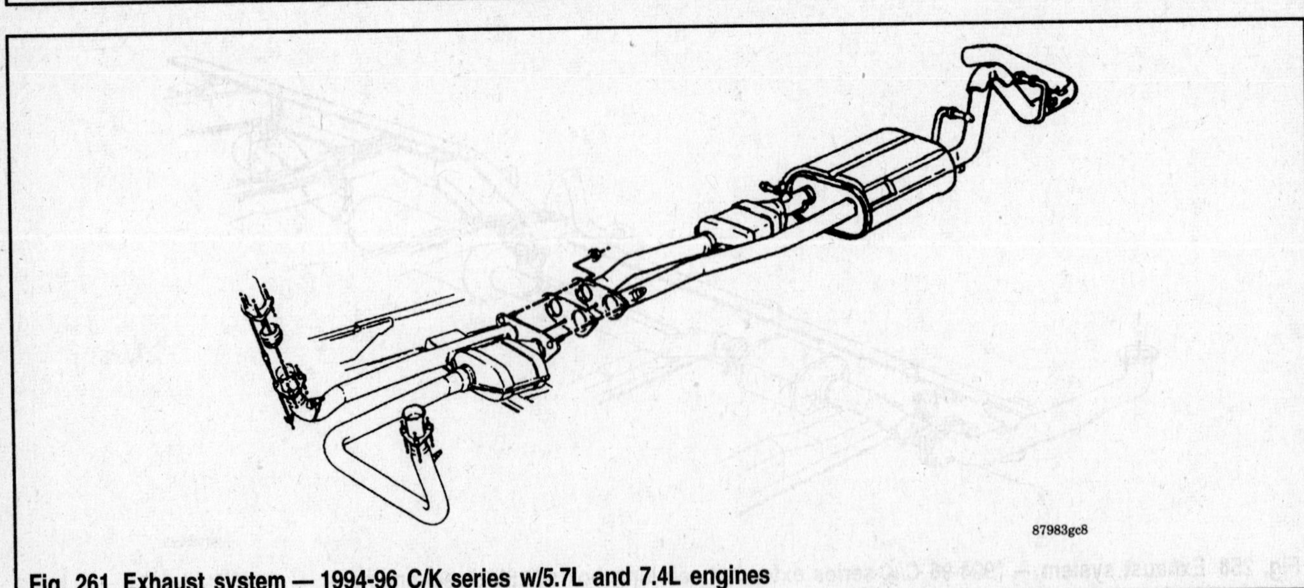

Fig. 261 Exhaust system — 1994-96 C/K series w/5.7L and 7.4L engines

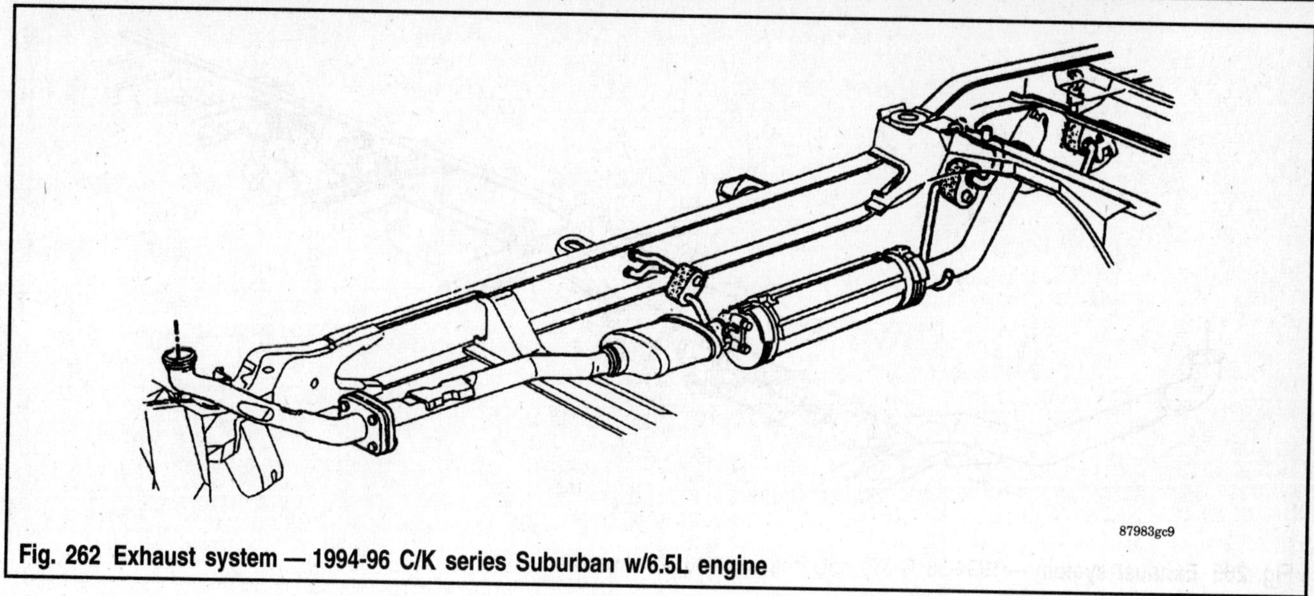

Fig. 262 Exhaust system — 1994-96 C/K series Suburban w/6.5L engine

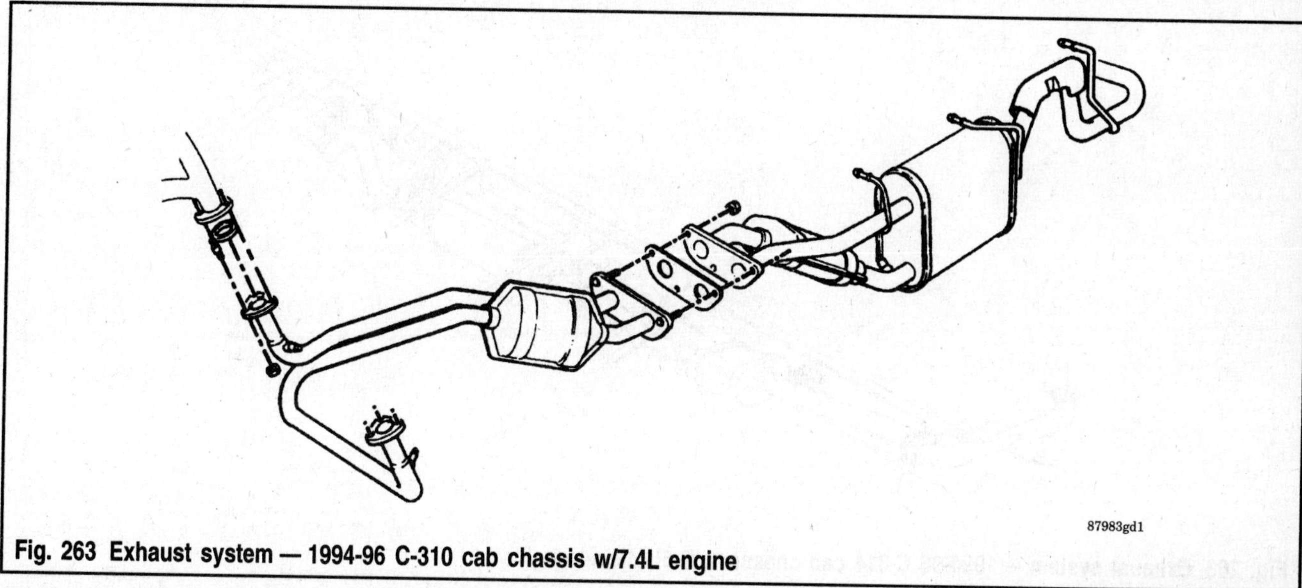

Fig. 263 Exhaust system — 1994-96 C-310 cab chassis w/7.4L engine

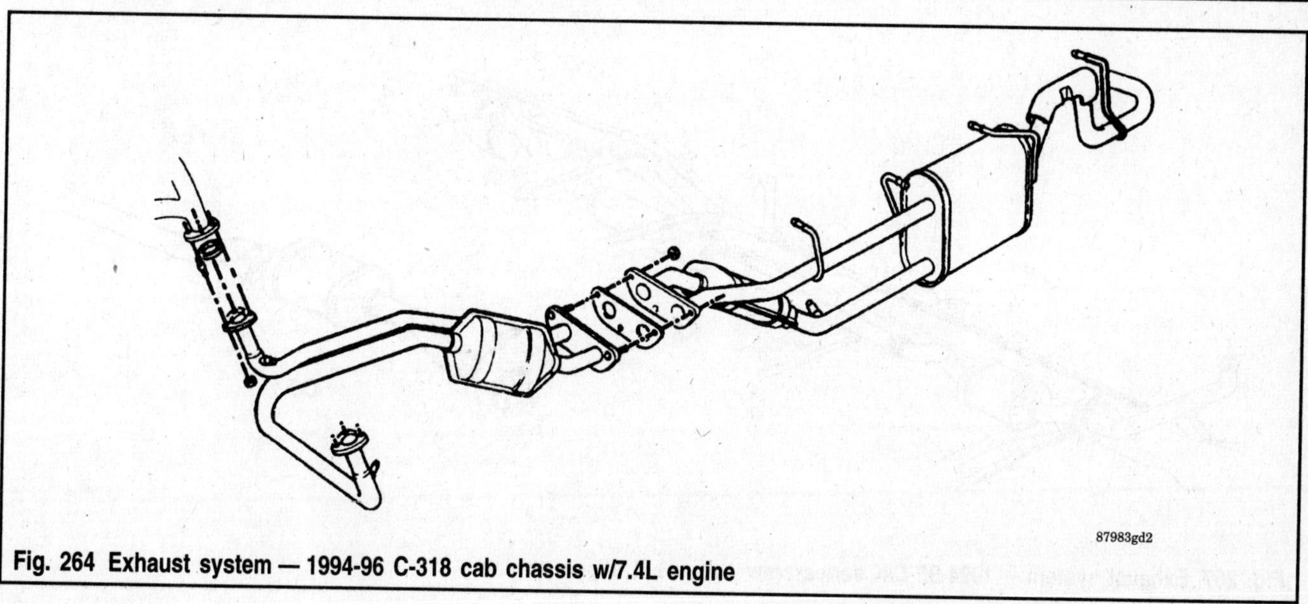

Fig. 264 Exhaust system — 1994-96 C-318 cab chassis w/7.4L engine

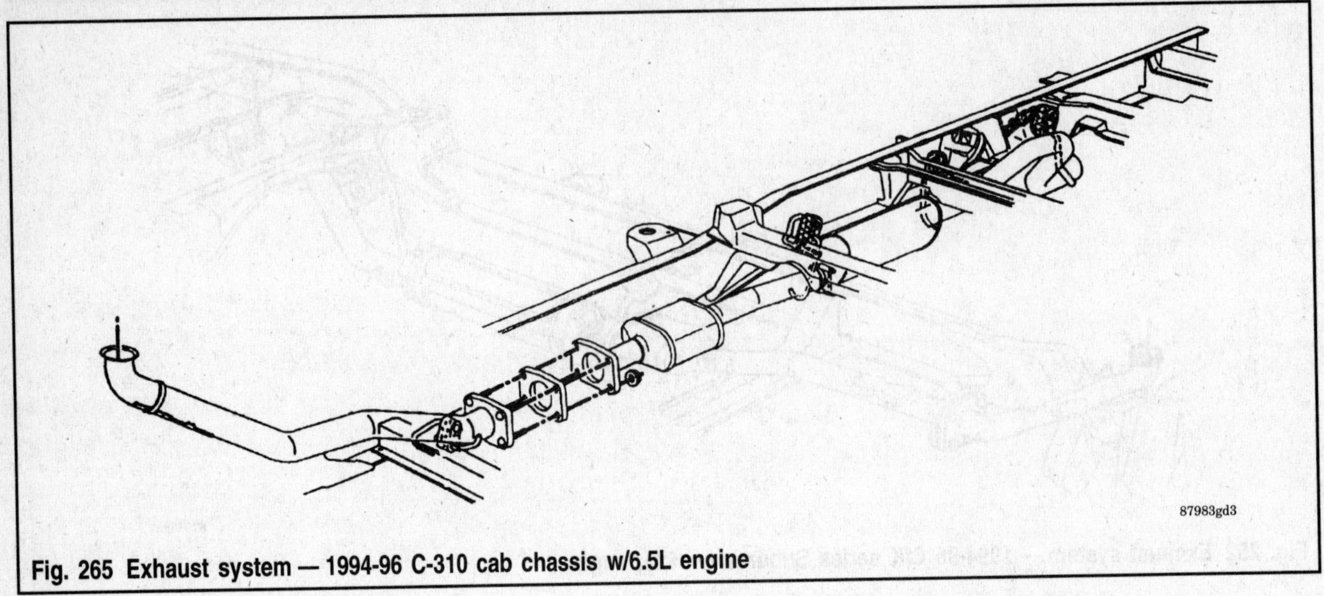

Fig. 265 Exhaust system — 1994-96 C-310 cab chassis w/6.5L engine

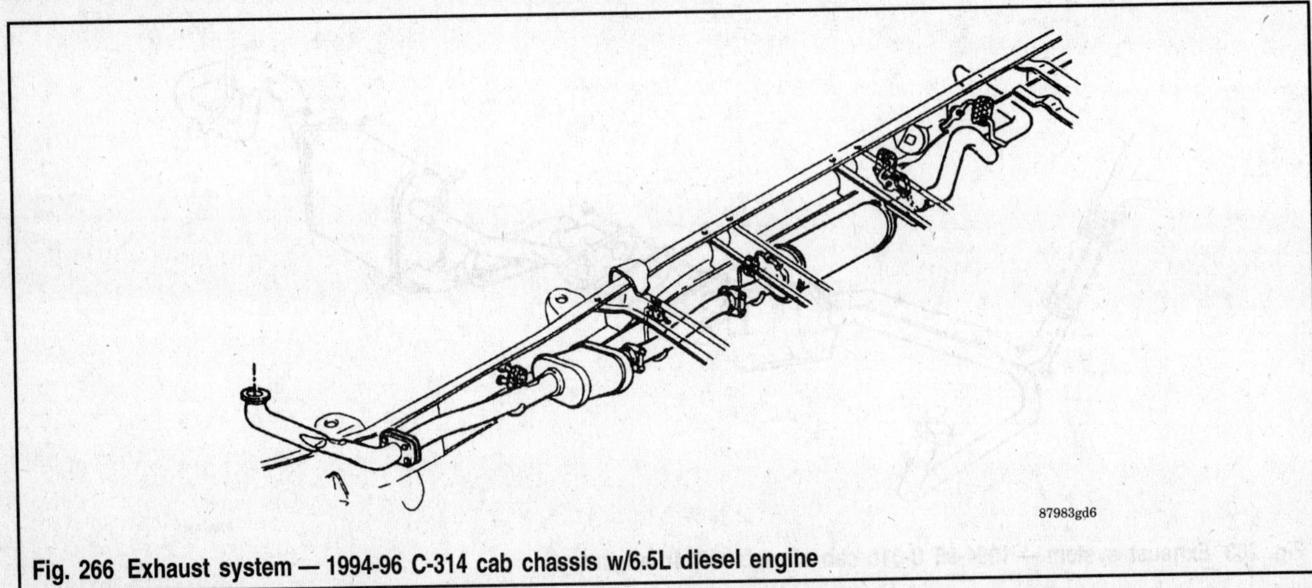

Fig. 266 Exhaust system — 1994-96 C-314 cab chassis w/6.5L diesel engine

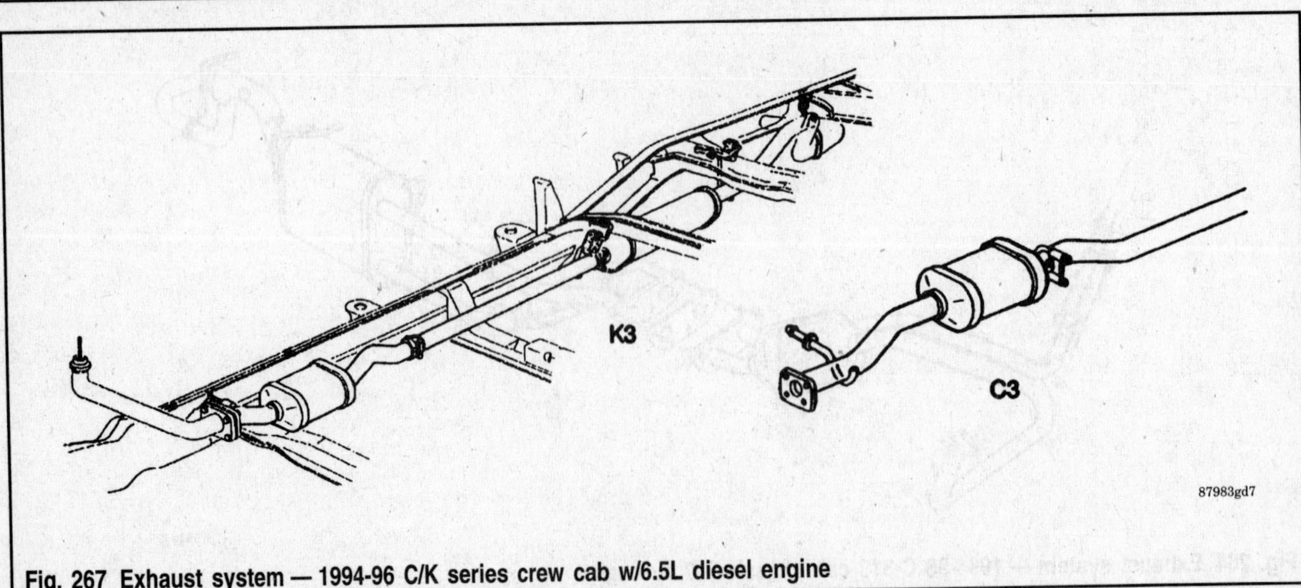

Fig. 267 Exhaust system — 1994-96 C/K series crew cab w/6.5L diesel engine

ENGINE REBUILDING SPECIFICATIONS

Component		US	Metric
Camshaft			
Intake Lobe lift			
4.3L Engines			
	1988-90	0.367 in.	9.07mm
	1991-94	0.234 in.	5.94mm
	1995-96	0.276 in.	7.02mm
Exhaust Lobe lift			
	1988-94	0.257 in.	6.53mm
	1995-96	0.285 in.	7.25mm
4.8L, 5.0L Engines			
Intake Lobe lift			
	1988-90	0.2484 in.	6.13mm
	1991-94	0.2336 in.	5.93mm
	1995-96	0.276 in.	7.02mm
Exhaust Lobe lift			
	1988-90	0.2667 in.	6.77mm
	1991-94	0.2565 in.	6.52mm
	1995-96	0.285 in.	7.25mm
5.7L Engines			
Intake Lobe lift			
	1988-90	0.2600 in.	6.60mm
	1991-94	0.2565 in.	6.52mm
	1995-96	0.276 in.	7.02mm
Exhaust Lobe lift			
	1988-90	0.2733 in.	6.94mm
	1991-94	0.2690 in.	6.83mm
	1995-96	0.285 in.	7.25mm
6.2L, 6.5L Engines			
Intake Lobe lift		0.2810 in.	7.13mm
Exhaust Lobe lift		0.2810 in.	7.13mm
7.4L Engines			
Intake Lobe lift			
	1988-95	0.2343 in.	5.95mm
	1996	0.2821 in.	7.16mm
Exhaust Lobe lift			
	1988-95	0.2530 in.	6.43mm
	1996	0.2843 in.	7.22mm
Journal Diameter			
4.3L, 5.0L, 5.7L Engines			
	1988-95	1.8682-1.8692 in.	47.45-47.48mm
	1996	1.8667-1.8697 in.	47.45-47.48mm
4.8L Engines		1.8682-1.8692 in.	47.44-47.49mm
6.2L, 6.5L Engines			
	1988-95		
	#1-#4	2.1644-2.1663 in.	54.98-55.03mm
	#5	2.0069-2.0089 in.	50.98-51.03mm
	1996		
	#1-#4	2.1658-2.1680 in.	55.01-55.06mm
	#5	2.0082-2.0104 in.	51.00-51.06mm

87983c20

ENGINE REBUILDING SPECIFICATIONS

Component	US	Metric
Camshaft		
7.4L Engines	1.9482-1.9492 in.	49.48-49.51mm
Runout		
4.8L Engines	0.020 in. (max)	0.51mm (max)
Endplay		
4.3L, 5.0L, 5.7L Engines	0.004-0.012 in.	0.10-0.31mm
4.8L Engines	0.003-0.008 in.	0.08-0.20mm
6.2L, 6.5L Engines	0.002-0.012 in.	0.05-0.31mm
Crankshaft/Connecting Rods		
Journal Diameter		
4.3L Engines		
1988-94		
#1	2.4484-2.4493 in.	62.19-62.21mm
#2, #3	2.4481-2.4490 in.	62.18-62.20mm
#4	2.2979-2.2994 in.	58.37-58.40mm
1995-96		
#1	2.4488-2.4495 in.	62.19-62.21mm
#2, #3	2.4485-2.4494 in.	62.19-62.21mm
#4	2.24480-2.4489 in.	62.18-62.20mm
4.8L Engines		
5.0L, 5.7L Engines		
1988-96		
#1	2.4484-2.4493 in.	62.19-62.21mm
#2, #4	2.4481-2.4490 in.	62.18-62.20mm
#5	2.4479-2.4488 in.	62.17-62.19mm
6.2L, 6.5L Engines		
1988-94		
#1-#4	2.9495-2.9504 in.	74.92-74.94mm
#5	2.9493-2.9502 in.	74.91-74.94mm
1995-96		
#1-#4	2.1658-2.1680 in.	54.97-55.02mm
#5	2.0082-2.0104 in.	50.97-51.02mm
7.4L Engines		
1988-90		
#1-#4	2.7481-2.7490 in.	69.80-69.83mm
#5	2.7476-2.7486 in.	69.79-69.81mm
1991-96	2.7482-2.7489 in.	69.80-69.82mm
Bearing Oil Clearance		
4.3L Engines		
1988-96		
#1	0.0008-0.0020 in.	0.02-0.05mm
#2, #3	0.0011-0.0023 in.	0.03-0.06mm
#4	0.0017-0.0032 in.	0.04-0.08mm

87983C21

ENGINE REBUILDING SPECIFICATIONS

Component	US	Metric
Crankshaft/Connecting Rods		
Bearing Oil Clearance		
4.8L Engines		
#1-#6	0.0010-0.0024 in.	0.03-0.06 mm
#7	0.0016-0.0035 in.	0.018-0.043mm
5.0L, 5.7L Engines		
#1	0.0008-0.0020 in.	0.02-0.05mm
#2, #4	0.0011-0.0023 in.	0.03-0.06mm
#5	0.0017-0.0032 in.	0.04-0.08mm
6.2L, 6.5L Engines		
#1-#4	0.002-0.003 in.	0.05-0.08mm
#5	0.002-0.004 in.	0.06-0.09mm
7.4L Engines		
1988-90		
#1-#4	0.0013-0.0025 in.	0.03-0.06mm
#5	0.0024-0.0040 in	0.06-0.10mm
1991-96		
#1-#4	0.0017-0.0030 in	0.04-0.08mm
#5	0.0025-0.0038 in.	0.06-0.10mm
Endplay		
4.3L, 5.0L, 5.7L Engines		
1988-95	0.002-0.006 in.	0.05-0.15mm
5.0L, 5.7L Engines		
1996	0.002-0.008 in.	
6.2L, 6.5L Engines	0.004-0.010 in.	0.10-0.25mm
7.4L Engines		
1988-90	0.006-0.010 in.	0.15-0.25mm
1991-96	0.005-0.011 in.	0.13-0.28mm
Runout		
4.3L Engines	0.001 in (max)	0.03mm (max)
Crankpin Diameter		
4.3L Engines	2.2487-2.2497 in.	57.12-57.14 mm
4.8L Engines	2.0009-2.1000 in.	53.32-53.34mm
5.0L, 5.7L Engines	2.0988-2.0998 in.	53.31-53.34mm
6.2L, 6.5L Engines	2.3981-2.3992 in.	60.91-60.94mm
7.4L Engines		
1988-90	2.1990-2.2000 in.	55.86-55.88mm
1991-96	2.1990-2.1996 in.	55.86-55.88mm
Connecting Rod Bearing Clearance		
4.3L, 5.0L, 5.7L Engines	0.0013-0.0035 in.	0.03-0.09mm
4.8L Engines	0.0010-0.0026 in.	0.03-0.07mm
7.4L Engines	0.0011-0.0029 in.	0.02-0.07mm
6.2L, 6.5L Engines	0.002-0.004 in.	0.05-0.10mm
Connecting Rod Side Clearance		
4.3L, 5.0L, 5.7L Engines	0.006-0.014 in.	0.16-0.35mm
4.8L Engines	0.006-0.017 in.	0.15-0.43mm
6.2L, 6.5L Engines	0.007-0.025 in.	0.17-0.63mm
7.4L Engines		
1988-90	0.0009-0.0025 in.	0.02-0.06mm
1991-96	0.0011-0.0029 in.	0.03-0.07mm

87983C22

ENGINE REBUILDING SPECIFICATIONS

Component		US	Metric
Cylinder Bore			
Diameter			
4.3L Engines			
	1988-90	3.9995-4.0025 in.	101.59-101.66mm
	1991-96	4.0007-4.0017 in.	101.62-101.64mm
4.8L Engines		3.8750-3.8780 in.	98.43-98.50mm
5.0L Engines		3.7350-3.7385 in.	94.87-94.96mm
5.7L Engines		3.9995-4.0025 in.	101.59-101.66mm
6.2L Engines			
	1988-90	3.9759-3.9789 in.	100.99-101.07mm
	1991-93	3.9759-.0025 in.	100.99-101.07mm
6.5L Engines		4.0541-4.0551 in.	102.97-103mm
7.4L Engines			
	1988-90	4.2495-4.2525 in.	107.94-108.01mm
	1991-96	4.2500-4.2507 in.	107.95-107.97mm
Out-of-Round			
4.3L, 5.0L, 5.7L, 7.4L Engines		0.001 in. (max)	0.03mm (max)
4.8L Engines		0.0005 in. (max)	0.01mm (max)
6.2L, 6.5L Engines		0.0008 in. (max)	0.02mm (max)
Taper			
4.3L, 5.0L, 5.7L, 7.4L Engines			
Thrust		0.0005 in. (max)	0.01mm (max)
Relief		0.001 in. (max)	0.03mm (max0
4.8L Engines		0.0005 in. (max)	0.01mm (max)
6.2L, 6.5L Engines		0.0008 in. (max)	0.02mm (max)
Pistons/Rings			
Piston Clearance			
4.3L, 5.0L, 5.7L, 7.4L Engines		0.0007-0.0017 in.	0.018-0.043mm
4.8L Engines		0.0026-0.0036 in.	0.07-0.09mm
6.2L, 6.5L Engines			
	#1-#6	0.0035-0.0045 in.	0.09-0.12mm
	#7-#8	0.0040-0.0050 in.	0.10-0.13mm
7.4L Engines		0.003-0.004 in.	0.08-0.10mm
Ring Groove Clearance			
4.3L, 5.0L, 5.7L, 7.4L Engines			
	1st	0.0012-0.0032 in.	0.031-0.081mm
	2nd	0.0012-0.0032 in.	0.031-0.081mm
	Oil	0.002-0.007 in.	0.05-0.18mm
4.8L Engines			
	1st	0.0020-0.0040 in.	0.05-0.10mm
	2nd	0.0020-0.0040 in.	0.05-0.10mm
	Oil	0.005-0.0055 in.	0.13-0.14mm
6.2L, 6.5L Engines			
	1st	0.0030-0.0070 in.	0.08-0.18mm
	2nd	0.030-0.040 in.	0.75-1.0mm
	Oil	0.002-0.004 in.	0.04-0.10mm
7.4L Engines			
	1988-90		
	1st	0.0017-0.0032 in.	0.04-0.08mm
	2nd	0.0017-0.0032 in.	0.04-0.08mm
	Oil	0.002-0.004 in.	0.04-0.10mm

87983C23

ENGINE REBUILDING SPECIFICATIONS

Component	US	Metric
Pistons/Rings		
Ring Groove Clearance		
7.4L Engines		
1991-96		
1st	0.012-0.0029 in.	0.03-0.07mm
2nd	0.012-0.0029 in.	0.03-0.07mm
Oil	0.0050-0.0065 in.	0.13-0.17mm
Ring End Gap		
4.3L Engines		
1st	0.010-0.020 in.	0.25-0.51mm
2nd	0.010-0.025 in.	0.25-0.64mm
Oil	0.015-0.055 in.	0.38-1.40mm
4.8L Engines		
1st	0.010-0.020 in.	0.25-0.51mm
2nd	0.010-0.025 in.	0.25-0.51mm
Oil	0.015-0.055 in.	0.38-1.40mm
5.0L, 5.7L Engines		
1st	0.010-0.020 in.	0.25-0.51mm
2nd		
1988-91	0.010-0.025 in.	0.25-0.64mm
1992-96	0.0018-0.0026 in.	0.046-0.066mm
Oil		
1988-91	0.015-0.055 in.	0.38-1.40mm
1992-96	0.010-0.030 in.	0.25-0.76mm
6.2L Engines		
1st	0.012-0.022 in.	0.30-0.55mm
2nd	0.003-0.040 in.	0.075-1.00mm
Oil	0.010-0.020 in.	0.25-0.51mm
6.5L Engines		
1st	0.010-0.020 in.	0.26-0.51mm
2nd	0.003-0.040 in.	0.075-1.00mm
Oil	0.010-0.024 in.	0.25-0.60mm
7.4L Engines		
1988-90		
1st	0.010-0.020 in.	0.25-0.51mm
2nd	0.010-0.020 in.	0.25-0.51mm
Oil	0.015-0.055 in.	0.38-1.40mm
1991-96		
1st	0.010-0.018 in.	0.25-0.46mm
2nd	0.016-0.024 in.	0.410.61mm
Oil	0.010-0.030 in.	0.38-0.76mm
Piston Pin Diameter		
4.3L, 4.8L, 5.0L, 5.7L Engines	0.9270-0.9273 in.	23.551-23.553mm
6.2L, 6.5L Engines	1.2230-1.2206 in.	30.996-31.004mm
7.4L Engines		
1988-90	0.9895-0.9898 in.	25.13-25.14mm
1991-96	0.9895-0.9897 in.	25.13-25.14mm

87983C24

ENGINE REBUILDING SPECIFICATIONS

Component		US	Metric
Pistons/Rings			
Piston Pin Clearance			
4.3L, 5.0L, 5.7L, 7.4L Engines		0.0002-0.0007 in.	0.0005-0.018mm
4.8L Engines		0.00015-0.00025 in.	0.004-0.006mm
6.2L, 6.5L Engines		0.0003-0.0012 in.	0.008-0.031mm
7.4L Engines			
	1988-90	0.00025-0.00035 in.	0.006-0.009mm
	1991-96	0.0002-0.0007 in.	0.005-0.018mm
Piston Pin Fit			
4.3L, 4.8L, 5.0L, 5.7L Engines		0.0008-00.0016 in. (interference)	0.020-0.041mm
6.2L, 6.5L Engines		0.0003-0.0012 in.	0.008-0.031mm
7.4L Engines			
	1988-90	0.0013-0.0021 in.	0.033-0.053mm
	1991-96	0.0031-0.0021 in.	0.079-0.053mm
Valves			
Face angle			
4.3L, 4.8L, 5.0L, 5.7L Engines		45°	45°
4.8L Engines		46°	46°
Seat Angle			
All Engines		46°	46°
Seat Runout			
All Engines		0.002 in. (max)	0.05mm
Stem Clearance			
Intake Valve			
All Engines		0.0010-0.0027 in.	0.025-0.069mm
Exhaust Valve			
4.3L, 4.8L, 5.0L, 5.7L, 6.2L, 6.5L Engines		0.0010-0.0027 in.	0.025-0.069mm
4.8L Engines		0.0015-0.0032 in.	0.038-0.081mm
7.4L Engines		0.0012-0.0029 in.	0.031-0.074mm
Spring Free Length			
4.3L, 5.0L, 5.7L Engines		2.03 in.	51.56mm
4.8L Engines		2.08 in.	52.83mm
7.4L Engines		2.12 in.	53.85mm
Spring Pressure			
Closed			
4.3L, 5.0L, 5.7L Engines		74-84 lbs. @ 1.70 in.	338-373N @ 43.18mm
4.8L Engines		78-86 lbs. @ 1.66 in.	347-383N @ 42.16mm
7.4L Engines		74-86 lbs. @ 1.80 in.	329-383N @ 45.72mm
Open			
4.3L, 5.0L, 5.7L Engines		194-206 lbs. @ 1.25 in.	862-916N @ 31.75mm
4.8L Engines		170-180 lbs. @ 1.26 in.	756-801N @ 35.56mm
7.4L Engines		195-215 lbs. @ 1.40 in.	
6.2L, 6.5L Engines			
Intake Valve		80 lbs. @ 1.81 in.	356N @ 45.97mm
Exhaust Valve		230 lbs. @ 1.39 in.	1023N @ 35.30mm
Spring Installed Height			
4.3L, 4.8L, 5.0L, 5.7L Engines		1.690-1.710 in.	42.93-43.43mm
6.2L, 6.5L Engines		1.81 in.	45.97mm
Spring Damper Length			
4.3L, 5.0L, 5.7L Engines		1.86 in.	47.24mm
4.8L Engines		1.94 in.	49.28mm

87983C25

TORQUE SPECIFICATIONS

Component	U.S.	Metric
Thermostat Housing Crossover		
6.2L, 6.5L Engines		
1988–91	35 ft. lbs.	47 Nm
1992–93	31 ft. lbs.	42 Nm
Turbocharger		
To manifold	37 ft. lbs.	50 Nm
Oil drain tube	19 ft. lbs.	26 Nm
Oil feed line	13 ft. lbs.	17 Nm
Exhaust elbow clamp	71 inch lbs.	8 Nm
Vacuum Pump		
6.2L Engines	20 ft. lbs.	27 Nm
6.5L Engines w/o AC		
Pump-to-bracket	20 ft. lbs.	27 Nm
Bracket-to-engine	30 ft. lbs.	40 Nm
6.5L Engines w/AC		
Bolts	30 ft. lbs.	40 Nm
Nuts	22 ft. lbs.	30 Nm
Vehicle Speed Sensor	97 inch lbs.	11 Nm
Water Pump		
4.8L Engines	15 ft. lbs.	20 Nm
4.3L, 5.0L, 5.7L, 7.4L Engines	30 ft. lbs.	41 Nm
6.2L, 6.5L Engines		
3 lower right bolts	31 ft. lbs.	42 Nm
All other bolts	17 ft. lbs.	23 Nm

84903260

Troubleshooting Engine Mechanical Problems

Problem	Cause	Solution
External oil leaks	• Cylinder head cover RTV sealant broken or improperly seated	• Replace sealant; inspect cylinder head cover sealant flange and cylinder head sealant surface for distortion and cracks
	• Oil filler cap leaking or missing	• Replace cap
	• Oil filter gasket broken or improperly seated	• Replace oil filter
	• Oil pan side gasket broken, improperly seated or opening in RTV sealant	• Replace gasket or repair opening in sealant; inspect oil pan gasket flange for distortion
	• Oil pan front oil seal broken or improperly seated	• Replace seal; inspect timing case cover and oil pan seal flange for distortion
	• Oil pan rear oil seal broken or improperly seated	• Replace seal; inspect oil pan rear oil seal flange; inspect rear main bearing cap for cracks, plugged oil return channels, or distortion in seal groove
	• Timing case cover oil seal broken or improperly seated	• Replace seal
	• Excess oil pressure because of restricted PCV valve	• Replace PCV valve
	• Oil pan drain plug loose or has stripped threads	• Repair as necessary and tighten
	• Rear oil gallery plug loose	• Use appropriate sealant on gallery plug and tighten
	• Rear camshaft plug loose or improperly seated	• Seat camshaft plug or replace and seal, as necessary
Excessive oil consumption	• Oil level too high	• Drain oil to specified level
	• Oil with wrong viscosity being used	• Replace with specified oil
	• PCV valve stuck closed	• Replace PCV valve
	• Valve stem oil deflectors (or seals) are damaged, missing, or incorrect type	• Replace valve stem oil deflectors
	• Valve stems or valve guides worn	• Measure stem-to-guide clearance and repair as necessary
	• Poorly fitted or missing valve cover baffles	• Replace valve cover
	• Piston rings broken or missing	• Replace broken or missing rings
	• Scuffed piston	• Replace piston
	• Incorrect piston ring gap	• Measure ring gap, repair as necessary
	• Piston rings sticking or excessively loose in grooves	• Measure ring side clearance, repair as necessary
	• Compression rings installed upside down	• Repair as necessary
	• Cylinder walls worn, scored, or glazed	• Repair as necessary

TCCS3C02

Troubleshooting Engine Mechanical Problems

Problem	Cause	Solution
Excessive oil consumption (cont.)	• Piston ring gaps not properly staggered • Excessive main or connecting rod bearing clearance	• Repair as necessary • Measure bearing clearance, repair as necessary
No oil pressure	• Low oil level • Oil pressure gauge, warning lamp or sending unit inaccurate • Oil pump malfunction • Oil pressure relief valve sticking • Oil passages on pressure side of pump obstructed • Oil pickup screen or tube obstructed • Loose oil inlet tube	• Add oil to correct level • Replace oil pressure gauge or warning lamp • Replace oil pump • Remove and inspect oil pressure relief valve assembly • Inspect oil passages for obstruction • Inspect oil pickup for obstruction • Tighten or seal inlet tube
Low oil pressure	• Low oil level • Inaccurate gauge, warning lamp or sending unit • Oil excessively thin because of dilution, poor quality, or improper grade • Excessive oil temperature • Oil pressure relief spring weak or sticking • Oil inlet tube and screen assembly has restriction or air leak • Excessive oil pump clearance • Excessive main, rod, or camshaft bearing clearance	• Add oil to correct level • Replace oil pressure gauge or warning lamp • Drain and refill crankcase with recommended oil • Correct cause of overheating engine • Remove and inspect oil pressure relief valve assembly • Remove and inspect oil inlet tube and screen assembly. (Fill inlet tube with lacquer thinner to locate leaks.) • Measure clearances • Measure bearing clearances, repair as necessary
High oil pressure	• Improper oil viscosity • Oil pressure gauge or sending unit inaccurate • Oil pressure relief valve sticking closed	• Drain and refill crankcase with correct viscosity oil • Replace oil pressure gauge • Remove and inspect oil pressure relief valve assembly
Main bearing noise	• Insufficient oil supply • Main bearing clearance excessive • Bearing insert missing • Crankshaft end-play excessive • Improperly tightened main bearing cap bolts • Loose flywheel or drive plate • Loose or damaged vibration damper	• Inspect for low oil level and low oil pressure • Measure main bearing clearance, repair as necessary • Replace missing insert • Measure end-play, repair as necessary • Tighten bolts with specified torque • Tighten flywheel or drive plate attaching bolts • Repair as necessary

TCCS3C03

Troubleshooting Engine Mechanical Problems

Problem	Cause	Solution
Connecting rod bearing noise	• Insufficient oil supply	• Inspect for low oil level and low oil pressure
	• Carbon build-up on piston	• Remove carbon from piston crown
	• Bearing clearance excessive or bearing missing	• Measure clearance, repair as necessary
	• Crankshaft connecting rod journal out-of-round	• Measure journal dimensions, repair or replace as necessary
	• Misaligned connecting rod or cap	• Repair as necessary
	• Connecting rod bolts tightened improperly	• Tighten bolts with specified torque
Piston noise	• Piston-to-cylinder wall clearance excessive (scuffed piston)	• Measure clearance and examine piston
	• Cylinder walls excessively tapered or out-of-round	• Measure cylinder wall dimensions, rebore cylinder
	• Piston ring broken	• Replace all rings on piston
	• Loose or seized piston pin	• Measure piston-to-pin clearance, repair as necessary
	• Connecting rods misaligned	• Measure rod alignment, straighten or replace
	• Piston ring side clearance excessively loose or tight	• Measure ring side clearance, repair as necessary
	• Carbon build-up on piston is excessive	• Remove carbon from piston
Valve actuating component noise	• Insufficient oil supply	• Check for: (a) Low oil level (b) Low oil pressure (c) Wrong hydraulic tappets (d) Restricted oil gallery (e) Excessive tappet to bore clearance
	• Rocker arms or pivots worn	• Replace worn rocker arms or pivots
	• Foreign objects or chips in hydraulic tappets	• Clean tappets
	• Excessive tappet leak-down	• Replace valve tappet
	• Tappet face worn	• Replace tappet; inspect corresponding cam lobe for wear
	• Broken or cocked valve springs	• Properly seat cocked springs; replace broken springs
	• Stem-to-guide clearance excessive	• Measure stem-to-guide clearance, repair as required
	• Valve bent	• Replace valve
	• Loose rocker arms	• Check and repair as necessary
	• Valve seat runout excessive	• Regrind valve seat/valves
	• Missing valve lock	• Install valve lock
	• Excessive engine oil	• Correct oil level

TCCS3C04

Troubleshooting Engine Performance

Problem	Cause	Solution
Hard starting (engine cranks normally)	• Faulty engine control system component	• Repair or replace as necessary
	• Faulty fuel pump	• Replace fuel pump
	• Faulty fuel system component	• Repair or replace as necessary
	• Faulty ignition coil	• Test and replace as necessary
	• Improper spark plug gap	• Adjust gap
	• Incorrect ignition timing	• Adjust timing
	• Incorrect valve timing	• Check valve timing; repair as necessary
Rough idle or stalling	• Incorrect curb or fast idle speed	• Adjust curb or fast idle speed (If possible)
	• Incorrect ignition timing	• Adjust timing to specification
	• Improper feedback system operation	• Refer to Chapter 4
	• Faulty EGR valve operation	• Test EGR system and replace as necessary
	• Faulty PCV valve air flow	• Test PCV valve and replace as necessary
	• Faulty TAC vacuum motor or valve	• Repair as necessary
	• Air leak into manifold vacuum	• Inspect manifold vacuum connections and repair as necessary
	• Faulty distributor rotor or cap	• Replace rotor or cap (Distributor systems only)
	• Improperly seated valves	• Test cylinder compression, repair as necessary
	• Incorrect ignition wiring	• Inspect wiring and correct as necessary
	• Faulty ignition coil	• Test coil and replace as necessary
	• Restricted air vent or idle passages	• Clean passages
	• Restricted air cleaner	• Clean or replace air cleaner filter element
Faulty low-speed operation	• Restricted idle air vents and passages	• Clean air vents and passages
	• Restricted air cleaner	• Clean or replace air cleaner filter element
	• Faulty spark plugs	• Clean or replace spark plugs
	• Dirty, corroded, or loose ignition secondary circuit wire connections	• Clean or tighten secondary circuit wire connections
	• Improper feedback system operation	• Refer to Chapter 4
	• Faulty ignition coil high voltage wire	• Replace ignition coil high voltage wire (Distributor systems only)
	• Faulty distributor cap	• Replace cap (Distributor systems only)
Faulty acceleration	• Incorrect ignition timing	• Adjust timing
	• Faulty fuel system component	• Repair or replace as necessary
	• Faulty spark plug(s)	• Clean or replace spark plug(s)
	• Improperly seated valves	• Test cylinder compression, repair as necessary
	• Faulty ignition coil	• Test coil and replace as necessary

TCCS3C05

Troubleshooting Engine Performance

Problem	Cause	Solution
Faulty acceleration (cont.)	• Improper feedback system operation	• Refer to Chapter 4
Faulty high speed operation	• Incorrect ignition timing	• Adjust timing (if possible)
	• Faulty advance mechanism	• Check advance mechanism and repair as necessary (Distributor systems only)
	• Low fuel pump volume	• Replace fuel pump
	• Wrong spark plug air gap or wrong plug	• Adjust air gap or install correct plug
	• Partially restricted exhaust manifold, exhaust pipe, catalytic converter, muffler, or tailpipe	• Eliminate restriction
	• Restricted vacuum passages	• Clean passages
	• Restricted air cleaner	• Cleaner or replace filter element as necessary
	• Faulty distributor rotor or cap	• Replace rotor or cap (Distributor systems only)
	• Faulty ignition coil	• Test coil and replace as necessary
	• Improperly seated valve(s)	• Test cylinder compression, repair as necessary
	• Faulty valve spring(s)	• Inspect and test valve spring tension, replace as necessary
	• Incorrect valve timing	• Check valve timing and repair as necessary
	• Intake manifold restricted	• Remove restriction or replace manifold
	• Worn distributor shaft	• Replace shaft (Distributor systems only)
	• Improper feedback system operation	• Refer to Chapter 4
Misfire at all speeds	• Faulty spark plug(s)	• Clean or relace spark plug(s)
	• Faulty spark plug wire(s)	• Replace as necessary
	• Faulty distributor cap or rotor	• Replace cap or rotor (Distributor systems only)
	• Faulty ignition coil	• Test coil and replace as necessary
	• Primary ignition circuit shorted or open intermittently	• Troubleshoot primary circuit and repair as necessary
	• Improperly seated valve(s)	• Test cylinder compression, repair as necessary
	• Faulty hydraulic tappet(s)	• Clean or replace tappet(s)
	• Improper feedback system operation	• Refer to Chapter 4
	• Faulty valve spring(s)	• Inspect and test valve spring tension, repair as necessary
	• Worn camshaft lobes	• Replace camshaft
	• Air leak into manifold	• Check manifold vacuum and repair as necessary
	• Fuel pump volume or pressure low	• Replace fuel pump
	• Blown cylinder head gasket	• Replace gasket
	• Intake or exhaust manifold passage(s) restricted	• Pass chain through passage(s) and repair as necessary
Power not up to normal	• Incorrect ignition timing	• Adjust timing
	• Faulty distributor rotor	• Replace rotor (Distributor systems only)

TCCS3C06

Troubleshooting Engine Performance

Problem	Cause	Solution
Power not up to normal (cont.)	• Incorrect spark plug gap	• Adjust gap
	• Faulty fuel pump	• Replace fuel pump
	• Faulty fuel pump	• Replace fuel pump
	• Incorrect valve timing	• Check valve timing and repair as necessary
	• Faulty ignition coil	• Test coil and replace as necessary
	• Faulty ignition wires	• Test wires and replace as necessary
	• Improperly seated valves	• Test cylinder compression and repair as necessary
	• Blown cylinder head gasket	• Replace gasket
	• Leaking piston rings	• Test compression and repair as necessary
	• Improper feedback system operation	• Refer to Chapter 4
Intake backfire	• Improper ignition timing	• Adjust timing
	• Defective EGR component	• Repair as necessary
	• Defective TAC vacuum motor or valve	• Repair as necessary
Exhaust backfire	• Air leak into manifold vacuum	• Check manifold vacuum and repair as necessary
	• Faulty air injection diverter valve	• Test diverter valve and replace as necessary
	• Exhaust leak	• Locate and eliminate leak
Ping or spark knock	• Incorrect ignition timing	• Adjust timing
	• Distributor advance malfunction	• Inspect advance mechanism and repair as necessary (Distributor systems only)
	• Excessive combustion chamber deposits	• Remove with combustion chamber cleaner
	• Air leak into manifold vacuum	• Check manifold vacuum and repair as necessary
	• Excessively high compression	• Test compression and repair as necessary
	• Fuel octane rating excessively low	• Try alternate fuel source
	• Sharp edges in combustion chamber	• Grind smooth
	• EGR valve not functioning properly	• Test EGR system and replace as necessary
Surging (at cruising to top speeds)	• Low fuel pump pressure or volume	• Replace fuel pump
	• Improper PCV valve air flow	• Test PCV valve and replace as necessary
	• Air leak into manifold vacuum	• Check manifold vacuum and repair as necessary
	• Incorrect spark advance	• Test and replace as necessary
	• Restricted fuel filter	• Replace fuel filter
	• Restricted air cleaner	• Clean or replace air cleaner filter element
	• EGR valve not functioning properly	• Test EGR system and replace as necessary
	• Improper feedback system operation	• Refer to Chapter 4

TCCS3C07

Troubleshooting the Serpentine Drive Belt

Problem	Cause	Solution
Tension sheeting fabric failure (woven fabric on outside circumference of belt has cracked or separated from body of belt)	• Grooved or backside idler pulley diameters are less than minimum recommended • Tension sheeting contacting (rubbing) stationary object • Excessive heat causing woven fabric to age • Tension sheeting splice has fractured	• Replace pulley(s) not conforming to specification • Correct rubbing condition • Replace belt • Replace belt
Noise (objectional squeal, squeak, or rumble is heard or felt while drive belt is in operation)	• Belt slippage • Bearing noise • Belt misalignment • Belt-to-pulley mismatch • Driven component inducing vibration • System resonant frequency inducing vibration	• Adjust belt • Locate and repair • Align belt/pulley(s) • Install correct belt • Locate defective driven component and repair • Vary belt tension within specifications. Replace belt.
Rib chunking (one or more ribs has separated from belt body)	• Foreign objects imbedded in pulley grooves • Installation damage • Drive loads in excess of design specifications • Insufficient internal belt adhesion	• Remove foreign objects from pulley grooves • Replace belt • Adjust belt tension • Replace belt
Rib or belt wear (belt ribs contact bottom of pulley grooves)	• Pulley(s) misaligned • Mismatch of belt and pulley groove widths • Abrasive environment • Rusted pulley(s) • Sharp or jagged pulley groove tips • Rubber deteriorated	• Align pulley(s) • Replace belt • Replace belt • Clean rust from pulley(s) • Replace pulley • Replace belt
Longitudinal belt cracking (cracks between two ribs)	• Belt has mistracked from pulley groove • Pulley groove tip has worn away rubber-to-tensile member	• Replace belt • Replace belt
Belt slips	• Belt slipping because of insufficient tension • Belt or pulley subjected to substance (belt dressing, oil, ethylene glycol) that has reduced friction • Driven component bearing failure • Belt glazed and hardened from heat and excessive slippage	• Adjust tension • Replace belt and clean pulleys • Replace faulty component bearing • Replace belt
"Groove jumping" (belt does not maintain correct position on pulley, or turns over and/or runs off pulleys)	• Insufficient belt tension • Pulley(s) not within design tolerance • Foreign object(s) in grooves	• Adjust belt tension • Replace pulley(s) • Remove foreign objects from grooves

tccs3c09

Troubleshooting the Cooling System

Problem	Cause	Solution
High temperature gauge indication—overheating	• Coolant level low	• Replenish coolant
	• Improper fan operation	• Repair or replace as necessary
	• Radiator hose(s) collapsed	• Replace hose(s)
	• Radiator airflow blocked	• Remove restriction (bug screen, fog lamps, etc.)
	• Faulty pressure cap	• Replace pressure cap
	• Ignition timing incorrect	• Adjust ignition timing
	• Air trapped in cooling system	• Purge air
	• Heavy traffic driving	• Operate at fast idle in neutral intermittently to cool engine
	• Incorrect cooling system component(s) installed	• Install proper component(s)
	• Faulty thermostat	• Replace thermostat
	• Water pump shaft broken or impeller loose	• Replace water pump
	• Radiator tubes clogged	• Flush radiator
	• Cooling system clogged	• Flush system
	• Casting flash in cooling passages	• Repair or replace as necessary. Flash may be visible by removing cooling system components or removing core plugs.
	• Brakes dragging	• Repair brakes
	• Excessive engine friction	• Repair engine
	• Antifreeze concentration over 68%	• Lower antifreeze concentration percentage
	• Missing air seals	• Replace air seals
	• Faulty gauge or sending unit	• Repair or replace faulty component
	• Loss of coolant flow caused by leakage or foaming	• Repair or replace leaking component, replace coolant
	• Viscous fan drive failed	• Replace unit
Low temperature indication—undercooling	• Thermostat stuck open	• Replace thermostat
	• Faulty gauge or sending unit	• Repair or replace faulty component
Coolant loss—boilover	• Overfilled cooling system	• Reduce coolant level to proper specification
	• Quick shutdown after hard (hot) run	• Allow engine to run at fast idle prior to shutdown
	• Air in system resulting in occasional "burping" of coolant	• Purge system
	• Insufficient antifreeze allowing coolant boiling point to be too low	• Add antifreeze to raise boiling point
	• Antifreeze deteriorated because of age or contamination	• Replace coolant
	• Leaks due to loose hose clamps, loose nuts, bolts, drain plugs, faulty hoses, or defective radiator	• Pressure test system to locate source of leak(s) then repair as necessary

tccs3c11

Troubleshooting the Cooling System (cont.)

Problem	Cause	Solution
Coolant loss—boilover	· Faulty head gasket · Cracked head, manifold, or block · Faulty radiator cap	· Replace head gasket · Replace as necessary · Replace cap
Coolant entry into crankcase or cylinder(s)	· Faulty head gasket · Crack in head, manifold or block	· Replace head gasket · Replace as necessary
Coolant recovery system inoperative	· Coolant level low · Leak in system · Pressure cap not tight or seal missing, or leaking · Pressure cap defective · Overflow tube clogged or leaking · Recovery bottle vent restricted	· Replenish coolant to FULL mark · Pressure test to isolate leak and repair as necessary · Repair as necessary · Replace cap · Repair as necessary · Remove restriction
Noise	· Fan contacting shroud · Loose water pump impeller · Glazed fan belt · Loose fan belt · Rough surface on drive pulley · Water pump bearing worn · Belt alignment	· Reposition shroud and inspect engine mounts **(on electric fans inspect assembly)** · Replace pump · Apply silicone or replace belt · Adjust fan belt tension · Replace pulley · Remove belt to isolate. Replace pump. · Check pulley alignment. Repair as necessary.
No coolant flow through heater core	· Restricted return inlet in water pump · Heater hose collapsed or restricted · Restricted heater core · Restricted outlet in thermostat housing · Intake manifold bypass hole in cylinder head restricted · Faulty heater control valve · Intake manifold coolant passage restricted	· Remove restriction · Remove restriction or replace hose · Remove restriction or replace core · Remove flash or restriction · Remove restriction · Replace valve · Remove restriction or replace intake manifold

NOTE: *Immediately after shutdown, the engine enters a condition known as heat soak. This is caused by the cooling system being inoperative while engine temperature is still high. If coolant temperature rises above boiling point, expansion and pressure may push some coolant out of the radiator overflow tube. If this does not occur frequently it is considered normal.*

tccs3c12

4 DRIVEABILITY AND EMISSION CONTROLS

AIR POLLUTION

The earth's atmosphere, at or near sea level, consists approximately of 78 percent nitrogen, 21 percent oxygen and 1 percent other gases. If it were possible to remain in this state, 100 percent clean air would result. However, many varied sources allow other gases and particulates to mix with the clean air, causing our atmosphere to become unclean or polluted.

Some of these pollutants are visible while others are invisible, with each having the capability of causing distress to the eyes, ears, throat, skin and respiratory system. Should these pollutants become concentrated in a specific area and under certain conditions, death could result due to the displacement or chemical change of the oxygen content in the air. These pollutants can also cause great damage to the environment and to the many man made objects that are exposed to the elements.

To better understand the causes of air pollution, the pollutants can be categorized into 3 separate types, natural, industrial and automotive.

Natural Pollutants

Natural pollution has been present on earth since before man appeared and continues to be a factor when discussing air pollution, although it causes only a small percentage of the overall pollution problem. It is the direct result of decaying organic matter, wind born smoke and particulates from such natural events as plain and forest fires (ignited by heat or lightning), volcanic ash, sand and dust which can spread over a large area of the countryside.

Such a phenomenon of natural pollution has been seen in the form of volcanic eruptions, with the resulting plume of smoke, steam and volcanic ash blotting out the sun's rays as it spreads and rises higher into the atmosphere. As it travels into the atmosphere the upper air currents catch and carry the smoke and ash, while condensing the steam back into water vapor. As the water vapor, smoke and ash travel on their journey, the smoke dissipates into the atmosphere while the ash and moisture settle back to earth in a trail hundreds of miles long. In some cases, lives are lost and millions of dollars of property damage result.

Industrial Pollutants

Industrial pollution is caused primarily by industrial processes, the burning of coal, oil and natural gas, which in turn produce smoke and fumes. Because the burning fuels contain large amounts of sulfur, the principal ingredients of smoke and fumes are sulfur dioxide and particulate matter. This type of pollutant occurs most severely during still, damp and cool weather, such as at night. Even in its less severe form, this pollutant is not confined to just cities. Because of air movements, the pollutants move for miles over the surrounding countryside, leaving in its path a barren and unhealthy environment for all living things.

Working with Federal, State and Local mandated regulations and by carefully monitoring emissions, big business has greatly reduced the amount of pollutant introduced from its industrial sources, striving to obtain an acceptable level. Because of the mandated industrial emission clean up, many land areas and streams in and around the cities that were formerly barren of vegetation and life, have now begun to move back in the direction of nature's intended balance.

Automotive Pollutants

The third major source of air pollution is automotive emissions. The emissions from the internal combustion engines were not an appreciable problem years ago because of the small number of registered vehicles and the nation's small highway system. However, during the early 1950's, the trend of the American people was to move from the cities to the surrounding suburbs. This caused an immediate problem in transportation because the majority of suburbs were not afforded mass transit conveniences. This lack of transportation created an attractive market for the automobile manufacturers, which resulted in a dramatic increase in the number of vehicles produced and sold, along with a marked increase in highway construction between cities and the suburbs. Multi-vehicle families emerged with a growing emphasis placed on an individual vehicle per family member. As the increase in vehicle ownership and usage occurred, so did pollutant levels in and around the cities, as suburbanites drove daily to their businesses and employment, returning at the end of the day to their homes in the suburbs.

It was noted that a smoke and fog type haze was being formed and at times, remained in suspension over the cities, taking time to dissipate. At first this "smog," derived from the words "smoke" and "fog," was thought to result from industrial pollution but it was determined that automobile emissions shared the blame. It was discovered that when normal automobile emissions were exposed to sunlight for a period of time, complex chemical reactions would take place.

It is now known that smog is a photo chemical layer which develops when certain oxides of nitrogen (NOx) and unburned hydrocarbons (HC) from automobile emissions are exposed to sunlight. Pollution was more severe when smog would become stagnant over an area in which a warm layer of air settled over the top of the cooler air mass, trapping and holding the cooler mass at ground level. The trapped cooler air would keep the emissions from being dispersed and diluted through normal air flows. This type of air stagnation was given the name "Temperature Inversion."

TEMPERATURE INVERSION

In normal weather situations, surface air is warmed by heat radiating from the earth's surface and the sun's rays. This causes it to rise upward, into the atmosphere. Upon rising it will cool through a convection type heat exchange with the cooler upper air. As warm air rises, the surface pollutants are carried upward and dissipated into the atmosphere.

When a temperature inversion occurs, we find the higher air is no longer cooler, but is warmer than the surface air, causing the cooler surface air to become trapped. This warm air blanket can extend from above ground level to a few hundred or even a few thousand feet into the air. As the surface air is trapped, so are the pollutants, causing a severe smog condition. Should this stagnant air mass extend to a few thousand feet high, enough air movement with the inversion takes place to allow the smog layer to rise above ground level but the pollutants still cannot dissipate. This inversion can remain for days over an area, with the smog level only rising or lowering from ground level to a few hundred feet high. Meanwhile, the pollutant levels increase, causing eye irritation, respiratory problems, reduced visibility, plant damage and in some cases, even disease.

This inversion phenomenon was first noted in the Los Angeles, California area. The city lies in terrain resembling a basin and with certain weather conditions, a cold air mass is held in the basin while a warmer air mass covers it like a lid.

Because this type of condition was first documented as prevalent in the Los Angeles area, this type of trapped pollution was named Los Angeles Smog, although it occurs in other areas where a large concentration of automobiles are used and the air remains stagnant for any length of time.

HEAT TRANSFER

Consider the internal combustion engine as a machine in which raw materials must be placed so a finished product comes out. As in any machine operation, a certain amount of wasted material is formed. When we relate this to the internal combustion engine, we find that through the input of air and fuel, we obtain power during the combustion process to drive the vehicle. The by-product or waste of this power is, in part, heat and exhaust gases with which we must dispose.

The heat from the combustion process can rise to over 4000°F (2204°C). The dissipation of this heat is controlled by a ram air effect, the use of cooling fans to cause air flow and a liquid coolant solution surrounding the combustion area to transfer the heat of combustion through the cylinder walls and into the coolant. The coolant is then directed to a thin-finned, multi-tubed radiator, from which the excess heat is transferred to the atmosphere by 1 of the 3 heat transfer methods, conduction, convection or radiation.

The cooling of the combustion area is an important part in the control of exhaust emissions. To understand the behavior of the combustion and transfer of its heat, consider the air/fuel charge. It is ignited and the flame front burns progressively across the combustion chamber until the burning charge reaches the cylinder walls. Some of the fuel in contact with the walls is not hot enough to burn, thereby snuffing out or quenching the combustion process. This leaves unburned fuel in the combustion chamber. This unburned fuel is then forced out of the cylinder and into the exhaust system, along with the exhaust gases.

Many attempts have been made to minimize the amount of unburned fuel in the combustion chambers due to quenching, by increasing the coolant temperature and lessening the contact area of the coolant around the combustion area. However, design limitations within the combustion chambers prevent the complete burning of the air/fuel charge, so a certain amount of the unburned fuel is still expelled into the exhaust system, regardless of modifications to the engine.

AUTOMOTIVE EMISSIONS

Before emission controls were mandated on internal combustion engines, other sources of engine pollutants were discovered along with the exhaust emissions. It was determined that engine combustion exhaust produced approximately 60 percent of the total emission pollutants, fuel evaporation from the fuel tank and carburetor vents produced 20 percent, with the final 20 percent being produced through the crankcase as a by-product of the combustion process.

Exhaust Gases

The exhaust gases emitted into the atmosphere are a combination of burned and unburned fuel. To understand the exhaust emission and its composition, we must review some basic chemistry.

When the air/fuel mixture is introduced into the engine, we are mixing air, composed of nitrogen (78 percent), oxygen (21 percent) and other gases (1 percent) with the fuel, which is 100 percent hydrocarbons (HC), in a semi-controlled ratio. As the combustion process is accomplished, power is produced to move the vehicle while the heat of combustion is transferred to the cooling system. The exhaust gases are then composed of nitrogen, a diatomic gas (N_2), the same as was introduced in the engine, carbon dioxide (CO_2), the same gas that is used in beverage carbonation, and water vapor (H_2O). The nitrogen (N_2), for the most part, passes through the engine unchanged, while the oxygen (O_2) reacts (burns) with the hydrocarbons (HC) and produces the carbon dioxide (CO_2) and the water vapors (H_2O). If this chemical process would be the only process to take place, the exhaust emissions would be harmless. However, during the combustion process, other compounds are formed which are considered dangerous. These pollutants are hydrocarbons (HC), carbon monoxide (CO), oxides of nitrogen (NOx) oxides of sulfur (SOx) and engine particulates.

HYDROCARBONS

Hydrocarbons (HC) are essentially fuel which was not burned during the combustion process or which has escaped into the atmosphere through fuel evaporation. The main sources of incomplete combustion are rich air/fuel mixtures, low engine temperatures and improper spark timing. The main sources of hydrocarbon emission through fuel evaporation on most vehicles used to be the vehicle's fuel tank and carburetor float bowl.

To reduce combustion hydrocarbon emission, engine modifications were made to minimize dead space and surface area in the combustion chamber. In addition, the air/fuel mixture was made more lean through the improved control which feedback carburetion and fuel injection offers and by the addition of external controls to aid in further combustion of the hydrocarbons outside the engine. Two such methods were the addition of air injection systems, to inject fresh air into the exhaust manifolds and the installation of catalytic converters, units that are able to burn traces of hydrocarbons without affecting the internal combustion process or fuel economy.

To control hydrocarbon emissions through fuel evaporation, modifications were made to the fuel tank to allow storage of the fuel vapors during periods of engine shut-down. Modifications were also made to the air intake system so that at specific times during engine operation, these vapors may be purged and burned by blending them with the air/fuel mixture.

CARBON MONOXIDE

Carbon monoxide is formed when not enough oxygen is present during the combustion process to convert carbon (C) to carbon dioxide (CO_2). An increase in the carbon monoxide (CO) emission is normally accompanied by an increase in the hydrocarbon (HC) emission because of the lack of oxygen to completely burn all of the fuel mixture.

Carbon monoxide (CO) also increases the rate at which the photo chemical smog is formed by speeding up the conversion of nitric oxide (NO) to nitrogen dioxide (NO_2). To accomplish this, carbon monoxide (CO) combines with oxygen (O_2) and nitric oxide (NO) to produce carbon dioxide (CO_2) and nitrogen dioxide (NO_2). ($CO + O_2 + NO = CO_2 + NO_2$).

The dangers of carbon monoxide, which is an odorless and colorless toxic gas are many. When carbon monoxide is inhaled into the lungs and passed into the blood stream, oxygen is replaced by the carbon monoxide in the red blood cells, causing a reduction in the amount of oxygen supplied to the many parts of the body. This lack of oxygen causes headaches, lack of coordination, reduced mental alertness and, should the carbon monoxide concentration be high enough, death could result.

NITROGEN

Normally, nitrogen is an inert gas. When heated to approximately 2500°F (1371°C) through the combustion process, this gas becomes active and causes an increase in the nitric oxide (NO) emission.

Oxides of nitrogen (NOx) are composed of approximately 97-98 percent nitric oxide (NO). Nitric oxide is a colorless gas but when it is passed into the atmosphere, it combines with oxygen and forms nitrogen dioxide (NO_2). The nitrogen dioxide then combines with chemically active hydrocarbons (HC) and when in the presence of sunlight, causes the formation of photo-chemical smog.

Ozone

To further complicate matters, some of the nitrogen dioxide (NO_2) is broken apart by the sunlight to form nitric oxide and oxygen. (NO_2 + sunlight = NO + O). This single atom of oxygen then combines with diatomic (meaning 2 atoms) oxygen (O_2) to form ozone (O_3). Ozone is one of the smells associated with smog. It has a pungent and offensive odor, irritates the eyes and lung tissues, affects the growth of plant life and causes rapid deterioration of rubber products. Ozone can be formed by sunlight as well as electrical discharge into the air.

The most common discharge area on the automobile engine is the secondary ignition electrical system, especially when inferior quality spark plug cables are used. As the surge of high voltage is routed through the secondary cable, the circuit builds up an electrical field around the wire, which acts upon the oxygen in the surrounding air to form the ozone. The faint glow along the cable with the engine running that may be visible on a dark night, is called the "corona discharge." It is the result of the electrical field passing from a high along the cable, to a low in the surrounding air, which forms the ozone gas. The combination of corona and ozone has been a major cause of cable deterioration. Recently, different and better quality insulating materials have lengthened the life of the electrical cables.

Although ozone at ground level can be harmful, ozone is beneficial to the earth's inhabitants. By having a concentrated ozone layer called the "ozonosphere," between 10 and 20 miles (16-32 km) up in the atmosphere, much of the ultra violet radiation from the sun's rays are absorbed and screened. If this ozone layer were not present, much of the earth's surface would be burned, dried and unfit for human life.

OXIDES OF SULFUR

Oxides of sulfur (SOx) were initially ignored in the exhaust system emissions, since the sulfur content of gasoline as a fuel is less than 1/10 of 1 percent. Because of this small amount, it was felt that it contributed very little to the overall pollution problem. However, because of the difficulty in solving the sulfur emissions in industrial pollutions and the introduction of catalytic converter to the automobile exhaust systems, a change was mandated. The automobile exhaust system, when equipped with a catalytic converter, changes the sulfur dioxide (SO_2) into the sulfur trioxide (SO_3).

When this combines with water vapors (H_2O), a sulfuric acid mist (H_2SO_4) is formed and is a very difficult pollutant to handle since it is extremely corrosive. This sulfuric acid mist that is formed, is the same mist that rises from the vents of an automobile battery when an active chemical reaction takes place within the battery cells.

When a large concentration of vehicles equipped with catalytic converters are operating in an area, this acid mist may rise and be distributed over a large ground area causing land, plant, crop, paint and building damage.

PARTICULATE MATTER

A certain amount of particulate matter is present in the burning of any fuel, with carbon constituting the largest percentage of the particulates. In gasoline, the remaining particulates are the burned remains of the various other compounds used in its manufacture. When a gasoline engine is in good internal condition, the particulate emissions are low but as the engine wears internally, the particulate emissions increase. By visually inspecting the tail pipe emissions, a determination can be made as to where an engine defect may exist. An engine with light gray or blue smoke emitting from the tail pipe normally indicates an increase in the oil consumption through burning due to internal engine wear. Black smoke would indicate a defective fuel delivery system, causing the engine to operate in a rich mode. Regardless of the color of the smoke, the internal part of the engine or the fuel delivery system should be repaired to prevent excess particulate emissions.

Diesel and turbine engines emit a darkened plume of smoke from the exhaust system because of the type of fuel used. Emission control regulations are mandated for this type of emission and more stringent measures are being used to prevent excess emission of the particulate matter. Electronic components are being introduced to control the injection of the fuel at precisely the proper time of piston travel, to achieve the optimum in fuel ignition and fuel usage. Other particulate after-burning components are being tested to achieve a cleaner emission.

Good grades of engine lubricating oils should be used, which meet the manufacturers specification. Cut-rate oils can contribute to the particulate emission problem because of their low flash or ignition temperature point. Such oils burn prematurely during the combustion process causing emission of particulate matter.

The cooling system is an important factor in the reduction of particulate matter. The optimum combustion will occur, with the cooling system operating at a temperature specified by the manufacturer. The cooling system must be maintained in the same manner as the engine oiling system, as each system is required to perform properly in order for the engine to operate efficiently for a long time.

Crankcase Emissions

Crankcase emissions are made up of water, acids, unburned fuel, oil fumes and particulates. These emissions are classified as hydrocarbons (HC) and are formed by the small amount of unburned, compressed air/fuel mixture entering the crankcase from the combustion area (between the cylinder walls and piston rings) during the compression and power strokes. The head of the compression and combustion help to form the remaining crankcase emissions.

Since the first engines, crankcase emissions were allowed into the atmosphere through a road draft tube, mounted on the lower side of the engine block. Fresh air came in through an open oil filler cap or breather. The air passed through the crankcase mixing with blow-by gases. The motion of the vehicle and the air blowing past the open end of the road draft tube caused a low pressure area (vacuum) at the end of the tube. Crankcase emissions were simply drawn out of the road draft tube into the air.

To control the crankcase emission, the road draft tube was deleted. A hose and/or tubing was routed from the crankcase to the intake manifold so the blow-by emission could be burned with the air/fuel mixture. However, it was found that intake manifold vacuum, used to draw the crankcase emissions into the manifold, would vary in strength at the wrong time and not allow the proper emission flow. A regulating valve was needed to control the flow of air through the crankcase.

Testing, showed the removal of the blow-by gases from the crankcase as quickly as possible, was most important to the longevity of the engine. Should large accumulations of blow-by gases remain and condense, dilution of the engine oil would occur to form water, soots, resins, acids and lead salts, resulting in the formation of sludge and varnishes. This condensation of the blow-by gases occurs more frequently on vehicles used in numerous starting and stopping conditions, excessive idling and when the engine is not allowed to attain normal operating temperature through short runs.

Evaporative Emissions

Gasoline fuel is a major source of pollution, before and after it is burned in the automobile engine. From the time the fuel is refined, stored, pumped and transported, again stored until it is pumped into the fuel tank of the vehicle, the gasoline gives off unburned hydrocarbons (HC) into the atmosphere. Through the redesign of storage areas and venting systems, the pollution factor was diminished, but not eliminated, from the refinery standpoint. However, the automobile still remained the primary source of vaporized, unburned hydrocarbon (HC) emissions.

Fuel pumped from an underground storage tank is cool but when exposed to a warmer ambient temperature, will expand. Before controls were mandated, an owner might fill the fuel tank with fuel from an underground storage tank and park the vehicle for some time in warm area, such as a parking lot. As the fuel would warm, it would expand and should no provisions or area be provided for the expansion, the fuel would spill out of the filler neck and onto the ground, causing hydrocarbon (HC) pollution and creating a severe fire hazard. To correct this condition, the vehicle manufacturers added overflow plumbing and/or gasoline tanks with built in expansion areas or domes.

However, this did not control the fuel vapor emission from the fuel tank. It was determined that most of the fuel evaporation occurred when the vehicle was stationary and the engine not operating. Most vehicles carry 5-25 gallons (19-95 liters) of gasoline. Should a large concentration of vehicles be parked in one area, such as a large parking lot, excessive fuel vapor emissions would take place, increasing as the temperature increases.

To prevent the vapor emission from escaping into the atmosphere, the fuel systems were designed to trap the vapors while the vehicle is stationary, by sealing the system from the atmosphere. A storage system is used to collect and hold the fuel vapors from the carburetor (if equipped) and the fuel tank when the engine is not operating. When the engine is started, the storage system is then purged of the fuel vapors, which are drawn into the engine and burned with the air/fuel mixture.

GASOLINE ENGINE EMISSION CONTROLS

Crankcase Ventilation System

OPERATION

➧ **See Figures 1 and 2**

The Positive Crankcase Ventilation (PCV) system is used to evacuate the crankcase vapors. Outside vehicle air is routed through the air cleaner to the crankcase where it mixes with the blow-by gases and is passed through the PCV valve. It is then routed into the intake manifold. The PCV valve meters the air flow rate which varies under engine operation depending on manifold vacuum. In order to maintain idle quality, the PCV valve limits the air flow when intake manifold vacuum is high. If abnormal operating conditions occur, the system will allow excessive blow-by gases to back flow through the crankcase vent tube into the air cleaner. These blow-by gases will then be burned by normal combustion.

A plugged PCV valve or hose may cause rough idle, stalling or slow idle speed, oil leaks, oil in the air cleaner or sludge in the engine. A leaking PCV valve or hose could cause rough idle, stalling or high idle speed.

Other than checking and replacing the PCV valve and associated hoses, there is not service required. Engine operating conditions that would direct suspicion to the PCV system are rough idle, oil present in the air cleaner, oil leaks and excessive oil sludging or dilution. If any of the above conditions exist, remove the PCV valve and shake it. A clicking sound indicates that the valve is free. If no clicking sound is heard, replace the valve. Inspect the PCV breather in the air cleaner. Replace the breather if it is so dirty that it will not allow gases to pass through. Check all the PCV hoses for condition and tight connections. Replace any hoses that have deteriorated.

TESTING

With the engine running, remove the PCV from the valve cover and place your thumb over the end of the valve. Check if vacuum is present at the valve. If vacuum is not present, check for plugged hoses, blockage of the manifold port at the throttle body/carburetor unit or a faulty PCV valve. Replace as necessary. With the engine not running, remove the PCV valve from the vehicle. Shake the valve and listen for the rattle of the check valve needle. If no rattle is heard the valve is defective and must be replaced.

REMOVAL & INSTALLATION

1. To replace the valve, gently pull the hose from the top of the valve, then pull the valve out of the cover grommet.
2. Installation is the reverse of removal.

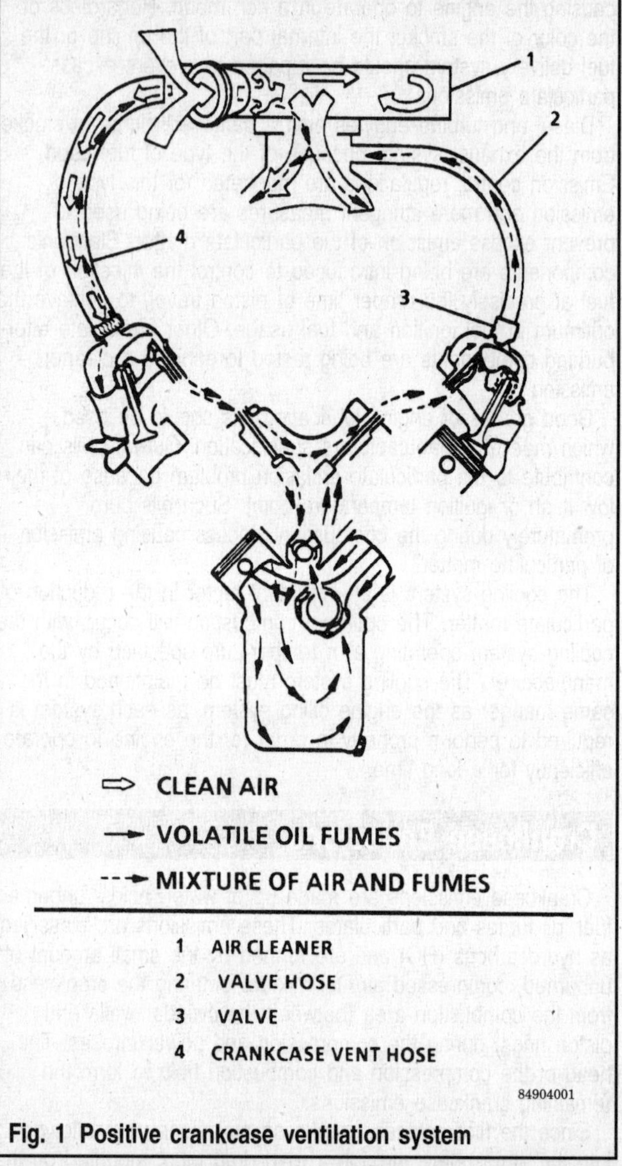

Fig. 1 Positive crankcase ventilation system

Evaporative Emission Control System

OPERATION

The Evaporative Emission Control System (EECS) is designed to prevent fuel tank vapors from being emitted into the atmosphere. Gasoline vapors are absorbed and stored by a fuel vapor charcoal canister. The charcoal canister absorbs the gasoline vapors and stores them until certain engine conditions are met and the vapors can be purged and burned by the engine.

The charcoal canister purge cycle is controlled either by a thermostatic vacuum switch or by a timed vacuum source. The thermostatic switch is installed in the coolant passage and prevents canister purge when engine operating temperature is below 115°F (46°C). The timed vacuum source uses a mani-

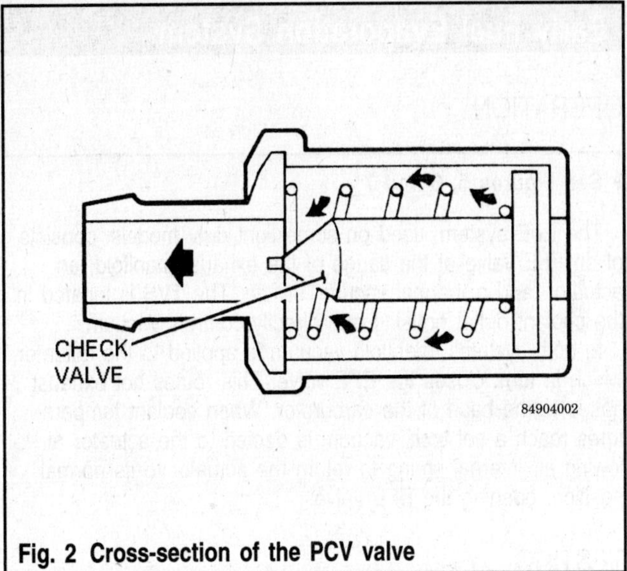

Fig. 2 Cross-section of the PCV valve

fold vacuum-controlled diaphragm to control canister purge. When the engine is running, full manifold vacuum is applied to the top tube of the purge valve which lifts the valve diaphragm and opens the valve.

A vent located in the fuel tank, allows fuel vapors to flow to the charcoal canister. A tank pressure control valve, used on high altitude applications, prevents canister purge when the engine is not running. The fuel tank cap does not normally vent to the atmosphere but is designed to provide both vacuum and pressure relief.

Poor engine idle, stalling and poor driveability can be caused by a damaged canister or split, damaged or improperly connected hoses.

Evidence of fuel loss or fuel vapor odor can be caused by a liquid fuel leak:

- A cracked or damaged vapor canister
- A disconnected, misrouted, kinked or damaged vapor pipe or canister hoses
- A damaged air cleaner or improperly seated air cleaner gasket

TESTING

Vapor Canister

See Figure 3

1. Apply a length of hose to the lower tube of the purge valve assembly and attempt to blow air through it. There should be little or no air should passing into the canister.

If the canister is equipped with a constant purge hole, a small amount of air will pass into the canister.

2. Using a hand-held vacuum pump, apply a vacuum of 15 in. Hg (51 kPa) to the control vacuum (upper) tube. If the vacuum does not hold for at least 20 seconds, the diaphragm is leaking. Replace the canister.
3. If the diaphragm holds vacuum, attempt to blow air through the hose connected to the PCV tube while vacuum is still being applied. An increase of air should be observed. If no increase is noted, the canister must be replaced.

Fuel Tank Pressure Control Valve

1. Attach a length of hose to the tank side of the valve assembly and try to blow air through it. Little or no air should pass into the canister.
2. Using a hand-held vacuum pump, apply vacuum equivalent to 15 in. Hg (51 kPa) to the control vacuum tube. If the diaphragm does not hold vacuum, the diaphragm is leaking. Replace the valve.
3. If the diaphragm holds vacuum, attempt to blow air through the hose connected to the valve while vacuum is still being applied. Air should pass. If no air is noted, the valve must be replaced.

Thermostatic Vacuum Switch

1. With engine temperature below 100°F (38°C), apply vacuum to the manifold side of the switch. The switch should hold vacuum.
2. Start and continue to run the engine until the engine temperature increases above 122°F (50°C). The vacuum should drop off.

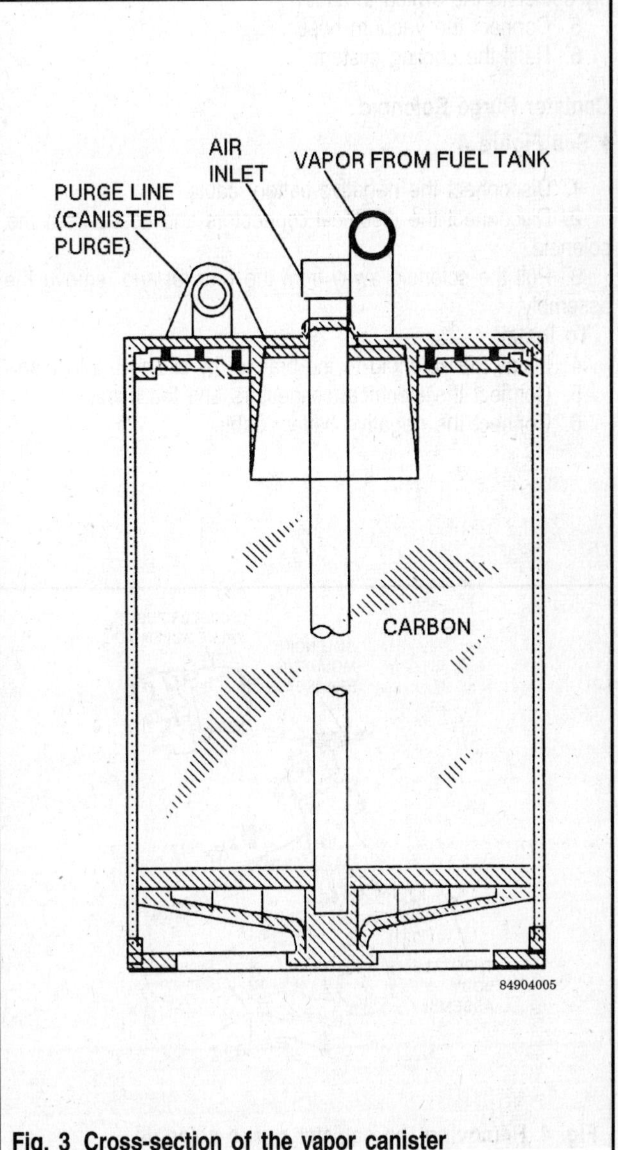

Fig. 3 Cross-section of the vapor canister

3. Replace the switch if it fails either test.

REMOVAL & INSTALLATION

Vapor Canister

1. Tag and disconnect the hoses from the canister.
2. Remove the vapor canister retaining nut.
3. Remove the canister from the vehicle.

To install:

4. Install the canister. If necessary refer to the vehicle emission control label, located in the engine compartment for proper routing of the vacuum hoses.

Thermostatic Vacuum Switch

1. Drain the cooling system to below the switch level.
2. Tag and disconnect the vacuum hoses from the switch.
3. Remove the thermostatic vacuum switch.

To install:

4. Install the thermostatic vacuum switch. Make sure to apply sealer to the switch threads.
5. Connect the vacuum hoses.
6. Refill the cooling system.

Canister Purge Solenoid

See Figure 4

1. Disconnect the negative battery cable.
2. Disconnect the electrical connectors and hoses from the solenoid.
3. Pull the solenoid away from the bracket and remove the assembly.

To install:

4. Install the solenoid to the bracket by sliding it into place.
5. Connect the electrical connectors and the hoses.
6. Connect the negative battery cable.

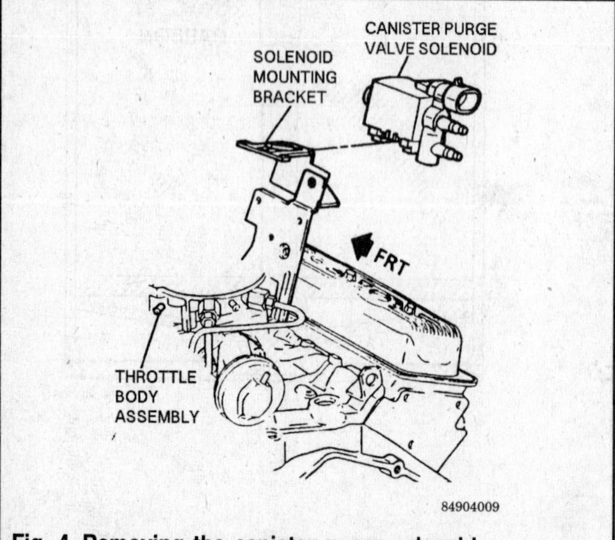

Fig. 4 Removing the canister purge solenoid

Early Fuel Evaporation System

OPERATION

See Figures 5, 6 and 7

The EFE system, used on some light duty models, consists of an EFE valve at the flange of the exhaust manifold, an actuator, and a thermal vacuum switch. The TVS is located in the coolant outlet housing and directly controls vacuum.

In both systems, manifold vacuum is applied to the actuator, which in turn, closes the EFE valve. This routes hot exhaust gases to the base of the carburetor. When coolant temperatures reach a set limit, vacuum is denied to the actuator allowing an internal spring to return the actuator to its normal position, opening the EFE valve.

TESTING

1. Locate the EFE valve on the exhaust manifold and not the position of the actuator arm. On some vehicles, the valve and arm are covered by a two-piece cover which must be removed for access. Make sure the engine is overnight cold.
2. Watch the actuator arm when the engine is started. The valve should close when the engine is started cold; the actuator link will be pulled into the diaphragm housing.
3. If the valve does not close, stop the engine. Remove the hose from the EFE valve and apply 10 in. Hg of vacuum by hand pump. The valve should close and stay closed for at least 20 seconds (you will hear it close). If the valve opens in less than 20 seconds, replace it. The valve could also be seized if it does not close; lubricate it with spray type manifold heat valve lube. If the valve does not close when vacuum is applied and when it is lubricated, replace the valve.
4. If the valve closes, the problem is not with the valve. Check for loose, cracked, pinched or plugged hoses, and replace as necessary. Test the EFE solenoid (located on the valve cover bracket); if it is working, the solenoid plunger will emit a noise when the current is applied.
5. Warm up the engine to operating temperature.
6. Watch the EFE valve to see if it has opened. It should now be open. If the valve is still closed, replace the solenoid if faulty, and/or check the engine thermostat; the engine coolant may not be reaching normal operating temperature.

REMOVAL & INSTALLATION

➡If the vehicle is equipped with an oxygen sensor, it is located near the EFE valve. Use care when removing the EFE valve as not to damage the oxygen sensor.

1. Disconnect the negative (-) battery cable and vacuum hose at the EFE valve.
2. Remove the exhaust pipe-to-manifold nuts, and the washers and tension springs if used.
3. Lower the exhaust cross-over pipe. On some models, complete removal of the pipe is not necessary.
4. Remove the EFE valve.

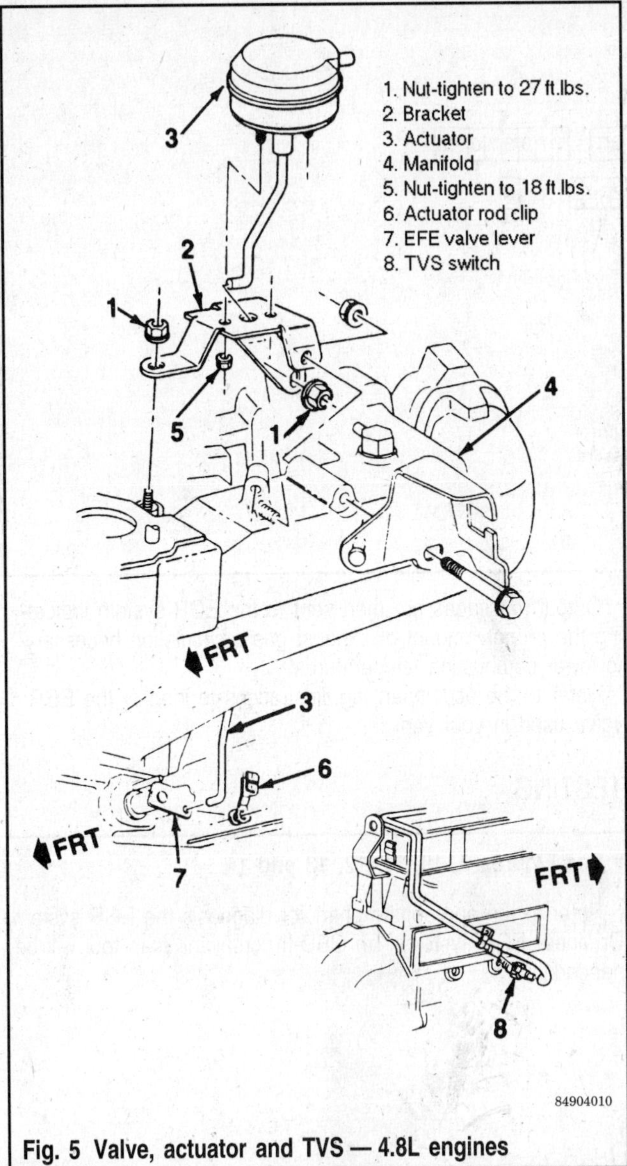

Fig. 5 Valve, actuator and TVS — 4.8L engines

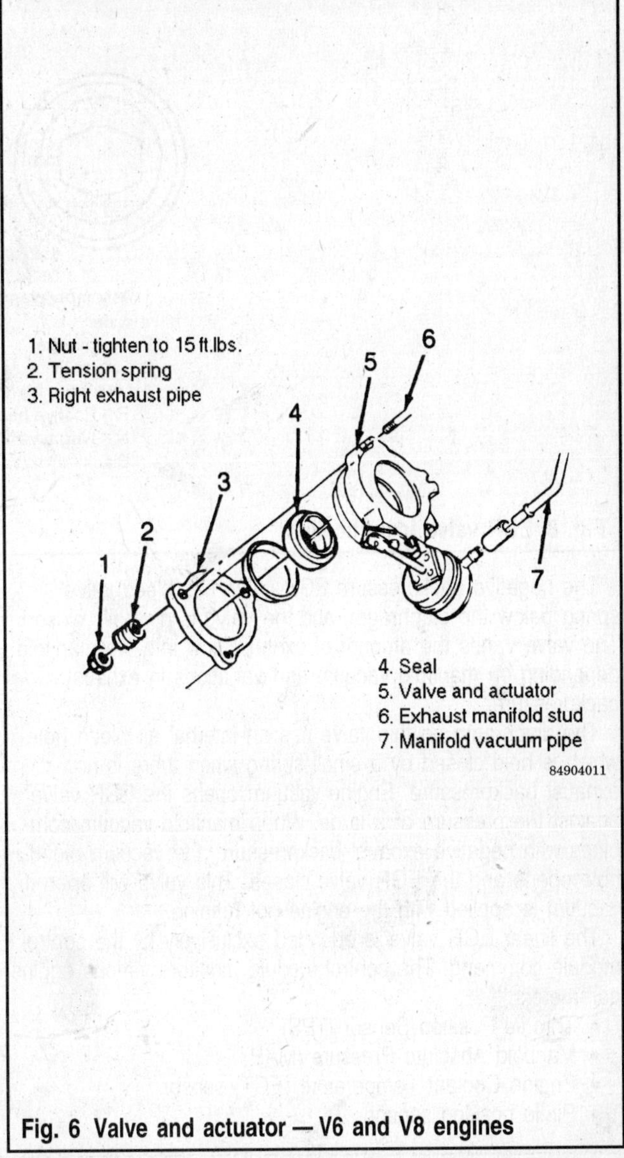

Fig. 6 Valve and actuator — V6 and V8 engines

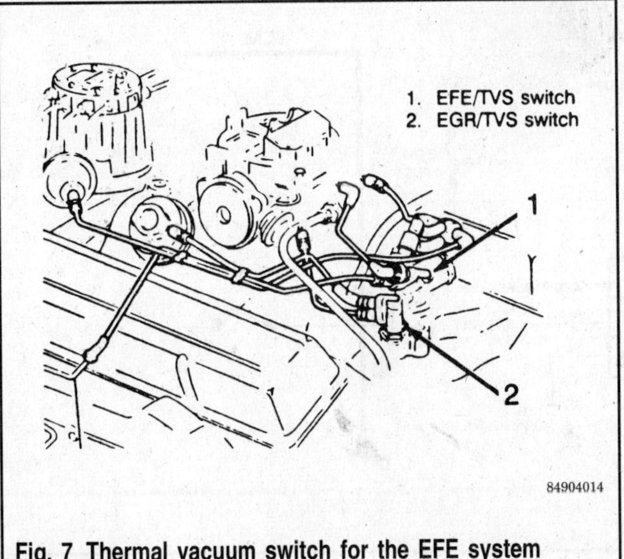

Fig. 7 Thermal vacuum switch for the EFE system

To install: Always install new seals and gaskets. Torque the exhaust nuts to 22 ft. lbs. (30 Nm). Connect the negative battery cable and vacuum hose to the valve.

Exhaust Gas Recirculation (EGR)

OPERATION

➧ **See Figure 8**

The EGR system's purpose is to control oxides of nitrogen which are formed during the peak combustion temperatures. The end products of combustion are relatively inert gases derived from the exhaust gases which are directed into the EGR valve to help lower peak combustion temperatures.

The port EGR valve is controlled by a flexible diaphragm which is spring loaded to hold the valve closed. Vacuum applied to the top side of the diaphragm overcomes the spring pressure and opens the valve which allows exhaust gas to be pulled into the intake manifold and enter the engine cylinders.

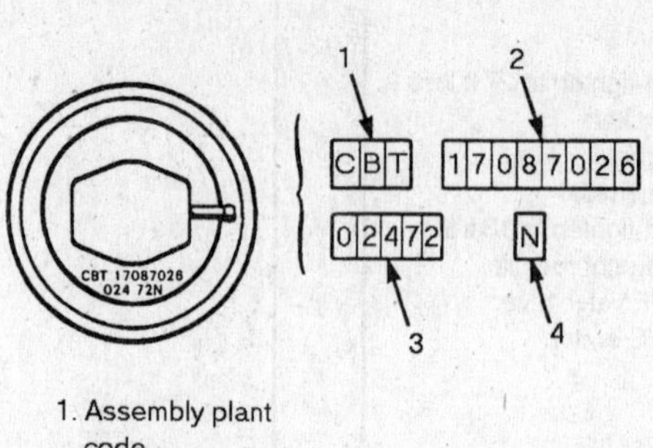

1. Assembly plant code
2. Part number
3. Date built
4. Look here for letter
   P = Postive back pressure
   N = Negative back pressure
   Blank = Port Valve

84904030

Fig. 8 EGR valve identification

The negative backpressure EGR valve has bleed valve spring below the diaphragm, and the valve is normally closed. The valve varies the amount of exhaust flow into the manifold depending on manifold vacuum and variations in exhaust backpressure.

The diaphragm on this valve has an internal air bleed hole which is held closed by a small spring when there is no exhaust backpressure. Engine vacuum opens the EGR valve against the pressure of a large. When manifold vacuum combines with negative exhaust backpressure, the vacuum bleed hole opens and the EGR valve closes. This valve will open if vacuum is applied with the engine not running.

The linear EGR valve is operated exclusively by the control module command. The control module monitors various engine parameters:

- Throttle Position Sensor (TPS)
- Manifold Absolute Pressure (MAP)
- Engine Coolant Temperature (ECT) sensor
- Pintle position sensor

Output messages are then sent to the EGR system indicating the proper amount of exhaust gas recirculation necessary to lower combustion temperatures.

Refer to the accompanying illustrations to identify the EGR valve used in your vehicle.

TESTING

See Figures 9, 10, 11, 12, 13 and 14

Refer to the appropriate chart for diagnosis the EGR system. On linear EGR systems, an OBD-II compliant scan tool will be needed.

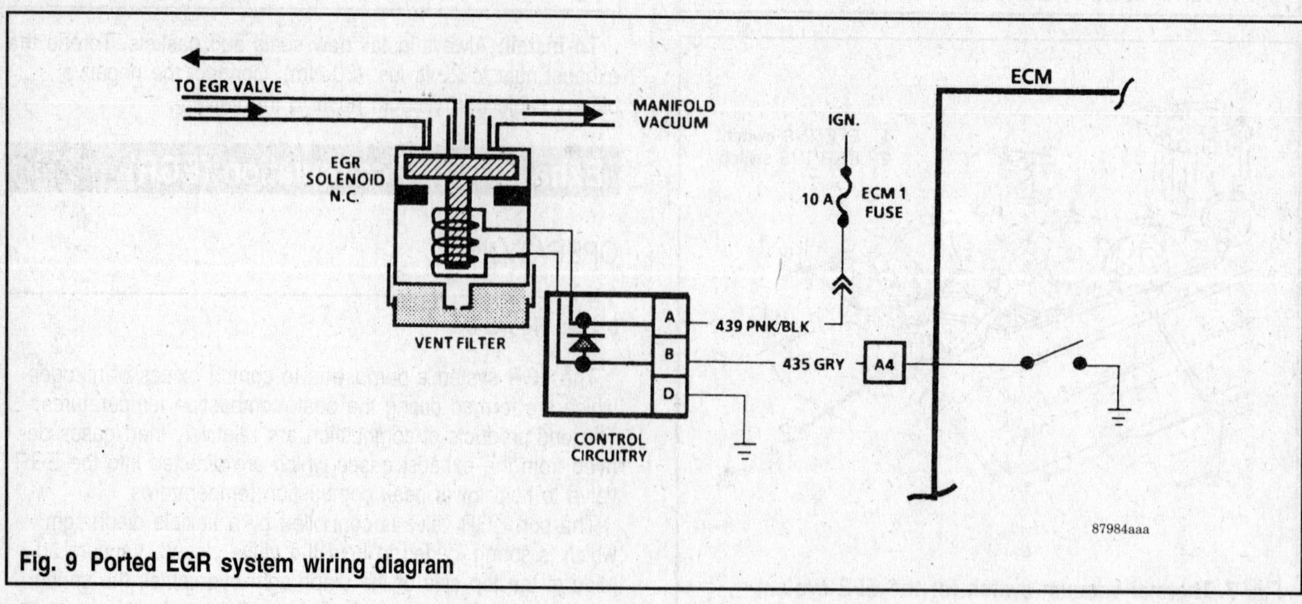

Fig. 9 Ported EGR system wiring diagram

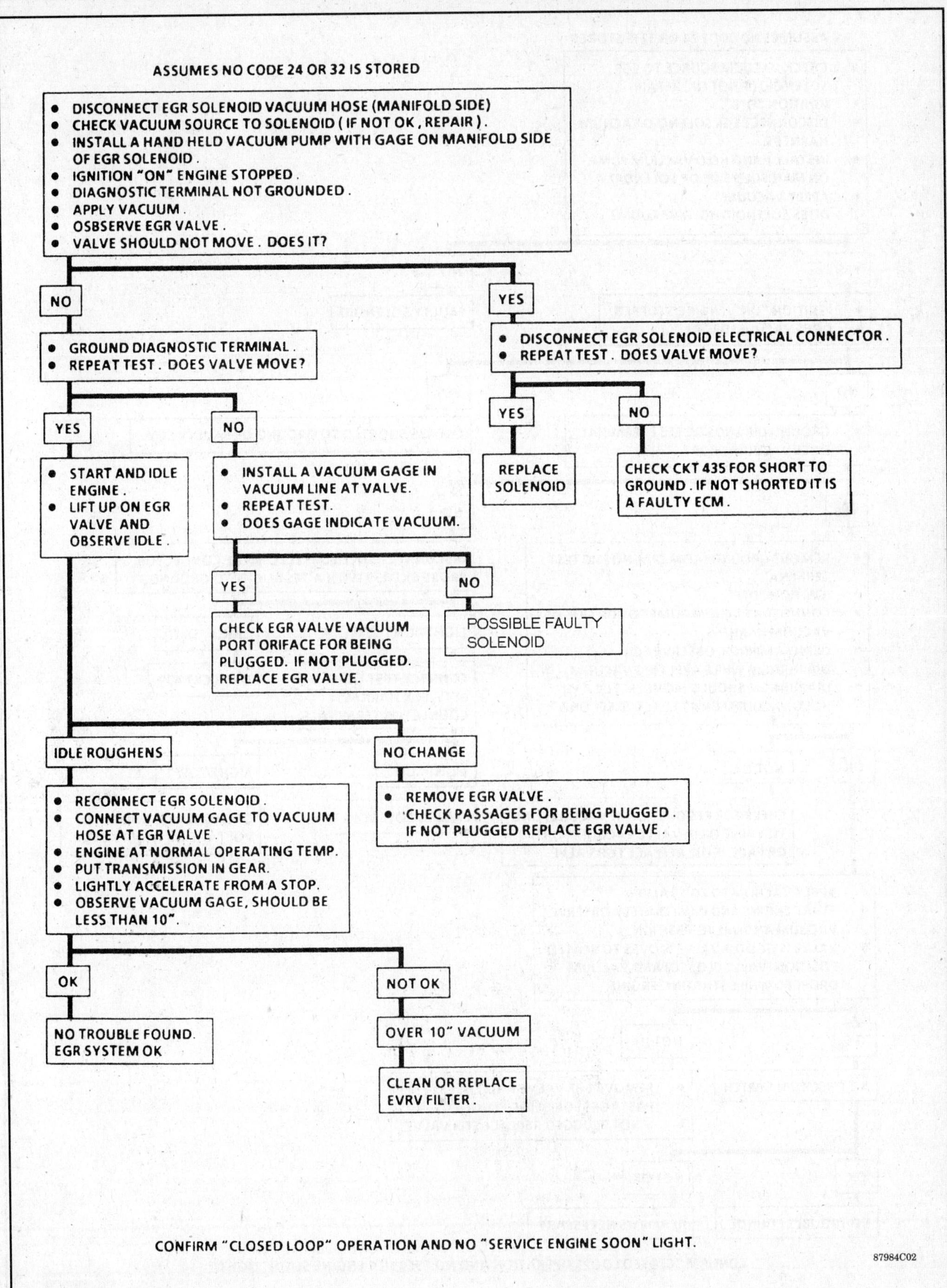

Fig. 10 Ported EGR system check

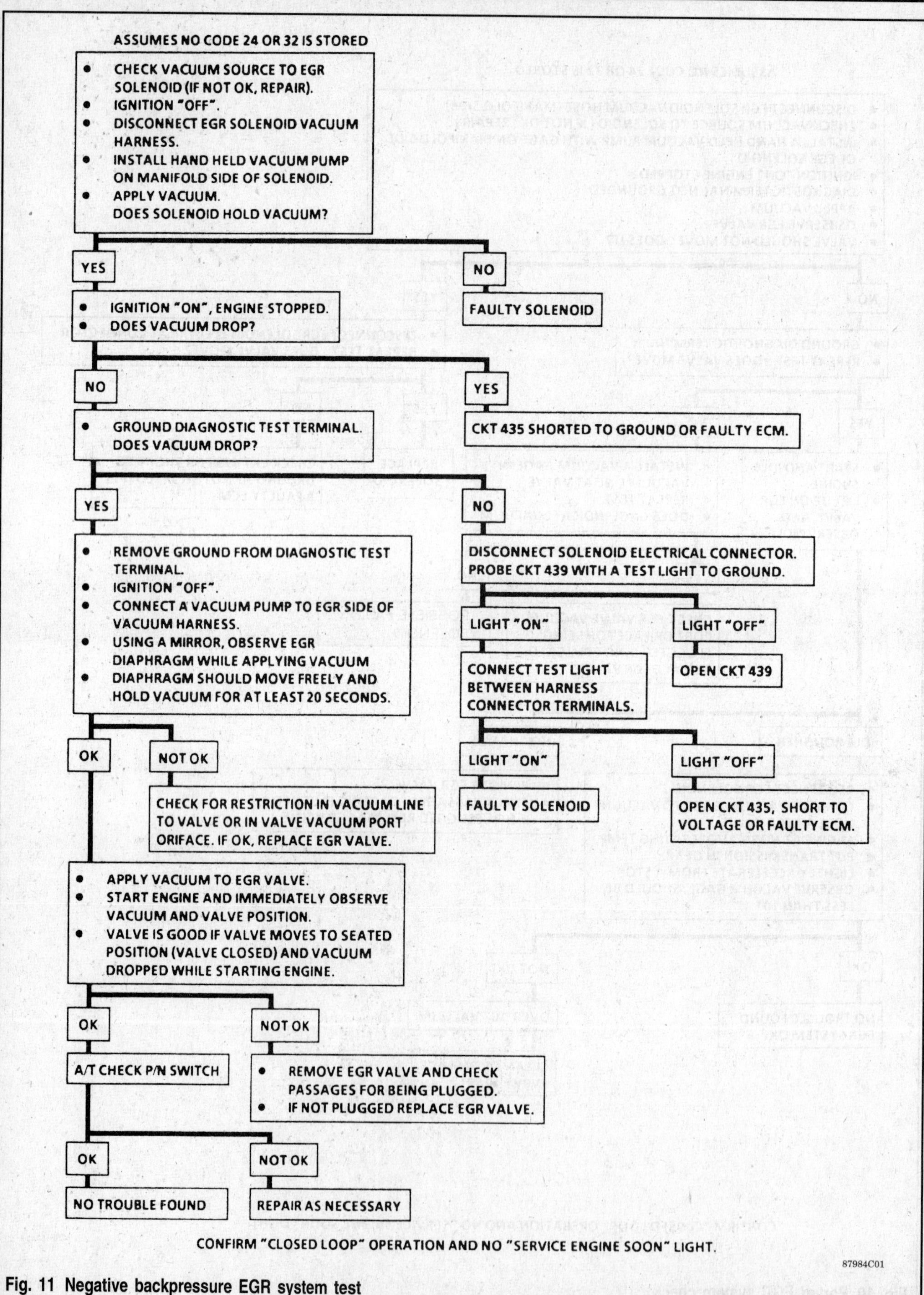

Fig. 11 Negative backpressure EGR system test

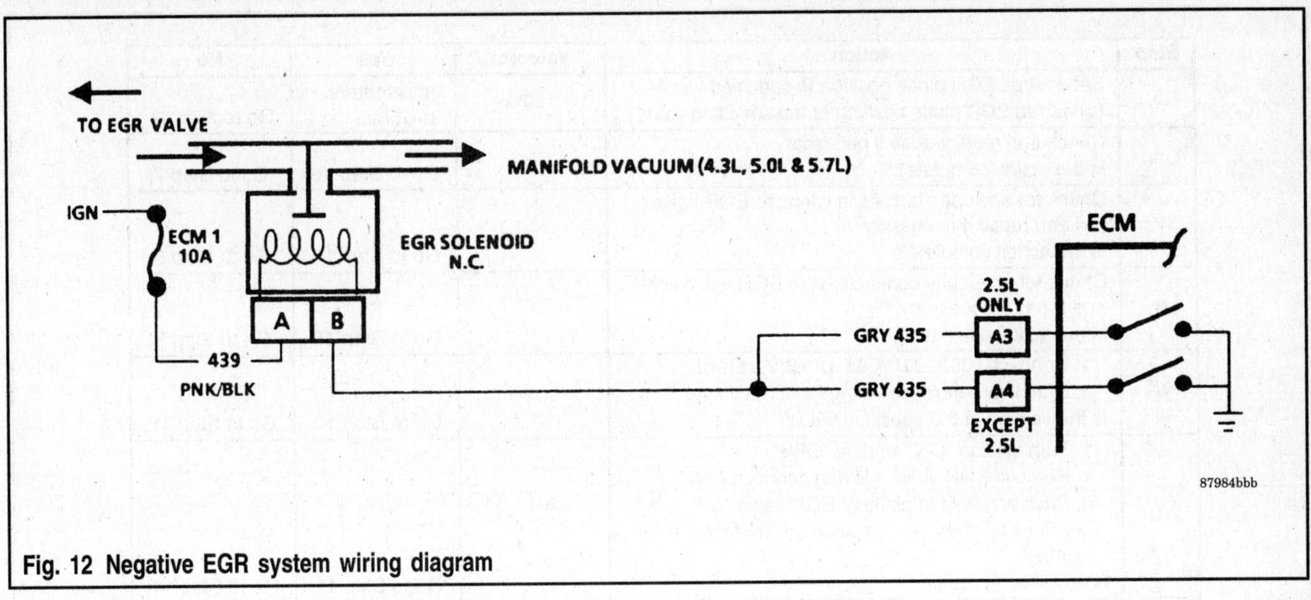

Fig. 12 Negative EGR system wiring diagram

Step	Action	Value(s)	Yes	No
1	Was the system checked for trouble codes?	—	Go to Step 2	Check for trouble codes
2	1. Set parking brake and block drive wheels. 2. Install scan tool. 3. Check Transmission Range (TR) switch position 4. Have engine idling at normal operating temperature. 5. With scan tool command EGR pintle position to specified value. 6. Increase RPM to specified value. Is actual EGR pintle position greater than the specified value?	0% 2000 3%	Go to Step 15	Go to Step 3
3	1. With scan tool command a 25% position step increase (0% To 25%, 25% To 50%, 50% To 75%, 75% To 100%). 2. Observe MAP and actual EGR pintle position for specified value. EGR should increase by about 25% of position, and MAP should also increase. Is actual EGR pintle position stable, and within 10% of position of desired EGR pintle position command after the specified value?	3 seconds 2 seconds	Go to Step 4	Go to Step 6
4	Set EGR pintle position to specified value. Did MAP increase when actual pintle responded?	25%	Go to Step 5	Go to Step 13

87984C04

Fig. 13 Linear EGR system test

Step	Action	Value(s)	Yes	No
5	Set desired EGR pintle position to specified value. Is desired EGR pintle position at the specified value?	100%	Intermittent problem	Go to Step 14
6	Check and replace fuse if necessary. Is the action complete?	—	Go to Step 16	Go to Step 7
7	Check for any open circuits in wiring to EGR valve coil and repair if necessary. Is the action complete?	—	Go to Step 16	Go to Step 8
8	Check for any faulty connections to EGR valve coil and repair if necessary. Is the action complete?	—	Go to Step 16	Go to Step 9
9	1. Connect J 39200 DVOM or equivalent. 2. Check for reference voltage at EGR valve. Is the voltage at the specified value?	5V	Go to Step 10	Go to Step 11
10	1. Turn ignition "ON," engine "OFF." 2. Remove EGR valve, leaving connector on. 3. Push and hold in pintle of EGR valve. 4. Check for voltage at position sensor signal from valve. Is any voltage present?	—	Go to Step 11	Go to Step 14
11	Check for an open in circuit from control module to EGR valve in the pintle position circuit and repair if necessary. Is the action complete?	—	Go to Step 16	Go to Step 12
12	Replace control module. Is the action complete?	—	Go to Step 16	—
13	Check and repair EGR valve passages for blockages if necessary. Is the action complete?	—	Go to Step 16	—
14	Replace EGR valve. Is the action complete?	—	Go to Step 16	—
15	EGR valve is stuck open. Replace EGR valve. Is the action complete?	—	Go to Step 16	—
16	1. Turn the ignition "ON," engine "OFF." 2. Using the scan tool, command the component "ON" and "OFF." Does the component operate properly?	—	System OK	Go to Step 2

87984C05

Fig. 14 Linear EGR system test (continued)

REMOVAL & INSTALLATION

EGR Valve

See Figures 15, 16 and 17

1. Disconnect the negative battery cable.
2. Remove the air cleaner assembly from the engine.
3. Remove the EGR valve vacuum tube from the valve.
4. Remove the EGR bolts and/or nuts and remove the EGR valve and gasket.

To install:

5. Install a new gasket to the EGR valve and install the EGR valve to the manifold.
6. Install the nuts and/or bolts. Tighten the bolts to 17 ft. lbs. (24 Nm) and the nuts to 15 ft. lbs. (20 Nm).
7. Connect the vacuum tube to the EGR valve.
8. Install the air cleaner and connect the negative battery cable.

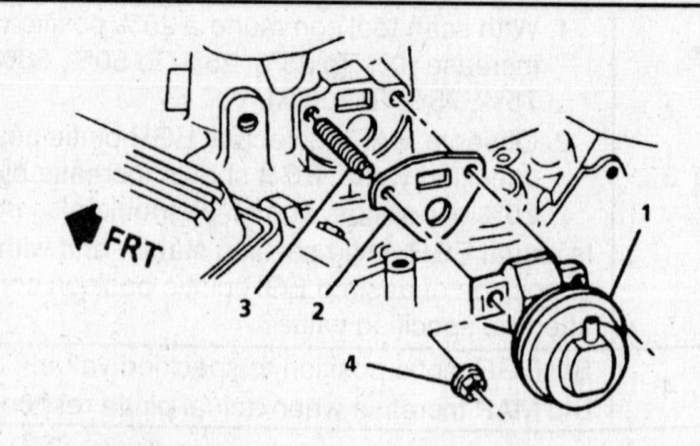

1. EGR valve
2. Gasket
3. Studs or bolts
4. Nut - tighten to 20 N·m (15 lb.ft.)

84904033

Fig. 15 EGR valve mounting — 4.3L engines

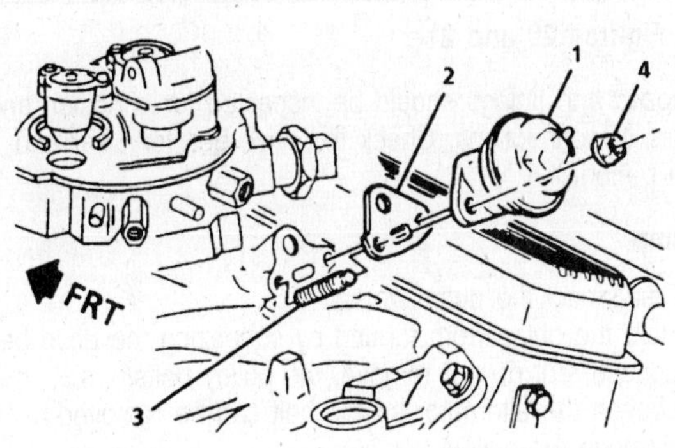

Fig. 16 EGR valve mounting — 5.0L and 5.7L engines

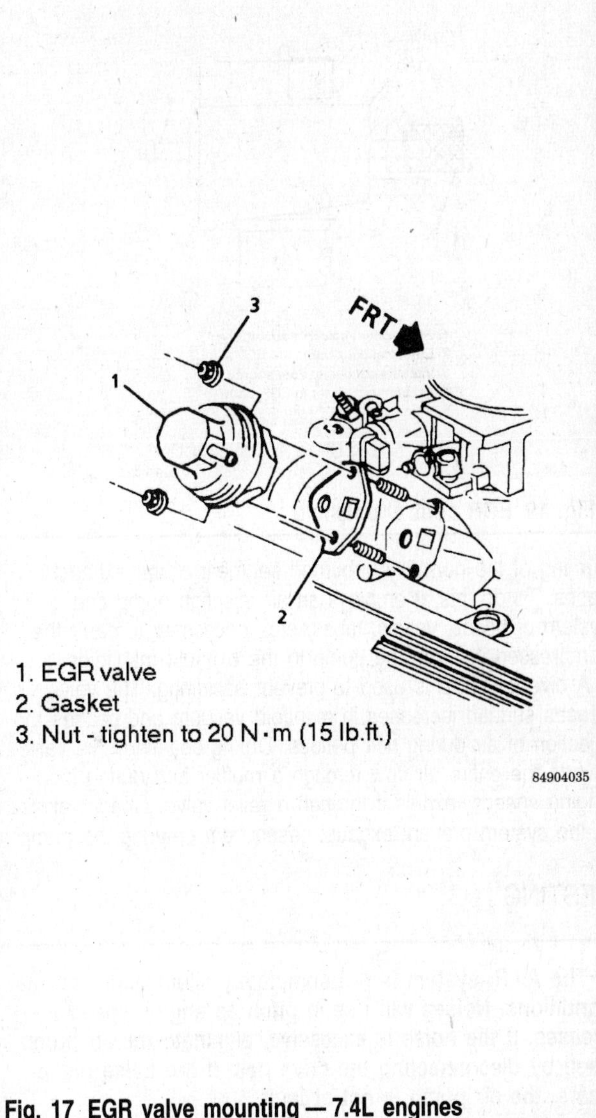

Fig. 17 EGR valve mounting — 7.4L engines

EGR Solenoid

➧ See Figures 18 and 19

1. Disconnect the negative battery cable.
2. Remove the air cleaner, as required.
3. Unplug the electrical connector at the solenoid.
4. Disconnect the vacuum hoses.
5. Remove the retaining bolts and the solenoid.
6. Remove the filter, as required.

To install:

7. If removed, install the filter.
8. Install the solenoid and retaining bolts.
9. Connect the vacuum hoses.
10. Engage the electrical connector.
11. If removed, install the air cleaner.
12. Connect the negative battery cable.

Air Injector Reactor (AIR) System

The AIR system injects compressed air into the exhaust system, near enough to the exhaust valves to continue the

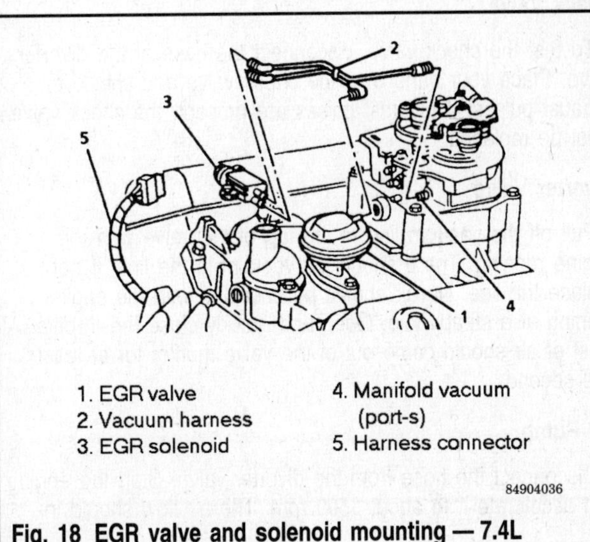

Fig. 18 EGR valve and solenoid mounting — 7.4L engine shown, others similar

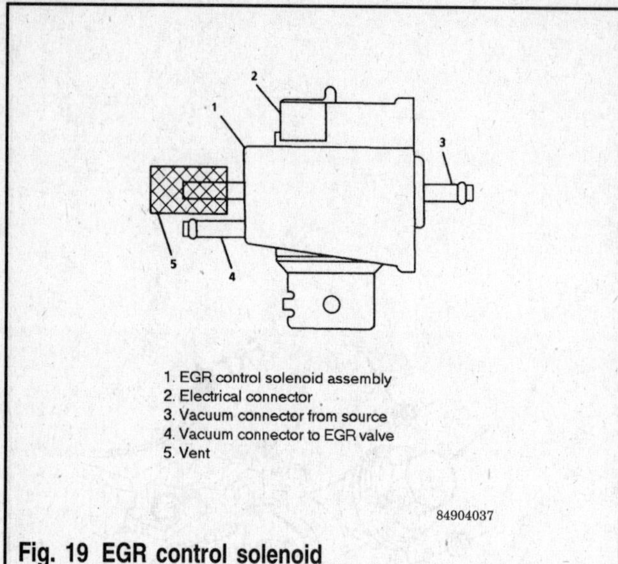

Fig. 19 EGR control solenoid

burning of the normally unburned segment of the exhaust gases. To do this, it employs an air injection pump and a system of hoses, valves, tubes, etc., necessary to carry the compressed air from the pump to the exhaust manifolds.

A diverter valve is used to prevent backfiring. The valve senses sudden increases in manifold vacuum and ceases the injection of air during rich periods. During coasting, this valve diverts the entire air flow through a muffler and during high engine speeds, expels it through a relief valve. Check valves in the system prevent exhaust gases from entering the pump.

TESTING

➡The A.I.R. system is not completely silent under normal conditions. Noises will rise in pitch as engine speed increases. If the noise is excessive, eliminate the air pump itself by disconnecting the drive belt. If the noise disappears, the air pump is not at fault.

Check Valve

To test the check valve, disconnect the hose at the diverter valve. Place your hand over the check valve and check for exhaust pulses. If exhaust pulses are present, the check valve must be replaced.

Diverter Valve

Pull off the vacuum line to the top of the valve with the engine running. There should be vacuum in the line, if not replace the line. No air should be escaping with the engine running at a steady idle. Open and quickly close the throttle. A blast of air should come out of the valve muffler for at least one second.

Air Pump

Disconnect the hose from the diverter valve. Start the engine and accelerate it to about 1500 rpm. The air flow should increase as the engine is accelerated. If no air flow is noted or it remains constant, check the following:

1. Drive belt tension.
2. Listen for a leaking pressure relief valve. If it is defective, replace the whole relief/diverter valve.
3. Foreign matter in pump filter openings. If the pump is defective or excessively noisy, it must be replaced.

REMOVAL & INSTALLATION

➧ See Figures 20 and 21

All hoses and fittings should be inspected for condition and tightness of connections. Check the drive belt for wear and tension periodically.

Air Pump

1. Disconnect the output hose.
2. Hold the pump from turning by squeezing the drive belt.
3. Loosen, but do not remove, the pulley bolts.
4. Loosen the alternator so the belt can be removed.
5. Remove the pulley.
6. Remove the pump mounting bolts and the pump.

To install:

7. Install the pump with the mounting bolts loose.
8. Install the pulley and tighten the bolts finger-tight.
9. Install the drive belt.
10. Squeeze the drive belt to prevent the pump from turning.
11. Tighten the pulley bolts to 25 ft. lbs. (33 Nm). Tighten the pump mountings.
12. Check and adjust the belt tension.
13. Connect the hose.
14. If any hose leaks are suspected, pour soapy water over the suspected area with the engine running. Bubbles will form wherever air is escaping.

Filter

1. Remove the pump and the diverter valve as an assembly.

✲✲WARNING

Do not clamp the pump in a vise or use a hammer or pry bar on the pump housing! Damage to the housing may result.

2. To change the filter, break the plastic fan from the hub. It is seldom possible to remove the fan without breaking it. Wear safety glasses.
3. Remove the remaining portion of the fan filter from the pump hub. Be careful that filter fragments do not enter the air intake hole.

To install:

4. Position the new centrifugal fan filter on the pump hub. Place the pump pulley against the fan filter and install the securing screws. Tighten the screws alternately to 95 inch lbs. (10 Nm). The fan filter will be pressed onto the pump hub.
5. Install the pump on the engine and adjust the drive belt.

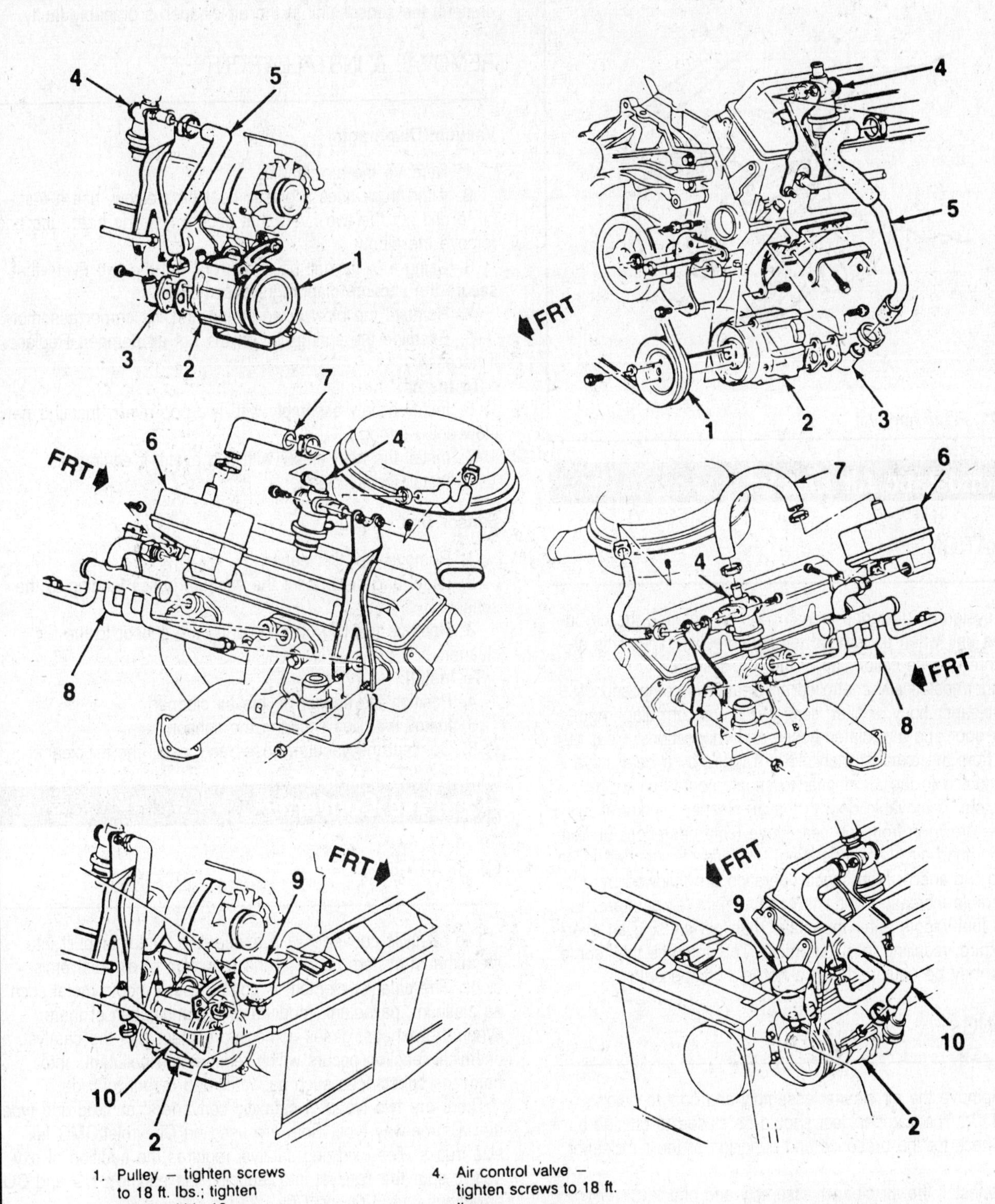

1. Pulley – tighten screws to 18 ft. lbs.; tighten again, within 10 minutes, to 18 ft. lbs.
2. AIR pump – tighten mounting screws to 22 ft. lbs.
3. Adapter – tighten screws to 98 inch lbs.
4. Air control valve – tighten screws to 18 ft. lbs.
5. Hose – pump-to-air control valve
6. Check valve – tighten nut to 74 ft. lbs.
7. Hose – air control valve-to-check valve
8. Air injection pipe – tighten nuts to 44 ft. lbs.
9. Filter – drain hole in inlet hose MUST point downward
10. Hose – filter-to-pump

84904017

Fig. 20 AIR system components

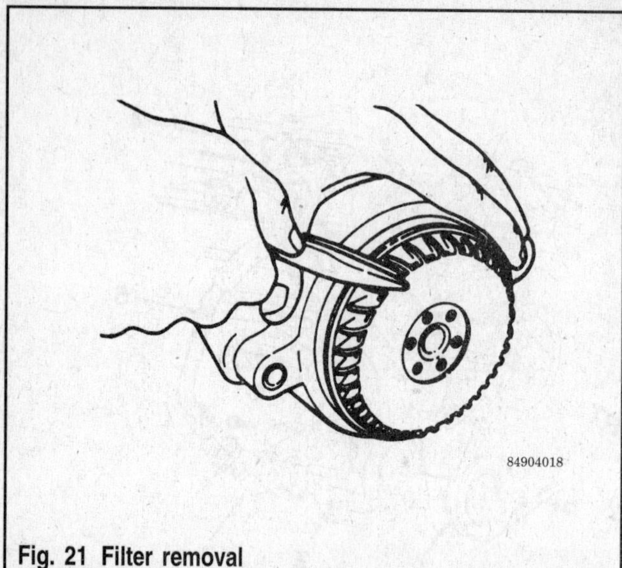

Fig. 21 Filter removal

Thermostatic Air Cleaner

OPERATION

This system is designed to warm the air entering the carburetor/TBI unit when underhood temperatures are low. This allows more precise calibration of the fuel system.

The thermostatically controlled air cleaner is composed of the air cleaner body, a filter, sensor unit, vacuum diaphragm, damper door and associated hoses and connections. Heat radiating from the exhaust manifold is trapped by a heat stove and is ducted to the air cleaner to supply heated air to the fuel system. A movable door in the air cleaner snorkel allows air to be drawn in from the heat stove (cold operation) or from the underhood air (warm operation). Periods of extended idling, climbing a grade or high speed operation are followed by a considerable increase in engine compartment temperature. Excessive fuel vapors enter the intake manifold causing an overrich mixture, resulting in a rough idle. To overcome this, some engines may be equipped with a hot idle compensator.

TESTING

1. Remove the air cleaner assembly and cool to below 40°F (4°C). The damper door should be closed to outside air.
2. Check for the presence and condition of the air cleaner gasket.
3. Reinstall the air cleaner assembly and check to make sure the heat stove tube is connected at the air cleaner snorkel and exhaust manifold.
4. Start the engine and watch the damper in the air cleaner snorkel. As the air cleaner warms up, the damper door should open slowly to the outside air.
5. If the damper fails to operate, check for vacuum at the port on the carburetor/TBI unit. If vacuum is not present, the port must be unclogged.
6. If vacuum was OK at the port, check for vacuum at the damper. If vacuum is present and the damper fails to operate, the vacuum diaphragm must be replaced. If vacuum is not present, the sensor unit in the air cleaner is probably faulty.

REMOVAL & INSTALLATION

Vacuum Diaphragm

1. Remove the air cleaner.
2. If the truck uses a plastic heat tube elbow, use a 1/8in. bit to drill out the two rivets that secure it to the heat tube and remove the elbow.
3. Using a 1/8 in. drill bit again, drill out the two rivets that secure the vacuum diaphragm assembly.
4. Remove the blow down spring and the carrier assembly.
5. Examine the spring clip on the hot air damper. Replace if necessary.

To install:

6. Install a new assembly with two pop rivets. Install a new blow down spring.
7. Install the heat elbow with two rivets, if equipped.
8. Install the air cleaner.

Sensor Unit

1. Remove the air cleaner.
2. Label and disconnect the vacuum hoses leading to the sensor.
3. Remove the two clips securing the sensor to the air cleaner.

To install:

4. Position the sensor on the air cleaner.
5. Install the clips securing the sensor.
6. Connect the vacuum hoses and install the air cleaner.

Catalytic Converter

OPERATION

The catalytic converter is a muffler-like container built into the exhaust system to aid in the reduction of exhaust emissions. The catalyst element is coated with a noble metal such as platinum, palladium, rhodium or a combination of them. When the exhaust gases come into contact with the catalyst, a chemical reaction occurs which reduces the pollutants into harmless substances such as water and carbon dioxide.

There are two types of catalytic converters: an oxidizing type and a three-way type. Both are used on Chevrolet/GMC full size trucks. The oxidizing catalyst requires the addition of oxygen to spur the catalyst into reducing the engine's HC and CO emissions into H_2O and CO_2.

PRECAUTIONS

1. Use only unleaded fuel.
2. Avoid prolonged idling; the engine should run no longer than 20 min. at curb idle and no longer than 10 min. at fast idle.
3. Don't disconnect any of the spark plug leads while the engine is running. If any engine testing procedure requires

disconnecting or bypassing a control component, perform the procedure as quickly as possible. A misfiring engine can overheat the catalyst and damage the oxygen sensor.

4. Make engine compression checks as quickly as possible.

5. Whenever under the vehicle or around the catalytic converter, remember that it has a very high outside or skin temperature. During operation, the catalyst must reach very high temperatures to work efficiently. Be very wary of burns, even after the engine has been shut off for a while. Additionally, because of the heat, never park the vehicle on or over flammable materials, particularly dry grass or leaves. Inspect the heat shields frequently and correct any bends or damage.

6. In the unlikely event that the catalyst must be replaced, DO NOT dispose of the old one where anything containing grease, gas or oil can come in contact with it. The catalytic action with these substances will result in heat which may start a fire.

DIESEL ENGINE EMISSIONS CONTROLS

Crankcase Ventilation

OPERATION

➧ See Figure 22

A Crankcase Depression Regulator Valve (CDRV) is used to regulate (meter) the flow of crankcase gases back into the engine to be burned. The CDRV is designed to limit vacuum in the crankcase as the gases are drawn from the valve covers through the CDRV and into the intake manifold (air crossover).

Fresh air enters the engine through the combination filter, check valve and oil fill cap. The fresh air mixes with blow-by gases and enters both valve covers. The gases pass through a filter installed on the valve covers and are drawn into connecting tubing.

Intake manifold vacuum acts against a spring loaded diaphragm to control the flow of crankcase gases. Higher intake vacuum levels pull the diaphragm closer to the top of the outlet tube. This reduces the amount of gases being drawn from the crankcase and decreases the vacuum level in the crankcase. As the intake vacuum decreases, the spring pushes the diaphragm away from the top of the outlet tube allowing more gases to flow to the intake manifold.

TESTING

Do not attempt to test the valve. If you suspect problems with the system, clean the filter and vent pipes with solvent. Be sure to dry the components before installing them.

REMOVAL & INSTALLATION

➧ See Figures 23 and 24

The components of this system can be removed by disconnecting the hoses and pulling the component from its mounting grommet. Be careful not to damage the grommet; replace if necessary.

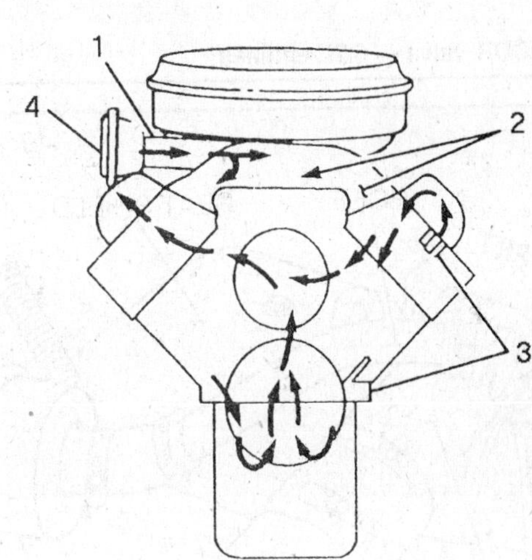

1. Crankcase vapors to induction system
2. Inlet manifold runners
3. Blowby leakage at valves and pistons
4. Crankcase depression regulator valve
↖ Crankcase vapors

84904112

Fig. 22 Crankcase vapor flow

Exhaust Gas Recirculation (EGR)

OPERATION

To lower the formation of nitrogen oxides (NOx) in the exhaust, it is necessary to reduce combustion temperatures. This

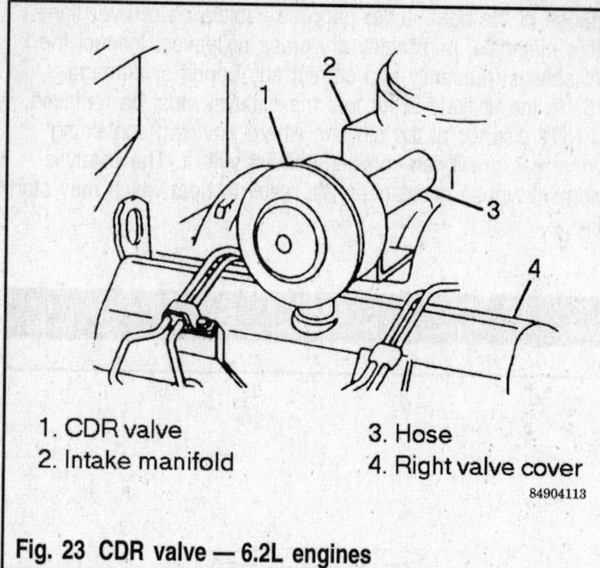

Fig. 23 CDR valve — 6.2L engines

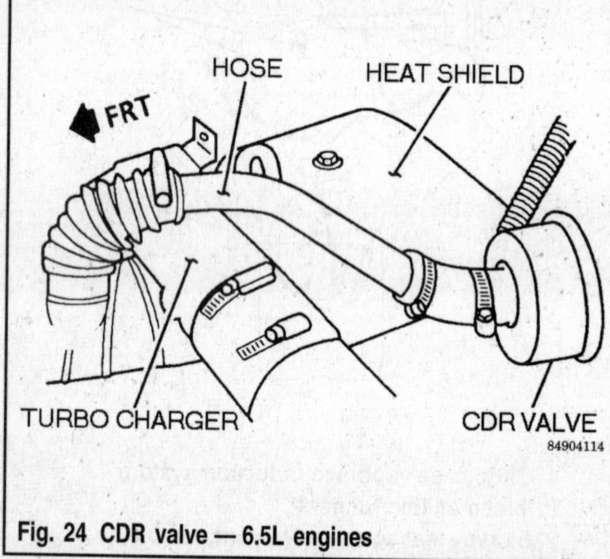

Fig. 24 CDR valve — 6.5L engines

is done in the diesel, as in the gasoline engine, by introducing exhaust gases into the cylinders through the EGR valve.

The Exhaust Pressure Regulator (EPR) valve and solenoid operate in conjunction with the EGR valve. The EPR valve's job is to increase exhaust backpressure in order to increase EGR flow. The EPR valve is usually open, and the solenoid is normally closed. When energized by the **B+** wire from the Throttle Position Switch (TPS), the solenoid opens, allowing vacuum to the EPR valve, closing it. This occurs at idle. As the throttle is opened, at a calibrated throttle angle, the TPS de-energizes the EPR solenoid, cutting off vacuum to the EPR valve, closing the valve. Two other solenoids are used for EGR valve control. The EGR solenoid allows vacuum to reach the EGR vent solenoid under certain conditions. The vent solenoid then controls the EGR valve to regulate the flow of gasses into the intake manifold.

TESTING

Exhaust Gas Recirculation (EGR) Valve

Apply vacuum to the EGR valve with a hand vacuum pump. The valve should be fully open at 11 in. Hg and closed below 6 in. Hg.

EPR Valve

1. Apply 11 in. Hg vacuum to the EPR valve tube with a hand vacuum pump. Observe the valve actuator lever for movement.
2. If it does not move, spray a penetrating lubricant on the lever and try to free the valve.

⁂CAUTION

Make sure the valve is not hot.

3. If the lubricant will not free the valve, it must be replaced.

REMOVAL & INSTALLATION

EGR Valve

➧ See Figure 25

1. Remove the air cleaner assembly and air intake tube.
2. Unplug the vacuum hose from the valve.
3. Remove the studs securing the valve to the intake manifold.
4. Installation is the reverse of removal. Tighten the studs until snug.

EPR Valve

➧ See Figure 26

1. Raise and safely support the vehicle.
2. Unplug the vacuum hose from the actuator.
3. Disconnect the exhaust pipe from the valve.

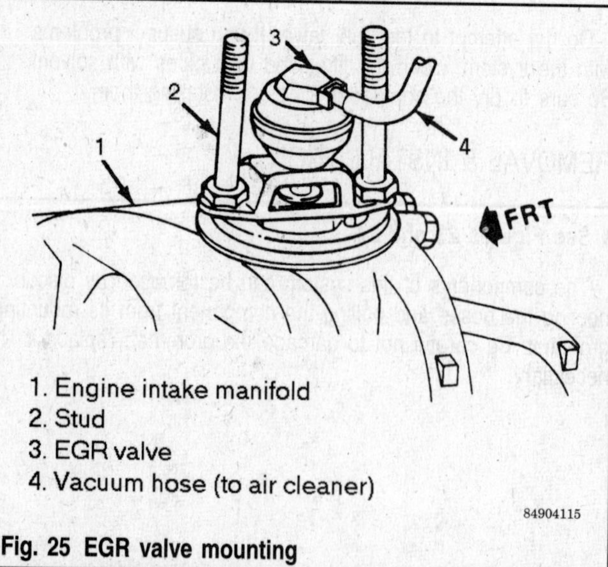

Fig. 25 EGR valve mounting

4. Remove the studs securing the valve to the exhaust manifold.
5. Installation is the reverse of removal.

EGR/EPR Solenoid Assembly

➧ **See Figure 27**

1. Disconnect the negative battery cable.
2. Label and disconnect the vacuum hoses from the assembly.
3. Unplug the solenoid electrical connectors.
4. Remove the retainers securing the assembly to the intake manifold.
5. Installation is the reverse of removal.

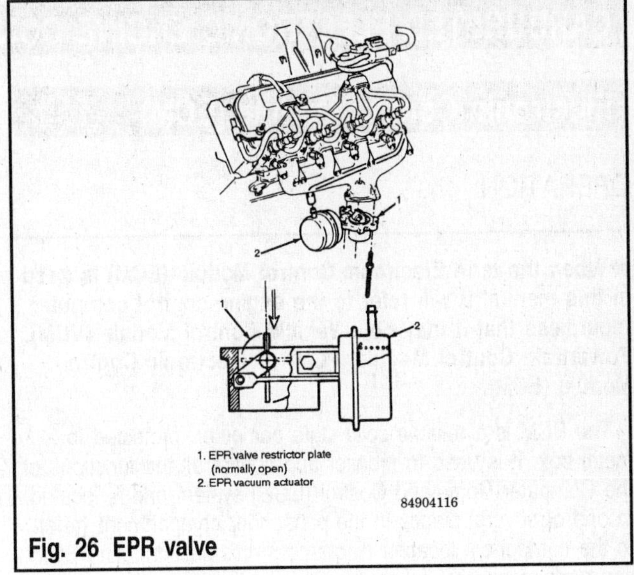

Fig. 26 EPR valve

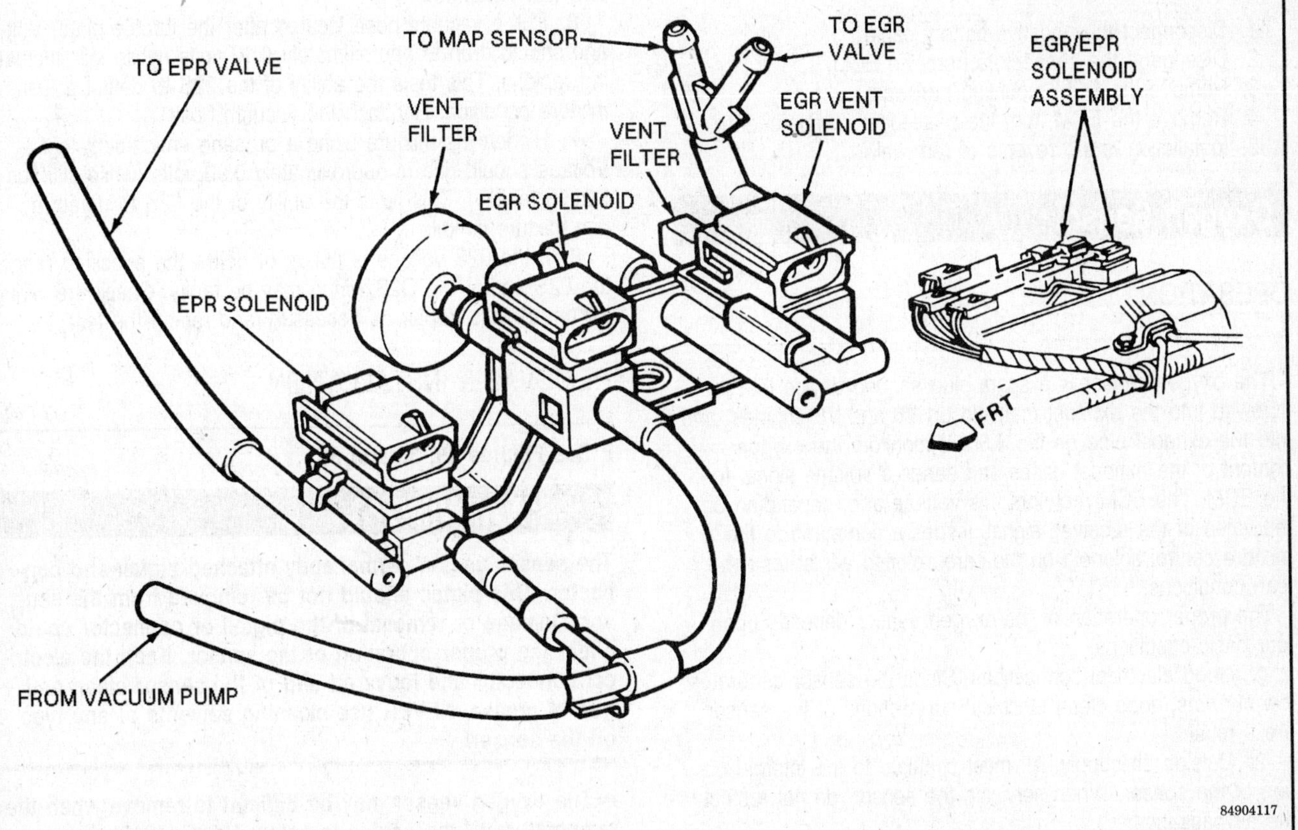

TO MAP SENSOR
TO EGR VALVE
EGR/EPR SOLENOID ASSEMBLY
TO EPR VALVE
VENT FILTER
VENT FILTER
EGR VENT SOLENOID
EGR SOLENOID
EPR SOLENOID
FRT
FROM VACUUM PUMP
84904117

Fig. 27 EGR/EPR solenoid assembly

CARBURETED ELECTRONIC ENGINE CONTROLS

Electronic Control Module (ECM)

OPERATION

➡When the term Electronic Control Module (ECM) is used in this manual it will refer to the engine control computer regardless that it may be a Vehicle Control Module (VCM), Powertrain Control Module (PCM) or Electronic Control Module (ECM).

The ECM is a reliable solid state computer, protected in a metal box. It is used to monitor and control all the functions of the Computer Command Control (CCC) system and is located in one of several places in the passenger compartment (refer to the component location diagrams in this section). The ECM can perform several on-car functions at the same time and has the ability to diagnose itself as well as other CCC system circuits.

REMOVAL & INSTALLATION

1. Disconnect the negative battery cable.
2. Disengage the connectors from the ECM.
3. Remove the ECM mounting hardware.
4. Remove the ECM from the passenger compartment.
5. Installation is the reverse of removal.

Oxygen Sensor

OPERATION

The oxygen sensor is a spark plug shaped device that is screwed into the exhaust manifold on V6 and V8 engines, and into the exhaust pipe on the 4.8L. It monitors the oxygen content of the exhaust gases and sends a voltage signal to the ECM. The ECM monitors this voltage and, depending on the value of the received signal, issues a command to the mixture control solenoid on the carburetor to adjust for rich or lean conditions.

The proper operation of the oxygen sensor depends upon four basic conditions:

1. Good electrical connections. Since the sensor generates low currents, good clean electrical connections at the sensor are a must.
2. Outside air supply. Air must circulate to the internal portion of the sensor. When servicing the sensor, do not restrict the air passages.
3. Proper operating temperatures. The ECM will not recognize the sensor's signals until the sensor reaches approximately 600°F (316°C).
4. Non-leaded fuel. The use of leaded gasoline will damage the sensor very quickly.

TESTING

➧ **See Figure 28**

1. Start the engine and bring it to normal operating temperature, then run the engine above 1200 rpm for two minutes.
2. Backprobe with a high impedance averaging voltmeter (set to the DC voltage scale) between the oxygen sensor (02S) and battery ground.
3. Verify that the 02S voltage fluctuates rapidly between 0.40-0.60 volts.
4. If the 02S voltage is stabilized at the middle of the specified range (approximately 0.45-0.55 volts) or if the 02S voltage fluctuates very slowly between the specified range (02S signal crosses 0.5 volts less than 5 times in ten seconds), the 02S may be faulty.
5. If the 02S voltage stabilizes at either end of the specified range, the ECM is probably not able to compensate for a mechanical problem such as a vacuum leak or a high float level. These types of mechanical problems will cause the 02S to sense a constant lean or constant rich mixture. The mechanical problem will first have to be repaired and then the 02S test repeated.
6. Pull a vacuum hose located after the throttle plate. Voltage should drop to approximately 0.12 volts (while still fluctuating rapidly). This tests the ability of the 02S to detect a lean mixture condition. Reattach the vacuum hose.
7. Richen the mixture using a propane enrichment tool. Voltage should rise to approximately 0.90 volts (while still fluctuating rapidly). This tests the ability of the 02S to detect a rich mixture condition.
8. If the 02S voltage is above or below the specified range, the 02S and/or the O2S wiring may be faulty. Check the wiring for any breaks, repair as necessary and repeat the test.

REMOVAL & INSTALLATION

➧ **See Figures 29, 30 and 31**

✲✲WARNING

The sensor uses a permanently attached pigtail and connector. This pigtail should not be removed from the sensor. Damage or removal of the pigtail or connector could affect the proper operation of the sensor. Keep the electrical connector and louvered end of the sensor clean and free of grease. NEVER use cleaning solvents of any type on the sensor!

➡The oxygen sensor may be difficult to remove when the temperature of the engine is below 120°F (49°C). Excessive force may damage the threads in the exhaust manifold or exhaust pipe.

1. Unplug the electrical connector and any attaching hardware.
2. Remove the sensor using an appropriate sized wrench or special socket.

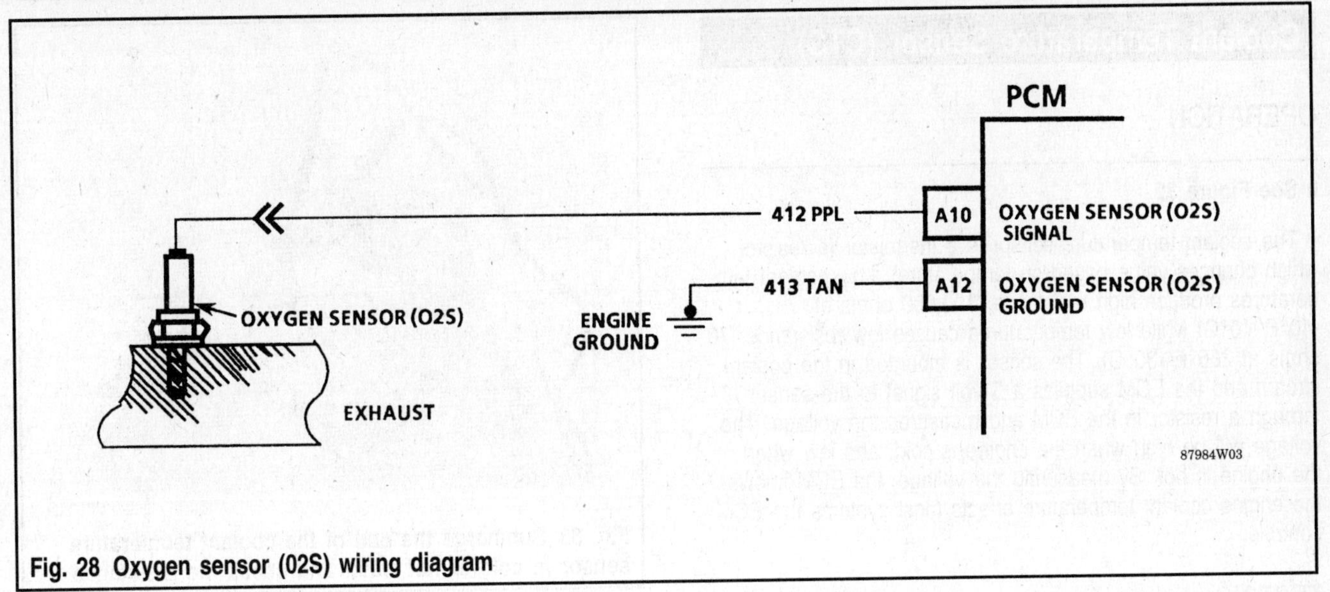

Fig. 28 Oxygen sensor (02S) wiring diagram

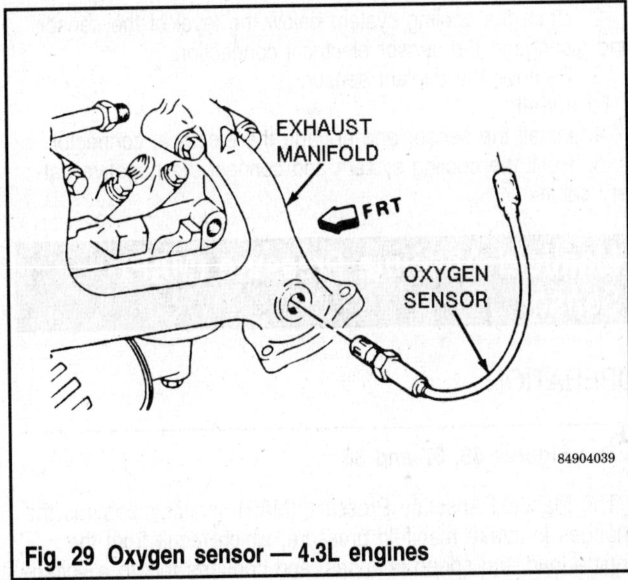

Fig. 29 Oxygen sensor — 4.3L engines

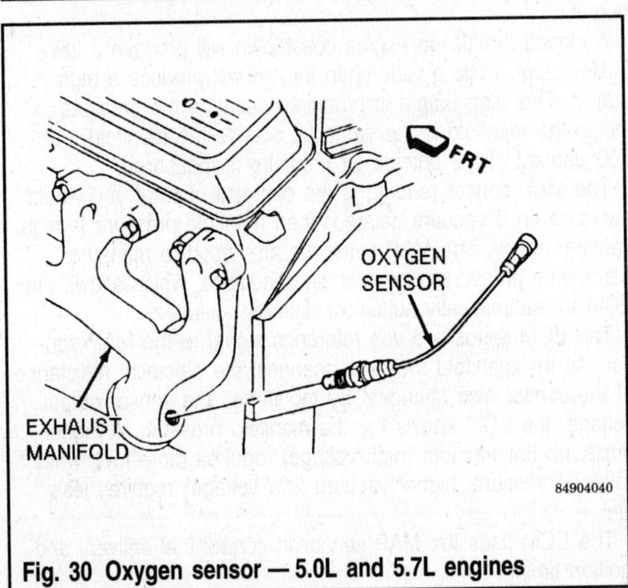

Fig. 30 Oxygen sensor — 5.0L and 5.7L engines

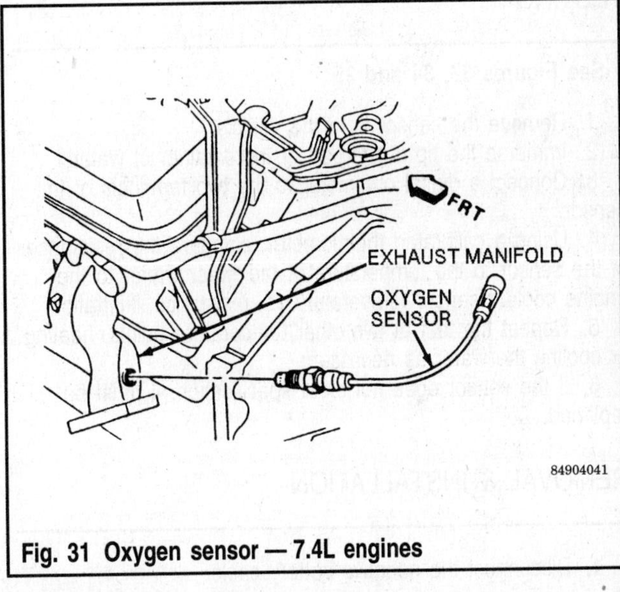

Fig. 31 Oxygen sensor — 7.4L engines

To install:

3. Coat the threads of the sensor with a GM anti-seize compound, part number 5613695, or its equivalent, before installation. New sensors are usually precoated with this compound.

➡The GM antiseize compound is NOT a conventional anti-seize paste. The use of a regular paste may electrically insulate the sensor, rendering it useless. The threads MUST be coated with the proper electrically conductive anti-seize compound.

4. Install the sensor and tighten to 30 ft. lbs. (40 Nm). Use care in making sure the silicone boot is in the correct position to avoid melting it during operation.

5. Engage the electrical connector and attaching hardware if used.

Coolant Temperature Sensor (CTS)

OPERATION

➧ See Figure 32

The coolant temperature sensor is a thermistor (a resistor which changes value based on temperature). Low coolant temperatures produce high resistance (100,000 ohms at -40°F/-40°C) while low temperatures causes low resistance (70 ohms at 266°F/130°C). The sensor is mounted in the coolant stream and the ECM supplies a 5 volt signal to the sensor through a resistor in the ECM and measures the voltage. The voltage will be high when the engine is cold, and low when the engine is hot. By measuring the voltage, the ECM knows the engine coolant temperature effects most systems the ECM controls.

TESTING

➧ See Figures 33, 34 and 35

1. Remove the sensor from the vehicle.
2. Immerse the tip of the sensor in container of water.
3. Connect a digital ohmmeter to the two terminals of the sensor.
4. Using a calibrated thermometer, compare the resistance of the sensor to the temperature of the water. Refer to the engine coolant sensor temperature vs. resistance illustration.
5. Repeat the test at two other temperature points, heating or cooling the water as necessary.
6. If the sensor does not meet specification, it must be replaced.

REMOVAL & INSTALLATION

1. Disconnect the negative battery cable.

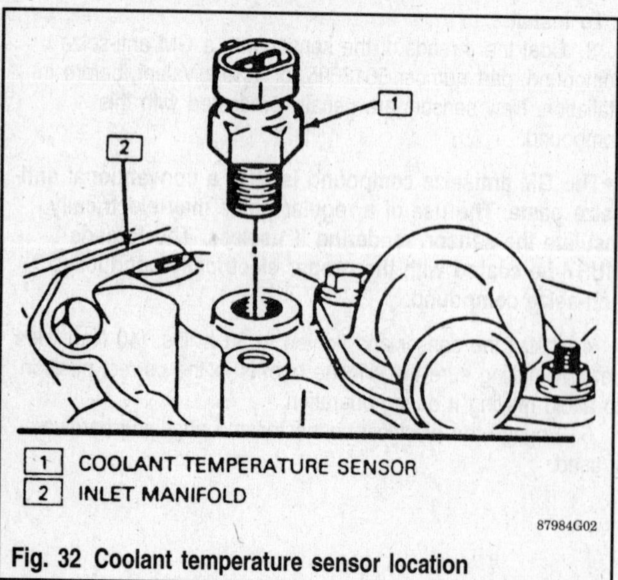

Fig. 32 Coolant temperature sensor location

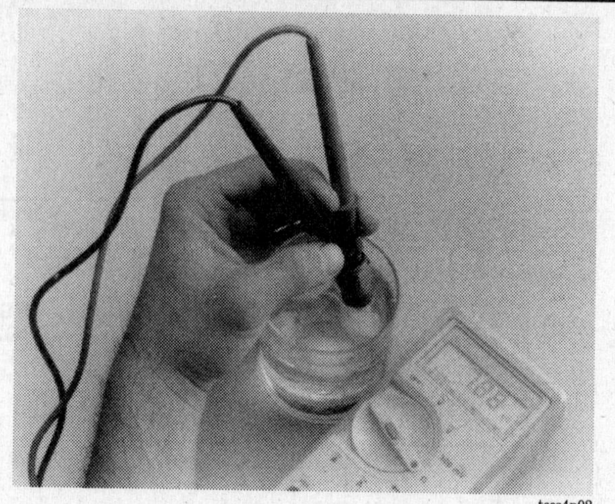

Fig. 33 Submerge the end of the coolant temperature sensor in cold or hot water and check the resistance

2. Drain the cooling system below the level of the sensor and disengage the sensor electrical connection.
3. Remove the coolant sensor.

To install:

4. Install the sensor and engage the electrical connector.
5. Refill the cooling system and connect the negative battery cable.

Manifold Absolute Pressure (MAP) Sensor

OPERATION

➧ See Figures 36, 37 and 38

The Manifold Absolute Pressure (MAP) sensor measures the changes in intake manifold pressure, which result from the engine load and speed changes, and converts this to a voltage output.

A closed throttle on engine coastdown will produce a low MAP output, while a wide-open throttle will produce a high output. This high output is produced because the pressure inside the manifold is the same as outside the manifold, so 100 percent of the outside air pressure is measured.

The MAP sensor reading is the opposite of what you would measure on a vacuum gauge. When manifold pressure is high, vacuum is low. The MAP sensor is also used to measure barometric pressure under certain conditions, which allows the ECM to automatically adjust for different altitudes.

The ECM sends a 5 volt reference signal to the MAP sensor. As the manifold pressure changes, the electrical resistance of the sensor also changes. By monitoring the sensor output voltage, the ECM knows the the manifold pressure. A higher pressure, low vacuum (high voltage) requires more fuel, while a lower pressure, higher vacuum (low voltage) requires less fuel.

The ECM uses the MAP sensor to control fuel delivery and ignition timing.

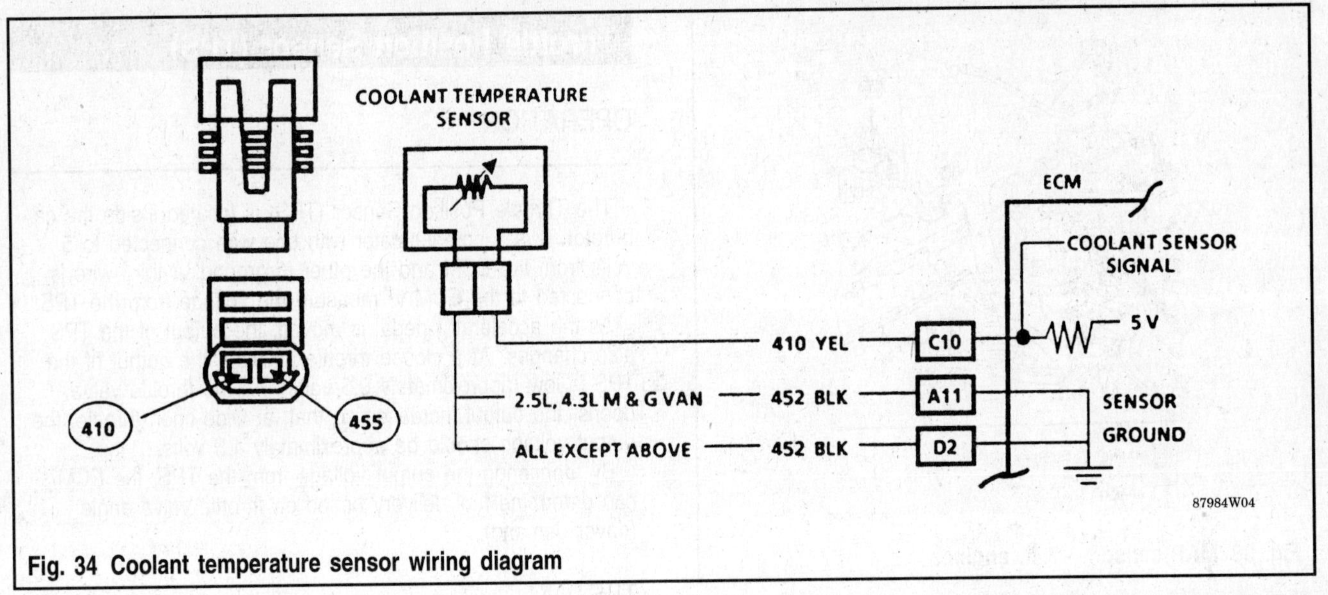

Fig. 34 Coolant temperature sensor wiring diagram

ENGINE COOLANT SENSOR		
TEMPERATURE VS. RESISTANCE VALUES (APPROXIMATE)		
°C	°F	OHMS
100	212	177
90	194	241
80	176	332
70	158	467
60	140	667
50	122	973
45	113	1188
40	104	1459
35	95	1802
30	86	2238
25	77	2796
20	68	3520
15	59	4450
10	50	5670
5	41	7280
0	32	9420
-5	23	12300
-10	14	16180
-15	5	21450
-20	-4	28680
-30	-22	52700
-40	-40	100700

87984G38

Fig. 35 Coolant temperature sensor temperature vs. resistance values

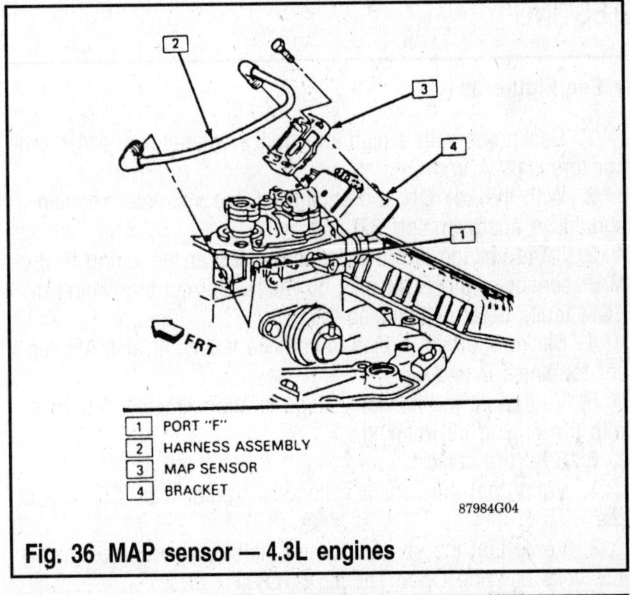

Fig. 36 MAP sensor — 4.3L engines

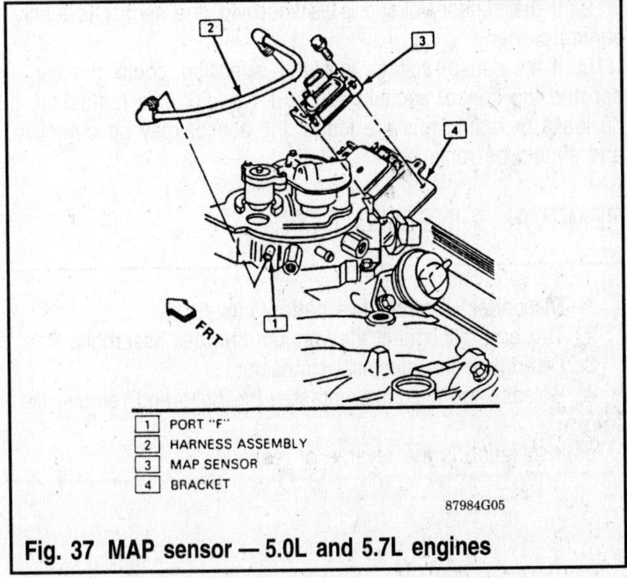

Fig. 37 MAP sensor — 5.0L and 5.7L engines

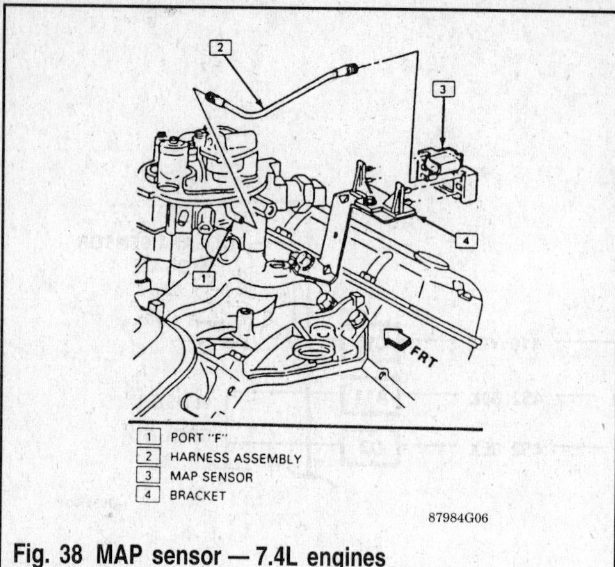

Fig. 38 MAP sensor — 7.4L engines

TESTING

See Figure 39

1. Backprobe with a high impedance voltmeter at MAP sensor terminals A and C.
2. With the key **ON** and engine off, the voltmeter reading should be approximately 5.0 volts.
3. If the voltage is not as specified, either the wiring to the MAP sensor or the ECM may be faulty. Correct any wiring or ECM faults before continuing test.
4. Backprobe with a high impotence voltmeter at MAP sensor terminals B and A.
5. Verify that the sensor voltage is approximately 0.5 volts with the engine not running.
6. Start the vehicle.
7. Verify that the sensor voltage is greater than 1.5 volts at idle.
8. Verify that the sensor voltage increases to approximately 4.5. volts at Wide Open Throttle (WOT).
9. If the sensor voltage is as specified, the sensor is functioning properly.
10. If the sensor voltage is not as specified, check the sensor and the sensor vacuum source for a leak or a restriction. If no leaks or restrictions are found, the sensor may be defective and should be replaced.

REMOVAL & INSTALLATION

1. Disconnect the negative battery cable.
2. Tag and disconnect the vacuum harness assembly.
3. Disengage the electrical connector.
4. Release the locktabs, unfasten the bolts and remove the sensor.
5. Installation is the reverse of removal.

Throttle Position Sensor (TPS)

OPERATION

The Throttle Position Sensor (TPS) is located inside the carburetor. It is a potentiometer with one wire connected to 5 volts from the ECM and the other to ground. A third wire is connected to the ECM to measure the voltage from the TPS.

As the accelerator pedal is moved, the output of the TPS also changes. At a closed throttle position, the output of the TPS is low (approximately 0.5 volts). As the throttle valve opens, the output increases so that, at wide-open throttle, the output voltage should be approximately 4.5 volts.

By monitoring the output voltage from the TPS, the ECM can determine fuel delivery based on throttle valve angle (driver demand).

TESTING

See Figure 40

1. Backprobe with a high impedance voltmeter at TPS terminals A and B.
2. With the key **ON** and engine off, the voltmeter reading should be approximately 5.0 volts.
3. If the voltage is not as specified, either the wiring to the TPS or the ECM may be faulty. Correct any wiring or ECM faults before continuing test.
4. Backprobe with a high impedance voltmeter at terminals C and B.
5. With the key **ON** and engine off and the throttle closed, the TPS voltage should be approximately 0.5-1.2 volts.
6. Verify that the TPS voltage increases or decreases smoothly as the throttle is opened or closed. Make sure to open and close the throttle very slowly in order to detect any abnormalities in the TPS voltage reading.
7. If the sensor voltage is not as specified, replace the sensor.

REMOVAL & INSTALLATION

The throttle position sensor is located in the carburetor. Please refer to Section 5 for the carburetor disassembly procedures to remove the TPS.

Vehicle Speed Sensor (VSS)

OPERATION

The vehicle speed sensor is sometimes located behind the speedometer or more commonly on the transmission. It sends a pulsing voltage signal to the ECM, which the ECM converts to vehicle speed. This sensor mainly controls the operation of the Torque Convertor Clutch (TCC) system, shift light and cruise control.

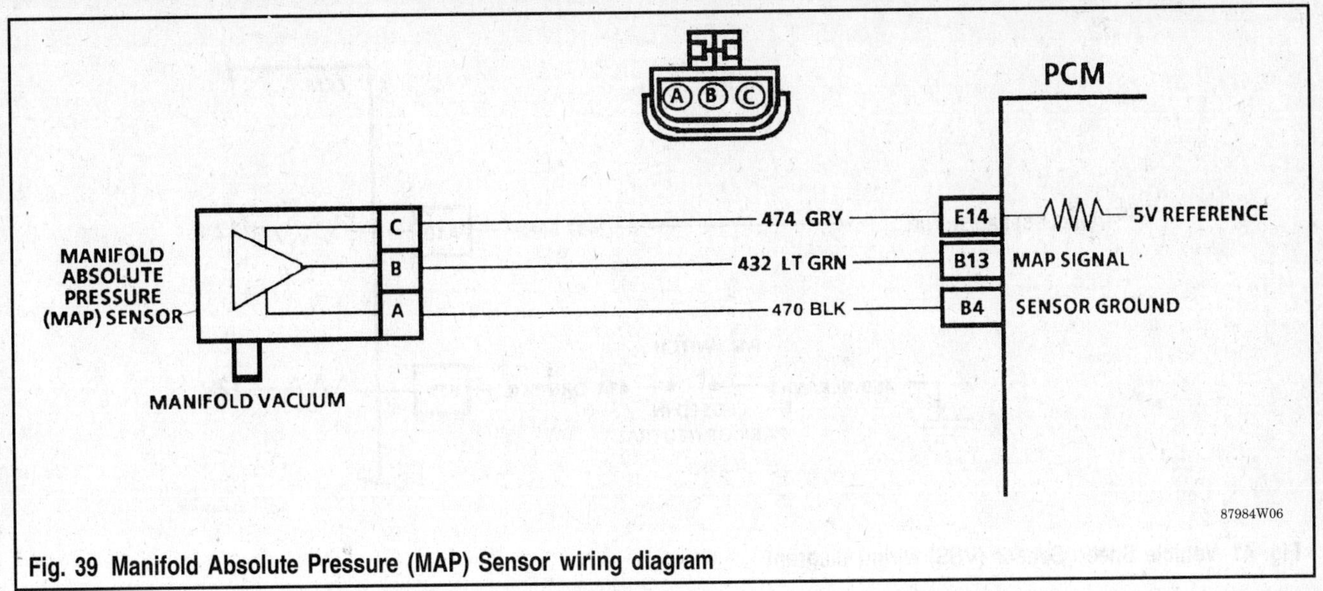

Fig. 39 Manifold Absolute Pressure (MAP) Sensor wiring diagram

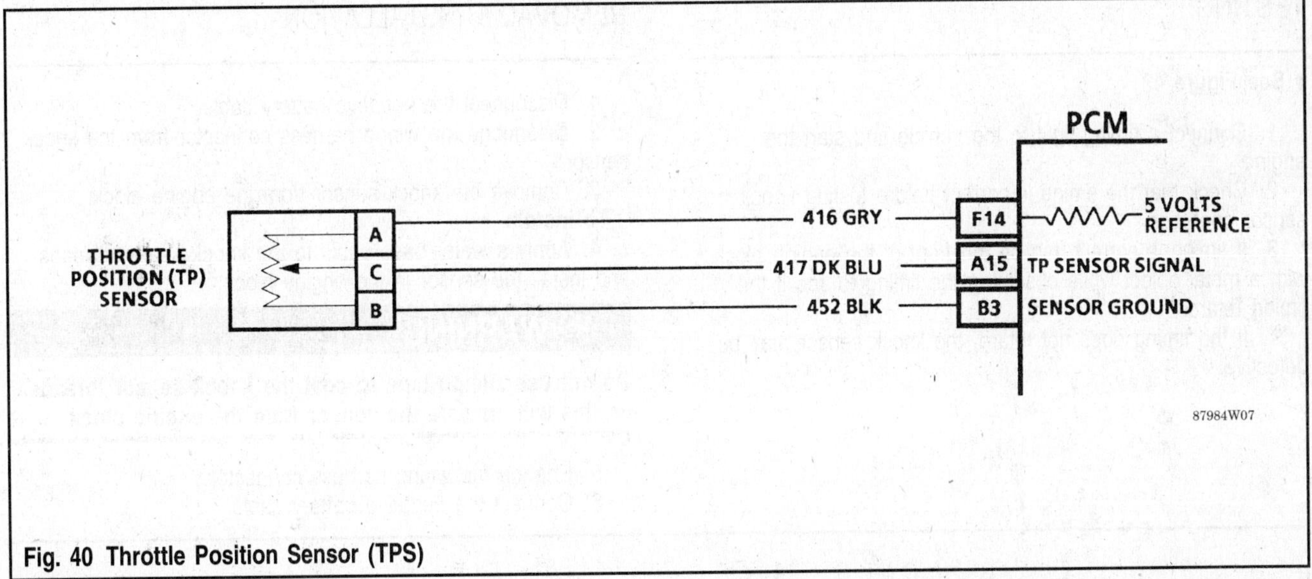

Fig. 40 Throttle Position Sensor (TPS)

TESTING

See Figure 41

1. Backprobe the VSS terminals with a high impedance voltmeter (set at the AC voltage scale).
2. Safely raise and support the entire vehicle using jackstands. Make absolutely sure the vehicle is secure.
3. Start the vehicle and place it in gear.
4. Verify that the VSS voltage increases as the speed increases.
5. If the VSS voltage is not as specified the VSS may be faulty.

REMOVAL & INSTALLATION

Speedometer Mounted

1. Disconnect the negative battery cable.
2. Remove the instrument cluster.
3. Remove the screws securing the sensor assembly.
4. Installation is the reverse of removal.

Transmission Mounted

1. Raise and safely support the vehicle.
2. Unplug the electrical connector.
3. Disconnect the speedometer cable from the sensor.
4. Remove the sensor from the transmission.
5. Installation is the reverse of removal.

Knock Sensor

OPERATION

Located in the engine block, the Knock Sensor (KS) retards ignition timing during a spark knock condition to allow the ECM to maintain maximum timing advance under most conditions.

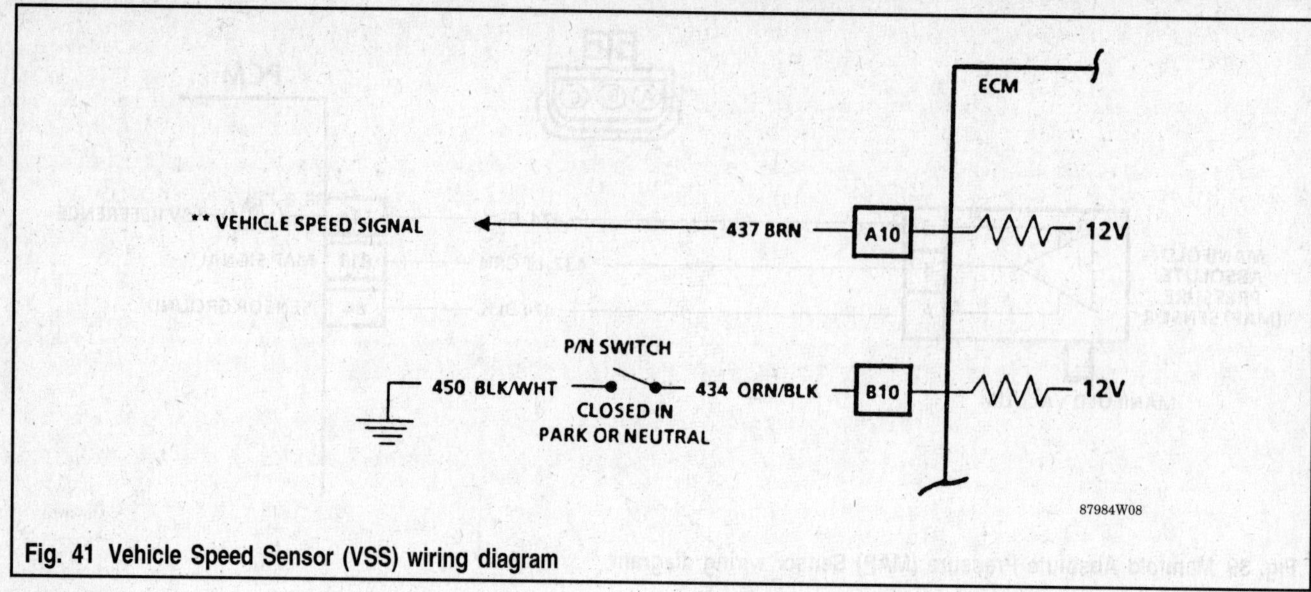

Fig. 41 Vehicle Speed Sensor (VSS) wiring diagram

TESTING

➧ See Figure 42

1. Connect a timing light to the vehicle and start the engine.
2. Check that the timing is correct before testing knock sensor operation.
3. If timing is correct, tap on the front of the engine block with a metal object while observing the timing to see if the timing retards.
4. If the timing does not retard, the knock sensor may be defective.

REMOVAL & INSTALLATION

1. Disconnect the negative battery cable.
2. Disengage the wiring harness connector from the knock sensor.
3. Remove the knock sensor from the engine block.

To install:

4. Apply a water base caulk to the knock sensor threads and install the sensor in the engine block.

⁂WARNING

Do not use silicon tape to coat the knock sensor threads as this will insulate the sensor from the engine block.

5. Engage the wiring harness connector.
6. Connect the negative battery cable.

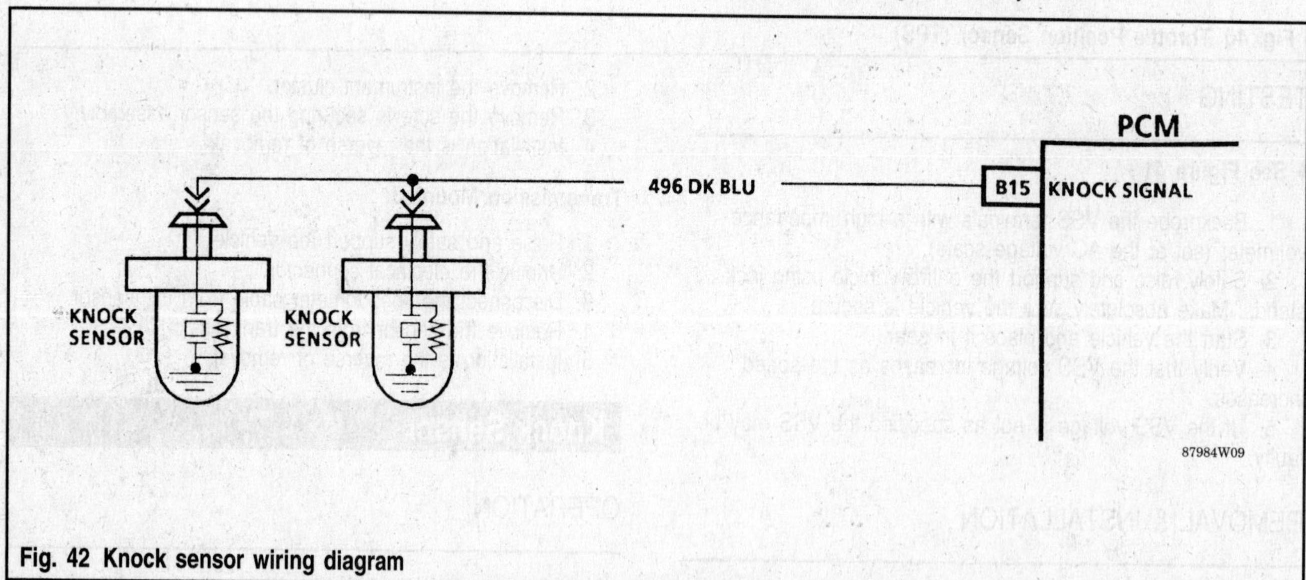

Fig. 42 Knock sensor wiring diagram

FUEL INJECTED ELECTRONIC ENGINE CONTROLS

Electronic Control Module (ECM)

OPERATION

➡When the term Electronic Control Module (ECM) is used in this manual it will refer to the engine control computer regardless that it may be a Vehicle Control Module (VCM), Powertrain Control Module (PCM) or Electronic Control Module (ECM).

The Electronic Control Module (ECM) is required to maintain the exhaust emissions at acceptable levels. The module is a small, solid state computer which receives signals from many sources and sensors; it uses these data to make judgments about operating conditions and then control output signals to the fuel and emission systems to match the current requirements.

Engines coupled to electronically controlled transmissions employ a Powertrain Control Module (PCM) or Vehicle Control Module (VCM) to oversee both engine and transmission operation. The integrated functions of engine and transmission control allow accurate gear selection and improved fuel economy.

In the event of an ECM failure, the system will default to a pre-programmed set of values. These are compromise values which allow the engine to operate, although at a reduced efficiency. This is variously known as the default, limp-in or back-up mode. Driveability is almost always affected when the ECM enters this mode.

REMOVAL & INSTALLATION

1. Disconnect the negative battery cable.
2. Disengage the connectors from the ECM.
3. Remove the spring retainer off and over the rail of the ECM.
4. Slide the ECM out of the bracket at an angle.
5. Remove the ECM.

To install:

6. Install the ECM into the bracket.
7. Install the spring retainer and engage the electrical connectors.
8. Connect the negative battery cable.

Oxygen Sensor

OPERATION

➧ See Figure 43

There are two types of oxygen sensor's used in these vehicles. They are the single wire oxygen sensor (02S) and the heated oxygen sensor (H02S). The oxygen sensor is a spark plug shaped device that is screwed into the exhaust manifold. It monitors the oxygen content of the exhaust gases and sends a voltage signal to the Electronic Control Module (ECM). The ECM monitors this voltage and, depending on the value of the received signal, issues a command to the mixture control solenoid on the carburetor to adjust for rich or lean conditions.

The heated oxygen sensor has a heating element incorporated into the sensor to aid in the warm up to the proper operating temperature and to maintain that temperature.

The proper operation of the oxygen sensor depends upon four basic conditions:

1. Good electrical connections. Since the sensor generates low currents, good clean electrical connections at the sensor are a must.
2. Outside air supply. Air must circulate to the internal portion of the sensor. When servicing the sensor, do not restrict the air passages.
3. Proper operating temperatures. The ECM will not recognize the sensor's signals until the sensor reaches approximately 600°F (316°C).
4. Non-leaded fuel. The use of leaded gasoline will damage the sensor very quickly.

TESTING

Single Wire Sensor

➧ See Figure 44

1. Start the engine and bring it to normal operating temperature, then run the engine above 1200 rpm for two minutes.
2. Backprobe with a high impedance averaging voltmeter (set to the DC voltage scale) between the oxygen sensor (02S) and battery ground.
3. Verify that the 02S voltage fluctuates rapidly between 0.40-0.60 volts.
4. If the 02S voltage is stabilized at the middle of the specified range (approximately 0.45-0.55 volts) or if the 02S voltage fluctuates very slowly between the specified range (02S signal crosses 0.5 volts less than 5 times in ten seconds), the 02S may be faulty.

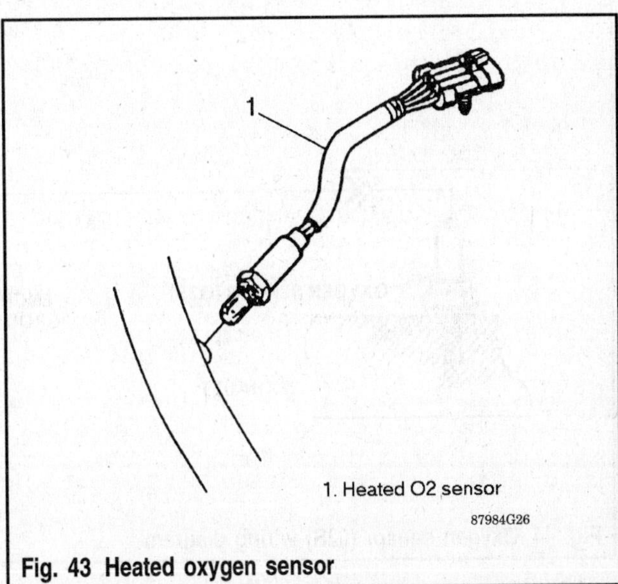

Fig. 43 Heated oxygen sensor

5. If the 02S voltage stabilizes at either end of the specified range, the ECM is probably not able to compensate for a mechanical problem such as a vacuum leak or a faulty pressure regulator. These types of mechanical problems will cause the 02S to sense a constant lean or constant rich mixture. The mechanical problem will first have to be repaired and then the 02S test repeated.

6. Pull a vacuum hose located after the throttle plate. Voltage should drop to approximately 0.12 volts (while still fluctuating rapidly). This tests the ability of the 02S to detect a lean mixture condition. Reattach the vacuum hose.

7. Richen the mixture using a propane enrichment tool. Voltage should rise to approximately 0.90 volts (while still fluctuating rapidly). This tests the ability of the 02S to detect a rich mixture condition.

8. If the 02S voltage is above or below the specified range, the 02S and/or the O2S wiring may be faulty. Check the wiring for any breaks, repair as necessary and repeat the test.

Heated Oxygen Sensor

See Figure 45

1. Start the engine and bring it to normal operating temperature, then run the engine above 1200 rpm for two minutes.

2. Turn the ignition **OFF** disengage the H02S harness connector.

3. Connect a test light between harness terminals A and B. With the ignition switch **ON** and the engine off, verify that the test light is lit. If the test light is not lit, either the supply voltage to the H02S heater or the ground circuit of the H02S heater is faulty. Check the H02S wiring and the fuse.

4. Next, connect a high impedance ohmmeter between the H02S terminals B and A and verify that the resistance is 3.5-14.0 ohms.

5. If the H02S heater resistance is not as specified, the H02S may be faulty.

6. Start the engine and bring it to normal operating temperature, then run the engine above 1200 rpm for two minutes.

7. Backprobe with a high impedance averaging voltmeter (set to the DC voltage scale) between the oxygen sensor (02S) and battery ground.

8. Verify that the 02S voltage fluctuates rapidly between 0.40-0.60 volts.

9. If the 02S voltage is stabilized at the middle of the specified range (approximately 0.45-0.55 volts) or if the 02S voltage fluctuates very slowly between the specified range (02S signal crosses 0.5 volts less than 5 times in ten seconds), the 02S may be faulty.

10. If the 02S voltage stabilizes at either end of the specified range, the ECM is probably not able to compensate for a mechanical problem such as a vacuum leak or a faulty fuel pressure regulator. These types of mechanical problems will cause the 02S to sense a constant lean or constant rich mixture. The mechanical problem will first have to be repaired and then the 02S test repeated.

11. Pull a vacuum hose located after the throttle plate. Voltage should drop to approximately 0.12 volts (while still fluctuating rapidly). This tests the ability of the 02S to detect a lean mixture condition. Reattach the vacuum hose.

12. Richen the mixture using a propane enrichment tool. Voltage should rise to approximately 0.90 volts (while still fluctuating rapidly). This tests the ability of the 02S to detect a rich mixture condition.

13. If the 02S voltage is above or below the specified range, the 02S and/or the O2S wiring may be faulty. Check the wiring for any breaks, repair as necessary and repeat the test.

REMOVAL & INSTALLATION

WARNING

The sensor uses a permanently attached pigtail and connector. This pigtail should not be removed from the sensor. Damage or removal of the pigtail or connector could affect the proper operation of the sensor. Keep the electrical connector and louvered end of the sensor clean and free of grease. NEVER use cleaning solvents of any type on the sensor!

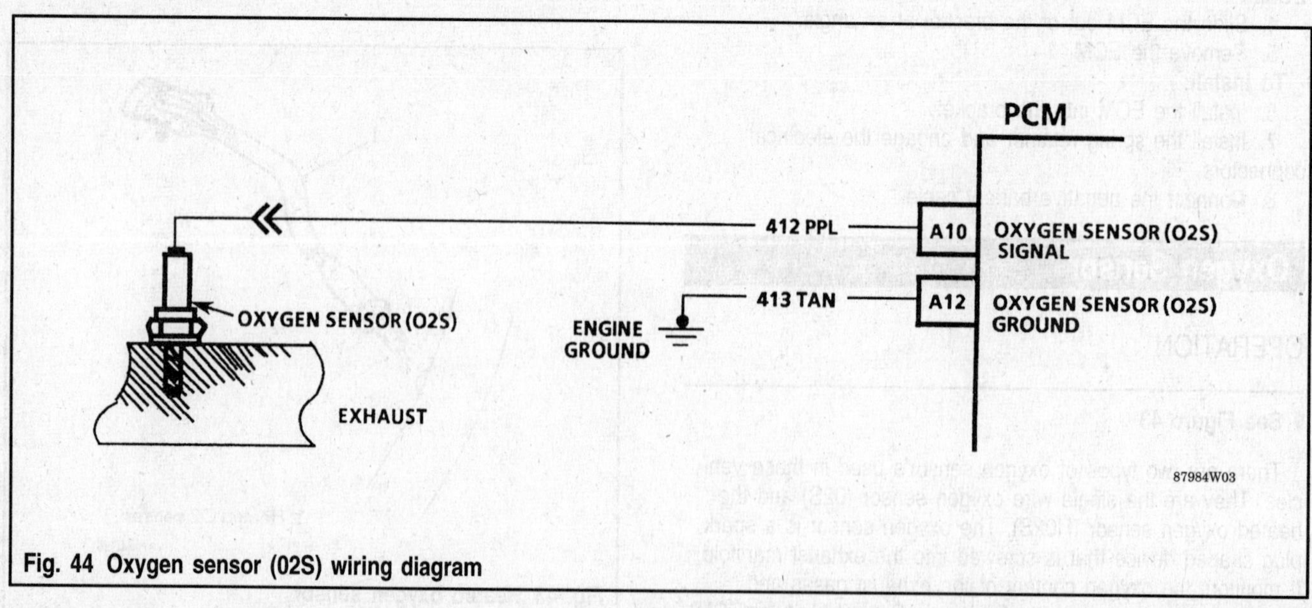

Fig. 44 Oxygen sensor (02S) wiring diagram

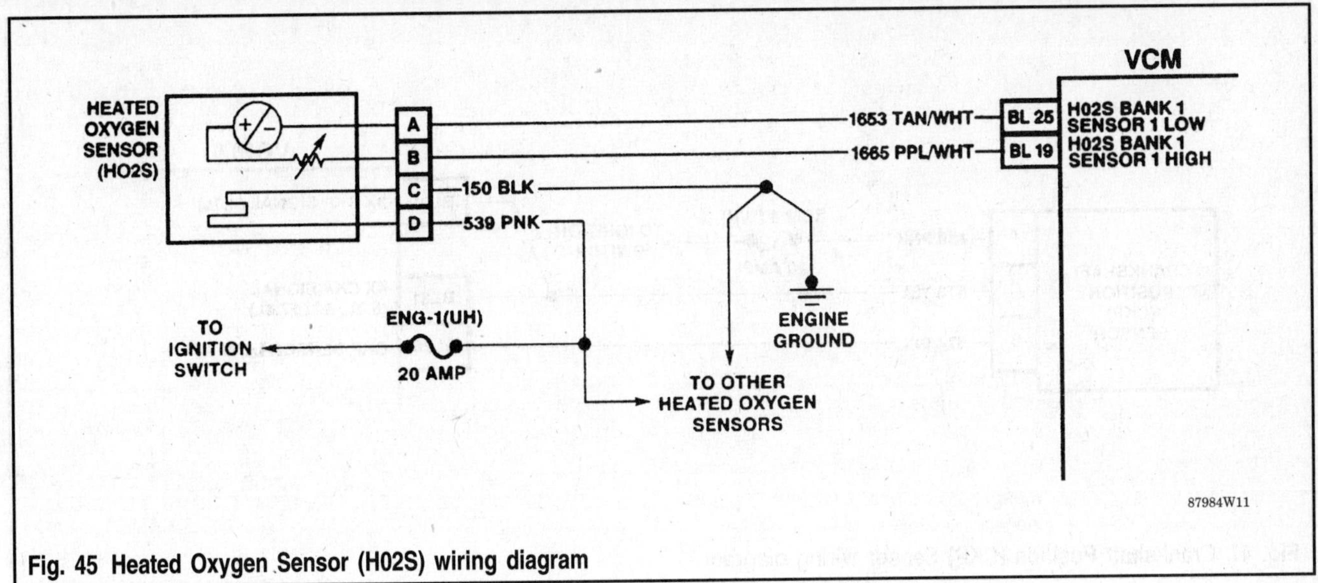

Fig. 45 Heated Oxygen Sensor (H02S) wiring diagram

➡The oxygen sensor may be difficult to remove when the temperature of the engine is below 120°F (49°C). Excessive force may damage the threads in the exhaust manifold or exhaust pipe.

1. Disconnect the negative battery cable.
2. Unplug the electrical connector and any attaching hardware.
3. Remove the sensor.

To install:

4. Coat the threads of the sensor with a GM anti-seize compound, part number 5613695, or its equivalent, before installation. New sensors are precoated with this compound.

➡The GM antiseize compound is NOT a conventional anti-seize paste. The use of a regular paste may electrically insulate the sensor, rendering it useless. The threads MUST be coated with the proper electrically conductive anti-seize compound.

5. Install the sensor and tighten to 30 ft. lbs. (40 Nm). Use care in making sure the silicone boot is in the correct position to avoid melting it during operation.
6. Engage the electrical connector.
7. Connect the negative battery cable.

Crankshaft Position (CKP) Sensor

OPERATION

See Figure 46

The Crankshaft Position (CKP) Sensor provides a signal through the ignition module which the ECM uses as a reference to calculate rpm and crankshaft position.

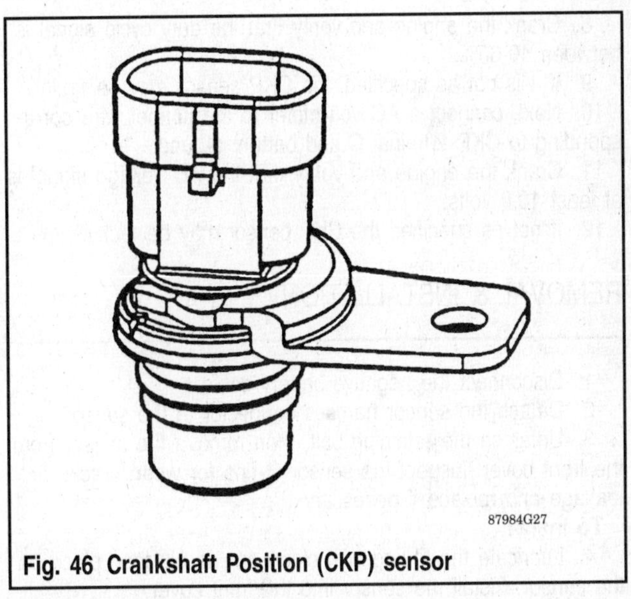

Fig. 46 Crankshaft Position (CKP) sensor

TESTING

See Figure 47

1. Disconnect the CKP sensor harness. Connect an LED test light between battery ground and CKP harness terminal A.
2. With the ignition **ON** and the engine off, verify that the test light illuminates.
3. If not as specified, repair or replace the fuse and/or wiring.
4. Carefully connect the test light between CKP harness terminal A and B. Verify that the test light illuminates.
5. If not as specified, repair the CKP harness ground circuit (terminal B).
6. Turn the ignition **OFF** and disconnect the test light.
7. Next, connect suitable jumper wires between the CKP sensor and CKP sensor harness. Connect a duty cycle meter to the jumper wire corresponding to CKP terminal C and battery ground.

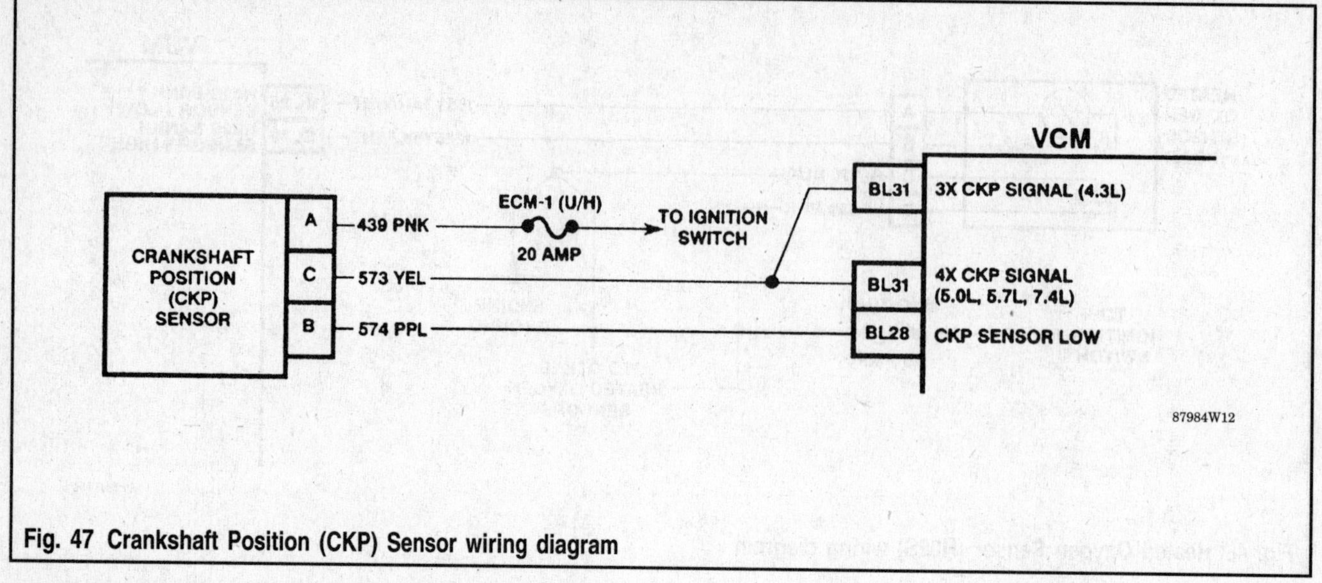

Fig. 47 Crankshaft Position (CKP) Sensor wiring diagram

8. Crank the engine and verify that the duty cycle signal is between 40-60%.
9. If it is not as specified, the CKP sensor may be faulty.
10. Next, connect a AC volt meter to the jumper wire corresponding to CKP terminal C and battery ground.
11. Crank the engine and verify that the AC voltage signal is at least 10.0 volts.
12. If not as specified the CKP sensor may be faulty.

REMOVAL & INSTALLATION

1. Disconnect the negative battery cable.
2. Detach the sensor harness connector at the sensor.
3. Unfasten the retaining bolt, then remove the sensor from the front cover. Inspect the sensor O-ring for wear, cracks or leakage and replace if necessary.

To install:

4. Lubricate the O-ring with clean engine oil, then place on the sensor. Install the sensor into the front cover.
5. Install the sensor and tighten the retaining bolt.
6. Attach the sensor harness connector.
7. Connect the negative battery cable.

Camshaft Position (CMP) Sensor

OPERATION

▶ See Figure 48

The ECM uses the camshaft signal to determine the position of the No. 1 cylinder piston during its power stroke. The signal is used by the ECM to calculate fuel injection mode of operation.

If the cam signal is lost while the engine is running, the fuel injection system will shift to a calculated fuel injected mode based on the last fuel injection pulse, and the engine will continue to run.

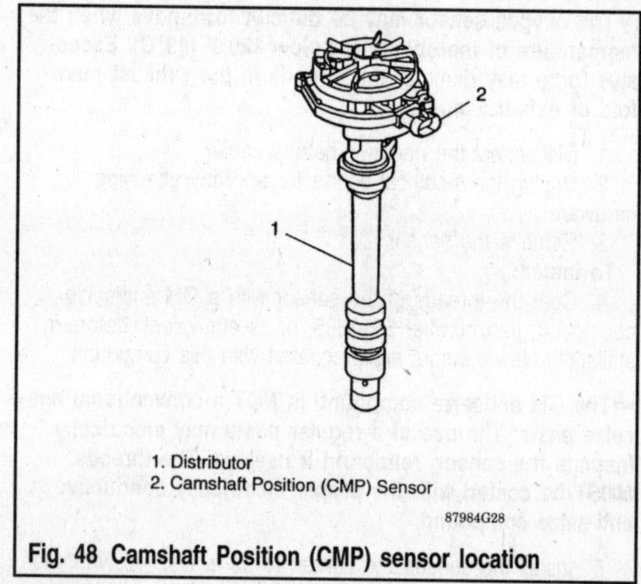

Fig. 48 Camshaft Position (CMP) sensor location

TESTING

▶ See Figure 49

1. Disconnect the CMP sensor wiring harness and connect an LED test light between CMP harness terminal C and battery ground.
2. With the ignition **ON** and the engine off, verify that the test light illuminates.
3. If not as specified, repair or replace the fuse and/or wiring.
4. Carefully connect the test light between CMP harness terminal A and C and verify that the test light illuminates.
5. If not as specified, repair the CMP harness ground circuit (terminal A).
6. Turn the ignition **OFF** and disconnect the test light.
7. Next, connect suitable jumper wires between the CMP sensor and CMP sensor harness. Connect a DC volt meter to the jumper wire corresponding to CMP terminal B and battery ground.

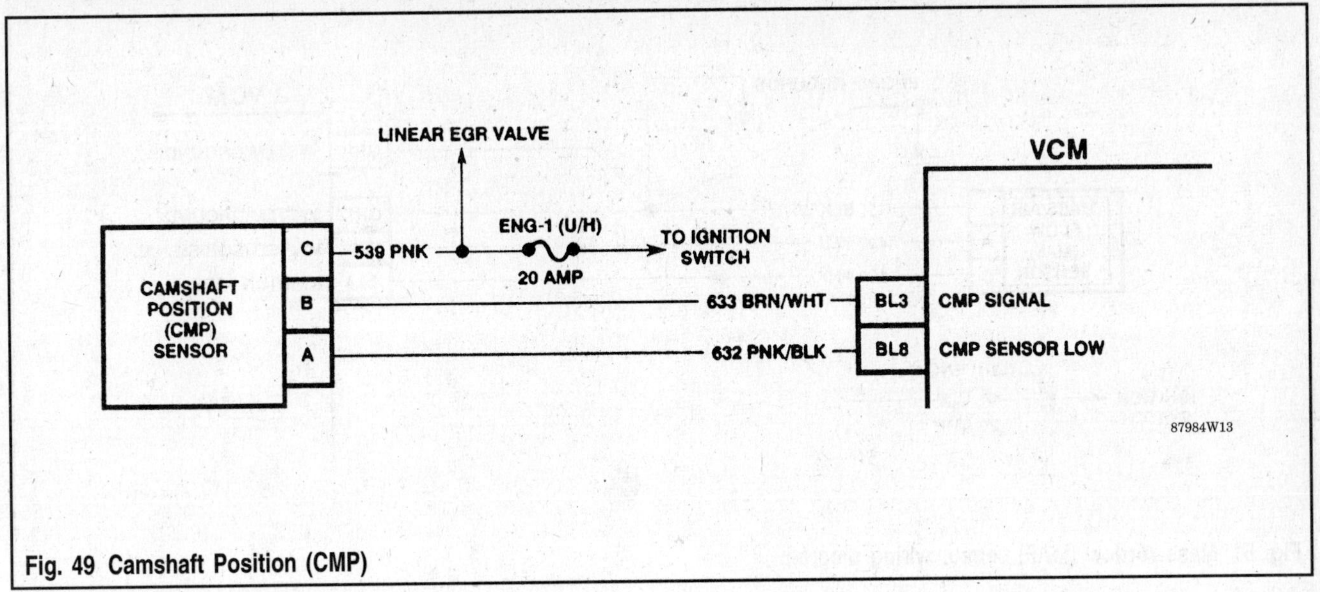

Fig. 49 Camshaft Position (CMP)

8. Start the engine and verify that the voltage signal is 5-7 volts.
9. If it is not as specified, the CMP sensor may be faulty.

REMOVAL & INSTALLATION

1. Disconnect the negative battery cable.
2. Detach the sensor harness connector at the sensor.
3. Unfasten the retaining bolt, then remove the sensor from the camshaft housing. Inspect the sensor O-ring for wear, cracks or leakage and replace if necessary.

To install:

4. Lubricate the O-ring with clean engine oil, then place on the sensor. Install the sensor into the camshaft housing.
5. Install the CMP sensor retaining bolt, then tighten to 88 inch lbs. (10 Nm).
6. Attach the sensor harness connector.
7. Connect the negative battery cable.

Mass Air Flow (MAF) Sensor

OPERATION

See Figure 50

The Mass Air Flow (MAF) Sensor measures the amount of air entering the engine during a given time. The ECM uses the mass airflow information for fuel delivery calculations. A large quantity of air entering the engine indicates an acceleration or high load situation, while a small quantity of air indicates deceleration or idle.

TESTING

See Figure 51

1. Backprobe with a high impedance voltmeter between MAF sensor terminals C and B.

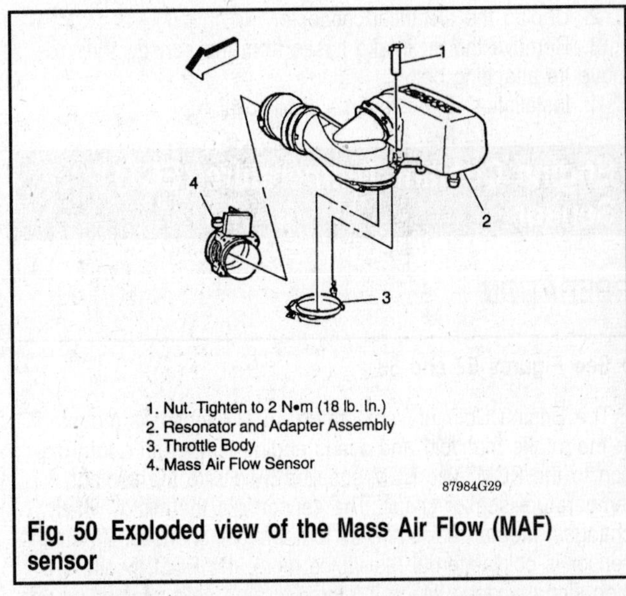

Fig. 50 Exploded view of the Mass Air Flow (MAF) sensor

2. With the ignition **ON** engine off, verify that battery voltage is present.
3. If the voltage is not as specified, either the wiring to the MAF sensor, fuse or the ECM may be faulty. Correct any wiring or ECM faults before continuing test.
4. Disconnect the voltmeter and backprobe with a frequency meter between MAF sensor terminals A and B.
5. Start the engine and wait until it reaches normal idle speed and verify that the MAF sensor output is approximately 2000 Hz.
6. Slowly raise engine speed up to maximum recommended rpm and verify that the MAF sensor output rises smoothly to approximately 8000 Hz.
7. If MAF sensor output is not as specified the sensor may be faulty.

REMOVAL & INSTALLATION

1. Disconnect the negative battery cable.

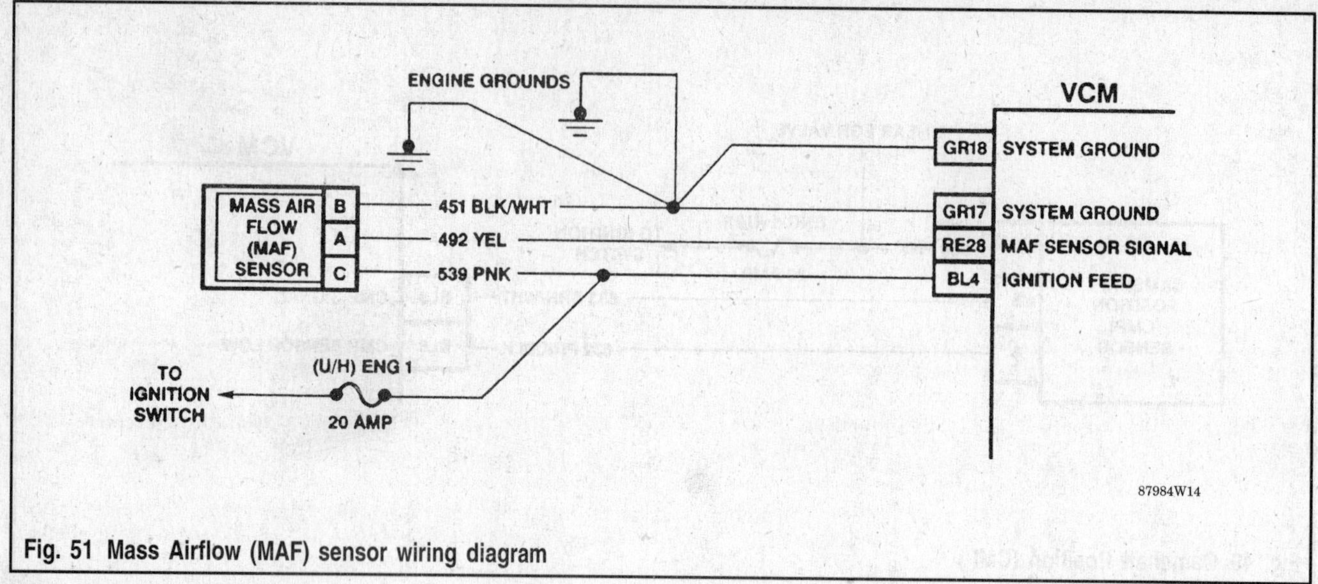

Fig. 51 Mass Airflow (MAF) sensor wiring diagram

2. Unplug the electrical connector.
3. Remove the air intake hoses from the sensor, then remove its attaching bolts.
4. Installation is the reverse of removal.

Engine Coolant Temperature (ECT) Sensor

OPERATION

▸ See Figures 52 and 53

The Engine Coolant Temperature (ECT) sensor is mounted in the intake manifold and sends engine temperature information to the ECM. The ECM supplies 5 volts to the coolant temperature sensor circuit. The sensor is a thermistor which changes internal resistance as temperature changes. When the sensor is cold (internal resistance high), the ECM monitors a high signal voltage which it interprets as a cold engine. As the sensor warms (internal resistance low), the ECM monitors a low signal voltage which it interprets as warm engine.

TESTING

▸ See Figures 54 and 55

1. Remove the ECT sensor from the vehicle.
2. Immerse the tip of the sensor in container of water.
3. Connect a digital ohmmeter to the two terminals of the sensor.
4. Using a calibrated thermometer, compare the resistance of the sensor to the temperature of the water. Refer to the engine coolant sensor temperature vs. resistance illustration.
5. Repeat the test at two other temperature points, heating or cooling the water as necessary.
6. If the sensor does not met specification, it must be replaced.

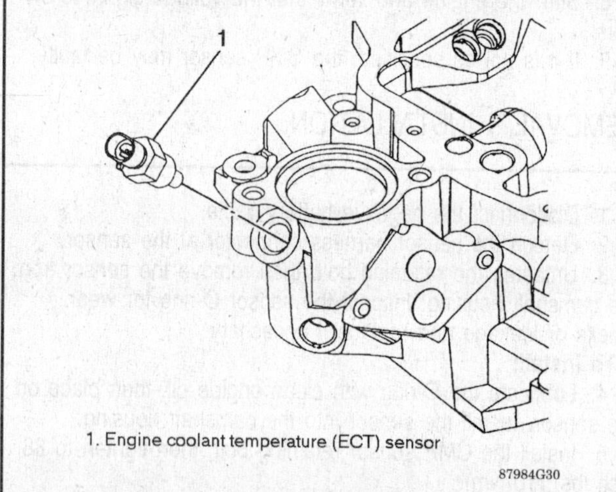

Fig. 52 Engine Coolant Temperature (ECT) sensor location — 4.3L, 5.0L and 5.7L engines

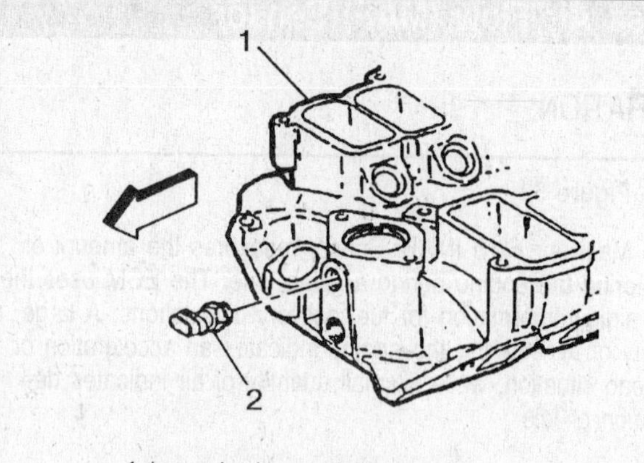

Fig. 53 Engine Coolant Temperature (ECT) sensor location — 7.4L engines

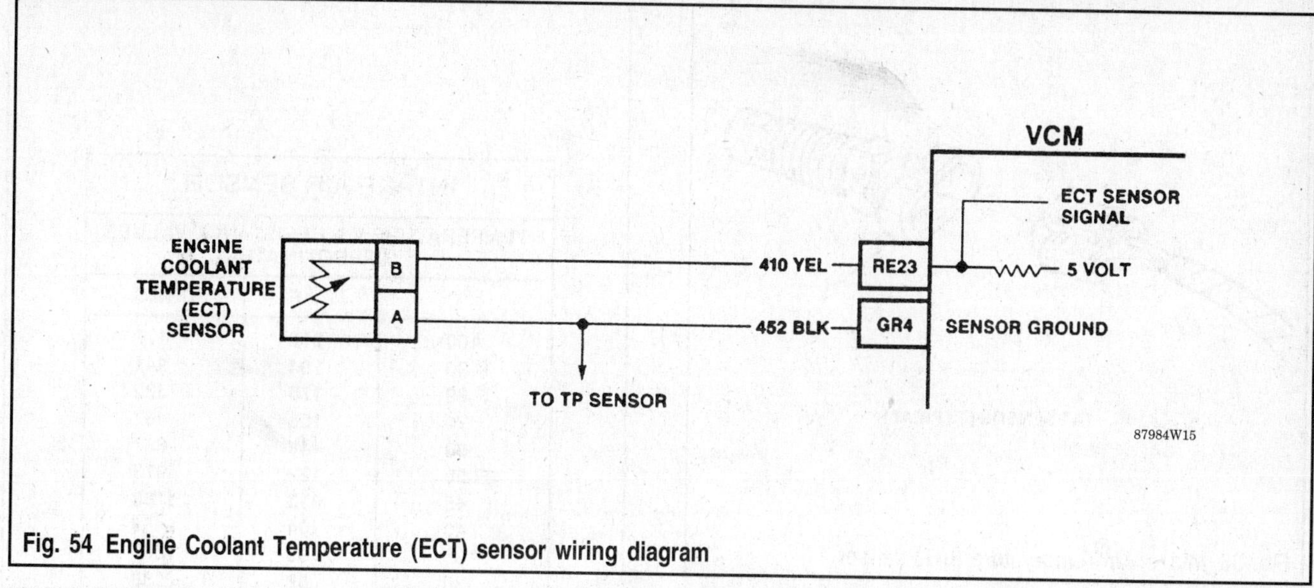

Fig. 54 Engine Coolant Temperature (ECT) sensor wiring diagram

ENGINE COOLANT SENSOR		
TEMPERATURE VS. RESISTANCE VALUES (APPROXIMATE)		
°C	°F	OHMS
100	212	177
90	194	241
80	176	332
70	158	467
60	140	667
50	122	973
45	113	1188
40	104	1459
35	95	1802
30	86	2238
25	77	2796
20	68	3520
15	59	4450
10	50	5670
5	41	7280
0	32	9420
-5	23	12300
-10	14	16180
-15	5	21450
-20	-4	28680
-30	-22	52700
-40	-40	100700

87984G38

Fig. 55 Engine Coolant Temperature (ECT) sensor temperature vs. resistance values

REMOVAL & INSTALLATION

1. Disconnect the negative battery cable.
2. Drain the cooling system below the level of the sensor and disengage the sensor electrical connection.
3. Remove the coolant sensor.

To install:

4. Install the sensor and engage the electrical connector.
5. Refill the cooling system and connect the negative battery cable.

Intake Air Temperature (IAT) Sensor

OPERATION

See Figure 56

the Intake Air Temperature (IAT) Sensor is a thermistor which changes value based on the temperature of the air entering the engine. Low temperature produces a high resistance, while a high temperature causes a low resistance. The ECM supplies a 5 volt signal to the sensor through a resistor in the ECM and measures the voltage. The voltage will be high when the incoming air is cold, and low when the air is hot. By measuring the voltage, the ECM calculates the incoming air temperature.

the IAT sensor signal is used to adjust spark timing according to incoming air density.

TESTING

See Figures 57 and 58

1. Remove the Intake Air Temperature (IAT) sensor.
2. Connect a digital ohmmeter to the two terminals of the sensor.
3. Using a calibrated thermometer, compare the resistance of the sensor to the temperature of the ambient air. Refer to the temperature vs. resistance illustration.

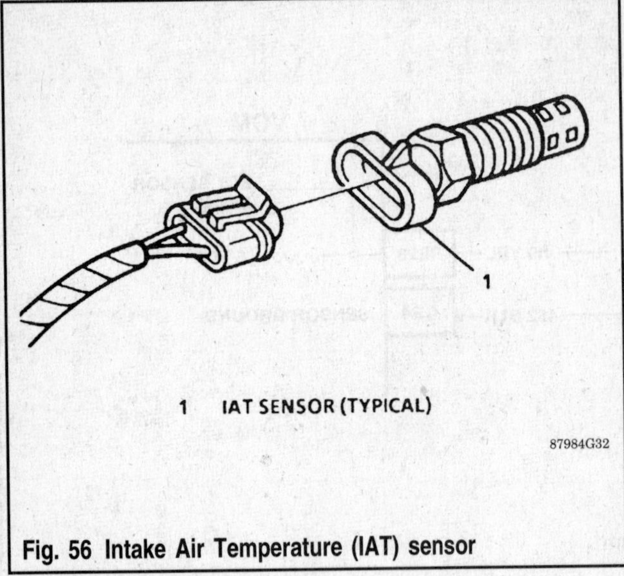

Fig. 56 Intake Air Temperature (IAT) sensor

4. Repeat the test at two other temperature points, heating or cooling the air as necessary with a hair dryer or other suitable tool.
5. If the sensor does not meet specification, it must be replaced.

REMOVAL & INSTALLATION

1. Disconnect the negative battery cable.
2. Disengage the sensor electrical connection.
3. Loosen and remove the IAT sensor.
4. Installation is the reverse of removal.

INTAKE AIR SENSOR

TEMPERATURE VS. RESISTANCE VALUES (APPROXIMATE)

°C	°F	OHMS
100	212	177
90	194	241
80	176	332
70	158	467
60	140	667
50	122	973
45	113	1188
40	104	1459
35	95	1802
30	86	2238
25	77	2796
20	68	3520
15	59	4450
10	50	5670
5	41	7280
0	32	9420
-5	23	12300
-10	14	16180
-15	5	21450
-20	-4	28680
-30	-22	52700
-40	-40	100700

87984G39

Fig. 58 Intake Air Temperature (IAT) sensor temperature vs. resistance values

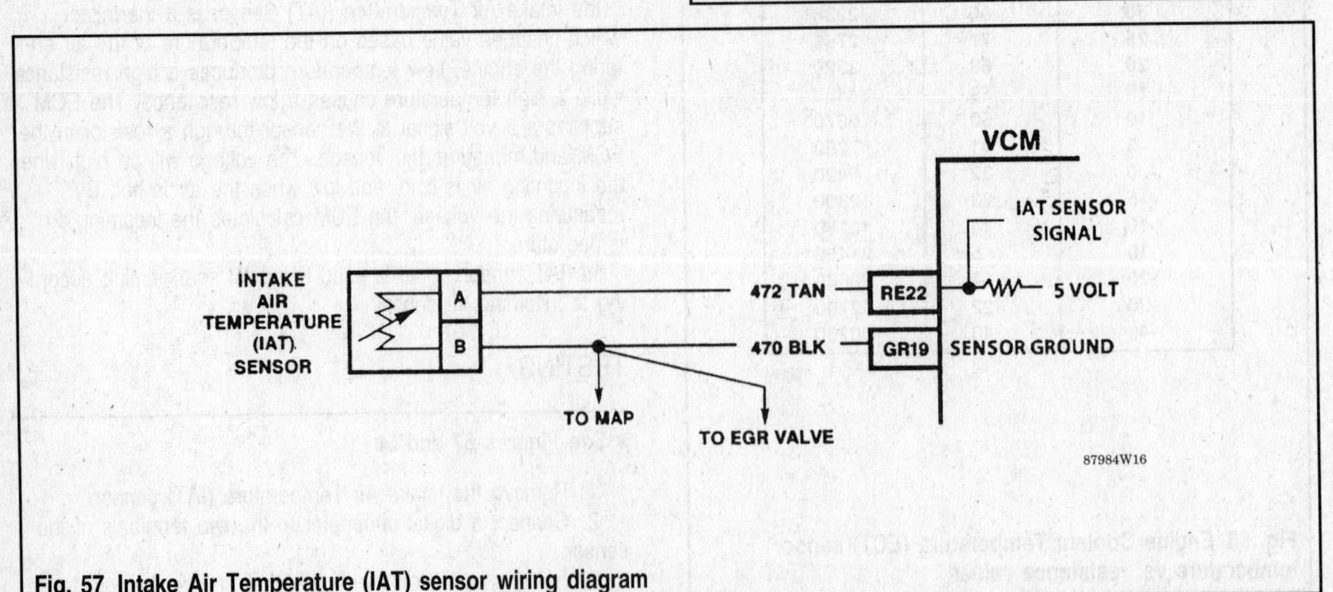

Fig. 57 Intake Air Temperature (IAT) sensor wiring diagram

Throttle Position Sensor (TPS)

OPERATION

➧ See Figure 59

The Throttle Position Sensor (TPS) is connected to the throttle shaft on the throttle body. It is a potentiometer with one end connected to 5 volts from the ECM and the other to ground.

A third wire is connected to the ECM to measure the voltage from the TPS. As the throttle valve angle is changed (accelerator pedal moved), the output of the TPS also changes. At a closed throttle position, the output of the TPS is low (approximately .5 volts). As the throttle valve opens, the output increases so that, at wide-open throttle, the output voltage should be approximately 4.5 volts.

By monitoring the output voltage from the TPS, the ECM can determine fuel delivery based on throttle valve angle (driver demand).

TESTING

➧ See Figure 60

1. Backprobe with a high impedance voltmeter at TPS terminals A and B.
2. With the key **ON** and engine off, the voltmeter reading should be approximately 5.0 volts.
3. If the voltage is not as specified, either the wiring to the TPS or the ECM may be faulty. Correct any wiring or ECM faults before continuing test.
4. Backprobe with a high impedance voltmeter at terminals C and B.
5. With the key **ON** and engine off and the throttle closed, the TPS voltage should be approximately 0.5-1.2 volts.
6. Verify that the TPS voltage increases or decreases smoothly as the throttle is opened or closed. Make sure to open and close the throttle very slowly in order to detect any abnormalities in the TPS voltage reading.
7. If the sensor voltage is not as specified, replace the sensor.

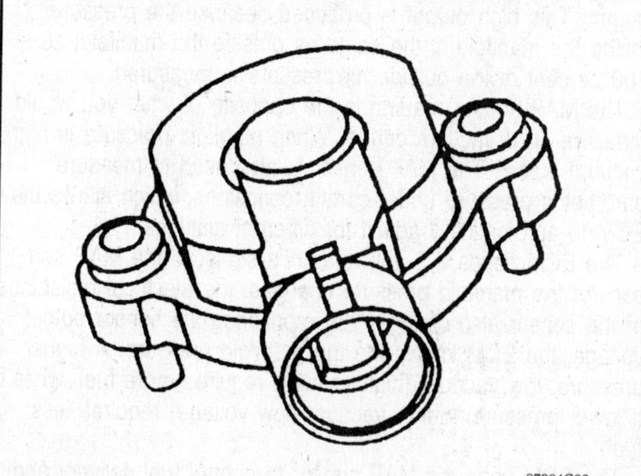

Fig. 59 Common Throttle Position Sensor (TPS) found on GM trucks

REMOVAL & INSTALLATION

1. Disconnect the negative battery cable and remove the air cleaner and gasket.
2. Disengage the electrical connector.
3. Unfasten the two TPS attaching screw assemblies.
4. Remove the TPS from the throttle body assembly.
5. Remove the TPS seal.

To install:

6. Install the TPS seal over the throttle shaft.
7. With the throttle valve closed, install the TPS on the throttle shaft. Rotate it counterclockwise, to align the mounting holes.
8. Install the two TPS attaching screw assemblies.
9. Engage the electrical connector.
10. Install the air cleaner and gasket.
11. Connect the negative battery cable.

Idle Air Control (IAC) Valve

OPERATION

➧ See Figure 61

The engine idle speed is controlled by the ECM through the Idle Air Control (IAC) valve mounted on the throttle body. The ECM sends voltage pulses to the IAC motor causing the IAC motor shaft and pintle to move in or out a given distance (number of steps) for each pulse, (called counts).

This movement controls air flow around the throttle plate, which in turn, controls engine idle speed, either cold or hot. IAC valve pintle position counts can be seen using a scan tool. Zero counts corresponds to a fully closed passage, while 140 or more counts (depending on the application) corresponds to full flow.

TESTING

➧ See Figure 62

1. Disengage the IAC electrical connector.
2. Using an ohmmeter, measure the resistance between IAC terminals A and B. Next measure the resistance between terminals C and D.
3. Verify that the resistance between both sets of IAC terminals is 20-80 ohms. If the resistance is not as specified, the IAC may be faulty.
4. Measure the resistance between IAC terminals B and C. Next measure the resistance between terminals A and D.
5. Verify that the resistance between both sets of IAC terminals is infinite. If the resistance is not infinite, the IAC may be faulty.

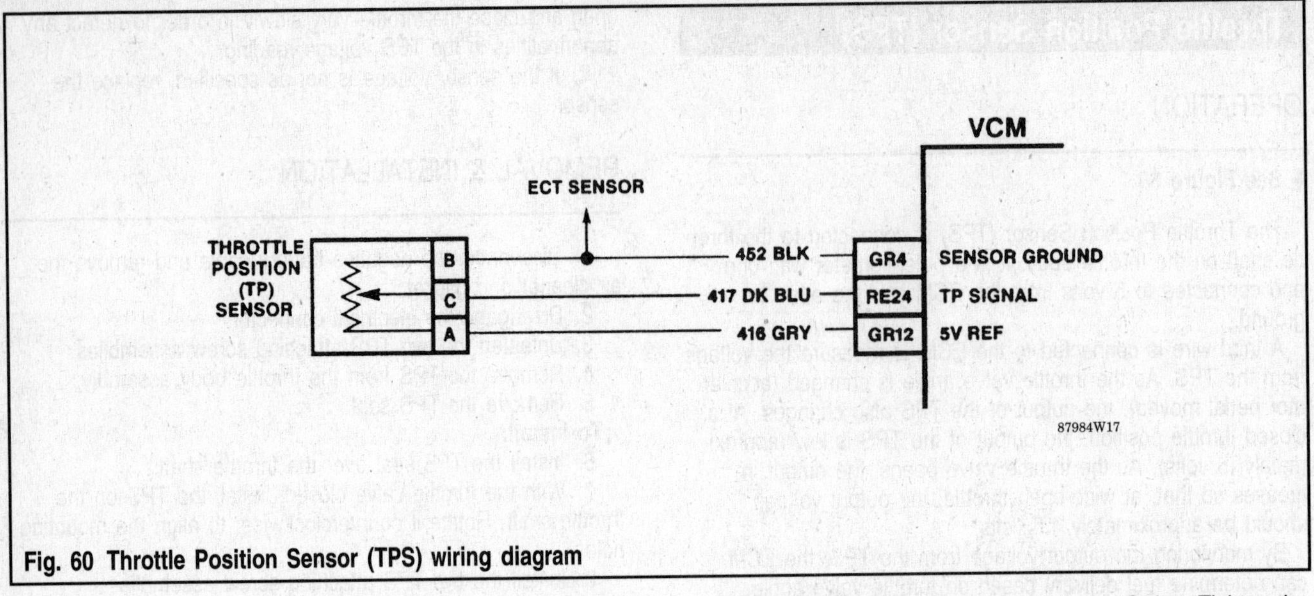

Fig. 60 Throttle Position Sensor (TPS) wiring diagram

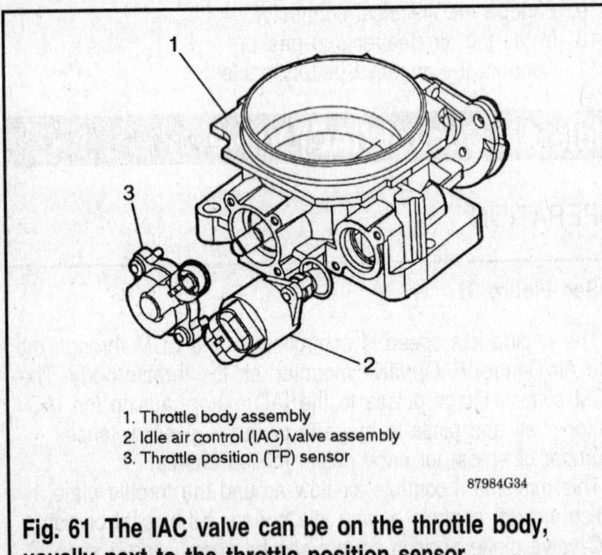

Fig. 61 The IAC valve can be on the throttle body, usually next to the throttle position sensor

6. Also, with a small mirror, inspect IAC air inlet passage and pintle for debris. Clean as necessary, as this can cause IAC malfunction.

REMOVAL & INSTALLATION

1. Disconnect the negative battery cable.
2. Disengage the electrical connection.
3. Remove the IAC valve. On thread-mounted units, use 1¼in. (32mm) wrench and on flange-mounted units, remove the screw assemblies.
4. Remove the IAC valve gasket or O-ring and discard it.

To install:

5. Clean the old gasket material from the surface of the throttle body assembly on the thread mounted valve. On the flange-mounted valve clean the surface to ensure proper O-ring sealing
6. Install the valve with a new gasket or O-ring. Tighten the thread mounted assembly 13 ft. lbs. (18 Nm) and tighten the flange mounted attaching screws to 28 inch. lbs. (3 Nm).
7. Engage the electrical connector to the IAC valve.
8. Connect the negative battery cable.

Manifold Absolute Pressure (MAP) Sensor

OPERATION

See Figure 63

The Manifold Absolute Pressure (MAP) sensor measures the changes in intake manifold pressure, which result from the engine load and speed changes, and converts this to a voltage output.

A closed throttle on engine coastdown will produce a low MAP output, while a wide-open throttle will produce a high output. This high output is produced because the pressure inside the manifold is the same as outside the manifold, so 100 percent of the outside air pressure is measured.

The MAP sensor reading is the opposite of what you would measure on a vacuum gauge. When manifold pressure is high, vacuum is low. The MAP sensor is also used to measure barometric pressure under certain conditions, which allows the ECM to automatically adjust for different altitudes.

The ECM sends a 5 volt reference signal to the MAP sensor. As the manifold pressure changes, the electrical resistance of the sensor also changes. By monitoring the sensor output voltage, the ECM knows the the manifold pressure. A higher pressure, low vacuum (high voltage) requires more fuel, while a lower pressure, higher vacuum (low voltage) requires less fuel.

The ECM uses the MAP sensor to control fuel delivery and ignition timing.

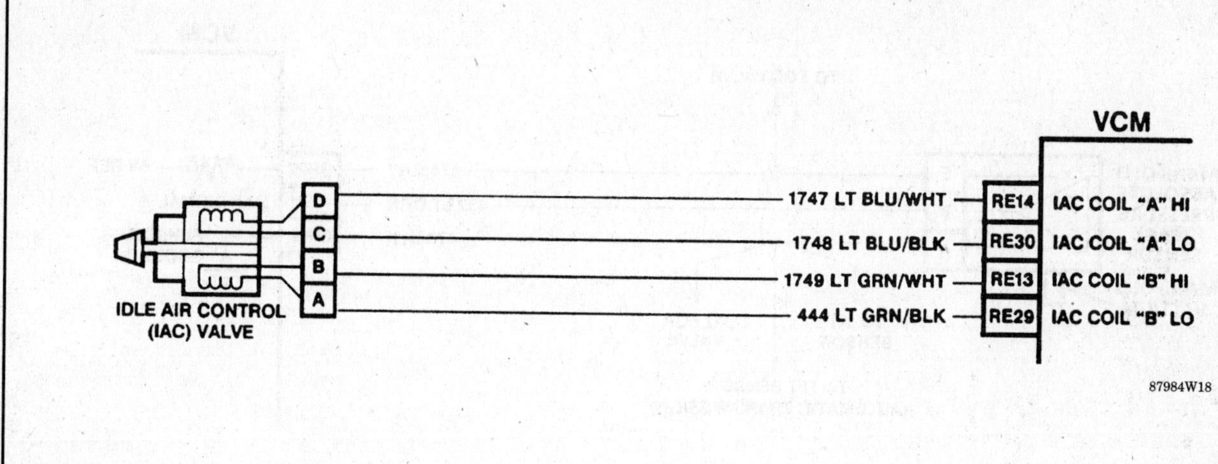

Fig. 62 Idle Air Control (IAC) valve wiring and terminal identification

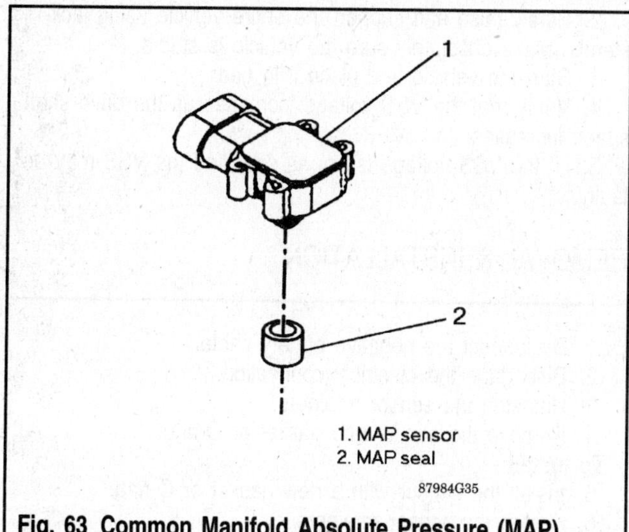

Fig. 63 Common Manifold Absolute Pressure (MAP) sensor

TESTING

➧ **See Figure 64**

1. Backprobe with a high impedance voltmeter at MAP sensor terminals A and C.
2. With the key **ON** and engine off, the voltmeter reading should be approximately 5.0 volts.
3. If the voltage is not as specified, either the wiring to the MAP sensor or the ECM may be faulty. Correct any wiring or ECM faults before continuing test.
4. Backprobe with the high impotence voltmeter at MAP sensor terminals B and A.
5. Verify that the sensor voltage is approximately 0.5 volts with the engine not running (at sea level).
6. Record MAP sensor voltage with the key **ON** and engine off.
7. Start the vehicle.
8. Verify that the sensor voltage is greater than 1.5 volts (above the recorded reading) at idle.
9. Verify that the sensor voltage increases to approximately 4.5. volts (above the recorded reading) at Wide Open Throttle (WOT).
10. If the sensor voltage is as specified, the sensor is functioning properly.
11. If the sensor voltage is not as specified, check the sensor and the sensor vacuum source for a leak or a restriction. If no leaks or restrictions are found, the sensor may be defective and should be replaced.

REMOVAL & INSTALLATION

1. Disconnect the negative battery cable.
2. Tag and disconnect the vacuum harness assembly.
3. Disengage the electrical connector.
4. Release the locktabs, unfasten the bolts and remove the sensor.
5. Installation is the reverse of removal.

Vehicle Speed Sensor (VSS)

OPERATION

➧ **See Figure 65**

The vehicle speed sensor is made up of a coil mounted on the transmission and a tooth rotor mounted to the output shaft of the transmission. As each tooth nears the coil, the coil produces an AC voltage pulse. As the vehicle speed increases the number of voltage pulses per second increases.

TESTING

➧ **See Figure 66**

1. To test the VSS, backprobe the VSS terminals with a high impedance voltmeter (set at the AC voltage scale).

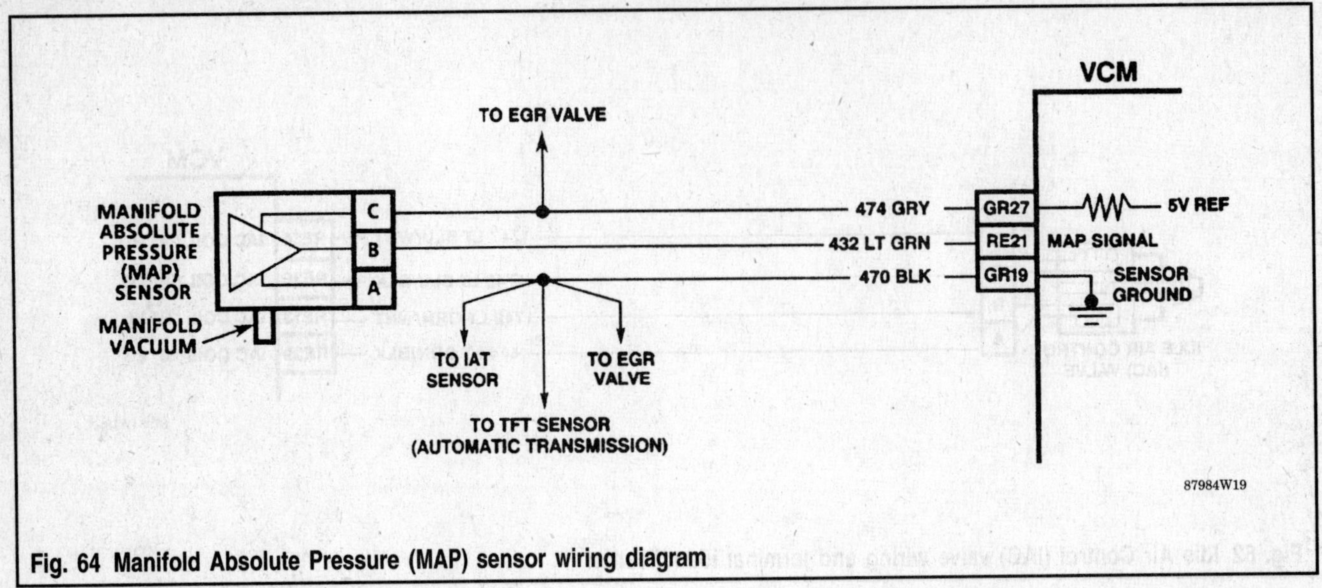

Fig. 64 Manifold Absolute Pressure (MAP) sensor wiring diagram

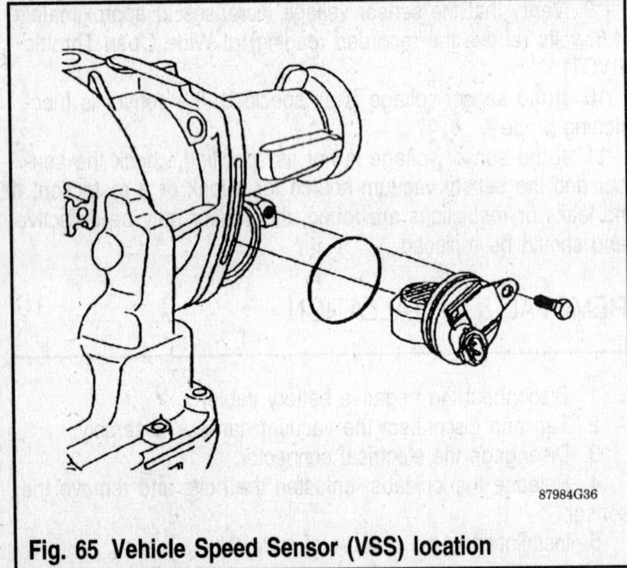

Fig. 65 Vehicle Speed Sensor (VSS) location

2. Safely raise and support the entire vehicle using jackstands. Make absolutely sure the vehicle is stable.
3. Start the vehicle and place it in gear.
4. Verify that the VSS voltage increases as the drive shaft speed increases.
5. If the VSS voltage is not as specified the VSS may be faulty.

REMOVAL & INSTALLATION

1. Disconnect the negative battery cable.
2. Disengage the electrical connection.
3. Unfasten the sensor retainers.
4. Remove the sensor and gasket or O-ring.

To install:

5. Install the sensor with a new gasket or O-ring.
6. Fasten the sensor retainers.
7. Engage the electrical connections.
8. Connect the negative battery cable.

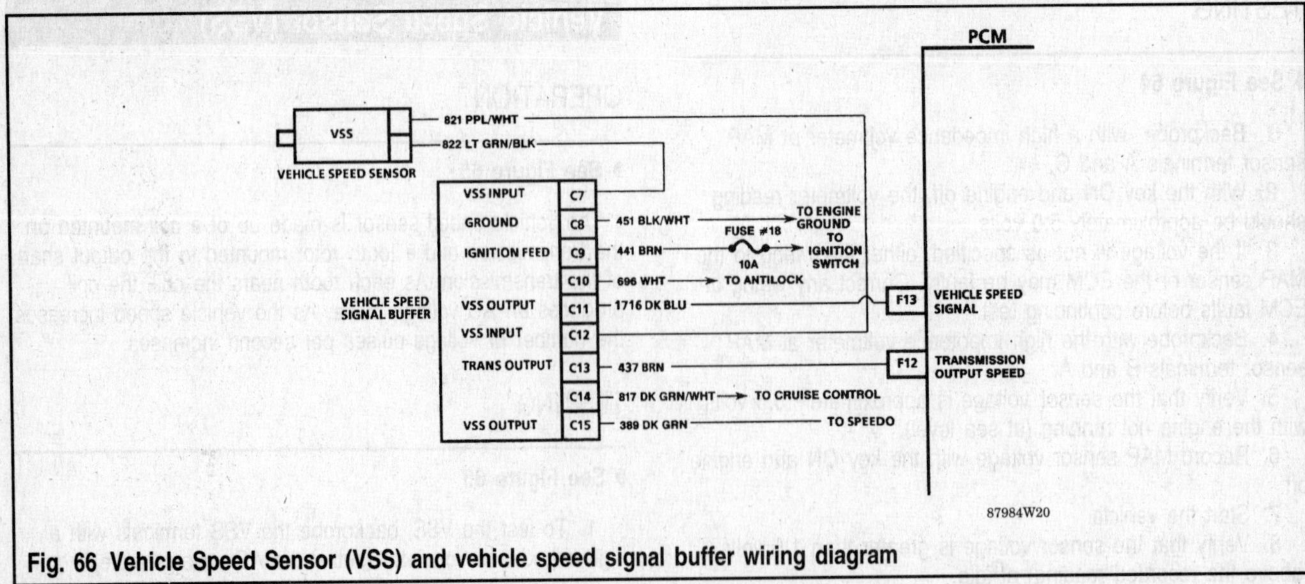

Fig. 66 Vehicle Speed Sensor (VSS) and vehicle speed signal buffer wiring diagram

Knock Sensor

OPERATION

➧ See Figure 67

Located in the engine block, the knock sensor retards ignition timing during a spark knock condition to allow the ECM to maintain maximum timing advance under most conditions.

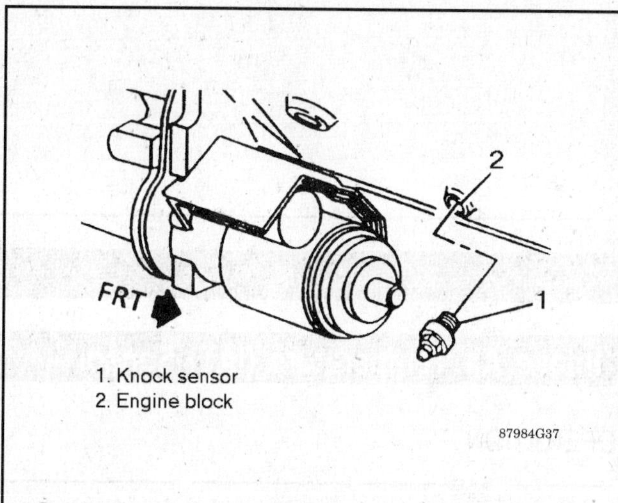

Fig. 67 Exploded view of the knock sensor location — 4.3L, 5.0L, 5.7L and 7.4L engines

TESTING

➧ **See Figures 68 and 69**

1. Connect a timing light to the vehicle and start the engine.
2. Check that the timing is correct before testing knock sensor operation.
3. If timing is correct, tap on the front of the engine block with a metal object while observing the timing to see if the timing retards.
4. If the timing does not retard the knock sensor may be defective.

REMOVAL & INSTALLATION

1. Disconnect the negative battery cable.
2. Disengage the wiring harness connector from the knock sensor.
3. Remove the knock sensor from the engine block.

To install:

4. Apply a water base caulk to the knock sensor threads and install the sensor in the engine block.

****WARNING**

Do not use silicon tape to coat the knock sensor threads as this will insulate the sensor from the engine block.

5. Engage the wiring harness connector.
6. Connect the negative battery cable.

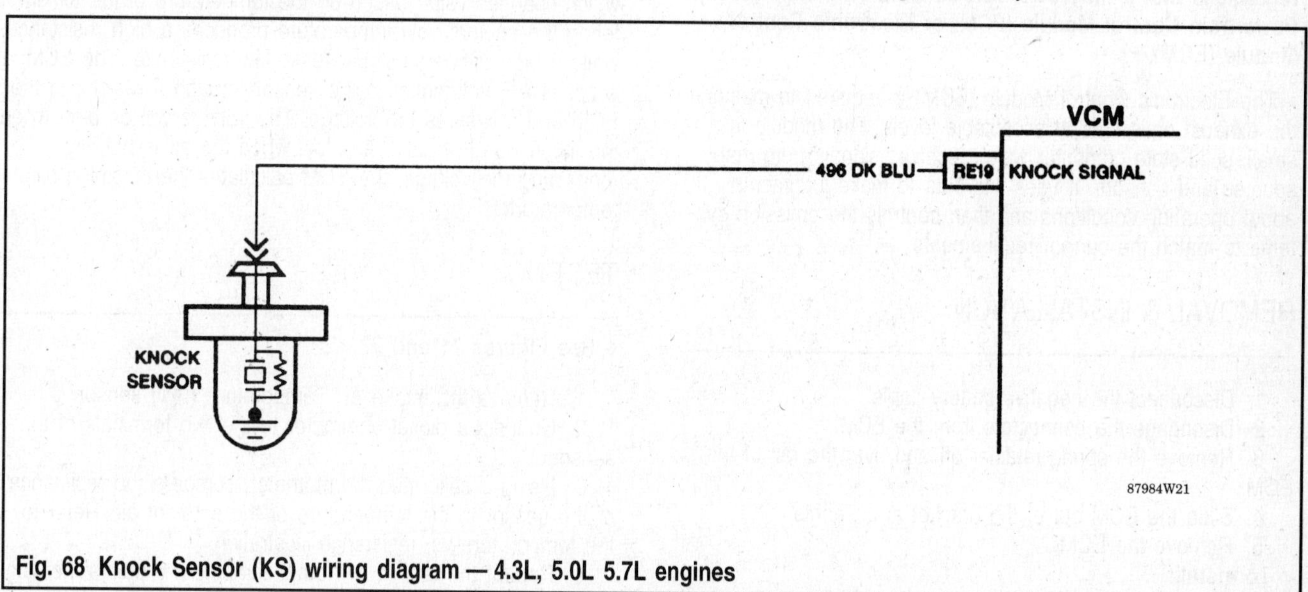

Fig. 68 Knock Sensor (KS) wiring diagram — 4.3L, 5.0L 5.7L engines

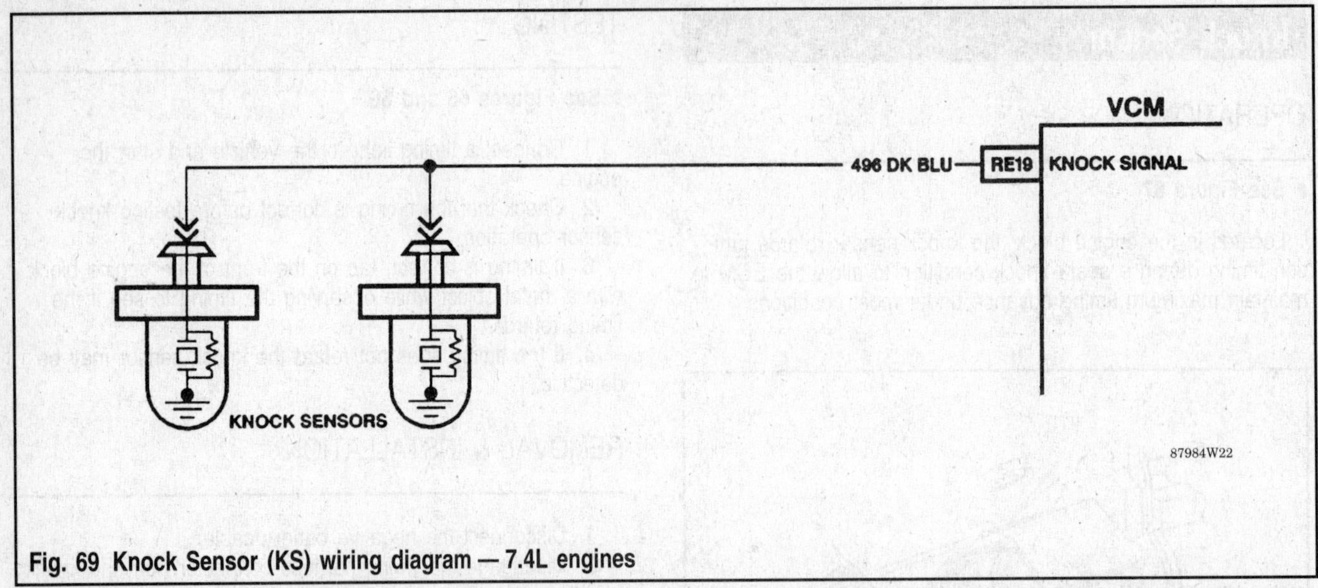

Fig. 69 Knock Sensor (KS) wiring diagram — 7.4L engines

DIESEL ELECTRONIC ENGINE CONTROLS

Electronic Control Module (ECM)

OPERATION

➡When the term Electronic Control Module (ECM) is used in this manual it will refer to the engine control computer regardless that it may be a Vehicle Control Module (VCM), Powertrain Control Module (PCM) or Electronic Control Module (ECM).

The Electronic Control Module (ECM) is required to maintain the exhaust emissions at acceptable levels. The module is a small, solid state computer which receives signals from many sources and sensors. It uses this data to make judgments about operating conditions and then controls the emission systems to match the current requirements.

REMOVAL & INSTALLATION

1. Disconnect the negative battery cable.
2. Disengage the connectors from the ECM.
3. Remove the spring retainer off and over the rail of the ECM.
4. Slide the ECM out of the bracket at an angle.
5. Remove the ECM.

To install:

6. Install the ECM into the bracket.
7. Install the spring retainer and engage the electrical connectors.
8. Connect the negative battery cable.

Intake Air Temperature (IAT) Sensor

OPERATION

➧ See Figure 70

the Intake Air Temperature (IAT) Sensor is a thermistor which changes value based on the temperature of the air entering the engine. Low temperature produces a high resistance, while a high temperature causes a low resistance. The ECM supplies a 5 volt signal to the sensor through a resistor in the ECM and measures the voltage. The voltage will be high when the incoming air is cold, and low when the air is hot. By measuring the voltage, the ECM calculates the incoming air temperature.

TESTING

➧ See Figures 71 and 72

1. Remove the Intake Air Temperature (IAT) sensor.
2. Connect a digital ohmmeter to the two terminals of the sensor.
3. Using a calibrated thermometer, compare the resistance of the sensor to the temperature of the ambient air. Refer to the temperature vs. resistance illustration.
4. Repeat the test at two other temperature points, heating or cooling the air as necessary with a hair dryer or other suitable tool.
5. If the sensor does not meet specification, it must be replaced.

REMOVAL & INSTALLATION

1. Unplug the sensor electrical connection.

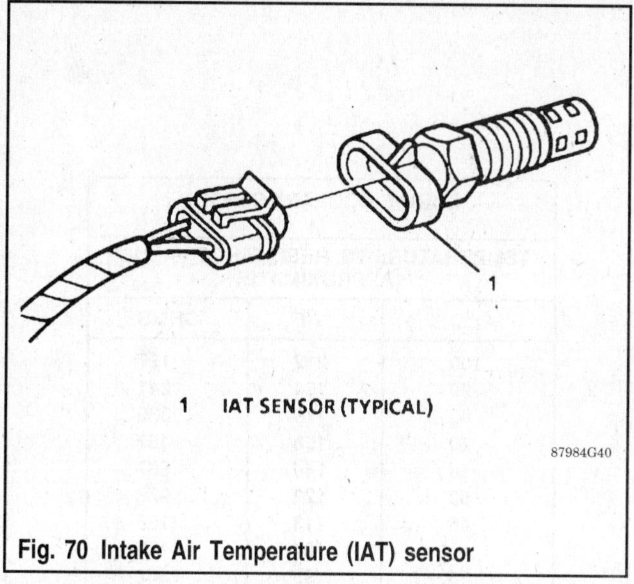

Fig. 70 Intake Air Temperature (IAT) sensor

2. Loosen and remove the sensor from the vehicle.
3. Installation is the reverse of removal.

Engine Coolant Temperature (ECT) Sensor

OPERATION

➧ See Figures 73 and 74

The Engine Coolant Temperature (ECT) sensor is mounted in the intake manifold and sends engine temperature information to the ECM. The ECM supplies 5 volts to the coolant temperature sensor circuit. The sensor is a thermistor which changes internal resistance as temperature changes. When the sensor is cold (internal resistance high), the ECM monitors a high signal voltage which it interprets as a cold engine. As the sensor warms (internal resistance low), the ECM monitors a low signal voltage which it interprets as warm engine.

INTAKE AIR SENSOR		
TEMPERATURE VS. RESISTANCE VALUES (APPROXIMATE)		
°C	°F	OHMS
100	212	177
90	194	241
80	176	332
70	158	467
60	140	667
50	122	973
45	113	1188
40	104	1459
35	95	1802
30	86	2238
25	77	2796
20	68	3520
15	59	4450
10	50	5670
5	41	7280
0	32	9420
-5	23	12300
-10	14	16180
-15	5	21450
-20	-4	28680
-30	-22	52700
-40	-40	100700

87984G39

Fig. 72 IAT sensor temperature vs. resistance values

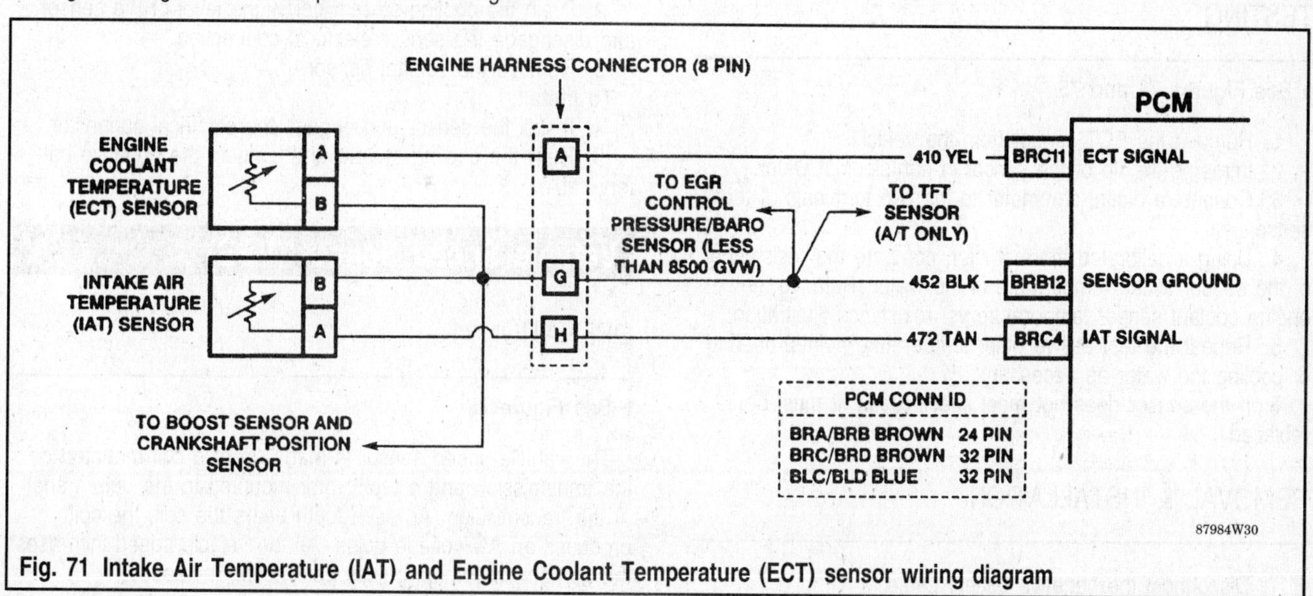

Fig. 71 Intake Air Temperature (IAT) and Engine Coolant Temperature (ECT) sensor wiring diagram

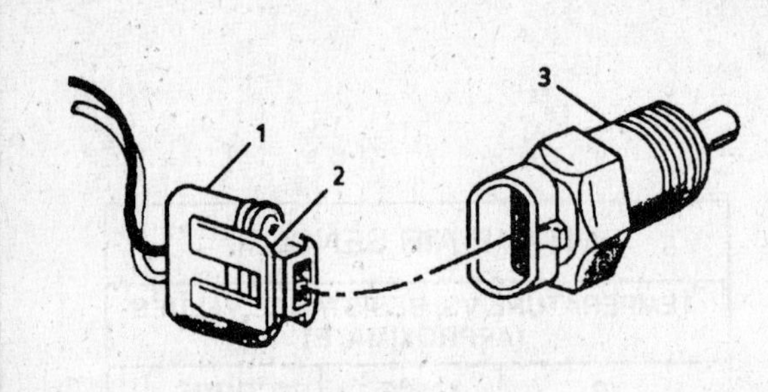

Fig. 73 View of the Engine Coolant Temperature (ECT) sensor

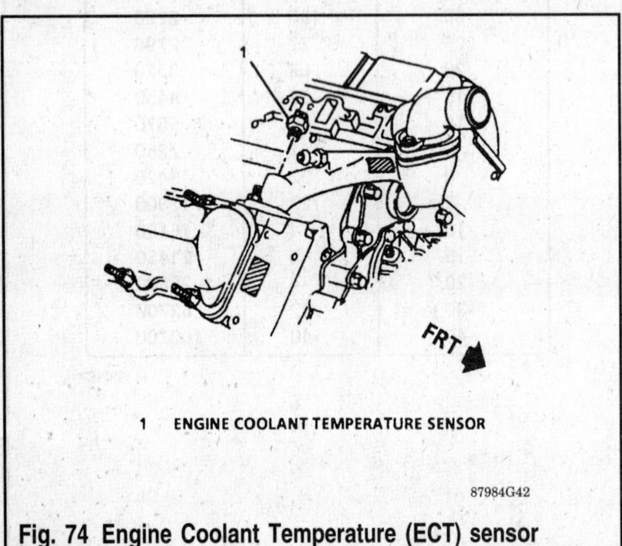

Fig. 74 Engine Coolant Temperature (ECT) sensor location

ENGINE COOLANT SENSOR		
TEMPERATURE VS. RESISTANCE VALUES (APPROXIMATE)		
°C	°F	OHMS
100	212	177
90	194	241
80	176	332
70	158	467
60	140	667
50	122	973
45	113	1188
40	104	1459
35	95	1802
30	86	2238
25	77	2796
20	68	3520
15	59	4450
10	50	5670
5	41	7280
0	32	9420
-5	23	12300
-10	14	16180
-15	5	21450
-20	-4	28680
-30	-22	52700
-40	-40	100700

87984G38

Fig. 75 ECT sensor temperature vs. resistance values

TESTING

➧ See Figures 71 and 75

1. Remove the ECT sensor from the vehicle.
2. Immerse the tip of the sensor in container of water.
3. Connect a digital ohmmeter to the two terminals of the sensor.
4. Using a calibrated thermometer, compare the resistance of the sensor to the temperature of the water. Refer to the engine coolant sensor temperature vs. resistance illustration.
5. Repeat the test at two other temperature points, heating or cooling the water as necessary.
6. If the sensor does not meet specification, it must be replaced.

REMOVAL & INSTALLATION

1. Disconnect the negative battery cable.
2. Drain the cooling system below the level of the sensor and disengage the sensor electrical connection.
3. Remove the coolant sensor.

To install:

4. Install the sensor and engage the electrical connector.
5. Refill the cooling system and connect the negative battery cable.

Vehicle Speed Sensor (VSS)

OPERATION

➧ See Figure 76

The vehicle speed sensor is made up of a coil mounted on the transmission and a tooth rotor mounted to the output shaft of the transmission. As each tooth nears the coil, the coil produces an AC voltage pulse. As the vehicle speed increases the number of voltage pulses per second increases.

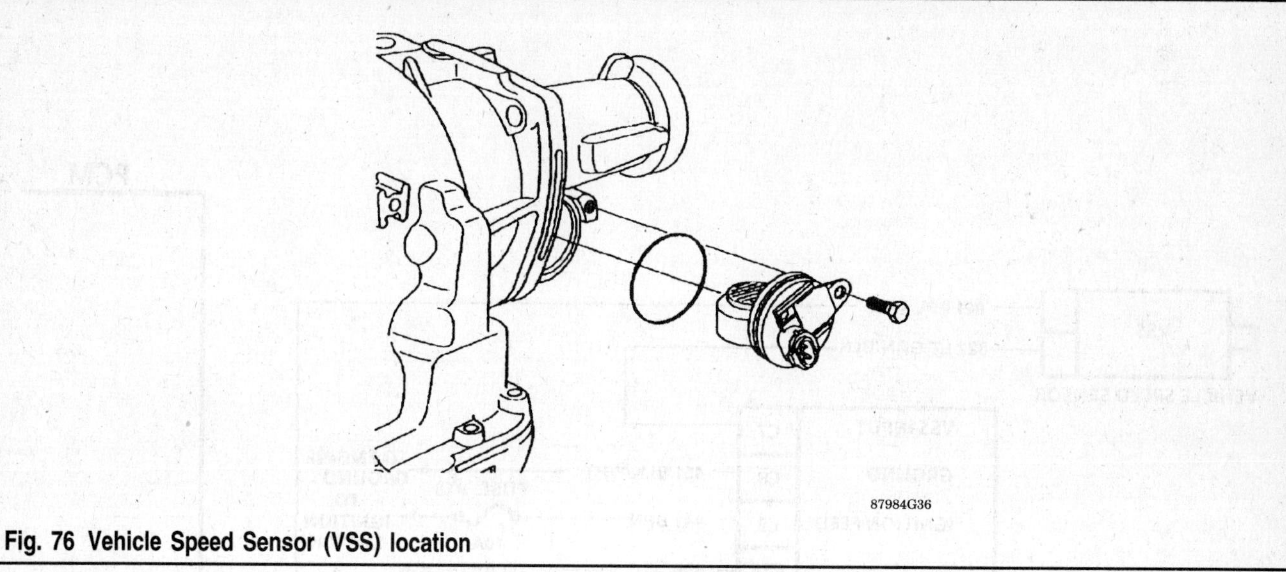

Fig. 76 Vehicle Speed Sensor (VSS) location

TESTING

➧ **See Figure 77**

1. To test the VSS, backprobe the VSS terminals with a high impedance voltmeter (set at the AC voltage scale).
2. Safely raise and support the entire vehicle using jackstands. Make absolutely sure the vehicle is stable.
3. Start the vehicle and place it in gear.
4. Verify that the VSS voltage increases as the drive shaft speed increases.
5. If the VSS voltage is not as specified the VSS may be faulty.

REMOVAL & INSTALLATION

1. Disconnect the negative battery cable.
2. Disengage the electrical connection.
3. Unfasten the sensor retainers.
4. Remove the sensor and gasket or O-ring.

To install:

5. Install the sensor with a new gasket or O-ring.
6. Fasten the sensor retainers.
7. Engage the electrical connections.
8. Connect the negative battery cable.

Accelerator Pedal Position (APP) Sensor Module

OPERATION

The APP sensor module contains three potentiometers (a device for measuring unknown voltage or potential difference by comparison to a standard voltage). Each of the APP sensors send a varying voltage to the ECM. By monitoring the output voltage from the Accelerator Pedal Position (APP) module, the ECM can determine fuel delivery based on the accelerator pedal position (driver demand).

TESTING

➧ **See Figure 78**

1. Backprobe with a high impedance voltmeter at APP sensor terminals G and A.
2. With the key **ON** and engine off, the voltmeter reading should be approximately 5.0 volts.
3. If the voltage is not as specified, either the wiring to the APP sensor or the ECM may be faulty. Correct any wiring or ECM faults before continuing test.
4. Backprobe with a high impedance voltmeter at terminals F and A.
5. With the key **ON** and engine idling, the APP sensor voltage should be approximately 0.5 volts.
6. Verify that the APP voltage increases or decreases smoothly as the throttle is opened or closed. Make sure to open and close the throttle very slowly in order to detect any abnormalities in the APP sensor voltage reading.
7. If the APP sensor voltage is not as specified, replace the APP sensor.
8. Backprobe with a high impedance voltmeter at APP sensor terminals D and B.
9. With the key **ON** and engine off, the voltmeter reading should be approximately 5.0 volts.
10. If the voltage is not as specified, either the wiring to the APP sensor or the ECM may be faulty. Correct any wiring or ECM faults before continuing test.
11. Backprobe with a high impedance voltmeter at terminals C and B.
12. With the key **ON** and engine idling, the APP sensor voltage should be approximately 4.5 volts.
13. Verify that the APP voltage decreases smoothly as the throttle is opened. Make sure to open and close the throttle very slowly in order to detect any abnormalities in the APP sensor voltage reading.
14. If the APP sensor voltage is not as specified, replace the APP sensor.
15. Backprobe with a high impedance voltmeter at APP sensor terminals E and J.

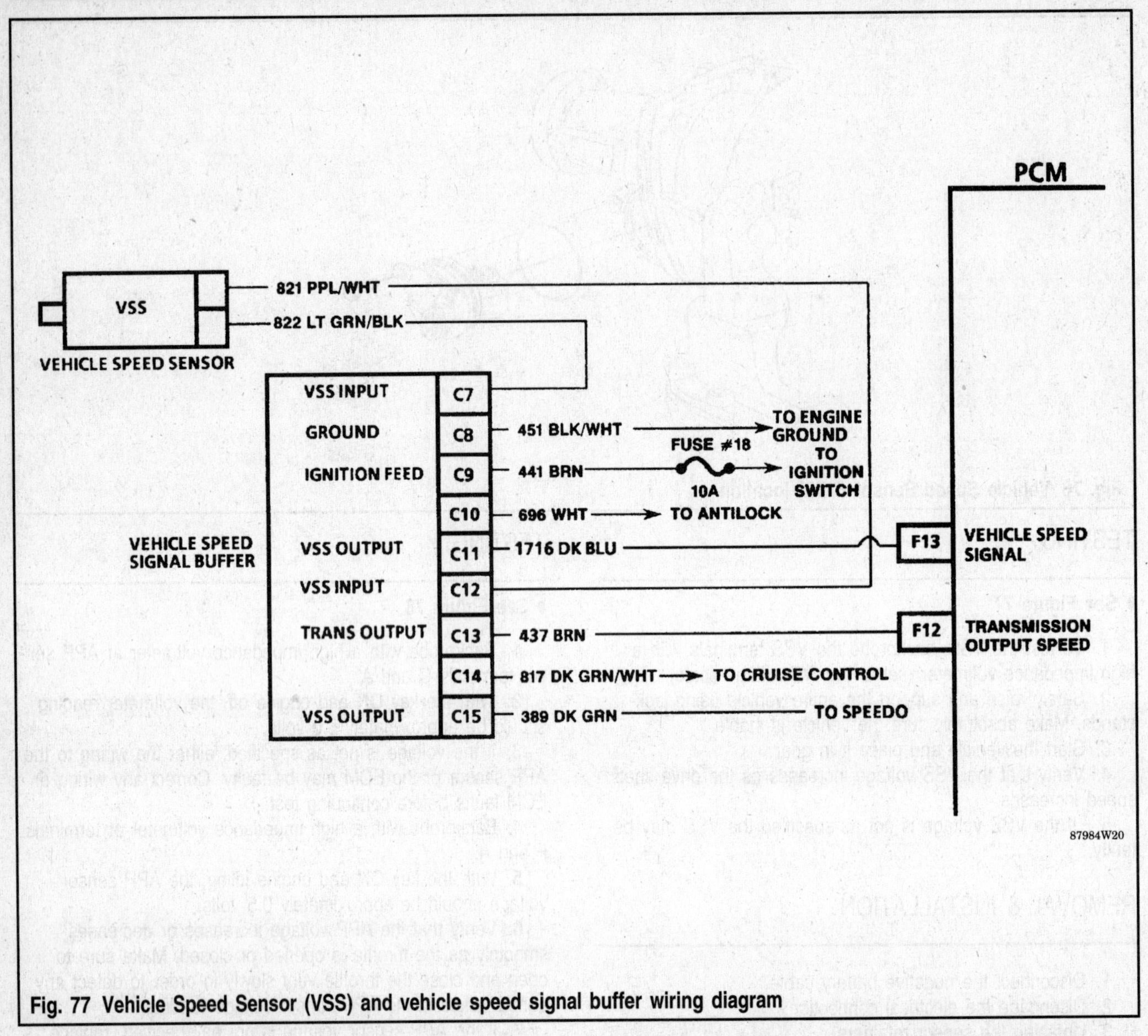

Fig. 77 Vehicle Speed Sensor (VSS) and vehicle speed signal buffer wiring diagram

16. With the key **ON** and engine off, the voltmeter reading should be approximately 5.0 volts.
17. If the voltage is not as specified, either the wiring to the APP sensor or the ECM may be faulty. Correct any wiring or ECM faults before continuing test.
18. Backprobe with a high impedance voltmeter at terminals K and J.
19. With the key **ON** and engine idling, the APP sensor voltage should be approximately 4.0 volts.
20. Verify that the APP voltage decreases smoothly to about 2.0 volts as the throttle is opened. Make sure to open and close the throttle very slowly in order to detect any abnormalities in the APP sensor voltage reading.
21. If the APP sensor voltage is not as specified, replace the APP sensor module.

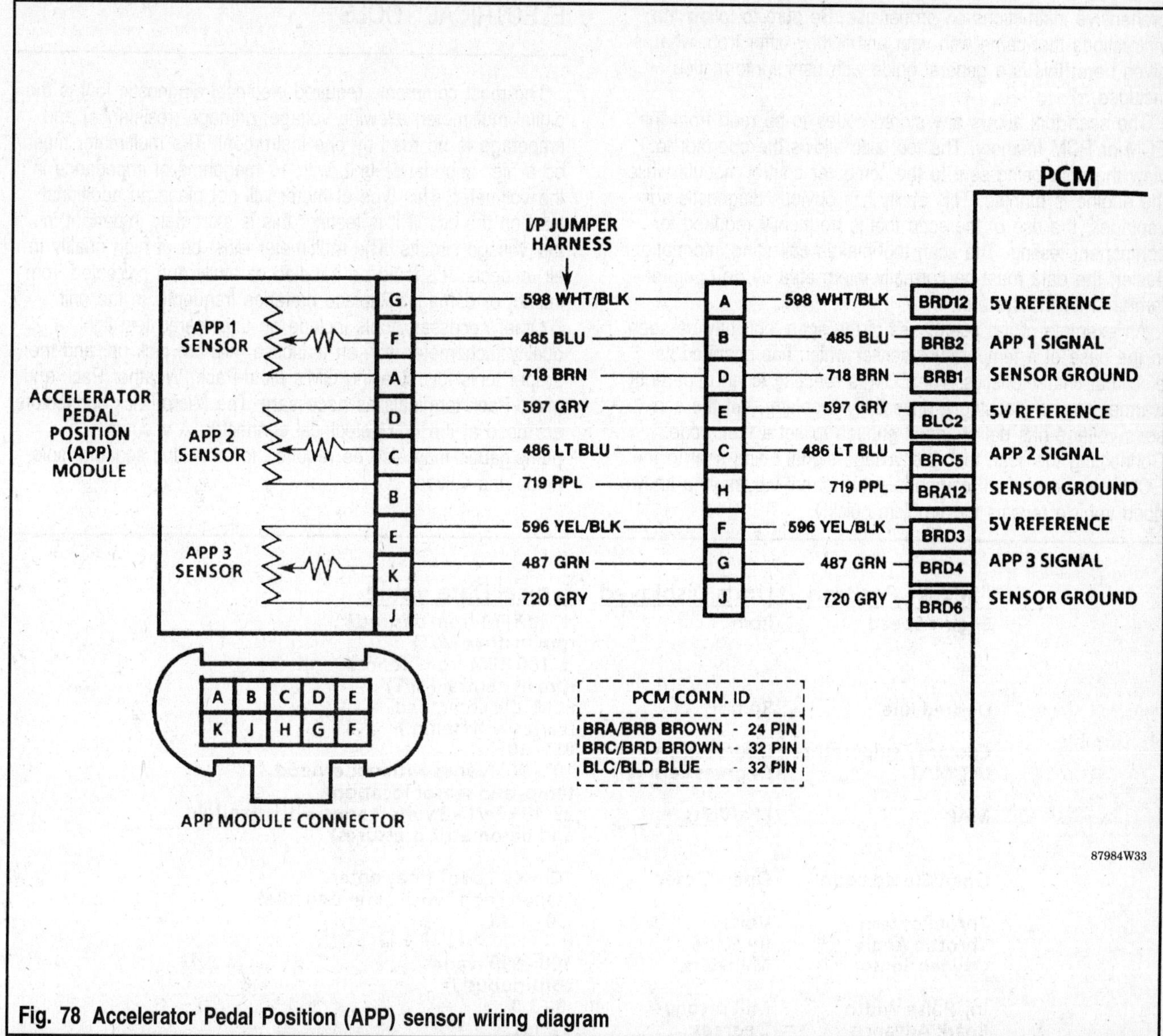

Fig. 78 Accelerator Pedal Position (APP) sensor wiring diagram

TROUBLE CODES

General Information

Since the control module is programmed to recognize the presence and value of electrical inputs, it will also note the lack of a signal or a radical change in values. It will, for example, react to the loss of signal from the vehicle speed sensor or note that engine coolant temperature has risen beyond acceptable (programmed) limits. Once a fault is recognized, a numeric code is assigned and held in memory. The dashboard warning lamp: CHECK ENGINE or SERVICE ENGINE SOON (SES), will illuminate to advise the operator that the system has detected a fault. This lamp is also known as the Malfunction Indicator Lamp (MIL).

More than one code may be stored. Keep in mind not every engine uses every code. Additionally, the same code may carry different meanings relative to each engine or engine family.

In the event of an computer control module failure, the system will default to a pre-programmed set of values. These are compromise values which allow the engine to operate, although possibly at reduced efficiency. This is variously known as the default, limp-in or back-up mode. Driveability is almost always affected when the ECM enters this mode.

SCAN TOOLS

➧ See Figure 79

On most models, the stored codes may be read with only the use of a small jumper wire, however the use of a hand-held scan tool such as GM's TECH-1® or equivalent is recommended. On 1996 models, an OBD-II compliant scan tool must be used. There are many manufacturers of these tools; a purchaser must be certain that the tool is proper for the intended use. If you own a scan type tool, it probably came with comprehensive instructions on proper use. Be sure to follow the instructions that came with your unit if they differ from what is given here; this is a general guide with useful information included.

The scan tool allows any stored codes to be read from the ECM or PCM memory. The tool also allows the operator to view the data being sent to the computer control module while the engine is running. This ability has obvious diagnostic advantages; the use of the scan tool is frequently required for component testing. The scan tool makes collecting information easier; the data must be correctly interpreted by an operator familiar with the system.

An example of the usefulness of the scan tool may be seen in the case of a temperature sensor which has changed its electrical characteristics. The ECM is reacting to an apparently warmer engine (causing a driveability problem), but the sensor's voltage has not changed enough to set a fault code. Connecting the scan tool, the voltage signal being sent to the ECM may be viewed; comparison to normal values or a known good vehicle reveals the problem quickly.

ELECTRICAL TOOLS

The most commonly required electrical diagnostic tool is the digital multimeter, allowing voltage, ohmage (resistance) and amperage to be read by one instrument. The multimeter must be a high-impedance unit, with 10 megohms of impedance in the voltmeter. This type of meter will not place an additional load on the circuit it is testing; this is extremely important in low voltage circuits. The multimeter must be of high quality in all respects. It should be handled carefully and protected from impact or damage. Replace batteries frequently in the unit.

Other necessary tools include an unpowered test light, a quality tachometer with an inductive (clip-on) pick up, and the proper tools for releasing GM's Metri-Pack, Weather Pack and Micro-Pack terminals as necessary. The Micro-Pack connectors are used at the ECM electrical connector. A vacuum pump/gauge may also be required for checking sensors, solenoids and valves.

"SCAN" Position	Units Displayed	Typical Data Value
Engine Speed	Rpm	± 50 RPM from desired rpm in drive (A/T) ± 100 RPM from desired rpm in neutral (M/T)
Desired Idle	Rpm	ECM idle command (varies with temp.)
Coolant Temperature	Degrees Celsius	85° - 105°
IAT/MAT	Degrees Celsius	10° - 90° (varies with underhood temp. and sensor location)
MAP	kPa/Volts	29-48 kPa/1 - 2 volts (varies with manifold and barometric pressures)
Open/Closed Loop	Open/Closed	"Closed Loop" (may enter "Open Loop" with extended idle)
Throt Position	Volts	.30 - 1.33
Throttle Angle	0 - 100%	0
Oxygen Sensor	Millivolts	100 - 999 (varies continuously)
Inj. Pulse Width	Milliseconds	.8 - 3.0
Spark Advance	Degrees	Varies
Engine Speed	Rpm	± 50 RPM from desired rpm in drive (A/T) ± 100 RPM from desired rpm in neutral (M/T)
Fuel Integrator	Counts	110-145
Block Learn	Counts	118-138
Idle Air Control	Counts (steps)	1 - 50
P/N Switch	P-N and R-D-L	Park/Neutral (P/N)
MPH/KPH	0-255	0
TCC	"ON"/"OFF"	"OFF"
Crank Rpm	Rpm	⟩796
Ign/Batt Voltage	Volts	13.5 - 14.5
Cooling Fan Relay	"ON"/"OFF"	"OFF" (coolant temperature below 102°C)
A/C Request	"YES"/"NO"	No
A/C Clutch	"ON"/"OFF"	"OFF"
Power Steering	Normal/High Pressure	Normal
Shift Light (M/T)	"ON"/"OFF"	"OFF"

84904059

Fig. 79 Example of scan tool data and typical or baseline values

Diagnosis and Testing

Diagnosis of a driveablility and/or emissions problems requires attention to detail and following the diagnostic procedures in the correct order. Resist the temptation to perform any repairs before performing the preliminary diagnostic steps. In many cases this will shorten diagnostic time and often cure the problem without electronic testing.

The proper troubleshooting procedure for these vehicles is as follows:

VISUAL/PHYSICAL INSPECTION

This is possibly the most critical step of diagnosis and should be performed immediately after retrieving any codes. A detailed examination of connectors, wiring and vacuum hoses can often lead to a repair without further diagnosis. Performance of this step relies on the skill of the technician performing it; a careful inspector will check the undersides of hoses as well as the integrity of hard-to-reach hoses blocked by the air cleaner or other component. Wiring should be checked carefully for any sign of strain, burning, crimping, or terminal pull-out from a connector. Checking connectors at components or in harnesses is required; usually, pushing them together will reveal a loose fit.

INTERMITTENTS

If a fault occurs intermittently, such as a loose connector pin breaking contact as the vehicle hits a bump, the ECM will note the fault as it occurs and energize the dash warning lamp. If the problem self-corrects, as with the terminal pin again making contact, the dash lamp will extinguish after 10 seconds but a code will remain stored in the computer control module's memory.

When an unexpected code appears during diagnostics, it may have been set during an intermittent failure that self-corrected; the codes are still useful in diagnosis and should not be discounted.

CIRCUIT/COMPONENT REPAIR

The fault codes and the scan tool data will lead to diagnosis and checking of a particular circuit. It is important to note that the fault code indicates a fault or loss of signal in an ECM-controlled system, not necessarily in the specific component.

Refer to the appropriate Diagnostic Code chart to determine the codes meaning. The component may then be tested following the appropriate component test procedures found in this section. If the component is OK, check the wiring for shorts or opens. Further diagnoses should be left to an experienced driveability technician.

If a code indicates the ECM to be faulty and the ECM is replaced, but does not correct the problem, one of the following may be the reason:

- There is a problem with the ECM terminal connections: The terminals may have to be removed from the connector in order to check them properly.
- The ECM or PROM is not correct for the application: The incorrect ECM or PROM may cause a malfunction and may or may not set a code.
- The problem is intermittent: This means that the problem is not present at the time the system is being checked. In this case, make a careful physical inspection of all portions of the system involved.
- Shorted solenoid, relay coil or harness: Solenoids and relays are turned on and off by the ECM using internal electronic switches called drivers. Each driver is part of a group of four called Quad-Drivers. A shorted solenoid, relay coil or harness may cause an ECM to fail, and a replacement ECM to fail when it is installed. Use a short tester, J34696, BT 8405, or equivalent, as a fast, accurate means of checking for a short circuit.
- The Programmable Read Only Memory (PROM) may be faulty: Although the PROM rarely fails, it operates as part of the ECM. Therefore, it could be the cause of the problem. Substitute a known good PROM.
- The replacement ECM may be faulty: After the ECM is replaced, the system should be rechecked for proper operation. If the diagnostic code again indicates the ECM is the problem, substitute a known good ECM. Although this is a very rare condition, it could happen.

Reading Codes

1988-95 MODELS

See Figures 80 and 81

Listings of the trouble for the various engine control system covered in this manual are located in this section. Remember that a code only points to the faulty circuit NOT necessarily to a faulty component. Loose, damaged or corroded connections may contribute to a fault code on a circuit when the sensor or component is operating properly. Be sure that the components are faulty before replacing them, especially the expensive ones.

The Assembly Line Diagnostic Link (ALDL) connector or Data Link Connector (DLC) may be located under the dash and sometimes covered with a plastic cover labeled DIAGNOSTIC CONNECTOR.

1. The diagnostic trouble codes can be read by grounding test terminal B. The terminal is most easily grounded by connecting it to terminal A (internal ECM ground). This is the terminal to the right of terminal B on the top row of the ALDL connector.
2. Once the terminals have been connected, the ignition switch must be moved to the **ON** position with the engine not running.
3. The Service Engine Soon or Check Engine light should be flashing. If it isn't, turn the ignition **OFF** and remove the jumper wire. Turn the ignition **ON** and confirm that light is now

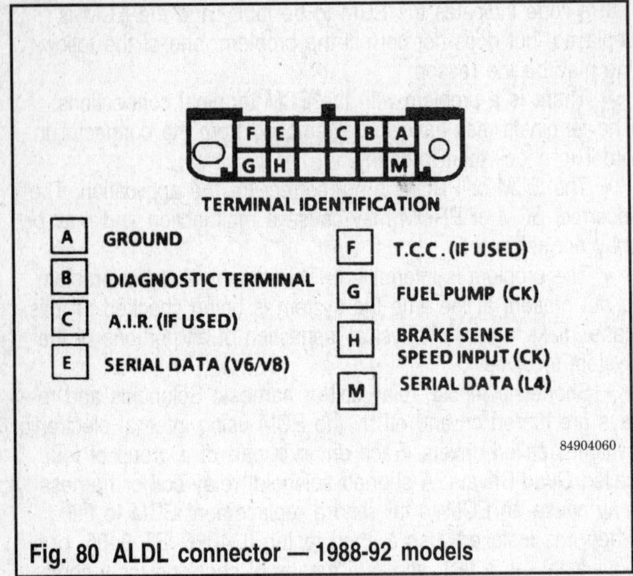

Fig. 80 ALDL connector — 1988-92 models

on. If it is not, replace the bulb and try again. If the bulb still will not light, or if it does not flash with the test terminal grounded, the system should be diagnosed by an experienced driveability technician. If the light is OK, proceed as follows.

4. The code(s) stored in memory may be read through counting the flashes of the dashboard warning lamp. The dash warning lamp should begin to flash Code 12. The code will display as one flash, a pause and two flashes. Code 12 is not a fault code. It is used as a system acknowledgment or handshake code; its presence indicates that the ECM can communicate as requested. Code 12 is used to begin every diagnostic sequence. Some vehicles also use Code 12 after all diagnostic codes have been sent.

5. After Code 12 has been transmitted 3 times, the fault codes, if any, will each be transmitted 3 times. The codes are stored and transmitted in numeric order from lowest to highest.

➡The order of codes in the memory does not indicate the order of occurrence.

6. If there are no codes stored, but a driveability or emissions problem is evident, the system should be diagnosed by an experienced driveability technician.

7. If one or more codes are stored, record them. Refer to the applicable Diagnostic Code chart in this section.

8. Switch the ignition **OFF** when finished with code retrieval or scan tool readings.

➡After making repairs, clear the trouble codes and operate the vehicle to see if it will reset, indicating further problems.

F E C B A
H J M

TERMINAL IDENTIFICATION

A GROUND
B DIAGNOSTIC TERMINAL
C AIR
E SERIAL DATA
F TCC
H BRAKE
J ELECTRIC SHIFT
M SERIAL DATA

ALL SYSTEMS NOT USED ON ALL ENGINES

84904061

Fig. 81 ALDL connector — 1993-95 models

1996 MODELS

On 1996 models, an OBD-II compliant scan tool must be used to retrieve the trouble codes. Follow the scan tool manufacturer's instructions on how to connect the scan tool to the vehicle and how to retrieve the codes.

Clearing Codes

Stored fault codes may be erased from memory at any time by removing power from the ECM for at least 30 seconds. It may be necessary to clear stored codes during diagnosis to check for any recurrence during a test drive, but the stored codes must be written down when retrieved. The codes may still be required for subsequent troubleshooting. Whenever a repair is complete, the stored codes must be erased and the vehicle test driven to confirm correct operation and repair.

✱✱WARNING

The ignition switch must be OFF any time power is disconnected or restored to the ECM. Severe damage may result if this precaution is not observed.

Depending on the electrical distribution of the particular vehicle, power to the ECM may be disconnected by removing the ECM fuse in the fusebox, disconnecting the in-line fuse holder near the positive battery terminal or disconnecting the ECM power lead at the battery terminal. Disconnecting the negative battery cable to clear codes is not recommended as this will also clear other memory data in the vehicle such as radio presets.

CODE IDENTIFICATION

The "Service Engine Soon" light will only be "ON" if the malfunction exists under the conditions listed below. If the malfunction clears, the light will go out and the code will be stored in the ECM. Any Codes stored will be erased if no problem reoccurs within 50 engine starts.

CODE AND CIRCUIT	PROBABLE CAUSE
Code 12 - No engine speed reference pulse.	No engine speed sensor reference pulses to the ECM. This code is not stored in memory and will only flash while the fault is present. Normal code with ignition "ON," engine not running.
Code 14 - Coolant Sensor High Temperature Indication	Sets if the sensor or signal line becomes grounded for 10 seconds.
Code 15 - Coolant Sensor Low Temperature Indication	Sets if the sensor, connections, or wires open for 10 seconds.
Code 21 - TPS Signal Voltage High	Throttle Position Sensor (TPS) circuit voltage high (open circuit or misadjusted TPS). Engine must run 30 seconds, at curb idle speed, before this code will set.
Code 22 - TPS Signal Voltage Low	Throttle Position Sensor (TPS) circuit voltage low (grounded circuit). Engine must run 2 minutes at 1250 rpm or above before this code will set.
Code 23 - TPS Not Calibrated	Throttle Position Sensor (TPS) circuit. Voltage not between .25 and 1.3 volts at curb idle speed. Engine must run for 30 seconds, at curb idle, before this code will set.
Code 24 - VSS No Vehicle Speed Indication	Vehicle speed sensor (VSS) circuit (open or grounded circuit). Vehicle must operate at road speed for 10 seconds before this code will set.
Code 31 - MAP Sensor Too Low	Absolute Pressure (MAP) circuit signal voltage too low. Engine must run at curb idle for 10 seconds before this code will set.
Code 32 - EGR Loop Error	Exhaust Gas Recirculation (EGR) vacuum circuit has seen improper EGR vacuum. Vehicle must be running at road speed approximately 30 mph (48 Km/h) for 10 seconds before this code will set.
Code 33 - MAP Sensor Too High	Absolute Pressure (MAP) circuit signal voltage too high. Engine must run at curb idle for 10 seconds before this code will set.
Code 51 - PROM	Faulty or improperly installed PROM. It takes approximately 10 seconds before this code will set.
Code 52 - ECM	Fault in ECM circuit. It takes 10 seconds before this code will set.
Code 53 - Five volt Reference Overload	5 volt reference (Vref) circuit overloaded (grounded circuit). It takes 10 seconds before this Code will set.

84904119

Fig. 82 Carbureted engine trouble codes

DIAGNOSTIC CODE IDENTIFICATION

The "Service Engine Soon" light will only be "ON" if the malfunction exists under the conditions listed below. If the malfunction clears, the light will go out and the code will be stored in the ECM/PCM. Any codes stored will be erased if no problem reoccurs within 50 engine starts.

CODE AND CIRCUIT	PROBABLE CAUSE
Code 13 - Oxygen O_2 Sensor Circuit (Open Circuit)	Indicates that the oxygen sensor circuit or sensor was open for one minute while off idle.
Code 14 - Coolant Temperature Sensor (CTS) Circuit (High Temperature Indicated)	Sets if the sensor or signal line becomes grounded for 3 seconds.
Code 15 - Coolant Temperature Sensor (CTS) Circuit (Low Temperature Indicated)	Sets if the sensor, connections, or wires open for 3 seconds.
Code 21 - Throttle Position Sensor (TPS) Circuit (Signal Voltage High)	TPS voltage greater than 2.5 volts for 3 seconds with less than 1200 RPM.
Code 22 - Throttle Position Sensor (TPS) Circuit (Signal Voltage Low)	A shorted to ground or open signal circuit will set code in 3 seconds.
Code 23 - Intake Air Temperature (IAT) Sensor Circuit (Low Temperature Indicated)	Sets if the sensor, connections, or wires open for 3 seconds.
Code 24 - Vehicle Speed Sensor (VSS)	No vehicle speed present during a road load decel.
Code 25 - Intake Air Temperature (IAT) Sensor Circuit (High Temperature Indicated)	Sets if the sensor or signal line becomes grounded for 3 seconds.
Code 32 - Exhaust Gas Recirculation (EGR) System	Vacuum switch shorted to ground on start up OR Switch not closed after the ECM/PCM has commanded EGR for a specified period of time. OR EGR solenoid circuit open for a specified period of time.

CODE AND CIRCUIT	PROBABLE CAUSE
Code 33 - Manifold Absolute Pressure (MAP) Sensor Circuit (Signal Voltage High- Low Vacuum)	MAP sensor output to high for 5 seconds or an open signal circuit.
Code 34 - Manifold Absolute Pressure (MAP) Sensor Circuit (Signal Voltage Low-High Vacuum)	Low or no output from sensor with engine running.
Code 35 - Idle Air Control (IAC) System	IAC error
Code 42 - Electronic Spark Timing (EST)	ECM/PCM has seen an open or grounded EST or bypass circuit.
Code 43 - Electronic Spark Control (ESC) Circuit	Signal to the ECM/ PCM has remained low for too long or the system has failed a functional check.
Code 44 - Oxygen (O_2) Sensor Circuit (Lean Exhaust Indicated)	Sets if oxygen sensor voltage remains below .2 volt for about 20 seconds.
Code 45 - Oxygen (O_2) Sensor Circuit (Rich Exhaust Indicated)	Sets if oxygen sensor voltage remains above .7 volt for about 1 minute.
Code 51 - Faulty MEM-CAL or PROM Problem	Faulty MEM-CAL, PROM, or ECM/PCM.
Code 52 - Fuel CALPAK Missing	Fuel CAL-PAK missing or faulty.
Code 53 - System Over Voltage	System overvoltage. Indicates a basic generator problem.
Code 54 - Fuel Pump Circuit (Low Voltage)	Sets when the fuel pump voltage is less than 2 volts when reference pulses are being received.
Code 55 - Faulty ECM/PCM	Faulty ECM/PCM

84904064

Fig. 83 Fuel injected engine trouble codes through 1995, except with 4L60E and 4L80E transmissions

DIAGNOSTIC TROUBLE CODE (DTC) IDENTIFICATION

The MIL (Service Engine Soon) will only be "ON" if the malfunction exists with the conditions listed below. If the malfunction clears, the lamp will go out and the DTC will be stored in the PCM. Any DTCs stored will be erased if no problem reoccurs within 50 engine starts.

DTC AND CIRCUIT	PROBABLE CAUSE	DTC AND CIRCUIT	PROBABLE CAUSE
DTC 13 - Oxygen O2S Sensor Circuit (Open Circuit)	Indicates that the oxygen sensor circuit or sensor was open for one minute while off idle.	DTC 33 - Manifold Absolute Pressure (MAP) Sensor Circuit (Signal Voltage High - Low Vacuum)	MAP sensor output high for 5 seconds or an open signal circuit.
DTC 14 - Engine Coolant Temperature (ECT) Sensor Circuit (High Temperature Indicated	Sets if the sensor or signal line becomes grounded or greater than 145°C (294°F) for 0.5 seconds.	DTC 34 - Manifold Absolute Pressure (MAP) Sensor Circuit (Signal Voltage Low- High Vacuum)	Low or no output from MAP sensor with engine operating.
DTC 15 - Engine Coolant Temperature (ECT) Sensor Circuit (Low Temperature Indicated)	Sets if the sensor, connections, or wires open or less than -33°C (-27°F) for 0.5 seconds.	DTC 35 - IAC	IAC error
DTC 16 - Transmission Output Speed Low	Open in CKT 1697/1716 or power loss to VSS buffer	*DTC 37 - Brake Switch Stuck On	With no voltage and vehicle speed is less than 5 mph for 6 seconds, then vehicle speed is 5 - 20 MPH for 6 seconds, then vehicle speed is greater than 20 MPH for 6 seconds, this must occur for 7 times.
DTC 21 - Throttle Position (TP) Sensor Circuit (Signal Voltage High)	TP voltage greater than 4.88 volts 4 seconds with less than 1200 RPM.	*DTC 38 - Brake Switch Stuck Off	With voltage and vehicle speed is greater than 20 MPH for 6 seconds, then vehicle speed is 5 - 20 MPH for 6 seconds. This must occur 7 times.
DTC 22 - Throttle Position (TP) Sensor Circuit (Signal Voltage Low)	A short to ground,open signal circuit, or TP voltage less than 0.16 volts for 4 seconds.		
DTC 24 - Vehicle Speed Sensor (VSS) Signal Low	No vehicle speed sensor signal present during a road load decel.	DTC 42 - Ignition Control (IC)	PCM detects an open or grounded IC or bypass circuit.
DTC 28 - Fluid Pressure Switch Assembly	PCM detects 1 of 2 invalid combinations of the fluid pressure switch range signals	DTC 43 - Knock Sensor (KS) Circuit	Signal to the PCM has remained low for too long, or the system has failed a functional system check.
DTC 32 - Exhaust Gas Recirculation (EGR) System	Vacuum switch shorted to ground on start up OR Switch not closed after the PCM has commanded EGR for a specified period of time. OR EGR solenoid circuit open for a specified period of time.	DTC 44 - Oxygen Sensor (O2S) Circuit (Lean Exhaust Indicated)	Sets if oxygen sensor voltage remains less than 0.2 volt for 20 seconds.
		DTC 45 - Oxygen Sensor (O2S) Circuit (Rich Exhaust Indicated)	Sets if oxygen sensor voltage remains greater than 0.7 volt for about 1 minute.

84904066

Fig. 84 Fuel injected engine trouble codes through 1995 with 4L60E transmissions

DIAGNOSTIC TROUBLE CODE (DTC) IDENTIFICATION

The MIL (Service Engine Soon) will only be "ON" if the malfunction exists with the conditions listed below. If the malfunction clears, the lamp will go out and the DTC will be stored in the PCM. Any DTCs stored will be erased if no problem reoccurs within 50 engine starts.

DTC AND CIRCUIT	PROBABLE CAUSE	DTC AND CIRCUIT	PROBABLE CAUSE
DTC 51 - Faulty PROM (MEM-CAL) Problem	Faulty PROM (MEM-CAL) or PCM.	*DTC 69 - TCC Stuck "ON"	Slip>-20 and slip 20 TCC is not locked gear=2, 3 or 4 TPS>25%, not in P/R/N for 4 seconds.
DTC 53 - System Voltage High	System overvoltage of 19.5 volts for 2 seconds	*DTC 72 - Vehicle Speed Sensor Loss	Not in P/N - Output speed changes greater than 1000 RPM • P/N - Output speed changes greater than - 2050 RPM • For 2 seconds
DTC 54 - Fuel Pump Circuit (Low Voltage)	Sets when the fuel pump voltage is less than 2 volts when reference pulses are being received.	*DTC 73 - Pressure Control Solenoid	If return amperage varies more than 0.16 amps. from commanded amperage
DTC 55 - Faulty PCM	Faulty PCM.	*DTC 75 - System Voltage Low	System voltage <7.3 at low temperature or <11.7 at high temperature for 4 seconds.
*DTC 58 - Transmission Fluid Temperature High	Transmission fluid temperature greater than 154°C (309°F) for one second.	*DTC 79 - Transmission Fluid Over Temperature	Transmission fluid Temperature >150°C and <154°C for 15 minutes.
*DTC 59 - Transmission Fluid Temperature Low	Transmission fluid temperature greater than -33°C (-27°F) for one second.	*DTC 81 - 2-3 Shift Solenoid Circuit Fault	2-3 shift solenoid is command "ON", and circuit voltage is high for two seconds OR 2-3 shift solenoid is command "OFF", and circuit voltage is low for two seconds.
*DTC 66 - 3-2 Control Solenoid Circuit Fault	At High Duty Cycle the circuit voltage is high OR at Low Duty Cycle the Circuit Voltage is low for four seconds.	*DTC 82 - 1-2 Shift Solenoid Circuit Fault	1-2 shift solenoid is command "ON," and circuit voltage is high for two seconds. OR 1-2 shift solenoid is command "OFF"and circuit voltage is low for two seconds.
*DTC 67 Torque Converter Clutch Circuit	TCC is commanded "ON"and circuit voltage remains high for two seconds OR TCC is commanded "OFF"and circuit voltage remains low for two seconds.		

84904067

Fig. 85 Fuel injected engine trouble codes through 1995 with 4L60E transmissions (continued)

DIAGNOSTIC TROUBLE CODE IDENTIFICATION

The MIL (Service Engine Soon) will only be "ON" if the malfunction exists with the conditions listed below. If the malfunction clears, the lamp will go out and the DTC will be stored in the PCM. Any DTCs stored will be erased if no problem reoccurs within 50 engine starts. Note: All DTC(S) with the sign * are transmission related DTC(S).

Remember, always start with the lowest numerical DTC first, when diagnosing some engine DTC(S) trigger other transmission DTC(S).

DTC AND CIRCUIT	PROBABLE CAUSE	DTC AND CIRCUIT	PROBABLE CAUSE
DTC 13 - Oxygen Sensor O2S Circuit (Open Circuit)	Indicates that the oxygen sensor circuit or sensor was open for one minute while off idle.	DTC 33 - Manifold Absolute Pressure (MAP) Sensor Circuit (Signal Voltage High - Low Vacuum)	MAP sensor output to high for 5 seconds or an open signal circuit.
DTC 14 - Engine Coolant Temperature (ECT) Sensor Circuit (High Temperature Indicated)	Signal voltage has been greater than 151°C (304°F) for 1 second.	DTC 34 - Manifold Absolute Pressure (MAP) Sensor Circuit (Signal Voltage Low - High Vacuum)	Low or no output from sensor with engine operating.
DTC 15 - Engine Coolant Temperature (ECT) Sensor Circuit (Low Temperature Indicated)	Signal voltage has been less than -37°C (-34°F) for 1 second.	DTC 39 - TCC Stuck "OFF"	
DTC 21 - Throttle Position (TP) Sensor Circuit (Signal Voltage High)	If signal voltage has been greater than 4.9 volts for 1 second.	DTC 42 - Ignition Control (IC)	PCM has an open or grounded IC or bypass circuit.
DTC 22 - Throttle Position (TP) Sensor Circuit (Signal Voltage Low)	DTC 22 will set if TP signal voltage is less than .2 volt for more than 1 second.	DTC 43 - Knock Sensor (KS) Circuit	Signal to the PCM has remained low for too long or the system has failed a functional check.
DTC 24 - Vehicle Speed Sensor (VSS)	With input speed at least 3000 RPM, output speed must read less than 200 RPM for 1.5 seconds.	DTC 44 - Oxygen Sensor O2S Circuit (Lean Exhaust Indicated)	Sets if oxygen sensor voltage remains less than .2 volt for 20 seconds.
DTC 28 - Fluid Pressure Switch Assembly*		DTC 45 - Oxygen Sensor O2S Circuit (Rich Exhaust Indicated)	Sets if oxygen sensor voltage remains greater than .7 volt for 1 minute.
DTC 32 - Exhaust Gas Recirculation (EGR) System	Vacuum switch shorted to ground on start up OR Switch not closed after the PCM has commanded EGR for a specified period of time OR EGR solenoid circuit open for a specified period of time.	DTC 51 - Faulty PROM (MEM-CAL) Problem	Faulty PROM or PCM.
		DTC 53 - System Over Voltage	Generator voltage is greater than 19.5 volts for 2 seconds.
		DTC 54 - Fuel Pump Circuit (Low Voltage)	Sets when the fuel pump voltage is less than 2 volts when reference pulses are being received.
		DTC 55 - Faulty PCM	Faulty PCM.

84904068

Fig. 86 Fuel injected engine trouble codes through 1995 with 4L80E transmissions

DIAGNOSTIC TROUBLE CODE IDENTIFICATION (Continued)

The MIL (Service Engine Soon) will only be "ON" if the malfunction exists with the conditions listed below. If the malfunction clears, the lamp will go out and the DTC will be stored in the PCM. Any DTCs stored will be erased if no problem reoccurs within 50 engine starts. Note: All DTC(S) with the sign * are transmission related DTC(S).

Remember, always start with the lowest numerical DTC first, when diagnosing some engine DTC(S) trigger other transmission DTC(S).

DTC AND CIRCUIT	PROBABLE CAUSE	DTC AND CIRCUIT	PROBABLE CAUSE
DTC 58 - Transmission Fluid Temperature High*		DTC 82 - 1-2 Shift Solenoid Circuit Fault*	
DTC 59 - Transmission Fluid Temperature Low*		DTC 83 - TCC Solenoid Circuit Fault*	
DTC 68 - Overdrive Ratio Error*		DTC 85 - Undefined Ratio*	
DTC 73 - Pressure Control Solenoid*		DTC 86 - Low Ratio*	
DTC 75 - System Voltage Low*		DTC 87 - High Ratio*	
DTC 81 - 2-3 Shift Solenoid Circuit Fault*			

84904069

Fig. 87 Fuel injected engine trouble codes through 1995 with 4L80E transmissions (continued)

DTC P0101 - Mass Air Flow (MAF) System Performance
DTC P0102 - Mass Air Flow (MAF) Sensor Circuit Low Frequency
DTC P0103 - Mass Air Flow (MAF) Sensor Circuit High Frequency
DTC P0106 - Manifold Absolute Pressure (MAP) System Performance
DTC P0107 - Manifold Absolute Pressure (MAP) Sensor Circuit Low Voltage
DTC P0108 - Manifold Absolute Pressure (MAP) Sensor Circuit High Voltage
P0112 - Intake Air Temperature (IAT) Sensor Circuit Low Voltage
P0113 - Intake Air Temperature (IAT) Sensor Circuit High Voltage
P0117 - Engine Coolant Temperature (ECT) Sensor Circuit Low Voltage
P0118 - Engine Coolant Temperature (ECT) Sensor Circuit High Voltage
P0121 - Throttle Position (TP) System Performance
P0122 - Throttle Position (TP) Sensor Circuit Low Voltage
P0123 - Throttle Position (TP) Sensor Circuit High Voltage
P0125 - Engine Coolant Temperature (ECT) Excessive Time to Closed Loop Fuel Control
P0131 - Heated Oxygen Sensor (HO2S) Circuit Low Voltage Bank 1, Sensor 1
P0132 - Heated Oxygen Sensor (HO2S) Circuit High Voltage Bank 1, Sensor 1
P0133 - Heated Oxygen Sensor (HO2S) Slow Response Bank 1, Sensor 1
P0134 - Heated Oxygen Sensor (HO2S) Circuit Insufficient Activity Bank 1, Sensor 1
P0135 - Heated Oxygen Sensor (HO2S) Heater Circuit Bank 1, Sensor 1
P0137 - Heated Oxygen Sensor (HO2S) Circuit Low Voltage Bank 1, Sensor 2
P0138 - Heated Oxygen Sensor (HO2S) Circuit High Voltage Bank 1, Sensor 2
P0140 - Heated Oxygen Sensor (HO2S) Circuit Insufficient Activity Bank 1, Sensor 2
P0141 - Heated Oxygen Sensor (HO2S) Heater Circuit Bank 1, Sensor 2
P0143 - Heated Oxygen Sensor (HO2S) Circuit Low Voltage Bank 1, Sensor 3
P0144 - Heated Oxygen Sensor (HO2S) Circuit High Voltage Bank 1, Sensor 3
P0146 - Heated Oxygen Sensor (HO2S) Circuit Insufficient Activity Bank 1, Sensor 3
P0147 - Heated Oxygen Sensor (HO2S) Heater Circuit Bank 1, Sensor 3
P0151 - Heated Oxygen Sensor (HO2S) Circuit Low Voltage Bank 2, Sensor 1
P0152 - Heated Oxygen Sensor (HO2S) Circuit High Voltage Bank 2, Sensor 1
P0153 - Heated Oxygen Sensor (HO2S) Slow Response Bank 2, Sensor 1
P0154 - Heated Oxygen Sensor (HO2S) Circuit Insufficient Activity Bank 2, Sensor 1
P0155 - Heated Oxygen Sensor (HO2S) Heater Circuit Bank 2, Sensor 1
P0157 - Heated Oxygen Sensor (HO2S) Circuit Low Voltage Bank 2, Sensor 2
P0158 - Heated Oxygen Sensor (HO2S) Circuit High Voltage Bank 2, Sensor 2
P0160 - Heated Oxygen Sensor (HO2S) Circuit Insufficient Activity Bank 2, Sensor 2
P0161 - Heated Oxygen Sensor (HO2S) Heater Circuit Bank 2, Sensor 2
P0171 - Fuel Trim System Lean Bank 1
P0172 - Fuel Trim System Rich Bank 1
P0174 - Fuel Trim System Lean Bank 2
P0175 - Fuel Trim System Rich Bank 2
P0300 - Engine Misfire Detected
P0301 - Cylinder 1 Misfire Detected
P0302 - Cylinder 2 Misfire Detected
P0303 - Cylinder 3 Misfire Detected
P0304 - Cylinder 4 Misfire Detected
P0305 - Cylinder 5 Misfire Detected
P0306 - Cylinder 6 Misfire Detected
P0307 - Cylinder 7 Misfire Detected
P0308 - Cylinder 8 Misfire Detected
P0325 - Knock Sensor (KS) Module Circuit
P0327 - Knock Sensor (KS) Circuit Low Voltage
P0336 - Crankshaft Position (CKP) Sensor Circuit Performance
P0337 - Crankshaft Position (CKP) Sensor Circuit Low Frequency
P0338 - Crankshaft Position (CKP) Sensor Circuit High Frequency
P0339 - Crankshaft Position (CKP) Sensor Circuit Intermittent
P0340 - Camshaft Position (CMP) Sensor Circuit
P0341 - Camshaft Position (CMP) Sensor Circuit Performance
P0401 - Exhaust Gas Recirculation (EGR) System
P0410 - AIR System
P0420 - Three Way Catalytic Converter (TWC) System Low Efficiency Bank 1
P0430 - Three Way Catalytic Converter (TWC) System Low Efficiency Bank 2
P0441 - Evaporative Emission (EVAP) System No Flow During Purge

87984g50

Fig. 88 Trouble code list for 1996 gasoline engines

P0500 - Vehicle Speed Sensor (VSS) Circuit
P0506 - Idle System Low - Idle Air Control (IAC) Responding
P0507 - Idle System High - Idle Air Control (IAC) Responding
P1106 - Manifold Absolute Pressure (MAP) Sensor Circuit Intermittent High Voltage
P1107 - Manifold Absolute Pressure (MAP) Sensor Circuit Intermittent Low Voltage
P1111 - Intake Air Temperature (IAT) Sensor Circuit Intermittent High Voltage
P1112 - Intake Air Temperature (IAT) Sensor Circuit Intermittent Low Voltage
P1114 - Engine Coolant Temperature (ECT) Sensor Circuit Intermittent Low Voltage
P1115 - Engine Coolant Temperature (ECT) Sensor Circuit Intermittent High Voltage
P1121 - Throttle Position (TP) Sensor Circuit Intermittent High Voltage
P1122 - Throttle Position (TP) Sensor Circuit Intermittent Low Voltage
P1133 - Heated Oxygen Sensor (HO2S) Insufficient Switching Bank 1, Sensor 1
P1134 - Heated Oxygen Sensor (HO2S) Transitior Time Ratio Bank 1, Sensor 1
P1153 - Heated Oxygen Sensor (HO2S) Insufficient Switching Bank 2, Sensor 1
P1154 - Heated Oxygen Sensor (HO2S) Transitior Time Ratio Bank 2, Sensor 1
P1345 - Crankshaft Position/Camshaft Position (CKP/CMP) Correlation
P1351 - Ignition Control (IC) Circuit High Voltage
P1361 - Ignition Control (IC) Circuit Low Voltage
P1380 - Electronic Brake Control Module (EBCM) DTC Detected - Rough Road Data Unusable
P1381 - Misfire Detected - No Electronic Brake Control Module (EBCM) VCM Serial Data
P1406 - Exhaust Gas Recirculation (EGR) Valve Pintle Position Circuit
P1415 - AIR System Bank 1
P1416 - AIR System Bank 2
P1441 - Evaporative Emission (EVAP) System Flow During Non-Purge
P1508 - Idle Air Control (IAC) System Low RPM
P1509 - Idle Air Control (IAC) System High RPM

87984g51

Fig. 89 Trouble code list for 1996 gasoline engines (continued)

CODE IDENTIFICATION

The "Service Engine Soon" light will only be "ON" if the malfunction exists under the conditions listed below. If the malfunction clears, the light will go out and the code will be stored in the ECM. Any Codes stored will be erased if no problem reoccurs within 50 engine starts.

CODE AND CIRCUIT	PROBABLE CAUSE
Code 12 - No engine speed reference pulse.	No engine speed sensor reference pulses to the ECM. This code is not stored in memory and will only flash while the fault is present. Normal code with ignition "ON," engine not running.
Code 14 - Coolant Sensor High Temperature Indication	Sets if the sensor or signal line becomes grounded for 5 minutes.
Code 15 - Coolant Sensor Low Temperature Indication	Sets if the sensor, connections, or wires open for 5 minutes.
Code 21 - TPS Signal Voltage High	Throttle Position Sensor (TPS) circuit voltage high (open circuit or misadjusted TPS). Engine must run 30 seconds, at curb idle speed, before this code will set.
Code 22 - TPS Signal Voltage Low	Throttle Position Sensor (TPS) circuit voltage low (grounded circuit). Engine must run 2 minutes at 1250 rpm or above before this code will set.
Code 23 - TPS Not Calibrated	Throttle Position Sensor (TPS) circuit. Voltage not between .25 and 1.3 volts at curb idle speed Engine must run for 30 seconds, at curb idle, before this code will set.
Code 24 - VSS No Vehicle Speed Indication	Vehicle speed sensor (VSS) circuit (open or grounded circuit). Vehicle must operate at road speed for 10 seconds before this code will set.
Code 31 - MAP Sensor Too Low	Absolute Pressure (MAP) circuit signal voltage too low. Engine must run at curb idle for 10 seconds before this code will set
Code 32 - EGR Loop Error	Exhaust Gas Recirculation (EGR) vacuum circuit has seen improper EGR vacuum Vehicle must be running at road speed approximately 30 mph (48 Km/h) for 10 seconds before this code will set.
Code 33 - MAP Sensor Too High	Absolute Pressure (MAP) circuit signal voltage too high. Engine must run at curb idle for 10 seconds before this code will set.
Code 51 - PROM	Faulty or improperly installed PROM. It takes approximately 10 seconds before this code will set.
Code 52 - ECM	Fault in ECM circuit. It takes 10 seconds before this code will set.
Code 53 - Five volt Reference Overload	5 volt reference (Vref) circuit overloaded (grounded circuit). It takes 10 seconds before this Code will set.

87984g55

Fig. 90 Trouble code list for 1988-93 diesel engines with manual transmissions and 1988-90 diesel engines with automatic transmissions

DIAGNOSTIC TROUBLE CODE (DTC) IDENTIFICATION

The MIL (Service Engine Soon) will only be "ON" if the malfunction exists with the conditions listed below. If the malfunction clears, the lamp will go out and the DTC will be stored in the PCM. Any DTCs stored will be erased if no problem reoccurs within 50 engine starts. Note: All DTCs with the sign * are transmission related DTCs.

Remember, always start with the lowest numerical DTC first, when diagnosing some engine DTCs trigger other transmission DTCs.

DTC AND CIRCUIT	PROBABLE CAUSE
DTC 14 - Engine Coolant Temperature (ECT) Sensor Circuit (High Temperature Indicated	Sets if the sensor or signal line becomes grounded or greater than 145°C (294°F) for 0.5 seconds.
DTC 15 - Engine Coolant Temperature (ECT) Sensor Circuit (Low Temperature Indicated)	Sets if the sensor, connections, or wires open or less than -33°C (-27°F) for 0.5 seconds.
DTC 16 - Transmission Output Speed Signal Low	Open in CKT 1716 or power loss to VSS buffer module.
DTC 21 - Throttle Position (TP) Sensor Circuit (Signal Voltage High)	TP voltage greater than 4.88 volts 4 seconds with less than 1200 RPM.
DTC 22 - Throttle Position (TP) Sensor Circuit (Signal Voltage Low)	A short to ground,open signal circuit, or TP voltage less than 0.16 volts for 4 seconds.
DTC 23 - Throttle Position (TP) Sensor Not Calibrated	Throttle Position TP sensor circuit voltage not between .25 and 1.3 volts at curb idle speed. Engine must run for 30 seconds, at curb idle, before this DTC will set.
*DTC 24 - Vehicle Speed Sensor (VSS) Signal Low	No vehicle speed sensor signal present during a road load decel.
*DTC 28 - Fluid Pressure Switch Assembly	PCM detects 1 of 2 invalid combinations of the fluid pressure switch range signals.
DTC 31 - MAP Sensor too low	MAP Sensor signal voltage too low. Engine must run at curb idle for 10 seconds before this DTC will set.
DTC 32 - Exhaust Gas Recirculation (EGR) System Error	Exhaust Gas Recirculation (EGR) vacuum circuit has seen improper EGR vacuum. Vehicle must be running at road speed approximately 30 mph (48 Km/h) for 10 seconds before this DTC will set.
DTC 33 - Manifold Absolute Pressure (MAP) Sensor Circuit (Signal Voltage High - Low Vacuum)	MAP sensor output high for 5 seconds or an open signal circuit.
*DTC 37 - Brake Switch Stuck On	With no voltage and vehicle speed is less than 5 mph for 6 seconds, then vehicle speed is 5 - 20 MPH for 6 seconds, then vehicle speed is greater than 20 MPH for 6 seconds, this must occur for 7 times.
*DTC 38 - Brake Switch Stuck Off	With voltage and vehicle speed is greater than 20 MPH for 6 seconds, then vehicle speed is 5 - 20 MPH for 6 seconds. This must occur 7 times.

87984g56

Fig. 91 Trouble code list for 1991-93 diesel engines with 4L60E automatic transmissions

DIAGNOSTIC TROUBLE CODE (DTC) IDENTIFICATION

The MIL (Service Engine Soon) will only be "ON" if the malfunction exists with the conditions listed below. If the malfunction clears, the lamp will go out and the DTC will be stored in the PCM. Any DTCs stored will be erased if no problem reoccurs within 50 engine starts. Note: All DTCs with the sign * are transmission related DTCs.

Remember, always start with the lowest numerical DTC first, when diagnosing some engine DTCs trigger other transmission DTCs.

DTC AND CIRCUIT	PROBABLE CAUSE
DTC 51 - Faulty PROM Problem	Faulty PROM or PCM.
*DTC 52 - Long System Voltage High	Generator Voltage is greater than 16V for 109 minutes.
*DTC 53 - System Voltage High	System overvoltage of 19.5 volts for 2 seconds
DTC 55 - Faulty PCM	Faulty PCM.
*DTC 58 - Transmission Fluid Temperature High	Transmission fluid temperature greater than 154°C (309°F) for one second.
*DTC 59 - Transmission Fluid Temperature Low	Transmission fluid temperature greater than -33°C (-27°F) for one second.
*DTC 66 - 3-2 Control Solenoid Circuit Fault	At High Duty Cycle the circuit voltage is high OR at Low Duty Cycle the Circuit Voltage is low for four seconds.
*DTC 67 Torque Converter Clutch Circuit	TCC is commanded "ON"and circuit voltage remains high for two seconds OR TCC is commanded "OFF"and circuit voltage remains low for two seconds.
*DTC 69 - TCC Stuck "ON"	Slip > -20 and slip 20 TCC is not locked gear = 2, 3 or 4 TPS > 25%, not in P/R/N for 4 seconds.
*DTC 72 - Vehicle Speed Sensor Loss	Not in P/N - Output speed changes greater than 1000 RPM • P/N - Output speed changes greater than - 2050 RPM • For 2 seconds
*DTC 73 - Pressure Control Solenoid	If return amperage varies more than 0.16 amps. from commanded amperage
*DTC 75 - System Voltage Low	System voltage < 7.3 at low temperature or < 11.7 at high temperature for 4 seconds.
*DTC 79 - Transmission Fluid Over Temperature	Transmission fluid Temperature > 150C and < 154C for 15 minutes.
*DTC 81 - 2-3 Shift Solenoid Circuit Fault	2-3 shift solenoid is command "ON", and circuit voltage is high for two seconds OR 2-3 shift solenoid is command "OFF", and circuit voltage is low for two seconds.
*DTC 82 - 1-2 Shift Solenoid Circuit Fault	1-2 shift solenoid is command "ON," and circuit voltage is high for two seconds. OR 1-2 shift solenoid is command "OFF"and circuit voltage is low for two seconds.

87984g57

Fig. 92 Trouble code list for 1991-93 diesel engines with 4L60E automatic transmissions (continued)

DIAGNOSTIC TROUBLE CODE (DTC) IDENTIFICATION

The MIL (Malfunction Indicator Lamp) will be "ON" if an emission malfunction exists. If the malfunction clears, the lamp will go "OFF" and the DTC will be stored in the PCM. Any DTC(s) stored will be cleared if no problem recurs within 50 engine starts.

Important

All DTC(s) with the sign * are transmission related DTC(s).
Remember, always start with the lowest numerical engine DTC first. When diagnosing some engine DTC(s), other transmission symptoms can occur.

DTC NUMBER AND NAME	DTC NUMBER AND NAME
DTC 13 - Engine Shutoff Solenoid Circuit Fault	* **DTC 28** - Trans Range Pressure Switch Circuit
DTC 14 - Engine Coolant Temperature (ECT) Sensor Circuit Low (High Temperature Indicated)	**DTC 29** - Glow Plug Relay Fault
DTC 15 - Engine Coolant Temperature (ETC) Sensor Circuit High (Low Temperature Indicated)	**DTC 31** - EGR Control Pressure/Baro Sensor Circuit Low (High Vacuum)
DTC 16 - Vehicle Speed Sensor Buffer Fault	**DTC 32** - EGR Circuit Error
DTC 17 - High Resolution Circuit Fault	**DTC 33** - EGR Control Pressure/Baro Sensor Circuit High
DTC 18 - Pump Cam Reference Pulse Error	**DTC 34** - Injection Timing Stepper Motor Fault
DTC 19 - Crankshaft Position Reference Error	**DTC 35** - Injection Pulse Width Error (Response Time Short)
DTC 21 - Accelerator Pedal Position 1 Circuit High	**DTC 36** - Injection Pulse Width Error (Response Time Long)
DTC 22 - Accelerator Pedal Position 1 Circuit Low	* **DTC 37** - TCC Brake Switch Stuck "ON"
DTC 23 - Accelerator Pedal Position 1 Circuit Range Fault	* **DTC 38** - TCC Brake Switch Stuck Stuck "OFF"
* **DTC 24** - Vehicle Speed Sensor Circuit Low (Output Speed Signal)	**DTC 41** - Brake Switch Circuit Fault
DTC 25 - Accelerator Pedal Position 2 Circuit High	**DTC 42** - Fuel Temperature Circuit Low (High Temp Indicated)
DTC 26 - Accelerator Pedal Position 2 Circuit Low	**DTC 43** - Fuel Temperature Circuit High (Low Temp Indicated)
DTC 27 - Accelerator Pedal Position 2 Circuit Range Fault	**DTC 44** - EGR Pulse Width Error
	DTC 45 - EGR Vent Error
	DTC 46 - Malfunction Indicator Lamp Circuit Fault

87984g58

Fig. 93 Trouble code list for 1994-95 diesel engines

DIAGNOSTIC TROUBLE CODE (DTC) IDENTIFICATION

The MIL (Malfunction Indicator Lamp) will be "ON" if an emission malfunction exists. If the malfunction clears, the lamp will go "OFF" and the DTC will be stored in the PCM. Any DTC(s) stored will be cleared if no problem recurs within 50 engine starts.

Important

All DTC(s) with the sign * are transmission related DTC(s).
Remember, always start with the lowest numerical engine DTC first. When diagnosing some engine DTC(s), other transmission symptoms can occur.

DTC NUMBER AND NAME	DTC NUMBER AND NAME
DTC 47 - Intake Air Temperature Sensor Circuit Low (High Temp Indicated)	* **DTC 72** - Vehicle Speed Sensor Circuit Loss (Output Speed Signal)
DTC 48 - Intake Air Temperature Sensor Circuit High (Low Temp Indicated)	* **DTC 73** - Pressure Control Solenoid Circuit
DTC 49 - Service Throttle Soon Lamp Circuit Fault	* **DTC 75** - System Voltage Low
DTC 51 - PROM Error	**DTC 76** - Resume/Accel Switch Fault
* **DTC 52** - System Voltage High Long	* **DTC 79** - Trans Fluid Overtemp
* **DTC 53** - System Voltage High	* **DTC 81** - 2-3 Shift Solenoid Circuit
DTC 56 - Injection Pump Calibration Resistor Error	* **DTC 82** - 1-2 Shift Solenoid Circuit
* **DTC 57** - PCM 5 Volt Shorted	**DTC 88** - TDC Offset Error
* **DTC 58** - Trans Fluid Temp Circuit Low	**DTC 91** - Cylinder Balance Fault #1 Cyl
* **DTC 59** - Trans Fluid Temp Circuit High	**DTC 92** - Cylinder Balance Fault #2 Cyl
DTC 63 - Accelerator Pedal Position 3 Circuit High	**DTC 93** - Cylinder Balance Fault #3 Cyl
DTC 64 - Accelerator Pedal Position 3 Circuit Low	**DTC 94** - Cylinder Balance Fault #4 Cyl
DTC 65 - Accelerator Pedal Position 3 Circuit Range Fault	**DTC 95** - Cylinder Balance Fault #5 Cyl
* **DTC 66** - 3-2 Control Solenoid Circuit	**DTC 96** - Cylinder Balance Fault #6 Cyl
* **DTC 67** - TCC Solenoid Circuit	**DTC 97** - Cylinder Balance Fault #7 Cyl
* **DTC 69** - TCC Stuck "ON"	**DTC 98** - Cylinder Balance Fault #8 Cyl
DTC 71 - Set/Coast Switch Fault	**DTC 99** - Accelerator Pedal Position 2 (5 Bolt Reference Fault)

87984g59

Fig. 94 Trouble code list for 1994-95 diesel engines (continued)

DTC	Description	Illuminate MIL
P0112	IAT Sensor Circuit Low Voltage	Yes
P0113	IAT Sensor Circuit High Voltage	Yes
P0117	ECT Sensor Circuit Low Voltage	Yes
P0118	ECT Sensor Circuit High Voltage	Yes
P0121	APP Sensor 1 Circuit Performance	No
P0122	APP Sensor 1 Circuit Low Voltage	No
P0123	APP Sensor 1 Circuit High Voltage	No
P0182	Fuel Temperature Sensor Circuit Low Voltage	Yes
P0183	Fuel Temperature Sensor Circuit High Voltage	Yes
P0215	Engine Shutoff Control Circuit	No
P0216	Injection Timing Control System	Yes
P0219	Engine Overspeed Condition	No
P0220	APP Sensor 2 Circuit	No
P0221	APP Sensor 2 Circuit Performance	No
P0222	APP Sensor 2 Circuit Low Voltage	No
P0223	APP Sensor 2 Circuit High Voltage	No
P0225	APP Sensor 3 Circuit	No
P0226	APP Sensor 3 Circuit Performance	No
P0227	APP Sensor 3 Circuit Low Voltage	No
P0228	APP Sensor 3 Circuit High Voltage	No
P0231	Lift Pump Secondary Circuit Low Voltage	Yes
P0236	TC Boost System	Yes
P0237	TC Boost Sensor Circuit Low Voltage	Yes
P0238	TC Boost Sensor Circuit High Voltage	Yes
P0251	Injection Pump Cam System	Yes
P0263	Cylinder 8 Balance System	No
P0266	Cylinder 7 Balance System	No
P0269	Cylinder 2 Balance System	No
P0272	Cylinder 6 Balance System	No
P0275	Cylinder 5 Balance System	No
P0278	Cylinder 4 Balance System	No
P0281	Cylinder 3 Balance System	No
P0284	Cylinder 1 Balance System	No
P0335	CKP Sensor Circuit Performance	Yes
P0370	Timing Reference High Resolution	Yes
P0380	Glow plug Circuit Performance	Yes
P0404	EGR System	Yes
P0405	EGR Sensor Circuit Low Voltage	Yes

87984g52

Fig. 95 Trouble code list for 1996 diesel engines

DTC	Description	Illuminate MIL
P0406	EGR Sensor Circuit High Voltage	Yes
P0501	Vehicle Speed Sensor Circuit	No
P0567	Cruise Resume Circuit	No
P0568	Cruise Set Circuit	No
P0571	Cruise Brake Switch Circuit	No
P0601	PCM Memory	No
P0602	PCM Not Programmed	No
P0606	PCM Internal Communication Interrupted	Yes
P1125	APP System	No
P1214	Injection Pump Timing Offset	Yes
P1216	Fuel Solenoid Response Time Too Short	No
P1217	Fuel Solenoid Response Time Too Long	No
P1218	Injection Pump Calibration Circuit	Yes
P1627	A/D Performance	Yes
P1635	5 Volt Reference Low	No
P1641	Malfunction Indicator Lamp (MIL) Control Circuit	No
P1653	EGR Vent Solenoid Control Circuit	Yes
P1654	Service Throttle Soon (STS) Lamp Control Circuit	No
P1655	EGR Solenoid Control Circuit	Yes
P1656	Wastegate Solenoid Control Circuit	Yes

87984g53

Fig. 96 Trouble code list for 1996 diesel engines (continued)

COMPONENT LOCATION DIAGRAMS

'C/K' SERIES RPO:LB4 ENGINE CODE:Z 4.3L V6

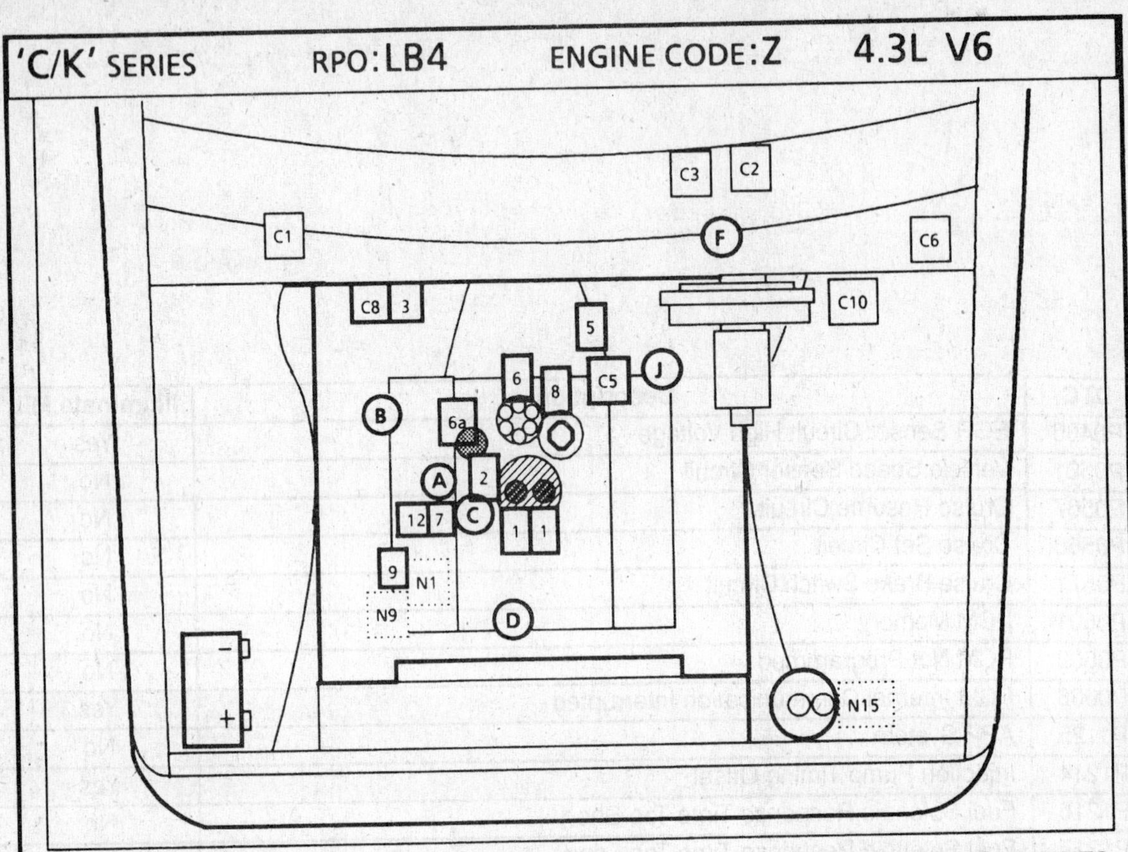

COMPUTER COMMAND CONTROL

- C1 Electronic Control Module (E.C.M.)
- C2 ALDL diagnostic connector
- C3 "SERVICE ENGINE SOON" light
- C5 ECM harness ground
- C6 Fuse panel
- C8 Fuel pump test connector

ECM CONTROLLED COMPONENTS

- 1 Fuel injector
- 2 Idle air control
- 3 Fuel pump relay
- 5 Transmission Converter Clutch Connector
- 6 Electronic Spark Timing Distributor (E.S.T.)
- 6a Remote ignition coil
- 7 Electronic Spark Control module (E.S.C.)
- 8 Oil pressure switch
- 9 Electric Air Control solenoid (E.A.C.)
- 12 Exhaust Gas Recirculation Vacuum Solenoid

ECM INFORMATION SENSORS

- A Manifold Absolute Pressure (M.A.P.)
- B Exhaust oxygen
- C Throttle position (T.P.S.)
- D Coolant temperature
- F Vehicle speed (V.S.S.)
- J Electronic Spark Control Knock (E.S.C.)

EMISSION COMPONENTS (NOT ECM CONTROLLED)

- N1 Crankcase vent valve (PCV)
- N9 Air Pump
- N15 Fuel Vapor Canister

84904042

Fig. 97 Component locations — 1988-90 C/K series with 4.3L engines

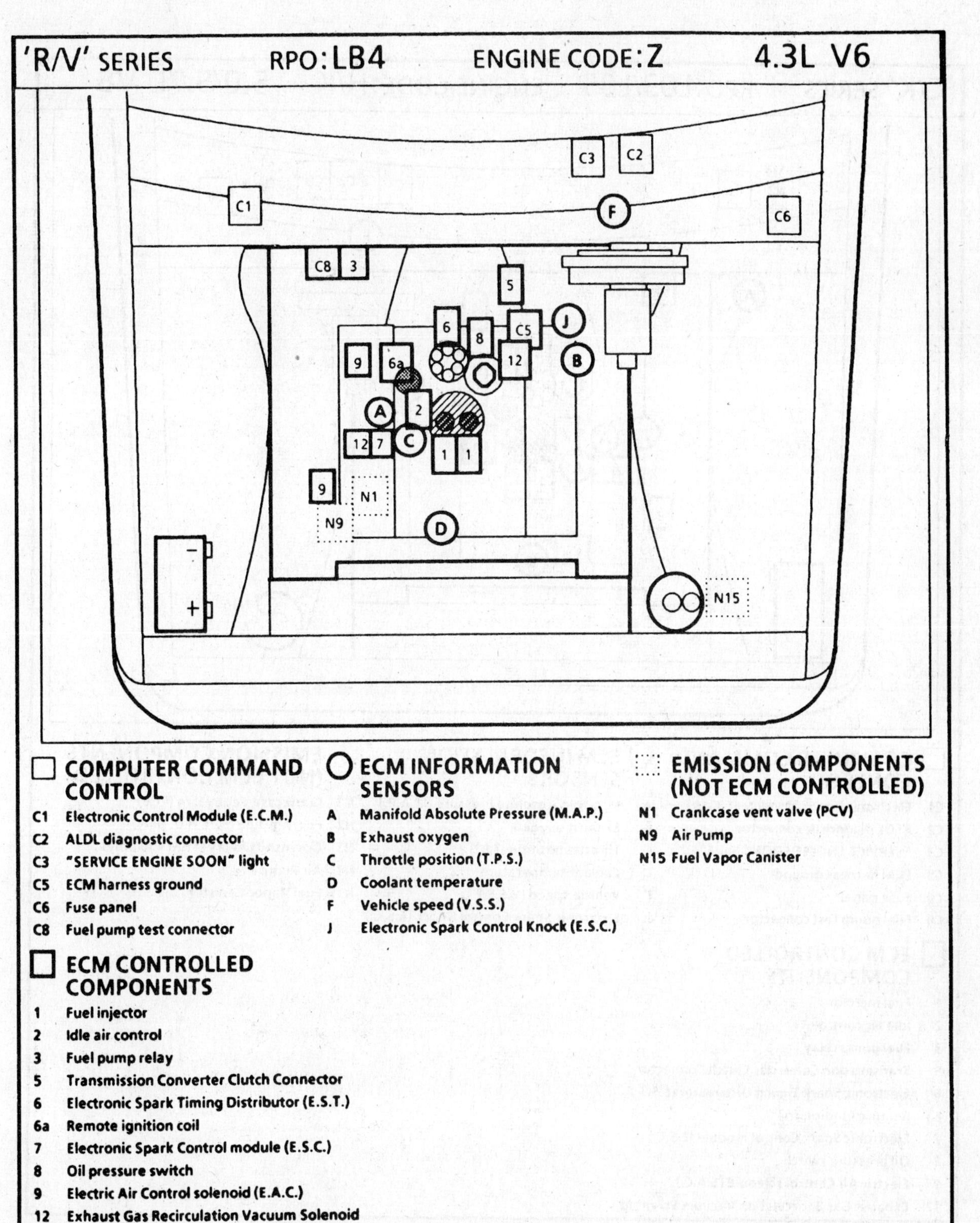

Fig. 98 Component locations — 1988-90 R/V series with 4.3L engines

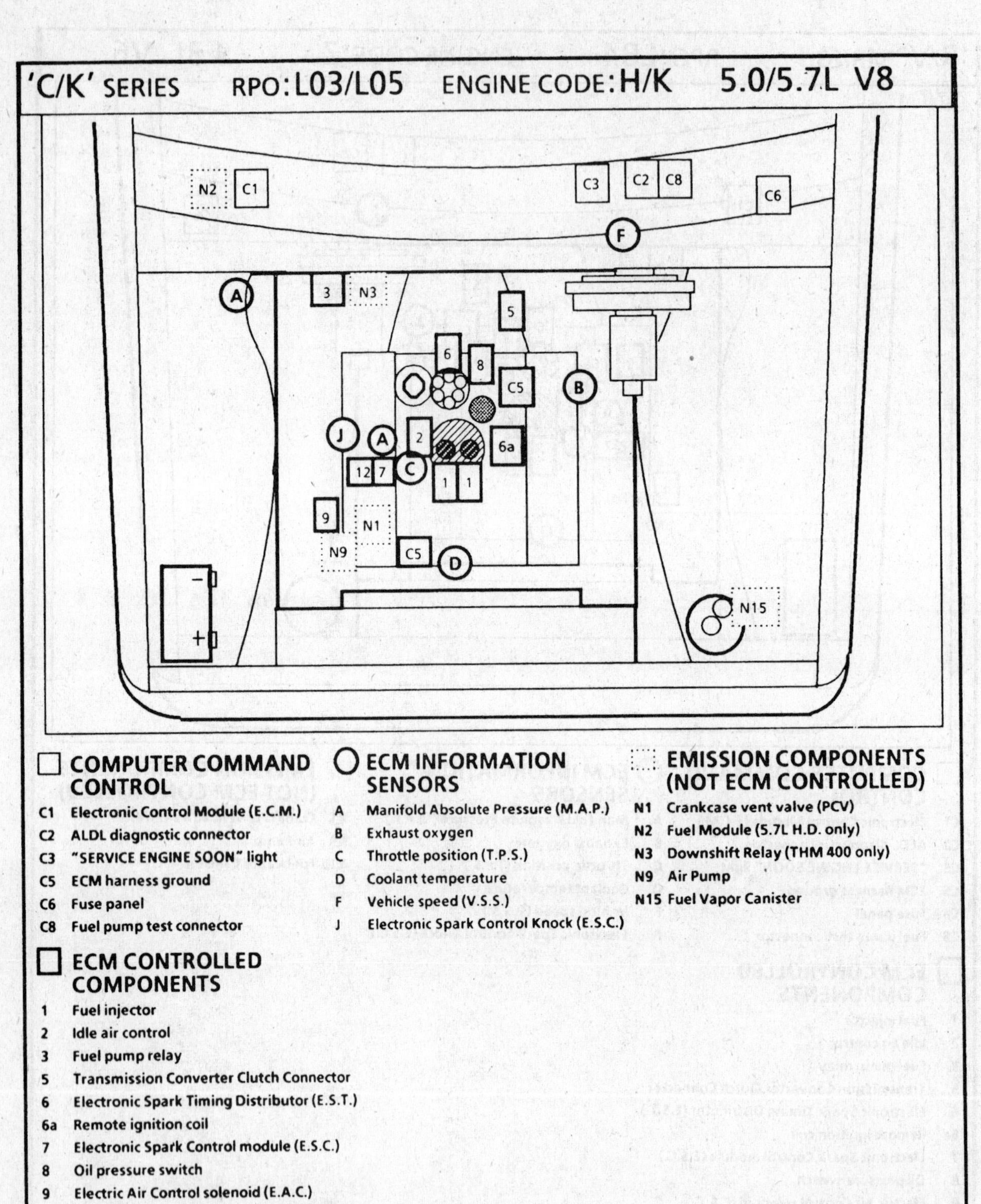

Fig. 99 Component locations — 1988-90 C/K series with 5.0L and 5.7L engines

'R/V' SERIES RPO: L03/L05 ENGINE CODE: H/K 5.0/5.7L V8

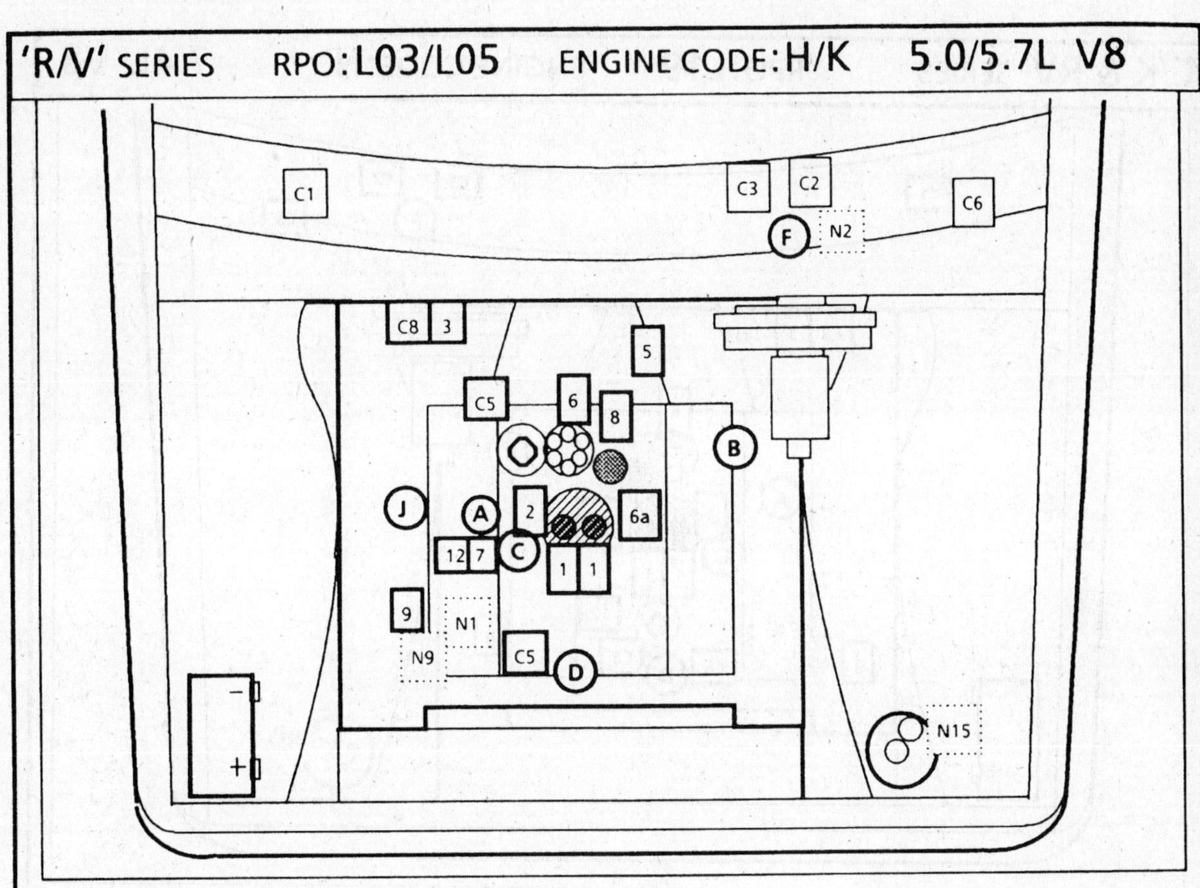

COMPUTER COMMAND CONTROL

C1 Electronic Control Module (E.C.M.)
C2 ALDL diagnostic connector
C3 "SERVICE ENGINE SOON" light
C5 ECM harness ground
C6 Fuse panel
C8 Fuel pump test connector

ECM CONTROLLED COMPONENTS

1 Fuel injector
2 Idle air control
3 Fuel pump relay
5 Transmission Converter Clutch Connector
6 Electronic Spark Timing Distributor (E.S.T.)
6a Remote ignition coil
7 Electronic Spark Control module (E.S.C.)
8 Oil pressure switch
9 Electric Air Control solenoid (E.A.C.)
12 Exhaust Gas Recirculation Vacuum Solenoid

ECM INFORMATION SENSORS

A Manifold Absolute Pressure (M.A.P.)
B Exhaust oxygen
C Throttle position (T.P.S.)
D Coolant temperature
F Vehicle speed (V.S.S.)
J Electronic Spark Control Knock (E.S.C.)

EMISSION COMPONENTS (NOT ECM CONTROLLED)

N1 Crankcase vent valve (PCV)
N2 Fuel Module (5.7L H.D. only)
N9 Air Pump
N15 Fuel Vapor Canister

84904045

Fig. 100 Component locations — 1988-90 R/V series with 5.0L and 5.7L engines

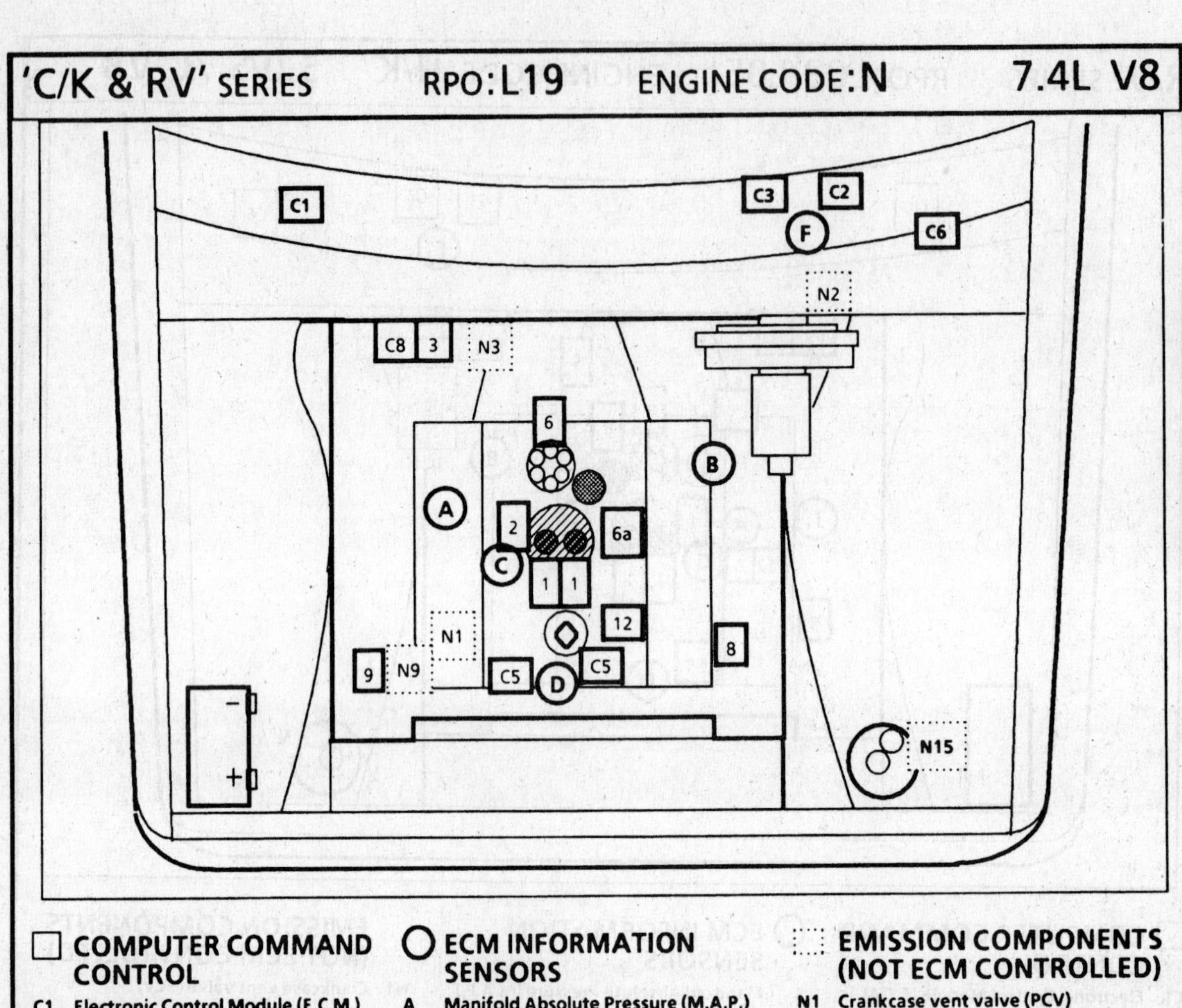

COMPUTER COMMAND CONTROL

C1 Electronic Control Module (E.C.M.)
C2 ALDL diagnostic connector
C3 "SERVICE ENGINE SOON" light
C5 ECM harness ground
C6 Fuse panel
C8 Fuel pump test connector

ECM CONTROLLED COMPONENTS

1 Fuel injector
2 Idle air control
3 Fuel pump relay
6 Electronic Spark Timing Distributor (E.S.T.)
6a Remote ignition coil
8 Oil pressure switch
9 Electric Air Control solenoid (E.A.C.)
12 Exhaust Gas Recirculation Vacuum Solenoid

ECM INFORMATION SENSORS

A Manifold Absolute Pressure (M.A.P.)
B Exhaust oxygen
C Throttle position (T.P.S.)
D Coolant temperature
F Vehicle speed (V.S.S.)

EMISSION COMPONENTS (NOT ECM CONTROLLED)

N1 Crankcase vent valve (PCV)
N2 Fuel Module
N3 Downshift Relay (THM 400 only)
N9 Air Pump
N15 Fuel Vapor Canister

84904046

Fig. 101 Component locations — 1988-90 with 7.4L engines

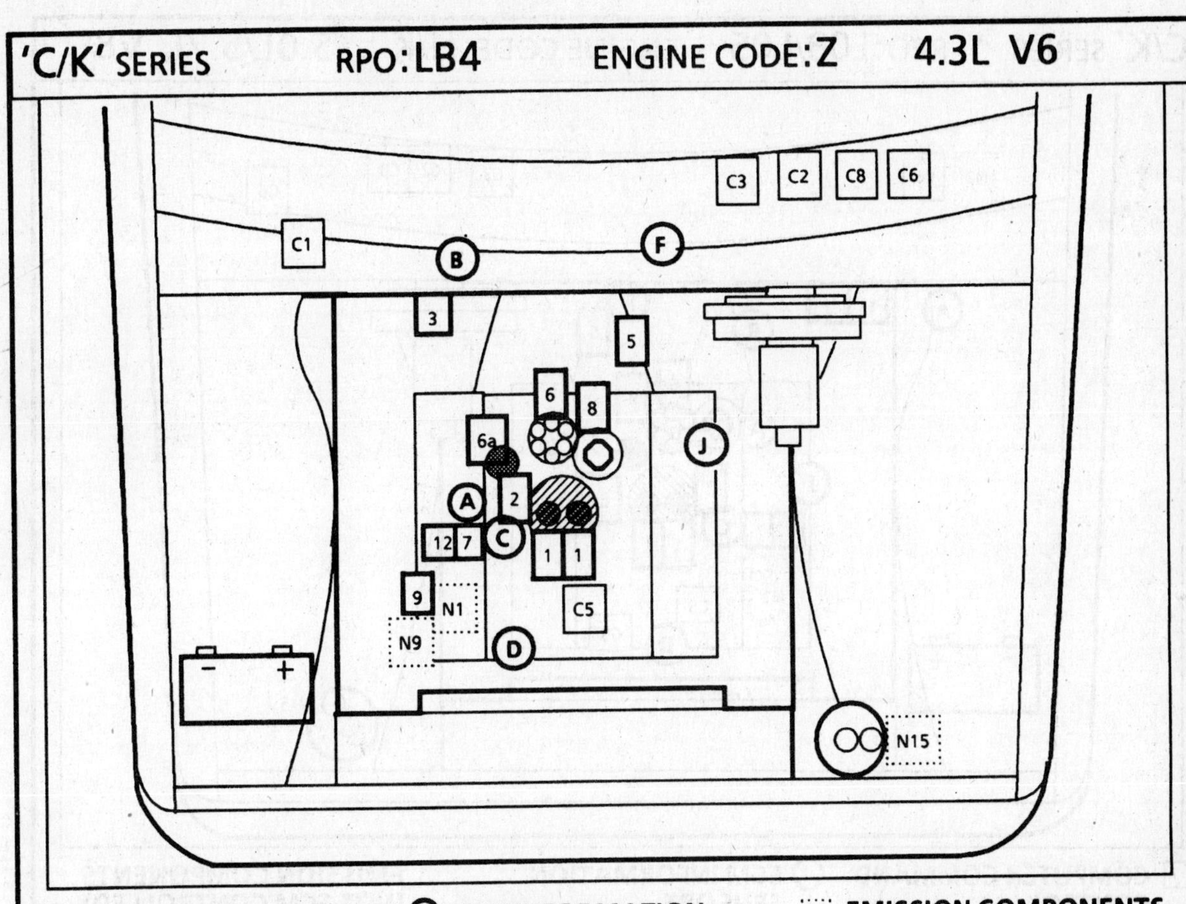

COMPUTER COMMAND CONTROL

- C1 Electronic Control Module (ECM)
- C2 ALDL diagnostic connector
- C3 "SERVICE ENGINE SOON" light
- C5 ECM harness ground
- C6 Fuse block
- C8 Fuel pump test connector

ECM CONTROLLED COMPONENTS

- 1 Fuel injector
- 2 Idle Air Control (IAC)
- 3 Fuel pump relay
- 5 Transmission connector
- 6 Electronic Spark Timing (EST) distributor
- 6a Remote ignition coil
- 7 Electronic Spark Control (ESC) module
- 8 Oil pressure switch
- 9 Electric Air Control (EAC) solenoid
- 12 Exhaust Gas Recirculation (EGR) vacuum solenoid

ECM INFORMATION SENSORS

- A Manifold Absolute Pressure (MAP)
- B Exhaust Oxygen (O_2) sensor
- C Throttle Position Sensor (TPS)
- D Coolant Temperature Sensor (CTS)
- F Vehicle Speed Sensor (VSS)
- J Electronic Spark Control (ESC) knock

EMISSION COMPONENTS (NOT ECM CONTROLLED)

- N1 Crankcase vent valve (PCV)
- N9 Air pump
- N15 Fuel vapor canister

84904047

Fig. 102 Component locations — 1991-92 C/K series with 4.3L engines

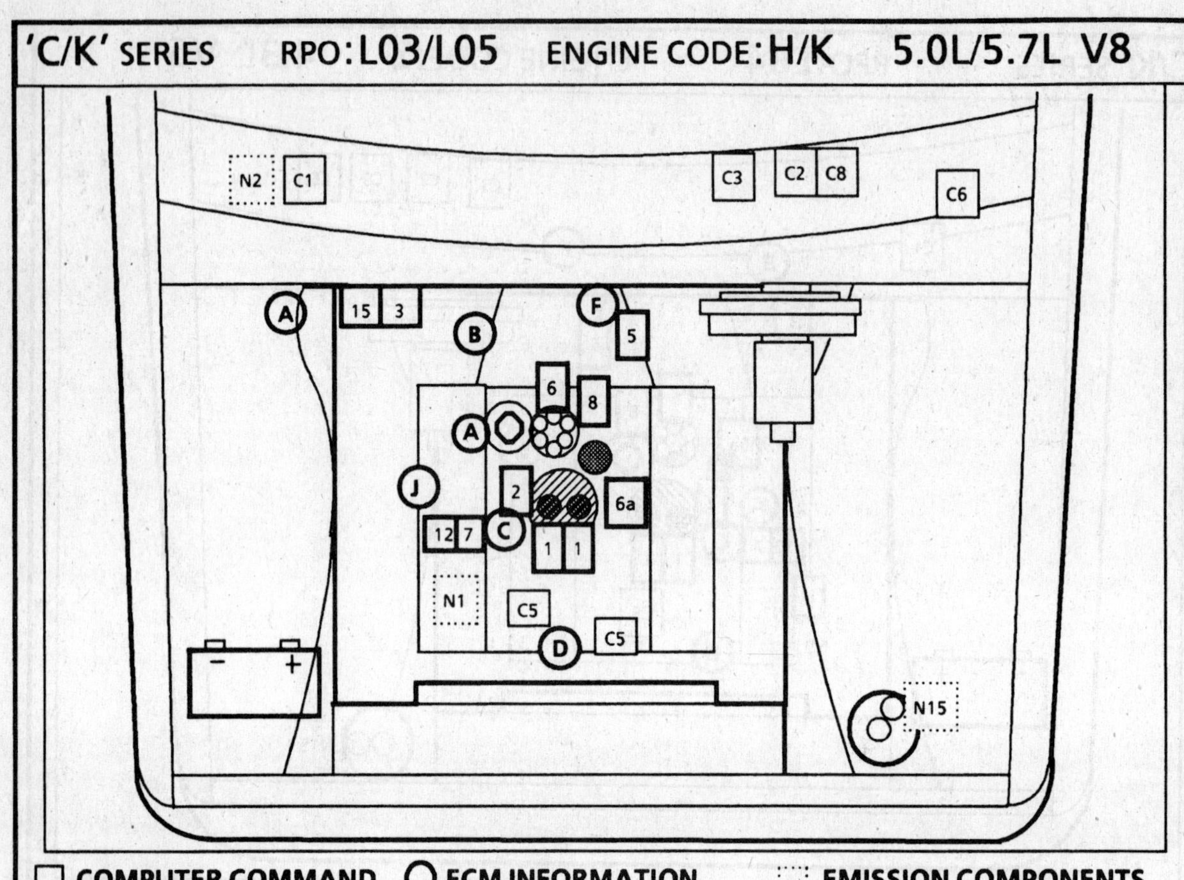

COMPUTER COMMAND CONTROL

- **C1** Electronic Control Module (ECM)
- **C2** ALDL diagnostic connector
- **C3** "SERVICE ENGINE SOON" light
- **C5** ECM harness ground
- **C6** Fuse block
- **C8** Fuel pump test connector

ECM INFORMATION SENSORS

- **A** Manifold Absolute Pressure (MAP)
- **B** Exhaust Oxygen (O_2)
- **C** Throttle Position Sensor (TPS)
- **D** Coolant Temperature Sensor (CTS)
- **F** Vehicle Speed Sensor (VSS)
- **J** Electronic Spark Control (ESC) Knock

EMISSION COMPONENTS (NOT ECM CONTROLLED)

- **N1** Crankcase Vent Valve (PCV)
- **N2** Fuel Module (5.7L H.D. only)
- **N15** Fuel Vapor Canister

ECM CONTROLLED COMPONENTS

- **1** Fuel injector
- **2** Idle Air Control (IAC)
- **3** Fuel pump relay
- **5** Transmission Converter Clutch Connector
- **6** Electronic Spark Timing (EST) Distributor
- **6a** Remote ignition coil
- **7** Electronic Spark Control (ESC) module
- **8** Oil pressure switch
- **12** Exhaust Gas Recirculation (EGR) Vacuum Solenoid
- **12** (EVRV) Vacuum Solenoid (5.7L H.D. only)
- **15** Fuel Pump Fuse

84904048

Fig. 103 Component locations — 1991-92 C/K series with 5.0L or 5.7L engines

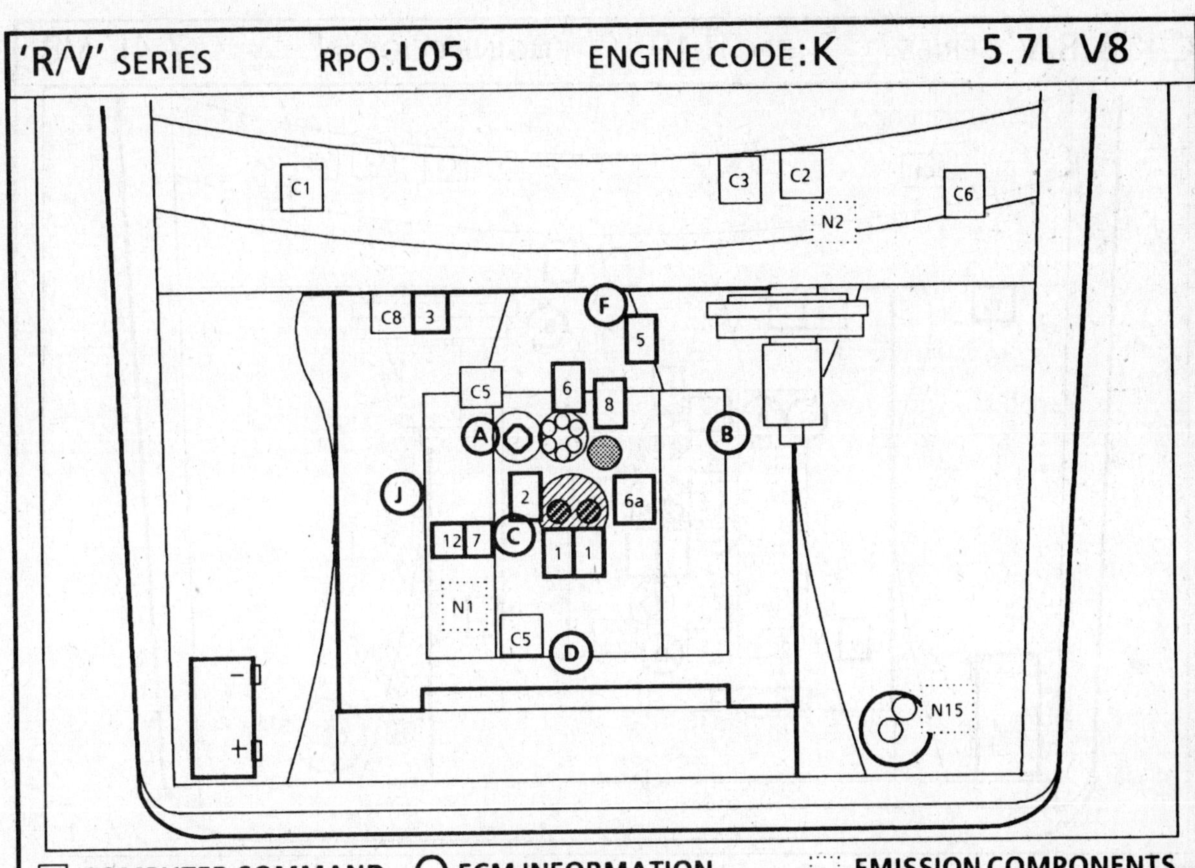

☐ COMPUTER COMMAND CONTROL

- C1 Electronic Control Module (ECM)
- C2 ALDL diagnostic connector
- C3 "SERVICE ENGINE SOON" light
- C5 ECM harness ground
- C6 Fuse panel
- C8 Fuel pump test connector

◯ ECM INFORMATION SENSORS

- A Manifold Absolute Pressure (MAP)
- B Exhaust Oxygen (O_2)
- C Throttle Position Sensor (TPS)
- D Coolant Temperature Sensor (CTS)
- F Vehicle Speed Sensor (VSS)
- J Electronic Spark Control (ESC) Knock

EMISSION COMPONENTS (NOT ECM CONTROLLED)

- N1 Crankcase Vent Valve (PCV)
- N2 Fuel Module (5.7L H.D. only)
- N15 Fuel Vapor Canister

☐ ECM CONTROLLED COMPONENTS

- 1 Fuel injector
- 2 Idle Air Control (IAC)
- 3 Fuel pump relay
- 5 Transmission Converter Clutch Connector
- 6 Electronic Spark Timing Distributor (EST)
- 6a Remote ignition coil
- 7 Electronic Spark Control (ESC) module
- 8 Oil pressure switch
- 12 Exhaust Gas Recirculation (EGR) Vacuum Solenoid

84904049

Fig. 104 Component locations — 1991-92 R/V series with 5.7L engines

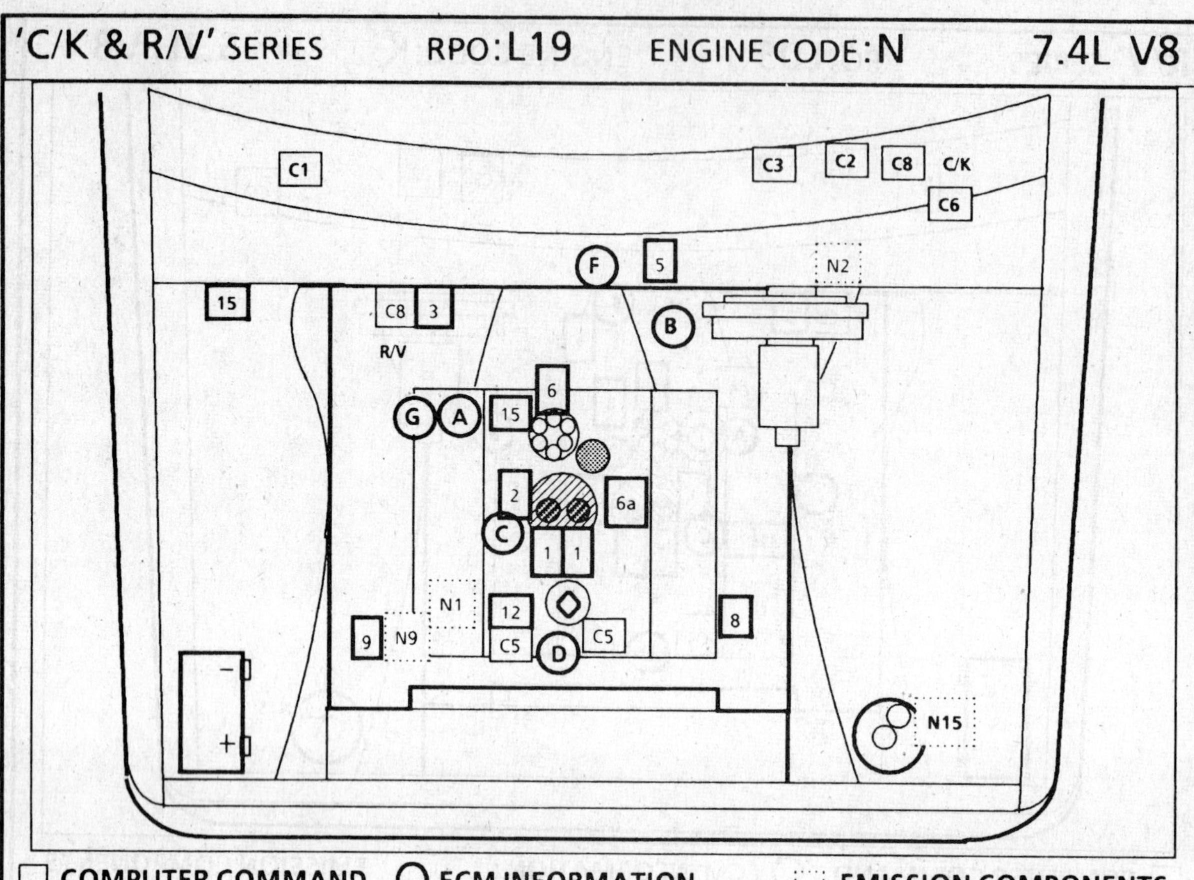

COMPUTER COMMAND CONTROL

- C1 Electronic Control Module (ECM)
- C2 ALDL diagnostic connector
- C3 "SERVICE ENGINE SOON" light
- C5 ECM harness ground
- C6 Fuse panel
- C8 Fuel pump test connector

ECM CONTROLLED COMPONENTS

- 1 Fuel injector
- 2 Idle Air Control (IAC)
- 3 Fuel pump relay
- 5 Trans connector
- 6 Electronic Spark Timing (EST) Distributor
- 6a Remote ignition coil
- 8 Oil pressure switch
- 9 Electric Air Control (EAC) solenoid
- 12 Exhaust Gas Recirculation (EGR) Vacuum Solenoid
- 15 Electronic Spark Control (ESC) Module

ECM INFORMATION SENSORS

- A Manifold Absolute Pressure (MAP)
- B Exhaust Oxygen (O_2) Sensor
- C Throttle Position Sensor (TPS)
- D Coolant Temperature Sensor (CTS)
- F Vehicle Speed Sensor (VSS)
- G Electronic Spark Control (ESC) knock

EMISSION COMPONENTS (NOT ECM CONTROLLED)

- N1 Crankcase Vent Valve (PCV)
- N2 Fuel Module
- N9 Air Pump
- N15 Fuel Vapor Canister

84904050

Fig. 105 Component locations — 1991-92 models with 7.4L engines

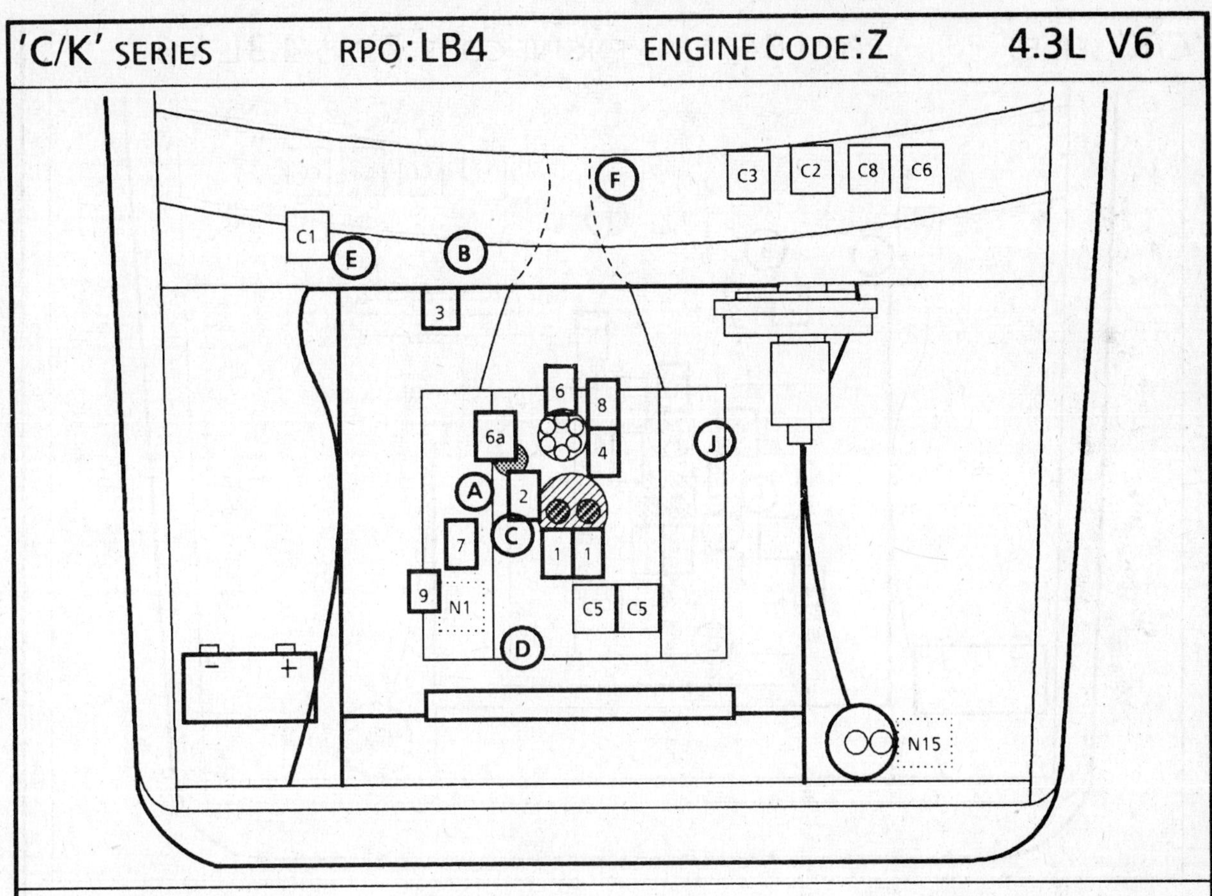

CONTROL MODULE SYSTEM

- C1 Engine Control Module (ECM)
- C2 Data Link Connector (DLC)
- C3 Malfunction Indicator Lamp (MIL)
- C5 ECM harness ground
- C6 Fuse block
- C8 Fuse pump prime terminal "G" of DLC

ECM CONTROLLED COMPONENTS

- 1 Fuel injector
- 2 Idle Air Control (IAC)
- 3 Fuel pump relay
- 4 EGR valve
- 6 Ignition Control (IC) distributor
- 6a Remote ignition coil
- 7 Knock Sensor (KS) Module
- 8 Oil pressure switch
- 9 AIR bypass valve
- 12 Exhaust Gas Recirculation (EGR) Vacuum Solenoid

ECM INFORMATION SENSORS

- A Manifold Absolute Pressure (MAP) sensor
- B Heated Oxygen Sensor (HO2S)
- C Throttle Position (TP) sensor
- D Engine Coolant Temperature (ECT) sensor
- E VSS buffer
- F Vehicle Speed Sensor (VSS)
- J Knock Sensor (KS)

EMISSION COMPONENTS (NOT ECM CONTROLLED)

- N1 Crankcase vent valve
- N15 Fuel vapor canister

84904051

Fig. 106 Component locations — 1993 models with 4.3L engines and MT

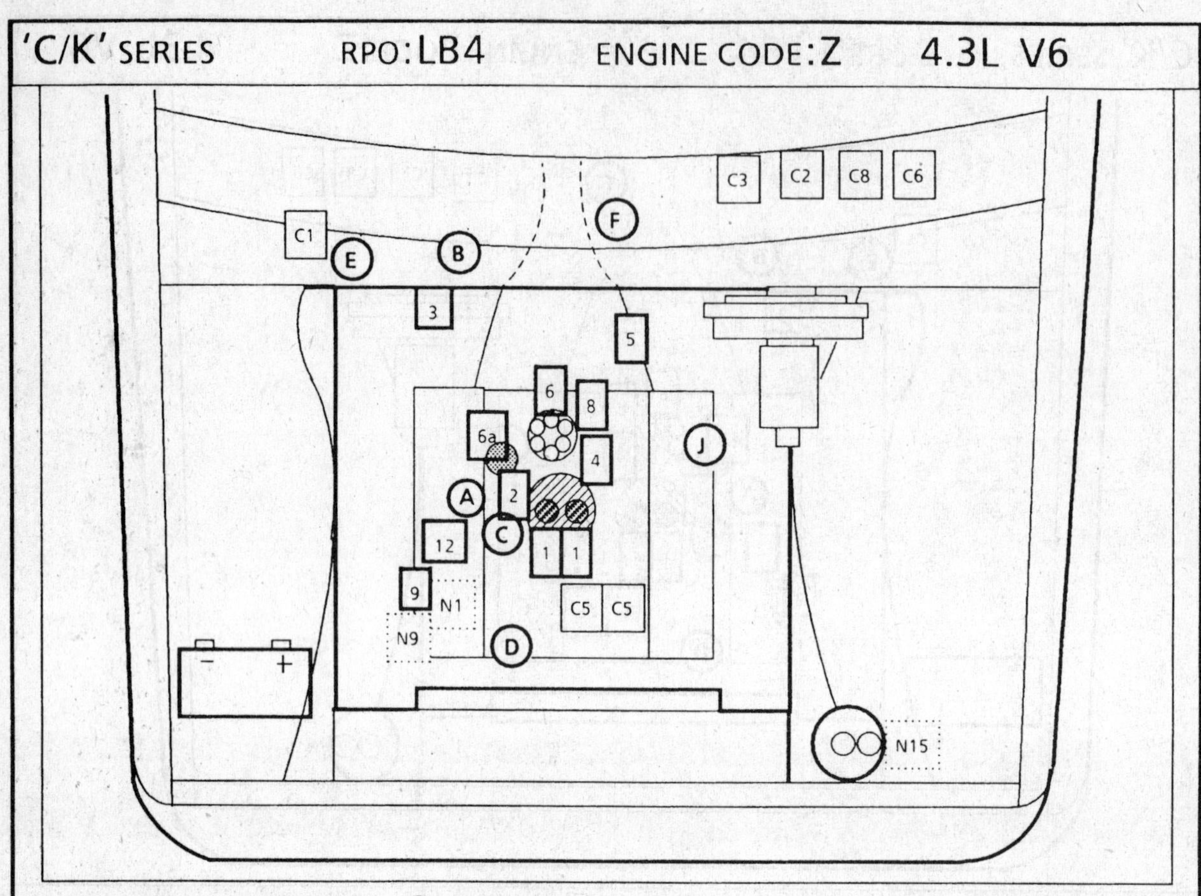

CONTROL MODULE SYSTEM

- C1 Powertrain Control Module (PCM)
- C2 Data Link Connector (DLC)
- C3 Malfunction Indicator Lamp (MIL)
- C5 PCM harness ground
- C6 Fuse block
- C8 Fuel pump test connector

PCM CONTROLLED COMPONENTS

- 1 Fuel injector
- 2 Idle Air Control (IAC)
- 3 Fuel pump relay
- 4 EGR valve
- 5 Transmission connector
- 6 Ignition Control (IC) distributor
- 6a Remote ignition coil
- 8 Oil pressure switch
- 9 AIR bypass valve
- 12 Exhaust Gas Recirculation (EGR) Vacuum Solenoid

PCM INFORMATION SENSORS

- A Manifold Absolute Pressure (MAP) sensor
- B Heated Oxygen Sensor (HO2S)
- C Throttle Position (TP) sensor
- D Engine Coolant Temperature (ECT) sensor
- E VSS buffer
- F Vehicle Speed Sensor (VSS)
- J Knock Sensor (KS)

EMISSION COMPONENTS (NOT PCM CONTROLLED)

- N1 Crankcase vent valve
- N9 AIR pump
- N15 Fuel vapor canister

84904052

Fig. 107 Component locations — 1993 models with 4.3L engines and AT. Less than 8500 lbs. GVW or without Tier 1 emissions

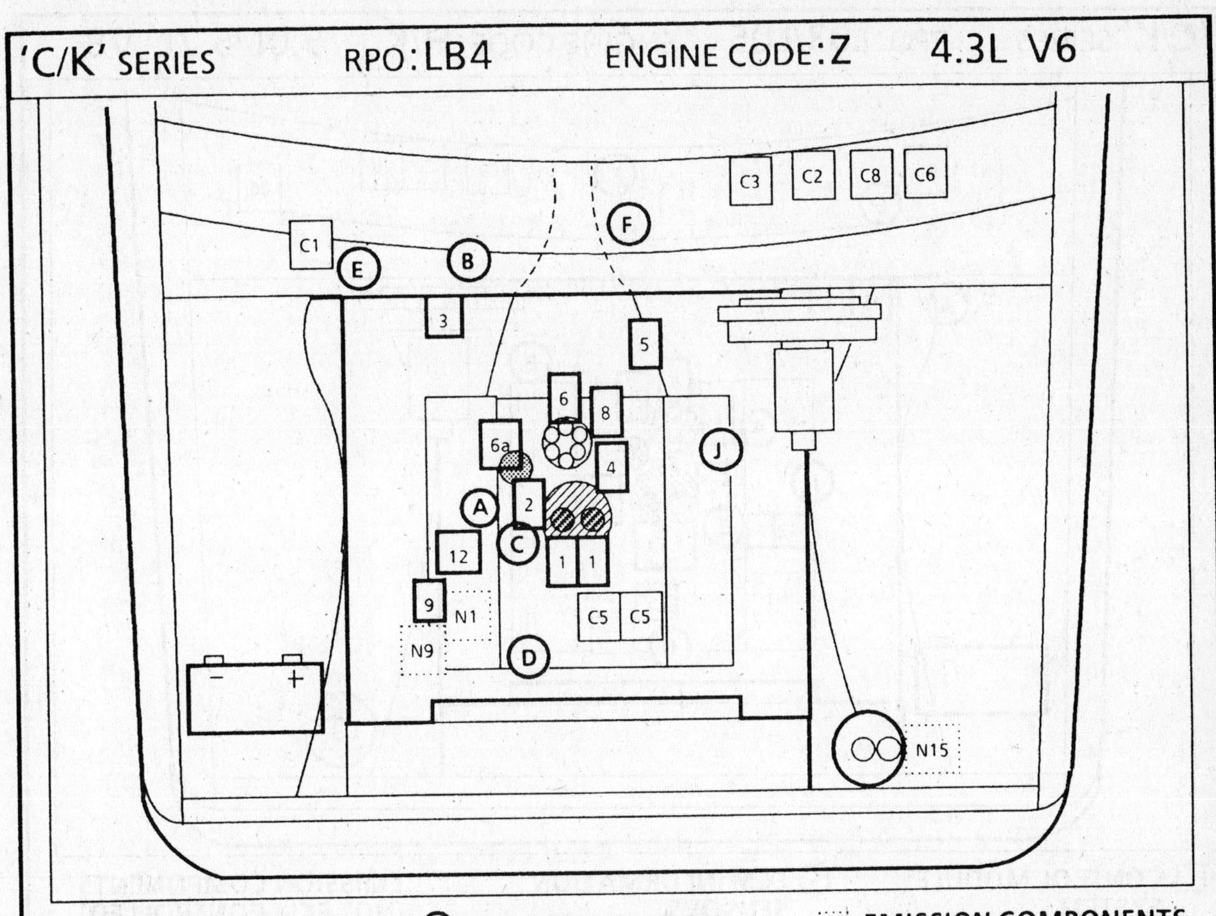

☐ CONTROL MODULE SYSTEM

- C1 Powertrain Control Module (PCM)
- C2 Data Link Connector (DLC)
- C3 Malfunction Indicator Lamp (MIL)
- C5 PCM harness ground
- C6 Fuse block
- C8 Fuel pump test connector

☐ PCM CONTROLLED COMPONENTS

- 1 Fuel injector
- 2 Idle Air Control (IAC)
- 3 Fuel pump relay
- 4 EGR valve
- 5 Transmission connector
- 6 Ignition Control (IC) distributor
- 6a Remote ignition coil
- 8 Oil pressure switch
- 9 AIR bypass valve
- 12 Exhaust Gas Recirculation (EGR) Vacuum Solenoid

○ PCM INFORMATION SENSORS

- A Manifold Absolute Pressure (MAP) sensor
- B Heated Oxygen Sensor (HO2S)
- C Throttle Position (TP) sensor
- D Engine Coolant Temperature (ECT) sensor
- E VSS buffer
- F Vehicle Speed Sensor (VSS)
- J Knock Sensor (KS)

EMISSION COMPONENTS (NOT PCM CONTROLLED)

- N1 Crankcase vent valve
- N9 AIR pump
- N15 Fuel vapor canister

84904053

Fig. 108 Component locations — 1993 models with 4.3L engines and Tier 1 emissions

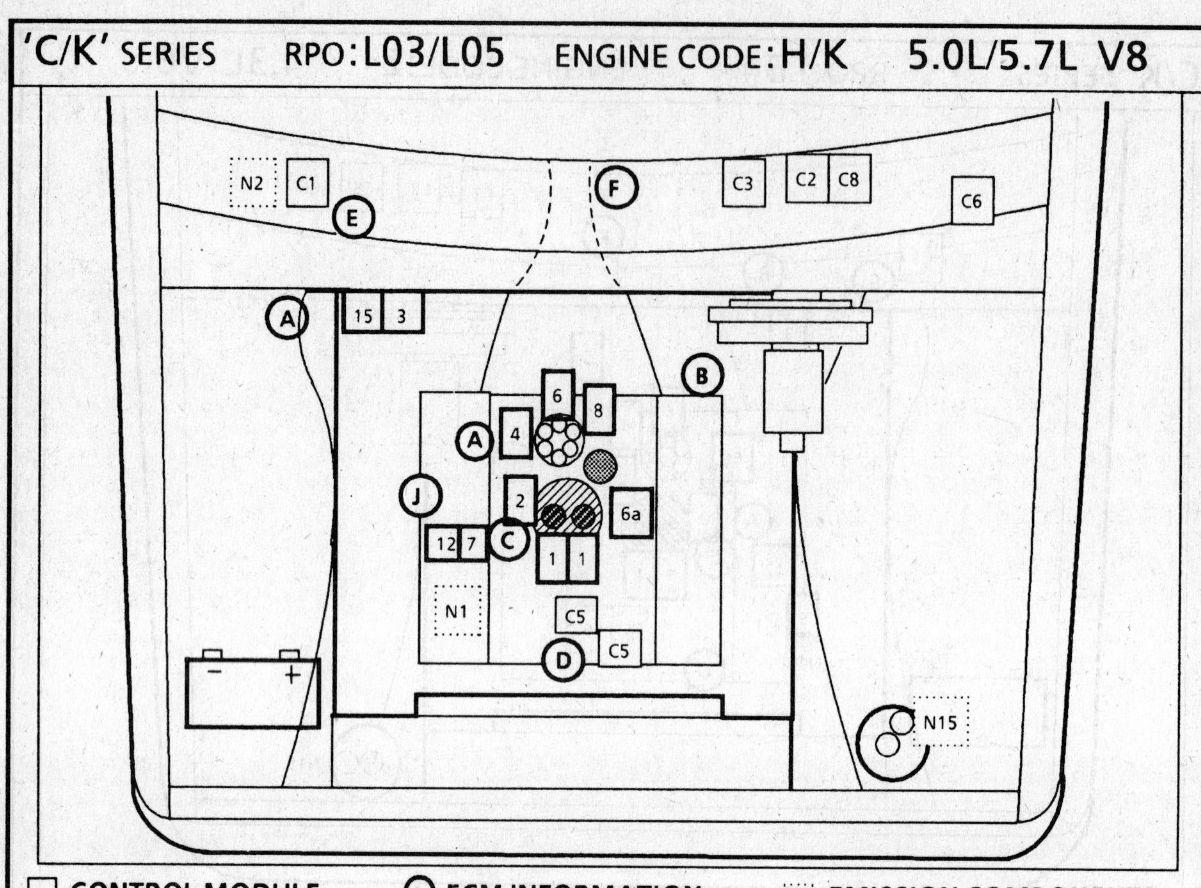

☐ CONTROL MODULE SYSTEM

- C1 Engine Control Module (ECM)
- C2 Data Link Connector (DLC)
- C3 Malfunction Indicator Lamp (MIL)
- C5 ECM harness ground
- C6 Fuse block
- C8 Fuel pump test connector terminal "G" of DLC

☐ ECM CONTROLLED COMPONENTS

- 1 Fuel injector
- 2 Idle Air Control (IAC)
- 3 Fuel pump relay
- 4 EGR valve
- 6 Ignition Control (IC) distributor
- 6a Remote ignition coil
- 7 Knock Sensor (KS) module
- 8 Oil pressure switch
- 12 Exhaust Gas Recirculation (EGR) Vacuum Solenoid
- 12 Exhaust Gas Recirculation (EGR) Electronic Vacuum Regulator Solenoid Valve (5.7L H.D. only)
- 15 Fuel pump fuse

◯ ECM INFORMATION SENSORS

- A Manifold Absolute Pressure (MAP) sensor
- B Oxygen Sensor (O2S)
- C Throttle Position (TP) sensor
- D Engine Coolant Temperature (ECT) sensor
- E VSS Buffer
- F Vehicle Speed Sensor (VSS)
- J Knock sensor (KS)

⬚ EMISSION COMPONENTS (NOT ECM CONTROLLED)

- N1 Crankcase vent valve
- N2 Fuel Module (5.7L H.D. only)
- N15 Fuel Vapor Canister

84904054

Fig. 109 Component locations — 1993 models with 5.0L/5.7L engines and MT

'C/K' SERIES RPO: L03/L05 ENGINE CODE: H/K 5.0L/5.7L V8

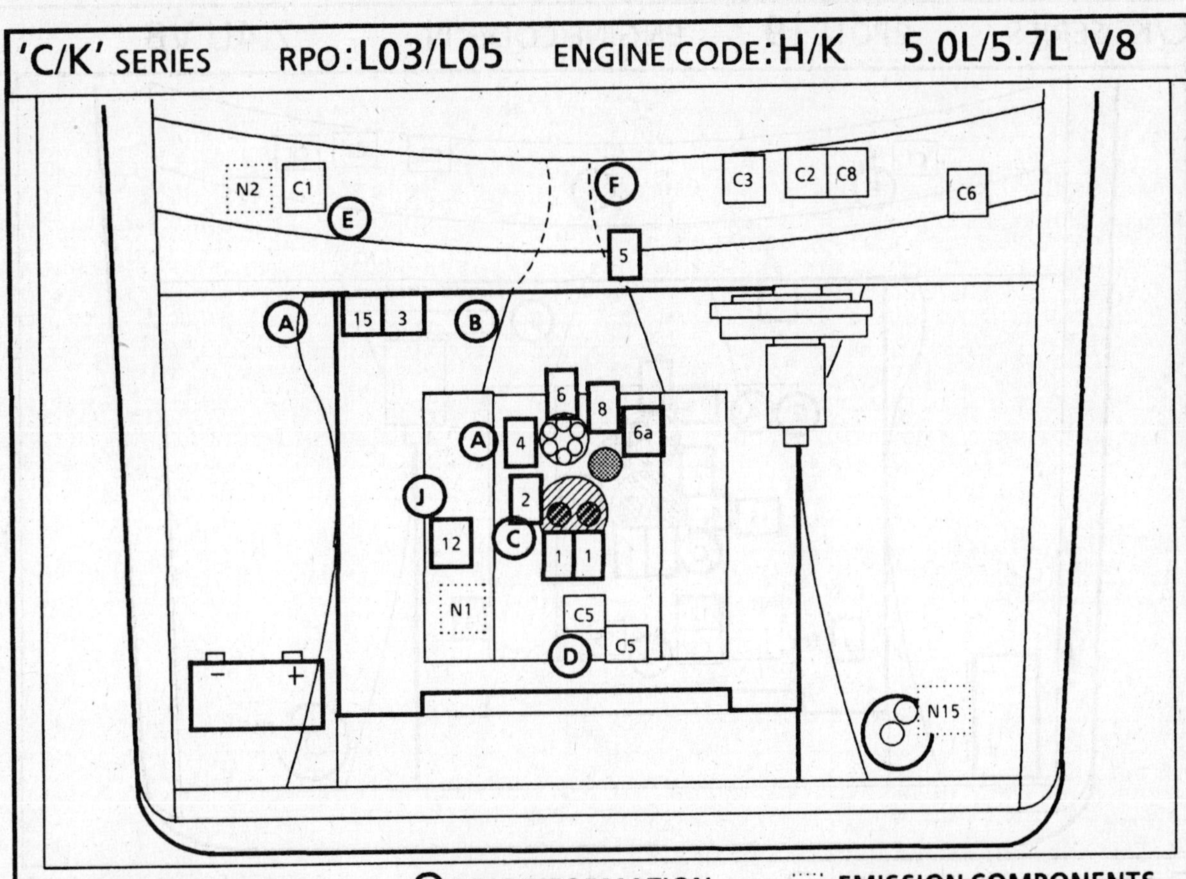

CONTROL MODULE SYSTEM

C1 Powertrain Control Module (PCM)
C2 Data Link Connector (DLC)
C3 Malfunction Indicator Lamp (MIL)
C5 PCM harness ground
C6 Fuse block
C8 Fuel pump test connector terminal "G" of DLC

PCM INFORMATION SENSORS

A Manifold Absolute Pressure (MAP) sensor
B Oxygen Sensor (O2S)
C Throttle Position (TP) sensor
D Engine Coolant Temperature (ECT) sensor
E VSS Buffer
F Vehicle Speed Sensor (VSS)
J Knock sensor (KS)

EMISSION COMPONENTS (NOT PCM CONTROLLED)

N1 Crankcase vent valve
N2 Fuel Module (5.7L H.D. only)
N15 Fuel vapor canister

PCM CONTROLLED COMPONENTS

1 Fuel injector
2 Idle Air Control (IAC)
3 Fuel pump relay
4 EGR valve
5 Transmission connector
6 Ignition Control (IC) distributor
6a Remote ignition coil
8 Oil pressure switch
12 Exhaust Gas Recirculation (EGR) Vacuum Solenoid
12 Exhaust Gas Recirculation (EGR) Electronic Vacuum Regulator Solenoid Valve (5.7L H.D. only)
15 Fuel pump fuse

84904055

Fig. 110 Component locations — 1993 models with 5.0L/5.7L engines and AT

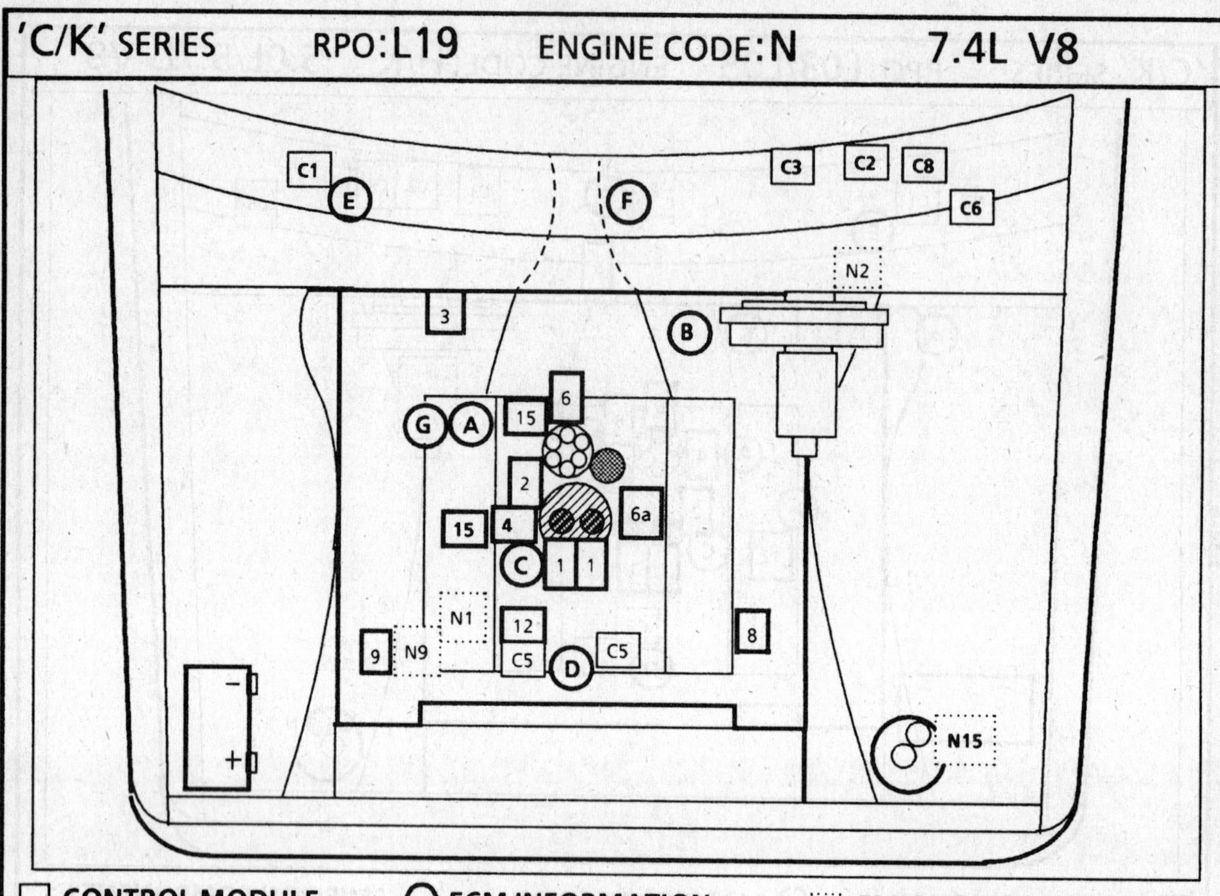

CONTROL MODULE SYSTEM

- C1 Engine Control Module (ECM)
- C2 Data Link Connector (DLC)
- C3 Malfunction Indicator Lamp (MIL)
- C5 ECM harness ground
- C6 Fuse block
- C8 Fuel pump test connector terminal "G" of DLC

ECM CONTROLLED COMPONENTS

- 1 Fuel injector
- 2 Idle Air Control (IAC)
- 3 Fuel pump relay
- 4 EGR valve
- 6 Ignition Control (IC) distributor
- 6a Remote ignition coil
- 8 Oil pressure switch
- 9 AIR bypass valve
- 12 Exhaust Gas Recirculation (EGR) electronic vacuum regulator solenoid valve
- 15 Knock Sensor (KS) module

ECM INFORMATION SENSORS

- A Manifold Absolute Pressure (MAP) sensor
- B Oxygen Sensor (O2S)
- C Throttle Position (TP) sensor
- D Engine Coolant Temperature (ECT) sensor
- E VSS Buffer
- F Vehicle Speed Sensor (VSS)
- G Knock Sensor (KS)

EMISSION COMPONENTS (NOT ECM CONTROLLED)

- N1 Crankcase vent valve
- N2 Fuel module
- N9 AIR pump
- N15 Fuel vapor canister

84904056

Fig. 111 Component locations — 1993 models with 7.4L engines and MT

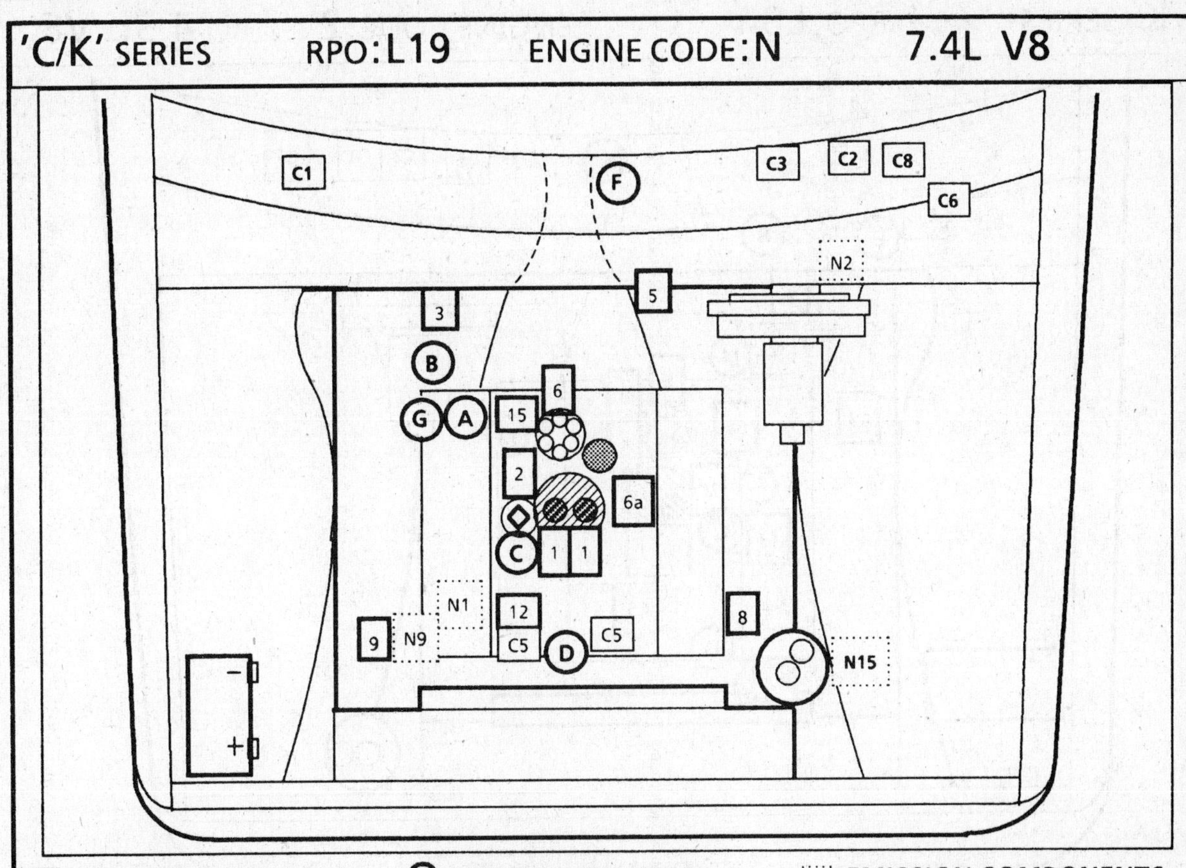

☐ CONTROL MODULE SYSTEM

- C1 Powertrain Control Module (PCM)
- C2 Data Link Connector (DLC)
- C3 Malfunction Indicator Lamp (MIL)
- C5 PCM harness ground
- C6 Fuse block
- C8 Fuel pump test connector (DLC Terminal "G")

☐ PCM CONTROLLED COMPONENTS

- 1 Fuel injector
- 2 Idle Air Control (IAC)
- 3 Fuel pump relay
- 5 Transmission connector
- 6 Ignition Control (IC) distributor
- 6a Remote ignition coil
- 8 Oil pressure switch
- 9 AIR bypass valve
- 12 Exhaust Gas Recirculation (EGR) electronic vacuum regulator solenoid valve

○ PCM INFORMATION SENSORS

- A Manifold Absolute Pressure (MAP) sensor
- B Oxygen Sensor (O2S)
- C Throttle Position (TP) sensor
- D Engine Coolant Temperature (ECT) sensor
- F Vehicle Speed Sensor (VSS)
- G Knock Sensor (KS)

⬚ EMISSION COMPONENTS (NOT PCM CONTROLLED)

- N1 Crankcase Vent Valve (PCV)
- N2 Fuel module
- N9 AIR pump
- N15 Fuel vapor canister

84904057

Fig. 112 Component locations — 1993 models with 7.4L engines and AT

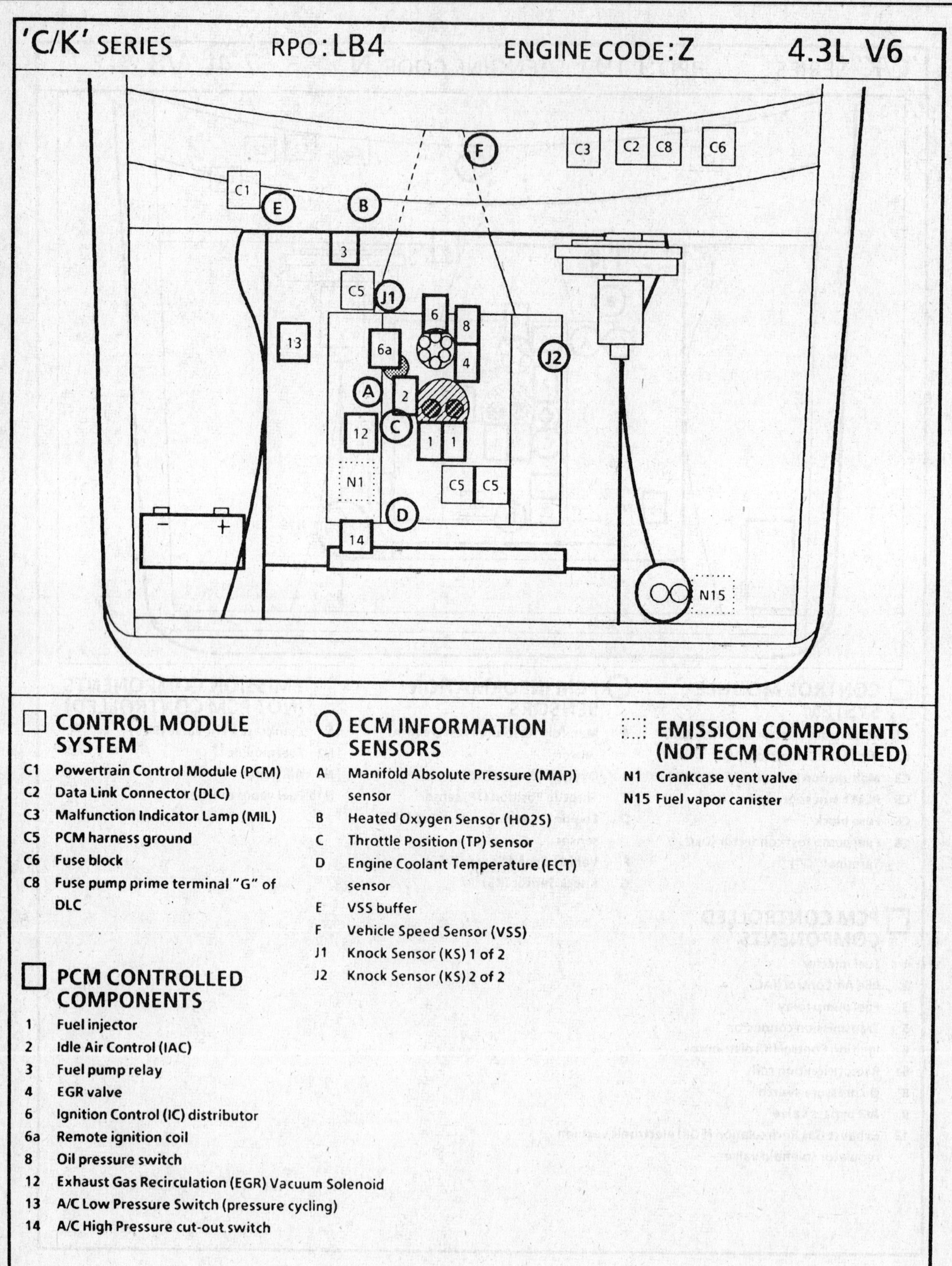

Fig. 113 Component locations — 1994 4.3L engines and MT

'C/K' SERIES RPO: LB4 ENGINE CODE: Z 4.3L V6

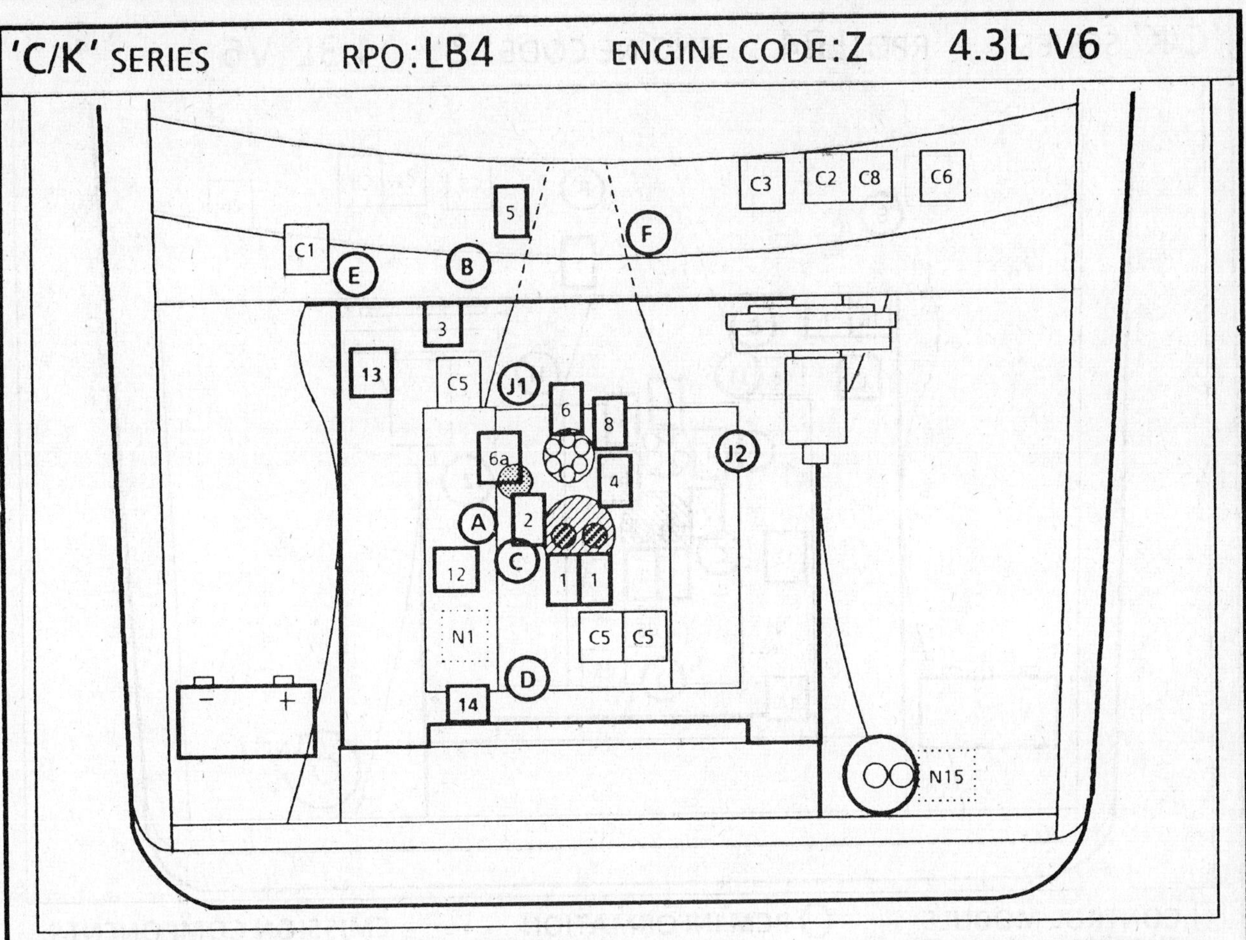

CONTROL MODULE SYSTEM

- C1 Powertrain Control Module (PCM)
- C2 Data Link Connector (DLC)
- C3 Malfunction Indicator Lamp (MIL)
- C5 PCM harness ground
- C6 Fuse block
- C8 Fuel pump test connector terminal "G" of DLC

PCM CONTROLLED COMPONENTS

- 1 Fuel injector
- 2 Idle Air Control (IAC)
- 3 Fuel pump relay
- 4 EGR valve
- 5 Transmission connector
- 6 Ignition Control (IC) distributor
- 6a Remote ignition coil
- 8 Oil pressure switch
- 12 Exhaust Gas Recirculation (EGR) Vacuum Solenoid
- 13 A/C Low Pressure Switch (Pressure Cycling)
- 14 A/C High Pressure Cut-Out Switch

PCM INFORMATION SENSORS

- A Manifold Absolute Pressure (MAP) sensor
- B Heated Oxygen Sensor (HO2S)
- C Throttle Position (TP) sensor
- D Engine Coolant Temperature (ECT) sensor
- E VSS buffer
- F Vehicle Speed Sensor (VSS)
- J1 Knock Sensor (KS) 1 of 2
- J2 Knock Sensor (KS) 2 of 2

EMISSION COMPONENTS (NOT PCM CONTROLLED)

- N1 Crankcase vent valve
- N15 Fuel vapor canister

87984G11

Fig. 114 Component locations — 1994 4.3L engines and AT

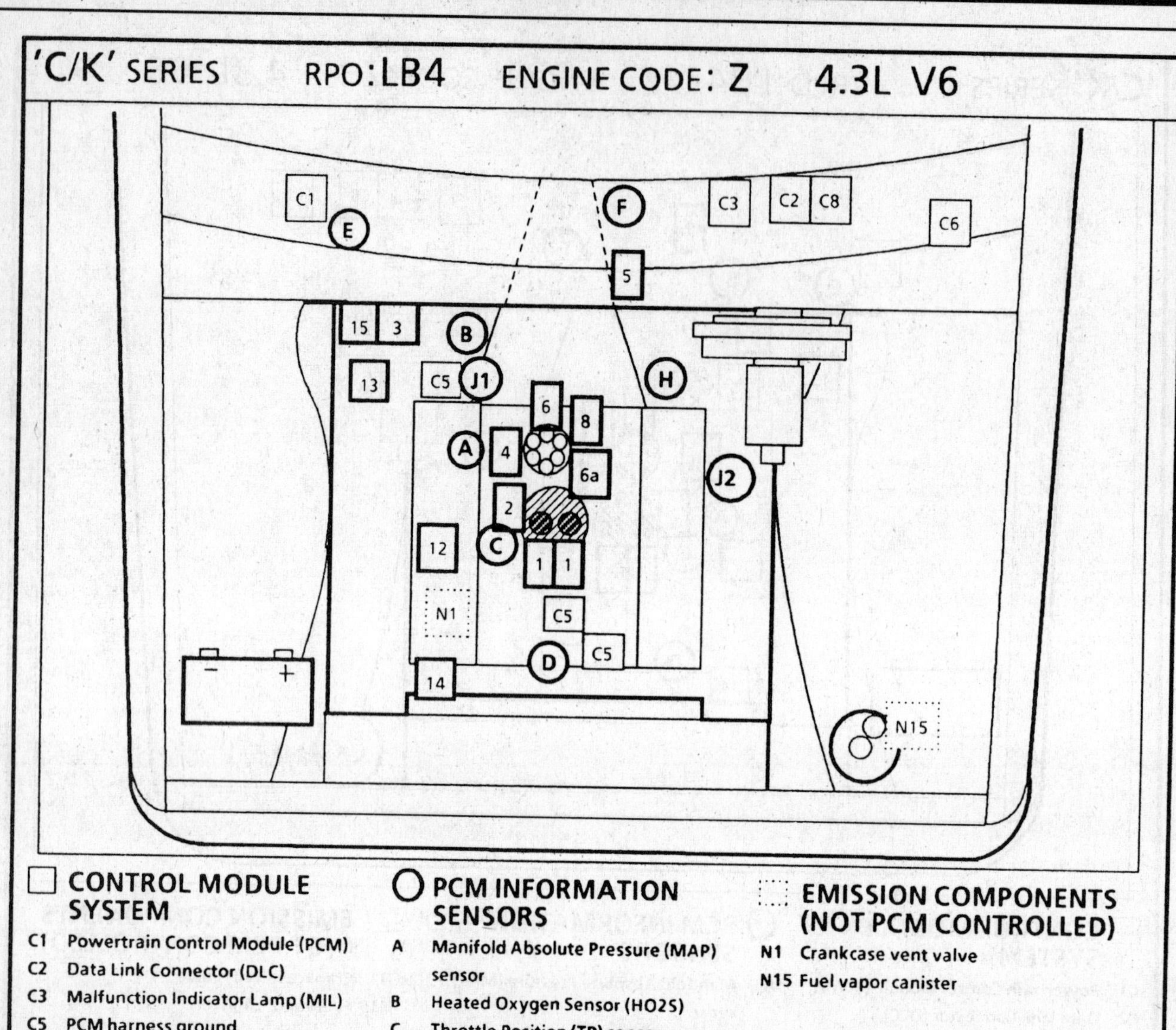

CONTROL MODULE SYSTEM

- C1 Powertrain Control Module (PCM)
- C2 Data Link Connector (DLC)
- C3 Malfunction Indicator Lamp (MIL)
- C5 PCM harness ground
- C6 Fuse block
- C8 Fuel pump test connector terminal "G" of DLC

PCM CONTROLLED COMPONENTS

- 1 Fuel injector
- 2 Idle Air Control (IAC)
- 3 Fuel pump relay
- 4 EGR valve
- 5 Transmission connector
- 6 Ignition Control (IC) distributor
- 6a Remote ignition coil
- 8 Oil pressure switch
- 12 Exhaust Gas Recirculation (EGR) electronic vacuum regulator solenoid valve
- 13 A/C low pressure switch (pressure cycling)
- 14 A/C high pressure cutout switch
- 15 Fuel pump fuse

PCM INFORMATION SENSORS

- A Manifold Absolute Pressure (MAP) sensor
- B Heated Oxygen Sensor (HO2S)
- C Throttle Position (TP) sensor
- D Engine Coolant Temperature (ECT) sensor
- E VSS buffer
- F Vehicle Speed Sensor (VSS) (output speed sensor)
- H Input speed sensor
- J1 Knock Sensor (KS) 1 of 2
- J2 Knock Sensor (KS) 2 of 2

EMISSION COMPONENTS (NOT PCM CONTROLLED)

- N1 Crankcase vent valve
- N15 Fuel vapor canister

87984G12

Fig. 115 Component locations — 1994 4.3L engines and AT (4L80E)

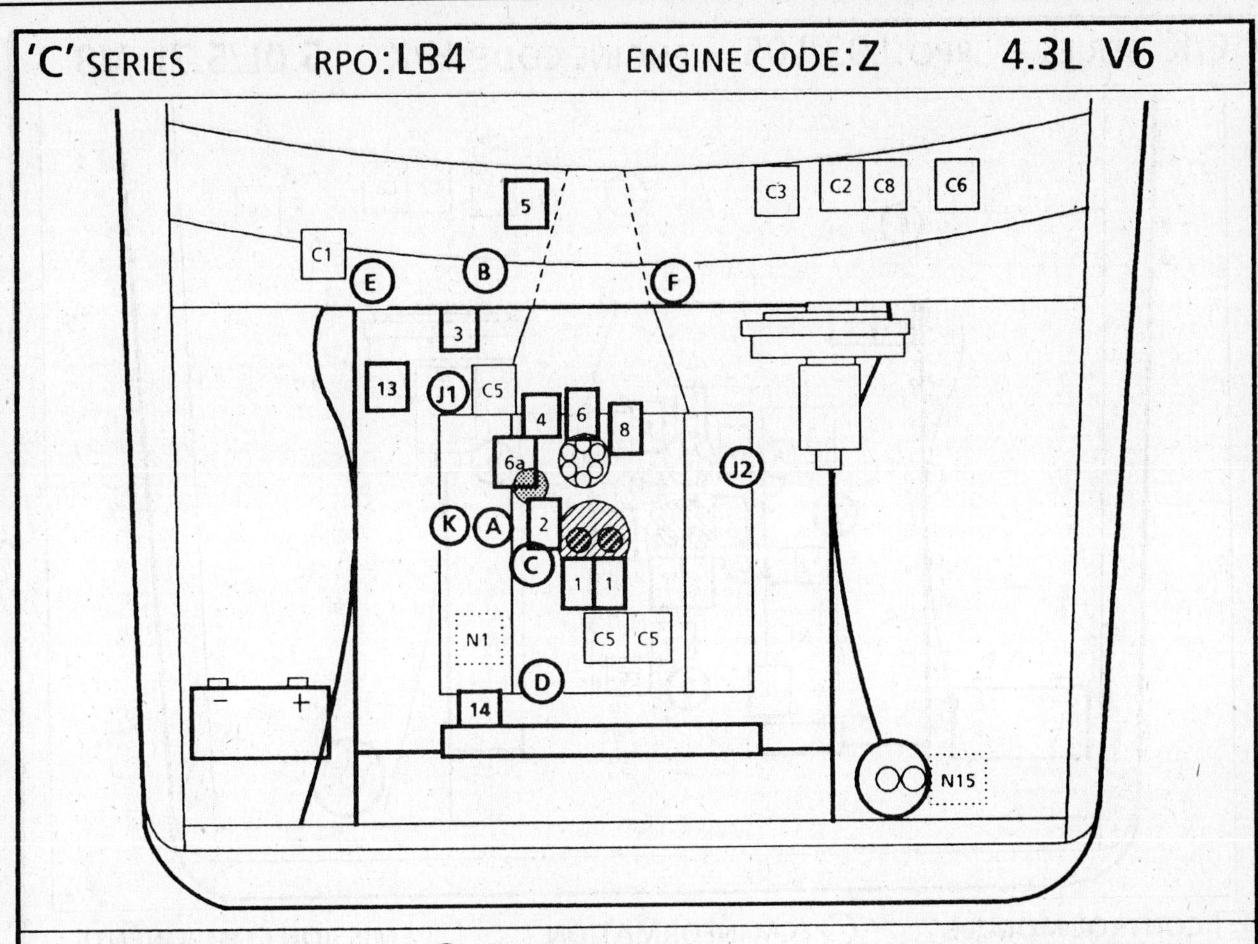

CONTROL MODULE SYSTEM

- C1 Powertrain Control Module (PCM)
- C2 Data Link Connector (DLC)
- C3 Malfunction Indicator Lamp (MIL)
- C5 PCM harness ground
- C6 Fuse block
- C8 Fuel pump test connector terminal "G" of DLC

PCM CONTROLLED COMPONENTS

- 1 Fuel injector
- 2 Idle Air Control (IAC)
- 3 Fuel pump relay
- 4 Linear Exhaust Gas Recirculation (EGR)
- 5 Transmission connector
- 6 Ignition Control (IC) distributor
- 6a Remote ignition coil
- 8 Oil pressure switch
- 13 A/C Low Pressure Switch (Pressure Cycling)
- 14 A/C High Pressure Cut-Out Switch

PCM INFORMATION SENSORS

- A Manifold Absolute Pressure (MAP) sensor
- B Heated Oxygen Sensor (HO2S)
- C Throttle Position (TP) sensor
- D Engine Coolant Temperature (ECT) sensor
- E VSS Buffer
- F Vehicle Speed Sensor (VSS)
- J1 Knock Sensor (KS) 1 of 2
- J2 Knock Sensor (KS) 2 of 2
- K Canister Purge Solenoid

EMISSION COMPONENTS (NOT PCM CONTROLLED)

- N1 Crankcase vent valve
- N15 Fuel vapor canister

87984G13

Fig. 116 Component locations — 1994 4.3L engines and California emissions

'C/K' SERIES RPO: L03/L05 ENGINE CODE: H/K 5.0L/5.7L V8

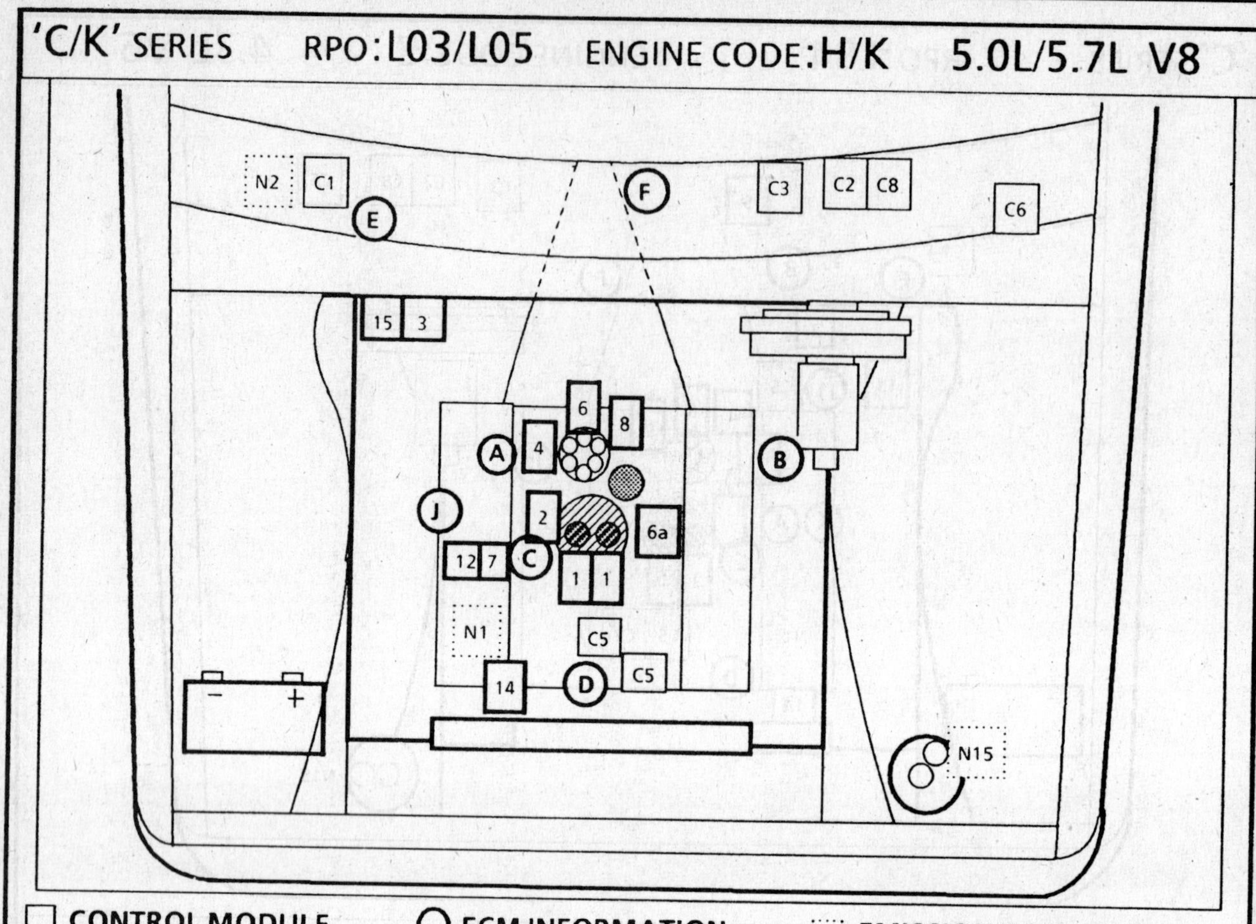

CONTROL MODULE SYSTEM

C1 Engine Control Module (ECM)
C2 Data Link Connector (DLC)
C3 Malfunction Indicator Lamp (MIL)
C5 ECM harness ground
C6 Fuse block
C8 Fuel pump test connector terminal "G" of DLC

ECM INFORMATION SENSORS

A Manifold Absolute Pressure (MAP) sensor
B Oxygen Sensor (O2S)
C Throttle Position (TP) sensor
D Engine Coolant Temperature (ECT) sensor
E VSS buffer
F Vehicle Speed Sensor (VSS)
J Knock Sensor (KS)

EMISSION COMPONENTS (NOT ECM CONTROLLED)

N1 Crankcase vent valve
N2 Fuel module (5.7L H.D. only)
N15 Fuel vapor canister

ECM CONTROLLED COMPONENTS

1 Fuel injector
2 Idle Air Control (IAC)
3 Fuel pump relay
4 EGR valve
6 Ignition Control (IC) distributor
6a Remote ignition coil
7 Knock Sensor (KS) module
8 Oil pressure switch
12 Exhaust Gas Recirculation (EGR) vacuum solenoid
12 Exhaust Gas Recirculation (EGR) electronic vacuum Regulator Solenoid Valve (5.7L H.D. only)
13 A/C low pressure switch (pressure cycling)
14 A/C high pressure cutout switch
15 Fuel pump fuse

87984G15

Fig. 117 Component locations — 1994 5.0L/5.7L engines and MT

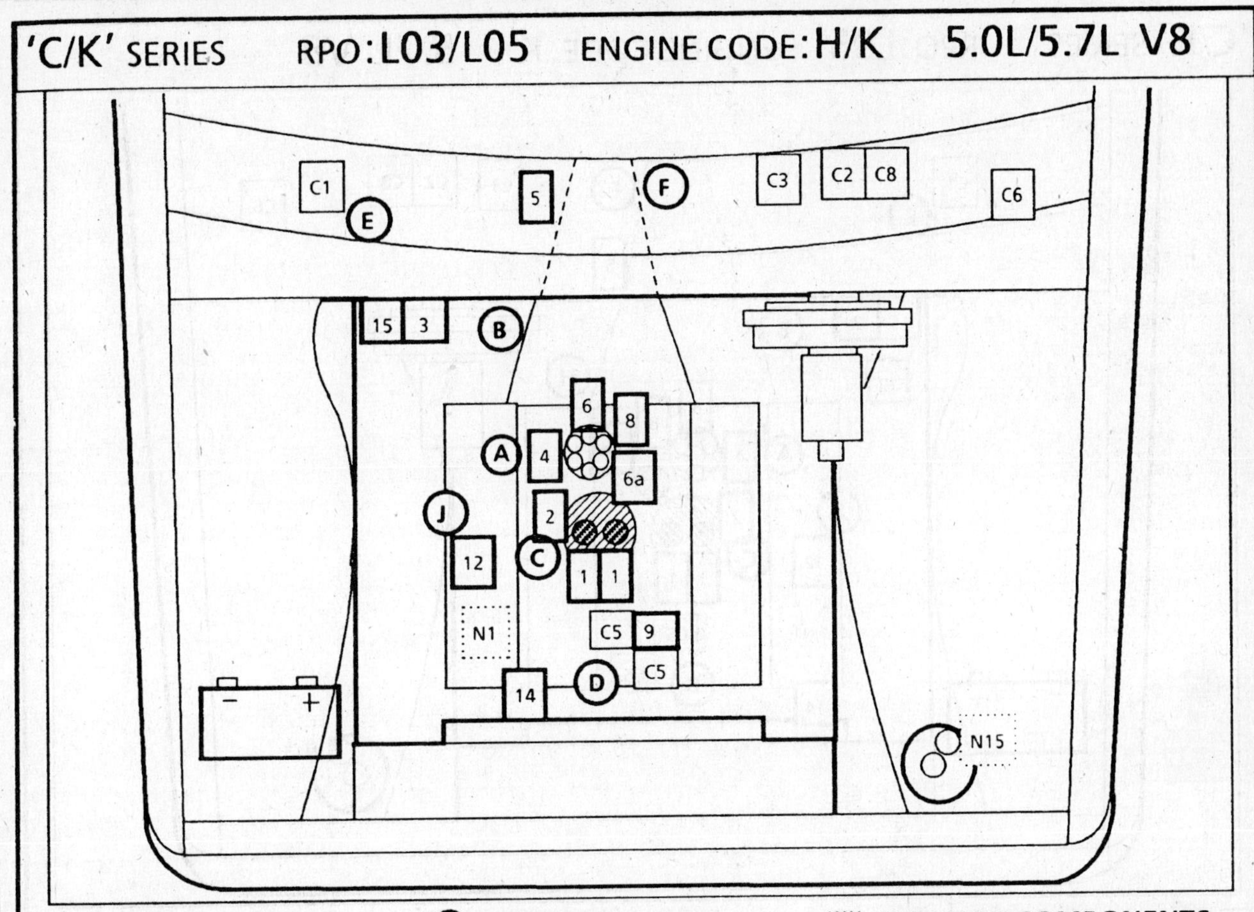

CONTROL MODULE SYSTEM

C1	Powertrain Control Module (PCM)
C2	Data Link Connector (DLC)
C3	Malfunction Indicator Lamp (MIL)
C5	PCM harness ground
C6	Fuse block
C8	Fuel pump test connector terminal "G" of DLC

PCM CONTROLLED COMPONENTS

1	Fuel injector
2	Idle Air Control (IAC)
3	Fuel pump relay
4	EGR valve
5	Transmission connector
6	Ignition Control (IC) distributor
6a	Remote ignition coil
8	Oil pressure switch
9	Canister purge solenoid
12	Exhaust Gas Recirculation (EGR) vacuum solenoid
13	A/C low pressure switch (pressure cycling)
14	A/C high pressure cutout switch
15	Fuel pump fuse

PCM INFORMATION SENSORS

A	Manifold Absolute Pressure (MAP) sensor
B	Heated Oxygen Sensor (HO2S)
C	Throttle Position (TP) sensor
D	Engine Coolant Temperature (ECT) sensor
E	VSS buffer
F	Vehicle Speed Sensor (VSS)
J	Knock Sensor (KS)

EMISSION COMPONENTS (NOT PCM CONTROLLED)

N1	Crankcase vent valve
N15	Fuel vapor canister

87984G16

Fig. 118 Component locations — 1994 5.0L/5.7L engines and AT (4L80E)

'C/K' SERIES RPO: L05 ENGINE CODE: K 5.7L V8

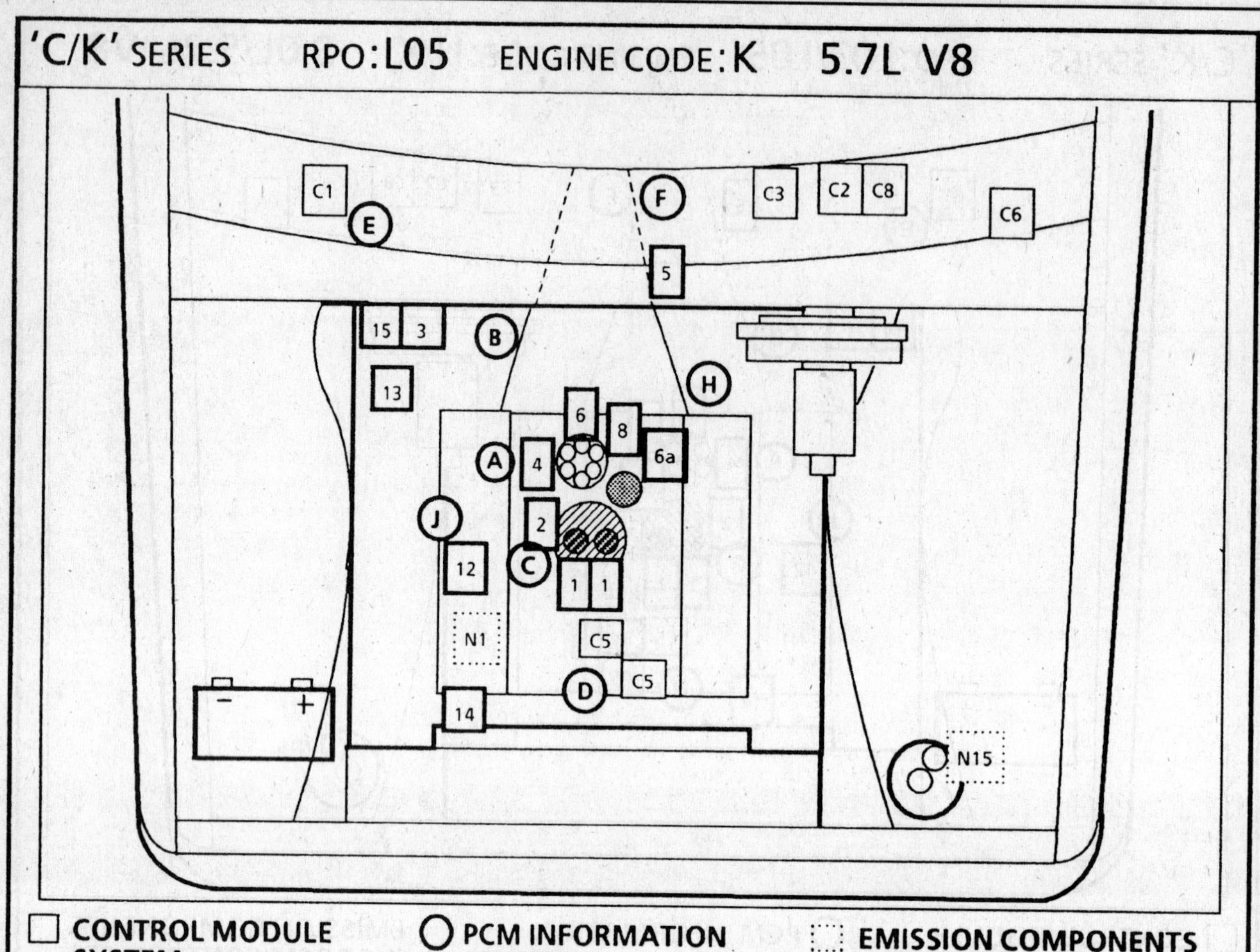

CONTROL MODULE SYSTEM

- C1 Powertrain Control Module (PCM)
- C2 Data Link Connector (DLC)
- C3 Malfunction Indicator Lamp (MIL)
- C5 PCM harness ground
- C6 Fuse block
- C8 Fuel pump test connector terminal "G" of DLC

PCM CONTROLLED COMPONENTS

1. Fuel injector
2. Idle Air Control (IAC)
3. Fuel pump relay
4. EGR valve
5. Transmission connector
6. Ignition Control (IC) distributor

- 6a Remote ignition coil
- 8 Oil pressure switch
- 12 Exhaust Gas Recirculation (EGR) electronic vacuum regulator solenoid valve
- 13 A/C low pressure switch (pressure cycling)
- 14 A/C high pressure cutout switch
- 15 Fuel pump fuse

PCM INFORMATION SENSORS

- A Manifold Absolute Pressure (MAP) sensor
- B Oxygen Sensor (O2S)
- C Throttle Position (TP) sensor
- D Engine Coolant Temperature (ECT) sensor
- E VSS buffer
- F Vehicle Speed Sensor (VSS) (output speed sensor)
- H Input speed sensor
- J Knock Sensor (KS)

EMISSION COMPONENTS (NOT PCM CONTROLLED)

- N1 Crankcase vent valve
- N15 Fuel vapor canister

87984G17

Fig. 119 Component locations — 1994 5.7L engines and AT (4L80E)

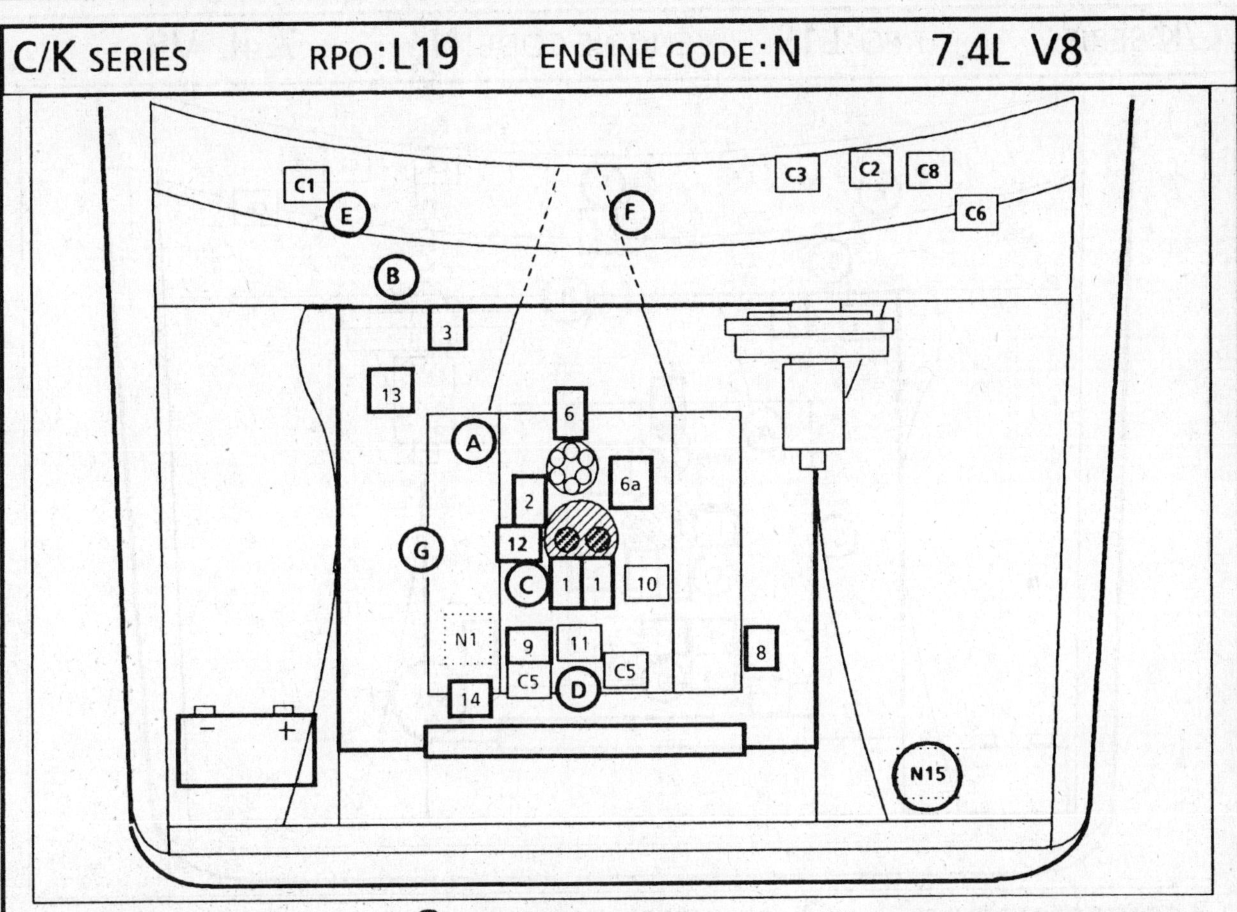

□ **CONTROL MODULE SYSTEM**

- C1 Powertrain Control Module (PCM)
- C2 Data Link Connector (DLC)
- C3 Malfunction Indicator Lamp (MIL)
- C5 PCM harness ground
- C6 Fuse block
- C8 Fuel pump test connector terminal "G" of DLC

□ **PCM CONTROLLED COMPONENTS**

- 1 Fuel injector
- 2 Idle Air Control (IAC)
- 3 Fuel pump relay
- 6 Ignition Control (IC) distributor
- 6a Remote ignition coil
- 8 Oil pressure switch
- 9 Idle speed control actuator solenoid
- 10 Idle speed control actuator
- 11 Canister purge solenoid
- 12 Linear Exhaust Gas Recirculation (EGR) valve
- 13 A/C low pressure switch (pressure cycling)
- 14 A/C high pressure cutout switch

○ **ECM INFORMATION SENSORS**

- A Manifold Absolute Pressure (MAP) sensor
- B Oxygen Sensor (O2S)
- C Throttle Position (TP) sensor
- D Engine Coolant Temperature (ECT) sensor
- E VSS buffer
- F Vehicle Speed Sensor (VSS)
- G Knock Sensor (KS)

EMISSION COMPONENTS (NOT ECM CONTROLLED)

- N1 Crankcase vent valve
- N15 Fuel vapor canister

87984G18

Fig. 120 Component locations — 1994 7.4L engines and MT

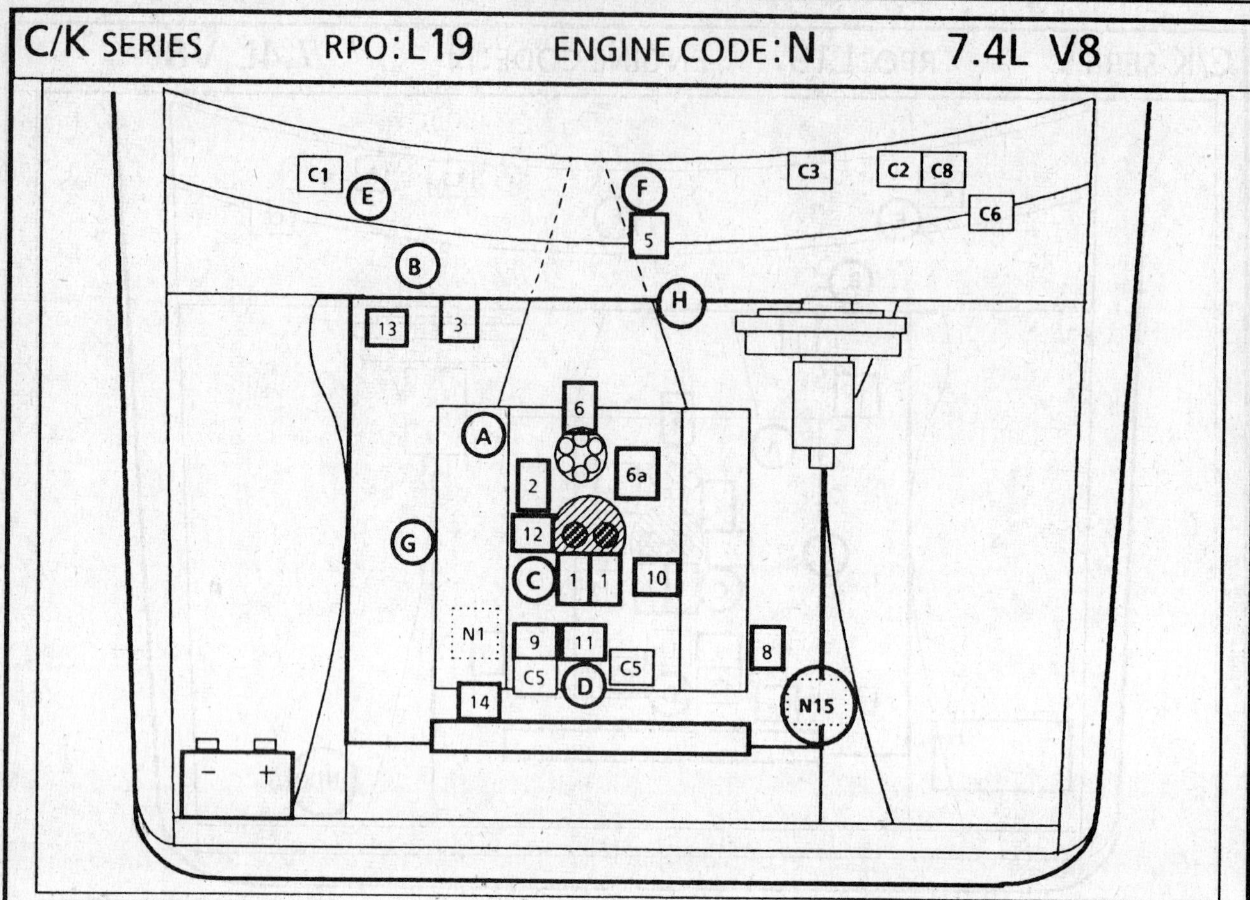

CONTROL MODULE SYSTEM

- C1 Powertrain Control Module (PCM)
- C2 Data Link Connector (DLC)
- C3 Malfunction Indicator Lamp (MIL)
- C5 PCM harness ground
- C6 Fuse block
- C8 Fuel pump test connector (DLC terminal "G")

PCM CONTROLLED COMPONENTS

- 1 Fuel injector
- 2 Idle Air Control (IAC)
- 3 Fuel pump relay
- 5 Transmission connector
- 6 Ignition Control (IC) distributor
- 6a Remote ignition coil
- 8 Oil pressure switch
- 9 Idle Speed Actuator Solenoid
- 10 Idle Speed Actuator
- 11 Canister Purge Solenoid
- 12 Linear Exhaust Gas Recirculation (EGR) valve
- 13 A/C Low Pressure Switch (pressure cycling)
- 14 A/C High Pressure Cut-out Switch

PCM INFORMATION SENSORS

- A Manifold Absolute Pressure (MAP) sensor
- B Oxygen Sensor (O2S)
- C Throttle Position (TP) sensor
- D Engine Coolant Temperature (ECT) sensor
- E VSS buffer
- F Vehicle Speed Sensor (VSS) (output speed sensor)
- G Knock Sensor (KS)
- H Input speed sensor

EMISSION COMPONENTS (NOT PCM CONTROLLED)

- N1 Crankcase vent valve
- N15 Fuel vapor canister

87984G19

Fig. 121 Component locations — 1994 7.4L engines and AT (4L80E)

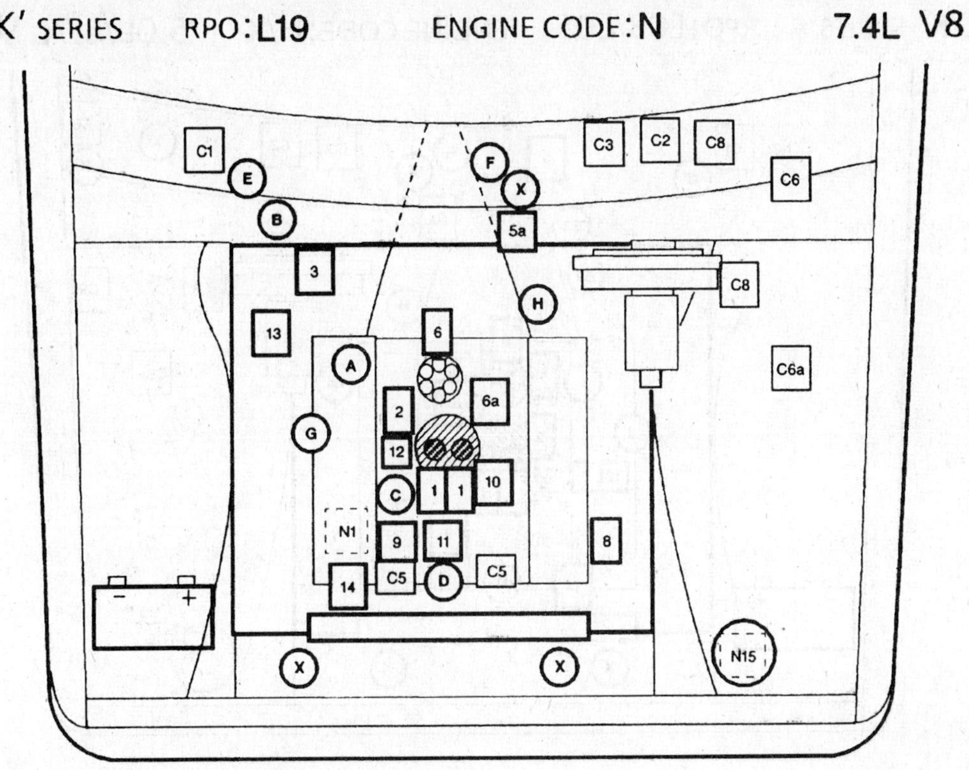

CONTROL MODULE SYSTEM

- C1 Powertrain Control Module (PCM)
- C2 Data Link Connector (DLC)
- C3 Malfunction Indicator Lamp (MIL)
- C5 PCM harness ground
- C6 Fuse block
- C6a Underhood electrical center
- C8 Fuel pump test connector terminal

PCM CONTROLLED COMPONENTS

- 1 Fuel injector
- 2 Idle Air Control (IAC)
- 3 Fuel pump relay
- 5a Transmission connector (4L80E Automatic transmission)
- 6 Ignition Control (IC) distributor
- 6a Remote ignition coil
- 8 Oil pressure switch
- 9 Idle speed control actuator solenoid
- 10 Idle speed control actuator
- 11 Canister purge solenoid
- 12 Linear Exhaust Gas Recirculation (EGR) valve
- 13 A/C low presure switch (pressure cycling)
- 14 A/C high pressure cut-out switch

PCM INFORMATION SENSORS

- A Manifold Absolute Pressure (MAP) sensor
- B Oxygen Sensor (O2S)
- C Throttle Position (TP) sensor
- D Engine Coolant Temperature (ECT) sensor
- E VSS buffer module
- F Output speed and Vehicle Speed Sensor (VSS)
- G Knock Sensor (KS)
- H Input speed sensor (4L80E Automatic transmission)

EMISSION COMPONENTS (NOT PCM CONTROLLED)

- N1 Crankcase vent valve
- N15 Fuel vapor canister

(X) SIR SYSTEM COMPONENTS

87984G20

Fig. 122 Component locations — 1995 7.4L engines

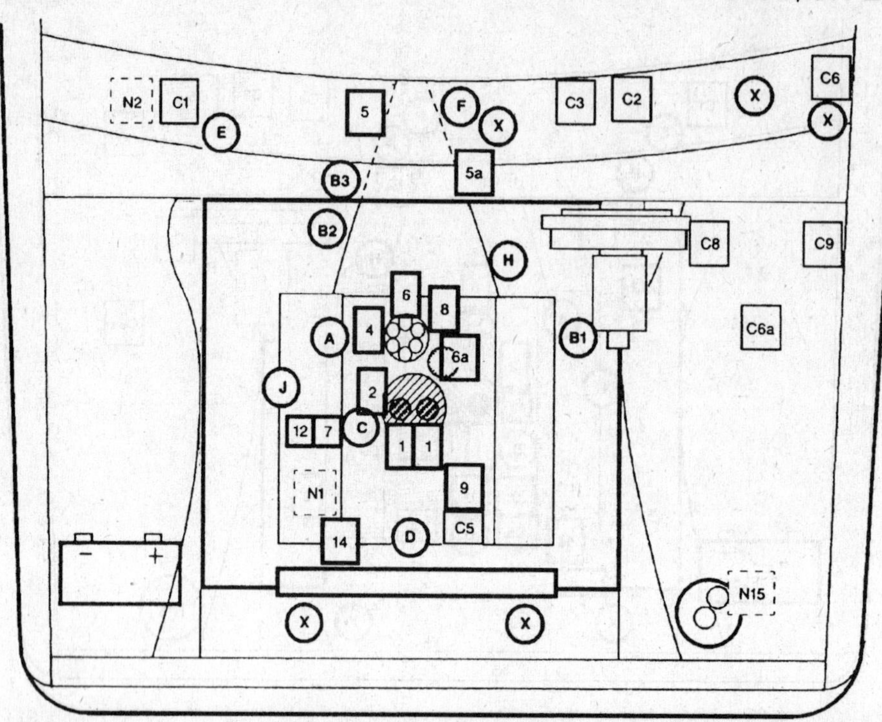

CONTROL MODULE SYSTEM

C1 Control Module Engine control Module (ECM)(Manual Transmission)/Powertrain Control Module (PCM)(Automatic Transmission)
C2 Data Link Connector (DLC)
C3 Malfunction Indicator Lamp (MIL)
C5 ECM harness ground
C6 Fuse block
C6a Underhood electrical center
C8 Fuel pump test connector terminal
C9 Underhood electrical center

ECM CONTROLLED COMPONENTS

1 Fuel injector
2 Idle Air Control (IAC)
4 EGR valve
5 Transmission connector (4L60E Automatic transmission)
5a Transmission connector (4L80E Automatic transmission)
6 Ignition Control (IC) distributor
6a Remote ignition coil
7 Knock Sensor (KS) module (manual transmission)
8 Oil pressure switch
9 Canister purge solenoid (less than 8500 GVW 4L60E Automatic Transmission)
12 Exhaust Gas Recirculation (EGR) vacuum solenoid (5.7L less than 8500 GVW)
12 Exhaust Gas Recirculation (EGR) electronic vacuum Regulator Solenoid Valve (EVRV) (5.7L greater than 8500 GVW)
13 A/C low pressure switch (pressure cycling)
14 A/C high pressure cut-out switch

CONTROL MODULE INFORMATION SENSORS

A Manifold Absolute Pressure (MAP) sensor
B1 Oxygen Sensor (O2S)
B2 Oxygen Sensor (O2S) (5.7L greater than 8500 GVW)
B3 Heated Oxygen Sensor (HO2S) (less than 8500 GVW 4L60E Automatic Transmission)
C Throttle Position (TP) sensor
D Engine Coolant Temperature (ECT) sensor
E VSS buffer module
F Vehicle Speed Sensor (VSS)
H Input Speed Sensor (4L80E Automatic Transmission)
J Knock Sensor (KS)

EMISSION COMPONENTS (NOT ECM/PCM CONTROLLED

N1 Crankcase vent valve
N2 Fuel module (5.7L greater than 8500 GVW)
N15 Fuel vapor canister

SIR SYSTEM COMPONENTS

87984G21

Fig. 123 Component locations — 1995 5.0L/5.7L engines

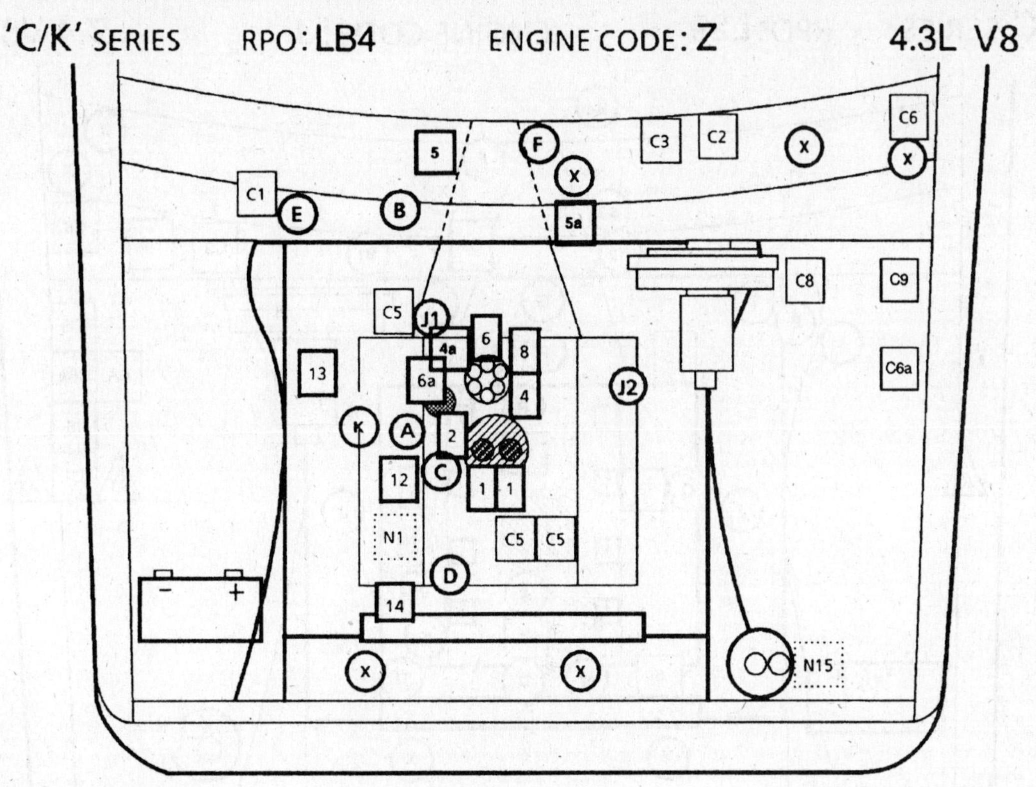

CONTROL MODULE SYSTEM

- C1 Powertrain Control Module (PCM)
- C2 Data Link Connector (DLC)
- C3 Malfunction Indicator Lamp (MIL)
- C5 PCM harness ground
- C6 Fuse block
- C6a Underhood electrical center
- C8 Fuel pump prime terminal
- C9 Underhood electrical center

PCM CONTROLLED COMPONENTS

- 1 Fuel injector
- 2 Idle Air Control (IAC)
- 4 EGR valve (Federal Emissions)
- 4a Linear Exhaust Gas Recirculation (EGR) Valve (California Emissions)
- 5 Transmission connector (4L60E Automatic transmission)
- 5a Transmission connector (4L80E Automatic transmission)
- 6 Ignition Control (IC) distributor
- 6a Remote ignition coil
- 8 Oil pressure switch
- 12 Exhaust Gas Recirculation (EGR) Vacuum Solenoid
- 13 A/C Low Presure Switch (pressing cycling)
- 14 A/C High Pressure cut-out switch

PCM INFORMATION SENSORS

- A Manifold Absolute Pressure (MAP) sensor
- B Heated Oxygen Sensor (HO2S)
- C Throttle Position (TP) sensor
- D Engine Coolant Temperature (ECT) sensor
- E VSS buffer module
- F Vehicle Speed Sensor (VSS)
- J1 Knock Sensor (KS) 1 of 2
- J2 Knock Sensor (KS) 2 of 2
- K Canister purge solenoid (California Emissions)

EMISSION COMPONENTS (NOT ECM CONTROLLED)

- N1 Crankcase vent valve
- N15 EVAP canister

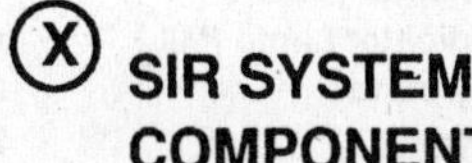

SIR SYSTEM COMPONENT

87984G22

Fig. 124 Component locations — 1995 4.3L engines

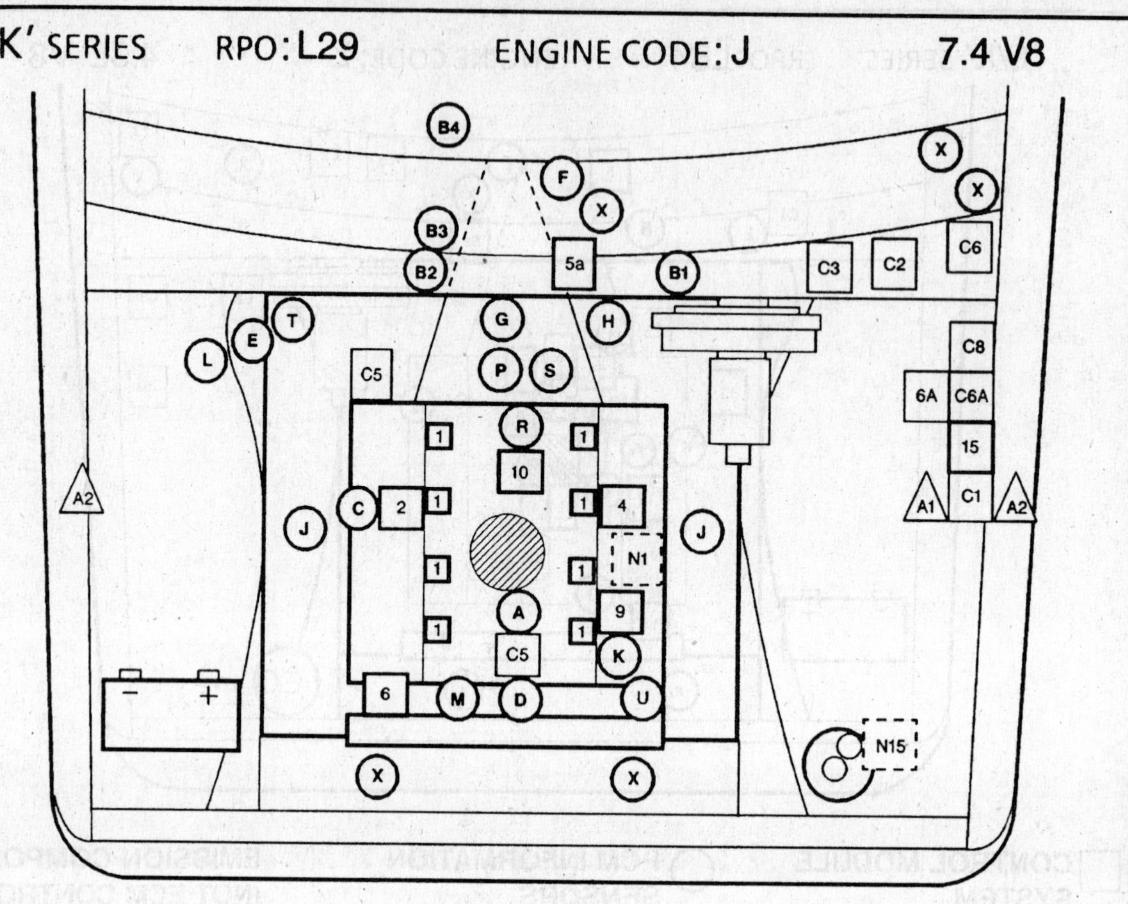

CONTROL MODULE SYSTEM

- C1 Vehicle Control Module (VCM)
- C2 Data Link Connector (DLC)
- C3 Malfunction Indicator Lamp (MIL)
- C5 VCM harness ground
- C6 Fuse block (I/P)
- C6a Underhood electrical center (U/H)
- C8 Fuel pump test connector terminal

VCM CONTROLLED COMPONENTS

- 1 Fuel injectors
- 2 Idle Air Control (IAC)
- 4 EGR valve
- 5a Transmission connector (4L80E Automatic transmission)
- 6 Air pump
- 6a Air relay/located in underhood electrical center
- 9 Canister purge solenoid
- 10 Coil driver module
- 15 Fuel pump relay/located in underhood electrical center

CONTROL MODULE INFORMATION SENSORS

- A Manifold Absolute Pressure (MAP) sensor
- B1 HO2S Bank 1 Sensor 1
- B2 HO2S Bank 2 Sensor 1
- B3 HO2S Bank 1 Sensor 2
- B4 HO2S Bank 2 Sensor 2
- C Throttle Position (TP) sensor
- D Engine Coolant Temperature (ECT) sensor
- E Mass Air Flow (MAF) sensor
- F Vehicle Speed Sensor (VSS)
- G Cam sensor
- H Input Speed Sensor (4L80E Automatic Transmission)
- J Knock Sensors (KS)
- K EVAP vacuum switch
- L Intake Air Temperature (IAT) sensor
- M Crankshaft Position (CKP) sensor
- P Distributor
- R Remote ignition coil
- S Fuel pump oil pressure switch
- T A/C low pressure switch (pressure cycling)
- U A/C high pressure cut-out switch

EMISSION COMPONENTS (NOT VCM CONTROLLED)

- N1 Crankcase ventilation valve
- N15 Fuel vapor canister

SIR SYSTEM COMPONENTS

ANTILOCK BRAKE COMPONENTS

- A1 Antilock module
- A2 Front wheel speed sensor

87984G23

Fig. 125 Component locations — 1996 7.4L engines

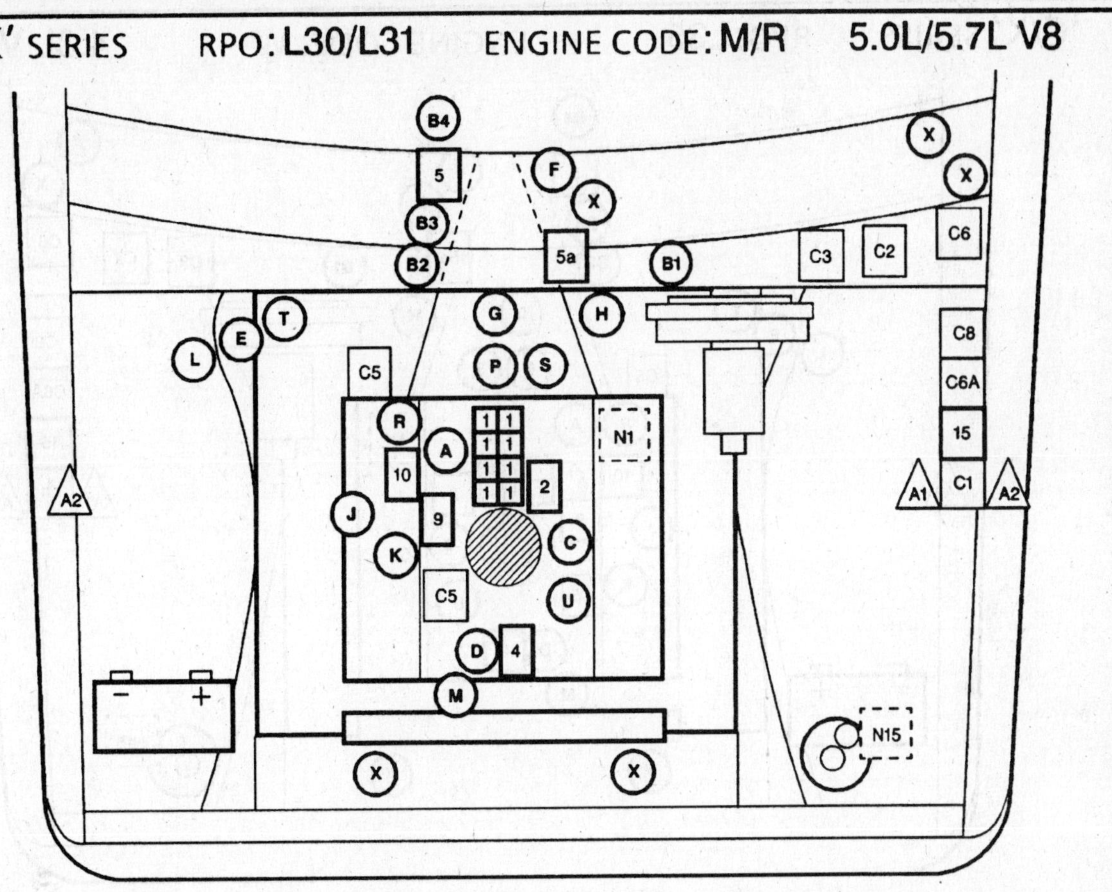

CONTROL MODULE SYSTEM

- C1 Vehicle Control Module (VCM)
- C2 Data Link Connector (DLC)
- C3 Malfunction Indicator Lamp (MIL)
- C5 VCM harness ground
- C6 Fuse block (I/P)
- C6a Underhood electrical center (U/H)
- C8 Fuel pump test connector terminal

VCM CONTROLLED COMPONENTS

- 1 Fuel injectors
- 2 Idle Air Control (IAC)
- 4 EGR valve
- 5 Transmission connector (4L60E Automatic transmission)
- 5a Transmission connector (4L80E Automatic transmission)
- 9 Canister purge solenoid
- 10 Coil driver module
- 15 Fuel pump relay/located in underhood electrical center

CONTROL MODULE INFORMATION SENSORS

- A Manifold Absolute Pressure (MAP) sensor
- B1 HO2S Bank 1 Sensor 1
- B2 HO2S Bank 2 Sensor 1
- B3 HO2S Bank 1 Sensor 2
- B4 HO2S Bank 2 Sensor 2 (5.7L) HO2S Bank 1 Sensor 3 (5.0L)
- C Throttle Position (TP) sensor
- D Engine Coolant Temperature (ECT) sensor
- E Mass Air Flow (MAF) sensor
- F Vehicle Speed Sensor (VSS)
- G Cam sensor
- H Input Speed Sensor (4L80E Automatic Transmission)
- J Knock Sensor (KS)
- K EVAP vacuum switch
- L Intake Air Temperature (IAT) sensor
- M Crankshaft Position (CKP) sensor
- P Distributor
- R Remote ignition coil
- S Fuel pump oil pressure switch
- T A/C low pressure switch (pressure cycling)
- U A/C high pressure cut-out switch

EMISSION COMPONENTS (NOT VCM CONTROLLED)

- N1 Crankcase ventilation valve
- N15 Fuel vapor canister

SIR SYSTEM COMPONENTS

ANTILOCK BRAKE COMPONENTS

- A1 Antilock module
- A2 Front wheel speed sensor

87984G24

Fig. 126 Component locations — 1996 5.0L/5.7L engines

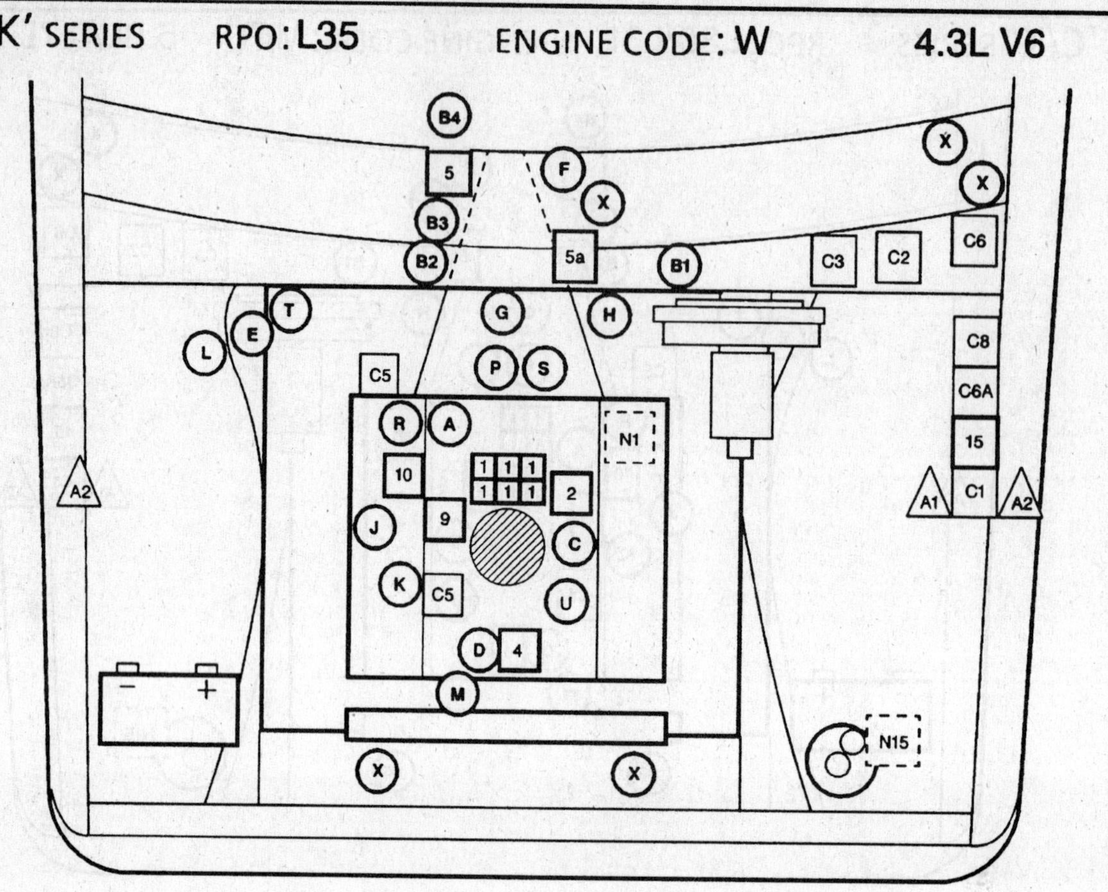

CONTROL MODULE SYSTEM

- C1 Vehicle Control Module (VCM)
- C2 Data Link Connector (DLC)
- C3 Malfunction Indicator Lamp (MIL)
- C5 VCM harness ground
- C6 Fuse block (I/P)
- C6a Underhood electrical center (U/H)
- C8 Fuel pump test connector terminal

VCM CONTROLLED COMPONENTS

- 1 Fuel injectors
- 2 Idle Air Control (IAC)
- 4 EGR valve
- 5 Transmission connector (4L60E Automatic transmission)
- 5a Transmission connector (4L80E Automatic transmission)
- 9 Canister purge solenoid
- 10 Coil driver module
- 15 Fuel pump relay/located in underhood electrical center

CONTROL MODULE INFORMATION SENSORS

- A Manifold Absolute Pressure (MAP) sensor
- B1 HO2S Bank 1 Sensor 1
- B2 HO2S Bank 2 Sensor 1
- B3 HO2S Bank 1 Sensor 2
- B4 HO2S Bank 1 Sensor 3
- C Throttle Position (TP) sensor
- D Engine Coolant Temperature (ECT) sensor
- E Mass Air Flow (MAF) sensor
- F Vehicle Speed Sensor (VSS)
- G Cam sensor
- H Input Speed Sensor (4L80E Automatic Transmission)
- J Knock Sensor (KS)
- K EVAP vacuum switch
- L Intake Air Temperature (IAT) sensor
- M Crankshaft Position (CKP) sensor
- P Distributor
- R Remote ignition coil
- S Fuel pump oil pressure switch
- T A/C low pressure switch (pressure cycling)
- U A/C high pressure cut-out switch

EMISSION COMPONENTS (NOT VCM CONTROLLED)

- N1 Crankcase ventilation valve
- N15 Fuel vapor canister

SIR SYSTEM COMPONENTS

ANTILOCK BRAKE COMPONENTS

- A1 Antilock module
- A2 Front wheel speed sensor

87984G25

Fig. 127 Component locations — 1996 4.3L engines

VACUUM DIAGRAMS

Following is a listing of vacuum diagrams for many of the engine and emissions package combinations covered by this manual. Because vacuum circuits will vary based on various engine and vehicle options, always refer first to the vehicle emission control information label. Should the label be missing, or should the vehicle be equipped with a different engine from the original equipment, refer to the diagrams below for the same or similar configuration.

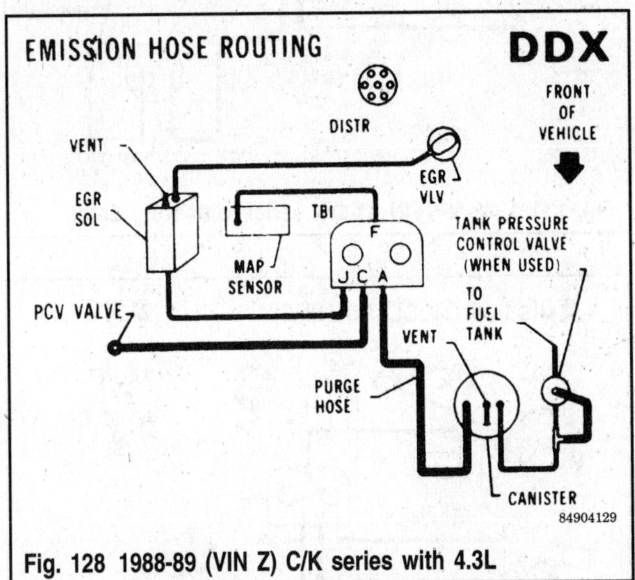

Fig. 128 1988-89 (VIN Z) C/K series with 4.3L

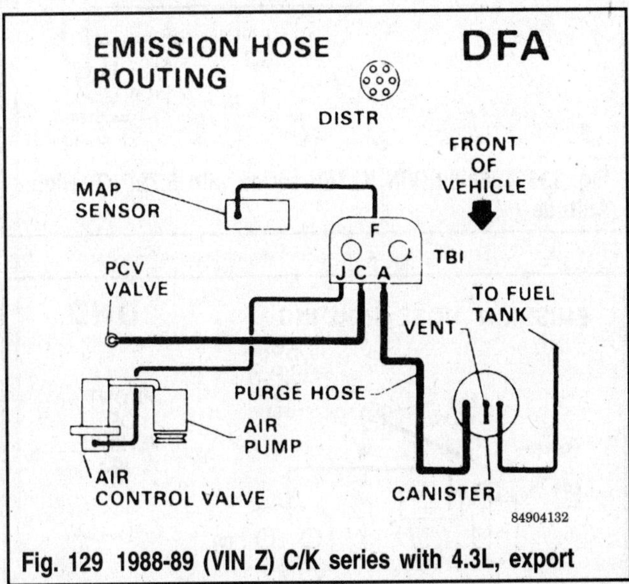

Fig. 129 1988-89 (VIN Z) C/K series with 4.3L, export

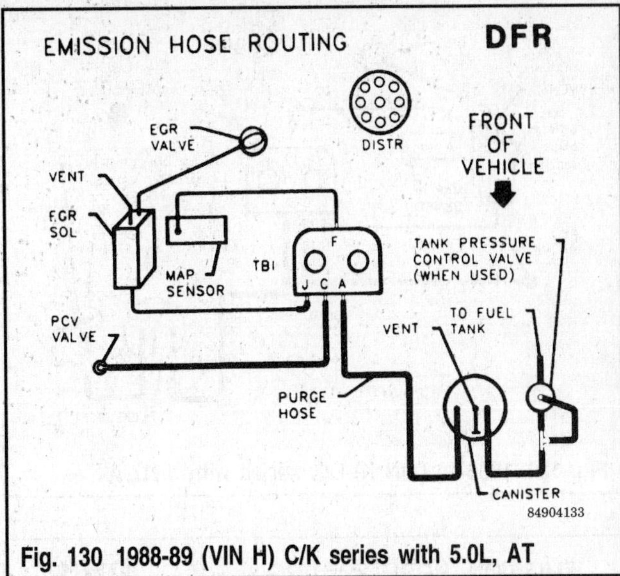

Fig. 130 1988-89 (VIN H) C/K series with 5.0L, AT

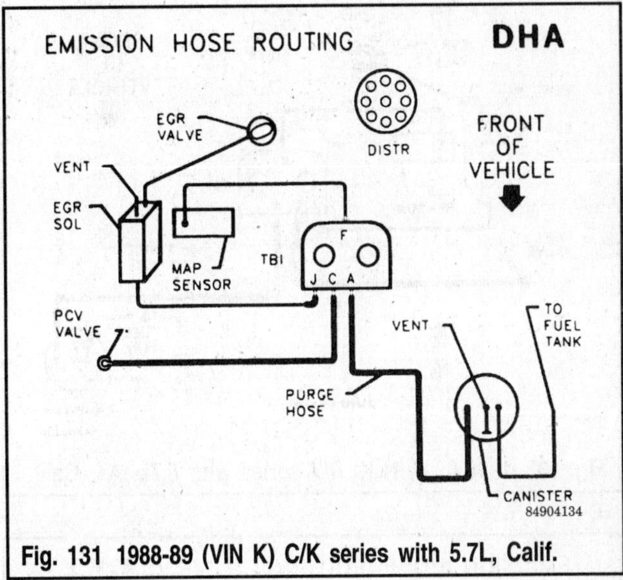

Fig. 131 1988-89 (VIN K) C/K series with 5.7L, Calif.

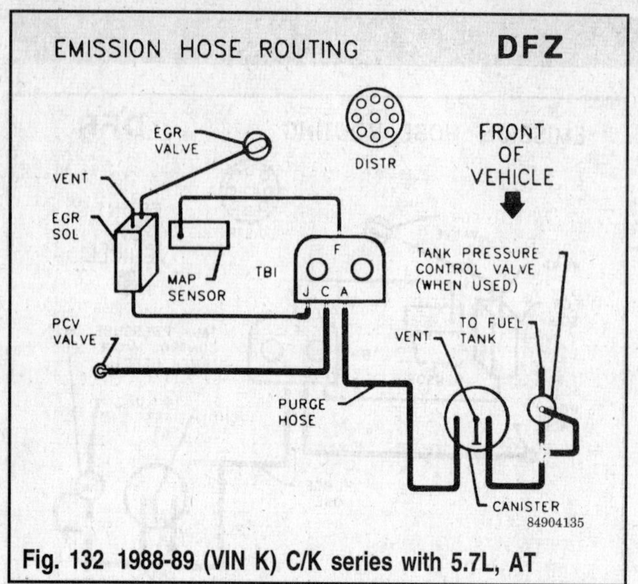

Fig. 132 1988-89 (VIN K) C/K series with 5.7L, AT

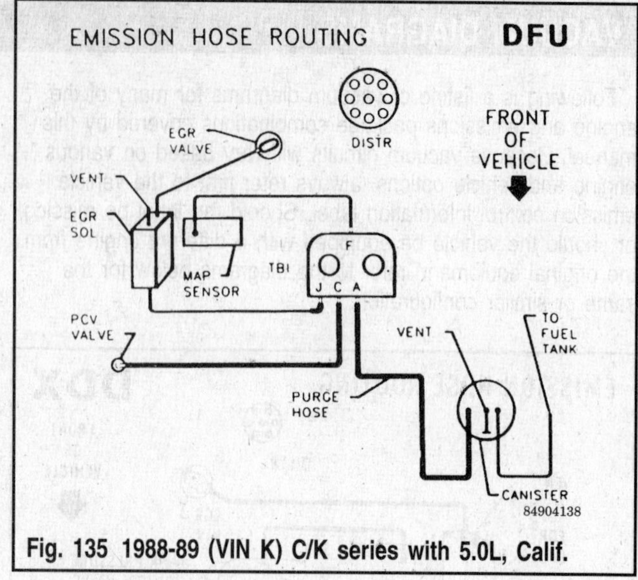

Fig. 135 1988-89 (VIN K) C/K series with 5.0L, Calif.

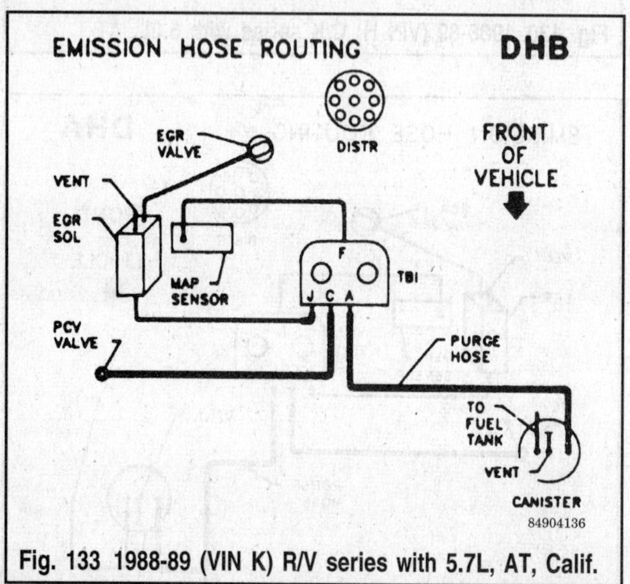

Fig. 133 1988-89 (VIN K) R/V series with 5.7L, AT, Calif.

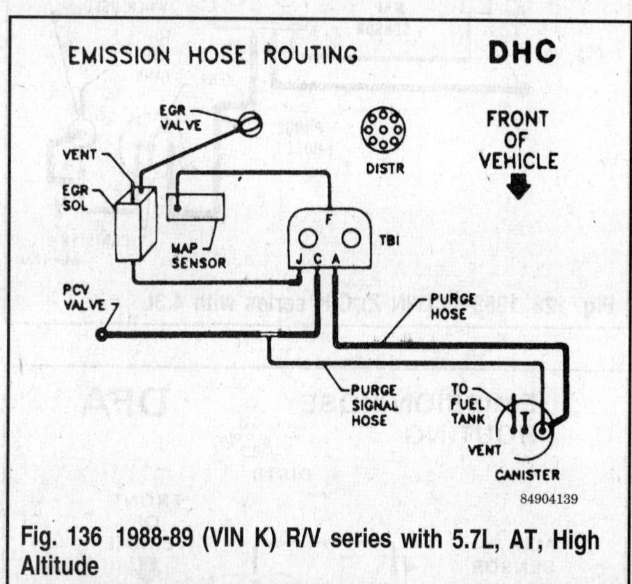

Fig. 136 1988-89 (VIN K) R/V series with 5.7L, AT, High Altitude

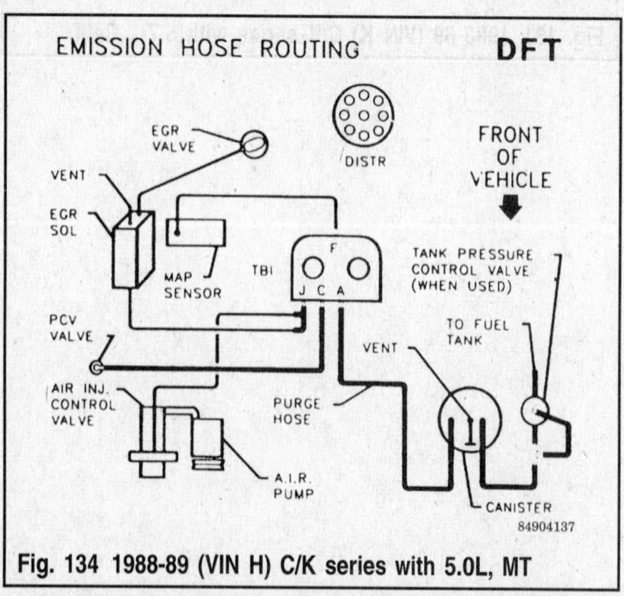

Fig. 134 1988-89 (VIN H) C/K series with 5.0L, MT

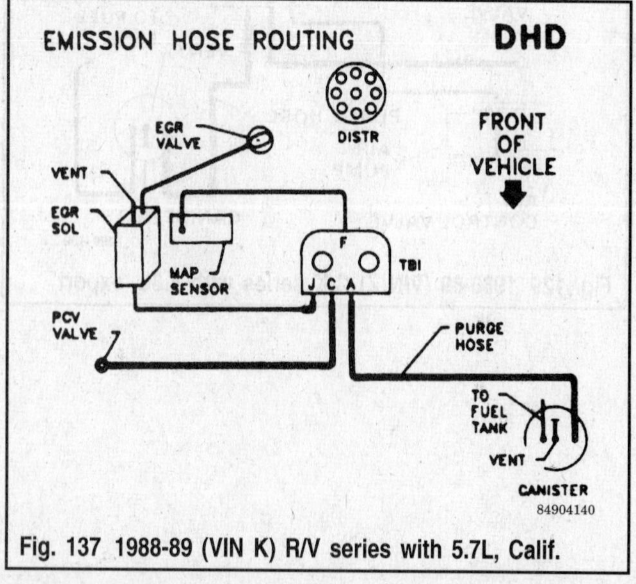

Fig. 137 1988-89 (VIN K) R/V series with 5.7L, Calif.

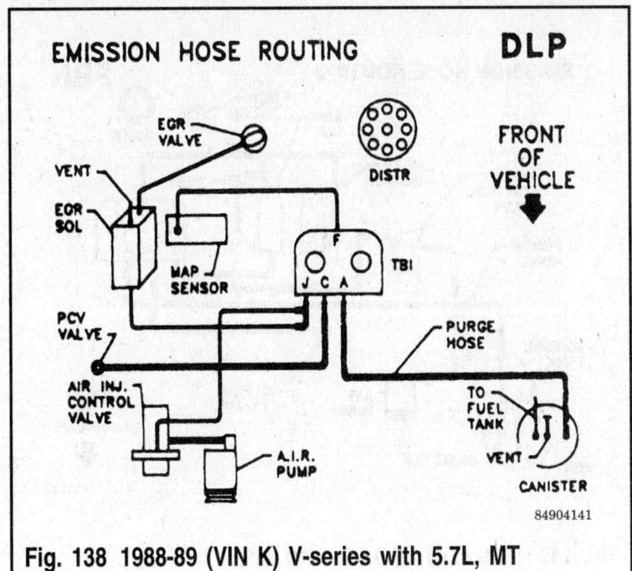

Fig. 138 1988-89 (VIN K) V-series with 5.7L, MT

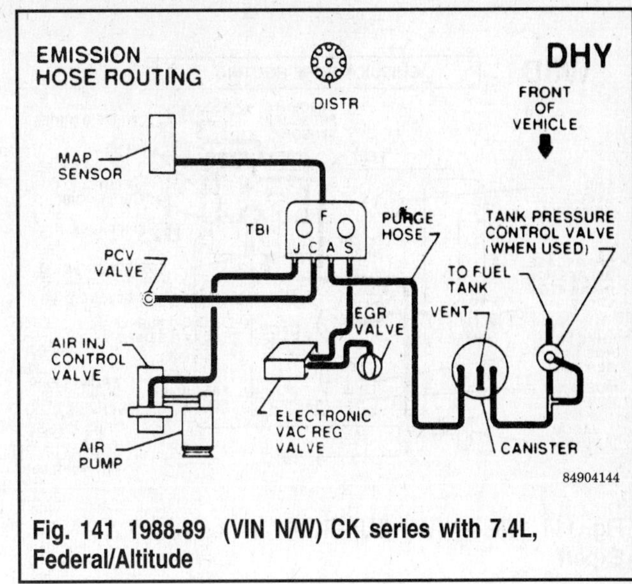

Fig. 141 1988-89 (VIN N/W) CK series with 7.4L, Federal/Altitude

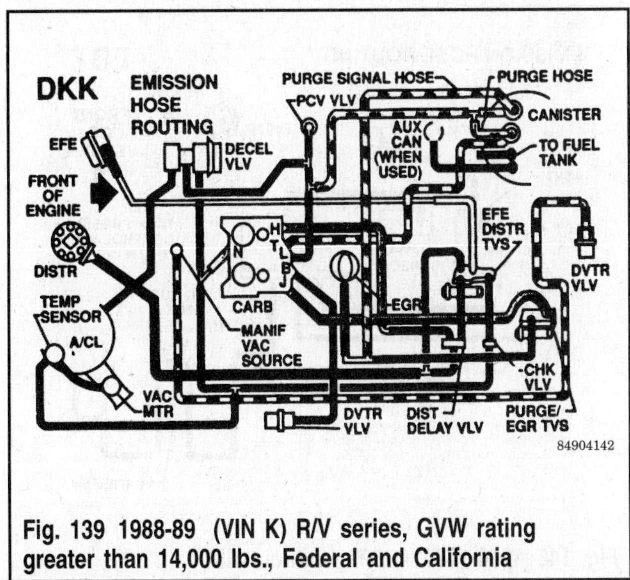

Fig. 139 1988-89 (VIN K) R/V series, GVW rating greater than 14,000 lbs., Federal and California

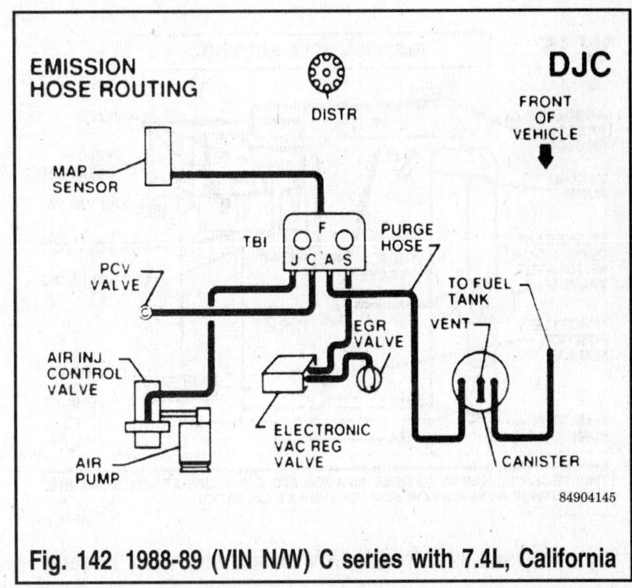

Fig. 142 1988-89 (VIN N/W) C series with 7.4L, California

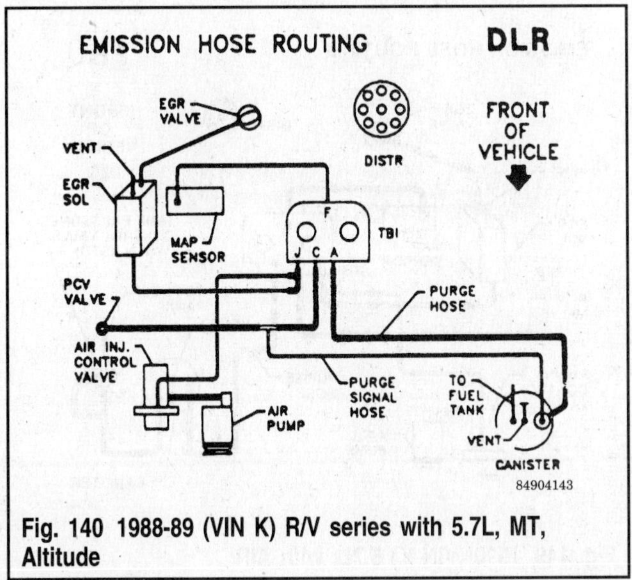

Fig. 140 1988-89 (VIN K) R/V series with 5.7L, MT, Altitude

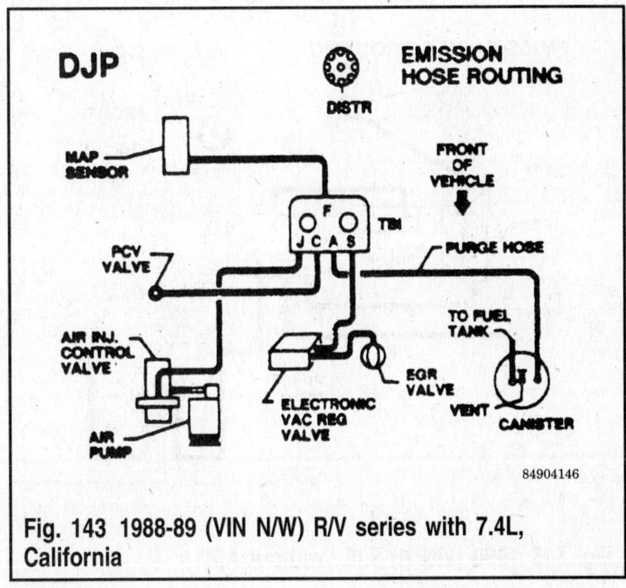

Fig. 143 1988-89 (VIN N/W) R/V series with 7.4L, California

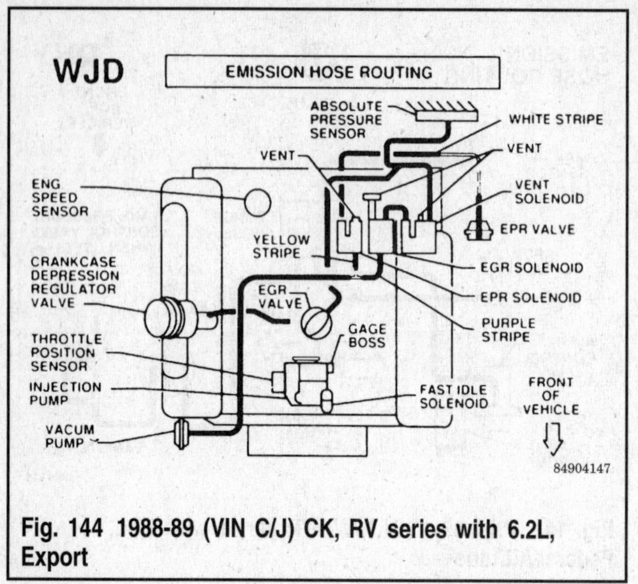

Fig. 144 1988-89 (VIN C/J) CK, RV series with 6.2L, Export

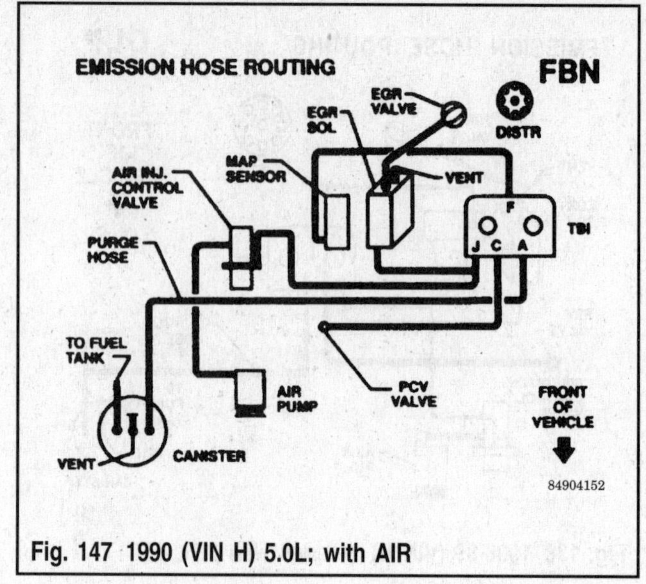

Fig. 147 1990 (VIN H) 5.0L; with AIR

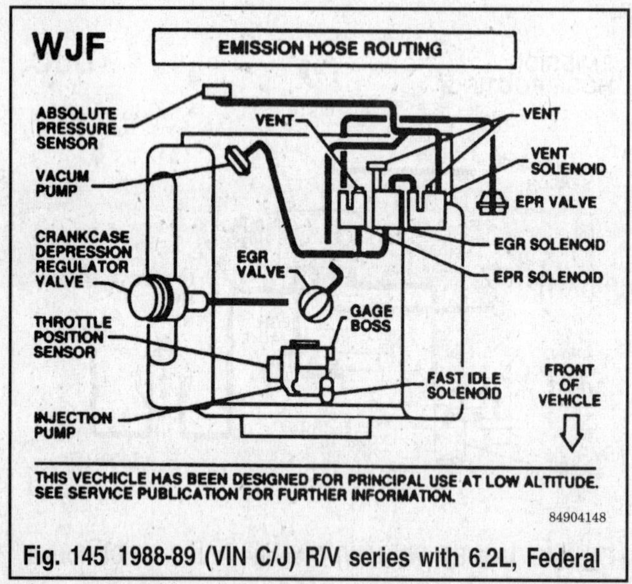

Fig. 145 1988-89 (VIN C/J) R/V series with 6.2L, Federal

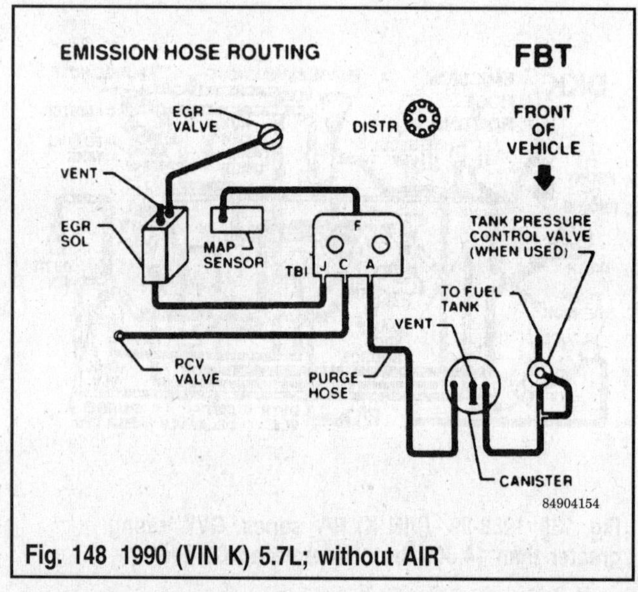

Fig. 148 1990 (VIN K) 5.7L; without AIR

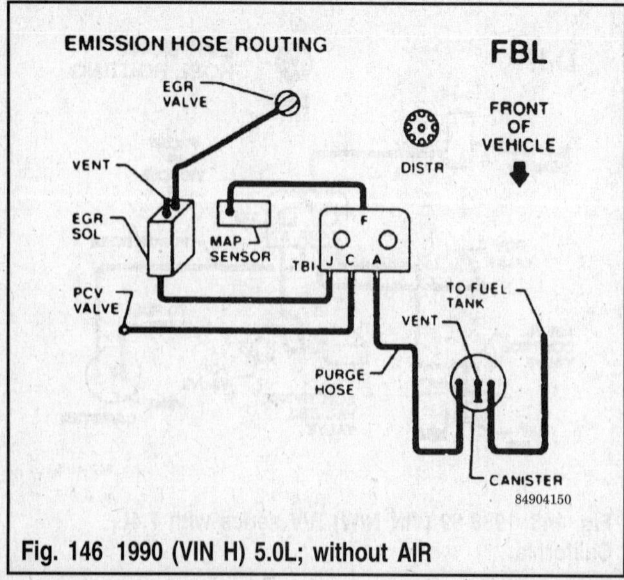

Fig. 146 1990 (VIN H) 5.0L; without AIR

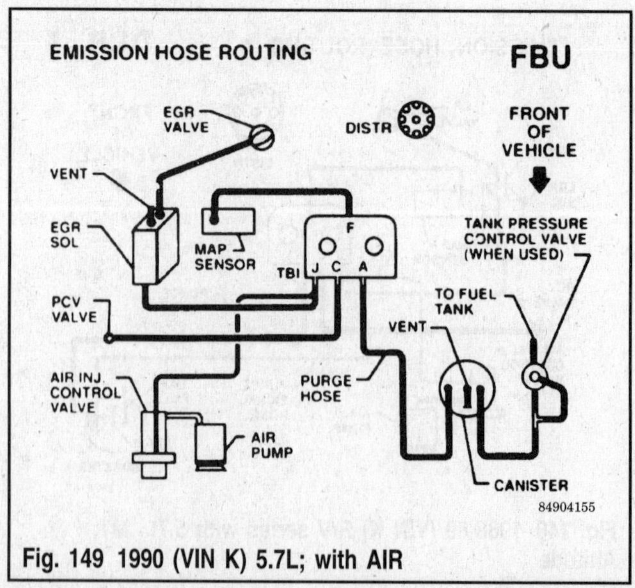

Fig. 149 1990 (VIN K) 5.7L; with AIR

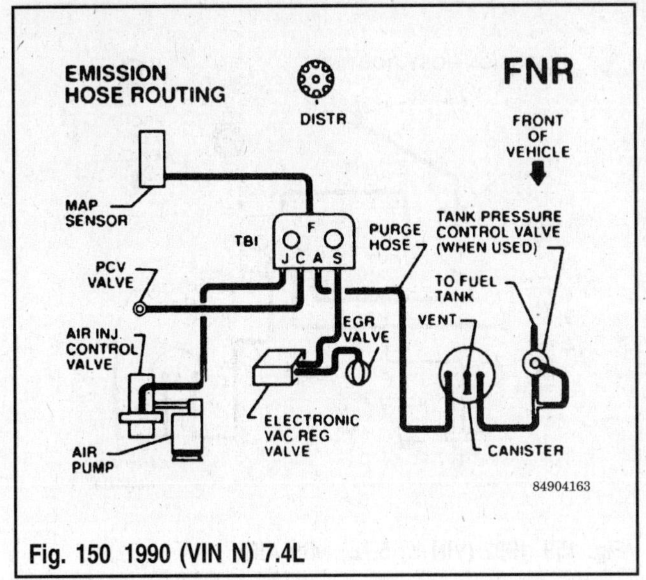

Fig. 150 1990 (VIN N) 7.4L

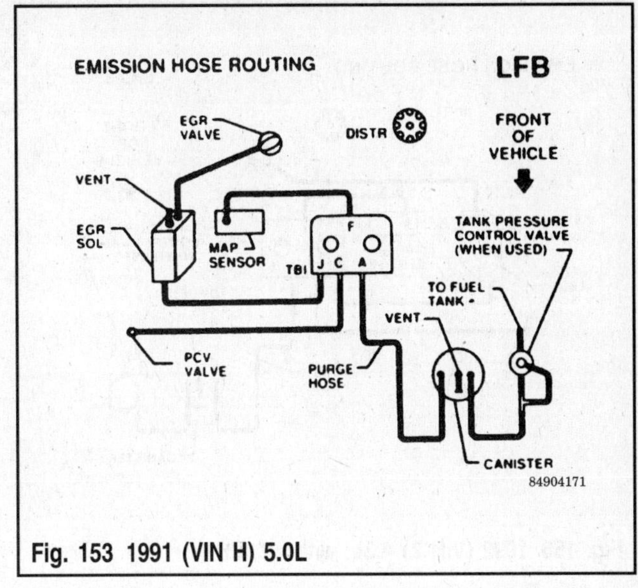

Fig. 153 1991 (VIN H) 5.0L

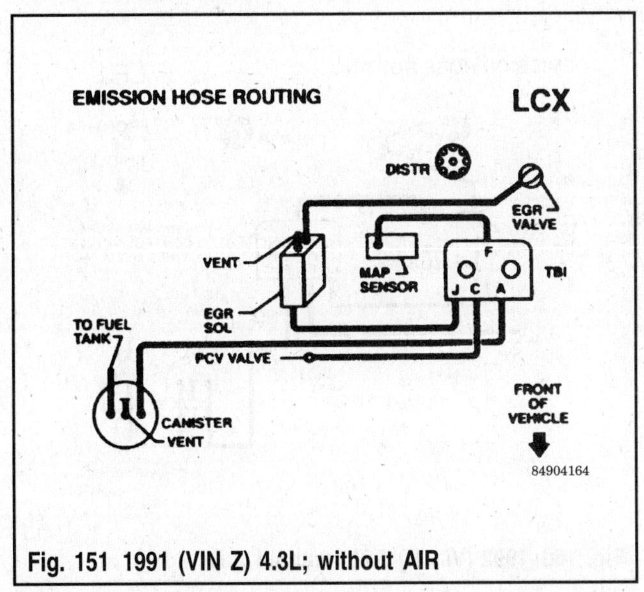

Fig. 151 1991 (VIN Z) 4.3L; without AIR

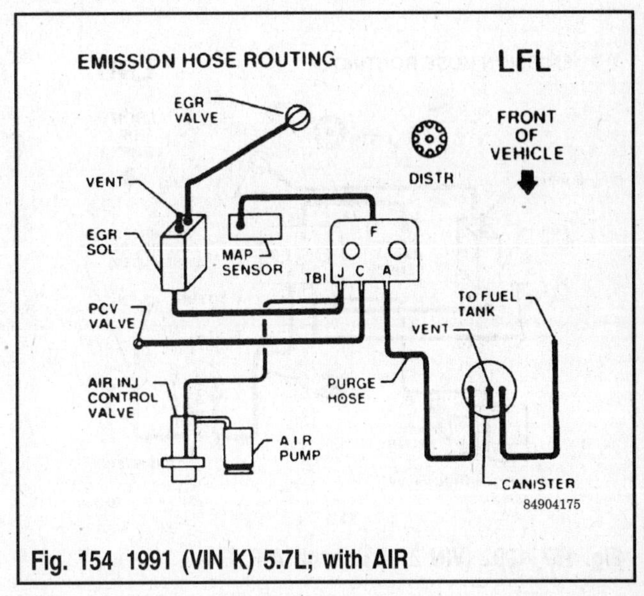

Fig. 154 1991 (VIN K) 5.7L; with AIR

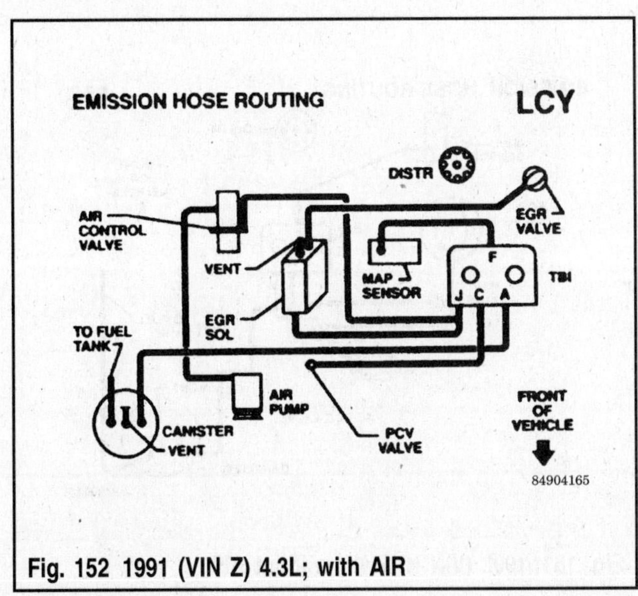

Fig. 152 1991 (VIN Z) 4.3L; with AIR

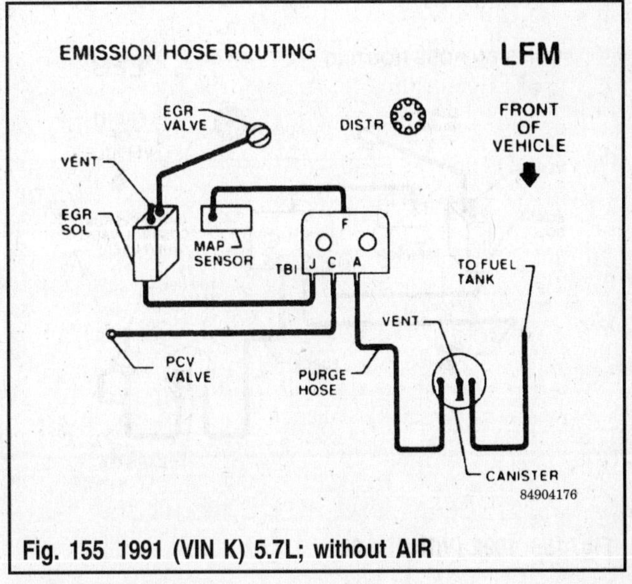

Fig. 155 1991 (VIN K) 5.7L; without AIR

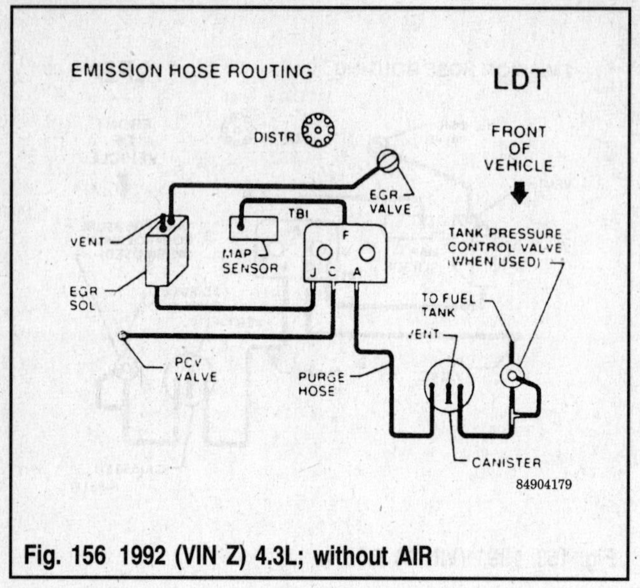

Fig. 156 1992 (VIN Z) 4.3L; without AIR

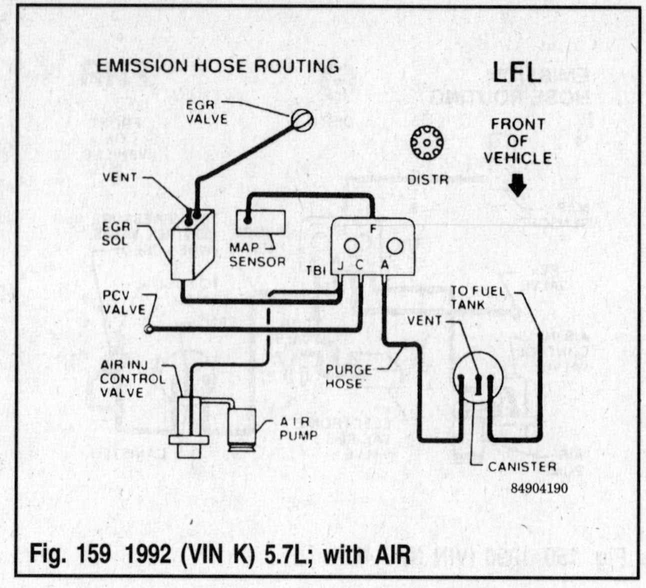

Fig. 159 1992 (VIN K) 5.7L; with AIR

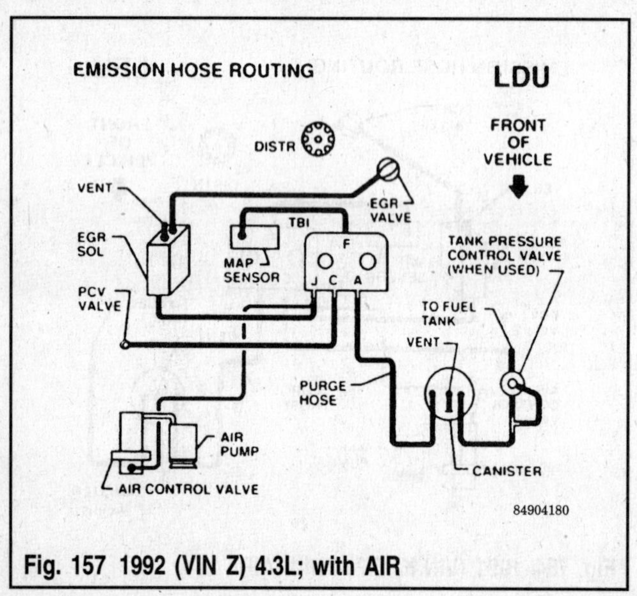

Fig. 157 1992 (VIN Z) 4.3L; with AIR

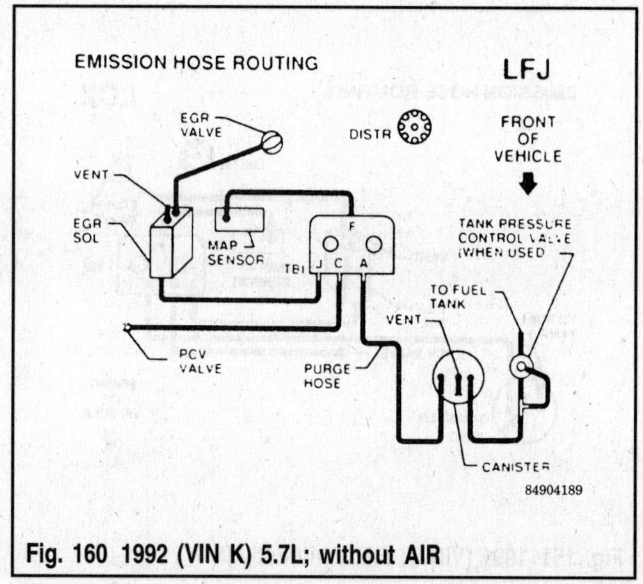

Fig. 160 1992 (VIN K) 5.7L; without AIR

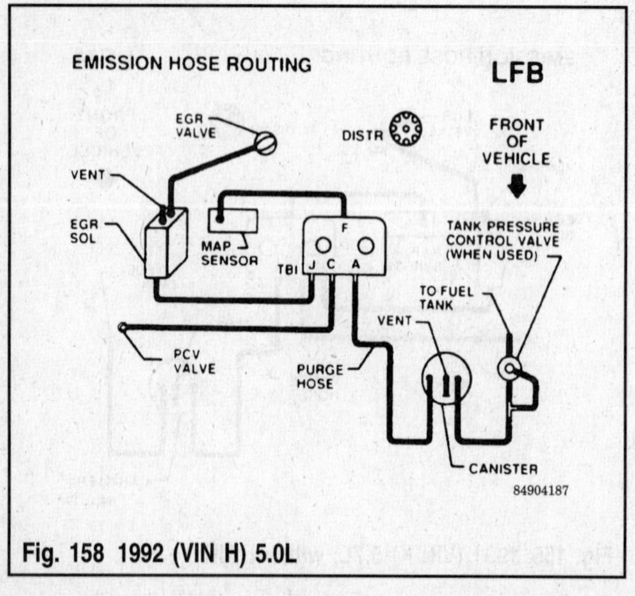

Fig. 158 1992 (VIN H) 5.0L

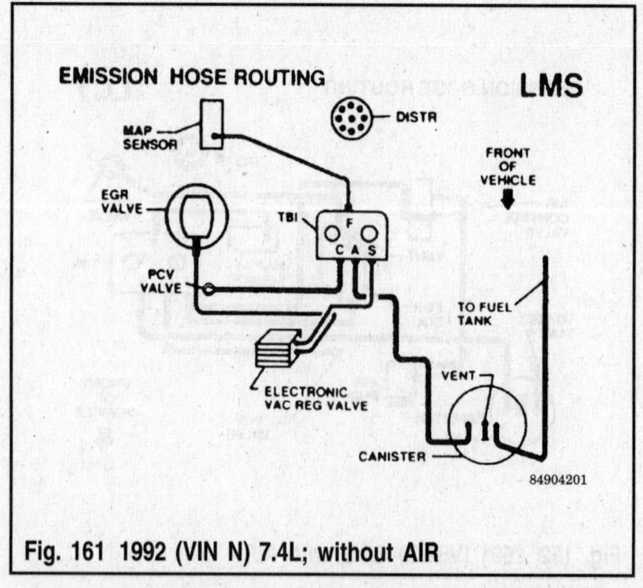

Fig. 161 1992 (VIN N) 7.4L; without AIR

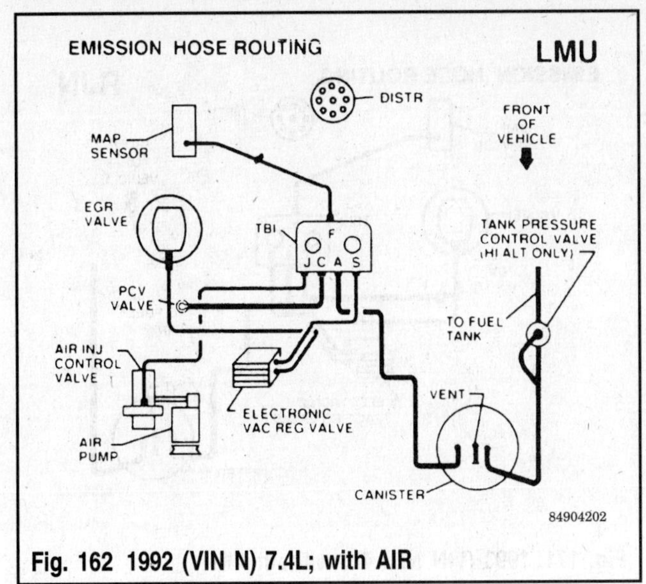

Fig. 162 1992 (VIN N) 7.4L; with AIR

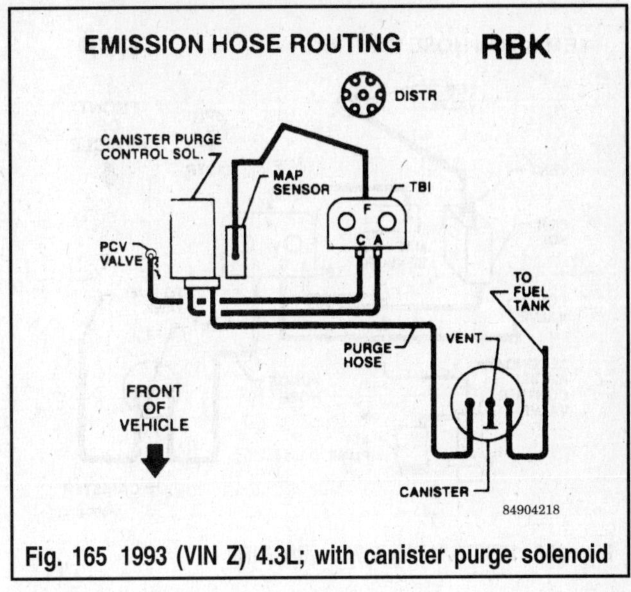

Fig. 165 1993 (VIN Z) 4.3L; with canister purge solenoid

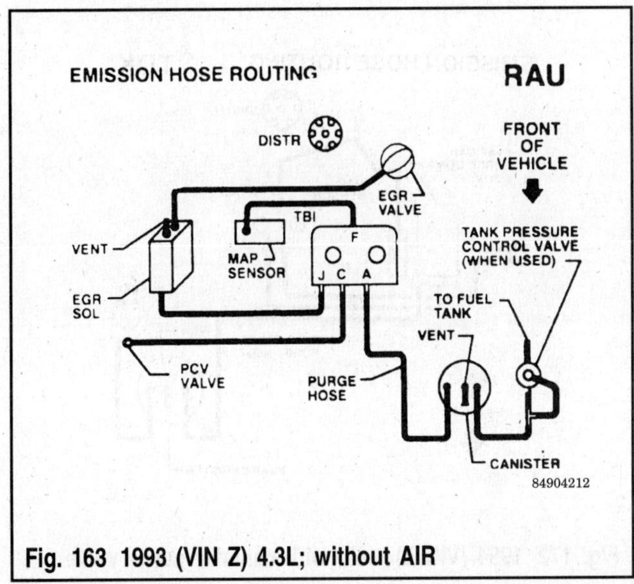

Fig. 163 1993 (VIN Z) 4.3L; without AIR

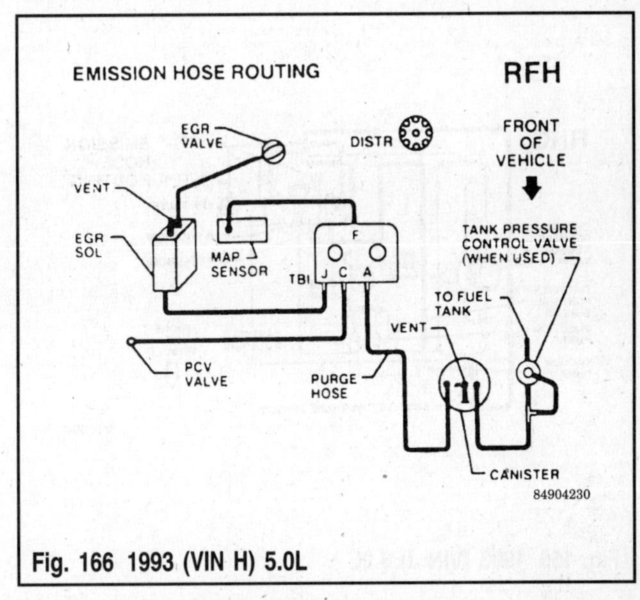

Fig. 166 1993 (VIN H) 5.0L

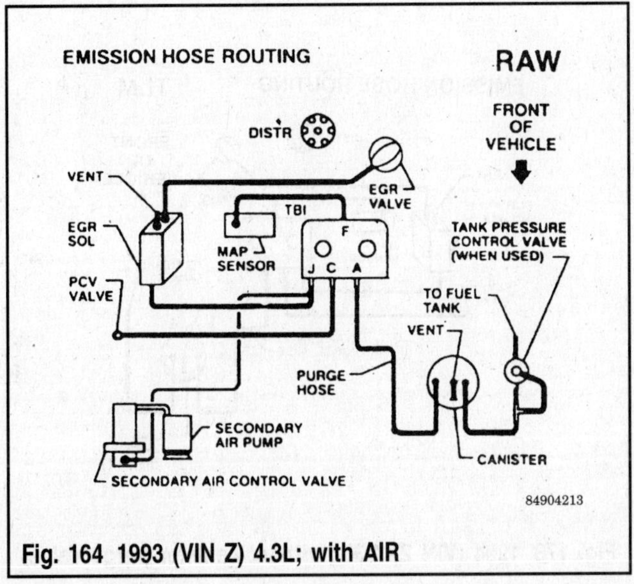

Fig. 164 1993 (VIN Z) 4.3L; with AIR

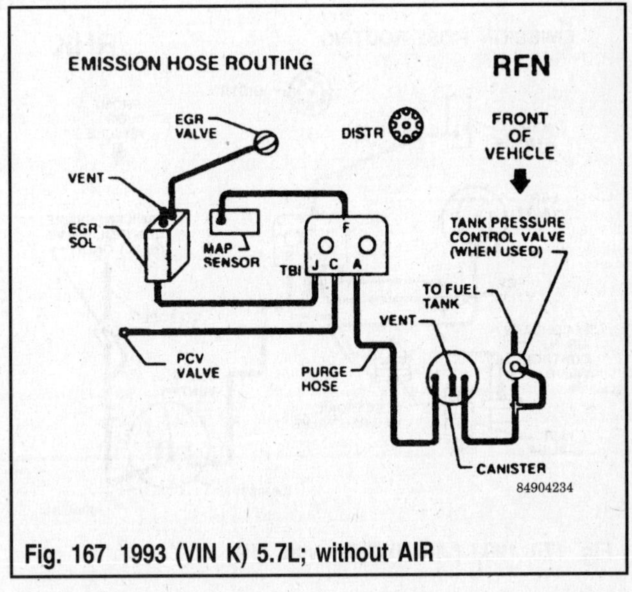

Fig. 167 1993 (VIN K) 5.7L; without AIR

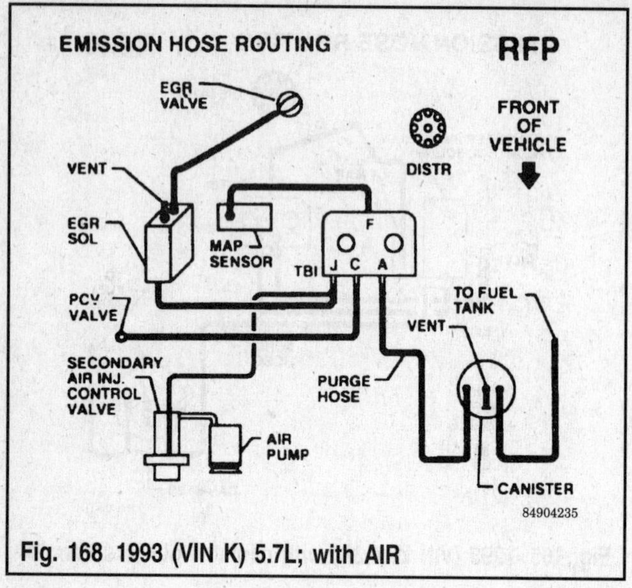

Fig. 168 1993 (VIN K) 5.7L; with AIR

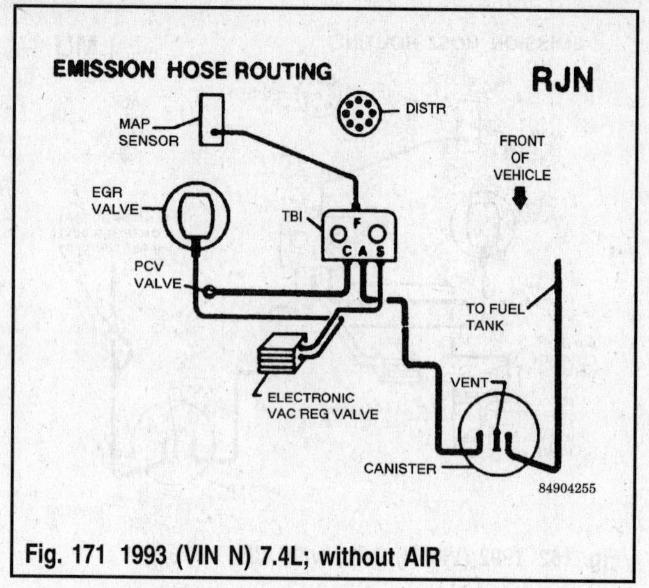

Fig. 171 1993 (VIN N) 7.4L; without AIR

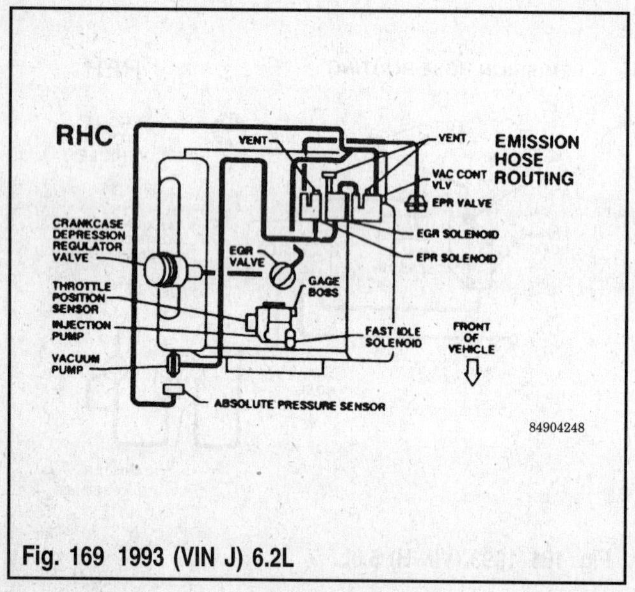

Fig. 169 1993 (VIN J) 6.2L

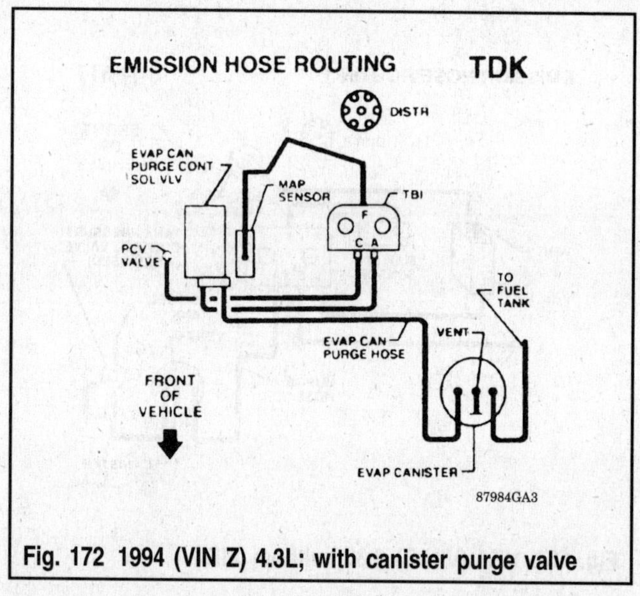

Fig. 172 1994 (VIN Z) 4.3L; with canister purge valve

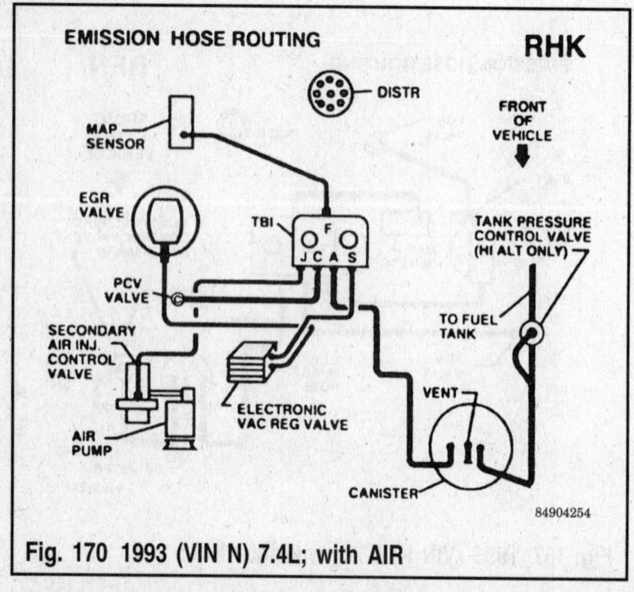

Fig. 170 1993 (VIN N) 7.4L; with AIR

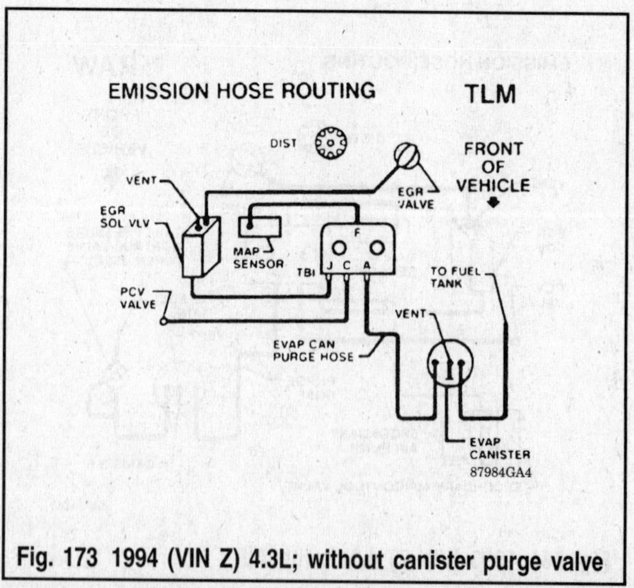

Fig. 173 1994 (VIN Z) 4.3L; without canister purge valve

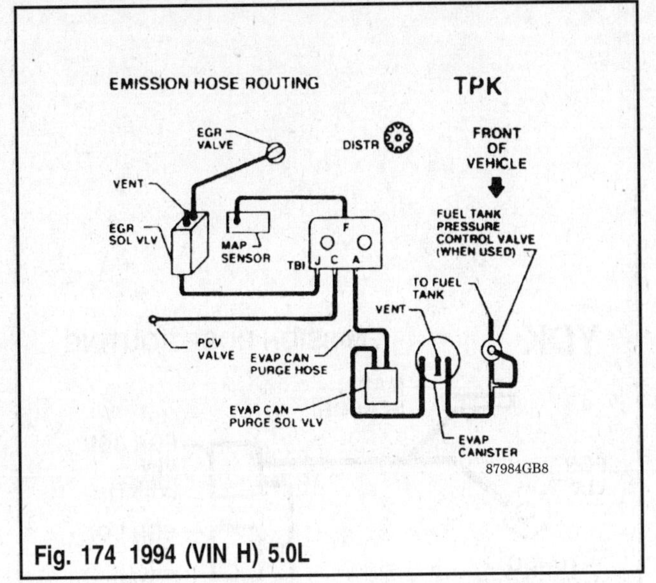

Fig. 174 1994 (VIN H) 5.0L

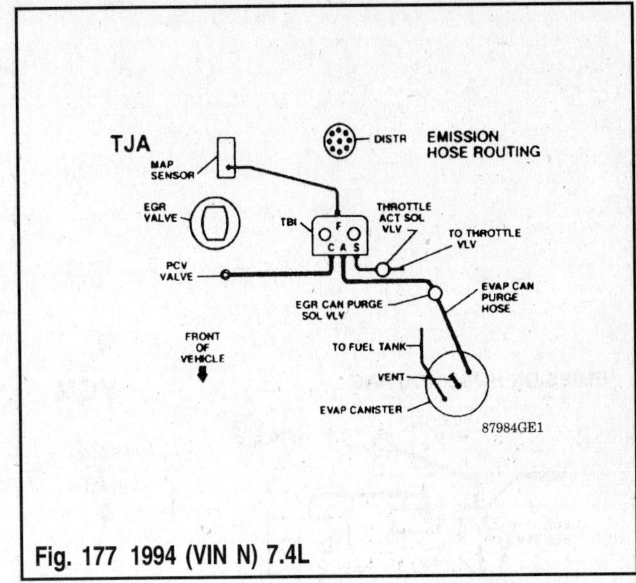

Fig. 177 1994 (VIN N) 7.4L

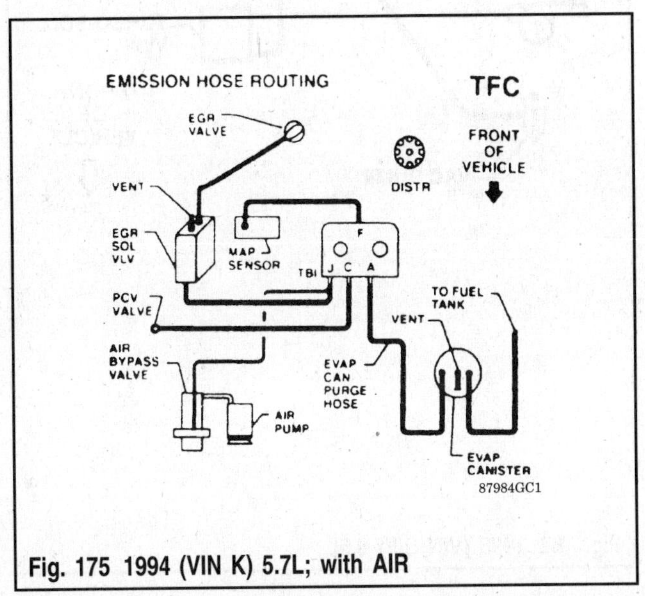

Fig. 175 1994 (VIN K) 5.7L; with AIR

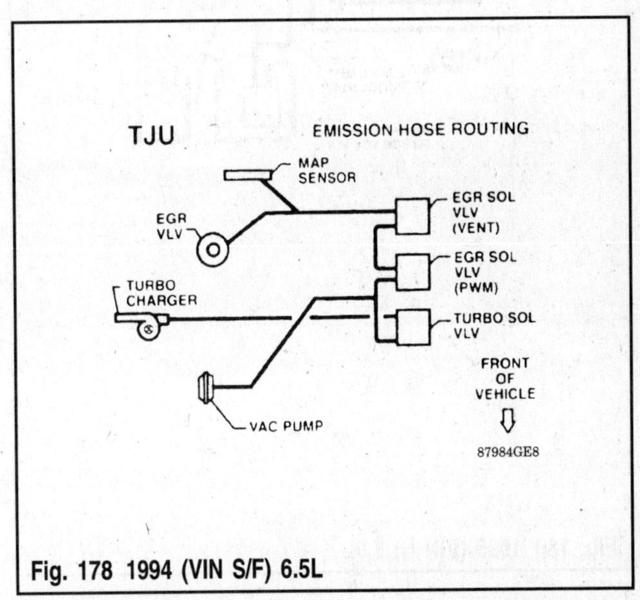

Fig. 178 1994 (VIN S/F) 6.5L

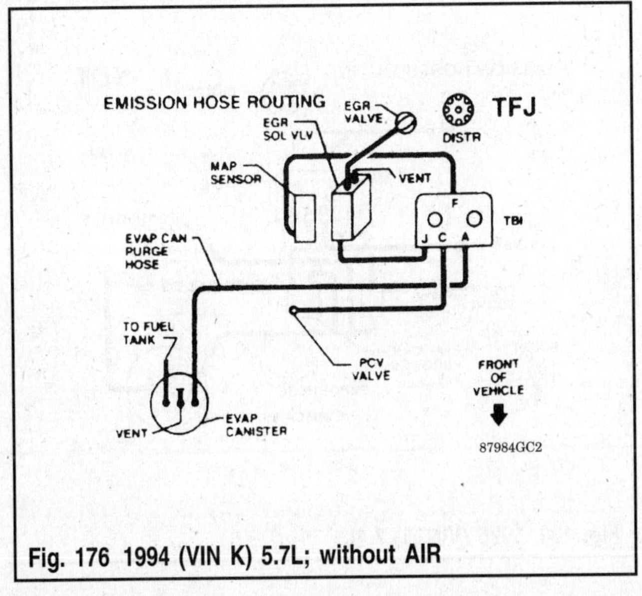

Fig. 176 1994 (VIN K) 5.7L; without AIR

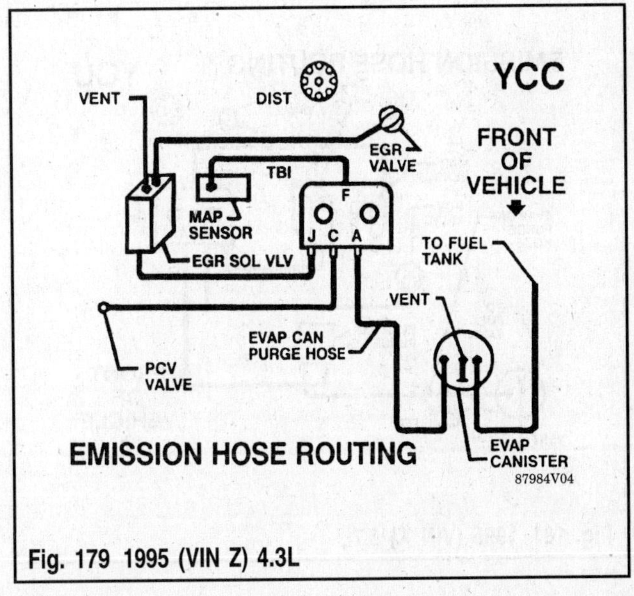

Fig. 179 1995 (VIN Z) 4.3L

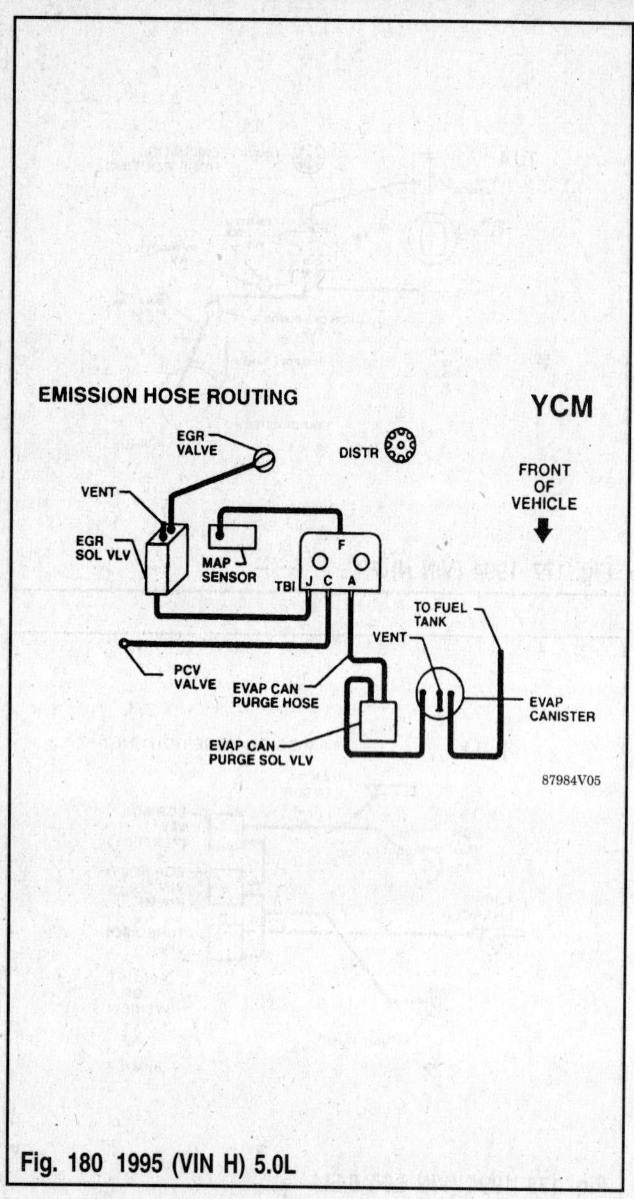

Fig. 180 1995 (VIN H) 5.0L

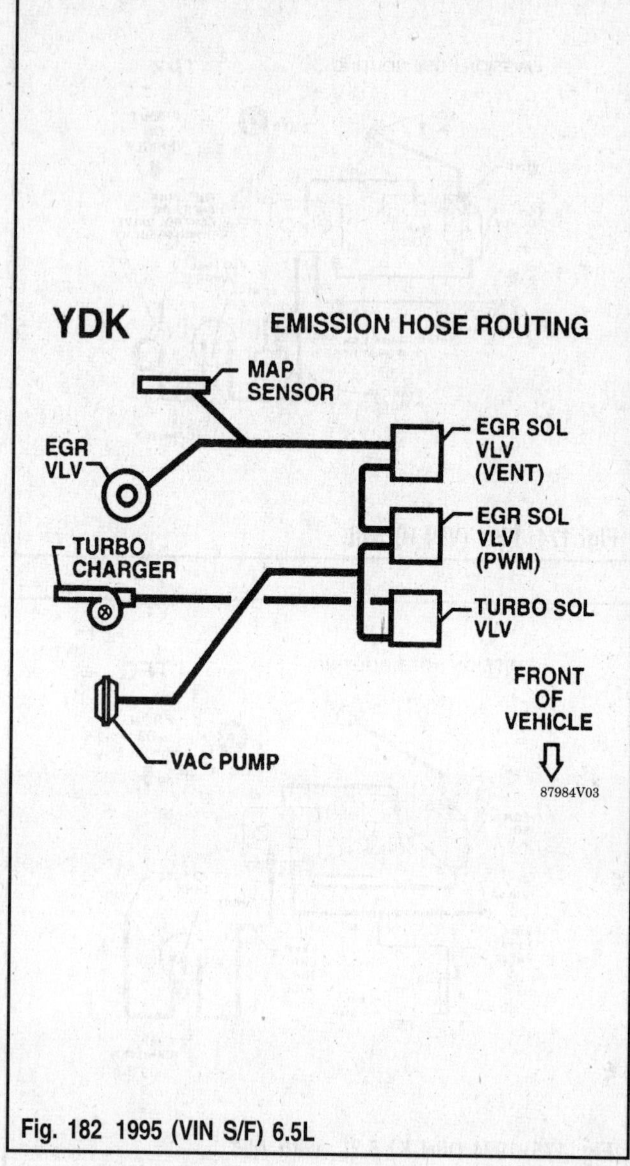

Fig. 182 1995 (VIN S/F) 6.5L

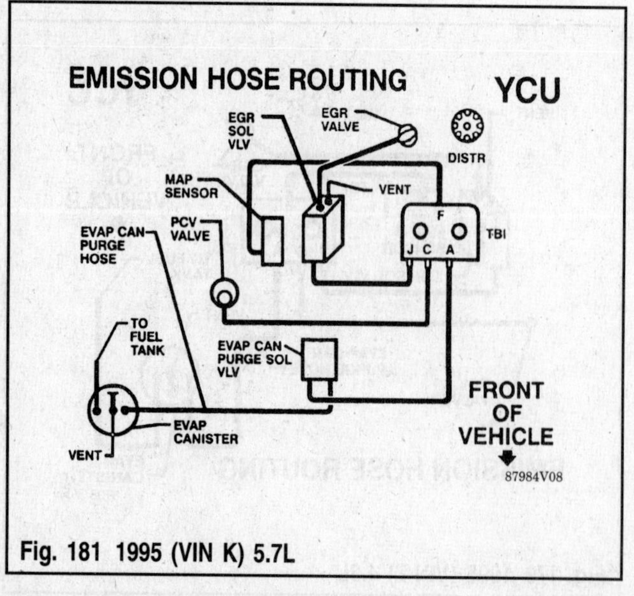

Fig. 181 1995 (VIN K) 5.7L

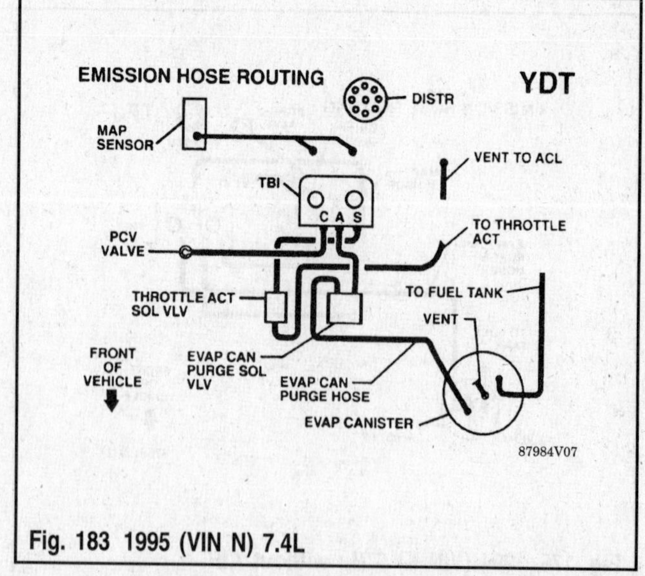

Fig. 183 1995 (VIN N) 7.4L

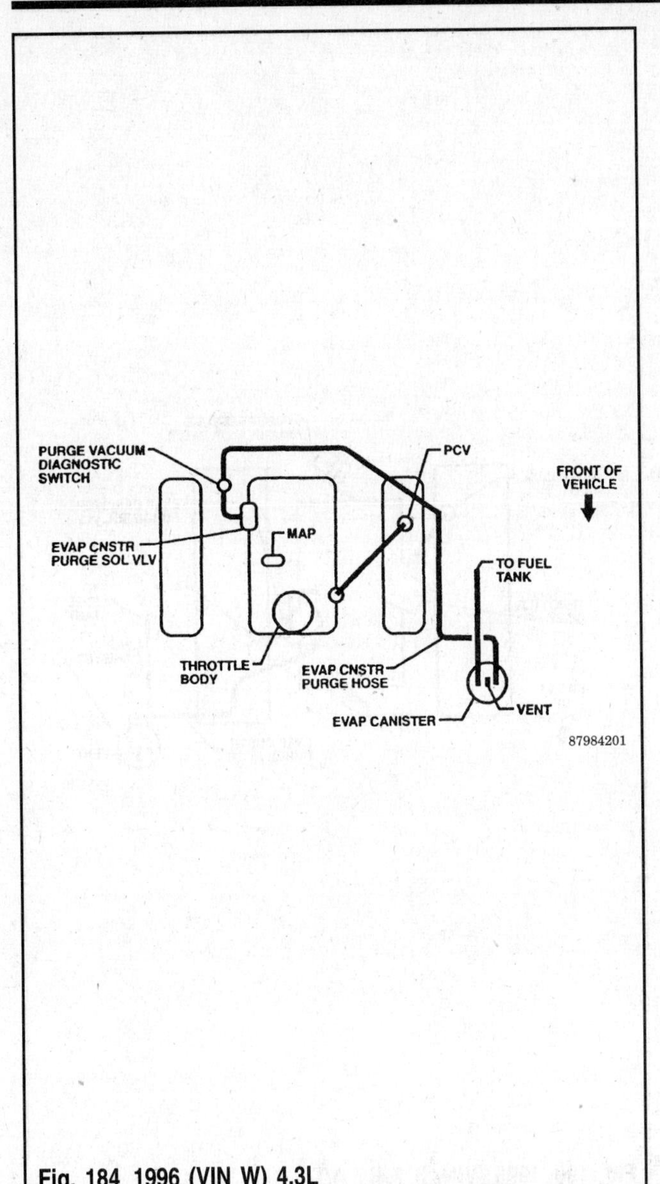

Fig. 184 1996 (VIN W) 4.3L

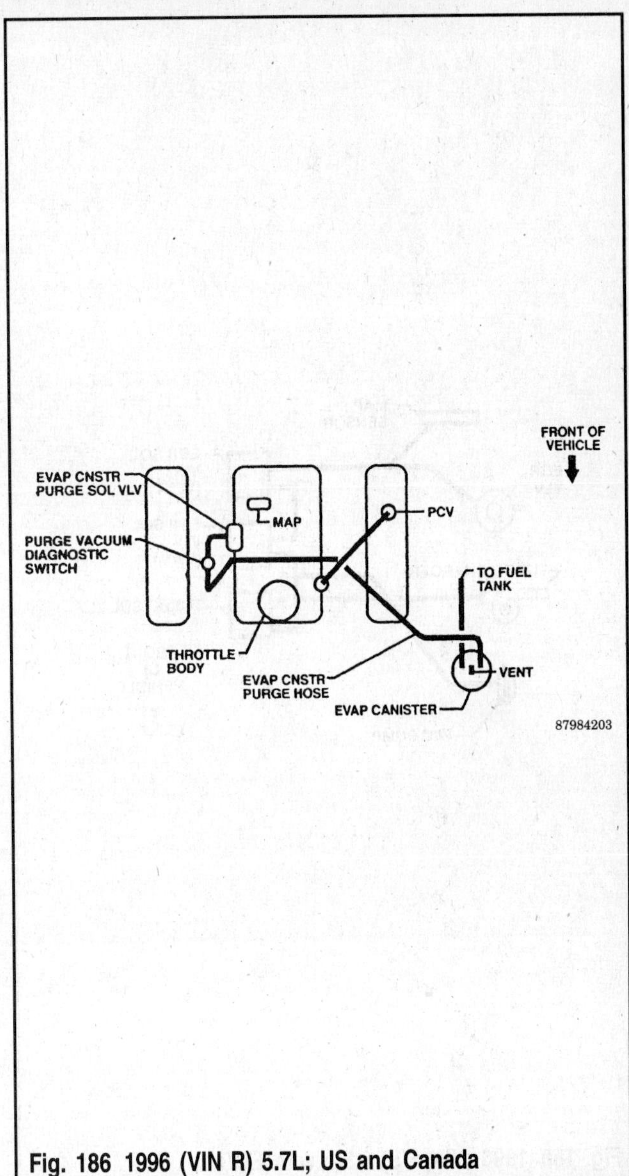

Fig. 186 1996 (VIN R) 5.7L; US and Canada

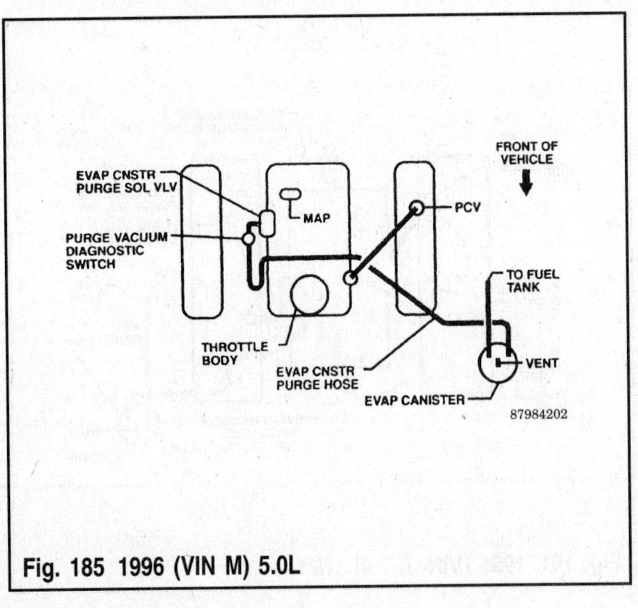

Fig. 185 1996 (VIN M) 5.0L

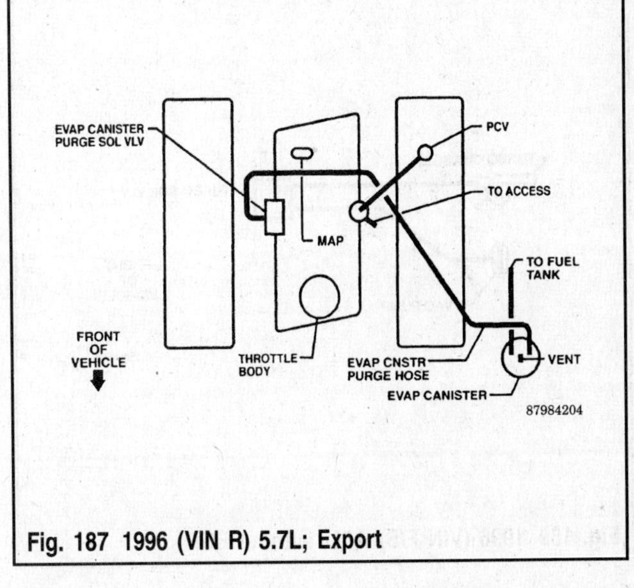

Fig. 187 1996 (VIN R) 5.7L; Export

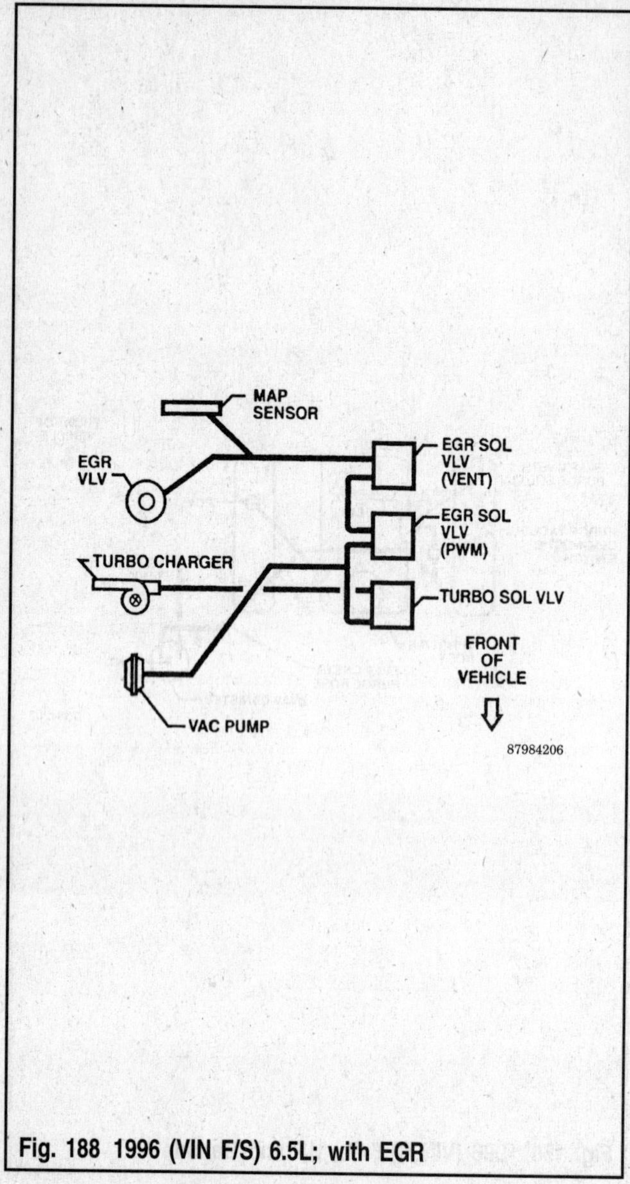

Fig. 188 1996 (VIN F/S) 6.5L; with EGR

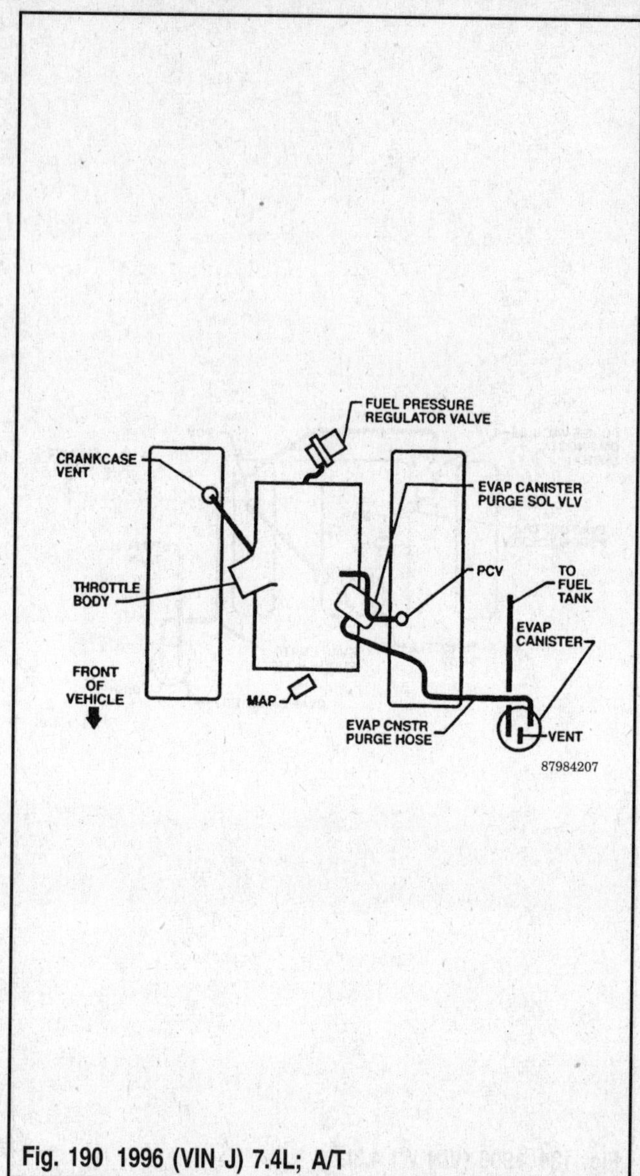

Fig. 190 1996 (VIN J) 7.4L; A/T

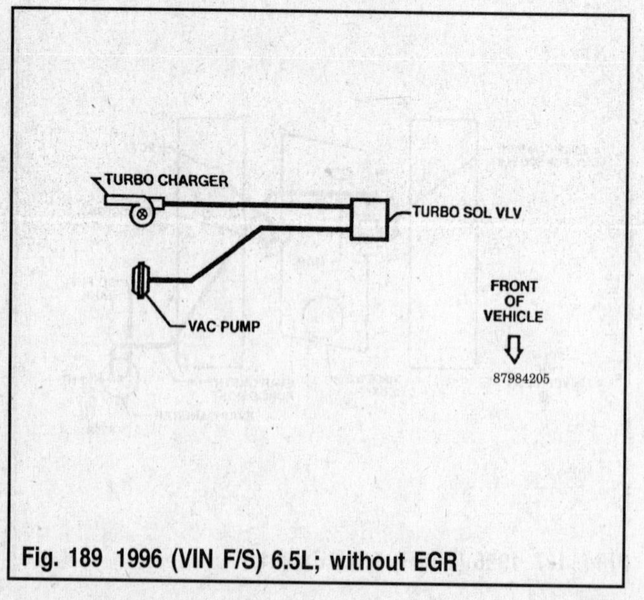

Fig. 189 1996 (VIN F/S) 6.5L; without EGR

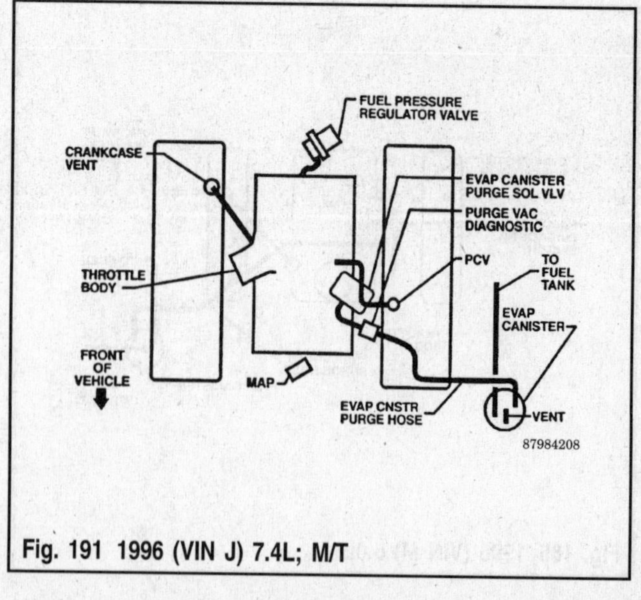

Fig. 191 1996 (VIN J) 7.4L; M/T

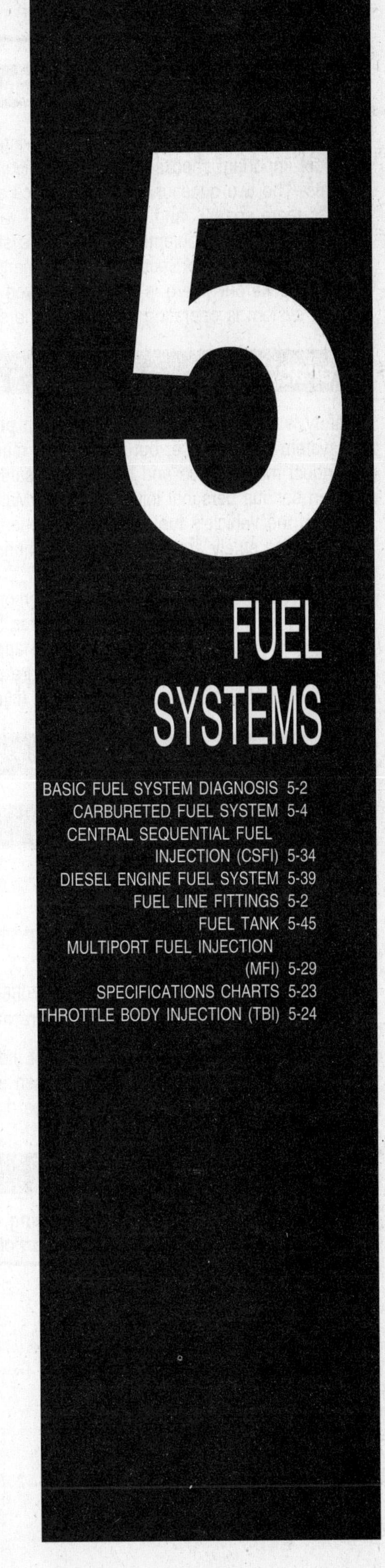

5 FUEL SYSTEMS

BASIC FUEL SYSTEM DIAGNOSIS

When there is a problem starting or driving a vehicle, two of the most important checks involve the ignition and the fuel systems. The two questions that mechanics attempt to answer first, "is there spark?" and "is there fuel?" will often lead to solving most basic problems. For ignition system diagnosis and testing, please refer to Section 2 of this manual. If the ignition system checks out (there is spark), then you must determine if the fuel system is operating properly (is there fuel?).

Precautions

Safety is the most important factor when performing not only fuel system maintenance, but any type of maintenance. Failure to conduct maintenance and repairs in a safe manner may result in serious personal injury or death. Maintenance and testing of the vehicle's fuel system components can be accomplished safely and effectively by adhering to the following rules and guidelines:

- To avoid the possibility of fire and personal injury, always disconnect the negative battery cable unless the repair or test procedure requires that battery voltage be applied.
- Always relieve the fuel system pressure prior to disconnecting any fuel system component (injector, fuel rail, pressure regulator, etc.), fitting or fuel line connection. Exercise extreme caution whenever relieving fuel system pressure to avoid exposing skin, face and eyes to fuel spray. Please be advised that fuel under pressure may penetrate the skin or any part of the body that it contacts.
- Always place a shop towel or cloth around the fitting or connection prior to loosening to absorb any excess fuel due to spillage. Ensure that all fuel spillage (should it occur) is quickly removed from engine surfaces. Ensure that all fuel soaked cloths or towels are deposited into a suitable waste container.
- Always keep a dry chemical (Class B) fire extinguisher near the work area.
- Do not allow fuel spray or fuel vapors to come into contact with a spark or open flame.
- Always use a backup wrench when loosening and tightening fuel line connection fittings. This will prevent unnecessary stress and torsion to fuel line piping. Always follow the proper torque specifications.
- Always replace worn fuel fitting O-rings with new ones. Do not substitute fuel hose or equivalent where fuel pipe is installed.
- Due to the possibility of a fire or explosion, never drain or store gasoline in an open container.

FUEL LINE FITTINGS

Quick-Connect Fittings

REMOVAL & INSTALLATION

➧ **See Figure 1**

➡**This procedure requires Tool Set J37088-A or its equivalent fuel line quick-connect separator.**

1. Grasp both sides of the fitting. Twist the female connector 1/4 turn in each direction to loosen any dirt within the fittings. Using compressed air, blow out the dirt from the quick-connect fittings at the end of the fittings.

✻✻CAUTION

Safety glasses MUST be worn when using compressed air to avoid eye injury due to flying dirt particles!

2. For plastic (hand releasable) fittings, squeeze the plastic retainer release tabs, then pull the connection apart.
3. For metal fittings, choose the correct tool from kit J37088-A or its equivalent for the size of the fitting to be disconnected. Insert the proper tool into the female connector, then push inward to release the locking tabs. Pull the connection apart.
4. If it is necessary to remove rust or burrs from the male tube end of a quick-connect fitting, use emery cloth in a radial motion with the tube end to prevent damage to the O-ring sealing surfaces. Using a clean shop towel, wipe off the male tube ends. Inspect all connectors for dirt and burrs. Clean and/or replace if required.

To install:

5. Apply a few drops of clean engine oil to the male tube end of the fitting.
6. Push the connectors together to cause the retaining tabs/fingers to snap into place.
7. Once installed, pull on both ends of each connection to make sure they are secure and check for leaks.

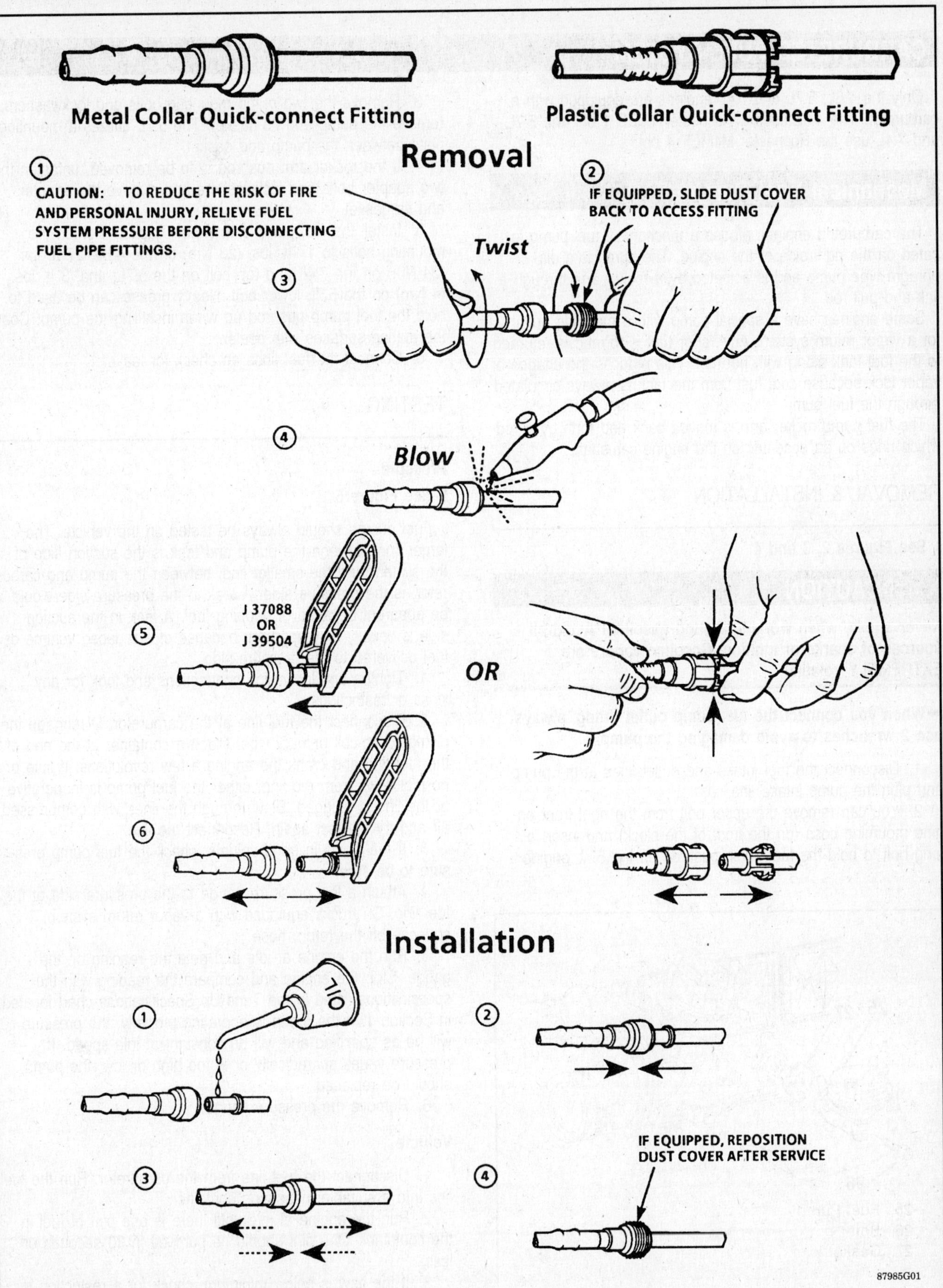

Fig. 1 Servicing quick connect fittings

CARBURETED FUEL SYSTEM

Only the 4.8L, 5.7L and 7.4L engines are equipped with a carburetor. The 4.8L uses a Rochester 1MEF 1 bbl; the 5.7L and 7.4L use the Rochester M4MEF 4 bbl.

Mechanical Fuel Pump

The carbureted engines all use a mechanical fuel pump located on the right side of the engine. The pump is a diaphragm type pump and is actuated by a rocker arm through a link and pull rod.

Some engines have a special pump with a metering outlet for a vapor return system. Any vapor that is formed is returned to the fuel tank along with hot fuel. This reduces the chance of vapor lock because cool fuel from the tank is always circulated through the fuel pump.

The fuel pump rocker arm is moved back and forth by a rod which rides on an eccentric on the engine camshaft.

REMOVAL & INSTALLATION

See Figures 2, 3 and 4

CAUTION

Never smoke when working around gasoline! Avoid all sources of sparks or ignition. Gasoline vapors are EXTREMELY volatile!

When you connect the fuel pump outlet fitting, always use 2 wrenches to avoid damaging the pump.

1. Disconnect the fuel intake and outlet lines at the pump and plug the pump intake line.
2. You can remove the upper bolt from the right front engine mounting boss (on the front of the block) and insert a long bolt to hold the fuel pump pushrod on the 5.7L engine.

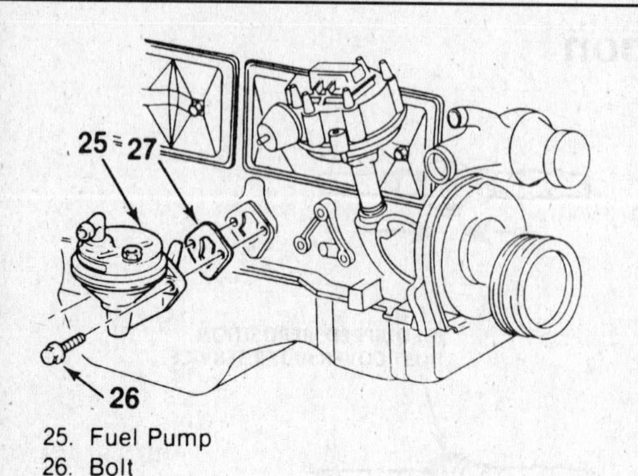

25. Fuel Pump
26. Bolt
27. Gasket

Fig. 2 Mechanical fuel pump — 4.8L engines

3. Remove the two pump mounting bolts and lockwashers; remove the pump and its gasket. The 5.7L utilizes a mounting plate between the pump and gasket.
4. If the rocker arm pushrod is to be removed, unfasten the two adapter bolts and lockwashers and remove the adapter and its gasket.
5. Install the fuel pump with a new gasket. Tighten the mounting bolts to 17 ft. lbs. (23 Nm) on the 4.8L; 27 ft. lbs. (34 Nm) on the 7.4L and top bolt on the 5.7L; and, 3 ft. lbs. (4 Nm) on the 5.7L lower bolt. Heavy grease can be used to hold the fuel pump pushrod up when installing the pump. Coat the mating surfaces with sealer.
6. Connect the fuel lines an check for leaks.

TESTING

Pressure

See Figure 5

Fuel pumps should always be tested on the vehicle. The larger line between the pump and tank is the suction side of the system and the smaller line, between the pump and carburetor, is the pressure side. A leak in the pressure side would be apparent because of dripping fuel. A leak in the suction side is usually only apparent because of a reduced volume of fuel delivered to the pressure side.

1. Tighten any loose line connections and look for any kinks or restrictions.
2. Disconnect the fuel line at the carburetor. Disengage the distributor-to-coil primary wire. Place a container at the end of the fuel line and crank the engine a few revolutions. If little or no fuel flows from the line, either the fuel pump is inoperative or the line is plugged. Blow through the lines with compressed air and try the test again. Reconnect the line.
3. If fuel flows in good volume, check the fuel pump pressure to be sure.
4. Attach a low pressure gauge to the pressure side of the fuel line. On trucks equipped with a vapor return system, squeeze off the return hose.
5. Run the engine at idle and note the reading on the gauge. Stop the engine and compare the reading with the specifications listed in the Tune-Up Specifications chart located in Section 1. If the pump is operating properly, the pressure will be as specified and will be constant at idle speed. If pressure varies sporadically or is too high or low, the pump should be replaced.
6. Remove the pressure gauge.

Volume

1. Disconnect the fuel line from the carburetor. Run the fuel line into a suitable measuring container.
2. Run the engine at idle until there is one pint of fuel in the container. One pint should be pumped in 30 seconds or less.
3. If the flow is below minimum, check for a restriction in the line. The only way to check fuel pump pressure is by connecting an accurate pressure gauge to the fuel line at the

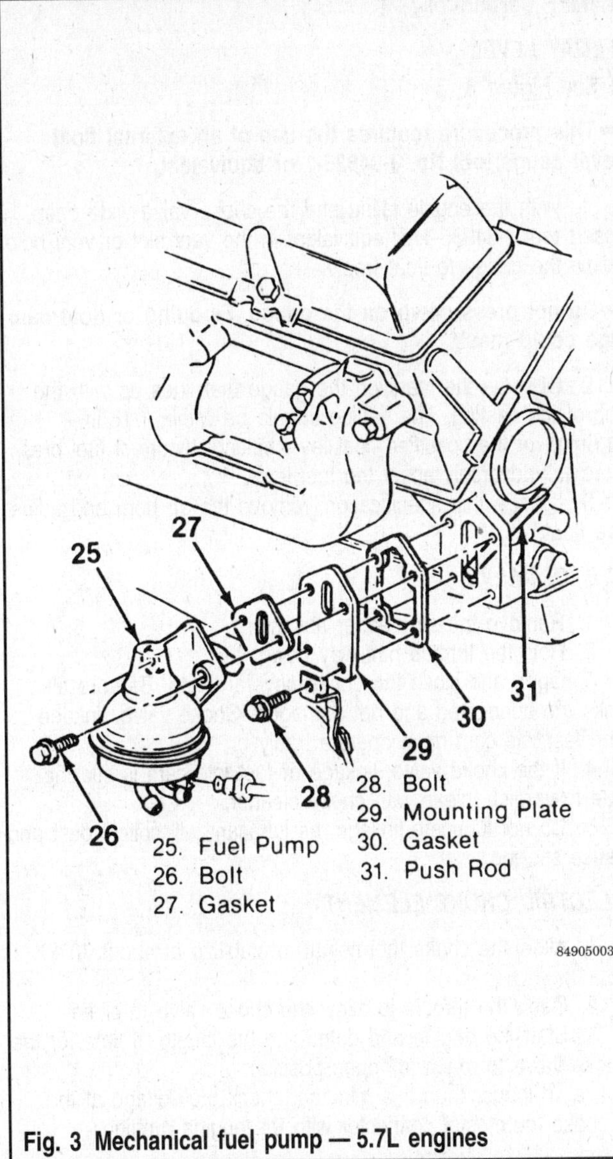

Fig. 3 Mechanical fuel pump — 5.7L engines

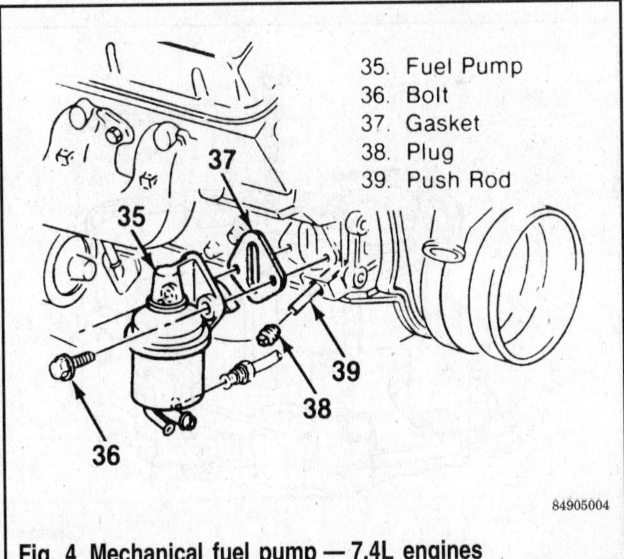

Fig. 4 Mechanical fuel pump — 7.4L engines

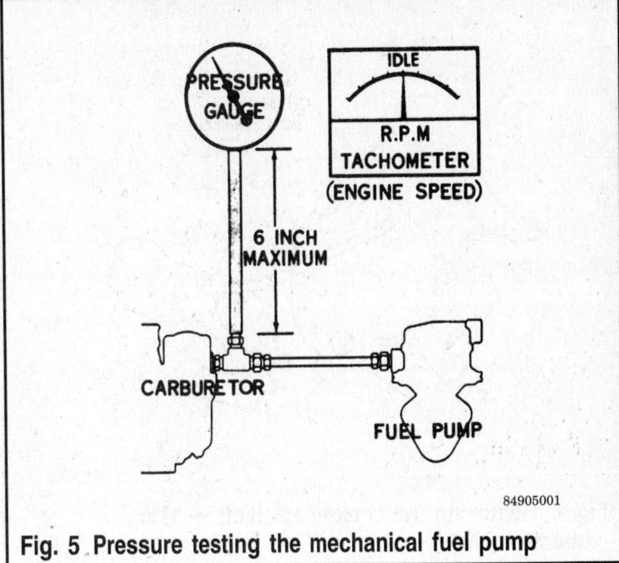

Fig. 5 Pressure testing the mechanical fuel pump

carburetor level. Never replace a fuel pump without performing this simple test. If the engine seems to be starving out, check the ignition system first. Also check for a plugged fuel filter or a restricted fuel line before replacing the pump.

Carburetor

PRELIMINARY CHECKS

1MEF Carburetor

CHOKE

➧ **See Figure 6**

1. Remove the air cleaner assembly.
2. Hold the throttle half way down.
3. Open and close the choke several times. Be sure all links are connected and not damaged. Choke valve, linkage and fast idle cam must operate freely.
4. If the choke valve, linkage or fast idle cam is sticking due to varnish, clean with choke cleaner.
5. Do not lubricate the linkage, as lubricant will collect dust and cause sticking.

VACUUM BREAK

➧ **See Figure 7**

➡A hand-operated vacuum pump such as J-23738-A or equivalent will be needed for this procedure.

1. If the vacuum break has an air bleed hole, plug it during this checking procedure.
2. Apply 15 in. Hg (103 kPa) of vacuum to the vacuum break with the hand pump.
   a. Apply finger pressure to see if the plunger has moved through full travel. If not, replace the vacuum break.
   b. Observe the vacuum gauge. Vacuum should hold for at least twenty seconds. If not, replace the vacuum break.
3. Replace vacuum break hoses that are cracked, cut or hardened.

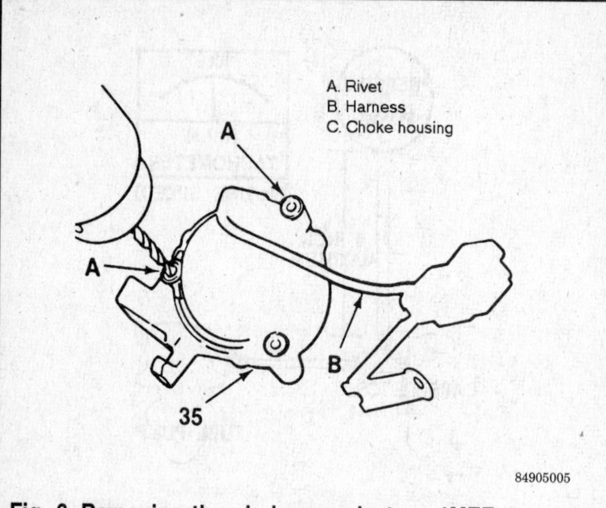

Fig. 6 Removing the choke cap rivets — 1MEF carburetor

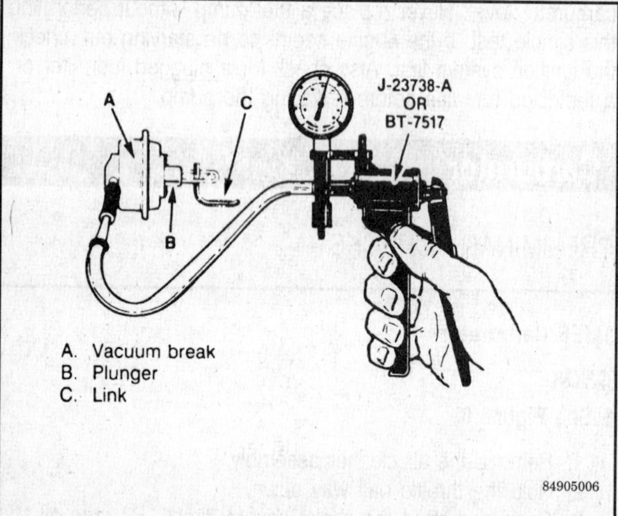

Fig. 7 Vacuum break functional test — 1MEF carburetor

IDLE STOP SOLENOID (ISS)

A non-functioning idle stop solenoid (if equipped) could cause stalling or rough idle.

1. Turn the ignition ON, but do not start the engine.
2. Open the throttle momentarily to allow the solenoid plunger to extend.
3. Disconnect the wire at the solenoid. The plunger should drop back from the throttle lever. If not, back out (counterclockwise) the 1/8 in. (3mm) hex screw 1 full turn. Reconnect the wire and repeat this step.
4. Connect the solenoid wire. The plunger should move out and contact the throttle lever.
5. If the plunger does not move in and out as the wire is disengaged and connected, or, if the plunger can be pushed back and forth with light finger pressure when the wire is engaged, check the voltage across the feed wire:
   a. If 12-15 volts are present in the feed wire, replace the solenoid.
   b. If the voltage is low, locate the cause of the open circuit in the solenoid feed wire and repair as necessary.

M4MEF Carburetor

FLOAT LEVEL

➧ See Figure 8

➡This procedure requires the use of an external float level gauge tool No. J-34935-1 or equivalent.

1. With the engine idling and the choke valve wide open, insert tool J-34935-1 or equivalent in the vent slot or vent hole. Allow the gauge to float freely.

➡Do not press down on the gauge. Flooding or float damage could result.

2. Observe the mark on the gauge that lines up with the top of the casting. The setting should be within 1/16 in. (1.6mm) of the specified float level setting. Incorrect fuel pressure will adversely affect the fuel level.
3. If not within specification, remove the air horn and adjust the float.

CHOKE VALVE

1. Remove the air cleaner assembly.
2. Hold the throttle half way down.
3. Open and close the choke several times. Be sure all links are connected and not damaged. Choke valve, linkage and fast idle cam must operate freely.
4. If the choke valve, linkage or fast idle cam is sticking due to varnish, clean with choke cleaner.
5. Do not lubricate linkage, as lubricant will collect dust and cause sticking.

ELECTRIC CHOKE ELEMENT

1. Allow the choke thermostat to stabilize at about 70°F (21°C).
2. Open the throttle to allow the choke valve to close.
3. Start the engine and determine the length of time for the choke valve to reach full open position:
   a. If longer than five minutes, check the voltage at the choke thermostat connector with the engine running.

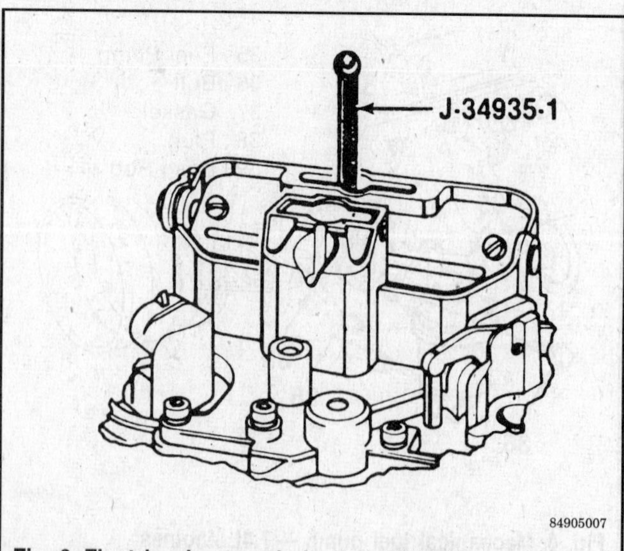

Fig. 8 Float level external check — M4MEF carburetor

b. If voltage is between 12-15 volts, check for proper ground between choke cover and choke housing. If correct, replace choke cover assembly.

c. If the voltage is low or zero, check all wires and connections.

VACUUM BREAK

➧ **See Figure 9**

➡**A hand-operated vacuum pump such as J-23738-A or equivalent will be needed for this procedure.**

1. If the vacuum break has an air bleed hole, plug it during this checking procedure.
2. Apply 15 in. Hg (103 kPa) of vacuum to the vacuum break with the hand pump.
   a. Apply finger pressure to see if the plunger has moved through full travel. If not, replace the vacuum break.
   b. Observe the vacuum gauge. Vacuum should hold vacuum for at least twenty seconds. If not, replace the vacuum break.
3. Replace vacuum break hoses that are cracked, cut or hardened.

IDLE STOP SOLENOID (ISS)

A non-functioning idle stop solenoid (if equipped) could cause stalling or rough idle.

1. Turn the ignition **ON**, but do not start the engine.
2. Open the throttle momentarily to allow the solenoid plunger to extend.
3. Disconnect the wire at the solenoid. The plunger should drop back from the throttle lever.
4. Connect the solenoid wire. The plunger should move out and contact the throttle lever.
5. If the plunger does not move in and out as the wire is disconnected and connected, check the voltage across the feed wire:
   a. If 12-15 volts are present in the feed wire, replace the solenoid.
   b. If the voltage is low, locate the cause of the open circuit in the solenoid feed wire and repair as necessary.

THROTTLE KICKER

➡**A hand-operated vacuum pump such as J-23738-A or equivalent will be needed for this procedure.**

1. Hold the throttle half way open to allow the plunger to extend fully.
2. Apply 20 in. Hg (68 kPa) of vacuum to the throttle kicker with the hand vacuum pump.
   a. Apply finger pressure to the plunger to see if it has extended fully. If not, replace the throttle kicker.
   b. Observe the vacuum gauge. Vacuum should hold for at least twenty seconds. If not, replace the throttle kicker.
3. Release the vacuum to the throttle kicker.
4. If the plunger does not retract to its starting position, replace kicker.

ADJUSTMENTS

1MEF Carburetor

MIXTURE

➧ **See Figure 10**

1. Set the parking brake and block the drive wheels.
2. Remove the carburetor from the engine.
3. Drain the fuel from the the carburetor into an approved container.
4. Remove the idle mixture needle plug as follows:
   a. Invert the carburetor and support it to avoid damaging external components.
   b. Make two parallel hacksaw cuts in the throttle body, between the locator points near one idle mixture needle plug. The distance between the cuts depends on the size of the punch to be used.
   c. Cut down to the plug, but not more than 1/8 in. (3mm) beyond the locator point.
   d. Place a flat punch at a point near the ends of the saw marks. Hold the punch at a 45° angle and drive it into the throttle body until the casting breaks away, exposing the steel plate.

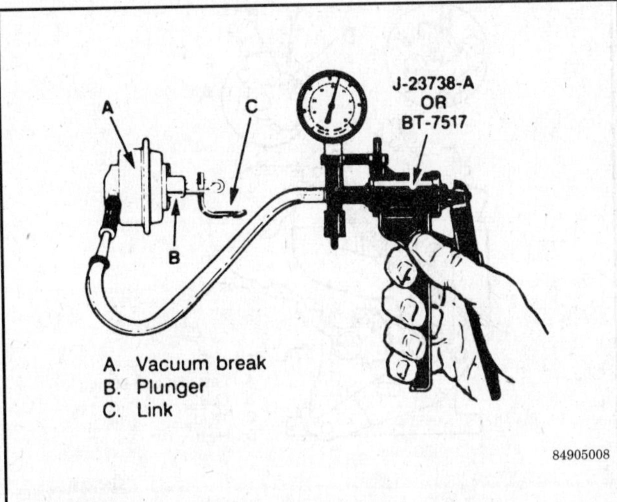

Fig. 9 Vacuum break functional test — M4MEF carburetor

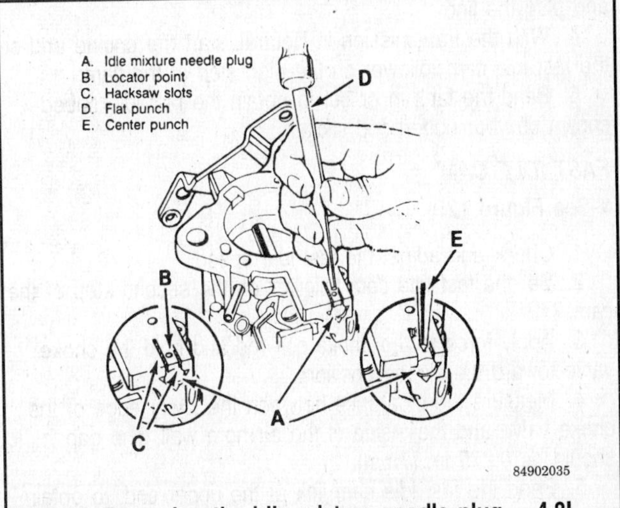

Fig. 10 Removing the idle mixture needle plug — 4.8L engines

e. Use a center punch to break the plug apart, uncover idle mixture needle. Remove all loose pieces of plug.

f. Repeat the previous steps for the other needle plug.

5. Use idle mixture needle socket J-29030-B or equivalent to lightly seat the idle mixture needle, then back it out 3 full turns.
6. Reinstall the carburetor on the engine.
7. Reinstall the air cleaner.
8. Place the transmission in Park (automatic transmission) or Neutral (manual transmission).
9. Start the engine and bring it to a normal operating temperature, choke valve open, and air conditioning off.
10. Connect a known, accurate tachometer to the engine.
11. Check ignition timing, and adjust if necessary, by following the procedure described on the Emission Control Information Label located under the hood on the vehicle.
12. Use idle mixture needle socket J-29030-B or equivalent to turn the mixture needle an 1/8 in. (3mm) turn at a time, in or out, to obtain the highest rpm (best idle).
13. Adjust the idle speed solenoid to obtain the curb idle speed specified on the underhood emission control information label.
14. Again try to readjust mixture needle to obtain the highest idle rpm. The adjustment is correct when the highest rpm (best idle) is reached with the minimum number of mixture needle turns from the seated position.
15. If necessary, readjust the idle stop solenoid to obtain the specified curb idle speed.
16. Check (and if necessary adjust) the base idle speed and fast idle speed. Refer to the underhood emission control information label.
17. Turn off the engine, remove all test equipment.
18. Remove the block from the drive wheels.

FAST IDLE

➧ See Figure 11

1. Check and adjust the idle speed.
2. With the engine at normal operating temperature, air cleaner installed, EGR valve signal line disconnected and plugged and the air conditioning off, connect a tachometer.
3. Disconnect the vacuum advance hose at the distributor and plug the line.
4. With the transmission in Neutral, start the engine and set the fast idle cam follower on the high step of the cam.
5. Bend the tank in or out to obtain the fast idle speed shown on your underhood sticker.

FAST IDLE CAM

➧ See Figure 12

1. Check and adjust the fast idle speed.
2. Set the fast idle cam follower on the second step of the cam.
3. Apply force to the choke coil rod and hold the choke valve toward the closed position.
4. Measure the clearance between the lower edge of the choke valve and the inside of the air horn wall. The gap should be 0.275 in. (7mm).
5. Bend the fast idle cam link at the upper end, to obtain the correct clearance.

CHOKE UNLOADER

➧ See Figure 13

1. Hold the choke valve down by applying light force to the choke coil lever.
2. Open the throttle valve to wide open.
3. Measure the clearance between the lower edge of the choke valve and the air horn wall. The gap should be 0.52 in. (13mm).
4. If adjustment is necessary, bend the unloader tang on the throttle lever.

CHOKE COIL ROD

1. Place the cam follower on the highest step of the fast idle cam.
2. Hold the choke valve completely closed.
3. A 0.120mm (3mm) plug gauge must pass through the hole in the lever attached to the choke coil housing and enter the hole in the casting.
4. Bend the choke link to adjust.

PRIMARY VACUUM BREAK

➧ See Figure 14

1. Place the fast idle cam follower on highest step of the fast idle cam.
2. Plug purge bleed hole in the vacuum break with masking tape. Not all models will have this hole.
3. Using an outside vacuum source, apply 15 in. Hg of vacuum to the primary vacuum break diaphragm. Push down on the choke valve. Make sure the plunger is fully extended.
4. Insert a 5mm (0.2 in.) gauge between the lower edge of the choke valve and the air horn wall.
5. Bend vacuum break rod for adjustment.
6. After adjustment, check for binding or interference. Remove tape.

FLOAT LEVEL

➧ See Figure 15

1. Remove the air horn and gasket.

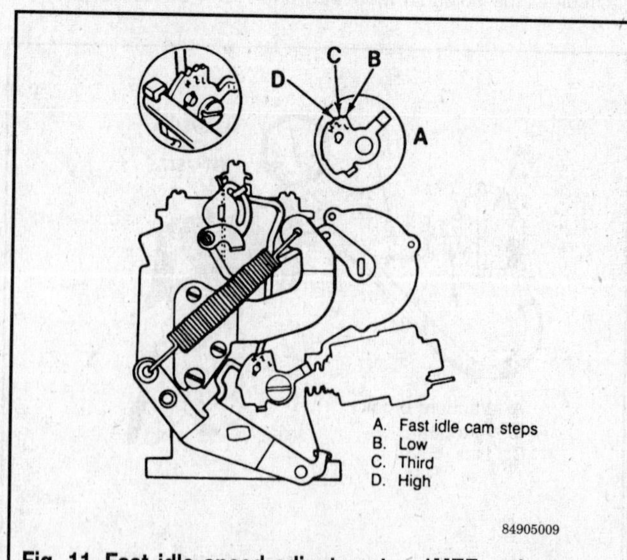

Fig. 11 Fast idle speed adjustment — 1MEF carburetor

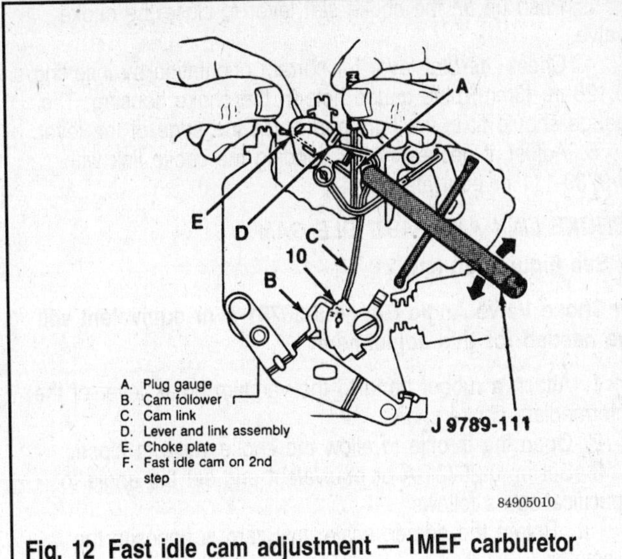

Fig. 12 Fast idle cam adjustment — 1MEF carburetor

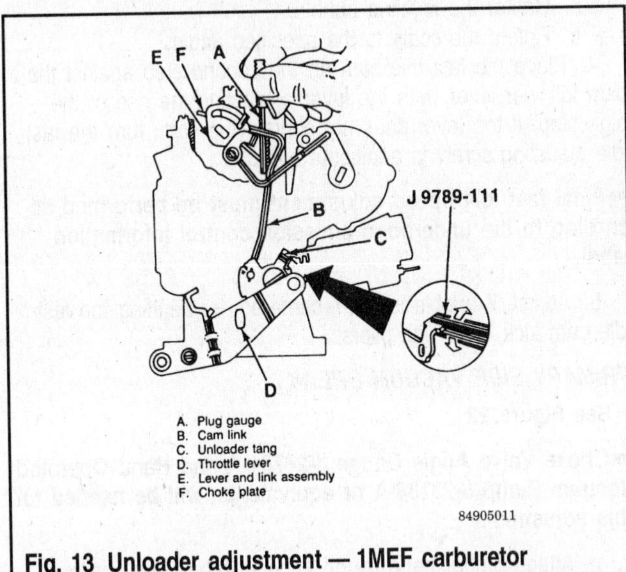

Fig. 13 Unloader adjustment — 1MEF carburetor

2. Hold the float retainer in place, and hold the float arm against the top of the float needle by pushing down on the float arm at the outer end toward the float bowl casting.

➡**A special tool is available to make this job a little easier, but it's not absolutely necessary.**

3. Using an adjustable T-scale, measure the distance from the toe of the float to the float bowl gasket surface. The distance should be $^{9}/_{32}$-$^{13}/_{32}$ in. (7.1-10.3mm).

➡**The gauge should be held on the index point on the float for accurate measurement.**

4. Adjust the float level by bending the float lever up or down at the float arm junction.

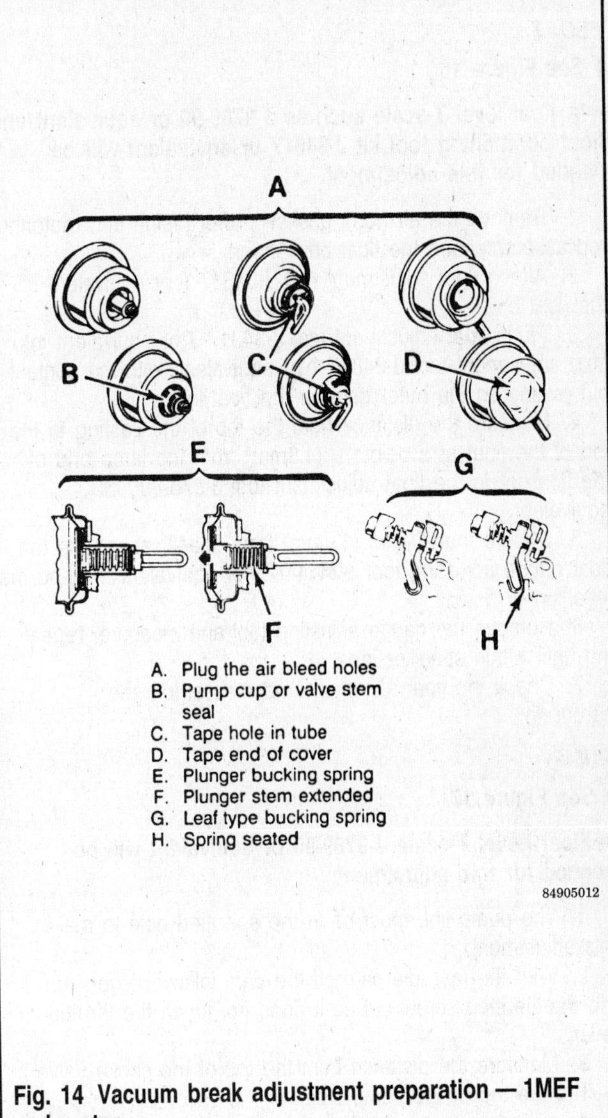

Fig. 14 Vacuum break adjustment preparation — 1MEF carburetor

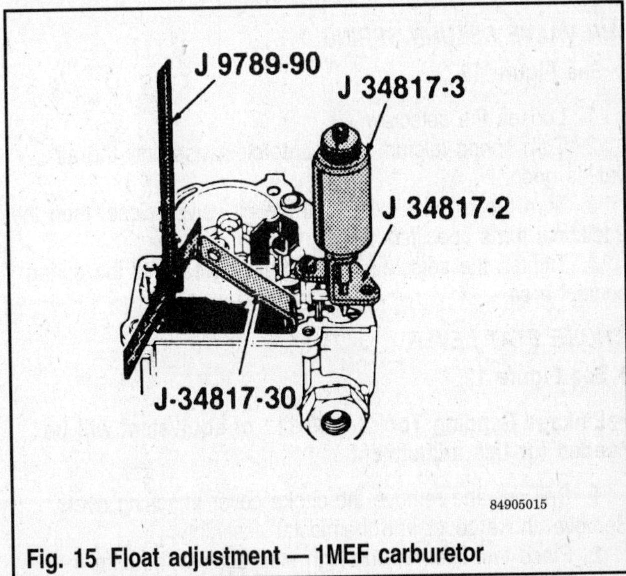

Fig. 15 Float adjustment — 1MEF carburetor

M4MEF Carburetor

FLOAT

➧ **See Figure 16**

➡A float level T-scale such as J-9789-90 or equivalent and float positioning tool kit J-34817 or equivalent will be needed for this adjustment.

1. Remove the air horn, gasket, power piston and metering rod assembly, and the float bowl insert.
2. Attach float adjustment tool J-34817-1 or equivalent to the float bowl.
3. Place float adjustment tool J-34817-3 or equivalent into float adjustment tool J-34817-1 or equivalent, with the contact pin resting on the outer edge of the float lever.
4. Measure the distance from the top of the casting to the top of the float at a point 3/16 (4.8mm) from the large end of the float using the float adjustment tool J-9789-90 or equivalent.
5. If more than 1/16 in. (1.6mm) from specification, use the float gauge adjusting tool J-34817-25 or equivalent to bend the lever up or down.
6. Remove the gauge adjusting tool and measure, repeating until within specifications.
7. Check the float alignment and reassemble the carburetor.

PUMP

➧ **See Figure 17**

➡Float Level T-scale J-9789-90 or equivalent will be needed for this adjustment.

1. The pump link must be in the specified hole to make this adjustment.
2. With the fast idle cam off the cam follower lever, turn the throttle stop screw out so it does not touch the throttle lever.
3. Measure the distance from the top of the choke valve wall to the top of the pump stem.
4. Adjust, if necessary, by supporting the pump lever with a screwdriver and bending it at the notch.

AIR VALVE RETURN SPRING

➧ **See Figure 18**

1. Loosen the setscrew.
2. Turn spring fulcrum pin counterclockwise until the air valves open.
3. Turn the pin clockwise until the air valves close, then the additional turns specified.
4. Tighten the setscrew. Apply lithium grease to the spring contact area.

CHOKE STAT LEVER

➧ **See Figure 19**

➡Linkage Bending Tool J-9789-111 or equivalent will be needed for this adjustment.

1. Drill out and remove the choke cover attaching rivets. Remove choke cover and thermostat assembly.
2. Place fast idle cam on high step against the cam follower lever.
3. Push up on the choke stat lever to close the choke valve.
4. Check the stat lever for correct orientation by inserting a 0.120 in. (3mm) plug gauge hole in the choke housing. The gauge should fit in the hole and touch the edge of the lever.
5. Adjust, if necessary, by bending the choke link with J-9789-111 or equivalent.

CHOKE LINK AND FAST IDLE CAM

➧ **See Figures 20 and 21**

➡Choke Valve Angle Gauge J-26701-A or equivalent will be needed for this adjustment.

1. Attach a rubber band to the vacuum break lever of the intermediate choke shaft.
2. Open the throttle to allow the choke valve to close.
3. Set up J-26701-A or equivalent and set the angle to specification as follows:
   a. Rotate the degree scale until zero is opposite the pointer.
   b. Center the leveling bubble.
   c. Rotate the scale to the specified angle.
4. Place the fast idle cam on the second step against the cam follower lever, with the lever contacting the rise of the high step. If the lever does not contact the cam, turn the fast idle adjusting screw in additional turn(s).

➡Final fast idle speed adjustment must be performed according to the underhood emission control information label.

5. Adjust, if bubble is not recentered, by bending the fast idle cam kick lever with pliers.

PRIMARY SIDE VACUUM BREAK

➧ **See Figure 22**

➡Choke Valve Angle Gauge J-26701-A and Hand Operated Vacuum Pump J-23738-A or equivalents, will be needed for this adjustment.

1. Attach rubber band to the vacuum break lever of the intermediate choke shaft.

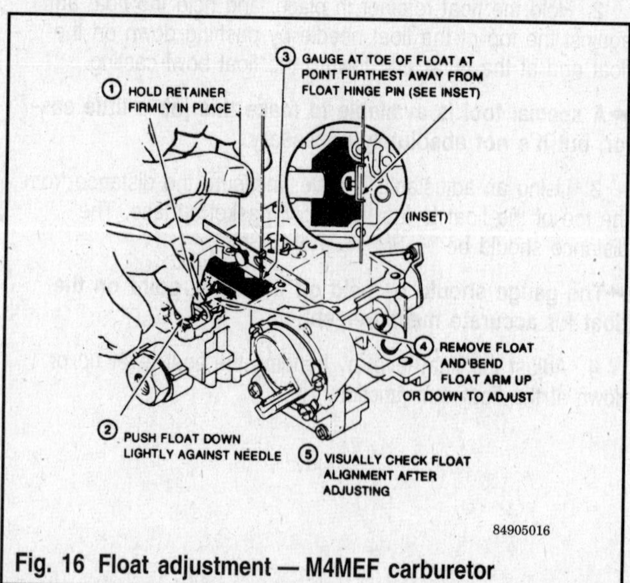

Fig. 16 Float adjustment — M4MEF carburetor

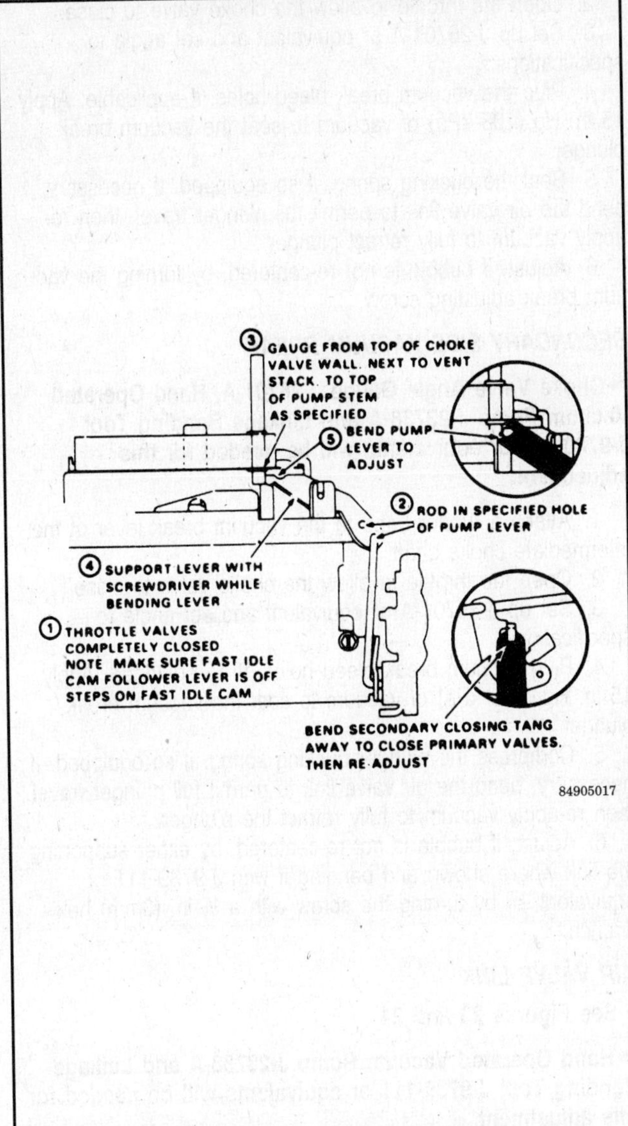

Fig. 17 Pump adjustment — M4MEF carburetor

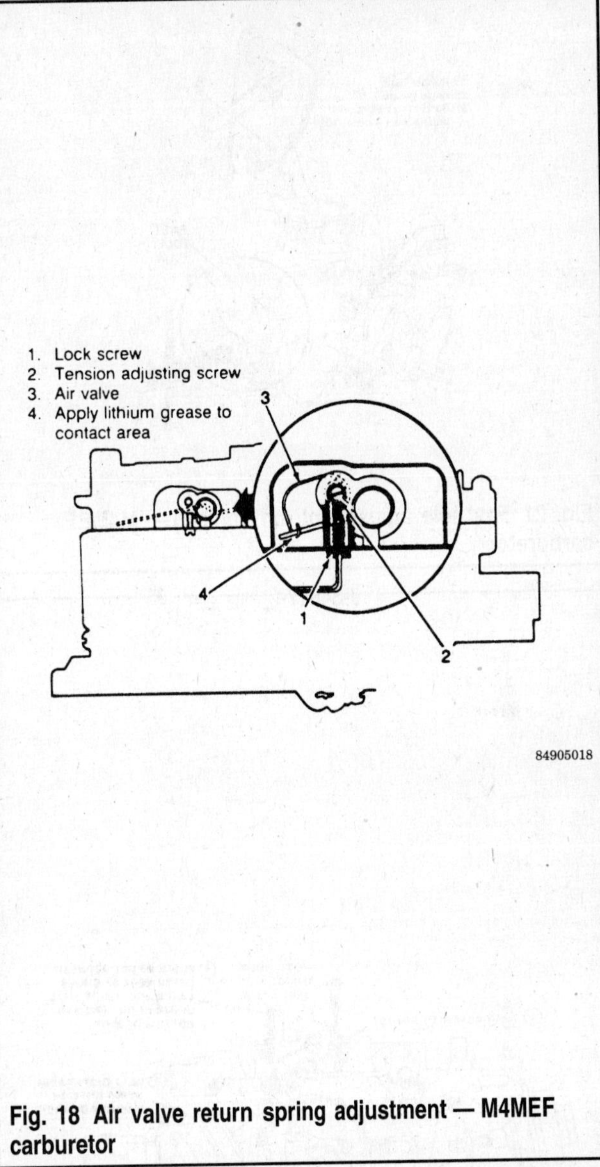

Fig. 18 Air valve return spring adjustment — M4MEF carburetor

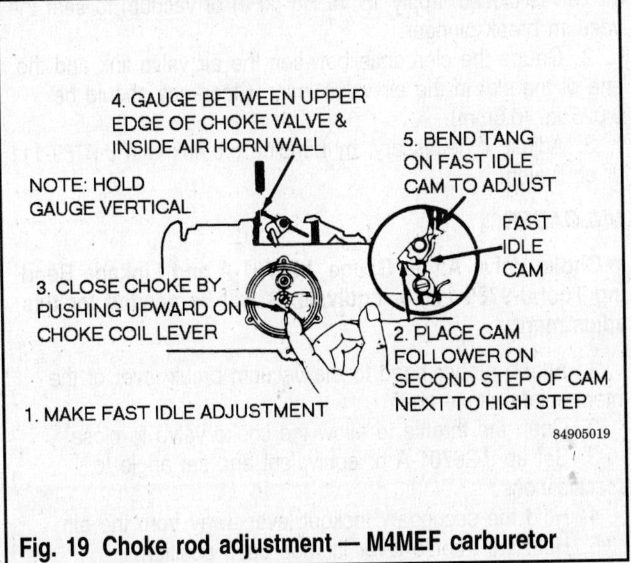

Fig. 19 Choke rod adjustment — M4MEF carburetor

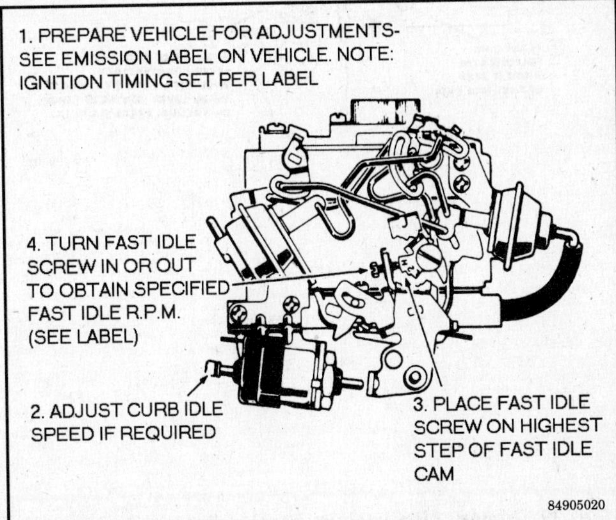

Fig. 20 Fast idle cam adjustment — M4MEF carburetor

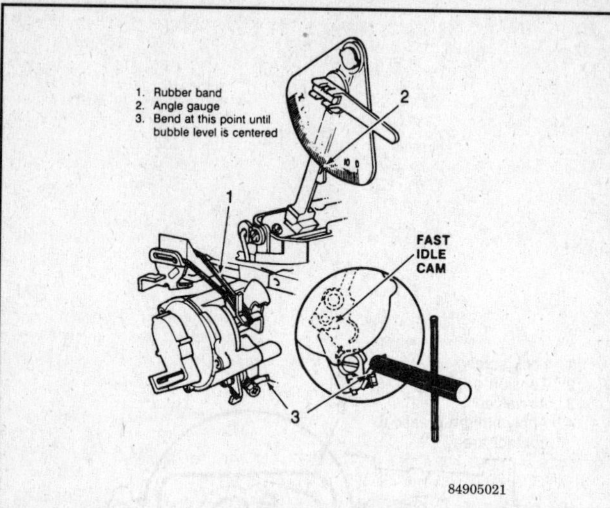

Fig. 21 Fast idle adjustment (on vehicle) — M4MEF carburetor

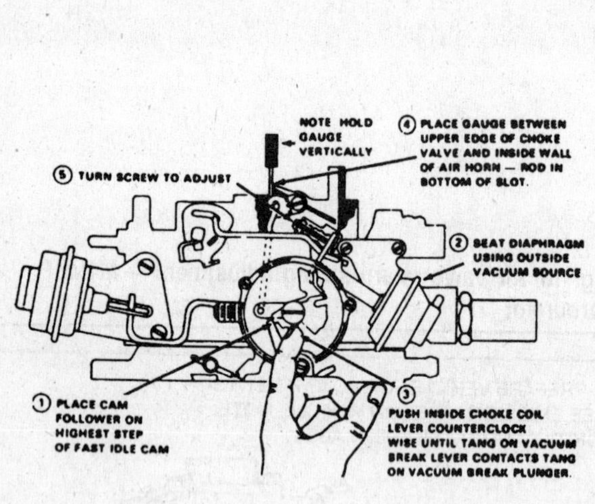

Fig. 22 Primary side vacuum break adjustment — M4MEF carburetor

2. Open the throttle to allow the choke valve to close.
3. Set up J-26701-A or equivalent and set angle to specifications.
4. Plug the vacuum break bleed holes, if applicable. Apply 15 in. Hg (103 kPa) of vacuum to seat the vacuum break plunger.
5. Seat the bucking spring, if so equipped. If necessary, bend the air valve link to permit full plunger travel, then re-apply vacuum to fully retract plunger.
6. Adjust, if bubble is not re-centered, by turning the vacuum break adjusting screw.

SECONDARY SIDE VACUUM BREAK

➡Choke Valve Angle Gauge J-26701-A, Hand Operated Vacuum Pump J-23738-A and Linkage Bending Tool J-9789-111 or equivalents will be needed for this adjustment.

1. Attach a rubber band to the vacuum break lever of the intermediate choke shaft.
2. Open the throttle to allow the choke valve to close.
3. Set up J-26701-A or equivalent and set angle to specification.
4. Plug vacuum break bleed holes, if so equipped. Apply 15 in. Hg (103 kPa) of vacuum to seat the vacuum break plunger.
5. Compress the plunger bucking spring, if so equipped. If necessary, bend the air valve link to permit full plunger travel, then re-apply vacuum to fully retract the plunger.
6. Adjust, if bubble is not re-centered, by either supporting the link where shown and bending it with J-9789-111 or equivalent, or by turning the screw with a ⅛ in. (3mm) hex wrench.

AIR VALVE LINK

➧ See Figures 23 and 24

➡Hand Operated Vacuum Pump J-23738-A and Linkage Bending Tool J-9789-111 or equivalents will be needed for this adjustment.

1. Plug vacuum break bleed holes, if applicable. With the air valves closed, apply 15 in. Hg (kPa) of vacuum to seat the vacuum break plunger.
2. Gauge the clearance between the air valve link and the end of the slot in the air valve lever. Clearance should be 0.025 in. (0.6mm).
3. Adjust, if necessary, by bending the link with J-9789-111 or equivalent.

UNLOADER

➡Choke Valve Angle Gauge J-26701-A and Linkage Bending Tool J-9789-111 or equivalents will be needed for this adjustment.

1. Attach rubber band to the vacuum break lever of the intermediate choke shaft.
2. Open the throttle to allow the choke valve to close.
3. Set up J-26701-A or equivalent and set angle to specifications.
4. Hold the secondary lockout lever away from the pin.
5. Hold the throttle lever in wide open position.
6. Adjust, if bubble is not re-centered, by bending fast idle lever with J-9789-111 or equivalent.

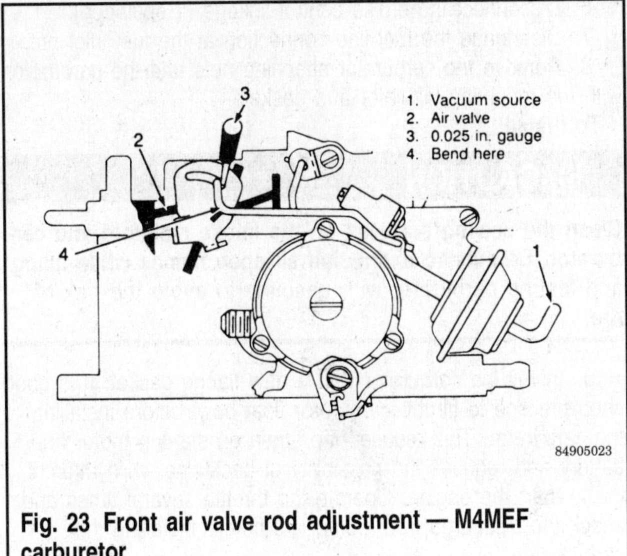

Fig. 23 Front air valve rod adjustment — M4MEF carburetor

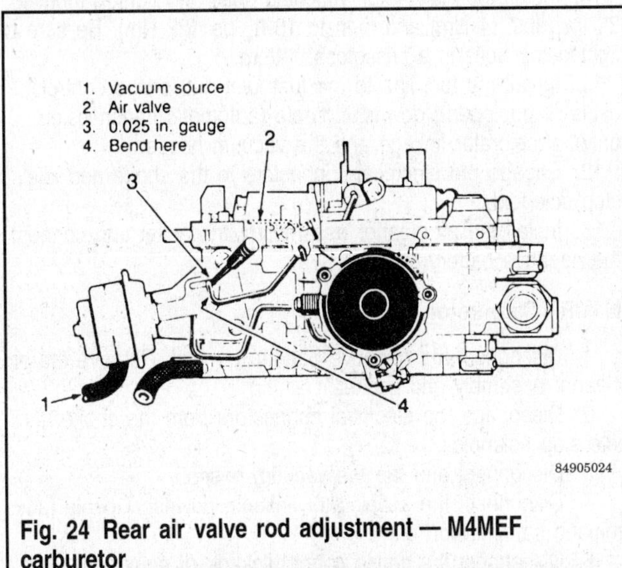

Fig. 24 Rear air valve rod adjustment — M4MEF carburetor

SECONDARY THROTTLE LOCKOUT

1. Place the fast idle cam on the high step against the cam follower lever.
2. Hold the throttle lever closed.
3. Gauge the clearance between the lockout lever and pin. It must be 0.015 inch ± 0.005 in. (0.38mm ± 0.13mm).
4. Adjust, if necessary, by bending pin.
5. Push down on tail of fast idle cam to move lockout lever away from pin.
6. Rotate the throttle lever to bring the lockout pin to the position of minimum clearance with the lockout lever.
7. Gauge the clearance between the lockout lever and pin. The minimum must be 0.015 in. (0.38mm).
8. Adjust, if necessary, by filing the end of the pin.

MIXTURE

➧ See Figure 25

1. Set the parking brake and block the drive wheels.
2. Remove the carburetor from the engine.

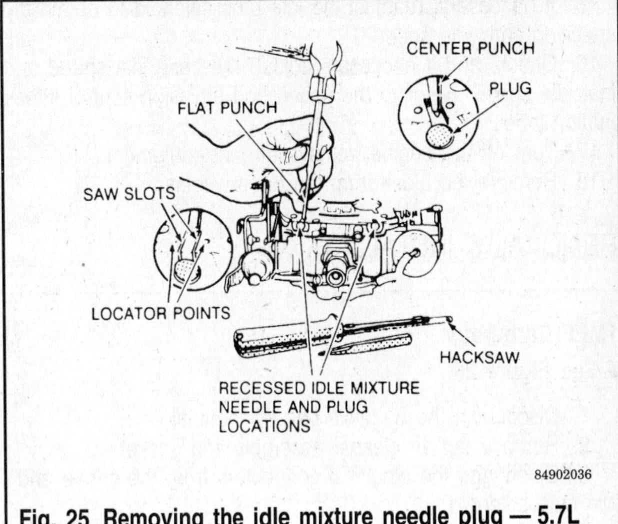

Fig. 25 Removing the idle mixture needle plug — 5.7L engines

3. Drain the fuel from the the carburetor into an approved container.
4. Remove the idle mixture needle plug as follows:
   a. Invert the carburetor and support it to avoid damaging external components.
   b. Make two parallel hacksaw cuts in the throttle body, between the locator points near one idle mixture needle plug. The distance between the cuts depends on the size of the punch to be used.
   c. Cut down to the plug, but not more than 1/8 in. (3mm) beyond the locator point.
   d. Place a flat punch at a point near the ends of the saw marks. Hold the punch at a 45° angle and drive it into the throttle body until the casting breaks away, exposing the steel plate.
   e. Use a center punch to break the plug apart, uncover idle mixture needle. Remove all loose pieces of plug.
   f. Repeat the previous steps for the other needle plug.
5. Use idle mixture needle socket J-29030-B or equivalent to lightly seat the idle mixture needle, then back it out 3 full turns.
6. Reinstall the carburetor on the engine.
7. Reinstall the air cleaner.
8. Place the transmission in Park (automatic transmission) or Neutral (manual transmission).
9. Start the engine and bring it to a normal operating temperature, choke valve open, and air conditioning off.
10. Connect a known, accurate tachometer to the engine.
11. Check ignition timing, and adjust if necessary, by following the procedure described on the Emission Control Information Label located under the hood on the vehicle.
12. Use idle mixture needle socket J-29030-B or equivalent to turn the mixture needle an 1/8 in. (3mm) turn at a time, in or out, to obtain the highest rpm (best idle).
13. Adjust the idle speed solenoid to obtain the curb idle speed specified on the underhood emission control information label.
14. Again try to readjust mixture needle to obtain the highest idle rpm. The adjustment is correct when the highest rpm (best idle) is reached with the minimum number of mixture needle turns from the seated position.

15. If necessary, readjust the idle stop solenoid to obtain the specified curb idle speed.
16. Check (and if necessary adjust) the base idle speed and fast idle speed. Refer to the underhood emission control information label.
17. Turn off the engine, remove all test equipment.
18. Remove the block from the drive wheels.

REMOVAL & INSTALLATION

1MEF Carburetor

See Figure 26

1. Disconnect the negative battery terminal.
2. Remove the air cleaner assembly and gasket.
3. Disengage the electrical connectors from the choke and idle stop solenoid.
4. Disconnect and tag the vacuum hoses.
5. Disconnect the accelerator linkage and the downshift cable (automatic transmission only).

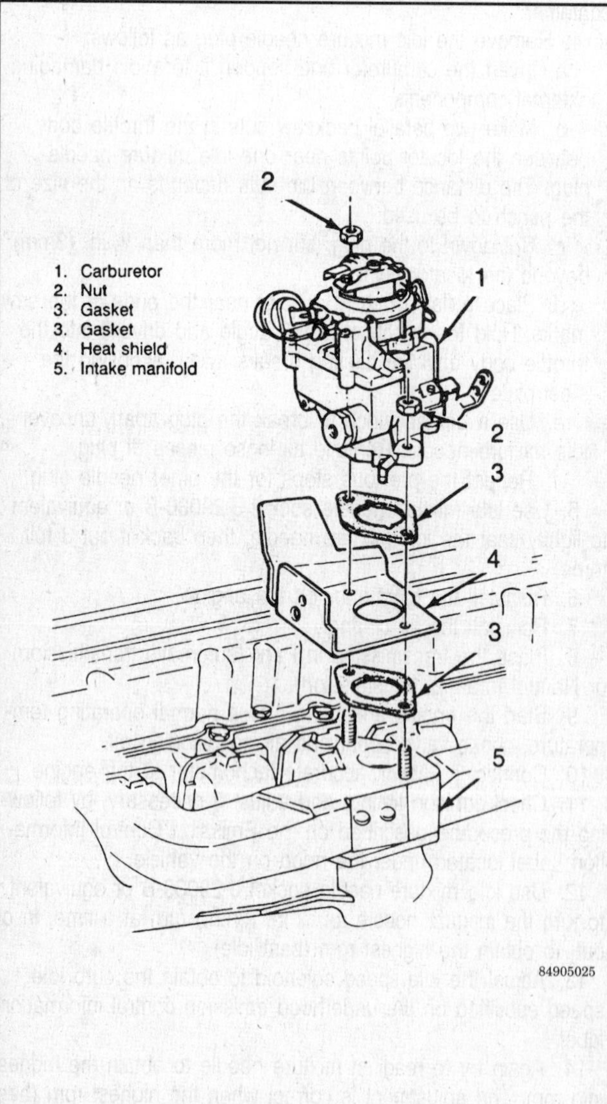

Fig. 26 Carburetor mounting — 1MEF carburetor

6. Disconnect the cruise control linkage (if equipped).
7. Disengage the fuel line connection at the fuel inlet nut.
8. Remove the carburetor attaching nuts and the carburetor with the mounting insulator and gaskets.

To install:

CAUTION

Clean the sealing surfaces on the intake manifold and carburetor. Be sure to extinguish all open flames while filling and testing carburetor with gasoline to avoid the risk of fire.

9. Install the carburetor with a new flange gasket. It is good shop practice to fill the carburetor float bowl before installing the carburetor. This reduces the strain on starting motor and battery and reduces the possibility of backfiring while attempting to start the engine. Operate the throttle several times and check the discharge from pump jets before installing the carburetor.
10. Install the carburetor attaching bolts and tighten them to 36 inch lbs. (4 Nm) and then to 16 ft. lbs. (22 Nm). Be sure to tighten the bolts in a crisscross pattern.
11. Install the fuel line to the fuel inlet nut, cruise control cable (if equipped), downshift cable (automatic transmission only), accelerator linkage and the vacuum hoses.
12. Engage the electrical connectors to the choke and idle stop solenoid.
13. Install the air cleaner assembly with gasket and connect the negative battery terminal.

M4MEF Carburetor

1. Disconnect the negative battery terminal. Remove the air cleaner assembly and gasket.
2. Disengage the electrical connectors from the choke and idle stop solenoid.
3. Disconnect and tag the vacuum hoses.
4. Disconnect the accelerator linkage, downshift cable (automatic transmission only).
5. Disconnect the cruise control linkage (if equipped).
6. Disengage the fuel line connection at the fuel inlet nut.
7. Remove the carburetor attaching bolts and the carburetor with the flange insulator.

To install:

CAUTION

Clean the sealing surfaces on the intake manifold and carburetor. Be sure to extinguish all open flames while filling and testing carburetor with gasoline to avoid the risk of fire.

8. Install the carburetor with a new flange gasket. It is good practice to fill the carburetor float bowl before installing the carburetor. This reduces the strain on starting motor and battery and reduces the possibility of backfiring while attempting to start the engine. Operate the throttle several times and check the discharge from pump jets before installing the carburetor.
9. Install the carburetor attaching bolts and tighten them to 12 ft. lbs. (16 Nm). Be sure to torque the bolts in a criss-cross pattern.

10. Install the fuel line to the fuel inlet nut, cruise control cable (if equipped), downshift cable (automatic transmission only), accelerator linkage and the vacuum hoses.
11. Disengage the electrical connectors to the choke and idle stop solenoid.
12. Install the air cleaner assembly with gasket and connect the negative battery terminal.

➡**When tightening the carburetor at recommended maintenance intervals, check the bolt torque. If less than 5 ft. lbs. (7 Nm), retighten to 8 ft. lbs. (11 Nm); but if greater than 5 ft. lbs. (7 Nm), do not retighten.**

OVERHAUL

Efficient carburetion depends greatly on careful cleaning and inspection during overhaul. Since dirt, gum, water, or varnish in or on the carburetor parts are often responsible for poor performance.

Overhaul your carburetor in a clean, dust free area. Carefully disassembly the carburetor, referring often to the exploded views and directions packaged with the rebuilding kit. Keep all similar and look alike parts segregated during disassembly and cleaning to avoid accidental interchange during assembly. Make a note of all jet sizes.

➡**Before performing any service on the carburetor, it is recommended that it be placed on a suitable holding fixture, such as Tool J-9789-118, BY-30-15 or equivalent. Without the use of the holding fixture, it is possible to damage throttle valves or other parts of the carburetor.**

When the carburetor is disassembled, wash all parts (except diaphragms, electric choke units, pump plunger, and any other plastic, leather, fiber, or rubber parts) in clean carburetor solvent. Do not leave parts in the solvent any longer than is necessary to sufficiently loosen the deposits. Excessive cleaning may remove the special finish from the float bowl and choke valve bodies, leaving these parts unfit for service. Soak all parts in clean solvent and blow them dry with compressed air or allow them to air dry. Wipe clean all cork, plastic, leather, and fiber parts with a clean, lint free cloth.

Blow out all passages and jets with compressed air and be sure that there are no restrictions or blockages. Never use wire or similar tools to clean jets, fuel passages, or air bleeds. Clean all jets and valves separately to avoid accidental interchange.

Check all parts for wear or damage. If wear or damage is found, replace the defective parts. Especially check the following:

1. Check the float needle and seat for wear. If wear is found, replace the complete assembly.
2. Check the float hinge pin for wear and the floats for dents or distortion. Replace the float if fuel has leaked into it.
3. Check the throttle and choke shaft bores for wear or an out-of-round condition. Damage or wear to the throttle arm, shaft, or shaft bore will often require replacement of the throttle body. These parts require a close tolerance of fit and wear may allow air leakage, which could affect starting and idling.

➡**Throttle shafts and bushings are not included in overhaul kits. They can be purchased separately.**

4. Inspect the idle mixture adjusting needles for burrs or grooves. Any such condition requires replacement of the needle, since you will not be able to obtain a satisfactory idle.
5. Test the accelerator pump check valves. They should pass air one way but not the other. Test for proper seating by blowing and sucking on the valve. Replace the valve as necessary. If the valve is satisfactory, wash the valve again to remove breath moisture.
6. Check the bowl cover for warped surfaces with a straightedge.
7. Closely inspect the valves and seats for wear and damage, replacing as necessary.
8. After the carburetor is assembled, check the choke valve for freedom of operation.

Carburetor overhaul kits are recommended for each overhaul. These kits may contain all gaskets and new parts to replace those which deteriorate most rapidly. Failure to replace all parts supplied with the kit (especially gaskets) can result in poor performance later.

Some carburetor manufacturers supply overhaul kits of three basic types: minor repair, major repair and gasket kits.

Refer to exploded view for parts identification. Always replace gaskets that are removed.

After cleaning and checking all components, reassemble the carburetor, using new parts and referring to the exploded view. When reassembling, make sure that all screws and jets are tight in their seats, but do not overtighten as the tips will be distorted. Tighten all screws gradually, in rotation. Do not tighten needle valves into their seats; uneven jetting will result. Always use new gaskets. Be sure to adjust the float level when reassembling.

1MEF Carburetor

➧ **See Figure 27**

1. Remove the fuel inlet nut, gasket, filter and spring.
2. Unscrew and remove the idle stop solenoid.
3. Remove the throttle return spring bracket.
4. Remove the vacuum break hose.
5. Remove the vacuum break attaching screws, disconnect the link and remove the vacuum break assembly. Allow the choke wire connector bracket to hang freely.
6. Remove the choke housing attaching screws and remove the housing and bearing.
7. Remove the fast idle cam attaching screw, cam and cam link.
8. Remove the air horn attaching screws and lift off the air horn. Discard the gasket.

➡**No further disassembly of the air horn is permitted. Under no circumstances should you remove the metering rod adjusting screw. Any attempt to turn this screw will cause illegal emission levels.**

9. Remove the float and hinge pin.
10. Remove the needle from the seat.
11. Remove the pump lever attaching screw.
12. Close the throttle plate.
13. Remove the pump and power rod lever from the end of the throttle shaft.
14. Press down on the power valve piston assembly and disconnect the power rod link from the power piston rod.

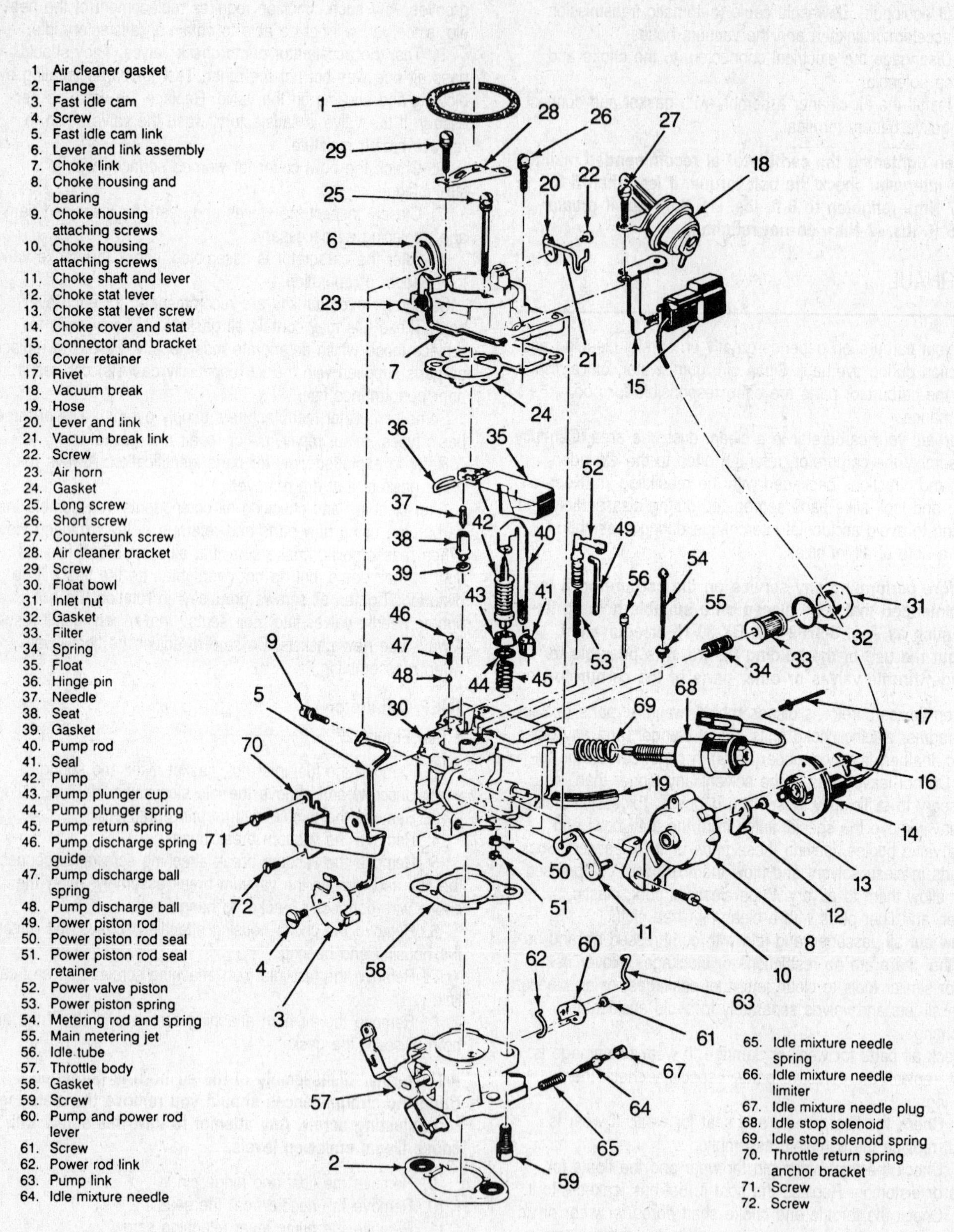

Fig. 27 Exploded view of the carburetor — 1MEF carburetor

15. Press down on the pump rod and disconnect the pump link from the slot in the rod.
16. Remove the plunger spring and cup from the pump rod and pump.
17. Remove the pump rod seal from the boss on the float bowl.
18. Remove the return spring from the pump well.
19. Remove the power valve piston assembly, metering rod and spring assembly and the power piston rod.
20. Remove the metering rod and spring assembly from the metering rod hanger.
21. Remove the power piston spring from the float bowl.
22. Remove the float needle seat and gasket.
23. Remove the main metering jet.
24. Turn the carburetor over and catch the idle tube.
25. Using needle-nose pliers, remove the pump discharge spring guide.
26. Turn the carburetor over and catch the pump discharge spring and ball.
27. Use hacksaw to make two parallel cuts in the throttle body, one on each side of the locator points near one idle mixture needle plug. The distance between the cuts will depend on the size of the punch to be used. Cuts should reach down to the steel plug, but should but extend more than 1/8 in. (3mm) beyond the locator point.
28. Place a flat punch at a point near the ends of the saw marks in the throttle body. Hold the punch at a 45° angle, and drive it into the throttle body until the casting breaks away, exposing the hardened steel plug. The plug will break, rather than remaining intact. Remove all the loose pieces.
29. Turn the idle mixture needle clockwise, slowly, counting the number of turns until it seats. Record this number for assembly purposes.
30. Remove the idle mixture needle.
31. Remove the float bowl-to-throttle body screws, separate the two pieces and discard the gasket.

➡No further disassembly of the throttle body is necessary. It is serviced as a unit.

32. Remove the power piston seal retainer from the float bowl with a small screwdriver.
33. Remove the power piston rod seal.

To assemble:

34. Install a new power piston rod seal.
35. Install a new power piston seal retainer in the float bowl, flush with the casting surface.
36. Using a new gasket, assemble the float bowl and throttle body. Tighten the screws to 15 ft. lbs. (20 Nm).
37. Install the idle mixture needle. Turn the idle mixture needle clockwise, slowly, until it seats and back it out the number of turns recorded.
38. Install the pump discharge spring and ball.
39. Install the pump discharge spring guide flush with the casting surface.
40. Install the idle tube. The tube should be flush with the casting surface.
41. Install the main metering jet.
42. Install the float needle seat and new gasket.
43. Install the power piston spring in the float bowl.
44. Install the power piston rod with the drive end facing away from the piston cavity.
45. Install the power valve piston assembly, without the metering rod.
46. Press down on the power valve piston assembly and connect the power rod link from the power piston rod.
47. Assemble the plunger spring and new cup to the pump rod and pump.
48. Install the return spring in the pump well.
49. Install a new pump rod seal on the boss in the float bowl.
50. Press down on the pump rod and connect the pump link with the slot in the rod.
51. Install the pump and power rod lever on the end of the throttle shaft.
52. Install the pump lever attaching screw.
53. Close the throttle plate.
54. Hold power piston down and swing metering rod holder over flat surface (gasket removed) of bowl casting next to carburetor bore.
55. Using a 0.09in. (2.3mm) gauge, measure the distance between the end of the metering rod holder and the mating surface of the float bowl.
56. Bend the hanger at the center point as necessary.
57. Hold the throttle wide open and position the metering rod in the main metering jet. Then, connect the rod to the power piston metering rod hanger with the metering rod spring on top of the hanger.
58. Install the float needle in the seat.
59. Install the float and hinge pin. Adjust the float as described earlier in this section.
60. Install the air horn and new gasket. Finger tighten the bolts at this time.
61. Install the fast idle cam and cam link.
62. Install the choke housing and bearing.
63. Install the vacuum break assembly. Install the choke wire connector bracket to hang freely.
64. Install the vacuum break hose.
65. Tighten all the air horn-to-float bowl screws.
66. Install the throttle return spring bracket.
67. Install the idle stop solenoid.
68. Install the fuel inlet nut, gasket, filter and spring.
69. Perform all the carburetor adjustments listed in this section.

M4MEF Carburetor

➧ See Figure 28

1. Cover internal bowl vents and air inlets to the bleed valve with masking tape.
2. Carefully align a 7/64 in. (0.109mm) drill bit on rivet head. Drill only enough to remove head of each rivet holding the idle air bleed valve cover.
3. Use a suitably sized punch to drive out the remainder of the rivet from the castings. Repeat procedure with other rivet.

✱✱CAUTION

For the next operation, safety glasses must be worn to protect eyes from possible metal shaving damage.

4. Lift off cover and remove any pieces of rivet still inside tower. Use shop air to blow out any remaining chips.
5. Remove idle air bleed valve from the air horn.

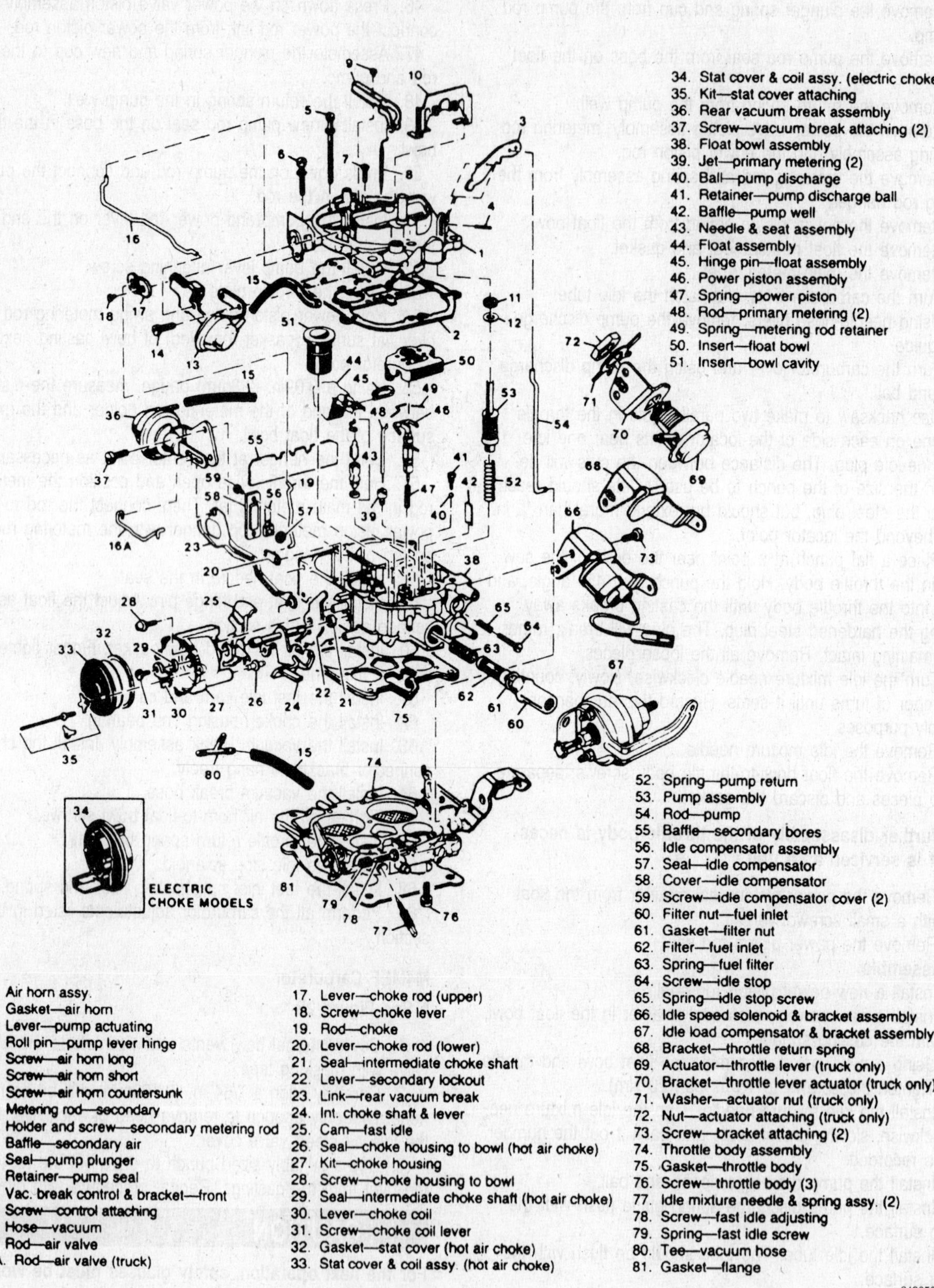

Fig. 28 Exploded view of the carburetor — M4MEF carburetor

6. Remove and discard O-ring seals from valve. New O-ring seals are required for reassembly. The idle air bleed valve is serviced as a complete assembly only.

7. Remove upper choke lever from the end of choke shaft by loosening retaining screw. Rotate upper choke lever to remove choke rod from slot in lever.

8. Remove choke rod from lower lever inside the float bowl casting.

9. Remove the rod by holding lower lever outward with small screwdriver and twisting rod counterclockwise.

10. Remove secondary metering rods by loosening the small screw in the top of the metering rod hanger. Lift upward on the metering rod hanger until the secondary metering rods are completely out of the air horn. Metering rods may be disassembled from the hanger by rotating the ends out of the holes in the end of the hanger.

11. Remove pump link retainer and remove link from pump lever.

➡Do not attempt to remove the lever, as damage to the air horn could result.

12. Remove the front vacuum break hose from tube on float bowl.

13. Unfasten air horn-to-bowl screws; then remove the countersunk attaching screws located next to the venturi. If used, remove secondary air baffle deflector from beneath the two center air horn screws.

14. Remove air horn from float bowl by lifting it straight up. The air horn gasket should remain on the float bowl for removal later.

➡When removing air horn from float bowl, use care to prevent damaging the mixture control solenoid connector, Throttle Position Sensor (TPS) adjustment lever, and the small tubes protruding from the air horn. These tubes are permanently pressed into the air horn casting. DO NOT remove them.

15. Remove the front vacuum break bracket attaching screws. The vacuum break assembly may now be removed from the air valve dashpot rod, and the dashpot rod from the air valve lever.

➡Do not place vacuum break assembly in carburetor cleaner, as damage to vacuum break will occur.

16. Remove Throttle Position Sensor (TPS) plunger by pushing plunger down through seal in air horn.

17. Remove TPS seal and pump plunger stem seal by inverting air horn and using a small screwdriver to remove staking holding seal retainers in place. Discard the retainers and seals.

➡Use care in removing the TPS plunger seal retainer and pump plunger stem seal retainer to prevent damage to air horn casting. New seals and retainers are required for reassembly.

18. Invert air horn, and use Tool J-28696-4, BT-7967A, or equivalent, to remove rich mixture stop screw and spring.

19. Use a suitable punch to drive the lean mixture screw plug and rich mixture stop screw plug out of the air horn. Discard the plugs.

20. Further disassembly of the air horn is not required for cleaning purposes.

➡The choke valve and choke valve screws, the air valves and air valve shaft should not be removed. However, if it is necessary to replace the air valve closing springs or center plastic eccentric cam, a repair kit is available. Instructions for assembly are included in the repair kit.

21. Remove the solenoid metering rod plunger by lifting straight up.

22. Remove the air horn gasket by lifting it from the dowel locating pins on float bowl. Discard the gasket.

23. Remove the pump plunger from the pump well.

24. Remove the staking holding the Throttle Position Sensor (TPS) in the bowl as follows:

a. Lay a flat tool or metal piece across the bowl casting to protect the gasket sealing surface.

b. Use a small screwdriver to depress the TPS sensor lightly and hold against spring tension.

c. Observing safety precautions, pry upward with a small chisel or equivalent to remove the bowl staking, making sure prying force is exerted against the metal piece and not against the bowl casting. Use care not to damage the TPS sensor.

d. Push up from bottom on electrical connector and remove the TPS and connector assembly from bowl. Use care in removing the sensor and connector assembly to prevent damage to this critical electrical part.

e. Remove the spring from bottom of the TPS well in float bowl.

25. Remove the plastic bowl insert from float bowl.

26. Carefully lift each metering rod out of the guided metering jet, checking to be sure the return spring is removed with each metering rod.

➡Use extreme care when handling these critical parts to avoid damage to the metering rod and spring.

27. Remove the mixture control solenoid from the float bowl as follows:

a. Remove the screw attaching the solenoid connector to the float bowl. Do not remove the solenoid connector from float bowl until called for in text.

b. Use Tool J-28696-10, BT-7928, or equivalent, to remove the lean mixture (solenoid) screw. Do not remove plunger return spring or connector and wires from the solenoid body. The mixture control solenoid, with plunger and connector, is only serviced as a complete assembly.

c. Remove the rubber gasket from top of the solenoid connector and discard.

d. Remove the solenoid screw tension spring (next to float hanger pin).

28. Remove the float assembly and float needle by pulling up on retaining pin. Remove the needle and seat and gasket using set remover Tool J-22769, BT-3006M, or equivalent.

29. Remove the large mixture control solenoid tension spring from the boss on bottom of float bowl located between the guided metering jets.

30. If necessary, remove the primary main metering jets using special Tool J-28696-4, BT-7928, or equivalent.

➡Use care installing the tool on jet, to prevent damage to the metering rod guide (upper area), and the locating tool over the vertical float sections on lower area of the jet. Also, no attempt should be made to remove the secondary metering jets (metering orifice plates). These jets are fixed and, if damaged, the entire bowl replacement is required.

31. Remove the pump discharge check ball retainer and turn bowl upside down, catching the discharge ball as if falls.
32. Remove the secondary air baffle.
33. Remove the pump well fill slot baffle only if necessary.

➡The tamper-resistant choke cover is used to discourage unnecessary readjustment of the choke thermostatic cover and coil assembly. However, it is necessary to remove the cover and coil assembly during normal carburetor disassembly for cleaning and overhaul.

34. Support the float bowl and throttle body, as an assembly, on a suitable holding fixture such as Tool J-9789-118, BT-30-15, or equivalent.
35. Carefully align a 5/32 in. (0.156mm) drill bit on the rivet head and drill only enough to remove the rivet head. Drill the remaining rivet heads, then use a drift and small hammer to drive the remainder of the rivets out of the choke housing.

➡Use care in drilling to prevent damage to the choke cover or housing.

36. Remove the conventional retainers, retainer with tab and choke cover assembly from choke housing.
37. Remove choke the housing assembly from the float bowl by removing retaining screw and washer inside the choke housing. The complete choke assembly can be removed from the float bowl by sliding outward.
38. Remove the secondary throttle valve lock-out lever from the float bowl.
39. Remove the lower choke lever from inside the float bowl cavity by inverting the bowl.
40. To disassemble the intermediate choke shaft from the choke housing, remove the coil lever retaining screw at end of the shaft inside the choke housing.
41. Remove the thermostatic coil lever from the flats on intermediate choke shaft.
42. Remove the intermediate choke shaft from the choke housing by sliding it outward. The fast idle cam can now be removed from the intermediate choke shaft. Remove the cup seal from the float bowl for cleaning purposes. DO NOT ATTEMPT TO REMOVE THE INSERT!
43. Remove the fuel inlet nut, gasket, check valve, filter assembly and spring. Discard the check valve filter assembly and gasket.
44. Remove the throttle body-to-bowl attaching screws and lockwashers and remove the throttle body assembly.
45. Remove the throttle body-to-bowl insulator gasket.

➡Place the throttle body assembly on carburetor holding fixture to avoid damage to throttle valves.

46. Remove the pump rod from the throttle lever by rotating the rod until the tang on the rod aligns with the slot in the lever.
47. Use hacksaw to make two parallel cuts in the throttle body, one on each side of the locator points near one idle mixture needle plug. The distance between the cuts will depend on the size of the punch to be used. Cuts should reach down to the steel plug, but should but extend more than ⅛ in. (3mm) beyond the locator point.
48. Place a flat punch at a point near the ends of the saw marks in the throttle body. Hold the punch at a 45° angle, and drive it into the throttle body until the casting breaks away, exposing the hardened steel plug. The plug will break, rather than remaining intact. Remove all the loose pieces.
49. Repeat the procedure for the other idle mixture needle plug.
50. Use Tool J-29030-B, BT-7610B or equivalent, to remove the idle mixture needles for thorough throttle body cleaning.
51. Further disassembly of the throttle body is not required for cleaning purposes. The throttle valve screws are permanently staked in place and should not be removed. The throttle body is serviced as a complete assembly.

To assemble:

52. Install the lower end of the pump rod in the throttle lever by aligning the tang on the rod with the slot in the lever. The end of the rod should point outward toward the throttle lever.
53. Install idle mixture needles and springs using Tool J-29030-B, BT-7610B or equivalent. Lightly seat each needle and then turn counterclockwise the number of specified turns. The final idle mixture adjustment is made on the vehicle.
54. If a new float bowl assembly is used, stamp or engrave the model number on the new float bowl. Install new throttle body-to-bowl insulator gasket over two locating dowels on bowl.
55. Install the throttle body making certain the throttle body is properly located over the dowels on float bowl. Install the throttle body-to-bowl screws and lockwashers and tighten evenly and securely.
56. Place the carburetor on a proper holding fixture such as J-9789-118, BT-30-15 or equivalent.
57. Install the fuel inlet filter spring, a new check valve filter assembly, new gasket and inlet nut. Tighten nut to 18 ft. lbs. (24 Nm).

➡When installing a service replacement filter, make sure the filter is the type that includes the check valve to meet government safety standard. New service replacement filters with check valve meet this requirement. When properly installed, the hole in the filter faces toward the inlet nut. Ribs on the closed end of the filter element prevent it from being installed incorrectly, unless forced. Tightening beyond the specified torque can damage the nylon gasket.

58. Install a new cup seal into the insert on the side of the float bowl for the intermediate choke shaft. The lip on the cup seal faces outward.
59. Install the secondary throttle valve lock-out lever on the boss of the float bowl, with the recess hole in the lever facing inward.
60. Install the fast idle cam on the intermediate choke shaft (steps on cam face downward).
61. Carefully install the fast idle cam and intermediate choke shaft assembly in the choke housing. Install the thermostatic coil lever on the flats on the intermediate choke shaft. Ensure the thermostatic choke coil lever is properly aligned when both the inside and outside levers face toward the fuel inlet. Install

inside lever retaining screw into the end of the intermediate choke shaft.

62. Install the lower choke rod (inner) lever into cavity in float bowl.

63. Install the choke housing to the bowl, sliding the intermediate choke shaft into the lower (inner) lever. Tool J-23417, BT-6911 or equivalent, can be used to hold the lower choke lever in the correct position while installing the choke housing. The intermediate choke shaft lever and fast idle cam are in correct position when the tang on lever is beneath the fast idle cam.

64. Install the choke housing retaining screws and washers. Check the linkage for freedom of movement. Do not install the choke cover and coil assembly until the inside coil lever is adjusted.

65. If removed, install air baffle in the secondary side of float bowl with the notches toward the top. The top edge of the baffle must be flush with the bowl casting.

66. If removed, install the baffle inside of the pump well with slot toward the bottom.

67. Install the pump discharge check ball and retainer screw in the passage next to the pump well.

68. If removed, carefully install the primary main metering jets in the bottom of the float bowl using or Tool J-28696-4, BT-7928 or equivalent.

➡Use care in installing jets to prevent damage to metering rod guide.

69. Install the large mixture control solenoid tension spring over the boss on bottom of the float bowl.

70. Install the needle seat assembly, with gasket, using seat installer J-22769, BT-3006M, or equivalent.

71. To make the adjustment easier, carefully bend the float arm before assembly.

72. Install the float needle onto the float arm by sliding the float lever under the needle pull clip. Proper installation of the needle pull clip is to hook the clip over the edge of the float on the float arm facing the float pontoon.

73. Install the float hinge pin into the float arm with end of loop of the pin facing the pump well.

74. Install the float assembly by aligning the needle in the seat, and float hinge pin into the locating channels in the float bowl. DO NOT install the float needle pull clip into the holes in float arm.

75. Make a float level adjustment as necessary.

76. Install the mixture control solenoid screw tension spring between the raised bosses next to float hanger pin.

77. Install the mixture control solenoid and the connector assembly as follows:

a. Install the new rubber gasket on top of the solenoid connector.

b. Install the solenoid carefully in the float chamber, aligning the pin on end of the solenoid with the hole in the raised boss at the bottom of bowl. Align the solenoid connector wires to fit in the slot in the bowl.

c. Install the lean mixture (solenoid) screw through the hole in the solenoid bracket and tension spring in the bowl, engaging the screw threads to assure proper thread Engagement.

d. Install the mixture control solenoid gauging Tool J-33815-1, BT-8253-A, or equivalent over the throttle side metering jet rod guide, and temporarily install the solenoid plunger.

e. Holding the solenoid plunger against the Solenoid Stop, use Tool J-28696-10, BT-7928, or equivalent, to turn the lean mixture (solenoid) screw slowly clockwise, until the solenoid plunger just contacts the gauging tool. The adjustment is correct when the solenoid plunger is contacting both the Solenoid Stop and the Gauging Tool.

f. Remove the solenoid plunger and gauging tool.

78. Install the connector attaching screw, but do not overtighten, as that could cause damage to the connector.

79. Install the TPS return spring in the bottom of the well in the float bowl.

80. Install the TPS and the connector assembly in the float bowl by aligning the groove in the electrical connector with slot in float bowl casting. Push down on the connector and sensor assembly so that the connector and wires are located below bowl casting surface.

81. Install the plastic bowl insert over the float valve, pressing downward until properly seated (flush with bowl casting surface).

82. Slide the metering rod return spring over the metering rod tip until the small end of spring stops against shoulder on rod. Carefully install the metering rod and spring assembly through the holding in the plastic bowl insert and gently lower the metering rod into the guided metering jet, until the large end of spring seats on the recess on end of jet guide.

✻✻CAUTION

Do not force the metering rod down in the jet. Use extreme care when handling these critical parts to avoid damage to rod and spring. If service replacement metering rods, springs and jets are installed, they must be installed in matched sets.

83. Install pump return spring in pump well.

84. Install pump plunger assembly in pump well.

85. Holding down on pump plunger assembly against return spring tension, install air horn gasket by aligning pump plunger stem with hole in gasket, and aligning holes in gasket over TPS plunger, solenoid plunger return spring metering rods, solenoid attaching screw and electrical connector. Position gasket over the two dowel locating pins on the float bowl.

86. Holding down on air horn gasket and pump plunger assembly, install the solenoid-metering rod plunger in the solenoid, aligning slot in end of plunger with solenoid attaching screw. Be sure plunger arms Engage top of each metering.

87. If a service replacement mixture control solenoid package is installed, the solenoid and plunger must be installed as a matched set.

88. If removed, install the TPS adjustment screw in the air horn using Tool J-28696-10, BT-7967A or equivalent. Final adjustment of the TPS is made on the vehicle.

89. Inspect the air valve shaft pin for lubrication. Apply a liberal quantity of lithium base grease to the air valve shaft pin, especially in the area contacted by the air valve spring.

90. Install new pump plunger and TPS plunger seals and retainers in air horn casting. The lip on the seal faces outward, away from the air horn mounting surface. Lightly stake the seal retainer in three places, choosing locations different from the original stakings.

91. Install the rich mixture stop screw and rich authority adjusting spring from bottom side of the air horn. Use Tool J-2869-4, BT-7967A or equivalent, to bottom the stop screw lightly, then back out ¼ turn.

92. Install TPS actuator plunger in the seal.

93. Carefully lower the air horn assembly onto the float bowl while positioning the TPS adjustment lever over the TPS sensor and guiding pump plunger stem through the seal in the air horn casting. To ease installation, insert a thin screwdriver between the air horn gasket and float bowl to raise the TPS adjustment lever, positioning it over the TPS sensor.

94. Make sure that the bleed tubes and accelerating well tubes are positioned properly through the holes in the air horn gasket. Do not force the air horn assembly onto the bowl, but lower it lightly into place over the two dowel locating pins.

95. Install two long air horn screws and lockwashers, nine short screws and lockwashers and two countersunk screws located next to the carburetor venturi area. Install secondary air baffle beneath the No. 3 and 4 screws. Tighten all screws evenly and securely.

96. Install air valve rod into slot in the lever on the end of the air valve shaft. Install the other end of the rod in hole in front vacuum break plunger. Install front vacuum break and bracket assembly on the air horn, using two attaching screws. Tighten screw securely. Connect pump link to pump lever and install retainer.

➡Use care installing the roll pin to prevent damage to the pump lever bearing surface and casting bosses.

97. Install two secondary metering rods into the secondary metering rod hanger (upper end of rods point toward each other). Install secondary metering rod holder, with rods, onto air valve cam follower. Install retaining screw and tighten securely. Work air valves up and down several times to make sure they remove freely in both directions.

98. Connect choke rod into lower choke lever inside bowl cavity. Install choke rod in slot in upper choke lever, and position lever on end of choke shaft, making sure flats on end of shaft align with flats in lever. Install attaching screw and tighten securely. When properly installed, the number on the lever will face outward.

99. Adjust the rich mixture stop screw as follows:

a. Insert external float gauging Tool J-34935-1, BT-8420A, or equivalent, in the vertical D-shaped vent hole in the air horn casting (next to the idle air bleed valve) and allow it to float freely.

b. Read (at eye level) the mark on the gauge, in inches, that lines up with the tip of the air horn casting.

c. Lightly press down on gauge, and again read and record the mark on the gauge that lines up with the top of the air horn casting.

d. Subtract gauge UP dimension, found in Step b, from gauge DOWN dimension, found in Step c, and record the difference in inches. This difference in dimension is the total solenoid plunger travel.

e. Insert Tool J-28696-10, BT-7928 or equivalent, in the access hole in the air horn, and adjust the rich mixture stop screw to obtain ⅛ in. (3mm) total solenoid plunger travel.

100. With the solenoid plunger travel correctly set, install the plugs supplied in the service kit into the air horn to retain the setting and prevent fuel vapor loss:

a. Install the plug, hollow end down, into the access hole to the lean mixture (solenoid) screw and use a suitably sized punch to drive the plug into the air horn until top of plug is even with the lower edge of the hole chamber.

b. In a similar manner, install the plug over the rich mixture screw access hole and drive the plug into place so that the tip of the plug is 1/16 in. (1.6mm) below the surface of the air horn casting.

101. Install the idle air bleed valve as follows:

a. Lightly coat two new O-ring seals with automatic transmission fluid, to aid in their installation on the idle air bleed valve body. The thick seal goes in the upper groove and the thin seal goes in the lower groove.

b. Install the idle air bleed valve in the air horn, making sure that there is proper thread engagement.

c. Insert idle air bleed valve gauging Tool J-33815-2, BT-8353B or equivalent, in throttle side D-shaped vent hole of the air horn casting. The upper end of the tool should be positioned over the open cavity next to the idle air bleed valve.

d. Hold the gauging tool down lightly so that the solenoid plunger is against the solenoid stop, then adjust the idle air bleed valve so that the gauging tool will pivot over and just contact the top of the valve.

e. Remove the gauging tool.

f. The final adjustment of the idle air bleed valve is made on the vehicle to obtain idle mixture control.

102. Perform the air valve spring adjustment and choke coil lever adjustment as outlined in this section.

103. Install the cover and coil assembly in the choke housing, as follows:

a. Place the cam follower on the highest step of the fast idle cam.

b. Install the thermostatic cover and coil assembly in the choke housing, making sure the coil tang Engages the inside coil pickup lever. Ground contact for the electric choke is provided by a metal plate located at the rear of the choke cover assembly. Do not install a choke cover gasket between the electric choke assembly and the choke housing.

c. A choke cover retainer kit is required to attach the choke cover to the choke housing. Follow the instructions found in the kit and install the proper retainer and rivets using a suitable blind rivet tool.

d. It may be necessary to use an adapter (tube) if the installing tool interferes with the electrical connector tower on the choke cover.

104. Install the hose on the front vacuum brake and on the tube on the float bowl.

105. Position the idle speed solenoid and bracket assembly on the float bowl, retaining it with two large countersunk screws.

106. Perform the choke rod-fast idle cam adjustment, primary (front) vacuum break adjustment, air valve rod adjustment-front, unloader adjustment and the secondary lockout adjustment as outlined in this section.

107. Reinstall the carburetor on the vehicle with a new flange gasket.

CARBURETOR SPECIFICATIONS
1MEF

Carb. Part No.	Float Level (in.)	Metering Rod (in.)	Choke Coil Lever (in.)	Choke Rod Cam Adj. (in.)	Vacuum Break (in.)	Unloader (in.)
17086101	11/32	0.090	0.120	0.275	0.200	0.520
17086096	11/32	0.090	0.120	0.275	0.200	0.520

84905064

CARBURETOR SPECIFICATIONS
M4MEF

Carb. Part No.	Float Level (in.)	Pump Rod Setting (in.)	Pump Rod Location	Air Valve Spring (turns)	Choke Coil Lever (in.)	Fast Idle Cam Choke Rod (±2.5°)	Vacuum Break Front (±2.5°)	Vacuum Break Rear (±3.5°)	Air Valve Rod (in.)	Unloader (±4°)
17085004	13/32	9/32	Inner	7/8	0.120	46°	23°	—	0.025	35°
17085212	13/32	9/32	Inner	7/8	0.120	46°	23°	—	0.025	35°
17088040	13/32	9/32	Inner	7/8	0.120	46°	27°	—	0.025	35°
17088041	13/32	9/32	Inner	7/8	0.120	46°	27°	—	0.025	35°

84905065

THROTTLE BODY INJECTION (TBI)

General Information

The electronic fuel injection system is a fuel metering system with the amount of fuel delivered by the Throttle Body Injectors (TBI) determined by an electronic signal supplied by the Electronic Control Module (ECM). The ECM monitors various engine and vehicle conditions to calculate the fuel delivery time (pulse width) of the injectors. The fuel pulse may be modified by the ECM to account for special operating conditions, such as cranking, cold starting, altitude, acceleration and deceleration.

The ECM controls the exhaust emissions by modifying fuel delivery to achieve, as near as possible, an air/fuel ratio of 14.7:1. The injector "on" time is determined by various inputs to the ECM. By increasing the injector pulse, more fuel is delivered, enriching the air/fuel ratio. Decreasing the injector pulse, leans the air/fuel ratio.

The basic TBI unit is made up of two major casting assemblies: (1) a throttle body with a valve to control airflow and (2) a fuel body assembly with an integral pressure regulator and fuel injector to supply the required fuel. An electronically operated device to control the idle speed and a device to provide information regarding throttle valve position are included as part of the TBI unit.

The fuel injector is a solenoid-operated device controlled by the ECM. The incoming fuel is directed to the lower end of the injector assembly which has a fine screen filter surrounding the injector inlet. The ECM actuates the solenoid, which lifts a normally closed ball valve off a seat. The fuel under pressure is injected in a conical spray pattern at the walls of the throttle body bore above the throttle valve. The excess fuel passes through a pressure regulator before being returned to the vehicle fuel tank.

The pressure regulator is a diaphragm-operated relief valve with injector pressure on one side and air cleaner pressure on the other. The function of the regulator is to maintain a constant pressure drop across the injector throughout the operating load and speed range of the engine.

The throttle body portion of the TBI may contain ports located at, above, or below the throttle valve. These ports generate the vacuum signals for the EGR valve, MAP sensor and the canister purge system.

Relieving Fuel System Pressure

The pressure regulator utilizes a constant bleed feature when the engine is turned off, but follow these general tips:

1. Always disconnect the negative battery terminal.
2. Loosen the fuel filler cap to relive the vapor pressure in the fuel tank.

Electric Fuel Pump

REMOVAL & INSTALLATION

➧ See Figure 29

✲✲CAUTION

The 220 TBI unit has a bleed in the pressure regulator to relieve pressure any time the engine is turned off, however a small amount of fuel may be released when the fuel line is disconnected. As a precaution, cover the fuel line with a cloth and dispose of properly.

1. With the engine turned **OFF**, relieve the fuel pressure at the pressure regulator. Refer to the fuel relief procedure in this section.
2. Disconnect the negative battery cable.
3. Raise and support the rear of the vehicle on jackstands.
4. Drain the fuel tank, then remove it.
5. Using a hammer and a drift punch, drive the fuel lever sending device and pump assembly locking ring (located on top of the fuel tank) counterclockwise. Lift the assembly from the tank and remove the pump from the fuel lever sending device.
6. Pull the pump up into the attaching hose while pulling it outward away from the bottom support. Be careful not to damage the rubber insulator and strainer during removal. After the pump assembly is clear of the bottom support, pull it out of the rubber connector.

To install:

7. Connect the fuel pump to the hose.

➡Be careful that you don't fold or twist the strainer when installing the sending unit, or you'll restrict fuel flow.

8. Install a new O-ring on the pump assembly and then position them into the fuel tank.

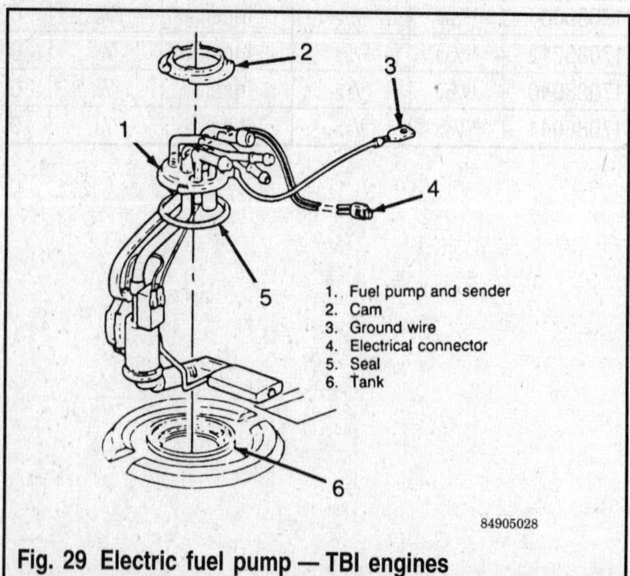

Fig. 29 Electric fuel pump — TBI engines

9. Turn the locking ring clockwise until its tight.
10. Install the fuel tank and connect the battery cable.

TESTING

➡Special tools J-29658-82 and J-29658, or their equivalents, will be necessary for this procedure.

1. Disconnect the negative battery cable.
2. Secure two sections of 3/8 in. x 10 in. (9.5mm x 254mm) steel tubing, with a double-flare on one end of each section.
3. Install a flare nut on each section of tubing, then connect each of the sections into the flare nut-to-flare nut adapter, while care included in the gauge adapter tool No. J-29658-82 or equivalent.
4. Attach the pipe and the adapter assembly to the gauge tool No. J-29658 or equivalent.
5. Raise and support the vehicle on jackstands.
6. Remove the air cleaner and plug the THERMAC vacuum port on the TBI.
7. Disconnect the fuel feed hose between the fuel tank and the filter, then secure the other ends of the 3/8 in. (9.5mm) tubing into the fuel hoses with hose clamps.
8. Reconnect the battery cable.
9. Start the engine, check for leaks and observe the fuel pressure, it should be 9-13 psi (62-89 kPa).
10. Depressurize the fuel system, remove the testing tool, remove the plug from the THERMAC vacuum port, reconnect the fuel line, start the engine and check for fuel leaks.

Throttle Body

REMOVAL & INSTALLATION

➧ See Figures 30, 31, 32, 33, 34 and 35

1. Release the fuel pressure. Refer to the fuel relief procedure in this section.
2. Disconnect the THERMAC hose from the engine fitting and remove the air cleaner.
3. Disengage the electrical connectors at the idle air control, throttle position sensor and the injector. Squeeze the plastic tabs on the injector connections and pull straight up.
4. Disconnect the grommet with wires from the throttle body.
5. Disconnect the throttle linkage, return spring, transmission control cable and cruise control (if equipped).
6. Disconnect the throttle body vacuum hoses, the fuel supply and fuel return lines.
7. Disconnect the bolts securing the throttle body, then remove it.

To install:

8. Replace the manifold gaskets and O-rings.
9. Install the TBI unit and tighten the bolts to 12 ft. lbs. (16 Nm).
10. Install new O-rings into the fuel line nuts and then screw them on by hand. Tighten them to 20 ft. lbs. (26 Nm).
11. Connect the vacuum hoses and bracket.
12. Connect the throttle linkage, transmission control cable, return springs and cruise control cable.

87985p20

Fig. 30 Tag and disconnect the vacuum lines

87985p21

Fig. 31 Tag and disengage the electrical connections

87985p22

Fig. 32 Disconnect the linkages

Fig. 33 Use a flare nut wrench to disconnect the fuel lines

Fig. 34 Loosen and remove the bolts securing the throttle body

Fig. 35 Remove the throttle body from the intake manifold

13. Install the grommet (with harness connected) to the TBI.
14. Reconnect all electrical leads. Press the accelerator pedal to the floor and make sure that it releases properly.
15. Turn the ignition switch ON (but don't start the engine!) and check for leaks around the fuel line nuts.
16. Install the air cleaner and start the engine — check for leaks.

ADJUSTMENT

▶ See Figure 36

Only if parts of the throttle body have been replaced should this procedure be performed; the engine should be at operating temperature.

1. Remove the air cleaner, adapter and gaskets. Discard the gaskets. Plug any vacuum line ports, as necessary.
2. Leave the IAC valve connected and ground the diagnostic terminal (ALDL connector).
3. Turn the ignition switch to the **ON** position, do not start the engine. Wait for at least 30 seconds (this allows the IAC valve pintle to extend and seat in the throttle body).
4. With the ignition switch still in the **ON** position, disconnect the IAC electrical connector.
5. Remove the ground from the diagnostic terminal and start the engine. Let the engine reach normal operating temperature.
6. Apply the parking brake and block the drive wheels. Remove the plug from the idle stop screw by piercing it first with a suitable tool, then applying leverage to the tool to lift the plug out.
7. Adjust the idle stop screw to the proper specifications
8. Turn the ignition **OFF** and reconnect the IAC valve connector. Unplug any plugged vacuum line ports and install the air cleaner, adapter and new gaskets.

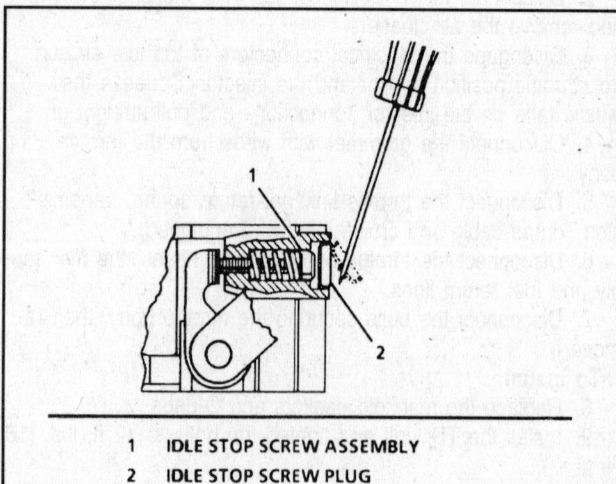

Fig. 36 Removing the idle stop screw

Fuel Meter Cover

REMOVAL & INSTALLATION

➧ See Figure 37

1. Relieve the fuel system pressure. Refer to the fuel relief procedure in this section.
2. Raise the hood, install fender covers and remove the air cleaner assembly.
3. Disconnect the negative battery cable.
4. Disengage electrical connector at the injector by squeezing the two tabs and pulling straight up.
5. Remove the five screws securing the fuel meter cover to the fuel meter body. Notice the location of the two short screws during removal.

****CAUTION**

Do not remove the four screws securing the pressure regulator to the fuel meter cover! The fuel pressure regulator includes a large spring under heavy tension which, if accidentally released, could cause personal injury! The fuel meter cover is serviced only as a complete assembly and includes the fuel pressure regulator preset and plugged at the factor.

6. Remove the fuel meter cover assembly from the throttle body.

****WARNING**

DO NOT immerse the fuel meter cover (with pressure regulator) in any type of cleaner! Immersion of cleaner will damage the internal fuel pressure regulator diaphragms and gaskets.

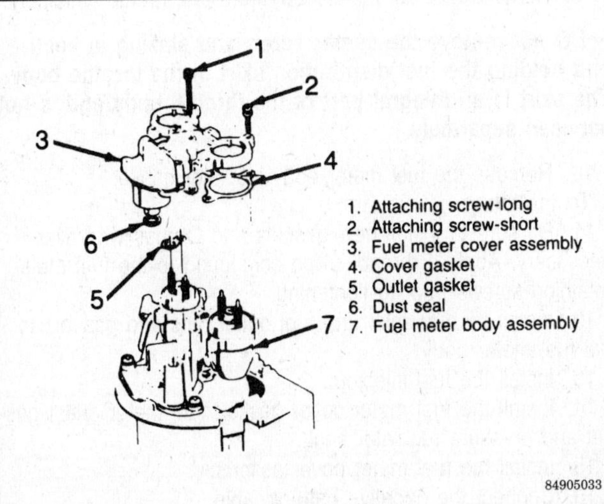

Fig. 37 Exploded view of the fuel meter cover mounting

To install:

7. Be sure to use new gaskets and then install the fuel meter cover. Tighten the attaching screws to 28 inch lbs. (3 Nm).

➡The service kits may include a small vial of thread locking compound with directions for use. If the material is not available, use part number 1054.3L4, Loctite® or equivalent. Do not use a higher strength locking compound than recommended, as this may prevent attaching screw removal or breakage of the screw head if removal is again required.

8. Reconnect all the fuel injectors, start the engine and check for leaks.

Fuel Injectors

REMOVAL & INSTALLATION

➧ See Figures 38, 39 and 40

****WARNING**

When removing the injectors, be careful not to damage the electrical connector pins (on top of the injector), the injector fuel filter and the nozzle. The fuel injector is serviced as a complete assembly ONLY. The injector is an electrical component and should not be immersed in any kind of cleaner.

1. Remove the air cleaner. Relieve the fuel system pressure. Refer to the fuel relief procedure in this section.
2. At the injector connector, squeeze the two tabs together and pull straight up.
3. Remove the fuel meter cover and leave the cover gasket in place.
4. Using a small pry bar or tool No. J-26868 or equivalent, carefully lift the injector until it is free from the fuel meter body.
5. Remove the small O-ring from the nozzle end of the injector. Carefully rotate the injector's fuel filter back and forth to remove it from the base of the injector.
6. Discard the fuel meter cover gasket.
7. Remove the large O-ring and back-up washer from the top of the counterbore of the fuel meter body injector cavity.

To install:

8. Lubricate the new lower O-rings with automatic transmission fluid and then push on the nozzle end of the injector until it presses against the injector fuel filter.
9. Position the injector back-up washer into the fuel meter bore.
10. Lubricate the new upper O-rings with automatic transmission fluid and then position it over the back-up washer so that it seats properly and is flush with the top of the meter body. Positioning must be correct or the injector will leak after installation.
11. Install the injector so that the raised lug on the injector base is aligned with the notch in the fuel meter body cavity. Press down on the injector until it is fully seated. The electrical terminals should be parallel with the throttle shaft.
12. Install the cover gasket and the meter cover.

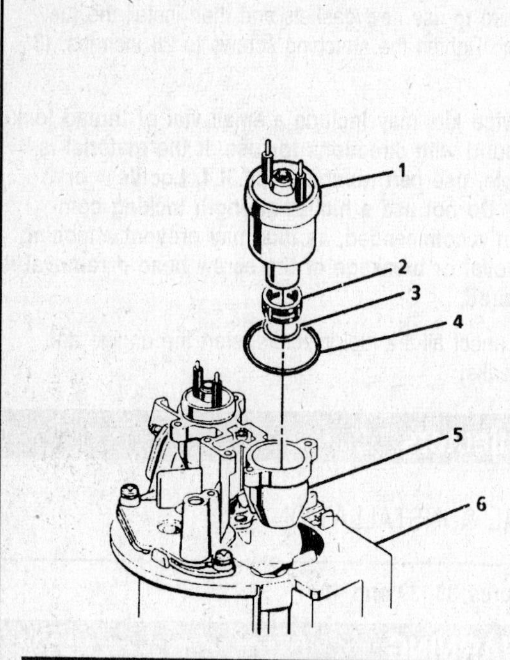

Fig. 38 Fuel injectors and components

Fig. 39 Removing the TBI injector

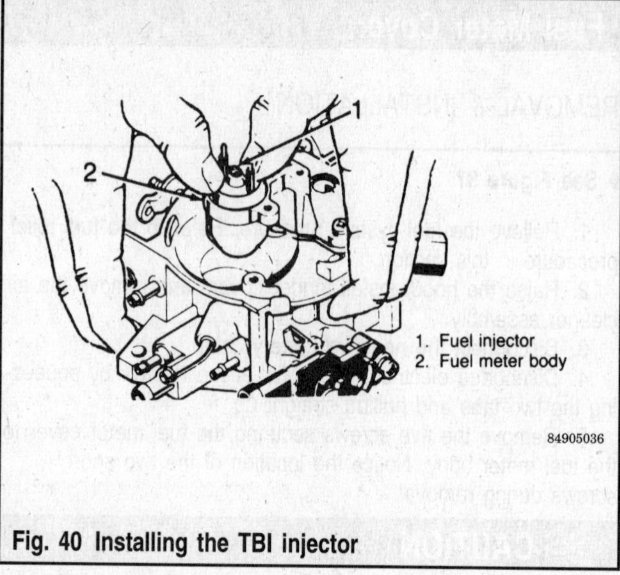

Fig. 40 Installing the TBI injector

13. Reconnect the electrical leads, start the engine and check for leaks.

Fuel Meter Body

REMOVAL & INSTALLATION

1. Relieve the fuel system pressure. Refer to the fuel relief procedure in this section.
2. Raise the hood, install fender covers and remove the air cleaner assembly.
3. Disconnect the negative battery cable.
4. Remove the fuel meter cover assembly.
5. Remove the fuel meter cover gasket, fuel meter outlet gasket and pressure regulator seal.
6. Remove the fuel injectors.
7. Remove the fuel inlet and outlet nuts and gaskets from the fuel meter body.
8. Remove the three screws and lockwashers.
9. Remove the fuel meter body from the throttle assembly.

➡DO not remove the center screw and staking at each end holding the fuel distribution skirt in the throttle body. The skirt is an integral part of the throttle body and is not serviced separately.

10. Remove the fuel meter body insulator gasket.

To install:

11. Be sure to install new gaskets and O-rings wherever necessary. Apply a threadlocking compound to the fuel meter retaining screws prior to tightening.
12. Install the fuel inlet and fuel outlet nuts and gaskets to the fuel meter body.
13. Install the fuel injectors.
14. Install the fuel meter cover gasket, fuel meter outlet gasket and pressure regulator seal.
15. Install the fuel meter cover assembly.
16. Connect the negative battery cable.
17. Install the air cleaner assembly.

MULTIPORT FUEL INJECTION (MFI)

General Information

In this system, the injectors are controlled individually. Each cylinder receives one charge every two revolutions just before the intake valve opens. This means that the mixture is never static in the intake manifold along with the mixture adjustments that can be made almost simultaneously between the firing of one injector and the next. A camshaft signal sensor or a special distributor reference pulse informs the ECM when the No. 1 cylinder is on the compression stroke. If the sensor fails or the distributor reference pulse is interrupted in any way, the system reverts to pulsing all the injectors simultaneously.

Relieving Fuel System Pressure

➡Fuel pressure gauge J 34730-1A or its equivalent is required to perform this procedure

1. Disconnect the negative battery cable.
2. Loosen the fuel filler cap to relieve fuel tank pressure.
3. Connect the fuel pressure gauge to the pressure connection. Wrap a shop towel around the fitting while connecting the gauge to prevent spillage.
4. Install the bleed hose into an approved container and open the valve to bleed the system. The system is now safe for servicing.
5. Drain any fuel remaining in the gauge into an approved container.

Electric Fuel Pump

➧ See Figure 41

All Chevrolet/GMC fuel-injected vehicles are equipped with an electric fuel pump. For a fuel injection system to work properly, the pump must develop pressures well above those of a mechanical fuel pump. This high pressure is maintained within the lines even when the engine is off. Extreme caution must be used to safely release the pressurized fuel before any work is begun.

****CAUTION**

Always relieve the fuel pressure within the system before any work is begun on any fuel component. Failure to safely relieve the pressure may result in fire and/or serious injury.

REMOVAL & INSTALLATION

➧ See Figures 42, 43 and 44

Single Tank

1. Disconnect the negative battery cable.
2. Relieve the fuel system pressure. Refer to the fuel system relief procedure in this section.
3. Raise the vehicle and support it safely with jackstands.
4. Drain the fuel system and remove the fuel tank. Refer to the fuel tank removal procedure in this section.
5. Remove the fuel sender assembly turning it counterclockwise using tool J 36608 or its equivalent.
6. Remove the assembly from the tank.
7. Pull the pump up into the attaching hose while pulling outward from the bottom support. Do not damage the rubber insulator or the strainer.
8. Inspect the fuel pump attaching hose and the rubber sound insulation for signs of deterioration.
9. Inspect the strainer for blockage and damage.

To install:

10. Install the fuel pump assembly into the attaching hose.

➡Be careful not to bend or fold over the fuel strainer when installing the fuel sender as this will restrict fuel flow.

11. Install the fuel sender into the fuel tank. Insert a new O-ring seal.
12. Install the camlock assembly turning it clockwise to lock it.
13. Install the fuel tank. Refer to the fuel tank installation procedure in this section.
14. Connect the negative battery cable.
15. Turn the ignition switch **ON** for 2 seconds then turn the switch **OFF** for 10 seconds. Again, turn the ignition switch **ON** and check for leaks.

Dual Tanks

1. Disconnect the negative battery cable.
2. Loosen the filler cap(s) to relieve fuel tank pressure.
3. Disconnect the fuel pipes from the pump.
4. Slide the pump out of the bracket.

To install:

5. Install new fuel pipe O-rings.
6. Position the pump in the pump bracket.
7. Connect the fuel feed pipe and suction pipe to the fuel pump.
8. Using a backup wrench to stop the fuel pump from turning, tighten the fittings to 22 ft. lbs. (30 Nm).
9. Engage the electrical connector.
10. Connect the negative battery cable.
11. Turn the ignition switch **ON** for 2 seconds then turn the switch **OFF** for 10 seconds. Again, turn the ignition switch **ON** and check for leaks.

Throttle Body

➧ See Figure 45

REMOVAL & INSTALLATION

1. Disconnect the negative battery cable.
2. Remove the air inlet duct.
3. Disengage the Idle Air Control (IAC) valve and the Throttle Position Sensor (TPS) electrical connectors.
4. Disconnect the throttle and cruise control cables.

1
2
3
4
5
6
7
8
9
10
11
12
13
14
15
16
87985G05

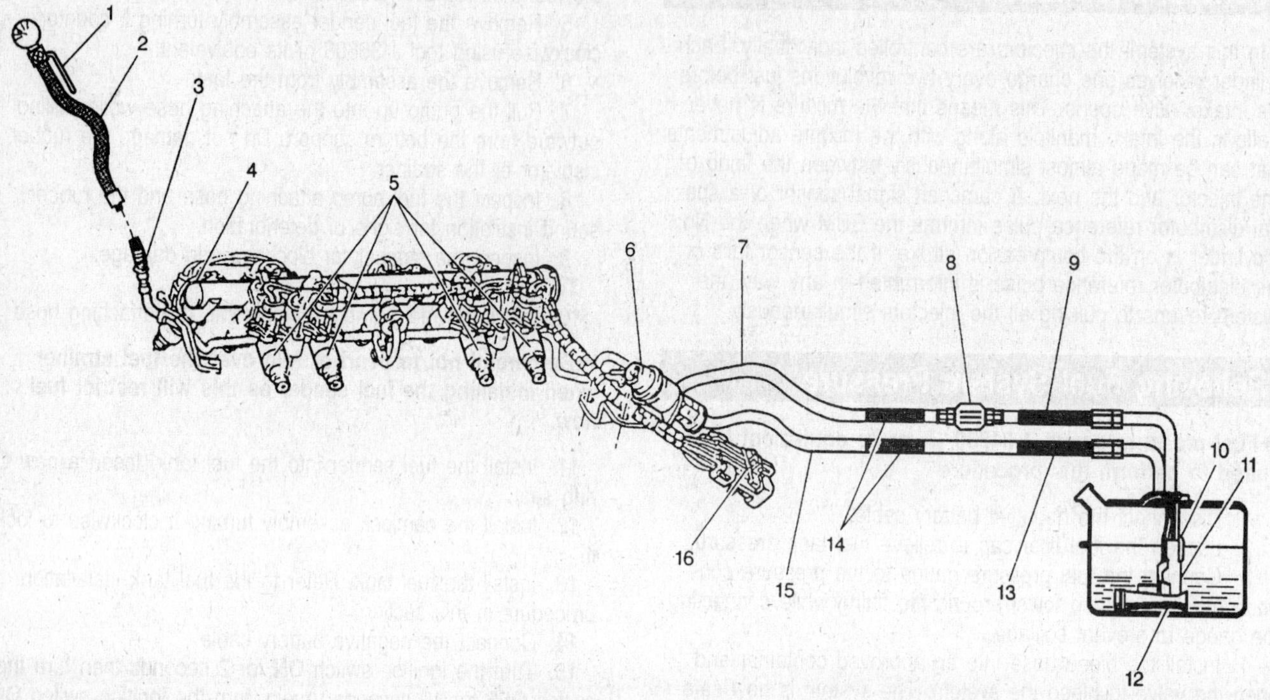

1. Bleed Hose
2. J 34730-1A Fuel Presure Gauge Assembly
3. Fuel Pressure Connection
4. Fuel Rail
5. Fuel Injectors
6. Fuel Pressure Regulator
7. Fuel Inlet Line
8. In-Line Fuel Filter
9. Pressure Line
10. Fuel Pump Feed Hose
11. In-Tank Pump
12. Fuel Pump Strainer
13. Return Line
14. Flexible Hose
15. Fuel Outlet
16. Injector Harness Connector

Fig. 41 Exploded view of the fuel supply system

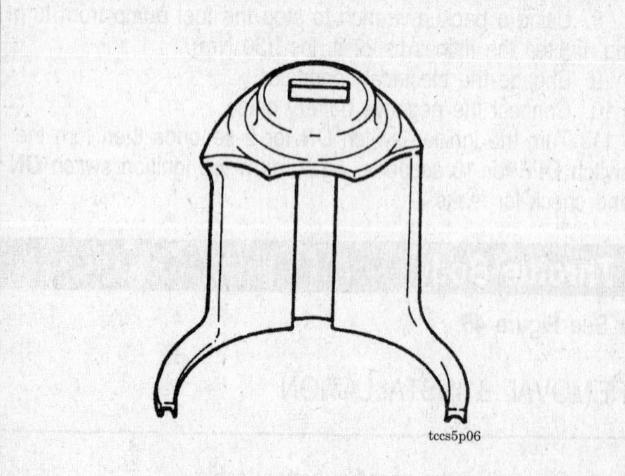

tccs5p06

Fig. 42 A special tool is usually available to remove or install the fuel pump locking cam

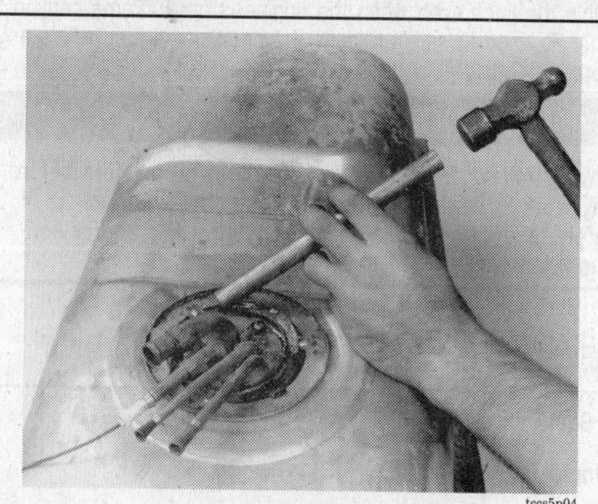

tccs5p04

Fig. 43 A brass drift and a hammer can also be used to loosen the fuel pump locking cam

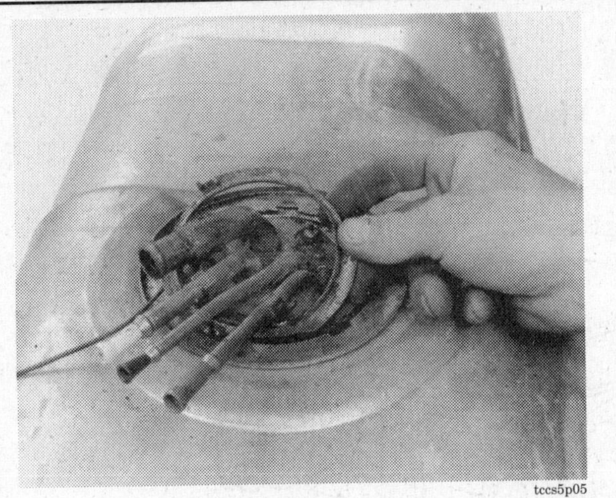

Fig. 44 Once the locking cam is released, it can be removed to free the fuel pump

5. Unfasten the throttle body retaining nuts and remove the throttle body.
6. Remove and discard the flange gasket.
7. Clean both gasket mating surfaces.

➡When cleaning the old gasket from the machined aluminum surfaces be careful as sharp tools may damage the sealing surfaces

To install:

8. Install the new flange gasket and the throttle body assembly.
9. Tighten the throttle body attaching nuts to 18 ft. lbs. (25 Nm).
10. Connect the throttle and cruise control cables.
11. Engage the IAC valve and the TPS electrical connectors.
12. Install the air inlet duct and connect the negative battery cable.

Fuel Injectors

REMOVAL & INSTALLATION

➧ See Figure 46

➡Use care when removing the injectors to prevent damage to the electrical connector pins on the injector and the nozzle. The fuel injector is serviced as a complete assembly only. Since the injector is an electrical component, it should not be immersed in any type of cleaner.

1. Disconnect the negative battery cable.
2. Relieve the fuel system pressure. Refer to the fuel system relief procedure in this section.
3. Remove the intake manifold plenum.
4. Remove the fuel rail assembly.
5. Disengage the electrical wiring harness.
6. Disassemble the injector clip and discard it.
7. Remove the injector o-ring seals from both ends of the injector. Save the o-ring backups for use on reassembly.

To install:

8. Install the o-ring backups before installing the O-rings.
9. Lubricate the new injector O-rings with clean engine oil and install them on the injector assembly.
10. Install the fuel injector into the fuel rail injector socket with the electrical connectors facing outward.
11. Install new injector retaining clips on the injector fuel rail assembly by sliding the clip into the injector groove as it snaps onto the fuel rail.
12. Install the fuel rail assembly.
13. Install the manifold plenum.
14. Engage the electrical wiring harness.
15. Connect the negative battery cable.

TESTING

➧ See Figure 47

➡This test requires the use of fuel injector tester J 34730-3 or its equivalent.

1. With the engine cool and the ignition turned **OFF**, install the fuel pressure gauge to the fuel pressure connection. Wrap a shop towel around the fitting while connecting the gauge to prevent spillage.
2. Disengage all the fuel injector electrical connectors. Engage the tester to one fuel injector.
3. Turn **ON** the ignition and bleed the air from the pressure gauge.
4. Turn **OFF** the ignition for ten seconds and then turn it **ON** again. This will bring the fuel pressure to its maximum pressure. Record this reading.
5. Press the tester button and record the lowest pressure reading. Subtract this reading from the initial reading obtained and record the result.
6. Connect the tester to each injector and repeat Steps 4 and 5.
7. Pressure should fall between 56-62 psi (430 kPa). Replace any injector that does not meet these specifications.

Fuel Pressure Regulator

REMOVAL & INSTALLATION

➧ See Figure 48

1. Disconnect the negative battery cable.
2. Relieve fuel system pressure. Refer to the fuel system relief procedure in this section.
3. Disconnect the ignition coil.
4. Remove the manifold plenum.
5. Disconnect the vacuum line to the regulator.
6. Remove the snapring from the regulator housing.
7. Place a towel under the regulator to absorb any spilled fuel and remove the pressure regulator from the fuel socket.
8. Remove the pressure regulator from the fuel rail.
9. Remove the pressure regulator o-ring filter, o-ring backup and o-ring and discard them.

To install:

10. Before installing the O-rings, lubricate them with clean engine oil and install them on the regulator inlet as a complete assembly.

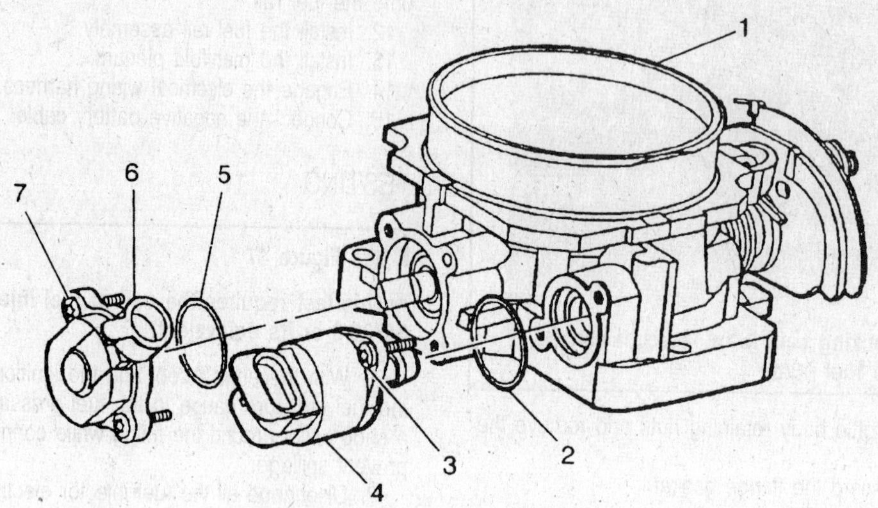

Fig. 45 Exploded view of throttle body

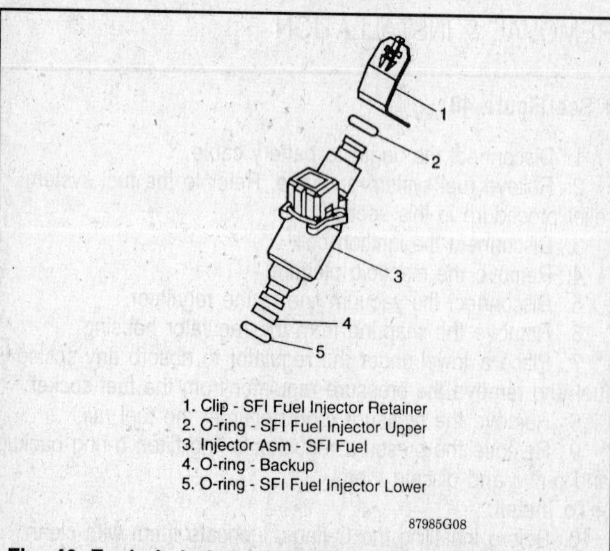

Fig. 46 Exploded view of the fuel injector assembly

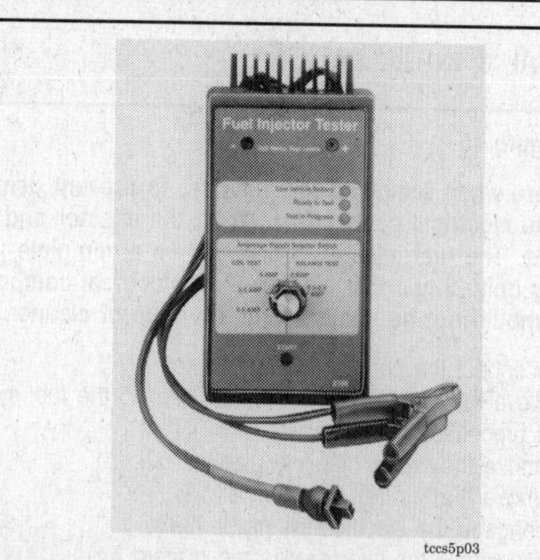

Fig. 47 Fuel injector testers can be purchased or sometimes rented

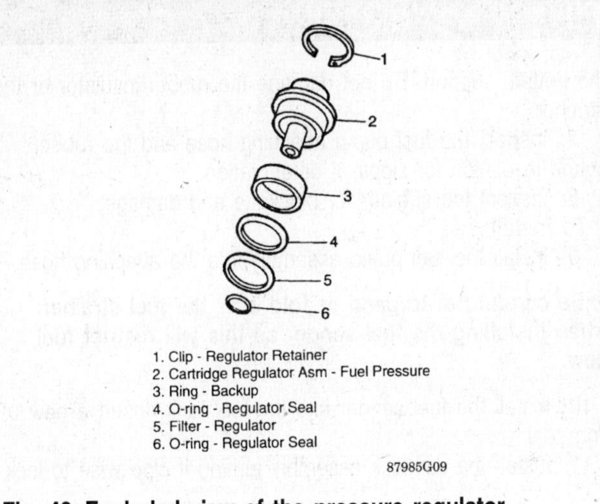

Fig. 48 Exploded view of the pressure regulator assembly

11. Install the snapring retainer into the slot on the regulator housing.
12. Connect the vacuum line to the regulator.

➡Ensure that the retainer is properly seated in the slot in the regulator housing. Pull on the regulator to make sure that it is properly seated.

13. Connect the negative battery cable.
14. Turn the ignition **ON** for 2 seconds and then turn it **OFF** for 10 seconds. Again turn the ignition **ON** and check for leaks.
15. Install the manifold plenum.

Fuel Rail Assembly

REMOVAL & INSTALLATION

➧ **See Figure 49**

➡Clean the fuel rail assembly before removal. The fittings should be capped to prevent dirt from entering open lines.

1. Disconnect the negative battery cable.
2. Relieve fuel system pressure. Refer to the fuel system relief procedure in this section.
3. Remove the manifold plenum.
4. Remove the distributor.
5. Disconnect the fuel lines at the rail.
6. Unfasten the fuel pipe bracket bolt.
7. Remove the fuel inlet and return line O-rings and discard them.
8. Disengage the fuel injector electrical connectors and remove from the coil bracket.
9. Unfasten the fuel rail retaining bolts.
10. Disconnect the vacuum line to the fuel pressure regulator.
11. Remove the fuel rail.
12. Remove the O-rings seals and backups from the injectors. Discard the old seals but retain the backups for reuse.

To install:

➡Ensure that the o-ring backups are on the injectors before installing the O-rings. Lubricate the O-rings with clean engine oil before installation.

13. Install the fuel rail in the intake manifold. Tilt the fuel rail assembly to install the injectors. Tighten the fuel rail retaining bolts to 89 inch. lbs. (10 Nm).
14. Engage the injector electrical connectors.
15. Install new O-rings on the fuel pipes.
16. Install the fuel return and feed lines.
17. Tighten the fuel pipe nuts to 20 ft. lbs. (27 Nm) using a back-up wrench to prevent the fittings from turning.
18. Connect the negative battery cable.
19. Turn the ignition **ON** for 2 seconds and then turn it **OFF** for 10 seconds. Again turn the ignition **ON** and check for leaks.
20. Install the manifold plenum.

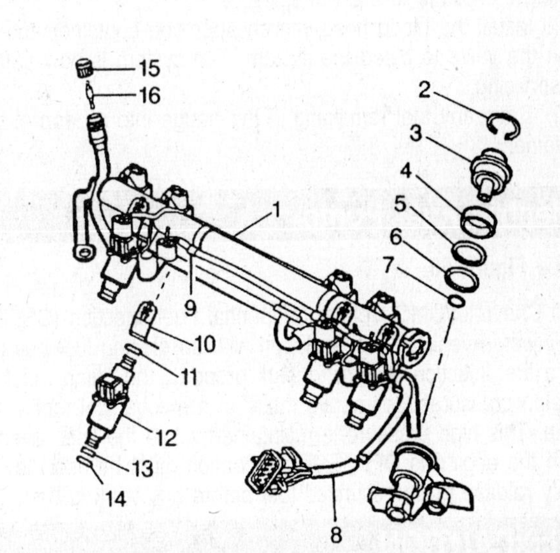

Fig. 49 Exploded view of the fuel rail assembly

CENTRAL SEQUENTIAL FUEL INJECTION (CSFI)

General Information

The 1996 trucks are equipped with the Central Sequential Fuel Injection (CSFI) system. Fuel is delivered to the engine by individual fuel injectors and poppet nozzles mounted in the intake manifold near each cylinder. Each is fired sequentially for accuracy and precise metering control.

Relieving Fuel System Pressure

➡**Fuel pressure gauge J 34730-1A or its equivalent is required to perform this procedure**

1. Disconnect the negative battery cable.
2. Loosen the fuel filler cap to relieve fuel tank pressure.
3. Engage the fuel pressure gauge to the fuel pressure connection. Wrap a shop towel around the fitting while connecting the gauge to prevent spillage.
4. Install the bleed hose into an approved container and open the valve to bleed the system. The system is now safe for servicing.
5. Drain any fuel remaining in the gauge into an approved container.

Electric Fuel Pump

See Figure 50

All Chevrolet/GMC Central Sequential Fuel Injection (CSFI) fuel-injected vehicles are equipped with an electric fuel pump. For a fuel injection system to work properly, the pump must develop pressures well above those of a mechanical fuel pump. This high pressure is maintained within the lines even when the engine is **OFF**. Extreme caution must be used to safely release the pressurized fuel before any work is begun.

***CAUTION

Always relieve the fuel pressure within the system before any work is begun on any fuel component. Failure to safely relieve the pressure may result in fire and/or serious injury.

REMOVAL & INSTALLATION

See Figures 51, 52 and 53

Single Tank

1. Disconnect the negative battery cable.
2. Relieve the fuel system pressure. Refer to the fuel system relief procedure in this section.
3. Raise the vehicle and support it safely with jackstands.
4. Drain the fuel system and remove the fuel tank. Refer to the fuel tank removal procedure in this section.
5. Remove the fuel sender assembly turning it counterclockwise using tool J 36608 or its equivalent.
6. Remove the fuel pump from the sender assembly. Pull the pump up into the attaching hose while pulling outward from the bottom support. Do not damage the rubber insulator or the strainer.
7. Inspect the fuel pump attaching hose and the rubber sound insulation for signs of deterioration.
8. Inspect the strainer for blockage and damage.

To install:

9. Install the fuel pump assembly into the attaching hose.

➡**Be careful not to bend or fold over the fuel strainer when installing the fuel sender as this will restrict fuel flow.**

10. Install the fuel sender into the fuel tank. Insert a new o-ring seal.
11. Install the camlock assembly turning it clockwise to lock it.
12. Install the fuel tank. Refer to the fuel tank installation procedure in this section.
13. Connect the negative battery cable.

Dual Tanks

1. Disconnect the negative battery cable.
2. Loosen the filler cap(s) to relieve fuel tank pressure.
3. Disconnect the fuel pipes from the pump.
4. Slide the pump out of the bracket.

To install:

5. Install new fuel pipe O-rings.
6. Position the pump in the pump bracket.
7. Connect the fuel feed pipe and suction pipe to the fuel pump.
8. Using a backup wrench to stop the fuel pump from turning, tighten the fittings to 22 ft. lbs. (30 Nm).
9. Engage the electrical connector.
10. Connect the negative battery cable.
11. Turn the ignition switch **ON** for 2 seconds then turn the switch **OFF** for 10 seconds. Again, turn the ignition switch **ON** and check for leaks.

Throttle Body

REMOVAL & INSTALLATION

1. Disconnect the negative battery cable.
2. Remove the air inlet fastener and duct.
3. Disengage the Idle Air Control (IAC) valve and the Throttle Position Sensor (TPS) electrical connectors.
4. Disconnect the throttle and cruise control cables.
5. Disconnect the accelerator cable bracket bolts and nuts.
6. Disengage the wiring harness fastener nut.
7. Unfasten the throttle body retaining nuts and remove the throttle body.
8. Remove and discard the flange gasket.
9. Clean both gasket mating surfaces.

➡**When cleaning the old gasket from the machined aluminum surfaces be careful as sharp tools may damage the sealing surfaces**

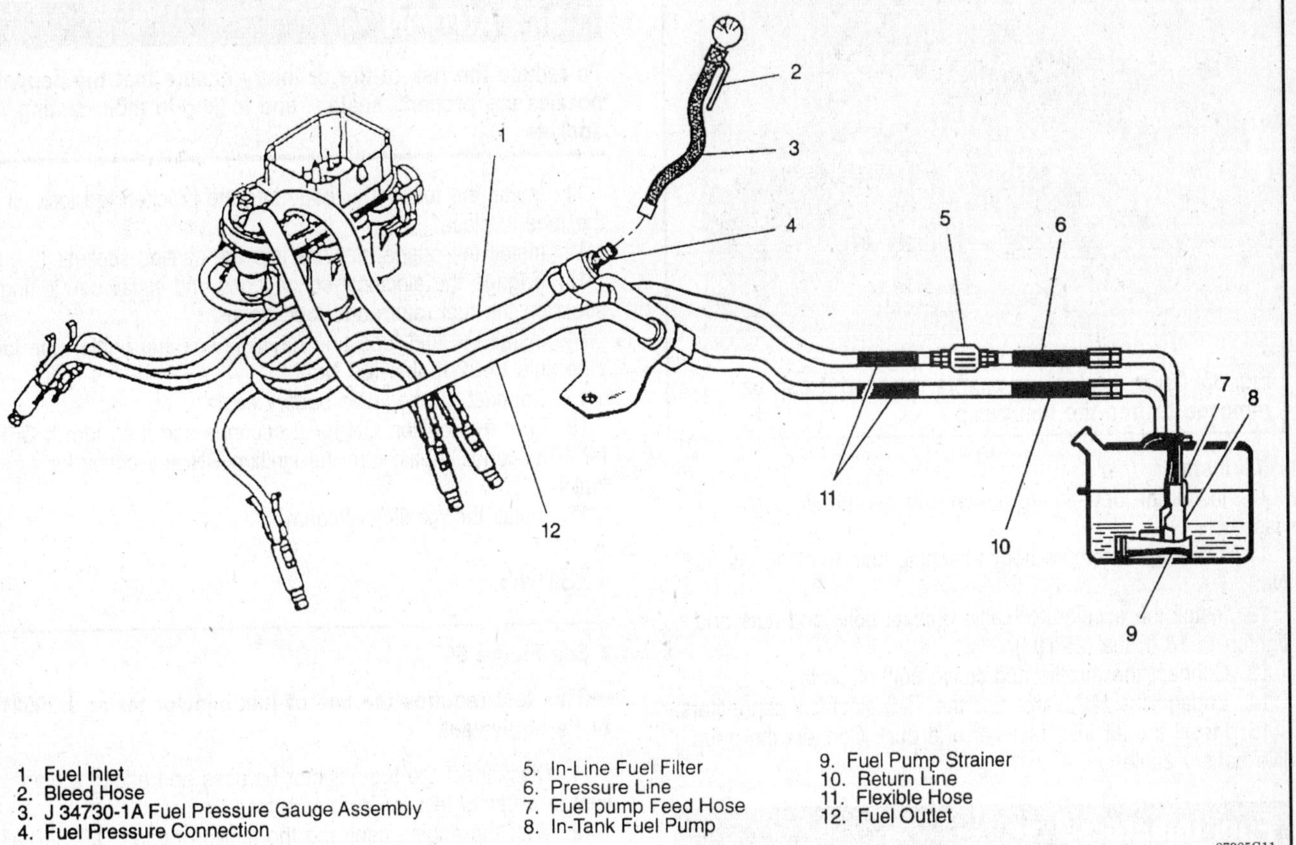

1
2
3
4
5
6
7
8
9
10
11
12
1. Fuel Inlet
2. Bleed Hose
3. J 34730-1A Fuel Pressure Gauge Assembly
4. Fuel Pressure Connection
5. In-Line Fuel Filter
6. Pressure Line
7. Fuel pump Feed Hose
8. In-Tank Fuel Pump
9. Fuel Pump Strainer
10. Return Line
11. Flexible Hose
12. Fuel Outlet
87985G11

Fig. 50 Exploded view of the fuel supply system

tccs5p06

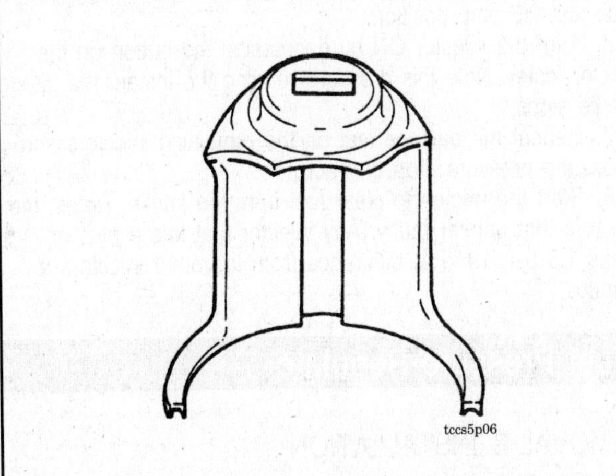

Fig. 51 A special tool is usually available to remove or install the fuel pump locking cam

tccs5p04

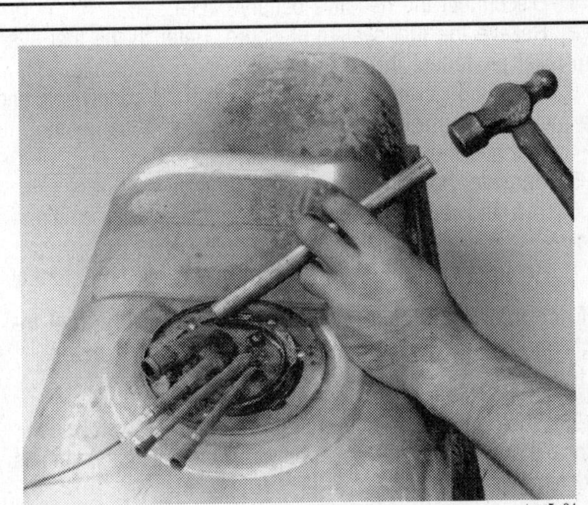

Fig. 52 A brass drift and a hammer can be used to loosen the fuel pump locking cam

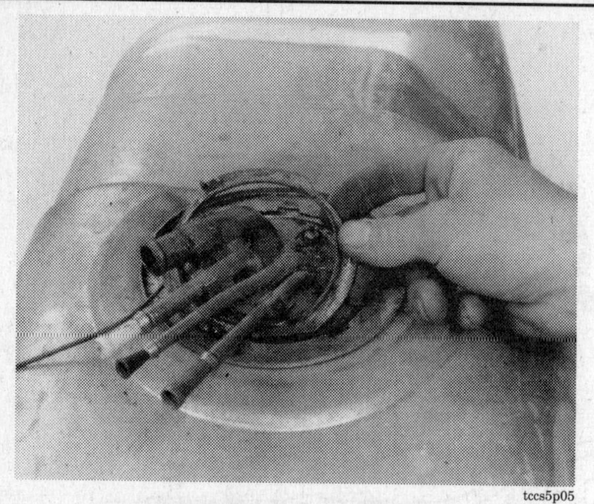

Fig. 53 Once the locking cam is released it can be removed to free the fuel pump

To install:

10. Install the new flange gasket and the throttle body assembly.
11. Tighten the throttle body attaching nuts to 18 ft. lbs. (25 Nm).
12. Install the accelerator cable bracket bolts and nuts and tighten to 18 ft. lbs (25 Nm).
13. Connect the throttle and cruise control cables.
14. Engage the IAC valve and the TPS electrical connectors.
15. Install the air inlet fastener and duct. Connect the negative battery cable.

Fuel Injectors

REMOVAL & INSTALLATION

➧ See Figures 54 and 55

1. Disconnect the negative battery cable.
2. Relieve the fuel system pressure. Refer to the fuel system relief procedure in this section.
3. Disengage the fuel meter body electrical connection and the fuel feed and return hoses from the engine fuel pipes.
4. Remove the upper manifold assembly.
5. Remove the upper manifold assembly.
6. Tag and remove the poppet nozzle out of the casting socket.
7. Remove the fuel meter body by releasing the locktabs.

➡Each injector is calibrated. When replacing the fuel injectors, be sure to replace it with the correct injector.

8. Disassemble the lower hold-down plate and nuts.
9. While pulling the poppet nozzle tube downward, push with a small screwdriver down between the injector terminals and remove the injectors.

To install:

10. Install the fuel meter body assembly into the intake manifold and tighten the fuel meter bracket retainer bolts to 88 inch. lbs. (10 Nm).

✱✱CAUTION

To reduce the risk of fire or injury ensure that the poppet nozzles are properly seated and locked in their casting sockets

11. Install the fuel meter body into the bracket and lock all the tabs in place.
12. Install the poppet nozzles into the casting sockets.
13. Engage the electrical connections and install new o-ring seals on the fuel return and feed hoses.
14. Install the fuel feed and return hoses and tighten the fuel pipe nuts to 22 ft. lbs. (30 Nm).
15. Connect the negative battery cable.
16. Turn the ignition **ON** for 2 seconds and then turn it **OFF** for 10 seconds. Again turn the ignition **ON** and check for leaks.
17. Install the manifold plenum.

TESTING

➧ See Figure 56

➡This test requires the use of fuel injector tester J 39021 or its equivalent.

1. Disconnect the fuel injector harness and attach a noid light in order to test for injector pulse.
2. With the engine cool and the ignition turned **OFF**, install the fuel pressure gauge to the fuel pressure connection. Wrap a shop towel around the fitting while connecting the gauge to prevent spillage.
3. Turn **ON** the ignition and record the fuel gauge pressure with the pump running.
4. Turn **OFF** the ignition. Pressure should drop and hold steady at this point.
5. To perform this test, set the selector switch to the balance test 2.5 amp position.
6. Turn the injector **ON** by depressing the button on the injector tester. Note this pressure reading the instant the gauge needle stops.
7. Repeat the balance test on the remaining injectors and record the pressure drop on each.
8. Start the engine to clear fuel from the intake. Retest the injectors that appear faulty. Any injector that has a plus or minus 1.5 psi (10 kPa) difference from the other injectors is suspect.

Fuel Pressure Regulator

REMOVAL & INSTALLATION

➧ See Figure 57

1. Disconnect the negative battery cable.

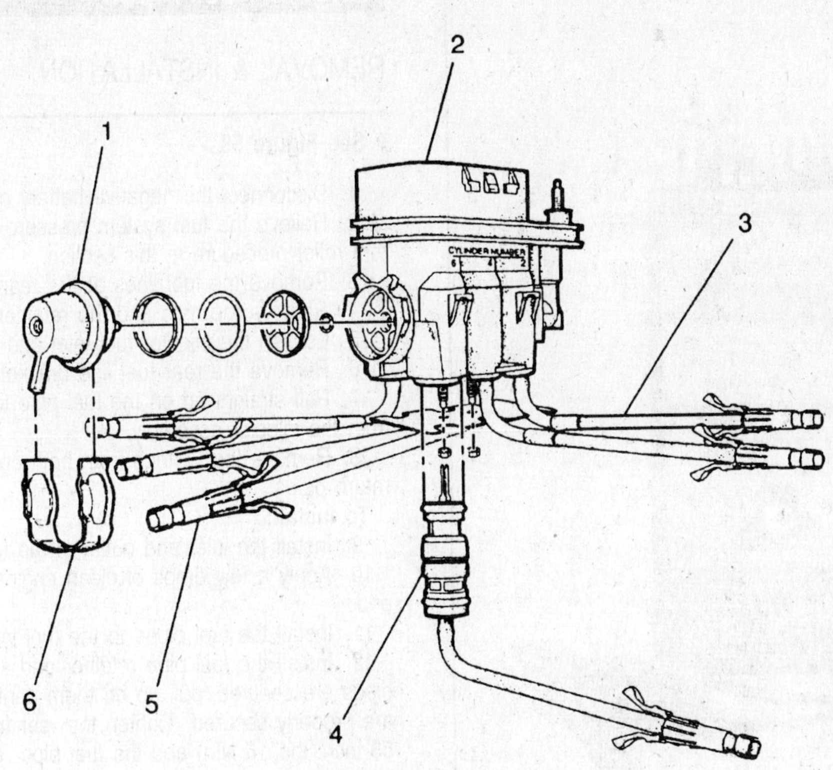

Fig. 54 Exploded view of the fuel meter body assembly

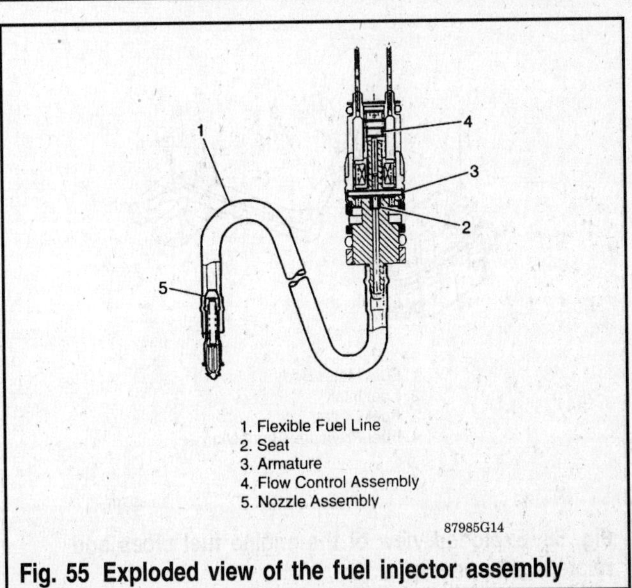

Fig. 55 Exploded view of the fuel injector assembly

2. Relieve the fuel system pressure. Refer to the fuel system relief procedure in this section.
3. Remove the upper manifold assembly.
4. Remove the fuel pressure regulator vacuum tube.
5. Disassemble the fuel pressure regulator snapring retainer.
6. Remove the fuel pressure regulator assembly and the O-rings. Discard the O-rings, filter and back-up O-rings.

To install:

7. Lubricate the O-rings with clean engine oil and install as an assembly.
8. Install the fuel pressure regulator, attach the vacuum tube.
9. Install the snapring retainer.
10. Install the upper manifold assembly.
11. Connect the negative battery cable.

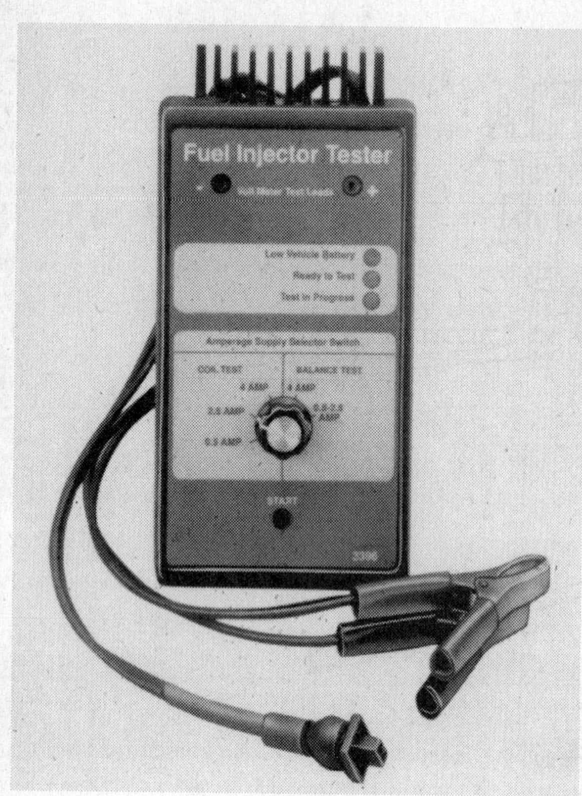

tccs5p03

Fig. 56 Fuel injector testers can be purchased or sometimes rented

Engine Fuel Pipes

REMOVAL & INSTALLATION

See Figure 58

1. Disconnect the negative battery cable.
2. Relieve the fuel system pressure. Refer to the fuel system relief procedure in this section.
3. Remove the fuel lines at the rear of the intake manifold.
4. Remove the nuts and the retainer.
5. Loosen the injector fuel inlet and outlet pipes.
6. Remove the rear fuel line bracket.
7. Pull straight up on the fuel pipe to remove the pipes from the injector assembly.
8. Remove the O-rings from both ends of the fuel feed and return pipes.

To install:

9. Install the inlet and outlet of the fuel injector assembly.
10. Apply a few drops of clean engine oil to the male tube ends.
11. Install the fuel pipes to the fuel injector assembly.
12. Install the fuel pipe retainer and attaching nuts. After the pipes are secured, pull up on them gently to ensure that they are properly secured. Tighten the rear fuel line bracket bolt to 53 inch. lbs. (6 Nm) and the fuel pipe retainer nuts to 27 inch. lbs. (3 Nm).
13. Tighten the fuel pipe nuts to 22 ft. lbs. (30 Nm) and connect the negative battery cable.
14. Turn the ignition **ON** for 2 seconds and then turn it **OFF** for 10 seconds. Again turn the ignition **ON** and check for leaks.

Fuel Pressure Connection

The fuel pressure connection is non-replaceable, but is serviceable.

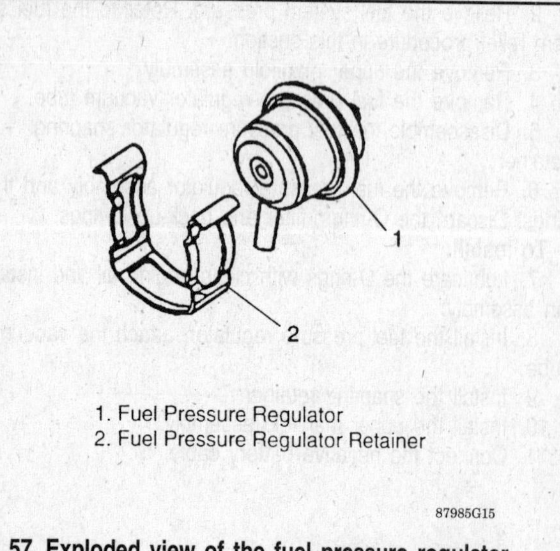

87985G15

Fig. 57 Exploded view of the fuel pressure regulator

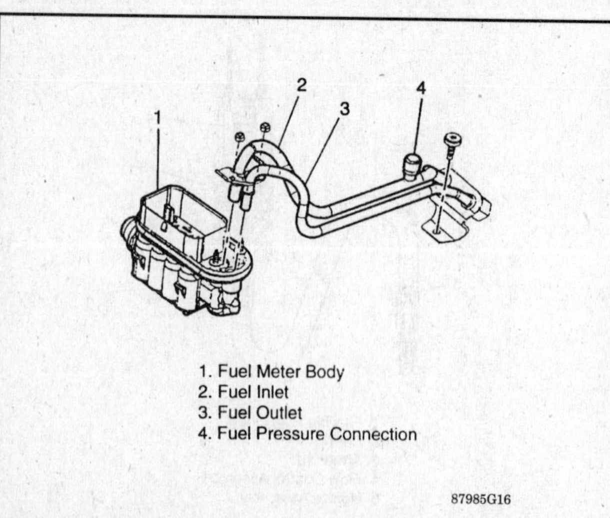

87985G16

Fig. 58 Exploded view of the engine fuel pipes and related components

SERVICE

1. Disconnect the negative battery cable.
2. Relieve the fuel system pressure. Refer to the fuel system relief procedure in this section.
3. Remove the fuel pressure connection cap.
4. Using a valve core removal tool remove the valve core assembly and discard it.

To install:

5. Install a new valve core assembly using a valve core removal tool.
6. Connect the negative battery cable.
7. Turn the ignition **ON** for 2 seconds and then turn it **OFF** for 10 seconds. Again turn the ignition **ON** and check for leaks.
8. Install the fuel pressure connection cap.

DIESEL ENGINE FUEL SYSTEM

Fuel Injection Lines

REMOVAL & INSTALLATION

See Figure 59

When the fuel lines are to be removed, clean all fuel line fittings thoroughly before loosening. Immediately cap the lines, nozzles and pump fittings to maintain cleanliness.

1. Disconnect both batteries.
2. Disconnect the air cleaner bracket at the valve cover.
3. Remove the crankcase ventilator bracket and move it aside.
4. Disconnect the secondary filter lines.
5. Remove the secondary filter adapter.
6. Loosen the vacuum pump hold-down clamp and rotate the pump in order to gain access to the intake manifold bolt. Remove the intake manifold bolts. The injection line clips are retained by the same bolts.
7. Remove the intake manifold. Install a protective cover (GM part no. J-29664-1 or equivalent) so no foreign material falls into the engine.
8. Remove the injection line clips at the loom brackets.
9. Remove the injection lines at the nozzles and cover the nozzles with protective caps.
10. Remove the injection lines at the pump and tag the lines for later installation.
11. Remove the fuel line from the injection pump.

To install:

12. Install the injection lines at the pump and nozzles. Tighten all fittings to 20 ft. lbs. (25 Nm).
13. Install the injection line clips at the loom bracket.
14. Install the intake manifold.
15. Install the alternator bracket and tighten the manifold bolts.
16. Install the fuel lines at the filter. Tighten the bolts to 9 inch lbs. (1 Nm).
17. Install the filter to the manifold and tighten the bolts to 30 ft. lbs. (40 Nm).
18. Install the air cleaner and the crankcase ventilator bracket.
19. Connect the batteries.

Fuel Injectors

REMOVAL & INSTALLATION

See Figure 60

Special tool J-29873, or its equivalent, an injection nozzle socket, will be necessary for this procedure.

1. Disconnect the batteries.

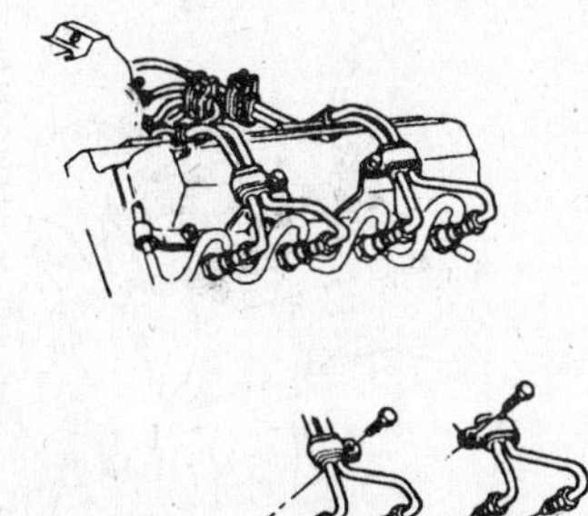
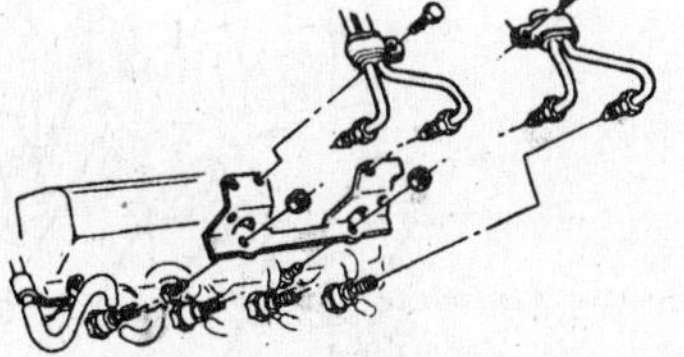
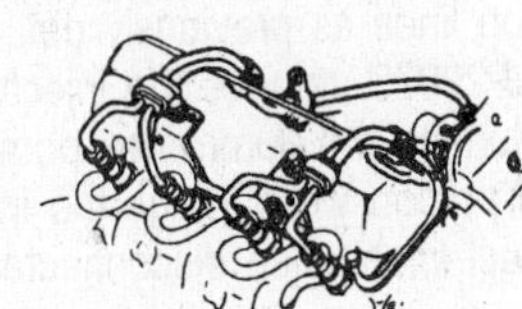

Fig. 59 Injection line routing — 6.2L and 6.5L engines

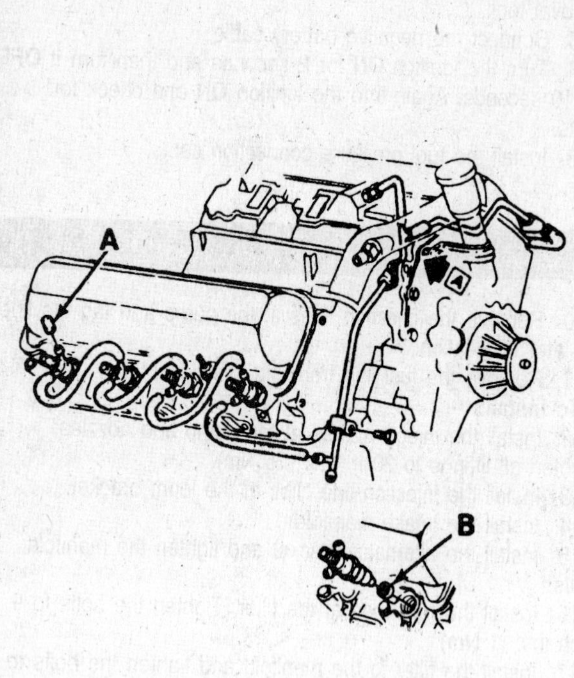

Fig. 60 Injection nozzles — 6.2L and 6.5L engines

2. Disconnect the fuel line clip, and remove the fuel return hose.
3. Remove the fuel injection lines as previously detailed.
4. Using GM special tool J-29873, remove the injector. Always remove the injector by turning the 30mm hex portion of the injector; turning the round portion will damage the injector. Always cap the injector and fuel lines when disconnected, to prevent contamination.
5. Install the injector with a new gasket and tighten to 50 ft. lbs. (70 Nm). Connect the injection line and tighten the nut to 20 ft. lbs. (25 Nm). Install the fuel return hose, fuel line clips, and connect the batteries.

TESTING

1. Install a suitable pressure gauge.
2. Open the shut-off valve on the gauge a ¼ turn.

CAUTION

When testing nozzle opening pressure, always keep your hands (or any exposed skin!) away from the nozzle. Diesel injectors have sufficient pressure to penetrate your skin!

3. Slowly depress the lever on the gauge. Note when the needle on the gauge stops — the maximum pressure is the opening pressure. Pressure should never fall below 1500 psi (10,342 kPa) on the 6.2L engine or 1700 psi (11,721 kPa) on the 6.5L engine.
4. Replace any injector which does not meets these pressures.

Fuel Supply Pump

REMOVAL & INSTALLATION

1988-90 6.2L Engines

See Figure 61

CAUTION

Never smoke when working around diesel fuel! Avoid all sources of sparks or ignition.

1. Disconnect the fuel intake and outlet lines at the pump and plug the pump intake line.
2. You can insert a long bolt to hold the fuel pump pushrod.
3. Remove the two pump mounting bolts and lockwashers; remove the pump and its gasket. The 6.2L utilizes a mounting plate between the pump and gasket.
4. If the rocker arm pushrod is to be removed, remove the two adapter bolts and lockwashers and remove the adapter and its gasket.
5. Install the fuel pump with a new gasket. Tighten the upper mounting bolts to 24 ft. lbs. (33 Nm) and the lower bolt

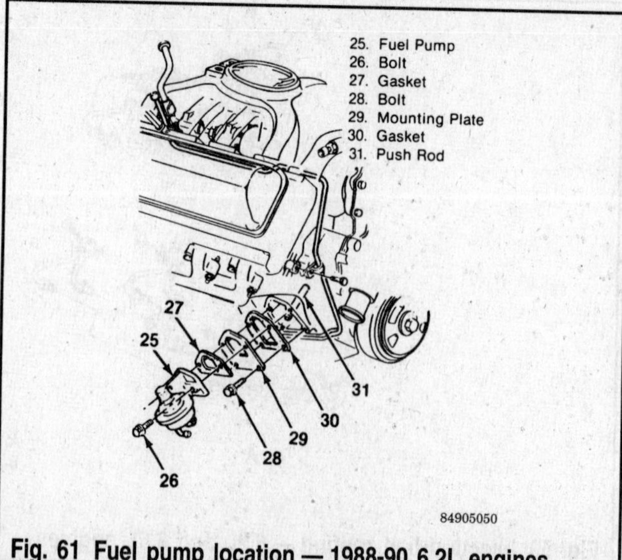

Fig. 61 Fuel pump location — 1988-90 6.2L engines

to 6 ft. lbs. (8 Nm). Heavy grease can be used to hold the fuel pump pushrod up when installing the pump. Coat the mating surfaces with sealant.

6. Connect the fuel lines an check for leaks.

1991-96 6.2L and 6.5L Engines

➧ See Figure 62

1. Disconnect the negative battery cables.
2. Locate the pump on the left frame rail and disconnect the electrical lead from the pump and the harness from the pump support bracket.
3. Use two open end wrenches and disconnect the fuel lines at the pump.
4. Remove the pump support bracket screws and remove it from the brake lines.
5. Remove the pump and bracket.

To install:

6. Attach the pump and bracket to the frame rail.
7. Attach the support bracket to the brake lines.
8. Connect the fuel lines to the pump.
9. Connect the harness to the bracket and then connect the lead to the pump.
10. Connect the batteries.

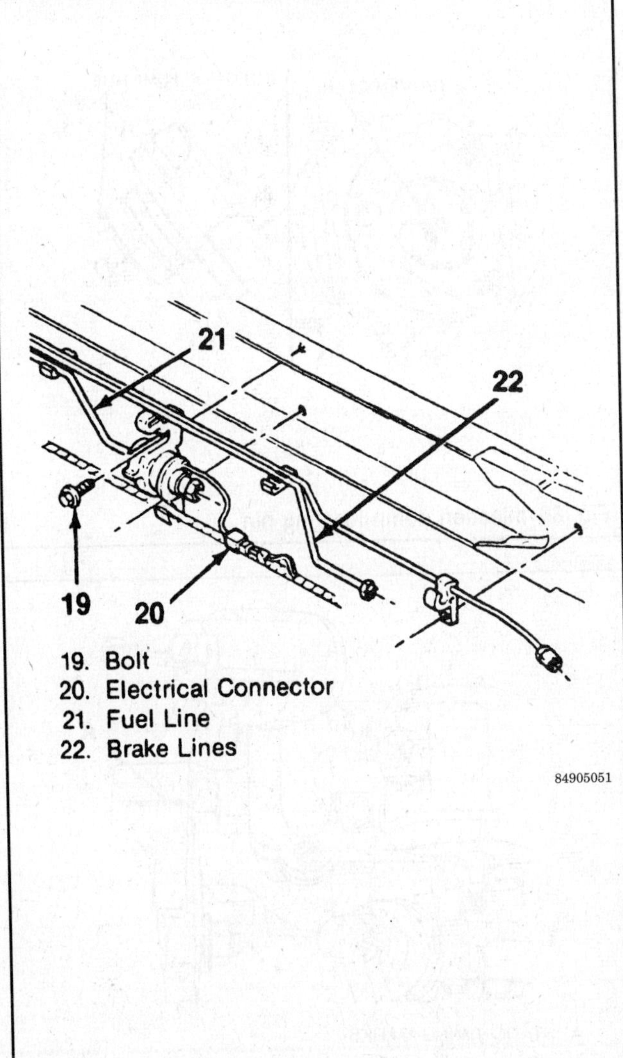

Fig. 62 Fuel pump location — 1991-96 6.2L and 6.5L engines

Fuel Injection Pump

REMOVAL & INSTALLATION

➧ See Figures 63, 64 and 65

1. Disconnect both batteries.
2. Remove the fan and fan shroud.
3. Remove the intake manifold.
4. Remove the fuel lines.
5. Disconnect the accelerator cable at the injection pump, and the detent cable (see illustration) where applicable.
6. Tag and disconnect the necessary wires and hoses at the injection pump.

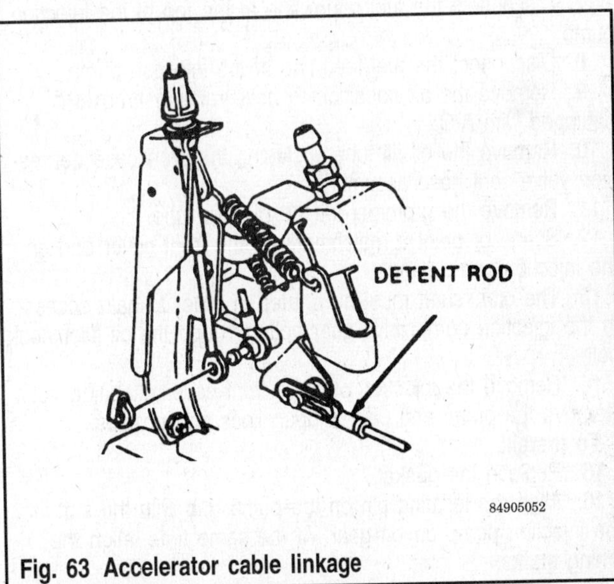

Fig. 63 Accelerator cable linkage

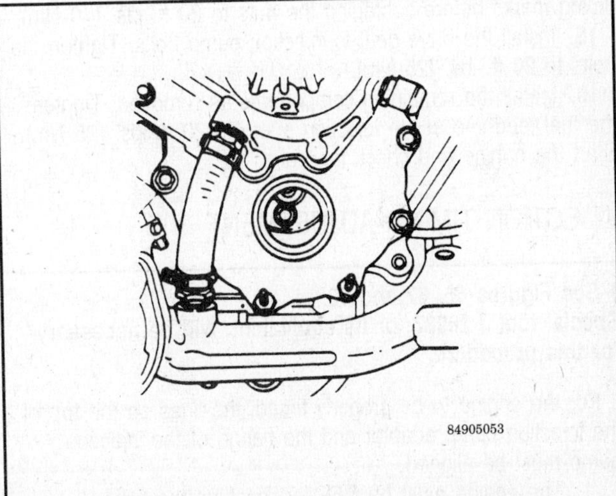

Fig. 64 Rotate the crankshaft so that the injection pump drive gear bolts become visible through the hole

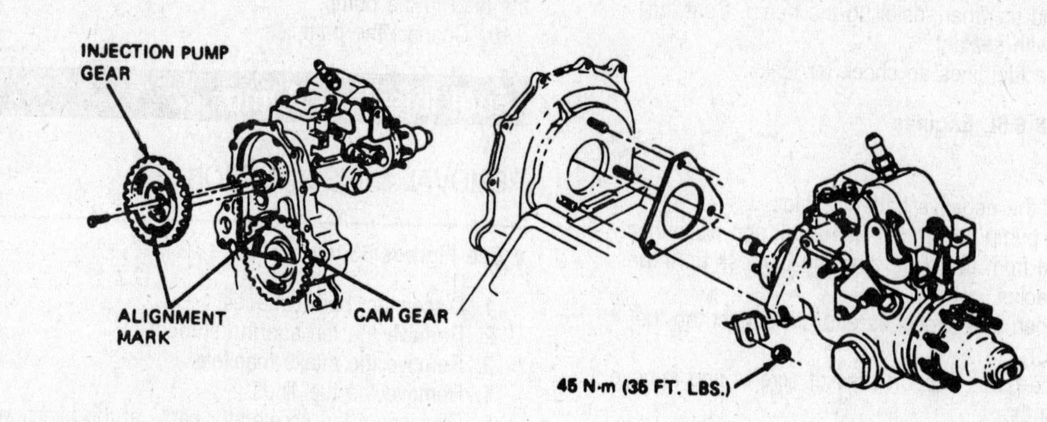

Fig. 65 Injection pump mounting

7. Disconnect the fuel return line at the top of the injection pump.
8. Disconnect the fuel feed line at the injection pump.
9. Remove the air conditioning hose retainer bracket if equipped with A/C.
10. Remove the oil fill tube, including the crankcase depression valve vent hose assembly.
11. Remove the grommet for the oil filler tube.
12. Scribe or paint a matchmark on the front cover and on the injection pump flange.
13. The crankshaft must be rotated in order to gain access to the injection pump drive gear bolts through the oil filler neck hole.
14. Remove the injection pump-to-front cover attaching nuts. Remove the pump and cap all open lines and nozzles.

To install:

15. Replace the gasket.
16. Align the locating pin on the pump hub with the slot in the injection pump driven gear. At the same time, align the timing marks.
17. Attach the injection pump to the front cover, aligning the timing marks before tightening the nuts to 30 ft. lbs. (40 Nm).
18. Install the drive gear-to-injection pump bolts. Tighten the bolts to 20 ft. lbs. (25 Nm).
19. Install the remaining components as removed. Tighten the fuel feed line at the injection pump to 20 ft. lbs. (25 Nm). Start the engine and check for leaks.

INJECTION TIMING ADJUSTMENT

➧ See Figures 66, 67 and 68
Special tool J-26987, or its equivalent, will be necessary for this procedure.

For the engine to be properly timed, the lines on the top of the injection pump adapter and the flange of the injection pump must be aligned.

1. The engine must be **OFF** for resetting the timing.
2. Loosen the three pump retaining nuts with tool J-26987, an injection pump intake manifold wrench, or its equivalent.

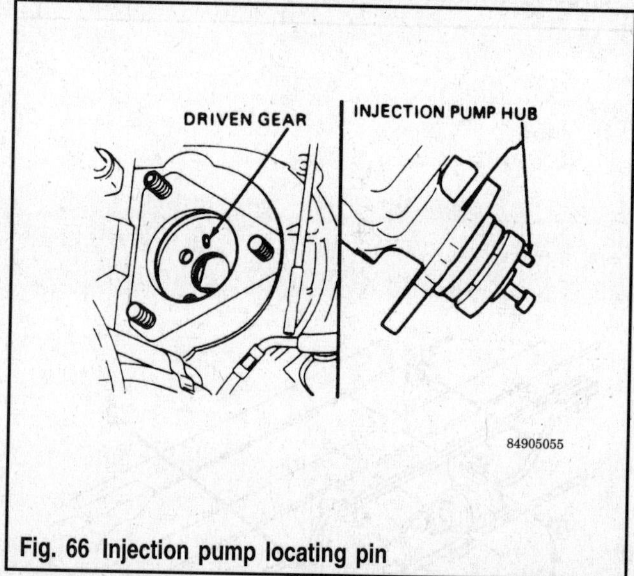

Fig. 66 Injection pump locating pin

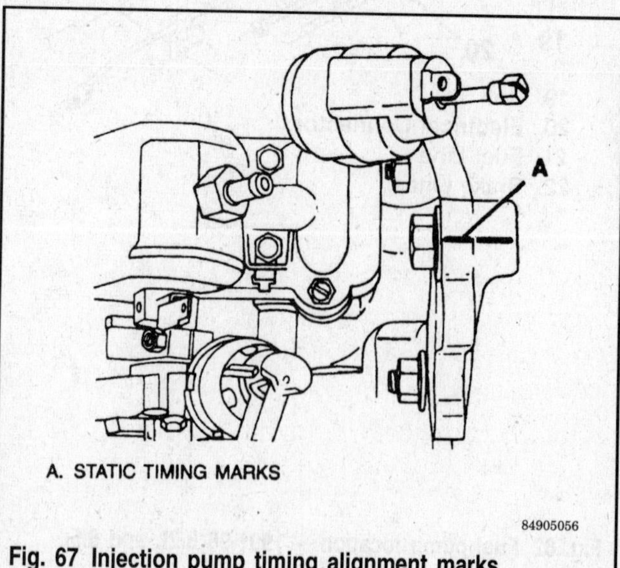

Fig. 67 Injection pump timing alignment marks

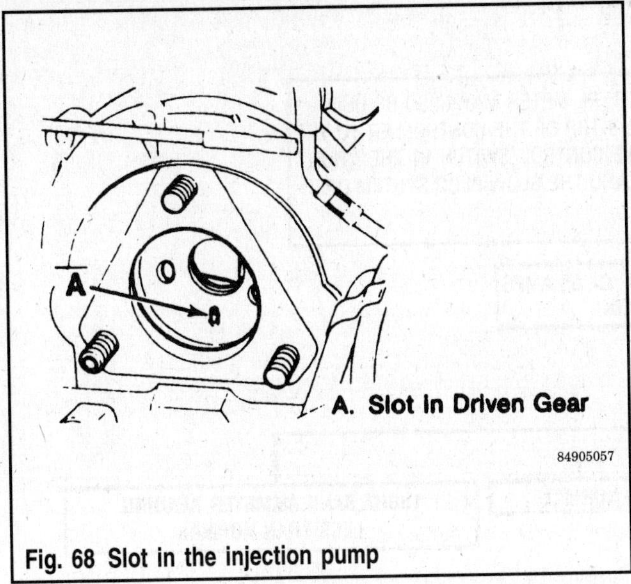

Fig. 68 Slot in the injection pump

3. Align the mark on the injection pump with the marks on the adapter and tighten the nuts. Tighten to 30 ft. lbs. (40 Nm). Use a ¾ in. (19.05mm) open-end wrench on the boss at the front of the injection pump to aid in rotating the pump to align the marks.
4. Adjust the throttle rod.

Glow Plugs

INSPECTION

➧ See Figure 69

1. Check all connections on the controller.
2. Check the upper copper stud nuts on the controller. Do not tighten them.
3. Check the engine harness ground connection and the wiring harness nuts. Tighten them to 44 inch lbs. (5 Nm).
4. Check that the four-wire connector at the controller is seated properly and latched.
5. Tighten the controller mounting nuts to 25 ft. lbs. (35 Nm).

REMOVAL & INSTALLATION

1. Disconnect the negative battery cables.
2. On the 6.2L engine and the left side only of the 6.5L, disconnect the glow plug lead wires and then remove the plugs. You'll need a 3/8 in. (9.525mm) deep-well socket.
3. On the right side of the 6.5L engine, raise the truck and support it with safety stands. Remove the right front tire.
4. Remove the inner splash shield from the fender well.
5. Remove the lead wire from the plug at the No. 2 cylinder. Remove the lead wires from plugs in the Nos. 4 and 6 cylinders at the harness connectors.
6. Remove the heat shroud for the plug in the No. 4 cylinder. Remove the heat shroud for the plug in the No. 6 cylinder. Slide the shrouds back just far enough to allow access so you can unplug the wires.
7. Remove the plugs in cylinders No. 2, 4 and 6.
8. Reach up under the vehicle and disconnect the lead wire at No. 8. Remove the glow plug. You may find that removing the exhaust down pipe make this a bit easier when working on Nos. 6 and 8.
9. Installation is the reverse of removal. Install all glow plugs and carefully tighten them to 13 ft. lbs. (17 Nm) for the right side on the 6.5L; 17 ft. lbs. (23 Nm) on all others.

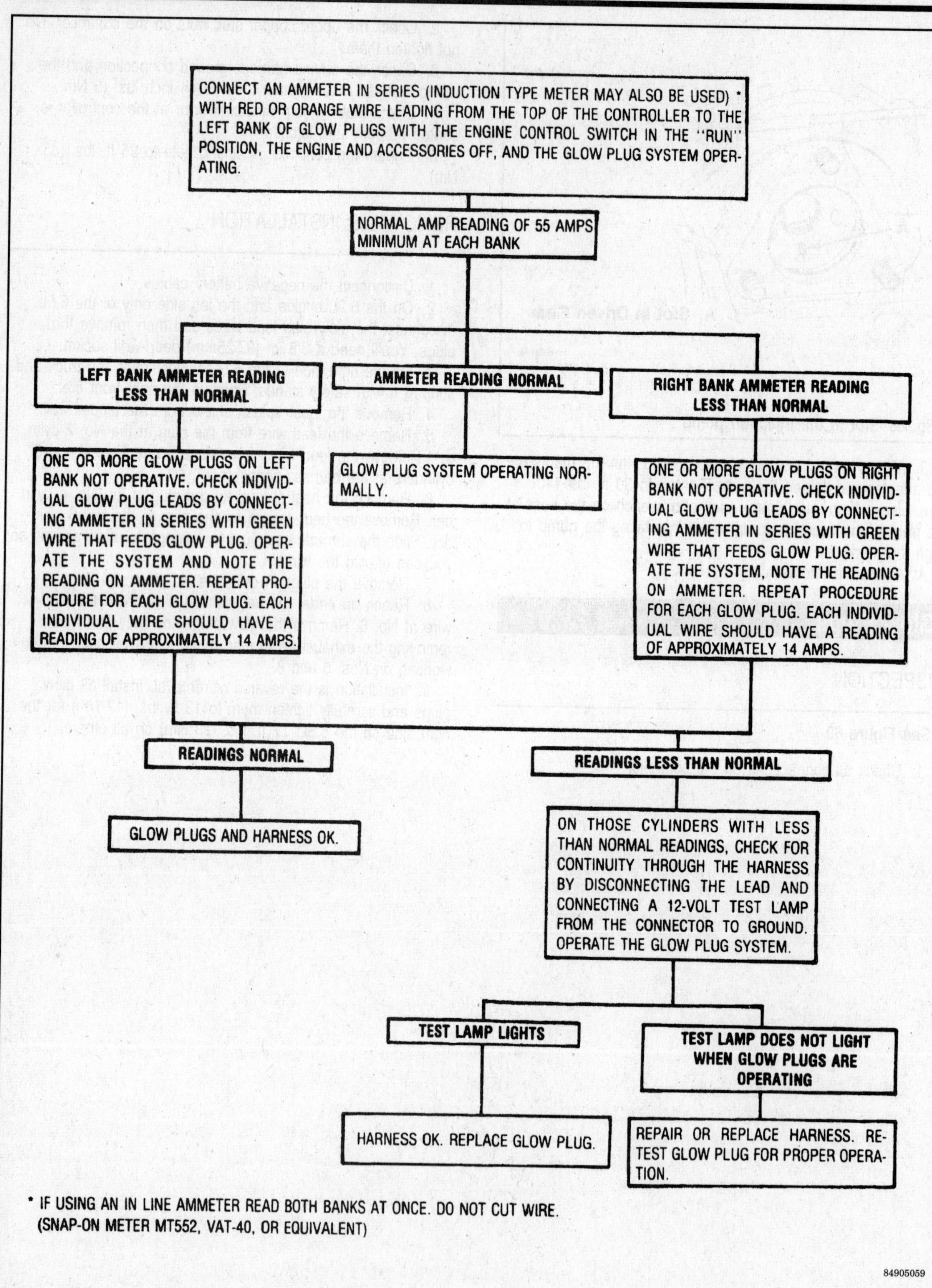

Fig. 69 Glow plug diagnosis with an ammeter

FUEL TANK

Tank Assembly

DRAINING

⁂CAUTION

Disconnect the battery before beginning the draining operation.

If the vehicle is not equipped with a drain plug, use the following procedure to remove the fuel.

1. Using a 10 ft. (305cm) piece of ³⁄₈ in. (9.5mm) hose, cut a flap slit 18 in. (45cm) from one end.
2. Install a pipe nipple, of slightly larger diameter than the hose, into the opposite end of the hose.
3. Install the nipple end of the hose into the fuel tank with the natural curve of the hose pointing downward. Keep feeding the hose in until the nipple hits the bottom of the tank.
4. Place the other end of the hose in a suitable container and insert a air hose pointing it in the downward direction of the slit and inject air into the line.

➡If the vehicle is to be stored, always drain the fuel from the complete fuel system including the carburetor or throttle body, fuel pump supply, fuel injection pump, fuel lines, and tank.

REMOVAL & INSTALLATION

1. Drain the tank.
2. Jack up your vehicle and support it with jackstands.
3. Remove the clamp on the filler neck and the vent tube hose.
4. Remove the gauge hose which is attached to the frame.
5. While supporting the tank securely, remove the support straps.
6. Lower the tank until the gauge wiring can be removed.
7. Remove the tank.

To install:

8. Install the unit and tighten the strap bolts to 115 inch lbs. (13 Nm). Make certain that the anti-squeak material is replaced during installation.
9. Lower the vehicle.

Fuel Tank Sending Unit

REMOVAL & INSTALLATION

➧ See Figure 70

1. With the engine turned **OFF**, relieve the fuel pressure.
2. Disconnect the negative battery cable.
3. Raise and support the rear of the vehicle on jackstands.
4. Drain the fuel tank, then remove it.
5. Using a hammer and a drift punch, drive the fuel lever sending device and pump assembly locking ring (located on top of the fuel tank) counterclockwise. Lift the assembly from the tank and remove the sending device.

To install:

6. Connect the fuel pump to the hose.

➡Be careful that you don't fold or twist the strainer when installing the sending unit, or you'll restrict fuel flow.

7. Install a new o-ring on the pump assembly. Install the sending unit and then position them into the fuel tank.
8. Turn the locking ring clockwise until it's tight.
9. Install the fuel tank and connect the battery cable.

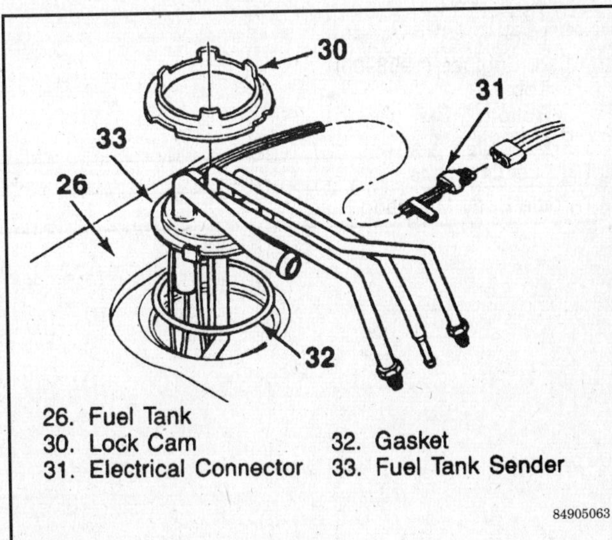

Fig. 70 Fuel tank sending unit

TORQUE SPECIFICATIONS

Component	U.S.	Metric
Carburetor Inlet Nut	18 ft. lbs.	24 Nm
Carburetor Mounting Bolts		
1 bbl		
1st	38 inch lbs.	4.1 Nm
2nd	16 ft. lbs.	22 Nm
4 bbl	12 ft. lbs.	16 Nm
Diesel Fuel Filter Mounting Bolts	30 ft. lbs.	40 Nm
Diesel Fuel Injector	50 ft. lbs.	70 Nm
Diesel Fuel Lines	9 inch lbs.	1 Nm
Diesel Injection Lines	20 ft. lbs.	25 Nm
Diesel Injection Pump-To-Drive Gear	20 ft. lbs.	25 Nm
Diesel Injection Pump Mounting Nuts	30 ft. lbs.	40 Nm
Float Bowl-To-Throttle Body Screws		
1 bbl	15 ft. lbs.	20 Nm
Fuel Meter Cover Mounting Screws	28 inch lbs.	3 Nm
Fuel Tank Strap Bolts	115 inch lbs.	13 Nm
Glow Plugs		
Right Side, 6.5L Engines	13 ft. lbs.	17 Nm
All Others	17 ft. lbs.	23 Nm
Glow Plug Controller Nuts	25 ft. lbs.	35 Nm
Glow Plug Harness Nuts	44 inch lbs.	5 Nm
Idle Air Control Valve		
Threaded	13 ft. lbs.	18 Nm
Flanged	28 inch lbs.	3 Nm
Mechanical Fuel Pump Mounting Bolts		
4.8L Engines	17 ft. lbs.	23 Nm
5.7L Engines		
Top	27 ft. lbs.	34 Nm
Bottom	3 ft. lbs.	4 Nm
6.2L Engines (1988–90)		
Top	24 ft. lbs.	33 Nm
Bottom	6 ft. lbs.	8 Nm
7.4L Engines	27 ft. lbs.	34 Nm
TBI Fuel Line Nuts	20 ft. lbs.	26 Nm
Throttle Body Mounting Nuts	12 ft. lbs.	16 Nm

84905066

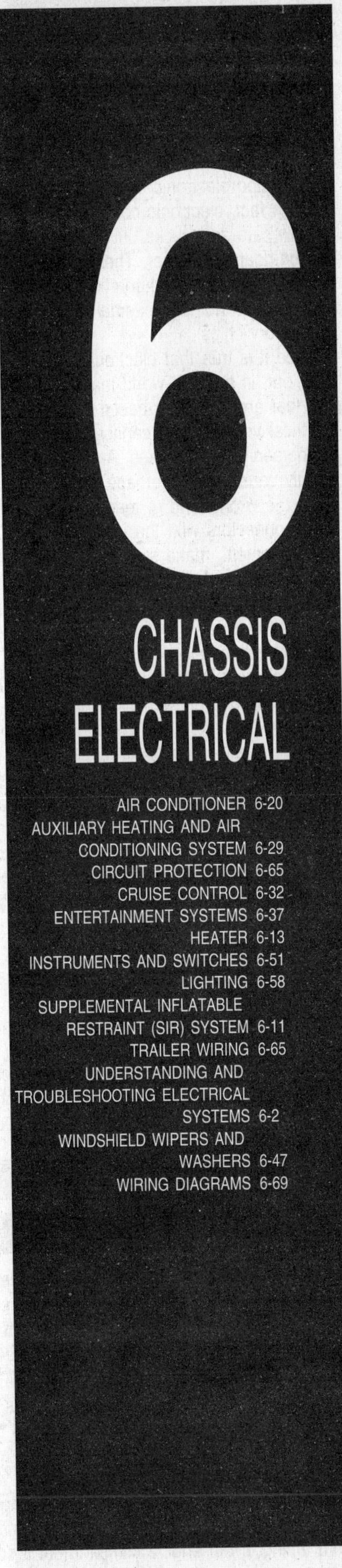

6 CHASSIS ELECTRICAL

UNDERSTANDING AND TROUBLESHOOTING ELECTRICAL SYSTEMS

Over the years import and domestic manufacturers have incorporated electronic control systems into their production lines. In fact, electronic control systems are so prevalent that all new cars and trucks built today are equipped with at least one on-board computer. These electronic components (with no moving parts) should theoretically last the life of the vehicle, provided that nothing external happens to damage the circuits or memory chips.

While it is true that electronic components should never wear out, in the real world malfunctions do occur. It is also true that any computer-based system is extremely sensitive to electrical voltages and cannot tolerate careless or haphazard testing/service procedures. An inexperienced individual can literally cause major damage looking for a minor problem by using the wrong kind of test equipment or connecting test leads/connectors with the ignition switch **ON**. When selecting test equipment, make sure the manufacturer's instructions state that the tester is compatible with whatever type of system is being serviced. Read all instructions carefully and double check all test points before installing probes or making any test connections.

The following section outlines basic diagnosis techniques for dealing with automotive electrical systems. Along with a general explanation of the various types of test equipment available to aid in servicing modern automotive systems, basic repair techniques for wiring harnesses and connectors are also given. Read the basic information before attempting any repairs or testing. This will provide the background of information necessary to avoid the most common and obvious mistakes that can cost both time and money. Although the replacement and testing procedures are simple in themselves, the systems are not, and unless one has a thorough understanding of all components and their function within a particular system, the logical test sequence these systems demand cannot be followed. Minor malfunctions can make a big difference, so it is important to know how each component affects the operation of the overall system in order to find the ultimate cause of a problem without replacing good components unnecessarily. It is not enough to use the correct test equipment; the test equipment must be used correctly.

Safety Precautions

****CAUTION**

Whenever working on or around any electrical or electronic systems, always observe these general precautions to prevent the possibility of personal injury or damage to electronic components.

- Never install or remove battery cables with the key **ON** or the engine running. Jumper cables should be connected with the key **OFF** to avoid power surges that can damage electronic control units. Engines equipped with computer controlled systems should avoid both giving and getting jump starts due to the possibility of serious damage to components from arcing in the engine compartment if connections are made with the ignition **ON**.
- Always remove the battery cables before charging the battery. Never use a high output charger on an installed battery or attempt to use any type of "hot shot" (24 volt) starting aid.
- Exercise care when inserting test probes into connectors to insure good contact without damaging the connector or spreading the pins. Always probe connectors from the rear (wire) side, NOT the pin side, to avoid accidental shorting of terminals during test procedures.
- Never remove or attach wiring harness connectors with the ignition switch **ON**, especially to an electronic control unit.
- Do not drop any components during service procedures and never apply 12 volts directly to any component (like a solenoid or relay) unless instructed specifically to do so. Some component electrical windings are designed to safely handle only 4 or 5 volts and can be destroyed in seconds if 12 volts are applied directly to the connector.
- Remove the electronic control unit if the vehicle is to be placed in an environment where temperatures exceed approximately 176°F (80°C), such as a paint spray booth or when arc/gas welding near the control unit location.

Understanding Basic Electricity

Understanding the basic theory of electricity makes electrical troubleshooting much easier. Several gauges are used in electrical troubleshooting to see inside the circuit being tested. Without a basic understanding, it will be difficult to understand testing procedures.

THE WATER ANALOGY

Electricity is the flow of electrons — hypothetical particles thought to constitute the basic stuff of electricity. Many people have been taught electrical theory using an analogy with water. In a comparison with water flowing in a pipe, the electrons would be the water. As the flow of water can be measured, the flow of electricity can be measured. The unit of measurement is amperes, frequently abbreviated amps. An ammeter will measure the actual amount of current flowing in the circuit.

Just as the water pressure is measured in units such as pounds per square inch, electrical pressure is measured in volts. When a voltmeter's two probes are placed on two live portions of an electrical circuit with different electrical pressures, current will flow through the voltmeter and produce a reading which indicates the difference in electrical pressure between the two parts of the circuit.

While increasing the voltage in a circuit will increase the flow of current, the actual flow depends not only on voltage, but on the resistance of the circuit. The standard unit for measuring circuit resistance is an ohm, measured by an ohmmeter. The ohmmeter is somewhat similar to an ammeter, but incorporates its own source of power so that a standard voltage is always present.

CIRCUITS

An actual electric circuit consists of four basic parts. These are: the power source, such as a generator or battery; a hot wire, which conducts the electricity under a relatively high voltage to the component supplied by the circuit; the load, such as a lamp, motor, resistor or relay coil; and the ground wire, which carries the current back to the source under very low voltage. In such a circuit the bulk of the resistance exists between the point where the hot wire is connected to the load, and the point where the load is grounded. In an automobile, the vehicle's frame or body, which is made of steel, is used as a part of the ground circuit for many of the electrical devices.

Remember that, in electrical testing, the voltmeter is connected in parallel with the circuit being tested (without disconnecting any wires) and measures the difference in voltage between the locations of the two probes; that the ammeter is connected in series with the load (the circuit is separated at one point and the ammeter inserted so it becomes a part of the circuit); and the ohmmeter is self-powered, so that all the power in the circuit should be off and the portion of the circuit to be measured contacted at either end by one of the probes of the meter.

For any electrical system to operate, it must make a complete circuit. This simply means that the power flow from the battery must make a complete circle. When an electrical component is operating, power flows from the battery to the component, passes through the component causing it to perform it to function (such as lighting a light bulb) and then returns to the battery through the ground of the circuit. This ground is usually (but not always) the metal part of the vehicle on which the electrical component is mounted.

Perhaps the easiest way to visualize this is to think of connecting a light bulb with two wires attached to it to your vehicle's battery. The battery in your vehicle has two posts (negative and positive). If one of the two wires attached to the light bulb was attached to the negative post of the battery and the other wire was attached to the positive post of the battery, you would have a complete circuit. Current from the battery would flow out one post, through the wire attached to it and then to the light bulb, where it would pass through causing it to light. It would then leave the light bulb, travel through the other wire, and return to the other post of the battery.

AUTOMOTIVE CIRCUITS

The normal automotive circuit differs from this simple example in two ways. First, instead of having a return wire from the bulb to the battery, the light bulb return the current to the battery through the chassis of the vehicle. Since the negative battery cable is attached to the chassis and the chassis is made of electrically conductive metal, the chassis of the vehicle can serve as a ground wire to complete the circuit. Secondly, most automotive circuits contain switches to turn components on and off.

Some electrical components which require a large amount of current to operate also have a relay in their circuit. Since these circuits carry a large amount of current, the thickness of the wire in the circuit (gauge size) is also greater. If this large wire were connected from the component to the control switch on the instrument panel, and then back to the component, a voltage drop would occur in the circuit. To prevent this potential drop in voltage, an electromagnetic switch (relay) is used. The large wires in the circuit are connected from the vehicle battery to one side of the relay, and from the opposite side of the relay to the component. The relay is normally open, preventing current from passing through the circuit. An additional, smaller wire is connected from the relay to the control switch for the circuit. When the control switch is turned on, it grounds the smaller wire from the relay and completes the circuit.

SHORT CIRCUITS

If you were to disconnect the light bulb (from the previous example of a light-bulb being connected to the battery by two wires) from the wires and touch the two wires together (please take our word for this; don't try it), the result will be a shower of sparks. A similar thing happens (on a smaller scale) when the power supply wire to a component or the electrical component itself becomes grounded before the normal ground connection for the circuit. To prevent damage to the system, the fuse for the circuit blows to interrupt the circuit — protecting the components from damage. Because grounding a wire from a power source makes a complete circuit — less the required component to use the power — the phenomenon is called a short circuit. The most common causes of short circuits are: the rubber insulation on a wire breaking or rubbing through to expose the current carrying core of the wire to a metal part of the car, or a shorted switch.

Some electrical systems on the vehicle are protected by a circuit breaker which is, basically, a self-repairing fuse. When either of the described events takes place in a system which is protected by a circuit breaker, the circuit breaker opens the circuit the same way a fuse does. However, when either the short is removed from the circuit or the surge subsides, the circuit breaker resets itself and does not have to be replaced as a fuse does.

Troubleshooting

When diagnosing a specific problem, organized troubleshooting is a must. The complexity of a modern automobile demands that you approach any problem in a logical, organized manner. There are certain troubleshooting techniques that are standard:

1. Establish when the problem occurs. Does the problem appear only under certain conditions? Were there any noises, odors, or other unusual symptoms?
2. Isolate the problem area. To do this, make some simple tests and observations; then eliminate the systems that are working properly. Check for obvious problems such as broken wires, dirty connections or split/disconnected vacuum hoses. Always check the obvious before assuming something complicated is the cause.
3. Test for problems systematically to determine the cause once the problem area is isolated. Are all the components functioning properly? Is there power going to electrical switches and motors? Is there vacuum at vacuum switches and/or actuators? Is there a mechanical problem such as bent linkage

or loose mounting screws? Performing careful, systematic checks will often turn up most causes on the first inspection without wasting time checking components that have little or no relationship to the problem.

4. Test all repairs after the work is done to make sure that the problem is fixed. Some causes can be traced to more than one component, so a careful verification of repair work is important in order to pick up additional malfunctions that may cause a problem to reappear or a different problem to arise. A blown fuse, for example, is a simple problem that may require more than another fuse to repair. If you don't look for a problem that caused a fuse to blow, a shorted wire (for example) may go undetected.

Experience has shown that most problems tend to be the result of a fairly simple and obvious cause, such as loose or corroded connectors or air leaks in the intake system. This makes careful inspection of components during testing essential to quick and accurate troubleshooting.

BASIC TROUBLESHOOTING THEORY

Electrical problems generally fall into one of three areas:

- The component that is not functioning is not receiving current.
- The component itself is not functioning.
- The component is not properly grounded.

Problems that fall into the first category are by far the most complicated. It is the current supply system to the component which contains all the switches, relay, fuses, etc.

The electrical system can be checked with a test light and a jumper wire. A test light is a device that looks like a pointed screwdriver with a wire attached to it. It has a light bulb in its handle. A jumper wire is a piece of insulated wire with an alligator clip attached to each end.

If a light bulb is not working, you must follow a systematic plan to determine which of the three causes is the villain.

1. Turn on the switch that controls the inoperable bulb.
2. Disconnect the power supply wire from the bulb.
3. Attach the ground wire to the test light to a good metal ground.
4. Touch the probe end of the test light to the end of the power supply wire that was disconnected from the bulb. If the bulb is receiving current, the test light will go on.

➡If the bulb is one which works only when the ignition key is turned on (turn signal), make sure the key is turned on.

If the test light does not go on, then the problem is in the circuit between the battery and the bulb. As mentioned before, this includes all the switches, fuses, and relays in the system. Turn to a wiring diagram and find the bulb on the diagram. Follow the wire that runs back to the battery. The problem is an open circuit between the battery and the bulb. If the fuse is blown and, when replaced, immediately blows again, there is a short circuit in the system which must be located and repaired. If there is a switch in the system, bypass it with a jumper wire. This is done by connecting one end of the jumper wire to the power supply wire into the switch and the other end of the jumper wire to the wire coming out of the switch. If the test light illuminates with the jumper wire installed, the switch or whatever was bypassed is defective.

➡Never substitute the jumper wire for the bulb, as the bulb is the component required to use the power from the power source.

5. If the bulb in the test light goes on, then the current is getting to the bulb that is not working in the car. This eliminates the first of the three possible causes. Connect the power supply wire and connect a jumper wire from the bulb to a good metal ground. Do this with the switch which controls the bulb works with jumper wire installed, then it has a bad ground. This is usually caused by the metal area on which the bulb mounts to the vehicle being coated with some type of foreign matter.

6. If neither test located the source of the trouble, then the light bulb itself is defective.

The above test procedure can be applied to any of the components of the chassis electrical system by substituting the component that is not working for the light bulb. Remember that for any electrical system to work, all connections must be clean and tight.

TEST EQUIPMENT

➡Pinpointing the exact cause of trouble in an electrical system can sometimes only be accomplished by the use of special test equipment. The following describes different types of commonly used test equipment and explains how to use them in diagnosis. In addition to the information covered below, the tool manufacturer's instructions booklet (provided with the tester) should be read and clearly understood before attempting any test procedures.

Jumper Wires

Jumper wires are simple, yet extremely valuable, pieces of test equipment. They are basically test wires which are used to bypass sections of a circuit. The simplest type of jumper wire is a length of multi-strand wire with an alligator clip at each end. Jumper wires are usually fabricated from lengths of standard automotive wire and whatever type of connector (alligator clip, spade connector or pin connector) that is required for the particular vehicle being tested. The well equipped tool box will have several different styles of jumper wires in several different lengths. Some jumper wires are made with three or more terminals coming from a common splice for special purpose testing. In cramped, hard-to-reach areas it is advisable to have insulated boots over the jumper wire terminals in order to prevent accidental grounding, sparks, and possible fire, especially when testing fuel system components.

Jumper wires are used primarily to locate open electrical circuits, on either the ground (-) side of the circuit or on the hot (+) side. If an electrical component fails to operate, connect the jumper wire between the component and a good ground. If the component operates only with the jumper installed, the ground circuit is open. If the ground circuit is good, but the component does not operate, the circuit between the power feed and component may be open. By moving the jumper wire successively back from the lamp toward the power source, you can isolate the area of the circuit where the open is located. When the component stops functioning, or the power is cut off, the open is in the segment of wire between the jumper and the point previously tested.

You can sometimes connect the jumper wire directly from the battery to the hot terminal of the component, but first make sure the component uses 12 volts in operation. Some electrical components, such as fuel injectors, are designed to operate on about 4 volts and running 12 volts directly to the injector terminals can cause damage.

By inserting an in-line fuse holder between a set of test leads, a fused jumper wire can be used for bypassing open circuits. Use a 5 amp fuse to provide protection against voltage spikes. When in doubt, use a voltmeter to check the voltage input to the component and measure how much voltage is normally being applied.

:*:*CAUTION

Never use jumpers made from wire that is of lighter gauge than that which is used in the circuit under test. If the jumper wire is of too small a gauge, it may overheat and possibly melt. Never use jumpers to bypass high resistance loads in a circuit. Bypassing resistances, in effect, creates a short circuit. This may, in turn, cause damage and fire. Jumper wires should only be used to bypass lengths of wire.

Unpowered Test Lights

The 12 volt test light is used to check circuits and components while electrical current is flowing through them. It is used for voltage and ground tests. Twelve volt test lights come in different styles but all have three main parts; a ground clip, a probe, and a light. The most commonly used 12 volt test lights have pick-type probes. To use a 12 volt test light, connect the ground clip to a good ground and probe wherever necessary with the pick. The pick should be sharp so that it can be probed into tight spaces.

:*:*CAUTION

Do not use a test light to probe electronic ignition spark plug or coil wires. Never use a pick-type test light to probe wiring on computer controlled systems unless specifically instructed to do so. Any wire insulation that is pierced by the test light probe should be taped and sealed with silicone after testing.

Like the jumper wire, the 12 volt test light is used to isolate opens in circuits. But, whereas the jumper wire is used to bypass the open to operate the load, the 12 volt test light is used to locate the presence of voltage in a circuit. If the test light glows, you know that there is power up to that point; if the 12 volt test light does not glow when its probe is inserted into the wire or connector, you know that there is an open circuit (no power). Move the test light in successive steps back toward the power source until the light in the handle does glow. When it glows, the open is between the probe and point which was probed previously.

➡The test light does not detect that 12 volts (or any particular amount of voltage) is present; it only detects that some voltage is present. It is advisable before using the test light to touch its terminals across the battery posts to make sure the light is operating properly.

Self-Powered Test Lights

The self-powered test light usually contains a 1.5 volt penlight battery. One type of self-powered test light is similar in design to the 12 volt unit. This type has both the battery and the light in the handle, along with a pick-type probe tip. The second type has the light toward the open tip, so that the light illuminates the contact point. The self-powered test light is a dual purpose piece of test equipment. It can be used to test for either open or short circuits when power is isolated from the circuit (continuity test). A powered test light should not be used on any computer controlled system or component unless specifically instructed to do so. Many engine sensors can be destroyed by even this small amount of voltage applied directly to the terminals.

Voltmeters

A voltmeter is used to measure voltage at any point in a circuit, or to measure the voltage drop across any part of a circuit. It can also be used to check continuity in a wire or circuit by indicating current flow from one end to the other. Analog voltmeters usually have various scales on the meter dial and a selector switch to allow the selection of different voltages. The voltmeter has a positive and a negative lead. To avoid damage to the meter, always connect the negative lead to the negative (-) side of the circuit (to ground or nearest the ground side of the circuit) and connect the positive lead to the positive (+) side of the circuit (to the power source or the nearest power source). Note that the negative voltmeter lead will always be black and that the positive voltmeter will always be some color other than black (usually red).

Depending on how the voltmeter is connected into the circuit, it has several uses. A voltmeter can be connected either in parallel or in series with a circuit and it has a very high resistance to current flow. When connected in parallel, only a small amount of current will flow through the voltmeter current path; the rest will flow through the normal circuit current path and the circuit will work normally. When the voltmeter is connected in series with a circuit, only a small amount of current can flow through the circuit. The circuit will not work properly, but the voltmeter reading will show if the circuit is complete or not.

Ohmmeters

The ohmmeter is designed to read resistance (which is measured in ohms or Ω) in a circuit or component. Although there are several different styles of ohmmeters, all analog meters will usually have a selector switch which permits the measurement of different ranges of resistance (usually the selector switch allows the multiplication of the meter reading by 10, 100, 1000, and 10,000). A calibration knob allows the meter to be set at zero for accurate measurement. Since all ohmmeters are powered by an internal battery, the ohmmeter can be used as a self-powered test light. When the ohmmeter is connected, current from the ohmmeter flows through the circuit or component being tested. Since the ohmmeter's internal resistance and voltage are known values, the amount of current flow through the meter depends on the resistance of the circuit or component being tested.

The ohmmeter can be used to perform a continuity test for opens or shorts (either by observation of the meter needle or as a self-powered test light), and to read actual resistance in a circuit. It should be noted that the ohmmeter is used to check the resistance of a component or wire while there is no voltage applied to the circuit. Current flow from an outside voltage source (such as the vehicle battery) can damage the ohmmeter, so the circuit or component should be isolated from the vehicle electrical system before any testing is done. Since the ohmmeter uses its own voltage source, either lead can be connected to any test point.

➡When checking diodes or other solid state components, the ohmmeter leads can only be connected one way in order to measure current flow in a single direction. Make sure the positive (+) and negative (-) terminal connections are as described in the test procedures to verify the one-way diode operation.

In using the meter for making continuity checks, do not be concerned with the actual resistance readings. Zero resistance, or any ohm reading, indicates continuity in the circuit. Infinite resistance indicates an open in the circuit. A high resistance reading where there should be none indicates a problem in the circuit. Checks for short circuits are made in the same manner as checks for open circuits except that the circuit must be isolated from both power and normal ground. Infinite resistance indicates no continuity to ground, while zero resistance indicates a dead short to ground.

Ammeters

An ammeter measures the amount of current flowing through a circuit in units called amperes or amps. Amperes are units of electron flow which indicate how fast the electrons are flowing through the circuit. Since Ohms Law dictates that current flow in a circuit is equal to the circuit voltage divided by the total circuit resistance, increasing voltage also increases the current level (amps). Likewise, any decrease in resistance will increase the amount of amps in a circuit. At normal operating voltage, most circuits have a characteristic amount of amperes, called "current draw" which can be measured using an ammeter. By referring to a specified current draw rating, measuring the amperes, and comparing the two values, one can determine what is happening within the circuit to aid in diagnosis. An open circuit, for example, will not allow any current to flow so the ammeter reading will be zero. More current flows through a heavily loaded circuit or when the charging system is operating.

An ammeter is always connected in series with the circuit being tested. All of the current that normally flows through the circuit must also flow through the ammeter; if there is any other path for the current to follow, the ammeter reading will not be accurate. The ammeter itself has very little resistance to current flow and therefore will not affect the circuit, but it will measure current draw only when the circuit is closed and electricity is flowing. Excessive current draw can blow fuses and drain the battery, while a reduced current draw can cause motors to run slowly, lights to dim and other components to not operate properly. The ammeter can help diagnose these conditions by locating the cause of the high or low reading.

Multimeters

Different combinations of test meters can be built into a single unit designed for specific tests. Some of the more common combination test devices are known as Volt/Amp testers, Tach/Dwell meters, or Digital Multimeters. The Volt/Amp tester is used for charging system, starting system or battery tests and consists of a voltmeter, an ammeter and a variable resistance carbon pile. The voltmeter will usually have at least two ranges for use with 6, 12 and/or 24 volt systems. The ammeter also has more than one range for testing various levels of battery loads and starter current draw. The carbon pile can be adjusted to offer different amounts of resistance. The Volt/Amp tester has heavy leads to carry large amounts of current and many later models have an inductive ammeter pickup that clamps around the wire to simplify test connections. On some models, the ammeter also has a zero-center scale to allow testing of charging and starting systems without switching leads or polarity. A digital multimeter is a voltmeter, ammeter and ohmmeter combined in an instrument which gives a digital readout. These are often used when testing solid state circuits because of their high input impedance (usually 10 megohms or more).

The tach/dwell meter that combines a tachometer and a dwell (cam angle) meter is a specialized kind of voltmeter. The tachometer scale is marked to show engine speed in rpm and the dwell scale is marked to show degrees of distributor shaft rotation. In most electronic ignition systems, dwell is determined by the control unit, but the dwell meter can also be used to check the duty cycle (operation) of some electronic engine control systems. Some tach/dwell meters are powered by an internal battery, while others take their power from the vehicle battery in use. The battery powered testers usually require calibration (much like an ohmmeter) before testing.

TESTING

Open Circuits

To use the self-powered test light or a multimeter to check for open circuits, first isolate the circuit from the vehicle's 12 volt power source by disconnecting the battery or wiring harness connector. Connect the test light or ohmmeter ground clip to a good ground and probe sections of the circuit sequentially with the test light. (start from either end of the circuit). If the light is out/or there is infinite resistance, the open is between the probe and the circuit ground. If the light is on/or the meter shows continuity, the open is between the probe and end of the circuit toward the power source.

Short Circuits

By isolating the circuit both from power and from ground, and using a self-powered test light or multimeter, you can check for shorts to ground in the circuit. Isolate the circuit from power and ground. Connect the test light or ohmmeter ground clip to a good ground and probe any easy-to-reach test point in the circuit. If the light comes on or there is continuity, there is a short somewhere in the circuit. To isolate the short, probe a test point at either end of the isolated circuit (the light should be on/there should be continuity). Leave the test light probe engaged and open connectors, switches, remove parts, etc., sequentially, until the light goes out/continuity is broken. When the light goes out, the short is between the last circuit component opened and the previous circuit opened.

➡The battery in the test light and does not provide much current. A weak battery may not provide enough power to illuminate the test light even when a complete circuit is made (especially if there are high resistances in the circuit). Always make sure that the test battery is strong. To check the battery, briefly touch the ground clip to the probe; if the light glows brightly the battery is strong enough for testing. Never use a self-powered test light to perform checks for opens or shorts when power is applied to the electrical system under test. The 12 volt vehicle power will quickly burn out the light bulb in the test light.

Available Voltage Measurement

Set the voltmeter selector switch to the 20V position and connect the meter negative lead to the negative post of the battery. Connect the positive meter lead to the positive post of the battery and turn the ignition switch **ON** to provide a load. Read the voltage on the meter or digital display. A well charged battery should register over 12 volts. If the meter reads below 11.5 volts, the battery power may be insufficient to operate the electrical system properly. This test determines voltage available from the battery and should be the first step in any electrical trouble diagnosis procedure. Many electrical problems, especially on computer controlled systems, can be caused by a low state of charge in the battery. Excessive corrosion at the battery cable terminals can cause a poor contact that will prevent proper charging and full battery current flow.

Normal battery voltage is 12 volts when fully charged. When the battery is supplying current to one or more circuits it is said to be "under load." When everything is off the electrical system is under a "no-load" condition. A fully charged battery may show about 12.5 volts at no load; will drop to 12 volts under medium load; and will drop even lower under heavy load. If the battery is partially discharged the voltage decrease under heavy load may be excessive, even though the battery shows 12 volts or more at no load. When allowed to discharge further, the battery's available voltage under load will decrease more severely. For this reason, it is important that the battery be fully charged during all testing procedures to avoid errors in diagnosis and incorrect test results.

Voltage Drop

When current flows through a resistance, the voltage beyond the resistance is reduced (the larger the current, the greater the reduction in voltage). When no current is flowing, there is no voltage drop because there is no current flow. All points in the circuit which are connected to the power source are at the same voltage as the power source. The total voltage drop always equals the total source voltage. In a long circuit with many connectors, a series of small, unwanted voltage drops due to corrosion at the connectors can add up to a total loss of voltage which impairs the operation of the normal loads in the circuit. The maximum allowable voltage drop under load is critical, especially if there is more than one high resistance problem in a circuit because all voltage drops are cumulative. A small drop is normal due to the resistance of the conductors.

INDIRECT COMPUTATION OF VOLTAGE DROPS

1. Set the voltmeter selector switch to the 20 volt position.
2. Connect the meter negative lead to a good ground.
3. While operating the circuit, probe all loads in the circuit with the positive meter lead and observe the voltage readings. A drop should be noticed after the first load. But, there should be little or no voltage drop before the first load.

DIRECT MEASUREMENT OF VOLTAGE DROPS

1. Set the voltmeter switch to the 20 volt position.
2. Connect the voltmeter negative lead to the ground side of the load to be measured.
3. Connect the positive lead to the positive side of the resistance or load to be measured.
4. Read the voltage drop directly on the 20 volt scale.

Too high a voltage indicates too high a resistance. If, for example, a blower motor runs too slowly, you can determine if perhaps there is too high a resistance in the resistor pack. By taking voltage drop readings in all parts of the circuit, you can isolate the problem. Too low a voltage drop indicates too low a resistance. Take the blower motor for example again. If a blower motor runs too fast in the MED and/or LOW position, the problem might be isolated in the resistor pack by taking voltage drop readings in all parts of the circuit to locate a possibly shorted resistor.

HIGH RESISTANCE TESTING

1. Set the voltmeter selector switch to the 4 volt position.
2. Connect the voltmeter positive lead to the positive post of the battery.
3. Turn on the headlights and heater blower to provide a load.
4. Probe various points in the circuit with the negative voltmeter lead.
5. Read the voltage drop on the 4 volt scale. Some average maximum allowable voltage drops are:
   - FUSE PANEL: 0.7 volts
   - IGNITION SWITCH: 0.5 volts
   - HEADLIGHT SWITCH: 0.7 volts
   - IGNITION COIL (+): 0.5 volts
   - ANY OTHER LOAD: 1.3 volts

➡Voltage drops are all measured while a load is operating; without current flow, there will be no voltage drop.

Resistance Measurement

The batteries in an ohmmeter will weaken with age and temperature, so the ohmmeter must be calibrated or "zeroed" before taking measurements. To zero the meter, place the selector switch in its lowest range and touch the two ohmmeter leads together. Turn the calibration knob until the meter needle is exactly on zero.

➡All analog (needle) type ohmmeters must be zeroed before use, but some digital ohmmeter models are automatically calibrated when the switch is turned on. Self-calibrating digital ohmmeters do not have an adjusting knob, but its a good idea to check for a zero readout before use by touching the leads together. All computer controlled systems require the use of a digital ohmmeter with at least 10 megohms impedance for testing. Before any test procedures are attempted, make sure the ohmmeter used is compatible with the electrical system or damage to the on-board computer could result.

To measure resistance, first isolate the circuit from the vehicle power source by disconnecting the battery cables or the harness connector. Make sure the key is **OFF** when disconnecting any components or the battery. Where necessary, also isolate at least one side of the circuit to be checked in order to avoid reading parallel resistances. Parallel circuit resistances will always give a lower reading than the actual resistance of either of the branches. When measuring the resistance of parallel circuits, the total resistance will always be lower than the smallest resistance in the circuit. Connect the meter leads to both sides of the circuit (wire or component) and read the actual measured ohms on the meter scale. Make sure the selector switch is set to the proper ohm scale for the circuit being tested to avoid misreading the ohmmeter test value.

⁂WARNING

Never use an ohmmeter with power applied to the circuit. Like the self-powered test light, the ohmmeter is designed to operate on its own power supply. The normal 12 volt automotive electrical system current could damage the meter!

Wiring Harnesses

The average automobile contains about ½ mile of wiring, with hundreds of individual connections. To protect the many wires from damage and to keep them from becoming a confusing tangle, they are organized into bundles, enclosed in plastic or taped together and called wiring harnesses. Different harnesses serve different parts of the vehicle. Individual wires are color coded to help trace them through a harness where sections are hidden from view.

Automotive wiring or circuit conductors can be in any one of three forms:

1. Single strand wire
2. Multi-strand wire
3. Printed circuitry

Single strand wire has a solid metal core and is usually used inside such components as alternators, motors, relays and other devices. Multi-strand wire has a core made of many small strands of wire twisted together into a single conductor. Most of the wiring in an automotive electrical system is made up of multi-strand wire, either as a single conductor or grouped together in a harness. All wiring is color coded on the insulator, either as a solid color or as a colored wire with an identification stripe. A printed circuit is a thin film of copper or other conductor that is printed on an insulator backing. Occasionally, a printed circuit is sandwiched between two sheets of plastic for more protection and flexibility. A complete printed circuit, consisting of conductors, insulating material and connectors for lamps or other components is called a printed circuit board. Printed circuitry is used in place of individual wires or harnesses in places where space is limited, such as behind instrument panels.

Since automotive electrical systems are very sensitive to changes in resistance, the selection of properly sized wires is critical when systems are repaired. A loose or corroded connection or a replacement wire that is too small for the circuit will add extra resistance and an additional voltage drop to the circuit. A ten percent voltage drop can result in slow or erratic motor operation, for example, even though the circuit is complete. The wire gauge number is an expression of the cross-section area of the conductor. The most common system for expressing wire size is the American Wire Gauge (AWG) system.

Gauge numbers are assigned to conductors of various cross-section areas. As gauge number increases, area decreases and the conductor becomes smaller. A 5 gauge conductor is smaller than a 1 gauge conductor and a 10 gauge is smaller than a 5 gauge. As the cross-section area of a conductor decreases, resistance increases and so does the gauge number. A conductor with a higher gauge number will carry less current than a conductor with a lower gauge number.

➡Gauge wire size refers to the size of the conductor, not the size of the complete wire. It is possible to have two wires of the same gauge with different diameters because one may have thicker insulation than the other.

12 volt automotive electrical systems generally use 10, 12, 14, 16 and 18 gauge wire. Main power distribution circuits and larger accessories usually use 10 and 12 gauge wire. Battery cables are usually 4 or 6 gauge, although 1 and 2 gauge wires are occasionally used. Wire length must also be considered when making repairs to a circuit. As conductor length increases, so does resistance. An 18 gauge wire, for example, can carry a 10 amp load for 10 feet without excessive voltage drop; however if a 15 foot wire is required for the same 10 amp load, it must be a 16 gauge wire.

An electrical schematic shows the electrical current paths when a circuit is operating properly. It is essential to understand how a circuit works before trying to figure out why it doesn't. Schematics break the entire electrical system down into individual circuits and show only one particular circuit. In a schematic, no attempt is made to represent wiring and components as they physically appear on the vehicle; switches and other components are shown as simply as possible. Face views of harness connectors show the cavity or terminal locations in all multi-pin connectors to help locate test points.

If you need to backprobe a connector while it is on the component, the order of the terminals must be mentally reversed. The wire color code can help in this situation, as well as a keyway, lock tab or other reference mark.

WIRING REPAIR

Soldering is a quick, efficient method of joining metals permanently. Everyone who has the occasion to make wiring repairs should know how to solder. Electrical connections that are soldered are far less likely to come apart and will conduct electricity much better than connections that are only "pig-tailed" together. The most popular (and preferred) method of soldering is with an electrical soldering gun. Soldering irons are available in many sizes and wattage ratings. Irons with higher wattage ratings deliver higher temperatures and recover lost heat faster. A small soldering iron rated for no more than 50 watts is recommended, especially on electrical systems where excess heat can damage the components being soldered.

There are three ingredients necessary for successful soldering; proper flux, good solder and sufficient heat. A soldering flux is necessary to clean the metal of tarnish, prepare it for soldering and to enable the solder to spread into tiny crevices. When soldering, always use a rosin core solder which is non-corrosive and will not attract moisture once the job is finished. Other types of flux (acid core) will leave a residue that will attract moisture and cause the wires to corrode. Tin is a unique metal with a low melting point. In a molten state, it dissolves and alloys easily with many metals. Solder is made by mixing tin with lead. The most common proportions are 40/60, 50/50 and 60/40, with the percentage of tin listed first. Low priced solders usually contain less tin, making them very difficult for a beginner to use because more heat is required to melt the solder. A common solder is 40/60 which is well suited for all-around general use, but 60/40 melts easier and is preferred for electrical work.

Soldering Techniques

Successful soldering requires that the metals to be joined be heated to a temperature that will melt the solder, usually 360-460°F (182-238°C). Contrary to popular belief, the purpose of the soldering iron is not to melt the solder itself, but to heat the parts being soldered to a temperature high enough to melt the solder when it is touched to the work. Melting flux-cored solder on the soldering iron will usually destroy the effectiveness of the flux.

➡Soldering tips are made of copper for good heat conductivity, but must be "tinned" regularly for quick transference of heat to the project and to prevent the solder from sticking to the iron. To "tin" the iron, simply heat it and touch the flux-cored solder to the tip; the solder will flow over the hot tip. Wipe the excess off with a clean rag, but be careful as the iron will be hot.

After some use, the tip may become pitted. If so, simply dress the tip smooth with a smooth file and "tin" the tip again. Flux-cored solder will remove oxides but rust, bits of insulation and oil or grease must be removed with a wire brush or emery cloth. For maximum strength in soldered parts, the joint must start off clean and tight. Weak joints will result in gaps too wide for the solder to bridge.

If a separate soldering flux is used, it should be brushed or swabbed on only those areas that are to be soldered. Most solders contain a core of flux and separate fluxing is unnecessary. Hold the work to be soldered firmly. It is best to solder on a wooden board, because a metal vise will only rob the piece to be soldered of heat and make it difficult to melt the solder. Hold the soldering tip with the broadest face against the work to be soldered. Apply solder under the tip close to the work, using enough solder to give a heavy film between the iron and the piece being soldered, while moving slowly and making sure the solder melts properly. Keep the work level or the solder will run to the lowest part and favor the thicker parts, because these require more heat to melt the solder. If the soldering tip overheats (the solder coating on the face of the tip burns up), it should be retinned. Once the soldering is completed, let the soldered joint stand until cool. Tape and seal all soldered wire splices after the repair has cooled.

Wire Harness Connectors

Most connectors in the engine compartment or that are otherwise exposed to the elements are protected against moisture and dirt which could create oxidation and deposits on the terminals.

These special connectors are weather-proof. All repairs require the use of a special terminal and the tool required to service it. This tool is used to remove the pin and sleeve terminals. If removal is attempted with an ordinary pick, there is a good chance that the terminal will be bent or deformed. Unlike standard blade type terminals, these weather-proof terminals cannot be straightened once they are bent. Make certain that the connectors are properly seated and all of the sealing rings are in place when connecting leads. On some models, a hinge-type flap provides a backup or secondary locking feature for the terminals. Most secondary locks are used to improve connector reliability by retaining the terminals if the small terminal lock tangs are not positioned properly.

Molded-on connectors require complete replacement of the connection. This means splicing a new connector assembly into the harness. All splices should be soldered to insure proper contact. Use care when probing the connections or replacing terminals in them as it is possible to short between opposite terminals. If this happens to the wrong terminal pair, it is possible to damage certain components. Always use jumper wires between connectors for circuit checking and never probe through weatherproof seals.

Open circuits are often difficult to locate by sight because corrosion or terminal misalignment are hidden by the connectors. Merely wiggling a connector on a sensor or in the wiring harness may correct the open circuit condition. This should always be considered when an open circuit or a failed sensor is indicated. Intermittent problems may also be caused by oxidized or loose connections. When using a circuit tester for diagnosis, always probe connections from the wire side. Be careful not to damage sealed connectors with test probes.

All wiring harnesses should be replaced with identical parts, using the same gauge wire and connectors. When signal wires are spliced into a harness, use wire with high temperature insulation only. It is seldom necessary to replace a complete harness. If replacement is necessary, pay close attention to insure proper harness routing. Secure the harness with suitable plastic wire clamps to prevent vibrations from causing the harness to wear in spots or contact any hot components.

➡Weatherproof connectors cannot be replaced with standard connectors. Instructions are provided with replacement connector and terminal packages. Some wire harnesses have mounting indicators (usually pieces of colored tape) to mark where the harness is to be secured.

In making wiring repairs, its important that you always replace damaged wires with wiring of the same gauge as the wire being replaced. The heavier the wire, the smaller the gauge number. Wires are color-coded to aid in identification and whenever possible the same color coded wire should be used for replacement. A wire stripping and crimping tool is necessary to install solderless terminal connectors. Test all crimps by pulling on the wires; it should not be possible to pull the wires out of a good crimp.

Wires which are open, exposed or otherwise damaged are repaired by simple splicing. Where possible, if the wiring harness is accessible and the damaged place in the wire can be located, it is best to open the harness and check for all possible damage. In an inaccessible harness, the wire must be bypassed with a new insert, usually taped to the outside of the old harness.

When replacing fusible links, be sure to use fusible link wire, NOT ordinary automotive wire. Make sure the fusible segment is of the same gauge and construction as the one being replaced and double the stripped end when crimping the terminal connector for a good contact. The melted (open) fusible link segment of the wiring harness should be cut off as close to the harness as possible, then a new segment spliced in as described. In the case of a damaged fusible link that feeds two harness wires, the harness connections should be replaced with two fusible link wires so that each circuit will have its own separate protection.

➡Most of the problems caused in the wiring harness are due to bad ground connections. Always check all vehicle ground connections for corrosion or looseness before performing any power feed checks to eliminate the chance of a bad ground affecting the circuit.

Hard-Shell Connectors

Unlike molded connectors, the terminal contacts in hard-shell connectors can be replaced. Weatherproof hard-shell connectors with the leads molded into the shell have non-replaceable terminal ends. Replacement usually involves the use of a special terminal removal tool that depresses the locking tangs (barbs) on the connector terminal and allows the connector to be removed from the rear of the shell. The connector shell should be replaced if it shows any evidence of burning, melting, cracks, or breaks. Replace individual terminals that are burnt, corroded, distorted or loose.

➡The insulation crimp must be tight to prevent the insulation from sliding back on the wire when the wire is pulled. The insulation must be visibly compressed under the crimp tabs, and the ends of the crimp should be turned in for a firm grip on the insulation.

The wire crimp must be made with all wire strands inside the crimp. The terminal must be fully compressed on the wire strands with the ends of the crimp tabs turned in to make a firm grip on the wire. Check all connections with an ohmmeter to insure a good contact. There should be no measurable resistance between the wire and the terminal when connected.

Fusible Links

The fuse link is a short length of special, Hypalon (high temperature) insulated wire, integral with the engine compartment wiring harness and should not be confused with standard wire. It is several wire gauges smaller than the circuit which it protects. Under no circumstances should a fuse link replacement repair be made using a length of standard wire cut from bulk stock or from another wiring harness.

To repair any blown fuse link use the following procedure:

1. Determine which circuit is damaged, its location and the cause of the open fuse link. If the damaged fuse link is one of three fed by a common No. 10 or 12 gauge feed wire, determine the specific affected circuit.
2. Disconnect the negative battery cable.
3. Cut the damaged fuse link from the wiring harness and discard it. If the fuse link is one of three circuits fed by a single feed wire, cut it out of the harness at each splice end and discard it.
4. Identify and procure the proper fuse link with butt connectors for attaching the fuse link to the harness.

➡Heat shrink tubing must be slipped over the wire before crimping and soldering the connection.

5. To repair any fuse link in a 3-link group with one feed:
   a. After cutting the open link out of the harness, cut each of the remaining undamaged fuse links close to the feed wire weld.
   b. Strip approximately ½ in. (13mm) of insulation from the detached ends of the two good fuse links. Insert two wire ends into one end of a butt connector, then carefully push one stripped end of the replacement fuse link into the same end of the butt connector and crimp all three firmly together.

➡Care must be taken when fitting the three fuse links into the butt connector as the internal diameter is a snug fit for three wires. Make sure to use a proper crimping tool. Pliers, side cutters, etc. will not apply the proper crimp to retain the wires and withstand a pull test.

   c. After crimping the butt connector to the three fuse links, cut the weld portion from the feed wire and strip approximately ½ in. (13mm) of insulation from the cut end. Insert the stripped end into the open end of the butt connector and crimp very firmly.
   d. To attach the remaining end of the replacement fuse link, strip approximately ½ in. (13mm) of insulation from the wire end of the circuit from which the blown fuse link was removed, and firmly crimp a butt connector or equivalent to the stripped wire. Then, insert the end of the replacement link into the other end of the butt connector and crimp firmly.
   e. Using rosin core solder with a consistency of 60 percent tin and 40 percent lead, solder the connectors and the wires at the repairs then insulate with electrical tape or heat shrink tubing.
6. To replace any fuse link on a single circuit in a harness, cut out the damaged portion, strip approximately ½ in. (13mm) of insulation from the two wire ends and attach the appropriate replacement fuse link to the stripped wire ends with two proper

size butt connectors. Solder the connectors and wires, then insulate.

7. To repair any fuse link which has an eyelet terminal on one end such as the charging circuit, cut off the open fuse link behind the weld, strip approximately ½ in. (13mm) of insulation from the cut end and attach the appropriate new eyelet fuse link to the cut stripped wire with an appropriate size butt connector. Solder the connectors and wires at the repair, then insulate.

8. Connect the negative battery cable to the battery and test the system for proper operation.

➡Do not mistake a resistor wire for a fuse link. The resistor wire is generally longer and has print stating, "Resistor-don't cut or splice."

When attaching a single No. 16, 17, 18 or 20 gauge fuse link to a heavy gauge wire, always double the stripped wire end of the fuse link before inserting and crimping it into the butt connector for positive wire retention.

Add-On Electrical Equipment

The electrical system in your vehicle is designed to perform under reasonable operating conditions without interference between components. Before any additional electrical equipment is installed, it is recommended that you consult your dealer or a reputable repair facility that is familiar with the vehicle and its systems.

If the vehicle is equipped with mobile radio equipment and/or mobile telephone, it may have an effect upon the operation of any on-board computer control modules. Radio Frequency Interference (RFI) from the communications system can be picked up by the vehicle's wiring harnesses and conducted into the control module, giving it the wrong messages at the wrong time. Although well shielded against RFI, the computer should be further protected by taking the following measures:

- Install the antenna as far as possible from the control module. For instance, if the module is located behind the center console area, then the antenna should be mounted at the rear of the vehicle.
- Keep the antenna wiring a minimum of eight inches away from any wiring running to control modules and from the module itself. NEVER wind the antenna wire around any other wiring.
- Mount the equipment as far from the control module as possible. Be very careful during installation not to drill through any wires or short a wire harness with a mounting screw.
- Insure that the electrical feed wire(s) to the equipment are properly and tightly connected. Loose connectors can cause interference.
- Make certain that the equipment is properly grounded to the vehicle. Poor grounding can damage expensive equipment.

SUPPLEMENTAL INFLATABLE RESTRAINT (SIR) SYSTEM

General Information

The Supplemental Inflatable Restraint (SIR) system offers protection in addition to that provided by the seat belt by deploying an air bag from the center of the steering wheel or dash panel. The air bag deploys when the vehicle is involved in a frontal crash of sufficient force up to 30° off the centerline of the vehicle. To further absorb the crash energy, there is also a knee bolster located beneath the instrument panel in the driver's area and the steering column is collapsible.

The system has an energy reserve, which can store a large enough electrical charge to deploy the air bag(s) for up to ten minutes after the battery has been disconnected or damaged. The system **MUST** be disabled before any service is performed on or around SIR components or SIR wiring.

SYSTEM OPERATION

The SIR system contains a deployment loop for each air bag and a Diagnostic Energy Reserve Module (DERM). The deployment loop supplies current through the inflator module which will cause air bag deployment in the event of a frontal collision of sufficient force. The DERM supplies the necessary power, even if the battery has been damaged.

The deployment loop is made up of the arming sensors, coil assembly, inflator module and the discriminating sensors. The inflator module is only supplied sufficient current when the arming sensor and at least one of the two discriminating sensors close simultaneously. The function of the DERM is to supply the deployment loop a 36 Volt Loop Reserve (36VLR) to assure sufficient voltage to deploy the air bag if ignition voltage is lost in a frontal crash.

The DERM, in conjunction with the sensor resistors, makes it possible to detect circuit and component malfunctions within the deployment loop. If the voltages monitored by the DERM fall outside expected limits, the DERM will indicate a malfunction by storing a diagnostic trouble code and illuminating the AIR BAG lamp.

SYSTEM COMPONENTS

Diagnostic Energy Reserve Module (DERM)

➧ See Figure 1

The DERM is designed to perform five main functions: energy reserve, malfunction detection, malfunction recording, driver notification and frontal crash recording.

The DERM maintains a reserve voltage supply to provide deployment energy for a few seconds when the vehicle voltage is low or lost in a frontal crash. The DERM performs diagnostic monitoring of the SIR system and records malfunctions in the form of diagnostic trouble codes, which can be obtained from a hand scan tool and/or on-board diagnostics. The DERM warns the driver of SIR system malfunctions by controlling the AIR BAG warning lamp and records SIR system status during a frontal crash.

Air Bag Warning Lamp

The AIR BAG warning/indicator lamp is used to verify lamp and DERM operation by flashing 7 times when the ignition is

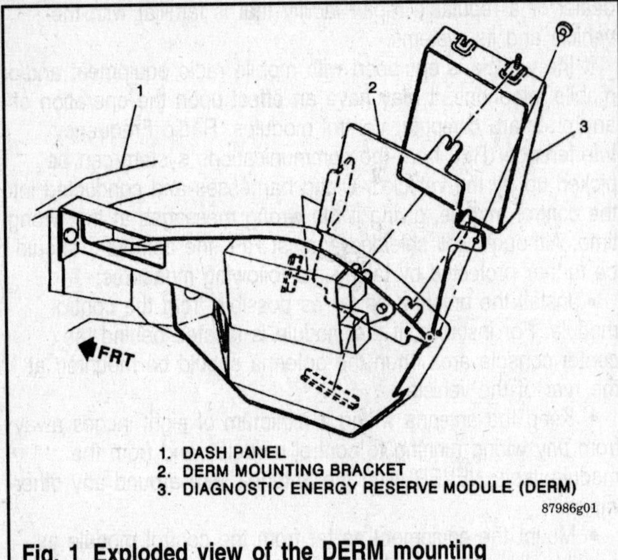

Fig. 1 Exploded view of the DERM mounting

first turned **ON**. It is also used to warn the driver of an SIR system malfunction.

Discriminating Sensors

➧ **See Figure 2**

There are two discriminating sensors in the SIR system, the LH forward and RH forward discriminating sensors. These sensors are located on the right frame rail for the RH sensor and the left front frame rail for the LH sensor.

The discriminating sensor consists of a sensing element, diagnostic resistor and normally open switch contacts. The sensing element closes the switch contact when vehicle velocity changes are severe enough to warrant air bag deployment.

Arming Sensor

➧ **See Figure 3**

The arming sensor is located on the left hand frame rail. The arming sensor is a switch located in the power side of the deployment loop. It is calibrated to close at low level velocity changes (lower than the discriminating sensors), assuring that the inflator module is connected directly to the 36VLR output of the DERM or Ignition 1 voltage when any discriminating sensor closes.

4WD SHOWN
2WD SIMILAR

1. RH FRAME RAIL
2. RH FORWARD DISCRIMINATING SENSOR
3. RH FORWARD DISCRIMINATING SENSOR HARNESS CONNECTOR

87986g02

Fig. 2 Exploded view of the RH forward discriminating sensor location

SIR Coil Assembly

The SIR coil assembly consists of two current carrying coils. They are attached to the steering column and allow rotation of the steering wheel while maintaining continuous deployment loop contact through the inflator module.

There is a shorting bar on the lower steering column connector that connects the SIR coil to the SIR wiring harness. The shorting bar shorts the circuit when the connector is disengaged. The circuit to the inflator module is shorted in this way to prevent unwanted air bag deployment when servicing the steering column or other SIR components.

Inflator Module

The inflator module is located on the steering wheel hub. The inflator module consists of an inflatable bag and an inflator (a canister of gas-generating material and an initiating device). When the vehicle is in a frontal crash of sufficient force to close the arming sensor and at least one discriminating sensor simultaneously, current flows through the deployment loop. Current passing through the initiator ignites the material in the inflator module, causing a reaction which produces a gas that rapidly inflates the air bag.

SERVICE PRECAUTIONS

- When performing service around the SIR system components or wiring, the SIR system **MUST** be disabled. Failure to do so could result in possible air bag deployment, personal injury or unneeded SIR system repairs.
- When carrying a live inflator module, make sure that the bag and trim cover are pointed away from you. Never carry the inflator module by the wires or connector on the underside

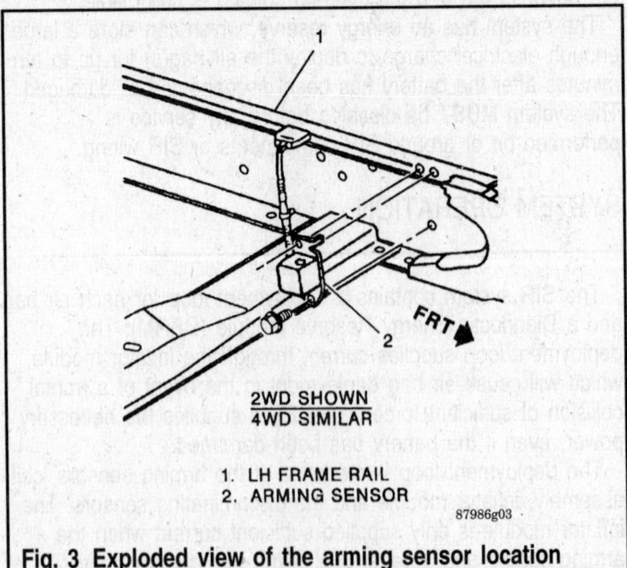

Fig. 3 Exploded view of the arming sensor location

of the module. In case of accidental deployment, the bag will then deploy with minimal chance of injury.

- When placing a live inflator module on a bench or other surface, always face the bag and trim cover up, away from the surface.

DISABLING THE SYSTEM

➡With the AIR BAG fuse removed and the ignition switch ON, the AIR BAG warning lamp will be on. This is normal and does not indicate any system malfunction.

1. Turn the steering wheel so that the vehicle's wheels are pointing straight ahead.
2. Turn the ignition switch to **LOCK**, remove the key, then disconnect the negative battery cable.
3. Remove the AIR BAG fuse from the fuse block.
4. Remove the steering column filler panel.
5. Disengage the Connector Position Assurance (CPA) and the yellow two way connector located at the base of the steering column.
6. Connect the negative battery cable.

ENABLING THE SYSTEM

1. Disconnect the negative battery cable.
2. Turn the ignition switch to **LOCK**, then remove the key.
3. Engage the yellow SIR connector and CPA located at the base of the steering column.
4. Install the steering column filler panel.
5. Install the AIR BAG fuse to the fuse block.
6. Connect the negative battery cable.
7. Turn the ignition switch to **RUN** and make sure that the AIR BAG warning lamp flashes seven times and then shuts off. If the warning lamp does not shut off, make sure that the wiring is properly connected. If the light remains on, take the vehicle to a reputable repair facility for service.

HEATER

Blower Motor

REMOVAL & INSTALLATION

Without Air Conditioning

➧ See Figure 4

1. Disconnect the negative battery terminal.
2. Mark the position of the blower motor in relation to its case.
3. Remove the electrical connection at the motor.
4. Remove the blower attaching screws and remove the assembly. Pry gently on the flange if the sealer sticks.
5. The blower wheel can be removed from the motor shaft by removing the nut at the center.

To install:

6. Install the blower wheel to the motor shaft and tighten the nut at the center.
7. Apply a bead of sealer to the blower mounting flange. Position the blower so that the marks are aligned and install the screws.
8. Engage the electrical connection at the motor.
9. Connect the negative battery terminal.

1988-91 R/V Series With Air Conditioning

➧ See Figures 5 and 6

GASOLINE ENGINES

1. Disconnect the negative battery terminal.
2. Mark the position of the blower motor in relation to its case.
3. Remove the electrical connection at the motor.
4. Disconnect the blower motor cooling tube.
5. Remove the blower attaching screws and remove the assembly. Pry gently on the flange if the sealer sticks.
6. The blower wheel can be removed from the motor shaft by removing the nut at the center.

To install:

7. Install the blower wheel to the motor shaft and tighten the nut at the center.
8. Apply a bead of sealer to the blower mounting flange. Position the blower so that the marks are aligned and install the screws.
9. Connect the motor cooling tube.
10. Engage the electrical connection at the motor.
11. Connect the negative battery terminal.

DIESEL ENGINES

1. Disconnect the negative battery terminal. Open the hood.
2. Remove the attaching bolts and nuts and remove the insulating shield from the case.
3. Mark the position of the blower motor in relation to its case.
4. Remove the electrical connection at the motor.
5. Disconnect the blower motor cooling tube.
6. Remove the blower attaching screws and remove the assembly. Pry gently on the flange if the sealer sticks.
7. The blower wheel can be removed from the motor shaft by removing the nut at the center.

To install:

8. Install the blower wheel to the motor shaft and tighten the nut at the center.
9. Apply a bead of sealer to the blower mounting flange. Position the blower so that the marks are aligned and install the screws.
10. Connect the motor cooling tube.
11. Engage the electrical connection at the motor.
12. Install the insulating shield.
13. Connect the negative battery terminal.

1988-90 C/K Series With Air Conditioning

1. Disconnect the negative battery terminal.
2. Remove the electrical connection at the motor.

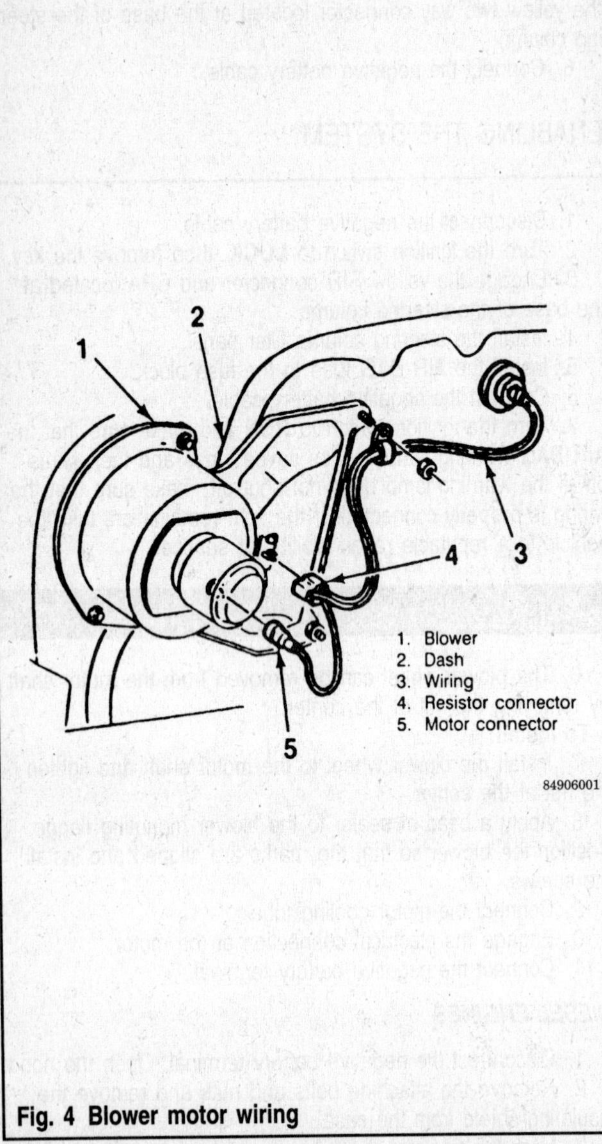

Fig. 4 Blower motor wiring

3. Remove the blower attaching screws and remove the assembly. Pry gently on the flange if the sealer sticks.
4. The blower wheel can be removed from the motor shaft by removing the nut at the center.

To install:

5. Install the blower wheel to the motor shaft and tighten the nut at the center.
6. Apply a bead of sealer to the blower mounting flange. Position the blower so that the marks are aligned and install the screws.
7. Connect the electrical connection at the motor.
8. Connect the negative battery terminal.

1991-96 C/K and 1992-96 R/V Series With Air Conditioning

1. Disconnect the negative battery cable.
2. Remove the instrument panel compartment.
3. Remove the forward-most screw in the right side door sill plate. Remove the trim panel from the right hinge pillar.
4. Disconnect the ECM wiring and remove the ECM.
5. Disconnect the electrical lead at the blower motor and remove the underdash courtesy lamp.
6. Remove the bolt from the right side lower dash support. Remove the blower cover and the cooling tube.
7. Remove the flange screws and pull out the blower — you may have to pry back the right side of the instrument panel slightly. Be careful!

To install:

8. Position the blower motor and install the mounting screws. Be careful not to catch the blower on anything when sliding it in.
9. Install the cooling tube and the blower shield. Install the bolt into the dash support.
10. Reconnect the courtesy lamp and the blower electrical lead.
11. Install the ECM and reconnect the wiring harness.
12. Install the trim panel on the pillar. Don't forget the screw in the sill plate!
13. Install the instrument panel compartment and connect the battery cable.

Heater Core

REMOVAL & INSTALLATION

CAUTION

When draining the coolant, keep in mind that cats and dogs are attracted by ethylene glycol antifreeze, and are quite likely to drink any that is left in an uncovered container or in puddles on the ground. This will prove fatal in sufficient quantity. Always drain the coolant into a sealable container. Coolant should be reused unless it is contaminated or several years old.

1988-91 R/V Series

WITHOUT AIR CONDITIONING

1. Disconnect the negative battery cable.
2. Disconnect the heater hoses at the core tubes and drain the engine coolant. Plug the core tubes to prevent spillage.
3. Remove the nuts from the distributor air ducts in the engine compartment.
4. Remove the glove compartment and door.
5. Disconnect the air-defrost and temperature door cables.
6. Remove the floor outlet and remove the defroster duct-to-heater distributor screw.
7. Remove the heater distributor-to-instrument panel screws. Pull the assembly rearward to gain access to the wiring harness and disconnect the wires attached to the unit.
8. Remove the heater distributor from the truck.
9. Remove the heater core retaining straps and remove the core from the truck.

To install:

10. Install the heater core. Be sure that the case-to-core and case-to-dash panel sealer is intact.
11. Position the heater distributor. Connect the wires attached to it and then install the heater distributor-to-instrument panel screws.

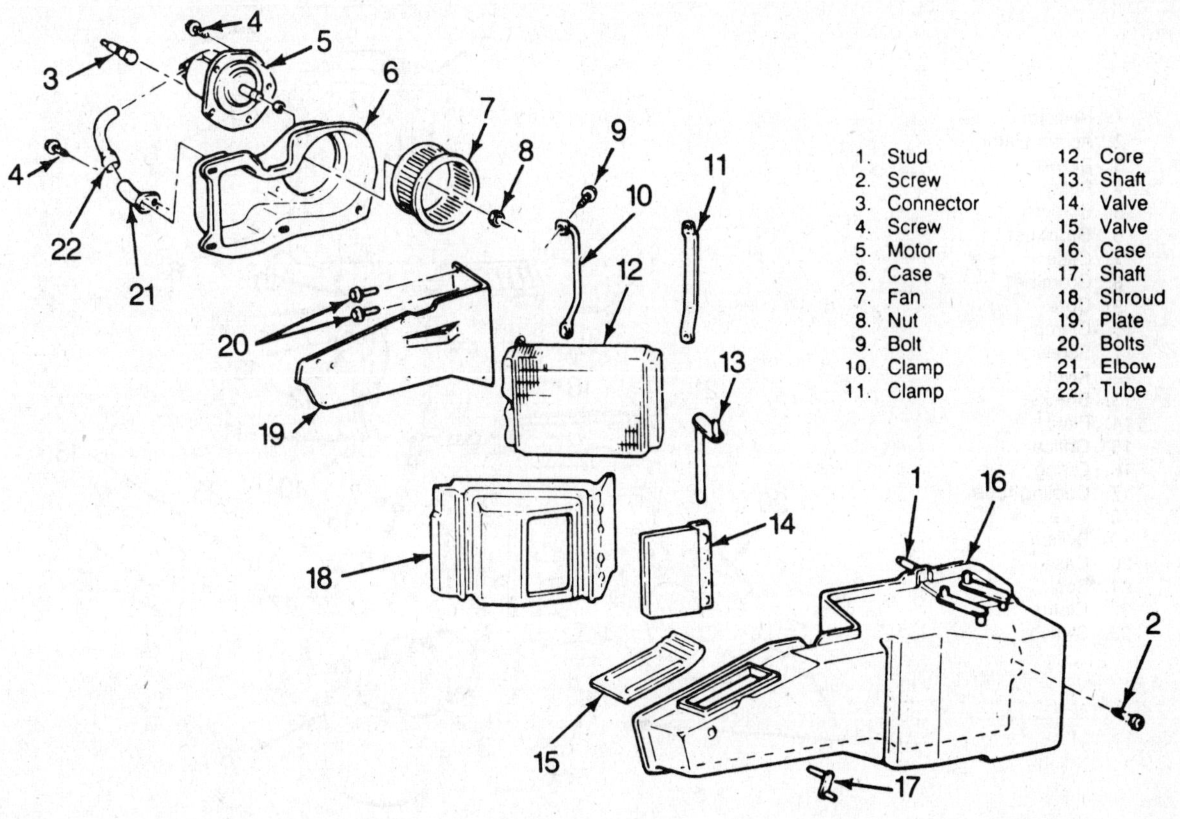

Fig. 5 Heater case and related parts

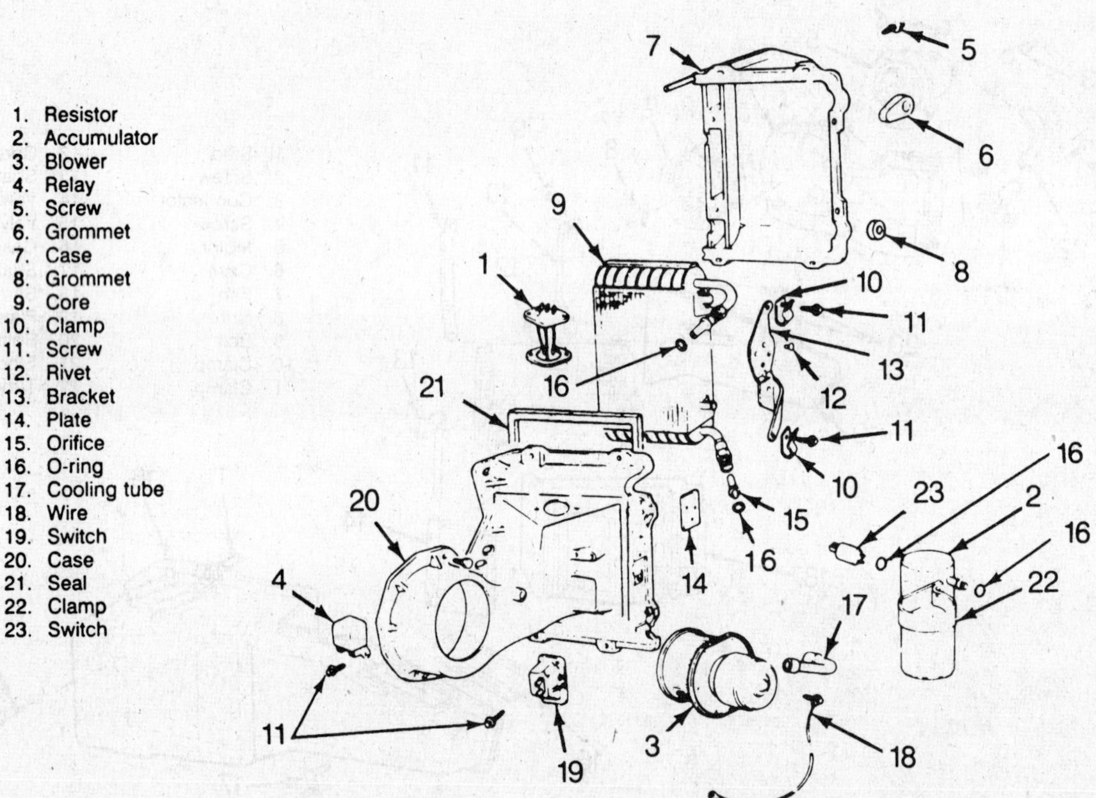

Fig. 6 Evaporator and blower motor

12. Install the floor outlet and tighten the defroster duct-to-heater distributor screw.
13. Connect the air-defrost and temperature door cables.
14. Install the glove compartment and door.
15. Install the nuts into the distributor air ducts (in the engine compartment).
16. Connect the heater hoses at the core tubes.
17. Connect the negative battery cable. Fill the cooling system and check for leaks.

WITH AIR CONDITIONING

1. Disconnect the negative battery cable.
2. Disconnect the heater hoses at the core tubes and drain the engine coolant. Plug the core tubes to prevent spillage.
3. Remove the glove compartment and door.
4. Disconnect the center duct from the defroster outlet duct.
5. Disconnect the center, lower air distributor and the center air outlet ducts.
6. Disconnect the temperature door cable.
7. Remove the nuts from the 3 selector duct studs that project into the engine compartment.
8. Remove the outlet duct-to-instrument panel screws. Pull the assembly rearward to gain access to the wiring harness and disconnect the wires and vacuum tubes attached to the unit.
9. Remove the heater distributor from the truck.
10. Remove the heater core retaining straps and remove the core from the case.

To install:

11. Install the heater core. Be sure that the core-to-core and case-to-dash panel sealer is intact.
12. Position the heater distributor. Connect the wires attached to it and then install the heater distributor-to-instrument panel screws.
13. Install the floor outlet and tighten the defroster duct-to-heater distributor screw.
14. Connect the temperature door cable.
15. Connect the center and lower air distributors and the center air outlet ducts.
16. Connect the center duct to the defroster outlet duct.
17. Install the glove compartment and door.
18. Connect the heater hoses at the core tubes.
19. Connect the negative battery cable. Fill the cooling system and check for leaks.

1988-90 C/K Series

1. Disconnect the negative battery cable.
2. Remove the coolant overflow bottle.
3. Drain the cooling system.
4. Disconnect the heater hoses at the core tubes.
5. In the engine compartment, remove the heater case-to-firewall screws.
6. Disconnect the antenna cable at the mast.
7. Remove the glove box.
8. Disconnect the wiring harness at the engine's Electronic Control Module (ECM).
9. Remove the ECM and bracket.
10. Remove the right side kick panel.
11. Remove the right side lower dash panel bolt and nut.
12. Remove the heater case mounting bolts.
13. While lifting the instrument panel slightly, remove the case assembly.
14. Lift the core from the case.

To install:

15. Lower the core into the case.
16. Position the case assembly against the firewall.
17. Install the heater case mounting bolts.
18. Install the right side lower dash panel bolt and nut.
19. Install the right side kick panel.
20. Install the ECM and bracket.
21. Connect the ECM wiring harness.
22. Install the glove box.
23. Connect the antenna cable at the mast.
24. Install the heater case-to-firewall screws.
25. Connect the heater hoses at the core tubes.
26. Fill the cooling system.
27. Install the coolant overflow bottle.
28. Connect the battery cable.

1991-92 R/V and 1991-96 C/K Series

1. Disconnect the negative battery cable.
2. Drain the cooling system.
3. Remove the instrument panel compartment.
4. Tag and disconnect all electrical leads as necessary.
5. Remove the center air distribution duct from the floor.
6. Remove the ECM and mounting tray. Remove the hinge pillar trim panels.
7. Remove the blower motor cover and then remove the motor.
8. Remove the steering wheel and tilt back the instrument panel slightly.
9. Remove the coolant overflow tank. Disconnect the heater hoses at the core connections.
10. Remove the attaching screws and nut and then remove the heater case.
11. Remove the 7 screws and lift off the heater case cover.
12. Remove the fasteners and brackets that hold the heater core to the case and lift the core from the case.

To install:

13. Install the heater core in the case.
14. Install the heater case bottom plate. Make sure there is a good seal.
15. Install the heater case into the truck. Tighten the 4 lower screws to 17 inch lbs. (2 Nm); the upper screw to 97 inch lbs. (11 Nm); and the nuts to 25 inch lbs. (2.8 Nm).
16. Connect the heater hoses at the core tubes.
17. Install the coolant overflow tank.
18. Install the instrument panel and the steering wheel.
19. Install the blower motor and cover.
20. Install the trim panels and the ECM. Install the air distribution duct and reconnect all electrical leads.
21. Install the instrument panel compartment. Fill the cooling system and connect the battery cable.

Control Cables

REMOVAL & INSTALLATION

Temperature Defrost/Mode Cable

➧ See Figures 7 and 8

1. Disconnect the negative battery cable.
2. Remove the instrument panel trim plate and then remove the control assembly.
3. Disconnect the cables at the control head. Remove the instrument panel compartment. Disconnect them at the heater case. Be sure to take note of their routing.
4. Connect the cables to the head and the heater case.
5. Install the control head and trim plate. Connect the battery cable.

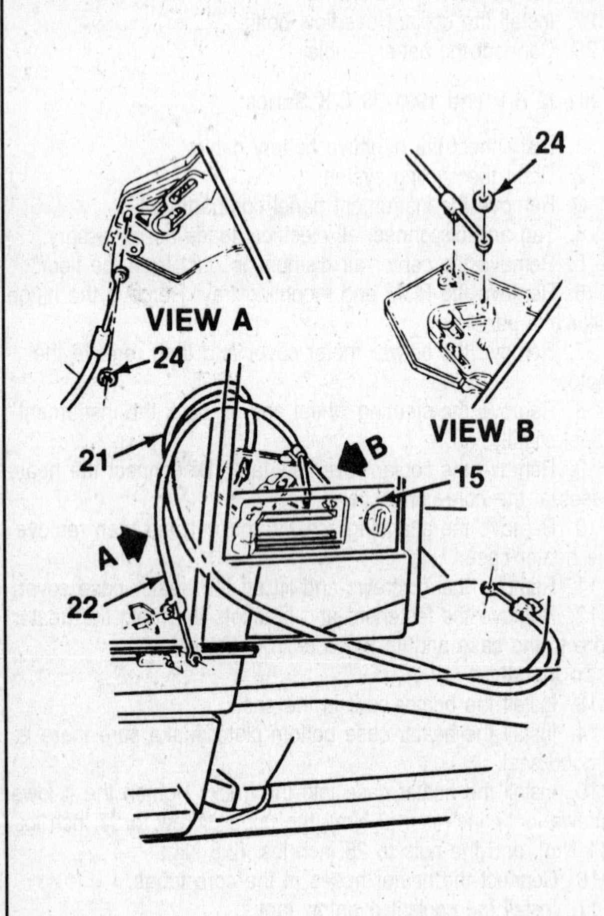

Fig. 7 Temperature and defroster control cables

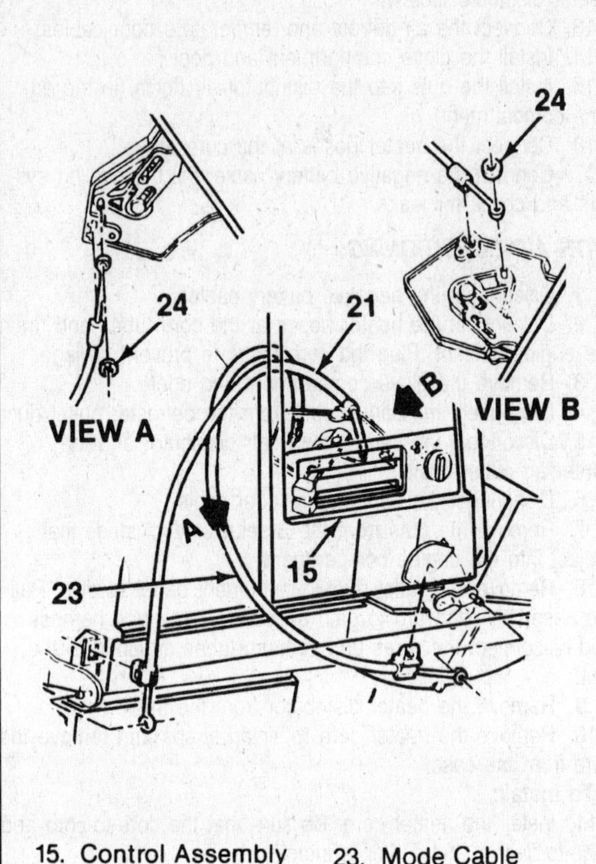

Fig. 8 Temperature and mode control cables

Vent Cable

➧ See Figure 9

1. Disconnect the negative battery cable.
2. Remove the instrument panel trim plate and then remove the control assembly.
3. Disconnect the cable at the control head, remove the instrument panel compartment and disconnect it at the vent door. Be sure to take note of the routing.

To install:

4. Connect the cable to the head and the door.
5. Install the control head and trim plate. Connect the battery cable.

ADJUSTMENT

1. Remove the instrument panel compartment and door.

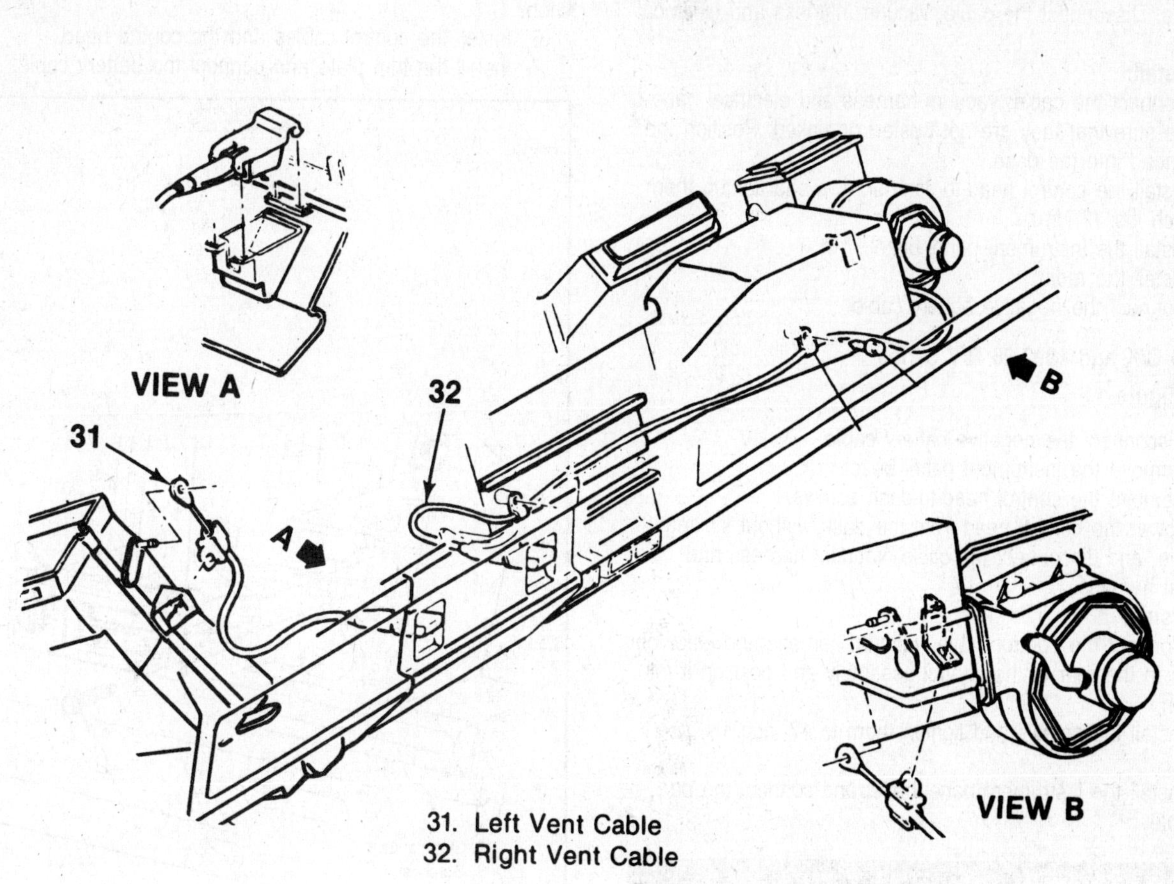

Fig. 9 Vent control cable

2. Loosen the cable attaching bolt at the heater case assembly.

➡**Ensure that the cable is installed in the bracket on the defroster duct assembly**

3. Place the temperature lever in the full **COLD** position and hold while tightening the cable attaching screw.
4. Install the instrument panel compartment and door.

Control Panel

REMOVAL & INSTALLATION

1988-91 R/V Series

➧ **See Figure 10**

1. Disconnect the negative battery cable.
2. Remove the radio.
3. Remove the instrument panel bezel.

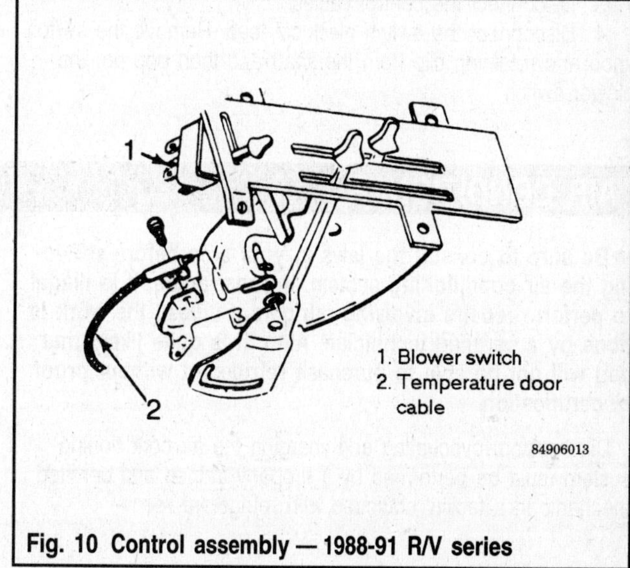

Fig. 10 Control assembly — 1988-91 R/V series

4. Remove the control head-to-dash screws.
5. Lower the control head from the dash, without kinking the cable. Disconnect the cable, vacuum harness and electrical harness.

To install:

6. Connect the cable, vacuum harness and electrical harness. Be sure that they are not twisted or kinked. Position the control head into the dash.
7. Install the control head-to-dash screws and tighten them to 17 inch lbs. (2 Nm).
8. Install the instrument panel bezel.
9. Install the radio.
10. Connect the negative battery cable.

1988-96 C/K and 1992-96 R/V Series

➧ See Figure 11

1. Disconnect the negative battery cable.
2. Remove the instrument panel bezel.
3. Remove the control head-to-dash screws.
4. Lower the control head from the dash, without kinking the cable, and disconnect the cable, vacuum harness and electrical harness.

To install:

5. Connect the control cable, vacuum harness and electrical harness to the rear of the control assembly and position it into the dash.
6. Install the screws and tighten them to 17 inch lbs. (2 Nm).
7. Install the instrument panel bezel and connect the battery cable.

Blower Switch

REMOVAL & INSTALLATION

1. Disconnect the negative battery cable.
2. Remove the instrument panel trim plate and remove the control head.
3. Disconnect the control cables.
4. Disconnect the switch electrical lead. Remove the switch knob and retaining clip from the shaft and then pop out the blower switch.

To install:

5. Position the switch and install the retaining clip and knob.
6. Install the control cables and the control head.
7. Install the trim plate and connect the battery cable.

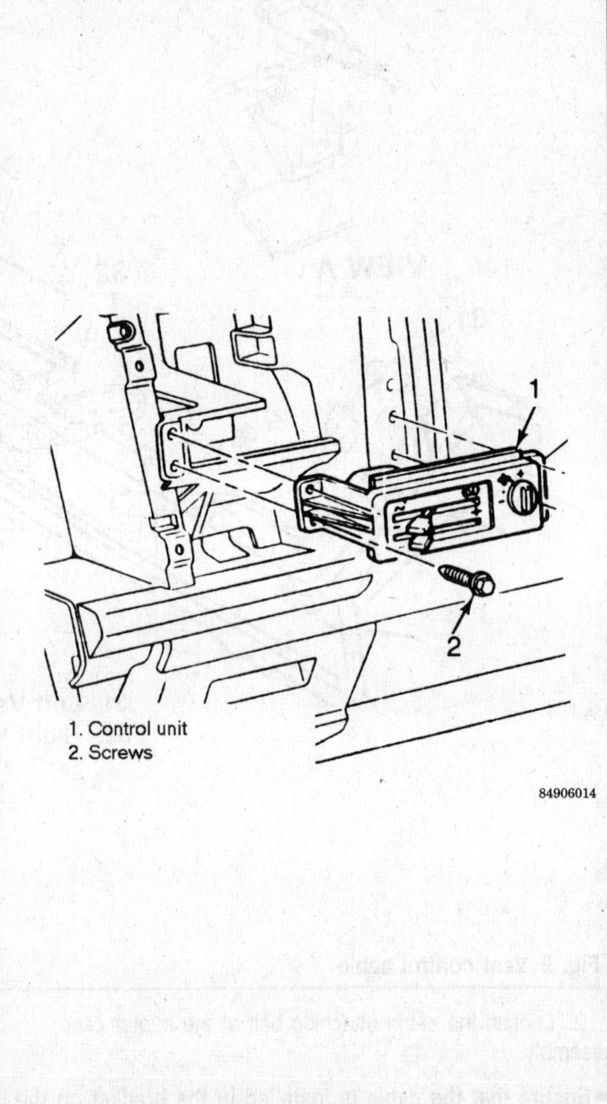

Fig. 11 Control assembly mounting

AIR CONDITIONER

➡Be sure to consult the laws in your area before servicing the air conditioning system. In most areas, it is illegal to perform repairs involving refrigerant unless the work is done by a certified technician. Also, it is quite likely that you will not be able to purchase refrigerant without proof of certification.

Discharging, evacuating and charging the air conditioning system must be performed by a properly trained and certified mechanic in a facility equipped with refrigerant recovery/recycling equipment that meets SAE standards for the type of system to be serviced.

If you don't have access to the necessary equipment, we recommend that you take your vehicle to a reputable service station to have the work done. If you still wish to perform repairs on the vehicle, have them discharge the system, then take your vehicle home and perform the necessary work. When you are finished, return the vehicle to the station for evacuation and charging. Just be sure to cap ALL A/C system fittings immediately after opening them and keep them protected until the system is recharged.

Compressor

REMOVAL & INSTALLATION

4.3L, 5.0L and 5.7L Engines

See Figure 12

1. Disconnect the negative battery cable. Discharge and recover the refrigerant from the air conditioning system.
2. Remove the drive belt.
3. Disconnect the refrigerant lines at the compressor. Cap all openings!
4. Disengage the electrical connections.
5. Remove the mounting bolts and nuts and lift the compressor from the bracket.
6. Drain and measure the compressor oil.

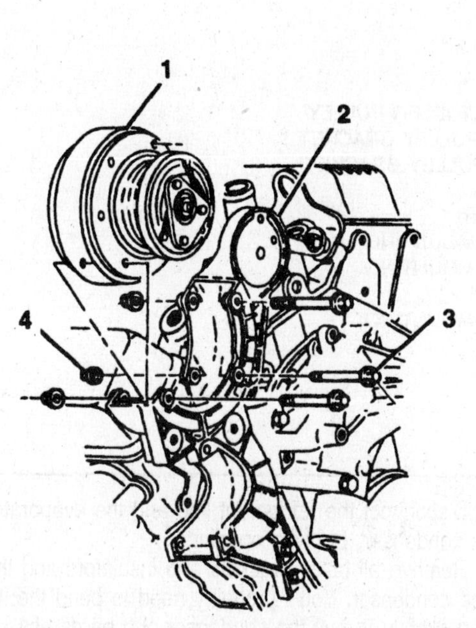

Fig. 12 Compressor installation — 4.3L, 5.0L and 5.7L engines

To install:

7. Replace the compressor oil as detailed later and position the compressor on the bracket. Tighten the bolts to 24 ft. lbs. (33 Nm).
8. Connect the electrical leads and the refrigerant lines.
9. Install and adjust the belt.
10. Connect the battery cable. Evacuate and charge the air conditioning system.

7.4L Engines

See Figure 13

1. Disconnect the negative battery cable. Discharge and recover the refrigerant from the air conditioning system.
2. Remove the drive belt.
3. Disconnect the refrigerant lines at the compressor. Cap all openings!
4. Disengage the electrical connections.
5. Remove the mounting bolts and nuts. Remove the compressor braces and then lift the compressor from the bracket.
6. Drain and measure the compressor oil.

To install:

7. Replace the compressor oil as detailed later and position the compressor on the bracket. Tighten the bolts to 37 ft. lbs. (50 Nm). Position the braces and tighten the compressor-to-brace bolts to 62 ft. lbs. (84 Nm) and the brace mounting bolt to 48 ft. lbs. (65 Nm).
8. Connect the electrical leads and the refrigerant lines.
9. Install and adjust the belt.
10. Connect the battery cable. Evacuate and charge the air conditioning system.

6.2L and 6.5L Engines

See Figure 14

1. Disconnect the negative battery cable. Discharge and recover the refrigerant from the air conditioning system.
2. Remove the fan belt.
3. Disconnect the refrigerant lines at the compressor. Cap all openings!
4. Disconnect any electrical leads.
5. Remove the mounting bolts and nuts and lift the compressor from the bracket.
6. Drain and measure the compressor oil.

To install:

7. Replace the compressor oil as detailed later and position the compressor on the bracket. Tighten the bolts to 30 ft. lbs. (40 Nm); tighten the nuts to 17 ft. lbs. (23 Nm).
8. Connect the electrical leads and the refrigerant lines.
9. Install and adjust the fan belt.
10. Connect the battery cable. Evacuate and charge the air conditioning system.

COMPRESSOR OIL REPLACEMENT

Drain and measure the oil when removing the old compressor. On R/V series trucks and 1988-90 C/K series, add 1 oz. (30 ml) to the quantity measured during draining; this is the amount to add to the compressor (old or new) when you install it.

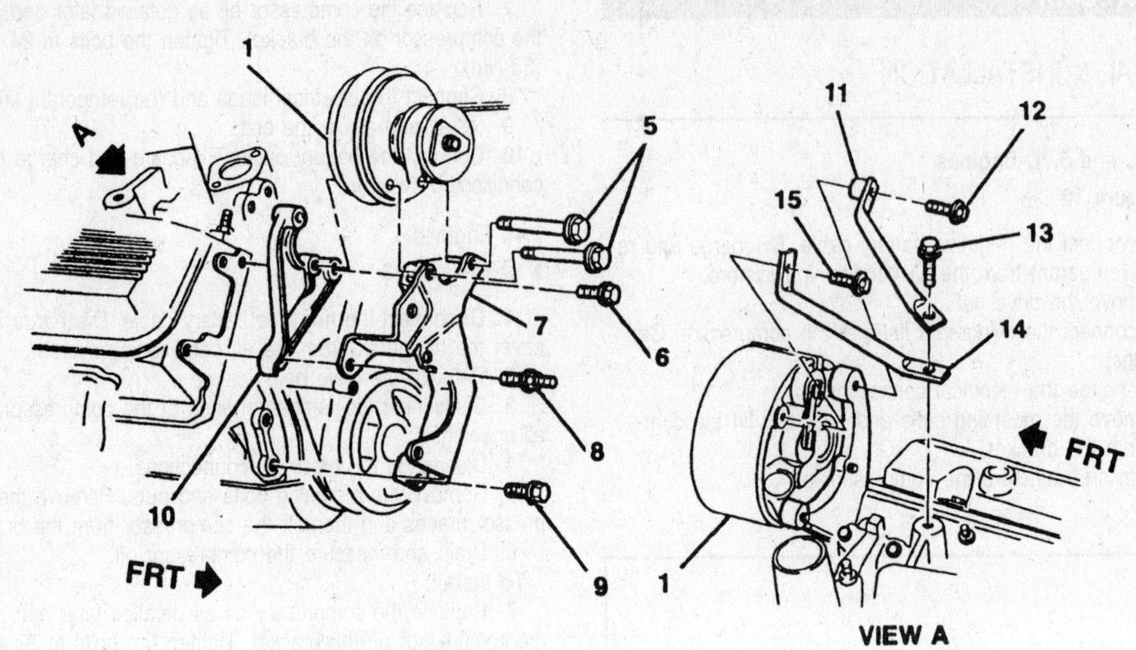

1. COMPRESSOR, A/C
5. BOLT, COMPRESSOR MOUNTING
6. BOLT, COMPRESSOR MOUNTING
7. BRACKET, A/C COMPRESSOR BELT IDLER PULLEY
8. STUD, A/C COMPRESSOR IDLER PULLEY BRACKET
9. BOLT, A/C COMPRESSOR IDLER PULLEY BRACKET
10. BRACE, A/C COMPRESSOR
11. BRACE, A/C COMPRESSOR OUTER
12. BOLT, A/C COMPRESSOR BRACE MOUNTING
13. BOLT, A/C COMPRESSOR BRACE MOUNTING
14. BRACE, A/C COMPRESSOR INNER
15. BOLT, A/C COMPRESSOR BRACE MOUNTING

84906020

Fig. 13 Compressor installation — 7.4L engines

On 1991-96 C/K series trucks, if less than 1 oz. was drained, add 1 oz. to that quantity for refilling. If more than 1 oz. was drained, add the exact amount for refilling.

Condenser

REMOVAL & INSTALLATION

See Figure 15

1. Disconnect the negative battery cable. Discharge and recover the refrigerant in the air conditioning system.
2. Remove the front grille and the hood primary latch support.
3. Remove the auxiliary cooling fan, if equipped.
4. Disconnect the refrigerant line and the evaporator tube at the condenser. Cap the openings.
5. Remove all bolts, brackets and insulators and then lift out the condenser. You'll probably need to bend the left grille support slightly to pull the condenser out; be careful.
6. Remove the lower insulators.

To install:

7. Install the lower insulators. Slide the condenser back into position with all the brackets and insulators and then tighten the bolts to 40 inch lbs. (5 Nm).
8. Reconnect the evaporator tube and refrigerant line at the condenser.
9. Install the auxiliary cooling fan, if equipped.
10. Bend the support back into place and install the grille and the hood primary latch support.
11. Connect the battery cable. Evacuate and charge the air conditioning system.

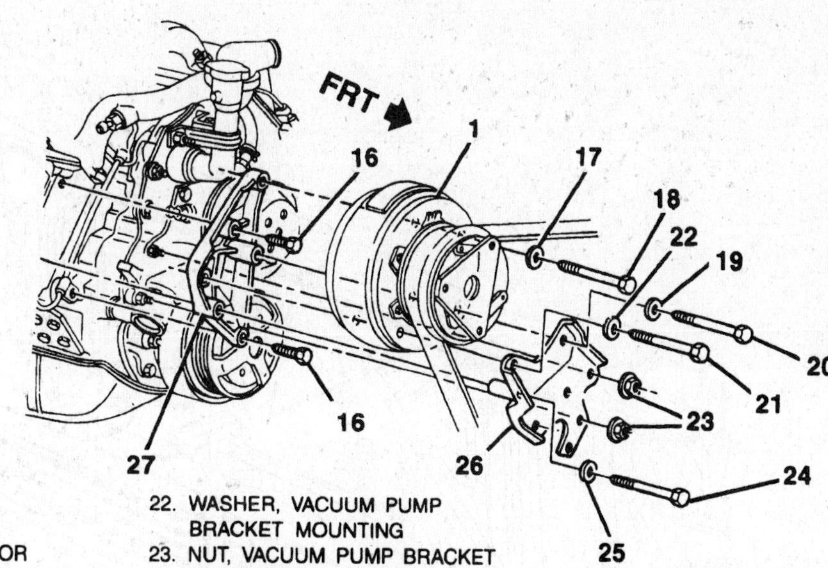

1. COMPRESSOR, A/C
16. BOLT, A/C COMPRESSOR SUPPORT MOUNTING
17. WASHER, A/C COMPRESSOR MOUNTING
18. BOLT, A/C COMPRESSOR MOUNTING
19. WASHER, VACUUM PUMP BRACKET MOUNTING
20. BOLT, VACUUM PUMP BRACKET MOUNTING
21. BOLT, VACUUM PUMP BRACKET MOUNTING
22. WASHER, VACUUM PUMP BRACKET MOUNTING
23. NUT, VACUUM PUMP BRACKET MOUNTING
24. BOLT, VACUUM PUMP BRACKET MOUNTING
25. WASHER, VACUUM PUMP BRACKET MOUNTING
26. BRACKET, A/C COMPRESSOR FRONT
27. SUPPORT, A/C COMPRESSOR

84906019

Fig. 14 Compressor installation — 6.2L and 6.5L engines

Evaporator Core

REMOVAL & INSTALLATION

CAUTION

When draining the coolant, keep in mind that cats and dogs are attracted by the ethylene glycol antifreeze, and are quite likely to drink any that is left in an uncovered container or in puddles on the ground. This will prove fatal in sufficient quantity. Always drain the coolant into a sealable container. Coolant should be reused unless it is contaminated or several years old.

1989-91 R/V Series

GASOLINE ENGINES

1. Disconnect the negative battery cable. Discharge and recover the refrigerant from the air conditioning system.
2. Unplug the wiring at the pressure switch.
3. Disconnect the refrigerant lines at the accumulator. Always use a back-up wrench! Cap all openings at once!
4. Remove the bracket screws and remove the accumulator and bracket. Drain the oil into a calibrated container and take note of the amount.
5. Remove the liquid line retaining screw.
6. Remove the liquid line from the evaporator. Cap all openings at once.
7. Remove the 8 bolts retaining the evaporator case halves and separate the case halves.
8. Remove the core.

To install:

9. Add 3 ounces of clean refrigerant oil to the core and position the core in the case.
10. Join the case halves.

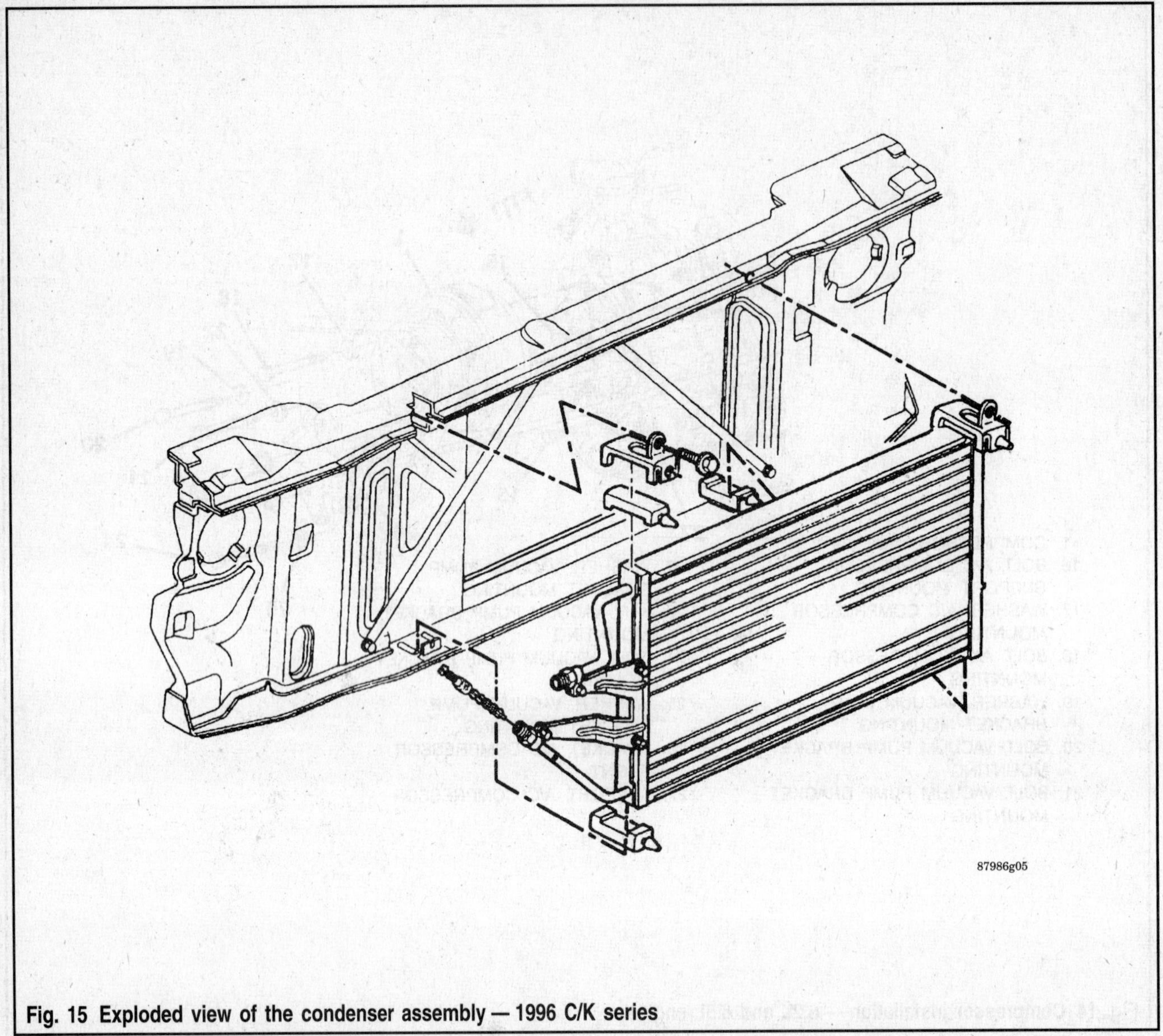

Fig. 15 Exploded view of the condenser assembly — 1996 C/K series

11. Install the liquid line at the evaporator.
12. Install the liquid line retaining screw.
13. Connect the refrigerant lines at the accumulator. Always use a back-up wrench! Use new O-rings coated with clean refrigerant oil.
14. Connect the wiring at the pressure switch.
15. Connect the battery cable. Evacuate and charge the air conditioning system.

DIESEL ENGINES

1. Disconnect the negative battery cable. Discharge and recover the refrigerant from the air conditioning system.
2. Drain the cooling system.
3. Remove the air cleaner and resonator.
4. Unplug the wiring at the pressure switch.
5. Disconnect the refrigerant lines at the accumulator. Always use a back-up wrench! Cap all openings at once!
6. Remove the bracket screws and remove the accumulator and bracket. Drain the oil into a calibrated container and take note of the amount.
7. Unbolt the fuel filter from the firewall and move it aside without disconnecting the fuel lines.
8. Remove the relay and resistors from the evaporator case.
9. Disconnect the heater hoses at the core tubes.
10. Remove the jack.
11. Remove the inner fender bolts and lower the fender to provide clearance.
12. Remove the nuts from the 2 studs on the firewall above the evaporator insulating shield.
13. Remove the bolt from the bottom of the insulating shield.
14. Remove the liquid line retaining screw.
15. Remove the liquid line from the evaporator. Cap all openings at once.
16. Remove the insulating shield.
17. Remove the 8 bolts retaining the evaporator case halves and separate the case halves.
18. Remove the core.

To install:

19. Add 3 ounces of clean refrigerant oil to the core and position the core in the case.

20. Join the case halves and install the bolts.
21. Install the liquid line at the evaporator.
22. Position the insulating shield on the case.
23. Install the liquid line at the evaporator. Always use a back-up wrench!
24. Install the liquid line retaining screw.
25. Install the bolt at the bottom of the insulating shield.
26. Install the nuts on the 2 studs on the firewall above the evaporator insulating shield.
27. Position the fender and install the inner fender bolts.
28. Install the jack.
29. Connect the heater hoses at the core tubes.
30. Install the relay and resistors on the evaporator case.
31. Install the fuel filter on the firewall.
32. Add the same amount of refrigerant oil drained from the accumulator, PLUS 2 ounces. Install the accumulator and bracket.
33. Connect the refrigerant lines at the accumulator. Always use a back-up wrench!
34. Connect the wiring at the pressure switch.
35. Install the air cleaner and resonator.
36. Fill the cooling system.
37. Connect the battery cable. Evacuate and charge the air conditioning system.

1988-90 C/K Series

1. Disconnect the negative battery cable. Discharge and recover the refrigerant from the air conditioning system.
2. Drain the cooling system.
3. Remove the coolant overflow tank.
4. Disconnect the heater hoses at the core tubes.
5. Disconnect the refrigerant lines at the evaporator. Always use a back-up wrench! Cap all openings at once!
6. Unplug the electrical connector at the temperature actuator.
7. Remove the 7 attaching screws and remove the heater case bottom plate.
8. Remove the screws and brackets that hold the heater core to the case and lift the core from the case.
9. Remove the 4 attaching screws and remove the evaporator core cover from the case.
10. Pull the evaporator core down and out of the case.

To install:

11. Position the evaporator core in the case.
12. Install the evaporator core cover.
13. Install the heater core in the case.
14. Install the heater case bottom plate.
15. Connect the electrical connector at the temperature actuator.
16. Connect the refrigerant lines at the evaporator. Always use a back-up wrench! Use new O-rings coated with clean refrigerant oil. Tighten the inlet line to 30 ft. lbs. (40 Nm); the outlet line to 18 ft. lbs. (24 Nm).
17. Connect the heater hoses at the core tubes.
18. Install the coolant overflow tank.
19. Fill the cooling system.
20. Connect the battery cable. Evacuate and charge the air conditioning system.

1991-96 C/K and 1992-96 R/V Series

1. Disconnect the negative battery cable. Discharge and recover the refrigerant from the air conditioning system.
2. Drain the cooling system.
3. Remove the instrument panel compartment.
4. Tag and disengage all electrical connections as necessary.
5. Remove the center air distribution duct from the floor.
6. Remove the ECM and mounting tray (diesel only). Remove the hinge pillar trim panels. Remove the blower motor cover and then remove the motor.
7. Remove the steering wheel and tilt back the instrument panel slightly.
8. Remove the coolant overflow tank. Disconnect the heater hoses at the core connections.
9. Remove the evaporator tube and the accumulator.
10. Remove the attaching screws and nut and then remove the heater case/module assembly.
11. Remove the 7 screws and lift off the heater case cover.
12. Remove the screws and brackets that hold the heater core to the case and lift the core from the case.
13. Remove the 4 screws that hold the evaporator case cover to the assembly and then remove the evaporator.

To install:

14. Install the evaporator. Install the case cover.
15. Install the heater core in the case.
16. Install the heater case bottom plate. Make sure there is a good seal.
17. Install the heater case/module assembly into the truck. Tighten the 4 lower screws to 17 inch lbs. (2 Nm), the upper screw to 97 inch lbs. (11 Nm) and the nuts to 25 inch lbs. (3 Nm).
18. Install the accumulator and evaporator tube.
19. Connect the heater hoses at the core tubes.
20. Install the coolant overflow tank.
21. Install the instrument panel and the steering wheel.
22. Install the blower motor and cover.
23. Install the trim panels and the ECM. Install the air distribution duct and reconnect all electrical leads.
24. Install the instrument panel compartment. Fill the cooling system.
25. Connect the battery cable. Evacuate and charge the air conditioning system.

Expansion Valve

REMOVAL & INSTALLATION

1. Disconnect the negative battery cable. Discharge and recover the refrigerant in the air conditioning system.
2. Remove the rear duct.
3. Disengage the blower motor harness connector and the ground wire.
4. Remove the lower to upper blower-evaporator case screws.
5. Remove the lower case with the motor assembly.
6. Remove the expansion valve sensing bulb clamps and the valve inlet and outlet lines. Cap the open lines.
7. Remove the expansion valve assembly.

To install:

8. Install a new expansion valve assembly.
9. Install new O-rings coated with clean refrigerant oil and attach the sensing bulb and clamps.
10. Install the lower case and blower motor.
11. Install the lower to upper case screws.
12. Engage the blower motor harness connector and ground wires.
13. Install the rear duct.
14. Connect the battery cable. Evacuate and charge the air conditioning system.

Accumulator

REMOVAL & INSTALLATION

➧ See Figure 16

1. Disconnect the negative battery cable. Discharge and recover the refrigerant in the air conditioning system.
2. Disengage any electrical connections, as necessary.
3. Remove the pressure cycling switch.
4. Disconnect the refrigerant line at the accumulator. Cap the opening.
5. Remove all bolts and brackets and then lift out the accumulator.

To install:

6. Install the accumulator to the bracket and tighten the screw to 53 inch lbs. (6 Nm).
7. Coat a new O-ring with refrigerant oil and attach the accumulator to the evaporator. Tighten the bolt to 30 ft. lbs. (40 Nm).
8. Reconnect the evaporator tube at the accumulator.
9. Engage any electrical connections that were removed.
10. Connect the battery cable. Evacuate and charge the air conditioning system.

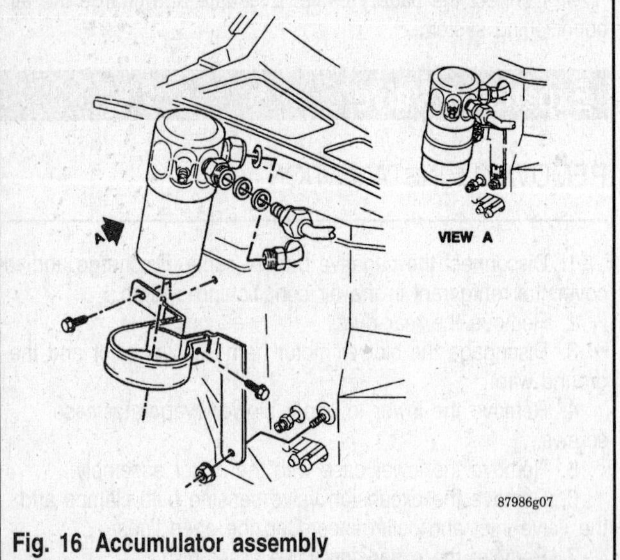

Fig. 16 Accumulator assembly

Refrigerant Lines

REMOVAL & INSTALLATION

➧ See Figures 17 and 18

1. Disconnect the negative battery cable. Discharge and recover the refrigerant in the air conditioning system.
2. Disengage any electrical connections, as necessary.
3. Disconnect the refrigerant line assembly at the rear of the compressor. Cap the opening.
4. Remove the sealing washers. Disconnect the lines from the accumulator and the condenser and remove the O-rings.

To install:

5. Always coat the new O-rings with refrigerant oil and tighten the line-to-accumulator to 30 ft. lbs. (41 Nm) or the line-to-condenser to 18 ft. lbs. (24 Nm).
6. Install the sealing washers and connect the line assembly to the rear of the compressor. Tighten the bolt to 25 ft. lbs. (34 Nm).
7. Connect the battery cable. Evacuate and charge the air conditioning system.

Vacuum Actuator

REMOVAL & INSTALLATION

1. Disconnect the vacuum hose from the actuator.
2. Disengage the valve return spring at the actuator end.
3. Remove the actuator mounting bracket fasteners.
4. Remove the cam-to-actuator arm fastener.
5. Remove the actuator and cam from the bracket.
6. Remove the actuator-to-bracket nuts.
7. Remove the actuator from the bracket.

To install:

8. Install the actuator to bracket.
9. Fasten the bracket nuts and install the actuator and bracket to the cam.
10. Install the cam-to-actuator arm fastener.
11. Install the valve return spring and the vacuum hose to the actuator.

Plenum Valve

REMOVAL & INSTALLATION

1. Raise the hood and remove the plastic cowl grille.
2. Remove the three cowl-to-valve assembly fasteners.
3. Remove the valve and actuator assembly from the vehicle.
4. Remove the actuator arm pushnut.
5. Remove the actuator-to-valve nuts and separate the valve and actuator.

To install:

6. Install the actuator-to-valve nuts and the actuator arm pushnut.

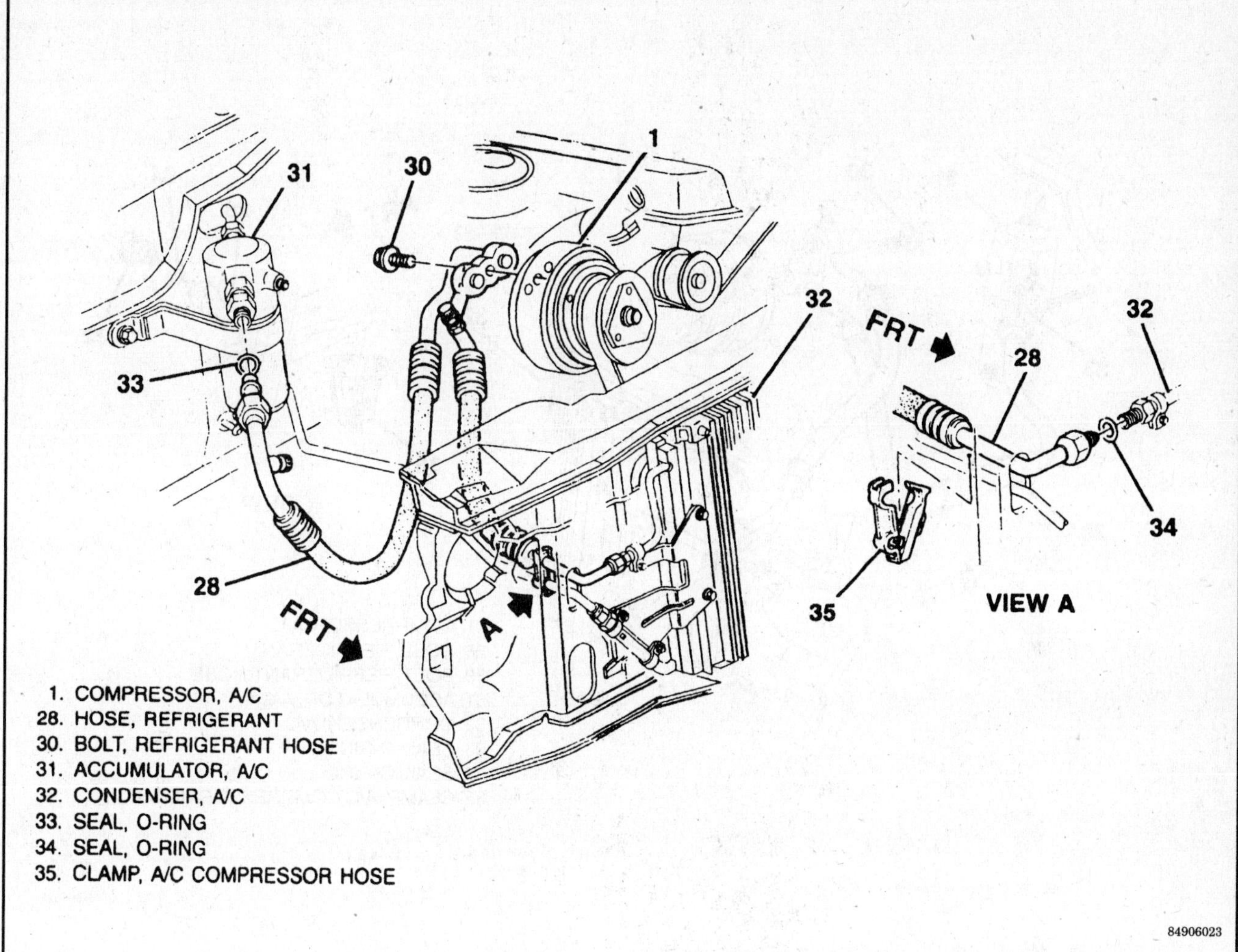

Fig. 17 Refrigerant line routing — except 7.4L engines with auxiliary system

7. Install the valve and actuator assembly.
8. Install the three cowl-to-valve assembly screws and the cowl panel.

Cycling Clutch Switch

REMOVAL & INSTALLATION

See Figure 19

1. Disconnect the negative battery cable. Discharge and recover the refrigerant from the air conditioning system.
2. Detach the electrical connector from the switch in the rear head of the compressor.
3. Remove the switch from the compressor. Remove the O-ring seal from the switch cavity.
4. Install the switch using new O-ring seals.
5. Connect the battery cable. Evacuate and charge the air conditioning system.

Expansion (Orifice) Tube

REMOVAL & INSTALLATION

1988-91 R/V Series

The expansion tube is located in the evaporator core inlet line.

1. Disconnect the negative battery cable. Discharge and recover the refrigerant from the air conditioning system.
2. Disconnect the condenser-to-evaporator line.

Use needle nose pliers to remove the orifice

3. Remove the expansion tube from the line.
4. Remove the old O-rings and discard.

To install:

5. Install new O-rings coated with clean refrigerant oil and the short screen and orifice into the evaporator inlet line.

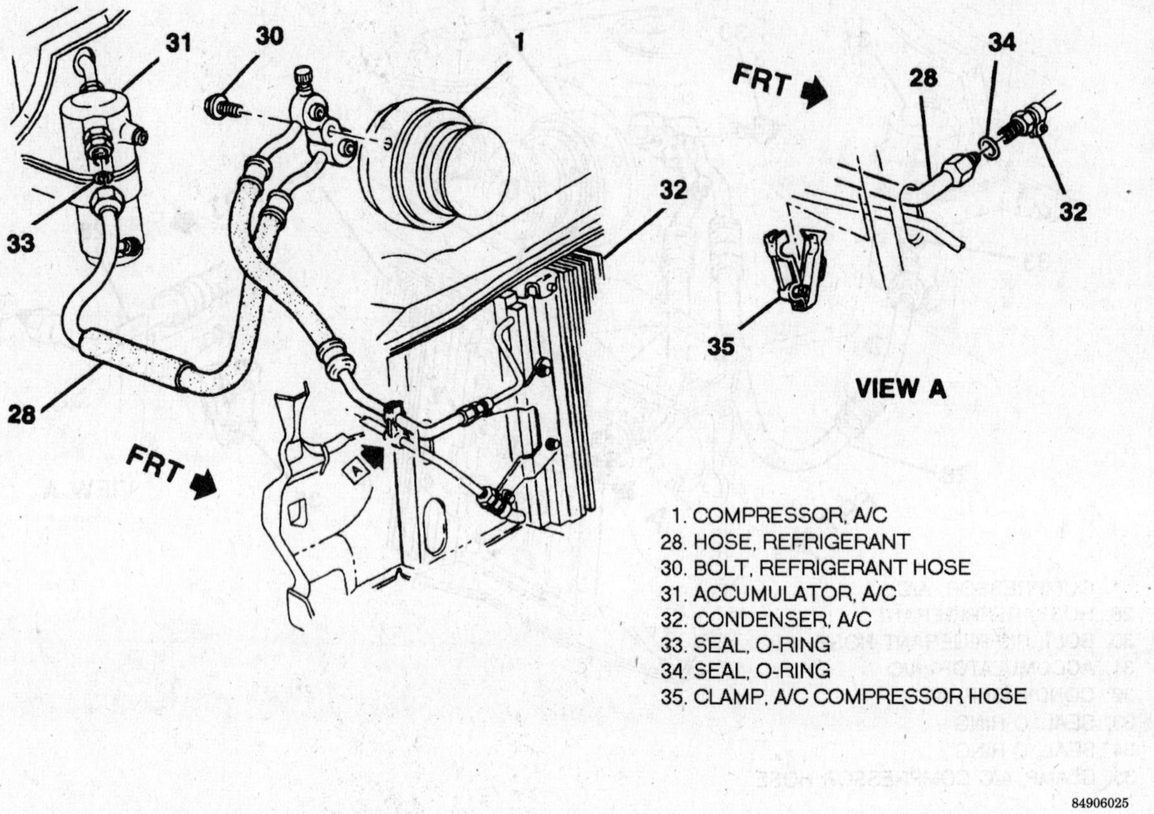

31
30
1
33
28
FRT
32
A
34
28
FRT
32
35
VIEW A
1. COMPRESSOR, A/C
28. HOSE, REFRIGERANT
30. BOLT, REFRIGERANT HOSE
31. ACCUMULATOR, A/C
32. CONDENSER, A/C
33. SEAL, O-RING
34. SEAL, O-RING
35. CLAMP, A/C COMPRESSOR HOSE
84906025

Fig. 18 Refrigerant line routing — 7.4L engines with auxiliary system

7.4L ENGINES
ALL OTHER ENGINES
87986g08

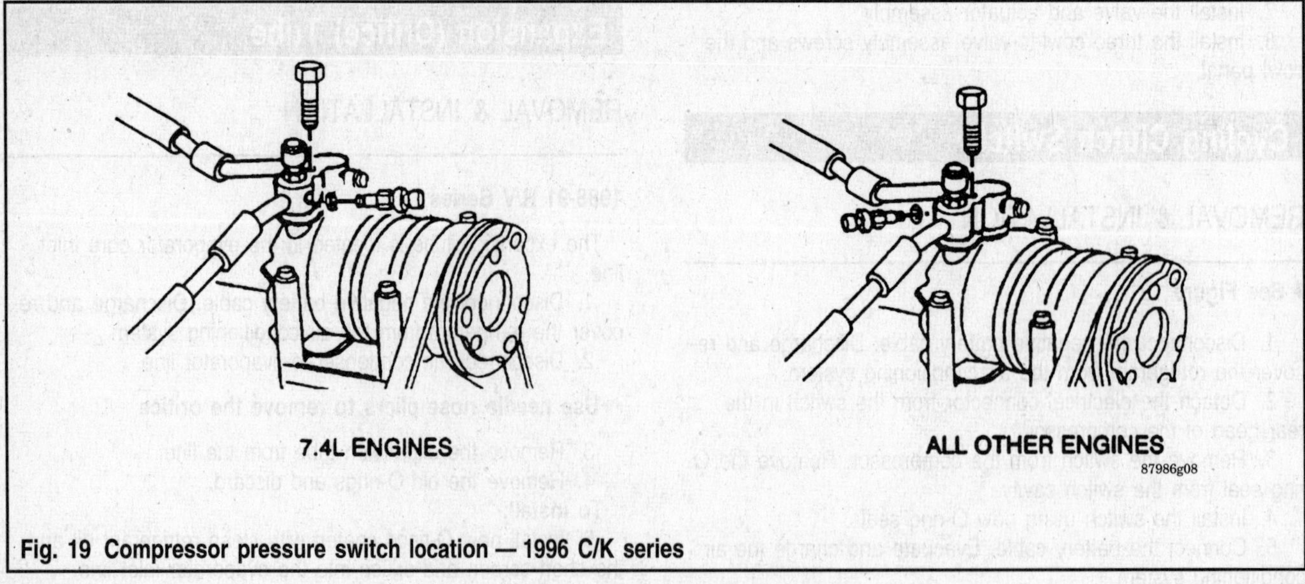

Fig. 19 Compressor pressure switch location — 1996 C/K series

6. Connect the expansion tube to the evaporator core inlet line.
7. Connect the condenser-to-evaporator line at the evaporator inlet.
8. Connect the battery cable. Evacuate and charge the air conditioning system.

Except 1988-91 R/V Series

➡To perform this procedure, orifice tube removal tool J 26549-E or equivalent is required

1. Have the system properly discharged by a repair shop with an approved recovery/recycling system.
2. Disconnect the negative battery cable.
3. Remove the grille and the disconnect the evaporator tube from the condenser.
4. Remove the O-ring seal and cap the lines.
5. Remove the expansion (orifice) tube from the condenser outlet pipe, using tool J 26549-E or equivalent.

To install:

6. Install the expansion tube into the condenser outlet pipe, using tool J 26549-E or equivalent.
7. Install a new O-ring seal lubricated with refrigerant oil.
8. Insert the short screen end of the new orifice into the evaporator tube.
9. Connect the evaporator tube to the condenser and install the grille.
10. Connect the battery cable. Evacuate and charge the air conditioning system.

AUXILIARY HEATING AND AIR CONDITIONING SYSTEM

Blower Motor

REMOVAL & INSTALLATION

1988-91 Models

WITHOUT AIR CONDITIONING

1. Disconnect the negative battery cable.
2. Disconnect the blower motor wiring harness.
3. Remove the blower motor clamp.
4. Remove the motor attaching screws and lift out the motor.

To install:

5. Install the motor and tighten the attaching screws.
6. Install the blower motor clamp.
7. Connect the blower motor wiring harness.
8. Connect the negative battery cable.

WITH AIR CONDITIONING

1. Disconnect the negative battery cable.
2. Remove the drain tube from the rear duct.
3. Remove the attaching screws and remove the rear duct from the roof panel.
4. Disconnect the blower motor wiring and remove the ground strap and wire.
5. Support the case and remove the lower-to-upper case half screws and lower the case and motor assemblies.
6. Remove the motor retaining strap and remove the motor and wheels.

To install:

7. Install the motor and wheels.
8. Install the motor retaining strap.
9. Raise the case and install the lower-to-upper case half screws.
10. Connect the blower motor wires.
11. Connect the blower motor ground straps at the center connector between the motors.
12. Install the duct.
13. Install the screws securing the duct to the roof and case.
14. Connect the drain tubes at the rear of the blower-evaporator duct.
15. Connect the battery cable.

1992-96 Models

➧ See Figure 20

1. Disconnect the negative battery cable.
2. Remove the right rear quarter panel trim.
3. Disconnect the electrical lead at the fan, remove the screws and the fan retaining nut and lift out the blower fan.
4. Remove the blower motor.

To install:

5. Install the blower motor and then position the fan.
6. Install the retaining nut and then tighten the mounting screws to 12 inch lbs. (2 Nm).
7. Connect the electrical lead. Install the quarter panel trim cover.
8. Connect the battery cable.

Heater Core

REMOVAL & INSTALLATION

⁂CAUTION

When draining the coolant, keep in mind that cats and dogs are attracted by ethylene glycol antifreeze, and are quite likely to drink any that is left in an uncovered container or in puddles on the ground. This will prove fatal in sufficient quantity. Always drain the coolant into a sealable container. Coolant should be reused unless it is contaminated or several years old.

1988-91 Models

1. Disconnect the negative battery cable.
2. Drain the cooling system.
3. Disconnect the heater hoses at the core tubes.
4. Disconnect the blower motor wiring harness.
5. Remove the blower motor clamp.
6. Remove the motor attaching screws and lift out the motor.

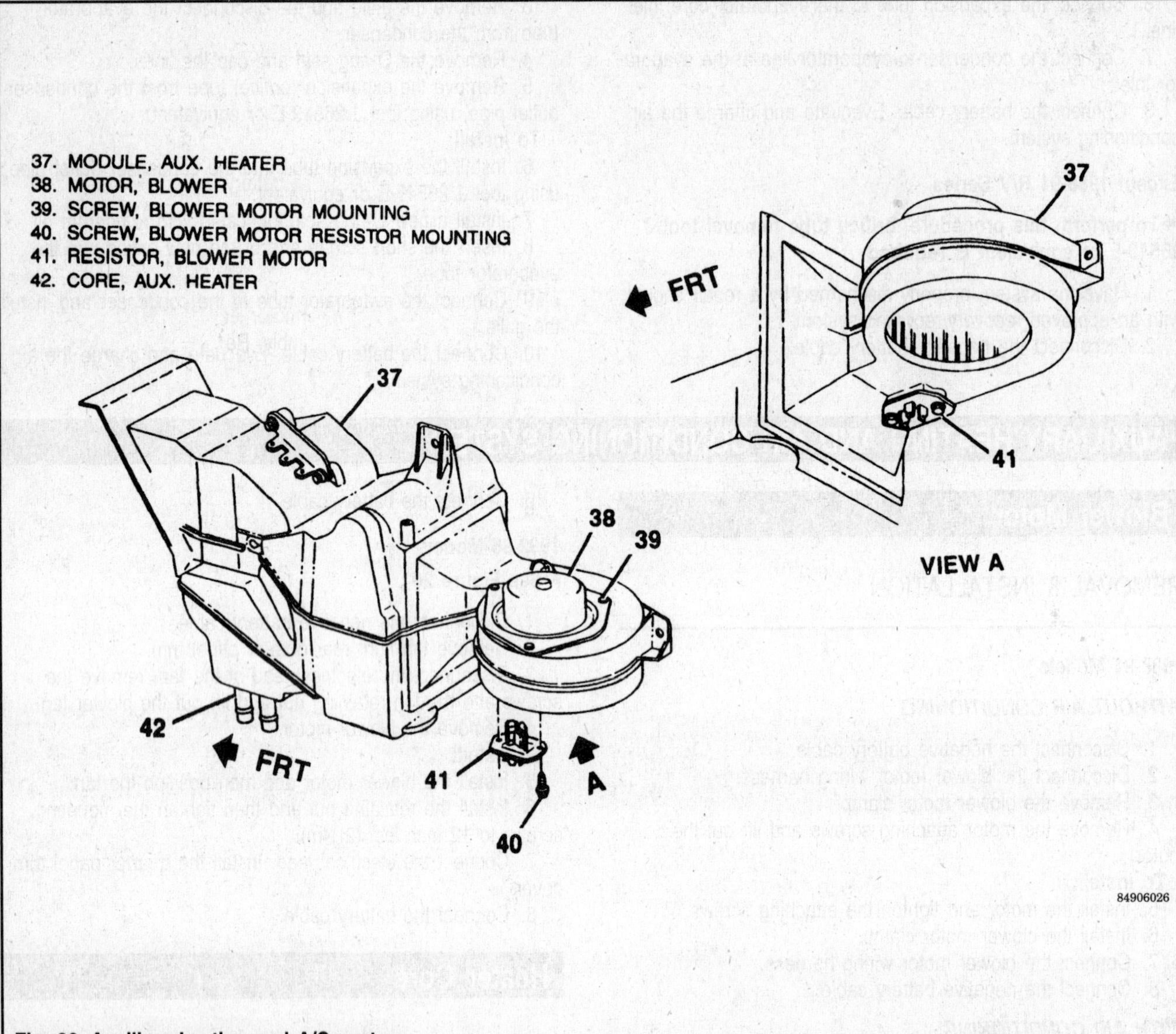

Fig. 20 Auxiliary heating and A/C system

7. Remove the upper-to-lower case half screws and remove the upper case half.
8. Remove the core seal.
9. Lift out the core.

To install:

10. Install the heater core.
11. Install the core seal.
12. Install the upper case half and then tighten the upper-to-lower case half screws.
13. Install the motor and then tighten the attaching screws.
14. Install the blower motor clamp.
15. Connect the blower motor wiring harness.
16. Connect the heater hoses at the core tubes.
17. Fill the cooling system.
18. Connect the negative battery cable.

1992-96 Models

1. Disconnect the negative battery cable and drain the engine coolant.
2. Remove the right rear quarter panel trim and then remove the panel itself.
3. Remove the right rear wheelhousing liner.
4. Disconnect the heater hoses from the core.
5. Disconnect the electrical lead. Remove the drain valve.
6. Remove the heater case mounting nuts and then remove the assembly.
7. Remove the blower motor.
8. Remove the heater case cover and then remove the heater core.

To install:

9. Install the heater core and then install the heater case cover.
10. Install the blower motor.
11. Install the heater case assembly and tighten the mounting nuts to 89 inch lbs. (10 Nm). Tighten the bolts to 13 inch lbs. (2 Nm).
12. Connect the electrical lead. Install the drain valve.
13. Connect the heater hoses to the core.
14. Install the right rear wheelhousing liner.
15. Install the right rear quarter panel and then install the trim.

16. Connect the negative battery cable and fill the engine with coolant.

Blower Switch

REMOVAL & INSTALLATION

➧ See Figure 21

1. Disconnect the negative battery cable.
2. Unplug the wiring at the switch.
3. Remove the attaching screws and bezel.
4. Remove the switch.
5. Installation is the reverse of the removal procedure.

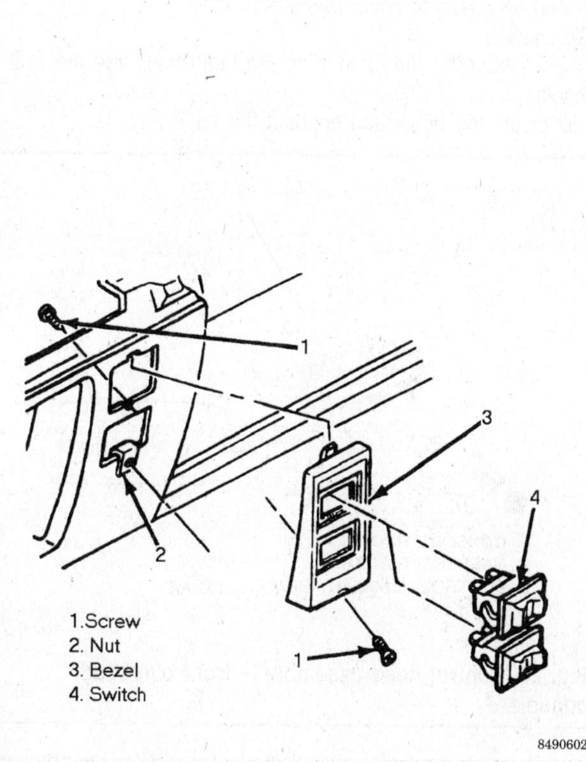

Fig. 21 Blower switch replacement — auxiliary system

Expansion Valve

REMOVAL & INSTALLATION

1. Disconnect the negative battery cable. Discharge and recover the refrigerant from the air conditioning system.
2. Remove the drain tube from the rear duct.
3. Remove the attaching screws and remove the rear duct from the roof panel.
4. Disconnect the blower motor lead and ground wires.
5. Support the case assembly. Remove the lower to upper blower/evaporator case screws. Lower the case and motor assembly.
6. Remove the expansion valve sensing bulb clamps.
7. Disconnect the valve inlet and outlet lines. Always use a back-up wrench! Cap the openings immediately.
8. Remove the expansion valve assembly.

To install:

9. Install the expansion valve assembly.
10. Connect the valve inlet and outlet lines.
11. Install the expansion valve sensing bulb clamps.
12. Install the case and motor assembly.
13. Connect the blower motor lead and ground wires.
14. Install the rear duct into the roof panel.
15. Install the drain tube to the rear duct.
16. Connect the battery cable. Evacuate and charge the air conditioning system.

Evaporator Core

REMOVAL & INSTALLATION

1988-91 Models

1. Disconnect the negative battery cable. Discharge and recover the refrigerant from the air conditioning system.
2. Disconnect the drain tubes at the rear of the blower-evaporator duct.
3. Remove the screws securing the duct to the roof and case.
4. Remove the duct.
5. Disconnect the blower motor ground straps at the center connector between the motors.
6. Disconnect the blower motor wires.
7. Disconnect the refrigerant lines at the case. Always use a back-up wrench! Cap all openings at once!
8. Support the case and remove the case-to-roof screws. Lower the case assembly.
9. Place the unit upside-down on a clean workbench.
10. Remove the screws and separate the case halves.
11. Remove the upper shroud and upper case from the evaporator core.
12. Disconnect the expansion valve lines. Always use a back-up wrench! Cap all openings at once!
13. Remove the expansion valve capillary bulbs from the evaporator outlet line and remove the valves.
14. Remove the screen from the core.

To install:

15. Always use new O-rings coated with clean refrigerant oil. Add 3 ounces of clean refrigerant oil to a new core.
16. Install the screen on the core.
17. Install the expansion valves.
18. Install the expansion valve capillary bulbs in the evaporator outlet line.
19. Connect the expansion valve lines.
20. Install the upper shroud and upper case.
21. Install the case screws.
22. Raise the case into position and install the case-to-roof screws.
23. Connect the refrigerant lines at the case.
24. Connect the blower motor wires.
25. Connect the blower motor ground straps at the center connector between the motors.
26. Install the shroud/duct.
27. Connect the drain tubes at the rear of the blower-evaporator shroud/duct.
28. Connect the battery cable. Evacuate and charge the air conditioning system.

1992-96 Models

1. Disconnect the negative battery cable. Discharge and recover the refrigerant from the air conditioning system.
2. Drain the engine coolant.
3. Remove the right rear quarter panel trim and then remove the panel itself.
4. Remove the right rear wheelhousing liner.
5. Disconnect the heater hoses from the core. Disconnect the refrigerant lines from the evaporator.
6. Disconnect the electrical lead.
7. Remove the heater/evaporator case cover.
8. Remove the evaporator core.

To install:

9. Install the evaporator core.
10. Install the heater/evaporator case cover.
11. Connect the electrical lead.
12. Connect the heater hoses to the core. Connect the refrigerant lines to the evaporator.
13. Install the right rear wheelhousing liner.
14. Install the right rear quarter panel and then install the trim.
15. Fill the engine with coolant.
16. Connect the battery cable. Evacuate and charge the air conditioning system.

Control Assembly

REMOVAL & INSTALLATION

Front Overhead

See Figure 22

1. Disconnect the negative battery cable.
2. Remove the roof console.
3. Pull the control head out slightly, disconnect the electrical lead and then remove the control head.

To install:

4. Connect the lead and slide the head back into the console.
5. Install the roof console and connect the battery cable.

Center Overhead

1. Disconnect the negative battery cable.
2. Remove the control head bezel.
3. Pull the control head out slightly, disconnect the electrical lead and then remove the control head.

To install:

4. Connect the lead and slide the head back into the console.
5. Install the bezel and connect the battery cable.

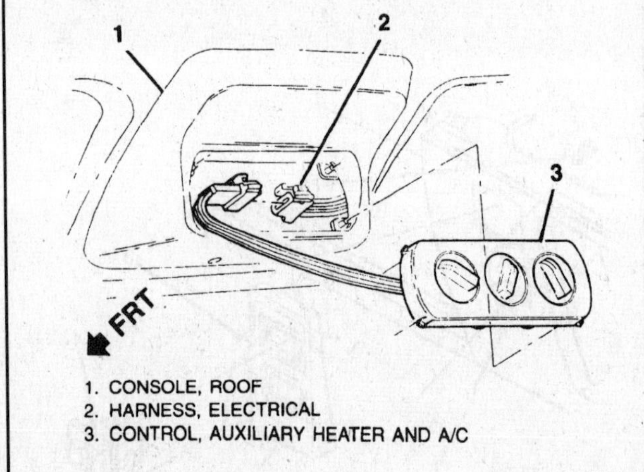

Fig. 22 Control head assembly — front overhead console

CRUISE CONTROL

Control Switches

REMOVAL & INSTALLATION

See Figure 23

The switch is located on the clutch pedal bracket.

1. Unplug the wiring connector and vacuum hose.
2. Turn the retainer counterclockwise and slide out the switch.

To install:

3. Place the switch in the retainer and turn the retainer clockwise to seat the switch.
4. Slide the switch into the retainer, with the clutch pedal fully depressed, as far as it will go. Clicking will be heard as the switch is pushed towards the pedal.
5. Pull the pedal fully rearwards against its stop until the clicking stops.

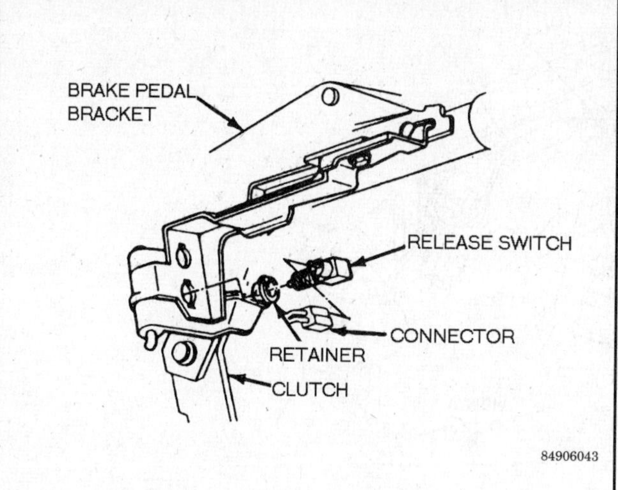

Fig. 23 Clutch release switch mounting — R/V series

6. Release the pedal and performs Steps 5 & 6 again to make sure the valve is correctly seated.

7. Connect the vacuum hose and wiring.

Engagement Switch

The cruise control engagement switch is part of the turn signal lever assembly and is not serviceable by itself. The turn signal lever and cruise control switch must be replaced as an assembly. Refer to the necessary service procedures in Section 8.

Vacuum Release Valve

REMOVAL & INSTALLATION

▸ See Figures 24 and 25

The valve is located on the brake pedal bracket.

1. Unplug the wiring connector (automatic transmission).
2. Disconnect the vacuum line.
3. Turn the retainer counterclockwise and slide out the valve.

To install:

4. Place the valve in the retainer and turn the retainer clockwise to seat the valve.
5. Slide the valve into the retainer, with the brake pedal fully depressed, as far as it will go. Clicking will be heard as the valve is pushed towards the pedal.
6. Pull the pedal fully rearwards against its stop until the clicking stops.
7. Release the pedal and make sure the valve is correctly seated.
8. Connect the vacuum hose and wiring.

Vehicle Speed Sensor (VSS)

REMOVAL & INSTALLATION

1. Disconnect the negative battery cable.
2. Raise and safely support the vehicle.
3. Detach the VSS electrical lead from the transmission.
4. Unfasten the retaining bolts, then remove the sensor from the housing. Remove and discard the sensor O-ring.
5. Installation is the reverse of the removal procedure.

Control Module

REMOVAL & INSTALLATION

1988-91 R/V Series

▸ See Figure 26

The module is mounted on the right side of the brake pedal bracket.

1. Unplug the harness connector.
2. Remove the module by prying back the retaining clip on the bracket and sliding off the module.

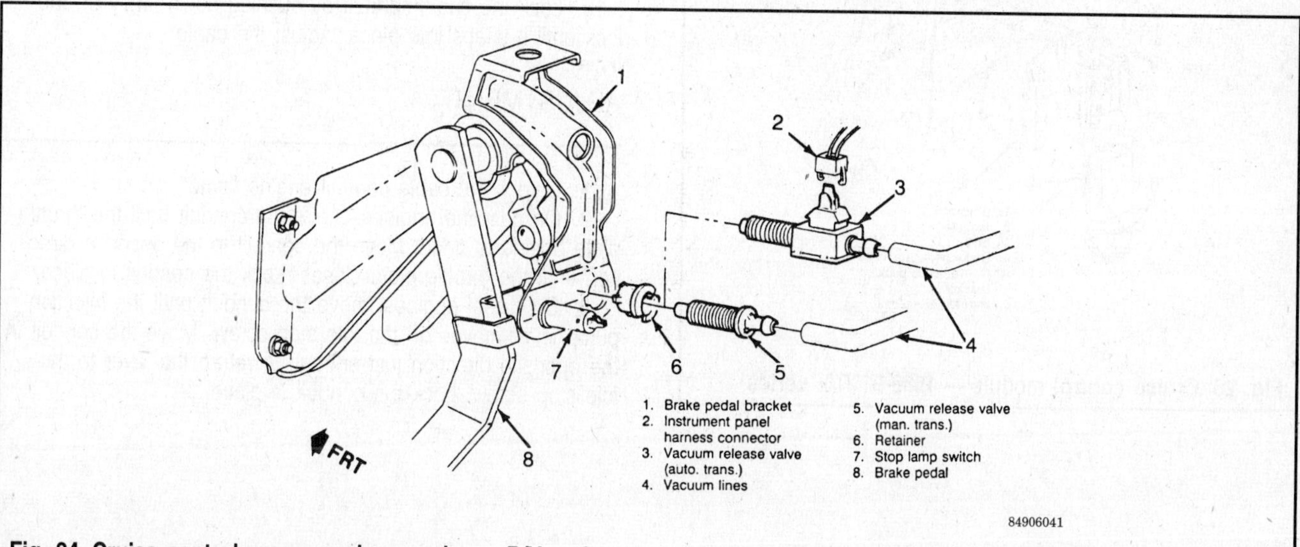

Fig. 24 Cruise control vacuum release valve — R/V series

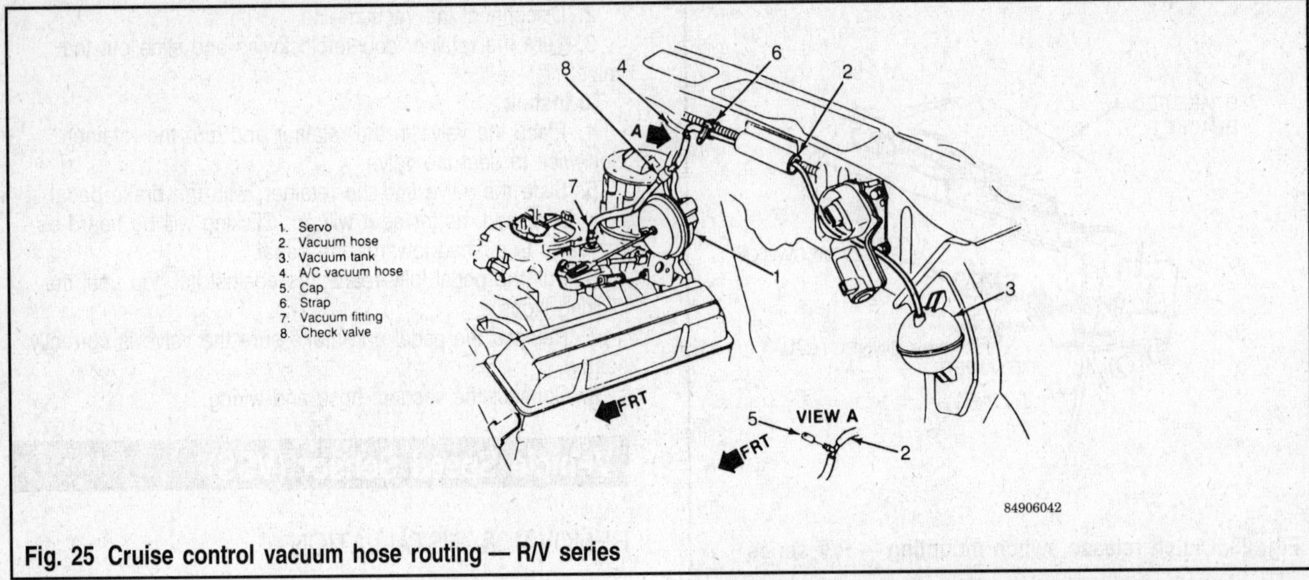

Fig. 25 Cruise control vacuum hose routing — R/V series

3. To install, pop the module back into the clip and reconnect the harness.

Except 1988-91 R/V Series

➧ See Figure 27

The module is located on the driver's side of the firewall, in the engine compartment.

1. Disconnect the negative battery cable.
2. Disconnect the control cable from the module.
3. Remove the attaching screws, lift off the module and unplug the wiring.
4. To install, screw the module back into the firewall, tighten the screws until snug and connect the control cable. Connect the negative battery cable.

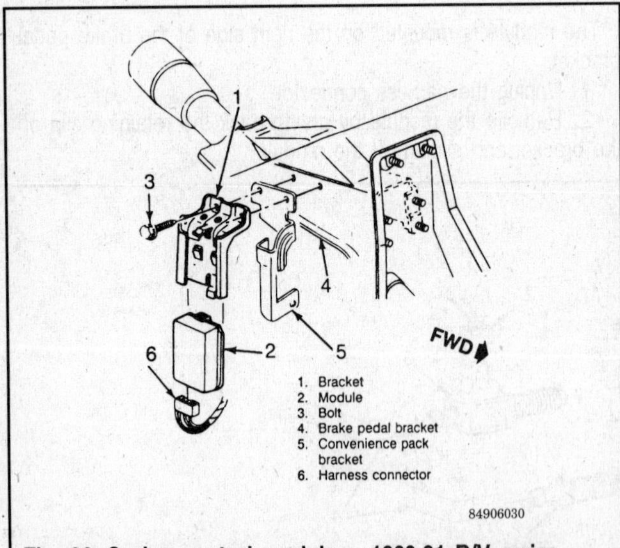

Fig. 26 Cruise control module — 1988-91 R/V series

Control Cable

REMOVAL & INSTALLATION

➧ See Figure 28

1. Remove the retaining clip.
2. Remove the engine end fitting from the lever stud.
3. Disconnect the cable conduit from the engine bracket.
4. Disconnect the cable conduit from the module housing.
5. Disconnect the cable bead from the end of the ribbon.

To install:

6. Connect the cable bead to the module ribbon fitting.
7. Pull the engine end of the cable until the cable is snug. Turn the engine end of the cable to straighten the ribbon, if necessary THE RIBBON MUST NOT BE TWISTED! Place the cable conduit over the ribbon and tangs, into the module housing.
8. Connect the end end of the conduit to the bracket.
9. Connect the engine end of the cable to the lever stud.
10. Lock the cable conduit by pushing down firmly on the lock until it snaps into place. Adjust the cable.

ADJUSTMENT

1. Unlock the cable conduit engine fitting.
2. On gasoline engines: move the conduit until the throttle plate begins to open. Move the conduit in the opposite direction until the throttle plate closes. Lock the conduit in place.
3. On diesel engines: move the conduit until the injection pump lever moves off the idle stop screw. Move the conduit in the opposite direction just enough to return the lever to the idle stop screw. Lock the conduit in place.

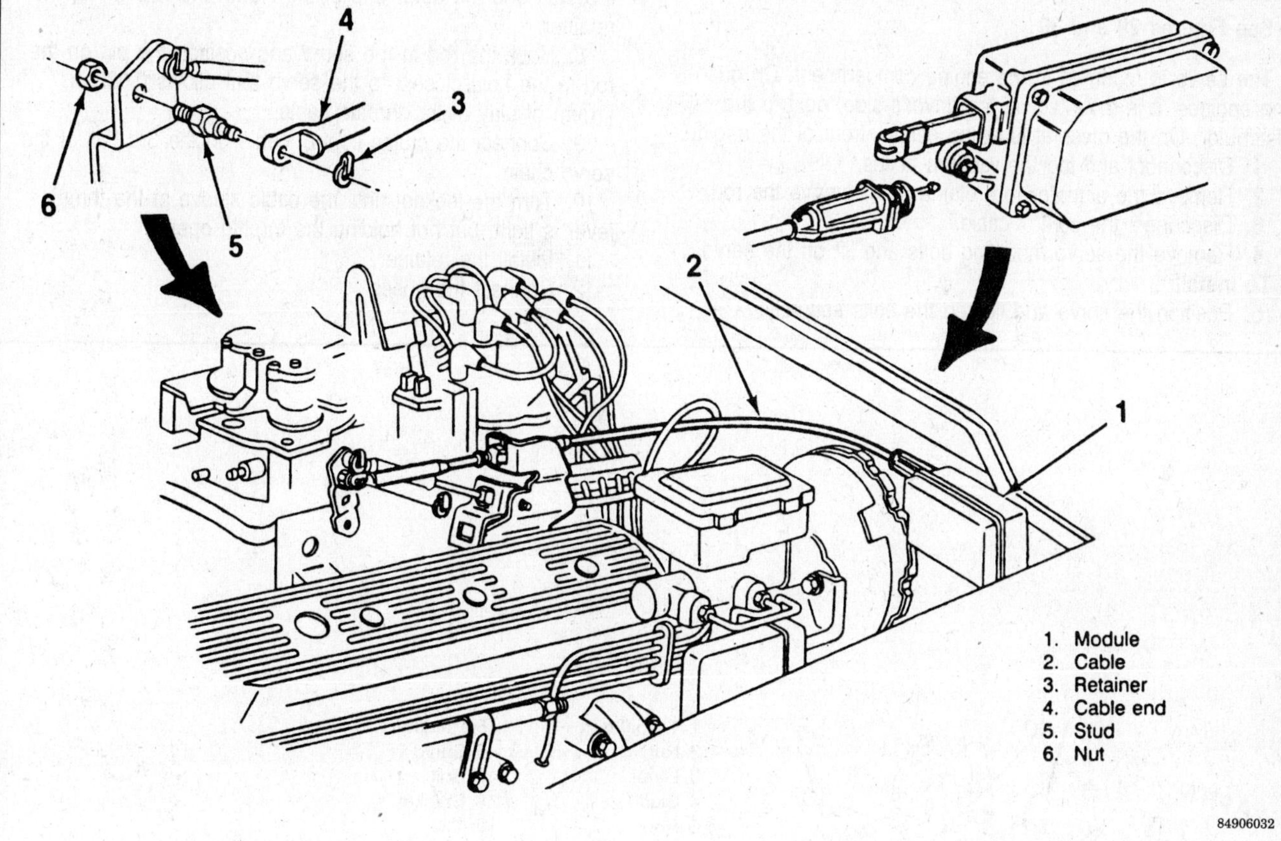

4
3
6
5
2
1
1. Module
2. Cable
3. Retainer
4. Cable end
5. Stud
6. Nut
84906032

Fig. 27 Cruise control module and cable routing — except 1988-91 R/V series

RIBBON MUST NOT BE TWISTED
84906034

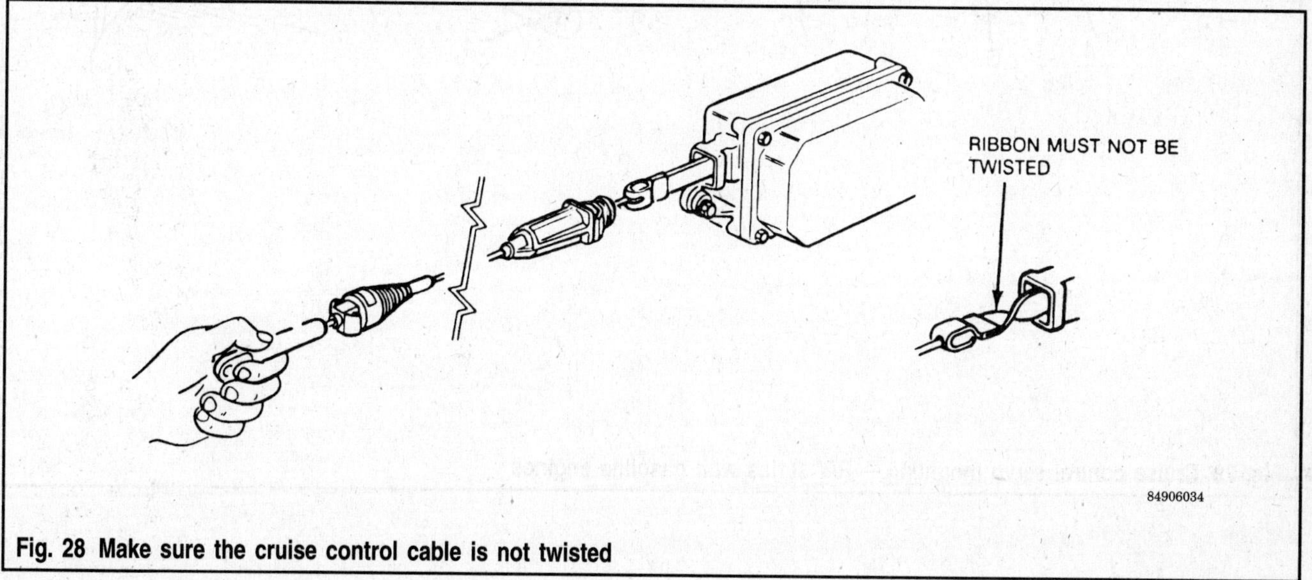

Fig. 28 Make sure the cruise control cable is not twisted

Servo

REMOVAL & INSTALLATION

➧ **See Figures 29 and 30**

The servo is mounted in the engine compartment. On gasoline engines, it is mounted on the driver's side, next to the distributor. On the diesel it is at the center, front of the engine.

1. Disconnect and tag the vacuum hoses.
2. Remove the actuator rod retainer and remove the rod.
3. Disconnect the control cable.
4. Remove the servo mounting bolts and lift off the servo.

To install:

5. Position the servo and tighten the bolts securely.
6. Connect the control cable.
7. On carbureted engines: With the ignition switch **OFF**, the fast idle cam not engaged, and the throttle fully closed, hook the rod in the servo and position over the stud. Position the rod so that there is a gap of 0.039-0.196 in. (1-5mm) between the stud and the outer end of the slot in the rod. Install the retainer.
8. Hook the rod in the servo and position the pin on the rod in the hole closest to the servo that allows 0.039 in. (1mm) of play at the throttle cable.
9. Connect the cruise control cable on the 3rd ball of the servo chain.
10. Turn the locknut until the cable sleeve at the throttle lever is tight, but not holding the throttle open.
11. Install the retainer.
12. Connect the hoses.

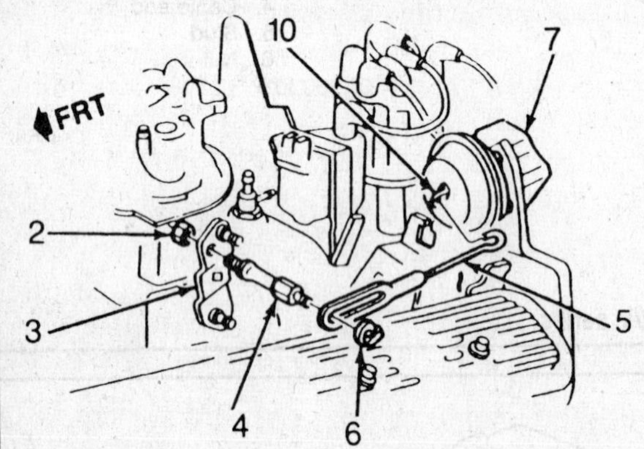

1. 1.0-5.0 mm
2. Nut
3. Lever
4. Stud
5. Rod
6. Retainer
7. Servo
8. Bolt
9. Bracket
10. Tab

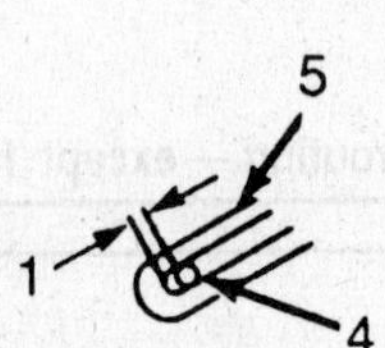

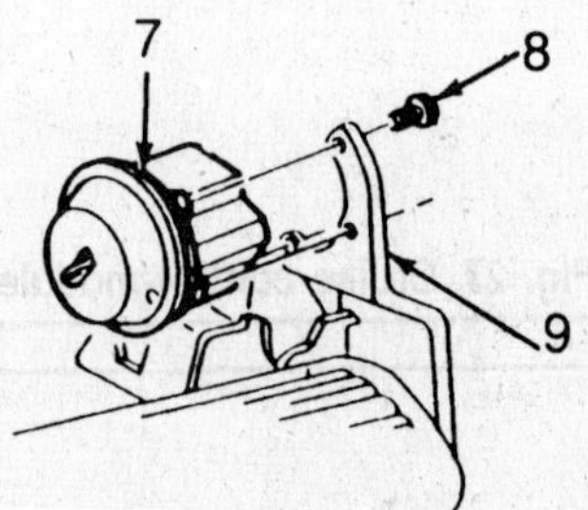

84906039

Fig. 29 Cruise control servo mounting — R/V series with gasoline engines

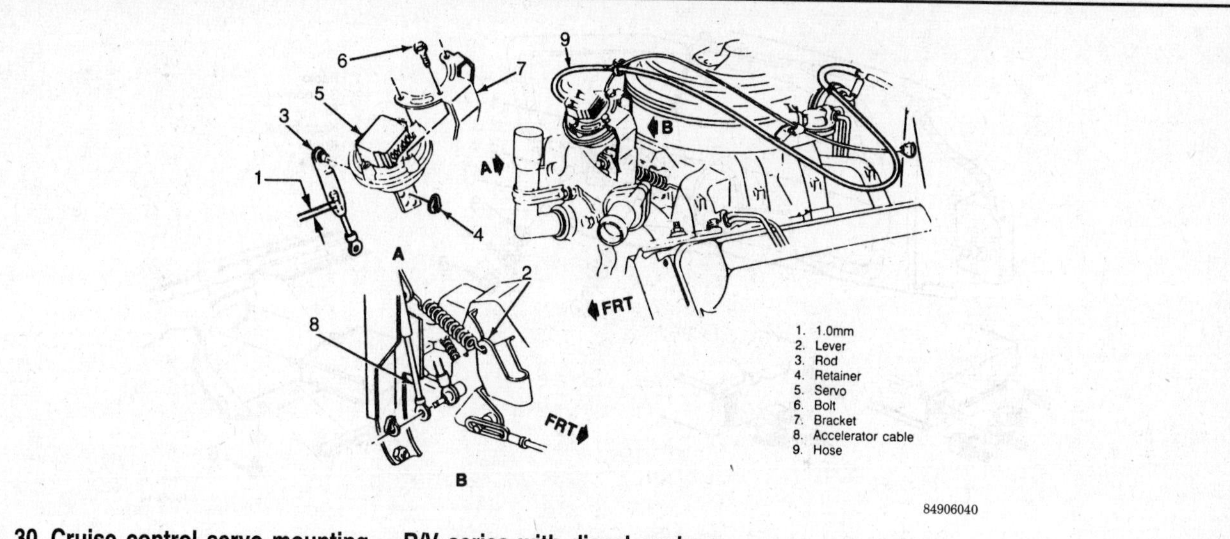

Fig. 30 Cruise control servo mounting — R/V series with diesel engines

ENTERTAINMENT SYSTEMS

Radio

REMOVAL & INSTALLATION

WARNING

Make certain that the speaker is attached to the radio before the unit is turned ON. If it is not, the output transistors may be damaged.

1988-91 R/V Series

See Figure 31

1. Disconnect the negative battery cable.
2. Remove the control knobs and the bezels from the radio control shafts.
3. Remove the nuts from the support shafts.
4. Remove the support bracket retaining screws.
5. Lifting the rear edge of the radio, push the radio forward until the control shafts clear the instrument panel. Then, lower the radio far enough so that the electrical connections can be unplugged.
6. Remove the power lead, speaker, and antenna wires and then pull out the unit.

To install:

7. Connect the power lead, speaker, and antenna wires and then install the unit.
8. Connect all electrical leads.
9. Install the support bracket retaining screws.
10. Install the nuts on the support shafts.
11. Press the control knobs and the bezels onto the radio control shafts.
12. Connect the negative battery cable.

Except 1988-91 R/V Series

RECEIVER

See Figure 32

1. Disconnect the negative battery cable.
2. Remove the steering column filler panel and the ashtray.
3. Disconnect any electrical leads.
4. Remove the screw from the receiver bracket and then remove the nut from the center support. Remove the receiver.
5. Remove the nut on the bracket and remove the bracket and clip from the receiver.

To install:

6. Attach the clip and bracket to the receiver. Tighten the nut to 22 inch lbs. (3 Nm).
7. Attach the receiver to the center support and tighten that nut to 22 inch lbs. (3 Nm).
8. Tighten the screw on the bracket to 17 inch lbs. (2 Nm). Connect the electrical lead.
9. Install the ashtray and steering column panel.
10. Connect the battery cable.

CD/TAPE PLAYER

See Figure 33

1. Disconnect the negative battery cable.
2. Remove the accessory trim plate.
3. Disconnect any electrical leads.
4. Remove the mounting screws and pull out the unit.
5. Remove the bumper and the clip from the unit.

To install:

6. Attach the bumper and clip to the unit and then slide it back into the slot. Make sure that the bumper fits into the hole in the bracket.
7. Tighten the mounting screws to 17 inch lbs. (2 Nm).
8. Connect the electrical lead and install the trim plate.
9. Connect the battery cable.

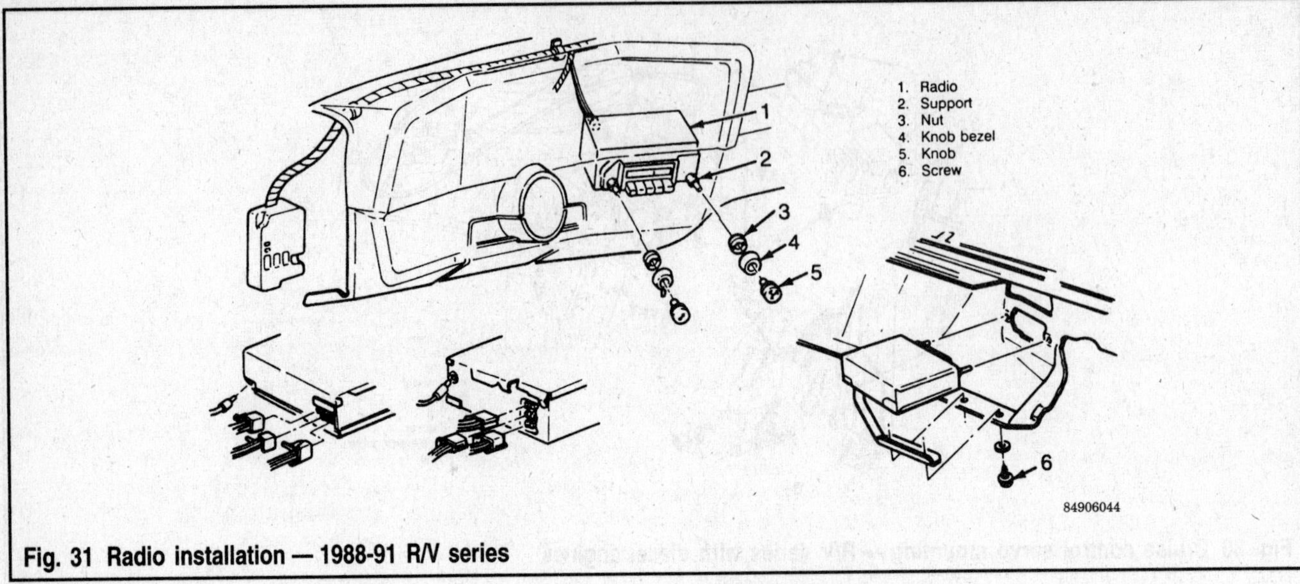

Fig. 31 Radio installation — 1988-91 R/V series

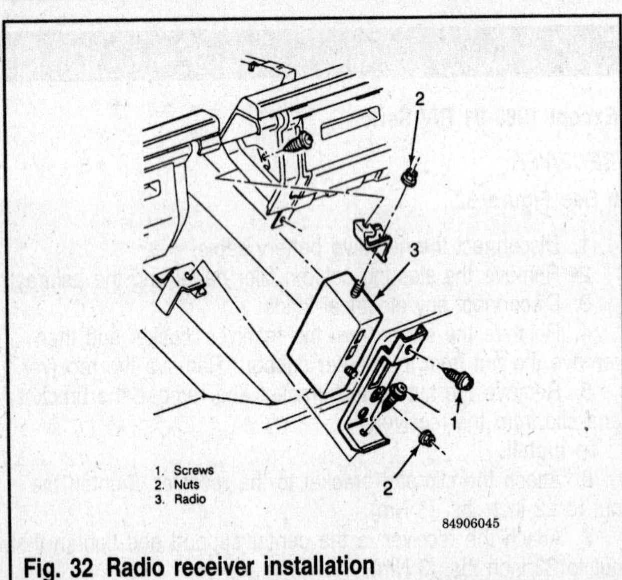

Fig. 32 Radio receiver installation

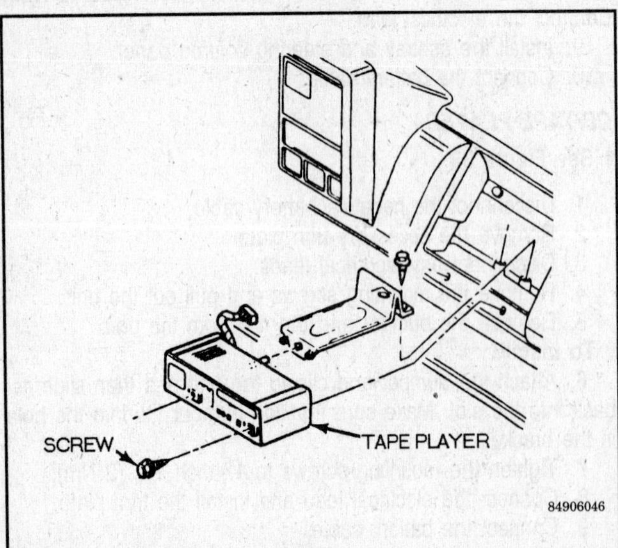

Fig. 33 Tape player installation

CONTROL HEAD

▶ See Figures 34, 35, 36, 37, 38 and 39

1. Disconnect the negative battery cable.
2. Remove the instrument cluster trim and bezel.
3. Remove the retainers or screws.
4. Pull the unit towards you just far enough to disconnect the wiring. Then, remove the unit.

To install:

5. Connect the wiring to the control head and then slide it into the hole. Fasten the retainers or snap the retainers into place.
6. Install the panel bezel.
7. Connect the battery cable.

Amplifier

REMOVAL & INSTALLATION

▶ See Figures 40 and 41

1. Disconnect the negative battery cable.
2. Locate the amplifier under the front seat, disconnect the wires and unbolt it from the bracket.
3. To install, mount the amplifier in the bracket and connect the wires.
4. Connect the battery cable.

Speakers

REMOVAL & INSTALLATION

1988-91 R/V Series

FRONT

▶ See Figure 42

1. Disconnect the negative battery cable.

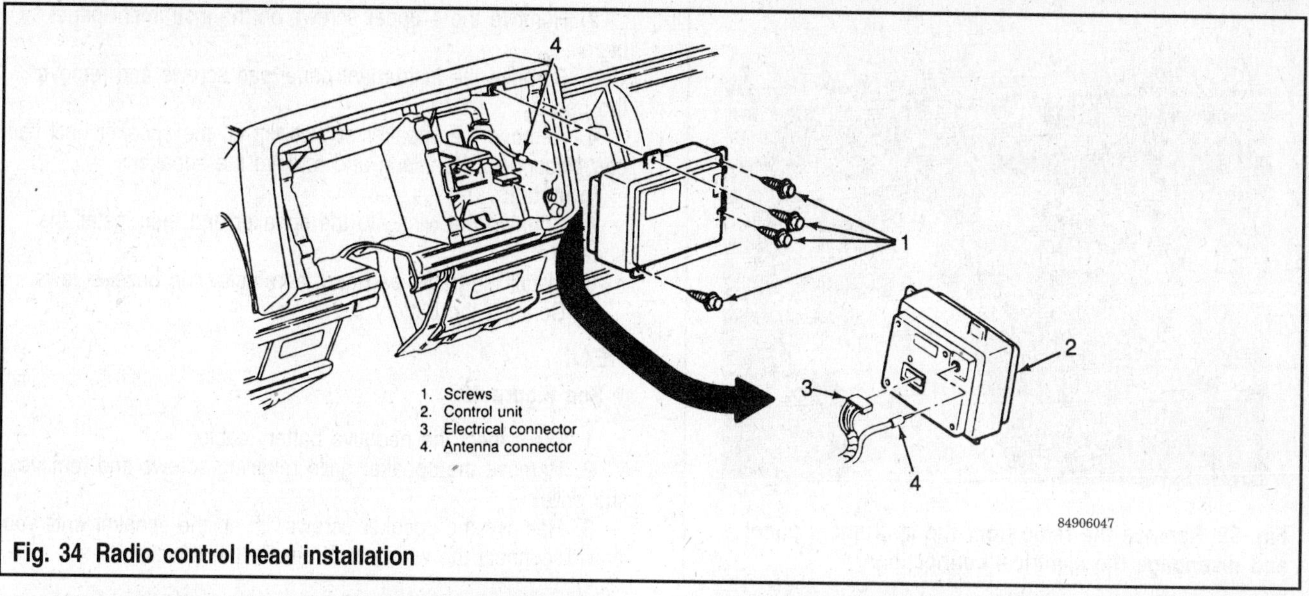

Fig. 34 Radio control head installation

Fig. 35 Remove the trim retaining screws

Fig. 37 Remove the audio component retaining fasteners

Fig. 36 Remove the trim plate

Fig. 38 Remove the tape player from the instrument panel and disengage the electrical connections

87986p05

Fig. 39 Remove the radio from the instrument panel and disengage the electrical connections

2. Remove the 4 upper screws on the instrument panel bezel.

3. Remove the instrument panel pad screws and remove the pad.

4. Remove the speaker screws, lift up the speaker until you can disconnect the wiring and remove the speaker.

To install:

5. Connect the wiring to the speaker and then install the speaker.

6. Install the panel pad and then install the bezel screws.

7. Connect the battery cable.

REAR

See Figure 43

1. Disconnect the negative battery cable.

2. Remove the speaker grille retaining screws and remove the grille.

3. Remove the speaker screws, lift up the speaker until you can disconnect the wiring and remove the speaker.

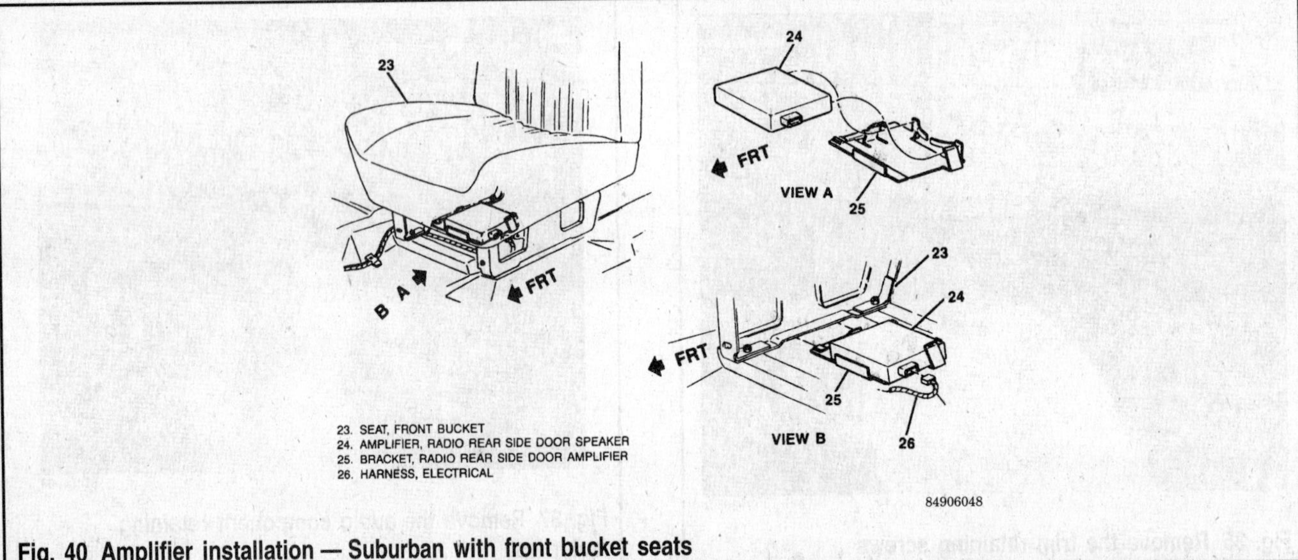

Fig. 40 Amplifier installation — Suburban with front bucket seats

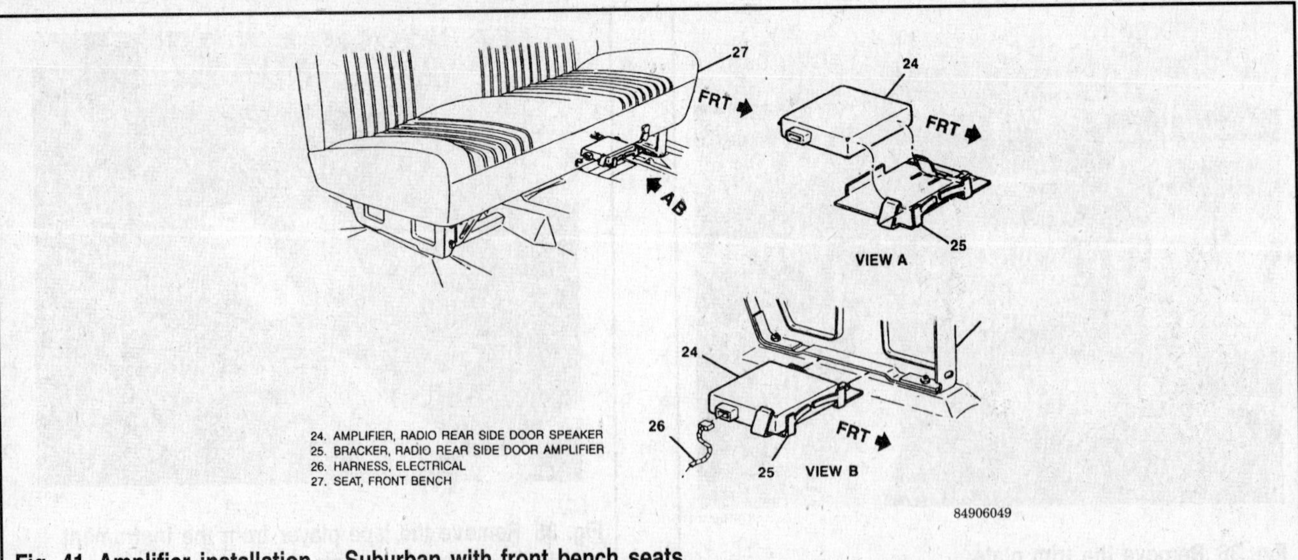

Fig. 41 Amplifier installation — Suburban with front bench seats

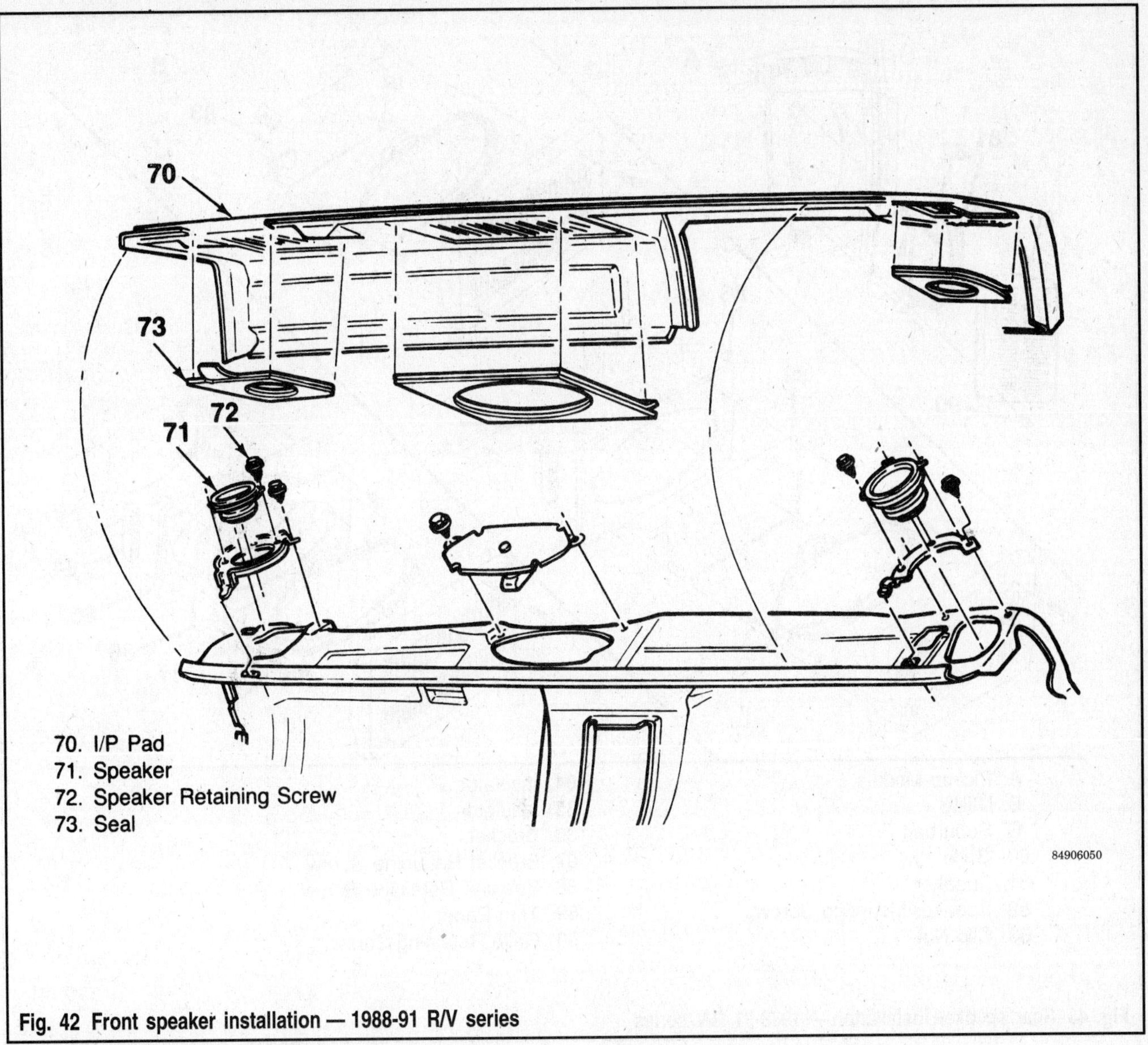

Fig. 42 Front speaker installation — 1988-91 R/V series

To install:

4. Connect the wiring to the speaker and then install the speaker.
5. Install the speaker grille and then install the screws.
6. Connect the battery cable.

1988-94 C/K and 1991-94 R/V Series

FRONT

➧ **See Figures 44, 45 and 46**

1. Disconnect the negative battery cable.
2. Remove the speaker grille retaining fasteners and remove the grille.
3. Remove the speaker screws, lift up the speaker until you can disconnect the wiring and remove the speaker.

To install:

4. Connect the wiring to the speaker and then install the speaker. Tighten the screws to 17 inch lbs. (2 Nm).
5. Install the speaker grille and then install the screws.
6. Connect the battery cable.

REAR

➧ **See Figures 47 and 48**

1. Disconnect the negative battery cable.
2. Remove the speaker grille or trim panel retaining screws and remove the grille.
3. Remove the speaker screws, lift up the speaker until you can disconnect the wiring and remove the speaker.

To install:

4. Connect the wiring to the speaker and then install the speaker. Tighten the screws to 17 inch lbs. (2 Nm).
5. Install the speaker grille or trim panel and then install the screws.
6. Connect the battery cable.

SIDE DOOR PANEL

➧ **See Figure 49**

1. Disconnect the negative battery cable.
2. Disconnect the speaker wiring.
3. Remove the side door map pocket.
4. Remove the speaker screws and remove the speaker.

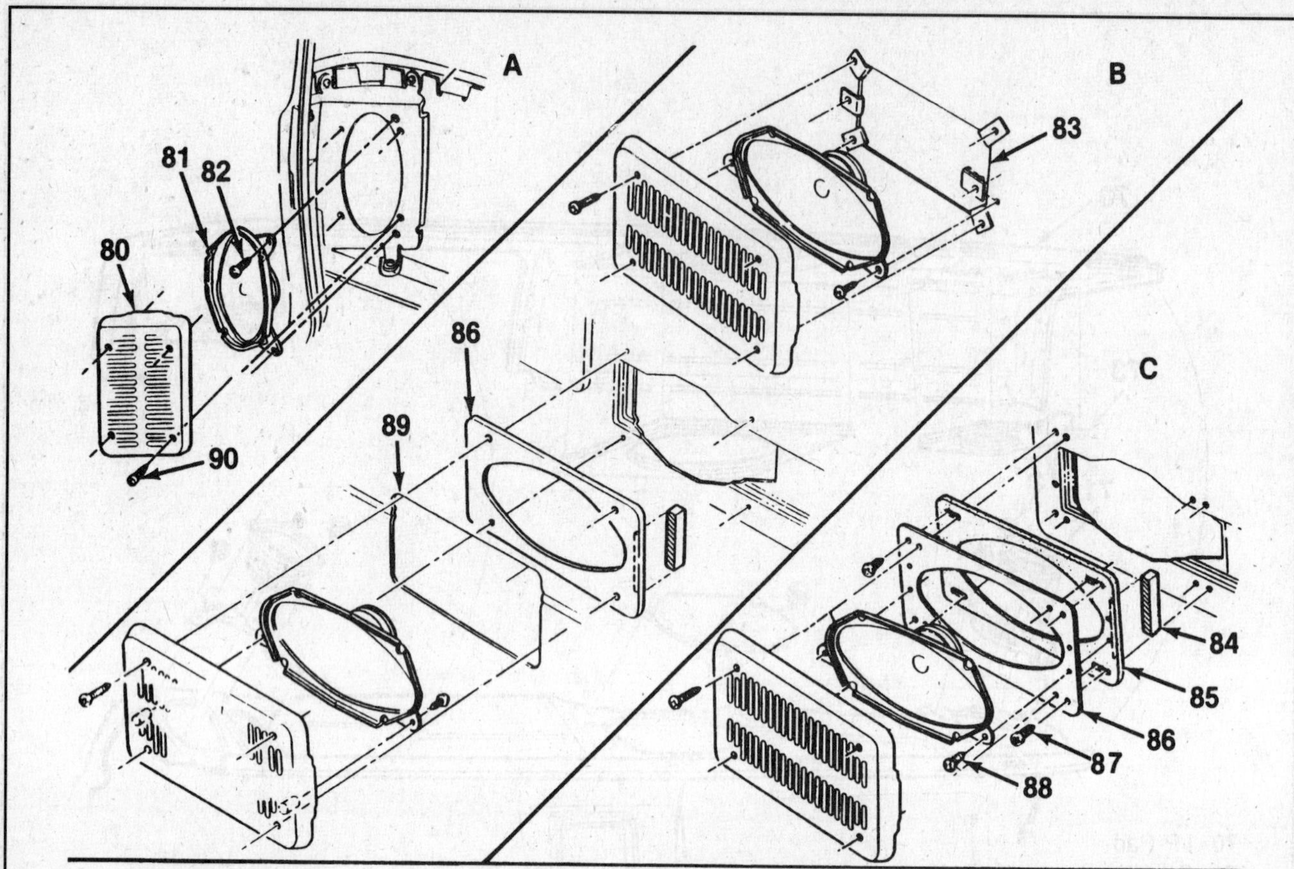

A. Pickup Models
B. Utility
C. Suburban
80. Grille
81. Speaker
82. Speaker Mounting Screw
83. Clip Nut
84. Insulator
85. Insulator
86. Bracket
87. Bracket Retaining Screw
88. Speaker Retaining Screw
89. Trim Panel
90. Grille Retaining Screw

84906051

Fig. 43 Rear speaker installation — 1988-91 R/V series

87986p06

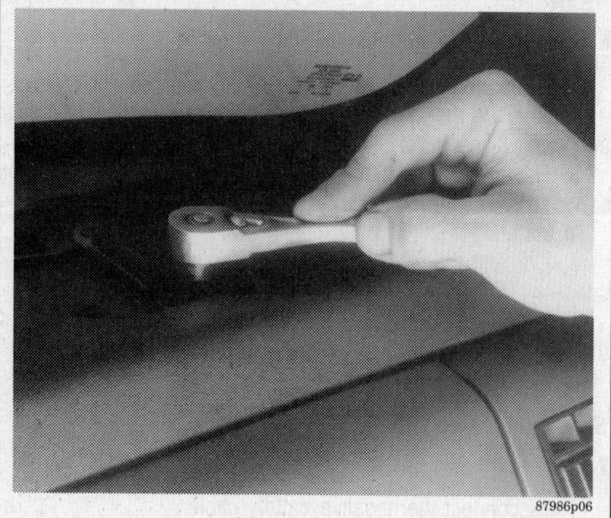

Fig. 44 Remove the speaker grille retaining fasteners

87986p07

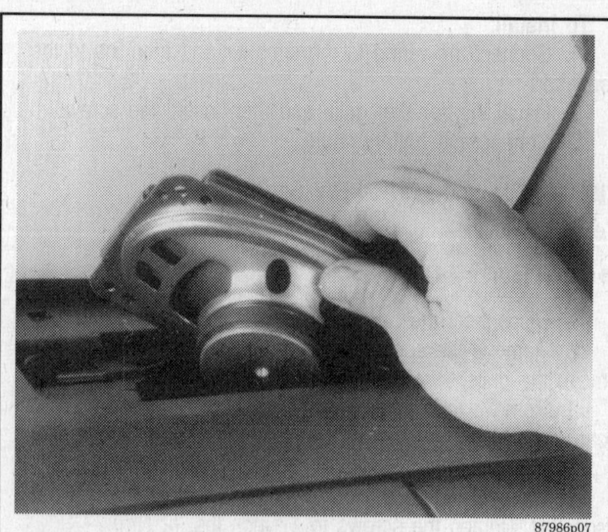

Fig. 45 Remove the speakers and disconnect the wiring

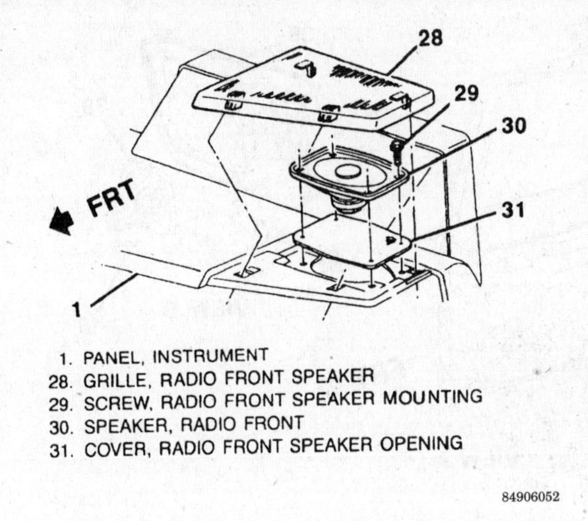

Fig. 46 Exploded view of the front speaker mounting

To install:

5. Connect the wiring to the speaker and then install the speaker. Tighten the screws to 14 inch lbs. (2 Nm).
6. Install the map pocket.
7. Connect the battery cable.

REAR OVERHEAD

See Figure 50

1. Disconnect the negative battery cable.
2. Remove the speaker grille or trim panel retaining screws and remove the grille.
3. Remove the speaker screws, lift up the speaker until you can disconnect the wiring and remove the speaker.

To install:

4. Connect the wiring to the speaker and then install the speaker. Tighten the screws to 17 inch lbs. (2 Nm).
5. Install the speaker grille or trim panel and then install the screws.
6. Connect the battery cable.

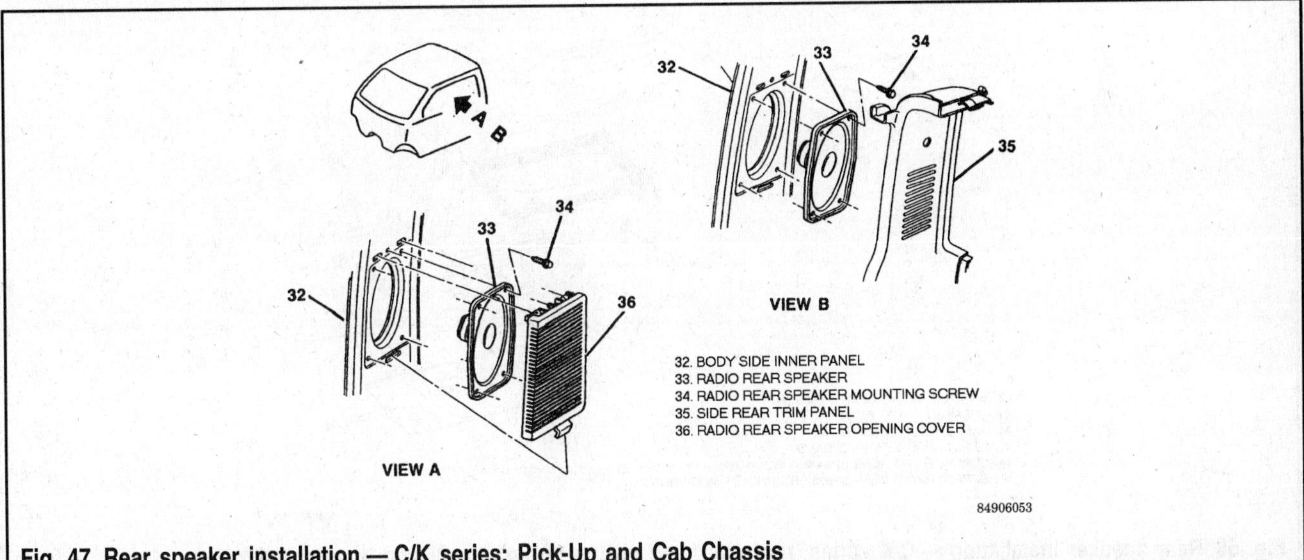

Fig. 47 Rear speaker installation — C/K series; Pick-Up and Cab Chassis

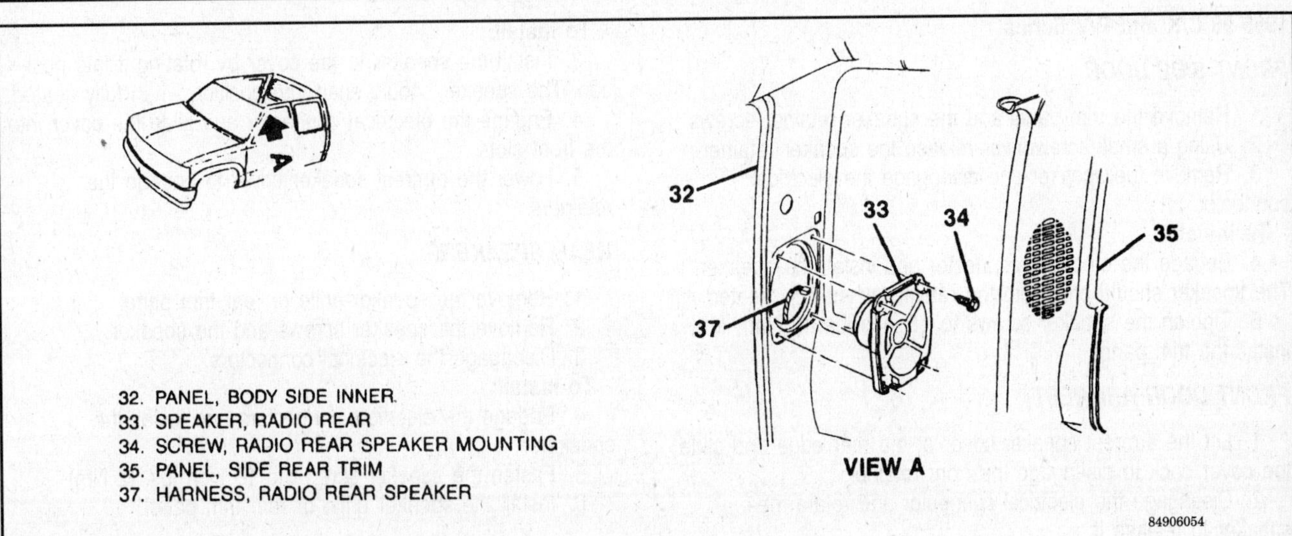

Fig. 48 Rear speaker installation — C/K series; Extended Cab and Crew Cab

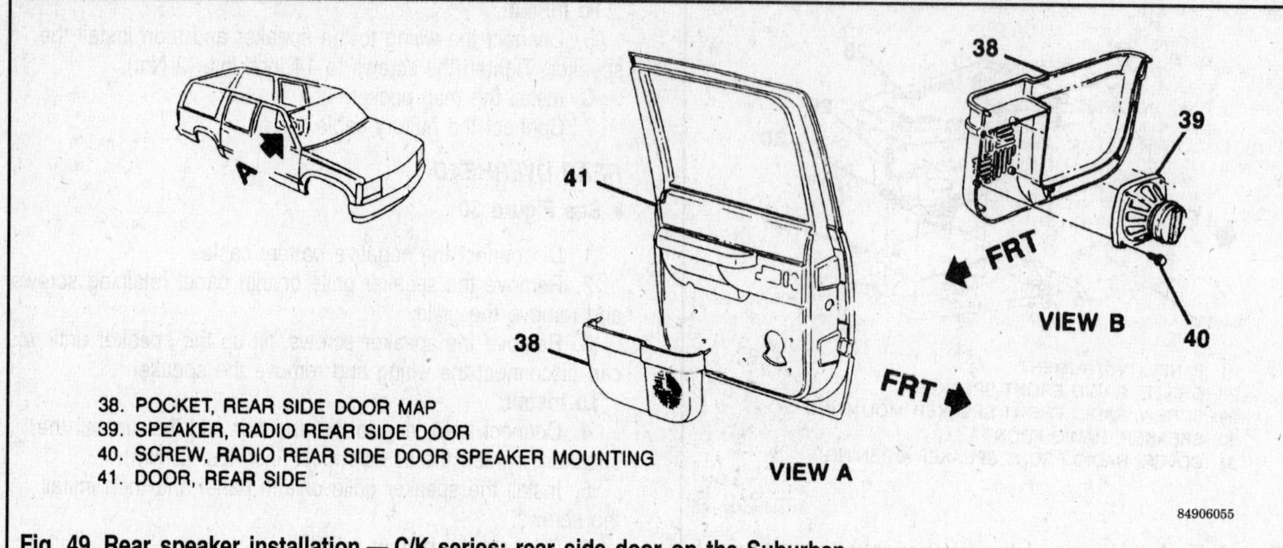

Fig. 49 Rear speaker installation — C/K series; rear side door on the Suburban

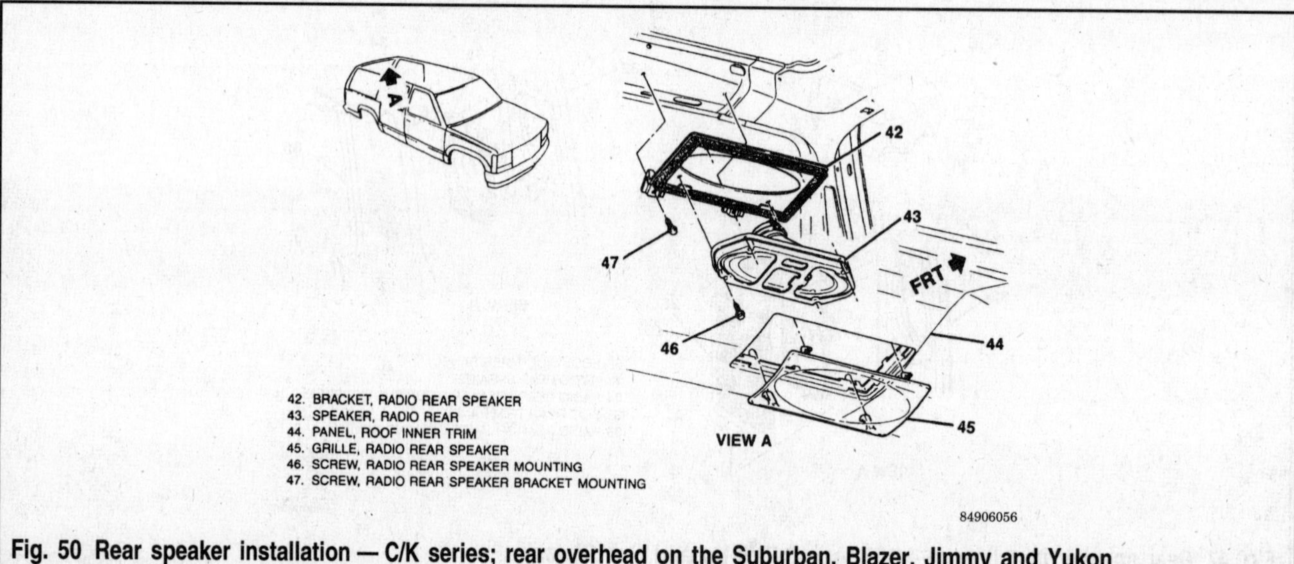

Fig. 50 Rear speaker installation — C/K series; rear overhead on the Suburban, Blazer, Jimmy and Yukon

1995-96 C/K and R/V Series

FRONT SIDE DOOR

1. Remove the trim panel and the speaker retainer screws.
2. Using a small screwdriver release the speaker retainer.
3. Remove the speaker and disengage the electrical connector.

To install:

4. Engage the electrical connector and install the speaker. The speaker should snap into the retainer when fully seated.
5. Tighten the speaker screws to 18 inch lbs. (2 Nm), and install the trim panel.

FRONT DOOR ARMREST

1. Lift the armrest speaker cover at the rear edge and slide the cover back to disengage the front retainer.
2. Disengage the electrical connector and rotate the speaker to release it.

To install:

3. Install the speaker to the cover by rotating it into position. The speaker should snap into position when fully seated.
4. Engage the electrical connector and slide the cover into the front slots.
5. Lower the armrest speaker cover to engage the retainers.

REAR SPEAKERS

1. Remove the speaker grille or rear trim panel.
2. Remove the speaker screws and the speaker.
3. Disengage the electrical connectors.

To install:

4. Engage the electrical connectors and install the speakers.
5. Fasten the speaker screws to 18 inch lbs. (2 Nm).
6. Install the speaker grille or rear trim panel.

SIDE DOOR

See Figures 51 and 52

1. Remove the speaker grille and retainers.
2. Remove the speaker and disengage the electrical connectors.

To install:

3. Engage the electrical connectors and install the speakers.
4. Install the speaker retainers and grille.

REAR OVERHEAD SPEAKERS

See Figure 53

1. Remove the speaker grille.
2. Remove the roof inner trim panel, if necessary.
3. Remove the speaker screws and the speaker.
4. Disengage the electrical connectors, as necessary.

To install:

5. Engage any electrical connectors that were removed.
6. Install the speaker and speaker screws. Tighten the screws to 18 inch lbs. (2 Nm).
7. Install the inner roof trim panel, if removed.
8. Install the speaker grille.

Antenna

REMOVAL & INSTALLATION

See Figure 54

1. Remove the antenna mast, nut and bezel.
2. Disconnect the antenna cable from the extension cable.
3. Remove the screws and antenna cable assembly.

To install:

4. Install the antenna cable assembly and the screws. Tighten the screws to 58 inch lbs. (5 Nm).
5. Connect the antenna cable to the extension cable.

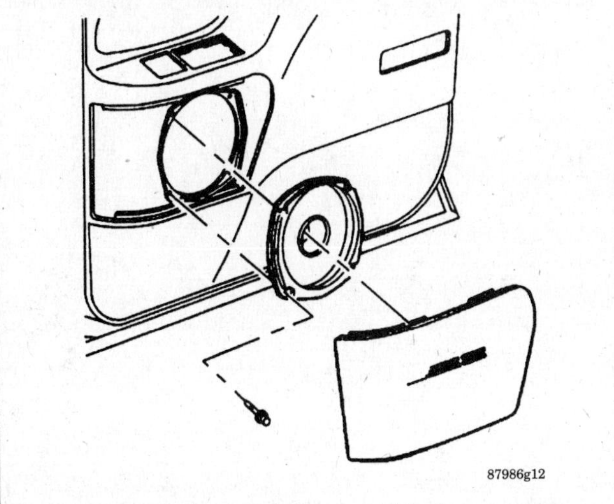

Fig. 51 Exploded view of the rear side door speaker assembly (Suburban models)

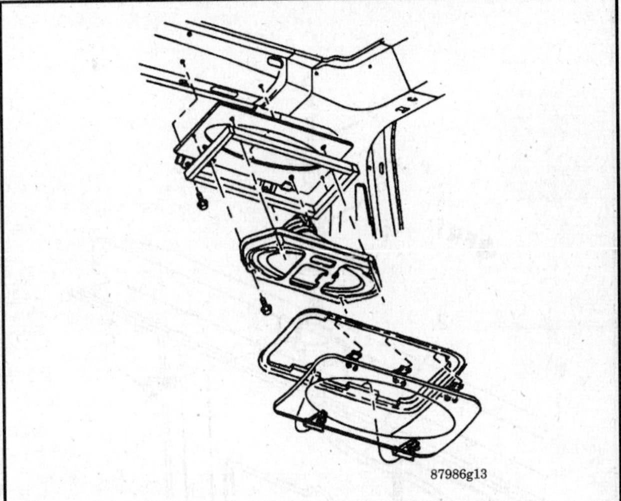

Fig. 53 Exploded view of the rear overhead speaker assembly (Suburban and utility models)

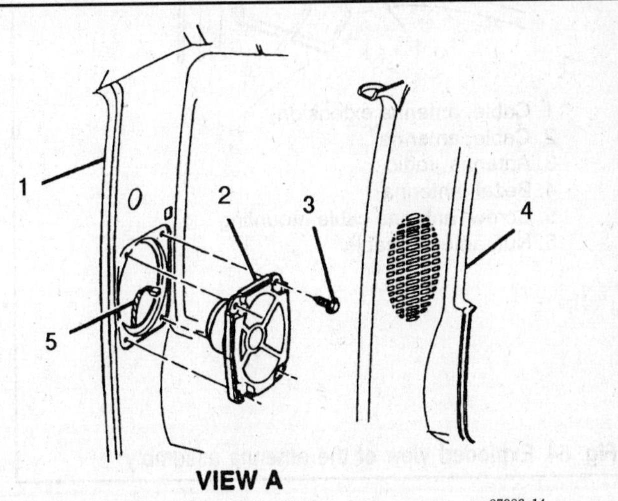

1. Panel, body side inner
2. Speaker, radio rear
3. Screw, radio rear speaker mounting
4. Panel, side rear trim
5. Harness, radio rear speaker

Fig. 52 Exploded view of the rear speaker assembly (Extended crew cab/cab models)

6. Install the bezel and nut. Tighten the nut to 58 inch lbs. (5 Nm).
7. Install the antenna mast.

Extension Cable

See Figure 55

1. Roll out the instrument panel and disconnect the extension cable from the radio.
2. Remove the extension cable from the HVAC duct.
3. Disconnect the extension cable from the antenna.

To install:

4. Connect the extension cable to the radio and to the routing around the HVAC duct.
5. Connect the extension cable to the antenna.
6. Install the instrument panel.

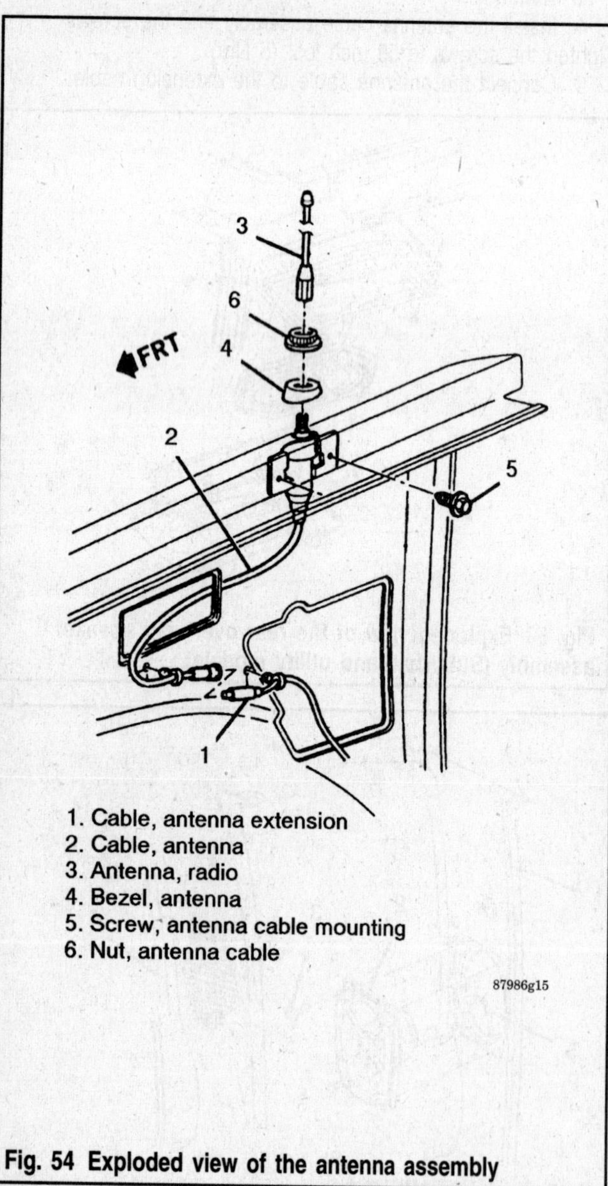

Fig. 54 Exploded view of the antenna assembly

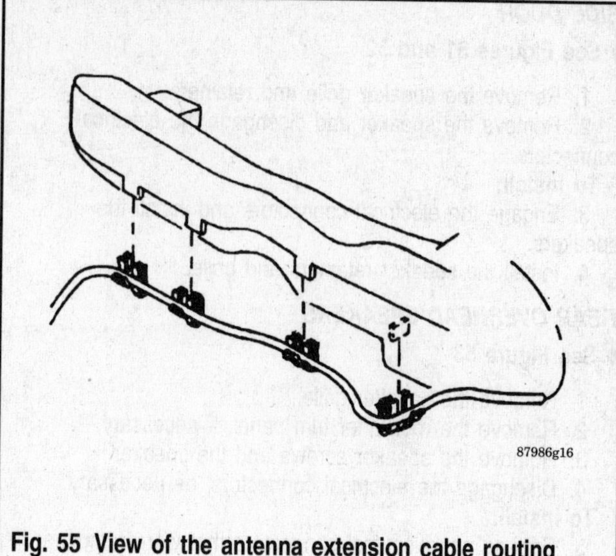

Fig. 55 View of the antenna extension cable routing

WINDSHIELD WIPERS AND WASHERS

Windshield Wiper Blade and Arm

REMOVAL & INSTALLATION

Wiper Blade

1. Insert a small prytool into the blade retaining slot over the spring.
2. Pivot the prytool so the blade tip presses downward on the retainer spring, releasing the pin of the wiper arm.
3. Remove the wiper blade.

To install:

4. Install the wiper blade by by pressing the pin of the wiper assembly into the blade retainer until the blade is engaged.

Wiper Arm

See Figure 56

1. Disconnect the washer hose.
2. Lift the wiper arm from the glass and pull the retaining latch.
3. Remove the wiper arm assembly.

To install:

4. Install the wiper arm onto the wiper motor driveshaft so that it will rest in the proper position when the wipers are turned off.
5. Lift the wiper arm extension and push in the retaining latch.
6. Connect the washer hose.

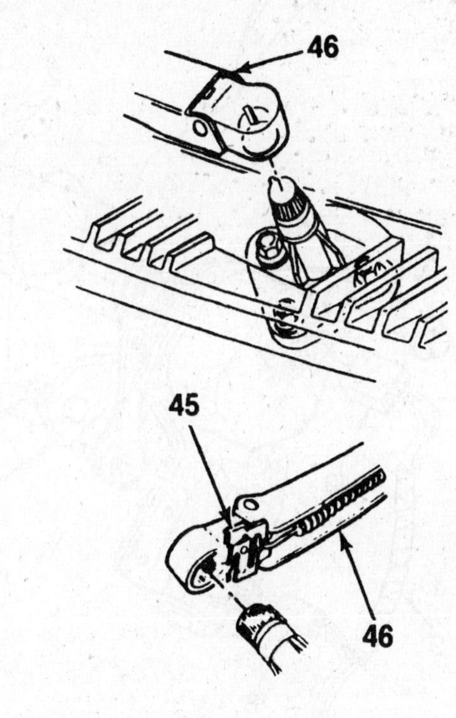

Fig. 56 Exploded view of the wiper arm mounting

Windshield Wiper Motor

REMOVAL & INSTALLATION

1988-91 R/V Series

See Figure 57

1. Make sure the wipers are parked.
2. Disconnect the negative battery cable.
3. Disconnect the wiring harness at the wiper motor and the hoses from the washer pump.
4. Reach down through the access hole in the plenum and loosen the wiper drive rod attaching screws. Remove the drive rod from the wiper motor crank arm.
5. Remove the wiper motor attaching screws and the motor assembly and linkage.
6. To install, reverse the removal procedure.

➡Lubricate the wiper motor crank arm pivot before reinstallation.

Except 1988-91 R/V Series

See Figures 58, 59, 60, 61, 62 and 63

1. Disconnect the negative battery cable.
2. Pivot the wiper arm away from the windshield, move the latch to the open position and lift the wiper arm off of the driveshaft.
3. Remove the cowl vent grille.
4. Disengage the wiring connector from the motor.
5. Remove the drive link-to-crank arm fasteners and slide the links from the arm. Do not remove the arm!
6. Remove the motor mounting bolts and lift the motor out.

To install:

7. Install the motor and tighten the bolts to 62 inch lbs. (7 Nm).
8. Install the drive link-to-crank arm fasteners and slide the links onto the arm.
9. Engage the wiring connector into the motor.
10. Install the cowl vent grille.
11. Install the wiper arm and move the latch to the closed position.
12. Connect the negative battery cable.

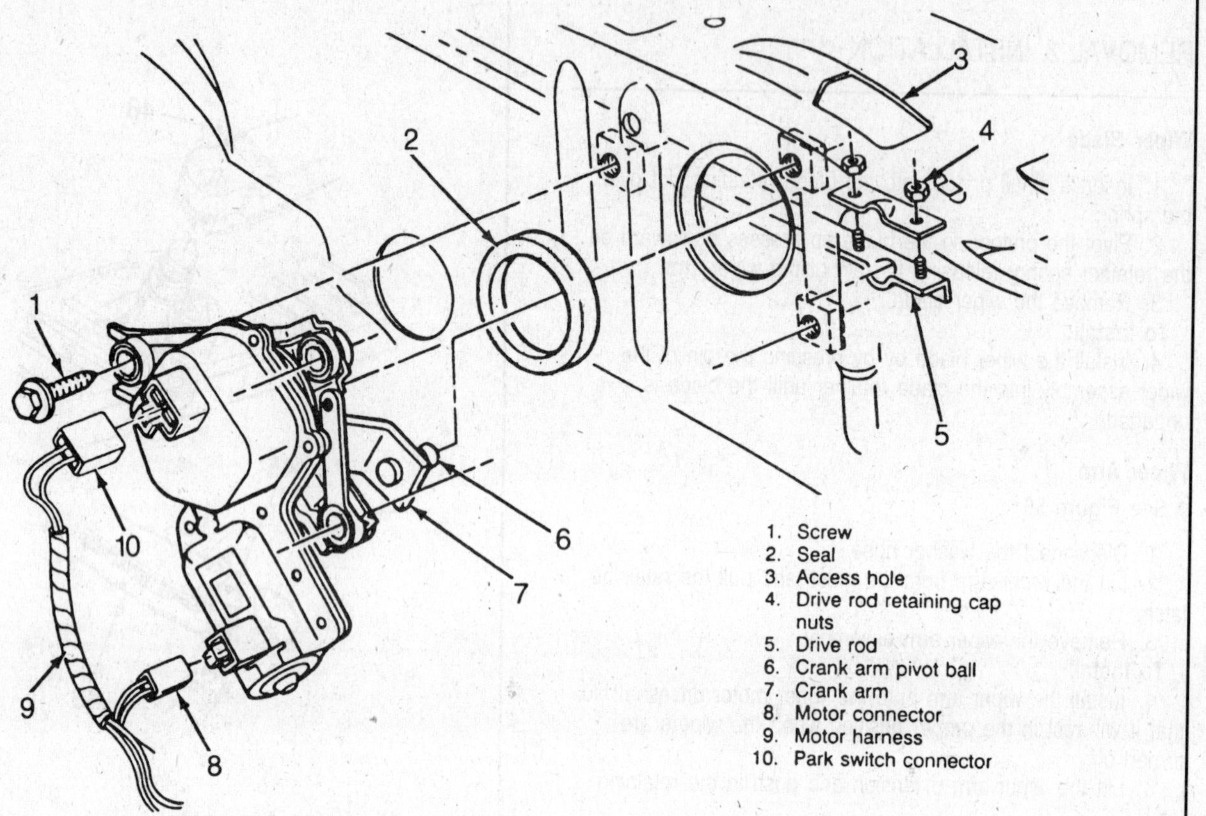

1. Screw
2. Seal
3. Access hole
4. Drive rod retaining cap nuts
5. Drive rod
6. Crank arm pivot ball
7. Crank arm
8. Motor connector
9. Motor harness
10. Park switch connector

84906058

Fig. 57 Windshield wiper motor — 1988-91 R/V series

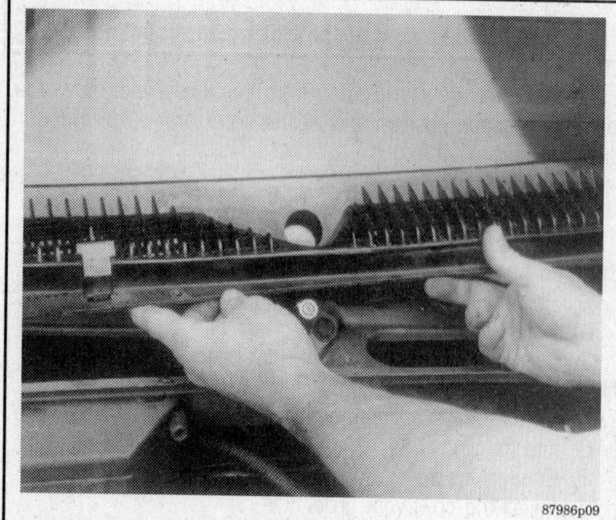

87986p09

Fig. 58 Remove the cowl vent grille

87986p10

Fig. 59 Disengage the wiring connector from the motor

87986p12

Fig. 60 Remove the drive link-to-crank arm fasteners

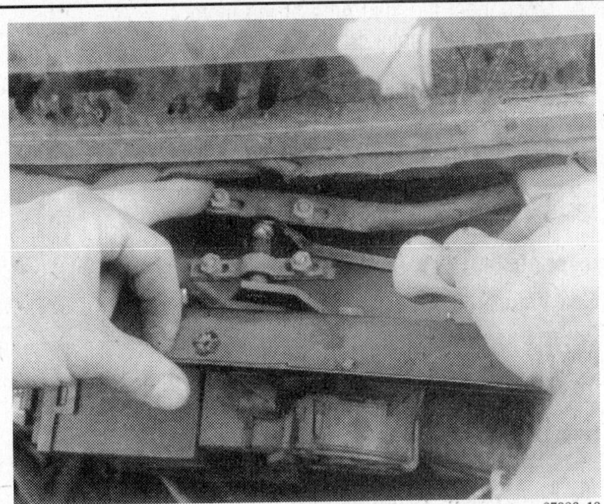
87986p13

Fig. 61 Slide the links from the arm

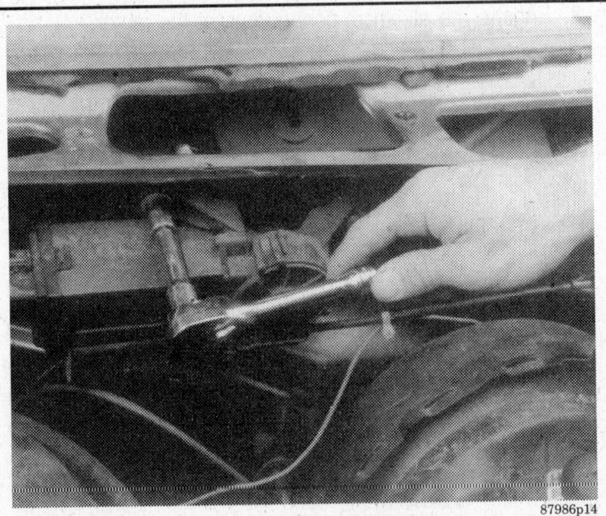
87986p14

Fig. 62 Remove the motor mounting bolts

87986p15

Fig. 63 Remove the motor from the vehicle

Rear Window Wiper Motor

REMOVAL & INSTALLATION

➧ **See Figure 64**

1. Disconnect the negative battery cable.
2. Remove the rear wiper arm.
3. Remove the motor cover and disconnect the wiring.
4. Remove the mounting bolts and nuts and lift out the motor.

To install:

5. Install the motor and tighten the bolts and nut to 53 inch lbs. (6 Nm).
6. Connect the wiring and install the cover.
7. Install the wiper blade and connect the battery cable.

Wiper Linkage

REMOVAL & INSTALLATION

1988-91 R/V Series

The linkage is removed with the motor. Please refer to the wiper motor removal and installation procedure.

Except 1988-91 R/V Series

1. Disconnect the negative battery cable.
2. Pivot the wiper arm away from the windshield, move the latch to the open position and lift the wiper arm off of the driveshaft.
3. Remove the cowl vent grille.
4. Remove the drive link-to-crank arm screws and slide the links from the arm.
5. Remove the linkage mounting bolts and lift the linkage out.

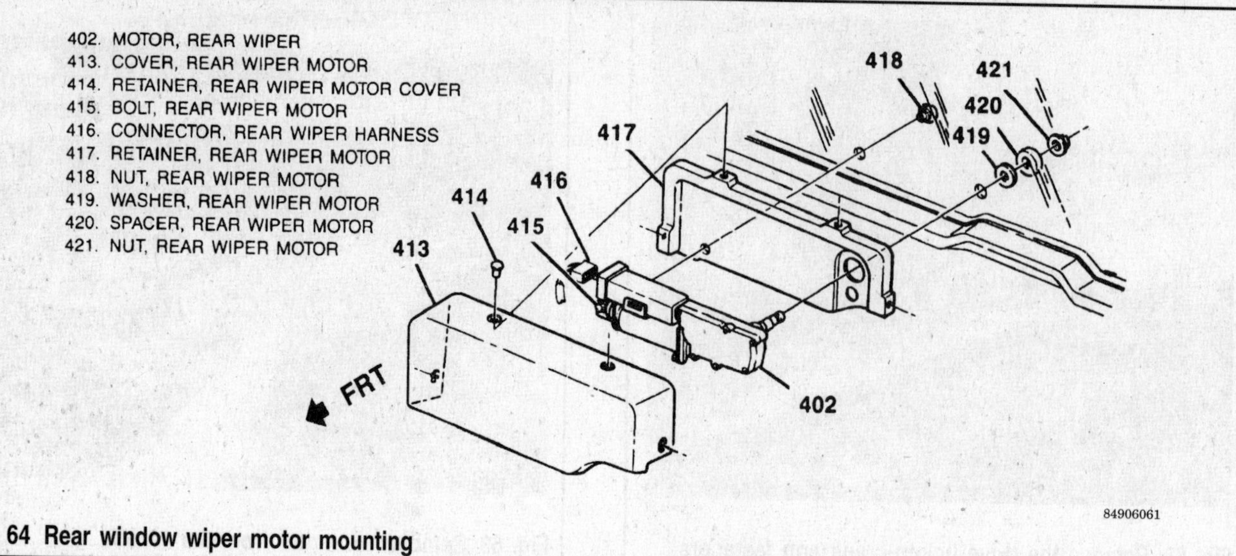

Fig. 64 Rear window wiper motor mounting

To install:

6. Position the linkage and tighten the mounting bolts to 62 inch lbs. (7 Nm).
7. Slide the links onto the arm. Install the drive link-to-crank arm screws and tighten them to 44 inch lbs. (5 Nm).
8. Install the cowl vent grille.
9. Install the wiper arm on the driveshaft and move the latch to the closed position.
10. Connect the negative battery cable.

Delay Module

REMOVAL & INSTALLATION

1988-91 R/V Series

1. Disconnect the negative battery cable.
2. Remove the steering column shrouds.
3. Unplug the harness connectors.
4. Slide the module off the bracket.
5. Installation is the reverse of removal.

Except 1988-91 R/V Series

1. Disconnect the negative battery cable.
2. Unplug the connector from the module.
3. Remove the module-to-motor screw.
4. Installation is the reverse of removal.

Windshield Washer Motor

REMOVAL & INSTALLATION

1988-91 R/V Series

1. Disconnect the negative battery cable.
2. Remove the 2 attaching screws and remove the reservoir.
3. Unplug the wiring at the motor.
4. Disconnect the fluid tube at the motor.
5. Remove the motor from the reservoir.

To install:

6. Install the motor into the reservoir.
7. Connect the fluid tube at the motor.
8. Connect the wiring at the motor.
9. Install the reservoir.
10. Connect the negative battery cable.

Except 1988-91 R/V Series

➧ See Figure 65

1. Disconnect the negative battery cable.
2. Disengage the wiring harness connector(s) from the pump.
3. Disconnect the hose(s) from the pump.
4. Remove the attaching fasteners and lift off the reservoir.
5. Remove the pump from the reservoir.

To install:

6. Install the motor into the reservoir.
7. Connect the hose(s) at the pump.
8. Engage the electrical connections at the motor.

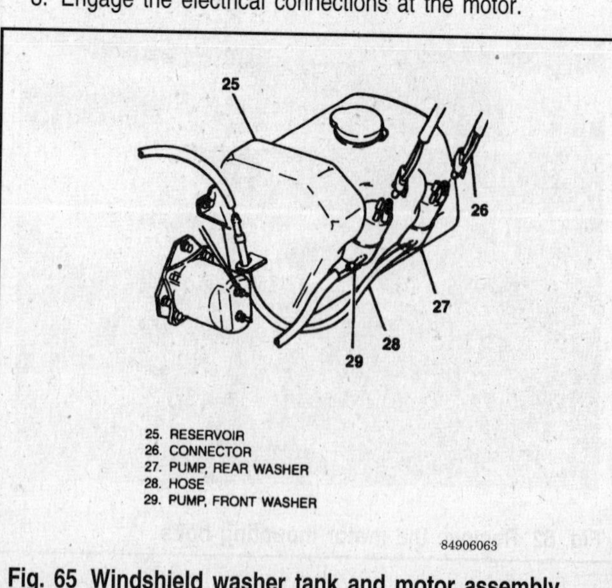

Fig. 65 Windshield washer tank and motor assembly

9. Install the reservoir.
10. Connect the negative battery cable.

INSTRUMENTS AND SWITCHES

Instrument Cluster

REMOVAL & INSTALLATION

1988-91 R/V Series

See Figure 66

1. Disconnect the negative battery cable.
2. Remove the headlamp switch control knob.
3. Remove the radio control knobs.
4. Remove the steering column cover (4 screws).
5. Remove eight screws and remove instrument bezel.
6. Reach under the dash, depress the speedometer cable tang, and remove the cable.
7. Pull instrument cluster out just far enough to disconnect all lines and wires.
8. Remove the cluster.

To install:

9. Install the cluster.
10. Connect all lines and wires.
11. Depress the speedometer cable tang, and reattach the cable.
12. Install the instrument bezel.
13. Install the steering column cover.
14. Press on the radio control knobs.
15. Install the headlamp switch control knob.

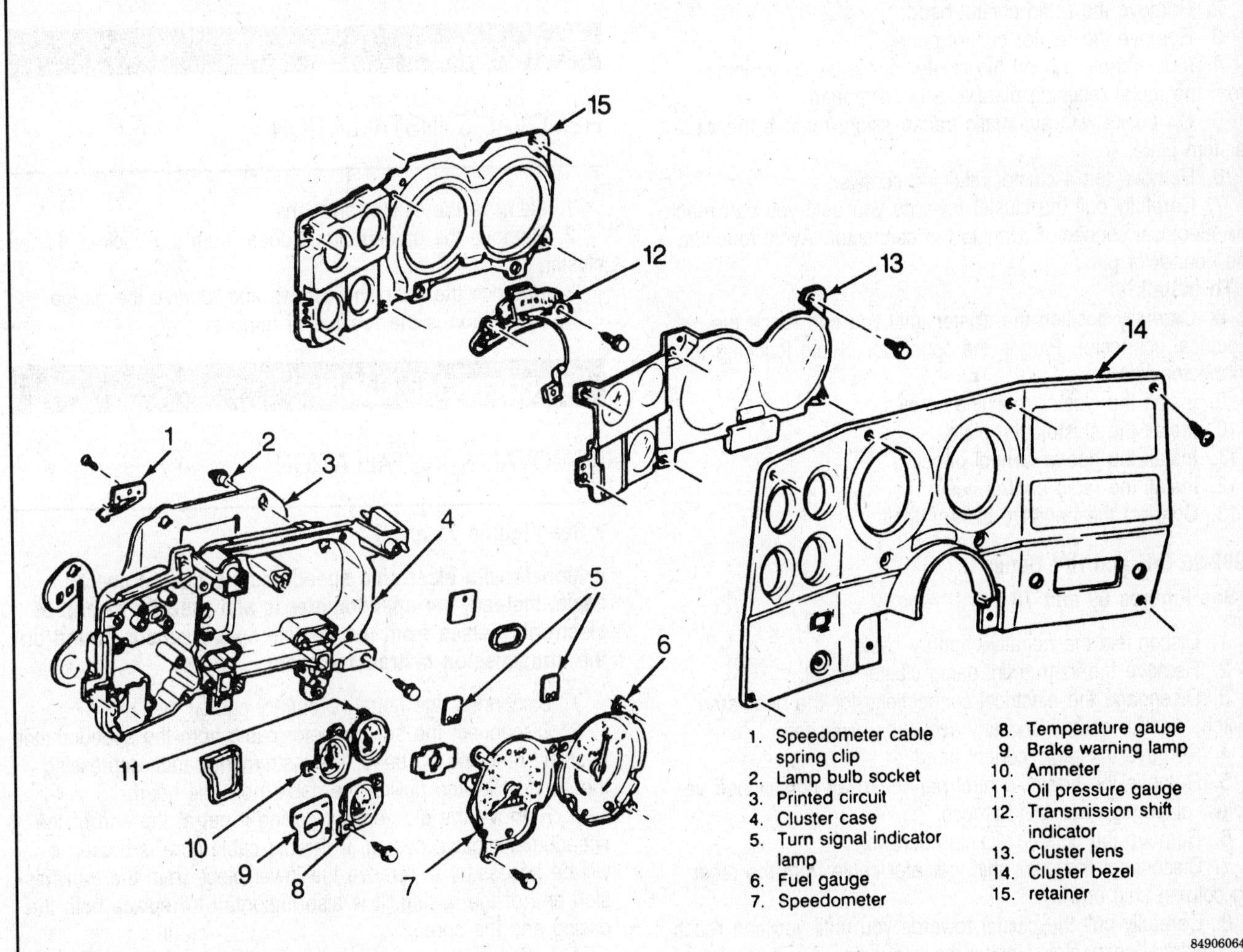

Fig. 66 Instrument cluster assembly — 1988-91 R/V series

16. Connect the negative battery cable.

WARNING

When replacing cluster components there are several steps which should be taken to avoid damage to Electrostatic Discharge Sensitive (EDS) parts. They are:

- Do not open the package until it is time to install the part
- Avoid touching the electrical terminals on the part
- Before removing the part from the package, ground the package to a known good ground on the truck
- Always touch a known good ground before handling the part. You should ground yourself occasionally while installing the part, especially after sliding across the seat, sitting down or walking a short distance

1988-91 C/K Series

See Figures 67 and 68

1. Disconnect the negative battery cable.
2. Remove the radio control head.
3. Remove the heater control panel.
4. Momentarily ground the cluster assembly by jumping from the metal retaining plate to a good ground.
5. On trucks with automatic transmission, remove the cluster trim plate.
6. Remove the 4 cluster retaining screws.
7. Carefully pull the cluster towards you until you can reach the electrical connector. Unplug the connector. Avoid touching the connector pins.

To install:

8. Carefully position the cluster until you can reach the electrical connector. Plug in the connector. Avoid touching the connector pins.
9. Install the cluster retaining screws.
10. Install the cluster trim plate.
11. Install the heater control panel.
12. Install the radio control head.
13. Connect the negative battery cable.

1992-96 C/K and R/V Series

See Figures 69 and 70

1. Disconnect the negative battery cable.
2. Remove the instrument panel cluster bezel.
3. Disengage the electrical connections for the headlamp switch, dimmer control and any accessory switches.
4. Remove the radio control head.
5. Remove the heater control panel. On air conditioned vehicles, disengage the A/C harness.
6. Remove the cluster retaining screws.
7. Disconnect the gear shift indicator cable from the steering column shift bowl.
8. Carefully pull the cluster towards you until you can reach the electrical connector. Unplug the connector. Avoid touching the connector pins. Turn the bulb assembly 1/2 turn to the left to remove.

To install:

9. Install the bulb assembly. Carefully position the cluster until you can reach the electrical connector. Plug in the connector. Avoid touching the connector pins.
10. Install the cluster retaining screws.
11. Connect the gear shift indicator cable.
12. Install the heater control panel and A/C harness (if removed).
13. Install the radio control head and any engage any electrical connections that were disengaged.
14. Install the bezel.
15. Connect the negative battery cable.

Speedometer

REMOVAL & INSTALLATION

1. Remove the cluster and lens.
2. Remove the speedometer mounting screws.
3. Carefully pull the speedometer from the circuit board. Avoid touching any of the circuit board pins.
4. Installation is the reverse of removal.

Tachometer

REMOVAL & INSTALLATION

1. Remove the cluster and lens.
2. Remove the printed circuit board from the back of the cluster.
3. Remove the attaching screws and remove the gauge.
4. Installation is the reverse of removal.

Speedometer Cable

REMOVAL & INSTALLATION

See Figures 71 and 72

Models with electronic speedometers do not use a cable. Instead, the speedometer is activated by means of electronic pulses from the vehicle speed sensor (found on the transmission or transfer case).

1. Disconnect the negative battery cable.
2. Disconnect the speedometer cable from the speedometer head by reaching up under the instrument panel, depressing the spring clip and pulling the cable from the head.
3. Remove the old core by pulling it out at the end of the speedometer cable casing. If the old cable core is broken it will be necessary to remove the lower piece from the transmission end of the casing. It is also important to replace both the casing and the core.
4. Lubricate the entire length of cable core with speedometer cable lubricant.
5. Install the new cable by reversing the steps above. Use care not to kink the cable core during installation.

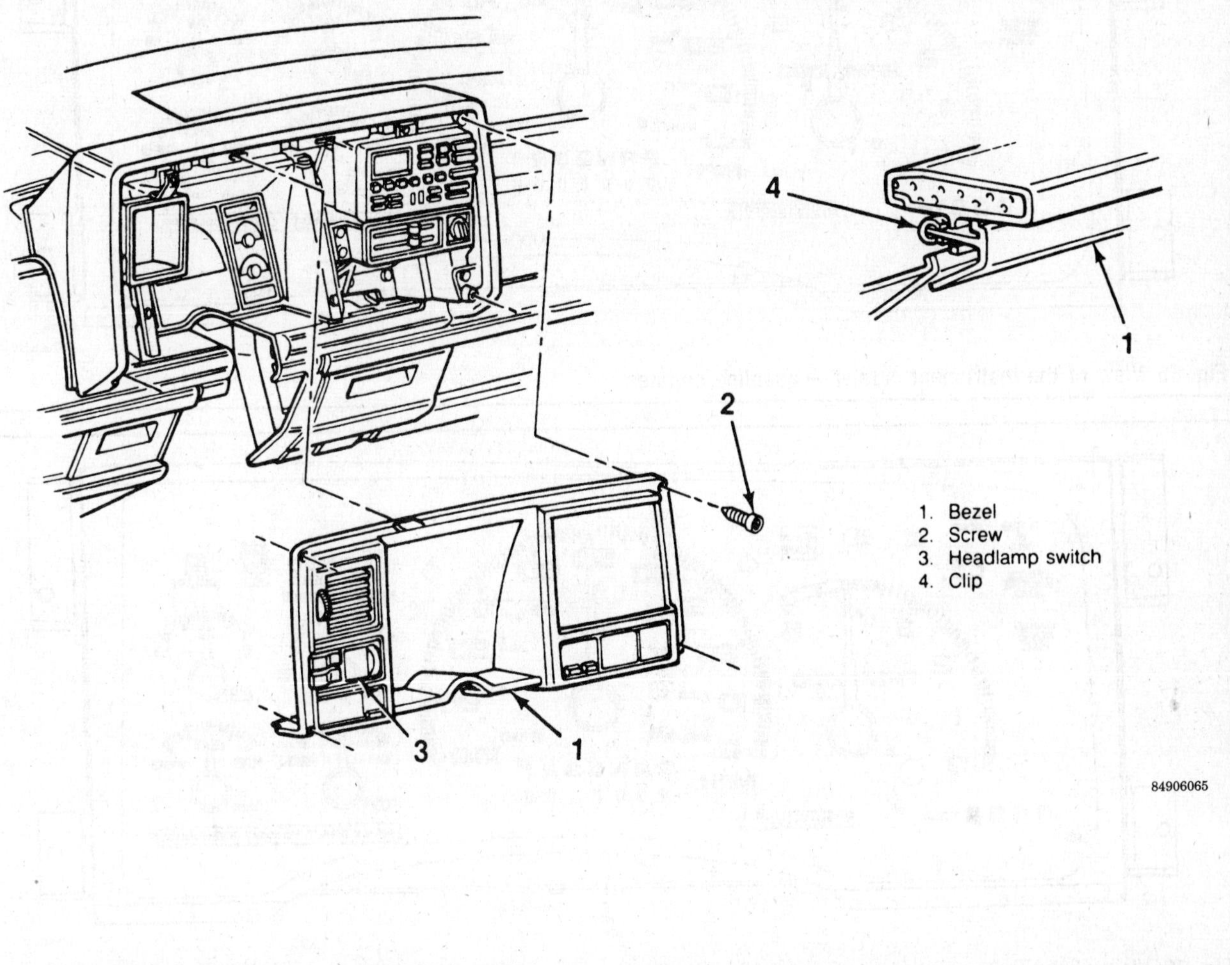

1. Bezel
2. Screw
3. Headlamp switch
4. Clip

84906065

Fig. 67 Instrument cluster bezel — 1988-91 C/K series

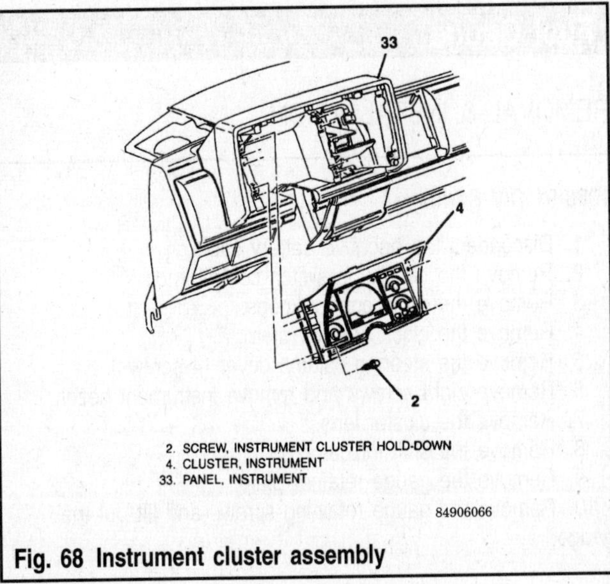

Fig. 68 Instrument cluster assembly

Oil Pressure Gauge

REMOVAL & INSTALLATION

1988-91 R/V Series

1. Disconnect the negative battery cable.
2. Remove the headlamp switch control knob.
3. Remove the radio control knobs.
4. Remove the clock adjuster stem.
5. Remove the steering column cover (4 screws).
6. Remove eight screws and remove instrument bezel.
7. Remove the cluster lens.
8. Remove the shift indicator.
9. Remove the gauge retainer plate.
10. Remove the gauge retaining screws and lift out the gauge.

To install:

11. Install the gauge and tighten the retaining screws.

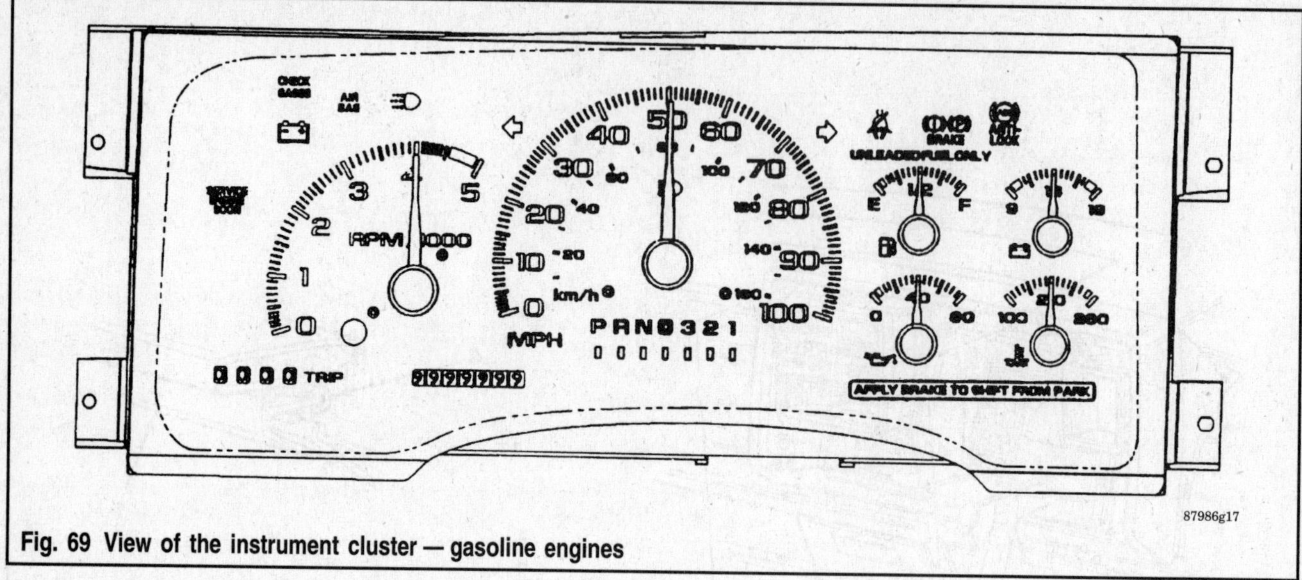

Fig. 69 View of the instrument cluster — gasoline engines

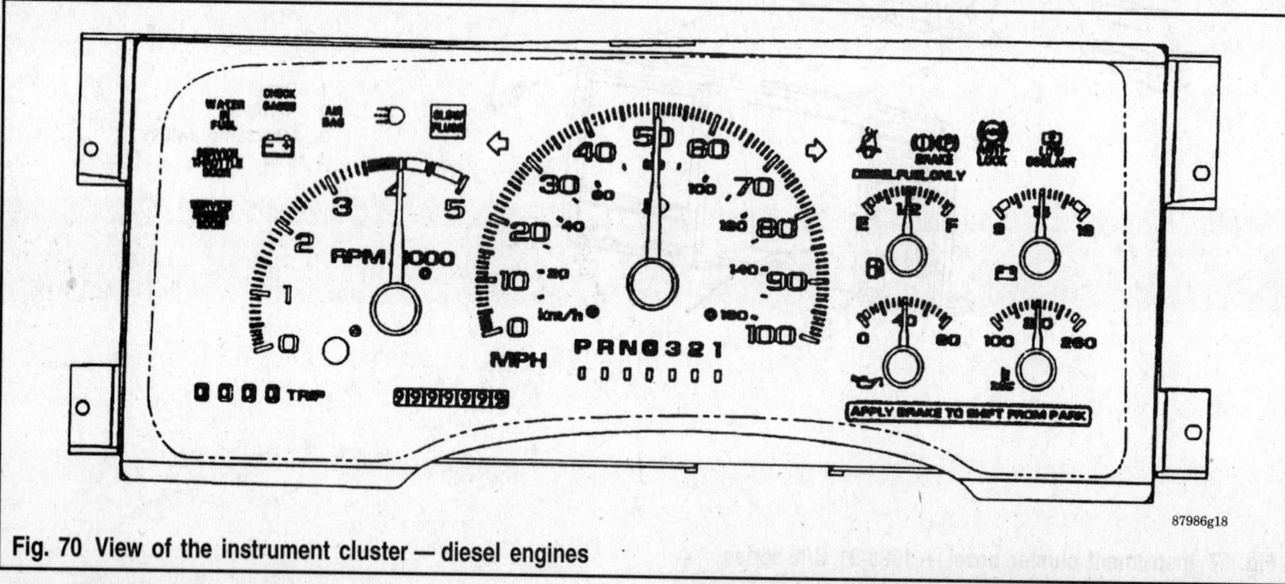

Fig. 70 View of the instrument cluster — diesel engines

12. Install the gauge retainer plate.
13. Connect the shift indicator.
14. Install the cluster lens.
15. Install instrument bezel.
16. Install the steering column cover (4 screws).
17. Insert the clock adjuster stem.
18. Press the radio control knobs and the headlamp switch control knob onto their shafts.
19. Connect the negative battery cable.

Except 1988-91 R/V Series

1. Remove the cluster.
2. Remove the gauge mounting screws.
3. Carefully pull the gauge from the circuit board. Avoid touching any of the circuit board pins.
4. Installation is the reverse of removal.

Fuel Gauge

REMOVAL & INSTALLATION

1988-91 R/V Series

1. Disconnect the negative battery cable.
2. Remove the headlamp switch control knob.
3. Remove the radio control knobs.
4. Remove the clock adjuster stem.
5. Remove the steering column cover (4 screws).
6. Remove eight screws and remove instrument bezel.
7. Remove the cluster lens.
8. Remove the shift indicator.
9. Remove the gauge retainer plate.
10. Remove the gauge retaining screws and lift out the gauge.

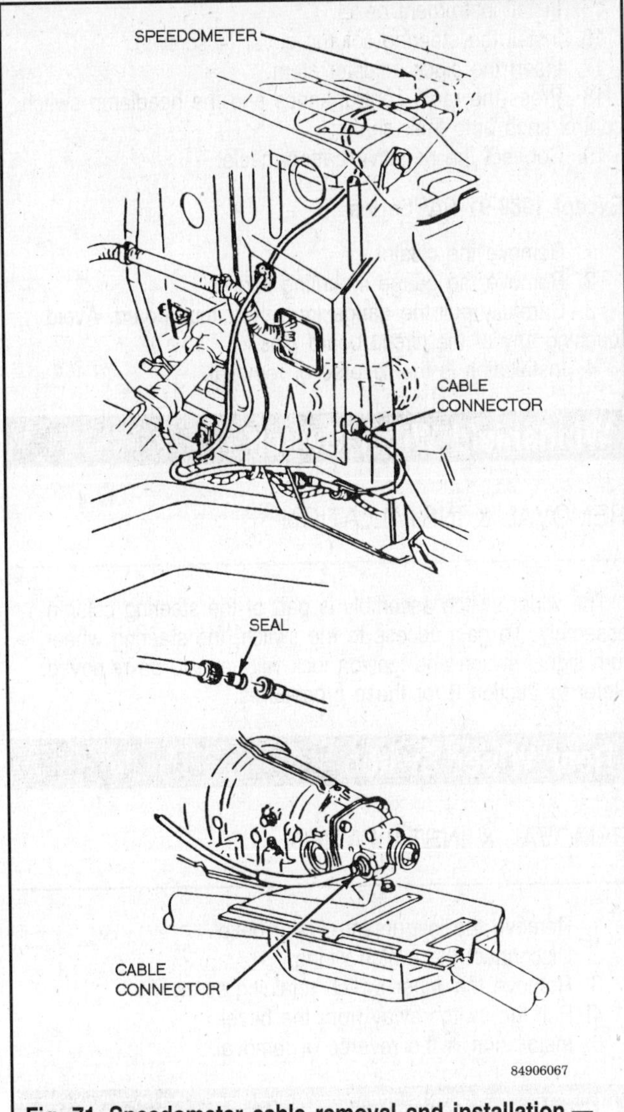

Fig. 71 Speedometer cable removal and installation — 2WD models

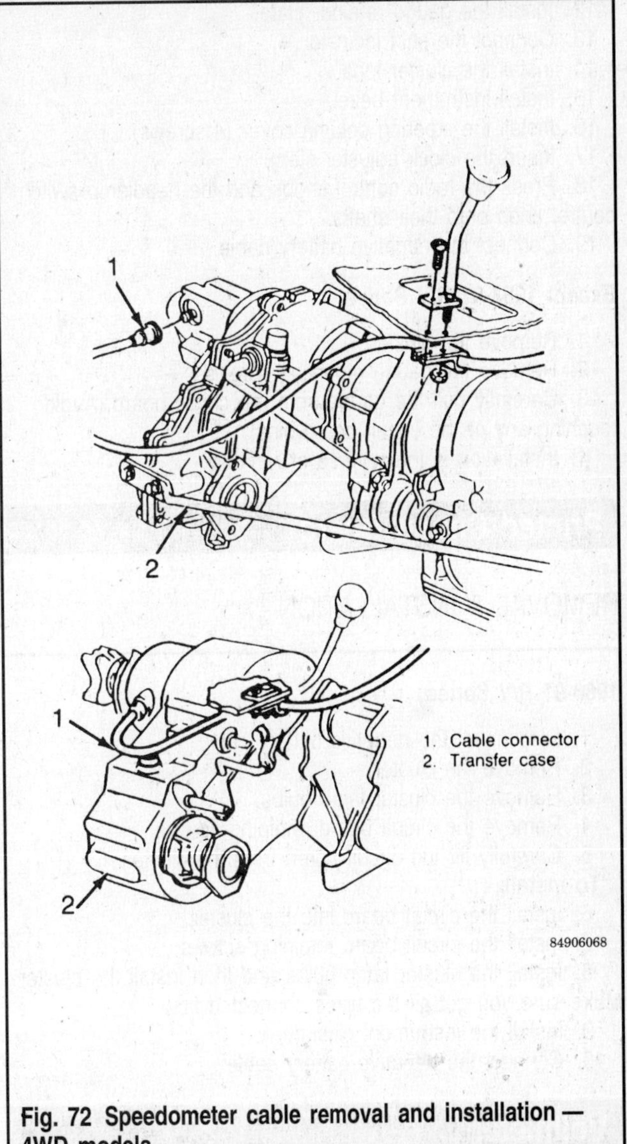

Fig. 72 Speedometer cable removal and installation — 4WD models

To install:

11. Install the gauge and tighten the retaining screws.
12. Install the gauge retainer plate.
13. Connect the shift indicator.
14. Install the cluster lens.
15. Install instrument bezel.
16. Install the steering column cover (4 screws).
17. Insert the clock adjuster stem.
18. Press the radio control knobs and the headlamp switch control knob onto their shafts.
19. Connect the negative battery cable.

Except 1988-91 R/V Series

1. Remove the cluster.
2. Remove the gauge mounting screws.
3. Carefully pull the gauge from the circuit board. Avoid touching any of the circuit board pins.
4. Installation is the reverse of removal.

Temperature Gauge

REMOVAL & INSTALLATION

1988-91 R/V Series

1. Disconnect the negative battery cable.
2. Remove the headlamp switch control knob.
3. Remove the radio control knobs.
4. Remove the clock adjuster stem.
5. Remove the steering column cover (4 screws).
6. Remove eight screws and remove instrument bezel.
7. Remove the cluster lens.
8. Remove the shift indicator.
9. Remove the gauge retainer plate.
10. Remove the gauge retaining screws and lift out the gauge.

To install:

11. Install the gauge and tighten the retaining screws.

12. Install the gauge retainer plate.
13. Connect the shift indicator.
14. Install the cluster lens.
15. Install instrument bezel.
16. Install the steering column cover (4 screws).
17. Insert the clock adjuster stem.
18. Press the radio control knobs and the headlamp switch control knob onto their shafts.
19. Connect the negative battery cable.

Except 1988-91 R/V Series

1. Remove the cluster.
2. Remove the gauge mounting screws.
3. Carefully pull the gauge from the circuit board. Avoid touching any of the circuit board pins.
4. Installation is the reverse of removal.

Printed Circuit Board

REMOVAL & INSTALLATION

1988-91 R/V Series

1. Disconnect the negative battery cable.
2. Remove the cluster.
3. Remove the cluster lamp bulbs.
4. Remove the circuit board retaining screws.
5. Carefully lift the circuit board from the cluster.

To install:

6. Install the circuit board into the cluster.
7. Install the circuit board retaining screws.
8. Install the cluster lamp bulbs and then install the cluster. Make sure you get all the wires connected first!
9. Install the instrument cluster.
10. Connect the negative battery cable.

Voltmeter

REMOVAL & INSTALLATION

1988-91 R/V Series

1. Disconnect the negative battery cable.
2. Remove the headlamp switch control knob.
3. Remove the radio control knobs.
4. Remove the clock adjuster stem.
5. Remove the steering column cover (4 screws).
6. Remove eight screws and remove instrument bezel.
7. Remove the cluster lens.
8. Remove the shift indicator.
9. Remove the gauge retainer plate.
10. Remove the gauge retaining screws and lift out the gauge.

To install:

11. Install the gauge and tighten the retaining screws.
12. Install the gauge retainer plate.
13. Connect the shift indicator.
14. Install the cluster lens.
15. Install instrument bezel.
16. Install the steering column cover (4 screws).
17. Insert the clock adjuster stem.
18. Press the radio control knobs and the headlamp switch control knob onto their shafts.
19. Connect the negative battery cable.

Except 1988-91 R/V Series

1. Remove the cluster.
2. Remove the gauge mounting screws.
3. Carefully pull the gauge from the circuit board. Avoid touching any of the circuit board pins.
4. Installation is the reverse of removal.

Windshield Wiper Switch

REMOVAL & INSTALLATION

The wiper switch assembly is part of the steering column assembly. To gain access to the switch, the steering wheel, turn signal switch and ignition lock will have to be removed. Refer to Section 8 for these procedures.

Rear Wiper Switch

REMOVAL & INSTALLATION

1. Remove the instrument cluster bezel.
2. Disconnect the switch wiring.
3. Remove the wiper switch retaining screws.
4. Pull the switch away from the bezel.
5. Installation is the reverse of removal.

Headlight Switch

REMOVAL & INSTALLATION

1988-91 R/V Series

➧ See Figure 73

1. Disconnect negative battery cable.
2. Reaching up behind instrument cluster, depress shaft retaining button and remove switch knob and rod.
3. Remove instrument cluster bezel screws on left end. Pull out on bezel and hold switch nut with a wrench.
4. Disconnect multiple wiring connectors at switch terminals.
5. Remove switch by rotating while holding switch nut.
6. Installation is the reverse of removal.

Except 1988-91 R/V Series

➧ See Figures 74 and 75

1. Remove the instrument cluster bezel.
2. Disconnect the switch wiring.
3. Remove the headlamp switch retaining screws.
4. Pull the switch away from the bezel.

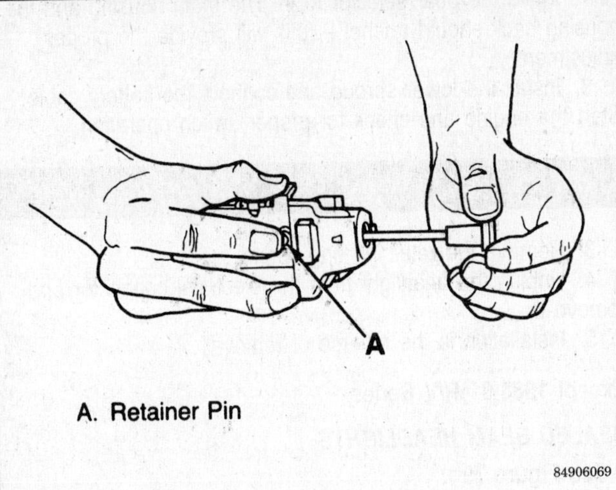

Fig. 73 Removing the headlight switch knob — R/V series

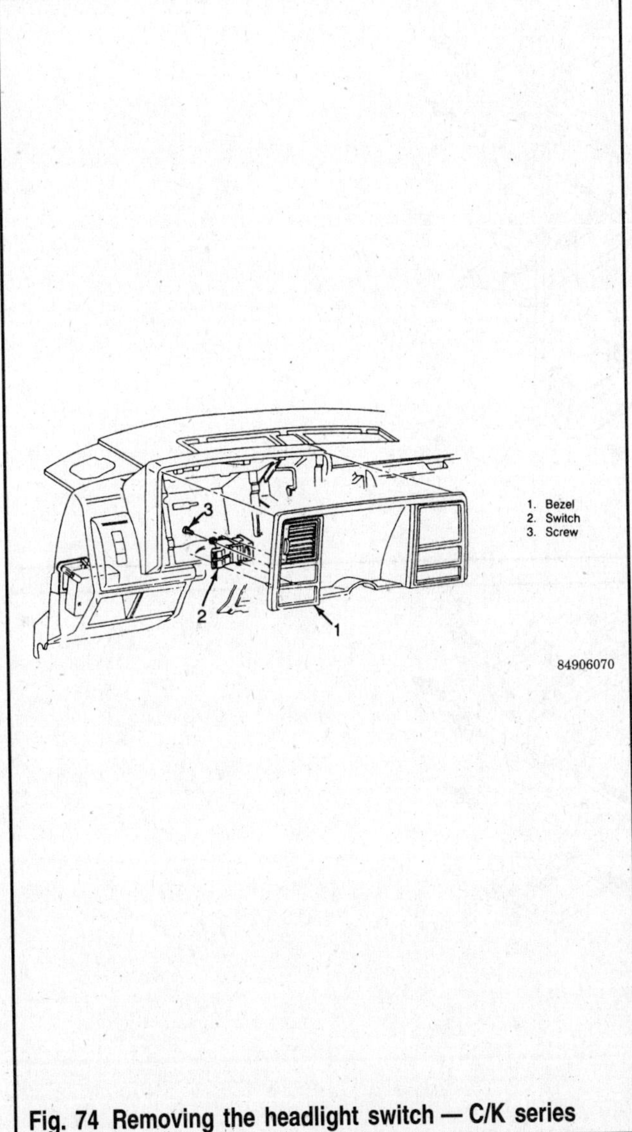

Fig. 74 Removing the headlight switch — C/K series

5. Installation is the reverse of removal.

Back-Up Light Switch

REMOVAL & INSTALLATION

➧ See Figure 76

➡The following procedures are for automatic transmission equipped vehicles only. For back-up light switch removal and installation on trucks with manual transmissions, please refer to Section 7.

1. Disconnect the negative battery cable.
2. Remove the lower steering column shroud and disconnect the wiring at the switch.
3. Pull the switch out from the steering column.

To install:

4. Align the actuator on the switch with the holes in the shifter tube.

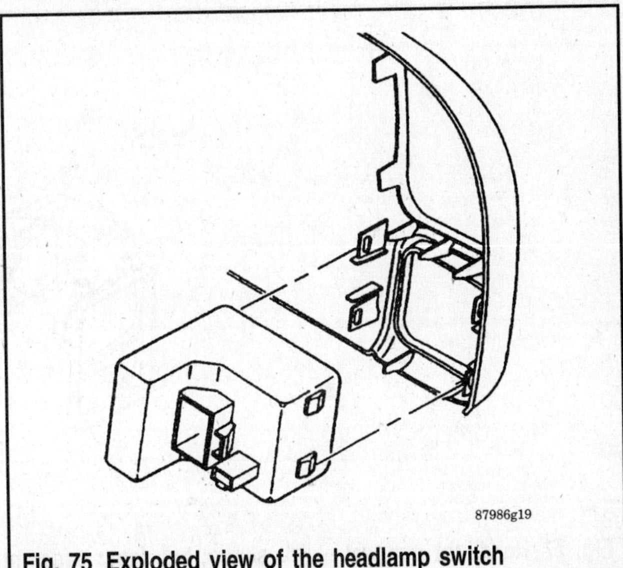

Fig. 75 Exploded view of the headlamp switch

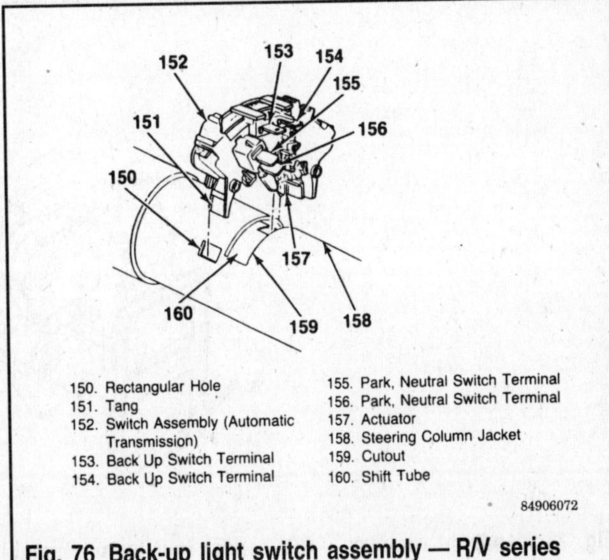

Fig. 76 Back-up light switch assembly — R/V series

5. Set the parking brake and move the gear selector to **N**. Press down on the front of the switch until the tangs snap into the rectangular holes in the steering column housing.
6. Connect the wiring.
7. Move the gear selector to **P**. The main housing and the housing back should ratchet — this will provide the proper adjustment.
8. Install the lower shroud and connect the battery cable. Start the engine and check for proper switch operation.

LIGHTING

Headlights

REMOVAL & INSTALLATION

1988-91 R/V Series

➧ See Figures 77 and 78

1. Remove the headlight bezel.
2. Remove the retaining ring screws and the retaining ring. Do not disturb the adjusting screws.
3. Remove the retaining ring spring.
4. Unplug the headlight from the electrical connector and remove it.
5. Installation is the reverse of removal.

Except 1988-91 R/V Series

SEALED BEAM HEADLIGHTS

➧ See Figure 79

1. Remove the headlight bezel.
2. Remove the retaining ring screws and the retaining ring. Do not disturb the adjusting screws.

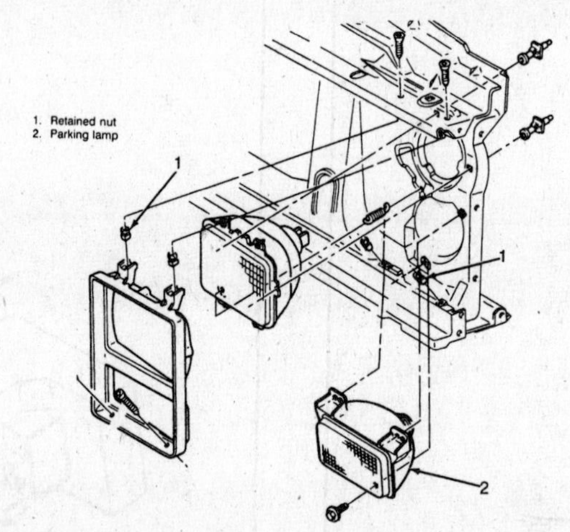

Fig. 77 Headlight removal — R/V series; two lamp assembly

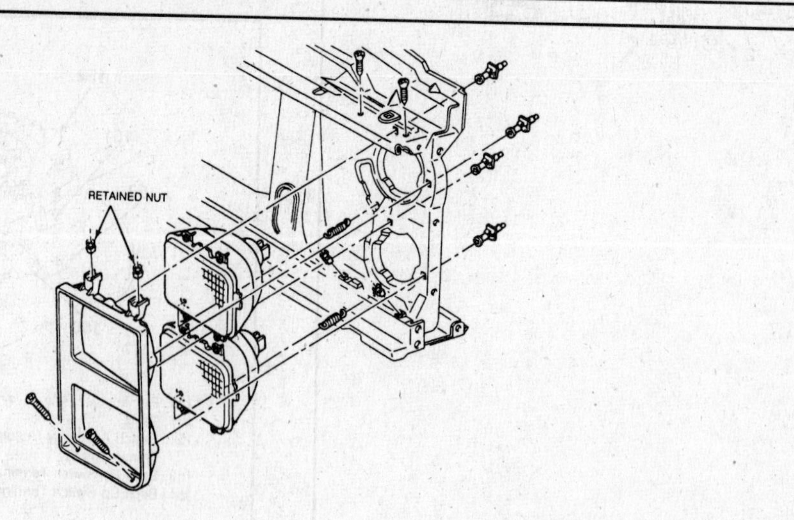

Fig. 78 Headlight removal — R/V series; four lamp assembly

3. Remove the headlamp from the mounting bracket.
4. Unplug the headlamp wiring connector.
5. Installation is the reverse of removal.

COMPOSITE HEADLIGHTS

See Figure 80

1. Disconnect the negative battery cable and make certain that the headlight switch is off.
2. Raise the hood.
3. Unplug the wiring connector.
4. Twist the retaining ring, then pull the bulb assembly from the unit.

To install:

5. Position the new bulb assembly into the unit and twist it to the right. The connector end should be facing down.

Always replace a high beam with a high beam, or a low beam with a low beam! The low beam should have a grey tip and a yellow gasket, while the high beam bulb uses a red gasket.

6. Connect the wiring harness to the bulb assembly.

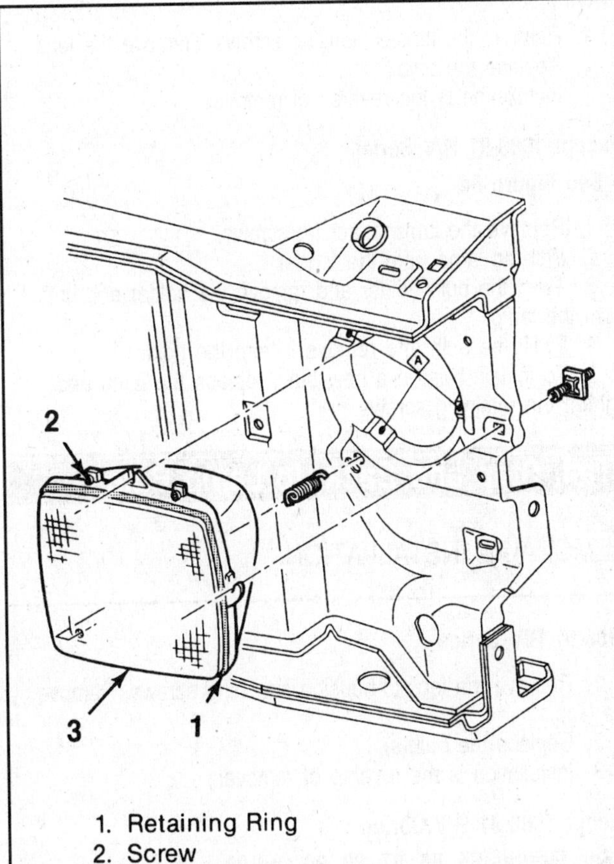

Fig. 79 Exploded view of the sealed beam headlight mounting

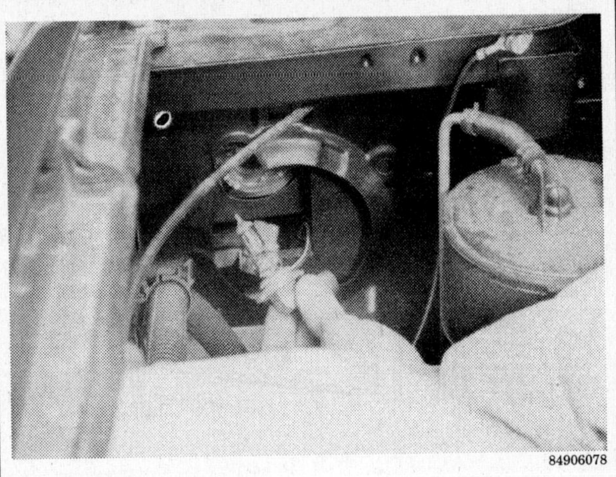

Fig. 80 After the retaining ring is unlocked, pull the bulb from the unit

7. Connect the battery cable.

HEADLIGHT AIMING

See Figures 81 and 82

The headlights must be properly aimed to provide the best, safest road illumination. The lights should be checked for proper aim, and adjusted if necessary, after installing a new sealed beam unit or if the front end sheet metal has been replaced. Certain state and local authorities have requirements for headlight aiming and you should check these before adjusting.

The truck's fuel tank should be about half full when adjusting the headlights. Tires should be properly inflated, and if a heavy load is carried in the pick-up bed, it should remain there.

Horizontal and vertical aiming of each sealed beam unit is provided by two adjusting screws, which move the mounting ring in the body against the tension of the coil spring. There is

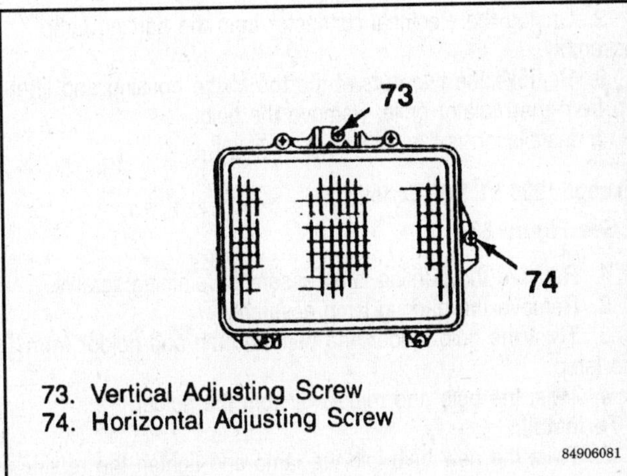

Fig. 81 Headlight adjustment screws — sealed beam lamp assemblies

Fig. 82 Adjusting screw locations — composite headlamps

no adjustment for focus; this is done during headlight manufacturing.

Front Parking Lamp Assembly

REMOVAL & INSTALLATION

1988-91 R/V Series

WITH TWO HEADLIGHTS

1. Disconnect the negative battery cable.
2. Remove the four bezel retaining screws and remove the bezel.
3. Remove the three parking lamp retaining screws. Unplug the electrical connector and remove the parking lamp. Remove the bulb.
4. Installation is the reverse of removal.

WITH FOUR HEADLIGHTS

1. Remove the radiator grille.
2. Unplug the electrical connector from the parking lamp assembly.
3. Remove the two nuts at the top of the housing and lift it up from the radiator grille. Remove the bulb.
4. Installation is the reverse of removal.

Except 1988-91 R/V Series

➧ See Figure 83

1. Remove the parking lamp assembly retaining screws.
2. Remove the parking lamp assembly.
3. Twist the bulb holder and pull the bulb and holder from the lamp.
4. Twist the bulb and remove it from the holder.

To install:

5. Twist the new bulb into the lamp and tighten the retaining screws.

Front Side Marker Lamp Bulb and/or Housing

REMOVAL & INSTALLATION

➧ See Figure 83

1. Remove the screws and the side marker lamp.
2. Remove the bulb from the lamp.
3. To install, twist the new bulb into the lamp and tighten the retaining screws.

Rear Side Marker Lamp Bulb and/or Housing

REMOVAL & INSTALLATION

1988-91 R/V Series

1. Remove the lens-to-housing screws. Remove the lens.
2. Replace the bulb.
3. Installation is the reverse of removal.

Except 1988-91 R/V Series

➧ See Figure 84

1. Remove the lamp attaching screws.
2. Pull the lamp from the fender.
3. Twist the bulb holder and remove the holder and bulb from the lamp.
4. Twist the bulb and remove it from the holder.
5. To install, twist in a new bulb, replace the lamp and tighten the retaining screws.

Tail, Stop and Back-Up Lamp Bulbs

REMOVAL & INSTALLATION

1988-91 R/V Series

1. Remove the lens-to-housing attaching screws. Remove the lens.
2. Replace the bulb(s).
3. Installation is the reverse of removal.

Except 1988-91 R/V Series

➧ See Figures 85, 86, 87, 88, 89 and 90

1. Lower the tailgate.
2. Remove the lamp assembly retaining screws.
3. Pull the lamp assembly from the truck and disconnect the wiring.
4. Remove the bulb holder fasteners.
5. Remove the bulb(s) from the lamp.
6. Install the bulb, connect the wiring and install the lamp.

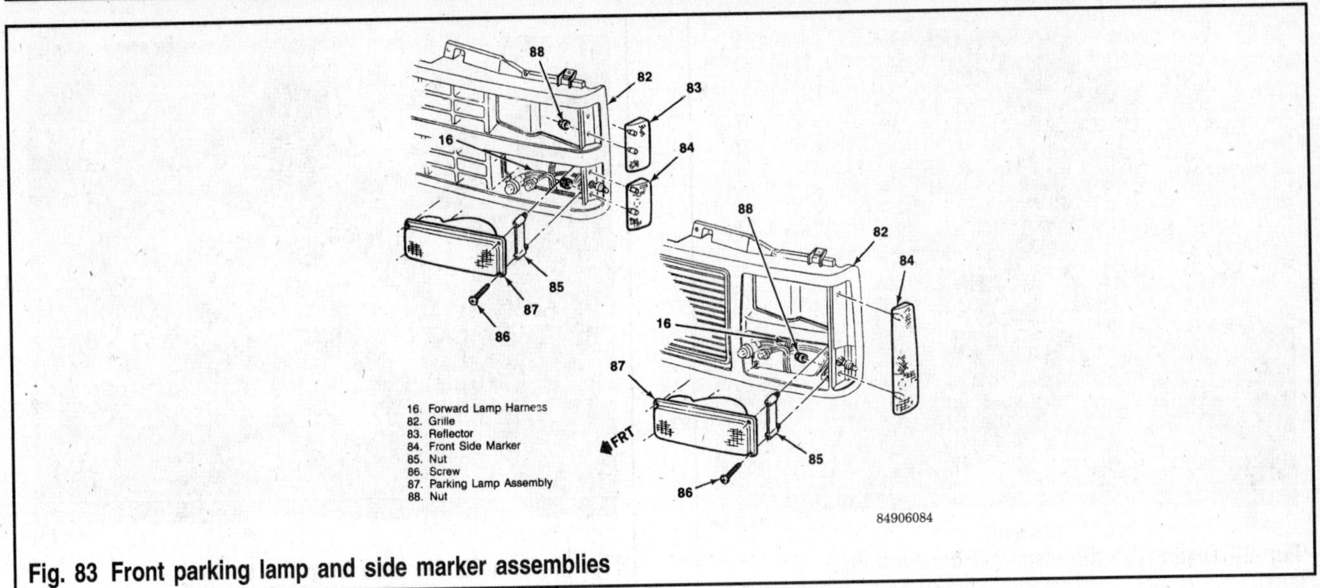

Fig. 83 Front parking lamp and side marker assemblies

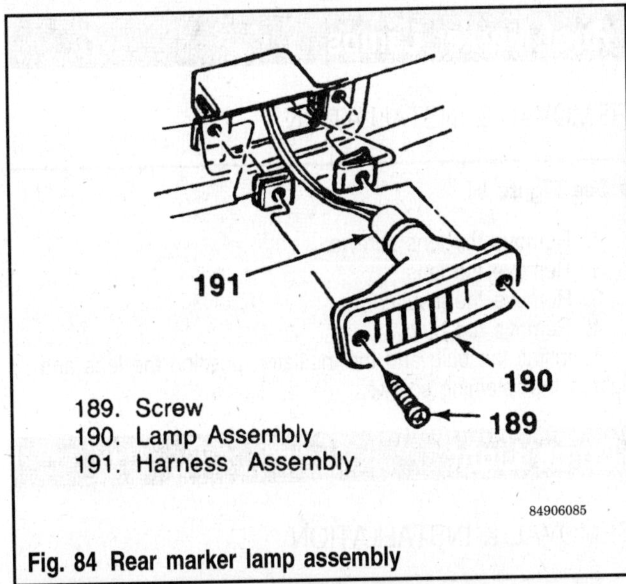

Fig. 84 Rear marker lamp assembly

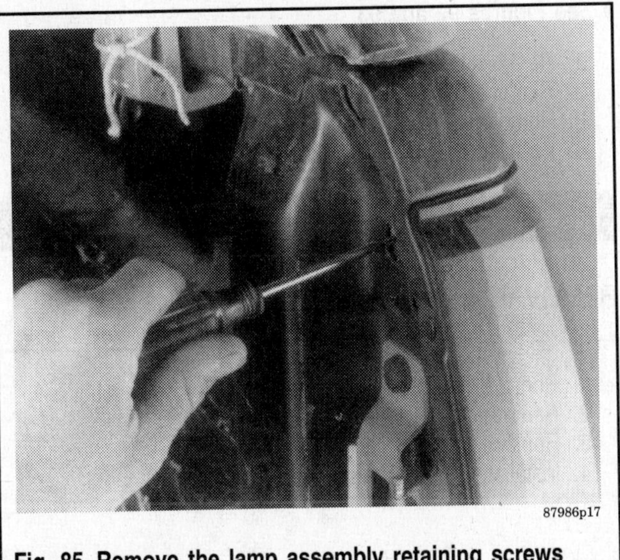

Fig. 85 Remove the lamp assembly retaining screws

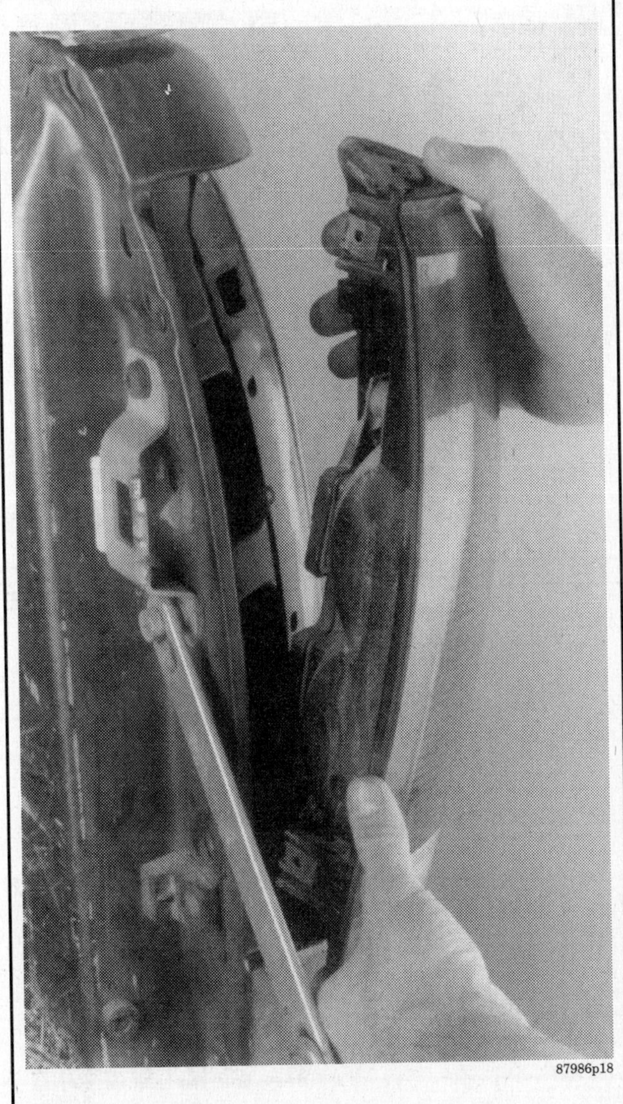

Fig. 86 Pull the lamp assembly from the truck

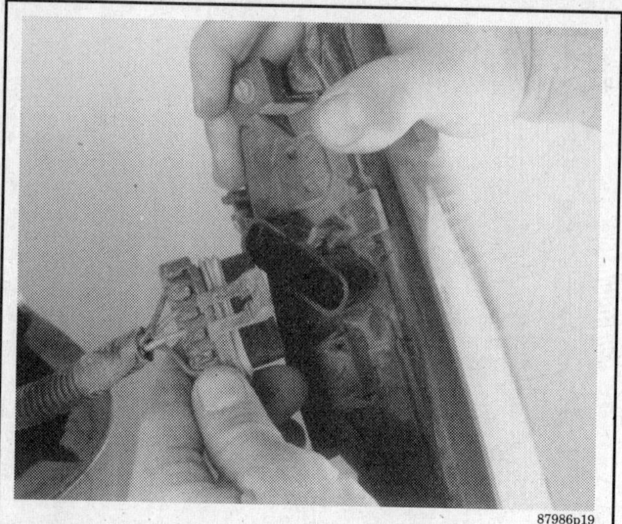

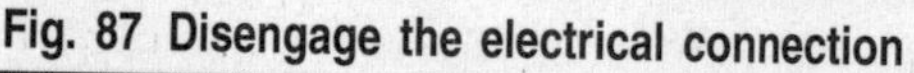
Fig. 87 Disengage the electrical connection

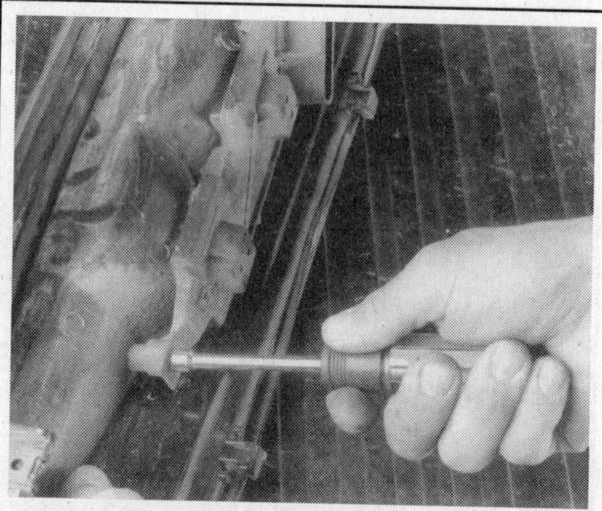

Fig. 88 Remove the bulb holder fasteners

Fig. 89 Remove the bulb holder

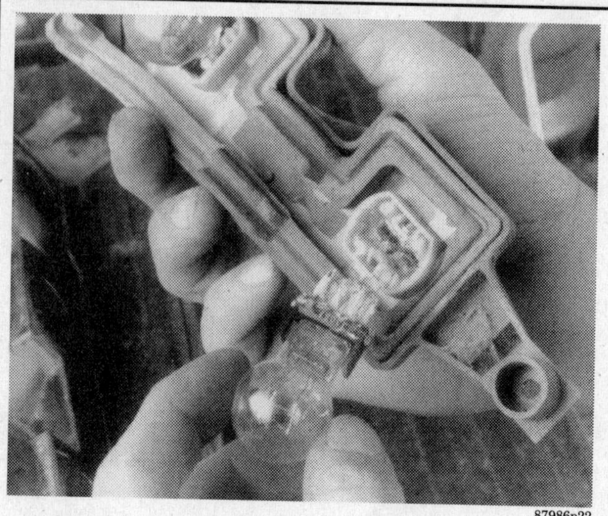

Fig. 90 Remove the bulb from the socket

Roof Marker Lamps

REMOVAL & INSTALLATION

➧ **See Figure 91**

1. Remove the lens screws.
2. Remove the lens.
3. Remove the insulator.
4. Remove the bulb.
5. Install the bulb and the insulator, position the lens and tighten the retaining screws.

Dome Light

REMOVAL & INSTALLATION

➧ **See Figures 92 and 93**

1. Remove the lens screws, if equipped.
2. Remove the lens.
3. Remove the bulb.
4. Installation is the reverse of removal.

License Plate Light

REMOVAL & INSTALLATION

1. Remove the lamp housing retaining screws or bolts.
2. Remove the lens.
3. Replace the bulb.
4. Installation is the reverse of removal.

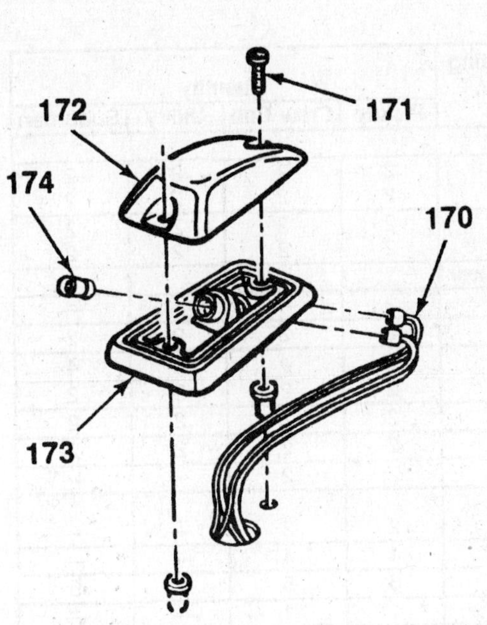

Fig. 91 Roof marker lamp assembly

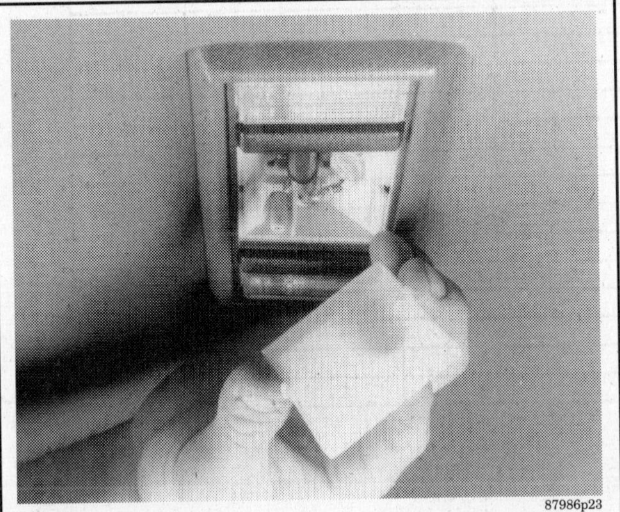

Fig. 92 Remove the lens cover from the dome light

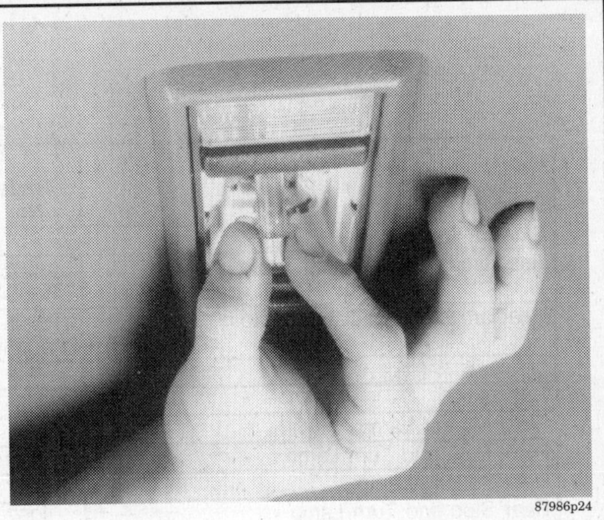

Fig. 93 Remove the bulb from the dome light

Fog Lights

REMOVAL & INSTALLATION

1. Disconnect the negative battery cable.
2. Make sure the headlamp and fog lamp switches are off.
3. Remove the two lens securing screws from the front of the lamp assembly.
4. Remove the bulb by twisting it to the left.

To install:

5. Insert the new bulb and screw the lens back into place.
6. Connect the battery cable.

AIMING

➧ See Figure 94

1. Park the truck on level ground, facing, perpendicular to, and about 25 ft. from a flat wall.
2. Remove any stone shields and switch on the fog lights.
3. Loosen the mounting hardware of the lights so you can aim them as follows:
   a. The horizontal distance between the light beams on the wall should be the same as between the lights themselves.
   b. The vertical height of the light beams above the ground should be 4 inches less than the distance between the ground and the center of the lamp lenses.
4. Tighten the mounting hardware.

Lamp or Bulb	Trade No.	Power Rating at 12.8V, Watts	Quantity			
			Pickup	Crew Cab	Utility	Suburban
Exterior Lights:						
Headlamps: 2 Headlamp System	6052	55/65	2	2	2	2
Halogen (Opt.)	H6054	35/65	2	2	2	2
Headlamps: 4 Headlamp System	9005	65	2	2	2	2
(Composite)	9006	55	2	2	2	2
		Candle Power				
Fog Lamp	H3	115	2	—	—	—
Front Marker Lamp	194	2	2	2	2	2
Front Park and Turn Lamp	2357NA	30/2	4	4	4	4
Rear Parking Lamp	3057	32-2	2	2	2	2
Rear Stop and Turn Lamp	3057	32-2	2	2	2	2
Backup Lamp	3156	32	2	2	2	2
Backup Lamp (Cab/Chassis Only)	1156	32	2	2	—	—
Rear Park, Stop, and Turn Lamp (Cab/Chassis Only)	1157	32-3	2	2	—	—
Fender Clearance Lamp	194	2	4	4	—	—
Roof Marker Lamp	194	2	5	5	—	5
Cargo Lamp	570	32	1	1	—	—
License Plate Lamp	194	2	2	2	2	2
Underhood Lamp	93	15	1	1	1	1
Reel Lamp	232	10	1	1	1	1
Interior Lights:						
Dome Lamps	211-2	12	1	2	2	2
Reading Lamps	211-2	12	2	4	4	4
Roof Console Lamps	168	3	—	2	2	2
Courtesy Lamp	1003	15	2	2	2	2
Heater or A/C Control Lamp	194	2	1	1	1	1
Four Wheel Drive Indicator	161	1	1	1	1	1
Four Wheel Drive Shift Lever	194	1	1	1	1	1
Instrument Panel Compartment Lamp	194	2	1	1	1	1
Ashtray Lamp	194	2	1	1	1	1
Sunshade Vanity Mirror	74	0.7	—	4	4	4
Instrument Panel Lights.						
Transmission Indicator (PRNDL)	161	1	1	1	1	1
Daytime Running Lights Indicator†	74	.7	1	1	1	1
Charging System Indicator Lamp	74	.7	1	1	1	1
Instrument Cluster Illuminating Lamps — Gage	194	.2	4	4	4	4
W. Tach	194	.2	6	6	6	6
Headlamp Beam Indicator	74	.7	1	1	1	1
Directional Signal Indicator	74	.7	2	2	2	2
Brake Warning Indicator	74	.7	1	1	1	1
Safety Belt Warning	74	.7	1	1	1	1
Check Gages Indicator	74	.7	1	1	1	1
Malfunction Indicator ("Service Engine Soon")	74	.7	1	1	1	1
Upshift Indicator	74	.7	1	1	1	—
ABS Warning Indicator	74	.7	—	—	1	1
Wait Lamp*	74	.7	1	1	—	—
Low Coolant Lamp*	74	.7	1	1	—	—
Service Fuel Filter Lamp*	74	.7	1	1	—	—

*Diesel only †Canadian Vehicles only

84906093

Fig. 94 Light bulb applications

TRAILER WIRING

Wiring the vehicle for towing is fairly easy. There are a number of good wiring kits available and these should be used, rather than trying to design your own.

All trailers will need brake lights and turn signals as well as tail lights and side marker lights. Most states require extra marker lights for overwide trailers. Also, most states have recently required back-up lights for trailers, and most trailer manufacturers have been building trailers with back-up lights for several years.

Additionally, some Class I, most Class II and just about all Class III trailers will have electric brakes. Add to this number an accessories wire, to operate trailer internal equipment or to charge the trailer's battery, and you can have as many as seven wires in the harness.

Determine the equipment on your trailer and buy the wiring kit necessary. The kit will contain all the wires needed, plus a plug adapter set which included the female plug, mounted on the bumper or hitch, and the male plug, wired into, or plugged into the trailer harness.

When installing the kit, follow the manufacturer's instructions. The color coding of the wires is usually standard throughout the industry. One point to note: some domestic vehicles, and most imported vehicles, have separate turn signals. On most domestic vehicles, the brake lights and rear turn signals operate with the same bulb. For those vehicles with separate turn signals, you can purchase an isolation unit so that the brake lights won't blink whenever the turn signals are operated, or, you can go to your local electronics supply house and buy four diodes to wire in series with the brake and turn signal bulbs. Diodes will isolate the brake and turn signals. The choice is yours. The isolation units are simple and quick to install, but far more expensive than the diodes. The diodes, however, require more work to install properly, since they require the cutting of each bulb's wire and soldering in place of the diode.

One, final point, the best kits are those with a spring loaded cover on the vehicle mounted socket. This cover prevent dirt and moisture from corroding the terminals. Never let the vehicle socket hang loosely; always mount it securely to the bumper or hitch.

CIRCUIT PROTECTION

Fuse Block and Convenience Center

➧ See Figures 95, 96, 97, 98 and 99

➡For 1988-93 models, refer to the wiring diagrams for fuse application and amperage ratings.

Fuses protect all the major electrical systems in the car. In case of an electrical overload, the fuse melts, breaking the circuit and stopping the flow of electricity.

The fuse block on most models covered by this manual is located under the instrument panel to the left of the steering column. The fuse block should be visible from underneath the steering column, near the pedal bracket.

Fig. 95 Some models may use an underhood fuse/relay panel

If the panel is not visible, check for a removable compartment door or trim panel which may used on later models to hide the block. This panel is usually located on the left end of the instrument panel.

The convenience center is located just below the instrument panel on the drivers side. It contains individual relays such as the seat belt and ignition key alarm, and flasher.

On newer model vehicles there is an underhood fuse/relay center contains both mini and maxi fuses, as well as some relays.

If a fuse blows, the cause should be investigated and corrected before the installation of a new fuse. This, however, is easier to say than to do. Because each fuse protects a limited number of components, your job is narrowed down somewhat. Begin your investigation by looking for obvious fraying, loose connections, breaks in insulation, etc. Use the techniques outlined at the beginning of this section. Electrical problems are almost always a real headache to solve, but if you are patient and persistent, and approach the problem logically (that is, don't start replacing electrical components randomly), you will eventually find the solution.

Each fuse block uses miniature fuses (normally plug-in blade terminal-type for these vehicles) which are designed for increased circuit protection and greater reliability. The compact plug-in or blade terminal design allows for fingertip removal and replacement.

Although most fuses are interchangeable in size, the amperage values are not. Should you install a fuse with too high a value, damaging current could be allowed to destroy the component you were attempting to protect by using a fuse in the first place. The plug-in type fuses have a volt number molded on them and are color coded for easy identification. Be sure to only replace a fuse with the proper amperage rated substitute.

87986p26

Fig. 96 Fuse panel cover — 1991 model shown

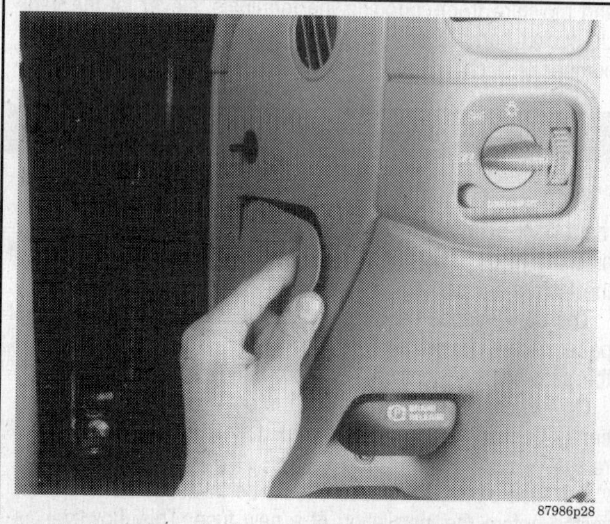

87986p28

Fig. 97 Fuse panel location — 1996 model shown

A blown fuse can easily be checked by visual inspection or by continuity checking.

➡**A special heavy duty turn signal flasher is required to properly operate the turn signals when a trailer's lights are connected to the system.**

REPLACEMENT

1. Locate the fuse for the circuit in question.

➡**When replacing the fuse, DO NOT use one with a higher amperage rating.**

2. Check the fuse by pulling it from the fuse block and observing the element. If it is broken, install a replacement fuse the same amperage rating. If the fuse blows again, check the circuit for a short to ground or faulty device in the circuit protected by the fuse.

3. Continuity can also be checked with the fuse installed in the fuse block with the use of a test light connected across the 2 test points on the end of the fuse. If the test light lights, replace the fuse. Check the circuit for a short to ground or faulty device in the circuit protected by the fuse.

Circuit Breakers

Circuit breakers differ from fuses in that they are reusable. Circuit breakers open when the flow of current exceeds specified value and will close after a few seconds when current flow returns to normal. Circuits breakers are used due to the fact that they must operate at times under prolonged high current flow due to demand even though there is not malfunction in the circuit.

There are 2 types of circuit breakers. The first type opens when high current flow is detected. A few seconds after the excessive current flow has been removed, the circuit breaker will close. If the high current flow is experienced again, the circuit will open again.

The second type is referred to as the Positive Temperature Coefficient (PTC) circuit breaker. When excessive current flow passes through the PTC circuit breaker, the circuit is not opened but its resistance increases. As the device heats ups with the increase in current flow, the resistance increases to the point where the circuit is effectively open. Unlike other circuit breakers, the PTC circuit breaker will not reset until the circuit is opened, removing voltage from the terminals. Once the voltage is removed, the circuit breaker will re-close within a few seconds.

Flashers

REMOVAL & INSTALLATION

The turn signal and hazard flasher units are usually located in the convenience center located just below the instrument panel on the drivers side. Replace the flasher by unplugging the old one and plugging in the new one. Confirm proper flasher operation.

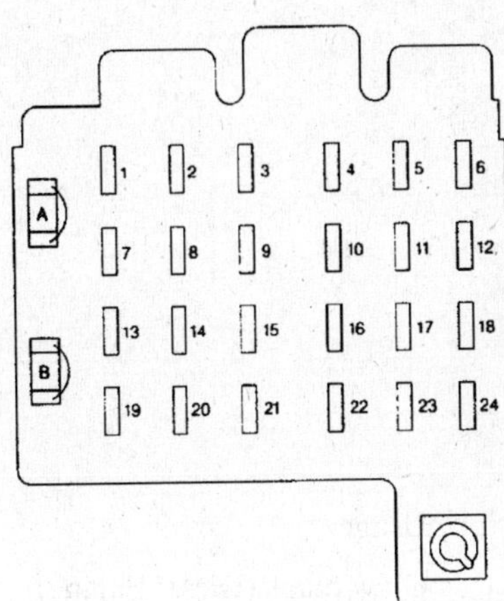

Fuse	Usage
1	Stop/TCC Switch, Buzzer, CHMSL, Hazard Lamps, Stoplamps
2	Transfer Case
3	Courtesy Lamps, Cargo Lamp, Glove Box Lamp, Dome/Reading Lamps, Vanity Mirrors, Power Mirrors

Fuse	Usage
4	Instrument Cluster, DRL Relay, Lamp Switch, Keyless Entry, Low Coolant Module, Illuminated Entry Module, DRAC (Diesel Engine)
5	Not Used
6	Cruise Control
7	Auxiliary Power Outlet
8	Air Bag System
9	License Lamp, Parking Lamps, Taillamps, Roof Marker Lamps, Tailgate Lamps, Front Sidemarkers, Fog Lamp Relay, Door Switch Illumination, Fender Lamps, Headlamp Switch Illumination
10	Air Bag System
11	Wiper Motor, Washer Pump
12	A/C, A/C Blower, High Blower Relay
13	Power Amp, Cigarette Lighter, Door Lock Relay, Power Lumbar Seat
14	4WD Indicator, Cluster, Comfort Controls, Instrument Switches, Radio Illumination, Chime Module

Fuse	Usage
15	DRL Relay, Fog Lamp Relay
16	Front and Rear Turn Signals, Back-Up Lamps, BTSI Solenoid
17	Radio (Ignition)
18	4WAL/VCM, ABS, Cruise Control
19	Radio (Battery)
20	PRNDL, Automatic Transmission, Speedometer, Check Gages Warning Light
21	Not Used
22	Not Used
23	Not Used
24	Front Axle, 4WD Indicator Lamp, TP2 Relay (Gasoline Engine)
A	Power Door Lock, Six-Way Power Seat, Keyless Entry Module
B	Power Windows

87986fxb

Fig. 98 Fuse application and amperage ratings — 1994-96 models. Refer to the wiring diagrams for 1988-93 models

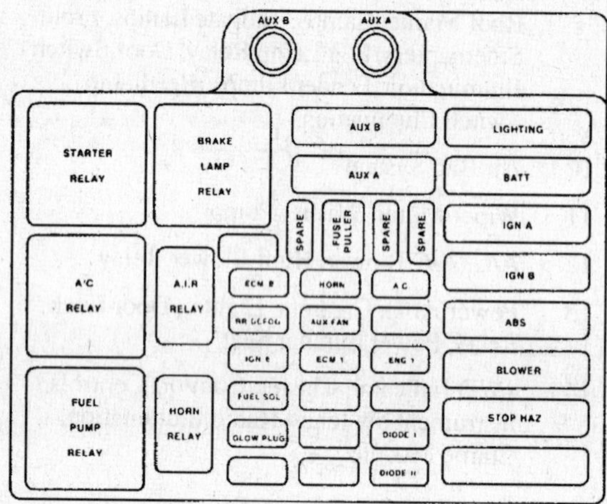

Fuse	Usage
ECM-B	Fuel Pump, PCM/VCM
RR DEFOG	Rear Window Defogger
IGN-E	Auxiliary Fan Relay Coil, A/C Compressor Relay, Hot Fuel Module, Dual Tanks
FUEL SOL	Fuel Solenoid (Diesel Engine)

Fuse	Usage
GLOW PLUG	Glow plugs (Diesel Engine)
HORN	Horn, Underhood Lamps
AUX FAN	Auxiliary Fan
ECM-1	Injectors, PCM/VCM
A/C	Air Conditioning
ENG-1	Ignition Switch, EGR, Canister Purge, EVRV Idle Coast Solenoid, Heated O_2, Fuel Heater (Diesel Engine), Water Sensor (Diesel Engine)
LIGHTING	Headlamp and Panel Dimmer Switch, Fog and Courtesy Fuses
BATT	Battery, Fuse Block Busbar
IGN-A	Ignition Switch
IGN-B	Ignition Switch
ABS	Anti-Lock Brake Module
BLOWER	Hi Blower Relay
STOP/HAZ	Stoplamps

87986fxa

Fig. 99 Underhood fuse/relay panel applications and ratings

WIRING DIAGRAMS

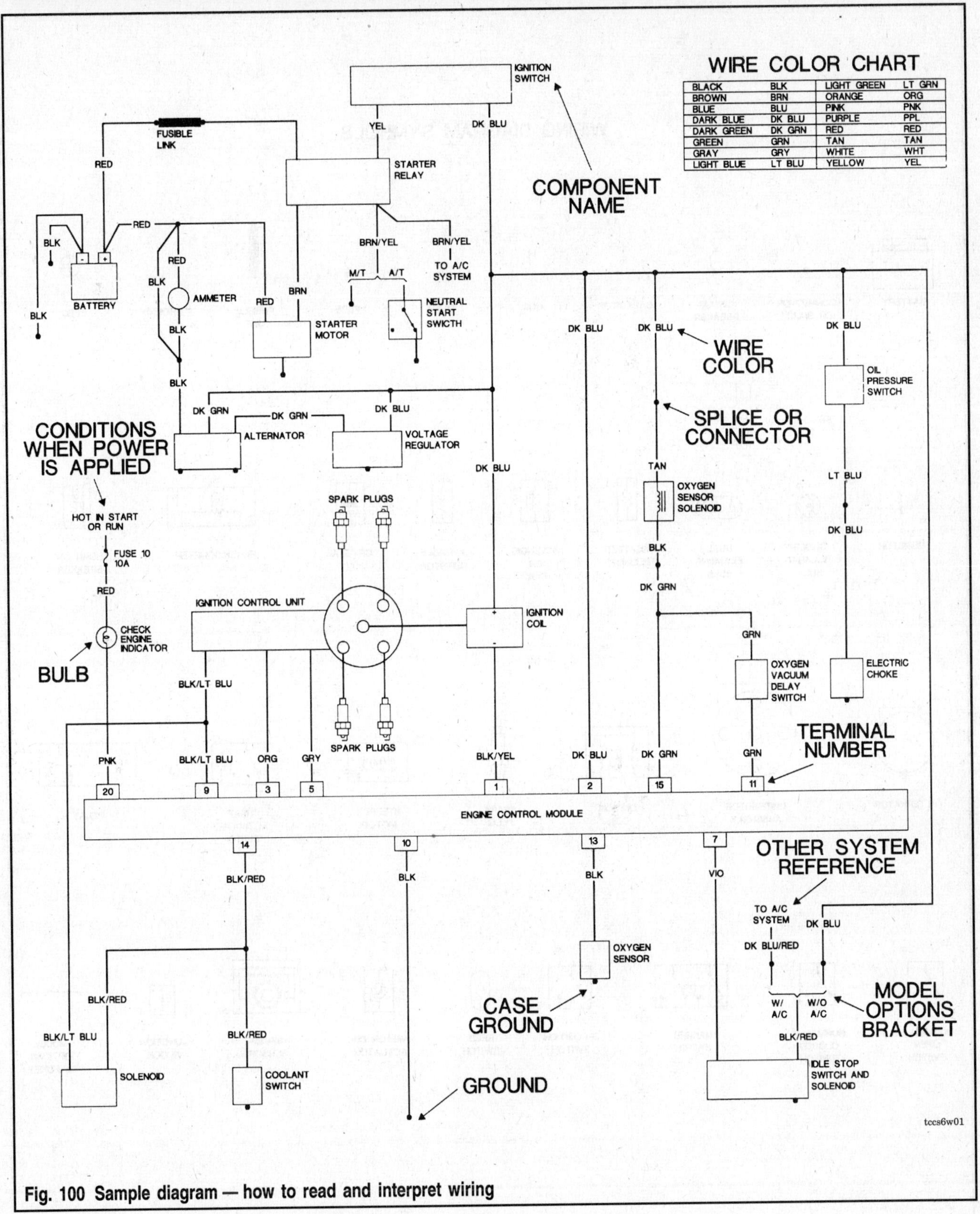

Fig. 100 Sample diagram — how to read and interpret wiring

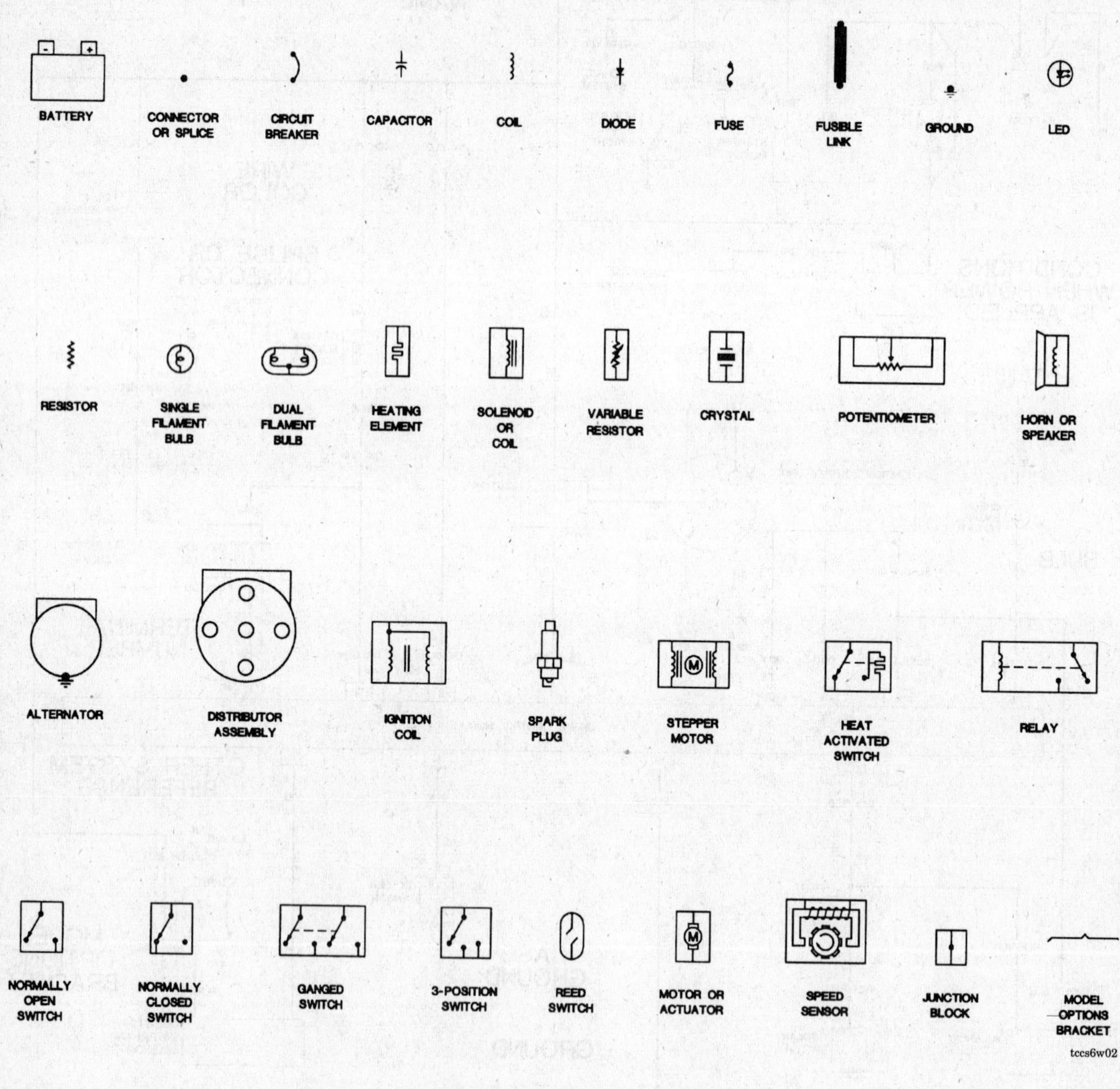

Fig. 101 Common wiring diagram symbols

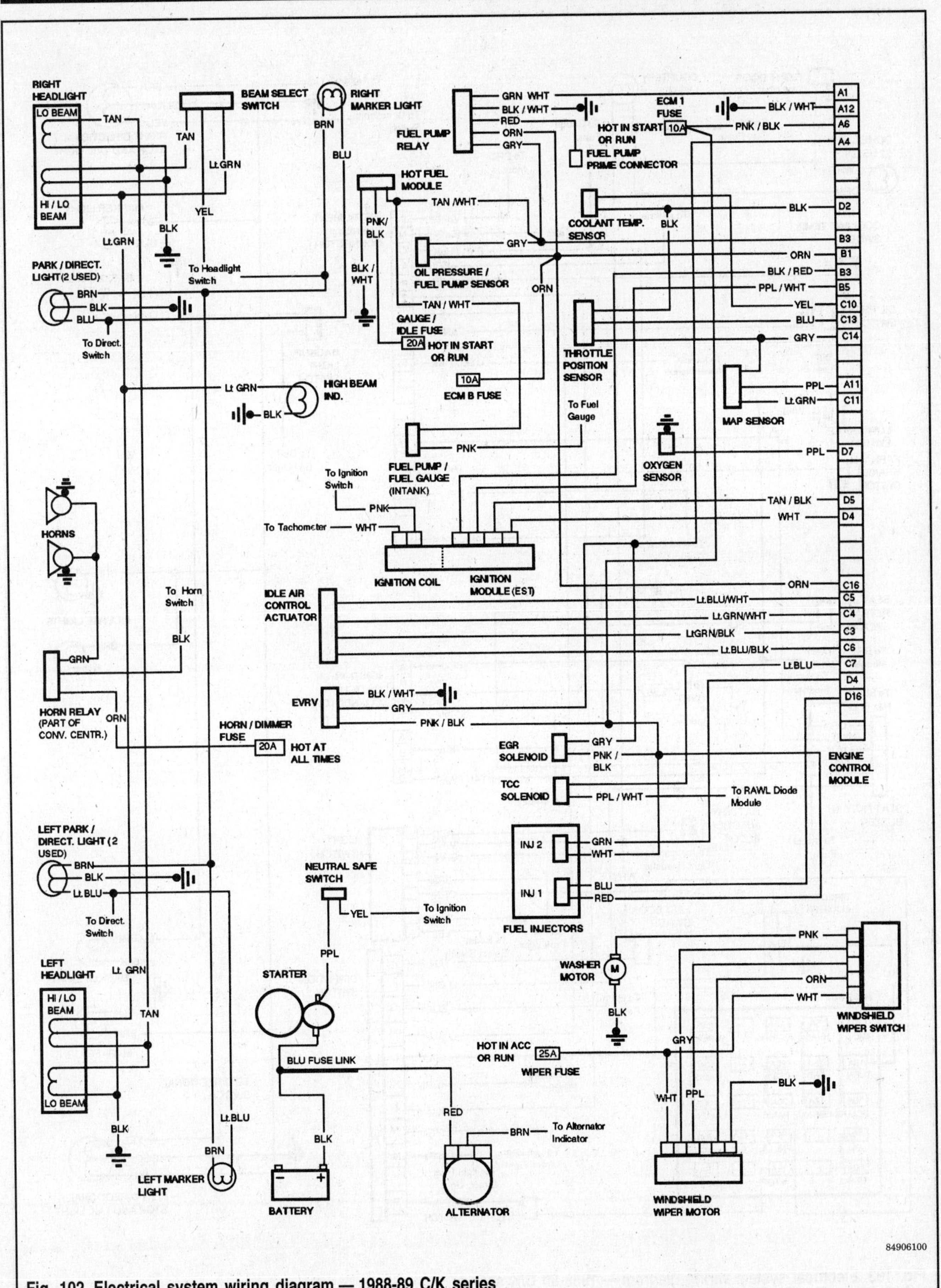

Fig. 102 Electrical system wiring diagram — 1988-89 C/K series

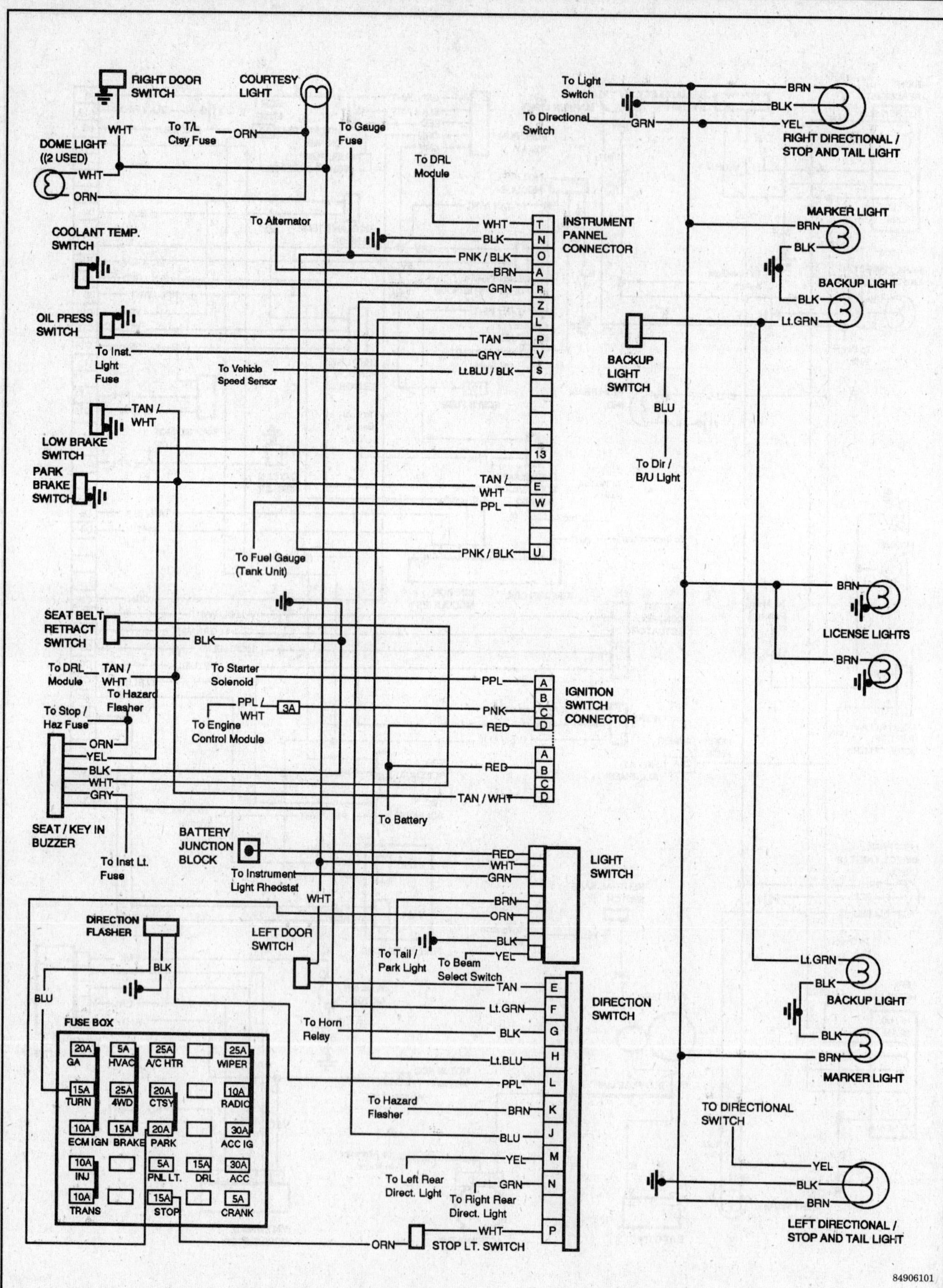

Fig. 103 Electrical system wiring diagram — 1988-89 C/K series

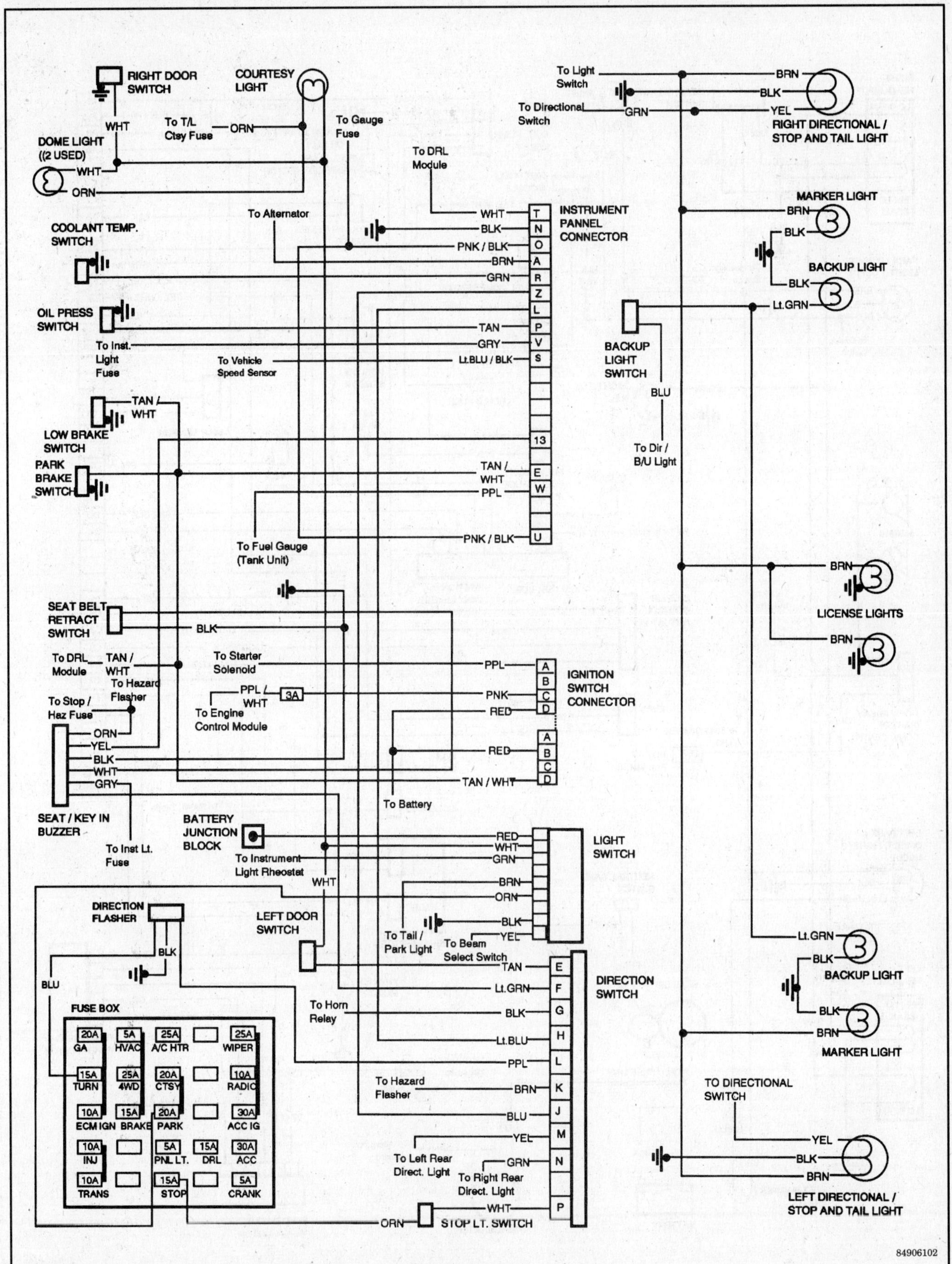

Fig. 104 Electrical system wiring diagram — 1990 C/K series

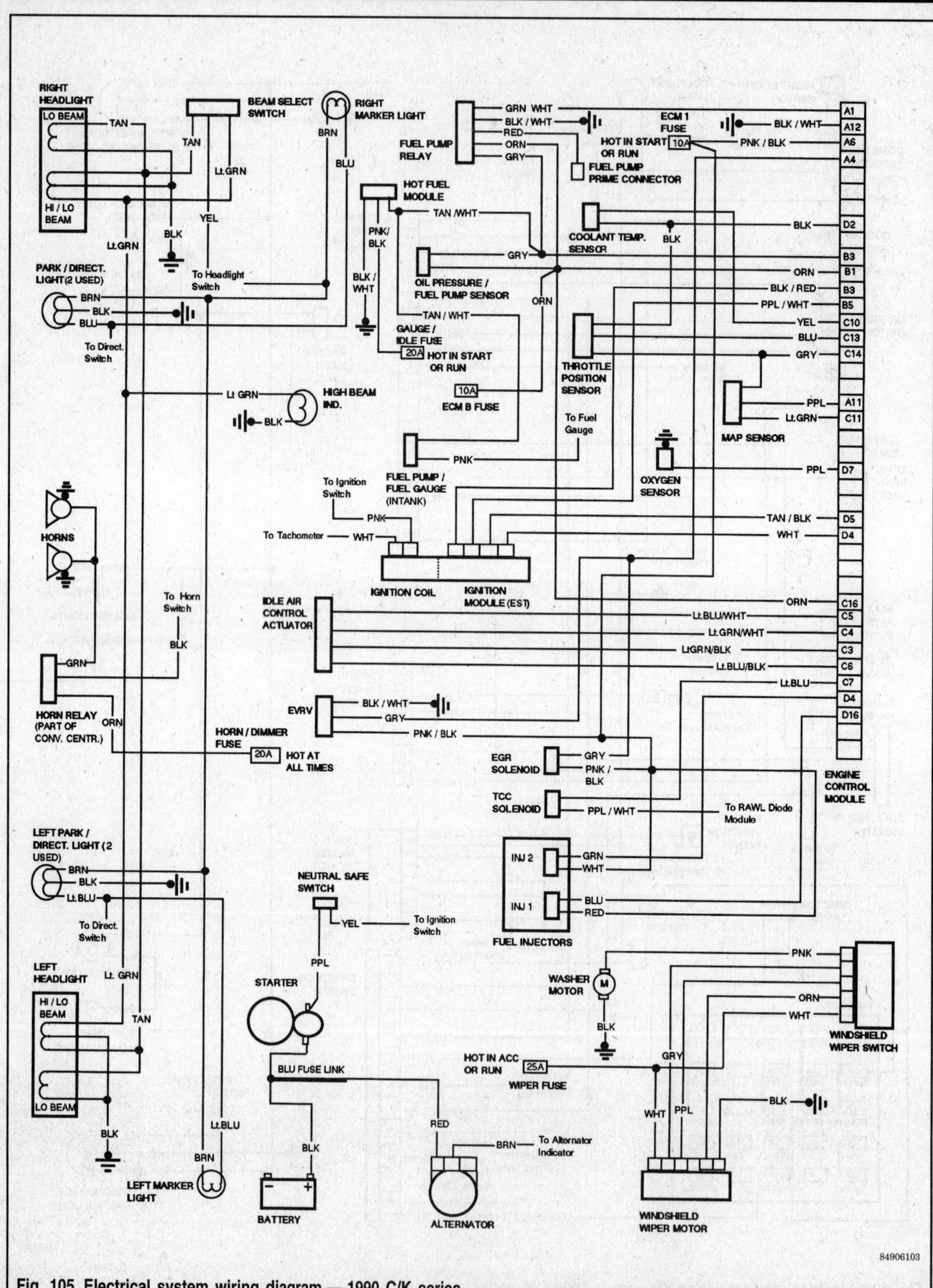

Fig. 105 Electrical system wiring diagram — 1990 C/K series

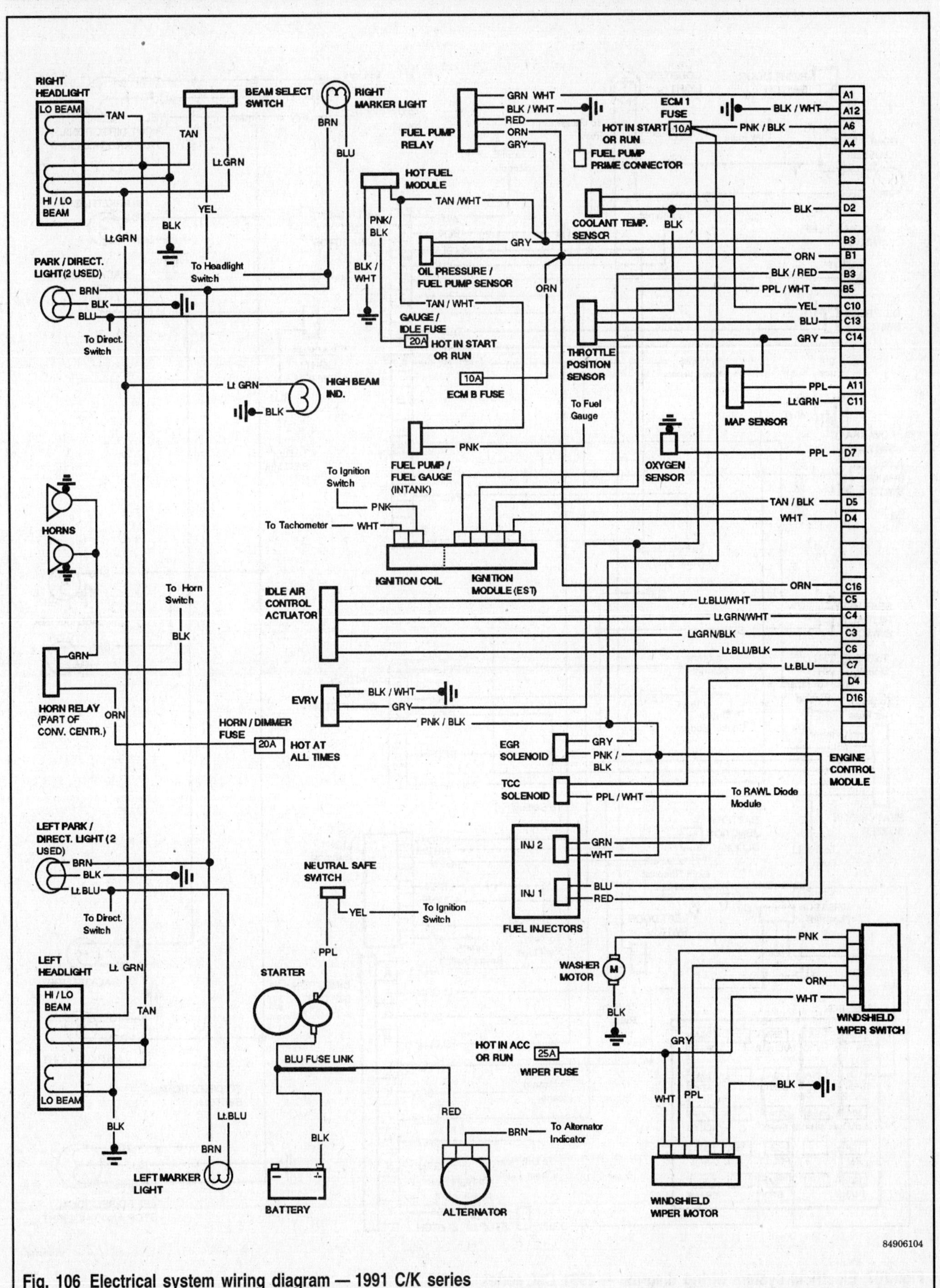

Fig. 106 Electrical system wiring diagram — 1991 C/K series

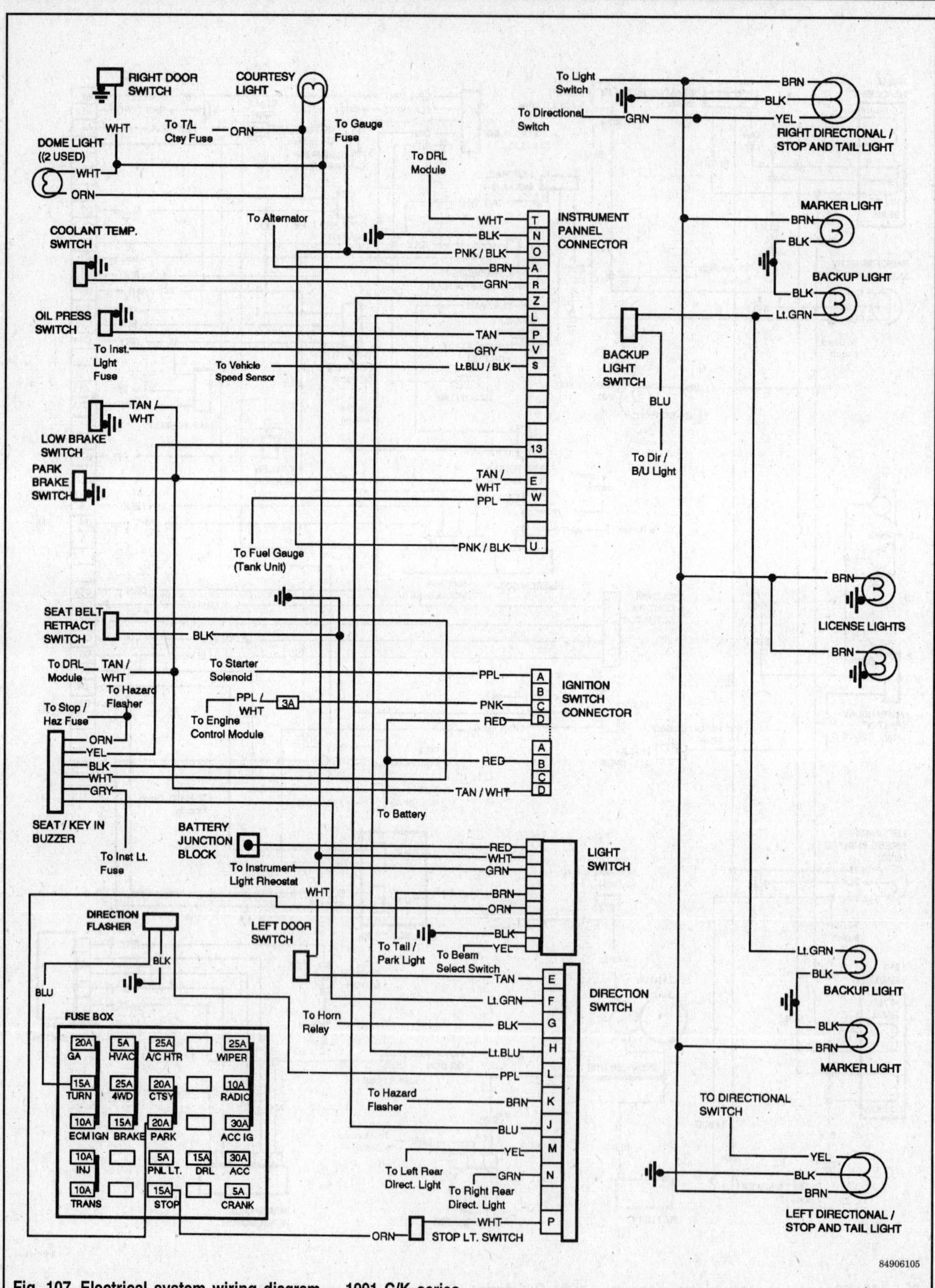

Fig. 107 Electrical system wiring diagram — 1991 C/K series

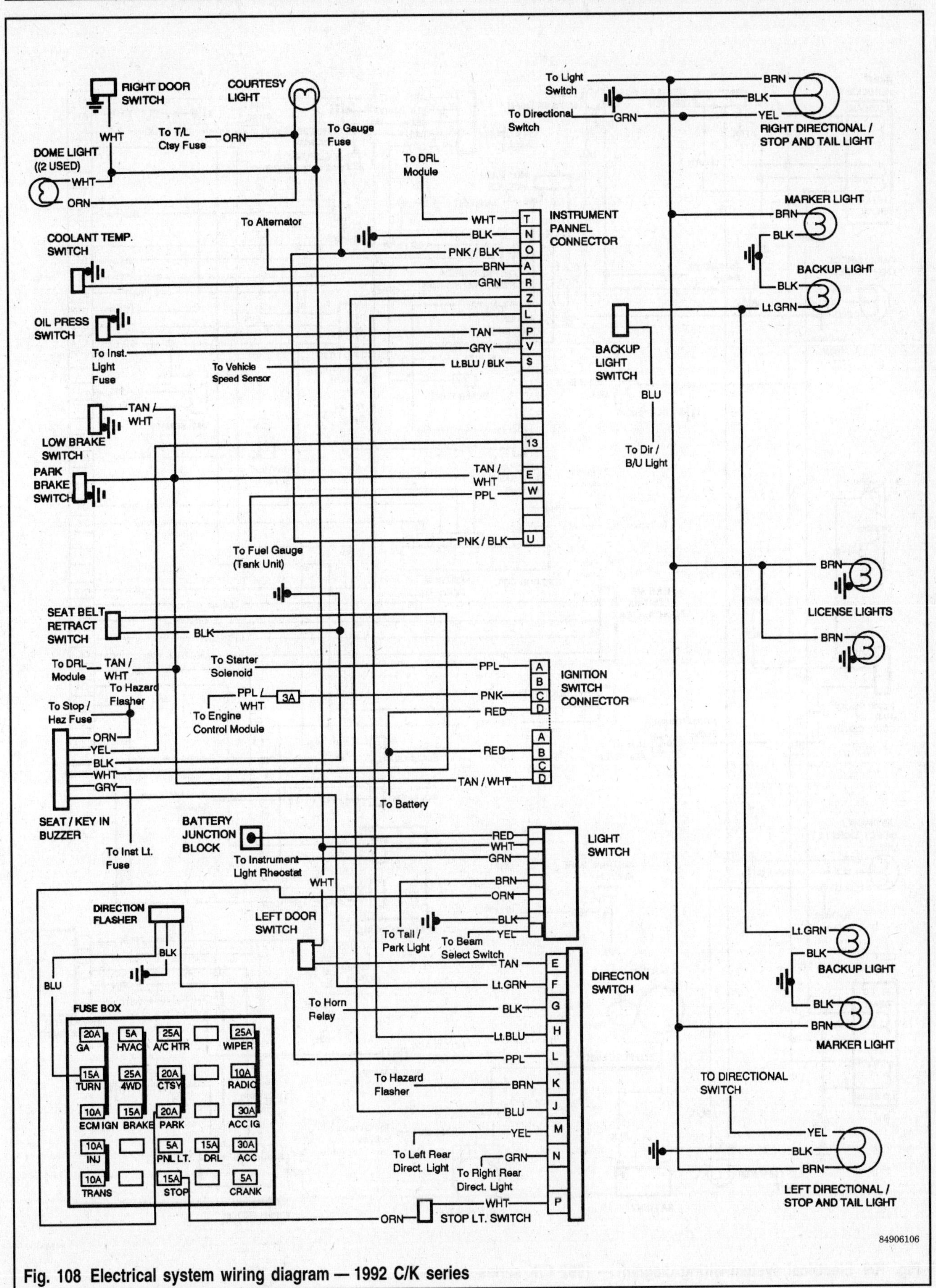

Fig. 108 Electrical system wiring diagram — 1992 C/K series

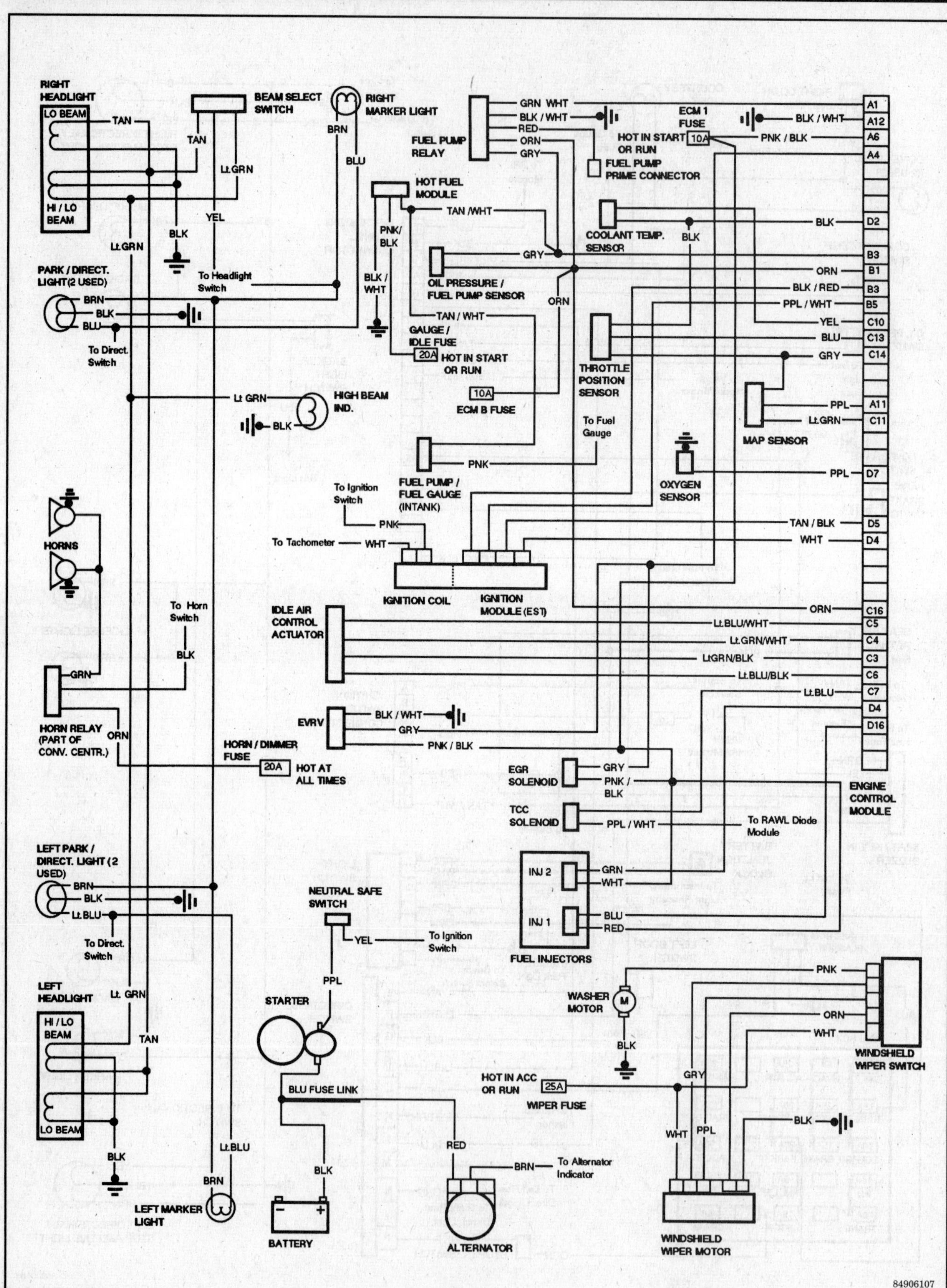

Fig. 109 Electrical system wiring diagram — 1992 C/K series

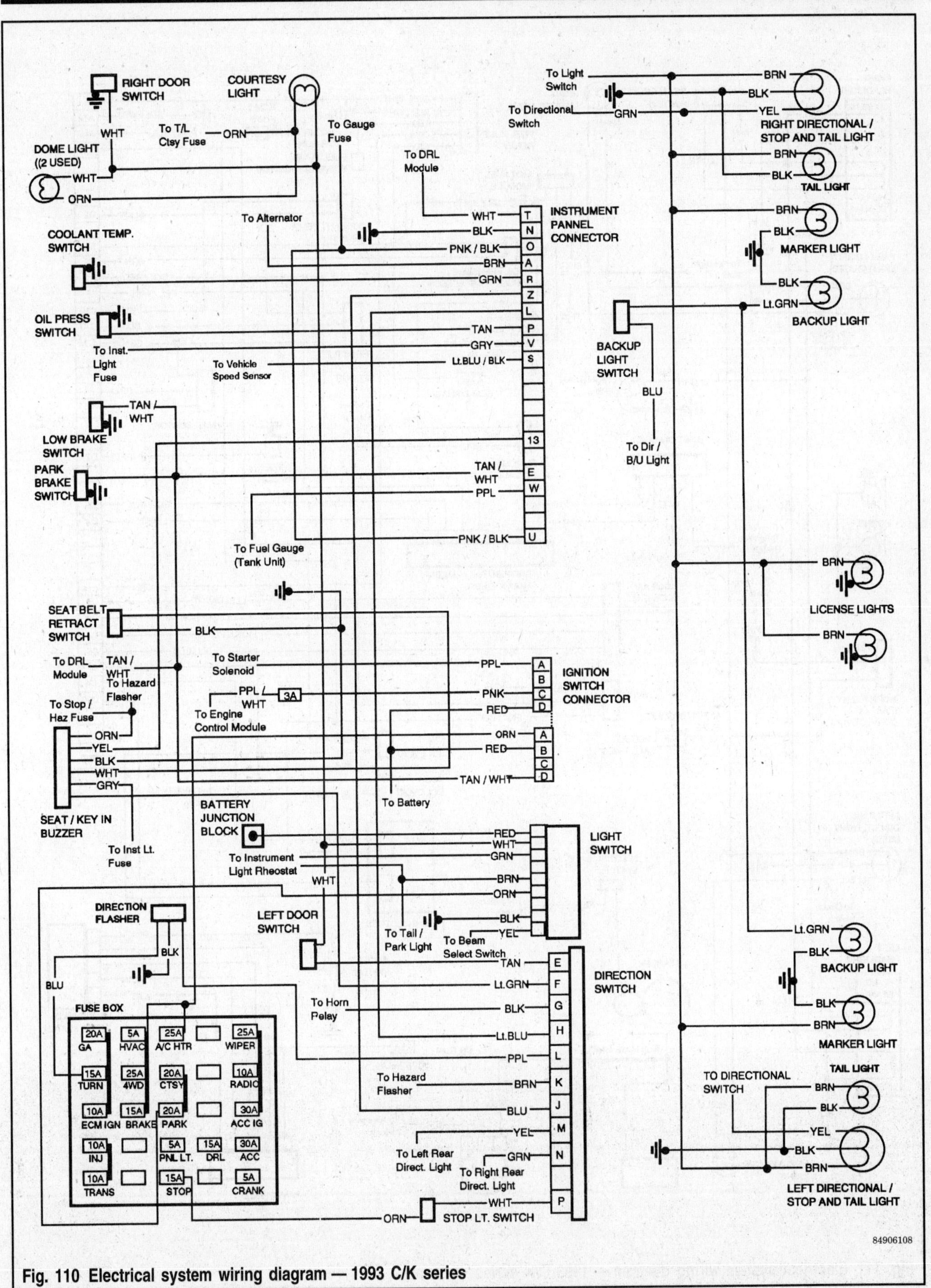

Fig. 110 Electrical system wiring diagram — 1993 C/K series

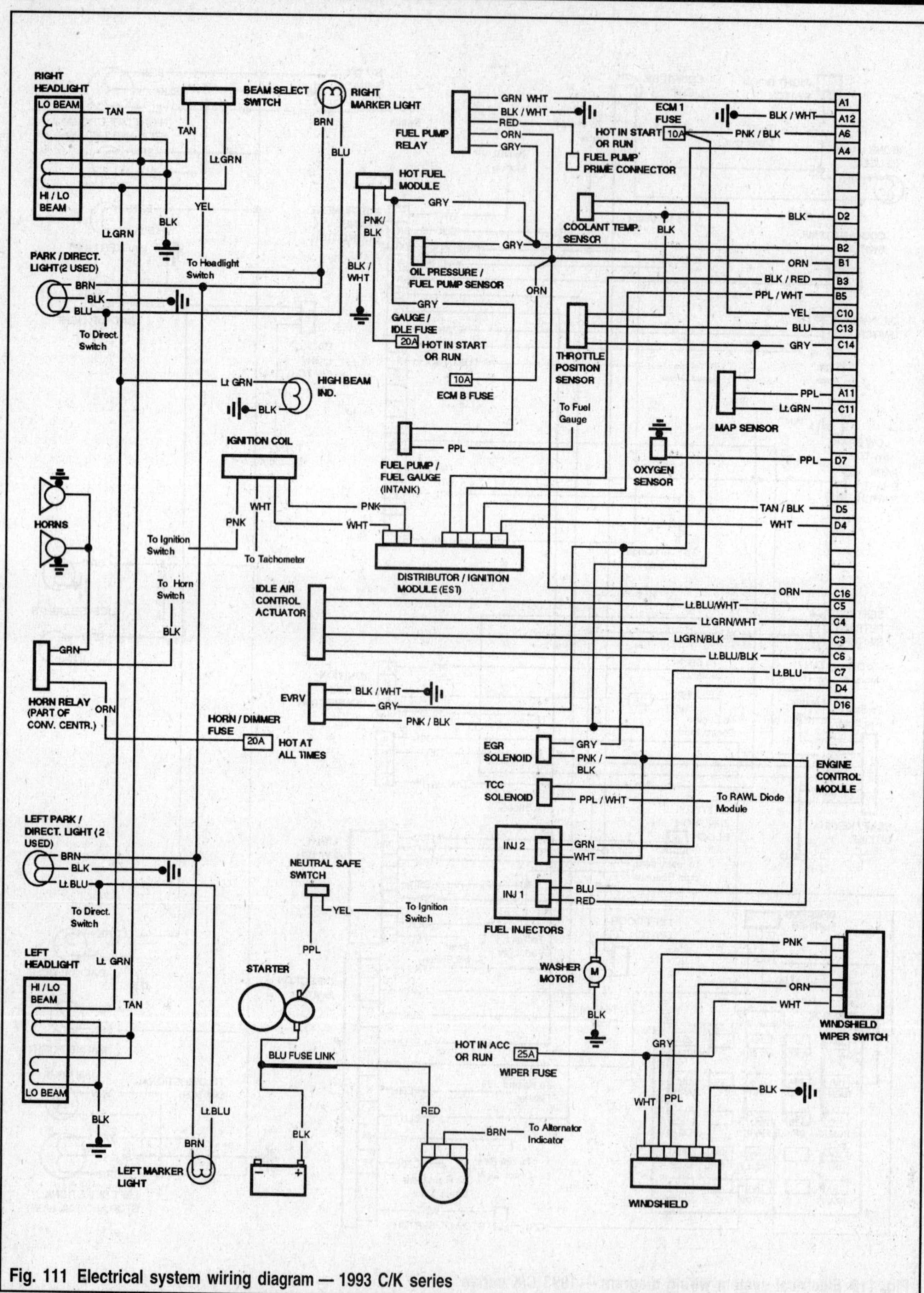

Fig. 111 Electrical system wiring diagram — 1993 C/K series

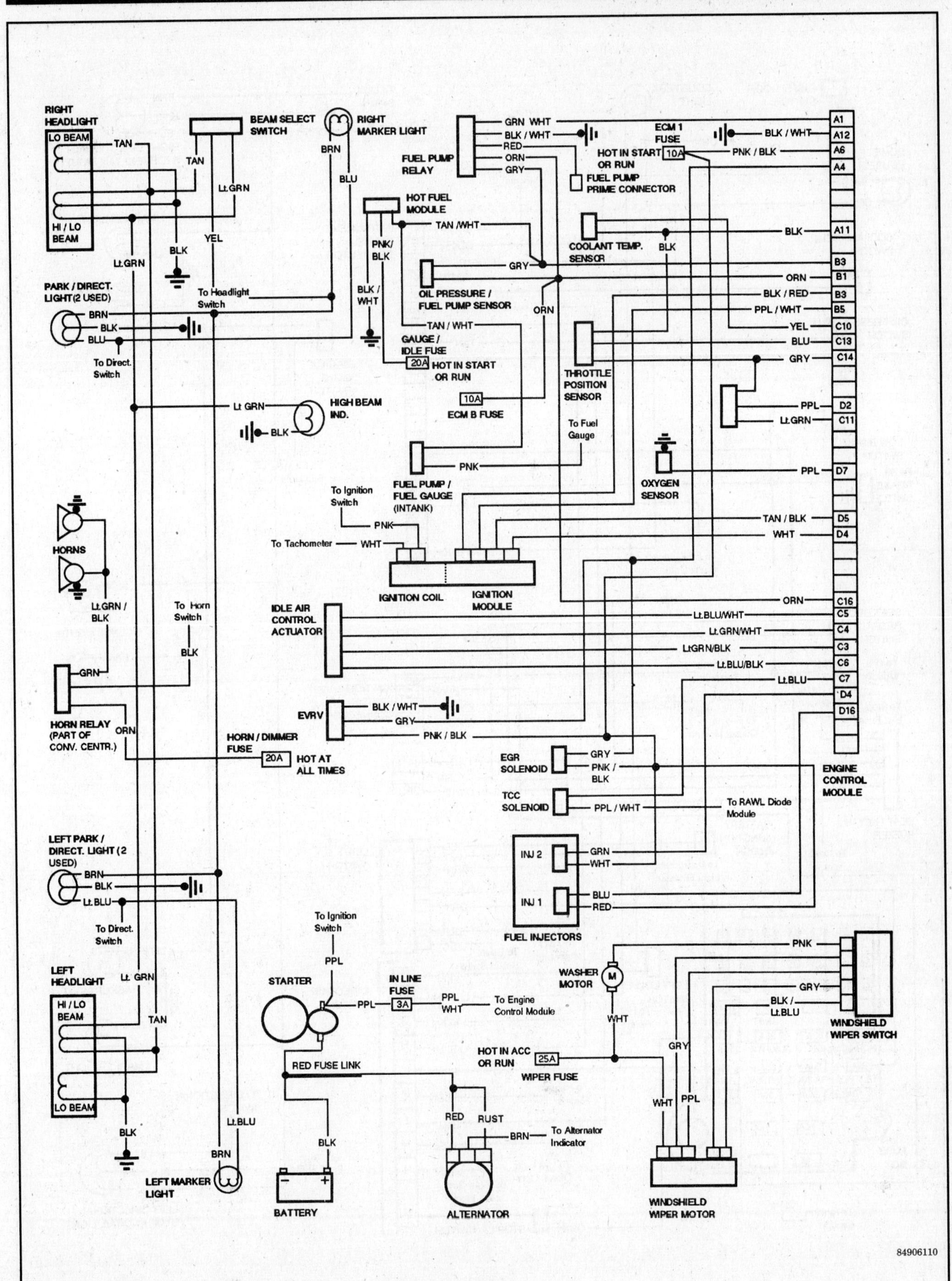

Fig. 112 Electrical system wiring diagram — 1988-89 R/V series

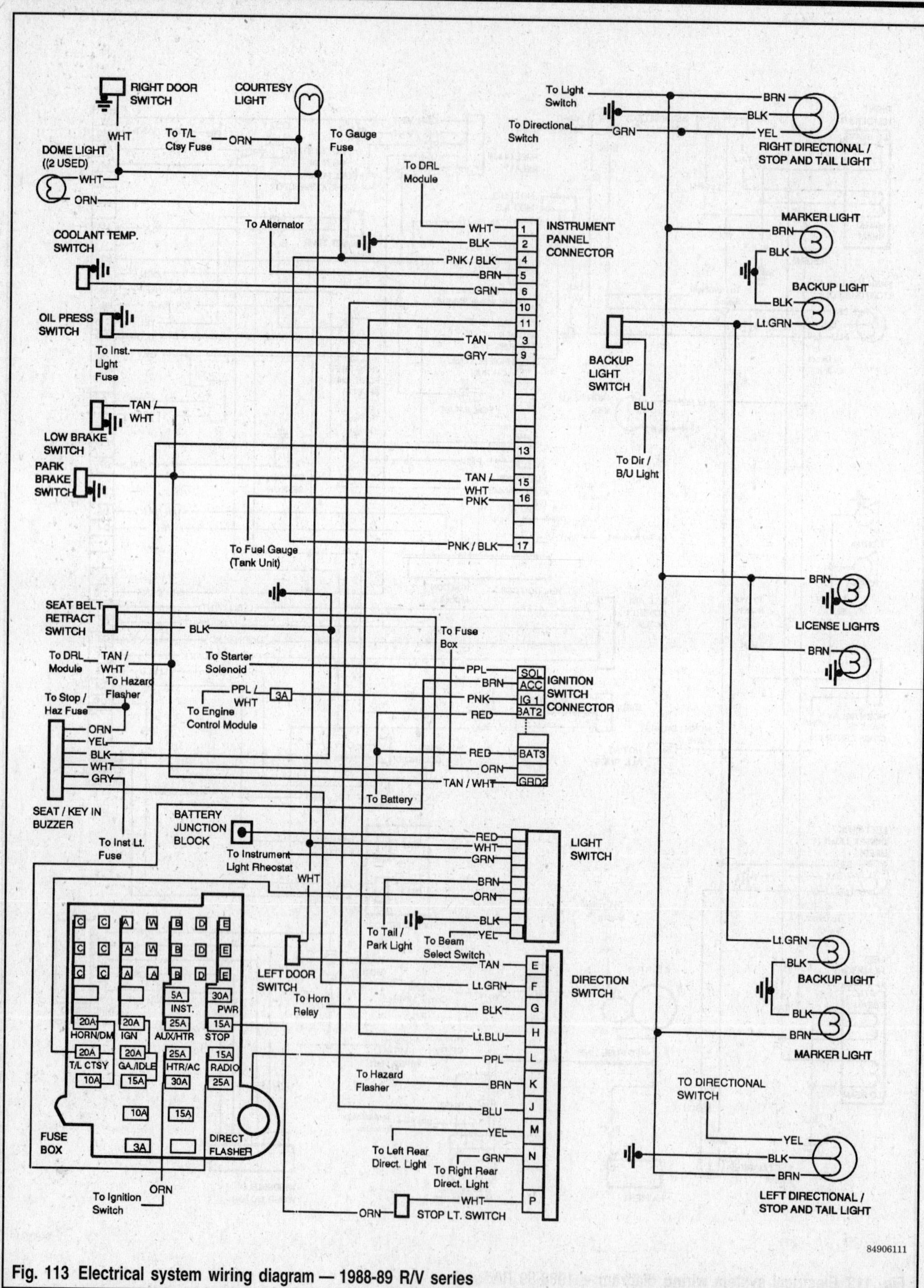

Fig. 113 Electrical system wiring diagram — 1988-89 R/V series

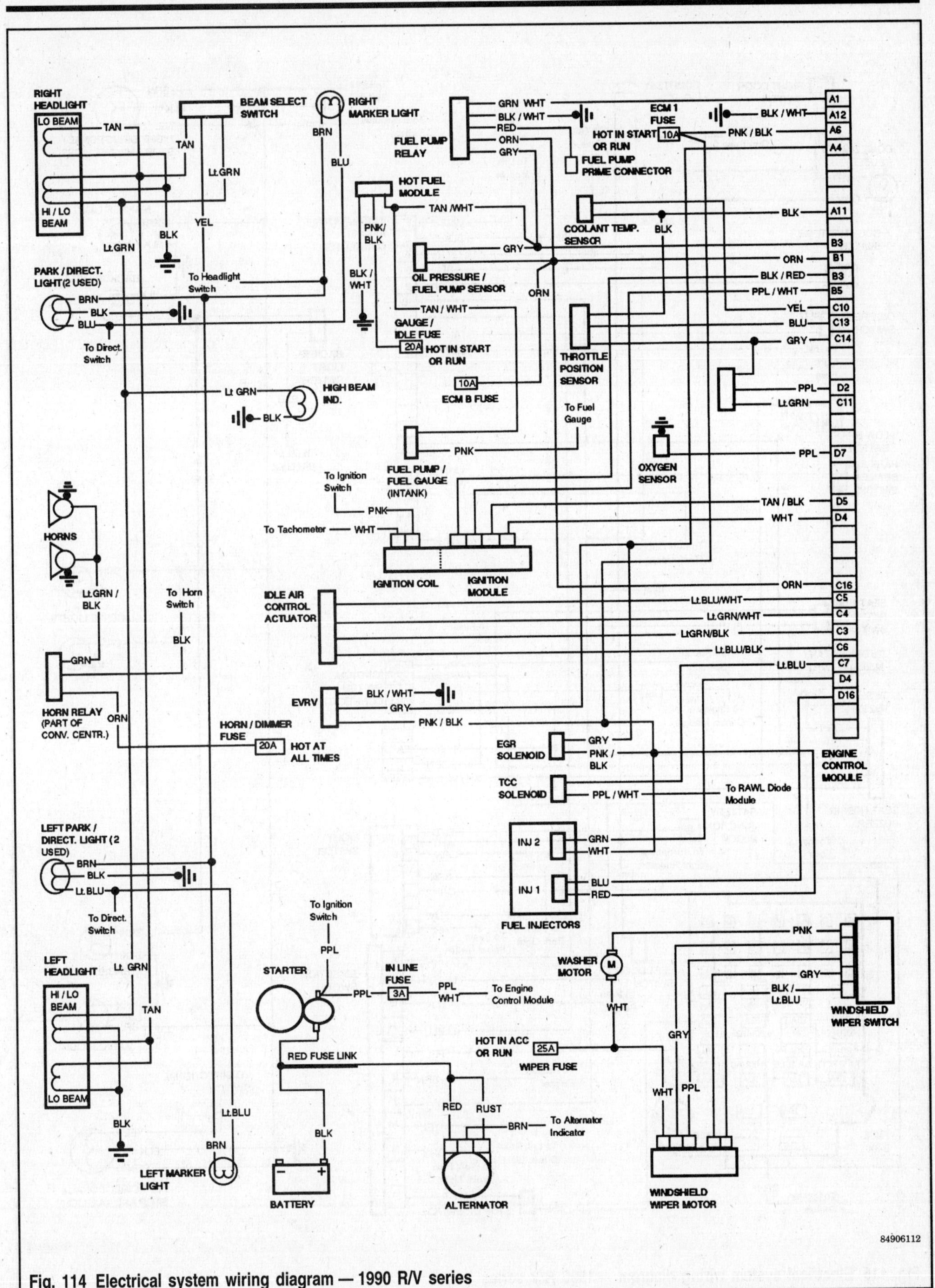

84906112

Fig. 114 Electrical system wiring diagram — 1990 R/V series

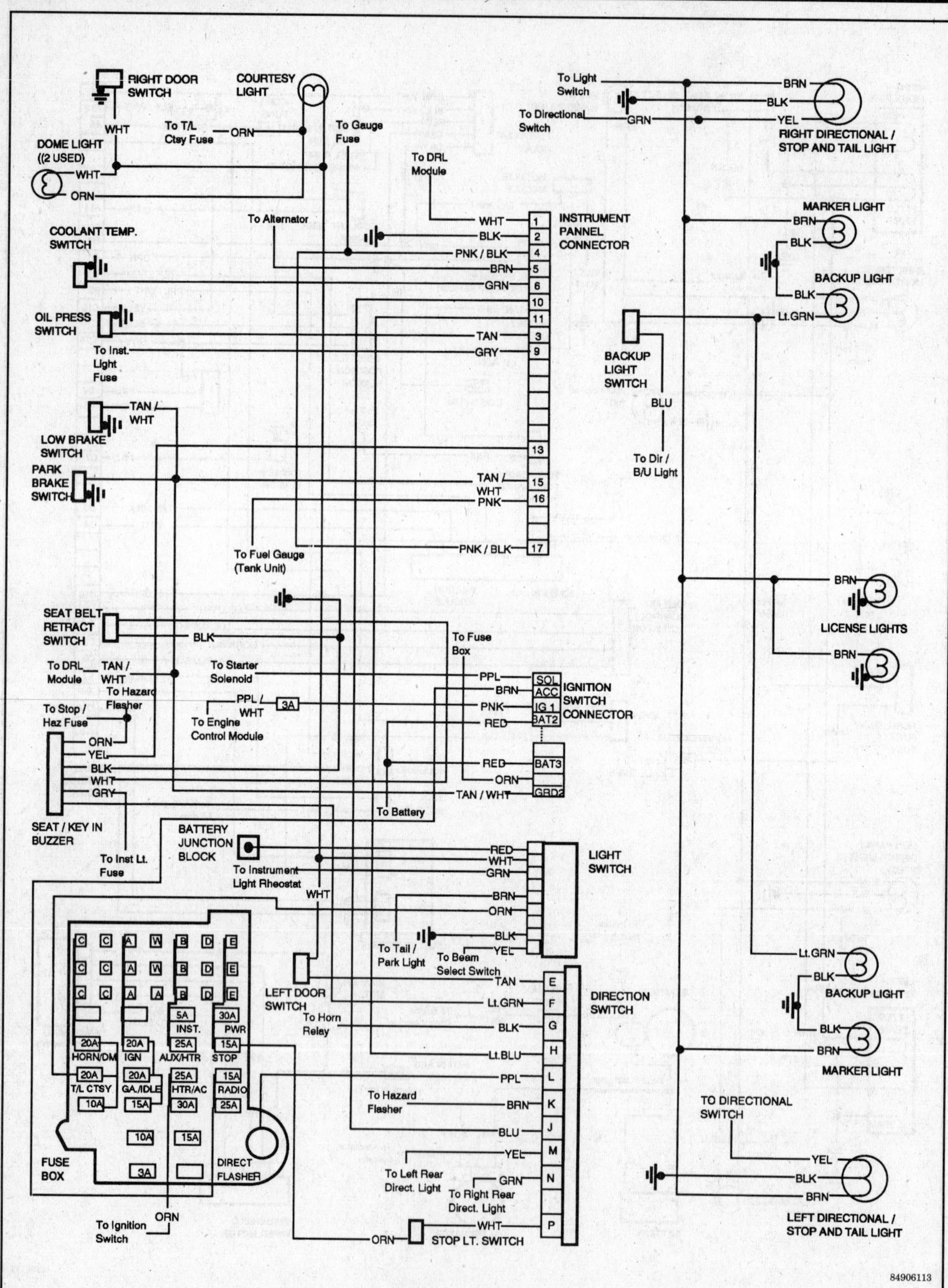

Fig. 115 Electrical system wiring diagram — 1990 R/V series

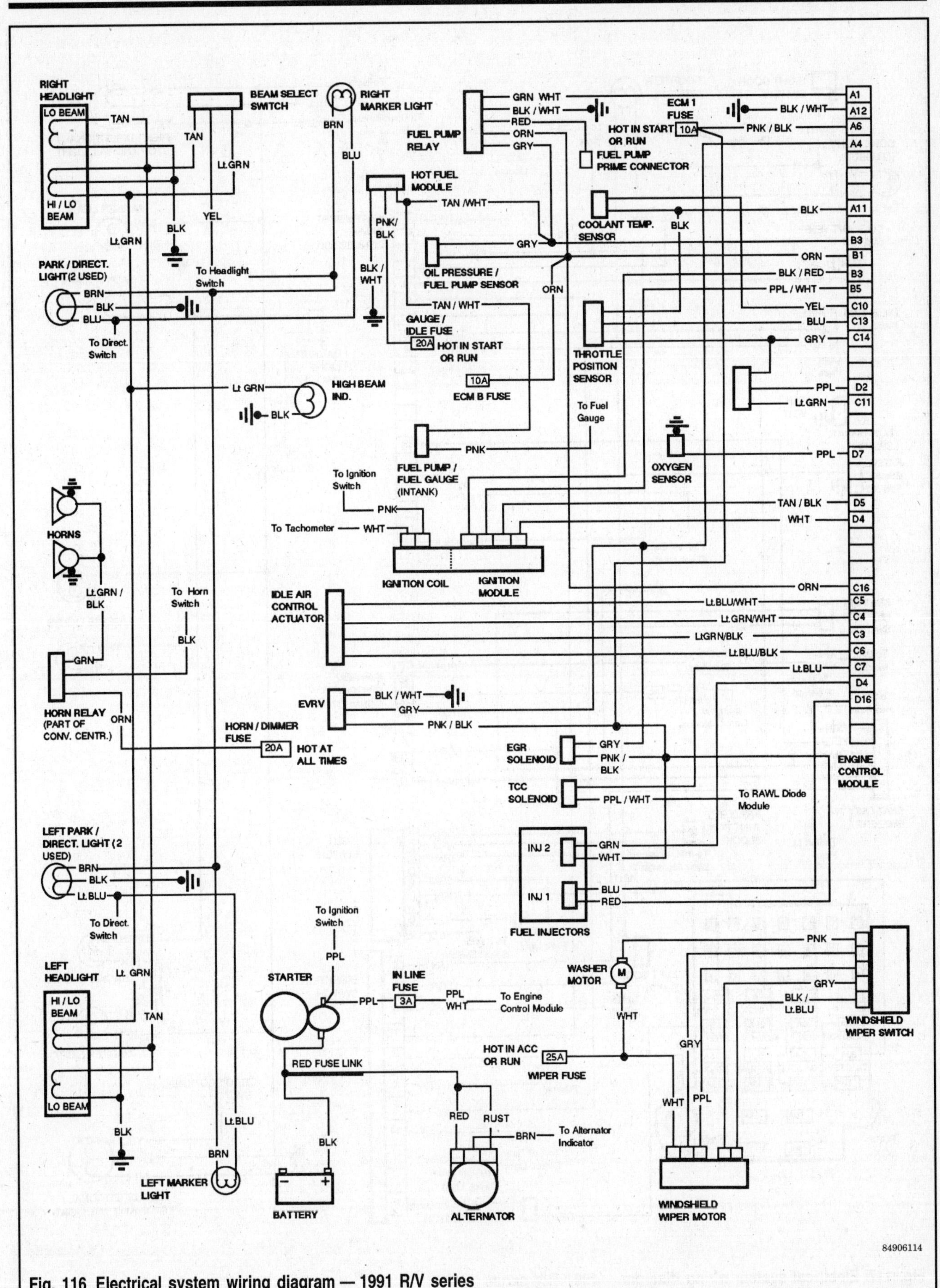

Fig. 116 Electrical system wiring diagram — 1991 R/V series

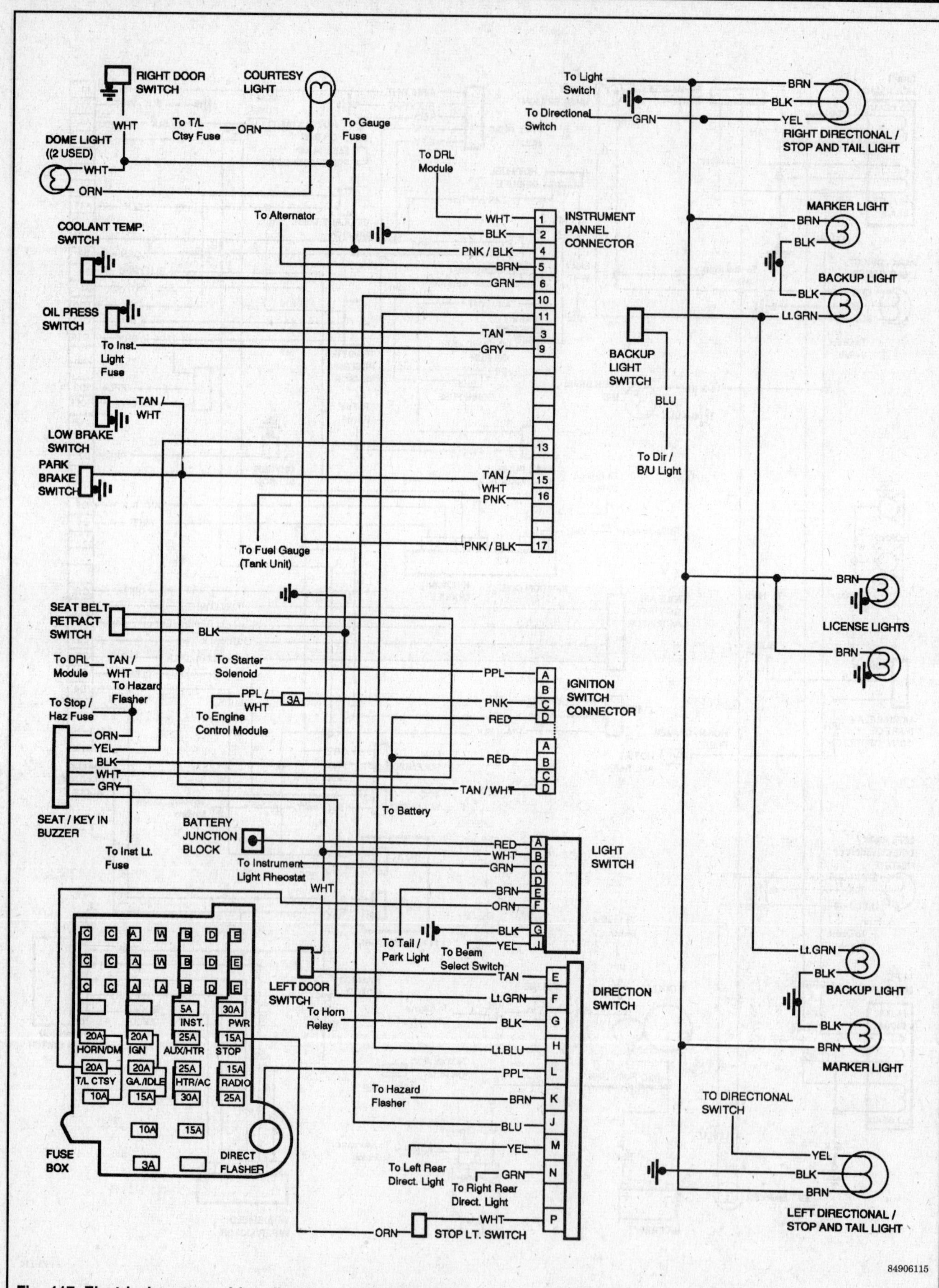

Fig. 117 Electrical system wiring diagram — 1991 R/V series

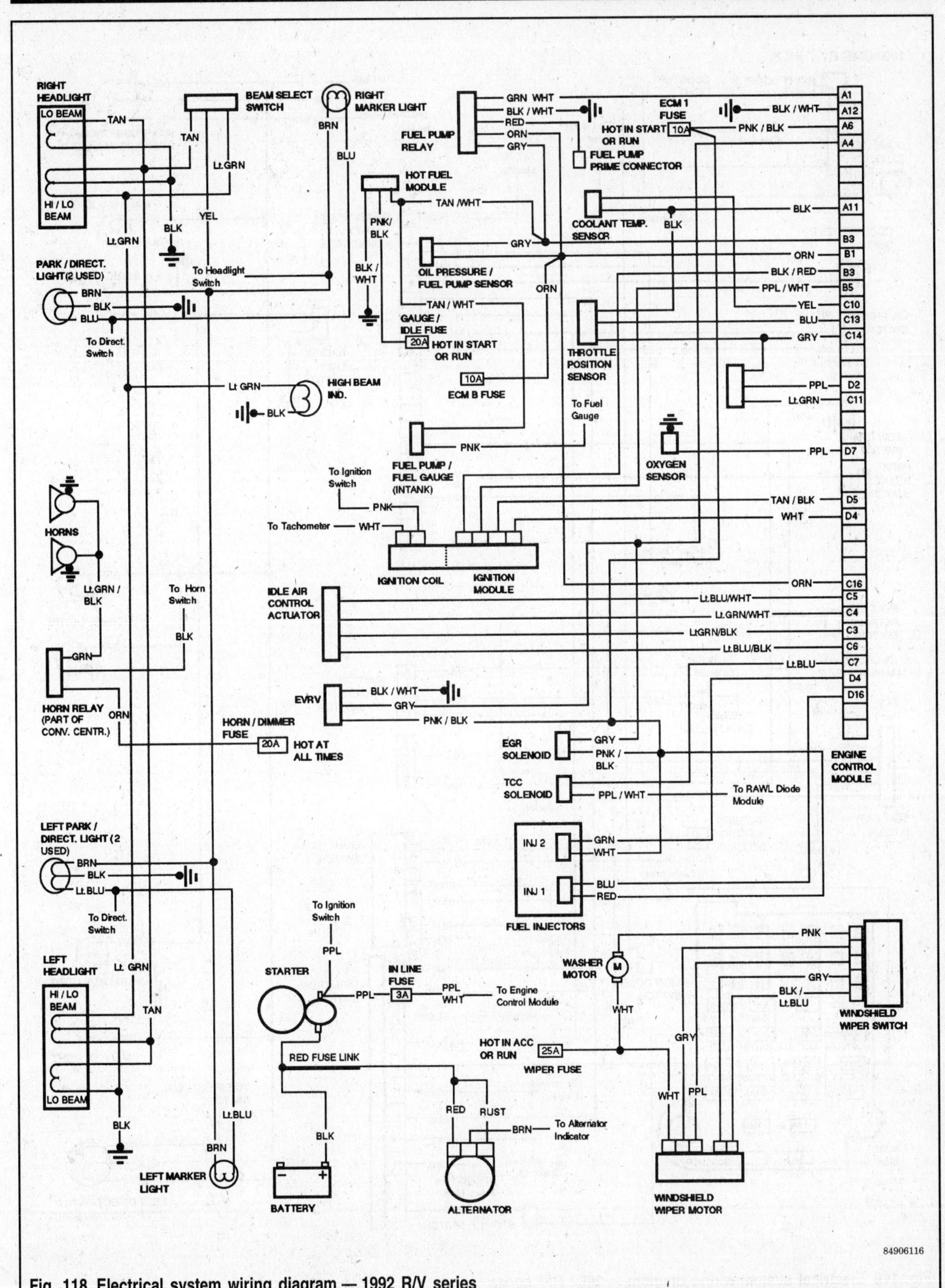

Fig. 118 Electrical system wiring diagram — 1992 R/V series

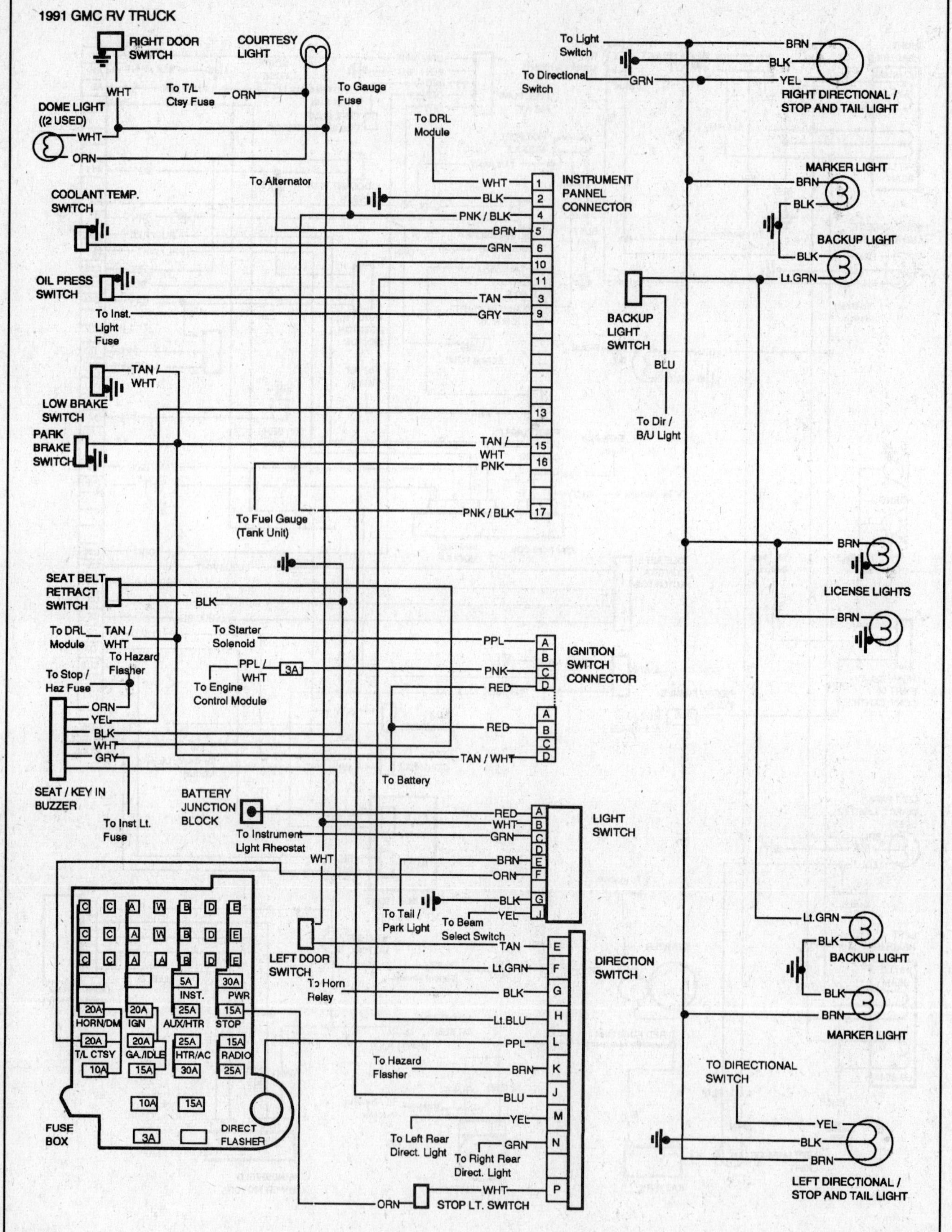

1991 GMC RV TRUCK

RIGHT DOOR SWITCH
COURTESY LIGHT
WHT
To T/L Ctsy Fuse
ORN
To Gauge Fuse
DOME LIGHT ((2 USED)
WHT
ORN
To DRL Module
To Alternator
COOLANT TEMP. SWITCH
OIL PRESS SWITCH
To Inst. Light Fuse
TAN / WHT
LOW BRAKE SWITCH
PARK BRAKE SWITCH
To Fuel Gauge (Tank Unit)
INSTRUMENT PANNEL CONNECTOR
WHT 1
BLK 2
PNK / BLK 4
BRN 5
GRN 6
10
11
TAN 3
GRY 9
13
TAN / WHT 15
PNK 16
PNK / BLK 17
To Light Switch
To Directional Switch
GRN
BRN
BLK
YEL
RIGHT DIRECTIONAL / STOP AND TAIL LIGHT
MARKER LIGHT
BRN
BLK
BACKUP LIGHT
BLK
Lt.GRN
BACKUP LIGHT SWITCH
BLU
To Dir / B/U Light
BRN
BRN
LICENSE LIGHTS
SEAT BELT RETRACT SWITCH
BLK
To DRL Module
TAN / WHT
To Starter Solenoid
To Hazard Flasher
To Stop / Haz Fuse
PPL / WHT
3A
To Engine Control Module
ORN
YEL
BLK
WHT
GRY
SEAT / KEY IN BUZZER
To Inst Lt. Fuse
IGNITION SWITCH CONNECTOR
PPL A
B
PNK C
RED D
A
RED B
C
TAN / WHT D
To Battery
BATTERY JUNCTION BLOCK
To Instrument Light Rheostat
WHT
LIGHT SWITCH
RED A
WHT B
GRN C
D
BRN E
ORN F
BLK G
YEL J
To Tail / Park Light
To Beam Select Switch
LEFT DOOR SWITCH
To Horn Relay
DIRECTION SWITCH
TAN E
Lt.GRN F
BLK G
Lt.BLU H
PPL L
To Hazard Flasher
BRN K
BLU J
YEL M
To Left Rear Direct. Light
To Right Rear Direct. Light
GRN N
WHT P
ORN
STOP LT. SWITCH
Lt.GRN
BLK
BACKUP LIGHT
BLK
BRN
MARKER LIGHT
TO DIRECTIONAL SWITCH
YEL
BLK
BRN
LEFT DIRECTIONAL / STOP AND TAIL LIGHT
FUSE BOX
C C A W B D E
C C A W B D E
C C A A B D E
5A INST.
30A PWR
20A HORN/DM
20A IGN
25A AUX/HTR
15A STOP
20A T/L CTSY
20A GA./IDLE
25A HTR/AC
15A RADIO
10A
15A
30A
25A
10A
15A
3A
DIRECT FLASHER

84906117

Fig. 119 Electrical system wiring diagram — 1992 R/V series

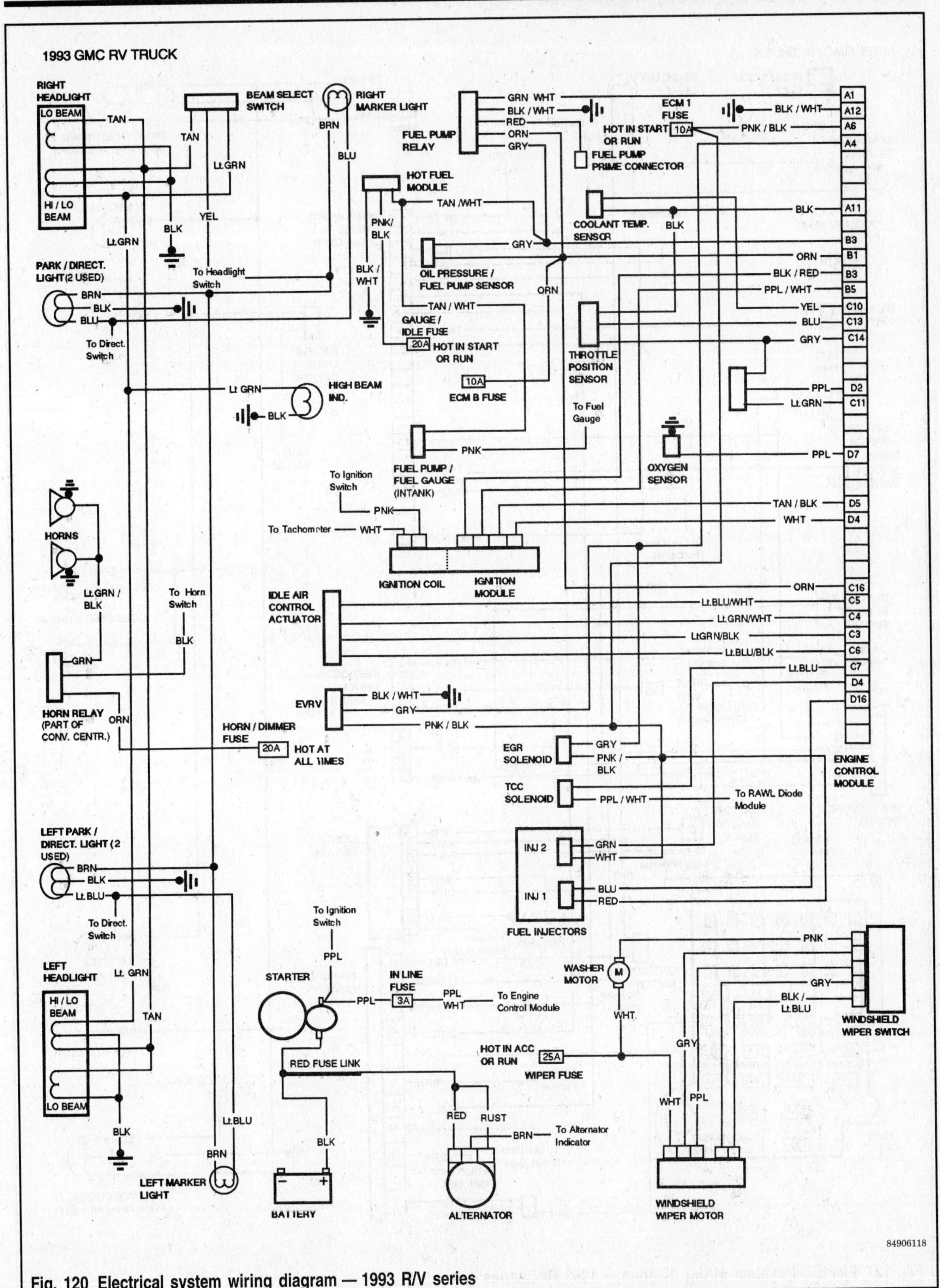

Fig. 120 Electrical system wiring diagram — 1993 R/V series

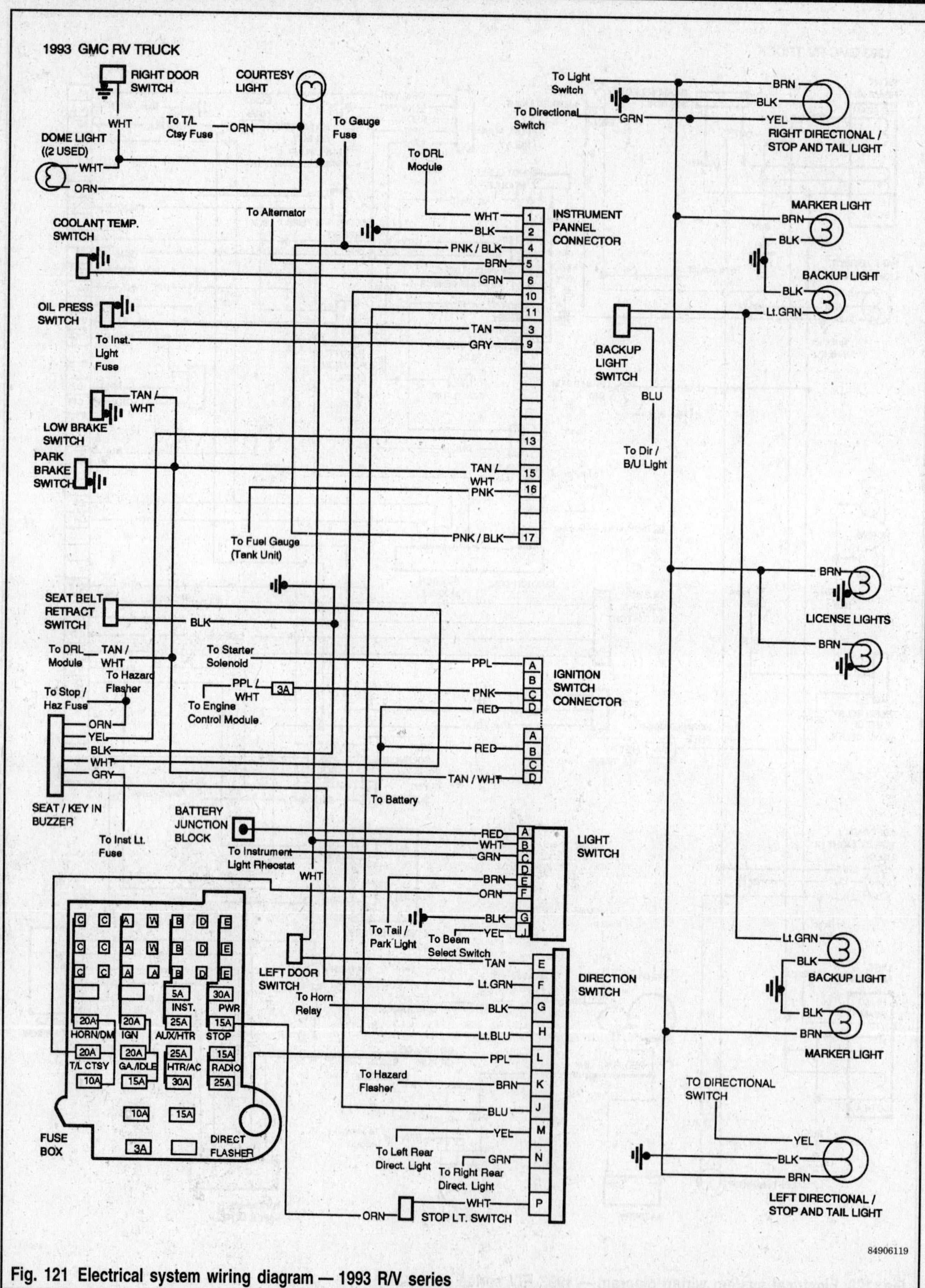

Fig. 121 Electrical system wiring diagram — 1993 R/V series

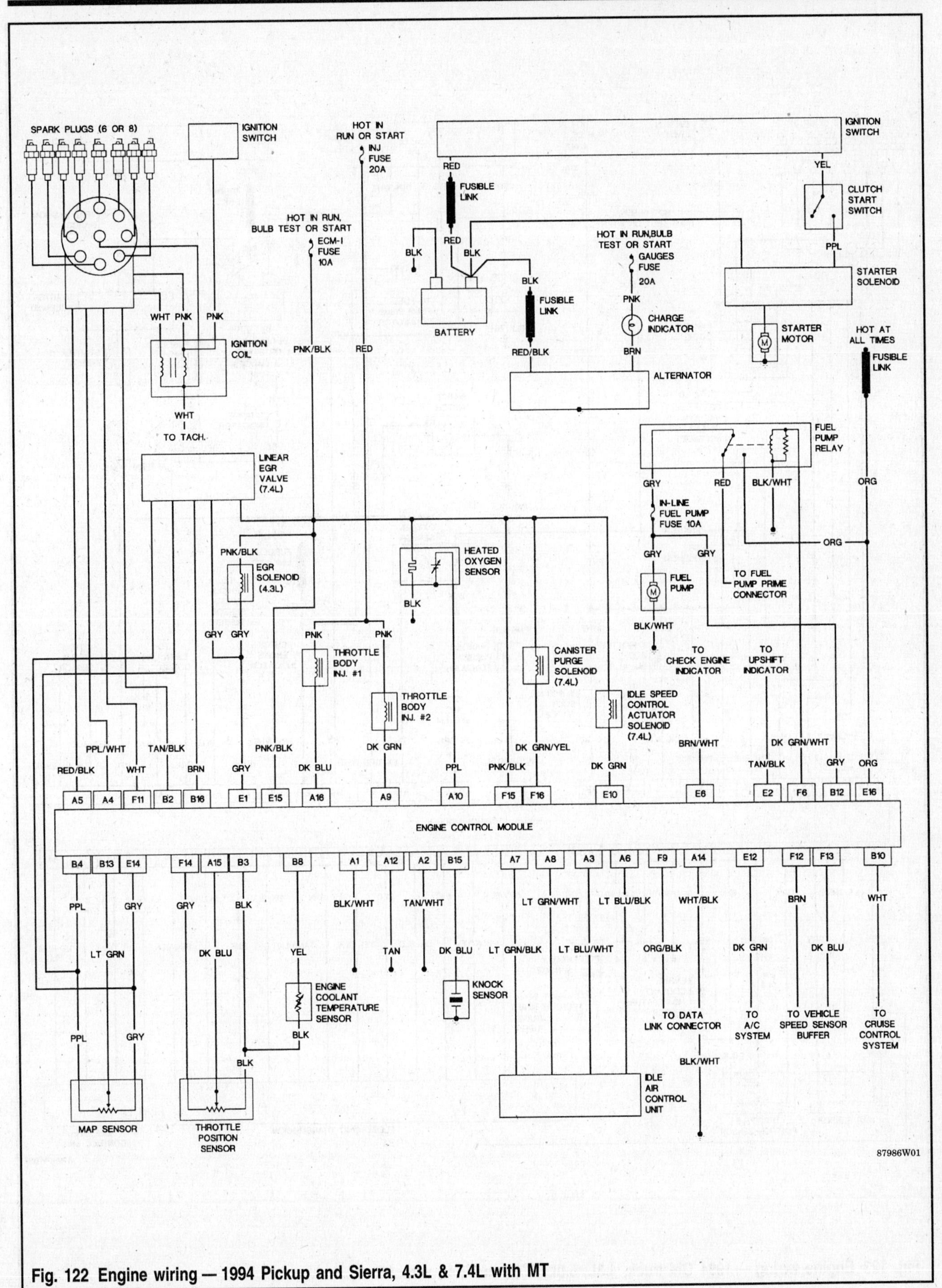

Fig. 122 Engine wiring — 1994 Pickup and Sierra, 4.3L & 7.4L with MT

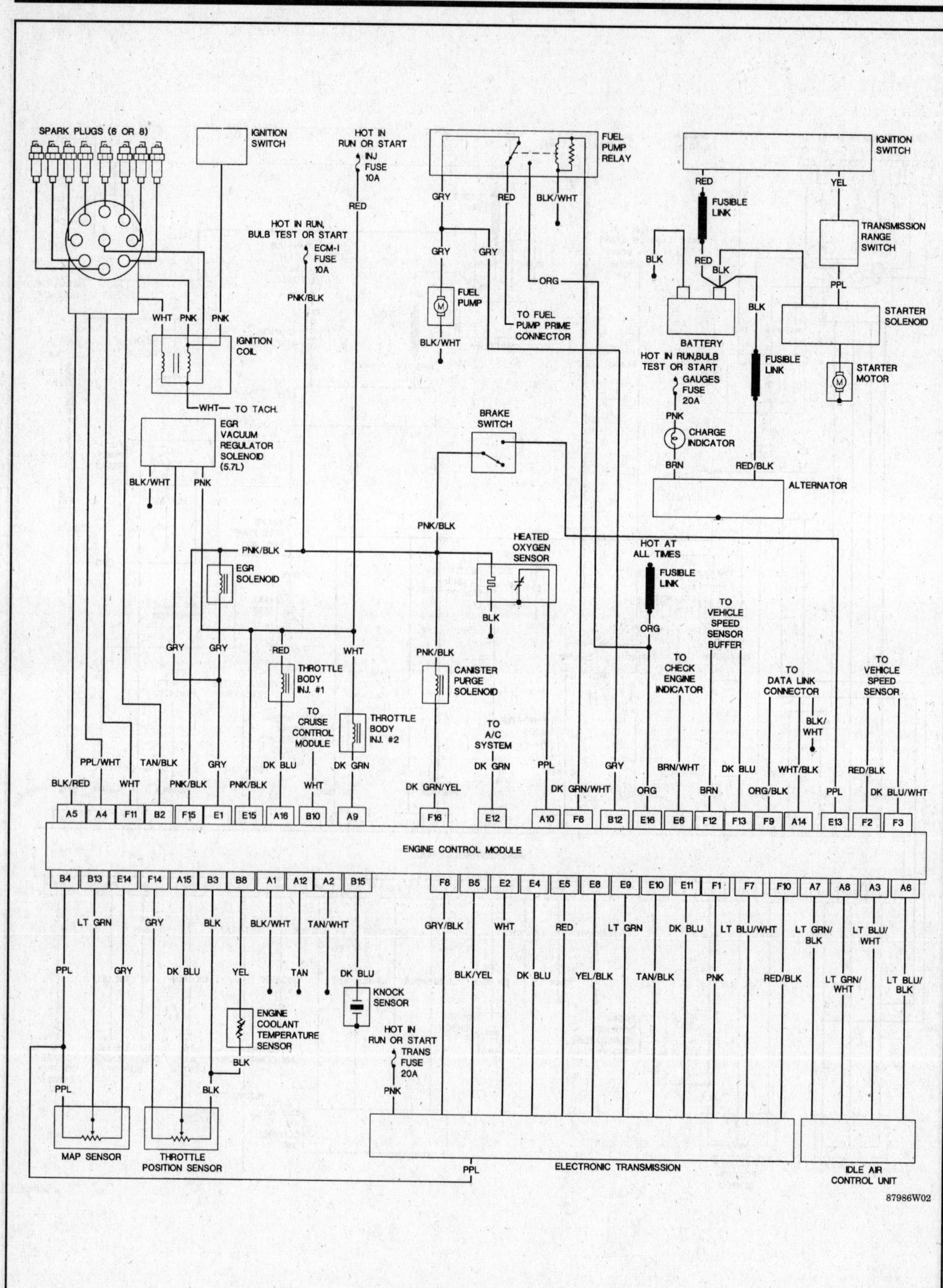

Fig. 123 Engine wiring — 1994 GM truck, 4.3L, 5.0L, 5.7L and 7.4L with AT

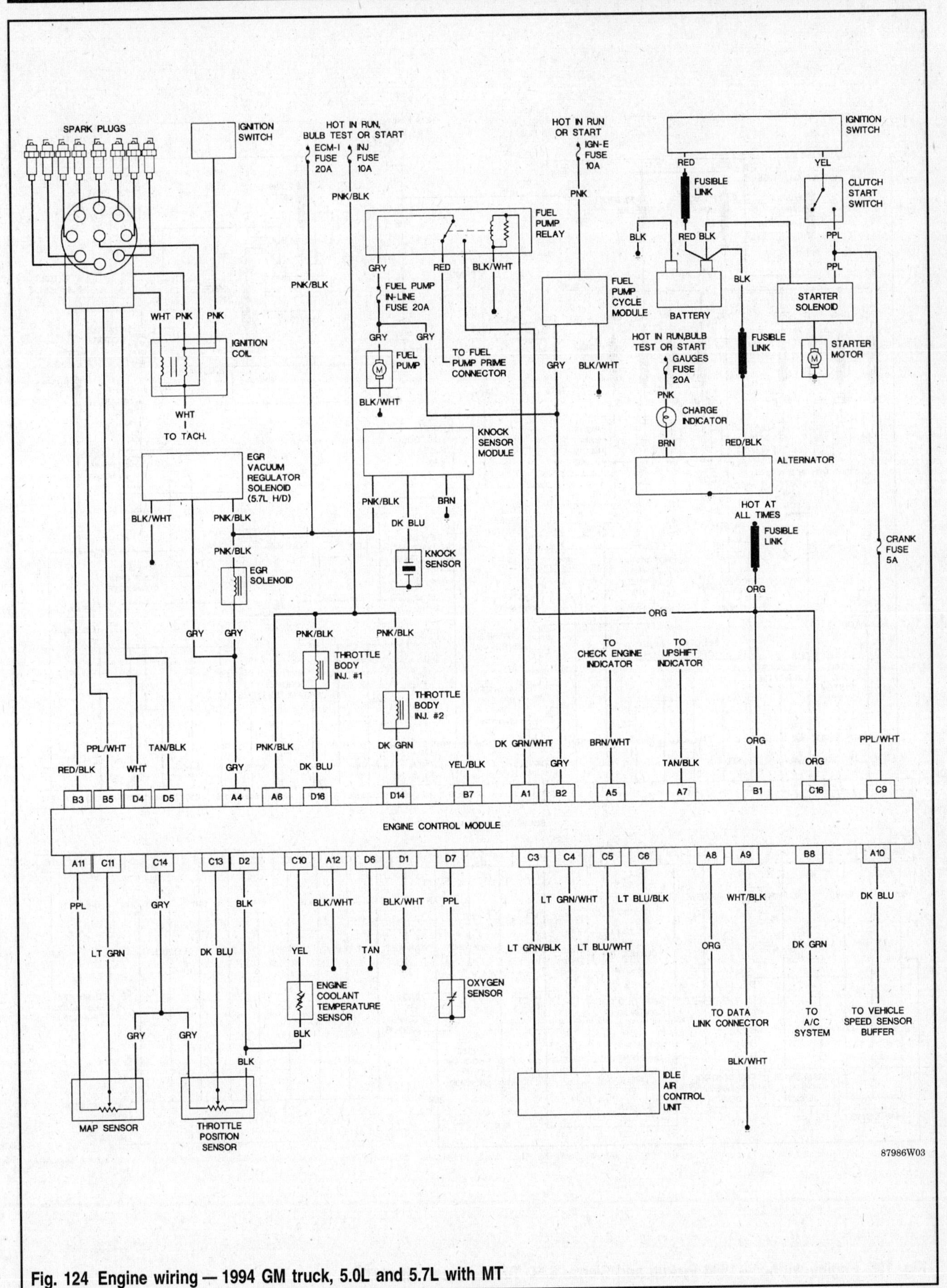

Fig. 124 Engine wiring — 1994 GM truck, 5.0L and 5.7L with MT

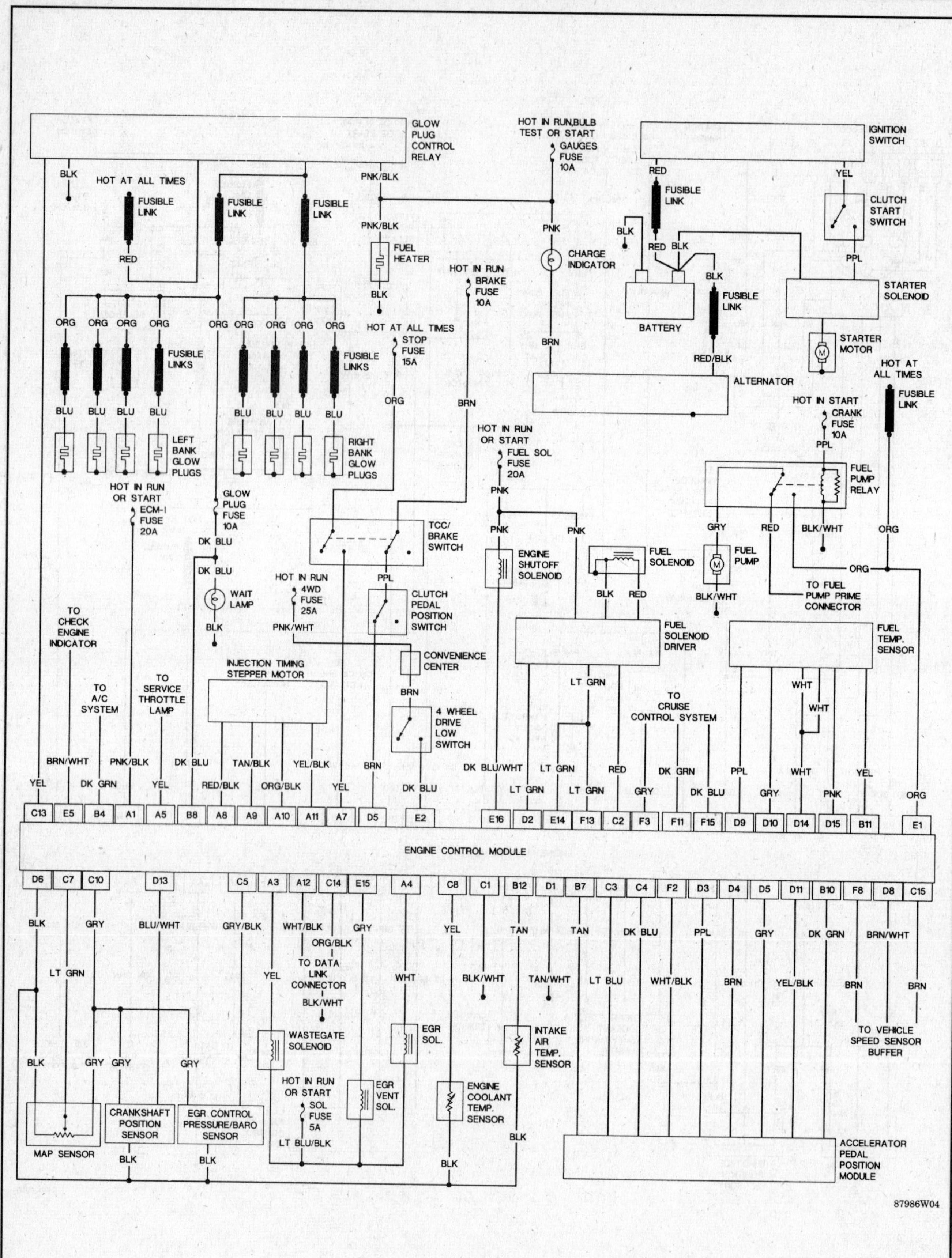

Fig. 125 Engine wiring — 1994 Pickup and Sierra, 6.5L Turbo Diesel with MT

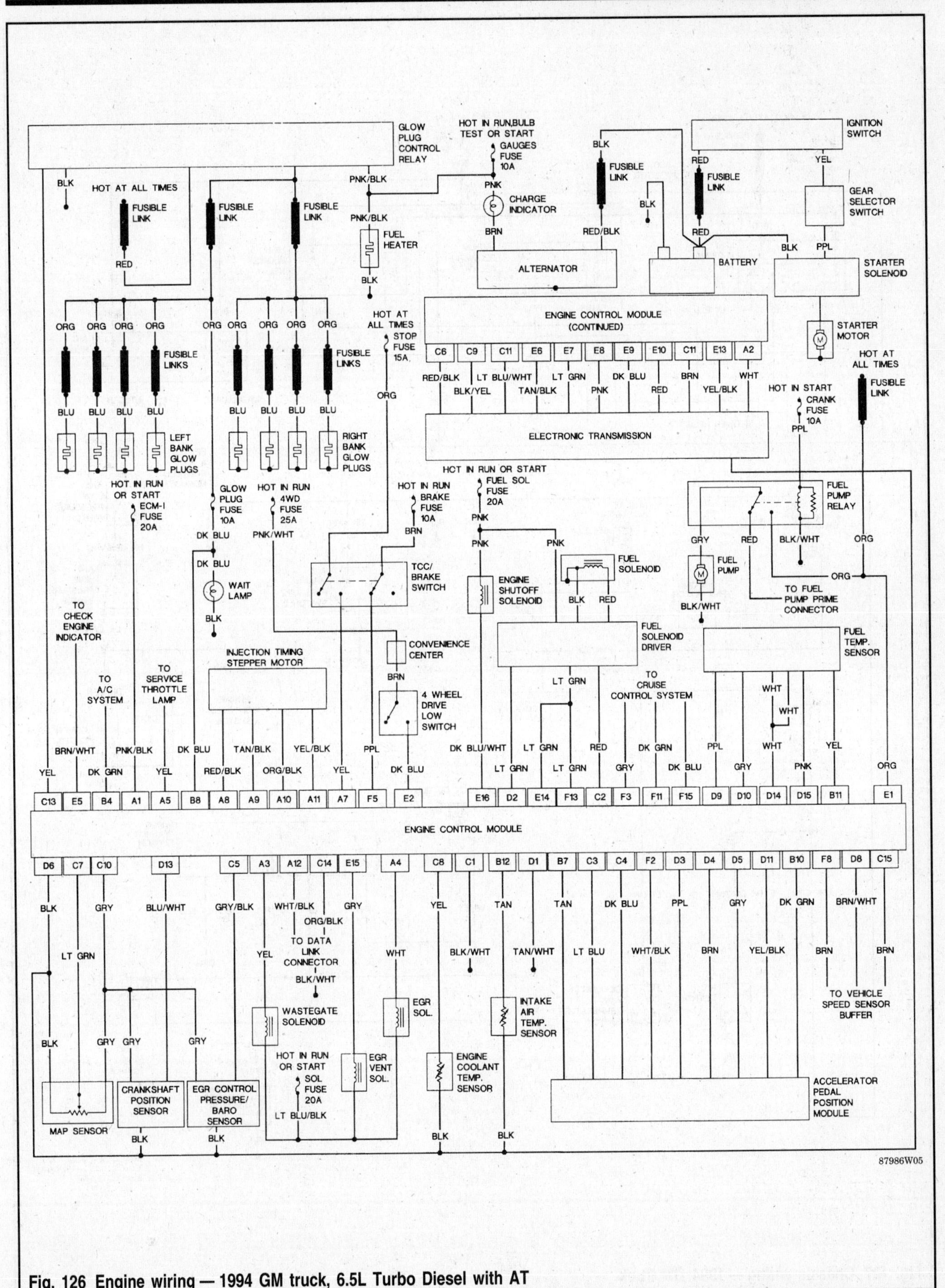

Fig. 126 Engine wiring — 1994 GM truck, 6.5L Turbo Diesel with AT

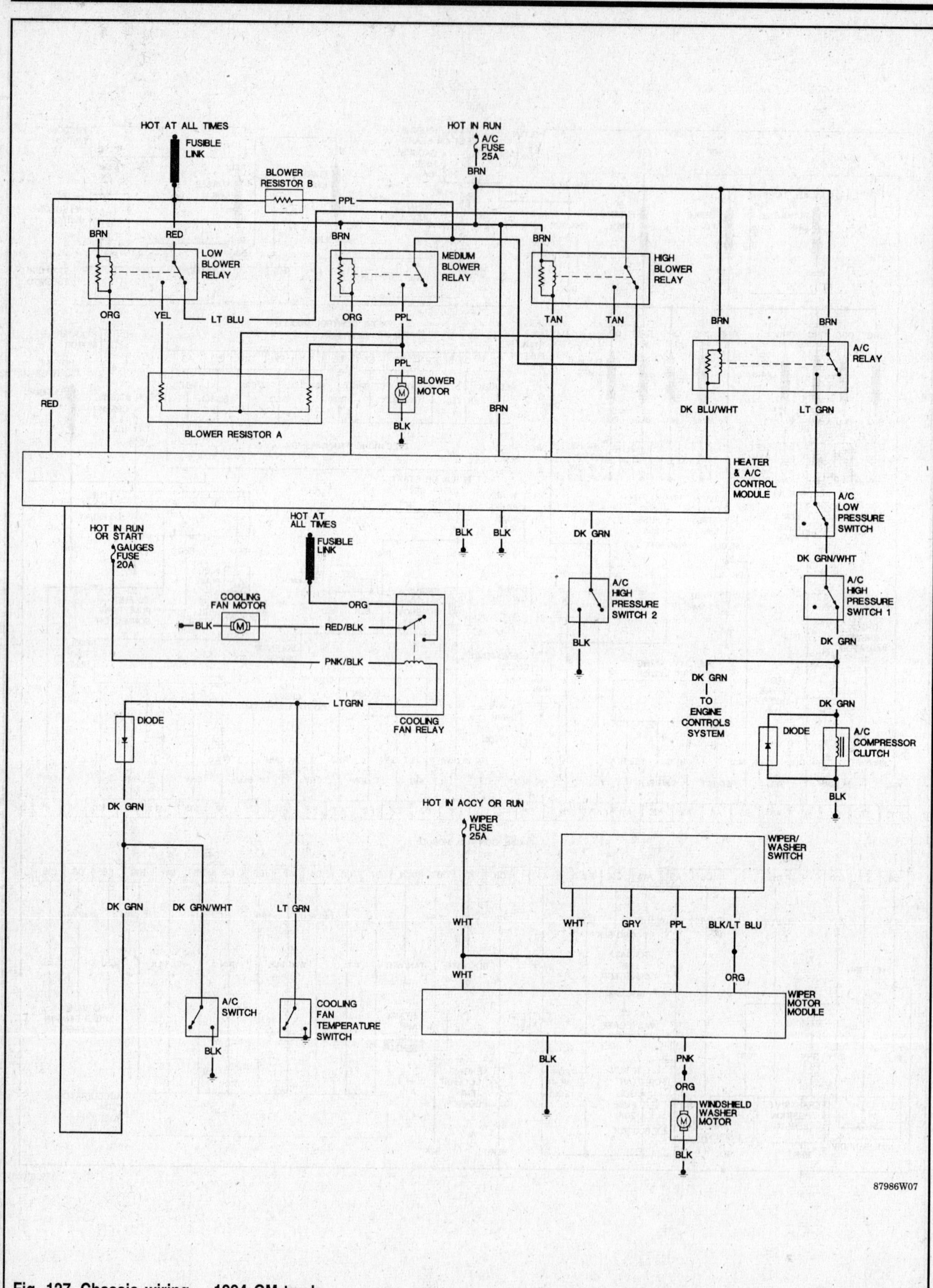

Fig. 127 Chassis wiring — 1994 GM truck

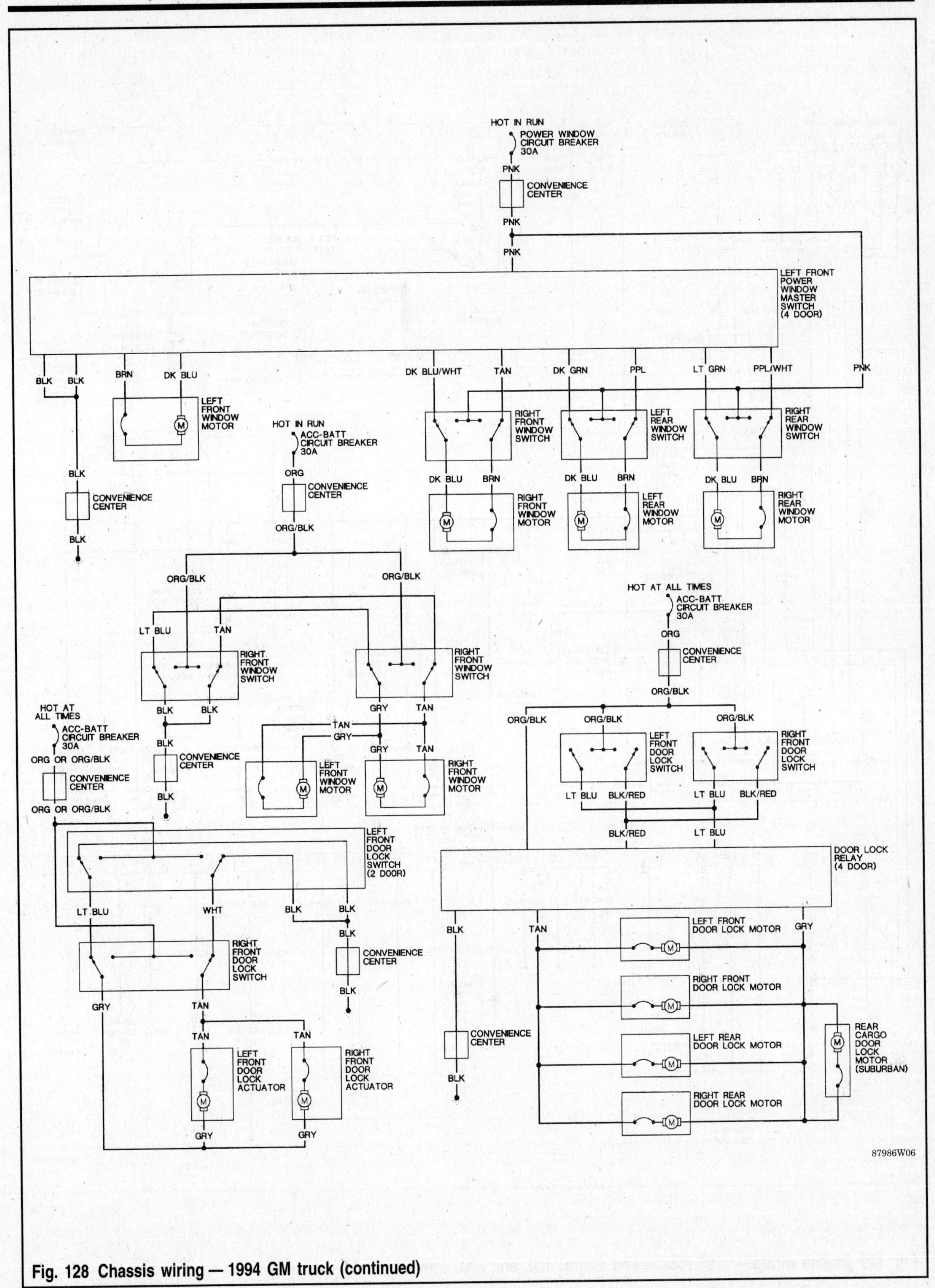

Fig. 128 Chassis wiring — 1994 GM truck (continued)

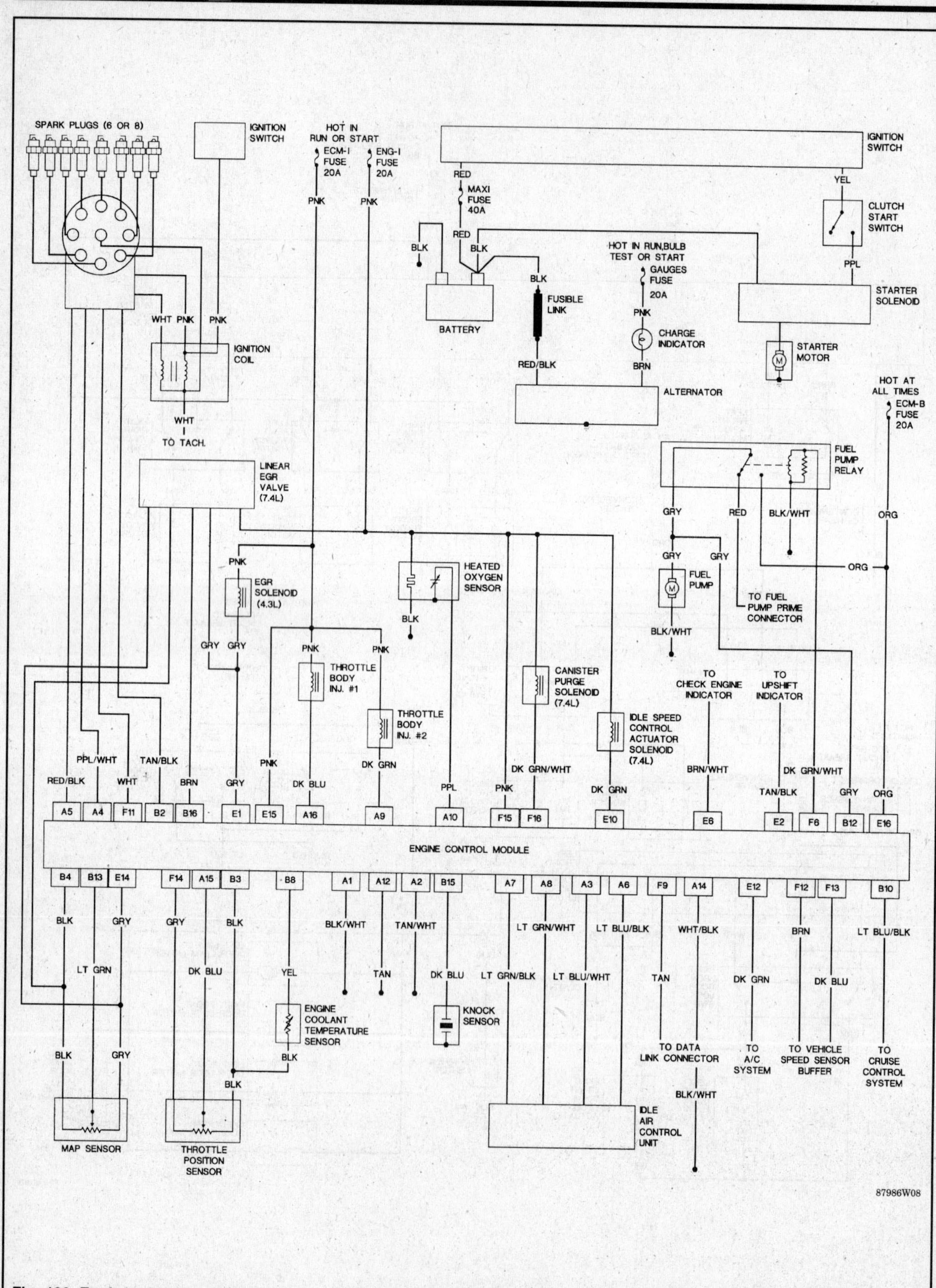

Fig. 129 Engine wiring — 1995 Pickup and Sierra, 4.3L and 7.4L with MT

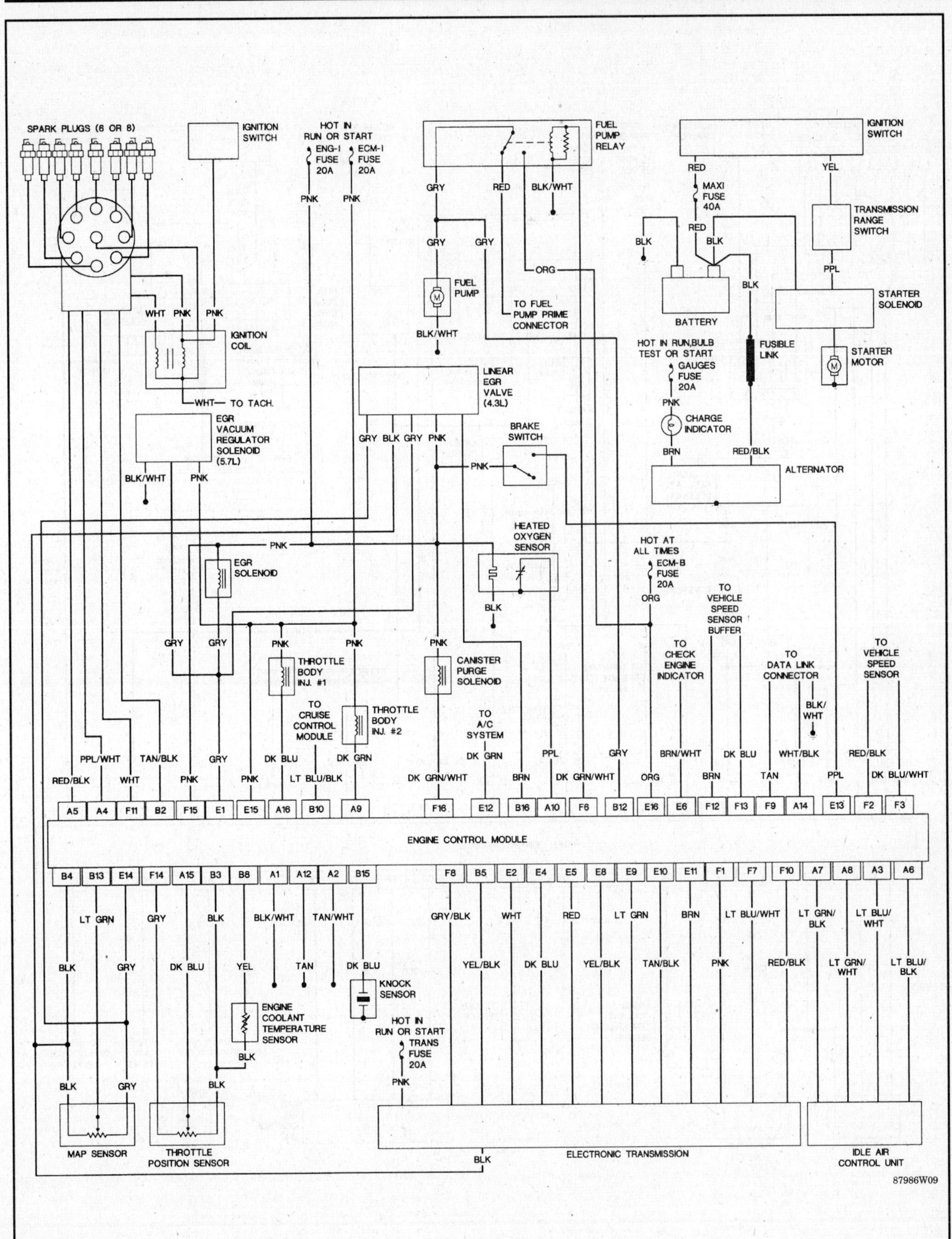

Fig. 130 Engine wiring — 1995 GM truck, 4.3L, 5.0L, 5.7L and 7.4L with AT

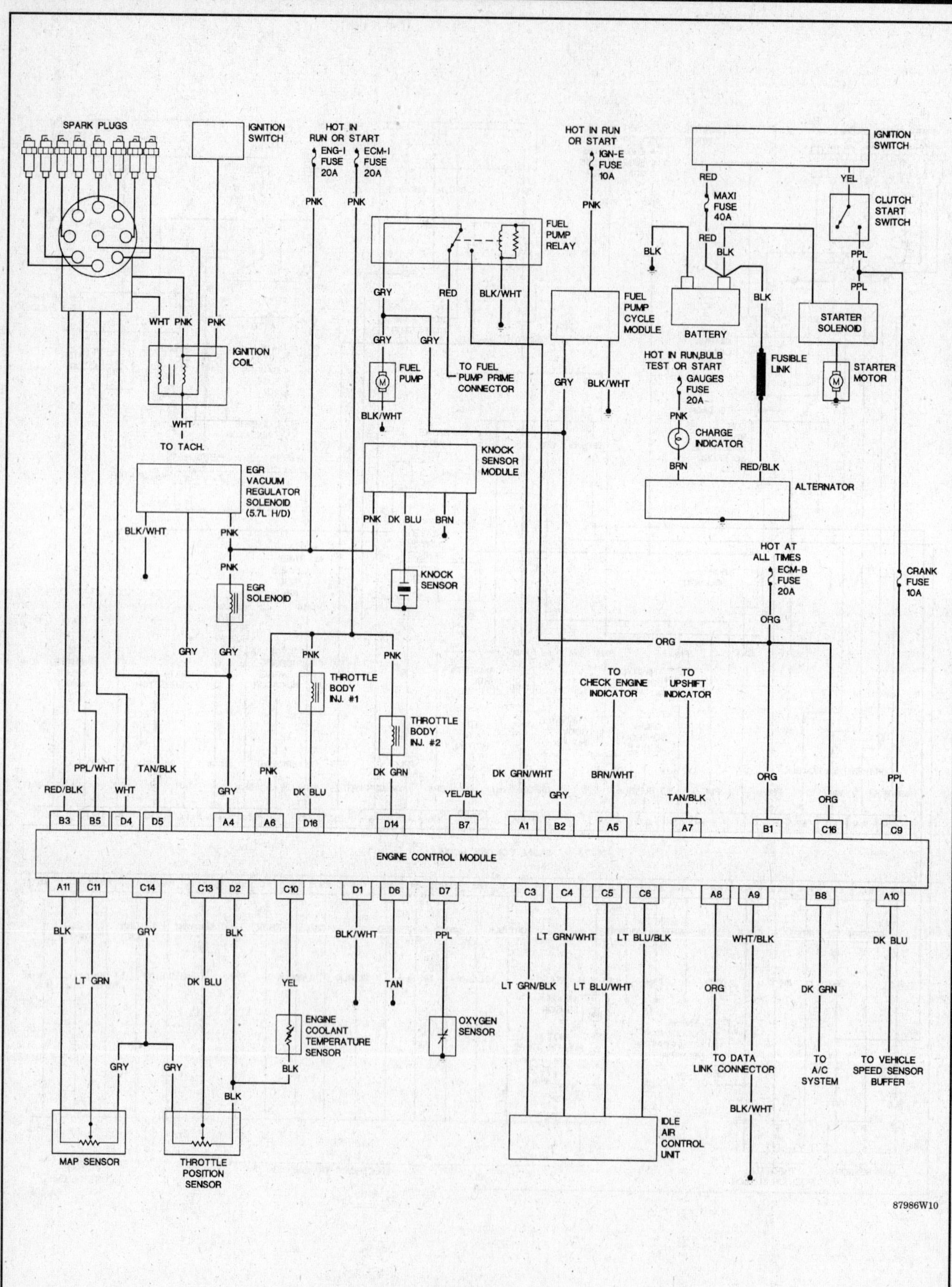

Fig. 131 Engine wiring — 1995 GM truck, 5.0L and 5.7L with MT

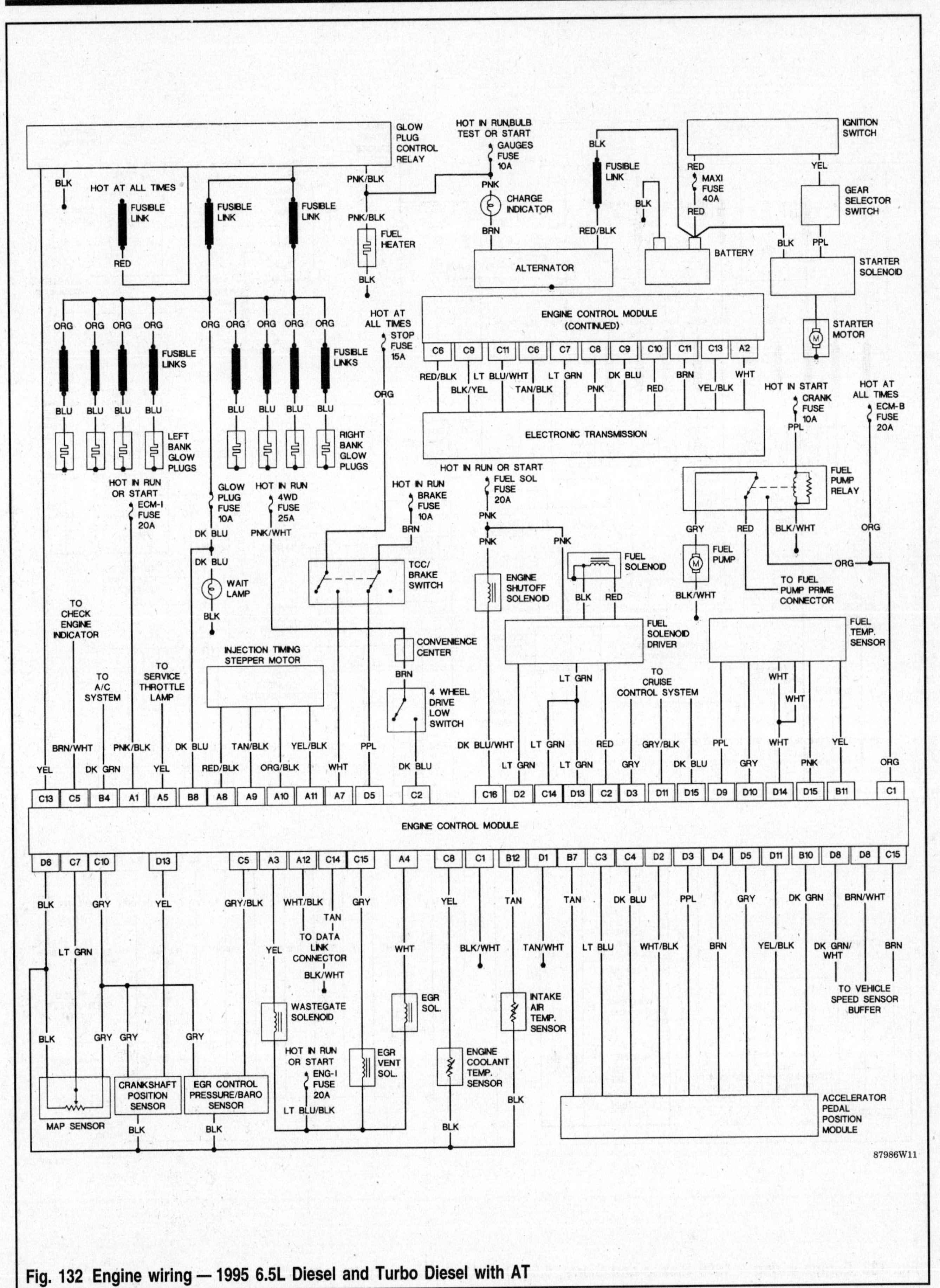

Fig. 132 Engine wiring — 1995 6.5L Diesel and Turbo Diesel with AT

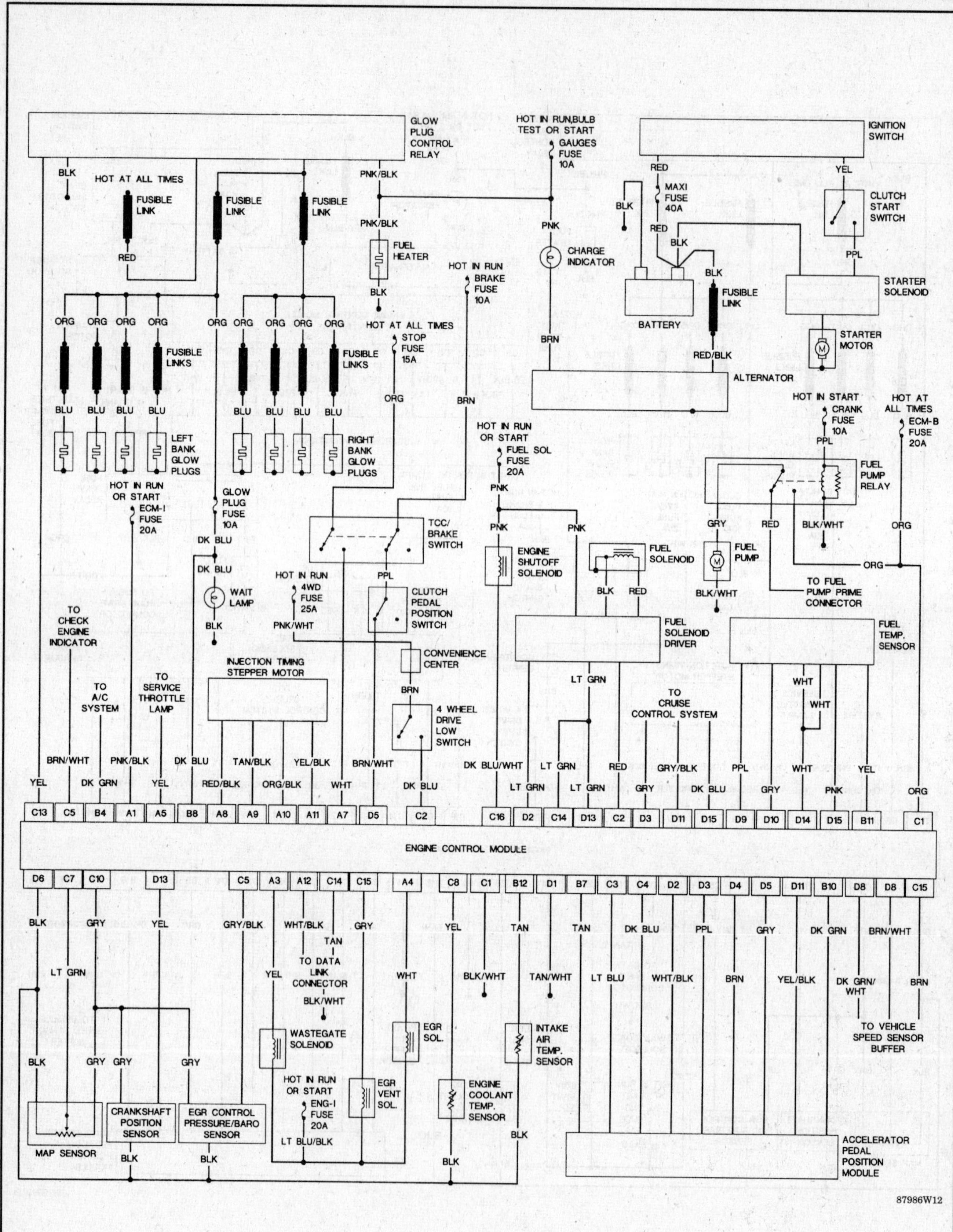

Fig. 133 Engine wiring — 1995 Pickup and Sierra, 6.5L Diesel and Diesel Turbo with MT

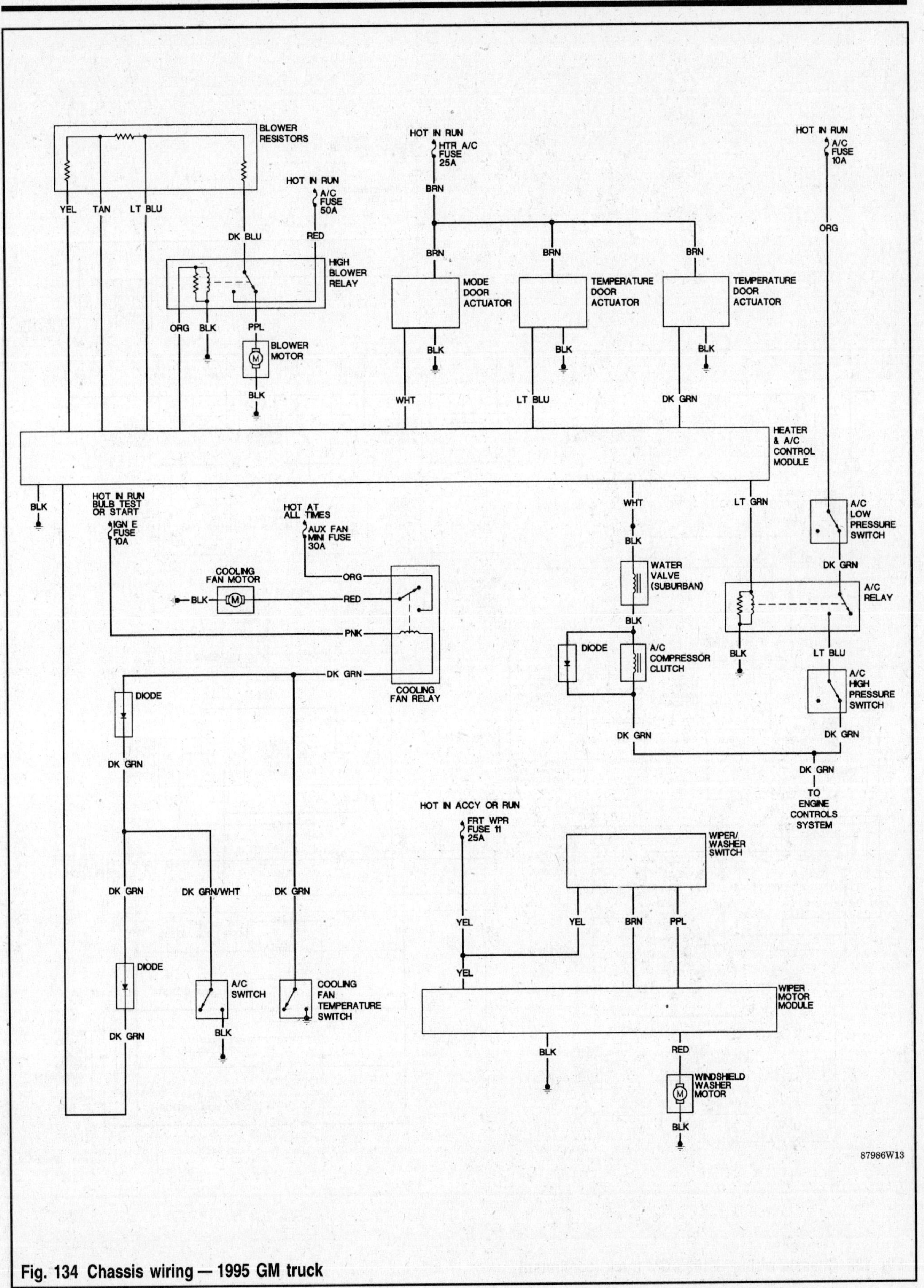

Fig. 134 Chassis wiring — 1995 GM truck

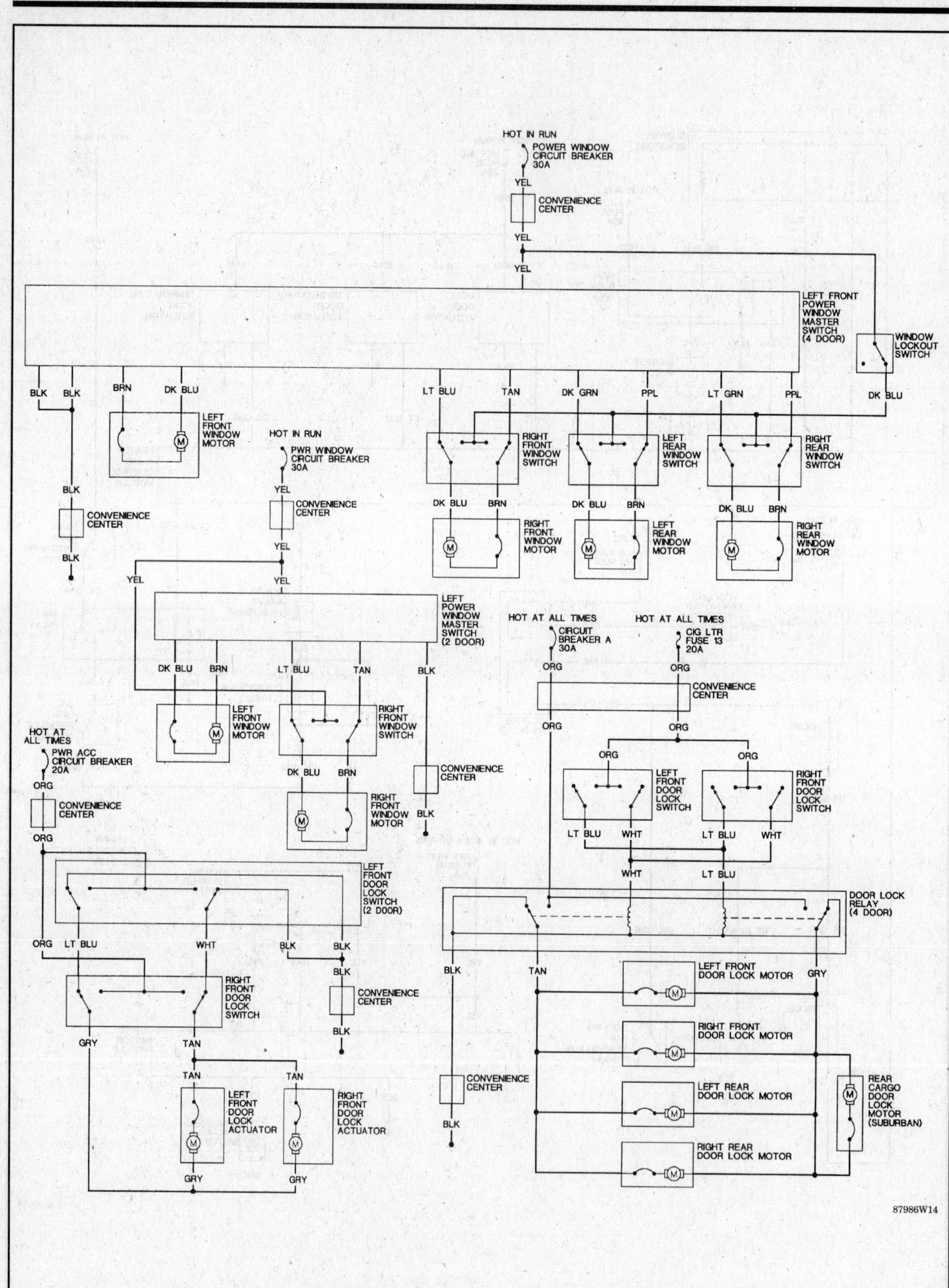

Fig. 135 Chassis wiring — 1995 GM truck (continued)

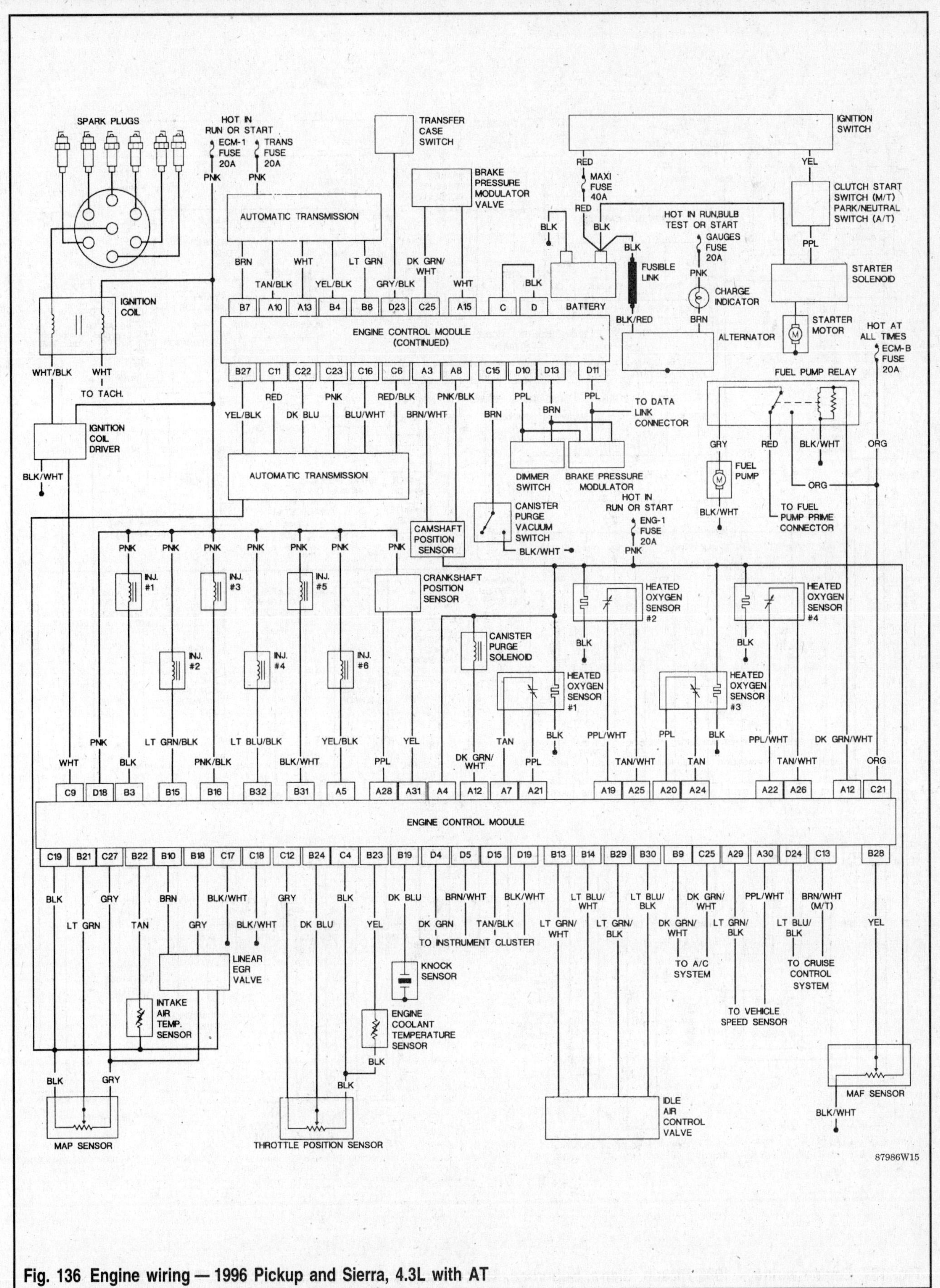

Fig. 136 Engine wiring — 1996 Pickup and Sierra, 4.3L with AT

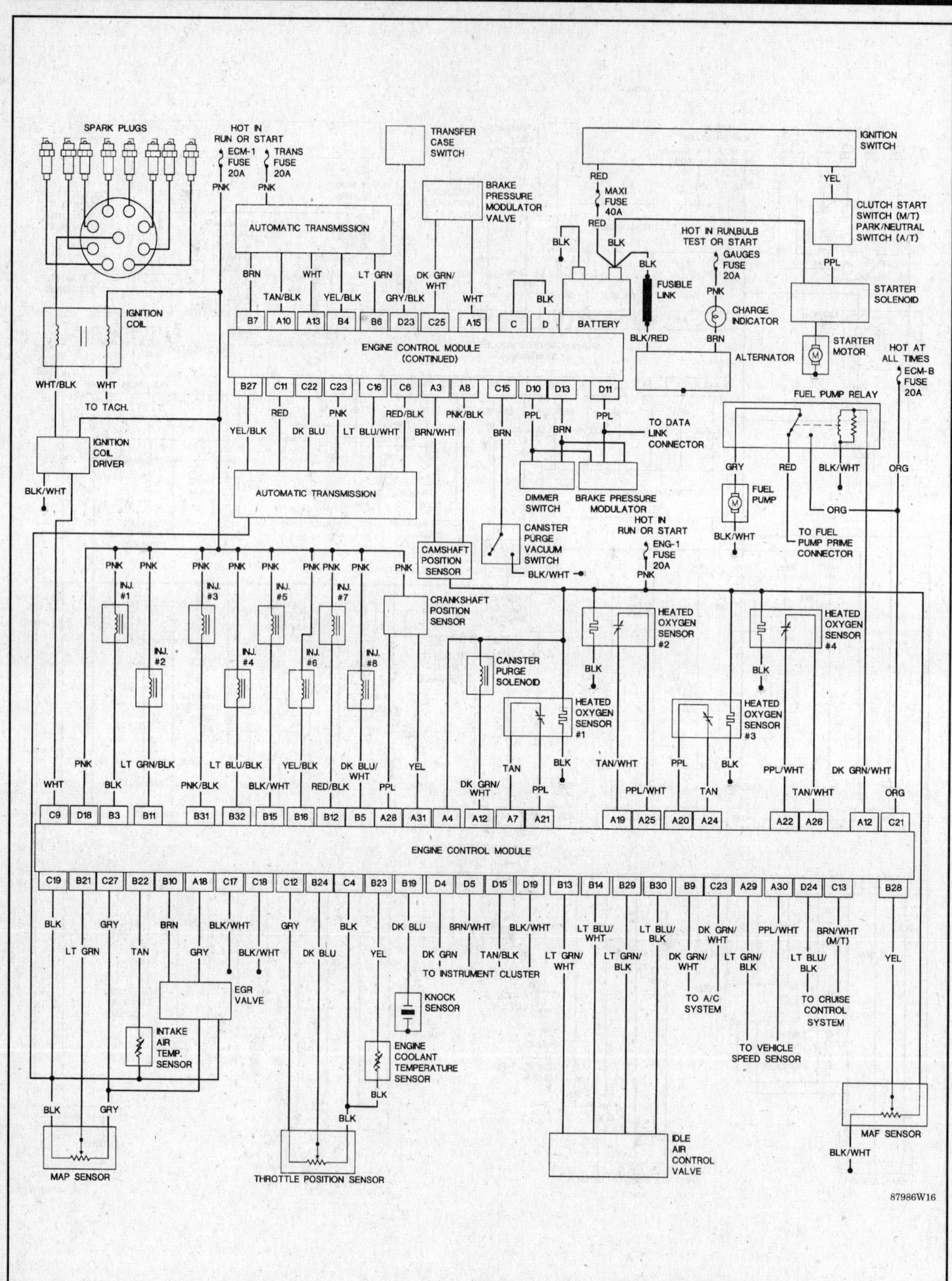

Fig. 137 Engine wiring — 1996 Pickup, Sierra, Suburban, Tahoe and Yukon, 5.0L and 5.7L with MT and AT

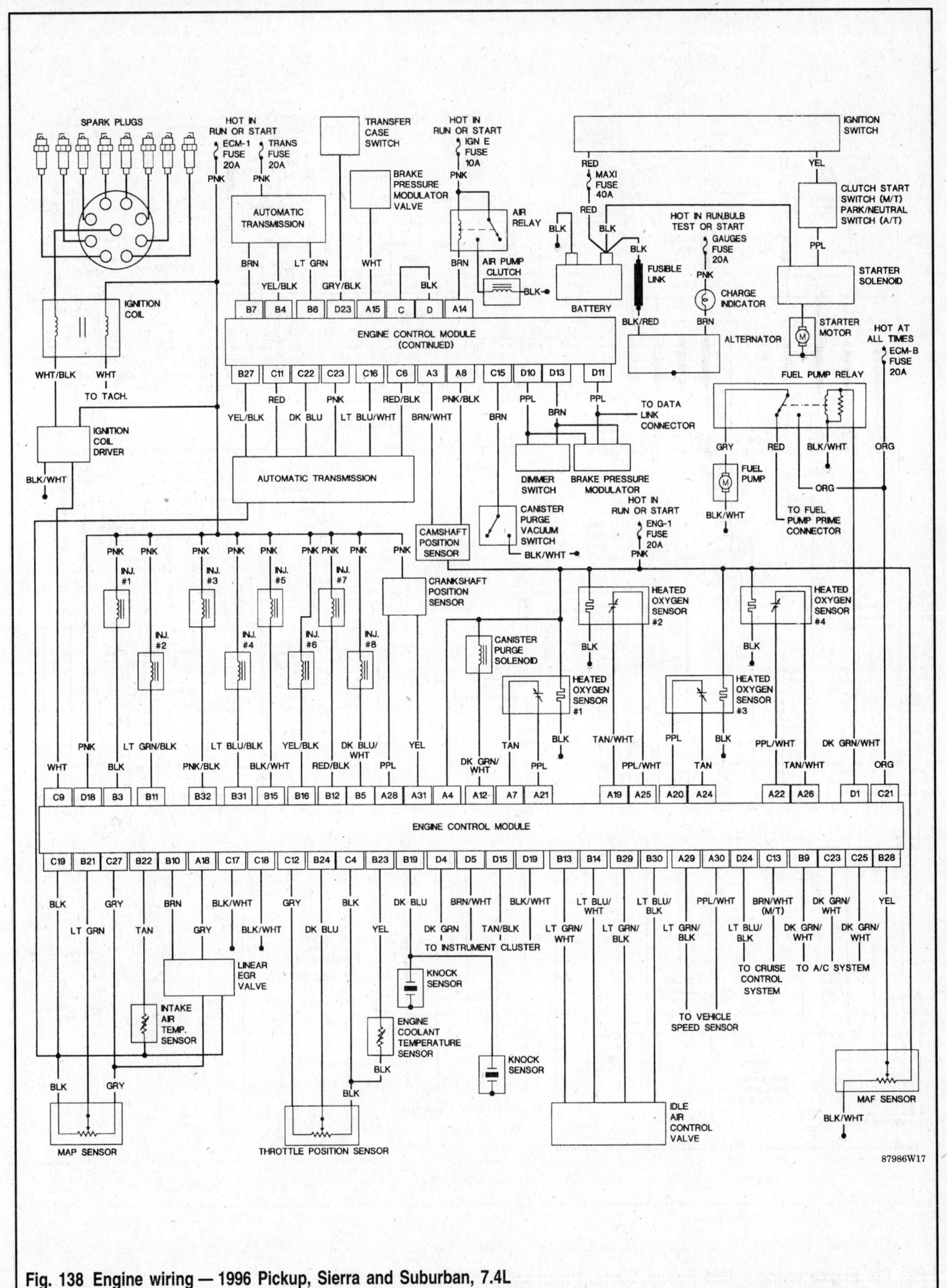

Fig. 138 Engine wiring — 1996 Pickup, Sierra and Suburban, 7.4L

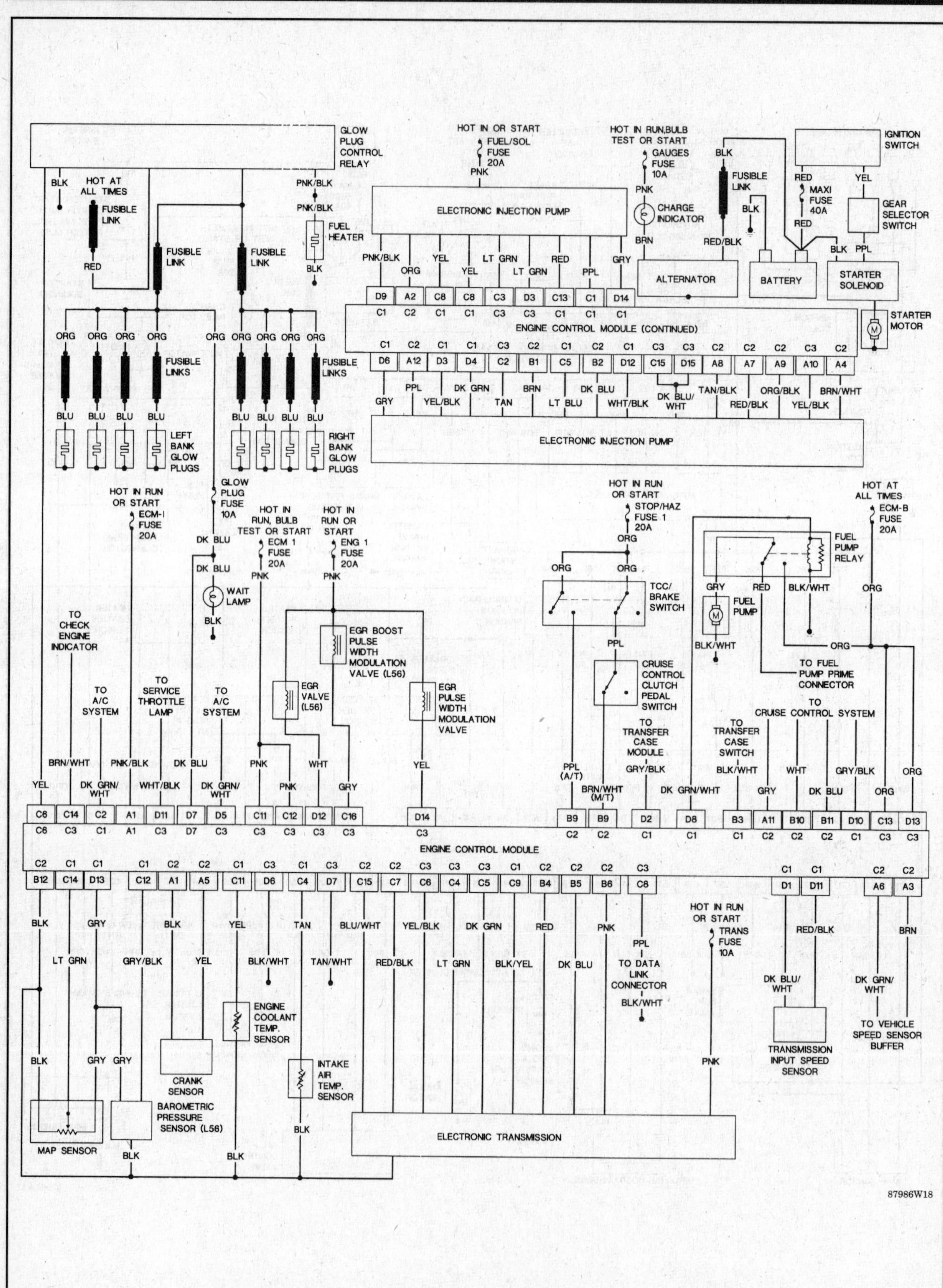

Fig. 139 Engine wiring — 1996 Pickup, Sierra, Yukon and Tahoe, 6.5 Turbo Diesel

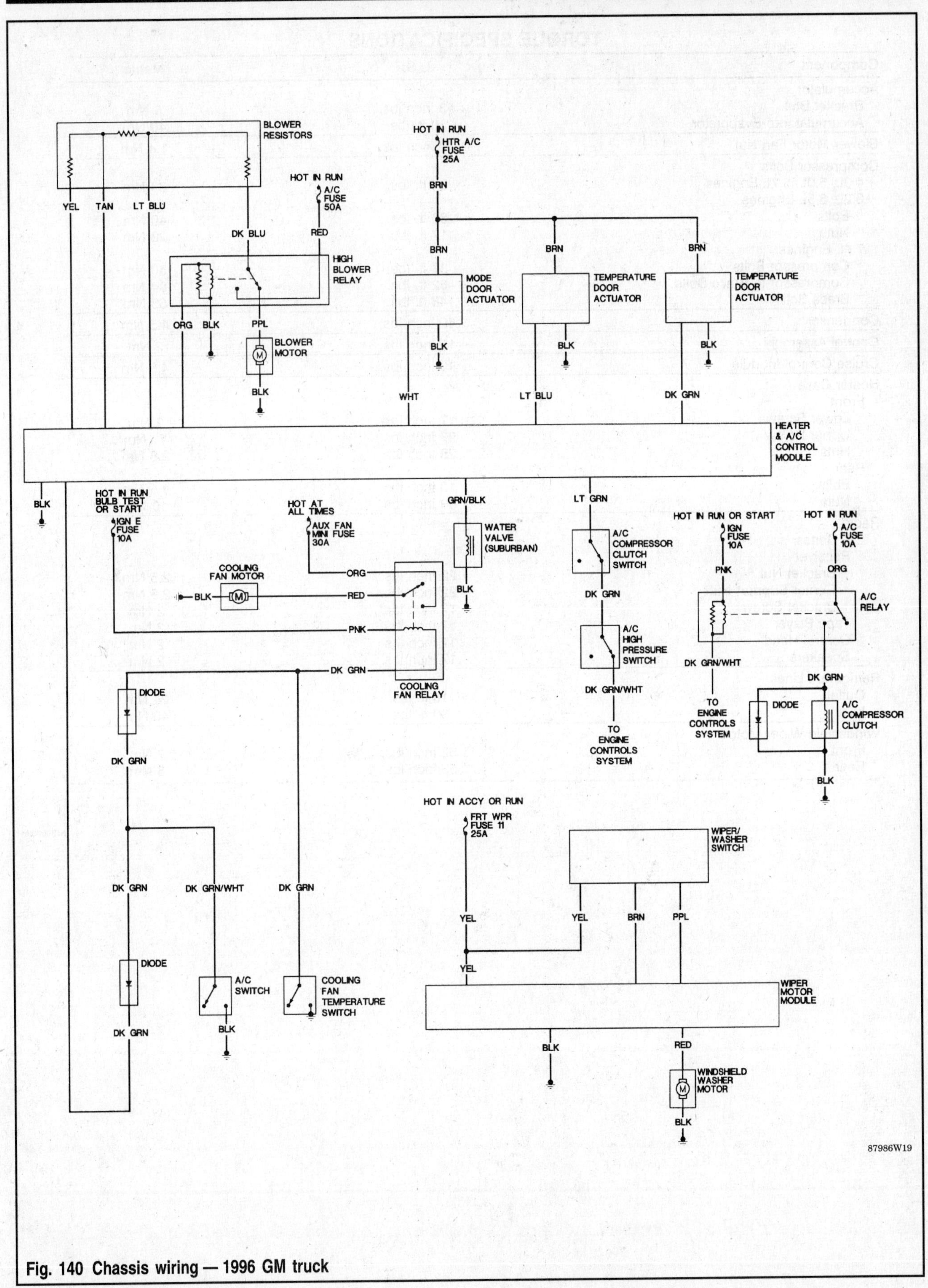

Fig. 140 Chassis wiring — 1996 GM truck

TORQUE SPECIFICATIONS

Component	U.S.	Metric
Accumulator		
Bracket Bolt	53 inch lbs.	6 Nm
Accumulator-to-Evaporator	30 ft. lbs.	40 Nm
Blower Motor Fan Nut	12 inch lbs.	1.4 Nm
Compressor Bolts		
4.3L, 5.0L, 5.7L Engines	24 ft. lbs.	33 Nm
6.2L, 6.5L Engines		
Bolts	30 ft. lbs.	40 Nm
Nuts	17 ft. lbs.	23 Nm
7.4L Engines		
Compressor Bolts	37 ft. lbs.	50 Nm
Compressor-to-Brace Bolts	62 ft. lbs.	84 Nm
Brace Bolt	48 ft. lbs.	65 Nm
Condenser	40 inch lbs.	4.5 Nm
Control Assembly	17 inch lbs.	2 Nm
Cruise Control Module	40 inch lbs.	4.5 Nm
Heater Case		
Front		
Lower Screws	17 inch lbs.	2 Nm
Upper Screw	97 inch lbs.	11 Nm
Nuts	25 inch lbs.	2.8 Nm
Rear		
Bolts	13 inch lbs.	1.5 Nm
Nuts	89 inch lbs.	10 Nm
Radio		
C/K Series		
Receiver		
Bracket Nut	22 inch lbs.	2.5 Nm
Center Support Nut	22 inch lbs.	2.5 Nm
Bracket Screw	17 inch lbs.	2 Nm
Tape Player	17 inch lbs.	2 Nm
Control Head	17 inch lbs.	2 Nm
Speakers	17 inch lbs.	2 Nm
Refrigerant Lines		
Outlet	18 ft. lbs.	24 Nm
Inlet	30 ft. lbs.	40 Nm
Windshield Wiper Motor		
Front	62 inch lbs.	7 Nm
Rear	53 inch lbs.	6 Nm

84906099

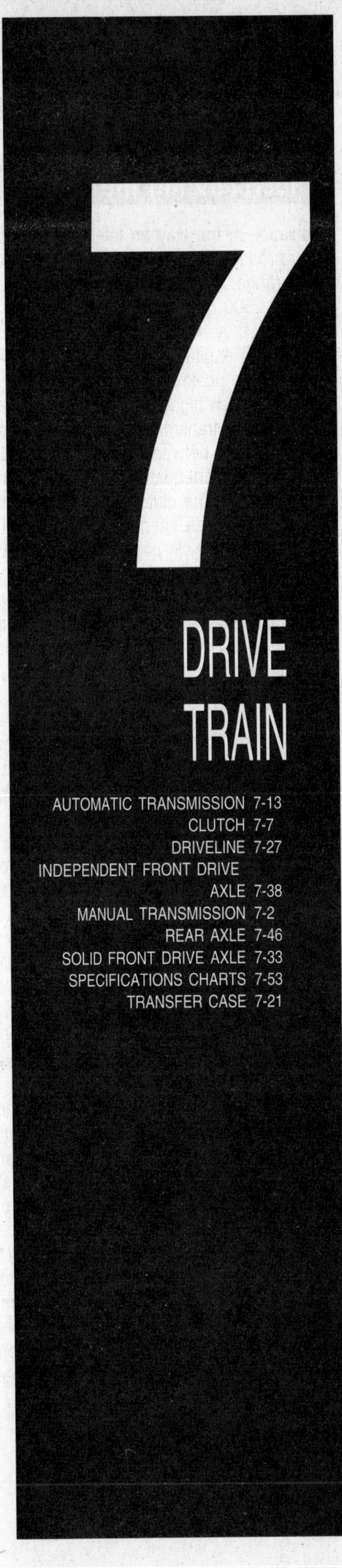

7 DRIVE TRAIN

MANUAL TRANSMISSION

Understanding the Manual Transmission

Because of the way an internal combustion engine breathes, it can produce torque (or twisting force) only within a narrow speed range. Most overhead valve pushrod engines must turn at about 2500 rpm to produce their peak torque. Often by 4500 rpm, they are producing so little torque that continued increases in engine speed produce no power increases.

The torque peak on overhead camshaft engines is, generally, much higher, but much narrower.

The manual transmission and clutch are employed to vary the relationship between engine RPM and the speed of the wheels so that adequate power can be produced under all circumstances. The clutch allows engine torque to be applied to the transmission input shaft gradually, due to mechanical slippage. The vehicle can, consequently, be started smoothly from a full stop.

The transmission changes the ratio between the rotating speeds of the engine and the wheels by the use of gears. 4-speed or 5-speed transmissions are most common. The lower gears allow full engine power to be applied to the rear wheels during acceleration at low speeds.

The clutch driveplate is a thin disc, the center of which is splined to the transmission input shaft. Both sides of the disc are covered with a layer of material which is similar to brake lining and which is capable of allowing slippage without roughness or excessive noise.

The clutch cover is bolted to the engine flywheel and incorporates a diaphragm spring which provides the pressure to engage the clutch. The cover also houses the pressure plate. When the clutch pedal is released, the driven disc is sandwiched between the pressure plate and the smooth surface of the flywheel, thus forcing the disc to turn at the same speed as the engine crankshaft.

The transmission contains a mainshaft which passes all the way through the transmission, from the clutch to the driveshaft. This shaft is separated at one point, so that front and rear portions can turn at different speeds.

Power is transmitted by a countershaft in the lower gears and reverse. The gears of the countershaft mesh with gears on the mainshaft, allowing power to be carried from one to the other. Countershaft gears are often integral with that shaft, while several of the mainshaft gears can either rotate independently of the shaft or be locked to it. Shifting from one gear to the next causes one of the gears to be freed from rotating with the shaft and locks another to it. Gears are locked and unlocked by internal dog clutches which slide between the center of the gear and the shaft. The forward gears usually employ synchronizers; friction members which smoothly bring gear and shaft to the same speed before the toothed dog clutches are engaged.

Adjustments

SHIFT LINKAGE

➧ See Figure 1

1. Loosen the nuts on either side of the swivel. Refer to the illustration of the floor shift linkage for component location.
2. Move the shift control lever to neutral and move the control levers to the front detent and then back one. This will place the transmission in neutral.
3. Place a 0.249-0.250 in. (6-7mm) gauge pin through the control levers and hold the shift rod levers forward tightly and tighten the nuts.
4. Remove the gauge pin and lubricate the levers.

Shift Linkage

REMOVAL & INSTALLATION

1. Remove the cotter pin and the washer.
2. Disconnect the shift rod from the control lever and remove the retainer and washer.
3. Disconnect the shift rod from the shift lever and remove the nuts and swivel.

To install:

4. Install but do not tighten the nuts and swivel.
5. Connect the shift rod to the shift lever.
6. Install the washer and new retainer.
7. Connect the shift rod to the control lever and install the washer and new retainer.
8. Adjust the shift linkage as outlined in this section.

Shift Lever

REMOVAL & INSTALLATION

117mm 4-Speed

➧ See Figure 2

1. On 4WD, remove the transfer case lever boot.
2. Remove the transmission lever boot retaining ring.
3. Remove the boot retaining screws.
4. Remove the boot.
5. Push downward on the cap at the bottom of the lever and turn it counterclockwise. Pull the lever from the transmission.
6. Installation is the reverse of removal.

NVG 4500/NVG 5LM60

➧ See Figures 3 and 4

1. On 4WD, remove the transfer case lever boot.
2. Remove the shift boot retaining ring.

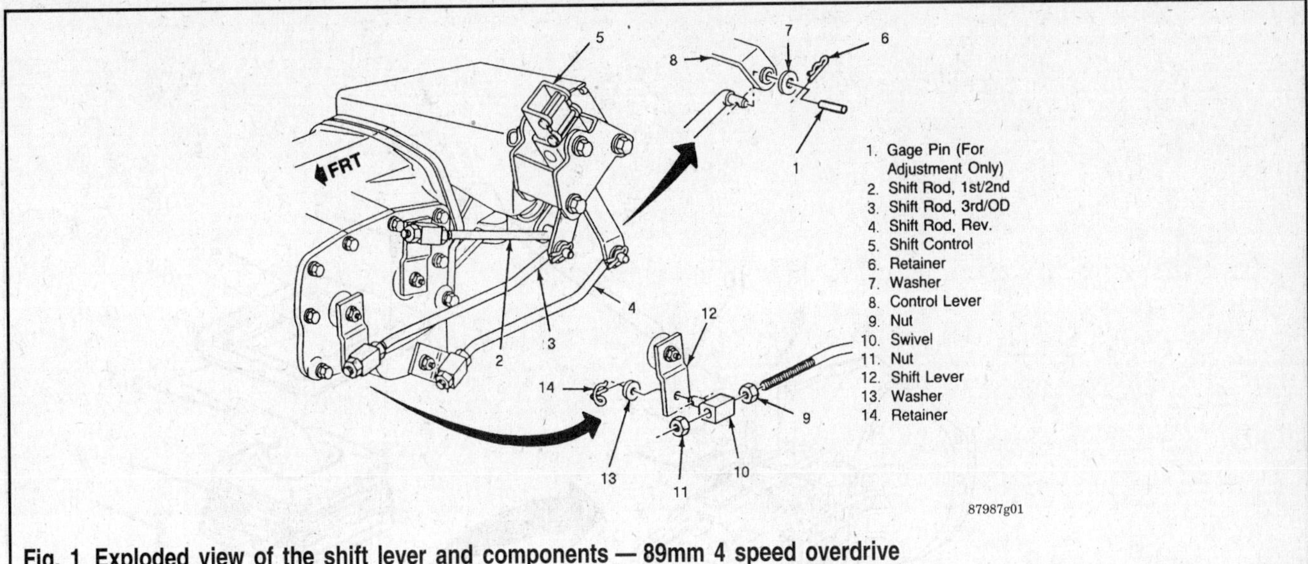

Fig. 1 Exploded view of the shift lever and components — 89mm 4 speed overdrive

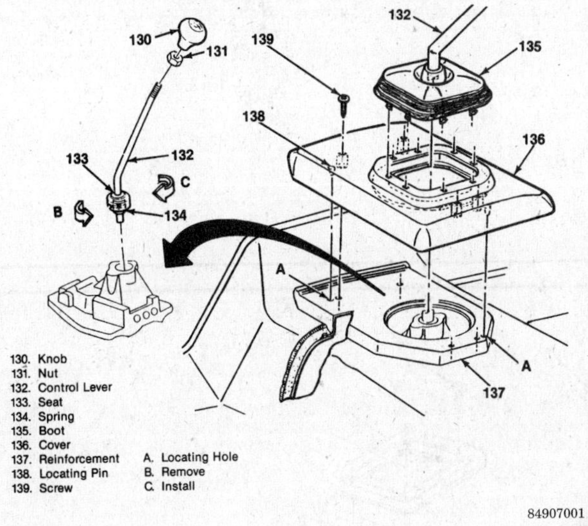

130. Knob
131. Nut
132. Control Lever
133. Seat
134. Spring
135. Boot
136. Cover
137. Reinforcement
138. Locating Pin
139. Screw

A. Locating Hole
B. Remove
C. Install

84907001

Fig. 2 Shift lever and components — 117mm

3. Remove the boot retaining screws and lift off the boot.
4. Loosen the jam nut and unscrew the lever.

Back-Up Light Switch

REMOVAL & INSTALLATION

➧ See Figures 5 and 6

1. Disconnect the negative battery cable.
2. Raise the vehicle and support it safely.
3. Unplug the electrical connector at the switch.
4. Unscrew the switch from the transmission case.
5. Installation is the reverse of removal.

Extension Housing Rear Seal

REMOVAL & INSTALLATION

➧ See Figure 7

1. Raise and support the truck end on jackstands.
2. Drain the transmission oil.
3. Matchmark and disconnect the driveshaft.
4. Deform the seal with a punch and pull it from the housing.
5. Install the seal. Coat the outside of the new seal with locking compound and fill the gap between the seal lips with chassis grease.

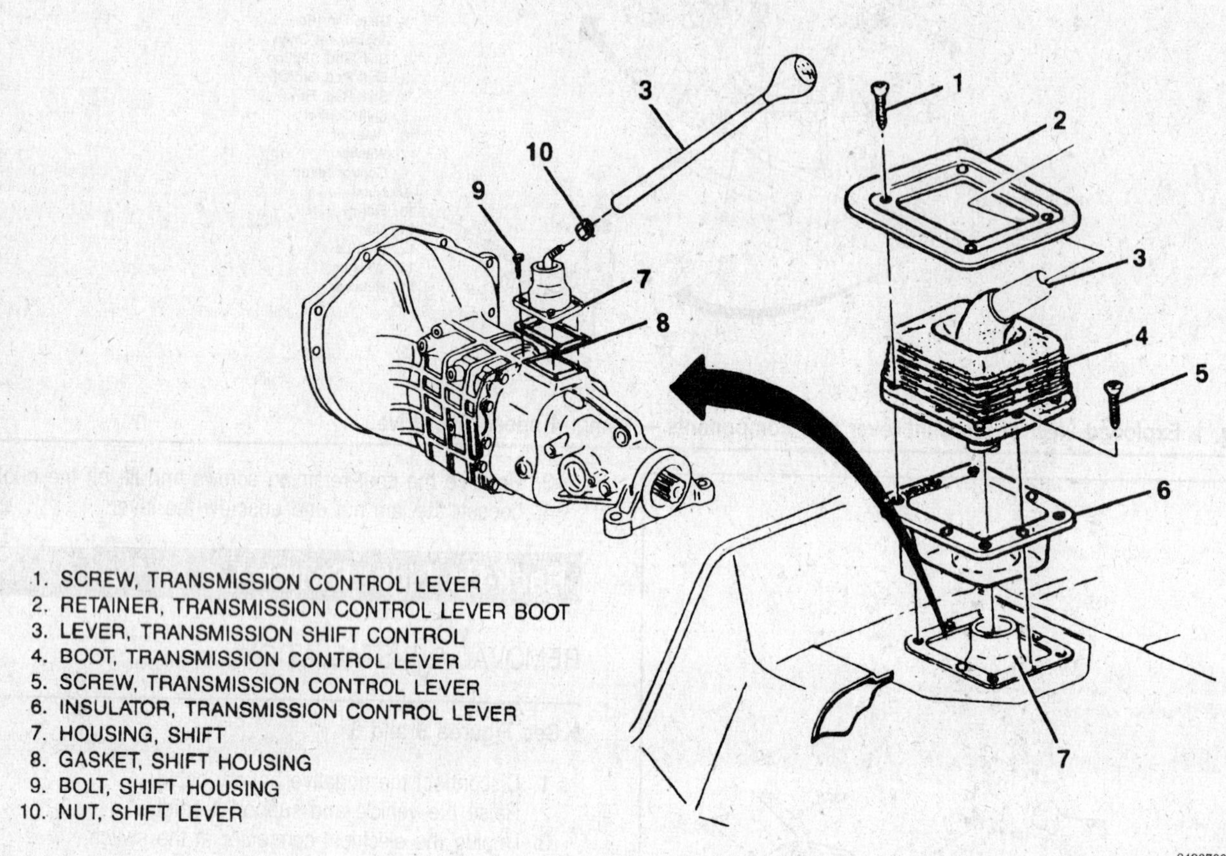

Fig. 3 Shift lever and components — NVG 4500

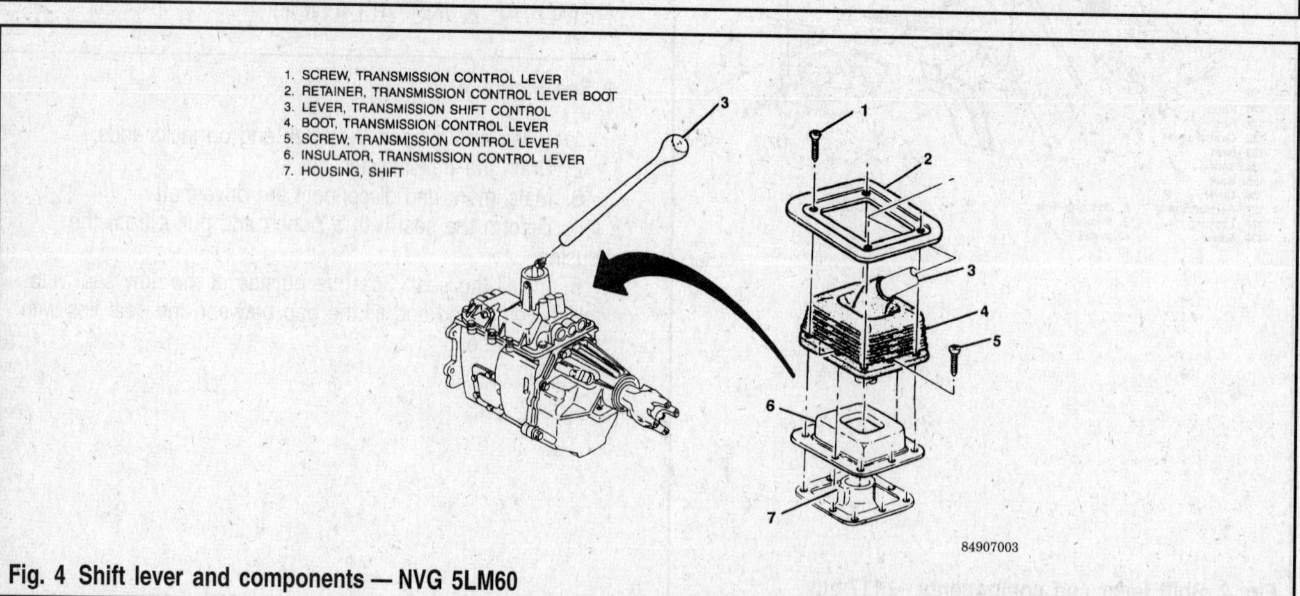

Fig. 4 Shift lever and components — NVG 5LM60

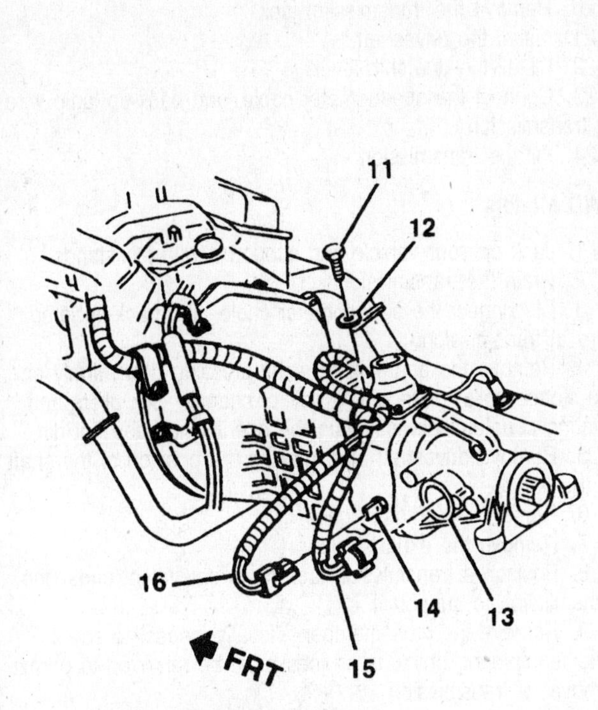

Fig. 5 Back-up light switch — NVG 4500

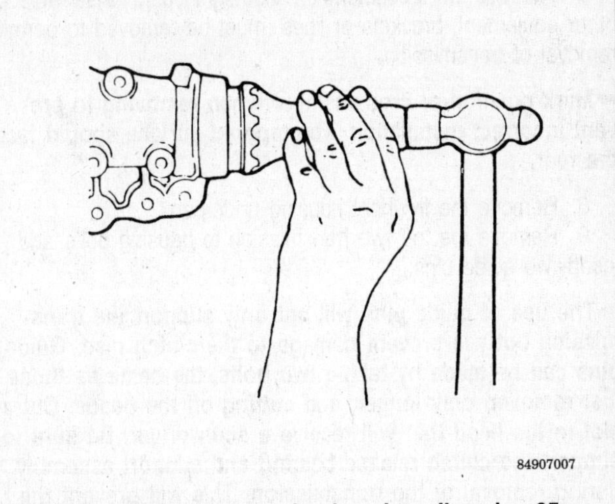

Fig. 7 Installing the extension housing oil seal — 85mm and NVG 4500

Transmission

REMOVAL & INSTALLATION

➧ See Figures 8 and 9

2WD Models

1. Jack up your vehicle and support it with jackstands.
2. Drain the transmission.
3. Disconnect the speedometer cable, and back-up lamp wire at transmission.
4. Remove the gearshift lever by pressing down firmly on the slotted collar plate with a pair of channel lock pliers and rotating counterclockwise. Plug the opening to keep out dirt.
5. Remove driveshaft after making the position of the shaft to the flange.
6. Position a transmission jack or its equivalent under the transmission to support it.

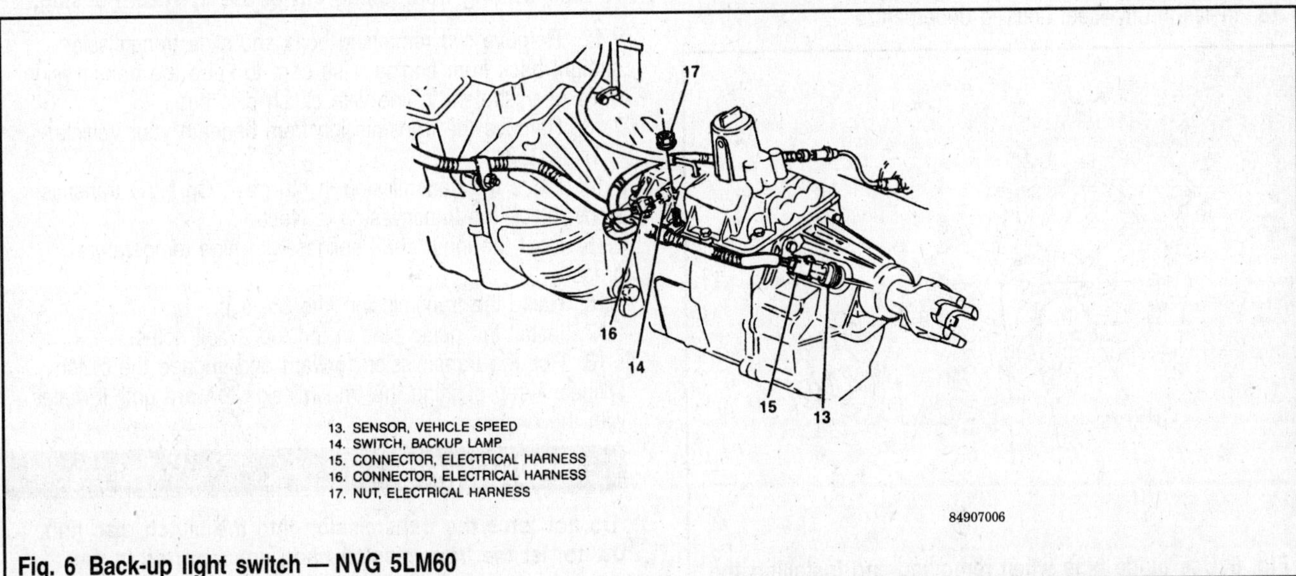

Fig. 6 Back-up light switch — NVG 5LM60

7. Remove the crossmember. Visually inspect to see if other equipment, brackets or lines, must be removed to permit removal of transmission.

➡Mark position of crossmember when removing to prevent incorrect installation. The tapered surface should face the rear.

8. Remove the flywheel housing underpan.
9. Remove the top two transmission to housing bolts and insert two guide pins.

➡The use of guide pins will not only support the transmission but will prevent damage to the clutch disc. Guide pins can be made by taking two bolts, the same as those just removed only longer, and cutting off the heads. Cut a slot in the head that will receive a screwdriver. Be sure to support the clutch release bearing and support assembly during removal of the transmission. This will prevent the release bearing from falling out of the flywheel housing.

10. Remove two remaining bolts and slide transmission straight back from engine. Use care to keep the transmission drive gear straight in line with clutch disc hub.
11. Remove the transmission from beneath your vehicle.

To install:

12. Place the transmission in 4th gear. On NVG transmissions, place the transmission in Neutral.
13. Coat the input shaft splines with high temperature grease.
14. Raise the transmission into position.
15. Install the guide pins in the top 2 bolt holes.
16. Roll the transmission forward and engage the clutch splines. Keep pushing the transmission forward until it mates with the engine.

WARNING

Do not force the transmission into the clutch disc hub. Do not let the transmission hang unsupported in the splined portion of the clutch disc.

17. Install the bolts, removing the guide pins.
18. Install the flywheel housing underpan.

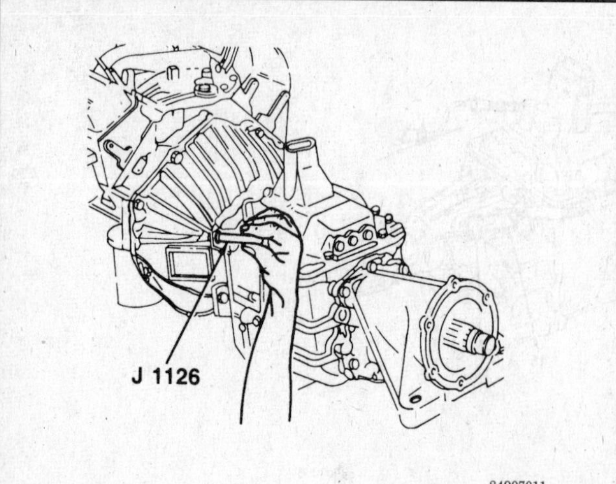

Fig. 8 Use guide pins when removing and installing the transmission

19. Install the crossmember.
20. Remove the transmission jack.
21. Install the driveshaft.
22. Install the gearshift lever.
23. Connect the speedometer cable, and back-up lamp wire at transmission.
24. Fill the transmission.

4WD Models

1. Jack up your vehicle and support it with jackstands.
2. Drain the transmission.
3. Disconnect the speedometer cable, and back-up lamp wire at transmission.
4. Remove the gearshift lever by pressing down firmly on the slotted collar plate with a pair of channel lock pliers and rotating counterclockwise. Plug the opening to keep out dirt.
5. Remove driveshaft after making the position of the shaft to the flange.
6. Remove the transfer case.
7. Remove the exhaust pipes.
8. Position a transmission jack or its equivalent under the transmission to support it.
9. Remove the crossmember. Visually inspect to see if other equipment, brackets or lines must be removed to permit removal of transmission.

➡Mark position of crossmember when removing to prevent incorrect installation. The tapered surface should face the rear.

10. Remove the flywheel housing underpan.
11. Remove the top two transmission-to-housing bolts and insert two guide pins.

➡The use of guide pins will not only support the transmission but will prevent damage to the clutch disc. Guide pins can be made by taking two bolts, the same as those just removed only longer, and cutting off the heads. Cut a slot in the head that will receive a screwdriver. Be sure to support the clutch release bearing and support assembly during removal of the transmission. This will prevent the release bearing from falling out of the flywheel housing.

12. Remove two remaining bolts and slide transmission straight back from engine. Use care to keep the transmission drive gear straight in line with clutch disc hub.
13. Remove the transmission from beneath your vehicle.

To install:

14. Place the transmission in 4th gear. On NVG transmissions, place the transmission in Neutral.
15. Coat the input shaft splines with high temperature grease.
16. Raise the transmission into position.
17. Install the guide pins in the top 2 bolt holes.
18. Roll the transmission forward and engage the clutch splines. Keep pushing the transmission forward until it mates with the engine.

WARNING

Do not force the transmission into the clutch disc hub. Do not let the transmission hang unsupported in the splined portion of the clutch disc.

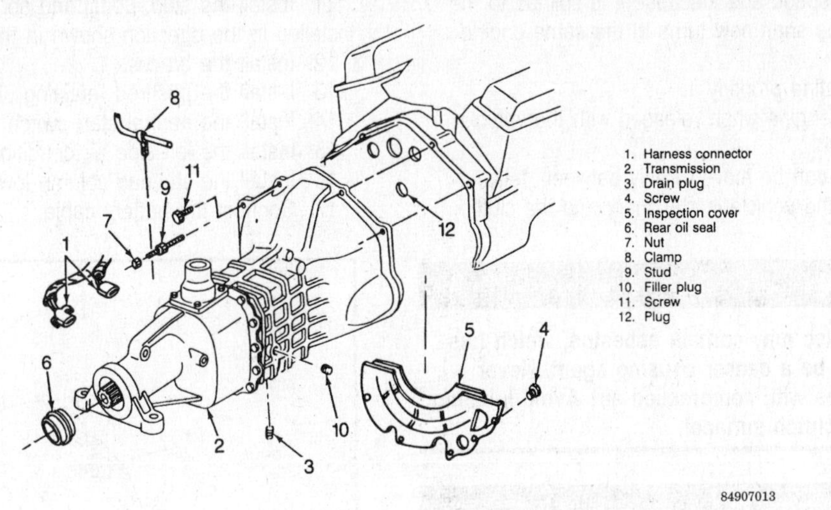

Fig. 9 Exploded view of the transmission mounting — 85mm 5-speed shown, others similar

19. Install the bolts, removing the guide pins.
20. Install the flywheel housing underpan.
21. Install the crossmember.
22. Install the transfer case.
23. Remove the transmission jack.
24. Install the exhaust system.
25. Install the driveshaft.
26. Install the gearshift lever.
27. Connect the speedometer cable, and back-up lamp wire at transmission.
28. Fill the transmission.

CLUTCH

Understanding the Clutch

The purpose of the clutch is to disconnect and connect engine power at the transmission. A vehicle at rest requires a lot of engine torque to get all that weight moving. An internal combustion engine does not develop a high starting torque (unlike steam engines) so it must be allowed to operate without any load until it builds up enough torque to move the vehicle. To a point, torque increases with engine rpm. The clutch allows the engine to build up torque by physically disconnecting the engine from the transmission, relieving the engine of any load or resistance.

The transfer of engine power to the transmission (the load) must be smooth and gradual; if it weren't, drive line components would wear out or break quickly. This gradual power transfer is made possible by gradually releasing the clutch pedal. The clutch disc and pressure plate are the connecting link between the engine and transmission. When the clutch pedal is released, the disc and plate contact each other (the clutch is engaged) physically joining the engine and transmission. When the pedal is pushed in, the disc and plate separate (the clutch is disengaged) disconnecting the engine from the transmission.

Most clutch assemblies consists of the flywheel, the clutch disc, the clutch pressure plate, the throw out bearing and fork, the actuating linkage and the pedal. The flywheel and clutch pressure plate (driving members) are connected to the engine crankshaft and rotate with it. The clutch disc is located between the flywheel and pressure plate, and is splined to the transmission shaft. A driving member is one that is attached to the engine and transfers engine power to a driven member (clutch disc) on the transmission shaft. A driving member (pressure plate) rotates (drives) a driven member (clutch disc) on contact and, in so doing, turns the transmission shaft.

There is a circular diaphragm spring within the pressure plate cover (transmission side). In a relaxed state (when the clutch pedal is fully released) this spring is convex; that is, it is dished outward toward the transmission. Pushing in the clutch pedal actuates the attached linkage. Connected to the other end of this is the throw out fork, which hold the throw out bearing. When the clutch pedal is depressed, the clutch linkage pushes the fork and bearing forward to contact the diaphragm spring of the pressure plate. The outer edges of the spring are secured to the pressure plate and are pivoted on rings so that when the center of the spring is compressed by the throw out bearing, the outer edges bow outward and, by so doing, pull the pressure plate in the same direction - away from the clutch disc. This action separates the disc from the plate, disengaging the clutch and allowing the transmission to be shifted into another gear. A coil type clutch return spring attached to the clutch pedal arm permits full release of the pedal. Releasing the pedal pulls the throw out bearing away from the diaphragm spring resulting in a reversal of spring position. As bearing pressure is gradually released from the spring center, the outer edges of the spring bow outward, pushing the pressure plate into closer contact with the clutch disc. As the disc and plate move closer together, friction between the two increases and slippage is reduced until, when full spring pressure is applied (by fully releasing the pedal) the speed of the disc and plate are the same. This stops all slipping, creating a direct connection between the plate and disc which results in the transfer of power from the engine to the transmission. The clutch disc is now rotating with the pressure plate at engine speed and, because it is splined to the transmission shaft, the shaft now turns at the same engine speed.

The clutch is operating properly if:

1. It will stall the engine when released with the vehicle held stationary.
2. The shift lever can be moved freely between 1st and reverse gears when the vehicle is stationary and the clutch disengaged.

CAUTION

The clutch driven disc may contain asbestos, which has been determined to be a cancer causing agent. Never clean clutch surfaces with compressed air! Avoid inhaling any dust from any clutch surface!

Clutch Pedal

REMOVAL & INSTALLATION

See Figures 10 and 11

1. Disconnect the negative battery cable.
2. Remove the steering column lower covers.
3. Remove the left side air conditioner duct.
4. Remove the neutral start switch.
5. Remove the pushrod retaining pin and washer.
6. Remove the nuts retaining the inboard and outboard braces.
7. Remove the braces from the stud.
8. Remove the stud, pedal and spring. Slide a long screwdriver or rod into the bracket while removing the stud. This will hold the bracket in place.
9. Remove the bushings and spacer. Replace the bumper if it's worn.

To install:

10. Install the bushings and spacer. Coat these parts with grease prior to assembly.

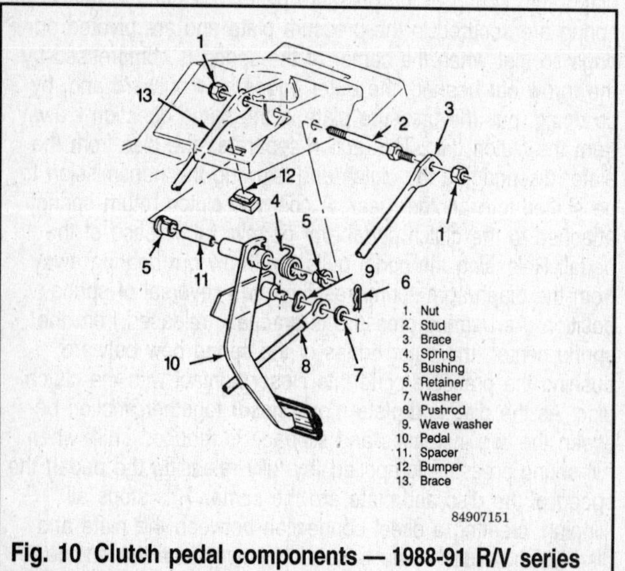

Fig. 10 Clutch pedal components — 1988-91 R/V series

11. Install the stud, pedal and spring. The stud must be installed in the direction shown in the illustration.
12. Install the braces.
13. Install the pushrod retaining pin and washer.
14. Install the neutral start switch.
15. Install the left side air conditioner duct.
16. Install the steering column lower covers.
17. Connect the battery cable.

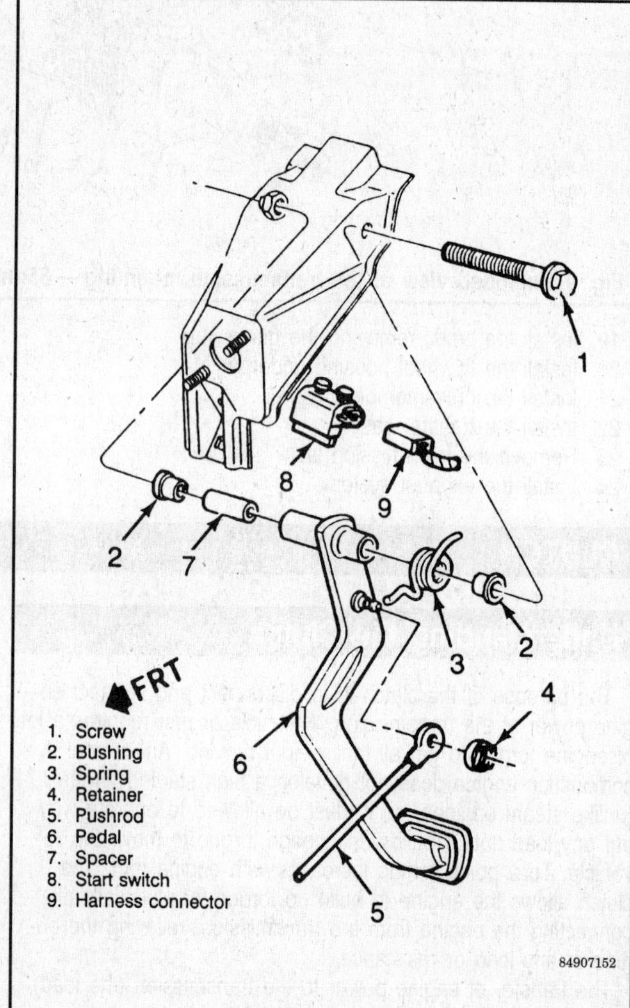

Fig. 11 Clutch pedal components — except 1988-91 R/V series

Driven Disc And Pressure Plate

REMOVAL & INSTALLATION

See Figures 12, 13, 14, 15, 16, 17, 18, 19 and 20

CAUTION

The clutch driven disc may contain asbestos, which has been determined to be a cancer causing agent. Never clean clutch surfaces with compressed air! Avoid inhaling any dust from any clutch surface! When cleaning clutch surfaces, use a commercially available brake cleaning fluid.

Before removing the bellhousing, the engine must be supported. This can be done by placing a hydraulic jack, with a board on top, under the oil pan.

1. Remove the transmission.
2. Remove the slave cylinder.
3. Remove the bellhousing cover.
4. Remove the bellhousing from the engine.
5. Remove the throwout spring and fork.
6. Remove the ballstud from the bellhousing.
7. Install a pilot tool (an old input shaft makes a good pilot tool) to hold the clutch while you are removing it.

Before removing the clutch from the flywheel, mark the flywheel, clutch cover and one pressure plate lug, so that these parts may be assembled in their same relative positions. They were balanced as an assembly.

8. Loosen the clutch attaching bolts one turn at a time to prevent distortion of the clutch cover until the tension is released.
9. Remove the clutch pilot tool and the clutch from the vehicle.
10. Check the pressure plate and flywheel for signs of wear, scoring, overheating, etc. If the clutch plate, flywheel, or pressure plate is oil-soaked, inspect the engine rear main seal and

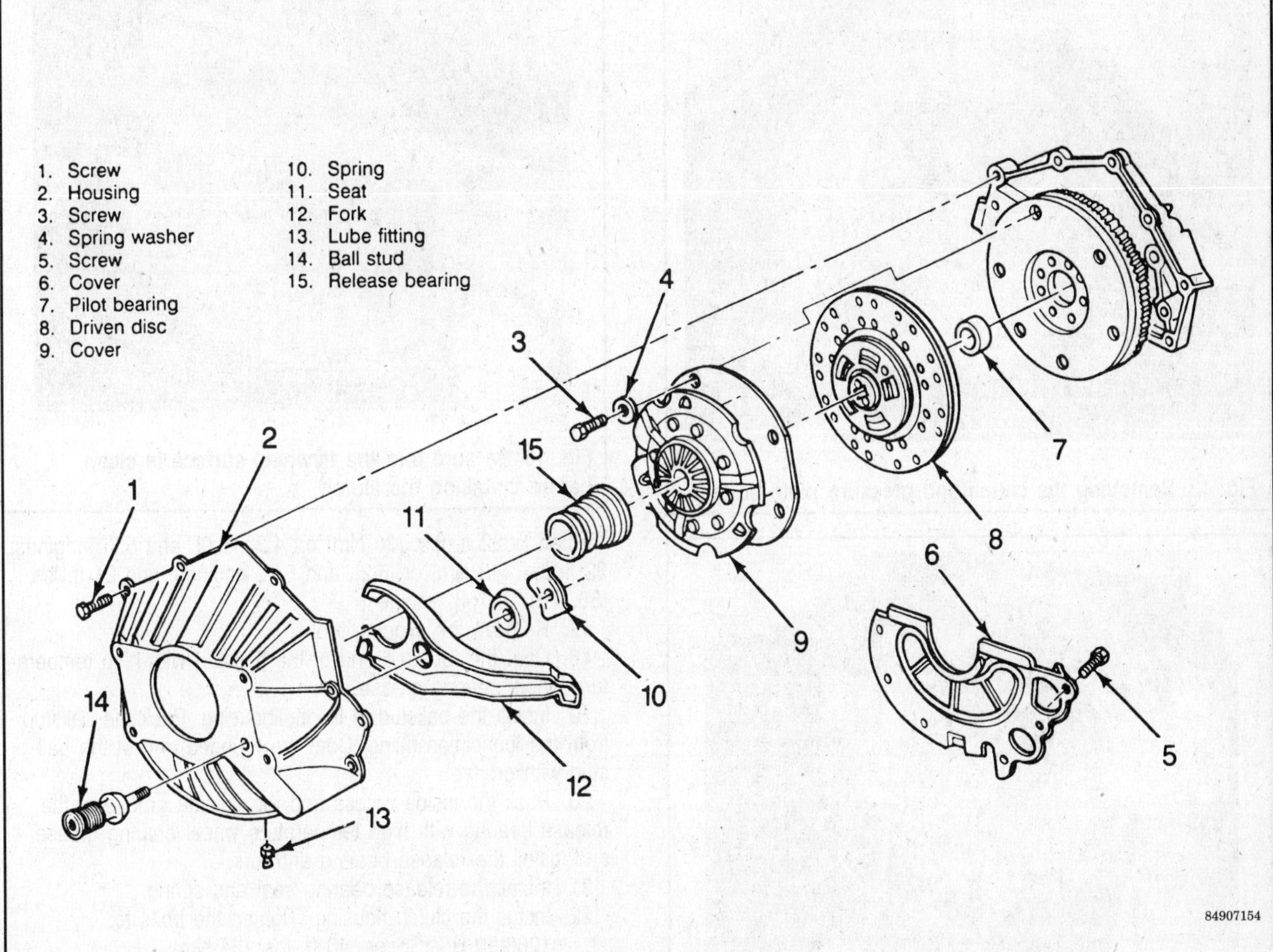

Fig. 12 Exploded view of the clutch

the transmission input shaft seal, and correct leakage as required. Replace any damaged parts.

To install:

11. Install a new pilot bearing. Lubricate with a few drops of machine oil.
12. Install the pressure plate in the cover assembly, aligning the notch in the pressure plate with the notch in the cover flange. Install pressure plate retracting springs, lockwashers and drive strap-to-pressure plate bolts. Tighten to 11 ft. lbs. (15 Nm). The clutch is now ready to be installed.

➡The manufacturer recommends that new pressure plate bolts and washers be used.

13. Turn the flywheel until the **X** mark is at the bottom.
14. Install the clutch disc, pressure plate and cover, using an old input shaft as an aligning tool.
15. Turn the clutch until the **X** mark or painted white letter on the clutch cover aligns with the **X** mark on the flywheel.
16. Install the attaching bolts and tighten them a little at a time in a crossing pattern until the spring pressure is taken up. Tighten to 22 ft. lbs. (30 Nm) on 4.3L, 5.0L and 5.7L engines; 32 ft. lbs. (43 Nm) on 6.2L and 6.5L engines; and 24 ft. lbs. (33 Nm) on 7.4L engines.

TCCS7118

Fig. 15 Removing the clutch and pressure plate

TCCS7116

Fig. 13 Removing the clutch and pressure plate bolts

TCCS7124

Fig. 16 Be sure that the flywheel surface is clean, before installing the clutch

TCCS7117

Fig. 14 Removing the clutch and pressure plate assembly

17. Remove the aligning tool.
18. Coat the rounded end of the ballstud with high temperature wheel bearing grease.
19. Install the ballstud in the bellhousing. Pack the ballstud from the lubrication fitting. Coat the rounded end of the ballstud with grease.
20. Pack the inside recess and the outside groove of the release bearing with high temperature wheel bearing grease and install the release bearing and fork.
21. Install the release bearing seat and spring.
22. Install the clutch housing. Tighten the bolts to:
    - 1988-90 R/V Series: 40 ft. lbs. (54 Nm)
    - 1988-90 C/K Series: 55 ft. lbs. (75 Nm)
    - 1991 Models: 31 ft. lbs. (43 Nm)
    - 1992-96 Models: 29 ft. lbs. (39 Nm)
23. Install the cover.

24. Install the slave cylinder. Tighten the bolt to 13 ft. lbs. (18 Nm).
25. Install the transmission.
26. Bleed the hydraulic system.

Clutch Master Cylinder and Reservoir

REMOVAL & INSTALLATION

See Figures 21 and 22

1. Disconnect the negative battery cable.
2. Remove the lower steering column covers.
3. Remove the lower left side air conditioning duct, if so equipped.
4. Disconnect the pushrod from the clutch pedal.
5. Disconnect the reservoir hose.
6. Disconnect the secondary cylinder hydraulic line to the master cylinder.

Fig. 17 Install a clutch alignment arbor, to align the clutch assembly during installation

Fig. 18 Apply a thread locking agent to clutch assembly bolts

Fig. 19 Be sure to use a torque wrench to tighten the bolts

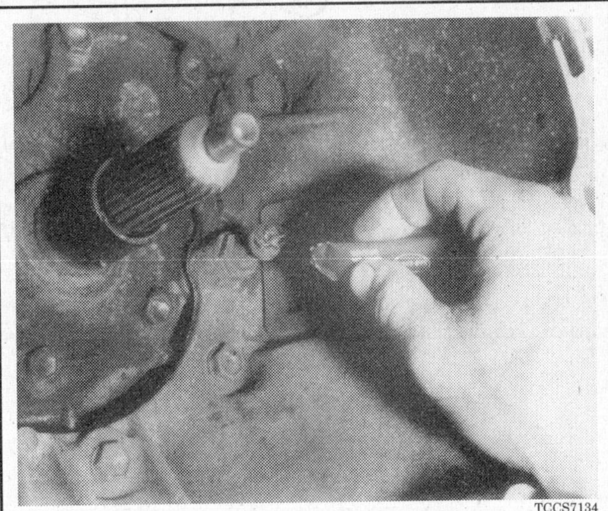

Fig. 20 Grease the clutch release fork ball

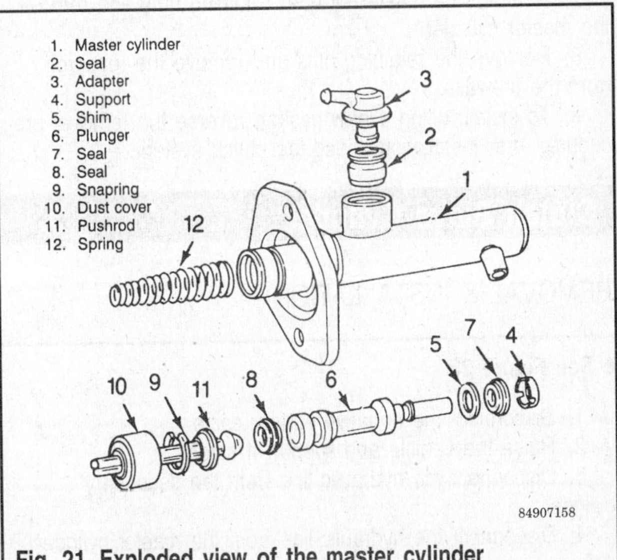

Fig. 21 Exploded view of the master cylinder

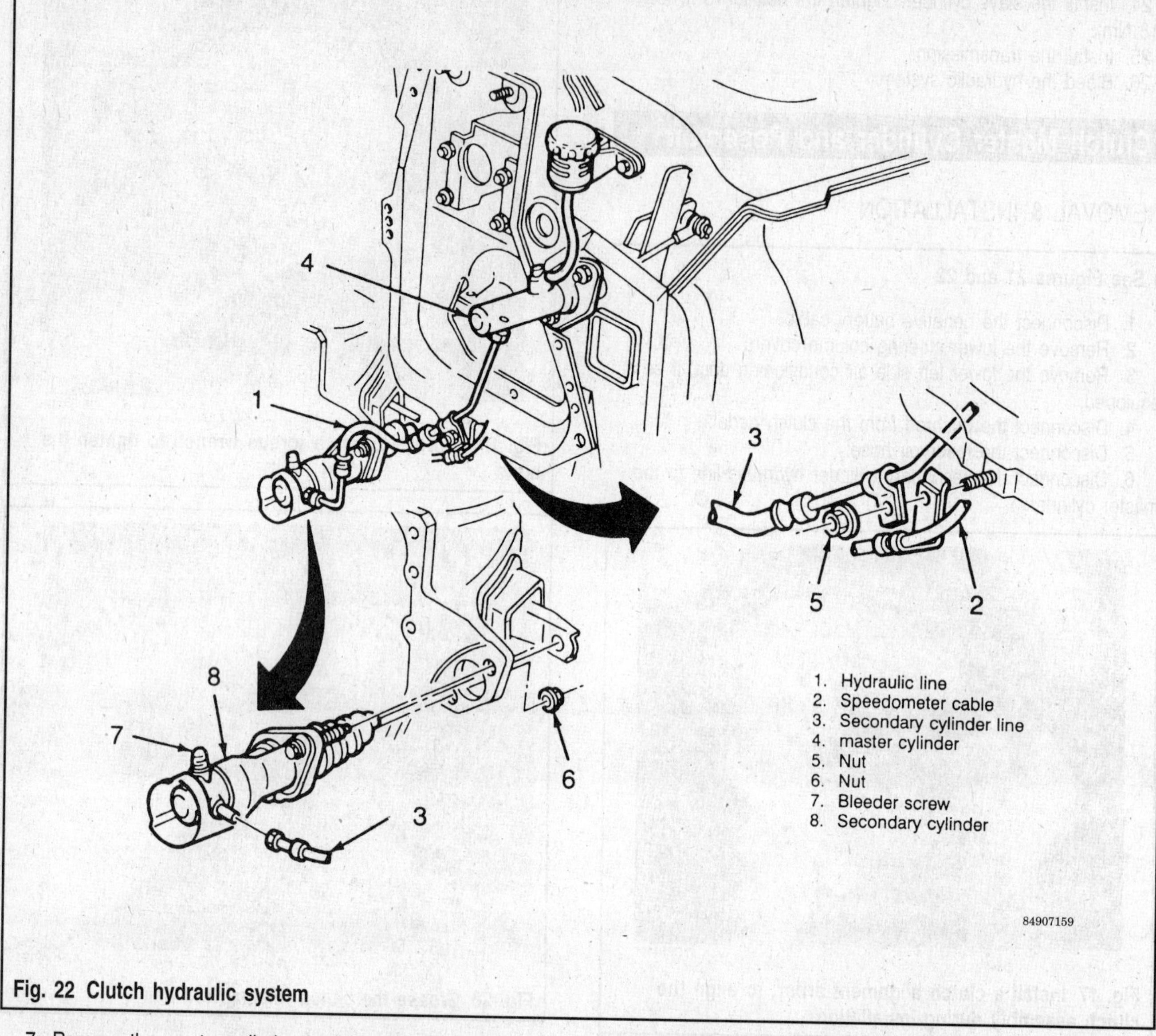

Fig. 22 Clutch hydraulic system

7. Remove the master cylinder retaining nuts and remove the master cylinder.

8. Remove the retaining nuts and remove the reservoir from the firewall.

9. To install, using a new gasket, reverse the removal procedure. After installation, bleed the clutch system.

Clutch Slave Cylinder

REMOVAL & INSTALLATION

➧ **See Figure 23**

1. Disconnect the negative battery cable.
2. Raise the vehicle and support it safely.
3. Disconnect the hydraulic line from the secondary cylinder.
4. Disconnect the hydraulic line from the master cylinder.
5. On 1988-91 R/V models, remove the nut retaining the hydraulic line and the speedometer cable to the cowl, than install the nut to hold the speedometer cable in place.
6. Cover all hydraulic lines to prevent dirt and moisture from entering the system.
7. Remove the bolts securing the cylinder and remove it from the transmission.
8. Installation is the reverse of removal. Bleed the clutch hydraulic system.

HYDRAULIC SYSTEM BLEEDING

1. Fill the clutch master cylinder with the proper grade and type fluid. See Section 1. Raise and support the vehicle safely.
2. Remove the slave cylinder retaining bolts. Hold the cylinder about 45° with the bleeder at the highest point.
3. Fully depress the clutch pedal and open the bleeder screw. Repeat until all air is expelled from the system.
4. Be sure that the fluid level remains full in the clutch master cylinder throughout the bleeding procedure.

AUTOMATIC TRANSMISSION

Adjustments

SHIFT LINKAGE

See Figures 24, 25, 26 and 27

1. Raise and support the front end on jackstands. Block the rear wheels.
2. Loosen the shift lever bolt or nut at the transmission lever so that the lever is free to move on the rod.
3. Set the column shift lever to the neutral gate notch, by rotating it until the shift lever drops into the Neutral gate. Do not use the indicator pointer as a reference to position the shift lever, as this will not be accurate.

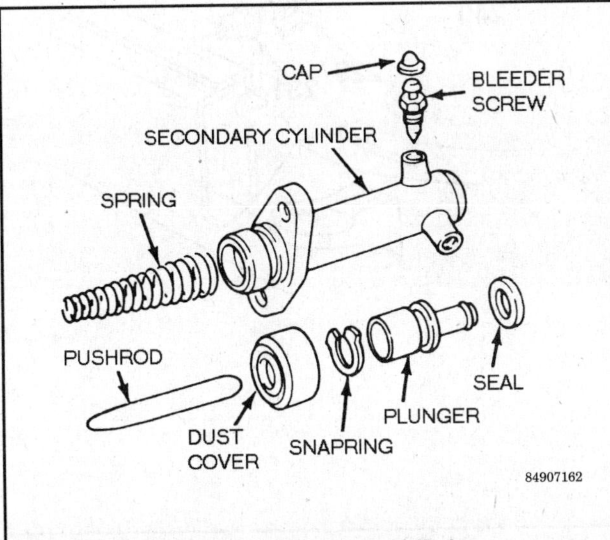

Fig. 23 Exploded view of the slave cylinder

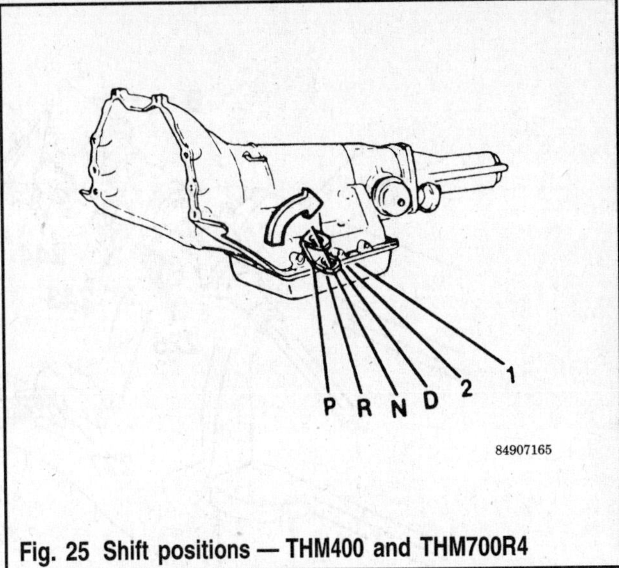

Fig. 25 Shift positions — THM400 and THM700R4

4. Set the transmission lever in the neutral position by moving it clockwise to the park detent, then counterclockwise 2 detents to neutral.
5. Hold the rod tightly in the swivel and tighten the nut or bolt to 17 ft. lbs. (23 Nm) on all but the 4L80E. On the 4L80E, tighten the bolt to 20 ft. lbs. (30 Nm).
6. Lower the vehicle.
7. Move the column shifter to park and check that the engine starts. Check the adjustment by moving the selector to each gear position.

SHIFT CABLE

➡This procedure applies to 4L60-E and 4L80-E transmissions.

1. Place the transmission in park and apply the parking brake.

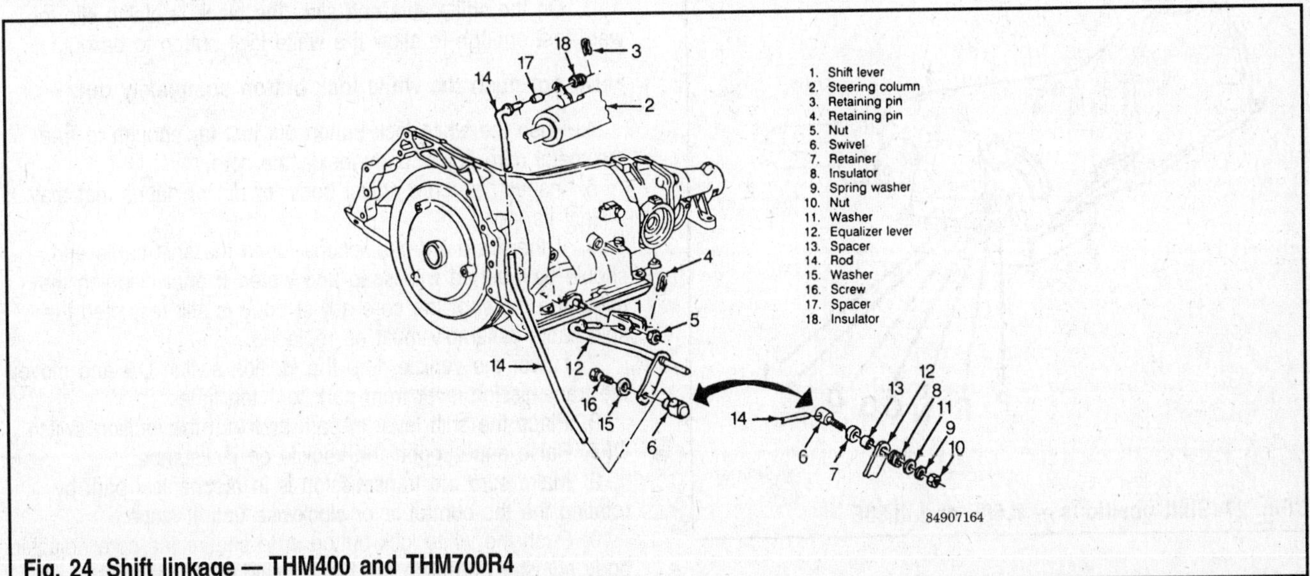

Fig. 24 Shift linkage — THM400 and THM700R4

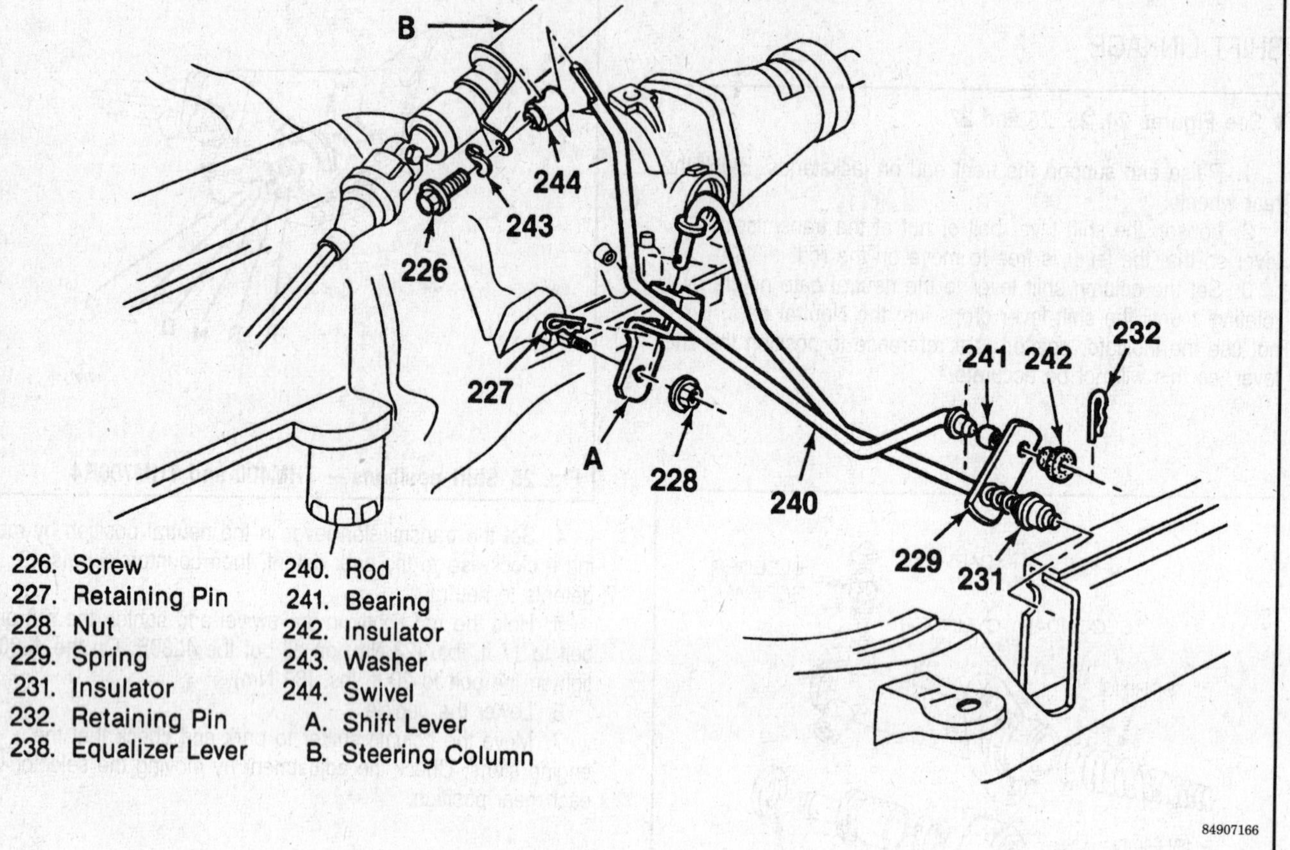

B
244
243
226
227
A
228
240
229
231
241
242
232
226. Screw
227. Retaining Pin
228. Nut
229. Spring
231. Insulator
232. Retaining Pin
238. Equalizer Lever
240. Rod
241. Bearing
242. Insulator
243. Washer
244. Swivel
A. Shift Lever
B. Steering Column
84907166

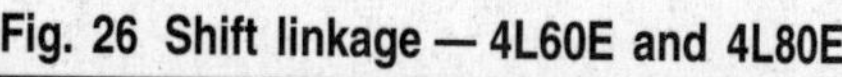

Fig. 26 Shift linkage — 4L60E and 4L80E

P
R
N
OD
D
2
1
84907167

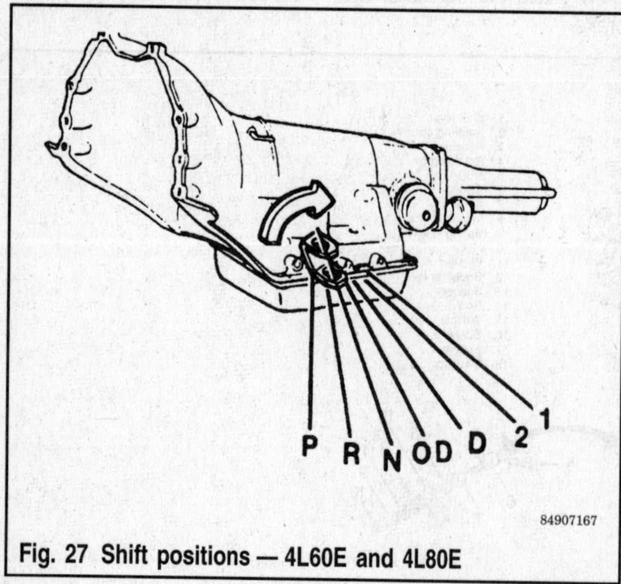

Fig. 27 Shift positions — 4L60E and 4L80E

2. Raise and support the vehicle on jackstands.
3. On the shift cable end slide the black retaining clip forward just enough to allow the white lock button to be out.

➡**Do not push the white lock button completely out.**

4. Push the white lock button out just far enough to free the metal core adjust body inside the core.
5. Inspect the core adjust body for dirt or debris that may restrict its travel.
6. If there are any restrictions found the shift cable end should be washed with soap and water. If after cleaning the cable the travel of the core adjust body is still restricted the shift cable assembly must be replaced.
7. Lower the vehicle, turn the ignition switch **ON** and move the transmission lever from park to 1 ten times.
8. Place the shift lever in park and turn the ignition switch **OFF**. Raise and support the vehicle on jackstands.
9. Make sure the transmission is in mechanical park by rotating the the control lever clockwise until it stops.
10. Push the white lock button in to secure the core adjuster body adjuster and slide the black retainer clip rearward until it

covers the white lock button and locks in place over the shift cable end.

11. Lower the vehicle and turn the ignition switch **ON**.
12. Move the shifter through the gear ranges and ensure that the light comes on under the shift column letter when the shifter is positioned under that letter.
13. Ensure that the engine starts only when the transmission is placed in park or neutral. Adjust the park/neutral switch if necessary. Refer to the park/neutral switch adjustment procedure in this section.
14. Turn the ignition switch to the **LOCK** position and ensure that the key can be removed in the park position only.
15. Release the parking brake, start the engine and check for proper transmission shift operation.

THROTTLE VALVE CABLE

➡This procedure applies to the THM 700R4 transmission.

The adjustment is made at the engine end of the cable with the engine off, by rotating the throttle lever by hand. DO NOT use the accelerator pedal to rotate the throttle lever.

1. Remove the air cleaner.
2. Depress and hold down the metal adjusting tab at the end of the cable.
3. Move the slider until it stops against the fitting.
4. Release the adjusting tab.
5. Rotate the throttle lever to the full extent of it travel.
6. The slider must move towards the lever when the lever is at full travel. Make sure that the cable moves freely.

➡The cable may appear to function properly with the engine cold. Recheck it with the engine hot.

7. Road test the truck.

NEUTRAL START/BACK-UP SWITCH

This adjustment is performed with the switch removed from the vehicle. Neutral position tool J 41364-A or its equivalent is required for this procedure.

1. Position tool J 41364-A or its equivalent onto the park/neutral switch. make sure that the slots on the switch are lined up with the lower tabs on the tool.
2. Rotate the tool until the upper locator pin on the tool is lined with the slot on the top of the switch.

➡Do not remove the tool from the switch

3. Install the switch and remove the tool.

Vacuum Modulator

REMOVAL & INSTALLATION

▸ See Figure 28

➡This applies to the THM 400 only.

1. Raise and support the front end on jackstands.
2. Disconnect the vacuum line at the modulator.
3. Remove the screw and retaining clamp.
4. Remove the modulator. Be careful, some fluid may run out.

To install:

5. Install the modulator.
6. Install the vacuum line. Be careful not to kink the vacuum line during installation. Replace any lost fluid.

Shift Linkage

REMOVAL & INSTALLATION

THM400 and 4L60E

▸ See Figures 24, 25, 26 and 27

1. Remove the linkage rod-to-column bolt and washer.
2. Remove the rod and swivel from the column.
3. Remove the control rod-to-equalizer lever retaining pin and disconnect the rod from the lever.
4. Remove the intermediate rod-to-transmission lever retaining pin and remove the rod and equalizer lever assembly. Don't lose the spring and bushing.
5. Install the linkage and adjust the linkage as described above.

THM700R4 and 4L80E

▸ See Figures 24, 25, 26 and 27

1. Remove the linkage rod-to-column retaining pin.
2. Remove the rod, bushing and spring from the column. Note any washers and/or spacers and their location(s).
3. Remove the control rod-to-equalizer lever bolt and swivel and disconnect the rod from the lever.
4. Remove the intermediate rod-to-transmission lever retaining pin and remove the rod and equalizer lever assembly. Don't lose the spring and bushing.
5. Install the linkage and adjust the linkage as described above.

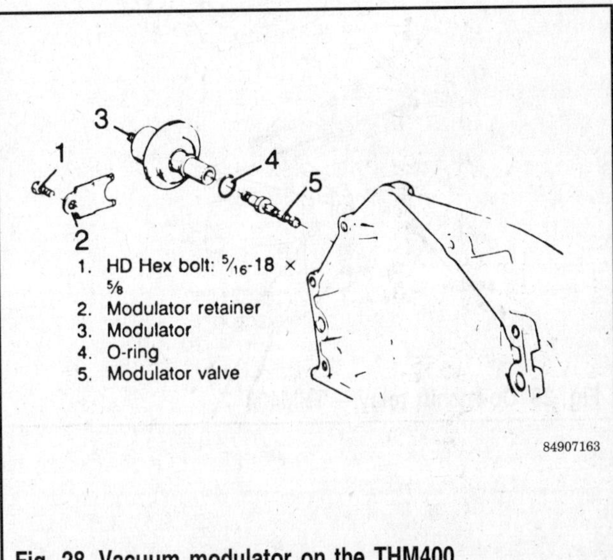

Fig. 28 Vacuum modulator on the THM400

Downshift Relay

REMOVAL & INSTALLATION

See Figure 29

This applies to the THM 400 only.

The relay is located just slightly to the passenger's side of center on the firewall.

1. Remove the wiring retainer and disconnect the wiring from the switch.
2. Remove the screws and remove the switch.
3. Installation the relay. No adjustment is necessary.

Throttle Valve Cable

REMOVAL & INSTALLATION

See Figure 30

This applies to the THM 700R4 only.

1. Remove the air cleaner.
2. Disconnect the cable from the throttle lever.
3. Compress the locking tangs and disconnect the cable housing from the bracket.
4. Remove all cable brackets and straps.
5. Remove the cable lower end retaining screw.
6. Disconnect the cable from the transmission link.
7. Installation is the reverse of removal. Take great care to avoid kinking the cable. Tighten the lower end retaining screw to 84 inch lbs. When connecting the cable to the throttle lever it should have a small amount of travel against the return spring and should easily return under spring pressure.
8. Adjust the cable.

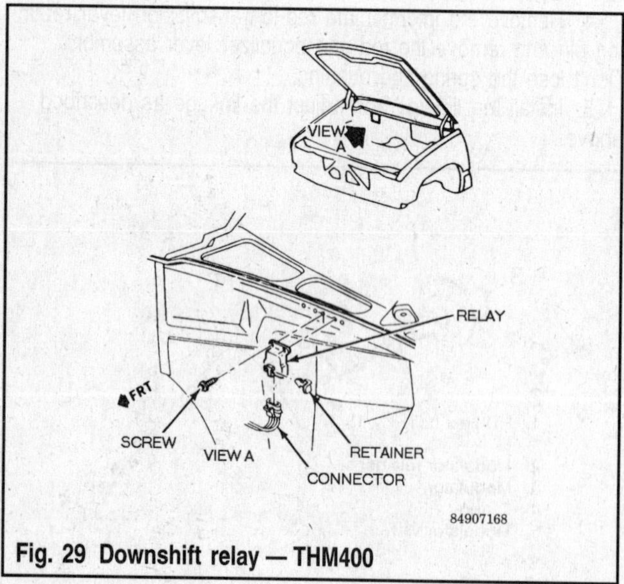

Fig. 29 Downshift relay — THM400

Neutral Start/Back-Up Switch

REMOVAL & INSTALLATION

1. Place the transmission in park and disconnect the negative battery cable.
2. Raise the vehicle and support it with jackstands.
3. Disconnect the shift cable end from the shift control lever and remove the nut securing the shift control lever to the manual shaft.
4. Disengage the electrical connector from the switch and remove the switch retainers.
5. Remove the switch from the transmission.

To install:

6. Adjust the switch as outlined in this section.
7. Install the switch and tighten the switch retainers. Tighten the switch retainers to 20ft. lbs. (27 Nm).
8. Engage the electrical connector and install the control lever to the manual shaft.
9. Install the control lever nut and tighten to 20 ft. lbs. (27 Nm).
10. Lower the vehicle and connect the negative battery cable.
11. Check the switch for proper operation. The vehicle should start in **P** or **N** only.
12. If adjustment is required, loosen the switch retaining bolts and rotate the switch slightly, tighten the bolts and check switch operation.

Extension Housing Rear Seal

REMOVAL & INSTALLATION

See Figure 31

1. Raise and support the truck on jackstands.
2. Matchmark and remove the driveshaft. Be careful! Some fluid may run out. You can avoid this by raising only the rear of the truck.
3. Centerpunch the seal to distort it and carefully pry it out.

To install:

4. Coat the outer edge of the new seal with non-hardening sealer.
5. Place the seal in the bore and carefully drive it into place. A seal installer makes this job easier.
6. Install the driveshaft. It's a good idea to coat the driveshaft end with grease to avoid damaging the seal.
7. Lower the truck and replace any lost fluid.

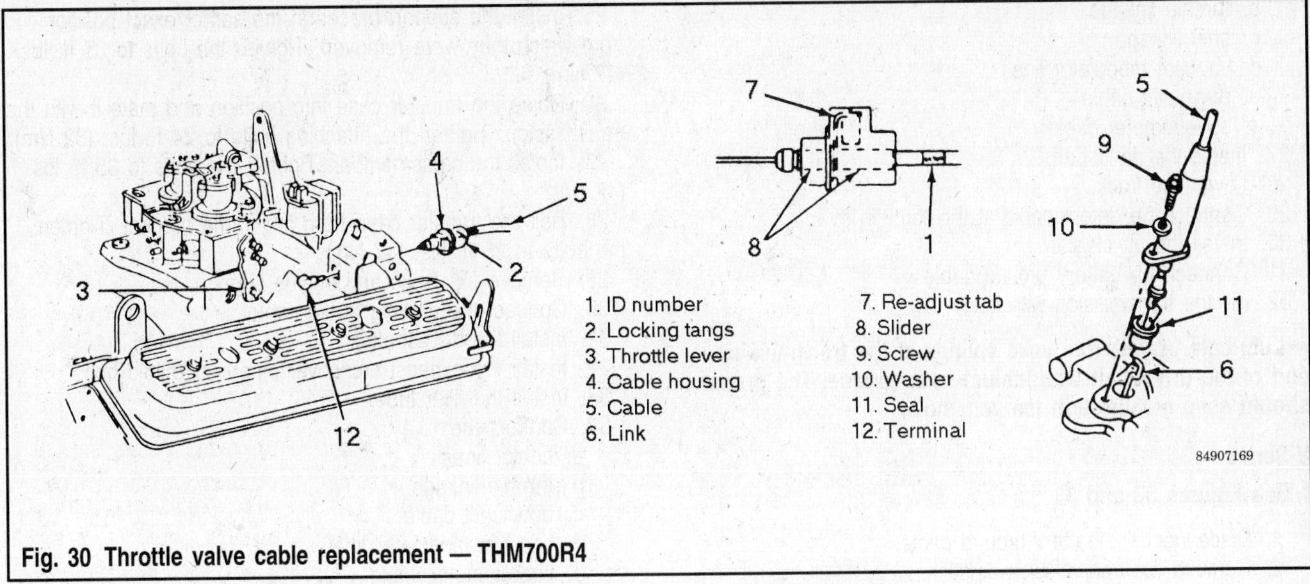

Fig. 30 Throttle valve cable replacement — THM700R4

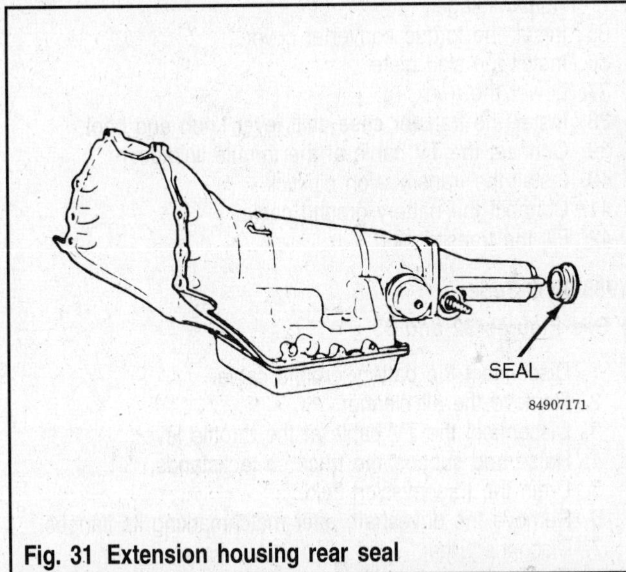

Fig. 31 Extension housing rear seal

Transmission

REMOVAL & INSTALLATION

➡It would be best to drain the transmission before starting. It may be necessary to disconnect and remove the exhaust crossover pipe on V8 engines, and to disconnect the catalytic converter and remove its support bracket.

R-Series

➧ See Figures 32 and 33

1. Disconnect the battery ground cable.
2. Remove the air cleaner.
3. Disconnect the detent cable at the throttle lever.
4. Raise and support the truck on jackstands.
5. Drain the transmission fluid.
6. Remove the driveshaft, after matchmarking its flanges.
7. Disconnect the:
   a. speedometer cable
   b. downshift cable
   c. vacuum modulator line
   d. shift linkage
   e. throttle linkage
   f. fluid cooler lines
8. Remove the filler tube.
9. Disconnect the support bracket at the catalytic converter.
10. Look around to see if there is anything else in the way.
11. Support the transmission on a transmission jack and unbolt the rear mount from the crossmember.
12. Remove the crossmember.
13. Remove any transmission support braces. Note their exact positions for installation.
14. Remove the torque converter underpan, matchmark the flywheel and converter, and remove the converter bolts.
15. Support the engine on a jack and lower the transmission slightly for access to the upper transmission to engine bolts.
16. Remove the transmission to engine bolts and pull the transmission back. Rig up a strap or keep the front of the transmission up so the converter doesn't fall out.

To install:

17. Raise the transmission into position.
18. Roll the unit forward and against the engine, engaging the locating dowels and aligning the torque converter marks. Install the transmission to engine bolts. Install all the bolts finger-tight, then tighten them to 35 ft. lbs. (47 Nm).
19. Install the converter bolts finger-tight. Then, tighten the bolts to 50 ft. lbs. (68 Nm).
20. Install the converter cover.
21. Install the transmission support braces. The braces must be installed in the exact positions from which they were removed! Tighten the bolts to 35 ft. lbs. (47 Nm).
22. Install the crossmember. Tighten all bolts to 35 ft. lbs. (47 Nm).
23. Remove the transmission jack and engine support jack.
24. Connect the support bracket at the catalytic converter.
25. Install the filler tube.
26. Connect the:
   a. fluid cooler lines

b. throttle linkage
c. shift linkage
d. vacuum modulator line
e. downshift cable
f. speedometer cable
27. Install the driveshaft.
28. Lower the truck.
29. Connect the detent cable at the throttle lever.
30. Install the air cleaner.
31. Connect the battery ground cable.
32. Fill the transmission with fluid.

➡**Lubricate the internal yoke splines at the transmission end of the driveshaft with lithium base grease. The grease should seep out through the vent hole.**

V-Series

➧ **See Figures 32 and 33**

1. Disconnect the battery ground cable.
2. Remove the transmission dipstick.
3. Detach the TV cable at the throttle linkage.
4. Remove the transfer case shift lever knob and boot.
5. Raise and support the truck on jackstands.
6. Remove the skid plate.
7. Remove the torque converter cover.
8. Matchmark the flywheel and torque converter, remove the bolts, and secure the converter so it doesn't fall out of the transmission.
9. Disconnect the:
a. shift linkage
b. speedometer cable
c. vacuum modulator line
d. downshift cable
e. throttle linkage
f. cooler times
10. Remove the filler tube.
11. Remove the exhaust crossover pipe-to-manifold bolts.
12. Unbolt the transfer case adapter from the crossmember.
13. Support the transmission with a floor jack and support the transfer case with a transmission jack.
14. Remove the crossmember.
15. Move the exhaust system aside.
16. Detach the driveshafts after matchmarking their flanges.
17. Disconnect the parking brake cable.
18. Unbolt the transfer case from the frame bracket. Support the engine.
19. Unbolt the transfer case from the transmission and remove it.
20. Remove any transmission support braces. Note their exact positions for installation.
21. Place the transmission jack under the transmission and secure it. Unbolt the transmission from the engine, pull the assembly back, and remove it.

To install:

22. Raise the transmission into position and roll it forward to engage the locating dowels on the engine. Make sure that the torque converter-to-flex plate matchmarks are aligned.
23. Install all engine-to-transmission bolts finger-tight. Then, tighten them to 35 ft. lbs. (47 Nm).
24. Install all the torque converter bolts finger-tight. Then, tighten them to 50 ft. lbs. (68 Nm).
25. Install the support braces in the same, exact position from which they were removed. Tighten the bolts to 35 ft. lbs. (47 Nm).
26. Raise the transfer case into position and mate it with the transmission. Tighten the attaching bolts to 24 ft. lbs. (32 Nm).
27. Install the crossmember. Tighten the bolts to 35 ft. lbs. (47 Nm).
28. Bolt the transfer case from the frame bracket. Tighten the bolts to 35 ft. lbs. (47 Nm).
29. Remove the jacks and engine support.
30. Connect the parking brake cable.
31. Install the driveshafts.
32. Install the exhaust crossover pipe-to-manifold bolts.
33. Install the filler tube.
34. Connect the:
a. cooler lines
b. throttle linkage
c. downshift cable
d. vacuum modulator line
e. speedometer cable
f. shift linkage
35. Install the torque converter cover.
36. Install the skid plate.
37. Lower the truck.
38. Install the transfer case shift lever knob and boot.
39. Connect the TV cable at the throttle linkage.
40. Install the transmission dipstick.
41. Connect the battery ground cable.
42. Fill the transmission.

1988-90 C-Series

➧ **See Figures 32 and 33**

1. Disconnect the battery ground cable.
2. Remove the air cleaner.
3. Disconnect the TV cable at the throttle lever.
4. Raise and support the truck on jackstands.
5. Drain the transmission fluid.
6. Remove the driveshaft, after matchmarking its flanges.
7. Disconnect the:
a. wiring harness at the transmission
b. vacuum modulator line
c. shift linkage
d. fluid cooler lines
8. Remove the filler tube.
9. Disconnect the support bracket at the catalytic converter.
10. Look around to see if there is anything else in the way.
11. Support the transmission on a transmission jack and unbolt the rear mount from the crossmember.
12. Remove the crossmember.
13. Remove any transmission support braces. Note their exact positions for installation.
14. Remove the torque converter underpan, matchmark the flywheel and converter, and remove the converter bolts.
15. Support the engine on a jack and lower the transmission slightly for access to the upper transmission to engine bolts.
16. Remove the transmission to engine bolts and pull the transmission back. Rig up a strap or keep the front of the transmission up so the converter doesn't fall out.

To install:

17. Raise the transmission into position.

1. Harness
2. Dipstick tube
3. Support brace
4. Cooler lines
5. Seal
6. Transmission
7. Transmission-to-engine bolts
8. Converter housing cover
9. Flywheel
10. Flywheel-to-converter bolt
11. Washer
12. Bolt
A
84907172

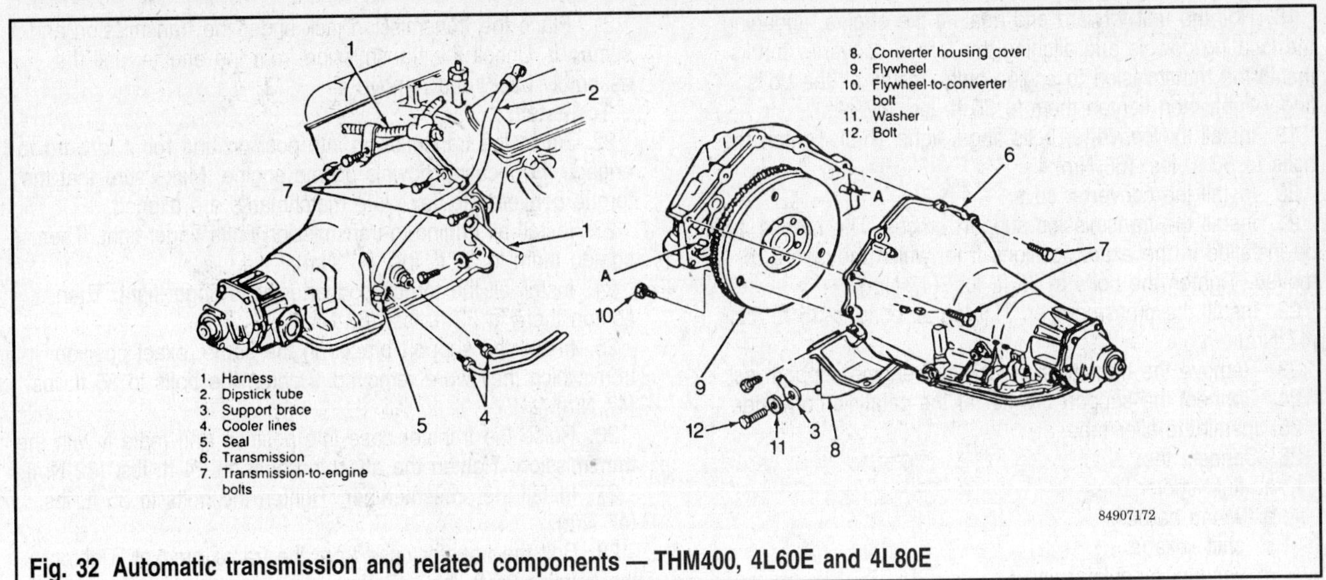

Fig. 32 Automatic transmission and related components — THM400, 4L60E and 4L80E

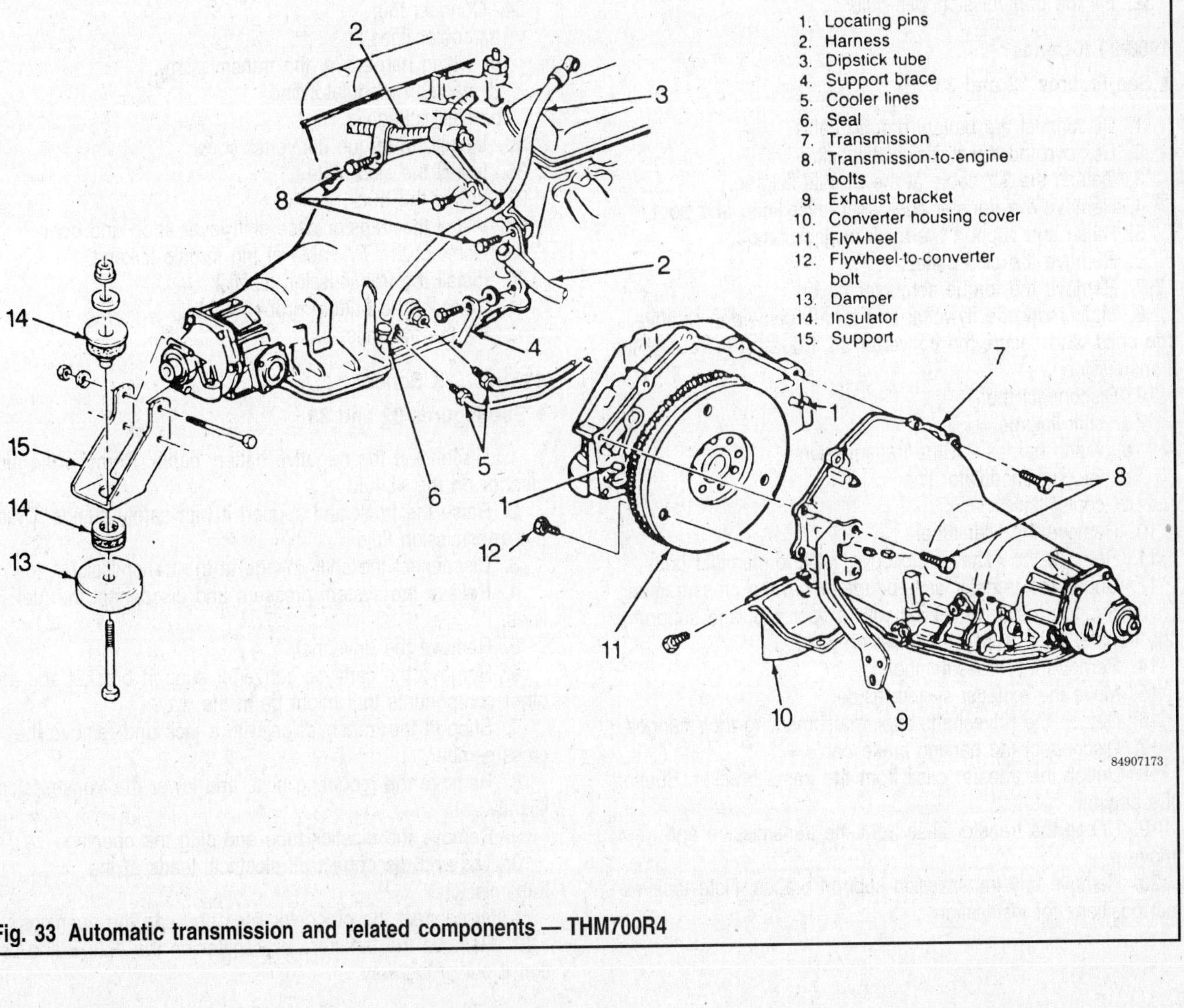

1. Locating pins
2. Harness
3. Dipstick tube
4. Support brace
5. Cooler lines
6. Seal
7. Transmission
8. Transmission-to-engine bolts
9. Exhaust bracket
10. Converter housing cover
11. Flywheel
12. Flywheel-to-converter bolt
13. Damper
14. Insulator
15. Support
84907173

Fig. 33 Automatic transmission and related components — THM700R4

18. Roll the unit forward and against the engine, engaging the locating dowels and aligning the torque converter marks. Install the transmission to engine bolts. Install all the bolts finger-tight, then tighten them to 35 ft. lbs. (47 Nm).
19. Install the converter bolts finger-tight. Then, tighten the bolts to 50 ft. lbs. (68 Nm).
20. Install the converter cover.
21. Install the transmission support braces. The braces must be installed in the exact positions from which they were removed. Tighten the bolts to 35 ft. lbs. (47 Nm).
22. Install the crossmember. Tighten all bolts to 35 ft. lbs. (47 Nm).
23. Remove the transmission jack and engine support jack.
24. Connect the support bracket at the catalytic converter.
25. Install the filler tube.
26. Connect the:
    a. fluid cooler lines
    b. wiring harness
    c. shift linkage
    d. vacuum modulator line
27. Install the driveshaft.
28. Lower the truck.
29. Connect the TV cable at the throttle lever.
30. Install the air cleaner.
31. Connect the battery ground cable.
32. Fill the transmission with fluid.

1988-90 K-Series

➧ See Figures 32 and 33

1. Disconnect the battery ground cable.
2. Remove the transmission dipstick.
3. Detach the TV cable at the throttle linkage.
4. Remove the transfer case shift lever knob and boot.
5. Raise and support the truck on jackstands.
6. Remove the skid plate.
7. Remove the torque converter cover.
8. Matchmark the flywheel and torque converter, remove the bolts, and secure the converter so it doesn't fall out of the transmission.
9. Disconnect the:
    a. shift linkage
    b. wiring harness at the transmission
    c. vacuum modulator line
    d. cooler lines
10. Remove the filler tube.
11. Remove the exhaust crossover pipe-to-manifold bolts.
12. Unbolt the transfer case adapter from the crossmember.
13. Support the transmission with a floor jack and support the transfer case with a transmission jack.
14. Remove the crossmember.
15. Move the exhaust system aside.
16. Detach the driveshafts after matchmarking their flanges.
17. Disconnect the parking brake cable.
18. Unbolt the transfer case from the frame bracket. Support the engine.
19. Unbolt the transfer case from the transmission and remove it.
20. Remove any transmission support braces. Note their exact positions for installation.
21. Place the transmission jack under the transmission and secure it. Unbolt the transmission from the engine, pull the assembly back, and remove it.

To install:

22. Raise the transmission into position and roll it forward to engage the locating dowels on the engine. Make sure that the torque converter-to-flex plate matchmarks are aligned.
23. Install all engine-to-transmission bolts finger-tight. Then, tighten them to 35 ft. lbs. (47 Nm).
24. Install all the torque converter bolts finger-tight. Then, tighten them to 50 ft. lbs. (68 Nm).
25. Install the support braces in the same, exact position from which they were removed. Tighten the bolts to 35 ft. lbs. (47 Nm).
26. Raise the transfer case into position and mate it with the transmission. Tighten the attaching bolts to 24 ft. lbs. (32 Nm).
27. Install the crossmember. Tighten the bolts to 35 ft. lbs. (47 Nm).
28. Bolt the transfer case from the frame bracket. Tighten the bolts to 35 ft. lbs. (47 Nm).
29. Remove the jacks and engine support.
30. Connect the parking brake cable.
31. Install the driveshafts.
32. Install the exhaust crossover pipe-to-manifold bolts.
33. Install the filler tube.
34. Connect the:
    a. cooler lines
    b. wiring harness at the transmission
    c. vacuum modulator line
    d. shift linkage
35. Install the torque converter cover.
36. Install the skid plate.
37. Lower the truck.
38. Install the transfer case shift lever knob and boot.
39. Connect the TV cable at the throttle linkage.
40. Install the transmission dipstick.
41. Connect the battery ground cable.
42. Fill the transmission.

1991-96 C/K Series

➧ See Figures 32 and 33

1. Disconnect the negative battery cable. Remove the air cleaner on the 4L80E.
2. Raise the truck and support it with safety stands. Drain the transmission fluid.
3. Disconnect the shift linkage at the transmission.
4. Relieve the system pressure and disconnect the fuel lines.
5. Remove the driveshaft.
6. Remove the catalytic converter support bracket and any other components that might be in the way.
7. Support the transmission with a jack and remove the crossmember.
8. Remove the mounting bolts and lower the transmission slightly.
9. Remove the dipstick tube and plug the opening.
10. Tag and disconnect all electrical leads at the transmission.
11. Disconnect the oil cooler lines and cap the openings.
12. Remove the transfer case shifter on the 4L80E and position it out of the way.

13. Mark the location of the transmission support braces and then remove them.

14. Remove the converter housing cover and mark the flywheel and torque converter for alignment.

15. Mark the location of any brackets or clips on the transmission screws, remove the screws. Slid the transmission straight back on the locating pins and remove it from the truck.

To install:

16. Slide the transmission onto the locating pins so that the marks on the flywheel and converter are in alignment. The torque converter **must** be flush with the flywheel and rotate free.

17. Install the transmission screws with all the brackets and clips and tighten them fingertight. Make sure that the converter is seated properly and then tighten them to 50 ft. lbs. (68 Nm) on the 4L60E; or 46 ft. lbs. (63 Nm) on the 4L80E.

18. Remove the jack and install the converter housing cover by hooking it under the lip of the oil pan.

19. Install the support braces in their original positions.

20. Install the transfer case shifter. Install the oil cooler lines.

21. Reconnect all electrical leads and install the dipstick tube. Tighten the screw to 23 ft. lbs. (32 Nm) on the 4L60E and 33 ft. lbs. (44 Nm) on the 4L80E.

22. Install the crossmember and mount.

23. Install the catalytic converter support bracket.

24. Install the driveshaft and then connect the fuel lines.

25. Install and adjust the shift linkage.

26. Fill the transmission with fluid and connect the battery cable.

TRANSFER CASE

On 1988 V-Series trucks, the New Process 205, 208 and 241 units were used. The 208 is used on ½ and ¾ ton models; the 205 on all 1 ton models.

On 1989-91 V-Series trucks the New Process 241 unit is used for all ½ and ¾ ton models; the 205 is still used on all 1 ton models.

On 1988 K-Series trucks, the NP 241 is used on all models.

On 1989-96 K and 1992-96 V-Series trucks the NP241 is used on all models except the 30 series with dual rear wheels; the Borg-Warner 1370, 4401 or 4470 is used on the 30 series with dual rear wheels.

Identification

Refer to Section 1 for transfer case identification

Adjustments

LINKAGE

NP205

No adjustment is necessary on the NP205. Periodically inspect the linkage for freedom of operation, proper engagement and loose bolts.

NP208

➧ See Figure 34

1. Raise and support the front end on jackstands.
2. Disconnect the shift rod from the case lever.
3. Place the shift lever in the 4H position.
4. Move the case lever forward to the 4H position.
5. Push the swivel into the lever.
6. Hang a 0.20 in. (5mm) gauge over the rod behind the swivel on the threaded portion.
7. Thread the nut down against the gauge and remove the gauge.
8. Push the swivel against the nut and tighten the nut.

NP241, BW 1370, BW 4401 and BW 4470

➧ See Figures 34, 35 and 36

1. Raise and support the front end on jackstands.
2. Place the shift lever in the 4H position.
3. Disconnect the linkage rod from the shift lever.
4. Move the case lever all the way forward to the 4H position.
5. Adjust the swivel so that the swivel stud will drop in the hole in the case lever. Connect the rod.

Electronic Synchronizer

SYSTEM CHECK

➡This applies to the BW 1370, BW 4401 and BW 4470 cases.

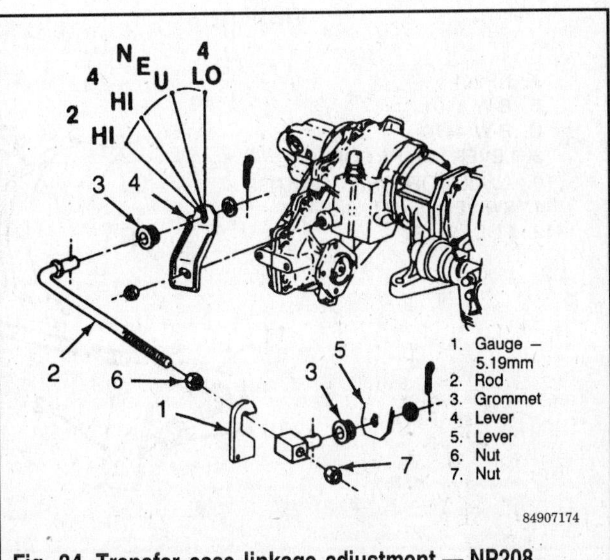

Fig. 34 Transfer case linkage adjustment — NP208

INSULATOR
ROD
SHIFT LEVER
INSULATOR
SWIVEL
84907175

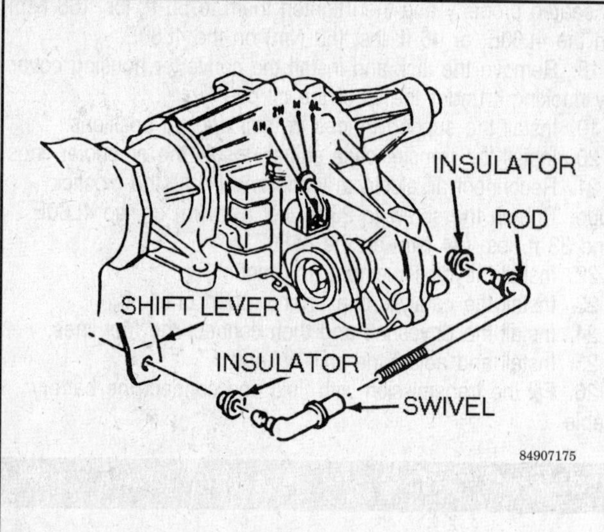

Fig. 35 Transfer case linkage adjustment — BW 1370

1. Turn the ignition switch to the **RUN** position with 4WD engaged.

➡It may be necessary to rotate the front wheels slightly to engage the axle.

2. Raise and support the front end on jackstands.
3. Disconnect the wiring plug at the transfer case.
4. Connect a test light from the red wire of the connector to a good ground. The light should come on. If it does not, check the circuit for opens. If no opens are found, replace the relay.
5. If the test lamp does light, check the synchronizer coil for continuity with an ohmmeter. If the coil is open, replace it. If the coil has continuity, it's okay. Recheck fluid levels, linkage adjustment, etc., before assuming the synchronizer is faulty.

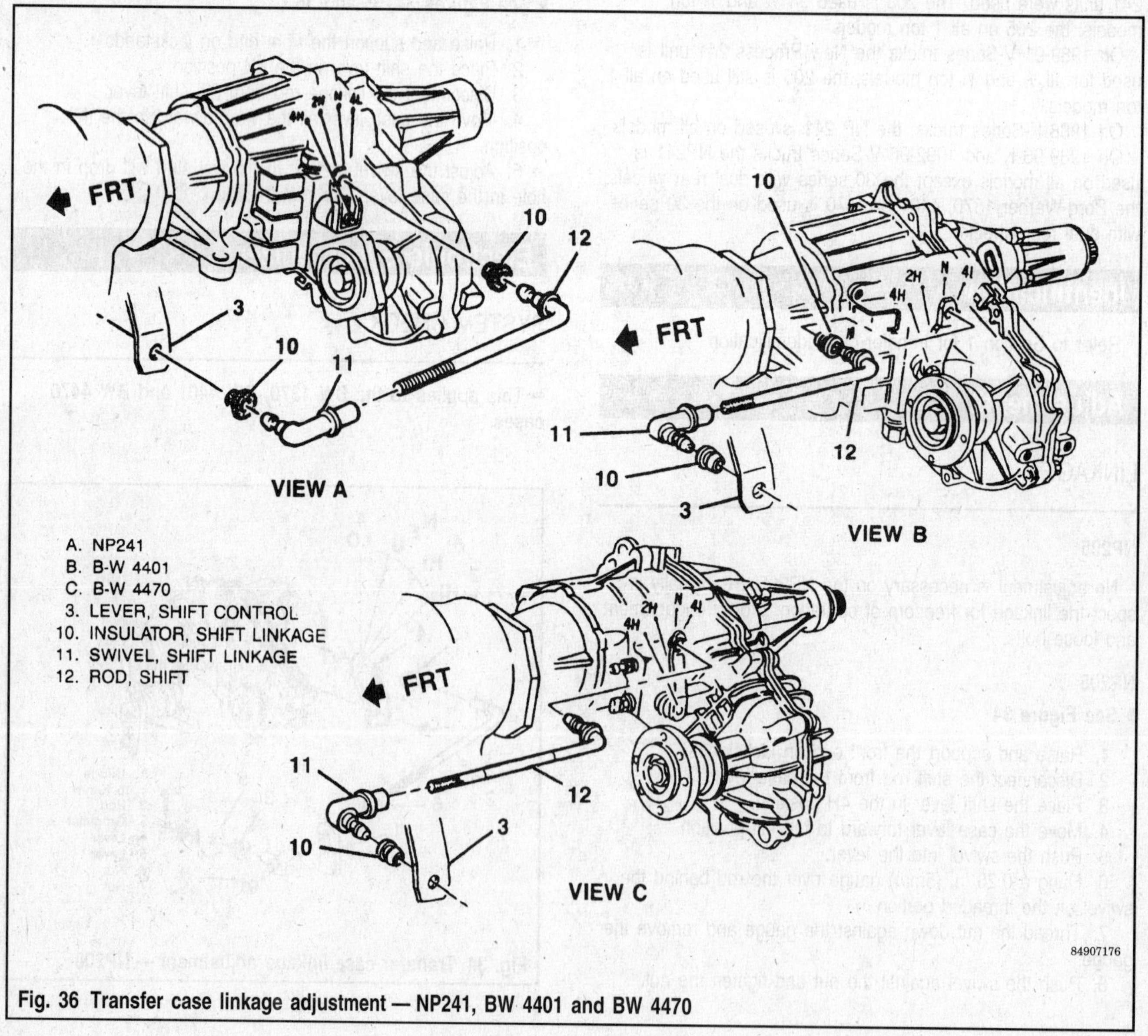

FRT
10
12
3
10
11
VIEW A
10
FRT
11
12
10
3
VIEW B
A. NP241
B. B-W 4401
C. B-W 4470
3. LEVER, SHIFT CONTROL
10. INSULATOR, SHIFT LINKAGE
11. SWIVEL, SHIFT LINKAGE
12. ROD, SHIFT
FRT
11
12
3
10
VIEW C
84907176

Fig. 36 Transfer case linkage adjustment — NP241, BW 4401 and BW 4470

Clutch Coil Relay

REMOVAL & INSTALLATION

➧ **See Figure 37**

➡**This applies to the BW 1370, BW 4401 and BW 4470 cases.**

The relay is mounted on the firewall, in the engine compartment.

1. Remove the connector retainer.
2. Unplug the harness connector.
3. Remove the retaining screws and remove the relay.
4. Installation is the reverse of removal.

Front or Rear Output Shaft Seal

REMOVAL & INSTALLATION

➧ **See Figures 38, 39 and 40**

1. Raise and support the truck on jackstands.
2. Remove the skid plate if necessary to gain access to the front seal.
3. Matchmark and remove the driveshaft.
4. Remove the nut, washer and yoke.

➡**Some models don't use a washer at the rear yoke nut.**

5. Some models employ a shield around the seal. Remove it.
6. Using a hammer and a punch, carefully distort the seal so that you can pull it out with a pliers. Be careful to avoid damage to the seal bore!

To install:

7. Coat the seal lips with clean oil fluid. Coat the outer edge of the seal with gasket sealer.

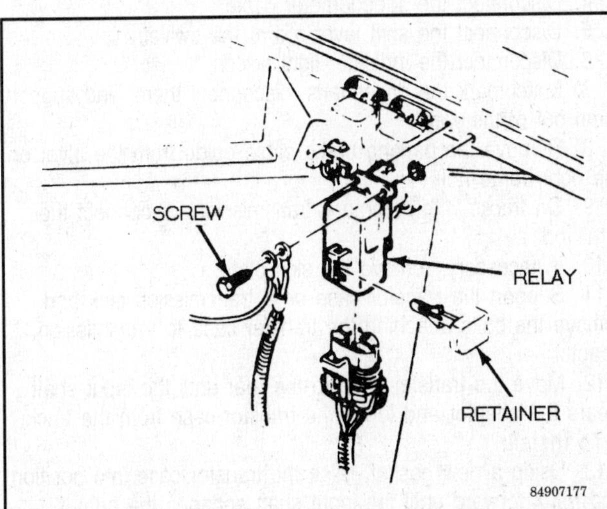

Fig. 37 Clutch coil relay — BW 1370, BW 4401 and BW 4470

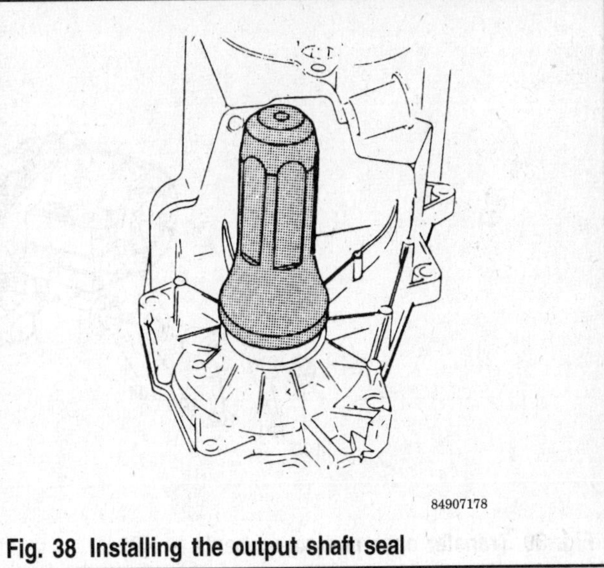

Fig. 38 Installing the output shaft seal

8. Position the seal in the bore and drive it into place by carefully tapping around it with a hammer. If you have access to one, a seal installer will make the job a little easier.
9. Install the shield, if used.
10. Coat the outer surface of the yoke neck with clean oil and slide it into place.
11. Install the nut and washer. Tighten the nut to:
    - NP205: 150 ft. lbs. (203 Nm)
    - NP208: 120 ft. lbs. (163 Nm)
    - NP241: 110 ft. lbs. (149 Nm)
    - BW 1370, BW 4401, BW 4470 front: 165 ft. lbs. (225 Nm)
    - BW 1370, BW 4401, BW 4470 rear: 125 ft. lbs. (170 Nm)
12. Install the driveshaft.
13. Install the skid plate.

Transfer Case Assembly

REMOVAL & INSTALLATION

NP205

➧ **See Figure 41**

1. Raise and support the truck on jackstands.
2. Drain the transfer case.
3. Disconnect the speedometer cable.
4. If necessary, remove the skid plate and crossmember support.
5. On trucks with automatic transmission, disconnect the strut rod.
6. Matchmark the driveshafts, disconnect them, and support them out of the way.
7. Disconnect the shift lever rod from the shift rail link.
8. Support the transfer case and remove the bolts attaching the transfer case to transmission adaptor.
9. Move the transfer case to the rear until the input shaft clears the adaptor and lower the transfer case from the truck.

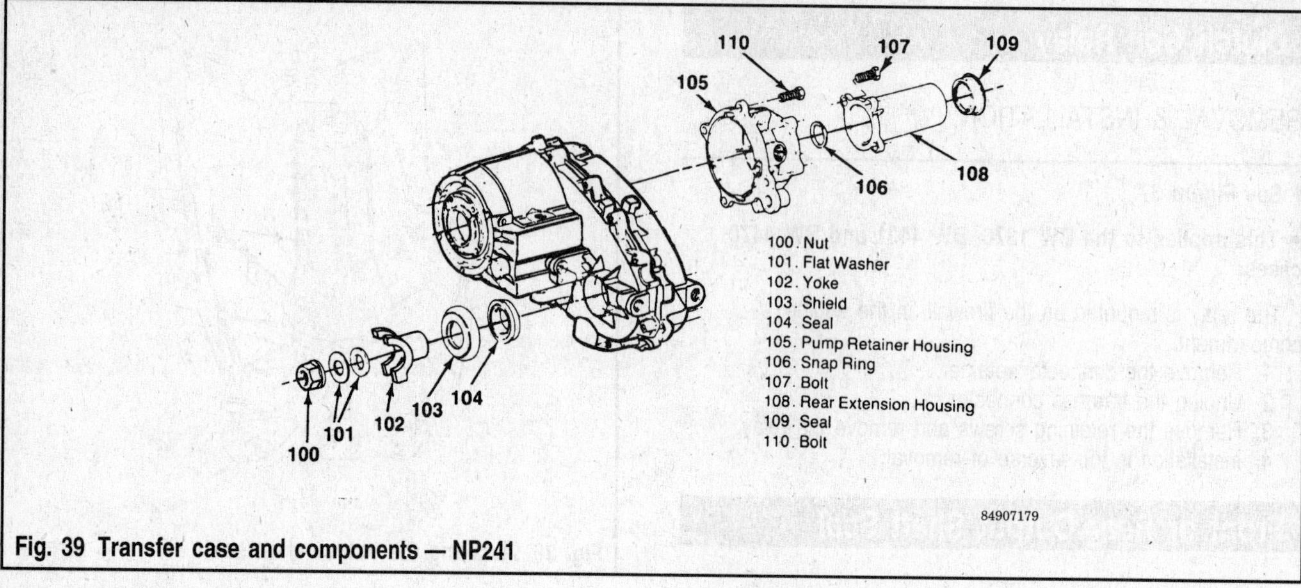

Fig. 39 Transfer case and components — NP241

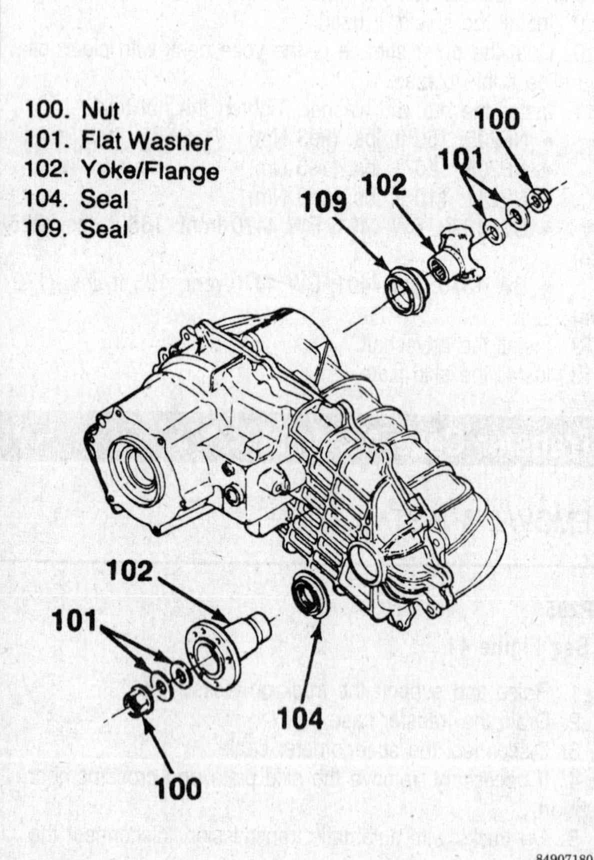

Fig. 40 Transfer case and components — BW 4401 and BW 4470

To install:

10. Raise the transfer case into position and roll it forward until the input shaft engages the adapter.
11. Install the bolts attaching the transfer case to transmission adaptor. Tighten them to 24 ft. lbs. (32 Nm).
12. Connect the shift lever rod to the shift rail link.
13. Connect the driveshafts.
14. On trucks with automatic transmission, connect the strut rod. Tighten the transmission end bolts to 129 ft. lbs. (175 Nm); the transfer case end bolts to 35 ft. lbs. (47 Nm).
15. Install the skid plate and crossmember support.
16. Remove the jack.
17. Connect the speedometer cable.
18. Fill the transfer case.

NP208

1. Raise and support the truck on jackstands.
2. Drain the transfer case.
3. Place the case in the 4H position.
4. Disconnect the speedometer cable.
5. Disconnect the shift lever rod at the swivel.
6. Disconnect the indicator light switch.
7. Matchmark the driveshafts, disconnect them, and support them out of the way.
8. Remove the parking brake cable guide from the pivot on the right frame rail.
9. On trucks with automatic transmission, disconnect the strut rod.
10. If necessary, remove the skid plate.
11. Support the transfer case on a transmission jack and remove the bolts attaching the transfer case to transmission adaptor.
12. Move the transfer case to the rear until the input shaft clears the adaptor and lower the transfer case from the truck.

To install:

13. Using a new gasket, raise the transfer case into position and roll it forward until the input shaft engages the output shaft. Make sure it's still in 4H.
14. Install the bolts attaching the transfer case to transmission adaptor. Make sure the transfer case is flush against the adapter. Tighten the bolts to 30 ft. lbs. (40 Nm).

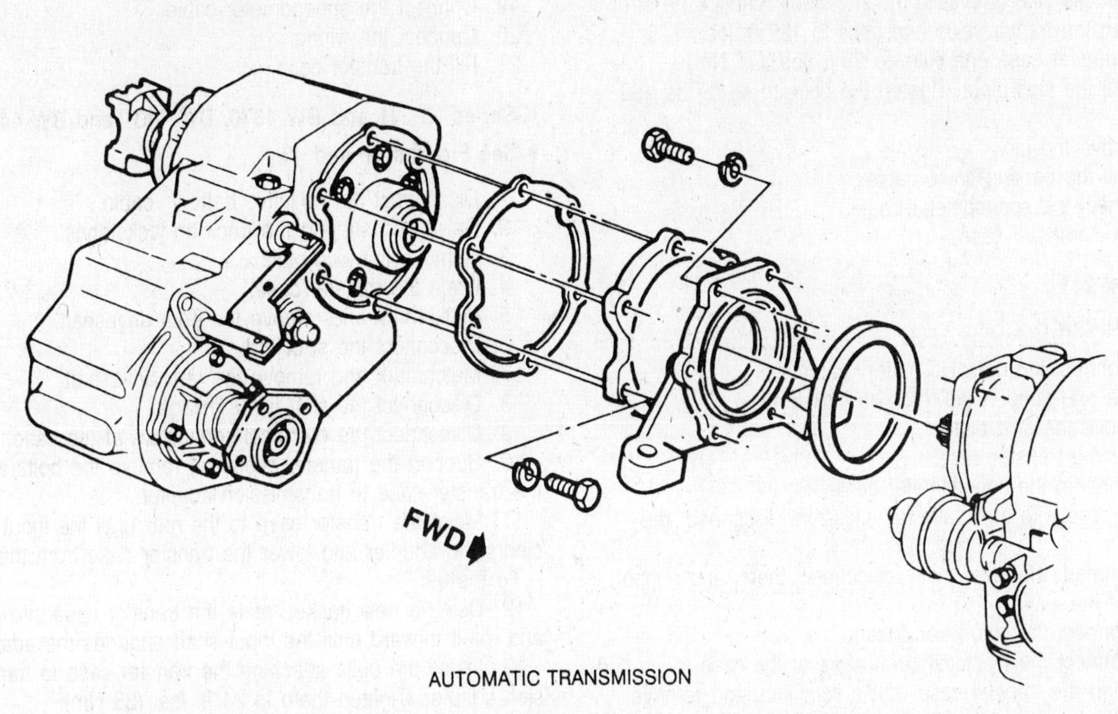

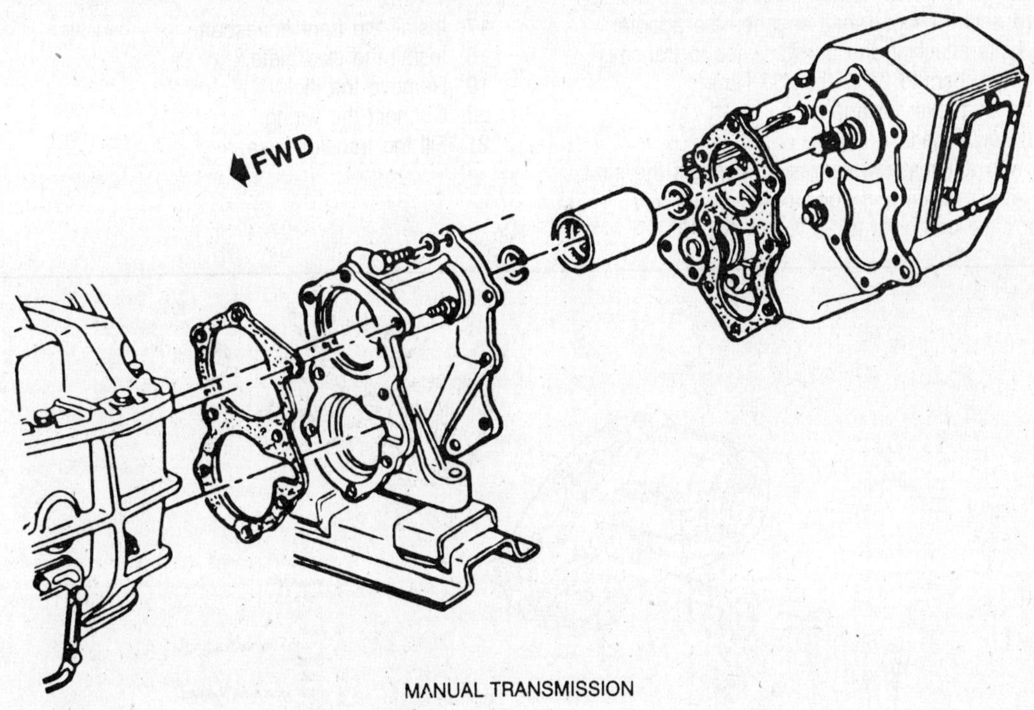

Fig. 41 Transfer case-to-transmission adapters — NP205

15. Connect the shift lever rod.
16. Connect the driveshafts.
17. On trucks with automatic transmission, connect the strut rod. Tighten the transmission end bolts to 129 ft. lbs. (175 Nm); the transfer case end bolts to 35 ft. lbs. (47 Nm)
18. Install the skid plate. Tighten the bolts to 46 ft. lbs. (62 Nm).
19. Remove the jack.
20. Install the parking brake cable.
21. Connect the speedometer cable.
22. Fill the transfer case.

V-Series NP241

➧ See Figure 42

1. Disconnect the negative battery cable.
2. Raise and support the truck on jackstands.
3. Remove the skid plate.
4. Drain the transfer case.
5. Disconnect the speedometer cable.
6. On trucks with automatic transmission, disconnect the strut rod.
7. Matchmark the driveshafts, disconnect them, and support them out of the way.
8. Disconnect the shift lever linkage.
9. Disconnect the electrical connectors at the case.
10. Support the transfer case with a floor jack and remove the bolts attaching the transfer case to transmission adapter.
11. Move the transfer case to the rear until the input shaft clears the adapter and lower the transfer case from the truck.

To install:

12. Using a new gasket, raise the transfer case into position and roll it forward until the input shaft engages the adapter.
13. Install the bolts attaching the transfer case to transmission adapter. Tighten them to 24 ft. lbs. (33 Nm).
14. Connect the shift lever linkage.
15. Connect the driveshafts.
16. On trucks with automatic transmission, connect the strut rod. Tighten the transmission end bolts to 129 ft. lbs. (175 Nm); the transfer case end bolts to 35 ft. lbs. (47 Nm).
17. Install the skid plate and crossmember support.
18. Remove the jack.
19. Connect the speedometer cable.
20. Connect the wiring.
21. Fill the transfer case.

K-Series NP241 and BW 1370, BW 4401 and BW 4470

➧ See Figures 42 and 43

1. Disconnect the negative battery cable.
2. Raise and support the truck on jackstands.
3. Remove the skid plate.
4. Drain the transfer case.
5. Matchmark and remove the front driveshaft.
6. Disconnect the strut rod.
7. Matchmark and remove the rear driveshaft.
8. Disconnect the shift lever linkage.
9. Disconnect the electrical connectors at the case.
10. Support the transfer case and remove the bolts attaching the transfer case to transmission adapter.
11. Move the transfer case to the rear until the input shaft clears the adapter and lower the transfer case from the truck.

To install:

12. Using a new gasket, raise the transfer case into position and roll it forward until the input shaft engages the adapter.
13. Install the bolts attaching the transfer case to transmission adapter. Tighten them to 24 ft. lbs. (33 Nm).
14. Connect the shift lever linkage.
15. Connect the rear driveshaft.
16. Connect the strut rod. Tighten the transmission end bolts to 129 ft. lbs. (175 Nm); the transfer case end bolts to 35 ft. lbs. (47 Nm).
17. Install the front driveshaft.
18. Install the skid plate.
19. Remove the jack.
20. Connect the wiring.
21. Fill the transfer case.

1. Nut
2. Washer
3. Yoke
4. Shield
5. Seal
6. Pump retainer housing
7. Snapring
8. Bolt
9. Rear extension housing
10. Seal
11. Bolt

84907183

Fig. 42 Transfer case and related components — NP241

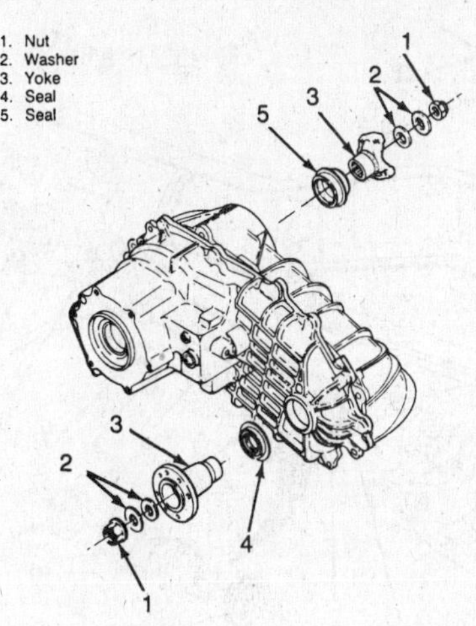

Fig. 43 Transfer case and related components — BW 1370, BW4401 and BW4470

DRIVELINE

Tubular driveshafts are used on all models, incorporating needle bearing U-joints. An internally splined sleeve at the forward end compensates for variation in distance between the rear axle and the transmission.

The number of rear driveshafts used is determined by the length of the wheelbase. On trucks that use a two-piece rear driveshaft there is a center support incorporating a rubber cushioned ball bearing mounted in a bracket attached to the frame crossmember. The ball bearing is permanently sealed and lubricated.

4WD models use a front driveshaft with a constant velocity joint or a U-joint.

Extended life U-joints have been incorporated on most models and can be identified by the absence of a lubrication fitting.

Front Driveshaft

REMOVAL & INSTALLATION

Solid Axle

See Figure 44

Chevrolet and GMC use U-bolts or straps to secure the driveshaft to the pinion flange. Use the following procedure to remove the driveshaft.

1. Jack up your vehicle and support it with jackstands.
2. Scribe aligning marks on the driveshaft and the pinion flange to aid in reassembly.
3. Remove the U-bolts or straps at the axle end of the shaft. Compress the shaft slightly and tape the bearings into place to avoid losing them.
4. Remove the U-bolts or flange bolts at the transfer case end of the shaft. Tape the bearings into place.
5. Remove the driveshaft.

To install:

6. Install the driveshaft. Make certain that the marks made earlier line up correctly to prevent possible imbalances. Be sure that the constant velocity joint is at the transfer case end. Tighten the U-bolts to 15 ft. lbs. (20 Nm); flange bolts to 75 ft. lbs. (101 Nm).

Independent Axle

See Figures 45, 46, 47, 48 and 49

1. Jack up your vehicle and support it with jackstands.
2. Scribe aligning marks on the driveshaft and each flange to aid in reassembly.
3. Remove the flange bolts and retainers at each end of the shaft. Remove the slip yoke from the front axle.
4. Push the driveshaft forward until it clears the transfer case flange and remove it. If the shaft is difficult to disengage from either flange, pry it loose; never hammer it loose!
5. Use a piece of tape to hold the U-joint caps in place. Remove the driveshaft.
6. Install the driveshaft. Make certain that the marks made earlier line up correctly to prevent possible imbalances. Be sure that the constant velocity joint is at the transfer case end. Tighten the axle end flange bolts to 15 ft. lbs. (20 Nm); the transfer case end flange bolts to 75 ft. lbs. (101 Nm).

Rear Driveshaft And Center Bearing

REMOVAL & INSTALLATION

See Figures 50, 51, 52, 53, 54, 55, 56 and 57

1. Jack up your truck and support it with jackstands.
2. Scribe alignment marks on the driveshaft and flange of the rear axle, and transfer case or transmission. If the truck is equipped with a two piece driveshaft, be certain to also scribe marks at the center joint near the splined connection. When reinstalling driveshafts, it is necessary to place the shafts in the same position from which they were removed. Failure to reinstall the driveshaft properly will cause driveline vibrations and reduced component life.

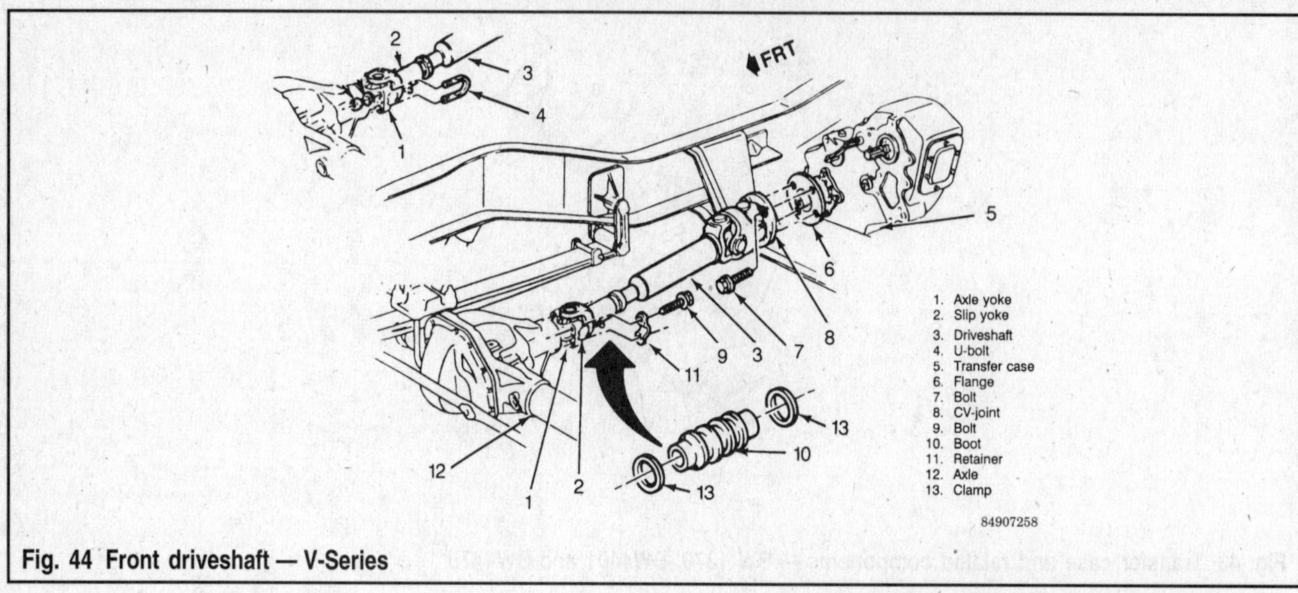

Fig. 44 Front driveshaft — V-Series

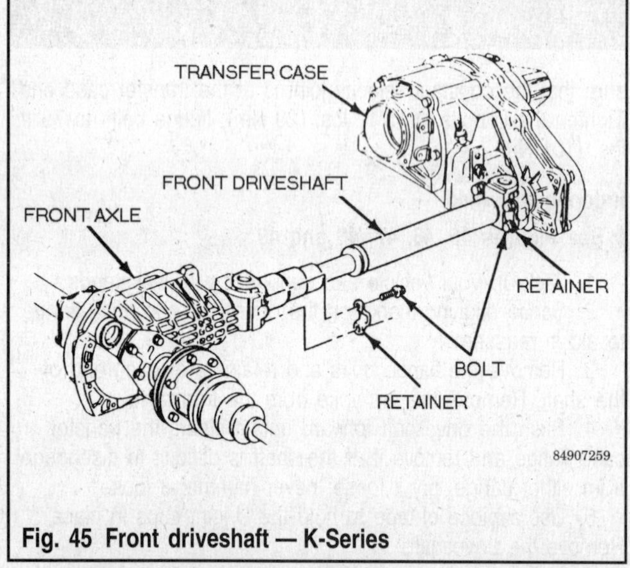

Fig. 45 Front driveshaft — K-Series

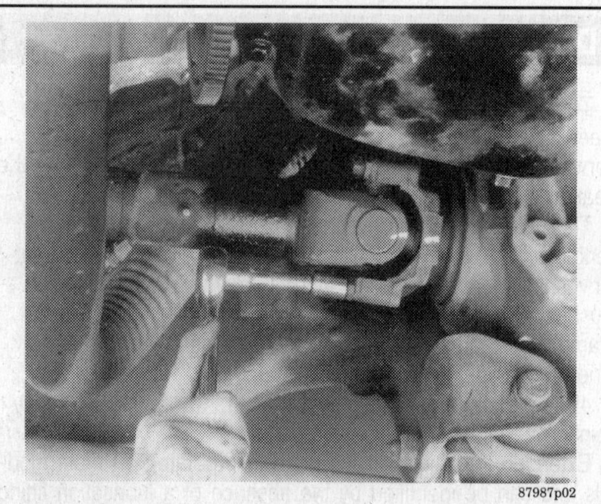

Fig. 47 Remove the flange bolts and retainers at each end of the shaft

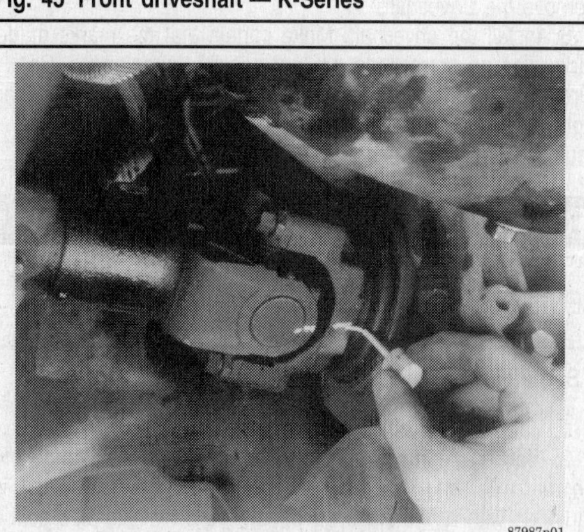

Fig. 46 Scribe aligning marks on the driveshaft and each flange to aid in reassembly

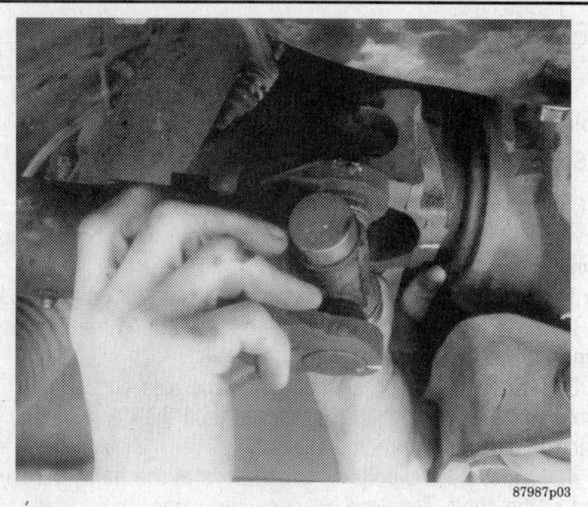

Fig. 48 Push the driveshaft forward until it clears the transfer case flange and remove it

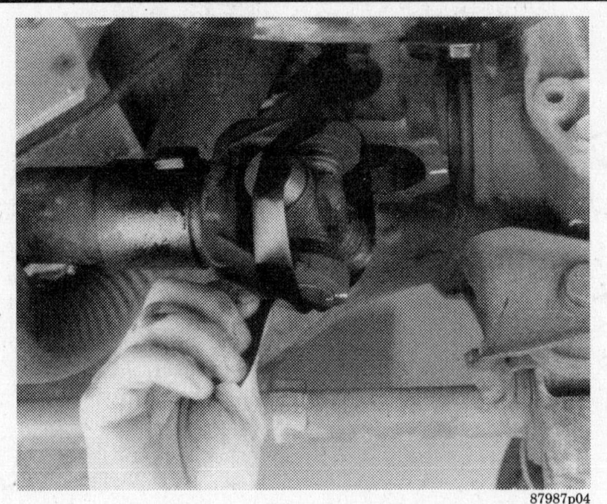
Fig. 49 Use a piece of tape to hold the u-joint caps in place.

3. Disconnect the rear universal joint by removing U-bolts or straps. Tape the bearings into place to avoid losing them.
4. If there are U-bolts or straps at the front end of the shaft, remove them. Tape the bearings into place. For trucks with two piece shafts, remove the bolts retaining the bearing support to the frame crossmember. Compress the shaft slightly and remove it.
5. If there are no fasteners at the front end of the transmission, there will only be a splined fitting. Slide the shaft forward slightly to disengage the axle flange, lower the rear end of the shaft, then pull it back out of the transmission. Most two wheel drive trucks are of this type. For trucks with two piece driveshafts, remove the bolts retaining the bearing support to the frame crossmember.
6. Reverse the procedure for installation. It may be tricky to get the scribed alignment marks to match up on trucks with two piece driveshafts. For those models only, the following

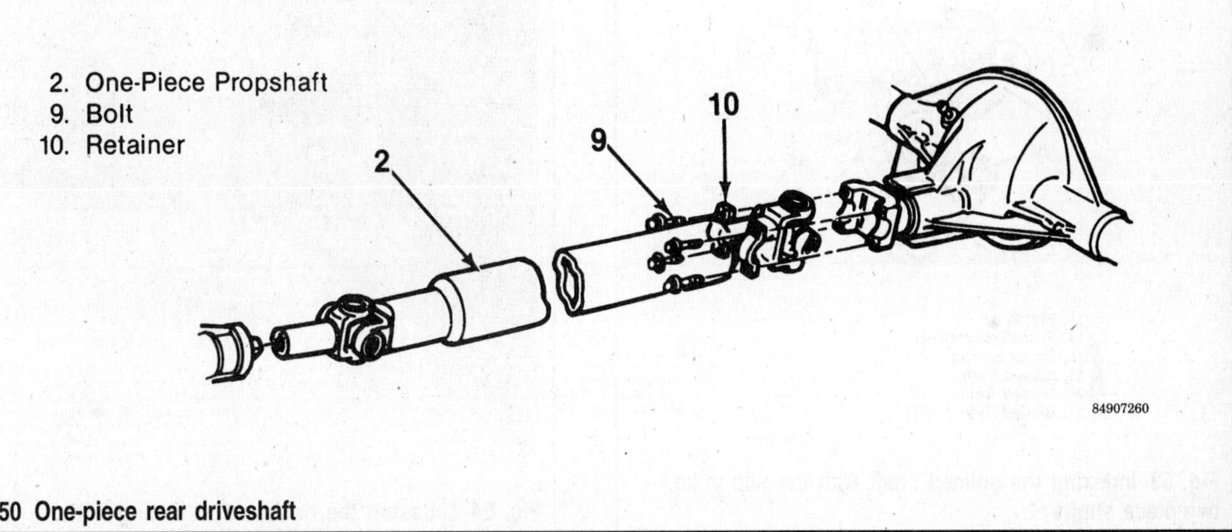

Fig. 50 One-piece rear driveshaft

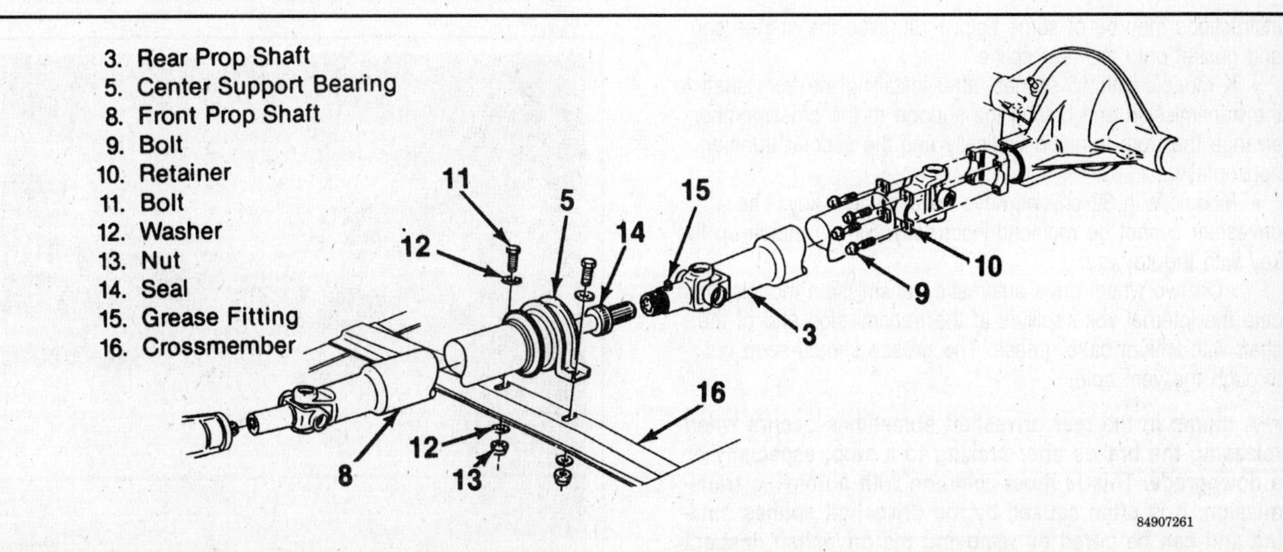

Fig. 51 Two-piece rear driveshaft with center bearing

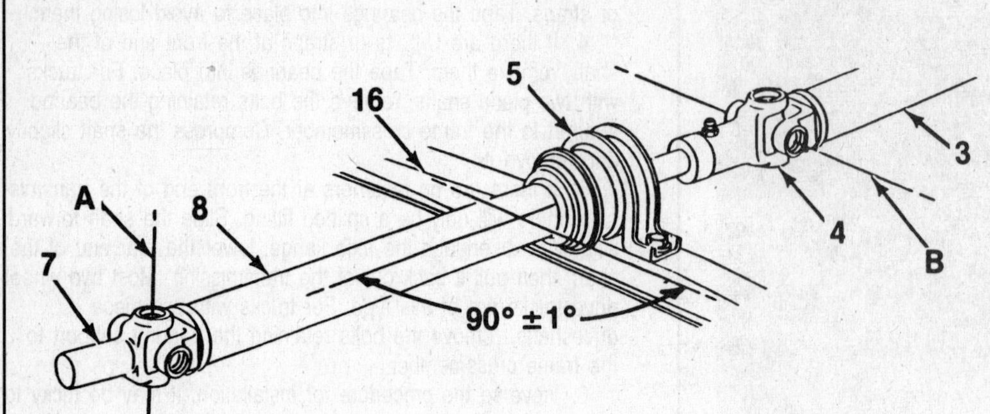

Fig. 52 Center bearing alignment

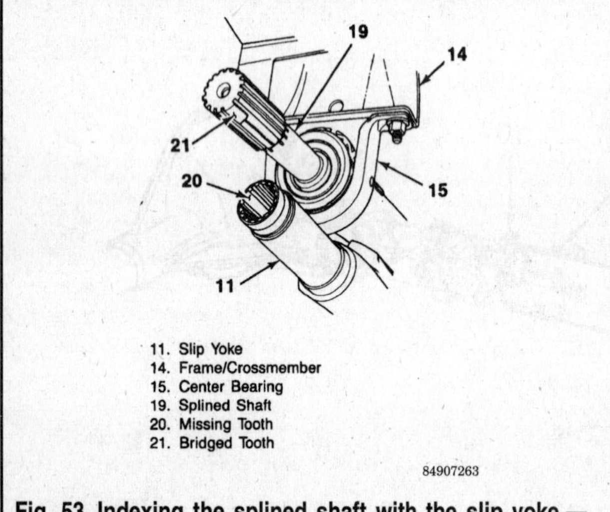

Fig. 53 Indexing the splined shaft with the slip yoke — two-piece shafts

Fig. 54 Unfasten the driveshaft retaining bolts

instructions may be of some help. First, slide the grease cap and gasket onto the rear splines.

- K models with 16 splines, after installing the front shaft to the transmission and bolting the support to the crossmember, arrange the front trunnion vertically and the second trunnion horizontally.
- Models with 32 splines have an alignment key. The driveshaft cannot be replaced incorrectly. Simply match up the key with the keyway.

7. On two wheel drive automatic transmission models, lubricate the internal yoke splines at the transmission end of the shaft with lithium base grease. The grease should seep out through the vent hole.

➡A thump in the rear driveshaft sometimes occurs when releasing the brakes after braking to a stop, especially on a downgrade. This is most common with automatic transmission. It is often caused by the driveshaft splines binding and can be cured by removing the driveshaft, inspecting the splines for rough edges, and carefully lubricating. A similar thump may be caused by the clutch plates in

Fig. 55 Remove the driveshaft retaining straps

Positraction limited slip rear axles binding. If this isn't caused by wear, it can be cured by draining and refilling the rear axle with the special lubricant and adding Positraction additive, both of which are available from dealers.

U-Joints

OVERHAUL

There are three types of U-joints used in these trucks. The first is held together by wire snaprings in the yokes. The second type is held together with injection molded plastic retainer rings. This type cannot be reassembled with the same parts, once disassembled. However, repair kits are available. The third type (4WD models only) is the large constant velocity joint which looks like a double U-joint, located at the transfer case end of the front driveshaft on V-Series trucks.

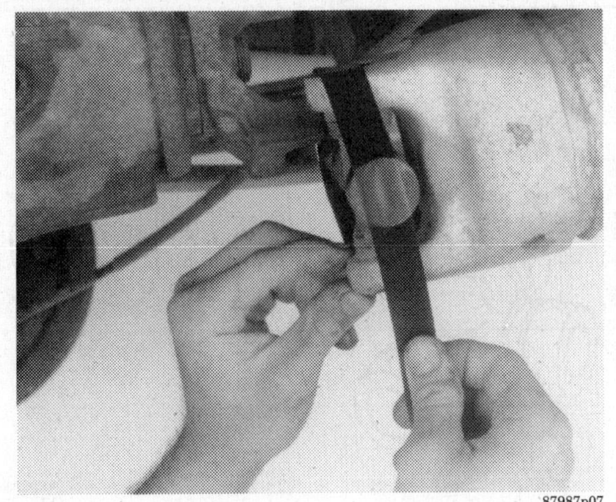

87987p07

Fig. 56 Tape the bearings into place to avoid losing them

87987p08

Fig. 57 Lower the rear end of the shaft, then pull it back out of the transmission

Snapring Type

➧ **See Figures 58, 59, 60 and 61**

1. Remove the driveshaft(s) from the truck.
2. Remove the lockrings from the yoke and remove the lubrication fitting.
3. Support the yoke in a bench vise. Never clamp the driveshaft tube.
4. Use a soft drift pin and hammer to drive against one trunnion bearing to drive the opposite bearing from the yoke.

➡The bearing cap cannot be driven completely out.

5. Grasp the cap and work it out.
6. Support the other side of the yoke and drive the other bearing cap from the yoke and remove as in Steps 4 and 5.
7. Remove the trunnion from the driveshaft yoke.
8. If equipped with a sliding sleeve, remove the trunnions bearings from the sleeve yoke in the same manner as above. Remove the seal retainer from the end of the sleeve and pull the seal and washer from the retainer.

To remove the bearing support:

9. Remove the dust shield, or, if equipped with a flange, remove the cotter pin and nut and pull the flange and deflector assembly from the shaft.
10. Remove the support bracket from the rubber cushion and pull the cushion away from the bearing.
11. Pull the bearing assembly from the shaft. If equipped, remove the grease retainers and slingers from the bearing.

Assemble the bearing support as follows:

12. Install the inner deflector on the driveshaft and punch the deflector on 2 opposite sides to be sure that it is tight.
13. Pack the retainers with special high melting grease. Insert a slinger (if used) inside one retainer and press this retainer over the bearing outer race.
14. Start the bearing and slinger on the shaft journal. Support the driveshaft and press the bearing and inner slinger against the shoulder of the shaft with a suitable pipe.
15. Install the second slinger on the shaft and press the second retainer on the shaft.
16. Install the dust shield over the shaft (small diameter first) and depress it into position against the outer slinger or, if equipped with a flange, install the flange and deflector. Align the centerline of the flange yoke with the centerline of the driveshaft yoke and start the flange straight on the splines of the shaft with the end of the flange against the slinger.
17. Force the rubber cushion onto the bearing and coat the outside diameter of the cushion with clean brake fluid.
18. Force the bracket onto the cushion.

Assemble the trunnion bearings:

19. Repack the bearings with grease and replace the trunnion dust seals after any operation that requires disassembly of the U-joint. But be sure that the lubricant reservoir at the end of the trunnion is full of lubricant. Fill the reservoirs with lubricant from the bottom.
20. Install the trunnion into the driveshaft yoke and press the bearings into the yoke over the trunnion hubs as far as it will go.
21. Install the lockrings.
22. Hold the trunnion in one hand and tap the yoke slightly to seat the bearings against the lockrings.

23. On the rear driveshafts, install the sleeve yoke over the trunnion hubs and install the bearings in the same manner as above.

Molded Retainer Type

See Figures 62, 63, 64 and 65

1. Remove the driveshaft.
2. Support the driveshaft in a horizontal position. Place the U-joint so that the lower ear of the shaft yoke is supported by a 1⅛in. socket. Press the lower bearing cup out of the yoke ear. This will shear the plastic retaining the lower bearing cup.

Never clamp the driveshaft tubing in a vise.

3. If the bearing cup is not completely removed, lift the cross, insert a spacer and press the cup completely out.
4. Rotate the driveshaft, shear the opposite plastic retainer, and press the other bearing cup out in the same manner.
5. Remove the cross from the yoke. Production U-joints cannot be reassembled. There are no bearing retainer grooves

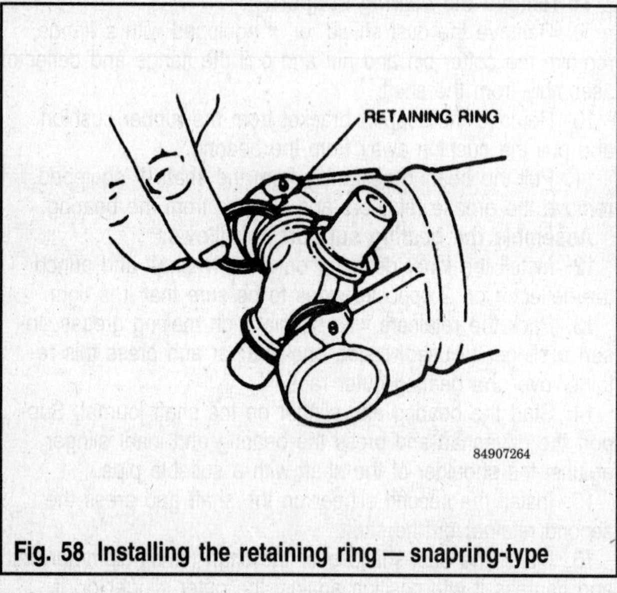

Fig. 58 Installing the retaining ring — snapring-type

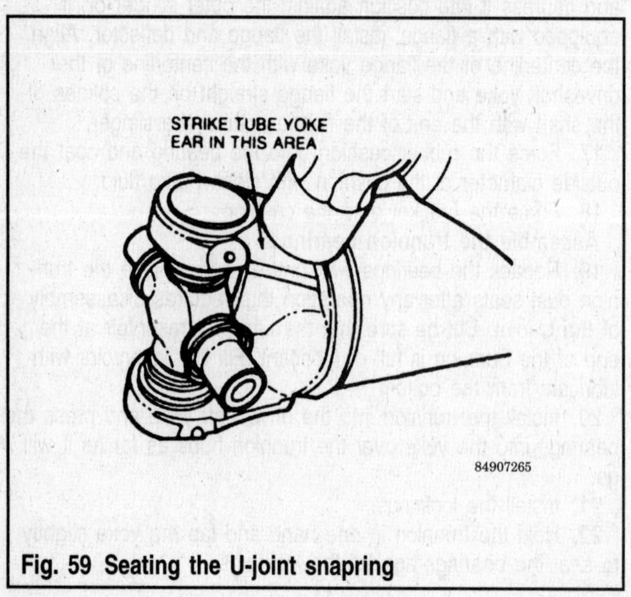

Fig. 59 Seating the U-joint snapring

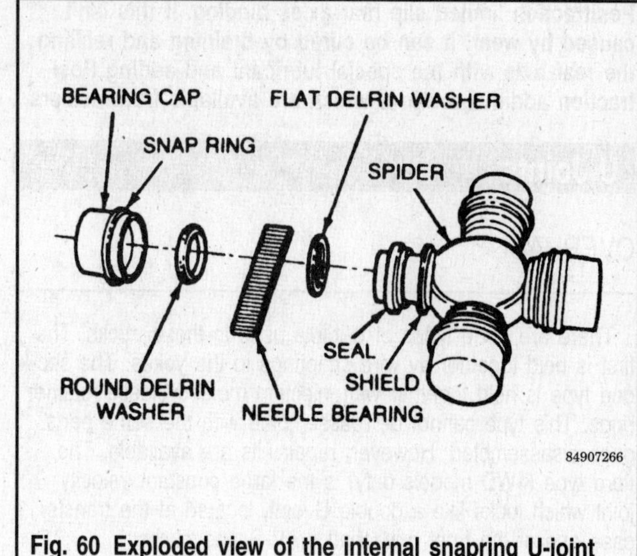

Fig. 60 Exploded view of the internal snapring U-joint

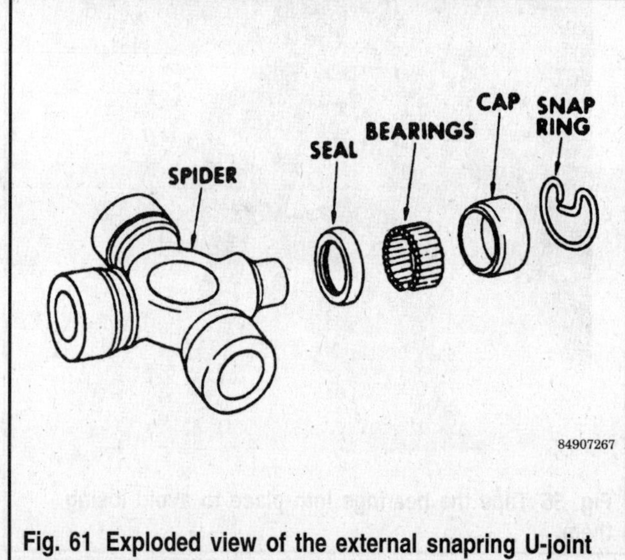

Fig. 61 Exploded view of the external snapring U-joint

in the cups. Discard all parts that we removed and substitute those in the overhaul kit.

6. Remove the sheared plastic bearing retainer. Drive a small pin or punch through the injection holes to aid in removal.
7. If the front U-joint is serviced, remove the bearing cups from the slip yoke in the manner previously described.
8. Be sure that the seals are installed on the service bearing cups to hold the needle bearings in place for handling. Grease the bearings if they aren't pregreased.
9. Install one bearing cup partway into one side of the yoke and turn this ear to the bottom.
10. Insert the opposite bearing cup partway. Be sure that both trunnions are started straight into the bearing cups.
11. Press against opposite bearing cups, working the cross constantly to be sure that it is free in the cups. If binding occurs, check the needle rollers to be sure that one needle has not become lodged under an end of the trunnion.
12. As soon as one bearing retainer groove is exposed, stop pressing and install the bearing retainer snapring.

13. Continue to press until the opposite bearing retainer can be installed. If difficulty installing the snaprings is encountered, tap the yoke with a hammer to spring the yoke ears slightly.

14. Assemble the other half of the U-joint in the same manner.

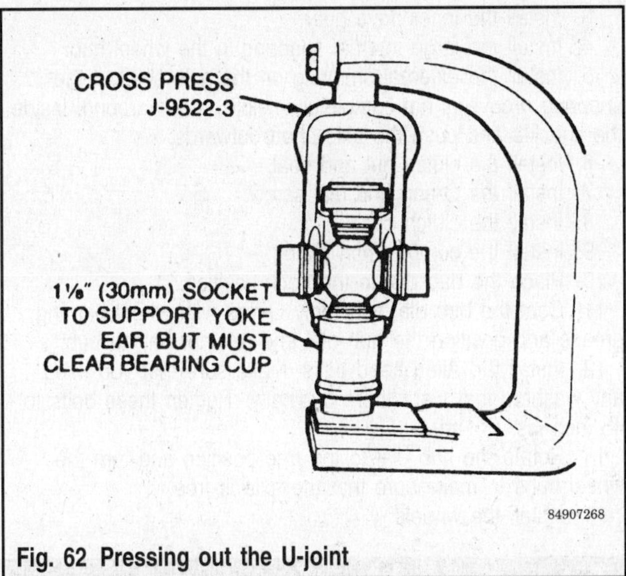

Fig. 62 Pressing out the U-joint

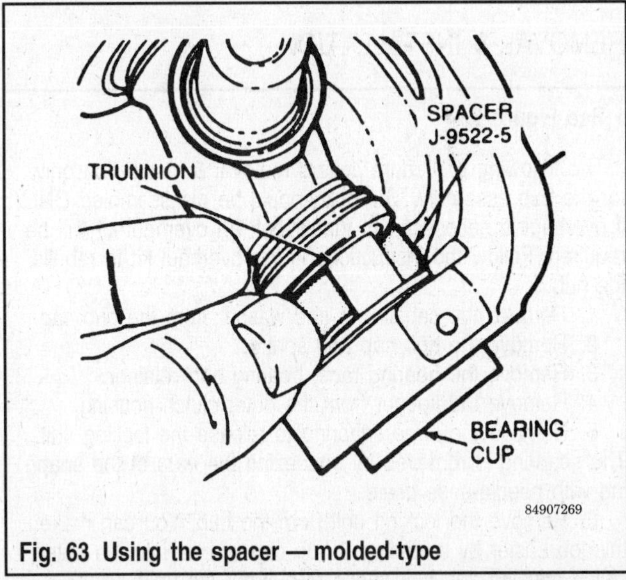

Fig. 63 Using the spacer — molded-type

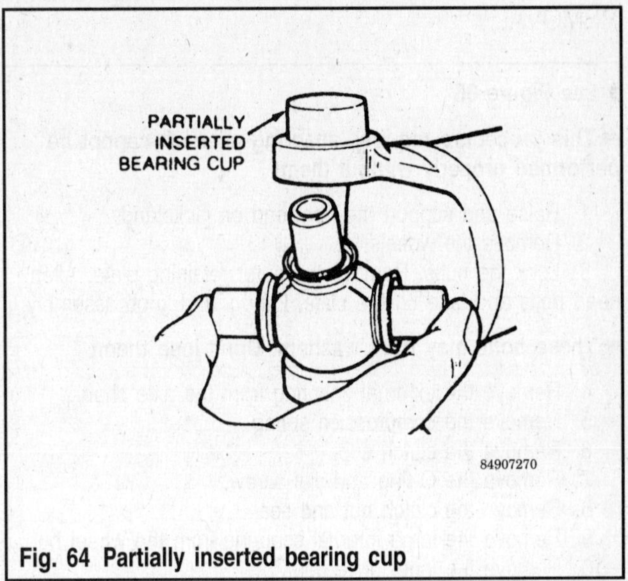

Fig. 64 Partially inserted bearing cup

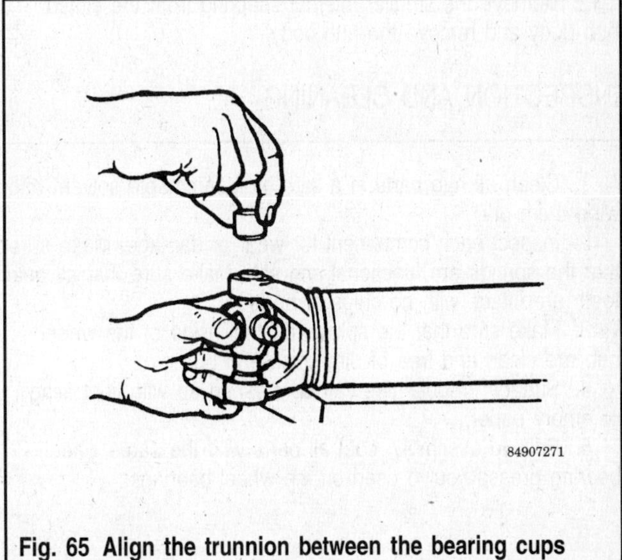

Fig. 65 Align the trunnion between the bearing cups

SOLID FRONT DRIVE AXLE

The 10/15 series and 20/25 series trucks use a GMC 8½ in. ring gear axle.

The 30/35 series trucks use a Dana 60, 9¾ in. ring gear axle.

Manual Locking Hubs

The engagement and disengagement of the hubs is a manual operation which must be performed at each hub assembly. The hubs should be placed FULLY in either Lock or Free position or damage will result.

⁂WARNING

Do not place the transfer case in either 4-wheel mode unless the hubs are in the Lock position!

Locking hubs should be run in the Lock position periodically for a few miles to assure proper differential lubrication.

REMOVAL

➧ See Figure 66

➡This procedure requires snapring pliers. It cannot be performed properly without them!

1. Raise and support the front end on jackstands.
2. Remove the wheels.
3. Lock the hubs. Remove the outer retaining plate, Allen head bolts and take off the plate, O-ring, and knob assembly.

➡These bolts may have washers. Don't lose them!

4. Remove the external snapring from the axle shaft.
5. Remove the compression spring.
6. Remove the clutch cup.
7. Remove the O-ring and dial screw.
8. Remove the clutch nut and seal.
9. Remove the large internal snapring from the wheel hub.
10. Remove the inner drive gear.
11. Remove the clutch ring and spring.
12. Remove the smaller internal snapring from the clutch hub body and remove the hub body.

INSPECTION AND CLEANING

1. Clean all hub parts in a safe, non-flammable solvent and wipe them dry.
2. Inspect each component for wear or damage. Make sure that the springs are functional and stiff. Make sure that all gear teeth are intact, with no chips or burrs.
3. Make sure that the splines on the inside of the wheel hub are clean and free of dirt, chips and burrs.
4. Surface irregularities can be cleaned up with light filing or emery paper.
5. Prior to assembly, coat all parts with the same wheel bearing grease you've used on the wheel bearings.

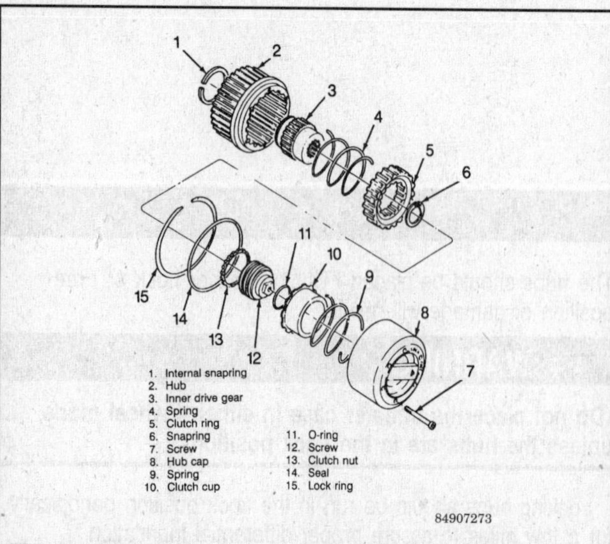

Fig. 66 Exploded view of the manual locking hubs

INSTALLATION

1. Install the hub body. Install the smaller internal snapring in the clutch hub body.
2. Install the clutch ring and spring.
3. Install the inner drive gear.
4. Install the large internal snapring in the wheel hub.
5. Install the external snapring on the axle shaft. If the snapring groove is not completely visible, reach around, inside the knuckle and push the axle shaft outwards.
6. Install the clutch nut and seal.
7. Install the O-ring and dial screw.
8. Install the clutch cup.
9. Install the compression spring.
10. Place the hub dial in the Lock position.
11. Coat the hub dial assembly O-ring with wheel bearing grease and position the hub dial and retainer on the hub.
12. Install the Allen head bolts. Make sure that you used any washers that were there originally. Tighten these bolts to 45 inch lbs. (5 Nm).
13. Rotate the hub dial to the free position and turn the wheel hubs to make sure that the axle is free.
14. Install the wheels.

Automatic Locking Hubs

REMOVAL & INSTALLATION

➧ See Figure 67

The following procedure covers removal & installation only, for the hub assembly. The hub should be disassembled ONLY if overhaul is necessary. In that event, an overhaul kit will be required. Follow the instructions in the overhaul kit to rebuild the hub.

1. Remove the capscrews and washer from the hub cap.
2. Remove the hub cap and spring.
3. Remove the bearing race, bearing and retainer.
4. Remove the keeper from the outer clutch housing.
5. Remove the large snapring to release the locking unit. The snapring is removed by squeezing the ears of the snapring with needle-nose pliers.
6. Remove the locking unit from the hub. You can make this job easier by threading 2 hub cap screws into the outer clutch housing and hold these to pull out the unit.

To install:

7. Wipe clean all parts and check for wear or damage.
8. Coat all parts with the same wheel bearing grease you've used on the bearings.
9. Position the locking unit in the hub and install the large snapring. Pull outward on the unit to make sure the snapring is fully seated in its groove.
10. Install the keepers.
11. Install the bearing retainer, bearing and race. Make sure that the bearing is fully pack with grease.
12. Coat the hub cap O-ring with wheel bearing grease and install the hub cap.
13. Install the capscrews and washers. Tighten the screws to 45 inch lbs. (5 Nm).

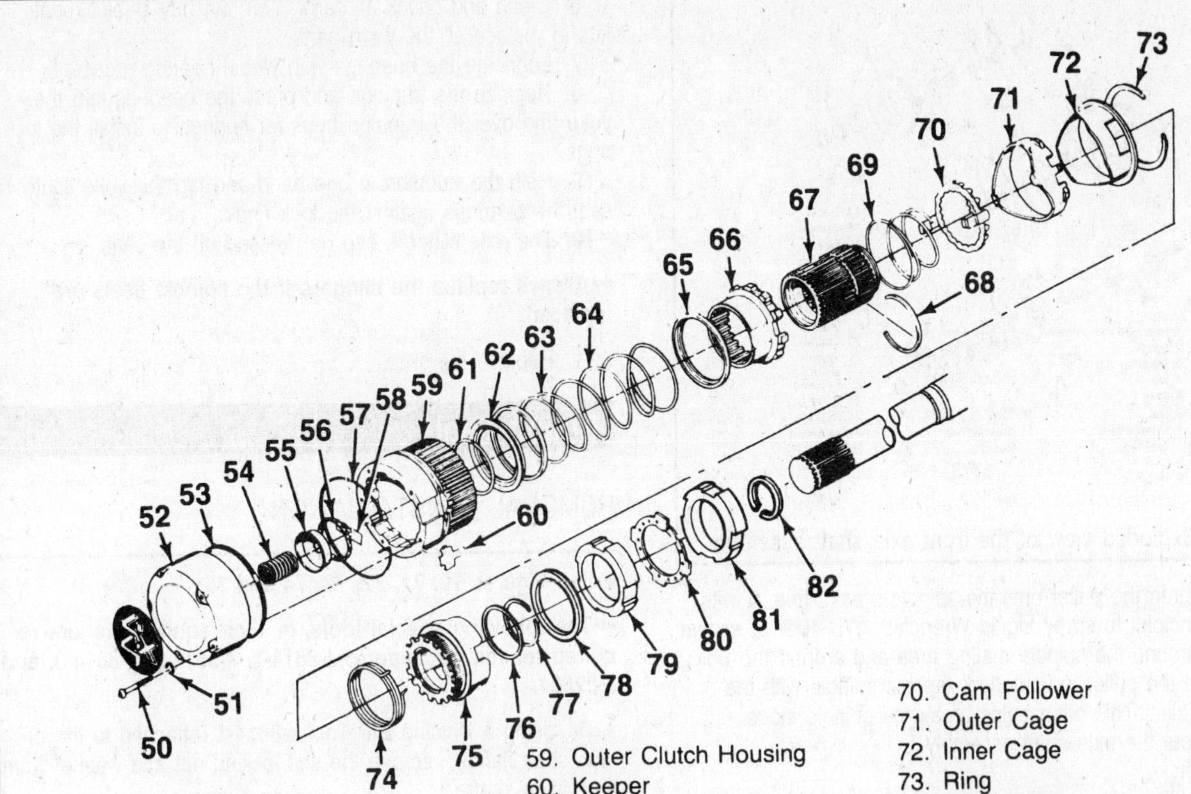

50. Screw
51. O-Ring Seal
52. Cover
53. Seal
54. Spring
55. Inner Race
56. Bearing
57. Ring
58. Retainer
59. Outer Clutch Housing
60. Keeper
61. Ring
62. Retainer Plate
63. Retainer
64. Return Spring
65. Retainer
66. Clutch Gear
67. Sleeve
68. Stop Ring
69. Conical Spring
70. Cam Follower
71. Outer Cage
72. Inner Cage
73. Ring
74. Brake Band
75. Drag Sleeve
76. Spacer
77. Retaining Ring
78. Washer
79. Adjusting Nut
80. Lock Ring
81. Nut
82. Ring

84907274

Fig. 67 Exploded view of the automatic locking hubs

Axle Shaft

REMOVAL & INSTALLATION

➧ **See Figures 68 and 69**

1. Raise and support the front end on jackstands.
2. Remove the wheel.
3. Remove the locking hub. Refer to the procedures in this section.
4. Remove the hub and bearing assembly. Refer to the procedures in this section.
5. Remove the nuts and remove the caliper mounting bracket and splash shield.
6. Tap the end of the spindle with a plastic mallet to break it loose from the knuckle. If tapping won't break it loose, you'll have to do the following:
   a. Thread the bearing locknut part way onto the spindle.
   b. Position a 2 or 3-jawed pull with the jaws grabbing the locknut and the screw bearing in the end of the axle shaft.

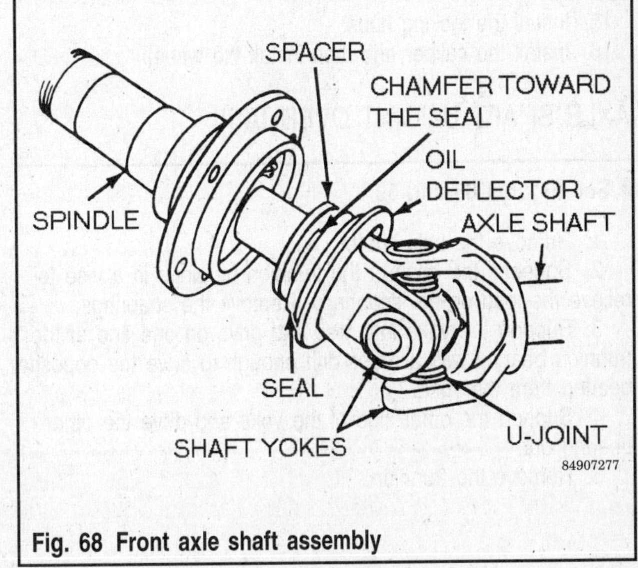

Fig. 68 Front axle shaft assembly

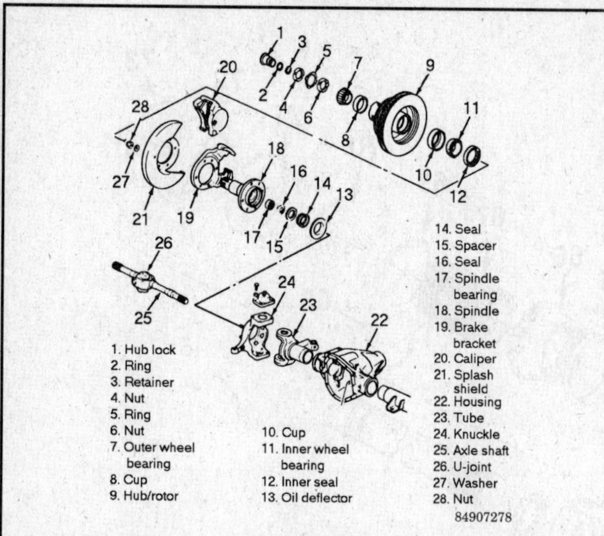

Fig. 69 Exploded view of the front axle shaft assembly

c. Tighten the puller until the spindle breaks free. It will be very helpful to spray Liquid Wrench®, WD-40® or similar solvent around the spindle mating area and around the bolt holes. As the puller is tightened, tap the spindle with the plastic mallet. This often helps break the spindle loose.

7. Pull out the axle shaft assembly.

To install:

8. Place the spacer and a new seal on the axle shaft.

➡The spacer's chamfer points towards the oil deflector.

9. Pack the spindle bearing with wheel bearing grease.
10. Slide the axle shaft into the housing. When installing the axle shaft, turn the shaft slowly to align the splines with the differential.
11. Place the spindle on the knuckle. Be sure the seal and oil deflector are in place.
12. Install the caliper bracket and splash shield.
13. Using new washers, install the nuts and tighten them to 65 ft. lbs. (88 Nm).
14. Install the hub and rotor assembly. Adjust the wheel bearings.
15. Install the locking hubs.
16. Install the caliper and then install the wheel.

AXLE SHAFT U-JOINT OVERHAUL

➧ See Figures 68 and 69

1. Remove the axle shaft.
2. Squeeze the ends of the trunnion bearings in a vise to relieve the load on the snaprings. Remove the snaprings.
3. Support the yoke in a vise and drive on one end of the trunnion bearing with a brass drift enough to drive the opposite bearing from the yoke.
4. Support the other side of the yoke and drive the other bearing out.
5. Remove the trunnion.
6. Clean and check all parts. You can buy U-joint repair kits to replace all the worn parts.
7. Lubricate the bearings with wheel bearing grease.
8. Replace the trunnion and press the bearings into the yoke and over the trunnion hubs far enough to install the lock rings.
9. Hold the trunnion in one hand and tap the yoke lightly to seat the bearings against the lock rings.
10. The axle slingers can be pressed off the shaft.

➡Always replace the slingers if the spindle seals are replaced.

11. Replace the shaft.

Pinion Seal

REMOVAL & INSTALLATION

➧ See Figures 70, 71, 72, 73, 74 and 75

➡The following special tools, or their equivalents, are required for this procedure: J-8614-1, J-8614-2, J-8614-3, and J-22804.

1. Using a Holding Bar Tool J-8614-1, attached to the pinion shaft flange, remove the self locking nut and washer from the pinion shaft.
2. Install Tool J-8614-2, and 3 into the holding bar and remove the flange from the drive pinion. Remove the drive pinion from the carrier.
3. With a long drift, tap on the inner race of the outer pinion bearing to remove the seal.
4. Install the oil seal, gasket and using Tool J-22804 install the oil seal.
5. Install the flange, washer and nut and tighten the nut to 270 ft. lbs. (366 Nm) for the GMC axle; 255 ft. lbs. (346 Nm) for the Dana axle.

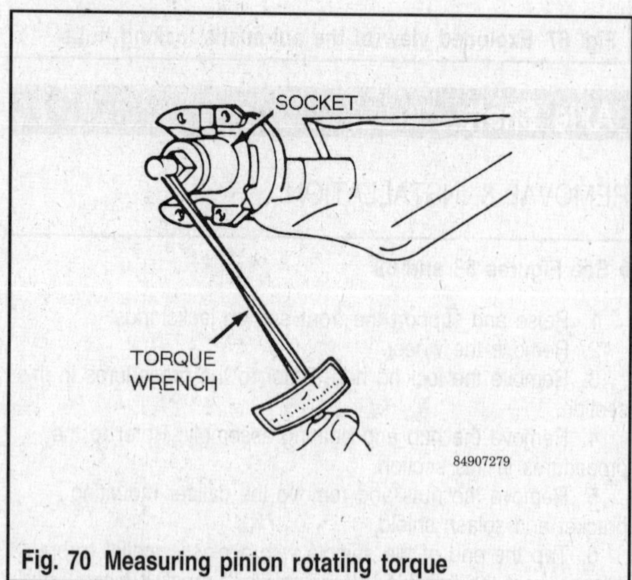

Fig. 70 Measuring pinion rotating torque

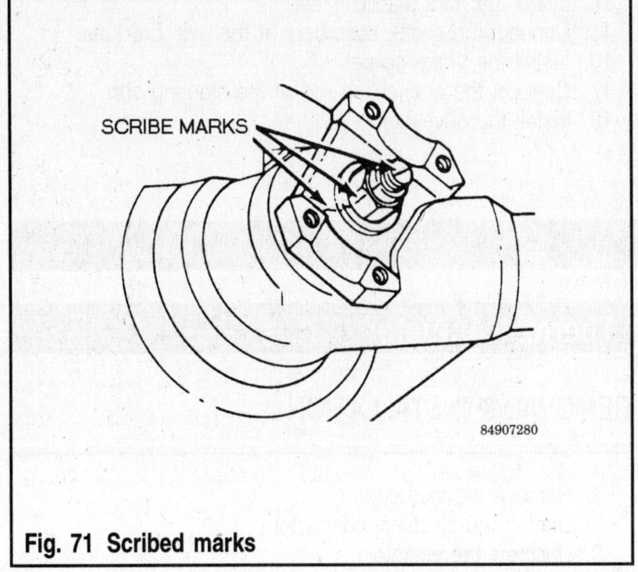

Fig. 71 Scribed marks

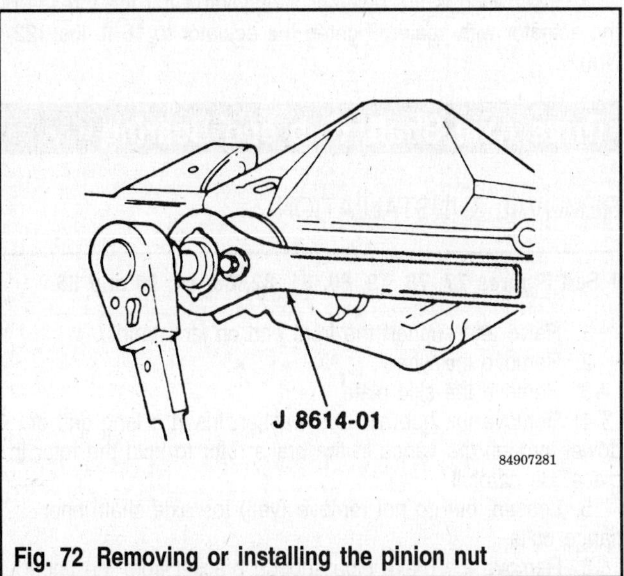

Fig. 72 Removing or installing the pinion nut

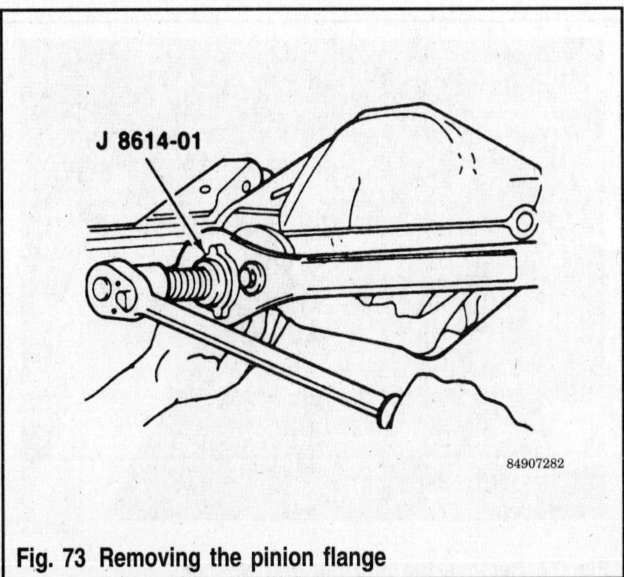

Fig. 73 Removing the pinion flange

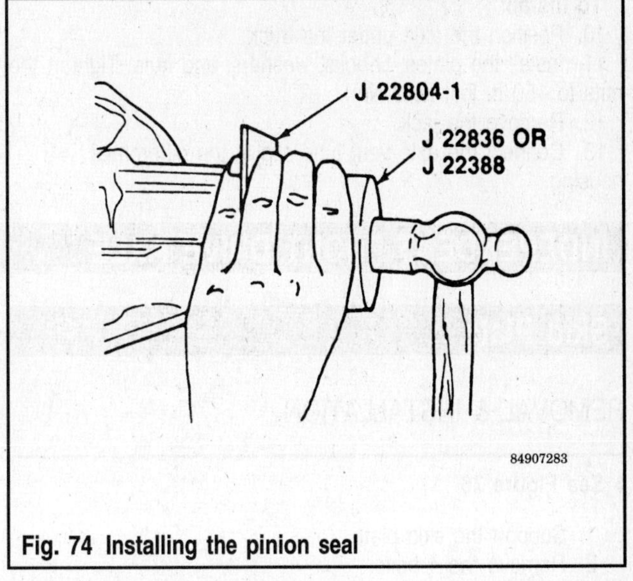

Fig. 74 Installing the pinion seal

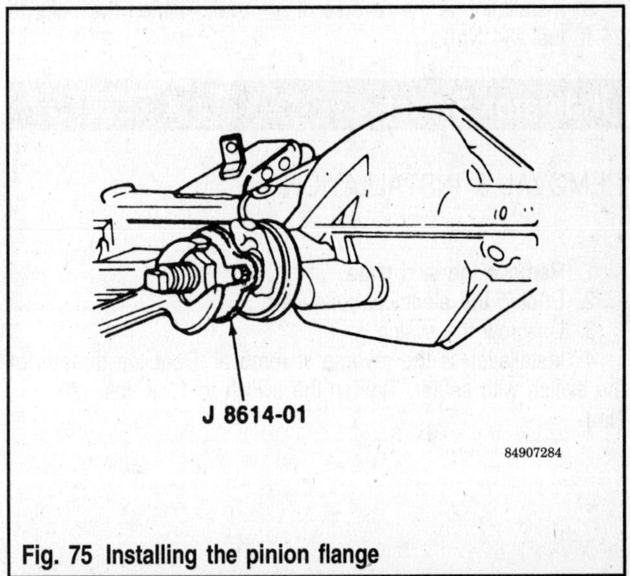

Fig. 75 Installing the pinion flange

Axle Housing

REMOVAL & INSTALLATION

1. Raise and support the vehicle safely.
2. Matchmark and remove the driveshaft.
3. Disconnect the connecting rod from the steering arm.
4. Disconnect the brake caliper and position it out of the way, without disconnecting the brake line.
5. Disconnect the shock absorbers from the axle brackets.
6. Remove the front stabilizer bar.
7. Disconnect the axle vent tube clip at the differential housing.
8. Take up the weight of the axle assembly using a suitable jack.
9. Remove the nuts, washers, U-bolts and plates from the axle and separate the axle from the springs. Remove the axle assembly from the vehicle.

To install:

10. Position the axle under the truck.
11. Install the plates, U-bolts, washers, and nuts. Tighten the nuts to 150 ft. lbs. (203 Nm).
12. Remove the jack.
13. Connect the axle vent tube clip at the differential housing.
14. Install the front stabilizer bar.
15. Connect the shock absorbers at the axle brackets.
16. Install the brake caliper
17. Connect the connecting rod at the steering arm.
18. Install the driveshaft.

INDEPENDENT FRONT DRIVE AXLE

Skid Plate

REMOVAL & INSTALLATION

➧ See Figure 76

1. Support the skid plate.
2. Remove the 4 bolts.
3. Installation is the reverse of removal. Tighten the bolts to 25 ft. lbs. (34 Nm).

Indicator Switch

REMOVAL & INSTALLATION

1. Remove the skid plate.
2. Unplug the electrical connector.
3. Unscrew the switch.
4. Installation is the reverse of removal. Coat the threads of the switch with sealer. Tighten the switch to 15 ft. lbs. (20 Nm).

Thermal Actuator

REMOVAL & INSTALLATION

1. Remove the skid plate.
2. Unplug the electrical connector.
3. Unscrew the actuator.
4. Installation is the reverse of removal. Coat the threads of the actuator with sealer. Tighten the actuator to 16 ft. lbs. (22 Nm).

Drive Axle Shaft, Hub and Bearing

REMOVAL & INSTALLATION

➧ See Figures 77, 78, 79, 80, 81, 82, 83, 84, 85 and 86

1. Raise and support the front end on jackstands.
2. Remove the wheel.
3. Remove the skid plate.
4. Remove the hub nut and washer. Insert a long drift or dowel through the vanes in the brake rotor to hold the rotor in place. Be careful!
5. Loosen, but do not remove (yet!) the axle shaft inner flange bolts.
6. Remove the brake pipe support bracket from the upper control arm.

1. Carrier
2. Washer
3. Nut
4. Bracket
5. Skid plate
6. Screw
7. Washer
8. Screw

84907285

Fig. 76 Skid plate — K-Series

87987p09

Fig. 77 Remove the hub nut and washer

Fig. 78 Using a puller, force the outer end of the axle shaft out of the hub

Fig. 81 Remove the drive axle from the vehicle

Fig. 79 Matchmark the flange

Fig. 80 Remove the inboard flange bolts

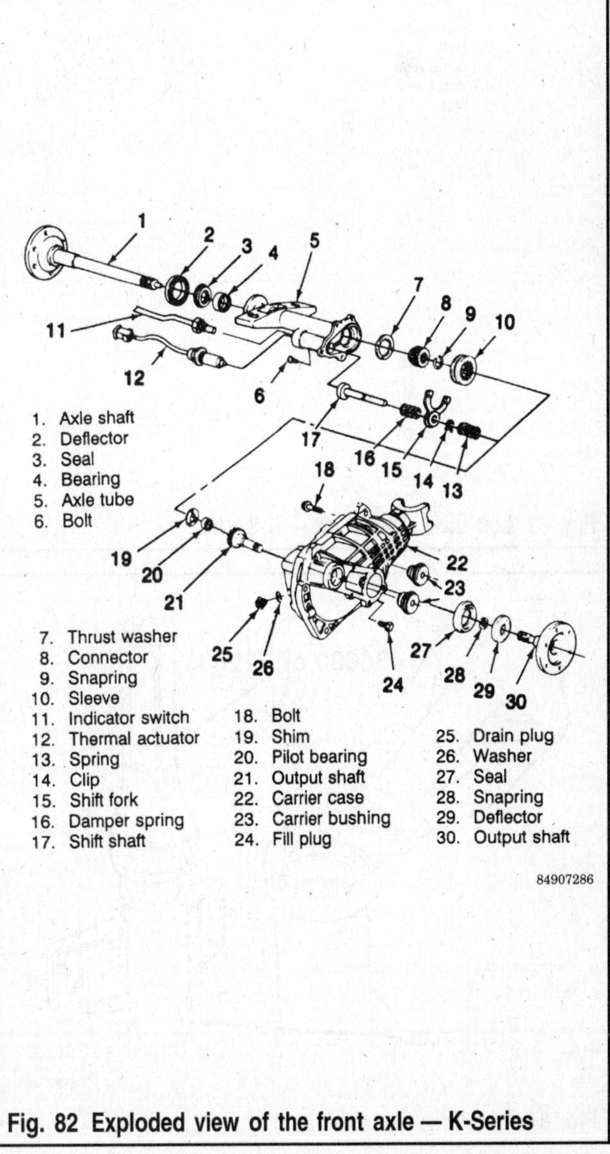

Fig. 82 Exploded view of the front axle — K-Series

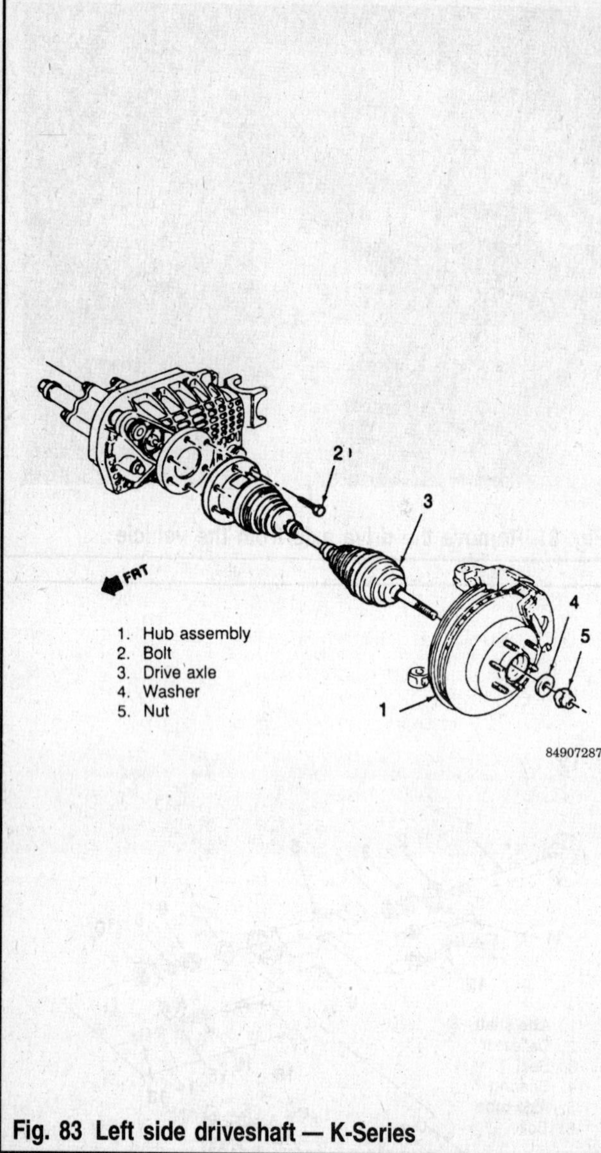

Fig. 83 Left side driveshaft — K-Series

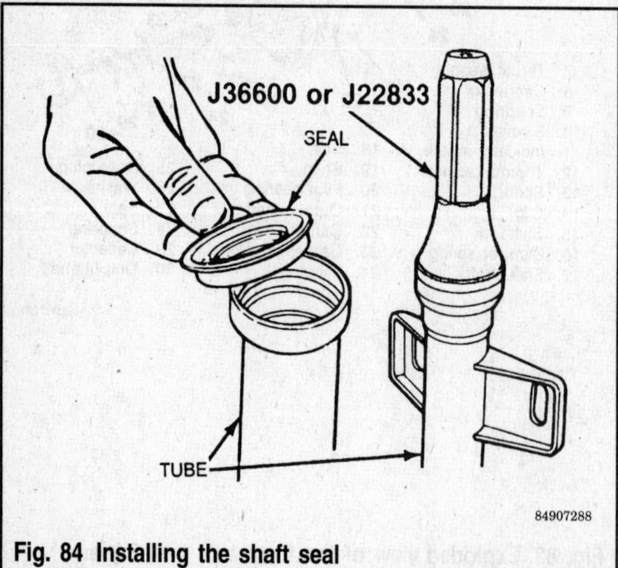

Fig. 84 Installing the shaft seal

7. Disconnect the tie rod end from the steering knuckle. Push the linkage to the other side of the truck and secure it out of the way.

8. Disconnect the lower shock absorber mounting bolt and swivel it out of the way.

9. Remove the stabilizer bar clamp. Remove the stabilizer bar bolt, spacer and bushings at the lower control arm.

10. Position a floor jack under the spring seat and lower control arm, this will relieve spring tension on the upper arm.

11. Remove the cotter pin on the upper ball joint and **loosen** the stud nut. Loosen the stud from the control arm and then remove the stud nut completely. Press the ball stud out of the knuckle.

12. Using a puller, force the outer end of the axle shaft out of the hub. Remove the inboard flange bolts and the remove the drive axle.

****WARNING**

Never allow the vehicle to rest on the wheels with the axle shaft removed!

To install:

13. Position the shaft in the hub and install the washer and hub nut finger tight. Install the inner flange bolts finger tight.

14. Connect the upper ball joint to the knuckle and tighten the stud nut to 61 ft. lbs. (83 Nm). Install a new cotter pin.

15. Install the stabilizer bar bolt, spacer and bushings at the lower control arm. Tighten the bolt to 24 ft. lbs. (33 Nm).

16. Install the stabilizer bar clamp. Tighten the bolts to 12 ft. lbs. (16 Nm).

17. Install the lower shock mounting bolt and tighten it to 54 ft. lbs. (73 Nm).

18. Connect the tie rod end at the steering knuckle. Tighten the nut to 35 ft. lbs. (47 Nm).

19. Install the brake support pipe and tighten the nut to 13 ft. lbs. (17 Nm).

20. Insert a drift into the brake rotor and tighten the inner flange bolts to 59 ft. lbs. (80 Nm). Tighten the outer hub nut to 173 ft. lbs. (235 Nm) on 1988-91 models and 180 ft. lbs. (245 Nm) on 1992-93 models.

21. Install the skid plate. Install the wheels and lower the truck.

CV JOINT

See Figures 87, 88, 89, 90, 91, 92, 93, 94, 95, 96, 97, 98, 99 and 100

Refer to the illustrations for CV joint overhaul.

Axle Tube Assembly

REMOVAL

1. Raise and support the front end on jackstands.
2. Remove the right wheel.
3. Position a drain pan under the axle.
4. Remove the stabilizer bar. See Section 8.
5. Remove the skid plate.

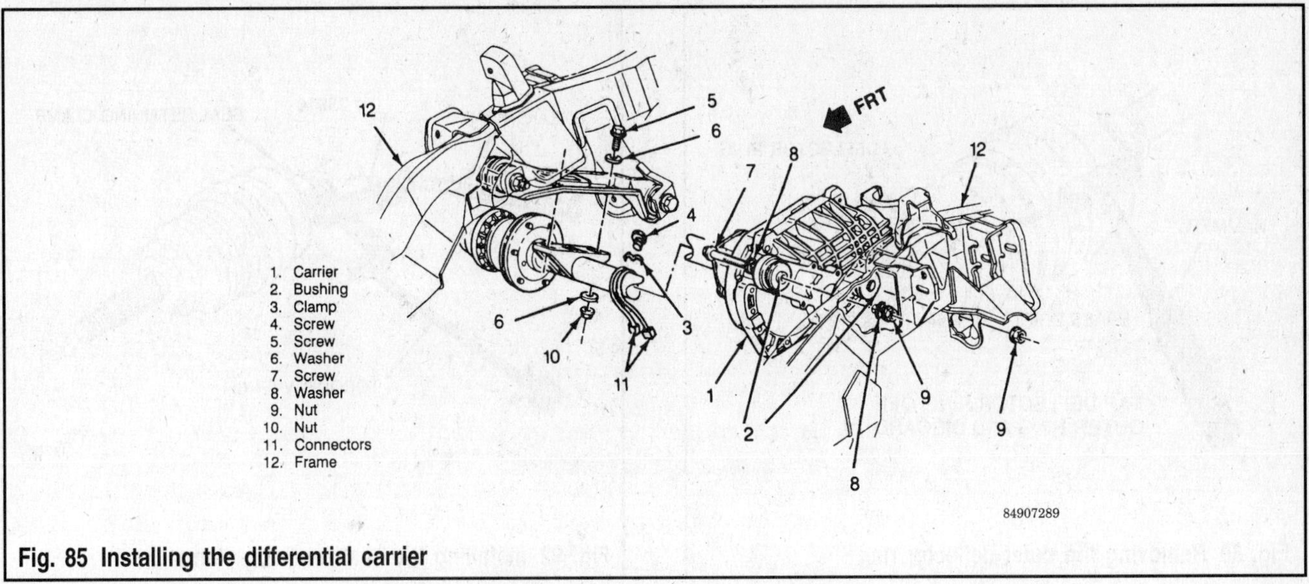

Fig. 85 Installing the differential carrier

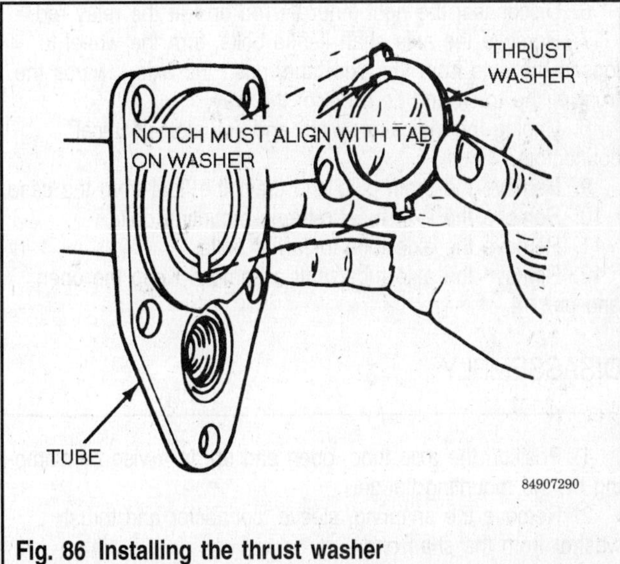

Fig. 86 Installing the thrust washer

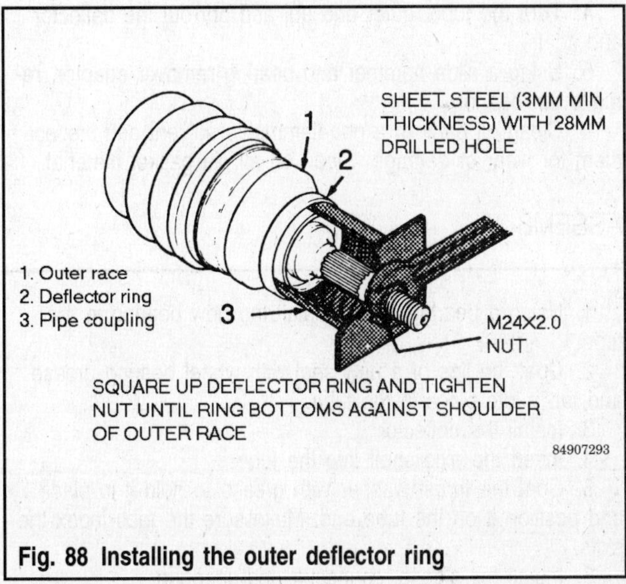

Fig. 88 Installing the outer deflector ring

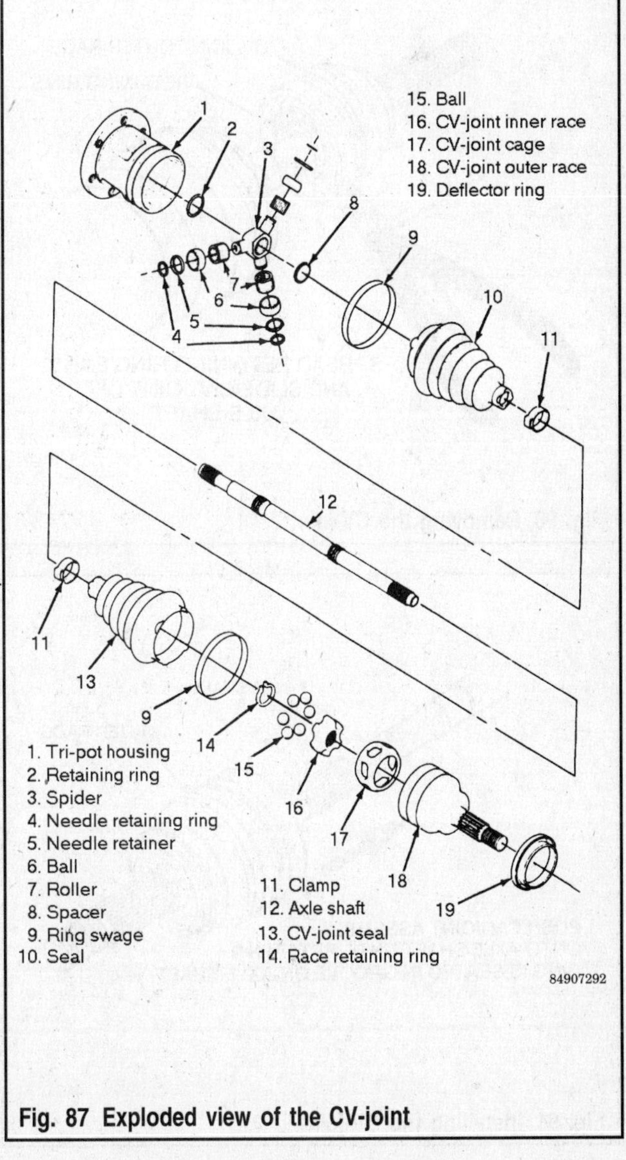

Fig. 87 Exploded view of the CV-joint

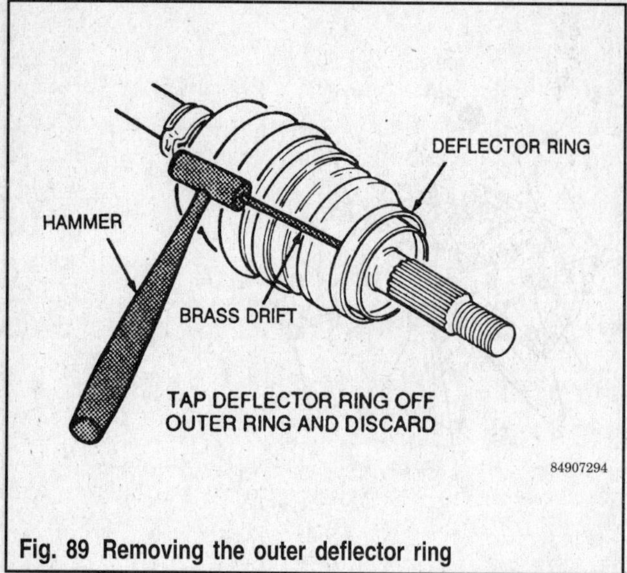

Fig. 89 Removing the outer deflector ring

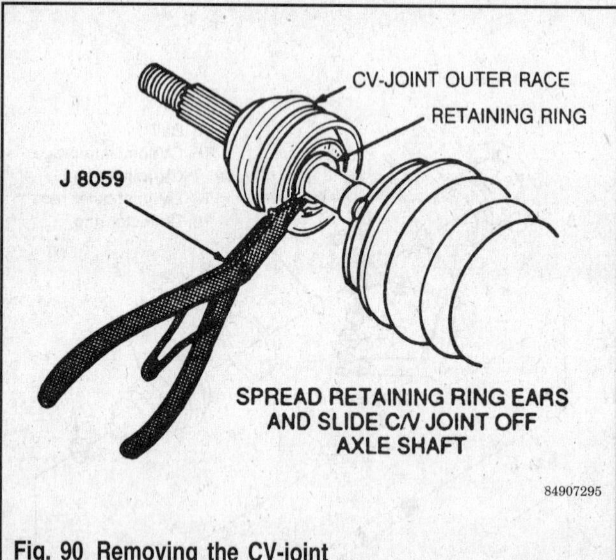

Fig. 90 Removing the CV-joint

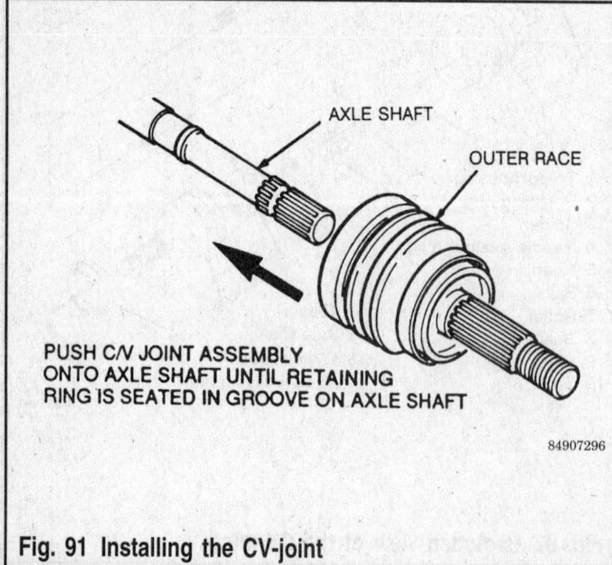

Fig. 91 Installing the CV-joint

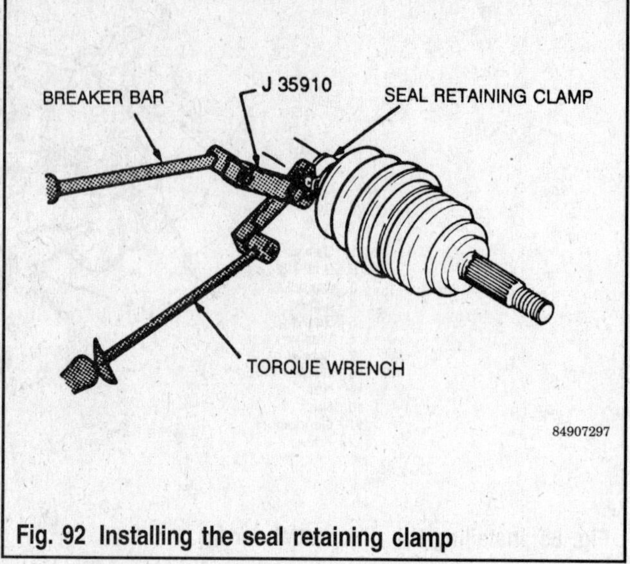

Fig. 92 Installing the seal retaining clamp

6. Disconnect the right inner tie rod end at the relay rod.
7. Remove the axle shaft flange bolts, turn the wheel to loosen the axle from the axle tube, push the axle towards the front of the truck and tie it out of the way.
8. Unplug the indicator switch and actuator electrical connectors.
9. Remove the drain plug and drain the fluid from the case.
10. Remove the axle tube-to-frame mounting bolts.
11. Remove the axle tube-to-carrier bolts.
12. Remove the axle tube/shaft assembly. Keep the open end up.

DISASSEMBLY

1. Position the axle tube, open end up, in a vise by clamping on the mounting flange.
2. Remove the snapring, sleeve, connector and thrust washer from the shaft end.
3. Tap out the axle shaft with a plastic mallet.
4. Turn the tube, outer end up, and pry out the deflector and seal.
5. Using a slide hammer and bearing remover adapter, remove the bearing.
6. Clean all parts in a non-flammable solvent and inspect them for wear or damage. Clean off all old gasket material.

ASSEMBLY

1. Using a bearing driver, install the new bearing in the tube.
2. Coat the lips of a new seal with wheel bearing grease and tap it into place in the tube.
3. Install the deflector.
4. Insert the axle shaft into the tube.
5. Coat the thrust washer with grease to hold it in place and position it on the tube end. Make sure the tabs index the slots.
6. Install the sleeve, connector and snapring.

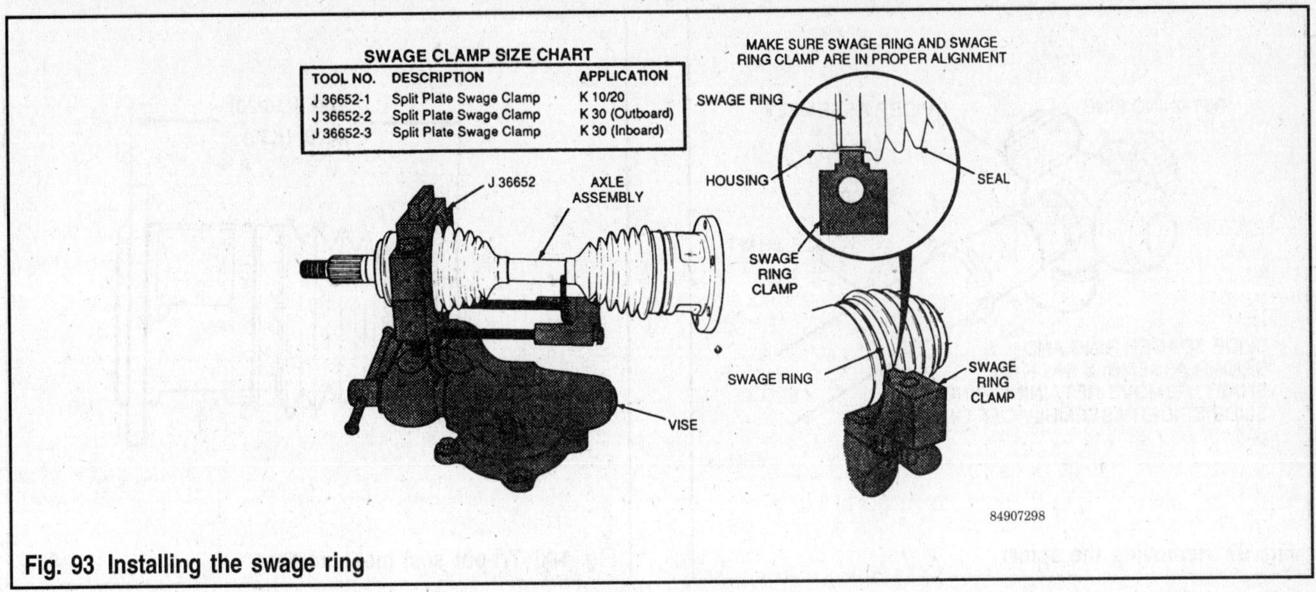

Fig. 93 Installing the swage ring

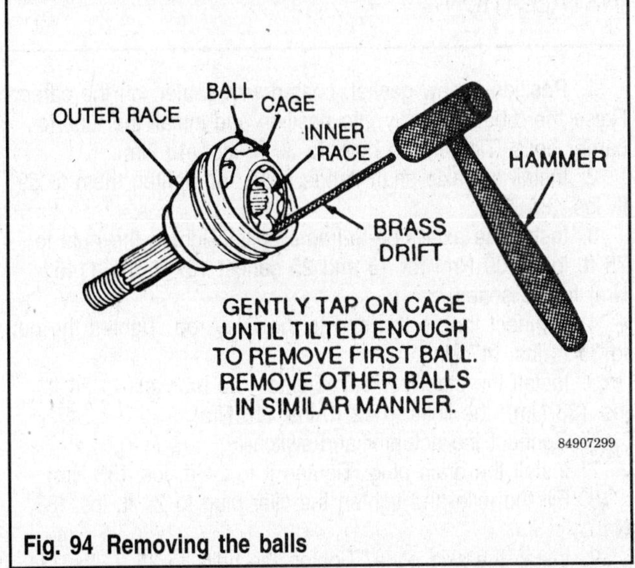

Fig. 94 Removing the balls

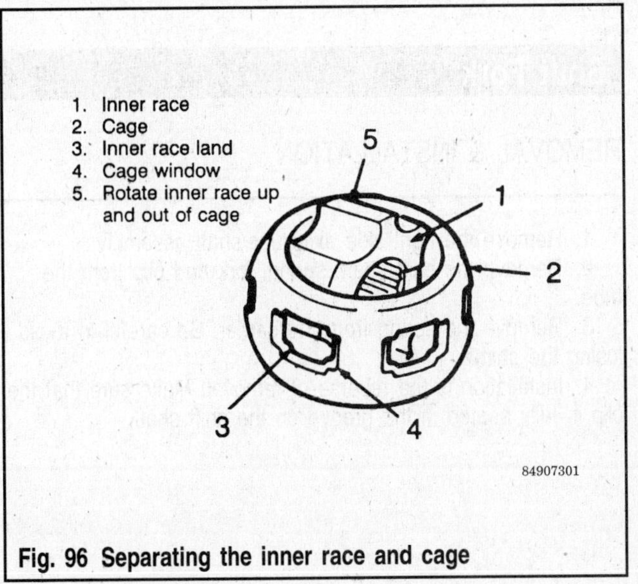

Fig. 96 Separating the inner race and cage

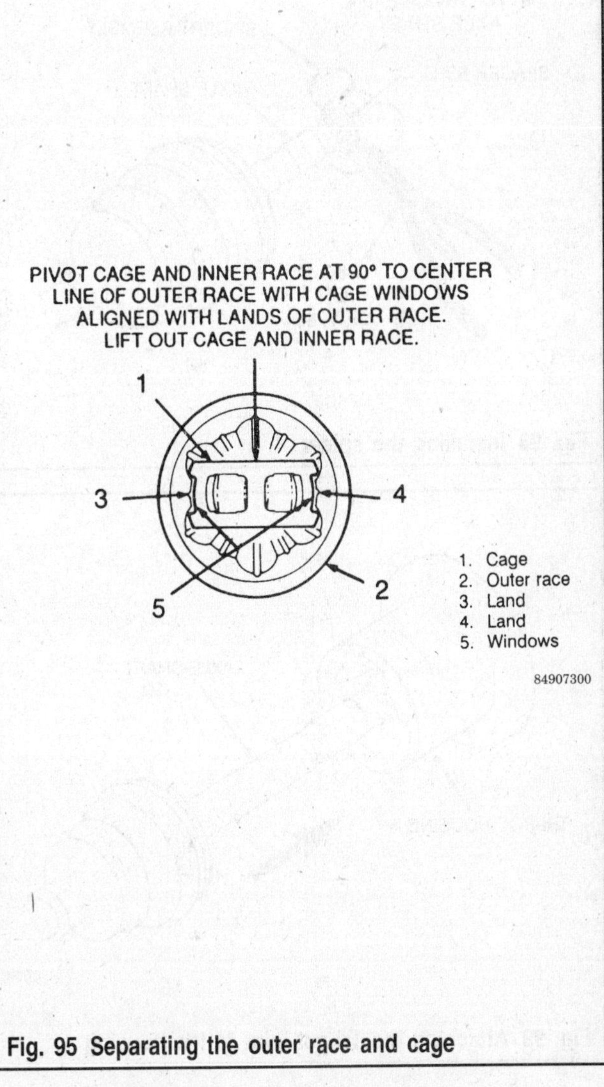

Fig. 95 Separating the outer race and cage

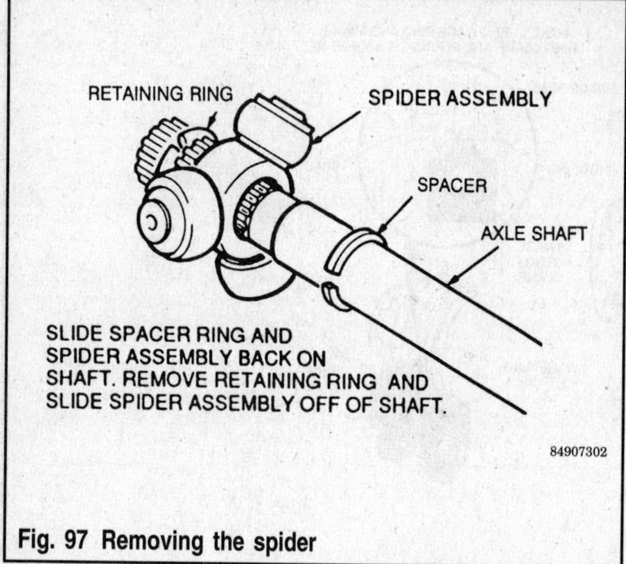

Fig. 97 Removing the spider

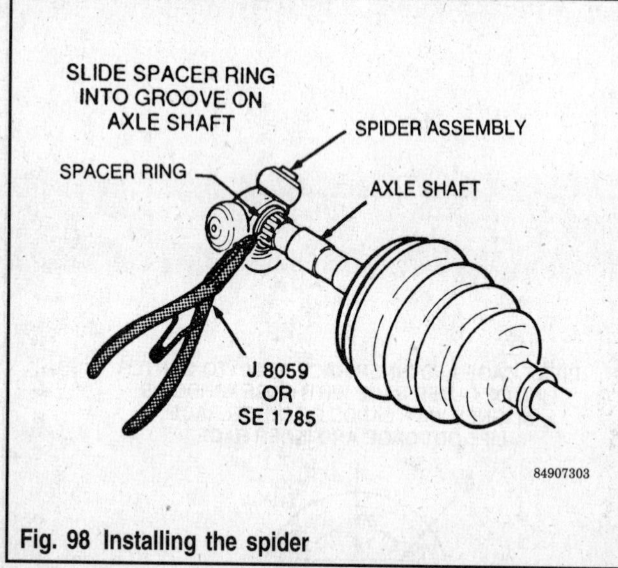

Fig. 98 Installing the spider

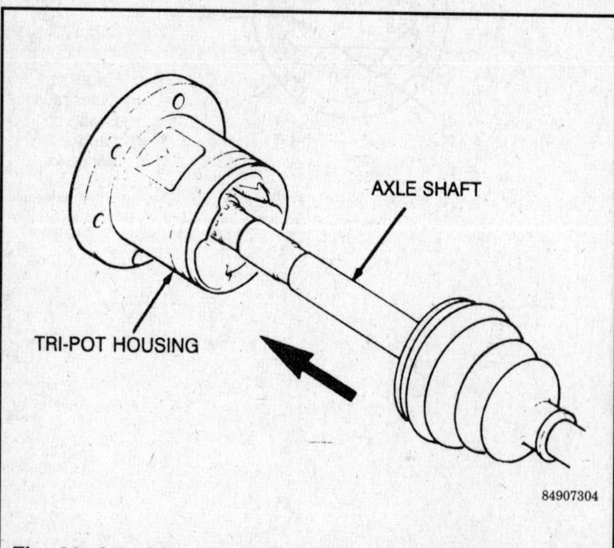

Fig. 99 Attaching the Tri-pot joint to the housing

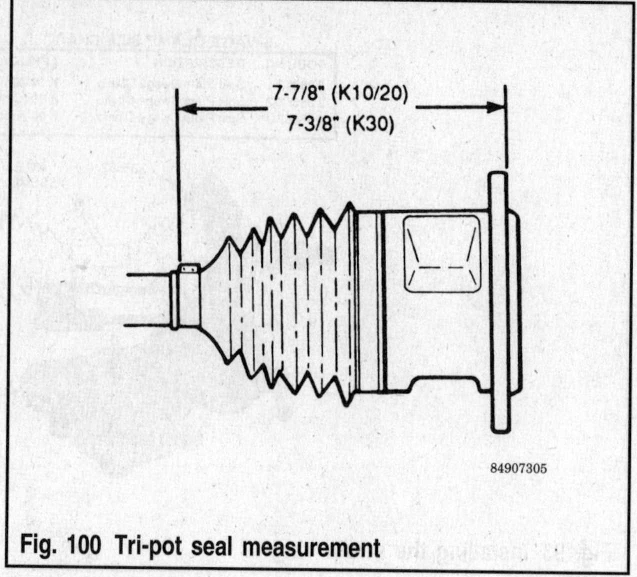

Fig. 100 Tri-pot seal measurement

INSTALLATION

1. Position a new gasket, coated with sealer, on the carrier. Raise the tube assembly into position and install the tube-to-carrier bolts. Tighten the bolts to 30 ft. lbs. (40 Nm).
2. Install the axle shaft flange bolts and tighten them to 59 ft. lbs. (80 Nm).
3. Install the axle tube-to-frame bolts. Tighten the nuts to 75 ft. lbs. (100 Nm) for 15 and 25 series; 107 ft. lbs. (145 Nm) for 35 series.
4. Connect the tie rod end to the relay rod. Tighten the nut to 35 ft. lbs. (47 Nm).
5. Install the stabilizer bar. Tighten the brackets to 24 ft. lbs. (33 Nm); the links to 12 ft. lbs. (16 Nm).
6. Connect the actuator and switch.
7. Install the drain plug. Tighten it to 24 ft. lbs. (33 Nm).
8. Fill the axle and tighten the filler plug to 24 ft. lbs. (33 Nm).
9. Install the skid plate. Tighten the bolts to 25 ft. lbs. (34 Nm).

Shift Fork

REMOVAL & INSTALLATION

1. Remove the right side axle tube/shaft assembly.
2. Remove the shift shaft, spring, fork and clip from the tube.
3. Remove the spring from the carrier. Be careful to avoid losing the shim!
4. Installation is the reverse of removal. Make sure that the clip is fully seated in the groove on the shift shaft.

Differential Pilot Bearing

REMOVAL & INSTALLATION

1. Remove the right side axle shaft tube/shaft assembly.
2. Remove the shim and pilot bearing from the carrier.
3. Dip the new bearing in axle fluid. Installation is the reverse of removal.

Output Shaft

REMOVAL & INSTALLATION

1. Raise and support the front end on jackstands.
2. Drain the axle.
3. Remove the left side axle shaft.
4. Remove the lower carrier mounting bolt.
5. CAREFULLY pry against the lower part of the carrier to provide clearance for the output shaft removal. While prying, insert a prybar between the output shaft flange and the carrier case. Pry the output shaft free. BE CAREFUL! It's possible to damage the carrier if you pry too hard.
6. Remove the deflector and seal from the carrier.

To install:

7. Lubricate the lips of a new seal with wheel bearing grease and drive it into place.
8. Install the deflector.
9. Pry against the case and position the output shaft in the carrier. Tap it into place with a plastic mallet.
10. Install the lower carrier mounting bolt, washer and nut. Tighten the bolt to 80 ft. lbs.
11. Install the left axle shaft.
12. Fill the axle.

Pinion Seal

REMOVAL & INSTALLATION

➧ **See Figures 101, 102, 103 and 104**

1. Raise and support the front end on jackstands.
2. Matchmark and disconnect the front driveshaft at the carrier.
3. Remove the wheels.
4. Dismount the calipers and wire them up, out of the way. See Section 9.
5. Position an inch pound torque wrench on the pinion nut. Measure the torque needed to rotate the pinion one full revolution. Record the figure.
6. Matchamrk the pinion flange, shaft and nut. Count and record the number of exposed threads on the pinion shaft.
7. Hold the flange and remove the nut and washer.
8. Using a puller, remove the flange.
9. Carefully pry the seal from its bore. Be careful to avoid scratching the seal bore.
10. Remove the deflector from the flange.

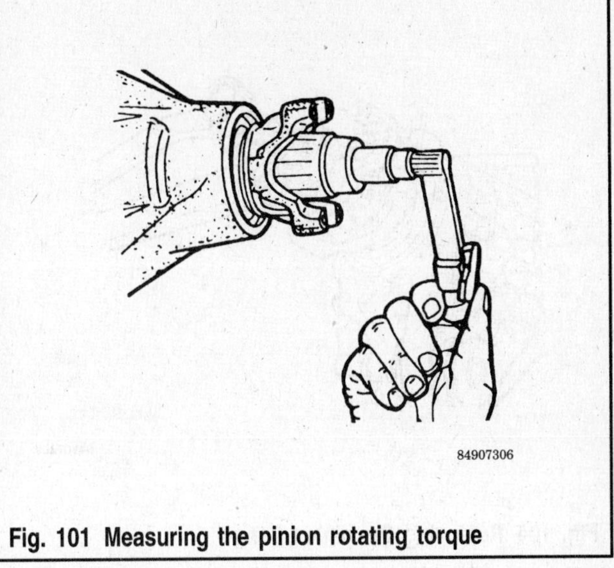

Fig. 101 Measuring the pinion rotating torque

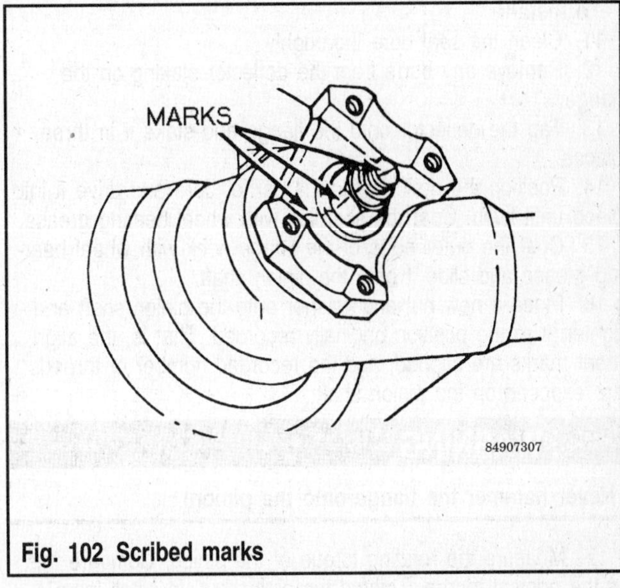

Fig. 102 Scribed marks

Fig. 103 Removing the pinion nut

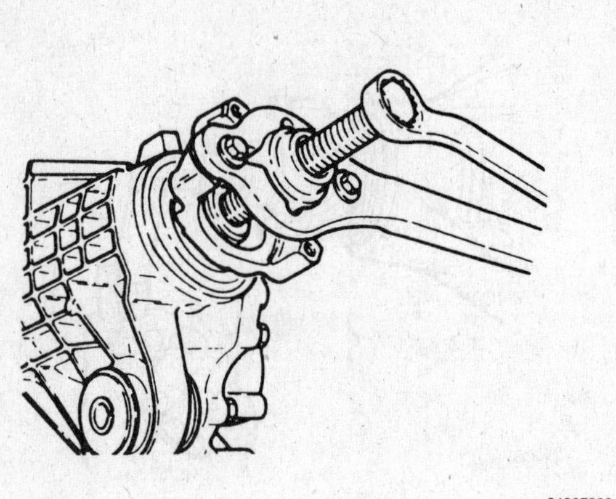

Fig. 104 Removing the pinion flange

To install:

11. Clean the seal bore thoroughly.
12. Remove any burrs from the deflector staking on the flange.
13. Tap the deflector onto the flange and stake it in three places.
14. Position the new seal in the carrier bore and drive it into place until flush. Coat the seal lips with wheel bearing grease.
15. Coat the outer edge of the flange neck with wheel bearing grease and slide it onto the pinion shaft.
16. Place a new nut and washer onto the pinion shaft and tighten it to the position originally recorded. That is, the alignment marks are aligned, and the recorded number of threads are exposed on the pinion shaft.

****WARNING**

Never hammer the flange onto the pinion!

17. Measure the rotating torque of the pinion. Compare this to the original torque. Tighten the pinion nut, in small increments, until the rotating torque is 3 inch lbs. GREATER than the original torque.
18. Install the driveshaft.
19. Install the calipers and install the wheels.

Differential Carrier

REMOVAL & INSTALLATION

1. Raise and support the front end on jackstands.
2. Remove the wheels.
3. Remove the skid plate.
4. Drain the carrier.
5. Matchmark and remove the front driveshaft.
6. Disconnect the right axle shaft at the tube flange.
7. Disconnect the left axle shaft at the carrier flange.
8. Wire both axle shafts out of the way.
9. Unplug the connectors at the indicator switch and actuator.
10. Disconnect the carrier vent hose.
11. Remove the axle tube-to-frame bolts, washers and nuts.
12. Remove the lower carrier mounting bolt.
13. Disconnect the right side inner tie rod end at the relay rod. See Section 8.
14. Depending on model, it may be necessary to remove the engine oil filter.
15. Support the carrier on a floor jack
16. Remove the upper carrier mounting bolt.
17. Lower the carrier assembly from the truck.

To install:

18. Raise the carrier into position.
19. Install the upper carrier mounting bolt, washers and nut. Then, install the lower carrier mounting bolt, washers and nut. Tighten the bolts to 80 ft. lbs. (110 Nm).
20. Remove the jack.
21. Install the oil filter.
22. Connect the tie rod end. Tighten the nut to 35 ft. lbs. (47 Nm).
23. Install the axle tube-to-frame bolts, washers and nuts. Tighten the nuts to 75 ft. lbs. (100 Nm) for 15 and 25 series; 107 ft. lbs. (145 Nm) for 35 series.
24. Connect the vent hose.
25. Connect the wiring.
26. Connect the axle shafts at the flanges. Tighten the bolts to 59 ft. lbs. (80 Nm).
27. Connect the driveshaft. Tighten the bolts to 15 ft. lbs. (20 Nm).
28. Fill the carrier with SAE 85W-90 gear oil.
29. Install the wheels.
30. Add any engine oil lost when the filter was removed.

REAR AXLE

Determining Axle Ratio

Axle ratios offered in these trucks vary from a heavy duty ratio of 4.57:1 to an economy ratio of 2.73:1.

The axle ratio is obtained by dividing the number of teeth on the drive pinion gear into the larger number of teeth on the ring gear. It is always expressed as a proportion and is a simple expression of gear speed reduction and torque multiplication.

To find a unknown axle ratio, make a chalk mark on a tire and on the driveshaft. Move the truck ahead (or back) slowly for one tire rotation and have an observer note the number of driveshaft rotations. The number of driveshaft rotations is the axle ratio. You can get more accuracy by going more than one tire rotation and dividing the result by the number of tire rotations. This can also be done by jacking up both rear wheels and turning them by hand.

The axle ratio is also identified by the axle serial number prefix on Chevrolet (GMC) axles. See Section 1 for serial number locations; the prefixes are listed in parts books. Dana axles usually have a tag under one of the cover bolts, giving either the ratio or the number of pinion ring gear teeth.

Axle Shaft, Bearing, and Seal

REMOVAL & INSTALLATION

Semi-Floating Axles

EXCEPT LOCKING DIFFERENTIAL

See Figures 105, 106, 107, 108, 109 and 110

1. Support the axle on jackstands.
2. Remove the wheels and brake drums.
3. Clean off the differential cover area, loosen the cover to drain the lubricant, and remove the cover.
4. Turn the differential until you can reach the differential pinion shaft lockscrew. Remove the lockscrew and the pinion shaft.

Fig. 105 Remove the differential pinon shaft lockscrew

Fig. 106 Remove the pinon shaft

Fig. 107 Remove the C-lock from the inner (button) end of the shaft

5. Push in on the axle end. Remove the C-lock from the inner (button) end of the shaft.
6. Remove the shaft, being careful of the oil seal.
7. You can pry the oil seal out of the housing by placing the inner end of the axle shaft behind the steel case of the seal, then prying it out carefully.
8. A puller or a slide hammer is required to remove the bearing from the housing.

To install:

9. Pack the new or reused bearing with wheel bearing grease and lubricate the cavity between the seal lips with the same grease.
10. The bearing has to be driven into the housing. Don't use a drift, you might cock the bearing in its bore. Use a piece of pipe or a large socket instead. Drive only on the outer bearing race. In a similar manner, drive the seal in flush with the end of the tube.
11. Slide the shaft into place, turning it slowly until the splines are engaged with the differential. Be careful of the oil seal.
12. Install the C-lock on the inner axle end. Pull the shaft out so that the C-lock seats in the counterbore of the differential side gear.
13. Position the differential pinion shaft through the case and the pinion gears, aligning the lockscrew hole. Install the lockscrew.
14. Install the cover with a new gasket and tighten the bolts evenly in a criss-cross pattern.
15. Fill the axle with lubricant as specified in Section 1.
16. Replace the brake drums and wheels.

LOCKING DIFFERENTIAL

See Figures 111 and 112

This axle uses a thrust block on the differential pinion shaft.

1. Support the axle on jackstands.
2. Remove the wheels and brake drums.
3. Clean off the differential cover area, loosen the cover to drain the lubricant, and remove the cover.
4. Rotate the differential case so that you can remove the lockscrew and support the pinion shaft so it can't fall into the housing. Remove the differential pinion shaft lockscrew.

Fig. 108 Remove the axle shaft from the from the vehicle

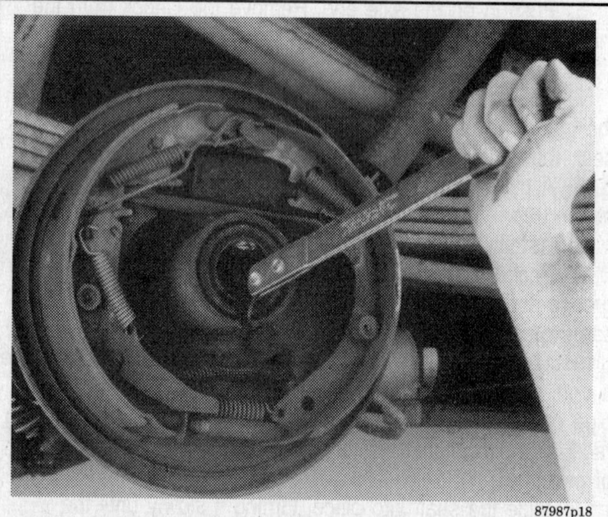

Fig. 109 Use a puller to remove the oil seal

Fig. 110 Install the oil seal using a seal installer

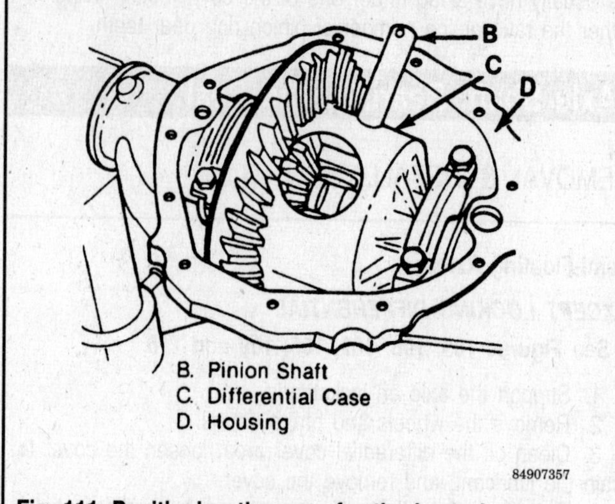

Fig. 111 Positioning the case for the best clearance — semi-floating axle w/locking differential

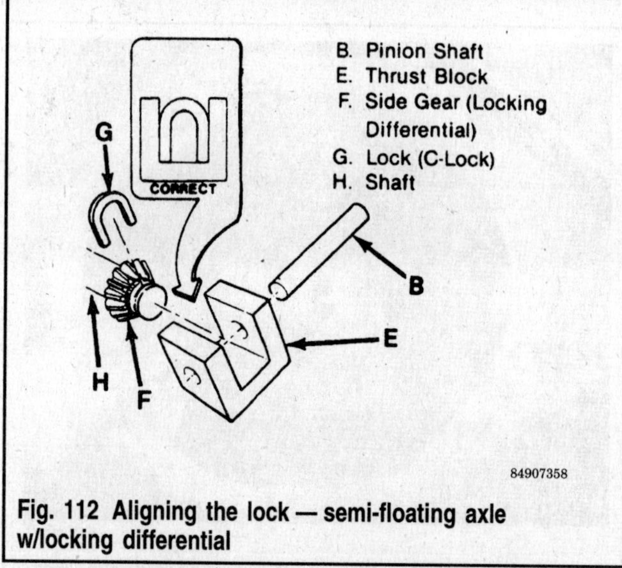

Fig. 112 Aligning the lock — semi-floating axle w/locking differential

5. Carefully pull the pinion shaft partway out and rotate the differential case until the shaft touches the housing at the top.
6. Use a screwdriver to position the C-lock with its open end directly inward. You can't push in the axle shaft till you do this.
7. Push the axle shaft in and remove the C-lock.
8. Remove the shaft, being careful of the oil seal.
9. You can pry the oil seal out of the housing by placing the inner end of the axle shaft behind the steel case of the seal, then prying it out carefully.
10. A puller or a slide hammer is required to remove the bearing from the housing.

To install:

11. Pack the new or reused bearing with wheel bearing grease and lubricate the cavity between the seal lips with the same grease.
12. The bearing has to be driven into the housing. Don't use a drift, you might cock the bearing in its bore. Use a piece of pipe or a large socket instead. Drive only on the outer bearing

race. In a similar manner, drive the seal in flush with the end of the tube.

13. Slide the shaft into place, turning it slowly until the splines are engaged with the differential. Be careful of the oil seal.

14. Keep the pinion shaft partway out of the differential case while installing the C-lock on the axle shaft. Put the C-lock on the axle shaft and carefully pull out on the axle shaft until the C-lock is clear of the thrust block.

15. Position the differential pinion shaft through the case and the pinion gears, aligning the lockscrew hole. Install the lockscrew.

16. Install the cover with a new gasket and tighten the bolts evenly in a criss-cross pattern.

17. Fill the axle with lubricant as specified in Section 1.

18. Replace the brake drums and wheels.

Full-Floating Axles

See Figures 113, 114, 115, 116, 117, 118 and 119

The procedures are the same for locking and non-locking axles.

The best way to remove the bearings from the wheel hub is with an arbor press. Use of a press reduces the chances of damaging the bearing races, cocking the bearing in its bore, or scoring the hub walls. A local machine shop is probably equipped with the tools to remove and install bearings and seals. However, if one is not available, the hammer and drift method outlined can be used.

1. Support the axles on jackstands.
2. Remove the wheels.
3. Remove the bolts and lock washers that attach the axle shaft flange to the hub.
4. Rap on the flange with a soft faced hammer to loosen the shaft. Grip the rib on the end of the flange with a pair of locking pliers and twist to start shaft removal. Remove the shaft from the axle tube.
5. The hub and drum assembly must be removed to remove the bearings and oil seals. You will need a large socket to remove and later adjust the bearing adjustment nut. There are also special tools available.
6. Disengage the tang of the locknut retainer from the slot or slat of the locknut, then remove the locknut from the housing tube.
7. Disengage the tang of the retainer from the slot or flat of the adjusting nut and remove the retainer from the housing tube.
8. Remove the adjusting nut from the housing tube.
9. Remove the thrust washer from the housing tube.
10. Pull the hub and drum straight off the axle housing.
11. Remove the oil seal and discard.
12. Use a hammer and a long drift to knock the inner bearing, cup, and oil seal from the hub assembly.
13. Remove the outer bearing snapring with a pair of pliers. It may be necessary to tap the bearing outer race away from the retaining ring slightly by tapping on the ring to remove the ring.
14. Drive the outer bearing from the hub with a hammer and drift.

To install:

15. Place the outer bearing into the hub. The larger outside diameter of the bearing should face the outer end of the hub.

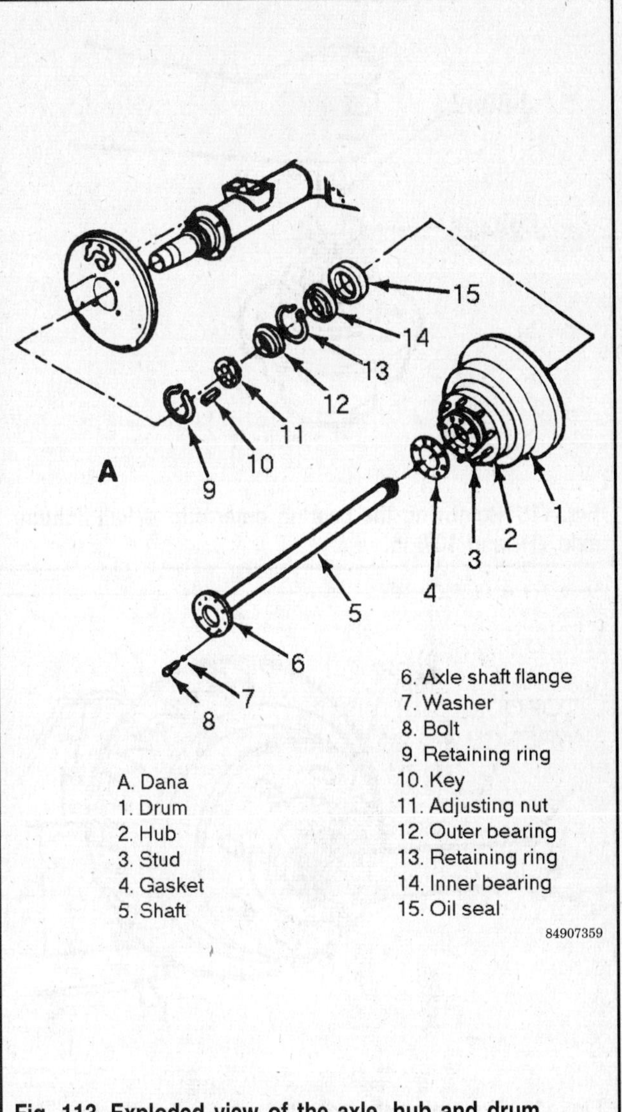

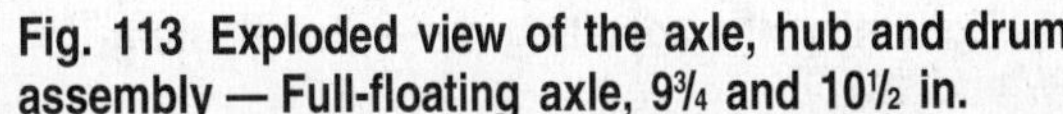

Fig. 113 Exploded view of the axle, hub and drum assembly — Full-floating axle, 9¾ and 10½ in.

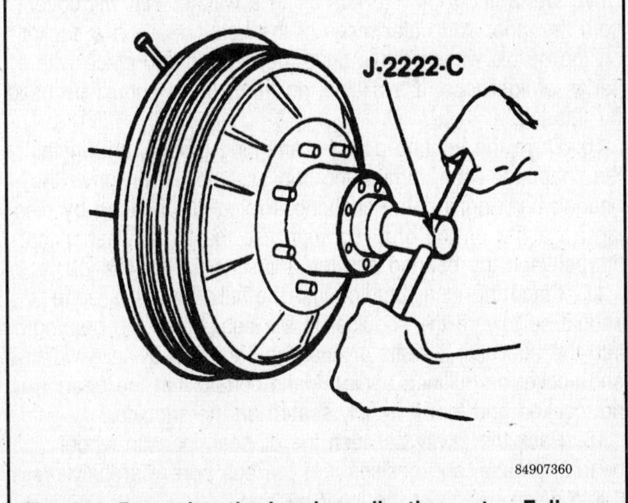

Fig. 114 Removing the bearing adjusting nut — Full-floating axle, 9¾ and 10½ in.

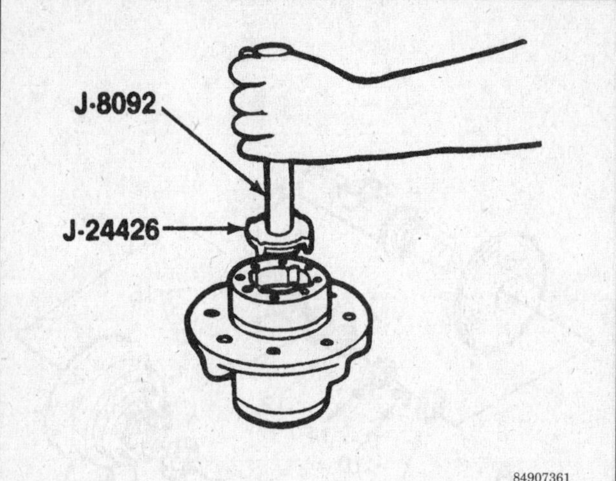

Fig. 115 Removing the bearing outer cup — Full-floating axle, 9¾ and 10½ in.

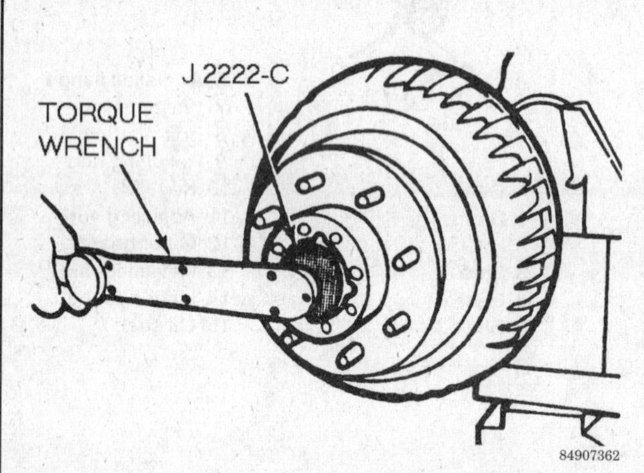

Fig. 116 Tightening the adjusting nut — Full-floating axle, 9¾ and 10½ in.

Drive the bearing into the hub using a washer that will cover both the inner and outer races of the bearing. Place a socket on top of this washer, then drive the bearing into place with a series of light taps. If available, an arbor press should be used for this job.

16. Drive the bearing past the snapring groove, and install the snapring. Then, turning the hub assembly over, drive the bearing back against the snapring. Protect the bearing by placing a washer on top of it. You can use the thrust washer that fits between the bearing and the adjusting nut for the job.

17. Place the inner bearing into the hub. The thick edge should be toward the shoulder in the hub. Press the bearing into the hub until it seats against the shoulder, using a washer and socket as outlined earlier. Make certain that the bearing is not cocked and that it is fully seated on the shoulder.

18. Pack the cavity between the oil seal lips with wheel bearing grease, and position it in the hub bore. Carefully press it into place on top of the inner bearing.

19. Pack the wheel bearings with grease, and lightly coat the inside diameter of the hub bearing contact surface and the outside diameter of the axle housing tube.

20. Make sure that the inner bearing, oil seal, axle housing oil deflector, and outer bearing are properly positioned. Install the hub and drum assembly on the axle housing, being careful so as not to damage the oil seal or dislocate other internal components.

21. Install the thrust washer so that the tang on the inside diameter of the washer is in the keyway on the axle housing.

22. Install the adjusting nut. Tighten to 50 ft. lbs. (68 Nm) while rotating the hub. Back off the nut and retighten to 35 ft. lbs. (47 Nm), then back off ¼ turn.

23. Install the tanged retainer against the inner adjusting nut. Align the adjusting nut so that the short tang of the retainer will engage the nearest slot on the adjusting nut.

24. Install the outer locknut and tighten to 65 ft. lbs. (88 Nm). Bend the long tang of the retainer into the slot of the outer nut. This method of adjustment should provide 0.001-0.010 in. (0.0254-0.254mm) end-play.

25. Place a new gasket over the axle shaft and position the axle shaft in the housing so that the shaft splines enter the differential side gear. Position the gasket so that the holes are in alignment, and install the flange-to-hub attaching bolts. Tighten to 115 ft. lbs. (156 Nm).

➡To prevent lubricant from leaking through the flange holes, apply a non-hardening sealer to the bolt threads. Use the sealer sparingly.

26. Replace the wheels.

Pinion Seal

REMOVAL & INSTALLATION

Semi-Floating Axles

➧ See Figures 120, 121, 122, 123 and 124

1. Raise and support the truck on jackstands. It would help to have the front end slightly higher than the rear to avoid fluid loss.
2. Matchmark and remove the driveshaft.
3. Release the parking brake.
4. Remove the rear wheels. Rotate the rear wheels by hand to make sure that there is absolutely no brake drag. If there is brake drag, remove the drums.
5. Using a torque wrench on the pinion nut, record the force needed to rotate the pinion.
6. Matchmark the pinion shaft, nut and flange. Count the number of exposed threads on the pinion shaft.
7. Install a holding tool on the pinion. A very large adjustable wrench will do, or, if one is not available, put the drums back on and set the parking brake as tightly as possible.
8. Remove the pinion nut.
9. Slide the flange off of the pinion. A puller may be necessary.
10. Centerpunch the oil seal to distort it and pry it out of the bore. Be careful to avoid scratching the bore.

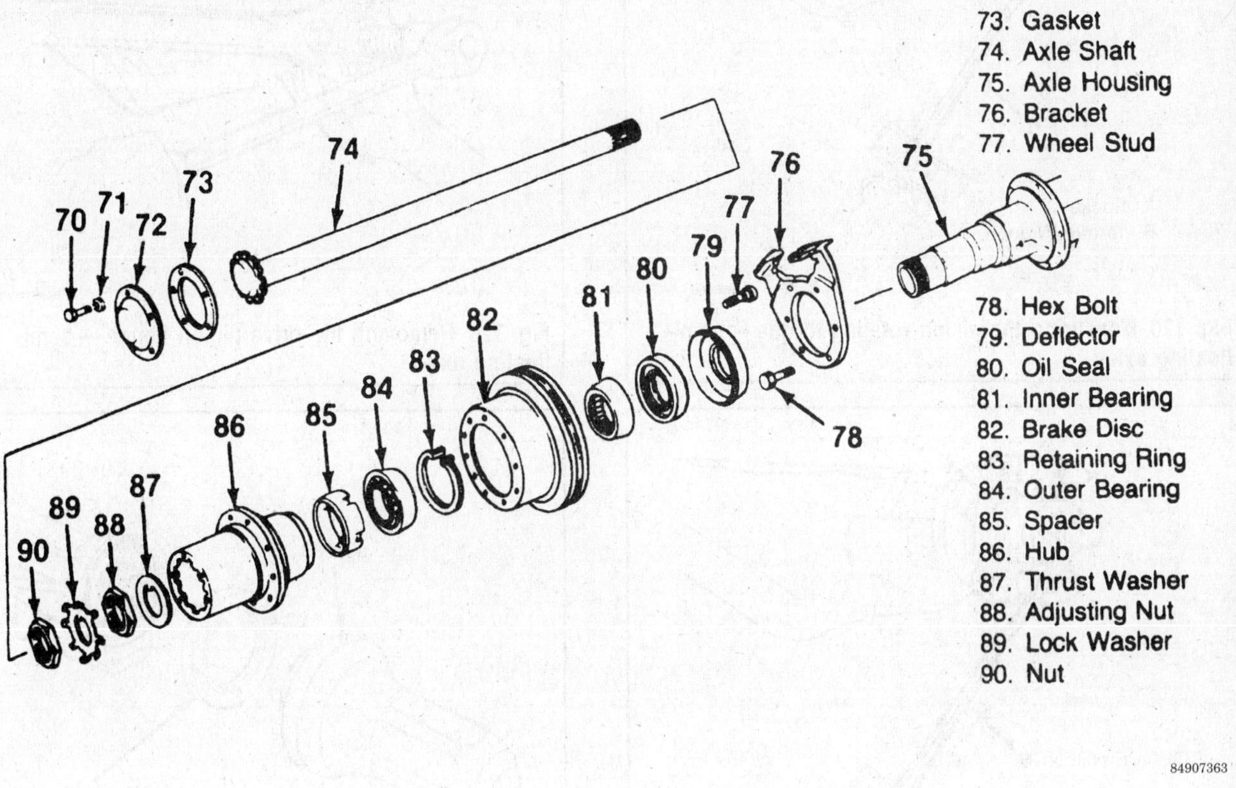

73. Gasket
74. Axle Shaft
75. Axle Housing
76. Bracket
77. Wheel Stud
78. Hex Bolt
79. Deflector
80. Oil Seal
81. Inner Bearing
82. Brake Disc
83. Retaining Ring
84. Outer Bearing
85. Spacer
86. Hub
87. Thrust Washer
88. Adjusting Nut
89. Lock Washer
90. Nut
84907363

Fig. 117 Exploded view of the axle and hub assembly — Full-floating axle, 12 in.

J 2919-01
84907364

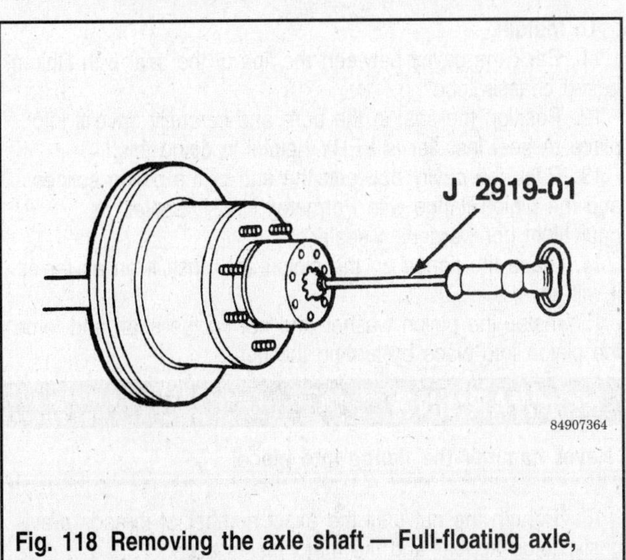

Fig. 118 Removing the axle shaft — Full-floating axle, 12 in.

J 25510
84907365

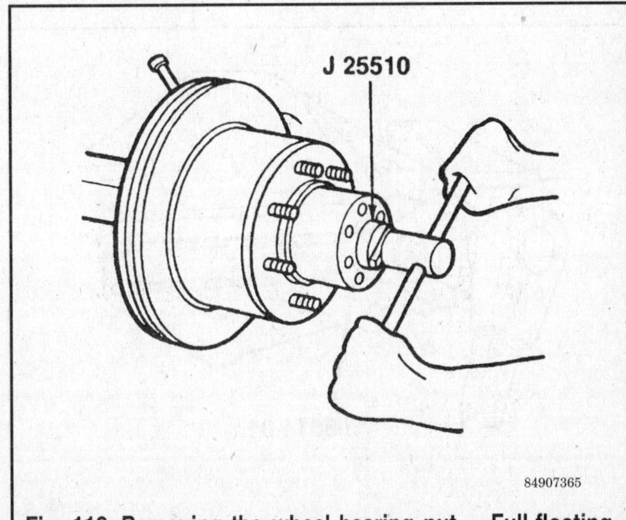

Fig. 119 Removing the wheel bearing nut — Full-floating axle, 12 in.

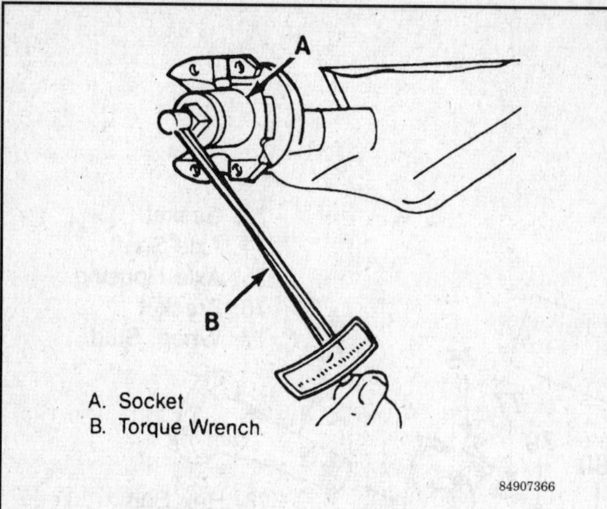

Fig. 120 Measuring the pinion rotating torque — semi-floating axles

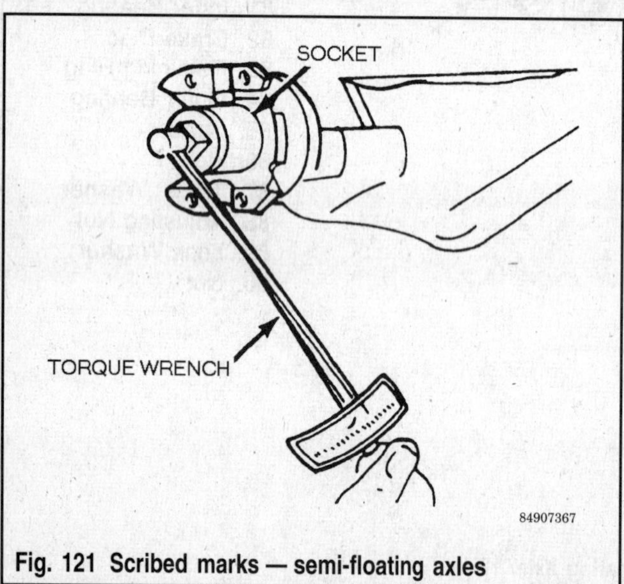

Fig. 121 Scribed marks — semi-floating axles

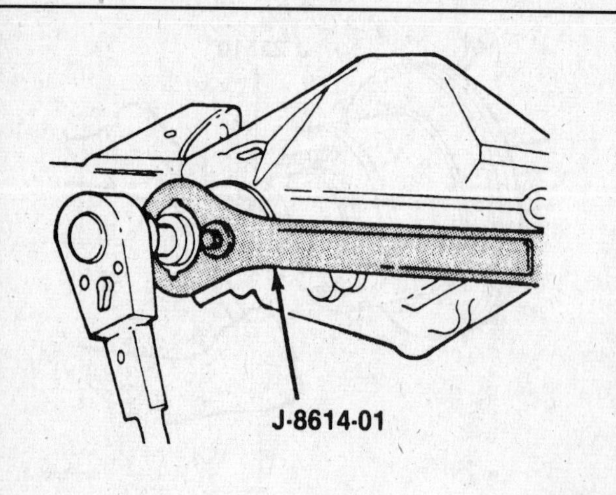

Fig. 122 Removing the drive pinion nut — semi-floating axles

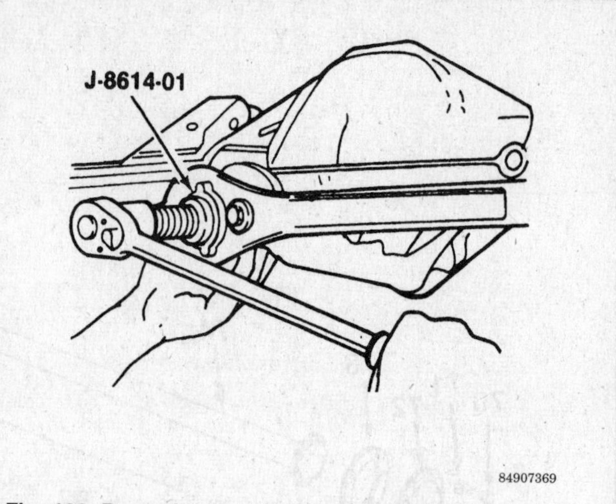

Fig. 123 Removing the drive pinion flange — semi-floating axles

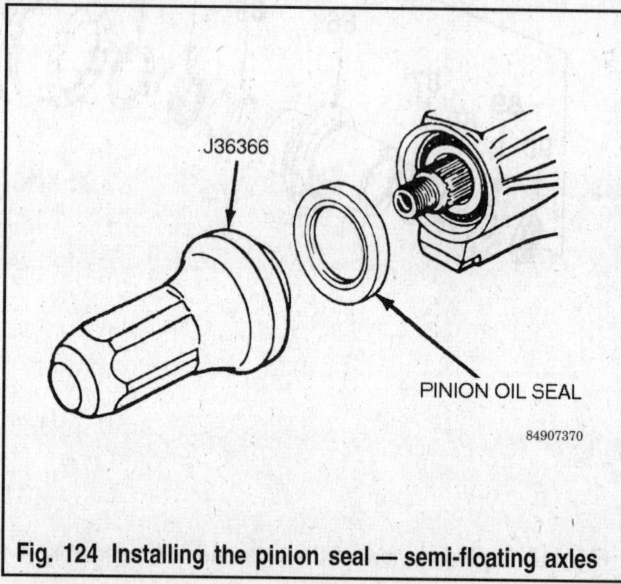

Fig. 124 Installing the pinion seal — semi-floating axles

To install:

11. Pack the cavity between the lips of the seal with lithium-based chassis lube.
12. Position the seal in the bore and carefully drive it into place. A seal installer is VERY helpful in doing this.
13. Pack the cavity between the end of the pinion splines and the pinion flange with Permatex No.2® sealer, or equivalent non-hardening sealer.
14. Place the flange on the pinion and push it on as far as it will go.
15. Install the pinion washer and nut on the shaft and force the pinion into place by turning the nut.

****WARNING**

Never hammer the flange into place!

16. Tighten the nut until the exact number of threads previously noted appear and the matchmarks align.
17. Measure the rotating torque of the pinion under the same circumstances as before. Compare the two readings. As

necessary, tighten the pinion nut in VERY small increments until the torque necessary to rotate the pinion is 3 inch lbs. higher than the originally recorded torque.

18. Install the driveshaft.

Full Floating Axles

1. Raise and support the truck on jackstands. It would help to have the front end slightly higher than the rear to avoid fluid loss.
2. Matchmark and remove the driveshaft.
3. Matchmark the pinion shaft, nut and flange. Count the number of exposed threads on the pinion shaft.
4. Install a holding tool on the pinion. A very large adjustable wrench will do, or, if one is not available, set the parking brake as tightly as possible.
5. Remove the pinion nut.
6. Slide the flange off of the pinion. A puller may be necessary.
7. Centerpunch the oil seal to distort it and pry it out of the bore. Be careful to avoid scratching the bore.

To install:

8. Pack the cavity between the lips of the seal with lithium-based chassis lube.
9. Position the seal in the bore and carefully drive it into place. A seal installer is VERY helpful in doing this.
10. Place the flange on the pinion and push it on as far as it will go.
11. Install the pinion washer and nut on the shaft and force the pinion into place by turning the nut.

⁂WARNING

Never hammer the flange into place!

12. Tighten the nut until the exact number of threads previously noted appear and the matchmarks align.
13. Install the driveshaft.

Axle Housing

REMOVAL & INSTALLATION

1. Raise and support the rear end on jackstands.
2. For the 9 ¾ in. ring gear and the 10 ½ in. ring gear axles, place jackstands under the frame side rails for support.
3. Drain the lubricant from the axle housing and remove the driveshaft.
4. Remove the wheel, the brake drum or hub and the drum assembly.
5. Disconnect the parking brake cable from the lever and at the brake flange plate.
6. Disconnect the hydraulic brake lines from the connectors.
7. Disconnect the shock absorbers from the axle brackets.
8. Remove the vent hose from the axle vent fitting (if used).
9. Disconnect the height sensing and brake proportional valve linkage (if used).
10. Support the stabilizer shaft assembly with a hydraulic jack and remove (if used).
11. Remove the nuts and washers from the U-bolts.
12. Remove the U-bolts, spring plates and spacers from the axle assembly.
13. Lower the jack and remove the axle assembly.

To install:

14. Raise the axle assembly into position.
15. Install the U-bolts, spring plates and spacers.
16. Install the nuts and washers on the U-bolts.
17. Install the stabilizer shaft.
18. Connect the height sensing and brake proportional valve linkage.
19. Install the vent hose at the axle vent fitting.
20. Connect the shock absorbers at the axle brackets.
21. Connect the hydraulic brake lines.
22. Connect the parking brake cable.
23. Install the wheels.
24. Install the driveshaft.
25. Fill the axle housing.

TORQUE SPECIFICATIONS

Component	US	Metric
Automatic Transmission		
Shift Linkage Nut		
4L80E	20 ft. lbs.	27 Nm
All Others	17 ft. lbs	23 Nm
R/V Series		
Mount Bolts	35 ft. lbs	47 Nm
Convertor Bolts	50 ft. lbs	68 Nm
Support Braces	35 ft. lbs	47 Nm
Crossmember	35 ft. lbs	47 Nm
Transfer Case-to-Transmission	24 ft. lbs	32 Nm
Transfer Case-to-Frame	35 ft. lbs	47 Nm
C/K Series		
Mount Bolts	35 ft. lbs	47 Nm
Convertor Bolts	50 ft. lbs	68 Nm
Support Braces	35 ft. lbs	47 Nm
Crossmember	35 ft. lbs	47 Nm
Transfer Case-to-Transmission	24 ft. lbs	32 Nm
Transfer Case-to-Frame	35 ft. lbs	47 Nm
Dipstick Tube		
4L60E	23 ft. lbs	32 Nm
4L80E	33 ft. lbs	44 Nm
Manual Transmission		
Clutch Bolts		
4.3L, 5.0L, 5.7L Engines	22 ft. lbs	30 Nm
6.2L, 6.5L Engines	32 ft. lbs	43 Nm
7.4L Engines	24 ft. lbs	33 Nm
Clutch Housing Bolts		
1988-90 R/V Series	40 ft.lbs.	54 Nm
1988-90 C/K Series	55 ft.lbs.	75 Nm
1991 Models	31 ft.lbs	43 Nm
1992-96 Models	29 ft. lbs.	39 Nm
Clutch Pedal Pivot Bolt	27 ft. lbs.	37 Nm
Clutch Slave Cylinder	13 ft. lbs.	18 Nm
Front Axle Housing		
R/V Series		
U-Bolt Nuts	150 ft. lbs.	203 Nm
Front Axle		
Pinion Seal Nut		
GMC Axle	270 ft. lbs.	366 Nm
Dana Axle	255 ft. lbs.	346 Nm
Series Front Axle tube		
Tube-to-Carrier	30 ft. lbs.	40 Nm
Axleshaft Flange Bolts	59 ft. lbs.	80 Nm
Tube-to-Frame Nuts		
15/25 Series	75 ft. lbs.	100 Nm
35 Series	107 ft. lbs.	145 Nm
Drain/Filler Plug	24 ft. lbs.	33 Nm
C/K Series Front Differntial Carrier		
Mount Bolts	80 ft. lbs.	110 Nm

87987c01

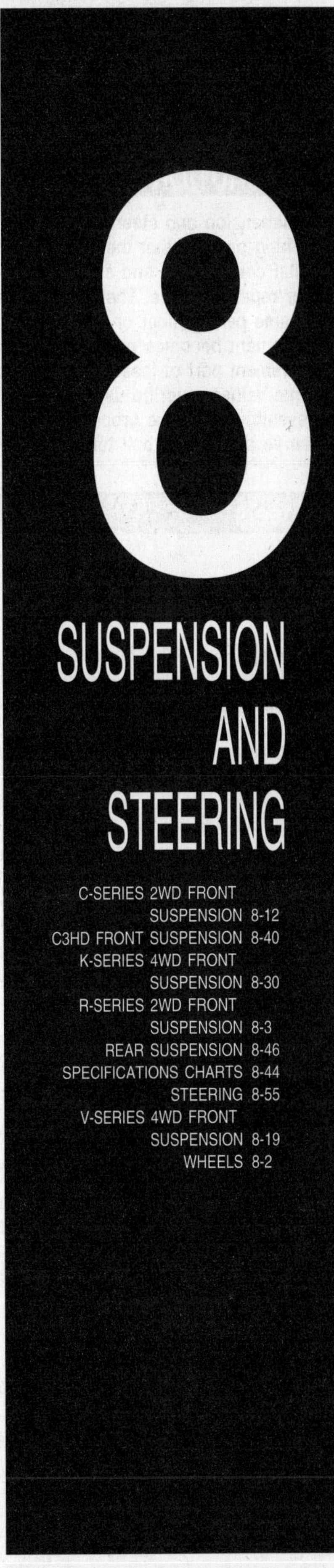

8 SUSPENSION AND STEERING

WHEELS

⁂CAUTION

All suspension and steering fasteners are important attaching parts in that they could affect the performance of vital components and systems, and/or could result in major repair expense. They must be replaced with one of the same part number or with an equivalent part if replacement becomes necessary. Do not use a replacement part of lesser quality or substitute design. Torque values must be used as specified during reassembly to assure proper retention of these parts. Observe all nut and bolt torque specifications.

Wheels

REMOVAL

1. Apply the parking brake and block the opposite wheel.
2. If equipped with an automatic transmission/transaxle, place the selector lever in **P**; with a manual transmission/transaxle, place the shifter in Reverse.
3. If equipped, remove the wheel cover or hub cap.
4. Break loose the lug nuts. If a nut is stuck, never use heat to loosen it or damage to the wheel and bearings may occur. If the nuts are seized, one or two heavy hammer blows directly on the end of the bolt head usually loosens the rust. Be careful as continued pounding will likely damage the brake drum or rotor.
5. Raise the vehicle until the tire is clear of the ground. Support the vehicle safely using jackstands.
6. Remove the lug nuts and the tire and wheel assembly.

INSPECTION

Check the wheels for any damage. They must be replaced if they are bent, dented, heavily rusted, have elongated bolt holes, or have excessive lateral or radial runout. Wheels with excessive runout may cause a high-speed vehicle vibration.

Replacement wheels must be of the same load capacity, diameter, width, offset and mounting configuration as the original wheels. Using the wrong wheels may affect wheel bearing life, ground and tire clearance, or speedometer and odometer calibrations.

INSTALLATION

➧ See Figure 1

Single Wheel

1. Lift the wheel onto the lugs.
2. Snug down the topmost nut, then snug down the rest of the nuts in a crisscross pattern.
3. When all nuts are snugged, torque them, in a crisscross pattern, to the specifications listed at the end of this procedure.

Dual Wheels

1. Install the inner and outer wheels, and clamp ring. Be sure that the pins on the clamp ring face outwards.
2. Install the nuts snugly, in a crisscross pattern. When all the lugs are snugged, tighten them in the sequence shown to the specifications listed.

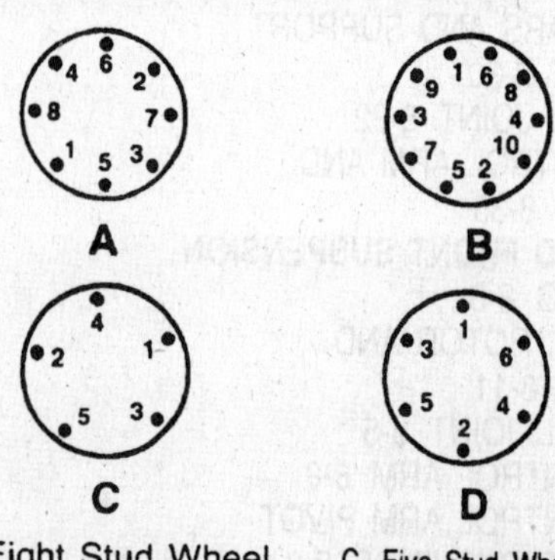

Fig. 1 Wheel lug nut tightening sequence — all models

Trucks with single front and rear wheels:

- R10/1500 w/5 studs and steel or aluminum wheels: 100 ft. lbs. (140 Nm)
- V10/1500 w/6 studs and steel wheels: 88 ft. lbs. (120 Nm)
- V10/1500 w/6 studs and aluminum wheels: 100 ft. lbs. (140 Nm)
- All C/K Series: 1988-90 — 90 ft. lbs. (123 Nm); 1991-93 — 120 ft. lbs. (160 Nm)
- All R/V Series with 8 studs: — 120 ft. lbs. (160 Nm)

Trucks with single front and dual rear wheels:

R/V Series with 8 studs — 140 ft. lbs. (190 Nm)
R/V Series with 10 studs — 175 ft. lbs. (240 Nm)
C/K Series: 1988-90 — 125 ft. lbs. (170 Nm).
C/K Series: 1991-96 with 8 studs — 140 ft. lbs. (190 Nm).
C/K Series: 1991-96 with 10 studs — 175 ft. lbs. (240 Nm)

R-SERIES 2WD FRONT SUSPENSION

CAUTION

All suspension and steering fasteners are important attaching parts in that they could affect the performance of vital components and systems, and/or could result in major repair expense. They must be replaced with one of the same part number or with an equivalent part if replacement becomes necessary. Do not use a replacement part of lesser quality or substitute design. Torque values must be used as specified during reassembly to assure proper retention of these parts. Observe all nut and bolt torque specifications.

Coil Spring

CAUTION

Coil springs are under considerable tension. Be very careful when removing and installing them; they can exert enough force to cause serious injury. Always use spring compressors or a safety chain when removing a coil spring or releasing spring tension!

REMOVAL & INSTALLATION

See Figure 2

1. Raise and support the truck under the frame rails. The control arms should hang freely.
2. Remove the wheel.
3. Disconnect the shock absorber at the lower end and move it aside.
4. Disconnect the stabilizer bar from the lower control arm.
5. Support the lower control arm and install a spring compressor on the spring, or chain the spring to the control arm as a safety precaution.

On trucks with an air cylinder inside the spring, remove the valve core from the cylinder and expel the air by compressing the cylinder with a prybar. With the cylinder compressed, replace the valve core so that the cylinder will stay in the compressed position. Push the cylinder as far as possible towards the top of the spring.

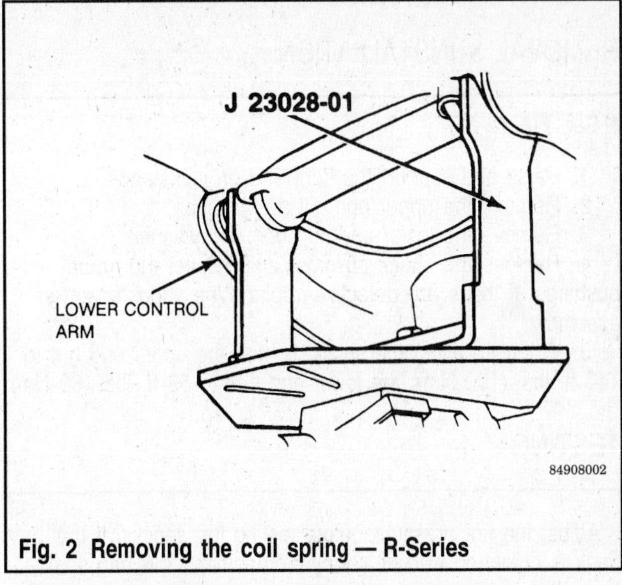

Fig. 2 Removing the coil spring — R-Series

6. Raise the jack to remove the tension from the lower control arm cross-shaft and remove the two U-bolts securing the cross-shaft to the crossmember.

CAUTION

The cross-shaft and lower control arm keeps the coil spring compressed. Use care when you lower the assembly.

7. Slowly release the jack and lower the control arm until the spring can be removed. Be sure that all compression is relieved from the spring.
8. If the spring was chained, remove the chain and spring. If you used spring compressors, remove the spring and slowly release the compressors.
9. Remove the air cylinder, if so equipped.

To install:

10. Install the air cylinder so that the protector plate is towards the upper control arm. The schrader valve should protrude through the hole in the lower control arm.
11. Install the chain and spring. If you used spring compressors, install the spring and compressors.
12. Slowly raise the jack and lower the control arm. Line up the indexing hole in the shaft with the crossmember attaching studs.
13. Install the two U-bolts securing the cross-shaft to the crossmember. Tighten the nuts to 85 ft. lbs. (115 Nm).
14. Remove the jack.

15. Connect the stabilizer bar to the lower control arm. Tighten the nuts to 24 ft. lbs. (32 Nm).
16. Connect the shock absorber at the lower end. Tighten the bolt to 59 ft. lbs. (80 Nm).
17. If equipped with air cylinders, inflate the cylinder to 60 psi.
18. Install the wheel.
19. Lower the truck. Once the weight of the truck is on the wheels, reduce the air cylinder pressure to 50 psi.
20. Have the alignment checked.

Shock Absorbers

REMOVAL & INSTALLATION

See Figure 3

1. Raise and support the front end on jackstands.
2. Remove the upper end nut and washer.
3. Remove the lower end nut, bolt and washer.
4. Remove the shock absorber and inspect the rubber bushings. If these are defective, replace the shock absorber assembly.
5. When installing the shock, tighten the upper end nut to 140 ft. lbs. (190 Nm); the lower end bolt to 59 ft. lbs. (80 Nm).

TESTING

Adjust the tire pressure before testing the shocks. If the truck is equipped with heavy duty equipment, this can sometimes be misleading. A stiff ride normally accompanies a stiff or heavy duty suspension. Be sure that all weight in the truck is distributed evenly.

Each shock absorber can be tested by bouncing the corner of the truck until maximum up and down movement is obtained. Let go of the truck. It should stop bouncing in 1-2 bounces. If not, the shock should be replaced.

Upper Ball Joint

INSPECTION

1. Raise and support the front end on jackstands so that the control arms hang freely.
2. Remove the wheel.
3. The upper ball joint is spring-loaded. Replace the ball joint if the is any lateral movement or if it can be twisted in its socket with your fingers.

REMOVAL & INSTALLATION

See Figures 4 and 5

1. Raise and support the truck with jackstands. Remove wheel.
2. Support the lower control arm with a floor jack.
3. Remove the cotter pin from the upper ball stud and loosen, but do not remove the stud nut.
4. Using a forcing-type ball joint separator tool, loosen the ball stud in the steering knuckle. When the stud is loose, remove the tool and the stud nut. It may be necessary to remove the brake caliper and wire it to the frame to gain clearance.
5. Drill out the rivets using a 1/8in. drill bit. Remove the ball joint assembly.

To install:

6. Install the replacement ball joint in the control arm, using the bolts and nuts supplied. Tighten the nuts to 18 ft. lbs. (24 Nm).

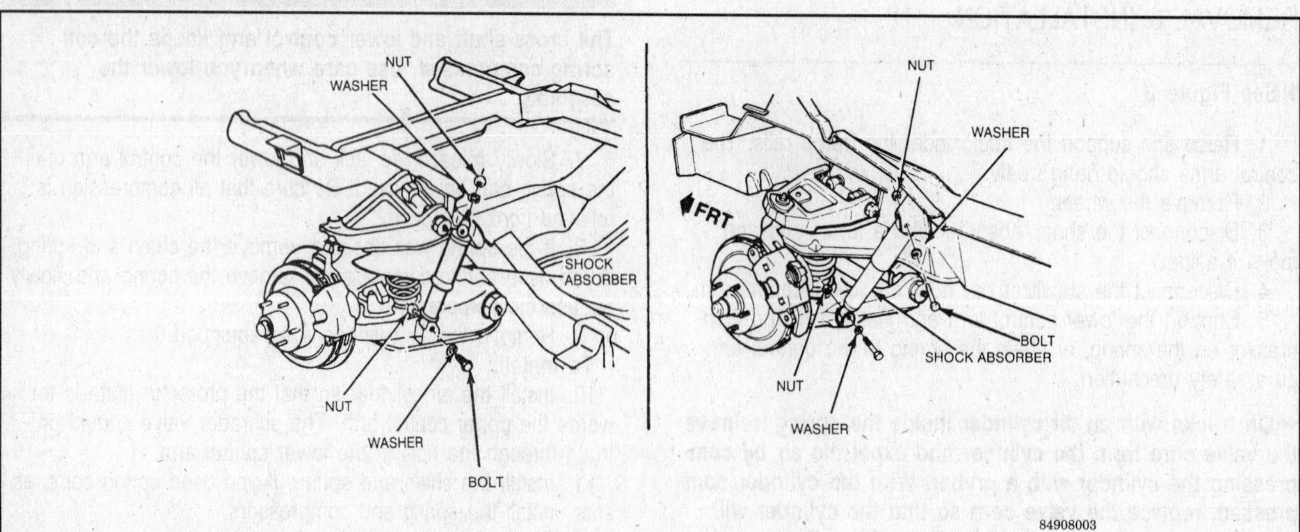

Fig. 3 Front shock absorber mounting — R-Series

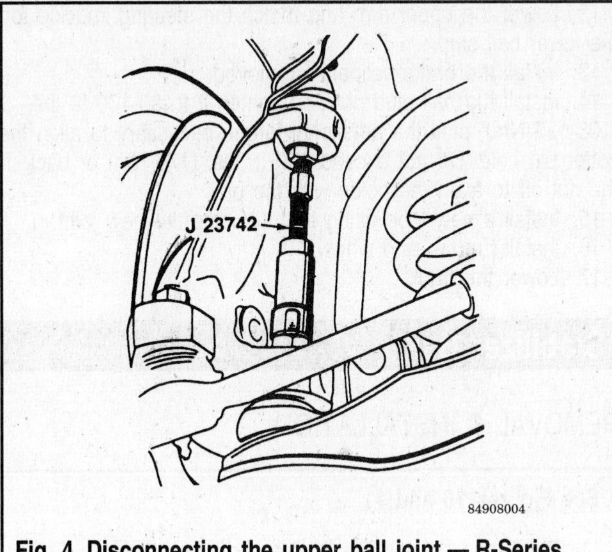

Fig. 4 Disconnecting the upper ball joint — R-Series

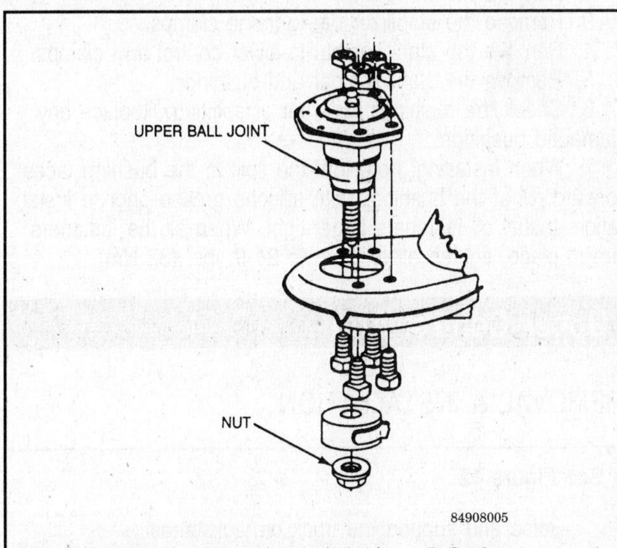

Fig. 5 Installing the upper ball joint — R-Series

7. Position the ball stud in the knuckle. Make sure it is squarely seated. Tighten the ball stud nut as follows:

- ½ ton trucks: 50 ft. lbs. (68 Nm), plus the additional torque to align the cotter pin. Do not exceed 90 ft. lbs. (122 Nm) and never back the nut off to align the pin.
- ¾ and 1 ton trucks: 90 ft. lbs. (122 Nm), plus additional torque necessary to align the cotter pin. Do not exceed 130 ft. lbs. (176 Nm) and never back off the nut to align the pin.

8. Install a new cotter pin.
9. Install a new lube fitting and lubricate the new joint.
10. If removed, install the brake caliper.
11. Install the wheel and lower the truck.

Lower Ball Joint

INSPECTION

➧ See Figure 6

1. Support the weight of the control arm at the wheel hub.
2. Measure the distance between the tip of the ball joint stud and the grease fitting below the ball joint.
3. Move the support to the control arm and allow the hub to hang free. Measure the distance again. If the variation between the two measurements exceeds $^{3}/_{32}$in. (2.4mm) the ball joint should be replaced.

REMOVAL & INSTALLATION

➧ See Figures 7, 8 and 9

1. Raise and support the front end on jackstands.
2. Support the lower control arm with a floor jack.
3. Remove the wheel.
4. Remove the lower stud cotter pin and loosen, but do not remove, the stud nut.
5. Loosen the ball joint with a forcing-type ball joint tool. It may be necessary to remove the brake caliper and wire it to the frame to gain enough clearance.
6. When the stud is loose, remove the tool and ball stud nut.
7. Install a spring compressor on the coil spring for safety.
8. Pull the brake disc and knuckle assembly up and off the ball stud and support the upper arm with a block of wood.
9. Remove the ball joint from the control arm with a ball joint fork or another suitable tool.

To install:

10. Start the new ball joint into the control arm. Position the bleed vent in the rubber boot facing inward.
11. Turn the screw until the ball joint is seated in the control arm.

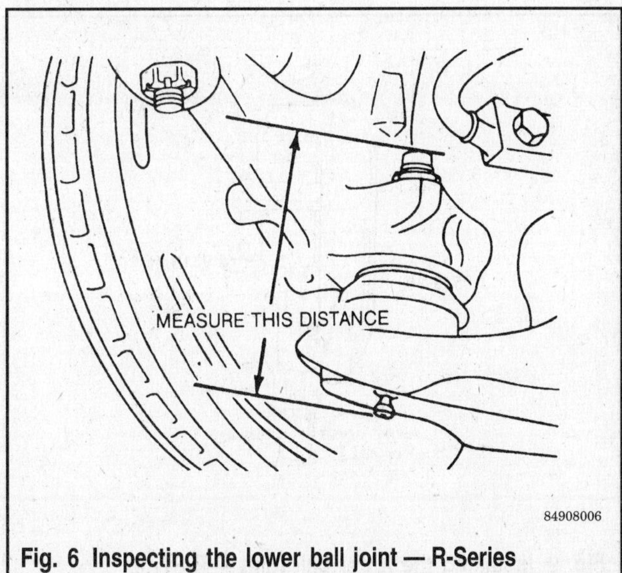

Fig. 6 Inspecting the lower ball joint — R-Series

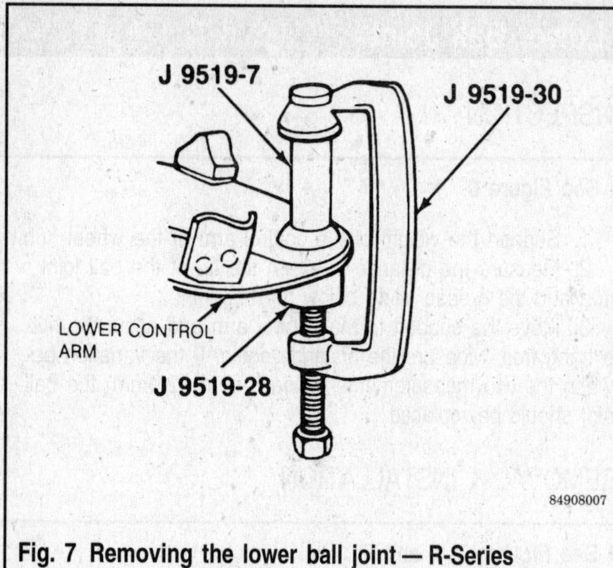

Fig. 7 Removing the lower ball joint — R-Series

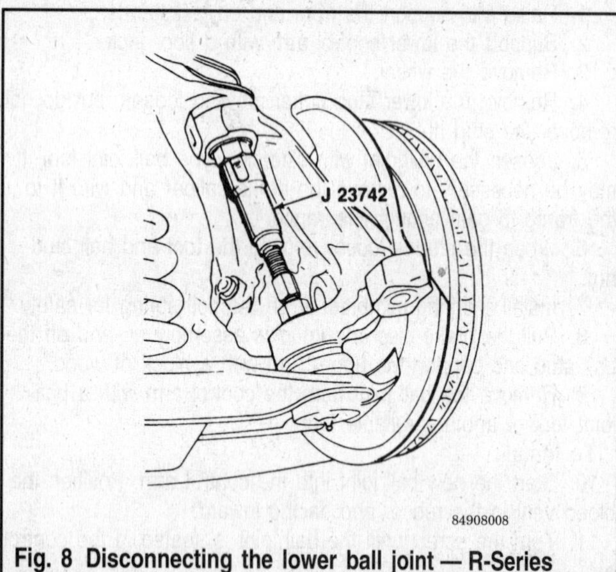

Fig. 8 Disconnecting the lower ball joint — R-Series

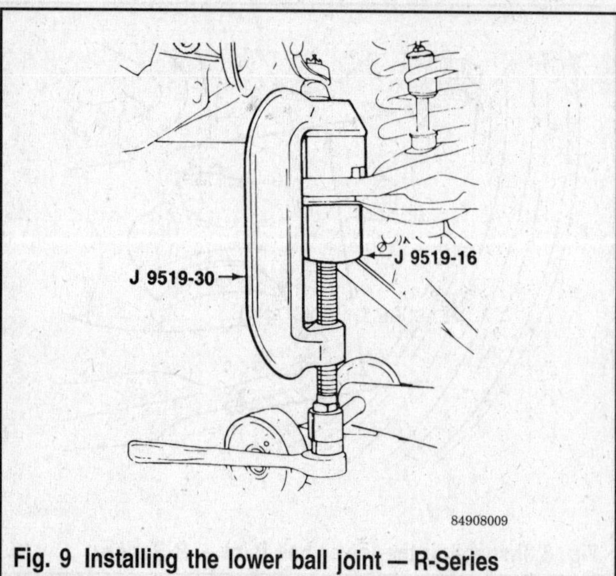

Fig. 9 Installing the lower ball joint — R-Series

12. Lower the upper arm and match the steering knuckle to the lower ball stud.
13. Install the brake caliper, if removed.
14. Install the ball stud nut and tighten it to 80-100 ft. lbs. (108-135 Nm), plus the additional torque necessary to align the cotter pin hole. Do not exceed 130 ft. lbs. (176 Nm) or back the nut off to align the holes with the pin.
15. Install a new lube fitting and lubricate the new joint.
16. Install the tire and wheel.
17. Lower the truck.

Stabilizer Bar

REMOVAL & INSTALLATION

See Figures 10 and 11

1. Raise and support the front end on jackstands.
2. Remove the wheels.
3. Remove the stabilizer bar-to-frame clamps.
4. Remove the stabilizer bar-to-lower control arm clamps.
5. Remove the stabilizer bar and bushings.
6. Check the bushings for wear or splitting. Replace any damaged bushings.
7. When installing, note that the split in the bushing faces forward. Coat the bushings with silicone grease prior to installation. Install all fasteners finger-tight. When all the fasteners are in place, tighten all of them to 24 ft. lbs. (32 Nm).

Upper Control Arm

REMOVAL & INSTALLATION

See Figure 12

1. Raise and support the truck on jackstands.
2. Support the lower control arm with a floor jack.
3. Remove the wheel.
4. Remove the cotter pin from the upper control arm ball stud and loosen the stud nut until the bottom surface of the nut is slightly below the end of the stud.
5. Install a spring compressor on the coil spring for safety.
6. Loosen the upper control arm ball stud in the steering knuckle using a ball joint stud removal tool. Remove the nut from the ball stud and raise the upper arm to clear the steering knuckle. It may be necessary to remove the brake caliper and wire it to the frame to gain clearance. Do not allow the caliper to hang by the brake hose.
7. Remove the nuts securing the control arm shaft studs to the crossmember bracket and remove the control arm.
8. Tape the shims and spacers together and tag for proper reassembly.

To install:

9. Place the control arm in position and install the nuts. Before tightening the nuts, insert the caster and camber shims in the same order as when installed.
10. Install the nuts securing the control arm shaft studs to the crossmember bracket. Tighten the nuts to 70 ft. lbs. (95

1. Nut
2. Washer
3. Bushing
4. Washer
5. Clamp
6. Bolt
7. Clamp
8. Bushing
9. Bolt
10. Washer
11. Washer
12. Nut
13. Stabilizer
84908015

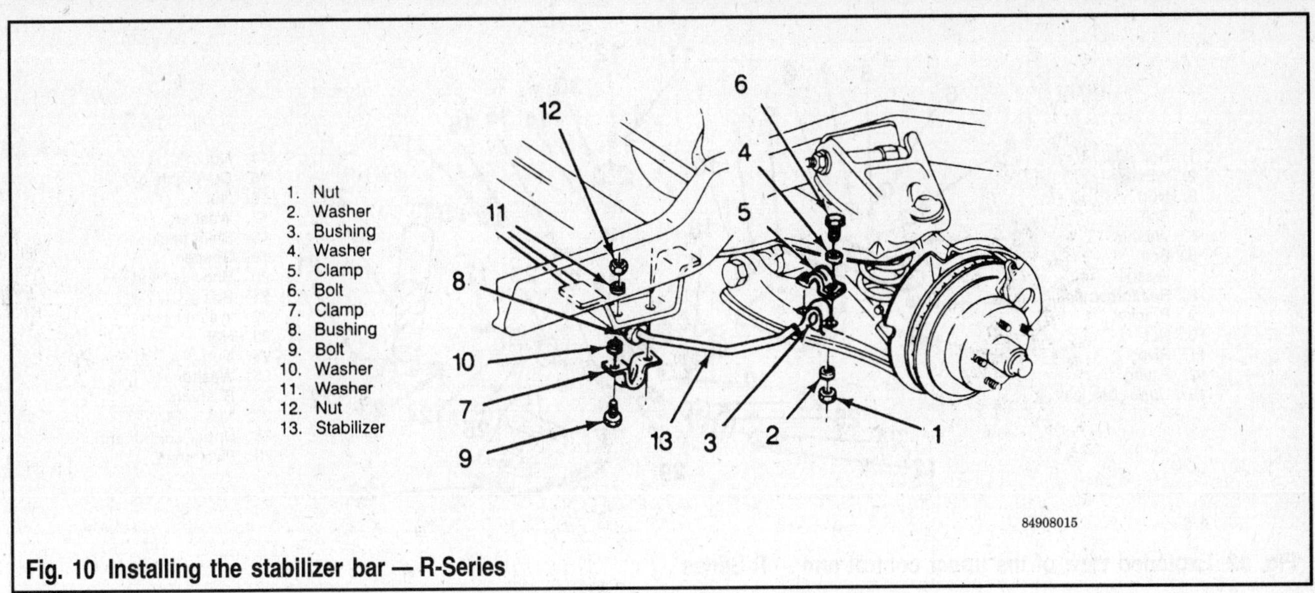

Fig. 10 Installing the stabilizer bar — R-Series

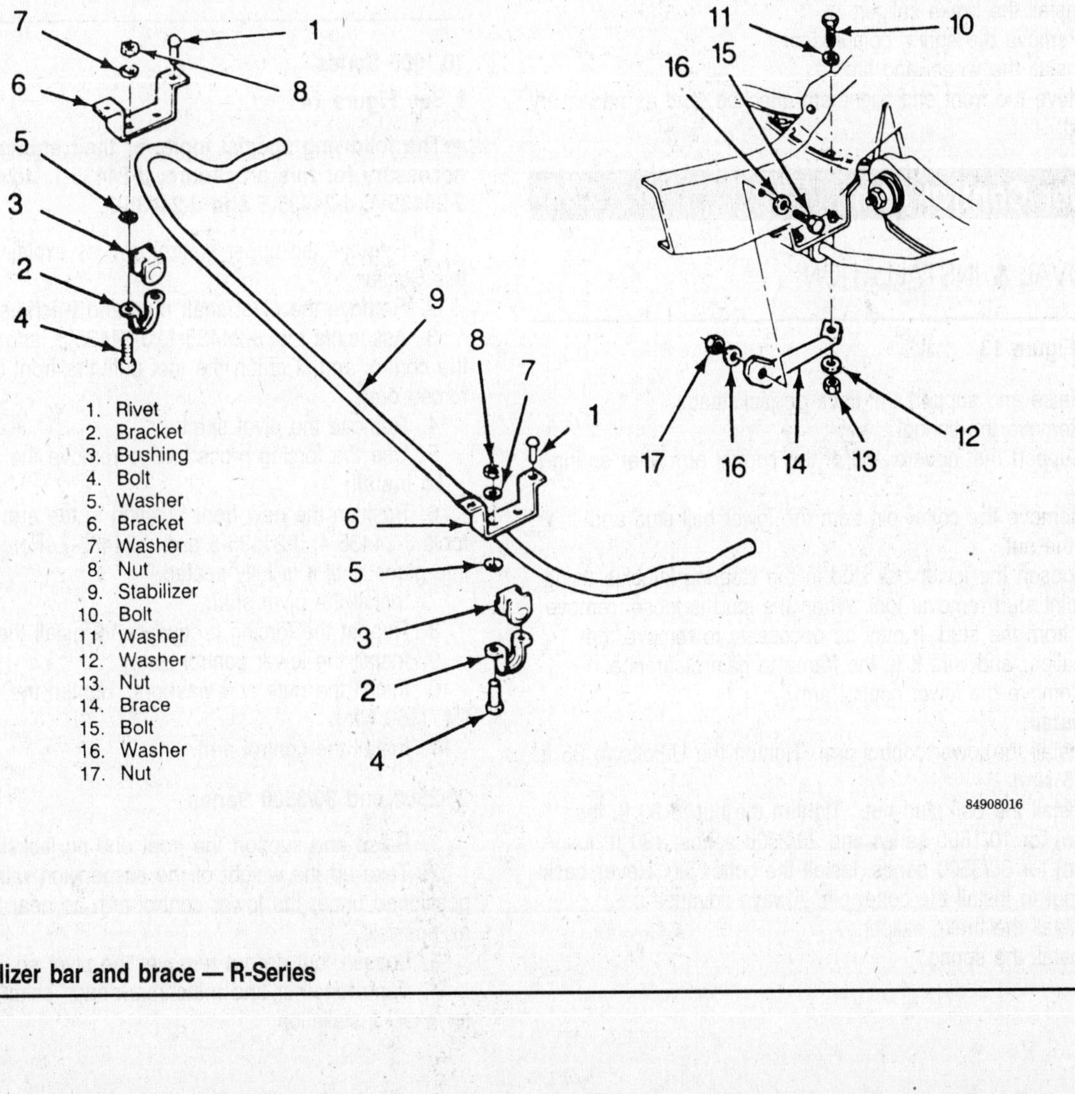

1. Rivet
2. Bracket
3. Bushing
4. Bolt
5. Washer
6. Bracket
7. Washer
8. Nut
9. Stabilizer
10. Bolt
11. Washer
12. Washer
13. Nut
14. Brace
15. Bolt
16. Washer
17. Nut
84908016

Fig. 11 Stabilizer bar and brace — R-Series

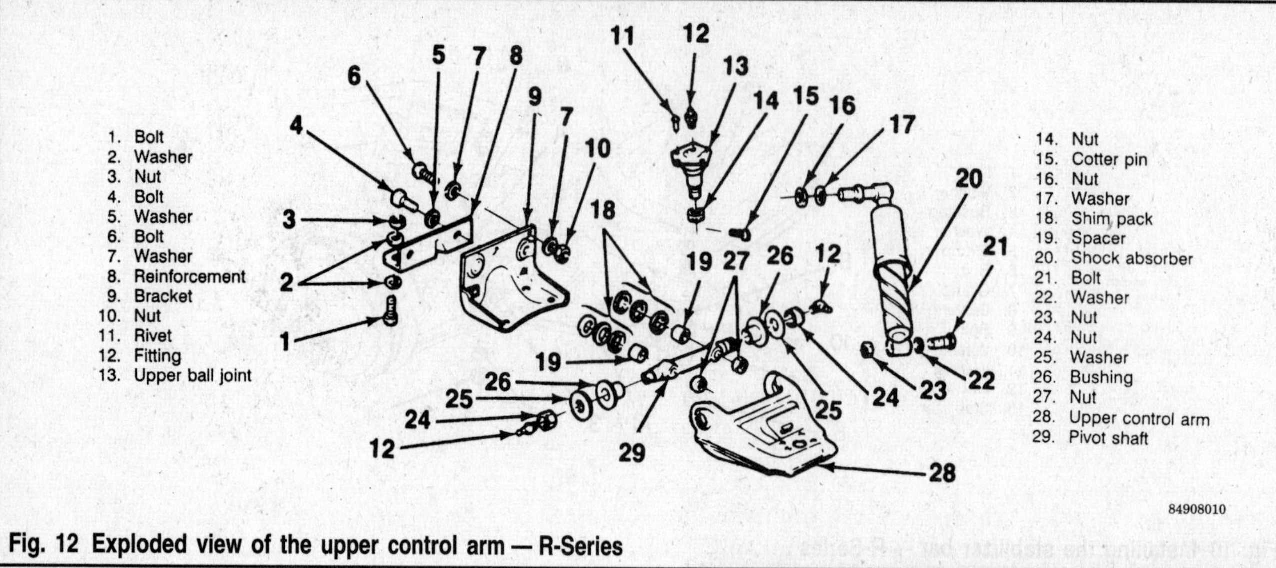

Fig. 12 Exploded view of the upper control arm — R-Series

Nm) for 10/1500 and 20/2500 series; 105 ft. lbs. (142 Nm) for 30/3500 series.

11. Install the ball stud nut. Tighten the nut to 90 ft. lbs. (122 Nm) for 10/1500 series and 20/2500 series; 130 ft. lbs. (176 Nm) for 30/3500 series. Install the cotter pin. Never back off the nut to install the cotter pin. Always advance it.
12. Install the brake caliper.
13. Remove the spring compressor.
14. Install the wheel and tire.
15. Have the front end alignment checked, and as necessary adjusted.

Lower Control Arm

REMOVAL & INSTALLATION

See Figure 13

1. Raise and support the truck on jackstands.
2. Remove the spring.
3. Support the inboard end of the control arm after spring removal.
4. Remove the cotter pin from the lower ball stud and loosen the nut.
5. Loosen the lower ball stud in the steering knuckle using a ball joint stud removal tool. When the stud is loose, remove the nut from the stud. It may be necessary to remove the brake caliper and wire it to the frame to gain clearance.
6. Remove the lower control arm.

To install:

7. Install the lower control arm. Tighten the U-bolts to 85 ft. lbs. (115 Nm).
8. Install the ball stud nut. Tighten the nut to 90 ft. lbs. (122 Nm) for 10/1500 series and 20/2500 series; 130 ft. lbs. (176 Nm) for 30/3500 series. Install the cotter pin. Never back off the nut to install the cotter pin. Always advance it.
9. Install the brake caliper.
10. Install the spring.

Upper Control Arm Pivot Shaft and Bushings

REMOVAL & INSTALLATION

10/1500 Series

See Figure 14

The following special tools, or their equivalents, are necessary for this procedure: J-24435-1, J-24435-3, J-24435-4, J-24435-5 and J-24435-7.

1. Remove the upper control arm as explained earlier in this Section.
2. Remove the pivot shaft nuts and washers.
3. Assemble tool J-24435-1. J-24435-3, and J-24435-7 on the control arm. Tighten the tool until the front bushing is forced out.
4. Remove the pivot shaft.
5. Use the forcing procedure to remove the rear bushing.

To install:

6. Position the new front bushing in the arm and assemble tools J-24435-4, J-24435-5 and J-24435-7. Force the bushing into place until it is fully seated.
7. Install the pivot shaft.
8. Repeat the forcing procedure to install the rear bushing.
9. Install the lower control arm.
10. Install the nuts and washers. Tighten the nuts to 115 ft. lbs. (156 Nm).
11. Install the control arm.

20/2500 and 30/3500 Series

1. Raise and support the front end on jackstands.
2. Take up the weight of the suspension with a floor jack positioned under the lower control arm as near to the ball joint as possible.
3. Loosen, but do not remove, the pivot shaft-to-frame nuts.
4. Tape together and matchmark each shim pack's position for exact installation.

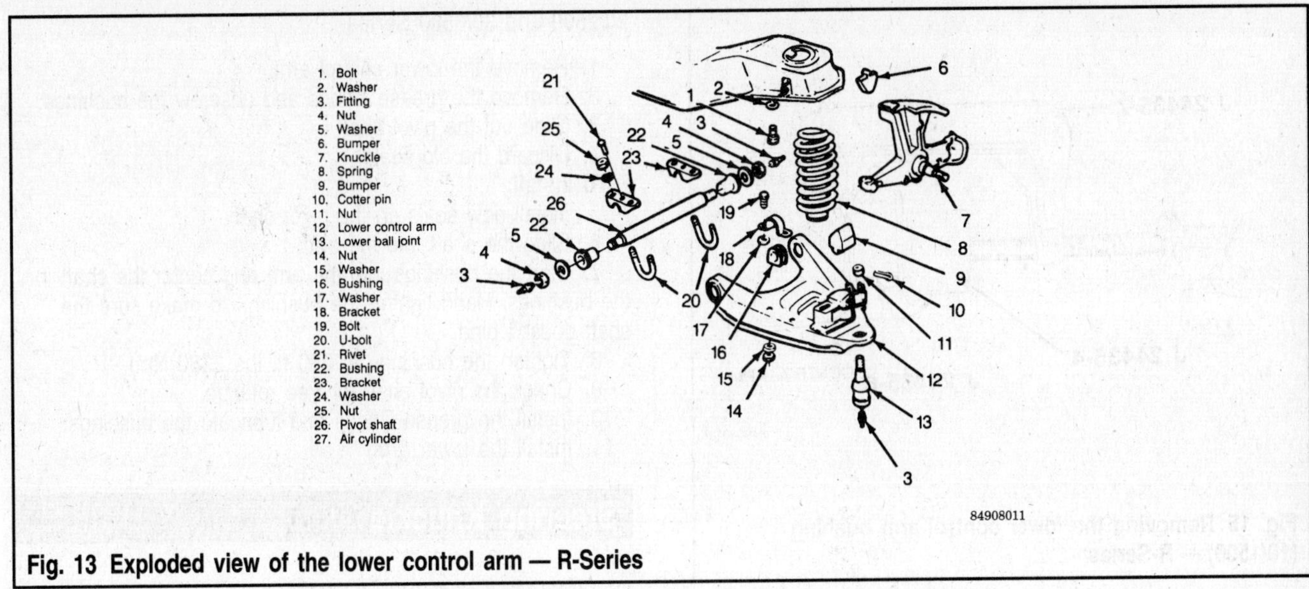

Fig. 13 Exploded view of the lower control arm — R-Series

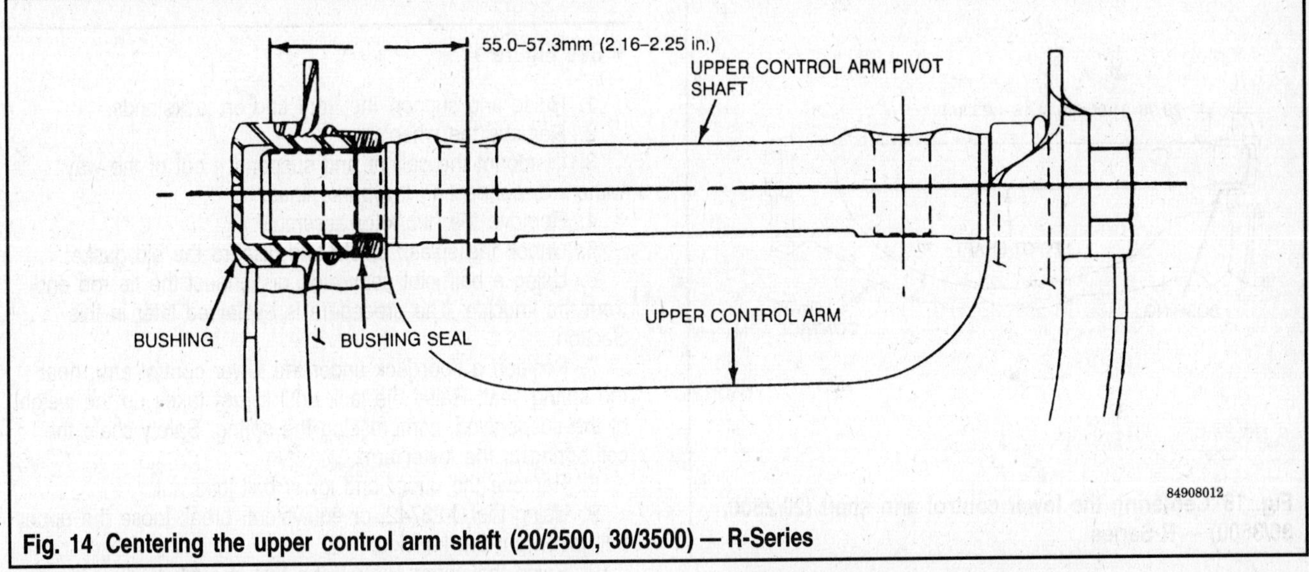

Fig. 14 Centering the upper control arm shaft (20/2500, 30/3500) — R-Series

5. Install a chain over the control arm, inboard of the stabilizer bar and outboard of the shock absorber to hold the control arm close to the crossmember.
6. Remove the pivot shaft nuts, bolts and spacers.
7. Remove the grease fittings and unscrew the bushings from the control arm.
8. Remove the pivot shaft. Discard the seals.

To install:

9. Install new seals on the pivot shaft.
10. Slide the shaft into the arm.
11. Start the bushings into the arm and center the shaft in the bushings. Hand tighten the bushings to make sure the shaft doesn't bind.
12. Tighten the bushings to 190 ft. lbs. (257 Nm).
13. Check the pivot shaft for free rotation.
14. Install the grease fittings and lubricate the bushings.
15. Position the control arm on the frame and install the shim packs, spacers, nuts and bolts. Tighten the nuts to 105 ft. lbs. (142 Nm).
16. Remove the chain and install the wheel.
17. Have the alignment checked.

Lower Control Arm Pivot Shaft and Bushings

REMOVAL & INSTALLATION

10/1500 Series

➧ See Figures 15 and 16

➡The following special tools, or their equivalents, are necessary for this procedure: J-22717, J-24435-7, J-24435-3, J-24435-2, J-24435-6, J-24435-4.

1. Remove the lower control arm as explained earlier in this Section.
2. Remove the pivot shaft nuts and washers.

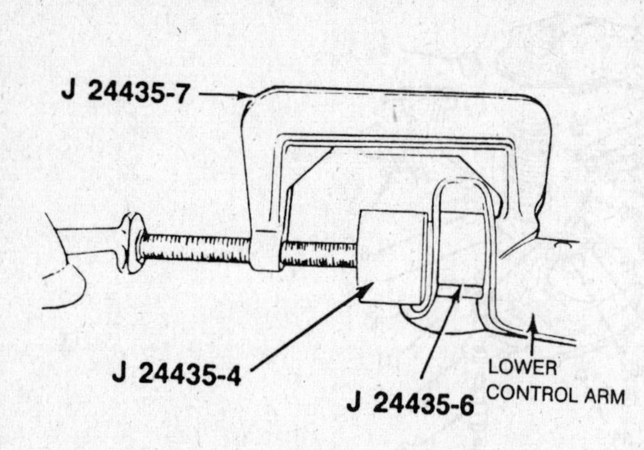

Fig. 15 Removing the lower control arm bushing (10/1500) — R-Series

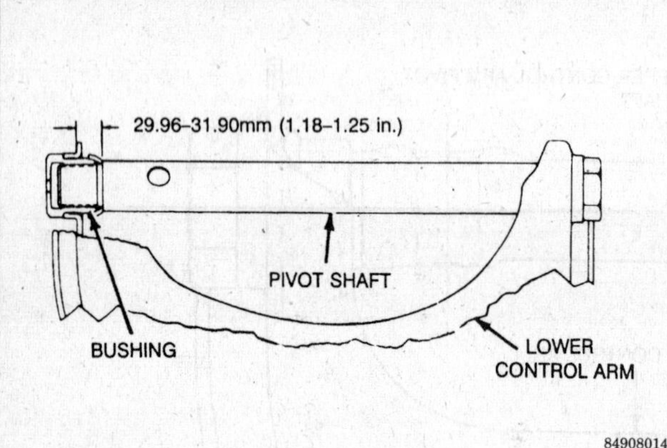

Fig. 16 Centering the lower control arm shaft (20/2500, 30/3500) — R-Series

3. Place the control arm in a press and press on the front end of the pivot shaft to remove the rear bushing.
4. Remove the pivot shaft.
5. Remove the front bushing stakes with tool J-22717, or equivalent.
6. Assemble tool J-24435-7. J-24435-3, J-24435-2 and J-24435-6 on the control arm. Tighten the tool until the bushing is forced out.

To install:

7. Position the new front bushing in the arm and assemble tools J-24435-6, J-24435-4 and J-24435-7. Force the bushing into place until it is fully seated. The outer tube hole must be lined up so that it faces the front, towards the staked bushing.
8. Stake the bushing in at least 2 places.
9. Install the pivot shaft.
10. Install the rear bushing.
11. Install the washers and pivot shaft nuts. Tighten the nuts to 70 ft. lbs. (94 Nm).
12. Install the lower control arm.

20/2500 and 30/3500 Series

1. Remove the lower control arm.
2. Remove the grease fittings and unscrew the bushings.
3. Slide out the pivot shaft.
4. Discard the old seals.

To install:

5. Install new seals on the pivot shaft.
6. Slide the shaft into the arm.
7. Start the bushings into the arm and center the shaft in the bushings. Hand tighten the bushings to make sure the shaft doesn't bind.
8. Tighten the bushings to 280 ft. lbs. (380 Nm).
9. Check the pivot shaft for free rotation.
10. Install the grease fittings and lubricate the bushings.
11. Install the lower arm.

Steering Knuckle

REMOVAL & INSTALLATION

➧ **See Figure 17**

1. Raise and support the front end on jackstands.
2. Remove the wheels.
3. Dismount the caliper and suspend it out of the way without disconnecting the brake lines.
4. Remove the hub/rotor assembly.
5. Unbolt the splash shield and discard the old gasket.
6. Using a ball joint separator, disconnect the tie rod end from the knuckle. The procedure is explained later in this Section.
7. Position a floor jack under the lower control arm, near the spring seat. Raise the jack until it **just** takes up the weight of the suspension, compressing the spring. Safety-chain the coil spring to the lower arm.
8. Remove the upper and lower ball joint nut.
9. Using tool J-23742, or equivalent, break loose the upper ball joint from the knuckle.
10. Raise the upper control arm just enough to disconnect the ball joint.
11. Using the afore-mentioned tool, break loose the lower ball joint.
12. Lift the knuckle off of the lower ball joint.
13. Inspect and clean the ball stud bores in the knuckle. Make sure that there are no cracks or burrs. If the knuckle is damaged in any way, replace it.
14. Check the spindle for wear, heat discoloration or damage. If at all damaged, replace it.

To install:

15. Maneuver the knuckle onto both ball joints.
16. Install both nuts. On 10/1500 series and 20/2500 series, tighten the upper nut to 50 ft. lbs. (68 Nm) and the lower nut to 90 ft. lbs. (122 Nm). On 30/3500 series, tighten both nuts to 90 ft. lbs. (122 Nm).
17. Install the cotter pins. Always advance the nut to align the cotter pin hole. NEVER back it off! On the upper nut which was originally tightened to 50 ft. lbs. (68 Nm), don't exceed 90 ft. lbs. (122 Nm) when aligning the hole. On nuts tightened originally to 90 ft. lbs. (122 Nm), don't exceed 130 ft. lbs. (176 Nm) to align the hole.

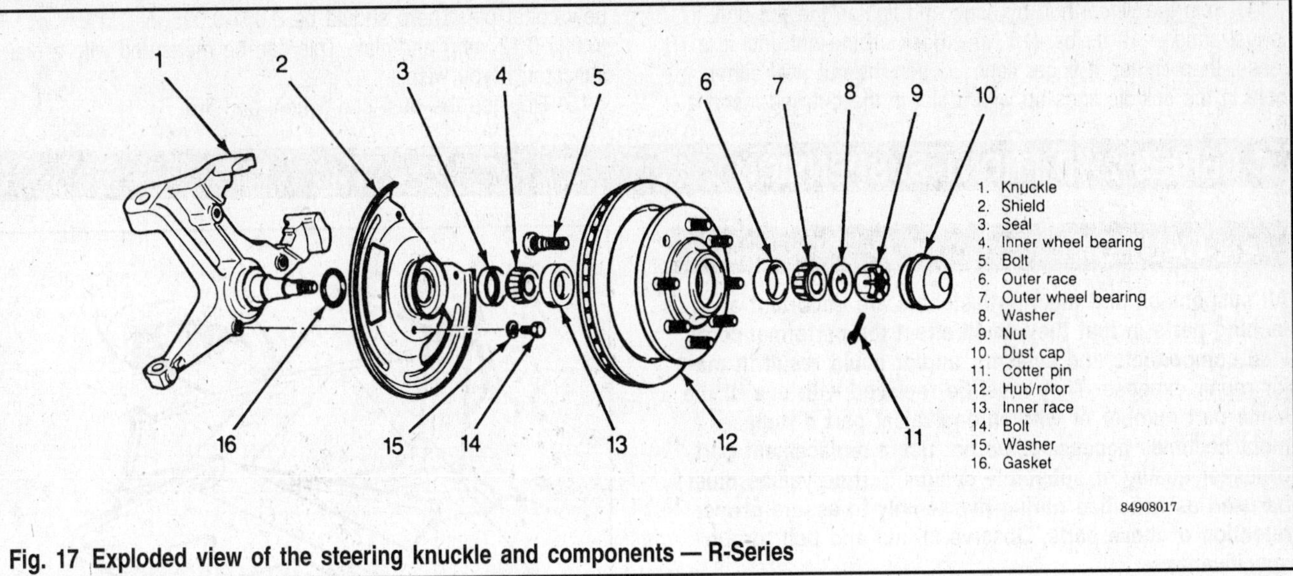

Fig. 17 Exploded view of the steering knuckle and components — R-Series

18. Remove the floor jack.
19. Install a new gasket and the splash shield. Tighten the bolts to 10 ft. lbs. (14 Nm).
20. Connect the tie rod end.
21. Install the hub/rotor assembly.
22. Install the caliper.
23. Adjust the wheel bearings.
24. Install the wheels.
25. Have the alignment checked.

Front Hub, Rotor and Bearings

Before handling the bearings, there are a few things that you should remember to do and not to do.

Remember to DO the following:

- Remove all outside dirt from the housing before exposing the bearing.
- Treat a used bearing as gently as you would a new one.
- Work with clean tools in clean surroundings.
- Use clean, dry canvas gloves, or at least clean, dry hands.
- Clean solvents and flushing fluids are a must.
- Use clean paper when laying out the bearings to dry.
- Protect disassembled bearings from rust and dirt. Cover them up.
- Use clean rags to wipe bearings.
- Keep the bearings in oil-proof paper when they are to be stored or are not in use.
- Clean the inside of the housing before replacing the bearing.

Do NOT do the following:

- Don't work in dirty surroundings.
- Don't use dirty, chipped or damaged tools.
- Try not to work on wooden work benches or use wooden mallets.
- Don't handle bearings with dirty or moist hands.
- Do not use gasoline for cleaning; use a safe solvent.
- Do not spin-dry bearings with compressed air. They will be damaged.
- Do not spin dirty bearings.
- Avoid using cotton waste or dirty cloths to wipe bearings.
- Try not to scratch or nick bearing surfaces.
- Do not allow the bearing to come in contact with dirt or rust at any time.

REMOVAL & INSTALLATION

1. Raise and support the front end on jackstands.
2. Remove the wheel.
3. Dismount the caliper and wire it out of the way.
4. Pry out the grease cap, remove the cotter pin, spindle nut, and washer.
5. Remove the hub. Do not drop the wheel bearings.
6. Remove the outer roller bearing assembly from the hub. The inner bearing assembly will remain in the hub and may be removed after prying out the inner seal. Discard the seal.
7. Using a hammer and drift, remove the bearing races from the hub. They are driven out from the inside out.

To install:

8. Clean all parts in a non-flammable solvent and let them air dry. Never spin-dry a bearing with compressed air! Check for excessive wear and damage.
9. When installing new races, make sure that they are not cocked and that they are fully seated against the hub shoulder.
10. Pack both wheel bearings using high melting point wheel bearing grease for disc brakes. Ordinary grease will melt and ooze out ruining the pads. Bearings should be packed using a cone-type wheel bearing greaser tool. If one is not available they may be packed by hand. Place a healthy glob of grease in the palm of one hand and force the edge of the bearing into it so that the grease fills the bearing. Do this until the whole bearing is packed.
11. Place the inner bearing in the hub and install a new inner seal, making sure that the seal flange faces the bearing race.
12. Carefully install the wheel hub over the spindle.
13. Using your hands, firmly press the outer bearing into the hub. Install the spindle washer and nut.

14. Spin the wheel hub by hand and tighten the nut until it is just snug — 12 ft. lbs. (16 Nm). Back off the nut until it is loose, then tighten it finger tight. Loosen the nut until either hole in the spindle lines up with a slot in the nut and insert a new cotter pin. There should be 0.001-0.005 in. (0.025-0.127mm) end-play. This can be measured with a dial indicator, if you wish.

15. Replace the dust cap, wheel and tire.

C-SERIES 2WD FRONT SUSPENSION

****CAUTION**

All suspension and steering fasteners are important attaching parts in that they could affect the performance of vital components and systems, and/or could result in major repair expense. They must be replaced with one of the same part number or with an equivalent part if replacement becomes necessary. Do not use a replacement part of lesser quality or substitute design. Torque values must be used as specified during reassembly to assure proper retention of these parts. Observe all nut and bolt torque specifications.

Coil Springs

****CAUTION**

Coil springs are under considerable tension. Be very careful when removing and installing them; they can exert enough force to cause serious injury. Always use spring compressors or a safety chain when removing a coil spring, or releasing spring tension!

REMOVAL & INSTALLATION

See Figures 18 and 19

1. Raise and support the truck under the frame rails. The control arms should hang freely.
2. Remove the wheel.
3. Remove the shock absorber.
4. Disconnect the stabilizer bar from the lower control arm.
5. Support the lower control arm and install a spring compressor on the spring, or chain the spring to the control arm as a safety precaution.
6. Raise the jack to remove the tension from the lower control arm pivot bolts. Remove the rear, then the front pivot bolts.

****CAUTION**

The lower control arm keeps the coil spring compressed. Use care when you lower the assembly.

7. Slowly release the jack and lower the control arm until the spring can be removed. Be sure that all compression is relieved from the spring.
8. Place a piece of tape on one of the lower coil so you can tell the top from the bottom during installation. If the spring was chained, remove the chain and spring. If you used spring compressors, remove the spring and slowly release the compressors.

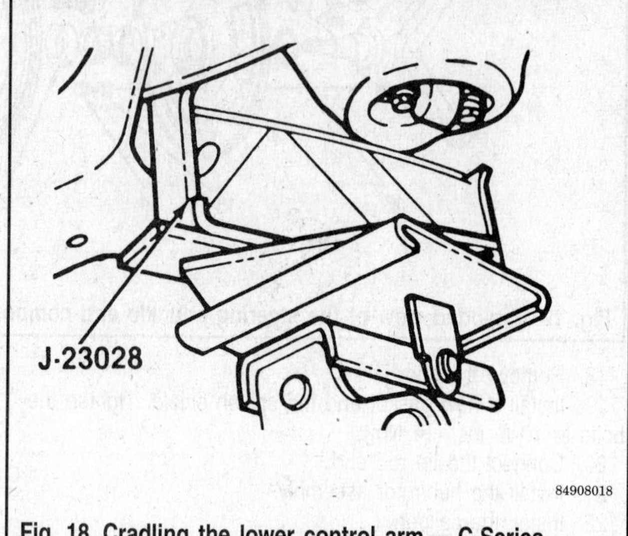

Fig. 18 Cradling the lower control arm — C-Series

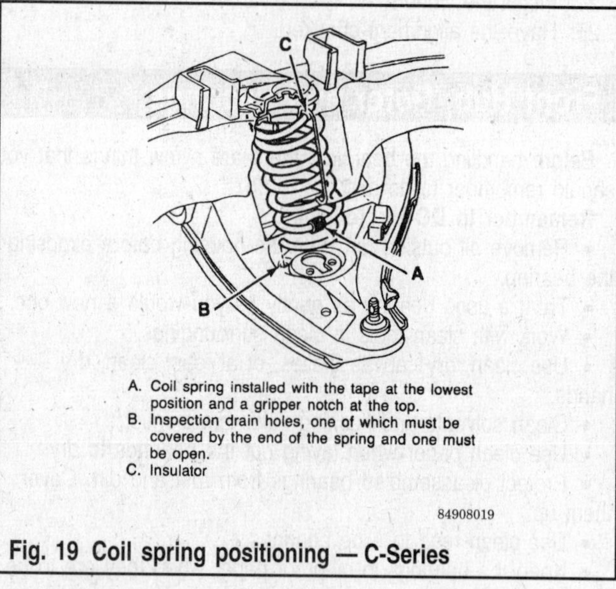

Fig. 19 Coil spring positioning — C-Series

To install:

9. Install the chain and spring. If you used spring compressors, install the spring and compressors.
   - Make sure that the insulator is in place.
   - Make sure that the tape is at the lower end. New springs will have an identifying tape.
   - Make sure that the gripper notch on the top coil is in the frame bracket.
   - Make sure that on drain hole in the lower arm is covered by the bottom coil and the other is open.
10. Slowly raise the jack and lower the control arm. Guide the control arm into place with a prybar.

11. Install the pivot shaft bolts, front one first. The bolts **must** be installed with the heads towards the front of the truck! Remove the safety chain or spring compressors.

➡Do not tighten the bolts yet. The bolts must be torqued with the truck at its proper ride height.

12. Remove the jack.
13. Connect the stabilizer bar to the lower control arm.
14. Install the shock absorber.
15. Install the wheel.
16. Lower the truck. Once the weight of the truck is on the wheels:
    a. Lift the front bumper about 38mm and let it drop.
    b. Repeat this procedure 2 or 3 more times.
    c. Draw a line on the side of the lower control arm from the centerline of the control arm pivot shaft, dead level to the outer end of the control arm.
    d. Measure the distance between the lowest corner of the steering knuckle and the line on the control arm. Record the figure.
    e. Push down about 38mm on the front bumper and let it return. Repeat the procedure 2 or 3 more times.
    f. Re-measure the distance at the control arm.
    g. Determine the average of the 2 measurements. The average distance should be 95.0mm ± 6mm.
    h. If the figure is correct, tighten the control arm pivot nuts to 96 ft. lbs. (130 Nm).
    i. If the figure is not correct, tighten the pivot bolts to 96 ft. lbs. (130 Nm) and have the front end alignment corrected.

Shock Absorbers

REMOVAL & INSTALLATION

➧ See Figure 20

1. Raise and support the front end on jackstands.
2. Remove the wheel.
3. Hold the stem with a wrench and back off the shock absorber upper nut.
4. Remove the nut, retainer and upper grommet.
5. Remove the lower mounting bolts and pull the shock absorber out through the lower control arm.
6. If the shock absorber is being reused, check the grommets for wear and damage. Replace them as needed.

To install:

7. Install the shock absorber onto the vehicle.
8. Tighten the upper nut to 100 inch. lbs. (11 Nm); tighten the lower mounting bolts to 20 ft. lbs. (27 Nm).

Upper Ball Joint

INSPECTION

1. Raise and support the front end on jackstands so that the control arms hang freely.
2. Remove the wheel.
3. The upper ball joint is spring-loaded. Replace the ball joint if there is any lateral movement or if it can be twisted in its socket with your fingers.

REMOVAL & INSTALLATION

➧ See Figures 21, 22, 23, 24 and 25

1. Raise and support the front end on jackstands.
2. Remove the wheel.
3. Support the lower control arm with a floor jack.
4. Remove the cotter pin from the upper ball stud and loosen, but do not remove the stud nut.
5. Using a forcing-type ball joint separator tool, loosen the ball stud in the steering knuckle. When the stud is loose, remove the tool and the stud nut. It may be necessary to remove the brake caliper and wire it to the frame to gain clearance.
6. Drill out the rivets using a ⅛in. drill bit to start a pilot hole. Drill out the rivets with a ½ in. bit. Remove the ball joint assembly using a screw-type forcing tool.

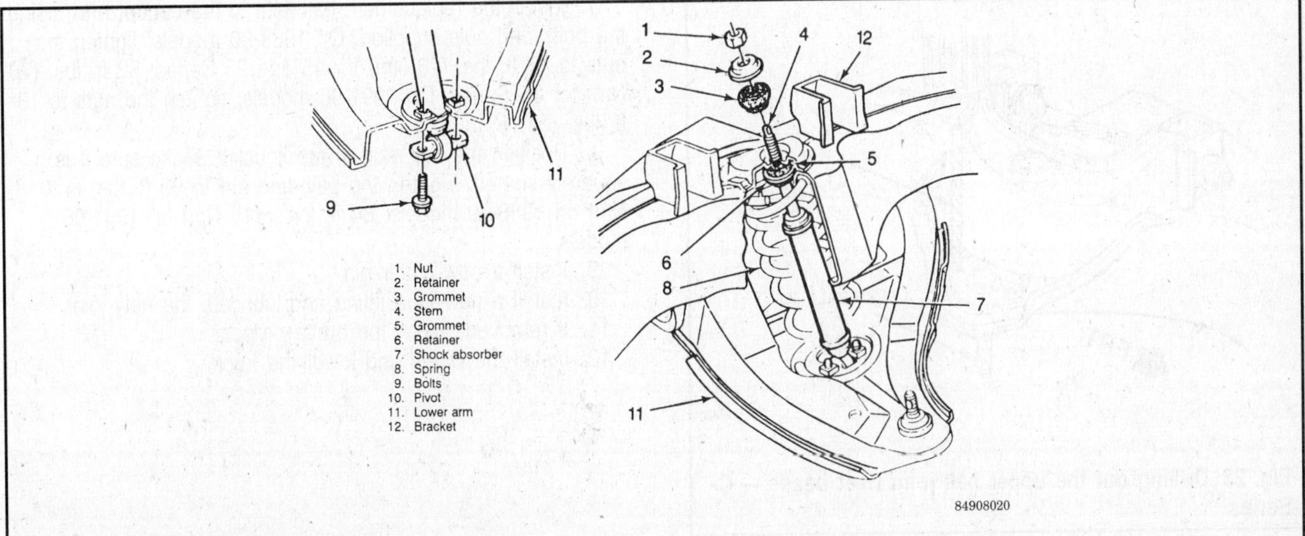

Fig. 20 Installing the shock absorber — C-Series

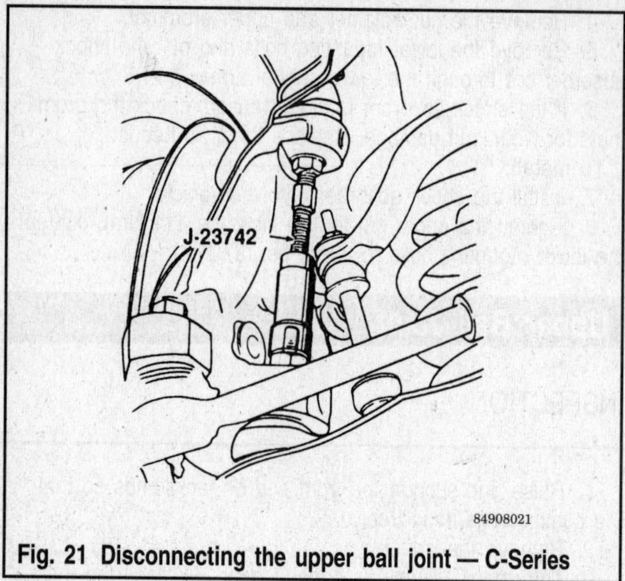

Fig. 21 Disconnecting the upper ball joint — C-Series

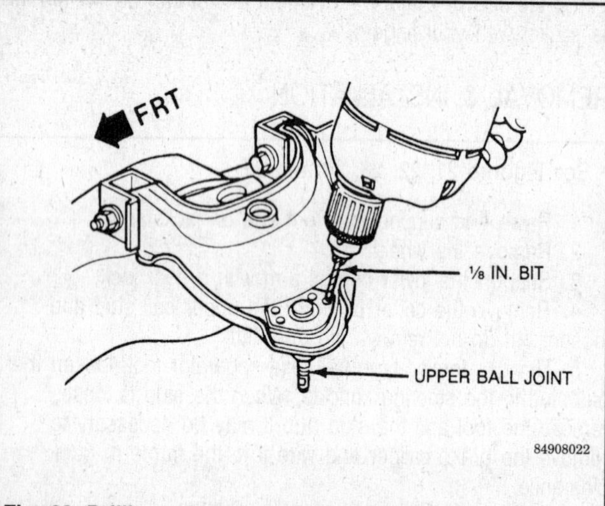

Fig. 22 Drilling out the upper ball joint rivets — C-Series

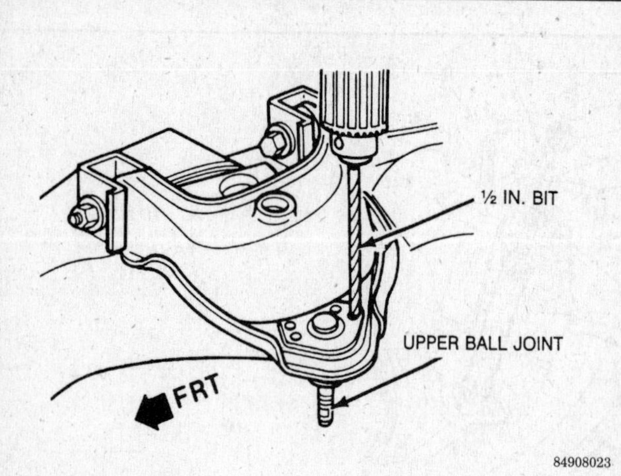

Fig. 23 Drilling out the upper ball joint rivet heads — C-Series

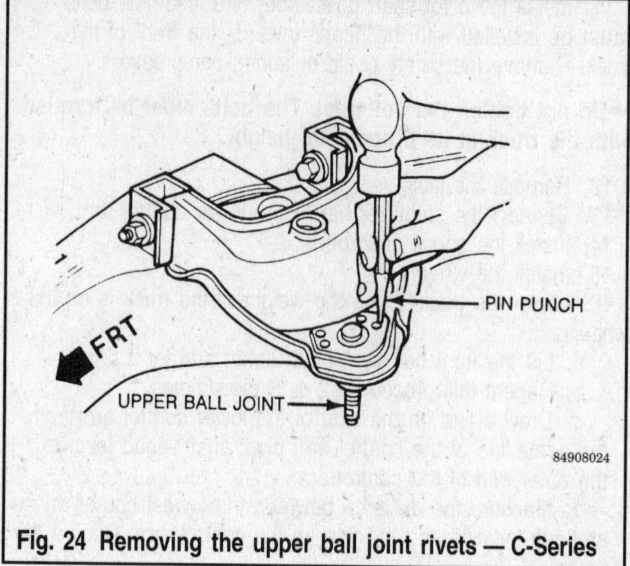

Fig. 24 Removing the upper ball joint rivets — C-Series

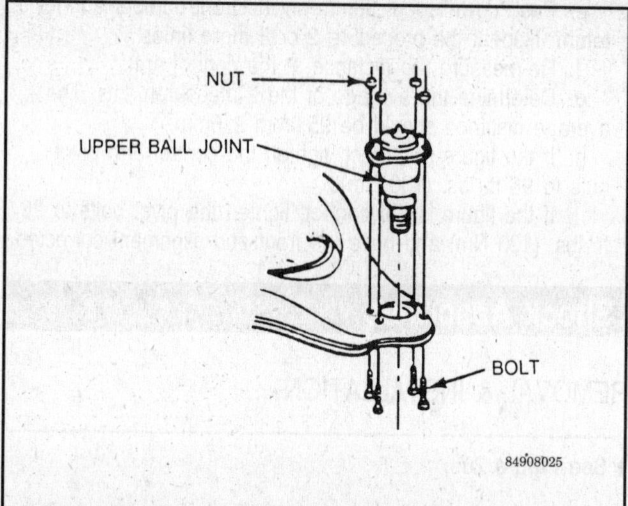

Fig. 25 Installing the upper ball joint (the kit comes with new nuts and bolts) — C-Series

To install:

7. Install the replacement ball joint in the control arm, using the bolts and nuts supplied. On 1988-90 models, tighten the nuts to 17 ft. lbs. (23 Nm) for 15 and 25 Series; 52 ft. lbs. (70 Nm) for 35 Series. On 1991-96 models, tighten the nuts to 18 ft. lbs. (24 Nm).
8. Position the ball stud in the knuckle. Make sure it is squarely seated. Tighten the ball stud nut to 90 ft. lbs. (120 Nm) on 1988-90 models; 84 ft. lbs. (115 Nm) on 1991-96 models.
9. Install a new cotter pin.
10. Install a new lube fitting and lubricate the new joint.
11. If removed, install the brake caliper.
12. Install the wheel and lower the truck.

Lower Ball Joint

INSPECTION

1. Support the weight of the control arm at the wheel hub.
2. Measure the distance between the tip of the ball joint stud and the grease fitting below the ball joint.
3. Move the support to the control arm and allow the hub to hang free. Measure the distance again. If the variation between the two measurements exceeds 3/32 in. (2.4mm) the ball joint should be replaced.

REMOVAL & INSTALLATION

➧ See Figures 26, 27 and 28

1. Raise and support the front end on jackstands.
2. Support the lower control arm with a floor jack.
3. Remove the wheel.
4. Install a spring compressor on the coil spring for safety.
5. Remove the lower stud cotter pin and stud nut.
6. Loosen the ball joint with a forcing-type ball joint tool. It may be necessary to remove the brake caliper and wire it to the frame to gain enough clearance.
7. When the stud is loose, remove the tool and guide the control arm out of the splash shield with a prybar, while lifting the upper control arm with a prybar. Block the knuckle assembly out of the way by placing a wood block between the frame and upper control arm.
8. Remove the ball joint from the control arm with a forcing-type ball joint remover.

To install:

9. Start the new ball joint into the control arm.
10. Force the ball joint into position using a screw-type forcing tool. The ball joint will bottom in the control arm. The grease seal should face inboard.
11. Start ball stud into the knuckle. Install the nut and tighten it to 90 ft. lbs. (122 Nm) on 1988-90 models; 84 ft. lbs. (115 Nm) on 1991-94 models; 94 ft. lbs. (128 Nm) on 1995-96 models. Advance the nut to align the cotter pin hole and insert the new cotter pin. NEVER back off the nut to align the cotter pin hole; always advance it!
12. Install the brake caliper, if removed.
13. Install a new lube fitting and lubricate the new joint.
14. Install the wheel.
15. Lower the truck.
16. Check the front end alignment.

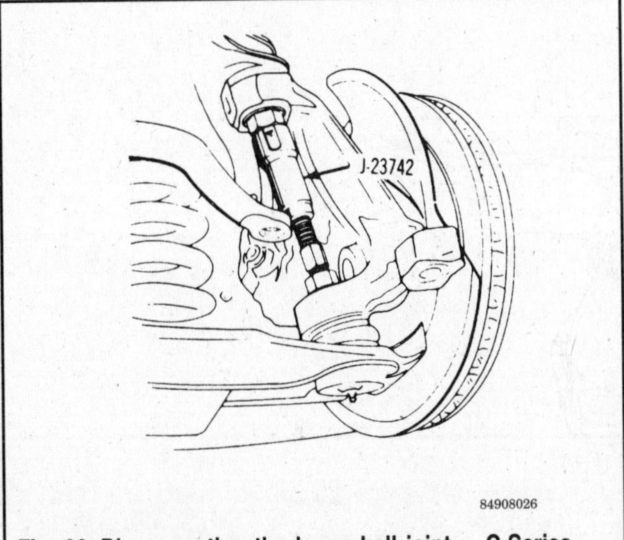

Fig. 26 Disconnecting the lower ball joint — C-Series

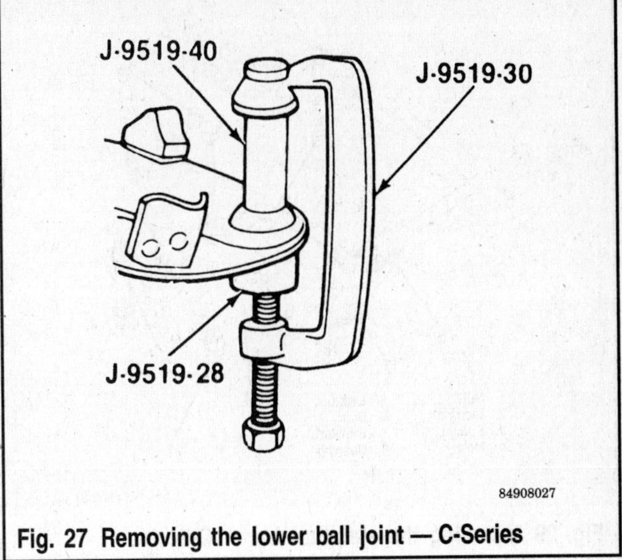

Fig. 27 Removing the lower ball joint — C-Series

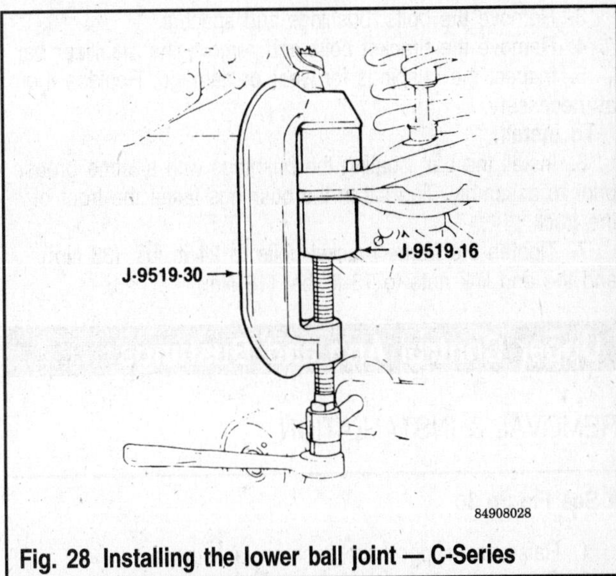

Fig. 28 Installing the lower ball joint — C-Series

Stabilizer Bar

REMOVAL & INSTALLATION

➧ See Figure 29

➡The end link bushings, bolts and spacers are not interchangeable from left to right, so keep them separate.

1. Raise and support the front end on jackstands.
2. Remove the nuts from the end link bolts.

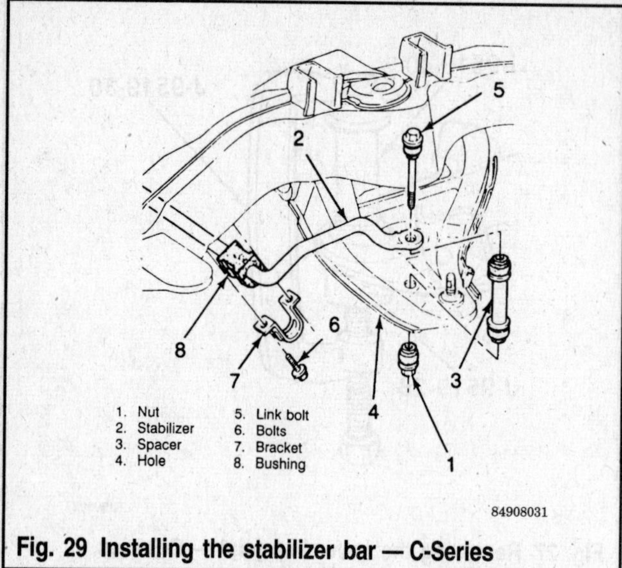

Fig. 29 Installing the stabilizer bar — C-Series

3. Remove the bolts, bushings and spacers.
4. Remove the bracket bolts and remove the stabilizer bar.
5. Inspect the bushings for wear or damage. Replace them as necessary.

To install:

6. Install the bar, coating the bushings with silicone grease prior to assembly. The slit in the bushings faces the front of the truck.
7. Tighten the frame bracket bolts to 24 ft. lbs. (33 Nm) and the end link nuts to 13 ft. lbs. (18 Nm).

Upper Control Arm and Bushings

REMOVAL & INSTALLATION

See Figure 30

1. Raise and support the truck on jackstands.
2. Support the lower control arm with a floor jack.
3. Remove the wheel.
4. Remove the air cleaner extension (if necessary).
5. Unbolt the brake hose bracket from the control arm.
6. Remove the cotter pin from the upper control arm ball stud and loosen the stud nut until the bottom surface of the nut is slightly below the end of the stud.
7. Install a spring compressor on the coil spring for safety.
8. Using a screw-type forcing tool, break loose the ball joint from the knuckle.
9. Remove the nuts and bolts securing the control arm to the frame brackets.
10. Tape the shims and spacers together and tag for proper reassembly. The 35 Series bushings are replaceable. The 15/25 Series bushings are welded in place.

To install:

11. Place the control arm in position and install the shims, bolts and new nuts. Both bolt heads **must** be inboard of the control arm brackets. Tighten the nuts finger tighten for now.

➡Do not tighten the bolts yet. The bolts must be torqued with the truck at its proper ride height.

12. Install the ball stud nut. Tighten the nut to 90 ft. lbs. (122 Nm). Install the cotter pin. Never back off the nut to install the cotter pin. Always advance it.
13. Install the brake caliper.
14. Remove the spring compressor or safety chain.
15. Install the wheel.
16. Install the brake hose.
17. Install the air cleaner extension.
18. Install the battery ground cable.
19. Lower the truck. Once the weight of the truck is on the wheels:
    a. Lift the front bumper about 38mm and let it drop.
    b. Repeat this procedure 2 or 3 more times.
    c. Draw a line on the side of the lower control arm from the centerline of the control arm pivot shaft, dead level to the outer end of the control arm.
    d. Measure the distance between the lowest corner of the steering knuckle and the line on the control arm. Record the figure.
    e. Push down about 38mm on the front bumper and let it return. Repeat the procedure 2 or 3 more times.

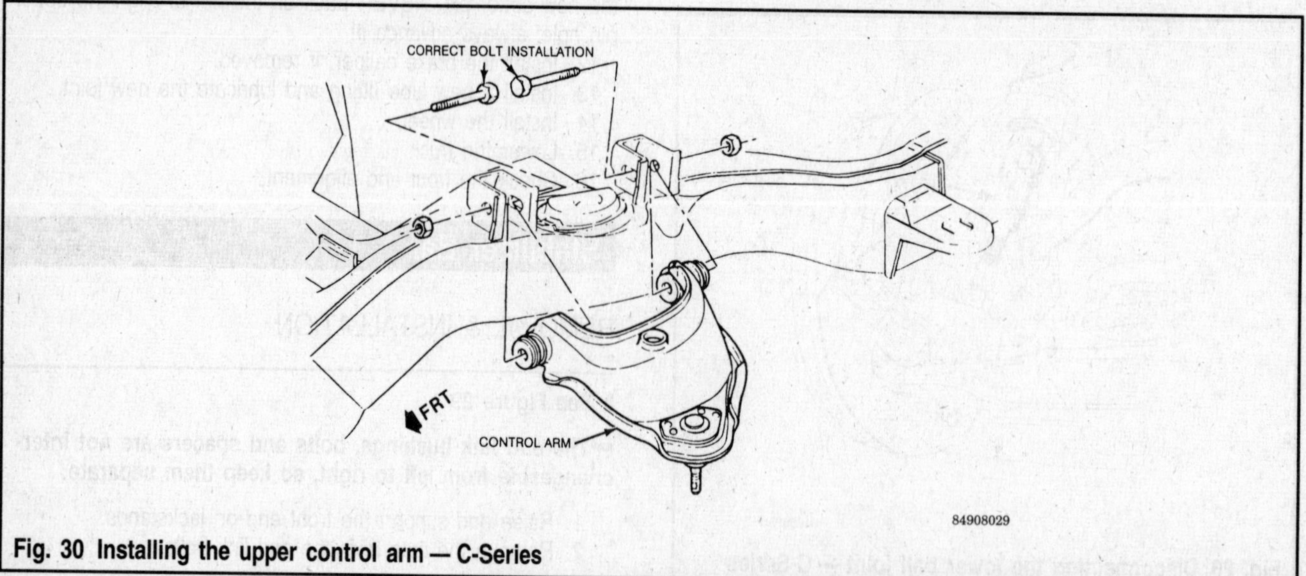

Fig. 30 Installing the upper control arm — C-Series

f. Re-measure the distance at the control arm.

g. Determine the average of the 2 measurements. The average distance should be 95.0mm ± 6mm.

h. If the figure is correct, tighten the control arm pivot nuts to 88 ft. lbs. (120 Nm) on 1988-90 models; 140 ft. lbs. (190 Nm) on 1991-96 models.

i. If the figure is not correct, tighten the pivot bolts to 88 ft. lbs. (120 Nm) on 1988-90 models; 140 ft. lbs. (190 Nm) on 1991-96 models and have the front end alignment corrected.

Lower Control Arm and Bushing

REMOVAL & INSTALLATION

▶ **See Figure 31**

1. Raise and support the truck on jackstands.
2. Remove the coil spring.
3. Support the inboard end of the control arm after spring removal.
4. Remove the cotter pin from the lower ball stud and loosen the nut.
5. Loosen the lower ball stud in the steering knuckle using a ball joint stud removal tool. When the stud is loose, remove the nut from the stud. It may be necessary to remove the brake caliper and wire it to the frame to gain clearance.
6. Remove the lower control arm.

To install:

7. Slowly raise the jack and lower the control arm. Guide the control arm into place with a prybar.
8. Install the pivot shaft bolts, front one first. The bolts **must** be installed with the heads towards the front of the truck! Remove the safety chain or spring compressors.

➡**Do not tighten the bolts yet. The bolts must be torqued with the truck at its proper ride height.**

9. Remove the jack.
10. Connect the stabilizer bar to the lower control arm. Tighten the nuts to 13 ft. lbs. (17 Nm).
11. Install the shock absorber.
12. Install the wheel.
13. Lower the truck. Once the weight of the truck is on the wheels:

a. Lift the front bumper about 38mm and let it drop.

b. Repeat this procedure 2 or 3 more times.

c. Draw a line on the side of the lower control arm from the centerline of the control arm pivot shaft, dead level to the outer end of the control arm.

d. Measure the distance between the lowest corner of the steering knuckle and the line on the control arm. Record the figure.

e. Push down about 38mm on the front bumper and let it return. Repeat the procedure 2 or 3 more times.

f. Re-measure the distance at the control arm.

g. Determine the average of the 2 measurements. The average distance should be 95.0mm ± 6mm.

h. If the figure is correct, tighten the control arm pivot nuts to 96 ft. lbs. (130 Nm) on 1988-90 models; 121 ft. lbs. (165 Nm) on 1991-94 models; 137 ft. lbs. (101 Nm) on 1991-96 models.

i. If the figure is not correct, tighten the pivot bolts to 96 ft. lbs. (130 Nm) on 1988-90 models; 121 ft. lbs. (165 Nm) on 1991-93 models and have the front end alignment corrected; 137 ft. lbs. (101 Nm) on 1991-96 models.

Steering Knuckle

REMOVAL & INSTALLATION

▶ **See Figures 32 and 33**

1. Raise and support the front end on jackstands. Let the control arms hang freely.
2. Remove the wheels.
3. Disconnect the tie rod end from the knuckle.
4. Dismount the caliper and suspend it out of the way without disconnecting the brake lines.
5. Remove the hub/rotor assembly.

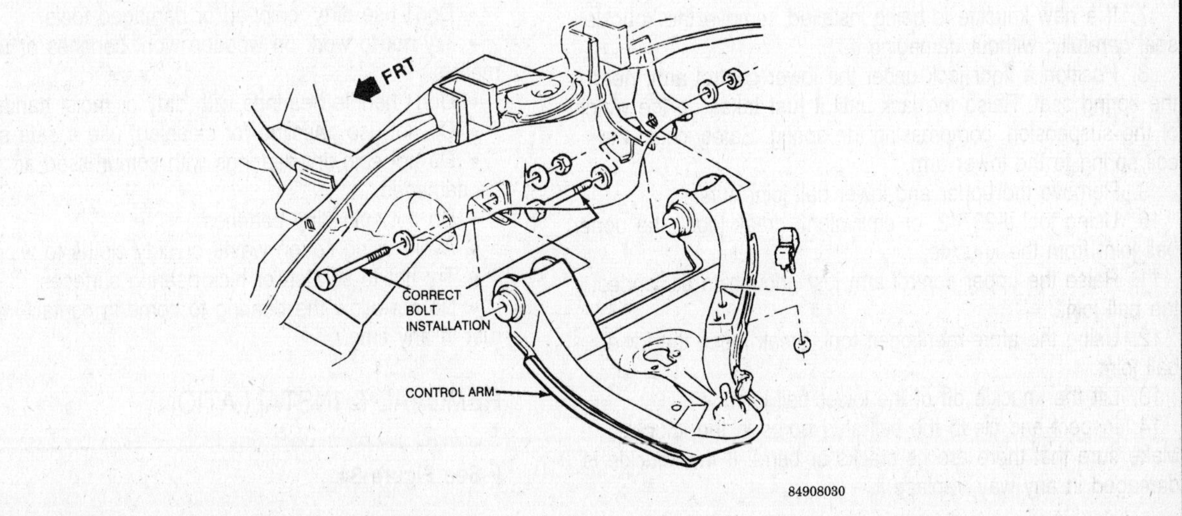

Fig. 31 Installing the lower control arm — C-Series

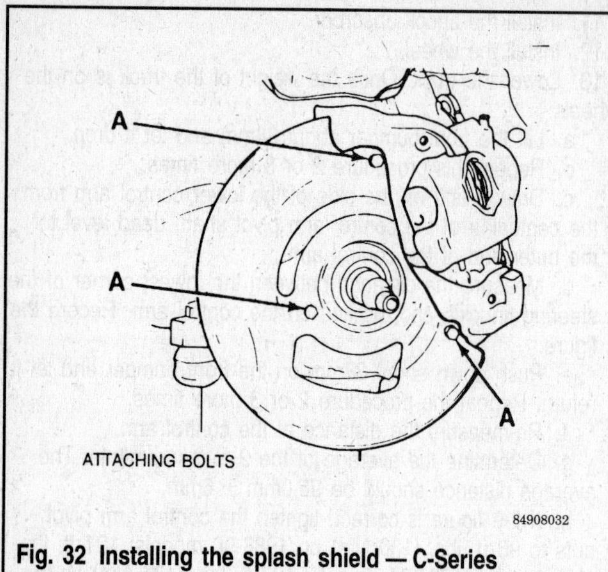

Fig. 32 Installing the splash shield — C-Series

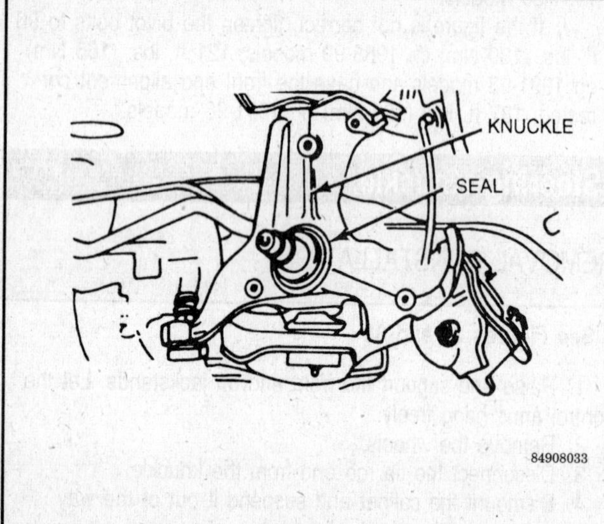

Fig. 33 Locating the seal on the yoke — C-Series

6. Unbolt the splash shield from the knuckle and discard the old gasket.
7. If a new knuckle is being installed, remove the knuckle seal carefully, without damaging it.
8. Position a floor jack under the lower control arm, near the spring seat. Raise the jack until it **just** takes up the weight of the suspension, compressing the spring. Safety-chain the coil spring to the lower arm.
9. Remove the upper and lower ball joint nuts.
10. Using tool J-23742, or equivalent, break loose the upper ball joint from the knuckle.
11. Raise the upper control arm just enough to disconnect the ball joint.
12. Using the afore-mentioned tool, break loose the lower ball joint.
13. Lift the knuckle off of the lower ball joint.
14. Inspect and clean the ball stud bores in the knuckle. Make sure that there are no cracks or burrs. If the knuckle is damaged in any way, replace it.
15. Check the spindle for wear, heat discoloration or damage. If at all damaged, replace it.

To install:

16. Maneuver the knuckle onto both ball joints.
17. Install both nuts. Tighten the nuts to 90 ft. lbs. (120 Nm) on 1988-90 models; 84 ft. lbs. (115 Nm) on 1991-96 models.
18. Install new cotter pins. Always advance the nut to align the cotter pin hole. NEVER back it off!
19. Install the knuckle seal.
20. Remove the floor jack.
21. Install a new gasket and the splash shield. Tighten the bolts to 12 ft. lbs. (16 Nm) on 1988-90 models; 19 ft. lbs. (26 Nm) on 1991-96 models.
22. Connect the tie rod end.
23. Install the hub/rotor assembly.
24. Install the caliper.
25. Adjust the wheel bearings.
26. Install the wheels.
27. Have the alignment checked.

Front Hub, Rotor and Bearings

Before handling the bearings, there are a few things that you should remember to do and not to do.

Remember to DO the following:

- Remove all outside dirt from the housing before exposing the bearing.
- Treat a used bearing as gently as you would a new one.
- Work with clean tools in clean surroundings.
- Use clean, dry canvas gloves, or at least clean, dry hands.
- Clean solvents and flushing fluids are a must.
- Use clean paper when laying out the bearings to dry.
- Protect disassembled bearings from rust and dirt. Cover them up.
- Use clean rags to wipe bearings.
- Keep the bearings in oil-proof paper when they are to be stored or are not in use.
- Clean the inside of the housing before replacing the bearing.

Do NOT do the following:

- Don't work in dirty surroundings.
- Don't use dirty, chipped or damaged tools.
- Try not to work on wooden work benches or use wooden mallets.
- Don't handle bearings with dirty or moist hands.
- Do not use gasoline for cleaning; use a safe solvent.
- Do not spin-dry bearings with compressed air. They will be damaged.
- Do not spin dirty bearings.
- Avoid using cotton waste or dirty cloths to wipe bearings.
- Try not to scratch or nick bearing surfaces.
- Do not allow the bearing to come in contact with dirt or rust at any time.

REMOVAL & INSTALLATION

➧ **See Figure 34**

1. Raise and support the front end on jackstands.
2. Remove the wheel.

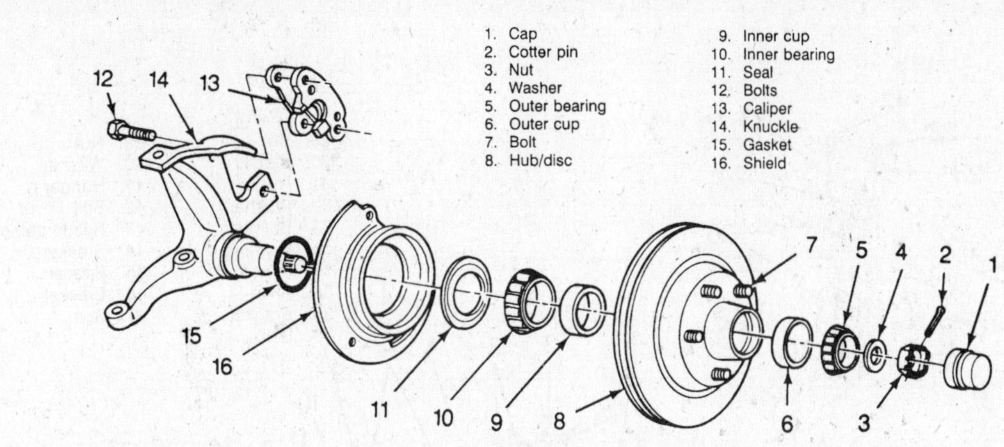

Fig. 34 Exploded view of the hub, knuckle and bearings — C-Series

3. Dismount the caliper and wire it out of the way.

4. Pry out the grease cap, remove the cotter pin, spindle nut, and washer, then remove the hub. Do not drop the wheel bearings.

5. Remove the outer roller bearing assembly from the hub. The inner bearing assembly will remain in the hub and may be removed after prying out the inner seal. Discard the seal.

6. Clean all parts in a non-flammable solvent and let them air dry. Never spin-dry a bearing with compressed air! Check for excessive wear and damage.

7. Using a hammer and drift, remove the bearing races from the hub. They are driven out from the inside out.

To install:

8. Install new bearing races, if required. When installing new races, make sure that they are not cocked and that they are fully seated against the hub shoulder.

9. Pack both wheel bearings using high melting point wheel bearing grease for disc brakes. Ordinary grease will melt and ooze out ruining the pads. Bearings should be packed using a cone-type wheel bearing greaser tool. If one is not available they may be packed by hand. Place a healthy glob of grease in the palm of one hand and force the edge of the bearing into it so that the grease fills the bearing. Do this until the whole bearing is packed.

10. Place the inner bearing in the hub and install a new inner seal, making sure that the seal flange faces the bearing race.

11. Carefully install the wheel hub over the spindle.

12. Using your hands, firmly press the outer bearing into the hub. Install the spindle washer and nut.

13. Spin the wheel hub by hand and tighten the nut until it is just snug — 12 ft. lbs. (16 Nm). Back off the nut until it is loose, then tighten it finger tight. Loosen the nut until either hole in the spindle lines up with a slot in the nut and insert a new cotter pin. There should be 0.001-0.008 in. (0.025-0.200mm) end-play. This can be measured with a dial indicator, if you wish.

14. Replace the dust cap, wheel and tire.

V-SERIES 4WD FRONT SUSPENSION

✲✲CAUTION

All suspension and steering fasteners are important attaching parts in that they could affect the performance of vital components and systems, and/or could result in major repair expense. They must be replaced with one of the same part number or with an equivalent part if replacement becomes necessary. Do not use a replacement part of lesser quality or substitute design. Torque values must be used as specified during reassembly to assure proper retention of these parts. Observe all nut and bolt torque specifications.

Leaf Spring

REMOVAL & INSTALLATION

See Figures 35, 36 and 37

1. Raise and support the vehicle so that all tension is taken off of the front suspension.

2. Remove the shackle retaining bolts, nuts and spacers.

3. Remove the front spring-to-frame bracket bolt, washer and nut.

4. On the 10/1500 and 20/2500 both sides and the 30/3500 left side: remove the U-bolt nuts, washers, U-bolts, plate and spacers.

5. On the 30/3500 right side: remove the inboard spring plate bolts, U-bolt nuts, washers, U-bolt, plate and spacers.

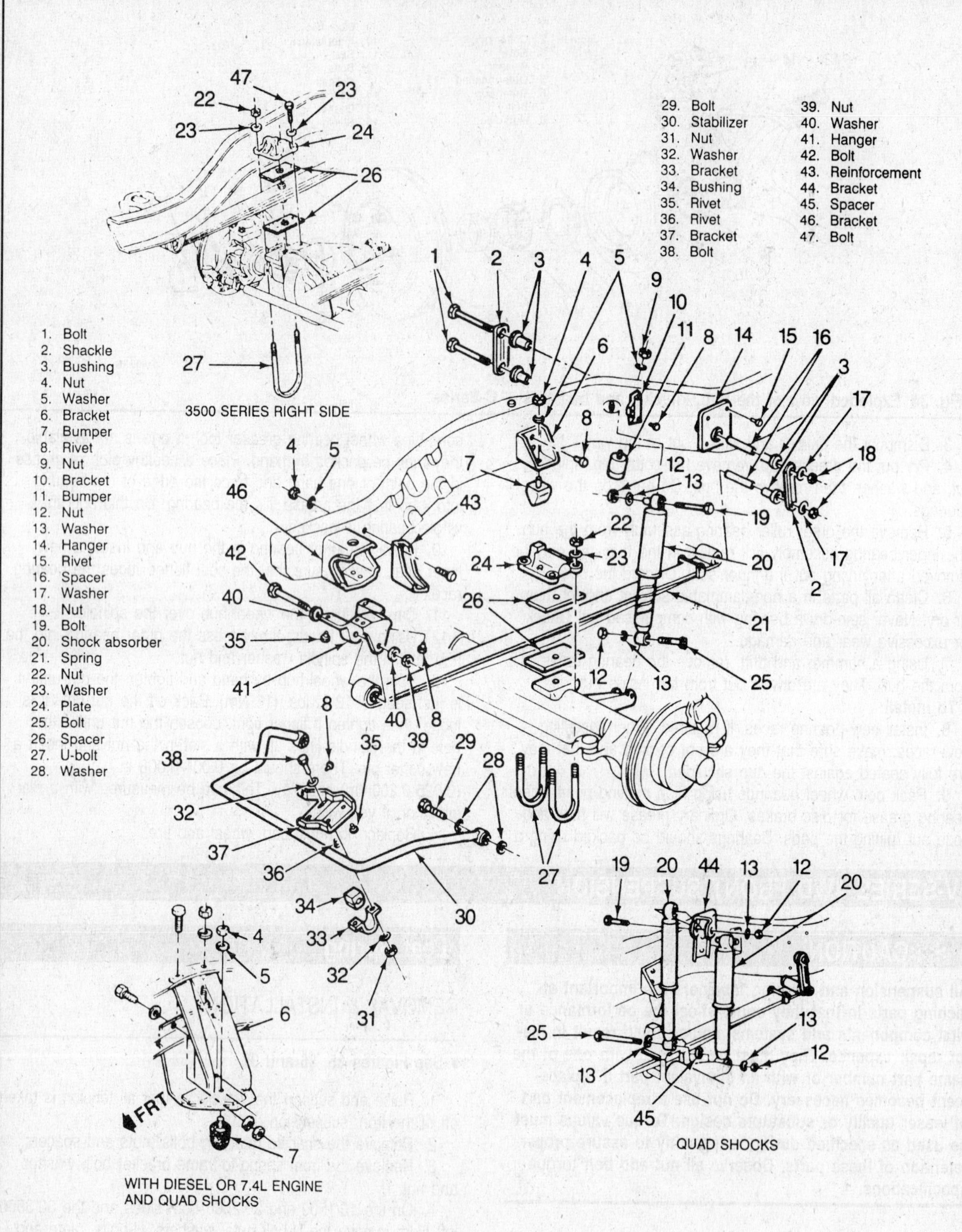

Fig. 35 Exploded view of the front suspension system — V-Series

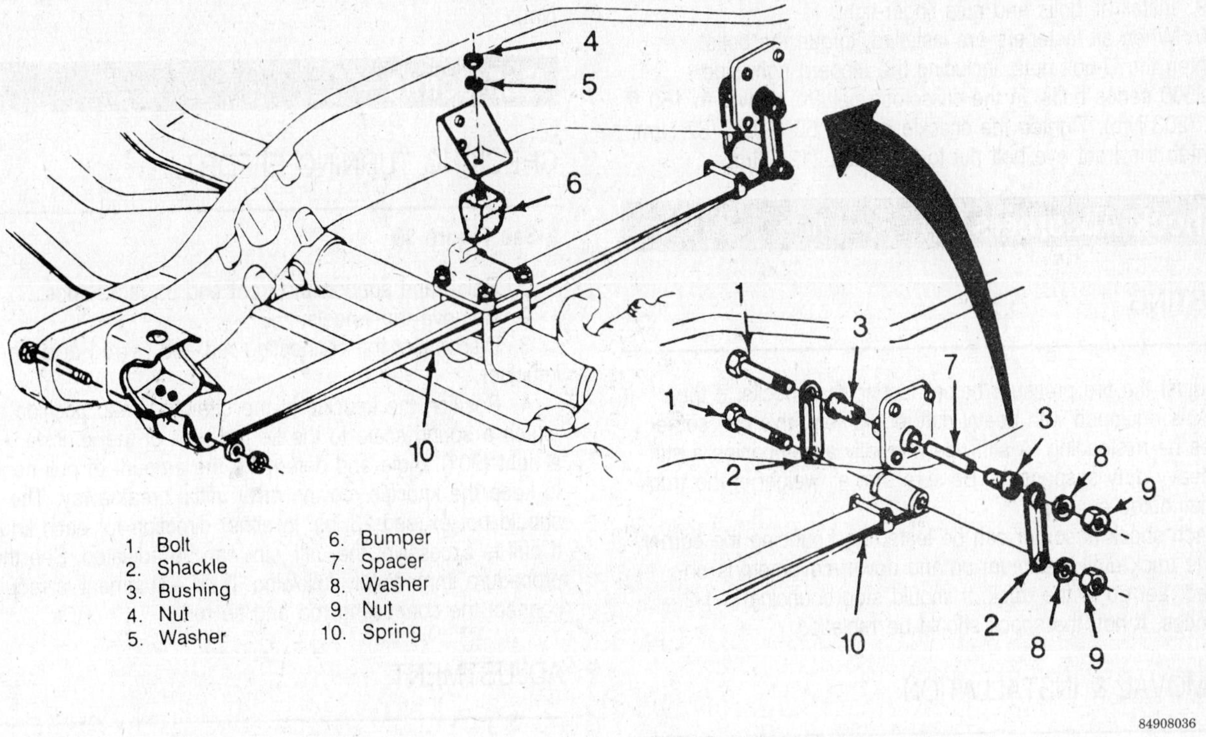

4
5
6
1
3
7
1
3
8
9
2
10
2
8
9
10
1. Bolt
2. Shackle
3. Bushing
4. Nut
5. Washer
6. Bumper
7. Spacer
8. Washer
9. Nut
10. Spring
84908036

Fig. 36 Installing the leaf spring — V-Series

FRT
3
2
4
1
3
1
1
4
3
2
1
FRT
2
2
1. Spring
2. U-bolt
3. Bolt
30/3500 SERIES RIGHT SIDE
ALL SERIES LEFT SIDE
84908037

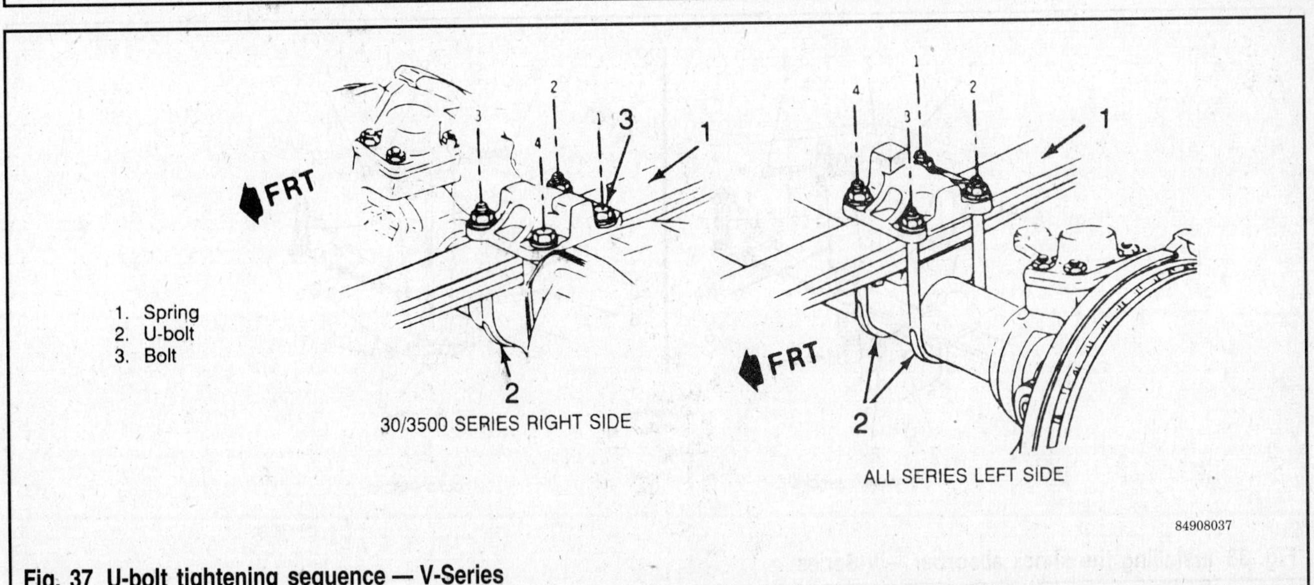

Fig. 37 U-bolt tightening sequence — V-Series

6. To replace the bushing, place the spring in a press or vise and press out the bushing.

To install:

7. Press in the new bushing. The new bushing should protrude evenly on both sides of the spring.
8. Install the spring. Coat all bushings with silicone grease prior to installation.
9. Install all bolts and nuts finger-tight.
10. When all fasteners are installed, torque the bolts. Tighten the U-bolt nuts, including the inboard right side 30/3500 series bolts, in the crisscross pattern shown, to 150 ft. lbs. (203 Nm). Tighten the shackle nuts to 50 ft. lbs. (67 Nm). Tighten the front eye bolt nut to 90 ft. lbs. (122 Nm).

Shock Absorbers

TESTING

Adjust the tire pressure before testing the shocks. If the truck is equipped with heavy duty equipment, this can sometimes be misleading. A stiff ride normally accompanies a stiff or heavy duty suspension. Be sure that all weight in the truck is distributed evenly.

Each shock absorber can be tested by bouncing the corner of the truck until maximum up and down movement is obtained. Let go of the truck. It should stop bouncing in 1-2 bounces. If not, the shock should be replaced.

REMOVAL & INSTALLATION

Dual or Quad Shocks

➧ See Figure 38

1. Raise and support the front end on jackstands.
2. Remove the nuts and eye bolts securing the upper and lower shock absorber eyes. Quad shocks have a spacer between the lower end bushings.
3. Remove the shock absorber(s) and inspect the rubber eye bushings. If these are defective, replace the shock absorber assembly.
4. Make sure that the spacer is installed at the bottom end on quad shocks. Tighten the upper end nut to 65 ft. lbs. (88 Nm). On dual shocks, tighten the lower end to 65 ft. lbs. (88 Nm). On quad shocks, tighten the lower end to 89 ft. lbs. (120 Nm).

Ball Joints

CHECKING TURNING EFFORT

➧ See Figure 39

1. Raise and support the front end on jackstands.
2. Remove the wheels.
3. Disconnect the connecting rod and tie rod at each knuckle.
4. Position the knuckle in the straight-ahead position and attach a spring scale to the tie rod hole of the knuckle. Pull at a right (90°) angle and determine the amount of pull necessary to keep the knuckle moving **after** initial break-away. The pull should not exceed 25 lbs. in either direction for each knuckle. If pull is excessive, the ball joint can be adjusted. See the procedure immediately following. If no adjustment is required, connect the connecting rod and tie rod.

ADJUSTMENT

➡Tool J-23447, or its equivalent, is necessary for this procedure.

1. Raise and support the front end on jackstands.
2. Remove the wheels.
3. Remove the cotter pin and nut from the upper ball joint.
4. Using tool J-23447, back off the adjusting ring no more than 2 threads, then, tighten the adjusting ring to 50 ft. lbs.

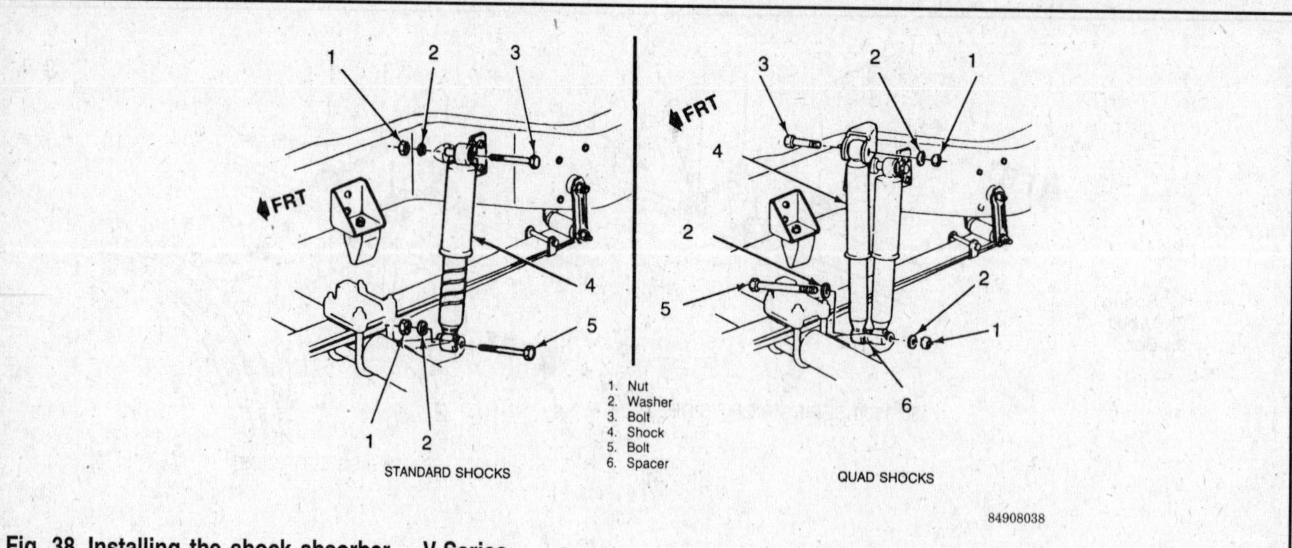

Fig. 38 Installing the shock absorber — V-Series

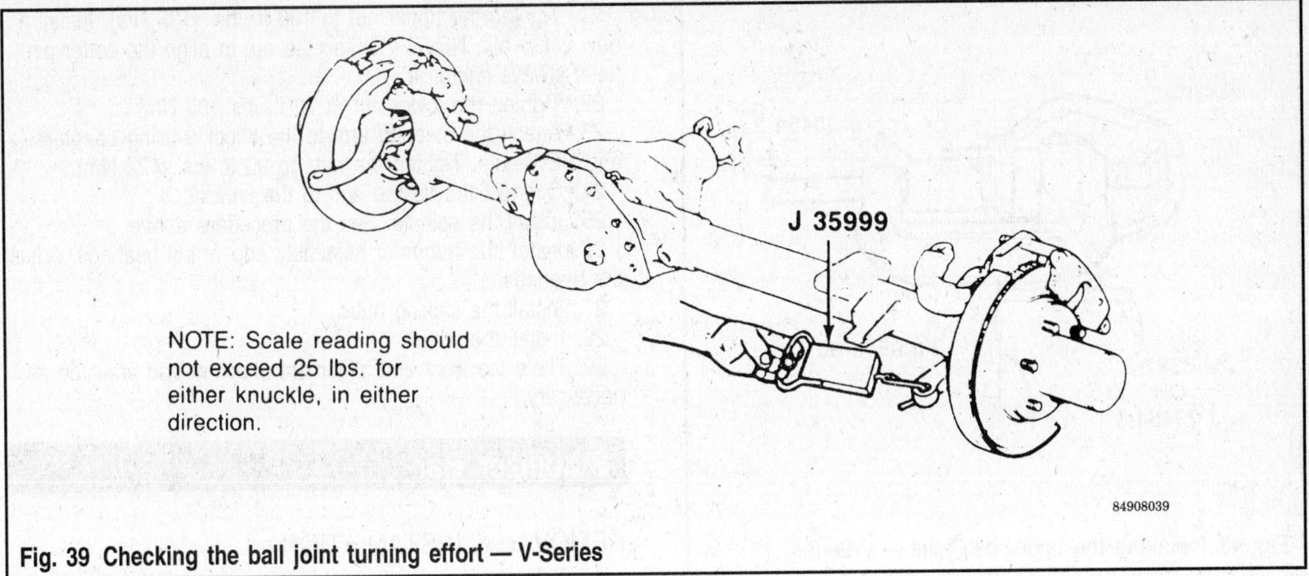

Fig. 39 Checking the ball joint turning effort — V-Series

5. Install the upper nut. Tighten the upper nut to 100 ft. lbs. Install a new cotter pin. NEVER loosen the nut to align the cotter pin hole; always tighten it.
6. Install the wheel.

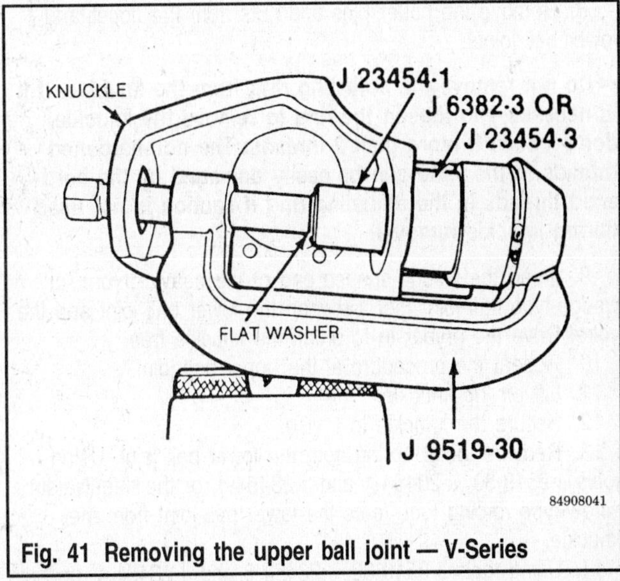

Fig. 41 Removing the upper ball joint — V-Series

REMOVAL & INSTALLATION

See Figures 40, 41, 42 and 43

The following special tools, or their equivalents, are necessary for this procedure: J-9519-30, J-23454-1, J-23454-4, J-23454-3, J-23454-2, J-23447.

1. Raise and support the front end on jackstands.
2. Remove the wheels.
3. Remove the locking hubs.
4. Remove the spindle.
5. Disconnect the tie rod end from the knuckle.
6. Remove the knuckle-to-steering arm nuts and adapters.
7. Remove the steering arm from the knuckle.

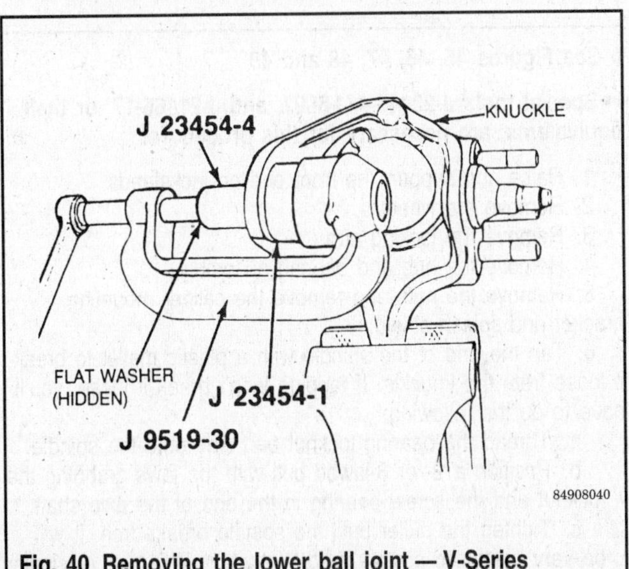

Fig. 40 Removing the lower ball joint — V-Series

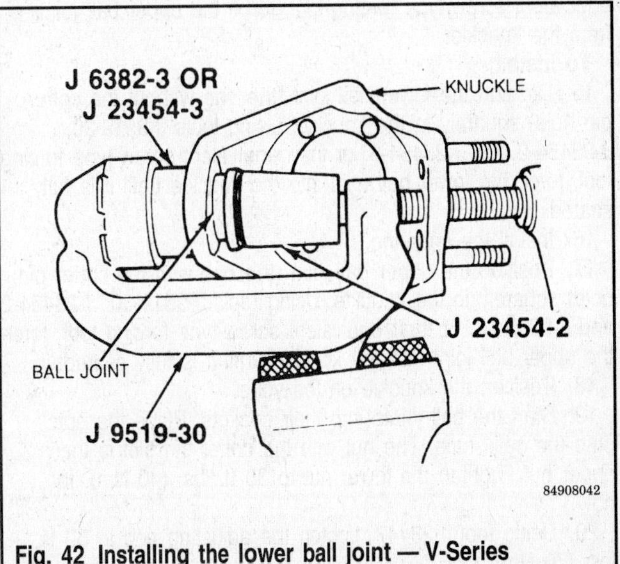

Fig. 42 Installing the lower ball joint — V-Series

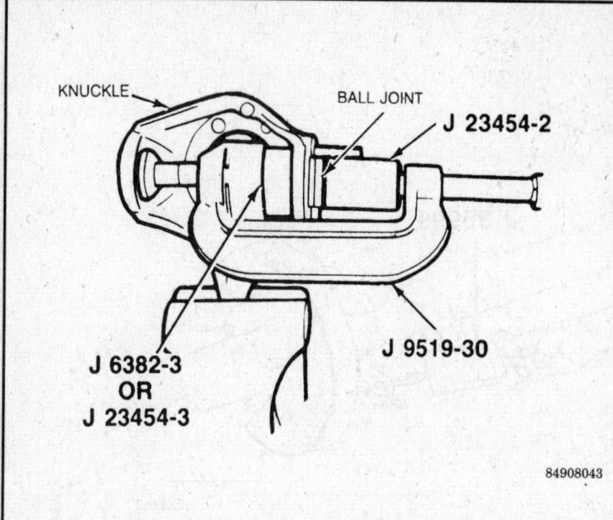

Fig. 43 Installing the upper ball joint — V-Series

8. Remove the cotter pins and nuts from the upper and lower ball joints.

➡Do not remove the adjusting ring from the knuckle. If it is necessary to loosen the ring to remove the knuckle, don't loosen it more than 2 threads. The non-hardened threads in the yoke can be easily damaged by the hardened threads in the adjusting ring if caution is not used during knuckle removal!

9. Insert the wedge-shaped end of the heavy prybar, or wedge-type ball joint tool, between the lower ball joint and the yoke. Drive the prybar in to break the knuckle free.
10. Repeat the procedure at the upper ball joint.
11. Lift off the knuckle.
12. Secure the knuckle in a vise.
13. Remove the snapring from the lower ball joint. Using tools J-9519-30, J-23454-1 and J-23454-4, or their equivalent screw-type forcing tool, force the lower ball joint from the knuckle.
14. Using tools J-9519-30, J-23454-3 and J-23454-4, or their equivalent screw-type forcing tool, force the upper ball joint from the knuckle.

To install:

15. Position the lower ball joint (the one without the cotter pin hole) squarely in the knuckle. Using tools J-9519-30, J-23454-2 and J-23454-3, or their equivalent screw-type forcing tool, force the lower ball joint into the knuckle until it is fully seated.
16. Install the snapring.
17. Position the upper ball joint (the one with the cotter pin hole) squarely in the knuckle. Using tools J-9519-30, J-23454-2 and J-23454-3, or their equivalent screw-type forcing tool, force the upper ball joint into the knuckle until it is fully seated.
18. Position the knuckle on the yoke.
19. Start the ball joints into their sockets. Place the nuts onto the ball studs. The nut with the cotter pin slot is the upper nut. Tighten the lower nut to 30 ft. lbs. (40 Nm), for now.
20. Using tool J-23447, tighten the adjusting ring to 50 ft. lbs. (70 Nm).
21. Tighten the upper nut to 100 ft. lbs. (135 Nm). Install a new cotter pin. NEVER loosen the nut to align the cotter pin hole; always tighten it.
22. Tighten the lower nut to 70 ft. lbs. (95 Nm).
23. Attach the steering arm to the knuckle using adapters and NEW nuts. Tighten the nuts to 90 ft. lbs. (122 Nm).
24. Connect the tie rod end to the knuckle.
25. Install the spindle. See the procedure above.
26. Install the hub/rotor assembly and wheel bearings. Adjust the bearings.
27. Install the locking hubs.
28. Install the wheel.
29. Have the front end alignment checked and adjusted as necessary.

Stabilizer Bar

REMOVAL & INSTALLATION

➧ See Figure 44

1. Raise and support the front end on jackstands.
2. Remove the wheels.
3. Remove the stabilizer bar-to-frame clamps.
4. Remove the stabilizer bar-to-spring plate bolts.
5. Remove the stabilizer bar and bushings.
6. Check the bushings for wear or splitting. Replace any damaged bushings.
7. When installing, note that the split in the bushing faces forward. Coat the bushings with silicone grease prior to installation. Install all fasteners finger-tight. When all the fasteners are in place, tighten the stabilizer bar-to-frame nuts to 52 ft. lbs. (70 Nm). Tighten the stabilizer bar-to-spring plate bolts to 133 ft. lbs. (180 Nm).

Spindle

REMOVAL & INSTALLATION

➧ See Figures 45, 46, 47, 48 and 49

➡Special tools J-23445-A/J-8092, and J-21465-17, or their equivalents, are necessary for this procedure.

1. Raise and support the front end on jackstands.
2. Remove the wheel.
3. Remove the locking hub.
4. Remove the hub and bearing assembly.
5. Remove the nuts and remove the caliper mounting bracket and splash shield.
6. Tap the end of the spindle with a plastic mallet to break it loose from the knuckle. If tapping won't break it loose, you'll have to do the following:
   a. Thread the bearing locknut part way onto the spindle.
   b. Position a 2- or 3-jawed pull with the jaws grabbing the locknut and the screw bearing in the end of the axle shaft.
   c. Tighten the puller until the spindle breaks free. It will be very helpful to spray Liquid Wrench®, WD-40® or similar solvent around the spindle mating area and around the bolt

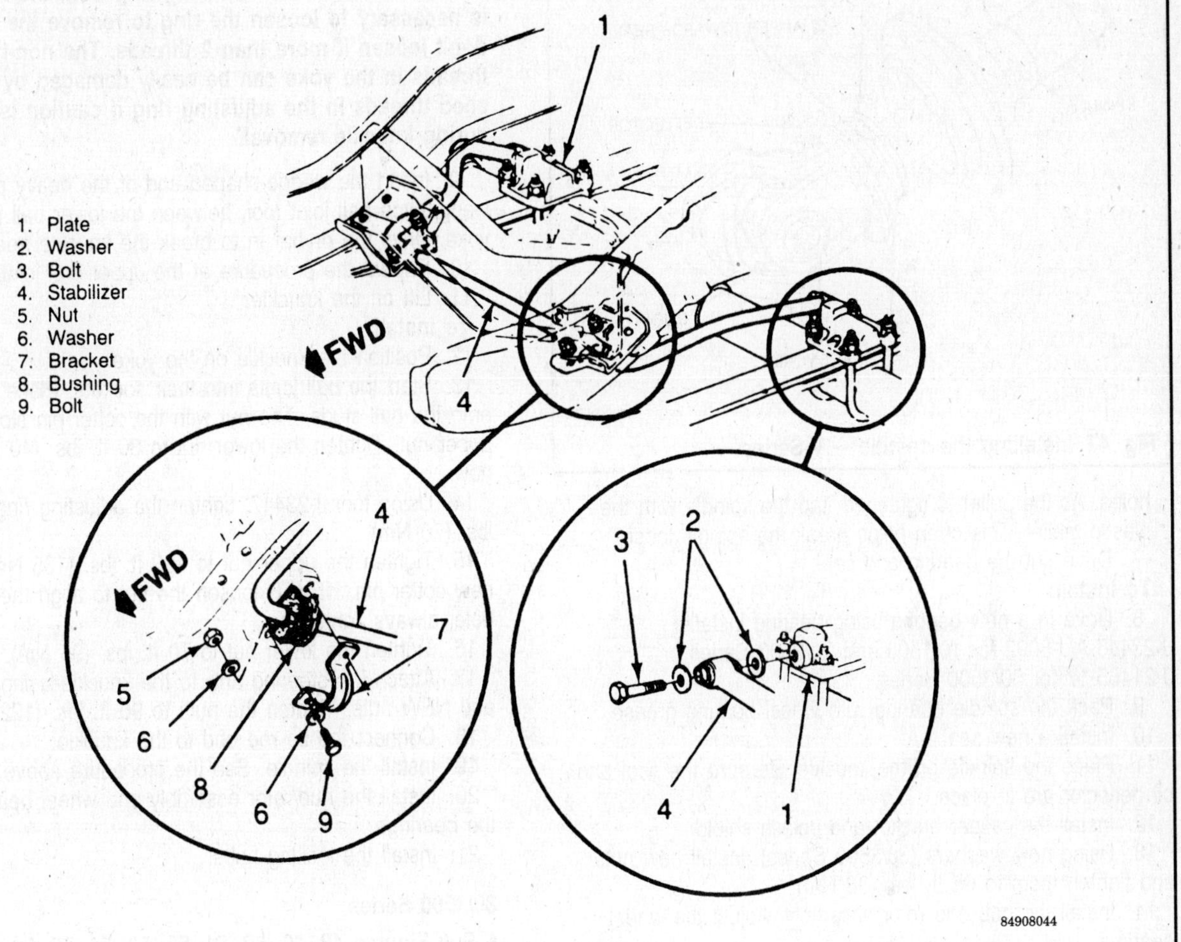

1. Plate
2. Washer
3. Bolt
4. Stabilizer
5. Nut
6. Washer
7. Bracket
8. Bushing
9. Bolt
FWD
1
4
FWD
4
7
5
6
8
6
9
3
2
4
1
84908044

Fig. 44 Installing the stabilizer bar — V-Series

J 6893-D OR
J 26878-A
84908045

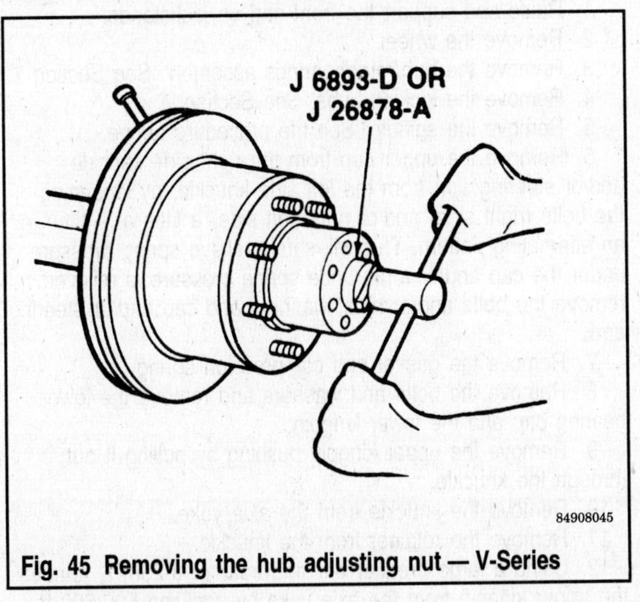

Fig. 45 Removing the hub adjusting nut — V-Series

274
265
265. Spindle
274. Steering Knuckle
84908046

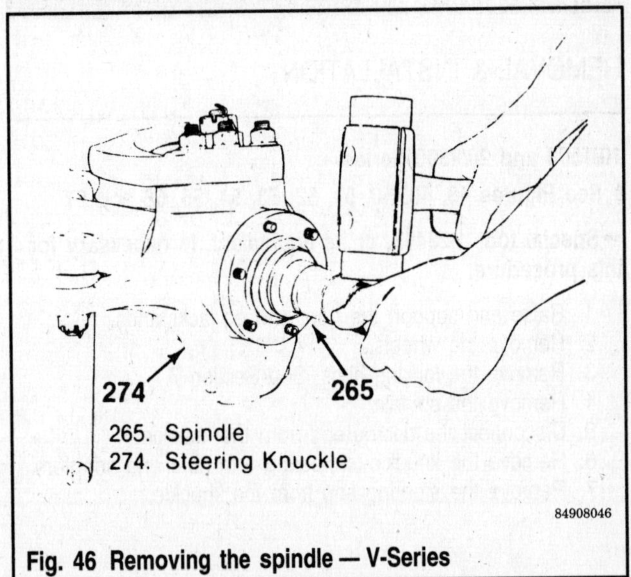

Fig. 46 Removing the spindle — V-Series

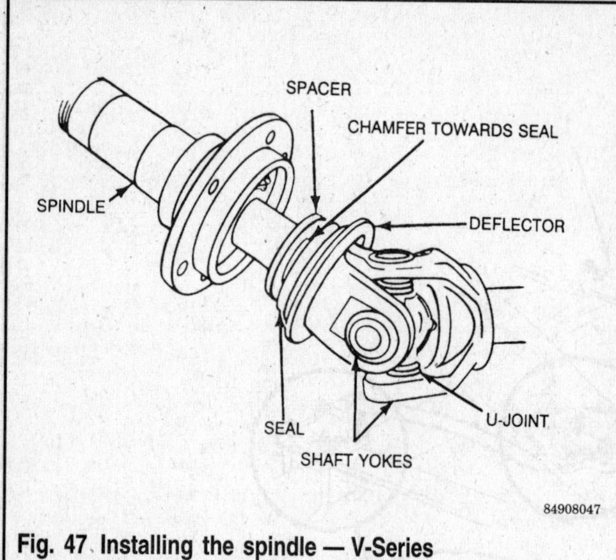

Fig. 47 Installing the spindle — V-Series

holes. As the puller is tightened, tap the spindle with the plastic mallet. This often helps break the spindle loose.

7. Drive out the bearing and seal.

To install:

8. Drive in a new bearing using bearing installer J-23445-A/J-8092 for 10/1500 and 20/2500 Series or J-21465-17 for 30/3500 Series.
9. Pack the spindle bearing with wheel bearing grease.
10. Install a new seal.
11. Place the spindle on the knuckle. Be sure the seal and oil deflector are in place.
12. Install the caliper bracket and splash shield.
13. Using new washers (30/3500 Series), install new nuts and tighten them to 65 ft. lbs. (88 Nm).
14. Install the hub and rotor assembly. Adjust the wheel bearings.
15. Install the locking hubs.
16. Install the caliper. Install the wheel.

Steering Knuckle

REMOVAL & INSTALLATION

10/1500 and 20/2500 Series

See Figures 48, 49, 50, 51, 52, 53, 54, 55, 56 and 57

Special tool J-23447, or its equivalent, is necessary for this procedure.

1. Raise and support the front end on jackstands.
2. Remove the wheels.
3. Remove the locking hubs. See Section 7.
4. Remove the spindle.
5. Disconnect the tie rod end from the knuckle.
6. Remove the knuckle-to-steering arm nuts and adapters.
7. Remove the steering arm from the knuckle.
8. Remove the cotter pins and nuts from the upper and lower ball joints.

Do not remove the adjusting ring from the knuckle. If it is necessary to loosen the ring to remove the knuckle, don't loosen it more than 2 threads. The non-hardened threads in the yoke can be easily damaged by the hardened threads in the adjusting ring if caution is not used during knuckle removal.

9. Insert the wedge-shaped end of the heavy prybar, or wedge-type ball joint tool, between the lower ball joint and the yoke. Drive the prybar in to break the knuckle free.
10. Repeat the procedure at the upper ball joint.
11. Lift off the knuckle.

To install:

12. Position the knuckle on the yoke.
13. Start the ball joints into their sockets. Place the nuts onto the ball studs. The nut with the cotter pin slot is the upper nut. Tighten the lower nut to 30 ft. lbs. (40 Nm), for now.
14. Using tool J-23447, tighten the adjusting ring to 50 ft. lbs. (70 Nm).
15. Tighten the upper nut to 100 ft. lbs. (135 Nm). Install a new cotter pin. NEVER loosen the nut to align the cotter pin hole; always tighten it.
16. Tighten the lower nut to 70 ft. lbs. (95 Nm).
17. Attach the steering arm to the knuckle using adapters and NEW nuts. Tighten the nuts to 90 ft. lbs. (122 Nm).
18. Connect the tie rod end to the knuckle.
19. Install the spindle. See the procedure above.
20. Install the hub/rotor assembly and wheel bearings. Adjust the bearings.
21. Install the locking hubs.

30/3500 Series

See Figures 48, 49, 50, 51, 52, 53, 54, 55, 56 and 57

The following special tools, or their equivalents, are necessary for this procedure: J-26871, J-7817, and J-22301.

1. Raise and support the front end on jackstands.
2. Remove the wheel.
3. Remove the hub/rotor/bearings assembly. See Section 7.
4. Remove the locking hubs. See Section 7.
5. Remove the spindle. See the procedure above.
6. Remove the upper cap from the right side knuckle and/or steering arm from the left side knuckle, by loosening the bolts (right side) and/or nuts (left side) a little at a time in an alternating pattern. This will safely relieve spring pressure under the cap and/or arm. Once spring pressure is relieved, remove the bolts and/or nuts, washers and cap and/or steering arm.
7. Remove the gasket and compression spring.
8. Remove the bolts and washers and remove the lower bearing cap and the lower kingpin.
9. Remove the upper kingpin bushing by pulling it out through the knuckle.
10. Remove the knuckle from the axle yoke.
11. Remove the retainer from the knuckle.
12. Using a large breaker bar and adapter J-26871, remove the upper kingpin from the axle yoke by applying 500-600 ft. lbs. of torque to the kingpin to break it free.

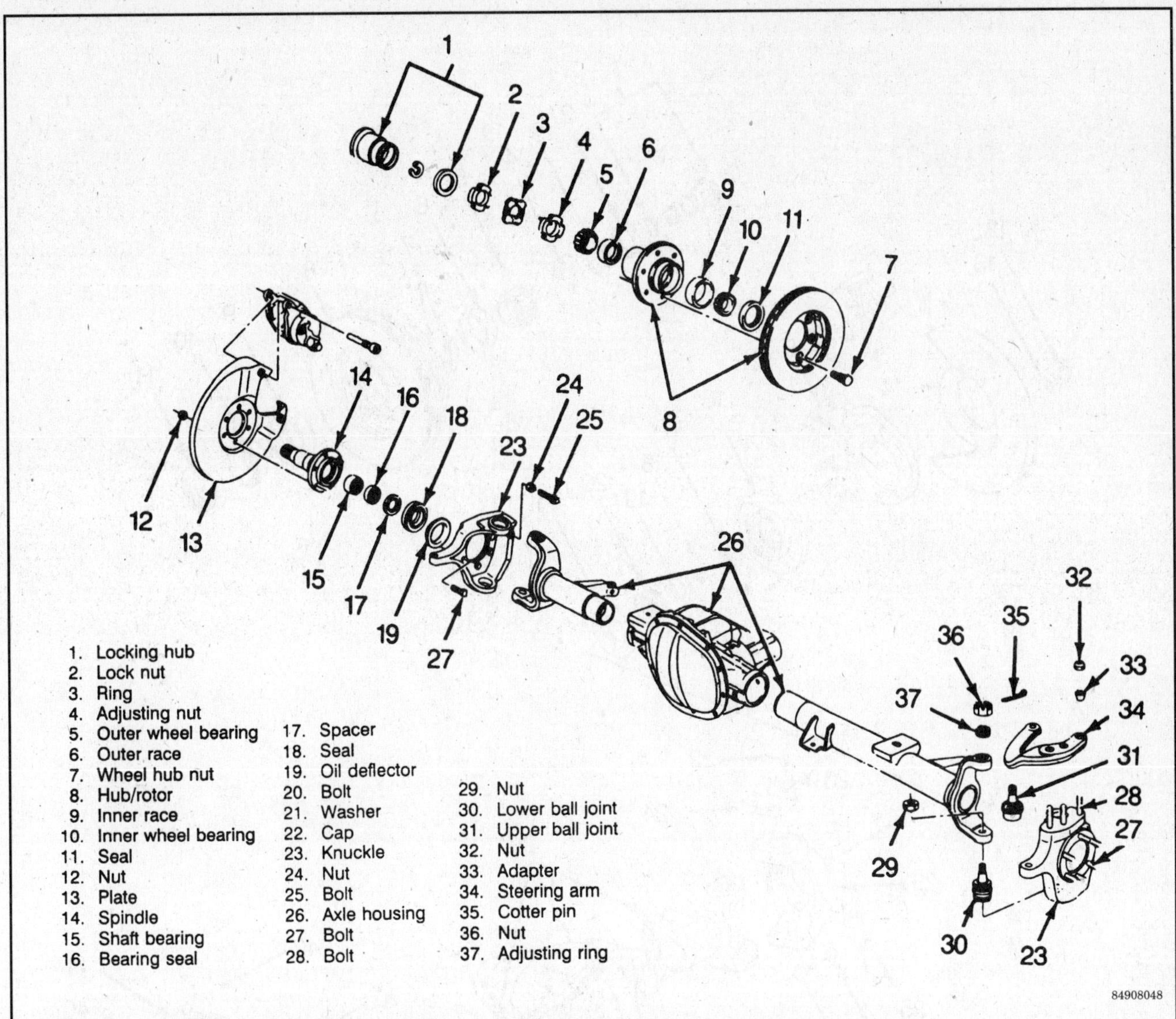

Fig. 48 Exploded view of the steering knuckle, hub and bearing (10/1500, 20/2500) — V-Series

13. Using a hammer and blunt drift, drive out the retainer, race bearing and seal from the axle yoke. These are driven out all at once.

To install:

14. Using tool J-7817, install a new retainer and race in the axle yoke.
15. Fill the recessed area in the retainer and race with the same grease used on the wheel bearings.
16. Completely pack the upper yoke roller bearing with wheel bearing grease. A cone-type bearing packer is preferable, but the bearing may be packed by hand.
17. Install the bearing and a new seal in the upper axle yoke, using a bearing driver such as J-22301. DON'T distort the seal. It should protrude slightly above the yoke when fully seated.
18. Using adapter tool J-28871, install the upper kingpin. The kingpin must be tightened to 550 ft. lbs. (745 Nm).
19. Position the knuckle in the yoke. Working through the knuckle, install a new felt seal over the kingpin and position the knuckle on the kingpin.
20. Install the bushing over the kingpin.
21. Install the compression spring, gasket, bearing cap and/or steering arm and bolts and/or nut and washer. Tighten the bolts and/or nuts, in an alternating pattern, to 80 ft. lbs. (108).
22. Install the lower bearing cap and kingpin. Tighten the bolts to 80 ft. lbs. (108 Nm) in an alternating pattern.
23. Thoroughly lube both kingpins through the grease fittings.
24. Install the spindle.
25. Install the hub/rotor/bearing assembly. Adjust the bearings.
26. Install the locking hubs.
27. Install the wheel.
28. Have the front end alignment checked and reset as necessary.

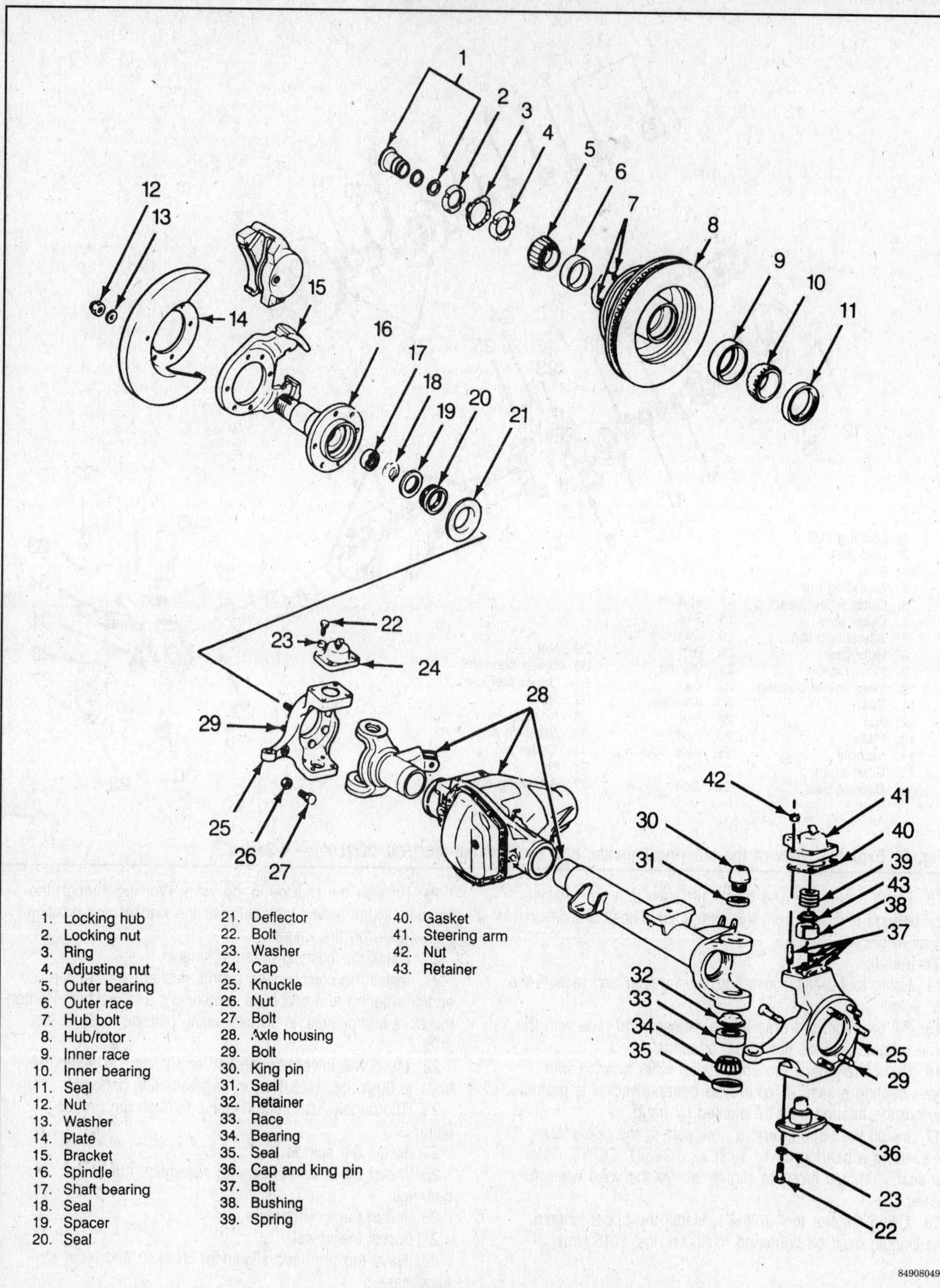

Fig. 49 Exploded view of the steering knuckle, hub and bearing (30/3500) — V-Series

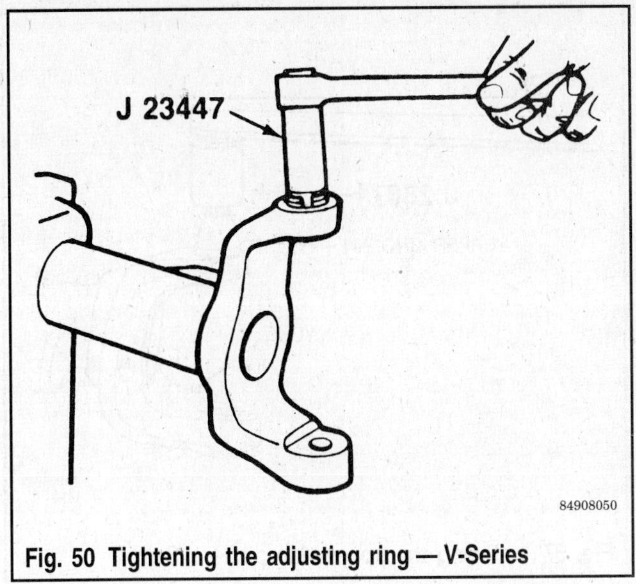

Fig. 50 Tightening the adjusting ring — V-Series

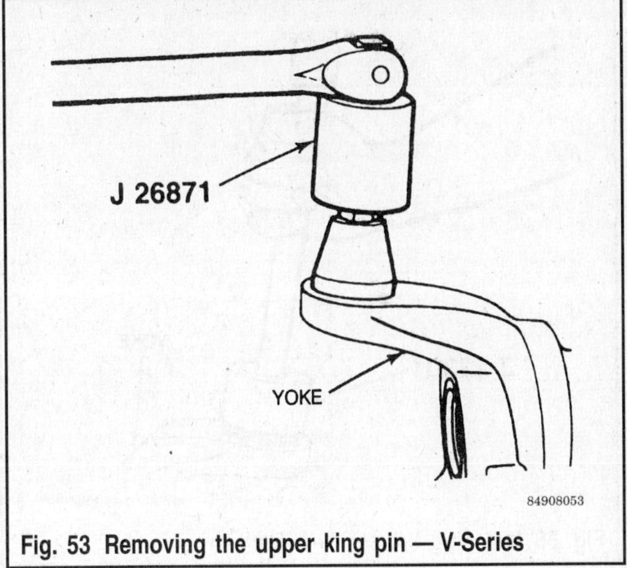

Fig. 53 Removing the upper king pin — V-Series

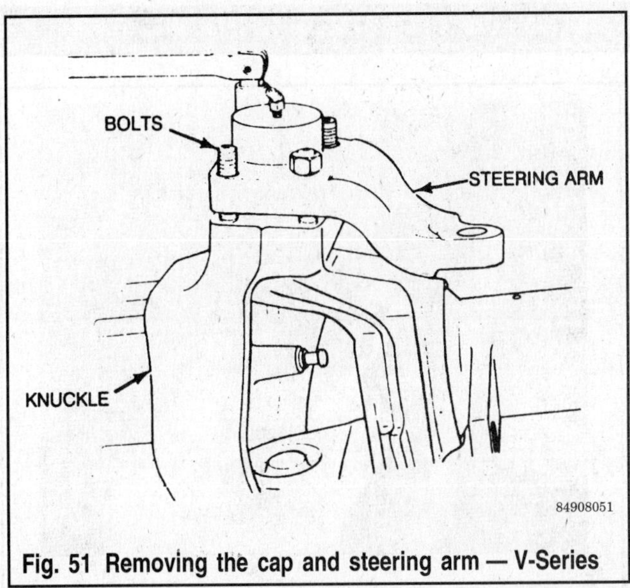

Fig. 51 Removing the cap and steering arm — V-Series

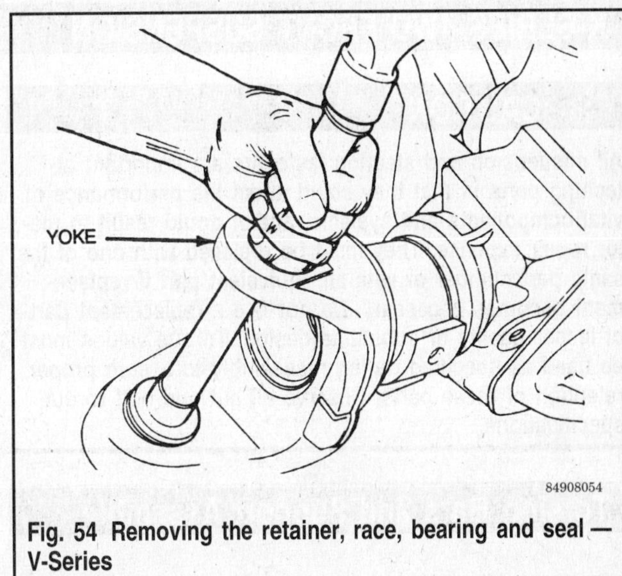

Fig. 54 Removing the retainer, race, bearing and seal — V-Series

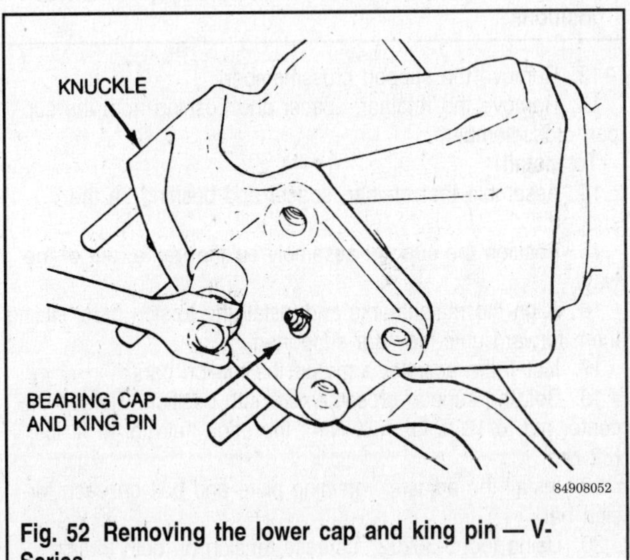

Fig. 52 Removing the lower cap and king pin — V-Series

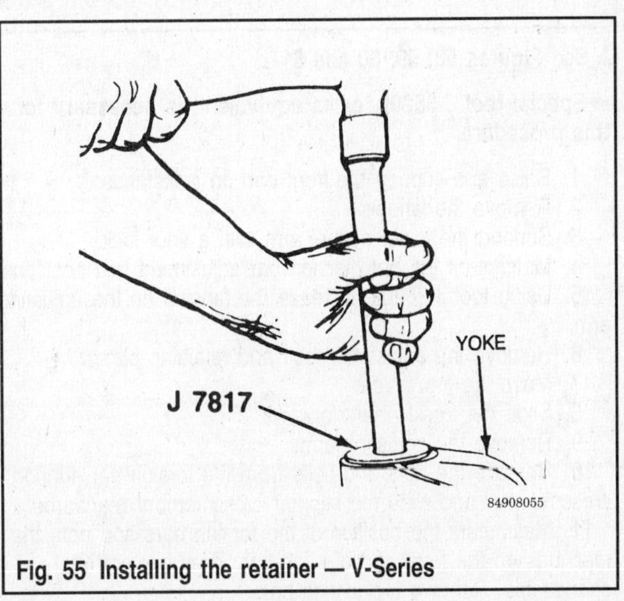

Fig. 55 Installing the retainer — V-Series

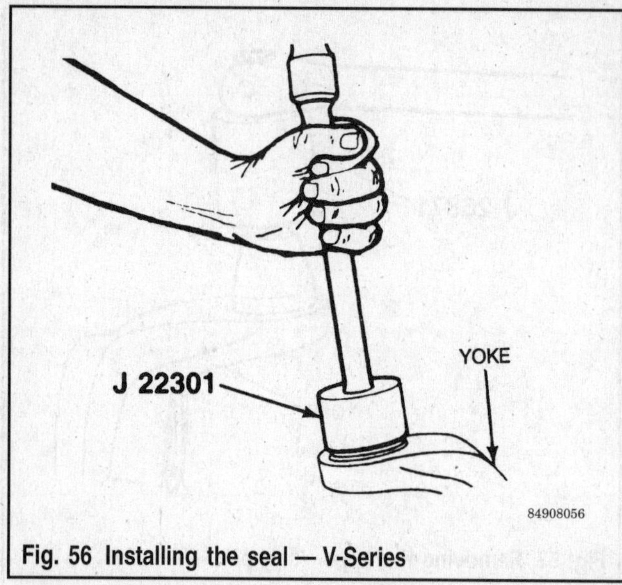

Fig. 56 Installing the seal — V-Series

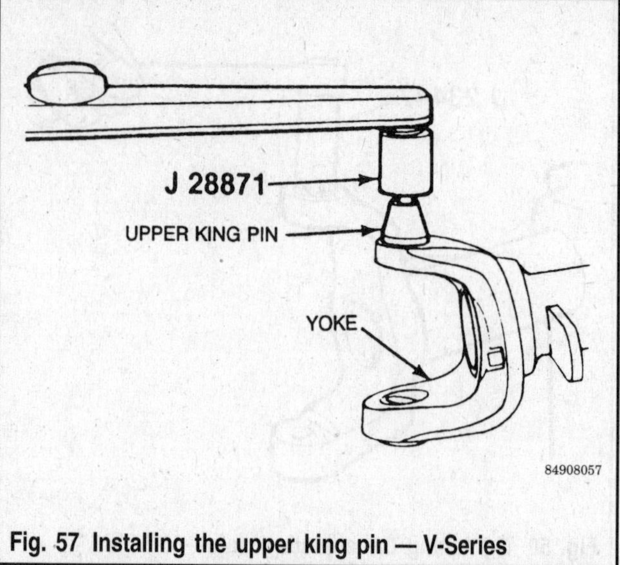

Fig. 57 Installing the upper king pin — V-Series

K-SERIES 4WD FRONT SUSPENSION

**CAUTION

All suspension and steering fasteners are important attaching parts in that they could affect the performance of vital components and systems, and/or could result in major repair expense. They must be replaced with one of the same part number or with an equivalent part if replacement becomes necessary. Do not use a replacement part of lesser quality or substitute design. Torque values must be used as specified during reassembly to assure proper retention of these parts. Observe all nut and bolt torque specifications.

Torsion Bars and Support Assembly

REMOVAL & INSTALLATION

See Figures 58, 59, 60 and 61

Special tool J-36202, or its equivalent, is necessary for this procedure.

1. Raise and support the front end on jackstands.
2. Remove the wheels.
3. Support the lower control arm with a floor jack.
4. Matchmark the both torsion bar adjustment bolt positions.
5. Using tool J-36202, increase the tension on the adjusting arm.
6. Remove the adjustment bolt and retaining plate.
7. Move the tool aside.
8. Slide the torsion bars forward.
9. Remove the adjusting arms.
10. Remove the nuts and bolts from the torsion bar support crossmember and slide the support crossmember rearwards.
11. Matchmark the position of the torsion bars and note the markings on the front end of each bar. They are not interchangeable. Remove the torsion bars.

Fig. 58 Matchmark the both torsion bar adjustment bolt positions

12. Remove the support crossmember.
13. Remove the retainer, spacer and bushing from the support crossmember.

To install:

14. Assemble the retainer, spacer and bushing on the support.
15. Position the support assembly on the frame, out of the way.
16. Align the matchmarks and install the torsion bars, sliding them forward until they are supported.
17. Install the adjuster arms on the torsion bars.
18. Bolt the support crossmember into position. Tighten the center nut to 18 ft. lbs. (24 Nm); the edge nuts to 46 ft. lbs. (62 Nm).
19. Install the adjuster retaining plate and bolt on each torsion bar.
20. Using tool J-36202, increase tension on both torsion bars.

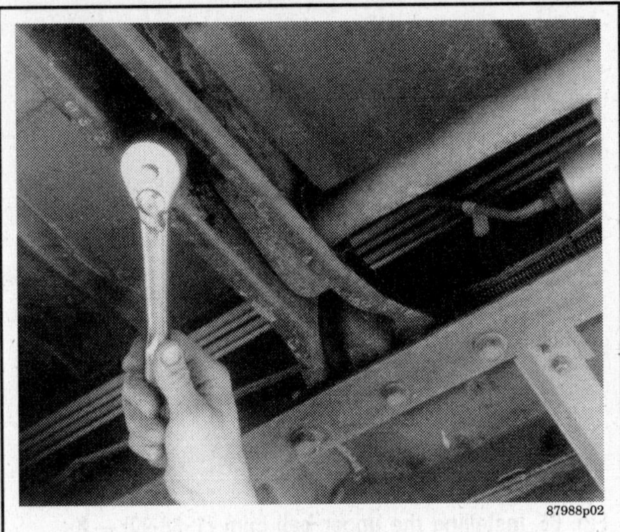

Fig. 59 Increase the tension on the adjusting arm

21. Install the adjustment retainer plate and bolt on both torsion bars.
22. Set the adjustment bolt to the marked position.
23. Release the tension on the torsion bar until the load is take up by the adjustment bolt.
24. Remove the tool.
25. Install the wheels.
26. Have the front end alignment checked.

Shock Absorbers

REMOVAL & INSTALLATION

➧ See Figures 62, 63 and 64

1. Raise and support the front end on jackstands.
2. Remove the upper end bolt, nut and washer.
3. Remove the lower end bolt, nut and washer.

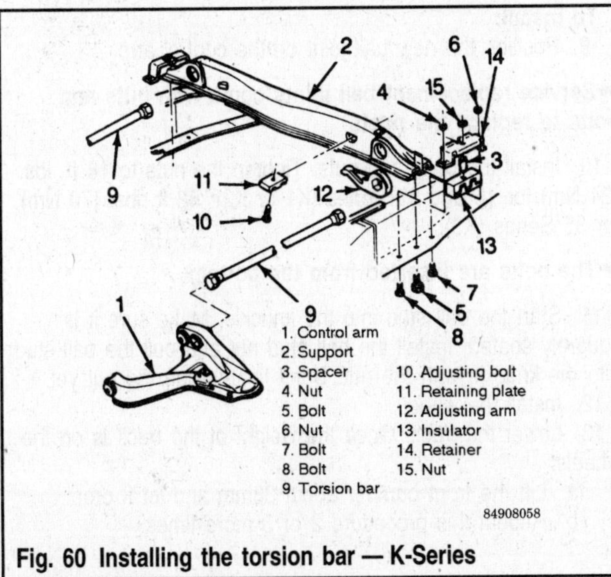

Fig. 60 Installing the torsion bar — K-Series

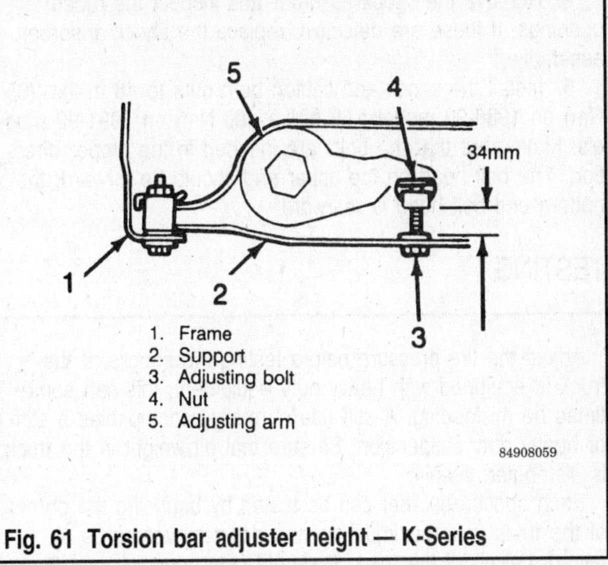

Fig. 61 Torsion bar adjuster height — K-Series

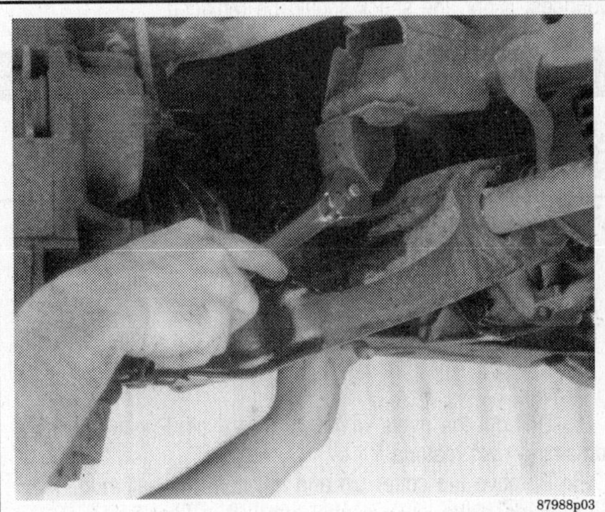

Fig. 62 Remove the lower end bolt, nut and washer

Fig. 63 Remove the shock absorber and inspect the rubber bushings

4. Remove the shock absorber and inspect the rubber bushings. If these are defective, replace the shock absorber assembly.

5. Install the shock and tighten both nuts to 48 ft. lbs. (65 Nm) on 1988-90 models; 66 ft. lbs. (90 Nm) on 1991-93 models. Make sure that the bolts are inserted in the proper direction. The bolt head on the upper end should be forward; the bottom end bolt head is rearward.

TESTING

Adjust the tire pressure before testing the shocks. If the truck is equipped with heavy duty equipment, this can sometimes be misleading. A stiff ride normally accompanies a stiff or heavy duty suspension. Be sure that all weight in the truck is distributed evenly.

Each shock absorber can be tested by bouncing the corner of the truck until maximum up and down movement is obtained. Let go of the truck. It should stop bouncing in 1-2 bounces. If not, the shock should be replaced.

Upper Ball Joint

REMOVAL & INSTALLATION

See Figures 65 and 66

1. Raise and support the front end on jackstands.
2. Remove the wheel.
3. Unbolt the brake hose bracket from the control arm.
4. Using a 1/8 in. drill bit, drill a pilot hole through each ball joint rivet.
5. Drill out the rivets with a 1/2 in. drill bit. Punch out any remaining rivet material.
6. Remove the cotter pin and nut from the ball stud.
7. Support the lower control arm with a floor jack.
8. Using a screw-type forcing tool, separate the ball joint from the knuckle.

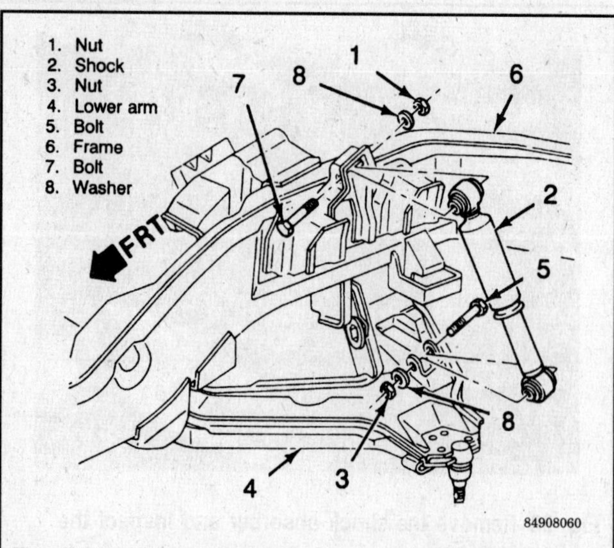

Fig. 64 Installing the shock absorber — K-Series

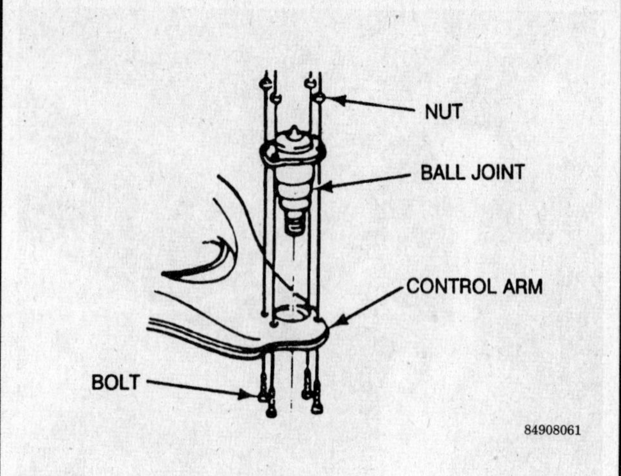

Fig. 65 Installing the upper ball joint (1988-90) — K-Series

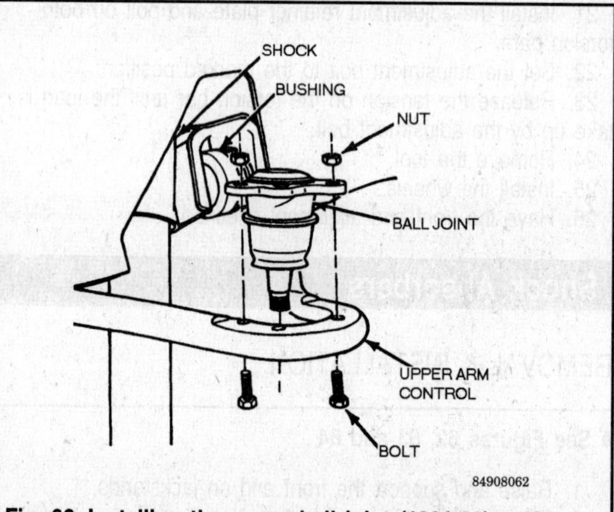

Fig. 66 Installing the upper ball joint (1991-93) — K-Series

To install:

9. Position the new ball joint on the control arm.

➡Service replacement ball joints come with nuts and bolts to replace the rivets.

10. Install the bolts and nuts. Tighten the nuts to 18 ft. lbs. (24 Nm) for 15 and 25 Series (K1 or K2); 52 ft. lbs. (70 Nm) for 35 Series (K3).

➡The bolts are inserted from the bottom.

11. Start the ball stud into the knuckle. Make sure it is squarely seated. Install the ball stud nut and pull the ball stud into the knuckle with the nut. Don't final-torque the nut yet.

12. Install the wheel.

13. Lower the truck. Once the weight of the truck is on the wheels:

a. Lift the front bumper about 38mm and let it drop.

b. Repeat this procedure 2 or 3 more times.

c. Draw a line on the side of the lower control arm from the centerline of the control arm pivot shaft, dead level to the outer end of the control arm.

d. Measure the distance between the lowest corner of the steering knuckle and the line on the control arm. Record the figure.

e. Push down about 38mm on the front bumper and let it return. Repeat the procedure 2 or 3 more times.

f. Re-measure the distance at the control arm.

g. Determine the average of the 2 measurements. The average distance should be:

- K15/25 without F60 option: 157.0mm ± 6.0mm
- K15/25 with F60 option: 183.0mm ± 6.0mm
- K35 without F60 option: 145.0mm ± 6.0mm
- K35 with F60 option: 173.0mm ± 6.0mm

h. If the figure is correct, tighten the control arm pivot nuts to 88 ft. lbs. (120 Nm) on 1988-90 models; 140 ft. lbs. (190 Nm) on 1991-96 models.

i. If the figure is not correct, tighten the pivot bolts to 88 ft. lbs. (120 Nm) on 1988-90 models; 140 ft. lbs. (190 Nm) on 1991-96 models and have the front end alignment corrected.

Lower Ball Joint

REMOVAL & INSTALLATION

See Figures 67, 68, 69 and 70

➡Special tool J-36202, or its equivalent, is necessary for this procedure.

1. Raise and support the front end on jackstands.
2. Remove the wheel.
3. Remove the splash shield from the knuckle.
4. Disconnect the the inner tie rod end from the relay rod using a ball joint separator.
5. Remove the hub nut and washer. Insert a long drift or dowel through the vanes in the brake rotor to hold the rotor in place.

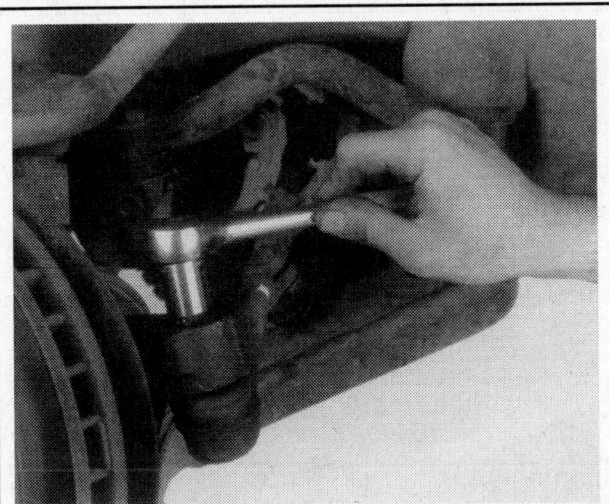

87988p06

Fig. 67 Remove the tie rod end bolt

87988p05

Fig. 68 Disconnect the the inner tie rod end from the relay rod using a ball joint separator

6. Remove the axle shaft inner flange bolts.
7. Using a puller, force the outer end of the axle shaft out of the hub. Remove the shaft.
8. Using a ⅛in. drill bit, drill a pilot hole through each ball joint rivet.
9. Drill out the rivets with a ½ in. drill bit. Punch out any remaining rivet material.
10. Remove the cotter pin and nut from the ball stud.
11. Support the lower control arm with a floor jack.
12. Matchmark both torsion bar adjustment bolt positions. This will aid in installation.
13. Using tool J-36202, increase the tension on the adjusting arm.
14. Remove the adjustment bolt and retaining plate.
15. Move the tool aside.
16. Slide the torsion bars forward.
17. Using a screw-type forcing tool, separate the ball joint from the knuckle.

To install:

18. Position the new ball joint on the control arm.

➡Service replacement ball joints come with nuts and bolts to replace the rivets.

19. Install the bolts and nuts. Tighten the nuts to 45 ft. lbs. (61 Nm).

➡The bolts are inserted from the bottom.

20. Start the ball stud into the knuckle. Make sure it is squarely seated. Install the ball stud nut and pull the ball stud into the knuckle with the nut. Don't final-torque the nut yet.
21. Using tool J-36202, increase tension on both torsion bars.
22. Install the adjustment retainer plate and bolt on both torsion bars.
23. Set the adjustment bolt to the marked position.
24. Release the tension on the torsion bar until the load is take up by the adjustment bolt.
25. Remove the tool.
26. Position the shaft in the hub and install the washer and hub nut. Leave the drift in the rotor vanes and tighten the hub nut to 173 ft. lbs. (235 Nm).

27. Install the flange bolts. Tighten them to 59 ft. lbs. (79 Nm). Remove the drift.

28. Connect the inner tie rod end at the steering relay rod. Tighten the nut to 35 ft. lbs. (47 Nm).

29. Install the splash shield.

30. Install the wheel.

31. Lower the truck. Once the weight of the truck is on the wheels:

a. Lift the front bumper about 38mm and let it drop.

b. Repeat this procedure 2 or 3 more times.

c. Draw a line on the side of the lower control arm from the centerline of the control arm pivot shaft, dead level to the outer end of the control arm.

d. Measure the distance between the lowest corner of the steering knuckle and the line on the control arm. Record the figure.

e. Push down about 38mm on the front bumper and let it return. Repeat the procedure 2 or 3 more times.

f. Re-measure the distance at the control arm.

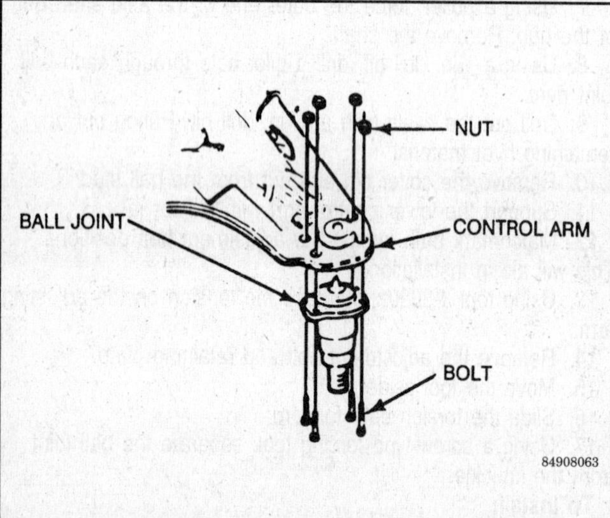

Fig. 69 Installing the lower ball joint — K-Series

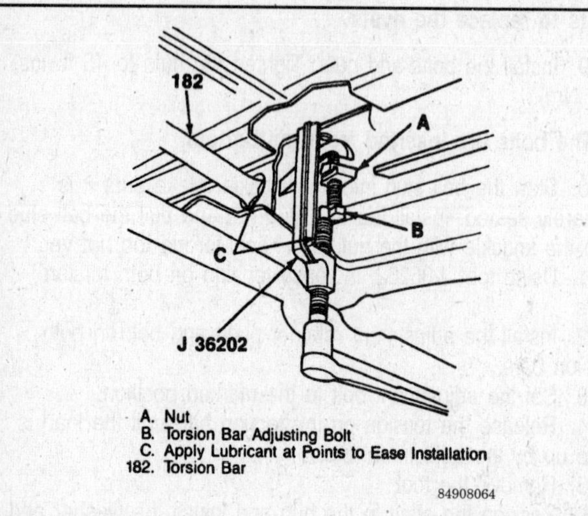

Fig. 70 Removing the torsion bar adjusting bolt — K-Series

g. Determine the average of the 2 measurements. The average distance should be:

- K15/25 without F60 option: 157.0mm ± 6.0mm
- K15/25 with F60 option: 183.0mm ± 6.0mm
- K35 without F60 option: 145.0mm ± 6.0mm
- K35 with F60 option: 173.0mm ± 6.0mm

h. If the figure is correct, tighten the control arm pivot nuts to 94 ft. lbs. (128 Nm).

i. If the figure is not correct, tighten the pivot bolts to 94 ft. lbs. (128 Nm) and have the front end alignment corrected.

Stabilizer Bar

REMOVAL & INSTALLATION

▸ See Figures 71, 72, 73 and 74

Special tool J-36202, or its equivalent, is necessary for this procedure.

1. Raise and support the front end on jackstands.
2. Remove the wheels.
3. Remove the stabilizer bar-to-frame clamps.
4. Remove the stabilizer bar-to-lower control arm bolts, nut/grommet assemblies and spacers.

➡The bolts, spacers and nuts are not interchangeable from side-to-side. Keep them separated.

5. Remove the stabilizer bar and bushings.
6. Check the bushings for wear or splitting. Replace any damaged bushings.

To install:

7. Matchmark the both torsion bar adjustment bolt positions.
8. Using tool J-36202, increase the tension on the adjusting arm.
9. Remove the adjustment bolt and retaining plate.
10. Move the tool aside.
11. Slide the torsion bars forward.
12. Coat the stabilizer bar bushings with silicone grease and install them on the stabilizer bar. Note, the split in the bushing faces forward.

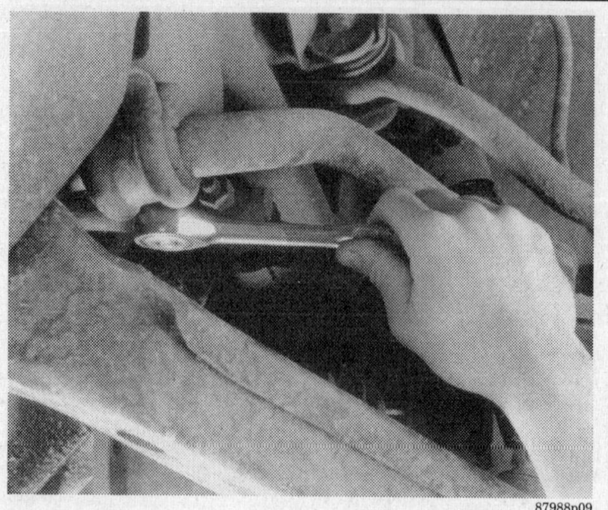

Fig. 71 Remove the stabilizer bar-to-frame clamps

Fig. 72 Remove the stabilizer bar-to-lower control arm bolts, nut/grommet assemblies and spacers

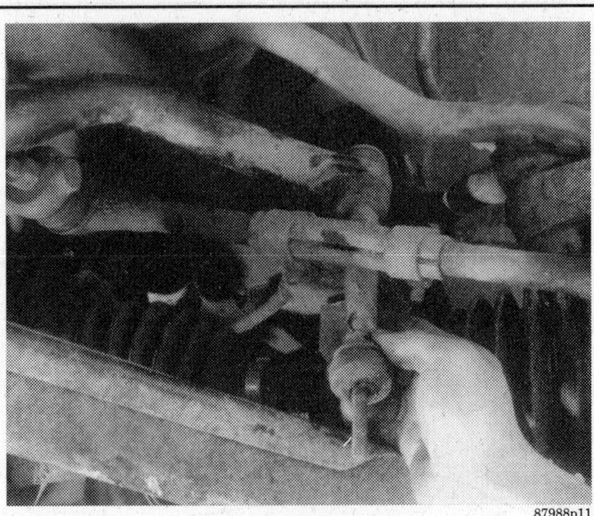

Fig. 73 Remove the stabilizer bar and bushings

13. Position the stabilizer bar and install the frame clamps. Make the bolts finger tight.
14. Install the end link bolts, spacers and nut/grommet assemblies. Make the bolts finger tight.
15. When all fasteners are installed, tighten the frame clamp bolts to 24 ft. lbs. (33 Nm); the end link bolts to 13 ft. lbs. (18 Nm).
16. Using tool J-36202, increase tension on both torsion bars.
17. Install the adjustment retainer plate and bolt on both torsion bars.
18. Set the adjustment bolt to the marked position.
19. Release the tension on the torsion bar until the load is take up by the adjustment bolt.
20. Remove the tool.
21. Install the wheels.
22. Have the front end alignment checked and adjusted as necessary.

Upper Control Arm and Bushings

REMOVAL & INSTALLATION

See Figure 75

1. Raise and support the truck on jackstands.
2. Support the lower control arm with a floor jack.
3. Remove the wheel.
4. Unbolt the brake hose bracket from the control arm.
5. Remove the air cleaner extension (if necessary).
6. Remove the cotter pin from the upper control arm ball stud and loosen the stud nut until the bottom surface of the nut is slightly below the end of the stud.
7. Using a screw-type forcing tool, break loose the ball joint from the knuckle.
8. Remove the nuts and bolts securing the control arm to the frame brackets.
9. Tape the shims and spacers together and tag for proper reassembly.

To install:

10. Place the control arm in position and install the shims, bolts and new nuts. Both bolt heads **must** be inboard of the control arm brackets. Tighten the nuts finger tight for now.

➡Do not tighten the bolts yet. The bolts must be torqued with the truck at its proper ride height.

11. Install the ball stud nut. Tighten the nut to 94 ft. lbs. (128 Nm) on 1988-90 models; 84 ft. lbs. (115 Nm) on 1991-94 models and 94 ft. lbs. (100 Nm) on 1995-96 models. Install the cotter pin. Never back off the nut to install the cotter pin. Always advance it. Never advance it more than 1/6 turn.
12. Install the brake caliper.
13. Install the wheel.
14. Install the brake hose.
15. Install the air cleaner extension.
16. Lower the truck. Once the weight of the truck is on the wheels:
    a. Lift the front bumper about 38mm and let it drop.
    b. Repeat this procedure 2 or 3 more times.
    c. Draw a line on the side of the lower control arm from the centerline of the control arm pivot shaft, dead level to the outer end of the control arm.
    d. Measure the distance between the lowest corner of the steering knuckle and the line on the control arm. Record the figure.
    e. Push down about 38mm on the front bumper and let it return. Repeat the procedure 2 or 3 more times.
    f. Re-measure the distance at the control arm.
    g. Determine the average of the 2 measurements. The average distance should be:
        - K15/25 without F60 option: 157.0mm ± 6.0mm
        - K15/25 with F60 option: 183.0mm ± 6.0mm
        - K35 without F60 option: 145.0mm ± 6.0mm
        - K35 with F60 option: 173.0mm ± 6.0mm
    h. If the figure is correct, tighten the control arm pivot nuts to 88 ft. lbs. (120 Nm) on 1988-90 models; 140 ft. lbs. (189 Nm) on 1991-93 models and 140 ft. lbs. (140 Nm) on 1995-96 models.

1. Lower arm
2. Frame
3. Nut
4. Spacer
5. Bolt
6. Stabilizer
7. Clamp
8. Bolt
9. Insulator
FRT
84908067

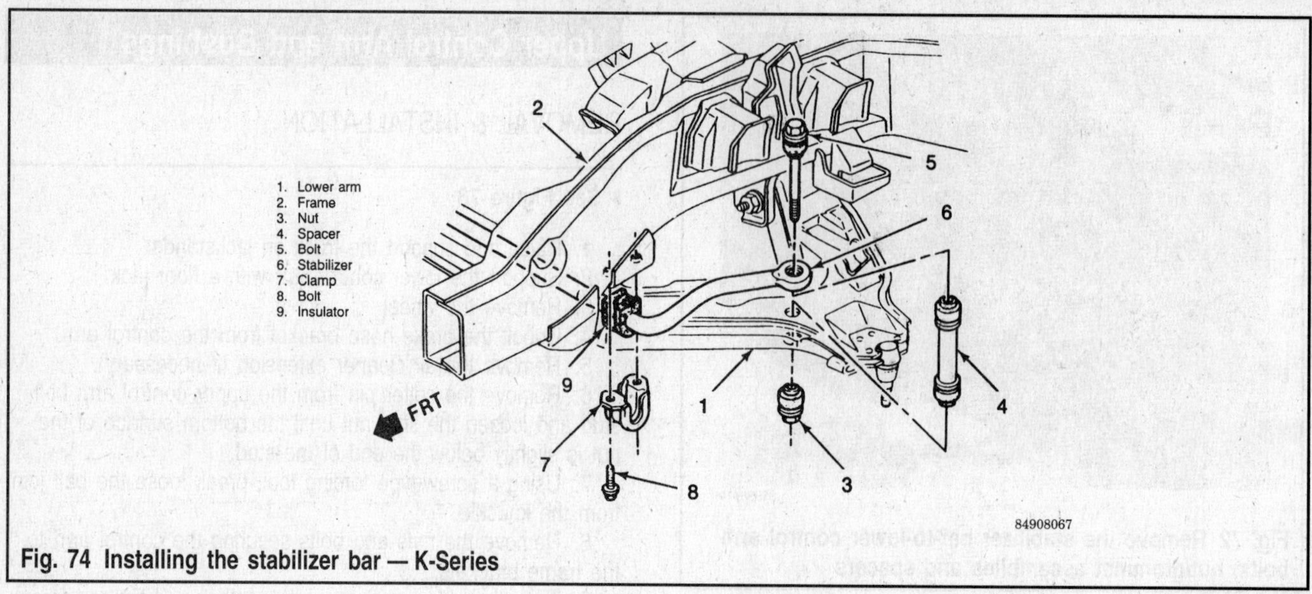

Fig. 74 Installing the stabilizer bar — K-Series

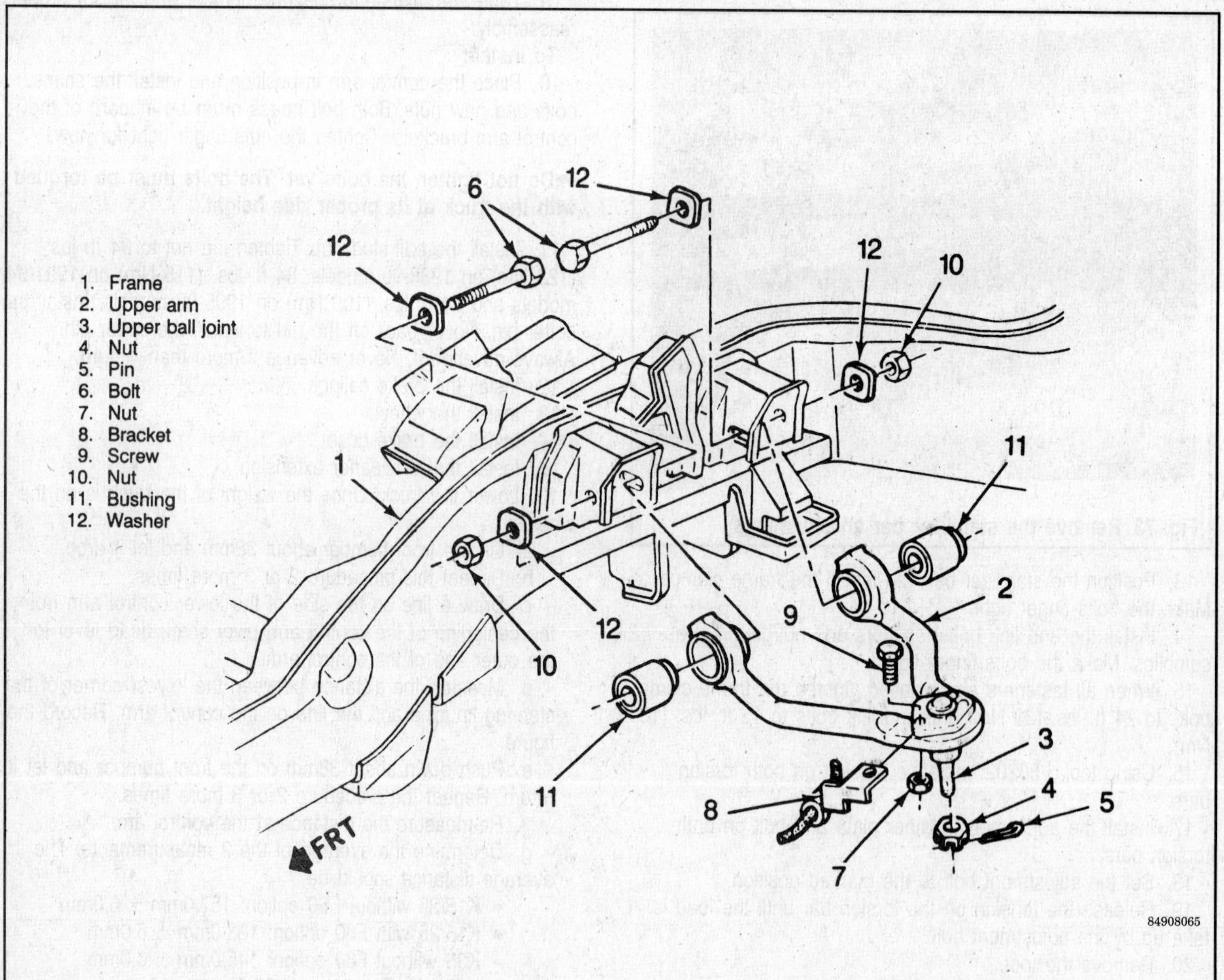

1. Frame
2. Upper arm
3. Upper ball joint
4. Nut
5. Pin
6. Bolt
7. Nut
8. Bracket
9. Screw
10. Nut
11. Bushing
12. Washer
FRT
84908065

Fig. 75 Installing the upper control arm — K-Series

i. If the figure is not correct, tighten the pivot bolts to 88 ft. lbs. (120 Nm) on 1988-90 models; 140 ft. lbs. (189 Nm) on 1991-94 models and 140 ft. lbs. (140 Nm) on 1995-96 models. Have the front end alignment corrected.

Lower Control Arm and Bushing

REMOVAL & INSTALLATION

See Figures 76, 77 and 78

➡Special tools J-36202, J-36618-1, J-36618-2, J-36618-3, J-36618-4, J-36618-5, and J-9519-23, or their equivalents, are necessary for this procedure.

1. Raise and support the truck on jackstands.
2. Remove the wheel.
3. Remove the splash shield from the knuckle.
4. Disconnect the stabilizer bar from the control arm.

87988p07

Fig. 76 Disconnect the tie rod end from the relay rod

87988p08

Fig. 77 Matchmark the torsion bar adjustment bolt positions

5. Remove the shock absorber.
6. Disconnect the tie rod end from the relay rod.
7. Remove the hub nut and washer. Insert a long drift or dowel through the vanes in the brake rotor to hold the rotor in place.
8. Remove the axle shaft inner flange bolts.
9. Using a puller, force the outer end of the axle shaft out of the hub. Remove the shaft.
10. Support the lower control arm with a floor jack.
11. Matchmark the both torsion bar adjustment bolt positions.
12. Using tool J-36202, increase the tension on the adjusting arm.
13. Remove the adjustment bolt and retaining plate.
14. Move the tool aside.
15. Slide the torsion bars forward.
16. Remove the adjusting arm.
17. Remove the cotter pin from the lower ball stud and loosen the nut.
18. Loosen the lower ball stud in the steering knuckle using a ball joint stud removal tool. When the stud is loose, remove the nut from the stud. It may be necessary to remove the brake caliper and wire it to the frame to gain clearance.
19. Remove the control arm-to-frame bracket bolts, nuts and washers.
20. Remove the lower control arm and torsion bar as a unit.
21. Separate the control arm and torsion bar.
22. On 15 and 25 Series, the bushings are not replaceable. If they are damaged, the control arm will have to be replaced. On 35 Series, proceed as follows:
    a. FRONT BUSHING: Unbend the crimps with a punch. Force out the bushings with tools J-36618-2, J-9519-23, J-36618-4 and 36618-1.
    b. REAR BUSHING: Force out the bushings with tools J-36618-5, J-9519-23, J-36618-3 and J-36618-2. There are no crimps.

To install:

23. On 35 Series, install a new front bushings, then a new rear bushing using the removal tools.
24. Assemble the control arm and torsion bar.
25. Raise the control arm assembly into position. Insert the front leg of the control arm into the crossmember first, then the rear leg into the frame bracket.
26. Install the bolts, front one first. The bolts **must** be installed with the front bolt head heads towards the front of the truck and the rear bolt head towards the rear of the truck!

➡Do not tighten the bolts yet. The bolts must be torqued with the truck at its proper ride height.

27. Start the ball joint into the knuckle. Make sure it is squarely seated. Tighten the nut to 96 ft. lbs. (130 Nm) and install a new cotter pin. Always advance the nut to align the cotter pin hole. NEVER back it off!
28. Install the adjuster arm.
29. Using tool J-36202, increase tension on both torsion bars.
30. Install the adjustment retainer plate and bolt on both torsion bars.
31. Set the adjustment bolt to the marked position.
32. Release the tension on the torsion bar until the load is take up by the adjustment bolt.
33. Remove the tool.

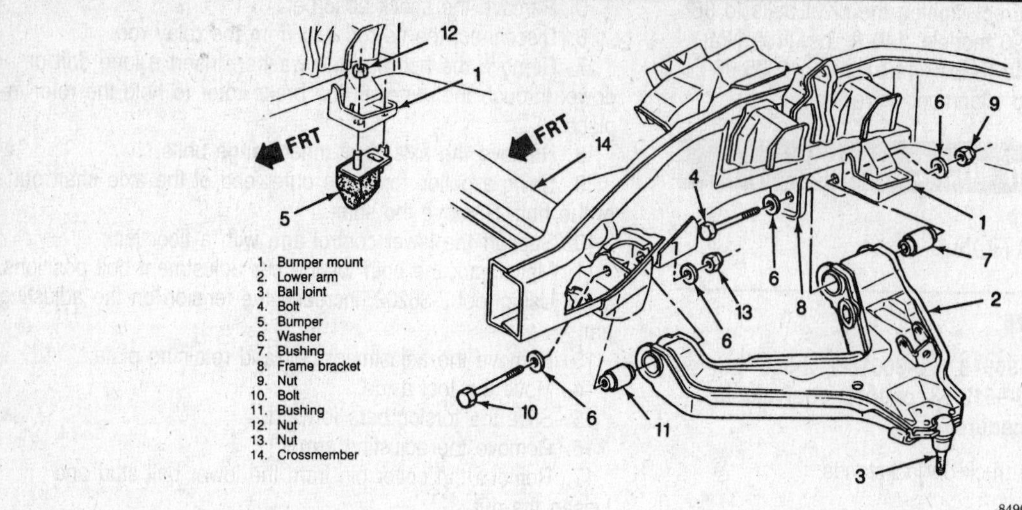

Fig. 78 Installing the lower control arm — K-Series

34. Position the shaft in the hub and install the washer and hub nut. Leave the drift in the rotor vanes and tighten the hub nut to 173 ft. lbs. (235 Nm).
35. Install the flange bolts. Tighten them to 59 ft. lbs. (79 Nm). Remove the drift.
36. Connect the inner tie rod end at the steering relay rod. Tighten the nut to 35 ft. lbs. (47 Nm).
37. Install the splash shield.
38. Connect the stabilizer bar to the lower control arm. Tighten the nuts to 13 ft. lbs. (17 Nm).
39. Install the shock absorber.
40. Install the wheel.
41. Lower the truck. Once the weight of the truck is on the wheels:
 a. Lift the front bumper about 38mm and let it drop.
 b. Repeat this procedure 2 or 3 more times.
 c. Draw a line on the side of the lower control arm from the centerline of the control arm pivot shaft, dead level to the outer end of the control arm.
 d. Measure the distance between the lowest corner of the steering knuckle and the line on the control arm. Record the figure.
 e. Push down about 38mm on the front bumper and let it return. Repeat the procedure 2 or 3 more times.
 f. Re-measure the distance at the control arm.
 g. Determine the average of the 2 measurements. The average distance should be:
  - K15/25 without F60 option: 157.0mm ± 6.0mm
  - K15/25 with F60 option: 183.0mm ± 6.0mm
  - K35 without F60 option: 145.0mm ± 6.0mm
  - K35 with F60 option: 173.0mm ± 6.0mm
 h. If the figure is correct, tighten the control arm nuts to 135 ft. lbs. (185 Nm).
 i. If the figure is not correct, tighten the pivot bolts to 135 ft. lbs. (185 Nm) and have the front end alignment corrected.

Steering Knuckle and Seal

REMOVAL & INSTALLATION

➧ **See Figures 79 and 80**

1. Raise and support the front end on jackstands.
2. Remove the wheel.
3. Remove the skid plate.
4. Remove the left stabilizer bar clamp.
5. Remove the left stabilizer bar bolt, spacer and bushings at the lower control arm.
6. Disconnect the left inner tie rod end from the steering relay rod.
7. Remove the caliper and suspend it out of the way.
8. Remove the brake disc. See Section 9.
9. Remove the hub nut and washer.
10. Using a puller, force the outer end of the axle shaft out of the hub. Remove the hub/bearing assembly.

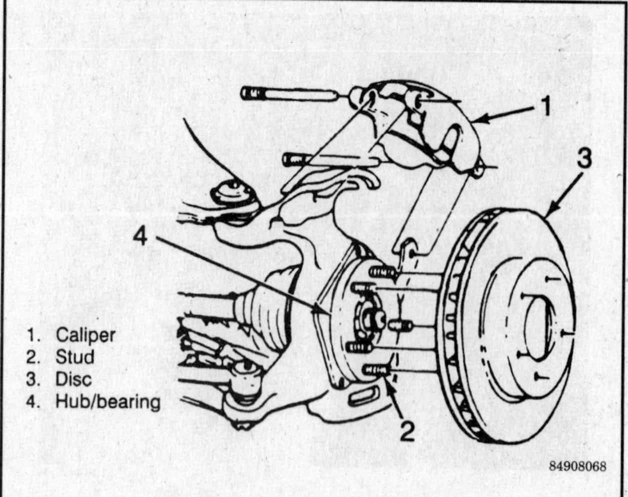

Fig. 79 Removing the brake disc — K-Series

11. Remove the axle shaft inner flange bolts. Remove the shaft.
12. Support the lower control arm with a floor jack.
13. Unbolt and remove the splash shield.
14. Remove the upper and lower ball joint nuts and cotter pins. Using a screw-type forcing tool, separate the upper, then the lower, ball joint from the knuckle.
15. Remove the knuckle and old seal.

To install:

16. Drive a new seal into the knuckle.
17. Position the knuckle on the ball joint studs and start the studs squarely into the knuckle. Install the nuts and tighten them to 94 ft. lbs. (128 Nm) on 1988-90 models; 84 ft. lbs. (115 Nm) on 1991-93 models.
18. Position the splash shield on the knuckle. Make sure it is properly aligned and tighten the bolts to 12 ft. lbs. (16 Nm) on 1988-90 models; 19 ft. lbs. (26 Nm) on 1991-93 models.
19. Position the axle shaft and install the flange bolts. Tighten them to 59 ft. lbs. (79 Nm).
20. Position the shaft in the hub and install the washer and hub nut. Position a drift in the rotor vanes and tighten the hub nut to 173 ft. lbs. (235 Nm).
21. Connect the left inner tie rod end at the steering relay rod. Tighten the nut to 35 ft. lbs. (47 Nm).
22. Install the stabilizer bar bolts and clamps.
23. Install the brakes and skid plate.

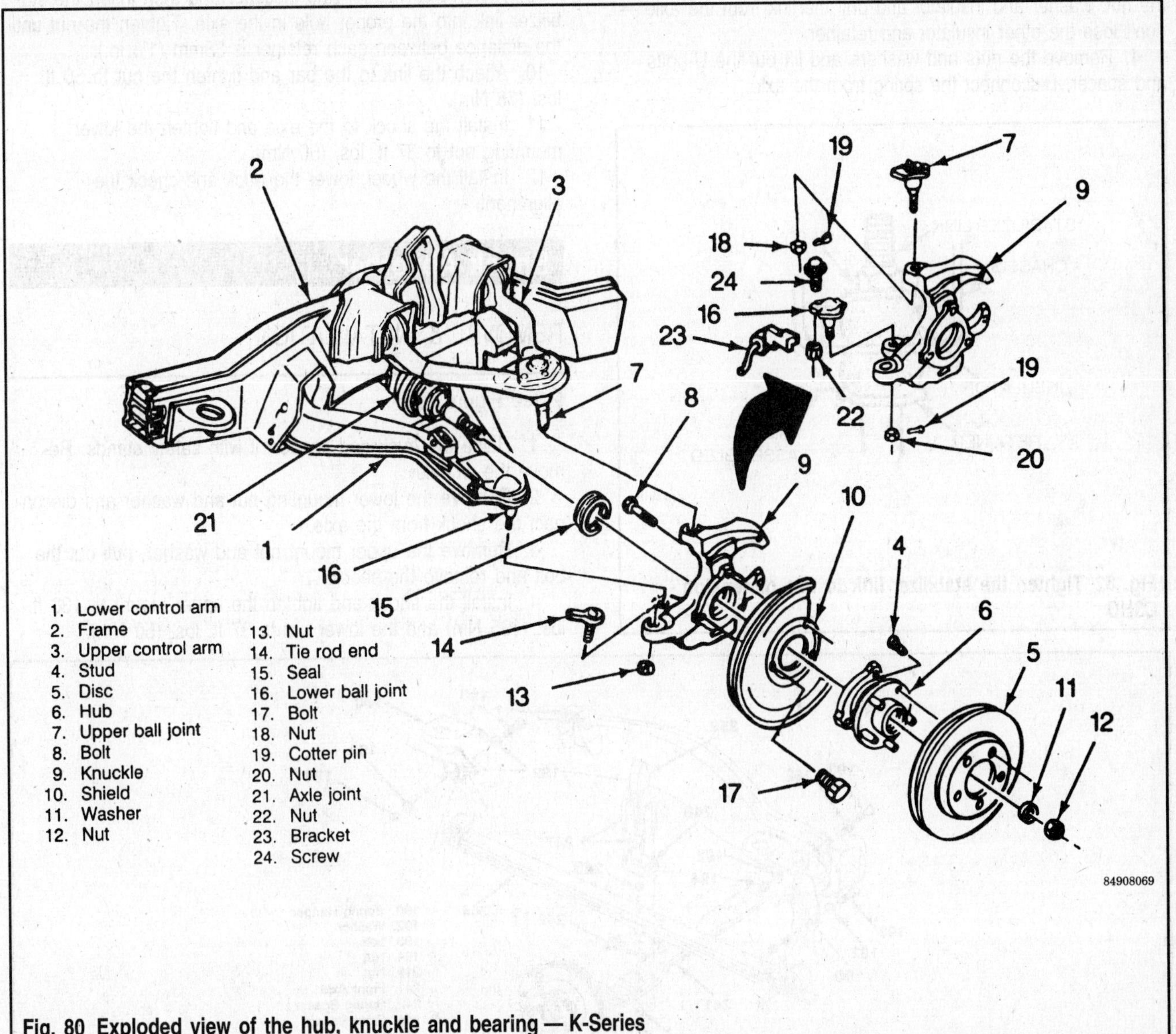

Fig. 80 Exploded view of the hub, knuckle and bearing — K-Series

C3HD FRONT SUSPENSION

Leaf Spring

REMOVAL & INSTALLATION

➧ **See Figures 81 and 82**

1. Raise the truck and support the axle with safety stands. Remove the tire.
2. Disconnect the lower shock absorber mount at the axle.
3. Disconnect the stabilizer bar link from the bar. Remove the nut, washer and insulator and pull the link from the axle — don't lose the other insulator and retainer.
4. Remove the nuts and washers and lift out the U-bolts and spacer. Disconnect the spring from the axle.

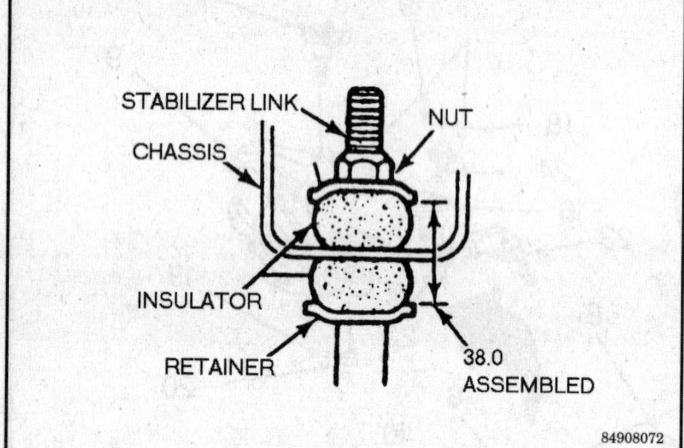

Fig. 82 Tighten the stabilizer link to this dimension — C3HD

5. Disconnect and separate the spring from the rear shackle and the front hanger. Remove the spring.

To install:

6. Position the spring so it lines up with the shackle and the hanger. The double wrap end should face forward.
7. Insert the hanger and shackle bolts and tighten to 92 ft. lbs. (125 Nm).
8. Position the spring spacer so that the aligning pin contacts the edge of the spring and tighten the U-bolt nuts, diagonally to 18 ft. lbs. (25 Nm). Retighten the nuts to 80 ft. lbs. (109 Nm).
9. Attach the retainer and insulator and then insert the stabilizer link into the proper hole in the axle. Tighten the nut until the distance between each retainer is 38mm (1½ in.).
10. Attach the link to the bar and tighten the nut to 50 ft. lbs. (68 Nm).
11. Install the shock to the axle and tighten the lower mounting nut to 37 ft. lbs. (50 Nm).
12. Install the wheel, lower the truck and check the alignment.

Shock Absorber

REMOVAL & INSTALLATION

➧ **See Figure 83**

1. Raise the truck and support it with safety stands. Remove the wheels.
2. Remove the lower mounting nut and washer and disconnect the shock from the axle.
3. Remove the upper mount nut and washer, pull out the bolt and remove the shock.
4. Install the shock and tighten the upper mount to 136 ft. lbs. (185 Nm) and the lower nut to 37 ft. lbs. (50 Nm).

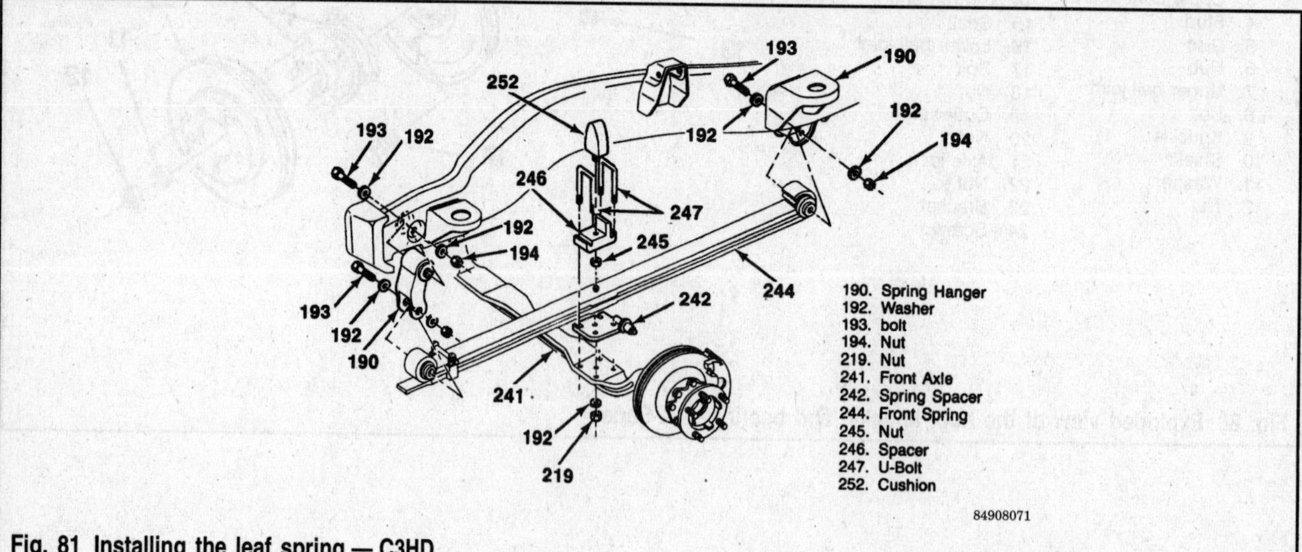

Fig. 81 Installing the leaf spring — C3HD

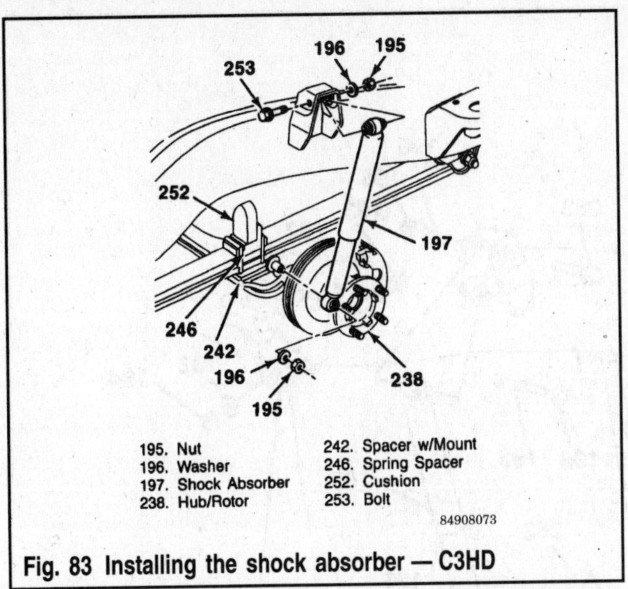

Fig. 83 Installing the shock absorber — C3HD

Stabilizer Bar

REMOVAL & INSTALLATION

➧ **See Figure 84**

1. Raise the truck and support the axle with safety stands. Remove the tire.
2. Disconnect the stabilizer bar link from the bar.
3. Remove the clamp bolts and disconnect the bar from the axle.
4. Remove the insulator from the bar.
5. Remove the nut, retainer and insulator and then pull the link from the frame bracket. An additional insulator and retainer will come off with it.

To install:

6. Slide a retainer and insulator onto the link and insert it into the proper hole in the frame bracket.
7. Install the other insulator and retainer and then tighten the nut until the distance between each retainer is 38mm (1½ in.)
8. Connect the bar to the front axle.
9. Slide the insulators onto the bar, install the clamps and bolts and tighten them to 21 ft. lbs. (28 Nm).
10. Connect the bar to the link and tighten the nut to 50 ft. lbs. (68 Nm).
11. Install the wheel and lower the truck.

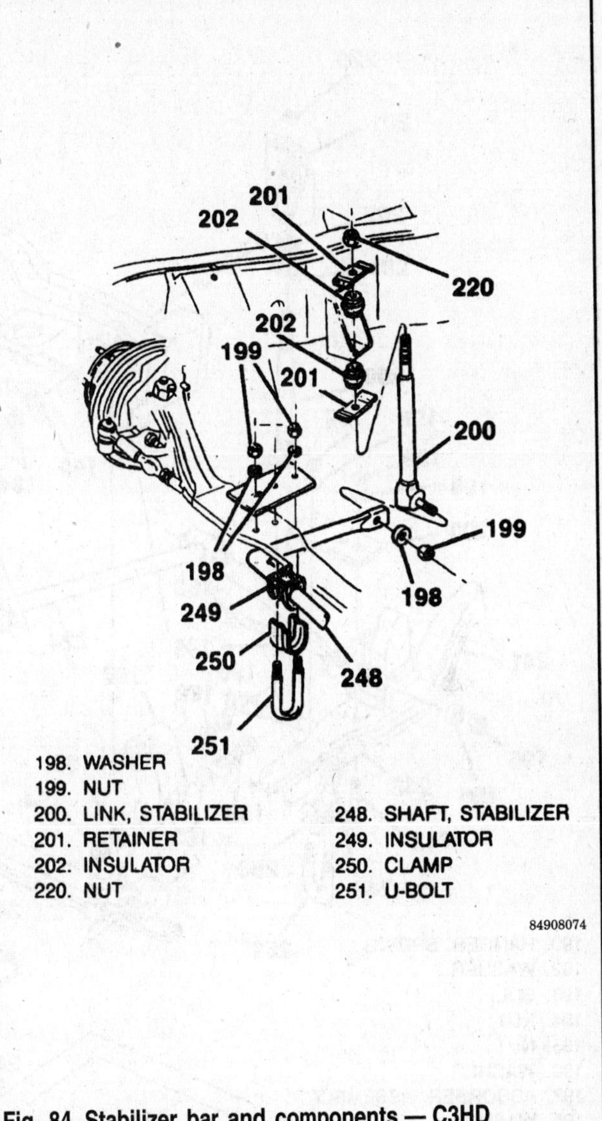

Fig. 84 Stabilizer bar and components — C3HD

Steering Arm, Knuckle and Spindle

REMOVAL & INSTALLATION

➧ **See Figure 85**

1. Raise the front of the truck and support it with safety stands. Remove the wheels.
2. Remove the brake caliper and hub/rotor assembly.
3. Loosen the mounting bolts and remove the anchor plate and splash shield. Press out the steering rod and let it hang by the rods.
4. Remove the brake hose bracket.
5. Remove the gaskets. Remove the caps from the knuckle.
6. Remove the nut, washer and lock pin and then drive the king pin out of the knuckle with a drift. Collect the spacers and bushings.
7. Disconnect the knuckle from the axle.

To install:

8. Install new bushings and ream them to 1.1804-1.1820 in. (29.982-30.022mm).
9. Install the knuckle to the axle and install the thrust bearing, shim and dust seal. Lubricate the king pin and install it with the spacers in the order in which they came out. Install the washer, nut and lock pin. Tighten the nut to 29 ft. lbs. (40 Nm).
10. Install the gaskets, caps and brake line bracket. Tighten the mounting bolts to 60 inch. lbs. (7 Nm).

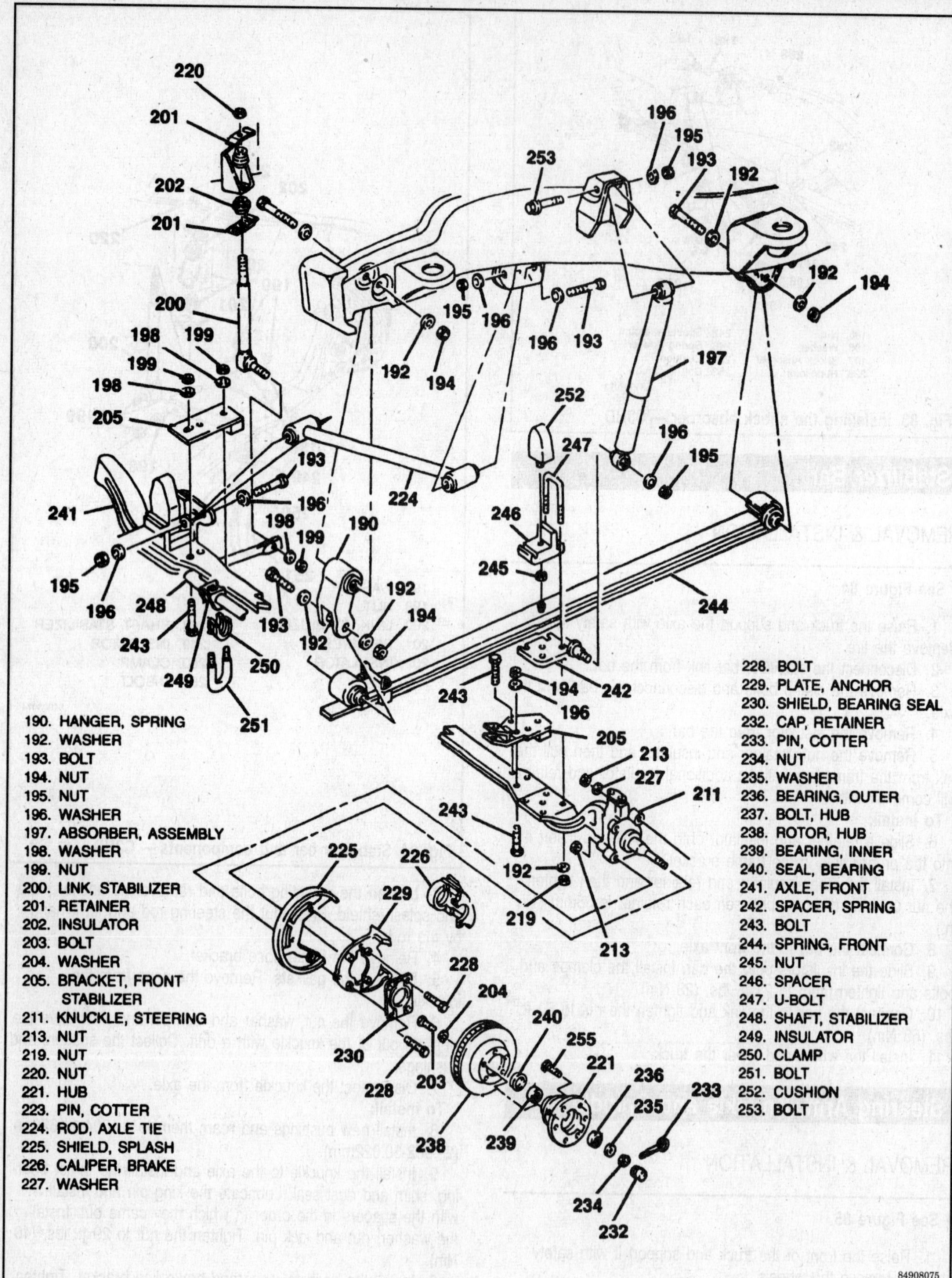

Fig. 85 Exploded view of the suspension system — C3HD

11. Connect the steering arm and install the splash shield and anchor plate. Tighten the bolts to 12 ft. lbs. (16 Nm) and the nuts to 230 ft. lbs. (312 Nm).

12. Install the hub assembly and adjust the wheel bearings. Install the caliper and wheels and then lower the truck. Check the alignment.

Front End Alignment

Correct alignment of the front suspension is necessary to provide optimum tire life and for proper and safe handling of the vehicle. Caster and camber cannot be set or measured accurately without professional equipment. Toe-in can be adjusted with some degree of success without any special equipment.

CASTER

Caster is the tilt of the front steering axis either forward or backward away from the vertical. A tilt toward the rear is said to be positive and a forward tilt is negative. Caster is calculated with a special instrument but one can see the caster angle by looking straight down from the top of the upper control arm. You will see that the ball joints are not aligned if the caster angle is more or less than 0 degrees. If the vehicle has positive caster, the lower ball joint would be ahead of the upper ball joint center line.

Caster is designed into the front axle on four wheel drive trucks and is not adjustable.

CAMBER

Camber is the slope of the front wheels from the vertical when viewed from the front of the vehicle. When the wheels tilt outward at the top, the camber is positive. When the wheels tilt inward at the top, the camber is negative. The amount of positive and negative camber is measured in degrees from the vertical and the measurement is called camber angle.

Camber is designed into the front axle of all four wheel drive vehicles and is not adjustable.

TOE-IN

Toe-in is the amount, measured in a fraction of an inch, that the wheels are closer together in front than at the rear. Some vehicles are set with toe-out, that is, the wheels are closer together at the rear, than the front, to prevent excessive toe-in under power.

WHEEL ALIGNMENT

Year	Model	Caster Range (deg.)	Caster Preferred Setting (deg.)	Camber Range (deg.)	Camber Preferred Setting (deg.)	Toe-in (in.)	Steering Axis Inclination (deg.)
1988	Blazer	-	4P	3/4P-2P	1 1/2P	0	NA
	C1500	2 3/4P-4 3/4P	4P	0-1P	1/2P	1/8P	NA
	C2500	2 3/4P-4 3/4P	4P	0-1P	1/2P	1/8P	NA
	C3500	2 3/4P-4 3/4P	4P	0-1P	1/2P	1/8P	NA
	K1500	3P-5P	4P	12/32P-1 13/32P	29/32P	1/16P	NA
	K2500	3P-5P	4P	12/32P-1 13/32P	29/32P	1/16P	NA
	K3500	3P-5P	4P	12/32P-1 13/32P	29/32P	1/16P	NA
	R20	2 3/4P-4 3/4P	4P	1/2N-1P	3/4P	3/16P	NA
	R30	2 3/4P-4 3/4P	4P	1/2N-1P	3/4P	3/16P	NA
	Suburban	2 3/4P-4 3/4P	4P	3/4P-2P	1 1/2P	0	NA
	V30	2 3/4P-4 3/4P	8P	3/4P-2P	1 3/8P	1/4P	NA
1989	Blazer	2 3/4P-4 3/4P	4P	3/4P-2P	1 1/2P	0	NA
	C1500	2 3/4P-4 3/4P	4P	0-1P	1/2P	1/8P	NA
	C2500	2 3/4P-4 3/4P	4P	0-1P	1/2P	1/8P	NA
	C3500	2 3/4P-4 3/4P	4P	0-1P	1/2P	1/8P	NA
	K1500	3P-5P	4P	12/32P-1 13/32P	29/32P	1/16P	NA
	K2500	3P-5P	4P	12/32P-1 13/32P	29/32P	1/16P	NA
	K3500	3P-5P	4P	12/32P-1 13/32P	29/32P	1/16P	NA
	R2500	2 3/4P-4 3/4P	4P	1/2N-1P	3/4P	3/16P	NA
	R3500	2 3/4P-4 3/4P	4P	1/2N-1P	3/4P	3/16P	NA
	Suburban	2 3/4P-4 3/4P	4P	3/4P-2P	1 1/2P	0	NA
	V3500	2 3/4P-4 3/4P	8P	3/4P-2P	1 3/8P	1/4P	NA
1990	Blazer	2 3/4P-4 3/4P	4P	3/4P-2P	1 1/2P	0	NA
	C1500	2 3/4P-4 3/4P	4P	0-1P	1/2P	1/8P	NA
	C2500	2 3/4P-4 3/4P	4P	0-1P	1/2P	1/8P	NA
	C3500	2 3/4P-4 3/4P	4P	0-1P	1/2P	1/8P	NA
	K1500	3P-5P	4P	12/32P-1 13/32P	29/32P	1/16P	NA
	K2500	3P-5P	4P	12/32P-1 13/32P	29/32P	1/16P	NA
	K3500	3P-5P	4P	12/32P-1 13/32P	29/32P	1/16P	NA
	R3500	2 3/4P-4 3/4P	4P	1/2N-1P	3/4P	3/16P	NA
	Suburban	2 3/4P-4 3/4P	4P	3/4P-2P	1 1/2P	0	NA
	V3500	2 3/4P-4 3/4P	4P	3/4P-2P	1 3/8P	1/4P	NA
1991	Blazer	2 3/4P-4 3/4P	4P	3/4P-2P	1 1/2P	0	NA
	C1500	2 3/4P-4 3/4P	3 3/4P	0-1P	1/2P	1/8P	NA
	C2500	2 3/4P-4 3/4P	3 3/4P	0-1P	1/2P	1/8P	NA
	C3500	2 3/4P-4 3/4P	3 3/4P	0-1P	1/2P	1/8P	NA
	K1500	3P-5P	4P	12/32P-1 13/32P	29/32P	1/16P	NA
	K2500	3P-5P	4P	12/32P-1 13/32P	29/32P	1/16P	NA
	K3500	3P-5P	4P	12/32P-1 13/32P	29/32P	1/16P	NA
	R3500	2 3/4P-4 3/4P	4P	1/2N-1P	3/4P	3/16P	NA
	Suburban	2 3/4P-4 3/4P	4P	3/4P-2P	1 1/2P	0	NA

87988C01

WHEEL ALIGNMENT

Year	Model	Caster Range (deg.)	Caster Preferred Setting (deg.)	Camber Range (deg.)	Camber Preferred Setting (deg.)	Toe-in (in.)	Steering Axis Inclination (deg.)
1992	Blazer	2 3/4P-4 3/4P	4P	3/4P-2P	1 1/2P	1/8P	NA
	C1500	3 3/4P-5 3/4P	4 3/4P	0-1P	1/2P	1/8P	NA
	C2500	3 3/4P-5 3/4P	4 3/4P	0-1P	1/2P	1/8P	NA
	C3500	3 3/4P-5 3/4P	4 3/4P	0-1P	1/2P	1/8P	NA
	K1500	1P-5P	3P	0-1P	1/2P	1/4P	NA
	K2500	1P-5P	3P	0-1P	1/2P	1/4P	NA
	K3500	1P-5P	3P	0-1P	1/2P	1/4P	NA
	Suburban	2 3/4P-4 3/4P	3P	3/4P-2P	1 1/2P	0	NA
1993	Blazer	2 3/4P-4 3/4P	3P	3/4P-2P	1 1/2P	0	NA
	C1500	3 3/4P-5 3/4P	4 3/4P	0-1P	1/2P	1/8P	NA
	C2500	3 3/4P-5 3/4P	4 3/4P	0-1P	1/2P	1/8P	NA
	C3500	3 3/4P-5 3/4P	4 3/4P	0-1P	1/2P	1/8P	NA
	K1500	1P-5P	3P	0-1P	1/2P	1/4P	NA
	K2500	1P-5P	3P	0-1P	1/2P	1/4P	NA
	K3500	1P-5P	3P	0-1P	1/2P	1/4P	NA
	Suburban	2 3/4P-4 3/4P	3P	3/4P-2P	1 1/2P	0	NA
1994	Blazer	2 3/4P-4 3/4P	3P	3/4P-2P	1 1/2P	0	NA
	C1500	3 3/4P-5 3/4P	4 3/4P	0-1P	1/2P	1/8P	NA
	C2500	3 3/4P-5 3/4P	4 3/4P	0-1P	1/2P	1/8P	NA
	C3500	3 3/4P-5 3/4P	4 3/4P	0-1P	1/2P	1/8P	NA
	K1500	1P-5P	3P	0-1P	1/2P	1/4P	NA
	K2500	1P-5P	3P	0-1P	1/2P	1/4P	NA
	K3500	1P-5P	3P	0-1P	1/2P	1/4P	NA
	Suburban	2 3/4P-4 3/4P	3P	3/4P-2P	1 1/2P	0	NA
1995	C1500	3 3/4P-5 3/4P	4 3/4P	0-1P	1/2P	1/8P	NA
	C2500	3 3/4P-5 3/4P	4 3/4P	0-1P	1/2P	1/8P	NA
	C3500	3 3/4P-5 3/4P	4 3/4P	0-1P	1/2P	1/8P	NA
	K1500	1P-5P	3P	0-1P	1/2P	1/4P	NA
	K2500	1P-5P	3P	0-1P	1/2P	1/4P	NA
	K3500	1P-5P	3P	0-1P	1/2P	1/4P	NA
	Suburban	2 3/4P-4 3/4P	3P	3/4P-2P	1 1/2P	0	NA
	Yukon/Tahoe	2 3/4P-4 3/4P	3P	3/4P-2P	1 1/2P	0	NA
1996	C1500	3 3/4P-5 3/4P	4 3/4P	0-1P	1/2P	1/8P	NA
	C2500	3 3/4P-5 3/4P	4 3/4P	0-1P	1/2P	1/8P	NA
	C3500	3 3/4P-5 3/4P	4 3/4P	0-1P	1/2P	1/8P	NA
	K1500	1P-5P	3P	0-1P	1/2P	1/4P	NA
	K2500	1P-5P	3P	0-1P	1/2P	1/4P	NA
	K3500	1P-5P	3P	0-1P	1/2P	1/4P	NA
	Suburban	2 3/4P-4 3/4P	3P	3/4P-2P	1 1/2P	0	NA
	Yukon/Tahoe	2 3/4P-4 3/4P	3P	3/4P-2P	1 1/2P	0	NA

87988C02

REAR SUSPENSION

⁂CAUTION

All suspension and steering fasteners are important attaching parts in that they could affect the performance of vital components and systems, and/or could result in major repair expense. They must be replaced with one of the same part number or with an equivalent part if replacement becomes necessary. Do not use a replacement part of lesser quality or substitute design. Torque values must be used as specified during reassembly to assure proper retention of these parts. Observe all nut and bolt torque specifications.

Leaf Spring

REMOVAL & INSTALLATION

R/V Series

See Figures 86, 87 and 88

1. Raise the vehicle and support it so that there is no tension on the leaf spring assembly.
2. Remove the stabilizer bar.
3. Loosen the spring-to-shackle retaining bolts. (Do not remove these bolts).
4. Remove the bolts which attach the shackle to the spring hanger.
5. Remove the nut and bolt which attach the spring to the front hanger.
6. Remove the U-bolt nuts.
7. Remove the stabilizer bar anchor plate, spacers, and shims. Take note of their positions.
8. If so equipped, remove the auxiliary spring.
9. Pull the spring from the vehicle.
10. Inspect the spring and replace any damaged components.

➡If the spring bushings are defective, use the following procedures for Removal & Installation. ¾ ton and 1 ton trucks use bushings that are staked in place. The stakes must first be straightened. When a new bushing is installed stake it in 3 equally spaced locations. Using a press or vise, remove the bushing and install the new one.

To install:

11. Place the spring assembly onto the axle housing. Position the front and rear of the spring at the hangers. Raise the axle with a floor jack as necessary to make the alignments. Install the front and rear hanger bolts loosely.
12. Install the spacers, shims, auxiliary spring and anchor plate or spring plate.
13. Install the U-bolts, washers and nuts.
14. Tighten the nuts, in a diagonal sequence, to 18 ft. lbs. (24 Nm). When the spring is evenly seated, Tighten the 10/15 and 20/25 Series nuts to 125 ft. lbs. (169 Nm). Tighten the 30/35 Series nuts to 147 ft. lbs. (200 Nm). Use the same diagonal sequence.
15. Make sure that the hanger and shackle bolts are properly installed. The front hanger bolt head is outboard as is the rear spring-to-shackle bolt head. The shackle-to-hanger bolt head faces inboard. When all the bolts, washers and nuts are installed, tighten them to 92 ft. lbs. (124 Nm) if you are torquing on the nut; 110 ft. lbs. (149 Nm) if your are torquing on the bolt head.
16. Install the stabilizer bar.

C/K Series

See Figures 89, 90, 91, 92, 93 and 94

1. Raise the vehicle and support it so that there is no tension on the leaf spring assembly.
2. Loosen the spring-to-shackle retaining bolts. (Do not remove these bolts).
3. Remove the U-bolt nuts, plates, and spacer(s).
4. Remove the bolts which attach the shackle to the spring hanger.
5. Remove the bolt which attaches the spring to the front hanger.
6. Pull the spring from the vehicle.
7. Inspect the spring and replace any damaged components.

➡If the spring bushings are defective, use the following procedures for replacement. On bushings that are staked in place, the stakes must first be straightened. Using a press or vise, remove the bushing and install the new one. When a new, previously staked bushing is installed, stake it in 3 equally spaced locations.

To install:

8. Place the spring assembly onto the axle housing. Position the front and rear of the spring at the hangers. Raise the axle with a floor jack as necessary to make the alignments. Install the front and rear hanger bolts loosely.
9. Install the spacers and spring plate.
10. Install the **NEW** U-bolts, washers and nuts.
11. Tighten the nuts, in a diagonal sequence, to 17 ft. lbs. (23 Nm). When the spring is evenly seated, tighten the nuts as follows:
    - 15/25 Series: 81 ft. lbs. (110 Nm)
    - 35 Series without dual wheels or 8-7.4L engine: 81 ft. lbs. (110 Nm)
    - 35 Series with dual wheels: 110 ft. lbs. (148 Nm)
    - 35 Series with 8-7.4L engine, without dual wheels: 110 ft. lbs. (148 Nm)
    - C3HD Series: 207 ft. lbs. (280 Nm)
12. Make sure that the hanger and shackle bolts are properly installed. All bolt heads should be inboard. Don't tighten them yet.
13. Using the floor jack, raise the axle until the distance between the bottom of the rebound bumper and its contact point on the axle is 182mm ± 6mm.
14. When the spring is properly positioned, tighten all the hanger and shackle nuts to 81 ft. lbs. (110 Nm) except on the C3HD. On the C3HD, tighten the nuts to 207 ft. lbs. (280 Nm).

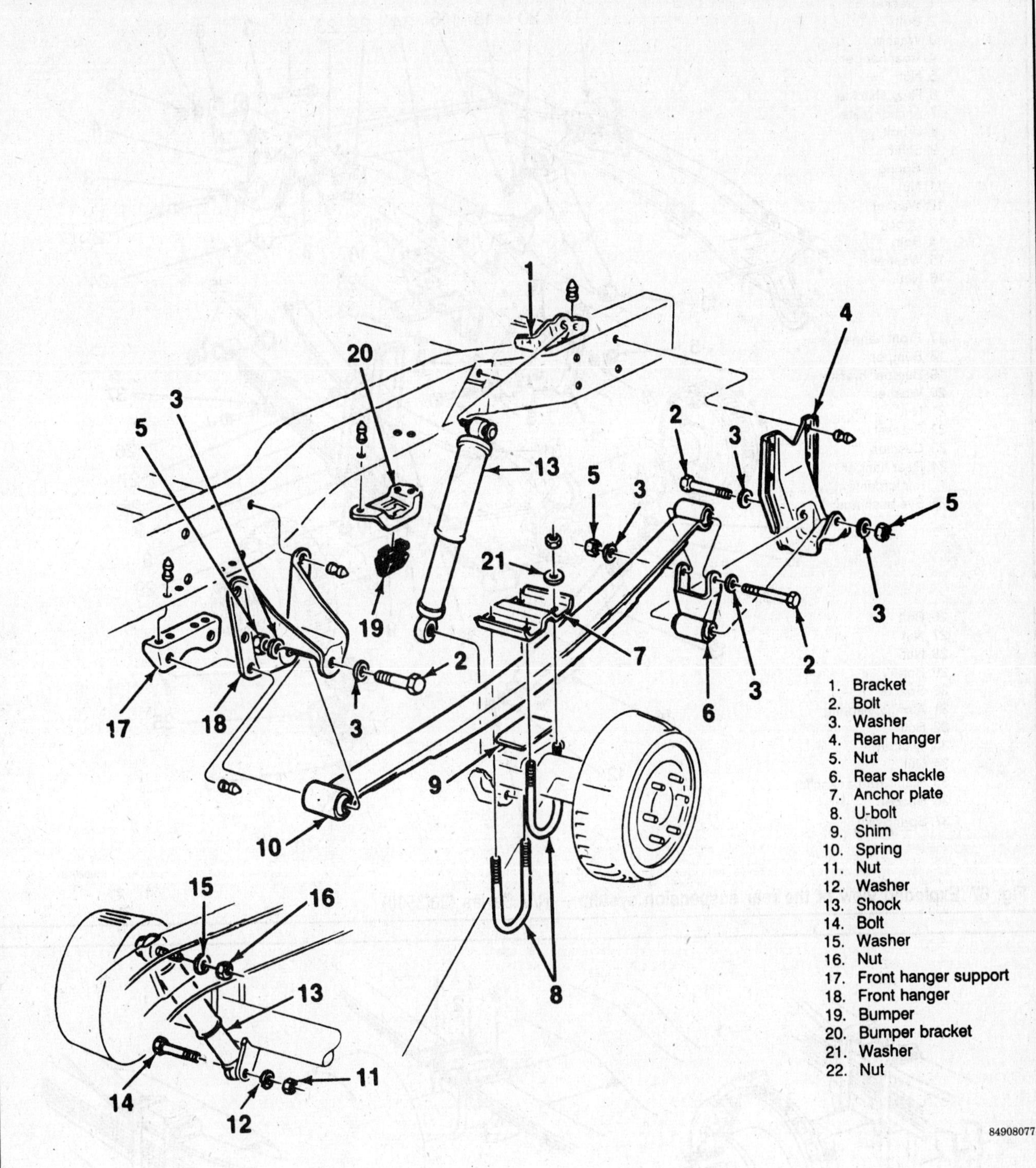

Fig. 86 Exploded view of the rear suspension system — R/V Series (exc. 30/3500)

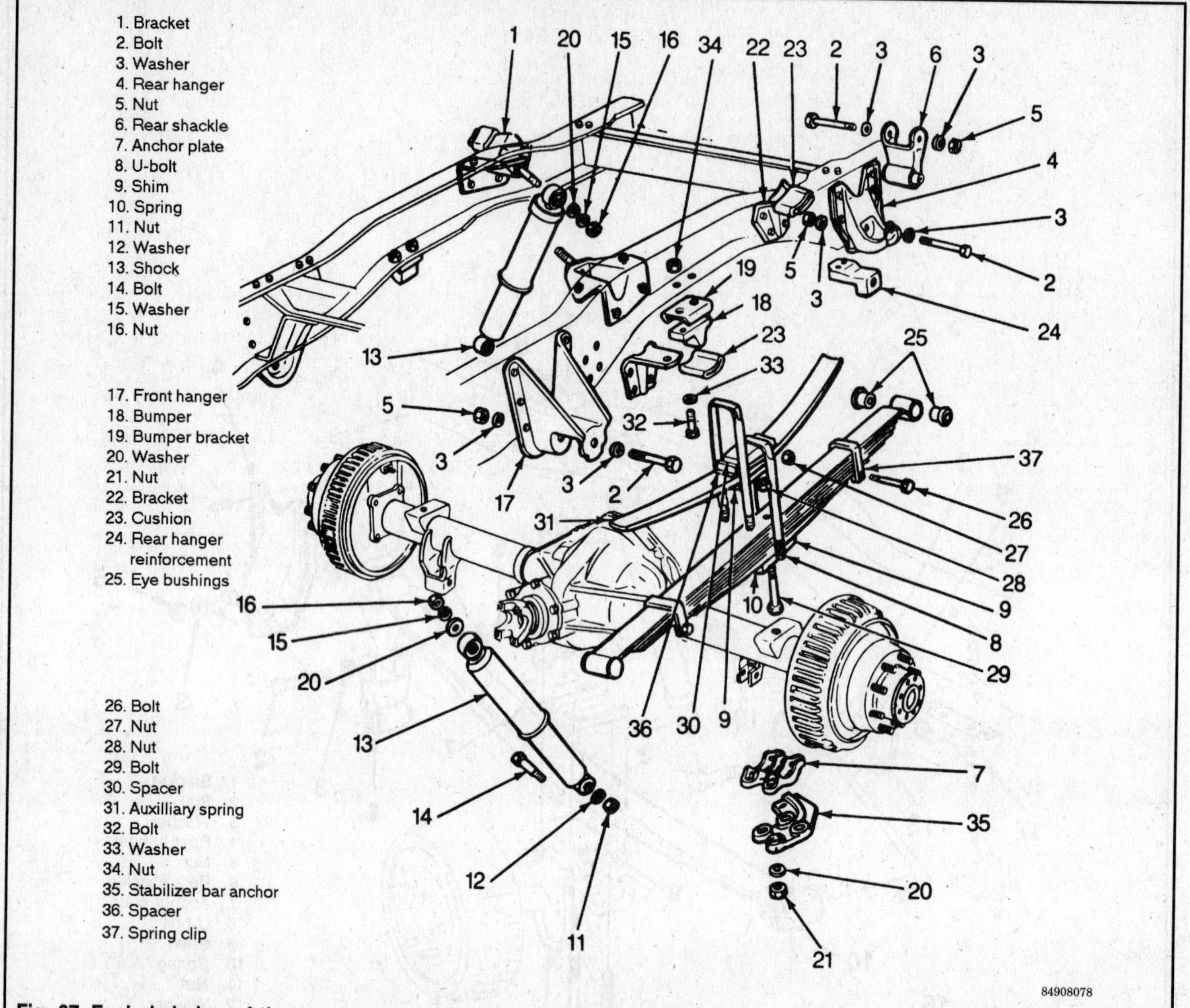

1. Bracket
2. Bolt
3. Washer
4. Rear hanger
5. Nut
6. Rear shackle
7. Anchor plate
8. U-bolt
9. Shim
10. Spring
11. Nut
12. Washer
13. Shock
14. Bolt
15. Washer
16. Nut
17. Front hanger
18. Bumper
19. Bumper bracket
20. Washer
21. Nut
22. Bracket
23. Cushion
24. Rear hanger reinforcement
25. Eye bushings
26. Bolt
27. Nut
28. Nut
29. Bolt
30. Spacer
31. Auxilliary spring
32. Bolt
33. Washer
34. Nut
35. Stabilizer bar anchor
36. Spacer
37. Spring clip

84908078

Fig. 87 Exploded view of the rear suspension system — R/V Series (30/3500)

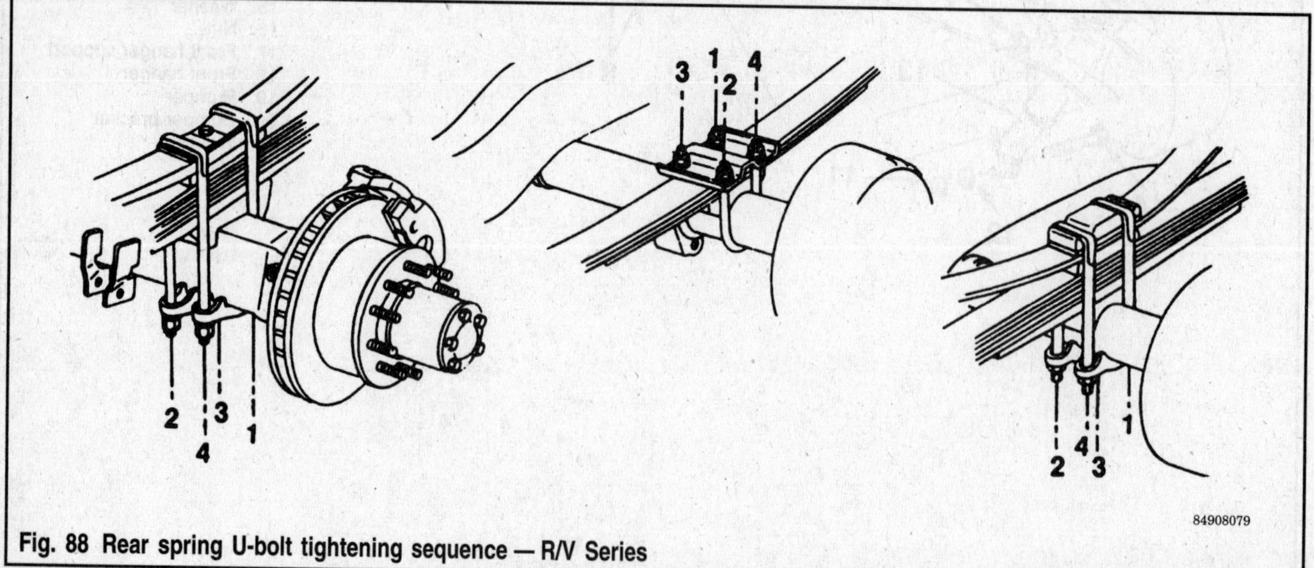

Fig. 88 Rear spring U-bolt tightening sequence — R/V Series

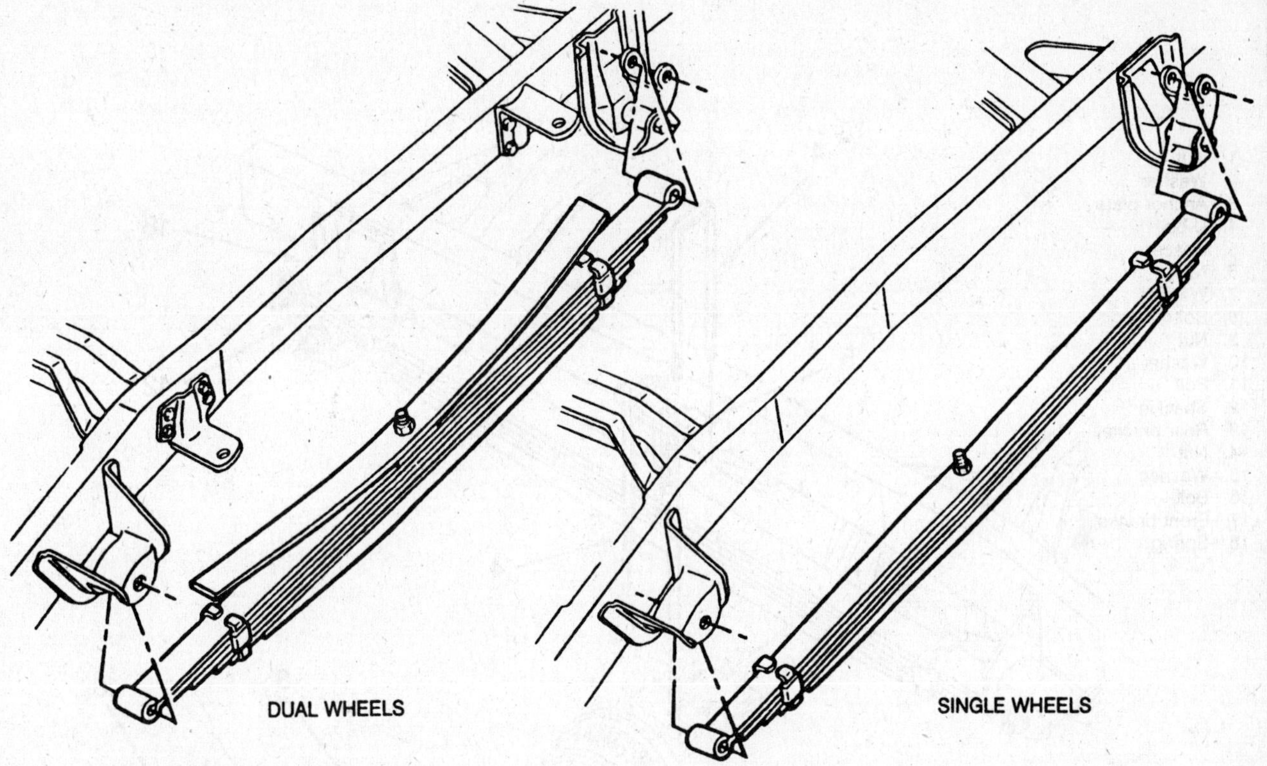

DUAL WHEELS
SINGLE WHEELS
84908080

Fig. 89 Rear leaf springs — 1988-90 C/K Series

A
B
C
A. Single Wheel Spring Assembly
B. Dual Wheel Spring Assembly
C. Heavy Duty Chassis C3HD Dual Wheel Spring Assembly
84908081

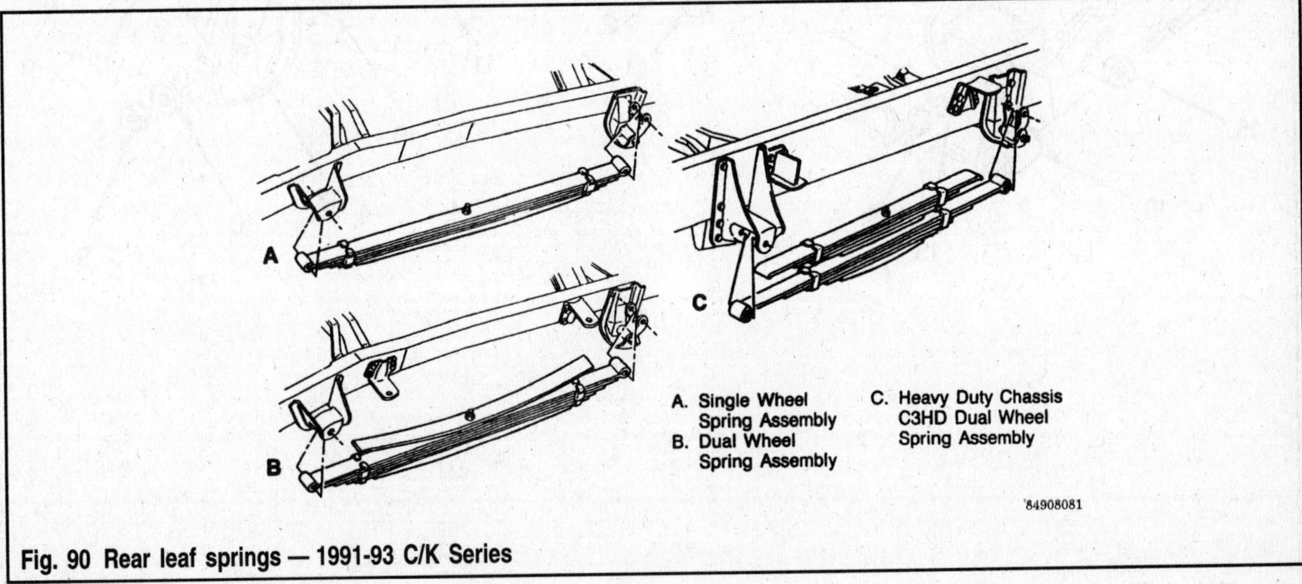

Fig. 90 Rear leaf springs — 1991-93 C/K Series

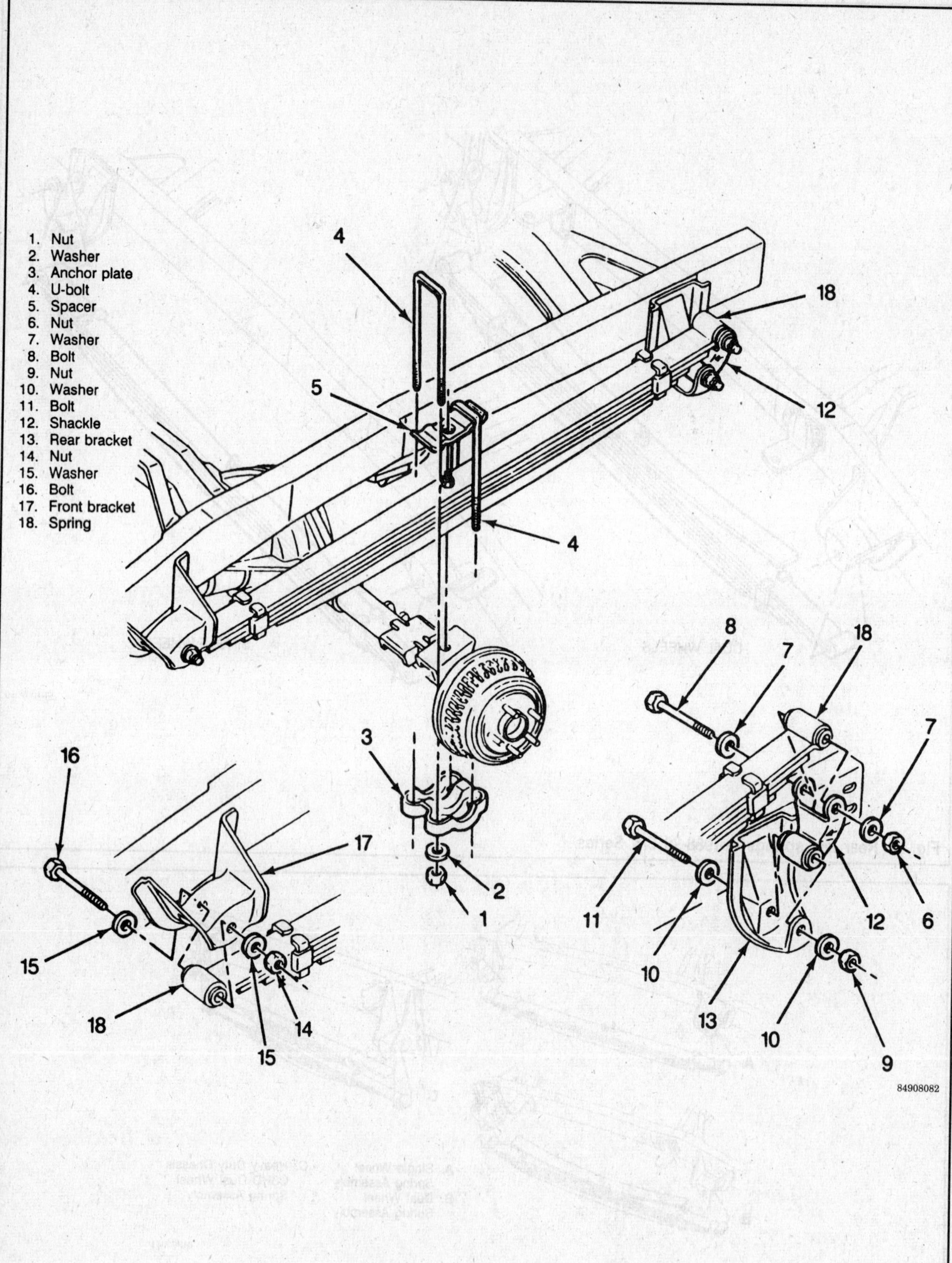

Fig. 91 Installing the rear leaf springs — 1988-90 C/K Series

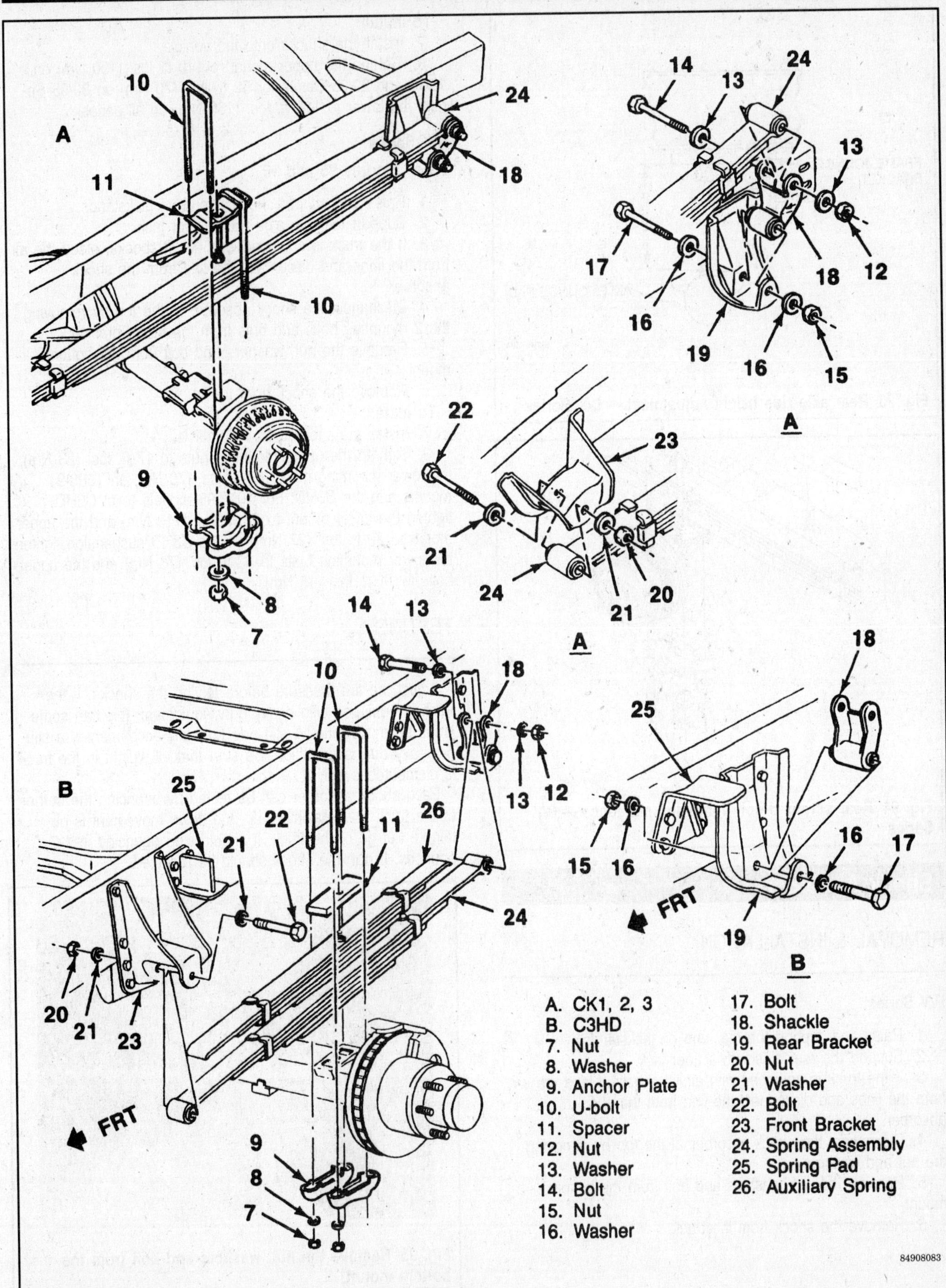

Fig. 92 Installing the rear leaf springs — 1991-93 C/K Series

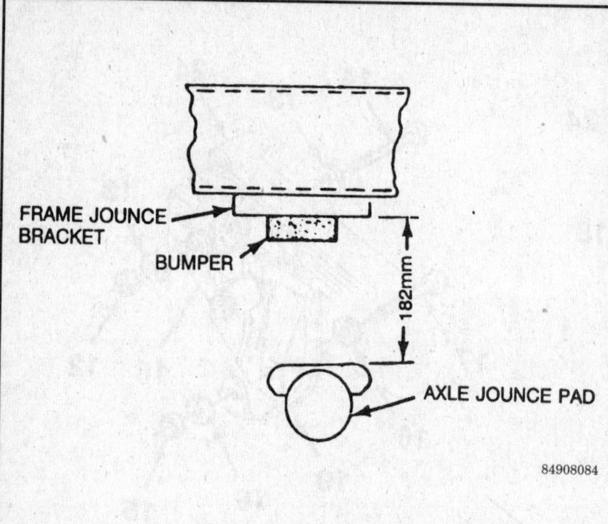

Fig. 93 Rear axle ride height adjustment — C/K Series

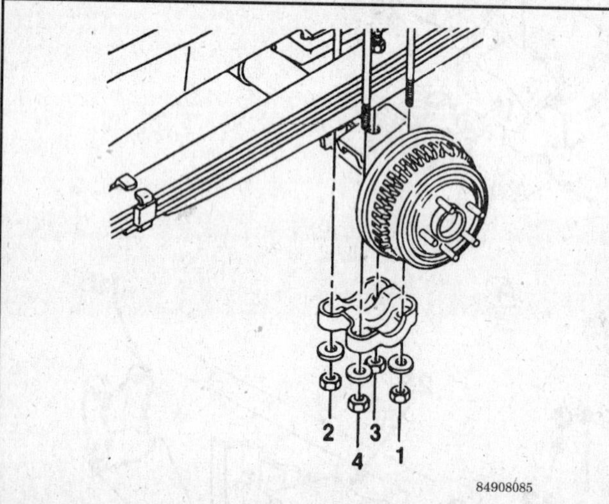

Fig. 94 Rear spring U-bolt tightening sequence — C/K Series

Shock Absorbers

REMOVAL & INSTALLATION

R/V Series

1. Raise and support the rear end on jackstands.
2. Support the rear axle with a floor jack.
3. If the truck is equipped with air lift shocks, bleed the air from the lines and disconnect the line from the shock absorber.
4. Disconnect the shock absorber at the top by removing the nut and washers.
5. Remove the nut, washers and bolt from the bottom mount.
6. Remove the shock from the truck.

To install:

7. Install the shocks onto the vehicle.
8. Tighten the upper mount to 140 ft. lbs. (190 Nm) on 10/15 and 20/25 Series, or 52 ft. lbs. (70 Nm) on 30/35 Series; the lower to 115 ft. lbs. (160 Nm) on all series.

C/K Series

➧ See Figures 95 and 96

1. Raise and support the rear end on jackstands.
2. Support the rear axle with a floor jack.
3. If the truck is equipped with air lift shocks, bleed the air from the lines and disconnect the line from the shock absorber.
4. Disconnect the shock absorber at the top by removing the 2 mounting bolts and nuts from the frame bracket.
5. Remove the nut, washers and bolt from the bottom mount.
6. Remove the shock from the truck.

To install:

7. Install the shock onto the vehicle.
8. Tighten the upper mounting nuts to 17 ft. lbs. (23 Nm); the lower mounting nut to 52 ft. lbs. (70 Nm) on 1988-91 models and the C3HD; For 1992-96 models (exc. C3HD), tighten the lower mount to 81 ft. lbs. (110 Nm) and the upper mount to 20 ft. lbs. (27 Nm) On the C3HD suspension tighten the lower mounting bolts to 52 ft. lbs. (70 Nm) and the upper bolts to 11 ft. lbs. (15 Nm).

TESTING

Adjust the tire pressure before testing the shocks. If the truck is equipped with heavy duty equipment, this can sometimes be misleading. A stiff ride normally accompanies a stiff or heavy duty suspension. Be sure that all weight in the truck is distributed evenly.

Each shock absorber can be tested by bouncing the corner of the truck until maximum up and down movement is obtained. Let go of the truck. It should stop bouncing in 1-2 bounces. If not, the shock should be replaced.

Fig. 95 Remove the nut, washers and bolt from the bottom mount

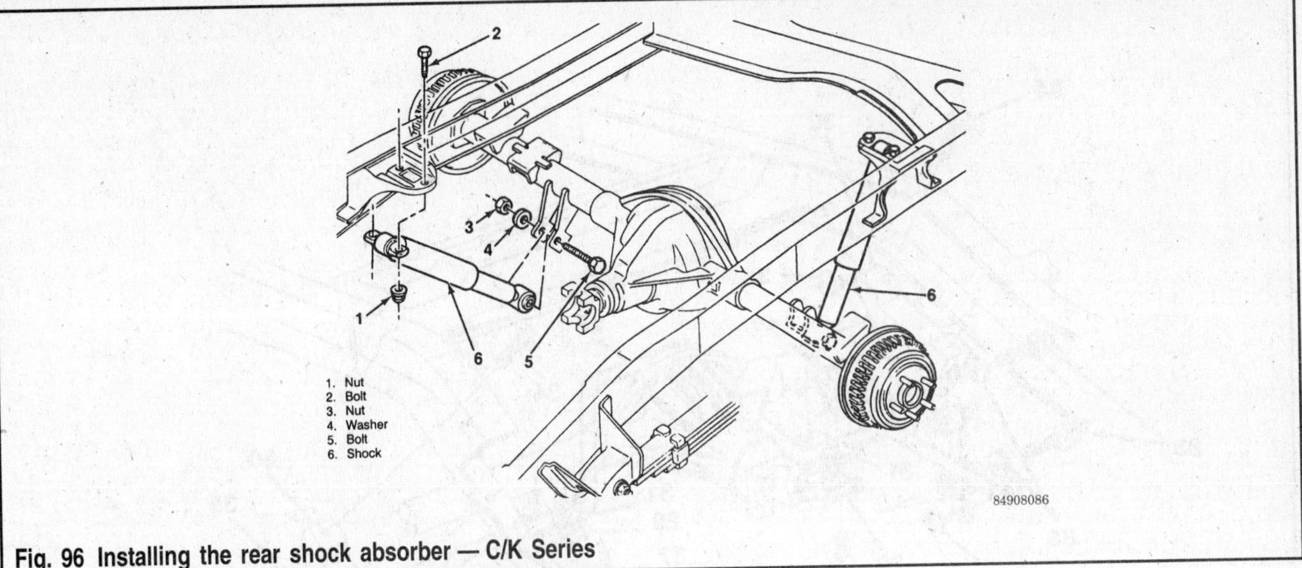

Fig. 96 Installing the rear shock absorber — C/K Series

Stabilizer Bar

REMOVAL & INSTALLATION

R/V Series

➧ See Figure 97

1. Raise and support the rear end on jackstands.
2. Remove the stabilizer bar end link nuts, bolts, washers, grommets and spacers. Take note of their respective positions for installation.
3. Remove the clamps securing the stabilizer bar to the anchor arms.
4. Remove the bar.
5. Remove the bushings from the clamps and check them for wear or damage. Replace them as necessary.

To install:

6. Install the bar onto the vehicle, coating the bushings and all rubber parts with silicone grease.
7. Tighten the end link nuts just until they reach the unthreaded part of the bolt.
8. Tighten the clamp-to-anchor bolts to 24 ft. lbs. (32 Nm).

CAUTION

Make sure that the parking brake cable is routed over the stabilizer bar!

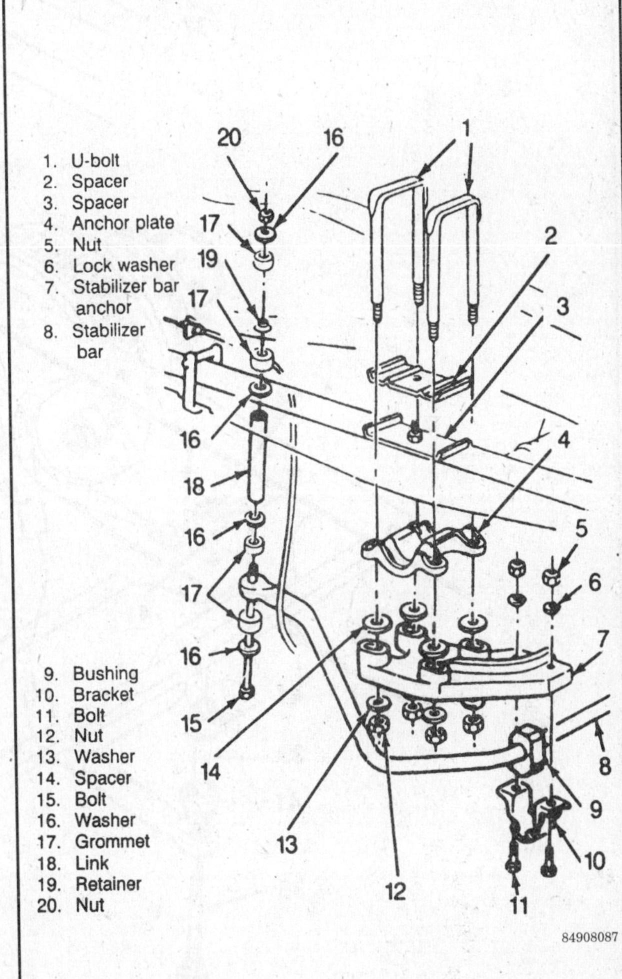

Fig. 97 Installing the rear stabilizer bar — 30/3500 R-Series

C3HD Series

➧ See Figure 98

1. Raise and support the vehicle on safety stands. Remove the wheels.
2. Remove the upper nut and insulator. Remove the bolts from the spacer and the bar.
3. Remove the U-bolt nuts, the U-bolts, clamps and lower insulators and lift out the bar.
4. Install the bar and tighten the U-bolt nuts to 22 ft. lbs. (30 Nm). Tighten the upper insulator nuts to 17 ft. lbs. (23 Nm).

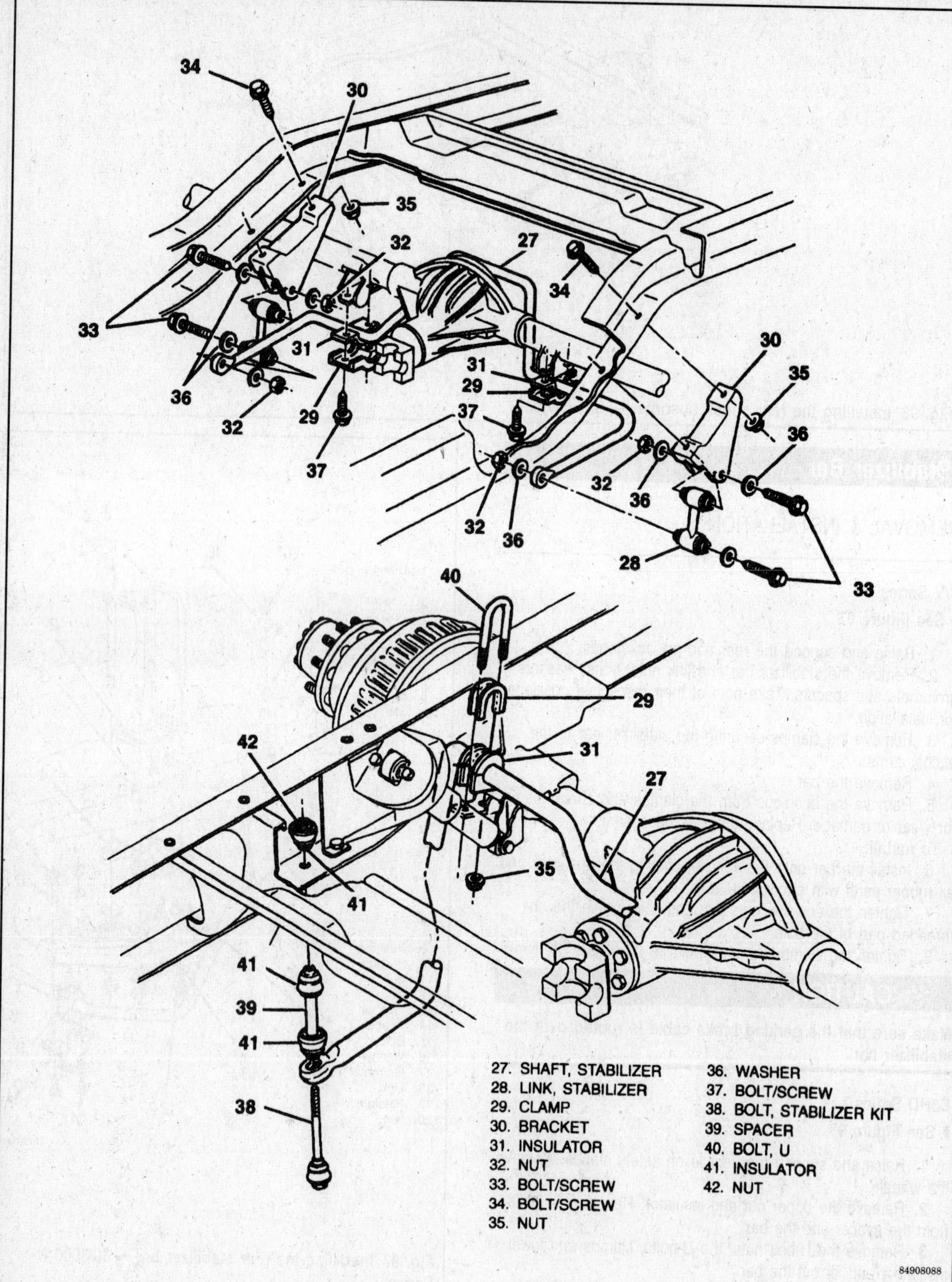

Fig. 98 Installing the rear stabilizer bar — C3HD

STEERING

Steering Wheel

REMOVAL & INSTALLATION

CAUTION

When performing service around the SIR system components or wiring, the SIR system MUST be disabled. Failure to do so could result in possible air bag deployment, personal injury or unneeded SIR system repairs.

All Series

See Figures 99, 100, 101, 102, 103, 104 and 105

1. Disconnect the battery ground cable.
2. Disable the Supplemental Restraint System (if equipped). Refer to Section 6 for this procedure.
3. Remove the horn button cap.
4. On some models, you'll have to disconnect the horn wires at this point.
5. Mark the steering wheel-to-steering shaft relationship.
6. Remove the snapring from the steering shaft.
7. Remove the nut and washer from the steering shaft.
8. Remove the steering wheel with a puller.

To install:

WARNING

Don't hammer on the steering shaft!

9. Install the wheel. The turn signal control assembly must be in the Neutral position to prevent damaging the canceling cam and control assembly. Tighten the nut to 30 ft. lbs. (40 Nm).

87988p13

Fig. 99 Remove the horn button cap

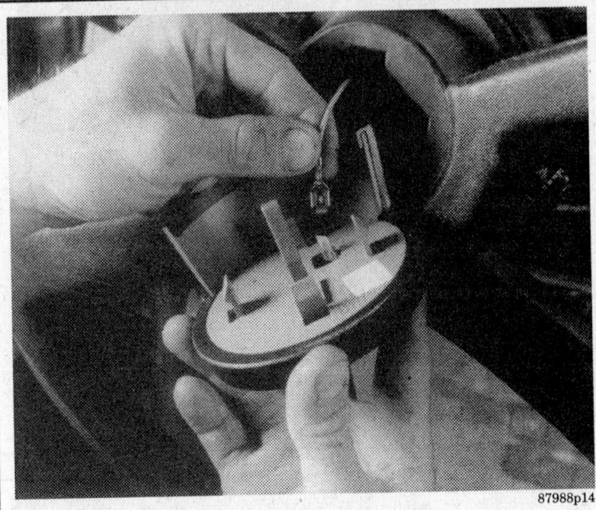

87988p14

Fig. 100 Disengage the horn wiring

87988p15

Fig. 101 Remove the snapring from the steering shaft

10. Install the horn pad and horn contact (if equipped).
11. Connect the battery ground cable and enable the SIR system (if equipped).

Turn Signal (Combination) Switch

REMOVAL & INSTALLATION

1988-94 Models

See Figures 106, 107, 108 and 109

1. Make sure the switch is in the off position.
2. Remove the steering wheel as outlined in this section.
3. Remove the instrument panel trim cover.

Fig. 102 Remove the nut and washer from the steering shaft

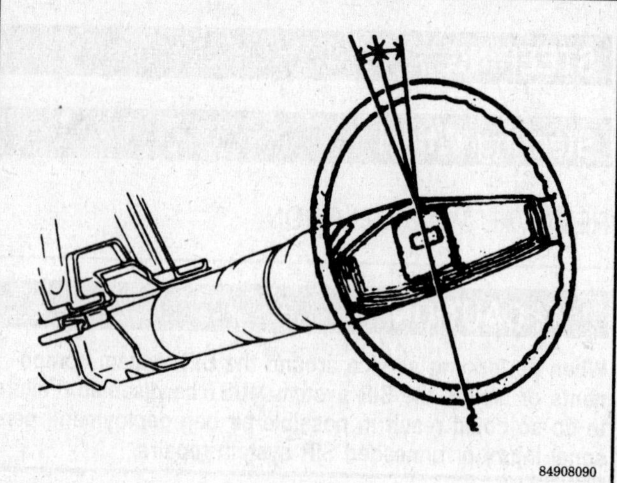

Fig. 105 Steering wheel alignment. Dimension A is 1 in. to either side of the centerline

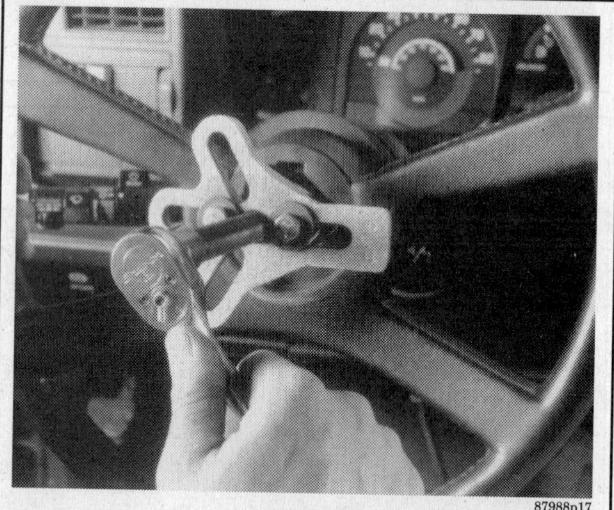

Fig. 103 Use a puller to remove the steering wheel

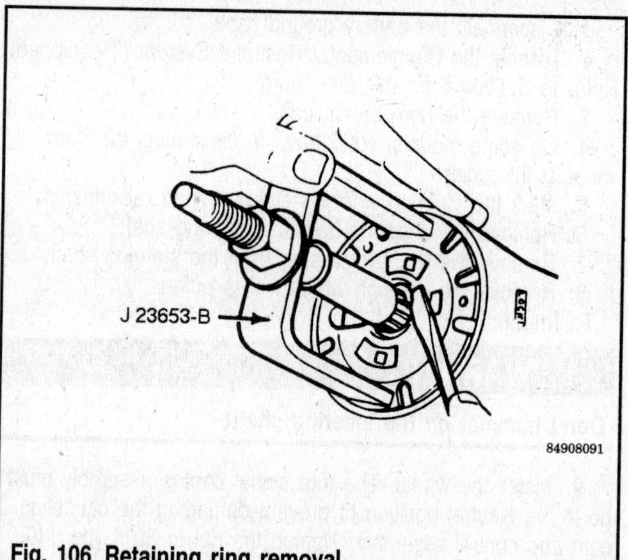

Fig. 106 Retaining ring removal

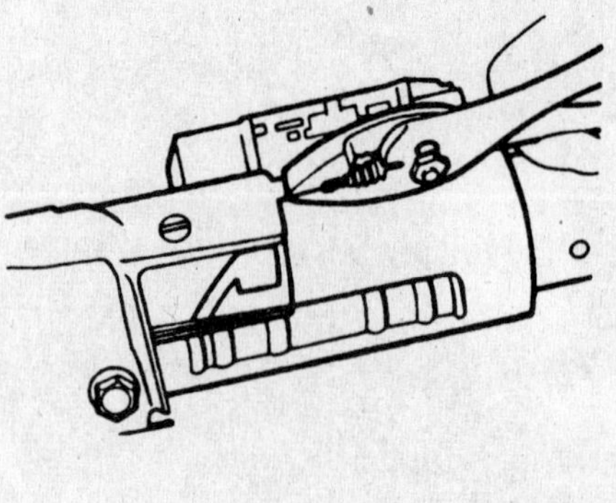

Fig. 104 Remove the steering wheel

84908092

Fig. 107 Removing the turn signal wire protector

Fig. 108 Removing the turn signal switch

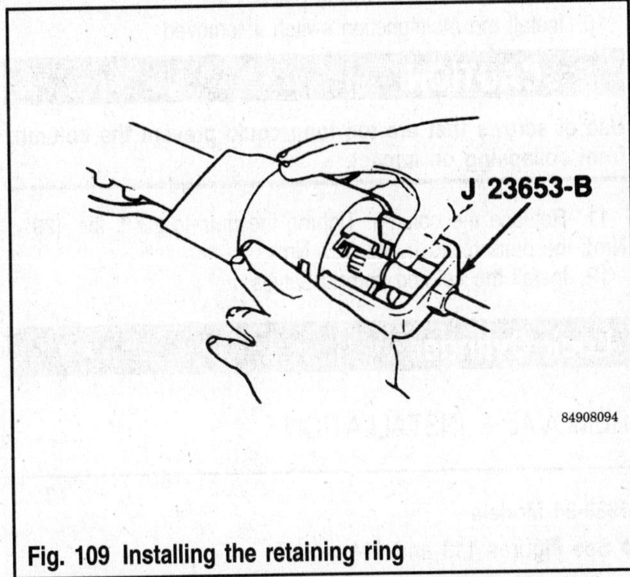

Fig. 109 Installing the retaining ring

4. Insert a screwdriver into the lockplate cover slot and pry out the cover. Remove the lockplate. A special tool is available to do this. The tool is an inverted U-shape, with a hole for the shaft. The shaft nut is used to force it down. Pry the wire snapring out of the shaft groove. Discard the snapring.
5. Remove the tool and lift the lockplate off the shaft.
6. Remove the turn signal lever screw and lever.
7. Press the hazard button inward and unscrew it.
8. Pull the switch connector out of the mast jacket and feed the switch connector through the column support bracket.
9. Position the turn signal lever and shifter housing in the downward, or 'low' position and pull downward on the lower end of the column using a pliers on the tab provided. Remove the wire protector.
10. Remove the switch mounting screws. Remove the switch by pulling it straight up while guiding the wiring harness cover through the column.

To install:

11. Install the replacement switch by working the connector and cover down through the housing and under the bracket.
12. Install the switch mounting screws and the connector on the mast jacket bracket. Install the column-to-dash trim plate.
13. Install the flasher knob and the turn signal lever.
14. With the turn signal lever in neutral and the flasher knob out, slide the thrust washer, upper bearing preload spring, and canceling cam into the shaft.
15. Position the lockplate on the shaft and press it down until a new snapring can be inserted in the shaft groove.
16. Install the cover and the steering wheel.

1995-96 Models

➧ See Figure 110

****CAUTION**

When performing service around the SIR system components or wiring, the SIR system MUST be disabled. Failure to do so could result in possible air bag deployment, personal injury or unneeded SIR system repairs.

1. Make sure the switch is in the off position.
2. Remove the steering wheel as outlined in this section.
3. Disconnect the tilt wheel lever by pulling it out.
4. Remove the knee bolster and the Torx® head screws from the lower column cover.
5. Lower the cover by tilting it down and then sliding it back to disengage the locking tabs.
6. Remove the Torx® head screws from the upper column cover.
7. Remove the steering column lock set and the upper cover.
8. Disconnect the wiring harness from the steering column wiring harness.
9. Remove the retainer from Connector Position Assurance (CPA) if equipped.
10. Disengage the connector from the Brake Transmission Shift Interlock (BTSI) if equipped.
11. Disengage the grey and black connectors from the bulkhead connector.
12. Unfasten the Torx® head screws from the switch and remove the switch.

To install:

13. Install the switch. Use a small blade screwdriver to compress the electrical contact and move the switch into position. The electrical contact must rest on the cancelling cam assembly.
14. Fasten the Torx® head screws on the switch. Tighten the screws to 53 inch. lbs. (6 Nm).
15. Engage the grey and black connectors to the bulkhead connector.
16. Engage the bulkhead connector to the vehicle wire harness.
17. Engage the connector to the Brake Transmission Shift Interlock (BTSI) if equipped..
18. Install the retainer to the Connector Position Assurance (CPA) if equipped.
19. Install the wire straps on the steering column harness.
20. Install the upper column cover and fasten the column bracket nuts. Tighten the nuts to 22 ft. lbs. (30 Nm).
21. Install the knee bolster and the steering column cylinder lock. Tighten the column cover Torx® screws to 12 inch. lbs. (1.4 Nm).

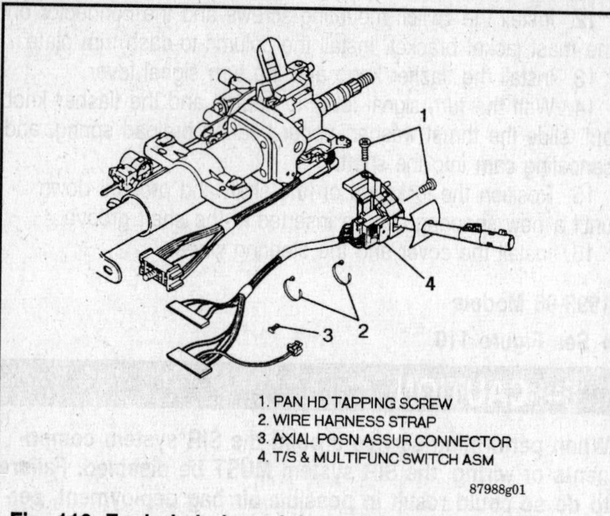

Fig. 110 Exploded view of the multifunction switch — 1996 C/K series

22. Install the lower column cover and tighten the Torx® screws 53 inch. lbs. (6 Nm).
23. Make sure the switch is in the off position and install the steering wheel.Refer to this section for this procedure.
24. Install the tilt wheel lever and connect the negative battery cable.
25. Enable the SIR system (if equipped). Refer to Section 6 for this procedure.

Ignition Switch

REMOVAL & INSTALLATION

➧ **See Figures 111 and 112**

1. Remove the column shroud halves.
2. Remove the column-to-dash attaching bolts and slowly lower the steering column, making sure that it is supported.
3. Remove the multifunction switch if necessary.

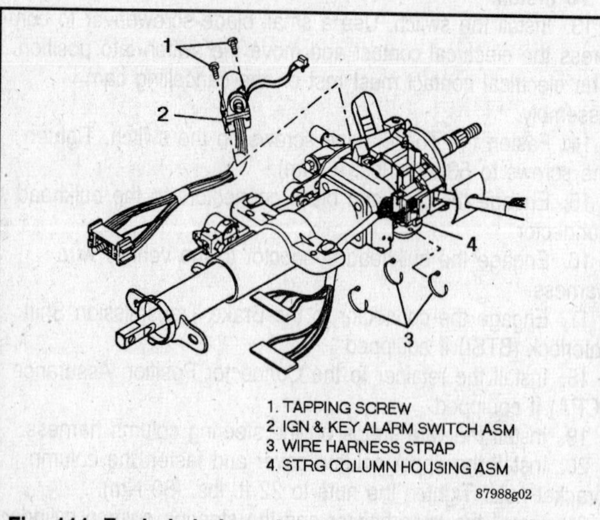

Fig. 111 Exploded view of the ignition and key alarm switch — 1996 C/K series

4. Remove the key alarm switch, if equipped by gently prying the alarm switch retaining clip with a small screwdriver. Rotate the alarm switch ¼ in. turn and remove.

WARNING

Extreme care is necessary to prevent damage to the collapsible column.

5. Make sure that the switch is in the Lock position. If the lock cylinder is out, pull the switch rod up to the stop, then go down one detent.
6. Remove the two screws and the switch.

To install:

7. Before installation, make sure the switch is in the Lock position.
8. Install the switch using the original screws. Tighten the screws to 12 inch. lbs. (1.4 Nm).
9. Install the key alarm switch, if equipped . Make sure the retaining clip is parallel to the lock cylinder. Rotate the alarm switch ¼ in. turn until locked in place.
10. Install the multifunction switch if removed.

CAUTION

Use of screws that are too long could prevent the column from collapsing on impact.

11. Replace the column. Tighten the nuts to 22 ft. lbs. (29 Nm); the bolts to 20 ft. lbs. (27 Nm).
12. Install the column shroud halves.

Lock Cylinder

REMOVAL & INSTALLATION

1988-94 Models

➧ **See Figures 113 and 114**

1. Remove the steering wheel.

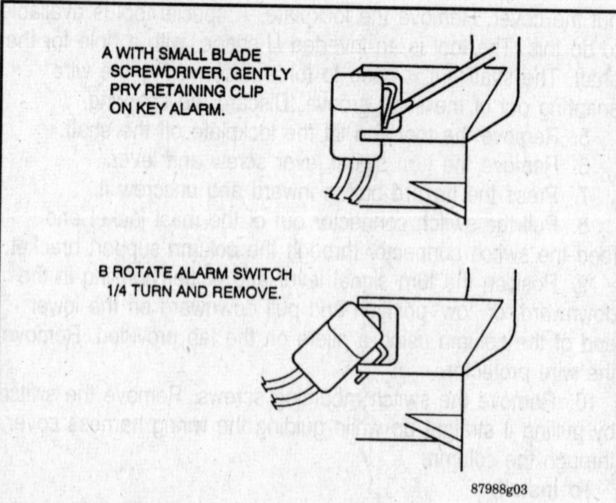

Fig. 112 Explode view of the alarm switch removal — 1996 C/K series

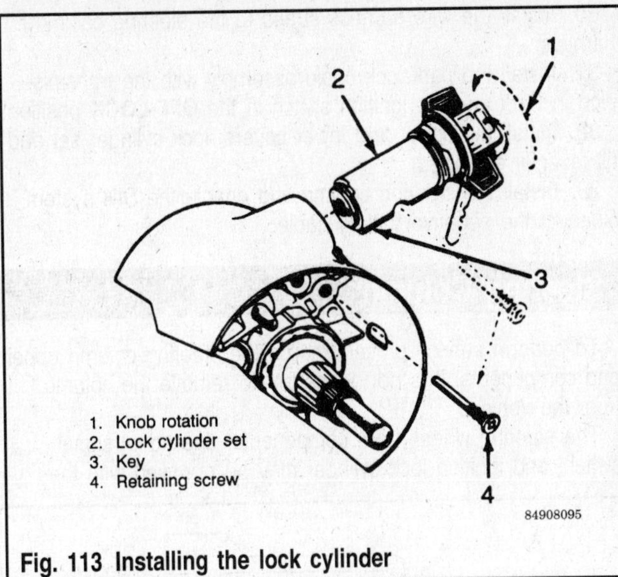

Fig. 113 Installing the lock cylinder

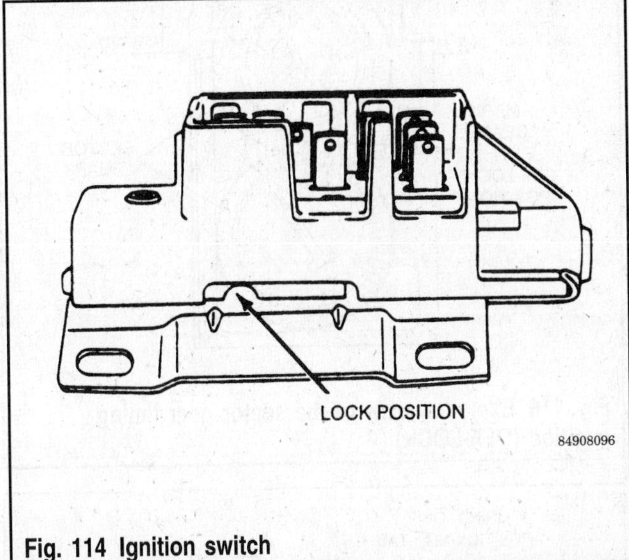

Fig. 114 Ignition switch

2. Remove the turn signal switch. It is not necessary to completely remove the switch from the column. Pull the switch rearward far enough to slip it over the end of the shaft, but do not pull the harness out of the column.
3. Turn the lock to Run.
4. Remove the lock retaining screw and remove the lock cylinder.

WARNING

If the retaining screw is dropped on removal, it may fall into the column, requiring complete disassembly of the column to retrieve the screw.

To install:

5. Rotate the key to the stop while holding onto the cylinder.
6. Push the lock all the way in.
7. Install the screw. Tighten the screw to 40 inch lbs. (5 Nm) for regular columns, 22 inch lbs. (2.5 Nm) for tilt columns.
8. Install the turn signal switch and the steering wheel.

1995-96 Models

See Figures 115, 116 and 117

CAUTION

When performing service around the SIR system components or wiring, the SIR system MUST be disabled. Failure to do so could result in possible air bag deployment, personal injury or unneeded SIR system repairs.

When carrying a live inflator module, make sure that the bag and trim cover are pointed away from you. Never carry the inflator module by the wires or connector on the underside of the module. In case of accidental deployment, the bag will then deploy with minimal chance of injury.

When placing a live inflator module on a bench or other surface, always face the bag and trim cover up, away from the surface.

1. Disconnect the negative battery cable and disable the SIR system. Refer to the procedure in Section 6.
2. Remove the upper and lower shroud, air bag module and the steering column.
3. Remove the retaining ring, SIR coil assembly, wave washer.
4. Remove the shaft lock retaining ring using tool J 23653-SIR or its equivalent to push down the shaft lock shield assembly. Discard the ring.
5. Remove the shaft lock shield and turn signal cancel cam assembly.
6. Remove the park lock cable assembly from the lock module assembly.
7. Remove the key alarm switch, if equipped by gently prying the alarm switch retaining clip with a small screwdriver. Rotate the alarm switch 1/4 in. turn and remove.

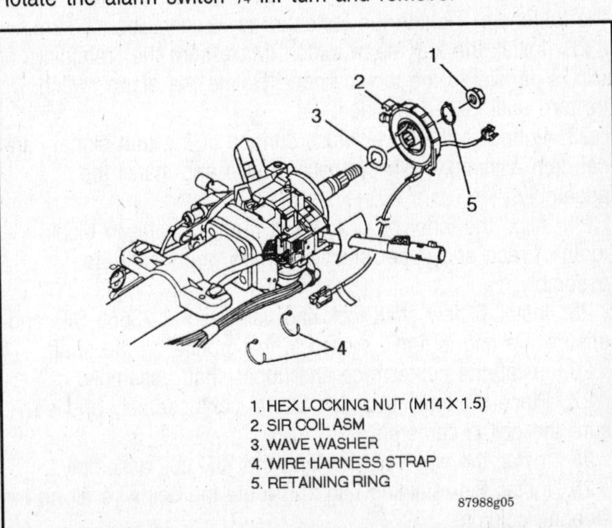

Fig. 115 Exploded view of the removal of the SIR coil assembly

8. Remove the two tapping screws and the ignition key and alarm assembly. Let the switch hang freely.

****CAUTION**

The lock assembly is under slight spring tension. Hold the lock bolt in place while removing the lock module assembly.

9. Remove the three pan head tapping screws and the lock module assembly.
10. Remove the backing plate from the module.

➡Mark the two sector gears at the OFF-LOCK position to ensure proper reassembly

11. Remove the sector gears.
12. Remove the positioning tab on the end of the lock cylinder using an ⅛ in. burring tool. Remove all burrs from the lock module and cylinder assembly.
13. Push on the locking tab of the lock cylinder from inside the the lock module assembly and remove the lock cylinder.

To install:

14. Align the marks on the sector gears and install the gears and the backing plate to the lock module assembly.
15. Install the lock cylinder set and ensure that the lock module assembly is in the **OFF-LOCK** position.
16. Install the key in the lock cylinder and ensure that it is in the **OFF-LOCK** position.
17. Line up the locking tab with the slots in the lock module assembly and push the cylinder into position.
18. Rotate the lock cylinder to the **ACC** position. The alignment arrows on the sector gears should be pointing towards each other.
19. Rotate the lock cylinder to the **LOCK** position. Push the lock bolt in until it is flush and align the lock module assembly with the head assembly and install the lock module assembly.
20. Install the three pan head screws and tighten to 53 inch. lbs. (6 Nm).
21. Install the ignition and key alarm switch assembly and the fasteners. Tighten the fasteners to 12 inch. lbs. (1 Nm).
22. Install the key alarm switch. Make sure the retaining clip is parallel to the lock cylinder. Rotate the alarm switch ¼ in. turn until locked in place.
23. Lubricate the lower brass surface of the turn signal cancel cam assembly with synthetic grease and install the assembly.
24. Align the inner block tooth of the lock plate to block tooth of race and upper shaft assembly and install the assembly.
25. Install a new shaft lock ring using tool J 23653-SIR and ensure the ring is firmly seated in the groove on the shaft.
26. Install the center race and upper shaft assembly.
27. Place the ignition switch to the lock assembly and ensure the coil is centered.
28. Install the wave washer and the SIR coil assembly.
29. Install the retaining ring and route the coil wire along the steering column.
30. Install the wire harness straps to the steering column harness.
31. Install the park lock cable assembly with the transmission in Park and the ignition switch in the **OFF-LOCK** position.
32. Install the upper and lower covers, lock cylinder set and tilt lever (if equipped).
33. Install the steering column and enable the SIR system. Connect the negative battery cable.

Steering Column

To perform service procedures on the steering column upper end components, it is not necessary to remove the column from the vehicle.

The steering wheel, horn components, directional signal switch, and ignition lock cylinder may be removed with the

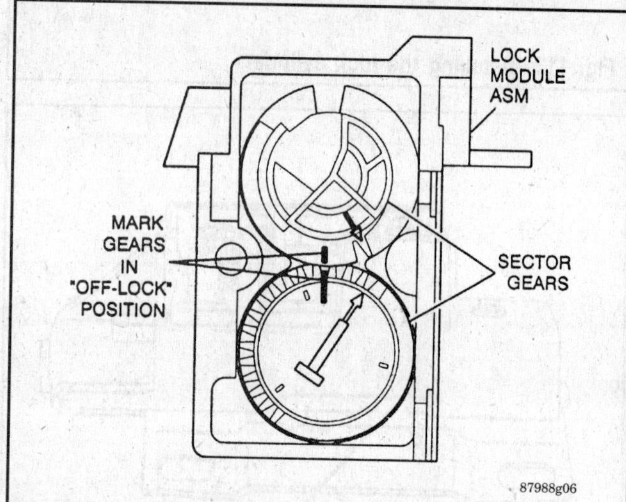

Fig. 116 Exploded view of the sector gear timing position (OFF-LOCK)

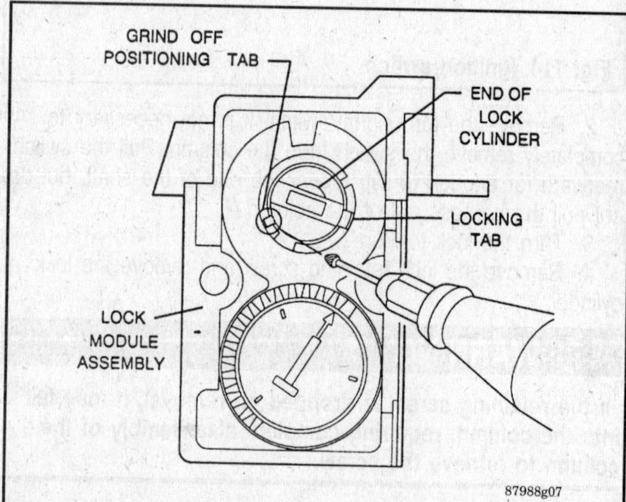

Fig. 117 Remove all burrs from the lock module and cylinder assembly

column remaining in the vehicle as described earlier in this section.

****WARNING**

The outer most jacket shift tube, steering shaft and instrument panel mounting bracket are designed as energy absorbing units. Because of the design of these components, it is absolutely necessary to handle the column with care when performing any service operation. Avoid hammering, jarring, dropping or leaning on any portion of the column. When reassembling the column components, use only the specified screws, nuts and bolts and tighten to specified torque. Care should be exercised in using over-length screws or bolts as they may prevent a portion of the column from compressing under impact.

INSPECTION

To determine if the energy absorbing steering column components are functioning as designed, or if repairs are required, a close inspection should be made. Inspection is called for in all cases where damage is evident or whenever the vehicle is being repaired due to a front end collision. Whenever a force has been exerted on the steering wheel or steering column, or its components, inspection should also be made. If damage is evident, the affected parts must be replaced.

The inspection procedure for the various steering column components are listed below.

Column Support Bracket

Damage in this area will be indicated by separation of the mounting capsules from the bracket. The bracket will have moved forward toward the engine compartment and will usually result in collapsing of the jacket section of the steering column.

Column Jacket

Inspect jacket section of column for looseness, and/or bends.

Shifter Shaft

Separation of the shifter shaft sections will be internal and cannot be visually identified. Hold lower end of the shifter shaft and move shift lever on column through its ranges and up and down. If there is little or no movement of the shifter shaft, the plastic joints are sheared.

Steering Shaft

If the steering shaft plastic pins have been sheared, the shaft will rattle when struck lightly from the side and some lash may be felt when rotating the steering wheel while holding the rag joint. It should be noted that if the steering shaft pins are sheared due to minor collision the vehicle can be safely steered; however, steering shaft replacement is recommended.

Because of the differences in the steering column types, be sure to refer to the set of instructions below which apply to the column being serviced.

REMOVAL & INSTALLATION

R/V Series

➧ **See Figures 118 and 119**

1. Disconnect the battery ground cable.
2. Remove the steering wheel as outlined under Steering Wheel Removal.
3. Remove the nuts and washers securing the flanged end of the steering shaft to the flexible coupling.
4. Disconnect the transmission control linkage from the column shift tube levers.
5. Disconnect the steering column harness at the connector. Disconnect the neutral start switch and back-up lamp switch connectors if so equipped.
6. Remove the floor pan trim cover screws and remove the cover.
7. Remove the transmission indicator cable, if so equipped.
8. Remove the screws securing the two halves of the floor pan cover, then remove the screws securing the halves and seal to the floor pan and remove the covers.
9. Move the front seat as far back as possible to provide maximum clearance.
10. Remove the two column bracket-to-instrument panel nuts and carefully remove from vehicle. Additional help should be obtained to guide the lower shift levers through the firewall opening.

To install:

11. Assemble the lower dash cover and upper dash cover to the seal with fasteners that are part of the seal.
12. Attach bracket to jacket and tighten four bolts to specified torque.
13. Position column in body and position flange to rag joint and install lock washers and nuts (May be tightened to specified torque at this time). Coupling on manual steering must be installed prior to column installation.
14. Loosely assemble (2) capsules nuts at the instrument panel bracket.
15. Position lower clamp and tighten attaching nuts to specified torque.
16. Tighten two nuts at capsules to specified torque.

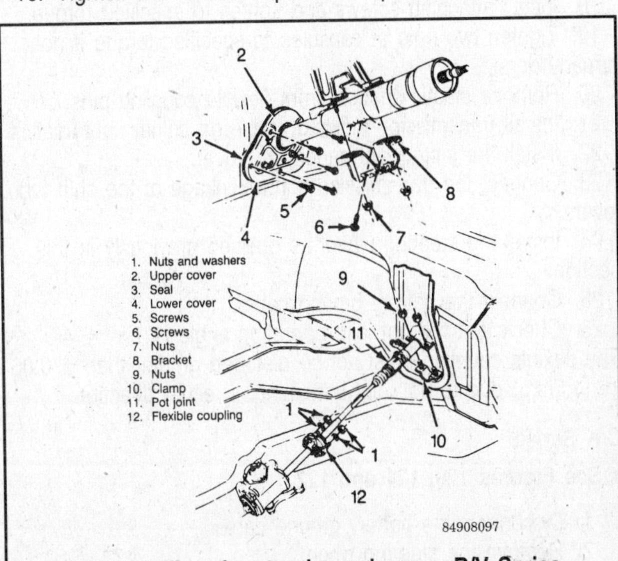

Fig. 118 Installing the steering column — R/V Series

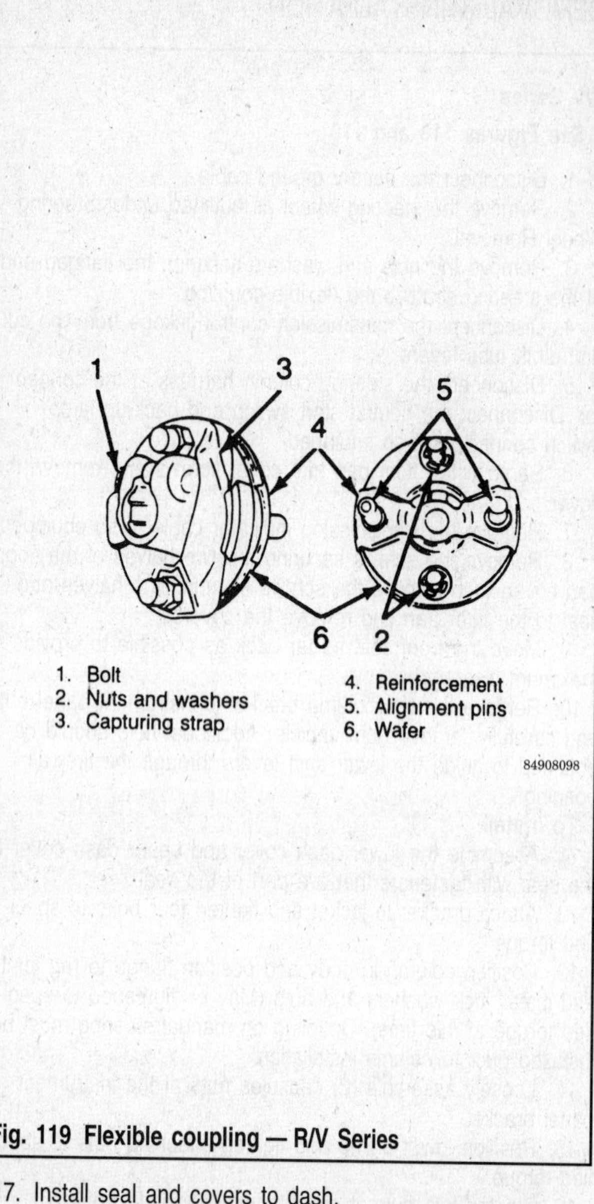

Fig. 119 Flexible coupling — R/V Series

17. Install seal and covers to dash.
18. Install attaching screws and tighten to specified torque.
19. Tighten two nuts at capsules to specified torque if not already done.
20. Remove plastic spacers from flexible coupling pins.
21. Install transmission indicator cable on column automatics.
22. Install the instrument panel trim cover.
23. Connect the transmission control linkage at the shift tube levers.
24. Install the steering wheel as outlined previously in this section.
25. Connect the battery ground cable.
26. Check that the pot joint operating angle is 1½° ± 4°. The flexible coupling must not be distorted greater than ± 0.06 in. (1.5mm) due to pot joint bottoming, in either direction.

C/K Series

➧ **See Figures 120, 121 and 122**

1. Disconnect the battery ground cable.
2. Remove the steering wheel.
3. Disconnect the transmission linkage at the column levers.
4. Matchmark the pot joint and steering shaft. Remove the pot joint bolt from the steering shaft.
5. Remove the steering column shrouds.
6. Remove the nuts, bolts and steering column support bracket.
7. Remove the column-to-floor plate bolts.
8. Disconnect the neutral start switch and back-up light switch wiring.
9. Lift out the column, rotating it as necessary for clearance.

To install:

10. Install the column, rotating it as necessary for clearance.
11. Install the nuts, bolts and steering column support bracket. Make them finger-tight, for now.
12. Guide the steering shaft into the pot joint, aligning the matchmarks. Install the pot joint bolt, passing through the cutout in the shaft. Tighten the bolt to 22 ft. lbs. (30 Nm).

➡The pot joint angle must not exceed 12½°.

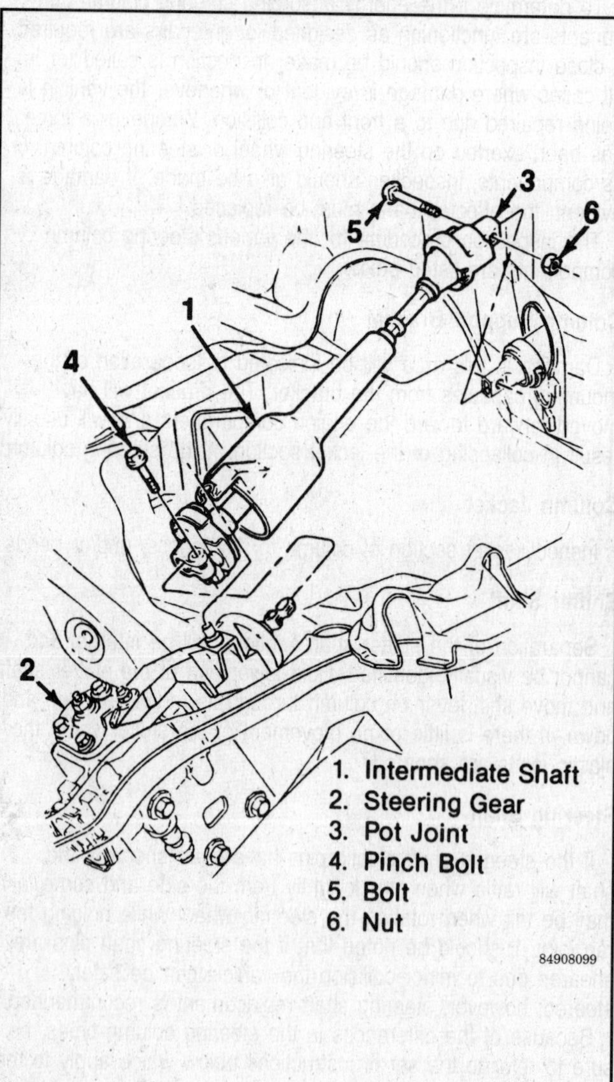

Fig. 120 Installing the intermediate shaft — 1988-91 C/K Series

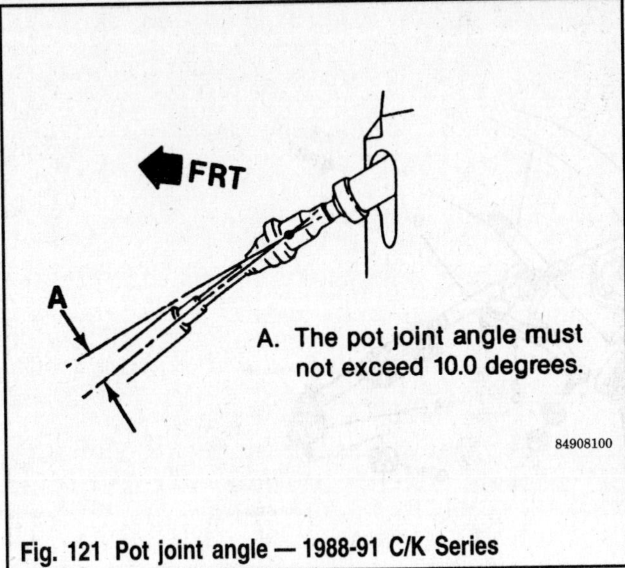

Fig. 121 Pot joint angle — 1988-91 C/K Series

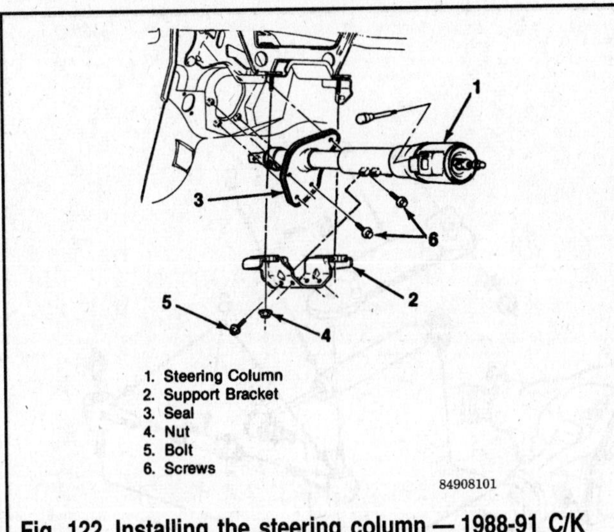

Fig. 122 Installing the steering column — 1988-91 C/K Series

13. Install the column-to-floor plate bolts. Tighten the bolts to 22 ft. lbs. (30 Nm). Tighten the nuts to 20 ft. lbs. (27 Nm).
14. Connect the neutral start switch and back-up light switch wiring.
15. Install the steering column shrouds.
16. Connect the transmission linkage at the column levers.
17. Install the steering wheel.
18. Connect the battery ground cable.

Steering Linkage

REMOVAL & INSTALLATION

Pitman Arm

R/V SERIES

See Figures 123, 124 and 125

1. Raise and support the front end on jackstands.
2. Remove nut from pitman arm ball stud.
3. Remove pitman arm or relay rod from ball stud by tapping on side of rod or arm (in which the stud mounts) with a hammer while using a heavy hammer or similar tool as a backing. Pull on linkage to remove from stud.
4. Remove pitman arm nut from pitman shaft or clamp bolt from pitman arm, and mark relation of arm position to shaft.
5. Remove pitman arm, using a large puller.

To install:

6. Install pitman arm on pitman shaft, lining up the marks made upon removal.

➡If a clamp type pitman arm is used, spread the pitman arm just enough, with a wedge, to slip arm onto pitman shaft. Do not spread pitman arm more than required to slip over pitman shaft with hand pressure. Do not hammer or damage to steering gear may result. Be sure to install the hardened steel washer before installing the nut.

7. Make sure that threads on ball studs and in ball stud nuts are clean and smooth. If threads are not clean and smooth, ball studs may turn in sockets when attempting to tighten nut. Check condition of ball stud seals; replace if necessary.
8. Install pitman shaft nut or pitman arm clamp bolt and tighten to 184 ft. lbs. (249 Nm) on R-Series; 125 ft. lbs. (169 Nm) on V-Series.
9. Position ball stud onto pitman arm or relay rod. Use a $^{5}/_{8}$in. - 18 free spinning nut to seat the tapers, as shown. Tighten the pitman arm-to-relay rod nut to 66 ft. lbs. (89 Nm). Always advance the nut to align the cotter pin hole. NEVER back it off!
10. Lubricate ball studs.
11. Lower the vehicle to the floor.

C/K SERIES

See Figures 126, 127 and 128

1. Raise and support the front end on jackstands.
2. Remove nut from pitman arm ball stud.
3. Break loose the pitman ball stud from the relay rod using a screw-type ball stud tool. Pull on the linkage to remove the stud.
4. Remove pitman arm nut from pitman shaft, and mark relation of arm position to shaft.
5. Remove pitman arm using a puller.

To install:

6. Install pitman arm on pitman shaft, lining up the marks made upon removal.
7. Make sure that threads on ball stud are clean and smooth.
8. Install pitman shaft nut and tighten it to 184 ft. lbs. (250 Nm).
9. Position ball stud into the relay rod. Tighten the pitman arm-to-relay rod nut to 40 ft. lbs. (54 Nm) on 1988-91 models; 48 ft. lbs. (62 Nm) on 1992-96 models. Always advance the nut to align the cotter pin hole. NEVER back it off!
10. Lubricate the ball stud.
11. Lower the vehicle to the floor.

1. Idler arm
2. Relay rod
3. Tie rod
4. Knuckle
5. Pitman arm
6. Steering gear
7. Idler arm frame support
FRT
84908126

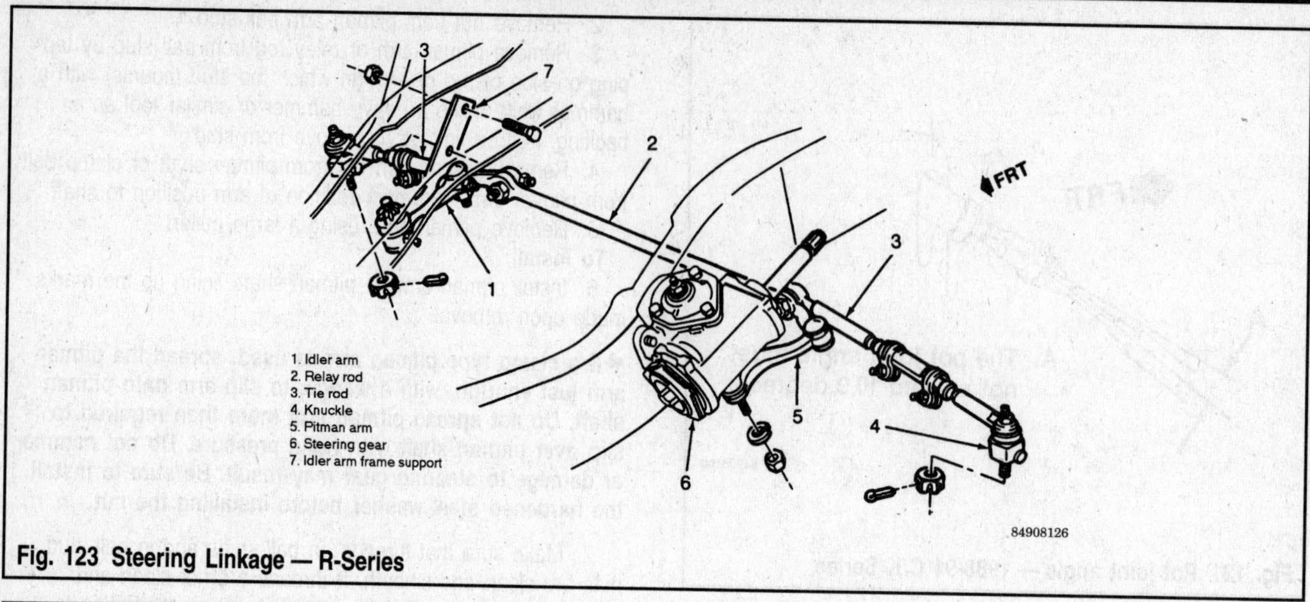

Fig. 123 Steering Linkage — R-Series

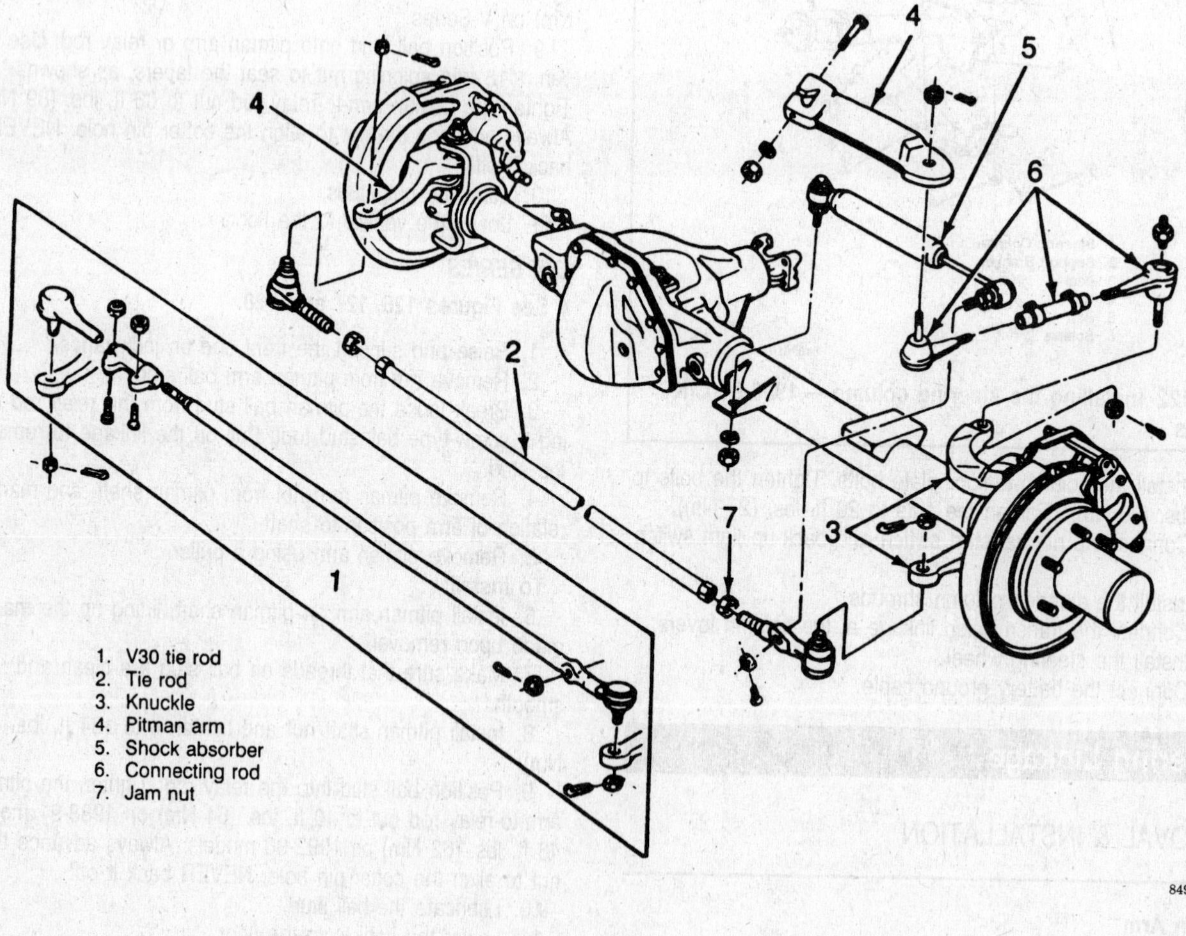

1. V30 tie rod
2. Tie rod
3. Knuckle
4. Pitman arm
5. Shock absorber
6. Connecting rod
7. Jam nut
84908127

Fig. 124 Steering Linkage — V-Series

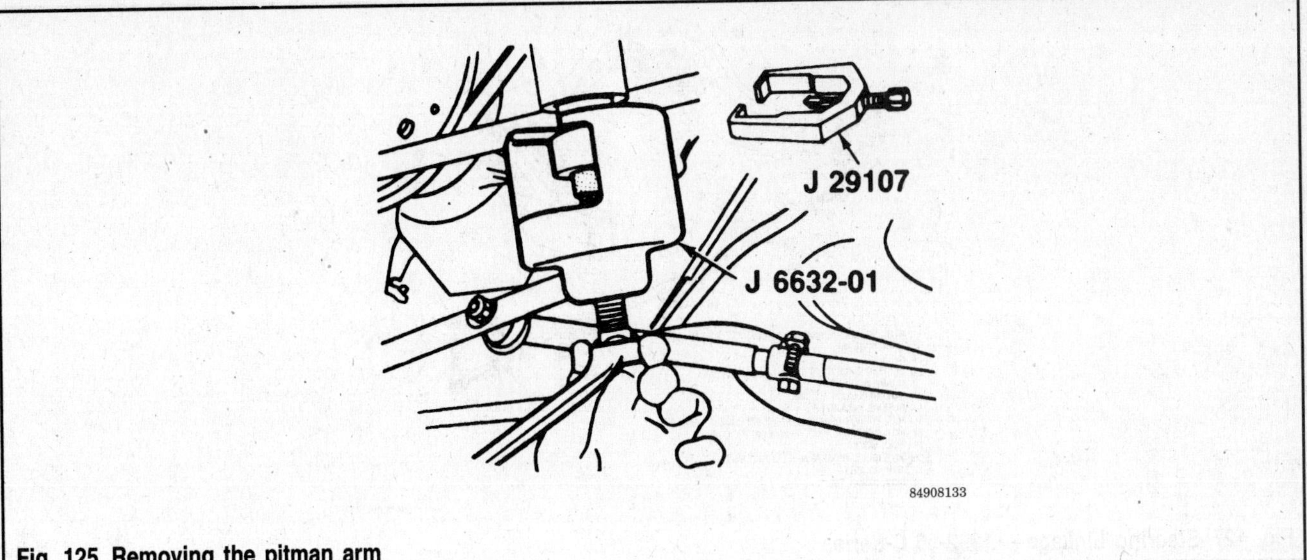

Fig. 125 Removing the pitman arm

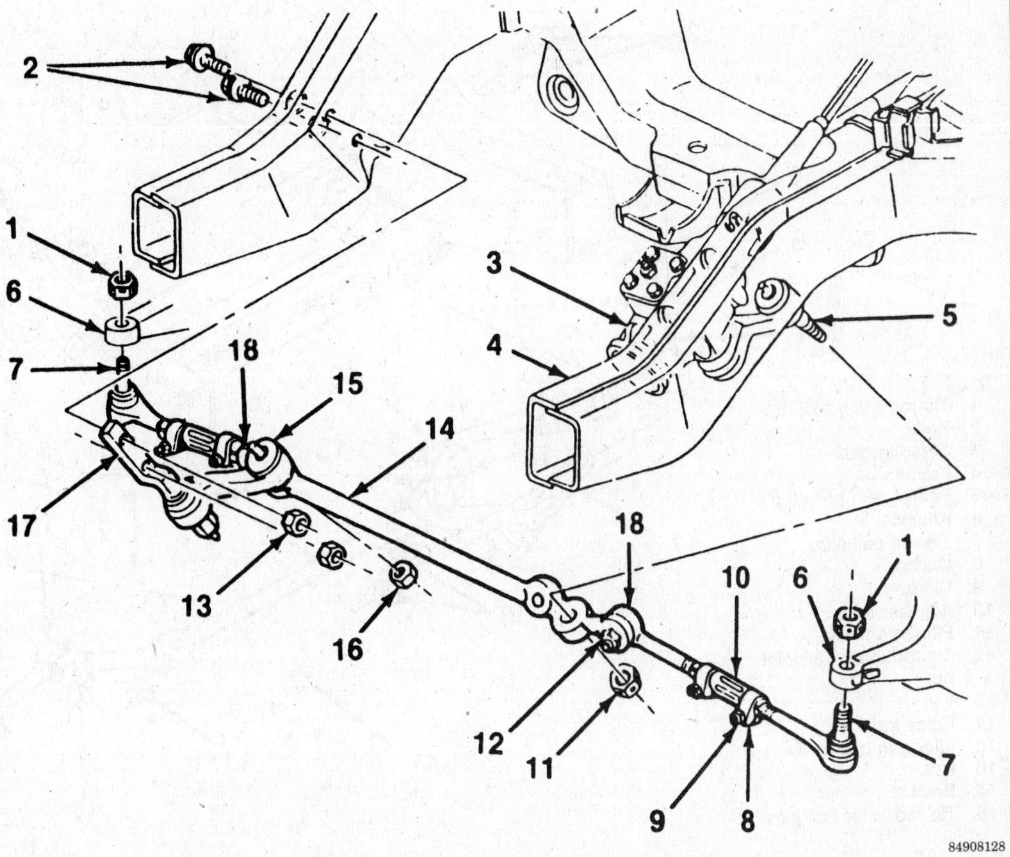

1. Tie rod outer ball nut
2. Bolts
3. Steering gear
4. Frame
5. Pitman arm ball stud
6. Knuckle
7. Tie rod ball stud
8. Clamp
9. Clamp nut
10. Adjuster tube
11. Pitman arm nut
12. Tie rod inner ball joint nut
13. Nut
14. Relay rod
15. Idler arm ball joint
16. Nut
17. Bracket
18. Tie rod inner ball joint

84908128

Fig. 126 Steering Linkage — 1988-91 C-Series

17
1
6
7
18
12
14
5
18
16
10
1
11
9
8
7
6
1. NUT, OUTER TIE ROD, 54 N·m (40 FT. LBS.)
5. ARM, PITMAN
6. KNUCKLE
7. TIE ROD BALL STUD
8. CLAMP ADJUSTER
9. NUT, 19 N·m (14 FT. LBS.)
10. SLEEVE, ADJUSTER
11. NUT, PITMAN ARM, 70 N·m (52 FT. LBS.)
12. NUT, INNER TIE ROD, 54 N·m (40 FT. LBS.)
14. ROD, RELAY
16. NUT, IDLER ARM, 70 N·m (52 FT. LBS.)
17. ARM, IDLER
18. ROD, INNER TIE
84908129

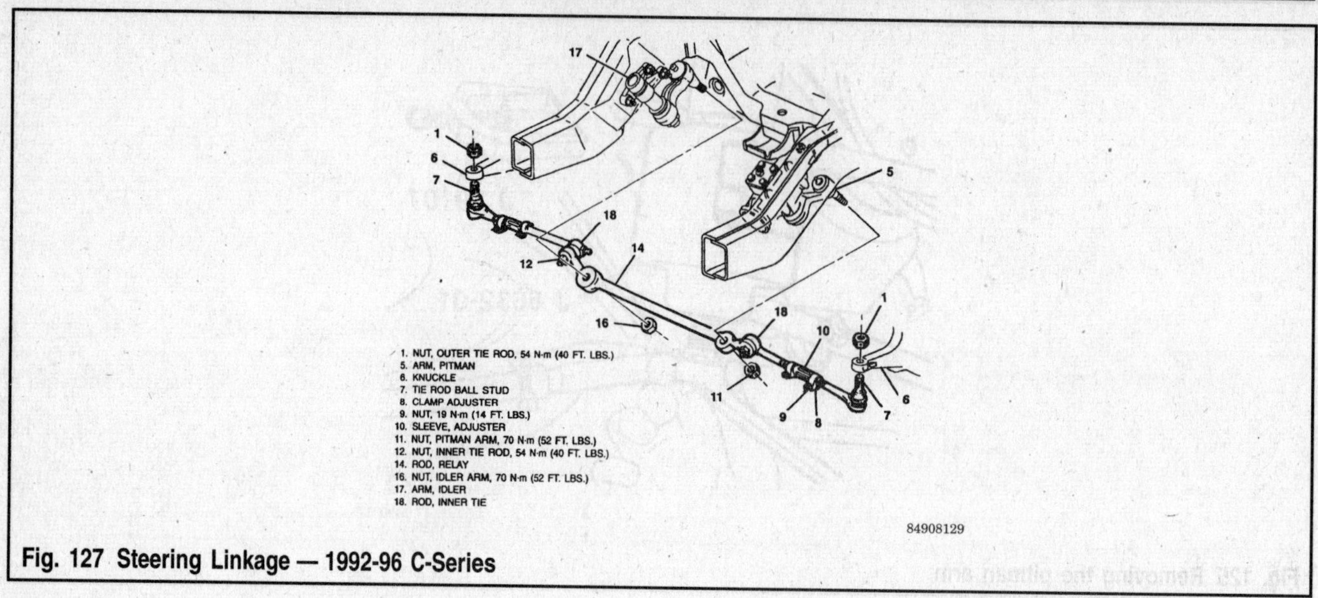

Fig. 127 Steering Linkage — 1992-96 C-Series

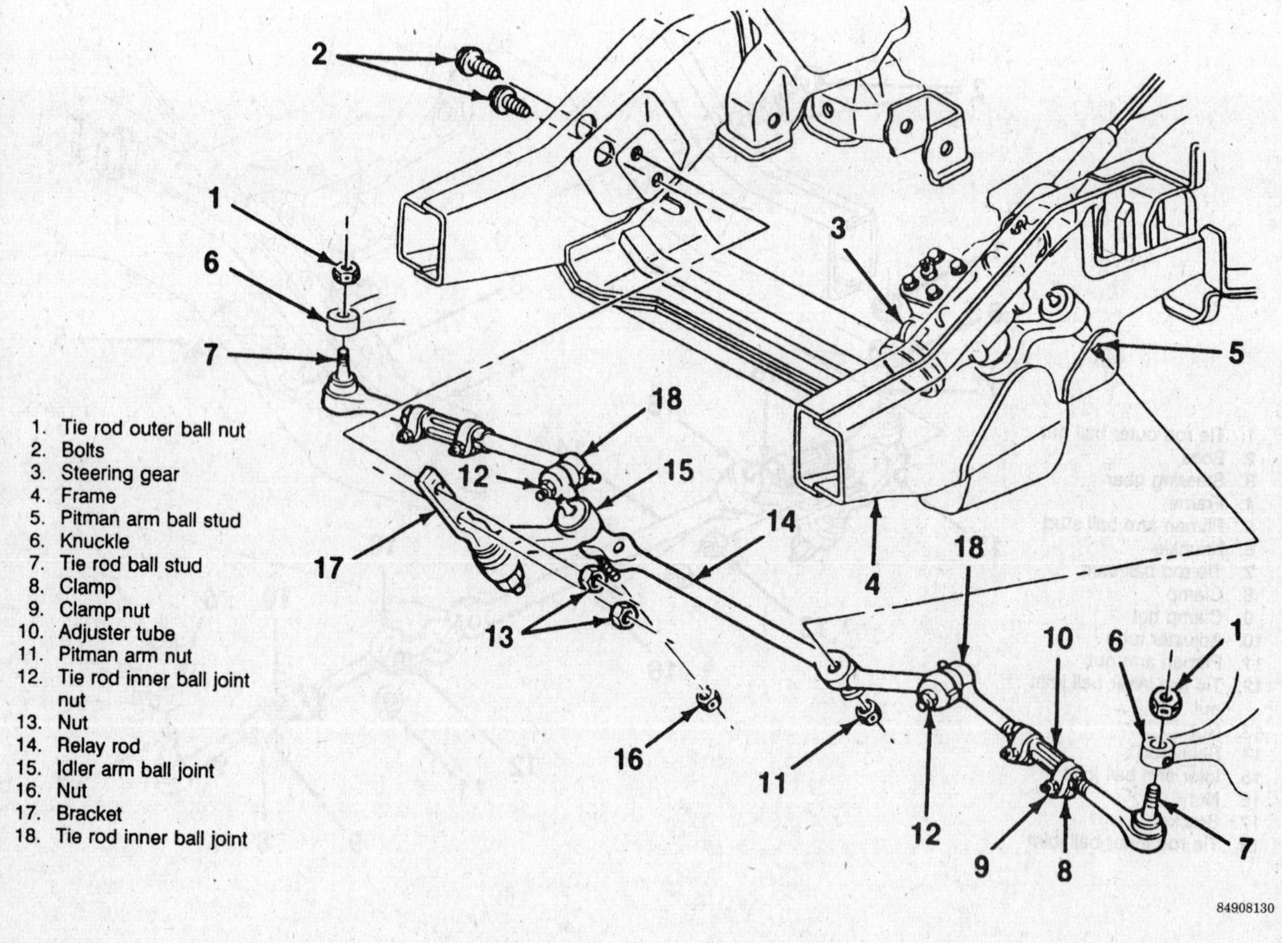

2
1
6
7
3
5
18
12
15
14
17
13
4
18
10
6
1
16
11
12
9
8
7
1. Tie rod outer ball nut
2. Bolts
3. Steering gear
4. Frame
5. Pitman arm ball stud
6. Knuckle
7. Tie rod ball stud
8. Clamp
9. Clamp nut
10. Adjuster tube
11. Pitman arm nut
12. Tie rod inner ball joint nut
13. Nut
14. Relay rod
15. Idler arm ball joint
16. Nut
17. Bracket
18. Tie rod inner ball joint
84908130

Fig. 128 Steering Linkage — 1988-91 K-Series

C3HD SERIES

➧ See Figure 129

1. Raise the front of the truck and support it with safety stands.
2. Disconnect the drag link from from the pitman arm ball stud.
3. Matchmark the pitman arm to the pitman shaft, remove the nut from the steering gear shaft and discard it.
4. Remove the pitman arm with the proper tool (ball joint puller).
5. Install the arm so the marks line up with those on the shaft. Tighten the nut to 184 ft. lbs. (250 Nm). Tighten the ball stud nut to 40 ft. lbs. (54 Nm).

Idler Arm

INSPECTION

➧ See Figure 130

1. Raise the vehicle in such a manner as to allow the front wheels to rotate freely and the steering mechanism freedom to turn. Position the wheels in a straight ahead position.
2. Using a spring scale located as near the relay rod end of the idler arm as possible, exert a 25 lb. force upward and then downward while noticing the total distance the end of the arm moves. This distance should not exceed $^{1}/_{16}$ in. (1.6mm) for a total acceptable movement of $^{1}/_{8}$in. (3mm). It is necessary to ensure that the correct load is applied to the arm since it will move more when higher loads are applied. It is also necessary that a scale or ruler be rested against the frame and used to determine the amount of movement since observers tend to over-estimate the actual movement when a scale is not

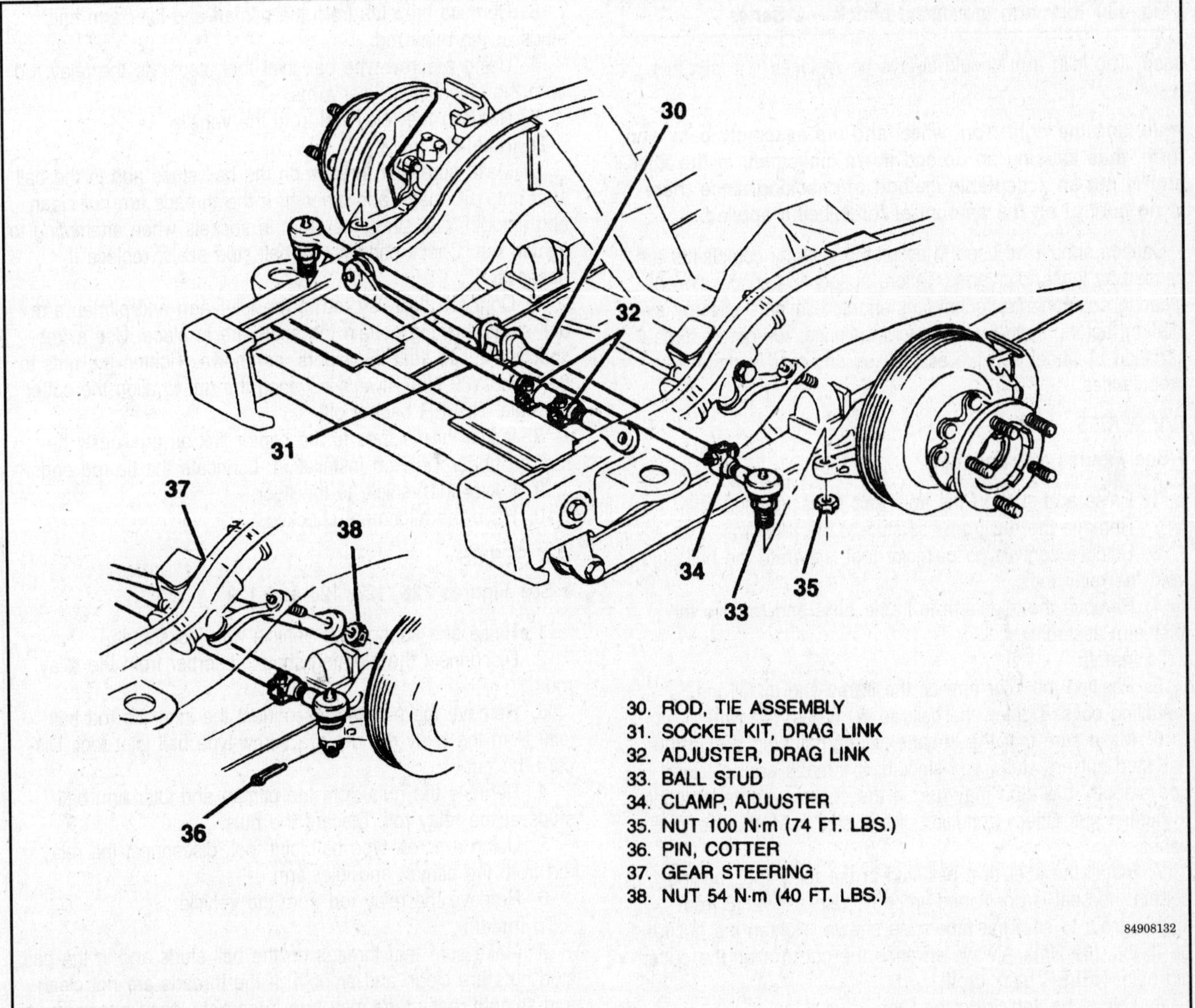

Fig. 129 Steering Linkage— C3HD Series

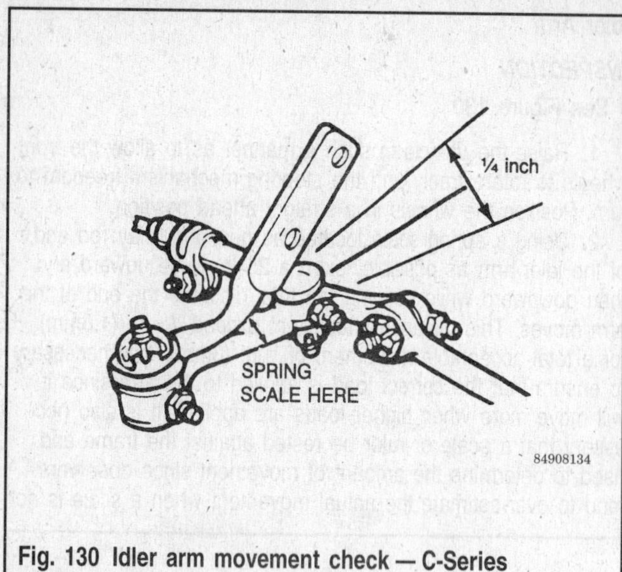

Fig. 130 Idler arm movement check — C-Series

used. The idler arm should always be replaced if it fails this test.

➡Jerking the right front wheel and tire assembly back and forth, thus causing an up and down movement in the idler arm is not an acceptable method of checking since there is no control on the amount of force being applied.

Caution should be used in assuming shimmy complaints are caused by loose idler arms. Before suspecting suspension or steering components, technicians should eliminate shimmy excitation factors, such as dynamic imbalance, run-out or force variation of wheel and tire assemblies and road surface irregularities.

R/V SERIES

See Figures 123 and 124

1. Raise and support the front end on jackstands.
2. Remove the nut from ball stud at the relay rod.
3. Using a screw-type ball joint tool; separate the ball stud from the relay rod.
4. Remove the idler arm to frame bolts and remove the idler arm assembly.

To install:

5. Position the idler arm on the frame and install the mounting bolts. Tighten the bolts to 30 ft. lbs. (40 Nm).
6. Make sure that the threads on the ball stud and in the ball stud nut are clean and smooth. If threads are not clean and smooth, ball stud may turn in the socket when attempting to tighten nut. Check condition of ball stud seal; replace if necessary.
7. Install the idler arm ball stud in the relay rod, making certain the seal is positioned properly. Use a ⅝in.-18 free-spinning nut to seat the tapers, as shown. Tighten the nut to 66 ft. lbs. (89 Nm). Always advance the nut to align the cotter pin hole. NEVER back it off!
8. Lower the vehicle to the floor.

C/K SERIES

See Figures 126, 127, 128 and 129

1. Raise and support the front end on jackstands.
2. Remove the idler arm bracket-to-frame bolts and nuts.
3. Remove the idler arm ball stud nut. Discard the nut.
4. Using a screw-type ball joint tool, separate the idler arm from the relay rod.
5. Install the arm and make sure the ball stud is positioned squarely in the relay rod before tightening the nut. Tighten the frame-to-bracket bolts to 59 ft. lbs. (80 Nm) on 1988-94 models and 71 ft. lbs. (96 Nm) on 1995-96 models. Tighten the new ball stud nut to 40 ft. lbs. (54 Nm) on all models.
6. Have the alignment checked and adjusted as necessary.

Relay Rod (Center Link)

R/V SERIES

See Figures 123 and 124

1. Raise and support the vehicle with jackstands.
2. Remove the inner ends of the tie rods from the relay rod.
3. Remove the nuts from the pitman and idler arm ball studs at the relay rod.
4. Using a screw-type ball joint tool, separate the relay rod from the pitman and idler arms.
5. Remove the relay rod from the vehicle.

To install:

6. Make sure that threads on the ball studs and in the ball stud nuts are clean and smooth. If the threads are not clean and smooth, ball studs may turn in sockets when attempting to tighten nut. Check condition of ball stud seals; replace if necessary.
7. Connect the relay rod to the idler arm and pitman arm ball studs, making certain the seals are in place. Use a free-spinning nut to seat the tapers, as shown. Tighten the nuts to 66 ft. lbs. (89 Nm).Always advance the nut to align the cotter pin hole. NEVER back it off!
8. Install the tie rods to the center link as previously described under Tie Rod Installation. Lubricate the tie rod ends.
9. Lower the vehicle to the floor.
10. Have the alignment checked.

C/K SERIES

See Figures 126, 127, 128 and 129

1. Raise and support the vehicle with jackstands.
2. Disconnect the steering shock absorber from the relay rod.
3. Remove the nut and disconnect the inner tie rod ball joint from the relay rod using a screw-type ball joint tool. Discard the nut.
4. Remove the nuts from the pitman and idler arm ball studs at the relay rod. Discard the nuts.
5. Using a screw-type ball joint tool, disconnect the relay rod from the pitman and idler arm.
6. Remove the relay rod from the vehicle.

To install:

7. Make sure that threads on the ball studs and in the ball stud nuts are clean and smooth. If the threads are not clean and smooth, ball studs may turn in sockets when attempting to tighten nut. Check condition of ball stud seals; replace if necessary.
8. Connect the relay rod to the idler arm and pitman arm ball studs, making certain the seals are in place. Use a free-spinning nut to seat the tapers, as shown. Tighten the new

nuts to 40 ft. lbs. (54 Nm) on 1988-90 models; 48 ft. lbs. (62 Nm) on 1991-93 models.

9. Install the tie rod to the center link. Tighten the new nut to 40 ft. lbs. (54 Nm) on 1988-90 models; 48 ft. lbs. (62 Nm) on 1991-96 models.

10. Install the shock absorber. Tighten the frame end nut to 30 ft. lbs. (40 Nm); the relay rod end nut to 46 ft. lbs. (62 Nm). Always advance the nut to align the cotter pin hole. NEVER back it off!

11. Lower the vehicle to the floor.

12. Have the alignment checked.

Drag Link

C3HD SERIES ONLY

➧ See Figure 129

1. Raise the front of the truck and support it on safety stands.

2. Remove the nuts from the pitman arm and drag link ball studs.

3. Press the link off the arm and the tie rod.

4. Install the link. Tighten the pitman arm ball stud to 48 ft. lbs. (62 Nm) to seat the tapers. Tighten both ball stud nuts to 40 ft. lbs. (54 Nm).

Steering Linkage Shock Absorber

R/V SERIES

➧ See Figures 123 and 124

1. Remove the cotter pins and nuts and remove the unit.

2. Installation is the reverse of removal. Tighten the tie rod end nut to 46 ft. lbs. (62 Nm); the frame end nut to 81 ft. lbs. (109 Nm). Always advance the nut to align the cotter pin hole. NEVER back it off!

C/K SERIES

➧ See Figures 131, 132 and 133

1. Raise and support the front end on jackstands.

2. Remove the frame end nut and bolt.

3. Remove the cotter pin and nut from the relay rod end. It may be necessary to separate the shock from the relay rod with a screw-type ball joint tool.

4. Install the shock and tighten the frame end nut and bolt to 33 ft. lbs. (45 Nm); the relay rod end nut to 46 ft. lbs. (62 Nm).Always advance the nut to align the cotter pin hole. NEVER back it off! A maximum torque of 59 ft. lbs. (80 Nm) is permissible to align the hole.

Tie Rod Ends

R-SERIES

➧ See Figure 134

1. Loosen the tie rod adjuster sleeve clamp nuts.

2. Remove the tie rod end stud cotter pin and nut.

3. Use a screw-type tie rod removal tool to loosen the stud.

4. Remove the inner stud in the same way.

5. Unscrew the tie rod end from the threaded sleeve. The threads may be left or right hand threads. Count the number of turns required to remove it.

To install:

6. Grease the threads and turn the new tie rod end in as many turns as were needed to remove it. This will give approximately correct toe-in.

7. Tighten the clamp bolts to 14 ft. lbs. (18 Nm).

8. Tighten the stud nuts to 45 ft. lbs. (61 Nm) and install new cotter pins. You may tighten the nut to align the cotter pin, but don't loosen it.

9. Adjust the toe-in.

Tie Rod

V-SERIES

1. Remove the cotter pins and nuts from the tie rod assembly.

2. Disconnect the steering shock absorber from the tie rod.

3. Use a screw-type tie rod removal tool to loosen the ball studs from the knuckles.

4. Count the number of exposed threads on each tie rod end and record it.

5. Loosen the tie rod end lock nuts and unscrew the tie rod ends.

6. When installing the tie rod ends, turn them in until the same number of threads previously visible are achieved. Tighten the locknuts.

7. Install the tie rod assembly in the knuckles and tighten the castellated nuts to 40 ft. lbs. (54 Nm). Always advance the nut to align the cotter pin hole. NEVER back it off!

8. Tighten the tie rod end locknuts to 175 ft. lbs. (237 Nm).

C/K SERIES

➧ See Figures 135, 136, 137 and 138

1. Raise and support the front end on jackstands.

2. Remove the nut from the knuckle end ball stud. Discard the nut.

3. Using a screw-type ball joint tool, separate the tie rod ball stud from the knuckle.

4. Remove the nut from the relay rod end ball stud.

5. Using a screw-type ball joint tool, separate the tie rod ball stud from the relay rod.

6. Clean the threaded parts of the tie rod ends thoroughly and count the exact number of threads exposed on each tie rod end. Measure the overall length of the tie rod assembly.

7. Loosen the clamp nuts, spread the clamps and unscrew each tie rod end.

To install:

8. Coat the threaded parts of the new tie rod ends with chassis grease. Screw the tie rod ends into the sleeve until the exact number of threads is exposed on each tie rod end. Check the overall length of the new assembly. Adjust as necessary. Don't tighten the clamp nuts yet.

9. Position the tie rod assembly in the relay rod and install a new nut on the ball stud. Tighten the nut to 40 ft. lbs. (54 Nm).

10. Position the other tie rod end in the knuckle. Install the new nut and tighten it to 40 ft. lbs. (54 Nm).

11. Before tightening the clamp nuts:

a. Each clamp must be positioned between the locating dimples at each end of the adjuster.

b. The clamps must be positioned with the nut facing forward and within 45 degrees of horizontal (60° on 1992-93 models).

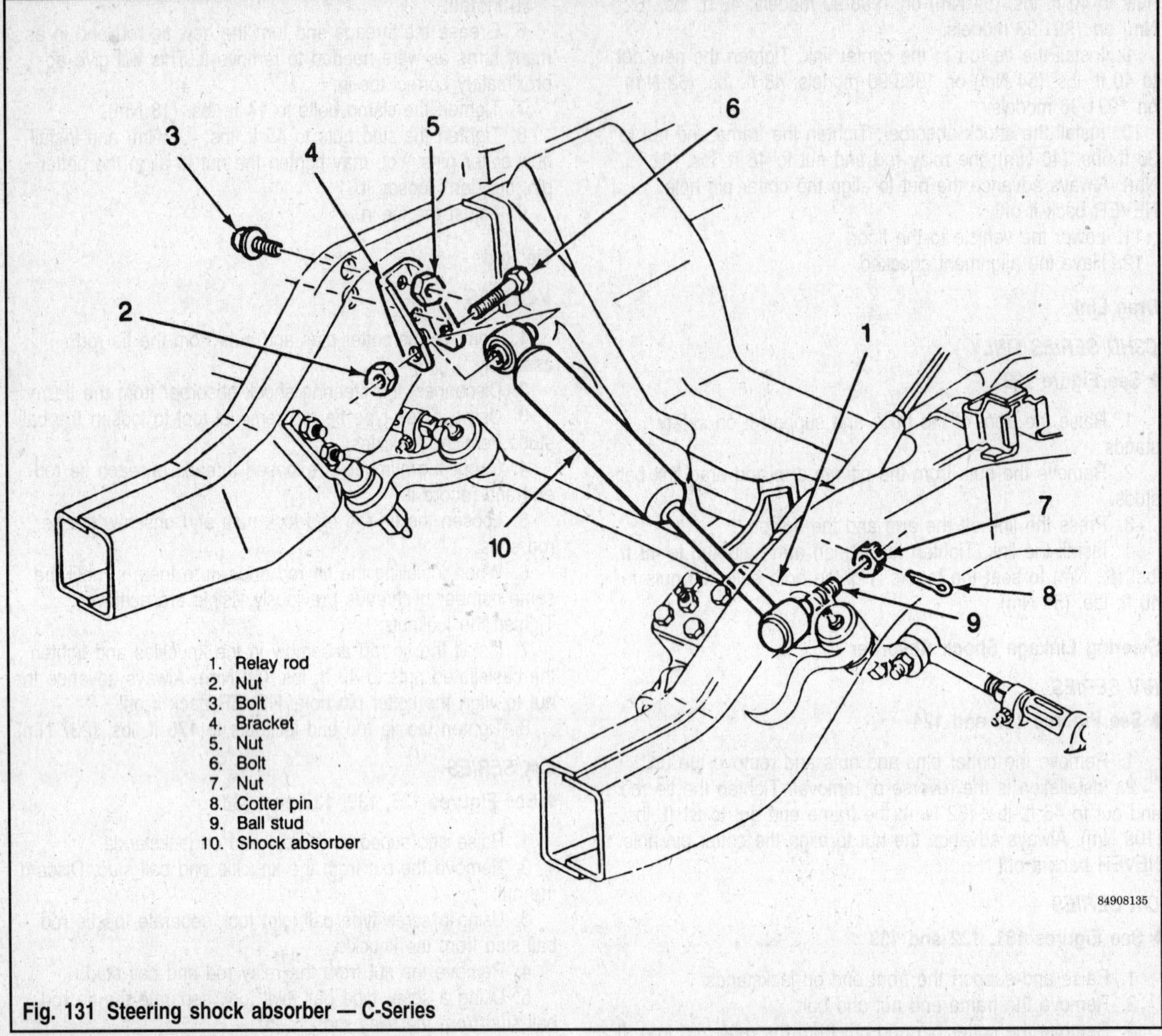

Fig. 131 Steering shock absorber — C-Series

c. The split in the sleeve must be position at a point just above the clamp nut.

12. Tighten the clamp nuts to 14 ft. lbs. (18 Nm). When the clamp nuts are tightened, the clamp ends may touch, but the split in the clamp, at the adjuster sleeve, must never be less than 0.127mm (0.005 in.).

Connecting Rod

V-SERIES

▶ See Figure 138

1. Remove the cotter pins and nuts from each end of the connecting rod.
2. Using a screw type remover tool, break loose the connecting rod from the pitman arm and steering knuckle.
3. If the connecting rod ends are being replaced, note the length of the complete assembly and record it. Also note the respective directions of the ends when installed.
4. Loosen the clamp bolts and unscrew the ends. If the bolts are rusted, replace them.
5. Install the rod and tighten the clamp bolts to 40 ft. lbs. (54 Nm); the ball stud nuts to 89 ft. lbs. (120 Nm). Always advance the nut to align the cotter pin hole. NEVER back it off!

Manual Steering Gear

ADJUSTMENT

Before any steering gear adjustments are made, it is recommended that the front end of the truck be raised and a thorough inspection be made for stiffness or lost motion in the steering gear, steering linkage and front suspension. Worn or damaged parts should be replaced, since a satisfactory adjustment of the steering gear cannot be obtained if bent or badly worn parts exist.

It is also very important that the steering gear be properly aligned in the truck. Misalignment of the gear places a stress on the steering worm shaft, therefore a proper adjustment is

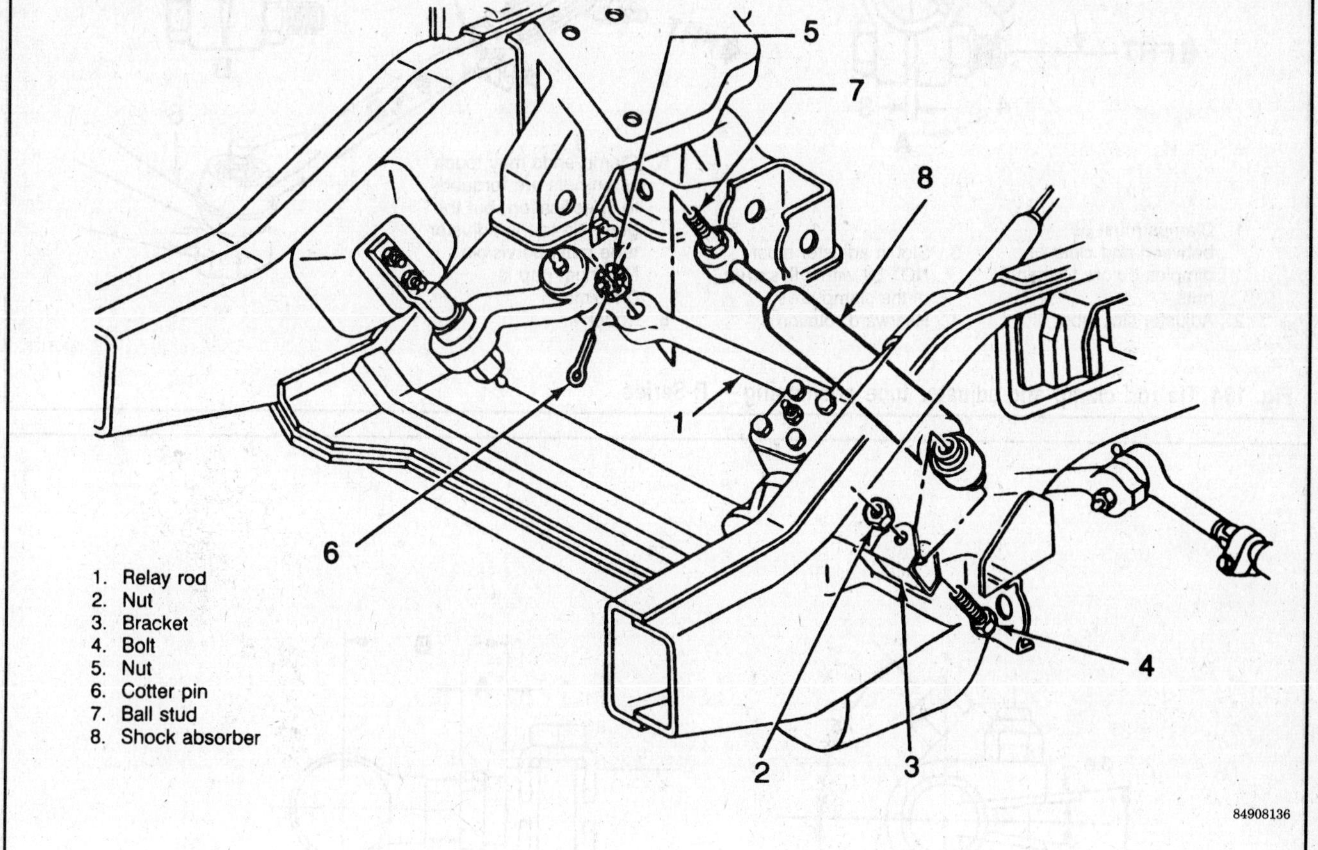

5
7
8
1
6
4
2
3
1. Relay rod
2. Nut
3. Bracket
4. Bolt
5. Nut
6. Cotter pin
7. Ball stud
8. Shock absorber
84908136

Fig. 132 Steering shock absorber — K-Series

40
40
39
42
41
42
40
41
39
42
39. Shock absorber
40. Bolt/screw
41. Washer
42. Nut 33 ft. lbs.(45 nm)
84908137

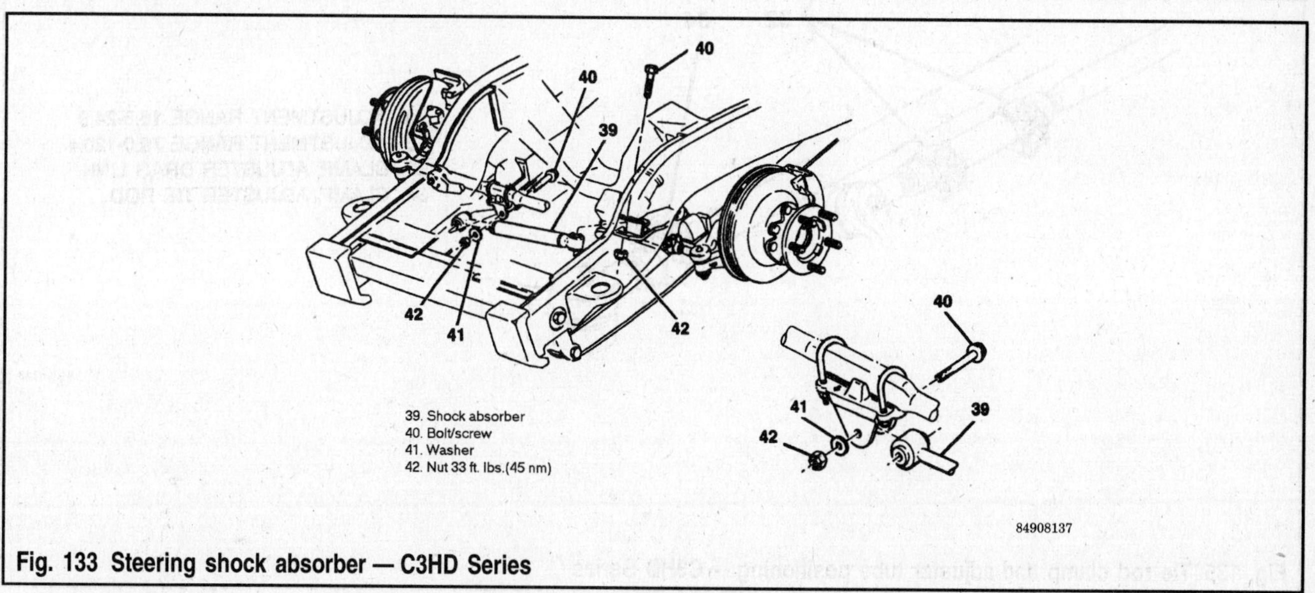

Fig. 133 Steering shock absorber — C3HD Series

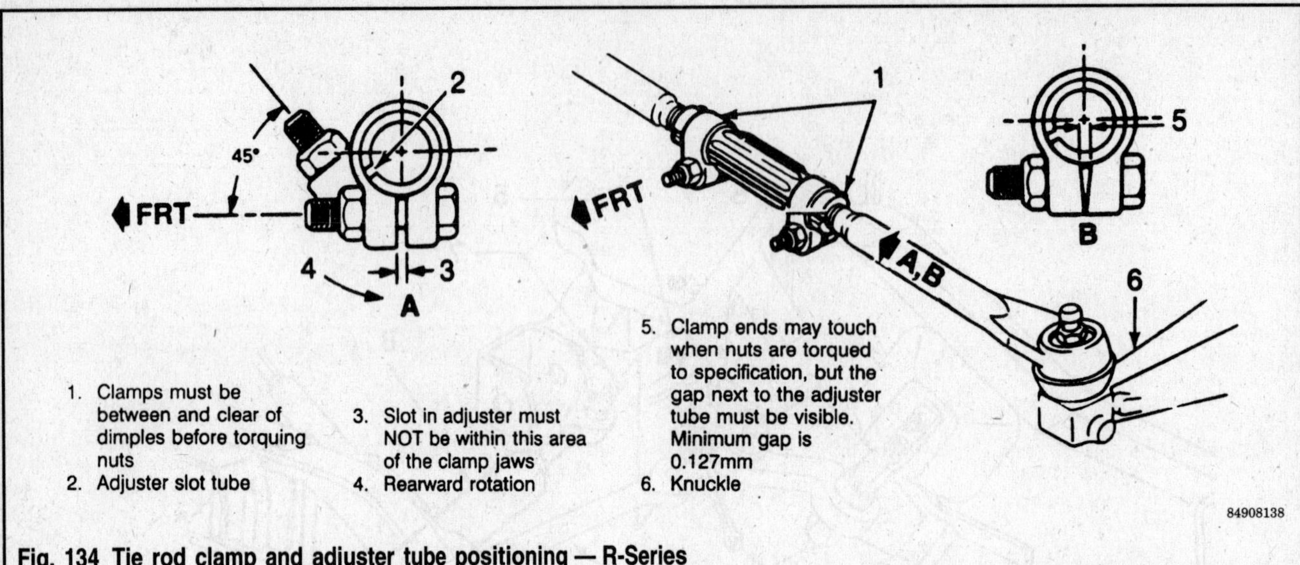

Fig. 134 Tie rod clamp and adjuster tube positioning — R-Series

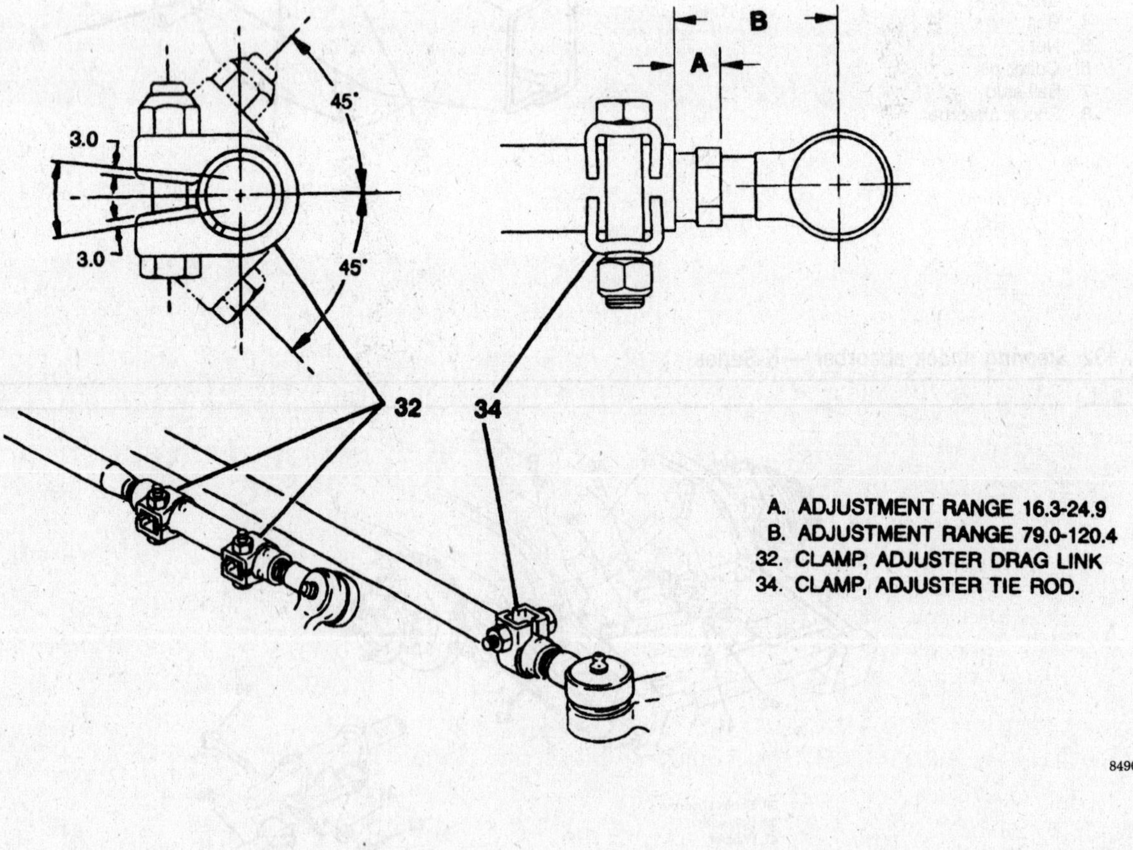

3.0

3.0

45°

45°

B

A

32

34

A. ADJUSTMENT RANGE 16.3-24.9
B. ADJUSTMENT RANGE 79.0-120.4
32. CLAMP, ADJUSTER DRAG LINK
34. CLAMP, ADJUSTER TIE ROD.

84908139

Fig. 135 Tie rod clamp and adjuster tube positioning — C3HD Series

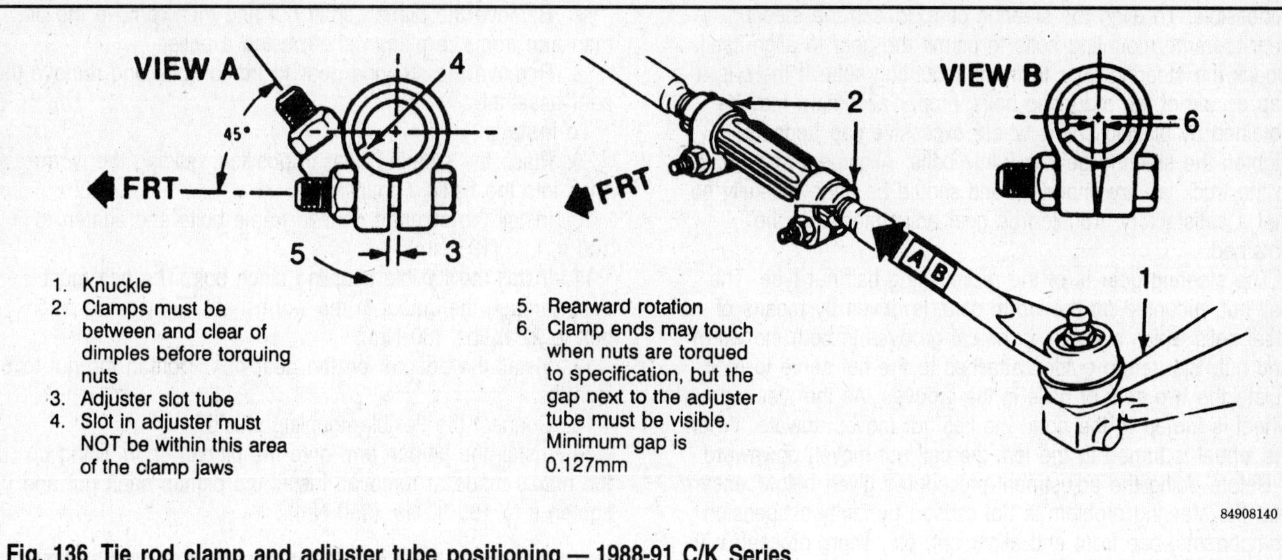

Fig. 136 Tie rod clamp and adjuster tube positioning — 1988-91 C/K Series

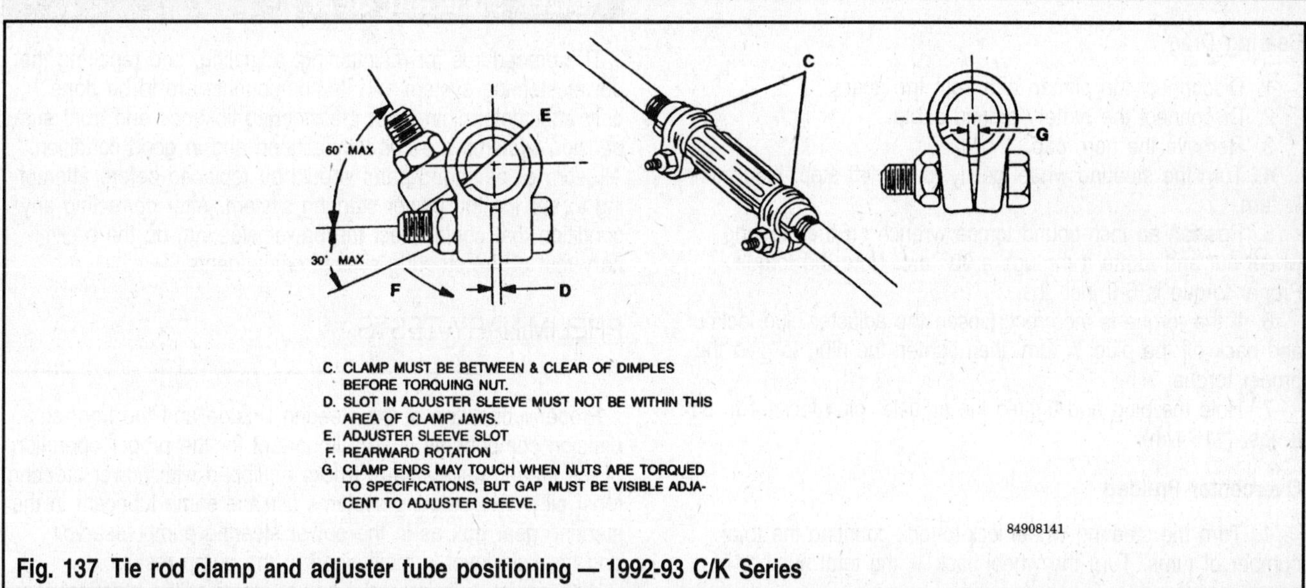

Fig. 137 Tie rod clamp and adjuster tube positioning — 1992-93 C/K Series

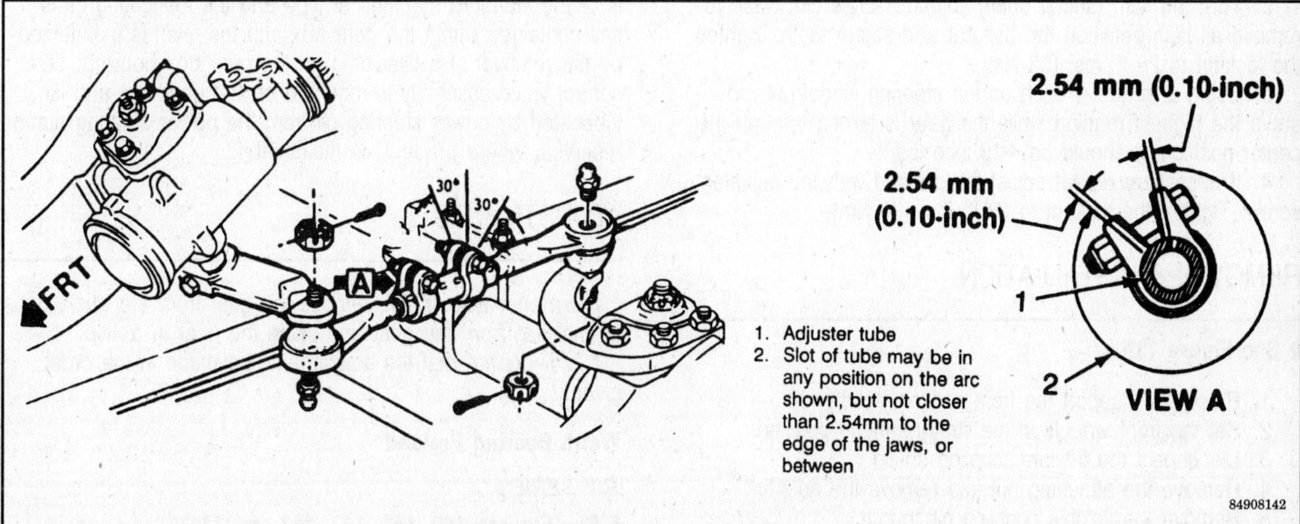

Fig. 138 Connecting rod clamp and adjuster tube positioning — R/V Series

impossible. To align the steering gear, loosen the steering gear-to-frame mounting bolts to permit the gear to align itself. Check the steering gear to frame mounting seat. If there is a gap at any of the mounting bolts, proper alignment may be obtained by placing shims where excessive gap appears. Tighten the steering gear-to-frame bolts. Alignment of the gear in the truck is very important and should be done carefully so that a satisfactory, trouble-free gear adjustment may be obtained.

The steering gear is of the recirculating ball nut type. The ball nut, mounted on the worm gear, is driven by means of steel balls which circulate in helical grooves in both the worm and nut. Ball return guides attached to the nut serve to recirculate the two sets of balls in the grooves. As the steering wheel is turned to the right, the ball nut moves upward. When the wheel is turned to the left, the ball nut moves downward.

Before doing the adjustment procedures given below, ensure that the steering problem is not caused by faulty suspension components, bad front end alignment, etc. Then, proceed with the following adjustments.

Bearing Drag

1. Disconnect the pitman arm from the gear.
2. Disconnect the battery ground cable.
3. Remove the horn cap.
4. Turn the steering wheel gently to the left stop, then back ½ turn.
5. Position an inch-pound torque wrench on the steering wheel nut and rotate it through a 90° arc. Note the torque. Proper torque is 5-8 inch lbs.
6. If the torque is incorrect, loosen the adjuster plug locknut and back off the plug ¼ turn, then tighten the plug to give the proper torque.
7. Hold the plug and tighten the adjuster plug locknut to 85 ft. lbs. (115 Nm).

Overcenter Preload

1. Turn the steering wheel lock-to-lock counting the total number of turns. Turn the wheel back ½ the total number of turns to center it.
2. Turn the lash (sector shaft) adjuster screw clockwise to remove all lash between the ball nut and sector teeth. Tighten the locknut to 25 ft. lbs. (33 Nm).
3. Using a torque wrench on the steering wheel nut, observe the highest reading while the gear is turned through the center position. It should be 4-10 inch lbs.
4. If necessary repeat adjust the preload with the adjuster screw. Tighten the locknut to 22 ft. lbs. (30 Nm).

REMOVAL & INSTALLATION

➧ See Figure 139

1. Raise and support the front end on jackstands.
2. Set the front wheels in the straight-ahead position.
3. Disconnect the flexible coupling shield.
4. Remove the attaching nut and remove the adapter.
5. Remove the flexible coupling pinch bolt.
6. Mark the relationship of the pitman arm to the pitman shaft.
7. Remove the pitman shaft nut and then remove the pitman arm from the pitman shaft, using a puller.
8. Remove the steering gear to frame bolts and remove the gear assembly.

To install:

9. Place the steering gear in position, guiding the wormshaft into the flexible coupling.
10. Install the steering gear to frame bolts and tighten to 100 ft. lbs. (135 Nm).
11. Install the flexible coupling pinch bolt. The bolt must pass through the cutout in the wormshaft. Tighten the pinch bolt to 22 ft. lbs. (30 Nm).
12. Install the adapter on the gear box. Tighten the nut to 5 inch lbs.
13. Connect the flexible coupling shield.
14. Install the pitman arm onto the pitman shaft, lining up the marks made at removal. Install the pitman shaft nut and tighten it to 185 ft. lbs. (250 Nm).

Power Steering Gear

The procedures for maintaining, adjusting, and repairing the power steering system and its components are to be done only after determining that the steering linkages and front suspension systems are correctly aligned and in good condition. All worn or damaged parts should be replaced before attempting to service the power steering system. After correcting any condition that could affect the power steering, do the preliminary test of the steering system components.

PRELIMINARY TESTS

Proper lubrication of the steering linkage and the front suspension components is very important for the proper operation of the steering systems of trucks equipped with power steering. Most all power steering systems use the same lubricant in the steering gear box as in the power steering pump reservoir, and the fluid level is maintained at the pump reservoir.

With power cylinder assist power steering, the steering gear is of the standard mechanical type and the lubricating oil is self contained within the gear box and the level is maintained by the removal of a filler plug on the gear box housing. The control valve assembly is mounted on the gear box and is lubricated by power steering oil from the power steering pump reservoir, where the level is maintained.

ADJUSTMENTS

For proper adjustment, remove the gear from the truck, drain all the fluid from the gear and place the gear in a vise.

It is important that the adjustments be made in the order given.

Worm Bearing Preload

R/V SERIES

➧ See Figures 140, 141, 142, 143 and 144

1. Remove the adjuster plug locknut.

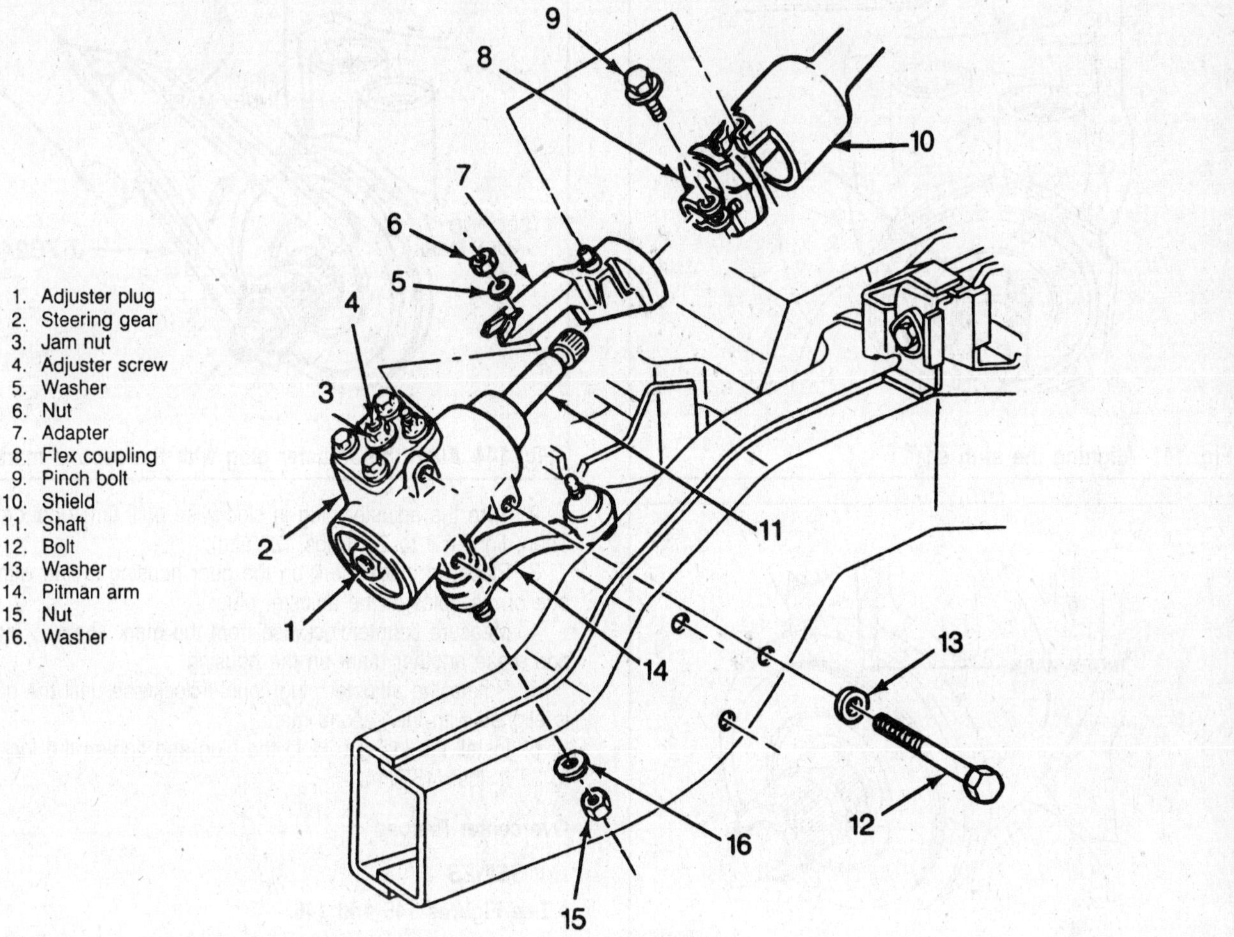

1. Adjuster plug
2. Steering gear
3. Jam nut
4. Adjuster screw
5. Washer
6. Nut
7. Adapter
8. Flex coupling
9. Pinch bolt
10. Shield
11. Shaft
12. Bolt
13. Washer
14. Pitman arm
15. Nut
16. Washer

84908143

Fig. 139 Manual steering gear — C/K Series

2. Turn the adjuster plug in clockwise until firmly bottomed. Then, tighten it to 20 ft. lbs. (27 Nm).
3. Place an index mark on the gear housing in line with one of the holes in the adjuster plug.
4. Measure counterclockwise from the mark about ¼ inch and make another mark on the housing.
5. Rotate the adjuster plug counterclockwise until the hole is aligned with the second mark.
6. Install the locknut. Hold the plug and tighten the locknut to 81 ft. lbs.
7. Place an inch pound torque wrench and 12-point deep socket on the stub shaft and measure the stub shaft rotating torque, starting with the torque wrench handle in a vertical position to a point ¼ turn to either side. Note your reading. The proper torque should be 4-10 inch lbs. If the reading is incorrect, whether your adjustment was done incorrectly or there is gear damage.

C/K SERIES

See Figures 140, 141, 142, 143 and 144

1. Remove the adjuster plug locknut.

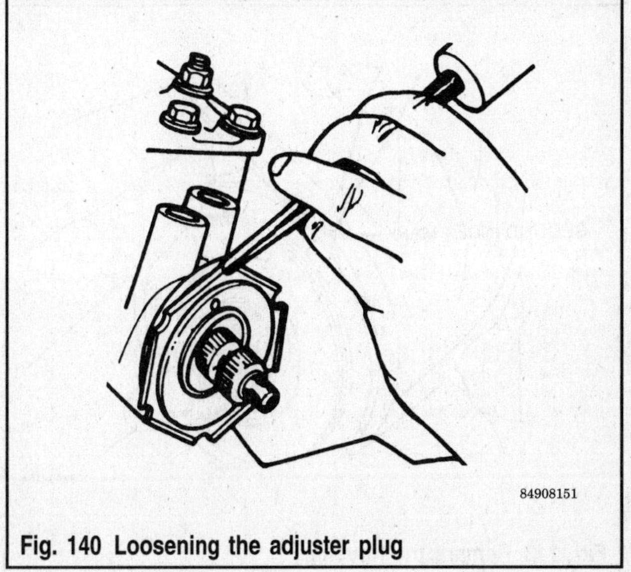

84908151

Fig. 140 Loosening the adjuster plug

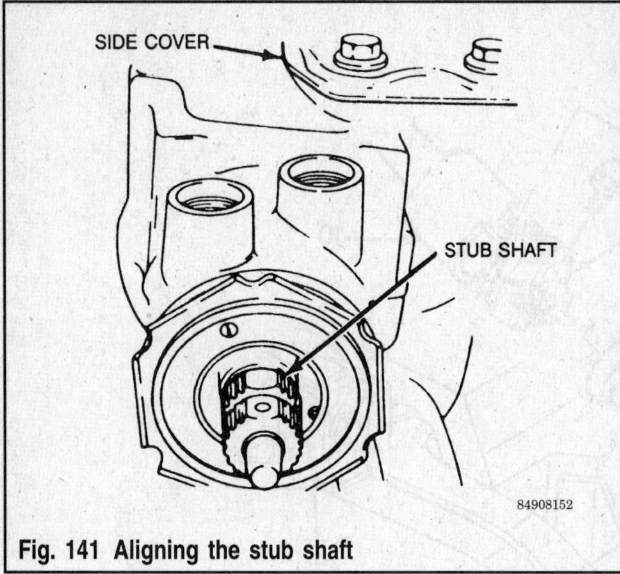

Fig. 141 Aligning the stub shaft

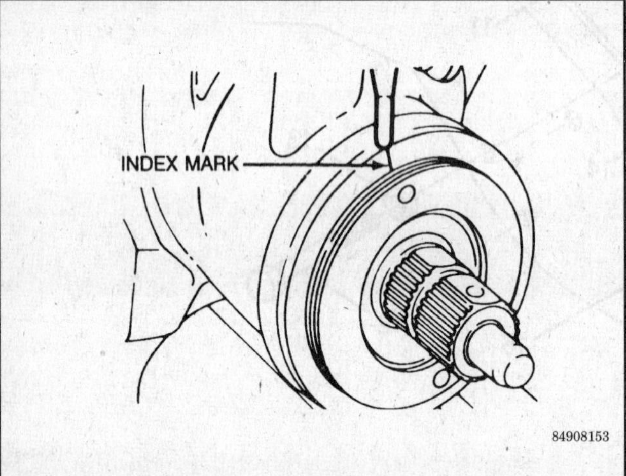

Fig. 142 Mark the housing so that it is even with the adjuster plug

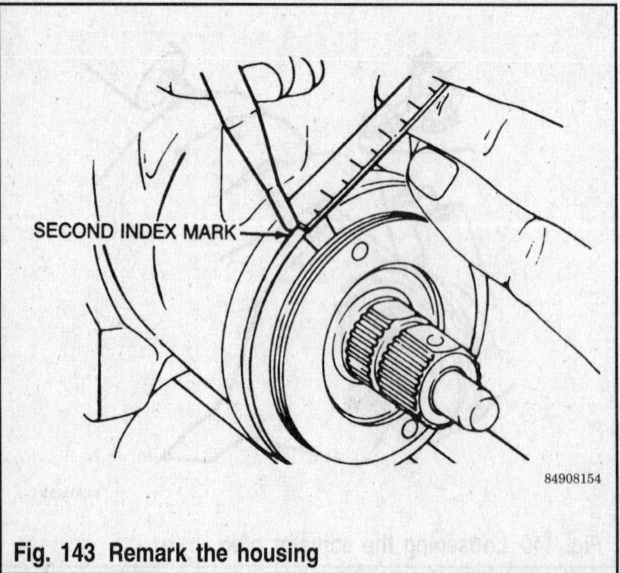

Fig. 143 Remark the housing

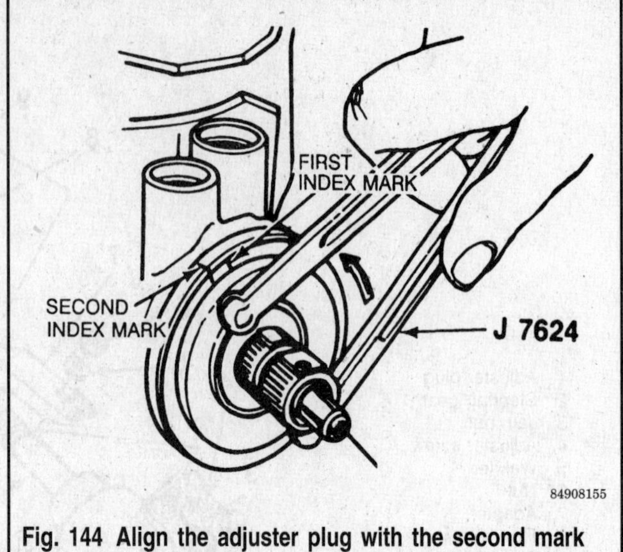

Fig. 144 Align the adjuster plug with the second mark

2. Turn the adjuster plug in clockwise until firmly bottomed. Then, tighten it to 20 ft. lbs. (27 Nm).

3. Place an index mark on the gear housing in line with one of the holes in the adjuster plug.

4. Measure counterclockwise from the mark about ½ inch and make another mark on the housing.

5. Rotate the adjuster plug counterclockwise until the hole is aligned with the second mark.

6. Install the locknut. Hold the plug and tighten the locknut to 32 ft. lbs. (43 Nm).

Overcenter Preload

R/V SERIES

See Figures 145 and 146

1. Loosen the locknut and turn the pitman shaft adjuster screw counterclockwise until it is all the way out. Then, turn it in ½ turn.

2. Rotate the stub shaft from stop to stop, counting the total number of turns, then turn it back ½ that number to center the gear.

3. Place an inch-pound torque wrench in a vertical position on the stub shaft and measure the torque necessary to rotate the shaft to a point 45° to either side of center. Record the highest reading. On gears with less than 400 miles, the reading should be 6-10 inch lbs. higher than the worm bearing preload torque previously recorded, but not to exceed 18 inch lbs. On gears with more than 400 miles, the reading should be 4-5 inch lbs. higher, but not to exceed 14 inch lbs.

4. If necessary, adjust the reading by turning the adjuster screw.

5, When the adjustment is made, hold the screw and tighten the locknut to 35 ft. lbs. (47 Nm).

6. Install the gear.

C/K SERIES

See Figures 145 and 146

1. Rotate the stub shaft from stop to stop, counting the total number of turns, then turn it back ½ that number to center the gear.

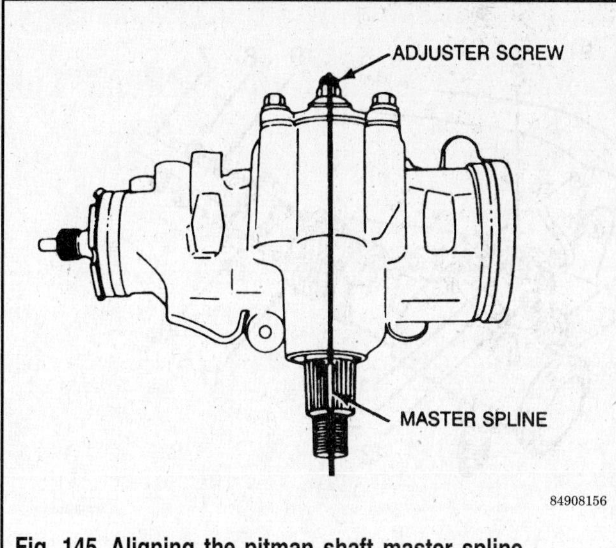

Fig. 145 Aligning the pitman shaft master spline

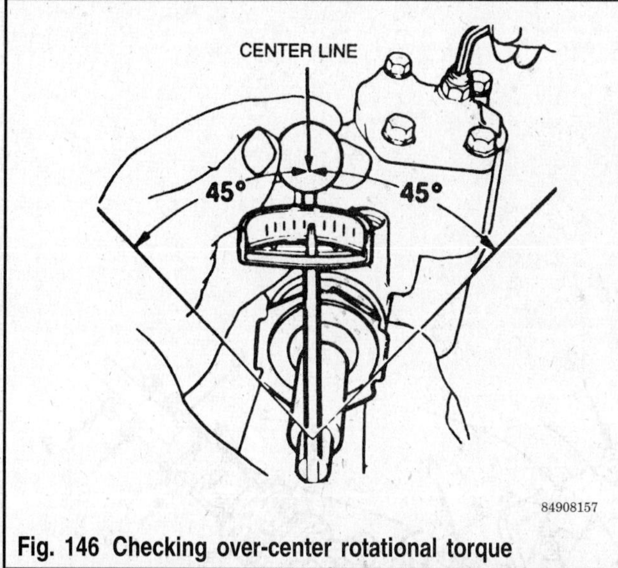

Fig. 146 Checking over-center rotational torque

2. Loosen the locknut and turn the pitman shaft adjuster screw counterclockwise until it is all the way out. Then, turn it in 1 full turn.
3. Place an inch-pound torque wrench in a vertical position on the stub shaft and measure the torque necessary to rotate the shaft to a point 45° to either side of center. Record the highest reading.
4. Turn the adjuster plug in until the torque required to rotate the shaft is 6-10 inch lbs. higher than the previously recorded torque.
5. When the adjustment is made, hold the screw and tighten the locknut to 32 ft. lbs. (43 Nm).

REMOVAL & INSTALLATION

R/V Series

➧ See Figures 147 and 148

1. Raise and support the front end on jackstands.
2. Set the front wheels in the straight ahead position.
3. Disconnect the battery ground cable.
4. Place a drain pan under the gear and disconnect the fluid lines. Cap the openings.
5. Remove the flexible coupling pinch bolt.
6. Mark the relationship of the pitman arm to the pitman shaft.
7. Remove the pitman shaft nut and then remove the pitman arm from the pitman shaft, using a puller.
8. Remove the steering gear to frame bolts and remove the gear assembly.

To install:

9. Place the steering gear in position, guiding the wormshaft into flexible coupling. Align the flat in the coupling with the flat on the wormshaft.
10. Install the steering gear to frame bolts and tighten to 66 ft. lbs. (89 Nm).
11. Install the flexible coupling pinch bolt. Tighten the pinch bolt to 30 ft. lbs. (40 Nm). Check that the relationship of the flexible coupling to the flange is 1/4-3/4 in. (6-19mm) of flat.
12. Install the pitman arm onto the pitman shaft, lining up the marks made at removal. Install the pitman shaft nut and tighten to 185 ft. lbs. (250 Nm).
13. Connect the fluid lines and refill the reservoir. Bleed the system.

C/K Series

➧ See Figure 149

1. Raise and support the front end on jackstands.
2. Set the front wheels in the straight ahead position.
3. Disconnect the battery ground cable.
4. Place a drain pan under the gear and disconnect the fluid lines. Cap the openings.
5. Remove the adapter and shield from the gear and flexible coupling.
6. Matchmark the flexible coupling clamp and wormshaft.
7. Remove the flexible coupling pinch bolt.
8. Mark the relationship of the pitman arm to the pitman shaft.
9. Remove the pitman shaft nut and then remove the pitman arm from the pitman shaft, using a puller.
10. Remove the steering gear to frame bolts and remove the gear assembly.

To install:

11. Place the steering gear in position, guiding the wormshaft into flexible coupling. Align the flat in the coupling with the flat on the wormshaft.
12. Install the steering gear-to-frame bolts and tighten to 69 ft. lbs. (93 Nm) on 1988-90 models; 100 ft. lbs. (135 Nm) on 1991-96 models.
13. Install the flexible coupling pinch bolt. Tighten the pinch bolt to 30 ft. lbs. (41 Nm) on 1988-90 models; 22 ft. lbs. (30 Nm) on 1991-96 models. Check that the relationship of the flexible coupling to the flange is 1/4-3/4 in. (6-19mm) of flat.
14. Install the pitman arm onto the pitman shaft, lining up the marks made at removal. Install the pitman shaft nut.
15. Install the adapter and shield.
16. Connect the fluid lines and refill the reservoir. Bleed the system.

1. Jam nut
2. Side cover
3. Bolt
4. Washer
5. Adjusting screw
6. Pinch bolt
7. Shaft
8. Nut
9. Spring washer
10. Flange
11. Coupling
12. Bolt
84908158

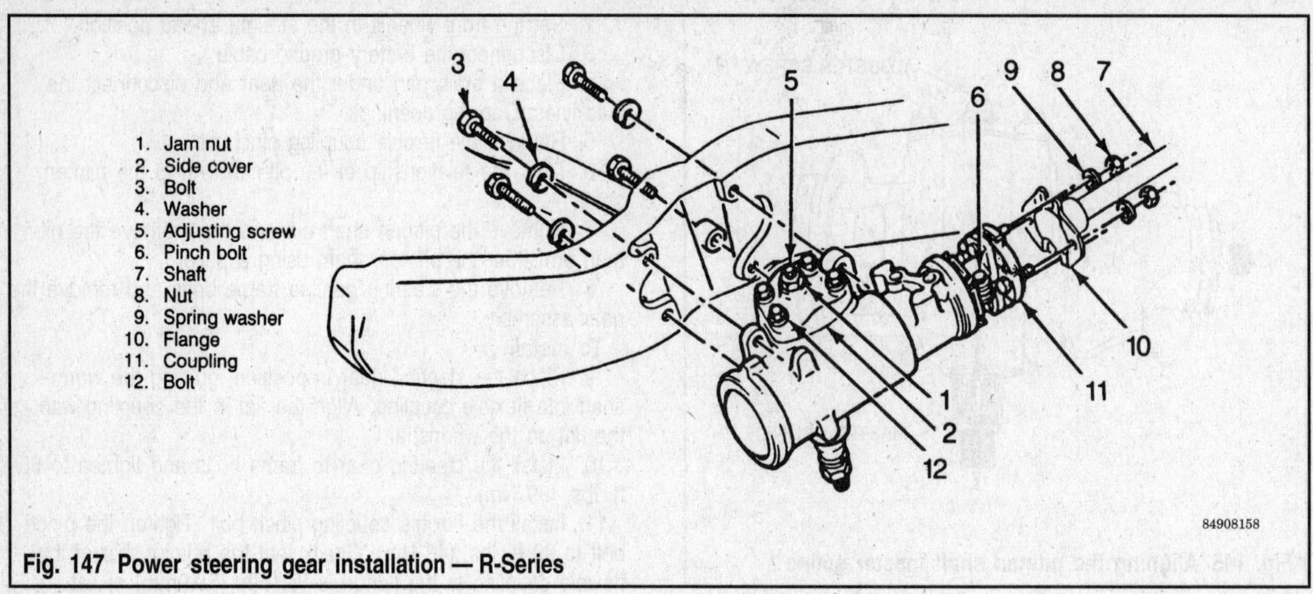

Fig. 147 Power steering gear installation — R-Series

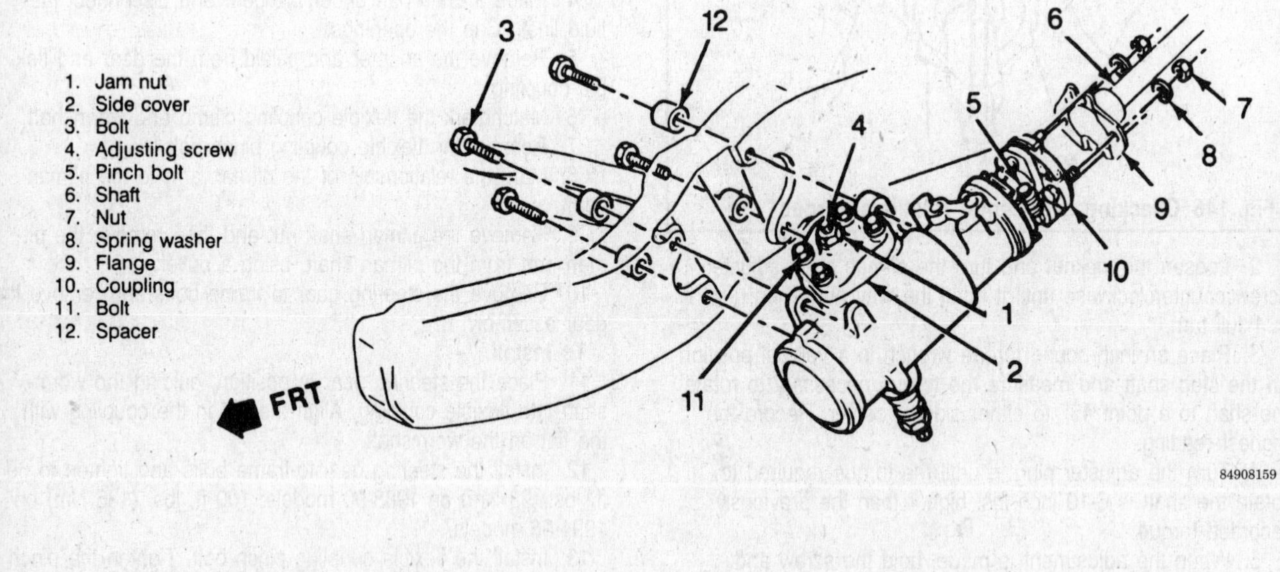

1. Jam nut
2. Side cover
3. Bolt
4. Adjusting screw
5. Pinch bolt
6. Shaft
7. Nut
8. Spring washer
9. Flange
10. Coupling
11. Bolt
12. Spacer
FRT
84908159

Fig. 148 Power steering gear installation — V-Series

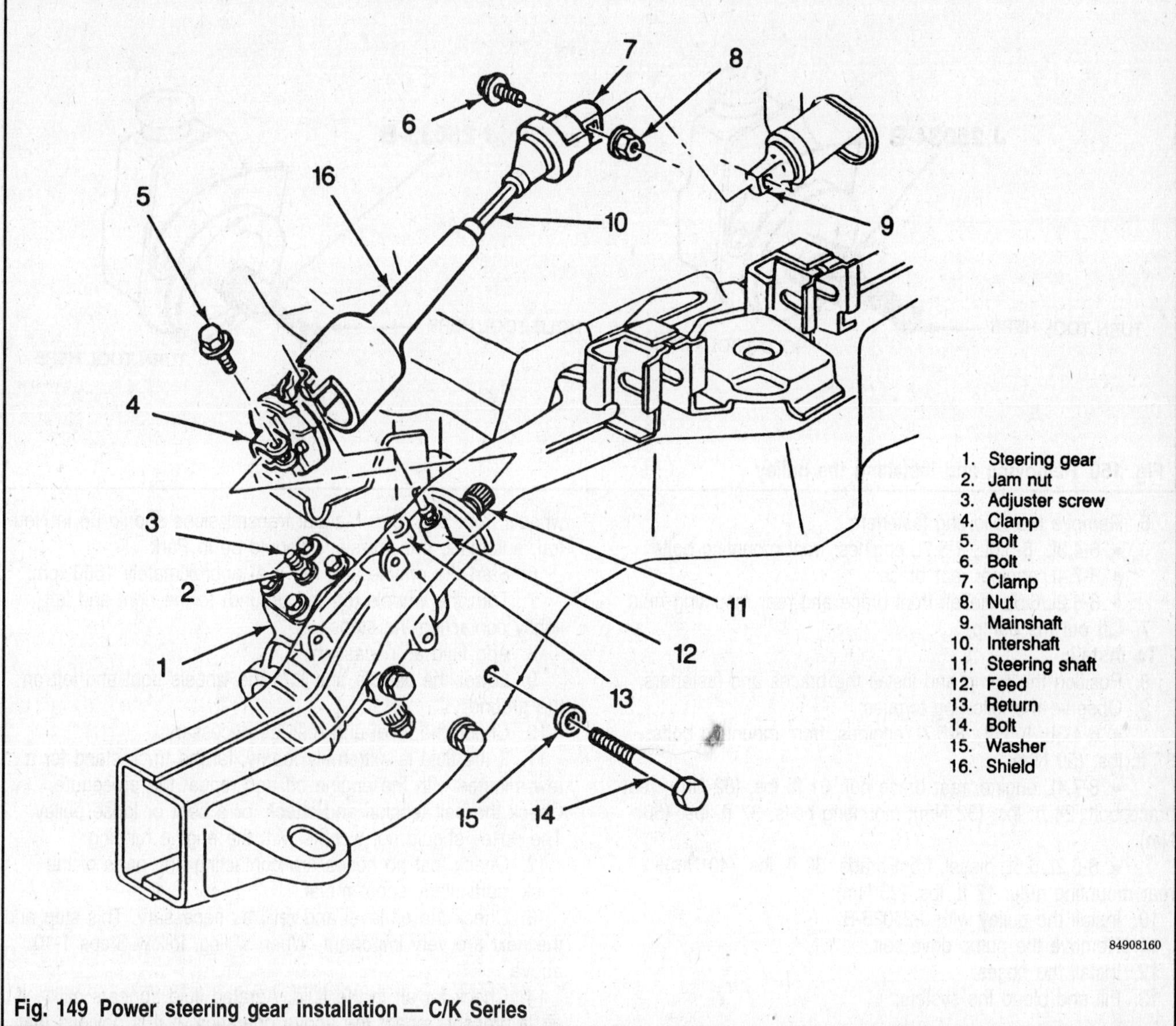

Fig. 149 Power steering gear installation — C/K Series

Power Steering Pump

REMOVAL & INSTALLATION

R/V Series

▶ See Figure 150

1. Disconnect the hoses at the pump. When the hoses are disconnected, secure the ends in a raised position to prevent leakage. Cap the ends of the hoses to prevent the entrance of dirt.
2. Cap the pump fittings.
3. Loosen the bracket-to-pump mounting nuts.
4. Remove the pump drive belt.
5. Remove the bracket-to-pump bolts and remove the pump from the truck.

To install:

6. If a new pump is being installed, remove the pulley with a pulley puller such as J-25034-B. Install the pulley on the new pump with a forcing screw and washer.
7. Install the pump and tighten all bolts and nuts securely.
8. Fill the reservoir and bleed the pump by turning the pulley counterclockwise (as viewed from the front) until bubbles stop forming.
9. Bleed the system as outlined following.

C/K Series

▶ See Figure 150

1. Disconnect the hoses at the pump. When the hoses are disconnected, secure the ends in a raised position to prevent leakage. Cap the ends of the hoses to prevent the entrance of dirt.
2. Cap the pump fittings.
3. Loosen the belt tensioner.
4. Remove the pump drive belt.
5. Remove the pulley with a pulley puller such as J-29785-A.

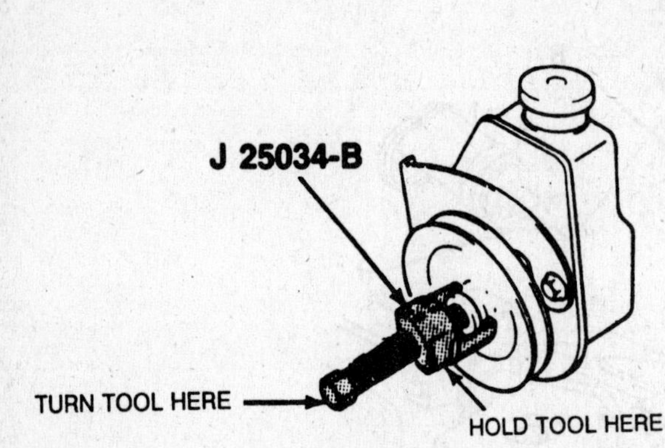

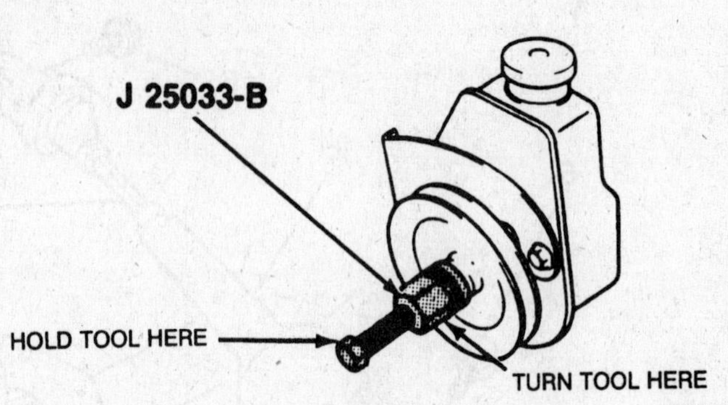

Fig. 150 Removing and installing the pulley

6. Remove the following fasteners:
   - 6-4.3L, 8-5.0L, 8-5.7L engines: front mounting bolts
   - 8-7.4L engine: rear brace
   - 8-6.2L/6.5L diesel: front brace and rear mounting nuts
7. Lift out the pump.

To install:

8. Position the pump and install the braces and fasteners.
9. Observe the following torques:
   - 6-4.3L, 8-5.0L, 8-5.7L engines, front mounting bolts: 37 ft. lbs. (50 Nm)
   - 8-7.4L engine, rear brace nut: 61 ft. lbs. (82 Nm); rear brace bolt: 24 ft. lbs. (32 Nm); mounting bolts: 37 ft. lbs. (50 Nm)
   - 8-6.2L/6.5L diesel, front brace: 30 ft. lbs. (40 Nm); rear mounting nuts: 17 ft. lbs. (23 Nm).
10. Install the pulley with J-25033-B.
11. Remove the pump drive belt.
12. Install the hoses.
13. Fill and bleed the system.

BLEEDING THE HYDRAULIC SYSTEM

1. Fill the reservoir to the proper level and let the fluid remain undisturbed for at least 2 minutes.
2. Start the engine and run it for only about 2 seconds.
3. Add fluid as necessary.
4. Repeat Steps 1-3 until the level remains constant.
5. Raise the front of the vehicle so that the front wheels are off the ground. Set the parking brake and block both rear wheels front and rear. Manual transmissions should be in Neutral; automatic transmissions should be in Park.
6. Start the engine and run it at approximately 1500 rpm.
7. Turn the wheels (off the ground) to the right and left, lightly contacting the stops.
8. Add fluid as necessary.
9. Lower the vehicle and turn the wheels right and left on the ground.
10. Check the level and refill as necessary.
11. If the fluid is extremely foamy, let the truck stand for a few minutes with the engine off and repeat the procedure. Check the belt tension and check for a bent or loose pulley. The pulley should not wobble with the engine running.
12. Check that no hoses are contacting any parts of the truck, particularly sheet metal.
13. Check the oil level and refill as necessary. This step and the next are very important. When willing, follow Steps 1-10 above
14. Check for air in the fluid. Aerated fluid appears milky. If air is present, repeat the above operation. If it is obvious that the pump will not respond to bleeding after several attempts, a pressure test may be required.

The procedures for maintaining, adjusting, and repairing the power steering systems and components discussed in this chapter are to be done only after determining that the steering linkages and front suspension systems are correctly aligned and in good condition. All worn or damaged parts should be replaced before attempting to service the power steering system. After correcting any condition that could affect the power steering, do the preliminary tests of the steering system components.

TORQUE SPECIFICATIONS

Component	US	Metric
C-Series Front Suspension		
Lower Control Arm		
Stud Nut		
1988-90	90 ft. lbs.	122 Nm
1991-94	84 ft. lbs.	115 Nm
1995-96	94 ft. lbs.	128 Nm
Pivot Shaft Nuts		
1988-90	96 ft. lbs.	130 Nm
1991-94	121 ft. lbs.	165 Nm
1995-96	101 ft. lbs.	137 Nm
Shock Absorber		
Lower	20 ft. lbs.	27 Nm
Upper	8 ft. lbs.	11 Nm
Stabilizer Bar-to-frame	24 ft. lbs.	32 Nm
Stabilizer Bar-to-lower Arm	13 ft. lbs.	17 Nm
Steering Knuckle Splash Shield		
1988-90	12 ft. lbs.	16 Nm
1991-96	19 ft. lbs.	26 Nm
Upper Ball Joint		
Nuts		
1988-90 15/25 Series	17 ft. lbs.	23 Nm
1988-90 35 Series	52 ft. lbs.	70 Nm
1991-96	18 ft. lbs.	24 Nm
Stud Nut		
1988-90	90 ft. lbs.	122 Nm
1991-96	84 ft. lbs.	115 Nm
Upper Control Arm		
Pivot Shaft Nuts		
1988-90	88 ft. lbs.	120 Nm
1991-96	140 ft. lbs.	190 Nm
C3HD Series Front Suspension		
Brake Line Bracket	6 ft. lbs	7 nm
King Pin Lock pin	29 ft. lbs.	40 Nm
Leaf Spring		
U-Bolt Nuts	80 ft. lbs.	109 Nm
Shackle Nuts	92 ft. lbs.	125 nm
Front Eye Bolt	92 ft. lbs.	125 Nm
Shock Absorber		
Lower	37 ft. lbs.	50 Nm
Upper	136 ft. lbs.	185 Nm
Stabilizer Bar-to-link	50 ft. lbs.	68 Nm
Stabilzer Bar clamp Bolt	21 ft. lbs.	28 nm
Steering Arm-to-Anchor Plate		
Bolts	12 ft. lbs.	16 Nm
Nuts	230 ft. lbs.	312 Nm
K-Series Front Suspension		
Drive Axle Flange Bolts	59 ft. lbs.	79 Nm
Hub Nut	173 ft. lbs.	235 Nm
Inner Tie Rod End Nut	35 ft. lbs.	47 Nm
Lower Ball Joint		
Nuts	45 ft. lbs.	61 Nm

87988C03

TORQUE SPECIFICATIONS

Component	US	Metric
Upper Control Arm		
Shaft Stud-to-Crossmember		
10/1500, 20/2500	90 ft. lbs.	122 Nm
30/3500	130 ft. lbs.	176 Nm
Ball Stud Nut		
10/1500, 20/2500	90 ft. lbs.	122 Nm
30/3500	130 ft. lbs.	176 Nm
Pivot Shaft Nuts		
10/1500	115 ft. lbs.	156 Nm
20/2500, 30/3500	105 ft. lbs.	142 Nm
Bushings		
20/2500, 30/3500	190 ft. lbs.	257 Nm
V-Series Front Suspension		
Ball Joint		
Adjusting Ring	50 ft. lbs.	70 Nm
Stud		
Upper Nut	100 ft. lbs.	135 Nm
Lower Nut	70 ft. lbs.	95 Nm
Leaf Spring		
U-Bolt Nuts	150 ft. lbs.	203 Nm
Shackle Nuts	50 ft. lbs.	67 Nm
Front Eye Bolt	90 ft. lbs.	122 Nm
Shock Absorber		
Lower		
Dual	65 ft. lbs.	88 Nm
Quad	89 ft. lbs.	120 Nm
Upper	65. ft. lbs.	88 Nm
Splash Shield Nuts	65. ft.lbs.	88 Nm
Stabilizer Bar-to-Frame	52 ft. lbs.	70 Nm
Stabilizer Bar-to-Spring Plate	133 ft. lbs.	180 Nm
Steering Arm-to-Knuckle	90 ft. lbs.	122 Nm
Idler Arm		
Ball stud Nut		
R/V Series	66 ft. lbs.	89 Nm
C/K Series	40 ft. lbs.	54 Nm
To Frame		
R/V Series	30 ft. lbs.	40 Nm
C/K Series	78 ft. lbs.	105 Nm

87988C05

TORQUE SPECIFICATIONS

Component	US	Metric
Lug Nuts		
Trucks with single front and rear wheels		
R10/1500 w/5 studs and steel or aluminum wheels	100 ft. lbs.	140 Nm
V10/1500 w/6 studs and steel wheels	88 ft. lbs.	120 Nm
V10/1500 w/6 studs and aluminum wheels	100 ft. lbs.	140 Nm
All C/K Series		
1988-90	90 ft. lbs.	123 Nm
1991-96	120 ft. lbs.	160 Nm
All R/V Series with 8 studs trucks with single front and dual rear wheels	120 ft.lbs.	160 Nm
R/V Series with 8 studs	140 ft. lbs.	190 Nm
R/V Series with 10 studs	175 ft. lbs.	240 Nm
C/K Series		
1988-90	125 ft. lbs.	170 Nm
1991-96 with 8 studs	140 ft. lbs.	190 Nm
1991-96 with 10 studs	175 ft. lbs.	240 Nm
Pitman Arm		
Arm-to-Relay Rod Nut		
R/V Series	66 ft. lbs.	89 Nm
C/K Series		
C3Hd Series	40 ft. lbs.	54 Nm
1988-90	40 ft. lbs.	54 Nm
1991-96	48 ft. lbs.	62 Nm
Shaft Nut/Clamp Bolt		
C/K Series	184 ft. lbs.	249 Nm
R-Series	184 ft. lbs.	249 Nm
V-Series	125 ft. lbs.	169 Nm
Pot Joint Bolt		
C/K Series	22 ft. lbs.	30 Nm
Rear Suspension		
Leaf springs		
U-Bolts		
R/V Series		
10/15, 20/25	125 ft. lbs.	169 Nm
30/35	147 ft. lbs.	200 Nm
C/K Series		
15/25 Series	81 ft. lbs.	110 Nm
35 Series w/o dual wheels or 7.4L engine	81 ft. lbs.	110 Nm
35 Series w/dual wheels	110 ft. lbs.	148 Nm
35 Series w/7.4L engine, w/o dual wheels	110 ft. lbs.	148 Nm
C3HD Series	207 ft. lbs.	280 Nm
Hangers/Shackles		
All exc. C3HD	81 ft. lbs.	
C3HD	136. ft. lbs.	185 Nm
Shock Absorbers		
R/V Series		
Lower	115 ft. lbs.	160 Nm
Upper		
10/15, 20/25	140 ft. lbs.	190 Nm
30/35	52 ft. lbs.	70 Nm

87988C06

TORQUE SPECIFICATIONS

Component	US	Metric
C/K Series		
Lower		
C3HD	52 ft. lbs.	70 Nm
1988-91	52 ft. lbs.	70 Nm
1992-94	81 ft. lbs.	70 Nm
1995-96	74 ft. lbs.	100 Nm
Upper		
1988-91	17 ft. lbs.	23 Nm
1992-94	20 ft. lbs.	27 Nm
1995-96	13 ft. lbs.	17 Nm
Stabilizer Bar Clamp		
R/V Series	24 ft. lbs.	32 Nm
C3HD Series		
U-Bolt	22 ft. lbs.	30 Nm
Upper Insulator	17 ft. lbs.	23 Nm
Relay Rod		
Ball stud Nut		
R/V Series	66 ft. lbs.	89 Nm
C/K Series		
1988-90	40 ft. lbs.	54 Nm
1991-96	48 ft. lbs.	62 Nm
Steering Column-to-Floor Plate		
C/K Series		
Bolts	22 ft. lbs.	30 Nm
Nuts	20 ft. lbs.	27 Nm
Steering Wheel Nut	30 ft. lbs.	40 nm
Tie Rod Nut		
C/K Series		
Stud Nut	40 ft. lbs.	54 Nm
Clamp Nut	14 ft. lbs.	18 Nm
R-Series		
Stud Nut	45 ft. lbs.	61 Nm
V-Series		
Castellated nut	40 ft. lbs.	54 Nm
Lock Nut	175 ft. lbs.	237 Nm

87988C07

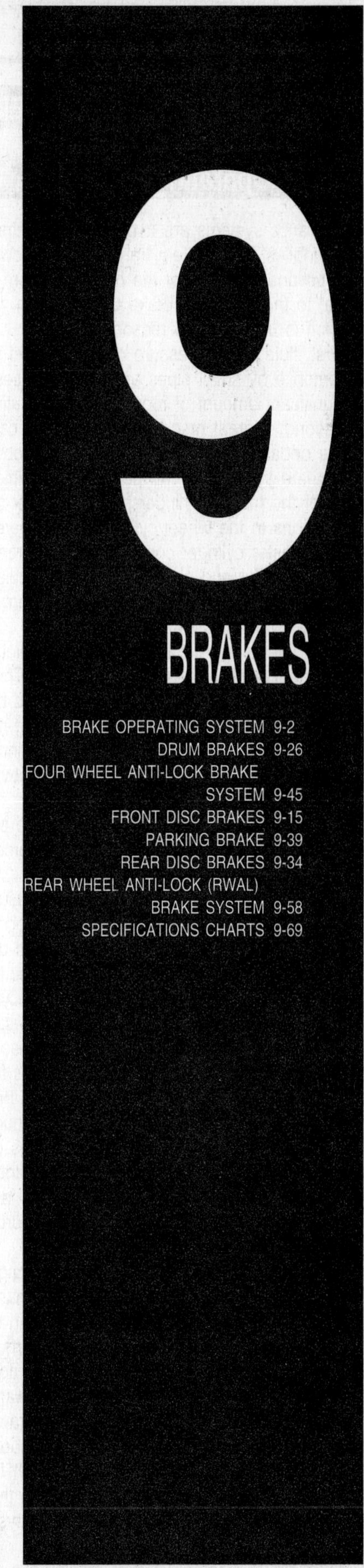

9 BRAKES

BRAKE OPERATING SYSTEM

Basic Operating Principles

Hydraulic systems are used to actuate the brakes of all automobiles. The system transports the power required to force the frictional surfaces of the braking system together from the pedal to the individual brake units at each wheel. A hydraulic system is used for two reasons.

First, fluid under pressure can be carried to all parts of an automobile by small pipes and flexible hoses without taking up a significant amount of room or posing routing problems.

Second, a great mechanical advantage can be given to the brake pedal end of the system, and the foot pressure required to actuate the brakes can be reduced by making the surface area of the master cylinder pistons smaller than that of any of the pistons in the wheel cylinders or calipers.

The master cylinder consists of a fluid reservoir and a double cylinder and piston assembly. Double type master cylinders are designed to separate the front and rear braking systems hydraulically in case of a leak.

Steel lines carry the brake fluid to a point on the vehicles frame near each of the vehicles wheels. The fluid is then carried to the calipers and wheel cylinders by flexible tubes in order to allow for suspension and steering movements.

In drum brake systems, each wheel cylinder contains two pistons, one at either end, which push outward in opposite directions.

In disc brake systems, the cylinders are part of the calipers. One cylinder in each caliper is used to force the brake pads against the disc.

All pistons employ some type of seal, usually made of rubber, to minimize fluid leakage. A rubber dust boot seals the outer end of the cylinder against dust and dirt. The boot fits around the outer end of the piston on disc brake calipers, and around the brake actuating rod on wheel cylinders.

The hydraulic system operates as follows: When at rest, the entire system, from the piston(s) in the master cylinder to those in the wheel cylinders or calipers, is full of brake fluid. Upon application of the brake pedal, fluid trapped in front of the master cylinder piston(s) is forced through the lines to the wheel cylinders. Here, it forces the pistons outward, in the case of drum brakes, and inward toward the disc, in the case of disc brakes. The motion of the pistons is opposed by return springs mounted outside the cylinders in drum brakes, and by spring seals, in disc brakes.

Upon release of the brake pedal, a spring located inside the master cylinder immediately returns the master cylinder pistons to the normal position. The pistons contain check valves and the master cylinder has compensating ports drilled in it. These are uncovered as the pistons reach their normal position. The piston check valves allow fluid to flow toward the wheel cylinders or calipers as the pistons withdraw. Then, as the return springs force the brake pads or shoes into the released position, the excess fluid reservoir through the compensating ports. It is during the time the pedal is in the released position that any fluid that has leaked out of the system will be replaced through the compensating ports.

Dual circuit master cylinders employ two pistons, located one behind the other, in the same cylinder. The primary piston is actuated directly by mechanical linkage from the brake pedal through the power booster. The secondary piston is actuated by fluid trapped between the two pistons. If a leak develops in front of the secondary piston, it moves forward until it bottoms against the front of the master cylinder, and the fluid trapped between the pistons will operate the rear brakes. If the rear brakes develop a leak, the primary piston will move forward until direct contact with the secondary piston takes place, and it will force the secondary piston to actuate the front brakes. In either case, the brake pedal moves farther when the brakes are applied, and less braking power is available.

All dual circuit systems use a switch to warn the driver when only half of the brake system is operational. This switch is located in a valve body which is mounted on the firewall or the frame below the master cylinder. A hydraulic piston receives pressure from both circuits, each circuit's pressure being applied to one end of the piston. When the pressures are in balance, the piston remains stationary. When one circuit has a leak, however, the greater pressure in that circuit during application of the brakes will push the piston to one side, closing the switch and activating the brake warning light.

In disc brake systems, this valve body also contains a metering valve and, in some cases, a proportioning valve. The metering valve keeps pressure from traveling to the disc brakes on the front wheels until the brake shoes on the rear wheels have contacted the drums, ensuring that the front brakes will never be used alone. The proportioning valve controls the pressure to the rear brakes to lessen the chance of rear wheel lock-up during very hard braking.

Warning lights may be tested by depressing the brake pedal and holding it while opening one of the wheel cylinder bleeder screws. If this does not cause the light to go on, substitute a new lamp, make continuity checks, and, finally, replace the switch as necessary.

The hydraulic system may be checked for leaks by applying pressure to the pedal gradually and steadily. If the pedal sinks very slowly to the floor, the system has a leak. This is not to be confused with a springy or spongy feel due to the compression of air within the lines. If the system leaks, there will be a gradual change in the position of the pedal with a constant pressure.

Check for leaks along all lines and at wheel cylinders. If no external leaks are apparent, the problem is inside the master cylinder.

DISC BRAKES

Instead of the traditional expanding brakes that press outward against a circular drum, disc brake systems utilize a disc (rotor) with brake pads positioned on either side of it. Braking effect is achieved in a manner similar to the way you would squeeze a spinning phonograph record between your fingers. The disc (rotor) is a casting with cooling fins between the two braking surfaces. This enables air to circulate between the braking surfaces making them less sensitive to heat buildup and more resistant to fade. Dirt and water do not affect braking action since contaminants are thrown off by the centrifugal action of the rotor or scraped off the by the pads.

Also, the equal clamping action of the two brake pads tends to ensure uniform, straight line stops. Disc brakes are inherently self-adjusting. There are three general types of disc brake:

1. A fixed caliper.
2. A floating caliper.
3. A sliding caliper.

The fixed caliper design uses two pistons mounted on either side of the rotor (in each side of the caliper). The caliper is mounted rigidly and does not move.

The sliding and floating designs are quite similar. In fact, these two types are often lumped together. In both designs, the pad on the inside of the rotor is moved into contact with the rotor by hydraulic force. The caliper, which is not held in a fixed position, moves slightly, bringing the outside pad into contact with the rotor. There are various methods of attaching floating calipers. Some pivot at the bottom or top, and some slide on mounting bolts. In any event, the end result is the same.

All the vehicles covered in this book employ the sliding caliper design.

DRUM BRAKES

Drum brakes employ two brake shoes mounted on a stationary backing plate. These shoes are positioned inside a circular drum which rotates with the wheel assembly. The shoes are held in place by springs. This allows them to slide toward the drums (when they are applied) while keeping the linings and drums in alignment. The shoes are actuated by a wheel cylinder which is mounted at the top of the backing plate. When the brakes are applied, hydraulic pressure forces the wheel cylinder's actuating links outward. Since these links bear directly against the top of the brake shoes, the tops of the shoes are then forced against the inner side of the drum. This action forces the bottoms of the two shoes to contact the brake drum by rotating the entire assembly slightly (known as servo action). When pressure within the wheel cylinder is relaxed, return springs pull the shoes back away from the drum.

Most modern drum brakes are designed to self-adjust themselves during application when the vehicle is moving in reverse. This motion causes both shoes to rotate very slightly with the drum, rocking an adjusting lever, thereby causing rotation of the adjusting screw.

WARNING

Clean, high quality brake fluid is essential to the safe and proper operation of the brake system. You should always buy the highest quality brake fluid that is available. If the brake fluid becomes contaminated, drain and flush the system and fill the master cylinder with new fluid. Never reuse any brake fluid. Any brake fluid that is removed from the system should be discarded.

Adjustments

DRUM BRAKES

These brakes are equipped with self-adjusters and no manual adjustment is necessary, except when brake linings are replaced.

DISC BRAKES

These brakes are inherently self-adjusting and no adjustment is ever necessary or possible.

BRAKE LIGHT SWITCH

R/V Series

The design of the switch and valve mounting provides for automatic adjustment when the brake pedal is manually returned to its mechanical stop as follows:

1. With brake pedal depressed, press the switch in until it firmly seats on the clip. Note that audible clicks can be heard as threaded portion of switch is pushed through the clip.
2. Pull brake pedal fully against pedal stop, until audible click sounds can no longer be heard.
3. Release brake pedal, then repeat Step 2 to assure that no audible click sounds remain.

Electrical contact should be made when the brake pedal is depressed 1.0-1.24 in. (25-31mm) from its fully released position.

C/K Series

1. Depress the brake pedal fully and hold it.
2. Pull the lever on the bottom of the switch, back to its stop.
3. Release the pedal.
4. The brake lamp switch will self-adjust when the pedal returns to its stop.

PEDAL TRAVEL

The stop light switch provides for an automatic adjustment for the brake pedal when it is returned to its stop. With pedal in fully released position, the stop light switch plunger should be fully depressed against the pedal shank. Adjust the switch by moving in or out as necessary.

R/V Series

➧ See Figure 1

Periodically check the pedal travel. With the engine off and the brakes cold, pump the pedal at least 3 times to expel all vacuum from the power brake booster. Use a yardstick to measure the distance between the lower edge of the steering wheel rim to the top of the pedal. Then measure the distance while holding the pedal in the fully depressed position — about 90 lbs. of force. Calculate the difference between the 2 readings. The distance should be 4.5 in. (115mm) for trucks with manual brakes; 3.5 in. (90mm) for trucks with power brakes.

C/K Series

See Figure 1

Periodically check the pedal travel. With the engine off and the brakes cold, pump the pedal at least 3 times to expel all vacuum from the power brake booster. Use a yardstick to measure the distance that the pedal can be depressed from the fully released position to the fully applied position — about 90 lbs. of force.

The distance should be 5.5 in. (140mm) for trucks with manual brakes; 5.5 in. (140mm) for trucks with vacuum type power brakes; 4.5 in. (114mm) for trucks with hydraulic type power brakes; 4 in. (102mm) for trucks with 4-wheel disc brakes; and, 4.5 in. (113mm) for trucks with anti-lock brakes.

Brake Pedal

REMOVAL & INSTALLATION

R/V Series

See Figure 2

1. Remove the retaining pin and washer, and disconnect the pushrod from the pedal arm.
2. Disconnect the return spring at the pedal arm.
3. Remove the brake pedal pivot bolt and nut and remove the pedal.

➡On trucks with manual transmission, as you pull out the pivot bolt, slide a rod in behind it to hold the clutch pedal in place.

4. Installation is the reverse of removal. Tighten the pivot bolt nut to 25 ft. lbs. (34 Nm).

C/K Series

See Figure 3

1. Disconnect the negative battery cable.
2. Disable the SIR system (if equipped).
3. Unplug the connector from the brake light switch.
4. Remove the retainer and bushing and slide the pedal pushrod off its stud.
5. Remove the pedal pivot bolt and nut, along with the spacer and bushings. Remove the pedal.

To install:

6. Install the pedal, spacer, bushings, pivot bolt and nut. Tighten the pivot bolt to 35 ft. lbs. (47 Nm).
7. Install the pushrod onto its stud.
8. Install the retainer and bushing, enable the SIR system and connect the negative battery cable.

Brake Light Switch

REMOVAL & INSTALLATION

1. Disconnect the negative battery cable.
2. Disable the SIR system (if equipped).
3. Remove the clip (R/V Series) or unclip the switch (C/K Series) and unplug the electrical connector from the brake light switch.
4. Remove the switch.
5. Installation is the reverse of removal.

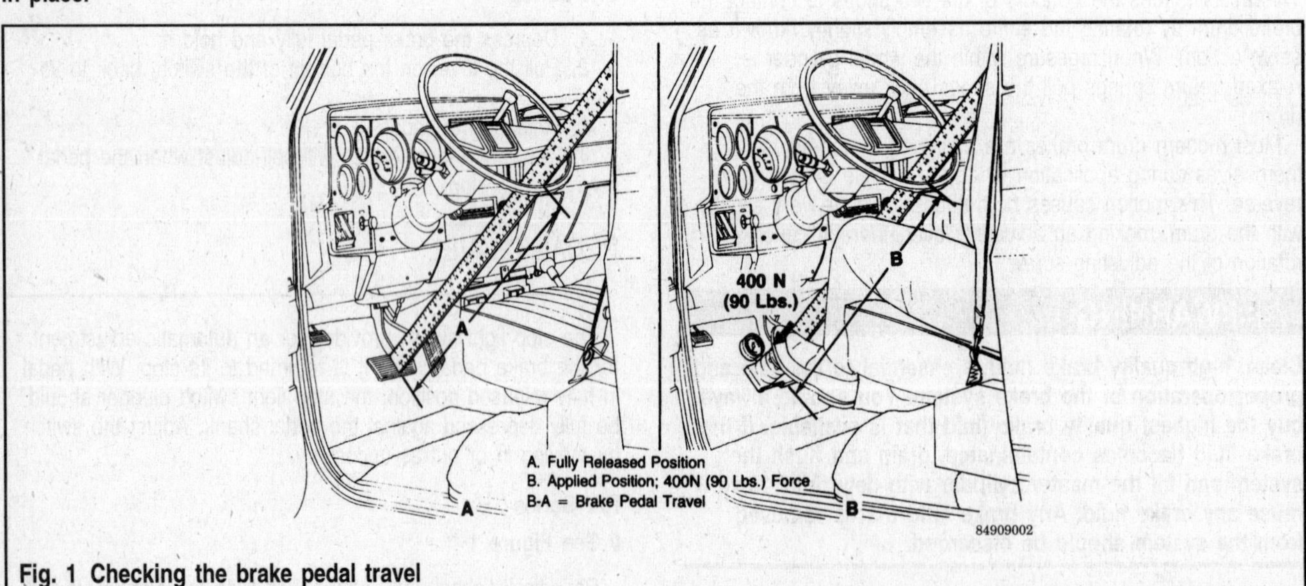

Fig. 1 Checking the brake pedal travel

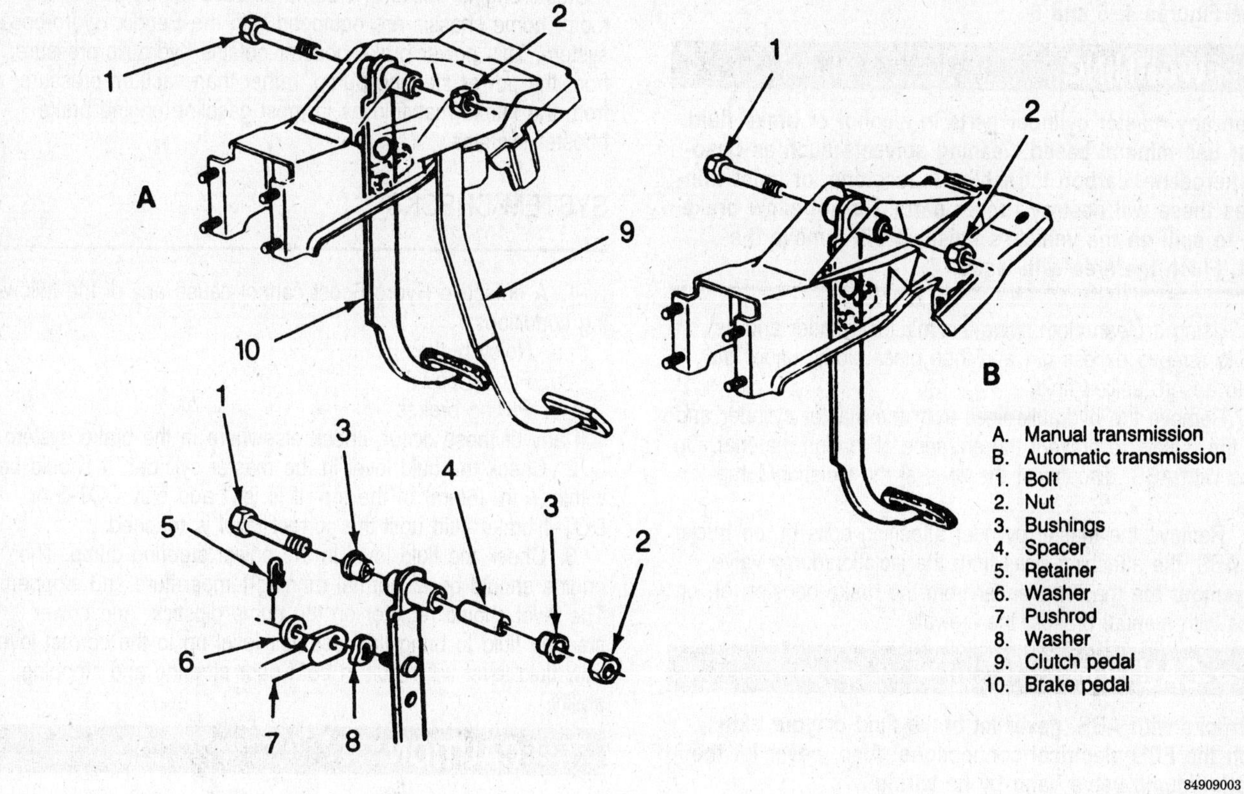

1
2
A
9
10
1
3
4
3
5
2
6
7
8
1
2
B
A. Manual transmission
B. Automatic transmission
1. Bolt
2. Nut
3. Bushings
4. Spacer
5. Retainer
6. Washer
7. Pushrod
8. Washer
9. Clutch pedal
10. Brake pedal
84909003

Fig. 2 Brake pedal components — R/V Series

4
6
5
5
1
2
3
8
7
1. Retainer
2. Bushing
3. Nut
4. Bolt
5. Bushings
6. Spacer
7. Brake pedal
8. Stoplamp switch
84909004

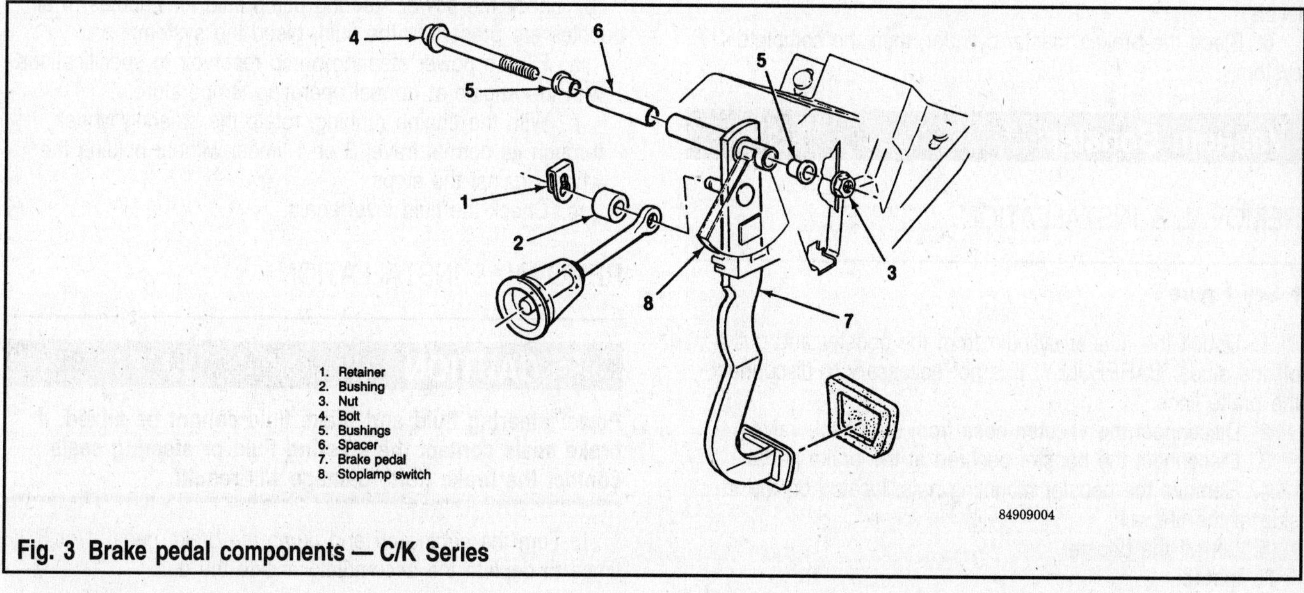

Fig. 3 Brake pedal components — C/K Series

Master Cylinder

REMOVAL & INSTALLATION

▶ See Figures 4, 5 and 6

****WARNING**

Clean any master cylinder parts in alcohol or brake fluid. Never use mineral based cleaning solvents such as gasoline, kerosene, carbon tetrachloride, acetone, or paint thinner as these will destroy rubber parts. Do not allow brake fluid to spill on the vehicle's finish, it will remove the paint. Flush the area with water.

1. Using a clean cloth, wipe the master cylinder and its lines to remove excess dirt and then place cloths under the unit to absorb spilled fluid.
2. Remove the hydraulic lines from the master cylinder and plug the outlets to prevent the entrance of foreign material. On trucks with ABS, disconnect the lines at the isolation/dump valve.
3. Remove the master cylinder attaching bolts or, on trucks with ABS, the attaching bolts from the isolation/dump valve, and remove the master cylinder from the brake booster, or, on trucks with manual brakes, the firewall.

****CAUTION**

On trucks with ABS, never let brake fluid or your skin touch the ECU electrical connections! Also, never let the isolation/dump valve hang by its wiring!

To install:

4. Position the master cylinder or, on trucks with ABS the master cylinder and isolation/dump valve, on the booster or firewall. Tighten the nuts to 20 ft. lbs. (27 Nm).
5. Connect the brake lines and tighten them to 13 ft. lbs. (17 Nm). Fill the master cylinder reservoirs to the proper levels.
6. Bleed the brakes master cylinder, then the complete system.

Vacuum Booster

REMOVAL & INSTALLATION

▶ See Figure 7

1. Unbolt the master cylinder from the booster and pull it off the studs, CAREFULLY! It is not necessary to disconnect the brake lines.
2. Disconnect the vacuum hose from the check valve.
3. Disconnect the booster pushrod at the brake pedal.
4. Remove the booster mounting nuts, located on the inside of the firewall.
5. Lift off the booster.

To install:

6. To install the the booster with a new gasket.
7. Tighten the booster mounting nuts to 21 ft. lbs. (29 Nm); the master cylinder nuts to 20 ft. lbs. (27 Nm).

Hydro-Boost

Diesel engine trucks and some 30/3500 series trucks and motor home chassis are equipped with the Bendix Hydro-boost system. This power brake booster obtains hydraulic pressure from the power steering pump, rather than vacuum pressure from the intake manifold as in most gasoline engine brake booster systems.

SYSTEM CHECKS

1. A defective Hydro-Boost cannot cause any of the following conditions:
   a. Noisy brakes
   b. Fading pedal
   c. Pulling brakes

   If any of these occur, check elsewhere in the brake system.
2. Check the fluid level in the master cylinder. It should be within 1/4 in. (6mm) of the top. If is isn't add only DOT-3 or DOT-4 brake fluid until the correct level is reached.
3. Check the fluid level in the power steering pump. The engine should be at normal running temperature and stopped. The level should register on the pump dipstick. Add power steering fluid to bring the reservoir level up to the correct level. Low fluid level will result in both poor steering and stopping ability.

****CAUTION**

The brake hydraulic system uses brake fluid only, while the power steering and Hydro-Boost systems use power steering fluid only. Don't mix the two!

4. Check the power steering pump belt tension, and inspect all the power steering/Hydro-Boost hoses for kinks or leaks.
5. Check and adjust the engine idle speed, as necessary.
6. Check the power steering pump fluid for bubbles. If air bubbles are present in the fluid, bleed the system:
   a. Fill the power steering pump reservoir to specifications with the engine at normal operating temperature.
   b. With the engine running, rotate the steering wheel through its normal travel 3 or 4 times, without holding the wheel against the stops.
   c. Check the fluid level again.

REMOVAL & INSTALLATION

****CAUTION**

Power steering fluid and brake fluid cannot be mixed. If brake seals contact the steering fluid or steering seals contact the brake fluid, damage will result!

1. Turn the engine off and pump the brake pedal 4 or 5 times to deplete the accumulator inside the unit.

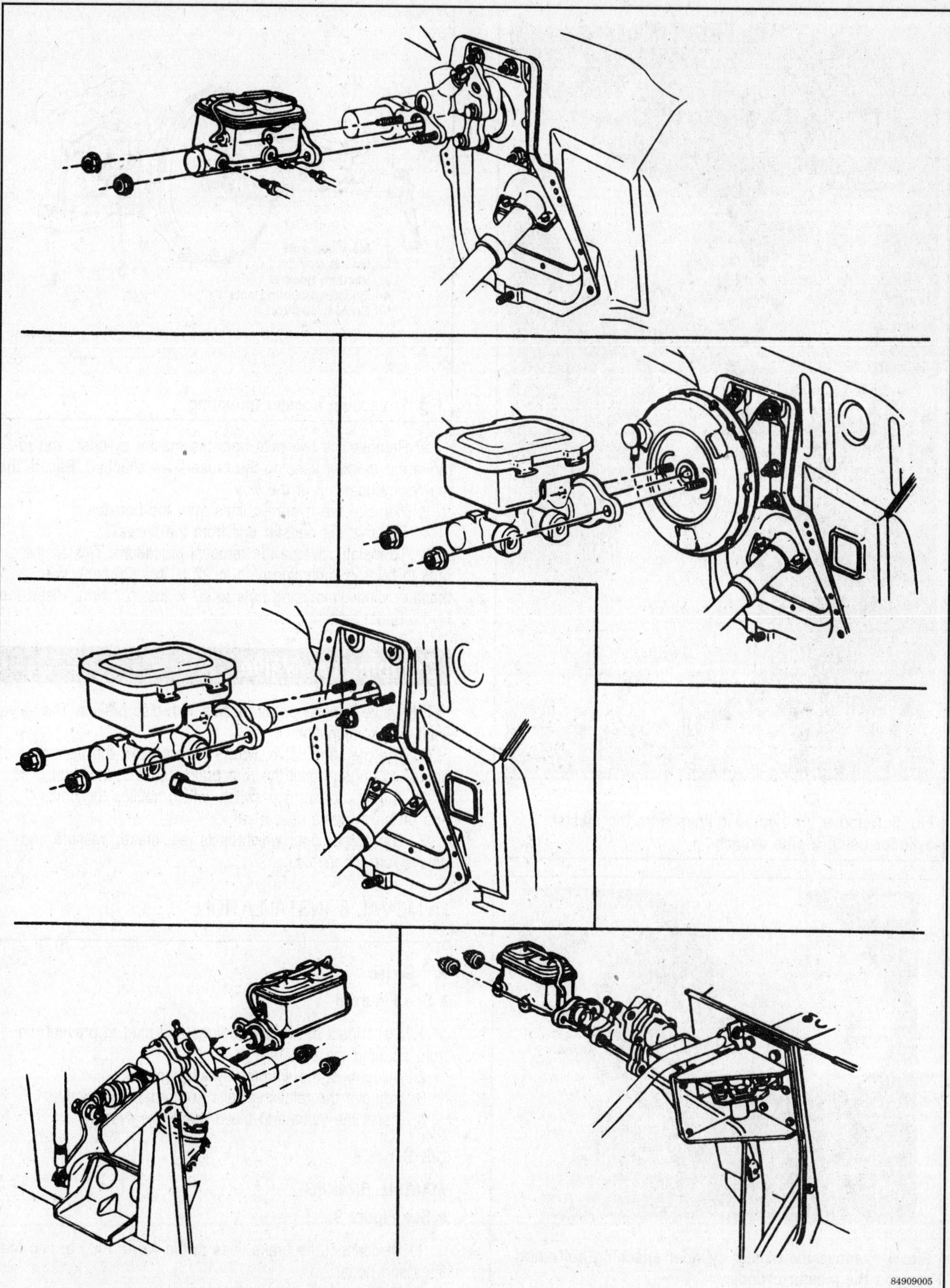

Fig. 4 Exploded view of the master cylinder mounting

Fig. 5 Remove the hydraulic lines from the master cylinder using a pipe wrench

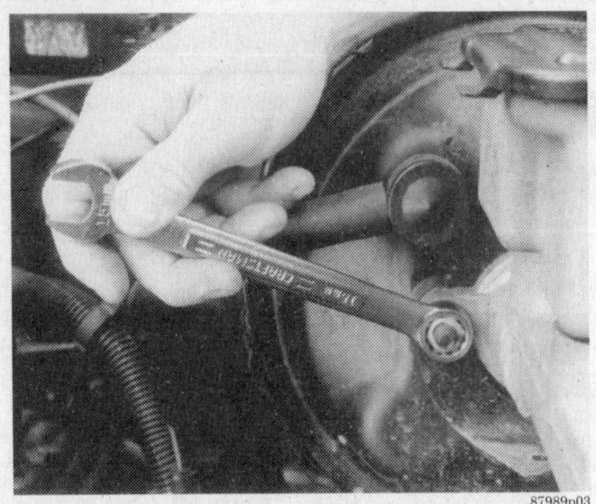

Fig. 6 Remove the master cylinder attaching bolts and remove the master cylinder

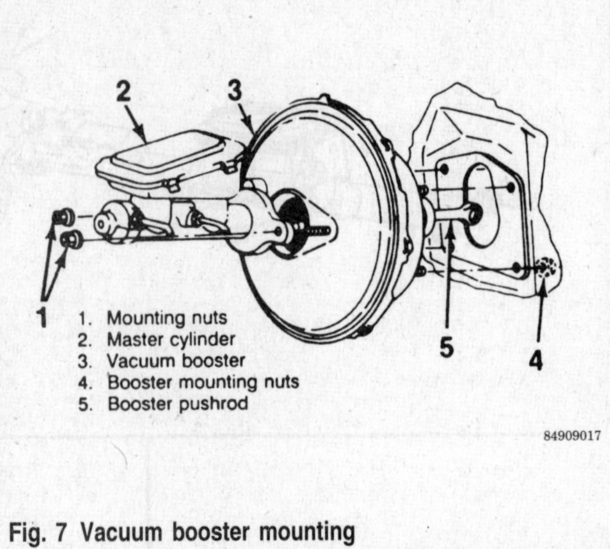

Fig. 7 Vacuum booster mounting

2. Remove the two nuts from the master cylinder, and remove the cylinder keeping the brake lines attached. Secure the master cylinder out of the way.

3. Remove the hydraulic lines from the booster.

4. Remove the booster unit from the firewall.

5. To install, reverse the removal procedure. Tighten the nuts to booster mounting nuts to 22 ft. lbs. (30 Nm); the master cylinder mounting nuts to 20 ft. lbs. (27 Nm). Bleed the Hydro-Boost system.

Combination Valve

This valve is used on all models with disc brakes. The valve itself is a combination of:

1. The metering valve, which will not allow the front disc brakes to engage until the rear brakes contact the drum.
2. The failure warning switch, which notifies the driver if one of the systems has a leak.
3. The proportioner which limits rear brake pressure and delays rear wheel skid.

REMOVAL & INSTALLATION

R/V Series

➧ See Figure 8

1. Disconnect the hydraulic lines and plug to prevent dirt from entering the system.
2. Disconnect the warning switch harness.
3. Remove the retaining bolts and remove the valve.
4. Install the valve and bleed the brake system.

C/K Series

MANUAL BRAKES

➧ See Figure 9

1. Disconnect the brake lines at the valve. Plug or cap the lines and ports.
2. Unplug the switch wiring connector.
3. Remove the valve-to-bracket bolts.

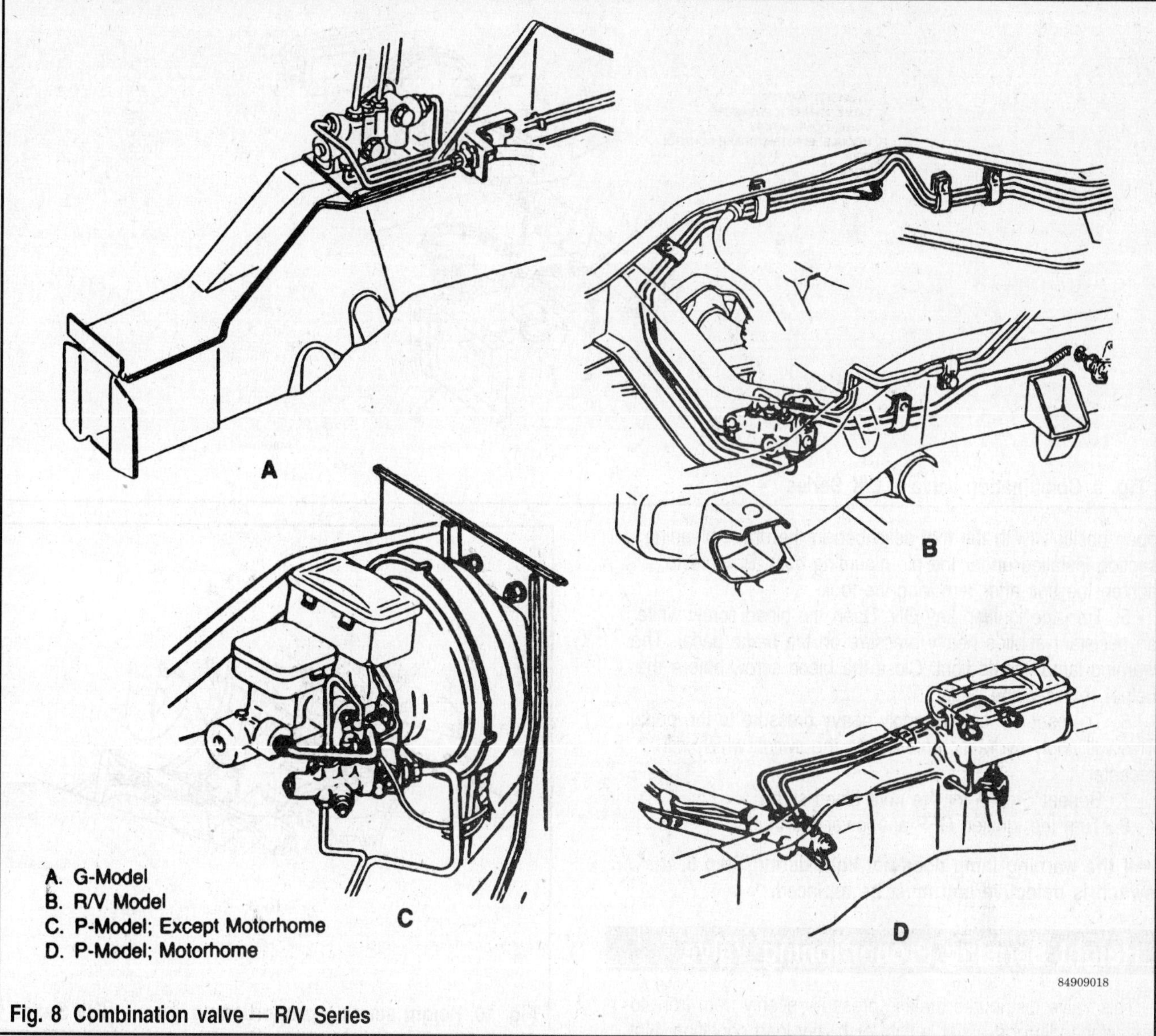

Fig. 8 Combination valve — R/V Series

To install:

4. Install the valve. Tighten the bolts to 20 ft. lbs. (27 Nm).
5. Bleed the system.

POWER BRAKES

➧ See Figure 9

1. Disconnect the brake lines at the switch. Plug or cap the lines and ports.
2. Unplug the warning switch wiring connector.
3. Remove the anit-lock brake system control module from the bracket. See the procedure later in this section.
4. Remove the bolts attaching the ABS isolation/dump valve to the bracket. See the procedure later in this section.
5. Remove the nuts that attach the master cylinder and bracket to the booster.
6. Remove the bracket and combination valve assembly.

To install:

7. Position the bracket/valve assembly and install the master cylinder-to-booster nuts. Tighten the nuts to 20 ft. lbs. (27 Nm).
8. Install the ABS isolation/dump valve nuts. Tighten them to 20 ft. lbs. (27 Nm).
9. Install the ABS control module.
10. Connect the wiring.
11. Connect the hydraulic lines.
12. Bleed the system.

SWITCH CENTERING

Whenever work on the brake system is done it is possible that the brake warning light will come on and refuse to go off when the work is finished. In this event, the switch must be centered.

1. Raise and support the truck.
2. Attach a bleeder hose to the rear brake bleed screw and immerse the other end of the hose in a jar of clean brake fluid.
3. Be sure that the master cylinder is full.
4. When bleeding the brakes, the pin in the end of the metering portion of the combination valve must be held in the

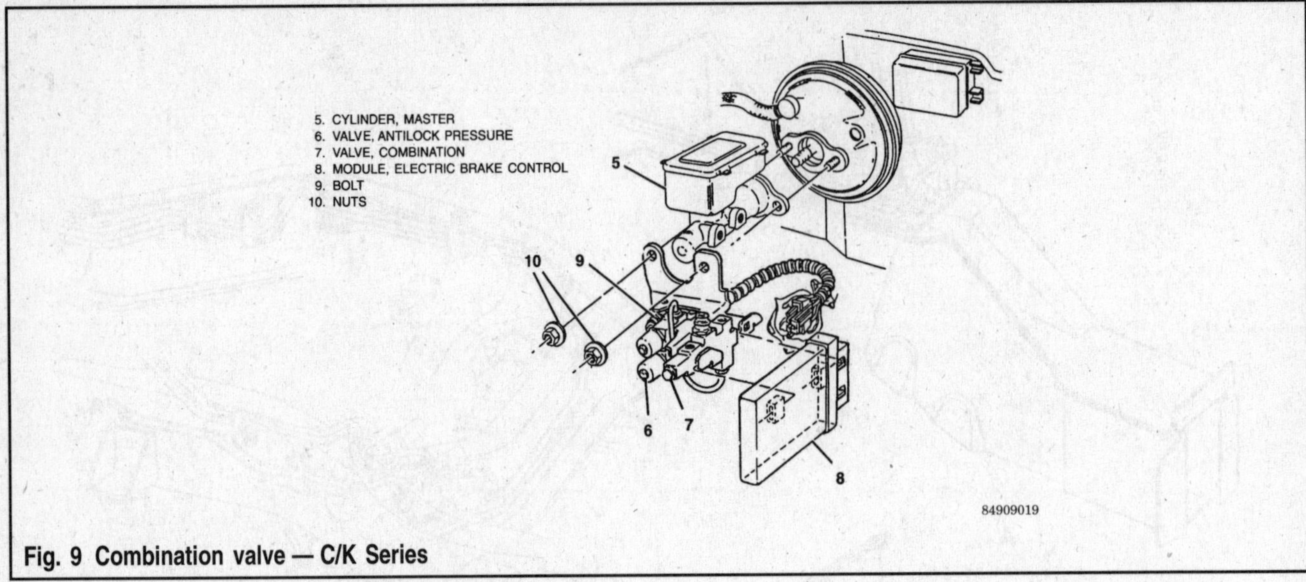

Fig. 9 Combination valve — C/K Series

open position (with the tool described in the brake bleeding section installed under the pin mounting bolt). Be sure to tighten the bolt after removing the tool.

5. Turn the ignition key ON. Open the bleed screw while an assistant applies heavy pressure on the brake pedal. The warning lamp should light. Close the bleed screw before the helper releases the pedal.
6. To reset the switch, apply heavy pressure to the pedal. This will apply hydraulic pressure to the switch which will recenter it.
7. Repeat Step 5 for the front bleed screw.
8. Turn the ignition OFF and lower the truck.

➡**If the warning lamp does not light during Step 5, the switch is defective and must be replaced.**

Height Sensing Proportioning Valve

This valve distributes braking pressure evenly from front-to-rear depending on either a light or heavy load condition. Not all models utilize this valve.

✻✻CAUTION

Adjustment of the valve is determined by the distance between the axle and frame. The addition of such aftermarket items as air shocks, lift kits and addition spring leaves will render the valve inoperable, resulting in unsatisfactory brake performance, accident and injury!

REMOVAL & INSTALLATION

➧ **See Figures 10 and 11**

➡**Special gauging tools are required for this job.**

1. Raise and support the rear end on jackstands under the frame, allowing the axle to hang freely.
2. Clean the exterior of the valve.
3. Disconnect the brake lines at the valve. Cap the lines.
4. Remove the valve shaft-to-lever nut.

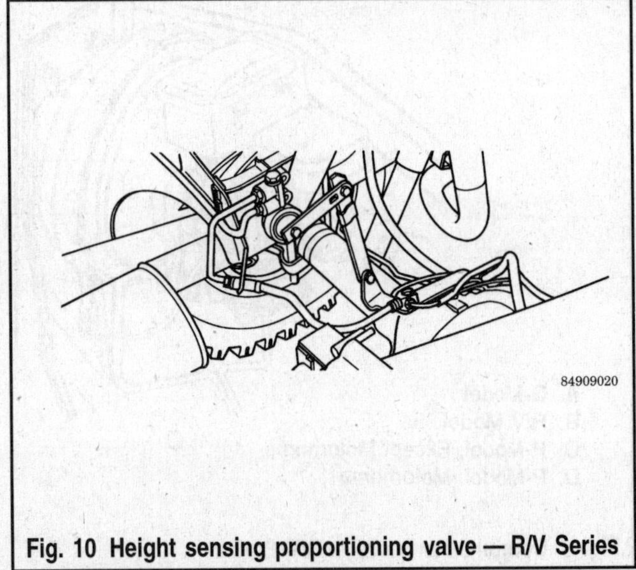

Fig. 10 Height sensing proportioning valve — R/V Series

5. Remove the valve-to-bracket bolts.

To install:

6. Position the valve on the bracket and tighten the bolts to 20 ft. lbs. (27 Nm).
7. Adjust the valve as described below.
8. Connect the lever to the valve shaft and tighten the nut to 89 inch lbs. (7 Nm).
9. Connect the brake lines and tighten them to 18 ft. lbs. (24 Nm).
10. Bleed the brakes.

ADJUSTMENT

➧ **See Figures 12, 13 and 14**

If front wheels lock-up at moderate brake pressure is experienced with the vehicle at or near maximum GVWR, or, whenever the valve is replaced, the valve must be adjusted.

➡**Special gauging tools are required for this job.**

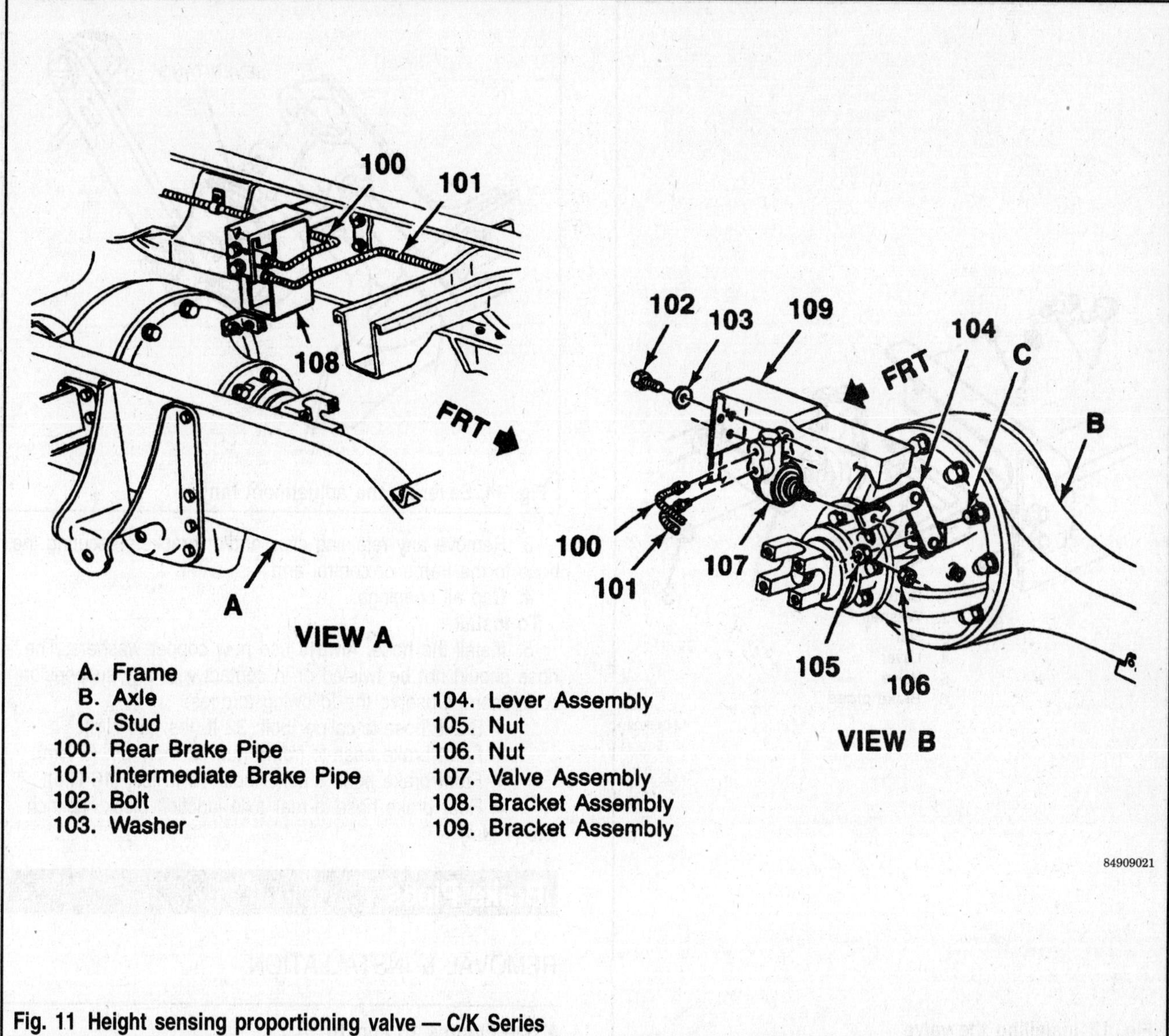

Fig. 11 Height sensing proportioning valve — C/K Series

1. Raise and support the rear end on jackstands under the frame, allowing the axle to hang freely.
2. Remove the shaft-to-lever nut and disconnect the lever from the shaft.
3. Obtain the proper gauge:
   - R and V with Extra Capacity Rear Spring option: part number 14061394; color green; code A
   - R Series without Extra Capacity Rear Spring option, and with either the 6-4.3L or 8-5.7L engine: part number 14061395; color black; code B.
   - V Series without Extra Capacity Rear Spring option and with the diesel engine or the 8-5.7L engine: part number 14061396; color blue; code C.
   - R and V Series with VD1 tire option: part number 15592484; color red; code D.
   - V Series, except above: part number 15548904; color yellow; code E.
   - C/K Series: part number 15592484.
4. Rotate the valve shaft to permit installation of the gauge. The center hole of the gauge must seat on the D-shape of the valve shaft. The gauge tang must seat in the valve mounting hole.
5. Install the lever on the shaft with a C-clamp to seat the nylon bushings on the serrated valve shaft. Don't force it into position.
6. Install the nut on the shaft and tighten it to 89 inch lbs. (7 Nm) on the R/V series; 8 ft. lbs. (9 Nm) on the C/K Series
7. Break off or cut the tang on the gauge.
8. Road test the truck. The gauge will stay in place.

Brake Hoses

REMOVAL & INSTALLATION

1. Clean the connection thoroughly before opening it.
2. Unscrew the connection at the steel pipe or junction block and/or remove the bolt at the caliper. Discard any copper washers.

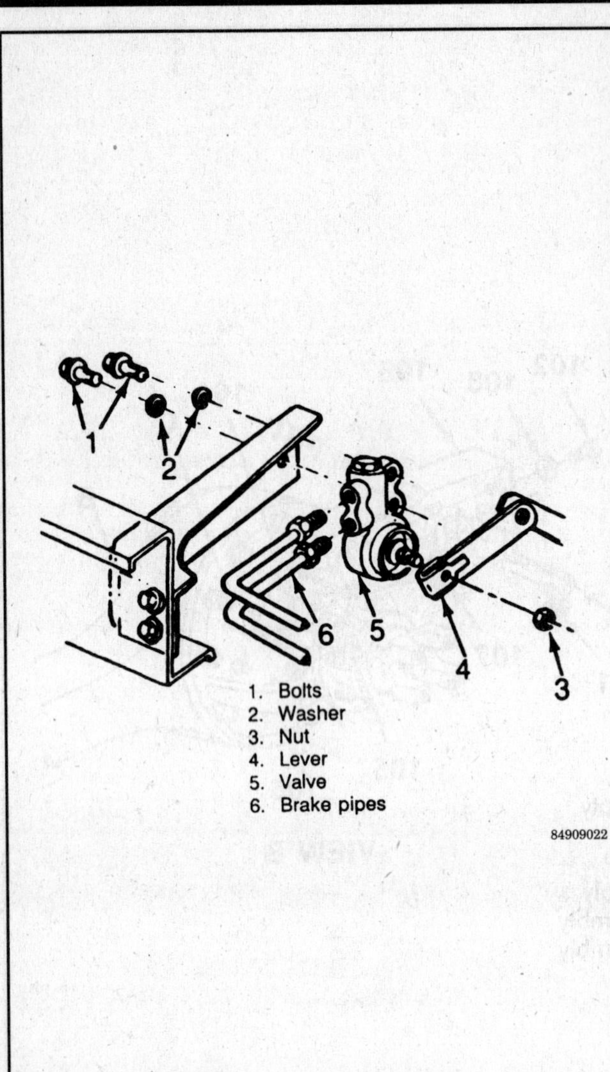

Fig. 12 Installing the valve

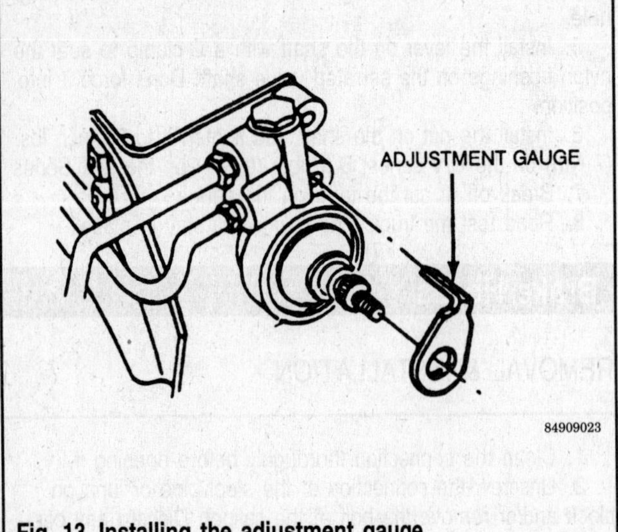

Fig. 13 Installing the adjustment gauge

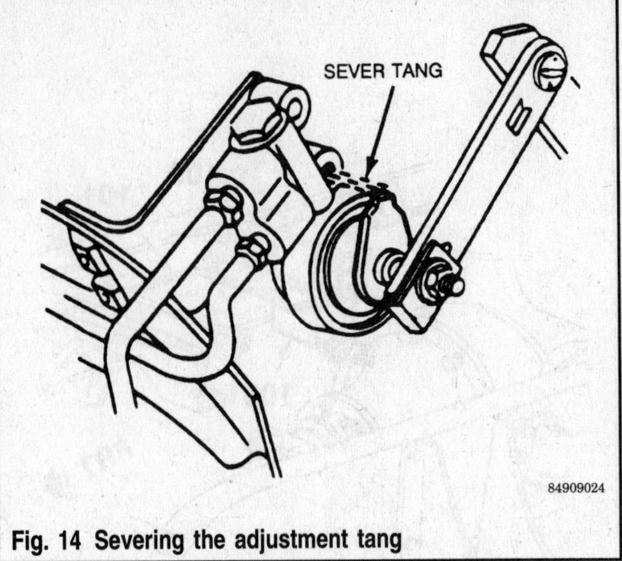

Fig. 14 Severing the adjustment tang

3. Remove any retaining clips and/or brackets securing the hose to the frame or control arm.

4. Cap all openings.

To install:

5. Install the hose. Always use new copper washers. The hose should not be twisted or in contact with any suspension component. Observe the following torques:

- Brake hose-to-caliper bolt: 32 ft. lbs. (44 Nm).
- Front brake hose-to-frame nut: 58 inch lbs. (5 Nm).
- Front brake hose bracket bolt: 12 ft. lbs. (16 Nm).
- Rear brake hose-to-rear axle junction block: 12 inch lbs. (1 Nm).

Brake Pipes

REMOVAL & INSTALLATION

➧ See Figures 15 and 16

⁂CAUTION

When replacing a steel brake pipe, always use steel tubing of the same pressure rating and corrosion resistance. The replacement pipe must be of the same diameter. Copper tubing must never be used as a replacement for steel brake pipes! Brake pipes running parallel must be separated by at least 1/4 in. (6mm) along their common run.

1. Clean the pipe fittings and disconnect the pipe at each end. Where necessary, always use a back-up wrench. Cap all openings.
2. Cut the new pipe to length, adding 1/8 inch for each flare.
3. Always double-flare the pipe ends. Single flaring cannot withstand the pressure.
4. Always use a tubing bender when bending the pipes.
5. All brake pipe nuts should be tightened to 13 ft. lbs. (17 Nm).

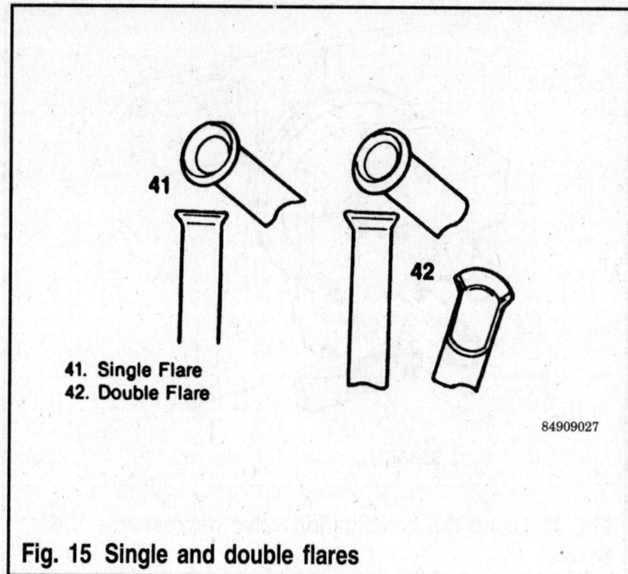

Fig. 15 Single and double flares

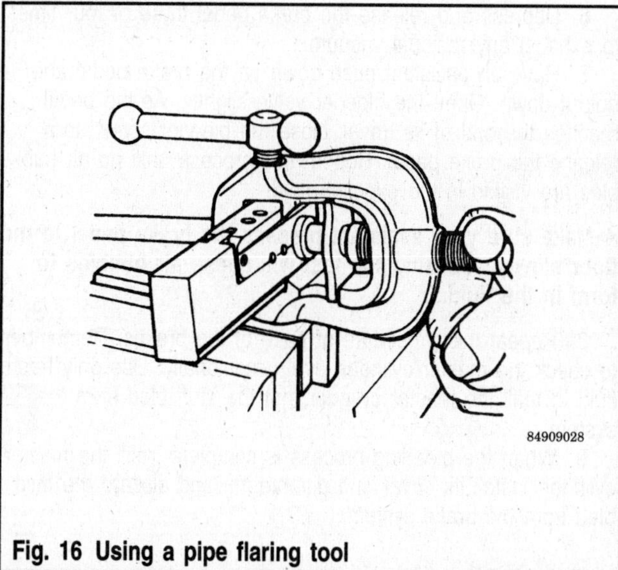

Fig. 16 Using a pipe flaring tool

BRAKE & PIPE FLARING

Use only brake line tubing approved for automotive use; never use copper tubing. Whenever possible, try to work with brake lines that are already cut to the length needed. These lines are available at most auto parts stores and have machine made flares, the quality of which is hard to duplicate with most of the available inexpensive flaring kits.

When the brakes are applied, there is a great amount of pressure developed in the hydraulic system. An improperly formed flare can leak with resultant loss of stopping power. If you have never formed a double-flare, take time to familiarize yourself with the flaring kit; practice forming double-flares on scrap tubing until you are satisfied with the results.

The following procedure applies to most commercially available double-flaring kits. If these instructions differ in any way from those in your kit, follow the instructions in the kit.

1. Cut the brake line to the necessary length using a tubing cutter.
2. Square the end of the tube with a file and chamfer the edges.
3. Insert the tube into the proper size hole in the bar until the end of the tube sticks out the thickness of the single flare adapter. Tighten the bar wing nuts tightly so the tube cannot move.
4. Place the single flare adapter into the tube and slide the bar into the yoke.
5. Position the yoke screw over the single flare adapter and tighten it until the bar is locked in the yoke. Continue tightening the yoke screw until the adapter bottoms on the bar. This should form the single flare.

➡Make sure the tube is not forced out of the hole in the bar during the single flare operation. If it is, the single flare will not be formed properly and the procedure must be repeated from Step 1.

6. Loosen the yoke screw and remove the single flare adapter.
7. Position the yoke screw over the tube and tighten until the taper contacts the single flare and the bar is locked in the yoke. Continue tightening to form the double flare.

➡Make sure the tube is not forced out of the hole in the bar during the double flare operation. If it is, the double flare will not be formed properly and the procedure must be repeated from Step 1.

8. Loosen the screw and remove the bar from the yoke. Remove the tube from the bar.
9. Check the flare for cracks or uneven flaring. If the flare is not perfect, cut it off and begin again at Step 1.

Bleeding the Brakes

EXCEPT HYDRO-BOOST OR ABS

▶ See Figures 17, 18, 19 and 20

The brake system must be bled when any brake line is disconnected or there is air in the system.

➡Never bleed a wheel cylinder when a drum is removed.

1. Clean the master cylinder of excess dirt and remove the cylinder cover and the diaphragm.
2. Fill the master cylinder to the proper level. Check the fluid level periodically during the bleeding process and replenish it as necessary. Do not allow the master cylinder to run dry, or you will have to start over.
3. Before opening any of the bleeder screws, you may want to give each one a shot of penetrating solvent. This reduces the possibility of breakage when they are unscrewed.
4. Attach a length of vinyl hose to the bleeder screw of the brake to be bled. Insert the other end of the hose into a clear jar half full of clean brake fluid, so that the end of the hose is beneath the level of fluid. The correct sequence for bleeding is to work from the brake farthest from the master cylinder to the one closest; right rear, left rear, right front, left front.
5. The combination valve must be held open during the bleeding process. A clip, tape, or other similar tool (or an assistant) will hold the metering pin in.

87989p04

Fig. 17 Bleeding the drum brake

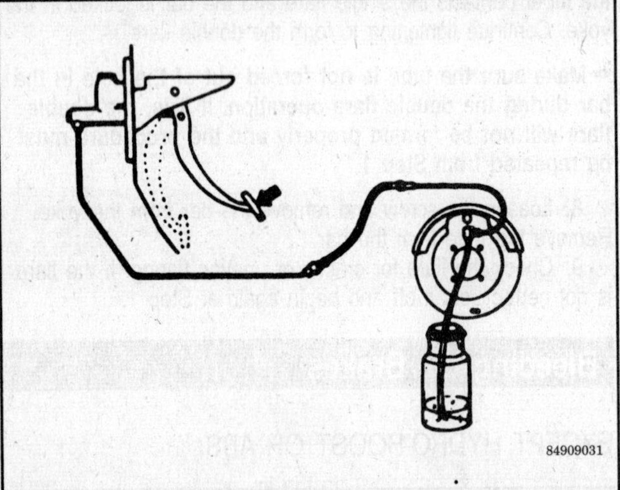
84909031

Fig. 18 Have an assistant pump, then hold in the brake pedal, while you bleed each wheel

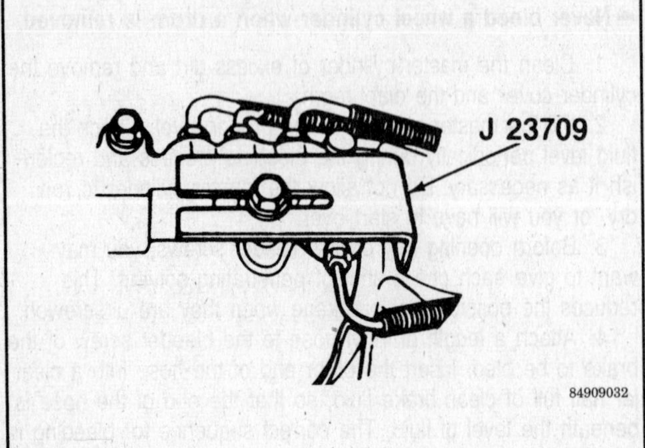

84909032

Fig. 19 Using the combination valve depressor — R/V Series

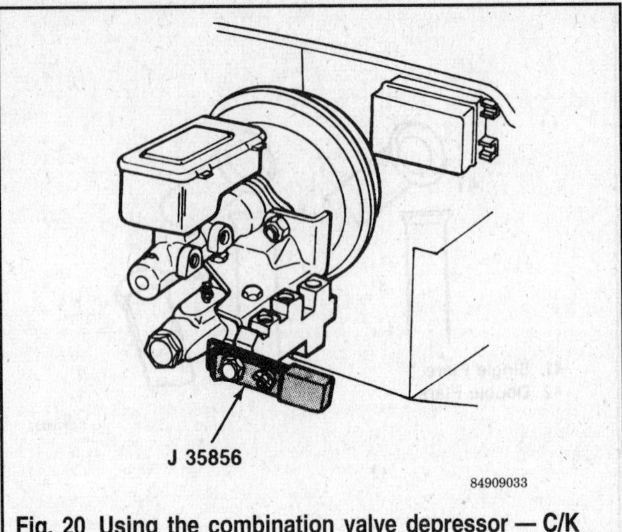

84909033

Fig. 20 Using the combination valve depressor — C/K Series

6. Depress and release the brake pedal three or four times to exhaust any residual vacuum.

7. Have an assistant push down on the brake pedal and hold it down. Open the bleeder valve slightly. As the pedal reaches the end of its travel, close the bleeder screw and release the brake pedal. Repeat this process until no air bubbles are visible in the expelled fluid.

➡Make sure your assistant presses the brake pedal to the floor slowly. Pressing too fast will cause air bubbles to form in the fluid.

8. Repeat this procedure at each of the brakes. Remember to check the master cylinder level occasionally. Use only fresh fluid to refill the master cylinder, not the stuff bled from the system.

9. When the bleeding process is complete, refill the master cylinder, install its cover and diaphragm, and discard the fluid bled from the brake system.

WITH ABS

➧ See Figures 17, 18, 19 and 20

The brake system must be bled when any brake line is disconnected or there is air in the system.

➡Never bleed a wheel cylinder when a drum is removed.

1. Clean the master cylinder of excess dirt and remove the cylinder cover and the diaphragm.

2. Fill the master cylinder to the proper level. Check the fluid level periodically during the bleeding process, and replenish it as necessary. Do not allow the master cylinder to run dry, or you will have to start over.

3. Before opening any of the bleeder screws, you may want to give each one a shot of penetrating solvent. This reduces the possibility of breakage when they are unscrewed.

4. Attach a length of vinyl hose to the bleeder screw of the brake to be bled. Insert the other end of the hose into a clear jar half full of clean brake fluid, so that the end of the hose is beneath the level of fluid. The correct sequence for bleeding is

to work from the brake farthest from the master cylinder to the one closest; right rear, left rear, right front, left front.

5. The combination valve must be held open during the bleeding process. A clip, tape, or other similar tool (or an assistant) will hold the metering pin in.

6. Depress and release the brake pedal three or four times to exhaust any residual vacuum.

7. Have an assistant push down on the brake pedal and hold it down. Open the bleeder valve slightly. As the pedal reaches the end of its travel, close the bleeder screw and release the brake pedal. Repeat this process until no air bubbles are visible in the expelled fluid.

➡Make sure your assistant presses the brake pedal to the floor slowly. Pressing too fast will cause air bubbles to form in the fluid.

8. Repeat this procedure at each of the brakes. Remember to check the master cylinder level occasionally. Use only fresh fluid to refill the master cylinder, not the stuff bled from the system.

9. When the bleeding process is complete, refill the master cylinder, install its cover and diaphragm, and discard the fluid bled from the brake system.

10. Perform 3 function tests with the TECH 1 scan tool. The brake pedal **must** be firmly applied.

11. On models with rear wheel ABS:

a. Refill the jar with clean brake fluid and attach the bleed hose to the bleed valve on the Isolation/Dump valve.

b. Have your assistant slowly depress the brake pedal and hold it. Loosen the bleed valve and expel the air. Tighten the valve and slowly release the pedal.

c. Wait 15 seconds and repeat this procedure. Repeat bleeding the Isolation/Dump valve until all the air is expelled.

12. On models with 4 wheel ABS, repeat Steps 1-9.

HYDRO-BOOST

The system should be bled whenever the booster is removed and installed.

1. Fill the power steering pump until the fluid level is at the base of the pump reservoir neck. Disconnect the battery lead from the distributor.

➡Remove the electrical lead to the fuel solenoid terminal on the injection pump before cranking the engine.

2. Jack up the front of the car, turn the wheels all the way to the left, and crank the engine for a few seconds.

3. Check steering pump fluid level. If necessary, add fluid to the "ADD" mark on the dipstick.

4. Lower the car, connect the battery lead, and start the engine. Check fluid level and add fluid to the "ADD" mark, as necessary. With the engine running, turn the wheels from side to side to bleed air from the system. Make sure that the fluid level stays above the internal pump casting.

5. The Hydro-Boost system should now be fully bled. If the fluid is foaming after bleeding, stop the engine, let the system set for one hour, then repeat the second part of Step 4.

The preceding procedures should be effective in removing the excess air from the system, however sometimes air may still remain trapped. When this happens the booster may make a gulping noise when the brake is applied. Lightly pumping the brake pedal with the engine running should cause this noise to disappear. After the noise stops, check the pump fluid level and add as necessary.

FRONT DISC BRAKES

Two different caliper designs are used. A Delco disc brake system is used on all models except R/V 30 Series and 3500 motorhome chassis and the C3HD. These trucks use a Bendix system.

CAUTION

Brake pads may contain asbestos, which has been determined to be a cancer causing agent. Never clean the brake surfaces with compressed air! Avoid inhaling any dust from any brake surface! When cleaning brake surfaces, use a commercially available brake cleaning fluid.

Brake Pads

INSPECTION

See Figures 21 and 22

Support the truck on jackstands and remove the wheels. Look in at the ends of the caliper to check the lining thickness of the outer pad. Look through the inspection hole in the top of the caliper to check the thickness of the inner pad. Minimum acceptable pad thickness is 1/32 in. (0.8mm) from the rivet heads on original equipment riveted linings and 1/2 in. (13mm) lining thickness on bonded linings.

➡These manufacturer's specifications may not agree with your state inspection law.

All original equipment pads are the riveted type; unless you want to remove the pads to measure the actual thickness from the rivet heads, you will have to make the limit for visual inspection 1/16 in. (1.6mm) or more. The same applies if you don't know what kind of lining you have. Original equipment pads and GM replacement pads have an integral wear sensor. This is a spring steel tab on the rear edge of the inner pad which produces a squeal by rubbing against the rotor to warn that the pads have reached their wear limit. They do not squeal when the brakes are applied.

The squeal will eventually stop if worn pads aren't replaced. Should this happen, replace the pads immediately to prevent expensive rotor (disc) damage.

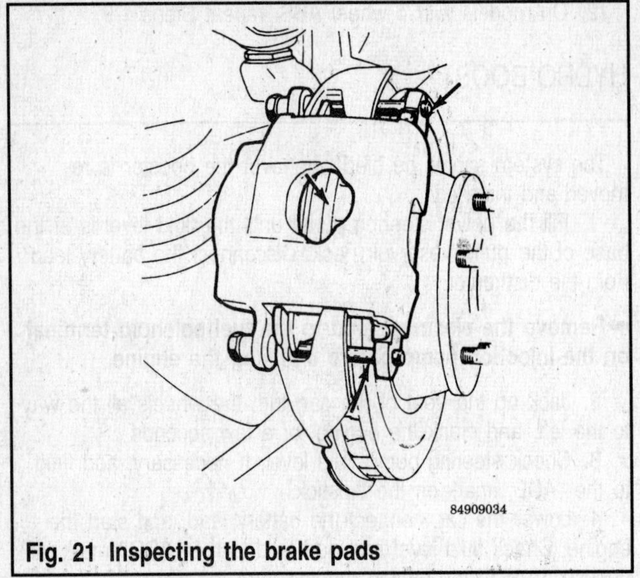
Fig. 21 Inspecting the brake pads

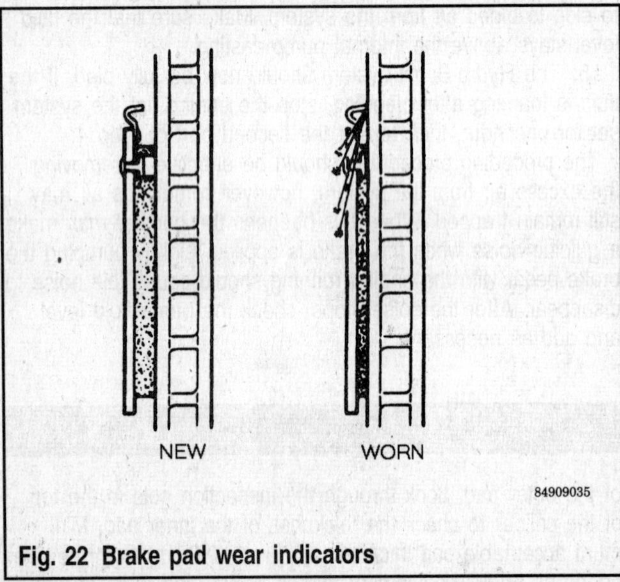

Fig. 22 Brake pad wear indicators

REMOVAL & INSTALLATION

Delco System

▶ See Figures 23, 24, 25, 26, 27, 28, 29, 30, 31, 32, 33, 34, 35, 36 and 37

1. Remove the cover on the master cylinder and siphon out ⅔ of the fluid. This step prevents spilling fluid when the piston is pushed back.
2. Raise and support the front end on jackstands.
3. Remove the wheels.
4. Push the brake piston back into its bore using a C-clamp to pull the caliper outward.
5. Remove the two bolts which hold the caliper and then lift the caliper off the disc.

****CAUTION**

Do not let the caliper assembly hang by the brake hose.

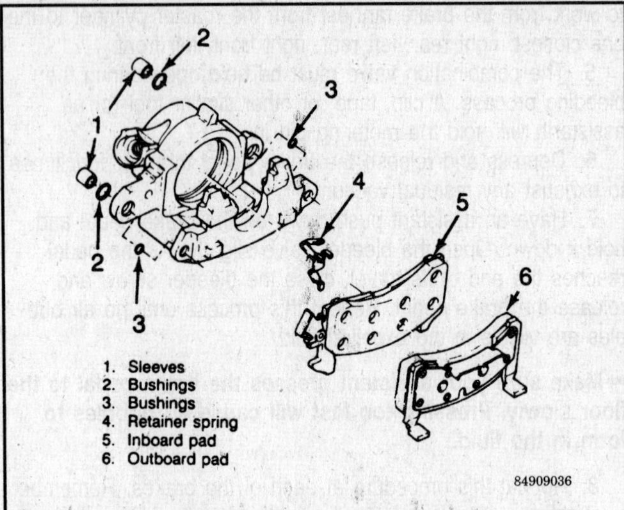

Fig. 23 Delco brake pad and caliper assembly — R/V Series

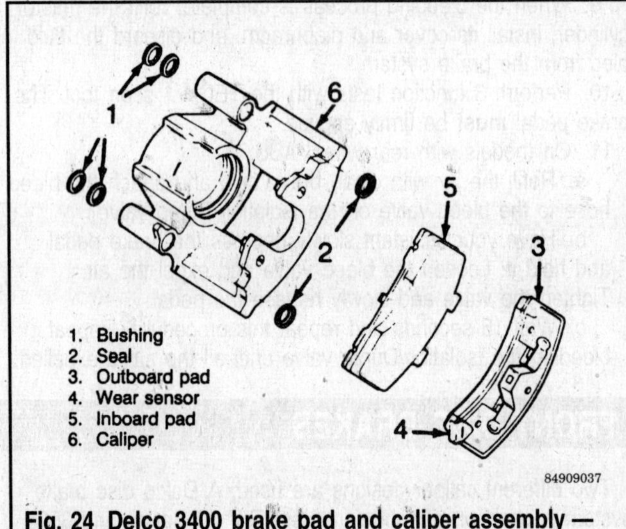

Fig. 24 Delco 3400 brake pad and caliper assembly — C/K Series

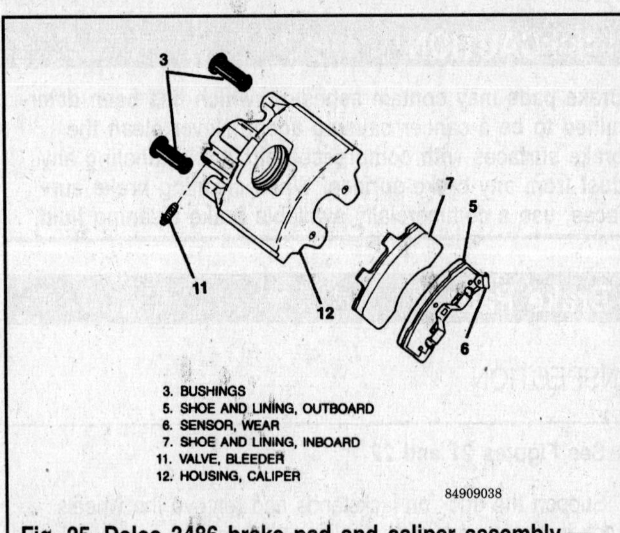

Fig. 25 Delco 3486 brake pad and caliper assembly — C/K Series

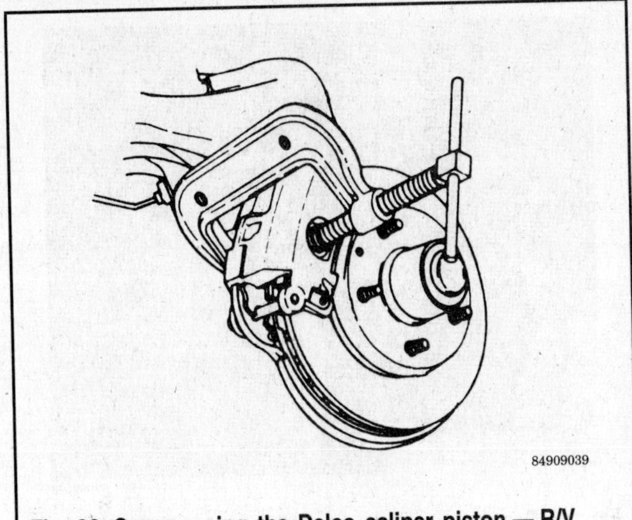

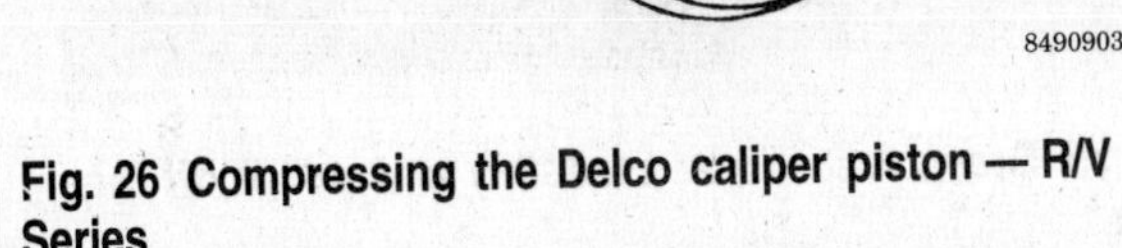
Fig. 26 Compressing the Delco caliper piston — R/V Series

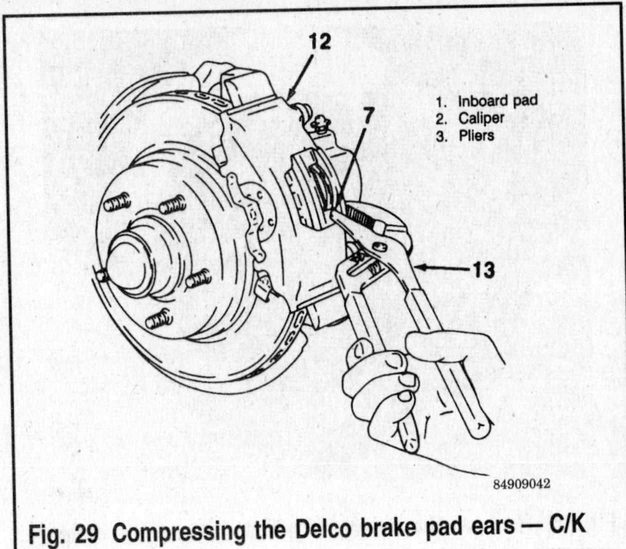

Fig. 29 Compressing the Delco brake pad ears — C/K Series

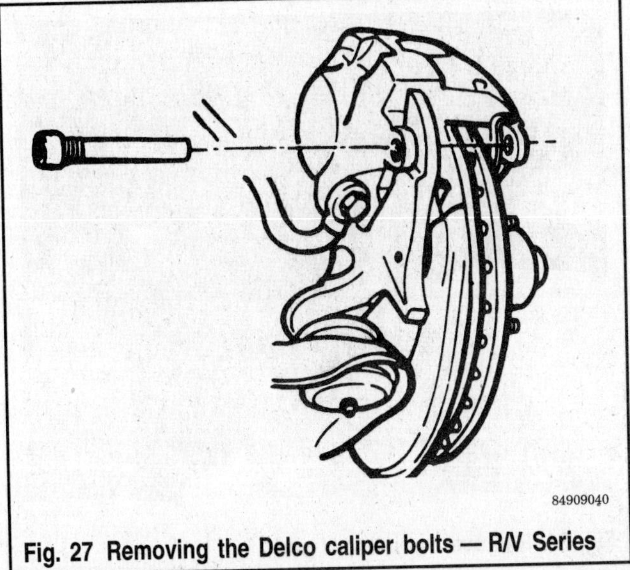

Fig. 27 Removing the Delco caliper bolts — R/V Series

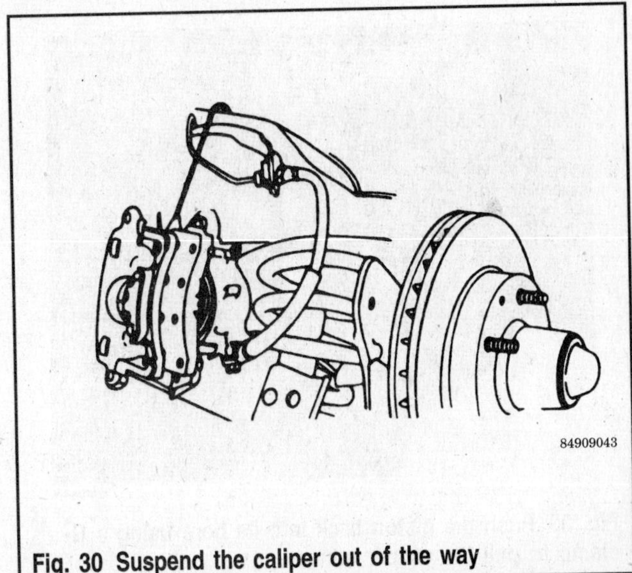

Fig. 30 Suspend the caliper out of the way

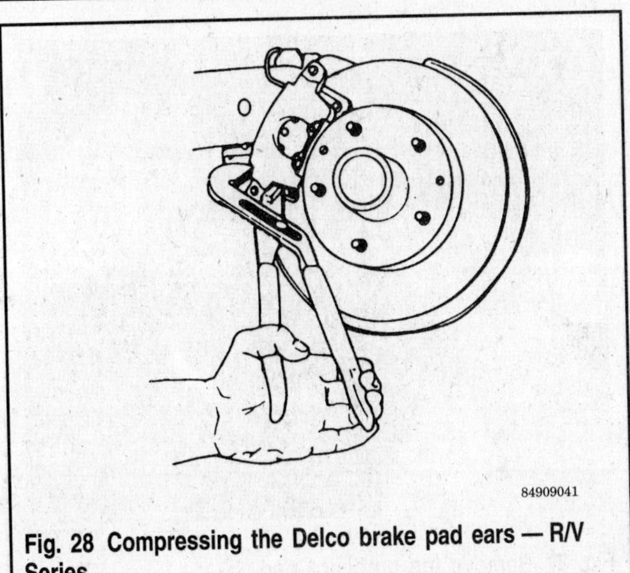

Fig. 28 Compressing the Delco brake pad ears — R/V Series

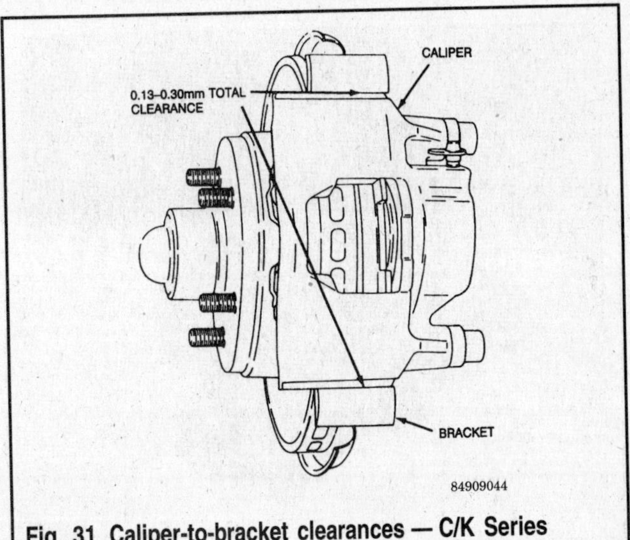

Fig. 31 Caliper-to-bracket clearances — C/K Series shown

87989p05

Fig. 32 Remove the wheel to gain access to the caliper and pad assembly

87989p07

Fig. 33 Push the piston back into its bore using a C-clamp to pull the caliper outward

87989p06

Fig. 34 Loosen and remove the caliper mounting bolts

87989p08

Fig. 35 Grasp the caliper assembly and pull it off the rotor

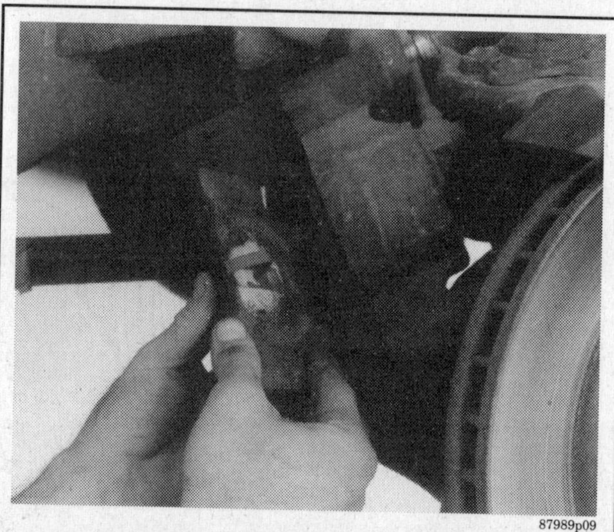
87989p09

Fig. 36 Remove the inboard pad

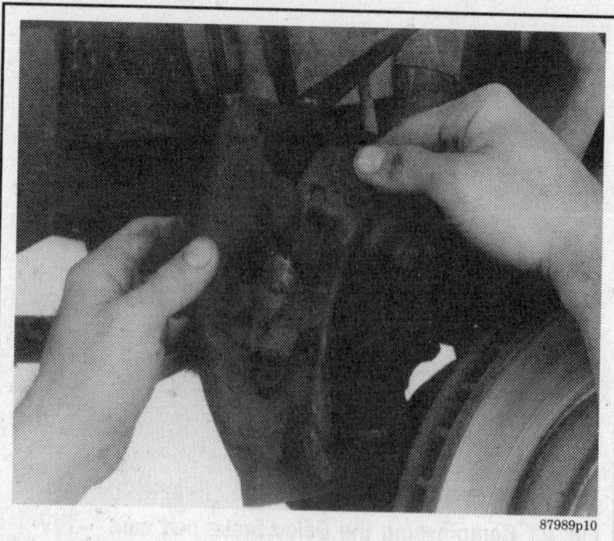
87989p10

Fig. 37 Remove the outboard pad

6. Remove the inboard and outboard shoe. Use a small prybar to disengage the buttons on the outboard shoe from the holes in the caliper housing.

➡If the pads are to be reinstalled, mark them inside and outside.

7. Remove the pad support spring from the piston.

To install:

8. Position the support spring and the inner pad into the center cavity of the piston, snap the retaining spring into the piston. The outboard pad has ears which are bent over to keep the pad in position while the inboard pad has ears on the top end which fit over the caliper retaining bolts. A spring which is inside the brake piston hold the bottom edge of the inboard pad.
9. Push down on the inner pad until it lays flat against the caliper. It is important to push the piston all the way into the caliper if new linings are installed or the caliper will not fit over the rotor.
10. Position the outboard pad with the ears of the pad over the caliper ears and the tab at the bottom engaged in the caliper cutout.
11. With the two pads in position, place the caliper over the brake disc and align the holes in the caliper with those of the mounting bracket.

✲✲CAUTION

Make certain that the brake hose is not twisted or kinked.

12. Install the mounting bracket bolts through the sleeves in the inboard caliper ears and through the mounting bracket, making sure that the ends of the bolts pass under the retaining ears on the inboard pad.

➡For best results, always use new bushings, bolt sleeves and bolt boot.

13. Tighten the mounting bolts to 35 ft. lbs. (47 Nm) for R/V Series; 28 ft. lbs. (38 Nm) for 1988-92 C/K Series and 38 ft. lbs. (51 Nm) for 1993-96 C/K Series.. Pump the brake pedal to seat the pad against the rotor. Don't do this unless both calipers are in place. Use a pair of channel lock pliers to bend over the upper ears of the outer pad so it isn't loose.

➡After tightening the mounting bolts, there must be clearance between the caliper and knuckle at both the upper and lower edge. On R/V Series, the clearance must be 0.010-0.024 in. (0.26-0.60mm); on C/K Series, it must be 0.005-0.012 in. (0.13-0.30mm) for 1988-91, and 0.010-0.028 in. (0.26-0.71mm). If not, loosen the bolts and reposition the caliper.

14. Install the wheel and lower the truck.
15. Add fluid to the master cylinder reservoirs so that they are 1/4 in. (6mm) from the top.
16. Test the brake pedal by pumping it to obtain a hard pedal. Check the fluid level again and add fluid as necessary. Do not move the vehicle until a hard pedal is obtained.

Bendix System

➧ See Figures 38, 39, 40, 41, 42 and 43

1. Remove approximately 1/3 of the brake fluid from the master cylinder. Discard the used brake fluid.
2. Jack up your vehicle and support it with jackstands.
3. Push the piston back into its bore. This can be done by suing a C-clamp.
4. Remove the bolt at the caliper support key. Use a brass drift pin to remove the key and spring.
5. Rotate the caliper up and forward from the bottom and lift it off the caliper support.
6. Tie the caliper out of the way with a piece of wire. Be careful not to damage the brake line.
7. Remove the inner pad from the caliper support. Discard the inner shoe clip.
8. Remove the outer pad from the caliper.

To install:

9. Lubricate the caliper support and support spring, with silicone.

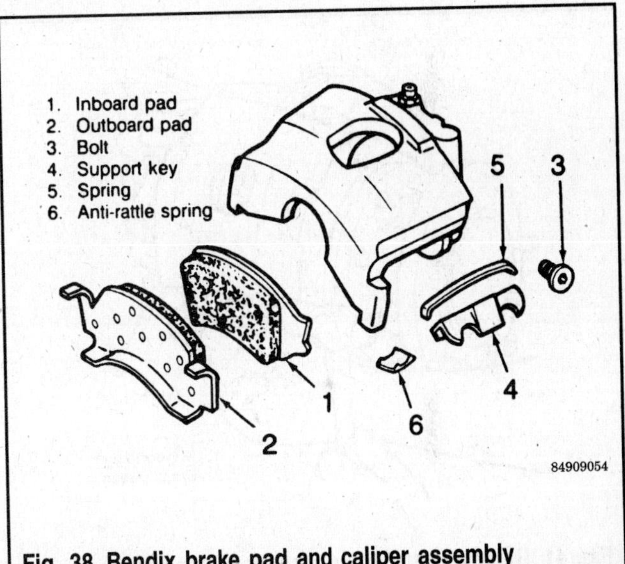

Fig. 38 Bendix brake pad and caliper assembly

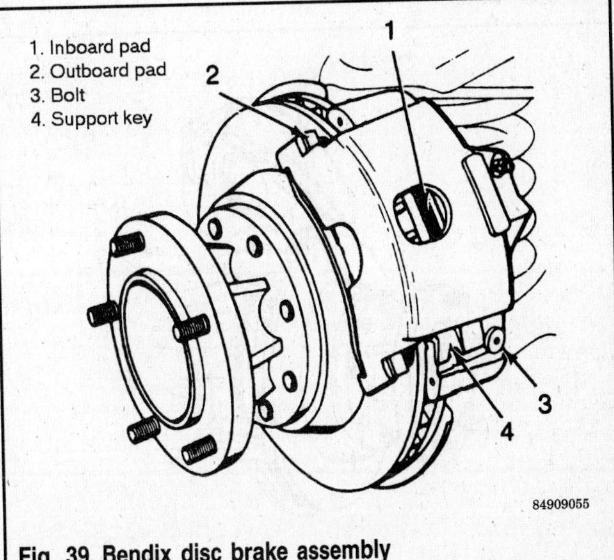

Fig. 39 Bendix disc brake assembly

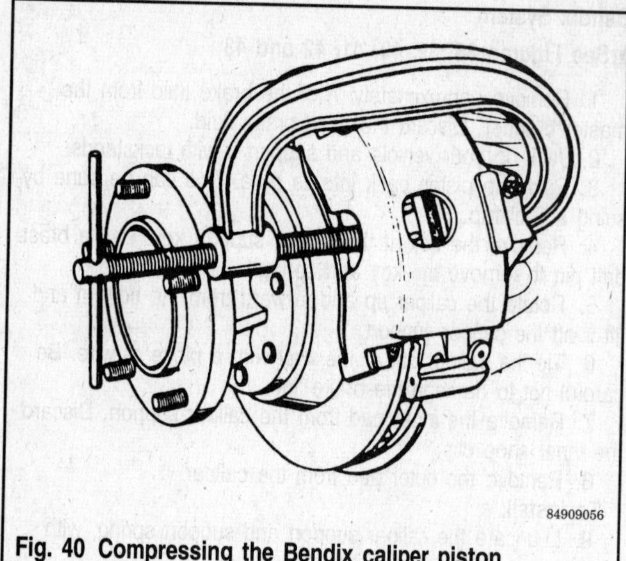
Fig. 40 Compressing the Bendix caliper piston

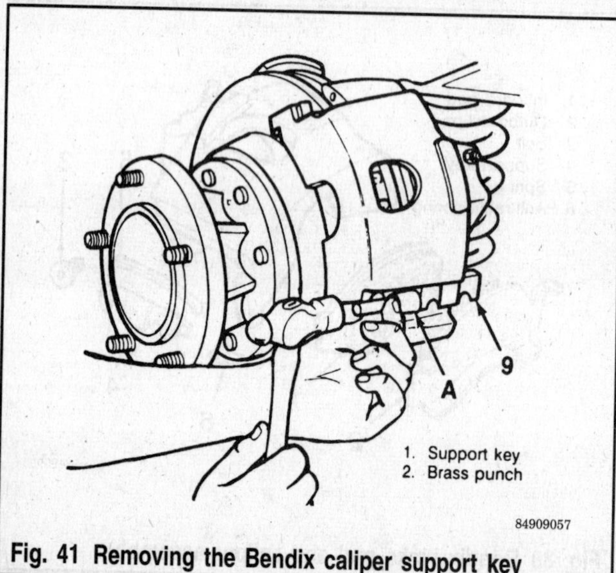

Fig. 41 Removing the Bendix caliper support key

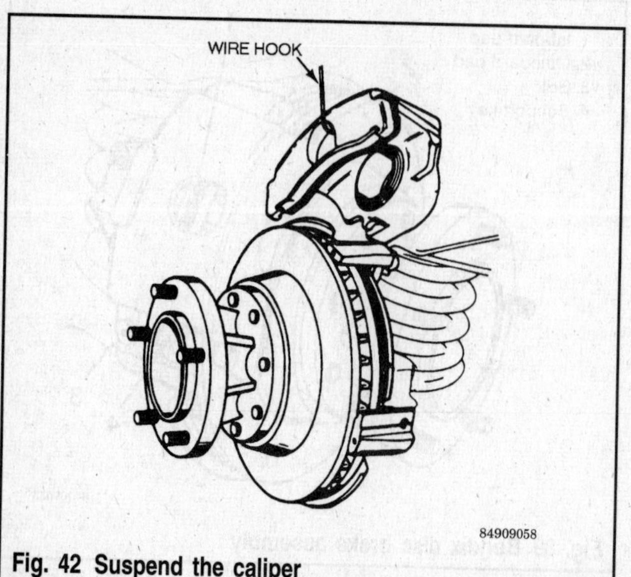

Fig. 42 Suspend the caliper

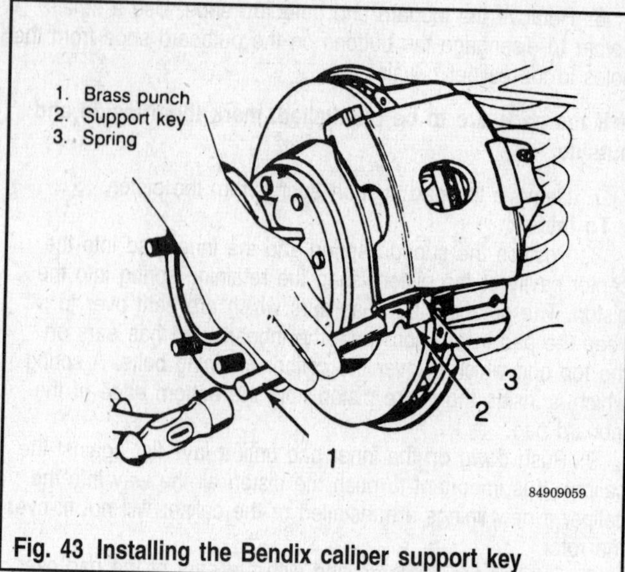

Fig. 43 Installing the Bendix caliper support key

10. Install a NEW inboard shoe clip on the shoe.
11. Install the lower end of the inboard shoe into the groove provided in the support. Slide the upper end of the shoe into position. Be sure the clip remains in position.
12. Position the outboard shoe in the caliper with the ears at the top of the shoe over the caliper ears and the tab at the bottom of the shoe engaged in the caliper cutout. If assembly is difficult, a C-clamp may be used. Be careful not to mar the lining.
13. Position the caliper over the brake disc, top edge first. Rotate the caliper downward onto the support.
14. Place the spring over the caliper support key, install the assembly between the support and lower caliper groove. Tap into place until the key retaining screw can be installed.
15. Install the screw and tighten to 15 ft. lbs. (20 Nm). The boss must fit fully into the circular cutout in the key.
16. Install the wheel and and add brake fluid as necessary.

Caliper

REMOVAL & INSTALLATION

Delco System

➧ See Figures 23, 24, 25, 26, 27, 28, 29, 30 and 31

1. Remove the cover on the master cylinder and siphon enough fluid out of the reservoirs to bring the level to ⅓ full. This step prevents spilling fluid when the piston is pushed back.
2. Raise and support the vehicle. Remove the front wheels and tires.
3. Push the brake piston back into its bore using a C-clamp to pull the caliper outward.
4. Remove the two bolts which hold the caliper and then lift the caliper off the disc.

✲✲CAUTION

Do not let the caliper assembly hang by the brake hose.

5. Remove the inboard and outboard shoe.

➡**If the pads are to be reinstalled, mark them inside and outside.**

6. Remove the pad support spring from the piston.
7. Remove the two sleeves from the inside ears of the caliper and the 4 rubber bushings from the grooves in the caliper ears.
8. Remove the hose from the steel brake line and tape the fittings to prevent foreign material from entering the line or the hoses.
9. Remove the retainer from the hose fitting.
10. Remove the hose from the frame bracket and pull off the caliper with the hose attached.
11. Check the inside of the caliper for fluid leakage; if so, the caliper should be overhauled.

CAUTION

Do not use compressed air to clean the inside of the caliper as this may unseat the dust boot.

To install:

12. Connect the brake line to start re-installation. Lubricate the sleeves, rubber bushings, bushing grooves, and the end of the mounting bolts using silicone lubricant.
13. Install new bushing in the caliper ears along with new sleeves. The sleeve should be replaced so that the end toward the shoe is flush with the machined surface of the ear.
14. Position the support spring and the inner pad into the center cavity of the piston, snap the retaining spring into the piston. The outboard pad has ears which are bent over to keep the pad in position while the inboard pad has ears on the top end which fit over the caliper retaining bolts. A spring which is inside the brake piston hold the bottom edge of the inboard pad.
15. Push down on the inner pad until it lays flat against the caliper. It is important to push the piston all the way into the caliper if new linings are installed or the caliper will not fit over the rotor.
16. Position the outboard pad with the ears of the pad over the caliper ears and the tab at the bottom engaged in the caliper cutout.
17. With the two pads in position, place the caliper over the brake disc and align the holes in the caliper with those of the mounting bracket.

CAUTION

Make certain that the brake hose is not twisted or kinked.

18. Fill the cavity between the bolt bushings with silicone grease. Install the mounting bracket bolts through the sleeves in the inboard caliper ears and through the mounting bracket, making sure that the ends of the bolts pass under the retaining ears on the inboard pad.

➡**For best results, always use new bushings, sleeves and bolt boots.**

19. Tighten the mounting bolts to 35 ft. lbs. (47 Nm) for R/V Series; 28 ft. lbs. (38 Nm) for 1988-92 C/K Series and 38 ft. lbs. (51 Nm) for 1993-96 C/K Series. Pump the brake pedal to seat the pad against the rotor. Don't do this unless both calipers are in place. Use a pair of channel lock pliers to bend over the upper ears of the outer pad so it isn't loose.

➡**After tightening the mounting bolts, there must be clearance between the caliper and knuckle at both the upper and lower edge. On R/V Series, the clearance must be 0.010-0.024 in. (0.26-0.60mm); on C/K Series, it must be 0.005-0.012 in. (0.13-0.30mm) for 1988-91, and 0.010-0.028 in. (0.26-0.71mm). If not, loosen the bolts and reposition the caliper.**

20. Install the front wheel and lower the truck.
21. Add fluid to the master cylinder reservoirs so that they are 1/4 in. (6mm) from the top.
22. Test the brake pedal by pumping it to obtain a hard pedal. Check the fluid level again and add fluid as necessary. Do not move the vehicle until a hard pedal is obtained.

Bendix System

➧ **See Figures 38, 39, 40, 41, 42 and 43**

1. Remove approximately 1/3 of the brake fluid from the master cylinder. Discard the used brake fluid.
2. Raise and support the front end on jackstands.
3. Push the piston back into its bore. This can be done by suing a C-clamp.
4. Remove the bolt at the caliper support key. Use a brass drift pin to remove the key and spring.
5. Rotate the caliper up and forward from the bottom and lift it off the caliper support.
6. Unscrew the brake line at the caliper. Plug the opening. Discard the copper washer. Be careful not to damage the brake line.
7. Remove the outer shoe from the caliper.

To install:

8. Using a new copper washer, connect the brake line at the caliper. Tighten the connector to 32 ft. lbs. (43 Nm)
9. Lubricate the caliper support and support spring with silicone.
10. Position the outboard shoe in the caliper with the ears at the top of the shoe over the caliper ears and the tab at the bottom of the shoe engaged in the caliper cutout. If assembly is difficult, a C-clamp may be used. Be careful not to mar the lining.
11. Position the caliper over the brake disc, top edge first. Rotate the caliper downward onto the support.
12. Place the spring over the caliper support key, install the assembly between the support and lower caliper groove. Tap into place until the key retaining screw can be installed.
13. Install the screw and tighten to 15 ft. lbs. (20 Nm). The boss must fit fully into the circular cutout in the key.
14. Install the wheel and and add brake fluid as necessary.

OVERHAUL

➧ **See Figures 44, 45, 46, 47, 48, 49, 50, 51, 52, 53, 54, 55 and 56**

The following procedure applies to both the Delco and Bendix types of calipers.

✻✻CAUTION

Use only denatured alcohol to clean metal parts and brake fluid to clean rubber parts. Never use any mineral based cleaning solvents such as gasoline or kerosene as these solvents will deteriorate rubber parts.

1. Remove the caliper, clean it and place it on a clean and level work surface.
2. Remove the brake hose from the caliper and discard the copper gasket. Check the brake hose for cracks or deterioration. Replace the hose as necessary.
3. Drain the brake fluid from the caliper.
4. Pad the interior of the caliper with cloth and then apply compressed air to the caliper inlet hose.

✻✻CAUTION

Do not place your hands or fingers in front of the piston in an attempt to catch it! Use just enough air pressure to ease the piston out of the bore.

5. Remove the piston dust boot by prying it out with a screwdriver. Use caution when performing this procedure.
6. Remove the piston seal from the caliper piston bore using a small piece of wood or plastic. DO NOT use any type of metal tool for this procedure.
7. Remove the bleeder valve from the caliper.

➡Dust boot, piston seal, rubber bushings, and sleeves are included in every rebuilding kit. These should be replaced at every caliper rebuild.

8. Clean all parts in the recommended solvent and dry them completely using compressed air if possible.

➡The use of shop air hoses may inject oil film into the assembly; use caution when using such hoses.

9. Examine the mounting bolts for rust or corrosion. Replace them as necessary.
10. Examine the piston for scoring, nicks, or worn plating. If any of these conditions are present, replace them as necessary.

✻✻CAUTION

Do not use any type of abrasive on the piston!

11. Check the piston bore. Small defects can be removed with crocus cloth. If the bore cannot be cleaned in this manner, replace the caliper.

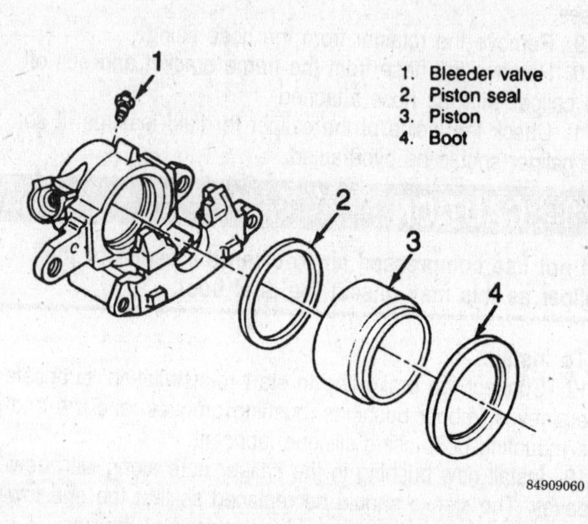

Fig. 44 Exploded view of the Delco caliper — R/V Series

12. Lubricate the piston bore and the new piston seal with brake fluid. Place the seal in the caliper bore groove.
13. Lubricate the piston in the same manner and position the new boot into the groove in the piston so that the fold faces the open end of the piston.
14. Place the piston into the caliper bore using caution not to unseat the seal. Force the piston to the bottom of the bore.
15. Place the dust boot in the caliper counterbore and seat the boot. Make sure that the boot in positioned correctly and evenly.
16. Install the brake hose in the caliper inlet using a new copper gasket.

➡The hose must be positioned in the caliper locating gate to assure proper positioning of the caliper.

17. Replace the bleeder screw.
18. Bleed the system.

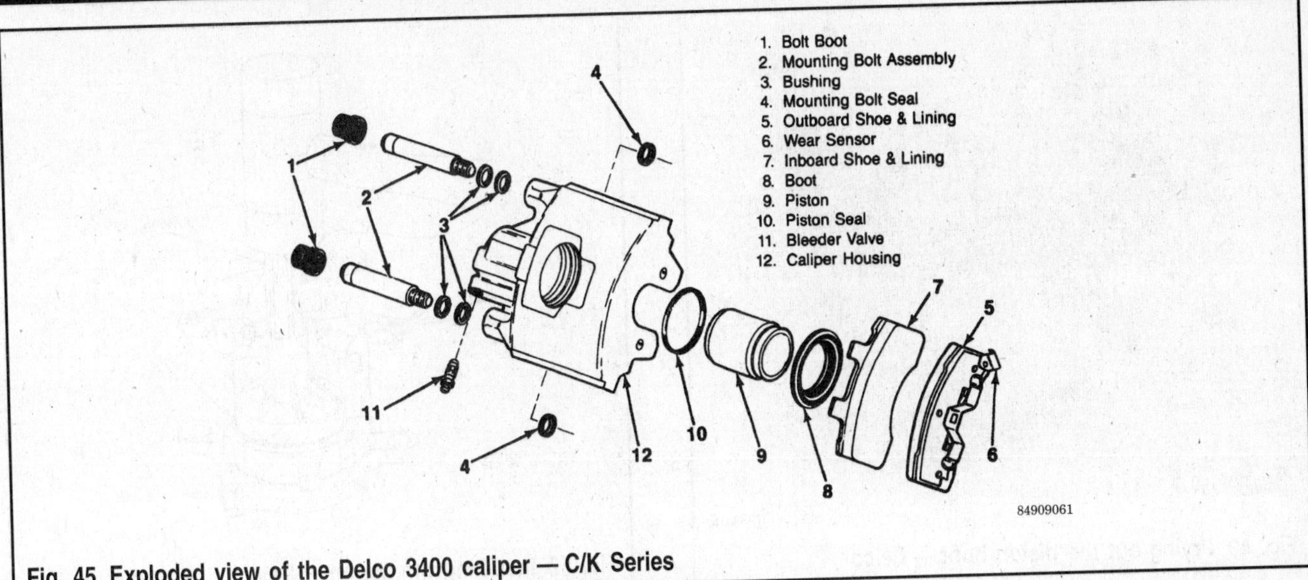

Fig. 45 Exploded view of the Delco 3400 caliper — C/K Series

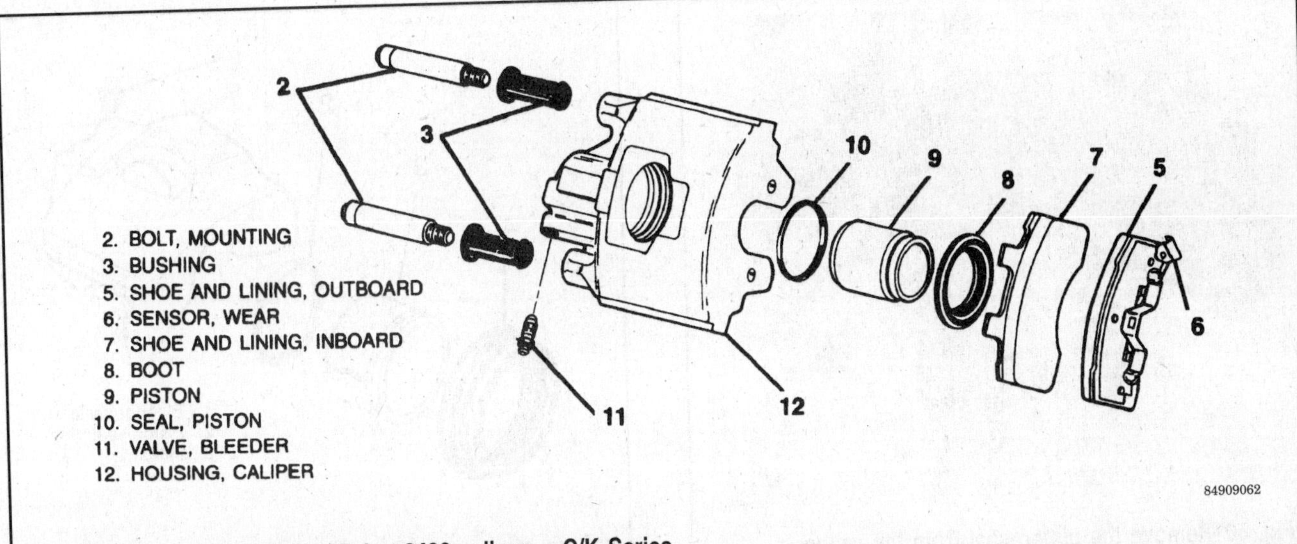

Fig. 46 Exploded view of the Delco 3486 caliper — C/K Series

Fig. 47 Force the piston out with compressed air — Delco

Fig. 48 Remove the piston from the caliper

Fig. 49 Prying out the piston boot — Delco

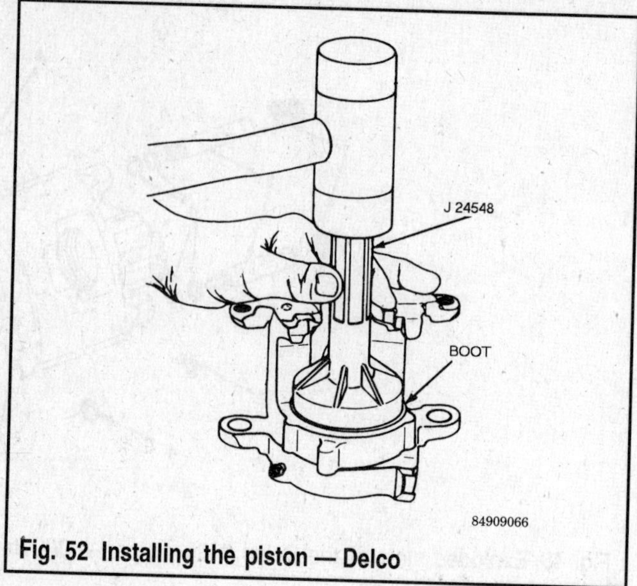

Fig. 52 Installing the piston — Delco

Fig. 50 Remove the piston seal from the caliper

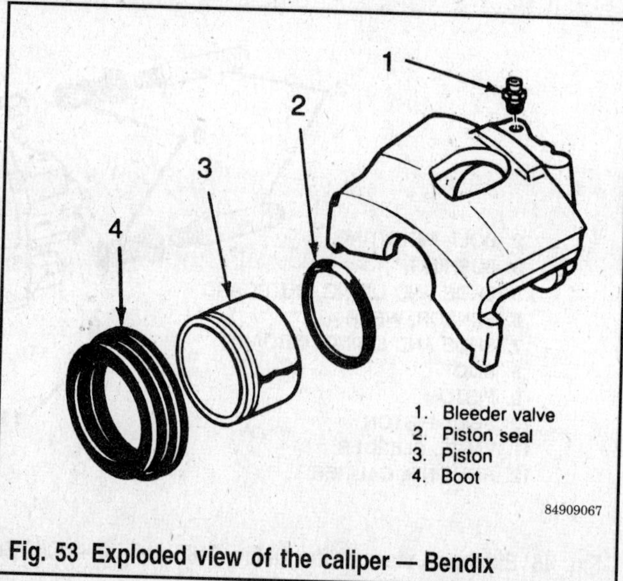

Fig. 53 Exploded view of the caliper — Bendix

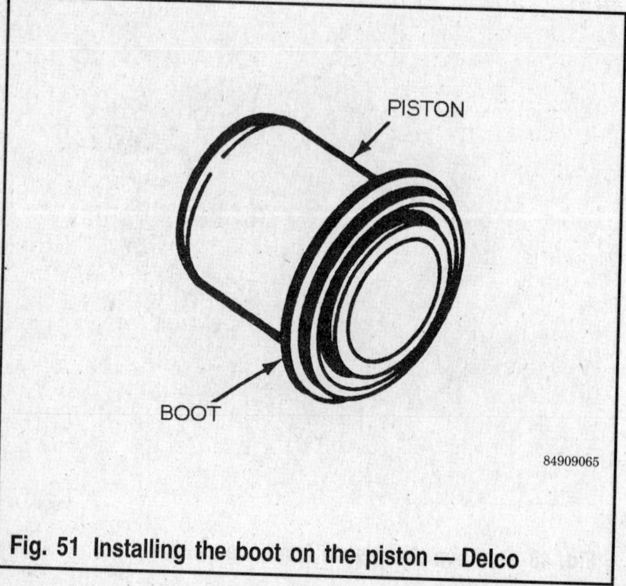

Fig. 51 Installing the boot on the piston — Delco

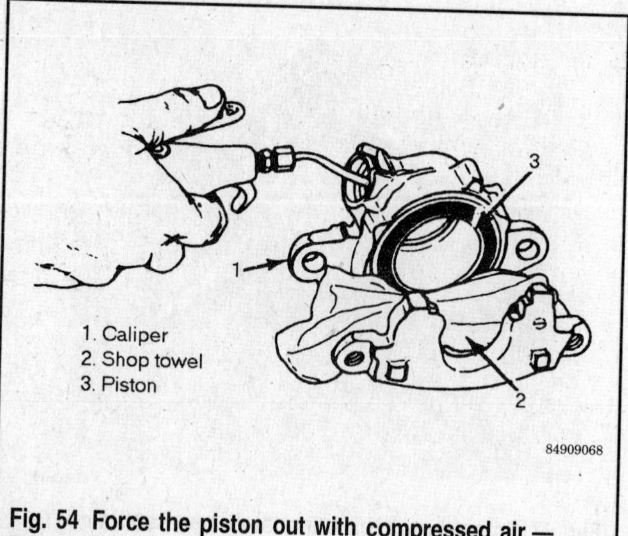

Fig. 54 Force the piston out with compressed air — Bendix

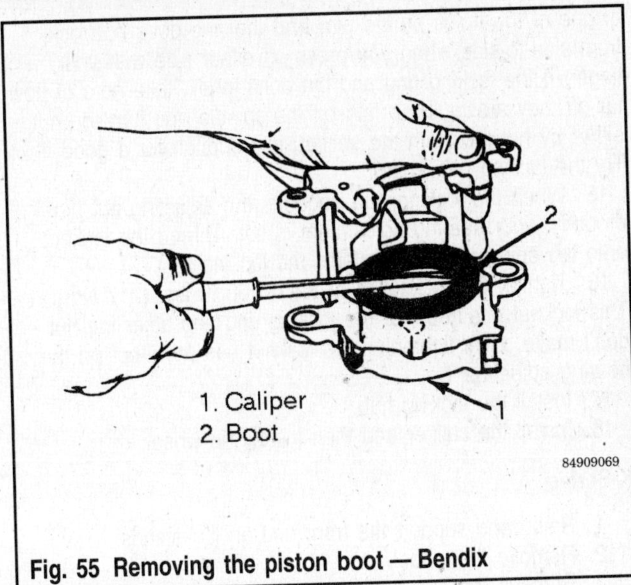

Fig. 55 Removing the piston boot — Bendix

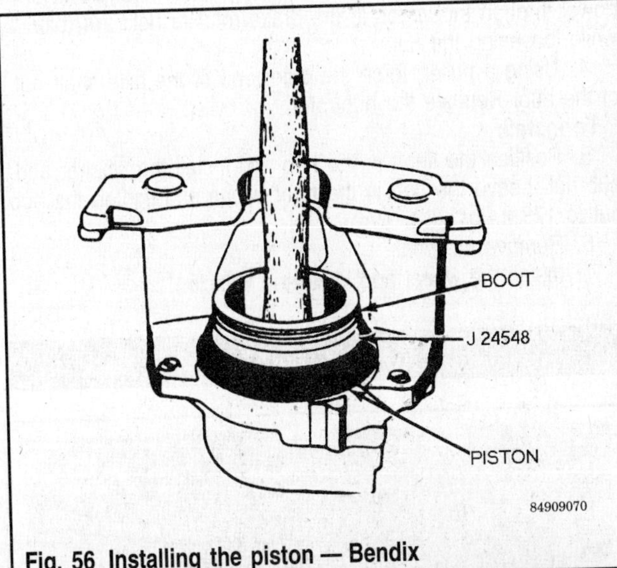

Fig. 56 Installing the piston — Bendix

Disc Brake (Rotor)

REMOVAL & INSTALLATION

R-Series and C-Series

See Figure 57

1. Remove the brake caliper as previously outlined.
2. Remove the outer wheel bearing. Refer to Section 1 for the proper procedure.
3. Remove the rotor from the spindle.
4. Reverse procedure to install. Adjust the bearings. Refer to Section 1 for the proper procedure.

V-Series

➡Before starting, you'll need a special wheel bearing nut socket for your ½ inch drive ratchet. These sockets are available through auto parts stores and catalogs. You can't do this job properly without it.

1. Raise and support the front end on jackstands.
2. Remove the wheels.
3. Remove the hubs. See the procedures above.
4. Wipe the inside of the hub to remove as much grease as possible.
5. Using your bearing nut socket, remove the locknut from the spindle.
6. With the locknut off you'll be able to see the locking ring on the adjusting nut. Remove the locking ring. A tool such as a dental pick will make this easier.
7. Using the special socket, remove the bearing adjusting nut.

➡You'll notice that the adjusting nut and the locknut are almost identical. The difference is, the adjusting nut has a small pin on one side which indexes with a hole in the locking ring. DO NOT CONFUSE THE TWO NUTS!

8. Dismount the brake caliper and suspend it out of the way, without disconnecting the brake line. See Section 9.
9. Pull the hub off of the spindle. The outer bearing will tend to fall out as soon as it clears the spindle, so have a hand ready to catch it.

The minimum wear thickness, 1.215 in. (30.86mm), is cast into each disc hub. This is a minimum wear dimension and not a refinish dimension. If the thickness of the disc after refinishing will be 1.230 in. (31.2mm) or less, it must be replaced. Refinishing is required whenever the disc surface shows scoring or severe rust scale. Scoring not deeper than 0.015 in. (0.38mm) in depth can be corrected by refinishing.

➡Some discs have an anti-squeal groove. This should not be mistaken for scoring.

Fig. 57 Remove the rotor from the vehicle

To install:

10. Carefully place the hub assembly on the spindle. Take care to avoid damaging the seal on the spindle threads. Make sure the hub is all the way on the spindle.

11. Place the outer bearing on the spindle and slide it into place in its race.

12. Thread the adjusting nut on the spindle until it contacts the outer bearing.

✲✲WARNING

Make sure you are using the adjusting nut. Remember, it has a small pin on one side. That pin must face outwards, towards you!

13. Using the special socket and the torque wrench:
    a. Tighten the adjusting nut to 50 ft. lbs. (68 Nm) while rotating the hub.
    b. Back off the adjusting nut until it is loose.
    c. While rotating the hub, tighten the adjusting nut to 35 ft. lbs. (47 Nm) for automatic locking hubs or 50 ft. lbs. (68 Nm) for manual locking hubs.
    d. Back off the adjusting nut ¼ to ⅜ of a turn for automatic hubs or ¼ turn for manual hubs.

14. Coat the locking ring with wheel bearing grease. Place the locking ring on the spindle. There is a tab on the inner diameter of the ring which must fit in the slot on the top of the spindle. Slide the locking ring in until it contacts the adjusting nut. The pin on the adjusting nut must enter one of the holes in the locking ring. You can tell that the locking ring is seated properly when you see the grease on the ring get pushed out of one of the holes by the pin, **and** the ring does not rock from side-to-side when you press on either side with your finger. If the locking ring and pin don't index, take note of how far off they are, pull the ring off the spindle and turn the nut, either by hand or with the socket, just enough for a good fit. Try the locking ring again.

15. When the locking ring engages the adjusting nut pin properly, your bearing adjustment is set. Thread the locknut onto the spindle until it contacts the locking ring.

16. Tighten the locknut to **at least** 160 ft. lbs. (217 Nm). This locknut ensures that the locking ring and adjusting nut don't move. Over-tightening the locknut has no effect on the bearing adjustment.

17. Install the locking hub.

18. Install the caliper and then install the wheel.

K-Series

1. Raise and support the front end on jackstands.
2. Remove the wheel.
3. Remove the hub nut and washer. Insert a long drift or dowel through the vanes in the brake rotor to hold the rotor while loosening the nut.
4. Using a puller, force the outer end of the axle shaft out of the hub. Remove the hub/rotor.

To install:

5. Position the shaft in the hub and install the washer and hub nut. Leave the drift in the rotor vanes and tighten the hub nut to 173 ft. lbs. (235 Nm).
6. Remove the drift.
7. Install the wheel and lower the vehicle.

DRUM BRAKES

✲✲CAUTION

Brake shoes may contain asbestos, which has been determined to be a cancer causing agent. Never clean the brake surfaces with compressed air! Avoid inhaling any dust from any brake surface! When cleaning brake surfaces, use a commercially available brake cleaning fluid.

Brake Drums

REMOVAL & INSTALLATION

Semi-Floating Axles

➧ **See Figure 58**

1. Raise and support the rear end on jackstands.
2. Remove the wheel.
3. Pull the drum from the brake assembly. If the brake drums have been scored from worn linings, the brake adjuster must be backed off so that the brake shoes will retract from the drum. The adjuster can be backed off by inserting a brake adjusting tool through the access hole provided. In some cases the access hole is provided in the brake drum. A metal cover plate is over the hole. This may be removed by using a hammer and chisel.

87989p16

Fig. 58 Pull the drum from the brake assembly

4. To install, reverse the removal procedure.

Full Floating Axles

To remove the drums from full floating rear axles, use the Axle Shaft Removal & Installation procedure in Section 7. Full floating rear axles can readily be identified by the bearing housing protruding through the center of the wheel.

➡Make sure all metal particles are removed from the brake drum before reassembly.

INSPECTION

When the drum is removed, it should be inspected for cracks, scores, or other imperfections. These must be corrected before the drum is replaced.

⁂CAUTION

If the drum is found to be cracked, replace it. Do not attempt to service a cracked drum.

Minor drum score marks can be removed with fine emery cloth. Heavy score marks must be removed by turning the drum. This is removing metal from the entire inner surface of the drum on a lathe in order to level the surface. Automotive machine shops and some large parts stores are equipped to perform this operation.

If the drum is not scored, it should be polished with fine emery cloth before replacement. If the drum is resurfaced, it should not be enlarged more than 0.060 in. (1.524mm).

➡Your state inspection law may disagree with this specification.

It is advisable, while the drums are off, to check them for out-of-round. An inside micrometer is necessary for an exact measurement, therefore unless this tool is available, the drums should be taken to a machine shop to be checked. Any drum which is more than 0.006 in. (0.1524mm) out-of-round will result in an inaccurate brake adjustment and other problems, and should be refinished or replaced.

➡Make all measurements at right angles to each other and at the open and closed edges of the drum machined surface.

Brake Shoes

REMOVAL & INSTALLATION

Full Floating Axle

➧ See Figures 59, 60, 61, 62, 63, 64, 65, 66, 67 and 68

1. Raise and securely support the vehicle using jackstands.
2. Loosen the parking brake equalizer enough to remove all tension on the brake cable.
3. Remove the brake drums.

⁂WARNING

The brake pedal must not be depressed while the drums are removed!

4. Using a brake tool, remove the shoe return springs. You can do this with ordinary tools, but it isn't easy.
5. Remove the self-adjuster actuator spring.
6. Remove the link from the secondary shoe by pulling it from the anchor pin.
7. Remove the hold-down pins. These are the brackets which run though the backing plate. They can be removed with a pair of pliers. Reach around the rear of the backing plate and hold the back of the pin. Turn the top of the pin retainer 45° with the plier. This will align the elongated tang with the slot in the retainer. Be careful, as the pin is spring loaded and may fly off when released. Use the same procedure for the other pin assembly.
8. Remove the adjuster actuator assembly.

➡Since the actuator, pivot, and override spring are considered an assembly it is not recommended that they be disassembled.

9. Remove the shoes from the backing plate. Make sure that you have a secure grip on the assembly as the bottom spring will still exert pressure on the shoes. Slowly let the tops of the shoes come together and the tension will decrease and the adjuster and spring may be removed.

➡If the linings are to be reused, mark them for identification.

10. Remove the rear parking brake lever from the secondary shoe. Using a pair of pliers, pull back on the spring which surrounds the cable. At the same time, remove the cable from the notch in the shoe bracket. Make sure that the spring does not snap back or injury may result.

To install:

11. Use a brake cleaning fluid to remove dirt from the brake drum. Check the drums for scoring and cracks. Have the drums checked for out-of-round and service the drums as necessary.
12. Check the wheel cylinders by carefully pulling the lower edges of the wheel cylinder boots away from the cylinders. If there is excessive leakage, the inside of the cylinder will be moist with fluid. If there is any leakage at all, a cylinder overhaul is in order. DO NOT delay, as a brake failure could result.

➡A small amount of fluid will be present to act as a lubricant for the wheel cylinder pistons.

13. Check the flange plate, which is located around the axle, for leakage of differential lubricant. This condition cannot be overlooked as the lubricant will be absorbed into the brake linings and brake failure will result. Replace the seals as necessary.

➡If new linings are being installed, check them against the old units for length and type.

14. Check the new linings for imperfections.

⁂CAUTION

It is important to keep your hands free of dirt and grease when handling the brake shoes. Foreign matter will be absorbed into the linings and result in unpredictable braking.

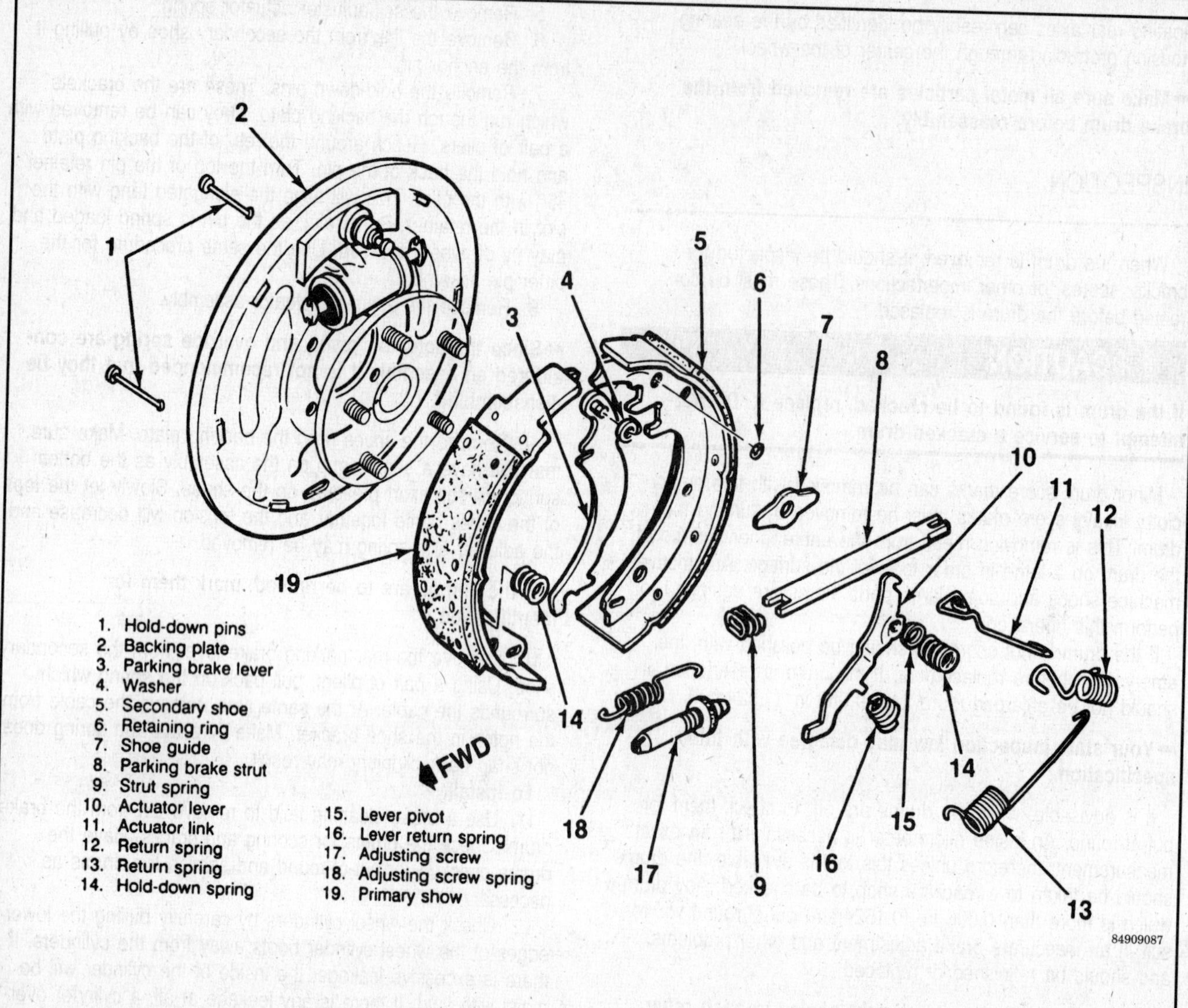

Fig. 59 Exploded view of the duo-servo drum brake — 1988-92

15. Lightly lubricate the parking brake and cable and the end of the parking brake lever where it enters the shoe. Use high temperature, waterproof, grease or special brake lube.

16. Install the parking brake lever into the secondary shoe with the attaching bolt, spring washer, lockwasher, and nut. It is important that the lever move freely before the shoe is attached. Move the assembly and check for proper action.

17. Lubricate the adjusting screw and make sure that it works freely. Sometimes the adjusting screw will not move due to lack of lubricant or dirt contamination and the brakes will not adjust. In this case, the adjuster should be disassembled, thoroughly cleaned, and lubricated before installation.

18. Connect the brake shoe spring to the bottom portion of both shoes. Make certain that the brake linings are installed in the correct manner, the primary and secondary shoe in the correct position. If you are not sure remove the other brake drum and check it.

19. Install the adjusting mechanism below the spring and separate the top of the shoes.

20. Make the following checks before installation:

a. Be certain that the right hand thread adjusting screw is on the left hand side of the vehicle and the left hand screw is on the right hand side of the vehicle.

b. Make sure that the star adjuster is aligned with the adjusting hole.

c. The adjuster should be installed with the starwheel nearest the secondary shoe and the tension spring away from the adjusting mechanism;

d. If the original linings are being reused, put them back in their original locations.

21. Install the parking brake cable.

22. Position the primary shoe (the shoe with the short lining) first. Secure it with the hold-down pin and with its spring by pushing the pin through the back of the backing plate and, while holding it with one hand, install the spring and the retainer using a pair of needlenose pliers. Install the adjuster actuator assembly.

23. Install the parking brake strut and the strut spring by pulling back the spring with pliers and engaging the end of the cable onto the brake strut and then releasing the spring.

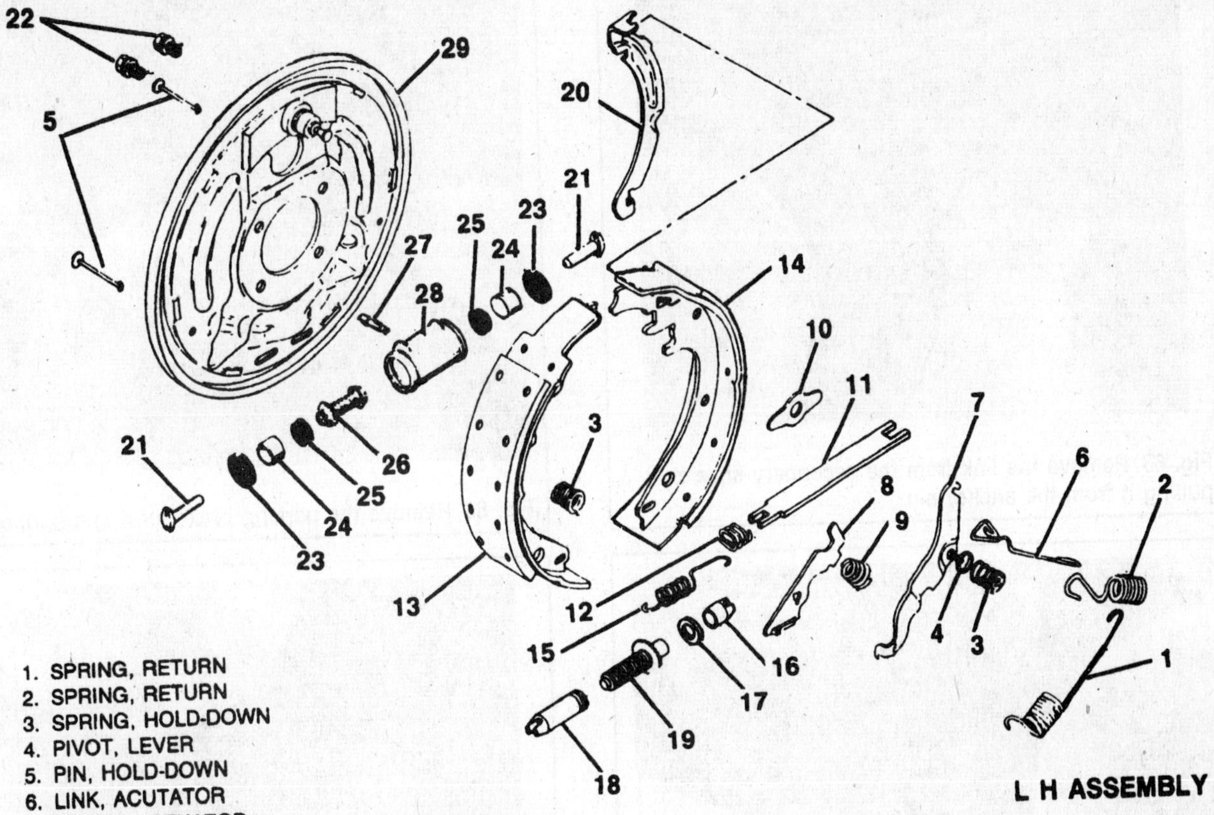

L H ASSEMBLY

1. SPRING, RETURN
2. SPRING, RETURN
3. SPRING, HOLD-DOWN
4. PIVOT, LEVER
5. PIN, HOLD-DOWN
6. LINK, ACUTATOR
7. LEVER, ACTUATOR
8. PAWL
9. SPRING, LEVER RETURN
10. GUIDE, SHOE
11. STRUT, PARKING BRAKE
12. SPRING, STRUT
13. SHOE, PRIMARY
14. SHOE, SECONDARY
15. SPRING, ADJUSTING SCREW
16. SOCKET
17. WASHER
18. NUT, PIVOT
19. SCREW, ADJUSTING
20. LEVER, PARKING BRAKE
21. LINK, CYLINDER
22. BOLT
23. BOOT
24. PISTON
25. SEAL
26. ASSEMBLY, SPRING
27. VALVE, BLEEDER
28. BODY, CYLINDER
29. PLATE, BACKING

84909088

Fig. 60 Exploded view of the duo-servo drum brake — 1993-96

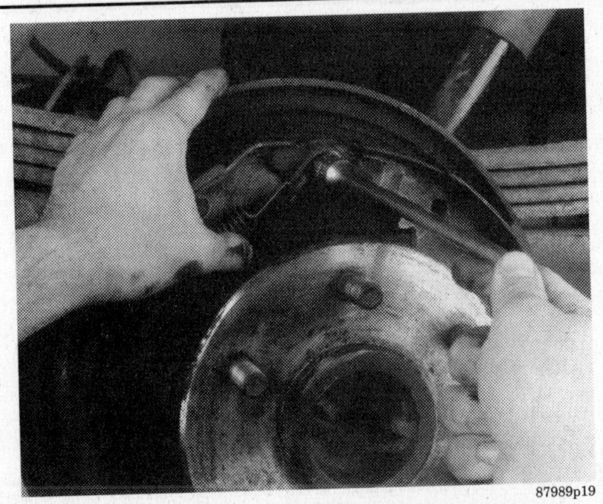

87989p19

Fig. 61 Using a brake tool, remove the shoe return springs

87989p20

Fig. 62 Remove the self-adjuster actuator spring

87989p21

Fig. 63 Remove the link from the secondary shoe by pulling it from the anchor pin

87989p18

Fig. 64 Remove the hold-down pins

87989p22

Fig. 65 Remove the shoes from the backing plate

87989p23

Fig. 66 Remove the parking brake strut and spring

87989p24

Fig. 67 Remove the rear parking brake lever from the secondary shoe using a pair of pliers

87989p17

Fig. 68 Its always a good idea to lay all the parts out as they come off

24. Place the small metal guide plate over the anchor pin and position the self-adjuster wire cable eye.

CAUTION

The wire should not be positioned with the conventional brake installation tool or damage will result. It should be positioned on the actuator assembly first and then placed over the anchor pin stud by hand with the adjuster assembly in full downward position.

25. Install the actuator return spring. DO NOT pry the actuator lever to install the return spring. Position it using the end of a screwdriver or another suitable tool.

➡If the return springs are bent or in any way distorted, they should be replaced.

26. Using the brake installation tool, place the brake return springs in position. Install the primary spring first over the anchor pin and then place the spring from the secondary show over the wire link end.
27. Pull the brake shoes away from the backing plate and apply a thin coat of high temperature, waterproof, grease or special brake lube in the brake shoe contact points.

CAUTION

Only a small amount is necessary. Keep the lubricant away from the brake linings.

28. Once the complete assembly has been installed, check the operation of the self-adjusting mechanism by moving the actuating lever by hand.
29. Adjust the brakes.
   a. Turn the star adjuster until the drum slides over the brakes shoes with only a slight drag. Remove the drum:
   b. Turn the adjuster back 1¼ turns.
   c. Install the drum and wheel and lower the vehicle.

CAUTION

Avoid overtightening the lug nuts to prevent damage to the brake drum. Alloy wheels can also be cracked by overtightening. Use of a torque wrench is highly recommended.

   d. If the adjusting hole in the drum has been punched out, make certain that the insert has been removed from the inside of the drum. Install a rubber hole cover to keep dirt out of the brake assembly. Also, be sure that the drums are installed in the same position as they were when removed, with the locating tang in line with the locating hole in the axle shaft flange.
   e. Make the final adjustment by backing the vehicle and pumping the brakes until the self-adjusting mechanisms adjust to the proper level and the brake pedal reaches satisfactory height.
30. Adjust the parking brake. Refer to the procedure in this section.

Semi-floating Axle

See Figures 69, 70 and 71

1. Jack up and securely support the vehicle using jackstands.
2. Loosen the parking brake equalizer enough to remove all tension on the brake cable.
3. Remove the brake drums. If difficulty is till encountered, remove the access hole plug in the backing plate and insert a metal rod to push the parking brake lever off its stop.

WARNING

The brake pedal must not be depressed while the drums are removed!

4. Raise the lever arm of the actuator until the upper end is clear of the slot in the adjuster screw. Slide the actuator off the adjuster pin.
5. Disconnect the actuator from the brake shoe.
6. Remove the hold-down pins. These are the brackets which run though the backing plate. They can be removed with a pair of pliers. Reach around the rear of the backing plate and hold the back of the pin. Turn the top of the pin retainer 45° with the plier. This will align the elongated tang with the slot in the retainer. Be careful, as the pin is spring loaded and may fly off when released. Use the same procedure for the other pin assembly.
7. Pull the lower ends of the shoes apart and lift the lower return spring over the anchor plate. Remove the spring from the shoes.
8. Lift the shoes and upper return spring along with the adjusting screw, from the backing plate. Some spreading of the shoes is necessary to clear the wheel cylinder and axle flange. Remove the upper spring.
9. Remove the retaining ring, pin, spring washer and parking brake lever.

➡If the linings are to be reused, mark them for identification.

To install:

10. Use a brake cleaning fluid to remove dirt from the brake drum. Check the drums for scoring and cracks. Have the drums checked for out-of-round and service the drums as necessary.
11. Check the wheel cylinders by carefully pulling the lower edges of the wheel cylinder boots away from the cylinders. If there is excessive leakage, the inside of the cylinder will be moist with fluid. If there is any leakage at all, a cylinder overhaul is in order. DO NOT delay, as a brake failure could result.

➡A small amount of fluid will be present to act as a lubricant for the wheel cylinder pistons.

12. Check the flange plate, which is located around the axle, for leakage of differential lubricant. This condition cannot be overlooked as the lubricant will be absorbed into the brake linings and brake failure will result. Replace the seals as necessary.

➡If new linings are being installed, check them against the old units for length and type.

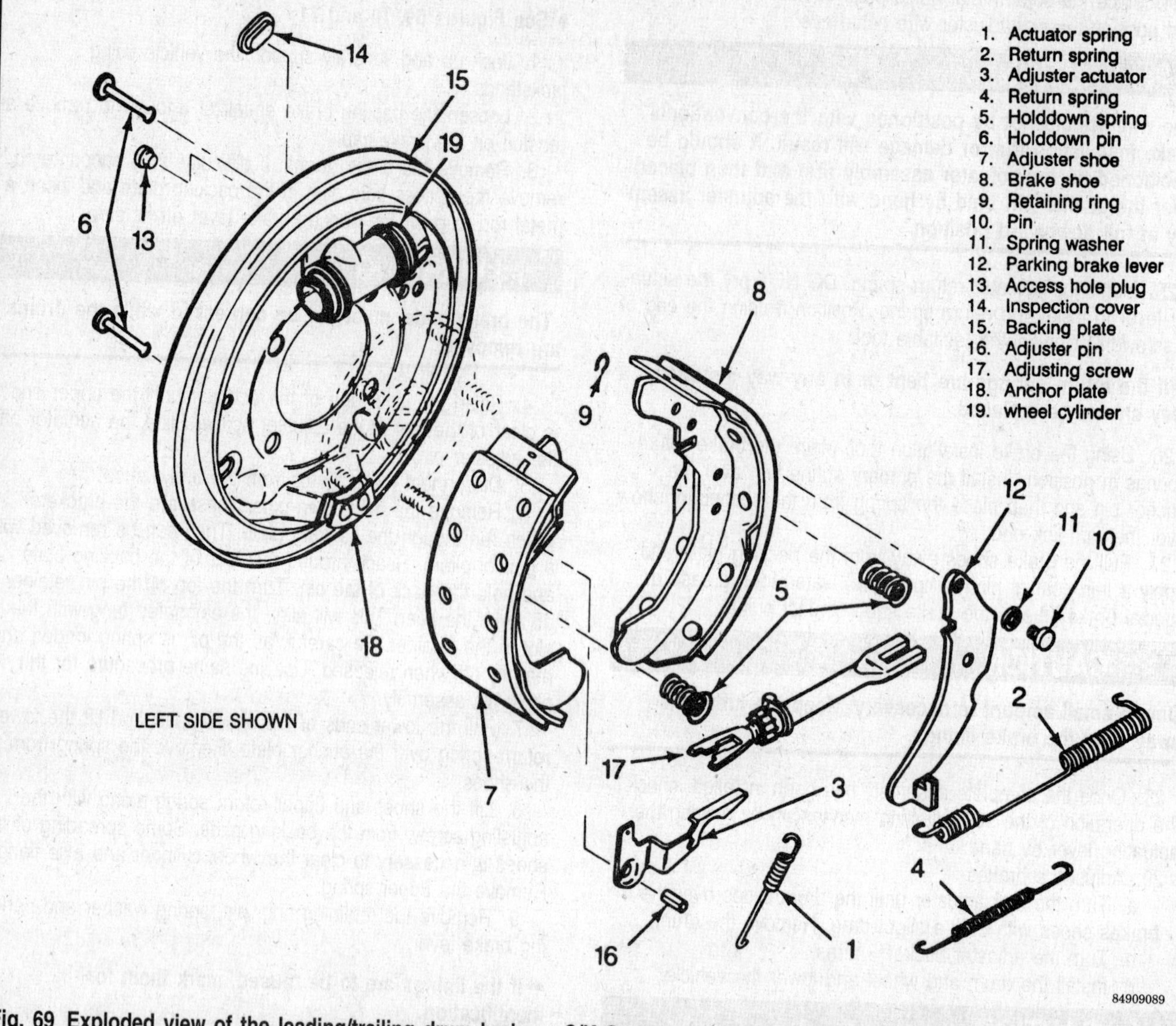

1. Actuator spring
2. Return spring
3. Adjuster actuator
4. Return spring
5. Holddown spring
6. Holddown pin
7. Adjuster shoe
8. Brake shoe
9. Retaining ring
10. Pin
11. Spring washer
12. Parking brake lever
13. Access hole plug
14. Inspection cover
15. Backing plate
16. Adjuster pin
17. Adjusting screw
18. Anchor plate
19. wheel cylinder
LEFT SIDE SHOWN
84909089

Fig. 69 Exploded view of the leading/trailing drum brake — C/K Series

LEFT SIDE SHOWN
BACKING PLATE
SCREWDRIVER
84909090

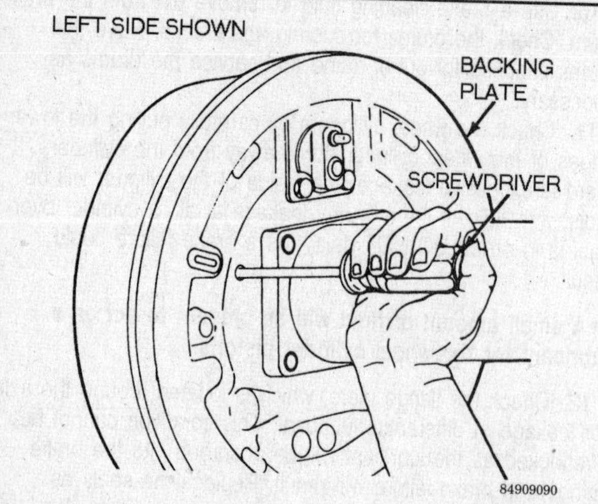

Fig. 70 Push the parking brake lever off its stop — C/K Series

13. Check the new linings for imperfections.

CAUTION

It is important to keep your hands free of dirt and grease when handling the brake shoes. Foreign matter will be absorbed into the linings and result in unpredictable braking.

14. Install the parking brake lever assembly The concave side of the washer should be against the shoe.
15. Install the adjuster pin in the shoe so that the pin projects 0.268-0.276 in. (6.8-7.0mm) from the side of the shoe where the actuator is installed.
16. Apply an approved brake lubricant grease to the threads of the adjuster screw, socket and socket face.
17. Make certain that the brake linings are positioned correctly and connect the upper spring. If you are not sure of which shoe goes where, remove the other brake drum and check it. Don't over-stretch the spring; you'll ruin it. The spring can't be stretched, safely, more than 8.04 in. (204mm).

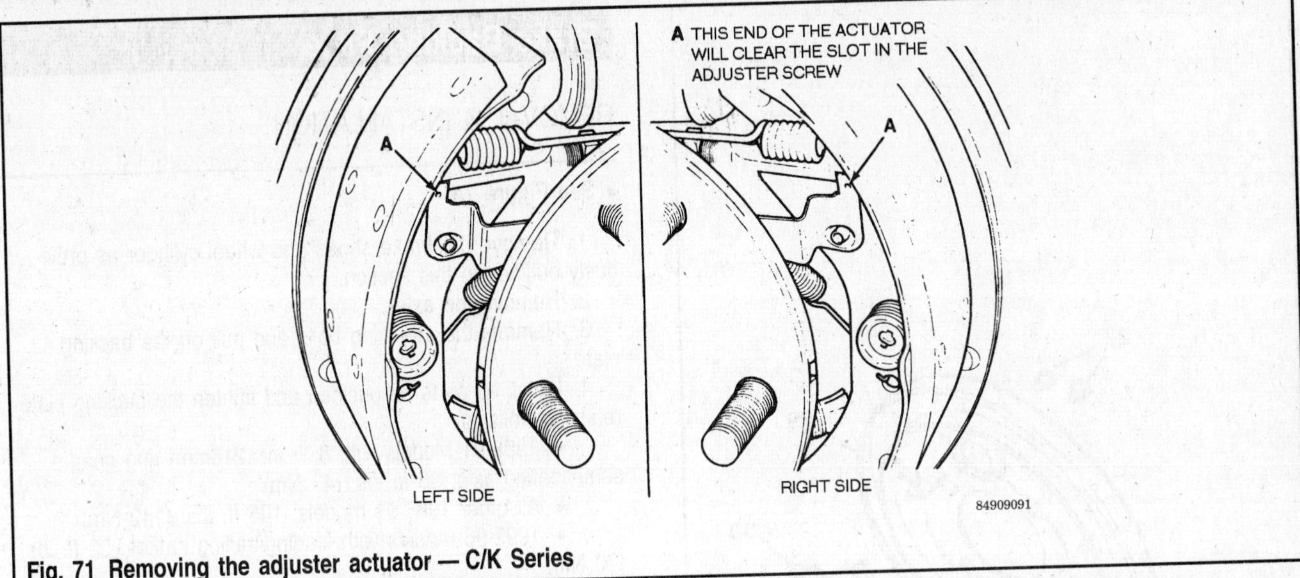

Fig. 71 Removing the adjuster actuator — C/K Series

18. Install the adjusting mechanism between the shoes. Make the following checks before installation:
   a. Be certain that the adjusting screw assembly engages the adjuster shoe and parking brake lever.
   b. Make sure that the spring clip is positioned towards the backing plate.
   c. The linings are in the correct positions. The shoe with the parking brake lever is the rear shoe.
19. Coat the shoe mounting pads on the backing plate with a thin coat of lithium grease.
20. Position the assembly on the backing plate, engaging the upper shoe ends with the wheel cylinder pushrods.
21. Hook the lower return spring into the shoe ends and spread the shoes, guiding the lower spring over the anchor plate. Don't over-stretch the spring; you'll ruin it. The spring can't be stretched, safely, more than 4¼ in. (108mm).
22. Install the hold-down spring assemblies.
23. Place the adjuster actuator over the end of the adjusting pin so its top leg engages the notch in the adjuster screw.
24. Install the actuator spring. Make sure that the free end of the actuator engage the notch of the adjuster nut. Don't over-stretch the spring. Its maximum stretch is 3¼ in. (83mm).
25. Connect the parking brake cable to the lever. Adjust the parking brake:
   a. Measure the brake drum inside diameter.
   b. Turn the adjuster nut until the brake shoe maximum diameter is 0.01-0.02 in. (0.25-50mm) less than the brake drum diameter.
   c. Make sure that the stops on the parking brake levers are against the edge of the brake shoe web. If the cable is holding the stops off the edge, loosen the adjustment.
   d. Tighten the cable at the adjuster nut until the lever stops begin to move off the shoe webs.
   e. Loosen the adjustment nut until the lever stops are **just** touching the shoe webs. There should be no more than 0.5mm clearance between the stops and the webs.
26. Install the drums and wheels.
27. Pump the brake pedal 30-35 times with normal force. Pause about 1 second between each stroke.
28. Depress the parking brake pedal 6 clicks. The wheels should be locked.
29. Release the parking brake. The wheels should rotate freely.

Wheel Cylinders

REMOVAL & INSTALLATION

➧ **See Figures 72 and 73**

1. Raise and support the vehicle using jackstands.
2. Remove the wheel and tire.
3. Back off the brake adjustment if necessary and remove the drum.
4. Disconnect and plug the brake line.
5. Remove the brake shoes as described above.
6. Remove the bolts securing the wheel cylinder to the backing plate.
7. Install the wheel cylinder. Tighten the mounting bolts to 15 ft. lbs. (20 Nm). Tighten the brake pipes to 13 ft. lbs. (17 Nm). Bleed the system.

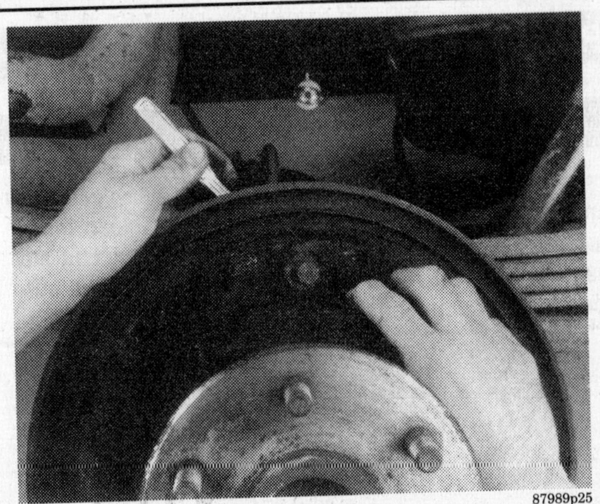

Fig. 72 Remove the bolts securing the wheel cylinder to the backing plate

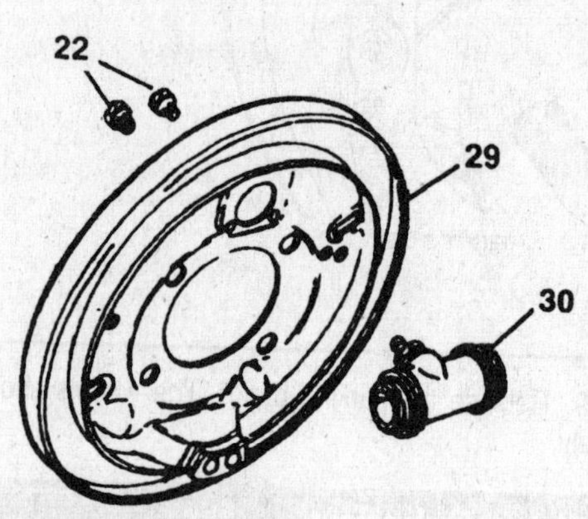

22. BOLTS, 20 N·m (15 FT. LBS.)
29. PLATE, BACKING
30. CYLINDER, WHEEL

84909101

Fig. 73 Wheel cylinder replacement

Brake Backing Plate

REMOVAL & INSTALLATION

➧ See Figure 74

1. Remove the brake shoes and wheel cylinder as previously outlined in this section.
2. Remove the axles.
3. Remove the attaching bolts and pull off the backing plate.
4. Install all parts as outlined and tighten the backing plate retaining bolts to:
    - 1988-91 Models with 8 ½ in. (216mm) ring gear, semi-floating axle: 35 ft. lbs. (47 Nm)
    - All other 1988-91 models: 105 ft. lbs. (142 Nm)
    - 1992-96 models with leading/trailing brakes: 52 ft. lbs. (70 Nm).
    - 1992-96 models w/duo-servo brakes: 118 ft. lbs. (160 Nm).

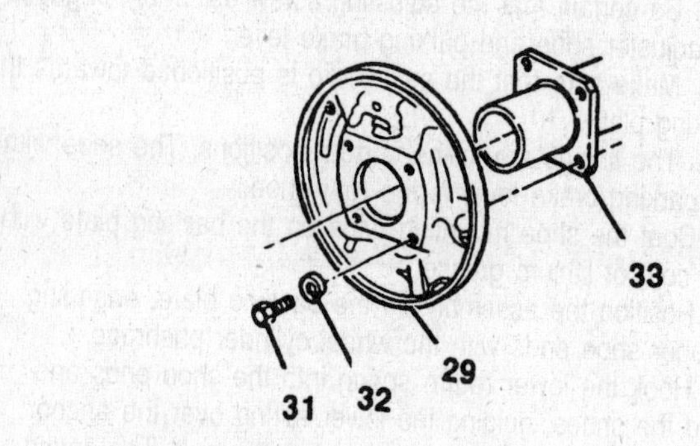

29. PLATE, BACKING
31. BOLT
32. WASHER, HELICAL SPRING
33. FLANGE, AXLE

84909103

Fig. 74 Brake backing plate

REAR DISC BRAKES

⁂CAUTION

Brake pads may contain asbestos, which has been determined to be a cancer causing agent. Never clean the brake surfaces with compressed air! Avoid inhaling any dust from any brake surface! When cleaning brake surfaces, use a commercially available brake cleaning fluid.

Brake Pads

INSPECTION

➧ See Figures 75 and 76

Support the truck on jackstands and remove the wheels. Look in at the ends of the caliper to check the lining thickness of the outer pad. Look through the inspection hole in the top of the caliper to check the thickness of the inner pad. Minimum acceptable pad thickness is 1/32 in. (0.8mm) from the rivet heads on original equipment riveted linings and ½ in. (13mm) lining thickness on bonded linings.

➡**These manufacturer's specifications may not agree with your state inspection law.**

All original equipment pads are the riveted type; unless you want to remove the pads to measure the actual thickness from the rivet heads, you will have to make the limit for visual inspection 1/16 in. (1.6mm) or more. The same applies if you don't know what kind of lining you have. Original equipment pads and GM replacement pads have an integral wear sensor. This is a spring steel tab on the rear edge of the inner pad which produces a squeal by rubbing against the rotor to warn that the pads have reached their wear limit. They do not squeal when the brakes are applied.

The squeal will eventually stop if worn pads aren't replaced. Should this happen, replace the pads immediately to prevent expensive rotor (disc) damage.

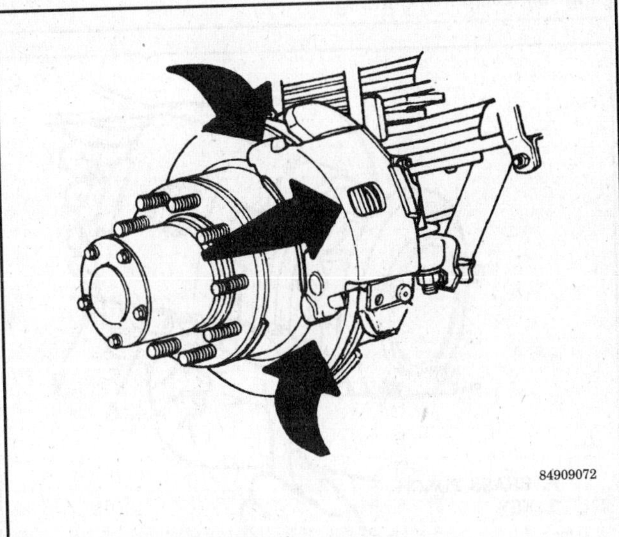

Fig. 75 Brake pad inspection points

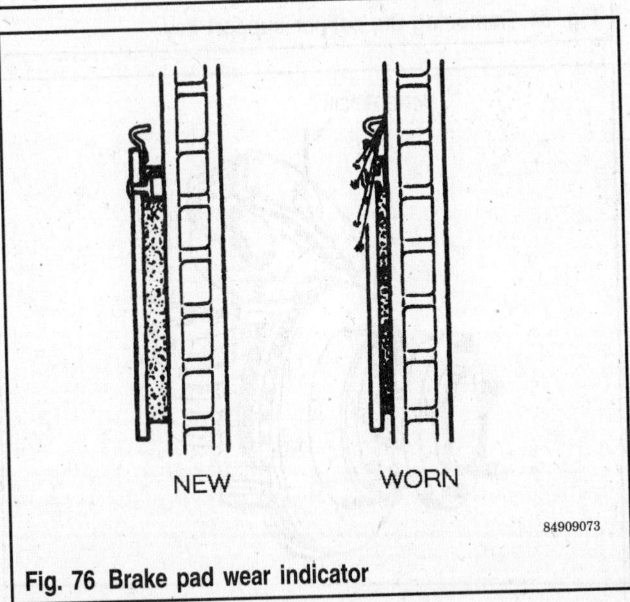

Fig. 76 Brake pad wear indicator

REMOVAL & INSTALLATION

See Figures 77, 78, 79, 80, 81, 82 and 83

1. Remove approximately ⅓ of the brake fluid from the master cylinder. Discard the used brake fluid.
2. Jack up your vehicle and support it with jackstands.
3. Push the piston back into its bore. This can be done by suing a C-clamp.
4. Remove the bolt at the caliper support key. Use a brass drift pin to remove the key and spring.
5. Rotate the caliper up and forward from the bottom and lift it off the caliper support.
6. Tie the caliper out of the way with a piece of wire. Be careful not to damage the brake line.
7. Remove the inner shoe from the caliper support. Discard the inner shoe clip.
8. Remove the outer shoe from the caliper.

To install:

9. Lubricate the caliper support and support spring, with silicone.
10. Install a NEW inboard shoe clip on the shoe.
11. Install the lower end of the inboard shoe into the groove provided in the support. Slide the upper end of the shoe into position. Be sure the clip remains in position.
12. Position the outboard shoe in the caliper with the ears at the top of the shoe over the caliper ears and the tab at the bottom of the shoe engaged in the caliper cutout. If assembly is difficult, a C-clamp may be used. Be careful not to mark the lining.
13. Position the caliper over the brake disc, top edge first. Rotate the caliper downward onto the support.
14. Place the spring over the caliper support key, install the assembly between the support and lower caliper groove. Tap into place until the key retaining screw can be installed.
15. Install the screw and tighten to 15 ft. lbs. (20 Nm). The boss must fit fully into the circular cutout in the key.
16. Install the wheel and and add brake fluid as necessary.

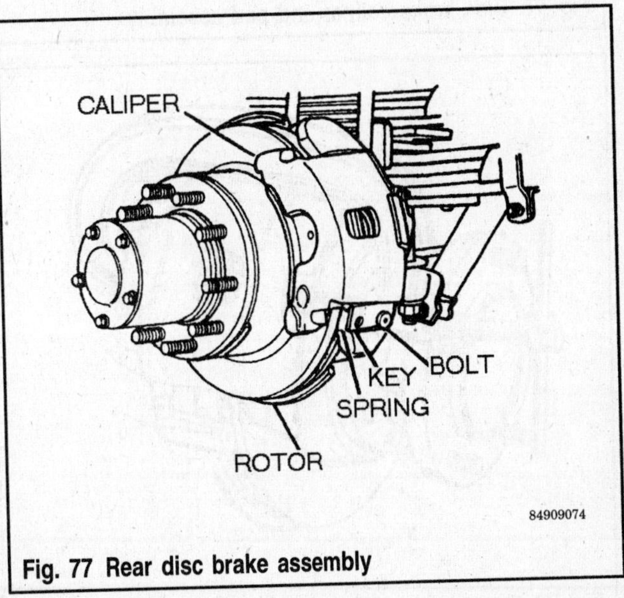

Fig. 77 Rear disc brake assembly

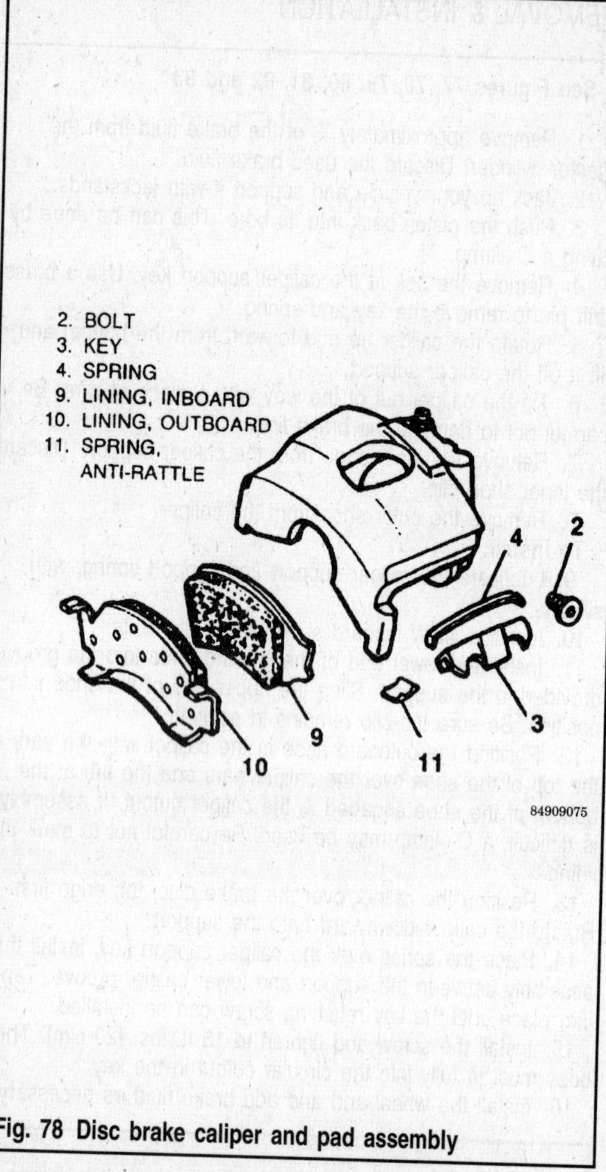

Fig. 78 Disc brake caliper and pad assembly

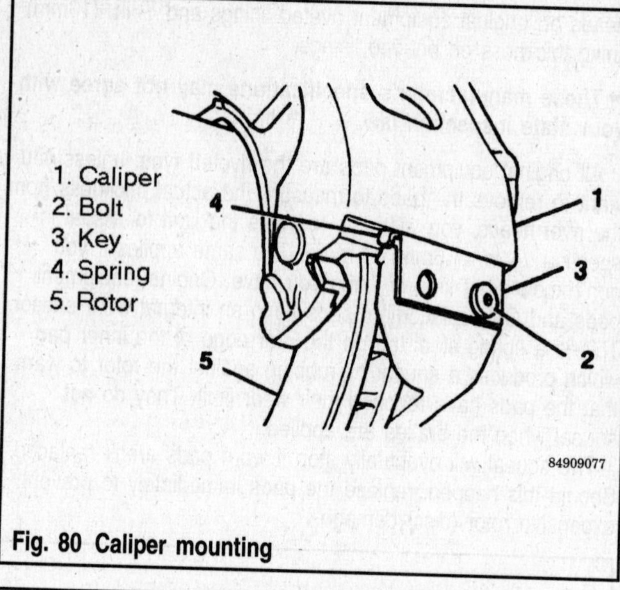

Fig. 80 Caliper mounting

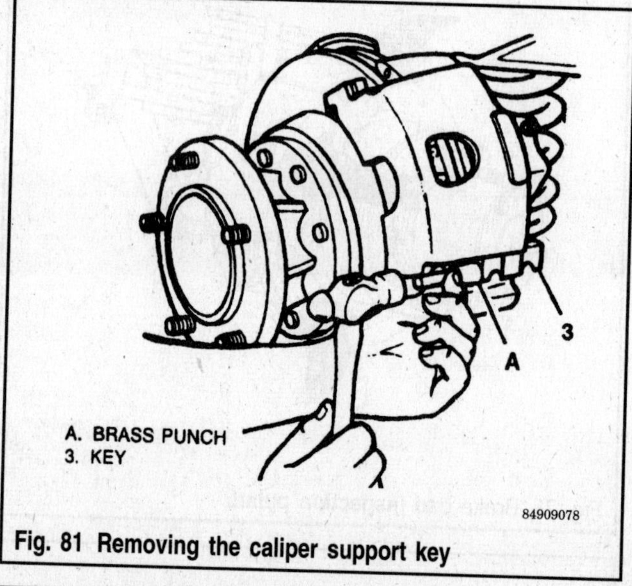

Fig. 81 Removing the caliper support key

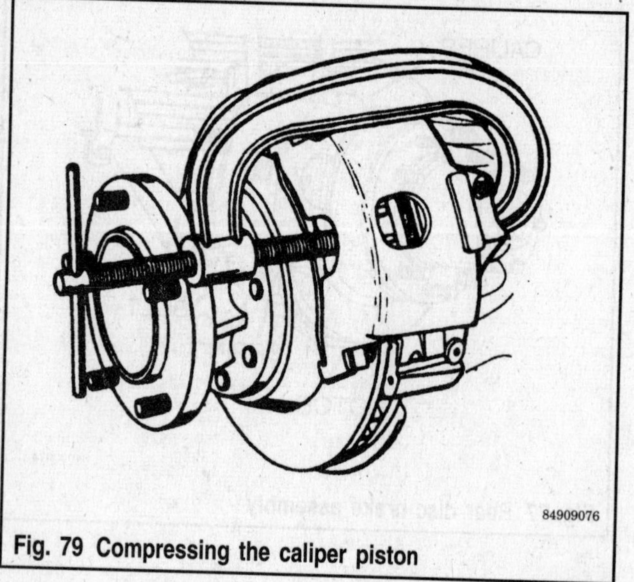

Fig. 79 Compressing the caliper piston

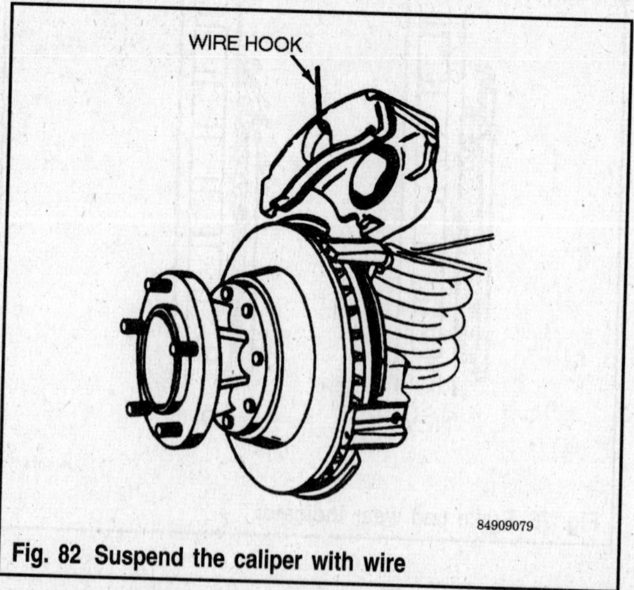

Fig. 82 Suspend the caliper with wire

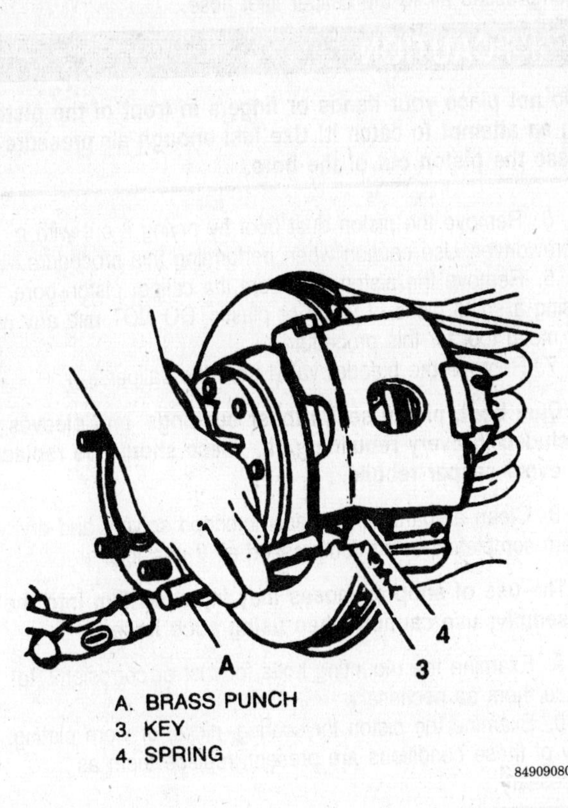

Fig. 83 Installing the caliper support key

Caliper

REMOVAL & INSTALLATION

➧ See Figures 77, 78, 79, 80, 81, 82 and 83

1. Remove approximately ⅓ of the brake fluid from the master cylinder. Discard the used brake fluid.
2. Raise and support the front end on jackstands.
3. Push the piston back into its bore. This can be done by suing a C-clamp.
4. Remove the bolt at the caliper support key. Use a brass drift pin to remove the key and spring.
5. Rotate the caliper up and forward from the bottom and lift it off the caliper support.
6. Unscrew the brake line at the caliper. Plug the opening. Discard the copper washer. Be careful not to damage the brake line.
7. Remove the outer shoe from the caliper.

To install:

8. Using a new copper washer, connect the brake line at the caliper. Tighten the connector to 33 ft. lbs. (45 Nm)
9. Lubricate the caliper support and support spring with silicone.
10. Position the outboard shoe in the caliper with the ears at the top of the shoe over the caliper ears and the tab at the bottom of the shoe engaged in the caliper cutout. If assembly is difficult, a C-clamp may be used. Be careful not to mar the lining.
11. Position the caliper over the brake disc, top edge first. Rotate the caliper downward onto the support.
12. Place the spring over the caliper support key, install the assembly between the support and lower caliper groove. Tap into place until the key retaining screw can be installed.
13. Install the screw and tighten to 15 ft. lbs. (20 Nm). The boss must fit fully into the circular cutout in the key.
14. Install the wheel and and add brake fluid as necessary.

OVERHAUL

➧ See Figures 84, 85, 86 and 87

The following procedure applies to both the Delco and Bendix types of calipers.

CAUTION

Use only denatured alcohol to clean metal parts and brake fluid to clean rubber parts. Never use any mineral based cleaning solvents such as gasoline or kerosene as these solvents will deteriorate rubber parts.

1. Remove the caliper, clean it and place it on a clean and level work surface.
2. Remove the brake hose from the caliper and discard the copper gasket. Check the brake hose for cracks or deterioration. Replace the hose as necessary.
3. Drain the brake fluid from the caliper.

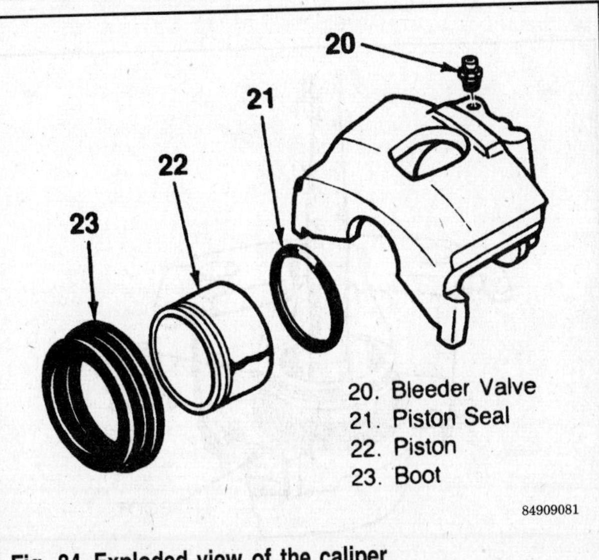

Fig. 84 Exploded view of the caliper

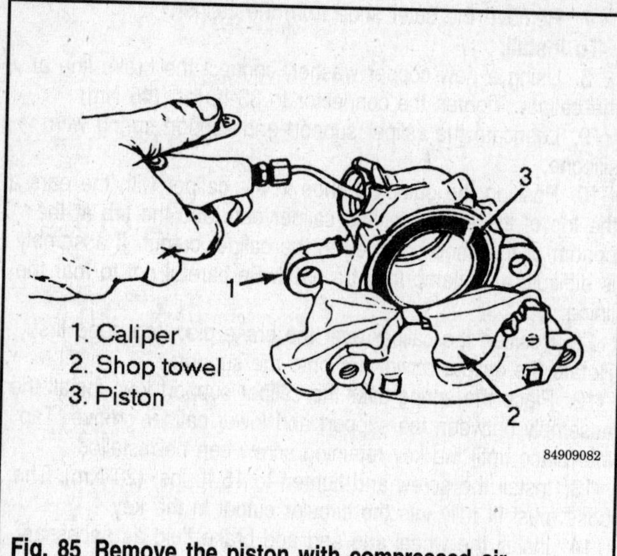

Fig. 85 Remove the piston with compressed air

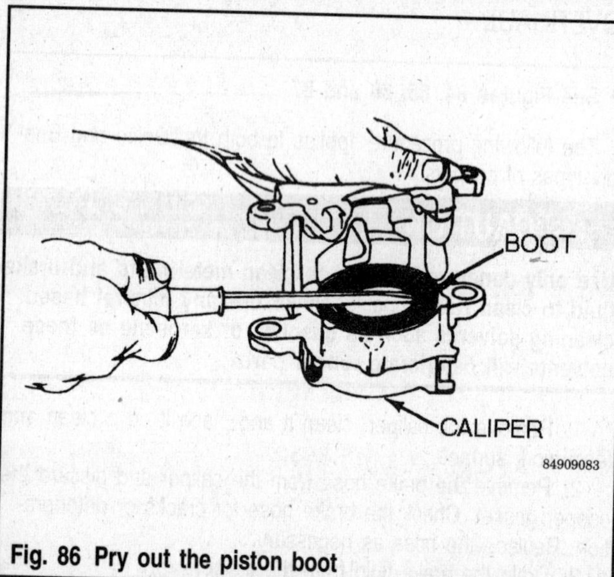

Fig. 86 Pry out the piston boot

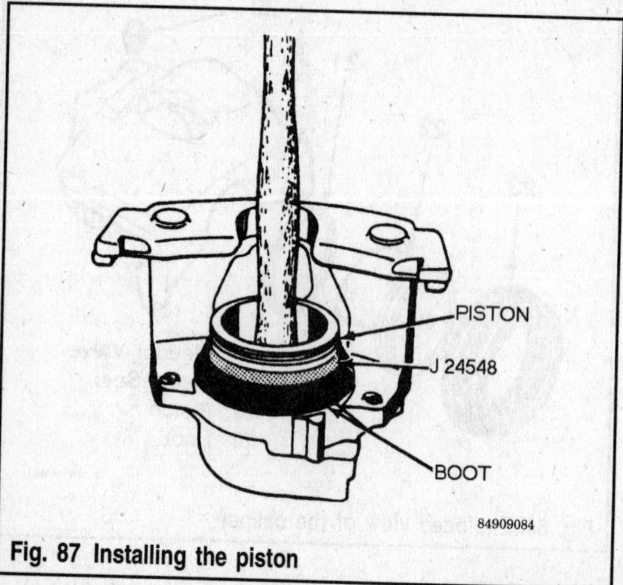

Fig. 87 Installing the piston

4. Pad the interior of the caliper with cloth and then apply compressed air to the caliper inlet hose.

CAUTION

Do not place your hands or fingers in front of the piston in an attempt to catch it! Use just enough air pressure to ease the piston out of the bore.

5. Remove the piston dust boot by prying it out with a screwdriver. Use caution when performing this procedure.
6. Remove the piston seal from the caliper piston bore using a small piece of wood or plastic. DO NOT use any type of metal tool for this procedure.
7. Remove the bleeder valve from the caliper.

➡Dust boot, piston seal, rubber bushings, and sleeves are included in every rebuilding kit. These should be replaced at every caliper rebuild.

8. Clean all parts in the recommended solvent and dry them completely using compressed air if possible.

➡The use of shop air hoses may inject oil film into the assembly; use caution when using such hoses.

9. Examine the mounting bolts for rust or corrosion. Replace them as necessary.
10. Examine the piston for scoring, nicks, or worn plating. If any of these conditions are present, replace them as necessary.

CAUTION

Do not use any type of abrasive on the piston!

11. Check the piston bore. Small defects can be removed with crocus cloth. If the bore cannot be cleaned in this manner, replace the caliper.
12. Lubricate the piston bore and the new piston seal with brake fluid. Place the seal in the caliper bore groove.
13. Lubricate the piston in the same manner and position the new boot into the groove in the piston so that the fold faces the open end of the piston.
14. Place the piston into the caliper bore using caution not to unseat the seal. Force the piston to the bottom of the bore.
15. Place the dust boot in the caliper counterbore and seat the boot. Make sure that the boot in positioned correctly and evenly.
16. Install the brake hose in the caliper inlet using a new copper gasket.

➡The hose must be positioned in the caliper locating gate to assure proper positioning of the caliper.

17. Replace the bleeder screw.
18. Bleed the system.

Disc Brake Rotor

REMOVAL & INSTALLATION

1. Remove the brake caliper as previously outlined.

2. Remove the outer wheel bearing. (Refer to Section 1 for the proper procedure).
3. Remove the rotor from the spindle.
4. Reverse procedure to install. Adjust the bearings. See Section 1.

PARKING BRAKE

Cables

REMOVAL & INSTALLATION

Front Cable

DRUM BRAKES

➧ See Figure 88

1. Raise vehicle and support it with safety stands.
2. Remove adjusting nut from equalizer.
3. Remove retainer clip from rear portion of front cable at frame and from lever arm.
4. Disconnect front brake cable from parking brake pedal or lever assemblies. Remove front brake cable. On some models, it may assist installation of new cable if a heavy cord is tied to other end of cable in order to guide new cable through proper routing.

To install:

5. Install cable by reversing removal procedure.
6. Adjust parking brake.

DISC BRAKES

➧ See Figure 89

1. Release the parking brake.
2. Raise the truck and support it with safety stands.

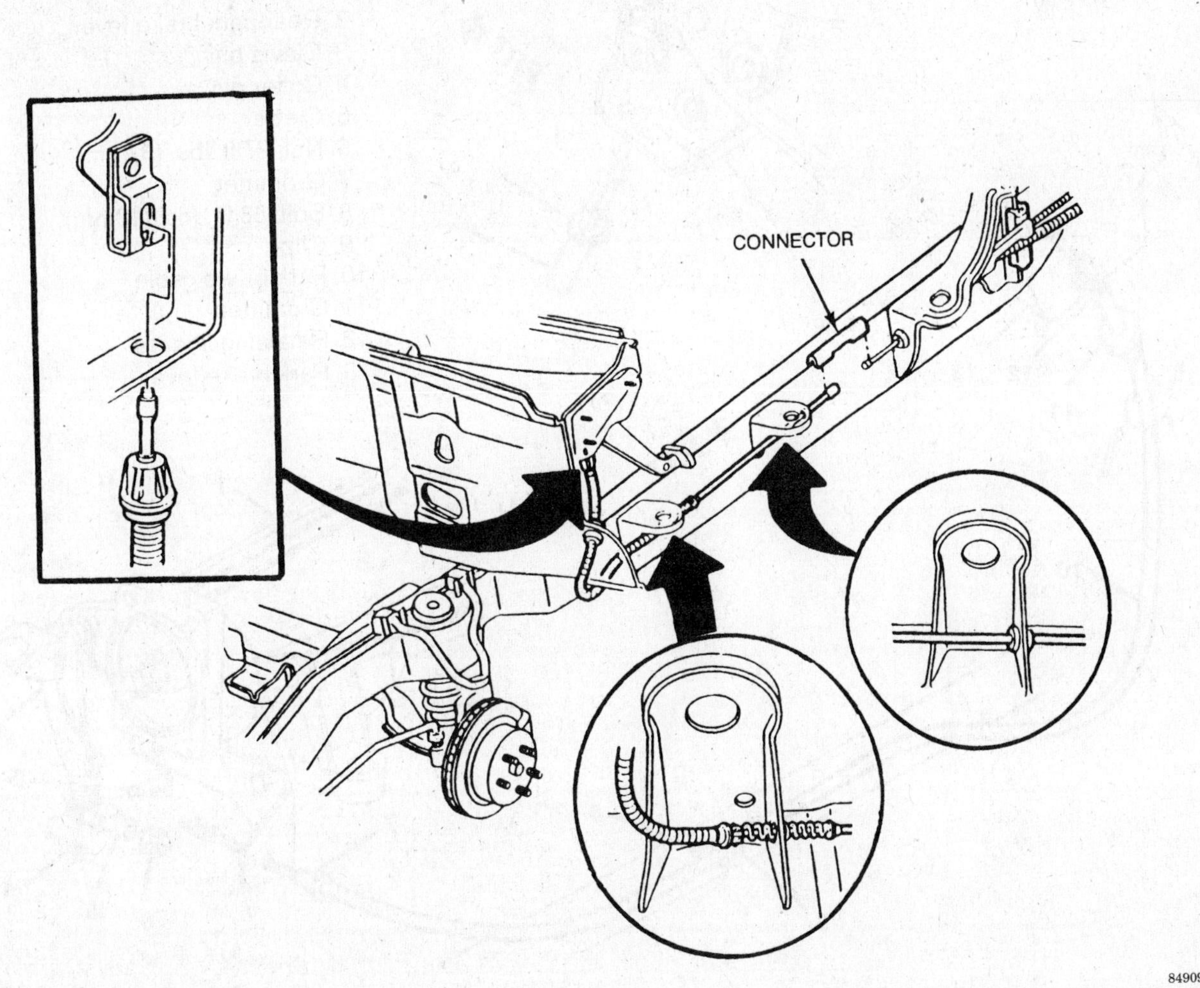

Fig. 88 Front parking brake cable — C/K Series

3. Remove the clevis pin from the brake lever and disconnect the clevis and lock nut from the end of the cable.
4. Pull the cable and grommet out of the lower bracket. Unscrew the bracket bolt on the frame rail.
5. Disconnect the end of the cable at the pedal lever, release the retaining fingers and remove the cable.
6. Install the cable and check the parking brake adjustment.

Center Cable

1. Raise vehicle on hoist.
2. Remove adjusting nut from equalizer.
3. Unhook connector at each end and disengage hooks and guides.
4. Install new cable by reversing removal procedure.
5. Adjust parking brake.
6. Apply parking brake 3 times with heavy pressure and repeat adjustment.

Rear Cable

➧ See Figure 90

1. Raise vehicle and support it on safety stands.
2. Remove rear wheel and brake drum.
3. Loosen adjusting nut at equalizer.
4. Disengage rear cable at connector.
5. Bend retainer fingers at the backing plate.
6. Disengage cable at brake shoe operating lever.
7. Install new cable.
8. Adjust parking brake.

ADJUSTMENT

Duo-Servo Drum Brakes

The rear brakes serve a dual purpose. They are used as service brakes and as parking brakes. To obtain proper adjust-

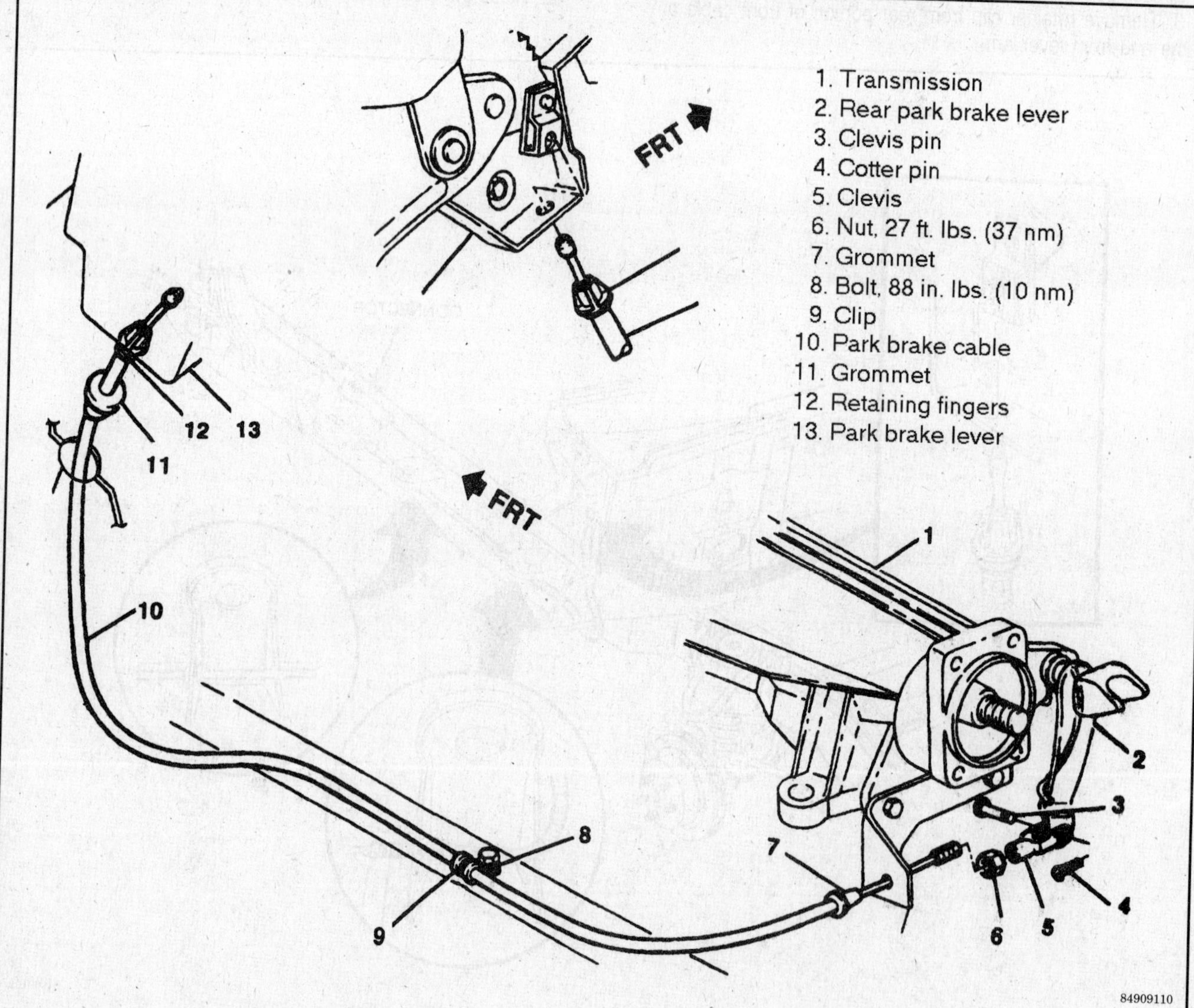

Fig. 89 Parking brake cable — rear disc brakes

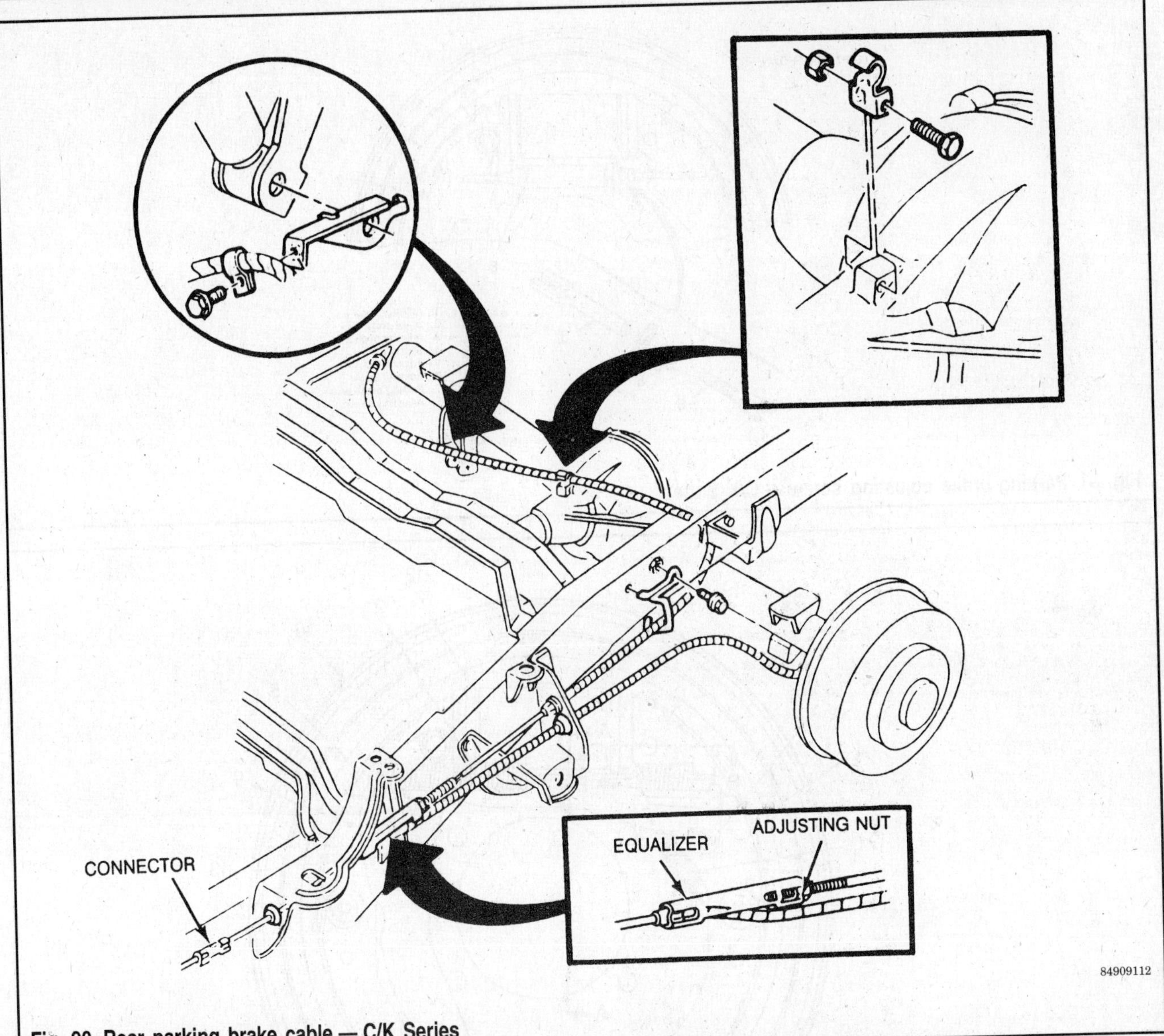

Fig. 90 Rear parking brake cable — C/K Series

ment of the parking brake, the service brakes must first be properly adjusted as outlined earlier.

1. Apply the parking brake 4 clicks from the fully released position.
2. Raise and support the vehicle.
3. Loosen the locknut at the equalizer.
4. Tighten or loosen the adjusting nut until a moderate drag is felt when the rear wheels are rotated forward.
5. Tighten the locknut.
6. Release the parking brake and rotate the rear wheels. No drag should be felt. If even a light drag is felt, readjust the parking brake.
7. Lower the vehicle.

➡If a new parking brake cable is being installed, pre-stretch it by applying the parking brake hard about three times before making adjustments.

Leading/Trailing Drum Brakes

See Figures 91 and 92

1. Raise the rear of the truck and support it with safety stands. Remove the wheels and brake drum.
2. Measure the brake drum inside diameter.
3. Turn the adjuster nut until the brake shoe maximum diameter is 0.01-0.02 in. (0.25-50mm) less than the brake drum diameter.
4. Make sure that the stops on the parking brake levers are against the edge of the brake shoe web. If the cable is holding the stops off the edge, loosen the adjustment.
5. Tighten the cable at the adjuster nut until the lever stops begin to move off the shoe webs.
6. Loosen the adjustment nut until the lever stops are **just** touching the shoe webs. There should be no more than 0.5mm clearance between the stops and the webs.
7. Install the drums and wheels.
8. Pump the brake pedal 30-35 times with normal force. Pause about 1 second between each stroke.

LEFT SIDE SHOWN
1
2
7
8
3
4
5
6
1. Adjuster shoe
2. Brake shoe
3. Adjuster socket
4. Spring
5. Adjuster nut
6. Adjuster screw
7. Parking brake lever
8. Adjusting screw
84909104

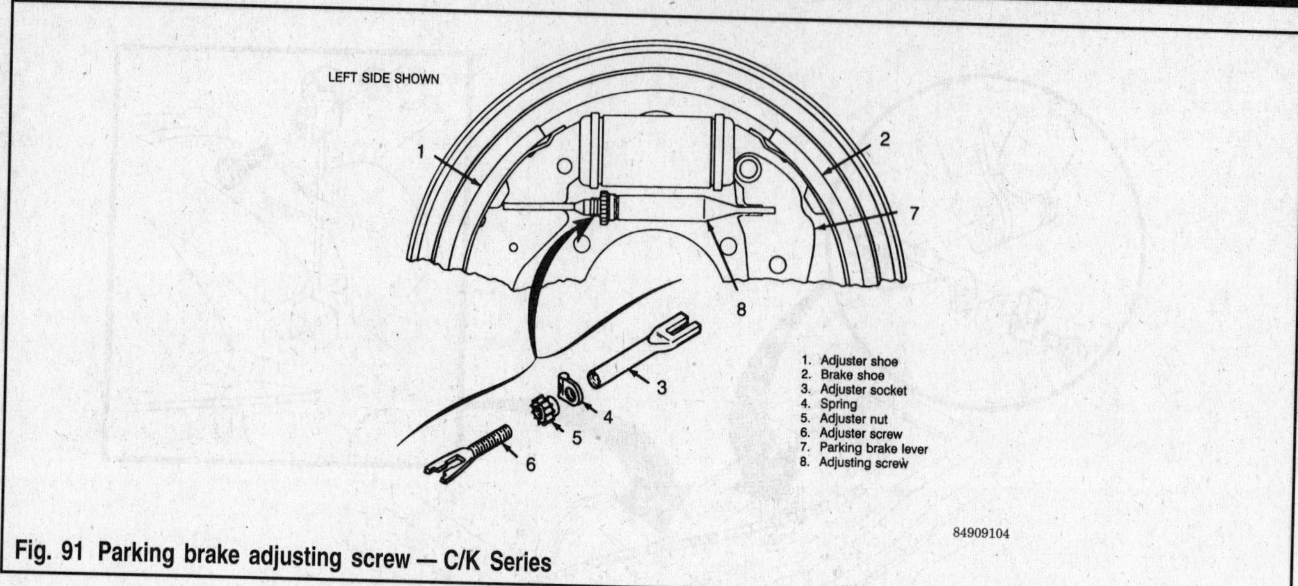

Fig. 91 Parking brake adjusting screw — C/K Series

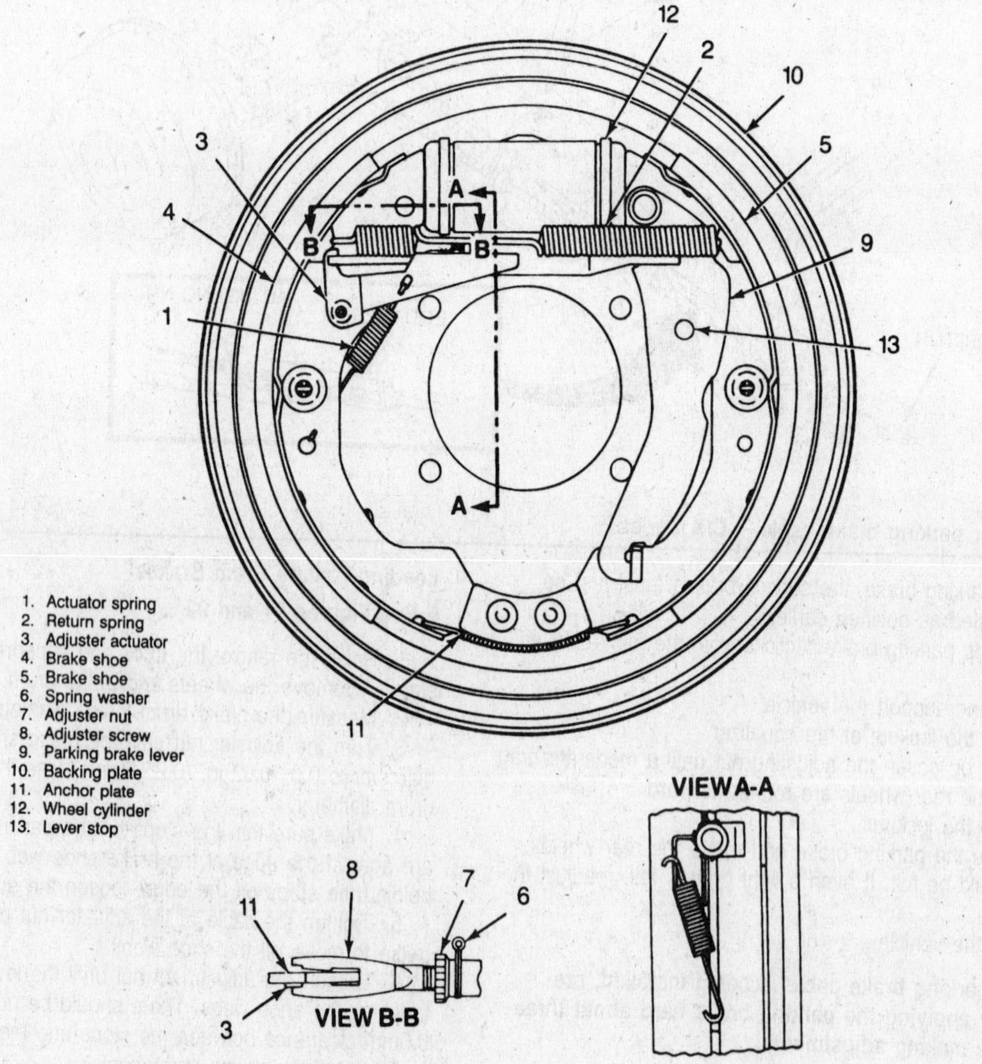

12
2
10
3
5
4
A
B
B
9
1
13
A
1. Actuator spring
2. Return spring
3. Adjuster actuator
4. Brake shoe
5. Brake shoe
6. Spring washer
7. Adjuster nut
8. Adjuster screw
9. Parking brake lever
10. Backing plate
11. Anchor plate
12. Wheel cylinder
13. Lever stop
11
VIEW A-A
8
7
11
6
3
VIEW B-B
84909105

Fig. 92 Left side parking brake assembly — C/K Series

9. Depress the parking brake pedal 6 clicks. The wheels should be locked.
10. Release the parking brake. The wheels should rotate freely.

Disc Brakes

➧ See Figure 93

1. Locate the parking brake drum assembly. Its at the back of the transmission extension housing. Remove the clevis pin from the parking brake lever.
2. Set the parking brake pedal to 4 clicks.
3. Connect a tension gauge to the frame of the truck with a small length of cable and a turn buckle.
4. Connect the tension gauge to the bottom of the parking brake lever and tighten it to 50 lbs. (222N).
5. Loosen the clevis lock nut and turn the clevis until the pin slides freely in the lever. There should be no slack in the cable.
6. Install the clevis pin and a new cotter pin. Tighten the lock nut to 27 ft. lbs. (27 Nm).
7. Remove the gauge and release the parking brake.

Parking Brake Pedal

REMOVAL & INSTALLATION

R/V Series

➧ See Figure 94

1. Fully release the parking brake.
2. Disconnect the release rod at the lever.
3. Remove the attaching bolt and stud nuts.
4. Disconnect the cable end.
5. Lift out the pedal assembly.
6. Installation is the reverse of removal. Tighten all fasteners to 100 inch lbs. (8 Nm).

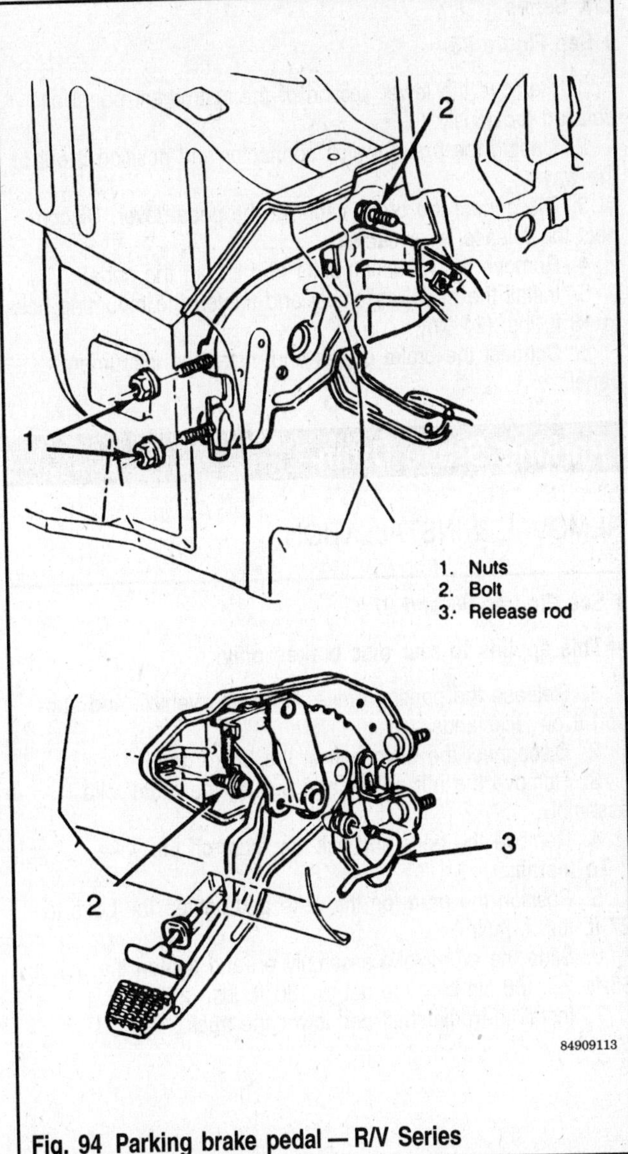

Fig. 94 Parking brake pedal — R/V Series

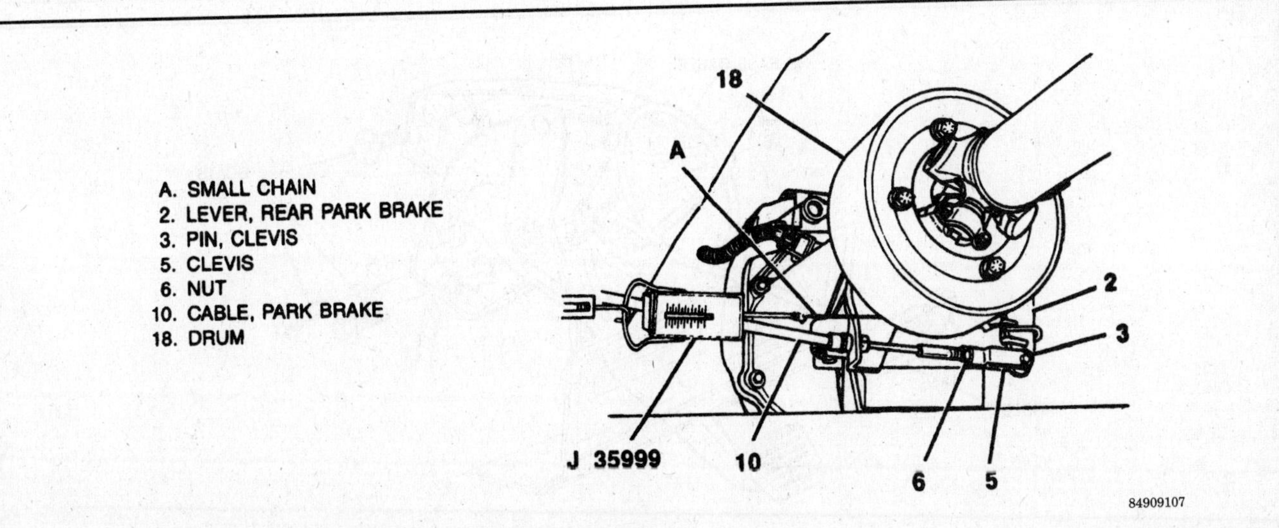

Fig. 93 Adjusting the parking brake on models with rear discs

C/K Series

➧ See Figure 95

1. Remove the lower section of the instrument panel as detailed previously.
2. Unplug the brake switch connector and position it out of the way.
3. Disconnect the brake cable at the pedal lever. Disconnect the release lever cable.
4. Remove the mounting bolts and lift out the pedal.
5. Install the pedal assembly and tighten the mounting bolts to 18 ft. lbs. (24 Nm).
6. Connect the brake cables and install the instrument panel.

Parking Brake Drum

REMOVAL & INSTALLATION

➧ See Figures 96 and 97

➡This applies to rear disc brakes only.

1. Release the parking brake. Raise the vehicle and support it on jackstands.
2. Disconnect the driveshaft at the brake drum.
3. Remove the nut or bolt and pull off the drum/yoke assembly.
4. Remove the bolts and pull the drum off the yoke.

To install:

5. Position the drum on the yoke and tighten the bolts to 27 ft. lbs. (37 Nm).
6. Slide the drum/yoke assembly on and tighten the bolt to 65 ft. lbs. (88 Nm), or the nut to 180 ft. lbs. (255 Nm).
7. Install the driveshaft and lower the truck.

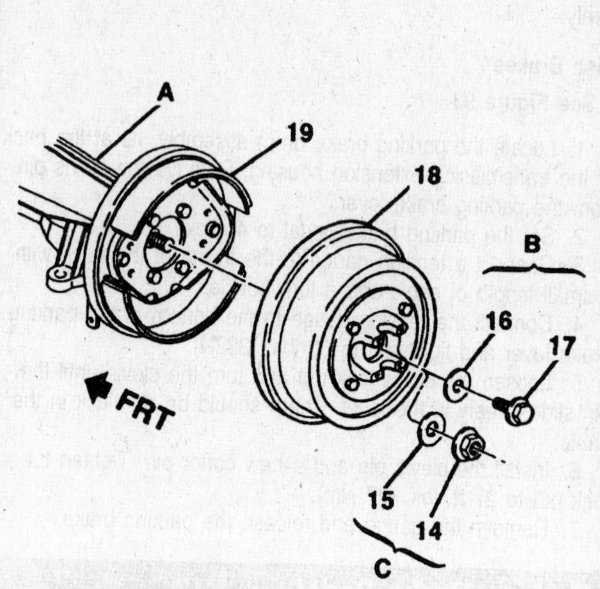

Fig. 96 Removing the parking brake drum on models with rear discs

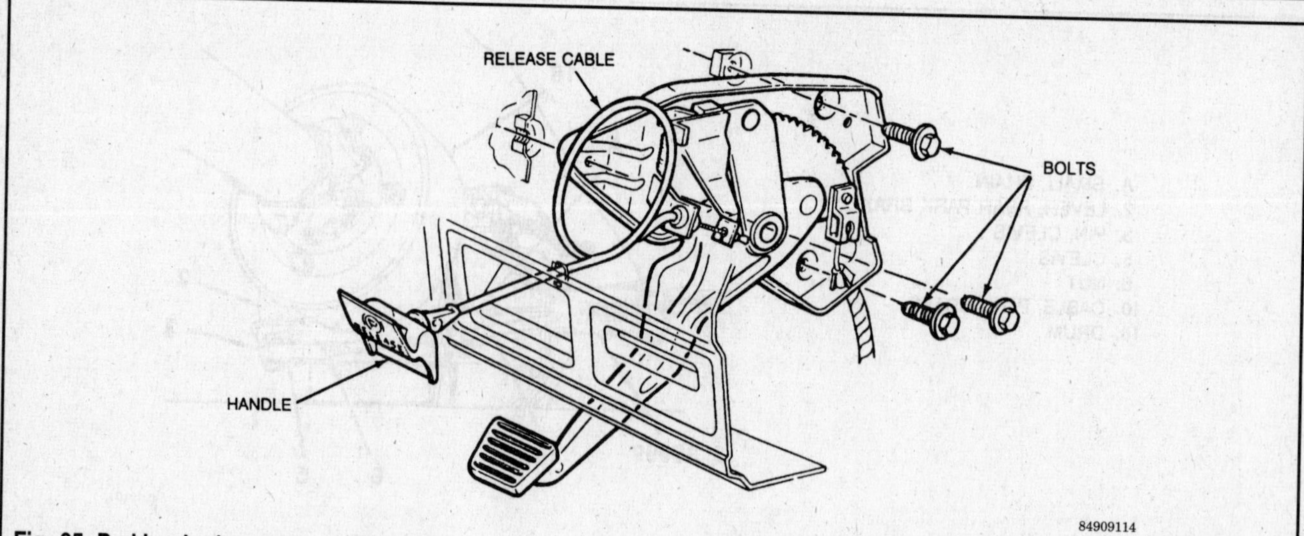

Fig. 95 Parking brake pedal — C/K Series

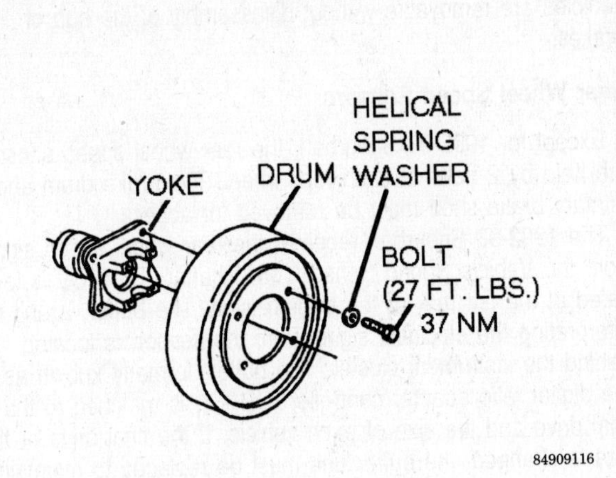

Fig. 97 Removing the drum and yoke assembly

Brake Shoes

REMOVAL & INSTALLATION

◆ See Figure 98

1. Remove the drum. Refer to the procedure in this section.
2. Remove the bolts and washers.
3. Disconnect the support plate and shoe kits.
4. Remove the springs and shoe kits.

To install:

5. Connect the shoe kits to the support plate.
6. Install the springs, support plate and shoe kits.
7. Install the bolts and washers. Tighten the washers to 77 ft. lbs. (105 Nm).
8. Install the drum. Refer to the procedure in this section.

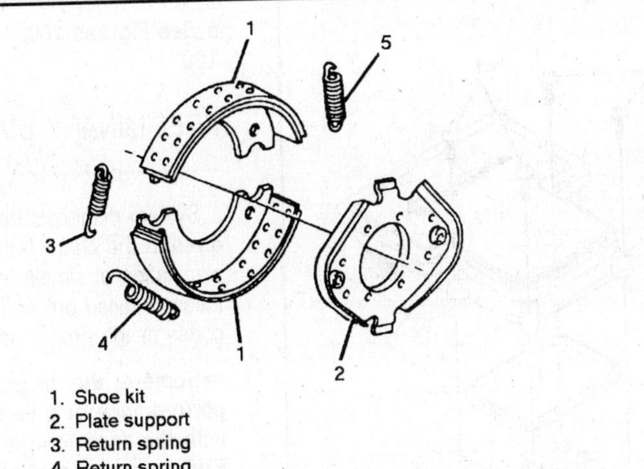

Fig. 98 Exploded view of the rear shoe assembly for the parking brake

FOUR WHEEL ANTI-LOCK BRAKE SYSTEM

General Description

The Kelsey Hayes four wheel anti-lock brake system is used on the 1992-96 Suburban, Jimmy, Yukon and Blazer and C/K Series trucks.

The 4 wheel anti-lock system is designed to reduce brake lock-up during severe brake application. The Electro-Hydraulic Control Unit (EHCU) valve — located near the master cylinder — controls the hydraulic pressure within the brake lines.

The control valve is made up of 2 types of valves. Each front wheel and the combined rear wheel circuit are served by a dedicated isolation valve and a dump valve. The isolation valves maintain pressure within their respective circuits; the dump valves release pressure within each circuit as commanded by the EHCU. The valves are controlled by a microcomputer within the EHCU valve.

SYSTEM OPERATION

In a severe brake application, the EHCU valve will either allow pressure to increase within the system or maintain (isolate) the pressure within the system or release existing pressure through the dump valves into the accumulators.

The EHCU valve operates by receiving signals from the speed sensors, located at each wheel, and from the brake lamp switch. The speed sensors connect directly to the EHCU valve through a multi-pin connector.

The system is connected to the ANTI-LOCK warning lamp on the dashboard. The warning lamp will illuminate for about 2 seconds every time the vehicle is started. The warning lamp will illuminate it the computer detects a problem within the anti-lock system during vehicle operation.

SYSTEM COMPONENTS

EHCU Valve

➧ See Figure 99

The EHCU valve is mounted near or under the master cylinder and combination valve. The valve is not serviceable and must be replaced if malfunctioning.

Front Wheel Speed Sensors

With one exception, on both 2WD and 4WD vehicles, the front wheel speed sensors are permanently mounted to the brake rotor splash shield. With the exception of the 1992-96 Suburban, if the sensor fails the rotor and splash shield must be removed. On 4WD vehicles, the hub and bearing assembly must also be removed for access.

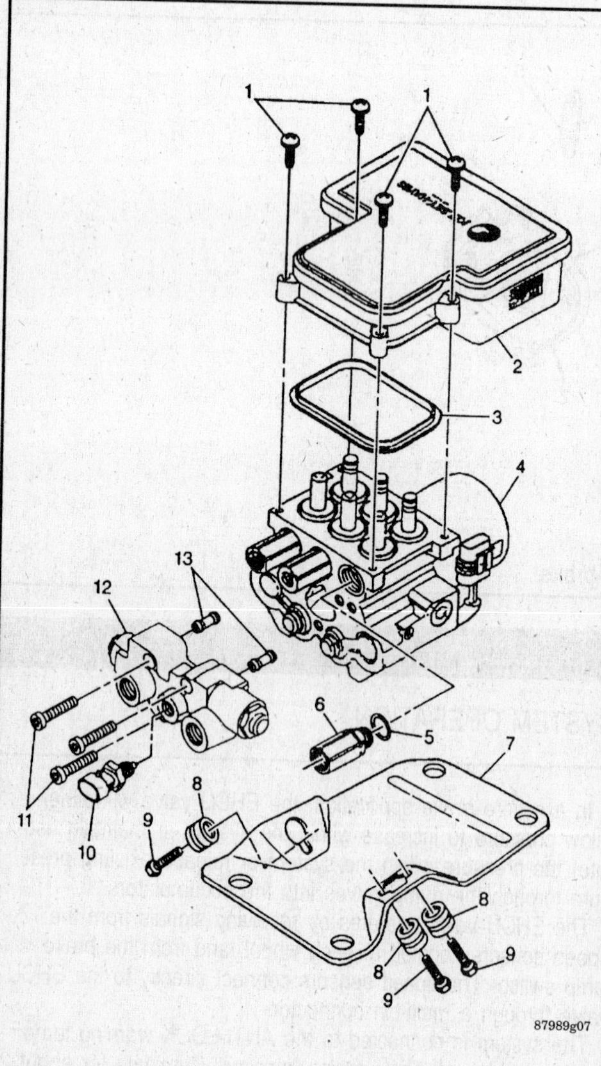

Fig. 99 Exploded view of the Electro-Hydraulic Control Unit (EHCU)

The front wheel speed sensors on 1992-96 4WD Suburban vehicles are removable without disassembly of the hub or brakes.

Rear Wheel Speed Sensors

Except for 1992-93 Suburban, the rear wheel speed sensors are held by 2 bolts at each rear wheel. The brake drum and primary brake shoe must be removed for access.

The 1992-93 Suburban receives the rear wheel speed signal from the Vehicle Speed Sensor (VSS) buffer. The VSS is located at the left rear of the transmission. The buffer, a unit for interpreting the electrical signal from the sensor, is located behind the instrument cluster. The buffer, formerly known as the digital ratio adapter controller (DRAC), is matched to the final drive and tire size of each vehicle. If the final drive or tire size is changed, the buffer unit must be replaced to maintain accurate speedometer/odometer readings and proper ABS function.

Diagnosis and Testing

➧ See Figures 100, 101, 102, 103, 104, 105, 106, 107 and 108

PRELIMINARY DIAGNOSIS

System diagnosis begins with the diagnostic circuit check as given in the chart. If the chart is used correctly, it will aid in elimination of simple, non-system problems such as blown fuses of failed bulbs. The chart will prompt the reading of codes at the proper point in the diagnosis.

➡Some of the diagnostic or repair procedures refer to the performance of a Function Test. This test is performed with the scan tool; it operates all components of the EHCU valve and checks their function. The test cannot be performed without the scan tool.

READING CODES

Stored trouble codes are transmitted through the flashing of the amber ANTI-LOCK dash warning lamp. The system may be put into diagnostic mode with a jumper wire, however, the use of the TECH-1 scan tool or its equivalent is highly recommended. The scan tool will allow performance of the specific system tests called for by the trouble tree for each code.

To read codes without the use of a hand scanner, use a jumper wire to connect Terminal H on the ALDL to either body ground or to terminal A. The terminals must be connected for a few seconds before the code(s) will transmit. Observe the ANTI-LOCK light on the dash and count the flashes in groups: a group of 4 flashes, a pause and a group of 3 flashes indicates Code 43. Codes 12 and 14 are not trouble codes, but may appear with them to indicate normal operation. Not all vehicles use Code 12 or 14.

After the trouble codes have been read, refer to the correct trouble tree for each code. After repairs, repeat the initial diagnostic circuit check to confirm normal operation of the system.

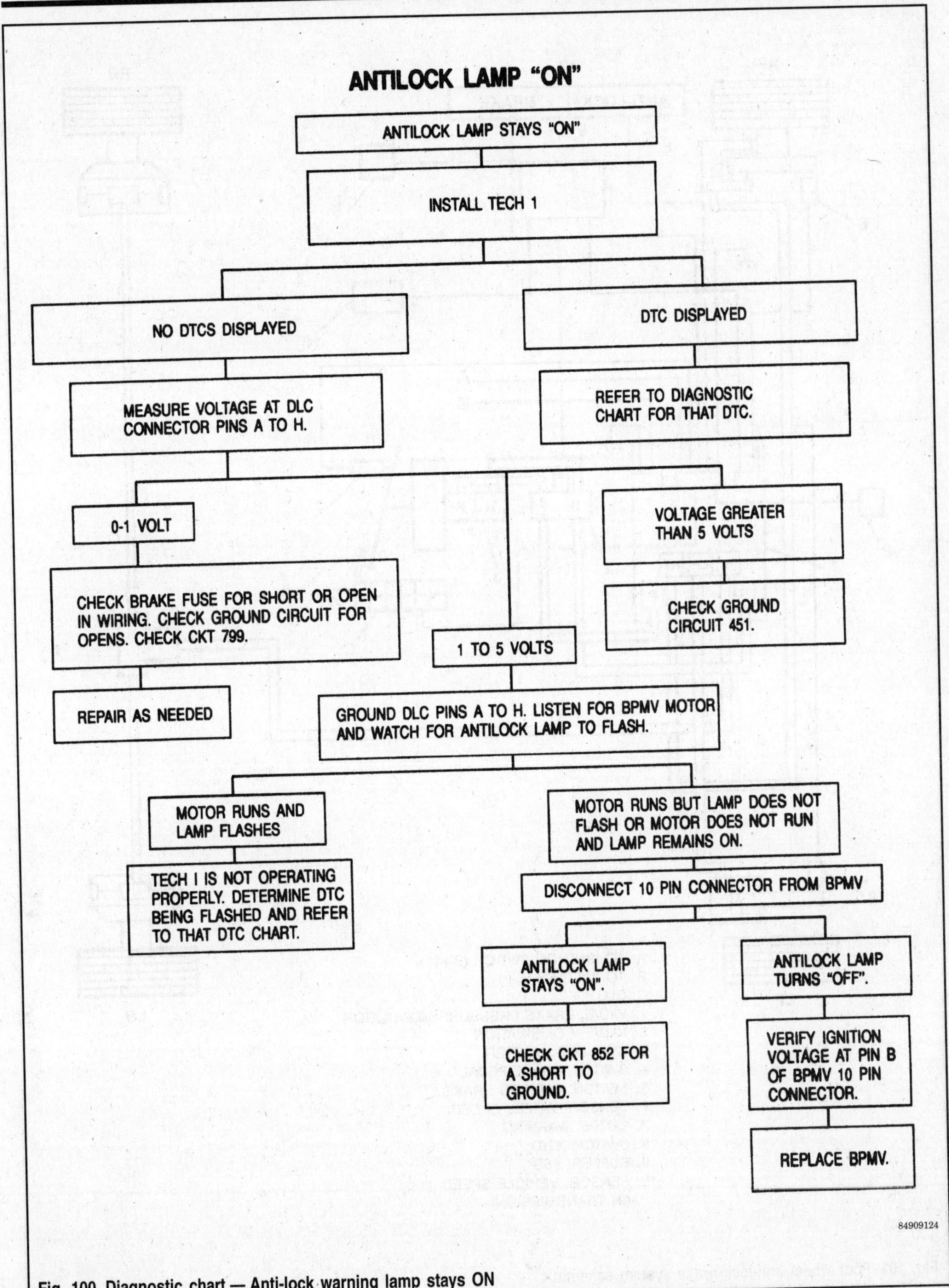

Fig. 100 Diagnostic chart — Anti-lock warning lamp stays ON

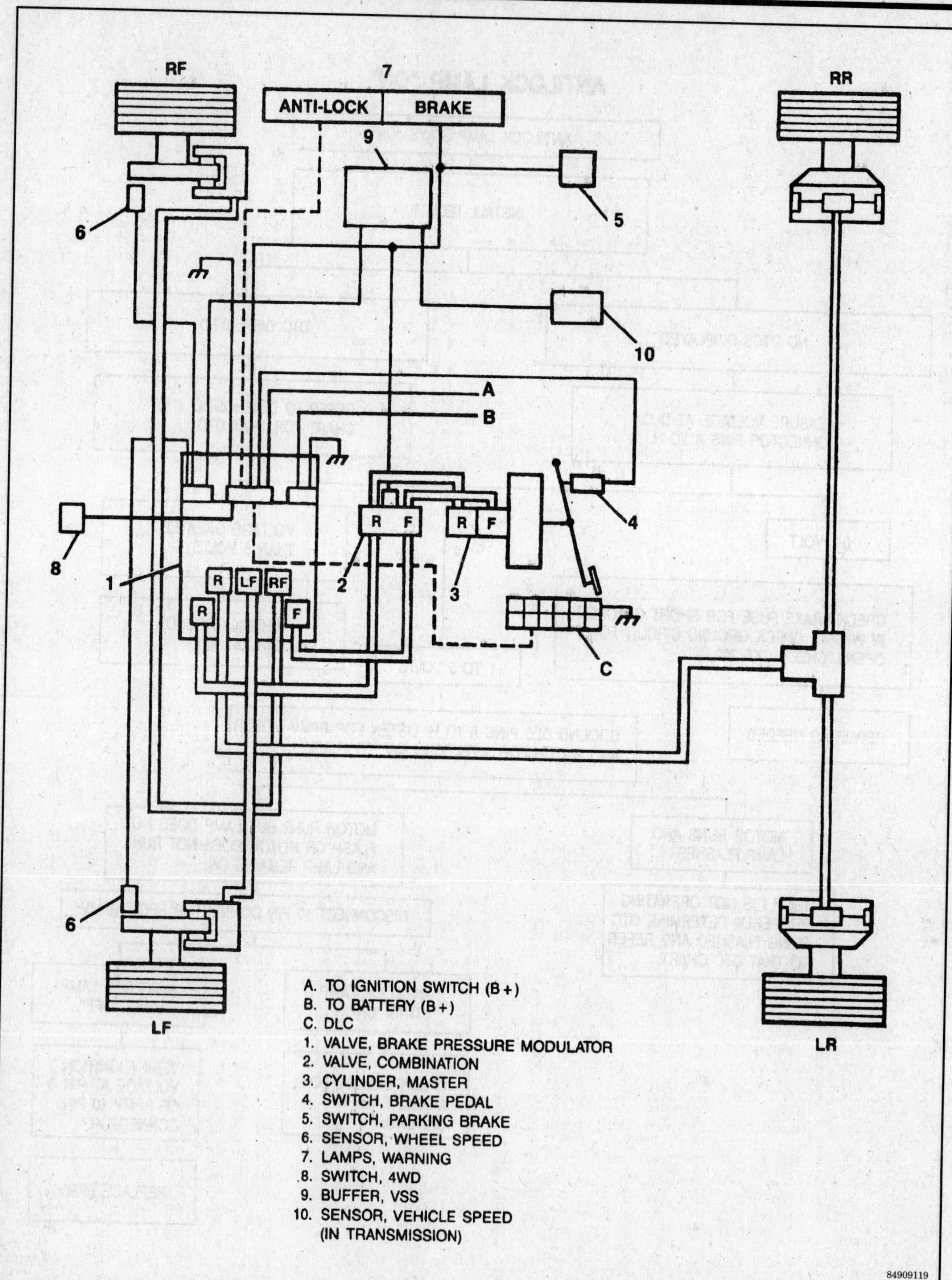

Fig. 101 Four wheel anti-lock brake system schematic

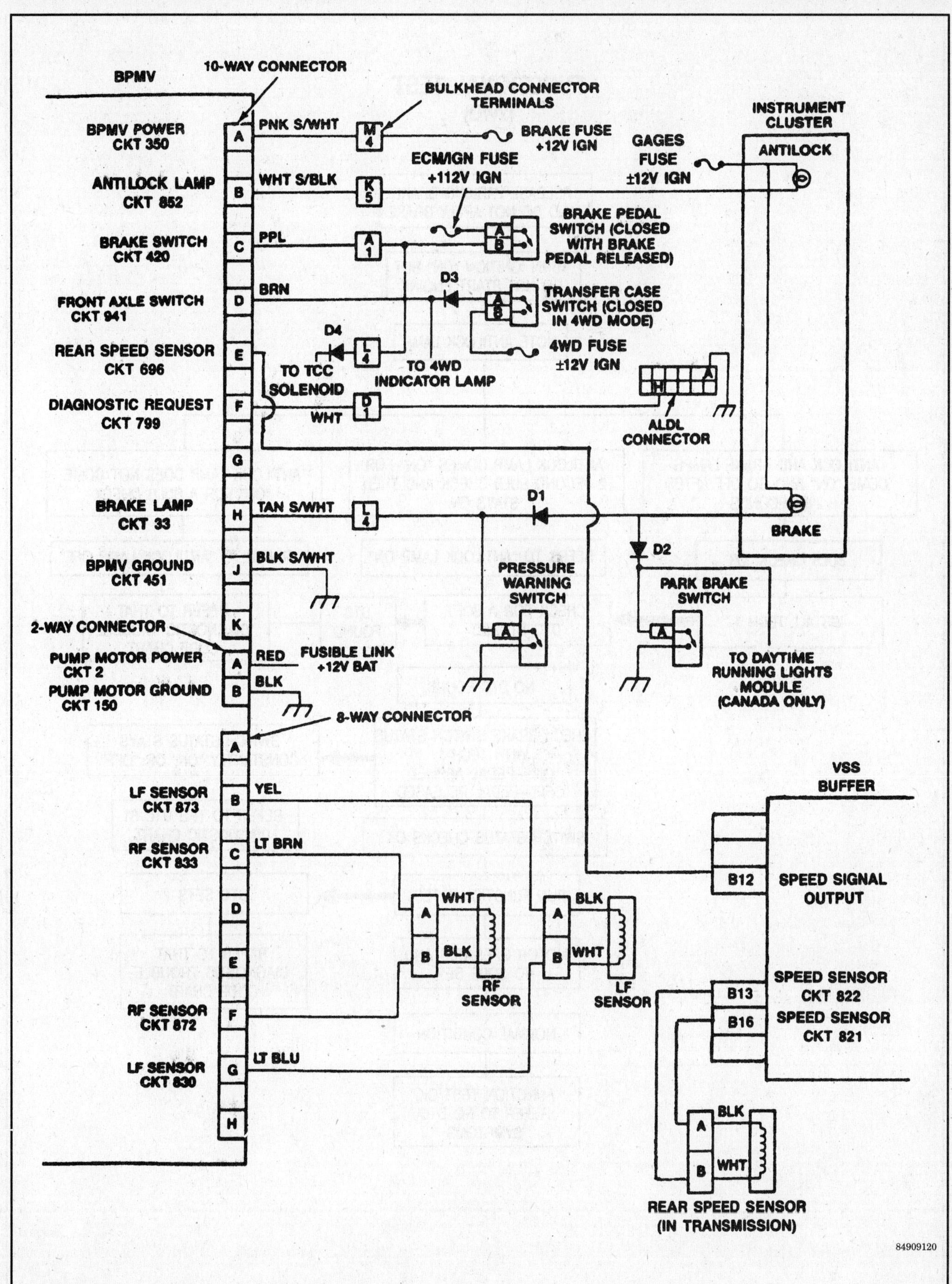

Fig. 102 Wiring diagram — Four wheel anti-lock brake system

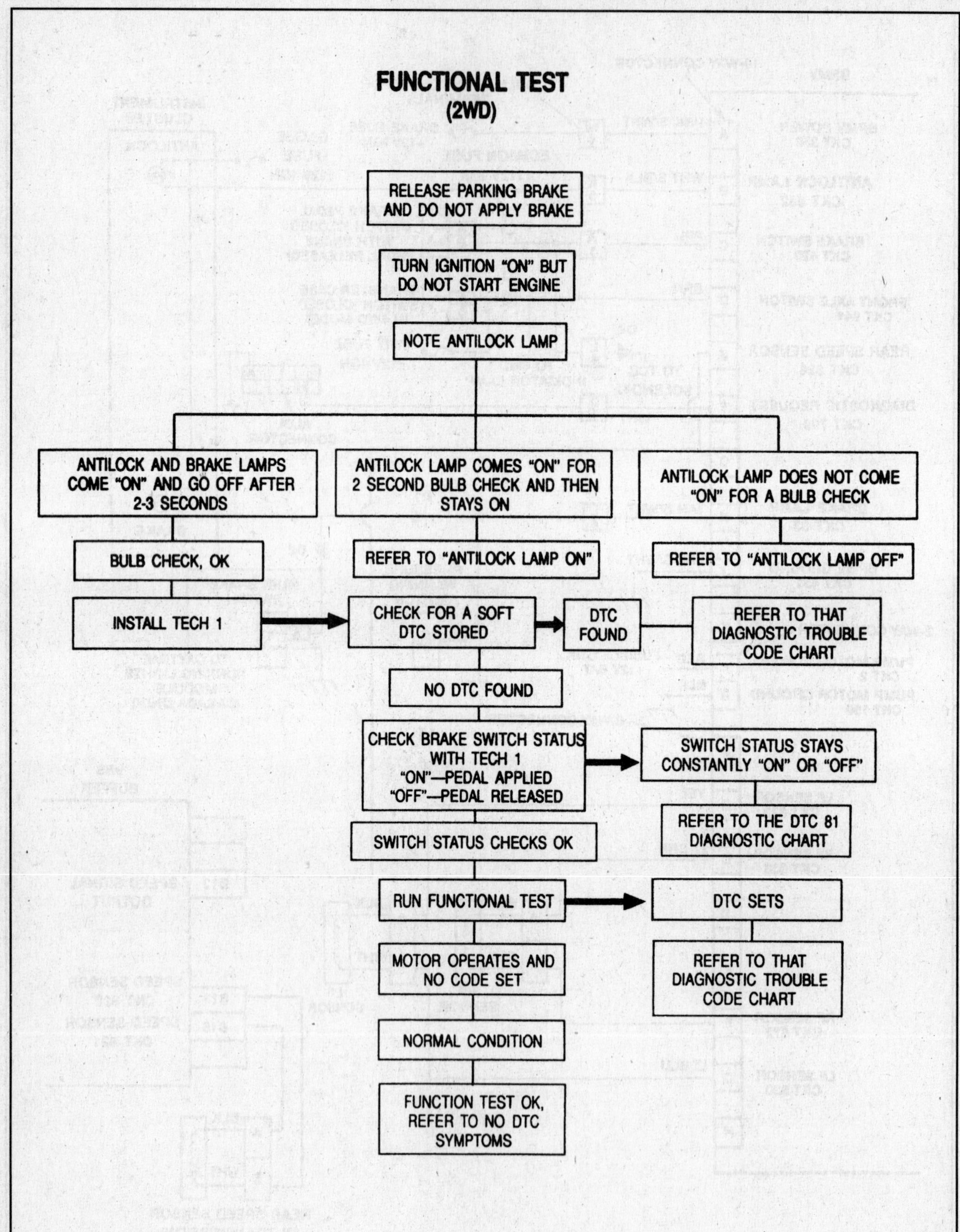

Fig. 103 Functional test — 2WD models

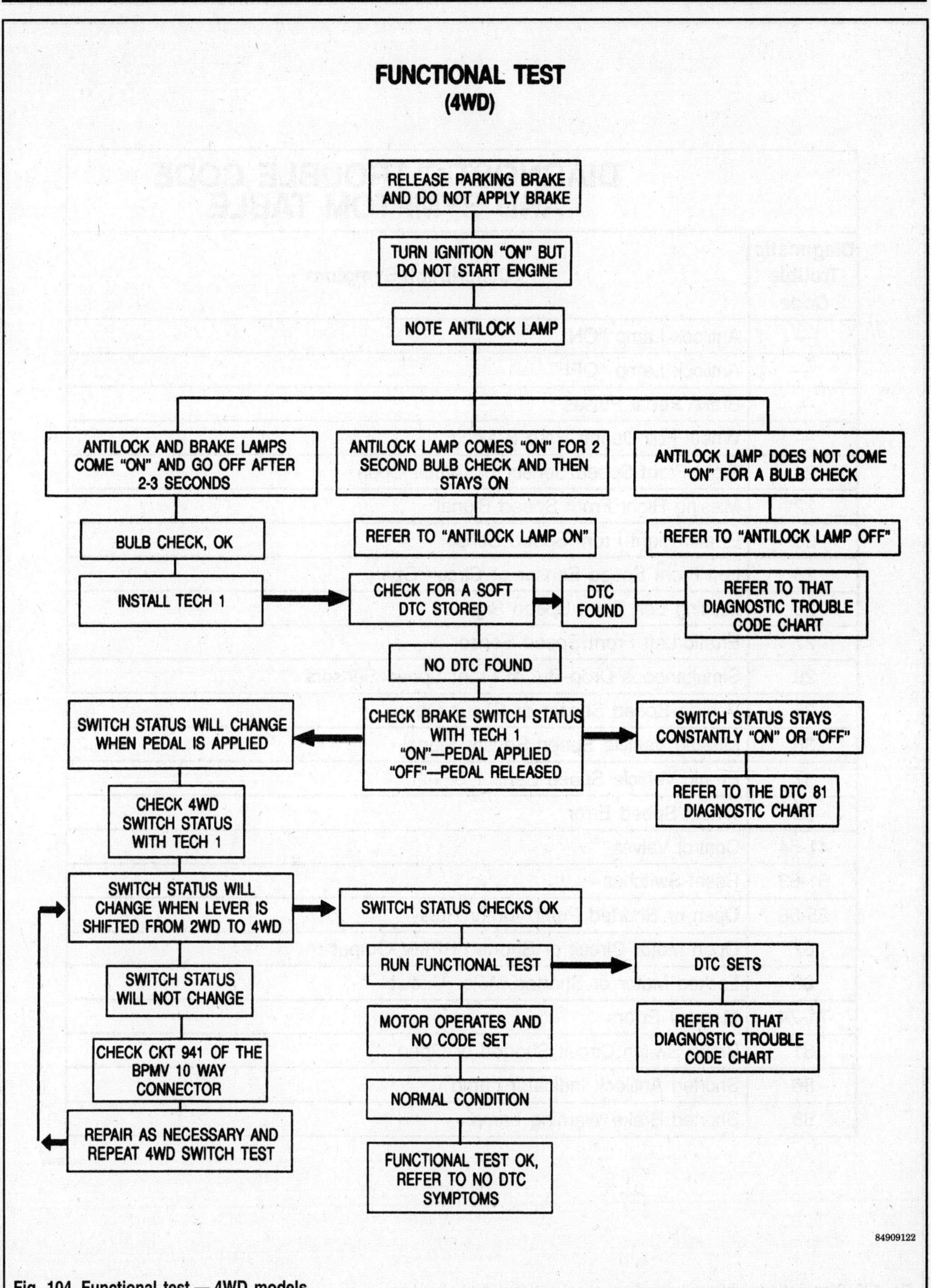

Fig. 104 Functional test — 4WD models

DIAGNOSTIC TROUBLE CODE AND SYMPTOM TABLE

Diagnostic Trouble Code	Description/Symptom
—	Antilock Lamp "ON"
—	Antilock Lamp "OFF"
—	Brake Pedal Pulses
—	Wheel Pull During Hard Braking
21	Right Front Speed Sensor or Circuit Open
22	Missing Right Front Speed Signal
23	Erratic Right Front Speed Sensor
25	Left Front Speed Sensor or Circuit Open
26	Missing Left Front Speed Signal
27	Erratic Left Front Speed Sensor
29	Simultaneous Drop-Out of Front Speed Sensors
35	Vehicle Speed Sensor or Circuit Open
36	Missing Vehicle Speed Sensor Signal
37	Erratic Vehicle Speed Sensor Signal
38	Wheel Speed Error
41-54	Control Valves
61-63	Reset Switches
65-66	Open or Shorted Pump Motor Relay
67	Open Motor Circuit or Shorted BPMV Output
68	Locked Motor or Shorted Motor Circuit
71-74	Memory Errors
81	Brake Switch Circuit Shorted or Open
86	Shorted Antilock Indicator Lamp
88	Shorted Brake Warning Lamp

84909123

Fig. 105 Diagnostic trouble codes — four wheel anti-lock brake system

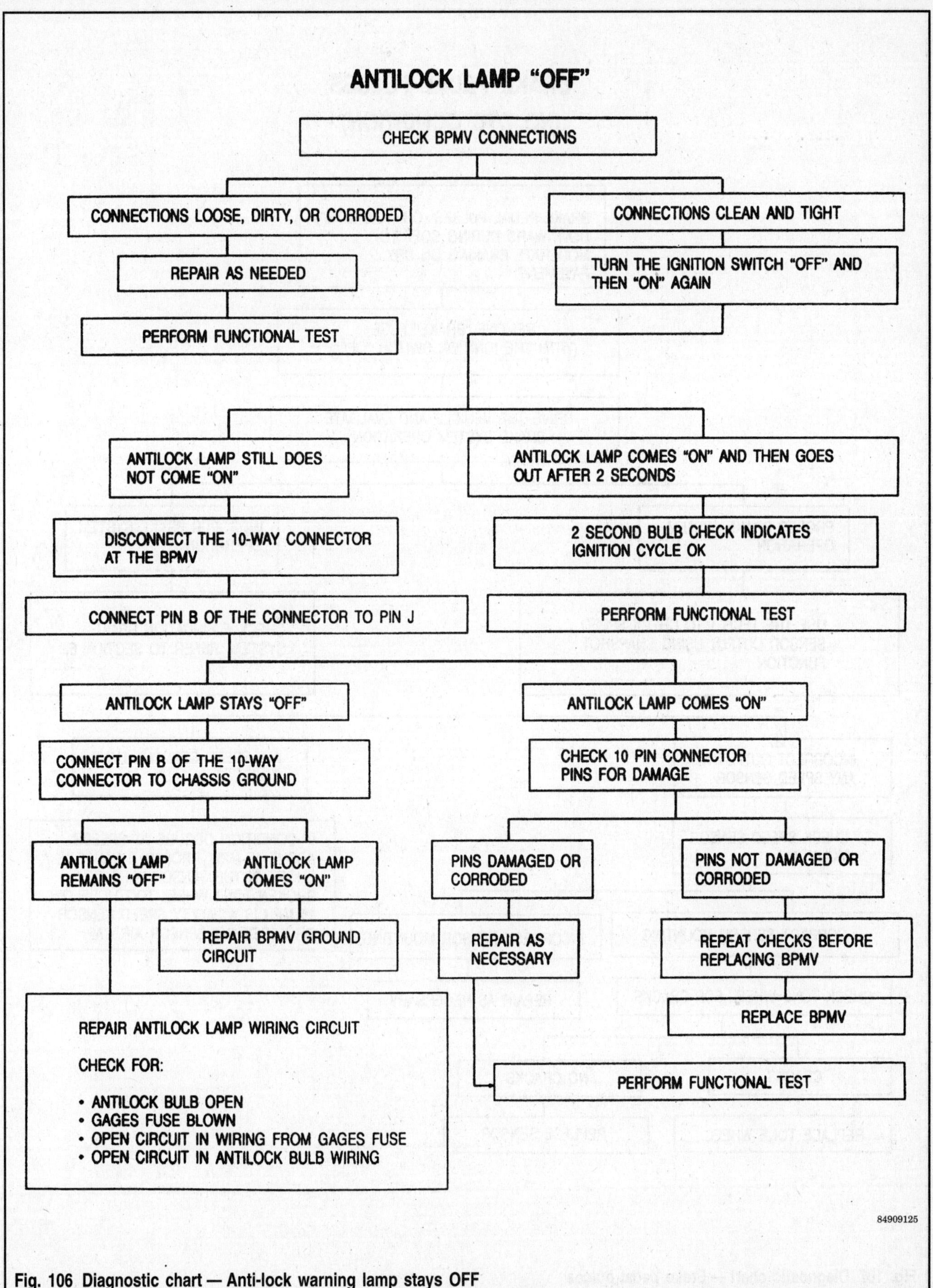

Fig. 106 Diagnostic chart — Anti-lock warning lamp stays OFF

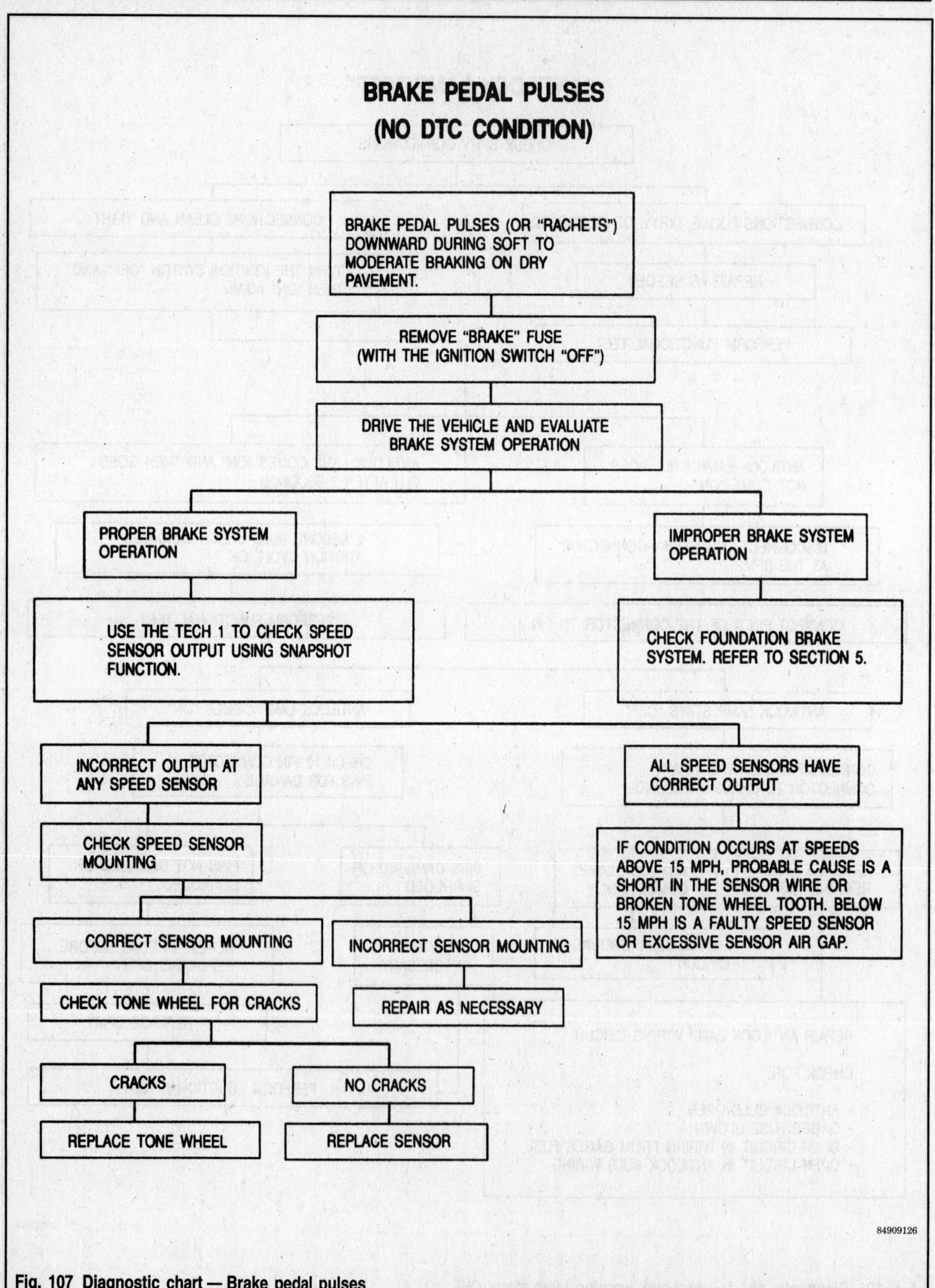

Fig. 107 Diagnostic chart — Brake pedal pulses

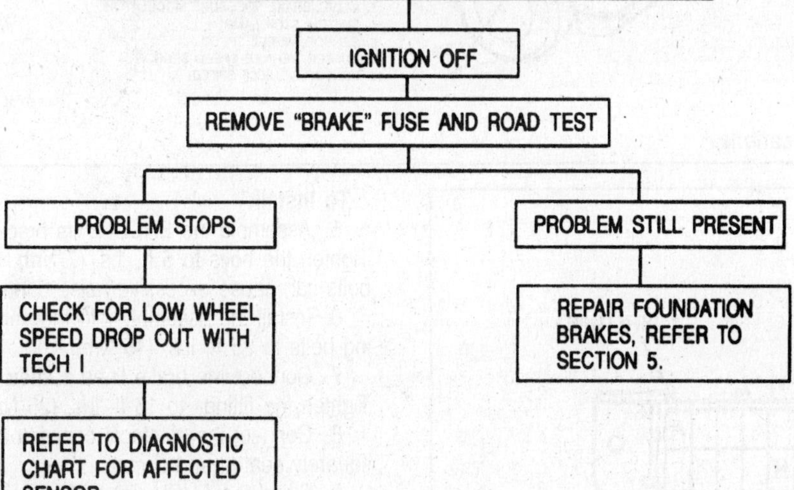

Fig. 108 Diagnostic chart — Wheels pull during hard braking

CLEARING CODES

Stored codes may be erased with the hand scanner if available. If not using a hand scanner, codes may be cleared as follows:

1. Turn the ignition switch **ON** but do not start the engine.
2. Use a jumper wire to ground ALDL terminal H to terminal A for 2 seconds.
3. Remove the jumper wire for 2 seconds.
4. Repeat the grounding and un-grounding two more times. Each connection and opening of the circuit should last 2 seconds.
5. Connect the jumper to terminals H and A for a longer time; no trouble codes should be displayed. If codes are displayed, the system was not properly erased.
6. If no trouble codes appear, the memory has been cleared. Turn the ignition switch **OFF**.

Component Replacement

See Figures 109, 110, 111 and 112

REMOVAL & INSTALLATION

Electro-Hydraulic Control Unit (EHCU) Valve

The EHCU valve is not serviceable and must never be disassembled or repaired. If tests indicate the unit is faulty, the EHCU must be replaced.

1. Label and disconnect the electrical connectors from the EHCU.
2. Label and disconnect the brake lines from the EHCU.
3. Remove the bolts holding the EHCU bracket to the vehicle. Remove the bracket and hydraulic unit as an assembly.
4. Once removed from the vehicle, separate the bracket from the EHCU.

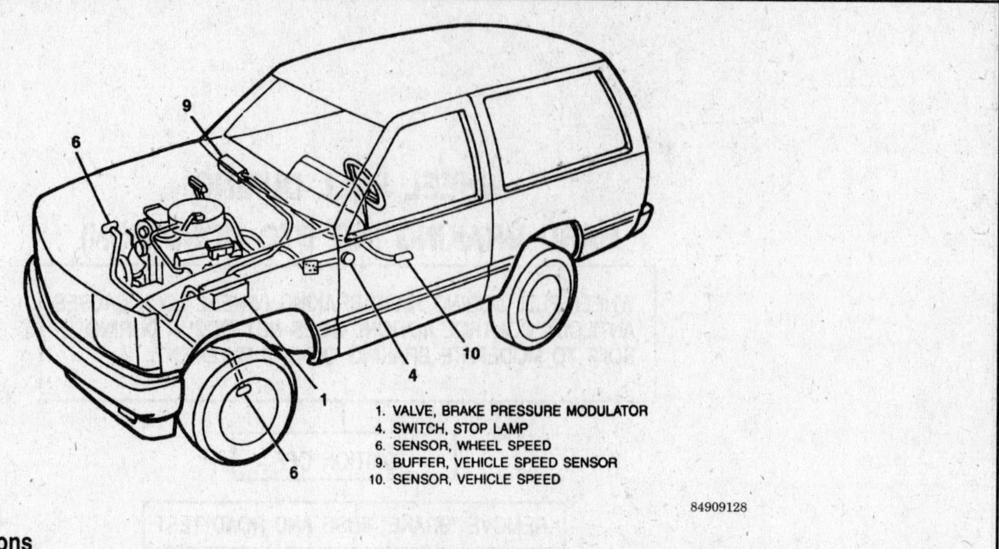

Fig. 109 Component locations

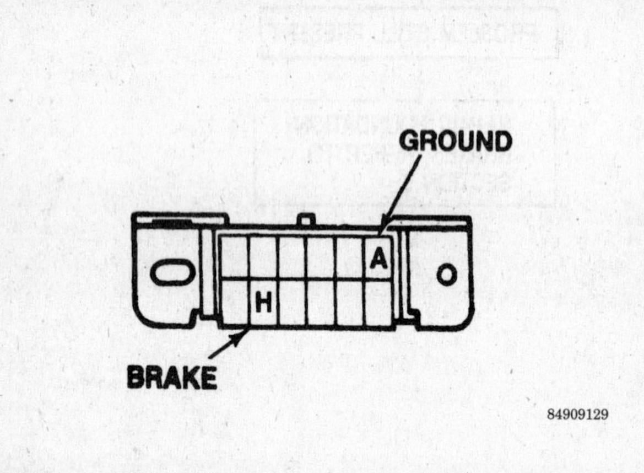

Fig. 110 Data link connector — four wheel anti-lock brake system

To install:

5. Assemble the EHCU to its bracket and install the bolts. Tighten the bolts to 5 ft. lbs. (7 Nm). Overtightening these bolts can cause excessive noise during system operation.
6. Install the assembly into the vehicle. Tighten the mounting bolts to 33 ft. lbs. (45 Nm).
7. Connect the brake lines in their original locations. Tighten the fittings to 16 ft. lbs. (25 Nm).
8. Connect the electrical connectors. Make certain each is squarely seated and secure.
9. Bleed the EHCU valve, then bleed the entire brake system.

Bleeding the EHCU

➡Bleeding the EHCU requires the use of the TECH-1 scanner or its equivalent and the appropriate cartridge. Additionally, 3 tools, J-39177 or equivalent, are required. Bleeding cannot be performed without this equipment.

The EHCU must be bled after replacement or if air is trapped within the unit. It must be bled after bleeding the

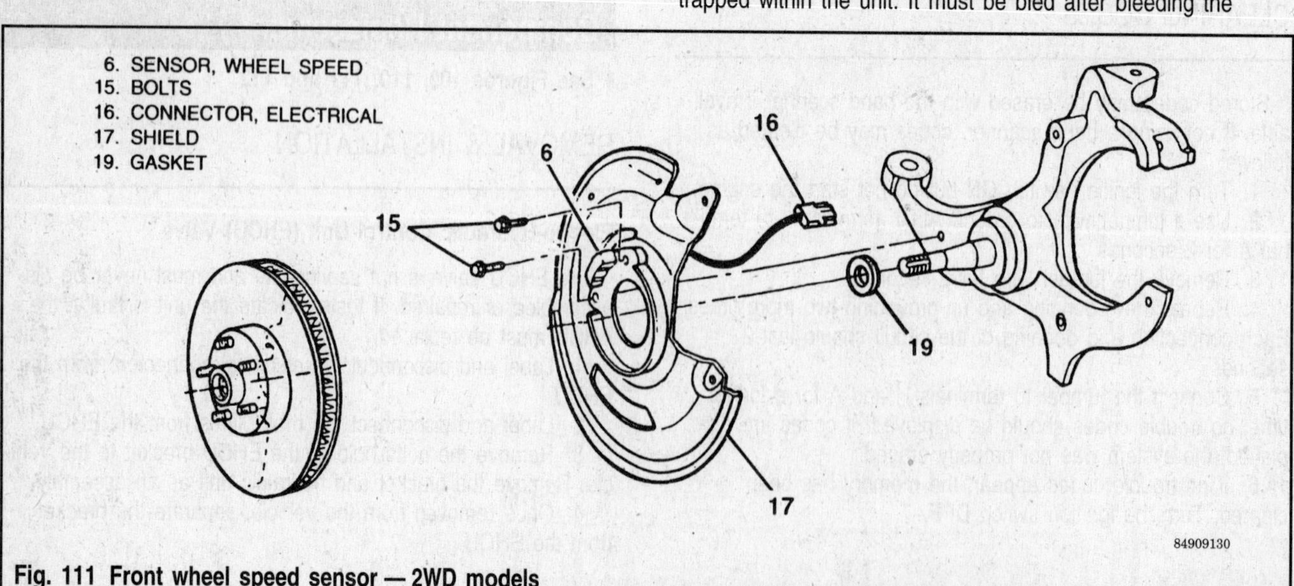

Fig. 111 Front wheel speed sensor — 2WD models

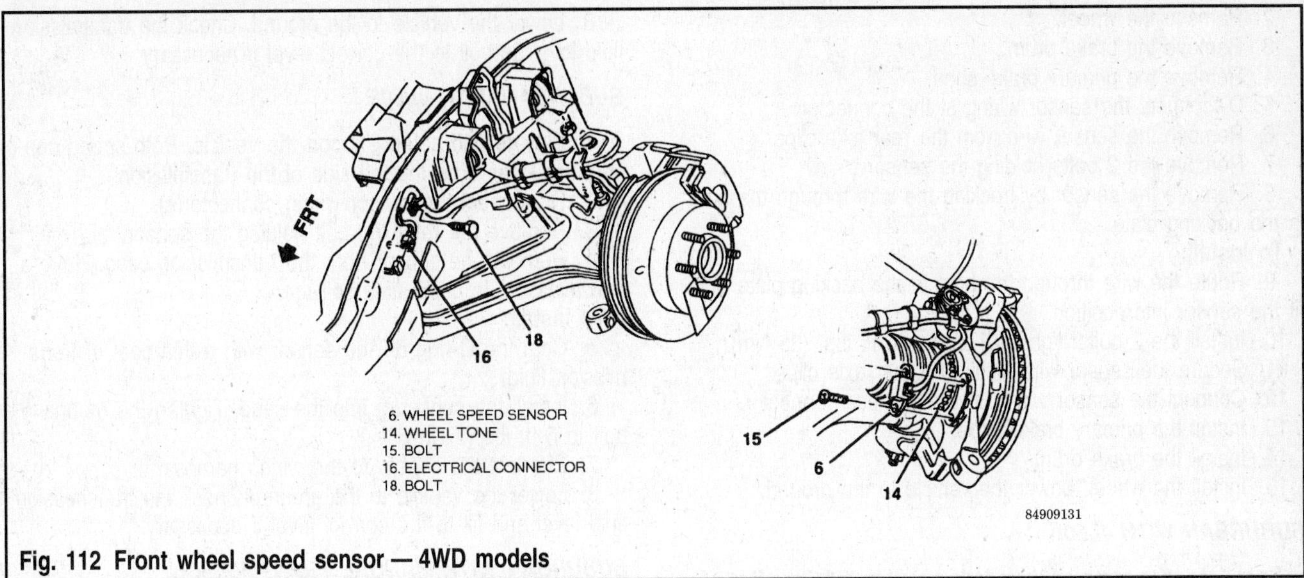

Fig. 112 Front wheel speed sensor — 4WD models

master cylinder and before bleeding the individual wheel circuits.

The Internal Bleed Valves on either side of the unit must be opened ¼-½ turn before bleeding begins. These valves open internal passages within the unit. Actual bleeding is performed at the two bleeders on the front of the EHCU module. The bleeders must not be opened when the system is not pressurized. The ignition switch must be **OFF** or false trouble codes may be set.

1. Open the internal bleed valve ¼-½ turn each.
2. Install one tool J-39177 on the left bleed stem of the EHCU. Install one tool on the right bleed stem and install the third tool on the combination valve.
3. Inspect the fluid level in the master cylinder, filling if needed.
4. Slowly depress the brake pedal and hold it down.
5. Open the left bleeder on the front of the unit. Allow fluid to flow until no air is seen or until the brake pedal bottoms.
6. Close the left bleeder, then slowly release the pedal. Wait 15 seconds.
7. Repeat Steps 4, 5 and 6, including the 15 second wait, until no air is seen in the fluid.
8. Tighten the left internal bleed valve to 5 ft. lbs (7 Nm).
9. Repeat Steps 3-7 at the right bleeder on the front of the unit.
10. When bleeding of the right port is complete, tighten the right internal bleed valve to 5 ft. lbs (7 Nm).
11. Remove the 3 special tools.
12. Check the master cylinder fluid level, refilling as necessary.
13. Bleed the individual brake circuits at each wheel.
14. Switch the ignition **ON**. Use the hand scanner to perform 3 function tests on the system.
15. Carefully test drive the vehicle at moderate speeds; check for proper pedal feel and brake operation. If any problem is noted in feel or function, repeat the entire bleeding procedure.

Front Wheel Speed Sensors

➧ See Figures 111 and 112

EXCEPT 1992-96 4WD SUBURBAN

1. Elevate and safely support the vehicle.
2. Remove the wheel.
3. Remove the brake caliper.
4. For 2WD vehicles, remove the hub and rotor assembly. On 4WD and AWD vehicles, remove the brake rotor and then remove the hub and bearing assembly.
5. Disconnect the sensor wire connector.
6. Disconnect the sensor wire from the clip(s) on the upper control arm.
7. Remove the bolts holding the splash shield.
8. Remove the splash shield and sensor assembly.

To install:

9. Mount the sensor and splash shield to the knuckle. Install the retaining bolts and tighten them to 11 ft. lbs. (15 Nm).
10. Connect the wiring to the clips on the upper control arm. Check the wiring for correct routing.
11. Connect the wiring connector.
12. Install the hub, bearing and rotor or the hub and rotor assembly.
13. Install the brake caliper.
14. Install the wheel. Lower the vehicle to the ground.

1992-96 4WD SUBURBAN

1. Elevate and safely support the vehicle.
2. Remove the wheel.
3. Disconnect the sensor electrical connector.
4. Release the sensor wire from the clip(s) on the upper control arm.
5. Remove the bolts holding the sensor; remove the sensor from its mount.
6. Reassemble in reverse order. Tighten the sensor mounting bolts to 11 ft. lbs. (15 Nm).

Rear Wheel Speed Sensor

EXCEPT SUBURBAN

1. Elevate and safely support the vehicle.

2. Remove the wheel.
3. Remove the brake drum.
4. Remove the primary brake shoe.
5. Disconnect the sensor wiring at the connector.
6. Remove the sensor wire from the rear axle clips.
7. Remove the 2 bolts holding the sensor.
8. Remove the sensor by tracking the wire through the hole in the backing plate.

To install:

9. Route the wire through the hole in the backing plate and fit the sensor into position.
10. Install the 2 bolts; tighten them to 26 ft. lbs. (35 Nm).
11. Secure the sensor wire within the rear axle clips.
12. Connect the sensor wiring to the harness connector.
13. Install the primary brake shoe.
14. Install the brake drum.
15. Install the wheel. Lower the vehicle to the ground.

SUBURBAN WITH 4L60E

➡Speed sensor removal/installation tool J-38417 or its equivalent is required for this procedure.

1. Elevate and safely support the vehicle. The speed sensor is located on the left side of the transmission.
2. Disconnect the sensor wiring connector.
3. Remove the retaining bolt holding the sensor.
4. Using the removal tool, remove the sensor from the transmission case. Have a pan available to catch fluid spillage.

To install:

5. Coat the O-ring on the sensor with a thin coat of transmission fluid.
6. Using the installation tool, install the sensor into the case. Tighten the mounting bolt to 8 ft. lbs (11 Nm).
7. Connect the sensor to the wiring harness.
8. Lower the vehicle to the ground. Check the transmission fluid level and fill to the correct level if necessary.

SUBURBAN WITH 4L80E

1. Elevate and safely support the vehicle. Both speed sensors are located on the left side of the transmission.
2. Disconnect the sensor wiring connector(s).
3. Remove the retaining bolt holding the sensor.
4. Remove the sensor from the transmission case. Have a pan available to catch fluid spillage.

To install:

5. Coat the O-ring on the sensor with a thin coat of transmission fluid.
6. Install the sensor(s) into the case. Tighten the mounting bolt to 5 ft. lbs (7 Nm).
7. Connect the sensor to the wiring harness.
8. Lower the vehicle to the ground. Check the transmission fluid level and fill to the correct level if necessary.

SUBURBAN WITH MANUAL TRANSMISSION

1. Elevate and safely support the vehicle. The speed sensor is located on the left side of the transmission.
2. Disconnect the sensor wiring connector.
3. Remove the retaining bolt holding the sensor.
4. Remove the sensor from the transmission case. Have a pan available to catch fluid spillage.

To install:

5. Coat the O-ring on the sensor with a thin coat of transmission fluid.
6. Install the sensor into the case. Tighten the mounting bolt to 5 ft. lbs (7 Nm).
7. Connect the sensor to the wiring harness.
8. Lower the vehicle to the ground. Check the transmission fluid level and fill to the correct level if necessary.

REAR WHEEL ANTI-LOCK (RWAL) BRAKE SYSTEM

General Description

➧ See Figures 113 and 114

The Kelsey Hayes RWAL system is found on Chevrolet and GMC products including Suburban and C/K Series pick-ups. The system is particularly useful because of the wide variations of loading the vehicle may experience. Preventing rear wheel lock-up often makes the difference in controlling the vehicle during hard or sudden stops.

Found on both 2WD and 4WD vehicles, the RWAL system is designed to regulate rear hydraulic brake line pressure, preventing wheel lock-up at the rear. Pressure regulation is managed by the control valve, located under the master cylinder. The control valve is capable of holding, increasing or decreasing brake line pressure based on electrical commands from the RWAL Electronic Control Unit (ECU) or Electronic Brake Control Module (EBCM).

The RWAL ECU is a separate and dedicated microcomputer mounted next to the master cylinder; it is not to be confused with the engine management ECU. The RWAL ECU receives signals from the speed sensor. The speed sensor sends its signals to the Vehicle Speed Sensor buffer (previously known as the Digital Ratio Adapter Controller or DRAC) within the instrument cluster. The buffer translates the sensor signal into a form usable by the ECU. The RWAL ECU reads this signal and commands the control valve to function. If commanded to release pressure, the dump valve releases pressurized fluid into the accumulator where it is held under pressure. If a pressure increase is called for, the isolator valve within the control valve pulses, releasing pressurized fluid into the system.

The RWAL system is connected to the BRAKE warning lamp on the instrument cluster. A RWAL self-check and a bulb test are performed every time the ignition switch is turned to **ON**. The BRAKE warning lamp should illuminate for about 2 seconds and then go off. Problems within the RWAL system will be indicated by the BRAKE warning lamp staying illuminated.

If a fault is detected within the system, the RWAL ECU will assign a fault code and store the code in memory. The code may be read to aid in diagnosis.

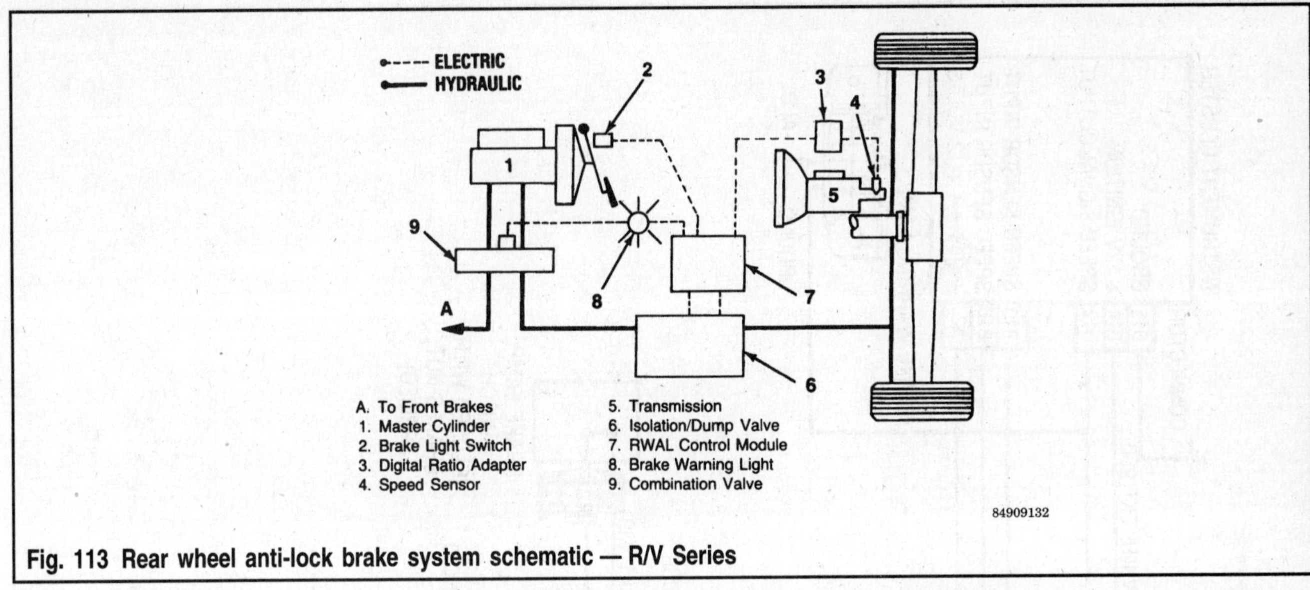

Fig. 113 Rear wheel anti-lock brake system schematic — R/V Series

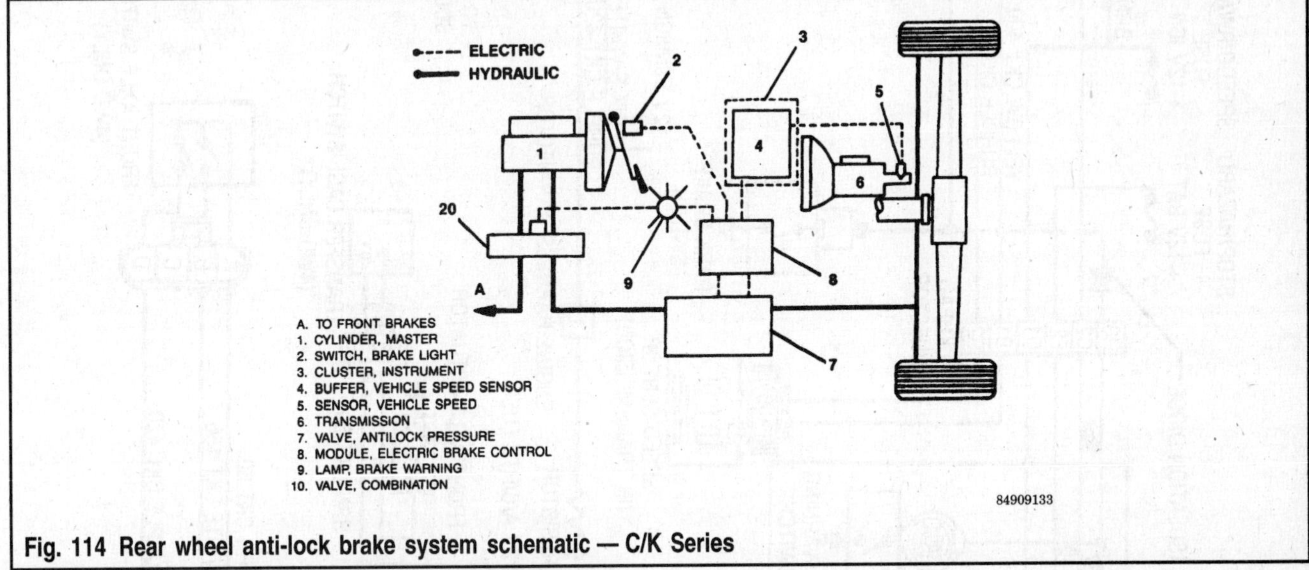

Fig. 114 Rear wheel anti-lock brake system schematic — C/K Series

Diagnosis and Testing

See Figures 115, 116, 117, 118, 119, 120, 121 and 122

SYSTEM PRECAUTIONS

- If the vehicle is equipped with air bag (SIR) system, always properly disable the system before commencing work on the ABS system.
- Certain components within the RWAL system are not intended to be serviced or repaired. Only those components with removal & Installation procedures should be serviced.
- Do not use rubber hoses or other parts not specifically specified for the RWAL system. When using repair kits, replace all parts included in the kit. Partial or incorrect repair may lead to functional problems.
- Lubricate rubber parts with clean, fresh brake fluid to ease assembly. Do not use lubricated shop air to clean parts; damage to rubber components may result.
- Use only brake fluid from an unopened container. Use of suspect or contaminated brake fluid can reduce system performance and/or durability.
- A clean repair area is essential. Perform repairs after components have been thoroughly cleaned; use only denatured alcohol to clean components. Do not allow components to come into contact with any substance containing mineral oil; this includes used shop rags.
- The RWAL ECU is a microprocessor similar to other computer units in the vehicle. Insure that the ignition switch is **OFF** before removing or installing controller harnesses. Avoid static electricity discharge at or near the controller.
- Never disconnect any electrical connection with the ignition switch **ON** unless instructed to do so in a test.
- Always wear a grounded wrist strap when servicing any control module or component labeled with a Electrostatic Discharge (ESD) symbol.
- Avoid touching module connector pins.
- Leave new components and modules in the shipping package until ready to install them.

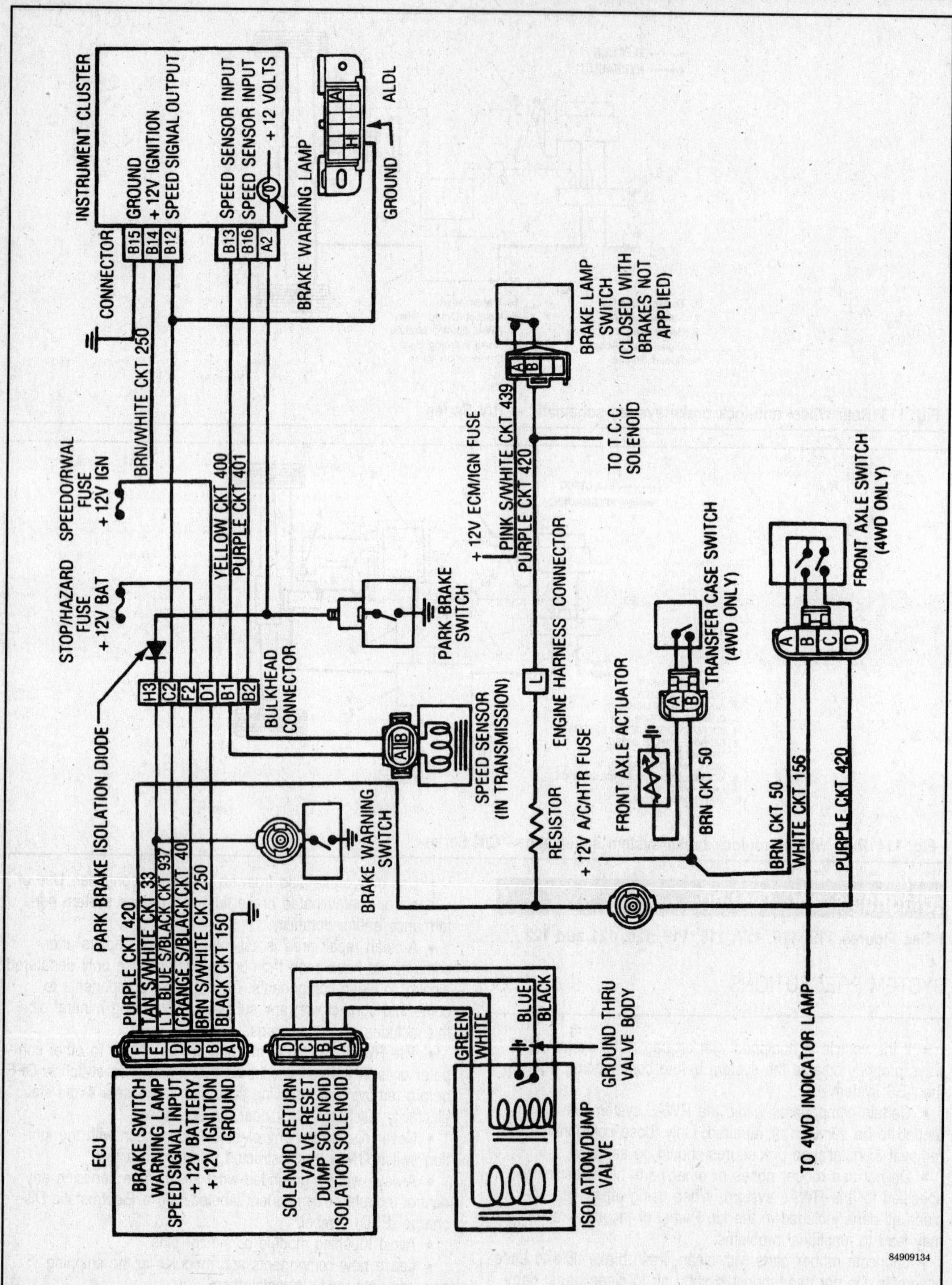

Fig. 115 Wiring diagram — rear wheel anti-lock brake system

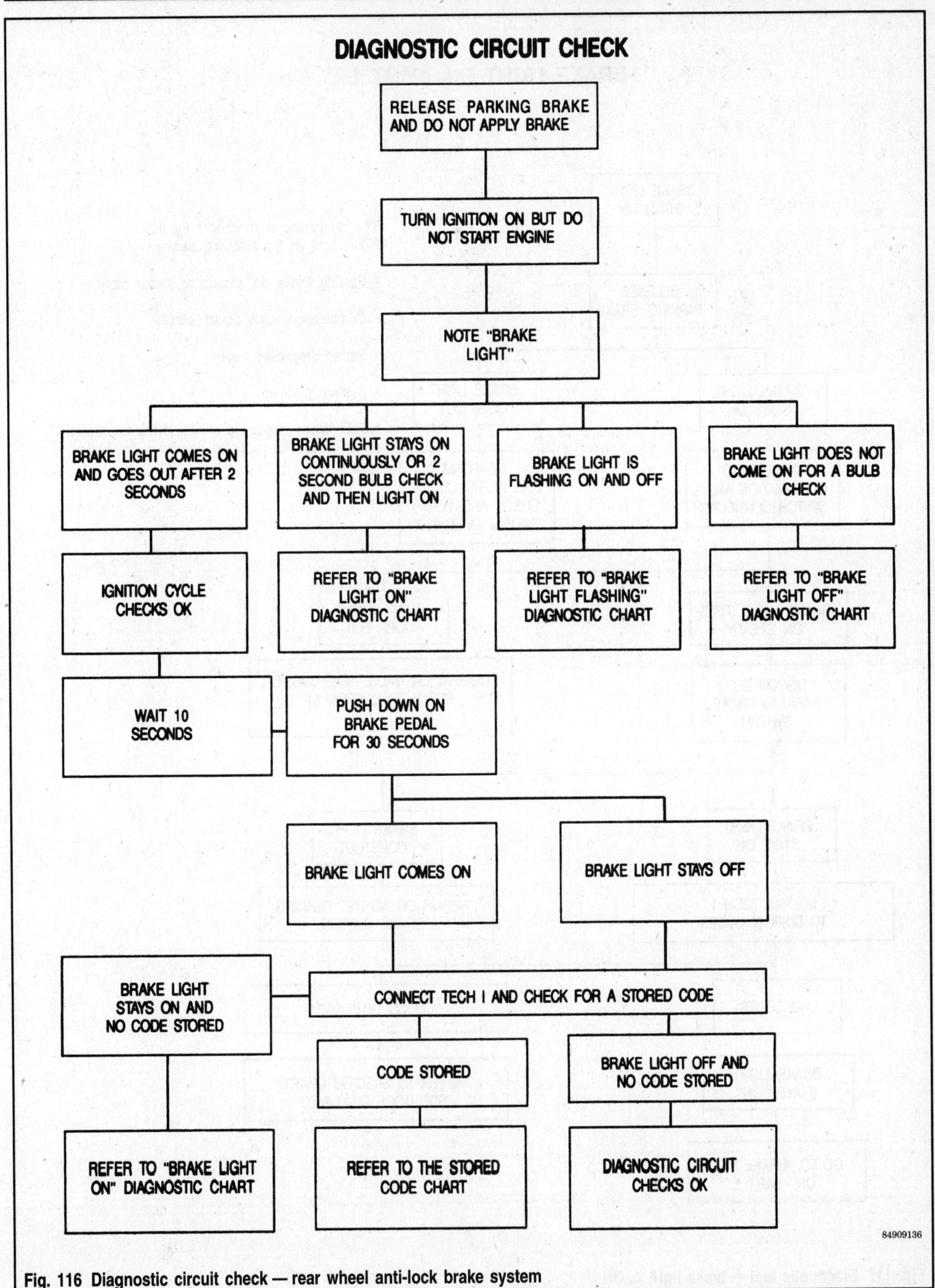

Fig. 116 Diagnostic circuit check — rear wheel anti-lock brake system

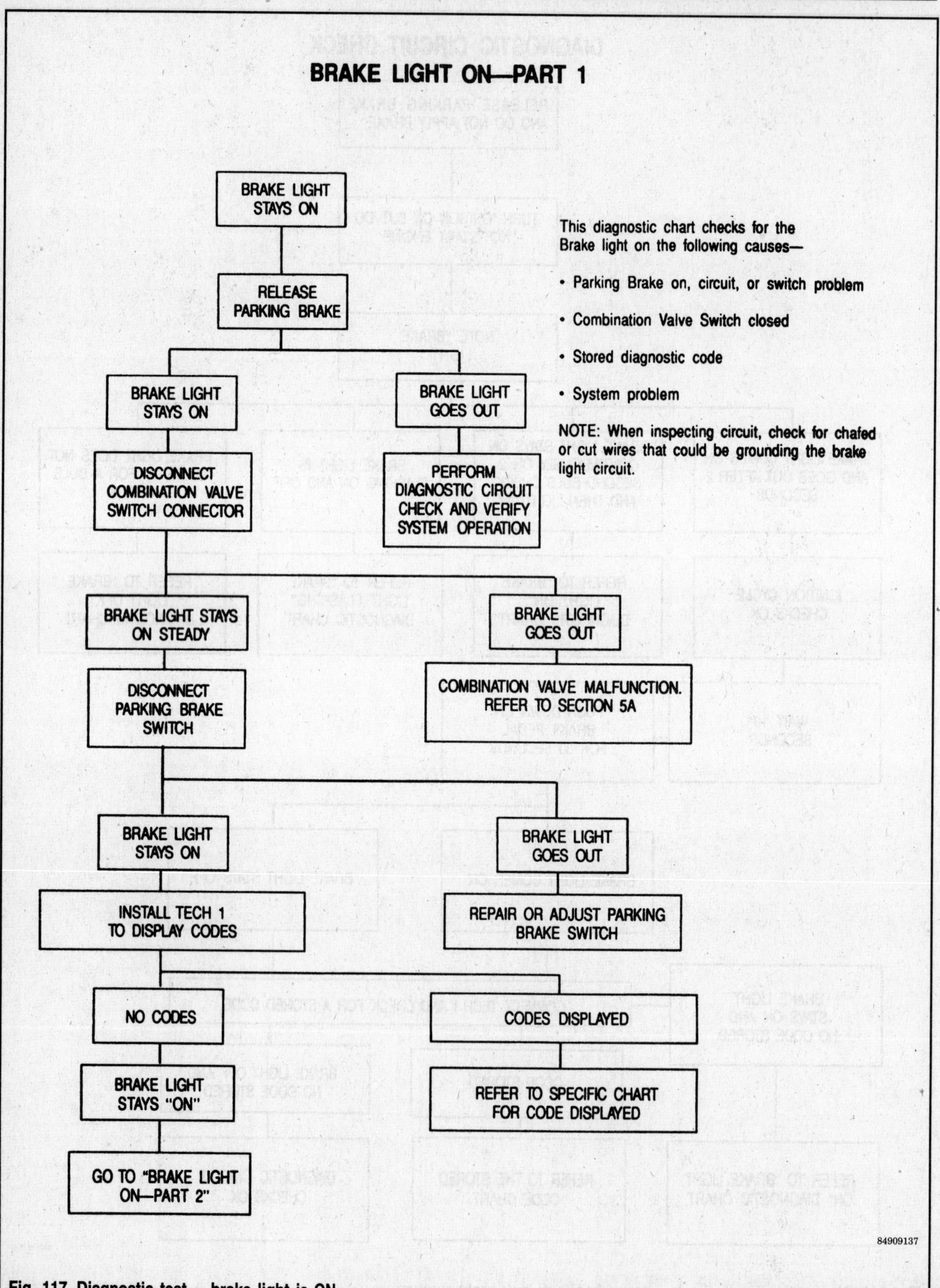

Fig. 117 Diagnostic test — brake light is ON

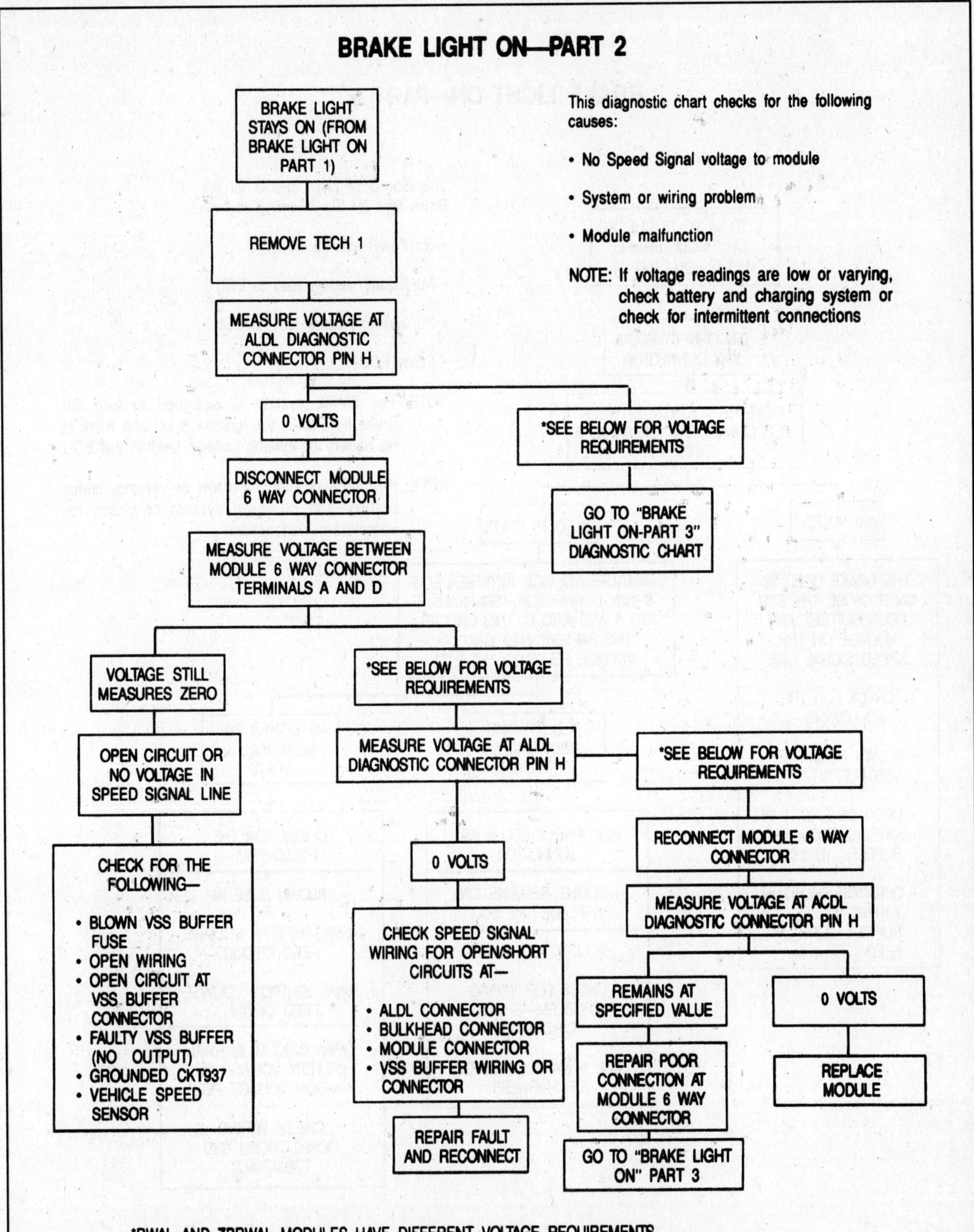

Fig. 118 Diagnostic test — brake light is ON

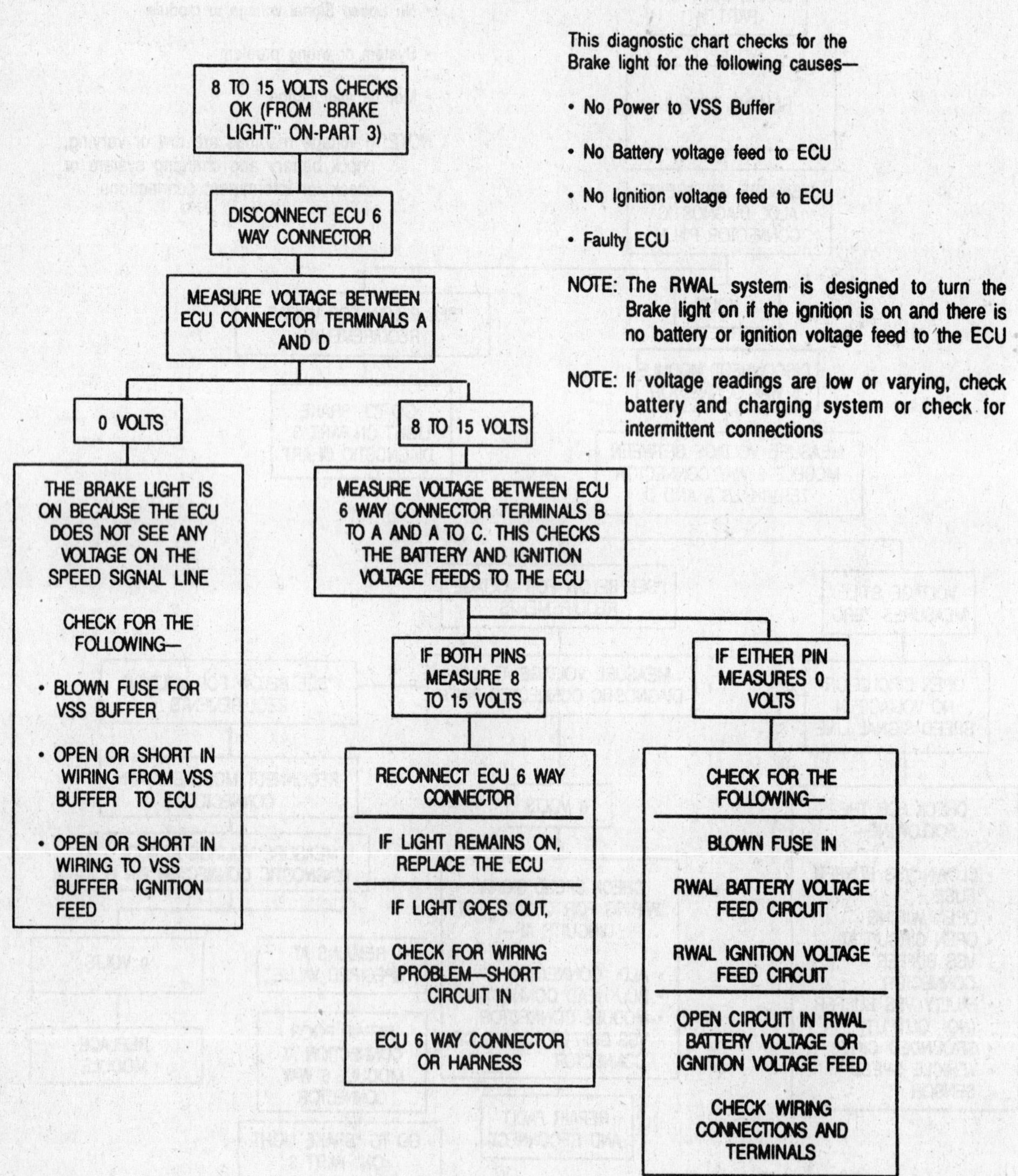

Fig. 119 Diagnostic test — brake light is ON

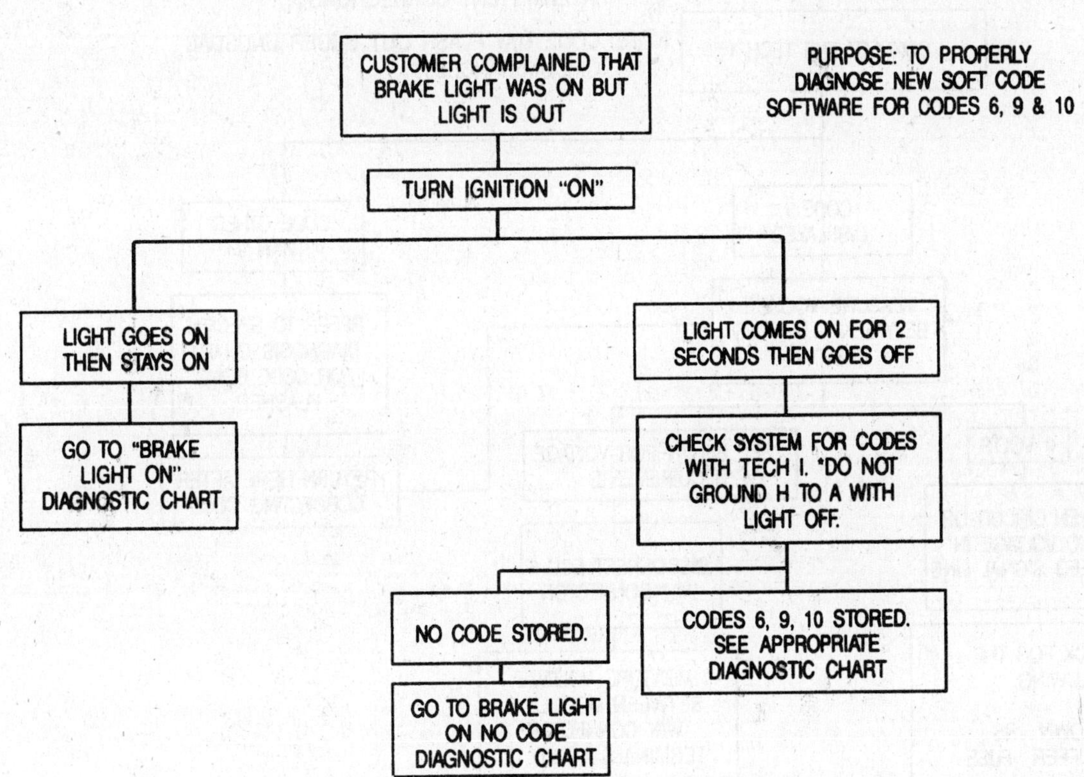

Fig. 120 Diagnostic test — brake light is intermittent

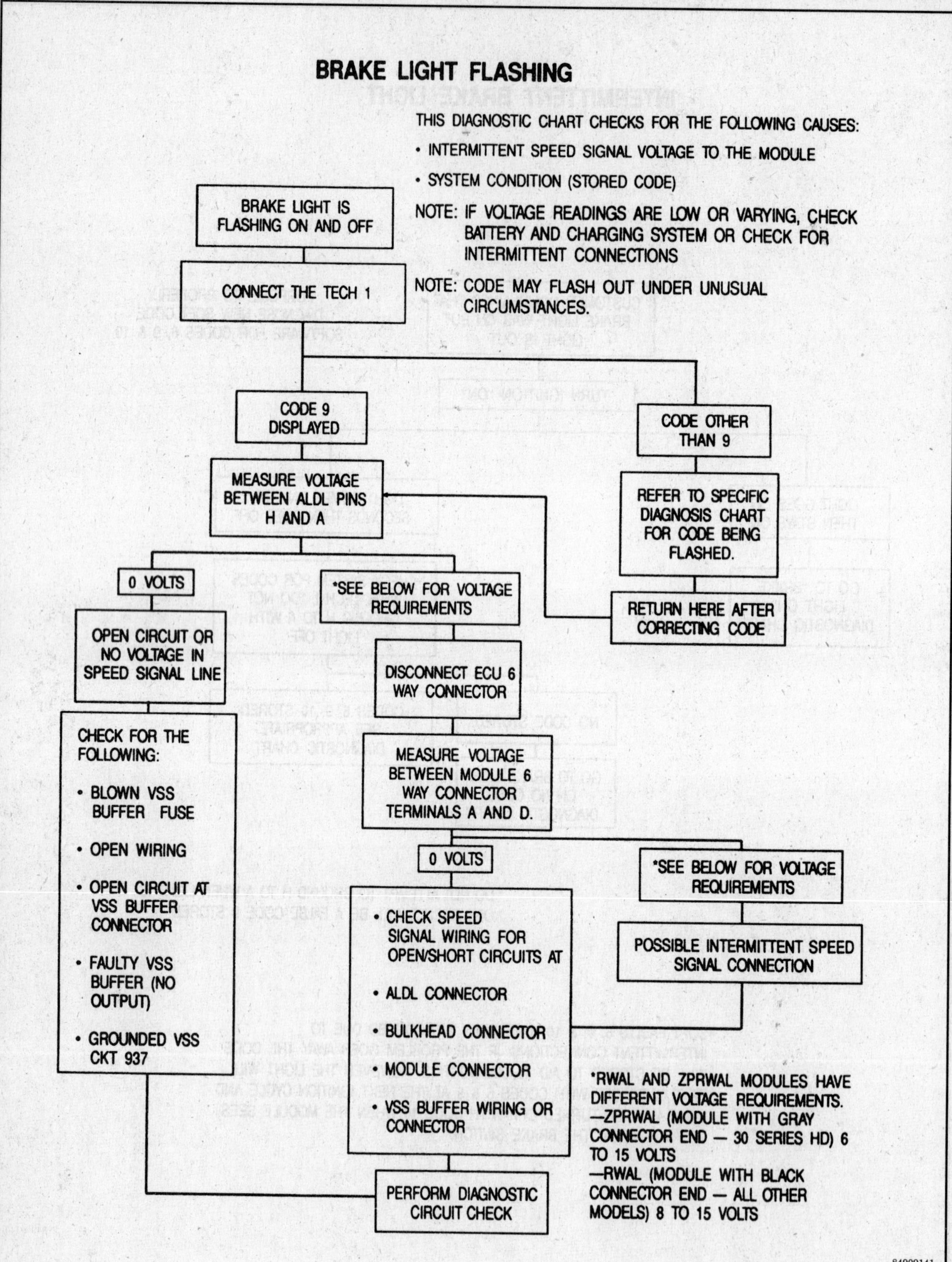

Fig. 121 Diagnostic test — brake light is flashing

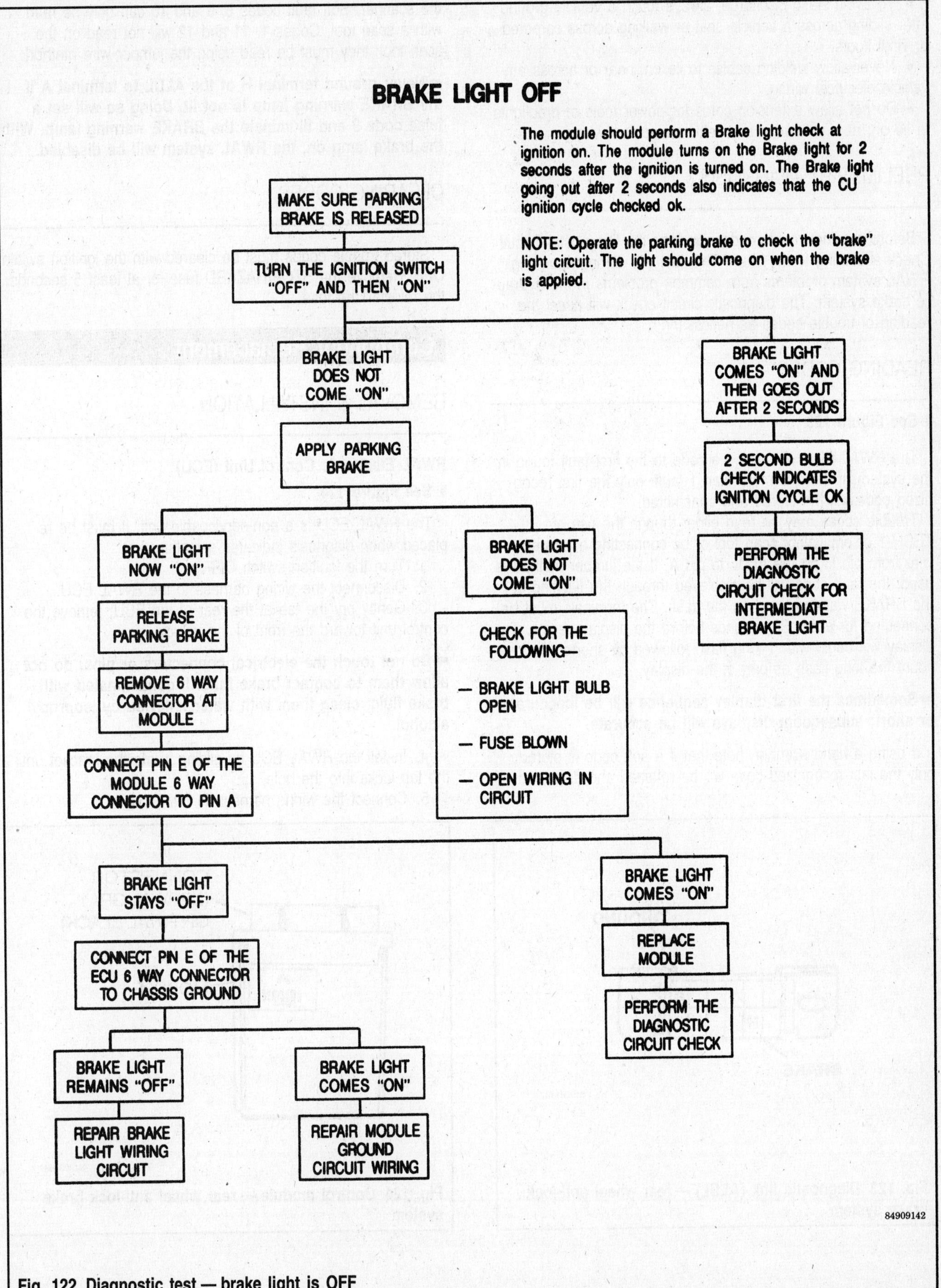

Fig. 122 Diagnostic test — brake light is OFF

• To avoid static discharge, always touch a vehicle ground after sliding across a vehicle seat or walking across carpeted or vinyl floors.

• Never allow welding cables to lie on, near or across any vehicle electrical wiring.

• Do not allow extension cords for power tools or droplights to lie on, near or across any vehicle electrical wiring.

PRELIMINARY DIAGNOSIS

Before reading trouble codes, perform the Diagnostic Circuit Check according to the chart. This test will aid in separating RWAL system problems from common problems in the hydraulic brake system. The diagnostic circuit check will direct the reading of trouble codes as necessary.

READING CODES

See Figure 123

The RWAL ECU will assign a code to the first fault found in the system. If there is more than 1 fault, only the first recognized code will the stored and transmitted.

Trouble codes may be read either though the use of TECH-1 or equivalent scan tool or by connecting a jumper wire from pin H on the ALDL to pin A. If the jumper method is used, the fault code will be displayed through the flashing of the BRAKE warning lamp on the dash. The terminals must be connected for about 20 seconds before the display begins. The display will begin with 1 long flash followed by shorter ones — count the long flash as part of the display.

➡Sometimes the first display sequence will be inaccurate or short; subsequent displays will be accurate.

If using a hand scanner, note that if a soft code is stored, only the last recognized code will be retained and displayed on the scanner. Soft fault codes 6, 9 and 10 can only be read with a scan tool. Codes 1, 11 and 12 will not read on the scan tool; they must be read using the jumper wire method.

➡Never ground terminal H of the ALDL to terminal A if the BRAKE warning lamp is not lit. Doing so will set a false code 9 and illuminate the BRAKE warning lamp. With the brake lamp on, the RWAL system will be disabled.

CLEARING CODES

Stored trouble codes must be cleared with the ignition switch **OFF**. Remove the STOP/HAZARD fuse for at least 5 seconds, the reinstall the fuse.

Component Replacement

REMOVAL & INSTALLATION

RWAL Electronic Control Unit (ECU)

See Figure 124

The RWAL ECU is a non-serviceable unit. It must be replaced when diagnosis indicates a malfunction.

1. Turn the ignition switch **OFF**.
2. Disconnect the wiring harness to the RWAL ECU.
3. Gently pry the tab at the rear of the ECU; remove the control unit toward the front of the vehicle.

➡Do not touch the electrical connectors or pins; do not allow them to contact brake fluid. If contaminated with brake fluid, clean them with water followed by isopropyl alcohol.

4. Install the RWAL ECU by sliding it into the bracket until the tab locks into the hole.
5. Connect the wiring harness to the ECU.

GROUND
A
H
BRAKE
84909143

Fig. 123 Diagnostic link (ALDL) — rear wheel anti-lock brake system

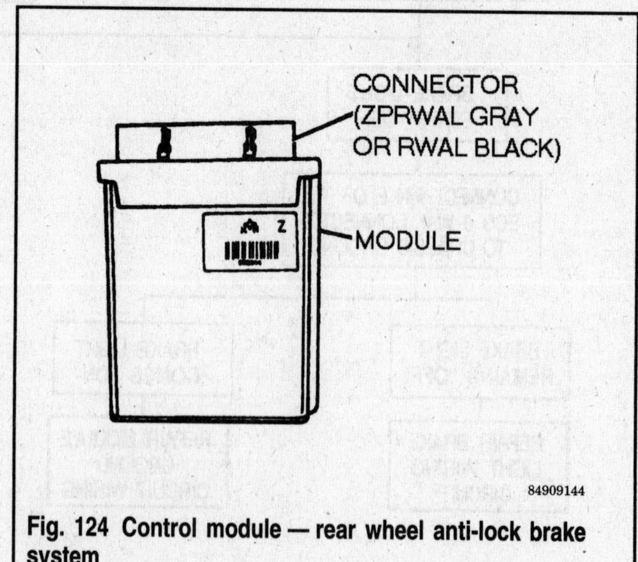

Fig. 124 Control module — rear wheel anti-lock brake system

Isolation/Dump Valve (Control Valve)

See Figure 125

1. Disconnect the brake line fittings at the valve. Protect surrounding paintwork from spillage.
2. Disconnect the electrical connectors from both the ECU and the isolation valve.
3. Remove the bolts holding the valve to the bracket.
4. Carefully remove the isolation/dump valve from the vehicle.

Do not touch the electrical connectors or pins; do not allow them to contact brake fluid. If contaminated with brake fluid, clean them with water followed by isopropyl alcohol.

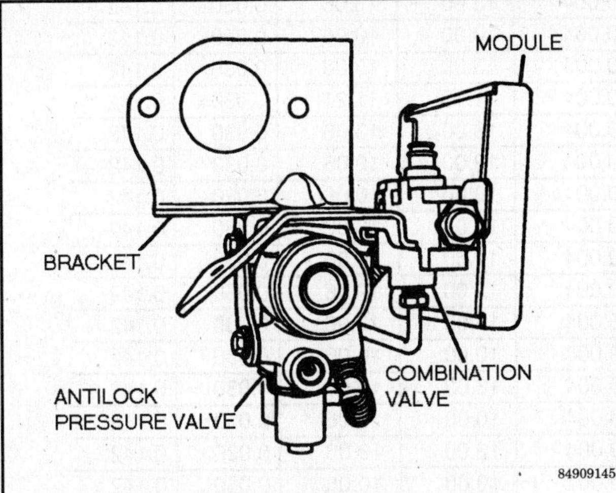

Fig. 125 Anti-lock pressure valve and module assembly — rear wheel anti-lock brake system

To install:

5. Place the valve in position and install the retaining bolts. Tighten the bolts to 21 ft. lbs. (29 Nm).
6. Connect the electrical connector to the RWAL ECU.
7. Install the brake lines; tighten the fittings to 20 ft. lbs. (27 Nm)
8. Bleed the brake system at all 4 wheels.

Speed Sensor

The speed sensor is not serviceable and must replaced if malfunctioning. The sensor is located in the left rear of the transmission case on 2WD vehicles and on the transfer case of 4WD vehicles.

The speed sensor may be tested with an ohmmeter; the correct resistance is 900-2000 ohms. To remove the speed sensor:

1. Disconnect the electrical connector from the speed sensor.
2. Remove the sensor retaining bolt if one is used.
3. Remove the speed sensor; have a container handy to catch transmission fluid when the sensor is removed.
4. Recover the O-ring used to seal the sensor; inspect it for damage or deterioration.

To install:

5. When installing, coat the new O-ring with a thin film of transmission fluid.
6. Install the O-ring and speed sensor.
7. If a retaining bolt is used, tighten the bolt to 8 ft. lbs. (11 Nm) in automatic transmissions or 9 ft. lbs. (12 Nm) for all other transmissions.
8. If the sensor is a screw-in unit, tighten it to 32 ft. lbs. (43 Nm).
9. Connect the wire harness to the sensor.

BRAKE SPECIFICATIONS

All measurements in inches unless noted

Year	Model	Brake Disc Original Thickness	Brake Disc Minimum Thickness	Brake Disc Maximum Runout	Brake Drum Diameter Original Inside Diameter	Brake Drum Diameter Max. Wear Limit	Minimum Lining Thickness Front	Minimum Lining Thickness Rear
1988	R/V 10, 15	1.000	0.979	0.004	11.15	11.21	0.030	0.142
	R/V 20, 25	1.250	1.230	0.004	13.00	13.06	0.030	0.142
	R/V 30, 35	1.260	1.240	0.004	13.00	13.06	0.030	0.142
	C/K 15, 25	1.000	0.979	0.004	10.00	10.06	0.030	0.142
	C/K 35	1.260	1.240	0.004	13.00	13.06	0.030	0.142
1989	R/V 10, 15	1.000	0.979	0.004	11.15	11.21	0.030	0.142
	R/V 20, 25	1.250	1.230	0.004	13.00	13.06	0.030	0.142
	R/V 30, 35	1.260	1.240	0.004	13.00	13.06	0.030	0.142
	C/K 15, 25	1.000	0.979	0.004	10.00	10.06	0.030	0.142
	C/K 35	1.260	1.240	0.004	13.00	13.06	0.030	0.142
1990	R/V 10, 15	1.000	0.979	0.004	11.15	11.21	0.030	0.142
	R/V 20, 25	1.250	1.230	0.004	13.00	13.06	0.030	0.142
	R/V 30, 35	1.260	1.240	0.004	13.00	13.06	0.030	0.142
	C/K 15, 25	1.000	0.979	0.004	10.00	10.06	0.030	0.142
	C/K 35	1.260	1.240	0.004	13.00	13.06	0.030	0.142
1991	R/V 10, 15	1.500	0.980	0.004	11.00	10.06	0.030	0.142
	R/V 20, 25	1.250	1.230	0.004	12.00	12.06	0.030	0.142
	R/V 30, 35	1.500	1.480	0.004	13.00	13.06	0.030	0.142
	C/K 15, 25	1.000	0.980	0.004	10.00	10.06	0.030	0.142
	C/K 35	1.500	1.480	0.004	13.00	13.06	0.030	0.142
1992	C/K 15, 25	1.250	1.230	0.004	10.00	10.05	0.030	0.142
	C/K 35	1.500	1.480	0.004	13.00	13.06	0.030	0.142
1993	C/K 15, 25	1.250	1.230	0.004	10.00	10.05	0.030	0.142
	C/K 35	1.500	1.480	0.004	13.00	13.06	0.030	0.142
1994	C/K 15, 25	1.250	1.230	0.004	10.00	10.00	0.030	0.142
	C/K 35	1.500	1.480	0.004	13.00	13.00	0.030	0.142
1995	C/K 15, 25	1.250	1.230	0.004	10.00	10.00	0.030	0.142
	C/K 35	1.500	1.480	0.004	13.00	13.00	0.030	0.142
1996	C/K 15, 25	1.250	1.230	0.004	10.00	10.00	0.030	0.142
	C/K 35	1.500	1.480	0.004	13.00	13.00	0.030	0.142

87988c04

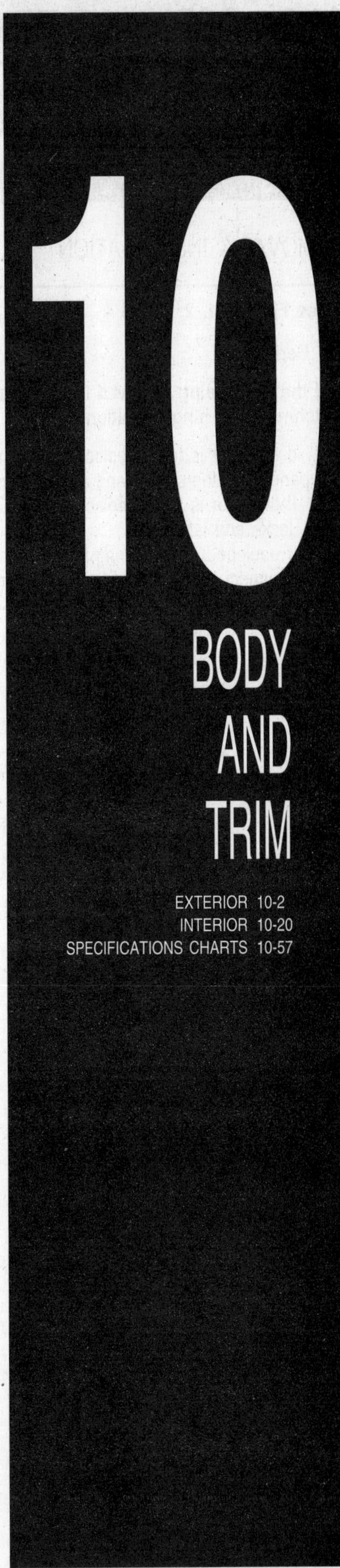

10 BODY AND TRIM

EXTERIOR

Doors

REMOVAL & INSTALLATION

➧ See Figures 1, 2, 3 and 4

R/V Series

➡If the door being removed is to be reinstalled, matchmark the hinge position.

1. If the door is to be replaced with a new one, remove the trim panels weathersheets and all molding.
2. If the door is to be replaced with a new one, remove the glass, locks and latches.
3. If equipped with a wiring harness, remove the trim panel and disconnect the harness. Guide the wiring out of the door.

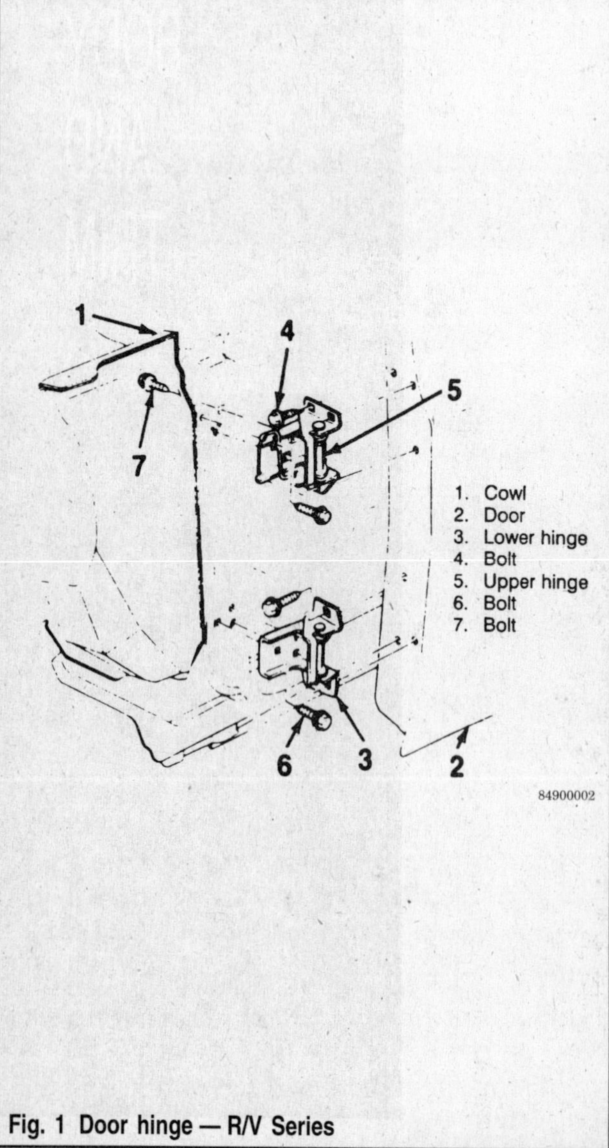

Fig. 1 Door hinge — R/V Series

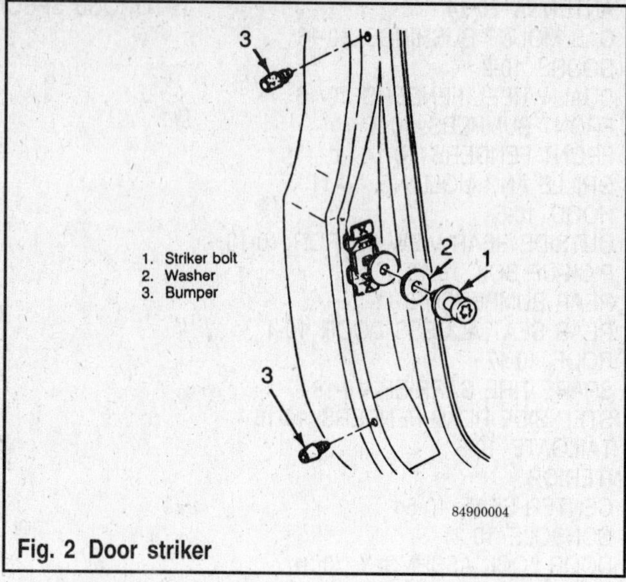

Fig. 2 Door striker

4. Support the door and remove the hinge-to-body attaching bolts. Lift the door from the truck.
5. Install the door.
6. Perform the alignment procedures indicated below.

C/K Series

1. On trucks with power components in the door, disconnect the battery ground cable.
2. On trucks with power components in the door, remove the cowl side vent cover.
3. On trucks with power components in the door, disconnect the wiring going to the door, under the dash panel. Feed the wiring through the door pillar.
4. Cover the door hinge spring with a heavy towel. Using tool J-36604 or its equivalent, insert the blades of the tool between the spring coils and turn the barrel nut to compress and hold the spring. Remove the spring using the tool.
5. Remove the lower hinge pin retainer.
6. Using a plastic or rubber mallet and locking pliers, remove the lower hinge pin.
7. Install a bolt through the lower hinges to hold the door while removing the upper hinge pin.
8. Remove the upper hinge pin retainer.
9. Remove the upper hinge pin.
10. Support the door and remove the bolt from the lower hinge.

To install:

11. Position the door and install the bolt in the lower hinge.
12. Install the upper hinge pin. with the pointed end up.
13. Install a new upper hinge pin retainer.
14. Remove the bolt from the lower hinges.
15. Install the lower hinge pin with the pointed end down.
16. Install a new lower hinge pin retainer.
17. Using tool J-36604, install the hinge spring.
18. On trucks with power components in the door, connect the wiring going to the door, under the dash panel. Feed the wiring through the door pillar.

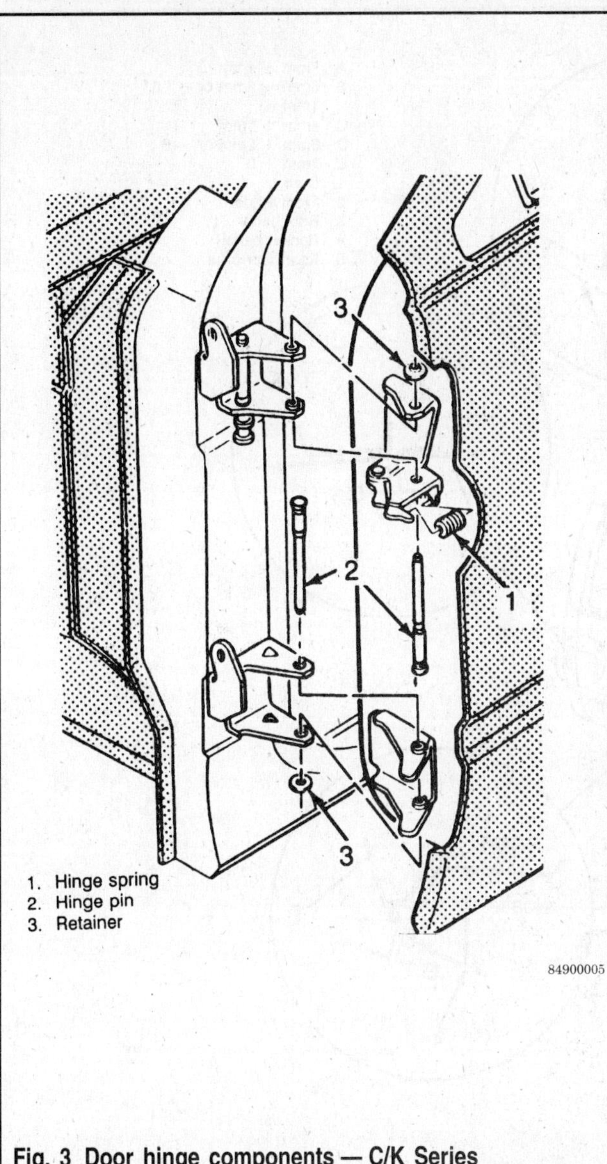

Fig. 3 Door hinge components — C/K Series

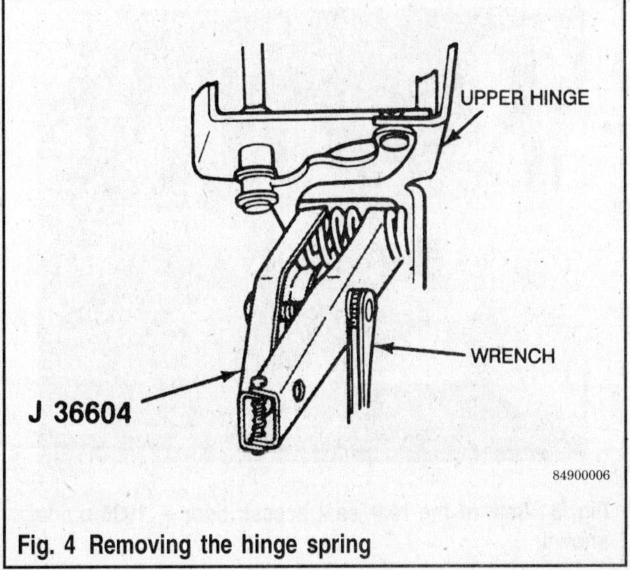

Fig. 4 Removing the hinge spring

19. On trucks with power components in the door, install the cowl side vent cover.

20. On trucks with power components in the door, connect the battery ground cable.

ADJUSTMENT

➡The holes for the hinges are oversized to provide for latitude in alignment. Align the door hinges first, then the striker.

Hinges

➧ See Figure 5

➡C/K series utilize hinges that are welded to the door and frame. No adjustment is possible except when replacement hinges have been installed.

1. If a door is being installed, first mount the door and tighten the hinge bolts lightly.

➡If the door has not been removed, determine which hinge bolts must be loosed to effect alignment.

2. Loosen the necessary bolts just enough to allow the door to be moved with a padded prybar.
3. Move the door in small movements and check the fit after each movement.

➡Be sure that there is no binding or interference with adjacent panels.

4. Repeat this procedure until the door is properly aligned.
R/V Series:
   - Door edge-to-rocker panel: 6mm
   - Door edge-to-roof panel: 5mm
   - Door edge-to-rear pillar: 5mm
   - Door edge-to-front pillar: 2mm

   C/K Series:
   - Door edge-to-rocker panel: 6mm
   - Door edge-to-roof panel: 6mm
   - Door edge-to-rear pillar: 4mm
   - Door edge-to-front pillar: 7mm
   - Door front edge-to-fender: 5mm
5. Tighten all the bolts to 26 ft. lbs. (35 Nm).

➡Shims may be either fabricated or purchased to install behind the hinges as an aid in alignment.

Striker Plate

➡The striker is attached to the pillar using oversized holes, providing latitude in movement. Striker plate bolt torque is 46 ft. lbs. (62 Nm).

Striker adjustment is made by loosening the bolts and moving the striker plate in the desired direction or adding or deleting the shims behind the plate, or both.

The striker is properly adjusted when the locking latch enters the striker without rubbing and the door closed fully and solidly, with no play when closed.

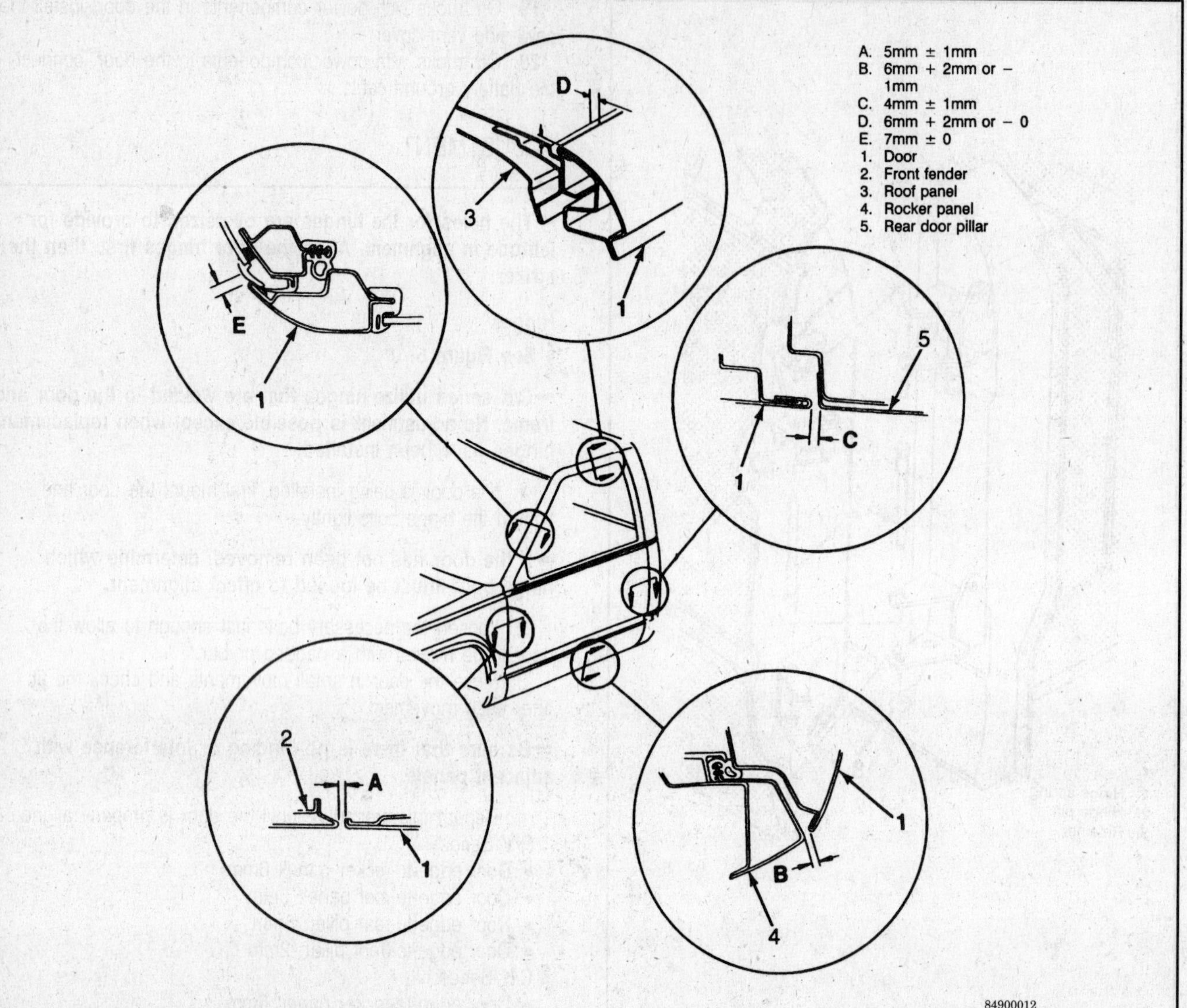

A. 5mm ± 1mm
B. 6mm + 2mm or − 1mm
C. 4mm ± 1mm
D. 6mm + 2mm or − 0
E. 7mm ± 0
1. Door
2. Front fender
3. Roof panel
4. Rocker panel
5. Rear door pillar

84900012

Fig. 5 Door adjustment check points

Rear Seat Access Door

REMOVAL & INSTALLATION

➧ **See Figure 6**

1. Remove the lower hinge pin retainer.
2. With pliers and a hammer, remove the lower hinge pin. Install a bolt through the lower hinges so as to hold the door in position while removing the upper hinge pin.
3. Remove the upper hinge pin retainer and the upper hinge pin.
4. Remove the bolt from the lower hinge.
5. Remove the door.

To install:

6. Install the door and temporarily install a bolt through the lower hinge pin holes.
7. Install the upper hinge pin and a new hinge pin retainer. Remove the temporary bolt from the lower hinge.
8. Install the lower hinge pin and a new hinge pin retainer.

87980p02

Fig. 6 View of the rear seat access door — 1996 model shown

ADJUSTMENT

➡The holes for the hinges are oversized to provide for latitude in alignment. Align the door hinges first, then the striker.

Hinges

➧ See Figures 7 and 8

1. If a door is being installed, first mount the door and tighten the hinge bolts lightly.

➡If the door has not been removed, determine which hinge bolts must be loosed to effect alignment.

2. Loosen the necessary bolts just enough to allow the door to be moved with a padded prybar.
3. Move the door in small movements and check the fit after each movement.

➡Be sure that there is no binding or interference with adjacent panels.

4. Keep repeating this procedure until the door is properly aligned.
    - Door panel lower edge-to-platform panel: 7mm ± 2mm
    - Door outer panel-to-platform panel (closed): 14mm ± 1.5mm
    - Door edge-to-roof panel: 5mm ± 2mm
    - Door edge-to-pillar: 5mm ± 2mm
    - Door edge-to-door edge (closed): 5mm ± 2mm
5. Tighten all the bolts to 26 ft. lbs. (35 Nm).

➡Shims may be either fabricated or purchased to install behind the hinges as an aid in alignment.

Striker Plate

➧ See Figure 9

➡The striker is attached to the pillar using oversized holes, providing latitude in movement. Striker plate bolt torque is 46 ft. lbs. (62 Nm).

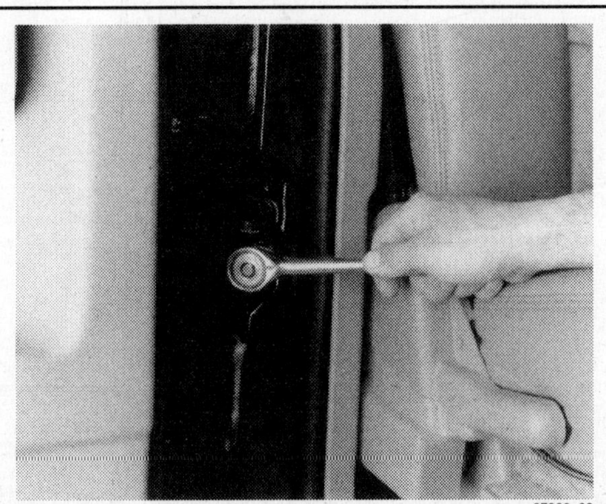

87980p03

Fig. 7 If a door is being installed, first mount the door and tighten the hinge bolts lightly

87980p04

Fig. 8 Adjusting the lower striker assembly

Striker adjustment is made by loosening the bolts and moving the striker plate in the desired direction or adding or deleting the shims behind the plate, or both.

The striker is properly adjusted when the locking latch enters the striker without rubbing and the door closed fully and solidly, with no play when closed.

Hood

REMOVAL & INSTALLATION

➡You are going to need an assistant for this job.

R/V Series

➧ See Figure 10

1. Open the hood and trace the outline of the hinges on the hood.
2. While an assistant holds the hood, remove the hinge-to-hood bolts and lift the hood off.

87980p05

Fig. 9 Loosen and adjust the door striker bolt so that it properly engages the door lock

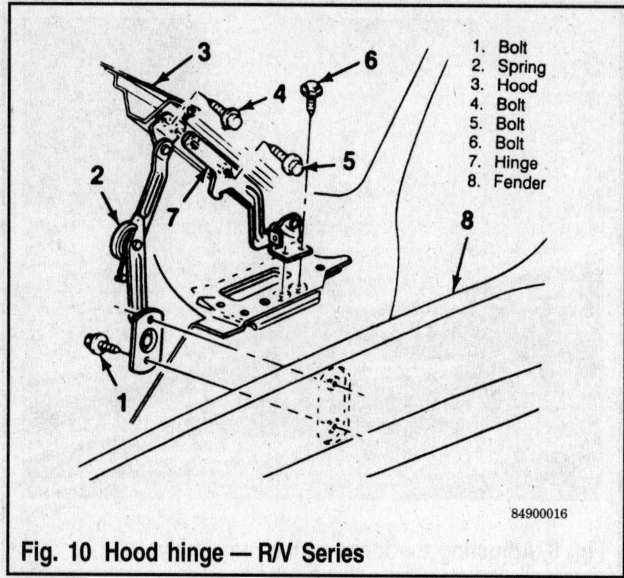

Fig. 10 Hood hinge — R/V Series

3. Install the hood and tighten the bolts to 18 ft. lbs. (24 Nm).
4. Adjust hood alignment, if necessary.

C/K Series

➧ See Figure 11

1. Open the hood and trace the outline of the hinges on the hood.
2. Remove the hood seals from the hinges.
3. While an assistant holds the hood, remove the hinge-to-link bolts and lower the hood.
4. Remove the outboard section of the cowl vent grille.
5. Remove the hinge-to-fender bracket bolts.
6. Lift off the hood.
7. Install the hood and tighten the bolts to 18 ft. lbs. (24 Nm).
8. Adjust hood alignment, if necessary.

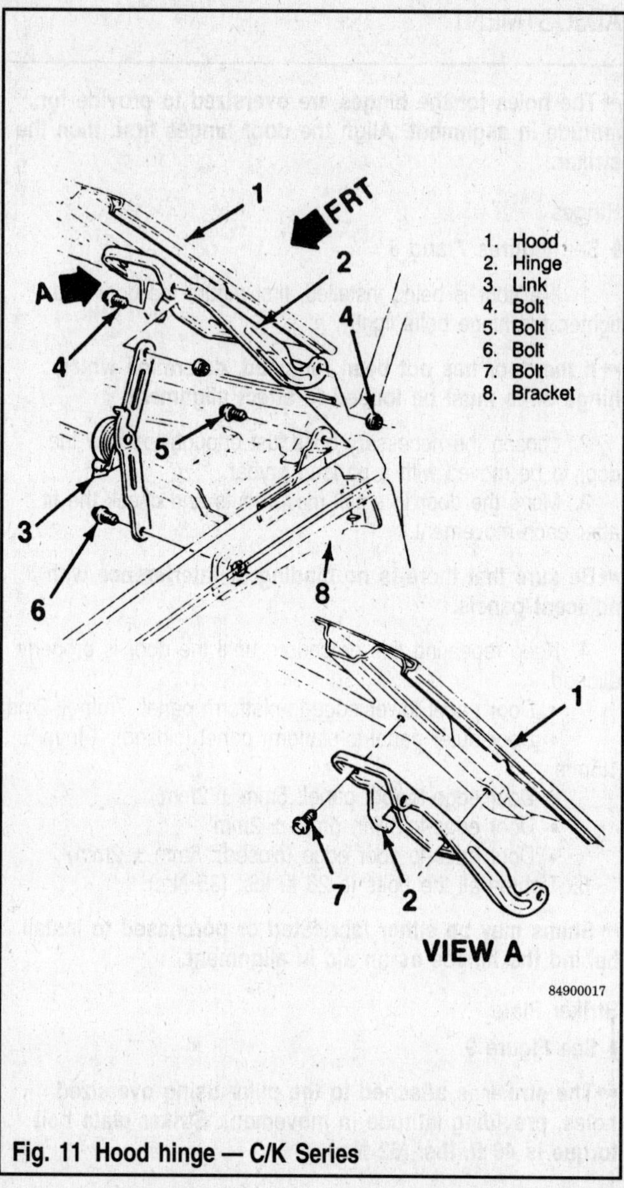

Fig. 11 Hood hinge — C/K Series

ALIGNMENT

1. Hood alignment can be adjusted front-to-rear or side-to-side by loosening the hood-to-hinge or hinge-to-body bolts.
2. The front edge of the hood can be adjusted for closing height by adding or deleting shims under the hinges.
3. The rear edge of the hood can be adjusted for closing height by raising or lowering the hood bumpers.

Tailgate

REMOVAL & INSTALLATION

Pick-Ups

1988-91 MODELS

➧ See Figure 12

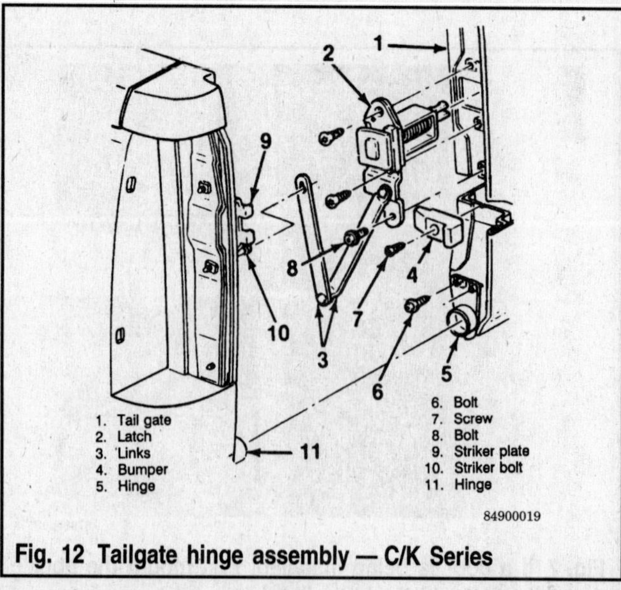

Fig. 12 Tailgate hinge assembly — C/K Series

1. Open the tailgate and support it with something like sawhorses.

2. Pull up on the side links at the joints.
3. Remove the attaching bolts and remove the link and striker plate from each end of the tailgate.
4. Remove the hinge-to-tailgate bolts.
5. Remove the tailgate.
6. Installation of the tailgate is the reverse of the removal procedure.

1992-96 MODELS

➧ See Figure 13

1. Lower the tailgate to the horizontal position.
2. Move the tailgate to the 45° position and support it while disconnecting the cable from each side at the striker bolts.
3. Disconnect the tailgate from the right and then the left side hinge and then remove the gate.
4. To install, position the tailgate into the hinges at 45° angle and then connect the cable.

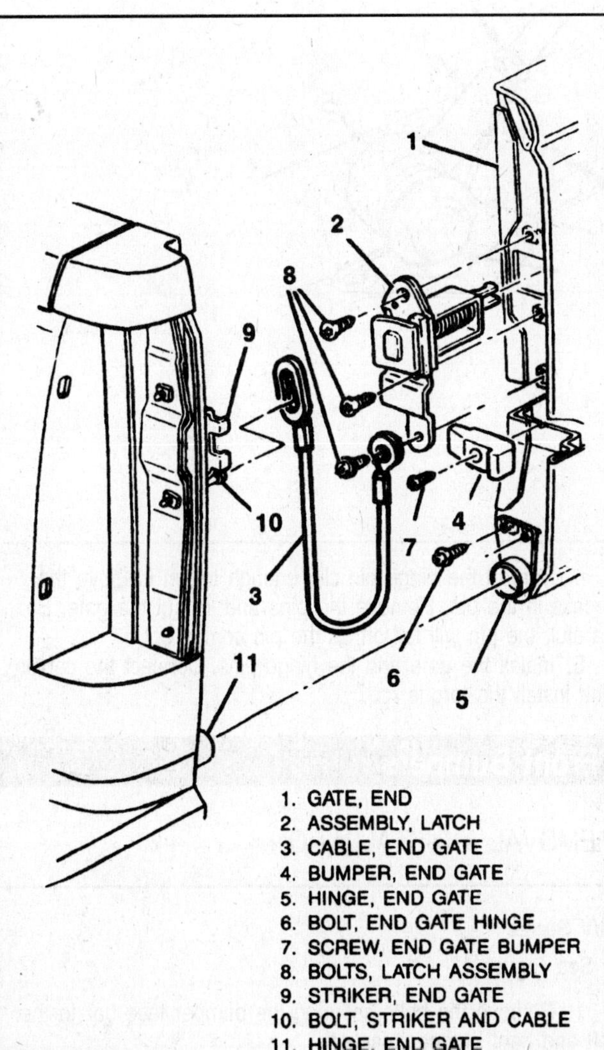

Fig. 13 End cable and latch components — 1992-96 C/K Series

Blazer/Jimmy/Yukon

1988-91 MODELS

➧ See Figure 14

1. Place the tailgate in the closed position and lower the window.
2. Remove the torque rod-to-frame stud and nut and allow the torque rod to swing down.
3. Open the tailgate and support it with something like a picnic table, so there is no tension on the support cables.
4. Remove the attaching screws and remove the tailgate inner cover.
5. Disconnect the wiring harness connectors in the tailgate.
6. Remove the support cables-to-pillar attaching bolts, spacers and washers.
7. Remove the torque rod brackets.
8. Remove the hinge-to-floor panel bolts.
9. Lift the tailgate off, guiding the torque rods over the gravel deflectors.

To install:

10. Position the tailgate, guiding the torque rods over the gravel deflectors. Insert the hinges into the floor panel slots.
11. Install the hinge-to-floor panel bolts. Make them snug.
12. Install the torque rod brackets.
13. Install the support cables-to-pillar attaching bolts, spacers and washers.
14. Connect the wiring harness connectors in the tailgate.
15. Install the tailgate inner cover.
16. Close the tailgate.
17. Install the torque rod-to-frame stud and nut.
18. Align the tailgate in the opening and tighten the hinge bolts securely.

1992-96 MODELS

➧ See Figure 15

1. Open the tailgate and remove the torque rod.
2. Disconnect the window electrical harness.
3. Support the gate and remove the cable support bolts and washers.
4. Spread the hinge pin clip enough to get it above the recess in the pin. Remove the pins and lift out the gate. Be careful, the pin will fall off as the pin comes out.
5. Install the gate and the hinge pins. Connect the cables and install the torque rod.

Suburban

1988-91 MODELS

➧ See Figure 16

1. Open the tailgate and support it with something like a picnic table, so there is no tension on the support cables.
2. Unbolt the torque rod bracket.
3. Remove the attaching screws and remove the tailgate inner cover.
4. Disconnect the wiring harness connectors in the tailgate.
5. Remove the hinge access cover and seal.
6. Lift the tailgate to the almost-closed position, hold it there, and remove the hinge-to-tailgate bolts.
7. Lower the tailgate and support it so there is no tension on the cables and remove the support cables-to-pillars attaching bolts and washers.

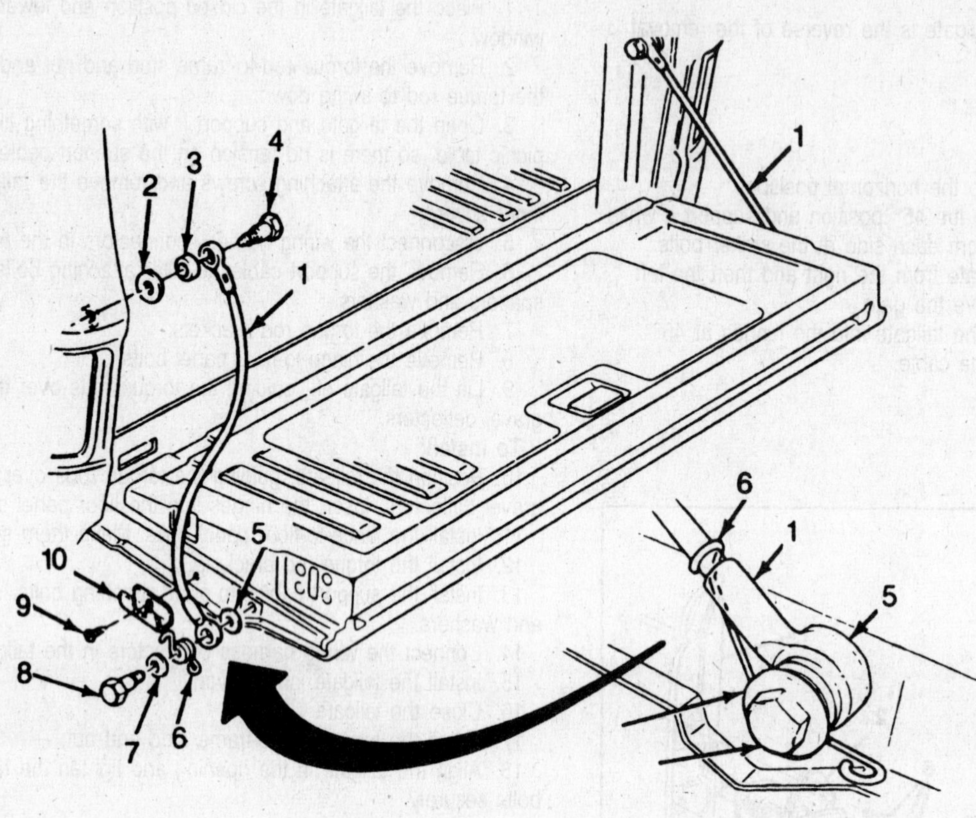

Fig. 14 Tailgate cable — 1988-91 Blazer/Jimmy

8. Lift the tailgate off, along with the torque rod.

To install:

9. Position the tailgate, along with the torque rods, in the opening, aligning the hinges.
10. Install the support cables-to-pillar attaching bolts, spacers and washers.
11. Install the hinge-to-floor panel bolts. Tighten them securely.
12. Install the hinge cover and seal.
13. Connect the wiring harness connectors in the tailgate.
14. Install the torque rod brackets.
15. Install the tailgate inner cover.

1992-96 MODELS

See Figure 15

1. Open the tailgate and remove the torque rod.
2. Disconnect the window electrical harness.
3. Support the gate and remove the cable support bolts and washers.
4. Spread the hinge pin clip enough to get it above the recess in the pin. Remove the pins and lift out the gate. Be careful, the pin will fall off as the pin comes out.
5. Install the gate and the hinge pins. Connect the cables and install the torque rod.

Front Bumpers

REMOVAL & INSTALLATION

R/V Series

See Figure 17

1. Remove the bolts securing the bumper face bar to the left and right bumper brackets.
2. Remove the bolts securing the bumper face bar to the left and right bumper braces and remove the bumper from the vehicle.

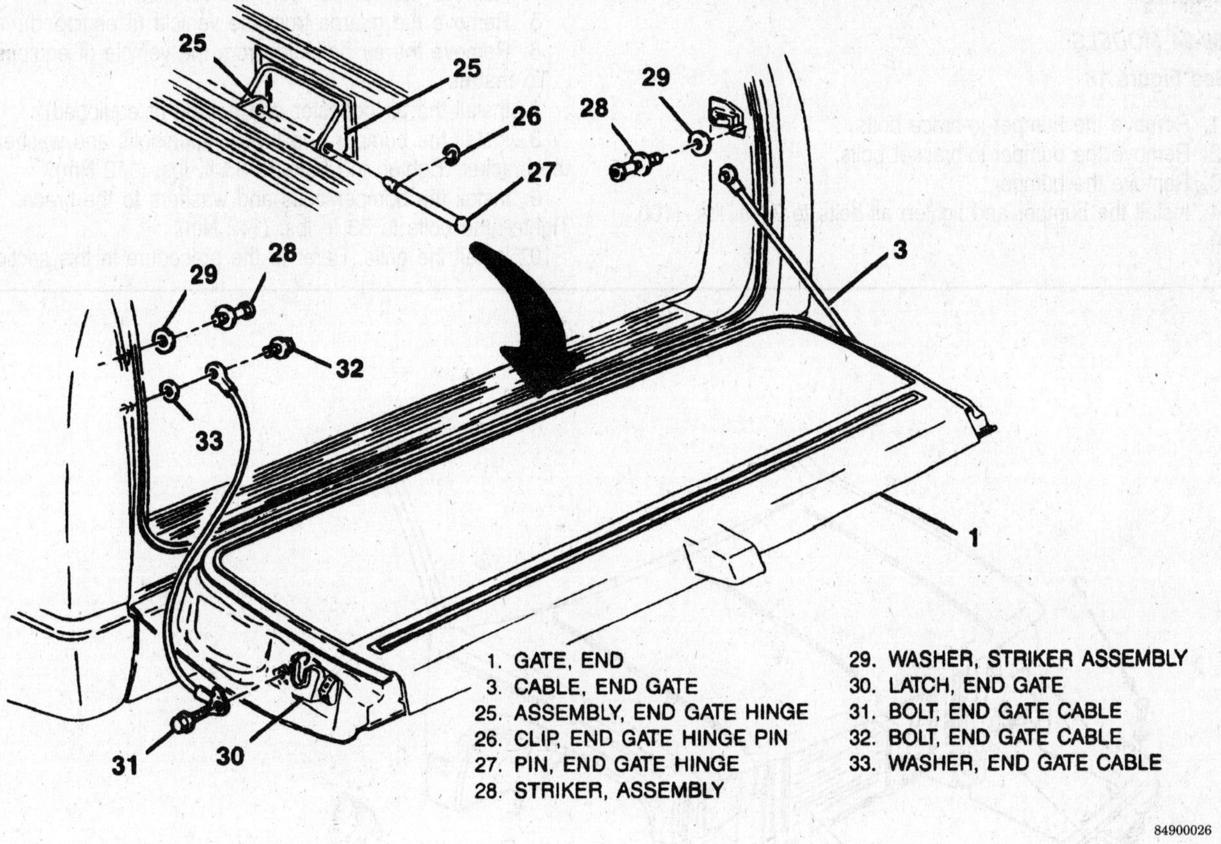

1. GATE, END
3. CABLE, END GATE
25. ASSEMBLY, END GATE HINGE
26. CLIP, END GATE HINGE PIN
27. PIN, END GATE HINGE
28. STRIKER, ASSEMBLY
29. WASHER, STRIKER ASSEMBLY
30. LATCH, END GATE
31. BOLT, END GATE CABLE
32. BOLT, END GATE CABLE
33. WASHER, END GATE CABLE
84900026

Fig. 15 Tailgate assembly

1. Striker
2. Washer
3. Screw
4. Cover
5. Seal
6. Bolt
7. Dolt
8. Hinge
84900029

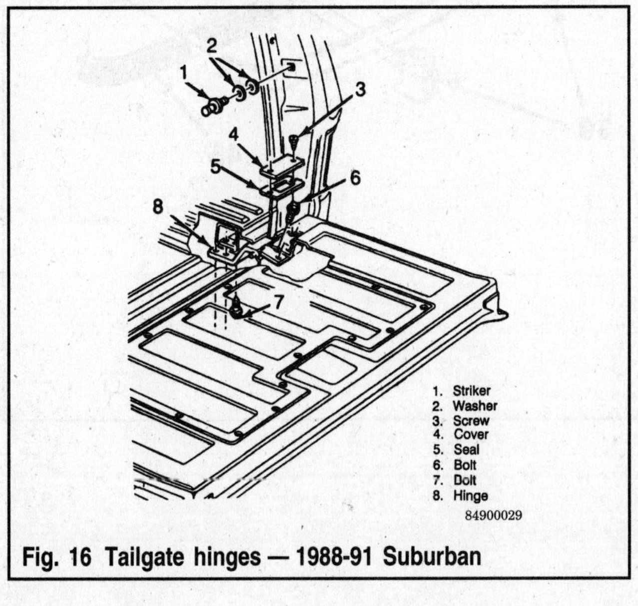

Fig. 16 Tailgate hinges — 1988-91 Suburban

1. Bumper
2. Nut
3. Guard
4. Bolt
5. Rub strip
84900032

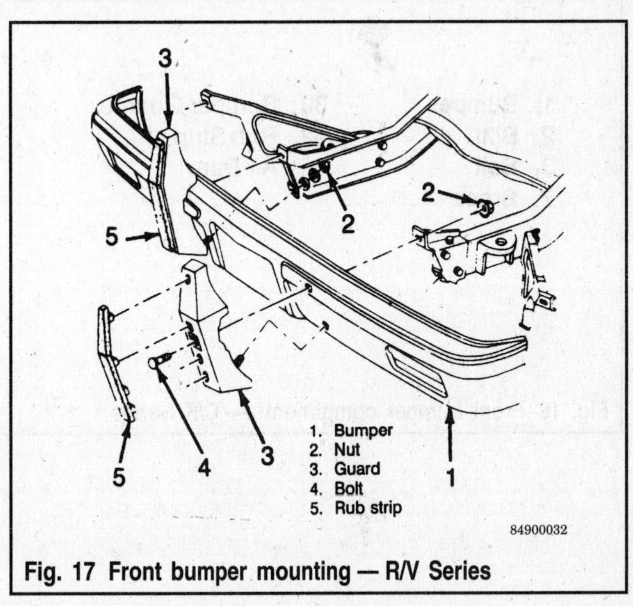

Fig. 17 Front bumper mounting — R/V Series

3. If necessary, the brackets and braces may be removed from the frame by removing the retaining bolts.

4. For ease of installation use something to support the bumper and tighten all nuts to 66 ft. lbs. (89 Nm).

C/K Series

1988-94 MODELS

See Figure 18

1. Remove the bumper-to-brace bolts.
2. Remove the bumper-to-bracket bolts.
3. Remove the bumper.
4. Install the bumper and tighten all bolts to 74 ft. lbs. (100 Nm).

1995-96 MODELS

1. Remove the grille. Refer to the procedure in this section.
2. Remove the bumper to brace bolts and washers.
3. Remove the bumper to bracket bolts and washers.
4. Remove the bumper from the vehicle.
5. Remove the guards from the vehicle (if equipped).
6. Remove the air deflector from the vehicle (if equipped).

To install:

7. Install the air deflector and guards (if equipped).
8. Install the bumper and the bumper bolts and washers to the bracket. Tighten the bolts to 83 ft. lbs. (112 Nm).
9. Install the bumper bolts and washers to the brace. Tighten the bolts to 83 ft. lbs. (112 Nm).
10. Install the grille. Refer to the procedure in this section.

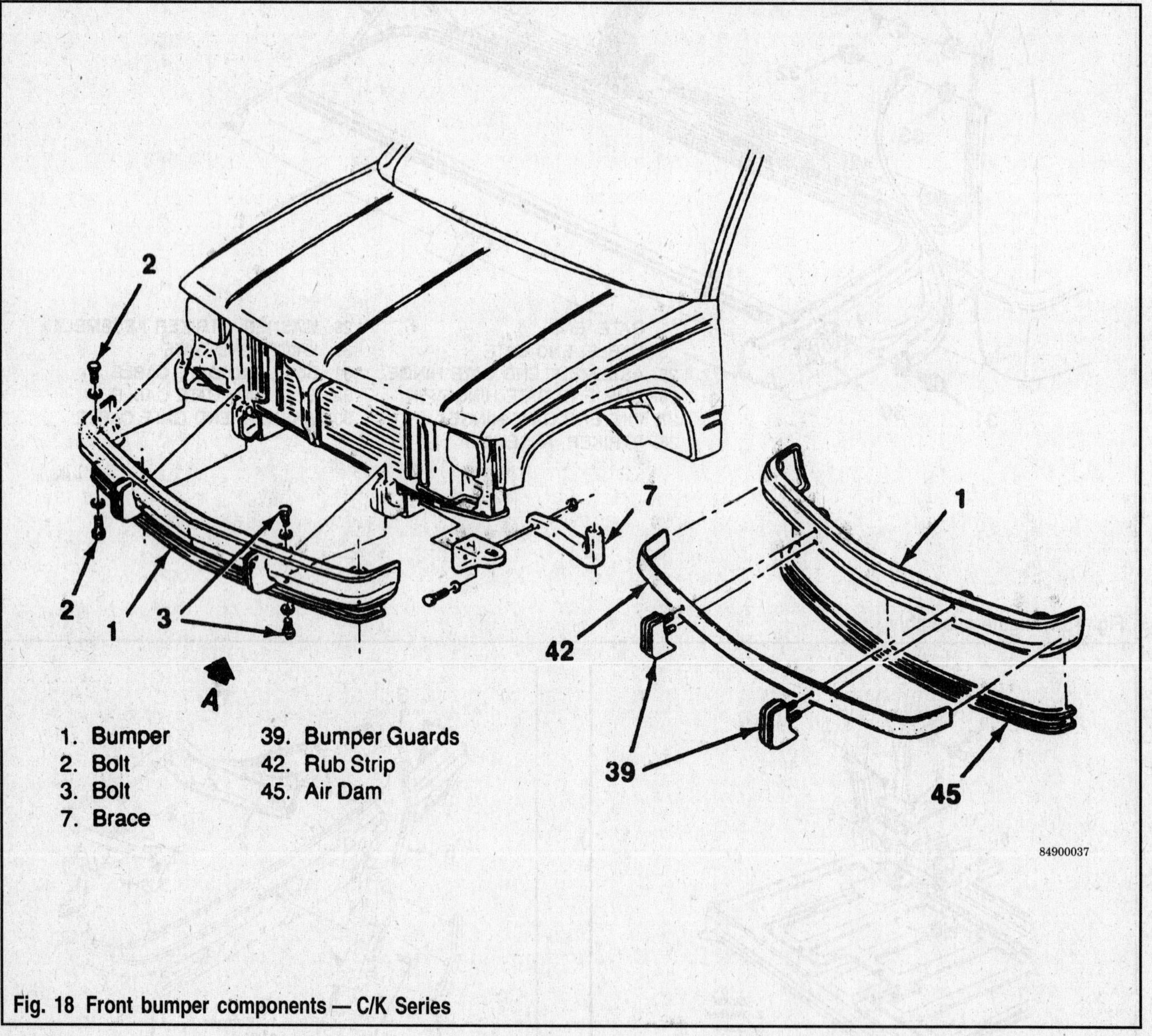

Fig. 18 Front bumper components — C/K Series

Rear Bumpers

REMOVAL & INSTALLATION

1988-91 R/V Series

EXCEPT STEP BUMPER

➧ See Figure 19

1. Remove the bolts securing the bumper face bar to the left and right bumper braces. Disconnect the license lamp wiring.
2. Remove the bolts securing the bumper face bar to the left and right bumper brackets and remove the bumper from the vehicle.
3. If necessary, the brackets, braces and rear stone shield may be removed from the frame by removing the retaining bolts.
4. For ease of installation use something to support the bumper. Tighten the bracket and brace nuts to 70 ft. lbs. (98 Nm). Connect the license lamp wiring.

STEP BUMPER

➧ See Figure 20

1. Remove the bracket-to-bumper nuts and bolts.
2. Remove the brace-to-bumper nuts, spring washers, washers and bolts.
3. Lift the bumper from the truck.
4. Install the bumper and tighten all nuts to 52 ft. lbs. (70 Nm).

Except 1988-91 R/V Series

➧ See Figure 21

1. Remove the bracket-to-bumper nuts and bolts.
2. Remove the brace-to-bumper nuts, washers and bolts.
3. Lift the bumper from the truck.
4. Install the bumper and tighten the brace and bracket bolts to 65 ft. lbs. (90 Nm).

Grille and Molding

REMOVAL & INSTALLATION

1988-91 R/V Series

➧ See Figure 22

1. Remove the lower radiator grille-to-grille bolts.
2. Remove the radiator support-to-grille bolts.
3. Slide the bottom of the grille out and lower the grille from the truck.
4. Remove the headlight bezels.
5. Remove the headlights.
6. Remove the nuts securing the molding to the fender, radiator support and lower grille panel.
7. Remove the molding.
8. Remove the molding clips.
9. Remove the lower radiator grille-to-fender bolts.
10. Remove the lower radiator grille-to-sheet metal support bolts.
11. Remove the lower radiator grille.

To install:

12. Position the lower radiator grille on the truck.
13. Install the lower radiator grille-to-sheet metal support bolts.
14. Install the lower radiator grille-to-fender bolts.
15. Install the upper molding on the radiator support with clips and nuts. Make the nuts finger-tight.
16. Install the lower molding. on the radiator support with clips and nuts. Make the nuts finger-tight.
17. Install the right and left moldings on the fenders.

➡The moldings must butt against the upper and lower moldings and are clipped to them.

18. Tighten the nuts securing the moldings.
19. Install the headlights.
20. Install the headlight bezels.
21. Insert the top of the grille into the underside of the radiator support, then, slide the bottom of the grille into place.

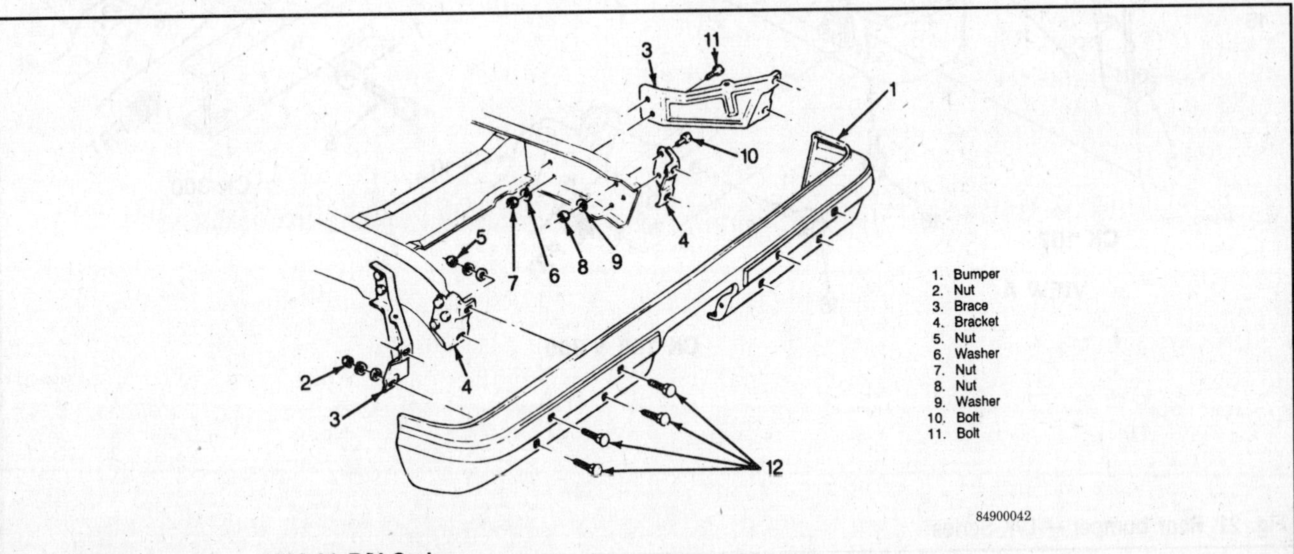

Fig. 19 Rear bumper — 1988-91 R/V Series

1. Bumper
2. Brace
3. Bracket
4. Nut
5. Bolt
6. Bolt
7. Bolt
8. Bolt
9. Reinforcement
10. Washer
11. Nut
12. Bolt
13. Nut
84900043

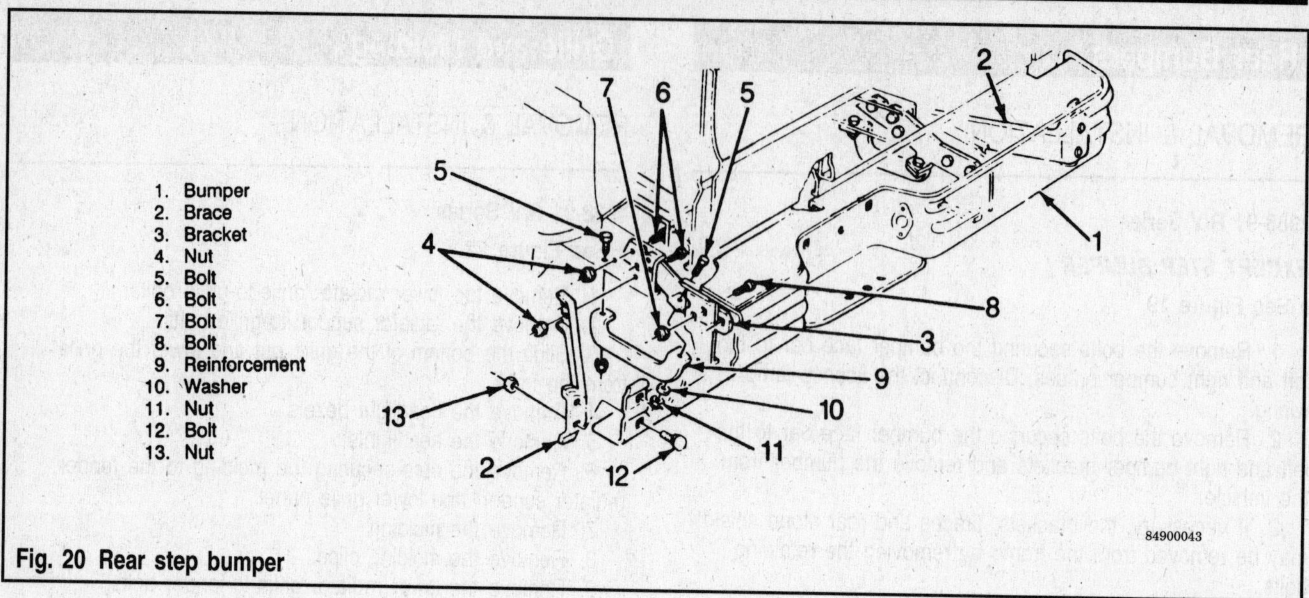

Fig. 20 Rear step bumper

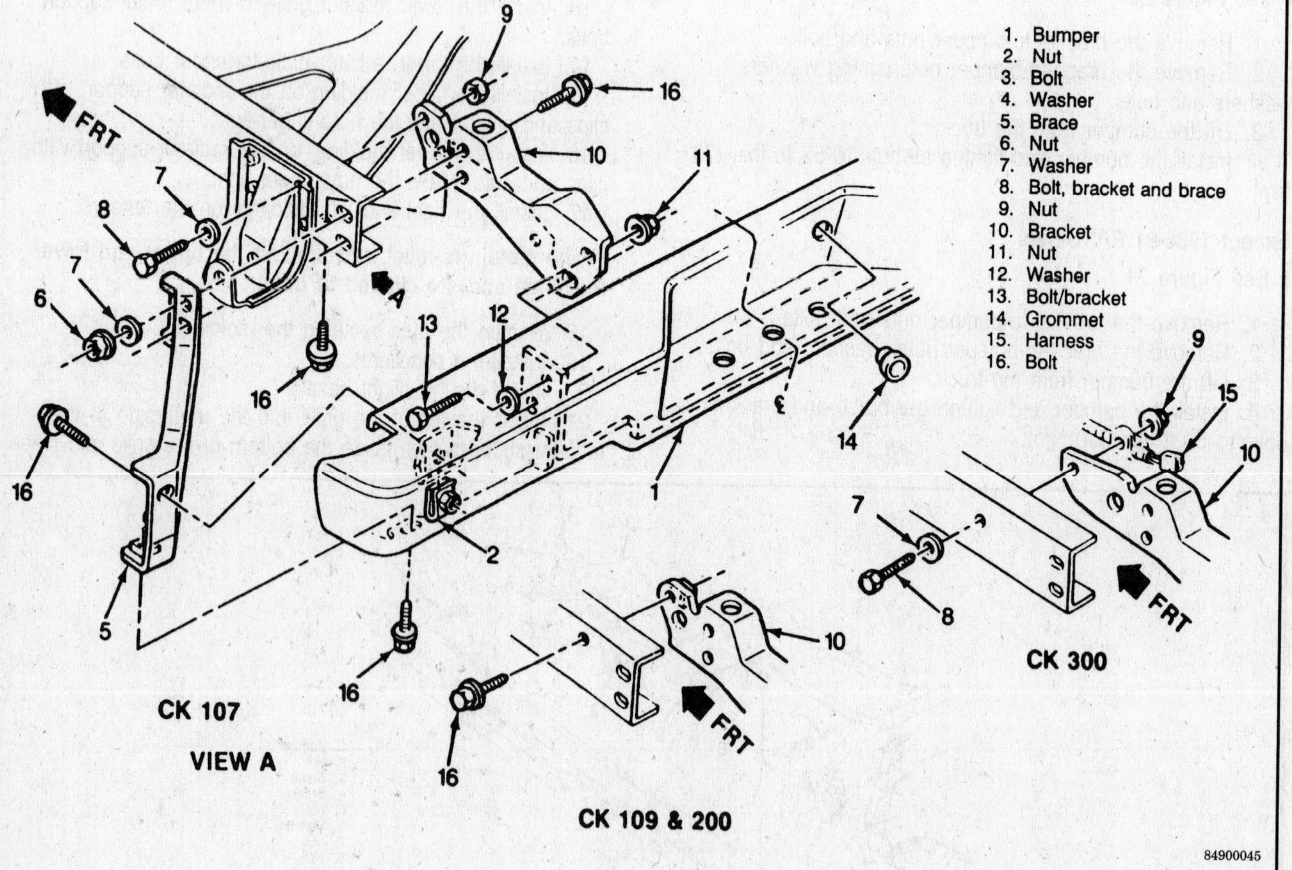

1. Bumper
2. Nut
3. Bolt
4. Washer
5. Brace
6. Nut
7. Washer
8. Bolt, bracket and brace
9. Nut
10. Bracket
11. Nut
12. Washer
13. Bolt/bracket
14. Grommet
15. Harness
16. Bolt
FRT
A
CK 107
VIEW A
CK 109 & 200
CK 300
84900045

Fig. 21 Rear bumper — C/K Series

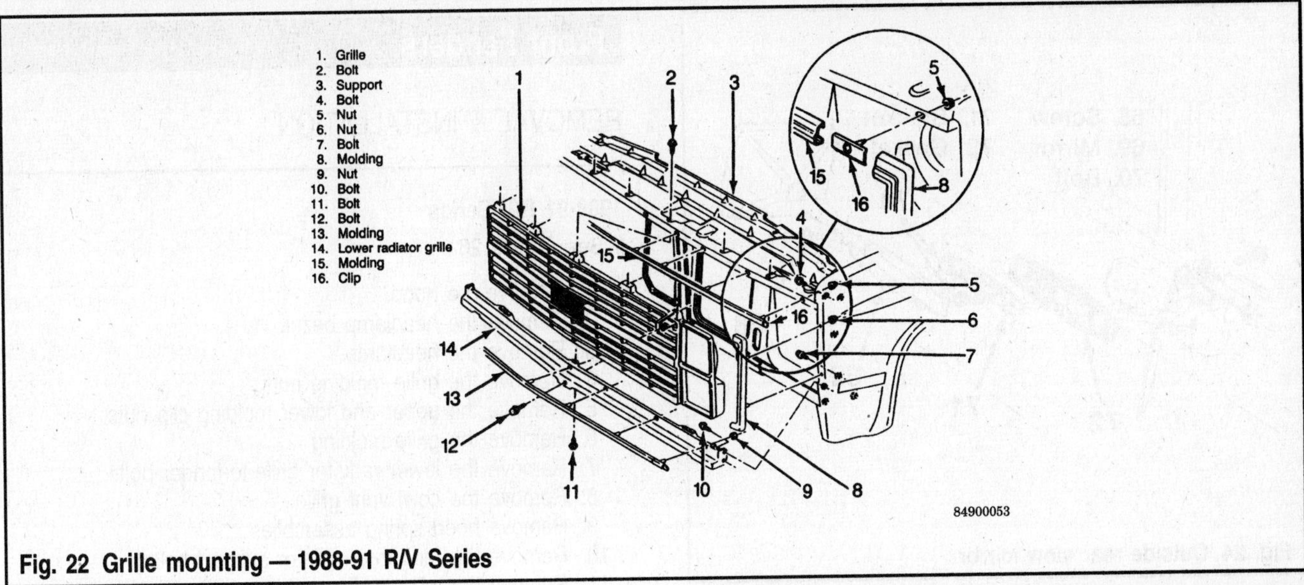

Fig. 22 Grille mounting — 1988-91 R/V Series

22. Install the radiator support-to-grille bolts.
23. Install the lower radiator grille-to-grille bolts.

Except 1988-91 R/V Series

➧ See Figure 23

1. Remove the parking lamps and side marker lamps.
2. Remove the 2 grille-to-latch support bolts.
3. Remove the 1 grille bracket-to-latch support bolt.
4. Remove the 6 grille-to-radiator support bolts.
5. Lift the grille and filler panels from the truck.
6. Install the grille.

Outside Rear View Mirror

REMOVAL & INSTALLATION

Standard Type

➧ See Figure 24

1. If you are replacing an electrically operated mirror it may be necessary to remove the trim panel upper extension.
2. Remove the mirror to bracket screw and remove the mirror from the door.
3. Remove the bracket to door bolts and remove the bracket and gasket from the vehicle.
4. Disengage the electrical connector.
5. Installation is the reverse of removal.

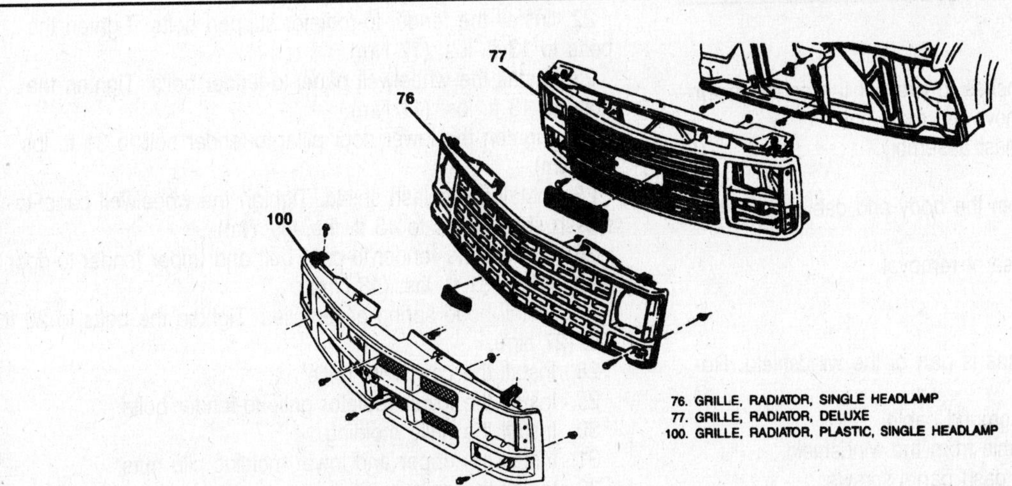

Fig. 23 Grille mounting — except 1988-91 R/V Series

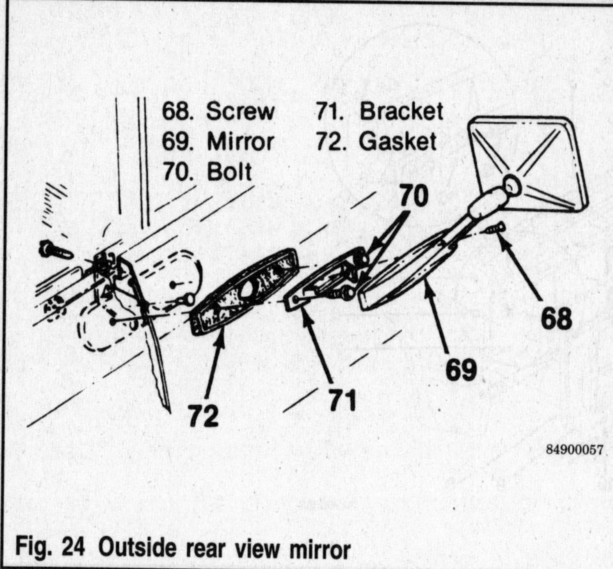

Fig. 24 Outside rear view mirror

Below Eyeline Type

➧ See Figure 25

1. Remove the mirror cover screw and lift the cover and pivot the mirror towards the window.
2. Remove the mirror to door bolts and remove the mirror and seal from the door.
3. To install, position the mirror and seal to the door and install the retaining bolts.
4. Pivot the mirror away from the window, and lower the mirror cover.
5. Installation is the reverse of removal.

Antenna

REMOVAL & INSTALLATION

Fender Mounted Type

1. Use two separate wrenches to prevent the cable assembly from turning and and remove the mast nut.
2. Remove the rod and mast assembly.
3. Remove the bezel.
4. Remove the screws from the body and cable assembly.
5. Remove the insulator.
6. Installation is the reverse of removal.

Windshield Type

On these models the antenna is part of the windshield. Replace the cable as follows:

1. Disconnect the battery ground cable.
2. Unsnap the antenna cable from the windshield.
3. Remove the bracket to dash panel screws.
4. Disconnect the cable at the rear of the radio receiver and remove the cable assembly.

Front Fenders

REMOVAL & INSTALLATION

1988-91 R/V Series

➧ See Figure 26

1. Remove the hood.
2. Remove the headlamp bezel.
3. Remove the headlamp.
4. Remove the grille molding nuts.
5. Remove the upper and lower molding clip nuts.
6. Remove the grille molding.
7. Remove the lower radiator grille-to-fender bolts.
8. Remove the cowl vent grille.
9. Remove hood spring assemblies.
10. Remove the fender-to-radiator support bolts.
11. Remove the wheelwell panel-to-splash shield bolts.
12. Carefully pry out the splash shield retainers and remove the shields.
13. Remove the wheelwell panel-to-fender bolts.
14. Remove the lower door pillar-to-fender bolt and any shims.
15. Open the door and remove the fender-to-cowl bolt and any shims.
16. Remove the upper fender-to-door pillar bolt and any shims.
17. Lift the fender from the truck.

To install:

18. Position the fender on the truck.
19. Install the upper fender-to-door pillar bolt and any shims. Make the bolt finger tight for now.
20. Install the fender-to-cowl bolt and any shims. Make the bolt finger-tight for now.
21. Install the lower door pillar-to-fender bolt and any shims. Make the bolt finger-tight for now.
22. Install the fender-to-radiator support bolts. Tighten the bolts to 13 ft. lbs. (17 Nm).
23. Install the wheelwell panel-to-fender bolts. Tighten the bolts to 13 ft. lbs. (17 Nm).
24. Tighten the lower door pillar-to-fender bolt to 31 ft. lbs. (42 Nm).
25. Install the splash shield. Tighten the wheelwell panel-to-splash shield bolts to 13 ft. lbs. (17 Nm).
26. Tighten the fender-to-cowl bolt and upper fender-to-door pillar bolt to 31 ft. lbs. (43 Nm).
27. Install hood spring assemblies. Tighten the bolts to 20 ft. lbs. (27 Nm).
28. Install the cowl vent grille.
29. Install the lower radiator grille-to-fender bolts.
30. Install the grille molding.
31. Install the upper and lower molding clip nuts.
32. Install the grille molding nuts.
33. Install the headlamp.
34. Install the headlamp bezel.
35. Install the hood.

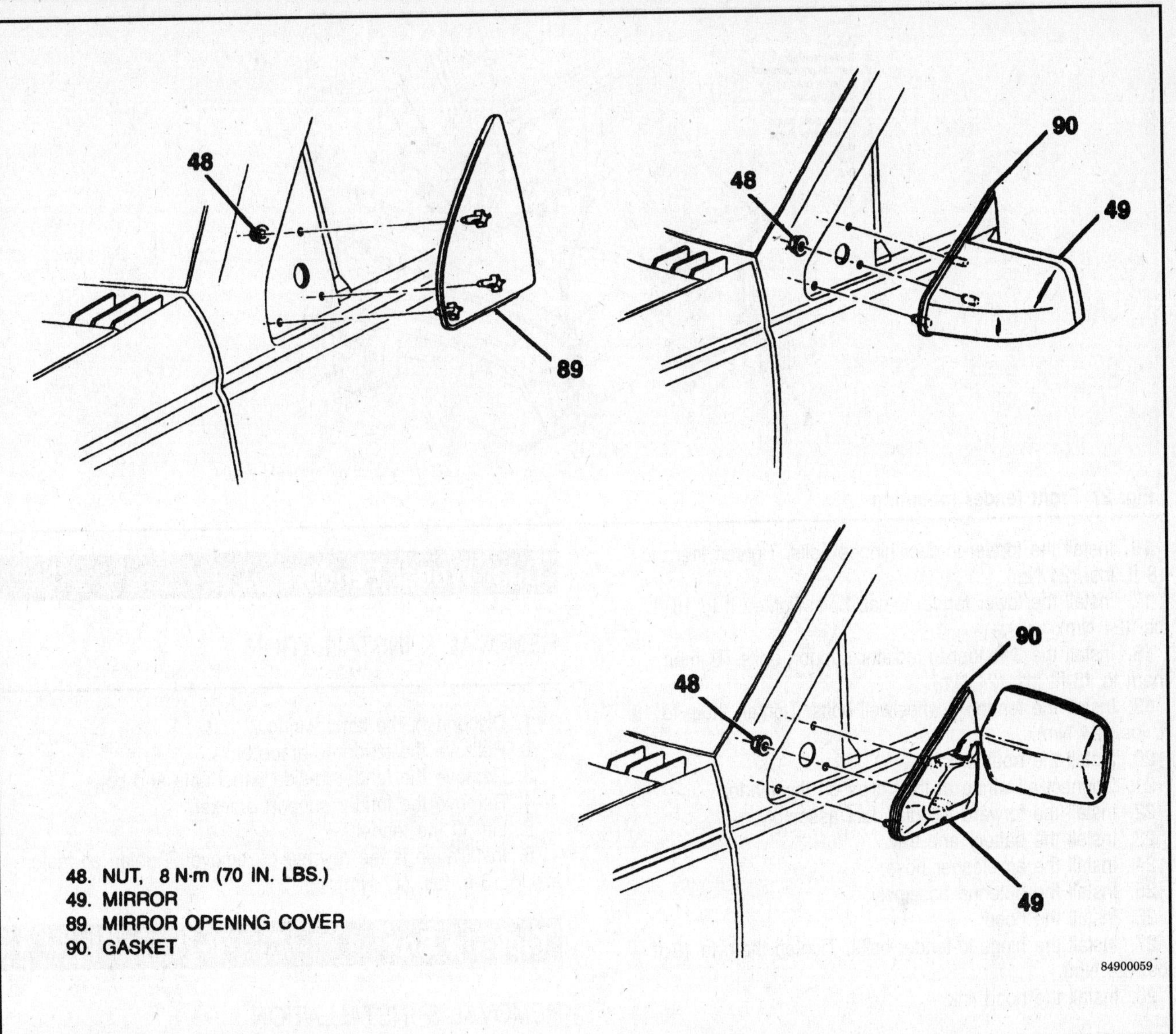

48
89
48
90
49
48
90
49
48. NUT, 8 N·m (70 IN. LBS.)
49. MIRROR
89. MIRROR OPENING COVER
90. GASKET
84900059

Fig. 25 Outside rear view mirror

5
4
3
1
6
2
3
1. Fender
2. Bolt
3. Shim
4. Bolt
5. Bolt
6. Bolt
84900061

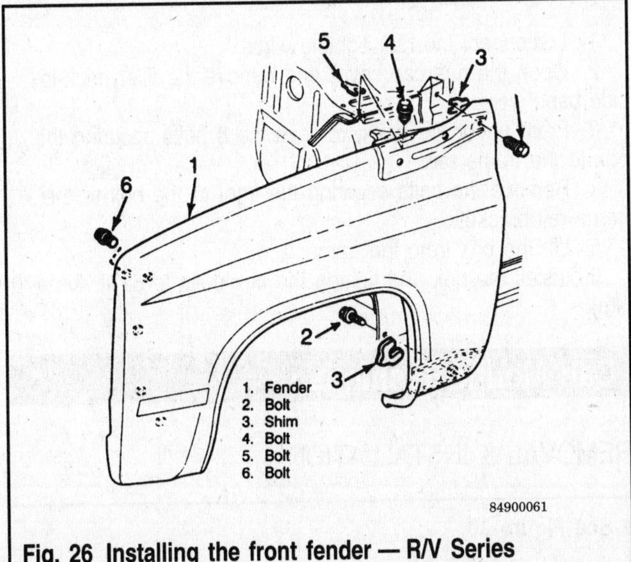

Fig. 26 Installing the front fender — R/V Series

Except 1988-91 R/V Series

➧ See Figure 27

1. Remove the hood link from the fender.
2. Remove the hinge-to-fender bolts.
3. Remove the hood.
4. Remove the antenna assembly.
5. Remove the air cleaner hose from the fender.
6. Remove the battery and tray.
7. Remove the forward air inlet duct assembly from the fender.
8. Disconnect all wiring at their clips on the fender.
9. Remove the trouble light.
10. Remove the fender-to-wheelwell bolts.
11. Remove the 3 fender-to-radiator support bolts.
12. Remove the lower fender-to-cab bolt.
13. Open the door and remove the fender-to-door hinges bolts.
14. Lift off the fender.

To install:

15. Position the fender.

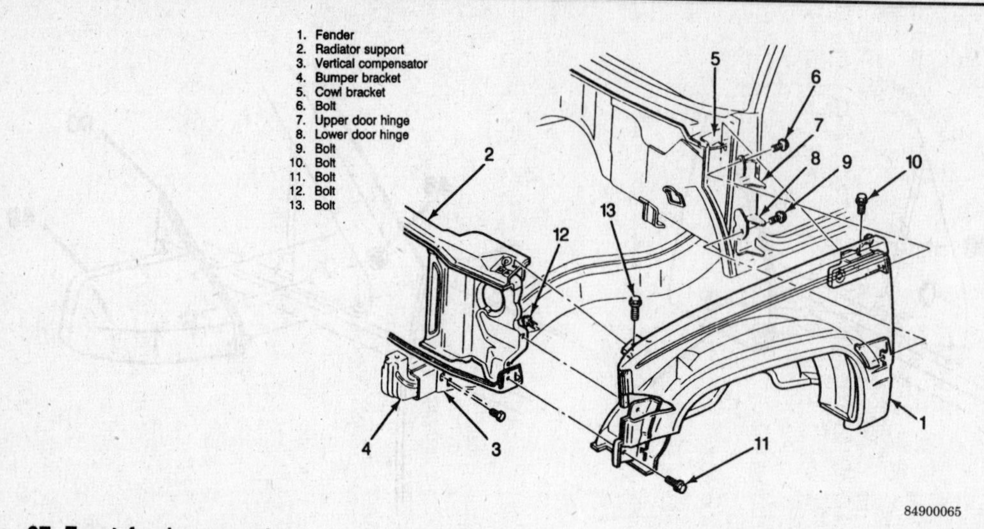

Fig. 27 Front fender mounting

16. Install the fender-to-door hinges bolts. Tighten them to 18 ft. lbs. (24 Nm).
17. Install the lower fender-to-cab bolt. Tighten it to 18 ft. lbs. (24 Nm).
18. Install the 3 fender-to-radiator support bolts. Tighten them to 18 ft. lbs. (24 Nm).
19. Install the fender-to-wheelwell bolts. Tighten them to 18 ft. lbs. (24 Nm).
20. Install the trouble light.
21. Connect all wiring at their clips on the fender.
22. Install the forward air inlet duct assembly.
23. Install the battery and tray.
24. Install the air cleaner hose.
25. Install the antenna assembly.
26. Install the hood.
27. Install the hinge-to-fender bolts. Tighten them to 18 ft. lbs. (24 Nm).
28. Install the hood link.

Step Side Rear Fenders

REMOVAL & INSTALLATION

See Figure 28

1. Remove the step pads.
2. Remove the fender-to-brace fasteners.
3. Remove the brace-to-support bolts.
4. Remove the fender-to-support screws.
5. Remove the tail light side panel screws.
6. Remove the fender-to-bracket screws.
7. Remove the fender-to-side panel screws.
8. Lift off the fender.
9. Install the fender and tighten the fender-to-bracket screw to 18 ft. lbs. (24 Nm) and all other screws to 13 ft. lbs. (17 Nm).

Dual Wheel Fenders

REMOVAL & INSTALLATION

1. Disconnect the lamp wiring.
2. Remove the fender-to-brace bolts.
3. Remove the fender-to-side panel nuts and bolts.
4. Remove the fender support bracket.
5. Lift off the fender.
6. Installation is the reverse of removal. Tighten all fasteners to 13 ft. lbs. (17 Nm).

Pick-Up Box

REMOVAL & INSTALLATION

See Figure 29

1. Disconnect the rear lighting wires.
2. Open the gas cap cover and remove the filler neck-to-side panel screws.
3. From under the truck, remove the 8 bolts securing the box to the frame rails.
4. Remove the bolts securing the front of the box to the frame rail brackets.
5. Lift the box from the frame.
6. Install the box and tighten the box bolts to 52 ft. lbs. (70 Nm)

Cab Mount Bushings

REMOVAL & INSTALLATION

See Figure 30

1. Raise the side of the truck to be worked on, with a floor jack.

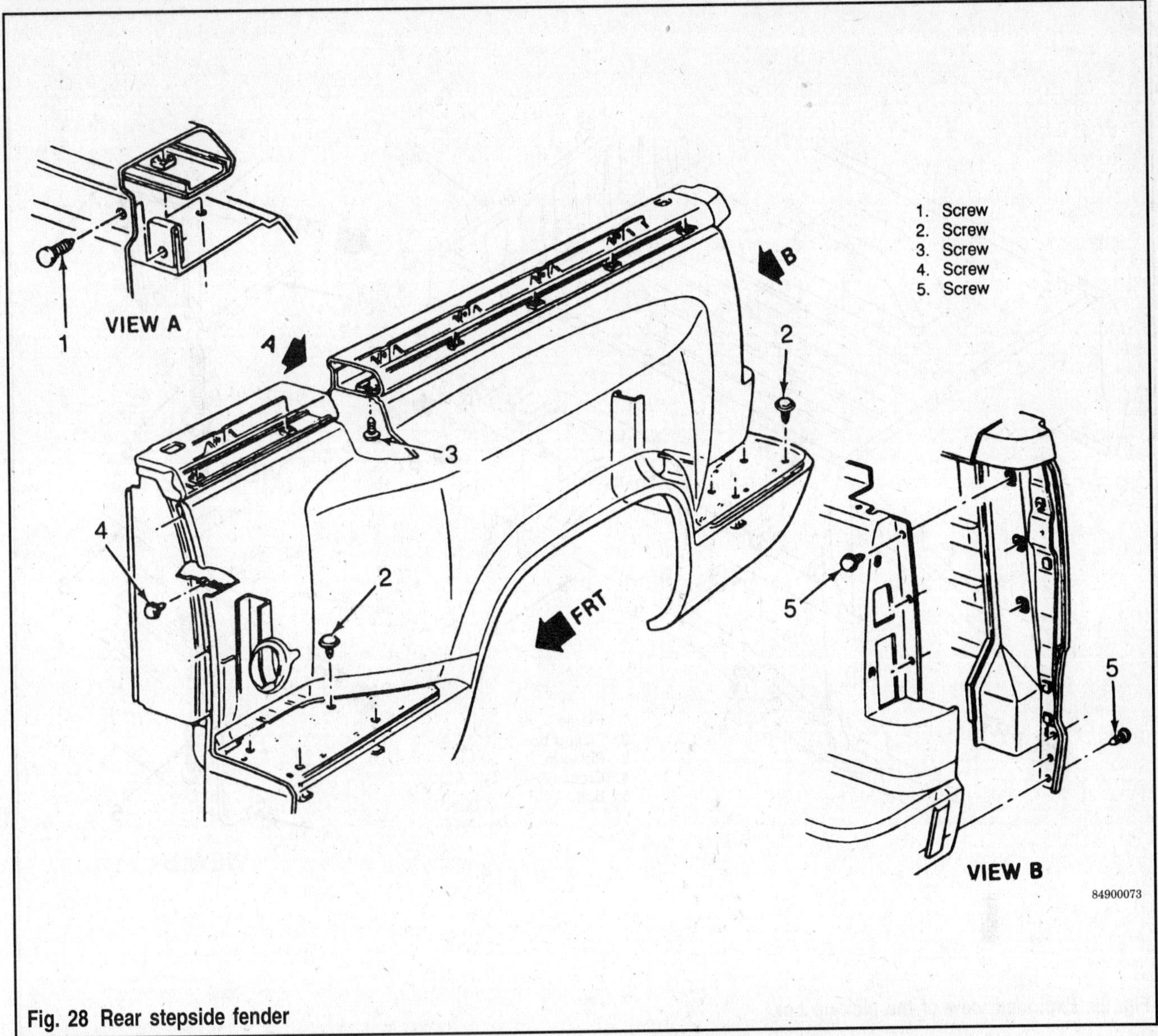

Fig. 28 Rear stepside fender

2. Place jackstands under the cab on that side.
3. Remove the bolt, bushing retainer and lower bushing.
4. Slowly and carefully, lower the truck so that the jackstand raises the cab. Replace the upper bushing.
5. Raise the truck and install the lower bushing, retainer and bolt. Tighten the bolt to 55 ft. lbs. (70 Nm).

Roof

REMOVAL & INSTALLATION

➡This applies to 1988-91 Blazer/Jimmy only.

1. Lower the rear window.
2. Remove the roof inner edge trim panels.
3. Remove the roof-to-body attaching bolts.
4. Using an assistant, break loose the roof from the insulating strips. Carefully lift the roof from the truck.

CAUTION

It is very heavy and awkward! Be careful to avoid flexing the roof or letting it crash into anything!

5. Without flexing the top, carefully place it on two 2·4 pieces of lumber.
6. Installation is the reverse of removal. Replace any damaged insulation.

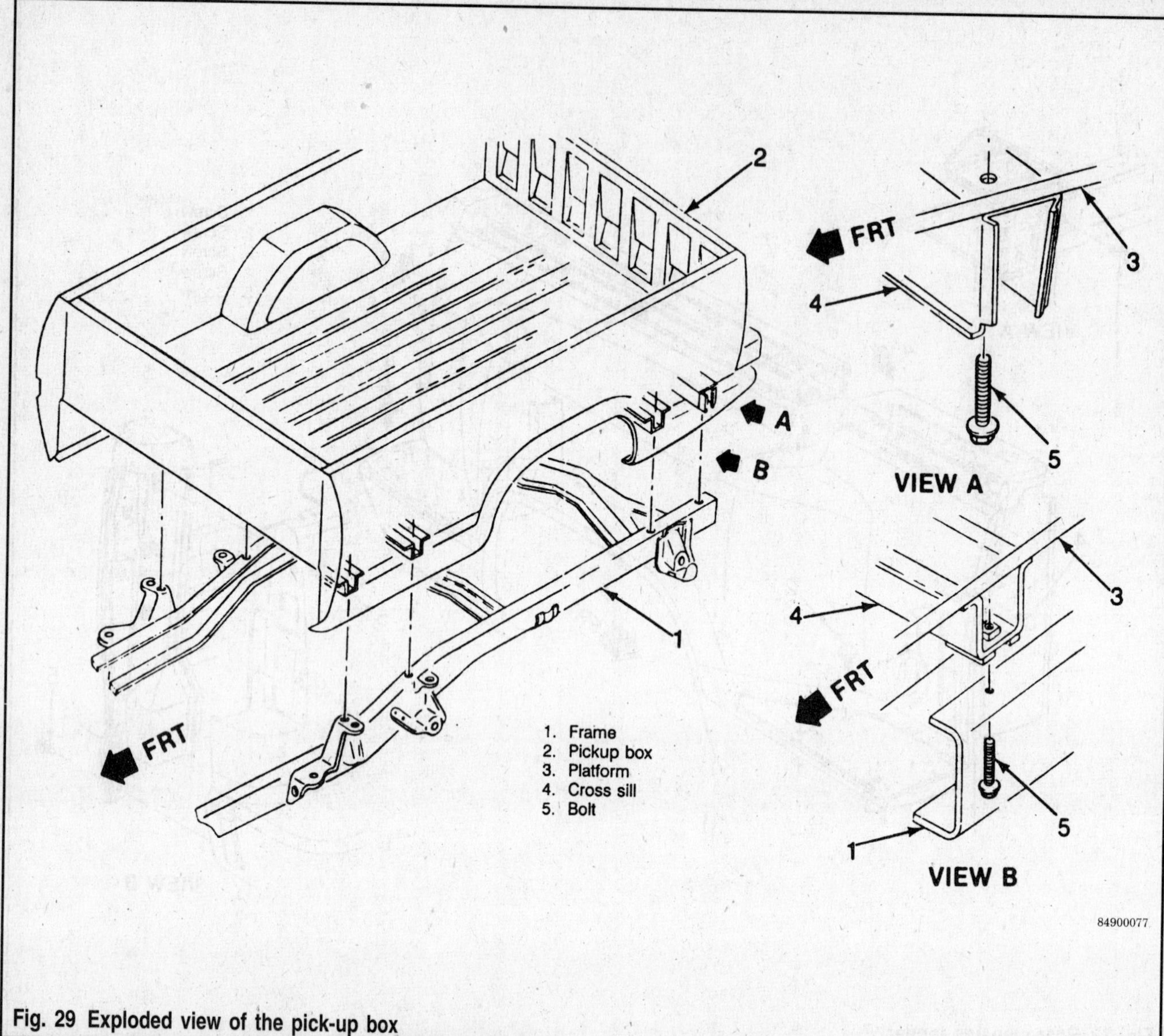

Fig. 29 Exploded view of the pick-up box

Spare Tire Carrier

REMOVAL & INSTALLATION

Suburban and Two Door Utility Models

The spare tire mounting for the Suburban and two door utility models is located at the left rear wheel well. The two door utility uses a bracket (carrier) for retention while the Suburban uses a mount (support) that is part of the body.

1. Remove the spare tire retaining nut and adapter.
2. Remove the spare tire.
3. Remove the bolts from the support (carrier).
4. Remove the support (carrier).

To install:

5. Install the support (carrier) and the bolts. Tighten the bolts to 44 inch. lbs. (5 Nm) on Suburban models and 32 ft. lbs. (40 Nm) on two door utility models.
6. Install the spare tire, adaptor and nut.

Pick-Up Models

The spare tire and mounting for the Pick-Up models is located behind the rear axle and forward of the rear bumper using a winch/cable system for stowage.

1. Remove the spare tire.
2. Remove the pin and retainer from the shaft.
3. Remove the bolts, nuts, and hoist from the crossmember.

To install:

4. Install the hoist to the crossmember.
5. Install the bolts and nuts. Tighten the bolts to 18 ft. lbs. (25 Nm).
6. Install the pin and retainer to the shaft.
7. Install the spare tire.

Four Door Utility Models

The spare tire and mounting for the Four Door Utility models is located behind the rear axle and forward of the rear bumper using a winch/cable system for stowage.

1. Remove the spare tire.

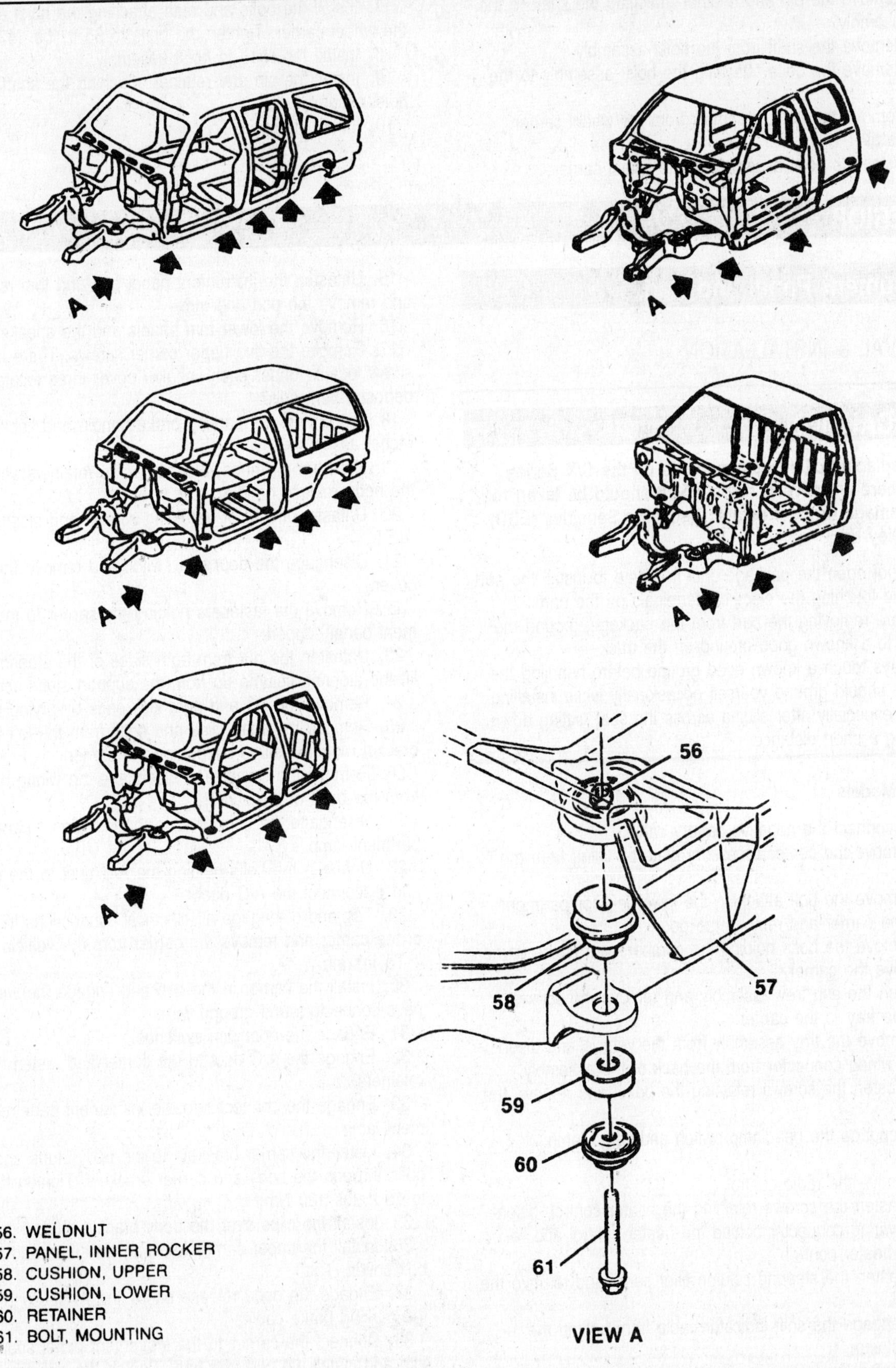

Fig. 30 Cab mount bushing locations

2. Remove the pin and retainer attaching the shaft to the hoist assembly.
3. Remove the shaft from the hoist assembly.
4. Remove the bolts attaching the hoist assembly to the carrier.
5. Remove the hoist assembly from the wheel carrier.

To install:

6. Install the hoist assembly to the wheel carrier.
7. Install the bolts and nuts attaching the hoist assembly to the wheel carrier. Tighten the bolts to 35 ft. lbs. (47 Nm).
8. Install the shaft to hoist assembly.
9. Install the pin and retainer attaching the shaft to the hoist assembly.
10. Install the spare tire.

INTERIOR

Instrument Panel and Pad

REMOVAL & INSTALLATION

⁂CAUTION

When replacing cluster components on the C/K Series trucks there are several steps which should be taken to avoid damage to Electrostatic Discharge Sensitive (ESD) parts. They are:

- Do not open the package until it is time to install the part
- Avoid touching the electrical terminals on the part
- Before removing the part from the package, ground the package to a known good ground on the truck
- Always touch a known good ground before handling the part. You should ground yourself occasionally while installing the part, especially after sliding across the seat, sitting down or walking a short distance

1988-94 Models

1. Disconnect the negative battery cable.
2. Remove the center accessory plate by lifting from the bottom.
3. Remove the bolt attaching the lower left compartment door to the carrier and remove the door.
4. Remove the bolts holding the compartment to the carrier and remove the carrier.
5. Open the ash tray assembly and remove the screws holding the tray to the carrier.
6. Remove the tray assembly from the vehicle and disengage the wiring connector from the back of the assembly.
7. Unfasten the screws retaining the bezel and remove the bezel.
8. Disengage the headlamp switch and cargo lamp connector.
9. Remove the radio control.
10. Unfasten the screws retaining the heater control, disengage the wiring connector behind the heater control and remove the heater control.
11. Unfasten the steering column filler panel and remove the filler panel.
12. Disengage the shift indicator cable from behind the instrument cluster.
13. Unfasten the instrument cluster retainers and remove the instrument cluster.
14. Unfasten the air duct retainers and disconnect the air duct.
15. Unfasten the instrument panel pod and trim retainers and remove the pod and trim.
16. Remove the lower trim panels and the speaker covers.
17. Remove the five upper carrier screws. There is one screw located under each speaker cover three located in the defroster vent grille.
18. Disconnect the parking brake handle and cable from the rachet assembly.
19. Unfasten the hood release handle retainers and remove the hood release handle.
20. Unfasten the ALDL retaining screws and disengage the ALDL.
21. Disengage the door jam switch and remove the fuse box cover.
22. Remove the fasteners holding the carrier to the instrument panel support.
23. Unfasten the nut from both sides of the steering column, lift the steering column up from the support studs and lower it.
24. Remove the left and right kick pads by prying them off.
25. Remove the snap clips and bolts from the left and right bracket mounted studs supporting the carrier.
26. Remove the carrier and disengage the wiring harness from the back of the carrier.
27. Disengage the connector to the instrument panel compartment lamp.
28. Unfasten the bolts holding the A/C duct to the carrier and disconnect the A/C duct.
29. Tag and disengage all electrical connections to the back of the carrier and remove the carrier from the vehicle.

To install:

30. Install the carrier in the cab and engage the wiring harness connectors and ground wire.
31. Engage the door jam switches.
32. Engage the A/C duct to the carrier and fasten the retainers.
33. Engage the connector to the instrument panel compartment lamp.
34. Install the carrier brackets to the body studs and the bolts through the body and carrier brackets. Tighten the bolts to 15 ft. lbs. (20 Nm).
35. Install the clips over the body bracket studs.
36. Install the upper carrier retaining fasteners and the fuse box cover.
37. Engage the hood release cable, the ALDL connector and the parking brake cable.
38. Connect the carrier to the instrument panel support and trim and install the pod and trim. Tighten the retainers.
39. Install the lower left and right trim panels.
40. Install the instrument cluster and tighten the fasteners.

41. Lift the steering column onto the mounting studs and install the two nuts.
42. Engage the shift indicator onto the steering column cover.
43. Connect the heater wiring to the heater control and engage the heater control to the carrier.Tighten the fasteners.
44. Engage the A/C duct to the pad and install the fasteners.
45. Install the speaker cover and the left and right kick trim panels.
46. Install the radio controls, engage the cargo lamp and headlamp electrical connectors.
47. Install the bezel on the carrier and tighten the screws.
48. Install the steering column filler panel and the ash tray assembly. Engage the electrical connectors to cigarette lighter and lamp.
49. Install the strap around the ash tray assembly. Engage the assembly to the carrier and tighten the fasteners.
50. Engage the instrument panel compartment to the right side carrier and tighten the fasteners.
51. Install the compartment door and stop cables.
52. Install the center accessory cover trim plate and connect the negative battery cable,

1995-96 Models

1. Disconnect the negative battery cable and disable the SIR system if equipped.
2. Remove the three relay center bolts from inside the wheel opening and set aside.
3. Disengage the cruise control harness, forward lamp harness, rear lamp harness, SIR system harness, relay center and unfasten the two screws retaining the convenience center to the cowl.
4. Disengage the antenna lead-in and unfasten the steering shaft bolt.
5. Remove the left and right hinge pillar trim panels and disconnect the brake release handle from the cable.
6. Remove the lower bolster fasteners
   a. Unsnap the bolster.
   b. Twist the brake release cable to disengage.
   c. Disengage the lap cooler hose.
7. Disconnect the reaction plate assembly and the tie bar.
8. Disengage the 8-way column connector and the 48-way connector to gain access to the lower column nuts.
9. Disconnect the shift cable (automatic transmission).
10. Remove the steering column.
11. Remove the shift levers
   a. Remove the transfer case lever by pulling straight up. 4WD models must be in 4-LO range.
   b. Manual transmission lever (if equipped).
12. Remove the left and right instrument panel bolts.
13. Remove the center support screws and the three upper instrument panel support screws.
14. Remove the instrument panel from the cowl.
15. Disconnect the parking brake release cable.
16. Tag disengage the following electrical connectors (as necessary).
   - DERM
   - HVAC
   - 22-way engine harness
   - Stoplamp switch
   - VSS calibrator module
   - Clutch or brake release switches
   - Electronic accelerator (diesel)
   - HVAC control cables (if equipped)
17. Remove the instrument panel from the vehicle.

To install:

18. Install the instrument panel in the vehicle and rest it on the lower pivot studs.
19. Connect the convenience center to the cowl and engage the lap cooler duct.
20. Connect the DERM to the center instrument panel support and fasten the nut to the steering column support.
21. Engage the parking brake cable and fasten the instrument panel pivot nuts.
22. Install the instrument panel support nuts.
23. Install the steering column and tighten the four nuts.
24. Install the 48-way connector and screw built onto the steering column.
25. Install the tie bar and tighten the fasteners.
26. Install shift cable (automatic transmission and the accelerator electrical connector (diesel).
27. Install the knee bolster close out panel and the reaction plate. Tighten the fasteners.
28. Install the shift knobs and the lap cooler hose.
29. Engage the park brake cable and install the knee bolster trim.
30. Install the bulkhead connector.
31. Engage all the electrical connections in the engine compartment.
32. Install the instrument panel storage compartment and the steering shaft and bolt.
33. Enable the SIR system and connect the negative battery cable.

Console

REMOVAL & INSTALLATION

Center Console

➧ See Figure 31

1. Remove the floor tray from the compartment.
2. Remove the storage bin and the plugs covering the screws.
3. Remove the screws and the storage compartment.
4. Installation is the reverse of removal.

Overhead Console

➧ See Figure 32

1. Remove the console retaining screws.
2. Disengage the console electrical connectors.
3. Remove the console.
4. Installation is the reverse of removal.

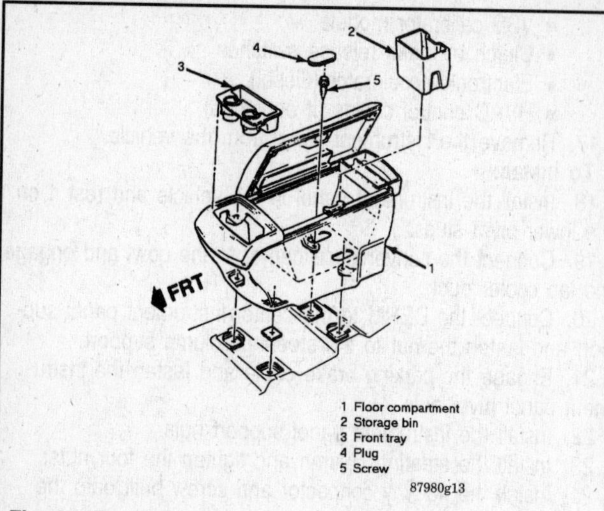

Fig. 31 Exploded view of the center console — 1996 model shown

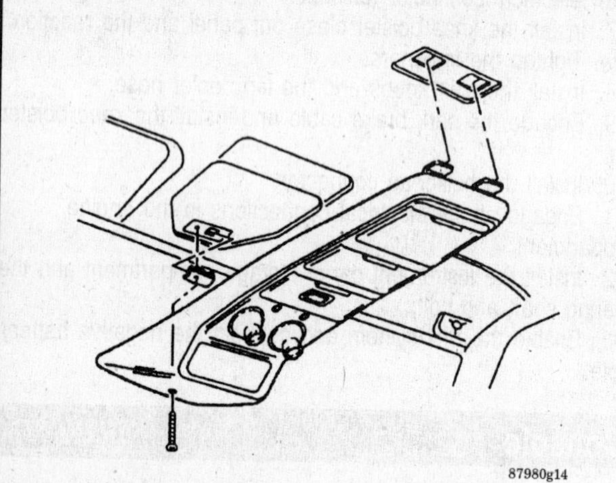

Fig. 32 Exploded view of the overhead console — 1996 model shown

Door Panels

REMOVAL & INSTALLATION

R/V Series

FRONT SIDE DOOR

➧ See Figures 33, 34 and 35

1. Remove the window handle by depressing the door panel and removing the retaining clip.
2. Remove the door lock knob.
3. Remove the arm rest.
4. Snap off the trim covers and remove the screws retaining the assist strap, if so equipped.
5. Remove the 4 screws securing the lower edge of trim panel.
6. Remove the screw at the door handle cover plate and the screw located under the arm rest pad.
7. Remove the trim panel by carefully prying out at the trim retainers located around the perimeter of the panel.

To install:

➡Before installing the door trim assembly, check that all trim retainers are securely installed to the assembly and are not damaged.

8. Pull the door inside handle inward, then position trim assembly to inner panel, inserting door handle through handle hole in panel.
9. Position rim assembly to door inner panel so trim retainers are aligned with attaching holes in panel and tap retainers into holes with a clean rubber mallet.
10. Install previously removed items.

REAR SIDE DOOR

➧ See Figure 36

1. Remove the window handle by depressing the door panel and removing the retaining clip.
2. Remove the door lock knob.
3. Remove the arm rest.
4. Snap off the trim covers and remove the screws retaining the assist strap, if so equipped.
5. Remove the 3 screws securing the lower edge of trim panel.
6. Remove the screw at the door handle cover plate and the screw located under the arm rest pad.
7. Remove the trim panel by carefully prying out at the trim retainers located around the perimeter of the panel.

To install:

➡Before installing the door trim assembly, check that all trim retainers are securely installed to the assembly and are not damaged.

8. Pull the door inside handle inward, then position trim assembly to inner panel, inserting door handle through handle hole in panel.
9. Position rim assembly to door inner panel so trim retainers are aligned with attaching holes in panel and tap retainers into holes with a clean rubber mallet.
10. Install previously removed items.

C/K Series

➧ See Figures 37, 38, 39, 40 and 41

1. Remove the window handle by depressing the door panel and removing the retaining clip.
2. Remove the door lock knob.
3. Remove the arm rest.
4. Snap off the trim covers and remove the screws retaining the assist strap, if so equipped.
5. Remove the electrical switch panel, if so equipped.
6. Remove the trim panel by carefully prying out at the trim retainers located around the perimeter of the panel.

To install:

➡Before installing the door trim assembly, check that all trim retainers are securely installed to the assembly and are not damaged.

7. Pull the door inside handle inward, then position trim assembly to inner panel, inserting door handle through handle hole in panel.

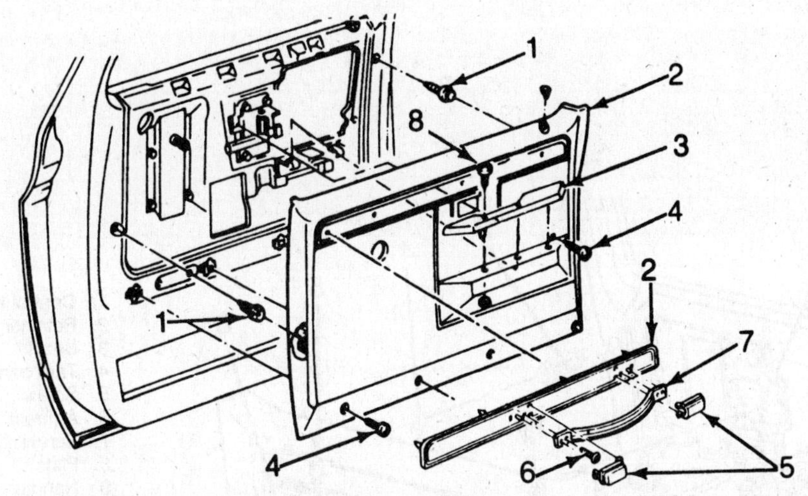

Fig. 33 Front door trim panel — R/V Series

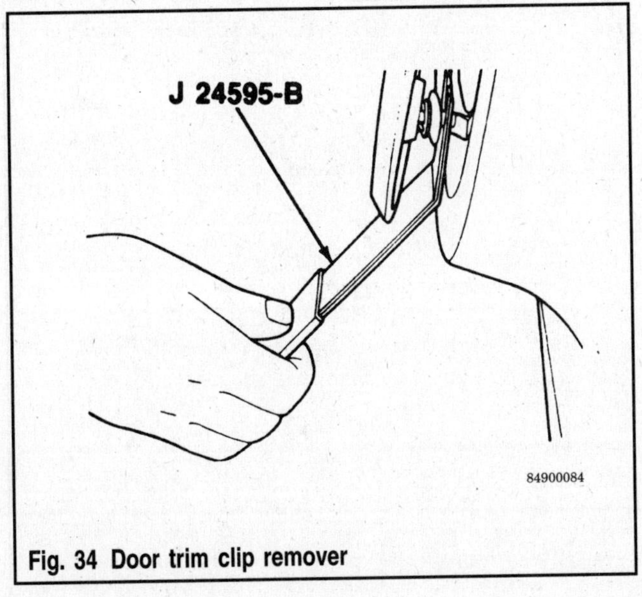

Fig. 34 Door trim clip remover

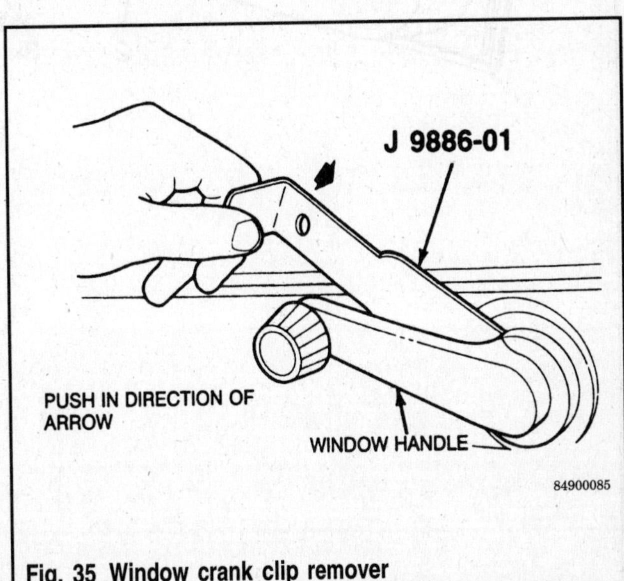

Fig. 35 Window crank clip remover

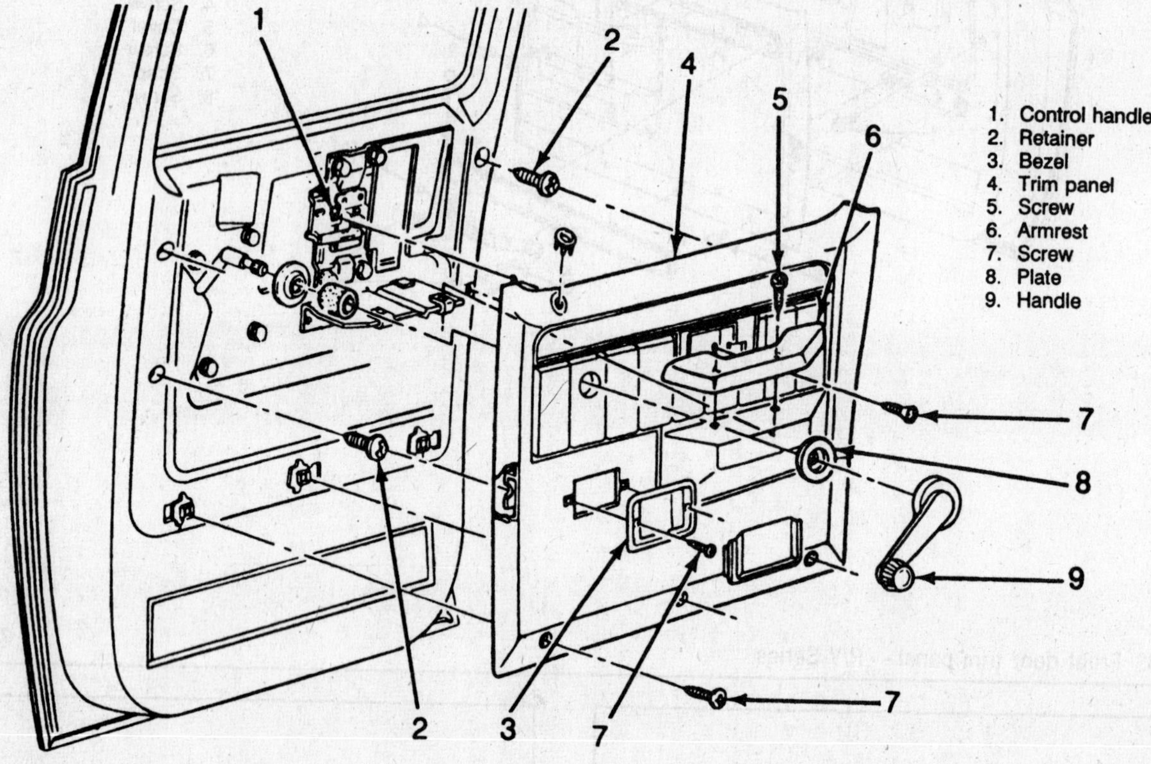

Fig. 36 Rear side door trim panel components — R/V Series

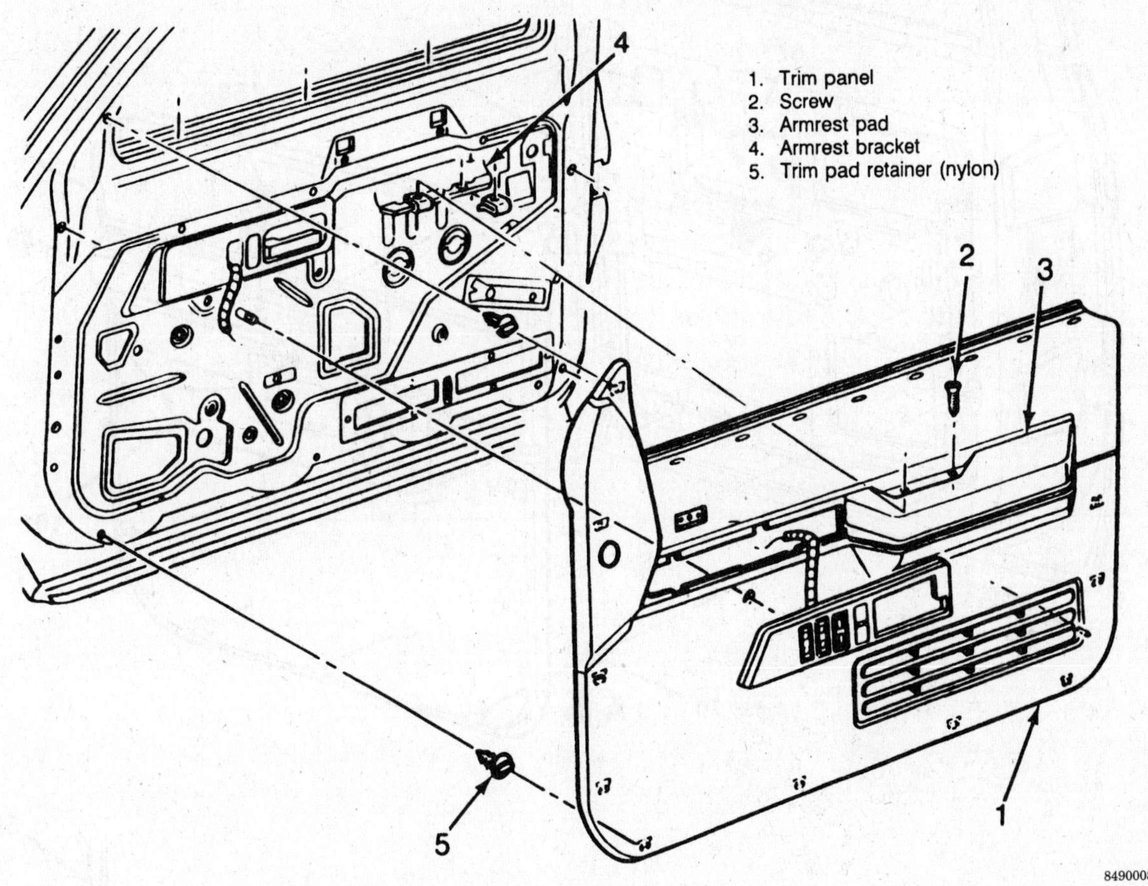

Fig. 37 Door trim panel — C/K Series

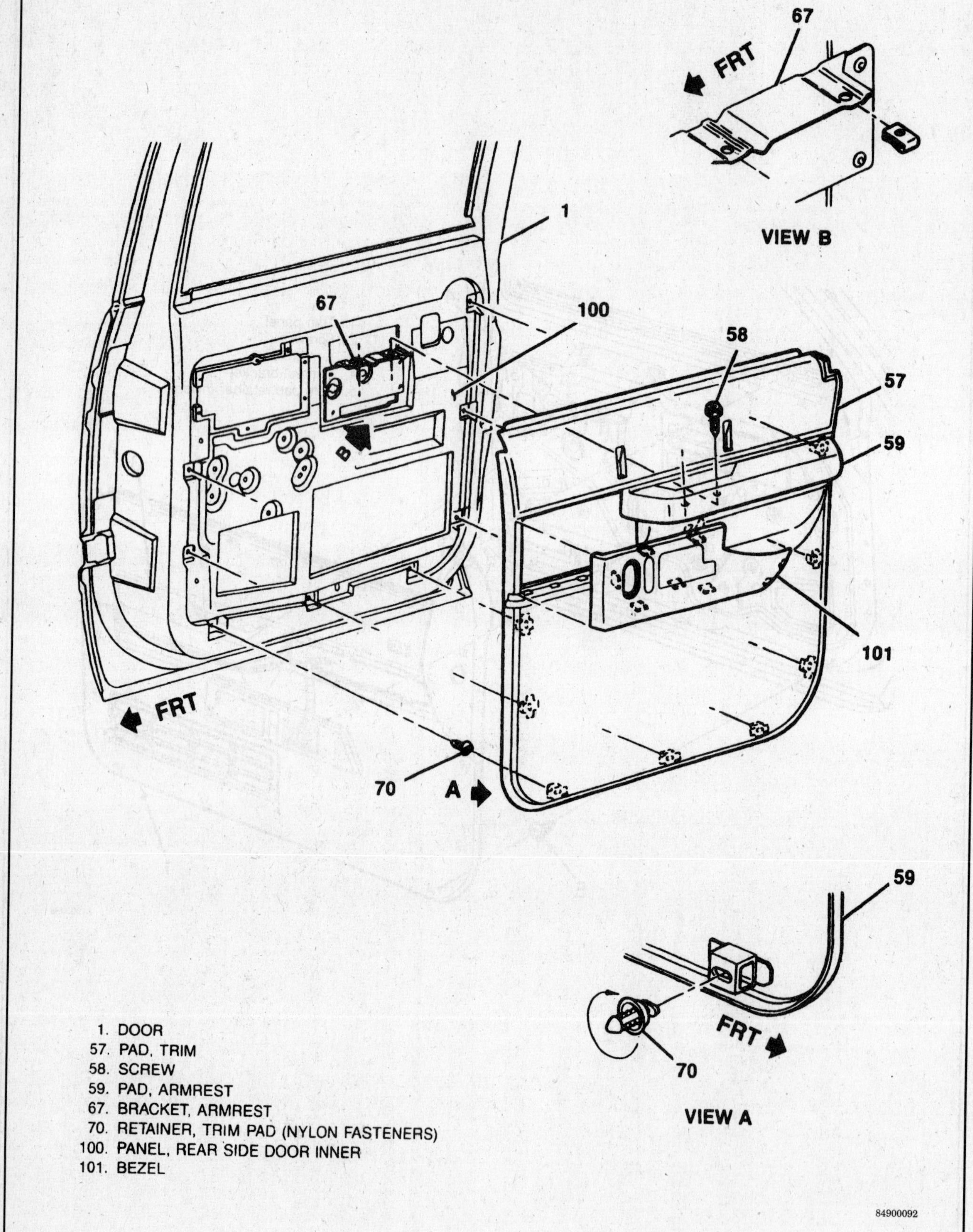

67
FRT
VIEW B
1
67
100
58
57
59
B
101
FRT
70
A
59
FRT
70
VIEW A
1. DOOR
57. PAD, TRIM
58. SCREW
59. PAD, ARMREST
67. BRACKET, ARMREST
70. RETAINER, TRIM PAD (NYLON FASTENERS)
100. PANEL, REAR SIDE DOOR INNER
101. BEZEL
84900092

Fig. 38 Rear side door trim panel — C/K Series

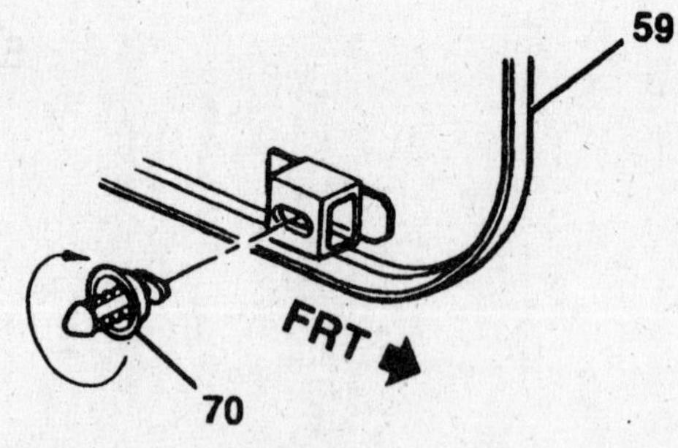

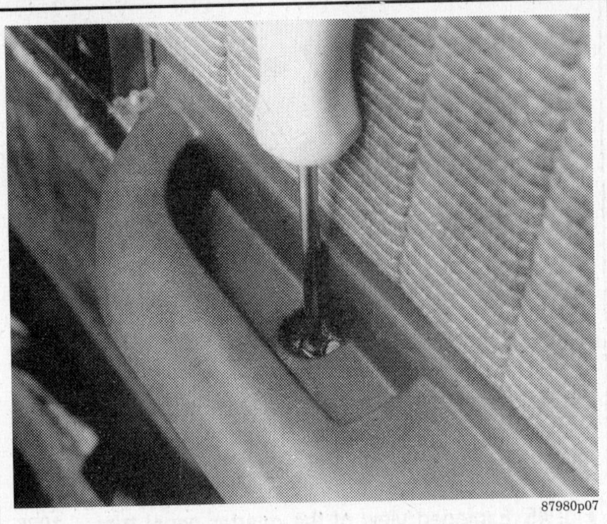
Fig. 39 Remove the arm rest

Fig. 40 Remove the electrical switch panel, if so equipped

Fig. 41 Remove the trim panel by carefully prying out at the trim retainers locations

8. Position rim assembly to door inner panel so trim retainers are aligned with attaching holes in panel and tap retainers into holes with a clean rubber mallet.
9. Install previously removed items.

Rear Seat Access Door (Extended Cab)

See Figures 42 and 43

1. Remove the armrest screws and the seatbelt retractor cover and "D" ring.
2. Remove the trim panel by carefully prying out at the trim retainers located around the perimeter of the panel.

To install:

3. Install the trim panel on the door and engage the trim retainers.
4. Install the seatbelt "D" ring and retractor cover.
5. Fasten the armrest screws.

Interior Trim Panels

REMOVAL & INSTALLATION

Quarter panel

PICK-UP, EXTENDED CAB AND CREW CAB

See Figures 44 and 45

1. Remove the coat hook retaining screw and the coat hook.
2. Remove the seat belt guide and retractor.
3. Remove the jack cover, jack, and jack tray on the right side.
4. Remove the rear window moulding retaining screws and the rear window moulding.
5. Quarter panel trim screws (pick-up and crew cab only).
6. Rear screw from the sill plate (pick-up and crew cab only).
7. Remove the quarter panel.

To install:

8. Install the quarter panel.

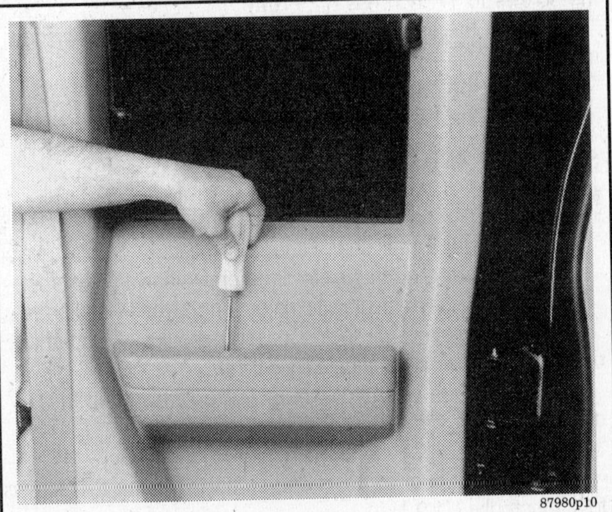
Fig. 42 Remove the armrest screws

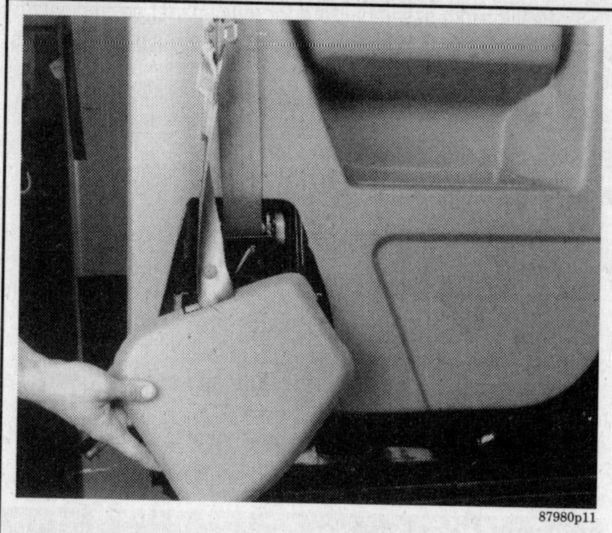

Fig. 43 Remove the seat belt retractor cover

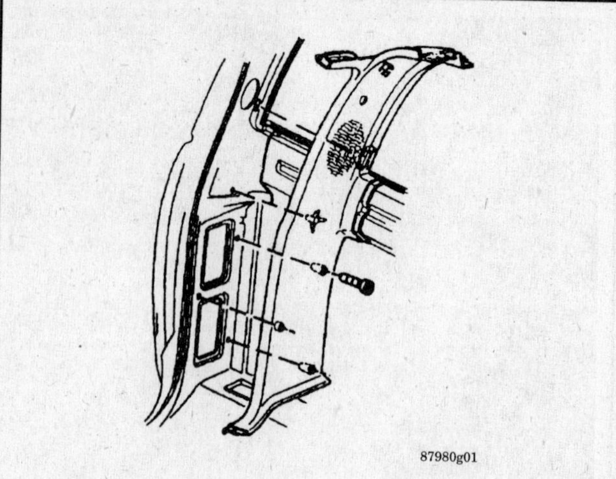

Fig. 45 Exploded view of the quarter panel trim — 1996 pick-up and crew cab shown

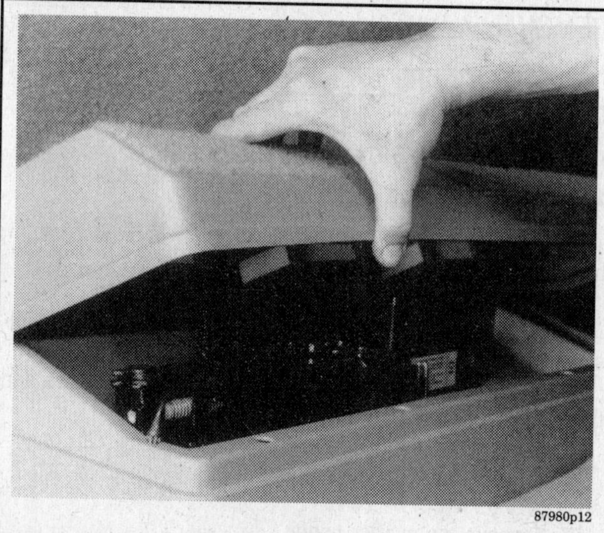

Fig. 44 Remove the jack cover

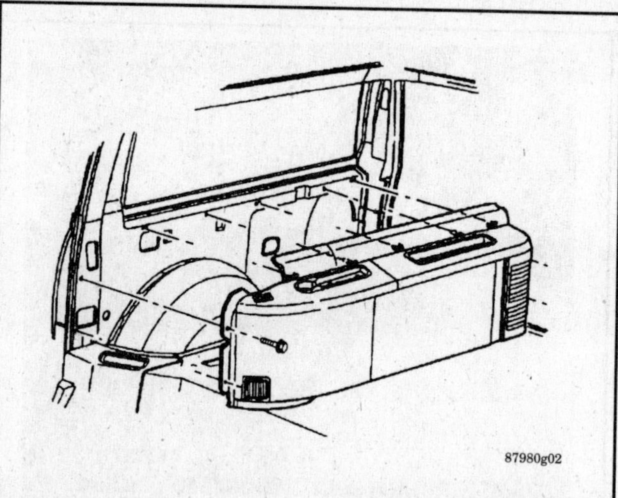

Fig. 46 Exploded view of the right quarter panel trim — 1996 Suburban shown

9. Fasten the screws (pick-up and crew cab only). Tighten the screws to 17 inch. lbs. (1.9 Nm).
10. Install the screw into the sill plate and the rear window moulding.
11. Install the jack tray, jack, and cover.
12. Install the seat belt retractor, guide and the coat hook.

SUBURBAN AND UTILITY (RIGHT SIDE)

See Figure 46

1. Remove the rear seat. Refer to procedure in this section.
2. Remove the armrest retaining screws and the armrest.
3. Remove the rear blower motor trim cover (if equipped).
4. Remove the cargo lock door pillar moulding (Suburban) or front door lock pillar moulding (utility).
5. Remove the quarter panel retaining screws and the quarter panel.

To install:

6. Install the quarter panel and screws. Tighten the screws to 17 inch. lbs. (1.9 Nm).
7. Install the cargo door lock pillar moulding (Suburban) or front door lock pillar moulding (utility).
8. Install the cargo door pillar trim moulding and the rear blower motor trim cover (if equipped).
9. Install the armrest and tighten the retaining screws to 17 inch. lbs. (1.9 Nm).
10. Install the rear seat. Refer to the procedure in this section.

SUBURBAN AND UTILITY (LEFT SIDE)

1. Remove the rear seat and spare tire cover.
2. Remove the spare tire and jack (utility).
3. Remove the spare tire rest trim covers, rest bolts, rest, and the tire holder from the floor.
4. Remove the spare tire I-bolt from the vehicle.
5. Remove the arm rest and the cargo door pillar mouldings.
6. Remove the intermediate seat belt to rear door pillar bolt and the seat belt anchor to the floor bolt.
7. Remove the rear door lock pillar moulding.

8. Remove the quarter panel retaining screws and quarter panel.

To install:

9. Install the quarter panel and retaining screws. Tighten the screws to 17 inch. lbs. (1.9 Nm).
10. Install the rear door lock pillar trim (Suburban) or front door lock pillar (Utility).
11. Install the intermediate seat belt anchor to floor bolt and the seat belt to rear door pillar bolt.
12. Install the cargo door trim panels to the pillar.
13. Install the arm rest and the spare tire I-bolt.
14. Install the spare tire holder and the tire rest.
15. Install the tire rest bolts and the tire rest covers and jack.
16. Install the spare tire and cover.

Lower Rear Quarter Trim Panel

PICK-UP AND EXTENDED CAB

1. Remove the arm rest (if equipped).
2. Remove the pocket from the lower panel (if equipped).
3. Remove the lower panel screws and the lower panel.

To install:

4. Install the panel and tighten the screws.
5. Install the pocket to the lower panel (if equipped).
6. Install the arm rest (if equipped).

Hinge Pillar Trim Panel

➧ **See Figure 47**

1. Remove the retaining screw and the trim panel from the retainers.
2. Installation is the reverse of removal.

Door Sill

1. Remove the door sill plate screws and the sill plates.
2. Installation is the reverse of removal.

Pillar Moulding

➧ **See Figures 48, 49 and 50**

1. Remove the door sill plate screws and sill plates.
2. Remove the seat belt to pillar anchors (side door lock pillars only).
3. Remove the pillar moulding screws and pillar moulding.

To install:

4. Install the pillar mouldings to the pillar and tighten the screws to 17 inch. lbs. (1.9 Nm).
5. Install the seat belt anchors.
6. Install the the sill plates and tighten the screws.

Headliner

REMOVAL & INSTALLATION

Pick-up, Extended Cab and Crew Cab

➧ **See Figures 51, 52 and 53**

1. Remove the sunshades and assist handles.
2. Remove the rear window lower moulding and the rear quarter panel trim.

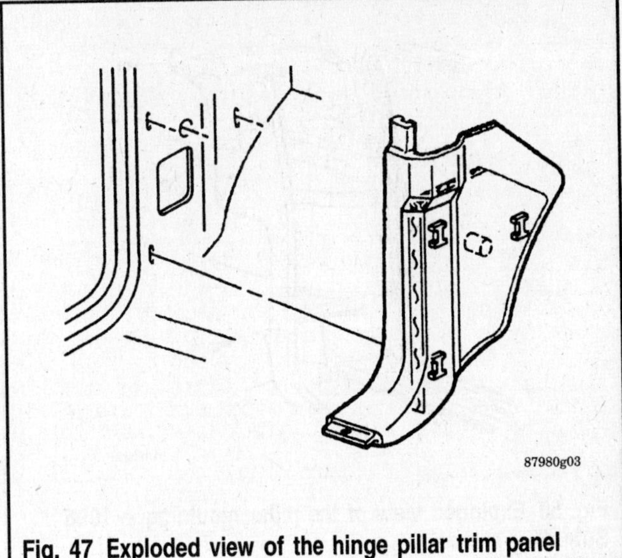

Fig. 47 Exploded view of the hinge pillar trim panel

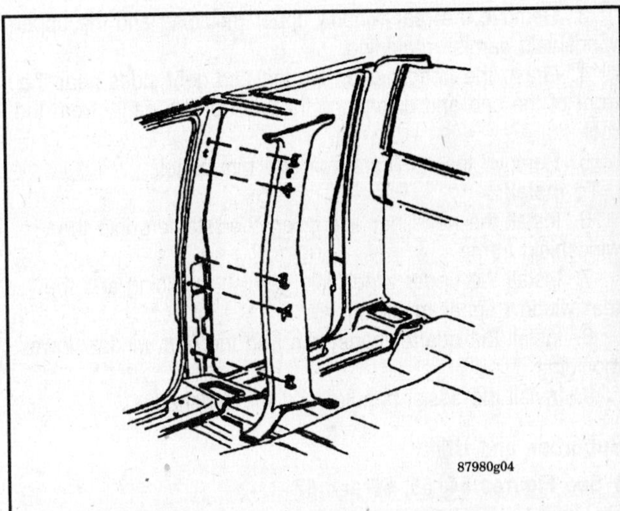

Fig. 48 Exploded view of the pillar moulding — 1996 crew cab shown

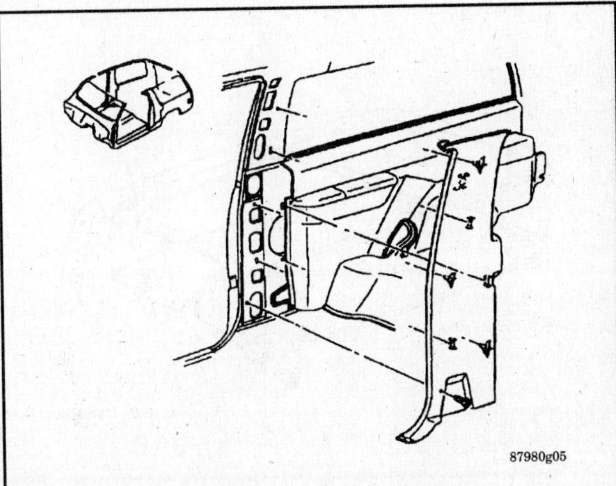

Fig. 49 Exploded view of the pillar moulding — 1996 two door utility shown

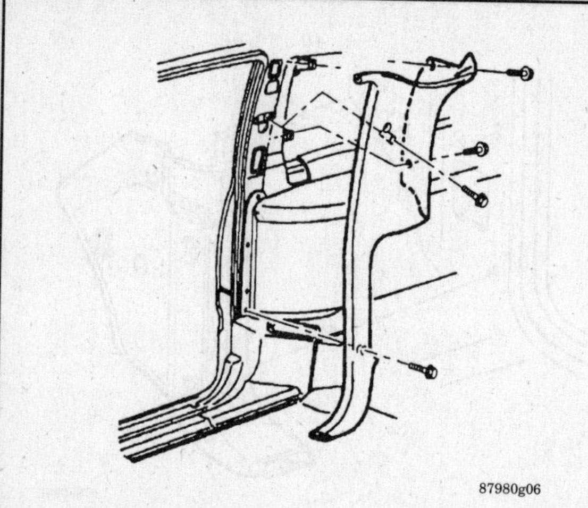

Fig. 50 Exploded view of the pillar moulding — 1996 Suburban shown

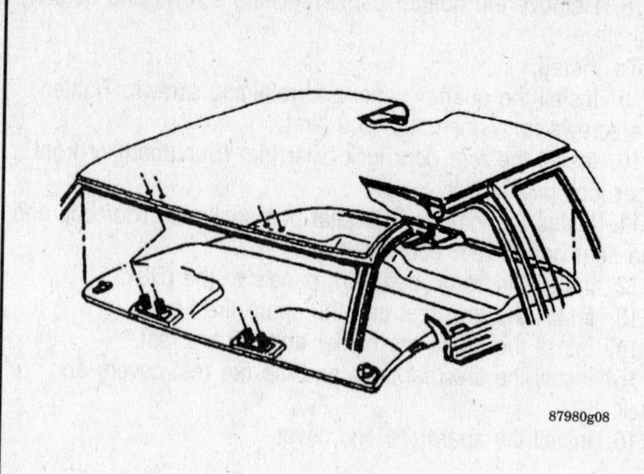

Fig. 52 Exploded view of the headliner — 1996 extended cab shown

3. Remove the rear window upper moulding and the upper windshield garnish moulding.
4. Grasp the headliner on the left and right sides near the front of the cab and disengage the front of the panel from the roof.
5. Remove the retainers from the trim panel.

To install:

6. Install the headliner and insert the retainers into the windshield frame.
7. Install the upper windshield garnish moulding and the rear window upper moulding.
8. Install the quarter panel trim and the rear window lower moulding.
9. Install the assist handles and the sunshades.

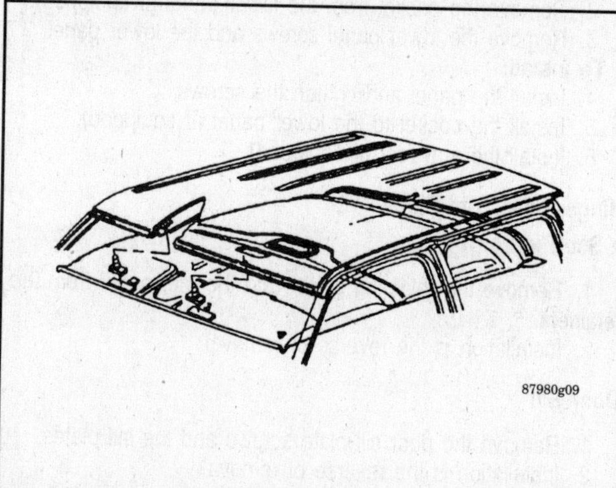

Fig. 53 Exploded view of the headliner — 1996 crew cab shown

Suburban and Utility

See Figures 54, 55, 56 and 57

1. Remove the sunshades and assist handles.
2. Remove the windshield garnish mouldings, coat hooks and dome lamp(s).
3. Remove the HVAC control assembly (if equipped).

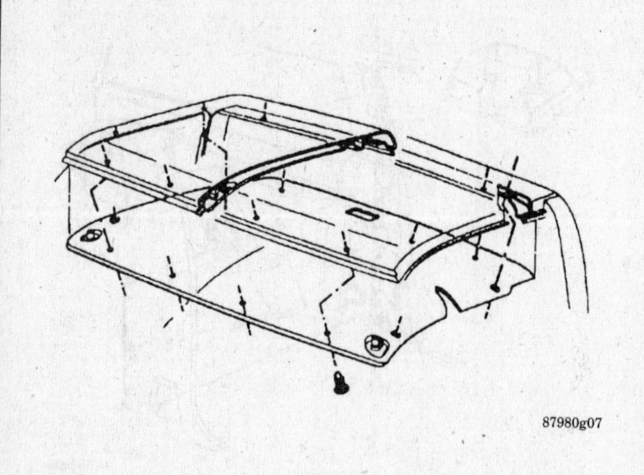

Fig. 51 Exploded view of headliner — 1996 pick-up shown

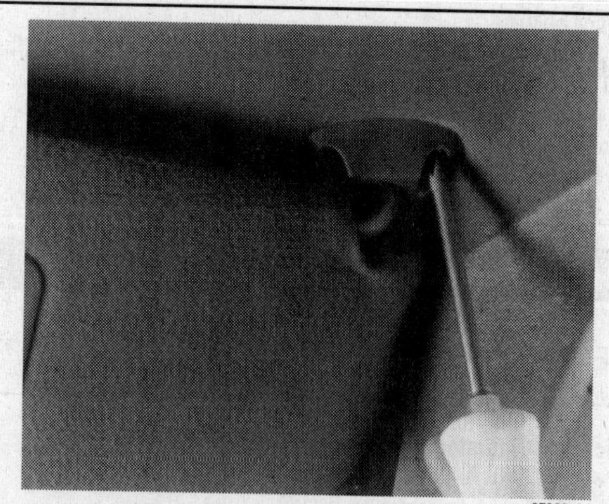

Fig. 54 Unfasten the sunshade retaining screws to remove the sunshade

4. Remove the upper windshield garnish mouldings and the rear seat belt upper trim covers.
5. Remove the side door lock pillar moulding and the upper center trim panel.
6. Remove overhead console and the headliner.

To install:

7. Install the headliner and the overhead console.
8. Install the window garnish mouldings, assist handles, coat hooks and the dome lamp(s).
9. Install the HVAC control assembly (if equipped).
10. Install the rear seat belt upper trim covers and the side door lock pillar moulding.
11. Install the upper center trim panel and the cargo door lock pillar moulding panel.
12. Install the sunshades and assist handles.

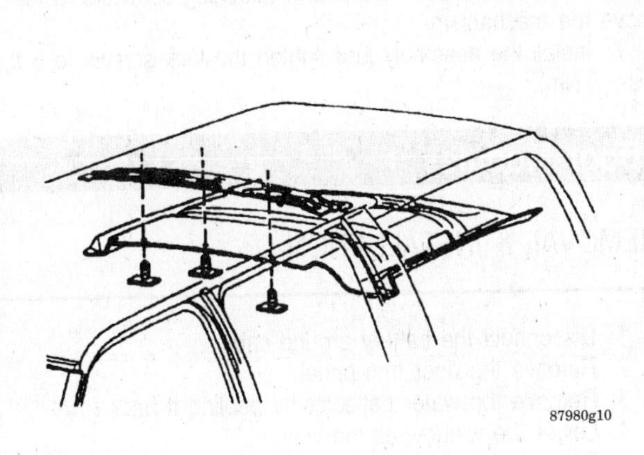

Fig. 55 Exploded view of the headliner — 1996 Suburban w/o rear A/C

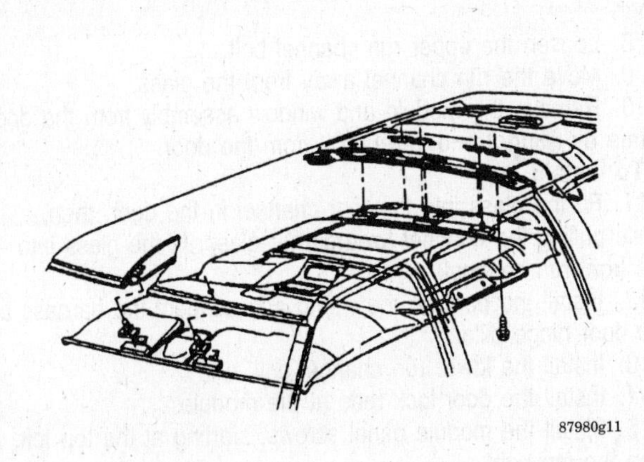

Fig. 56 Exploded view of the headliner — 1996 Suburban w/rear A/C

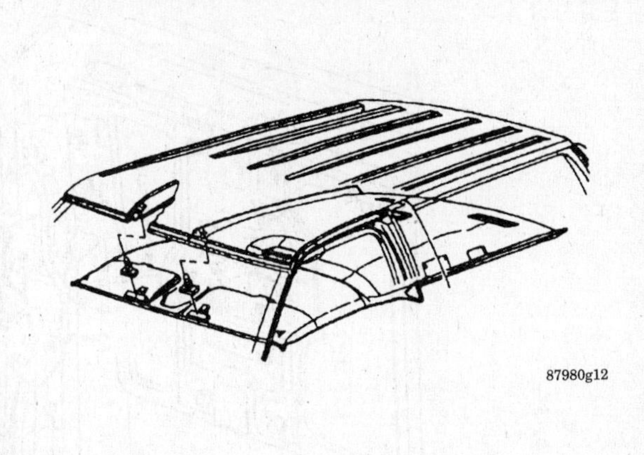

Fig. 57 Exploded view of the headliner — 1996 two door utility shown

Door Lock Cylinder

REMOVAL & INSTALLATION

➡A key code is stamped on the lock cylinder to aid in replacing lost keys.

1. Raise the window.
2. Remove the door trim panel.
3. Slide the lock cylinder retaining clip off of the cylinder.
4. Remove the lock cylinder from the door.
5. Installation is the reverse of removal.

Door Lock Assembly

REMOVAL & INSTALLATION

R/V Series

➧ See Figures 58 and 59

1. Raise the window completely.
2. Remove the door trim panel.
3. Using a suitable flat bladed tool, push on the top of the door lock rod clips and pivot the clip away from the rod.
4. Disconnect the door handle to lock rod from the lock.
5. Disconnect the outside door handle to lock rod clip, using the same procedure as in Step 3.
6. Remove the inside door lock knob.
7. Remove the door to lock assembly screws, then tilt the lock assembly away from the outside lock cylinder. Pull the lock assembly downward to make clearance for the inside lock rod and remove the lock assembly from the door.

To install:

8. Align the lock rod to the hole in the door panel. Tilt the lock assembly onto the outside lock cylinder.
9. Install the door to lock assembly screws.
10. Install the inside door lock knob.

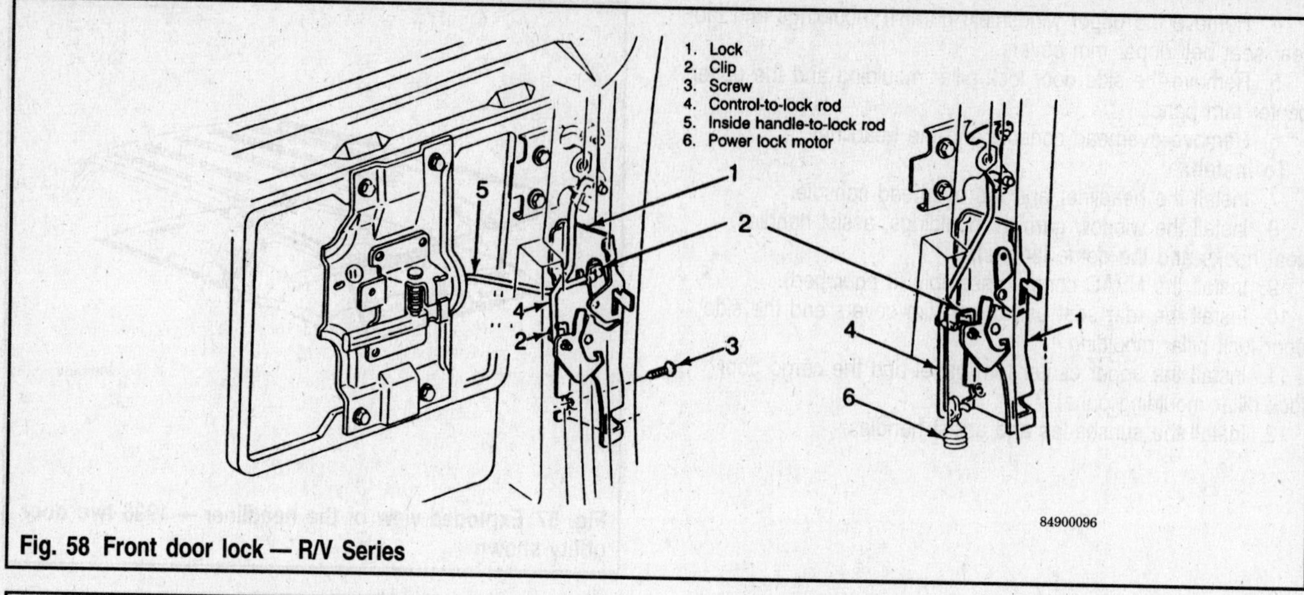

Fig. 58 Front door lock — R/V Series

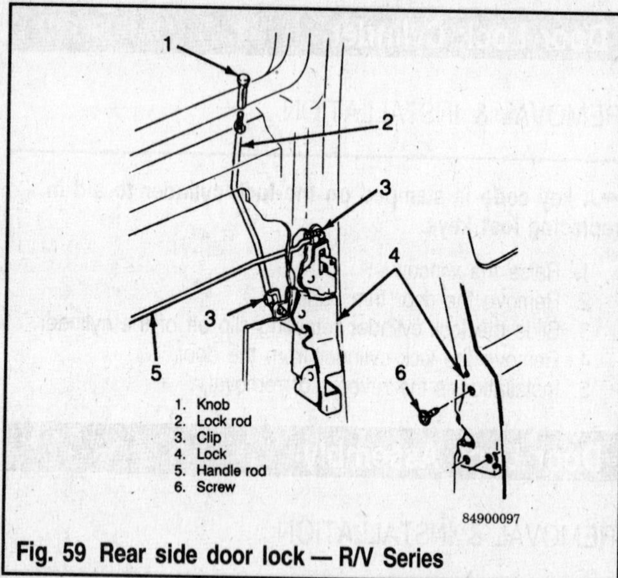

Fig. 59 Rear side door lock — R/V Series

11. Install the outside door handle to lock rod onto the lock assembly.
12. Pivot the clip up and onto the lock rod.
13. Install the inside door handle to the lock rod onto the lock assembly.
14. Pivot the clip up and onto the lock rod.
15. Install the door trim panel.

C/K Series

➧ See Figures 60 and 61

1. Door trim panel.
2. Peel off the water deflector.
3. Remove the door module attaching screws and tilt the module out at the top.
4. Disconnect the outside handle lock rod from the lock mechanism.
5. Using a screwdriver, reach between the glass and door and press down on the top of the lock cylinder assembly to disengage the lock cylinder rod from the cylinder.
6. Remove the lock mechanism attaching screws and remove the mechanism.
7. Install the assembly and tighten the lock screws to 5 ft. lbs. (7 Nm).

Door Module

REMOVAL & INSTALLATION

1. Disconnect the battery ground cable.
2. Remove the door trim panel.
3. Remove the water deflector by peeling it back.
4. Lower the window all the way.
5. Remove the module attaching screws.
6. Disconnect the door lock rods at the module and tape them to the door.
7. Pull the wiring harness towards the door to reach the connector. Remove the boot from the wiring and disconnect the harness at the door hinge pillar. Push the harness into the door.
8. Loosen the upper run channel bolt.
9. Move the run channel away from the glass.
10. Remove the module and window assembly from the door frame by tilting it and lowering it from the door.

To install:

11. Fit the glass into the rear channel in the door, then, while pulling the channel towards the glass, fit the glass into the front run channel.
12. Install the boot on the wiring and connect the harness at the door hinge pillar.
13. Install the lower run channel bolt.
14. Install the door lock rods at the module.
15. Install the module panel screws, starting at the top left, then the top right.
16. Install the water deflector.
17. Tighten the upper run channel bolt.
18. Install the trim panel on the door.

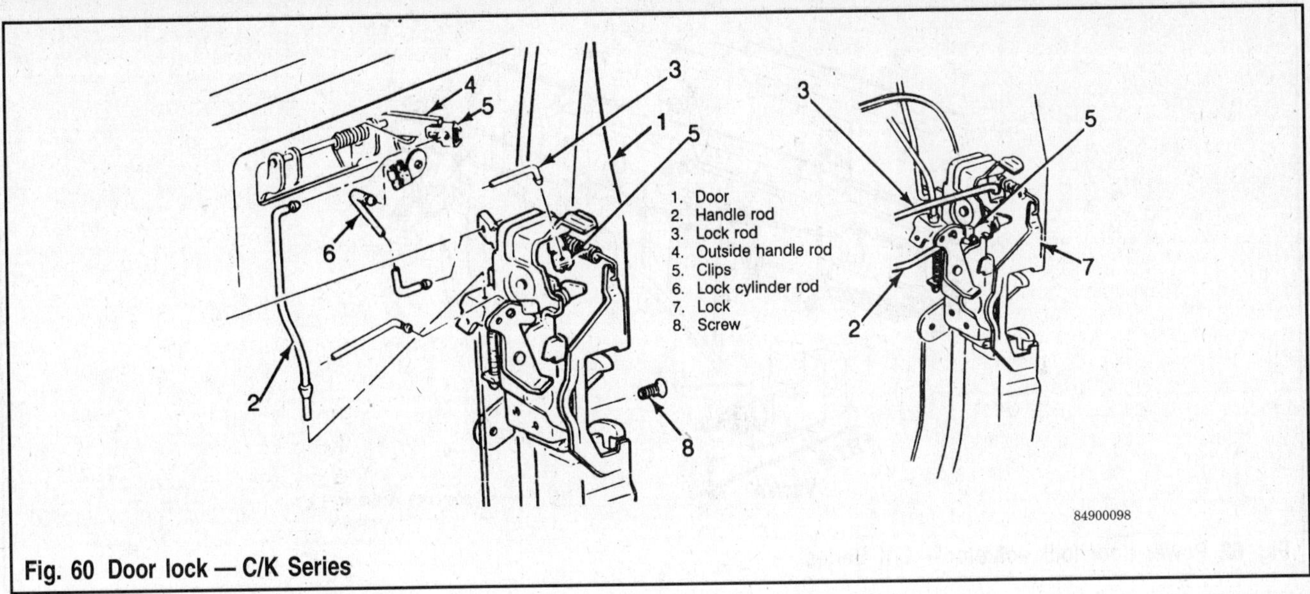

Fig. 60 Door lock — C/K Series

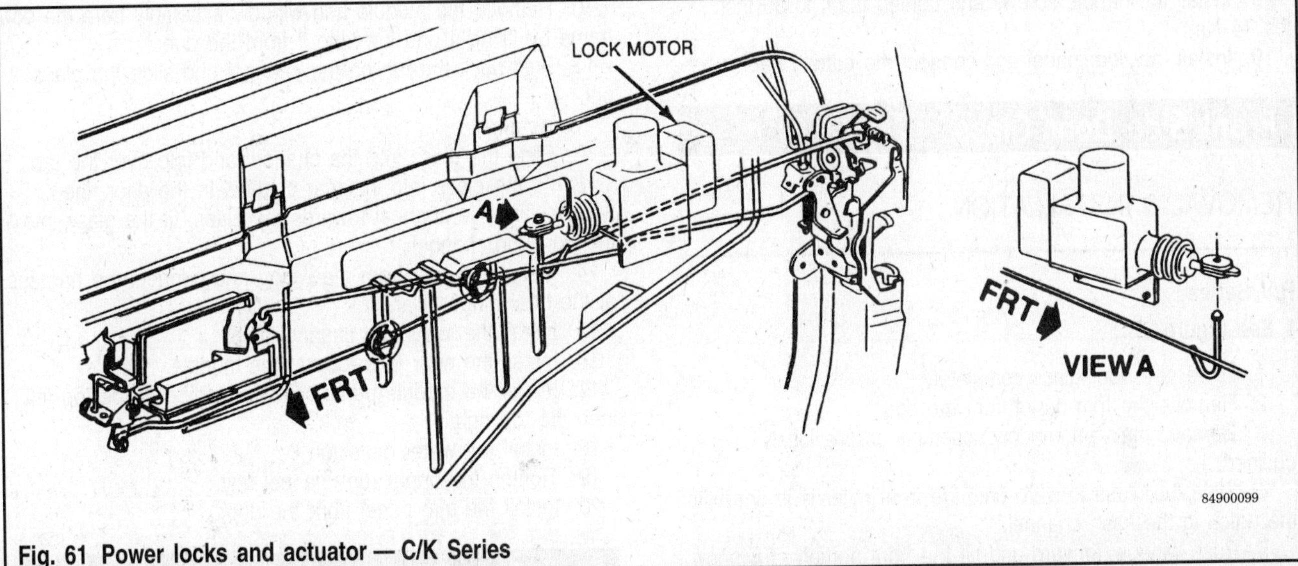

Fig. 61 Power locks and actuator — C/K Series

Power Door Lock Actuator

REMOVAL & INSTALLATION

➧ See Figure 62

1. Disconnect the negative battery cable.
2. Remove the door trim panel and the water shield.
3. Remove the module panel.
4. Locate the actuator mounting rivets and drill them out.
5. Disconnect the remote lock rod from the actuator arm.
6. Disconnect the wiring harness and remove the actuator from the panel.

To install:

7. Install the actuator and pop in new rivets.
8. Connect the wiring harness and lock rod.
9. Install the module and the water shield.
10. Install the door panel and connect the battery cable.

Rear Door Lock Cylinder, Rod and Handle

REMOVAL & INSTALLATION

➧ See Figures 63, 64, 65 and 66

1. Disconnect the negative battery cable.
2. Remove the door panel, module and window.
3. Disconnect the outside door handle rod from the clip.
4. Disconnect the lock cylinder rod from the clip.
5. Remove the handle mounting screws and pull the cylinder out of the handle housing. Remove the handle.

To install:

6. Install the handle and press the cylinder into the housing.
7. Connect the lock cylinder rod to the clip.
8. Connect the handle rod to the handle clip.

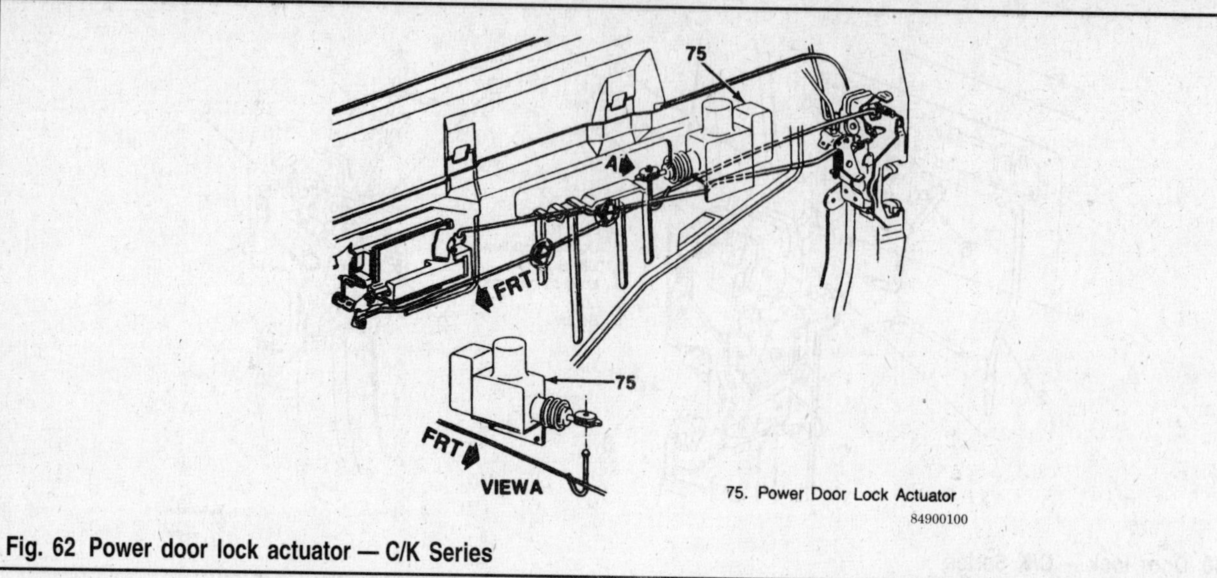

Fig. 62 Power door lock actuator — C/K Series

9. Install the handle screws and tighten them to 35 inch lbs. (4 Nm).
10. Install the door panel and connect the battery cable.

Front Side Door Glass

REMOVAL & INSTALLATION

R/V Series

See Figure 67

1. Lower the door glass completely.
2. Remove the trim panel from the door.
3. Remove the vent window assembly as previously outlined.
4. Slide the glass forward until the front roller is in line with the notch in the sash channel.
5. Push window forward and tilt the front portion of window up until rear roller is disengaged.
6. Put window assembly in normal position (level) and raise straight up and out.
7. Tilt the window into position and install it.

C/K Series

See Figure 68

1. Lower the door glass completely.
2. Remove the trim panel from the door.
3. Remove the water deflector by peeling it back.
4. Remove the module panel screws.
5. Remove the door lock rods from the module and tape them to the door.
6. Remove the lower run channel bolt.
7. Loosen the upper run channel bolt.
8. Move the run channel away from the glass.
9. Pull the wiring harness towards the door to reach the connector. Remove the boot from the wiring and disconnect the harness at the door hinge pillar.
10. Remove the module and window assembly from the door frame by tilting it and lowering it from the door.
11. Fold back the tab on the channel and slide the glass out.

To install:

12. Slide the glass into the channel and fold over the tab.
13. Fit the glass into the rear channel in the door, then, while pulling the channel towards the glass, fit the glass into the front run channel.
14. Install the boot from the wiring and connect the harness at the door hinge pillar.
15. Install the lower run channel bolt.
16. Install the door lock rods at the module.
17. Install the module panel screws, starting at the top left, then the top right.
18. Install the water deflector.
19. Tighten the upper run channel bolt.
20. Install the trim panel from the door.

Rear Side Door Stationary Glass

REMOVAL & INSTALLATION

1. Place the window in the fully lowered position.
2. Remove the door trim panel.
3. Pull out the glass run channel molding.
4. Remove the door panel-to-run channel bolt.
5. Remove the door frame-to-run channel screw.
6. Pull the stationary glass/run channel assembly from the door, by pulling the top of the channel rearwards away from the door frame while rotating it out of the door.
7. Install the window, frame and trim panel.

➡The door frame-to-run channel screw must pass through the run channel molding slot.

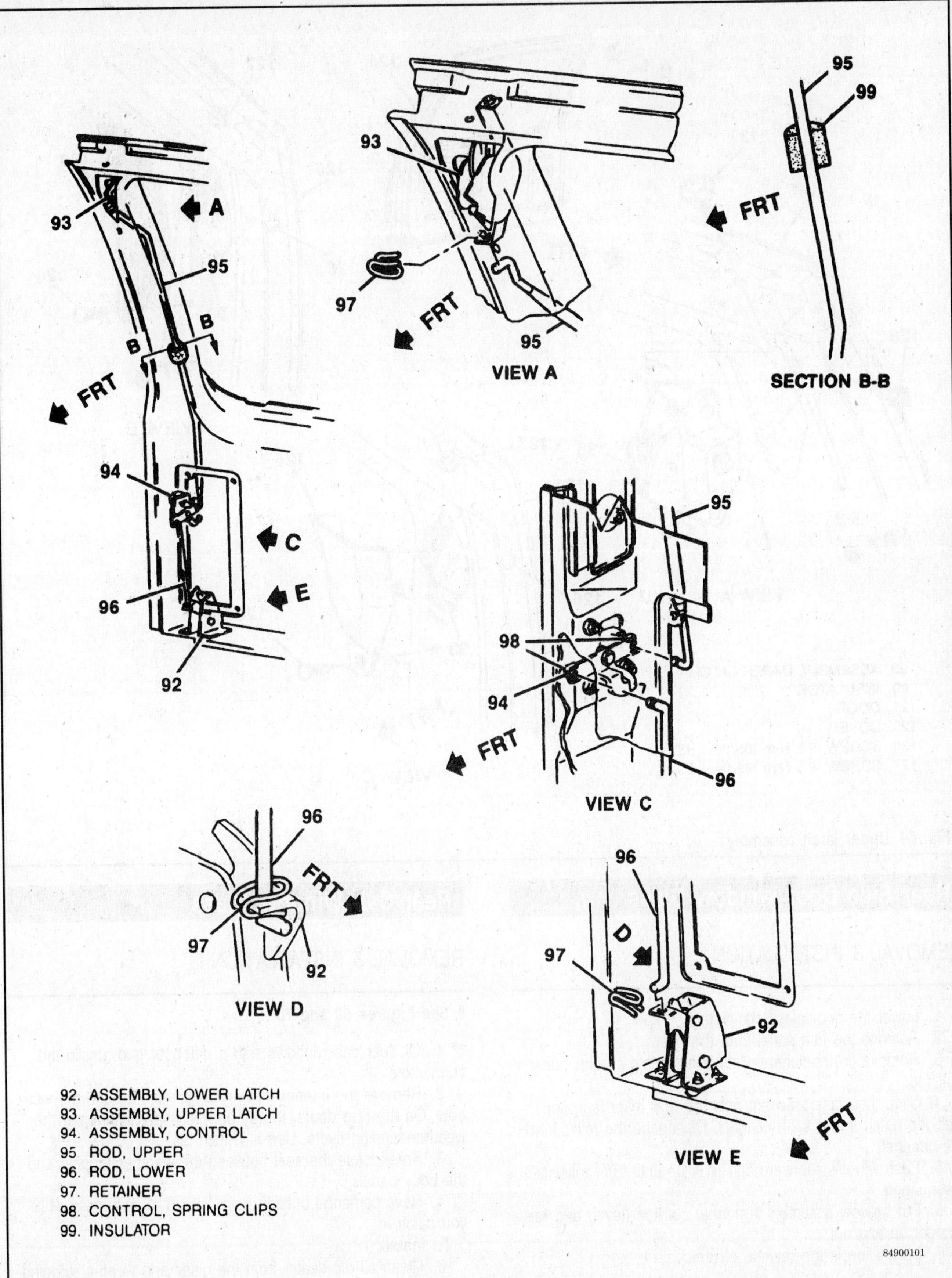

Fig. 63 Rear door latch

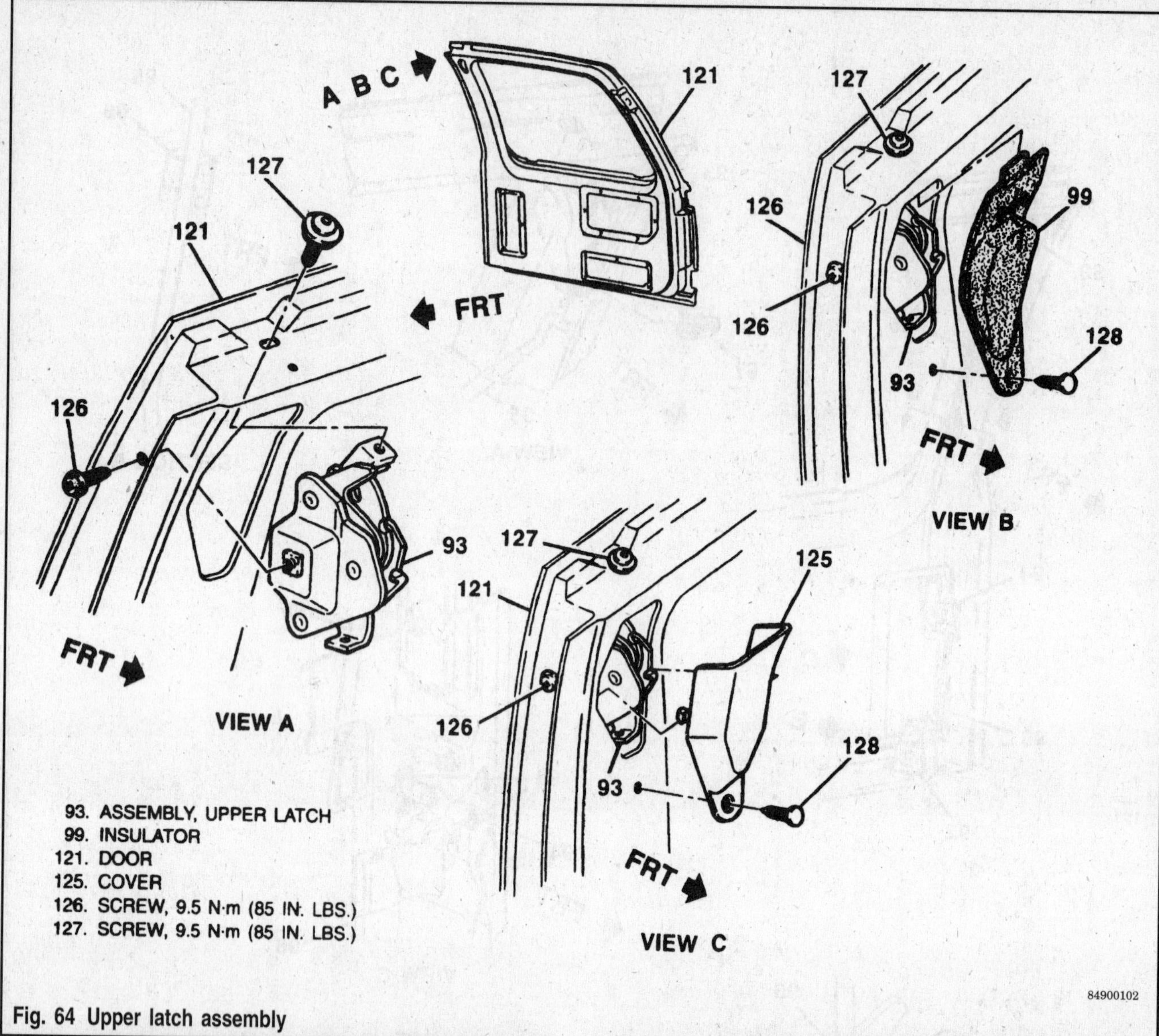

Fig. 64 Upper latch assembly

Rear Side Door Window Glass

REMOVAL & INSTALLATION

1. Lower the door glass completely.
2. Remove the trim panel from the door.
3. Remove the stationary window assembly as previously outlined.
4. Slide the glass rearward until the rear roller is in line with the notch in the sash channel. Disengage the roller from the channel.
5. Push window rearward and tilt it up until front roller is disengaged.
6. Put window assembly in normal position (level) and raise straight up and out.
7. Installation is the reverse of removal.

Rear Cab Window Glass

REMOVAL & INSTALLATION

See Figures 69 and 70

1. On rear cab windows with a defogger grid, unclip the connectors.
2. Remove the interior trim moldings from around the window. On the rear doors, it may be necessary to drill out the weatherstripping rivets. Use a ¼ inch bit.
3. Break loose the seal between the weatherstripping and the body panels.
4. Have someone outside push inward on the glass while you catch it.

To install:

5. Clean all old sealer from the glass and weatherstripping.
6. Fill the glass channel in the weatherstripping with a 3/16 in. (5mm) bead of sealer.

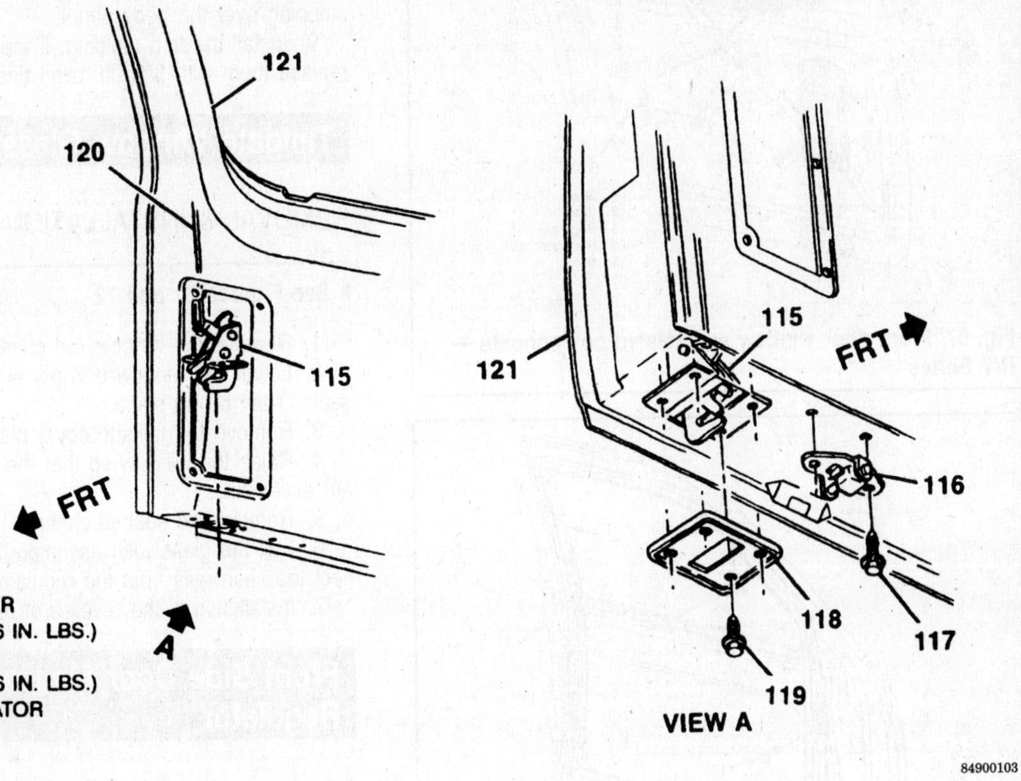

115. ASSEMBLY, LOCK
116. ASSEMBLY, BUMPER
117. SCREW 7.5 N·m (66 IN. LBS.)
118. REINFORCEMENT
119. SCREW 7.5 N·m (66 IN. LBS.)
120. ROD, LOCK ACTUATOR
121. DOOR

VIEW A

84900103

Fig. 65 Rear door lock

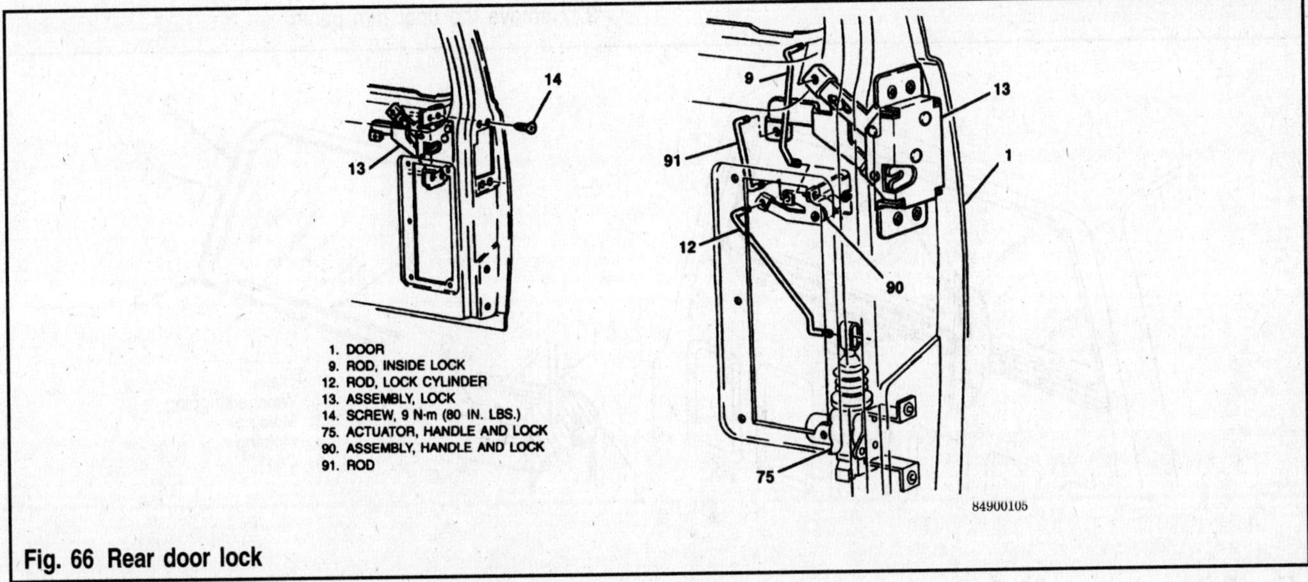

Fig. 66 Rear door lock

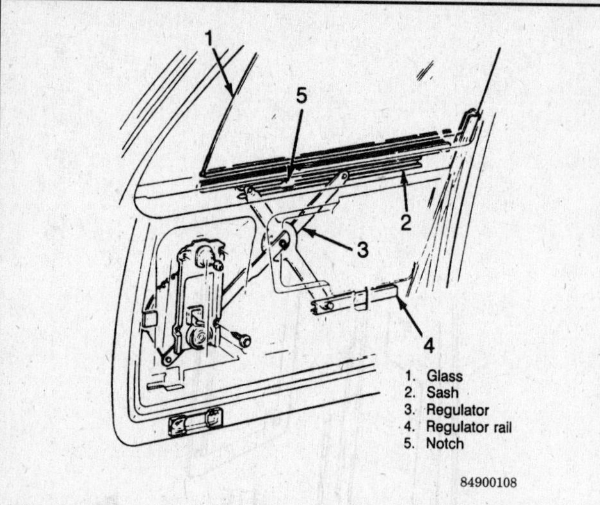

Fig. 67 Front door window and related components — R/V Series

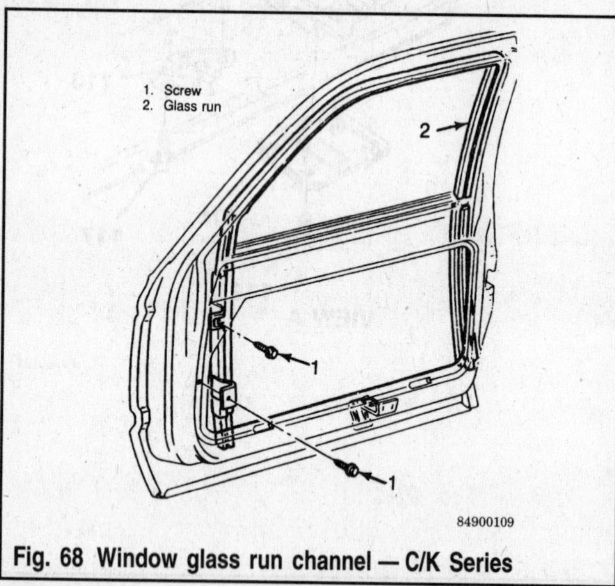

Fig. 68 Window glass run channel — C/K Series

7. Fit the glass in the weatherstripping and place a 1/4 in. (6mm) diameter cord in the frame cavity around the outside diameter of the weatherstripping. Allow the ends of the cord to hang down the outside of the glass from the top center.
8. Place the glass and weatherstripping in the vehicle opening. Pull on the cord ends to pull the lip of the weatherstripping over the body panel.
9. Install the trim molding. If the trim was held by rivets, replace them with 3/16 in. blind rivets and a rivet gun.

Tailgate Window Glass

REMOVAL & INSTALLATION

➧ See Figures 71 and 72

1. Remove the window run channel caps.
2. Lower the window and pry out the inner and outer glass seals. They clip in place.
3. Remove the tailgate cover plate.
4. Raise the window so that the window sash channel bolts are accessible.
5. Remove the sash-to-channel bolts.
6. Pull the glass/sash assembly from the tailgate. Disconnect the sash rails from the regulator.
7. Installation is the reverse of removal.

Front Side Door Manual Window Regulator

REMOVAL & INSTALLATION

R/V Series

➧ See Figure 73

1. Place the window in the full up position and hold it there with heavy tape.
2. Remove the door trim panel.

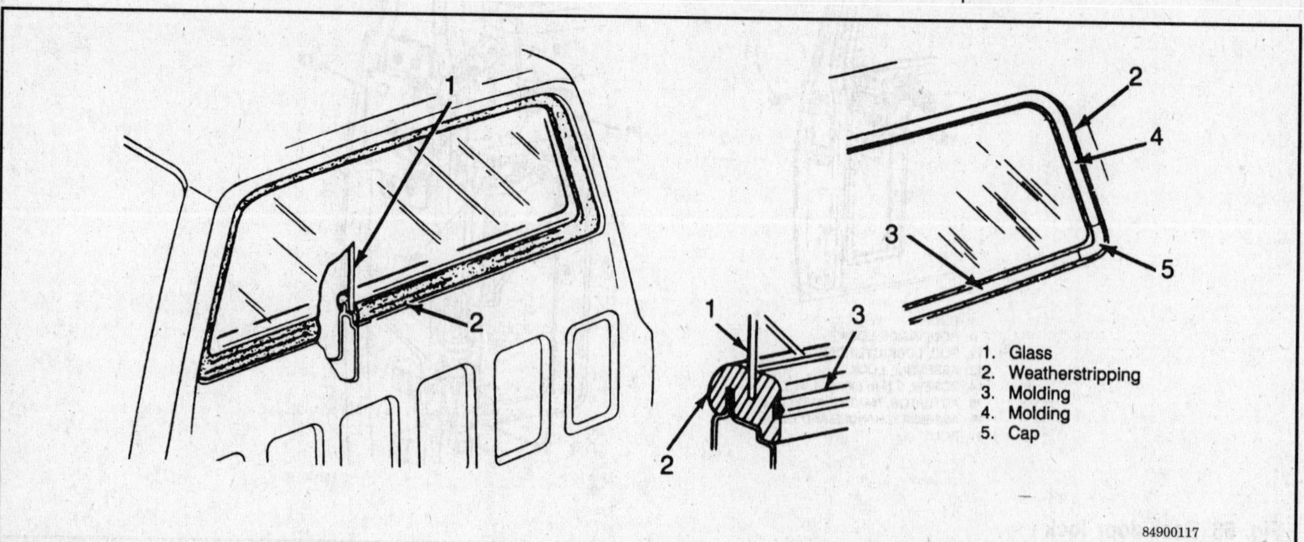

Fig. 69 Rear window — R/V Series

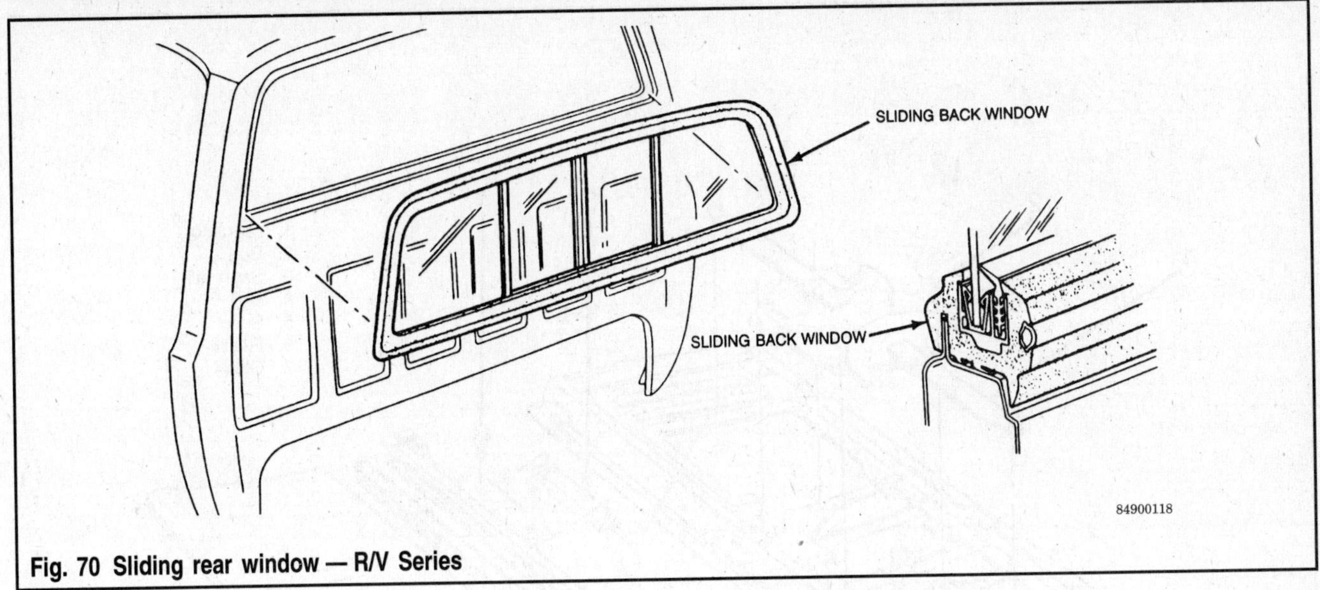

Fig. 70 Sliding rear window — R/V Series

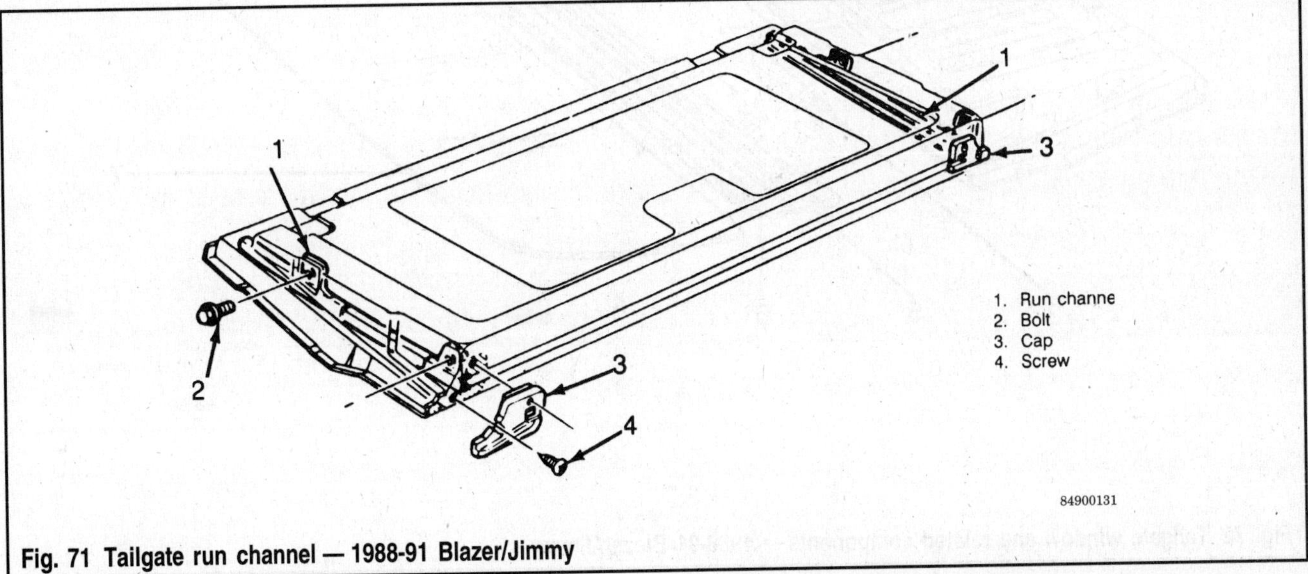

Fig. 71 Tailgate run channel — 1988-91 Blazer/Jimmy

3. Remove the regulator attaching bolts.
4. Slide the regulator rearward to disengage the rear roller from the sash channel.
5. Disengage the lower roller from the regulator rail.
6. Disengage the forward roller from the sash channel at the notch.
7. Fold the regulator down and remove it.
8. Installation is the reverse of removal.

C/K Series

See Figure 74

1. Remove the door trim panel.
2. Remove the water deflector by peeling it back.
3. Disconnect the door lock linkage.
4. Loosen the upper run channel bolt.
5. Move the run channel away from the glass.
6. Remove the window assembly from the door frame by tilting it and lowering it from the door.
7. Fold back the tab on the channel and slide the glass out.
8. Drill out the regulator assembly rivets.
9. Remove the regulator.

To install:

10. Install the regulator. Use bolts and nuts to replace the rivets.
11. Disconnect the door lock linkage.
12. Install the water deflector by peeling it back.
13. Slide the glass into the channel and fold over the tab.
14. Fit the glass into the rear channel in the door, then, while pulling the channel towards the glass, fit the glass into the front run channel.
15. Install the lower run channel bolt.
16. Install the door lock linkage.
17. Install the door trim panel.

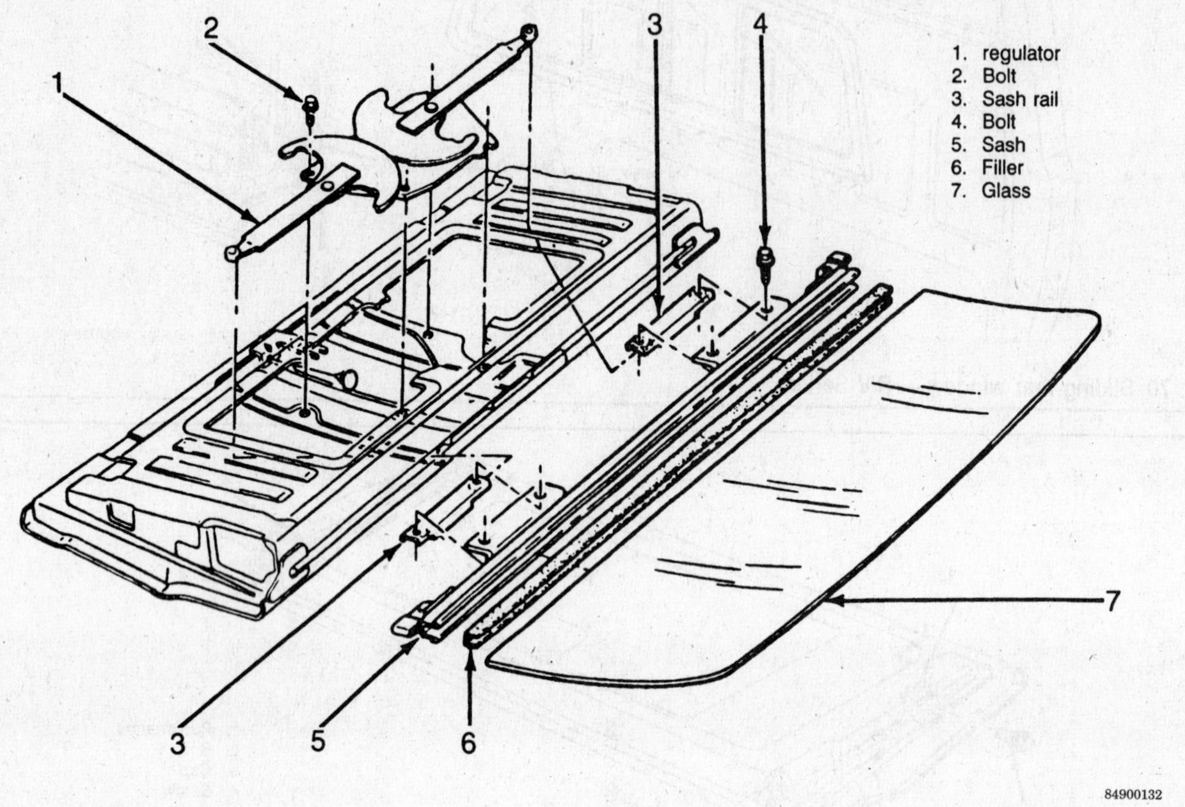

1. regulator
2. Bolt
3. Sash rail
4. Bolt
5. Sash
6. Filler
7. Glass
84900132

Fig. 72 Tailgate window and related components — 1988-91 Blazer/Jimmy

1. Sash
2. Regulator
3. Rail
4. Bolt
84900111

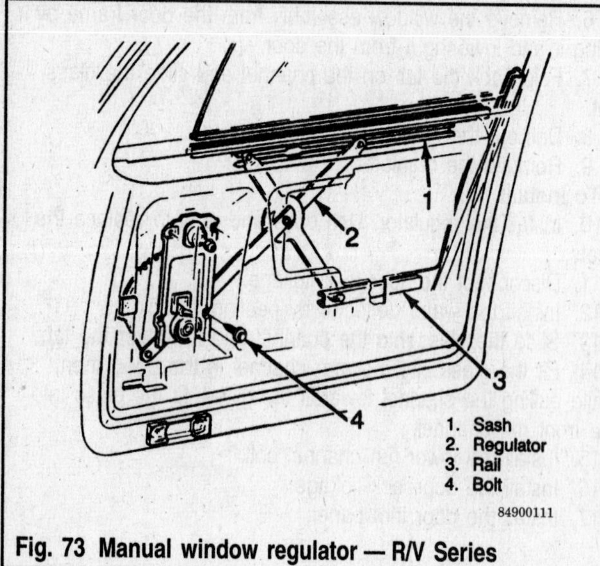

Fig. 73 Manual window regulator — R/V Series

Rear Side Door Manual Window Regulator

REMOVAL & INSTALLATION

See Figure 75

1. Remove the door trim panel.
2. Remove the window glass as described above.
3. Remove the regulator attaching bolts.
4. Fold the regulator down and remove it.
5. Installation is the reverse of removal.

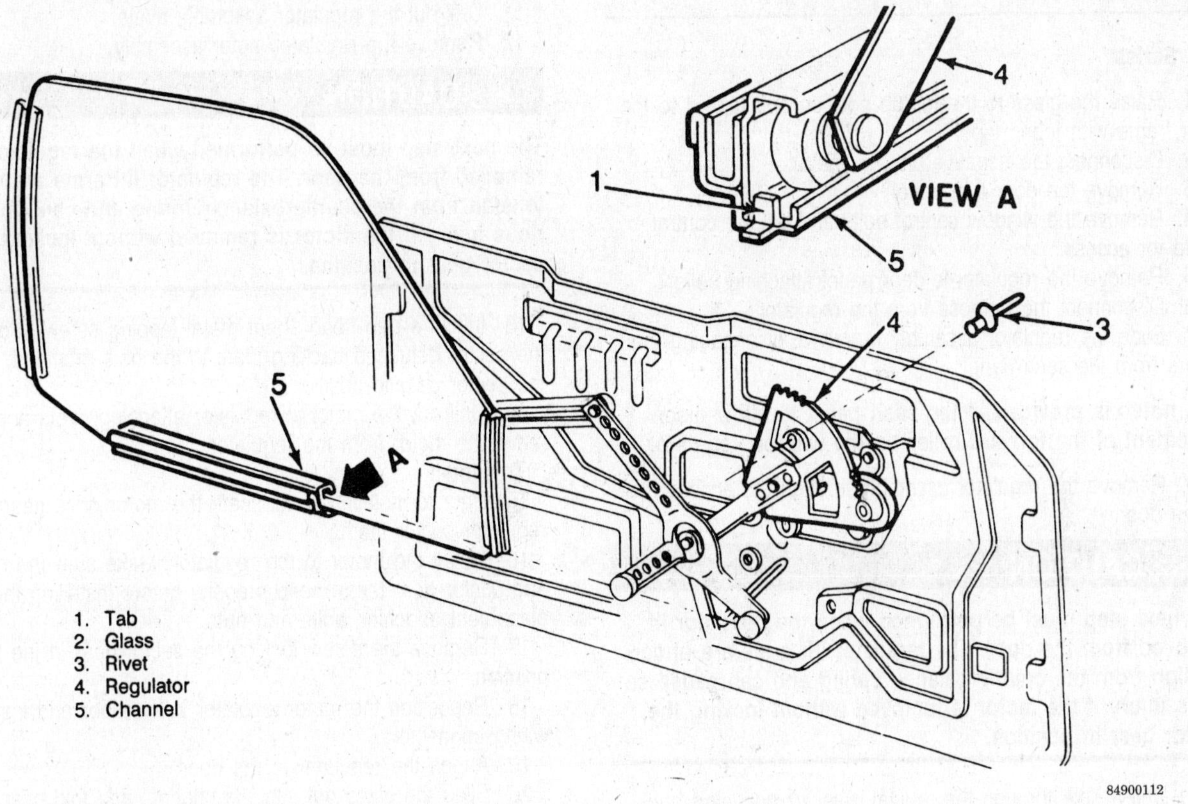

4
1
VIEW A
5
4
3
5
A
1. Tab
2. Glass
3. Rivet
4. Regulator
5. Channel
84900112

Fig. 74 Window regulator — C/K Series

1
6
2
4
3
5
1. Glass
2. Filler
3. Sash
4. Regulator
5. Bolt
6. Notch
84900113

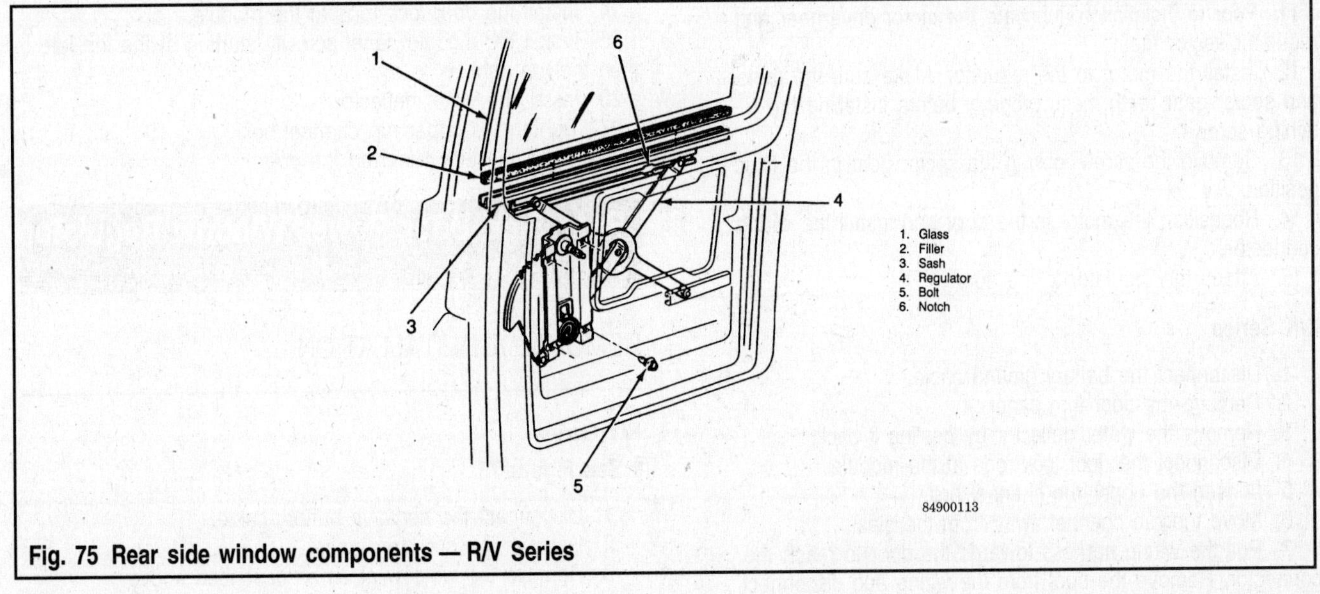

Fig. 75 Rear side window components — R/V Series

Front Side Door Power Window Regulator and Motor

REMOVAL & INSTALLATION

R/V Series

1. Raise the glass to the full up position and tape it to the door frame with fabric tape.
2. Disconnect the negative battery cable.
3. Remove the door trim panel.
4. Remove the window control bolts and lay the control aside for access.
5. Remove the regulator-to-door panel attaching bolts.
6. Disconnect the harness from the regulator.
7. Slide the regulator assembly rearward, disengaging the rollers from the sash panel.

➡A notch is provided in the sash panel to allow disengagement of the forward roller on the window regulator.

8. Remove the regulator assembly through the access hole in the door.

CAUTION

The next step must be performed when the regulator is removed from the door. The regulator lift arms are under tension from the counterbalance spring and can cause serious injury if the motor is removed without locking the sector gear in position.

9. Drill a hole through the regulator sector gear and back plate. DO NOT drill a hole closer than ½ in. (13mm) to the edge of the sector gear or back plate. Install a pan head sheet metal tapping screw (No. 10-12·¾ in.) in the drilled hole to lock the sector gear in position.
10. Remove the motor-to-regulator attaching screws and remove the motor from the regulator.

To install:

11. Prior to installation, lubricate the motor drive gear and regulator sector teeth.
12. Install the motor to the regulator. Make sure the motor and sector gear teeth mesh properly before installing the retaining screws.
13. Remove the screw locking the sector gear in the fixed position.
14. Reposition the motor in the door and install the wiring connector.
15. Attach the regulator to the door.

C/K Series

1. Disconnect the battery ground cable.
2. Remove the door trim panel.
3. Remove the water deflector by peeling it back.
4. Disconnect the door lock rods at the module.
5. Loosen the upper run channel bolt.
6. Move the run channel away from the glass.
7. Pull the wiring harness towards the door to reach the connector. Remove the boot from the wiring and disconnect the harness at the door hinge pillar.
8. Remove the module and window assembly from the door frame by tilting it and lowering it from the door.
9. Fold back the tab on the channel and slide the glass out.
10. On trucks with power components, drill out the rivets from the inner handle housing.
11. Drill out the regulator assembly rivets.
12. Remove the regulator/motor assembly.

CAUTION

The next step must be performed when the regulator is removed from the door. The regulator lift arms are under tension from the counterbalance spring and can cause serious injury if the motor is removed without locking the sector gear in position.

13. Install a pan head sheet metal tapping screw through the sector gear and backing plate in the hole provided, to lock the sector gear in position.
14. Drill out the motor-to-regulator attaching rivets and remove the motor from the regulator.

To install:

15. Prior to installation, lubricate the motor drive gear and regulator sector teeth.
16. Install the motor to the regulator. Make sure the motor and sector gear teeth mesh properly before installing the replacement attaching bolts and nuts.
17. Remove the screw locking the sector gear in the fixed position.
18. Reposition the motor/regulator in the door and install the wiring connector.
19. Attach the regulator to the door.
20. Slide the glass out into the channel and fold over the tab.
21. Fit the glass into the rear channel in the door, then, while pulling the channel towards the glass, fit the glass into the front run channel.
22. Install the boot from the wiring and connect the harness at the door hinge pillar.
23. Install the lower run channel bolt.
24. Install the door lock rods at the module.
25. Install the module panel screws, starting at the top left, then the top right.
26. Install the water deflector.
27. Tighten the upper run channel bolt.
28. Install the trim panel on the door.

Rear Side Door Power Window Regulator and Motor

REMOVAL & INSTALLATION

R/V Series

➧ See Figure 76

1. Disconnect the negative battery cable.
2. Remove the door trim panel.
3. Remove the window glass as described above.
4. Remove the regulator-to-door panel attaching bolts.

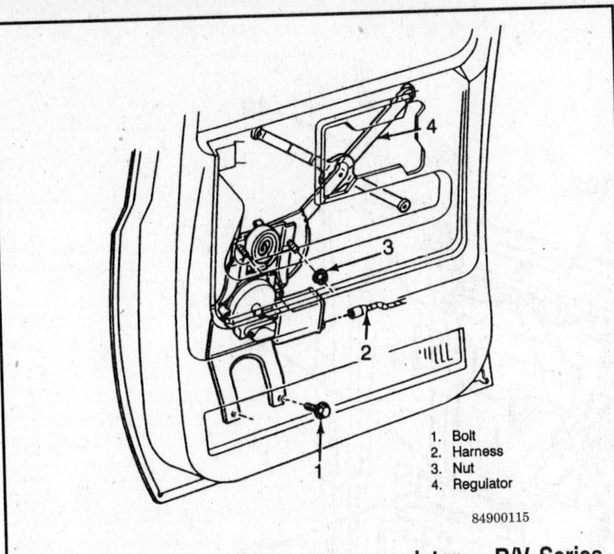

Fig. 76 Rear side window power regulator — R/V Series

5. Disconnect the harness from the regulator.
6. Remove the regulator assembly through the access hole in the door.

✻✻CAUTION

The next step must be performed when the regulator is removed from the door. The regulator lift arms are under tension from the counterbalance spring and can cause serious injury if the motor is removed without locking the sector gear in position.

7. Drill a hole through the regulator sector gear and back plate. DO NOT drill a hole closer than ½ in. (13mm) to the edge of the sector gear or back plate. Install a pan head sheet metal tapping screw (No. 10-12·¾ in.) in the drilled hole to lock the sector gear in position.
8. Remove the motor-to-regulator attaching screws and remove the motor from the regulator.

To install:

9. Prior to installation, lubricate the motor drive gear and regulator sector teeth.
10. Install the motor to the regulator. Make sure the motor and sector gear teeth mesh properly before installing the retaining screws.
11. Remove the screw locking the sector gear in the fixed position.
12. Reposition the motor in the door and install the wiring connector.
13. Attach the regulator to the door.
14. The remainder of installation is the reverse of removal.

C/K Series

➧ See Figure 77

1. Disconnect the battery ground cable.
2. Remove the door trim panel.
3. Remove the water deflector by peeling it back.
4. Disconnect the door lock rods at the module.
5. Loosen the upper run channel bolt.
6. Move the run channel away from the glass.
7. Pull the wiring harness towards the door to reach the connector. Remove the boot from the wiring and disconnect the harness at the door hinge pillar.
8. Remove the module and window assembly from the door frame by tilting it and lowering it from the door.
9. Fold back the tab on the channel and slide the glass out.
10. On trucks with power components, drill out the rivets from the inner handle housing.
11. Drill out the regulator assembly rivets.
12. Remove the regulator/motor assembly.

✻✻CAUTION

The next step must be performed when the regulator is removed from the door. The regulator lift arms are under tension from the counterbalance spring and can cause serious injury if the motor is removed without locking the sector gear in position.

13. Install a pan head sheet metal tapping screw through the sector gear and backing plate in the hole provided, to lock the sector gear in position.
14. Drill out the motor-to-regulator attaching rivets and remove the motor from the regulator.

To install:

15. Prior to installation, lubricate the motor drive gear and regulator sector teeth.
16. Install the motor to the regulator. Make sure the motor and sector gear teeth mesh properly before installing the replacement attaching bolts and nuts.
17. Remove the screw locking the sector gear in the fixed position.
18. Reposition the motor/regulator in the door and install the wiring connector.
19. Attach the regulator to the door.
20. Slide the glass out into the channel and fold over the tab.
21. Fit the glass into the rear channel in the door, then, while pulling the channel towards the glass, fit the glass into the front run channel.
22. Install the boot from the wiring and connect the harness at the door hinge pillar.
23. Install the lower run channel bolt.
24. Install the door lock rods at the module.
25. Install the module panel screws, starting at the top left, then the top right.
26. Install the water deflector.
27. Tighten the upper run channel bolt.
28. Install the trim panel on the door.

Tailgate Manual Window Regulator

REMOVAL & INSTALLATION

1. Remove the tailgate cover plate.
2. Disconnect the tailgate handle control rod from the handle.
3. Remove the handle.

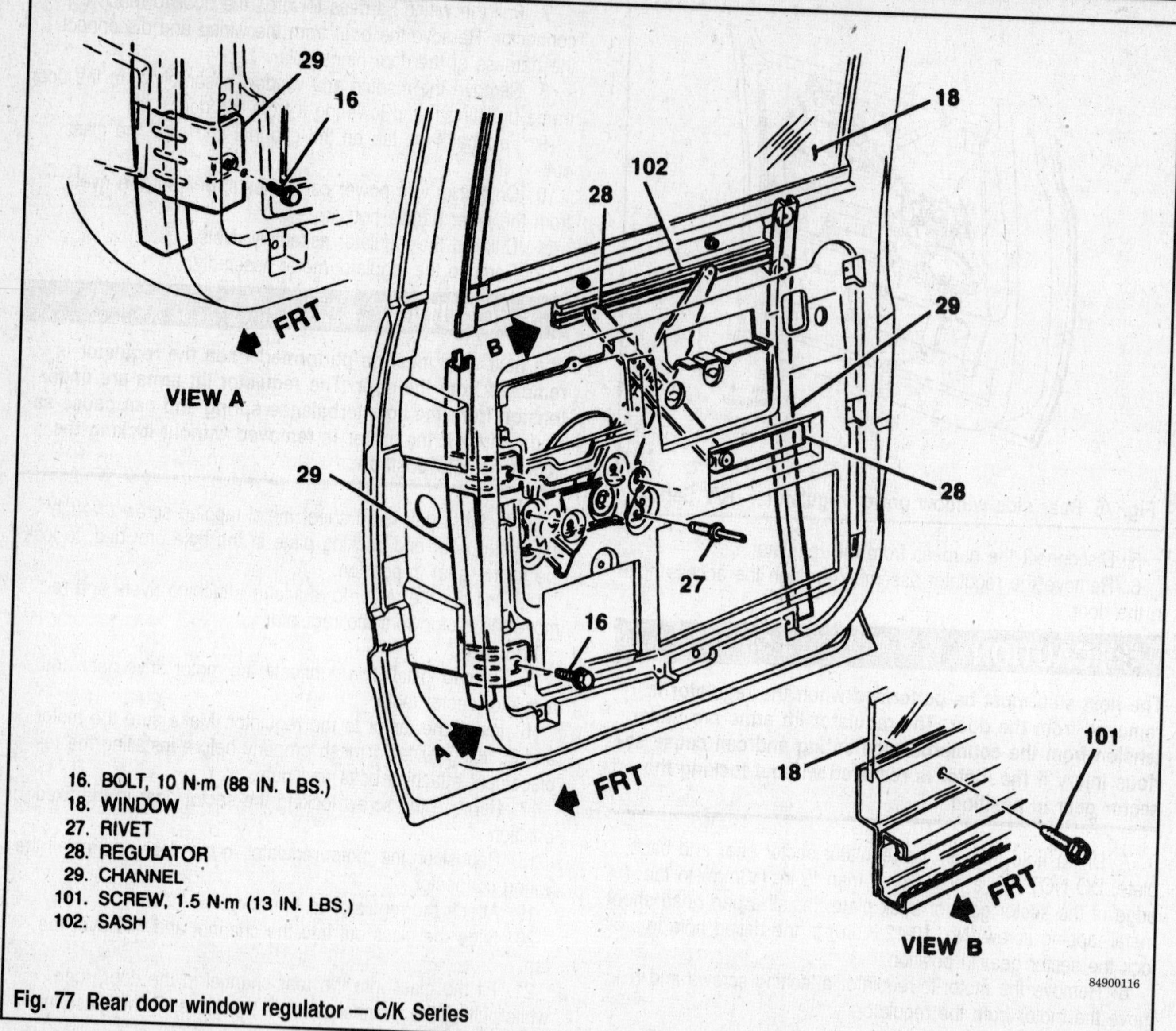

Fig. 77 Rear door window regulator — C/K Series

4. Disconnect the right and left latch rods from the control assembly.
5. Remove the attaching bolts and lift the control assembly from the tailgate.
6. Remove the window glass as described above.
7. Remove the attaching bolts and lift the regulator from the tailgate.
8. Installation is the reverse of removal.

Tailgate Power Window Regulator

REMOVAL & INSTALLATION

➧ See Figure 78

1. Remove the tailgate cover plate.
2. Disconnect the tailgate handle control rod from the handle.
3. Remove the handle.
4. Disconnect the right and left latch rods from the control assembly.
5. Remove the attaching bolts and lift the control assembly from the tailgate.
6. Remove the window glass as described above.

✲✲CAUTION

The next step must be performed before if the gearbox is removed or disengaged from the regulator arms. The regulator lift arms are under tension from the counterbalance spring and can cause serious injury if the gearbox is removed without locking the sector gear in position.

7. Drill a ⅛ in. hole through the regulator sector gear and back plate. Install a pan head sheet metal tapping screw in the drilled hole to lock the sector gear in position.
8. Disconnect the drive cable at the regulator.
9. Remove the attaching bolts and lift the regulator from the tailgate.
10. Unbolt the gear assembly from the regulator.

To install:

11. Assemble the gearbox and regulator.
12. Install the regulator in the tailgate.
13. Connect the drive cable at the regulator.
14. Remove the head sheet metal tapping screw used to lock the sector gear in position.
15. Install the window glass as described above.
16. Install the control assembly in the tailgate.
17. Connect the right and left latch rods at the control assembly.
18. Install the handle.
19. Connect the tailgate handle control rod at the handle.
20. Install the tailgate cover plate.

Windshield

➡**Bonded windshields require special tools and special removal procedures to be removed without being broken. For this reason we recommend that you refer all removal & installation to a qualified technician.**

CAUTION

Always wear heavy gloves when handling glass to reduce the risk of injury.

When replacing a cracked windshield, it is important that the cause of the crack be determined and the condition corrected, before a new glass is installed.

The cause of the crack may be an obstruction or a high spot somewhere around the flange of the opening; cracking may not occur until pressure from the high spot or obstruction becomes particularly high due to winds, extremes of temperature, or rough terrain.

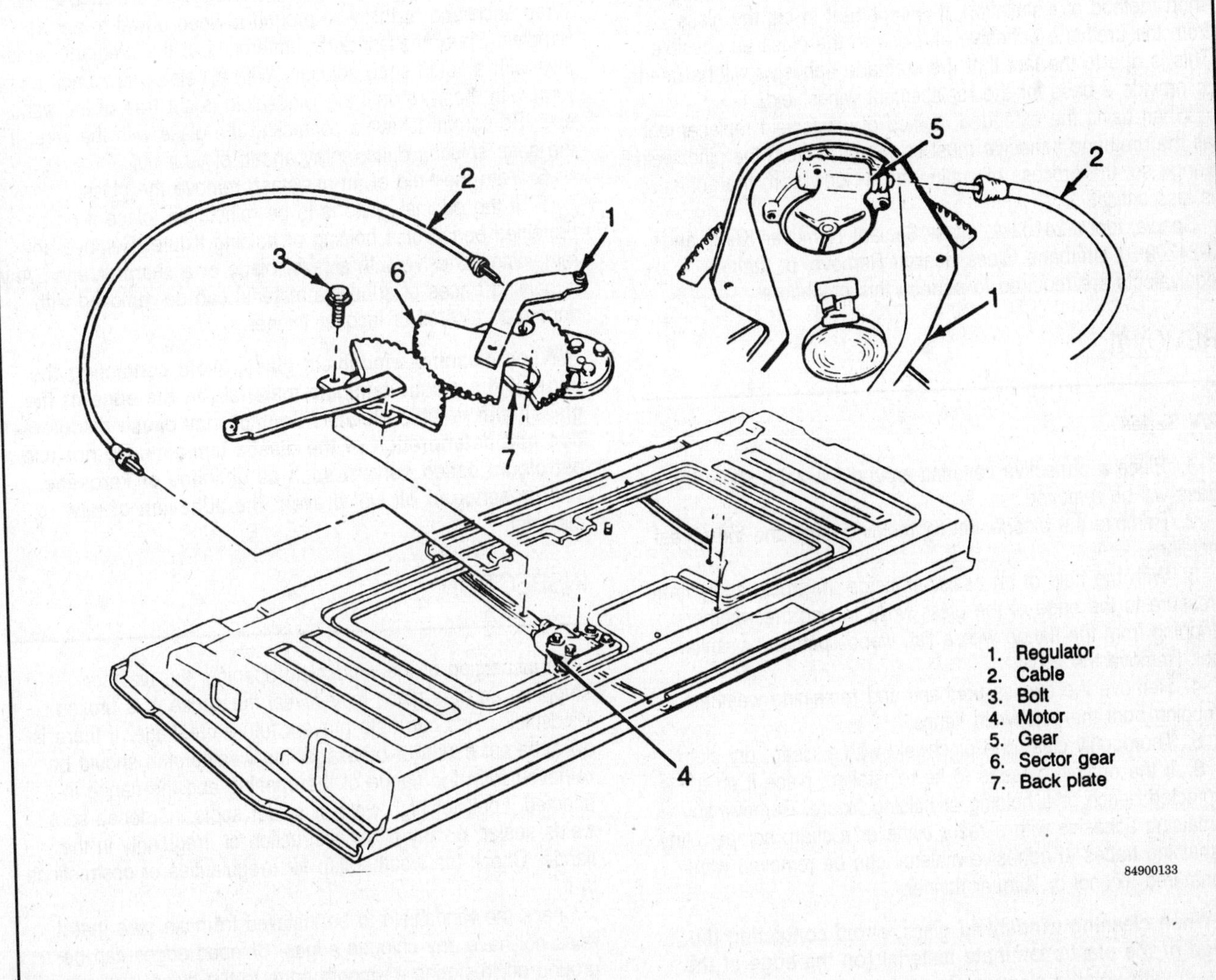

Fig. 78 Tailgate power window regulator — R/V Series

Suggestions of what to look for are described later in this section under inspection.

When a windshield is broken, the glass may have already have fallen or been removed from the weatherstrip. Often, however, it is necessary to remove a cracked or otherwise imperfect windshield that is still intact. In this case, it is a good practice to crisscross the glass with strips of masking tape before removing the it; this will help hold the glass together and minimize the risk of injury.

If a crack extends to the edge of the glass, mark the point where the crack meets the weather strip. (Use a piece of chalk and mark the point on the cab, next to the weatherstrip.) Later, when examining the flange of the opening for a cause of the crack start at the point marked.

The higher the temperature of the work area, the more pliable the weather strip will be. The more pliable the weather strip, the more easily the windshield can be removed.

Before removing the glass, cover the instrument panel, and the surrounding sheet metal with protective covering and remove the wiper arms.

There are two methods of windshield removal, depending on the method of windshield replacement chosen. When using the short method of installation, it is important to cut the glass from the urethane adhesive as close to the glass as possible. This is due to the fact that the urethane adhesive will be used to provide a base for the replacement windshield.

When using the extended method of windshield replacement, all the urethane adhesive must be removed from the pinchweld flange so, the process of cutting the window from the adhesive is less critical.

Special tool J-24402-A, Glass Sealant Remover Knife, and J-24709-01 Urethane Glass Sealant Remove, or their equivalents are required to perform this procedure.

REMOVAL

R/V Series

1. Place a protective covering around the area where the glass will be removed.
2. Remove the exterior reveal molding caps and the reveal moldings.
3. With the help of an assistant inside the truck, apply firm pressure to the edge of the glass while forcing the weatherstripping from the flange with a flat, wood spatula, or similar tool. Remove the glass.
4. Remove the excess urethane and remaining weatherstripping from the pinchweld flange.
5. Thoroughly clean the pinchweld with a clean, dry cloth.
6. If the original glass is to be reinstalled, place it on a protected bench or a holding or holding fixture. Remove any remaining adhesive with a razor blade or a sharp scraper. Any remaining traces of adhesive material can be removed with denatured alcohol or lacquer thinner.

➡When cleaning windshield glass, avoid contacting the edge of the plastic laminate material (on the edge of the glass) with volatile cleaner. Contact may cause discoloration and deterioration of the plastic laminate. Do not use a petroleum based solvent such as gasoline or kerosene. The presence of oil will prevent the adhesion of new material.

C/K Series

➧ See Figures 79, 80 and 81

1. Place the protective covering around the area where the glass will be removed.
2. Remove the windshield wiper arms, antenna mast, and the interior moldings. Pull the door seal back from the windshield area.
3. Remove the cowl vent grille, rear view mirror, windshield stop screws and speaker grilles.
4. If the windshield is broken: Using J-24402-A cut the windshield from the urethane adhesive. If the short method of glass replacement is to be used, keep the knife as close to the glass as possible in order to leave a base for the replacement glass.
5. If the windshield is unbroken: Cut a 6 ft. (183mm) length of 0.02 in. (0.5mm) piano wire and insert it through the urethane sealer at any point on the lower edge of the windshield. Wrap each end of the wire around a wood dowel to act as handles. Spray the entire circumference of the urethane adhesive with a liquid soap solution. With a helper, saw back and forth with the wire until the windshield is cut free of the adhesive. Be careful to avoid contacting the glass with the wire. If the soap solution dries, spray ahead of your cut.
6. With the help of an assistant, remove the glass.
7. If the original glass is to be reinstalled, place it on a protected bench or a holding or holding fixture. Remove any remaining adhesive with a razor blade or a sharp scraper. Any remaining traces of adhesive material can be removed with denatured alcohol or lacquer thinner.

➡When cleaning windshield glass, avoid contacting the edge of the plastic laminate material (on the edge of the glass) with volatile cleaner. Contact may cause discoloration and deterioration of the plastic laminate. Do not use a petroleum based solvent such as gasoline or kerosene. The presence of oil will prevent the adhesion of new material.

INSPECTION

An inspection of the windshield opening, the weatherstripping, and the glass may reveal the cause of a broken windshield. This can help prevent future breakage. If there is no apparent cause of breakage, the weatherstrip should be removed from the flange of the opening and the flange inspected. Look for high weld or solder spots, hardened spot welds sealer, or any other obstruction or irregularity in the flange. Check the weatherstrip for irregularities or obstructions in it.

Check the windshield to be installed to make sure that it does not have any chipped edges. Chipped edges can be ground off, restoring a smooth edge to the glass, and minimizing concentrations of pressure that cause breakage. Remove no more than necessary, in an effort to maintain the original shape of the glass and the proper clearance between it and the flange of the opening.

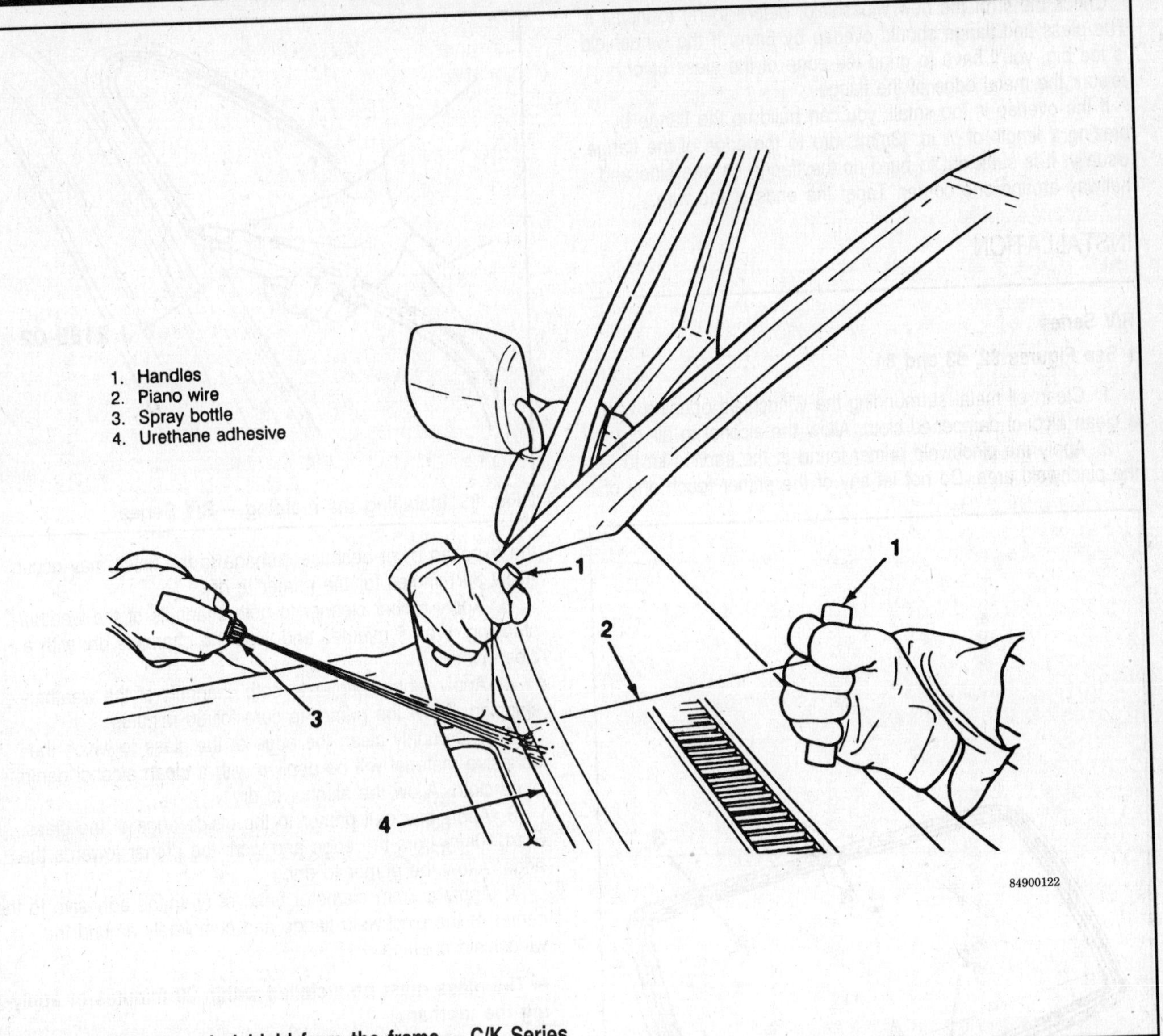

1. Handles
2. Piano wire
3. Spray bottle
4. Urethane adhesive

84900122

Fig. 79 Cutting the windshield from the frame — C/K Series

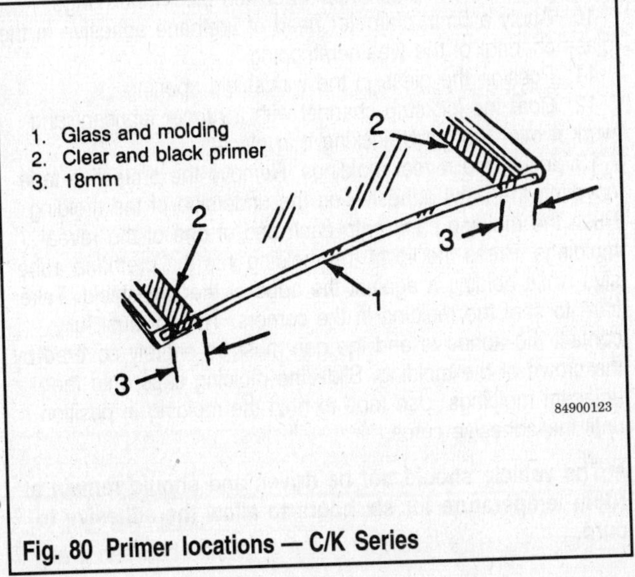

Fig. 80 Primer locations — C/K Series

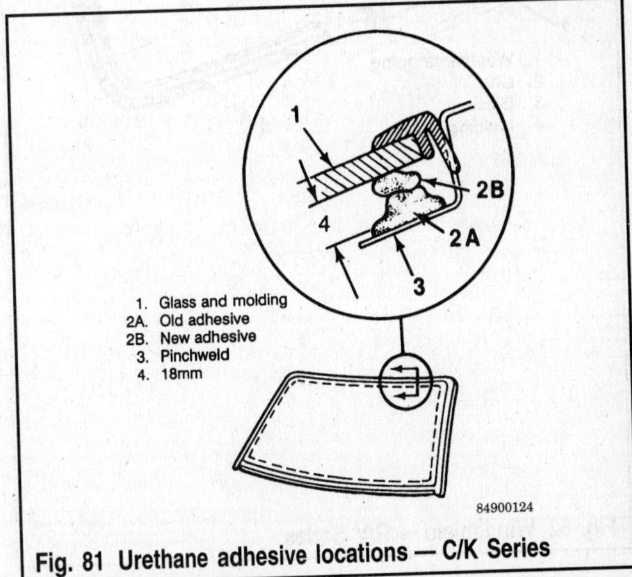

Fig. 81 Urethane adhesive locations — C/K Series

Check the fit of the new windshield, before trying to install it. The glass and flange should overlap by 5mm. If the windshield is too big, you'll have to grind the edge of the glass or or rework the metal edge of the flange.

If the overlap is too small, you can build up the flange by brazing a length of 1/8 in. (3mm) wire to the edge of the flange. Usually, it is sufficient to build up the flange on one side and halfway around one corner. Taper the ends of the wire.

INSTALLATION

R/V Series

See Figures 82, 83 and 84

1. Clean all metal surrounding the windshield opening with a clean alcohol dampened cloth. Allow the alcohol to air dry.
2. Apply the pinchweld primer found in the service kit to the pinchweld area. Do not let any of the primer touch any of the exposed paint because damage to the finish may occur. Allow 30 minutes for the primer to dry.

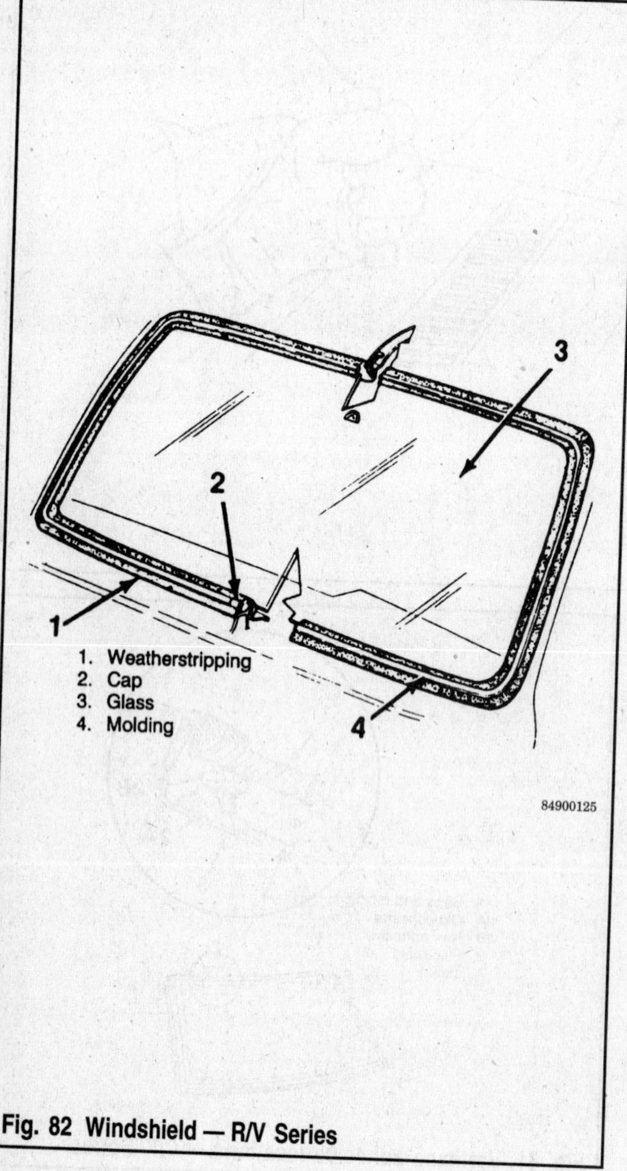

Fig. 82 Windshield — R/V Series

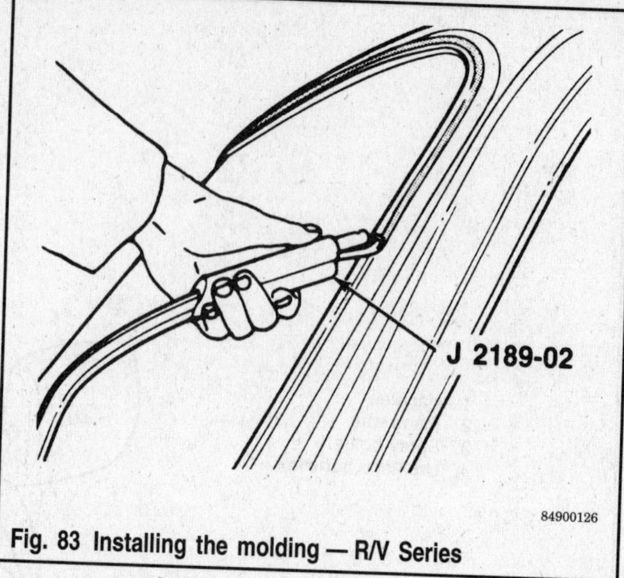

Fig. 83 Installing the molding — R/V Series

3. Apply rubber cleaner to both channels of the weatherstripping. Wait 5 minutes and wipe the channels dry with a clean cloth.
4. Apply rubber primer to both channels of the weatherstripping. Allow the primer to cure for 30 minutes.
5. Thoroughly clean the edge of the glass to which the adhesive material will be applied with a clean alcohol dampened cloth. Allow the alcohol to dry.
6. Apply blackout primer to the inside edge of the glass. Start 10mm from the edge and work the primer towards the edge. Allow the primer to dry.
7. Apply a 6mm diameter bead of urethane adhesive to the center of the pinchweld flange and completely around the windshield opening.

➡The glass must be installed within 20 minutes of applying the urethane!

8. Spray the urethane with water, wetting it completely.
9. Install the weatherstripping on the pinchweld flange.
10. Apply a 5mm diameter bead of urethane adhesive in the glass channel of the weatherstripping.
11. Position the glass in the windshield opening.
12. Coat the lockstrip channel with a rubber lubricant and work it over the glass, locking it in place.
13. Install the reveal moldings. Remove the protective tape covering the butyl adhesive on the underside of the molding. Push the molding caps onto each end of one of the reveal moldings. Press the lip of the molding into the urethane adhesive while holding it against the edge of the windshield. Take care to seat the molding in the corners. The lip must fully contact the adhesive and the gap must be entirely covered by the crown of the molding. Slide the molding caps onto the adjacent moldings. Use tape to hold the molding in position until the adhesive cures.

➡The vehicle should not be driven and should remain at room temperature for six hours to allow the adhesive to cure.

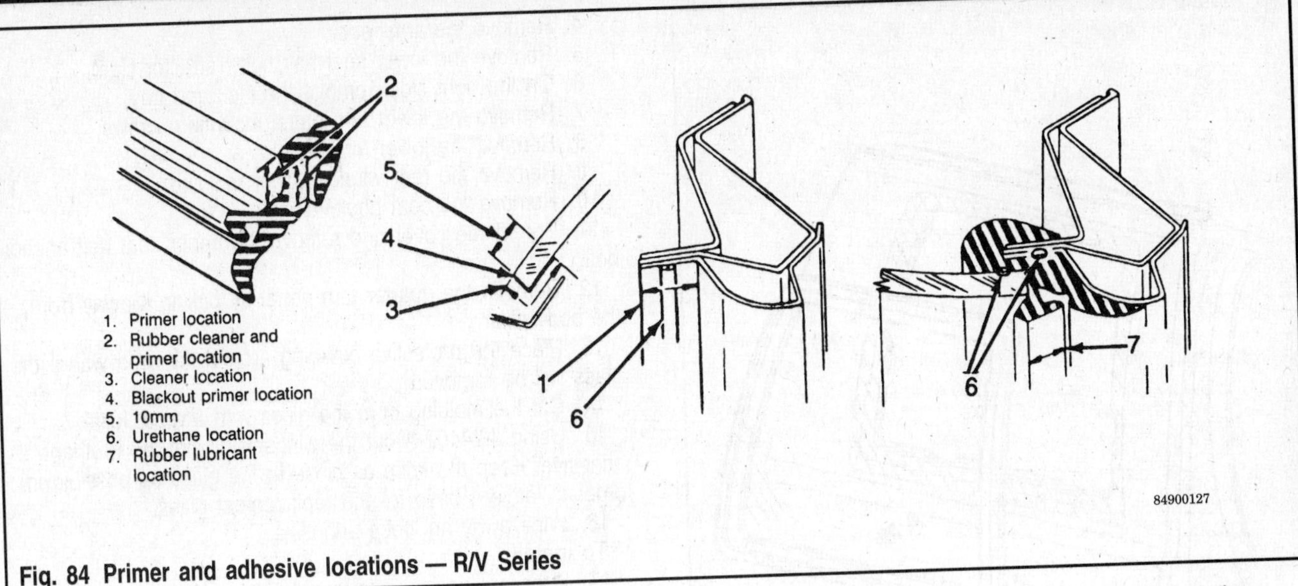

Fig. 84 Primer and adhesive locations — R/V Series

C/K Series

To replace a urethane adhered windshield, GM adhesive service kit No. 1052420 contains the materials needed, and must be used to insure the original integrity of the windshield design.

EXTENDED METHOD

1. Clean all metal surrounding the windshield opening with a clean alcohol dampened cloth. Allow the alcohol to air dry.
2. Apply the pinchweld primer found in the service kit to the pinchweld area. Do not let any of the primer touch any of the exposed paint because damage to the finish may occur. Allow thirty minutes for the primer to dry.
3. Follow the steps listed under Short Method for the remainder of the procedure.

SHORT METHOD

1. Thoroughly clean the edge of the glass to which the adhesive material will be applied with a clean alcohol dampened cloth. Allow the alcohol to dry.
2. Apply the clear glass primer in the kit to the inner edge of the windshield from the edge of the glass inward ¾ in. (19mm). Apply the primer around the entire perimeter of the glass. Allow the primer to cure for thirty minutes.
3. Apply the blackout primer to the glass in the same area as the clear primer. Allow the blackout primer to dry to the touch.
4. Apply a bead of urethane, 1mm high, over the primer.
5. Drill or punch a hole in the center of each tab at the bottom of the windshield.
6. With the aid of a helper, lift the glass into the opening. Align the groove in each upper, outer edge of the windshield molding with the door edge.
7. Install the windshield stop screws.
8. Cut the tip of the adhesive cartridge approximately 3/16 in. (5mm) from the end of the tip.
9. Apply a smooth continuous bead of adhesive into the gap between the glass edge and the sheet metal. Use a flat bladed tool to paddle the material into position if necessary. Be sure that the adhesive contacts the entire edge of the glass, and extends to fill the gap between the glass and the primer sheet metal (extended method) or solidified urethane base (short method).
10. Spray a mist of water onto the urethane. Water will assist in the curing process.
11. Install the wiper arms.
12. Install the interior garnish moldings.
13. Install the rear view mirror.
14. Install the speaker grilles, cowl vent grille and antenna mast.

➡Leave the door window open to prevent air pressure from dislodging the windshield when the doors are closed. The vehicle should not be driven and should remain at room temperature for six hours to allow the adhesive to cure.

Stationary Body Side And Rear Cab Window

REMOVAL & INSTALLATION

C/K Series

➧ See Figures 85, 86 and 87

➡Bonded windows require special tools and special removal procedures to be removed without being broken. For this reason we recommend that you refer all REMOVAL & installation to a qualified technician.

CAUTION

Always wear heavy gloves when handling glass to reduce the risk of injury.

Special tool J-24402-A, Glass Sealant Remover Knife, or its equivalent is required to perform this procedure.

1. Remove the latch trim cover from the quarter trim panel.
2. Remove the seat mounting bolts and lift out the rear seat.
3. Remove the ashtray and panel pocket.

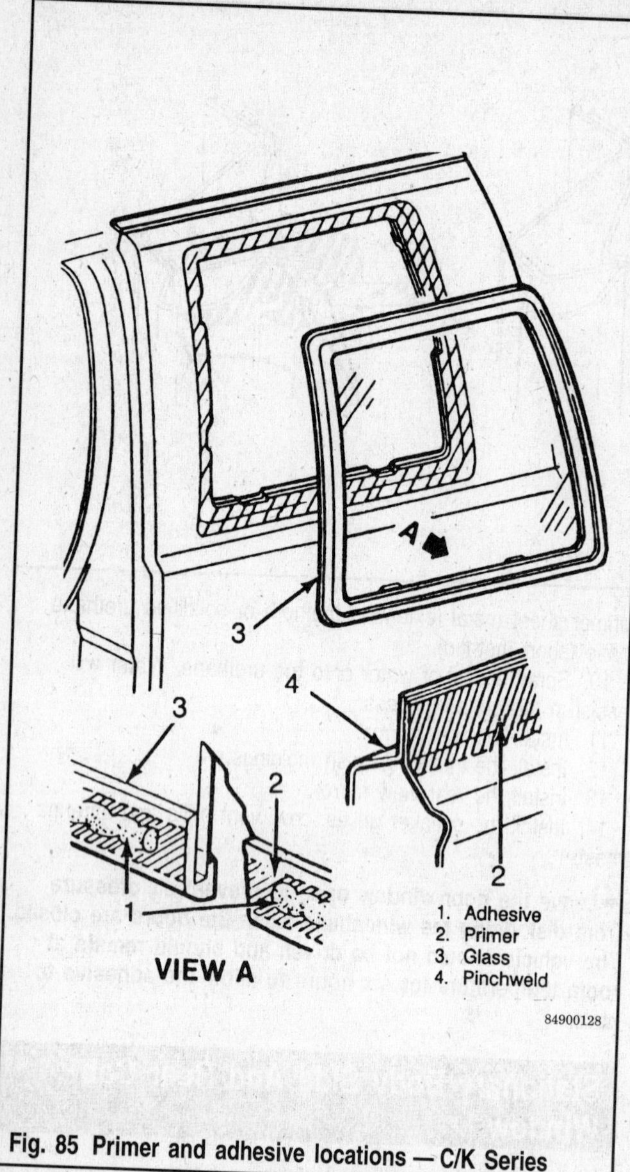

Fig. 85 Primer and adhesive locations — C/K Series

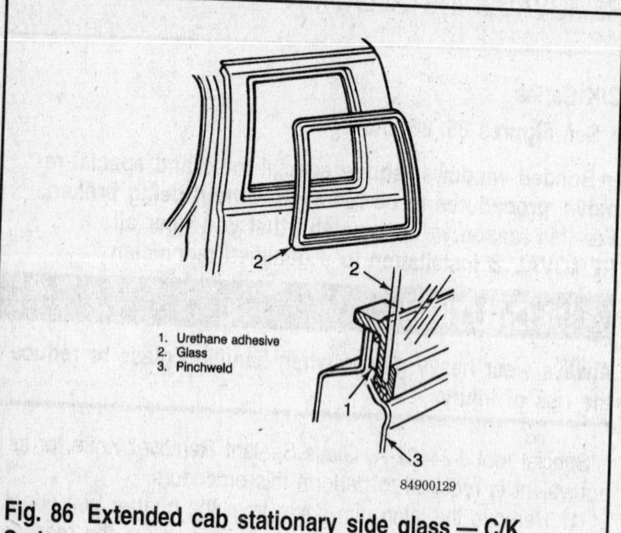

Fig. 86 Extended cab stationary side glass — C/K Series

4. Remove the arm rest.
5. Remove the lower seat belt bolt (retractor side).
6. On the right side, remove the jack and tray.
7. Remove the lower trim panel mounting screws.
8. Remove the lower trim panel.
9. Remove the rear window lower molding.
10. Remove the coat hook.
11. Pry off the cover and remove the upper seat belt anchor bolt.
12. Remove the quarter trim panel by pulling it away from the body pillar.
13. Place the protective covering around the area where the glass will be removed.
14. Cut the molding from the glass with a razor knife.
15. Using J-24402-A cut the windshield from the urethane adhesive. Keep the knife as close to the glass as possible in order to leave a base for the replacement glass.
16. Wipe away an loose adhesive.

To install:

17. If the original glass is to be reinstalled, place it on a protected bench or a holding or holding fixture. Remove any remaining adhesive with a razor blade or a sharp scraper. Any remaining traces of adhesive material can be removed with denatured alcohol or lacquer thinner.

➡When cleaning windshield glass, avoid contacting the edge of the plastic laminate material (on the edge of the glass) with volatile cleaner. Contact may cause discoloration and deterioration of the plastic laminate. Do not use a petroleum based solvent such as gasoline or kerosene. The presence of oil will prevent the adhesion of new material.

To replace the glass, GM adhesive service kit No. 1052420 contains the materials needed.

18. Thoroughly clean the edge of the glass to which the adhesive material will be applied with a clean alcohol dampened cloth. Allow the alcohol to dry.
19. Apply the clear glass primer in the kit to the inner edge of the windshield from the edge of the glass inward ¾ in. (19mm). Apply the primer around the entire perimeter of the glass. Allow the primer to cure for thirty minutes.
20. Apply the blackout primer to the glass in the same area as the clear primer. Allow the blackout primer to dry to the touch.
21. Lift the glass into the opening. Center the glass in the opening, on top of the support molding.
22. Cut the tip of the adhesive cartridge approximately 3/16 in. (5mm) from the end of the tip.
23. Apply a smooth continuous bead of adhesive into the gap between the glass edge and the sheet metal. Use a flat bladed tool to paddle the material into position if necessary. Be sure that the adhesive contacts the entire edge of the glass, and extends to fill the gap between the glass and the solidified urethane base.
24. Spray a mist of water onto the urethane. Water will assist in the curing process.

➡The vehicle should not be driven and should remain at room temperature for six hours to allow the adhesive to cure.

25. Position the quarter trim panel on the body pillar.
26. Install the upper seat belt anchor bolt and cover.

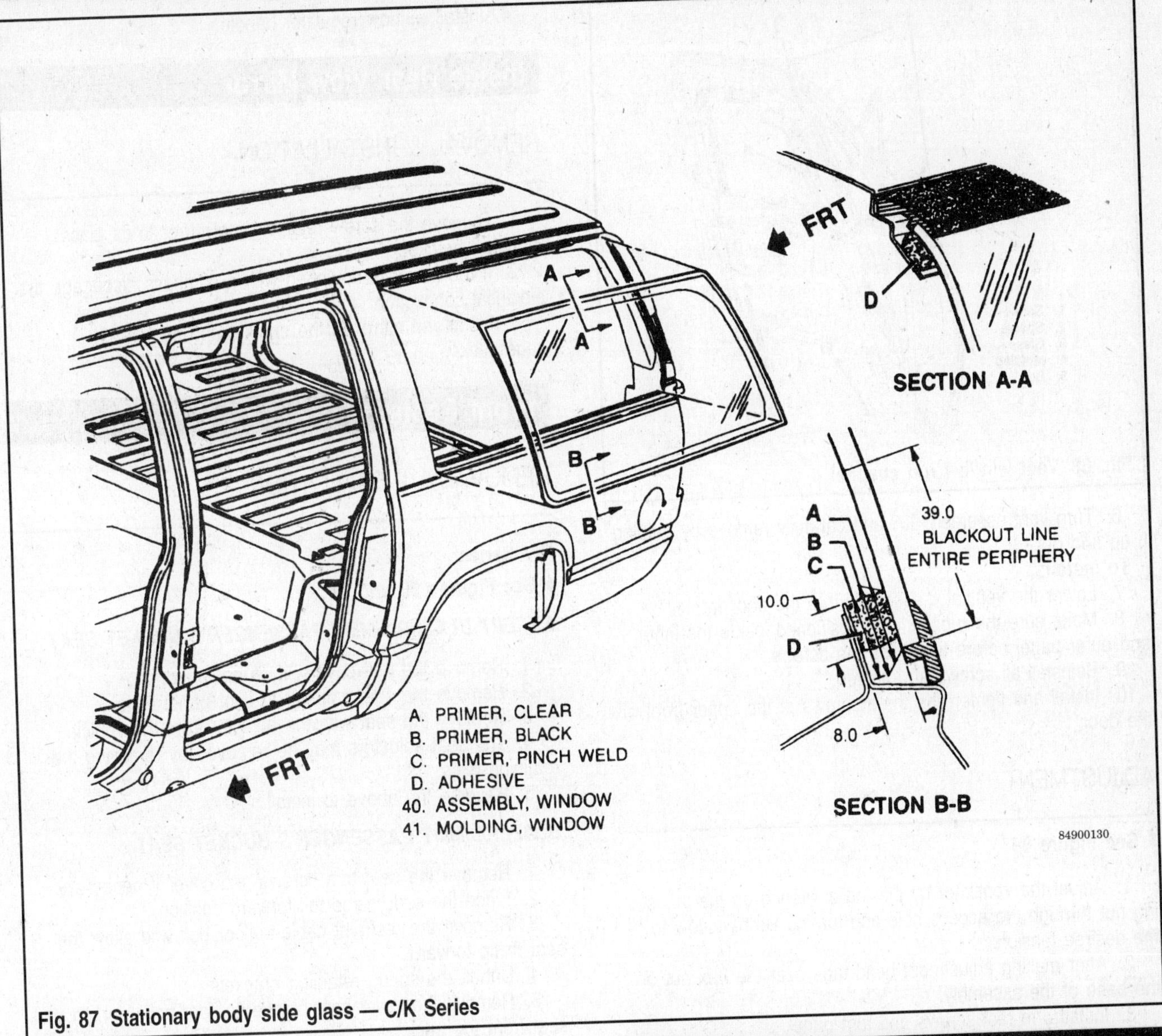

Fig. 87 Stationary body side glass — C/K Series

27. Install the coat hook.
28. Install the rear window lower molding.
29. Install the lower trim panel.
30. Install the lower trim panel mounting screws.
31. On the right side, install the jack and tray.
32. Install the lower seat belt bolt.
33. Install the arm rest.
34. Install the ashtray and panel pocket.
35. Install the seat.
36. Install the latch trim cover.

Vent Window Assembly

REMOVAL & INSTALLATION

R/V Series

See Figure 88

The channel between the door window glass and door vent is removed as part of the vent assembly.

1. Place the door window glass in the full down position.
2. Remove the door trim panel.
3. Remove the glass run channel molding from the vent window area.
4. Remove the screws at the upper front of the door frame which secure the vent assembly.
5. Pull upper portion of the vent assembly rearward and upward while rotating it counterclockwise.

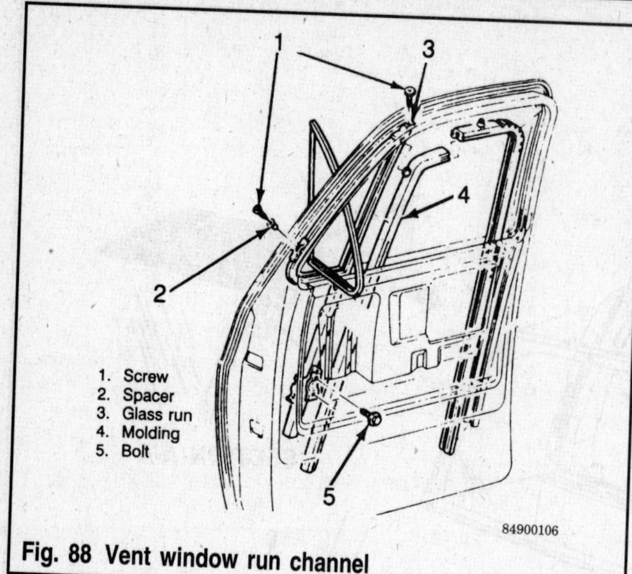

Fig. 88 Vent window run channel

6. Turn vent assembly 90° and carefully remove by guiding it up and out.

To install:

7. Lower the ventilator assembly into the door frame.
8. Make sure the rubber lip is positioned inside the inner and outer panel before tightening the screws.
9. Reinstall all screws and tighten.
10. Install and tighten the three screws at the upper front of the door.

ADJUSTMENT

See Figure 89

1. Adjust the ventilator by placing a wrench on the adjusting nut through the access hole and turning vent window to the desired tension.
2. After making adjustment bend tabs over the hex nut on the base of the assembly.
3. Install arm rest screws and trim panel.

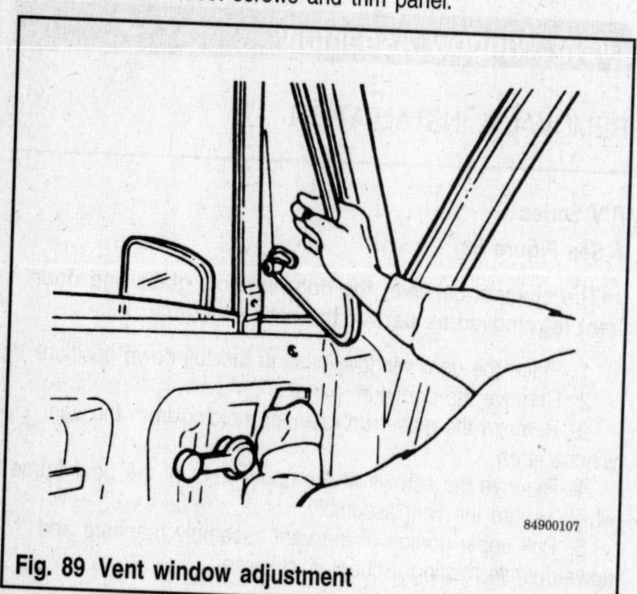

Fig. 89 Vent window adjustment

4. Install window regulator handle.

Inside Rear View Mirror

REMOVAL & INSTALLATION

1. Remove the screw retaining the mirror to its glass mounted bracket.
2. If the mirror is equipped with a compass disengage the electrical connection.
3. Install the mirror to the bracket and tighten as necessary.

Front Seats

REMOVAL & INSTALLATION

R/V Series

See Figures 90 and 91

EXCEPT BLAZER/JIMMY PASSENGER'S BUCKET SEAT

1. Remove the bolt covers, if so equipped.
2. Remove the seat adjuster to floor panel bolts.
3. Remove the seat with the adjuster from the vehicle.
4. The seat adjusters may be removed by removing the retaining bolts.
5. Reverse the above to install.

BLAZER/JIMMY PASSENGER'S BUCKET SEAT

1. Remove the seat trim screws and cover if necessary.
2. Place the seat in the full forward position.
3. Remove the restraint cable-to-floor bolt and allow the seat to tip forward.
4. Unbolt the spring retaining brackets.
5. Remove the lower seat bracket-to-floor bolts and lift the seat from the truck.
6. Installation is the reverse of removal. Tighten the bolts to 41 ft. lbs. (55 Nm).

C/K Series

BUCKET SEAT

See Figure 92

1. Remove the seat trim screws and cover if necessary.
2. Remove the seat-to-floor bolts.
3. Lift out the seat.
4. Installation is the reverse of removal. Tighten the bolts to 41 ft. lbs. (55 Nm).

SPLIT BENCH SEAT

1. Remove the seat trim screws and cover if necessary.
2. Remove the seat-to-floor bolts.
3. Remove the seat belt retaining bolts.
4. Lift out the seat/seat belt assembly.
5. Installation is the reverse of removal. Tighten the seat and belt bolts to 41 ft. lbs. (55 Nm).

1. Wire
2. Adjuster
3. Screw
4. Cover
5. Spring
6. Bolt
7. Bolt
8. Seat
84900134

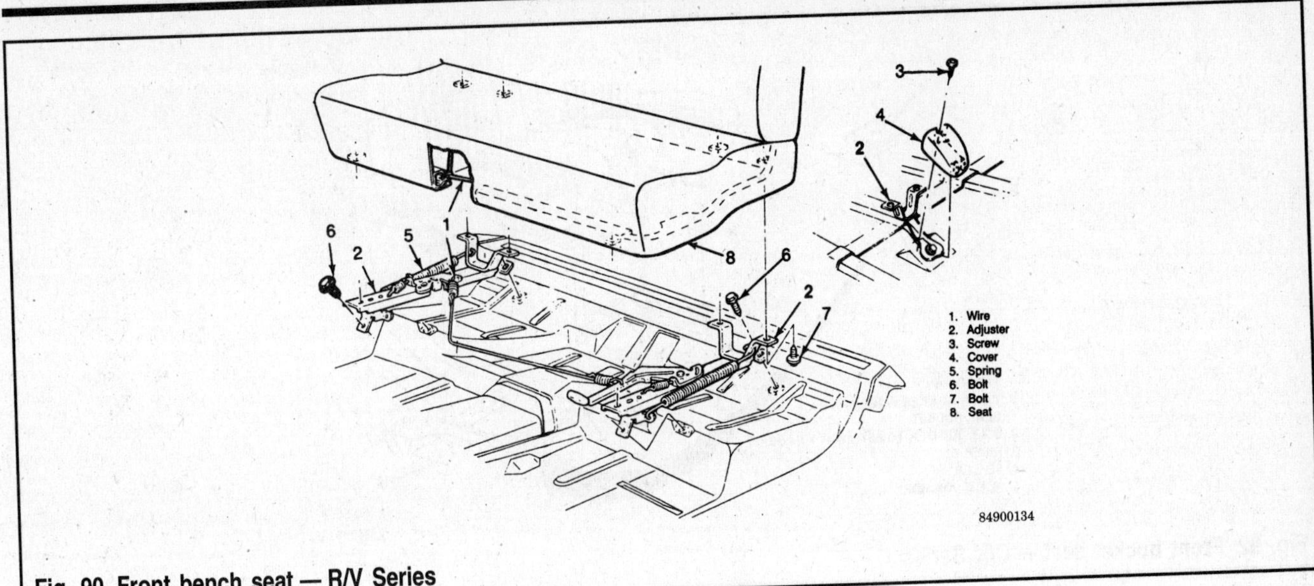

Fig. 90 Front bench seat — R/V Series

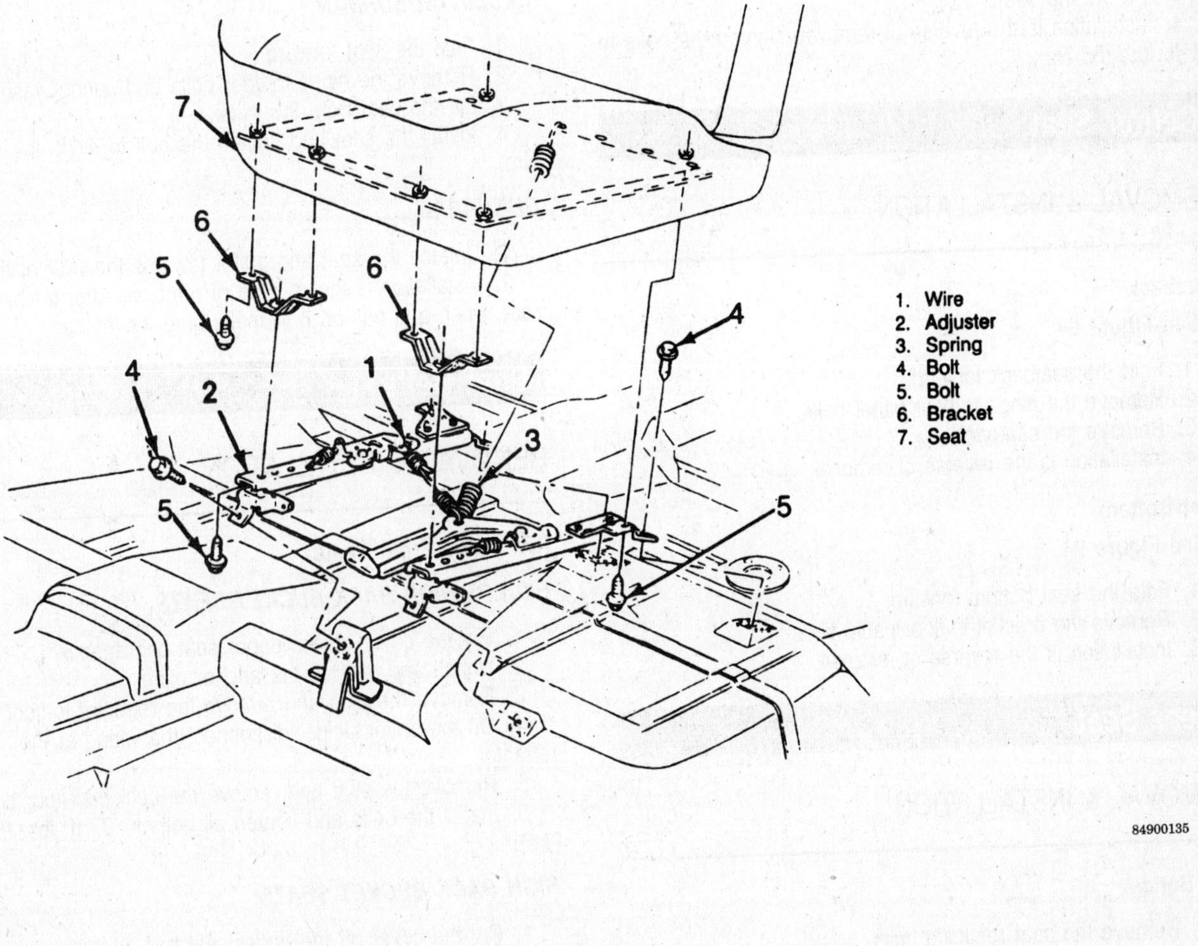

1. Wire
2. Adjuster
3. Spring
4. Bolt
5. Bolt
6. Bracket
7. Seat
84900135

Fig. 91 Front bucket seat — R/V Series

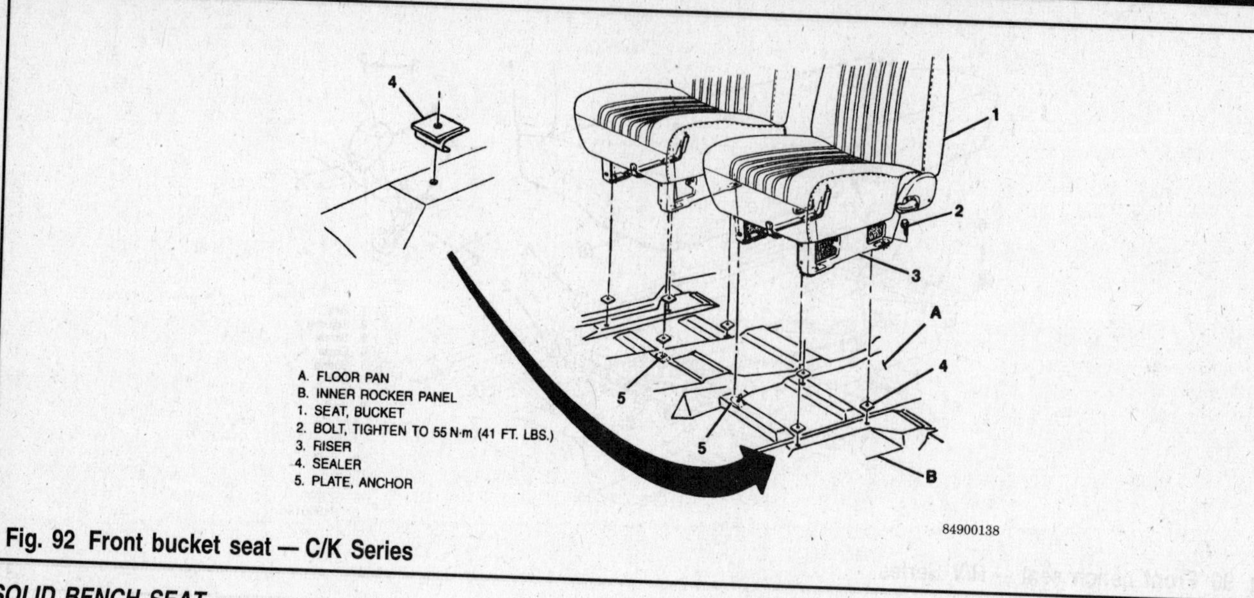

Fig. 92 Front bucket seat — C/K Series

SOLID BENCH SEAT

➧ **See Figure 93**

1. Remove the seat trim screws and cover if necessary.
2. Remove the seat-to-floor bolts.
3. Lift out the seat.
4. Installation is the reverse of removal. Tighten the bolts to 41 ft. lbs. (55 Nm).

Center Seat

REMOVAL & INSTALLATION

Seatback

➧ **See Figure 94**

1. Fold the seatback forward.
2. Remove the hinge-to-floor panel bolts.
3. Remove the seatback.
4. Installation is the reverse of removal.

Seat Bottom

➧ **See Figure 94**

1. Fold the seat bottom forward.
2. Remove the bracket-to-floor panel bolts.
3. Installation is the reverse of removal.

Rear Seat

REMOVAL & INSTALLATION

C/K Series

1. Remove the seat retaining bolts.
2. Lift out the seat.
3. Installation is the reverse of removal. Tighten the bolts to 41 ft. lbs. (55 Nm).

R/V Series

EXCEPT SUBURBAN

1. Fold the seat forward.
2. Remove the hinge-to-floor bolts and spring washers.
3. Lift the seat from the truck.
4. Install the seat and tighten the bolt to 41 ft. lbs. (55 Nm).

SUBURBAN

1. Unlatch the seat and pull it towards the rear of the truck.
2. Installation is the reverse of removal. After latching the seat. Push and pull on it to make sure it's latched.

Seat Belts

REMOVAL & INSTALLATION

R/V Series Front Seats

EXCEPT HIGH BACK BUCKET SEATS

1. Pry the cover off the upper seat belt anchor.
2. Unbolt and remove the anchor plate.
3. Remove the plug and remove the retractor-to-floor bolt.
4. On the driver's side, disconnect the wiring at the retractor.
5. Remove the plug and remove the buckle-to-floor bolt.
6. Install the belts and tighten all bolts to 37 ft. lbs. (50 Nm).

HIGH BACK BUCKET SEATS

1. Pry the cover off the upper seat belt anchor.
2. Unbolt and remove the anchor plate.
3. Remove the retractor lower flap and remove the retractor-to-pillar bolt.

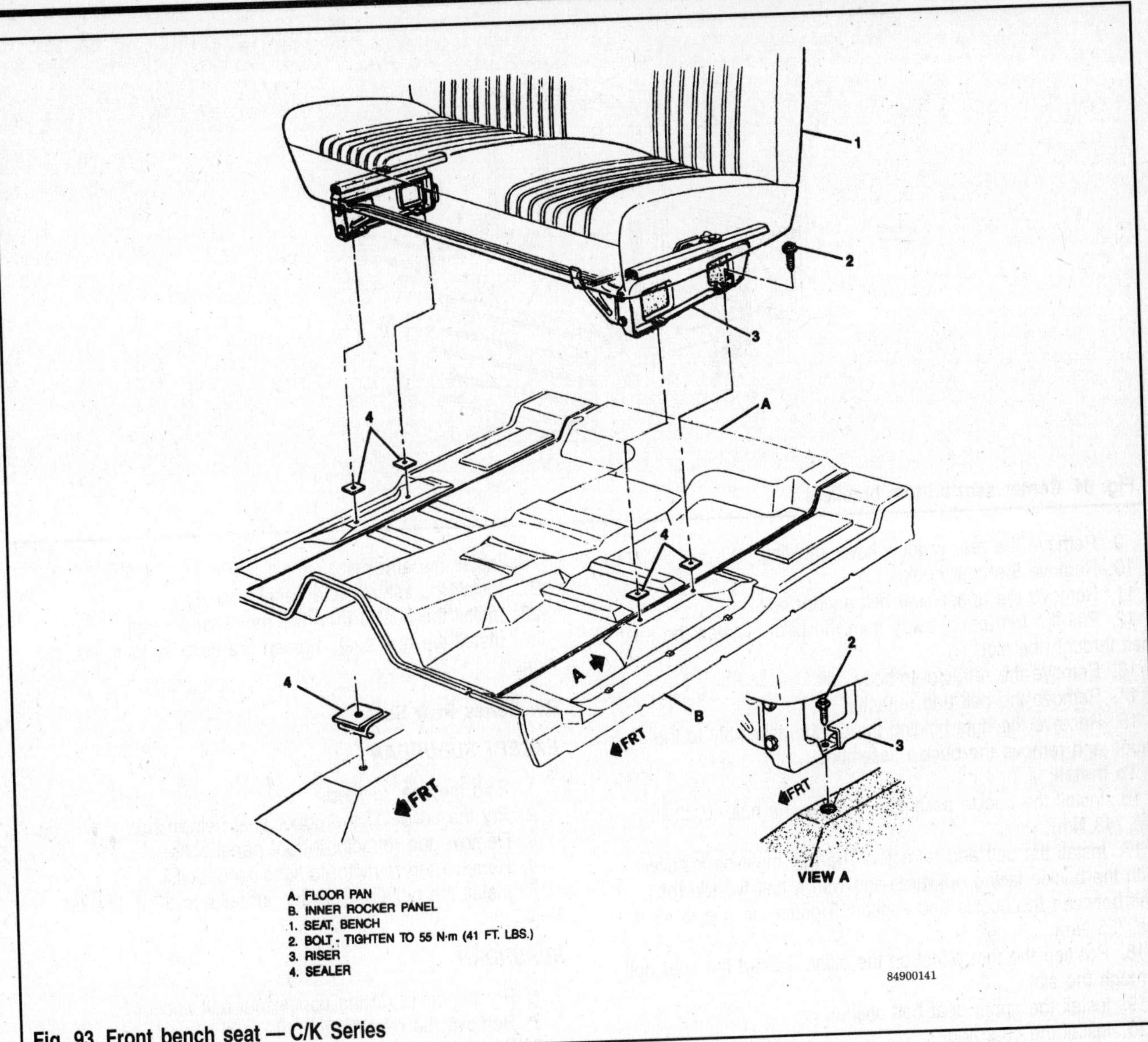

Fig. 93 Front bench seat — C/K Series

4. Remove the lower anchor bolt.
5. Remove the retractor.
6. On the driver's side, disconnect the wiring at the retractor.
7. Remove the plug and remove the buckle-to-floor bolt.
8. Install the belts and tighten all bolts to 37 ft. lbs. (50 Nm).

C/K Series Front Seat

1. Pry the cover off the upper seat belt anchor.
2. Unbolt and remove the anchor plate.
3. Remove the retractor attaching bolts.
4. Unbolt the buckle assemblies from the floor panel.
5. On the driver's side, disconnect the wiring at the retractor.
6. Install the belts. On Regular Cabs, torque the buckle-to-floor panel stud nut to 32 ft. lbs. (43 Nm). Tighten all nuts and bolts to 41 ft. lbs. (55 Nm).

Suburban Center Seat

1. Fold the seat bottoms forward.
2. Take note of the belt positions.
3. Pry the cover off the upper seat belt anchor.
4. Remove the anchor bolt.
5. Remove the retractor.
6. Remove the guide assemblies.
7. Remove the buckle and latch plate assemblies.
8. Install the belts and tighten all bolts to 37 ft. lbs. (43 Nm).

C/K Series Rear Seats

1. Remove the rear seat.
2. Remove the buckle from the rear seat support.
3. Remove the ashtray and panel pocket.
4. Remove the arm rest.
5. Remove the retractor side, lower seat belt bolt.
6. On the right side, remove the jack and tray.
7. Remove the lower trim panel mounting screws.
8. Remove the lower quarter trim panel.

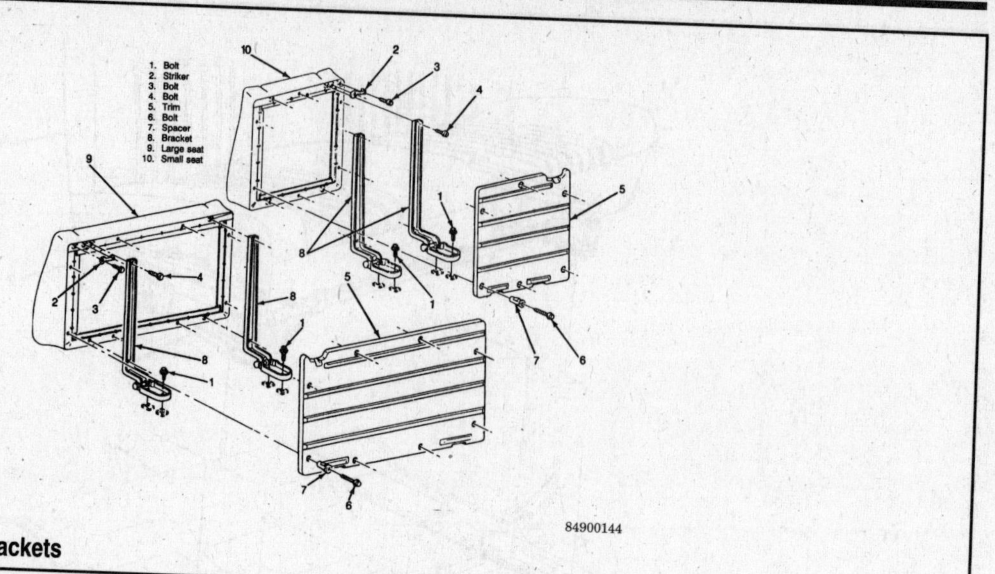

Fig. 94 Center seat bottom brackets

9. Remove the rear window lower molding.
10. Remove the coat hook.
11. Remove the upper seat belt anchor bolt.
12. Pull the trim panel away from the pillar. Thread the seat belt through the slot.
13. Remove the retractor-to-body bolt.
14. Remove the belt and retractor.
15. Remove the nuts holding the buckle assembly to the studs and remove the buckle assembly.

To install:

16. Install the buckle assembly. Tighten the nuts to 32 ft. lbs. (43 Nm).
17. Install the belt and retractor. The belt must be installed with the buckle facing outwards and with a half twist in the belt between the buckle and support. Tighten the bolt to 41 ft. lbs. (55 Nm).
18. Position the trim panel on the pillar. Thread the seat belt through the slot.
19. Install the upper seat belt anchor.
20. Install the coat hook.
21. Install the rear window lower molding.
22. Install the lower quarter trim panel.
23. Install the lower trim panel mounting screws.
24. On the right side, install the jack and tray.
25. Install the retractor side, lower seat belt bolt. Tighten the bolt to 41 ft. lbs. (55 Nm).
26. Install the arm rest.
27. Install the ashtray and panel pocket.
28. Install the buckle from the rear seat support.
29. Install the rear seat. Tighten the bolts to 12 ft. lbs. (17 Nm).

R/V Series Rear Seat

EXCEPT SUBURBAN

1. Fold the seat forward.
2. Pry the cover off the upper seat belt anchor.
3. Remove the retractor-to-roof panel bolts.
4. Remove the retractor-to-floor panel bolts.
5. Install the belts and tighten all bolts to 37 ft. lbs. (50 Nm).

SUBURBAN

1. Pry the cover off the upper seat belt anchor.
2. Remove the retractor-to-roof panel bolts.
3. Remove the retractor-to-floor panel bolts.
4. Remove the retractor cover and remove the retractor-to-body panel bolts.
5. Install the belts. Tighten all the retractor-to-body panel bolts to 49 ft. lbs. (66 Nm). Tighten all other bolts to 37 ft. lbs. (50 Nm).

TORQUE SPECIFICATIONS

Component	U.S.	Metric
Cab Mount Bushings	55 ft. lbs.	70 Nm
Center Seats	41 ft. lbs.	55 Nm
Dead Weight Tow Hitch		
R/V Series		
Bracket-to-Frame Bolts	52 ft. lbs.	70 Nm
Bar-to-Bracket Bolt	70 ft. lbs.	100 Nm
Bar-to-Support Nuts	52 ft. lbs.	70 Nm
Support-to-Bumper Nuts	24 ft. lbs.	32 Nm
Door Lock Assembly		
C/K Series	5 ft. lbs.	7 Nm
Front Bumpers		
R/V Series	66 ft. lbs.	89 Nm
C/K Series	74 ft. lbs.	100 Nm
Front Door Hinge Bolts	26 ft. lbs.	35 Nm
Front Fenders		
R/V Series		
Fender-to-Radiator Support	13 ft. lbs.	17 Nm
Wheelwell Panel-to-Fender	13 ft. lbs.	17 Nm
Door Pillar-to-Fender	31 ft. lbs.	42 Nm
Wheelwell Panel-to-Splash Shield	13 ft. lbs.	17 Nm
Fender-to-Cowl	31 ft. lbs.	42 Nm
Upper Fender-to-Door Pillar	31 ft. lbs.	42 Nm
Hood Spring Assemblies	20 ft. lbs.	27 Nm
C/K Series		
All	18 ft. lbs.	24 Nm
Front Seats	41 ft. lbs.	55 Nm
Hood Hinge Bolts	18 ft. lbs.	24 Nm
Pick-Up Box		
C/K Series	52 ft. lbs.	70 Nm
Rear Bumpers		
R/V Series		
Regular	70 ft. lbs.	98 Nm
Step	52 ft. lbs.	70 Nm
C/K Series		
CK107	65 ft. lbs.	90 Nm
CK109, 201, 300	31 ft. lbs.	42 Nm
Rear Door Handle		
C/K Series	35 inch lbs.	4 Nm
Rear Fenders		
Stepside		
Fender-to-Bracket Screws	18 ft. lbs.	24 Nm
All Others	13 ft. lbs.	17 Nm
Dual Rear Wheel		
C/K Series	18 ft. lbs.	24 Nm
R/V Series	13 ft. lbs.	17 Nm
Raer Seats		
C/K Series Extended Cab	12 ft. lbs.	17 Nm
All Others	41 ft. lbs.	55 Nm
Rear Side Door Hinge Bolts	26 ft. lbs.	35 Nm

84900161

GLOSSARY

AIR/FUEL RATIO: The ratio of air-to-gasoline by weight in the fuel mixture drawn into the engine.

AIR INJECTION: One method of reducing harmful exhaust emissions by injecting air into each of the exhaust ports of an engine. The fresh air entering the hot exhaust manifold causes any remaining fuel to be burned before it can exit the tailpipe.

ALTERNATOR: A device used for converting mechanical energy into electrical energy.

AMMETER: An instrument, calibrated in amperes, used to measure the flow of an electrical current in a circuit. Ammeters are always connected in series with the circuit being tested.

AMPERE: The rate of flow of electrical current present when one volt of electrical pressure is applied against one ohm of electrical resistance.

ANALOG COMPUTER: Any microprocessor that uses similar (analogous) electrical signals to make its calculations.

ARMATURE: A laminated, soft iron core wrapped by a wire that converts electrical energy to mechanical energy as in a motor or relay. When rotated in a magnetic field, it changes mechanical energy into electrical energy as in a generator.

ATMOSPHERIC PRESSURE: The pressure on the Earth's surface caused by the weight of the air in the atmosphere. At sea level, this pressure is 14.7 psi at 32°F (101 kPa at 0°C).

ATOMIZATION: The breaking down of a liquid into a fine mist that can be suspended in air.

AXIAL PLAY: Movement parallel to a shaft or bearing bore.

BACKFIRE: The sudden combustion of gases in the intake or exhaust system that results in a loud explosion.

BACKLASH: The clearance or play between two parts, such as meshed gears.

BACKPRESSURE: Restrictions in the exhaust system that slow the exit of exhaust gases from the combustion chamber.

BAKELITE: A heat resistant, plastic insulator material commonly used in printed circuit boards and transistorized components.

BALL BEARING: A bearing made up of hardened inner and outer races between which hardened steel balls roll.

BALLAST RESISTOR: A resistor in the primary ignition circuit that lowers voltage after the engine is started to reduce wear on ignition components.

BEARING: A friction reducing, supportive device usually located between a stationary part and a moving part.

BIMETAL TEMPERATURE SENSOR: Any sensor or switch made of two dissimilar types of metal that bend when heated or cooled due to the different expansion rates of the alloys. These types of sensors usually function as an on/off switch.

BLOWBY: Combustion gases, composed of water vapor and unburned fuel, that leak past the piston rings into the crankcase during normal engine operation. These gases are removed by the PCV system to prevent the buildup of harmful acids in the crankcase.

BRAKE PAD: A brake shoe and lining assembly used with disc brakes.

BRAKE SHOE: The backing for the brake lining. The term is, however, usually applied to the assembly of the brake backing and lining.

BUSHING: A liner, usually removable, for a bearing; an anti-friction liner used in place of a bearing.

CALIPER: A hydraulically activated device in a disc brake system, which is mounted straddling the brake rotor (disc). The caliper contains at least one piston and two brake pads. Hydraulic pressure on the piston(s) forces the pads against the rotor.

CAMSHAFT: A shaft in the engine on which are the lobes (cams) which operate the valves. The camshaft is driven by the crankshaft, via a belt, chain or gears, at one half the crankshaft speed.

CAPACITOR: A device which stores an electrical charge.

CARBON MONOXIDE (CO): A colorless, odorless gas given off as a normal byproduct of combustion. It is poisonous and extremely dangerous in confined areas, building up slowly to toxic levels without warning if adequate ventilation is not available.

CARBURETOR: A device, usually mounted on the intake manifold of an engine, which mixes the air and fuel in the proper proportion to allow even combustion.

CATALYTIC CONVERTER: A device installed in the exhaust system, like a muffler, that converts harmful byproducts of combustion into carbon dioxide and water vapor by means of a heat-producing chemical reaction.

CENTRIFUGAL ADVANCE: A mechanical method of advancing the spark timing by using flyweights in the distributor that react to centrifugal force generated by the distributor shaft rotation.

CHECK VALVE: Any one-way valve installed to permit the flow of air, fuel or vacuum in one direction only.

CHOKE: A device, usually a moveable valve, placed in the intake path of a carburetor to restrict the flow of air.

CIRCUIT: Any unbroken path through which an electrical current can flow. Also used to describe fuel flow in some instances.

CIRCUIT BREAKER: A switch which protects an electrical circuit from overload by opening the circuit when the current flow exceeds a predetermined level. Some circuit breakers must be reset manually, while most reset automatically.

COIL (IGNITION): A transformer in the ignition circuit which steps up the voltage provided to the spark plugs.

COMBINATION MANIFOLD: An assembly which includes both the intake and exhaust manifolds in one casting.

COMBINATION VALVE: A device used in some fuel systems that routes fuel vapors to a charcoal storage canister instead of venting them into the atmosphere. The valve relieves fuel tank pressure and allows fresh air into the tank as the fuel level drops to prevent a vapor lock situation.

COMPRESSION RATIO: The comparison of the total volume of the cylinder and combustion chamber with the piston at BDC and the piston at TDC.

CONDENSER: 1. An electrical device which acts to store an electrical charge, preventing voltage surges. 2. A radiator-like device in the air conditioning system in which refrigerant gas condenses into a liquid, giving off heat.

CONDUCTOR: Any material through which an electrical current can be transmitted easily.

CONTINUITY: Continuous or complete circuit. Can be checked with an ohmmeter.

COUNTERSHAFT: An intermediate shaft which is rotated by a mainshaft and transmits, in turn, that rotation to a working part.

CRANKCASE: The lower part of an engine in which the crankshaft and related parts operate.

CRANKSHAFT: The main driving shaft of an engine which receives reciprocating motion from the pistons and converts it to rotary motion.

CYLINDER: In an engine, the round hole in the engine block in which the piston(s) ride.

CYLINDER BLOCK: The main structural member of an engine in which is found the cylinders, crankshaft and other principal parts.

CYLINDER HEAD: The detachable portion of the engine, usually fastened to the top of the cylinder block and containing all or most of the combustion chambers. On overhead valve engines, it contains the valves and their operating parts. On overhead cam engines, it contains the camshaft as well.

DEAD CENTER: The extreme top or bottom of the piston stroke.

DETONATION: An unwanted explosion of the air/fuel mixture in the combustion chamber caused by excess heat and compression, advanced timing, or an overly lean mixture. Also referred to as "ping".

DIAPHRAGM: A thin, flexible wall separating two cavities, such as in a vacuum advance unit.

DIESELING: A condition in which hot spots in the combustion chamber cause the engine to run on after the key is turned off.

DIFFERENTIAL: A geared assembly which allows the transmission of motion between drive axles, giving one axle the ability to turn faster than the other.

DIODE: An electrical device that will allow current to flow in one direction only.

DISC BRAKE: A hydraulic braking assembly consisting of a brake disc, or rotor, mounted on an axle, and a caliper assembly containing, usually two brake pads which are activated by hydraulic pressure. The pads are forced against the sides of the disc, creating friction which slows the vehicle.

DISTRIBUTOR: A mechanically driven device on an engine which is responsible for electrically firing the spark plug at a predetermined point of the piston stroke.

DOWEL PIN: A pin, inserted in mating holes in two different parts allowing those parts to maintain a fixed relationship.

DRUM BRAKE: A braking system which consists of two brake shoes and one or two wheel cylinders, mounted on a fixed backing plate, and a brake drum, mounted on an axle, which revolves around the assembly.

DWELL: The rate, measured in degrees of shaft rotation, at which an electrical circuit cycles on and off.

ELECTRONIC CONTROL UNIT (ECU): Ignition module, module, amplifier or igniter. See Module for definition.

ELECTRONIC IGNITION: A system in which the timing and firing of the spark plugs is controlled by an electronic control unit, usually called a module. These systems have no points or condenser.

END-PLAY: The measured amount of axial movement in a shaft.

ENGINE: A device that converts heat into mechanical energy.

EXHAUST MANIFOLD: A set of cast passages or pipes which conduct exhaust gases from the engine.

FEELER GAUGE: A blade, usually metal, of precisely predetermined thickness, used to measure the clearance between two parts.

FIRING ORDER: The order in which combustion occurs in the cylinders of an engine. Also the order in which spark is distributed to the plugs by the distributor.

FLOODING: The presence of too much fuel in the intake manifold and combustion chamber which prevents the air/fuel mixture from firing, thereby causing a no-start situation.

FLYWHEEL: A disc shaped part bolted to the rear end of the crankshaft. Around the outer perimeter is affixed the ring gear. The starter drive engages the ring gear, turning the flywheel, which rotates the crankshaft, imparting the initial starting motion to the engine.

FOOT POUND (ft. lbs. or sometimes, ft.lb.): The amount of energy or work needed to raise an item weighing one pound, a distance of one foot.

FUSE: A protective device in a circuit which prevents circuit overload by breaking the circuit when a specific amperage is present. The device is constructed around a strip or wire of a lower amperage rating than the circuit it is designed to protect. When an amperage higher than that stamped on the fuse is present in the circuit, the strip or wire melts, opening the circuit.

GEAR RATIO: The ratio between the number of teeth on meshing gears.

GENERATOR: A device which converts mechanical energy into electrical energy.

HEAT RANGE: The measure of a spark plug's ability to dissipate heat from its firing end. The higher the heat range, the hotter the plug fires.

HUB: The center part of a wheel or gear.

HYDROCARBON (HC): Any chemical compound made up of hydrogen and carbon. A major pollutant formed by the engine as a byproduct of combustion.

HYDROMETER: An instrument used to measure the specific gravity of a solution.

INCH POUND (inch lbs.; sometimes in.lb. or in. lbs.): One twelfth of a foot pound.

INDUCTION: A means of transferring electrical energy in the form of a magnetic field. Principle used in the ignition coil to increase voltage.

INJECTOR: A device which receives metered fuel under relatively low pressure and is activated to inject the fuel into the engine under relatively high pressure at a predetermined time.

INPUT SHAFT: The shaft to which torque is applied, usually carrying the driving gear or gears.

INTAKE MANIFOLD: A casting of passages or pipes used to conduct air or a fuel/air mixture to the cylinders.

JOURNAL: The bearing surface within which a shaft operates.

KEY: A small block usually fitted in a notch between a shaft and a hub to prevent slippage of the two parts.

MANIFOLD: A casting of passages or set of pipes which connect the cylinders to an inlet or outlet source.

MANIFOLD VACUUM: Low pressure in an engine intake manifold formed just below the throttle plates. Manifold vacuum is highest at idle and drops under acceleration.

MASTER CYLINDER: The primary fluid pressurizing device in a hydraulic system. In automotive use, it is found in brake and hydraulic clutch systems and is pedal activated, either directly or, in a power brake system, through the power booster.

MODULE: Electronic control unit, amplifier or igniter of solid state or integrated design which controls the current flow in the ignition primary circuit based on input from the pick-up coil. When the module opens the primary circuit, high secondary voltage is induced in the coil.

NEEDLE BEARING: A bearing which consists of a number (usually a large number) of long, thin rollers.

OHM:(Ω) The unit used to measure the resistance of conductor-to-electrical flow. One ohm is the amount of resistance that limits current flow to one ampere in a circuit with one volt of pressure.

OHMMETER: An instrument used for measuring the resistance, in ohms, in an electrical circuit.

OUTPUT SHAFT: The shaft which transmits torque from a device, such as a transmission.

OVERDRIVE: A gear assembly which produces more shaft revolutions than that transmitted to it.

OVERHEAD CAMSHAFT (OHC): An engine configuration in which the camshaft is mounted on top of the cylinder head and operates the valve either directly or by means of rocker arms.

OVERHEAD VALVE (OHV): An engine configuration in which all of the valves are located in the cylinder head and the camshaft is located in the cylinder block. The camshaft operates the valves via lifters and pushrods.

OXIDES OF NITROGEN (NOx): Chemical compounds of nitrogen produced as a byproduct of combustion. They combine with hydrocarbons to produce smog.

OXYGEN SENSOR: Used with the feedback system to sense the presence of oxygen in the exhaust gas and signal the computer which can reference the voltage signal to an air/fuel ratio.

PINION: The smaller of two meshing gears.

PISTON RING: An open-ended ring which fits into a groove on the outer diameter of the piston. Its chief function is to form a seal between the piston and cylinder wall. Most automotive pistons have three rings: two for compression sealing; one for oil sealing.

PRELOAD: A predetermined load placed on a bearing during assembly or by adjustment.

PRIMARY CIRCUIT: The low voltage side of the ignition system which consists of the ignition switch, ballast resistor or resistance wire, bypass, coil, electronic control unit and pick-up coil as well as the connecting wires and harnesses.

PRESS FIT: The mating of two parts under pressure, due to the inner diameter of one being smaller than the outer diameter of the other, or vice versa; an interference fit.

RACE: The surface on the inner or outer ring of a bearing on which the balls, needles or rollers move.

REGULATOR: A device which maintains the amperage and/or voltage levels of a circuit at predetermined values.

RELAY: A switch which automatically opens and/or closes a circuit.

RESISTANCE: The opposition to the flow of current through a circuit or electrical device, and is measured in ohms. Resistance is equal to the voltage divided by the amperage.

RESISTOR: A device, usually made of wire, which offers a preset amount of resistance in an electrical circuit.

RING GEAR: The name given to a ring-shaped gear attached to a differential case, or affixed to a flywheel or as part of a planetary gear set.

ROLLER BEARING: A bearing made up of hardened inner and outer races between which hardened steel rollers move.

ROTOR: 1. The disc-shaped part of a disc brake assembly, upon which the brake pads bear; also called, brake disc. 2. The device mounted atop the distributor shaft, which passes current to the distributor cap tower contacts.

SECONDARY CIRCUIT: The high voltage side of the ignition system, usually above 20,000 volts. The secondary includes the ignition coil, coil wire, distributor cap and rotor, spark plug wires and spark plugs.

SENDING UNIT: A mechanical, electrical, hydraulic or electro-magnetic device which transmits information to a gauge.

SENSOR: Any device designed to measure engine operating conditions or ambient pressures and temperatures. Usually electronic in nature and designed to send a voltage signal to an on-board computer, some sensors may operate as a simple on/off switch or they may provide a variable voltage signal (like a potentiometer) as conditions or measured parameters change.

SHIM: Spacers of precise, predetermined thickness used between parts to establish a proper working relationship.

SLAVE CYLINDER: In automotive use, a device in the hydraulic clutch system which is activated by hydraulic force, disengaging the clutch.

SOLENOID: A coil used to produce a magnetic field, the effect of which is to produce work.

SPARK PLUG: A device screwed into the combustion chamber of a spark ignition engine. The basic construction is a conductive core inside of a ceramic insulator, mounted in an outer conductive base. An electrical charge from the spark plug wire travels along the conductive core and jumps a preset air gap to a grounding point or points at the end of the conductive base. The resultant spark ignites the fuel/air mixture in the combustion chamber.

SPLINES: Ridges machined or cast onto the outer diameter of a shaft or inner diameter of a bore to enable parts to mate without rotation.

TACHOMETER: A device used to measure the rotary speed of an engine, shaft, gear, etc., usually in rotations per minute.

THERMOSTAT: A valve, located in the cooling system of an engine, which is closed when cold and opens gradually in response to engine heating, controlling the temperature of the coolant and rate of coolant flow.

TOP DEAD CENTER (TDC): The point at which the piston reaches the top of its travel on the compression stroke.

TORQUE: The twisting force applied to an object.

TORQUE CONVERTER: A turbine used to transmit power from a driving member to a driven member via hydraulic action, providing changes in drive ratio and torque. In automotive use, it links the driveplate at the rear of the engine to the automatic transmission.

TRANSDUCER: A device used to change a force into an electrical signal.

TRANSISTOR: A semi-conductor component which can be actuated by a small voltage to perform an electrical switching function.

TUNE-UP: A regular maintenance function, usually associated with the replacement and adjustment of parts and components in the electrical and fuel systems of a vehicle for the purpose of attaining optimum performance.

TURBOCHARGER: An exhaust driven pump which compresses intake air and forces it into the combustion chambers at higher than atmospheric pressures. The increased air pressure allows more fuel to be burned and results in increased horsepower being produced.

VACUUM ADVANCE: A device which advances the ignition timing in response to increased engine vacuum.

VACUUM GAUGE: An instrument used to measure the presence of vacuum in a chamber.

VALVE: A device which control the pressure, direction of flow or rate of flow of a liquid or gas.

VALVE CLEARANCE: The measured gap between the end of the valve stem and the rocker arm, cam lobe or follower that activates the valve.

VISCOSITY: The rating of a liquid's internal resistance to flow.

VOLTMETER: An instrument used for measuring electrical force in units called volts. Voltmeters are always connected parallel with the circuit being tested.

WHEEL CYLINDER: Found in the automotive drum brake assembly, it is a device, actuated by hydraulic pressure, which, through internal pistons, pushes the brake shoes outward against the drums.

MASTER
INDEX